Butch
BREWER

LOUISIANA CRIMINAL LAW AND MOTOR VEHICLE HANDBOOK

—including—

Legislative Highlights and Legal Guidelines
R.S. Title 14–Criminal Law
R.S. Title 15–Criminal Procedure
R.S. Title 32–Motor Vehicle and Traffic Regulations
R.S. Title 37–Professions and Occupations
R.S. Title 40–Public Health and Safety
R.S. Title 47–Revenue and Taxation
Code of Criminal Procedure
Children's Code

1999

(Includes the enactments of the 1998 First Extraordinary Session through Act 170 and the 1998 Regular Session through Act 76)

GOULD PUBLICATIONS of Florida, Inc.

RECYCLED PAPER

Published by
GOULD PUBLICATIONS of Florida, Inc.
1333 North U.S. Hwy. 17-92
Longwood, FL 32750-3724
(407) 695-9500
World Wide Web—http://www.gouldlaw.com
E-mail—info@gouldlaw.com

ISBN 0-87526-367-4

Every attempt has been made to ensure the accuracy and the completeness of the law contained herein. No express or implied guarantees or warranties are made.

Since laws change very often and vary from jurisdiction to jurisdiction, it is very important to check the timeliness and applicability of the laws contained herein.

FOREWORD

The material presented herewith in convenient form is the **Louisiana Criminal Law and Motor Vehicle Handbook**, as currently amended to include the enactments of the 1998 First Extraordinary Session through Act 170 and the 1998 Regular Legislative Session through Act 76 for use in 1999. All changes to these laws have been incorporated in text, and effective dates have been added where applicable. Also included are Legislative Highlights, Legal Guidelines, and a comprehensive index.

At the end of this book is Gould's handy ***Quick Find Locator***™ which helps you find the law you need.

Updated pages are supplied periodically to keep your book current. Please send back the **"IMPORTANT"** card at the front of this book to ensure that you are on our subscription list.

Comments from users of this book and ways to improve it to facilitate its use would be appreciated by the publisher.

This product is also available on ***computer disk*** *as* ***Louisiana Criminal & Motor Vehicle Laws DiskLaw***™. *For details on how to obtain the laws you need and enforce for use on a single computer or on a network, please contact the publisher.*

This page intentionally left blank.

1998 Legislative Changes to the LOUISIANA CRIMINAL LAW AND MOTOR VEHICLE HANDBOOK
(for use in 1999)

Section	*Change*	*Act*	*Eff. Date*
R.S. TITLE 14			
14:32.1(B)	Amend	82X(1)	6/16/98
14:90.4	New	162X(1)	6/16/98
14:93.20	Repeal	71(2)	6/25/98
14:98(C)(intro)	Amend	4X(1)	6/16/98
R.S. TITLE 15			
15:587(A)(1)(c)	Add	137X(1)	5/5/98
15:1181(2)	Amend	110X(1)	5/5/98
15:1181(4)	Add	110X(1)	5/5/98
15:1181(4)	Redesignate	110X(1)	5/5/98
15:1181(5)	Redesignate/Amend	110X(1)	5/5/98
15:1181(6)–(9)	Redesignate	110X(1)	5/5/98
15:1183(A)	Amend	110X(1)	5/5/98
15:1184(A)–(C)	Amend	110X(1)	5/5/98
15:1184(E)	Amend	110X(1)	5/5/98
15:1185(A)	Amend	110X(1)	5/5/98
15:1186(C)	Amend	110X(1)	5/5/98
15:1187 to 15:1189	Amend	110X(1)	5/5/98
R.S. TITLE 32			
32:7	New	37X(1)	4/24/98
32:168	Amend	83X(1)	3/1/99
32:169(E), (F)	Add	122X(1)	6/16/98
32:171(A)(5)	Add	122X(1)	6/16/98
32:171(E)–(G)	Add	122X(1)	6/16/98
32:172	Amend	121X(1)	6/16/98
32:176	New	87X(1)	6/16/98
32:289	Repeal	148X(10)	6/16/98
32:298.1	New	98X(1)	5/5/98
32:301(3)	Amend	118X(1)	5/5/98
32:402.1(A)(2)(intro)	Amend	80X(2)	6/16/98
32:402.2	Amend	82X(2)	6/16/98
32:407(A)(2)	Amend	80X(2)	6/16/98
32:408(A)(1), (3)	Amend	80X(2)	6/16/98
32:408(H)(1)(h)	Amend	80X(2)	6/16/98
32:409.1(A)(2)(d)(vi)	Add	8X(2)	4/24/98
32:409.1(A)(2)(d)(viii)	Amend	8X(2)	4/24/98
32:410(A)(3)(a)(viii)	Amend	8X(2)	4/24/98

(continued)

1998 Legislative Changes to the LOUISIANA CRIMINAL LAW AND MOTOR VEHICLE HANDBOOK

(Continued)

Section	*Change*	*Act*	*Eff. Date*
32:414(A)(3)(a)	Amend	148X(4)	6/16/98
32:414(A)(3)(b)	Amend	148X(4)	6/16/98
32:661.2	New	81X(1)	6/16/98
32:863(A)(3)	Amend	159X(1)	6/16/98
32:874(B)(1)	Amend	40X(1)	6/16/98

R.S. TITLE 40

Section	Change	Act	Eff. Date
40:964(Sch. III)(B)(9)	Add	129X(1)	6/16/98

CODE OF CRIMINAL PROCEDURE

Section	Change	Act	Eff. Date
211.3(A)	Amend	148X(9)	6/16/98
408.1	Amend	124X(1)	6/16/98
895.1(B)(7)	Add	138X(1)	6/16/98

HIGHLIGHTS OF THE 1998 LOUISIANA LEGISLATIVE SESSION

CONTROLLED DANGEROUS SUBSTANCES

Schedules
Ketamine hydrochloride is added to Schedule III depressants. (R.S. 40:964)

CRIMINAL PROCEDURE

General Venire
Sources other than voter registration lists may be used to provide names of prospective grand or petit jurors. (C.Cr.P. Art. 408.1)

DRIVING WHILE INTOXICATED

Second Offense
The total sentence of imprisonment cannot exceed 6 months. Home incarceration may be ordered. (R.S. 14:98)

GAMBLING

Video Draw Poker
Persons under twenty-one years of age are prohibited from playing video draw poker devices. (R.S. 14:90.4)

MOTOR VEHICLE AND TRAFFIC REGULATIONS

Railroad and Highway Grade Crossing Safety
Locomotive engines must be equipped with signal audible for a quarter mile. The signal must be sounded when approaching within a quarter mile of a highway and continue until the engine has crossed the roadway. Operation of locomotive engine constitutes implied consent to chemical tests following collisions. Officer investigating crossing accident must be notified whether the train has an event recorder. Additional stop signs and traffic control devices to be installed at particularly dangerous crossings. Driver education and driver license examination to include railroad crossing safety. Penalties provided for drivers who fail to safely yield at crossings. (R.S. 14:32.1, 32:168, 32:169, 32:171, 32:172, 32:176, 32:402.1, 32:402.2, 32:407, 32:408, 32:661.2)

This page intentionally left blank.

TABLE OF CONTENTS

LOUISIANA CRIMINAL LAW AND MOTOR VEHICLE HANDBOOK

This page intentionally left blank.

LOUISIANA LEGAL GUIDELINES

(Editor's Note: This section provides an overview of selected topics in criminal procedure. This is a reference tool only and must not be relied upon for specific guidance in daily law enforcement activities. Statutes and case law do change. Therefore, readers must always check for the most current law. Readers must also check their local ordinances and police procedures and seek the advice of their appropriate legal counsel.)

LIST OF TOPICS

I. INVESTIGATIVE DETENTIONS

A. Officers free to approach individuals in public place for questioning.

An officer may question any person in a public place as long as the person is free to leave and free to refuse to answer. "There is nothing in the Constitution which prevents a policeman from addressing questions to anyone on the streets". *Terry v. Ohio*, 392 U.S. 1, 26, 88 S.Ct. 1868, 1882 (1968).

While on patrol in a high crime area at 2:00 a.m., an officer observed the defendant in a car talking to a pedestrian. As the officer drove up alongside the defendant's car, the pedestrian left. After the defendant exited his car, the officer questioned him. This officer and the defendant had a consensual encounter because the defendant voluntarily exited his car. *State v. Barre*, 592 So. 2d 440 (La. App. 5 Cir. 1991). However, after the officer shined his light in the defendant's car and observed a knife in the car, the consensual encounter was transformed into an "investigatory stop". *State v. Barre*, supra.

Often an officer will approach a person in a public place (i.e. airport, bus station, train, plane or bus, etc.) *Florida v. Bostick*, 501 U.S. 429; 115 L.Ed. 2d 389 (U.S. 1991). An officer needs no reasonable suspicion to ask questions, or ask for a person's identification, as long as a reasonable person would understand that he or she could refuse to cooperate. *Florida v. Bostick*, supra.

Undercover officers suspected that an individual in an airport was involved in drug trafficking. The officers approached him. They identified themselves as police and asked to speak with him. He agreed to speak with them. They asked him where he was arriving from and what was his purpose for being there. They also asked him to produce his ticket and his identification. This was a consensual encounter with the defendant. They were allowed to ask these questions and to ask for his tickets and identification. He could refuse to answer their questions. He could refuse to provide the tickets and identification and was free to walk away. *State v. Garriga*, 592 So. 2d 453 (La. App. 5 Cir. 1991).

However, when they asked him for his permission to search his luggage for drugs, this consensual encounter was transformed into an "Investigatory Stop". The officers would need a reasonable suspicion of criminal activity before they could ask for permission to search the bag. *State v. Garriga*, supra.

B. Definition of reasonable suspicion for investigatory detention: *Terry* Stop.

The Fourth Amendment only forbids unreasonable searches and seizures. *Terry v. Ohio*, supra. An officer may stop and briefly detain a person to investigate for possible criminal activity if the officer has reasonable suspicion supported by facts that criminal activity may be occurring. This stop and detention of a person may occur even if the officer lacks probable cause. *U.S. v. Sokolow*, 490 U.S. 1, 109 S.Ct. 1581 (1989). In addition, the validity of the stop must be evaluated by considering "the totality of the circumstances - the whole picture." *U.S. v. Sokolow*, supra.

In Louisiana, an "investigatory stop" to question a suspect is allowed under certain circumstances. (LSA-C.Cr.P.) Art. 215.1(A) states that:

"A law enforcement officer may stop a person in a public place whom he suspects is committing, has committed, or is about to commit an offense and may demand of him his name, address, and an explanation of his actions."

In other words, if an officer reasonably believes that a suspect is involved with criminal activity, that officer can temporarily detain that suspect for questioning and identification.

C. Cases illustrating Reasonable Suspicion for purposes of investigative detention.

The following cases demonstrate the reasonable suspicion that the suspects have participated, are participating or are about to participate in criminal activity. Only a reasonable suspicion of a suspect's involvement in criminal activity will warrant an investigative detention.

Officers observed the defendant on a street corner at 12:00 a.m., raising a small dark glass bottle and examining its contents under the street lights. The defendant placed the bottle in his pocket as the officers approached. These officers knew from previous experience that drug users and sellers use this type of bottle to protect perishable PCP liquid from light. Reasonable suspicion that the bottle might contain PCP warranted detention. This reasonable suspicion was increased when the officers smelled the odor of PCP immediately after exiting their vehicle. *State v. Fleming*, 676 So. 2d 1141 (La. App. 4 Cir. 1996).

Officers approached the defendants standing on side patio of apartment building in a known drug area. The defendants who did not live at that location failed to explain why they were at that location. The officers had the authority to detain and question the defendants. *State v. Johnson*, 675 So. 2d 1175 (La. App. 5 Cir. 1996).

Officer received a complaint that someone was prowling around a closed medical center late at night. This medical center had recently been burglarized. The officer then saw the defendant between the medical center and the sidewalk. There was no justification for the defendant's presence other than criminal activity. Thus, the officer lawfully stopped the defendant. *State v. Rodriquez*, 476 So. 2d 994 (La. App. 1 Cir. 1985).

The defendant had just exited a car he was driving at night in an area with a high amount of crime and drug dealing. An officer, while shining his light into the defendant's car, observed a knife inside. An investigative stop was justified by a reasonable suspicion that the defendant was engaged in, or about to become engaged in, criminal activity. The time, the location, and the knife in the defendant's car provided the reasonable suspicion. *State v. Barre*, 592 So. 2d 440 (La. App. 5 Cir. 1991).

Officers knew of armed robberies, in the area, in which two persons would ride a bicycle. One person sat on the handlebars so he could jump off and pull a gun on the victim. The officers saw the defendant and another person riding a bicycle in this manner at 4:45 a.m., in this area. The defendant, wearing a heavy coat in warm weather, which could be used to conceal a weapon, appeared startled and scared when he saw the officers. The officers were entitled to detain the defendant because of their reasonable suspicion that he was engaged in criminal activity. *State v. Martin*, 643 So. 2d 830 (La. App. 4 Cir. 1994).

An officer, patrolling an area known for drug trafficking, observed the defendant flag down a minivan. When it stopped, the defendant talked to the driver and the two engaged in a "hand-to-hand" transaction consistent with the sale of drugs. At this point, the officer could legally detain the defendant due to reasonable suspicion of a drug deal. *State v. Collins*, 637 So. 2d 741 (La. App. 1 Cir. 1994).

D. Cases illustrating No Reasonable Suspicion for purposes of investigative detention.

The following cases demonstrate insufficient suspicion that the suspects have participated, are participating, or are about to participate in criminal activity so that an investigative detention is not warranted.

Officers observed four young people walking about on a street late at night. This observation alone did not constitute a lawful basis for an investigative stop. There was no reasonable suspicion that the four young people were involved in criminal activity. *State v. Phipps*, 429 So. 2d 445 (La. 1983).

While patrolling a high-crime area, an officer observed a group of individuals, including the defendant, sitting in front of a closed bar at 9:30 a.m. The officer exited his car and approached this group. As he asked these persons why they were there, he noticed that the defendant had a black case in his hand. The officer detained him and asked him what was in his hand. The detention was illegal because there was no suspicion that the defendant was involved in criminal activity. *State v. Thibodeaux*, 531 So. 2d 284 (La. App. 3 Cir. 1987).

Officers observed the defendant carrying a tire pump and walking a small bicycle in a public housing development in a high-crime area. He looked nervous when he saw the officers. They detained him. The officers did not have reasonable suspicion to believe that the defendant was involved in criminal activity. It was unreasonable to assume that a person walking a small bicycle and carrying a tire pump was a thief. Criminality could not be inferred because the incident occurred in a public housing development. It was unreasonable to assume that only a criminal would be nervous in the presence of two officers at 7:00 a.m. in a public housing development. Thus, the officers illegally detained him. *State v. Daniels*, 631 So. 2d 1281 (La. App. 4 Cir. 1994).

A stop of the defendant's car was not supported by reasonable belief that the defendant was involved in criminal activity. The officers testified that the defendant had done nothing suspicious. The defendant was stopped as part of a systematic roadblock in which every fourth vehicle was stopped in order to check for drivers' licenses. *State v. Ellis*, 662 So. 2d 159 (La. App. 4 Cir. 1995).

Wildlife law enforcement officers had a general suspicion of illegal duck hunting in a certain area. They stopped as many boats as possible in this area to check hunting licenses and inquire about game in the boaters' possession. These officers stopped the defendant's boat. Because the officers did not have any reasonable basis to suspect the defendant's of criminal activity, they did not have a legal basis to stop the defendant's boat. *State v. McHugh*, 630 So. 2d 1259 (La. 1994).

E. Detention of persons by roadblocks in Louisiana.

Another form of detention used by law enforcement officers is the "roadblock" or "checkpoint". Often these roadblocks are unannounced and used to check for intoxicated drivers. In *Michigan Dept. of State Police v. Sitz*, 496 U.S. 444, 110 S.Ct. 2481 (1990), the U.S. Supreme Court upheld the use of unannounced roadblocks for the purpose of checking for intoxicated drivers. These roadblocks are valid under the Fourth Amendment *Michigan Dept. of State Police v. Sitz*, supra.

There are several cases in Louisiana in which roadblocks were held in violation of Article 1, Section 5 of the Louisiana Constitution.

Stop of the defendant's car and protective sweep of the passenger's compartment were not supported by reasonable belief that the defendant was dangerous and might gain immediate control of weapon. The defendant had done nothing suspicious before the search. The defendant was stopped as part of a systematic roadblock in which every fourth vehicle was stopped in order to check for drivers' licenses. Thus, the stop of the defendant's car was illegal. *State v. Ellis*, supra.

Officers set up a DWI roadblock to stop all drivers. The defendant was not stopped because of any violation of the law. The officers had no reasonable suspicion that the defendant had committed, was about to commit, or was engaged in violation of the law. *State v. Church*, 538 So. 2d 993 (La. 1989).

A DWI roadblock at which all drivers were stopped involved seizure without reasonable suspicion to believe the driver engaged in criminal activity in violation of Article 1, Section 5 of the Louisiana Constitution. Evidence of the defendant's intoxication derived from the DWI roadblock was suppressed because there was no observed legal violation nor any reasonable suspicion of criminal activity. *State v. Church*, supra.

When analyzed as seizures without probable cause or reasonable suspicion and as invasions of privacy, roadblocks are unconstitutional under Article 1, Section 5 of the Louisiana Constitution. *State v. Parms*, 523 So. 2d 1293 (La. 1988). Thus, roadblocks which are constitutional under *Michigan Dept. of State Police v. Sitz*, supra, will likely be in violation of the Louisiana Constitution.

F. Detention of persons for possession of contraband on premises of correctional institution.

La. C. Cr. P. Art. 215.2 provides that certain correctional institution employees may detain a person at a correctional institution for up to one hour, when that employee has reasonable cause to believe that the person is carrying contraband as defined in R.S. § 14:402(A). This employee may detain such a person for questioning, procurement of a search warrant, or arrest by a peace officer.

G. Detention for theft of goods for sale in stores.

Under certain circumstances a merchant, employee, or agent of a merchant has the right to detain a person reasonably suspected of stealing goods held for sale by the merchant. La. C. Cr. P. Art. 215A(1) provides:

"A peace officer, merchant, or a specifically authorized employee or agent of a merchant, may use reasonable force to detain a person for questioning on the merchant's premises, for a length of time not to exceed 60 minutes, unless it is reasonable under the circumstances that the person be detained longer, when he has reasonable cause to believe that the person has committed a theft of goods held for sale by the merchant... The merchant or his employee may also detain such a person for arrest by a peace officer. The detention shall not constitute an arrest."

"Reasonable under the circumstances" includes the value of the merchandise in question, the store's location, the cooperation of the person detained, and the length of time for the law enforcement officers to respond. La. C. Cr. P. Art. 215C.

A merchant is also permitted to detain someone when electronic devices used to detect the unauthorized removal of merchandise indicates that such merchandise has been removed from the store. Sufficient notice must be provided to patrons that such a device is being utilized. La. C. Cr. P. Art. 215B.

H. Recent U.S. Supreme Court Cases.

Several recent U.S. Supreme Court cases dealt with detentions of vehicle occupants as well as warrantless searches of vehicles.

An officer lawfully stopped a car for speeding. After issuing a verbal warning and returning the driver's license, the officer asked the driver if he had any weapons in the car. The driver said "No". The officer asked for and obtained the driver's consent to search the car. Some illegal drugs were found in the car. The driver's consent was valid. The officer did not need to tell the defendant that he could refuse to consent to the search. The Fourth Amendment does not require a lawfully detained defendant to be advised that he is "free to go" before his consent to search is recognized as voluntary. *Ohio v. Robinette*, ____ U.S. ____, 117 S. Ct. 417, 136 L. Ed. 2d 347 (1996).

The principle that an officer can order a validly detained driver out of a car, *Pennsylvania v. Mimms*, 434 U.S. 106, 54 L. Ed. 2d 331, 98 S. Ct. 330 (1977), was extended to all the occupants of a car in *Maryland v. Wilson*, ____ U.S. ____, 117 S. Ct. 882, 137 L. Ed. 2d 41 (1997). In this case, the officer, after noticing a passenger's nervousness, ordered him out of the car. As the passenger exited the car, some cocaine fell to the ground. Since the intrusion of ordering the passenger out of a car is minimal, an officer may order any passenger out of a car during a valid detention. Thus the cocaine was admissible.

When an officer, who was following the defendant during a drug investigation, observed the defendant's car turn without using a turn signal, in violation of Washington D.C. law, the officer stopped the car. On approaching the car, the officer observed some bags of cocaine in the car. The officer seized the drugs. The officer's observation of the minor traffic violation entitled him to stop the car and to lawfully be in the position where he observed the drugs. The temporary detention of a driver upon violation of a minor traffic ordinance, such as turning without using a signal, does not violate a person's Fourth Amendment rights even if a reasonable officer would not have stopped the motorist for such a violation. *Whren v. U.S.*, 517 U.S. 806, 116 S. Ct. 1769, 135 L. Ed. 2d 89 (1996).

In other words, an officer can use any observed traffic law violation to stop a vehicle; can order the driver or any of the occupants out of the vehicle during the investigation; can, without advising the driver of his or her right to refuse to consent, request permission from the driver to search the vehicle.

II. FRISK

A. Frisks allowed when suspect is armed or sufficient evidence of criminal activity exists.

In Louisiana, a frisk is permitted after an investigatory stop under La.C.Cr.P Art. 215.1 if the following circumstances are met:

When a law enforcement officer has stopped a person for questioning pursuant to this Article and reasonably suspects that he is in danger, he may frisk the outer clothing of such person for a dangerous weapon. If the law enforcement officer reasonably suspects the person possesses a dangerous weapon, he may search the person. La.C.Cr.P Art. 215.1(B).

La.C.Cr.P Art. 215.1 also contains a section on what the officer can do to the suspect and what the officer can do with the weapon.

If the law enforcement officer finds a dangerous weapon, he may take and keep it until the completion of the questioning, at which time he shall either return it, if lawfully possessed, or arrest such person. La.C.Cr.P Art. 215.1(C).

B. Plain Touch.

Evidence, other than a weapon, may be seized when an officer is conducting a lawful frisk and the nature of the contraband is immediately apparent to the officer based on his sense of touch. *Minnesota v. Dickerson*, 508 U.S. 366, 113 S. Ct. 2130, 124 L. Ed. 2d 334 (1993). The "plain touch" doctrine is analogous to the "plain view" doctrine in searches and seizures. If an officer conducts a lawful protective frisk of a suspect's outer clothing and feels a bulge whose contour or mass makes its identity immediately apparent, the officer is justified in seizing the object. Whether the officer detects the contraband by sight or touch the Fourth Amendment requires that the officer have probable cause to believe the item is contraband before seizing it. *Minnesota v. Dickerson*, 508 U.S. 366, 113 S. Ct. 2130, 124 L. Ed. 2d 334 (1993).

Minnesota v. Dickerson, supra, set out the three requirements for "Plain Touch". First, the officer must be lawfully in the touching area. Second, the officer must have some independent constitutional justification for placing his hands on the person or property in question. Third, upon touching the area the officer must, through the process of touching, garner probable cause to believe the object which he or she is touching constitutes evidence of crime, or contraband. The probable cause must be reasonably contemporaneous with the initial touching. Any evidence obtained as a result of an illegal pat down or frisk is inadmissible under the "Exclusionary Rule". *Minnesota v. Dickerson*, 508 U.S. 366, 113 S. Ct. 2130, 124 L. Ed. 2d 334 (1993).

State v. Anderson, 696 So. 2d 105 (La. App. 4 Cir. 1997) is a Louisiana case which adopted the holding of *Minnesota v. Dickerson*, 508 U.S. 366, 113 S. Ct. 2130, 124 L. Ed. 2d 334 (1993).

C. When Frisks are allowed.

The officer was lawfully permitted to frisk in the following cases:

An officer observed the defendant drop a glass pipe and step on it at a spot where a drug transaction had just occurred. As the defendant moved to enter a house, the officer frisked him for weapons. The officer was justified in frisking the defendant because people who deal in drugs frequently carry weapons. *State v. Matthews*, 654 So. 2d 868 (La. App. 4 Cir. 1995).

Officers had lawfully detained the defendant because his clothing and his physical characteristics matched those of an armed robber who had been described to the officers. As the officers approached the defendant from behind and informed him that they were police, he looked over his shoulder and reached towards his pocket. The officers frisked him. The defendant's action in reaching towards his pocket gave the officers reasonable cause to believe that he was armed. Thus, the officers were justified in frisking the defendant for a weapon. *State v. Evans*, 388 So. 2d 774 (La. 1980).

An officer lawfully detained the defendant because he matched the description given by an anonymous caller of a man engaged in suspicious activity at a street corner. After the officer noticed a bulge in the defendant's pocket, he frisked him. The officer had a right to frisk the defendant after noticing a bulge in his pocket. *State v. Herbert*, 669 So. 2d 499 (La. App. 4 Cir. 1996), writ denied, 675 So. 2d 1117 (La. 1996).

An Officer received a complaint that someone was prowling around a closed medical center late at night. This medical center previously was burglarized. The encounter with the defendant occurred between the medical center and the sidewalk. There was no reason for the defendant's presence other than criminal activity. When the officer was alone with the defendant late at night in a secluded area, the officer was reasonably justified in his belief that his safety and possibly that the defendant was in danger. The officer's frisk of the defendant was lawful. *State v. Rodriquez*, 476 So. 2d 994 (La. App. 1 Cir. 1985).

Officers were investigating the defendant for narcotics. The defendant immediately made a spontaneous, unsolicited admission that he had "some stuff". This admission provided officers with probable cause to believe that the defendant possessed contraband. Thus, the officers were justified in frisking the defendant. *State v. Lee*, 475 So. 2d 1116 (La. App. 4 Cir. 1985).

A frisk is also permitted of the passenger compartment of a vehicle if there is a reasonable suspicion that the passenger compartment contains a gun. In *State v. Davis*, 612 So. 2d 256(La. App. 4 Cir. 1992), as a speeding car was being pulled over, an officer observed the defendant make a motion like he was putting something under his seat. This motion gave the officers a reasonable suspicion that the defendant had a gun under his seat because many suspects hide guns under their seats when stopped. After he exited his car, the officers searched under his seat and found drugs. Because there was reasonable suspicion that he had a gun in a location where he could gain immediate control of it, the officers could conduct a frisk under the front seat. Thus, a frisk for weapons is permitted of the passenger area of a car, even if the defendant has exited the car. *State v. Davis*, supra.

While conducting a valid frisk of the defendant, the officer felt a square shaped object inside one of the defendant's pockets. Although the officer did not know what this square shaped box-like object was, he was justified in looking at this object to determine whether the object contained any weapon. The object was big enough to carry a weapon. *State v. Clausen*, 697 So. 2d 1066 (La. App. 4 Cir. 1997).

D. When Frisks are not allowed or exceeding the scope of a frisk.

The following are cases in which the officer was either not entitled to frisk the defendant or when the officer exceeded the scope of the frisk. The officer exceeds the scope of a frisk when the frisk does not reveal a weapon or the likelihood of contraband.

An officer observed the defendant, in a high-crime area, place an object in the back of his waistband. Although the officer did not believe that the defendant was armed, the officer frisked him. This observation did not give the officer the right to conduct a pat-down search because the officer did not believe that the defendant was armed. *State v. Denis*, 691 So. 2d 1295 (La. App. 4 Cir. 1997).

After the officers stopped the defendant, they frisked him for weapons. They did not feel or find any weapons but instead felt a matchbox. They further detained the defendant, seized the matchbox and found cocaine inside it. The seizure or search of the matchbox was not authorized or reasonable because the matchbox was not a weapon. *State v. Williams*, 613 So. 2d 259 (La. App. 1 Cir. 1992).

Officers observed the defendant exchange currency for a packet in an area known for drug trafficking. The officers illegally went beyond the scope of a legal frisk when they frisked the defendant, seized the packet, and opened it. *State v. Thornton*, 621 So. 2d 173 (La. App 4 Cir. 1993), writ denied 642 So. 2d 1307 (La. 1994).

Even if the officers felt that they were in danger after stopping the defendant's car, their search exceeded the scope of a pat-down when they searched thoroughly enough to locate money, and determine that the bills were marked. *State v. Fogan*, 609 So. 2d 1016 (La. App. 4 Cir. 1992).

Officer exceeded scope of pat-down search for weapons when he asked the defendant to empty his pockets. *State v. Bohn*, 668 So. 2d 756 (La. App. 1 Cir 1996).

III. SEARCH WARRANTS

A. Requirements of search warrants.

La. C. Cr. P. Art. 161A lists the property which may be subject to seizure under a search warrant. "A judge may issue a warrant authorizing the search for and seizure of any thing within the territorial jurisdiction of the court which:

"(1) Has been the subject of theft.

"(2) Is intended for use or has been used as a means of committing an offense.

"(3) May constitute evidence tending to prove the commission of an offense." La. C. Cr. P. Art. 161A.

The phrase "within the territorial jurisdiction of the court" has been construed by several courts. A city court judge did not have authority to issue warrant to search a trailer that was admittedly outside the city's boundaries. *State v. Case*, 363 So. 2d 486 (La. 1978).

On the other hand, in *State v. Matthieu*, 506 So. 2d 1209 (La. 1987), the Court permitted a search, of the defendant's home, conducted outside the territorial limits of the issuing court. There was confusion in regard to the parish where the defendant's home was located, due to the convergence of three parishes in that area. Although the search violated La. C. Cr. P. Art. 161A, it was constitutional because the warrant could easily have been obtained from a court within the proper judicial district. *State v. Matthieu*, supra.

Likewise, searches authorized outside of a judicial district are valid under other circumstances. When all the judges of any judicial district are absent from the district or otherwise unable to act, a district judge of an adjoining district can issue a search warrant that the absent or incapacitated judges could grant, if present. R.S. § 13:586; *State v. Loera*, 530 So. 2d 1271 (La. App. 2 Cir. 1988), writ denied 536 So. 2d 1252 (La. 1988). In this case, the officers could not reach any judge in their district. They were told that one of the judges might be out of town. The officers obtained a search warrant from a judge in an adjoining district. Thus the search warrant was valid and the evidence obtained from it was admissible. *State v. Loera*, supra.

A search warrant may also be issued upon oral testimony via phone, radio, and other electronic methods of communication pursuant to La. C. Cr. P. Art. 162.1. Look at the requirements of La. C. Cr. P. Art. 162.1.

There are several other statutes that permit search warrants. R.S. § 14:102.3 provides for search warrants for animal cruelty offenses, while R.S. § 14:102.7 provides for search warrants for dogfighting offenses. R.S. § 40:985 provides for search warrants relating to offenses involving controlled dangerous substances. R.S. § 40:986 provides for administrative inspection warrants.

An important point to remember is that making material and intentional misrepresentations in a search warrant affidavit to a magistrate involves fraud upon the court and will result in the invalidation of the search warrant and suppression of the items seized. *State v. Ceasar,* 700 So. 2d 242 (La. App. 4 Cir. 1977).

B. Judicial officers who may issue search warrants.

La. C. Cr. P. Art. 161A provides the situations in which a judge may issue a search warrant and the property subject to seizure. La. C. Cr. P. Art. 161C provides that a judge may issue a search warrant in all other cases specifically provided by law, but that a justice of the peace may issue a search warrant only in those cases specifically provided by law. La. C. Cr. P. Art. 161C. In other words, a justice of the peace cannot issue a search warrant pursuant to La. C. Cr. P. Art. 161A.

La. C. Cr. P. Art. 161B provides that certain judges of city courts within municipalities may, with the consent of the judicial district court, issue a warrant authorizing the search for and seizure of anything allowed under La. C. Cr. P. Art. 161A, within the territorial jurisdiction of the district court.

Usually, the magistrate or judge that issued a search warrant cannot rule on the validity of the search warrant. Federal cases have held that the issuing authority must be a neutral and detached person and cannot participate in the search, investigation or prosecution. *Lo-Ji Sales, Inc. v. New York,* 442 U.S. 319, 99 S.Ct. 2319 (1979); *Coolidge v. New Hampshire,* 403 U.S. 443 (1971); *Shadwick v. City of Tampa,* 407 U.S. 345 (1972).

C. Particularity of search warrants.

Search warrants must particularly describe the person or place to be searched and the thing to be seized, and the reasons for the search or seizure. *State v. Harper,* 660 So. 2d 537 (La. App. 2 Cir. 1995). See also, La. C. Cr. P. Art. 162 and Article 1, Section 5 of the Louisiana Constitution.

A search warrant that authorized the seizure of all computer software as well as a particular software program on a floppy disk was not overly broad. After being unable to find the software program on a floppy disk, the officer found the program on the hard drive. Accordingly, the officer was entitled to seize the computer which contained the hard drive even though the warrant did not mention the hard drive or the computer. *State v. Tanner,* 534 So. 2d 535 (La. App. 5 Cir. 1988).

If the description in the warrant is not particular enough, the evidence obtained pursuant to the warrant can be suppressed. In *State v. Ockman,* 446 So. 2d 658 (La. App. 5 Cir. 1985), a description in affidavit and search warrant describing the home to be searched was inadequate and did not particularly describe the house to be searched as required by law. The home was described as a white brick home with an asphalt shingle roof and a garage. The description further indicated a Christmas tree in the front window and that the house was located off a certain street. There was no indication in the affidavit or in the warrant that the officer knew the place to be searched or had the home under surveillance.

D. Probable Cause Requirement for Search Warrant.

A court will consider the totality of the circumstances to determine whether the information contained in a search warrant affidavit establishes a fair probability that a place contains contraband or evidence of a crime. *Illinois v. Gates,* 462 U.S. 233, 103 S. Ct. 2329, 76 L. Ed. 2d 545 (1983); *State v. Smith,* 663 So. 2d 845 (La. App. 4 Cir. 1995). In situations where the officer relies upon an informer's statement, the "totality-of-the-circumstances test" is used . This test considers the contents of the informant's statement as well as independent investigations or corroboration of details. *Illinois v. Gates,* supra.

The totality of the circumstances test often requires several different sources of information to establish probable cause for a search warrant.

Often it is difficult for a magistrate to determine if the search warrant affidavit establishes the existence of probable cause. Doubtful or marginal cases are to be resolved by the preference to be accorded to written affidavits. *United States v. Ventresca,* 380 U.S. 102, 111, 85 S.Ct. 741, 747 (1965).

La. C. Cr. P. Art. 162 provides the circumstances under which a judge may issue a search warrant. A search warrant may issue:

"only upon probable cause established to the satisfaction of the judge, by the affidavit of a credible person, reciting facts establishing the cause of the issuance of the warrant." La. C. Cr. P. Art. 162.

Probable cause exists when the affiant has trustworthy information or knowledge of facts and circumstances that support a reasonable belief that evidence or contraband will be found at the place to be searched. *State v. Duncan*, 420 So. 2d 1105 (La. 1982); *State v. Williams*, 619 So. 2d 650 (La. App. 4 Cir. 1993). The facts relied upon by the magistrate must be contained within the four corners of the affidavit. *State v. Williams*, 619 So. 2d 650 (La. App. 4 Cir. 1993).

E. Probable Cause for Search Warrant - illustrative cases

The following cases indicate the circumstances under which there was sufficient evidence of probable cause in a search warrant affidavit.

The search warrant affidavit related the following: a citizen observed the defendant unloading commodities from school board trucks and bringing them into his home. This observation was corroborated by videotape. Probable cause was established for a search warrant on the defendant's house. *State v. Bailey*, 639 So. 2d 860 (La. App. 5 Cir. 1994).

A judge can rely solely on the observations of an informer in a search warrant affidavit to establish probable cause for a search warrant. Even though the informer's statements in the affidavit are hearsay, such statements may still establish probable cause. However, the reliability of the informant's statements need to be shown before such statements can establish probable cause.

The search warrant affidavit related the following: an informant went to the defendant's home and personally observed an occupant selling as preludin some pink pills marked BI62. This informant also observed the defendant's husband in possession of pills which he was selling for $20 per tablet. The informant's tips had been responsible for at least five previous convictions. There was probable cause for a warrant to search the defendant's home for controlled substances. Probable cause was established because the informant was reliable in the past and because the informant's observations were detailed enough to show controlled substances were on the premises. *State v. Sheppard*, 466 So. 2d 493 (La. App. 1 Cir. 1985).

A judge can rely solely on an affidavit by an officer which mentions a victim's observations to establish probable cause for a search warrant. Even though the victim's statements in the affidavit are hearsay, such statements may still establish probable cause. A victim's statement is presumed more reliable than an informant's statement.

A robbery victim gave a description of the robbery suspects and the car they drove in. The search warrant affidavit listed the victim's description and the defendant's vehicle which corresponded to the victim's description. There was probable cause for a search warrant to search the defendant's vehicle because there was no indication that the victim's statement was unreliable. *State v. Reed*, 483 So. 2d 1278 (La. App. 4 Cir. 1986).

Often, a search warrant affidavit will include an informant's statements which by themselves are unreliable. If such statements are not corroborated by other evidence, then there would be no probable cause for a search warrant.

An informant told an officer that the defendant returned from Houston that day with a large shipment of illegal drugs. The officer told this information to other officers. The officers went to the defendant's trailer. The defendant allowed the officers to enter. While they were inside the defendant's trailer, the officers observed a marijuana cigarette in plain view. After the defendant was arrested, the officers put this information in an affidavit to search the trailer for illegal drugs. *State v. Williams*, 608 So. 2d 266 (La. App. 3 Cir 1992).

The affidavit showed no basis for believing that the informant's tip was trustworthy. The affidavit did not explain if the informant had first-hand knowledge of the defendant's illegal drug activity or if the informant learned of the activity through hearsay. The informant's tip alone failed to provide probable cause for a warrant to search the defendant's trailer for illegal drugs. *State v. Williams*, supra.

Nevertheless, probable cause was established for a search warrant. The independent observation of illegal drugs in the defendant's dwelling by the affiant officer corroborated

 ZL

sufficient details of the informant's tip to indicate that the information was not fabricated. *State v. Williams*, supra.

The search warrant affidavit related the following. An informant tipped the police that the defendant was a drug dealer. A controlled purchase of narcotics was made from the defendant at a location other than the defendant's home. Probable cause existed for a warrant to search the defendant's home. *State v. Smith*, 546 So. 2d 538 (La. App. 1 Cir. 1989), writ denied 552 So. 2d 393 (La. 1989).

The search warrant affidavit related the following. The officer-affiant had attended a neighborhood watch meeting in which residents told him about drug sales at the defendant's home and the adjacent vacant home. This officer observed hand-to-hand transactions for cash outside of the defendant's home. Officers discovered drugs on a customer after one such transaction. The affiant also observed the defendant make many trips from his home to the vacant home. These circumstances established probable cause for a warrant to search the vacant home. *State v. Smith*, 663 So. 2d 845 (La. App. 4 Cir. 1995).

F. Lack of Probable Cause for Search Warrant - illustrative cases.

The following cases indicate the circumstances under which there was not sufficient evidence of probable cause for a search warrant.

If the length of time between the observation of contraband and the search warrant application is too long, then there is no probable cause to expect to find the contraband at the premises. The search warrant affidavit stated that two former employees of the cattery to be searched provided information about animal abuse at the cattery. No probable cause was established for the issuance of the search warrant. One of the employees last worked at the cattery more than one year prior to the time the search warrant was sought. This information was stale. The other employee did not give specific indications of what type of evidence might be found. *State v. Lazarus*, 633 So. 2d 225 (La. App. 1 Cir. 1993).

If the length of time between the observation of contraband and the search warrant application is too long or is not indicated in a search warrant affidavit, then there is no probable cause to expect to find the contraband at the premises.

The search warrant affidavit to search the defendant's car for marijuana related the following: an informant, who had provided reliable information two months earlier, informed the affiant-officer that the defendant uses marijuana and sells marijuana out of his car to local teenagers. "Other sources" reported that the defendant has used and possessed marijuana. The defendant has been suspected of using and distributing marijuana for more than a year. *State v. Humble*, 309 So. 2d 138 (La. 1975).

The affidavit failed to establish probable cause that marijuana would be in the car. First, the affidavit did not contain specific details that stated how or when the informant obtained this information. Second, the affidavit does not indicate any attempt by the affiant to corroborate the informer's information. Third, the "other sources" are not identified or rendered reliable. Fourth, the accusation of unidentified "sources" is not sufficiently detailed. Fifth, the affidavit did not provide any information to establish that there was probable cause that marijuana would still be in the car. The only time element mentioned in the affidavit was that the defendant has been selling marijuana for a year or more. This information was stale. Therefore, affidavit failed to establish probable cause for a search warrant. *State v. Humble*, supra.

There is a good possibility that a supporting affidavit for a search warrant will include statements from an informant that are not reliable. If such statements are not corroborated by other evidence, then there would be no probable cause for a search warrant.

The search warrant affidavit stated the following. The affiant-officer received a tip from a confidential informant that the defendant trafficked in cocaine and possessed a large amount of it at his residence. This informant had proved reliable in the past because his information led to arrests and convictions. *State v. Melbert*, 649 So. 2d 740 (La. App. 3 Cir. 1994).

This affidavit also stated that the officer searched and seized some crack cocaine in a boot bag located in the house where the defendant was staying. However, since this evidence was illegally seized, the discovery of the crack cocaine could not be used to establish probable cause for a search warrant. *State v. Melbert*, supra.

The informant's information did not provide sufficient evidence to establish probable cause on which a search warrant could be issued. The general allegation of drug trafficking made by the informant did not have any specific details. Neither was the general allegation of drug trafficking corroborated by investigation or surveillance. Therefore, the cocaine found in the boot bag was suppressed. *State v. Melbert*, supra.

The search warrant affidavit stated the following. An informant stated to the affiant-officer that a female used her house to distribute heroin. This informant also stated that the defendant, who lived in another house, supplied the female with heroin. According to the informant, the defendant previously lived with the female. The informant also stated that he purchased heroin from the defendant at his house and from the female at her house. *State v. Nelson*, 381 So. 2d 477 (La. 1980).

There was no probable cause to believe that heroin was located at the defendant's residence. The informant never mentioned when he had purchased the heroin from the defendant at the defendant's house. *State v. Nelson*, supra.

G. Execution and Return of Search Warrant.

A search warrant must be executed by a peace officer. After the peace officer executes it, he or she will return the property seized before the Court issuing the warrant. A search warrant must be lawfully executed within 10 days of its issuance or it is not valid. Moreover, a search or seizure cannot be made during the nighttime or on Sunday, unless the warrant expressly directs such. La. C. Cr. P. Art. 163.

A peace officer may use such force and means as are authorized for arrests in La. C. Cr. P. Art. 201 to La. C. Cr. P. Art. 232 in order to execute a search warrant. La. C. Cr. P. Art. 164.

Generally, an officer must announce his or her presence when executing a search warrant. There are certain situations that courts have recognized as instances where police may enter the dwelling of a suspect unannounced. These are instances where knocking and announcing may precipitate a likelihood of violence or lead to a destruction of evidence. As in other areas implicating Fourth Amendment concerns, the courts will conduct an inquiry into the reasonableness of the unannounced entry. The courts will consider such factors as officer safety, risk of evidence being destroyed, and recent pursuit (see *Wilson v. Arkansas*, 514 U.S. ___ (1995); *United States v. Ramirez*, ___ U.S. ___; No. 96-1469, (U.S. Supreme Court, March 4, 1998); *Richards v. Wisconsin*, 520 U.S. ___; 117 S. Ct. 1416; 137 L. Ed. 2d 615 (1997)).

"A no-knock entry" by officers into the defendant's apartment was justified for two reasons: First by probable cause to believe that illegal drugs that could easily be disposed of were in the apartment. Second by the officer's knowledge that the defendant was violent and known to carry guns. *State v. Johnson*, 665 So. 2d 1237 (La. App. 2 Cir. 1995).

The police officers unannounced entry into a private residence, in broad daylight, using a battering ram, to execute a search warrant was unreasonable for the following reasons. The officers did not have any specific information about anyone in the residence being armed. Moreover, there was no indication that there was anyone in the residence who could have destroyed the drugs. Likewise, there was no indication that anyone was in a position to spot the officers and warn the occupants of the officers' approach. Therefore, the evidence found during the search was suppressed. *State v. Thompson*, 693 So. 2d 282 (La. App. 4 Cir. 1997).

La. C. Cr. P. Art. 165 provides that an officer while in the course of executing a search warrant may seize items not described in the search warrant in plain view if it constitutes evidence tending to prove the commission of any offense.

The requirements for the execution and return of search warrants are contained in La. C. Cr. P. Art. 161 to La. C. Cr. P. Art. 167.

H. The Exclusionary Rule - General.

The "Exclusionary Rule" was first applied by the U.S. Supreme Court in *Weeks v. U.S.*, 232 U.S. 383, 34 S. Ct. 341, 58 L. Ed. 652 (1914), which merely applied this rule to federal courts. In *Mapp v. Ohio*, 367 U.S. 643, 81 S. Ct. 1684, 6 L. Ed. 2d 1081 (1961), the U.S. Supreme Court applied the "Exclusionary Rule" to state courts as well as federal courts. In this case, the Court held that the Fourth Amendment forbids the use of illegally obtained evidence in state courts.

Subsequent to the decision in *Mapp v. Ohio*, 367 U.S. 643, 81 S. Ct. 1684, 6 L. Ed. 2d 1081 (1961), the U.S. Supreme Court has allowed various exceptions to the "Exclusionary Rule".

These exceptions include: the "Good Faith" Exception, the "Inevitable Discovery" Exception, and the "Independent Source" Exception.

The exclusionary rule does not extend to parole revocation hearings. *Pennslyvania Board of Probation & Parole v. Scott*, ____ U.S. ____, No. 97-561 (U.S. Supreme Court June 22, 1998).

I. The Exclusionary Rule - Good Faith Exception.

In *United States v. Leon*, 468 U.S. 897, 104 S. Ct. 3405 (1984), the U.S. Supreme Court adopted the "Good Faith" exception to the "Exclusionary Rule". This exception will not bar the admissibility of evidence obtained from the execution of a search warrant subsequently found to be defective, if the officer in good faith reasonably relied on such warrant. *United States v. Leon*, supra.

The defendant operated an outpatient clinic for chemically dependent patients. An informant told an officer that the defendant was defrauding insurance companies by overbilling for services rendered and billing for therapy sessions never conducted. The officer put this information in a search warrant affidavit. The judge issued a search warrant to search the clinic. The search pursuant to the warrant produced records which established the operation of the fraudulent scheme. There was not probable cause for the search warrant based on the affidavit because it failed to comply with Article 162 of the Louisiana Code of Criminal Procedure. The affidavit failed to mention why the informant was reliable or how the informant obtained this information. *State v. Barrilleaux*, 620 So. 2d 1317 (La. 1993).

The affiant-officer withheld the name of the informant in the affidavit because the officer feared that the defendant might threaten the informant. However, this officer told the judge the following: that the informant was the admissions coordinator at the clinic; and that the informant produced some of the defendant's business records which showed that the defendant charged for certain patients on days on which the patients had not been treated. Moreover, this officer told the judge the reason for not including the informant's name in the affidavit. The information in the affidavit along with the information the officer told the judge would have been sufficient to establish probable cause. The officer reasonably believed in good faith that he had valid justification for withholding the name of the informant who had a close relationship with the defendant. *State v. Barrilleaux*, supra.

On the other hand, if evidence from an illegal warrantless search is used to establish probable cause for the search warrant, then the evidence obtained from the search must be suppressed. The officer's good faith belief that the warrantless search was legal will not fall under the good faith exception to the exclusionary rule. *State v. Scull*, 639 So. 2d 1239 (La. App. 4 Cir. 1994).

In this case, officers received a tip from a reliable informant that a Spanish male named "Raul" stored drugs at an apartment and sold the drugs at a house. The informant alleged that he had purchased drugs from Raul at the house within the last 72 hours. Officers observed two unidentified men enter the apartment mentioned by the informant and leave it. These two men drove by car and stopped at the house mentioned by the informant. The officers saw one of these men place an object in the glove compartment. The officers stopped the car, searched the glove compartment and found $3,400. A canine unit alerted to the presence of drugs on the money. *State v. Scull*, supra.

There was not probable cause to search the car's glove compartment because there was not probable cause to believe that it contained contraband or the evidence of a crime. Moreover, the officers were not able to establish that either of the two men was the "Raul" mentioned in the tip. In addition, the officers did not observe any drug activities with respect to the apartment. *State v. Scull*, supra.

The officers used the information obtained from the informant, their observations and the search of the car in their search warrant affidavit. The search warrant was granted and cocaine was found in the apartment. Under the exclusionary rule, the evidence from the apartment had to be excluded because it was based on evidence obtained from an illegal search of the car. Search of the apartment could not be upheld under the good faith exception on the theory that the officers believed the warrant was good when they executed it. The drug-tainted money that was the critical factor in supplying probable cause for the warrant was gleaned as a result of a unlawful search. Therefore the good faith exception to the exclusionary rule could not be used to render the evidence found in the apartment admissible. *State v. Scull*, supra.

J. The Exclusionary Rule - Independent Source Exception.

In *Murray v. United States*, 487 U.S. 533, 108 S. Ct. 2529 (1988), the U. S. Supreme Court adopted the "Independent Source" exception to the Exclusionary Rule which admits evidence discovered during a legal search even if such evidence was obtained during a prior illegal search. An independent source, other than the illegal search, must furnish probable cause for the search warrant. The illegal search must not have contributed to the issuance of the warrant or the discovery of the evidence during the lawful search that occurred pursuant to the warrant.

A credible informant told the officers that cocaine was being sold from a certain house by several people. He told the officers that he observed cocaine in this house within the last 72 hours. The officers' surveillance of the house indicated activity consistent with drug trafficking. When the informant exited the house, he told the officers that the defendant had just spoken about leaving to do a drug deal. After the defendant and another man left the house, they were arrested. The officers then illegally entered the house and secured it until they obtained a search warrant. Even without this illegal entry, there was probable cause to obtain a search warrant for the house. The evidence seized in the house was not remotely related to the illegal entry into the house. Rather, the evidence in the house was seized as a result of an independent source, the search warrant. Thus, this evidence was admissible. *State v. Williams*, 619 So. 2d 650 (La. App. 4 Cir. 1993).

K. The Exclusionary Rule - Inevitable Discovery Exception.

In *Nix v. Williams*, 467 U.S. 431, 104 S. Ct. 2501 (1984), the U.S. Supreme Court adopted the "Inevitable Discovery" exception to the Exclusionary Rule in which evidence discovered illegally can be admitted under this exception. At a motion to suppress hearing, the state must prove, by a preponderance of the evidence, that such evidence would have been inevitably discovered by legal means. *Nix v. Williams*, supra.

In *Nix v. Williams*, supra, a preponderance of the evidence indicated that the girl's body would have inevitably been discovered without the defendant's confession. The evidence produced from the lower court indicated that the girl's body was found in a ditch beside a gravel road. Moreover, a search party of 200 had stopped within two and one half miles of the location of the girl's body. The Court held that the search party, under these facts, would have discovered the girl's body.

An informant told officers that the defendant's husband was selling narcotics. After they observed the defendant's husband, on two successive days, drive from his home to conduct what appeared to be drug transactions at different locations, they arrested him. They went back to the home with the intention of securing it while they obtained a search warrant. When the defendant opened the front door, they told her what had happened, and asked for permission to secure the home. The defendant refused to allow them to enter and walked back into the home. One of the officers entered the home and saw the defendant pouring cocaine into a toilet. This officer recovered the cocaine. The officers subsequently secured a search warrant for the home. *State v. Knapper*, 626 So. 2d 395 (La. App. 4 Cir. 1993).

The officer's entry into the house was illegal. Under the exclusionary rule, the cocaine, and the evidence found in the search conducted pursuant to the search warrant would not be admissible. When the officers observed what appeared to be a second illegal drug transaction, they had probable cause to believe that illegal drugs were in the defendant's home. It was more probable than not that a search warrant would have been issued to search the home for drugs, even if the officer had not illegally entered the home. Thus, the cocaine would have inevitably been discovered. Therefore, the cocaine and the evidence obtained pursuant to the search warrant were admissible. *State v. Knapper*, supra.

IV. WARRANTLESS SEARCHES AND SEIZURES

A. Warrantless searches - Prerequisites.

A warrantless search and seizure of property is per se unreasonable unless the search falls within a well-delineated exception to the warrant requirement. Louisiana and federal courts have, however, defined limited exceptions to permit warrantless searches. The basic categories may be stated as: searches based on reasonable suspicion, searches based on probable cause, searches based on consent, and situations not legally considered searches since the items are in public view and there can be no expectation of privacy.

To justify a warrantless search, the state must show that the search falls into one of the narrowly drawn exceptions to warrant requirement. *State v. Crews*, 674 So. 2d 1082 (La. App. 2d 1996).

The "preference for warrants" rule encourages officers to obtain judicial authorization to conduct a search. The Fourth Amendment imposes a warrant requirement on government agents who seek to enter a house for purposes of search or arrest. *Welsh v. Wisconsin*, 466 U.S. 740, 748, 104 S.Ct. 2097 (1984).

In a doubtful or marginal case, a search under a warrant may be sustainable where without one it would fail. *United States v. Ventresca*, 308 U.S. 102, 85 S.Ct. 741 (1965); *Aguilar v. Texas*, 378 U.S. 108, 84 S.Ct. 1509 (1964); *Jones v. United States*, 362 U.S. 257, 80 S.Ct. 725 (1960).

The Fourth Amendment protects a person's privacy in many settings, particularly in a person's home: "the right of the people to be secure in their houses...shall not be violated". Probable cause that certain items subject to seizure are in a dwelling cannot of itself justify a warrantless search. Absent exigent circumstances, the house may not be entered without a warrant. *Payton v. New York*, 445 U.S. 573, 100 S.Ct. 1371 (1979). Obviously, what is found in an unlawful search will not justify the illegal search.

Probable cause for a warrantless search exists when the totality of the circumstances allow the conclusion that there is fair probability that contraband or evidence of crime will be found in a particular location. *State v. Pittman*, 683 So. 2d 748 (La. App. 5 Cir. 1996).

B. Warrantless searches - Cases establishing probable cause.

In order to search someone or some place without a warrant, an officer needs probable cause and exigent circumstances. The following cases demonstrate the probable cause needed for warrantless searches.

A reliable informant told an officer that the defendant regularly carried drugs from a house to his girlfriend's apartment in the late afternoon. One day at 4:10 p.m., some officers observed the defendant leave this house carrying a brown paper bag. He drove to his girlfriend's apartment. As he exited his car, he looked back and forth before retrieving the bag from his car. After he entered his girlfriend's apartment, he placed the bag inside the apartment, and returned to his car. When they approached him at his car, they asked him if he stayed at the apartment. He replied that he did not. After they told him that they saw him enter the apartment with a key, he told them that he stayed there with his girlfriend. They entered the apartment and searched the bag. *State v. Sterling*, 641 So. 2d 696 (La. App. 4 Cir. 1994).

The following circumstances provided probable cause to believe that the brown paper bag contained contraband, i.e. narcotics: Information provided by a reliable informant was corroborated by the independent surveillance by the police; the officers knew that the defendant had been arrested in the past for narcotics violations; they knew that the apartment was located in a high drug trafficking area; and the defendant's initial statement was contradicted by the officer's surveillance, and then changed by the defendant. Therefore, there was probable cause to search the bag for narcotics. *State v. Sterling*, supra.

A confidential informant told an officer that a black male carrying cocaine would arrive at Lake Charles around 8:30 p.m., from Houston, by way of a Greyhound Bus. The informant described this black male as a man of medium build in his early 20's who would be wearing a baseball cap and carrying a handbag . At 8:15 p.m., the officers in Lake Charles observed a man matching this description exit the Greyhound Bus from Houston and enter a taxi cab. After the officers stopped the cab, they searched the suspect's luggage. *State v. Hutchinson*, 620 So. 2d 1205 (La. App. 3 Cir. 1993).

They knew that the informant was reliable because this informant provided information in the past which led to narcotics arrests. They had probable cause to search the suspect's luggage because the informant predicted future acts of the suspect and those acts occurred and were corroborated by police surveillance. Thus, there was probable cause to believe that the informant's unverified allegations of drug possession were true. *State v. Hutchinson*, supra.

A neighbor at the defendant's request called the police to report a stabbing and to request that they go to the defendant's apartment. The defendant allowed the police officers to enter into her apartment. They found the defendant's boyfriend dead outside the bathroom. She told the officers that, after he had staggered into the apartment, he said that he had been stabbed in another residence. Then, she told the officers that the victim collapsed in the hall outside the bathroom. They noticed, in the bathroom, a bloody towel in the lavatory as well as blood on a handle of a closet door next to the lavatory. They opened the closet door. The officers had a fair probability to believe that evidence of a homicide would be found in the closet because they had evidence of a stabbing, a bloody towel in the lavatory next to the closet, and blood on the closet door. The officers had probable cause to conduct a warrantless search of the closet. *State v. Brady*, 585 So. 2d 524 (La. 1991).

Officers were flagged down by a pedestrian who said that a black male, on a bicycle, was selling drugs on a nearby street corner. This person was wearing a white T-shirt and purple pants with the letters LSU on the side. The officers found the defendant, on a bicycle, who matched the description given by the pedestrian at that street corner. They approached and told him to open his clenched fist. He did so and the officers found crack cocaine. There was probable cause to search the defendant's fist because they were told moments before that a person exactly matching the defendant description was selling drugs and because the defendant's clenched fist probably held the drugs. *State v. Parker*, 645 So. 2d 1309 (La. App. 4 Cir. 1994).

C. Warrantless searches - Cases not establishing probable cause.

The following cases indicate insufficient evidence of probable cause for a warrantless search.

While patrolling a high-crime area, an officer observed a group of individuals, including the defendant, sitting in front of a closed bar at 9:30 a.m. The officer exited his vehicle and approached the defendant and the others. As the officer was asking these persons what they were doing there, he noticed that the defendant had a black case in his left hand. The officer asked the defendant what was in his left hand. When the defendant refused to answer him and began to turn away, the officer seized the item from the defendant. The search of the defendant's left hand was illegal because there was not probable cause that the search would uncover contraband. *State v. Thibodeaux*, 531 So. 2d 284 (La. App. 3 Cir. 1987).

An informant told officers that the defendant sold narcotics, from his apartment, to the informant within the last 72 hours. The officers went to the private apartment complex where the defendant lived. One of the officers pushed open an unlocked solid black gate in order to secure entry into the courtyard and in turn enter into this private apartment building. After entering, he concealed himself on a balcony to watch the activity below. He observed what appeared to be a drug transaction involving the defendant. The officer entered and searched the courtyard without probable cause of finding any evidence of a crime or finding any contraband. The informant's tip was not reliable enough to establish probable cause because the informant was never tested before, and the tip was not corroborated prior to the illegal search. Therefore, the results of the search were suppressed. *State v. Karston*, 588 So. 2d 165 (La. App. 4 Cir. 1991).

After the officers stopped the defendant, they frisked him for weapons. They did not feel or find any weapons but instead felt a matchbox. They further detained the defendant, searched him, seized the matchbox and found cocaine inside it. There was no probable cause to believe that the matchbox contained any contraband. Therefore, there was no probable cause to search or seize the matchbox. *State v. Williams*, 613 So. 2d 259 (La. App. 1 Cir. 1992).

While on routine patrol, officers saw four men and the defendant standing in a parking lot. Two of the men turned away, removed their hands from their pockets, and put their hands back into their pockets. Neither of these persons actions were indicative of criminal activity. There were no signs of criminal activity, yet the officers still searched the defendant. The officers lacked probable cause to search the defendant as well as the reasonable suspicion to frisk him. *State v. Bourgeois*, 609 So. 2d 1003 (La. App. 5 Cir. 1992).

D. Warrantless searches - Valid Consent - Prerequisites.

An individual may waive his or her Fourth Amendment rights by giving voluntary and intelligent consent to a warrantless search of his or her person, property, or premises. *Bumper v. North Carolina*, 391 U.S. 543 (1968).

There is no bright line test of voluntariness and no one factor that in itself will be determinative. The form of the consent itself is not determinative since a valid consent can be oral, written or implied by specific conduct. In determining "consent", the Courts will assess various factors: whether the defendant is in custody, whether he has been threatened or coerced, any deception by the police, and the defendant's background.

Consent to search a container will generally give permission to search the items found within the container. *United States v. Smith*, 901 F.2d 1116 (D.C. Cir. 1990). Officers should use a written signed consent form prior to the search to specify the place to be searched and all items within that place.

Consensual search is an exception to both warrant and probable cause requirements for a warrantless search. *State v. Crews*, 674 So. 2d 1082 (La. App. 2d 1996). The state has the burden of proof to show that the consent to search was freely and voluntarily given. *State v. Crews*, supra. An oral consent to search is valid. *State v. Crews*, supra.

E. Warrantless searches - Valid Consent - By Defendant.

The defendant can consent to a search by signing a consent form or by orally consenting to an officer's request to search.

After the officer completed the background check on the driver, the officer asked the driver for his consent to search his motor home. The driver signed the consent form after having it explained to him and silently reading the form itself. The driver's consent to search his motor home was freely and voluntarily given. *State v. Bostic*, 637 So. 2d 591 (La. App. 2 Cir. 1994), writ denied 643 So. 2d 159 (La. 1994).

An informant told an officer that the defendant returned from Houston that day with a shipment of illegal drugs. This officer told this information to some other officers who went to the defendant's trailer. When these officers asked the defendant if they could enter, he allowed them to enter. While they were in the defendant's trailer, they observed a marijuana cigarette in an ashtray on a coffee table. The defendant consented to the officers' entry. *State v. Williams*, 608 So. 2d 266 (La. App. 3 Cir 1992).

F. Warrantless searches - Valid Consent - By Third Party.

A related area of "consent" is whether or not a third party's consent to enter is valid. In *Illinois v. Rodriquez*, 497 U.S. 177, 110 S.Ct. 2793, the Supreme Court held that a third party's consent was valid when the officers reasonably (though erroneously) believed that the consenting person was a resident of the premises or had common authority over the premises. Generally, a third party who has joint access or control over the premises can consent to a search of areas where he or she exercises joint control but not over areas where the defendant has exclusive control. *United States v. Matlock*, 415 U.S. 14 (1974).

A case in which a third party provided consent was in *State v. Melbert*, 649 So. 2d 740 (La. App. 3 Cir. 1994). An officer received a tip from an informant, who previously provided reliable tips which led to arrests and convictions, that the defendant trafficked in cocaine and possessed a large amount of it where he lived. The officer who talked to the owner of the house where the defendant lived, told her this information and obtained her consent to search her house. He found a closed boot bag in the defendant's room. The officer searched the boot bag and found some cocaine inside. *State v. Melbert*, supra.

Homeowner could give permission for police to search a room in which the defendant was staying as a guest. Defendant did not have any expectation of privacy for three reasons. His room was open to the rest of the house at all times. He shared storage space in the room with other household members. Moreover, he could stay solely at the discretion of the homeowner. Had the officer seen any contraband or evidence of a crime in plain view in the room, the officer would have been entitled to take such evidence because the officer was entitled to be there. *State v. Melbert*, supra.

On the other hand, the homeowner's consent to search the defendant's room did not give the officer the right to search through the defendant's boot bag. Although he was a guest in the home of another who had use of the room, the defendant could expect his personal belongings kept in a boot bag not to be searched by the police without his permission. Thus, the cocaine found in the boot bag was suppressed. *State v. Melbert*, supra.

G. Warrantless searches - Incident to Lawful Arrest - Person.

A warrantless search without probable cause is permitted incident to a lawful arrest. There must be probable cause to arrest that person before they can be searched pursuant to a lawful arrest. Often such a search will reveal contraband or evidence of another crime.

The U.S. Supreme Court in *Chimel v. California*, 395 U.S. 752 (1969) ruled that warrantless searches are permitted on persons arrested. There are several requirements for these searches incident to arrest. First, the arrest itself must be valid (based on probable cause). Then the items to be searched must be associated with the arrestee and under the exclusive control of the arrestee. The search incident to arrest may then be based on: a need to locate identification of a suspect; exigent circumstances demanding location of weapons used in a crime; or safeguarding evidence that may be discarded or destroyed. *Chimel v. California*, supra.

An "accelerated booking search" will not justify a search incident to arrest. A delayed station house search may, however, be considered justified under some circumstances when the search incident to the arrest could not be conducted in the field. *Illinois v. Lafayette*, 462 U.S. 640 (1983).

A search incident to an arrest must take place "contemporaneously" (during or immediately after) the arrest. *United States v. Chadwick*, 433 U.S. 1 (1977). As long as probable cause for an arrest exists prior to the undertaking of any search of the person, it does not matter whether the search immediately precedes the formal arrest. *Rawlings v. Kentucky*, 448 U.S. 98 (1980).

The officers lawfully arrested the defendant. As an officer handcuffed the defendant's left arm, he felt a bulge in the defendant's left sleeve. Then, the button of this sleeve ripped open, allowing money to spill out. Then, this officer saw a clear plastic bag containing cocaine in the defendant's clenched right hand. Because the officer was entitled to search the defendant's left wrist area and the defendant's right hand, the money and the bag containing cocaine could be searched and seized. *State v. Lassere*, 683 So. 2d 812 (La. App. 5 Cir. 1996).

An officer lawfully detained the defendant. The officer noticed a bulge in the defendant's pocket. Then, the defendant was seen putting something into his mouth. At that point, the officer had probable cause to arrest the defendant for drug possession. The officer ordered the defendant to spit out what was in his mouth. The defendant spit out packets of heroin. The officer ordering the defendant to spit out what was in his mouth was a search incident to a lawful arrest because there was probable cause to arrest the defendant. *State v. Herbert*, 669 So. 2d 499 (La. App. 4 Cir. 1996), writ denied, 675 So. 2d 1117 (La. 1996).

H. Warrantless searches - Incident to Lawful Arrest - Areas and Items around Person Arrested.

When a warrantless search is permitted on a person just arrested, the area around that person may be searched.

There is a need to make a contemporaneous search incident to a lawful custodial arrest based on the need to remove any weapons and to prevent concealment or destruction of evidence. *Chimel v. California*, supra. The scope of the search is the area within the "immediate control" of the defendant; the area from within which a defendant might gain possession of a weapon or destructible evidence. That area includes a room in which an arrest might occur, but not a search of all the desk drawers or concealed areas in the room.

When law enforcement officers effect a lawful custodial arrest of an occupant of a car, they may search the passenger compartment. They may search the contents of any containers, found within the passenger compartment, regardless of whether such containers are opened or closed. A glove compartment is considered a container. *New York v. Belton*, 453 U.S. 454 (1981).

While officers were executing an arrest warrant, they arrested the defendant at the front door of his apartment. A gun was found behind some objects on a shelf in a closet in the apartment. The gun, because it was not readily accessible or in immediate control of the defendant, could not be seized incident to a lawful arrest. Therefore, the gun was suppressed. *State in the Interest of Jynes*, 626 So. 2d 457 (La. App. 4 Cir. 1993).

I. Warrantless searches - Exigent Circumstances.

An officer often has probable cause to search but because of the urgency of the situation does not have time to obtain a warrant. The State has the burden of proving the specific exigency that justified the entry of a building or vehicle.

Exigent circumstances are those circumstances that would cause a reasonable officer to believe that entry was necessary to prevent physical harm to the officer or others, the destruction of relevant evidence, the escape of the suspect, or some other situation that might frustrate law enforcement efforts.

The fact that exigent circumstances existed at some point during an investigation will not necessarily justify a warrantless entry "if there is a period of unnecessary delay during which the exigency evaporates or the police might have obtained a warrant." *Vale v. Louisiana*, 399 U.S. 30, 90 S.Ct. 1969 (1970).

"If the exigency arises because of unreasonable and deliberate delay by the officer, it is not an exigent circumstance capable of dispensing with the requirement of a warrant." *United States v. Curran*, 498 F.2d 30, 34 (9th Cir. 1974).

Under the Exigent Circumstances exceptions to a search warrant requirement, officers may make a warrantless entry into building only if two conditions are met. First, there must be probable cause to believe the building contains contraband or evidence of crime. Second, there must be exigent circumstances to justify a warrantless entry. *State v. Ennis*, 676 So. 2d 196 (La. App. 4 Cir. 1996).

The potential escape of a suspect, avoidance of a violent confrontation that could cause injury, and destruction of evidence may be exigent circumstances that justify a warrantless entry into a building. *State v. Laird*, 674 So. 2d 425 (La. App. 4 Cir. 1996).

An informant told the police that the defendant had a large quantity of marijuana in his home that he was planning to sell to others soon after the informant left. Officers who were unable to secure a search warrant in time, decided to act to prevent loss of narcotics and "buy money" marked for later identification. An officer standing at the front door of the defendant's home viewed objects that he recognized as contraband. "Exigent circumstances" justified warrantless entry into the defendant's home. *State v. Killian*, 677 So. 2d 487 (La. App. 3 Cir. 1996).

Officers had probable cause to arrest the suspect based on the informant's information and the suspect's discarding of what appeared to be cocaine while fleeing from the officers. Exigent circumstances existed in that the suspect might escape or destroy evidence if the officers did not follow him into the house. The officers were also justified in entering the house to search and arrest the defendant because she slammed the door on the officer and thereby assisted the suspect in attempting his escape. *State v. Byas*, 648 So. 2d 37 (La. App. 4 Cir. 1994), supra.

Another type of exception similar to exigent circumstances is the emergency exception to the search warrant. Probable cause is not required to enter a residence pursuant to the emergency exception. This exception is demonstrated in *State v. Copeland*, 631 So. 2d 1223 (La. App. 5 Cir. 1994) when backup officers arrived on the scene two minutes after the detective investigating gunshots exited the apartment. The detective had checked the victim for pulse and found none. It was reasonable for the backup officers to enter the apartment to ascertain the need for medical assistance or to confirm the death. Also the officers had to enter the apartment because there was a two-year-old in it for whom immediate assistance was necessary. *State v. Copeland*, supra.

J. Warrantless searches - Abandoned Property.

Police can conduct a warrantless search on property that is voluntarily abandoned. The police need no probable cause for such a search. However, a person does not voluntarily abandon property when the abandonment results from police misconduct. *United States v. Lara*, 638 F.2d 892, 895 (5th Cir. 1981).

When an individual abandons an item of personal property, he relinquishes a reasonable expectation of privacy in the discarded item. When persons fleeing from police officers drop contraband, the contraband is admissible as abandoned property. *California v. Hodari*, 499 U.S. 621, 111 S.Ct. 1547 (1991). Likewise, the contents of a trash can found in the defendant's hotel room after the defendant checked out, is abandoned property. Thus, officers could search the trash can without a warrant. *Abel v. United States*, 362 U.S. 217, 80 S.Ct. 683 (1960).

Another situation where property is deemed abandoned is when a person discards garbage by setting it out on the street. This discarded garbage is abandoned property that may be seized without a warrant. *California v. Greenwood*, 486 U.S. 35, 40, 108 S.Ct. 1625, 1628 (1988).

A bank bag discovered in a trash bin located near a trailer where the defendant had been staying was abandoned property and subject to seizure without warrant. *State v. Strickland*, 683 So. 2d 218 (La. 1996), rehearing denied.

The defendant saw flashing lights on an unmarked squad car, walked off toward the alley, and threw a brown object with a white lid onto the street. Because this evidence was abandoned by the defendant prior to the alleged unlawful intrusion, such evidence was legally obtained by the police. *State v. Bell*, 709 So. 2d 921 (La. App. 5 Cir. 1998).

On the other hand, the discovery of a bag containing a gun was a direct result of an illegal stop and could not be lawfully seized. The defendant had placed the bag under the police car after being unlawfully stopped. The defendant only abandoned the property after being stopped. *State v. McBarry*, 699 So. 2d 127 (La. App. 4 Cir. 1997).

K. Warrantless searches - Administrative searches.

An administrative search is conducted pursuant to a regulatory scheme designed to further specific governmental goals. The search is conducted by the government to regulate activities that historically and typically are subject to scrutiny by the government. The Courts will consider factors such as whether the intrusion on privacy interest was minimal, whether the governmental interest is substantial, whether there are safeguards to ensure an individual's expectation of privacy and whether these safeguards are subject to unregulated or unlimited discretionary inspection.

Saacks v. City of New Orleans, 687 So. 2d 432 (La. App. 4 Cir. 1996), rehearing denied, demonstrates a valid warrantless administrative search based on less than probable cause. The defendant was a police officer under investigation for illegal involvement in gambling. An anonymous phone call indicated that records of the defendant's private detail business would be found in his police department office. The department's operational manual provided that as a condition of employment, a police department office was subject to search upon the request of a superior. Since the defendant's supervisor agreed to the search and supervised it and since the defendant was already under investigation, the search of the defendant's office was a legal administrative search. There was no need for probable cause to conduct the search. The public's interest in stopping police misconduct outweighed the defendant's privacy interest. *Saacks v. City of New Orleans*, supra.

Administrative safety searches of airports, courthouses, and schools may also be authorized. *New York v. Burger*, 479 U.S. 812 (1987); *Donovan v. Dewey*, 452 U.S. 594 (1981); *Camara v. Municipal Court*, 387 U.S. 523 (1967).

L. Warrantless searches - Border searches.

A long-standing exception to the warrant requirement permits a warrantless inspection, without probable cause, of individuals who enter the country. *United States v. Ramsey*, 431 U.S. 606, 619, 97 S.Ct. 1972, 1980 (1977).

A person's luggage and other belongings may be routinely searched at a border without a warrant and without probable cause. A border search that goes beyond the routine may be justified by reasonable suspicion, a lesser standard than probable cause. *United States v. Oriakhi*, 57 F.3d 1290 (4th Cir. 1995).

The border search exception extends to routine searches at the nation's borders, irrespective of whether persons or effects are entering or exiting the country. *United States v. Oriakhi*, supra. Also see *Julian v. United States*, 463 U.S. 1308, 103 S.Ct. 3522 (1983).

M. Warrantless searches - Open fields.

The protection of the Fourth Amendment, generally, does not extend to open fields and land where an individual does not take precautions to exclude the public from entry. An officer can search open fields without a warrant and without probable cause because there is no expectation of privacy for items contained in open fields. This is demonstrated in *State v. Green*, 683 So. 2d 1292 (La. App. 3 Cir. 1996).

In this case a plastic bottle containing crack cocaine was first discovered in a vacant lot by a police officer, who placed his initials and badge number on it. It was next seen in, and recovered from, the defendant's hands by the same officer after he saw the defendant retrieve the container from underneath a tire in the lot. The defendant could not have a reasonable expectation of privacy in an article left in such a location. Warrantless search and seizure yielding bottle containing crack cocaine fell within the "open fields" exception to the search warrant requirement. *State v. Green*, 683 So. 2d 1292 (La. App. 3 Cir. 1996).

N. Warrantless seizures - Plain View - General.

Under the "plain view" doctrine, officers can make a warrantless seizure of contraband, evidence or instruments of a crime, when these items are in open view and the officer makes his observation from a lawful vantage point. Two requirements for "plain view" seizures are:

1) an officer must have the right to be in the position from which he makes his observation; and 2) it must be immediately apparent that the items are evidence of a crime, contraband, or otherwise subject to seizure. *Arizona v. Hicks*, 480 U.S. 321 (1987). Prior to *Arizona v. Hicks*, supra, there was another requirement that the discovery of the item seized in plain view be inadvertent. This means that the officers must not have intended to discover the item. Rather, the discovery must have been accidental.

Although some courts in Louisiana have eliminated the requirement that the item seized be discovered inadvertently, *State v. Williams*, 608 So. 2d 266 (La. App. 3 Cir 1992), other courts still require that the discovery of the item seized be inadvertent. *State v. Laird*, 674 So. 2d 425 (La. App. 4 Cir. 1996).

In Louisiana, therefore, it is safe to meet the three conditions of the "plain view" doctrine. There must be prior justification for intrusion into the protected area. It must be immediately apparent without close inspection that the items are evidence or contraband. The evidence must be discovered "inadvertently". Then, an officer can safely seize evidence seen in plain view. *State v. Laird*, 674 So. 2d 425 (La. App. 4 Cir. 1996).

The area of the search is limited to that within the immediate control of the defendant, *Chimel v. California*, supra, or the "lunge, reach, and grasp of the defendant". *New York v. Belton*, 453 U.S. 454 (1981). The area of the search may be extended by the movement of the arrested person. *Washington v. Chrisman*, 455 U.S. 1 (1982). In this case, where the defendant entered his home after his arrest, the police were authorized "to remain literally at the arrestee's elbow and seize any contraband in plain view". *Washington v. Chrisman*, supra.

O. Warrantless seizures - Plain View - Right of officer to be where he was at the time of discovery.

Under the "plain view" doctrine, the officer must have the right to be in the position from which he makes his observation. In other words, the officer must make his observations from a lawful vantage point. One of the ways in which an officer can be at a lawful vantage point is demonstrated in *State v. Williams*, 608 So. 2d 266 (La. App. 3 Cir 1992).

In this case an informant told an officer that the defendant had returned from Houston that day with a shipment of illegal drugs. The officer told this information to some other officers who went to the defendant's trailer. When these officers asked the defendant if they could enter, he allowed them. While in the defendant's trailer, they observed a marijuana cigarette in an ashtray on a coffee table. The officers had a right to be where they observed the marijuana cigarette because the defendant had consented to their entry and the defendant agreed to talk to them in the room where the ashtray was located. *State v. Williams*, supra.

Another way in which an officer can be in a lawful vantage point is when the officer is executing a search warrant in a residence. This is demonstrated in *State in the Interest of Jynes*, 626 So. 2d 457 (La. App. 4 Cir. 1993).

In this case, a hat and plaque that were in plain view of officers in the living room of an apartment where officers were executing an arrest warrant were lawfully seized. The officers had a right to be where they were because of the arrest warrant. *State in the Interest of Jynes*, supra.

In *State v. Karston*, 588 So. 2d 165 (La. App. 4 Cir. 1991), (see discussion supra, "IV. Warrantless Searches and Seizures, C. Warrantless searches - Cases not establishing probable cause"), the officer did not have a right to be in the area where he observed a crime. Thus, because the officer did not have a right to be where he was at the time of discovery, the evidence had to be suppressed. *State v. Karston*, supra.

P. Warrantless seizures - Plain View - Immediate apparency of the illegality of seized items.

When an officer is in a place where he has a right to be, items in plain view can only be seized when it is immediately apparent without close inspection that the items are evidence or contraband. This is demonstrated in *State v. Williams*, supra. In this case, an informant told an officer that the defendant returned from Houston that day with a shipment of illegal drugs. The officer told this information to some other officers who went to the defendant's trailer. When these officers asked the defendant if they could enter, he allowed them. While they were in the defendant's trailer, one of the officers observed a marijuana cigarette in an ashtray on a coffee table. This officer knew immediately that the cigarette was a marijuana cigarette. Therefore the marijuana cigarette could be seized. *State v. Williams*, supra.

Q. Warrantless seizures - Plain View - Inadvertent discovery.

Louisiana case law in the area of inadvertent discovery, indicates that when there is a planned search, the seizure of items may not be in plain view.

The officers were specifically called by a neighbor to inspect the defendant's property. The neighbor suspected that some of the plants that the defendant was growing on his property were marijuana plants. The officers did not visit the neighbor for some other reason, and then happen to notice the marijuana. This was a planned search. Therefore, the marijuana plants could not be justly seized pursuant to the plain view doctrine. *State v. Fearn*, 345 So. 2d 468 (La. 1977).

On the other hand, *State v. Howard*, 448 So. 2d 713 (La. App. 1 Cir. 1984), cert. den. 449 So. 2d 1355 (La. 1984) does permit a seizure of items seen in plain view when the finding of items is not wholly unexpected. In this case, the initial intrusion into the defendant's home was supported by a warrant authorizing a search of the entire home for marijuana previously observed in the defendant son's bedroom. Thus, officers were permitted to search the master bedroom where closed suitcases and wrapped bales of marijuana were found. The opening of the suitcases was valid, even though the officers suspected that the suitcases contained other drugs brought in by the defendant and the search was delayed until the defendant arrived home with the suitcases. The seizing of the cocaine in the suitcases was therefore valid under the plain view rule. *State v. Howard*, supra.

State v. Howard, supra, gives a definition of "inadvertancy" for the purpose of the plain view exception. "Inadvertancy," means that the police must not have probable cause to believe that the evidence not listed in the warrant will be found, but the finding be not wholly unexpected. *State v. Howard*, supra.

R. Warrantless searches - Caretaker Doctrine.

The U.S. Supreme Court adopted the community caretaker function in *Cady v. Dombrowski*, 413 U.S. 433, 93 S. Ct. 2523 (1973). In this case the Court stated:

"Local police officers, unlike federal officers, frequently investigate vehicle accidents in which there is no claim of criminal liability and engage in what, for want of a better term, may be described as community caretaking functions, totally divorced from the detection, investigation, or acquisition of evidence relating to the violation of a criminal statute." *Cady v. Dombrowski*, supra.

S. Warrantless searches - Protective Sweep.

A limited protective sweep of the premises is permitted based on the exigent circumstance surrounding a particular arrest. A protective sweep is a very quick and limited pass through the premises to check for third persons who may destroy evidence or pose a threat to the officers. It is normally conducted after an arrest or detention occurs inside the premises but has been permitted when the arrest or detention occurs immediately outside the premises.

Under *Maryland v. Buie*, 494 U.S. 325 (1990), the Supreme Court ruled that a protective sweep is permitted if the officer reasonably believes that the area harbors a person posing a danger to the officer or to the destruction of contraband or evidence. Facts and rational inferences from those facts warrant a reasonable officer to believe that an individual posing a danger is in the area to be swept. *Maryland v. Buie*, supra.

There is no crime scene exception to the warrant requirement. Therefore, when a crime occurs inside premises, the police are limited to a preliminary warrantless search related to the exigencies of the situation. *Mincey v. Arizona*, 437 U.S. 385, 98 S.Ct. 2408 (1978).

When officers receive information that shooting has occurred in the area, they are entitled to make a prompt warrantless search of such area to see if other persons are in need of aid or if the perpetrator is still on the premises. The officers are entitled to conduct such a warrantless search of a residence, if the shooting occurred outside the residence. *State v. Aspin*, 449 So. 2d 49 (La. App. 1 Cir. 1984).

As demonstrated in *State v. Ludwig*, 423 So. 2d 1073 (La. 1982), the protective sweep is very similar to the emergency exception to the search warrant requirement. In this case, officers, who learned that the murder victim and the suspect had been in a recent altercation, observed blood and a shell casing outside the suspect's motel room. The officers searched the suspect's motel room. The warrantless limited search of the room, to determine whether anyone was present, was valid as an emergency exception to the warrant requirement. *State v. Ludwig*, 423 So. 2d 1073 (La. 1982).

In *State in the Interest of Jynes*, supra, the officers went beyond the scope of a protective sweep. In this case, the officers were executing an arrest warrant. They arrested the defendant at the front door of his apartment. A gun found in the closet of the apartment was not the product of a permissive protective sweep. The gun was found behind some objects on a shelf in a closet. The need for the protective sweep ceased once the officers made the arrest at the front door. The gun, therefore was suppressed. *State in the Interest of Jynes*, supra.

T. Warrantless searches - Probationers and parolees.

In Louisiana, an officer does not need probable cause to search a probationer or a parolee. A warrantless search of a probationer is permitted if there is reasonable suspicion of criminal activity. *State v. Thomas*, 683 So. 2d 885 (La. App. 4 Cir. 1996).

Reasonable suspicion of criminal activity justifying a warrantless search is illustrated in *State v. Thomas*, supra. In this case, the defendant-probationer drove to his probation officer's office to take a drug test. After the defendant failed the drug test, he was arrested and his car was searched for controlled substances. The probation officer had reasonable suspicion that drug paraphernalia or drugs would be in the car because the defendant who just failed a drug test recently drove the car. The probation officer's warrantless search of the probationer's car was reasonable when the search was conducted after the probationer had been placed under arrest for testing positive for cocaine during a recent urine test. *State v. Thomas*, supra.

U. Warrantless searches - Vehicles - General.

Once the police have probable cause, they may search a vehicle as thoroughly as a magistrate could authorize in a search warrant. *United States v. Ross*, 456 U.S. 798, 102 S.Ct. 2157 (1982). Probable cause permits contraband goods concealed and illegally transported in a vehicle to be searched for, without a warrant. *Carroll v. United States*, 267 U.S. 132, 45 S.Ct. 280 (1925). The Automobile Exception doctrine was developed from these cases.

The Automobile Exception developed from two concepts. First, there is a reduced expectation of privacy for vehicles on public highways. The second concept is related to the exigent circumstances exception. It may not be practical to obtain a warrant since the vehicle can be quickly moved. The Automobile Exception does not permit the search of the trunk or any area outside of the passenger compartment without probable cause.

Courts have consistently upheld warrantless searches of motor vehicles based on the reduced expectation of privacy (use and open viewing on the public highways) and based on the mobility and need to act quickly when acting on probable cause to search for and seize contraband.

Under the Automobile Exception, the police may search a vehicle and the containers within it when they have probable cause to believe contraband or evidence of a crime is contained within the vehicle. *United States v. Ross*, 456 U.S. 798 (1982) and *California v. Acevedo*, 500 U.S. 565, 111 S.Ct. 1982 (1991).

If there is probable cause to search a vehicle when it is stopped on a highway, then the officers may either make a warrantless search on the highway or take the car to the station. *Chambers v. Maroney*, 399 U.S. 42, 90 S.Ct. 1975 (1970) and *California v. Carney*, 471 U.S. 386, 105 S.Ct. 2066 (1985).

Under the Automobile Exception, if there is probable cause to search a car, the car may be searched even if it has been immobilized. A warrantless search of the car was conducted 6 hours after the drug defendant's arrest. The search was conducted after the car was stored in a wrecker yard. This warrantless search was reasonable and justified under the automobile exception to the warrant requirement. Justification to conduct such search did not vanish once the car was immobilized. *State v. Laviolette*, 576 So. 2d 1000 (La. App. 3 Cir. 1991), writ denied 581 So. 2d 683 (La. 1991).

Under limited circumstances a car may be searched when there is not probable cause that the car contains contraband. This occurs when there is reasonable suspicion that the person stopped or one of the passengers has immediate access to a gun (i.e. the gun is in the passenger compartment of the vehicle). A frisk of the passenger compartment of a vehicle is permitted if there is a reasonable suspicion that the passenger compartment contains a gun.

Officers, pulling over a speeding car, observed the driver make a motion like he was putting something under his seat. This motion gave the officers reasonable suspicion that the driver hid a gun under the front seat of his car because many suspects hide guns under their seats when stopped. After he exited his car, the officers searched under his seat and found drugs. Because they had reasonable suspicion that the driver had a gun in a location in his car where he could gain immediate control of it, the officers could conduct a frisk search under the seat for a gun. A frisk for weapons is permitted of the passenger area of a car, even if the defendant exited the car. *State v. Davis*, 612 So. 2d 256 (La. App. 4 Cir. 1992).

There was no reasonable expectation of privacy in a vehicle identification number (VIN). A motorist must expect that the State will on occasion need to determine the VIN of his vehicle. The reasonable expectation of privacy in the VIN is thereby diminished. This is especially true when a driver committed a traffic violation. *New York v. Class*, 475 U.S. 106, 106 S.Ct. 960 (1986).

V. Warrantless searches - Vehicles - Cases illustrating Probable Cause.

The following cases indicate probable cause for a warrantless search of the vehicle.

Officers validly stopped the defendant's car for having tinted windows. They received conflicting stories as to where the defendant and her passenger had been and their relationship to each other. Both the defendant and passenger appeared nervous. Upon checking their criminal records, the officers noticed that the passenger had numerous narcotics violations. A narcotics dog already on the scene gave a positive indication of narcotics in the car. The officers then searched the car. The nervousness of the defendant and the passenger, their conflicting stories, the prior narcotics violations of the passenger, and the positive identification of narcotics in the car gave the officers probable cause to search the car for narcotics. *State v. Dillon*, 670 So. 2d 278 (La. App. 3 Cir. 1996).

An officer, while examining evidence for an unrelated crime, may accidentally find in plain view some evidence which may then provide the probable cause for the warrantless search of a vehicle.

The defendant just exited a car he was driving. He was in an area at night with a high amount of crime and drug dealing. An officer, by shining his light into the defendant's car, observed a knife in plain view. The officer was justified in entering the car to secure this knife and to conduct a search limited to those areas in which weapons could be placed or hidden. As the officer reached inside the car to retrieve the knife, he observed near the knife plastic wrappings with a white powdery residue that looked like cocaine. The officer was justified in seizing the plastic wrapping because the weapon and the plastic wrapping gave him probable cause to believe that the vehicle contained contraband. *State v. Barre*, 592 So. 2d 440 (La. App. 5 Cir. 1991).

Often, a statement by an occupant of the car, alone, can supply probable cause to search the car.

An officer stopped a car for being without a required inspection sticker. He found during a computer check that the driver did not have a license. After he arrested the driver for driving without a license, the officer told him that the car would be impounded and searched. When the officer asked if there were any drugs in the car, he told the officer that there were. At this point the officer had probable cause to search the car. This probable cause was augmented when the other passengers admitted that there were drugs in the car. *State v. St. Martin*, 644 So. 2d 773 (La. App. 1 Cir. 1994).

Sometimes, an odor alone can furnish probable cause that the vehicle contains contraband.

The officer stopped a car for speeding. When standing at the driver's side window, he noticed a strong smell of air freshener and a faint smell of marijuana. This smell of marijuana, when coupled with the use of air freshener to hide it, established probable cause to search the vehicle for marijuana. *State v. Reynaga*, 643 So. 2d 431 (La. App. 3 Cir. 1994).

Wildlife agents stopped a car leaving an area under watch for killing deer out of season. On approaching the car, these agents saw what appeared to be blood on the trunk of the car as well as rifles and a bloody knife in the car. The blood on the knife and on the trunk of the car, and the presence of the rifles, established probable cause that a deer carcass was inside the car. Thus, the agents had probable cause to search the car for a deer carcass. *State v. Alderman*, 285 So. 2d 193 (La. 1973).

W. Warrantless searches - Vehicles - Cases illustrating No Probable Cause.

The following cases indicate where there was insufficient evidence of probable cause for a warrantless search of a vehicle.

See *State v. Scull*, 639 So. 2d 1239 (La. App. 4 Cir. 1994) (see discussion supra, "III. Search Warrants, I. The Exclusionary Rule - Good Faith Exception") as to why there was no probable cause to search the car.

There was not probable cause to search a vehicle where an officer merely observed something transpiring between a pedestrian and the defendant, after which the defendant drove away in a reckless manner. *State v. Harris*, 504 So. 2d 156 (La. App. 2 Cir. 1987).

An officer stopped and detained the defendant for speeding. As this officer wrote out a traffic ticket (summons), another officer appeared on the scene. This second officer searched the defendant's car and found a beer can. Then this officer searched the defendant and found some marijuana on him. The defendant was arrested for possession of marijuana. The warrantless search of a motorist during a temporary detention after the motorist was stopped for speeding and after the officer decided to issue a summons for the traffic offense was unconstitutional. Thus, the marijuana found in the motorist's pocket could not be used against him. *State v. Breaux*, 329 So. 2d 696 (La. 1976).

X. Warrantless searches - Vehicles - Incident to lawful arrest.

A warrantless search of a vehicle is valid when incident to a lawful arrest. There need not be probable cause to search the vehicle. There must only be probable cause to arrest the defendant. However, the search is limited to areas under the reach or control of the arrestee. The search is based on the need to remove weapons and prevent the concealment or destruction of evidence. *New York v. Belton*, 453 U.S. 454, 101 S.Ct. 2860 (1981) and *Chimel v. California*, 395 U.S. 752, 89 S.Ct. 2034 (1969). A search of the passenger compartment and any containers, including the glove compartment, found within the passenger compartment is authorized. *United States v. McCraw*, 920 F.2d 224, 228 (4th Cir. 1990). The rule in *New York v. Belton*, supra, applies even if the person arrested was separated from the vehicle before the passenger compartment is searched. *United States v. Mans*, 999 F.2d 966 (6th Cir.), cert. denied, 114 S. Ct. 567 (1993).

The following cases demonstrate the application of the search of motor vehicles incident to a lawful arrest.

An officer attempted to stop the defendant's car for failure to have a license plate, but the defendant's car sped away. During the chase, the defendant failed to stop at a stop sign. When the officer finally stopped the defendant's car, the defendant was arrested for failure to have a license plate, failure to stop at a stop sign, and failure to obey a police officer. The officer searched the driver's side of the defendant's car. Because of the officer's reasonable suspicion that the defendant's flight was the result of the commission of another crime, and because of the various traffic offenses committed by the defendant, a warrantless search of the driver's side of the car was justified as a lawful search incident to arrest. *State v. Carter*, 663 So. 2d 152 (La. App. 3 Cir. 1995).

Seizure of marijuana from the defendant's car could not be justified as a contemporaneous search incident to a lawful custodial arrest of the defendant. The marijuana was found inside a container locked in the trunk of the car and not in the passenger compartment of the car. *State v. Carey*, 499 So. 2d 283 (La. App. 1 Cir. 1986).

Y. Warrantless searches and seizures - Vehicles - Impounding and Inventory of vehicle.

Officers may search a vehicle on the spot where it is located, if they have probable cause. However, even when they think they have probable cause, they may impound the vehicle and place it in storage until a magistrate determines that there is probable cause for a search warrant to search the vehicle.

For constitutional purposes, there is no difference between seizing and holding a vehicle before presenting a probable cause issue to a magistrate and carrying out an immediate search without a warrant. Given probable cause to search, either course is reasonable under the Fourth Amendment and the State Constitution. *State v. Pittman*, 683 So. 2d 748 (La. App. 5 Cir. 1996).

A warrantless search of an impounded car was constitutional where the warrantless search at the scene of arrest would have been constitutional and the arresting officer chose not to search the car on the scene because the location was dangerous. *State v. Redfern*, 441 So. 2d 200 (La. 1983).

An inventory search of the defendant's car pursuant to a valid arrest was proper despite the fact that the search took place in a field rather than a storage area. There was no indication that the search was a pretext for the officers to look for illegal drugs. Moreover, there were no passengers who could drive the defendant's car home after he was arrested. In addition, the car was stopped in an unsafe area of a private driveway. Furthermore, the officers had called a tow truck to impound the car for safekeeping. *State v. Cousin*, 700 So. 2d 1016 (La. App. 1 Cir. 1997).

V. ARRESTS

A. Definitions of arrest.

La. C. Cr. P. Art 201 defines "Arrest" as follows:

"Arrest is the taking of one person into custody by another. To constitute arrest there must be an actual restraint of the person. The restraint may be imposed by force or may result from the submission of the person arrested to the custody of the one arresting him or her." La. C. Cr. P. Art 201.

An "Arrest" occurs when there is actual restraint of a person and circumstances indicate the intent to effect extended restraint on the liberty of the accused. *State v. Wimberly*, 678 So. 2d 577 (La. App. 4 Cir. 1996).

An example of "actual restraint" is demonstrated in *State v. Davis*, 558 So. 2d 1379 (La. App. 5 Cir. 1990) where an arrest, rather than investigatory stop, occurred when officers who observed a suspected drug transaction drove their car into the parking lot where the transaction had taken place and ordered the defendant and his companion to put their hands on their car.

B. Statutory Authority to Arrest.

La. C. Cr. P. Art 213 provides the situations when an officer may arrest a person without a warrant. Under La. C. Cr. P. Art 213, a peace officer may, without a warrant, arrest a person when:

(1) The person to be arrested has committed an offense in his presence, If the arrest is for a misdemeanor it must be made immediately or on close pursuit;

(2) The person to be arrested has committed a felony, although not in the presence of the officer;

(3) The peace officer has reasonable cause to believe the person to be arrested has committed an offense, although not in the presence of the officer; or

(4) The peace officer received positive and reliable information that another peace officer from this state holds an arrest warrant, or a peace officer of another state or the federal government holds an arrest warrant for a felony offense.

A peace officer in close pursuit of a person to be arrested, who is making an arrest pursuant to this article, may enter another jurisdiction in this state and make the arrest. La. C. Cr. P. Art 213.

C. Right to resist illegal arrest.

A suspect has a limited right to resist arrest in Louisiana. A suspect can use such force as is necessary to resist arrest when the police have no probable cause to arrest the suspect.

Officers responded to a unrelated incident at an apartment complex of teenagers drinking and reportedly using a gun. Officers sought to clear an area, approximately 50 yards away, where a group of bystanders were gathered. All of the bystanders, except for the defendant, cleared out of the way. The officer told the defendant to move with the others. The defendant still refused to move and told the officer that "the only problem was with the police". The officer then arrested him for the misdemeanor charges of criminal trespass and interfering with a police officer. However, as the officer was arresting him, the defendant pulled back from the officer. Other officers and a police dog came to subdue the defendant. During the ensuing struggle when the defendant lashed out at one officer, the defendant's ring accidentally hit an officer's face and caused a long cut. The defendant had a right to use such force as was necessary to resist arrest when the officers lacked probable cause to arrest him for the misdemeanor charges. Moreover, the defendant was not guilty of battery under these circumstances. *City of Monroe v. Goldston*, 661 So. 2d 428 (La. 1995).

D. Requirements for arrest pursuant to a warrant.

La. C. Cr. P. Art 203 deals with the form and contents of the arrest warrant. La. C. Cr. P. Art 202 deals with the time when a warrant of arrest may be issued. La. C. Cr. P. Art 202 provides that a warrant of arrest may be issued by a magistrate when:

(1) The person making the complaint executes an affidavit specifying, to his best knowledge and belief, the nature, date, and place of the offense, and the name and surname of the offender if known, and of the person injured if any; and

(2) The magistrate has probable cause to believe that an offense was committed and that the person against whom the complaint was made, committed it.

Probable cause to believe that the suspect committed the offense charged for purposes of an arrest warrant is demonstrated in *State v. Haynie*, 395 So. 2d 669 (La. 1981), concurred 401 So. 2d 965 (La. 1981) where the affidavit for the arrest warrant contained the date, location, and nature of the offense, and the name of the offender. The affidavit also contained the following information: the victim had $500 taken from her on the night of the rape; a former officer and an acquaintance of the defendant saw the defendant with a large sum of money; the defendant's acquaintance told the affiant that the defendant stated that the victim gave him money on the night of the offense. *State v. Haynie*, supra.

E. Statutory Authority to Arrest - Other statutes

Other than the general statutes dealing with a warrantless arrest, La. C. Cr. P. Art 213, and arrest by warrant, La. C. Cr. P. Art 202, there are many other statutes permitting arrests. For example, under La. C. Cr. P. Art 214 a private person is allowed to make an arrest when the person arrested committed a felony, whether in or out of his presence.

A private person is not permitted to arrest a person who commits a misdemeanor. An agent of the Louisiana Department of Wildlife and Fisheries acted outside the scope of his authority in arresting defendants for possession of marijuana. Likewise, the arrest was not a valid arrest by a private citizen since marijuana possession was a misdemeanor. Therefore, evidence seized as a result of the arrest should have been suppressed. *State v. Longlois*, 374 So. 2d 1208 (La. 1979).

La. C. Cr. P. Art 226 provides that a private person who makes an arrest shall immediately turn the prisoner and all effects removed from the prisoner over to a peace officer.

Another statute, La. C. Cr. P. Art 214(2), permits a peace officer to arrest shoplifters under the following circumstances:

"A peace officer may, without a warrant, arrest a person when he has reasonable grounds to believe the person has committed a theft of goods held for sale by a merchant .... A complaint made to a police officer by a merchant or a merchant's employee or agent shall constitute reasonable cause for the officer making the arrest."

A complaint made by a merchant to a police officer alone may constitute reasonable cause to arrest a shoplifter. An officer may arrest a suspected shoplifter upon the complaint of a merchant without independently ascertaining facts supporting the merchant's complaint. *State ex re. Bailey v. City of West Monroe*, 418 So. 2d 570 (La. 1982).

La.C.Cr.P Art. 215.1C which provides that an officer can make an arrest when he finds a dangerous weapon, unlawfully possessed, during a frisk or an investigatory detention states:

"If the law enforcement officer finds a dangerous weapon, he may take and keep it until the completion of the questioning, at which time he shall either return it, if lawfully possessed, or arrest such person."

The actions of the defendant in concealing a weapon justified the stop of defendant. Officers had probable cause to arrest the defendant after they received information from police headquarters that the gun found in the defendant's possession was reported stolen. *State v. Daley*, 459 So. 2d 66 (La. App. 2 Cir. 1984), writ denied 462 So. 2d 1264 (La. 1984).

La. C. Cr. P. Art 227 permits an officer, without a warrant, to rearrest anywhere within the state any person who escapes from the officer. The defendant was placed under arrest, on a street, after he struck his brother during a fight. The defendant ran inside a house following this initial arrest. La. C. Cr. P. Art 227 authorized officers to pursue and retake the defendant inside his mother's house without a warrant. *State v. Mackey*, 519 So. 2d 162 (La. App. 4 Cir. 1987).

La. C. Cr. P. Art 106 permits limited powers to arrest for coroners; La. C. Cr. P. Art 340 permits limited powers to arrest by sureties and bailbondsmen; La. C. Cr. P. Art 231 grants limited powers to peace officers from another state who enter in close pursuit of a suspect to arrest the suspect; and R.S. § 15:1355 provides that no person shall be arrested without a warrant under the provisions of the Drug Racketeering Act, except in emergency circumstances.

F. Summons in lieu of arrest.

La. C. Cr. P. Art 208 to La. C. Cr. P. Art 211.4 provide officers the opportunity to issue a summons for defendants to appear in court instead of being arrested. A magistrate may issue a summons instead of a warrant of arrest, if he has reasonable ground to believe that the person against whom the complaint is made will appear upon a summons. La. C. Cr. P. Art 209. A summons can also be issued to order the defendant to appear for violation of probation. La. C. Cr. P. Art 899.

An officer who arrests any person for a violation of the Louisiana Highway Regulatory Act, R.S. § 32:1 to 32:399, shall issue a summons in writing to appear at a specified time and place. R.S. § 32:391. Even an arrest for purposes of a traffic violation is not like a full-scale custodial arrest.

In *State v. Breaux*, 329 So. 2d 696 (La. 1976) (see discussion supra, "IV. Warrantless Searches and Seizures, W. Warrantless searches - Vehicles - Cases illustrating No Probable Cause"), not every detention constitutes an "arrest" which justifies a search incident to an arrest. The arrests which do justify a search of the person incident to it are full custody arrests made with the purpose of booking the person for the offense charged. Although a temporary detention for issuing a speeding ticket is a type of arrest, it is not a full-scale custody arrest. In *State v. Breaux*, supra, since the defendant was only subject to a temporary detention for a speeding ticket, he was not subject to a search incident to a full-scale arrest. *State v. Breaux*, supra.

When the officer has reasonable ground to believe that the defendant committed one of the following crimes, the officer can under certain circumstances issue a written summons to the offender:

(1) Misdemeanor crime, La. C. Cr. P. Art 211; La. C. Cr. P. Art 497.

(2) Theft or illegal possession of stolen things worth at least $100 but less than $500, La. C. Cr. P. Art 211.

(3) Criminal trespass, La. C. Cr. P. Art 211.1;

(4) Issuing worthless checks, La. C. Cr. P. Art 211.2;

(5) Littering, La. C. Cr. P. Art 211.3;

(6) Driving without possession of a driver's license, La. C. Cr. P. Art 211.4;

G. Probable cause for a warrantless arrest.

Probable cause for a warrantless arrest is similar to probable cause needed for an arrest warrant.

In Louisiana, probable cause for a warrantless arrest exists when facts and circumstances known to the officer or of which he has trustworthy information are sufficient to justify a cautious man in the belief that the person to be arrested has committed a crime. *State v. White*, 674 So. 2d 1018 (La. App. 2 Cir. 1996).

H. Probable cause for a warrantless arrest - illustrative cases.

The following cases illustrate the probable cause needed for a warrantless arrest.

An informant told an officer that a black male carrying cocaine would arrive at Lake Charles around 8:30 p.m., from Houston, on a Greyhound Bus. The informant described this black male, as a man of medium build in his early 20's, who would be wearing a baseball cap and carrying a handbag . At 8:15 p.m., the Lake Charles officers observed a man matching this description exit the Greyhound Bus from Houston and enter a taxi cab. After they stopped the cab, they arrested the suspect. The informant was reliable because the informant gave information in the past which led to narcotics arrests. *State v. Hutchinson*, 620 So. 2d 1205 (La. App. 3 Cir. 1993).

The officers had probable cause to arrest the suspect because the informant's prediction of the suspect's future acts occurred. The corroborations of these acts gave them a reasonable basis to believe that the informant's unverified allegation of drug possession was true. *State v. Hutchinson*, supra.

Officers lawfully detained the defendant and a group of other people in a high drug use area. A police officer noticed the defendant trying to conceal rocklike objects under his tongue. The officers then arrested the defendant. These officers had probable cause to arrest the defendant because they had probable cause to believe that the defendant was trying to conceal crack cocaine. *State v. Johnson*, 675 So. 2d 1175 (La. App. 5 Cir. 1996).

A female, who was assaulted, notified the police with a physical description of her assailant and the make, model, color and license plate number of the assailant's car. The officers had probable cause to arrest the defendant after determining that he and the car matched the victim's description of the assailant, car, and license plate. *State v. White*, 674 So. 2d 1018 (La. App. 2 Cir. 1996).

Officers had probable cause to arrest the defendant after narcotics dogs alerted the officers to bags of cocaine found in the folds of the vinyl top in the defendant's car. *State v. Bruser*, 661 So. 2d 152 (La. App. 4 Cir. 1996).

An officer, while patrolling an area known as a place for drug trafficking, observed the defendant flag down a minivan. When it stopped, the defendant talked to the driver. These two had some type of "hand-to-hand" transaction consistent with the sale of drugs. When the officer approached the defendant, he began to run. While the officer was chasing him, he opened a matchbox and tossed it to the ground. This officer knew that matchboxes are often used by drug traffickers to store drugs. As the matchbox fell to the ground, the officer observed some small packages, containing a white powder, fall from the matchbox. At this point, the officer had probable cause to arrest the defendant for possession of drugs. *State v. Collins*, 637 So. 2d 741 (La. App. 1 Cir. 1994).

Probable cause to arrest was established because of an observed hand-to-hand transaction consistent with the sale of drugs, the defendant's flight upon seeing the officer, the defendant's abandonment of a container often used to store drugs, and the sight of packages that apparently contained drugs. *State v. Collins*, supra.

An officer observed the defendant take what appeared to be a gun from his waistband area and throw it to the ground. The officer then picked up the item and determined it to be a gun. At this point, the officer had probable cause to arrest the defendant for carrying a concealed weapon. *State v. Johnson*, 660 So. 2d 942 (La. App. 4 Cir. 1995), writ denied 666 So. 2d 1092 (La. 1996).

I. No Probable cause for a warrantless arrest - illustrative cases.

The following cases indicate the circumstances under which there was not sufficient evidence of probable cause for a warrantless arrest.

Officers arranged for an informant to make a controlled purchase of marijuana from the defendant. After he allegedly met with the defendant to purchase marijuana, the informant told the officers that the defendant was going to a house to get a scale to weigh the marijuana. The officers followed the defendant to that house. When the defendant exited the house, he was carrying a large brown paper bag. After he entered his car, the officers stopped him. The officers seized a beeper visible in the car. A search of the paper bag revealed a scale. *State v. Fogan*, 609 So. 2d 1016 (La. App. 4 Cir. 1992).

This information did not establish probable cause to arrest the defendant for attempted distribution of marijuana. There was no information as to the untested informant's reliability. Also, the officers did not witness the alleged meeting between the informant and the defendant. *State v. Fogan*, supra.

Officers at an airport observed the defendant, who carried only a purse and a carry-on bag, exit a plane from Miami. As they followed her, she walked hurriedly, and looked nervously over her shoulders. She did not claim any luggage when she passed through the baggage claim area. After she exited the airport, they asked her for her ticket. She possessed a seating stub assigned to another person. She told the officers that she bought her ticket from a man at the Miami airport. She consented to a search of her luggage which only uncovered some clothing. When asked why she carried so little; she replied that she left her belongings back in Miami. They asked her to consent to a full body search. She refused to allow a warrantless full body search. They took her into custody and forced her to walk toward their office. When they took her into custody, she was arrested. She was illegally arrested because there were not sufficient facts to justify the officers' belief that she had committed a crime. *State v. Moreno*, 619 So. 2d 62 (La. 1993).

Officers, in an area known for drugs, observed the defendant exchange currency with another man for an unknown object wrapped in white paper. The officers did not know either of the individuals. Neither individual tried to elude the police. Neither acted in a suspicious manner. The officers arrested the defendant. The officers had no probable cause to arrest the defendant because they were not justified in believing that a crime had been committed. *State v. Thornton*, 621 So. 2d 173 (La. App 4 Cir. 1993), writ denied 642 So. 2d 1307 (La. 1994).

In *City of Monroe v. Goldston*, 661 So. 2d 428 (La. 1995) (see discussion supra, "V. Arrests, C. Right to resist illegal arrest"), the officer lacked probable cause to arrest the defendant for interfering with a police officer when the defendant refused a request to clear an area 50 yards away from the site of a police investigation. At the time the officer made the request, the defendant was neither under arrest nor suspected of any crime. The ongoing investigation did not involve the defendant. Moreover, there was no evidence that his reluctance to move obstructed the investigation or the officer's efforts at crowd control. Furthermore, the investigation became delayed only after the officer grabbed his arm and attempted to arrest him.

The officer lacked probable cause to arrest him for criminal trespass when he refused a request to clear an area 50 yards away from the site of a police investigation. A month prior to this incident, another officer told the defendant to leave the apartment complex and not to return. However, there was no evidence that the officer who arrested the defendant sought to enforce this ban when he told the defendant to clear the immediate area. The officer did not ask the defendant to leave the apartment complex but rather to leave the immediate area. *City of Monroe v. Goldston*, supra.

A vehicle was stopped for a traffic violation. After the vehicle stopped, the driver fled on foot. The officer ordered the passenger out of the vehicle. After the passenger refused to exit the vehicle, the officer opened the car door, forced the passenger out of the vehicle, and arrested him. A search of the defendant incident to arrest revealed drug paraphernalia. The officer did not have probable cause to arrest the defendant for resisting an officer, when the defendant, a passenger in a vehicle stopped for a traffic violation, refused to leave the vehicle when ordered to do so by the officer. Although the defendant was interfering with the officer's investigation, the officer was not engaged in serving process, seizing property, or making an arrest pursuant to R.S. § 14:108. *State v. Green*, 706 So. 2d 536 (La. App. 5 Cir. 1997).

When an officer is not engaged in attempting to seize property, serve process, or make an arrest, then the defendant who opposes the officer is not resisting the officer within the definition of the crime of resisting an officer R.S. §14:108. *State v. Green*, 706 So. 2d 536 (La. App. 5 Cir. 1997).

VI. CONFESSIONS AND SELF-INCRIMINATION

A. *Miranda* Warnings: General overview.

The Fifth Amendment of the U.S. Constitution provides that "no person shall... be compelled in any criminal case to be a witness against himself." This provision prohibits the use of coerced confessions as evidence against the defendant.

In *Miranda v. Arizona*, 384 U.S. 436, 86 S. Ct. 1602 (1966), the U.S. Supreme Court ruled that the Fifth Amendment as applied to the states by the Fourteenth Amendment requires the state, its police officers or state attorneys to issue a warning to a suspect in custody when they wish to question this suspect. This warning, called the "*Miranda* Warning", states:

"Prior to any questioning, the person must be warned that he has the right to remain silent, that any statement he does make [can and will] be used [against him in a court of law], and that he has a right to the presence of an attorney,.... and that if he cannot afford an attorney, one will be appointed for him prior to any questioning, if he so desires." *Miranda v. Arizona*, supra.

A person is in custody for purposes of *Miranda v. Arizona*, supra, when that person has been taken into custody or otherwise deprived of his freedom of action in a significant way. Thus, any questioning begun when a person is in custody must be preceded by the *Miranda* warning. *Miranda v. Arizona*, supra.

The defendant, under investigation for murder, was handcuffed, placed in a patrol car, and taken to the homicide office. Officers later determined, before a statement was taken, that he was no longer under investigation for murder. However, the defendant was never told that he was not under investigation. He was never told that he was not under arrest, but actually was free to go. Since the defendant did not reasonably believe that he was free to leave the homicide office, he was in custody for purposes of the *Miranda* warning. Therefore, his statement must be suppressed because he had not been given a *Miranda* warning before making the statement. *State v. Garner*, 621 So. 2d 1203 (La. App. 4 Cir. 1993).

A valid inventory search was done on the defendant's car after his arrest. He remarked, after seeing an officer pull a bag of crack cocaine from the car during the inventory search, "just that little bit; you're going to charge me with just that little bit". This was a spontaneous comment that was not part of a custodial interrogation. Therefore, Miranda warnings were not necessary. *State v. Cousin*, 700 So. 2d 1016 (La. App. 1 Cir. 1997).

The defendant was not entitled to Miranda warnings because he was not in custody when he indicated that the substance found in the apartment during the consensual search was marijuana and that it belonged to him. The defendant was not the focus of investigation. Moreover, the officer asked all three occupants, in the room where the marijuana was found, at the same time, what the substance was. After the other persons said nothing, the defendant said that the substance was marijuana and that it was his. The defendant was free to leave at the time he answered the officer's questions. A warrant for his arrest was not issued until the police received a report from the drug lab confirming that the substance was marijuana. Therefore, the defendant's statement could be used against him. *State v. Nguyen*, 707 So. 2d 66 (La. App. 4 Cir. 1998).

Custodial interrogation must cease when the accused requests an attorney. It may not be resumed by officers without an attorney present unless the interrogation is thereafter initiated by the accused. *Edwards v. Arizona*, 451 U.S. 477, 101 S. Ct. 1880, 68 L. Ed. 2d 378 (1981).

The officers may obtain the consent of a defendant to waive his or her rights to remain silent as well as his or her right to have counsel present. However such consent must be made voluntarily, knowingly, and intelligently. It must not be coerced. *Miranda v. Arizona*, supra. The officers may obtain oral or written consent from the defendant after reading him or her the *Miranda* warnings. This consent can be done with a written consent form or on an audio cassette or a videotape.

A defendant's knowing and voluntary waiver of his *Miranda* rights is demonstrated in *State v. Johnson*, 595 So. 2d 789 (La. App. 2 Cir. 1992). The defendant was twice informed of, and validly waived his *Miranda* rights within four to five hours before he gave a statement. The defendant did not request a lawyer at any time. *State v. Johnson*, supra.

When the defendant is informed of and validly waives his *Miranda* rights during initial questioning by the police, those rights need not be repeated before every subsequent interrogation. Only if the evidence shows a significant break in the interrogation process, such as a specific request for counsel, or police coercion, do *Miranda* rights need to be repeated. *State v. Johnson*, supra.

The failure to obtain the defendant's signature on a written Miranda waiver form does not require that the confession is voluntary in deciding whether the inculpatory statement or commission is admissible. *State v. Parker*, 696 So. 2d 599 (La. App. 4 Cir. 1997); *State v. McCorkle*, 708 So. 2d 1212 (La. App. 5 Cir. 1998). The waiver of Miranda rights need not be explicit but may be inferred from the words or the actions of the defendant. An oral or express waiver of rights is strong proof of a valid waiver. *State v. Parker*, 696 So. 2d 599 (La. App. 4 Cir. 1997).

In *State v. Fernandez*, No. 96-KK-2719 (La. April 14, 1998), the Louisiana Supreme Court vacated a prior decision in *State in the Interest of Dino*, 359 So. 2d 586 (La. 1978) which required that a juvenile's confession in a custodial interrogation would not be admissible unless the juvenile first consulted with an attorney or an adult interested in the welfare of the juvenile (i.e parent or relative). Now, the totality of the circumstances need to be considered to determine whether the juvenile's confession was knowing and voluntary. *State v. Fernandez*, No. 96-KK-2719 (La. April 14, 1998).

B. Statements allowed after the defendant reinitiated questioning.

Once a subject has expressed a desire to deal with the police only through counsel, he or she is not subject to further interrogation by the police until counsel is made available to him or her. *State v. Pierce*, 681 So. 2d 478 (La. App. 4 Cir. 1996).

When the defendant asserts his right to remain silent, the assertion of this right does not create a permanent barrier to further discussions. *State v. Gaspard*, 685 So. 2d 151 (La. App. 3

Cir. 1996). In *State v. Gaspard*, supra, the defendant's request to wait over the weekend before he told police about his participation in a murder was an invocation of his right to remain silent. However, the defendant himself later initiated resumption of contact with a detective. Thus, defendant's subsequent recorded confession was not taken in violation of his right to remain silent. *State v. Gaspard*, supra.

Even after the subject has expressed a desire to deal with the police only through counsel or even after the defendant's attorney tells the police not to question his or her client in the attorney's absence, the police can still interrogate the subject. This only occurs if the subject later initiates further communication. At that point, he or she is subject to further interrogation by the police. *State v. Pierce*, supra.

In *State v. Pierce*, supra, the defendant's attorney told the police not to question the defendant in the attorney's absence. The defendant indicated that he was aware of his right to have an attorney present but waived that right. The defendant knowingly and voluntarily waived his right to have counsel present. He turned himself in and told the officers that he wanted to make a statement. This statement did not result from questioning initiated by the police but was made at the request of the defendant. *State v. Pierce*, supra.

VII. LIABILITY OF LAW ENFORCEMENT OFFICERS

A. Criminal Liability of officers - 18 U.S.C. 241.

Under 18 U.S.C. 241, an officer may be criminally liable if he enters into a conspiracy to deprive any citizen of any right or privilege guaranteed by the Constitution.

This section requires that the plaintiff be a citizen and that two or more persons act together with the specific intent to deny that citizen his rights under the law. *U.S. v. Reese*, 2 F. 3d 870 (9th Cir. 1993), cert. denied 114 S.Ct. 928; *U.S. v. Ehrlichman*, 546 F. 2d 910 (D.C. Cir. 1976), cert. denied 97 S.Ct. 1155, 429 U.S. 1120; *U.S. v. Liddy*, 542 F.2d 76 (D.C. Cir. 1976), cert. denied 97 S.Ct. 1155, 429 U.S. 1120.

A jail inmate is a "citizen" under 18 U.S.C. 241. It was a felony to conspire to interfere with a citizen in the free exercise or enjoyment of his or her constitutional or federal rights despite the fact that he was a convicted felon *U.S. v. King*, 587 F.2d 209, (C.A. Ga. 1979), cert. denied 99 S.Ct. 972.

The mere acquiescence, silence, or failure of an officer to perform a duty does not make him or her a participant in a conspiracy. Participation is evidenced if he or she acts, or fails to act, with the knowledge of purpose for the conspiracy and with an intent to protect and aid it. *Luteran v. U.S.*, 93 F.2d 395, (C.A. Mo. 1938).

Rights protected under 18 U.S.C. 241 and 18 U.S.C. 242 include rights expressly defined in the Constitution and rights judicially determined to be fundamental within the due process and equal protection clauses of the Fourteenth Amendment. *U.S. v. Anderson*, 481 F.2d 685 (4th Cir. 1973), affirmed 94 S.Ct. 2253, 417 U.S. 211; *U.S. v. City of Philadelphia*, 644 F. 2d 187 (3rd Cir. 1980).

Proof that a person knew there was a violation or conspiracy against a constitutional right is not essential for a conviction under 18 U.S.C. 241 and 18 U.S.C. 242. *U.S. v. O'Dell*, 462 F. 224 (6th Cir. 1972).

B. Criminal Liability of officers - Deprivation of rights under 18 U.S.C. 242.

An officer may be held criminally liable under 18 U.S.C. 242 if he or she acts under the color of law to willfully deprive any inhabitant of the United States of rights guaranteed by the Constitution or the laws of the United States. Elements of an offense under 18 U.S.C. 242 are:

(1) the accused's acts must have deprived someone of a right secured or protected by the Constitution or the laws of the United States;

(2) the defendant's illegal acts must have been committed under the color of law;

(3) the person whose rights were violated must have been an inhabitant of a state, territory, or district; and

(4) the defendant must have acted willfully.

See *U.S. v. Senak*, 477 F.2d 304, (C.A. Ind. 1973), cert. denied 94 S.Ct. 157, 414 U.S. 856.

The definition of "wilfulness" is an act done voluntarily and intentionally and with the specific intent to do something the law forbids. "With intent to violate a specific protected right." *U.S. v. Reese*, 2 F.3d 870 (9th Cir. 1993)., cert. denied 114 S.Ct. 928.

To act "under the color of law", for purposes of this section, does not require that the accused be an officer of the state. It is sufficient that the accused is a willful participant in a joint activity with the state or its agents *U.S. v. Price*, 383 U.S. 787, 86 S.Ct. 1152 (1986).

An officer was convicted of a civil rights violation when he continued to strike the arrestee after the arrestee no longer posed a threat. *U.S. v. Koon*, 833 F.Supp. 769 (C.D. Cal. 1993), affirmed in part, vacated in part 34 F.3d 1416, rehearing and suggestion for rehearing en banc denied 45 F. 3d 1303, as amended, cert. granted in part 116 S.Ct. 39.

Several Louisiana Statutes provide for criminal liability of peace officers. R.S. § 14:134.1 covers Malfeasance in office, sexual conduct prohibited with persons confined in correctional institutions; R.S. § 14:134.2 covers tampering with evidence.

C. Civil Liability of officers - General overview.

Under 42 U.S.C. 1983, (commonly referred to as a "1983" action), any person:

"who, under color of any statute, ordinance, regulation, custom, or usage, of any State ...subjects or causes to be subjected, any citizen of the United States or other person within the jurisdiction thereof to the deprivation of any rights, privileges, or immunities secured by the Constitution and laws, shall be liable to the party injured in an action at law, suit in equity, or other proper proceeding for redress."

An officer (and the department) may be sued for money damages in a "1983" action by the victim of an unlawful arrest, *Malley v. Briggs*, 475 U. S. 335, 106 S.Ct. 1092 (1986). In *Malley v. Briggs*, supra, the defendants claimed the arrest warrant was obtained and executed without probable cause. The test to apply is whether a reasonable officer would have known that his or her affidavit failed to establish probable cause and that he or she should not have applied for the warrant. If such was the case, his arrest warrant application was not reasonable, because it created the unnecessary danger of an unlawful arrest. *Malley v. Briggs*, 475 U. S. 335, 106 S.Ct. 1092 (1986).

The same civil liability for an objectively unreasonable arrest will also apply to an objectively unreasonable search. *Anderson v. Creighton*, 483 U.S. 635, 107 S.Ct. 3034 (1987). An officer was not found in violation of the Fourth Amendment when "a reasonable officer could have believed the search to be lawful in light of clearly established law and the information the searching officers possessed." *Anderson v. Creighton*, supra.

Any action brought under 42 U.S.C. 1983 must have the elements that the actions complained about were performed under (1) color of state law; and (2) by one who is a state official; i.e., "a peace officer"; *Dahl v. Akin*, 630 F. 2d 277, (5th Cir. 1980); *West v. Atkins*, 487 U.S. 42, 108 S.Ct. 2250 (1988).

The liability of police officers under this statute is not dependent upon whether their actions are legal under state law. *Ellenburg v. Shepherd*, 406 F.2d 1331 (D.C. Tenn. 1966).

A police officer's intent in making a false arrest is not material to an action, for deprivation of civil rights, brought under this statute. *Caballero v. City of Concord*, 956 F.2d 204 (9th Cir. 1992). Any collateral bad motive or intent on the part of the arresting officer is immaterial. *Caballero v. City of Concord*, supra.

As a general rule, once probable cause to arrest is established, an officer cannot be held liable for false arrest under state laws. *Hunter v. Clardy*, 558 F.2d 290, (C.A. Ga. 1977). A subsequent dismissal of a charge for any reason is irrelevant to the officer's liability under this statute if the officer arrested with probable cause or under a facially valid bench warrant. *Mitchell v. Aluisi*, 872 F.2d 577 (4th Cir. 1989).

A municipality may be liable for damages, in a Section 1983 claim, only if the municipality causes the constitutional violation. *Monell v. New York City Dept. of Social Services*, 436 U.S. 658, 98 S.Ct. 2018 (1978). A municipality was liable for a failure to train its officers when to call for medical care. *City of Canton, Ohio v. Harris*, 489 U. S. 37, 109 S.Ct. 1197 (1989). The municipality's liability does not depend necessarily or automatically on any officer's liability. *Fagan v. City of Vineland*, 22 F.3d 1296 (1994).

"High-speed chases with no intent to harm suspects physically or to worsen their legal plight do not give rise to liability under the 14th Amendment redressable by an action under 42 U.S.C. § 1983." *City of Sacramento v. Lewis*, Case 96-1337 (U.S. Supreme Court, May 26, 1998).

D. Qualified Immunity - Affirmative defense to claim under 42 U.S.C. 1983.

Qualified Immunity is an affirmative defense against Section 1983 claims. Its purpose is to shield public officials from undue interference with their duties and from potentially disabling threats of liability when the official acts objectively and reasonably in the good faith performance of his or her duties. This defense not only relieves liability from suit, but provides immunity. Its purpose is to spare defendants the burden of going to trial. *Wilson v. Weeks*, 52 F.3d 1547, 1552 (10th Cir. 1995). In *Hunter v. Bryant*, 502 U.S. 224, 227 (1991) the Supreme Court stated:

"When government officials are performing discretionary functions, they will not be held liable for their conduct unless their actions violate clearly established statutory or constitutional rights of which a reasonable person would have known."

Also see *Baker v. Chapman*, 517 N.W.2d 911 (Minn. 1994), cert. denied 115 S.Ct. 723.; *Osabutey v. Welch*, 857 F.2d 220 (4th Cir. 1988).

Qualified immunity will generally apply to the police and others involved in the investigative phase of a crime. Absolute immunity will generally apply to judges, prosecutors, other judicial, and quasi-judicial persons closely associated with judicial process.

E. Absolute Immunity - Affirmative defense to claim under 42 U.S.C. 1983.

Absolute immunity has long been recognized by the Courts for "all persons-governmental or otherwise- who were integral parts of the judicial process." *Valdez v. City and County of Denver*, 878 F.2d 1285 (10th Cir. 1989); *Forrester v. White*, 484 U.S. 219, 108 S.Ct. 538, 542, 544 (1988). This includes a "quasi-judicial civil immunity" of prosecutors, grand jurors, witnesses, agency officials, and those officials carrying out an order of the court. Yet, in *Burns v. Reed*, 500 U.S. 478, 111 S.Ct. 1934 (1991) a prosecuting attorney is not absolutely immune from liability for damages under Section 1983 when advising the police in the investigative phase of a criminal case.

Absolute immunity will generally apply to persons intimately associated with the judicial process or acting pursuant to an order of the court. It is given for officers acting at the direction of a judge. *Valdez v. City and County of Denver*, supra. Courts will look at factors such as the need for the assurance that the person can perform his or her functions without intimidation or harassment, insulation from political influence, correctability of error on appeal, and safeguards already in existence to reduce the need for private damage claims. *Young v. Selsky*, 41 F.3d 47 (2nd. Cir. 1994), cert. denied 115 S.Ct. 1837.

Under Louisiana law, there is an absolute immunity for prosecutors. A prosecutor acting within the scope of his prosecutorial duties is entitled to absolute immunity from suit for malicious prosecution as a consequence of conduct associated with the judicial phase of the criminal process. *Knapper v. Connick*, 681 So. 2d 994 (La. 1996). The prosecutor is not entitled to absolute immunity for administrative duties and those investigative functions that do not relate to the preparation for the initiation of prosecution or for judicial proceedings. *State v. Walls*, 670 So. 2d 382 (La. App. 3 Cir. 1996).

F. Cases brought under 42 U.S.C. 1983.

The following are examples of the types of cases which have been brought under 42 U.S.C. 1983:

(a) Failure to advise the grounds for arrest and detention. *Tilson v. Forrest City Police Dept.*, 28 F.3d 802, cert. denied 115 S.Ct. 1315 (1994).

(b) Detaining, the person arrested, for too long a period. *Tilson v. Forrest City Police Dept.*, supra.

(c) Assaulting the person arrested. *Jones v. Ziegler*, 894 F.Supp. 880 (D.Md. 1995).

(d) Failure to prevent the suicide of a person jailed. *Litz v. City of Allentown*, 896 F.Supp. 1401 (E.D. Pa. 1995); *Belcher v. City of Foley, Ala.*; 30 F.3d 1390 (11th Cir. 1994).

(e) Failure to intercede and prevent crime. *Jonelis v. Russo*, 863 F.Supp. 84 (D.Conn. 1994); *Gazette v. City of Pontiac*, 41 F.3d 1061 (6th Cir. 1994).

(f) Performing an illegal search or seizure upon the person or property of an arrestee. *O'Brien v. City of Grand Rapids*, 23 F.3d 990 (6th Cir. 1994).

(g) Failure to provide the person arrested with medical attention. *Hogan v. Franco*, 896 F. Supp. 1313 (N.D. N.Y. 1995).

(h) Improper identification. *Campbell v. City of San Antonio*, 43 F.3d 973 (5th Cir. 1995).

(i) Failure to protect the victim's anonymity or safety. *Piotrowski v. City of Houston*, 51 F.3d 512 (5th Cir. 1995).

(j) Use of unreasonable or excessive force during an arrest or detention. *Matthews v. Jones*, 35 F.3d 1046 (C.A. Ky, 1994); *Hogan v. Franco*, 896 F. Supp. 1313 (N.D. N.Y. 1995).

(k) Verbal abuse or coercion during an arrest or detention. *Cooper v. Dupnik*, 963 F.2d 1220 (9th Cir. 1992); *Haussman v. Fergus*, 894 F.Supp. 142 (S.D. N.Y. 1995).

(*l*) Damage to a house during the execution of a search warrant. *Bonds v. Cox*, 20 F.3d 973 (10th Cir. 1993).

(m) Failure to train: *Zuchel v. City and County of Denver Colorado*, 997 F.2d 730 (10th Cir. 1993) on use of deadly force; *Diloreto v. Burough of Oaklyn*, 744 F.Supp., 610 (D.N.J. 1990) on subject of strip searches; *Fagan v. City of Vineland*, 22 F.2d 1296 (1994) on subject of vehicle pursuit.

(n) False arrest. *Cook v. Sheldon*, 41 F.3d 73 (C.A. 2 N.Y. 1994).

G. Conspiracy to interfere with civil rights.

If two or more persons conspire for the purpose of depriving either directly or indirectly any person, or class of persons, of the equal protection of the laws, or of equal privileges and immunities under the laws, they can be liable under 42 U.S.C. 1985(3). To make out a valid cause of action for damages under 42 U.S.C. 1985(3), the plaintiff must allege:

(1) a conspiracy;

(2) an intent to deprive, either directly or indirectly, any person, or class of persons, of equal protection of the laws, or of equal privileges and immunities under the laws;

(3) an act in furtherance of the conspiracy; and

(4) injury to the person or property of the plaintiff or deprivation of any right or privilege of a citizen of the United States.

See *Quinones v. Szorc*, 771 F.2d 289, (7th Cir. 1985); *Munson v. Friske*, 754 F.2d 683, (C.A. Wis. 1985); *Mass v. McClenahan*, 893 F.Supp. 225 (S.D. N.Y. 1995).

Aliens, who are entitled to the equal protection of law, may bring an action for damages under this section, *Vietnamese Fishermen's Association v. Knights of Ku Klux Klan*, 518 F.Supp. 993, (D.C. Tex. 1981).

Under 42 U.S.C. 1986 an action may be presented for "neglect to prevent conspiracy." The elements under this section are:

(1) The defendant had actual knowledge of a Section 1985 conspiracy.

(2) The defendant had the power to prevent or aid in preventing the conspiracy.

(3) The defendant neglected or refused to prevent the conspiracy.

(4) A wrongful act was committed.

See *Clark v. Clabaugh*, 20 F.3d 1290 (C.A. 3 Pa, 1994). The plaintiff must show that the defendant had actual knowledge of a conspiracy to prove neglect.

VIII. CRIMINAL OFFENSES - ELEMENTS OF CRIMES

Here are the elements of a crime for several selected crimes.

A. Simple Arson (R.S. § 14:52)

1) Intentional;
2) damaging;
3) by any explosive substance or by setting fire to;
4) any property;
5) of another;
6) without the consent of the owner.

B. Simple Burglary (R.S. § 14:62)

1) Unauthorized;
2) entering;
3) of any dwelling, vehicle, watercraft, or other structure, movable or immovable;
4) with the intent to commit a felony or any theft therein.

C. Theft (R.S. § 14:67)

1) Taking of anything;
2) of value;
3) which belongs to another;
4) with an intent to deprive the other permanently;
5) without the consent of the other to the misappropriation or taking; or by means of fraudulent conduct, practices, or representations.

D. Illegal possession of stolen things (R.S. § 14:69)

1) Intentional;
2) possessing, procuring, receiving, concealing;
3) anything of value;
4) which has been the subject of any robbery or theft;
5) under circumstances which indicate that the offender knew or had good reason to believe that the thing was the subject of these offenses.

E. Unauthorized use of a motor vehicle (R.S. § 14:68.4)

1) Intentional;
2) taking or use of a motor vehicle;
3) which belongs to another;
4) without the owner's consent or by means of fraudulent conduct, practices, or representations;
5) without any intention to deprive the other of the motor vehicle permanently.

F. Simple Robbery (R.S. § 14:65)

1) Taking of anything;
2) of value;
3) which belongs to another;
4) from the person of another or that is in the immediate control of another;
5) by the use of force or intimidation.

G. False Imprisonment (R.S. § 14:46)

1) Intentional;
2) confinement or detention;
3) of another;
4) without his consent;
5) without proper legal authority.

H. Rape (R.S. § 14:41)

1) Act of anal or vaginal intercourse;
2) with a male or female person;
3) committed without the person's lawful consent.

Note: Any sexual penetration, vaginal or anal, however slight is sufficient to complete the crime.

I. Battery (R.S. § 14:33 and R.S. § 14:35)

1) Intentional;
2) use of force or violence;
3) upon the person of another;
4) without that person's consent.

or

1) Intentional;
2) administration of a poison or other noxious liquid or substance;
3) to another;
4) without that person's consent.

J. Assault (R.S. § 14:36)

1) Attempt;
2) to commit a battery.

 ZL

or

1) Intentional;
2) placing of another;
3) in reasonable apprehension of receiving a battery.

K. Criminal Trespass (R.S. § 14:63)

1) Intentionally;
2) entering any structure, watercraft, or moveable;
3) without authorization.

or

1) Intentionally;
2) entering immovable property;
3) owned by another
4) when he knows his entry is unauthorized, or under circumstances when he reasonably should know his entry is unauthorized.

L. Operating a vehicle while intoxicated (R.S. § 14:98)

1) Operating any motor vehicle, aircraft, watercraft, vessel, or other means of conveyance when;
2) a) the operator is under the influence of alcoholic beverages; or
 b) the operator's blood alcohol concentration is 0.10 percent or more by weight, or is 0.04 percent or more by weight if the operator is under 18 years of age; or
 c) the operator is under the influence of any controlled substance listed in Schedule I, II, III, IV, or V as set forth in R.S. § 40:964.

M. Simple criminal damage to property (R.S. § 14:56)

1) Intentional;
2) damaging;
3) of any property;
4) of another;
5) without the consent of the owner;
6) by any means other than fire or explosion.

N. Interference with the custody of a child (R.S. § 14:45.1)

1) Intentional;
2) taking, enticing, or decoying away;
3) of a minor child;
4) by a parent not having a right of custody;
5) with intent to detain or conceal such child
6) from a parent having a right of custody pursuant to a court order; or from a person entrusted with the child's care by a parent having custody pursuant to a court order.

O. Stalking (R.S. § 14:40.2)

1) willful;
2) malicious;
3) repeated following or harassing of another person;
4) with the intent to place that person in fear of death or bodily injury.

P. First Degree Murder (R.S. § 14:30)

First degree murder is the killing of a human being:

(1) When the offender has specific intent to kill or to inflict great bodily harm and is engaged in the perpetration or attempted perpetration of aggravated kidnapping, second degree kidnapping, aggravated escape, aggravated arson, aggravated rape, forcible rape, aggravated burglary, armed robbery, drive-by shooting, first degree robbery, or simple robbery.

2) When the offender has a specific intent to kill or to inflict great bodily harm upon a fireman or peace officer engaged in the performance of his lawful duties;

3) When the offender has a specific intent to kill or to inflict great bodily harm upon more than one person; or

4) When the offender has specific intent to kill or inflict great bodily harm and offered, was offered, gave, or received anything in value for the killing;

5) When the offender has the specific intent to kill or to inflict great bodily harm upon a victim under the age of twelve or sixty-five years of age or older;

6) When the offender has the specific intent to kill or to inflict great bodily harm while engaged in the distribution, exchange, sale, or purchase, or any attempt thereof, of a controlled dangerous substance listed in Schedules I, II, III, IV, or V of the Uniformed Controlled Dangerous Substances Law.

7) When the offender has specific intent to kill and is engaged in ritualistic acts prohibited by R.S. § 14:107.1(C) (1).

IX. MISCELLANEOUS CASES

R.S. § 40:981.4 the **Drug-traffic loitering** statute was found unconstitutionally vague and overbroad by the Supreme Court of Louisiana in *State v. Muschkat*, No. 96-KA-2922 (La. 1998).

LOUISIANA REVISED STATUTES

TITLE 14
CRIMINAL LAW
(Complete Title)

CHAPTER 1. CRIMINAL CODE

PART I. GENERAL PROVISIONS

SUBPART A. PRELIMINARY PROVISIONS

SUBPART B. ELEMENTS OF CRIMES

SUBPART C. CULPABILITY

SUBPART D. PARTIES

SUBPART E. INCHOATE OFFENSES

PART II. OFFENSES AGAINST THE PERSON

SUBPART A. HOMICIDE

SUBPART A-1. FETICIDE

SUBPART A-2. SUICIDE

SUBPART B. ASSAULT AND BATTERY (WITH RELATED OFFENSES)

SUBPART C. RAPE AND SEXUAL BATTERY

SUBPART D. KIDNAPPING AND FALSE IMPRISONMENT

SUBPART E. DEFAMATION

PART III. OFFENSES AGAINST PROPERTY

SUBPART A. BY VIOLENCE TO BUILDINGS AND OTHER PROPERTY

1. ARSON AND USE OF EXPLOSIVES

2. CRIMINAL DAMAGE TO PROPERTY

3. BURGLARY

4. CRIMINAL TRESPASS

PART IV. OFFENSES AFFECTING THE FAMILY

SUBPART A. CRIMINAL NEGLECT OF FAMILY

SUBPART B. SEX OFFENSES AFFECTING THE FAMILY

SUBPART C. DOMESTIC VIOLENCE OFFENSES

SUBPART D. CRIMINAL ABANDONMENT

PART V. OFFENSES AFFECTING THE PUBLIC MORALS

SUBPART A. OFFENSES AFFECTING SEXUAL IMMORALITY

1. SEXUAL OFFENSES AFFECTING MINORS

2. OFFENSES CONCERNING PROSTITUTION

3. ABORTION

4. CRIME AGAINST NATURE

SUBPART B. OFFENSES AFFECTING GENERAL MORALITY

1. GAMBLING

2. OFFENSES AFFECTING THE HEALTH AND MORALS OF MINORS

3. OFFENSES AFFECTING THE HEALTH AND SAFETY OF THE INFIRMED

4. UNLAWFUL SALE, PURCHASE, AND POSSESSION OF ALCOHOLIC BEVERAGES

PART VI. OFFENSES AFFECTING THE PUBLIC GENERALLY

SUBPART A. OFFENSES AFFECTING THE PUBLIC SAFETY

1. ILLEGAL CARRYING AND DISCHARGE OF WEAPONS

2. OBSTRUCTING HIGHWAYS OF COMMERCE

3. DRIVING OFFENSES

4. OBSTRUCTING PUBLIC PASSAGES

SUBPART B. OFFENSES AFFECTING THE PUBLIC SENSIBILITY

SUBPART C. OFFENSES AFFECTING THE GENERAL PEACE AND ORDER

SUBPART D. OFFENSES AFFECTING LAW ENFORCEMENT

108. Resisting an officer.
108.1. Flight from an officer; aggravated flight from an officer.
110. Simple escape; aggravated escape.
110.1. Jumping bail.
111. Assisting escape.
112. False personation.
112.1. False personation of a peace officer.

PART VII. OFFENSES AFFECTING ORGANIZED GOVERNMENT

SUBPART A. TREASON AND DISLOYAL ACTS

113. Treason.
114. Misprision of treason.
115. Criminal anarchy.
116. Flag desecration.
117. Flag desecration; exceptions.
117.1. Paramilitary organizations; prohibitions.

SUBPART B. BRIBERY AND INTIMIDATION

118. Public bribery.
118.1. Bribery of sports participants.
118.2. Falsifying information on racing license applications.
119. Bribery of voters.
119.1. Bribery of parents of school children.
120. Corrupt influencing.
121. Informers granted immunity.
122. Public intimidation.
122.1. Intimidation and interference in the operation of schools.
122.2. Threatening a public official; penalties; definitions.

SUBPART C. PERJURY

123. Perjury.
124. Inconsistent statements; perjury.
125. False swearing.
125.1. False swearing in paternity cases.
126. Inconsistent statements; false swearing.
126.1. False swearing for purpose of violating public health or safety.
126.2. False statements concerning denial of constitutional rights.
126.3. False statements concerning employment in a nursing or health care facility.
127. Limitation of defenses.
128. Completion of affidavit.

SUBPART D. MISCELLANEOUS OFFENSES AFFECTING JUDICIAL FUNCTIONS AND PUBLIC RECORDS

129. Jury tampering.
129.1. Intimidating, impeding or injuring witnesses; injuring officers; penalties.
129.2. Recording, listening to, or observing proceedings of grand or petit juries while deliberating or voting.
130. Jury misconduct.
130.1. Obstruction of justice.
131. Compounding a felony.
132. Injuring public records.
133. Filing or maintaining false public records.
133.1. Obstruction of court orders.
133.2. Misrepresentation during booking.
133.3. Falsification of drug tests.

SUBPART E. OFFICIAL MISCONDUCT AND CORRUPT PRACTICES

PART VIII. CONCLUDING PROVISIONS

PART I. GENERAL PROVISIONS

SUBPART A. PRELIMINARY PROVISIONS

§1. Method of citation.

This Chapter shall be known as the Louisiana Criminal Code. The provisions hereunder may be referred to or cited either as Articles of the Criminal Code or as Sections of the Revised Statutes. Thus Article 30 of Louisiana Criminal Code may also be referred to or cited as R.S. 14:30.

Whenever reference is made herein to an Article of the Criminal Code, the same shall also relate to the corresponding Section of the Revised Statutes.

§2. Definitions.

In this Code the terms enumerated shall have the designated meanings:

(1) "Another" refers to any other person or legal entity, including the state of Louisiana or any subdivision thereof.

(2) "Anything of value" must be given the broadest possible construction, including any conceivable thing of the slightest value, movable or immovable, corporeal or incorporeal, public or private, and including transportation, telephone and telegraph services, or any other service available for hire. It must be construed in the broad popular sense of the phrase, not necessarily as synonymous with the traditional legal term "property." In all cases involving shoplifting the term "value" is the actual retail price of the property at the time of the offense.

(3) "Dangerous weapon" includes any gas, liquid or other substance or instrumentality, which, in the manner used, is calculated or likely to produce death or great bodily harm.

(4) "Felony" is any crime for which an offender may be sentenced to death or imprisonment at hard labor.

(5) "Foreseeable" refers to that which ordinarily would be anticipated by a human being of average reasonable intelligence and perception.

(6) "Misdemeanor" is any crime other than a felony.

(7) "Person" includes a human being from the moment of fertilization and implantation and also includes a body of persons, whether incorporated or not.

(8) "Property" refers to both public and private property, movable and immovable, and corporeal and incorporeal property.

(9) "Public officer," "public office," "public employee" or "position of public authority" means and applies to any executive, ministerial, administrative, judicial, or legislative officer, office, employee or position of authority respectively, of the state of Louisiana or any parish, municipality, district, or other political subdivision thereof, or of any agency, board, commission, department or institution of said state, parish, municipality, district, or other political subdivision.

(10) "State" means the state of Louisiana, or any parish, municipality, district, or other political subdivision thereof, or any agency, board, commission, department or institution of said state, parish, municipality, district or other political subdivision.

(11) "Unborn child" means any individual of the human species from fertilization and implantation until birth.

(12) "Whoever" in a penalty clause refers only to natural persons insofar as death or imprisonment is provided, but insofar as a fine may be imposed "whoever" in a penalty clause refers to any person.

(13) "Crime of violence" means an offense that has, as an element, the use, attempted use, or threatened use of physical force against the person or property of another, and that, by its very nature, involves a substantial risk that physical force against the person or property of another may be used in the course of committing the offense or an offense that involves the possession or use of a dangerous weapon. The following enumerated offenses and attempts to commit any of them are included as "crimes of violence":

(a) Solicitation for murder
(b) First degree murder
(c) Second degree murder
(d) Manslaughter
(e) Aggravated battery
(f) Second degree battery
(g) Aggravated assault
(h) Mingling harmful substances
(i) Aggravated rape
(j) Forcible rape
(k) Simple rape
(*l*) Sexual battery
(m) Aggravated sexual battery
(n) Oral sexual battery
(*o*) Aggravated oral sexual battery
(p) Intentional exposure to AIDS virus
(q) Aggravated kidnapping
(r) Second degree kidnapping
(s) Simple kidnapping
(t) Aggravated arson
(u) Aggravated criminal damage to property
(v) Aggravated burglary
(w) Armed robbery
(x) First degree robbery
(y) Simple robbery
(z) Purse snatching
(aa) Extortion
(bb) Assault by drive-by shooting
(cc) Aggravated crime against nature
(dd) Carjacking
(ee) Illegal use of weapons or dangerous instrumentalities

(Chgd. by Acts 1992 No. 1015, §1; Acts 1994 Third Ex. Sess. No. 73, §1; Acts 1995 No. 650, §1, No. 1223, §1, eff. 8/15/95.)

§3. Interpretation.

The articles of this Code cannot be extended by analogy so as to create crimes not provided for herein; however, in order to promote justice and to effect the objects of the law, all of its provisions shall be given a genuine construction, according to the fair import of their words, taken in their usual sense, in connection with the context, and with reference to the purpose of the provision.

§4. Conduct made criminal under several articles; how prosecuted.

Prosecution may proceed under either provision, in the discretion of the district attorney, whenever an offender's conduct is:

(1) Criminal according to a general article of this Code or Section of this Chapter of the Revised Statutes and also according to a special article of this Code or Section of this Chapter of the Revised Statutes; or

(2) Criminal according to an article of the Code or Section of this Chapter of the Revised Statutes and also according to some other provision of the Revised Statutes, some special statute, or some constitutional provision.

§5. Lesser and included offenses.

An offender who commits an offense which includes all the elements of other lesser offenses, may be prosecuted for and convicted of either the greater offense or one of the lesser and included offenses. In such case, where the offender is prosecuted for the greater offense, he may be convicted of any one of the lesser and included offenses.

§6. Civil remedies not affected.

Nothing in this Code shall affect any civil remedy provided by the law pertaining to civil matters, or any legal power to inflict penalties for contempt.

SUBPART B. ELEMENTS OF CRIMES

§7. Crime defined.

A crime is that conduct which is defined as criminal in this Code, or in other acts of the legislature, or in the constitution of this state.

§8. Criminal conduct.

Criminal conduct consists of:

(1) An act or a failure to act that produces criminal consequences, and which is combined with criminal intent; or

(2) A mere act or failure to act that produces criminal consequences, where there is no requirement of criminal intent; or

(3) Criminal negligence that produces criminal consequences.

§9. Criminal consequences.

Criminal consequences are any set of consequences prescribed in the various articles of this Code or in the other acts of the legislature of this state as necessary to constitute any of the various crimes defined therein.

§10. Criminal intent.

Criminal intent may be specific or general:

(1) Specific criminal intent is that state of mind which exists when the circumstances indicate that the offender actively desired the prescribed criminal consequences to follow his act or failure to act.

(2) General criminal intent is present whenever there is specific intent, and also when the circumstances indicate that the offender, in the ordinary course of human experience, must have adverted to the prescribed criminal consequences as reasonably certain to result from his act or failure to act.

§11. Criminal intent; how expressed.

The definitions of some crimes require a specific criminal intent, while in others no intent is required. Some crimes consist merely of criminal negligence that produces criminal consequences. However, in the absence of qualifying provisions, the terms "intent" and "intentional" have reference to "general criminal intent."

§12. Criminal negligence.

Criminal negligence exists when, although neither specific nor general criminal intent is present, there is such disregard of the interest of others that the offender's conduct amounts to a gross deviation below the standard of care expected to be maintained by a reasonably careful man under like circumstances.

SUBPART C. CULPABILITY

§13. Infancy.

Those who have not reached the age of ten years are exempt from criminal responsibility. However, nothing in this article shall affect the jurisdiction of juvenile courts as established by the constitution and statutes of this state.

§14. Insanity.

If the circumstances indicate that because of a mental disease or mental defect the offender was incapable of distinguishing between right and wrong with reference to the conduct in question, the offender shall be exempt from criminal responsibility.

§15. Intoxication.

The fact of an intoxicated or drugged condition of the offender at the time of the commission of the crime is immaterial, except as follows:

(1) Where the production of the intoxicated or drugged condition has been involuntary, and the circumstances indicate this condition is the direct cause of the commission of the crime, the offender is exempt from criminal responsibility.

(2) Where the circumstances indicate that an intoxicated or drugged condition has precluded the presence of a specific criminal intent or of special knowledge required in a particular crime, this fact constitutes a defense to a prosecution for that crime.

§16. Mistake of fact.

Unless there is a provision to the contrary in the definition of a crime, reasonable ignorance of fact or mistake of fact which precludes the presence of any mental element required in that crime is a defense to any prosecution for that crime.

§17. Mistake of law.

Ignorance of the provision of this Code or of any criminal statute is not a defense to any criminal prosecution. However, mistake of law which results in the lack of an intention that consequences which are criminal shall follow, is a defense to a criminal prosecution under the following circumstances:

(1) Where the offender reasonably relied on the act of the legislature in repealing an existing criminal provision, or in otherwise purporting to make the offender's conduct lawful; or

(2) Where the offender reasonably relied on a final judgment of a competent court of last resort that a provision making the conduct in question criminal was unconstitutional.

§18. Justification; general provisions.

The fact that an offender's conduct is justifiable, although otherwise criminal, shall constitute a defense to prosecution for any crime based on that conduct. This defense of justification can be claimed under the following circumstances:

(1) When the offender's conduct is an apparently authorized and reasonable fulfillment of any duties of public office; or

(2) When the offender's conduct is a reasonable accomplishment of an arrest which is lawful under the Code of Criminal Procedure; or

(3) When for any reason the offender's conduct is authorized by law; or

(4) When the offender's conduct is reasonable discipline of minors by their parents, tutors or teachers; or

(5) When the crime consists of a failure to perform an affirmative duty and the failure to perform is caused by physical impossibility; or

(6) When any crime, except murder, is committed through the compulsion of threats by another of death or great bodily harm, and the offender reasonably believes the person making the threats is present and would immediately carry out the threats if the crime were not committed; or

(7) When the offender's conduct is in defense of persons or of property under any of the circumstances described in Articles 19 through 22.

§19. Use of force or violence in defense.

The use of force or violence upon the person of another is justifiable, when committed for the purpose of preventing a forcible offense against the person or a forcible offense or trespass against property in a person's lawful possession; provided that the force or violence used must be reasonable and apparently necessary to prevent such offense, and that this article shall not apply where the force or violence results in a homicide.

§20. Justifiable homicide.

A homicide is justifiable:

(1) When committed in self-defense by one who reasonably believes that he is in imminent danger of losing his life or receiving great bodily harm and that the killing is necessary to save himself from that danger.

(2) When committed for the purpose of preventing a violent or forcible felony involving danger to life or of great bodily harm by one who reasonably believes that such an offense is about to be committed and that such action is necessary for its prevention. The circumstances must be sufficient to excite the fear of a reasonable person that there would be serious danger to his own life or person if he attempted to prevent the felony without the killing.

(3) When committed against a person whom one reasonably believes to be likely to use any unlawful force against a person present in a dwelling or a place of business, or when committed against a person whom one reasonably believes is attempting to use any unlawful force against a person present in a motor vehicle as defined in R.S. 32:1(40), while committing or attempting to commit a burglary or robbery of such dwelling, business, or motor vehicle. The homicide shall be justifiable even though the person does not retreat from the encounter.

(4) When committed by a person lawfully inside a dwelling, a place of business, or a motor vehicle as defined in R.S. 32:1(40), against a person who is attempting to make an unlawful entry into the dwelling, place of business, or motor vehicle, or who has made an unlawful entry into the dwelling, place of business, or motor vehicle, and the person committing the homicide reasonably believes that the use of deadly force is necessary to prevent the entry or to compel the intruder to leave the premises or motor vehicle. The homicide shall be justifiable even though the person committing the homicide does not retreat from the encounter.

(Chgd. by Acts 1993 No. 516, §1; Acts 1997 No. 1378, §1, eff. 8/15/97.)

§21. Aggressor cannot claim self defense.

A person who is the aggressor or who brings on a difficulty cannot claim the right of self-defense unless he withdraws from the conflict in good faith and in such a manner that his adversary knows or should know that he desires to withdraw and discontinue the conflict.

§22. Defense of others.

It is justifiable to use force or violence or to kill in the defense of another person when it is reasonably apparent that the person attacked could have justifiably used such means himself, and when it is reasonably believed that such intervention is necessary to protect the other person.

SUBPART D. PARTIES

§23. Parties classified.

The parties to crimes are classified as:

(1) Principals; and

(2) Accessories after the fact.

§24. Principals.

All persons concerned in the commission of a crime, whether present or absent, and whether they directly commit the act constituting the offense, aid and abet in its commission, or directly or indirectly counsel or procure another to commit the crime, are principals.

§25. Accessories after the fact.

An accessory after the fact is any person who, after the commission of a felony, shall harbor, conceal, or aid the offender, knowing or having reasonable ground to believe that he has committed the felony, and with the intent that he may avoid or escape from arrest, trial, conviction, or punishment.

An accessory after the fact may be tried and punished, notwithstanding the fact that the principal felon may not have been arrested, tried, convicted, or amenable to justice.

Whoever becomes an accessory after the fact shall be fined not more than five hundred dollars, or imprisoned, with or without hard labor, for not more than five years, or both; provided that in no case shall his punishment be greater than one-half of the maximum provided by law for a principal offender.

SUBPART E. INCHOATE OFFENSES

§26. Criminal conspiracy.

A. Criminal conspiracy is the agreement or combination of two or more persons for the specific purpose of committing any crime; provided that an agreement or combination to commit a crime shall not amount to a criminal conspiracy unless, in addition to such agreement or combination, one or more of such parties does an act in furtherance of the object of the agreement or combination.

If the intended basic crime has been consummated, the conspirators may be tried for either the conspiracy or the completed offense, and a conviction for one shall not bar prosecution for the other.

B. Whoever is a party to a criminal conspiracy to commit any crime shall be fined or imprisoned, or both, in the same manner as for the offense contemplated by the conspirators; provided, however, whoever is a party to a criminal conspiracy to commit a crime punishable by death or life imprisonment shall be imprisoned at hard labor for not more than thirty years.

C. Whoever is a party to a criminal conspiracy to commit any other crime shall be fined or imprisoned, or both, in the same manner as for the offense contemplated by the conspirators; but such fine or imprisonment shall not exceed one-half of the largest fine, or one-half the longest term of imprisonment prescribed for such offense, or both.

§27. Attempt.

A. Any person who, having a specific intent to commit a crime, does or omits an act for the purpose of and tending directly toward the accomplishing of his object is guilty of an attempt to commit the offense intended; and it shall be immaterial whether, under the circumstances, he would have actually accomplished his purpose.

B. Mere preparation to commit a crime shall not be sufficient to constitute an attempt; but lying in wait with a dangerous weapon with the intent to commit a crime, or searching for the intended victim with a dangerous weapon with the intent to commit a crime, shall be sufficient to constitute an attempt to commit the offense intended.

C. An attempt is a separate but lesser grade of the intended crime; and any person may be convicted of an attempt to commit a crime, although it appears on the trial that the crime intended or attempted was actually perpetrated by such person in pursuance of such attempt.

D. Whoever attempts to commit any crime shall be punished as follows:

(1) If the offense so attempted is punishable by death or life imprisonment, he shall be imprisoned at hard labor for not less than ten nor more than fifty years without benefit of parole, probation, or suspension of sentence;

(2) If the offense so attempted is theft or receiving stolen things, and is not punishable as a felony, he shall be fined not more than two hundred dollars, or imprisoned for not more than six months, or both. If the offense so attempted is receiving stolen things, and is punishable as a felony, he shall be fined not more than two hundred dollars, or imprisoned not more than one year, or both. If the offense so attempted is theft, and is punishable as a felony, he shall be fined not more than five hundred dollars, or imprisoned not more than one year or both;

(3) In all other cases he shall be fined or imprisoned or both, in the same manner as for the offense attempted; such fine or imprisonment shall not exceed one-half of the largest fine, or one-half of the longest term of imprisonment prescribed for the offense so attempted, or both. *(Chgd. by Acts 1995 No. 988, §1, eff. 8/15/95.)*

§28. Inciting a felony.

A. Inciting a felony is the endeavor by one or more persons to incite or procure another person to commit a felony.

B. Whoever commits the crime of inciting a felony shall be fined not more than one thousand dollars, or imprisoned, with or without hard labor, for not more than two years, or both.

C. If an offender over the age of seventeen years commits the crime of inciting a felony by endeavoring to incite or procure a person under the age of seventeen years to commit a felony,

the offender shall be fined not more than one thousand dollars and imprisoned at hard labor for not more than five years.
(Chgd. by Acts 1994 Third Ex. Sess. No. 131, §1, eff. 8/27/94.)

§28.1. Solicitation for murder.

A. Solicitation for murder is the intentional solicitation by one person of another to commit or cause to be committed a first or second degree murder.

B. Whoever commits the crime of solicitation for murder shall be imprisoned at hard labor for not less than five years nor more than ten years.

PART II. OFFENSES AGAINST THE PERSON

SUBPART A. HOMICIDE

§29. Homicide.

Homicide is the killing of a human being by the act, procurement, or culpable omission of another. Criminal homicide is of five grades:

(1) First degree murder.
(2) Second degree murder.
(3) Manslaughter.
(4) Negligent homicide.
(5) Vehicular homicide.

§30. First degree murder.

A. First degree murder is the killing of a human being:

(1) When the offender has specific intent to kill or to inflict great bodily harm and is engaged in the perpetration or attempted perpetration of aggravated kidnapping, second degree kidnapping, aggravated escape, aggravated arson, aggravated rape, forcible rape, aggravated burglary, armed robbery, drive-by shooting, first degree robbery, or simple robbery.

(2) When the offender has a specific intent to kill or to inflict great bodily harm upon a fireman or peace officer engaged in the performance of his lawful duties;

(3) When the offender has a specific intent to kill or to inflict great bodily harm upon more than one person; or

(4) When the offender has specific intent to kill or inflict great bodily harm and has offered, has been offered, has given, or has received anything of value for the killing.

(5) When the offender has the specific intent to kill or to inflict great bodily harm upon a victim under the age of twelve or sixty-five years of age or older.

(6) When the offender has the specific intent to kill or to inflict great bodily harm while engaged in the distribution, exchange, sale, or purchase, or any attempt thereof, of a controlled dangerous substance listed in Schedules I, II, III, IV, or V of the Uniform Controlled Dangerous Substances Law*.

**R.S. 40:961 et seq.*

(7) When the offender has specific intent to kill and is engaged in the activities prohibited by R.S. 14:107.1(C)(1).

B. For the purposes of Paragraph A(2) of this Section, the term "peace officer" means any peace officer, as defined in R.S. 40:2402, and includes any constable, marshal, deputy marshal, sheriff, deputy sheriff, local or state policeman, commissioned wildlife enforcement agent, federal law enforcement officer, jail or prison guard, parole officer, probation officer, judge, attorney general, assistant attorney general, attorney general's investigator, district attorney, assistant district attorney, or district attorney's investigator.

C. Whoever commits the crime of first degree murder shall be punished by death or life imprisonment at hard labor without benefit of parole, probation, or suspension of sentence in accordance with the determination of the jury.
(Chgd. by Acts 1992 No. 296, §1; Acts 1993 No. 244, §1, No. 496, §1, eff. 8/15/93.)

§30.1. Second degree murder.

A. Second degree murder is the killing of a human being:

(1) When the offender has a specific intent to kill or to inflict great bodily harm; or

(2) (a) When the offender is engaged in the perpetration or attempted perpetration of aggravated rape, forcible rape, aggravated arson, aggravated burglary, aggravated

kidnapping, second degree kidnapping, aggravated escape, drive-by shooting, armed robbery, first degree robbery, or simple robbery, even though he has no intent to kill or to inflict great bodily harm.

(b) When the offender is engaged in the perpetration of cruelty to juveniles, even though he has no intent to kill or to inflict great bodily harm.

(3) When the offender unlawfully distributes or dispenses a controlled dangerous substance listed in Schedule I or II of the Uniform Controlled Dangerous Substances Law* which is the direct cause of the death of the recipient who ingested or consumed the controlled dangerous substance.

(4) When the offender unlawfully distributes or dispenses a controlled dangerous substance listed in Schedules I or II of the Uniform Controlled Dangerous Substances Law* to another who subsequently distributes or dispenses such controlled dangerous substance which is the direct cause of the death of the person who ingested or consumed the controlled dangerous substance.

**R.S. 40:961 et seq.*

B. Whoever commits the crime of second degree murder shall be punished by life imprisonment at hard labor without benefit of parole, probation, or suspension of sentence.
(Chgd. by Acts 1993 No. 496, §1; Acts 1997 No. 563, §1, No. 899, §1, eff. 8/15/97.)

§§30.2 to 30.5. *(Renumbered as R.S. 14:32.5 to 14:32.8.)*

§31. Manslaughter.

A. Manslaughter is:

(1) A homicide which would be murder under either Article 30 (first degree murder) or Article 30.1 (second degree murder), but the offense is committed in sudden passion or heat of blood immediately caused by provocation sufficient to deprive an average person of his self-control and cool reflection. Provocation shall not reduce a homicide to manslaughter if the jury finds that the offender's blood had actually cooled, or that an average person's blood would have cooled, at the time the offense was committed; or

(2) A homicide committed, without any intent to cause death or great bodily harm.

(a) When the offender is engaged in the perpetration or attempted perpetration of any felony not enumerated in Article 30 or 30.1, or of any intentional misdemeanor directly affecting the person; or

(b) When the offender is resisting lawful arrest by means, or in a manner, not inherently dangerous, and the circumstances are such that the killing would not be murder under Article 30 or 30.1.

B. Whoever commits manslaughter shall be imprisoned at hard labor for not more than forty years. However, if the victim was killed as a result of receiving a battery and was under the age of ten years, the offender shall be imprisoned at hard labor, without benefit of probation or suspension of sentence, for not less than ten years nor more than forty years.
(Chgd. by Acts 1991 No. 864, §1; Acts 1992 No. 306, §1; Acts 1994 Third Ex. Sess. No. 115, §1, eff. 8/27/94.)

§32. Negligent homicide.

A. Negligent homicide is the killing of a human being by criminal negligence.

B. The violation of a statute or ordinance shall be considered only as presumptive evidence of such negligence.

C. Whoever commits the crime of negligent homicide shall be imprisoned with or without hard labor for not more than five years, fined not more than five thousand dollars, or both. However, if the victim was killed as a result of receiving a battery and was under the age of ten years, the offender shall be imprisoned at hard labor, without benefit of probation or suspension of sentence, for not less than two nor more than five years.
(Chgd. by Acts 1991 No. 864, §1, eff. 9/6/91.)

§32.1. Vehicular homicide.

A. Vehicular homicide is the killing of a human being caused proximately or caused directly by an offender engaged in the operation of, or in actual physical control of, any motor vehicle, aircraft, watercraft, or other means of conveyance, whether or not the offender had the intent to cause death or great bodily harm, whenever any of the following conditions exists:

(1) The operator is under the influence of alcoholic beverages as determined by chemical tests administered under the provisions of R.S. 32:662.

(2) The operator's blood alcohol concentration is 0.08 percent or more by weight based upon grams of alcohol per one hundred cubic centimeters of blood.

(3) The operator is under the influence of any controlled dangerous substance listed in Schedule I, II, III, IV, or V as set forth in R.S. 40.964.

(4) The operator is under the influence of alcoholic beverages and has fled the scene of the accident.

B. Whoever commits the crime of vehicular homicide shall be fined not less than two thousand dollars nor more than fifteen thousand dollars and shall be imprisoned with or without hard labor for not less than two years nor more than fifteen years. At least one year of the sentence of imprisonment shall be imposed without benefit of probation, parole, or suspension of sentence. The court shall require the offender to participate in a court-approved substance abuse program or a court-approved driver improvement program, or both. All driver improvement courses required under this Section shall include instruction on railroad grade crossing safety.

(Chgd. by Acts 1993 No. 410, §1, No. 415, §1; Acts 1995 No. 1120, §1; Acts 1997 No. 1019, §1; Acts 1998 First Ex. Sess. No. 82, §1, eff. 6/16/98.)

SUBPART A-1. FETICIDE

§32.5. Feticide defined; exceptions.

A. Feticide is the killing of an unborn child by the act, procurement, or culpable omission of a person other than the mother of the unborn child. The offense of feticide shall not include acts which cause the death of the unborn child if those acts were committed during any abortion to which the pregnant woman or her legal guardian has consented or which was performed in an emergency as defined in R.S. 40:1299.35.12. Nor shall the offense of feticide include acts which are committed pursuant to usual and customary standards of medical practice during diagnostic testing or therapeutic treatment.

B. Criminal feticide is of three grades:

(1) First degree feticide.

(2) Second degree feticide.

(3) Third degree feticide.

§32.6. First degree feticide.

A. First degree feticide is:

(1) The killing of an unborn child when the offender has a specific intent to kill or to inflict great bodily harm.

(2) The killing of an unborn child when the offender is engaged in the perpetration or attempted perpetration of aggravated rape, forcible rape, aggravated arson, aggravated burglary, aggravated kidnapping, aggravated escape, armed robbery, first degree robbery, or simple robbery, even though he has no intent to kill or inflict great bodily harm.

B. Whoever commits the crime of first degree feticide shall be imprisoned at hard labor for not more than fifteen years.

§32.7. Second degree feticide.

A. Second degree feticide is:

(1) The killing of an unborn child which would be first degree feticide, but the offense is committed in sudden passion or heat of blood immediately caused by provocation of the mother of the unborn child sufficient to deprive an average person of his self control and cool reflection. Provocation shall not reduce a first degree feticide to second degree feticide if the jury finds that the offender's blood had actually cooled, or that an average person's blood would have cooled, at the time the offense was committed.

(2) A feticide committed without any intent to cause death or great bodily harm:

(a) When the offender is engaged in the perpetration or attempted perpetration of any felony not enumerated in Article 32.6 (first degree feticide), or of any intentional misdemeanor directly affecting the person; or

(b) When the offender is resisting lawful arrest by means, or in a manner, not inherently dangerous, and the circumstances are such that the killing would not be first degree feticide under Article 32.6.

B. Whoever commits the crime of second degree feticide shall be imprisoned at hard labor for not more than ten years.

§32.8. Third degree feticide.

A. Third degree feticide is:

(1) The killing of an unborn child by criminal negligence. The violation of a statute or ordinance shall be considered only as presumptive evidence of such negligence.

(2) The killing of an unborn child caused proximately or caused directly by an offender engaged in the operation of, or in actual physical control of, any motor vehicle, aircraft, vessel, or other means of conveyance whether or not the offender had the intent to cause death or great bodily harm whenever any of the following conditions exist:

(a) The offender is under the influence of alcoholic beverages as determined by chemical tests administered under the provisions of R.S. 32:662.

(b) The offender's blood alcohol concentration is 0.10 percent or more by weight based upon grams of alcohol per one hundred cubic centimeters of blood.

(c) The offender is under the influence of narcotic drugs, central nervous system stimulants, hallucinogenic drugs, methaqualone, or barbiturates and such condition was a contributing factor to the killing.

B. Whoever commits the crime of third degree feticide shall be fined not less than two thousand dollars and shall be imprisoned with or without hard labor for not more than five years.

§32.9. Partial birth abortion.

A. (1) Partial birth abortion is the performance of a procedure on a female by a licensed physician or any other person whereby a living fetus or infant is partially delivered or removed from the female's uterus by vaginal means and with specific intent to kill or do great bodily harm is then killed prior to complete delivery or removal.

(2) As used in this Section, the terms "fetus" and "infant" are used interchangeably to mean the biological offspring of human parents.

B. It shall not be unlawful for a licensed physician to perform a partial birth abortion where the procedure is necessary to save the life of the mother because her life is endangered by a physical disorder, physical illness, or physical injury, and further provided that no other medical procedure would suffice for that purpose.

C. As used in this Section, the term "person" shall not include the female upon whom the partial birth abortion is performed, and she shall not be subject to prosecution hereunder or as accessory to the offense or as a co-conspirator thereto.

D. Whoever commits the crime of partial birth abortion shall be imprisoned at hard labor for not less than one nor more than ten years or fined not less than ten thousand nor more than one hundred thousand dollars.
(Added by Acts 1997 No. 906, §1, eff. 7/10/97.)

SUBPART A-2. SUICIDE

(Added by Acts 1995 No. 384, §1, eff. 6/16/95.)

§32.12. Criminal assistance to suicide.

A. Criminal assistance to suicide is:

(1) The intentional advising or encouraging of another person to commit suicide or the providing of the physical means or the knowledge of such means to another person for the purpose of enabling the other person to commit or attempt to commit suicide.

(2) The intentional advising, encouraging, or assisting of another person to commit suicide, or the participation in any physical act which causes, aids, abets, or assists another person in committing or attempting to commit suicide.

B. For the purposes of this Section, "suicide" means the intentional and deliberate act of taking one's own life through the performance of an act intended to result in death.

C. The provisions of this Section shall not apply to any licensed physician or other authorized licensed health care professional who either:

(1) Withholds or withdraws medical treatment in accordance with the provisions of R.S. 40:1299.58.8.

(2) Prescribes, dispenses, or administers any medication, treatment, or procedure if the intent is to relieve the patient's pain or suffering and not to cause death.

D. Whoever commits the crime of criminal assistance to suicide shall be imprisoned, with or without hard labor, for not more than ten years or fined not more than ten thousand dollars, or both.
(Added by Acts 1995 No. 384, §1, eff. 6/16/95.)

SUBPART B. ASSAULT AND BATTERY (WITH RELATED OFFENSES)

§33. Battery defined.

Battery is the intentional use of force or violence upon the person of another; or the intentional administration of a poison or other noxious liquid or substance to another.

§34. Aggravated battery.

Aggravated battery is a battery committed with a dangerous weapon.

Whoever commits an aggravated battery shall be fined not more than five thousand dollars, imprisoned with or without hard labor for not more than ten years, or both.

§34.1. Second degree battery.

Second degree battery is a battery committed without the consent of the victim when the offender intentionally inflicts serious bodily injury.

For purposes of this article, serious bodily injury means bodily injury which involves unconsciousness, extreme physical pain or protracted and obvious disfigurement, or protracted loss or impairment of the function of a bodily member, organ, or mental faculty, or a substantial risk of death.

Whoever commits the crime of second degree battery shall be fined not more than two thousand dollars or imprisoned, with or without hard labor, for not more than five years, or both.

§34.2. Battery of a police officer.

A. (1) Battery of a police officer is a battery committed without the consent of the victim when the offender has reasonable grounds to believe the victim is a police officer acting in the performance of his duty.

(2) For purposes of this Section, "police officer" shall include commissioned police officers, sheriffs, deputy sheriffs, marshals, deputy marshals, correctional officers, constables, wildlife enforcement agents, and probation and parole officers.

(3) For purposes of this Section, "battery of a police officer" includes the use of force or violence upon the person of the police officer by throwing feces, urine, blood, saliva, or any form of human waste by an offender while the offender is incarcerated by a court of law and is being detained in any jail, prison, correctional facility, juvenile institution, temporary holding center, halfway house, or detention facility.

B. (1) Whoever commits the crime of battery of a police officer shall be fined not more than five hundred dollars and imprisoned not less than fifteen days nor more than six months without benefit of suspension of sentence.

(2) If at the time of the commission of the offense the offender is under the jurisdiction and legal custody of the Department of Public Safety and Corrections, or is being detained in any jail, prison, correctional facility, juvenile institution, temporary holding center, halfway house, or detention facility, the offender shall be fined not more than one thousand dollars and imprisoned with or without hard labor without benefit of parole, probation, or suspension of sentence for not less than one year nor more than five years. Such sentence shall be consecutive to any other sentence imposed for violation of the provisions of any state criminal law.

(3) If the battery produces an injury that requires medical attention, the offender shall be fined not more than one thousand dollars or imprisoned with or without hard labor for not less than one year nor more than five years, or both.
(Chgd. by Acts 1990 No. 84, §1; Acts 1991 No. 132, §1; Acts 1993 No. 438, §1; Acts 1994 Third Ex. Sess. No. 16, §1; Acts 1997 No. 486, §1, eff. 8/15/97.)

§34.3. Battery of a school teacher.

A. (1) Battery of a school teacher is a battery committed without the consent of the victim when the offender has reasonable grounds to believe the victim is a school teacher acting in the performance of employment duties.

(2) For purposes of this Section, "school teacher" shall include any teacher or instructor, administrator, staff person, or employee of any public or private elementary, secondary, vocational-technical training, special, or post-secondary school or institution.

B. Whoever commits the crime of battery of a school teacher shall be fined not more than one thousand dollars or imprisoned not less than two months nor more than six months or both.

(Chgd. by Acts 1994 Third Ex. Sess. No. 44, §1, eff. 8/27/94.)

§34.4. Battery of a school athletic contest official.

A. (1) Battery of a school athletic contest official is a battery committed without the consent of the victim when the offender has reasonable grounds to believe the victim is a school athletic contest official.

(2) For purposes of this Section, "school athletic contest official" means any referee, umpire, coach, instructor, administrator, staff person, or school or school board employee of any public or private secondary school while actively engaged in the conducting, supervising, refereeing, or officiating of a school sanctioned interscholastic athletic contest.

B. (1) Whoever commits the crime of battery of a school athletic contest official shall be fined not more than five hundred dollars and imprisoned not less than fifteen days nor more than six months without benefit of suspension of sentence.

(2) The court, in its discretion, may suspend the imposition of the sentence and place the offender on probation with the condition that he shall serve two days in jail or perform five days of community service work. Failure to successfully complete the community service work, as determined by the supervisor of the program to which he is assigned, may result in revocation of probation.

(Added by Acts 1990 No. 675, §1, eff. 9/7/90.)

§34.5. Battery of a correctional facility employee.

A. (1) Battery of a correctional facility employee is a battery committed without the consent of the victim when the offender has reasonable grounds to believe the victim is a correctional facility employee acting in the performance of his duty.

(2) For purposes of this Section, "correctional facility employee" means any employee of any jail, prison, correctional facility, juvenile institution, temporary holding center, halfway house, or detention facility.

(3) For purposes of this Section, "battery of a correctional facility employee" includes the use of force or violence upon the person of the employee by throwing feces, urine, blood, saliva, or any form of human waste on an offender while the offender is incarcerated by a court of law and is being detained in any jail, prison, correctional facility, juvenile institution, temporary holding center, halfway house, or detention facility.

B. (1) Whoever commits the crime of battery of a correctional facility employee shall be fined not more than five hundred dollars and imprisoned not less than fifteen days nor more than six months without benefit of suspension of sentence.

(2) If at the time of the commission of the offense the offender is under the jurisdiction and legal custody of the Department of Public Safety and Corrections, or is being detained in any jail, prison, correctional facility, juvenile institution, temporary holding center, halfway house, or detention facility, the offender shall be fined not more than one thousand dollars and imprisoned with or without hard labor without benefit of parole, probation, or suspension of sentence for not less than one year nor more than five years. Such sentence shall be consecutive to any other sentence imposed for violation of the provisions of any state criminal law.

(Added by Acts 1997 No. 486, §1, eff. 8/15/97.)

§34.6. Disarming of a peace officer.

A. (1) Disarming of a peace officer is committed when an offender, through use of force or threat of force, and without the consent of the peace officer, takes possession of a firearm from the person of a peace officer or from an area within the peace officer's immediate control, when the offender has reasonable grounds to believe that the victim is a peace officer acting in the performance of his duty.

(2) For purposes of this Section, "peace officer" shall include commissioned police officers, sheriffs, deputy sheriffs, marshals, deputy marshals, correctional officers, constables, wildlife enforcement agents, and probation and parole officers.

B. Whoever commits the crime of disarming of a peace officer shall be imprisoned at hard labor for not more than five years.

(Added by Acts 1997 No. 558, §1, eff. 8/15/97.)

§34.7. Aggravated second degree battery.

A. (1) Aggravated second degree battery is a battery committed with a dangerous weapon when the offender intentionally inflicts serious bodily injury.

(2) For purposes of this Section, "serious bodily injury" means bodily injury which involves unconsciousness, extreme physical pain or protracted and obvious disfigurement, or protracted loss or impairment of the function of a bodily member, organ, or mental faculty, or a substantial risk of death.

B. Whoever commits the crime of aggravated second degree battery shall be fined not more than ten thousand dollars or imprisoned, with or without hard labor, for not more than fifteen years, or both.

(Added by Acts 1997 No. 1318, §1, eff. 7/15/97.)

§35. Simple battery.

Simple battery is a battery committed without the consent of the victim.

Whoever commits a simple battery shall be fined not more than five hundred dollars, or imprisoned for not more than six months, or both.

§35.1. Simple battery of a child welfare worker.

A. (1) Simple battery of a child welfare worker is a battery, other than a second degree battery or an aggravated battery, committed without the consent of the victim when the offender has reasonable grounds to believe the victim is a child welfare worker working in the performance of employment duties who has presented proper identification.

(2) For purposes of this Section, "child welfare worker" shall include any child protection investigator, family services worker, foster care worker, adoption worker, any supervisor of the above, or any person authorized to transport clients for the agency.

B. Whoever commits the crime of simple battery of a child welfare worker shall be fined not more than five hundred dollars and imprisoned not less than fifteen days nor more than six months without benefit of suspension of sentence.

§36. Assault defined.

Assault is an attempt to commit a battery, or the intentional placing of another in reasonable apprehension of receiving a battery.

§37. Aggravated assault.

A. Aggravated assault is an assault committed with a dangerous weapon.

B. Whoever commits an aggravated assault shall be fined not more than one thousand dollars or imprisoned for not more than six months, or both.

C. If the offense is committed upon a store's or merchant's employee while the offender is engaged in the perpetration or attempted perpetration of theft of goods, the offender shall be imprisoned for not less than one hundred twenty days without benefit of suspension of sentence nor more than six months and may be fined not more than one thousand dollars.

(Chgd. by Acts 1992 No. 985, §1, eff. 8/21/92.)

§37.1. Assault by drive-by shooting.

A. Assault by drive-by shooting is an assault committed with a firearm when an offender uses a motor vehicle to facilitate the assault.

B. Whoever commits an assault by drive-by shooting shall be imprisoned for not less than one year nor more than five years, with or without hard labor, and without benefit of suspension of sentence.

C. As used in this Section and in R.S. 14:30(A)(1) and 30.1(A)(2), the term "drive-by shooting" means the discharge of a firearm from a motor vehicle on a public street or highway with the intent either to kill, cause harm to, or frighten another person.

(Added by Acts 1993 No. 496, §1, eff. 8/15/93.)

§37.2. Aggravated assault upon a peace officer with a firearm*.

A. Aggravated assault upon a peace officer with a firearm* is an assault committed upon a peace officer with a firearm**.

B. For purposes of this Section, "firearm" is defined as an instrument used in the propulsion of shot, shell, or bullets by the action of gunpowder exploded within it.

C. Whoever commits an aggravated assault with a firearm*** shall be fined not more than five thousand dollars or imprisoned for not more than five years, with or without hard labor.

(Added by Acts 1995 No. 881, §1; chgd. by Acts 1997 No. 936, §1, eff. 8/15/97.)

**Probably should be "Aggravated assault with a firearm upon a peace officer".*

***Probably should be "assault committed with a firearm upon a peace officer".*

****Probably should be "aggravated assault with a firearm upon a peace officer".*

§38. Simple assault.

Simple assault is an assault committed without a dangerous weapon.

Whoever commits a simple assault shall be fined not more than two hundred dollars, or imprisoned for not more than ninety days, or both.

§38.1. Mingling harmful substances.

Mingling harmful substances is the intentional mingling of any harmful substance or matter with any food, drink or medicine with intent that the same shall be taken by any human being to his injury.

Whoever commits the crime of mingling harmful substances shall be imprisoned, with or without hard labor, for not more than two years or fined not more than one thousand dollars, or both.

§38.2. Assault on a school teacher.

A. (1) Assault on a school teacher is an assault committed when the offender has reasonable grounds to believe the victim is a school teacher acting in the performance of his duties.

(2) For purposes of this Section, "school teacher" means any teacher, instructor, administrator, staff person, or employee of any public or private elementary, secondary, vocational-technical training, special, or postsecondary school or institution.

B. Whoever commits the crime of assault on a school teacher shall be fined not more than five hundred dollars or imprisoned not less than thirty days nor more than ninety days, or both.

(Added by Acts 1994 Third Ex. Sess. No. 44, §1, eff. 8/27/94.)

§39. Negligent injuring.

Negligent injuring is the inflicting of any injury upon the person of another by criminal negligence.

The violation of a statute or ordinance shall be considered only as presumptive evidence of such negligence.

Whoever commits the crime of negligent injuring shall be fined not more than five hundred dollars, or imprisoned for not more than six months, or both.

§39.1. Vehicular negligent injuring.

A. Vehicular negligent injuring is the inflicting of any injury upon the person of a human being when caused proximately or caused directly by an offender engaged in the operation of, or in actual physical control of any, motor vehicle, aircraft, watercraft, or other means of conveyance whenever any of the following conditions exists:

(1) The offender is under the influence of alcoholic beverages.

(2) The offender's blood alcohol concentration is 0.10 percent or more by weight based upon grams of alcohol per one hundred cubic centimeters of blood.

(3) The offender is under the influence of any controlled dangerous substance listed in Schedule I, II, III, IV, or V as set forth in R.S. 40:964.

B. The violation of a statute or ordinance shall be considered only as presumptive evidence of negligence as set forth in Subsection A.

C. Whoever commits the crime of vehicular negligent injuring shall be fined not more than one thousand dollars or imprisoned for not more than six months, or both.

(Chgd. by Acts 1997 No. 1020, §1, eff. 7/11/97.)

§39.2. First degree vehicular negligent injuring.

A. First degree vehicular negligent injuring is the inflicting of serious bodily injury upon the person of a human being when caused proximately or caused directly by an offender engaged in the operation of, or in actual physical control of, any motor vehicle, aircraft, watercraft, or other means of conveyance whenever any of the following conditions exists:

(1) The offender is under the influence of alcoholic beverages.

(2) The offender's blood alcohol concentration is 0.08 percent or more by weight based upon grams of alcohol per one hundred cubic centimeters of blood.

(3) The offender is under the influence of any controlled dangerous substance listed in Schedule I, II, III, IV, or V as set forth in R.S. 40:964, or any abused substance.

B. The violation of a statute or ordinance shall be considered only as presumptive evidence of negligence as set forth in Subsection A.

C. For purposes of this Section, "serious bodily injury" means bodily injury which involves unconsciousness, extreme physical pain or protracted and obvious disfigurement, or protracted loss or impairment of the function of a bodily member or organ or a mental faculty, or a substantial risk of death.

D. Whoever commits the crime of first degree vehicular negligent injuring shall be fined not more than two thousand dollars or imprisoned with or without hard labor for not more than five years, or both.

(Added by Acts 1995 No. 403, §1; chgd. by Acts 1997 No. 1021, §1, eff. 7/11/97.)

§40. Intimidation by officers.

Intimidation by officers is the intentional use, by any police officer or other person charged with the custody of parties accused of a crime or violation of a municipal ordinance, of threats, violence, or any means of inhuman treatment designed to secure a confession or incriminating statement from the person in custody.

Whoever commits the crime of intimidation by officers shall be fined not more than five hundred dollars, or imprisoned for not more than six months, or both.

§40.1. Terrorizing.

A. Terrorizing is the intentional communication of information, known by the offender to be false, that the commission of a crime of violence is imminent or in progress or that a circumstance dangerous to human life exists or is about to exist, thereby causing any person to be in sustained fear for his or another person's safety; causing evacuation of a building, a public structure, or a facility of transportation; or causing other serious disruption to the public.

B. Whoever commits the offense of terrorizing shall be fined not more than fifteen thousand dollars or imprisoned with or without hard labor for not more than fifteen years, or both.

(Chgd. by Acts 1997 No. 1318, §2, eff. 7/15/97.)

§40.2. Stalking.

A. Stalking is the willful, malicious, and repeated following or harassing of another person with the intent to place that person in fear of death or bodily injury.

B. (1) Whoever commits the crime of stalking may be imprisoned for not more than one year or fined not more than two thousand dollars, or both.

(2) Any person who commits the offense of stalking and who is found by the trier of fact, whether the jury at a jury trial, the judge in a bench trial, or the judge at a sentencing hearing following a jury trial, beyond a reasonable doubt to have placed the victim of the stalking in fear of death or bodily injury by the actual use of or the defendant's having in his possession during the instances which make up the crime of stalking, a dangerous weapon, shall be fined one thousand dollars or imprisoned with or without hard labor for one year, or both. Whether or not the defendant's use of or his possession of the dangerous weapon is a crime or, if a crime, whether or not he is charged for that offense separately or in addition to the crime of stalking shall have no bearing or relevance as to the enhanced sentence under the provisions of this Paragraph.

(3) Any person who commits the offense of stalking against a person for whose benefit a protective order, a temporary restraining order, or an injunction is in effect in either a civil or criminal proceeding, protecting the victim of the stalking from acts by the offender which otherwise constitute the crime of stalking, shall be punished by imprisonment for not less

than ninety days and not more than two years and fined not more than five thousand dollars, or both.

(4) Upon a second conviction occurring within seven years of a prior conviction for stalking of the same victim, the offender shall be imprisoned with or without hard labor for not less than one hundred eighty days and not more than three years, and may be fined not more than five thousand dollars, or both.

(5) Upon a third or subsequent conviction occurring within seven years of a prior conviction for stalking, the offender shall be imprisoned with or without hard labor for not less than two years and not more than five years, and may be fined not more than five thousand dollars, or both.

(6) (a) Any person thirteen years of age or older who commits the crime of stalking against a child twelve years of age or younger and who is found by the trier of fact, whether the jury at a jury trial, the judge in a bench trial, or the judge at a sentencing hearing following a jury trial, beyond a reasonable doubt to have placed the child in reasonable fear of death or bodily injury, or in reasonable fear of the death or bodily injury of a family member of the child shall be punished by imprisonment for not less than one year and not more than three years and fined not less than fifteen hundred dollars and not more than five thousand dollars, or both.

(b) Lack of knowledge of the child's age shall not be a defense.

C. For the purposes of this Section, the following words shall have the following meanings:

(1) "Harassing" means engaging in a knowing and willful pattern of conduct directed at a specific person which seriously alarms, annoys, or distresses the person, and which serves no legitimate purpose. The conduct must be such as would cause a reasonable person to suffer substantial emotional distress and must actually cause substantial emotional distress to the person.

(2) "Pattern of conduct" means a series of acts over a period of time, however short, evidencing an intent to inflict a continuity of emotional distress upon the person. Constitutionally protected activity is not included within the meaning of pattern of conduct.

(3) *(Repealed.)*

D. As used in this Section, when the victim of the stalking is a child twelve years old or younger:

(1) "Pattern of conduct" includes repeated acts of nonconsensual contact involving the victim or a family member.

(2) "Family member" includes:

(a) A child, parent, grandparent, sibling, uncle, aunt, nephew, or niece, of the victim, whether related by blood, marriage, or adoption.

(b) A person who lives in the same household as the victim.

(3) (a) "Nonconsensual contact" means any contact with a child twelve years old or younger that is initiated or continued without that child's consent, that is beyond the scope of the consent provided by that child, or that is in disregard of that child's expressed desire that the contact be avoided or discontinued.

(b) "Nonconsensual contact" includes:

(i) Following or appearing within the sight of that child.

(ii) Approaching or confronting that child in a public place or on private property.

(iii) Appearing at the residence of that child.

(iv) Entering onto or remaining on property occupied by that child.

(v) Contacting that child by telephone.

(vi) Sending mail or electronic communications to that child.

(vii) Placing an object on, or delivering an object to, property occupied by that child.

(c) "Nonconsensual contact" does not include any otherwise lawful act by a parent, tutor, caretaker, mandatory reporter, or other person having legal custody of the child as those terms are defined in the Louisiana Children's Code.

(4) "Victim" means the child who is the target of the stalking.

(Chgd. by Acts 1993 No. 125, §§1, 2; Acts 1994 Third Ex. Sess. No. 30, §1; Acts 1995 No. 416, §1, No. 645, §1; Acts 1997 No. 1231, §1, eff. 7/15/97.)

SUBPART C. RAPE AND SEXUAL BATTERY

§41. Rape; defined.

A. Rape is the act of anal or vaginal sexual intercourse with a male or female person committed without the person's lawful consent.

B. Emission is not necessary and any sexual penetration, vaginal or anal, however slight is sufficient to complete the crime.

C. *(Repealed.)*

(Chgd. by Acts 1990 No. 722, §§1, 2, eff. 9/7/90.)

§42. Aggravated rape.

A. Aggravated rape is a rape committed upon a person sixty-five years of age or older or where the anal or vaginal sexual intercourse is deemed to be without lawful consent of the victim because it is committed under any one or more of the following circumstances:

(1) When the victim resists the act to the utmost, but whose resistance is overcome by force.

(2) When the victim is prevented from resisting the act by threats of great and immediate bodily harm, accompanied by apparent power of execution.

(3) When the victim is prevented from resisting the act because the offender is armed with a dangerous weapon.

(4) When the victim is under the age of twelve years. Lack of knowledge of the victim's age shall not be a defense.

(5) When two or more offenders participated in the act.

(6) When the victim is prevented from resisting the act because the victim suffers from a physical or mental infirmity preventing such resistance.

B. For purposes of Paragraph (5), "participate" shall mean:

(1) Commit the act of rape.

(2) Physically assist in the commission of such act.

C. For purposes of this Section, the following words have the following meanings:

(1) "Physical infirmity" means a person who is a quadriplegic or paraplegic.

(2) "Mental infirmity" means a person with an intelligence quotient of seventy or lower.

D. Whoever commits the crime of aggravated rape shall be punished by life imprisonment at hard labor without benefit of parole, probation, or suspension of sentence.

(1)* However, if the victim was under the age of twelve years, as provided by Paragraph A(4) of this Section:

(a) And if the district attorney seeks a capital verdict, the offender shall be punished by death or life imprisonment at hard labor without benefit of parole, probation, or suspension of sentence, in accordance with the determination of the jury. The provisions of C.Cr.P. Art. 782 relative to cases in which punishment may be capital shall apply.

(b) And if the district attorney does not seek a capital verdict, the offender shall be punished by life imprisonment at hard labor without benefit of parole, probation, or suspension of sentence. The provisions of C.Cr.P. Art. 782 relative to cases in which punishment is necessarily confinement at hard labor shall apply.

**So in original. No paragraph D(2) has been enacted.*

(Chgd. by Acts 1993 No. 630, §1; Acts 1995 No. 397, §1; Acts 1997 No. 757, §1, No. 898, §1, eff. 8/15/97.)

§42.1. Forcible rape.

A. Forcible rape is rape committed when the anal or vaginal sexual intercourse is deemed to be without the lawful consent of the victim because it is committed under any one or more of the following circumstances:

(1) When the victim is prevented from resisting the act by force or threats of physical violence under circumstances where the victim reasonably believes that such resistance would not prevent the rape.

(2) When the victim is incapable of resisting or of understanding the nature of the act by reason of stupor or abnormal condition of the mind produced by a narcotic or anesthetic agent or other controlled dangerous substance administered by the offender and without the knowledge of the victim.

B. Whoever commits the crime of forcible rape shall be imprisoned at hard labor for not less than five nor more than forty years. At least two years of the sentence imposed shall be without benefit of probation, parole, or suspension of sentence.
(Chgd. by Acts 1997 No. 862, §1, eff. 8/15/97.)

§43. Simple rape.

A. Simple rape is a rape committed when the anal or vaginal sexual intercourse is deemed to be without the lawful consent of a victim who is not the spouse of the offender because it is committed under any one or more of the following circumstances:

(1) When the victim is incapable of resisting or of understanding the nature of the act by reason of a stupor or abnormal condition of mind produced by an intoxicating agent or any cause, other than the administration by the offender, and without the knowledge of the victim, of any narcotic or anesthetic agent or other controlled dangerous substance and the offender knew or should have known of the victim's incapacity.

(2) When the victim is incapable, through unsoundness of mind, whether temporary or permanent, of understanding the nature of the act and the offender knew or should have known of the victim's incapacity.

(3) When the female victim submits under the belief that the person committing the act is her husband and such belief is intentionally induced by any artifice, pretense, or concealment practiced by the offender.

B. For purposes of this Section, a person shall not be considered to be a spouse if a judgment of separation from bed and board has been rendered, or if the person and the offender are not legally separated but are living separate and apart and the offender knows that a temporary restraining order, preliminary or permanent injunction, or other order or decree has been issued prohibiting or restraining the offender from sexually or physically abusing, intimidating, threatening violence against, or in any way physically interfering with the person.

C. Whoever commits the crime of simple rape shall be imprisoned, with or without hard labor, without benefit of parole, probation, or suspension of sentence, for not more than twenty-five years.
(Chgd. by Acts 1990 No. 722, §1; Acts 1995 No. 946, §2; Acts 1997 No. 862, §1, eff. 8/15/97.)

§43.1. Sexual battery.

A. Sexual battery is the intentional engaging in any of the following acts with another person, who is not the spouse of the offender, where the offender acts without the consent of the victim, or where the other person has not yet attained fifteen years of age and is at least three years younger than the offender:

(1) The touching of the anus or genitals of the victim by the offender using any instrumentality or any part of the body of the offender; or

(2) The touching of the anus or genitals of the offender by the victim using any instrumentality or any part of the body of the victim.

B. Lack of knowledge of the victim's age shall not be a defense. However, where the victim is under seventeen, normal medical treatment or normal sanitary care of an infant shall not be construed as an offense under the provisions of this Section.

C. Whoever commits the crime of sexual battery shall be punished by imprisonment, with or without hard labor, without benefit of parole, probation, or suspension of sentence, for not more than ten years.
(Chgd. by Acts 1991 No. 654, §1; Acts 1995 No. 946, §2, eff. 8/15/95.)

§43.2. Aggravated sexual battery.

A. Aggravated sexual battery is the intentional engaging in any of the following acts with another person when the offender intentionally inflicts serious bodily injury on the victim:

(1) The touching of the anus or genitals of the victim by the offender using any instrumentality or any part of the body of the offender; or

(2) The touching of the anus or genitals of the offender by the victim using any instrumentality or any part of the body of the victim.

B. For the purposes of this Section, serious bodily injury means bodily injury which involves unconsciousness, extreme physical pain or protracted and obvious disfigurement, or protracted loss or impairment of the function of a bodily member, organ, or mental faculty, or a substantial risk of death.

C. Whoever commits the crime of aggravated sexual battery shall be punished by imprisonment, with or without hard labor, without benefit of parole, probation, or suspension of sentence, for not more than fifteen years.
(Chgd. by Acts 1995 No. 946, §2, eff. 8/15/95.)

§43.3. Oral sexual battery.

A. Oral sexual battery is the intentional engaging in any of the following acts with another person, who is not the spouse of the offender, when the offender either compels the other person to submit by placing the person in fear of receiving bodily harm, or when the other person has not yet attained fifteen years of age and is at least three years younger than the offender:

(1) The touching of the anus or genitals of the victim by the offender using the mouth or tongue of the offender; or

(2) The touching of the anus or genitals of the offender by the victim using the mouth or tongue of the victim.

B. Lack of knowledge of the victim's age shall not be a defense.

C. Whoever commits the crime of oral sexual battery shall be punished by imprisonment, with or without hard labor, without benefit of parole, probation, or suspension of sentence, for not more than fifteen years.
(Chgd. by Acts 1995 No. 946, §2, eff. 8/15/95.)

§43.4. Aggravated oral sexual battery.

A. Aggravated oral sexual battery is an oral sexual battery committed when the intentional touching of the genitals or anus of one person and the mouth or tongue of another is deemed to be without the lawful consent of the victim because it is committed under any one or more of the following circumstances:

(1) When the victim resists the act to the utmost, but whose resistance is overcome by force.

(2) When the victim is prevented from resisting the act by threats of great and immediate bodily harm, accompanied by apparent power of execution.

(3) When the victim is prevented from resisting the act because the offender is armed with a dangerous weapon.

(4) When the victim is under the age of twelve years. Lack of knowledge of the victim's age shall not be a defense.

(5) When two or more offenders participated in the act without the consent of the victim.

(6) When the victim is prevented from resisting the act because the victim suffers from a physical or mental infirmity preventing such resistance.

B. For purposes of Paragraph (5) of Subsection A of this Section, "participate" shall mean:

(1) Commit the act of oral sexual battery.

(2) Physically assist in the commission of such act.

C. Whoever commits the crime of aggravated oral sexual battery shall be punished by imprisonment, with or without hard labor, without benefit of parole, probation, or suspension of sentence, for not more than twenty years.

D. For purposes of this Section, the following words have the following meanings:

(1) "Physical infirmity" means a person who is a quadriplegic or paraplegic.

(2) "Mental infirmity" means a person with an intelligence quotient of seventy or lower.
(Chgd. by Acts 1995 No. 946, §2; Acts 1997 No. 757, §1, eff. 8/15/97.)

§43.5. Intentional exposure to AIDS virus.

A. No person shall intentionally expose another to any acquired immunodeficiency syndrome (AIDS) virus through sexual contact without the knowing and lawful consent of the victim.

B. No person shall intentionally expose another to any acquired immunodeficiency syndrome (AIDS) virus through any means or contact without the knowing and lawful consent of the victim.

C. No person shall intentionally expose a police officer to any AIDS virus through any means or contact without the knowing and lawful consent of the police officer when the offender has reasonable grounds to believe the victim is a police officer acting in the performance of his duty.

D. For purposes of this Section, the following words have the following meanings:

(1) "Means or contact" is defined as spitting, biting, stabbing with an AIDS contaminated object, or throwing of blood or other bodily substances.

(2) "Police officer" includes a commissioned police officer, sheriff, deputy sheriff, marshal, deputy marshal, correctional officer, constable, wildlife enforcement agent, and probation and parole officer.

E. (1) Whoever commits the crime of intentional exposure to AIDS virus shall be fined not more than five thousand dollars, imprisoned with or without hard labor for not more than ten years, or both.

(2) Whoever commits the crime of intentional exposure to AIDS virus against a police officer shall be fined not more than six thousand dollars, imprisoned with or without hard labor for not more than eleven years, or both.

(Chgd. by Acts 1993 No. 411, §1, eff. 8/15/93.)

SUBPART D. KIDNAPPING AND FALSE IMPRISONMENT

§44. Aggravated kidnapping.

Aggravated kidnapping is the doing of any of the following acts with the intent thereby to force the victim, or some other person, to give up anything of apparent present or prospective value, or to grant any advantage or immunity, in order to secure a release of the person under the offender's actual or apparent control:

(1) The forcible seizing and carrying of any person from one place to another; or

(2) The enticing or persuading of any person to go from one place to another; or

(3) The imprisoning or forcible secreting of any person.

Whoever commits the crime of aggravated kidnapping shall be punished by life imprisonment at hard labor without benefit of parole, probation, or suspension of sentence.

§44.1. Second degree kidnapping.

A. Second degree kidnapping is the doing of any of the acts listed in Subsection B wherein the victim is:

(1) Used as a shield or hostage;

(2) Used to facilitate the commission of a felony or the flight after an attempt to commit or the commission of a felony;

(3) Physically injured or sexually abused;

(4) Imprisoned or kidnapped for seventy-two or more hours, except as provided in R.S. 14:45(A)(4) or (5); or

(5) Imprisoned or kidnapped when the offender is armed with a dangerous weapon or leads the victim to reasonably believe he is armed with a dangerous weapon.

B. For purposes of this Section, kidnapping is:

(1) The forcible seizing and carrying of any person from one place to another; or

(2) The enticing or persuading of any person to go from one place to another; or

(3) The imprisoning or forcible secreting of any person.

C. Whoever commits the crime of second degree kidnapping shall be imprisoned at hard labor for not less than five nor more than forty years. At least two years of the sentence imposed shall be without benefit of parole, probation, or suspension of sentence.

§45. Simple kidnapping.

A. Simple kidnapping is:

(1) The intentional and forcible seizing and carrying of any person from one place to another without his consent; or

(2) The intentional taking, enticing or decoying away, for an unlawful purpose, of any child not his own and under the age of fourteen years, without the consent of its parent or the person charged with its custody; or

(3) The intentional taking, enticing or decoying away, without the consent of the proper authority, of any person who has been lawfully committed to any orphan, insane, feeble-minded or other similar institution.

(4) The intentional taking, enticing or decoying away and removing from the state, by any parent of his or her child, from the custody of any person whom custody has been awarded by any court of competent jurisdiction of any state, without the consent of the legal custodian, with intent to defeat the jurisdiction of the said court over the custody of the child.

(5) The taking, enticing or decoying away and removing from the state, by any person, other than the parent, of a child temporarily placed in his custody by any court of competent jurisdiction in the state, with intent to defeat the jurisdiction of said court over the custody of the child.

B. Whoever commits the crime of simple kidnapping shall be fined not more than five thousand dollars, imprisoned with or without hard labor for not more than five years, or both.

§45.1. Interference with the custody of a child.

A. Interference with the custody of a child is the intentional taking, enticing, or decoying away of a minor child by a parent not having a right of custody, with intent to detain or conceal such child from a parent having a right of custody pursuant to a court order or from a person entrusted with the care of the child by a parent having custody pursuant to a court order.

It shall be an affirmative defense that the offender reasonably believed his actions were necessary to protect the welfare of the child.

B. Whoever commits the crime of interference with the custody of a child shall be fined not more than five hundred dollars or be imprisoned for not more than six months, or both. Costs of returning a child to the jurisdiction of the court shall be assessed against any defendant convicted of a violation of this Section, as court costs as provided by the Louisiana Code of Criminal Procedure.

§46. False imprisonment.

False imprisonment is the intentional confinement or detention of another, without his consent and without proper legal authority.

Whoever commits the crime of false imprisonment shall be fined not more than two hundred dollars, or imprisoned for not more than six months, or both.

§46.1. False imprisonment; offender armed with dangerous weapon.

A. False imprisonment while armed with a dangerous weapon is the unlawful intentional confinement or detention of another while the offender is armed with a dangerous weapon.

B. Whoever commits the crime of false imprisonment while armed with a dangerous weapon shall be imprisoned, with or without hard labor, for not more than ten years.

SUBPART E. DEFAMATION

§47. Defamation.

Defamation is the malicious publication or expression in any manner, to anyone other than the party defamed, of anything which tends:

(1) To expose any person to hatred, contempt, or ridicule, or to deprive him of the benefit of public confidence or social intercourse; or

(2) To expose the memory of one deceased to hatred, contempt, or ridicule; or

(3) To injure any person, corporation, or association of persons in his or their business or occupation.

Whoever commits the crime of defamation shall be fined not more than five hundred dollars, or imprisoned for not more than six months, or both.

§48. Presumption of malice.

Where a non-privileged defamatory publication or expression is false it is presumed to be malicious unless a justifiable motive for making it is shown.

Where such a publication or expression is true, actual malice must be proved in order to convict the offender.

§49. Qualified privilege.

A qualified privilege exists and actual malice must be proved, regardless of whether the publication is true or false, in the following situations:

(1) Where the publication or expression is a fair and true report of any judicial, legislative, or other public or official proceeding, or of any statement, speech, argument, or debate in the course of the same.

(2) Where the publication or expression is a comment made in the reasonable belief of its truth, upon,

(a) The conduct of a person in respect to public affairs; or

(b) A thing which the proprietor thereof offers or explains to the public.

(3) Where the publication or expression is made to a person interested in the communication, by one who is also interested or who stands in such a relation to the former as to afford a reasonable ground for supposing his motive innocent.

(4) Where the publication or expression is made by an attorney or party in a judicial proceeding.

§50. Absolute privilege.

There shall be no prosecution for defamation in the following situations:

(1) When a statement is made by a legislator or judge in the course of his official duties.

(2) When a statement is made by a witness in a judicial proceeding, or in any other legal proceeding where testimony may be required by law, and such statement is reasonably believed by the witness to be relevant to the matter in controversy.

(3) Against the owner, licensee or operator of a visual or sound broadcasting station or network of stations or the agents or employees thereof, when a statement is made or uttered over such station or network of stations by one other than such owner, licensee, operator, agents, or employees.

§50.1. Perpetration or attempted perpetration of crimes against a victim sixty-five years of age or older.

Notwithstanding any other provisions of law to the contrary, any person who is convicted of manslaughter, simple rape, forcible rape, aggravated assault, aggravated battery, simple battery, aggravated kidnapping, simple kidnapping, or false imprisonment or any attempt to commit the aforementioned crimes where a victim of any such crime is sixty-five years of age or older shall in addition to any other penalty imposed, serve a minimum of five years without benefit of parole, probation or suspension of sentence and adjudication of guilt or imposition of sentence shall not be suspended, and lack of knowledge of the victim's age shall not be a defense.

Such sentence shall be consecutive to any other sentence imposed for violation of the provisions of any state criminal law.

PART III. OFFENSES AGAINST PROPERTY

SUBPART A. BY VIOLENCE TO BUILDINGS AND OTHER PROPERTY

1. ARSON AND USE OF EXPLOSIVES

§51. Aggravated arson.

Aggravated arson is the intentional damaging by any explosive substance or the setting fire to any structure, watercraft, or movable whereby it is foreseeable that human life might be endangered.

Whoever commits the crime of aggravated arson shall be imprisoned at hard labor for not less than six nor more than twenty years, and shall be fined not more than twenty-five thousand dollars. Two years of such imprisonment at hard labor shall be without benefit of parole, probation, or suspension of sentence.

§52. Simple arson.

A. Simple arson is the intentional damaging by any explosive substance or the setting fire to any property of another, without the consent of the owner and except as provided in R.S. 14:51.

B. Whoever commits the crime of simple arson, where the damage done amounts to five hundred dollars or more, shall be fined not more than fifteen thousand dollars and imprisoned at hard labor for not less than two years nor more than fifteen years.

C. Where the damage is less than five hundred dollars, the offender shall be fined not more than twenty-five hundred dollars or imprisoned with or without hard labor for not more than five years, or both.

§52.1. Simple arson of a religious building.

A. Simple arson of a religious building is the intentional damaging, by any explosive substance or by setting fire, of any church, synagogue, mosque, or other building, structure, or place primarily used for religious worship or other religious purpose.

B. Whoever commits the crime of simple arson of a religious building shall be fined not more than fifteen thousand dollars and imprisoned at hard labor for not less than two years nor more than fifteen years. At least two years of the sentence of imprisonment shall be imposed without benefit of probation, parole, or suspension of sentence.
(Added by Acts 1997 No. 404, §1, No. 1362, §1, eff. 8/15/97.)

§53. Arson with intent to defraud.

Arson with intent to defraud is the setting fire to, or damaging by any explosive substance, any property, with intent to defraud.

Whoever commits the crime of arson with intent to defraud shall be fined not more than ten thousand dollars, imprisoned with or without hard labor for not more than five years, or both.

§54. Placing combustible materials.

The placing of any combustible or explosive material in or near any structure, watercraft, movable, or forestland, with the specific intent eventually to set fire to such structure, watercraft, movable, or forestland, shall constitute an attempt to commit arson within the meaning of the attempt article of this Code, and the Court shall look at Articles 51 through 53 of this Code in order to determine which type of arson was attempted.

§54.1. Communicating of false information of planned arson.

A. Communicating of false information of arson or attempted arson is the intentional impartation or conveyance, or causing the impartation or conveyance by the use of the mail, telephone, telegraph, word of mouth, or other means of communication, of any threat or false information knowing the same to be false, including bomb threats or threats involving fake explosive devices, concerning an attempt or alleged attempt being made, or to be made, to commit either aggravated or simple arson.

B. Whoever commits the crime of communicating of false information of arson or attempted arson shall be imprisoned at hard labor for not more than twenty years.
(Chgd. by Acts 1990 No. 321, §1, eff. 9/7/90.)

§54.2. Manufacture and possession of delayed action incendiary devices; penalty.

It shall be unlawful for any person, without proper license as required by R.S. 40:1471.1 et seq. to knowingly and intentionally possess or have under his control any instrument, device, chemical or explosive substance which is arranged, manufactured, mixed, or so made up as to be a device or substance which, when exposed to heat, humidity, air, or foreign elements, will after prolongation of time burst into flame, ignite, cause to be ignited, or explode.

This section shall not apply to fireworks possessed within the meaning and contemplation of R.S. 51:650 et seq.

Whoever violates this Section shall be fined not more than ten thousand dollars or be imprisoned at hard labor for not more than twenty years, or both.

§54.3. Manufacture and possession of a bomb.

A. It shall be unlawful for any person without proper license as required by R.S. 40:1471.1 et seq. knowingly and intentionally to manufacture, possess, or have under his control any bomb.

B. A "bomb", for the purposes of this Section, is defined as an explosive compound or mixture with a detonator or initiator, or both, but does not include small arms ammunition. The term "bomb", as used herein, shall also include any of the materials listed in Subsection C present in an unassembled state but which could, when assembled, be ignited in the same manner as described in Subsection C, when possessed with intent to manufacture or assemble a bomb.

C. As used herein the term "explosive" means gunpowders, powders used for blasting, all forms of high explosives, blasting materials, fuses (other than electric circuit breakers), detonators, and other detonating agents, smokeless powders, and any chemical compounds, mechanical mixture, or device that contains any oxidizing and combustible units, or other ingredients, in such proportions, quantities, or packing that ignition by fire, by friction, by concussion, by percussion, or by detonation of the compound, mixture, or device or any part thereof may cause an explosion.

D. This Section shall not apply to fireworks possessed within the meaning and contemplation of R.S. 51:650 et seq.

E. Whoever violates this Section shall be fined not more than ten thousand dollars or be imprisoned at hard labor for not more than twenty years, or both.

§54.4. Forfeitures.

A. The following contraband shall be subject to seizure and forfeiture and no property right shall exist therein:

(1) Any instrument, device, chemical or explosive substance which is arranged, manufactured, mixed or so made up as to be a device or substance which, when exposed to heat, humidity, air or foreign elements will after prolongation of time burst into flame, ignite, cause to be ignited or explode, or raw materials used or intended to be used in the manufacture of such instrument, device, chemical or explosive substance;

(2) Any bomb as proscribed and defined in R.S. 14:54.3;

(3) All property which is used, or intended for use as a container for property described in Paragraphs (1) and (2) of this Subsection;

(4) All conveyances including aircraft, vehicles, or vessels, which are used or intended for use, to transport, or in any manner to facilitate the transportation, possession, production, manufacture, dispensation or concealment of property described in Paragraphs (1) and (2) of this Subsection, except that:

(a) No conveyance used by any person as a common carrier in transaction of business as a common carrier shall be seized or forfeited under the provisions of this Section unless it shall appear that the owner or other person in charge of such conveyance was knowingly and intentionally a consenting party or privy to a violation of R.S. 14:54.2 and 54:3; and

(b) No vessel, vehicle or aircraft shall be seized or forfeited under the provisions of this Section by reason of any act or omission established by the owner thereof to have been committed or omitted, without the owner's knowledge, consent, or permission by any person other than such owner while such vessel, vehicle or aircraft was in the possession of such person.

B. Any property subject to forfeiture under this Section may be seized under process issued by any court of record having jurisdiction over the property except that seizure without such process may be made when:

(1) The seizure is incident to an arrest with probable cause or a search under a valid search warrant or with probable cause or an inspection under valid administrative inspection warrant;

(2) The property subject to seizure has been the subject of a prior judgment in favor of the state in a criminal injunction or forfeiture proceeding under this Section.

C. After seizure, all conveyances taken or detained under this Section shall be immediately returned to the owner when the charges of violation R.S. 14:54.2 and 54.3 in which the conveyance was involved are dismissed by the district attorney or dismissed by the district court, on the basis of a preliminary hearing or other preliminary proceedings, or when the accused is acquitted following a trial in the district court of the parish in which the violation is alleged to have occurred. Vehicles seized under this Section shall be forfeited upon:

(1) A showing by the district attorney of a conviction for a violation under which seizure is authorized by this Section; and

(2) A showing by the district attorney that the seizure was made incident to an arrest with probable cause or a search under a valid search warrant or with probable cause or an inspection under a valid administrative inspection warrant; and

(3) A showing by the district attorney that the owner of the conveyance was knowingly and intentionally a consent party or privy to a violation of R.S. 14:54.2 or R.S. 14:54.3.

D. Property taken or detained under this Section shall not be repleviable, but shall be deemed to be in the custody of the law enforcement agency making the seizure subject only to the orders and decrees of the court of record having jurisdiction thereof. Whenever property is seized under provisions of this Section, the law enforcement officer or employee making the seizure shall:

(1) Place the property under seal;

(2) Remove the property to a place designated by the valid warrant under which such property was seized; or

(3) Request that the Department of Public Safety take custody of the property and remove it to an appropriate location for disposition in accordance with law.

E. Whenever property is forfeited under this Section, the law enforcement agency making the seizure may:

(1) Retain the property for official use except the conveyances described in R.S. 14:54.4(A)(4); or

(2) Sell any forfeited property, which is not required to be destroyed by law and which is not harmful to the public, provided that the proceeds be used for payment of all costs of the proceedings for forfeiture and sale including expenses of seizure, maintenance of custody, advertising, and court costs; or

(3) Request that the Department of Public Safety take custody of the property and remove it for disposition in accordance with law.

F. Any law enforcement agency is empowered to authorize, or designate officers, agents, or other persons to carry out the seizure provisions of this Section.

G. The district attorney within whose jurisdiction the vessel, vehicle, or aircraft or other property has been seized because of its use, attempted use in violation of R.S. 14:54.2 or R.S. 14:54.3, shall proceed against the vessel, vehicle, or aircraft or other property as provided in Subsection C in the district court having jurisdiction over the offense and have it forfeited to the use of or the sale by the law enforcement agency making the seizure.

H. Where it appears by affidavit that the residence of the owner of the vessel, vehicle, aircraft or other property is out of state or is unknown to the district attorney, the court shall appoint an attorney at law to represent the absent owner, against whom the rule shall be tried contradictorily within ten days after its filing. This affidavit may be made by the district attorney or one of his assistants. The attorney so appointed may waive service and citation of the petition or rule but shall not waive time nor any legal defenses.

I. Whenever the head of the law enforcement agency effecting the forfeiture deems it necessary or expedient to sell the property forfeited, rather than retain it for the use of the law enforcement agency, he shall cause an advertisement to be inserted in the official journal of the parish where the seizure was made, and after ten days, shall dispose of said property at public auction to the highest bidder, for cash and without appraisal.

J. The proceeds of all funds collected from any such sale, except as provided in R.S. 14:54.4(E)(2), shall be paid into the state treasury.

K. The rights of any mortgage or lien holder or holder of a vendor's privilege on the property seized shall not be affected by the seizure.

§54.5. Fake explosive device.

A. It shall be unlawful for any person to manufacture, possess, have under his control, buy, sell, mail, send to another person, or transport a fake explosive device, if the offender knowingly and intentionally:

(1) Influences the official conduct or action of an official or any personnel of a public safety agency; or

(2) Threatens to use the fake explosive device while committing or attempting to commit any felony.

B. For purposes of this Section the following words shall have the following meanings:

(1) A "fake explosive device" means any device or object that by its design, construction, content, or characteristics appears to be or to contain an explosive, an explosive compound or mixture with a detonator or initiator, or both, but is, in fact, an inoperative facsimile or imitation of such a destructive device, bomb, or explosive as defined in R.S. 14:54.3.

(2) A "public safety agency" means the Department of Public Safety and Corrections, a fire department, an emergency medical or rescue service, a law enforcement agency, or a volunteer agency organized to deal with emergencies.

C. Whoever violates the provisions of this Section shall be imprisoned at hard labor for not more than five years and shall be fined an amount equal to the costs of any law enforcement investigation or emergency response which results from the commission of the offense.

D. Provisions of this Section shall not apply to authorized military, police, and fire operations and training exercises.

(Added by Acts 1991 No. 832, §1, eff. 7/23/91.)

2. CRIMINAL DAMAGE TO PROPERTY

§55. Aggravated criminal damage to property.

Aggravated criminal damage to property is the intentional damaging of any structure, watercraft, or movable, wherein it is foreseeable that human life might be endangered, by any means other than fire or explosion.

Whoever commits the crime of aggravated criminal damage to property shall be fined not more than ten thousand dollars, imprisoned with or without hard labor for not less than one nor more than fifteen years, or both.

§56. Simple criminal damage to property.

A. Simple criminal damage to property is the intentional damaging of any property of another, without the consent of the owner, and except as provided in R.S. 14:55, by any means other than fire or explosion.

B. Whoever commits the crime of simple criminal damage to property, where the damage is less than five hundred dollars, shall be fined not more than five hundred dollars, or imprisoned for not more than six months, or both.

Where the damage amounts to five hundred dollars but less than fifty thousand dollars, the offender shall be fined not more than one thousand dollars, or imprisoned, with or without hard labor, for not more than two years, or both.

Where the damage amounts to fifty thousand dollars or more, the offender shall be fined not more than ten thousand dollars, or imprisoned with or without hard labor for not less than one nor more than ten years, or both.

§56.1. Criminal damage to coin-operated devices.

Criminal damage to a coin-operated device is the intentional damaging of any coin-operated device belonging to another.

Coin-operated device means any parking meter, pay telephone, vending machine, money-changing machine, or any other coin activated device designed to accept money for a privilege, service, or product.

For purposes of this Section, the value of damages shall be determined by the actual cost of repair, or replacement if necessary.

Whoever commits the crime of criminal damage to a coin-operated device, when the damage done amounts to one hundred dollars or more, shall be fined not more than two thousand dollars or imprisoned for not more than two years, or both.

Whoever commits the crime of criminal damage to a coin-operated device, when the damage amounts to a value of less than one hundred dollars shall be fined not more than five hundred dollars or imprisoned for not more than six months, or both.

§56.2. Criminal damage of a pipeline facility.

A. Criminal damage of a pipeline facility is the intentional damaging of a pipeline facility as defined in this Section.

B. For purposes of this Section, a pipeline facility shall include:

(1) Any pipeline, including but not limited to flow lines, transmission, distribution, or gathering lines regardless of size or length, which transmits or transports oil, gas, petrochemicals, minerals, or water in a solid, liquid, or gaseous state, and

(2) Any pipeline, flow line, transmission, distribution, or gathering line which meets the requirements of Paragraph (1) preceding and which is under construction or repair.

C. Whoever commits the crime of criminal damage of a pipeline facility may be imprisoned for not more than five years or fined not more than ten thousand dollars, or both.

D. Whoever commits the crime of criminal damage of a pipeline facility wherein it is foreseeable that human life might be threatened as a result of such conduct shall be imprisoned at hard labor without benefit of suspension of sentence for not less than two years nor more than ten years and shall be fined not more than ten thousand dollars.

§57. Damage to property with intent to defraud.

Damage to property with intent to defraud is the damaging of any property, by means other than fire or explosion, with intent to defraud.

Whoever commits the crime of damage to property with intent to defraud shall be fined not more than ten thousand dollars, imprisoned with or without hard labor for not more than four years, or both.

§58. Contaminating water supplies.

Contaminating water supplies is the intentional performance of any act tending to contaminate any private or public water supply.

Whoever commits the crime of contaminating water supplies, when the act foreseeably endangers the life or health of human beings, shall be fined not more than one thousand dollars, or imprisoned, with or without hard labor, for not more than twenty years, or both.

Whoever commits the crime of contaminating water supplies, when the act does not foreseeably endanger the life or health of human beings, shall be fined not more than five hundred dollars, or imprisoned, with or without hard labor, for not more than five years, or both.

§59. Criminal mischief.

A. Criminal mischief is the intentional performance of any of the following acts:

(1) Tampering with any property of another, without the consent of the owner, with the intent to interfere with the free enjoyment of any rights of anyone thereto, or with the intent to deprive anyone entitled thereto of the full use of the property.

(2) Giving of any false alarm of fire or notice which would reasonably result in emergency response.

(3) Driving of any tack, nail, spike or metal over one and one-half inch in length into any tree located on lands belonging to another, without the consent of the owner, or without the later removal of the object from the tree.

(4) The felling, topping or pruning of trees or shrubs within the right of way of a state highway, without prior written approval of the assistant secretary of the Department of Transportation and Development who supervises the office of highways of that department or his representative, provided prior written approval is not required for agents or employees of public utility companies in situations of emergency where the person or property of others is endangered.

(5) Giving of any false report or complaint to a sheriff, or his deputies, or to any officer of the law relative to the commission of, or an attempt to commit, a crime.

(6) Throwing any stone or any other missile in any street, avenue, alley, road, highway, open space, public square, or enclosure, or throwing any stone, missile, or other object from any place into any street, avenue, road, highway, alley, open space, public square, enclosure, or at any train, railway car, or locomotive.

(7) Taking temporary possession of any part or parts of a place of business, or remaining in a place of business after the person in charge of such business or portion of such business has directed such person to leave the premises and to desist from the temporary possession of any part or parts of such business.

(8) The communication to any person for the purpose of disrupting any public utility water service, when the communication causes any officer, employee, or agent of the service reasonably to be placed in sustained fear for his or another person's safety, or causes the evacuation of a water service building, or causes any discontinuance of any water services.

(9) The discharging of any firearm at a train, locomotive, or railway car.

(10) Placing graffiti upon immovable or movable property, whether publicly or privately owned, without the consent of the owner, by means of the use of spray paint, ink, marking pens containing a nonwater soluble fluid, brushes, applicators, or other materials for marking, scratching, or etching. "Graffiti" includes but is not limited to any sign, inscription, design, drawing, diagram, etching, sketch, symbol, lettering, name, or marking placed upon immovable or movable property in such a manner and in such a location as to deface the property and be visible to the general public.

B. Whoever commits the crime of criminal mischief shall be fined not more than five hundred dollars, or be imprisoned for not more than six months in the parish jail, or both. *(Chgd. by Acts 1994 Third Ex. Sess. No. 118, §1; Acts 1995 No. 882, §1, eff. 8/15/95.)*

3. BURGLARY

§60. Aggravated burglary.

Aggravated burglary is the unauthorized entering of any inhabited dwelling, or of any structure, water craft, or movable where a person is present, with the intent to commit a felony or any theft therein, if the offender,

(1) Is armed with a dangerous weapon; or

(2) After entering arms himself with a dangerous weapon; or

(3) Commits a battery upon any person while in such place, or in entering or leaving such place.

Whoever commits the crime of aggravated burglary shall be imprisoned at hard labor for not less than one nor more than thirty years.

§62. Simple burglary.

Simple burglary is the unauthorized entering of any dwelling, vehicle, watercraft, or other structure, movable or immovable, with the intent to commit a felony or any theft therein, other than as set forth in Section 60.

Whoever commits the crime of simple burglary shall be fined not more than two thousand dollars, imprisoned with or without hard labor for not more than twelve years, or both.

§62.1. Simple burglary of a pharmacy.

A. Simple burglary of a pharmacy is the unauthorized entry of any building, warehouse, physician's office, hospital, pharmaceutical house, or other structure used in whole or in part for the sale, storage and/or dispensing of controlled dangerous substances, as defined in R.S. 40:961(7), with the intent to commit the theft of any drug which is defined as a controlled dangerous substance in R.S. 40:961(7) other than set forth in R.S. 14:60.

B. Whoever commits the crime of burglary of a pharmacy shall be imprisoned at hard labor for not less than one nor more than nine years without benefit of parole, probation or suspension of sentence.

C. On a second or subsequent conviction, the offender shall be imprisoned at hard labor for not less than two nor more than ten years without benefit of parole, probation or suspension of sentence.

§62.2. Simple burglary of an inhabited dwelling.

Simple burglary of an inhabited home is the unauthorized entry of any inhabited dwelling, house, apartment or other structure used in whole or in part as a home or place of abode by a person or persons with the intent to commit a felony or any theft therein, other than as set forth in Article 60.

Whoever commits the crime of simple burglary of an inhabited dwelling shall be imprisoned at hard labor for not less than one year, without benefit of parole, probation or suspension of sentence, nor more than twelve years.

§62.3. Unauthorized entry of an inhabited dwelling.

A. Unauthorized entry of an inhabited dwelling is the intentional entry by a person without authorization into any inhabited dwelling or other structure belonging to another and used in whole or in part as a home or place of abode by a person.

B. Whoever commits the crime of unauthorized entry of an inhabited dwelling shall be fined not more than one thousand dollars or imprisoned with or without hard labor for not more than six years, or both.

§62.4. Unauthorized entry of a place of business.

A. Unauthorized entry of a place of business is the intentional entry by a person without authority into any structure belonging to another and used in whole or in part as a place of business.

B. Whoever commits the crime of unauthorized entry of a place of business shall be fined not more than one thousand dollars or imprisoned with or without hard labor for not more than six years, or both.

§62.5. Looting.

A. Looting is the intentional entry by a person without authorization into any dwelling or other structure belonging to another and used in whole or in part as a home or place of abode by a person, or any structure belonging to another and used in whole or in part as a place of business, or any vehicle, watercraft, building, plant, establishment, or other structure, movable or immovable, in which normal security of property is not present by virtue of a hurricane, flood, fire, act of God, or force majeure of any kind, or by virtue of a riot, mob, or other human agency, and the obtaining or exerting control over or damaging or removing property of the owner.

B. Whoever commits the crime of looting shall be fined not more than ten thousand dollars or imprisoned at hard labor for not more than fifteen years, or both.
(Added by Acts 1993 No. 667, §1, eff. 8/15/93.)

§62.6. Simple burglary of a religious building.

A. Simple burglary of a religious building is the unauthorized entering of any church, synagogue, mosque, or other building, structure, or place primarily used for religious worship or other religious purpose with the intent to commit a felony or any theft therein, other than as set forth in R.S. 14:60.

B. Whoever commits the crime of simple burglary of a religious building shall be fined not more than two thousand dollars and imprisoned with or without hard labor for not less than two years nor more than twelve years. At least two years of the sentence of imprisonment shall be imposed without benefit of probation, parole, or suspension of sentence.
(Added by Acts 1997 No. 405, §1, eff. 8/15/97.)

4. CRIMINAL TRESPASS

§63. Criminal trespass.

A. No person shall without authorization intentionally enter any structure, watercraft, or movable.

B. No person shall intentionally enter immovable property owned by another:

(1) When he knows his entry is unauthorized, or

(2) Under circumstances where he reasonably should know his entry is unauthorized.

C. (1) It shall be an affirmative defense to a prosecution pursuant to Subsection B(2) that the person was unarmed and entered immovable property for the sole purpose of retrieving a dog or livestock.

(2) It shall be an affirmative defense to a prosecution pursuant to Subsection B(2) to show that property was not adequately posted in accordance with Subsections D or E, and F of this Section.

D. In order for forest land to be adequately posted the owner, lessee, or person having the written permission of the owner or lessee shall post the property by any one of the following methods:

(1) Placing identifying paint marks on trees or posts around the area to be posted. Each paint mark shall be a vertical line of at least eight inches in length, and the bottom of the mark shall be no less than three feet nor more than five feet high. Such paint marks shall be placed no more than one hundred feet apart and shall be readily visible to any person approaching the property.

(2) Placing signs around the area to be posted at no more than one hundred feet apart and at normal points of ingress and egress. The signs shall bear the words "Posted", "No Trespassing", or "No" in letters at least three and one-half inches high and shall be so placed as to be readily visible to any person approaching the property.

(3) Constructing a fence around the area to be posted of not less than three strand wire, or its equivalent, and placing signs that bear the words "Posted", "No Trespassing", or "No" in letters at least three and one-half inches high at normal points of ingress and egress.

E. In order for any immovable property other than forest land to be adequately posted, including cultivated land, orchards, pasture lands, impoundments, or other immovable property, the owner, lessee, or person having the written permission of the owner or lessee shall post the property by any one of the following methods:

(1) Placing identifying paint marks on posts around the area to be posted. Each paint mark shall be a vertical line of at least eight inches in length, and the bottom of the mark shall be no less than three feet nor more than five feet high. Such paint marks shall be placed no more than one thousand feet apart and at normal points of ingress and egress and shall be readily visible to any person approaching the property.

(2) Placing signs around the area to be posted at points no more than one thousand feet apart and at each normal point of ingress and egress. The signs shall bear the words "Posted", "No Trespassing", or "No" in letters at least three and one-half inches high and shall be so placed as to be readily visible to any person approaching the property.

(3) Constructing a fence around the area to be posted of not less than three strand wire, or its equivalent, and placing signs that bear the words "Posted", "No Trespassing", or "No" in letters at least three and one-half inches high at normal points of ingress and egress.

F. The type of color of the paint to be used for posting shall be prescribed by regulation by the Louisiana Forestry Commission, which shall not select a color that is presently being used by the timber industry in this state to mark land line or property lines. The color of paint prescribed shall not be used on trees or posts for any other purpose.

G. Affirmative defenses to a prosecution pursuant to Subsection B of this Section shall be:

(1) That the entry was by a registered land surveyor, and his personnel, engaged in the "Practice of Land Surveying", as defined in R.S. 37:682, or a person employed by a public utility acting in the course and scope of his employment relating to operation, repair, or maintenance of a public utility facility, or

(2) That the entry was by an employee or agent of the Louisiana Department of Agriculture and Forestry and was for the purpose of locating and suppressing wildfire in accordance with the rules and regulations of the department.

H. Whoever commits the crime of criminal trespass shall be fined not more than five hundred dollars.

I. (1) Upon a second conviction, regardless of whether the second offense occurred before or after the first conviction, the offender shall be imprisoned for not more than six months, or shall be fined not more than five hundred dollars, or both.

(2) Upon a third or subsequent conviction, whether trespass has been committed in each previous offense upon land belonging to the same landowner or landowners, regardless of the time sequence of the occurrence of the offenses, the offender shall be imprisoned for not more than one year, or shall be fined not more than one thousand dollars, or both.

J. The provisions of this Section shall not be applicable to marshland which shall be governed by the provisions of R.S. 14:63.12.

K. The provisions of this Section shall not prohibit the governing authority of any parish from adopting an ordinance in accordance with the provisions of R.S. 33:1236(14).

L. The owner or lessee shall be immune from liability as a result of trespassing by any person upon forest land, cultivated land, orchards, pasturelands, swamplands, marshlands, and impoundments.

M. No person shall knowingly paint such color prescribed by the Louisiana Forest Commission for posting immovable property on any tree or post for any purpose other than posting immovable property pursuant to Paragraph (1) of Subsection D or Paragraph (1) of Subsection E of this Section. Any person who violates the provisions of this Subsection shall be fined not more than five hundred dollars.

(Chgd. by Acts 1991 No. 438, §1; Acts 1993 No. 887, §1, eff. 8/15/93.)

§63.1. Illegal posting.

A. Illegal posting is the posting or the placing and/or maintaining of posted signs on property by anyone other than:

(1) The owner or his duly authorized agent or representative.

(2) The lessee or his duly authorized agent or representative.

(3) A person having the written permission of the owner or lessee.

B. Whoever commits the crime of illegal posting shall be fined not more than five hundred dollars.

(Chgd. by Acts 1991 No. 438, §1, eff. 9/6/91.)

§63.2. Destruction, defacing or removal of posted signs.

No person shall intentionally and without authority destroy, deface or remove posted signs, or signs designating or purporting to designate the boundary lines of immovable property.

Whoever violates the provisions of this Section shall be fined not less than fifty dollars, nor more than three hundred dollars, or imprisoned for not more than sixty days, or both.

§63.3. Entry on or remaining in places or on land after being forbidden.

A. No person shall without authority go into or upon or remain in or upon or attempt to go into or upon or remain in or upon any structure, watercraft, or any other movable, or immovable property, which belongs to another, including public buildings and structures, ferries, and bridges, or any part, portion, or area thereof, after having been forbidden to do so, either orally or in writing, including by means of any sign hereinafter described, by any owner, lessee, or custodian of the property or by any other authorized person. For the purposes of this Section, the above mentioned sign means a sign or signs posted on or in the structure, watercraft, or any other movable, or immovable property, including public buildings and structures, ferries and bridges, or part, portion or area thereof, at a place or places where such sign or signs may be reasonably expected to be seen.

B. Whoever violates the provisions of this Section shall be guilty of a misdemeanor and upon conviction thereof shall be fined not more than five hundred dollars or imprisoned in the parish jail for not more than six months, or both.

§63.4. Aiding and abetting others to enter or remain on premises where forbidden.

A. No person shall incite, solicit, urge, encourage, exhort, instigate, or procure any other person to go into or upon or to remain in or upon any structure, watercraft, or any other movable which belongs to another, including public buildings and structures, ferries, and bridges, or any part, portion, or area thereof, knowing that such other person has been forbidden to go or remain there, either orally or in writing, including by means of any sign hereinafter described, by the owner, lessee, or custodian of the property or by any other authorized person.

For the purposes of this Section, the above mentioned sign means a sign or signs posted on or in the structure, watercraft or any other movable, including public buildings and structures, ferries and bridges, or part, portion or area thereof, at a place or places where such sign or signs may be reasonably expected to be seen.

B. Any law enforcement officer investigating a complaint that the provisions of this Section are being or have been violated or any such officer making any arrest for violation of the provisions of this Section, is hereby vested with authority to require any person involved in such investigation or arrest to identify himself to such officer. Upon demand of such officer, the person involved shall inform the officer of his true name and address.

C. Whoever violates the provisions of Sub-section A or Sub-section B above, shall be guilty of a misdemeanor and upon conviction thereof shall be fined not more than five hundred dollars or be imprisoned in the parish jail for not more than six months, or both.

§63.5. Unauthorized access to railroad property.

A. No person shall without authorization intentionally access into or upon any railroad movable property when he knows such access is unauthorized, or under circumstances where he reasonably should know such access is unauthorized.

B. As used herein:

(1) "Access" means to enter by any means and includes but is not limited to the attaching or holding by any means onto any train, locomotive, or railroad car.

(2) "Railroad movable property" means any rolling stock owned, leased, operated, or possessed by a railroad, including but not limited to any train, locomotive, or railway car located or operated upon any railroad property.

C. Whoever violates the provisions of this Section shall be fined not more than five hundred dollars or imprisoned for not more than six months, or both.

§63.6. Unauthorized entry upon railroad property.

A. No person shall without authorization intentionally enter any property of a railroad when he knows his entry is unauthorized, or under circumstances where he reasonably should know his entry is unauthorized, and when such entry is with the intent to interfere with, interrupt, or prevent the operation of any train, locomotive, or railway car.

B. No person shall remain in or upon any property of a railroad when authorization for his entry was not given, or has been withdrawn, and when his continued presence interferes with, interrupts, or prevents the operation of any train, locomotive, or railway car.

C. "Property of a railroad" as used herein means any movable or immovable property owned or leased by a railroad, or any immovable property possessed by a railroad upon which is placed a railroad track and the land adjacent thereto.

D. Whoever violates the provisions of Subsection A or Subsection B herein, upon first conviction, shall be fined not more than five hundred dollars or imprisoned for not more than ninety days, or both, and, upon second or subsequent conviction, shall be fined not more than five hundred dollars or imprisoned for not more than six months, or both.

§63.7. Criminal trespass; crawfish ponds; penalty.

A. No person shall intentionally enter upon immovable property owned by another on which crawfish ponds are located when the offender knows the entry is unauthorized or when the entry is under circumstances where the offender reasonably should know that the entry is unauthorized.

B. Whoever violates the provisions of this Section shall be imprisoned for not more than ninety-one days, or shall be fined not more than five hundred dollars, or both. Upon a second or subsequent conviction, regardless of whether the second or subsequent offense occurred before or after the previous conviction, the offender shall be imprisoned for not more than six months, or shall be fined not more than five hundred dollars, or both.

§63.8. Criminal trespass; catfish ponds; penalty.

A. No person shall intentionally enter upon immovable property owned by another on which catfish ponds are located when the offender knows the entry is unauthorized or when the entry is under circumstances where the offender reasonably should know that the entry is unauthorized.

B. Whoever violates the provisions of this Section shall be imprisoned for not more than ninety-one days or shall be fined not more than five hundred dollars, or both. Upon a second or subsequent conviction, regardless of whether the second or subsequent offense occurred before or after the previous conviction, the offender shall be imprisoned for not more than six months or shall be fined not more than five hundred dollars, or both.

§63.9. Criminal trespass; agricultural row crop land; penalty.

A. No person shall intentionally enter upon immovable property owned by another and in use as agricultural land for the production of row crops without the written permission of the owner or the lessee of the property.

B. Affirmative defenses to a prosecution pursuant to this Section shall include the following:

(1) The person was unarmed and entered immovable property for the sole purpose of retrieving a dog or livestock.

(2) The entry was by a registered land surveyor and his personnel, engaged in the "Practice of Land Surveying", as defined in R.S. 37:682, or a person employed by a public utility acting in the course and scope of his employment relating to operation, repair, or maintenance of a public utility facility.

(3) The entry was by an employee or agent of the Louisiana Department of Agriculture and Forestry and was for the purpose of locating and suppressing wildfire in accordance with the rules and regulations of the department.

C. The provisions of this Section shall not prohibit the governing authority of any parish from adopting an ordinance in accordance with the provisions of R.S. 33:1236(14).

D. The owner or lessee shall be immune from liability as a result of trespassing by any person upon immovable property in use as agricultural land for the production of row crops.

E. Whoever violates the provisions of this Section may be imprisoned for not more than ninety days or fined not more than five hundred dollars, or both. Upon a second or subsequent conviction, regardless of whether the second or subsequent offense occurred before or after the previous conviction, the offender may be imprisoned for not more than six months or fined not more than one thousand dollars, or both.

(Added by Acts 1993 No. 425, §1, eff. 8/15/93.)

§63.10. Vehicular trespass.

A. No person shall knowingly enter into or upon the motor vehicle, boat, or aircraft of another, without the consent of its owner or of any person who has a right to possession superior to that of the entrant, when the entrant is not otherwise privileged to do so.

B. "Enter into or upon" means:

(1) To open or unlock any door, window, or other access opening of any motor vehicle, boat, or aircraft.

(2) To be astride of any motor vehicle, boat, or aircraft.

(3) To be supported by any motor vehicle, boat, or aircraft.

C. An entrant is privileged to enter if:

(1) He is attempting to render aid or assistance to an ill or injured person.

(2) He reasonably believes that the entry is necessary to prevent injury to person or property.

(3) He is a state or local law enforcement officer in the performance of his official duties.

D. Whoever commits the crime of vehicular trespass shall be fined not more than five hundred dollars or imprisoned for not more than six months, or both.
(Added by Acts 1995 No. 1056, §1, eff. 8/15/95.)

§63.12. Criminal trespass upon marshlands.

A. Criminal trespass upon marshlands is:

(1) The unauthorized and intentional taking possession of any tract of marshland or structure thereon without the consent of the owner thereof; or

(2) The unauthorized and intentional entry upon any:

(a) Plot of marshland in excess of one acre which is posted but not enclosed, unless said property is situated in an open range area; or

(b) Plot of marshland which is posted and enclosed, including property situated in open range areas; or

(c) Posted marshland belonging to public institutions; or

(d) Structure, water craft or movable located upon marshland, except where an entry is made from a waterway for emergency purposes the party in distress may use the banks of said waterway without violating the provisions of Paragraph 2.

B. Definitions

For purposes of criminal trespass upon marshland the following definitions are adopted:

(1) "Posted" marshland means any marshland which is designated as such by the owner, lessee or other person lawfully authorized to take such action, provided the following requirements are satisfied:

(a) The owner or person seeking to post the property shall place and maintain signs along the boundaries of the property or area to be posted, which signs shall be written in the English language, and said signs shall contain the words "Posted", or, "Private Property", "No Trespassing", "No Hunting", "No Fishing", or words to that effect.

(b) The signs shall have letters at least two and one-half inches in height and shall be of sufficient size and clarity to give notice to the public of the location and boundary of the posted property. The signs shall be placed and maintained at intervals of not more than one thousand five hundred feet and at all points of ingress or egress and shall be at least three but not more than nine feet above the ground or water level.

(c) The party seeking to post the marshlands shall include his name and address on the posted signs, in addition to the words required by Subparagraph (a) hereof, which name and address shall be indicated by letters at least three-fourths of an inch in height.

(2) "Enclosed" marshland means any marshland which is surrounded or encompassed by natural and/or artificial barriers.

Natural barriers include:

(a) The Gulf of Mexico,

(b) Lakes or ponds or other bodies of water which hold water during twelve months of the year,

(c) Any river, stream, bayou or canal in which water is held or runs during twelve months of the year,

(d) Other similar natural barriers.

Artificial barriers include:

(e) Any wall or wire, stone, metal or wooden fence,

(f) Any cattle-guard being used as part of a fence,

(g) Other similar barriers.

(3) "Open Range" area means any area in which livestock are not prohibited by law to freely rove, provided that any road or highway which is required by law to be fenced, and which passes through any area in which livestock are not otherwise prohibited by law to freely rove, shall not prevent such area from being classified as "open range".

(4) "Marshland" shall include any levee or spoil bank situated on or adjacent to marshland.

C. Penalties

(1) Whoever commits the crime of criminal trespass upon marshland shall be fined not more than five hundred dollars, or imprisoned for not more than ninety-one days, or both.

(2) On a second or subsequent conviction, regardless of whether the second offense occurred before or after the first conviction, the offender shall be fined not more than five hundred dollars, or imprisoned for not more than six months, or both.

D. For the purposes of this Section the personnel of and a professional land surveyor qualified and currently registered by the State Board of Registered Professional Engineers and Land Surveyors in accordance with R.S. 37:681 et seq. are exempt from these penalties while performing the practice of land surveying as defined in R.S. 37:682. Nor shall criminal trespass under this Section include the mere exercise of the right of passage to an enclosed estate as otherwise provided by law.

SUBPART B. BY MISAPPROPRIATION WITH VIOLENCE TO THE PERSON

§64. Armed robbery.

A. Armed robbery is the taking of anything of value belonging to another from the person of another or that is in the immediate control of another, by use of force or intimidation, while armed with a dangerous weapon.

B. Whoever commits the crime of armed robbery shall be imprisoned at hard labor for not less than five years and for not more than ninety-nine years, without benefit of parole, probation or suspension of sentence.

§64.1. First degree robbery.

A. First degree robbery is the taking of anything of value belonging to another from the person of another, or that is in the immediate control of another, by use of force or intimidation, when the offender leads the victim to reasonably believe he is armed with a dangerous weapon.

B. Whoever commits the crime of first degree robbery shall be imprisoned at hard labor for not less than three years and for not more than forty years, without benefit of parole, probation or suspension of imposition or execution of sentence.

§64.2. Carjacking.

A. Carjacking is the intentional taking of a motor vehicle, as defined in R.S. 32:1(40), belonging to another person, in the presence of that person, or in the presence of a passenger, or any other person in lawful possession of the motor vehicle, by the use of force or intimidation.

B. Whoever commits the crime of carjacking shall be imprisoned at hard labor for not less than two years and for not more than twenty years, without benefit of parole, probation, or suspension of sentence.

(Added by Acts 1993 No. 488, §1, eff. 8/15/93.)

§65. Simple robbery.

A. Simple robbery is the taking of anything of value belonging to another from the person of another or that is in the immediate control of another, by use of force or intimidation, but not armed with a dangerous weapon.

B. Whoever commits the crime of simple robbery shall be fined not more than three thousand dollars, imprisoned with or without hard labor for not more than seven years, or both.

§65.1. Purse snatching.

A. Purse snatching is the theft of anything of value contained within a purse or wallet at the time of the theft, from the person of another or which is in the immediate control of another, by use of force, intimidation, or by snatching, but not armed with a dangerous weapon.

B. Whoever commits the crime of purse snatching shall be imprisoned, with or without hard labor, for not less than two years and for not more than twenty years.

§66. Extortion.

Extortion is the communication of threats to another with the intention thereby to obtain anything of value or any acquittance, advantage, or immunity of any description. The following kinds of threats shall be sufficient to constitute extortion:

(1) A threat to do any unlawful injury to the person or property of the individual threatened or of any member of his family or of any other person held dear to him;

(2) A threat to accuse the individual threatened or any member of his family or any other person held dear to him of any crime;

(3) A threat to expose or impute any deformity or disgrace to the individual threatened or to any member of his family or to any other person held dear to him;

(4) A threat to expose any secret affecting the individual threatened or any member of his family or any other person held dear to him;

(5) A threat to do any other harm.

Whoever commits the crime of extortion shall be imprisoned at hard labor for not less than one nor more than fifteen years.

SUBPART C. BY MISAPPROPRIATION WITHOUT VIOLENCE

§67. Theft.

A. Theft is the misappropriation or taking of anything of value which belongs to another, either without the consent of the other to the misappropriation or taking, or by means of fraudulent conduct, practices, or representations. An intent to deprive the other permanently of whatever may be the subject of the misappropriation or taking is essential.

B. (1) Whoever commits the crime of theft when the misappropriation or taking amounts to a value of five hundred dollars or more shall be imprisoned, with or without hard labor, for not more than ten years, or may be fined not more than three thousand dollars, or both.

(2) When the misappropriation or taking amounts to a value of one hundred dollars or more, but less than a value of five hundred dollars, the offender shall be imprisoned, with or without hard labor, for not more than two years, or may be fined not more than two thousand dollars, or both.

(3) When the misappropriation or taking amounts to less than a value of one hundred dollars, the offender shall be imprisoned for not more than six months, or may be fined not more than five hundred dollars, or both. If the offender in such cases has been convicted of theft two or more times previously, upon any subsequent conviction he shall be imprisoned, with or without hard labor, for not more than two years, or may be fined not more than one thousand dollars, or both.

C. When there has been a misappropriation or taking by a number of distinct acts of the offender, the aggregate of the amount of the misappropriations or takings shall determine the grade of the offense.

(Chgd. by Acts 1990 No. 118, §1, eff. 9/7/90.)

§67.1. Theft of livestock.

A. Theft of livestock is the misappropriation or taking of livestock belonging to another, either without the consent of the other to the misappropriation or taking, or by means of fraudulent conduct, practices, or representations. An intent to deprive the other permanently of the livestock is essential. It shall not be necessary to prove defendants killed the animal; the mere taking of meat from the animal shall constitute theft hereunder. Transportation of livestock to a slaughterhouse or an auction sale barn and assignment in a record book in a name other than that of the owner shall also be theft of livestock. An intent to deprive the owner permanently of funds derived from sale is essential.

B. "Livestock" means any animal, hybrid, mixture, or mutation of the species of horses, mules, donkeys, asses, cattle, swine, sheep, goats, domesticated deer, buffalo, bison, beefalo, or oxen.

C. Whoever commits the crime of theft of livestock shall be fined not more than five thousand dollars, or imprisoned, with or without hard labor, for not more than ten years, or both.

D. The Livestock Brand Commission of the State of Louisiana shall have primary responsibility for the collection of information in such cases and shall aid all police agencies in such investigations.

E. Whenever there is a prosecution under this Section as a second or third offense not more than one offense committed prior to the enactment of this Section may be used to establish the second or third offense as the case may be.

F. The Livestock Brand Commission of the state of Louisiana shall have primary responsibility for collection of information in such cases and shall aid all police agencies in such investigations.

§67.2. Theft of animals.

A. Theft of animals is the misappropriation or taking of any animal which belongs to another, either without consent of the other to the misappropriation or taking, or by means of fraudulent conduct, practices, or representations. An intent to deprive the other permanently of the animal or an intent to ransom it for the purpose of extorting money or favor is essential.

B. (1) Whoever commits the crime of theft of animals, when the misappropriation or taking amounts to a value of five hundred dollars or more, shall be imprisoned, with or without hard labor, for not more than ten years, or may be fined not more than three thousand dollars, or both.

(2) When the misappropriation or taking amounts to a value of one hundred dollars or more, but less than a value of five hundred dollars, the offender shall be imprisoned, with or without hard labor, for not more than two years, or may be fined not more than two thousand dollars, or both.

(3) When the misappropriation or taking amounts to less than a value of one hundred dollars, the offender shall be imprisoned for not more than six months, or may be fined not more than five hundred dollars, or both. If the offender in such a case has been convicted of misdemeanor theft of an animal two or more times previously, upon any subsequent conviction he shall be imprisoned, with or without hard labor, for not more than two years, or may be fined not more than one thousand dollars, or both.

C. The value of the animal which was misappropriated or taken shall be decided by the court, or the jury in a jury trial, based upon the evidence establishing the value beyond a reasonable doubt, including but not limited to the following:

(1) The amount of money which was acquired from the sale, use, or other disposal of the animal.

(2) Expert testimony as to the amount of money which may be acquired from the sale, use, or other disposal of the animal.

(3) In cases of a pet, testimony by the owner as to the strength of the bond between the owner and the animal and the emotional attachment between the animal and the owner or person with whom the animal is attached.

D. The provisions of Subsection C of this Section do not apply when the state proves beyond a reasonable doubt that the animal is a dog and a pet, and the theft of such animal shall be punishable as provided in Paragraph B(1) of this Section.

E. For the purposes of this Section, "animal" means any non-human living creature except for livestock as defined in R.S. 14:67.1.

(Chgd. by Acts 1995 No. 1183, §1, eff. 8/15/95.)

§67.3. Unauthorized use of "access card" as theft; definitions.

A. (1) "Access card" shall mean and include any card, plate, account number, paper, book, or any other device, issued to a person which authorizes such person to obtain credit, money, goods, services, or anything of value, whether contemporaneously or not, by use of any credit or deferred payment plan with the issuer or by use of debiting or charging such person's demand deposit or savings or time account with the issuer or by debiting or charging any other funds such person has on deposit with the issuer.

(2) "Revoked Access Card" as used herein shall mean an Access Card which has been cancelled or terminated by the issuer of said Access Card.

(3) "Person" as used herein shall mean and include natural persons, or any organization, or other entity.

(4) "Issuer" as used herein shall be the depository and/or creditor issuing the Access Card, directly or through another entity.

(5) The aggregate amount or value of credit, money, goods, services or anything else of value obtained shall determine the value of the misappropriation or taking in determining the penalty under R.S. 14:67 when the offender has obtained the credit, money, goods, services or anything else of value from any one issuer or the offender has used an Access Card, or referred to a nonexistent Access Card on two or more occasions within any consecutive ninety day period.

B. Whoever, directly or indirectly, by agent or otherwise, with intent to defraud, (1) uses a forged Access Card, (2) makes reference by number or other description to a nonexistent Access Card, (3) steals or wrongfully appropriates an Access Card, or (4) uses an Access Card belonging to another person without authority of said person; thereby obtaining, whether contemporaneously or not, credit, money, goods, services or anything of value shall be guilty of theft and shall be subject to the penalties provided for the crime of theft in R.S. 14:67.

C. Whoever, directly or indirectly, by agent or otherwise, with intent to defraud, uses a revoked Access Card, thereby obtaining, whether contemporaneously or not, credit, money, goods, services or anything of value shall be guilty of theft and shall be subject to the penalties provided for the crime of theft in R.S. 14:67. For purposes of this Subsection, it shall be presumptive evidence that a person used a revoked Access Card with intent to defraud if the said person, directly or indirectly, by agent or otherwise, uses the said Access Card after actually receiving oral or written notice that the Access Card has been cancelled or terminated, or if said person, directly or indirectly, by agent or otherwise, uses the said Access Card at a time period more than five days after written notice of the termination or cancellation of said Access Card has been deposited by registered or certified mail in the United States mail system. Said notice shall be addressed to the person to whom such Access Card has been issued at the last known address for such person as shown on the records of the issuer.

D. Whoever, directly or indirectly, by agent or otherwise, with the intent to defraud, uses an Access Card to obtain, whether contemporaneously or not, money, goods, services or anything of value, and the final payment for said items is to be made by debiting or charging said person's demand deposit or savings or time account with issuer, or by debiting or charging any other funds said person has on deposit with issuer, and there are not sufficient funds on deposit to the credit of said person with the issuer to make payment in full of said items obtained, said person shall have committed the crime of theft in R.S. 14:67. Said person's failure to pay the amount due on said items obtained:

(1) Within ten days after written notice of said amount due has been deposited by certified or registered mail in the United States mail system addressed to the person to whom such Access Card has been issued at the last known address for such person as shown on the records of issuer; or

(2) Within ten days of delivery or personal tender of said written notice shall be presumptive evidence of said person's intent to defraud.

E. As used herein and in R.S. 14:67, the Access Card itself shall be a thing of value, with a value less than one hundred dollars.

F. In addition to any other fine or penalty imposed under this Section or under R.S. 14:67, the court may, at its discretion, order as a part of the sentence, restitution.

§67.4. Theft of domesticated fish from fish farm; penalty.

On and after July 29, 1970, it shall be unlawful for any person, other than the owner thereof, to fish or to take any domesticated fish from any fish farm or private pond, except with the consent of the owner thereof.

Any person violating the provisions of this section shall, upon conviction thereof, be subject to a fine or imprisonment or both, as provided for in accordance with the penalties prescribed for violation of R.S. 14:67 based on the value of the domesticated fish unlawfully taken or misappropriated.

§67.5. Theft of crawfish; penalty.

A. No person shall knowingly, willfully and intentionally fish or take any commercial crawfish from any crawfish farm, except with the consent of the owner thereof.

B. Any person violating the provisions of this Section shall, upon conviction thereof, be subject to a fine or imprisonment or both, the same as provided for violations of R.S. 14:67 based on the value of the crawfish unlawfully taken or misappropriated.

§67.6. Theft of utility service; inference of commission of theft; penalties.

A. Theft of utility service is the misappropriation, taking, or use of any electricity, gas, water, or telecommunications which belongs to another, is held for sale by another, or is being distributed by another, without the consent of the owner, seller, or distributor or by means of fraudulent conduct, practices, or representations. A taking, misappropriation, or use includes the diversion by any means or device of any quantity of electricity, gas, water, or telecommunications from the wires, cables, pipes, mains, or other means of transmission of such person, or by directly or indirectly preventing a metering device from properly registering the quantity of electricity, gas, water, or telecommunications actually used, consumed, or transmitted.

B. The trier of fact may infer that there was a misappropriation, taking, or using without the consent of the owner, seller, or distributor, or that there was fraudulent conduct, practices, or representations when:

(1) There is on or about any wire, cable, pipe, main, or meter, or the equipment to which said wire, cable, pipe, main, or meter is affixed or attached, any device or any other means resulting in the diversion of electricity, gas, water, or telecommunications, or any device or

any other means resulting in the prevention of the proper action or accurate registration of the meter or meters used to measure the quantity of electricity, gas, water, or telecommunications actually used, consumed, or transmitted, or interfering with the proper action or accurate registration of such meter or meters;

(2) The person charged had custody or control of the room, structure, or place where such device, other means, or such wire, cable, pipe, main, meter, or equipment affixed or attached thereto was located; and

(3) The person charged benefited from the misappropriation of such utility service; or

(4) The person charged intentionally supplied false information in applying for such utility service.

C. (1) On a first conviction, the offender shall be fined not less than one hundred dollars nor more than five hundred dollars or imprisoned for not more than six months, or both.

(2) On a second or subsequent conviction, regardless of whether the second or subsequent offense occurred before or after an earlier conviction, the offender shall be fined not less than one hundred dollars nor more than three thousand dollars or imprisoned with or without hard labor, for not more than two years, or both.

D. The provisions of this Section shall not apply to the attachment on the customer's side of the customer's main electric disconnect of any device which lowers the quantity of utilities actually used and does not divert such utilities or prevent their proper registration.

§67.7. Theft of petroleum products; penalties.

Any person who shall unlawfully make or cause to be made any connection with or in any way tap or cause to be tapped, or drill or cause to be drilled a hole in any pipe or pipeline or tank laid or used for the conduct or storage of crude oil, naptha, gas or casinghead gas, or any of the manufactured or natural products thereof, with intent to deprive the owner thereof of any of said crude oil, naptha, gas, casinghead gas or any of the manufactured or natural products thereof, shall be guilty of a felony, and upon conviction shall be punished by forfeiture of the instrumentality of the crime and by a fine of not less than one hundred dollars and not more than fifty thousand dollars, or imprisoned, with or without hard labor, for a term of not less than one year nor more than ten years, or both.

§67.8. Theft of oilfield geological survey, seismograph, and production maps; penalties.

Any person who shall unlawfully take or misappropriate any oilfield geological survey, seismograph, production maps, or any similar or related items, with the intent to deprive the owner thereof of any of said maps or items, shall be guilty of a felony, and upon conviction shall be punished by a fine of not less than one hundred dollars nor more than fifty thousand dollars, or imprisonment, with or without hard labor, for a term of not less than one year nor more than ten years, or both.

§67.9. Theft of oil and gas equipment; penalties.

Any person who shall unlawfully take or misappropriate any machinery, drilling mud, welding equipment, pipe, fittings, pumps, or any other oil and gas equipment used in connection with the drilling, production, or maintenance of oil or gas wells, with the intent to deprive the owner or lessee thereof of said items shall:

(1) When the misappropriation or taking amounts to a value of five hundred dollars or more, be fined not less than one hundred or more than fifty thousand dollars or be imprisoned for not less than one year or more than ten years, with or without hard labor, or both.

(2) When the misappropriation or taking amounts to a value of one hundred dollars or more but less than five hundred dollars, be fined not more than two thousand dollars or be imprisoned, with or without hard labor, for not more than two years, or both.

(3) When the misappropriation or taking amounts to less than a value of one hundred dollars, be fined not more than five hundred dollars or be imprisoned for not more than six months, or both.

§67.10. Theft of goods.

A. Theft of goods is the misappropriation or taking of anything of value which is held for sale by a merchant, either without the consent of the merchant to the misappropriation or taking, or by means of fraudulent conduct, practices, or representations. An intent to deprive the merchant permanently of whatever may be the subject of the misappropriation or taking is essential and may be inferred when a person:

(1) Intentionally conceals, on his person or otherwise, goods held for sale.

(2) Alters or transfers any price marking reflecting the actual retail price of the goods.

(3) Transfers goods from one container or package to another or places goods in any container, package, or wrapping in a manner to avoid detection.

(4) Willfully causes the cash register or other sales recording device to reflect less than the actual retail price of the goods.

(5) Removes any price marking with the intent to deceive the merchant as to the actual retail price of the goods.

(6) Damages or consumes foods or property so as to render it unmerchantable.

B. (1) Whoever commits the crime of theft of goods when the misappropriation or taking amounts to a value of five hundred dollars or more shall be imprisoned, with or without hard labor, for not more than ten years or may be fined not more than three thousand dollars, or both.

(2) When the misappropriation or taking amounts to a value of one hundred dollars or more, but less than a value of five hundred dollars, the offender shall be imprisoned, with or without hard labor, for not more than two years or may be fined not more than two thousand dollars, or both.

(3) When the misappropriation or taking amounts to less than a value of one hundred dollars, the offender shall be imprisoned for not more than six months or may be fined not more than five hundred dollars, or both. If the offender in such cases has been convicted of theft or theft of goods two or more times previously, upon any subsequent conviction he shall be imprisoned, with or without hard labor, for not more than two years or may be fined not more than one thousand dollars, or both.

(4) When there has been a misappropriation or taking by a number of distinct acts of the offender, the aggregate of the amount of the misappropriations or takings shall determine the grade of the offense.

(Chgd. by Acts 1992 No. 701, §1, eff. 8/21/92.)

§67.11. Credit card fraud by persons authorized to provide goods and services.

A. As used in this Section the following terms have the following meanings:

(1) "Acquirer" means a business organization including without limitation a merchant, financial institution, or an agent of a business organization or financial institution that authorizes a merchant to accept payment by credit card for money, goods, services, or anything else of value.

(2) "Cardholder" means the person or organization named on the face of a credit card to whom or for whose benefit the credit card is issued by an issuer.

(3) "Credit card" means any instrument or device whether known as a credit card, credit plate, bank service card, banking card, check guarantee card, debit card, or by any other name, including an account number, issued with or without fee by an issuer for the use of a cardholder in obtaining money, goods, services, or anything of value on credit or for use in an automated banking device to obtain any of the services offered through the device.

(4) "Issuer" means the business organization or financial institution, or its duly authorized agent, which issues a credit card.

(5) "Provider" means a person who is authorized by an issuer or an acquirer to furnish money, goods, services, or anything else of value upon presentation of a credit card by the cardholder, or any agent or employee of such person.

(6) "Revoked credit card" means a credit card which is no longer valid because permission to use it has been suspended or terminated by the issuer.

B. No provider shall, with intent to defraud an issuer, an acquirer, or a cardholder, furnish money, goods, services, or anything else of value upon presentation of a credit card obtained or retained in violation of this Section, or a credit card which the provider knows is forged or revoked.

C. No provider shall, with intent to defraud an issuer, an acquirer, or a cardholder, fail to furnish money, goods, services, or anything else of value which the provider represents in writing, electronically or otherwise, to an issuer or an acquirer that such provider has furnished.

D. No provider shall, with intent to defraud an issuer, an acquirer, or a cardholder, present to an issuer or acquirer for payment a credit card transaction record which is not the result of an act between the cardholder and the provider.

E. No person shall employ, solicit, or otherwise cause a provider's employee or authorized agent or representative to remit to an acquirer a credit card transaction record of a sale that was not originated as a result of an act between the cardholder and such provider.

F. Any person who violates the provisions of this Section may be imprisoned, with or without hard labor, for not more than fifteen years, or fined not more than fifty thousand dollars, or both.
(Added by Acts 1990 No. 691, §1, eff. 9/7/90.)

§67.12. Theft of timber; information and investigations.

The enforcement division of the office of forestry within the Department of Agriculture and Forestry shall have primary responsibility for collection, preparation, and central registry of information relating to theft of timber and shall assist all law enforcement agencies in investigations of violations of R.S. 14:67. *(Added by Acts 1990 No. 118, §1, eff. 9/7/90.)*

§67.13. Theft of an alligator.

A. Theft of an alligator is the misappropriation or taking of an alligator, an alligator's skin, or a part of an alligator, whether dead or alive, belonging to another, either without the consent of the other to the misappropriation or taking, or by means of fraudulent conduct, practices, or representations. An intent to deprive the other permanently of the alligator, the alligator's skin, or a part of an alligator is essential.

B. (1) Whoever commits the crime of theft of an alligator when the misappropriation or taking amounts to a value of five hundred dollars or more shall be imprisoned, with or without hard labor, for not more than ten years, or may be fined not more than three thousand dollars, or both.

(2) When the misappropriation or taking amounts to a value of one hundred dollars or more, but less than a value of five hundred dollars, the offender shall be imprisoned, with or without hard labor, for not more than two years, or may be fined not more than two thousand dollars, or both.

(3) When the misappropriation or taking amounts to less than a value of one hundred dollars, the offender shall be imprisoned for not more than six months, or may be fined not more than five hundred dollars, or both. If the offender in such cases has been convicted of theft of an alligator two or more times previously, upon any subsequent conviction he shall be imprisoned, with or without hard labor, for not more than two years, or may be fined not more than one thousand dollars, or both.
(Added by Acts 1992 No. 410, §1, eff. 8/21/92.)

§67.14. Fraudulent acquisition of a rental motor vehicle.

A. Fraudulent acquisition of a rental motor vehicle is the lease or rental of a motor vehicle from a commercial lessor by the intentional giving or communicating payment information to the commercial lessor relating to how the lessee will pay the rental fee, or part thereof, when the lessee knows or reasonably should know that the payment information is or was false, fraudulent, insufficient, or incorrect. For purposes of this Section, incorrect payment information includes but is not limited to the presentation or tender of a credit card or check, when the credit card spending authorization or funds in the checking account are insufficient to cover the payment of the rental vehicle.

B. Whoever violates the provisions of this Section may be imprisoned for up to six months, or fined one thousand dollars, or both.
(Added by Acts 1992 No. 986, §1, eff. 8/21/92.)

§67.15. Theft of a firearm.

A. Theft of a firearm is the misappropriation or taking of a firearm which belongs to another, either without the consent of the other to the misappropriation or taking or by means of fraudulent conduct, practices, or representations. An intent to deprive the other permanently of the firearm is essential.

B. For purposes of this Section, "firearm" means a shotgun or rifle, or a pistol, revolver, or other handgun.

C. (1) For a first offense, the penalty for theft of a firearm shall be imprisonment with or without hard labor for not less than one year nor more than five years and a fine of one thousand dollars.

(2) For a second offense, the penalty for theft of a firearm shall be imprisonment with or without hard labor for not less than four years nor more than five years, and a fine of two thousand dollars.

(3) For a third and subsequent offense, the penalty for theft of a firearm shall be imprisonment at hard labor for not less than ten years nor more than twelve years, and a fine of five thousand dollars.

(Added by Acts 1994 Third Ex. Sess. No. 122, §1, eff. 8/27/94.)

§68. Unauthorized use of a movable.

A. Unauthorized use of a movable is the intentional taking or use of a movable which belongs to another, either without the other's consent, or by means of fraudulent conduct, practices, or representations, but without any intention to deprive the other of the movable permanently. The fact that the movable so taken or used may be classified as an immovable, according to the law pertaining to civil matters, is immaterial.

B. Whoever commits the crime of unauthorized use of a movable having a value of one thousand dollars or less shall be fined not more than five hundred dollars, or imprisoned for not more than six months, or both. Whoever commits the crime of unauthorized use of a movable having a value in excess of one thousand dollars shall be fined not more than five thousand dollars, or imprisoned with or without hard labor for not more than five years, or both.

(Chgd. by Acts 1993 No. 419, §1, eff. 8/15/93.)

§68.1. Unauthorized removal of shopping cart, basket, or dairy case.

A. It shall be a misdemeanor for any person to remove a shopping cart, basket, or dairy case belonging to another from the parking area or grounds of any store without authorization therefor.

B. Whoever commits the crime of unauthorized removal of a shopping cart, basket, or dairy case from the parking area or grounds of a store shall be fined not more than one hundred dollars, or imprisoned for not more than six months, or both.

§68.2. Unauthorized use of food stamp coupons, food stamp authorization cards, or food stamp access devices.

A. As used in this Section the following terms have the following meanings:

(1) "Food stamp coupon" means any coupon, stamp, or type of certificate issued pursuant to the provisions of the Federal Food Stamp Act, 7 USC §2011 et seq.

(2) "Food stamp authorization card" means the document issued by the Department of Social Services to an eligible household which shows the allotment of food stamp coupons the household is entitled to be issued.

(3) "Food stamp access device" means any card, plate, code account access number, or other means of access that can be used, alone or in conjunction with another access device, to obtain payment, allotments, benefits, money, goods, or other things of value or that can be used to initiate a transfer of funds pursuant to the provisions of the Federal Food Stamp Act.

B. The unauthorized use of food stamp coupons, food stamp authorization cards, or food stamp access devices is:

(1) To knowingly use, transfer, acquire, alter, or possess food stamp coupons, food stamp authorization cards, or food stamp access devices contrary to the provisions of the Federal Food Stamp Act or the federal or state regulations issued pursuant thereto.

(2) To knowingly counterfeit, alter, transfer, acquire, or possess counterfeited or altered food stamp coupons, food stamp authorization cards, or food stamp access devices.

(3) To present or cause to be presented food stamp coupons for payment or redemption, knowing the same to have been counterfeited, altered, received, transferred, or used in any manner contrary to the provisions of the Federal Food Stamp Act or the federal or state regulations issued pursuant thereto.

(4) To knowingly appropriate food stamp coupons, food stamp authorization cards, or food stamp access devices with which a person has been entrusted or of which a person has gained possession by virtue of his position as a public employee.

C. (1) Whoever commits the crime of unauthorized use of food stamp coupons, food stamp authorization cards, or food stamp access devices when the coupons, authorization cards, or access devices amount to a value of five hundred dollars or more shall be imprisoned, with or without hard labor, for not more than ten years, or may be fined not more than three thousand dollars, or both.

(2) When the coupons, authorization cards, or access devices amount to a value of one hundred dollars or more, but less than five hundred dollars, the offender shall be imprisoned, with or without hard labor, for not more than two years, or may be fined not more than two thousand dollars, or both.

(3) When the coupons, authorization cards, or access devices amount to less than a value of one hundred dollars, the offender shall be imprisoned for not more than six months, or may be fined not more than five hundred dollars, or both.

D. If the offender in such cases has been convicted under this Section two or more times previously, upon any subsequent conviction he shall be imprisoned, with or without hard labor, for not more than two years, or may be fined not more than one thousand dollars, or both.

E. In addition to the foregoing penalties, a person convicted under this Section shall be ordered to make restitution in the total amount found to be the value of the coupons which form the basis for the conviction. If a person ordered to make restitution pursuant to this Section is found to be indigent and therefore unable to make restitution in full at the time of conviction, the court shall order a periodic payment plan consistent with the person's financial ability.

(Added by Acts 1991 No. 187, §1, eff. 7/2/91.)

§68.3. Unauthorized removal of a motor vehicle; penalties.

A. No one, except upon court order, shall remove a motor vehicle from a garage, repair shop, or vehicle storage facility when there is a charge due such garage, repair shop, or vehicle storage facility for repair work, mechanical service, or storage rendered to such vehicle without paying the charge or making arrangements acceptable to the management of the garage, repair shop, or vehicle storage facility to pay the charge.

B. Whoever violates this Section shall be imprisoned for not more than six months or fined not more than five hundred dollars, or both.

(Added by Acts 1991 No. 568, §1, eff. 9/6/91.)

§68.4. Unauthorized use of a motor vehicle.

A. Unauthorized use of a motor vehicle is the intentional taking or use of a motor vehicle which belongs to another, either without the other's consent, or by means of fraudulent conduct, practices, or representations, but without any intention to deprive the other of the motor vehicle permanently.

B. Whoever commits the crime of unauthorized use of a motor vehicle shall be fined not more than five thousand dollars or imprisoned with or without hard labor for not more than ten years or both.

(Added by Acts 1995 No. 904, §1, eff. 8/15/95.)

§68.5. Unauthorized removal of property from governor's mansion and the state capitol complex.

A. It shall be unlawful for any person to remove any property of the state from the grounds of the governor's mansion without the authorization of the property manager designated for the executive office of the governor, as provided for in R.S. 39:322, after consultation with the Louisiana Governor's Mansion Foundation.

B. It shall be unlawful for any person to remove any property of the Louisiana Governor's Mansion Foundation from the grounds of the governor's mansion without the authorization of the Louisiana Governor's Mansion Foundation.

C. It shall be unlawful for any person to remove any property of the state which has been catalogued pursuant to R.S. 24:43 from the state capitol complex without the authorization of the Legislative Budgetary Control Council.

D. Whoever commits the crime of unauthorized removal of property from the governor's mansion or from the state capitol complex as provided for in this Section shall, upon conviction, be subject to a fine or imprisonment or both, as provided for in accordance with the penalties prescribed for violation of R.S. 14:67 based on the value of the property unlawfully removed.

(Added by Acts 1997 No. 1153, §1, eff. 8/15/97.)

§69. Illegal possession of stolen things.

A. Illegal possession of stolen things is the intentional possessing, procuring, receiving, or concealing of anything of value which has been the subject of any robbery or theft, under circumstances which indicate that the offender knew or had good reason to believe that the thing was the subject of one of these offenses.

B. (1) Whoever commits the crime of illegal possession of stolen things, when the value of the things is five hundred dollars or more, shall be imprisoned, with or without hard labor, for not more than ten years, or may be fined not more than three thousand dollars, or both.

(2) When the value of the stolen things is one hundred dollars or more, but less than five hundred dollars, the offender shall be imprisoned, with or without hard labor, for not more than two years, or may be fined not more than two thousand dollars, or both.

(3) When the value of the stolen things is less than one hundred dollars, the offender shall be imprisoned for not more than six months, or may be fined not more than five hundred dollars, or both. If the offender in such cases has been convicted of receiving stolen things or illegal possession of stolen things two or more times previously, upon any subsequent conviction he shall be imprisoned, with or without hard labor, for not more than two years, or may be fined not more than one thousand dollars, or both.

(4) When the offender has committed the crime of illegal possession of stolen things by a number of distinct acts, the aggregate of the amount of the things so received shall determine the grade of the offense.

C. It shall be an affirmative defense to a violation of this Section committed by means of possessing, that the accused, within seventy-two hours of his acquiring knowledge or good reason to believe that a thing was the subject of robbery or theft, reports that fact or belief in writing to the district attorney in the parish of his domicile.

§70. False accounting.

False accounting is the intentional rendering of a financial statement of account which is known by the offender to be false, by anyone who is obliged to render an accounting by the law pertaining to civil matters.

Whoever commits the crime of false accounting shall be fined not more than five hundred dollars or imprisoned for not more than six months, or both.

§70.1. Medicaid fraud.

A. The crime of Medicaid fraud is the act of any person, who, with intent to defraud the state through any medical assistance program created under the federal Social Security Act and administered by the Department of Health and Hospitals:

(1) Presents for allowance or payment any false or fraudulent claim for furnishing services or merchandise; or

(2) Knowingly submits false information for the purpose of obtaining greater compensation than that to which he is legally entitled for furnishing services or merchandise; or

(3) Knowingly submits false information for the purpose of obtaining authorization for furnishing services or merchandise.

B. Whoever commits the crime of Medicaid fraud shall be imprisoned, with or without hard labor, for not more than five years, or may be fined not more than twenty thousand dollars, or both. A sentence of at least one year of imprisonment shall be imposed without benefit of probation, parole, or suspension of sentence if the loss to the state is in excess of twenty-five thousand dollars.

(Chgd. by Acts 1997 No. 1018, §1, eff. 8/15/97.)

§70.2. Refund or access device application fraud.

A. No person shall with the intent to defraud use a false or fictitious name or any other identifying information as his own or use the name or any other identifying information of any other person without that person's knowledge and consent for the purpose of:

(1) Obtaining or attempting to obtain a refund for merchandise returned to a business establishment or a refund on a ticket or other document that is evidence of services purchased from a business establishment; or

(2) Obtaining or attempting to obtain an access device.

B. For the purposes of this Section, "any other identifying information" shall include, but not be limited to, an address, telephone number, social security number, account number, or any other information through which the identity of a person may be ascertained. "Access device" means any card, plate, code, account number, or other means of account access that can be used to obtain anything of value, whether contemporaneously or not.

C. (1) Whoever commits the crime of refund fraud shall be fined not more than five hundred dollars or imprisoned for not more than six months, or both.

(2) Whoever commits the crime of access device application fraud when the misappropriation or taking amounts to a value of five hundred dollars or more shall be imprisoned, with or without hard labor, for not more than ten years, or may be fined not more than three thousand dollars, or both.

(3) When the misappropriation or taking amounts to a value of one hundred dollars or more, but less than a value of five hundred dollars, the offender shall be imprisoned, with or without hard labor, for not more than two years, or may be fined not more than two thousand dollars, or both.

(4) When the misappropriation or taking amounts to less than a value of one hundred dollars, the offender shall be imprisoned for not more than six months, or may be fined not more than five hundred dollars, or both. If the offender in such cases has been convicted of theft two or more times previously, upon any subsequent conviction he shall be imprisoned, with or without hard labor, for not more than two years, or may be fined not more than one thousand dollars, or both.

D. When there has been a misappropriation or taking by a number of distinct acts of the offender, the aggregate amount of the misappropriation or taking shall determine the grade of the offense.

(Chgd. by Acts 1997 No. 1255, §1, eff. 8/15/97.)

§70.3. Fraud in selling agricultural equipment.

A. As used in this Section, the term "security device" means any legal act which confers an interest in property to secure the payment of an obligation and includes liens, pawns, privileges, mortgages, and chattel mortgages.

B. The crime of fraud in selling agricultural equipment is the sale of any piece of agricultural equipment which is subject to a security device without informing the purchaser of the existence of the security device that is known to the vendor at the time of the sale.

C. Each person who sells farm equipment which is subject to a security device and who does not inform the purchaser of the existence of the security device shall have an affirmative defense to any prosecution under this Section if he satisfies the obligation secured by the security device within ten days of demand for payment by the purchaser.

D. Whoever commits the crime of fraud in selling agricultural equipment shall be fined not more than five hundred dollars or imprisoned for not more than six months, or both.

§70.4. Access device fraud.

A. No person shall without authorization and with the intent to defraud transfer an access device to another person.

B. No person shall without authorization and with the intent to defraud possess an access device issued to another person.

C. No person shall with the intent to defraud use, possess, or transfer device-making equipment or a counterfeit access device.

D. As used herein:

(1) "Access device" means any card, plate, code, account number, or other means of account access that can be used to obtain anything of value, whether contemporaneously or not.

(2) "Counterfeit access device" means an access device that is fictitious, altered, or forged.

(3) "Device-making equipment" means any instrumentality, mechanism, or impression designed or primarily used for making an access device or counterfeit access device.

(4) "Transfer" means sell, give, provide, or transmit.

E. Whoever violates any provision of this Section shall be fined not more than two thousand dollars or imprisoned with or without hard labor for not more than two years, or both.

F. In addition to any other penalty imposed under this Section, the court may, in its discretion, order restitution as a part of the sentence.

§71. Issuing worthless checks.

A. (1)(a) Issuing worthless checks is the issuing, in exchange for anything of value, whether the exchange is contemporaneous or not, with intent to defraud, of any check, draft or order for the payment of money upon any bank or other depository, knowing at the time of the issuing that the offender has not sufficient credit with the bank, or other depository for the payment of such check, draft, or order in full upon its presentation.

(b) This Section shall apply to a check, draft, or order tendered for satisfaction, in whole or in part, of payments due on installment contracts, open accounts, or any other obligation for which the creditor has authorized periodic payments or the extension of time in which to pay.

(c) This Section shall apply to a check, draft, or order for the payment of money given for a motor vehicle when such payment is conditioned upon delivery of documents necessary for transfer of a valid title to the purchaser.

(d) For purposes of this Section, an open account shall include accounts where checks are tendered as payment:

(i) In advance of receipt, in whole or in part, for telecommunication facilities or services.

(ii) For deposits, prepayments, or payments for the lease or rent of a rental motor vehicle, pursuant to a lease or rental agreement.

(2) The offender's failure to pay a check, draft, or order, issued for value, within ten days after notice of its nonpayment upon presentation has been deposited by certified mail in the United States mail system addressed to the issuer thereof either at the address shown on the instrument or the last known address for such person shown on the records of the bank upon which such instrument is drawn or within ten days after delivery or personal tender of the written notice to said issuer by the payee or his agent, shall be presumptive evidence of his intent to defraud.

B. Issuing worthless checks is also the issuing, in exchange for anything of value, whether the exchange is contemporaneous or not, with intent to defraud, of any check, draft, or order for the payment of money, when the offender knows at the time of the issuing that the account designated on the check, draft, or order has been closed, or is nonexistent or fictitious, or is one in which the offender has no interest or on which he has no authority to issue such check, draft, or order.

C. Whoever commits the crime of issuing worthless checks, when the amount of the check or checks is five hundred dollars or more, shall be imprisoned, with or without hard labor, for not more than ten years, or may be fined not more than three thousand dollars, or both.

D. When the amount of the check or checks is one hundred dollars or more, but less than five hundred dollars, the offender shall be imprisoned, with or without hard labor, for not more than two years, or may be fined not more than two thousand dollars, or both.

E. When the amount of the check or checks is less than one hundred dollars, the offender shall be imprisoned for not more than six months, or may be fined not more than five hundred dollars, or both. If the offender in such cases has been convicted of issuing worthless checks two or more times previously, upon any subsequent conviction he shall be imprisoned, with or without hard labor, for not more than two years, or be fined not more than one thousand dollars, or both.

F. When the offender has issued more than one worthless check within a one hundred eighty-day period, the amount of several or all worthless checks issued during that one hundred eighty-day period may be aggregated to determine the grade of the offense.

G. In addition to any other fine or penalty imposed under this Section, the court shall order as part of the sentence restitution in the amount of the check or checks, plus a fifteen dollar per check service charge payable to the person or entity that initially honored the worthless check or checks, an authorized collection agency, or justice of the peace. In the event the fifteen dollar per check service charge is paid to a person or entity other than one who initially honored the worthless check or checks, the court shall also order as part of the sentence restitution equal to the amount that the bank or other depository charged the person or entity who initially honored the worthless check, plus the actual cost of notifying the offender of nonpayment as required in Paragraph A(2).

(Chgd. by Acts 1990 No. 1003, §1; Acts 1991 No. 135, §1, No. 171, §1; Acts 1993 No. 670, §1; Acts 1994 Third Ex. Sess. No. 125, §1, eff. 8/27/94.)

§71.1. Bank fraud.

A. Whoever knowingly executes, or attempts to execute, a scheme or artifice to do any of the following shall be imprisoned, with or without hard labor, for not more than ten years, or may be fined not more than one hundred thousand dollars, or both:

(1) To defraud a financial institution.

(2) To obtain any of the monies, funds, credits, assets, securities, or other property owned by or under the custody or control of a financial institution by means of false or fraudulent pretenses, practices, transactions, representations, or promises.

B. As used in this Section, the term "financial institution" has the same meaning as in R.S. 6:2(8).

(Added by Acts 1992 No. 104, §1, eff. 9/1/92.)

§71.2. Failure to pay bridge or bridge-causeway toll.

A. Failure to pay bridge or bridge-causeway toll is the intentional driving or towing of a motor vehicle through a toll collection facility without payment of a required toll, where appropriate signs have been erected to notify that it is subject to payment of the tolls beyond such sign.

B. The registered owner of any vehicle who has failed to contest a notice of liability or pay the toll and administrative fees provided by R.S. 47:820.5.1, upon notice from the public entity which owns and administers the bridge or the bridge-causeway, and who has failed to pay the demand for payment served by the public entity which owns and administers the bridge or the bridge-causeway within thirty days after the demand for payment has been deposited, by certified mail, in the United States mail system addressed to the registered owner of the vehicle as shown by the records of the Louisiana Department of Public Safety and Corrections, office of motor vehicles, shall be presumptive evidence of the vehicle owner's intent to defraud.

C. Whoever commits the crime of failing to pay bridge or bridge-causeway tolls shall be imprisoned for not more than six months or may be fined not more than one hundred dollars for each violation, or both.

D. In addition to any fine or penalty imposed under this Section, the court shall order payment of the toll and administrative cost provided by R.S. 47:820.5.1.

(Added by Acts 1995 No. 720, §1, eff. 8/15/95.)

§72. Forgery.

Forgery is the false making or altering, with intent to defraud, of any signature to, or any part of, any writing purporting to have legal efficacy.

Issuing or transferring, with intent to defraud, a forged writing, known by the offender to be a forged writing, shall also constitute forgery.

Whoever commits the crime of forgery shall be fined not more than five thousand dollars, or imprisoned, with or without hard labor, for not more than ten years, or both.

§72.1. Use of forged academic records.

A. A "forged academic record" shall mean a transcript, diploma, grade report, or similar document which is presented as being a bona fide record of an institution of secondary or higher education, but which is, in fact, false, forged, altered, or counterfeit.

B. "Use of a forged academic record" shall mean the knowing and intentional offering, presentation, or other use of a forged academic record to a public or private institution of higher education in the state for the purpose of seeking admission to that institution, or one of its colleges or other academic branches, or for the purposes of securing a scholarship or other form of financial assistance from the institution itself or from other public or private sources of financial assistance for education purposes including, without limitation, loans, grants, fellowships, assistantships, or other forms of financial aid.

C. Whoever commits the crime of the use of forged academic records may be fined not in excess of five thousand dollars or imprisoned for not in excess of six months, or both.

§72.2. Monetary instrument abuse.

A. Whoever makes, issues, possesses, sells, or otherwise transfers a counterfeit or forged monetary instrument of a state or a political subdivision thereof or of an organization, with intent to deceive another person, shall be fined not more than one million dollars but not less than five thousand dollars and imprisoned, with or without hard labor, for not more than ten years but not less than six months, or both.

B. Whoever makes, issues, possesses, sells, or otherwise transfers an implement designed for or particularly suited for making a counterfeit or forged monetary instrument with the intent to deceive a person, shall be fined not more than one million dollars but not less than five thousand dollars, and imprisoned, with or without hard labor, for not more than ten years but not less than six months, or both.

C. For purposes of this Section:

(1) "Counterfeit" means a document or writing that purports to be genuine but is not, because it has been falsely made, manufactured, or composed.

(2) "Forged" means the false making or altering, with intent to defraud, of any signature to, or any part of, any writing purporting to have legal efficacy.

(3) "Monetary instrument" means:

(a) A note, stock certificate, treasury stock certificate, bond, treasury bond, debenture, certificate of deposit, interest coupon, warrant, debit instrument, access device or means of electronic fund transfer, money order, bank check, teller's check, cashier's check, traveler's check, letter of credit, warehouse receipt, negotiable bill of lading, certificate of interest in or participation in any profit-sharing agreement, collateral-trust certificate, pre-organization certificate of subscription, transferable share, investment contract, voting trust certificate, or certificate of interest in tangible or intangible property.

(b) An instrument evidencing ownership of goods, wares, or merchandise.

(c) Any other written instrument commonly known as a security.

(d) A certificate of interest in, certificate of participation in, certificate for, receipt for, or warrant or option or other right to subscribe to or purchase, any of the foregoing.

(e) A blank form of any of the foregoing.

(4) "Organization" means a legal entity, other than a government, established or organized for any purpose, and includes a corporation, company, association, firm, partnership, joint stock company, foundation, institution, society, union, or any other association of persons which operates in or the activities of which effect intrastate, interstate, or foreign commerce.

(5) "State" includes a state of the United States, the District of Columbia, Puerto Rico, Guam, the Virgin Islands, and any other territory or possession of the United States.

(Added by Acts 1997 No. 674, §1, eff. 8/15/97.)

§73. Commercial bribery.

Commercial bribery is the giving or offering to give, directly or indirectly, anything of apparent present or prospective value to any private agent, employee, or fiduciary, without the knowledge and consent of the principal or employer, with the intent to influence such agent's, employee's, or fiduciary's action in relation to the principal's or employer's affairs.

The agent's, employee's or fiduciary's acceptance of or offer to accept, directly or indirectly, anything of apparent present or prospective value under such circumstances shall also constitute commercial bribery.

The offender under this article who states the facts, under oath, to the district attorney charged with prosecution of the offense, and who gives evidence tending to convict any other offender under this article, may, in the discretion of the district attorney, be granted full immunity from prosecution for commercial bribery, in respect to the particular offense reported.

Whoever commits the crime of commercial bribery shall be fined not more than five hundred dollars, or imprisoned for not more than six months, or both.

SUBPART D. COMPUTER RELATED CRIME

§73.1. Definitions.

As used in this Subpart unless the context clearly indicates otherwise:

(1) "Access" means to program, to execute programs on, to communicate with, store data in, retrieve data from, or otherwise make use of any resources, including data or programs, of a computer, computer system, or computer network.

(2) "Computer" includes an electronic, magnetic, optical, or other high-speed data processing device or system performing logical, arithmetic, and storage functions, and includes any property, data storage facility, or communications facility directly related to or operating in conjunction with such device or system. "Computer" shall not include an automated typewriter or typesetter, a machine designed solely for word processing, or a portable hand-held calculator, nor shall "computer" include any other device which might contain components similar to those in computers but in which the components have the sole function of controlling the device for the single purpose for which the device is intended.

(3) "Computer network" means a set of related, remotely connected devices and communication facilities including at least one computer system with capability to transmit data through communication facilities.

(4) "Computer program" means an ordered set of data representing coded instructions or statements that when executed by a computer cause the computer to process data.

(5) "Computer services" means providing access to or service or data from a computer, a computer system, or a computer network.

(6) "Computer software" means a set of computer programs, procedures, and associated documentation concerned with operation of a computer system.

(7) "Computer system" means a set of functionally related, connected or unconnected, computer equipment, devices, or computer software.

(8) "Financial instrument" means any check, draft, money order, certificate of deposit, letter of credit, bill of exchange, access card as defined in R.S. 14:67.3, or marketable security.

(9) "Intellectual property" includes data, computer programs, computer software, trade secrets as defined in R.S. 51:1431(4), copyrighted materials, and confidential or proprietary information, in any form or medium, when such is stored in, produced by, or intended for use or storage with or in a computer, a computer system, or a computer network.

(10) "Proper means" include:

(a) Discovery by independent invention;

(b) Discovery by "reverse engineering", that is by starting with the known product and working backward to find the method by which it was developed. The acquisition of the known product must be by lawful means;

(c) Discovery under license or authority of the owner;

(d) Observation of the property in public use or on public display; or

(e) Discovery in published literature.

(11) "Property" means property as defined in R.S. 14:2(8) and shall specifically include but not be limited to financial instruments, electronically stored or produced data, and computer programs, whether in machine readable or human readable form.

§73.2. Offenses against intellectual property.

A. An offense against intellectual property is the intentional:

(1) Destruction, insertion, or modification, without consent, of intellectual property; or

(2) Disclosure, use, copying, taking, or accessing, without consent, of intellectual property.

B. (1) Whoever commits an offense against intellectual property shall be fined not more than five hundred dollars, or imprisoned for not more than six months, or both, for commission of the offense.

(2) However, when the damage or loss amounts to a value of five hundred dollars or more, the offender may be fined not more than ten thousand dollars, or imprisoned with or without hard labor, for not more than five years, or both.

C. The provisions of this Section shall not apply to disclosure, use, copyright, taking, or accessing by proper means as defined in this Subpart.

§73.3. Offenses against computer equipment or supplies.

A. An offense against computer equipment or supplies is the intentional modification or destruction, without consent, of computer equipment or supplies used or intended to be used in a computer, computer system, or computer network.

B. (1) Whoever commits an offense against computer equipment or supplies shall be fined not more than five hundred dollars, or be imprisoned for not more than six months, or both.

(2) However, when the damage or loss amounts to a value of five hundred dollars or more, the offender may be fined not more than ten thousand dollars, or imprisoned with or without hard labor, for not more than five years, or both.

§73.4. Offenses against computer users.

A. An offense against computer users is the intentional denial to an authorized user, without consent, of the full and effective use of or access to a computer, a computer system, a computer network, or computer services.

B. (1) Whoever commits an offense against computer users shall be fined not more than five hundred dollars, or be imprisoned for not more than six months, or both, for commission of the offense.

(2) However, when the damage or loss amounts to a value of five hundred dollars or more, the offender may be fined not more than ten thousand dollars, or imprisoned with or without hard labor, for not more than five years, or both.

§73.5. Computer fraud.

A. Computer fraud is the accessing or causing to be accessed of any computer, computer system, computer network, or any part thereof with the intent to:

(1) Defraud; or

(2) Obtain money, property, or services by means of false or fraudulent conduct, practices, or representations, or through the fraudulent alteration, deletion, or insertion of programs or data.

B. Whoever commits computer fraud shall be fined not more than ten thousand dollars, or imprisoned with or without hard labor for not more than five years, or both.

PART IV. OFFENSES AFFECTING THE FAMILY

SUBPART A. CRIMINAL NEGLECT OF FAMILY

§74. Criminal neglect of family.

A. (1) Criminal neglect of family is the desertion or intentional nonsupport:

(a) By a spouse of his or her spouse who is in destitute or necessitous circumstances; or

(b) By either parent of his minor child who is in necessitous circumstances, there being a duty established by this Section for either parent to support his child.

(2) Each parent shall have this duty without regard to the reasons and irrespective of the causes of his living separate from the other parent. The duty established by this Section shall apply retrospectively to all children born prior to the effective date of this Section.

(3) For purposes of this Subsection, the factors considered in determining whether "necessitous circumstances" exist are food, shelter, clothing, health, and with regard to minor children only, adequate education, including but not limited to public, private, or home schooling, and comfort.

B. (1) Whenever a husband has left his wife or a wife has left her husband in destitute or necessitous circumstances and has not provided means of support within thirty days thereafter, his or her failure to so provide shall be only presumptive evidence for the purpose of determining the substantive elements of this offense that at the time of leaving he or she intended desertion and nonsupport. The receipt of assistance from the Family Independence Temporary Assistance Program (FITAP) shall constitute only presumptive evidence of necessitous circumstances for purposes of proving the substantive elements of this offense. Physical incapacity which prevents a person from seeking any type of employment constitutes a defense to the charge of criminal neglect of family.

(2) Whenever a parent has left his minor child in necessitous circumstances and has not provided means of support within thirty days thereafter, his failure to so provide shall be only presumptive evidence for the purpose of determining the substantive elements of this offense that at the time of leaving the parent intended desertion and nonsupport. The receipt of assistance from the Familiy Independence Temporary Assistance Program(FITAP) shall constitute only presumptive evidence of necessitous circumstances of proving the substantive elements of this offense. Physical incapacity which prevents a person from seeking any type of employment constitutes a defense to the charge of criminal neglect of family.

C. Laws attaching a privilege against the disclosure of communications between husband and wife are inapplicable to proceedings under this Section. Husband and wife are competent witnesses to testify to any relevant matter.

D. (1) Whoever commits the offense of criminal neglect of family shall be fined not more than five hundred dollars or be imprisoned for not more than six months, or both, and may be placed on probation pursuant to R.S. 15:305.

(2) If a fine is imposed, the court shall direct it to be paid in whole or in part to the spouse or to the tutor or custodian of the child, to the court approved fiduciary of the spouse or child, or to the Louisiana Department of Health and Human Resources in an AFDC case or in a non-AFDC case in which the said department is rendering services, whichever is applicable; hereinafter, said payee shall be referred to as the "applicable payee." In addition, the court may issue a support order, after considering the circumstances and financial ability of the defendant, directing the defendant to pay a certain sum at such periods as the court may direct.

This support shall be ordered payable to the applicable payee. The amount of support as set by the court may be increased or decreased by the court as the circumstances may require.

(3) The court may also require the defendant to enter into a recognizance, with or without surety, in order that the defendant shall make his or her personal appearance in court whenever required to do so and shall further comply with the terms of the order or of any subsequent modification thereof.

E. For the purposes of this Section, "spouse" shall mean a husband or wife.
(Chgd. by Acts 1997 No. 1402, §1, eff. 8/15/97.)

§74.1. Right of action.

The provisions of Art. 242 of the Louisiana Revised Civil Code of 1870 shall not apply to any proceeding brought under the provisions of R.S. 14:74.

§§75 to 75.2. *(Repealed by Acts 1993 No. 442, §4, eff. 6/9/93.)*

SUBPART B. SEX OFFENSES AFFECTING THE FAMILY

§76. Bigamy.

Bigamy is the marriage to another person by a person already married and having a husband or wife living; or the habitual cohabitation, in this state, with such second husband or wife, regardless of the place where the marriage was celebrated.

The provisions of this article shall not extend:

(1) To any person whose former husband or wife has been absent, at the time of the second marriage, for five successive years without being known to such person, within that time, to be living; or

(2) To any person whose former marriage has been annulled or dissolved at the time of the second marriage, by the judgment of a competent court; or

(3) To any person who has, at the time of the second marriage, a reasonable and honest belief that his or her former husband or wife is dead, or that a valid divorce or annulment has been secured, or that his or her former marriage was invalid.

Whoever commits the crime of bigamy shall be fined not more than one thousand dollars, or imprisoned, with or without hard labor, for not more than five years, or both.

§77. Abetting in bigamy.

Abetting in bigamy is the marriage of an unmarried person to the husband or wife of another, with knowledge of the fact that the party is married and without a reasonable and honest belief that such party is divorced or his marriage annulled, or that the party's husband or wife is dead.

Whoever commits the crime of abetting in bigamy shall be fined not more than one thousand dollars, or imprisoned, with or without hard labor, for not more than five years, or both.

§78. Incest.

A. Incest is the marriage to, or sexual intercourse with, any ascendant or descendant, brother or sister, uncle or niece, aunt or nephew, with knowledge of their relationship.

B. The relationship must be by consanguinity, but it is immaterial whether the parties to the act are legitimate or illegitimate or related to one another by the whole or half blood.

C. This Section shall not apply where one, not a resident of this state at the time of the celebration of his marriage, shall have contracted a marriage lawful at the place of celebration and shall thereafter have removed to this state.

D. (1) Whoever commits incest, where the crime is between an ascendant and descendant, or between brother and sister, shall be imprisoned at hard labor for not more than fifteen years.

(2) Whoever commits incest, where the crime is between uncle and niece, or aunt or nephew, shall be fined not more than one thousand dollars, or imprisoned, with or without hard labor, for not more than five years, or both.

§78.1. Aggravated incest.

A. Aggravated incest is the engaging in any prohibited act enumerated in Subsection B with a person who is under eighteen years of age and who is known to the offender to be related to the offender as any of the following biological, step, or adoptive relatives: child, grandchild of any degree, brother, sister, half-brother, half-sister, uncle, aunt, nephew, or niece.

B. The following are prohibited acts under this Section:

(1) Sexual intercourse, sexual battery, aggravated sexual battery, carnal knowledge of a juvenile, indecent behavior with juveniles, pornography involving juveniles, molestation of a juvenile, crime against nature, cruelty to juveniles, parent enticing a child into prostitution, or any involvement of a child in sexual activity constituting a crime under the laws of this state.

(2) Any lewd fondling or touching of the person of either the child or the offender, done or submitted to with the intent to arouse or to satisfy the sexual desires of either the child, the offender, or both.

C. Consent is a defense under this Section to aggravated incest with or upon a stepson or stepdaughter unless the victim is less than eighteen years of age.

D. A person convicted of aggravated incest shall be fined an amount not to exceed fifty thousand dollars, or imprisoned, with or without hard labor, for a term not less than five years nor more than twenty years, or both.

E. (1) In addition to any sentence imposed under Subsection D, the court shall, after determining the financial resources and future ability of the offender to pay, require the offender, if able, to pay the victim's reasonable costs of counseling that result from the offense.

(2) The amount, method, and time of payment shall be determined by the court either by ordering that documentation of the offender's financial resources and future ability to pay restitution and of the victim's pecuniary loss submitted by the victim be included in the presentence investigation and report, or the court may receive evidence of the offender's ability to pay and the victim's loss at the time of sentencing.

(3) The court may provide for payment to a victim up to but not in excess of the pecuniary loss caused by the offense. The offender may assert any defense that he could raise in a civil action for the loss sought to be compensated by the restitution order.

(Added by Acts 1993 No. 525, §1, eff. 6/10/93.)

SUBPART C. DOMESTIC VIOLENCE OFFENSES

§79. Violation of protective orders.

A. (1) Violation of protective orders is the willful disobedience of a preliminary or permanent injunction or protective order issued pursuant to R.S. 9:361 et seq., R.S. 9:372, R.S. 46:2131 et seq., Children's Code Article 1564 et seq., or Code of Civil Procedure Article 3604 after a contradictory court hearing, or the willful disobedience of a temporary restraining order or any ex parte protective order issued pursuant to R.S. 9:361 et seq., R.S. 9:372, R.S. 46:2131 et seq., Children's Code Article 1564 et seq., or Code of Civil Procedure Article 3604 if the defendant has been given notice of the temporary restraining order or ex parte protective order by service of process as required by law.

(2) An order for protection from abuse issued by a foreign state shall be afforded full faith and credit. This order shall contain a certification by the issuing court confirming both of the following:

(a) That the issuing court has jurisdiction over the parties and subject matter under the law of the issuing state.

(b) That reasonable notice and opportunity to be heard were given to the defendant sufficient to protect the defendant's right to due process before the order was issued; or, if the order was issued ex parte, the court ordered that the defendant be given reasonable notice and an opportunity to be heard as required in the issuing state.

B. (1) On a first conviction for violation of protective orders which does not involve a battery to the person protected by the protective order, the offender shall be fined not more than five hundred dollars or imprisoned for not more than six months, or both.

(2) On a second conviction for violation of protective orders which does not involve a battery to the person protected by the protective order, regardless of whether the second offense occurred before or after the first conviction, the offender shall be fined not more than one thousand dollars and imprisoned for not less than forty-eight hours nor more than six months. At least forty-eight hours of the sentence of imprisonment imposed under this Paragraph shall be without benefit of probation, parole, or suspension of sentence. If a portion of the sentence is imposed with benefit of probation, parole, or suspension of sentence, the court shall require the offender to participate in a court-approved domestic abuse counseling program.

(3) On a third or subsequent conviction for violation of protective orders which does not involve a battery to the person protected by the protective order, regardless of whether the current offense occurred before or after the earlier convictions, the offender shall be fined not more than one thousand dollars and imprisoned for not less than fourteen days nor more than six months. At least fourteen days of the sentence of imprisonment imposed under this Paragraph shall be without benefit of probation, parole, or suspension of sentence. If a portion of the sentence is imposed with benefit of probation, parole, or suspension of sentence, the court shall require the offender to participate in a court-approved domestic abuse counseling program, unless the offender has previously been required to participate in such program and, in the discretion of the judge, the offender would not benefit from such counseling.

C. (1) Whoever is convicted of the offense of violation of protective orders where the violation involves a battery to the person protected by the protective order, and who has not been convicted of violating a protective order or of an assault or battery upon the person protected by the protective order within the five years prior to commission of the instant offense, shall be fined not more than five hundred dollars and imprisoned for not less than fourteen days nor more than six months. At least fourteen days of the sentence of imprisonment imposed under this Paragraph shall be without benefit of probation, parole, or suspension of sentence. If a portion of the sentence is imposed with benefit of probation, parole, or suspension of sentence, the court shall require the offender to participate in a court-approved domestic abuse counseling program as part of that probation.

(2) Whoever is convicted of the offense of violation of protective orders where the violation involves a battery to the person for whose benefit the protective order is in effect, and who has been convicted not more than one time of violating a protective order or of an assault or battery upon the person for whose benefit the protective order is in effect within the five-year period prior to the commission of the instant offense, regardless of whether the instant offense occurred before or after the earlier convictions, shall be fined not more than one thousand dollars and imprisoned for not less than three months nor more than six months. At least fourteen days of the sentence of imprisonment imposed under this Paragraph shall be without benefit of probation, parole, or suspension of sentence. If a portion of the sentence is imposed with benefit of probation, parole, or suspension of sentence, the court shall require the offender to participate in a court-approved domestic abuse counseling program, unless the offender has previously been required to participate in such program and, in the discretion of the court, the offender would not benefit from such counseling.

(3) Whoever is convicted of the offense of violation of protective orders where the violation involves a battery to the person for whose benefit the protective order is in effect, and who has more than one conviction of violating a protective order or of an assault or battery upon the person for whose benefit the protective order is in effect during the five-year period prior to commission of the instant offense, regardless of whether the instant offense occurred before or after the earlier convictions, the offender shall be fined not more than two thousand dollars and imprisoned with or without hard labor for not less than one year nor more than five years. At least one year of the sentence of imprisonment imposed under this Paragraph shall be without benefit of probation, parole, or suspension of sentence.

D. If, as part of any sentence imposed under this Section, a fine is imposed, the court may direct that the fine be paid for the support of the spouse or children of the offender.

E. Law enforcement officers shall use every reasonable means, including but not limited to immediate arrest of the violator, to enforce a preliminary or permanent injunction or protective order obtained pursuant to R.S. 9:306, R.S.9:372, R.S. 46:2131 et seq., Children's Code Article 1564 et seq., or Code of Civil Procedure Article 3604 after a contradictory court hearing, or to enforce a temporary restraining order or ex parte protective order issued pursuant to R.S. 9:306, R.S. 9:372, R.S. 46:2131 et seq., Children's Code Article 1564 et seq., or Code of Civil Procedure Article 3604 if the defendant has been given notice of the temporary restraining order or ex parte protective order by service of process as required by law.

F. This Section shall not be construed to limit the effect of any other criminal statute or civil remedy.

G. "Instant offense" as used in this Section means the offense which is before the court.

H. An offender ordered to participate in a domestic abuse counseling program under the provision of this Section shall pay the cost incurred in participating in the program, unless the court determines that the offender is unable to pay. Failure to make payment under this Subsection shall subject the offender to revocation of probation.

(Chgd. by Acts 1994 Third Ex. Sess. No. 70, §1; Acts 1995 No. 905, §1; Acts 1997 No. 1156, §6, eff. 8/15/97.)

SUBPART D. CRIMINAL ABANDONMENT

§79.1. Criminal abandonment.

A. Criminal abandonment is the intentional physical abandonment of a minor child under the age of ten years by the child's parent or legal guardian by leaving the minor child unattended and to his own care when the evidence demonstrates that the child's parent or legal guardian did not intend to return to the minor child or provide for adult supervision of the minor child.

B. Whoever commits the crime of criminal abandonment shall be fined not more than one thousand dollars, or be imprisoned for not more than one year, or both.

PART V. OFFENSES AFFECTING THE PUBLIC MORALS

SUBPART A. OFFENSES AFFECTING SEXUAL IMMORALITY

1. SEXUAL OFFENSES AFFECTING MINORS

§80. Carnal knowledge of a juvenile.

A. Carnal knowledge of a juvenile is committed when:

(1) A person over the age of seventeen has sexual intercourse, with consent, with any person of the age of twelve years or more, but under the age of seventeen years, when there is an age difference of greater than two years between the two persons and the victim is not the spouse of the offender; or

(2) A person over the age of seventeen has anal or oral sexual intercourse, with consent, with a person of the age of twelve years or more, but under the age of seventeen years, when there is an age difference of greater than two years between the two persons.

B. Lack of knowledge of the juvenile's age shall not be a defense. Emission is not necessary; and penetration, however slight, is sufficient to complete the crime.

C. Whoever commits the crime of carnal knowledge of a juvenile shall be imprisoned, with or without hard labor, for not more than ten years, provided that the defendant shall not be eligible to have his conviction set aside or his prosecution dismissed in accordance with the provisions of Code of Criminal Procedure Article 893.

(Chgd. by Acts 1990 No. 590, §1; Acts 1995 No. 241, §1, eff. 8/15/95.)

§81. Indecent behavior with juveniles.

A. Indecent behavior with juveniles is the commission of any lewd or lascivious act upon the person or in the presence of any child under the age of seventeen, where there is an age difference of greater than two years between the two persons, with the intention of arousing or gratifying the sexual desires of either person. Lack of knowledge of the child's age shall not be a defense.

B. The trial judge shall have the authority to issue any necessary orders to protect the safety of the child during the pendency of the criminal action and beyond its conclusion.

C. Whoever commits the crime of indecent behavior with juveniles shall be fined not more than five thousand dollars, or imprisoned with or without hard labor for not more than seven years, or both, provided that the defendant shall not be eligible to have his conviction set aside or his prosecution dismissed in accordance with the provisions of Code of Criminal Procedure Article 893.

(Chgd. by Acts 1990 No. 590, §1; Acts 1997 No. 743, §1, eff. 8/15/97.)

§81.1. Pornography involving juveniles.

A. Pornography involving juveniles is any of the following:

(1) The photographing, videotaping, filming, or otherwise reproducing visually of any sexual performance involving a child under the age of seventeen.

(2) The solicitation, promotion, or coercion of any child under the age of seventeen for the purpose of photographing, videotaping, filming, or otherwise reproducing visually any sexual performance involving a child under the age of seventeen.

(3) The intentional possession, sale, distribution, or possession with intent to sell or distribute of any photographs, films, videotapes, or other visual reproductions of any sexual performance involving a child under the age of seventeen.

(4) The consent of a parent, legal guardian, or custodian of a child under the age of seventeen for the purpose of photographing, videotaping, filming, or otherwise reproducing visually any sexual performance involving the child.

B. For purposes of this Section the following definitions shall apply:

(1) "Sexual performance" means any performance or part thereof that includes sexual conduct involving a child under the age of seventeen.

(2) "Performance" means any play, motion picture, photograph, dance, or other visual presentation.

(3) "Sexual conduct" means actual or simulated sexual intercourse, deviate sexual intercourse, sexual bestiality, masturbation, sadomasochistic abuse, or lewd exhibition of the genitals.

(4) "Promote" means to procure, manufacture, issue, sell, give, provide, lend, mail, deliver, transfer, transmute, publish, distribute, circulate, disseminate, prevent, exhibit, or advertise, or to offer or agree to do the same.

C. Possession of three or more of the same photographs, films, videotapes, or other visual reproductions shall be prima facie evidence of intent to sell or distribute.

D. Lack of knowledge of the juvenile's age shall not be a defense.

E. Whoever commits the crime of pornography involving juveniles shall be fined not more than ten thousand dollars and be imprisoned at hard labor for not less than two years or more than ten years, without benefit of parole, probation, or suspension of sentence.

F. Each photograph, film, videotape, or other reproduction of any sexual conduct involving a child under the age of seventeen shall be contraband and shall be seized and disposed of in accordance with law.

G. In prosecutions for violations of this Section, the trier of fact may determine, utilizing the following factors, whether or not the person displayed or depicted in any photograph, videotape, film, or other video reproduction introduced in evidence was under the age of seventeen years at the time of filming or recording:

(1) The general body growth, bone structure, and bone development of the person.

(2) The development of pubic or body hair on the person.

(3) The development of the person's sexual organs.

(4) The context in which the person is placed or the age attributed to the person in any accompanying video, printed, or text material.

(5) Available expert testimony and opinion as to the chronological age or degree of physical or mental maturity or development of the person.

(6) Such other information, factors, and evidence available to the trier of fact which the court determines is probative and reasonably reliable.

(Chgd. by Acts 1992 No. 305, §1, eff. 8/21/92.)

§81.2. Molestation of a juvenile.

A. Molestation of a juvenile is the commission by anyone over the age of seventeen of any lewd or lascivious act upon the person or in the presence of any child under the age of seventeen, where there is an age difference of greater than two years between the two persons, with the intention of arousing or gratifying the sexual desires of either person, by the use of force, violence, duress, menace, psychological intimidation, threat of great bodily harm, or by the use of influence by virtue of a position of control or supervision over the juvenile. Lack of knowledge of the juvenile's age shall not be a defense.

B. Whoever commits the crime of molestation of a juvenile shall be fined not more than five thousand dollars, or imprisoned, with or without hard labor, for not less than one nor more than ten years, or both, provided that the defendant shall not be eligible to have his conviction set aside or his prosecution dismissed in accordance with the provisions of Code of Criminal Procedure Article 893.

C. Whoever commits the crime of molestation of a juvenile when the offender has control or supervision over the juvenile shall be fined not more than ten thousand dollars, or imprisoned, with or without hard labor, for not less than one nor more than fifteen years, or both, provided that the defendant shall not be eligible to have his conviction set aside or his prosecution dismissed in accordance with Code of Criminal Procedure Article 893.

D. (1) Whoever commits the crime of molestation of a juvenile when the incidents of molestation recur during a period of more than one year shall, on first conviction, be fined not more than ten thousand dollars or imprisoned, with or without hard labor, for not less than five nor more than fifteen years, or both. At least five years of the sentence imposed shall be without benefit of parole, probation, or suspension of sentence. After five years of the sentence have been served, the offender, who is otherwise eligible, may be eligible for parole if a licensed psychologist or a board certified social worker or a board certified psychiatrist, after psychological examination, including testing, approves.

(2) Conditions of parole shall include treatment in a qualified sex offender program for a minimum of five years, or until expiration of sentence, whichever comes first. The state shall be responsible for the cost of testing but the offender shall be responsible for the cost of the treatment program. It shall also be a condition of parole that the offender be prohibited from being alone with a child without the supervision of another adult.

(3) For purposes of this Subsection, a "qualified sex offender program" means one which includes both group and individual therapy and arousal reconditioning. Group therapy shall be conducted by two therapists, one male and one female, at least one of whom is licensed as a psychologist or is board certified as a psychiatrist or clinical social worker.

(4) On a subsequent conviction, the offender shall be imprisoned for twenty years at hard labor without benefit of parole, probation, or suspension of sentence.

(Chgd. by Acts 1990 No. 590, §1; Acts 1991 No. 925, §1, eff. 9/6/91.)

2. OFFENSES CONCERNING PROSTITUTION

§82. Prostitution; definition; penalties; enhancement.

A. Prostitution is:

(1) The practice by a person of indiscriminate sexual intercourse with others for compensation.

(2) The solicitation by one person of another with the intent to engage in indiscriminate sexual intercourse with the latter for compensation.

B. (1) Whoever commits the crime of prostitution shall be fined not more than five hundred dollars or be imprisoned for not more than six months, or both.

(2) On a second conviction, the offender shall be fined not less than two hundred fifty dollars nor more than two thousand dollars or be imprisoned, with or without hard labor, for not more than two years, or both.

(3) On a third and subsequent conviction the offender shall be imprisoned, with or without hard labor, for not less than two nor more than four years and shall be fined not less than five hundred dollars nor more than four thousand dollars.

C. Any offense under this Section committed more than five years prior to the commission of the offense with which the defendant is charged shall not be considered in the assessment of penalties under this Section.

D. If the offense occurred as a result of a solicitation by the offender while the offender was located on a public road or highway, or the sidewalk, walkway, or public servitude thereof, the court shall sentence the offender to imprisonment for a minimum of ninety-days which, except as provided in this Subsection, shall not be suspended. The court may suspend imposition of forty-five days of the ninety-day imprisonment and place the offender upon supervised probation if the offender agrees, as a condition of probation, to perform two hundred forty hours of community service work collecting or picking up litter and trash on the public roads, streets, and highways, under conditions specified by the court.

E. All persons who are convicted of the offense of prostitution shall be referred to the parish health unit for counseling concerning Acquired Immune Deficiency Syndrome. The counseling shall be provided by existing staff of the parish health unit whose duties include such counseling.

§82.1. Prostitution; persons under seventeen; additional offenses.

A. It shall be unlawful:

(1) For any person over the age of seventeen to engage in sexual intercourse with any person under the age of seventeen who is practicing prostitution, and there is an age difference of greater than two years between the two persons. Lack of knowledge of the latter person's age shall not be a defense.

(2) For any parent or tutor of any person under the age of seventeen knowingly to consent to the person's entrance or detention in the practice of prostitution.

B. Whoever violates the provisions of this Section shall be fined not more than five thousand dollars or imprisoned, with or without hard labor, for not less than two years nor more than ten years, or both.

§83. Soliciting for prostitutes.

Soliciting for prostitutes is the soliciting, inviting, inducing, directing or transporting a person to any place with the intention of promoting prostitution.

Whoever commits the crime of soliciting for prostitutes shall be fined not more than five hundred dollars, imprisoned for not more than six months, or both.

§83.1. Inciting prostitution.

A. Inciting prostitution is the aiding, abetting, or assisting in an enterprise for profit in which:

(1) Customers are charged a fee for services which include prostitution, regardless of what portion of the fee is actually for the prostitution services,

(2) When the person knows or when a reasonable person in such a position should know that such aiding, abetting, or assisting is for prostitution, and

(3) When the proceeds or profits are to be in any way divided by the prostitute and the person aiding, abetting, or assisting the prostitute.

B. Whoever commits the crime of inciting prostitution shall be fined not more than one thousand dollars or imprisoned for not more than one year, or both.

§83.2. Promoting prostitution.

A. Promoting prostitution is the knowing and willful control of, supervision of, or management of an enterprise for profit in which customers are charged a fee for services which include prostitution, regardless of what portion of the fee is actually for the prostitution services.

B. Whoever commits the crime of promoting prostitution shall be fined not more than five thousand dollars or imprisoned with or without hard labor for not more than two years, or both.

§83.3. Prostitution by massage.

A. Prostitution by massage is the erotic stimulation of the genital organs of another by any masseur, masseuse, or any other person, whether resulting in orgasm or not, by instrumental manipulation, touching with the hands, or other bodily contact exclusive of sexual intercourse or unnatural carnal copulation, when done for money.

B. As used in this Section, the terms:

(1) "Masseur" means a male who practices massage or physiotherapy, or both.

(2) "Masseuse" means a female who practices massage or physiotherapy, or both.

C. Whoever commits the crime of prostitution by massage shall be fined not more than five hundred dollars or imprisoned not more than six months, or both.

§83.4. Massage; sexual conduct prohibited.

A. It shall be unlawful for any masseur, masseuse, or any other person, while in a massage parlor or any other enterprise used as a massage parlor, by stimulation in an erotic manner, to:

(1) Expose, touch, caress, or fondle the genitals, anus, or pubic hairs of any person or the nipples of the female breast; or

(2) To perform any acts of sadomasochistic abuse, flagellation, or torture in the context of sexual conduct.

B. Whoever violates this Section shall be fined not more than five hundred dollars or imprisoned for not more than six months, or both.

§84. Pandering.

Pandering is the intentional:

(1) enticing, placing, persuading, encouraging, or causing the entrance of any person into the practice of prostitution, either by force, threats, promises, or by any other device or scheme;

(2) maintaining a place where prostitution is habitually practiced;

(3) detaining any person in any place of prostitution by force, threats, promises, or by any other device or scheme;

(4) receiving or accepting by a person as a substantial part of support or maintenance anything of value which is known to be from the earnings of any person engaged in prostitution;

(5) consenting, on the part of any parent or tutor of any person, to the person's entrance or detention in the practice of prostitution; or

(6) transporting any person from one place to another for the purpose of promoting the practice of prostitution.

Whoever commits the crime of pandering shall be fined not more than five thousand dollars, imprisoned with or without hard labor for not more than five years, or both.

§85. Letting premises for prostitution.

Letting premises for prostitution is the granting of the right of use or the leasing of any premises, knowing that they are to be used for the practice of prostitution, or allowing the continued use of the premises with such knowledge.

Whoever commits the crime of letting premises for prostitution shall be fined not more than five hundred dollars, or imprisoned for not more than six months, or both.

§85.1. Letting premises for obscenity.

Letting premises for obscenity is the granting of the right of use or the leasing of any premises, knowing that they are to be used for the practice of obscenity as defined in R.S. 14:106—Criminal Code Article 106, or allowing the continued use of the premises with such knowledge.

Whoever commits the crime of letting premises for obscenity shall be fined not more than five hundred dollars, or imprisoned for not more than six months, or both.

§86. Enticing persons into prostitution.

Enticing persons into prostitution is committed when any person over the age of seventeen entices, places, persuades, encourages, or causes the entrance of any other person under the age of twenty-one into the practice of prostitution, either by force, threats, promises, or by any other device or scheme. Lack of knowledge of the other person's age shall not be a defense.

Whoever commits the crime of enticing persons into prostitution shall be imprisoned, with or without hard labor, for not less than two years nor more than ten years.

3. ABORTION

§87. Abortion.

A. (1) Abortion is the performance of any of the following acts, with the specific intent of terminating a pregnancy:

(a) Administering or prescribing any drug, potion, medicine, or any other substance to a female; or

(b) Using any instrument or external force whatsoever on a female.

(2) This Section shall not apply to the female who has an abortion.

B. It shall not be unlawful for a physician to perform any of the acts described in Subsection A of this Section if performed under the following circumstances:

(1) The physician terminates a pregnancy in order to preserve the life or health of the unborn child or to remove a dead unborn child.

(2) The physician terminates a pregnancy for the express purpose of saving the life of the mother.

(3) The physician terminates a pregnancy which is the result of rape as defined in either R.S. 14:42, R.S. 14:42.1, or R.S. 14:43 and in which all of the following requirements are met prior to the pregnancy termination:

(a) The rape victim obtains a physical examination and/or treatment from a physician other than the physician who is to terminate the pregnancy within five days of the rape to determine whether she was pregnant prior to the rape and to prevent pregnancy and venereal disease, unless the rape victim is incapacitated to such degree that she is unable to obtain this examination. If the victim is unable to obtain the examination due to such incapacity, then an examination shall be performed within five days after the incapacity is removed; and

(b) The rape victim reports the rape to law enforcement officials within seven days of the rape unless the victim is incapacitated to such a degree that she is unable to report the rape. If the victim is unable to report the rape due to such incapacity, then a report shall be made within seven days after the incapacity is removed; and

(c) The abortion is performed within thirteen weeks of conception.

(4) The physician terminates a pregnancy which is the result of incest as defined in R.S. 14:78, provided the crime is reported to law enforcement officials and the abortion is performed within thirteen weeks of conception.

C. (1) Prior to the performance of any abortion under Subsection (B)(3) or (B)(4) of this Section, the physician who is to perform the abortion shall obtain from the victim a statement in writing verifying that she has obtained the physical examination and shall obtain written verification by a law enforcement official that the victim reported the rape to law enforcement officials as required under this Section.

(2) Every physician who conducts a physical examination of a rape victim within five days of the rape shall immediately, upon written request of either the victim or the physician who is to perform the abortion on the victim, provide to the victim or the requesting physician written verification of his examination.

(3) Every law enforcement official who receives a report of a rape victim within seven days of the rape or receives a report of incest shall immediately, upon written request of either the victim or the physician who is to perform the abortion, provide to the victim or requesting physician written verification of the report which was made to the official.

D. As used in this Section, the following words and phrases are defined as follows:

(1) "Law enforcement official or officer" means any peace officer or agency empowered to enforce the law in criminal matters within his or its respective jurisdiction, including but not limited to a state police officer, sheriff, constable, local police officer, and district attorney.

(2) "Physician" means any person licensed to practice medicine in this state.

(3) "Unborn child" means the unborn offspring of human beings from the moment of conception until birth.

(4) "Conception" means the contact of spermatozoan with the ovum.

E. (1) Whoever commits the crime of abortion shall be imprisoned at hard labor for not less than one nor more than ten years and shall be fined not less than ten thousand dollars nor more than one hundred thousand dollars.

(2) This penalty shall not apply to the female who has an abortion.

(Chgd. by Acts 1991 No. 26, §2, eff. 9/6/91.)

 ZL

§87.1. Killing a child during delivery.

Killing a child during delivery is the intentional destruction, during parturition of the mother, of the vitality or life of a child in a state of being born and before actual birth, which child would otherwise have been born alive; provided, however, that the crime of killing a child during delivery shall not be construed to include any case in which the death of a child results from the use by a physician of a procedure during delivery which is necessary to save the life of the child or of the mother and is used for the express purpose of and with the specific intent of saving the life of the child or of the mother.

Whoever commits the crime of killing a child during delivery shall be imprisoned at hard labor in the penitentiary for life.

§87.2. Human experimentation.

Human experimentation is the use of any live born human being, without consent of that live born human being, as hereinafter defined, for any scientific or laboratory research or any other kind of experimentation or study except to protect or preserve the life and health of said live born human being, or the conduct, on a human embryo or fetus in utero, of any experimentation or study except to preserve the life or to improve the health of said human embryo or fetus.

A human being is live born, or there is a live birth, whenever there is the complete expulsion or extraction from its mother of a human embryo or fetus, irrespective of the duration of pregnancy, which after such separation, breathes or shows any other evidence of life such as beating of the heart, pulsation of the umbilical cord, or movement of voluntary muscles, whether or not the umbilical cord has been cut or the placenta is attached.

Whoever commits the crime of human experimentation shall be imprisoned at hard labor for not less than five nor more than twenty years, or fined not more than ten thousand dollars, or both.

§87.4. Abortion advertising.

Abortion advertising is the placing or carrying of any advertisement of abortion services by the publicizing of the availability of abortion services.

Whoever commits the crime of abortion advertising shall be imprisoned, with or without hard labor, for not more than one year or fined not more than five thousand dollars, or both.

§87.5. Intentional failure to sustain life and health of aborted viable infant.

The intentional failure to sustain the life and health of an aborted viable infant shall be a crime. The intentional failure to sustain the life and health of an aborted viable infant is the intentional failure, by any physician or person performing or inducing an abortion, to exercise that degree of professional care and diligence, and to perform such measures as constitute good medical practice, necessary to sustain the life and health of an aborted viable infant, when the death of the infant results. For purposes of this Section, "viable" means that stage of fetal development when the life of the unborn child may be continued indefinitely outside the womb by natural or artificial life-supporting systems. Any person who commits the crime of intentional failure to sustain the life and health of an aborted viable infant shall be imprisoned at hard labor for not more than twenty-one years.

§88. Distribution of abortifacients.

Distribution of abortifacients is the intentional:

(1) Distribution or advertisement for distribution of any drug, portion, instrument, or article for the purpose of procuring an abortion; or

(2) Publication of any advertisement or account of any secret drug or nostrum purporting to be exclusively for the use of females, for preventing conception or producing abortion or miscarriage.

Whoever commits the crime of distribution of abortifacients shall be fined not more than five hundred dollars, or imprisoned for not more than six months, or both.

4. CRIME AGAINST NATURE

§89. Crime against nature.

A. Crime against nature is:

(1) The unnatural carnal copulation by a human being with another of the same sex or opposite sex or with an animal, except that anal sexual intercourse between two human beings shall not be deemed as a crime against nature when done under any of the circumstances described in R.S. 14:41, 14:42, 14:42.1 or 14:43. Emission is not necessary; and, when committed by a human being with another, the use of the genital organ of one of the offenders of whatever sex is sufficient to constitute the crime.

(2) The solicitation by a human being of another with the intent to engage in any unnatural carnal copulation for compensation.

B. Whoever violates the provisions of this Section shall be fined not more than two thousand dollars, or imprisoned, with or without hard labor, for not more than five years, or both.

§89.1. Aggravated crime against nature.

A. Aggravated crime against nature is crime against nature committed under any one or more of the following circumstances:

(1) When the victim resists the act to the utmost, but such resistance is overcome by force;

(2) When the victim is prevented from resisting the act by threats of great and immediate bodily harm accompanied by apparent power of execution;

(3) When the victim is prevented from resisting the act because the offender is armed with a dangerous weapon; or

(4) When through idiocy, imbecility, or any unsoundness of mind, either temporary or permanent, the victim is incapable of giving consent and the offender knew or should have known of such incapacity;

(5) When the victim is incapable of resisting or of understanding the nature of the act, by reason of stupor or abnormal condition of mind produced by a narcotic or anesthetic agent, administered by or with the privity of the offender; or when he has such incapacity, by reason of a stupor or abnormal condition of mind from any cause, and the offender knew or should have known of such incapacity; or

(6) When the victim is under the age of seventeen years and the offender is at least three years older than the victim.

B. Whoever commits the crime of aggravated crime against nature shall be imprisoned at hard labor for not less than three nor more than fifteen years, such prison sentence to be without benefit of suspension of sentence, probation or parole.

SUBPART B. OFFENSES AFFECTING GENERAL MORALITY

1. GAMBLING

§90. Gambling.

A. (1)(a) Gambling is the intentional conducting, or directly assisting in the conducting, as a business, of any game, contest, lottery, or contrivance whereby a person risks the loss of anything of value in order to realize a profit.

(b) Whoever commits the crime of gambling shall be fined not more than five hundred dollars, or imprisoned for not more than six months, or both.

(2) Whoever conducts, finances, manages, supervises, directs, or owns all or part of an illegal gambling business shall be fined not more than twenty thousand dollars, or imprisoned with or without hard labor, for not more than five years, or both when:

(a) R.S. 14:90 is violated.

(b) Five or more persons are involved who conduct, finance, manage, supervise, direct, or own all or part of an illegal gambling business.

(c) Such business has been in or remains in substantially continuous operation for a period of thirty days or more or, if the continuous operation is for less than thirty days, has a gross revenue of two thousand dollars in any single day.

B. The conducting, or directly assisting in the conducting, as a business, of any game, contest, lottery, or contrivance on board a commercial cruiseship used for the international carriage of passengers whereby a person risks the loss of anything of value in order to realize a profit is not gambling and shall not be suppressed by any law enforcement officer of the state of Louisiana or any of its political subdivisions. This Subsection shall apply only to commercial cruiseships for the carriage of passengers which are sailing from a port outside the continental limits of the United States to a port in any parish of this state having a population of more than four hundred seventy-five thousand or any such ship which is sailing from a port in such a parish to a port outside the continental limits of the United States, provided that the ship is not docked or anchored but is navigating en route between such ports.

C. The conducting or assisting in the conducting of authorized lottery activities or operations in accordance with provisions of R.S. 47:9000 through 9081 shall not be considered gambling for purposes of this Section.

D. The intentional conducting or assisting in the conducting of gaming activities upon a riverboat as defined and authorized in R.S. 4:501 through R.S. 4:562, whereby a person risks the loss of anything of value in order to realize a profit is not gambling and shall not be suppressed by any state or local law enforcement officer.

E. The intentional conducting or assisting in the conducting of gaming operations at the official gaming establishment as defined and authorized in Chapter 10 of Title 4 of the Louisiana Revised Statutes of 1950 shall not constitute gambling.

(Chgd. by Acts 1990 No. 1045, §2; Acts 1991 No. 158, §1, No. 289, §6, No. 753, §2; Acts 1992 No. 384, §2, eff. 6/18/92.)

§90.1. Seizure and disposition of evidence; gambling.

Upon conviction of a person for the crime of gambling, the evidence, property, and paraphernalia seized as instruments of such crime shall, upon order of the Court, be destroyed when it is no longer needed as evidence and all such evidence, property, and paraphernalia found to be in use in the conduct of such unlawful activity and having a value for lawful purposes, shall be sold under the orders of the Court at public auction by a duly licensed auctioneer and the proceeds paid into the Court. Upon conviction, as aforesaid, any monies and other things of value, except as herein provided, shall be transferred to the state general fund.

§90.2. Gambling in public.

A. Gambling in public is the aiding or abetting or participation in any game, contest, lottery, or contrivance, in any location or place open to the view of the public or the people at large, such as streets, highways, vacant lots, neutral grounds, alleyway, sidewalk, park, beach, parking lot, or condemned structures whereby a person risks the loss of anything of value in order to realize a profit.

B. This Section shall not prohibit activities authorized under the Charitable Raffles, Bingo and Keno Licensing Law*, nor shall it apply to bona fide fairs and festivals conducted for charitable purposes.

**R.S. 33:4861.1 et seq.*

C. Whoever commits the crime of gambling in public shall be fined not more than five hundred dollars, or imprisoned for not more than six months, or both.

§90.3. Gambling by computer.

A. The Legislature of Louisiana, desiring to protect individual rights, while at the same time affording opportunity for the fullest development of the individual and promoting the health, safety, education, and welfare of the people, including the children of this state who are our most precious and valuable resource, finds that the state has a compelling interest in protecting its citizens and children from certain activities and influences which can result in irreparable harm. The legislature has expressed its intent to develop a controlled well-regulated gaming industry. The legislature is also charged with the responsibility of protecting and assisting its citizens who suffer from compulsive or problem gaming behavior which can result from the increased availability of legalized gaming activities. The legislature recognizes the development of the Internet and the information super highway allowing communication and exchange of information from all parts of the world and freely encourages this exchange of information and ideas. The legislature recognizes and encourages the beneficial effects computers, computer programming, and use of the Internet resources have had on the children of the state of Louisiana by expanding their educational horizons. The legislature further recognizes that it has an obligation and responsibility to protect its citizens, and in particular its youngest citizens, from the pervasive nature of gambling which can occur via the Internet and the use of computers connected to the Internet. Gambling has long been recognized as a crime in the state of Louisiana and despite the enactment of many legalized gaming activities remains a crime. Gambling which occurs via the Internet embodies the very activity that the legislature seeks to prevent. The legislature further recognizes that the state's constitution and that of the United States are declarations of rights which the drafters intended to withstand time and address the wrongs and injustices which arise in future years. The legislature hereby finds and declares that it has balanced its interest in protecting the citizens of this state with the protection afforded by the First Amendment, and the mandates of Article XII, Section 6 of the Constitution of Louisiana and that this Section is a product thereof.

B. Gambling by computer is the intentional conducting, or directly assisting in the conducting as a business of any game, contest, lottery, or contrivance whereby a person risks the loss of anything of value in order to realize a profit when accessing the Internet, World Wide Web, or any part thereof by way of any computer, computer system, computer network, computer software, or any server.

C. For purposes of this Section the following definitions apply:

(1) "Client" means anyone using a computer to access a computer server.

(2) "Computer" includes an electronic, magnetic, optical, or other high-speed data processing device or system performing logical, arithmetic, and storage functions, and includes any property, data storage facility, or communications facility directly related to or operating in conjunction with such device or system. "Computer" shall not include an automated typewriter or typesetter, a machine designed solely for word processing, or a portable hand-held calculator, nor shall "computer" include any other device which might contain components similar to those in computers but in which the components have the sole function of controlling the device for the single purpose for which the device is intended.

(3) "Computer network" means a set of related, remotely connected devices and communication facilities including at least one computer system with capability to transmit data through communication facilities.

(4) "Computer services" means providing access to or service or data from a computer, a computer system, or a computer network.

(5) "Computer software" means a set of computer programs, procedures, and associated documentation concerned with operation of a computer system.

(6) "Computer system" means a set of functionally related, connected or unconnected, computer equipment, devices, or computer software.

(7) "Home Page" means the index or location for each computer site on the World Wide Web.

(8) "Internet" means the global information system that is logically linked together by a globally unique address space based on the Internet Protocol or its subsequent extensions, is able to support communications using the Transmission Control Protocol/Internet Protocol suite or its subsequent extensions, and other Internet Protocol compatible protocols, and provides, uses or makes accessible, either publicly or privately, high level services layered on the communications and related infrastructure described herein.

(9) "Server" means a computer that listens for and services a client.

(10) "World Wide Web" means a server providing connections to mega lists of information on the Internet; it is made up of millions of individual web sites linked together.

D. Whoever commits the crime of gambling by computer shall be fined not more than five hundred dollars, or imprisoned for not more than six months, or both.

E. Whoever designs, develops, manages, supervises, maintains, provides, or produces any computer services, computer system, computer network, computer software, or any server providing a Home Page, Web Site, or any other product accessing the Internet, World Wide Web, or any part thereof offering to any client for the primary purpose of the conducting as a business of any game, contest, lottery, or contrivance whereby a person risks the loss of anything of value in order to realize a profit shall be fined not more than twenty thousand dollars, or imprisoned with or without hard labor, for not more than five years, or both.

F. The conducting or assisting in the conducting of gaming activities or operations upon a riverboat, at the official gaming establishment, by operating an electronic video draw poker device, by a charitable gaming licensee, or at a pari-mutuel wagering facility or the operation of a state lottery which is licensed for operation and regulated under the provisions of Chapter 4 of Title 4, Chapters 4, 5, and 6 of Title 27, or Part V-A of Chapter 14 of Title 33 or Subtitle XI of Title 47 of the Louisiana Revised Statutes of 1950, shall not be considered gambling by computer for the purposes of this Section, so long as the wagering is done on the premises of the licensed establishment.

G. The conducting or assisting in the conducting of pari-mutuel wagering at licensed racing facilities under the provisions of Chapter 4 of Title 4 of the Louisiana Revised Statutes of 1950, shall not be considered gambling by computer for the purposes of this Section so long as the wagering is done on the premises of the licensed establishment.

H. Nothing in this Section shall prohibit, limit, or otherwise restrict the purchase, sale, exchange, or other transaction related to stocks, bonds, futures, options, commodities, or other similar instruments or transactions occurring on a stock or commodities exchange, brokerage house, or similar entity.

I. The providing of Internet or other on-line access, transmission, routing, storage, or other communication related services, or Web Site design, development, storage, maintenance, billing, advertising, hypertext linking, transaction processing, or other site related services, by telephone companies, Internet Service Providers, software developers, licensors, or other such parties providing such services to customers in the normal course of their business, shall not be considered gambling by computer even though the activities of such customers using such services to conduct a prohibited game, contest, lottery, or contrivance may constitute gambling by computer for the purposes of this Section. The provisions of this Subsection shall not exempt from criminal prosecution any telephone company, Internet Service Provider, software developer, licensor, or other such party if its primary purpose in providing such service is to conduct gambling as a business.
(Added by Acts 1997 No. 1467, §1, eff. 8/15/97.)

§90.4. Unlawful play of video draw poker devices by persons under the age of twenty-one; penalty.

A. It is unlawful for any person under twenty-one years of age to play video draw poker devices.

B. For purposes of this Section, "video draw poker device" means a device, as defined in R.S. 27:301(B)(15), placed in an establishment licensed for operation and regulated under the applicable provisions of Chapter 6 of Title 27 of the Louisiana Revised Statutes of 1950.

C. Whoever violates the provisions of this Section shall be fined not more than one hundred dollars for the first offense, two hundred fifty dollars for the second offense, and five hundred dollars for the third offense.

D. A gaming licensee, or a specifically authorized employee or agent of a gaming licensee, may use reasonable force to detain a person for questioning on the premises of the gaming establishment, for a length of time, not to exceed sixty minutes, unless it is reasonable under the circumstances that the person be detained longer, when he has reasonable cause to

believe that the person has violated the provisions of this Section. The licensee or his employee or agent may also detain such a person for arrest by a peace officer. The detention shall not constitute an arrest.
(Added by Acts 1998 First Ex. Sess. No. 162, §1, eff. 6/16/98.)

2. OFFENSES AFFECTING THE HEALTH AND MORALS OF MINORS

§91. Unlawful sales of weapons to minors.

A. Unlawful sales of weapons to minors is the selling or otherwise delivering for value of any firearm or other instrumentality customarily used as a dangerous weapon to any person under the age of eighteen. Lack of knowledge of the minor's age shall not be a defense.

B. Whoever commits the crime of unlawful sales of weapons to minors shall be fined not more than three hundred dollars or imprisoned for not more than six months, or both.
(Chgd. by Acts 1994 Third Ex. Sess. No. 84, §1; Acts 1995 No. 639, §1; Acts 1996 First Ex. Sess. No. 78, §1, eff. 6/18/96.)

§§91.1 to 91.5. *(Repealed by Acts 1995 No. 639, §3; Acts 1996 First Ex. Sess. No. 78, §3, eff. 6/18/96.)*

§91.6. Unlawful distribution of sample tobacco products to persons under age eighteen; penalty.

A. No person shall distribute or cause to be distributed to persons under eighteen years of age a promotional sample of any tobacco product.

B. For purposes of this Section, the following definitions apply:

(1) "Tobacco product" means any cigar, cigarette, smokeless tobacco, or smoking tobacco.

(2) "Cigar" means any roll of tobacco for smoking, irrespective of size or shape, and irrespective of the tobacco being flavored, adulterated, or mixed with any other ingredients, where such roll has a wrapper made chiefly of tobacco.

(3) "Cigarette" means any roll for smoking made wholly or in part of tobacco, irrespective of size or shape and irrespective of the tobacco being flavored, adulterated, or mixed with any other ingredient, where such roll as a wrapper or cover made of paper, or any other material, except where such wrapper is wholly or in greater part made of tobacco.

(4) "Smokeless tobacco" means any finely cut, ground, powdered, or leaf tobacco that is intended to be placed in the oral or nasal cavity.

(5) "Smoking tobacco" means granulated, plug cut, crimp cut, ready rubbed, and any other kind and form of tobacco prepared in such manner as to be suitable for smoking in a pipe or cigarette.

C. Whoever violates a provision of this Section shall be fined not less than one hundred dollars nor more than five hundred dollars upon conviction.

§91.7. Unauthorized possession or consumption of alcoholic beverages on public school property.

A. No person shall intentionally possess or consume alcoholic beverages upon public school property unless authorized by the principal or person in charge of the public school property at the time.

B. For purposes of this Section:

(1) "School" means any public elementary or secondary school.

(2) "School property" means all property used for school purposes, including but not limited to school playgrounds, buildings, and parking lots.

C. Whoever violates the provisions of this Section shall be fined not more than one thousand dollars and imprisoned not less than fifteen days nor more than six months without benefit of suspension of sentence.
(Added by Acts 1991 No. 866, §1; chgd. by Acts 1994 Third Ex. Sess. No. 93, §1, eff. 8/27/94.)

§91.8. Unlawful sale, purchase, or possession of tobacco; signs required; penalties.

A. This Section shall be known and may be cited as the "Prevention of Youth Access to Tobacco Law".

B. It is the intent of the legislature that enforcement of this Section shall be implemented in an equitable manner throughout the state. For the purpose of equitable and uniform implementation and application of state and local laws and regulations, the provisions of this Section shall supersede existing or subsequently adopted local ordinances or regulations which relate to the sale, promotion, and distribution of tobacco products. It is the intent of the legislature that this Section shall be equitably enforced so as to ensure the eligibility for and receipt of any federal funds or grants the state now receives or may receive relating to the provisions of this Section.

C. It is unlawful for any manufacturer, distributor, retailer, or other person knowingly to sell or distribute any tobacco product to a person under the age of eighteen. However, it shall not be unlawful for a person under the age of eighteen to accept receipt of a tobacco product from an employer when required in the performance of such person's duties. At the point of purchase, a sign in type not less than 30-point type shall be displayed that reads "LOUISIANA LAW PROHIBITS THE SALE OF TOBACCO TO PERSONS UNDER AGE 18".

D. It is unlawful for a vending machine operator to place in use a vending machine to vend any tobacco product automatically, unless the machine displays a sign or sticker in not less than 22-point type on the front of the machine stating, "LOUISIANA LAW PROHIBITS THE SALE OF TOBACCO TO PERSONS UNDER AGE 18", or words of similar meaning.

E. It is unlawful for any person under the age of eighteen to buy any tobacco product.

F. (1) It is unlawful for any person under the age of eighteen to possess any tobacco product.

(2) However, it shall not be unlawful for a person under the age of eighteen to possess a tobacco product under any of the following circumstances:

(a) When a person under eighteen years of age is accompanied by a parent, spouse, or legal guardian twenty-one years of age or older.

(b) In private residences.

(c) When the tobacco product is handled during the course and scope of his employment and required in the performance of such person's duties.

G. For purposes of this Section, the following definitions apply:

(1) "Tobacco product" means any cigar, cigarette, smokeless tobacco, or smoking tobacco.

(2) "Cigar" means any roll of tobacco for smoking, irrespective of size or shape, and irrespective of the tobacco being flavored, adulterated, or mixed with any other ingredients, where such roll has a wrapper made chiefly of tobacco.

(3) "Cigarette" means any roll for smoking made wholly or in part of tobacco, irrespective of size or shape and irrespective of the tobacco being flavored, adulterated, or mixed with any other ingredient, where such roll has a wrapper or cover made of paper, or any other material, except where such wrapper is wholly or in greater part made of tobacco.

(4) "Smokeless tobacco" means any finely cut, ground, powdered, or leaf tobacco that is intended to be placed in the oral or nasal cavity.

(5) "Smoking tobacco" means granulated, plug cut, crimp cut, ready rubbed, and any other kind and form of tobacco prepared in such manner as to be suitable for smoking in a pipe or cigarette.

H. (1) A person who violates the provisions of this Section by selling or buying tobacco products shall be fined not more than fifty dollars for the first violation. The penalties for subsequent violations shall be a fine of not more than one hundred dollars for the second violation, a fine of not more than two hundred fifty dollars for the third violation, and a fine of not more than four hundred dollars for any violation thereafter.

(2) A person who violates the provisions of this Section by possessing tobacco products shall be fined not more than fifty dollars for each violation.

I. A violation of the signage requirement of Subsection C of this Section shall be deemed to be a violation by the owner of the establishment where the violation occurred. A violation of the signage requirement of Subsection D of this Section shall be deemed to be a violation by the owner of the vending machine. For the first such violation, the owner shall be fined not more than fifty dollars. The penalties for subsequent violations shall be a fine of not more than one hundred dollars for the second violation, a fine of not more than two hundred fifty dollars for the third violation, and a fine of not more than five hundred dollars for any violation thereafter.

J. The law enforcement agency issuing the citation or making the arrest or the clerk of the court in which a prosecution is initiated, as the case may be, shall notify the commissioner of the office of alcohol and tobacco control of the action and the final disposition of the matter. *(Added by Acts 1991 No. 919, §1; chgd. by Acts 1994 Third Ex. Sess. No. 64, §1; Acts 1997 No. 1010, §1, eff. 8/15/97.)*

§91.11. Sale, exhibition, or distribution of material harmful to minors.

A. (1) The unlawful sale, exhibition, rental, leasing, or distribution of material harmful to minors is the intentional sale, allocation, distribution, advertisement, dissemination, exhibition, or display of material harmful to minors, to any unmarried person under the age of seventeen years, or the possession of material harmful to minors with the intent to sell, allocate, advertise, disseminate, exhibit, or display such material to any unmarried person under the age of seventeen years, at a newsstand or any other commercial establishment which is open to persons under the age of seventeen years.

(2) "Material harmful to minors" is defined as any paper, magazine, book, newspaper, periodical, pamphlet, composition, publication, photograph, drawing, picture, poster, motion picture film, video tape, figure, phonograph record, album, cassette, compact disc, wire or tape recording, or other similar tangible work or thing which exploits, is devoted to or principally consists of, descriptions or depictions of illicit sex or sexual immorality for commercial gain, and when the trier of fact determines that the average person applying contemporary community standards would find that the work or thing is presented in a manner to provide or arouse lust, passion, or perversion or exploits sex.

(3) For the purposes of this Section, "descriptions or depictions of illicit sex or sexual immorality" includes the depiction, display, description, exhibition or representation of:

(a) Ultimate sexual acts, normal or perverted, actual, simulated, or animated, whether between human beings, animals, or an animal and a human being;

(b) Masturbation, excretory functions, or exhibition, actual, simulated, or animated, of the genitals, pubic hair, anus, vulva, or female breast nipples;

(c) Sadomasochistic abuse, meaning actual, simulated, or animated, flagellation or torture by or upon a person who is nude or clad in undergarments or in a costume which reveals the pubic hair, anus, vulva, genitals, or female breast nipples, or the condition of being fettered, bound, or otherwise physically restrained, on the part of one so clothed;

(d) Actual, simulated, or animated, touching, caressing, or fondling of, or other similar physical contact with, a pubic area, anus, female breast nipple, covered or exposed, whether alone or between human, animals or a human and an animal, of the same or opposite sex, in an act of apparent sexual simulation or gratification; or

(e) Actual, simulated, or animated, stimulation of the human genital organs by any device whether or not the device is designed, manufactured, and marketed for such purpose.

B. It shall be unlawful to invite or permit any unmarried person under the age of seventeen years of age to be in any commercial establishment that exhibits or displays any item, material, work or thing of any kind that is described in Subsection A of this section.

Lack of knowledge of age or marital status shall not constitute a defense, unless the defendant shows that he had reasonable cause to believe that the minor involved was either married or seventeen years of age or more and that the minor exhibited to the defendant a draft card, driver's license, birth certificate or other official or apparently official document purporting to establish that such a minor was either married or seventeen years of age or more.

For the purpose of Subsections A and B of this section, "exhibition or display" means the exhibition or display of material harmful to minors as defined in Subsection A so that, as displayed, depictions and representations of illicit sex or sexual immorality are visible to minors, or that an unmarried person under the age of seventeen years is permitted to see or examine the contents of the material harmful to minors.

A commercial establishment shall not be in violation of this section if the commercial establishment provides for a separate area for the exhibition or display of material harmful to minors and designates said area "NOT FOR MINORS" or similar words and the commercial establishment prohibits unmarried minors under the age of seventeen years from seeing or examining the contents of material harmful to minors.

C. This section does not preempt, nor shall anything in this section be construed to preempt, the regulation of obscenity by municipalities, parishes and consolidated city-parish governments; however, in order to promote uniform obscenity legislation throughout the state, the regulation of obscenity by municipalities, parishes and consolidated city-parish governments shall not exceed the scope of the regulatory prohibitions contained in the provisions of this section.

D. Whoever is found guilty of violating the provisions of this section shall be fined not less than one hundred dollars nor more than two thousand dollars or imprisoned for not more than one year, or both.

§91.12. Sale, distribution or making available to minors publications encouraging, advocating, or facilitating the illegal use of controlled dangerous substances.

No person shall sell, distribute or make available to a person under eighteen years of age any publication which has as its dominant theme articles or a substantial number of advertisements encouraging, advocating, or facilitating the illegal use of any substance classified as a controlled dangerous substance pursuant to Title 40 of the Louisiana Revised Statutes of 1950.

No employee acting within the course and scope of his employment and who has no proprietary interest in the business shall be guilty of a violation of this Section unless he has actual knowledge of the contents of the publication.

Whoever violates this Section shall be fined not more than five hundred dollars or imprisoned for not more than six months, or both.

§91.13. Illegal use of controlled dangerous substances in the presence of persons under seventeen years of age.

A. It shall be unlawful for any person over the age of seventeen, while in the presence of any person under the age of seventeen and when there is an age difference of greater than two years between the two persons, to use, consume, possess, or distribute any controlled dangerous substance in violation of the Uniform Controlled Dangerous Substances Act*.

**R.S. 40:961 et seq.*

B. Whoever violates the provisions of this Section shall be fined not more than five hundred dollars or imprisoned for more than six months, or both.

§91.21. Sale of poisonous reptiles to minors; penalty.

It shall be unlawful for any person to sell any type of poisonous reptile to a minor.

Any person violating the provision of this section shall be guilty of a misdemeanor and, upon conviction thereof, shall be fined not more than one hundred dollars or imprisoned for not more than six months, or both, for each such offense.

§92. Contributing to the delinquency of juveniles.

A. Contributing to the delinquency of juveniles is the intentional enticing, aiding, soliciting, or permitting, by anyone over the age of seventeen, of any child under the age of seventeen, and no exception shall be made for a child who may be emancipated by marriage or otherwise, to:

(1) Beg, sing, sell any article or play any musical instrument in any public place for the purpose of receiving alms.

(2) Associate with any vicious or disreputable persons, or frequent places where the same may be found.

(3) Visit any place where beverages of either high or low alcoholic content are the principal commodity sold or given away.

(4) Visit any place where any gambling device is found, or where gambling habitually occurs.

(5) Habitually trespass where it is recognized he has no right to be.

(6) Use any vile, obscene or indecent language.

(7) Perform any sexually immoral act.

(8) Absent himself or remain away, without authority of his parents or tutor, from his home or place of abode.

(9) Violate any law of the state or ordinance of any parish or village, or town or city of the state.

(10) Visit any place where sexually indecent and obscene material, of any nature, is offered for sale, displayed or exhibited.

(11) (a) Become involved in the commission of a crime of violence as defined in R.S. 14:2(13) which is a felony or a violation of the Uniform Controlled Dangerous Substances Law* which is a felony.

**R.S. 40:961 et seq.*

(b) Become involved in the commission of any other felony not enumerated in Subparagraph (a) of this Paragraph.

B. Lack of knowledge of the juvenile's age shall not be a defense.

C. Whoever commits the crime of contributing to the delinquency of a juvenile shall be fined not more than five hundred dollars, or imprisoned for not more than six months, or both.

D. Whoever is charged and convicted of contributing to the delinquency of a juvenile under Paragraph (7) of Subsection A of this Section shall be fined not more than one thousand dollars, or imprisoned with or without hard labor for not more than two years, or both.

E. (1) Whoever is charged and convicted of contributing to the delinquency of a juvenile under Subparagraph (a) of Paragraph (11) of Subsection A of this Section shall be imprisoned at hard labor for not less than two years and for not more than ten years or imprisoned according to the sentence of imprisonment for the underlying felony, whichever is less.

(2) Whoever is charged and convicted of contributing to the delinquency of a juvenile under Subparagraph (b) of Paragraph (11) of Subsection A of this Section shall be fined not more than one thousand dollars or imprisoned with or without hard labor for not more than two years, or both.

(Added by Acts 1993 No. 526, §1; chgd. by Acts 1994 Third Ex. Sess. No. 74, §1; Acts 1995 No. 1290, §1, eff. 8/15/95.)

§92.1. Encouraging or contributing to child delinquency, dependency, or neglect; penalty; suspension of sentence; definitions.

A. (1) In all cases where any child shall be a delinquent, dependent, or neglected child, as defined in the statutes of this state or by this Section, irrespective of whether any former proceedings have been had to determine the status of such child, the parent or parents, legal guardian, or any person having the custody of such child, or any other person or persons who shall by any act encourage, cause or contribute to the dependency or delinquency of such child, or who acts in conjunction with such child in the acts which cause such child to be dependent or delinquent, shall be punished by a fine not exceeding one thousand dollars, or by imprisonment for not more than six months, or by both fine and imprisonment.

(2) The court in which the case is heard may suspend the sentence for violation of the provisions of this Section, and impose conditions upon the defendant as to his future conduct, and may make such suspension dependent upon the fulfillment by the defendant of such conditions. In the case of the breach of such conditions or any part of them, the court may impose sentence as though there had been no such suspension.

(3) The court may also, as a condition of such suspension, require a bond in such sum as the court may designate, to be approved by the judge requiring it, to secure the performance by such person of the conditions placed by the courts on such suspension. The bond by its terms shall be made payable to the district judge of the parish in which the prosecution is pending, and any money received from a breach of any of the provisions of the bond shall be paid into the parish treasury. The provisions of law regulating forfeiture of appearance bonds shall govern so far as they are applicable.

(4) Exclusive jurisdiction of the offense defined in this Section is hereby conferred on juvenile courts, in accordance with the provisions of law establishing such courts.

B. By the term "delinquency", as used in this section, is meant any act which tends to debase or injure the morals, health or welfare of a child; drinking beverages of low alcoholic content or beverages of high alcoholic content; the use of narcotics, going into or remaining in any bawdy house, assignation house, disorderly house or road house, hotel, public dance hall, or other gathering place where prostitutes, gamblers or thieves are permitted to enter and ply their trade; or associating with thieves and immoral persons, or enticing a minor to leave home or to leave the custody of its parents, guardians or persons standing in lieu thereof, without first receiving the consent of the parent, guardian, or other person; or begging, singing, selling any article; or playing any musical instrument in any public place for the purpose of receiving alms; or habitually trespassing where it is recognized he has no right to be; or using any vile, obscene, or indecent language; or performing any sexually immoral act; or violating any law of the state ordinance of any village, town, city, or parish of the state.

The term "juvenile", as used in this section, refers to any child under the age of seventeen. Lack of knowledge of the juvenile's age shall not be a defense.
(Chgd. by Acts 1991 No. 667, §1, eff. 9/6/91.)

§92.2. Improper supervision of a minor by parent or legal custodian; penalty.

A. Improper supervision of a minor by a parent or legal custodian, who has care and control of the minor, includes any of the following activities:

(1) Through criminal negligence, the permitting of the minor to associate with a person known by the parent or custodian:

(a) To be a member of a known criminal street gang as defined in R.S. 15:1404(A).

(b) To have been convicted of a felony offense.

(c) To be a known user or distributor of drugs in violation of the Uniform Controlled Dangerous Substances Law*.

**R.S. 40:961 et seq.*

(d) To be a person who possesses or has access to an illegal firearm, weapon, or explosive.

(2) Through criminal negligence, the permitting of the minor:

(a) To enter premises known by the parent or custodian to be a place where sexually indecent activities or prostitution is practiced.

(b) To violate a local or municipal curfew ordinance.

(c) To habitually be a truant from school without valid excuse.

(d) To enter the premises known by the parent or legal custodian as a place of illegal drug use or distribution activity.

(e) To enter the premises known by the parent or legal custodian as a place of underage drinking or gambling.

(f) To enter the premises known by the parent or legal custodian as a place which stores or has a person present who possesses an illegal firearm, weapon, or explosive.

B. Whoever violates the provisions of this Section shall be fined not less than twenty-five dollars and not more than two hundred fifty dollars for each offense, or imprisoned for not more than thirty days, or both. Imposition of sentence shall not be suspended unless the offender is placed on probation with a minimum condition that he participate in forty hours of court-approved community service activities, or a combination of forty hours of court-approved community service and attendance at a court-approved family counseling program by both a parent or legal custodian and the minor.

C. The provisions of Subparagraph A(1)(b) shall not apply to an immediate family member who lives in the household with the minor or other relative who is supervised by the parent or legal custodian when visiting with the minor.

D. No parent or legal guardian shall be guilty of a violation of this Section if, upon acquiring knowledge that the minor has undertaken acts as described in Paragraphs (1) and (2) of Subsection A, the parent or legal guardian seeks the assistance of local, parish, or state law enforcement officials, school officials, social services officials, or other appropriate authorities in either leading the child to modify his or her behavior, or in referring the child to appropriate treatment or corrective facilities.
(Added by Acts 1995 No. 702, §2, eff. 8/15/95.)

§92.3. Retaliation by a minor against a parent, legal custodian, witness, or complainant.

A. Retaliation by a minor against a parent, legal custodian, witness, or complainant is the willful, malicious, and repeated threats of force against or harassment of a person or his property by a minor under the age of seventeen accompanied by an overt act on the part of the minor or by the apparent capability of the minor to carry out the threat or harassment, against a parent, legal custodian, person who filed a complaint against the minor, or a witness in a criminal case in which the minor is the defendant or charged with a delinquency and the minor intends to place that person in a reasonable fear of death, serious bodily injury, or damage to property.

B. The provisions of Subsection A do not apply if the conduct of the parent, legal custodian, person who filed a complaint against the minor, or a witness in a criminal case in which the minor is the defendant or charged with a delinquency is acting in violation of any criminal law.

C. A minor who violates the provisions of this Section shall be placed in the custody of the Department of Public Safety and Corrections for a period not to exceed six months.

Imposition of sentence shall not be suspended unless the minor is placed on probation with a minimum condition that he participate in forty hours of court-approved community service activities or a combination of forty hours of court-approved community service and attendance at a court-approved family counseling program by both a parent or legal custodian and the minor.
(Added by Acts 1995 No. 702, §2, eff. 8/15/95.)

§93. Cruelty to juveniles.

A. Cruelty to juveniles is the intentional or criminally negligent mistreatment or neglect, by anyone over the age of seventeen, of any child under the age of seventeen whereby unjustifiable pain or suffering is caused to said child. Lack of knowledge of the child's age shall not be a defense.

B. The providing of treatment by a parent or tutor in accordance with the tenets of a well-recognized religious method of health, in lieu of medical treatment, shall not for that reason alone be considered to be criminally negligent mistreatment or neglect of a child. The provisions of this Subsection shall be an affirmative defense to a prosecution under this Section. Nothing herein shall be construed to limit the provisions of R.S. 40:1299.36.1.

C. The trial judge shall have the authority to issue any necessary orders to protect the safety of the child during the pendency of the criminal action and beyond its conclusion.

D. Whoever commits the crime of cruelty to juveniles shall be fined not more than one thousand dollars or imprisoned with or without hard labor for not more than ten years, or both.

§93.1. Model glue; use of; abuse of toxic vapors; unlawful sales to minors; penalties.

A. Definitions:

(1) The term "model glue" shall mean any glue or cement of the type commonly used in the building of model airplanes, boats and automobiles and which contains one or more of the following volatile solvents: (a) toluol, (b) hexane, (c) trichlorethylene, (d) acetone, (e) toluene, (f) ethyl acetate, (g) methyl ethyl ketone, (h) trichlorochthane, (i) isopropanol, (j) methyl isobutyl ketone, (k) methyl cellosolve acetate, (*l*) cyclohexanone, or (m) any other solvent, material, substance, chemical or combination thereof having the property of releasing toxic vapors.

(2) "Abuse of toxic vapors" shall mean to smell or inhale the fumes of any solvent, material, substance, chemical or combinations thereof having the property of releasing toxic vapors for the purpose of causing a condition of, or inducing a symptom included in Subsection B of this Section.

B. It shall be unlawful for any person to intentionally smell or inhale the fumes of any type of model glue or toxic vapors for the purpose of causing a condition of, or inducing symptoms of intoxication, elation, euphoria, dizziness, excitement, irrational behavior, exhilaration, paralysis, stupefaction or dulling of the senses or nervous system; or for the purpose of, in any manner, changing, distorting or disturbing the audio, visual or mental processes. This Section shall not apply to the inhalation of any anesthesia for medical or dental purposes.

C. It shall be unlawful for any person to sell any type of model glue to a minor for any reason whatsoever.

D. It shall be unlawful for any person to sell or otherwise transfer possession of any type of model glue to any minor for any purpose whatsoever, unless the minor receiving possession of the model glue is the child or ward of and under the lawful custody of the vendor, donor or transferor of the glue.

E. Any person violating any provisions of this Section shall be guilty of a misdemeanor and, upon conviction thereof, shall be fined not less than twenty-five dollars nor more than one hundred dollars or imprisoned for not more than ninety days for each such offense or both.
(Chgd. by Acts 1997 No. 659, §1, eff. 8/15/97.)

§93.2. Tattooing and body piercing of minors; prohibition.

A. It is unlawful for any person to tattoo or body pierce any other person under the age of eighteen without the consent of an accompanying parent or tutor of such person.

B. It is unlawful for any business entity to pierce the body of any person under the age of eighteen without the consent of a parent or legal custodian of such person.

C. Whoever is found guilty of violating the provisions of this Section shall be fined not less than one hundred dollars nor more than five hundred dollars or be imprisoned for not less than thirty days nor more than one year, or both.
(Chgd. by Acts 1997 No. 743, §1, No. 684, §1, eff. 8/15/97.)

§93.2.1. Child desertion.

A. Child desertion is the intentional or criminally negligent exposure of a child under the age of ten years, by a person who has the care, custody, or control of the child, to a hazard or danger against which the child cannot reasonably be expected to protect himself, or the desertion or abandonment of such child, knowing or having reason to believe that the child could be exposed to such hazard or danger.

B. (1) Whoever commits the crime of child desertion shall be fined not more than five hundred dollars or be imprisoned for not more than six months, or both.

(2) On a second and subsequent conviction the offender shall be fined not less than five hundred dollars nor more than one thousand dollars and imprisoned for not less than six months nor more than one year.

§93.2.2. Unlawful placement of gold fillings, caps, and crowns; minors.

It is unlawful for any person to replace a tooth or part of a tooth or associated tissue by means of a filling, cap, or crown made of any gold substance on any person under the age of eighteen without the consent of the parents or guardian of such person. Whoever violates the provisions of this Section shall be fined not less than five hundred dollars nor more than five thousand dollars. *(Added by Acts 1995 No. 1101, §1, eff. 8/15/95.)*

3. OFFENSES AFFECTING THE HEALTH AND SAFETY OF THE INFIRMED

§93.3. Cruelty to the infirmed.

A. Cruelty to the infirmed is the intentional or criminally negligent mistreatment or neglect by any person, including a caregiver, whereby unjustifiable pain, malnourishment, or suffering is caused to the infirmed, a disabled adult, or an aged person, including but not limited to a person who is a resident of a nursing home, mental retardation facility, mental health facility, hospital or other residential facility.

B. "Caregiver" is defined as any person or persons who temporarily or permanently is responsible for the care of the infirmed, physically or mentally disabled adult, or aged person, whether such care is voluntarily assumed or is assigned. Caregiver includes, but is not limited to, adult children, parents, relatives, neighbors, daycare institutions and facilities, adult congregate living facilities, and nursing homes which or who have voluntarily assumed or been assigned the care of an aged or infirmed person or disabled adult, or have assumed voluntary residence with an aged or infirmed person or disabled adult.

C. For the purposes of this Section, an aged person is any individual sixty years of age or older.

D. The providing of treatment by a caregiver in accordance with a well-recognized spiritual method of healing, in lieu of medical treatment, shall not for that reason alone be considered the intentional or criminally negligent mistreatment or neglect of an infirmed, a disabled adult, or an aged person. The provisions of this Subsection shall be an affirmative defense to a prosecution under this Section.

E. Whoever commits the crime of cruelty to the infirmed, disabled adults, or aged persons shall be fined not more than ten thousand dollars or imprisoned with or without hard labor for not more than ten years, or both.
(Chgd. by Acts 1994 Third Ex. Sess. No. 26, §1; Acts 1995 No. 841, §1, No. 883, §1, eff. 8/15/95.)

§93.4. Exploitation of the infirmed.

A. Exploitation of the infirmed is:

(1) The intentional expenditure, diminution, or use by any person, including a caregiver, of the property or assets of the infirmed, a disabled adult, or an aged person, including but not limited to a resident of a nursing home, mental retardation facility, mental health facility, hospital, or other residential facility without the express voluntary consent of the resident or the consent of the resident or the consent of a legally authorized representative of an incompetent resident, or by means of fraudulent conduct, practices, or representations.

(2) The use of an infirmed person's, or aged person's, or disabled adult's power of attorney or guardianship for one's own profit or advantage by means of fraudulent conduct, practices, or representations.

B. Whoever commits the crime of exploitation of the infirmed shall be fined not more than ten thousand dollars or imprisoned, with or without hard labor, for not more than ten years, or both.

(Added by Acts 1992 No. 309, §1; chgd. by Acts 1994 Third Ex. Sess. No. 26, §1; Acts 1995 No. 883, §1, eff. 8/15/95.)

§93.5. Sexual battery of the infirmed.

A. Sexual battery of the infirm* is the intentional engaging in any of the sexual acts listed in Subsection B with another person, who is not the spouse of the offender, when:

(1) The offender compels the victim, who is physically incapable of preventing the act because of advanced age or physical infirmity, to submit by placing the victim in fear of receiving bodily harm.

(2) The victim is incapable of resisting or of understanding the nature of the act by reason of stupor or abnormal condition of the mind produced by an intoxicating, narcotic, or anesthetic agent administered by or with the privity of the offender.

(3) The victim has such incapacity, by reason of a stupor or abnormal condition of mind from any cause, and the offender knew or should have known of the victim's incapacity.

(4) The victim is incapable, through unsoundness of mind, whether temporary or permanent, of understanding the nature of the act, and the offender knew or should have known of the victim's incapacity.

B. For purposes of this Section, "sexual acts" mean the following:

(1) The touching of the anus or genitals of the victim by the offender using any instrumentality or any part of the body of the offender; or

(2) The touching of the anus or genitals of the offender by the victim using any instrumentality or any part of the body of the victim.

C. Normal medical treatment and normal sanitary care shall not be construed as an offense under the provisions of this Section.

D. Whoever commits the crime of sexual battery of the infirm* shall be punished by imprisonment, with or without hard labor, for not more than ten years.

(Added by Acts 1992 No. 617, §1, eff. 8/21/92.)

**Probably should be "infirmed".*

4. UNLAWFUL SALE, PURCHASE, AND POSSESSION OF ALCOHOLIC BEVERAGES

(Added by Acts 1995 No. 639, §1, eff. 8/15/95.)

§93.10. Definitions.

For purposes of R.S. 14:93.10 through 93.14, the following definitions shall apply:

(1) "Purchase" means acquisition by the payment of money or other consideration. Purchase does not include such acquisition for medical purposes either when purchased as over the counter medication or when prescribed or administered by a licensed physician, pharmacist, dentist, nurse, hospital, or medical institution.

(2) "Public possession" means the possession of any alcoholic beverage for any reason, including consumption, on any street or highway or in any public place or any place open to the public, including a club which is de facto open to the public. "Public possession" does not include the following:

(a) The possession or consumption of any alcoholic beverage:

(i) For an established religious purpose.

(ii) When a person under twenty-one years of age is accompanied by a parent, spouse, or legal guardian twenty-one years of age or older.

(iii) For medical purposes when purchased as an over the counter medication, or when prescribed or administered by a licensed physician, pharmacist, dentist, nurse, hospital, or medical institution.

(iv) In private residences.

(b) The sale, handling, transport, or service in dispensing of any alcoholic beverage pursuant to lawful ownership of an establishment or to lawful employment of a person under twenty-one years of age by a duly licensed manufacturer, wholesaler, or retailer of beverage alcohol.

(3) "Alcoholic beverage" means beer, distilled spirits, and wine containing one-half of one percent or more of alcohol by volume. Beer includes but is not limited to ale, lager, porter, stout, sake, and other similar fermented beverages brewed or produced from malt wholly or in part or from any substitute therefor. Distilled spirits include alcohol, ethanol, or spirits or wine in any form, including all dilutions and mixtures thereof from whatever process produced.
(Added by Acts 1995 No. 639, §1; chgd. by Acts 1996 First Ex. Sess. No. 78, §1, eff. 6/18/96.)

§93.11. Unlawful sales to persons under twenty-one.
A. Unlawful sales to persons under twenty-one is the selling or otherwise delivering for value of any alcoholic beverage to any person under twenty-one years of age unless such person is the lawful owner or lawful employee of an establishment to which the sale is being made and is accepting such delivery pursuant to such ownership or employment. Lack of knowledge of the person's age shall not be a defense.

B. Whoever violates the provisions of this Section shall be fined not more than one hundred dollars or imprisoned for not more than six months, or both.
(Added by Acts 1995 No. 639, §1; chgd. by Acts 1996 First Ex. Sess. No. 78, §1, eff. 6/18/96.)

§93.12. Purchase and public possession of alcoholic beverages; exceptions; penalties.
A. It is unlawful for any person under twenty-one years of age to purchase or have public possession of any alcoholic beverage.

B. (1) Whoever violates the provisions of this Section shall be fined not more than one hundred dollars or imprisoned for not more than six months, or both.

(2) Any person apprehended while violating the provisions of this Section shall be issued a citation by the apprehending law enforcement officer, which shall be paid in the same manner as provided for the offenders of local traffic violations.
(Added by Acts 1995 No. 639, §1; chgd. by Acts 1996 First Ex. Sess. No. 78, §1, eff. 6/18/96.)

§93.13. Unlawful purchase of alcoholic beverages by persons on behalf of persons under twenty-one.
A. It is unlawful for any person, other than a parent, spouse, or legal guardian, as specified in R.S. 14:93.10(2)(a)(ii), to purchase on behalf of a person under twenty-one years of age any alcoholic beverage.

B. Whoever violates the provisions of this Section shall be fined not more than five hundred dollars or imprisoned for not more than thirty days, or both.
(Added by Acts 1995 No. 639, §1; chgd. by Acts 1996 First Ex. Sess. No. 78, §1, eff. 6/18/96.)

§93.14. Responsibilities of retail dealers not relieved.
Nothing in R.S. 14:93.10 through 93.13 shall be construed as relieving any licensed retail dealer in alcoholic beverages any responsibilities imposed under the provisions of Title 26 of the Louisiana Revised Statutes of 1950. *(Added by Acts 1995 No. 639, §1; chgd. by Acts 1996 First Ex. Sess. No. 78, §1, eff. 6/18/96.)*

§93.20. *(Repealed by Acts 1998 No. 71, §2, eff. 6/25/98.)*

PART VI. OFFENSES AFFECTING THE PUBLIC GENERALLY

SUBPART A. OFFENSES AFFECTING THE PUBLIC SAFETY

1. ILLEGAL CARRYING AND DISCHARGE OF WEAPONS

§94. Illegal use of weapons or dangerous instrumentalities.
A. Illegal use of weapons or dangerous instrumentalities is the intentional or criminally negligent discharging of any firearm, or the throwing, placing, or other use of any article, liquid, or substance, where it is foreseeable that it may result in death or great bodily harm to a human being.

B. Except as provided in Subsection E, whoever commits the crime of illegal use of weapons or dangerous instrumentalities shall be fined not more than one thousand dollars, or imprisoned with or without hard labor for not more than two years, or both.

C. Except as provided in Subsection E, on a second or subsequent conviction, the offender shall be imprisoned at hard labor for not less than five years nor more than seven years, without benefit of probation or suspension of sentence.

D. The enhanced penalty upon second and subsequent convictions provided for in Subsection C of this Section shall not be applicable in cases where more than five years have elapsed since the expiration of the maximum sentence, or sentences, of the previous conviction or convictions, and the time of the commission of the last offense for which he has been convicted. The sentence to be imposed in such event shall be the same as may be imposed upon a first conviction.

E. Whoever commits the crime of illegal use of weapons or dangerous instrumentalities by discharging a firearm from a motor vehicle located upon a public street or highway, where the intent is to injure, harm, or frighten another human being, shall be imprisoned at hard labor for not less than five nor more than ten years without benefit of probation or suspension of sentence.

F. Whoever commits the crime of illegal use of weapons or dangerous instrumentalities by discharging a firearm while committing, attempting to commit, conspiring to commit, or soliciting, coercing, or intimidating another person to commit a crime of violence or violation of the Uniform Controlled Dangerous Substances Law*, shall be imprisoned at hard labor for not less than ten years nor more than twenty years, without benefit of parole, probation, or suspension of sentence, If the firearm used in violation of this Subsection is a machine gun or is equipped with a firearm silencer or muffler, as defined by R.S. 40:1751 and R.S. 40:1781, respectively, the offender shall be sentenced to imprisonment for not less than twenty years nor more than thirty years, without benefit of parole, probation, or suspension of sentence. Upon a second or subsequent conviction, under this Subsection, such offender shall be sentenced to imprisonment for not less than twenty years. If the violation of this Subsection, upon second or subsequent conviction, involves the use of a machine gun or a firearm equipped with a firearm silencer or muffler, such offender shall be sentenced to imprisonment for life without benefit of parole, probation, or suspension of sentence.

(Chgd. by Acts 1991 No. 904, §1; Acts 1992 No. 1015, §1; Acts 1995 No. 748, §1, eff. 8/15/95.)
**R.S. 40:961 et seq.*

§95. Illegal carrying of weapons.

A. Illegal carrying of weapons is:

(1) The intentional concealment of any firearm, or other instrumentality customarily used or intended for probable use as a dangerous weapon, on one's person; or

(2) The ownership, possession, custody or use of any firearm, or other instrumentality customarily used as a dangerous weapon, at any time by an enemy alien; or

(3) The ownership, possession, custody or use of any tools, or dynamite, or nitroglycerine, or explosives, or other instrumentality customarily used by thieves or burglars at any time by any person with the intent to commit a crime; or

(4) The manufacture, ownership, possession, custody or use of any switchblade knife, spring knife or other knife or similar instrument having a blade which may be automatically unfolded or extended from a handle by the manipulation of a button, switch, latch or similar contrivance.

(5) (a) The intentional possession or use by any person of a dangerous weapon on a school campus during regular school hours or on a school bus. "School" means any elementary, secondary, high school, or vo-tech school in this state and "campus" means all facilities and property within the boundary of the school property. "School bus" means any motor bus being used to transport children to and from school or in connection with school activities.

(b) The provisions of this Paragraph shall not apply to:

(i) A state or local law enforcement officer in the performance of his official duties.

(ii) A school official or employee acting during the normal course of his employment or a student acting under the direction of such school official or employee.

(iii) Any person having the written permission of the principal or school board and engaged in competition or in marksmanship or safety instruction.

B. (1) Whoever commits the crime of illegal carrying of weapons shall be fined not more than five hundred dollars, or imprisoned for not more than six months, or both.

(2) Whoever commits the crime of illegal carrying of weapons with any firearm used in the commission of a crime of violence as defined in R.S. 14:2(13), shall be fined not more than two thousand dollars, or imprisoned, with or without hard labor, for not less than one year nor

more than two years, or both. Any sentence issued pursuant to the provisions of this Paragraph and any sentence issued pursuant to a violation of a crime of violence as defined in R.S. 14:2(13) shall be served consecutively.

C. On a second conviction, the offender shall be imprisoned with or without hard labor for not more than five years.

D. On third and subsequent convictions, the offender shall be imprisoned with or without hard labor for not more than ten years without benefit of parole, probation, or suspension of sentence.

E. If the offender uses, possesses, or has under his immediate control any firearm, or other instrumentality customarily used or intended for probable use as a dangerous weapon, while committing or attempting to commit a crime of violence or while in the possession of or during the sale or distribution of a controlled dangerous substance, the offender shall be fined not more than ten thousand dollars and imprisoned at hard labor for not less than five nor more than ten years without the benefit of probation, parole, or suspension of sentence. Upon a second or subsequent conviction, the offender shall be imprisoned at hard labor for not less than twenty years nor more than thirty years without the benefit of probation, parole, or suspension of sentence.

F. The enhanced penalty upon second, third, and subsequent convictions shall not be applicable in cases where more than five years have elapsed since the expiration of the maximum sentence, or sentences, of the previous conviction or convictions, and the time of the commission of the last offense for which he has been convicted; the sentence to be imposed in such event shall be the same as may be imposed upon a first conviction.

G. The provisions of this Section except Paragraph (4) of Subsection A shall not apply to sheriffs and their deputies, state and city police, constables and town marshals, or persons vested with police power when in the actual discharge of official duties or, if not actually discharging official duties, when such sheriffs and their deputies and state and city police are full-time, active, or retired from full-time active law enforcement service with at least sixteen years of service upon retirement, excluding medical retirees, and certified by the Council on Peace Officer Standards and Training and have on their persons valid identification as duly commissioned or retired law enforcement officers. The retired law enforcement officer must be retired from full-time active law enforcement service with at least sixteen years service upon retirement. The retired law enforcement officer must be certified annually in the use of firearms by the Council on Peace Officer Standards and Training and have proof of such certification.

H. The provisions of this Section shall not prohibit active justices or judges of the supreme court, courts of appeal, district courts, parish courts, juvenile courts, family courts, city courts, and traffic courts, constables, and justices of the peace from possessing and concealing a handgun on their person when the justice or judge, constable or justice of the peace is certified by the Council on Peace Officer Standards and Training.

I. The provisions of this Section shall not prohibit the carrying of a concealed handgun by a person who is a college or university police officer under the provisions of R.S. 17:1805 and who is carrying a concealed handgun in accordance with the provisions of that statute.

J. The provisions of this Section shall not prohibit the ownership of rescue knives by commissioned full-time law enforcement officers. The provisions of this Section shall not prohibit the carrying of rescue knives by commissioned full-time law enforcement officers who are in the actual discharge of their official duties. The provisions of this Section shall not prohibit the sale of rescue knives to commissioned full-time law enforcement officers. The provisions of this Section shall not prohibit the ownership or possession of rescue knives by merchants who own or possess the knives solely as inventory to be offered for sale to commissioned full-time law enforcement officers. As used in this Subsection, a "rescue knife" is a folding knife, which can be readily and easily opened with one hand and which has at least one blade which is designed to be used to free individuals who are trapped by automobile seat belts, or at least one blade which is designed for a similar purpose. No blade of a rescue knife shall exceed five inches in length.

(Chgd. by Acts 1992 No. 1017, §1; Acts 1993 No. 636, §1, No. 844, §1; Acts 1994 Third Ex. Sess. No. 143, §1; Acts 1995 No. 636, §1, No. 930, §1, No. 1195, §1, No. 1199, §1; Acts 1997 No. 508, §1, No. 611, §1, No. 1064, §1, eff. 8/15/97.)

§95.1. Possession of firearm or carrying concealed weapon by a person convicted of certain felonies.

A. It is unlawful for any person who has been convicted of a crime of violence as defined in R.S. 14:2(13) which is a felony or simple burglary, burglary of a pharmacy, burglary of an inhabited dwelling, unauthorized entry of an inhabited dwelling, felony illegal use of weapons or dangerous instrumentalities, manufacture or possession of a delayed action incendiary device, manufacture or possession of a bomb, or any violation of the Uniform Controlled Substances Law* which is a felony, or any crime defined as an attempt to commit one of the above enumerated offenses under the laws of this state, or who has been convicted under the laws of any other state or of the United States or of any foreign government or country of a crime which, if committed in this state, would be one of the above enumerated crimes, to possess a firearm or carry a concealed weapon.

**R.S. 40:961 et seq.*

B. Whoever is found guilty of violating the provisions of this Section shall be imprisoned at hard labor for not less than ten nor more than fifteen years without the benefit of probation, parole, or suspension of sentence and be fined not less than one thousand dollars nor more than five thousand dollars.

C. Except as otherwise specifically provided, this Section shall not apply to the following cases:

(1) The provisions of this Section prohibiting the possession of firearms and carrying concealed weapons by persons who have been convicted of certain felonies shall not apply to any person who has not been convicted of any felony for a period of ten years from the date of completion of sentence, probation, parole, or suspension of sentence.

(2) Upon completion of sentence, probation, parole, or suspension of sentence the convicted felon shall have the right to apply to the sheriff of the parish in which he resides, or in the case of Orleans Parish the superintendent of police, for a permit to possess firearms. The felon shall be entitled to possess the firearm upon the issuing of the permit.

(3) The sheriff or superintendent of police, as the case may be, shall immediately notify the Department of Public Safety, in writing, of the issuance of each permit granted under this Section.

(Chgd. by Acts 1990 No. 328, §1; Acts 1992 No. 403, §1; Acts 1994 Third Ex. Sess. No. 28, §1; Acts 1995 No. 987, §1, eff. 8/15/95.)

§95.2. Carrying a firearm, or dangerous weapon, by a student or nonstudent on school property, at school sponsored functions or firearm-free zone.

A. Carrying a firearm, or dangerous weapon as defined in R.S. 14:2, by a student or nonstudent on school property, at a school sponsored function or in a firearm-free zone is unlawful and shall be defined as possession of any firearm or dangerous weapon, on one's person, at any time while on a school campus, on school transportation, or at any school sponsored function in a specific designated area including but not limited to, athletic competitions, dances, parties, or any extracurricular activities, or within one thousand feet of any school campus.

B. For purposes of this Section, the following words have the following meanings:

(1) "School" means any elementary, secondary, high school, vocational-technical school, college, or university in this state.

(2) "Campus" means all facilities and property within the boundary of the school property.

(3) "School bus" means any motor bus being used to transport children to and from school or in connection with school activities.

(4) "Nonstudent" means any person not registered and enrolled in that school or a suspended student who does not have permission to be on the school campus.

C. The provisions of this Section shall not apply to:

(1) A federal, state, or local law enforcement officer in the performance of his official duties.

(2) A school official or employee acting during the normal course of his employment or a student acting under the direction of such school official or employee.

(3) Any person having the written permission of the principal.

(4) The possession of a firearm occurring within one thousand feet of school property and entirely on private property, or entirely within a private residence, or in accordance with a concealed handgun permit issued pursuant to R.S. 40:1379.1.

(5) Any constitutionally protected activity which cannot be regulated by the state, such as a firearm contained entirely within a motor vehicle.

(6) Any student carrying a firearm to or from a class, in which he is duly enrolled, that requires the use of the firearm in the class.

(7) A student enrolled or participating in an activity requiring the use of a firearm including but not limited to any ROTC function under the authorization of a university.

(8) A student who possesses a firearm in his dormitory room or while going to or from his vehicle or any other person with permission of the administration.

D. Whoever commits the crime of carrying a firearm by a student or nonstudent on school property or in a firearm-free zone shall be imprisoned at hard labor for not more than five years.

E. Lack of knowledge that the prohibited act occurred on or within one thousand feet of school property shall not be a defense.

F. (1) School officials shall notify all students and parents of the impact of this legislation and shall post notices of the impact of this Section at each major point of entry to the school. These notices shall be maintained as permanent notices.

(2) (a) If a student is detained by the principal or other school official for violation of this Section or the school principal or other school official confiscates or seizes a firearm or concealed weapon from a student while upon school property, at a school function, or on a school bus, the principal or other school official in charge at the time of the detention or seizure shall immediately report the detention or seizure to the police department or sheriff's department where the school is located and shall deliver any firearm or weapon seized to that agency.

(b) The confiscated weapon shall be disposed of or destroyed as provided by law.

(3) If a student is detained pursuant to Paragraph (2) of this Subsection for carrying a concealed weapon on campus, the principal shall immediately notify the student's parents.

(4) If a person is arrested for carrying a concealed weapon on campus by a university or college police officer, the weapon shall be given to the sheriff, chief of police, or other officer to whom custody of the arrested person is transferred as provided by R.S. 17:1805(B).

G. Any principal or school official in charge who fails to report the detention of a student or the seizure of a firearm or concealed weapon to a law enforcement agency as required by Paragraph F(2) of this Section within seventy-two hours of notice of the detention or seizure may be issued a misdemeanor summons for a violation hereof and may be fined not more than five hundred dollars or sentenced to not more than forty hours of community service, or both. Upon successful completion of the community service or payment of the fine, or both, the arrest and conviction shall be set aside as provided for in Code of Criminal Procedure Article 894(B).

(Added by Acts 1991 No. 833, §1; chgd. by Acts 1992 No. 197, §1; Acts 1993 No. 844, §1, No. 1031, §1; Acts 1994 Third Ex. Sess. No. 25, §1, No. 38, §1, No. 107, §1, eff. 8/27/94.)

§95.3. Unlawful use of body armor.

A. No person shall use or wear body armor while committing or attempting to commit the crimes of first or second degree murder, manslaughter, armed robbery, aggravated rape, sexual battery, aggravated battery, aggravated assault, aggravated kidnapping, aggravated arson, aggravated burglary, aggravated escape, or illegal carrying of weapons.

B. Whoever violates the provisions of this Section shall be fined not more than two thousand dollars or imprisoned with or without hard labor for not more than two years, or both.

C. For the purposes of this Section, "body armor" shall mean bullet resistant metal or other material intended to provide protection from weapons or bodily injury.

§95.4. Consent to search; alcoholic beverage outlet.

A. Any person entering an alcoholic beverage outlet as defined herein, by the fact of such entering, shall be deemed to have consented to a reasonable search of his person for any firearm by a law enforcement officer or other person vested with police power, without the necessity of a warrant.

B. For purposes of this Section, "alcoholic beverage outlet" means any commercial establishment in which alcoholic beverages of either high or low alcoholic content are sold in individual servings for consumption on the premises, whether or not such sales are the primary purpose or are an incidental purpose of the business of the establishment.

C. An "alcoholic beverage outlet" licensed to sell firearms or containing an indoor shooting gallery shall be exempt from the provisions of this Section in those areas designated for the sale of firearms or the shooting gallery.

D. An "alcoholic beverage outlet" shall not include a restaurant if a majority of its gross receipts are from sales of food and non-alcoholic beverages.

E. The owner of the alcoholic beverage outlet shall post a sign, at or near the entrance, that states that by the fact of entering these premises a person shall be deemed to have consented to a reasonable search of his person for any firearm by a law enforcement officer or other person vested with police power, without the necessity of a warrant.

§95.5. Possession of firearm on premises of alcoholic beverage outlet.

A. No person shall intentionally possess a firearm while on the premises of an alcoholic beverage outlet.

B. "Alcoholic beverage outlet" as used herein means any commercial establishment in which alcoholic beverages of either high or low alcoholic content are sold in individual servings for consumption on the premises, whether or not such sales are a primary or incidental purpose of the business of the establishment.

C. The provisions of this Section shall not apply to the owner or lessee of an alcoholic beverage outlet, or to an employee of such owner or lessee, or to a law enforcement officer or other person vested with law enforcement authority acting in the performance of his official duties.

D. Whoever violates the provisions of this Section shall be fined not more than five hundred dollars or imprisoned for not more than six months, or both.

§95.6. Firearm-free zone; notice; signs; crime; penalties.

A. A "Firearm-free zone" is an area inclusive of any school campus and within one thousand feet of any such school campus, and within a school bus.

B. The provisions of this Section shall not apply to:

(1) A federal, state, or local law enforcement building.

(2) A military base.

(3) A commercial establishment which is permitted by law to have firearms or armed security.

(4) Private premises where a firearm is kept pursuant to law.

(5) Any constitutionally protected activity within the firearm-free zone, such as a firearm contained entirely within a motor vehicle.

C. For purposes of this Section:

(1) "School" means any public or private elementary, secondary, high school, or vocational-technical school, college, or university in this state.

(2) "School campus" means all facilities and property within the boundary of the school property.

(3) "School bus" means any motor bus being used to transport children to and from school or in connection with school activities.

D. The local governing authority which has jurisdiction over zoning matters in which each firearm-free zone is located shall publish a map clearly indicating the boundaries of each firearm-free zone in accordance with the specifications in Subsection A. The firearm-free zone map shall be made an official public document and placed with the clerk of court for the parish or parishes in which the firearm-free zone is located.

E. The state superintendent of education, with the approval of the State Board of Elementary and Secondary Education, and the commissioner of higher education, with the approval of the Board of Regents, shall develop a method by which to mark firearm-free zones, including the use of signs or other markings suitable to the situation. Signs or other markings shall be located in a visible manner on or near each school and on and in each school bus indicating that such area is a firearm-free zone and that such zone extends to one thousand feet from the boundary of school property. The state Department of Education shall assist each approved school with the posting of notice as required in this Subsection.

F. (1) It is unlawful for any person to cover, remove, deface, alter, or destroy any sign or other marking identifying a firearm-free zone as provided in this Section.

(2) Whoever violates the provisions of this Subsection shall be fined not more than one thousand dollars or imprisoned for not more than six months, or both.

(Added by Acts 1992 No. 197, §1; chgd. by Acts 1993 No. 844, §1, No. 1031, §1, eff. 8/15/93.)

§95.7. Possession of or dealing in firearms with obliterated number or mark.

A. No person shall intentionally receive, possess, carry, conceal, buy, sell, or transport any firearm from which the serial number or mark of identification has been obliterated.

B. This Section shall not apply to any firearm which is an antique or war relic and is inoperable or for which ammunition is no longer manufactured in the United States and is not readily available in the ordinary channels of commercial trade, or which was originally manufactured without such a number.

C. Whoever violates the provisions of this Section shall be fined not more than one thousand dollars and may be imprisoned for not more than six months.
(Added by Acts 1993 No. 85, §1, eff. 8/15/93.)

2. OBSTRUCTING HIGHWAYS OF COMMERCE

§96. Aggravated obstruction of a highway of commerce.

Aggravated obstruction of a highway of commerce is the intentional or criminally negligent placing of anything, or performance of any act, on any railway, railroad, navigable waterway, road, highway, thoroughfare, or runway of an airport, wherein it is foreseeable that human life might be endangered.

Whoever commits the crime of aggravated obstruction of a highway of commerce shall be imprisoned, with or without hard labor, for not more than fifteen years.

§97. Simple obstruction of a highway of commerce.

Simple obstruction of a highway of commerce is the intentional or criminally negligent placing of anything or performance of any act on any railway, railroad, navigable waterway, road, highway, thoroughfare, or runway of an airport, which will render movement thereon more difficult.

Whoever commits the crime of simple obstruction of a highway of commerce shall be fined not more than two hundred dollars, or imprisoned for not more than six months, or both.

§97.1. Solicitation on an interstate highway.

A. Solicitation on an interstate highway is the intentional act of soliciting, begging, panhandling or otherwise requesting anything of value on any interstate highway, or on any entrance or exit ramp of an interstate highway.

B. Whoever commits the crime of solicitation on an interstate highway shall be fined not more than two hundred dollars, or imprisoned for not more than six months, or both.
(Added by Acts 1997 No. 1099, §1, eff. 8/15/97.)

3. DRIVING OFFENSES

§98. Operating a vehicle while intoxicated.

A. (1) The crime of operating a vehicle while intoxicated is the operating of any motor vehicle, aircraft, watercraft, vessel, or other means of conveyance when:

(a) The operator is under the influence of alcoholic beverages; or

(b) The operator's blood alcohol concentration is 0.10 percent or more by weight based on grams of alcohol per one hundred cubic centimeters of blood; or

(c) The operator is under the influence of any controlled dangerous substance listed in Schedule I, II, III, IV, or V as set forth in R.S. 40:964.

(2) A valid driver's license shall not be an element of the offense, and the lack thereof shall not be a defense to a prosecution for operating a vehicle while intoxicated.

B. On a first conviction, notwithstanding any other provision of law to the contrary, the offender shall be fined not less than three hundred dollars nor more than one thousand dollars, and may be imprisoned for not less than ten days nor more than six months. Imposition or execution of sentence shall not be suspended unless:

(1) The offender is placed on probation with a minimum condition that he serve two days in jail and participate in a court-approved substance abuse program and participate in a court-approved driver improvement program; or

(2) The offender is placed on probation with a minimum condition that he perform four eight-hour days of court-approved community service activities, at least half of which shall consist of participation in a litter abatement or collection program, participate in a court-approved substance abuse program, and participate in a court-approved driver

improvement program. An offender, who participates in a litter abatement or collection program pursuant to this Paragraph, shall have no cause of action for damages against the entity conducting the program or supervising his participation therein, including a municipality, parish, sheriff, or other entity, nor against any official, employee, or agent of such entity, for any injury or loss suffered by him during or arising out of his participation in the program, if such injury or loss is a direct result of the lack of supervision or act or omission of the supervisor, unless the injury or loss was caused by the intentional or grossly negligent act or omission of the entity or its official, employee, or agent.

C. On a conviction of a second offense, notwithstanding any other provision of law to the contrary, regardless of whether the second offense occurred before or after the first conviction, the offender shall be fined not less than seven hundred fifty dollars, nor more than one thousand dollars, and shall be imprisoned for not less than thirty days nor more than six months. At least forty-eight hours of the sentence imposed shall be served without the benefit of parole, probation, or suspension of sentence. Nothing herein shall prohibit a court from sentencing a defendant to home incarceration, if otherwise allowed under the provisions of Article 894.2 of the Code of Criminal Procedure. Imposition or execution of the remainder of the sentence shall not be suspended unless:

(1) The offender is placed on probation with a minimum condition that he serve fifteen days in jail and participate in a court-approved substance abuse program and participate in a court-approved driver improvement program; or

(2) The offender is placed on probation with a minimum condition that he perform thirty eight-hour days of court-approved community service activities, at least half of which shall consist of participation in a litter abatement or collection program, and participate in a court-approved substance abuse program, and participate in a court-approved driver improvement program. An offender, who participates in a litter abatement or collection program pursuant to this Paragraph, shall have no cause of action for damages against the entity conducting the program or supervising his participation therein, including a municipality, parish, sheriff, or other entity, nor against any official, employee, or agent of such entity, for any injury or loss suffered by him during or arising out of his participation therein, if such injury or loss is a direct result of the lack of supervision or act or omission of the supervisor, unless the injury or loss was caused by the intentional or grossly negligent act or omission of the entity or its official, employee, or agent.

D. 1. On a conviction of a third offense, notwithstanding any other provision of law to the contrary and regardless of whether the offense occurred before or after an earlier conviction, the offender shall be imprisoned with or without hard labor for not less than one year nor more than five years, and shall be fined two thousand dollars. At least six months of the sentence of imprisonment imposed shall be without benefit of probation, parole, or suspension of sentence. If a portion of the sentence is imposed with benefit of probation, parole, or suspension of sentence, the court shall require the offender to participate in a court-approved substance abuse program and/or participate in a court-approved driver improvement program.

(2) (a) In addition, the court shall order that the vehicle being driven by the offender at the time of the offense shall be seized and impounded, and sold at auction in the same manner and under the same conditions as executions of writ of seizures and sale as provided in Book V, Title II, Chapter 4 of the Code of Civil Procedure.

(b) The vehicle shall be exempt from sale if it was stolen, or if the driver of the vehicle at the time of the violation was not the owner and the owner did not know that the driver was operating the vehicle while intoxicated. If this exemption is applicable, the vehicle shall not be released from impoundment until such time as towing and storage fees have been paid.

(c) In addition, the vehicle shall be exempt from sale if all towing and storage fees are paid by a valid lienholder.

(d) The proceeds of the sale shall first be used to pay court costs and towing and storage costs, and the remainder shall be forwarded to the Council on Automobile Insurance Rates and Enforcement for its use in studying other ways to reduce drunk driving and insurance rates.

E. (1) On a conviction of a fourth or subsequent offense, notwithstanding any other provision of law to the contrary and regardless of whether the fourth offense occurred before or after an earlier conviction, the offender shall be sentenced to imprisonment at hard labor for not less than ten nor more than thirty years, and shall be fined five thousand dollars.

(2) (a) In addition, the court shall order that the vehicle being driven by the offender at the time of the offense be seized and impounded, and be sold at auction in the same manner and

under the same conditions as executions of writ of seizure and sale as provided in Book V, Title II, Chapter 4 of the Code of Civil Procedure.

(b) The vehicle shall be exempt from sale if it was stolen, or if the driver of the vehicle at the time of the violation was not the owner and the owner did not know that the driver was operating the vehicle while intoxicated. If this exemption is applicable, the vehicle shall not be released from impoundment until such time as towing and storage fees have been paid.

(c) In addition, the vehicle shall be exempt from sale if all towing and storage fees are paid by a valid lienholder.

(d) The proceeds of the sale shall first be used to pay court costs and towing and storage costs, and the remainder shall be forwarded to the Council on Automobile Insurance Rates and Enforcement for its use in studying other ways to reduce drunk driving and insurance rates.

(3) (a) At least two years of the sentence shall be imposed without benefit of suspension of sentence, probation, or parole. In the discretion of the court, any additional portion or all of the sentence may be imposed without benefit of suspension of sentence, probation, or parole. If a portion of the sentence is imposed with benefit of suspension of sentence, probation, or parole, the court shall require the offender to participate in a court-approved substance abuse program and a court-approved driver improvement program.

(b) If the offender has previously been required to participate in either or both of such programs pursuant to Subsection D of this Section, at least three years of the sentence shall be imposed without benefit of suspension of sentence, probation, or parole.

(c) If the offender has previously been required to participate in either or both of such programs under Subsection B or C of this Section, but not under Subsection D, at least two years of the sentence shall be imposed without benefit of suspension of sentence, probation, or parole.

(d) If the offender has previously received the benefit of suspension of sentence, probation, or parole as a fourth offender, no part of the sentence may be imposed with benefit of suspension of sentence, probation, or parole, and no portion of the sentence shall be imposed concurrently with the remaining balance of any sentence to be served for a prior conviction for any offense.

F. (1) For purposes of determining whether a defendant has a prior conviction for violation of this Section, a conviction under either R.S. 14:32.1, vehicular homicide, R.S. 14:39.1, vehicular negligent injuring, or R.S. 14:39.2, first degree vehicular negligent injuring, or a conviction under the laws of any state or an ordinance of a municipality, town, or similar political subdivision of another state, which prohibits the operation of any motor vehicle, aircraft, watercraft, vessel, or other means of conveyance while intoxicated, while impaired, or while under the influence of alcohol, drugs, or any controlled dangerous substance shall constitute a prior conviction. This determination shall be made by the court as a matter of law.

(2) For purposes of this Section, a prior conviction shall not include a conviction for an offense under this Section or R.S. 14:32.1 or R.S. 14:39.1 or under a comparable statute or ordinance of another jurisdiction, as described in Paragraph (1) of this Subsection, if committed more than ten years prior to the commission of the crime for which the defendant is being tried and such conviction shall not be considered in the assessment of penalties hereunder. However, periods of time during which the offender was incarcerated in a penal institution in this or any other state shall be excluded in computing the ten-year period. Subsections B and C shall include a screening procedure to determine the portions of the program which may be applicable and appropriate for individual offenders.

G. Court-approved substance abuse programs provided for in Subsections (B) and (C) shall include a screening procedure to determine the portions of the program which may be applicable and appropriate for individual offenders.

H. "Community service activities" as used in this Section may include duty in any morgue, coroner's office, or emergency treatment room of a state-operated hospital or other state-operated emergency treatment facility, with the consent of the administrator of the morgue, coroner's office, hospital, or facility.

I. An offender ordered to participate in a substance abuse program shall pay the cost incurred in participating in the program. Failure to make such payment shall subject the offender to revocation of probation, unless the court determines that the offender is unable to pay.

J. This subsection shall be cited as the "Child Endangerment Law". When the state proves in addition to the elements of the crime as set forth in Subsection A of this Section that a minor

child twelve years of age or younger was a passenger in the motor vehicle, aircraft, watercraft, vessel, or other means of motorized conveyance at the time of the commission of the offense, of the sentence imposed by the court, the execution of the minimum mandatory sentence provided by Subsection B, C, or D of this Section, as appropriate, shall not be suspended. For the fourth conviction, at least two years of the sentence shall be imposed without benefit of suspension of sentence.
(Chgd. by Acts 1991 No. 83, §1, No. 454, §1; Acts 1992 No. 69, §1, No. 679, §1, No. 697, §1; Acts 1993 No. 247, §1, No. 403, §1, No. 669, §1; Acts 1994 Third Ex. Sess. No. 20, §1; Acts 1995 No. 316, §1, No. 520, §1; Acts 1997 No. 1296, §2; Acts 1998 First Ex. Sess. No. 4, §1, eff. 6/16/98.)

§98.1. Underage driving under the influence.

A. The crime of underage operating a vehicle while intoxicated is the operating of any motor vehicle, aircraft, watercraft, vessel, or other means of conveyance when the operator's blood alcohol concentration is 0.02 percent or more by weight if the operator is under the age of twenty-one based on grams of alcohol per one hundred cubic centimeters of blood.

B. Any underage person whose blood alcohol concentration is found to be in violation of R.S. 14:98(A)(1)(b) shall be charged under its provisions rather than under this Section.

C. On a first conviction, the offender shall be fined not less than one hundred nor more than two hundred fifty dollars, and participate in a court-approved substance abuse and driver improvement program.

D. On a second or subsequent conviction, regardless of whether the second offense occurred before or after the first conviction, the offender shall be fined not less than one hundred fifty dollars nor more than five hundred dollars, and imprisoned for not less than ten days nor more than three months. Imposition or execution of sentence shall not be suspended unless:

(1) The offender is placed on probation with a minimum condition that he serve forty-eight hours in jail and participate in a court-approved substance abuse and driver improvement program; or

(2) The offender is placed on probation with a minimum condition that he perform ten eight-hour days of court-approved community service activities, at least half of which shall consist of participation in a litter abatement or collection program and participate in a court-approved substance and driver improvement program.

E. Court programs regarding substance abuse provided for in Subsections C and D shall include a screening procedure to determine the portions of the program which may be applicable and appropriate for individual offenders.

F. An offender ordered to participate in a substance abuse program shall pay the cost incurred in participating in the program. Failure to make such payment shall subject the offender to revocation of probation, unless the court determines that the offender is unable to pay.
(Added by Acts 1997 No. 1296, §2, eff. 7/15/97.)

§99. Reckless operation of a vehicle.

Reckless operation of a vehicle is the operation of any motor vehicle, aircraft, vessel, or other means of conveyance in a criminally negligent or reckless manner.

Whoever commits the crime of reckless operation of a vehicle shall be fined not more than two hundred dollars, or imprisoned for not more than ninety days, or both.

On a second or subsequent conviction the offender shall be fined not less than twenty-five nor more than five hundred dollars, or imprisoned for not less than ten days nor more than six months, or both.

§100. Hit-and-run driving.

A. Hit and run driving is the intentional failure of the driver of a vehicle involved in or causing any accident, to stop such vehicle at the scene of the accident, to give his identity, and to render reasonable aid.

B. For the purpose of this Section:

(1) "To give his identity", means that the driver of any vehicle involved in any accident shall give his name, address, and the license number of his vehicle, or shall report the accident to the police.

(2) "Serious bodily injury" means bodily injury which involves unconsciousness, extreme physical pain, or protracted and obvious disfigurement, or protracted loss or

impairment of the function of a bodily member, organ, or mental faculty, or a substantial risk of death.

(3) "Vehicle" includes a watercraft.

C. (1) Whoever commits the crime of hit and run driving where there is no death or serious bodily injury shall be fined not more than five hundred dollars or imprisoned for not more than six months, or both.

(2) Whoever commits the crime of hit and run driving, when death or serious bodily injury is a direct result of the accident and when the driver knew or should have known that death or serious bodily injury has occurred, shall be fined not more than five thousand dollars or imprisoned with or without hard labor for not more than ten years, or both.
(Chgd. by Acts 1997 No. 561, §1, eff. 8/15/97.)

4. OBSTRUCTING PUBLIC PASSAGES

§100.1. Obstructing public passages.

No person shall willfully obstruct the free, convenient and normal use of any public sidewalk, street, highway, bridge, alley, road, or other passageway, or the entrance, corridor or passage of any public building, structure, water craft or ferry, by impeding, hindering, stifling, retarding or restraining traffic or passage thereon or therein.

Whoever violates the provisions of this Section shall be guilty of a misdemeanor and upon conviction thereof shall be fined not more than five hundred dollars or imprisoned for not more than six months, or both fined and imprisoned.

This Section shall not be applicable to the erection or construction of any barricades or other forms of obstructions as a safety measure in connection with construction, excavation, maintenance, repair, replacement or other work, in or adjacent to any public sidewalk, street, highway, bridge, alley, road, or other passageway, nor to the placing of barricades or other forms of obstruction by governmental authorities, or any officer or agent thereof, in the proper performance of duties.

SUBPART B. OFFENSES AFFECTING THE PUBLIC SENSIBILITY

§101. Desecration of graves.

Desecration of graves is the:

(1) Unauthorized opening of any place of interment, or building wherein the dead body of a human being is located, with the intent to remove or to mutilate the body or any part thereof, or any article interred or intended to be interred with the said body; or

(2) Intentional or criminally negligent damaging in any manner, of any grave, tomb, or mausoleum erected for the dead.

Whoever commits the crime of desecration of graves shall be fined not more than five hundred dollars, or imprisoned for not more than six months, or both.

§101.1. Purchase or sale of human organs.

A. No person shall intentionally acquire, receive, sell, or otherwise transfer in exchange for anything of value any human organ for use in human transplantation.

B. For purposes of Subsection A:

(1) The term "human organ" means the human kidney, liver, heart, lung, pancreas, bone marrow, cornea, eye, bone, skin, and any other human organ.

(2) The term "anything of value" shall not include the reasonable payments associated with the removal, transportation, implantation, processing, preservation, quality control, and storage of a human organ or the expenses of travel, housing, and lost wages incurred by the donor of a human organ in connection with the donation of the organ.

C. Whoever violates the provisions of this Section shall be fined not more than fifty thousand dollars or imprisoned with or without hard labor not more than five years, or both.

§102. Definitions; cruelty to animals.

The following words, phrases, and terms as used in R.S. 14:102.1 through R.S. 14:102.4 shall be defined and construed as follows:

(1) "Cruel" means every act or failure to act whereby unjustifiable physical pain or suffering is caused or permitted.

(2) "Abandons" means to completely forsake and desert an animal previously under the custody or possession of a person without making reasonable arrangements for its proper care, sustenance, and shelter.

(3) "Proper food" means providing each animal with daily food of sufficient quality and quantity to prevent unnecessary or unjustifiable suffering by the animal.

(4) "Proper water" means providing each animal with daily water of sufficient quality and quantity to prevent unnecessary or unjustifiable suffering by the animal.

(5) "Proper shelter" means providing each animal with adequate shelter from the elements as required to prevent unnecessary or unjustifiable suffering by the animal.

(6) "Proper veterinary care" means providing each animal with veterinary care sufficient to prevent unnecessary or unjustifiable physical pain or suffering by the animal.

(7) "Livestock" means cattle, sheep, swine, goats, horses, mules, burros, asses, other livestock of all ages, farm raised cervidae species, and farm raised ratite species.

(8) "Public livestock exhibition" means any place, establishment, or facility commonly known as a "livestock market", "livestock auction market", "sales ring", "stockyard", or the like, operated for compensation or profit as a public market for livestock, consisting of pens, or other enclosures, and their appurtenances, in which livestock are received, held, sold, or kept for sale or shipment. "Public livestock exhibition" also means any public exhibition or sale of livestock or a livestock show.

(9) "Tampers" means any of the following:

(a) The injection, use, or administration of any drug or other internal or external administration of any product or material, whether gas, solid, or liquid, to livestock for the purpose of concealing, enhancing, transforming, or changing the true conformation, configuration, condition, natural color, or age of the livestock or making the livestock appear more sound than they actually are.

(b) The use or administration, for cosmetic purposes, of steroids, growth stimulants, or internal artificial filling, including paraffin, silicone injection, or any other substance.

(c) The use or administration of any drug or feed additive affecting the central nervous system of the livestock, unless administered or prescribed by a licensed veterinarian for the treatment of an illness or an injury.

(d) The use or administration of diuretics for cosmetic purposes.

(e) The surgical manipulation or removal of tissue so as to change, transform, or enhance the true conformation, configuration, or natural color of the livestock unless the procedure is considered an accepted livestock management practice.

(Chgd. by Acts 1997 No. 461, §2, eff. 8/15/97.)

§102.1. Cruelty to animals; simple and aggravated.

A. (1) Any person who intentionally or with criminal negligence commits any of the following shall be guilty of simple cruelty to animals:

(a) Overdrives, overloads, drives when overloaded, or overworks a living animal.

(b) Torments, cruelly beats, or unjustifiably injures any living animal, whether belonging to himself or another.

(c) Having charge, custody, or possession of any animal, either as owner or otherwise, unjustifiably fails to provide it with proper food, proper drink, proper shelter, or proper veterinary care.

(d) Abandons any animal. A person shall not be considered to have abandoned an animal if he delivers to an animal control center an animal which he found running at large.

(e) Impounds or confines or causes to be impounded or confined in a pound or other place, a living animal and fails to supply it during such confinement with proper food, proper drink, and proper shelter.

(f) Carries, or causes to be carried, a living animal in or upon a vehicle or otherwise, in a cruel or inhumane manner.

(g) Unjustifiably administers any poisonous or noxious drug or substance to any domestic animal or unjustifiably exposes any such drug or substance, with intent that the same shall be taken or swallowed by any domestic animal.

(h) Injures any animal belonging to another person without legal privilege or consent of the owner.

(i) Mistreats any living animal by any act or omission whereby unnecessary or unjustifiable physical pain, suffering, or death is caused to or permitted upon the animal.

(j) Causes or procures to be done by any person any act enumerated in this Subsection.

(2) (a) Whoever commits the crime of simple cruelty to animals shall be fined not more than one thousand dollars, or imprisoned for not more than six months, or both.

(b) In addition to any other penalty imposed, a person who commits the crime of cruelty to animals shall be ordered to perform five eight-hour days of court-approved community service. The community service requirement shall not be suspended.

B. (1) Any person who intentionally or with criminal negligence tortures, maims, or mutilates any living animal, whether belonging to himself or another, shall be guilty of aggravated cruelty to animals.

(2) Any person who tampers with livestock at a public livestock exhibition or at a private sale shall also be guilty of aggravated cruelty to animals.

(3) Any person who causes or procures to be done by any person any act designated in this Subsection shall also be guilty of aggravated cruelty to animals.

(4) Whoever commits the crime of aggravated cruelty to animals shall be fined not less than five thousand dollars nor more than twenty-five thousand dollars or imprisoned, with or without hard labor, for not less than one year nor more than ten years, or both.

(5) For purposes of this Subsection, where more than one animal is tortured, maimed, mutilated, or maliciously killed* or where more than one head of livestock is tampered with, each act comprises a separate offense.

** "maliciously kills" was deleted from the definition of "aggravated cruelty to animals" in paragraph (1) of this subsection by Acts 1997 No. 1212, §1.*

C. This Section shall not apply to the lawful hunting or trapping of wildlife as provided by law, herding of domestic animals, accepted veterinary practices, and activities carried on for scientific or medical research governed by accepted standards.

D. For purposes of this Section, fowl shall not be defined as animals. Only the following birds shall be identified as animals for purposes of this Section:

(1) Order Psittaciformes-parrots, parakeets, lovebirds, macaws, cockatiels or cockatoos.

(2) Order Passeriformes-canaries, starlings, sparrows, flycatches, mynah or myna.

(Chgd. by Acts 1995 No. 1165, §1, No. 1246, §1; Acts 1997 No. 461, §2, No. 1212, §1, eff. 8/15/97.)

§102.2. Seizure and disposition of animals cruelly treated.

A. When a person is charged with cruelty to animals, said person's animal may be seized by the arresting officer and held pursuant to this Section.

B. (1) The seizing officer shall notify the owner of the seized animal of the provisions of this Section by posting written notice at the location where the animal was seized or by leaving it with a person of suitable age and discretion residing at that location within twenty-four hours of the seizure.

(2) The seizing officer shall photograph the animal within fifteen days after posting of the notice of seizure and shall cause an affidavit to be prepared in order to document its condition in accordance with R.S. 15:436.2.

(3) The seizing officer shall appoint a licensed veterinarian or other suitable custodian to care for any such animal. The custodian shall retain custody of the animal in accordance with this Section.

(4) The seized animal shall be held by the custodian provided for in Paragraph (3) for a period of fifteen consecutive days including weekends and holidays, after such notice of seizure is given. Thereafter, if a person who claims an interest in such animal has not posted bond in accordance with Subsection C, the animal may be humanely disposed of by sale, adoption, or euthanasia.

C. A person claiming an interest in any animal seized pursuant to this Section may prevent the disposition of the animal as provided for in Subsection B by posting a bond with the court within fifteen days after receiving notice of such seizure in an amount sufficient to secure payment for all reasonable costs incurred in the boarding and treatment for any seized animal for a thirty day period commencing on the date of initial seizure. Such bond shall not prevent the department, agency, humane society, or other custodian of the animal from disposing of the animal in accordance with Subsection B at the end of the thirty day period covered by bond, unless the person claiming an interest posts an additional bond for such reasonable expenses for an additional thirty day period. In addition, such bond shall not prevent disposition of the animal for humane purposes at any time, in accordance with Subsection E of this Section. The amount of the bond shall be determined by the department, agency, humane society or other custodian of the animal as authorized by the court in accordance with the current rate for board and on the condition of the animal after examination by a licensed veterinarian.

D. Upon a person's conviction of cruelty to animals, it shall be proper for the court, in its discretion, to order the forfeiture and final determination of the custody of any animal found to be cruelly treated in accordance with this Section and the forfeiture of the bond posted pursuant to Subsection C as part of the sentence. The court may, in its discretion, order the payment of any reasonable or additional costs incurred in the boarding or veterinary treatment of any seized animal prior to its disposition, whether or not a bond was posted by the defendant. In the event of the acquittal or final discharge, without conviction of the accused, the court shall, on demand, direct the delivery of any animal held in custody to the owner thereof and order the return of any bond posted pursuant to Subsection C, less reasonable administrative costs.

E. Nothing in this Section shall prevent the euthanasia of any seized animal, at any time, whether or not any bond was posted, if a licensed veterinarian determines that the animal is not likely to survive and is suffering, as a result of any physical condition. In such instances, the court, in its discretion, may order the return of any bond posted, less reasonable costs, at the time of trial.

(Chgd. by Acts 1997 No. 1212, §1, eff. 8/15/97.)

§102.3. Search warrant; animal cruelty offenses.

If the complaint is made, by affidavit, to any magistrate authorized to issue search warrants in criminal cases, that the complainant has reason to believe that an animal has been or is being cruelly treated in violation of R.S. 14:102.1, in any building or place, such magistrate, if satisfied that there is reasonable cause for such belief, shall issue a search warrant to any law enforcement officer authorized by law to make arrests for such offenses, authorizing any such officer to make a search of said building or place, and to arrest any person found violating R.S. 14:102.1. Said warrant may also authorize said officer to seize any animal believed to be cruelly treated and to take custody thereof. This section shall not be construed as a limitation on the power of law enforcement officers to seize animals as evidence at the time of the arrest.

§102.4. Confined animals; necessary food and water.

When a living animal is impounded or confined, and continues without necessary food and water for more than twenty-four consecutive hours, any law enforcement officer may, as often as is necessary, enter any place in which the animal is impounded or confined and supply it with necessary food and water so long as it shall remain impounded or confined.

§102.5. Dogfighting.

A. No person shall intentionally do any of the following:

(1) For amusement or gain, cause any dog to fight with another dog, or cause any dogs to injure each other.

(2) Permit any act in violation of Paragraph (1) to be done on any premises under his charge or control, or aid or abet any such act.

(3) Promote, stage, advertise, or be employed at a dogfighting exhibition.

(4) Sell a ticket of admission or receive money for the admission of any person to any place used, or about to be used, for any activity described in Paragraph (2).

(5) Own, manage, or operate any facility kept or used for the purpose of dogfighting.

(6) Knowingly attend as a spectator at any organized dogfighting event.

B. "Dogfighting" means an organized event wherein there is a display of combat between two or more dogs in which the fighting, killing, maiming, or injuring of a dog is the significant feature, or main purpose, of the event.

C. Whoever violates any provision of Paragraphs (1) through (5) of Subsection A shall, upon first conviction, be fined not more than one thousand dollars or be imprisoned with or without hard labor for not more than one year, or both. Upon a second or subsequent conviction, the offender shall be fined not more than three thousand dollars or be imprisoned with or without hard labor for not more than three years or both.

D. Whoever violates Paragraph (6) of Subsection A of this Section shall be fined not more than five hundred dollars or be imprisoned for not more than six months, or both.

(Chgd. by Acts 1993 No. 1002, §1, eff. 8/15/93.)

§102.6. Seizure and destruction or disposition of dogs and equipment used in dogfighting.

A. (1) Any law enforcement officer making an arrest under R.S. 14:102.5 may lawfully take possession of all fighting dogs on the premises where the arrest is made or in the immediate possession or control of the person being arrested, whether or not the dogs are actually engaged in a fight at the time, and all paraphernalia, implements, equipment, or other property or things used or employed in violation of that Section.

(2) The legislature finds and declares that fighting dogs used or employed in violation of that Section are dangerous, vicious, and a threat to the health and safety of the public. Therefore, fighting dogs seized in accordance with this Section are declared to be contraband and, notwithstanding R.S. 14:102.1, the officer may cause them to be humanely euthanized as soon as possible by a licensed veterinarian or a qualified technician and shall not be civilly or criminally liable for so doing. Fighting dogs not destroyed immediately shall be disposed of in accordance with R.S. 14:102.2.

B. (1) The officer, after taking possession of any dogs other than those destroyed or disposed of pursuant to Subsection A and of the other paraphernalia, implements, equipment, or other property or things, shall file with the district court of the parish within which the alleged violation occurred an affidavit stating therein the name of the person charged, a description of the property so taken and the time and place of the taking thereof, together with the name of the person who claims to own such property, if known, and that the affiant has reason to believe and does believe, stating the ground of such belief, that the property so taken was used or employed in such violation.

(2) The seizing officer shall dispose of any dogs or other animals seized in the manner provided for in R.S. 14:102.2.

(3) He shall thereupon deliver the other property so taken to such court which shall, by order in writing, place such paraphernalia, implements, equipment, or other property in the custody of a suitable custodian, to be kept by such custodian until the conviction or final discharge of the accused, and shall send a copy of such order without delay to the district attorney of the parish. The custodian so named and designated in such order shall immediately thereupon assume the custody of such property and shall retain the same, subject to the order of the court before which the accused shall be required to appear for trial.

C. Any person claiming an interest in a seized animal may post a bond with the court in accordance with the provisions of R.S. 14:102.2(C) in order to prevent the disposition of such animal.

D. Upon conviction of the person so charged, all dogs so seized shall be adjudged by the court to be forfeited and the court shall order a humane disposition of the same in accordance with R.S. 14:102.2. The court may also in its discretion, order the forfeiture of the bond posted, as well as payment of any reasonable or additional costs incurred in the boarding or veterinary treatment of any seized dog, as provided in R.S. 14:102.2. In the event of the acquittal or final discharge, without conviction, of the accused, the court shall, on demand, direct the delivery of the animals and other property so held in custody to the owner thereof and order the return of any bond posted pursuant to R.S. 14:102(C), less reasonable administrative costs.

(Added by Acts 1993 No. 1002, §1; chgd. by Acts 1997 No. 1212, §1, eff. 8/15/97.)

§102.7. Search warrant for dogfighting offenses.

If complaint is made, by affidavit, to any magistrate authorized to issue search warrants in criminal cases, that the complainant has reason to believe that R.S. 14:102.5 has been violated within the past forty-eight hours, is being, or will be violated in any building or place, such magistrate, if satisfied that there is reasonable cause for such belief, shall issue a search warrant authorizing any law enforcement officer competent by law to make arrests for such offenses to make a search of said building or place, and to arrest any person found violating R.S. 14:102.5. This Section shall not be construed as a limitation on the power of law enforcement officers to seize animals or evidence at the time of arrest.

§102.8. Injuring or killing of a police animal.

A. Injuring or killing of a police animal is the intentional infliction of great bodily harm, permanent disability, or death upon a police animal.

B. For purposes of this Section, "police animal" means:

(1) Any dog which is owned, or the service of which is employed, by any state or local law enforcement agency for the principal purpose of aiding in the detection of criminal activity, enforcement of laws, or apprehension of offenders.

(2) Any dog trained in accordance with the standards of a national or regional search and rescue association to respond to instructions from its handler in the search and rescue of lost or missing individuals and which dog, together with its handler, is prepared to render search and rescue services at the request of law enforcement.

(3) Any horse which is used by a state or local law enforcement officer in the course of his official duty.

C. It shall be an affirmative defense to a prosecution under this Section when the injuring or killing of a police animal is committed with the reasonable belief by one not involved in or being apprehended for the commission of any offense or by one taken into custody that:

(1) He is in imminent danger of losing his life or receiving great bodily harm and that the injuring or killing is necessary to save himself from that danger.

(2) Another person not involved in or being apprehended for the commission of any offense is in imminent danger of losing his life or receiving great bodily harm and that the injury or killing is necessary to save that person from that danger.

(3) His animal or other property not involved in the commission of any offense or in the apprehension of any person for an offense is in imminent danger of being destroyed or receiving grave injury or damage that may result in its destruction.

D. (1) Whoever commits the crime of injuring or killing of a police animal shall be fined not less than two thousand five hundred dollars nor more than three thousand five hundred dollars, or imprisoned with or without hard labor for not less than one year nor more than three years, or both.

(2) Upon a second or subsequent conviction, regardless of whether the second or subsequent offense occurred before or after the first conviction, the offender shall be fined not less than two thousand five hundred dollars and not more than three thousand five hundred dollars, or imprisoned with or without hard labor for not less than five years nor more than seven years, or both.

(Chgd. by Acts 1992 No. 921, §1; Acts 1994 Third Ex. Sess. No. 82, §1; Acts 1995 No. 208, §1; Acts 1997 No. 130, §1, eff. 8/15/97.)

§102.9. Interference with animal research; research laboratory or farm.

A. Interference with animal research is any of the following:

(1) The unauthorized entry of any research laboratory or research farm with the intent of releasing or causing the release of any animal housed or kept within such research facility.

(2) The intentional or criminally negligent damaging of any research laboratory or research farm.

(3) The intentional or criminally negligent unauthorized release of any animal housed or kept within any research laboratory or research farm.

B. Whoever commits the crime of interference with animal research shall, upon conviction, be fined not less than one thousand nor more than five thousand dollars and may be imprisoned, with or without hard labor, for not more than one year.

§102.10. Bear wrestling; penalty.

A. Any person who intentionally commits any of the following shall be guilty of bear wrestling:

(1) Promotes, engages in, or is employed by anyone who conducts a bear wrestling match.

(2) Receives money for the admission of another person to a place kept for bear wrestling matches.

(3) Sells, purchases, possesses, or trains a bear for a bear wrestling match.

B. For purposes of this Section, a "bear wrestling match" means a match or contest between one or more persons and a bear for the purpose of fighting or engaging in a physical altercation.

C. Whoever commits the crime of bear wrestling shall be fined not more than five hundred dollars or imprisoned for not more than six months, or both.

(Added by Acts 1992 No. 740, §1, eff. 8/21/92.)

§102.11. Illegal contact sports; penalty.

A. Any person who intentionally commits any of the following shall be guilty of illegal contact sports:

(1) Promotes, engages or participates in, judges, or referees a tough-man competition or is employed by anyone who conducts a tough-man competition.

(2) Receives money for the admission of another person to a place which holds or has held tough-man competitions.

B. For the purposes of this Section, a "tough-man contest or competition" means any boxing match, wrestling event, or contest or competition, or combination thereof, between two or more persons, whether professional or amateur, who use their hands, with or without gloves, or their feet, or both, in any manner unauthorized by the State Boxing and Wrestling Commission, and compete for money, financial prize, or any item of pecuniary or nonpecuniary value or compete at an event where a fee is charged whereby either participant may obtain pecuniary gain. "Tough-man contest or competition" shall not include, nor shall the provisions of this Section apply to any contest, competition, or exhibition of any of the recognized martial arts including karate, judo, kung fu, tae kwan do, jujitsu, kickboxing, or any substantially similar tradition.

C. Whoever commits the crime of illegal contact sports shall be fined not more than five hundred dollars or imprisoned, with or without hard labor, for not more than one year, or both.
(Added by Acts 1995 No. 1275, §2, eff. 8/15/95.)

SUBPART C. OFFENSES AFFECTING THE GENERAL PEACE AND ORDER

§103. Disturbing the peace.

A. Disturbing the peace is the doing of any of the following in such manner as would foreseeably disturb or alarm the public:

(1) Engaging in a fistic encounter; or

(2) Addressing any offensive, derisive, or annoying words to any other person who is lawfully in any street, or other public place; or call him by any offensive or derisive name, or make any noise or exclamation in his presence and hearing with the intent to deride, offend, or annoy him, or to prevent him from pursuing his lawful business, occupation, or duty; or

(3) Appearing in an intoxicated condition; or

(4) Engaging in any act in a violent and tumultuous manner by any three or more persons; or

(5) Holding of an unlawful assembly; or

(6) Interruption of any lawful assembly of people; or

(7) *(Repealed.)*

Whoever commits the crime of disturbing the peace shall be fined not more than one hundred dollars or imprisoned for not more than ninety days, or both.

B. *(Repealed.)*

§103.1. Emanation of excessive sound or noise; exceptions; penalties.

A. No person shall operate or permit the operation of any sound amplification system which emanates unreasonably loud or excessive sound or noise which is likely to cause inconvenience or annoyance to persons of ordinary sensibilities, when both the following exist:

(1) The sound amplification system is located in or on any motor vehicle on a public street, highway, or public park.

(2) The sound or noise emanating from the sound amplification system is audible at a distance of greater than twenty-five feet which exceeds eighty-five decibels.

B. The provisions of this Section do not apply to the use of a horn, alarm, or other warning device which has as its purpose the signaling of unsafe or dangerous situations or to summon the assistance of law enforcement when used for such purpose, or when used in conjunction with a permitted event.

C. Whoever violates a provision of this Section shall be fined one hundred dollars for a first offense, and not less than two hundred dollars nor more than five hundred dollars for second and subsequent offenses.
(Added by Acts 1997 No. 811, §1, eff. 1/1/98.)

§104. Keeping a disorderly place.

Keeping a disorderly place is the intentional maintaining of a place to be used habitually for any illegal purpose.

Whoever commits the crime of keeping a disorderly place shall be fined not more than five hundred dollars, or imprisoned for not more than six months, or both.

§105. Letting a disorderly place.

Letting a disorderly place is the granting of the right to use any premises knowing that they are to be used as a disorderly place, or allowing the continued use of the premises with such knowledge.

Whoever commits the crime of letting a disorderly place shall be fined not more than five hundred dollars, or imprisoned for not more than six months, or both.

§106. Obscenity.

A. The crime of obscenity is the intentional:

(1) Exposure of the genitals, pubic hair, anus, vulva, or female breast nipples in any public place or place open to the public view with the intent of arousing sexual desire or which appeals to prurient interest or is patently offensive.

(2) (a) Participation or engagement in, or management, operation, production, presentation, performance, promotion, exhibition, advertisement, sponsorship, or display of, hard core sexual conduct when the trier of fact determines that the average person applying contemporary community standards would find that the conduct, taken as a whole, appeals to the prurient interest; and the hard core sexual conduct, as specifically defined herein, is presented in a patently offensive way; and the conduct taken as a whole lacks serious literary, artistic, political, or scientific value.

(b) Hard core sexual conduct is the public portrayal, for its own sake, and for ensuing commercial gain of:

(i) Ultimate sexual acts, normal or perverted, actual, simulated, or animated, whether between human beings, animals, or an animal and a human being; or

(ii) Masturbation, excretory functions or lewd exhibition, actual, simulated, or animated, of the genitals, pubic hair, anus, vulva, or female breast nipples; or

(iii) Sadomasochistic abuse, meaning actual, simulated or animated flagellation, or torture by or upon a person who is nude or clad in undergarments or in a costume that reveals the pubic hair, anus, vulva, genitals, or female breast nipples, or in the condition of being fettered, bound, or otherwise physically restrained, on the part of one so clothed; or

(iv) Actual, simulated, or animated touching, caressing, or fondling of, or other similar physical contact with a pubic area, anus, female breast nipple, covered or exposed, whether alone or between humans, animals, or a human and an animal, of the same or opposite sex, in an act of apparent sexual stimulation or gratification; or

(v) Actual, simulated, or animated stimulation of a human genital organ by any device whether or not the device is designed, manufactured, or marketed for such purpose.

(3) Sale, allocation, consignment, distribution, dissemination, advertisement, exhibition, or display of obscene material, or the preparation, manufacture, publication, or printing of obscene material for sale, allocation, consignment, distribution, advertisement, exhibition, or display.

Obscene material is any tangible work or thing which the trier of fact determines (a) that the average person applying contemporary community standards would find, taken as a whole, appeals to the prurient interest, and (b) depicts or describes in a patently offensive way, hard core sexual conduct specifically defined in Paragraph (2) above, and (c) the work or thing taken as a whole lacks serious literary, artistic, political, or scientific value.

(4) Requiring as a condition to a sale, allocation, consignment, or delivery for resale of any paper, magazine, book, periodical, or publication to a purchaser or consignee that such purchaser or consignee also receive or accept any obscene material, as defined in Paragraph (3) above, for resale, distribution, display, advertisement, or exhibition purposes; or denying or threatening to deny a franchise to, or imposing a penalty, on or against a person by reason of his refusal to accept, or his return of, such obscene material.

(5) Solicitation or enticement of an unmarried person under the age of seventeen years to commit any act prohibited by Paragraphs (1), (2), or (3) above.

(6) Advertisement, exhibition, or display of sexually violent material. "Violent material" is any tangible work or thing which the trier of facts determines depicts actual or simulated patently offensive acts of violence, including but not limited to, acts depicting sadistic conduct, whippings, beatings, torture, and mutilation of the human body, as described in Sub-Subparagraph (b)(iii) of Paragraph (2) of Subsection A herein.

B. Lack of knowledge of age or marital status shall not constitute a defense.

C. If any employee of a theatre or bookstore acting in the course or scope of his employment, is arrested for an offense designated in this Section, the employer shall reimburse the employee for all attorney's fees and other costs of defense of such employee.

Such fees and expenses may be fixed by the court exercising criminal jurisdiction after contradictory hearing or by ordinary civil process.

D. (1) The provisions of this Section do not apply to recognized and established schools, churches, museums, medical clinics, hospitals, physicians, public libraries, governmental agencies, quasi-governmental sponsored organizations and persons acting in their capacity as employees or agents of such organizations, or a person solely employed to operate a movie projector in a duly licensed theatre.

(2) For the purpose of this Paragraph, the following words and terms shall have the respective meanings defined as follows:

(a) "Recognized and established schools" means schools having a full time faculty and pupils, gathered together for instruction in a diversified curriculum.

(b) "Churches" means any church, affiliated with a national or regional denomination.

(c) "Physicians" means any licensed physician or psychiatrist.

(d) "Medical clinics and hospitals" means any clinic or hospital of licensed physicians or psychiatrists used for the reception and care of the sick, wounded or infirm*.

**Probably should be "infirmed".*

E. This Section does not preempt, nor shall anything in this Section be construed to preempt, the regulation of obscenity by municipalities, parishes, and consolidated city-parish governments; however, in order to promote uniform obscenity legislation throughout the state, the regulation of obscenity by municipalities, parishes, and consolidated city-parish governments shall not exceed the scope of the regulatory prohibitions contained in the provisions of this Section.

F. (1) Except for those motion pictures, printed materials, and photographic materials showing actual ultimate sexual acts or simulated or animated ultimate sexual acts when there is an explicit, closeup depiction of human genital organs so as to give the appearance of the consummation of ultimate sexual acts, no person, firm, or corporation shall be arrested, charged, or indicted for any violations of a provision of this Section until such time as the material involved has first been the subject of an adversary hearing under the provisions of this Section, wherein such person, firm, or corporation is made a defendant and, after such material is declared by the court to be obscene, such person, firm, or corporation continues to engage in the conduct prohibited by this Section. The sole issue at the hearing shall be whether the material is obscene.

(2) The hearing shall be held before the district court having jurisdiction over the proceedings within seventy-two hours after receipt of notice by the person, firm, or corporation. The person, firm, or corporation shall be given notice of the hearing by registered mail or by personal service on the owner, manager, or other person having a financial interest in the material; provided, if there is no such person on the premises, then notice may be given by personal service on any employee of the person, firm, or corporation on such premises. The notice shall state the nature of the violation, the date, place, and time of the hearing, and the right to present and cross-examine witnesses.

(3) The state or any defendant may appeal from a judgment. Such appeal shall not stay the judgment. Any defendant engaging in conduct prohibited by this Section subsequent to notice of the judgment, finding the material to be obscene, shall be subject to criminal prosecution notwithstanding the appeal from the judgment.

(4) No determination by the district court pursuant to this Section shall be of any force and effect outside the judicial district in which made and no such determination shall be res judicata in any proceeding in any other judicial district. In addition, evidence of any hearing held pursuant to this Section shall not be competent or admissible in any criminal action for the violation of any other Section of this Title; provided, however, that in any criminal action, charging the violation of any other Section of this Title, against any person, firm, or corporation that was a defendant in such hearing, involving the same material declared to be obscene under the provisions of this Section, then evidence of such hearing shall be competent and admissible as bearing on the issue of scienter only.

G. (1) On a first conviction, whoever commits the crime of obscenity shall be fined not less than one thousand dollars nor more than two thousand five hundred dollars, or imprisoned, with or without hard labor, for not less than six months nor more than three years, or both.

(2) (a) On a second conviction, the offender shall be imprisoned with or without hard labor for not less than six months nor more than three years, without benefit of probation, parole, or suspension of sentence, and in addition may be fined not less than two thousand five hundred dollars nor more than five thousand dollars.

(b) The imprisonment provided for in Subparagraph (a), may be imposed at court discretion if the court determines that the offender, due to his employment, could not avoid engagement in the offense. This Subparagraph (b) shall not apply to the manager or other person in charge of an establishment selling or exhibiting obscene material.

(3) On a third or subsequent conviction, the offender shall be imprisoned with or without hard labor for not less than two years nor more than five years, without benefit of probation, parole, or suspension of sentence, and in addition may be fined not less than five thousand dollars nor more than ten thousand dollars.

(4) When a violation of Paragraph (1), (2), or (3) of Subsection A of this Section is with or in the presence of an unmarried person under the age of seventeen years, the offender shall be fined not more than ten thousand dollars and shall be imprisoned, with or without hard labor, for not less than two years nor more than five years, without benefit of parole, probation, or suspension of sentence.

H. (1) When a corporation is charged with violating this Section, the corporation, the president, the vice president, the secretary, and the treasurer may all be named as defendants. Upon conviction for a violation of this Section, a corporation shall be sentenced in accordance with Subsection G hereof. All corporate officers who are named as defendants shall be subject to the penalty provisions of this Section as set forth in Subsection G.

(2) If the corporation is domiciled in this state, upon indictment or information filed against the corporation, a notice of arraignment shall be served upon the corporation, or its designated agent for service of process, which then must appear before the district court in which the prosecution is pending to plead to the charge within fifteen days of service. If no appearance is made within fifteen days, an attorney shall be appointed by the court to represent the defendant corporation with respect to the charge or to show cause why the corporation should not be enjoined from continuing in business during the pendency of the criminal proceedings. Appearance for arraignment may be made through private counsel.

(3) If the corporation is domiciled out of state and is registered to do business in Louisiana, notice of arraignment shall be served upon the corporate agent for service of process or the secretary of state, who shall then notify the corporation charged by indictment or information to appear before the district court in which the prosecution is pending for arraignment within sixty days after the notice is mailed by the secretary of state. If no appearance is made within sixty days the court shall appoint an attorney to represent the defendant corporation with respect to the charge or to show cause why the corporation should not be enjoined from continuing in business during the pendency of the criminal proceedings. Appearance for arraignment may be made by private counsel.

(4) If the corporation is domiciled out of state and is not registered to do business in Louisiana, notice of arraignment of the corporation shall be served upon the secretary of state and an employee, officer, or agent for service of process of the corporation found within the parish where the violation of this Section has allegedly occurred. Such notice shall act as a bar to that corporation registering to do business in Louisiana until it appears before the district court in which the prosecution is pending to answer the charge.

§106.1. Promotion or wholesale promotion of obscene devices.

A. For the purposes of this Section, the following definitions shall apply unless the context clearly requires otherwise:

(1) "Obscene device" means a device, including an artificial penis or artificial vagina, which is designed or marketed as useful primarily for the stimulation of human genital organs.

(2) "Promote" means to manufacture, issue, sell, give, provide, lend, mail, deliver, transfer, transmit, distribute, circulate, disseminate, present, or exhibit, including the offer or agreement to do any of these things, for the purpose of sale or resale.

B. No person shall knowingly and intentionally promote an obscene device.

C. (1) On a first conviction, whoever commits the crime of promoting an obscene device shall be fined not less than one thousand dollars nor more than two thousand dollars five hundred dollars or imprisoned with or without hard labor for not less than six months nor more than three years, or both.

(2) On a second conviction, the offender shall be imprisoned with or without hard labor for not less than six months nor more than three years, without benefit of probation, parole, or suspension of sentence, and in addition may be fined not less than two thousand five hundred dollars nor more than five thousand dollars.

§107. Vagrancy.

The following persons are and shall be guilty of vagrancy:

(1) Habitual drunkards; or

(2) Persons who live in house of ill fame or who habitually associate with prostitutes; or

(3) Able-bodied persons who beg or solicit alms, provided that this article shall not apply to persons soliciting alms for bona fide religious, charitable or eleemosynary organizations with the authorization thereof; or

(4) Habitual gamblers or persons who for the most part maintain themselves by gambling; or

(5) Able-bodied persons without lawful means of support who do not seek employment and take employment when it is available to them; or

(6) Able-bodied persons of the age of majority who obtain their support gratis from persons receiving old age pensions or from persons receiving welfare assistance from the state; or

(7) Persons who loaf the streets habitually or who frequent the streets habitually at late or unusual hours of the night, or who loiter around any public place of assembly, without lawful business or reason to be present; or

(8) Persons found in or near any structure, movable, vessel, or private grounds, without being able to account for their lawful presence therein; or

(9) Prostitutes.

Whoever commits the crime of vagrancy shall be fined not more than two hundred dollars, or imprisoned for not more than six months, or both.

§107.1. Ritualistic acts.

A. (1) The legislature hereby finds that this enactment is necessary for the immediate preservation of the public peace, health, morals, safety, and welfare and for the support of state government and its existing public institutions.

(2) The legislature further recognizes that:

(a) The preamble to the Constitution of Louisiana affirmatively states, "We, the people of Louisiana, grateful to Almighty God for the civil, political, economic, and religious liberties we enjoy, and desiring to protect individual rights to life, liberty, and property; afford opportunity for the fullest development of the individual; assure equality of rights, promote the health, safety, education, and welfare of the people; maintain a representative and orderly government; ensure domestic tranquility; provide for the common defense; and secure the blessings of freedom and justice to ourselves and our posterity, do ordain and establish this constitution."

(b) The state, under its police power, may enact in order to promote public peace, health, morals, and safety.

B. (1) For purposes of this Subsection, "ritualistic acts" means those acts undertaken as part of a ceremony, rite, initiation, observance, performance, or practice that result in or are intended to result in:

(a) The mutilation, dismemberment, torture, abuse, or sacrifice of animals.

(b) The ingestion of human or animal blood or human or animal waste.

(2) The acts defined in this Subsection are hereby determined to be destructive of the peace, health, morals, and safety of the citizens of this state and are hereby prohibited.

(3) Any person committing, attempting to commit, or conspiring with another to commit a ritualistic act may be sentenced to imprisonment for not more than five years or fined not more than five thousand dollars, or both.

C. (1) No person shall commit ritualistic mutilation, dismemberment, or torture of a human as part of a ceremony, rite, initiation, observance, performance, or practice.

(2) No person shall commit ritualistic sexual abuse of children or of physically or mentally disabled adults as part of a ceremony, rite, initiation, observance, performance, or practice.

(3) No person shall commit ritualistic psychological abuse of children or of physically or mentally disabled adults as part of a ceremony, rite, initiation, observance, performance, or practice.

(4) Any person who commits, attempts to commit, or conspires with another to commit a violation of this Subsection shall be sentenced to imprisonment for not less than five nor more than twenty-five years and may be fined not more than twenty-five thousand dollars.

D. Each violation that occurs under the provisions of this Section shall be considered a separate violation.

E. The provisions of this Section shall not be construed to apply to generally accepted agricultural or horticultural practices and specifically the branding or identification of livestock.

F. The provisions of this Section shall not be construed to apply to any state or federally approved, licensed, or funded research project.

§107.2. Hate crimes.

A. It shall be unlawful for any person to select the victim of the following offenses against person and property because of actual or perceived race, age, gender, religion, color, creed, disability, sexual orientation, national origin, or ancestry of that person or the owner or occupant of that property or because of actual or perceived membership or service in, or employment with, an organization: first or second degree murder; manslaughter; battery; aggravated battery; second degree battery; aggravated assault with a firearm; terrorizing; mingling harmful substances; simple, forcible, or aggravated rape; sexual battery, aggravated sexual battery; oral sexual battery; aggravated oral sexual battery; carnal knowledge of a juvenile; indecent behavior with juveniles; molestation of a juvenile; simple, second degree, or aggravated kidnapping; simple or aggravated arson; placing combustible materials; communicating of false information of planned arson; simple or aggravated criminal damage to property; contamination of water supplies; simple or aggravated burglary; criminal trespass; simple, first degree, or armed robbery; purse snatching; extortion; theft; desecration of graves; institutional vandalism; or assault by drive-by-shooting.

B. If the underlying offense named in Subsection A of this Section is a misdemeanor, and the victim of the offense listed in Subsection A of this Section is selected in the manner proscribed by that Subsection, the offender may be fined not more than five hundred dollars or imprisoned for not more than six months, or both. This sentence shall run consecutively to the sentence for the underlying offense.

C. If the underlying offense named in Subsection A of this Section is a felony, and the victim of the offense listed in Subsection A of this Section is selected in the manner proscribed by that Subsection, the offender may be fined not more than five thousand dollars or imprisoned with or without hard labor for not more than five years, or both. This sentence shall run consecutively to the sentence for the underlying offense.

D. "Organization", as used in this Section, means all of the following:

(1) Any lawful corporation, trust, company, partnership, association, foundation, or fund.

(2) Any lawful group of persons, whether or not incorporated, banded together for joint action on any subject or subjects.

(3) Any entity or unit of federal, state, or local government.

(Added by Acts 1997 No. 1479, §2, eff. 7/15/97.)

SUBPART D. OFFENSES AFFECTING LAW ENFORCEMENT

§108. Resisting an officer.

A. Resisting an officer is the intentional interference with, opposition or resistance to, or obstruction of an individual acting in his official capacity and authorized by law to make a lawful arrest or seizure of property or to serve any lawful process or court order when the offender knows or has reason to know that the person arresting, seizing property, or serving process is acting in his official capacity.

B. (1) The phrase "obstruction of" as used herein shall, in addition to its common meaning, signification, and connotation mean the following:

(a) Flight by one sought to be arrested before the arresting officer can restrain him and after notice is given that he under arrest.

(b) Any violence toward or any resistance or opposition to the arresting officer after the arrested party is actually placed under arrest and before he is incarcerated in jail.

(c) Refusal by the arrested party to give his name and make his identity known to the arresting officer.

(d) Congregation with others on a public street and refusal to move on or when ordered by the officer.

(2) The word "officer" as used herein means any peace officer, as defined in R.S. 40:2402, and includes deputy sheriffs, municipal police officers, probation and parole officers, city marshals and deputies, and wildlife enforcement agents.

C. Whoever commits the crime of resisting an officer shall be fined not more than five hundred dollars or be imprisoned for not more than six months, or both.
(Chgd. by Acts 1991 No. 677, §1; Acts 1992 No. 302, §1; Acts 1993 No. 860, §1; Acts 1997 No. 565, §1, eff. 8/15/97.)

§108.1. Flight from an officer; aggravated flight from an officer.

A. No driver of a motor vehicle shall intentionally refuse to bring a vehicle to a stop knowing that he has been given a visual and audible signal to stop by a police officer when the officer has reasonable grounds to believe that the driver has committed an offense. The signal shall be given by an emergency light and a siren on a vehicle marked as a police vehicle.

B. Whoever commits the crime of flight from an officer shall be fined not less than one hundred fifty dollars, nor more than five hundred dollars, or imprisoned for not more than six months, or both.

C. Aggravated flight from an officer is the intentional refusal of a driver to bring a vehicle to a stop, under circumstances wherein human life is endangered, knowing that he has been given a visual and audible signal to stop by a police officer when the officer has reasonable grounds to believe that the driver has committed an offense. The signal shall be given by an emergency light and a siren on a vehicle marked as a police vehicle.

D. Circumstances wherein human life is endangered shall be any situation where the operator of the fleeing vehicle commits at least two of the following acts:

(1) Leaves the roadway or forces another vehicle to leave the roadway.

(2) Collides with another vehicle.

(3) Exceeds the posted speed limit by at least twenty-five miles per hour.

(4) Travels against the flow of traffic.

E. Whoever commits aggravated flight from an officer shall be imprisoned at hard labor for not more than two years.
(Chgd. by Acts 1997 No. 865, §1, eff. 8/15/97.)

§110. Simple escape; aggravated escape.

A. Simple escape shall mean any of the following:

(1) The intentional departure, under circumstances wherein human life is not endangered, of a person imprisoned, committed, or detained from a place where such person is legally confined, from a designated area of a place where such person is legally confined, or from the lawful custody of any law enforcement officer or officer of the Department of Public Safety and Corrections.

(2) The failure of a criminal serving a sentence and participating in a work release program authorized by law to report or return from his planned employment or other activity under the program at the appointed time.

(3) The failure of a person who has been granted a furlough under the provisions of R.S. 15:833 or R.S. 15:908 to return to his place of confinement at the appointed time.

B. (1) A person who is participating in a work release program as defined in Paragraph A(2) of this Section and who commits the crime of simple escape shall be imprisoned with or without hard labor for not less than six months nor more than one year and any such sentence shall not run concurrently with any other sentence.

(2) A person who fails to return from an authorized furlough as defined in Paragraph A(3) of this Section shall be imprisoned with or without hard labor for not less than six months nor more than one year and any such sentence shall not run concurrently with any other sentence.

(3) A person imprisoned, committed, or detained who commits the crime of simple escape as defined in Paragraph A(1) of this Section shall be imprisoned with or without hard labor for not less than two years nor more than five years; provided that such sentence shall not run concurrently with any other sentence.

C. (1) Aggravated escape is the intentional departure of a person from the legal custody of any officer of the Department of Public Safety and Corrections or any law enforcement officer or from any place where such person is legally confined when his departure is under circumstances wherein human life is endangered.

(2) Whoever commits an aggravated escape as herein defined shall be imprisoned at hard labor for not less than five years nor more than ten years and any such sentence shall not run concurrently with any other sentence.

D. For purposes of this Section, a person shall be deemed to be in the lawful custody of a law enforcement officer or of the Department of Public Safety and Corrections and legally confined when he is in a rehabilitation unit, a work release program, or any other program under the control of a law enforcement officer or the department.

E. The provisions of this Section shall be applicable to all penal, correctional, rehabilitational, and work release centers and any and all prison facilities under the control of the sheriffs of the respective parishes of the state of Louisiana. The prison facilities shall include but are not limited to parish jails, correctional centers, work release centers, and rehabilitation centers, hospitals, clinics, and any and all facilities where inmates are confined under the jurisdiction and control of the sheriffs of the respective parishes.

§110.1. Jumping bail.

A. Jumping bail is the intentional failure to appear at such time and place as designated by the judge or committing magistrate who has fixed the amount of the bail bond. The fact that no loss shall result to any surety or bondsman is immaterial.

B. Whoever commits the crime of jumping bail when the bail is to assure the presence of the defendant for those cases defined as misdemeanors in this Title and in the Uniform Controlled Dangerous Substances Law* shall be imprisoned for not more than six months, or fined not more than five hundred dollars, or both.

C. Whoever commits the crime of jumping bail when the bail is to assure the presence of the defendant for those cases defined as felonies in this Title and in the Uniform Controlled Dangerous Substances Law* shall be imprisoned at hard labor for not more than two years.
(Chgd. by Acts 1993 No. 501, §1, eff. 8/15/93.)
**R.S. 40:961 et seq.*

§111. Assisting escape.

Assisting escape is the:

(1) Permitting, by any public officer, of the escape of any prisoner in his custody, by virtue of his active assistance or intentional failure to act; or

(2) The active assistance given by any person to one in legal custody with intent to aid him in escaping therefrom.

Whoever commits the crime of assisting escape shall be fined not more than three thousand dollars, or imprisoned, with or without hard labor, for not more than five years or both.

§112. False personation.

False personation is the performance of any of the following acts with the intent to injure or defraud, or to obtain or secure any special privilege or advantage:

(1) Impersonating any public officer, or private individual having special authority by law to perform an act affecting the rights or interests of another, or the assuming, without authority, of any uniform or badge by which such officer or person is lawfully distinguished; or

(2) Performing any act purporting to be official in such assumed character.

Whoever commits the crime of false personation shall be fined not more than one hundred dollars, or imprisoned for not more than ninety days, or both.

§112.1. False personation of a peace officer.

A. False personation of a peace officer is the performance of any one or more of the following acts with the intent to injure or defraud or to obtain or secure any special privilege or advantage:

(1) Impersonating any peace officer or assuming, without authority, any uniform or badge by which a peace officer is lawfully distinguished.

(2) Performing any act purporting to be official in such assumed character.

(3) Making, altering, possession, or use of a false document or document containing false statements which purports to be a training program certificate or in-service training certificate or other documentation issued by the Council on Peace Officer Standards and Training, pursuant to R.S. 40:2405, which certifies the peace officer has successfully completed the requirements necessary to exercise his authority as a peace officer.

B. Whoever commits the crime of false personation of a peace officer shall be fined not more than one thousand dollars or imprisoned with or without hard labor for not more than two years, or both.
(Added by Acts 1993 No. 673, §1, eff. 8/15/93.)

PART VII. OFFENSES AFFECTING ORGANIZED GOVERNMENT

SUBPART A. TREASON AND DISLOYAL ACTS

§113. Treason.

Treason is the levying of war against the United States or the State of Louisiana, adhering to enemies of the United States or of the State of Louisiana, or giving such enemies aid and comfort.

No person shall be convicted of treason except on the testimony of two witnesses to the same overt act, or on his own confession in open court.

Whoever commits the crime of treason shall be punished by death.

§114. Misprision of treason.

Misprision of treason is the concealment of treason, or the failure to disclose immediately all pertinent facts to proper authorities, by a person who has knowledge of the commission of the crime of treason.

Whoever commits misprision of treason shall be fined not more than one thousand dollars, and imprisoned at hard labor for not more than ten years.

§115. Criminal anarchy.

Criminal anarchy is:

(1) The advocating or teaching, in any manner, in public or private, of the subversion, opposition, or destruction of the government of the United States or of the State of Louisiana by violence or other unlawful means; or

(2) The organizing or becoming a member of any organization or society which is known to the offender to advocate, teach, or practice the subversion, opposition, or destruction of the government of the United States or of the State of Louisiana by violence or other unlawful means.

Whoever commits the crime of criminal anarchy shall be imprisoned at hard labor for not more than ten years.

§116. Flag desecration.

Flag desecration is the act of any person who shall intentionally, in any manner, for exhibition or display:

(1) Place or cause to be placed any word, mark, design or advertisement of any nature upon any flag; or

(2) Expose to public view any flag, upon which has been printed or otherwise produced, or to which shall have been attached any such word, mark, design, or advertisement; or

(3) Expose to public view, or have in possession for sale or any other purpose, any article of merchandise, or thing for holding or carrying merchandise, upon or to which shall have been produced or attached any flag, in order to advertise, call attention to or decorate such article; or

(4) Publicly mutilate, defile, or by word or act cast contempt upon any flag.

The word "flag" as used herein shall mean any duly authorized flag, shield, standard, color or ensign of the United States, the State of Louisiana, or the Confederate States of America, or any copy thereof.

Whoever commits the crime of flag desecration shall be fined not more than one hundred dollars, or imprisoned for not more than ninety days, or both.

§117. Flag desecration; exceptions.

The flag desecration section shall not apply to any act permitted by the statutes of the United States or of Louisiana, or by the United States army and navy regulations; nor shall it apply to the depicting of a flag upon any document, stationery, ornament, picture, or jewelry, with no design or words thereon and disconnected with any advertisement.

§117.1. Paramilitary organizations; prohibitions.

A. No paramilitary organization, or any member thereof, shall train in this state.

B. Whoever violates the provisions of this Section shall be fined not more than five hundred dollars, or be imprisoned for not more than six months, or both.

C. (1) For the purposes of this Section, "paramilitary organization" shall mean a group organized in a military or paramilitary structure, consisting of two or more persons who knowingly possess firearms or other weapons and who train in the use of such firearms or weapons, or knowingly teach or offer to teach the use of such firearms or weapons to others, for the purpose of committing an offense under the laws of this state or any political subdivision thereof.

(2) It shall not include a law enforcement agency, the armed services or reserve forces of the United States, the Louisiana National Guard, or any other organization that may possess firearms and train with such firearms, or teach or offer to teach the use of such firearms to others, for a lawful purpose.

SUBPART B. BRIBERY AND INTIMIDATION

§118. Public bribery.

A. (1) Public bribery is the giving or offering to give, directly or indirectly, anything of apparent present or prospective value to any of the following persons, with the intent to influence his conduct in relation to his position, employment, or duty:

(a) Public officer, public employee, or person in a position of public authority.

(b) Election official at any general, primary, or special election.

(c) Grand or petit juror.

(d) Witness, or person about to be called as a witness, upon a trial or other proceeding before any court, board, or officer authorized to hear evidence or to take testimony.

(e) Any person who has been elected or appointed to public office, whether or not said person has assumed the title or duties of such office.

(2) The acceptance of, or the offer to accept, directly or indirectly, anything of apparent present or prospective value, under such circumstances, by any of the above named persons, shall also constitute public bribery.

B. For purposes of this Section, "public officer", "public employee", or "person in a position of public authority", includes those enumerated in R.S. 14:2(9), and also means any public official, public employee, or person in a position of public authority, in other states, the federal government, any foreign sovereign, or any subdivision, entity, or agency thereof.

C. Whoever commits the crime of public bribery shall be fined not more than one thousand dollars, or imprisoned, with or without hard labor, for not more than five years, or both.

§118.1. Bribery of sports participants.

A. Bribing of sports participants is the giving or offering to give, directly or indirectly, anything of apparent present or prospective value to any professional or amateur baseball, football, hockey, polo, tennis or basketball player or boxer or any person or player who participates or expects to participate in any professional or amateur game or sport or any contest of skill, speed, strength or endurance of man or beast or any jockey, driver, groom or any person participating or expecting to participate in any horse race, including owners of race tracks and their employees, stewards, trainers, judges, starters or special policemen, or to any owner, manager, coach or trainer of any team or participant in any such game, contest or sport, with the intent to influence him to lose or cause to be lost, or corruptly to affect or influence the result thereof, or to limit his or his team's or his mount or beast's margin of victory in any baseball, football, hockey or basketball game, boxing, tennis or polo match or horse race or any professional amateur sport or game in which such player or participant or jockey or driver is taking part or expects to take part, or has any duty in connection therewith.

The acceptance of, or the offer to accept directly or indirectly anything of apparent present or prospective value under such circumstances by any of the above named persons shall also constitute bribery of sports participants.

Whoever commits the crime of bribery of sports participants is guilty of a felony and shall be punished by a fine of not more than ten thousand dollars and imprisoned for not less than one year nor more than five years, with or without hard labor, or both.

B. The offender under this Section, who states the facts under oath to the district attorney charged with the prosecution of the offense, and who gives evidence tending to convict any other offender under that Section, may, in the discretion of such district attorney be granted full immunity from prosecution in respect to the offense reported, except for perjury in giving such testimony.

§118.2. Falsifying information on racing license applications.

A. Falsifying racing license applications is the intentional falsification of any information required on an application for a Louisiana racing license.

B. Whoever commits the crime of falsifying racing license applications shall be fined not more than five hundred dollars, or imprisoned for not more than six months, or both.

C. For the purpose of this Section, the term "racing license" shall mean any license issued by the Louisiana State Racing Commission including, but not limited to those licenses issued to persons applying for jobs as cooks, nurses, stand girls, and other miscellaneous employees along with persons actually involved in racing.

§119. Bribery of voters.

A. Bribery of voters is the giving or offering to give, directly or indirectly, any money, or anything of apparent present or prospective value to any voter at any general, primary, or special election, or at any convention of a recognized political party, with the intent to influence the voter in the casting of his ballot.

The acceptance of, or the offer to accept, directly or indirectly, any money, or anything of apparent present or prospective value, by any such voters under such circumstances shall also constitute bribery of voters.

B. Whoever commits the crime of bribery of voters shall be fined not more than two thousand dollars or imprisoned with or without hard labor for not more than two years, or both, for the first offense. On a second offense, or any succeeding offense, the penalty shall be a fine of not more than five thousand dollars or imprisonment at hard labor for not more than five years, or both.

C. In the trial of persons charged with bribery of voters either the bribe-giver or the bribe-taker may give evidence, or make affidavit against the other, with immunity from prosecution in favor of the first informer, except for perjury in giving such testimony.

D. Any fine imposed and collected from the convicted person or persons under the provisions of this Section shall be paid to the informer or informers who shall give information resulting in the conviction of said person or persons, provided that the informer or informers shall not have been party to the violation of this Section as either the bribe-giver or the bribe-taker. No penalty imposed under the provisions of this Section shall be suspended or remitted by any court or other authority, provided that this provision shall not be construed against the right of suspensive appeal granted by the constitution and laws of this state.

§119.1. Bribery of parents of school children.

A. Bribery of parents of school children is the giving or offering to give, directly or indirectly, any money, or anything of apparent present or prospective value to any parent, to any tutor or guardian, to any person having legal or actual custody of, or to any person standing in loco parentis to, any child eligible to attend a public school in this State, as an inducement to encourage, influence, prompt, reward or compensate any such person to permit, prompt, force, or cause any such child to attend any such school in violation of any law of this state.

The acceptance of, or the offer to accept, directly or indirectly, any money, or anything of apparent present or prospective value, by any such person under any such circumstances, shall also constitute bribery of parents of school children.

B. Whoever commits the crime of bribery of parents of school children shall be fined not less than five hundred dollars, nor more than one thousand dollars, and imprisoned for not more than one year.

C. In the trial of persons charged with bribery of parents of school children, either the bribe-giver or the bribe-taker may give evidence, or make affidavit against the other, with immunity from prosecution in favor of the first informer, except for perjury in giving such testimony.

D. Any fine imposed and collected from the convicted person or persons under the provisions of this Section shall be paid to the informer or informers who shall give information resulting in the conviction of said person or persons. No penalty imposed under the provisions of this Section shall be suspended or remitted by any court.

§120. Corrupt influencing.

Corrupt influencing is the giving or offering to give anything of apparent present or prospective value to, or the accepting or offering to accept anything of apparent present or prospective value by, any person, with the intention that the recipient shall corruptly influence the conduct of any of the persons named in R.S. 14:118 (public bribery) in relation to such person's position, employment or duty.

Whoever commits the crime of corrupt influencing shall be imprisoned for not more than five years with or without hard labor or shall be fined not more than five thousand dollars or both.

§121. Informers granted immunity.

The offender, under the public bribery, bribery of voters or corrupt influencing articles, who states the facts under oath to the district attorney charged with the prosecution of the offense, and who gives evidence tending to convict any other offender under those articles, may, in the discretion of such district attorney, be granted full immunity from prosecution in respect to the offense reported, except for perjury in giving such testimony.

§122. Public intimidation.

Public intimidation is the use of violence, force, or threats upon any of the following persons, with the intent to influence his conduct in relation to his position, employment, or duty:

(1) Public officer or public employee.

(2) Grand or petit juror.

(3) Witness, or person about to be called as a witness upon a trial or other proceeding before any court, board or officer authorized to hear evidence or to take testimony.

(4) Voter or election official at any general, primary, or special election.

(5) School bus operator.

Whoever commits the crime of public intimidation shall be fined not more than one thousand dollars, or imprisoned, with or without hard labor, for not more than five years, or both.

§122.1. Intimidation and interference in the operation of schools.

A. Intimidation and interference in the operation of public schools is the offering to do or doing of any act, or threatening to do any act, directly or indirectly, to any child enrolled in a public school, to any parent, tutor or guardian, or person having lawful custody of or standing in loco parentis to any such child, the purpose and intent of which is to intimidate, induce, influence, reward, compensate or cause any such person, or any school teacher, school principal, transfer operator, or any other school employee, to do or perform any act in violation of any law of this state.

B. Whoever commits the crime of intimidation and interference in the operation of schools shall be fined not less than five hundred dollars, nor more than one thousand dollars, and imprisoned for not more than one year.

C. In the trial of persons charged with public intimidation and interference in the operation of schools, either the person doing or offering to do or the person or persons sought to be influenced, coerced, intimidated, threatened, or forced, may give evidence, or make affidavit against the other, with immunity from prosecution in favor of the first informer, except for perjury in giving such testimony.

D. Any fine imposed and collected from the convicted person or persons under the provisions of this Section shall be paid to the informer or informers who shall give information resulting in the conviction of said person or persons. No penalty imposed under the provisions of this Section shall be suspended or remitted by any court.

§122.2. Threatening a public official; penalties; definitions.

A. (1) Threatening a public official is engaging in any verbal or written communication which threatens serious bodily injury or death to a public official.

(2) Except as provided in Subsection B, whoever commits the crime of threatening a public official shall be fined not more than five hundred dollars, or imprisoned for not more than six months, or both.

B. Whoever commits the crime of threatening a public official with the intent to influence his conduct in relation to his position, employment, or official duty, or in retaliation as reprisal for his previous action in relation to his position, employment, or official duty, shall be fined not more than five hundred dollars, or imprisoned for not more than six months, or both.

C. For the purpose of this Section, "public official" is defined as any executive, ministerial, administrative, judicial, or legislative officer of the state of Louisiana.

SUBPART C. PERJURY

§123. Perjury.

A. Perjury is the intentional making of a false written or oral statement in or for use in a judicial proceeding, any proceeding before a board or official, wherein such board or official is authorized to take testimony, or before any committee or subcommittee of either house or any joint committee or subcommittee of both houses of the legislature. In order to constitute perjury the false statement must be made under sanction of an oath or an equivalent affirmation and must relate to matter material to the issue or question in controversy.

B. It is a necessary element of the offense that the accused knew the statement to be false, but an unqualified statement of that which one does not know or definitely believe to be true is equivalent to a statement of that which he knows to be false.

C. Whoever commits the crime of perjury shall be punished as follows:

(1) When committed on a trial in which a sentence of death or life imprisonment may be imposed, the offender shall be fined not more than one hundred thousand dollars or imprisoned at hard labor for not less than five years, without benefit or parole, probation, or suspension of sentence, nor more than forty years, or both.

(2) When committed on a trial in which a sentence of imprisonment necessarily at hard labor for any period less than a life sentence may be imposed, the offender shall be fined not more than fifty thousand dollars or imprisoned at hard labor for not less than one year, without benefit of parole, probation, or suspension of sentence, nor more than twenty years, or both.

(3) When committed in all other cases in which any other sentence may be imposed, the offender shall be fined not more than ten thousand dollars or imprisoned at hard labor for not more than five years, or both.

(4) In all other cases by a fine of not more than ten thousand dollars or imprisonment at hard labor for not more than five years, or both.

(Chgd. by Acts 1995 No. 820, §1; Acts 1997 No. 1312, §1, eff. 8/15/97.)

§124. Inconsistent statements; perjury.

It shall constitute perjury whenever any person, having taken an oath required by law, or made an equivalent affirmation, swears of affirms any fact or state of facts material to the issue or question in controversy; and thereafter in the same or other proceedings, where such matter is material to the issue or question in controversy, swears or affirms in a manner materially contradictory of or inconsistent with his former sworn or affirmed statement. It shall not be necessary for the prosecution, in such case, to show which of the contradictory or inconsistent statements was false; but it shall be an affirmative defense that at the time he made them, the accused honestly believed both statements to be true.

This article shall only be applicable in cases where at least one of the contradictory or inconsistent statements was made in, or for use in, a judicial proceeding or a proceeding before a board or official wherein such board or official is authorized to take testimony.

§125. False swearing.

False swearing is the intentional making of a written or oral statement, known to be false, under sanction of an oath or an equivalent affirmation, where such oath or affirmation is required by law; provided that this article shall not apply where such false statement is made in, or for use in, a judicial proceeding or any proceeding before a board or official, wherein such board or official is authorized to take testimony.

Whoever commits the crime of false swearing shall be fined not more than five hundred dollars, or imprisoned for not more than one year, or both.

§125.1. False swearing in paternity cases.

A. False swearing in paternity cases is the intentional making of a written or oral statement, known to be false, under sanction of oath or equivalent statement, where such oath or affirmation is given for use in any judicial proceeding filed by or on behalf of the state of Louisiana to establish paternity.

B. Whoever commits the crime of false swearing in paternity cases shall be fined not more than five hundred dollars, or imprisoned for not more than six months, or both.

(Added by Acts 1992 No. 722, §1, eff. 8/21/92.)

§126. Inconsistent statements; false swearing.

It shall constitute false swearing whenever any person, having made a statement under sanction of an oath, or an equivalent affirmation, required by law, shall thereafter swear or affirm in a manner materially contradictory of or inconsistent with his former sworn or affirmed statement. It shall not be necessary for the prosecution, in such case, to show which of the contradictory or inconsistent statements was false; but it shall be an affirmative defense that at the time he made them, the accused honestly believed both statements to be true.

§126.1. False swearing for purpose of violating public health or safety.

No person shall make a false statement, report or allegation concerning the commission of a crime for the purpose of violating, disrupting, interfering with or endangering the public health or safety, or to deprive any person or persons of any right, privilege or immunity secured by the United States Constitution and laws or by the Louisiana Constitution and laws, or cause such false statement or report to be made to any official or agency of the state or any parish, city or political subdivision thereof, or to any judicial, executive or legislative body or subdivision thereof within this state, knowing or having reason to believe the same or any material part thereof to be false and with the intent to cause an investigation of or any other action to be taken as a result thereof.

Any person or persons convicted of violating the provisions of this Section shall be punished by imprisonment for not less than one year nor more than five years, with or without hard labor, or by a fine of not less than one hundred dollars nor more than one thousand dollars, or by both such fine and imprisonment.

§126.2. False statements concerning denial of constitutional rights.

No person shall wilfully and knowingly, whether orally or in writing, make or cause to be made to any agency, board, commission, member, officer, official, appointee, employee or representative thereof, of the executive, legislative or judicial department of the United States or any subdivision thereof, which may be now in existence, or who may be now appointed, or hereafter created or appointed, including but not limited to any commissioner, referee or voting referee now appointed or who may be hereafter appointed by any court of the United States or any judge thereof, and further including but not limited to any member of the Federal Bureau of Investigation and any agent or representative, investigator or member of the Commission of Civil Rights of the United States, or the Advisory Committee or Board of the Commission of Civil Rights of the United States appointed in and for the state of Louisiana, any false or fictitious or fraudulent statement or statements, or to use any false writing or document asserting or claiming that such person or persons, or any other person or persons have been or are about to be denied or deprived of any right, privilege or immunity granted or secured to them, or to any of them, by the United States Constitution and laws, or by the Louisiana Constitution and laws, by any officer, agency, employee, representative, board or commission or any member thereof of the state of Louisiana, or of any parish or municipality of the state of Louisiana, or of any other political subdivision of the state of Louisiana, or by the state of Louisiana.

Any person or persons violating the provisions of this Section shall, upon conviction thereof, be punished by imprisonment for not less than one year nor more than five years with or without hard labor, or by a fine of not less than one hundred dollars nor more than one thousand dollars or by both such fine and imprisonment.

§126.3. False statements concerning employment in a nursing or health care facility.

A. The crime of health care facility application fraud is the knowing and intentional offering of a false written or oral statement in any employment application or in an effort to obtain employment as a caretaker in any nursing home, mental retardation facility, mental health facility, hospital, home health agency, hospice, or other residential facility required to be licensed or operated under the laws of this state or established by the laws of this state. Such false statement must be relevant to the caretaking obligation of such employee, but shall specifically apply to but not be limited to educational and professional background and licensing and credential qualifications.

B. Any person who violates the provisions of this Section shall be fined not more than five hundred dollars or imprisoned for not more than six months, or both.

(Added by Acts 1995 No. 788, §1, eff. 8/15/95.)

§127. Limitation of defenses.

It is no defense to a prosecution for perjury or false swearing:

(1) That the oath, or affirmation, was administered or taken in an irregular manner; or

(2) That the accused was not competent to give the testimony, deposition, affidavit or certificate of which falsehood is alleged; or

(3) That the accused did not know the materiality of the false statement made by him, or that it did not in fact affect the proceeding in or for which it was made.

§128. Completion of affidavit.

The making of a deposition, affidavit or certificate is deemed to be complete, within the provisions of this chapter, from the time when it is delivered by the accused to any other person, with intent that it be uttered or published as true.

SUBPART D. MISCELLANEOUS OFFENSES AFFECTING JUDICIAL FUNCTIONS AND PUBLIC RECORDS

§129. Jury tampering.

A. Jury tampering is any verbal or written communication or attempted communication, whether direct or indirect, made to any juror in a civil or criminal cause, including both grand and petit jurors, for the purpose of influencing the juror in respect to his verdict or indictment in any cause pending or about to be brought before him, otherwise than in the regular course of proceedings upon the trial or other determination of such cause. To constitute the offense of jury tampering, the influencing or attempt to influence the juror must be either:

(1) For a corrupt or fraudulent purpose, or

(2) By violence or force, by threats whether direct or indirect.

B. (1) Whoever commits the crime of jury tampering in a civil case shall be fined not more than five thousand dollars, or imprisoned, with or without hard labor, for not more than five years, or both.

(2) Whoever commits the crime of jury tampering in a criminal case shall be punished as follows:

(a) If the offense charged in the trial for which the jury has been impaneled is punishable by death or life imprisonment, the offender shall be imprisoned at hard labor for not more than ninety-nine years.

(b) In all other cases the offender shall be fined or imprisoned, or both, to the same extent and in the same manner as for the offense charged in the trial for which the jury has been impaneled.

(Chgd. by Acts 1995 No. 823, §1, eff. 8/15/95.)

§129.1. Intimidating, impeding or injuring witnesses; injuring officers; penalties.

No person shall intentionally:

(a) Intimidate or impede, by threat of force or force, or attempt to intimidate or impede, by threat of force or force, a witness with intent to influence his testimony, his reporting of criminal conduct or his appearance at a judicial proceeding;

(b) Injure or attempt to injure a witness in his person or property with intent to influence his testimony, his reporting of criminal conduct or his appearance at a judicial proceeding; or

(c) Injure or attempt to injure an officer of a court of this state in his person or property because of the performance of his duties as an officer of a court of this state or with intent to influence the performance of his duties as an officer of a court of this state.

For purposes of this Section a "witness" is a person (a) who is a victim of conduct defined as a crime under the laws of this state, another state or the United States, or (b) whose declaration under oath has been received in evidence in any court of this state, another state or the United States, or (c) who has reported a crime to a peace officer, prosecutor, probation or parole officer, correctional officer or judicial officer of this state, another state or the United States, or (d) who has been served with a subpoena issued under authority of any court of this state, another state or the United States.

A witness also shall include a person who reasonably would be believed by an offender to be a witness as previously defined in this Section.

Whoever violates the provisions of this Section shall be fined not more than five thousand dollars, imprisoned, with or without hard labor, for not more than five years, or both.

§129.2. Recording, listening to, or observing proceedings of grand or petit juries while deliberating or voting.

It shall be unlawful for any person knowingly and intentionally, by any means or device whatsoever:

(1) to record or attempt to record, the proceedings of any grand or petit jury in any court of the state of Louisiana while such jury is deliberating or voting; or

(2) to listen to or observe, or attempt to listen to or observe, the proceedings of any grand or petit jury of which he is not a member in any court of the state of Louisiana while such jury is deliberating or voting.

Whoever violates the provisions of this Section shall be fined not more than five hundred dollars, or imprisoned for not more than six months, or both.

§130. Jury misconduct.

A. Jury misconduct is committed when:

(1) Any petit or grand juror shall make any promise or agreement to give a verdict or finding for or against any party.

(2) Any petit juror shall intentionally permit any person to influence him, or attempt to influence him, in respect to his verdict in any cause pending, or about to be brought before him, otherwise than in the regular course of proceedings upon the trial of such cause.

(3) Any petit juror shall either use or consume any beverage of low or high alcoholic content during the time he is in actual service as juror.

(4) Any petit juror accepts or offers to accept anything of apparent present or prospective value, before he is discharged from his services as a juror, even if the thing of value is not to be received, delivered, or come to fruition until after discharge from jury service, for his interpretation, impression, analysis or narrative, verbal or written, regarding any element of the criminal trial or jury deliberations.

B. Whoever commits the crime of jury misconduct, shall be fined not more than five hundred dollars, or imprisoned for not more than six months, or both.

(Chgd. by Acts 1991 No. 967, §1, eff. 9/6/91.)

§130.1. Obstruction of justice.

A. The crime of obstruction of justice is any of the following when committed with the knowledge that such act has, reasonably may, or will affect an actual or potential present, past, or future criminal proceeding as hereinafter described:

(1) Tampering with evidence with the specific intent of distorting the results of any criminal investigation or proceeding which may reasonably prove relevant to a criminal investigation or proceeding. Tampering with evidence shall include the intentional alteration, movement, removal, or addition of any object or substance either:

(a) At the location of any incident which the perpetrator knows or has good reason to believe will be the subject of any investigation by state, local, or United States law enforcement officers; or

(b) At the location of storage, transfer, or place of review of any such evidence.

(2) Using or threatening force toward the person or property of another with the specific intent to:

(a) Influence the testimony of any person in any criminal proceeding;

(b) Cause or induce the withholding of testimony or withholding of records, documents, or other objects from any criminal proceeding;

(c) Cause or induce the alteration, destruction, mutilation, or concealment of any object with the specific intent to impair the object's integrity or availability for use in any criminal proceeding;

(d) Evade legal process or the summoning of a person to appear as a witness or to produce a record, document, or other object in any criminal proceeding;

(e) Cause the hindrance, delay, or prevention of the communication to a peace officer, as defined in R.S. 14:30, of information relating to an arrest or potential arrest or relating to the commission or possible commission of a crime or parole or probation violation.

(3) Retaliating against any witness, victim, juror, judge, party, attorney, or informant by knowingly engaging in any conduct which result in bodily injury to or damage to the property of any such person or the communication of threats to do so with the specific intent to retaliate against any person for:

(a) The attendance as a witness, juror, judge, attorney, or a party to any criminal proceeding or for producing evidence or testimony for use or potential use in any criminal proceeding, or

(b) The giving of information, evidence, or any aid relating to the commission or possible commission of a parole or probation violation or any crime under the laws of any state or of the United States.

B. Whoever commits the crime of obstruction of justice shall be subject to the following penalties:

(1) When the obstruction of justice involves a criminal proceeding in which a sentence of death or life imprisonment may be imposed, the offender shall be fined not more than one hundred thousand dollars, imprisoned for not more than forty years at hard labor, or both.

(2) When the obstruction of justice involves a criminal proceeding in which a sentence of imprisonment necessarily at hard labor for any period less than a life sentence may be imposed, the offender may be fined not more than fifty thousand dollars, or imprisoned for not more than twenty years at hard labor, or both.

(3) When the obstruction of justice involves any other criminal proceeding, the offender shall be fined not more than ten thousand dollars, imprisoned for not more than five years, with or without hard labor, or both.

§131. Compounding a felony.

Compounding a felony is the accepting of anything of apparent present or prospective value which belongs to another, or of any promise thereof, by a person having knowledge of the commission of a felony, upon an agreement, express or implied, to conceal such offense, or not to prosecute the same, or not to reveal or give evidence thereof.

Whoever commits the offense of compounding a felony shall be fined not more than one thousand dollars or imprisoned, with or without hard labor, for not more than two years, or both.

§132. Injuring public records.

Injuring public records is the intentional removal, mutilation, destruction, alteration, falsification, or concealment of any record, document, or other thing, filed or deposited, by authority of law, in any public office or with any public officer.

Whoever commits the crime of injuring public records shall be imprisoned for not more than five years with or without hard labor or shall be fined not more than five thousand dollars or both.

§133. Filing or maintaining false public records.

A. Filing false public records is the filing or depositing for record in any public office or with any public official, or the maintaining as required by law, regulation, or rule, with knowledge of its falsity, of any of the following:

(1) Any forged document.

(2) Any wrongfully altered document.

(3) Any document containing a false statement or false representation of a material fact.

B. The good faith inclusion of any item of cost on a Medical Assistance Program cost report which is later determined by audit to be nonreimbursable under state and federal regulations shall be an affirmative defense to a violation of this Section.

C. Whoever commits the crime of filing false public records shall be imprisoned for not more than five years with or without hard labor or shall be fined not more than five thousand dollars, or both.

(Chgd. by Acts 1992 No. 539, §1; Acts 1995 No. 787, §1, eff. 8/15/95.)

§133.1. Obstruction of court orders.

Whoever, by threats or force, or wilfully prevents, obstructs, impedes, or interferes with, or wilfully attempts to prevent, obstruct, impede, or interfere with, the due exercise of rights or the performance of duties under any order, judgment, or decree of a court of the state of Louisiana, shall be fined not more than $1,000 or imprisoned not more than one year, or both.

No injunctive or other civil relief against the conduct made criminal by this Section shall be denied on the ground that such conduct is a violation of criminal law, and, when granted, the order, judgment or decree granting such relief as to conduct which does constitute a violation of criminal law shall be construed as a mandate to all law enforcement officers to take such affirmative action as may be necessary to apprehend, arrest and charge any person or persons who engage in such conduct.

§133.2. Misrepresentation during booking.

A. Misrepresentation during booking is the misrepresentation of, or refusal by a person being booked to provide his name, age, sex, residence, or social security number to any law enforcement officer or official who is booking him pursuant to a lawful arrest, or the refusal of such person to submit to fingerprinting or photographing.

B. Whoever commits the crime of misrepresentation during booking shall be imprisoned for not more than six months, provided that any such sentence shall be made to run concurrently with any other sentence.

§133.3. Falsification of drug tests.

A. (1) No person who submits to court-ordered drug testing, either after arrest for an offense and as a condition of pretrial release or after conviction of, or plea of guilty to, an offense and as a condition of probation, shall intentionally falsify or alter or attempt to falsify or alter the results of such a drug test by the substitution of urine or other samples or specimens or the use of any device in order to obscure or conceal the presence of a substance the presence of which the test is administered to detect.

(2) No person shall knowingly and intentionally deliver, possess with intent to deliver, or manufacture with intent to deliver a substance or device designed or intended solely to falsify or alter drug test results.

B. Whoever violates the provisions of this Section shall be fined not more than five hundred dollars or imprisoned for not more than six months, or both.

(Added by Acts 1995 No. 250, §1, eff. 8/15/95.)

SUBPART E. OFFICIAL MISCONDUCT AND CORRUPT PRACTICES

§134. Malfeasance in office.

Malfeasance in office is committed when any public officer or public employee shall:

(1) Intentionally refuse or fail to perform any duty lawfully required of him, as such officer or employee; or

(2) Intentionally perform any such duty in an unlawful manner; or

(3) Knowingly permit any other public officer or public employee, under his authority, to intentionally refuse or fail to perform any duty lawfully required of him, or to perform any such duty in an unlawful manner.

Any duty lawfully required of a public officer or public employee when delegated by him to a public officer or public employee shall be deemed to be a lawful duty of such public officer or employee. The delegation of such lawful duty shall not relieve the public officer or employee of his lawful duty.

Whoever commits the crime of malfeasance in office shall be imprisoned for not more than five years with or without hard labor or shall be fined not more than five thousand dollars or both.

§134.1. Malfeasance in office; sexual conduct prohibited with persons confined in correctional institutions.

A. It shall be unlawful and constitute malfeasance in office for any person who is a law enforcement officer, officer of the Department of Corrections, or employee of a prison, jail, or correctional institution, to engage in sexual intercourse or any other sexual conduct with a person confined in a prison, jail or correctional institution.

B. Whoever violates a provision of this Section shall be fined not more than ten thousand dollars, or imprisoned for not more than ten years, or both.

§134.2. Malfeasance in office; tampering with evidence.

A. It shall be unlawful and constitute malfeasance in office for a peace officer to tamper with evidence.

(1) For purposes of this Section, "a peace officer" shall be defined as a commissioned state, parish, or municipal police officer, a sheriff, or a deputy sheriff.

(2) For purposes of this Section, "tampering with evidence" is the intentional alteration, movement, removal, or addition of any object or substance when the peace officer:

(a) Knows or has good reason to believe that such object or substance will be the subject of any investigation by state, local, or federal law enforcement officers, and

(b) Acts with the intent of distorting the results of such an investigation.

B. Whoever violates this Section shall be fined not more than ten thousand dollars, or be imprisoned, with or without hard labor, for not more than three years, or both.

§135. Public salary deduction.

Public salary deduction is committed when any public officer or public employee shall retain or divert for his own use or the use of any other person or political organization, any part of the salary or fees allowed by law to any other public officer or public employee.

Whoever commits the crime of public salary deduction shall be imprisoned for not more than five years with or without hard labor or shall be fined not more than five thousand dollars or both.

§136. Public salary extortion.

Public salary extortion is committed when any person shall:

(1) Solicit or receive, or attempt to solicit or receive, either directly or indirectly, the payment of any money or other thing of value from any public officer or public employee to himself or any other person or political organization, through any means or form whatsoever and for any purpose whatsoever, when such payment is obtained or solicited upon suggestion or threat that the failure to make such payment shall result in the loss or impairment of value to such officer or employee of his office or employment, or when such payment shall be a reward or remuneration for securing such office or employment; and proof that such payments were collected from or paid by such officers or employees on a uniform or progressive percentage or amount basis, shall be presumptive evidence that payments were made under duress or upon the consideration set forth hereinbefore; or

(2) Solicit or receive or attempt to solicit or receive, either directly or indirectly, the contribution of any money or other thing of value for any general, primary or special election or for any other political purpose, from any person holding any office or employment for remuneration or profit, including those persons who work on a commission basis, with the state, who receive a remuneration of two hundred dollars per month or less from such employment; provided that this Subdivision shall not apply where the person solicited or whose contribution was received was an elective public officer or a candidate for any elective public office.

Whoever commits the crime of public salary extortion shall be imprisoned for not more than five years with or without hard labor or shall be fined not more than five thousand dollars or both.

§138. Public payroll fraud.

A. Public payroll fraud is committed when:

(1) Any person shall knowingly receive any payment or compensation, or knowingly permit his name to be carried on any employment list or payroll for any payment or compensation from the state, for services not actually rendered by himself, or for services grossly inadequate for the payment or compensation received or to be received according to such employment list or payroll; or

(2) Any public officer or public employee shall carry, cause to be carried, or permit to be carried, directly or indirectly, upon the employment list or payroll of his office, the name of any person as employee, or shall pay any employee, with knowledge that such employee is receiving payment or compensation for services not actually rendered by said employee or for services grossly inadequate for such payment or compensation.

B. This Section shall not apply in the following situations:

(1) When a bona fide public officer or public employee, who is justifiably absent from his job or position for a reasonable time, continues to receive his usual compensation or a part thereof.

(2) When arrangements between firefighters to swap work or perform substitute work with or for each other is done in compliance with the provisions of the federal Fair Labor Standards Act, 29 U.S.C. 207(p)(3) and the associated regulations found in the Code of Federal Regulations and in accordance with rules and regulations adopted by the appointing authority.

C. Whoever commits the crime of public payroll fraud shall be fined not more than one thousand dollars, or imprisoned, with or without hard labor, for not more than two years, or both.

(Chgd. by Acts 1997 No. 538, §1, eff. 8/15/97.)

§139. Political payroll padding.

Political payroll padding is committed when any public officer or public employee shall, at any time during the six months preceding any election for governor:

(1) Increase the number of public employees in his office, department, board, agency, or institution more than five percent over the average number of such employees for each of the first six months of the twelve months next preceding said election; or

(2) Increase the payroll or other operating expenses of his office, department, board, agency, or institution more than fifteen percent over its average amount of such expenditures for each of the months of the first six months of the twelve months next preceding said election.

The provisions of this Article shall not apply where the increases are necessitated by flood, invasion by a common enemy, or other public emergency.

Whoever commits the crime of political payroll padding shall be imprisoned for not more than five years with or without hard labor or shall be fined not more than five thousand dollars or both.

§139.1. Political payroll padding by sheriff; sale of assets of sheriff's office prohibited.

A. During the six months preceding a gubernatorial election and during the time interval between the gubernatorial election and the first day of July following election, it shall be unlawful for any sheriff to:

(1) Increase the number of deputies or employees in his office by more than five percent over the average number of such employees for each of the first six months of the twelve months preceding said election; or

(2) Increase the payroll or other operating expenses of his office more than fifteen percent over its average amount of such expenditures for each of the months of the first six months of the twelve months preceding said election; or

(3) Transfer title and ownership of the capital assets of his office of a value in excess of ten percent of the total value of said assets as reflected in the current inventory filed in the office of the sheriff on date of the first primary election under the provisions of Section 513 of Title 24.

B. In determining whether any surplus or deficit exists in the office of any sheriff at the expiration of a term of office, the current market value of the capital assets of the office as set forth in the inventory filed in accordance with Section 513 of Title 24 shall be included in the total assets of the sheriff's office.

C. The provisions of this Section shall not apply where the increases or decreases are necessitated by flood, invasion by common enemy, or other public emergency.

D. Whoever violates the provisions of Subsection A of this Section shall be imprisoned, with or without hard labor, for not more than five years or shall be fined not more than five thousand dollars, or both.

§139.2. Transfer of capital assets of clerk of court's office prohibited.

A. It shall be unlawful for any clerk of court, during a period beginning on the second Saturday in April of a year in which a regular gubernatorial election is scheduled and ending on the first day of July of the following year, to transfer title and ownership of any capital assets of his office which have an aggregate value greater than ten percent of the total value of the capital assets of his office.

B. For purposes of this Section, the capital assets of the office of a clerk of court shall include all general fixed assets over which the clerk has custody and control, regardless of whether such assets are carried as assets by the clerk or by the parish governing authority.

C. The value of the capital assets shall be the value of such assets as reflected in the current inventory filed under the provisions of R.S. 24:513 prior to the beginning day of the period specified in Subsection A or, if no such inventory is filed, the value of the assets as carried on the records of the clerk or the parish governing authority on the day prior to the beginning day of the period specified in Subsection A.

D. The provisions of this Section shall not apply to a transfer necessitated by flood, invasion by common enemy, or other public emergency.

E. Whoever violates the provisions of Subsection A of this Section shall be imprisoned, with or without hard labor, for not more than five years or shall be fined not more than five thousand dollars, or both.

§140. Public contract fraud.

A. Public contract fraud is committed:

(1) When any public officer or public employee shall use his power or position as such officer or employee to secure any expenditure of public funds to himself, or to any partnership of which he is a member, or to any corporation of which he is an officer, stockholder, or director; or

(2) When any member of any public board, body, or commission charged with the custody, control, or expenditure of any public funds votes for or uses his influence to secure any expenditure of such funds to himself, or to any partnership of which he is a member, or to any corporation of which he is an officer, director, or stockholder.

(3) When any sheriff charged with the duties of enforcing the laws of this state or any political subdivision thereof shall enter into a contract, either written or oral, individually or as a member or stockholder of any partnership, company, or corporation, with any such person whereby such sheriff or partnership, company, or corporation, of which he is a member or stockholder is to perform any services of a law enforcement nature; provided, however, a deputy sheriff may, as an employee only, perform services of a law enforcement nature for any person, partnership, company, or corporation, but only if said deputy sheriff fulfills his employee performance requirements while not on official duty.

The fact that an expenditure has been made to any party named in Paragraphs (1) and (2) of this Section, or to any partnership of which he is a member, or to any corporation of which he is an officer, stockholder, or director, shall be presumptive evidence that such person has used his power, position, or influence to secure such expenditure.

B. Whoever commits the crime of public contract fraud shall be fined not more than one thousand dollars, or imprisoned, with or without hard labor, for not more than two years, or both.

§141. Prohibited splitting of profits, fees or commissions; exceptions.

A. For the purposes of this section, splitting of profits, fees or commissions means the giving, offering to give, receiving or offering to receive, directly or indirectly, anything of apparent present or prospective value by or to a public officer or public employee or to any fund or fiduciary existing for the benefit of or use by such public officer or employee, when such value is derived from any agreement or contract to which the state or any subdivision thereof is a party.

B. There shall be no splitting of profits, fees or commissions, past or present, derived from the sale of any commodity, goods, services, insurance, or anything of value to the state or any subdivision thereof from which a public official or employee, representing the state in his official capacity in the contract negotiations, receives or offers to receive a portion of the profits, fees and/or commissions, unless the amount thereof and the conditions therefor are included in detail in the contract of sale or the insurance contract and said contract is filed by the public official or employee hereinabove described with the secretary of state at least ten days prior to execution of said contract. The ten-day filing period shall be waived in the event of an emergency in which such filing is not reasonable. Upon filing thereof, the secretary of state shall immediately release to the news media the details of such contract and, upon written request, furnish a copy of such contract to the news media.

C. Whoever commits the crime of failure to report the splitting of profits, fees or commissions, and to contain such fee arrangement in the contract of sale or in the insurance contract as provided by this act shall upon conviction be fined not more than one thousand dollars or shall be imprisoned, with or without hard labor, for not more than two years, or both.

PART VIII. CONCLUDING PROVISIONS

§142. Offenses committed prior to effective date of Code.

This Code shall not apply to any crimes committed before July 29, 1942. Crimes committed before that time shall be governed by the law existing at the time the crime was committed.

§143. Preemption of state law.

No governing authority of a political subdivision shall enact an ordinance defining as an offense conduct that is defined and punishable as a felony under state law.

CHAPTER 2. MISCELLANEOUS CRIMES AND OFFENSES

PART I. OFFENSES AGAINST PROPERTY

PART II. OFFENSES AFFECTING PUBLIC MORALS

PART III. OFFENSES AFFECTING THE PUBLIC GENERALLY

311. Discharging fire-works or explosives within one thousand feet of hospital prohibited; penalty.
312. Jumping from state bridge for publicity prohibited; penalty.
313. Masks or hoods, wearing in public places prohibited; penalty; exceptions; permit to conduct Mardi Gras festivities, how obtained.
314. Mississippi River, making unauthorized cut-offs prohibited; penalty.
315. Mississippi River, stopping outlets or bayous prohibited; reopening; penalty.
316. Naming public buildings, etc., in honor of living person prohibited; removal and change of name; penalty.
318. Sale of fireworks containing white or yellow phosphorus prohibited; penalty.
319. Sale of toy pistols prohibited; penalty; exceptions.
320. Telegrams, divulging or obtaining knowledge of contents prohibited; penalty.
321. Unauthorized signals to persons in charge of locomotives, etc., prohibited; penalty.
322. Wire-tapping prohibited; penalty.
322.1, 322.2. *(Repealed.)*
324. Abandoning or discarding ice boxes or other air tight containers; penalty.
325. Annual registration of conductors of public opinion polls; penalty for failure.
326. Processions, marches, parades or demonstrations; permits; liability; bond; exemptions; penalty.
327. Obstructing a fireman.
328. Obstruction or interference with members of staff, faculty, or students of educational institutions; trespass, damage to property; felony; penalties.
329.1. Riot.
329.2. Inciting to riot.
329.3. Command to disperse; who may give; failure to comply.
329.4. Wrongful use of public property; permits for use of public property.
329.5. Prohibition of interference with educational process; certain activities excepted.
329.6. Proclamation of state of emergency; conditions therefore; effect thereof.
329.7. Punishment.
329.8. Applicability of other acts.
330. Motion picture ratings; definitions; prohibition on advertising coming attraction with more restrictive rating.
331. Prohibition of debt adjusting when conducted for profit.
332. Interference with medical treatment.
333. Misrepresentation of age to obtain alcoholic beverages or gain entry to licensed premises prohibited; penalties.
334. Ignition interlock device offenses.
335. Checks; requiring certain information to be recorded on; prohibited; penalties.

PART IV. OFFENSES AFFECTING ORGANIZED GOVERNMENT

351. Bail, sale, etc. of real estate securing, prohibited; penalty.
352. Bribery of withdrawn candidates for office prohibited; penalty; immunity of witnesses; fine to be paid informer.
353. Documents simulating official court papers for collection purposes, sale or purchase prohibited; use prohibited; penalty.
354. Fiduciaries, failure to file accounts in court; penalty.
355. Property exempt from execution; penalty for deprivation of rights.
356. Sheriffs, etc., solicitation of legal business prohibited; penalty.
356.1. Unlawful referrals by wrecker drivers and others; penalty.
356.2. Unlawful appearance bond procurement.
356.3. Unlawful referrals by ambulance drivers and others; penalty.
357. Candies, selling without payment of license tax; penalty.
358. Subversive activities and communist control law; legislative finding of fact and declaration of necessity.
359. Definitions.
360. Due process determination of facts.
361. Venue.
362. Registration of organizations.
363. Registration of individuals.

PART V. OFFENSES AFFECTING LAW ENFORCEMENT

PART VI. OFFENSES AGAINST THE PERSON

PART VII. LOANSHARKING

PART I. OFFENSES AGAINST PROPERTY

§201. Collateral securities, unauthorized use or withdrawal prohibited; penalty; proof of intent; of personal advantage.

No customer, nor any officer, member, or employee of any person who is a customer of any bank or banking institution, savings bank, or trust company organized under the laws of this state, of the United States, or of any foreign country, or of a private banker or of a person, or association that loans money on collateral security, doing business in this state, who is allowed to withdraw any collateral pledged by him, either personally or in his representative capacity, on a trust receipt or other form of receipt, shall:

(1) Use, sell, repledge, or otherwise dispose of the collateral so withdrawn, for any other purpose other than that of paying the indebtedness for the security of which the collateral was pledged; or,

(2) Fail or refuse to return the collateral on demand; or,

(3) Fail or refuse in lieu of the return of the collateral to make the pledgee a cash payment equivalent to the full value of the collateral so withdrawn; or,

(4) If the collateral exceeds in value the indebtedness it secures, fail or refuse to make a cash payment to the pledgee equal to the full amount of the indebtedness; or,

(5) If the delivery of the collateral was to be made in the future and the customer has taken possession or control of the collateral, fails or refuses to deliver the collateral on demand.

Whoever violates this Section shall be imprisoned with or without hard labor, for not more than ten years.

Proof of any of the acts set forth in this Section shall be considered prima facie evidence of criminal intent. The state may proceed further and prove criminal intent by any competent evidence in its possession.

Where the person doing the acts denounced by this Section was an officer, agent, or employee of any person, who was a customer of any lender (as mentioned in the first paragraph of this Section) loaning money on collateral security, it shall not be necessary, to complete the proof of the crime charged, for the state to prove that the person derived any personal benefit, advantage, or profit from the transaction. The state may always prove the crime charged by any competent evidence it may have in its possession.

§202. Contractors, misapplication of payments prohibited; penalty.

A. No person, contractor, subcontractor, or agent of a contractor or subcontractor, who has received money on account of a contract for the construction, erection, or repair of a building, structure, or other improvement, including contracts and mortgages for interim financing, shall knowingly fail to apply the money received as necessary to settle claims for material and labor due for the construction or under the contract.

B. When the amount misapplied is one thousand dollars or less, whoever violates the provisions of this Section shall be fined not less than one hundred dollars nor more than five hundred dollars, or imprisoned for not less than ninety days nor more than six months, or both.

C. When the amount misapplied is greater than one thousand dollars, whoever violates this Section shall be fined not less than one hundred dollars nor more than five hundred dollars, or imprisoned with or without hard labor for not less than ninety days nor more than six months, or both, for each one thousand dollars in misapplied funds, provided that the aggregate imprisonment shall not exceed five years.

D. Any person, contractor, subcontractor, or agent of a contractor or subcontractor who knowingly fails properly to apply construction contract payments as required in Subsection A shall pay to the court, and the court shall transfer to the person whose construction contract payments were misapplied, an amount equal to the sum of the payments not properly applied and any additional legal costs resulting from the misapplication of construction fund payments, including a fee charged by the clerk of court for handling such payments.
(Chgd. by Acts 1990 No. 690, §1, eff. 9/7/90.)

§203. Electrical appliances, sale without original factory serial number prohibited; penalty.

No person shall offer to sell or cause to be sold or distributed either retail or wholesale, new household appliances, such as radios, television sets, refrigerators, washing machines, ironers, dryers, gas or electric ranges, air conditioners, without the appliance having the original factory serial number indicated thereon provided it is the custom of the manufacturer to place serial numbers on the appliances.

Whoever violates this Section shall be fined not more than one hundred dollars or imprisoned for not more than ninety days, or both.

§204. Fire-raising on lands of another by criminal negligence; penalty.

Fire-raising on lands of another by criminal negligence is the performance of any of the following acts:

(1) The setting fire to any grass, leaves, brush or debris on lands by the owner, or by the owner's agent or lessee, and allowing the fire to spread or pass to lands of another.

(2) The starting of fire with wood or other fuel on lands of another, without malice, for camping or other purposes, with failure to exercise sufficient precautions so as to prevent the fire from spreading to grass, leaves, brush or other debris on the lands.

(3) The setting fire to grass, leaves, brush or other debris on lands of another by means of casting aside a lighted match or lighted cigar or cigarette stub.

(4) The burning over or causing burning over to be done on any land which adjoins woodlands of another within the boundaries of any parish of this state wherein an organized fire protection unit is maintained by the state or federal government, or both, without first giving the protecting agency written notice of intention to burn over the lands, giving a description of the property which will reasonably describe the location where the burning shall begin, and the date on which the lands are to be burned over. For the purpose of this Section, an "organized fire protection unit" is defined to be any area in which an organized system of fire prevention and control is in effect.

Whoever commits the crime of fire-raising on lands of another by criminal negligence shall be fined not more than three hundred dollars or imprisoned for not more than thirty days, or both.

§205. Fire-raising on lands of another with malice; penalty.

Fire-raising on lands of another with malice is the malicious setting fire to any grass, leaves, brush or debris on lands of another, or the procuring same to be done.

Whoever commits the crime of fire-raising on lands of another with malice shall be fined not more than five hundred dollars, or imprisoned for not more than six months, or both.

§206. Fire prevention interference; penalty.

Fire prevention interference is the intentional performance of any of the following acts:

(1) Defacing or destroying fire warning notices or posters.

(2) Injuring, destroying, removing or in any manner interfering with the use of any tools, equipment, towers, buildings or telephone lines used in the detection, reporting or suppression of fire.

Whoever commits the crime of fire prevention interference shall be fined not more than five hundred dollars or imprisoned for a period of not more than six months, or both.

§207. Motor vehicles, alteration or removal of identifying numbers prohibited; sale, etc., of motor vehicle with altered identifying numbers prohibited; penalty; application of Section.

A. No person shall cover, remove, deface, alter, or destroy the manufacturer's number or any other distinguishing number or identification mark on any motor vehicle or motor vehicle part for the purpose of concealing or misrepresenting its identity; nor shall any person buy, sell, receive, dispose of, conceal, or knowingly have in his possession any motor vehicle or motor vehicle part from or on which the manufacturer's number or any other distinguishing number or identification mark has been covered, removed, defaced, altered, or destroyed for the purpose of concealing or misrepresenting its identity.

B. Whoever violates this Section shall be fined not more than two thousand dollars, or imprisoned with or without hard labor for not more than twenty-four months, or both, and, in default of fine, imprisoned with or without hard labor for not more than twelve months additional.

C. This Section shall apply to all vehicles propelled otherwise than by muscular power, except motor vehicles running upon rails or tracks.

§208. Operas, performance or representation without consent of owner prohibited; penalty.

No person or company shall take part in or cause to be publicly performed or represented for profit any unpublished or undedicated dramatic or musical composition known as an opera without the consent of its owner or proprietor, or knowing an opera is unpublished or undedicated, shall permit, aid, or take part in a public performance or representation without the consent of the owner or proprietor.

Whoever violates this Section shall, for every performance, be fined not less than one hundred dollars nor more than five hundred dollars or imprisoned for not less than thirty days.

§209. Seals, breaking prohibited; penalty.

No person shall, without legal authority, break any seal placed, in accordance with law, on the effects or any place or thing containing the effects or property of any deceased person.

Whoever violates this Section shall be fined not more than one thousand dollars and imprisoned with or without hard labor for not more than two years.

§210. Taxicabs, tampering with meter forbidden; penalty.

No person shall, without the written consent of the owner, tamper with or alter in any manner or form the fare-registering device of any taxicab or automobile for hire.

Whoever violates this Section shall be fined not less than fifty dollars nor more than two hundred dollars, or imprisoned for not less than six months nor more than one year, or both.

§211. Sale of forest products; failure to remit payment to owner; penalty.

A. (1) Any person who acquires, with the consent of an owner, any forest product from that owner and who receives payment for the forest product, shall within thirty days of such receipt, make payment in full to the owner.

(2) If the owner has not received payment within the required thirty days, the owner shall notify the offender of his demand for payment at the offender's last known address, by certified mail, or by personal delivery of the written notice to the offender. The offender's failure to make payment in full within ten days after the mailing or personal delivery shall be presumptive evidence of the offender's intent to violate this Section.

B. A written agreement signed by the owner providing for a means of payment contrary to this Section shall constitute an affirmative defense.

C. As used in this Section:

(1) "Forest product" means any tree, shrub, plant, or related vegetation, or any part thereof.

(2) "Owner" means any person, partnership, corporation, unincorporated association, or other legal entity having any interest in any forest product, any land upon which a forest product is growing, or any land from which a forest product has been removed.

D. Whoever violates this Section where the value of the forest product is five hundred dollars or less shall be fined not more than one thousand dollars, or imprisoned for not more than one year, or both. When the value of the forest product is more than five hundred dollars, the violator shall be fined not more than five thousand dollars, or imprisoned with or without hard labor for not more than ten years, or both.

E. When the offender has violated this Section by a number of distinct acts, the aggregate of the amount of the forest products involved shall determine the grade of the offense.

(Chgd. by Acts 1997 No. 978, §1, eff. 8/15/97.)

§212. Forest products, false statement prohibited; penalty.

A. No person, in the course of a sale, attempted sale, delivery, or other completed or attempted transaction involving forest products, shall willfully or knowingly make a false statement or cause a false statement to be made with regard to ownership of the forest products, with regard to ownership of the land where the forest products were harvested, or with regard to location of the land where the forest products were harvested.

B. Whoever violates this Section shall be fined not more than one thousand dollars or imprisoned for not more than one year, or both.

(Chgd. by Acts 1997 No. 108, §1, eff. 8/15/97.)

§213. False packing of cotton bales and other agricultural products; penalty.

The false packing of cotton bales or other agricultural products is the packing of a bale or bales of cotton or other agricultural products in such manner as is calculated to deceive persons with regard to quantity, weight, or quality of the product therein contained, whether said false packing of cotton bales or other agricultural products be accompanied by the wetting of the product packed, or by concealing in the interior of the packed product another substance, or by plating the product by concealing in the interior thereof material inferior in grade or quality to that on the exterior thereof, or by any other means.

Whoever commits the crime of false packing of cotton bales or other agricultural products shall be punished, for the first offense, by a fine of five hundred dollars, or imprisoned for not less than sixty days nor more than six months, or both. For any offense beyond the first, the offender shall be punished by a fine of one thousand dollars, or imprisoned for not less than sixty days nor more than six months, or both.

§214. Fishing or hunting contest fraud.

A. The crime of fishing or hunting contest fraud is the act of any person, who, with the intent to defraud, knowingly makes a false representation in an effort to win any prize awarded in any fishing or hunting contest.

B. When the most valuable prize offered in the contest amounts to a value of less than one hundred dollars, the offender shall be fined not more than five hundred dollars, imprisoned for not more than six months, or both.

C. When the most valuable prize offered in the contest amounts to a value of one hundred dollars or more, the offender shall be fined not more than three thousand dollars, imprisoned, with or without hard labor, for not more than one year, or both.

§217. Purchase or sale of seafoods prohibited under certain conditions; penalties.

A. It shall be unlawful for any person:

(1) Who is engaged commercially in catching or taking fish, shrimp, oysters, or other seafood in a joint adventure or other undertaking whereby he receives a percentage of the proceeds of the sale of the catch, or a share of the catch itself, to sell or offer for sale any of such products, obtained in the joint adventure, except as provided for and in accordance with the terms and conditions of such joint adventure, without the express or implied consent of his co-adventurer or co-adventurers, or

(2) Who is employed on a salary or any other basis in the commercial catching or taking of fish, shrimp, oysters, or other seafood, to sell or offer for sale such products without the express or implied consent of his employer, or

(3) To purchase any fish, shrimp, oysters, or other seafood, knowing it is offered for sale in violation of Paragraph (1) or (2) of this Subsection.

B. Any person who violates any provision of this Section shall be, for the first offense, fined not less than one hundred dollars nor more than two hundred dollars and, for the second and subsequent offenses, shall be fined not less than five hundred dollars nor more than two thousand dollars, or be sentenced to serve not less than five days nor more than six months in the parish jail, or shall be punished by both such fine and imprisonment.

§218. Seafood sales and purchases; commercial license required of seller; penalties.

A. It shall be unlawful for any person, firm, or corporation to offer to sell or to sell any shrimp, oyster, fish, or other seafood without having first obtained a valid commercial fishing, retail, or wholesale license as provided in Subpart A of Part VII of Chapter 1 of Title 56 of the Louisiana Revised Statutes of 1950*. It shall be unlawful for any person, firm, or corporation, including any restaurant or retail establishment, to purchase any shrimp, oyster, fish, or other seafood from any person who does not possess a valid commercial fishing, retail, or wholesale license lawfully issued in his name or his employer's name as provided in the above-referenced Subpart A. The commercial fishing license required herein shall be one which authorizes the bearer to sell his catch. Such license or a copy thereof shall be in the possession of the seller and conspicuously displayed at all times when transacting any sale.
**R.S. 56:311 et seq.*

B. The provisions of this Section shall be enforceable by all law enforcement agencies throughout the state, in addition to agents of the Department of Wildlife and Fisheries and including but not limited to law enforcement officers of local governmental subdivisions.

C. (1) The following penalties shall be imposed for violation of the provisions of Subsection A of this Section:

(a) For the first offense, the fine shall be not less than five hundred dollars nor more than seven hundred fifty dollars, or imprisonment for not more than one hundred twenty days, or both.

(b) For the second offense, the fine shall be not less than seven hundred fifty dollars nor more than three thousand dollars and imprisonment for not less than ninety days nor more than one hundred eighty days.

(c) For the third offense, the fine shall be not less than one thousand dollars nor more than five thousand dollars and imprisonment for not less than one hundred eighty days nor more than two years.

(2) The above penalties in all cases shall include forfeiture of anything seized in connection with the violation and may include revocation of any applicable fishing, retail, or wholesale license under which the violation occurred for the period for which it is issued.

§219. Removal of building or structure from immovable property subject to a conventional mortgage or vendor's privilege.

Any person who wilfully or knowingly removes from any immovable property subject to a conventional mortgage or vendor's privilege affecting the immovable property, any building or other structure, or any part of a building or other structure, or any item which was so attached to or connected with any such building or structure as to become subject to a conventional mortgage or vendor's privilege affecting the immovable property at the time of the execution of the mortgage or act creating the vendor's privilege, with intent to defraud and without first obtaining the written consent of all holders of conventional mortgages or vendor's privileges affecting the immovable property shall be guilty of a misdemeanor and, upon conviction, shall be fined not more than two thousand dollars, or imprisoned for not more than one (1) year, or both, at the discretion of the Court.

§220. Rented or leased motor vehicles; obtaining by false representation, etc.; failure to return; defenses; penalties.

A. If any person rents or leases a motor vehicle and obtains or retains possession of the motor vehicle by means of any false or fraudulent representation including but not limited to a false representation as to his name, residence, employment, or operator's license, or by means of fraudulent concealment, or false pretense or personation, or trick, artifice, or device; or, if the person with fraudulent intent willfully refuses to return the leased vehicle to the lessor after the expiration of the lease term as stated in the lease contract, the person shall be guilty of a felony and upon conviction thereof shall be subject to the penalty provided for in Subsection B of this Section. Except as provided in Subsection D, the offender's failure to return or surrender the motor vehicle within seven calendar days after notice to make such return or surrender has been sent by certified mail to the offender's last known address shall be presumptive evidence of his intent to defraud and the lessor may report to any law enforcement agency that the rented or leased motor vehicle has been stolen.

B. Any person found guilty of violating the provisions of this Section shall be fined not more than five hundred dollars or imprisoned not more than five years with or without hard labor, or both.

C. It shall be a complete defense to any civil action arising out of or involving the arrest or detention of any person renting or leasing a motor vehicle that any representation made by him in obtaining or retaining possession of the vehicle is contrary to the fact.

D. It shall be a complete defense to any civil action arising out of or involving the arrest or detention of any person, upon whom such demand was personally made or personally served, that he failed to return the vehicle to the place specified in the rental agreement within such seventy-two hour period.

(Chgd. by Acts 1997 No. 790, §1, eff. 8/15/97.)

§220.1. Leased movables; obtaining by false representation; failure to return or surrender; penalties; restitution.

A. No person leasing a movable shall obtain or retain possession of the movable by:

(1) Making a false statement or false representation of a material fact, where such false statement or false representation is made with the intent to obtain or retain possession of the movable; or

(2) Intentionally failing to return or surrender the movable when obligated under the terms of the lease, or after the expiration or cancellation of the lease. The lessee's failure to return or surrender the movable within fifteen calendar days or the number of days for which the movable was leased, whichever is less, after the date written notice requesting return or surrender of the movable was delivered or tendered to the lessee's last known address shall be presumptive evidence that the failure to return or surrender the movable was intentional. In order for the presumption to arise, the written notice must be sent by the lessor or the district attorney by means of registered or certified mail.

B. Whoever violates the provisions of this Section shall be fined not more than five hundred dollars, or imprisoned for not more than six months, or both.

C. When a defendant is convicted of violating Paragraph A(2) and the notice requirements of Paragraph A(2) are complied with, a court shall order, in addition to or in lieu of the penalty in Subsection B, upon proof established by a preponderance of the evidence, that defendant pay restitution to the victim for all acknowledged appropriate fees assessed for intentional failure to return or surrender the leased movable after the agreed rental period or lease term or in the amount of lost profit resulting from the defendant's failure to return or surrender the movable as stated under the terms of the lease, or after the expiration or cancellation of the lease. The court may permit the prosecuting attorney to present evidence of the amount of the victim's lost profits either at the trial of the matter or at the sentencing of the defendant.

D. The offender's failure to return or surrender a video cassette film or tape that has been rented from a facility which rents video cassette films or tapes within thirty calendar days after notice to make such return or surrender has been sent by certified mail to the offender's last known address shall be presumptive evidence of his intent to defraud and the lessor may report to any law enforcement agency that the rented video cassette film or tape has been stolen.

(Added by Acts 1992 No. 981, §1; chgd. by Acts 1997 No. 790, §1, eff. 8/15/97.)

§221. Avoiding payment for telecommunications services, cable television services, or multipoint distribution system service.

A. Avoidance of payment for telecommunication, cable television, or multipoint distribution system services is the avoidance, attempt to avoid, or the causing of another person to avoid, the lawful charges, in whole or in part, for any telephone, telegraph, cable, or multipoint distribution system service utilized or for the transmission of a message, signal, or other communication over telephone, telegraph, cable facilities, or multipoint distribution system:

(1) By the use of a code, prearranged scheme, or other similar strategem* or device whereby such person, in effect, sends or receives information; or

**So in original. Probably should be "stratagem".*

(2) By rearranging, tampering or interfering with, or making unauthorized connection with any facilities or equipment of a telephone or telegraph company, whether physically, inductively, acoustically, or otherwise; or

(3) By intercepting and decoding a transmission by a multipoint distribution system without the authorization of the provider of the service, the person intentionally or knowingly attaches to, causes to be attached to, or incorporates in a television set, video tape recorder, or other equipment designed to receive a television transmission a device that intercepts and decodes the transmission.

(4) By the use of any other fraudulent means, method, trick, or device.

B. (1) On a first conviction, the offender shall be fined not more than five hundred dollars, or imprisoned for not more than six months, or both.

(2) On a second conviction, the offender shall be fined not more than five thousand dollars, or imprisoned, with or without hard labor, for not more than five years, or both.

C. Nothing herein shall prohibit the use of earth station receivers to receive satellite communications.

§222. Possession, manufacture, sale or transfer of devices for avoidance of payment for telecommunications services or related offenses; seizure of devices.

A. It shall be unlawful for any person knowingly to:

(1) Make or possess any instrument, apparatus, equipment or device designed, adapted or which can be used

(a) For commission of a crime in violation of R.S. 14:67, R.S. 14:67.3 or R.S. 14:221 or

(b) To conceal, or to assist another to conceal, from any supplier of telecommunications services or from any lawful authority the existence or place of origin or destination of any telecommunications:

(2) Sell, give, transport, or otherwise transfer to another, or offer or advertise to sell, give, or otherwise transfer, any instrument, apparatus, equipment, or device described in (1) above, or plans or instructions for making or assembling the same; under circumstances evincing an intent to use or employ such instrument, apparatus, equipment, or device, or to allow the same to be used or employed, for a purpose described in (1)(a) or (1)(b) above, or knowing or having reason to believe that the same is intended to be so used, or that the aforesaid plans or instructions are intended to be used for making or assembling such instrument, apparatus, equipment, or device.

B. Whoever violates any provision of this Section shall, on first conviction, be fined not more than one thousand dollars, or imprisoned for not more than six months, or both.

On a second conviction, the offender shall be fined not more than two thousand dollars, or imprisoned for not more than one year, or both.

C. Any such instrument, apparatus, equipment, device or plans or instructions therefor, may be seized by court order under a search warrant or incident to a lawful arrest; and upon the conviction of any person for a violation of any provision of this Section, or R.S. 14:67, R.S. 14:67.3 or R.S. 14:221, such instrument, apparatus, equipment, device, plans or instructions shall either be destroyed as contraband by the sheriff of the parish in which such person was convicted or turned over to the telephone company in whose territory such instrument, apparatus, equipment, device, plans or instructions were seized.

D. The provisions of this Section shall not apply to privately owned communications equipment which is not connected with, or does not use the equipment or facilities of a telecommunications supplier regulated by a duly constituted governmental authority; nor shall the provisions of this Section apply to privately owned communications equipment which is connected with or does use the equipment or facilities of such telecommunications supplier when such connection or use is lawful and in accord with the tariffs of such supplier or is made with the consent of such supplier.

E. Nothing herein shall apply to public service and emergency communications performed by holders of valid Federal Communications Commission radio amateur licenses without charge on the part of such licensees; provided that nothing herein shall excuse any person from compliance with lawful tariffs or any telecommunications company.

F. Nothing herein shall apply to the sale of premises reception equipment by other than an operating cable company, so long as the equipment sold is not capable of descrambling cable signals.

G. Nothing herein shall be construed to allow, permit, or encourage the unauthorized interception of cable services.

§222.1. Unauthorized interception of cable television services.

A. No person shall knowingly:

(1) Connect, attach, modify, alter, remove, or tamper with, any equipment, device, or television or radio component for the purpose of intercepting or receiving without the authorization of a cable television system any program or other service carried by that system; or

(2) Manufacture, sell, transfer, rent, or distribute any electronic equipment, or a kit for making such equipment, designed specifically to decode or descramble any programming or other services carried by a cable television system licensed and franchised in accordance with federal and state law.

B. Whoever violates the provisions of Subsection A(1) of this Section shall:

(1) On first offense, be fined not more than one hundred dollars; and

(2) On second or subsequent offense, be fined not more than five hundred dollars, or imprisoned for not more than sixty days, or both.

C. Whoever violates the provisions of Subsection A(2) of this Section shall:

(1) On first offense, be fined not more than five hundred dollars; and

(2) On second or subsequent offense, be fined not more than one thousand dollars, be imprisoned for not more than sixty days, or both.

D. The provisions of this Section shall not apply to cable television companies licensed and franchised in accordance with federal and state law, or multipoint distribution systems licensed in accordance with federal law, or to the use of earth station receivers to receive satellite communications.

§222.2. Cellular telephone counterfeiting.

A. For purposes of this Section:

(1) "Cellular telephone" means a communication device containing a unique electronic serial number that is programmed into its computer chip by its manufacturer and the operation of which is dependent on the transmission of that electronic serial number along with a mobile identification number, which is assigned by the cellular telephone carrier, in the form of radio signals through cell sites and mobile switching stations.

(2) "Cloned cellular telephone" or "counterfeit cellular telephone" means a cellular telephone the electronic serial number of which has been altered from the electronic serial number that was programmed in the phone by the manufacturer.

(3) "Cloning paraphernalia" means materials that, when possessed in combination, are necessary for and capable of the creation of a cloned cellular telephone. These materials include scanners to intercept the electronic serial number and mobile identification number, cellular telephones, cables, EPROM chips, EPROM burners, software for programming the

microchip of the cloned cellular telephone with a false electronic serial number and mobile identification number combination, a computer containing such software, and lists of electronic serial number and mobile identification number combinations.

(4) "Electronic serial number" means the unique numerical algorithm that is programmed into the microchip of each cellular telephone by the manufacturer and is vital to the successful operation and billing of the telephone.

(5) "Intercept" means to electronically capture, record, reveal, or otherwise access the signals emitted or received during the operation of a cellular telephone without the consent of the sender or receiver thereof, by means of any instrument, device, or equipment.

(6) "Mobile identification number" means the cellular telephone number assigned to the cellular telephone by the cellular telephone carrier.

(7) "Possess" means to have physical possession or otherwise to exercise dominion or control over tangible property.

B. It is unlawful for any person to knowingly possess a cloned cellular telephone. Any person found guilty of knowingly possessing a cloned cellular telephone shall be fined not more than two thousand dollars or imprisoned with or without hard labor for not more than two years, or both.

C. It is unlawful for any person to knowingly sell a cloned cellular telephone. Any person found guilty of knowingly selling a cloned cellular telephone shall be fined not more than five thousand dollars or imprisoned with or without hard labor for not less than two years nor more than five years, or both.

D. It is unlawful for any person to knowingly possess an instrument capable of intercepting electronic serial number and mobile identification number combinations or other cloning paraphernalia under circumstances evidencing an intent to clone a cellular telephone. Any person violating this provision shall be fined not more than seven thousand five hundred dollars and imprisoned with or without hard labor for not less than five years nor more than seven years.

E. On a second and subsequent conviction of any of the offenses provided for in this Section, the offender shall be fined not less than ten thousand dollars nor more than fifteen thousand dollars and imprisoned with or without hard labor for not more than ten years.

F. Nothing herein shall make unlawful the possession or use of cloning paraphernalia, a cloned cellular telephone, or any intercept by a law enforcement officer or persons acting pursuant to a lawful court order in the course of a criminal investigation.

(Added by Acts 1997 No. 1014, §1, eff. 8/15/97.)

§223. Sound reproductions without consent prohibited.

Any person who, for commercial gain, knowingly transfers or causes to be transferred, sells, distributes, circulates or causes to be sold, distributed or circulated, directly or indirectly, or possesses for such purposes, any sounds recorded on any article for a consideration without the consent of the owner within the State of Louisiana shall be guilty of a criminal offense and punished as provided in R.S. 14:223.3. This Section applies only to sound recordings initially fixed prior to February 15, 1972, and does not apply to motion pictures or other audiovisual works. *(Chgd. by Acts 1990 No. 122, §1, eff. 9/7/90.)*

§223.1. Terms defined.

The following terms have the meanings indicated:

(1) As used in R.S. 14:223 and 223.6,* "owner" means the person who owns the sounds fixed in the master phonograph record, master disc, master tape, master film, master audio or video cassette, or other device now known or later developed, used for reproducing recorded sounds or images on phonograph records, discs, tapes, films, video cassettes, or other articles or media on which sound is or may be recorded and from which the transferred recorded sounds are directly or indirectly derived. As used in R.S. 14:223.5, "owner" means the person who owns the sounds and images or the rights to authorize the recording of the sounds or images of any performance not fixed in a tangible medium of expression.

**So in original.*

(2) "Person" means any individual, partnership, corporation, association, or any other legal entity.

(3) "Recording" and "article" mean any original phonograph record, disc, tape, audio or visual cassette, wire, film, or other medium known or later developed on which sounds or images are recorded or otherwise stored, or any copy or reproduction which duplicates, in whole or in part, the original.

Printed in the U.S.A. ZL

(4) "Audiovisual work" means a series of related images intended to be shown through the use of mechanical or electronic devices, together with accompanying sounds, if any.

(5) "Motion picture" means an audiovisual work consisting of a series of images which, when shown in succession, impart an impression of motion together with accompanying sounds, if any.

(6) "Phonorecord" means a material object in which sounds other than those accompanying a motion picture or other audiovisual work are fixed by any method now known or later developed, and from which the sounds can be perceived, reproduced, or otherwise communicated directly or with the aid of a machine or device. Phonorecord includes the material object in which the sound is first fixed.

(7) "Counterfeit label" means an identifying label or container that appears to be genuine but is not.

(Chgd. by Acts 1990 No. 122, §1, eff. 9/7/90.)

§223.2. Exceptions.

R.S. 14:223 through 223.8 shall not apply to any person engaged in radio or television broadcasting who transfers or causes to be transferred any such sounds intended for or in connection with broadcast transmissions or related uses or for archival purposes. *(Chgd. by Acts 1990 No. 122, §1, eff. 9/7/90.)*

§223.3. Penalties.

Any person, any member of a partnership, or any officer or employee of a corporation found guilty of violating any provision of R.S. 14:223 through 223.8 shall be punished as follows:

(1) For the first offense of a violation of R.S. 14:223, 223.5, or 223.6 involving fewer than one thousand phonorecords; a violation of R.S. 14:223.7 involving fewer than one thousand counterfeit labels affixed or designed to be affixed to phonorecords; a violation of R.S. 14:223.6 involving fewer than one hundred articles upon which motion pictures or other audiovisual words are recorded; or a violation of R.S. 14:223.7 involving fewer than one hundred counterfeit labels affixed or designed to be affixed to articles upon which motion pictures or other audiovisual works are or are to be recorded, the offender shall be punished by a fine of not more than five thousand dollars, or by imprisonment not exceeding six months, or both.

(2) For the first offense of a violation of R.S. 14:223.8, the offender shall be punished by a fine not exceeding twenty-five thousand dollars, or by imprisonment for not more than two years with or without hard labor, or both.

(3) For any offense of a violation of R.S. 14:223, 223.5, or 223.6 involving one thousand or more phonorecords; a violation of R.S. 14:223.7 involving one thousand or more counterfeit labels affixed or designed to be affixed to phonorecords; a violation of R.S. 14:223.6 involving one hundred or more articles upon which motion pictures or other audiovisual works are recorded; or a violation of R.S. 14:223.7 involving one hundred or more counterfeit labels affixed or designed to be affixed to articles upon which motion pictures or other audiovisual works are or are to be recorded, the offender shall be punished by a fine not exceeding fifty thousand dollars, or by imprisonment for not more than five years with or without hard labor, or both.

(4) For the second and subsequent violations of R.S. 14:223 through 223.8, the offender shall be punished by a fine not exceeding one hundred thousand dollars, or by imprisonment for not less than two years nor more than five years with or without hard labor, or both.

(5) Whenever any person is convicted of any violation of R.S. 14:223 through 223.8, the court in its judgment of conviction may, in addition to any other penalty, order the forfeiture and destruction or other disposition of all unlawful recordings, counterfeit labels, and all implements, devices, and equipment used or intended to be used in the manufacture of the unlawful recordings or counterfeit labels. The court may enter an order preserving such recordings, labels, implements, devices, or equipment as evidence for use in other cases or pending the final determination of an appeal.

(Chgd. by Acts 1990 No. 122, §1, eff. 9/7/90.)

§223.4. Civil remedies preserved.

Nothing in R.S. 14:223 through 223.8 shall be construed to abrogate or modify any civil action for any of the acts referred to herein. *(Chgd. by Acts 1990 No. 122, §1, eff. 9/7/90.)*

§223.5. Recording of performances without consent prohibited.

Any person who, without the consent of the owner and for commercial gain, knowingly transfers or causes to be transferred to any article, or sells, distributes, circulates, or causes to be sold, distributed, or circulated, directly or indirectly, or possesses for such purposes, a recording of any performance whether live before an audience or transmitted by wire or through the air by radio or television with intent to sell or cause to be sold or used to promote the sale of any article or product within the state of Louisiana shall be guilty of a criminal offense and punished as provided in R.S. 14:223.3. *(Added by Acts 1990 No. 122, §1, eff. 9/7/90.)*

§223.6. Rental or sale of improperly labeled articles prohibited.

Any person who advertises, offers for rental, sale, resale, distribution, or circulation, or rents, sells, resells, distributes, or circulates, or causes to be sold, resold, distributed, or circulated, or possesses for such purposes, any recording the cover, label, or jacket of which fails to conspicuously display thereon in clearly readable print, the true name and address of the manufacturer and the name of any actual performer or group thereof shall be guilty of a criminal offense and punished as provided in R.S. 14:223.3. *(Added by Acts 1990 No. 122, §1, eff. 9/7/90.)*

§223.7. Counterfeiting or possessing counterfeit labels prohibited.

Any person who has in his possession for any illegal purpose or who makes, sells, issues, distributes, circulates, or puts in circulation a counterfeit label affixed or designed to be affixed to a recording within the state of Louisiana shall be guilty of a criminal offense and punished as provided in R.S. 14:223.3. *(Added by Acts 1990 No. 122, §1, eff. 9/7/90.)*

§223.8. Possessing of tools and equipment used for manufacturing unauthorized sound recordings prohibited.

Any person who, for any of the purposes mentioned in R.S. 14:223 through 223.7, possesses or controls any electronic, mechanical, or other device for manufacturing or reproducing recordings or counterfeit labels, or who possesses or controls any tool, implement, instrument, or thing, used, fitted, or intended to be used for such purposes within the state of Louisiana shall be guilty of a criminal offense and punished as provided in R.S. 14:223.3. *(Added by Acts 1990 No. 122, §1, eff. 9/7/90.)*

§224. Transportation of water from St. Tammany Parish prohibited; penalties.

A. No person, firm, corporation, public body, quasi-public body or political subdivision shall transport underground water or surface water from the parish of St. Tammany to any person, firm, corporation, municipality or city located outside of said parish; provided, however, that the provisions of this section shall not be construed to prohibit any person, firm or corporation engaged in the business of selling or furnishing to consumers bottled water from wells which are situated within the said parish.

B. Any violation of this law shall be punishable by a fine of not more than five thousand dollars or by a jail sentence of not more than six months, and each day of continued violation shall constitute a separate offense.

§225. Institutional vandalism.

A. A person commits the crime of institutional vandalism by knowingly vandalizing, defacing, or otherwise damaging the following:

(1) Any church, synagogue, or other building, structure, or place used for religious worship or other religious purpose.

(2) Any cemetery, mortuary, or other facility used for the purpose of burial or memorializing the dead.

(3) Any school, educational facility, or community center.

(4) The grounds adjacent to and owned or rented by any institution, facility, building, structure, or place described in Paragraphs (1), (2) or (3) above.

(5) Any personal property contained in any institution, facility, building, structure, or place described in Paragraphs (1), (2), or (3) above.

(6) Any building owned by the United States, state of Louisiana, or a political subdivision of this state.

B. Institutional vandalism is punishable as follows:

(1) When the damage is less than five hundred dollars, the offender shall be fined not more than five hundred dollars, or imprisoned for not more than six months, or both.

(2) When the damage amounts to five hundred dollars but less than fifty thousand dollars, the offender shall be fined not more than one thousand dollars, or imprisoned, with or without hard labor, for not more than two years or both.

(3) When the damage amounts to fifty thousand dollars or more, the offender shall be fined not more than ten thousand dollars, or imprisoned, with or without hard labor, for not less than one nor more than ten years, or both.

C. In determining the amount of damage to or loss of property, damage includes the cost of repair or replacement of the property that was damaged or lost.

§226. Protection of owners of crayfish farms; penalties.

A. It shall be unlawful for any person, other than the owner thereof, to fish for or to take crayfish from any domestic crayfish farm, unless the express consent of the owner is first obtained.

B. A domestic crayfish farm for the purposes of this section means an earthen reservoir constructed so as to prevent the free ingress and egress of crayfish from public waters and on which the owner of private property cultivates, grows, harvests and markets domesticated crayfish that are spawned, grown, cultivated, managed, harvested and marketed on an annual, biennial or short term basis in privately owned waters which do not form a part of natural streams or lakes.

C. Whoever violates Subsection (A) of this section shall, upon conviction thereof, be imprisoned for not more than one year or be subject to a fine of not less than fifty dollars nor more than three hundred dollars, or both.

§227. Identification number, personal property, alteration or removal prohibited.

A. No person shall cover, remove, deface, alter, or destroy the manufacturer's number or any other distinguishing number or identification mark on any pipeline or oil and gas equipment for the purpose of concealing or misrepresenting its identity; nor shall any person knowingly buy, sell, receive, dispose of, conceal, or knowingly have in his possession any pipeline or oil and gas equipment from or on which the manufacturer's number or any other distinguishing number or identification mark has been covered, removed, defaced, altered, or destroyed, for the purpose of concealing or misrepresenting its identity.

B. The following definitions shall apply for the purpose of this Section, unless the context clearly requires otherwise:

(1) "Pipeline equipment" means all pipe, fittings, pumps, telephone and telegraph lines, and all other material and equipment used or intended to be used as part of or incident to the construction, maintenance, and operation of a pipeline for the transportation of oil, gas, water, or other liquid or gaseous substance.

(2) "Oil and gas equipment" means equipment and materials that are part of or incident to the development, maintenance, and operation of oil and gas properties, and includes equipment and materials that are part of or incident to the construction, maintenance, and operation of oil and gas wells, oil and gas leases, gasoline plants, and refineries.

C. Whoever violates this Section shall be fined not more than one thousand dollars or imprisoned for not more than twelve months, or both; and in default of fine, shall be imprisoned for not more than twelve additional months.

§228. Interference with animal research facilities or animal management facilities.

A. It shall be unlawful for any person:

(1) To intentionally release, steal, or otherwise cause the loss of any animal from an animal research facility or an animal management facility.

(2) To damage, vandalize, or steal any property from or on an animal research facility or an animal management facility.

(3) To obtain access to an animal research facility or an animal management facility by false pretenses for the purpose of performing acts described in Paragraphs (1) and (2) of this Subsection.

(4) To break and enter into any animal research facility or animal management facility with the intent to destroy, alter, duplicate, or obtain unauthorized possession of records, data, materials, equipment, or animals.

(5) To enter or remain on an animal research facility or an animal management facility with the intent to commit an act prohibited in Paragraphs (1) and (2) of this Subsection.

(6) To knowingly obtain or exert unauthorized control, by theft or deception, over records, data, material, equipment, or animals of any animal research facility or animal management facility for the purpose of depriving the legal owner of an animal research facility or animal management facility of records, material, data, equipment, or animals or for the purpose of using, concealing, abandoning, or destroying such records, material, data, equipment, or animals.

(7) To possess or use records, material, data, equipment, or animals or in any way to copy or reproduce records or data of an animal research facility or animal management facility, knowing or reasonably believing such records, material, data, equipment, or animals to have been obtained by theft or deception or without authorization of that facility.

B. (1) "Animal research facility" as used herein means that portion of the premises of an accredited institution of higher learning located within the state that is engaged in legitimate scientific, medical, or veterinary medicine research involving the use of animals.

(2) "Animal management facility" as used herein means that portion of any vehicle, building, structure, or premises, where an animal is kept, handled, housed, exhibited, bred, or offered for sale, and any agricultural trade association properties. Animal management facility also means that portion of any vehicle, building, structure, premises, property, or equipment used in the conduction of authorized wildlife management practices, including but not limited to the control of animals that damage property, natural resources, or human health and safety.

C. Whoever violates any provision of this Section shall be fined not more than five thousand dollars or imprisoned, with or without hard labor, for not more than one year, or both.

(Chgd. by Acts 1990 No. 445, §1, eff. 9/7/90.)

§228.1. Unauthorized release of certain animals, birds, or aquatic species.

A. It shall be unlawful for any person to intentionally and without permission, release any animal, bird, or aquatic species which has been lawfully confined for agriculture, science, research, commerce, public propagation, protective custody, or education.

B. Whoever violates the provisions of this Section shall be fined not more than one thousand dollars, imprisoned for not more than one year, or both.

(Added by Acts 1990 No. 205, §2, eff. 9/7/90.)

§229. Illegal use of counterfeit trademark; penalties.

A. No person shall knowingly sell or otherwise transfer for compensation anything of value having a counterfeit trademark.

B. For the purposes of this Section:

(1) "Person" shall include an individual, corporation, partnership, association, or other body of persons, whether incorporated or not.

(2) "Counterfeit trademark" shall mean a false trademark that is identical to or substantially indistinguishable from:

(a) A genuine trademark registered on the principal register in the United States Patent and Trademark Office and used or intended for use on or in connection with goods or services; or

(b) A genuine trademark specifically protected by any state or federal statute.

C. Whoever violates the provisions of this Section shall be fined not more than ten thousand dollars, or be imprisoned with or without hard labor for not more than five years, or both.

D. In lieu of a fine otherwise authorized by law, any person convicted of engaging in conduct in violation of the provisions of this Section through which said person derived pecuniary value, or by which said person caused personal injury or property damage or other loss, may be sentenced to pay a fine that does not exceed three times the gross value gained or three times the gross loss caused, whichever is greater. The court shall hold a hearing to determine the amount of the fine authorized by this Subsection.

§230. Money laundering; transactions involving proceeds of criminal activity.

A. As used in this Section:

(1) "Criminal activity" means any offense, including conspiracy and attempt to commit the offense, that is classified as a felony under the laws of this state or the United States or that is punishable by confinement for more than one year under the laws of another state.

(2) "Funds" means any of the following:

(a) Coin or paper money of the United States or any other country that is designated as legal tender and that circulates and is customarily used and accepted as a medium of exchange in the country of issue.

(b) United States silver certificates, United States Treasury notes, and Federal Reserve System notes.

(c) Official foreign bank notes that are customarily used and accepted as a medium of exchange in a foreign country and foreign bank drafts.

(3) "Peace officer" has the same meaning as in R.S. 40:2402(1)(a).

(4) "Proceeds" means funds acquired or derived directly or indirectly from or produced or realized through an act.

B. It is unlawful for any person knowingly to do any of the following:

(1) Conduct, supervise, or facilitate a financial transaction involving proceeds known to be derived from criminal activity, when the transaction is designed in whole or in part to conceal or disguise the nature, location, source, ownership, or the control of proceeds known to be derived from such violation or to avoid a transaction reporting requirement under state or federal law.

(2) Give, sell, transfer, trade, invest, conceal, transport, maintain an interest in, or otherwise make available anything of value known to be for the purpose of committing or furthering the commission of any criminal activity.

(3) Direct, plan, organize, initiate, finance, manage, supervise, or facilitate the transportation or transfer of proceeds known to be derived from any violation of criminal activity.

(4) Receive or acquire proceeds derived from any violation of criminal activity, or knowingly or intentionally engage in any transaction that the person knows involves proceeds from any such violations.

(5) Acquire or maintain an interest in, receive, conceal, possess, transfer, or transport the proceeds of criminal activity.

(6) Invest, expend, or receive, or offer to invest, expend, or receive, the proceeds of criminal activity.

C. It is a defense to prosecution under this Section that the person acted with intent to facilitate the lawful seizure, forfeiture, or disposition of funds or other legitimate law enforcement purpose pursuant to the laws of this state or the United States.

D. It is a defense to prosecution under this Section that the transaction was necessary to preserve a person's right to representation as guaranteed by the Sixth Amendment of the Constitution of the United States and by Article I, Section 13 of the Constitution of Louisiana or that the funds were received as bona fide legal fees by a licensed attorney and, at the time of their receipt, the attorney did not have actual knowledge that the funds were derived from criminal activity.

E. (1) Whoever violates the provisions of this Section, if the value of the funds is less than three thousand dollars, may be imprisoned for not more than six months or fined not more than one thousand dollars, or both.

(2) Whoever violates the provisions of this Section, if the value of the funds is three thousand dollars or more but less than twenty thousand dollars, may be imprisoned with or without hard labor for not less than two years nor more than ten years and may be fined not more than ten thousand dollars.

(3) Whoever violates the provisions of this Section, if the value of the funds is twenty thousand dollars or more but less than one hundred thousand dollars, shall be imprisoned at hard labor for not less than two years nor more than twenty years and may be fined not more than twenty thousand dollars.

(4) Whoever violates the provisions of this Section, if the value of the funds is one hundred thousand dollars or more, shall be imprisoned at hard labor for not less than five years nor more than ninety-nine years and may be fined not more than fifty thousand dollars.
(Added by Acts 1994 Third Ex. Sess. No. 78, §1, eff. 8/27/94.)

PART II. OFFENSES AFFECTING PUBLIC MORALS

§281. Disorderly place, maintaining of prohibited; penalty.

No person shall maintain a place of public entertainment or a public resort or any place, room, or part of a building open to the public in such a manner as to disturb the public peace and quiet of the neighborhood, or in which lewd dancing is permitted, or in which lewd pictures are accessible to view.

Whoever violates this Section shall be fined not less than twenty-five dollars nor more than one hundred dollars or imprisoned for not less than thirty days nor more than ninety days, or both.

§282. Operation of places of prostitution prohibited; penalty.

No person shall maintain, operate, or knowingly own any place or any conveyance used for the purpose of lewdness, assignation, or prostitution, or shall rent or let any place or conveyance to any person with knowledge of or good or good reason to believe that the lessee intends to use the place or conveyance for the purpose of lewdness, assignation, or prostitution, or reside in, enter, or remain in any place for the purpose of lewdness, assignation, or prostitution.

Whoever violates or aids, abets, or participates in the violation of this Section shall be fined not less than twenty-five dollars nor more than five hundred dollars, imprisoned for not less than thirty days nor more than six months, or both.

§284. Peeping Tom; penalty.

No person shall perform such acts as will make him a "Peeping Tom" on or about the premises of another, or go upon the premises of another for the purpose of becoming a "Peeping Tom."

"Peeping Tom" as used in this Section means one who peeps through windows or doors, or other like places, situated on or about the premises of another for the purpose of spying upon or invading the privacy of persons spied upon without the consent of the persons spied upon. It is not a necessary element of this offense that the "Peeping Tom" be upon the premises of the person being spied upon.

Whoever violates this Section shall be fined not more than five hundred dollars, or imprisoned for not more than six months, or both.

§285. Telephone communications; improper language; harassment; penalty.

A. No person shall:

(1) Engage in or institute a telephone call, telephone conversation, or telephone conference, with another person, anonymously or otherwise, and therein use obscene, profane, vulgar, lewd, lascivious, or indecent language, or make any suggestion or proposal of an obscene nature or threaten any illegal or immoral act with the intent to coerce, intimidate, or harass another person.

(2) Make repeated telephone communications anonymously or otherwise in a manner reasonably expected to annoy, abuse, torment, harass, embarrass, or offend another whether or not conversation ensues.

(3) Make a telephone call and intentionally fail to hang up or disengage the connection.

(4) Engage in a telephone call, conference, or recorded communication by using obscene language, when by making a graphic description of a sexual act, and the offender knows or reasonably should know that such obscene or graphic language is directed to, or will be heard by, a minor. Lack of knowledge of age shall not constitute a defense.

(5) Knowingly permit any telephone under his control to be used for any purpose prohibited by this Section.

B. Any offense committed by use of a telephone as set forth in this Section shall be deemed to have been committed at either the place where the telephone call or calls originated or at the place where the telephone call or calls were received.

C. Whoever violates the provisions of this Section shall be fined not more than five hundred dollars, or imprisoned for not more than six months, or both.

D. Upon second or subsequent offenses, the offender shall be fined not more than five thousand dollars, or imprisoned with or without hard labor for not more than two years, or both.

§286. Sale of minor children; penalties.

A. Except as provided by law, it shall be unlawful for any person to sell or surrender a minor child to another person for money or anything of value, or to receive a minor child for such payment of money or anything of value.

B. (1) Nothing in this Section shall be construed to prohibit any person contemplating adopting a minor child, not yet born, from paying necessary, actual prenatal care and living expenses of the mother of the minor child adopted, nor of paying necessary, actual living and medical expenses of such mother or child for a reasonable period of time, not to exceed thirty days, after the child is born, nor of paying legal fees of the surrendering parent or parents in connection with a voluntary surrender.

(2) "Legal fees" as used herein shall include anything of value paid or received for rendering of legal services in connection with an act of voluntary surrender of a child for adoption and shall not include a broker's fee paid in connection with an act of voluntary surrender.

(3) "Broker's fees" as used herein shall include anything of value paid or received for the procurement, attempted procurement, or assistance in the procurement of a party to an act of voluntary surrender of a child for adoption.

C. None of the provisions of this Section shall apply to the fees charged by nonprofit adoption agencies licensed by the state of Louisiana.

D. A person convicted of violating any of the provisions of this Section shall be punished by a fine not to exceed five thousand dollars or imprisonment with or without hard labor for not more than five years, or both.

PART III. OFFENSES AFFECTING THE PUBLIC GENERALLY

§311. Discharging fire-works or explosives within one thousand feet of hospital prohibited; penalty.

No person shall shoot, discharge, explode, or cause to be shot, discharged or exploded any fire-crackers, fire-works or other explosives within one thousand feet of any hospital in Louisiana.

Whoever violates this Section shall be fined not more than one dollar or imprisoned for not more than one day, or both.

§312. Jumping from state bridge for publicity prohibited; penalty.

No person shall dive or jump off of any public bridge, constructed or owned by the state or any of its political subdivisions, where the object and purpose of the act is to gain publicity.

Whoever violates this Section shall be fined not more than twenty-five dollars, or imprisoned for not more than thirty days, or both.

§313. Masks or hoods, wearing in public places prohibited; penalty; exceptions; permit to conduct Mardi Gras festivities, how obtained.

No person shall use or wear in any public place of any character whatsoever, or in any open place in view thereof, a hood or mask, or anything in the nature of either, or any facial disguise of any kind or description, calculated to conceal or hide the identity of the person or to prevent his being readily recognized.

Whoever violates this Section shall be imprisoned for not less than six months nor more than three years.

This Section shall not apply:

(1) To activities of children on Hallowe'en, to persons participating in any public parade or exhibition of an educational, religious, or historical character given by any school, church, or public governing authority, or to persons in any private residence, club, or lodge room; or,

(2) To persons participating in masquerade balls or entertainments, to persons participating in carnival parades or exhibitions during the period of Mardi Gras festivities, to persons participating in the parades or exhibitions of minstrel troupes, circuses, or other dramatic or amusement shows, or to promiscuous masking on Mardi Gras which are duly authorized by the governing authorities of the municipality in which they are held or by the sheriff of the parish if held outside of an incorporated municipality.

All persons having charge or control of any of the festivities set forth in paragraph (2) of this Section shall, in order to bring the persons participating therein within the exceptions contained in paragraph (2), make written application for and shall obtain in advance of the festivities from the mayor of the city, town, or village in which the festivities are to be held, or when the festivities are to be held outside of an incorporated city, town, or village, from the sheriff of the parish, a written permit to conduct the festivities. A general public proclamation by the mayor or sheriff authorizing the festivities shall be equivalent to an application and permit.

§314. Mississippi River, making unauthorized cut-offs prohibited; penalty.

No person shall make or cause to be made any cut-off in the Mississippi River without authority of law.

Whoever violates this Section shall be fined not less than one hundred dollars nor more than one thousand dollars and imprisoned for not less than one week nor more than twelve months.

§315. Mississippi River, stopping outlets or bayous prohibited; reopening; penalty.

No person shall stop any outlet or natural bayou of the Mississippi River. If any outlet or natural bayou is closed the opening of it may be ordered by the state engineer at any time.

Whoever violates this Section shall be fined not less than one thousand dollars nor more than ten thousand dollars and shall be liable for all expenses necessary for the reopening of the bayou or outlet.

This Section shall not apply to bayous already closed, or that may be hereafter opened by crevasses.

§316. Naming public buildings, etc., in honor of living person prohibited; removal and change of name; penalty.

No public building, public bridge, public park, public fish or game preserve, or public wildlife refuge built, constructed, and maintained in whole or in part with public funds and title to which stands in the name of the state or any of its subdivisions or in the name of any institution receiving its support in whole or in part from the state shall be named in honor of any living person.

The officer, officers, board, or commissioner in charge of a public building, public park, public fish or game preserve, or public wildlife refuge named in honor of any person who is still living shall change the name and destroy, deface, or remove all plaques, signs, or other evidence of the old name appearing on the building, bridge, park, preserve, or refuge.

Whoever violates this Section or fails to perform the duties imposed by this Section shall be fined not less than one hundred dollars nor more than two hundred dollars and, in default of fine, imprisoned for not less than thirty days nor more than sixty days.

§318. Sale of fireworks containing white or yellow phosphorous prohibited; penalty.

No person shall sell, exchange, barter, or in any other manner dispose of any friction firework containing white or yellow phosphorus and explosives, which makes a noise and resembles a piece of candy in size and general appearance.

Whoever violates this Section shall be fined not less than fifty dollars or imprisoned for not more than sixty days, or both.

§319. Sale of toy pistols prohibited; penalty; exceptions.

No person shall sell or offer to sell any toy pistol constructed so as to accommodate blank powder cartridges, blank cartridges, or shells used in firing or discharging toy pistols.

Whoever violates this Section shall be fined not less than ten dollars nor more than fifty dollars, or imprisoned for not more than ten days, or both.

Paper cap pistols and other toy pistols not constructed so as to accommodate blank powder cartridges or shells are not included within the provisions of this Section.

§320. Telegrams, divulging or obtaining knowledge of contents prohibited; penalty.

No person shall wrongfully obtain, or attempt to obtain, any knowledge of a private telegraphic message by connivance with a clerk, operator, messenger or other employee of a telegraph company. No clerk, operator, messenger or other employee shall use, or suffer or permit to be used, or wilfully divulge to anyone but the person to whom it was addressed or his agent, or a duly authorized United States Government official or under due process of any court of record, the contents of a telegraphic message or dispatch intrusted to him for transmission or delivery, or the nature thereof.

Whoever violates this Section shall be fined not more than two hundred and fifty dollars or imprisoned for not more than four months, or both.

§321. Unauthorized signals to persons in charge of locomotives, etc., prohibited; penalty.

No person without authority and in the absence of apparent danger shall, out of the spirit of mischief, or with any purpose other than to prevent or give information of an accident, make or cause to be made any signal to persons in charge of a locomotive, railroad train, or railroad cars, or to any of these persons or in their sight, with intent to cause the stopping of the locomotive, train, or cars.

Whoever violates this Section shall be fined not less than ten dollars nor more than two hundred dollars or imprisoned for not more than three months.

§322. Wire-tapping prohibited; penalty.

No person shall tap or attach any devices for the purpose of listening in on wires, cables, or property owned and used by any person, for the transmission of intelligence by magnetic telephone or telegraph, without the consent of the owner.

Whoever violates this Section shall be fined not less than ten dollars nor more than three hundred dollars, or imprisoned for not more than three months.

This Section shall not be construed to prevent officers of the law, while in the actual discharge of their duties, from tapping in on wires or cables for the purpose of obtaining information to detect crime.

§§322.1, 322.2. *(Repealed by Acts 1991 No. 795, §3, eff. 7/22/91.)*

§324. Abandoning or discarding ice boxes or other air tight containers; penalty.

A. It shall be unlawful for any person, firm or corporation to leave outside of any building or dwelling in a place accessible to children, any abandoned, unattended or discarded ice box, refrigerator, or any other container of any kind which has an airtight door or doors, or which may not be released for opening from the inside of said icebox, refrigerator or container. It shall further be unlawful for any person, firm or corporation, to leave outside of any building or dwelling in a place accessible to children any abandoned, unattended or discarded icebox, refrigerator, or any other container of any kind which is airtight and has a snap lock or other device thereon without first removing said snap lock or locks, or door or doors, from said icebox, refrigerators or containers.

B. Should any person, firm or corporation violate any of the provisions of this Section they shall be deemed guilty of a misdemeanor, and upon conviction thereof shall be fined not exceeding $1,000.00, or imprisoned for not in excess of six months, or both, at the discretion of the court.

§325. Annual registration of conductors of public opinion polls; penalty for failure.

A. Any persons, associations, partnerships or corporations who offer themselves to the public as professional poll takers shall register with the secretary of state before commencing such activity and annually thereafter not later than February 15 of each year. Only the managing or overseeing party responsible for conducting the poll must register under this act, and it will not be necessary for individuals hired by the managing or overseeing party to register on an individual basis.

Such registration shall state that the person, association, partnership or corporation is engaging in the making of public opinion polls or samplings in the State of Louisiana; the name and current mailing address of the person, association, partnership or corporation under which the polls are conducted; the name and current mailing address of the principal executive officer thereof, and the year for which the registration is filed. It shall be signed by the principal executive officer thereof. The secretary of state is directed to collect a registration fee of five dollars for each such registration.

B. Failure to comply with the provisions of this section shall be punishable, for the first offense, by a fine of one hundred dollars or ten days in jail, or both; for the second offense, by a fine of two hundred dollars or ten days in jail, or both; and for the third offense, by a fine of five hundred dollars or ten days in jail, or both.

C. The secretary of state shall keep the registrations filed with him under this section as a part of the permanent public records of his office and may cause same to be published annually.

§326. Processions, marches, parades or demonstrations; permits; liability; bond; exemptions; penalty.

A. Any procession, march, parade or public demonstration of any kind or for whatever purpose is prohibited by any group, association or organization on any public sidewalk, street, highway, bridge, alley, road or other public passageway of any municipality or unincorporated town or village unless there first has been obtained a permit therefor, and in all cases the person or persons or the group, association or organization to whom the permit is issued shall be liable for all damage to property or persons which may arise out of or in connection with any such procession, march, parade or public demonstration for which a permit is issued.

B. Application for the permit required herein shall be made to the mayor and governing authority of the municipality or to the governing authority of the parish in which the unincorporated town or village in which the procession, march, parade or public demonstration is located, as the case may be. Permits may be granted by the authority to which application is made, provided, however, that bond in the amount of ten thousand dollars has first been filed with the mayor and municipal governing authority or with parish governing authority, as the case may be, as security for the payment of any damage or injury which may occur as the result of or in connection with such procession, march, parade or public demonstration.

C. The provisions of this Section shall apply to all groups, associations, or organizations regardless of race, creed, disability as defined in R.S. 51:2232(11), color, or political beliefs of its members; however, nothing contained herein shall apply to a bona fide legitimate labor organization or to any lawful activity of a labor union permitted by law, nor shall these provisions apply to any procession or parade directly held or sponsored by the governing authority of any municipality or the governing authority of any parish, nor shall these provisions apply to any procession, march, or parade directly held or sponsored by a bona fide organization specifically for the celebration of Mardi Gras and/or directly related prelenten or carnival festivities, school parades or other functions, parish parades or other functions, state, parish, or municipal fairs or other such related activities. However, the provisions of this Section shall apply only to parishes with a population of more than four hundred fifty thousand.

D. Whoever violates any provision of this Section shall be guilty of a misdemeanor and upon conviction shall, for each offense, be fined not more than one thousand dollars or be imprisoned for not more than six months, or both.
(Chgd. by Acts 1993 No. 672, §1, No. 820, §2, eff. 8/15/93.)

§327. Obstructing a fireman.

A. It shall be unlawful for any person intentionally to obstruct any fireman while in the performance of his official duties. Obstructing a fireman is hereby defined as intentionally hindering, delaying, hampering, interfering with, or impeding the progress of, any regularly employed member of a fire department of any municipality, parish or fire protection district of the State of Louisiana, or any volunteer fireman of the State of Louisiana while in the performance of his official duties; or cursing, reviling or using any opprobrious language directed at any such fireman while in the performance of his official duties.

B. Whoever commits the crime of obstructing a fireman shall be punished as follows:

(1) If the act constituting the offense is equivalent to manslaughter or attempted murder as those crimes are defined in the Louisiana Criminal Code, he shall be imprisoned at hard labor for not less than one nor more than twenty years;

(2) If the act constituting the offense is equivalent to aggravated battery as that crime is defined in the Louisiana Criminal Code, he shall be imprisoned with or without hard labor for not less than six months nor more than ten years;

(3) If the act constituting the offense is equivalent to simple battery, aggravated assault, or false imprisonment, as those crimes are defined in the Louisiana Criminal Code, he shall be fined not less than one hundred dollars nor more than three hundred dollars, or imprisoned for not less than ninety days nor more than two years, or both;

(4) If the act constituting the offense is equivalent to simple assault as that crime is defined in the Louisiana Criminal Code, he shall be fined not less than twenty-five dollars nor

more than fifty dollars, or imprisoned for not less than thirty days nor more than ninety days, or both;

(5) In all other cases, he shall be fined not less than twenty-five dollars nor more than one hundred dollars, or imprisoned for not less than thirty days nor more than one year, or both.

C. Whoever attempts to commit the crime of obstructing a fireman shall be fined not less than one-half of the minimum fine nor more than one-half of the maximum fine provided in Subsection B hereof, or imprisoned for not less than one-half of the minimum term nor more than one-half of the maximum term as provided in Subsection B hereof, or both.

For the purposes of this subsection, an attempt shall be defined as provided in R.S. 14:27.

D. The penalties provided in this section for the crime of obstructing a fireman shall be in addition to any other penalties provided by existing law.

§328. Obstruction or interference with members of staff, faculty, or students of educational institutions; trespass, damage to property; felony; penalties.

A. No person shall, on the campus or grounds of any state or public owned and operated junior college, college, university or branch thereof or any high school or junior high school in this state, hereinafter referred to as "educational institutions", or at any or in any building or other facility thereof, willfully deny to students, school officials, teachers or other employees and invitees and guests thereof:

(1) Lawful freedom of movement on the campus or grounds;

(2) Lawful use of any property or facilities of any educational institution; or

(3) Their right of lawful ingress and egress to and from the physical facilities of such educational institution.

B. No person shall, on the campus or grounds of any educational institution or at or in any building or other facility owned, operated, controlled or administered by the governing authority of any such institution, willfully obstruct or impede any member of the faculty or administrative staff or other personnel of such institution in the lawful performance of their duties, or willfully obstruct or impede any student of such institution in the lawful pursuit of his educational activities or activities related thereto or a part thereof, through the use of restraint, abduction, coercion or intimidation, or by any action as a result of which force and/or violence are present or threatened.

C. No person shall willfully refuse or fail to leave the property of or any building or other facility owned, operated, controlled or administered by the governing authority of any such institution of higher education upon being requested to do so by the chief administrative officer or his designee charged with maintaining order on the campus or grounds and in the facilities thereon, if such person is committing, threatens to commit or incites others to commit any act which would disrupt, impair, interfere with or obstruct the lawful missions, processes, procedures or functions of the educational institution.

D. Nothing in this section shall be construed to prevent lawful assembly and peaceful and orderly petition for the redress of grievances, including any labor dispute between an educational institution and its employees, or any contractor or subcontractor or any employees thereof. Providing that nothing herein contained shall apply to a bona fide legal labor organization or to any of its legal activities such as picketing, lawful assembly or concerted activities in the interest of its members for the purpose of accomplishing or securing more favorable wage standards, hours of employment and working conditions.

E. Whoever violates any provision of this section shall be punished by a fine of not to exceed five hundred dollars or be imprisoned for not more than six months, or both.

F. The provisions of this section shall be supplemental and in addition to any other applicable laws of this state.

§329.1. Riot.

A.* A riot is a public disturbance involving an assemblage of three or more persons acting together or in concert which by tumultuous and violent conduct, or the imminent threat of tumultuous and violent conduct, results in injury or damage to persons or property or creates a clear and present danger of injury or damage to persons or property.

**So in original. No subsection B has been enacted.*

§329.2. Inciting to riot.

Inciting to riot is the endeavor by any person to incite or procure any other person to create or participate in a riot.

§329.3. Command to disperse; who may give; failure to comply.

Any law enforcement or peace officer or public officer responsible for keeping the peace may issue a command to disperse under the authority of R.S. 14:329.1—14:329.8 if he reasonably believes that riot is occurring or about to occur. The command to disperse shall be given in a manner reasonably calculated to be communicated to the assemblage.

Whoever willfully fails to comply with a lawful command to disperse shall be punished in accordance with the provisions of R.S. 14:329.7.

§329.4. Wrongful use of public property; permits for use of public property.

Wrongful use of public property is

(1) The intentional entering of or onto any public property without the permission of the lawful custodian thereof, or his designated representative, at any time when the public property is not open to the public and the remaining in or occupying of any public property after having been requested to leave by the lawful custodian thereof, or his designated representative, or any law enforcement or peace officer, and

(2) The depriving of the general public of the intended use of public property without a permit.

In accordance with R.S. 14:329.1—14:329.8, permits to occupy or use public property may be obtained from the lawful custodian thereof, or his designated representative, upon written application therefor. All such applications shall (1) describe the public property sought to be occupied or used, and (2) state the period of time during which the public property will be occupied or used.

The lawful custodian, or his designated representative, may issue the permit if he determines that the use or occupation of the public property will not reasonably interfere with the intended or customary use of the public property by the general public and that the intended use will not destroy or damage the public property.

For the purposes of this section, the term "public property" means any public land, building, facility, structure or enclosure used for a public purpose or as a place of public gathering, owned and/or under the control of the state or one of its agencies or political subdivisions.

§329.5. Prohibition of interference with educational process; certain activities excepted.

A. No person shall, on the campus or lands of any university, college, junior college, trade or vocational-technical school, special school, elementary or secondary school in this state, hereinafter referred to as "institutions of learning," or at or in any building or other facility thereof owned, operated or controlled by the state or any of its agencies or political subdivisions, willfully deny to students, school officials, faculty, employees, invitees and guests thereof:

(1) Lawful freedom of movement on the campus or lands; or

(2) Lawful use of the property, facilities or parts of any institution of learning; or

(3) The right of lawful ingress and egress to and from the institution's physical facilities.

B. No person shall, on the campus of any institution of learning or at or in any building or other facility thereof owned, operated or controlled by the state or any agency or political subdivision thereof, willfully impede the staff or faculty of such institution in the lawful performance of their duties, or willfully impede a student of such institution in lawful pursuit of his educational activities, through use of restraint, abduction, coercion, or intimidation, or when force and violence are present or threatened.

C. No person shall willfully refuse or fail to leave the property of, or any building or other facility owned, operated or controlled by the state or any agency or political subdivision thereof, upon being requested to do so by the chief administrative officer thereof, or by his designee charged with maintaining order on the campus or grounds and in its facilities, or a dean of such institution of learning, if such person is committing, threatens to commit, or incites others to commit, any act which would or is likely to disrupt, impair, interfere with or obstruct the lawful missions, processes, procedures or functions of such institutions of learning.

D. Nothing contained in R.S. 14:329.1—14:329.8 shall apply to a bona fide legitimate labor organization or to any of its legal activities such as lawful picketing, lawful assembly or concerted activity in the interest of its members for the purpose of accomplishing or securing more favorable wage standards, hours of employment or working conditions.

§329.6. Proclamation of state of emergency; conditions therefor; effect thereof.

A. During times of great public crisis, disaster, rioting, catastrophe or similar public emergency within the territorial limits of any municipality or parish, or in the event of reasonable apprehension of immediate danger thereof, and upon a finding that the public safety is imperiled thereby, the chief executive officer of any political subdivision or the district judge, district attorney or the sheriff of any parish of this state, or the public safety director of a municipality, may request the governor to proclaim a state of emergency within any part or all of the territorial limits of such local government. Following such proclamation by the governor, and during the continuance of such state of emergency, the chief law enforcement officer of the political subdivision affected by the proclamation may, in order to protect life and property and to bring the emergency situation under control, promulgate orders affecting any part or all of the territorial limits of the municipality or parish:

(1) Establishing a curfew and prohibiting and/or controlling pedestrian and vehicular traffic, except essential emergency vehicles and personnel;

(2) Designating specific zones within which the occupancy and use of buildings and the ingress and egress of vehicles and persons shall be prohibited or regulated;

(3) Regulating and closing of places of amusement and assembly;

(4) Prohibiting the sale and distribution of alcoholic beverages;

(5) Prohibiting and controlling the presence of persons on public streets and places;

(6) Regulating and controlling the possession, storage, display, sale, transport and use of firearms, other dangerous weapons and ammunition;

(7) Regulating and controlling the possession, storage, display, sale, transport and use of explosives and flammable materials and liquids, including but not limited to the closing of all wholesale and retail establishments which sell or distribute gasoline and other flammable products;

(8) Regulating and controlling the possession, storage, display, sale, transport and use of sound apparatus, including but not limited to public address systems, bull horns and megaphones.

(9) Prohibiting the sale or offer for sale of goods or services within the designated emergency area for value exceeding the prices ordinarily charged for comparable goods and services in the same market area at, or immediately before, the time of the state of emergency. However, the value received may include reasonable expenses and a charge for any attendant business risk in addition to the cost of the goods and services which necessarily are incurred in procuring the goods and services during the state of emergency, pursuant to the provisions of R.S. 29:701 through 716.

B. Such orders shall be effective from the time and in the manner prescribed in such orders and shall be published as soon as practicable in a newspaper of general circulation in the area affected by such order and transmitted to the radio and television media for publication and broadcast. Such orders shall cease to be in effect five days after their promulgation or upon declaration by the governor that the state of emergency no longer exists, whichever occurs sooner; however, the chief law enforcement officer, with the consent of the governor, may extend the effect of such orders for successive periods of not more than five days each by republication of such orders in the manner hereinabove provided.

C. All orders promulgated pursuant to this section shall be executed in triplicate and shall be filed with the clerk of court of the parish affected and with the secretary of state of this state.

D. During any period during which a state of emergency exists the proclaiming officer may appoint additional peace officers or firemen for temporary service, who need not be in the classified lists of such departments. Such additional persons shall be employed only for the time during which the emergency exists.

E. During the period of the existence of the state of emergency the chief law enforcement officer of the political subdivision may call upon the sheriff, mayor or other chief executive officer of any other parish or municipality to furnish such law enforcement or fire protection personnel, or both, together with appropriate equipment and apparatus, as may be necessary to preserve the public peace and protect persons and property in the requesting area. Such aid shall be furnished to the chief law enforcement officer requesting it insofar as possible without withdrawing from the political subdivision furnishing such aid the minimum police and fire protection appearing necessary under the circumstances. In such case, law enforcement and fire protection personnel acting outside the territory of their regular employment shall be considered as performing services within the territory of their regular employment for purposes of compensation, pension and other rights or benefits to which they may be entitled as incidents of their regular employment. The political subdivision receiving

such aid shall reimburse the cost thereof to the other political subdivision which furnished the aid, including the cost of compensation of personnel, expenses incurred by reason of the injury or death of any such personnel while rendering such aid, expenses of furnishing equipment and apparatus, compensation for damages to or loss of equipment or apparatus while in service outside the territory of its regular use, and such other reasonable expenses as may be incurred by any such political subdivision furnishing such aid. Law enforcement officers acting pursuant to this Section outside the territory of their regular employment have the same authority to enforce the law as when acting within the territory of their own employment.
(Chgd. by Acts 1990 No. 152, §1, eff. 7/1/90.)

§329.7. Punishment.

A. Whoever willfully is the offender or participates in a riot, or is guilty of inciting a riot, or who fails to comply with a lawful command to disperse, or who is guilty of wrongful use of public property, or violates any other provision hereof shall be fined not more than five hundred dollars or be imprisoned not more than six months, or both.

B. Where as a result of any willful violation of the provisions of R.S. 14:329.1—14:329.8 there is any serious bodily injury or any property damage in excess of five thousand dollars, such offender shall be imprisoned at hard labor for not more than five years.

C. Where, as a result of any willful violation of the provisions of R.S. 14:329.1—14:329.8, the death of any person occurs, such offender shall be imprisoned at hard labor for not to exceed twenty-one years.

§329.8. Applicability of other acts.

The provisions of R.S. 14:329.1 to 14:329.8 shall be supplemental and in addition to any other applicable laws of this state, including but not limited to the Louisiana Disaster Act of 1974, R.S. 29:701 through 716. *(Chgd. by Acts 1990 No. 152, §1, eff. 7/1/90.)*

§330. Motion picture ratings; definitions; prohibition on advertising coming attraction with more restrictive rating.

A. An owner or operator of any motion picture theatre, including a drive-in theatre, shall spell out on the face of all motion picture advertisements the rating of the advertised attraction, each in conspicuous and legible type in contrast by typography, layout, or color with other printed matter appearing on the advertisement.

B. No owner or operator of any motion picture theatre, including a drive-in theatre, shall advertise, or permit to be advertised by film a coming attraction which has a more restrictive rating than the motion picture currently engaged at the aforementioned establishments. For the purposes of this section a restrictive rating is one which excludes certain people from the viewing audience on the basis of age and the subject matter of the motion picture.

C. Any person who violates the provisions of this section shall be fined not less than one hundred dollars nor more than five hundred dollars or be imprisoned for not more than six months, or both.

§331. Prohibition of debt adjusting when conducted for profit.

A. Except as otherwise provided herein, no person shall engage in the business of debt adjusting.

B. As used in this section, the following words and phrases shall have the following meaning, unless the context clearly indicates otherwise:

(1) "Person" means an individual, corporation, partnership, trust, firm, association or other legal entity.

(2) "Debt adjusting" means the making of a contract, express or implied, with a debtor whereby the debtor agrees to pay a certain amount of money or other thing of value periodically to the person engaged in the debt adjusting business who shall, for a consideration, distribute the same among certain specified creditors in accordance with a plan agreed upon. The term includes debt adjustment, budget counseling, debt management or debt pooling service or the holding of oneself out, by words of similar import, as providing services to debtors in the management of their debts and contracting with the debtor for a fee to (a) effect the adjustment, compromise, or discharge of any account, note, or other indebtedness, of the debtor, or (b) receive from the debtor and disperse to his creditors any money or other thing of value.

C. This section shall not apply to:

(1) Situations involving debt adjusting incurred incidentally in the lawful practice of law in this state;

(2) Banks and fiduciaries, as duly authorized and admitted to transact business in this state and performing credit and financial adjusting service in the regular course of their principal business;

(3) Title insurers and abstract companies, while doing an escrow business;

(4) Judicial officers or others acting under court orders;

(5) Nonprofit or charitable corporations or associations engaged in debt adjusting;

(6) Situations involving debt adjusting incurred incidentally in connection with lawful practice as a certified public accountant;

(7) Bona fide trade or mercantile associations in the course of arranging adjustment of debts with business establishments;

(8) Employers for their employees;

(9) Any person who, at the request of a debtor, arranges for or makes a loan to the debtor, and who, at the authorization of the debtor, acts as an adjuster of the debtor's debts in the disbursement of the proceeds of the loan, without compensation for services rendered in adjusting the debts.

D. Whoever shall engage in the business of debt adjusting shall be guilty of a misdemeanor and upon conviction thereof shall be fined not more than five hundred dollars or imprisoned for not more than six months, or both.

§332. Interference with medical treatment.

A. Interference with medical treatment is the intentional and willful interference with a physician, physician's trained assistant, nurse, nurse's aid, paramedic, emergency medical technician, or other medical or hospital personnel in the performance of their duties relating to the care and treatment of patients in any hospital, clinic, other medical facility, or at the scene of a medical emergency.

B. Whoever violates the provisions of this Section shall be fined not less than one hundred dollars or more than two hundred and fifty dollars upon conviction of a first offense, and not less than two hundred fifty dollars or more than five hundred dollars or ten days in jail or both upon conviction of any subsequent offense.

§333. Misrepresentation of age to obtain alcoholic beverages or gain entry to licensed premises prohibited; penalties.

A. It is unlawful for any person under the age of twenty-one years to present or offer to any person having a license or permit to sell alcoholic beverages, under Title 26 of the Louisiana Revised Statutes of 1950, or to his agent or employee any written, printed, or photostatic evidence of age and identity which is false, fraudulent, or not actually his own for the purpose of obtaining or purchasing alcoholic beverages or attempting to enter the licensed premises.

B. Whoever violates the provisions of this Section shall be punishable by one or more of the following:

(1) A fine of not more than two hundred dollars.

(2) An appropriate amount of community service not to exceed thirty hours.

(3) Suspension of the violator's driver's license for ninety days.

C. As used in this Section, "licensed premises" means an establishment licensed under Title 26 of the Louisiana Revised Statutes of 1950 where the sale of alcoholic beverages constitutes its main business.

(Added by Acts 1992 No. 947, §1, eff. 8/21/92.)

§334. Ignition interlock device offenses.

A. No person who, as a condition of probation, is prohibited from operating a motor vehicle unless it is equipped with an ignition interlock device as provided in R.S. 15:306 shall:

(1) Operate, lease, or borrow a motor vehicle unless that vehicle is equipped with a functioning ignition interlock device.

(2) Request or solicit any other person to blow into an ignition interlock device or to start a motor vehicle equipped with the device for the purpose of providing the person so restricted with an operable motor vehicle.

B. No person shall blow into an ignition interlock device or start a motor vehicle equipped with the device for the purpose of providing an operable motor vehicle to a person who is prohibited from operating a motor vehicle without an ignition interlock device.

C. No person shall intentionally attempt to tamper with, defeat, or circumvent the operation of an ignition interlock device.

D. Any person convicted of a violation of this Section may be punished by imprisonment for not more than six months or a fine of not more than five hundred dollars, or both.
(Added by Acts 1992 No. 982, §2, eff. 1/1/93.)

§335. Checks; requiring certain information to be recorded on; prohibited; penalties.

A. No retail or wholesale merchant shall demand the race of any customer for the purposes of recording such on the customer's personal check which has been tendered for the payment of goods or services or for cashing.

B. No retail or wholesale merchant shall cause the race of any customer to be recorded on a personal check tendered by such customer for the payment of goods or services or for cashing.

C. Any person convicted of a violation of this Section may be assessed civil damages in an amount not to exceed two hundred fifty dollars.
(Added by Acts 1993 No. 399, §1, eff. 8/15/93.)

PART IV. OFFENSES AFFECTING ORGANIZED GOVERNMENT

§351. Bail, sale, etc. of real estate securing, prohibited; penalty.

No person shall, with intent to defraud, sell, transfer, donate, give, mortgage, hypothecate, or in any way encumber to the prejudice of the state any real estate offered as security to the state on any bail or appearance bond for the release of any person charged with crime.

Whoever violates this Section shall be imprisoned with or without hard labor for not less than six months nor more than twelve months.

§352. Bribery of withdrawn candidates for office prohibited; penalty; immunity of witnesses; fine to be paid informer.

No person shall give or offer to give, directly or indirectly, any money or property to any person, who was a candidate for public office in any primary election held or to be held under the laws of this state who may have withdrawn, or who was eliminated prior or subsequent to the first primary election as a candidate for public office, for the purpose of securing or giving his political support to any remaining candidate or candidates for public office in the first or succeeding second primary election held under the laws of this state.

No candidate who has withdrawn or was eliminated prior or subsequent to the first primary election as a candidate for public office shall accept or offer to accept, directly or indirectly, any money or property which is given for the purpose of securing or giving his political support to any remaining candidate or candidates for public office in the first or succeeding second primary election for public office held under the laws of this state.

Whoever violates this Section shall be fined not less than one thousand dollars nor more than ten thousand dollars and imprisoned for not more than one year.

In the trial of persons charged with a violation of this Section either the bribe giver or the bribe taker may give evidence, or make affidavit against the other, with immunity from prosecution in favor of the first informer, except for perjury in giving the testimony.

No penalty imposed under the provisions of this Section shall be suspended or remitted by any court or other authority. This provision shall not be construed against the right of suspensive appeal granted by the Constitution and laws of this state.

§353. Documents simulating official court papers for collection purposes, sale or purchase prohibited; use prohibited; penalty.

(A) No person shall, either as principal or agent, in any manner sell or offer to sell, cause to be sold or offer to be sold, or solicit for or offer to purchase, any paper or document, except a paper or document intended for use by a court or a judicial or administrative tribunal or unit, which simulates or purports to be an official paper or document, such as is issued by or from any court or judicial tribunal within the United States and intended or calculated to secure or collect any sum of money or other thing of value.

(B) No person, either as principal or agent, other than a court or a judicial or administrative tribunal or unit shall make use of any paper or document which simulates or purports to be an official paper or document, such as is issued by or from any court or judicial tribunal within the United States and intended or calculated to secure or collect any sums of money or other thing of value.

(C) Whoever violates any provisions of this Section shall be fined not more than one hundred dollars, or imprisoned for not more than sixty days, or both.

§354. Fiduciaries, failure to file accounts in court; penalty.

No administrator, tutor, executor, or other person holding fiduciary trusts shall neglect, fail, or refuse, after having been ordered by a court of competent jurisdiction, to file in the court where such trust is exercised, once between the first day of January and the thirty-first day of December of each calendar year, a full and complete account and statement of the trust.

Whoever violates this Section shall be fined not more than five hundred dollars and, in default of fine, imprisoned for not more than six months.

§355. Property exempt from execution; penalty for deprivation of rights.

No person shall make any seizures prohibited under Article 644 of the Code of Practice* or shall, by any artifice or subterfuge, induce or procure another to sign away, by contract or otherwise, any of the rights he may have under Article 644 of the Code of Practice.*

**So in original. See R.S. 13:3881.*

Whoever violates this Section shall be fined not more than two hundred dollars, or imprisoned for not more than six months, or both.

§356. Sheriffs, etc., solicitation of legal business prohibited; penalty.

No sheriff, clerk of court, constable, or their deputies, or any police officer or detective, whether commissioned without pay or otherwise, shall procure or solicit any legal business for any attorney at law under the expectation or promise, whether express or implied, of being paid in any manner.

Whoever violates this Section shall be imprisoned with or without hard labor for not more than two years.

Proof of solicitation or procurement of any legal business for any attorney at law shall be considered prima facie evidence that the solicitation or procurement has been done for pecuniary reward.

§356.1. Unlawful referrals by wrecker drivers and others; penalty.

A. It shall be unlawful for any wrecker driver, owner, or any other person engaged in providing wrecker services to refer to an attorney at law any person involved in an accident in connection with which he has provided wrecker services, when the wrecker driver, owner, or other person receives any compensation for such referral.

B. Whoever violates the provisions of this Section shall be fined not more than five thousand dollars or imprisoned for not more than five years, with or without hard labor, or both.

(Chgd. by Acts 1993 No. 420. §1, eff. 8/15/93.)

§356.2. Unlawful appearance bond procurement.

A. No police officer, employee of any police department, sheriff, deputy sheriff, employee of any sheriff's office, employee of a district attorney's or clerk of court's office, or any law enforcement personnel or employee or agent of any law enforcement agency shall negotiate for, procure, solicit, sell, or in any way participate in the negotiation for, procuration, solicitation, or sale of a bond taken to secure the appearance of any person before any court with criminal jurisdiction in the state of Louisiana for any fee, commission, or the receipt of anything of value.

B. Whoever violates any provision of this Section shall upon conviction be fined not more than five thousand dollars, imprisoned for not more than six months, or both.

§356.3. Unlawful referrals by ambulance drivers and others; penalty.

A. It shall be unlawful for any ambulance driver, owner, or any other person engaged in providing ambulance services to refer to an attorney at law any person involved in an accident in connection with which he has provided ambulance services, when the ambulance driver, owner, or other person receives any compensation for such referral.

B. Whoever violates the provisions of this Section shall be fined not more than five thousand dollars or imprisoned for not more than five years, with or without hard labor, or both.

(Added by Acts 1993 No. 421, §1, eff. 8/15/93.)

§357. Candies, selling without payment of license tax; penalty.

No manufacturer of candies or sweets or transient vendor selling candies or sweets, shall consign to or leave any candies or manufactured sweets on consignment with any person, firm or corporation other than schools, churches, religious societies and civil organization, who has not paid the privilege or license tax, required by law in order to obtain a license to sell and dispose of the articles.

Whoever violates this Section, for the first offense, shall be fined not more than one hundred dollars, and for the second offense, not more than five hundred dollars.

§358. Subversive activities and communist control law; legislative finding of fact and declaration of necessity.

There exists a world communist movement, directed by the Union of Soviet Socialist Republics and the other communist bloc nations, which has as its declared objective, world control. Such world control is to be brought about by aggression, force and violence, and is to be accomplished in large by infiltrating tactics involving the use of fraud, espionage, sabotage, infiltration, subversion, propaganda, terrorism and treachery. The state of Louisiana, as a sovereign political entity under the constitution of the United States, and as a functioning representative State government which is responsible solely to the people of this state under the constitutions of this state and nation, is a most probable and obvious target for those who seek by force, violence and other unlawful means to overthrow constitutional government, and is in imminent danger of communist espionage, infiltration, subversion and sabotage. Communist control of a country is characterized by an absolute denial of the right of self-government and by the abolition of those personal liberties which are cherished and held sacred in the state of Louisiana and in the United States of America.

The direction and control of the world communist movement is vested in and exercised by the communist dictatorships of the various communist bloc nations which, in furthering the purposes of the world communist movement, have established or caused the establishment of various action organizations and "front" organizations which are not free and independent, but are sections of a world wide communist organization or apparatus and are controlled and directed by and subject to the discipline of the various communist dictatorships.

These communist action organizations and front organizations so established and utilized in the state of Louisiana, and acting under such control, direction and discipline, endeavor to carry out the objectives of the world communist movement by bringing about the overthrow of existing governments, both national and state, by any available means, including force if necessary, and to set up communist totalitarian dictatorships which will be subservient to the world communist movement.

The agents of the world communist movement who knowingly participate in the conspiratorial subversive work of the world communist movement, by so doing, in effect repudiate their allegiance and loyalty to the state of Louisiana and in effect transfer their allegiance and loyalty to the foreign countries in which is vested the direction and control of the world communist movement. By clever and ruthless tactics of espionage, sabotage, infiltration, fraud, propaganda and subversion, the agents of the world communist movement in many instances in some form or manner successfully evade existing law. Any action organization or front organization managed, operated or controlled by communists, no matter what outward guise, cover, or public image it may assume, is in fact an arm, or tool, or agent organization, of the world communist movement, and its continued operation is a threat and a clear and present danger to the state of Louisiana and the citizens of the state of Louisiana. The effective regulation of such organizations and the control of Communist personalities is in the best interests of the state of Louisiana because the world communist movement is not a legitimate political effort, but is in fact a dangerous criminal conspiracy.

The world communist movement constitutes a clear and present danger to the citizens of the state of Louisiana and is a dangerous enemy of the state of Louisiana. This makes it necessary that the Legislature, in order to protect the people of the state, to preserve the sovereignty of the state under the constitutions of the United States and the state of Louisiana, and to guarantee to the State a republican form of government, enact appropriate legislation recognizing the existence of the world communist movement and preventing it from the accomplishment of its purposes in the state of Louisiana.

There exists a clear difference between natural persons protected by full constitutional freedoms, and organizations which are artificial entities. With this difference in mind and considering the paramount right and interest of the state to protect itself from subversion, the issue of due process is satisfied in R.S. 14:358—14:373 by the legal test of a preponderance of the evidence in a civil proceeding, R.S. 14:358—14:373 being intended as regulatory rather than punitive. The paramount interest of the state to control a clear and present danger demands the broadest possible venue provisions in such regulations. The guarantees of sovereignty and freedom enjoyed by this state and its citizens are certain to vanish if the United States and its constitution are destroyed by the communists, and any communist effort or attack against the United States is and should rightly be considered an attack upon and a clear and present danger to the state of Louisiana and its citizens.

The Legislature of Louisiana does not intend that R.S. 14:358—14:373 shall in any way regulate or control race relations in the state of Louisiana, the question of race being irrelevant for the purposes of R.S. 14:358—14:373, which is written and passed solely for the purpose of regulating subversive activities directed against the state and people of Louisiana. Nothing in R.S. 14:358—14:373 is in any way intended to improperly infringe upon the constitutionally protected right of freedom of expression, for this right, strong though it may be, is not absolute, and falls short of the right to shout "fire" in a crowded movie theater. The protections afforded by the right to freedom of speech do not extend to acts which are by their very nature a clear and present danger to the state of Louisiana and its citizens and the carrying on of communist propaganda activity and other communist controlled activities in the state of Louisiana is such a danger and is therefore an intolerable abuse of the right to freedom of expression which can and should be regulated by statute for the safety of the people of this state. The public good, and the general welfare of the citizens of this state require the immediate enactment of this measure.

§359. Definitions.

As used in R.S. 14:358—14:373:

(1) An "organization" is any corporation, trust, company, partnership, association, foundation, or fund, and includes any group of persons, whether or not incorporated, banded together for joint action on any subject or subjects.

(2) A "Communist Action Organization" is the Communist Party Of The United States, the communist party of any state or foreign nation, the Progressive Labor Movement, or any other organization (other than a diplomatic representative or mission of a foreign government accredited as such by the U.S. Department of State), which is substantially directed, controlled or dominated by any of the foreign governments controlling the world Communist movement described in R.S. 14:358, and shall include any section, branch, fraction or cell of any such organization as is described in this Section.

(3) A "Communist" is any person who has accepted the discipline of or has become a member of a communist action organization and has remained under the discipline thereof or remained a member thereof knowing it to be such an organization.

(4) A "Communist Front Organization" is any organization other than a communist action organization which is directed, controlled or dominated by a communist action organization or is primarily operated for the purpose of giving aid and support to a communist action organization, a Communist foreign government, or the world Communist movement referred to in R.S. 14:358.

(5) A "Communist Infiltrated Organization" is any organization (other than a communist action organization or a communist front organization) which is substantially directed, controlled or dominated by any person who is a communist or persons who are communists.

(6) A "Communist Organization" is any communist action organization, communist front organization or communist infiltrated organization.

(7) The term "world Communist movement" means a revolutionary movement, the purpose of which is to establish eventually a communist totalitarian dictatorship in any or all the countries of the world through the medium of an internationally coordinated Communist movement.

(8) A "Subversive Organization" is any organization which advocates the overthrow or destruction of the United States, the state of Louisiana, or any political subdivision thereof by revolution, force, violence or other unlawful means, and performs or carries out as a function

of the organization, known, agreed to, or knowingly performed by any of the officers of the organization, any affirmative act, including abetting, materially assisting, advising or teaching such overthrow or destruction, with the intent to incite action rather than engage in the mere exposition of theory.

(9) A "Subversive Person" is any person who knowingly is a member of a subversive organization knowing the said organization to be subversive within the meaning of R.S. 14:358—14:373 or any person who commits any act intended to bring about the overthrow or destruction of the United States, the state of Louisiana or any political subdivision thereof by revolution, force, violence or other unlawful means.

§360. Due process determination of facts.

In determining that any organization or individual is in fact a communist action organization, a communist front organization, a communist infiltrated organization, a subversive organization, a communist or a subversive person, the following procedure shall be the legal method of such determination:

Upon any district attorney or the attorney general being reasonably informed that an organization or person is or should be subject to the regulation of R.S. 14:358—14:373, the district attorney having proper jurisdiction, or the attorney general, shall institute in the appropriate district court a civil proceeding in the name of the state of Louisiana against such organization or individual, setting forth the relevant and pertinent facts pertaining to said organization or individual under the definitions provided in R.S. 14:358—14:373, and praying for a judgment of the court determining, from the facts presented concerning said organization or individual, whether or not said organization or individual is in fact a communist action organization, a communist front organization, a communist infiltrated organization, a subversive organization, a communist or a subversive person, as the case may be. All such suits shall be procedurally handled as an adversary proceeding the same as any other civil action. The judgment of the court in such actions shall be based upon a preponderance of the evidence, as in all other civil cases. No determination of fact as provided in this Section concerning any organization or individual shall be made by any other way than by judgment of a district court of this state, which judgment shall, when so justified by the facts presented, by rendered as prayed for by the district attorney or attorney general, as the case may be, identifying the defendant in the terms defined in R.S. 14:359. The provisions of Articles 1871 through 1883, of the Louisiana Code of Civil Procedure, concerning declaratory judgments, shall apply to all civil actions provided for in this Section.

§361. Venue.

The action provided in R.S. 14:360 may properly be brought in any parish where the organization in question is domiciled, owns property of any kind, is doing business, is soliciting or has solicited funds, is sending or has sent printed propaganda or other printed materials, an agent duly appointed for the service of process resides, or where any agent appointed by action of law for the service of process resides, has officers or members living therein or in which any officer can be found for personal service, or in the case of an individual, in any parish where such individual may be domiciled, temporarily living, be employed, carry on any propaganda activities, solicit or pay out any funds or money, or be found for personal service of process.

§362. Registration of organizations.

Upon final definitive judgment under the provisions of R.S. 14:358—14:373 that an organization is a communist action organization, a communist front organization, a communist infiltrated organization or a subversive organization, the president, vice president, secretary or treasurer, or in their absence any director or other officer of the organization, shall file or cause to be filed, within five days thereafter and annually thereafter between the 1st and 15th of January, with the commissioner of public safety, or his designated representative, a registration statement, and for the purposes of filing this registration statement only, any member of the bar of this state may be employed. Except with respect to the disclosures required to be made in this registration statement, the legal privileges of the attorney-client relationship shall be observed. The said registration statement shall contain the following information:

The names and current home and office addresses of all current officers, plus all officers during the year preceding the date of the statement, with a designation of the title of the officer and a brief description of the duties of said officers.

The names and current home and office addresses of all persons or organizations which have contributed funds to said organization in the year preceding the date of the statement plus a statement of the amount and date of each contribution received from each contributor during the year preceding the date of the statement, the qualifications for membership in the organization, a detailed statement of the aims, purposes and activities of the organization and all the means by which they are carried out.

In the case of a communist action organization or a subversive organization, the name and last known address of each person who was a member of the organization at any time during the year preceding the date of the statement.

(In the case of any officer or member listed above who is or has been known by more than one name, each name which such officer or member uses or by which he has been known must be listed to comply with R.S. 14:358—14:373).

An inventory of all property and assets owned by the said organization listing brief description, location and approximate values.

Registrants under this Section shall attach to their registration statements copies of all publications of any kind, including written transcripts of any radio or television broadcasts, published or disseminated by the registering organization during the year preceding the date of the statement, plus, a copy of the Charter, articles of incorporation, bylaws and rules of the organization.

The registration statement of any organization under this Section shall be submitted under oath or by affirmation.

§363. Registration of individuals.

Upon final definitive judgment under the provisions of R.S. 14:358—14:373 that any individual is a communist or a subversive person, that individual shall, within five days thereafter, register with the commission of public safety by filing in person a statement under oath or affirmation setting forth his or her name, including any other names used or in use, address, occupation, date and place of birth, features of identification, and name of spouse, if any. All such individual registrants shall be fingerprinted for positive identification at the time of each registration and shall re-register annually between the 1st and 15th of January, for so long as they remain in the state of Louisiana. If a person found to be a communist or subversive person under the terms of R.S. 14:358—14:373 shall leave the state of Louisiana for a period as long as fifteen days or longer, he or she shall re-register as provided above within five days after he or she shall return to the state.

§364. Registration statements to be public records.

All registration statements of both organizations and individuals under R.S. 14:358—14:373 shall be considered public records and shall be kept open for public inspection at any reasonable time.

§365. Election ballots.

No organization finally determined under the provisions of R.S. 14:358—14:373 to be a communist organization or a subversive organization shall have its name or the name of any of its nominees printed on any election ballot used in any primary or general election in the state of Louisiana.

§366. Public office and public support, disqualification.

It shall be the public policy of this state to discourage the public employment of persons legally determined under the provisions of R.S. 14:358—14:373 to be Communists or Subversive Persons, and no official or employee of the state of Louisiana or any political subdivision thereof having the authority to hire and fire other employees shall hire or retain on the official payrolls any person about whom the courts have made any such determination under R.S. 14:358—14:373, and further, no official or employee of the state of Louisiana or any political subdivision thereof who has the authority and responsibility to pay out any public funds for any purpose shall pay out any such funds in any amount for any purpose to any person about whom the courts have made any such determination under R.S. 14:358—14:373.

§367. Labeling of propaganda.

Any publication of any type whatsoever of any organization finally determined to be a communist action organization, a communist front organization, a communist infiltrated organization or a subversive organization under the provisions of R.S. 14:358—14:373, which publication is intended to be, or which is, circulated or disseminated among two or more persons, shall be marked plainly in block letters in red ink. "Disseminated by _____ , a Communist Organization" (or Subversive Organization if the organization has been so designated) inserting in the blank space the full name of the organization.

§368. Acts prohibited.

It shall be a felony for any person knowingly and wilfully to:

1. Fail to register as required in R.S. 14:363, when required to so register by the terms of R.S. 14:358—14:373.

2. Fail as an officer of a communist action organization, a communist front organization, a communist infiltrated organization or a subversive organization to perform and carry out the obligations set forth and provided in R.S. 14:362.

3. File any false registration statement under the provisions of R.S. 14:362 and 14:363.

4. Violate the provisions of R.S. 14:367 in regard to the labeling and dissemination of propaganda material.

§369. Penalties.

Any person convicted of violating any of the provisions of R.S. 14:368 shall be fined not more than ten thousand dollars or imprisoned at hard labor for not more than five years, or both. Any organization which shall fail to register as provided in R.S. 14:362 when required to so under the terms of R.S. 14:358—14:373 shall, on the motion of the district attorney or the attorney general as the case may be, have all assets of said organization frozen by preliminary restraining order and injunction of the district court having jurisdiction in the matter and held secure under the jurisdiction of said court and unavailable to said organization until the required registration is completed or until the owners of the organization petition the said court for a distribution of the assets following a dissolution of the organization.

§370. Additional penalties.

Any person convicted by a court of competent jurisdiction of violating any of the provisions of R.S. 14:368 in addition to all other penalties herein provided shall from the date of such conviction be barred from:

(1) Holding any office, elective or appointive, or any other position of profit or trust in or employment by the government of the state of Louisiana or of any agency thereof or of any parish, municipal corporation or other political subdivision of said state;

(2) Filing or offering for election to any public office in the state of Louisiana; or

(3) Voting in any election in this state.

§371. Screening of prospective public officials and employees.

Every person and every board, commission, council, department, court or other agency of the state of Louisiana or any political subdivision thereof, who or which appoints or employs or supervises in any manner the appointment or employment of public officials or employees, shall establish by rules, regulations or otherwise, procedures designed to reasonably ascertain before any person, including teachers and other employees of any public educational institution in this state, is appointed or employed, that he or she is not a communist or a subversive person, and that there are no reasonable grounds to believe such person is a communist or a subversive person. In the event such reasonable grounds exist, he or she shall not be appointed or employed. In securing any facts necessary to ascertain the information herein required, the applicant may be required to sign a written affidavit containing answers to such inquiries as may be reasonably material.

§372. Candidates for public office; filing of nonsubversive affidavits.

No person shall become a candidate nor shall be certified by any political party as a candidate for election to any public office created by the constitution or laws of this state unless such candidate for certification by the political party shall have attached to the qualifying papers, the nominating petition or nominating papers filed with the appropriate party committee of this state or the secretary of state, whichever the case may be, a sworn affidavit that the candidate is not and never has been a communist or a subversive person as defined in R.S. 14:359. No qualification of candidates, nominating petition or nominating papers for such office shall be received for filing by the official aforesaid unless the same shall be accompanied by the affidavit aforesaid and there shall not be entered upon any ballot or voting machine at any election the name of any person who has failed or refused to make the affidavit as required above.

§373. Citation of subversive activities and communist control law.

R.S. 14:358 through R.S. 14:373 may be cited as the Subversive Activities and Communist Control Law.

§374. Failure to report bail bonds.

A. It shall be a misdemeanor offense for any agent of a commercial surety company, who posted a criminal bail bond through a power of attorney issued by that company, to fail to report and remit the premium and any fees or taxes due to the commercial surety company within fifteen days of posting the bail bond.

B. Whoever violates any provisions of this Section shall be fined not more than five hundred dollars and imprisoned for not more than six months or both.

(Added by Acts 1993 No. 834, §3, eff. 6/22/93.)

§375. Illegal consideration for criminal bail bonds.

A. It shall be unlawful for any person to:

(1) Charge a fee or to receive anything of value to act as a personal surety on a criminal bail bond or to procure another to act as a personal surety on a criminal bail bond in the state of Louisiana.

(2) Charge a fee for or to receive anything of value for obtaining a release of a criminal defendant on a bail without surety.

B. An attorney at law admitted to practice in the state of Louisiana, in the course of his representation of his client, shall not be affected by this Section.

C. Whoever violates the provisions of this Section:

(1) When the amount charged or received is valued at five hundred dollars or more, shall be imprisoned with or without hard labor for not more than five years or may be fined not more than five thousand dollars, or both.

(2) When the amount charged or received is valued at one hundred dollars or more, but less than five hundred dollars, shall be imprisoned with or without hard labor for not more than two years or may be fined two thousand dollars or both.

(3) When the amount received or charged is valued at less than one hundred dollars, shall be imprisoned for not more than six months or fined not more than five hundred dollars, or both.

(Added by Acts 1993 No. 834, §3, eff. 6/22/93.)

§385. Organizations engaged in social, educational or political activities; Communist affiliations prohibited.

Non-trading corporations, partnerships and associations of persons operating in the state of Louisiana and engaged in social, educational or political activities are prohibited from being affiliated with any foreign or out of state non-trading corporations, partnerships or associations of persons, any of the officers or members of the board of directors of which are members of Communist, Communist-front or subversive organizations, as cited by the House of Congress un-American Activities Committee, or the United States Attorney. Reports or information from the files of the Committee on un-American Activities of the U.S. House of Representatives shall constitute prima facie evidence of such membership in said organizations.

§386. Affidavits.

As a condition precedent to being authorized to operate or conduct any activities in the state of Louisiana, every non-trading corporation, partnership or association of persons engaged in social, educational or political activities, affiliated with any similar non-trading corporation, partnership or association of persons, chartered, created or operating under the laws of any other state, shall file with the secretary of state yearly, on or before December 31, an affidavit attesting to the fact that none of the officers of such out of state or foreign corporation, partnership or association of persons with which it is affiliated, is a member of any such organization cited by the House of Congress un-American Activities Committee, or the United States Attorney General, as Communist, Communist-front or subversive.

§387. Failure to file affidavit; penalty.

Failure to file the affidavit required by R.S. 14:386 shall constitute a misdemeanor, and the officers and members of such non-trading corporation, partnership or association of persons operating in this state and affiliated with such out of state or foreign organizations, failing to file such affidavit, shall be deemed guilty of a misdemeanor and upon conviction by a court of competent jurisdiction shall be fined $100.00 and imprisoned 30 days in the parish jail.

§388. False statements in affidavit as perjury.

Any false statement under oath contained in the affidavit required by R.S. 14:386 filed with the secretary of state shall constitute perjury and shall be punished as provided by R.S. 14:123.

§390. Declaration of public policy.

In the interpretation and application of R.S. 14:390 and the Subsections thereof, and as a result of certain evidence having been presented to the Joint Legislative Committee on Un-American Activities of this Legislature, the public policy of this state is declared to be as follows:

There exists a clear, present and distinct danger to the security of the state of Louisiana and the well-being and security of the citizens of Louisiana arising from the infiltration of a significant amount of communist propaganda into the state. In addition, this state is a stopping place or "way station" for sizeable shipments of dangerous communist propaganda to the rest of the United States and to many foreign countries.

The danger of communist propaganda lies not in its being "different" in the philosophy it expresses from the philosophy generally held in this state and nation, but instead in the fact that it is a specific tool or weapon used by the communists for the express purpose of bringing about the forcible total destruction or subjugation of this state and nation and the total eradication of the philosophy of freedom upon which this state and nation were founded. "Words are bullets" and the communists know it and use them so. Whatever guarantees of sovereignty and freedom are enjoyed by this state and its citizens are certain to vanish if the United States of America is destroyed or taken over by the communists, and we therefore declare that any communist effort by propaganda infiltration or otherwise against the United States is and should rightly be considered an attack upon or clear and present danger to the state of Louisiana and its citizens. Such attacks should therefore be the subject of concurrent jurisdiction through remedial legislation such as is now in effect on both the state and federal level concerning such dangers as the narcotics traffic, bank robbery, kidnapping, etc. We hereby declare that the danger of communist propaganda infiltration is even greater than the danger from narcotics, pornographic literature, switch blade knives, burglar tools or illicit alcohol in dry jurisdictions, all of which have been the subject of valid statutory regulation by the States within the constitutional framework. The federal legislation on this subject matter is either inadequate in its scope, or not being effectively enforced, as much communistic propaganda material unlabeled and unidentified as such, is in fact entering the state of Louisiana at this time.

We further declare that communist propaganda, properly identified in terms similar to those used in the Foreign Agents Registration Act of the United States, is hereby identified as illicit dangerous contraband material. We further declare that certain exemptions hereinafter provided are for the purpose of allowing bona fide students of foreign languages, foreign affairs or foreign political systems, other interested individuals, and also bona fide educational institutions, to obtain this contraband upon specifically requesting its delivery for the purpose of personal or institutional use in the due course of the educational process. We do not believe that the possession or use of such material by knowing and informed individuals for their personal use is any significant danger, and in fact it might be of some benefit in informing such individuals of the cynical and insidious nature of the communist party line. In view of these facts and so that any user of such materials will be adequately forewarned, we declare that all such material in any way entering the state of Louisiana should be required to be clearly labeled as communist propaganda as hereinafter provided.

§390.1. Definition of communist propaganda.

(1) "Communist propaganda" means any oral, visual, graphic, written, pictorial or other communication which is issued, prepared, printed, procured, distributed or disseminated by the Soviet Union, any of its satellite countries, or by the government of any other communist

country or any agent of the Soviet Union, its satellite countries or any other communist country, wherever located, or by any communist organization, communist action organization, communist front organization, communist infiltrated organization or communist controlled organization or by any agent of any such organization, which communication or material from any of the above listed sources is

(a) reasonably adopted to, or which the person disseminating the same believes will, or which he intends to, prevail upon, indoctrinate, convert, induce, or in any way influence a recipient or any section of the public with reference to the political or public interests, policies or relations of a government of a foreign country or a foreign political party, or promote in the United States or the state of Louisiana, any attitude or state of mind that tends to undermine the determination of any citizen of the United States or of any of the various states to uphold and defend the Constitution of the United States or the constitutions of the respective states, or tends to create or encourage disrespect for duly constitutional legal authority, either federal or state, or

(b) which advocates, advises, instigates or promotes any racial, social, political or religious disorder, civil riot, or other conflict involving the use of force or violence in the United States, the state of Louisiana or any other American republic, or the overthrow of any government or political subdivision of the United States, the state of Louisiana or any other American republic by any means involving the use of force or violence.

(2) For the purposes of R.S. 14:390—14:390.8, the fact that an organization has been officially cited or identified by the attorney general of the United States, the subversive activities control board of the United States or any committee of the United States Congress as a communist organization, a communist action organization, a communist front organization or a communist infiltrated organization or has been in any other way officially cited or identified by any of these aforementioned authorities as a communist controlled organization, shall be considered presumptive evidence of the factual status of any such organization.

§390.2. Acts prohibited.

It shall be a felony for any person to knowingly, willfully and intentionally deliver, distribute, disseminate or store communist propaganda in the state of Louisiana except under the specific exemptions hereinafter provided.

§390.3. Legitimate procurement of contraband.

Bona fide students of foreign languages, foreign affairs, or foreign political systems, other interested individuals, and also bona fide officially accredited educational institutions may obtain communist propaganda and have the same legally delivered to them within the state of Louisiana upon specifically requesting the delivery of the same for the purpose of personal or institutional use in the due course of the educational process. All such communist propaganda legally entering this state under this exemption shall be clearly and legibly labeled on both the front and back cover thereof, or on the front if not covered, with the words "Communist Propaganda" printed or stamped conspicuously in red ink, and failure to so label said material shall constitute a violation of R.S. 14:390—14:390.8 on the part of the sender or distributor thereof, the violation to be considered to take place at the point of actual delivery to the ultimate user who requested the material.

§390.4. Venue.

Violations of R.S. 14:390—14:390.8 are considered to take place at the location where the prohibited contraband material is found, either stored in bulk or placed in the hands of the ultimate user.

§390.5. Warehousing and storage.

It is the duty of the sheriffs of the respective parishes, upon the finding of any bulk storage of any communist propaganda, to enter upon the premises where the material is found, clear the premises of all human occupants, and padlock the premises until judicially ordered to reopen them. The owner of any padlocked premises may, upon application to the district court of proper jurisdiction and upon showing the court that the premises can be immediately cleared of the prohibited contraband material, obtain an order from the court to the sheriff, authorizing him to supervise the removal of the contraband by the owner of the premises and to re-open the premises thereafter.

§390.6. Destruction of contraband.

All communist propaganda discovered in the state of Louisiana in violation of R.S. 14:390—14:390.8 shall be seized and after proper identification and upon summary order of the district court of proper jurisdiction, destroyed, unless needed for official purposes.

§390.7. Penalties.

Any person who violates any of the provisions of R.S. 14:390—14:390.6 shall be fined not more than ten thousand dollars or imprisoned at hard labor for not more than six years, or both.

§390.8. Short title.

R.S. 14:390 through 14:390.7 may be cited as the "Communist Propaganda Control Law."

PART V. OFFENSES AFFECTING LAW ENFORCEMENT

§401. Demonstrations in or near building housing a court or occupied as residence by judge, juror, witness or court officer.

Whoever, with the intent of interfering with, obstructing, or impeding the administration of justice, or with the intent of influencing any judge, juror, witness, or court officer, in the discharge of his duty pickets or parades in or near a building housing a court of the State of Louisiana, or in or near a building or residence occupied or used by such judge, juror, witness, or court officer, or with such intent uses any sound-truck or similar device or resorts to any other demonstration in or near any such building or residence, shall be fined not more than five thousand dollars or imprisoned not more than one year, or both.

Nothing in this section shall interfere with or prevent the exercise by any court of the State of Louisiana of its power to punish for contempt.

§402. Contraband defined; taking to and from penal institutions prohibited; penalty; disposition of seized contraband.

A. No person shall introduce contraband into or upon the grounds of any state correctional institution.

B. No person shall possess contraband upon the grounds of any state correctional institution.

C. No person shall send contraband from any state correctional institution.

D. "Contraband" as used herein means:

(1) Any controlled dangerous substance as defined in R.S. 40:961, et seq., or any other drug or substance that if taken internally, whether separately or in combination with another drug or substance, produces or may produce an hypnotic effect. The provisions of this Paragraph shall not apply to a drug or substance that has been prescribed by a physician, if the drug or substance is in a container issued by the pharmacy or other place of dispensation, the container identifies the prescription number, prescribing physician, and issuing pharmacist or other person, and the container is not concealed upon the body of the person.

(2) A dangerous weapon, or other instrumentality customarily used or intended for probable use as a dangerous weapon or to aid in an escape, unless authorized by the warden of the institution.

(3) Explosives or combustibles, unless authorized by the warden of the institution.

(4) Plans for the making or manufacturing of a dangerous weapon or other instrumentality customarily used or intended for probable use as a dangerous weapon or to aid in an escape, or for the making or manufacturing of explosives or combustibles, or for an escape from an institution, unless authorized by the warden of the institution.

(5) An alcoholic beverage or other beverage which produces or may produce an intoxicating effect.

(6) Stolen property.

(7) Any currency or coin, unless authorized by the warden of the institution.

(8) Any article of food, toiletries, or clothing, unless authorized by the warden of the institution.

E. It shall be unlawful to possess or to introduce or attempt to introduce into or upon the premises of any municipal or parish prison or jail or to take or attempt to take or send therefrom, or to give or to attempt to give to an inmate of any municipal or parish prison or jail, any of the following articles which are hereby declared to be contraband for the purpose of this Section, to wit:

(1) Any currency or coin which is legal tender;

(2) Any stolen property;

(3) Any article of food or clothing;

(4) Any intoxicating beverage or beverages which cause or may cause any intoxicating effects;

(5) Any narcotic or hypnotic or excitive drug or any drugs of whatever kind or nature, including nasal inhalators of any variety, sleeping pills or barbiturates of any variety that create or may create a hypnotic effect if taken internally, or any other controlled dangerous substance as defined in R.S. 40:961, et seq.; and

(6) Any firearm or any instrumentality customarily used as a dangerous weapon, including explosives or combustibles, except through regular channels as authorized by the officer in charge of any institution herein, or any plans for the making or manufacturing of such weapons or devices; however, the definition of contraband is not restricted to those articles set forth hereinabove.

F. Any contraband which is seized may be destroyed, donated to a charitable organization, or put to lawful use within the institution, unless it is needed as evidence in a criminal prosecution. However, any money seized which is legal tender shall be placed in a fund at the institution at which the money was seized to be used solely for the purchase of contraband detection and escape chase team equipment. A record of the disposition of all contraband shall be maintained.

G. Whoever violates any provision of this Section shall be imprisoned with or without hard labor for not more than five years.

(Chgd. by Acts 1991 No. 191, §1, eff. 9/6/91.)

§402.1. Taking of contraband to state owned hospitals unlawful; penalty.

A. It shall be unlawful for any person to introduce or attempt to introduce into or upon the grounds or buildings of any state owned and administered hospital or related facility, except through regular channels as authorized by the administrator of the hospital, any of the following articles which are hereby declared contraband for the purposes of this Part, namely: Any intoxicating beverage or beverage which causes or may cause an intoxicating effect; any narcotic or hypnotic or exciting drug of whatever kind or nature including nasal inhalators of any variety, sleeping pills or barbiturates of any variety that create or may create a hypnotic effect if taken internally; and any firearm or other instrumentality customarily considered a dangerous weapon.

B. Whoever violates any provision of this Section shall upon conviction be imprisoned with or without hard labor for not more than three years without being eligible for a suspended sentence or for a parole.

§403. Abuse of children; reports; waiver of privilege.

A. (1) Any person who, under Children's Code Article 609(A), is required to report the abuse or neglect or sexual abuse of a child and knowingly and willfully fails to so report shall be guilty of a misdemeanor and upon conviction shall be fined not more than five hundred dollars or imprisoned for not more than six months, or both.

(2) Any person, any employee of a local child protection unit of the Department of Social Services, any employee of any local law enforcement agency, any employee or agent of any state department, or any school employee who knowingly and willfully violates the provisions of Chapter 5 of Title IV of the Children's Code, or who knowingly and willfully obstructs the procedures for receiving and investigating reports of child abuse or neglect or sexual abuse, or who discloses without authorization confidential information about or contained within such reports shall be guilty of a misdemeanor and upon conviction shall be fined not more than five hundred dollars or imprisoned for not more than six months, or both.

(3) Any person who reports a child as abused or neglected or sexually abused to the department or to any law enforcement agency, knowing that such information is false, shall be guilty of a misdemeanor and upon conviction shall be fined not more than five hundred dollars or imprisoned for not more than six months, or both.

B. In any proceeding concerning the abuse or neglect or sexual abuse of a child or the cause of such condition, evidence may not be excluded on any ground of privilege, except in the case of communications between an attorney and his client or between a priest, rabbi, duly ordained minister or Christian Science practitioner and his communicant.

(Chgd. by Acts 1990 No. 439, §1; Acts 1992 No. 705, §3, eff. 7/6/92.)

§403.1. Substance abuse in schools; definitions; confidential reports; immunity; penalty.

A. The purpose of this Section is to protect teachers, administrators, school support personnel, and employees of the public school systems of this state from liability for damages as a result of reporting substance abuse on school campuses. It is intended that as a result of such reporting, the children attending schools in this state shall not be exposed to substance abuse while on campus, and law enforcement shall be aided in efforts to eradicate substance abuse by students.

B. For the purposes of this Section, the following terms shall mean:

(1) "Person" is any employee of a public school system including, but not limited to, teachers, administrators, school bus drivers, janitors, lunch room workers, maintenance employees, and coaches of athletic teams.

(2) "Student" is any person enrolled at school, including any person so enrolled but on temporary suspension, and any person physically on campus, whether a student or non-student.

(3) "School" is any public elementary or secondary school in the state of Louisiana.

(4) "Campus" is all facilities and property within the boundary of the school property and all vehicles used for public transportation of students.

(5) "Controlled dangerous substance" is any substance regulated or defined in the Uniform Controlled Dangerous Substance Law, Part X, Chapter IV of Title 40 of the Louisiana Revised Statutes of 1950, except where prescribed by a physician and possessed and consumed by the person for whom prescribed.

(6) "Substance Abuse Prevention Team," hereafter sometimes referred to as "the team," is a panel of not less than six members consisting of at least one (a) administrator, (b) teacher, (c) guidance counselor, (d) parent representative, and (e) school support person. The team shall be trained by personnel from the Substance Abuse Prevention Education Program of the Louisiana Department of Education.

In the absence of the availability of a team trained by personnel from the Substance Abuse Prevention Education Program, the principal of a school may establish a substantially similar panel which shall be considered a substance abuse prevention team.

C. (1) Any person having reasonable cause to believe that a student possesses a controlled dangerous substance or an alcoholic beverage on a school campus, under circumstances other than those described in Paragraph (2) of this Subsection, shall report such fact to the principal of the school or to the chairman of the Substance Abuse Prevention Team on a report form prepared by the Department of Education or on a substantially similar form. If the report is to the principal, the principal immediately shall forward it to the chairman of the team.

The team shall discuss the circumstances of the report with the student reported without disclosing the name of the reporting person and shall also meet with the parents of the student reported. The team shall thereafter report to the principal of the school and make recommendations for treatment, counseling, or other appropriate action.

(2) Any person having factual knowledge that a student has manufactured, distributed, or possessed with intent to distribute a controlled dangerous substance shall report such fact to the principal of the school who, upon a finding that there is reasonable cause to believe that the student has manufactured, distributed, or possessed with intent to distribute a controlled dangerous substance, shall report such information to the appropriate law enforcement agency. If the principal determines that there are reasonable grounds to believe the student possessed a controlled dangerous substance but did not manufacture, distribute, or possess with intent to distribute a controlled dangerous substance, he shall refer the matter to the Substance Abuse Prevention Team chairman.

(3) The report required in Paragraphs (1) and (2) of this Subsection shall be written and shall include the name of the person making the report, the name of the student suspected of committing the act so reported, and the specific incident which caused the reporting person to believe the act had occurred. Sufficient detail shall be included to allow the report to be adequately reviewed. When appropriate, the report shall include a behavioral profile of the student since his enrollment in class.

D. (1) The provisions of Subsection C of this Section shall not preclude any person from making a report of conduct to a law enforcement agency when that person has reasonable cause to believe that the manufacture or distribution of a controlled dangerous substance has taken or is taking place and that delay would jeopardize or impair the ability to control the manufacture or distribution of a controlled dangerous substance on a campus.

(2) The provisions of Subsection C of this Section shall not preclude any person from making a report of conduct to a law enforcement agency when that person has reasonable cause to believe that a student on campus is under the influence of alcoholic beverages and that delay would jeopardize or impair the ability to operate the school or result in the student's being a danger to himself or others.

(3) A law enforcement agency receiving a report under the provisions of this Subsection may conduct an investigation of the report. Such investigation may include the administering, upon the school grounds and after consent has been obtained from student's parent or legal tutor, of a breath or urine test for the presence of alcohol or a controlled dangerous substance, if the investigating officer has reasonable cause to believe the student is or recently was on campus while under the influence of alcoholic beverages or a controlled dangerous substance. The methods for the administration and analysis of a breath or urine test under the provisions of this Subsection shall be the same as for chemical testing and analysis authorized under R.S. 32:663. The results of a breath or urine test authorized under this Subsection shall be provided solely to the student, the parent or legal tutor of the student, the principal of the school, and the chairman of the Substance Abuse Prevention Team, and shall not be used as the basis for any disciplinary proceeding against the student. The law enforcement agency may keep a copy of the test results which copy shall not be a public record and shall not be open for public inspection but shall be kept confidential under lock and key and maintained only for internal record keeping purposes to preserve the integrity of said agency's file and shall not be used for any investigative purpose. The test results shall be exempt from the Public Records Act* and shall not be admissible as evidence in any civil or criminal trial, hearing, or other proceeding.

**R.S. 44:1 et seq.*

E. All reports filed pursuant to this Section shall be confidential. The identity of the reporting person shall not be disclosed except when the constitution of the State of Louisiana or the United States so requires. All reports shall be exempt from the Public Records Act.

F. Any person who makes a report in good faith, pursuant to Subsections C and D of this Section, shall have immunity from civil liability that otherwise might be incurred. Such immunity shall extend to testimony in any judicial proceeding resulting from such report.

G. The willful failure by a person with permanent status to make a report required by Subsection C of this Section shall constitute willful neglect of duty which may subject the person to dismissal pursuant to R.S. 17:443, R.S. 17:462, R.S. 17:493, R.S. 17:523, or R.S. 17:533, as appropriate. Any person without permanent status may be dismissed for willful neglect of duty under this Section after a hearing in accordance with the procedures set forth in R.S. 17:443.

§403.2. Abuse and neglect of adults; reports; investigation; waiver of privileges; penalties; immunity.

A. (1) The purpose of this Section is to protect adults who cannot physically or mentally protect themselves and who are harmed or threatened with harm through action or inaction by themselves or by the individuals responsible for their care or by other parties, by requiring mandatory reporting of suspected cases of abuse or neglect by any person having reasonable cause to believe that such a case exists. It is intended that, as a result of such reports, protective services shall be provided by the adult protection agency. Such services shall be available as needed without regard to income.

(2) It is the further intent of the legislature to authorize only the least possible restriction on the exercise of personal and civil rights consistent with the person's need for services and to require that due process be followed in imposing such restrictions.

B. For the purposes of this Section, the following definitions shall apply:

(1) "Abuse" is the infliction of physical or mental injury on an adult by other parties, including but not limited to such means as sexual abuse, exploitation, or extortion of funds or other things of value, to such an extent that his health, self-determination, or emotional well-being is endangered.

(2) "Adult" is any person sixty years of age or older, any disabled person eighteen years of age or older, or an emancipated minor.

(3) "Adult protection agency" is the office of elderly affairs in the office of the governor, for any individual sixty years of age or older in need of adult protective services as provided in this Section. Adult protection agency is the Department of Health and Hospitals for any individual between the ages of eighteen and fifty-nine years of age in need of adult protective services as provided in this Section. The secretary of the Department of Health and Hospitals

may assign the duties and powers provided in this Section to any office of the department for provision of adult protective services, as provided in subsection E(1).

(4) "Capacity to consent" means the ability to understand and appreciate the nature and consequences of making decisions concerning one's person, including but not limited to provisions for health or mental health care, food, shelter, clothing, safety, or financial affairs. This determination may be based on assessment or investigative findings, observation, or medical or mental health evaluations.

(5) "Caregiver" is any person or persons, either temporarily or permanently, responsible for the care of an aged person or a physically or mentally disabled adult. Caregiver includes but is not limited to adult children, parents, relatives, neighbors, daycare personnel, adult foster home sponsors, personnel of public and private institutions and facilities, adult congregate living facilities, and nursing homes which have voluntarily assumed the care of an aged person, or disabled adult, have assumed voluntary residence with an aged person or disabled adult, or have assumed voluntary use or tutelage of an aged or disabled person's assets, funds, or property, and specifically shall include city, parish, or state law enforcement agencies.

(6) "Exploitation" is the illegal or improper use or management of an aged person's or disabled adult's funds, assets, or property, or the use of an aged person's or disabled adult's power of attorney or guardianship for one's own profit or advantage.

(7) "Extortion" is the acquisition of a thing of value from an unwilling or reluctant adult by physical force, intimidation, or abuse of legal or official authority.

(8) "Neglect" is the failure, by a caregiver responsible for an adult's care or by other parties, to provide the proper or necessary support or medical, surgical, or any other care necessary for his well-being. No adult who is being provided treatment in accordance with a recognized religious method of healing in lieu of medical treatment shall for that reason alone be considered to be neglected or abused.

(9) "Protective services" include but are not limited to:

(a) Conducting investigations and assessments of complaints of possible abuse, neglect, or exploitation to determine if the situation and condition of the adult warrant further action.

(b) Preparing a social services plan utilizing community resources aimed at remedying abuse, neglect, and exploitation.

(c) Case management to assure stabilization of the situation.

(d) Referral for legal assistance to initiate any necessary extrajudicial remedial action.

(10) "Self-neglect" is the failure, either by the adult's action or inaction, to provide the proper or necessary support or medical, surgical, or any other care necessary for his own well-being. No adult who is being provided treatment in accordance with a recognized religious method of healing in lieu of medical treatment shall for that reason alone be considered to be self-neglected.

(11) "Disabled person" is a person with a mental, physical, or developmental disability that substantially impairs the person's ability to provide adequately for his own care or protection.

C. Any person, including but not limited to a health, mental health, and social service practitioner, having cause to believe that an adult's physical or mental health or welfare has been or may be further adversely affected by abuse, neglect, or exploitation shall report in accordance with Subsection D of this Section.

D. (1) Reports reflecting the reporter's belief that an adult has been abused or neglected shall be made to any adult protection agency or to any local or state law enforcement agency. These reports need not name the persons suspected of the alleged abuse or neglect.

(2) All reports shall contain the name and address of the adult, the name and address of the person responsible for the care of the adult, if available, and any other pertinent information.

(3) All reports received by a local or state law enforcement agency shall be referred to the appropriate adult protection agency.

(4) *(Repealed.)*

E. (1) The adult protection agency shall make prompt investigation and assessment. When the report concerns care in a facility or program under the supervision of the Department of Health and Hospitals, the secretary of the department may assign the duties and powers enumerated in Paragraph (2) of this Subsection to any office or entity within the department to carry out the purposes of this Section.

(2) The investigation and assessment shall include the nature, extent, and cause of the abuse and neglect, the identity of the person or persons responsible for the abuse and neglect, if known, and an interview with the adult and a visit to the adult's home, if possible.

Consultation with others having knowledge of the facts of the particular case shall also be included in the investigation.

(3) In the event that admission to the adult's home is refused, the adult protection agency may apply to a court of competent civil jurisdiction for an order to enter the home to make such an investigation.

(4) To secure further information and coordinate community service efforts, the adult protection agency shall contact other appropriate local or state agencies.

(5) The adult protection agencies shall convene a regional level coordinating council composed of representatives of both public and private agencies providing services, with the objectives of identifying resources, increasing needed supportive services, avoiding duplication of effort, and assuring maximum community coordination of effort.

(6) If it appears after investigation that an adult has been abused and neglected by other parties and that the problem cannot be remedied by extrajudicial means, the adult protection agency shall refer the matter to the appropriate district attorney's office. Evidence that abuse or neglect has occurred must be presented together with an account of the protective services given or available to the adult and a recommendation as to what services, if ordered, would eliminate the abuse or neglect.

(7) Protective services may not be provided in cases of self-neglect to any adult having the capacity to consent, who does not consent to such service or who, having consented, withdraws such consent. Nothing herein shall prohibit the adult protection agency, the district attorney, the coroner, or the judge from petitioning for interdiction pursuant to Civil Code Articles 389 through 426 or petitioning for an order for protective custody or for judicial commitment pursuant to R.S. 28:50 et seq. seeking an order for emergency protective services pursuant to Subsection N of this Section, or prohibit the district attorney from seeking an order for involuntary protective services pursuant to Subparagraph F(*l*)(e) of this Section.

(8) Information contained in the case records of the adult protection agency shall be confidential and shall not be released without a written authorization from the adult or his legal representative, except that the information may be released to law enforcement agencies and social service agencies who are providing services to the adult or pursuing enforcement of criminal statutes related to the abuse of the adult.

F. (1) The district attorney shall notify the adult of the hearing and any action proposed with respect to the alleged abuse or neglect. He shall advise the adult of his right to be represented by an attorney. The district attorney may apply to a court of competent civil jurisdiction for an order to:

(a) Provide mandatory counseling for the parties involved to prevent further abuse or neglect of the adult.

(b) Enjoin the parties contributing to the abuse or neglect of the adult from continuing such acts.

(c) Have the adult receive a medical examination or psychiatric/psychological evaluation which will help to determine the least restrictive setting the adult may need.

(d) Enjoin any party interfering with the provision of protective services to an adult from continuing such interference.

(e) Provide protective services, if the adult lacks the capacity to consent to services, and the adult is suffering harm or deterioration or is likely to suffer harm or deterioration from abuse, neglect, or self-neglect, if protective services are not provided, and no other person authorized by law or by court order to give consent for the adult is available or willing to arrange for protective services. Such an order shall specify the services needed to protect the adult, which may include medical treatment, social services, temporary placement in a safer living situation, and other services needed to protect the adult. Such an order shall be effective for a period of not more than thirty days, but an order may be renewed one time for another thirty days upon a showing to the court that continuation of the order is necessary to prevent further harm to the adult. However, admission to a mental health treatment facility shall be made only in accordance with the provisions of R.S. 28:1 et seq.

(2) The district attorney may likewise institute any criminal proceedings he deems appropriate in accordance with existing laws.

(3) Pursuant to Code of Criminal Procedure Art. 66, the district attorney or the attorney general may cause to be issued a subpoena or subpoena duces tecum for the purpose of requiring a person having knowledge, written material, or other evidence pertinent to alleged abuse, neglect, or exploitation of the adult to produce such evidence to the district attorney, attorney general or the adult protection agency.

G. Upon application by the district attorney under the provisions of Subsection F, the court shall fix a date for a hearing to be held not more than twenty days, excluding Saturdays, Sundays, and legal holidays from receipt of the petition. If the alleged abused or neglected adult has no attorney, the court shall appoint an attorney to represent him. The adult's attorney shall be granted access to all records of the adult.

H. The court shall cause the alleged abused or neglected adult and his attorney to be served with notice of the appointment and of the time, date, and place of the hearing no later than five days prior to the hearing. The notice shall inform such respondent that he has a right to be present at the hearing, that he has a right to choose his own privately retained and paid counsel or have a court-appointed attorney if he cannot afford one, that he has a right to subpoena witnesses to testify on his behalf, and that he has a right to cross-examine any witness testifying against him. The alleged abused or neglected adult shall have the right to attend the hearing; however, this may be waived by his attorney for cause with approval of the court.

I. (1) The adult protection agency may adopt such rules and regulations as may be necessary in carrying out the provisions of this Section. Specifically, such rules shall provide for cooperation with local agencies, including but not limited to hospitals, clinics, and nursing homes, and cooperation with other states. The adult protection agencies may enter into cooperative agreements with other state agencies or contractual agreements with private agencies to carry out the purposes of this Section. The immunity granted to the staff of the adult protection agencies defined in Paragraph (3) of this Subsection shall extend to the staff of those agencies carrying out the provisions of this Section through cooperative or contractual agreement.

(2) (a) The adult protection agencies shall implement adult protective services for aged and disabled adults in accordance with an agency plan and shall submit an annual funding request in accordance with its plan. No funds shall be expended to implement the plan until the budget is approved by the commissioner of administration and by the legislature in the annual state appropriations act, with the exception of Subparagraph (c) of Paragraph I(2) providing for initial implementation during the course of a state fiscal year by transition of funds and positions across programs.

(b) Subject to the availability of funds and positions appropriated, the office of elderly affairs shall implement an adult protective services program for persons sixty years of age or older during state Fiscal Year 1992-1993.

(c) Subject to state funds and positions becoming available with the transfer of specialized investigations of allegations of abuse and/or neglect involving class members under the jurisdiction of the federal court in the Gary W., et al. vs. Louisiana, et al. class action back under the state's authority from court authority, those state funds and positions currently authorized and funded for court-ordered administration and compliance in the Gary W. case which are budgeted in the Department of Health and Hospitals shall be used to implement a protective services program for disabled adults age eighteen to fifty-nine as provided in this Section. The Department of Health and Hospitals may submit this plan for approval to the federal court and the commissioner of administration. Upon approval by the court, the commissioner of administration and the secretary of the department shall be authorized to transfer the positions and funds appropriated in the secretary's budget for court-ordered Gary W. administration and compliance to implement protective services for disabled adults.

(3) When the adult protection agency's staff is not sufficient to respond promptly to all reported cases, the aged protection agency shall set priorities for case response and allocate staff resources to cases in accordance with the rules and regulations promulgated in accordance with Paragraph (1) of this Subsection. Until the funding becomes available for a protective services program for disabled adults within the Department of Health and Hospitals and in view of the office of elderly affairs' earlier implementation date for adult protective service, this office shall have the authority to intervene, as provided in this Section, on an emergency basis in reported cases of imminent life-threatening circumstances involving disabled adults age eighteen to fifty-nine. Absent evidence of willful or intentional misconduct or gross negligence in carrying out the investigative functions of the adult protective services program, caseworkers, supervisors, program managers, and agency heads shall be immune from civil or criminal liability in any legal action arising from any decision by the adult protection agency relative to the setting of priorities for cases and targeting of staff resources.

J. (1) Any person who knowingly and willfully fails to report as provided by Subsection C, shall be fined not more than five hundred dollars or imprisoned not more than six months, or both.

(2) Any person who knowingly files a false report of abuse or neglect shall be fined not more than one thousand dollars, imprisoned with or without hard labor for not more than one year, or both.

K. No cause of action shall exist against any person who in good faith makes a report, cooperates in an investigation by an adult protective agency, or participates in judicial proceedings authorized under the provisions of this Section, or any adult protective services caseworker who in good faith conducts an investigation or makes an investigative judgment or disposition, and such person shall have immunity from civil or criminal liability that otherwise might be incurred or imposed. This immunity shall not be extended to:

(1) Any alleged principal, conspirator, or accessory to an offense involving the abuse or neglect of the adult.

(2) Any person who makes a report known to be false or with reckless disregard for the truth of the report.

(3) Any person charged with direct or constructive contempt of court, any act of perjury as defined in Subpart C of Part VII of Chapter 1 of this Title, or any offense affecting judicial functions and public records as defined in Subpart D of Part VII of Chapter 1 of this Title.

L. The adult protection agency shall also be responsible for ongoing inservice training for its staff which assures adequate performance.

M. In any proceeding concerning the abuse, neglect, or self-neglect of an adult, evidence may not be excluded on any ground of privilege, except in the case of communications between an attorney and his client or between a priest, rabbi, duly ordained minister, or Christian Science practitioner and his communicant.

N. (1) If the adult protection agency has reasonable cause to believe that an adult is at immediate and present risk of substantial harm or deterioration from abuse, neglect, or self-neglect, and the adult lacks the capacity to consent, or with the consent of an adult who has capacity, the agency or any entity named in Paragraph E(7) of this Section may petition a court of competent civil jurisdiction for an ex parte order to provide emergency protective services. The petition shall contain an affidavit setting forth the facts upon which the agency relied in making the determination.

(2) Such an order shall specify the services needed to protect the adult, which may include medical treatment, social services, temporary placement in a safer living situation, and other services needed to protect the adult and may contain any remedy outlined in Subsection F of this Section or any remedy deemed by the court as needed to protect the adult. However, admission to a mental health treatment facility shall be made only in accordance with the provisions of R.S. 28:1 et seq.

(3) Such an order shall extend for a period not to exceed fifteen days.

(4) (a) Within three days of the issuance of the ex parte court order, there shall be a hearing held by the court issuing the order. The hearing may be continued for up to three additional days upon motion and with good cause shown.

(b) The adult has the right to be represented by an attorney. If the alleged abused or neglected adult has no attorney, the court shall appoint an attorney to represent him.

(c) At the hearing, the adult protection agency has the burden to prove that the adult lacks the capacity to consent, and that the adult is at immediate and present risk of substantial harm or deterioration from abuse, neglect, or self-neglect.

(d) The adult shall have the right to present evidence, call witnesses, be heard on his own behalf, and cross-examine witnesses called by the adult protection agency.

(e) Reasonable notice of the hearing and rights set forth in this Section shall be given to the adult.

(Chgd. by Acts 1990 No. 534, §1; Acts 1991 No. 408, §1; Acts 1992 No. 975, §1; Acts 1995 No. 841, §1; Acts 1997 No. 1183, §1, eff. 8/15/97.)

§403.3. Reports of missing children; procedures; false reports or communications; penalties.

A. (1) Any state or local law enforcement agency receiving a report of a missing child and having reasonable grounds to believe such report is accurate shall within forty-eight hours after the date of receipt of the report notify each of the following of the fact and contents of such report:

(a) The Department of Health and Human Resources.

(b) The Department of Public Safety and Corrections, if it did not originally receive the report.

(c) The office of the sheriff for the parish in which such report was received, if it did not originally receive the report.

(d) The office of the sheriff for all parishes adjacent to the parish in which such report was received.

(e) The National Crime Information Computer System.

(2) The law enforcement agency may also notify any other appropriate local, state, or federal agency of the fact and contents of such report.

B. No person shall knowingly file a false missing child report with a law enforcement agency.

C. No person shall intentionally communicate false information concerning a missing child to a law enforcement agency when such information is communicated with the specific intent to delay or otherwise hinder an investigation to locate the child.

D. Whoever violates the provisions of Subsections B or C herein shall be fined not more than five hundred dollars or be imprisoned for not more than six months, or both.

§403.4. Burn injuries and wounds; reports; registry; immunity; penalties.

A. The purpose of this Section is to combat arson through the rapid identification and apprehension of suspected arsonists who may suffer burn injuries during the commission of their crimes. It is the further intent of this Section to provide for a central registry for burn injuries and wounds data from which effective fire and arson prevention and fire safety education programs may be developed.

B. In every case of a burn injury or wound in which the victim sustains second or third degree burns to five percent or more of the body or any burns to the upper respiratory tract or laryngeal edema due to the inhalation of super-heated air, and every case of a burn injury or wound which is likely to or may result in death shall be reported to the office of the state fire marshal, code enforcement and building safety hereinafter sometimes referred to as the "office". That office shall then immediately notify the appropriate local or state investigatory agency or law enforcement agency of the receipt of such report and its contents.

C. (1) An oral report shall be made within twenty-four hours of the examination or treatment of the victim. The report shall be made by the physician attending or treating the case, or by the manager, superintendent, director, or other person in charge whenever such case is treated in a hospital, burn center, sanitarium, or other medical facility. The report may be recorded electronically or in any other suitable manner, by the office of the state fire marshal, code enforcement and building safety.

(2) The oral report shall contain the following information if known:

(a) Victim's name, address, and date of birth.

(b) Address where the burn injury occurred.

(c) Date and time of the burn injury.

(d) Degree of burns and percent of body burned.

(e) Area of body injured.

(f) Injury severity.

(g) Apparent cause of burn injury.

(h) Name and address of reporting facility.

(i) Name of the attending physician.

D. (1) The office shall maintain a central registry of all reported cases of the treatment or examination of persons with burn injuries or wounds. The registry may be used to provide information to those agencies whose duties include the investigation into possible arson activities.

(2) The office of the state fire marshal, code enforcement and building safety may adopt rules and regulations as may be necessary in carrying out the provisions of this Section. Specifically such rules shall provide for cooperation with local investigatory and law enforcement agencies and may also authorize law enforcement personnel and the state fire marshal to review those medical records of reported victims which relate to the burn without the consent of the victim.

E. No cause of action shall exist against any person who in good faith makes a report pursuant to this Section, cooperates in an investigation by any agency, or participates in any judicial proceeding resulting from such report.

F. Any person who knowingly files a false report shall be fined not more than five hundred dollars or imprisoned for not more than six months, or both.
(Chgd. by Acts 1991 No. 657, §1, eff. 9/6/91.)

§403.5. Gunshot wounds; mandatory reporting.

A. The purpose of this Section is to aid law enforcement in combating violent crime through the rapid identification and reporting of all gunshot wounds or injuries treated by any medical professionals, practitioners, or associated persons.

B. In every case of a gunshot wound or injury presented for treatment to a medical professional, practitioner, or associated person, that professional, practitioner, or associated person shall make an oral notification to either the sheriff of the parish in which the wounded person was presented for treatment, or the chief or superintendent of police in the municipality in which the wounded person was presented for treatment immediately after complying with all applicable state and federal laws, rules, and regulations related to the treatment of emergencies and before the wounded person is released from the hospital. A written notation of this action shall be made on the emergency record.

C. The provisions of this Section shall not apply to any wounds or injuries received from the firing of an air gun.

D. Any report of a gunshot wound or injury required to be reported by this Section, which does not result in criminal prosecution shall not become public record and shall be destroyed by the law enforcement agency receiving the information.

E. Any person who fails to file a report under this Section shall be fined not more than five hundred dollars or imprisoned for not more than six months, or both. Any person who knowingly files a false report under this Section shall be fined not more than five hundred dollars or imprisoned for not more than six months, or both.
(Added by Acts 1997 No. 1309, §1, eff. 8/15/97.)

§404. Self-mutilation by a prisoner.

A. Self-mutilation by a prisoner is the intentional infliction of injuries to himself by a prisoner incarcerated in any state penitentiary or any local penal or correctional institution or while in the lawful custody of a peace officer, or the procuring or permitting of another person to inflict injury on such prisoner by means of shooting, stabbing, cutting, applying chemicals or other substances to the body, drinking or eating poisonous or toxic substances, or in any manner, when such results in permanent or temporary injury.

B. Whoever commits the crime of self-mutilation by a prisoner shall be imprisoned at hard labor for a term not exceeding two years. Any sentence imposed under this Section shall run consecutively to any other sentence being served by the offender at the time of the offense.
(Chgd. by Acts 1997 No. 179, §1, eff. 8/15/97.)

PART VI. OFFENSES AGAINST THE PERSON

§501. Killing or injuring a person while hunting; penalty for failure to render aid.

Whoever, while taking any bird or mammal, kills or injures another person by the use of any firearm, bow and arrow, spear, slingshot, or other weapon or device used in such taking, and who knowingly either abandons such person or fails to render to such injured person all necessary aid possible under the circumstances, shall be punished by a fine of not more than five hundred dollars.

PART VII. LOANSHARKING

§511. Loansharking; penalty.

A. A person is guilty of loansharking when he knowingly solicits, or receives any money or anything of value, including services, as interest or compensation for a loan, or as forbearance of any right to money or other property, at a rate exceeding forty-five percentum per annum or the equivalent rate for a longer or shorter period. This Section shall not apply to any transaction under Title 6, Title 9, or Sections 1751 through 1770 of Title 37 of the Louisiana Revised Statutes of 1950 or under Revised Civil Code Article 2924.

B. Whoever commits the crime of loansharking is guilty of a felony and shall be punished by a fine of not more than ten thousand dollars or imprisoned for not less than one year nor more than five years with or without hard labor, or both.

C. For the purposes of this Part, the term "person" shall mean any individual, partnership, corporation, or combination of individuals.

§512. Aggravated loansharking; penalty.

A. A person is guilty of aggravated loansharking when, in the commission of loansharking or any attempt thereof, he engages in acts which do injury to the person or property of another, or which places that other person in fear that such injury will be done.

B. Whoever commits the crime of aggravated loansharking is guilty of a felony and shall be punished by a fine of not more than twenty thousand dollars or imprisoned for not less than five nor more than thirty years with or without hard labor, or both.

§513. Possession of loanshark records; penalty.

A. A person is guilty of possession of loanshark records when, with knowledge of the contents thereof, he possesses any writing, paper, instrument or article used to record loansharking transactions.

B. Whoever commits the crime of possession of loanshark records shall be fined not less than five hundred dollars nor more than one thousand dollars or imprisoned for not more than one year, or both.

This page intentionally left blank.

TITLE 15
CRIMINAL PROCEDURE
(Complete Title)

CHAPTER 1. CODE OF CRIMINAL PROCEDURE ANCILLARIES

CODE TITLE II. DISTRICT ATTORNEY AND ATTORNEY GENERAL

Section	
22.	*(Repealed.)*

CODE TITLE III. THE CORONER AND OTHER OFFICERS

30.	Returns.
31.	Confiscation and destruction of gambling devices.
31.1.	Antique slot machines.
32.	Disposition of money used as evidence in criminal cases.

CODE TITLE IV. SEARCH WARRANTS

41.	Disposition of property seized in connection with criminal proceedings.
42.	News media, restrictions on search warrants.
43.	Attorneys; restrictions on search warrants.

CODE TITLE VIII. BAIL

81.	Bond for release for violation of municipal ordinances; parole or release of prisoners; penalty.
82.	Guaranteed arrest bond certificates as cash bail; forfeiture; sureties.
84.	*(Repealed.)*
85.	Forfeiture; procedure; notice; enforcement; and collection.
85.1.	*(Repealed.)*
86.	Forfeiture of cash, checks or securities.
86.1.	Unclaimed bail bonds; disposition; return to owner.
86.2.	City Court of Thibodaux; unclaimed bail bonds; disposition; return to owner.
86.3.	City courts: unclaimed bail bonds; disposition; return to owner.
87.	Non-forfeiture situations.

88. Appearance bond defined.
89. Prescription of forfeiture judgment; revival.

CODE TITLE XI. QUALIFICATIONS AND SELECTION OF GRAND AND PETIT JURORS

111. Parish of Orleans; salary of jury commissioners; vacancy; appointment of secretary.
112. Parish of Orleans; process servers.
113. Duty of Orleans registrar to furnish jury commission lists of voters added to or deleted from rolls.
114. Parish of Orleans; rotation and selection of grand jury; control of grand jury.
115. Service of jury commission process; general rule.
116. Preparation of general venire list; assistance.
117. Discharge of grand jury; review of discharge by supreme court.

CODE TITLE XII. THE GRAND JURY

121. Duty to inspect prisons and hospitals; reports.

CODE TITLE XIV. RIGHT TO COUNSEL

144. Judicial district indigent defender board.
145. Powers and duties of the judicial district indigent defender boards.
146. Judicial district indigent defender fund.
147. Proceedings to determine indigency.
148. Partial reimbursement by indigents.
149. Appointment of counsel at parole revocation and prerevocation hearings.
150. Regional defense service centers.
151. Indigent Defense Assistance Board.
151.1. Quorum; compensation; officers; records.
151.2. Powers; duties; responsibilities; limitations.
151.3. Special reporting requirements.
151.4. Limited effect.

CODE TITLE XVII. TIME LIMITATIONS

171. *(Repealed.)*

CODE TITLE XIX. JURISDICTION AND VENUE

191. Place of trial of criminal neglect of family cases.

CODE TITLE XXI. INSANITY PROCEEDINGS

211. Procedures in handling defendants committed to mental institutions because of lack of capacity to stand trial.

CODE TITLE XXII. RECUSATION OF JUDGES AND DISTRICT ATTORNEYS

221. Appointment of substitute judge by supreme court.

CODE TITLE XXIV. PROCEDURES PRIOR TO TRIAL

241. Medical, psychological, psychiatric examination of certain victims under age eighteen; prohibition.
242. Pretrial diversion for driving while intoxicated; reporting.

CODE TITLE XXV. COMPULSORY PROCESS

252. Witnesses' fees and mileage.
253. Witnesses not residents of parish.
254. Sheriffs, jurors and law enforcement officers not entitled to witness fees.
254.1. Compensation of off-duty law enforcement officers; City Court of New Iberia.

CODE TITLE XXVI. TRIAL PROCEDURE

CODE TITLE XXVIII. BILL OF EXCEPTIONS

CODE TITLE XXX. SENTENCE

CODE TITLE II. DISTRICT ATTORNEY AND ATTORNEY GENERAL

§22. *(Repealed by Acts 1992 No. 315, §1, eff. 6/17/92.)*

CODE TITLE III. THE CORONER AND OTHER OFFICERS

§30. Returns.

Unless otherwise provided by law, a sheriff, marshal, constable or other officer or person who serves a subpoena, summons, writ, notice, order or other process of a court, of a jury commission or of a coroner shall make a return showing the date and manner in which service was made. The return shall become part of the record and shall be considered prima facie correct. Failure to make such return shall not invalidate the service.

§31. Confiscation and destruction of gambling devices.

A. (1) All law enforcement officers of municipal police forces, sheriffs' departments, and the division of state police are hereby authorized and empowered and it is made mandatory and compulsory on their part to confiscate and immediately destroy all gambling devices or machines used for gambling that come to their attention.

(2) Any gaming device or equipment in possession of a licensed manufacturer, seller, distributor, transporter, or repairman in this state shall not be subject to confiscation and destruction unless such device or equipment is being used for unlawful gambling activities. If such confiscated device or equipment is considered an antique under Louisiana law, the device may be sold and such proceeds shall go to the office of state police fund as provided in R.S. 47:7001.

B. As used in this section the term "gambling device" means:

(1) any slot machine; or (2) any machine, mechanical or electronic device of any sort whatsoever with a cash automatic payout device; or (3) a pinball or other ball machine, mechanical or electronic device equipped with a mechanism to release the number of free games or replays and a mechanism to record the free games or free plays so released.

C. Whenever any other machine, mechanical or electronic device, including but not limited to roulette wheels and similar devices, designed and manufactured primarily for use in connection with gambling, and (1) which, when operated, may deliver, as the result of the application of an element of chance, any money or property, or (2) by the operation of which a person may become entitled to receive, as the result of the application of an element of chance, any money or property, is used to conduct gambling, then following the conviction of any person for the crime of gambling by use of any such machine or device, the court wherein the verdict of guilty was returned shall order the immediate destruction of the machine or device by the proper law enforcement agency of the parish wherein the machine or device was used for gambling.

D. Whenever any machine or other mechanical or electronic device of any kind whatsoever, not designed and manufactured primarily for use in connection with gambling, including specifically but not limited to coin-operated bowling games, shuffle alleys, mechanical baseball games, pinball games, mechanical guns, electronic ray guns, digger type machines, iron claws, and all similar types of coin-operated games, is used to conduct gambling, then following the conviction of any person for the crime of gambling by use of any such machine or device, the court wherein the verdict of guilty was returned shall order the immediate destruction of the machine or device by the proper law enforcement agency of the parish wherein the machine or device was used for gambling.

E. The ownership of a federal gambling stamp for any machine or device, other than a machine commonly known as an "iron claw" or a "digger" machine, shall be absolute proof of its use for purposes of gambling, and neither the State of Louisiana nor any subdivision, agency, agent or enforcement officer shall be liable civilly or criminally for the destruction of any gambling device or gambling machine for which a federal gambling stamp has been issued.

§31.1. Antique slot machines.

A. For the purposes of this Section, a slot machine is an antique if at least twenty-five years have elapsed since it was manufactured.

B. Notwithstanding any provisions of Section 31 of this Title, or R.S. 14:90.1, or any other provisions of law to the contrary, an antique slot machine may be owned and possessed in this state and shall not be subject to confiscation or destruction without a judgment of court as provided in this Section, but may be seized as evidence when operated for unlawful gambling purposes.

C. An antique slot machine, antique gambling device, or antique gaming machine seized as evidence in connection with unlawful gambling shall not be destroyed, altered, or sold until the owner has been afforded a reasonable opportunity to present testimony and other evidence in court that his antique slot machine was not operated for unlawful gambling, and until the court determines by a final and definitive judgment that such slot machine was operated for unlawful gambling, in which event the court shall order the destruction of the slot machine. Otherwise, if the judgment is in favor of the owner, such antique slot machine shall be returned to its owner.

D. An antique slot machine may be owned, possessed, used, and operated in this state under the following conditions:

(1) Within a private dwelling, an antique slot machine may be owned, possessed, used, and operated, provided the operation of the machine is for the purpose of fostering esthetic interest, and the use of the machine does not subject a person to loss of money or property on the element of chance of winning money or property as a result.

(2) An antique slot machine may be offered for sale except at a place licensed to sell alcoholic beverages. When a machine is offered for sale it may be operated and used, provided a prospective buyer is not subjected to loss of money or property on the element of chance of winning money or property as a result.

(3) An antique slot machine, as an item of historic interest, may be presented for public viewing and inspection at any place, provided it is sealed and locked such that is rendered inoperable and all openings for coin deposits and payouts are blocked.

E. It is the purpose of this Section to protect and foster the collection and restoration of antique slot machines not used for gambling purposes, due to their esthetic value and importance in Louisiana history.

(Chgd. by Acts 1990 No. 987, §1, eff. 9/7/90.)

§32. Disposition of money used as evidence in criminal cases.

Whenever any money used as evidence of a crime in criminal cases and thereafter deposited with the clerk of the district court is not disposed of by the district attorney or the district judge within five years after final disposition of the case, the clerk of the district court shall remit all of such funds to the governing authority of the parish to be placed to the credit of the general fund of the parish.

CODE TITLE IV. SEARCH WARRANTS

§41. Disposition of property seized in connection with criminal proceedings.

A. If there is a specific statute concerning the disposition of the seized property, the property shall be disposed of in accordance with the provisions thereof.

B. If there is no such specific statute, the following governs the disposition of property seized in connection with a criminal proceeding, which is not to be used as evidence or is no longer needed as evidence:

(1) The seized property shall be returned to the owner, unless a statute declares the property to be contraband, in which event the court shall order the property destroyed if the court determines that its destruction is in the public interest; otherwise, Paragraph (2) of this Section shall apply.

(2) If the seized property is contraband, and the court determines that it should not be destroyed, or if the owner of noncontraband property does not claim it within two years after its seizure, the court shall order:

(a) A sale of the property at a nonjudicial public sale or auction, if the court concludes that such a sale will probably result in a bid greater than the costs of the sale. The proceeds of the sale shall be administered by the court and used exclusively for the maintenance, renovation, preservation, or improvement of the court building, facilities, or records system.

(b) If the court concludes that the cost of a public sale would probably exceed the highest bid, the court may order the property transferred to a public or a nonprofit institution or destroyed or may make such other court ordered disposition as it deems appropriate.

C. Where the release of seized property is sought by a person claiming to be the owner, it shall be released only upon motion contradictorily with the clerk of court. In all other cases the court may either render an ex parte order for the disposition of the property as herein provided on motion of any interested person, or on its own motion, or the court may require a motion contradictorily with the apparent owner or the person in possession of the property at the time of the seizure.

D. Notwithstanding any provision of law to the contrary, an official criminalistics laboratory may destroy any controlled dangerous substance, controlled dangerous substance paraphernalia, or both, in its possession without an order of court after a period of five years from the date of seizure. Any criminalistics laboratory intending to destroy a controlled dangerous substance, controlled dangerous substance paraphernalia, or both, pursuant to this Subsection shall give the seizing agency and the district attorney thirty days notice prior to such destruction. In the case that the seizing agency or the district attorney object to such destruction, no destruction shall occur.

§42. News media, restrictions on search warrants.

A. No search warrant shall issue directing the seizure of property belonging to, or directing the search of the premises occupied by, any person engaged in the business of collecting, writing, editing, or disseminating news through a news media unless there is probable cause, established by affidavit, to believe that such person or an employee thereof has committed a criminal offense and that the search or seizure is directed toward that offense.

B. As used in this Section, "news media" means newspapers or other periodicals issued at regular intervals, press associations, wire services, radio, and television.

§43. Attorneys; restrictions on search warrants.

A. The court may issue a subpoena when requested by either the defendant or the state, as provided for in Code of Criminal Procedure Articles 731 through 737, when an attorney is believed to be in possession of evidence of the commission of a crime by a client or a third party. In response to the subpoena, the attorney may assert any objection or privilege he may have under law, and the court shall, after hearing, grant or deny the objection or privilege in accordance with law.

B. A search warrant may issue, directing the seizure of property belonging to a client of an attorney which is in the possession of such attorney, or directing the search of the premises occupied by the attorney, on probable cause, established by affidavit, that the attorney or his employee has committed a criminal offense and that the search or seizure is directed toward obtaining evidence relative to that offense.

C. No search warrant shall issue directing the seizure of property belonging to a client of an attorney which is in the possession of an attorney, or directing the search of the premises occupied by the attorney, except under the circumstances provided for in Subsection B.

CODE TITLE VIII. BAIL

§81. Bond for release for violation of municipal ordinances; parole or release of prisoners; penalty.

At the earliest practicable time after arrest of a person imprisoned or detained for violation of any ordinance of any village, town, city, or municipality an order admitting to bail shall be made. Upon execution of the bond in due form and with proper surety the arrested person shall be released pending trial.

Except in municipalities or wards in which a city court vested with criminal jurisdiction exists, no bond for release shall exceed one hundred dollars. In municipalities having criminal jurisdiction it shall not exceed twenty-five hundred dollars.

A person unable to furnish other surety may deposit the amount of the bond in cash. The officer taking the money shall give him a receipt for the deposit. Upon his appearance before any court in compliance with the condition of the bond, the money deposited shall be refunded to him.

Within one-half hour after arrest, the captain, police clerk, or arresting officer of the station where the person is being detained shall have the name of the arrested person placed on a placard visible for public display in the main office of the police station. The placard must be presented to any and all persons inquiring or requesting a view or perusal of it.

The parole or release from custody of any person arrested or detained for violation or alleged violation of an ordinance of any village, town, city, or other municipality shall be executed in accordance with the provisions of this Section. A municipality, by ordinance, may specifically grant the power of parole and release to the presiding judges and officers of its municipal courts.

In cities having a population of more than 300,000 the parish parole officer of the state board of parole and each of the members of the jury commission of the parish in which the municipality is located shall have the power to parole and release persons arrested or detained for alleged violation of any of such municipalities' ordinances.

Whoever violates or advises, consents, aids, or abets in the violation of this Section shall be fined not less than one hundred dollars nor more than five hundred dollars or imprisoned for not less than sixty days nor more than twelve months, or both.

§82. Guaranteed arrest bond certificates as cash bail; forfeiture; sureties.

A. A guaranteed arrest bond certificate with respect to which a fidelity and surety company has become surety as provided in Subsection B of this section, when posted by the person whose signature appears thereon, shall be accepted in lieu of cash bail in an amount not to exceed two hundred dollars, as a bail bond, to guarantee the appearance of such person, in any court in this state at such time as may be required by the court, when such person is arrested for violation of any motor vehicle law of this state or ordinance of any municipality or parish in this state, except for the offense of driving while intoxicated or for any felony, and the alleged violation was committed prior to the date of expiration shown on such guaranteed arrest bond certificate.

Any such guaranteed arrest bond certificate so posted as a bail bond in any court in this state shall be subject to the forfeiture and collection provisions of law applicable to a bail bond, except that any judgment forfeiting a guaranteed arrest bond certificate rendered under said forfeiture and collection provisions shall, at any time within thirty days after rendition, be set aside upon the surrender, or the appearance and trial and conviction or acquittal of the defendant, or upon a continuance granted upon motion of the district attorney after such appearance.

B. Any domestic or foreign insurance company which has qualified to transact fidelity and surety insurance business in this state may, in any year, become surety in an amount not to exceed two hundred dollars with respect to each guaranteed arrest bond certificate issued in such year by an automobile club, automobile association or insurance company authorized to transact automobile liability insurance business within this state or by the fidelity and surety company itself.

The term "guaranteed arrest bond certificate," as used herein, means a printed card or other certificate issued by an automobile club, automobile association, insurance company authorized to transact automobile liability insurance business within this state, or an insurance company authorized to transact fidelity and surety insurance business within this state to any of its members or insureds, which is signed by such member or insured, and contains a printed statement that a fidelity and surety company authorized to do business in this state guarantees the appearance of the person whose signature appears on the card or certificate, and that such company will, in the event of the failure of said person to appear in court at the time of trial, pay any fine or forfeiture imposed on such person in an amount not to exceed two hundred dollars.

The issuance of a "guaranteed arrest bond certificate," as hereinabove defined, by an automobile club, automobile association or insurance company not authorized to transact fidelity and surety insurance business in this state shall not be construed as engaging in fidelity and surety insurance business in this state by such automobile club, automobile association or insurance company.

§84. *(Repealed by Acts 1993 No. 834, §6, eff. 6/22/93.)*

§85. Forfeiture; procedure; notice; enforcement; and collection.

All bonds taken to secure the appearance of any person before any court executed in the state of Louisiana shall be forfeited and collected as follows:

(1) FAILURE TO APPEAR AND ANSWER. If at the time fixed for appearance the defendant fails to appear and answer when called, the judge, on motion of the prosecuting attorney, upon hearing of proper evidence including: the bail contract; the power of attorney if any; and the notice to the defendant and the surety as required by Article 344 of the Code of Criminal Procedure, shall immediately and forthwith issue a warrant for the arrest of the person failing to appear and order a judgment decreeing the forfeiture of the bond and against the defendant and his sureties in solido for the full amount of the bond.

(2) SIGNING OF THE JUDGMENT OF BOND FORFEITURE. Following the defendant's failure to appear, the court shall sign a written judgment of bond forfeiture.

(3) NOTICE OF JUDGMENT.

(a) After entering the fact of the signing of the judgment of bond forfeiture in the court minutes, the clerk of court shall promptly mail notice of the signing of the judgment of bond forfeiture. The notice of the signing of the judgment shall be mailed by United States certified mail with return receipt to all the following:

(i) The defendant at the address designated pursuant to Code of Criminal Procedure Art. 322.

(ii) The personal sureties at the addresses designated pursuant to Code of Criminal Procedure Art. 322.

(iii) The agent or bondsman who posted the bond for the commercial sureties at the address designated pursuant to Code of Criminal Procedure Art. 322.

(iv) The commercial sureties at the addresses designated pursuant to Code of Criminal Procedure Art. 322. Notice to the commercial sureties shall include the power of attorney number used to execute the bond.

(b) After mailing the notice of the signing of the judgment of bond forfeiture, the clerk of court shall execute an affidavit of the mailing and place the affidavit and the return receipts in the record.

(c) Failure to mail proper notice of the signing of the judgment within sixty days after the defendant's failure to appear shall release the sureties of any and all obligations under the bond.

(4) RECORDATION OF JUDGMENT. After mailing notice of the signing of the judgment of bond forfeiture, the district attorney shall cause the judgment to be recorded in every parish in which he thinks the recordation is proper. Every such recordation shall be without cost and shall operate as a judicial mortgage against the defendant and all his sureties.

(5) SUMMARY PROCEEDINGS. The defendant and his sureties shall be entitled to bring defenses and actions in nullity by use of summary proceedings in the criminal matter before the trial court which issued the judgment of bond forfeiture within sixty days from mailing the notice of the signing of the judgment of bond forfeiture. Any summary proceeding brought by the defendant or his sureties within the sixty-day period shall be determined by the court within one hundred and eighty days of mailing the notice of signing of the judgment of bond forfeiture. The defendant and his sureties shall be entitled to bring defenses pursuant to Code of Criminal Procedure Art. 345 and R.S. 15:87 by use of summary proceedings in the criminal matter before the trail court which issued the judgment of bond forfeiture within six months from mailing the notice of the signing of the judgment of bond forfeiture.

(6) APPEALS.

(a) The defendant and his sureties shall have the right to an appeal that suspends the effect or the execution of the judgment of bond forfeiture. The security to be furnished for this suspensive appeal shall be equal to the bail obligation.

(b) The defendant and his sureties shall have the right to a devolutive appeal of the judgment of bond forfeiture.

(c) All appeals shall be to the appellate court having general civil appellate jurisdiction over the court issuing the judgment of bond forfeiture.

(7) ENFORCEMENT AND COLLECTION OF JUDGMENT. No judgment of bond forfeiture rendered on or after August 15, 1997, shall be enforced or collected until ten days after the expiration of six months after the mailing of proper notice of the signing of the judgment of bond forfeiture. The timely filing of a suspensive appeal shall suspend the enforcement or collection of the judgment of the bond forfeiture. In addition, the court may provide by court rule for the filing of an offset claim against the principal with the secretary of the Department of Revenue, in accordance with R.S. 47:299.1 through 299.20. If after six months and ten days from the mailing of proper notice of the signing of the judgment, a judgment of bond forfeiture against a commercial surety company has not been suspensively appealed nor satisfied or proceedings challenging the bond forfeiture have not been timely filed, the prosecuting attorney may either file a rule to show cause with the commissioner of insurance in accordance with R.S. 22:658.1 or collect the judgment in the same manner as a civil judgment.

(8) COLLECTION BY INSURANCE COMMISSIONER. Within thirty days of the filing of a rule to show cause by the prosecuting attorney with the commissioner of insurance, the commissioner of insurance shall notify the insurance company, the surety or Lloyd's association, in writing, at the address of the home office of that organization by certified mail, setting a time, place, and date of the commissioner's hearing, which shall not be more than sixty days from the date of receipt of notice from the prosecuting attorney. If after the hearing, the insurance commissioner finds that there is no just cause or legal reason for the surety's nonpayment, the commissioner shall take any action deemed necessary for collection of the amount owed, including suspension of the surety from doing business in the state of Louisiana.

(9) NULLITY ACTIONS. Nullity actions pursuant to Code of Civil Procedure Art. 2001 et seq. not filed within the sixty days provided for filing summary proceedings shall be brought by the use of ordinary civil proceedings.

(10) SATISFACTION OF JUDGMENT OF BOND FORFEITURE. Any judgment forfeiting the appearance bond rendered according to this Section shall at any time, within six months, after mailing of the notice of the signing of the judgment of bond forfeiture, be fully satisfied and set aside upon the surrender or the appearance of the defendant. The appearance of the defendant shall operate as a satisfaction of the judgment and the surrender shall operate as a satisfaction of the judgment and shall fully and finally relieve the surety of any and all obligations under the bond. Any judgment forfeiting the appearance bond rendered according

to this Section shall at any time, within ten days after the expiration of the six month period provided to surrender the defendant, be fully satisfied by the payment of the amount of the bail obligation without incurring any interest, costs, or fees.

(11) FAILURE TO SATISFY JUDGMENT OF BOND FORFEITURE.

(a) If a judgment of bond forfeiture rendered after June 22, 1993, against a commercial surety company has not been satisfied within two hundred ten days from mailing the notice of the signing of the judgment of bond forfeiture, nor has a suspensive appeal or other proceeding challenging the bond forfeiture been timely filed, the prosecuting attorney may file with the appropriate court a rule to show cause why that commercial surety company should not be prohibited from executing criminal bail bonds before the court issuing the judgment of bond forfeiture. The appropriate court is the court where the bond is posted, whether in a district court or a court other than a district court composed of more than one judge. If the appropriate court is not a district court, it shall sit en banc on such a rule to show cause. If the bond is posted in a court other than a district court and composed of only one judgeship position, then the rule shall be filed in the appropriate district court.

(b) At the rule to show cause, the court may consider only issues which would interrupt the enforceability of the judgment. Should the court find:

(i) A judgment of bond forfeiture has been rendered after June 22, 1993, against the commercial surety;

(ii) Proper notice pursuant to this Section has been mailed;

(iii) No suspensive appeal has been taken;

(iv) The defendant has neither been surrendered nor appeared within six months of mailing of the notice of the signing of the judgment of bond forfeiture;

(v) Two hundred ten days have passed since the mailing of proper notice of the signing of the judgment of bond forfeiture; and

(vi) The judgment of bond forfeiture has not been satisfied by payment, then the court may issue an order enjoining the commercial surety company from posting criminal bail bonds before the court issuing the judgment of bond forfeiture if the judgment is not satisfied within the ten days.

(c) The burden of proof at the hearing shall be upon the commercial surety by a preponderance of evidence and shall be limited to documents contained in the official court record where the judgment was rendered. The surety company may use evidence not contained in the record to show that it did not receive post-forfeiture notice or the post-forfeiture notice required pursuant to this Section was not properly mailed.

(Chgd. by Acts 1993 No. 834, §4; Acts 1994 Third Ex. Sess. No. 52, §3; Acts 1997 No. 813, §1, No. 815, §1, eff. 8/15/97.)

§85.1. *(Repealed by Acts 1993 No. 834, §6, eff. 6/22/93.)*

§86. Forfeiture of cash, checks or securities.

When the court declares a forfeiture of cash, a check, a negotiable bond or a money order which has been deposited as bail, the court shall order the disposition of such security in satisfaction of the bail obligation.

When the bail undertaking is discharged, the court shall order the security returned to the depositor. Upon presentation of a certified copy of the order, the custodian of the security shall pay or deliver it to the person named therein or to his order.

§86.1. Unclaimed bail bonds; disposition; return to owner.

A. Notwithstanding any other provision of law to the contrary, any sheriff having possession or control of cash bail bonds which have been discharged and which remain unclaimed for more than three years, or which belong to an owner who is unknown or who has not been heard from for more than three years, shall deposit the same into the general fund of the sheriff, and thereafter the sheriff shall assume liability therefor. However, in the parishes of Caddo, Plaquemines, East Baton Rouge, Bossier, and St. Mary, the sheriff shall pay such funds to the treasurer of the governing authority, who shall collect and receive this money and deposit it to the credit of the general fund, and thereafter the sheriff shall be relieved of all liability therefor.

B. Any owner who claims a cash bail bond which has been deposited in the general fund of the sheriff or, in Caddo, Plaquemines, East Baton Rouge, Bossier, and St. Mary Parishes, in the governing authority's general fund, pursuant to this Section shall be reimbursed from the sheriff's general fund or said governing authority's general fund upon establishing his claim thereto by a judgment of a court of competent jurisdiction. Upon being presented with a certified copy of the judgment, the sheriff or, in Caddo, Plaquemines, East Baton Rouge, Bossier, and St. Mary Parishes, the treasurer, shall draw a warrant and pay out of the general fund of the sheriff or, in Caddo, Plaquemines, East Baton Rouge, Bossier and St. Mary Parishes, the general fund of the governing authority, the amount of the judgment.

§86.2. City Court of Thibodaux; unclaimed bail bonds; disposition; return to owner.

A. Notwithstanding any other provision of law to the contrary, the City Court of the city of Thibodaux having in its control or possession cash bail bonds which have been discharged and which remain unclaimed for more than three years, or which belong to an owner who is unknown or has not been heard from for more than three years, shall pay the same, in cases involving the violation of state law, to the treasurer of the governing authority of Lafourche Parish for deposit in the criminal court's fund of the parish, or in cases involving a violation of a city ordinance, to the trustee of public finance or director of finance of the governing authority for the city of Thibodaux for deposit in the general fund of the city of Thibodaux, and in both instances thereafter the City of Thibodaux shall be relieved of all liability therefor.

B. Where the cash bail bond involves the violation of a state law the treasurer of the governing authority of Lafourche Parish shall collect and receive this money and shall deposit it to the credit of the Lafourche Parish criminal court's fund. Where the cash bail bond involves the violation of a city ordinance, the trustee of public finance or director of finance of the governing authority for the city of Thibodaux shall collect and receive this money and shall deposit it to the credit of the general fund of the city of Thibodaux.

C. Any owner who claims a cash bail bond which has been deposited in either the Lafourche Parish general fund or the criminal court's fund of the city of Thibodaux pursuant to this section shall be reimbursed from the general fund or the criminal court's fund involved, upon establishing his claim thereto by a judgment of a court of competent jurisdiction. Upon being presented with a certified copy of the judgment either the parish treasurer or the trustee of public finance or director of finance, as the case may be, shall draw a warrant and pay out of the appropriate general fund the amount of the judgment without the necessity of an appropriation by the respective governing authority.

§86.3. City courts: unclaimed bail bonds; disposition; return to owner.

A. Notwithstanding any other provision of law to the contrary, any city court having in its control or possession cash bail bonds which have been discharged and which remain unclaimed for more than three years, after notice by certified mail, or which belong to an owner who is unknown or has not been heard from for more than three years, shall pay the same, in cases involving the violation of state law, to the treasurer of the governing authority of the parish in which the city court is located for deposit in the criminal court's fund of the parish, or in cases involving a violation of a city ordinance, to the treasurer or chief financial officer of the city for deposit in the general fund of the city, and in both instances thereafter the city court shall be relieved of all liability therefor.

B. If the cash bail bond involves the violation of a state law the treasurer of the governing authority of the parish in which the city court is located shall collect and receive this money and shall deposit it to the credit of the parish's criminal court's fund. If the cash bail bond involves the violation of a city ordinance, the treasurer or chief financial officer of the city shall collect and receive this money and shall deposit it to the credit of the general fund of the city.

C. Any owner who claims a cash bail bond which has been deposited in either a parish criminal court's fund or the general fund of a city pursuant to this Section shall be reimbursed from the general fund or the criminal court's fund involved, upon establishing his claim thereto by a judgment of a court of competent jurisdiction. Upon being presented with a certified copy of the judgment either the treasurer or chief financial officer, as the case may be, shall draw a warrant and pay out of the appropriate general fund the amount of the judgment without the necessity of an appropriation by the respective governing authority. *(Added by Acts 1995 No. 996, §1, eff. 8/15/95.)*

§87. Non-forfeiture situations.

A. No judgment decreeing the forfeiture of an appearance bond shall be rendered, if it is shown to the satisfaction of the court that the defendant, principal in such bond, is prevented from attending because of any of the following:

(1) He has a physical disability, illness, or injury.

(2) He is being detained in the jail or penitentiary of another jurisdiction.

(3) He is serving in the armed forces of the United States.

B. A sworn affidavit of the jailer, warden, physician, commanding officer, or other responsible officer where the principal is detained, who attests to the cause of the defendant's failure to appear shall be considered adequate proof of the defendant/principal's inability to appear.

C. If a judgment of bond forfeiture is rendered while the defendant is prevented from appearing for reasons enumerated in this Section, the court shall declare the judgment of bond forfeiture null and void if the defendant or his sureties file a motion to set aside the judgment of bond forfeiture within six months of the mailing of notice of the signing of the judgment of bond forfeiture, and it is shown to the satisfaction of the court that the defendant was prevented from attending for the causes enumerated in this Section.

(Chgd. by Acts 1993 No. 834, §4, eff. 6/22/93.)

§88. Appearance bond defined.

The term "appearance bond" shall be taken and intended to mean every bail bond, recognizance or other obligation, or deposit of cash, checks, negotiable bonds or money orders made or taken to secure the appearance of any person before any court, but in all cases where cash, checks, negotiable securities or money orders have been deposited in lieu of bond with a surety, in case of discharge or forfeiture, the same shall be disposed of as otherwise provided by law.

§89. Prescription of forfeiture judgment; revival.

Every judgment decreeing the forfeiture of any appearance bond, and every mortgage resulting from the recordation of such judgment, shall be prescribed by the lapse of ten years from the rendition of such judgment; provided, however, that the district attorney or any party in interest may have such judgment revived at any time before it is prescribed by taking, in the court which rendered said judgment, a rule upon the persons against whom said judgment was rendered, to show cause why the same should not be revived and unless, upon the trial of said rule, such cause be shown, said judgment shall be revived.

Any judgment revived as above provided shall continue in full force for ten years from the date of the order of court reviving the same, and any such judgment may be revived as often as the district attorney or any party interested may desire.

CODE TITLE XI. QUALIFICATIONS AND SELECTION OF GRAND AND PETIT JURORS

§111. Parish of Orleans; salary of jury commissioners; vacancy; appointment of secretary.

Each of the jury commissioners for the Parish of Orleans shall receive a salary of not less than four thousand two hundred dollars per annum.

The commissioners shall select a secretary of the board of jury commissioners. The secretary of the board shall receive a salary of not less than four thousand dollars per annum.

The salaries of the jury commissioners and the secretary shall be payable monthly by the City of New Orleans; provided that the City of New Orleans shall be required to budget and continue to pay to the jury commissioners and the secretary the amount presently budgeted and that any increase in the amount of salaries presently paid by the City of New Orleans occasioned by the passage of this bill shall not be effective unless and until ratified and approved by the City Council.

In the case of absence or inability to act for any cause, there shall be no quorum of the board of commissioners, the Governor shall appoint commissioners to fill said temporary vacancy or vacancies, who shall have the power of jury commissioner under the Code of Criminal Procedure.

§112. Parish of Orleans; process servers.

Unless otherwise provided by law, all subpoenas, notices, process, orders and papers issued by the jury commissioners in the parish of Orleans shall be served by a chief process server or one of his deputies, which said chief process server and as many deputy process servers as may be necessary shall be appointed by the said jury commissioners. The chief process server shall be paid not less than two hundred and fifty dollars per month, and the deputy process servers shall each be paid not less than one hundred seventy-five dollars per month plus fifty dollars per month automobile allowance. The city of New Orleans shall appropriate and pay to the jury commissioners an amount not to exceed the amount presently budgeted for the salaries of the commissioners, chief process server, deputy process servers, automobile allowance, office help, supplies and printing. Said sums shall be included in the budget of the city of New Orleans.

§113. Duty of Orleans registrar to furnish jury commission lists of voters added to or deleted from rolls.

The registrar of voters for the Parish of Orleans shall prepare and furnish to the jury commission for the Parish of Orleans quarterly a list containing the names of persons added to and deleted from the voter registration rolls for the Parish of Orleans during the preceding quarter, which list the jury commission may use, together with other information, for the purpose of discharging its duties.

§114. Parish of Orleans; rotation and selection of grand jury; control of grand jury.

Each judge of the criminal district court for the Parish of Orleans shall, in rotation, select the grand jury for the Parish of Orleans. The order of rotation among the judges in the selection of the grand jury prevailing at the time this Section goes into effect shall be preserved and continued. The judge of the section of the criminal district court who shall have appointed said grand jury shall have control and instruction over the grand jury, exclusive of all other judges of the criminal district court, and such grand jury shall make all findings and returns in open court to said judge; and in addition thereto may make reports and requests in open court as provided by law; provided that if the judge to whom the control of the grand jury shall belong shall not be from any cause in the actual discharge of his duties as judge, the judges of the criminal district court then present shall designate some other judge to impanel and instruct said grand jury, or to receive its returns and findings, as the case may be, and the judge so designated shall continue to act for the judge to whom the control of such grand jury shall belong until said last-mentioned judge shall return to the discharge of duties; provided, further, that the grand jury in office at the time of the adoption of this Section shall, until the expiration of that term of office, be under the control of the presiding judge of the section by whom it was selected and shall return all indictments and findings to said judge in open court.

§115. Service of jury commission process; general rule.

Unless otherwise provided by law, a subpoena, notice, process, order or document issued by a jury commission shall be served by the sheriff.

§116. Preparation of general venire list; assistance.

The clerk of court and the jury commission may avail themselves of the services of a deputy clerk or of a stenographer in the preparation of the general venire list, the slips for use in the general venire box, the proces verbal of the meetings and in all other proceedings of the jury commission. All names, lists, slips, or other papers may be typewritten.

§117. Discharge of grand jury; review of discharge by supreme court.

Upon being discharged for legal cause, the discharged grand jury or any of the discharged members may make applications for review directly to the supreme court. Such application must be made within two days from the date that the district judge ordered a discharge for legal cause, and shall be taken up by the supreme court, by preference, immediately over all other matters.

If, after the discharge by the district judge is ordered, application is made by the discharged grand jury or any of the discharged members as prescribed by law said grand jury or the members making application shall serve as before; and should the supreme court affirm the order of discharge or deny the application of the grand jury or any of its members, the validity of indictments shall in no wise be affected because they were brought in by the grand jury between the time that the district judge ordered a discharge for legal cause of the grand jury or any of its members and the time that the supreme court affirmed that order or denied the application.

Within two days after the order of the district judge discharging for legal cause, the grand jury or any of its members, is affirmed by the supreme court, or becomes final, the district judge shall make the necessary appointments to fill vacancies caused thereby as prescribed by law.

CODE TITLE XII. THE GRAND JURY

§121. Duty to inspect prisons and hospitals; reports.

Each grand jury, except those impaneled pursuant to Code of Criminal Procedure Article 415.1, shall inspect every prison, place of detention, asylum, and hospital within the parish and report to the district judge how the prisoners and inmates of every such institution are treated. Every such report shall state the number of prisoners and inmates in every such public institution, and the costs of maintenance, and shall state the length of time that each prisoner awaiting trial, at the time of said report, has been so held for trial. *(Chgd. by Acts 1990 No. 74, §2, eff. 9/7/90.)*

CODE TITLE XIV. RIGHT TO COUNSEL

§144. Judicial district indigent defender board.

A. An indigent defender board, hereinafter referred to as the district board, shall be established in each judicial district, domiciled at a place approved by a majority of the district court judges. In the event of a tie vote, the chief judge shall determine where the board shall be domiciled.

B. Each district board shall be composed of no less than three nor more than seven members as determined by the district court. Board members shall be selected by the district court (in Orleans Parish, the criminal district court) from nominees provided by each bar association within the judicial district. In the event no nominations are submitted by the bar association within a judicial district, a majority of the district court judges shall select a board member. Each parish within the judicial district shall have a representative on the board. The board shall select a chairman from its members. Elected officials, district attorneys, their employees, including assistant district attorneys, or prosecutors in any court shall not be permitted to serve on the district board.

C. A majority of the members of the district board shall constitute a quorum for the transaction of business, and all official action shall require the favorable vote of a majority of the members present.

D. The judges of each judicial district shall adopt rules and regulations to establish policy regarding the appointment of members to the indigent defender board, which shall at a minimum include provisions for requiring that the racial and gender makeup of the board reflect the racial and gender makeup of the judicial district involved. Any citizen of majority age shall have a cause of action to enjoin the activities of the board for failure to comply with this provision.

(Chgd. by Acts 1990 No. 1044, §1, eff. 9/7/90.)

§145. Powers and duties of the judicial district indigent defender boards.

A. Each district board shall maintain a current panel of volunteer attorneys licensed to practice law in this state and shall additionally maintain a current panel of nonvolunteer attorneys under the age of fifty-five licensed to practice law in this state and residing in the judicial district. The panel of nonvolunteer attorneys shall not include any attorney who has been licensed to practice in this state for thirty or more years.

B. Each district board shall select one of the following procedures or any combination thereof for providing counsel for indigent defendants.

(1) (a) Appointment by the court from a list provided by the district board of volunteer attorneys licensed to practice law in this state. In the event of an inadequate number of volunteer attorneys, appointment shall be from a list provided by the district board of nonvolunteer attorneys as provided in Subsection A of this Section. The court may delegate appointing power to the district board.

(b) All appointments shall be on a successive basis. Deviations from the panel list shall be permitted only to comply with Article 512 of the Code of Criminal Procedure and in exceptional circumstances upon approval of the district board.

(2) (a) The district board may employ a chief indigent defender and such assistants and supporting personnel as it deems necessary. The chief indigent defender shall be appointed for a period of three years and may not be a member of the board. The salaries of the chief indigent defender and all assistants and supporting personnel shall be fixed by the district board. All employees of the board shall possess such powers and duties as prescribed by the district board and consistent with the Code of Professional Responsibility.

(b) The chief indigent defender may in the event of conflicts of interest, inadequate personnel or for any other reason approved by the board request that the court appoint counsel to represent indigent defendants pursuant to Section 145(B)(1).

(3) The district board may enter into a contract or contracts, on such terms and conditions as it deems advisable, with one or more attorneys licensed to practice law in this state and residing in the judicial district to provide counsel for indigent defendants.

(4) In a judicial district comprising more than one parish, the board may select the method of providing counsel for indigents on an individual parish basis.

C. The district board shall adopt rules for the transaction of business and shall keep an accurate record of all its proceedings and official actions. All papers, documents, and records of the board shall be filed at the domicile of the board.

D. The district board shall keep accurate records of the information set forth in R.S. 15:143(B) and shall furnish such information to the state board upon request.

E. The district board may expend funds for its necessary expenses, including compensating its employees and reimbursing the district board members for actual expenses in traveling to and from district board meetings and otherwise incurred while on district board business.

F. The district board may accept, receive, and use public or private grants. Copies of applications for public or private grants shall be forwarded to the state board.

G. The district board shall possess such other authority as is necessary to carry out the intent and purposes of this Code Title.

H. Each indigent defender board shall adopt rules to establish a policy of selecting a proportionate number of minority and women lawyers in accordance with the makeup of the general population of the district, to the extent that minority and women lawyers are available and otherwise eligible for selection within the district in accordance with the provisions of this Section. Any citizen of majority age shall have a cause of action to enjoin the activities of a board for failure to comply with this provision.

(Chgd. by Acts 1990 No. 1044, §1, eff. 9/7/90.)

§146. Judicial district indigent defender fund.

A. There is hereby created within each judicial district an indigent defender fund which shall be administered by the district board and composed of funds provided for by this Section and such funds as may be appropriated or otherwise made available to it.

B. (1) Every court of original criminal jurisdiction, except in the town of Jonesville, in the city of Plaquemine, and in mayors' courts in municipalities having a population of less than four thousand, shall remit the following special costs to the district indigent defender fund for the following violations, under state statute as well as under parish or municipal ordinance. The following costs shall be assessed in cases in which a defendant is convicted after a trial, a plea of guilty or nolo contendere, or after forfeiting bond, and shall be in addition to all other fines, costs, or forfeitures imposed:

(a) Not less than the sum of seventeen dollars and fifty cents for each offense, except a parking violation. Upon recommendation of the district board and by a majority vote of the judges of the courts of original jurisdiction within the district, this sum may be increased to not more than thirty dollars. Notwithstanding the provisions of this Section, the City Court of Port Allen shall not impose an amount in excess of twelve dollars for each offense, except a parking violation.

(b) In the Twenty-Seventh Judicial District, the sum of seventeen dollars and fifty cents for each felony and each misdemeanor, except a parking violation. Such sum shall be remitted to the fund until the indigent defender board certifies to the court that sufficient amounts are in the fund to pay timely the volunteer counsel appointed by the court to represent indigent defendants. After such certification, the court of the Twenty-Seventh Judicial District shall have the authority, from time to time as the needs of the fund require, to decrease and increase again the amount of special costs authorized by this Section. The amount of such costs shall not exceed twenty-five dollars and fifty cents for each felony and for each misdemeanor, except a parking violation, and shall be not less than four dollars and fifty cents for each misdemeanor, except a parking violation, and not less than ten dollars for each felony.

(2) Such amounts shall be remitted by the respective recipients thereof to the judicial district indigent defender fund monthly by the tenth day of the succeeding month.

C. In addition to the funds provided for in Subsection B hereof the state shall pay to each district indigent defender board, on the warrant of its chairman, the sum of ten thousand dollars per annum.

D. The funds provided for in this Section and all interest or other income earned from the investment of such funds shall be used and administered by the district board.

(Chgd. by Acts 1990 No. 1044, §1; Acts 1991 No. 549, §1; Acts 1995 No. 1286, §1, eff. 8/15/95.)

§147. Proceedings to determine indigency.

A. (1)(a) A preliminary inquiry and determination of indigency of any accused person shall be made by the court not later than arraignment and such determination may be reviewed by the court at any other stage of the proceedings.

(b) If the court makes the preliminary determination that the accused is or may be indigent, the court shall require the accused to make application to the local indigent defender office or an attorney appointed or under contract to provide indigent defender services, who shall inquire further into the accused's economic status and, upon determining that the accused is indigent, shall file a certification thereof, in such form as the court may require and without paying costs in advance, in the record of the proceeding or enroll as counsel.

(c) The accused shall be responsible for applying for indigent defense counsel and for establishing his indigency and entitlement to appointment of counsel. Any oral or written statements made by the accused in or for use in the criminal proceeding and material to the issue of his indigency shall be made under oath or an equivalent affirmation.

(2) The chief indigent defender or his assistants, or a member of the indigent defender panel appointed by the board or the court for such purpose, or an attorney providing indigent defender services pursuant to a contract with the district board shall be allowed to summon witnesses to testify before the court concerning the financial ability of any accused person to employ counsel for his defense.

(3) Failure of the judge to comply with provisions of this Section shall result in deduction of reasonable criminal defense costs from the Judicial Expense Fund.

B. (1) In determining whether or not a person is indigent and entitled to the appointment of counsel, the court shall consider whether the person is a needy person and the extent of his ability to pay. The court may consider such factors as income or funds from employment or any other source, including public assistance, to which the accused is entitled, property owned by the accused or in which he has an economic interest, outstanding obligations, the number and ages of dependents, employment and job training history, and level of education.

(2) Release on bail alone shall not disqualify a person for appointment of counsel. In each case, the person subject to the penalty of perjury shall certify in writing such material factors relating to his ability to pay as the court prescribes.

(Chgd. by Acts 1994 Third Ex. Sess. No. 105, §1; Acts 1997 No. 1361, §1, eff. 12/31/97.)

§148. Partial reimbursement by indigents.

A. To the extent that a person is financially able to provide for an attorney, other than necessary services and facilities of representation and court costs, the court shall order him to pay for these items. The court may order payment in installments, or in any manner which it believes reasonable and compatible with the defendant's financial ability.

B. Payments so made shall be transmitted to and become a part of the indigent defender fund of the district in which the person is prosecuted.

C. (1) When an accused is initially determined to be indigent and appointed counsel but subsequently hires private counsel, the court shall conduct a contradictory hearing to determine the expenses of representing the accused incurred by the indigent defender board. Upon determining the expenses incurred, the accused shall, within the discretion of the court, be liable to reimburse the board those expenses, upon a determination that the accused was in fact not initially indigent. A judgment for the amount owed may be recorded in the mortgage records in favor of the board for the payment of money against the accused and may be enforced as provided by law.

(2) All funds received by the board shall be deposited into the indigent defender fund.

(3) Failure of the accused to disclose the full amount involved in the hiring shall constitute grounds for contempt of court.

§149. Appointment of counsel at parole revocation and prerevocation hearings.

A. The Department of Corrections shall provide legal representation for each indigent parolee who is charged with violating the conditions of his parole with respect to which he has the right to a parole revocation or prerevocation hearing, if the indigent parolee is entitled by law to representation by counsel and if the parolee requests such representation.

B. The department may appoint counsel or may request that a district court judge in the parish where a parole revocation or prerevocation hearing is to be held appoint counsel to represent the indigent parolee. When requested to do so, the court shall have counsel appointed.

C. Attorneys appointed under the provisions of this Section shall be paid reasonable compensation and reimbursement for expenses necessarily incurred, which shall be fixed and paid by the Department of Corrections.

§150. Regional defense service centers.

A. Any district indigent defender board may contract with one or more other district indigent defender boards for the establishment of a regional defense service center. A district indigent defender board may enter into only one contract for a regional center in a particular field of practice.

B. As used in this Section, the term "regional defense service center" means:

(1) A regional appellate resource center.

(2) A regional death penalty center.

C. (1) A regional defense service center may be granted authority to contract with counsel for death penalty defense, appeals, other specific functions, and operation of an office, library, and other reasonably necessary authority as the contracting boards deem appropriate.

(2) A regional death penalty center may retain a supervising attorney or chief defender, whose job description and compensation shall be specifically set out in the contract by the districts which establishes the regional defense service center. No attorney with less than five years criminal trial practice shall serve as lead counsel in any death penalty case assigned to the regional death penalty center.

(3) A regional defense service center may apply for grants from any source of funding for the center's operation. The funds from such grants shall belong to the regional center.

D. A contract among district indigent defender boards shall provide for adequate supervision of the regional defense service center established, with periodic reports to each of the contracting boards, at least every six months, regarding the following:

(1) Information on the center's caseload and the status of each case.

(2) Receipts and disbursements.

(3) Comparison of budget to actual expenses.

(4) Assessment of the effectiveness of the center.

E. (1) The contract establishing a regional defense service center shall further provide for the specifics of contracts with attorneys, the method of staffing, and the contract amount. If a center is intended to retain full-time counsel, that condition shall be specified in the contract establishing the center.

(2) Regional defense service centers shall operate on a calendar year budget and shall be subject to the rules and regulations of the legislative auditor.

(3) A regional defense service center shall have an established caseload limit beyond which counsel at the center may decline to provide representation in its assigned area of criminal defense.

(4) The contract for a regional defense service center shall provide for contribution by the contracting districts for a period not more than five nor less than three calendar years, which commitment shall be binding on the contracting boards. The basis of the contribution may be any rational basis, including population, caseload, or other criteria agreed to by the respective boards. The contracting boards shall be required by the contract to contribute to the regional service center for a period of not less than three nor more than five years, and the contract shall be noncancellable.

F. (1) The purpose of regional defense service centers shall be to improve services and reduce cost by creating a regional defense service center for appellate work, death penalty defense, and such other specific related purposes as the districts involved shall define by the contract.

(2) Nothing herein shall be interpreted as creating a duty on the part of such regional defense service centers to do any act, or provide any service, beyond that contemplated in the establishment of the center by the district indigent defender boards and present jurisprudence. *(Added by Acts 1993 No. 532, §1, eff. 8/15/93.)*

§151. Indigent Defense Assistance Board.

A. There is hereby established in the office of the governor the Indigent Defense Assistance Board.

B. (1) The board shall consist of nine members. No individual may be recommended, appointed, or serve on the board if he is an elected official, or employed by a law enforcement agency, or an office having any prosecutorial authority, or employed full-time by a court.

(2) Each member of the board shall be admitted to the practice of law in this state for at least five years prior to appointment.

(3) The members shall be selected as follows:

(a) The governor shall appoint three members, and shall designate the chairman.

(b) The president of the Senate and the speaker of the House of Representatives shall each appoint three members.

(4) A vacancy on the board shall be filled in the same manner as the original appointment.

(5) Members of the board shall serve staggered terms of four years, after initial terms as follows:

(a) Two members shall be appointed for four-year terms by the governor.

(b) One member shall be appointed for a two-year term by the governor.

(c) Three members appointed by the speaker of the House of Representatives shall be appointed for a three-year term.

(d) Three members appointed by the president of the Senate shall be appointed for a three year term.

(6) In addition there shall be three ex officio, nonvoting members of the board who shall not be counted or be permitted to be counted for purposes of the number of members necessary to take board action or the number of members necessary to establish a quorum. In all other respects they have all the duties, authority, requirements and benefits, except per diem, of any other board member. Each of the following organizations shall appoint one such member:

(a) the Louisiana Association of Criminal Defense Lawyers.

(b) the Louisiana Public Defender's Association.

(c) the Louisiana Trial Lawyers Association

(Added by Acts 1997 No. 1361, §1, eff. 12/31/97.)

§151.1. Quorum; compensation; officers; records.

A. Five voting members shall constitute a quorum for transacting business. A vote of a majority of the membership of the board shall be required to take action.

B. Members of the board shall receive per diem at the same rate as members of the legislature for each day the board meets. They shall also receive reimbursement for travel, lodging, and other expenses at the rate established for state employees.

C. The board shall elect a vice chairman. The chairman and the vice chairman shall serve two-year terms. The board shall select other necessary officers from among its membership.

D. All meetings of the board shall be open and subject to the provisions of R.S. 42:4.1 et seq. A record of all proceedings at regular and special meetings of the board shall be kept and shall be open to public inspection, except as otherwise provided by R.S. 42:6.1.
(Added by Acts 1997 No. 1361, §1, eff. 12/31/97.)

§151.2. Powers; duties; responsibilities; limitations.

A. The board may provide supplemental funds, when appropriated by the legislature for that purpose, to judicial district indigent defender boards only as authorized herein for the purposes of complying with the requirements of the Constitution of Louisiana and the Constitution of the United States of America and specific statutory provisions affording the right to counsel to indigent defendants in criminal cases.

B. The board may set the terms of employment and compensation of a director and such staff as it determines to be necessary. The board may enter into contracts in accordance with law for the purpose of maintaining and operating an office and performing the functions enumerated herein.

C. Except as provided in Paragraph D(10), the board shall not provide supplemental funds to a judicial district indigent defender board, unless the judicial district:

(1) Has assessed court costs, pursuant to R.S. 15:146, of at least twenty-five dollars.

(2) Has instituted and is complying with a system to assure that defense services are limited only to those who meet indigency standards after reasonable inquiry, including compliance with R.S. 15:147.

D. The board shall adopt rules for providing supplemental assistance to the judicial district indigent defender boards, which address the following:

(1) Guidelines for supplemental assistance that take into account the provision of defense services by the judicial district indigent defender board for misdemeanor offenses.

(2) Guidelines for supplemental assistance that take into account the employment by the judicial district indigent defender board of other than trial counsel or counsel from within the judicial district to provide services for appeals.

(3) Guidelines for supplemental assistance that take into account the failure of the judicial district indigent defender board to provide local counsel in capital cases.

(4) Guidelines for supplemental assistance relating to expenses of scientific testing and expert witnesses.

(5) Guidelines for supplemental assistance that take into account the administrative expenses and management practices and efficiencies of the judicial district indigent defender board.

(6) Guidelines for supplemental assistance for compensation when the judicial district indigent defender board compensates a lawyer retained to handle a specific case or cases.

(7) Guidelines for supplemental assistance that take into account the providing by the judicial district indigent defender board of financial and other information and cooperation reasonably necessary to carry out the enumerated powers of the board.

(8) Guidelines for supplemental assistance that take into account capital cases, appellate cases, expert witnesses, specialized testing and other clearly demonstrated needs.

(9) Guidelines for supplemental assistance to judicial district indigent defender boards which participate in regional defense service centers.

(10) Guidelines for supplemental assistance in specific capital cases for judicial district indigent defender boards which are not otherwise qualified to receive supplemental assistance. The limitations of Paragraph (C)(1) shall not apply to such assistance.

E. The board shall have authority by rule, to develop and maintain such programs as necessary to implement the guidelines for supplemental assistance.

F. The board shall adopt its rules pursuant to the Administrative Procedure Act, and the rules shall be only those necessary to carry out the enumerated powers granted to the board by R.S. 15:151 through 151.4.

(Added by Acts 1997 No. 1361, §1, eff. 12/31/97.)

§151.3. Special reporting requirements.

In addition to the general oversight requirements provided by law, the board shall submit an annual report to the legislature not later than February first of each year, commencing in 1999. The report shall include a comprehensive status report on the board's activities, the number of meetings of the board and attendance, expenditures, decisions, and actions for the previous fiscal year. The report shall be directed to the chairmen of the standing committees of the Senate and the House of Representatives with subject matter jurisdiction over criminal justice matters. *(Added by Acts 1997 No. 1361, §1, eff. 12/31/97.)*

§151.4. Limited effect.

The provisions of R.S. 15:151 through 151.3 are intended to facilitate the providing of legal services and related expenses only to the extent required by the Constitution of Louisiana or the Constitution of the United States of America and specific statutory provisions affording the right of counsel to indigent defendants in criminal cases. No provision of R.S. 15:151 through 151.3 or rule adopted pursuant thereto creates or shall be construed to confer substantive or procedural rights in favor of any person accused of an offense. *(Added by Acts 1997 No. 1361, §1, eff. 12/31/97.)*

CODE TITLE XVII. TIME LIMITATIONS

§171. *(Repealed by Acts 1997 No. 713, §1, eff. 7/8/97.)*

CODE TITLE XIX. JURISDICTION AND VENUE

§191. Place of trial of criminal neglect of family cases.

When any person shall desert or intentionally not support his family in violation of R.S. 14:74, the offense may be prosecuted and punished:

(1) In the parish where the person owing the duty of support resides or is found, or

(2) In the parish where the last matrimonial domicile was established, or

(3) In the parish where the person (or persons) to whom the duty of support is owed establishes a bona fide residence, provided that this provision shall be effective only if the person to whom the duty of support was owed was justified in establishing a separate residence.

CODE TITLE XXI. INSANITY PROCEEDINGS

§211. Procedures in handling defendants committed to mental institutions because of lack of capacity to stand trial.

A. The medical staff of a mental institution to which a defendant is committed after he has been found not guilty by reason of insanity or after a court determines that he lacks mental capacity to proceed with a criminal trial shall review the defendant's record after the first sixty days and after one hundred twenty days of commitment and every one hundred eighty days thereafter to determine his present mental condition and whether he is presently capable of being discharged, conditionally or unconditionally, or being placed on probation, without being a danger to others or himself, or presently capable of standing trial. The superintendent of the institution shall make such recommendations to the review panel or the court as provided for in Title XXI relating to insanity proceedings of the Code of Criminal Procedure.

B. The medical staff shall, as long as the defendant remains in the mental institution, have full authority to determine whether his condition in such as to require that he be confined in a security ward or place designated pursuant to R.S. 28:25 for the confinement of patients charged with crimes or misdemeanors, or should be transferred into a different type of ward in the institution.

CODE TITLE XXII. RECUSATION OF JUDGES AND DISTRICT ATTORNEYS

§221. Appointment of substitute judge by supreme court.

Whenever any district judge is prevented by any cause whatever from holding court, and that fact is made to appear, by the certificate of the clerk under the seal of the court, to the supreme court or to any justice thereof, if in the judgment of the court or any justice the public interest so requires, the court or such justice shall designate and appoint any district judge of any other district to hold said court and discharge all the duties of the judge so disabled during such disability. Such appointment shall be filed in the clerk's office of and entered on the minutes of said district court, and a certified copy thereof, under the seal of the court, shall be transmitted by the clerk of the district court to the district judge so designated and appointed.

CODE TITLE XXIV. PROCEDURES PRIOR TO TRIAL

§241. Medical, psychological, psychiatric examination of certain victims under age eighteen; prohibition.

If the defendant is charged with a violation of R.S. 14:93 or any provision of Subpart C of Part II, Subpart B of Part IV, or Subpart A(1) or A(4) of Part V of Chapter 1 of Title 14 of the Louisiana Revised Statutes of 1950, and the victim was under the age of eighteen at the time of the offense, the defendant shall not be entitled to compel the victim to submit to a medical, psychological, or psychiatric examination, unless the court finds, after a contradictory hearing with the state, that such an examination is necessary and appropriate and will not cause the victim undue emotional stress and is not being sought for the purpose of harassing or intimidating the victim. At such a hearing the defendant shall not be entitled to compel the attendance of the victim. *(Added by Acts 1995 No. 754, §1, eff. 8/15/95.)*

§242. Pretrial diversion for driving while intoxicated; reporting.

Notwithstanding any provision of law to the contrary, if a person is placed in a pretrial diversion program following an arrest for a violation of R.S. 14:98, operating a vehicle while intoxicated, or a parish or municipal ordinance that prohibits operating a vehicle while intoxicated, while impaired, or while under the influence of alcohol, drugs, or any controlled dangerous substance, then the prosecuting authority shall maintain a record consisting of the name of the person, the arrest date, and a description of the pretrial intervention or diversion program in which the person was placed. Such record shall become a public record when the person has successfully completed the intervention program or is terminated from the program. *(Added by Acts 1997 No. 714, §1, eff. 8/15/97.)*

CODE TITLE XXV. COMPULSORY PROCESS

§252. Witnesses' fees and mileage.

Witnesses subpoenaed in all preliminary criminal trials or proceedings, for attendance before grand juries and upon final trials shall receive a per diem of three dollars per day and mileage of not more than five cents for each mile necessarily traveled in going to and returning from court, the exact amount to be fixed by the police juries of the several parishes, provided, however, that in the parishes of Acadia and Vermilion witnesses shall not be allowed any fees, per diem or mileage in all preliminary criminal trials or proceedings and for attendance before grand juries, provided further, however, that witnesses subpoenaed in the parishes of Acadia and Vermilion upon final trials shall receive a per diem of three dollars per day and mileage of not more than five cents for each mile necessarily travelled in going to and returning from court, the exact amount to be fixed by the police juries of the parties of Acadia and Vermillion.

§253. Witnesses not residents of parish.

Witnesses who are summoned to testify in prosecutions pending in other parishes than those in which they reside, shall receive a compensation of five cents for every mile they may necessarily travel in going and returning, and five dollars for every day they may be necessarily in attendance upon the court.

§254. Sheriffs, jurors and law enforcement officers not entitled to witness fees.

No sheriff, deputy sheriff or juror, and no law enforcement officer except as otherwise provided by R.S. 15:254.1 and R.S. 15:255 while attending court as such, shall be allowed any compensation for attendance as a witness in any criminal case.

§254.1. Compensation of off-duty law enforcement officers; City Court of New Iberia.

A. Any sheriff, deputy sheriff, city or state police officer, or other law enforcement officer subpoenaed to testify in a traffic, criminal, or juvenile case before the City Court of New Iberia on a date or at a time when such an officer is off duty shall be paid the sum of twenty-five dollars per case per day by the clerk of the city of New Iberia.

B. (1) The maximum allowable fee to be received by an officer on any given day when he is summoned in an off-duty status shall be seventy-five dollars per day, no matter how many summonses he receives per specific day. Said sum shall be in addition to any other compensation the law enforcement officer is eligible to receive from his or her employer.

(2) Witness fees provided by this Subsection shall be paid from costs of court which shall be assessed and collected in individual cases in which there is a plea of guilty or a conviction, in accordance with a schedule of costs adopted by the judge or judges of the City Court of New Iberia. The costs so collected shall be placed in a special fund maintained and administered by the governing authority, the city of New Iberia, and from which the governing authority shall pay the witness fees provided for herein.

(3) The judge or judges of the City Court of New Iberia may adjust the schedule of costs from time to time as the need for funds may require.

C. As a condition precedent to receipt of the compensation provided in this Section, the law enforcement officer and his superior shall be required to certify to the clerk of the City Court of New Iberia that the officer was summoned to testify on a day while he was off duty and did in fact appear in court as commanded in the subpoena.
(Chgd. by Acts 1992 No. 667, §1, eff. 8/21/92.)

§254.2. Compensation of off-duty law enforcement officers; Fifteenth Judicial District Court, Lafayette Parish.

Any sheriff, deputy sheriff, city or state police officer, or other law enforcement officer subpoenaed to testify in a criminal case in Lafayette Parish before the Fifteenth Judicial District Court on a date or at a time when such officer is off duty shall be paid the sum of fifteen dollars per day by the clerk of court of Lafayette Parish. Said sum shall be in addition to any other compensation the aforesaid law enforcement officer is eligible to receive. Provided that as a condition precedent to receipt of the compensation provided in this Section, the aforesaid law enforcement officer and his superior shall be required to certify to the clerk of court issuing the subpoena that the officer was summoned to testify on a day while he was off duty and did in fact appear in court as commanded in the subpoena. Said sum shall not be taxed as court costs.

§254.3. Compensation of off-duty law enforcement officers; City Court of Lafayette.

Any sheriff, deputy sheriff, city or state police officer, or other law enforcement officer subpoenaed to testify in a traffic or criminal case before the City Court of Lafayette on a date or at a time when such officer is off duty shall be paid the sum of five dollars per day by the clerk of the City Court of Lafayette. Provided that as a condition precedent to receipt of the compensation provided in this Section, the aforesaid law enforcement officer and his superior shall be required to certify to the clerk of the City Court of Lafayette that the officer was summoned to testify on a day while he was off duty and did in fact appear in court as commanded in the subpoena. The maximum allowable fee to be received by an officer on any given day when he is summoned in an off-duty status will be five dollars, no matter how many summons he receives for the specific day. Said sum shall be in addition to any other compensation the aforesaid law enforcement officer is eligible to receive. Said sum shall not be taxed as court costs.

§254.4. Compensation of off-duty law enforcement officers; Twenty-Seventh Judicial District Court, St. Landry Parish.

A. Any deputy sheriff, city or state police officer, or other law enforcement officer subpoenaed to testify in a criminal case before the Twenty-Seventh Judicial District Court on a date or at a time when such officer is off duty shall be paid the sum of fifteen dollars per day by the clerk of court. Said sum shall be in addition to any other compensation the aforesaid law enforcement officer is eligible to receive. Provided that as a condition precedent to receipt of the compensation provided in this Subsection, the aforesaid law enforcement officer and his superior shall be required to certify to the clerk of court issuing the subpoena that the officer was summoned to testify on a day while he was off duty and did in fact appear in court as commanded in the subpoena. Said sum shall not be taxed as court costs.

B. Any deputy sheriff, city or state police officer, or other law enforcement officer subpoenaed to testify in a traffic or criminal case before the city court of Opelousas or Eunice on a date or at a time when such officer is off duty shall be paid the sum of five dollars per day by the clerk of the respective city courts. Provided that as a condition precedent to receipt of the compensation provided in this Subsection, the aforesaid law enforcement officer and his superior shall be required to certify to the clerk of the respective city courts that the officer was summoned to testify on a day while he was off duty and did in fact appear in court as commanded in the subpoena. The maximum allowable fee to be received by an officer on any given day when he is summoned in an off duty status will be five dollars, regardless of how many summons he receives for the specific day. Said sum shall be in addition to any other compensation the aforesaid law enforcement officer is eligible to receive. Said sum shall not be taxed as court costs.

§254.5. Plans for witness fees to off-duty law enforcement officers; Ascension Parish.

A. The governing authority of Ascension Parish shall adopt a plan under which each law enforcement officer who, because of his official connections with any criminal case as the arresting officer or in some other official capacity, is required to be present as a witness in any criminal case which is being tried in the Ascension Parish Court, during any time when he otherwise is not required to report to work or perform the duties of his job, shall be paid witness fees in the amount of fifteen dollars for each case for which his presence in the court is required and for which he was present. No officer shall be allowed more than thirty dollars in any one day regardless of the number of cases for which he is required to be present.

B. The plan adopted for the payment of witness fees to law enforcement officers shall be applicable to all law enforcement officers alike and shall be paid whenever any law enforcement officer is required to be present and is present in one or more cases in such court during his regular time off.

C. Compensation allowed law enforcement officers as witnesses in accordance with the provisions of this Section shall not be deemed to be in lieu of, or to constitute any portion of, the salary or compensation paid to such law enforcement officers for the performance of the duties of their jobs, nor shall the payment of such witness fees be taken into consideration in determining the salary, any salary increase or any supplemental pay by the state to which any law enforcement officer is or becomes entitled.

D. Witness fees provided for by this Section shall be paid from costs of court collected in individual cases tried in the parish court, which shall be assessed as a part of the costs of court to be collected in such cases, and shall be collected for each case in which there is a plea of guilty or in which there is a conviction. When the governing authority adopts a plan for the payment of these witness fees, the judge or judges of the parish court shall adopt a schedule of costs which shall be applicable in each case to which such costs are applicable. All of such costs shall be placed, as they are collected, in a special fund which shall be maintained and be administered by the parish governing authority and from which the witness fees herein provided for shall be paid. The judge or judges shall have authority, from time to time as the needs of the fund require, to adjust the schedule of costs.

(Chgd. by Acts 1993 No. 705, §1, eff. 8/15/93.)

§254.6. Compensation of off-duty law enforcement officers; mayor's court, town of Welsh.

A. Any sheriff, deputy sheriff, city or state police officer, or other law enforcement officer subpoenaed to testify in a case before the mayor's court of Welsh on a date or at a time when such an officer is off duty shall be paid the sum of twenty-five dollars per case per day by the clerk of the town of Welsh.

B. (1) The maximum allowable fee to be received by an officer on any given day when he is summoned in an off-duty status shall be seventy-five dollars per day, no matter how many summonses he receives per specific day. This fee shall be in addition to any other compensation the law enforcement officer is eligible to receive from his or her employer.

(2) Notwithstanding the provisions of R.S. 33:441(A), witness fees provided by this Subsection shall be paid from costs of court which shall be assessed and collected in individual cases in which there is a plea of guilty or a conviction, in accordance with a schedule of costs adopted by the mayor's court. The costs so collected shall be placed in a special fund maintained and administered by the clerk of the town of Welsh, and from which the governing authority shall pay the witness fees provided for herein.

(3) The mayor's court of the town of Welsh may adjust the schedule of costs from time to time as the need for funds may require.

C. As a condition precedent to receipt of the compensation provided in this Section, the law enforcement officer and his superior shall be required to certify to the clerk of the town of Welsh that the officer was summoned to testify on a day while he was off duty and did in fact appear in court as commanded in the subpoena.

(Added by Acts 1995 No. 775, §1, 8/15/95.)

§255. Witness fees to off-duty law enforcement officers.

A. (1) Whenever a law enforcement officer is required to be present, in his official capacity, as a witness in any criminal case or delinquency adjudication in any district or parish court or any court exercising juvenile jurisdiction, during any time he is not required to report to work or perform the duties of his office, the governing authority of the parish shall pay him the sum of twenty-five dollars for each day per case, but no more than seventy-five dollars in any one day, regardless of the number of cases for which he is required to be present or whether he actually testified in the case, and which sum shall be paid pursuant to the provisions of R.S. 15:255(D)(1). The fee shall be provided to the law enforcement officer within sixty days from the date of appearance. This fee shall not be paid, however, to any law enforcement officer who is compensated by his employer for his appearance as a witness pursuant to the provisions of the federal Fair Labor Standards Act, as amended*.

**29 U.S.C. 201 et seq.*

(2) In the city of New Orleans, the Civil Service Commission shall establish rules for the payment of each law enforcement officer who because of his official connection with any criminal case as the arresting officer or in some other official capacity, is required to be present as a witness in any criminal case which is being tried in the Criminal District Court for the parish of Orleans during any time when he otherwise is not required to report to work or perform the duties of his job.

B. The plan adopted for the payment of witness fees to law enforcement officers shall be applicable to all law enforcement officers alike and shall be paid for each day any law enforcement officer is required to be present and is present in one or more cases in such courts during his regular time off.

C. Compensation allowed law enforcement officers as witnesses in accordance with the provisions of this Section shall not be deemed to be in lieu of, or to constitute any portion of, the salary or compensation paid to such law enforcement officers for the performance of the duties of their jobs, nor shall the payment of such witness fees be taken into consideration in determining the salary, any salary increase or any supplemental pay by the state to which any law enforcement officer is or becomes entitled.

D. (1) Witness fees provided for by this Section shall be paid from costs of court collected in individual cases tried in district or parish courts or in any court exercising juvenile jurisdiction which shall be assessed as a part of the costs of court to be collected in such cases, and shall be collected for each case in which there is a plea of guilty or in which there is a conviction. The judge or judges of court for the judicial district wherein the parish, or City of New Orleans, is situated shall adopt a schedule of costs that shall be applicable in each case before that court to which such costs are applicable. All of such costs shall be placed, as they are collected, in a special fund that shall be maintained and be administered by the governing authority and said authority shall pay out of said fund the witness fees herein provided for.

(2) The judge or judges shall, as the needs of the special fund require, adjust the schedule of costs to insure that the proceeds are adequate to fully pay the witness fees herein provided.

E. (1) The governing authority of each municipality having a city court shall pay to each law enforcement officer who, because of his official connections with any criminal case being tried in the city court, as the arresting officer or in some other official capacity, is required to be present as a witness in the case during any time when he is otherwise not required to report to work or perform the duties of his office, the sum of twenty-five dollars for each day per case for which his presence in the court is required and for which he is present. No officer shall be allowed more than seventy-five dollars in any one day, regardless of the number of cases for which he is required to be present. This fee shall not be paid, however, to any law enforcement officer who is compensated by his employer for his appearance as a witness pursuant to the provisions of the federal Fair Labor Standards Act, as amended.

(2) Witness fees provided by this Subsection shall be paid from costs of court which shall be assessed and collected in individual cases in which there is a plea of guilty or a conviction, in accordance with a schedule of costs adopted by the judge or judges of the city court. The costs so collected shall be placed in a special fund maintained and administered by the governing authority and from which the governing authority shall pay the witness fees provided for herein.

(3) The judge or judges of the city court may adjust the schedule of costs from time to time as the needs of the fund may require.

(4) The governing authority of the city of Baton Rouge is authorized to pay each law enforcement officer who, because of his official connections with any criminal case being tried in the city court, as the arresting officer or in some other official capacity, is required to be present as a witness in the case during any time when he is otherwise not required to report to work or perform the duties of his office, the sum of twenty-five dollars for each day per case for which his presence in the court is required and for which he is present. No officer shall be allowed more than fifty dollars in any one day, regardless of the number of cases for which he is required to be present.

F. For the purposes of this Section only, "law enforcement officer" as used herein shall include a person who withdraws blood for the purpose of determining the alcoholic content therein under the provisions of R.S. 32:664. However, no such person shall be eligible for a witness fee pursuant to this Section if he is paid by his employer for his time in court.
(Chgd. by Acts 1990 No. 318, §1, eff. 9/7/90.)

§256. Fees where more than one case on same day.

Except as provided in R.S. 15:255, no person shall be allowed, for attendance as a witness in criminal cases, more than is allowed in one case on the same day, or mileage for more than one case at a time. The provisions of this section shall not apply to the city of New Orleans.

§257. Placing material witness under bond.

Whenever it shall appear, upon motion of the district attorney or upon motion of a defendant supported by his affidavit, that the testimony of any witness is essential to the prosecution or the defense, as the case may be, and that there are good grounds to fear that said witness may depart or be taken from the jurisdiction of the court, a judge, as defined in Article 931 of the Code of Criminal Procedure, shall issue a warrant for the arrest of the witness. The witness shall be arrested and held in the parish jail, or such other suitable place as shall be designated by the court, until he gives an appearance bond as provided for defendants when admitted to bail, or until his testimony shall have been given in the cause or dispensed with.

§258. Taking deposition of witness imprisoned in default of bond.

When any witness in any criminal case, imprisoned in default of giving bond for his appearance, shall wish to have his testimony taken and to be enlarged, he shall apply to the judge of the court in which such prosecution is pending to have his testimony taken in writing; and thereupon the judge shall order said testimony to be taken in writing before him in court or in chambers or before any officer authorized by law to administer oaths, after giving forty-eight hours personal notice to the accused and to the district attorney to be present at the time and place of the taking of said testimony; provided, that with the consent of the district attorney and of the accused any and all delays for the taking of said testimony may be waived. If the accused is in jail, the sheriff shall be notified and shall produce the accused at the time and place designated to be confronted with the witness. The testimony when so taken shall be sworn to and signed by the witness if he knows how to write, if not, by his ordinary mark attested by the officer taking the testimony; and the said testimony so certified to shall be without delay returned by the officer taking the same into the court in which said prosecution is pending, together with the said notice and the officer's return of service annexed thereto, and thereupon the said witness shall be discharged from custody.

The taking of this testimony shall be without expense to the witness, but shall be taxed as a part of the costs of the prosecution.

§259. Admissibility of depositions taken in jail.

The testimony taken as provided for in R.S. 15:258, when certified to by the officer before whom taken, shall, in case of the death or departure of the witness from the parish or other inability to attend court, be admissible before the grand jury as well as on the trial of the accused, subject to all legal objections, but shall not be admissible when the presence of the witness can be procured by subpoena; provided that whenever an accused, not in jail, shall have been duly notified to be present, at the taking of said testimony and shall not attend, he shall not be allowed to set up the plea that he had been deprived of his right to be confronted with the witnesses against him.

§260. Production of certain records of victim under age eighteen; conditions.

If the defendant is charged with a violation of R.S. 14:93 or any provision of Subpart C of Part II, Subpart B of Part IV, or Subpart A(1) or A(4) of Part V of Chapter 1 of Title 14 of the Louisiana Revised Statutes of 1950, and the victim was under the age of eighteen at the time of the offense, a subpoena or court order compelling the production of medical, psychological, school, or other records pertaining to the victim shall not be issued upon request of the defendant unless the subpoena or court order identifies the records sought with particularity and is reasonably limited as to subject matter, and the court finds, after a contradictory hearing with the state, that the requested records are likely to be relevant and admissible at trial and are not sought for the purpose of harassing the victim. *(Added by Acts 1995 No. 755, §1, eff. 8/15/95.)*

§261. Disposition of witness or appearance fees for off-duty law enforcement officers.

A. Notwithstanding any other provision of law to the contrary, whenever by reason of the enforcement or imposition of any federal law or rule or for any other reason, an off-duty municipal law enforcement officer is compensated by his governmental employer for an appearance in court in his official capacity as a witness in any criminal case or delinquency adjudication in any city court during any time he would not otherwise be required to report to work or perform the duties of his office, then the officer of the court responsible for the disposition of any witness or appearance fee provided in law to compensate or reimburse for the cost of such officer's appearance shall pay the fee to the fiscal officer or other person designated by the officer's governmental employer to receive revenues on behalf of the governmental body.

B. The governmental employer may retain such portion of the appearance fee as is necessary to reimburse it for salary, benefits, and other expenses it expends in making its employee available for the appearance. If the witness or appearance fee exceeds the amount the employer is required to pay in salary, benefits, and expenses for such appearance, the employer shall transmit the difference to the officer who made the appearance. In no case, however, shall the officer receive less than he would have been compensated if he had received the fee directly.

(Added by Acts 1997 No. 918, §1, eff. 8/15/97.)

CODE TITLE XXVI. TRIAL PROCEDURE

§270. Interpreters for deaf or severely hearing-impaired persons.

A. In all criminal prosecutions, where the accused is deaf or severely hearing-impaired, he shall have the proceedings of the trial interpreted to him in a language that he can understand by a qualified interpreter appointed by the court. In all cases where the mental condition of a person is being considered and where such person may be committed to a mental institution, and where such person is deaf or severely hearing-impaired, all of the court proceedings pertaining to him shall be interpreted by a qualified interpreter appointed by the court. The qualification of an interpreter as an expert witness is governed by the Louisiana Code of Evidence.

B. (1) In any case where an interpreter is required to be appointed by the court under this Section, the court shall not commence proceedings until the appointed interpreter is in court.

(2) The interpreter appointed in accordance with this Section shall be required to take an oath or affirmation that he will make a true interpretation to the deaf or severely hearing-impaired person accused or being examined of all the proceedings of his case in a language that he understands, and that he will repeat said deaf or severely hearing-impaired person's answer to questions to counsel, court or jury, to the best of his skill and judgment.

(3) Interpreters appointed in accordance with this Section shall receive for their services an amount to be fixed by the judge presiding. When travel of the interpreter is necessary, all the actual expenses of travel, lodging and meals incurred by the interpreter in connection with the case at which he is appointed to serve shall be paid at the same rate applicable to state employees.

§271. Plea of not guilty; burden of proof.

The plea of not guilty throws upon the state the burden of proving beyond a reasonable doubt each element of the crime necessary to constitute the defendant's guilt.

§272. Order for substitution of certified copy of missing document.

The judge shall, upon proof of the loss, destruction or abstraction from the court of any indictment, information or bail bond, order that a certified copy from the judicial record of such lost, destroyed or abstracted document shall be substituted for the original and that the trial and all further proceedings in the cause be had as on the original.

§273. Right of accused to be confronted with witnesses.

The accused shall have the right to be confronted with the witnesses against him and the depositions of witnesses shall not be evidence either for or against him except as provided by law.

§§274, 275. *(Repealed.)*

§276. Self-incrimination of witness.

No witness can be forced to criminate himself, but the judge is not bound by the witness' statement that the answer would criminate him, when from the nature of the question asked and the circumstances of the case such statement can not be true.

§§277 to 282. *(Repealed.)*

§283. Victims of child abuse; testimony taken outside courtroom.

A. On its own motion or on the motion of the attorney for any party, a court may order that the testimony of a child under fourteen years of age who may have been physically or sexually abused be taken in a room other than the courtroom and be simultaneously televised by closed circuit television to the court and jury, when the court makes a specific finding of necessity based upon both of the following:

(1) Expert testimony that the child would be likely to suffer serious emotional distress if forced to give testimony in open court.

(2) Expert testimony that, without such simultaneous televised testimony, the child cannot reasonably communicate his testimony to the court or jury.

B. The court shall ensure that the child cannot see or hear the accused unless such viewing or hearing is requested for purposes of identification. However, the court shall ensure that the accused is afforded the ability to consult with his attorney during the testimony of the child.

C. The only persons who may be present in the room with the child are the person or persons operating the audio-video equipment, the presiding judge, the attorneys for the state, the attorneys for the defendant, and any person, other than a relative of the child, whose presence is determined by the court to be necessary to the welfare and well-being of the child during his testimony. The persons operating the equipment shall be confined to an adjacent room or behind a screen or mirror that permits them to see and hear the child during his testimony but does not permit the child to see or hear them.

D. Only the attorneys, or the presiding judge as authorized by law, may question the child.

(Chgd. by Acts 1991 No. 500, §1, eff. 9/6/91.)

CODE TITLE XXVIII. BILL OF EXCEPTIONS

§291. Right of accused to have testimony taken down; provision for paying.

The testimony of the witnesses on the question of guilt or innocence may be taken down under the supervision of the court and in order to explain any bill of exception which may be taken by counsel for the accused, the accused shall have the right, if he chooses, to have all of the testimony so taken made a part of the transcript; provided, that any accused desiring to send up the testimony of all of the witnesses so taken, shall pay for the same, and provided further, that the said testimony shall be considered only in explanation of the bills of exception reserved during the trial on behalf of the accused.

CODE TITLE XXX. SENTENCE

§301. Remittance of fine or imprisonment.

Any fine or imprisonment, imposed for violation of state laws or municipal or parish ordinances, which is alleged to be excessive or that for any reason should be abated or remitted in whole or in part shall be abated or remitted in the following manner:

Fines or imprisonment imposed under state laws shall be abated or remitted in the manner directed by law.

Fines or imprisonment imposed under ordinances of police juries may be abated or remitted only upon the recommendation of the judge of the parish and the consent of the police jury.

Fines or imprisonment imposed under ordinances of any city or other municipal corporation may be remitted only upon the recommendation of the mayor or other chief magistrate and the consent of the least numerous branch of the municipal legislative body.

§302. Sentences to prison districts; persons excluded.

Whenever prison districts have been established the rules of sentencing set forth below shall be followed:

A. The following persons shall be sentenced to prison districts:

(1) All persons convicted of misdemeanors and sentenced to imprisonment by any state court within the judicial district.

(2) All persons convicted of violations of state or parish laws by any municipal court within the judicial district.

B. The following persons may be sentenced to prison districts:

(1) Persons convicted of felonies by any state court within the judicial district notwithstanding the conviction ordinarily requires imprisonment in the penitentiary.

(2) Persons convicted of violations of municipal ordinances and sentenced to imprisonment by the municipal courts of those municipalities which have contracted with the governing authority of the prison district for the keeping of such persons.

C. The following persons shall not be imprisoned in any prison district:

(1) Persons sentenced to life imprisonment.

(2) Persons convicted of treason, aggravated or simple rape, aggravated or simple arson, aggravated or simple kidnapping.

(3) Bank and homestead officials convicted of theft by reason of misusing funds of depositors or other funds entrusted to them.

(4) Notaries public who are defaulters.

(5) Second or third offenders.

(6) Persons whose sentences exceed five years.

§303. Maximum fine or imprisonment when not specified.

Whenever the punishment of fine and imprisonment are left by law to the discretion of any court, the fine shall not exceed one thousand dollars, nor the imprisonment two years.

§304. Expenses to be paid by parishes; juror's fee in city of New Orleans.

All expenses incurred in the different parishes of the state or in the city of New Orleans by the arrest, confinement, and prosecution of persons accused or convicted of crimes, their removal to prison, the pay of witnesses specifically provided for by law, jurors and all prosecutorial expenses whatever attending criminal proceedings shall be paid by the respective parishes in which the offense charged may have been committed or by the city of New Orleans, as the case may be. The expenses shall be paid by the parish treasurer or by the city of New Orleans after an account of the expenses shall be duly certified to be correct by the presiding judge and the clerk of court. The fees, salaries, and expenses to be paid shall be fixed and regulated by the parish or city authority unless otherwise provided by law; however, those persons serving as jurors in the trial of criminal cases in the city of New Orleans shall be entitled to compensation of sixteen dollars for each and every day or part of a day on which they serve as jurors in any criminal case to be paid by the city of New Orleans; provided further that this shall not become effective until the council of the city of New Orleans will have appropriated sufficient funds for this purpose. Notwithstanding the provisions of this Section, the city of New Orleans shall only pay the above expenses after the special account created pursuant to R.S. 15:571.11(D), and to the extent authorized thereby, shall have been depleted. Nothing in this Section shall be construed to make the parishes or the city of New Orleans responsible for the expenses associated with the costs, expert fees, or attorney fees of a defendant in a criminal proceeding. *(Chgd. by Acts 1994 Third Ex. Sess. No. 81, §1, eff. 7/7/94.)*

§305. Probation in neglect of family cases.

A. (1) Whenever a person has pleaded guilty or been found guilty of the misdemeanor of criminal neglect of family or has been found in contempt of court for failing to pay support as ordered under the provisions of Children's Code Art. 1353, the judge may suspend the execution or imposition of sentence and release the offender on unsupervised probation or probation under the supervision of the Department of Social Services. The judge may suspend the sentence and place the defendant on probation although he has begun to serve the sentence imposed and may impose any specific conditions reasonably related to the offender's rehabilitation, including but not limited to the conditions of probation as set forth in Code of Criminal Procedure Article 895.

(2) The period of probation or of suspension of sentence shall be fixed by the court at not less than six months nor more than five years, subject to renewal by the court for fixed periods not exceeding five years. The period of probation or suspended sentence may be continued in this manner as long as the responsibility for support continues or as long as an arrearage is owed.

B. As a condition of probation authorized by this Section, the defendant may be required to provide for the support of any persons for whose support he is legally responsible. The court may also require the defendant to enter into a recognizance, with or without surety, in order to insure the payment of the support. The condition of the recognizance shall be such that the defendant shall make his or her personal appearance at court whenever required to do so, and shall further comply with the terms of the order or of any subsequent modification thereof.

C. In placing such an offender on probation, the court may place the offender under the supervision of the department. However, separate juvenile courts now or hereinafter established may use their own probation services.

D. The clerk of court shall give notice to the Department of Health and Human Resources in every case in which an offender is placed on probation under this Section.

E. (1) If the court finds that the defendant has violated a condition of his probation, it shall order that the probation be revoked and shall sentence the defendant to imprisonment for not more than six months. The court shall also order the defendant to pay the total amount of unpaid support to the spouse, to the tutor or custodian of the child, to the court-approved fiduciary of the spouse or child, or to the Department of Health and Human Resources in an AFDC case or in a non-AFDC case in which the department is rendering services, whichever is applicable; hereinafter, said payee shall be referred to as the applicable payee. Such judgment shall have the same force and effect as a final judgment for money damages against the defendant. This judgment may be made executory by any Louisiana court of competent jurisdiction on petition of the department or the district attorney.

(2) (a) At the discretion of the judge, the sentence may be suspended by the court upon payment of:

(i) The amount of the order for unpaid support;

(ii) The amount of unpaid support accrued since the date of the said order; and

(iii) The amount of all attendant court costs.

(b) Upon recommendation of the state attorney or the support enforcement officer, or both, the remainder of the sentence may be suspended upon payment of a lesser amount plus attendant court costs. Such payment shall apply toward but not extinguish the total amount due.

(c) In addition, if the defendant has entered into a recognizance in the amount fixed by the court to insure the payment of the support, the court may order the forfeiture of such recognizance and enforcement thereof by execution. The sum recovered shall be paid in whole or in part to the applicable payee. However, should the court order both the forfeiture of the recognizance and at the same time order the accused to pay all unpaid support under the sentence for violation of probation, the amount of unpaid support plus attendant court costs shall be the maximum amount payable.

(Chgd. by Acts 1993 No. 429, §2, eff. 8/15/93.)

§306. Operating a vehicle while intoxicated; additional conditions of probation; ignition interlock devices.

A. As an additional condition of probation, the court shall require that any person convicted of a second or subsequent violation of R.S. 14:98 and placed on probation in accordance with that Section shall not operate a motor vehicle during the period of probation unless that vehicle is equipped with a functioning ignition interlock device as provided in R.S. 15:307.

B. When the court imposes the use of an ignition interlock device as a condition of probation upon a person whose driving privileges are not suspended or revoked, the court shall require the person to provide proof of installation of such a device to the court or a probation officer within thirty days. If the person fails to provide proof of installation within that period, absent a finding by the court of good cause for that failure which is entered into the court record, the court shall revoke the person's probation.

C. The person whose driving privileges are restricted pursuant to this Section shall have the system on his vehicle monitored by the manufacturer for proper use at least semiannually or more frequently as the court may order. A report of any monitoring shall be issued by the manufacturer to the court within fourteen days after the monitoring.

D. If a person is required in the course and scope of his employment to operate a motor vehicle which does not have an approved ignition interlock device, and if the vehicle is owned by the employer, the court may allow the person to operate the employer's vehicle. Any person authorized to operate an employer's vehicle without an ignition interlock device shall be required to obtain and present to the court written permission from the employer for the employee to operate a specific vehicle or vehicles. Such permission shall be in the possession of such person when he operates the employer's vehicle. A motor vehicle owned by a business entity which is in whole or in part owned or controlled by a person otherwise subject to this Section is not a motor vehicle owned by the employer.

(Added by Acts 1992 No. 982, §1; chgd. by Acts 1997 No. 581, §1, eff. 8/15/97.)

§307. Ignition interlock devices; installation and certification.

A. As used in R.S. 15:306, "ignition interlock device" means a constant monitoring device that prevents a motor vehicle from being started at any time without first determining the equivalent blood alcohol level of the operator through the taking of a breath sample for testing. The system shall be calibrated so that the motor vehicle may not be started if the blood alcohol level of the operator, as measured by the test, reaches a level established by the court and consistent with the rules promulgated by the secretary of the Department of Public Safety and Corrections, hereafter referred to as the "secretary".

B. The secretary shall certify or cause to be certified ignition interlock devices required by R.S. 15:306 and shall publish a list of approved devices. All reasonable costs of certification shall be borne by the manufacturer. The manufacturer of the system shall be responsible for the installation or the training of installers and shall educate users and service and maintain the system.

C. The secretary shall formulate and promulgate a set of rules and regulations for the proper approval, installation, and use of ignition interlock devices in full compliance with this Section and R.S. 15:306. The standards shall include but not be limited to requirements that the devices or systems:

(1) Do not impede the safe operation of the vehicle.

(2) Correlate with established measures of alcohol impairment.

(3) Work accurately and reliably in an unsupervised environment.

(4) Resist tampering and give evidence if tampering is attempted.

(5) Are difficult to circumvent.

(6) Minimize inconvenience to a sober user.

(7) Require a proper, deep lung breath sample or other accurate measure of blood alcohol content equivalence.

(8) Operate reliably over the range of automobile environments.

(9) Are manufactured by a party who will provide product liability insurance and a bond against malfunction of the device.

D. The secretary may adopt in whole or relevant part the guidelines, rules, regulations, studies, or independent laboratory tests performed or relied upon by other states, their agencies or commissions.

E. The secretary shall design and adopt by regulation a warning label which shall be affixed to each ignition interlock device upon installation. The label shall contain a warning that any person tampering with, defeating, or otherwise circumventing the device is guilty of a criminal offense and subject to criminal penalty and civil liability.

(Added by Acts 1992 No. 982, §1, eff. 1/1/93.)

CHAPTER 1-A. LOUISIANA SENTENCING COMMISSION

Section

§321. Purpose.

A. The enactment of statutes defining criminal offenses and the establishment of ranges of penalties for those offenses is a matter of substantive law solely within the prerogative of the legislature. The determination and imposition of sentence in particular cases is generally the function of the sentencing court, subject to appellate review and to mandatory sentences provided by law.

B. The legislature has determined that the best interest of the state would be served by the development and implementation of a uniform sentencing policy for use by the Louisiana judiciary. The purpose of the Louisiana Sentencing Commission is to assist the judiciary and the legislature in formulating such policy.

C. The commission shall conduct an annual review of the state's sentencing structure based upon existing criminal law and law relative to criminal procedure. The commission may recommend such legislation as may be necessary and appropriate to achieve a uniform sentencing policy.

(Chgd. by Acts 1995 No. 942, §2, eff. 8/15/95.)

§322. Louisiana Sentencing Commission.

The Louisiana Sentencing Commission is hereby created and established under the jurisdiction of the Louisiana Commission on Law Enforcement and Administration of Criminal Justice in the office of the governor.

§323. Composition of commission.

A. The commission shall be composed of twenty-three members. Nineteen members shall be voting members as designated in Subsection B and four members shall be nonvoting members as designated in Subsection D.

B. (1) Four voting members of the commission shall be as follows:

(a) A member of the House of Representatives appointed by the speaker of the House of Representatives.

(b) The chairman of the House Committee on Administration of Criminal Justice.

(c) One member of the Senate appointed by the president of the Senate.

(d) The chairman of the Senate Committee on Judiciary, Section C.

(2) Fifteen voting members shall be appointed by the governor as follows:

(a) Two district attorneys.

(b) Two attorneys specializing primarily in the defense of persons charged with criminal offenses.

(c) Two sheriffs.

(d) One judge of a court of appeal.

(e) Five district court judges, at least four of whom must be active.

(f) One city court judge.

(g) One justice of the Louisiana Supreme Court.

(h) One Louisiana citizen who is not an attorney, who is not formally associated with the criminal justice system, and who is a felony crime victim or a member of the immediate family of a felony crime victim, from a list of three names submitted by Victims and Citizens Against Crime, Inc.

C. Except as provided in R.S 15:323(B)(1), voting members shall serve for a term concurrent with that of the governor.

D. A representative of the Louisiana State Law Institute as designated by its president, a representative of the Louisiana Commission on Law Enforcement and Administration of Criminal Justice as designated by its chairman, the secretary of the Department of Public Safety and Corrections, or his designee, and one professional having a doctorate degree in a social science or criminal justice field appointed by the governor shall serve as the four nonvoting members of the commission.

E. Each appointment by the governor shall be subject to Senate confirmation.

F. Legislative members of the commission shall receive the same per diem and reimbursement of travel expense as is provided for legislative committees under the rules of the respective house. Nonlegislative commission members shall serve without compensation or per diem.

(Chgd. by Acts 1995 No. 548, §1, eff. 8/15/95.)

§324. Officers; meetings; staff.

A. The governor shall designate one voting member to serve as chairman at the pleasure of the governor. The chairman shall serve as chief executive officer of the commission.

B. The domicile of the commission shall be in Baton Rouge. The commission shall hold public meetings monthly except as otherwise provided by vote of the commission or by order of the chairman.

C. A simple majority of the voting membership of the commission shall constitute a quorum for the transaction of business.

D. The Louisiana Commission on Law Enforcement and Administration of Criminal Justice shall provide to the sentencing commission such clerical, administrative, and technical assistance and support as may be necessary in order to enable the sentencing commission to accomplish its goals.

§§325 to 329. *(Repealed by Acts 1995 No. 942, §3, eff. 8/15/95.)*

CHAPTER 2. EVIDENCE

PART I. THINGS THAT NEED NOT BE PROVED—PRIMA FACIE EVIDENCE—PRESUMPTIONS

PART II. GENERAL RULES OF EVIDENCE

SUBPART I. GENERAL

SUBPART II. ELECTRONIC RECORDING: CHILD ABUSE VICTIMS

PART III. RELEVANCY

PART IV. KNOWLEDGE AND INTENT

PART VI. ADMISSIONS AND CONFESSIONS

PART VII. DOCUMENTARY EVIDENCE

PART VIII. COMPETENCY OF WITNESSES

PART XI. EVIDENCE FROM CRIMINALISTICS LABORATORIES

PART XII. COURT REPORTERS, NOTES AND RECORDINGS

PART I. THINGS THAT NEED NOT BE PROVED—PRIMA FACIE EVIDENCE—PRESUMPTIONS

§423. Proof of registration of physicians and surgeons.

This list of the registered physicians and surgeons in this state published by the Department of Health and Human Resources and duly certified by the secretary of said office shall be received by the courts of the state as proof that the physicians and surgeons therein named are duly registered as required by law, provided that this method of proof shall not be considered exclusive.

§424. Statute law of other states.

The published statutes and digests of the other states and territories shall be prima facie evidence of the statute laws of the state or territory from which they purport to emanate, without being filed in evidence.

§425. Recitals in report of lunacy commissions.

The report of every commission of lunacy shall be prima facie evidence of the facts recited in such report and of the correctness of the findings of such commission.

§426. Proof of signature of articles of vessels.

A copy of the articles of any vessels, authenticated by the affidavit of the captain, shall be prima facie evidence that any seaman whose name appears subscribed thereto has actually signed articles.

§427. Recitals in act of protest of commercial paper.

Whenever any commercial paper shall have been protested, either in or out of this state, for nonpayment, the act of protest, or a certified copy thereof, shall be prima facie evidence of the facts recited in said act.

§428. Dishonored checks and drafts prima facie evidence of insufficient funds in bank.

Whenever any check or draft shall have been drawn on any bank, whether such bank be in or out of this state, and payment shall have been refused, such check or draft with its endorsements shall be prima facie evidence, that at the time of the presentation of said check or draft, the drawer did not have the money in said bank with which to pay said check or draft.

§429. Corporate existence presumed unless affidavit of denial filed before trial.

On trial of any criminal case it shall not be necessary to prove the incorporation of any corporation mentioned in the indictment, unless the defendant, before entering upon such trial, shall have filed his affidavit specifically denying the existence of such corporation.

§430. Proof of truth of recitals in copy of registry of birth, baptism or circumcision.

In all criminal prosecutions for the violation of any law relative to the employment of children or young persons, a copy of the registry of the birth, baptism or circumcision of such child or young person, duly certified to by the person in whose custody such registry may be kept, shall be prima facie evidence of the truth of the facts recited in such certified copy.

§431. Theft by public officer.

The failure, neglect, or refusal on the part of any public officer to pay over, at the time and in the manner required by law and to the authority designated by law to receive such payment, any public money in his hands, shall be prima facie evidence of the theft by such public officer of any public money not so paid over.

§432. Effect of legal presumptions; rebutting evidence; illustrations.

A legal presumption relieves him in whose favor it exists from the necessity of any proof; but may none the less be destroyed by rebutting evidence; such is the presumption attaching to the regularity of judicial proceedings; that the grand jury was legally constituted; that public officers have done their duty; that a relation or subject-matter once established, continues, but not that it pre-existed; that the defendant intended the natural and probable consequence of his act; that the defendant is innocent; that the defendant is sane and responsible for his actions; that the person in the unexplained possession of property recently stolen is the thief; that evidence under the control of a party and not produced by him was not produced because it would not have aided him; that the witnesses have told the truth.

§433. Conclusive presumption defined; illustration.

A conclusive presumption is one against which no proof can be admitted, such as the presumption that attaches to res adjudicata, to the recitals contained in legislative acts and to the official journals of legislative proceedings.

PART II. GENERAL RULES OF EVIDENCE

SUBPART I. GENERAL

§436.1. Photographs of objects of theft; affidavit of value and ownership; notice to defendant.

A. A photograph of property alleged to be the object of a theft, otherwise admissible, may be admitted as evidence without regard to the availability of the property itself.

B. An affidavit of the value and ownership of property which is alleged to be the object of a theft shall be admissible in evidence under the following circumstances:

(1) The affidavit shall be upon personal knowledge and shall state the basis for such knowledge;

(2) The affidavit shall be paraphed for identification with the photograph taken pursuant to Subsection A, and

(3) The state shall give written notice of its intent to introduce the affidavit, along with a copy of the affidavit and photograph, not less than ten days prior to commencement of the trial.

C. An affidavit admitted pursuant to Subsection B shall be deemed prima facie evidence of the value and ownership of the property alleged to be the object of a theft. Provided, however, that if the defendant files a written objection to the admission of the affidavit within three days prior to the commencement of trial, the affidavit shall not be admissible and shall not be deemed to be prima facie evidence of the value and ownership of the property.

§436.2. Photographs of animals cruelly treated; affidavit of condition; notice to defendant.

A. A photograph of an animal alleged to be cruelly treated, otherwise admissible, may be admitted as evidence without regard to the availability of the animal itself.

B. An affidavit of the condition of the animal which is alleged to be cruelly treated, shall be admissible in evidence when all of the following circumstances exist:

(1) The affidavit shall be upon personal knowledge and shall state the basis for such knowledge.

(2) The affidavit shall be paraphed for identification with the photograph taken pursuant to Subsection A.

C. An affidavit admitted pursuant to Subsection B shall be deemed prima facie evidence of the condition of the animal alleged to be cruelly treated.

D. Nothing in this Section shall prohibit the defendant from using photographs as part of his defense, nor shall the defendant be prohibited from using the animal as part of his defense, except if there has been a prior disposition of the animal as provided by R.S. 14:102.2 or 102.6.

(Added by Acts 1997 No. 1212, §2, eff. 8/15/97.)

§437. *(Repealed.)*

§438. Circumstantial evidence.

The rule as to circumstantial evidence is: assuming every fact to be proved that the evidence tends to prove, in order to convict, it must exclude every reasonable hypothesis of innocence.

§439. Burden of proof.

The burden of proof is upon him alleging the existence of a fact.

§440. Relative weight of positive and negative testimony.

Positive testimony on a given point must be given greater weight than negative testimony on the same point.

SUBPART II. ELECTRONIC RECORDING: CHILD ABUSE VICTIMS

§440.1. Purpose.

It is declared to be in the best interest of the state that children be spared from crimes of violence, and that persons who commit such crimes be prosecuted with a minimum of additional intrusion into the lives of such children.

§440.2. Authorization.

A. (1) A court with original criminal jurisdiction or juvenile jurisdiction may, on its own motion or on motion of the district attorney, a parish welfare unit or agency, or the Department of Health and Human Resources, require that a statement of a child under fourteen who has been physically or sexually abused be recorded on videotape.

(2) Further, the coroner may, in conjunction with the district attorney and appropriate hospital personnel and pursuant to their duties in R.S 40:2109.1 and 40:2113.4, provide for the videotaping of children who are rape victims or who have been otherwise physically or sexually abused.

(3) Such a videotape shall be available for introduction as evidence in a juvenile proceeding or adult criminal proceeding.

B. For purposes of this part, "videotape" means the visual recording on a magnetic tape together with the associated oral record.

§440.3. Videotape; admissibility; exception to hearsay rule.

The videotape authorized by this Subpart is hereby admissible in evidence as an exception to the hearsay rule.

§440.4. Method of recording videotape; competency.

A. A videotape of a child fourteen years of age or under may be offered in evidence either for or against a defendant charged with the rape or physical or sexual abuse of a child. To render such a videotape competent evidence, it must be satisfactory proved:

(1) That electronic recording was voluntarily made by the victim of the physical or sexual abuse.

(2) That no relative of the victim of the physical or sexual abuse was present in the room where the recording was made.

(3) That such recording was not made of answers to interrogatories calculated to lead the child to make any particular statement.

(4) That the recording is accurate, has not been altered, and reflects what the witness or victim said.

(5) That the taking of the child's statement was supervised by a physician, a board-certified social worker, a law enforcement officer, a licensed psychologist, or an authorized representative of the Department of Health and Human Resources.

B. The department shall develop and promulgate regulations on or before September 12, 1984, regarding training requirements and certification for department personnel designated in Paragraph (A)(5) who supervise the taking of the child's statement.

§440.5. Admissibility of videotaped statements; discovery by defendant.

A. The videotape of an oral statement of the child made before the proceeding begins may be admissible into evidence if:

(1) No attorney for either party was present when the statement was made;

(2) The recording is both visual and oral and is recorded on film or videotape or by other electronic means;

(3) The recording is accurate, has not been altered, and reflects what the witness or victim said;

(4) The statement was not made in response to questioning calculated to lead the child to make a particular statement;

(5) Every voice on the recording is identified;

(6) The person conducting the interview of the child in the recording is present at the proceeding and available to testify or be cross-examined by either party;

(7) The defendant or the attorney for the defendant is afforded an opportunity to view the recording before it is offered into evidence; and

(8) The child is available to testify.

B. The admission into evidence of the videotape of a child as authorized herein shall not preclude the prosecution from calling the child as a witness or from taking the child's testimony outside of the courtroom as authorized in R.S. 15:283. Nothing in this Section shall be construed to prohibit the defendant's right of confrontation.

C. In a criminal prosecution, when the state intends to offer as evidence a copy of a videotaped oral statement of a child made pursuant to the provisions of this Subpart, the defendant may be provided a copy of the videotape if the court determines it necessary to prepare a proper defense. If the court orders the defendant be provided a copy of the videotaped statement, only the attorney and the defendant shall be permitted to view the tape and no copies shall be made by any person. The copy shall be returned to the court immediately upon conclusion of the case. Any violation of this Subsection shall be punished as contempt of court.

(Added by Acts 1990 No. 654, §1, eff. 9/7/90.)

§440.6. Confidentiality.

Videotapes which are a part of the court record shall be preserved under a protective order of the court in order to protect the privacy of the child. The court shall order the destruction of the videotapes after five years have elapsed from the date of entry of judgment. However, if an appeal is filed, the videotapes shall not be destroyed until a final judgment on appeal has been rendered.

PART III. RELEVANCY

§441.1. DNA, blood, and saliva testing; relevance.

Evidence of deoxyribonucleic acid profiles, genetic markers of the blood, and secretor status of the saliva offered to establish the identity of the offender of any crime is relevant as proof in conformity with the Louisiana Code of Evidence.

§442. *(Repealed.)*

§443. Prosecutions for defamation.

In all prosecutions for defamation, the truth thereof may be given in evidence.

PART IV. KNOWLEDGE AND INTENT

§444. Proof of intent unnecessary in statutory crimes; inadmissible evidence.

If a statute has made it a crime to do a particular act, no further proof of intent is required than that accused voluntarily did the act; and any evidence that he did not know such act to be forbidden by law is inadmissible.

PART VI. ADMISSIONS AND CONFESSIONS

§449. Applicability.

The term "admission" is applied to those matters of fact which do not involve criminal intent; the term "confession" is applied only to an admission of guilt, not to an acknowledgment of facts merely tending to establish guilt.

§450. Use of confession, admission or declaration in entirety.

Every confession, admission or declaration sought to be used against any one must be used in its entirety, so that the person to be affected thereby may have the benefit of any exculpation or explanation that the whole statement may afford.

§451. Condition precedent to use of confession; free and voluntary rule.

Before what purposes* to be a confession can be introduced in evidence, it must be affirmatively shown that it was free and voluntary, and not made under the influence of fear, duress, intimidation, menaces, threats, inducements or promises.

**So in original. Probably should be "purports".*

§452. Rights of arrested person as to confession.

No person under arrest shall be subjected to any treatment designed by effect on body or mind to compel a confession of crime.

§453. Confessions obtained by questions and answers.

A confession need not be the spontaneous act of the accused and may be obtained by means of questions and answers.

§454. Inapplicability of free and voluntary rule to admissions not involving criminal intent.

The rule that a confession produced by threat or promise is inadmissible in evidence does not apply to admissions not involving the existence of a criminal intent.

§455. Effect of declarations and acts of coconspirators.

Each coconspirator is deemed to assent to or to commend whatever is said or done in furtherance of the common enterprise, and it is therefore of no moment that such act was done or such declaration was made out of the presence of the conspirator sought to be bound thereby, or whether the conspirator doing such act or making such declaration be or be not on trial with his codefendant. Such evidence is controlled by the provisions of the Louisiana Code of Evidence.

PART VII. DOCUMENTARY EVIDENCE

§459. Use of records or documents of trial court as evidence.

Whenever, during the trial of any criminal case, either party may desire to offer in evidence any record, paper or document belonging to the files or records of the court in which the trial is proceeding, the presiding judge shall, at the request of such party, direct the clerk to produce such record, document or paper, in order that the same may be used in evidence; and it shall not be necessary for the clerk in any such case to make a copy of such record, document or paper.

PART VIII. COMPETENCY OF WITNESSES

§461. *(Repealed by Acts 1992 No. 376, §6, eff. 1/1/93.)*

§§462 to 467. *(Repealed.)*

§468. Duty to testify as to bribery or corruptly influencing voters; immunity.

Any person may be compelled to testify in any lawful proceeding against another charged with commercial bribery, public bribery, bribery of voters or corrupt influencing, and shall not be permitted to withhold his testimony upon the ground that it may incriminate him or expose him to public infamy; but such testimony shall not afterwards be used against him in any judicial proceeding, except for perjury in giving such testimony.

§469. *(Repealed.)*

§469.1. Receipt of testimony from victims of certain crimes who are fifteen years of age or younger; closed session of court or in chambers; procedure.

In cases of simple rape, attempted simple rape, aggravated rape, attempted aggravated rape, forcible rape, attempted forcible rape, or carnal knowledge of a juvenile in which the victim is a child of fifteen years of age or younger, the court, upon its own motion or that of the defendant or state, may order that the testimony of such victim be heard either in closed session of court or in the judge's chambers, in the presence of the judge or jury, the defendant, counsel for the defendant, the family of the defendant, the parents or parent of the victim, the attorney for the state, a reasonable but limited number of members of the public which the court may allow in its discretion under these circumstances, and any other party which the court determines has a valid interest in the proceedings.

§470. *(Repealed.)*

§471. Grand jurors and district attorneys incompetent to testify as to grand jury proceedings; perjury cases.

No grand juror or district attorney is competent to testify as to anything that took place before the grand jury during its sessions, or to testify upon what evidence any indictment was found, or that it was found upon insufficient evidence, or without evidence; but the grand jurors and the district attorney are competent witnesses both for the state and for the defense in any prosecution for perjury or false swearing, alleged to have been committed before the grand jury, and as authorized by Louisiana Code of Evidence Article 606.

§§472 to 474. *(Repealed.)*

§§475 to 477. *(Repealed by Acts 1992 No. 376, §6, eff. 1/1/93.)*

§477.1. Privileged communications to "crime stoppers" organizations.

A. As used in this Section, the following terms shall have the following meanings unless the context clearly requires otherwise:

(1) "Crime stoppers organization" means a private, nonprofit organization that accepts and expends donations for rewards to persons who report to the organization information concerning criminal activity and that forwards the information to the appropriate law enforcement agency.

(2) "Privileged communication" means a statement by any person, in any manner whatsoever, to a crime stoppers organization for the purpose of reporting alleged criminal activity.

B. No person shall be required to disclose, by way of testimony or otherwise, a privileged communication between a person who submits a report of alleged criminal activity to a crime stoppers organization and the person who accepts the report on behalf of a crime stoppers organization or to produce, under subpoena, any records, documentary evidence, opinions, or decisions relating to such privileged communication:

(1) In connection with any criminal case or proceeding.

(2) By way of any discovery procedure.

C. Any person arrested or charged with a criminal offense may petition the court for an in camera inspection of the records of a privileged communication concerning such person made to a crime stoppers organization. The petition shall allege facts showing that such records would provide evidence favorable to the defendant and relevant to the issue of guilt or punishment. If the court determines that the person is entitled to all or any part of such records, it may order production and disclosure as it deems appropriate.

§478. *(Repealed by Acts 1992 No. 376, §6, eff. 1/1/93.)*

PART XI. EVIDENCE FROM CRIMINALISTICS LABORATORIES

§499. Certificates of analysis.

A. All criminalistics laboratories established by laws of this state or by laws of the United States, and all coroners, forensic pathologists, and other persons, partnerships, corporations, and other legal entities practicing in fields of knowledge and expertise in the gathering, examination, and analysis of evidence by scientific means are authorized to make proof of examination and analysis of physical evidence by the certificate of the person in charge of the facility in which such examination and analysis is made. Such certificate shall list:

(1) The date and time such evidence was delivered to such facility.

(2) The name of the person making such delivery, and the person receiving same.

(3) A brief description of the evidence.

(4) The type of examination or analysis requested.

(5) The name of the person making the examination or analysis.

(6) The date or dates of the examination or analysis.

(7) The results of the examination or analysis.

B. The certificate shall give the name and address of the facility in which the examination or analysis was made, and shall be signed by the person making the examination or analysis and by the person in charge of the facility.

§500. Admissibility.

In all criminal cases and in all cases in juvenile or family courts which are of a criminal nature, and in civil forfeiture proceedings arising from criminal activity, the courts of this state shall receive as evidence any certificate made in accordance with R.S. 15:499 subject to the conditions contained in this Section and R.S. 15:501. The certificate shall be received in evidence as prima facie proof of the facts shown thereon, and as prima facie proof of proper custody of the physical evidence listed thereon from time of delivery of said evidence to the facility until its removal therefrom.

§501. Notice of opposing party and opportunity to cross-examine expert; certification of subpoena request.

A. The party seeking to introduce a certificate made in accordance with R.S. 15:499 shall, not less than ten days prior to the commencement of the trial, give written notice of intent to offer proof by certificate. Such notice shall include a copy of the certificate.

B. (1) The party against whom such certificate is offered shall be permitted to subpoena on cross-examination, the person who performed the examination or analysis of the evidence. If the subpoena is requested at least five days prior to the commencement of trial or the person subpoenaed responds to the subpoena, the certificate shall not be prima facie proof of its contents or of proper custody.

(2) When the attorney for the defendant, or the defendant acting in his own defense, requests that a subpoena issue to the person who performed the examination or analysis, the

request shall be in writing and shall contain a certification that the attorney or the defendant intends in good faith to conduct the cross-examination.
(Chgd. by Acts 1990 No. 850, §1, eff. 9/7/90.)

PART XII. COURT REPORTERS, NOTES AND RECORDINGS

§511. Court reporters, retention and destruction of notes and recordings of criminal cases.

A. The court reporter shall retain indefinitely all notes and tape recordings of a criminal case. However, if the record of the trial or other criminal proceeding is fully transcribed, the court reporter shall retain all notes and tape recordings which have been fully transcribed for a period of not less than two years after transcription is completed. In criminal cases where all defendants are acquitted, the court reporter need not retain the notes and tape recordings. The court reporter shall destroy any notes and tape recordings of any matter upon order of a court of competent jurisdiction.

B. The notes and tape recordings of any criminal case which are retained by a court reporter pursuant to the provisions of this Section shall be the property of the court in which the case was heard. The court reporter shall have the duty to retain and maintain all such notes and tape recordings pursuant to the provisions of this Section, although the notes and tape recordings shall remain the property of the court.

CHAPTER 3. HABITUAL OFFENDER LAW

§529.1. Sentences for second and subsequent offenses; certificate of warden or clerk of court in the state of Louisiana as evidence.

A. (1) Any person who, after having been convicted within this state of a felony or adjudicated a delinquent under Title VIII of the Louisiana Children's Code for the commission of a felony-grade violation of either the Louisiana Controlled Dangerous Substances Law* involving the manufacture, distribution, or possession with intent to distribute a controlled dangerous substance or a crime of violence as listed in Paragraph (2) of this Subsection, or who, after having been convicted under the laws of any other state or of the United States, or any foreign government or country of a crime which, if committed in this state would be a felony, thereafter commits any subsequent felony within this state, upon conviction of said felony, shall be punished as follows:
**R.S. 40:961 et seq.*

(a) If the second felony is such that upon a first conviction the offender would be punishable by imprisonment for any term less than this natural life, then the sentence to imprisonment shall be for a determinate term not less than one-half the longest term and not more than twice the longest term prescribed for a first conviction;

(b) If the third felony is such that upon a first conviction, the offender would be punishable by imprisonment for any term less than his natural life then:

(i) The person shall be sentenced to imprisonment for a determinate term not less than two-thirds of the longest possible sentence for the conviction and not more than twice the longest possible sentence prescribed for a first conviction; or

(ii) If the third felony or either of the two prior felonies is a felony defined as a crime of violence under R.S. 14:2(13) or as a violation of the Uniform Controlled Dangerous Substances Law punishable by imprisonment for more than five years or any other crime punishable by imprisonment for more than twelve years, the person shall be imprisoned for the remainder of his natural life, without benefit of parole, probation, or suspension of sentence.

(c) If the fourth or subsequent felony is such that, upon a first conviction the offender would be punishable by imprisonment for any term less than his natural life then:

(i) The person shall be sentenced to imprisonment for the fourth or subsequent felony for a determinate term not less than the longest prescribed for a first conviction but in no event less than twenty years and not more than his natural life; or

(ii) If the fourth or subsequent felony or any of the prior felonies is a felony defined as a crime of violence under R.S. 14:2(13) or as a violation of the Uniform Controlled Dangerous Substances Law punishable by imprisonment for more than five years or of any other crime punishable by imprisonment for more than twelve years, the person shall be imprisoned for the remainder of his natural life, without benefit of parole, probation, or suspension of sentence.

(2) (a) Attempted first degree murder.

(b) Attempted second degree murder.

(c) Manslaughter.

(d) Armed robbery.

(e) Forcible rape.

(f) Simple rape.

(g) Second degree kidnapping.

(h) A second or subsequent aggravated battery.

(i) A second or subsequent aggravated burglary.

(j) A second or subsequent offense of burglary of an inhabited dwelling.

B. It is hereby declared to be the intent of this Section that an offender need not have been adjudged to be a second offender in a previous prosecution in order to be charged as and adjudged to be a third offender, or that an offender has been adjudged in a prior prosecution to be a third offender in order to be convicted as a fourth offender in a prosecution for a subsequent crime.

C. This Section shall not be applicable in cases where more than ten years have elapsed since the expiration of the maximum sentence or sentences of the previous conviction or convictions, or adjudication or adjudications of delinquency, and the time of the commission of the last felony for which he has been convicted. In computing the period of time as provided herein, any period of servitude by a person in a penal institution, within or without the state, shall not be included in the computation of any of said ten-year periods.

D. (1)(a) If, at any time, either after conviction or sentence, it shall appear that a person convicted of a felony has previously been convicted of a felony under the laws of this state or adjudicated a delinquent under Title VIII of the Louisiana Children's Code for the commission of a felony-grade violation of either the Louisiana Controlled Dangerous Substances Law involving the manufacture, distribution, or possession with intent to distribute a controlled dangerous substance or a crime of violence as listed in Paragraph (2) of Subsection A of this Section, or has been convicted under the laws of any other state, or of the United States, or of any foreign government or country, of a crime, which, if committed in this state would be a felony, the district attorney of the parish in which subsequent conviction was had may file an information accusing the person of a previous conviction or adjudication of delinquency. Whereupon the court in which the subsequent conviction was had shall cause the person, whether confined in prison or otherwise, to be brought before it and shall inform him of the allegation contained in the information and of his right to be tried as to the truth thereof according to law and shall require the offender to say whether the allegations are true. If he denies the allegation of the information or refuses to answer or remains silent, his plea or the fact of his silence shall be entered on the record and he shall be given fifteen days to file particular objections to the information, as provided by Subparagraph (b). The judge shall fix a day to inquire whether the offender has been convicted of a prior felony or felonies, or adjudicated a delinquent for an offense or offenses specified above as set forth in the information.

(b) Except as otherwise provided in this Subsection, the district attorney shall have the burden of proof beyond a reasonable doubt on any issue of fact. The presumption of regularity of judgment shall be sufficient to meet the original burden of proof. If the person claims that any conviction or adjudication of delinquency alleged is invalid, he shall file a written response to the information. A copy of the response shall be served upon the prosecutor. A person claiming that a conviction or adjudication of delinquency alleged in the information was obtained in violation of the Constitutions of Louisiana or of the United States shall set forth his claim, and the factual basis therefor, with particularity in his response to the information. The person shall have the burden of proof, by a preponderance of the evidence, on any issue of fact raised by the response. Any challenge to a previous conviction or adjudication of delinquency which is not made before sentence is imposed may not thereafter be raised to attack the sentence.

(2) Following a contradictory hearing, the court shall find that the defendant is:

(a) A second offender upon proof of a prior felony conviction or adjudication of delinquency as authorized in Subsection A.

(b) A third offender, upon proof of two prior felony convictions or adjudications of delinquency as authorized in Subsection A, or any combination thereof.

(c) A fourth offender, upon proof of three or more prior felony convictions or adjudications of delinquency as authorized in Subsection A, or any combination thereof.

(3) When the judge finds that he has been convicted of a prior felony or felonies or adjudicated a delinquent as authorized in Subsection A, or if he acknowledges or confesses in open court, after being duly cautioned as to his rights, that he has been so convicted or adjudicated, the court shall sentence him to the punishment prescribed in this Section, and shall vacate the previous sentence if already imposed, deducting from the new sentence the time actually served under the sentence so vacated. The court shall provide written reasons for its determination. Either party may seek review of an adverse ruling.

E. Whenever it shall become known to any superintendent or prison, probation, parole, police, or other peace officer, that any person charged with or convicted of a felony has been previously convicted or adjudicated delinquent within the meaning of this Section, he shall immediately report the fact to the district attorney of the parish in which the charge lies, or the conviction has been had.

F. The certificates of the warden or other chief officer of any state prison, or of the superintendent or other chief officer of any penitentiary of this state or any other state of the United States, or of any foreign country, or of any chief officer of any parish or county jail in this state or any other state of the United States, or of the clerk of court of the place of conviction in the state of Louisiana, under the seal of his office, if he has a seal, containing the name of the person imprisoned, the photograph, and the fingerprints of the person as they appear in the records of his office, a statement of the court in which a conviction was had, the date and time of sentence, length of time imprisoned, and date of discharge from prison or penitentiary, shall be prima facie evidence of the imprisonment and of the discharge of the person, either by a pardon or expiration of his sentence as the case may be under the conviction stated and set forth in the certificate.

G. Any sentence imposed under the provisions of this Section shall be without benefit of probation or suspension of sentence.

H. A person shall not be qualified to be a candidate for elected public office or take elected office if that person has been convicted of a felony, whether convicted within this state or convicted under the laws of any other state or of the United States of a crime which, if committed in this state would be a felony, and has not received a pardon therefor.

(Chgd. by Acts 1991 No. 405, §1; Acts 1993 No. 853, §1, No. 896, §1; Acts 1994 Third Ex. Sess. No. 23, §1, No. 85, §1, No. 144, §1; Acts 1995 No. 839, §1, No. 1245, §1, eff. 8/15/95.)

CHAPTER 3-A. SEXUAL OFFENDER LAW

Section

§535. Blood and saliva testing; AIDS, and sexually transmitted diseases; victim's testing and services.

A. When a sexual offender is convicted, the court shall order and direct the offender to submit to a blood and saliva test, to be made by qualified physicians or other qualified persons, under such restrictions and direction as the court deems proper.

B. The test must include chemical testing of his blood to determine its genetic markers and of his saliva to determine its secretor status. The court shall order that the results of the test be submitted to the Louisiana Bureau of Criminal Identification and Information.

C. The court shall also order the person convicted of or adjudicated a delinquent for a sexual offense as defined in R.S. 14:42 through 43.4 to submit to a test designed to determine whether the person is infected with a sexually transmitted disease, or is infected with acquired immune deficiency syndrome (AIDS), the human immuno deficiency virus (HIV), HIV-1 antibodies, or any other probable causative agent of AIDS. The procedure or test shall be performed by a qualified physician or other qualified person who shall report any positive result to the Department of Public Safety and Corrections, make the notification of the test results to the victim of the alleged offense, and notify the victim or the parent or custodian of the victim of the alleged offense, regardless of the results.

D. If the offender tested under the provisions of Subsection C of this Section tests positive for AIDS, HIV, HIV-1 antibodies, or any other probable causative agent of AIDS, the victim shall be provided with HIV testing, if such testing is requested by the victim, or in the case of a minor, by the victim's parent or legal custodian, at a state hospital or other facility as determined by the Department of Health and Hospitals or as provided by law. If the victim tested under to provisions of this Subsection tests positive for AIDS, HIV, HIV-1 antibodies, or any other probable causative agent of AIDS, the victim shall, upon request, be provided with all of the following services:

(1) Counseling regarding HIV disease.

(2) Referral to appropriate health care and support services. These services shall be provided in accordance with applicable state law and the regulations governing the specific programs under which the services are to be provided.

(Chgd. by Acts 1991 No. 419, §1; Acts 1993 No. 904, §1, eff. 8/15/93.)

§536. Definitions.

For purposes of this Chapter, "sexual offender" means a person who has violated any provision of Subpart C of Part II, Subpart B of Part IV, or Subpart A(1) or A(4) of Part V, of Chapter 1 of Title 14 of the Louisiana Revised Statutes of 1950.

§537. Sentencing of sexual offenders.

If a person is convicted of or pleads guilty to a violation of any provision of Subpart C of Part II, Subpart B of Part IV, or Subpart A(1) or A(4) of Part V, of Chapter 1 of Title 14 of the Louisiana Revised Statutes of 1950, and is sentenced to imprisonment for a stated number of years or months, the sentencing court may deny or place conditions on eligibility for diminution of sentence for good behavior unless diminution of sentence is prohibited by R.S. 15:571.3(C) or (D). *(Added by Acts 1994 Third Ex. Sess. No. 110, §1, eff. 8/27/94.)*

§538. Conditions of probation, parole, and suspension or diminution of sentence.

A. No sexual offender, whose offense involved a minor child, shall be eligible for probation, parole, or suspension of sentence unless, as a condition thereof, the sexual offender is prohibited from engaging in any business or volunteer work activity which provides goods, services, instruction, or care to and requires the offender to engage in a significant amount of direct contact with minor children.

B. No sexual offender shall be eligible for probation, parole, or suspension of sentence unless, as a condition thereof, the sexual offender is prohibited from engaging in any unsupervised business or volunteer work activity which provides goods, services, instruction, or care to and requires the offender to engage in a significant amount of direct contact with potential victims who are minor children.

C. (1) No sexual offender, whose offense involved a minor child who is twelve years old or younger or who is convicted two or more times of a violation of R.S. 14:42, R.S. 14:42.1, R.S. 14:43, R.S. 14:43.1, R.S. 14:43.2, R.S. 14:43.3, R.S. 14:43.4, R.S. 14:78, R.S. 14:78.1, or R.S. 14:89.1 shall be eligible for probation, parole, or suspension of sentence or diminution of sentence if imposed as a condition by the sentencing court pursuant to R.S. 15:537, unless, as a condition thereof, the offender undergoes a treatment plan based upon a mental health evaluation which plan shall effectively deter recidivist sexual offenses by the offender, thereby reducing risk of reincarceration of the offender and increasing safety of the public, and under which the offender may reenter society.

(2)(a) "Mental health evaluation", as used in this Subsection, means an examination by a qualified mental health professional with experience in treating sexual offenders.

(b) The treatment plan may include:

(i) The utilization of medroxyprogesterone acetate treatment or its chemical equivalent as a preferred method of treatment.

(ii) A component of defined behavioral intervention if the evaluating qualified mental health professional determines that is appropriate for the offender.

(3)(a) The provisions of this Subsection shall only apply if parole, probation, or suspension or diminution of sentence is permitted by law and the offender is otherwise eligible.

(b) If on probation or parole or subject to a sentence that has been suspended, the offender shall begin medroxyprogesterone acetate, or chemically equivalent treatment as ordered by the court.

(c) If medroxyprogesterone acetate or chemically equivalent treatment is part of an incarcerated offender's treatment plan, the offender shall begin such treatment six weeks prior to release.

(d) The offender shall continue treatments during incarceration and any suspended sentence, probation, or parole, unless it is determined that the treatment is no longer necessary.

(4) Before beginning medroxyprogesterone acetate or chemical equivalent therapy as required by the provisions of this Subsection, the offender shall be informed about the uses and side effects of medroxyprogesterone therapy, and provide the department with a written acknowledgment that he has received this information.

(5) The offender shall be responsible for the costs of the evaluation, the treatment plan, and the treatment.

(6) (a) Chemical treatment pursuant to this Subsection shall be administered by the state through a licensed medical practitioner.

(b) Any physician or qualified mental health professional who acts in good faith in compliance with this Subsection in the administration of treatment shall be immune from civil or criminal liability for his actions in connection with such treatment.

(7) Failure to continue or complete treatment pursuant to this Subsection shall be a ground for revocation of probation, parole, or suspension of sentence. Good time earned may be forfeited pursuant to R.S. 15:571.4.

(8) If an offender voluntarily undergoes a permanent, surgical alternative to hormonal chemical treatment for sex offenders, he shall not be subject to the provisions of this Subsection.

(9) The Department of Public Safety and Corrections shall promulgate rules and regulations to implement the provisions of this Subsection.

(Added by Acts 1994 Third Ex. Sess. No. 126, §1; chgd. by Acts 1995 No. 1265, §1; Acts 1997 No. 746, §1, eff. 8/15/97.)

CHAPTER 3-B. REGISTRATION OF SEX OFFENDERS, SEXUALLY VIOLENT PREDATORS, AND CHILD PREDATORS

(Added by Acts 1992 No. 388, §1; chgd. by Acts 1997 No. 1147, §1, eff. 7/14/97.)

Section

§540. Findings; purpose.

A. The legislature finds that sex offenders, sexually violent predators, and child predators often pose a high risk of engaging in sex offenses, and crimes against victims who are minors even after being released from incarceration or commitment and that protection of the public from sex offenders, sexually violent predators, and child predators is of paramount governmental interest. The legislature further finds that local law enforcement officers' efforts to protect their communities, conduct investigations, and quickly apprehend offenders who commit sex offenses and crimes against victims who are minors, are impaired by the lack of information available to law enforcement agencies about convicted sex offenders, sexually violent predators, and child predators who live within the agency's jurisdiction, and the penal and mental health components of our justice system are largely hidden from public view and that lack of information from either may result in failure of both systems to meet this paramount concern of public safety. Restrictive confidentiality and liability laws governing the release of information about sexual offenders, sexually violent predators, and child predators have reduced willingness to release information that could be appropriately released under the public disclosure laws, and have increased risks to public safety. Persons found to have committed a sex offense or a crime against a victim who is a minor have a reduced expectation of privacy because of the public's interest in public safety and in the effective operation of government. Release of information about sex offenders, sexually violent predators, and child predators to public agencies, and under limited circumstances to the general public, will further the governmental interests of public safety and public scrutiny of the criminal and mental health systems so long as the information released is rationally related to the furtherance of those goals.

B. Therefore, this state's policy is to assist local law enforcement agencies' efforts to protect their communities by requiring sex offenders, sexually violent predators, and child predators to register with state and local law enforcement agencies and to require the exchange of relevant information about sex offenders, sexually violent predators, and child predators among state, local, and federal public agencies and officials and to authorize the release of necessary and relevant information about sex offenders, sexually violent predators, and child predators to members of the general public as provided in this Chapter.

(Added by Acts 1992 No. 388, §1; chgd. by Acts 1997 No. 1147, §1, eff. 7/14/97.)

§541. Definitions.

For the purposes of this Chapter, the definitions of terms in this Section shall apply.

(1) "The administration of criminal justice" means performance of any of the following activities: detection, apprehension, detention, pretrial release, post-trial release, prosecution, adjudication, correctional supervision, or rehabilitation of accused persons or criminal offenders. The term also includes criminal identification activities, the collection, storage, and dissemination of criminal history record information, and the compensation of victims of crime.

(2) "Conviction or other disposition adverse to the subject" means any disposition of charges, except a decision not to prosecute, a dismissal, or an acquittal, except when the acquittal is due to a finding of not guilty by reason of insanity and the person was committed. However, a dismissal entered after a period of probation, suspension, or deferral of sentence shall be considered a disposition adverse to the subject.

(3) "Conviction record" means criminal history record information relating to an incident which has led to a conviction or other disposition adverse to the subject.

(4) "Criminal history record information" means information contained in records collected by criminal justice agencies, other than courts, on individuals, consisting of identifiable descriptions and notations of arrests, detention, indictments, information, or other formal criminal charges, and any disposition arising therefrom, including sentences, correctional supervision, and release. The term includes information contained in records maintained by or obtained from criminal justice agencies, other than courts, which records provide individual identification of a person together with any portion of the individual's record of involvement in the criminal justice system as an alleged or convicted offender, except:

(a) Posters, announcements, or lists for identifying or apprehending fugitives or wanted persons.

(b) Original records of entry maintained by criminal justice agencies to the extent that such records are compiled and maintained chronologically and are accessible only on a chronological basis.

(c) Court indices and records of public judicial proceedings, court decisions, and opinions, and information disclosed during judicial proceedings.

(d) Records of traffic violations which are not punishable by a maximum term of imprisonment of more than ninety days.

(e) Records of any traffic offenses as maintained by the office of motor vehicles for the purpose of regulating the issuance, suspension, revocation, or renewal of drivers' or other operators' licenses.

(f) Records of any aviation violation or offenses as maintained by the Department of Transportation and Development for the purpose of regulating pilots or other aviation operators.

(g) Announcement of pardons.

(5) "Criminal justice agency" means:

(a) A court.

(b) A government agency which performs the administration of criminal justice pursuant to a statute or executive order and which allocates a substantial part of its annual budget to the administration of criminal justice.

(6) "Disposition" means the formal conclusion of a criminal proceeding at whatever stage it occurs in the criminal justice system.

(7) "Dissemination" means disclosing criminal history record information or disclosing the absence of criminal history record information to any person or agency outside the agency possessing the information, subject to the following exceptions:

(a) When criminal justice agencies jointly participate in the maintenance of a single recordkeeping department as an alternative to maintaining separate records, the furnishing of information by that department to personnel of any participating agency.

(b) The furnishing of information by any criminal justice agency to another for the purpose of processing a matter through the criminal justice system, such as a police department providing information to a prosecutor for use in preparing a charge.

(c) The reporting of an event to a recordkeeping agency for the purpose of maintaining the record.

(8) "Nonconviction data" consists of all criminal history record information relating to an incident which has not led to a conviction or other disposition adverse to the subject, and for which proceedings are no longer actively pending. There shall be a rebuttable presumption that proceedings are no longer actively pending if more than one year has elapsed since arrest, citation, or service of warrant and no disposition has been entered.

(9) "Mental abnormality" means a congenital or acquired condition of a person that affects the emotional or volitional capacity of the person in a manner that predisposes that person to the commission of criminal sexual acts to a degree that makes the person a menace to the health and safety of others. Nothing in this definition is intended to supersede or apply to the definitions found in R.S. 14:10 or R.S. 14:14 in reference to criminal intent or insanity.

(10) "Sexually violent predator" means a person who has been convicted of a sex offense as defined in R.S. 15:542(E) and who has a mental abnormality or anti-social personality disorder that makes the person likely to engage in predatory sexually violent offenses as determined by the sentencing court upon receipt and review of relevant information including the recommendation of the sexual predator commission as defined in Paragraph (12).

(11) "Predatory" means an act directed at a stranger or a person with whom a relationship has been established or promoted for the primary purpose of victimization.

(12) "Sexual predator commission", the commission, means an advisory panel containing not less than two nor more than three physicians who are licensed to practice medicine in Louisiana, who have been in the actual practice of medicine for not less than three consecutive years immediately preceding the appointment, and who are qualified by training or experience in forensic evaluations of sex offenders. The court may appoint in lieu of one physician, a psychologist who is licensed to practice psychology in Louisiana, who has been engaged in the practice of clinical or counseling psychology for not less than three consecutive years immediately preceding the appointment, and who is qualified by training or experience in forensic evaluations of sex offenders. A list of qualified physicians and psychologists shall be provided to the court by the Department of Health and Hospitals.

(13) "Court determination" means a determination that a person is a sexually violent predator or a determination that a person is no longer a sexually violent predator that shall be made by the sentencing court after receiving a report by the commission.

(14) "Criminal offense against a victim who is a minor" for the purposes of this Chapter means conviction for the perpetration or attempted perpetration of:

(a) A violation of Subpart D of Part II of Chapter 1 of Title 14 of the Louisiana Revised Statutes of 1950 when the victim is under eighteen years of age and the defendant is not the parent of the victim.

(b) A violation of any of the following provisions when the victim is under eighteen years of age: R.S. 14:82, R.S. 14:82.1, R.S. 14:83, R.S. 14:84(1), (3), (5), (6), R.S. 14:86, R.S. 15:542(E) or R.S. 23:251(A)(4).

(15) "Child predator" means a person who has been convicted of a criminal offense against a victim who is a minor, as defined in Paragraph (14).

(16) "Bureau" means the Louisiana Bureau of Criminal Identification and Information as established in Chapter 6 of Title 15 of the Louisiana Revised Statutes of 1950.

(Added by Acts 1992 No. 388, §1; chgd. by Acts 1997 No. 1147, §1, eff. 7/14/97.)

§542. Registration of sex offenders.

A. Any adult residing in this state who has pled guilty or has been convicted of any sex offense and any juvenile who has pled guilty or has been convicted of a sex offense as provided for in Ch.C. Art. 857 shall register with the sheriff of the parish of the person's residence. If the adult or juvenile resides in a parish with a population in excess of four hundred fifty thousand, he shall register with the police department of his municipality of residence.

B. The person and the juvenile sex offender shall, within thirty days of establishing residence in Louisiana, or if a current resident, within fifteen days after conviction or release from confinement, whichever occurs later, provide the sheriff or, if required under Subsection A, the police department with the following information: his name, address, and place of employment; the crime for which he was convicted; the date and place of such conviction; any aliases used by the person; and the person's social security number. Excluding the juvenile sex offender, the person shall also:

(1) Give notice of the crime for which he was convicted, his name, and address to:

(a) At least one person in every residence or business within a one mile radius in a rural area and a three square block area in an urban or suburban area of the address where the defendant will reside upon release.

(b) The superintendent of the school district where the defendant will reside, who shall notify the principal of every school located within a one-mile radius of the address where the offender will reside and may notify the principals of other schools as he deems appropriate. The principal of any such school upon receipt of the notification shall post notices in conspicuous areas at the school which state the defendant's name, address, and the crime for which he was convicted. Failure of the superintendent or principal to comply with the provisions of this Subparagraph shall not be construed to impose civil liability on any person.

(c) The lessor, landlord, or owner of the residence or the property on which he resides.

(2)(a) Give notice of the crime for which he was convicted, his name, and his address by mail to all people residing within the designated area within thirty days of the sentencing or release from confinement or within twenty-one days of setting up residency in the locale where the offender plans to have his domicile, and that the notice shall be published on two separate days within the applicable period provided for herein, without cost to the state, in the official journal of the governing authority of the parish where the defendant plans to reside and, if ordered by the sheriff or police department, in a newspaper which meets the requirements of R.S. 43:140(3) for qualification as an official journal and which has a larger or smaller circulation in the parish than the official journal.

(b) In the parish of St. Tammany, the sheriff or police department may order that the notice be published in a newspaper which meets the requirements of R.S. 43:140(3) for qualification as an official journal and which has a larger circulation in the parish than the official journal.

(3) Give any other notice deemed appropriate by the court in which the defendant was convicted of the offense that subjects him to the duty to register, including but not limited to signs, handbills, bumper stickers, or clothing labeled to that effect.

(4) State under oath where he will reside after sentencing or release.

C. If any person required to register pursuant to this Section changes his residence address within the same parish, the person shall send written notice of the change of address to the sheriff or, if required under Paragraph A, the police department, within ten days of establishing the new residence. If any person required to register pursuant to this Section moves to a new parish, the person shall register with the sheriff or, if required under Paragraph A, the police department, in the new parish within ten days of establishing the new residence. The person shall also send written notice, within ten days after the change of address in the new parish, to the sheriff or, if required under Paragraph A, the police department with whom the person last registered.

D. The sheriff or police department shall obtain a photograph of the person and shall obtain a copy of the person's fingerprints.

E. "Sex offense" for the purpose of this Chapter means conviction for the perpetration or attempted perpetration of any provision of R.S. 14:92(A)(7), of Subpart C of Part II, Subpart B of Part IV, or Subpart A(1) or A(4) of Part V, of Chapter 1 of Title 14 of the Louisiana Revised Statutes of 1950, committed on or after June 18, 1992, or committed prior to June 18, 1992 if the person, as a result of the offense, is under the custody of the Department of Public Safety and Corrections on or after June 18, 1992. A conviction for any offense provided in this definition includes a conviction for the offense under the laws of another state which is equivalent to an offense provided for in this Chapter.

F. (1) A person who fails to register as required by this Section shall, upon first conviction, be fined not more than one thousand dollars or imprisoned for not more than one year, or both.

(2) Upon second or subsequent convictions, whoever fails to register as required by this Section, shall be sentenced to imprisonment for not more than three years without benefit of parole, probation, or suspension of sentence.

(Added by Acts 1992 No. 388, §1; chgd. by Acts 1995 No. 928, §1, No. 1290, §2; Acts 1997 No. 134, §2, No. 137, §2, eff. 8/15/97, No. 928, §1, eff. 7/10/97, No. 1135, §1, No. 1148, §2, eff. 7/14/97.)

§542.1. Registration of sexually violent predators and child predators.

A. DUTIES. Any person convicted of a sex offense as defined in R.S. 15:542(E) or of a criminal offense against a victim who is a minor as defined in R.S. 15:541(14) after July 1, 1997 shall have the duty to register and report under the provisions of this Chapter.

B. SEXUALLY VIOLENT PREDATOR DETERMINATION.

(1) At any time after a person has been convicted of a sex offense as defined in R.S. 15:542(E) but before the satisfaction of the sentence arising from that conviction, the sentencing court, shall on its own motion or upon the motion of the prosecuting attorney, may refer the case to the sexual predator commission as defined in R.S. 15:541(12) for review and recommendation as to whether or not the defendant is a sexually violent predator as defined in R.S. 15:541(10).

(2) The sexual predator commission shall conduct its review and make a recommendation to the court as to whether the defendant is a sexually violent predator. Such recommendation shall include the factual basis upon which the recommendation is made.

(3) Upon receiving a recommendation from the sexual predator commission, the court shall make a determination as to whether or not an offender is a sexually violent predator.

(4) A defendant determined to be a sexually violent predator under this Section may petition the sentencing court for review of this determination on an annual basis, provided the defendant is currently receiving treatment from a court-approved treatment provider, and good cause for such reconsideration is shown by the defendant. If the court grants the petition for review, the court shall refer the case to the sexual predator commission for a recommendation as to whether or not the defendant remains a sexually violent predator. After receiving the recommendation of the sexual predator commission, and providing notification to the prosecutor, who will be allowed an opportunity to oppose any change in status, the sentencing court shall make a determination as to whether or not the defendant is a sexually violent predator.

C. NOTICE TO THE OFFENDER. If a person who is required to register under this Section is released from prison, or placed under parole, supervised release, or probation, a Department of Public Safety and Corrections officer, or the court if the offender is not placed in the jurisdictional custody of the Department of Public Safety and Corrections, shall:

(1) Inform the person of the duty to register and report, and obtain the information required for such registration.

(2) Inform the person that if the person changes residence address, the person shall give the new address in writing to the Louisiana Bureau of Criminal Identification and Information, hereinafter referred to as "the bureau", within ten days from the date of the change of address.

(3) Inform the person that if the person changes residence to another state, the person shall notify in writing both the bureau and the law enforcement agency designated for sex offender reporting under the laws of state in which the new address is located if that state has a registration requirement, within ten days from the date the person establishes residence in the new state.

(4) Obtain fingerprints and a photograph of the person if these have not already been obtained in connection with the offense that triggers registration.

(5) Require the person to read and sign a form stating that the duty of the person to register and report under this Section and the penalty for failure to comply has been explained.

D. INFORMATION TO BE COLLECTED FROM THE OFFENDER. The Department of Public Safety and Corrections officer, or the court if the offender is not placed in the jurisdictional custody of the Department of Public Safety and Corrections, shall obtain the following information as part of the registration from any person required to register under this Section: name of the offender, address of offender's place of residence upon release from confinement, crime for which the offender was convicted which gave rise to the requirement to register under this Section, date and place of such conviction, any aliases used by the offender, the offender's social security number, and other such information as may be required by the Department of Public Safety and Corrections to carry out the purposes of this Chapter. In all cases where an offender has been determined by a court of competent jurisdiction as a sexually violent predator, a notation shall be made as to whether or not the offender has received treatment as a sex offender.

E. TRANSFER OF INFORMATION TO THE BUREAU. Within three days of obtaining the information necessary for registration and giving notice to the offender in accordance with Subsections C and D, the Department of Public Safety and Corrections officer or the court which received the offender's registration information shall transmit that information along with the applicable reporting requirements under Paragraphs (H)(1) and (2) and (I)(1) and (2) of this Section, the offender's criminal history, photograph, identifying factors and fingerprints to the bureau.

F. STATE SEX OFFENDER AND CHILD PREDATOR REGISTRY.

(1) The central registry of sex offenders maintained by the bureau as defined in R.S. 15:545 shall hereafter be known as the State Sex Offender and Child Predator Registry and shall include the information transmitted to the bureau under Subsection E for any person subject to registration under this Section.

(2) Upon receipt of the registration and information of any person subject to the provisions of this Section, the bureau shall immediately enter the information in the State Sex Offender and Child Predator Registry.

G. NOTIFICATION OF LOCAL LAW ENFORCEMENT AND THE FEDERAL BUREAU OF INVESTIGATION.

(1) Immediately upon entry of the required information into the State Sex Offender and Child Predator Registry, the bureau shall notify the sheriff of the parish in which the offender's address of residence is located, and the chief of police if the address is located in an incorporated area which has a police department.

(2) Immediately upon entry of the required information into the State Sex Offender and Child Predator Registry, the bureau shall transmit to the Federal Bureau of Investigation the conviction data and fingerprints of the offender registered.

H. DUTY TO REGISTER.

(1) A person required to register under this Section as a sex offender or child predator shall register and maintain his registration pursuant to the provisions of this Section for a period of ten years after the date on which the person was released from prison, placed on parole, supervised release or probation for a conviction giving rise to the requirement to register.

(2) A person required to register under this Section where there has been a determination that the person is a sexually violent predator according to the provisions of Subsection B, shall continue to register for life, or until there has been a determination by the court that the person is no longer a sexually violent predator. If a person has been determined by the court pursuant to Subsection B to no longer be a sexually violent predator, the person shall register according to the duty for a sex offender or child predator as specified in Paragraph (1).

I. VERIFICATION OF ADDRESS.

(1) Once each year during the required period of registration as defined in Subsection H, provided the offender has not been determined to be a sexually violent predator, not less than five days prior to the anniversary of the date of the offender's initial registration under the conviction giving rise to the duty to register under Subsection A, the bureau shall mail a non-forwardable verification form to the last reported address of the person.

(2) The bureau shall mail a non-forwardable verification form to the last reported address of the sexually violent predator every ninety days following the receipt of the initial registration information.

(3) The person subject to registration shall mail the verification to the bureau within ten days of receipt. For purposes of this Section, it shall be assumed that the person subject to registration shall have received the non-forwardable verification form ten days from the date of mailing by the bureau.

(4) If the person fails to mail the verification form to the bureau within ten days of receipt of the form, the person shall be in violation of this Section and subject to the penalties specified in R.S. 15:542 (F) unless the person proves that the person has not changed the

residence address and can show good cause why the person failed to mail the verification form to the bureau within the specified ten days.

(5) If the bureau does not receive the verification form from the person within thirty days from the date of mailing by the bureau, the bureau shall immediately notify the sheriff of the parish in which the person's last reported address of residence is located, or in the case of a person residing in a parish with a population in excess of four hundred and fifty thousand the police department of his municipality of residence. If the offender is under the supervision of Department of Public Safety and Corrections, the bureau shall also immediately notify the Department of Public Safety and Corrections.

J. (1) DUTY TO REPORT CHANGE OF ADDRESS, PENALTY FOR FAILURE TO COMPLY AND TRANSFER OF INFORMATION. Any person required to register under this Section shall notify the bureau in writing of any change of address within ten days of the change. If a person required to register under this Section fails to register, keep registration current, or notify the bureau of any change of address within ten days, the person shall be in violation of this Section and subject to the penalties provided in R.S. 15:542(F).

(2) Transfer of information by the Louisiana Bureau of Criminal Identification and Information.

(a) If the bureau receives notice of a change of address from a person subject to registration under this Section, it shall immediately notify the sheriff of the parish in which the new address is located, and, if the address is located in a municipality with a police department, the chief of police.

(b) If the offender is under the supervision of the Department of Public Safety and Corrections, the bureau shall also immediately notify the Department of Public Safety and Corrections of any change of address.

(c) If the bureau receives notice of a change of address to another state from a person subject to registration under this Section, the bureau shall immediately notify the law enforcement agency with which the person must register in the new state, if the new state has a registration requirement.

K. SEX OFFENDERS FROM OTHER STATES.

(1) Any sex offender, or offender subject to registration for a criminal offense against a victim who is a minor, or sexually violent predator, who has been convicted or determined to be a sexually violent predator under the laws of another state or the United States, who establishes residence in Louisiana shall be subject to the registration and reporting requirements of this Section.

(2) The Louisiana Bureau of Criminal Identification and Information is hereby designated as the state law enforcement agency to receive sex offender, child predator, and sexually violent predator registrations from other states.

(3) A sex offender, child predator, or sexually violent predator subject to registration under the laws of another state or the United States, shall notify the bureau within ten days of establishing residence in Louisiana, and shall present himself for registration in accordance with R.S. 15:542.

(4) When the bureau receives notification that a sex offender, child predator, or sexually violent predator subject to registration under the similar laws of another state or the United States, is establishing residence in Louisiana, it shall immediately notify the sheriff of the parish in which the address of residence is located and the chief of police if that address is within a municipality with a police department.

L. COMMUNITY NOTIFICATION.

(1) Persons subject to registration as a sex offender, child predator, or sexually violent predator shall comply with the requirements of R.S. 15:542(B)(1), (2), (3), and (4).

(2) Persons giving community notification under this Section shall do so under the supervision of the Department of Public Safety and Corrections, and if not sentenced to the custody or supervision of the state, under the supervision of the sentencing court.

M. NOTIFICATION. All notification requirements specified in R.S. 15:549 relative to sex offenders shall apply to child predators and sexually violent predators as defined in R.S. 15:541.

(Added by Acts 1997 No. 1147, §1, eff. 7/14/97.)

§543. Offender notification.

A. The court shall provide written notification to any defendant charged with a sex offense of the registration requirements of R.S. 15:542. Such notice shall be included on any guilty plea forms and judgment and sentence forms provided to the defendant.

B. The Department of Public Safety and Corrections shall provide written notification to an inmate convicted of a sex offense of the registration requirements of R.S. 15:542 at the time of the inmate's release from confinement and shall receive and retain a signed acknowledgment of receipt.

C. The Department of Public Safety and Corrections shall provide written notification to an individual convicted of a sex offense from another state of the registration requirements of R.S. 15:542 at the time the department accepts supervision and has legal authority of the individual under the terms and conditions of the interstate compact agreement under R.S. 15:574.14.

D. A person having charge of a jail shall notify in writing any confined person who is in the custody of the jail for a conviction of any sex offense at the time of the inmate's release from confinement, and shall obtain written acknowledgment of such notification.

E. At the time a person renews his driver's license or identification card, or surrenders a driver's license from another jurisdiction and makes an application for a driver's license or an identification card, the Department of Public Safety and Corrections shall provide the applicant with written information on the registration requirements of R.S. 15:542.
(Added by Acts 1992 No. 388, §1, eff. 6/18/92.)

§544. Duty to register.

A. A person required to register and give notice under R.S. 15:542 shall comply with the requirement for a period of ten years after the conviction, if not imprisoned during that period in a penal institution, full-time residential treatment facility, hospital, or other facility or institution pursuant to the conviction. If the person required to register and give notice is imprisoned or confined to a penal institution, full-time residential facility, hospital, or other facility or institution pursuant to the conviction, he shall comply with the registration and notice provisions for a period of ten years after release from his confinement or imprisonment. A convicted sex offender's duty to register and give notice terminates at the expiration of ten years from the date of initial registration, provided that during the ten-year period the convicted sex offender does not again become subject to this Chapter.

B. Any person having the duty to register and give notice under R.S. 15:542 may petition the court to be relieved of that duty. The petition shall be made to the court in which the petitioner was convicted of the offense that subjects him to the duty to register, or, in the case of conviction in other states, to the district court of the parish in which the person is registered. The district attorney of the parish shall be named and served as the defendant in any such petition. The court shall consider the nature of the sex offense committed and the criminal and relevant noncriminal behavior of the petitioner, both before and after conviction, and may consider other factors. The court may relieve the petitioner of the duty to register and give notice only if the petitioner shows, with clear and convincing evidence, that future registration of the petitioner will not serve the purposes of this Chapter.

C. Unless relieved of the duty to register and give notice in the manner prescribed in Subsection B, a violation of R.S. 15:542 is an ongoing offense for purposes of prescription.

D. The discharge of an offender pursuant to any other law shall not be construed as operating to relieve the offender of his duty to register and give notice pursuant to R.S. 15:542.
(Added by Acts 1992 No. 388, §1; chgd. by Acts 1995 No. 928, §1, eff. 8/15/95.)

§545. Duty of law enforcement.

A. It shall be the duty of the sheriff of every parish, the chief of police of each municipality, and every chief officer of every other law enforcement agency operating within this state, to record the fingerprints of all persons held in or remanded to their custody when convicted of any sex offense for which the penalty of imprisonment might be imposed and to disseminate and file such fingerprints in the same manner as those recorded upon every arrest. The sheriff shall forward the fingerprints and information obtained pursuant to R.S. 15:542 to the Louisiana Bureau of Criminal Identification and Information, hereinafter referred to as "the bureau" within five working days. The bureau shall maintain a central registry of sex offenders required to register under R.S. 15:542 and shall adopt rules, regulations, and policies in accordance with the provisions set forth pursuant to R.S. 15:547.

B. Every time a furlough is authorized, the Department of Public Safety and Corrections shall notify, forty-eight hours prior to the beginning of such furlough, the bureau that the named prisoner has been granted a furlough, the place to which furloughed, and the dates and times during which the prisoner will be on furlough status. In the case of an emergency furlough the forty-eight hour time period shall not be required but notification shall be made as promptly as possible and before the prisoner is released on furlough. Upon receipt of furlough information pursuant to this Subsection, the bureau shall notify the sheriff of the parish or the chief of police of the municipality to which the prisoner is being furloughed, the nearest Louisiana state police troop unit wherein the furloughed prisoner shall be residing, and such other criminal justice agencies as the bureau may deem necessary.

C. Disposition of the charge for which the arrest was made shall be reported to the bureau at whatever stage in the proceedings a final disposition occurs by the arresting law enforcement agency, district attorney, parish attorney, city attorney, or court having jurisdiction over the offense.

D. Whenever a person serving a sentence for a term of incarceration in a state correctional facility for convicted felons, pursuant to court commitment, is released on an order of the Board of Parole or office of adult services, or is discharged from custody on expiration of sentence, the Department of Public Safety and Corrections shall promptly notify the bureau that the named person has been released or discharged, and the conditions of his release or discharge, and shall additionally notify the bureau of change in residence or conditions of release or discharge of a person on active parole supervision, and shall notify the bureau when the person is discharged from active parole supervision. Any person released or discharged shall register with the sheriff pursuant to R.S. 15:542. In addition, nothing in this Chapter shall be construed to prevent any local law enforcement agency from recording the residency and other information concerning any convicted felon or other person convicted of a criminal offense when such information is obtained from a source other than from registration pursuant to R.S. 15:542, which source may include any law enforcement officer or other agency or subdivision of the state.

(Added by Acts 1992 No. 388, §1, eff. 6/18/92.)

§546. Release of information.

A. Criminal justice agencies shall release relevant and necessary information regarding sex offenders, child predators, and sexually violent predators to the public when the release of the information is necessary for public protection, according to the provisions set forth by the board pursuant to R.S. 15:547(C).

B. (1) An elected* official, public employee, public agency, or criminal justice agency shall be immune from civil liability for damages for any discretionary decision to release relevant and necessary information, unless it is shown that the official, employee, or agency acted with gross negligence or in bad faith. The authorization and immunity in this Chapter apply to information regarding:

(a) A person convicted of a sex offense or criminal offense against a victim who is a minor, or who has been determined to be a sexually violent predator as defined in this Chapter.

(b) A person found not guilty of a sex offense or criminal offense against a victim who is a minor by reason of insanity.

(c) A person found incompetent to stand trial for a sex offense or criminal offense against a victim who is a minor and subsequently committed to a treatment facility or institution or hospital.

(2) The immunity provided under this Section applies to the release of relevant information to other employees or officials or to the general public.

(3) The identity of a victim, or information leading to the identity of a victim, of an offense that requires registration under this Section shall not be released.

C. Nothing in this Chapter, except as otherwise provided, shall impose any liability upon a public* official, public employee, or public agency for failing to release information as provided in this Chapter.

D. An offender's pending appeal or writ of habeas corpus shall not restrict the agency's, official's, or employee's authority to release relevant information concerning an offender's prior criminal history. However, the agency shall release the latest dispositions of the charges as they are provided.

(Added by Acts 1992 No. 388, §1; chgd. by Acts 1997 No. 1147, §1, eff. 7/14/97.)
**So in original.*

§547. Board of Parole.

A. The Board of Parole, hereinafter referred to as "the board," shall cause a complete record to be kept of every prisoner released on parole. Such records shall be organized in accordance with the most modern methods of filing and indexing so that there will be always immediately available complete information about such prisoner. The board may make rules as to the privacy of such records and their use by persons other than the board and its staff. In determining the rules regarding dissemination of information regarding convicted sex offenders, child predators, or persons determined to be sexually violent predators under the board's jurisdiction, the board shall institute rules pursuant to the provisions of R.S. 15:546, and shall be immune from liability for the release of information concerning any sex offender, sexually violent predator, or child predator.

B. In addition to any other information required to be released under this Chapter, the board may, pursuant to R.S. 15:546, release information concerning any inmate under the jurisdiction of the board who is convicted of any sex offense or criminal offense against a victim who is a minor, or who has been determined to be a sexually violent predator.

C. (1) The board shall conduct one public hearing in each municipality with a population of not less than fifty thousand and otherwise in accordance with the provisions of the Administrative Procedure Act, and receive information and input from the public and shall establish and promulgate rules, regulations, policy, and guidelines governing the disclosure and dissemination of information regarding sex offenders, sexually violent predators, and child predators to the public pursuant to the intent and purposes of this Chapter.

(2) Every criminal justice agency and other agency, board, office, or other entity of the state or any political subdivision thereof, shall cooperate, consult with, and otherwise assist the board in the promulgation, implementation, and enforcement of the rules, regulations, guidelines, and policy required and established pursuant to the full implementation of this Chapter.

(Added by Acts 1992 No. 388, §1; chgd. by Acts 1997 No. 1147, §1, eff. 7/14/97.)

§548. Dissemination policy.

A. Conviction records may be disseminated without restriction.

B. Any criminal history record information which pertains to an incident for which a person is currently being processed by the criminal justice system, including the entire period of correctional supervision extending through final discharge from parole, when applicable, may be disseminated without restriction.

C. Criminal history record information which includes non-conviction data may be disseminated by a criminal justice agency to another criminal justice agency for any purpose associated with the administration of criminal justice, or in connection with the employment of the subject of the record by a criminal justice or juvenile justice agency. A criminal justice agency may respond to any inquiry from another criminal justice agency without any obligation to ascertain the purpose for which the information is to be used by the agency making the inquiry.

D. Criminal history record information which includes non-conviction data may be disseminated by a criminal justice agency to implement a statute, ordinance, executive order, or a court rule, decision, or order which expressly refers to records of arrest, charges, or allegations of criminal conduct or other non-conviction data and authorizes or directs that it be available or accessible for a specific purpose.

E. Criminal history record information which includes non-conviction data may be disseminated to individuals and agencies pursuant to a contract with a criminal justice agency to provide services related to the administration of criminal justice. Such contract must specifically authorize access to criminal history record information, but need not specifically state that access to non-conviction data is included. The agreement must limit the use of the criminal history record information to stated purposes and insure the confidentiality and security of the information consistent with state law and any applicable federal statutes and regulations.

F. Criminal history record information which includes non-conviction data may be disseminated to individuals and agencies for the express purpose of research, evaluative, or statistical activities pursuant to an agreement with a criminal justice agency. Such agreement must authorize the access to non-conviction data, limit the use of that information which identifies specific individuals to research, evaluative, or statistical purposes, and contain provisions giving notice to the person or organization to which the records are disseminated that the use of information obtained therefrom and further dissemination of such information are subject to this Chapter and applicable federal statutes and regulations, which shall be cited with express reference to the penalties provided for a violation thereof.

G. (1) Every criminal justice agency that maintains and disseminates criminal history record information shall maintain information pertaining to each dissemination of criminal history record information, except a dissemination to the effect that the agency has no record concerning an individual. Information pertaining to disseminations shall include:

(a) An indication as to which agency or person to whom the criminal history record information was disseminated.

(b) The date on which the information was disseminated.

(c) The individual to whom the information relates.

(d) A brief description of the information disseminated.

(2) The information pertaining to dissemination required to be maintained shall be retained for a period of not less than one year.

H. In addition to the other provisions in this Chapter allowing dissemination of criminal history record information, R.S. 15:546 governs dissemination of information concerning any offender who commits a sex offense or criminal offense against a victim who is a minor, or who has been determined to be a sexually violent predator. Criminal justice agencies, their employees, and officials shall be immune from civil liability for dissemination on criminal history record information concerning sex offenders, sexually violent predators, or child predators as provided in this Chapter.

(Added by Acts 1992 No. 388, §1; chgd. by Acts 1997 No. 1147, §1, eff. 7/14/97.)

§549. Notification.

A. At the earliest possible date, and in no event later than ten days before release, except in the event of escape or emergency furloughs, the Department of Public Safety and Corrections shall send written notice of parole, community placement, work release placement, furlough, or escape, about a specific inmate convicted of a sex offense, to all of the following:

(1) The chief of police of the municipality, in which the inmate will reside or in which placement will be made in a work release program.

(2) The sheriff of the parish in which the inmate will reside or in which placement will be made in the work release program.

B. The same notice as required in Subsection A of this Section shall be sent to the following if such notice has been requested in writing about a specific inmate convicted of a sex offense:

(1) The victim of the crime for which the inmate was convicted.

(2) Any witnesses who testified against the inmate in any court proceedings involving the offense.

(3) Any person specified in writing by the prosecuting district attorney.

C. Information regarding any victim, a relative of the victim, or witness requesting the notice, information regarding any other person specified in writing by the prosecuting district attorney to receive the notice, and the notice are confidential and shall not be available to the inmate.

D. If an inmate convicted of a sex offense escapes from a correctional facility, the Department of Public Safety and Corrections shall immediately notify, by the most reasonable and expedient means available, the chief of police of the municipality and the sheriff of the parish in which the inmate resided immediately before the inmate's arrest and conviction. If previously requested, the department shall also notify the witnesses and the victim of the crime for which the inmate was convicted. If the inmate is recaptured, the department shall send notice to the persons designated in this Subsection as soon as possible but in no event later than two working days after the department learns of such recapture.

E. If the victim or any witness is under the age of sixteen, the notice required by this Section shall be sent to the parents, tutor or legal guardian of the child.

F. The Department of Public Safety and Corrections shall send the notices required by this Chapter to the last address provided to the department by the requesting party. The requesting party shall furnish the department with a current address.

G. Nothing in this Section shall impose any liability upon a chief of police of a municipality or sheriff of a parish for failing to request in writing a notice as provided in this Section.

(Added by Acts 1992 No. 388, §1, eff. 6/18/92.)

CHAPTER 4. EXECUTION OF SENTENCE

PART I. IN GENERAL

PART II. CAPITAL CASES

PART IV. DIMINUTION AND COMMUTATION OF SENTENCE FOR GOOD BEHAVIOR

PART V. VENUE FOR ACTIONS CONTESTING COMPUTATION OF SENTENCE, DISCHARGE, PAROLE, GOOD TIME DATES

PART VI. PROBATION AND PAROLE MANAGEMENT

PART VII. INCARCERATION ALTERNATIVES

PART I. IN GENERAL

§565. Duty of sheriff.

The sheriff, as soon as any sentence to imprisonment, without hard labor, or to imprisonment without hard labor in default of the payment of fine and costs, shall have become final, shall, unless the governor shall have reprieved the person convicted, proceed forthwith to the execution of said sentence.

§566. Pendency of appeal, payments; delivery to penitentiary.

A. The Department of Corrections shall pay the sum of eighteen dollars and twenty-five cents per day to the sheriff of each parish, or to the governing authority of those parishes in which said authority operates the parish jail, for feeding and maintaining each prisoner who has been convicted of a crime and sentenced to imprisonment at a state penitentiary, who is held in the parish jail without bail, pending an appeal. Each sheriff shall file a monthly report with the Department of Corrections and the local governing authority and shall be paid for such charges on a monthly basis by the Department of Corrections. However, in the parish of Orleans, said payment shall be to the criminal sheriff of the parish of Orleans, to be reimbursed to the city of New Orleans.

When the Department of Corrections makes payment in accordance with this Subsection, no additional compensation from the parish governing authority shall be paid for the care of such prisoners.

B. The sheriff or his duly qualified deputy, within thirty days of the date upon which sentence to imprisonment at hard labor has been imposed, shall deliver the prisoner to the state correctional institution designated by the Department of Corrections, unless:

(1) The governor shall have reprieved said prisoner; or

(2) The prisoner is retained in the parish pursuant to R.S. 15:824(B) or R.S. 15:832; or

(3) The prisoner has been admitted to post-conviction bail; or

(4) The prisoner has obtained an order of appeal and the secretary of the Department of Corrections agrees to take custody of the prisoner. In other cases in which an order of appeal is obtained, the sheriff shall deliver the prisoner to the department within fifteen days of the date upon which the highest court of the state to which the prisoner may appeal as of right has affirmed the conviction and sentence. If the prisoner has filed a timely application for rehearing, the sheriff shall deliver the prisoner within fifteen days of the date upon which the rehearing is denied. Application for writs of certiorari or review to the state supreme court shall not prevent transfer under the provisions of this Subparagraph, or

(5) The court, for good cause, stays for a specified period a transfer to the Department of Corrections pursuant to Paragraph (4) above.

C. The sheriff of the parish in which the prisoner has been convicted, or his duly qualified and regularly employed deputy, shall deliver with the prisoner all documents and statements required by Article 892 of Chapter 1 of Title 30 of the Louisiana Code of Criminal Procedure. If said documents are not tendered with the prisoner, the Department of Corrections shall refuse delivery of said prisoner.

§566.2. Commencing of sentence to state penitentiary.

Whenever a prisoner is sentenced to imprisonment in the state penitentiary, and has not been released on bail or perfected a suspensive appeal, such sentence shall be considered as commencing on the day following the day on which such prisoner is sentenced without regard to the actual date of incarceration in the state penitentiary.

PART II. CAPITAL CASES

§567. Conditions precedent to execution.

A. Whenever the Supreme Court of Louisiana affirms a sentence of death, after review on appeal provided by Louisiana Code of Criminal Procedure Article 905.9, the court of original jurisdiction shall cause to be forwarded to the secretary of the Department of Public Safety and Corrections a certified copy of the indictment, verdict, sentence, and the judgment of the Supreme Court of Louisiana affirming the sentence of death.

B. The court of original jurisdiction shall also issue a warrant commanding the secretary to cause the execution of the person condemned as provided by law. The warrant shall specify the date upon which the person condemned shall be put to death, which date shall be not less than sixty days nor more than ninety days from the date the warrant is issued. Upon receipt of the warrant the secretary shall cause a copy of the warrant to be delivered to the person condemned. A certified copy of the warrant shall be mailed, return receipt requested, to the governor and the return receipt filed in the record.

C. If any federal or Louisiana court grants a stay of execution, or if the governor of Louisiana grants a reprieve, the trial court shall reset the execution date at not less than thirty days nor more than forty-five days from the dissolution of the stay order, or termination or expiration of the reprieve.

D. The execution of a female who has been clinically diagnosed as being pregnant shall be suspended. The trial court shall reset the execution date at not less than ninety days nor more than one hundred twenty days from the date of delivery of the baby, a miscarriage, or voluntary termination of the pregnancy.

E. The failure of the trial court to fix an execution date within the time limits of this Section shall not affect the validity of a sentence of death. In such a case, the attorney general shall bring a mandamus proceeding in any court of competent jurisdiction to have the trial court set the execution date at not less than thirty days nor more then forty-five days from the date of issuance of the mandamus order.

§568. Execution of death sentence; prior confinement of offender.

The director of the Department of Corrections, or a competent person selected by him, shall execute the offender in conformity with the death warrant issued in the case. Until the time of his execution, the Department of Corrections shall incarcerate the offender in a manner affording maximum protection to the general public, the employees of the department, and the security of the institution.

§569. Place for execution of death sentence; manner of execution.

A. Every sentence of death executed in this state prior to September 15, 1991 shall be by electrocution, that is, causing to pass through the body of the person convicted a current of electricity of sufficient intensity to cause death, and the application and continuance of such current through the body of the person convicted until such person is dead. Every sentence of death imposed in this state shall be executed at the Louisiana State Penitentiary at Angola. Every execution shall be made in a room entirely cut off from view of all except those permitted by law to be in said room.

B. Every sentence of death executed on or after September 15, 1991 shall be by lethal injection; that is, by the intravenous injection of a substance or substances in a lethal quantity into the body of a person convicted until such person is dead. Every sentence of death imposed in this state shall be executed at the Louisiana State Penitentiary at Angola. Every execution shall be made in a room entirely cut off from view of all except those permitted by law to be in said room.

C. No licensed health care professional shall be compelled to administer a lethal injection.

(Chgd. by Acts 1990 No. 717, §1; Acts 1991 No. 159, §1, eff. 9/6/91.)

§569.1. Hours for execution of death sentence.

Every sentence of death imposed in this state shall be executed between the hours of 12:00 o'clock midnight and 3:00 A.M. upon the date set for the execution by the court of original jurisdiction.

§570. Execution; officials and witnesses; minors excluded; time; notice to victim's relatives.

A. Every execution of the death sentence shall take place in the presence of:

(1) The warden of the Louisiana State Penitentiary at Angola, or a competent person selected by him.

(2) The coroner of the parish of West Feliciana, or his deputy.

(3) A physician summoned by the warden of the Louisiana State Penitentiary at Angola.

(4) the operator of the electric chair, who shall be a competent electrician, who shall have not been previously convicted of a felony, or a competent person selected by the warden of the Louisiana State Penitentiary to administer the lethal injection.

(5) A priest or minister of the gospel, if the convict so requests it.

(6) Not less than five nor more than seven other witnesses, all citizens of the state of Louisiana.

B. No person under the age of eighteen years shall be allowed within the execution room during the time of execution.

C. Notwithstanding any other provision of law to the contrary, every execution of the death sentence shall take place between the hours of 6:00 p.m. and 11:59 p.m.

D. The secretary of the Department of Public Safety and Corrections shall, at least ten days prior to the execution, give written notice of the date and time of execution to the victim's parents, or guardian, spouse, and any adult children who have indicated to the secretary that they desire such notice. The secretary, in such notice, shall give the named parties the option of attending the execution. The victim's parents, or guardian, spouse, and any adult children who desire to attend the execution shall, within three days of their receipt of the secretary's notification, notify, either verbally or in writing, the secretary's office of their intention to attend. The number of victim relationship witnesses may be limited to two. If more than two of the aforementioned parties desire to attend the execution, then the secretary is authorized to select, from the interested parties, the two victim relationship witnesses who will be authorized to attend. In no event shall failure to give notice to the victim's parents, or guardian, spouse, or any adult children have any effect as to execution of sentence.

(Chgd. by Acts 1990 No. 717, §1; Acts 1997 No. 1260, §1, eff. 8/15/97.)

§571. Proces verbal of execution; attesting and filing.

When the sentence shall have been executed, the warden of the Louisiana State Penitentiary at Angola, or his deputy performing the execution, shall make a proces verbal of said execution immediately thereafter, which proces verbal shall recite the manner and date of said execution and shall be attested by said warden, or his deputy, and by all of the witnesses, and said proces verbal, when so signed, shall be filed with the clerk of court of the parish in which the sentence shall have been imposed.

PART IV. DIMINUTION AND COMMUTATION OF SENTENCE FOR GOOD BEHAVIOR

§571.3. Diminution of sentence for good behavior.

A. (1) Every prisoner in a parish prison convicted of an offense and sentenced to imprisonment without hard labor, except a prisoner convicted a second time of a crime of violence as defined by R.S. 14:2(13) or when the sentencing court has denied or conditioned eligibility for "good time" as provided in R.S. 15:537, may earn a diminution of sentence, to be known as "good time", by good behavior and performance of work or self-improvement activities, or both. The amount of diminution of sentence allowed under this Paragraph shall be at the rate of thirty days for every thirty days in actual custody, except for a prisoner convicted a first time of a crime of violence, as defined in R.S. 14:2(13), who shall earn diminution of sentence at the rate of three days for every seventeen days in actual custody, including in either case time spent in custody with good behavior prior to sentence for which the prisoner is given credit.

(2) The sheriff of the parish in which the conviction was had shall have the sole authority to determine when good time has been earned in accordance with the sheriff's regulations which shall be approved by the secretary of the Department of Public Safety and Corrections before such regulations are implemented.

(3) In the event that the prisoner is confined in a parish or multiparish correctional facility not operated by the sheriff, the superintendent of the correctional facility shall have the sole power to determine when good time has been earned or which diminution of sentence may be allowed in accordance with the superintendent's regulations which shall be approved by the secretary of the Department of Public Safety and Corrections before such regulations are implemented.

B. (1) Every inmate in the custody of the department who has been convicted of a felony, except an inmate convicted a second time of a crime of violence as defined by R.S. 14:2(13), and sentenced to imprisonment for a stated number of years or months or when the sentencing court has denied or conditioned eligibility for "good time" as provided in R.S. 15:537 or Code of Criminal Procedure Art. 890.1, may earn, in lieu of incentive wages, a diminution of sentence by good behavior and performance of work or self-improvement activities, or both, to be known as "good time". Those inmates serving life sentences will be credited with good time earned which will be applied toward diminution of their sentences at such time as the life sentences might be commuted to a specific number of years. The secretary shall establish regulations for awarding and recording of good time and shall determine when good time has been earned toward diminution of sentence. The amount of diminution of sentence allowed under the provisions of this Section shall be at the rate of thirty days for every thirty days in actual custody except for an inmate convicted a first time of a crime of violence as defined in R.S. 14:2(13), who shall earn diminution of sentence at a rate of three days for every seventeen days in actual custody, including time spent in custody with good behavior prior to sentence for which the defendant is given credit. Under the provisions of this Section, no inmate shall receive more than thirty days of good time or thirty days of jail credit for any calendar month while serving a term for consecutive sentences.

(2) Any inmate not opting for good time in lieu of incentive wages may earn diminution for sentence under the provisions of this Section at the rate of fifteen days per thirty days in actual custody, including time spent in custody with good behavior prior to sentence for which the defendant is given credit.

C. Diminution of sentence shall not be allowed an inmate in the custody of the Department of Public Safety and Corrections if:

(1) The inmate has been convicted one or more times under the laws of this state of any one or more of the following crimes:

(a) First degree murder.
(b) Second degree murder.
(c) Manslaughter.
(d) Aggravated battery.
(e) Aggravated rape.
(f) Forcible rape.
(g) Simple rape.
(h) Aggravated kidnapping.
(i) Aggravated burglary.
(j) Simple burglary.
(k) Armed robbery.
(*l*) Simple robbery.
(m) A violation of R.S. 14:67 which is a felony.
(n) A violation of R.S. 14:95 which is a felony.
(*o*) A violation of R.S. 14:95.1 which is a felony.
(p) A violation of Chapter 9 of Title 40 of the Louisiana Revised Statutes of 1950 which is a felony.
(q) Any crime of violence as defined by R.S. 14:2(13).
(r) A violation of the Louisiana Controlled Dangerous Substances Law* which is a felony; or

**R.S. 40:961 et seq.*

(s) Any felony which is defined as an attempt to commit one of the crimes enumerated in Subparagraphs (a) through (r) of this Paragraph, and

(2) The inmate has been sentenced as an habitual offender under the Habitual Offender Law as set forth in R.S. 15:529.1, and

(3) The inmate's last conviction for the purposes of the Habitual Offender Law, was for a crime: (a) Committed during the period beginning September 16, 1975 through September 9, 1977, inclusive of both dates, and the sentence of the court specifically denies eligibility for diminution of sentence, or (b) committed on or after September 10, 1977.

(4) The inmate has been convicted two or more times under the laws of this state of any one or more of the following crimes:

(a) Carnal knowledge of a juvenile.
(b) Indecent behavior with juveniles.
(c) Molestation of a juvenile.
(d) Incest.
(e) Aggravated incest.

D. Diminution of sentence shall not be allowed an inmate in the custody of the Department of Public Safety and Corrections if the instant offense is a second offense crime of violence as defined by R.S. 14:2(13) or was committed during a period of time that the inmate was under the jurisdiction of the department or placed on probation as a juvenile.

(Chgd. by Acts 1991 No. 138, §1; Acts 1992 No. 1011, §1; Acts 1994 Third Ex. Sess. No. 110, §1, No. 149, §1, No. 150, §1; Acts 1995 No. 946, §3, No. 1099, §1; Acts 1997 No. 832, §1, eff. 8/15/97.)

§571.4. Forfeiture of diminution of sentence.

A. Determination shall be made by the secretary on a monthly basis as to whether good time has been earned by inmates in the department's custody. Good time which has been earned by inmates in the custody of the Department of Public Safety and Corrections, hereinafter referred to as the "department", shall not be forfeited except as provided in Subsection C of this section.

B. (1) An inmate who is sentenced to the custody of the Department of Public Safety and Corrections and who commits a simple or aggravated escape from any correctional facility or from the lawful custody of any law enforcement officer or officer of the department may forfeit all good time earned on that portion of his sentence served prior to his escape.

(2) An inmate who has been returned to the custody of the department because of a violation of the terms of parole granted by the Board of Parole shall forfeit all good time earned on that portion of the sentence served prior to the granting of parole.

(3) An inmate who is sentenced to the custody of the department and who commits a battery on an employee of the Department of Public Safety and Corrections or any police officer as defined in R.S. 14:34.2 may forfeit good time earned on that portion of the sentence served prior to committing the battery of such person, up to a maximum of one hundred eighty days.

(4) In all other cases, forfeiture of good time may include up to a maximum of one hundred eighty days.

C. The department shall, in accordance with the Administrative Procedure Act*, promulgate and adopt rules and regulations for the forfeiture of good time as provided in Subsection B herein. The rules and regulations shall include but not be limited to the following:

**R.S. 49:950 et seq.*

(1) That written notification of the forfeiture be provided to the inmate and that the inmate within fifteen days after such notification may make a written request for a hearing to review the forfeiture of good time.

(2) That, upon request of the inmate, a hearing shall be conducted to review the finding that the inmate committed an escape and other facts relevant to the forfeiture. The hearing shall be conducted as a disciplinary proceeding. The inmate shall have the right to be present, to be represented by counsel, and to offer exculpatory evidence or evidence in mitigation.

(3) That, upon request of the inmate, a hearing shall be conducted to review the finding that the inmate committed a battery on an employee of the Department of Public Safety and Corrections or on a police officer as defined in R.S. 14:34.2, and other facts relevant to the forfeiture. The hearing shall be conducted as a disciplinary proceeding. The inmate shall have the right to be present, to be represented by counsel, and to offer exculpatory evidence or evidence in mitigation.

(4) That, at the conclusion of such hearing, a determination shall be made to either affirm the forfeiture of good time, reject the forfeiture, or make such modification to the forfeiture as may be appropriate.

(Chgd. by Acts 1991 No. 138, §1; Acts 1992 No. 689, §1, No. 1011, §1; Acts 1993 No. 78, §1, No. 854, §1; Acts 1995 No. 980, §1; Acts 1997 No. 820, §1, eff. 8/15/97.)

§571.5. Supervision upon release after diminution of sentence for good behavior; conditions of release; revocation.

A. (1) When a prisoner committed to the Department of Public Safety and Corrections is released because of diminution of sentence pursuant to this Part, he shall be released as if released on parole.

(2) At least three months prior to the anticipated release due to diminution of sentence, the secretary of the department shall notify the parole board and provide such information as is necessary to allow the board to establish such conditions as provided in R.S. 15:574.4(H) as may be reasonably necessary to facilitate supervision. If diminution of sentence is not prohibited by R.S. 15:571.3(C)(1) and the sentence is for a sexual offense as enumerated in R.S. 15:574.4(H)(2), then the provisions of R.S. 15:574.4(H)(2)(a) and (b) and (3) apply.

B. (1) Before any prisoner is released on parole upon diminution of sentence, he shall be issued a certificate of parole that enumerates the conditions of parole. These conditions shall be explained to the prisoner and the prisoner shall agree in writing to such conditions prior to his release on parole.

(2) The person released because of diminution of sentence pursuant to this Part shall be supervised in the same manner and to the same extent as if he were released on parole. The

supervision shall be for the remainder of the original full term of sentence. If a person released because of diminution of sentence pursuant to this Part violates a condition imposed by the parole board, the board shall proceed in the same manner as it would to revoke parole to determine if the release upon diminution of sentence should be revoked.

C. If such person's parole is revoked by the parole board for violation of the terms of parole, the person shall be recommitted to the department for the remainder of the full term. *(Chgd. by Acts 1991 No. 138, §1; Acts 1992 No. 690, §1, No. 962, §2, eff. 8/21/92.)*

§571.6. Report of persons eligible for discharge.

On any day not later than the twentieth day of each month, the superintendent of the state penitentiary shall forward to the Governor a report directed to him of any convict who may be discharged the following month by reason of the diminution of his sentence.

§571.7. Supervision upon release from parish prison after diminution of sentence for good behavior; conditions of release; revocation.

A. When a prisoner who has been sentenced to a parish prison in a parish having a population in excess of four hundred seventy-five thousand people is released because of diminution of sentence pursuant to this Part, he shall be released as if released on parole.

B. A prisoner released in accordance with Subsection A herein shall be supervised by the sheriff, the keeper of the parish prison if not the sheriff, or, in Orleans Parish, the criminal sheriff of Orleans Parish. Such supervision shall be for the remainder of the original full term of the prisoner's sentence and shall be performed in the same manner and to the same extent as supervision of a prisoner committed to the Department of Corrections who is released on parole.

C. The supervisor may make rules for the conduct of a prisoner while he is on release and may also require, either at the time of release or at any time while on release, that the prisoner conform to any of the following conditions:

(1) Residence in a community rehabilitation center.

(2) Restitution to a victim of the crime for which release is being sought, if such victim has suffered a direct pecuniary loss as a result of the crime. The supervisor shall take into account the prisoner's ability to pay and shall not revoke release based upon this condition unless the prisoner has willfully failed to comply.

(3) Community service work, as determined by the supervisor.

(4) Payment into a victim compensation fund, if such fund is established, in a manner and amount specified by law.

(5) Obtaining gainful employment.

(6) Continuing education or vocational training.

(7) Participation in a substance abuse treatment facility program or other counseling program.

(8) Any other condition which may presently be applied under R.S. 15:574.4(H) and (L) to a prisoner committed to the Department of Public Safety and Corrections who is released on parole.

D. A prisoner released in accordance with this Section shall be subject to having the release revoked for violation of the release conditions. The supervisor shall establish rules and regulations governing the revocation of release.

E. Upon revocation of release, the prisoner shall be recommitted to the parish prison and shall serve the remaining full term of his sentence.
(Chgd. by Acts 1991 No. 289, §7, eff. 9/6/91.)

§571.8. Forfeiture of good behavior allowance or commutation.

If any prisoner who has received commutation of sentence or earned diminution of sentence escapes, the prisoner shall thereby automatically forfeit all claims to commutation of sentence previously granted or diminution of sentence previously earned. *(Chgd. by Acts 1979 No. 490, §1.)*

§§571.9, 571.10. *(Repealed by Acts 1991 No. 138, §3, eff. 1/31/92.)*

§571.11. Dispositions of fines and forfeitures.

A. (1)(a) All fines and forfeitures, except for forfeitures of criminal bail bonds posted by a commercial security imposed by district courts and district attorneys, conviction fees in criminal cases, and prosecutions for violations of state law or parish ordinances, upon collection by the sheriff or executive officer of the court, shall be paid into the treasury of the parish in which the court is situated and deposited in a special "Criminal Court Fund" account, which, on motion by the district attorney and approval order of the district judge, may be used or paid out in defraying the expenses of the criminal courts of the parish as provided in Ch.C. Articles 419 and 421 and R.S. 16:6, in defraying the expenses of those courts in recording and transcribing of testimony, statements, charges and other proceedings in the trial of indigent persons charged with the commission of felonies, in defraying their expenses in the preparation of records in appeals in such cases, for all expenses and fees of the petit jury and grand jury, for witness fees, for attendance fees of the sheriff and clerk of court, for costs and expenses of a parish law library, and for other expenses related to the judges of the criminal courts and the office of the district attorney. In the Second Judicial District, the criminal court fund shall be used to defray the expenses of the criminal court system.

(b) The sheriffs throughout the state, the parish of Orleans excepted, shall retain twelve percent of the amount of fines collected to go into the sheriff's general fund in each parish and an additional twelve percent of the amount of fines collected shall be transmitted to the district attorney of the judicial district or be used by the district attorney in defraying such expenses of his office as in his discretion may be necessary.

(c) Prior to the making of any payment in accordance with this Section, beginning January 1, 1996, two-thirds of all fines collected for violations of parking restrictions established pursuant to R.S. 40:1742 and two-thirds of all fines collected for false certification of mobility impairment by a physician as provided by R.S. 47:463.4(G)(4) shall be forwarded in accordance with the provisions of R.S. 46:2583(A).

(2) All fines and forfeitures, except for forfeitures of criminal bail bonds posted by a commercial surety imposed by district courts and collected by the sheriff or executive officer of the court for violations of municipal ordinances shall be disbursed as follows, except in the case of violations of any of the provisions of Title 32 of the Louisiana Revised Statutes of 1950, wherein such proceeds shall be distributed in accordance with Subparagraph A (1)(a) of this Section:

(a) Twelve percent thereof shall be remitted to the office of the district attorney.

(b) Twelve percent shall be remitted to the sheriff's general fund.

(c) The remainder shall be transmitted to the municipality for deposit in its treasury.

B. Notwithstanding the provisions of R.S. 13:692, 13:1587 and R.S. 16:6 and the other provisions of this section, a district judge of the state of Louisiana, except in the parishes of Calcasieu and Cameron, shall have the right to order the sheriff of the parish wherein his principal office is domiciled, to pay, on the voucher of that district judge alone, without the concurrence of the other judges of his district, and without motion of the district attorney, a salary for a secretary for that district judge's office, which amount shall be paid by the sheriff prior to depositing the fines and forfeitures into the treasury of the parish.

C. (1) One-half of any surplus remaining in the special account or fund on December 31 of each year shall be transferred to the parish general fund. No money shall be paid out of the special account except upon the order or warrant of the district judge and district attorney as above provided.

(2) Notwithstanding any other provision of the law to the contrary, the Criminal Court Fund for the Sixteenth Judicial District shall be operated as a single fund, and one-half of any surplus remaining in the single special account or fund on December 31 of each year shall be transferred to the general funds of the parishes of the district in the same proportion as the revenues in the fund were produced from the parishes.

(3) Notwithstanding any other provision of law to the contrary, the Criminal Court Fund accounts for the Second Judicial District shall be operated as a single account or fund. One-half of any surplus remaining in the single account or fund on December 31 of each year shall be transferred to the general funds of the parishes of the district in the same proportion as the revenues in the single account or fund were produced from the parishes.

(4) (a) Notwithstanding any other provision of law to the contrary, the criminal court fund for the Fifth Judicial District shall be operated as a single fund. Except as provided in this Paragraph, one-half of any surplus remaining in the single fund on December thirty-first of each year shall be transferred to the general fund of the parishes of the district in the same proportion as the revenues in the fund were produced from the parishes.

(b) Upon motion of the district attorney, with the concurrence of the chief judge of the Fifth Judicial District, a certain amount of the surplus monies remaining in the single fund on December thirty-first of each year shall be deposited into a special excessive costs account for the Fifth Judicial District. The total amount of monies deposited into the special excessive costs account, in any calendar year, shall not exceed fifty thousand dollars.

(c) No money shall be paid out of the special excessive costs account except upon the order or warrant of the chief judge and district attorney of the Fifth Judicial District. Monies in the account shall only be used to defray excessive costs incurred in first degree murder cases or very serious felony trials wherein venue has been changed.

D. All fines and forfeitures, including forfeitures of criminal bail bonds, imposed in criminal cases and prosecutions by the courts of Orleans Parish and any payments ordered as a condition of probation under Code of Criminal Procedure Art. 895.1(B)(2) shall, upon collection, be paid to the criminal sheriff of Orleans Parish who shall deposit same in a special account, and shall thereafter be divided equally between the district attorney of Orleans Parish and the criminal district court of Orleans Parish in two special accounts, one account to be administered by the judges of the criminal district court of Orleans Parish, and the other account to be administered by the district attorney of Orleans Parish to be used in defraying the expenses of the criminal courts of the parish, extraditions, and such other expenses pertaining to the operation of the criminal court of Orleans Parish and the office of the district attorney of Orleans Parish. Disbursements from the account to the criminal district court and district attorney shall be made on an equal basis. Said accounts shall be annually audited by the director of finance of the city of New Orleans.

E. Notwithstanding any provision herein contained to the contrary, the fines and forfeitures, except for forfeitures of criminal bail bonds, collected by the district courts of the parishes of Iberia and Vermilion as a result of a conviction for a violation of R.S. 14:98 occurring within the territorial limits of a municipality shall be remitted to the city treasury of the municipality in accordance with the provisions of R.S. 13:1894.1.

F. Notwithstanding any other provision of law to the contrary, the governing authority of Grant Parish is hereby authorized to pay all or part of the expenses of the offices of judge; but not the salary of the judge, and district attorney for the Thirty-fifth Judicial District, and all or part of the salaries of the employees of those offices, including assistant district attorneys, from the Criminal Court Fund of the Thirty-fifth Judicial District.

G. Notwithstanding any other provision of the law to the contrary, the governing authorities of the parishes of Iberia, St. Martin, and St. Mary are hereby authorized to pay all or part of the salaries of those persons employed as law clerks by the Sixteenth Judicial District out of the Criminal Court Fund of the Sixteenth Judicial District. Those persons employed as law clerks shall be employed to perform general duties as such and shall not be limited to those duties connected with criminal cases.

H. Notwithstanding any other provision of law to the contrary, the governing authority of Red River Parish is hereby authorized to pay all or part of the expenses of the office of judge, but not the salary of the judge, and the expenses of office of district attorney for the judicial district in which Red River Parish is located, and also all or part of the salaries of the employees of those offices, including assistant district attorneys, from the Criminal Court Fund of the judicial district in which Red River Parish is located.

I. Notwithstanding any other provision of law to the contrary, the governing authorities of the parishes of Acadia, Lafayette, and Vermilion are hereby authorized to pay all or part of the salaries of those persons employed as law clerks by the Fifteenth Judicial District out of the Criminal Court Fund of the Fifteenth Judicial District. Those persons employed as law clerks shall be employed to perform general duties as such and shall not be limited to those duties connected with criminal cases.

J. In addition to the authority heretofore granted and authorized by any other provision, the Criminal Court Fund of the Seventeenth Judicial District, parish of Lafourche, may be used to pay for the office expenses, operating expenses, equipment costs, and salaries of juvenile officers, employees of the offices of the district judges, district attorney, indigent defender, and juvenile officers of the Seventeenth Judicial District, parish of Lafourche. The fund shall not be used to pay the salaries of the district judges. The fund may be used to pay the salaries of law clerks for the judicial district and to provide for transportation and the cost of maintaining and operating the transportation for the grand jury and petit juries of the judicial district. The fund may also be used to provide for planning, maintenance, and operating expenses for the juvenile justice facility for the parish of Lafourche.

K. (1) Notwithstanding any other provision of law to the contrary, the Ninth Judicial District Court and the office of the district attorney for the Ninth Judicial District shall cause to be prepared a comprehensive budget presenting their financial plan for expenditure of monies deposited to the Criminal Court Fund for the Ninth Judicial District for the ensuing fiscal year. Such proposed budget shall be completed and submitted by the court and district attorney to the governing authority of Rapides Parish, hereinafter referred to as the governing authority, no later than thirty-five days prior to the beginning of each fiscal year.

(2) No later than fifteen days prior to the beginning of each fiscal year, the governing authority shall cause a notice to be published in the official journal of Rapides Parish stating that the proposed budget of the court and district attorney is available for public inspection at the office of the governing authority. The notice shall also state that a public hearing on the proposed budget shall be held, with the date, time, and place of the hearing specified in the notice. At least one public hearing shall be conducted on the proposal.

(3) The governing authority of the parish shall monitor the expenditures from the budget on a quarterly basis during the year.

L. All judgments of bond forfeiture rendered after June 22, 1993 resulting from the posting of a commercial surety bond in a criminal proceeding in the state of Louisiana upon collection by the prosecuting attorney for the jurisdiction in which the bond was posted shall be paid to the prosecuting attorney who shall, as attorney of record in the proceeding, distribute the funds as follows:

(1) District courts. (a) In all judicial district courts of the state of Louisiana, except in the parish of Orleans, where the district attorney collects on a judgment of bond forfeiture, the proceeds shall be distributed as follows:

(i) Thirty percent of all funds collected by the district attorney shall be paid to the general operating account of the district attorney for the parish where the bond was posted.

(ii) Twenty-five percent of all funds collected by the district attorney shall be paid to the criminal court fund of the parish where the bond was posted.

(iii) Twenty-five percent of all funds collected by the district attorney shall be paid to the operating fund of the sheriff of the parish where the bond was posted.

(iv) Twenty percent of all funds collected by the district attorney shall be paid to the Indigent Defenders Program for the parish where the bond was posted.

(b) In cases of violation of the provisions of Title 32 of the Louisiana Revised Statutes of 1950, the proceeds shall be distributed in accordance with Paragraph A (1) of this Section.

(2) Parish courts. (a) In all parish courts throughout the state of Louisiana, where the prosecuting attorney collects on a judgment of bond forfeiture, the proceeds shall be deposited into the parish general fund.

(b) In cases of violation of the provisions of Title 32 of the Louisiana Revised Statutes of 1950, the proceeds shall be distributed in accordance with Paragraph A (1) of this Section.

(3) City and municipal courts. In all city and municipal courts throughout the state of Louisiana, except in municipal and traffic courts in the city of New Orleans, where the prosecuting attorney collects on a judgment of bond forfeiture, the proceeds shall be distributed as follows:

(a) Twenty-five percent of all funds collected by the prosecuting attorney shall be paid to the general operating account of the prosecuting attorney for the political subdivision where the bond was posted.

(b) Twenty-five percent of all funds collected by the prosecuting attorney shall be paid to the judicial court fund of the court issuing the judgment of bond forfeiture.

(c) Twenty-five percent of all funds collected by the prosecuting attorney shall be paid to the law enforcement agency of the political subdivision responsible for executing orders of the court where the judgment was rendered.

(d) Twenty-five percent of all funds collected by the prosecuting attorney shall be paid to the Indigent Defenders Program of the court where the judgment was rendered. In the event the political subdivision does not have an Indigent Defenders Program, the funds shall be paid to the Indigent Defenders Program of the parish in which the bond was posted.

(4) Municipal and traffic courts for the city of New Orleans. Where the prosecuting attorney for municipal and traffic courts for the city of New Orleans collects on a judgment of bond forfeiture the proceeds shall be distributed in accordance with city ordinance.

M. In all cases where the attorney general collects on judgments of bond forfeiture, fifty percent of the funds collected shall be turned over to the attorney general for deposit in his operating account, and the remaining fifty percent of the funds collected shall be distributed as follows:

(1) Ten percent of all funds collected by the attorney general shall be paid to the court fund of the parish where the bond was posted, as determined by the local rules of court.

(2) Ten percent of all funds collected by the attorney general shall be paid to the operating fund of the sheriff of the parish where the bond was posted.

(3) Thirty percent of all funds collected by the attorney general shall be paid to the Indigent Defenders Program for the parish where the bond was posted.
(Chgd. by Acts 1992 No. 488, §1; Acts 1993 No. 834, §4; Acts 1994 Third Ex. Sess. No. 52, §3; Acts 1995 No. 573, §4, eff. 8/15/95.)

§571.12. Louisiana Society for the Prevention of Cruelty to Children to receive fines.

All fines, penalties, and forfeitures incurred and appearance bonds forfeited in prosecutions instituted or conducted by the Louisiana Society for the Prevention of Cruelty to Children shall be turned over to the Society.

The Society shall have a right of action to recover all fines, penalties, and forfeitures, and forfeited appearance bonds in its own name in the civil courts of this state when they are not collected in the court in which incurred or the existing laws do not provide for their collection.

§571.13. Supervised release of parish prisoners; rules of conduct; revocation.

A. When a prisoner who has been sentenced to a parish prison is released pursuant to this Part, he may be released as if on parole.

B. A prisoner released in accordance with Subsection A herein shall be supervised by the sheriff, the keeper of the parish prison if not the sheriff, the keeper of the parish prison if not the sheriff, or, in Orleans Parish, the criminal sheriff of Orleans Parish. Such supervision shall be for the remainder of the original full term of the prisoner's sentence and shall be performed in the same manner and to the same extent as supervision of a prisoner committed to the Department of Public Safety and Correction who is released on parole.

C. The supervisor may make rules for the conduct of a prisoner while he is on release and may also require, either at the time of release or at any time while on release, that the prisoner conform to the following conditions:

(1) Residence in a community rehabilitation or work release center.

(2) Restitution to a victim of the crime for which release is being sought, if such victim has suffered a direct pecuniary loss as a result of the crime.

(3) Community service work, as determined by the supervisor.

(4) Payment into a victim compensation or service fund.

(5) Obtaining gainful employment.

(6) Continuing education or vocational training.

(7) Participation in a substance abuse treatment facility program or other counseling program.

(8) Defraying the cost, or any portion thereof, of his supervision by making payments to the supervisor in a sum and manner to be determined by the supervisor, based on his ability to pay.

(9) Any other condition which may be applied under R.S. 15:574.4(H) to a prisoner committed to the Department of Public Safety and Corrections who is released on parole.

D. A prisoner released in accordance with this Section shall be subject to having the release revoked for violation of the release conditions. The supervisor shall establish rules and regulations governing the revocation of release.

E. Upon revocation of release, the prisoner shall be recommitted to the parish prison in order to serve the full term of his sentence.

§571.14. *(Repealed by Acts 1991 No. 138, §3, eff. 1/31/92.)*

PART V. VENUE FOR ACTIONS CONTESTING COMPUTATION OF SENTENCE, DISCHARGE, PAROLE, GOOD TIME DATES

§571.15. Venue.

Venue in any action in which an individual committed to the Department of Public Safety and Corrections contests the computation of his sentence or sentences, discharge, good time dates, or any action concerning parole shall be in the parish of East Baton Rouge. Venue in a suit contesting the actions of the Board of Parole shall be controlled by this Part and R.S. 15:574.2 and 574.11 and not by the Code of Criminal Procedure, Title XXXI-A, Post Conviction Relief, or Title IX, Habeas Corpus, regardless of the captioned pleadings stating the contrary. *(Chgd. by Acts 1990 No. 670, §1, eff. 9/7/90.)*

PART VI. PROBATION AND PAROLE MANAGEMENT

§571.20. Work units; assignment limits.

A. Beginning July 1, [1986] *1995*, the number of work units assigned to each probation and parole specialist performing the supervisory and investigative functions and duties required by law of the Department of Public Safety and Corrections shall be reduced at a rate determined by the secretary of the department until the number of work units assigned does not exceed fifty.

B. Beginning July 1, [1989] *1997*, the department shall not assign more than fifty work units to any probation and parole specialist [unless otherwise specifically authorized in writing by the secretary of the department based upon regulations adopted by the director of probation and parole].

(Chgd. by Acts 1995 No. 394, §1, eff. 8/15/95 only if funding is available. Matter in brackets eff. only until funding is available. Matter in italics eff. if funding is available.)

§571.21. Deposit of fees and assessments.

A. All probation supervision fees received by the department pursuant to Code of Criminal Procedure Art. 895.1(C) shall be deposited immediately upon receipt into the state treasury.

B. Twelve percent of the amount of any monetary assessments imposed as a condition of probation or parole except fines, any court costs, restitution, or compensation to the victim or his family, collected by the division of probation and parole for disbursement to any governmental or judicial entity shall be deposited immediately upon receipt into the state treasury.

(Chgd. by Acts 1992 No. 984, §5, eff. 8/21/92.)

§571.22. Limitation of liability; release of information.

Any probation and parole officer or specialist who releases or uses information contained in the case files of criminal offenders under his supervision, after first obtaining written consent of the district manager having jurisdiction over the offender, for the purpose of protecting the public shall be immune from civil or criminal liability that may otherwise be incurred or imposed. The immunity provided by this Section shall only apply when the officer or specialist acts in good faith and shall not extend to any such person who releases or uses information which is known to be false or releases or uses information with reckless disregard for its truth. *(Added by Acts 1997 No. 1437, §1, eff. 8/15/97.)*

PART VII. INCARCERATION ALTERNATIVES

(Added by Acts 1990 No. 553, §1, eff. 9/7/90.)

§571.31. Alternatives to traditional imprisonment; findings; purposes.

A. The legislature finds that the safety and welfare of the people of this state; the interests of the criminal justice community in prisoner security, humane and just conditions for prisoners, reduced recidivism, and rehabilitation of criminal offenders; and the need for more efficient and effective use of limited state resources may all be well served by the use of nontraditional approaches to the incarceration of prisoners.

B. In view of Subsection A of this Section, it is the purpose of this Part to assure that a practical examination of the use of such nontraditional approaches is undertaken by the Department of Public Safety and Corrections and considered by the legislature and the governor.

(Added by Acts 1990 No. 553, §1, eff. 9/7/90.)

§571.32. Alternatives to traditional imprisonment; pilot projects; mandated inclusions; evaluation; reporting.

A. Not later than October 1, 1990, contingent upon legislative appropriation, the Department of Public Safety and Corrections shall implement a pilot project in using an alternative mode of incarceration to traditional imprisonment for executing the sentences of first offenders. The project shall provide for active monitoring of the prisoner as well as for intense probation.

B. (1) The pilot project undertaken pursuant to this Section shall be implemented in not less than three areas of the state. Each area shall be unique from the others regarding its location and the size of its population.

(2) The pilot project undertaken pursuant to this Section may include the use of electronic and telephone monitoring devices.

C. (1) The pilot project undertaken pursuant to this Section shall be evaluated with regard to security, beneficial and detrimental effects on the prisoner, projected probable effects on deterrence, cost, labor intensiveness, and other relevant measures of effectiveness. Such evaluation shall provide the required information on a project basis as well as in comparison with traditional imprisonment.

(2) All evaluations shall be presented to the members of the Joint Legislative Committee on the Budget, the House Committee on the Administration of Criminal Justice, and the Senate Committee on the Judiciary, Section C, as well as the governor. The first such evaluation shall be reported not later than thirty days prior to the first day of the 1991 Regular Session of the Legislature.
(Added by Acts 1990 No. 553, §1, eff. 9/7/90.)

§571.33. Extension or alteration of pilot; approval of the budget committee; statewide implementation.

The pilot project undertaken as required in this Part may be varied, extended, or dissolved prior to evaluation only if approved by the Joint Legislative Committee on the Budget and the governor. *(Added by Acts 1990 No. 553, §1, eff. 9/7/90.)*

§571.34. Alternative to traditional imprisonment; pilot project; mandated inclusions; evaluation; reporting.

A. Not later than October 1, 1997, contingent upon legislative appropriation, the Department of Public Safety and Corrections shall implement a pilot project using an alternative mode of incarceration to traditional imprisonment involving electronic monitoring for executing the sentences of certain elderly or infirm offenders as determined by the department. The project shall provide for active electronic monitoring of the prisoner.

B. (1) The pilot project undertaken pursuant to this Section shall be implemented in not less than three areas of the state. Each area shall be unique from the others regarding its location and the size of its population.

(2) The pilot project undertaken pursuant to this Section shall include the use of electronic monitoring devices.

C. (1) The pilot project undertaken pursuant to this Section shall be evaluated with regard to security, beneficial and detrimental effects on the prisoner, projected probable effects on deterrence, cost, labor intensiveness, and other relevant measures of effectiveness. Such evaluation shall provide the required information on a project basis as well as in comparison with traditional imprisonment.

(2) All evaluations shall be presented to the Joint Legislative Committee on the Budget, the House Committee on the Administration of Criminal Justice, and the Senate Committee on the Judiciary, Section C, as well as the governor. The first such evaluation shall be reported not later than thirty days prior to the first day of the 1998 Regular Session of the Legislature.
(Added by Acts 1997 No. 1180, §1, eff. 7/14/97.)

CHAPTER 5. REPRIEVE, PARDON, AND PAROLE

PART I. REPRIEVE AND PARDON

Section

PART II. PAROLE

(1) BOARD OF PAROLE AND RULES OF PAROLE

(2) OUT OF STATE PAROLEE SUPERVISION

(3) VIOLATIONS OF MUNICIPAL ORDINANCES

(4) MEDICAL PAROLE

(5) PAROLE RISK ASSESSMENT PILOT PROGRAM

PART I. REPRIEVE AND PARDON

§572. Powers of governor to grant reprieves and pardons; automatic pardon for first offender.

A. The governor may grant reprieves to persons convicted of offenses against the state and, upon recommendation of the Board of Pardons as hereinafter provided for by this Part, may commute sentences, pardon those convicted of offenses against the state, and remit fines and forfeitures imposed for such offenses.

B. A first offender never previously convicted of a felony shall be pardoned automatically upon completion of his sentence without a recommendation of the Board of Pardons and without action by the governor.

C. For the purposes of this Section, "first offender" means a person convicted within this state of a felony but never previously convicted of a felony within this state or convicted under the laws of any other state or of the United States or of any foreign government or country of a crime which, if committed in this state, would have been a felony, regardless of any previous convictions for any misdemeanors. Convictions in other jurisdictions which do not have counterparts in this state will be classified according to the laws of the jurisdiction of conviction.

D. On the day that an individual completes his sentence the Division of Probation and Parole of the Department of Corrections, after satisfying itself that (1) the individual is a first offender as defined herein and (2) the individual has completed his sentence shall issue a certificate recognizing and proclaiming that the petitioner is fully pardoned for the offense, and that he has all rights of citizenship and franchise, and shall transmit a copy of the certificate to the individual and to the clerk of court in and for the parish where the conviction occurred. This copy shall be filed in the record of the proceedings in which the conviction was obtained. However, once an automatic pardon is granted under the provisions of this Section, the individual who received such pardon shall not be entitled to receive another automatic pardon.

E. Notwithstanding any provision herein contained to the contrary, any person receiving a pardon under the provisions of Subparagraph (1) of Paragraph (E) of Section 5 of Article IV of the Louisiana Constitution of 1974 and this Section may be charged and punished as a second or multiple offender as provided in R.S. 15:529.1.

§572.1. Board of Pardons; membership; domicile; session; quorum.

A. The Board of Pardons shall consist of five electors, who shall be appointed by the governor to serve terms concurrent with the governor making the appointments, or until their successors are appointed and take office. At least one of the members may be appointed from a list of three names submitted by the membership of Victims and Citizens Against Crime, Inc. All appointments shall be subject to confirmation by the Senate. The governor shall designate the chairman of the board.

B. The domicile of the board shall be in the city of Baton Rouge, and the board shall establish its office at its domicile, but may hold meetings at other places within the state.

C. The board shall meet on regularly scheduled dates determined by it, and at such other times as the chairman may determine are necessary for the purpose of reviewing and taking action on applications for pardons pending before it and to transact such other business as it deems necessary.

D. The board shall select a vice chairman from its membership and shall select and fix the salary of an executive secretary, who need not be a member of the board, and who shall serve at the pleasure of the board. All meetings of the board shall be open to the public.

E. Four members of the board shall constitute a quorum for the transaction of business, and all actions of the board shall require the favorable vote of at least four members of the board.

F. Each member of the board shall devote full time to the duties of his office, and shall be prohibited from holding any elective, appointive, or public employment; or from engaging in any private business or employment which is in conflict with his duties as a member of the board.

(Chgd. by Acts 1995 No. 1150, §1; Acts 1997 No. 828, §1, eff. 8/15/97.)

§572.2. Compensation of board members.

The chairman of the board shall receive an annual salary of forty-two thousand dollars and each of the other members of the board shall receive an annual salary of thirty-six thousand dollars payable on his own warrant, and each member shall be reimbursed for necessary travel and other expenses actually incurred in the discharge of his duties. *(Chgd. by Acts 1991 No. 1012, §1, eff. 9/6/91.)*

§572.3. Powers of the board.

In addition to the other powers, duties, and functions set forth in this Part, the board may:

(1) Adopt rules and regulations necessary to carry out the provisions of this Part and its duties and functions in connection therewith.

(2) Employ a staff, including such administrative, clerical and legal personnel, and other professional personnel with training or past experience in criminology or related fields such as sociology, psychology, or psychiatry, as it finds are necessary to effectuate its purposes, powers, and duties. The board shall fix the compensation and duties of its staff, in conformity with applicable civil service and other laws.

(3) Do such other things as are necessary to carry out its powers, duties, and functions.

(4) Sanction the applicant's disorderly, threatening, or insolent behavior, or use of insulting, abusive, or obscene language or written communication in connection with the application before the board. A decision to sanction may result in the immediate termination of the proceedings and a recommendation against the relief sought by the applicant. The applicant shall be informed of the sanction at the commencement of the proceedings. *(Chgd. by Acts 1997 No. 1196, §1, eff. 8/15/97.)*

§572.4. Board of Pardons; rules, regulations, and procedures; notice to district attorneys and sheriffs, applicants, injured victim, spouse, or next of kin of injured or deceased victim, and other interested persons; publication of notice of intent; restrictions on applications of certain inmates; time periods for additional review.

A. Written rules, regulations and procedures for consideration or clemency applications shall be adopted by the Board of Pardons by January 1, 1980. Such rules, regulations and procedures shall be adopted in accordance with the procedures of R.S. 49:953(A)(1) and (2) and shall become effective upon approval of the governor.

B. (1) Before considering the application for pardon of any person the board shall give written notice of the date and time at which the application will be heard and considered, at least thirty days prior to the hearing, to the following:

(a) The district attorney, the sheriff of the parish in which the applicant was convicted, and in Orleans Parish, the superintendent of police.

(b) The applicant.

(c) A victim who has been physically or psychologically injured by the applicant, and the victim's spouse or next of kin, unless the injured victim or his spouse or next of kin advises the board in writing that such notification is not desired.

(d) The spouse or next of kin of a deceased victim when the offender responsible for the death is the applicant, unless the spouse or next of kin advises the board in writing that such notification is not desired.

(e) Any other interested persons.

(2) The district attorney, injured victim, spouse or next of kin, and any other persons who desire to do so shall be given a reasonable opportunity to attend the meeting and be heard.

C. Before setting a hearing on an application for pardon or commutation of sentence, notice of application to the board for clemency or commutation of sentence shall be published on three separate days within a thirty-day period of time, without cost to the state, in any newspaper recognized, at any time during the six-month period prior to or following the publication of the first notice, as the official journal of the governing authority of the parish where the offense occurred for which the person was convicted.

D. Notwithstanding any provisions of law to the contrary, any applicant who has been sentenced to life imprisonment shall not be eligible to apply to the board for a pardon or commutation of sentence for a period of fifteen years after being sentenced by the trial court. If the application is denied, the applicant shall be notified in writing of the reason for the denial and thereafter may file a new application to the board no earlier than six years from the date of action by the board. A third application shall not be filed earlier than three years from the date of action taken by the board on the second application. Any subsequent applications shall not be filed earlier than two years after the immediately preceding action taken by the board. However, the provisions of this Subsection shall not apply when the board determines that new and material evidence that, notwithstanding the exercise of reasonable diligence by the applicant, was not discovered before or during his trial, is available and if it had been introduced at the trial it would probably have changed the verdict or judgment of guilty. *(Chgd. by Acts 1990 No. 535, §1; Acts 1997 No. 822, §1, No. 828, §1, eff. 8/15/97.)*

§572.5. Information to be provided to Board of Pardons.

Upon request of the Board of Pardons, the Department of Corrections and the Department of Public Safety shall provide the Board of Pardons with such records of the fact and circumstances of the offense for which the person applying for a pardon was convicted, the offender's past criminal record, his social history, the prison record, and the physical, mental, or psychiatric condition of the person applying for a pardon, and any other records or other reports that may be requested.

§572.6. Finality of clemency determinations.

No person shall have a right of appeal from a decision of the Board of Pardons or the governor regarding clemency.

§572.7. Representation of applicants before board; prohibitions.

A.* (1) The following persons shall not represent any person, directly or indirectly, for compensation before the board:

(a) The executive counsel to the governor.

(b) The executive secretary to the governor.

(c) Any member of the immediate staff of the governor.

(d) Any member of a law firm, law partnership, or law corporation of which a member, associate, or partner is the executive counsel to the governor, the executive secretary to the governor, or a member of the immediate staff of the governor.

(2) If an executive counsel, executive secretary, or member of the immediate staff of the governor violates the provisions of this Section, such person shall forfeit the office or position held and all emoluments of the office or position. In addition, if a member of a law firm, partnership, or corporation of which such a person is a member, associate, or partner violates the provisions of this Section, the office or position held with the governor and all emoluments of said office or position shall be forfeited.

**So in original. No subsection B has been enacted.*

§573. Sessions of Board of Pardons open.

All sessions of the Board of Pardons shall be public.

§573.1. Prohibited contact with Board of Pardons; penalties; public record.

A. Notwithstanding the provisions of R.S. 15:574.12, or any other provision of law to the contrary, no person shall contact or communicate with the Board of Pardons or any of its members urging pardon, clemency, or commutation of sentence, or otherwise regarding any inmate except in the following ways:

(1) In an open hearing as provided in this Part.

(2) By written letter addressed to the Board of Pardons.

B. Any communication with the Board of Pardons urging pardon, clemency, or commutation of sentence, or otherwise regarding an inmate as provided in Paragraph A(2) of this Section shall be deemed a public record and subject to public inspection as provided by the provisions of R.S. 44:1 et seq.

C. Any member of the Board of Pardons improperly contacted by an individual shall immediately notify the individual in writing accompanied by a copy of this Section of law that such contact is illegal and inappropriate, cease the inappropriate communication with the individual, and report the contact to the other board members.

D. Any person who violates the provisions of this Section after being informed of the inappropriate contact as provided in Subsection C of this Section shall be fined not more than five hundred dollars or imprisoned for not more than six months, or both.

E. This Section does not apply to any letter written by, or on behalf of, any victim of a crime committed by the inmate under consideration for pardon, clemency, or commutation of sentence, or any letter written in opposition to pardon, clemency, or commutation of sentence. The exception provided by this Subsection shall not apply to any elected or appointed public official.

F. The Board of Pardons shall adopt rules and regulations to provide for uniform notification procedures pursuant to Subsection C of this Section, and a method of documenting which persons have received such notification.
(Added by Acts 1997 No. 821, §1, eff. 8/15/97.)

§573.2. Telephone communications by certain persons.

Notwithstanding any law to the contrary the crime victim or the victim's family, a victim advocacy group, and the district attorney or his representatives, may appear before the Board of Pardons by means of telephone communication from the office of the local district attorney.
(Added by Acts 1997 No. 870, §1, eff. 8/15/97.)

§574. Adoption of rules by Board of Pardons.

The Board of Pardons may adopt for its governance such rules as it may deem proper, not contrary to law; provided that the board shall not take up for consideration any application for a pardon, until the district attorney of the parish in which the person applying for the pardon shall have been convicted, shall have been notified, and shall have had ample opportunity to attend the session at which said application shall be considered. In addition, the board shall not take up any consideration of an application for a pardon until it has made reasonable efforts to contact the victim or the surviving family members of the victim, including correspondence mailed at least ten days prior to the date of the hearing to the last known address of the victim or the surviving family members of the victim, and it has notified the Crime Victims Services Bureau of the Department of Public Safety and Corrections. *(Chgd. by Acts 1997 No. 828, §1, eff. 8/15/97.)*

§574.1. Expenses of members of Board of Pardons; reimbursement.

Members of the Board of Pardons, whose expenses are not now provided for by law, shall be reimbursed their actual traveling expenses and hotel bills incurred in attending meetings of the Board of Pardons. The reimbursement shall be made on the warrant of the member, in the same manner and from the same source as that from which he receives his salary.

PART II. PAROLE

(1) BOARD OF PAROLE AND RULES OF PAROLE

§574.2. Board of Parole; membership; qualifications; vacancies; compensation; domicile; venue; meetings; quorum; panels; powers and duties; transfer of property to board; representation of applicants before the board; prohibitions.

A. (1) A Board of Parole, hereinafter referred to as "the board", is hereby created in the Department of Public Safety and Corrections. It shall consist of seven members appointed by the governor, one of whom shall be the chairman of the board, and all of whom shall serve at the pleasure of the governor. One of the seven members shall be appointed from a list of at least three names submitted by Victims and Citizens Against Crime, Inc. Each appointment by the governor shall be submitted to the Senate for confirmation.

(2) Each member shall devote full time to the duties of his office and shall not engage in any other business or profession or hold any other public office.

(3) The chairman of the board shall receive an annual salary of forty-two thousand dollars and each of the other members of the board shall receive an annual salary of thirty-six thousand dollars payable on his own warrant, and shall be reimbursed for necessary travel and other expenses actually incurred in the discharge of his duties.

B. (1) The domicile of the board shall be in the parish of East Baton Rouge, city of Baton Rouge, Louisiana. The board shall meet in a minimum of three-member panels at the adult correctional institutions on regular scheduled dates, not less than every three months. Such dates are to be determined by the chairman. Three votes of a three-member panel shall be required to grant parole, or, if the number exceeds a three-member panel, a unanimous vote of those present shall be required to grant parole.

(2) Venue in any action in which an individual committed to the Department of Public Safety and Corrections contests any action of the board is East Baton Rouge Parish. Venue in a suit contesting the actions of the board shall be controlled by this Part and R.S. 15:571.15 and not the Code of Criminal Procedure, Title XXXI-A, Post Conviction Relief, or Title IX, Habeas Corpus, regardless of the captioned pleadings stating the contrary.

C. In accordance with the provisions of this Part, the Board of Parole shall have the following powers and duties:

(1) To determine the time and conditions of release on parole of any person who has been convicted of a felony and sentenced to imprisonment, and confined in any penal or correctional institution in this state.

(2) To determine and impose sanctions for violation of the conditions of parole.

(3) To keep a record of its acts and to notify each institution of its decisions relating to the persons who are or have been confined therein.

(4) To transmit annually, on or before the first day of February, a report to the secretary of public safety and corrections, for inclusion in his report to the governor, which report shall include statistical and other data with respect to the determinations and work of the board for the preceding calendar year, research studies which the board may make of sentencing, parole or related functions, and may include a recommendation of legislation to further improve the parole system of this state.

(5) To apply to a district court to issue subpoenas, compel the attendance of witnesses, and the production of books, papers and other documents pertinent to the subject of its inquiry; to take testimony under oath, either at a hearing or by deposition; and to pay all costs in connection with the board hearings.

(6) To consider all pertinent information with respect to each prisoner who is incarcerated in any penal or correctional institution in this state at least one month prior to the parole eligible date and thereafter at such other intervals as it may determine, which information shall be a part of the inmate's consolidated summary record and which shall include:

(a) The circumstances of his offense.

(b) The reports filed under Articles 875 and 876 of the Louisiana Code of Criminal Procedure.

(c) His previous social history and criminal record.

(d) His conduct, employment, and attitude in prison.

(e) His participation in vocational training, adult education, literacy, or reading programs.

(f) Any reports of physical and mental examinations which have been made.

(7) To adopt such rules not inconsistent with law as it deems necessary and proper, with respect to the eligibility of prisoners for parole and to the conditions imposed on persons released on parole.

(8) When requested, to notify the chief of police, where such exists, and the sheriff and district attorney of the parish where the individual resides and the conviction occurred. The notification shall be in writing and shall be issued at least seven days prior to the release of any parolees residing within the jurisdiction of the agency.

(9)(a) To notify the victim, or the spouse or next of kin of a deceased victim, when the offender is scheduled for a parole hearing. The notification shall be in writing and sent no less than thirty days prior to the hearing date. The written notice shall advise the victim, spouse, or next of kin, that the hearing is open to the public, that he or she may remain in the hearing room during the entire hearing, and that he or she may speak to the Board of Parole prior to its making a decision in the case. The written notice is not required when the victim, the spouse, or next of kin advises the board in writing that such notification is not desired.

(b) To mail written notification to the injured victim at his last known address at least seven days prior to the hearing before the Board of Parole. The written notice shall inform the victim that the Board of Parole hearing is public, and the victim can present testimony to the board. The notice shall also indicate that the victim can be present during the proceedings, as long as he conducts himself properly, and does not cause a disturbance which interrupts the hearing.

(10) To adopt rules and regulations to encourage voluntary participation by inmates committed to the Department of Public Safety and Corrections in vocational training, adult education, literacy, and reading programs, through programs established by the department under R.S. 15:828(B). The rules and regulations may include provisions for accelerated parole release time, in addition to the provisions of R.S. 15:574.4(A)(1), for persons who are not otherwise ineligible in R.S. 15:574.4(B) and who are otherwise eligible, but no offender shall receive more than ten additional days per month or one hundred eighty days total accelerated parole release time for program participation.

(11) To sanction the applicant's disorderly, threatening, or insolent behavior, or use of insulting, abusive, or obscene language or written communication in connection with the

application before the board. A decision to sanction may result in the immediate and unfavorable termination of the proceedings and the applicant's right to make future application for parole may be suspended for not more than two years. The applicant shall be informed of the sanction of the board at the commencement of the proceedings.

(12) To adopt such rules as it deems necessary and proper with respect to the conduct of parole hearings for the purpose of excluding any person or persons in order to protect the privacy of the victim or victims during parole hearings.

D. The Board of Parole established by Act No. 162 of 1952, as last amended by Act No. 90 of 1967, is hereby abolished and all books, papers, records, monies and other property heretofore used or possessed by said board shall be transferred to the Board of Parole established by the provisions of this Part.

E. (1) The following persons shall not represent any applicant directly or indirectly, before the board:

(a) The executive counsel to the governor.

(b) The executive secretary to the governor.

(c) Any member of the immediate staff of the governor.

(d) Any member of a law firm, law partnership, or law corporation of which a member, associate, or partner is the executive counsel to the governor, the executive secretary to the governor, or a member of the immediate staff of the governor.

(2) If an executive counsel, executive secretary, or member of the immediate staff of the governor violates the provisions of this Subsection, such person shall forfeit the office or position held and all emoluments of the office or position. In addition, if a member of a law firm, partnership, or corporation of which such a person is a member, associate, or partner, violates the provisions of this Subsection, the office or position held with the governor and all emoluments of said office or position shall be forfeited.

F. (1) On and after August 15, 1997, no member of the Board of Parole shall transmit any correspondence to, or otherwise confer with, a judge before whom a convicted offender is awaiting sentence to request or recommend any action relating to the sentence imposed upon the offender.

(2) Violation of the provisions of this Subsection shall immediately disqualify the member from serving on the board and a vacancy shall be declared.

(3) However, no decision of the board shall be nullified or otherwise affected by the participation of a member who has violated this Subsection, except as to a decision that involves the offender or any decision rendered after the board is notified of the violation and the violation is determined to have occurred.

(Chgd. by Acts 1990 No. 670, §1; Acts 1991 No. 116, §1, No. 766, §1, No. 1012, §1; Acts 1995 No. 303, §1, No. 1011, §1; Acts 1997 No. 730, §1, No. 960, §1, No. 1196, §1, No. 1273, §1, eff. 8/15/97, No. 1358, §1, eff. 7/15/97.)

§574.2.1. Prohibited contact with Board of Parole; penalties; public record.

A. Notwithstanding the provisions of R.S. 15:574.12, or any other provision of law to the contrary, no person shall contact or communicate with the Board of Parole or any of its members urging parole, or otherwise regarding any inmate except in the following ways:

(1) In an open hearing as provided in this Part.

(2) By written letter addressed to the Board of Parole.

B. Any communication with the Board of Parole regarding an inmate as provided in Paragraph A(2) of this Section shall be deemed a public record and subject to public inspection as provided by the provisions of R.S. 44:1 et seq.

C. Any member of the Board of Parole improperly contacted by an individual shall immediately notify the individual in writing accompanied by a copy of this Section of law that such contact is illegal and inappropriate, cease the inappropriate communication with the individual, and report the contact to the other board members.

D. Any person who violates the provisions of this Section after being informed of the inappropriate contact as provided in Subsection C of this Section shall be fined not more than five hundred dollars or imprisoned for not more than six months, or both.

E. This Section does not apply to any letter written by, or on behalf of, any victim of a crime committed by the inmate eligible for parole, or any letter written in opposition to the inmate's being placed on parole. The exception provided by this Subsection shall not apply to any elected or appointed public official.

F. The Board of Parole shall adopt rules and regulations to provide for uniform notification procedures pursuant to Subsection C of this Section, and a method of documenting which persons have received such notification.
(Added by Acts 1997 No. 821, §1, eff. 8/15/97.)

§574.3. Personnel and reports to be furnished by the Department of Public Safety and Corrections to the Board of Parole; reports to be provided to the Board of Pardons; intensive incarceration and intensive parole supervision program data compilation; annual report.

A. The Department of Public Safety and Corrections shall provide the necessary clerical and administrative personnel, equipment, office space, and facilities for the Board of Parole and its members.

B. The Department of Public Safety and Corrections shall see that every offender is interviewed and explained the rules with respect to release on parole. It shall secure all relevant data and shall assist the offender in formulating a parole plan. Whenever the board orders a parole hearing to be held, the Department of Public Safety and Corrections shall secure a report with respect to the personality of the offender, his social history, his adjustment to authority, and his prison record, and may include any recommendation with reference to the release of the offender on parole.

C. In an application for pardon or commutation, the Department of Public Safety and Corrections shall provide the Board of Pardons and the governor with such records of the facts and circumstances of the offense for which the offender was confined, the offender's past criminal record and his social history, the prison record, the physical, mental, or psychiatric condition of the offender, and any other records or other reports that may be requested.

D. The department shall compile statistical data to document successful program completions and program failures by offenders assigned to the intensive incarceration and intensive parole supervision program. The department shall utilize the statistical data to evaluate the operation of the program, define policies, and formulate eligibility standards. The secretary of the department shall establish regulations for the administration of the intensive incarceration and intensive parole supervision program.

E. The department shall prepare and submit an annual report to the legislature and to the governor, which shall include the following:

(1) An overall assessment of the intensive incarceration and intensive parole supervision program.

(2) An evaluation of the extent to which program goals and objectives are being met.

(3) A statement regarding the fiscal impact of the program.

§574.4. Parole; intensive incarceration and intensive parole supervision; eligibility for consideration; consideration and hearings; consideration of clinical reports; decisions of board; nature of parole; order of parole; conditions of parole; rules of conduct; reading proficiency test; transferred parolees; offenders convicted of crimes of violence; eligibility.

A. (1) Except as provided for in Subsection B of this Section, a person, otherwise eligible for parole, convicted of a first felony offense and committed to the Department of Public Safety and Corrections shall be eligible for parole consideration upon serving one-third of the sentence imposed; upon conviction of a second felony offense, such person shall be eligible for parole consideration upon serving one-half of the sentence imposed. A person convicted of a third or subsequent felony and committed to the Department of Public Safety and Corrections shall not be eligible for parole.

(2) (a) Notwithstanding the provisions of Paragraph A(1) of this Section, a person, otherwise eligible for parole, convicted of a nonviolent first felony offense and committed to the Department of Public Safety and Corrections, or of a nonviolent second felony offense and committed to the Department of Public Safety and Corrections but never having served time in a state prison, may be eligible for intensive parole supervision upon successful completion of intensive incarceration. The intensive incarceration and intensive parole supervision program shall be established and administered by the department. The offender may be considered for participation in the program if all of the following conditions are met:

(i) The offender is sentenced to be committed to the Department of Public Safety and Corrections to serve seven years or less.

(ii) The department, through the division of probation and parole within the office of adult services, recommends to the sentencing court that the offender is particularly likely to respond affirmatively to participation in the program.

(iii) The court at sentencing recommends that the offender be considered for participation in the program.

(iv) The secretary of the department, or his designee, finds, after an evaluation, that the offender is particularly likely to respond affirmatively to participation in the program.

(v) The offender voluntarily enrolls in the program after having been advised by the department of rules and regulations governing participation in the program.

(b) Notwithstanding the provisions of Paragraph A(1) of this Section, an offender who is otherwise eligible for intensive incarceration and intensive parole supervision, but who has not been recommended for participation in the intensive incarceration and intensive parole supervision program by the division of probation and parole of the office of adult services and the sentencing judge, as provided for in Paragraphs A(2)(a)(ii) and (iii) of this Section, may additionally be placed in the intensive incarceration and intensive parole supervision program if all of the following conditions are met:

(i) The staff at the adult reception and diagnostic center, after a thorough evaluation, determines that the offender is suitable and appropriate for participation.

(ii) The warden at the adult reception and diagnostic center concurs with the staff recommendation.

(iii) The warden of the facility where the offender would be placed concurs with the recommendation of the staff and warden of the adult reception and diagnostic center.

(iv) The offender meets other conditions of participation as set forth in Paragraphs A(2)(a)(i), (iv), and (v) of this Section.

(c) (i) Notwithstanding the provisions of Paragraph A(1), a person, otherwise eligible for parole, convicted of a first felony offense and committed to the Department of Public Safety and Corrections, or of a second felony offense and committed to the Department of Public Safety and Corrections but never having served time in a state prison, may be eligible for intensive parole supervision upon successful completion of intensive incarceration. The intensive incarceration and intensive parole supervision program shall be established and administered by the department.

(ii) The court may sentence an offender directly to the program if the court commits the offender to the Department of Public Safety and Corrections to serve seven years or less.

(d) For purposes of this Section, a "first offender" shall not have been convicted previously of another felony as provided in R.S. 15:572(C) and shall not have been granted an automatic pardon as provided in R.S. 15:572(B).

(e) The duration of intensive incarceration shall not be less than one hundred eighty calendar days.

(f) The participating offender shall be evaluated by the program staff on a continual basis throughout the entire period of intensive incarceration. The evaluation shall include the offender's performance while incarcerated, the likelihood of successful adjustment on parole, and other factors deemed relevant by the Board of Parole or the program staff. The evaluation shall provide the basis for the recommendations by the department to the Board of Parole upon the offender's completion of intensive incarceration. Violation of any institutional or program rules or regulations may subject the participant to removal from the program by the department.

(g) (i) If an offender is denied entry into the intensive incarceration program for physical or mental health reasons or for failure to meet the department's suitability criteria, the department shall notify the sentencing court, and based upon the court's order, shall either return the offender to court for resentencing in accordance with the provisions of the Code of Criminal Procedure Art. 881.1 or return the offender to a prison to serve the remainder of his sentence as provided by law.

(ii) If an offender enters the intensive incarceration program and is subsequently removed for physical or mental health reasons or for failure to meet the department's suitability criteria, the department shall notify the sentencing court and, based upon the court's order, shall either return the offender to court for resentencing in accordance with the provisions of Code of Criminal Procedure Article 881.1 or return the offender to a prison to serve the remainder of his sentence as provided by law. If an offender enters the intensive incarceration program and is removed for violating any institutional or program rules or regulations, the offender shall be assigned to the general population to serve the remainder of his sentence as provided by law.

(h) When an offender completes intensive incarceration, the Board of Parole shall review the case of the offender and recommend either that the offender be released on intensive parole supervision or that the offender serve the remainder of his sentence as provided by law. When the offender is released to intensive parole supervision by the board, the board shall require the offender to comply with the following conditions of intensive parole supervision in addition to any other conditions of parole ordered by the board:

(i) Be subject to multiple weekly visits with his supervising officers without prior notice.

(ii) Abide by any curfew set by his supervising officers.

(iii) Perform at least one hundred hours of unpaid community service work during the period of intensive parole supervision and, if unemployed, perform additional hours as instructed by his supervising officers.

(iv) Refrain from using or possessing any controlled dangerous substance or alcoholic beverage and submit, at his own expense, to screening, evaluation, and treatment for controlled dangerous substance or alcohol abuse as directed by his supervising officers.

(v) Pay any costs as ordered by the sentencing court or Board of Parole.

(i) In cases in which the Board of Parole determines that there is victim opposition to parole, that the offender has a questionable disciplinary record, or that other extraordinary circumstances exist, the board may conduct a hearing to consider intensive parole supervision for the offender having successfully completed intensive incarceration, which shall be public and conducted in the same manner as parole hearings as otherwise provided in this Part. Otherwise the decision shall be made upon the approval or disapproval of a majority of the members of the board without necessity of a hearing, after a review of all available information on the offender, including the pre-parole report prepared by the department.

(3) Notwithstanding the provisions of Paragraph (A)(1) or any other law to the contrary, unless eligible for parole at an earlier date, a person committed to the Department of Public Safety and Corrections for a term or terms of imprisonment with or without benefit of parole for thirty years or more shall be eligible for parole consideration upon serving at least twenty years of the term or terms of imprisonment in actual custody and upon reaching the age of forty-five. This provision shall not apply to a person serving a life sentence unless the sentence has been commuted to a fixed term of years.

B. No person shall be eligible for parole consideration who has been convicted of armed robbery and denied parole eligibility under the provisions of R.S. 14:64. No prisoner serving a life sentence shall be eligible for parole consideration until his life sentence has been commuted to a fixed term of years. No prisoner may be paroled while there is pending against him any indictment or information for any crime suspected of having been committed by him while a prisoner. Notwithstanding any other provisions of law to the contrary, a person convicted of a crime of violence and not otherwise ineligible for parole shall serve at least eighty-five percent of the sentence imposed, before being eligible for parole. The victim or victim's family shall be notified whenever the offender is to be released.

C. (1) At such intervals as it determines, the board or a member thereof shall consider all pertinent information with respect to each prisoner eligible for parole, including the nature and circumstances of the prisoner's offense, his prison records, the presentence investigation report, any recommendations of the chief probation and parole officer, and any information and reports of data supplied by the staff. A parole hearing shall be held if, after such consideration, the board determines that a parole hearing is appropriate or if such hearing is requested in writing by its staff.

(2) (a) In cases where the offender has been convicted of a violation of any provision of R.S. 14:92(A)(7), Subpart C of Part II, Subpart B of Part IV, or Subpart A(1) or A(4) of Part V of Chapter 1 of Title 14 of the Louisiana Revised Statutes of 1950, and parole is permitted by law and the offender is otherwise eligible, the board shall consider reports, assessments, and clinical information, as available, including any testing and recommendations by mental health professionals, as to all of the following:

(i) Whether the offender has successfully completed the sex offender program.

(ii) Whether, in the expert's opinion, there is a likelihood that the offender will or will not repeat the criminal conduct and that the offender will or will not be a danger to society.

(b) The board shall render its decision ordering or denying the release of the prisoner on parole only after considering this clinical evidence where such clinical evidence is available.

D. (1) The parole hearings shall be conducted in a formal manner in accordance with the rules formulated by the board and with the provisions of this Part. Before the parole of any prisoner is ordered, such prisoner shall appear before and be interviewed by the board, except those incarcerated in parish prisons or parish correctional centers, in which case one board member may conduct the interview. The board may order a reconsideration of the case or a rehearing at any time.

(2) The crime victim or the victim's family, a victim advocacy group, and the district attorney or his representatives, may appear before the Board of Parole by means of telephone communication from the office of the local district attorney.

E. The board shall render its decision ordering or denying the release of the prisoner on parole within thirty days after the hearing. A parole shall be ordered only for the best interest of society, not as an award of clemency, and upon determination by the board that there is reasonable probability that the prisoner is able and willing to fulfill the obligations of a law-abiding citizen so that he can be released without detriment to the community or to himself.

F. All paroles shall issue upon order of the board and each order of parole shall recite the conditions thereof; provided, however, that before any prisoner is released on parole he shall be provided with a certificate of parole that enumerates the conditions of parole. These conditions shall be explained to the prisoner and the prisoner shall agree in writing to such conditions.

G. The release date of the prisoner shall be fixed by the board, but such date shall not be later than six months after the parole hearing or the most recent reconsideration of the prisoner's case.

H. (1) The Board of Parole may make rules for the conduct of persons heretofore or hereafter granted parole. When a prisoner is released on parole, the board shall require as a condition of his parole that he refrain from engaging in criminal conduct.

(2) In cases where the offender has been convicted of a violation of any provision of R.S. 14:92(A)(7), Subpart C of Part II, Subpart B of Part IV, or Subpart A(1) or A(4) of Part V of Chapter 1 of Title 14 of the Louisiana Revised Statutes of 1950, including criminal sexual offenders under the supervision and legal authority of the Department of Public Safety and Corrections pursuant to the terms and conditions of the interstate compact agreement provided for in R.S. 15:574.14, and parole is permitted by law and the offender is otherwise eligible, and when the board releases an offender on parole, and the victim was under eighteen years of age at the time of the commission of the offense, the board shall order the following:

(a) As a condition of parole, that the offender give notice of the crime for which he was convicted and paroled, his name, and address to:

(i) People who live within a one-mile radius in a rural area or a three-square block area in an urban or suburban area of the address where the offender will reside upon release on parole.

(ii) The superintendent of the school district within the designated area where the offender will reside, who shall notify the principal of whichever schools the superintendent thinks should be notified of the offender's name, address, and crime for which he was convicted and paroled. The superintendent shall also notify the principal and headmaster of each nonpublic school located within the designated area where the offender will reside. The notice sent by the superintendent shall be accompanied by two clear, recent photographs or a clear photocopy of the offender. The photographs, which shall be provided by the offender, shall be taken after release and within sufficient time to accompany the notification which is a required condition of parole.

(iii) The superintendent of the park, playground, and recreation districts within the designated area where the offender will reside, who shall notify the custodians of whichever parks, playgrounds, and recreational facilities of the offender's name, address, and the crime for which he was convicted. The notice sent by the superintendent shall be accompanied by two clear, recent photographs or a clear photocopy of the offender. The photographs, which shall be provided by the offender, shall be taken after release and within sufficient time to accompany the notification which is a required condition of parole.

(b) That the offender give notice of the crime for which he was convicted and paroled, his name, and his address, by mail, to all people residing within the designated area, including the superintendent of the park, playground, and recreation districts and the superintendent of the school district within the designated area, within thirty days of the release on parole or within thirty days of setting up residency in the locale where the offender plans to have his domicile, and that the notice be published on two separate days within this thirty-day period of time, without cost to the state, in the official journal of the governing authority of the parish where the offender will reside and in a newspaper which meets the requirements of R.S. 43:140(3) for qualification as an official journal and which has a larger or smaller circulation in the parish than the official journal. This notice which shall be provided to the superintendent of the school district, the superintendent of the park, playground, and recreational districts and the official journal and other designated newspaper shall also include a recent photograph or a clear photocopy of the offender. The board may order any other form of notice which it deems appropriate, including but not limited to signs, handbills, bumper stickers, or clothing labeled to that effect.

(c) For offenders who will reside in the parish of St. Tammany, the board may order that the notice be published in a newspaper which meets the requirements of R.S. 43:140(3) for qualification as an official journal and which has a larger circulation in the parish than the official journal.

(3) The board shall mail notice within three days after it makes a decision to release a sexual offender, as enumerated and pursuant to the circumstances in Paragraph (2) of this Subsection, on parole. The notice shall contain the address where the defendant will reside, a statement that the offender will be released on parole, and the date he will be released and shall be mailed to the victim or the victim's parent or guardian if the victim or a relative was not present at the parole hearing of the offender, and the notice shall be sent to their last known address by registered or certified letter, unless the victim or relative has signed a written waiver of notification.

(4) The board may also require, either at the time of his release on parole or at any time while he remains on parole, that he conform to any of the following conditions of parole which are appropriate to the circumstances of the particular case:

(a) Report immediately to the division of probation and parole office, Department of Public Safety and Corrections, which is listed on the face of the certificate of parole.

(b) Remain within the limits fixed by the certificate of parole. If he has good cause to leave these limits, he will obtain written permission from the parole officer and the approval of the division of probation and parole before doing so.

(c) Between the first and fifth days of each month, until his final release, and also on the final day of his parole, make a full and truthful written report upon the form provided for that purpose and that he will take or mail his report to his parole officer. He will report to the probation and parole officer when directed to do so.

(d) Avoid injurious or vicious habits and places of disreputable or harmful character.

(e) Will not associate with persons known to be engaged in criminal activities or with persons known to have been convicted of a felony, without written permission of his parole officer.

(f) In all respects conduct himself honorably, work diligently at a lawful occupation, and support his dependents, if any, to the best of his ability.

(g) Promptly and truthfully answer all inquiries directed to him by the probation and parole officer.

(h) Live and remain at liberty and refrain from engaging in any type of criminal conduct.

(i) Live and work at the places stated in his parole plan and not change residence or employment until after he has permission to do so from his parole officer.

(j) Shall not have in his possession or control any firearms or dangerous weapons.

(k) Submit himself to available medical, psychiatric, mental health, or substance abuse examination or treatment or both when deemed appropriate and ordered to do so by the probation and parole officer.

(*l*) Waive extradition to the state of Louisiana from any jurisdiction in or outside the United States where he may be found and also agree that he will not contest any effort by any jurisdiction to return him to the state of Louisiana.

(m) Will be subject to visits by his parole officer at his home or place of employment without prior notice.

(n) Such other specific conditions as are appropriate, stated directly and without ambiguity so as to be understandable to a reasonable man.

(*o*) Defray the cost, or any portion thereof, of his parole supervision by making payments to the Board of Parole in a sum and manner determined by the board, based upon his ability to pay.

(p) Perform at least one hundred hours of unpaid community service work during the period of parole supervision and, if unemployed, perform additional hours as instructed by his supervising officers.

(q) Devote himself to an approved reading program at his cost if he is unable to read the English language.

(5) No offender, who is the parent, stepparent, or has legal custody and physical custody of the child who is the victim, shall be released on parole unless the victim has received psychological counseling prior to the offender's release if the offender is returning to the

residence or community in which the child resides. Such psychological counseling shall include an attempt by the health care provider to ease the psychological impact upon the child of the notice required under Paragraph (2) of this Subsection, including assisting the child in coping with potential insensitive comments and actions by the child's neighbors and peers. The cost of such counseling shall be paid by the offender.

I. At the time these written conditions are given, the board shall notify the parolee that:

(1) If he is arrested while on parole, the board has the authority to place a detainer against him which will in effect prevent him from making bail pending any new charges against him; and

(2) Should his parole be revoked for any reason, good time earned prior to parole and good time that would have been earned if parole had not been granted will be forfeited, as required by R.S. 15:571.4.

J. (1) When a victim of the crime for which parole is being considered has suffered a direct pecuniary loss other than damage to or loss of property, the parole board may impose as a condition of parole that restitutions to the victim be made. When such a condition is imposed, the board shall take into account the defendant's ability to pay and shall not revoke parole based upon this condition unless the parolee has willfully failed to comply. When the victim's loss consists of damage to or loss of property, the board shall impose as a condition of parole payment of restitution, either in a lump sum or in monthly installments based on the earning capacity and assets of the defendant. If the victim was paid for such property loss or damage with monies from the Crime Victims Reparations Fund, the board shall order the parolee to make such payments as reimbursement to the fund in the same amount as was paid from the fund to the victim. This condition of parole shall continue until such time as the restitution is paid or the parolee is discharged from parole in accordance with R.S. 15:574.6.

(2) Nothing herein shall affect a victim's civil remedy except that funds actually received shall be credited to any civil judgment arising out of the same offense.

K. If the prisoner has not paid and is liable for any costs of court or costs of the prosecution or proceeding in which he was convicted or any fine imposed as a part of his sentence, the Board of Parole shall require as a condition of parole the payment of such costs or fine, either in a lump sum or according to a schedule of payments established by the board and based upon the prisoner's ability to pay.

L. *(Repealed.)*

M. Before the Board of Parole places a person on parole, the board shall determine if he has a high school degree or its equivalent and, if he does not, the board shall condition parole upon the parolee's enrolling in and attending an adult education or reading program until he obtains a GED, or until he completes such educational programs required by the board, and has attained a sixth grade reading level, or until his term of parole expires, whichever occurs first. All costs shall be paid by the parolee. If the board finds that there are no adult education or reading programs in the parish in which the parolee is domiciled, the parolee is unable to afford such a program, or attendance would create an undue hardship on the parolee, the board may suspend this condition of parole. The provisions of this Subsection shall not apply to those parolees who are mentally, physically, or by reason of age, infirmity, dyslexia, or other such learning disorders, unable to participate.

N. The collection of the supervision fee imposed pursuant to R.S. 15:574.4(H)(15) shall be suspended upon the transfer of an offender to another state for parole supervision in that state, pursuant to the interstate compact for out of state parolee supervision as provided in R.S. 15:574.14.

O. (1) Before having a parole hearing for any offender who has been convicted of a violation of any provision of R.S. 14:92(A)(7), Subpart C of Part II, Subpart B of Part IV, or Subpart A(1) or A(4) of Part V of Chapter 1 of Title 14 of the Louisiana Revised Statutes of 1950, when the victim was under eighteen years of age at the time of the offense, when the law permits parole consideration for that offense, and when according to law an offender convicted of one of those offenses is otherwise eligible for parole, the board shall give written notice of the date and time of the parole hearing at least three days prior to the hearing to the victim or the victim's parent or guardian, unless the victim, parent, or guardian has advised the Board of Parole in writing that such notification is not desired.

(2) The victim or the victim's parent or guardian who desires to do so shall be given a reasonable opportunity to attend the hearing and to be heard.

P. If a person who is otherwise eligible for intensive parole supervision pursuant to Paragraph (2) of Subsection A of this Section, has been convicted of one of the sexual offenses enumerated in Paragraph (2) of Subsection H and Paragraph (1) of Subsection O of this

Section and the intensive parole supervision is applicable to any of those enumerated crimes, then Subsections H and O of this Section shall apply.

Q. If a person, who is otherwise eligible for diminution of sentence for good behavior pursuant to R.S. 15:571.3, has been convicted of one of the sexual offenses enumerated in Paragraph (2) of Subsections H and O of this Section and the diminution of sentence for good behavior is applicable to any of those enumerated crimes, then Paragraphs (2) and (3) of Subsection H of this Section shall apply.

(Chgd. by Acts 1990 No. 566, §1, No. 790, §1; Acts 1991 No. 119, §1; Acts 1992 No. 413, §1, No. 962, §2, No. 1122, §1; Acts 1993 No. 484, §1, No. 671, §1, No. 678, §1, No. 874, §1, No. 922, §1; Acts 1994 Third Ex. Sess. No. 58, §1; Acts 1995 No. 605, §2, No. 1099, §1, No. 1290, §2, No. 1303, §1; Acts 1997 No. 134, §2, No. 137, §2, No. 820, §1, No. 870, §1, eff. 8/15/97, No. 1148, §2, eff. 7/14/97, No. 1396, §1, eff. 7/15/97.)

§574.5. Intensive incarceration and parole supervision of persons held by sheriffs in eligible parishes.

A. An offender sentenced to the custody of the Department of Public Safety and Corrections but held by the sheriff of an eligible parish, as defined in Subsection E, and who is otherwise eligible for the intensive incarceration and parole supervision program of the department as provided for in R.S. 15:574.4, may be considered for an intensive incarceration program administered by the sheriff of that parish if all the following conditions are met:

(1) The offender is sentenced to be committed to the department to serve seven years or less.

(2) The court at sentencing recommends that the offender be considered for participation in an intensive incarceration and parole supervision program.

(3) The sheriff's office of the parish finds, after an evaluation, that the offender is particularly likely to respond affirmatively to participation in such a program.

(4) The offender voluntarily enrolls in such a program after having been advised by the sheriff's office of the rules and regulations governing participation in such a program.

B. The provisions of the intensive incarceration program of the department as set forth in R.S. 15:574.4(A) and Code of Criminal Procedure Article 901.1 shall apply to any intensive incarceration program administered by the sheriff of any eligible parish except for the following:

(1) The duration of any intensive incarceration shall not be less than ninety nor more than one hundred eighty calendar days.

(2) The participating offender shall be evaluated by the program staff of the sheriff conducting the program on a continual basis throughout the entire period of intensive incarceration. The evaluation shall include the offender's performance while incarcerated, the likelihood of successful adjustment on parole, and other factors deemed relevant by the Board of Parole and the program staff. The evaluation shall provide the basis for recommendations by the sheriff's office to the Board of Parole upon the offender's successful completion of any intensive incarceration program. Violation of any institutional or program rules or regulations may subject the participant to removal from an intensive incarceration program.

(3) Upon completion of any intensive incarceration program, the Board of Parole shall review the case of the offender and recommend that the offender by released on intensive parole supervision or that the offender serve the remainder of his sentence as provided by law.

C. Notwithstanding the provisions of R.S. 15:574.4(A)(1), offenders who have successfully completed an intensive incarceration program as provided for in this Section shall be eligible for intensive parole supervision as provided for in R.S. 15:574.4(A)(2).

D. In the event an offender sentenced to be committed to the custody of the department participates in an intensive incarceration program of any eligible parish, the sheriff's office shall be reimbursed by the department for his participation in the program in the amount appropriated by the legislature.

E. As used in this Section, "eligible parish" means a parish with a population of five hundred thousand persons as determined by the latest United States census.

§574.6. Parole term; automatic discharge.

The parole term, when the board orders a prisoner released on parole, shall be for the remainder of the prisoner's sentence, without any diminution of sentence for good behavior. When the parolee has completed his full parole term, he shall be discharged from parole by the Department of Public Safety and Corrections without any order of the board, provided that:

(1) No warrant has been issued by the board for the arrest of the parolee.

(2) No detainer has been issued by the parole officer for the detention of the parolee pending revocation proceedings.

(3) No indictment or bill of information is pending for any felony the parolee is suspected to have committed while on parole.

(Chgd. by Acts 1991 No. 117, §1, eff. 9/6/91.)

§574.7. Custody and supervision of parolees; modification or suspension of supervision; violation of conditions of parole; sanctions; alternative conditions.

A. Each parolee shall remain in the legal custody of the Department of Public Safety and Corrections, office of corrections services, and shall be subject to the orders and supervision of the board. At the direction of the board, the chief probation and parole officer shall be responsible for the investigation and supervision of all parolees. The board may modify or suspend such supervision upon a determination that a parolee who had conducted himself in accordance with the conditions of his parole no longer needs the guidance and supervision originally imposed.

B. (1) If the chief probation and parole officer, upon recommendation by a parole officer, has reasonable cause to believe that a parolee has violated the conditions of parole, he shall notify the board, and shall cause the appropriate parole officer to submit the parolee's record to the board. After consideration of the record submitted, and after such further investigation as it may deem necessary, the board may order:

(a) The issuance of a reprimand and warning to the parolee.

(b) That the parolee be required to conform to one or more additional conditions of parole which may be imposed in accordance with R.S. 15:574.4.

(c) That the parolee be arrested, and upon arrest be given a prerevocation hearing within a reasonable time, at or reasonably near the place of the alleged parole violation or arrest, to determine whether there is probable cause to detain the parolee pending orders of the parole board.

(2) Upon receiving a summary of the prerevocation proceeding, the board may order the following:

(a) The parolee's return to the physical custody of the Department of Public Safety and Corrections, office of corrections services, to await a hearing to determine whether his parole should be revoked.

(b) As an alternative to revocation, that the parolee, as a condition of parole, be committed to a community rehabilitation center or a substance abuse treatment program operated by, or under contract with, the department, for a period of time not to exceed six months, without benefit of good time, provided that such commitment does not extend the period of parole beyond the full parole term. Upon written request of the department that the offender be removed for violations of the rules or regulations of the community rehabilitation center or substance abuse program, the board shall order that the parole be revoked, with credit for time served in the community rehabilitation center.

(Chgd. by Acts 1992 No. 301, §1, eff. 8/21/92.)

§574.8. Parole officers; powers of arrest; summary arrest and detention of parolees.

A. Incidental to the supervision of parolees, parole officers shall be deemed to be peace officers and shall have the same powers with respect to criminal matters and the enforcement of the law relating thereto as sheriffs, constables and police officers have in their respective jurisdictions. They have all the immunities and matters of defense now available or hereafter made available to sheriffs, constables and police officers in any suit brought against them in consequence of acts done in the course of their employment.

B. If a parole officer has reasonable cause to believe that a parolee has violated or is attempting to violate a condition of his parole and that an emergency exists, so that awaiting action by the board under R.S. 15:574.7 would create an undue risk to the public or to the parolee, such parole officer may arrest the parolee without a warrant, or may authorize any peace officer to do so. The authorization may be in writing or oral, but if not written, shall be subsequently confirmed by a written statement. The written authorization or subsequent confirmation shall set forth that, in the judgment of the parole officer, the person to be arrested has violated or was attempting to violate a condition of his parole. The parolee arrested hereunder shall be detained in a local jail or other detention facility, pending action by the board. Immediately after such arrest and detention, the parole officer concerned shall notify the chief probation and parole officer and submit a written report of the reason for the arrest. After consideration of the written report, the chief probation and parole officer shall, with all practicable speed, make a preliminary determination, and shall either order the parolee's release from detention or proceed promptly in accordance with R.S. 15:574.7.

§574.9. Revocation of parole for violation of condition; board panels; return to custody hearing; duration of reimprisonment and reparole after revocation; credit for time served.

A. When a parolee has been returned to the physical custody of the Department of Public Safety and Corrections, office of corrections services, the board shall hold a hearing to determine whether his parole should be revoked, unless said hearing a expressly waived in writing by the parolee. A waiver shall constitute an admission of the findings of the prerevocation proceeding and result in immediate revocation. If the revocation hearing is not waived, the parolee shall be permitted to consult with and be advised and represented by his own legal counsel or legal counsel appointed under the provisions of R.S. 15:149. At the hearing the parolee may admit, deny, or explain the violation charged, and he may present proof, including affidavits and other evidence, in support of his contentions. Upon request of the parolee, the parole board may postpone the rendering of its decision for a specified reasonable time pending receipt of further information necessary to a final determination.

B. The board may order revocation of parole upon a determination that:

(1) The parolee has failed, without a satisfactory excuse, to comply with a condition of his parole; and

(2) The violation of condition involves the commission of another felony, or misconduct indicating a substantial risk that the parolee will commit another felony, or misconduct indicating that the parolee is unwilling to comply with proper conditions of parole.

C. Other than for conviction of a felony committed while on parole, action revoking a parolee's parole and recommitting him for violation of the condition of parole must be initiated before the expiration of his parole term. When a warrant for arrest is issued by the Board of Parole or a detainer is issued by the parole officer, the running of the period of parole shall cease as of the time the warrant or detainer is issued. A parolee under supervision in this state or another state, who has absented himself from the supervising jurisdiction, or from his place of residence, without proof of permission for such absence, shall be deemed a fugitive from justice and shall be returned to the physical custody of the Department of Public Safety and Corrections for a revocation hearing by the Board of Parole, without necessity of a prerevocation or probable cause hearing, at or near the place of the arrest or violation. No credit shall be applied toward completing the full parole term for the period of time the parolee was a fugitive from justice.

D. Parole revocation shall require two votes of a three-member panel of parole board members or, if the number of members present exceeds a three-member panel, a majority vote of those members present and voting, and the order of revocation shall be reduced to writing and preserved.

E. When the parole of a parolee has been revoked by the board for the violation of the conditions of parole, the parolee shall be returned to the physical custody of the Department of Public Safety and Corrections, office of corrections services, and serve the remainder of his sentence as of the date of his release on parole, subject to consideration by the board of any commutation of the sentence, and any diminution of sentence earned for good behavior while in the institution. The parolee shall be given credit for time served prior to the revocation hearing whether such time is served in a local detention facility, state institution, or out-of-state institution, except that the parolee shall not receive credit for such time served prior to the revocation hearing where such hearing does not result in revocation, or the revocation is based on the subsequent conviction of a crime, in which case the parolee will receive credit for time served for the subsequent conviction pursuant to Code of Criminal Procedure Article 880.

F. Any such prisoner whose parole has been revoked may be considered by the board for re-parole in accordance with the provisions of this Part.

(Chgd. by Acts 1990 No. 330, §1; Acts 1991 No. 116, §1, No. 118, §1; Acts 1995 No. 1011, §1, eff. 8/15/95.)

§574.10. Conviction of a felony while on parole.

When a person is convicted in this state of a felony committed while on parole or is convicted under the laws of any other state or of the United States or any foreign government or country of an offense committed while on parole and which if committed in this state would be a felony, his parole shall be deemed revoked as of the date of the commission of the felony or such offense under the laws of the other jurisdiction. His parole officer shall inform the sentencing judge of the fact that the convicted defendant is a parole violator. The term for which the defendant shall be imprisoned as a parole violator shall be the same as that provided in cases of revocation of parole for violation of the conditions of parole. The new sentence of imprisonment shall be served consecutively to the term of imprisonment for violation of parole unless a concurrent term of imprisonment is expressly directed by the court. An appeal by the defendant on the new conviction or sentence shall not suspend the revocation provisions of this Section, unless the defendant has been admitted to post-conviction bail on the new sentence of imprisonment. In the event of a successful appeal of the new conviction or sentence, the state shall be liable for any loss of income sustained by the defendant due to such revocation of parole. *(Chgd. by Acts 1993 No. 104, §1, eff. 8/15/93.)*

§574.11. Finality of board determinations; venue.

A. Parole is an administrative device for the rehabilitation of prisoners under supervised freedom from actual restraint, and the granting, conditions or revocation of parole rest in the discretion of the Board of Parole. No prisoner or parolee shall have a right of appeal from a decision of the board regarding release or deferment of release on parole, the imposition or modification of authorized conditions of parole, the termination or restoration of parole supervision or discharge from parole before the end of the parole period, or the revocation or reconsideration of revocation of parole, except for the denial of a revocation hearing under R.S. 15:574.9.

B. Venue in any action in which an individual committed to the Department of Public Safety and Corrections contests any action of the board shall be in the parish of East Baton Rouge. Venue in a suit contesting the actions of the board shall be controlled by this Part and R.S. 15:571.15 and not the Code of Criminal Procedure, Title XXXI-A, Post Conviction Relief, or Title IX, Habeas Corpus, regardless of the captioned pleadings stating the contrary. *(Chgd. by Acts 1990 No. 670, §1, eff. 9/7/90.)*

§574.12. Information as to offenders and ex-offenders; confidentiality.

A. The presentence investigation report, the pre-parole report, the clemency report, the information and data gathered by the staffs of the boards of pardons and parole, the prison record, and any other information obtained by the boards or the Department of Public Safety and Corrections, office of corrections services, in the discharge of their official duties shall be confidential and shall not be subject to public inspection nor be disclosed directly or indirectly to anyone except as provided by this Section.

B. Information may be released upon request without special authorization to the Board of Parole, the Board of Pardons, the governor, the sentencing judge, a district attorney or law enforcement agency, the personnel and legal representatives of the Department of Public Safety and Corrections, office of corrections services, including student interns, appropriate governmental agencies, or officials when access to such information is imperative for discharge of the requesting agency's or official's responsibilities and the information is not reasonably available through any other means, and court officers with court orders specifying the information requested.

C. Fingerprints, photographs and information pertaining to arrests and dispositions of criminal charges may be released to criminal justice agencies without special authorization.

D. The secretary of the Department of Public Safety and Corrections or his designated representative may approve the reading of confidential information by the following:

(1) Social service agencies assisting in the treatment of the offender or ex-offender.

(2) Approved researchers who have guaranteed in writing anonymity of all subjects.

E. The secretary of the Department of Public Safety and Corrections or his designated representative may approve the selective reading of information to a private citizen or organization aiding in the rehabilitation of an offender or ex-offender or directly involved in the hiring of the offender or ex-offender under the following conditions:

(1) It appears that the withholding of the information would be to the offender's or ex-offender's disadvantage.

(2) The requested information is necessary to further the rehabilitation or the likelihood of hiring the offender or ex-offender.

(3) The requested information is not reasonably available through other means.

(4) The offender or ex-offender has given his written consent to the release of the information.

F. (1) Whenever records covered by this Section are subpoenaed, the records shall be submitted to the appropriate court for a ruling as to whether the information should be turned over to the party who caused the subpoena to be issued. The court shall make this determination in camera. Should the court find:

(a) That the information is not relevant to the proceedings, or

(b) That the information was derived from communications which were obviously made in the confidence that they would not be disclosed, or

(c) That confidentiality is essential to future useful relations between the source and the recorder of the information,

the information shall be withheld.

(2) Should the court authorize disclosure of the records in accordance with the subpoena, the party who caused the subpoena to be issued shall pay a fee for the cost of production of the records in accordance with R.S. 39:241, unless the court determines that the party has been granted pauper status in accordance with law.

G. (1)(a) Notwithstanding the provisions of Subsection (A) of this Section, following an application for pardon or parole, all information pertaining to an individual's misconduct while incarcerated, statistical information, information pertaining to disposition of criminal charges and incarcerations, and information of a general nature including an individual's age, offense, date of conviction, length of sentence, any correspondence by a public official which requests, or may be determined to be in support of, or in opposition to, the pardon or parole of an individual, and discharge date shall be released to the general public at any time upon request.

(b) Each piece of correspondence by a public official which requests, or may be determined to be in support of, or in opposition to, the pardon or parole of an individual shall be recorded in a central register by the board which received the correspondence. The register shall contain the name of the individual whose pardon or parole is the subject of the letter, the name of the public official who is the author of the letter, and the date the letter was received by the board.

(2) The provisions of Paragraph (1) shall not apply to any correspondence submitted which requests, or may be determined to be in support of, or in opposition to, the pardon or parole of an individual received before August 15, 1997.

H. The secretary of the Department of Public Safety and Corrections is authorized to establish rules and regulations to provide for the orderly administration of this Section.

I. It shall be a misdemeanor, punishable by a fine of not more than two thousand dollars or imprisonment for not more than one year, or both, for any member of the boards of pardon and parole or their employees to make public any confidential information.

(Chgd. by Acts 1997 No. 1273, §1, eff. 8/15/97.)

§574.13. General applicability; juveniles in correctional institutions excepted.

A. The provisions of this Part shall apply to all persons who, on July 31, 1968, are sentenced to or serving prison sentences, are on parole, or are eligible to be placed on parole, with the same force and effect as if it had been in operation at the time such persons were sentenced, imprisoned, placed on parole, or became eligible to be placed on parole, as the case may be provided that prisoners on parole prior to July 31, 1968 shall continue on parole subject to the provisions of this Part.

B. The provisions of this Part shall not apply to parole from any correctional institution for juveniles now in operation or which may be established hereafter.

(2) OUT OF STATE PAROLEE SUPERVISION

§574.14. Compact for out of state parolee supervision; fees.

A. The governor of this state may enter into a compact, on behalf of the State of Louisiana with any of the United States legally joining therein in the form substantially as follows:

A COMPACT

Entered into by and among the contracting states, signatories hereto, with the consent of the Congress of the United States of America, granted by an Act entitled "An Act Granting the Consent of Congress to any two or more States to enter into Agreements or Compacts for Cooperative Effort and Mutual Assistance in the Prevention of Crime and for other purposes".

The contracting states solemnly agree:

(1) That it shall be competent for the duly constituted judicial and administrative authorities of a state party to this compact, (herein called "sending state") to permit any person convicted of an offense within that state and placed on probation or released on parole to reside in any other state party to this compact, (herein called "receiving state") while on probation or parole, if

(a) The person is in fact a resident of or has his family residing within the receiving state and can obtain employment there;

(b) Though not a resident of the receiving state and not having his family residing there, the receiving state consents to the person being sent there.

Before granting permission, opportunity shall be granted to the receiving state to investigate the home and prospective employment of the person.

A resident of the receiving state, within the meaning of this section, is one who has been an actual inhabitant of the state continuously for more than one year prior to his coming to the sending state and has not resided within the sending state more than six continuous months immediately preceding the commission of the offense for which he has been convicted.

(2) That each receiving state will assume the duties of visitation of and supervision over probationers or parolees of any sending state and in the exercise of those duties will be governed by the same standards that prevail for its own probationers and parolees.

(3) That duly accredited officers of a sending state may at all times enter a receiving state and there apprehend and retake any person on probation or parole. For that purpose no formalities will be required other than establishing the authority of the officer and the identity of the person to be retaken. All legal requirements to obtain extradition of fugitives from justice are hereby expressly waived on the part of states party hereto, as to such persons. The decision of the sending state to retake a person on probation or parole shall be conclusive upon and not reviewable within the receiving state. If at the time when a state seeks to retake a probationer or parolee there should be pending against him within the receiving state any criminal charge, or he should be suspected of having committed within the State a criminal offense, he shall not be retaken without the consent of the receiving state until discharged from prosecution or from imprisonment for the offense.

(4) That the duly accredited officers of the sending state will be permitted to transport prisoners being retaken through any and all states parties to this compact, without interference.

(5) That the governor of each state may designate an officer who, acting jointly with like officers of other contracting states, if and when appointed, shall promulgate all rules and regulations which may be deemed necessary to more effectively carry out the terms of this compact.

(6) That this compact shall become operative immediately upon its ratification by any state as between it and any other state or states so ratifying. When ratified it shall have the full force and effect of law within the state, the form of ratification to be in accordance with the laws of the ratifying state.

(7) That this compact shall continue in force and remain binding upon each ratifying state until renounced by it. The duties and obligations hereunder of a renouncing state shall continue as to parolees or probationers residing therein at the time of withdrawal until retaken or finally discharged by the sending state. Renunciation of this compact shall be by the same authority which ratified it, by sending six months' notice in writing of its intention to withdraw from the compact to the other states parties hereto.

B. It is hereby declared that the term "state" as used in this section means any one of the several states and Alaska, Hawaii, the Commonwealth of Puerto Rico, the Virgin Islands, and the District of Columbia. It is hereby recognized and further declared that pursuant to the consent and authorization contained in Section III(b) of Title 4 of the United States Code as added by Public Law 970–84th Congress, Chapter 941–2d Session, this state shall be a party to said Interstate Compact for the supervision of parolees and probationers with any additional jurisdiction legally joining therein when such jurisdiction shall have enacted said compact in accordance with the terms thereof.

C. The interstate compact administrator appointed pursuant to R.S. 15:574.14(A)(5) shall promulgate rules and regulations for the assessment of a supervision fee not to exceed one hundred dollars to be paid by an out of state offender transferred into this state for supervision, pursuant to the provisions of the Compact for Out of State Parole Supervision, as enacted in R.S. 15:574.14. The collection of the fee shall be to defray the costs associated with supervision and terms of the compact.
(Chgd. by Acts 1991 No. 119, §1, eff. 9/6/91.)

(3) VIOLATIONS OF MUNICIPAL ORDINANCES

§574.15. Power of elected state, parochial, or municipal officials to parole persons arrested for violation of municipal ordinances.

A. (1) Every elected officer of the state or any parish or municipality in the state shall have the power to parole a person who is under arrest and detention for the violation of any criminal or quasi criminal ordinance, not enumerated in Paragraph (2) of this Subsection, of any municipality in any parish, within the territorial jurisdiction of the state or parish elected officer, and within the municipality wherein the municipal officer exercises his jurisdiction, whenever any municipality has a population of more than four hundred fifty thousand inhabitants according to the census of the United States for 1980 or any subsequent year.

(2) Persons arrested for any of the following violations of municipal ordinances shall not be eligible for parole by any elected officer:

(a) Any violations of municipal ordinances defining criminal battery and assault.

(b) Any violations of other municipal ordinances including criminal trespass, criminal damage to property, or disturbing the peace, if they occurred at the arrestee's residence or if they result from an obvious domestic dispute.

(c) Any violations of Article VII of Chapter 42 of the City Code of the City of New Orleans dealing with domestic violence as enumerated below:

(i) Attempting to cause or causing physical harm to another family or household member.

(ii) Placing another family or household member in fear of physical harm.

(iii) Causing another family or household member to engage in involuntary sexual activity by force, threat of force, or duress.

(iv) Committing one or more of the following crimes against another family or household member.

(aa) Arson, of any grade.

(bb) Assault, of any grade.

(cc) Burglary, of any grade.

(dd) Criminal damage to property.

(ee) Homicide, of any grade.

(ff) Kidnapping, of any grade.

(gg) Sex offenses, of any grade.

(hh) Any offense involving stolen property.

(ii) Any weapon law violation.

(jj) Disorderly conduct.

(kk) Stalking.

(*ll*) Criminal trespass of property.

(3) The following persons shall not be eligible for parole by any elected officer:

(a) Persons arrested for two or more felony violations.

(b) Persons arrested for five or more misdemeanors or felony arrests.

(c) Persons arrested for illegal possession or carrying of a firearm.

B. (1) Any such officer may notify the parish sheriff or municipal authority detaining such a person that he desires that the person be paroled pending arraignment on his own recognizance. The officer shall notify the parish sheriff or municipal authority detaining said individual. The notice from the officer may be verbal only if the officer is contacted at his residence or office and can state an identifying number or word as may be prescribed for securing proper identification of such officer. Prior to authorizing release, the officer shall be informed of the nature of the charges pending against the intended parolee.

(2) If the officer cannot be contacted at his residence or office, the notice shall be in writing only and on a form supplied by the parish sheriff or municipal authority. The form shall contain a place for the signature of the elected officer, the identification of his elected position, the name of the person paroled, the nature of the charge pending against the person paroled, and the date the parole is requested. This written form shall be signed by the officer and all information called for therein correctly completed and the form delivered to the parish sheriff or the municipal authority either by the officer or on his behalf before any parole request may be honored.

(3) At the time of authorizing a release, the officer shall be informed of the criminal history of the intended parolee. If the authorization is verbal, then the information shall be given verbally. If the authorization is written, then the information shall be contained upon the form supplied by the parish sheriff's office or municipal authority as indicated in Paragraph (2) of this Subsection.

C. (1) For the purposes of this Section, members of the state central committee, parish executive committees, and municipal executive committees of political parties shall be deemed to be elected state, parochial, or municipal officials, as the case may be, as hereinabove set forth.

(2) For purposes of accurate recordkeeping, each of the committees listed above, shall supply the parish sheriff or municipal authority with a list of membership additions and deletions, to include the names, addresses, phone numbers and other information as requested, within thirty days of any changes in committee membership. If this information is not supplied within thirty days, the membership in question shall not be permitted to exercise any parole powers until five days after such information has been supplied to the proper authorities.

D. (1) No elected official shall have any business arrangement with a bail bonding company.

(2) In any sixty-day period if three persons paroled by an elected official granted parole power, as described in Subsections A and C, fail to appear for arraignment at the appointed time, the parish sheriff or the municipal authority may suspend the parole power of said elected official for a period of sixty days.

(Chgd. by Acts 1995 No. 918, §1, eff. 8/15/95.)

§574.16. Refusal to parole; penalty.

Should any officer of any such municipality described in R.S. 15:574.15 refuse to parole any such person or persons upon the verbal request, or otherwise, of any such officer herein mentioned, such officer of the municipality shall upon conviction before the criminal district court of such parish be condemned to pay a fine of not less than one hundred dollars, nor more than one thousand dollars, or suffer imprisonment of not less than thirty days, nor more than six months, or both, as the judge of said criminal district court of said parish shall deem expedient.

§574.17. Kenner; power of elected municipal officials to parole or release persons in custody for violations of ordinances.

A. Every elected municipal official of the city of Kenner may parole and authorize the release from custody of any person who is under arrest or in custody in the city of Kenner for the violation of any ordinance of the city of Kenner by notifying the head or acting head of the parish or municipal law enforcement agency holding the person to be released.

B. The notice from the elected official may be verbal if the elected official authorizing the release or parole is contacted at his office or his place of residence; otherwise, the notice shall be in writing on a form supplied by the office of the law enforcement agency holding the person to be released. The form shall contain a place for the elected official's signature, the name of his office, the name of the person to be released or paroled, the nature of the charge or charges pending against the person to be released, and the date his release is requested. The form shall be signed by the elected official and all information called for therein correctly completed. The form shall be delivered by the elected official, or someone acting on his behalf, to the parish or municipal officer in charge of holding or detaining the person to be released.

C. In any sixty-day period, if three persons paroled or released by an elected official described in Subsection A above fail to appear for any court proceeding of which the released person had been properly notified, the authority of that official to parole or release persons in accordance with this Section may be suspended for a period of sixty days by the chief officer of any parish or municipal law enforcement agency having jurisdiction in the city of Kenner.

§574.18. Prohibition of city council members to parole or release persons.

Notwithstanding any other law to the contrary, no member of a city council or the chief of police in a municipality with a population under eighty thousand shall have the power or authority to parole or authorize the release from custody of any person who is under arrest or in custody for the violation of an ordinance of that municipality. The chief of police shall not have the authority to suspend the parole power of the mayor or his designated magistrate of such municipality. *(Added by Acts 1991 No. 758, §1, eff. 9/6/91.)*

(4) MEDICAL PAROLE

§574.20. Medical parole program; eligibility; revocation.

A. (1) Notwithstanding the provisions of this Part or any other law to the contrary, any person sentenced to the custody of the Department of Public Safety and Corrections may, upon referral by the department, be considered for medical parole by the Board of Parole. Medical parole consideration shall be in addition to any other parole for which an inmate may be eligible, but shall not be available to any inmate who is awaiting execution or who has a contagious disease.

(2) Medical parole shall not be available to any inmate serving time for the violation of R.S. 14:30, first degree murder, or R.S. 14:30.1, second degree murder.

B. The Parole Board shall establish the medical parole program to be administered by the Department of Public Safety and Corrections. An inmate eligible for consideration for release under the program shall be any person who, because of an existing medical or physical condition, is determined by the department to be within one of the following designations:

(1) "Permanently incapacitated inmate" which shall mean any person who, by reason of an existing physical or medical condition, is so permanently and irreversibly physically incapacitated that he does not constitute a danger to himself or to society; or

(2) "Terminally ill inmate" which shall mean any person who, because of an existing medical condition, is irreversibly terminally ill, and who by reason of the condition does not constitute a danger to himself or to society.

C. The authority to grant medical parole shall rest solely with the Parole Board, and the board shall establish additional conditions of the parole in accordance with the provisions of this Subpart. The Department of Public Safety and Corrections shall identify those inmates who may be eligible for medical parole based upon available medical information. In considering an inmate for medical parole, the board may require that additional medical evidence be produced or that additional medical examinations be conducted.

D. The parole term of an inmate released on medical parole shall be for the remainder of the inmate's sentence, without diminution of sentence for good behavior. Supervision of the parolee shall consist of periodic medical evaluations at intervals to be determined by the board at the time of release.

E. If it is discovered through the supervision of the medical parolee that his condition has improved such that he would not then be eligible for medical parole under the provisions of this Subpart, the board may order that the person be returned to the custody of the Department of Public Safety and Corrections to await a hearing to determine whether his parole shall be revoked. Any person whose medical parole is revoked due to an improvement in his condition shall resume serving the balance of his sentence with credit given for the duration of the medical parole. If the person's medical parole is revoked due to an improvement in his condition shall resume serving the balance of his sentence with credit given for the duration of the medical parole. If the person's medical parole is revoked due to an improvement in his condition, and he would be otherwise eligible for parole, he may then be considered for parole under the provisions of R.S. 15:574.4. Medical parole may also be revoked for violation of any condition of the parole as established by the Parole Board.

F. The Parole Board shall promulgate such rules as are necessary to effectuate this Subpart, including rules relative to the conduct of medical parole hearings, and the conditions of medical parole release.

(Added by Acts 1990 No. 563, §1; chgd. by Acts 1993 No. 938, §1, eff. 8/15/93.)

(5) PAROLE RISK ASSESSMENT PILOT PROGRAM

§574.21. Parole risk assessment pilot program; statistical system; agency cooperation; rules promulgation.

A. The Board of Parole shall establish a parole risk assessment pilot program which shall incorporate risk assessment analysis into the parole decision making process. The risk assessment analysis shall be designed to enhance objectivity and consistency in the parole decision making process. The program shall include the development of objective parole criteria consisting of statistical evaluation of the threat to society posed by parole candidates based on past patterns of recidivism.

B. The board shall utilize in the program, an offender risk assessment scoring system designed to measure the threat of risk of new criminal activity in general and the specific threat of new violence.

C. The pilot program shall conclude on April 15, 1995, unless the legislature extends this date or establishes a similar program prior to that date. The Board of Parole shall report annually to the legislature on the progress of the program, with such information on the impact of the use of objective criteria on the parole rate, prison population levels, and public protection as may be available from the Department of Public Safety and Corrections and the Louisiana Commission on Law Enforcement and the Administration of Criminal Justice.

D. Contingent upon the availability of funding, the Department of Public Safety and Corrections and the Louisiana Commission on Law Enforcement and the Administration of Criminal Justice shall provide the necessary resources, including clerical and administrative personnel, required by the Board of Parole to establish, implement and evaluate the risk assessment pilot program. Specifically, the Department of Public Safety and Corrections, the Louisiana Commission on Law Enforcement and the Administration of Criminal Justice, the Louisiana Sentencing Commission, and the Louisiana Bureau of Criminal Identification and Information shall provide technical assistance to the Board of Parole, and shall make available all facts, records, information, data and data processing assistance required by the board.

E. The Board of Parole is hereby authorized to promulgate rules necessary to effectuate this Subpart.

(Added by Acts 1990 No. 411, §1, eff. 9/7/90.)

CHAPTER 6. LOUISIANA BUREAU OF CRIMINAL IDENTIFICATION AND INFORMATION

Section

§575. Legislature findings and objectives.

The legislature hereby finds and declares that:

(1) The improvement of public safety and sound law enforcement and administration of criminal justice requires the complete and timely collection, processing, and dissemination of available information on crime, offenders, and the operations of the criminal justice system through a centralized system.

(2) It is in the public interest that to the greatest extent possible, government agencies at all levels concerned with the detection, apprehension, prosecution, sentencing, confinement, and rehabilitation of criminal offenders share among themselves available information relating to such offenders.

(3) Available computer and communications technology now enables the coordination, collection, storage, and dissemination of relevant information heretofore dispersed in separate files throughout the state.

(4) The reduction of crime, the protection of citizens and enforcement officers, and the need to improve the efficiency of the criminal justice system mandates the development and operation of a computer-based criminal justice information system in Louisiana.

§576. Definitions.

As used in this Chapter:

(1) The term "bureau" means the Louisiana Bureau of Criminal Identification and Information.

(2) The terms "criminal history record" or "criminal history record information" means information collected by criminal justice agencies on individuals consisting of identifiable descriptions and notations of arrests, detentions, indictments, bills of information, or any formal criminal charges, and any disposition arising therefrom, including sentencing, correctional supervision, and release. The terms do not include intelligence or investigatory purposes, nor does it include any identification information which does not indicate involvement of the individual in the criminal justice system.

(3) The term "criminal justice agency" means any government agency or subunit thereof, or private agency which, through statutory authorization or a legal formal agreement with a governmental unit or agency has the power of investigation, arrest, detention, prosecution, adjudication, treatment, supervision, rehabilitation or release of persons suspected, charged, or convicted of a crime; or which collects, stores, processes, transmits, or disseminates criminal history record or crime information.

(4) The term "criminal justice system" means that body of agencies at the federal, state, or local level, which may legally arrest, detain, prosecute, adjudicate, treat, supervise, rehabilitate or release, or collect, store, process, transmit, or disseminate criminal history record or crime information.

(5) The term "criminal justice information system" means all agencies, procedures, mechanisms, media, and forms as well as the information itself which are or become involved in the origination, collection, transmittal, storage, retrieval, and dissemination of information related to offenses or offenders in Louisiana.

§577. Bureau of criminal identification and information; creation and organization.

A. There is hereby created within the Department of Public Safety as a part of the office of state police, the Louisiana Bureau of Criminal Identification and Information. The bureau shall be administered by the deputy secretary who shall employ qualified commissioned officers of the state police to supervise the activities of the bureau under such terms and conditions as he may direct. The deputy secretary may appoint such other employees and employ such consultants as he deems necessary for the efficient operation of the bureau. The Louisiana Bureau of Criminal Identification and Information shall assume the functions, powers, and duties of the Bureau of Identification which prior to July 1, 1981 operated as a part of the office of state police.

B. Within the bureau, the following sections are hereby established:

(1) Criminal Records and Identification Section.

(2) Field Services and Quality Assurance Section.

(3) Latent Fingerprint Section.

The bureau may establish such units within each section as are necessary to carry out the provisions of this Chapter.

C. All data processing and related communications needs of the bureau shall be provided by the Data Processing Center and other facilities of the Department of Public Safety unless otherwise agreed by the deputy secretary.

§578. Functions, powers, and duties of the bureau; crime laboratory.

A. The bureau shall perform the following functions:

(1) To establish and maintain a central repository of criminal history record information and to adopt regulations and procedures to prescribe the terms and conditions under which the Department of Insurance, section on fraud, and the Department of Revenue, office of alcohol and tobacco control, shall have direct access to this information and adopt regulations and procedures to prescribe the terms and conditions under which other eligible individuals or agencies may gain access to such information.

(2) To establish and implement a uniform system for reporting criminal history record information from any state or local criminal justice agency.

(3) To adopt and promulgate regulations to protect the privacy and security of criminal history record information exchanged with the bureau by any state or local criminal justice agency.

(4) To establish, maintain, and regulate a modern system of telecommunication and data processing for the efficient collection, storage, and rapid transmission of criminal history record information and relevant statistics maintained by the bureau. To serve qualified agencies concerned with the administration of criminal justice throughout the state.

(5) To establish a system of fingerprint identification and analysis for use in the maintenance of criminal history record information; to aid in official investigations by eligible agencies; and to establish identification where authorized by law.

(6) *(Repealed.)*

(7) To establish and maintain a central registry of sex offenders and to adopt regulations and procedures to prescribe the terms and conditions under which information shall be released in accordance with the provisions of R.S. 15:540 through 549.

(8) To automate the criminal histories of all persons treated in the forensic conditional release program as well as all persons committed as not guilty by reason of insanity or unrestorably incompetent to stand trial pursuant to Chapters 1 and 2 of Title XXI of the Code of Criminal Procedure, and to establish an "alert flag" on criminal information records of such persons which would appear on state police computer records, as follows:

"This subject is under the supervision of the Department of Public Safety and Corrections, division of probation and parole, pursuant to a conditional release order from the district court. If in your custody, contact the division of probation and parole immediately."

B. Upon request the bureau shall assist any sheriff, chief police officer, or any governmental unit to do the following:

(1) Establish local identification and records systems.

(2) Investigate the circumstances of any crime and the identification, apprehension, and conviction of the perpetrator or perpetrators of any crime, and for this purpose may detail any employee or employees of the bureau for any length of time the deputy secretary may deem fit.

(3) Without request the deputy secretary shall, at the direction of the governor, detail any employee or employees, for any length of time which the governor may deem fit, to investigate any crime within the state for the purpose of identifying, apprehending, and convicting the perpetrator or perpetrators.

C. For the purpose of expediting local, state, national, and international efforts in the detection and apprehension of criminals, the bureau may operate and coordinate all communication systems which may be required in the normal conduct of its duties.

D. The Louisiana Commission on Law Enforcement and the Administration of Criminal Justice shall be assigned the functions, powers, and duties of the bureau related to the gathering and dissemination of data concerning parish prison population statistics and uniform crime reports. Any assignment shall relieve the bureau of responsibility for such responsibilities and duties.

E. Upon written request, the bureau shall provide specified criminal history information to the Department of Health and Human Resources to provide for the well-being of children, as provided in R.S. 15:587.1.

F. Upon written request, the bureau shall provide mental health agencies providing treatment and supervision to patients pursuant to Chapter 1 and 2 of Title XXI of the Code of Criminal Procedure with access to criminal histories with all case disposition data. Treatment and supervision staff who have access to these criminal histories shall maintain the confidentiality of this information and shall sign a statement, to be developed by the Department of Public Safety and Corrections, which informs them of this obligation.
(Chgd. by Acts 1991 No. 509, §1; Acts 1992 No. 388, §2; Acts 1993 No. 678, §1; Acts 1994 Third Ex. Sess. No. 50, §1; Acts 1995 No. 800, §2, eff. 8/15/95, No. 1188, §1, eff. 6/29/95.)

§578.1. Pretrial diversion program for driving while intoxicated; criminal history records.

Pursuant to the provisions of R.S. 15:242, the prosecuting authority shall maintain a list of all persons arrested for a violation of R.S. 14:98, operating a vehicle while intoxicated, or a parish or municipal ordinance that prohibits operating a vehicle while intoxicated, while impaired, or while under the influence of alcohol, drugs, or any controlled dangerous substance, and placed by the prosecuting authority into a pretrial diversion program. The arrest record and placement into the pretrial diversion or intervention program shall become a public record when the person successfully completes the pretrial diversion or intervention program or is terminated from the program. Such record shall be maintained for a period of five years from the date of arrest and shall not be subject to expungement or destruction during the period. *(Added by Acts 1997 No. 714, §1, eff. 8/15/97.)*

§579. Rules and regulations.

The bureau shall issue rules and regulations, consistent with United States Department of Justice requirements, governing the maintenance of privacy and security of criminal history records; governing access to and use of records maintained by the central repository; governing restrictions to access and use by authorized agencies or individuals of any state owned or operated system of communications utilized for transmitting criminal history record information to or from the bureau; and governing the purging of any information maintained by the bureau as permitted by law.

§580. Forms; procedures; training; assistance.

The bureau shall develop, print, and distribute forms and/or related procedures and regulations for the collection of any information or statistics which it is empowered to obtain to insure the correct reporting of data to the bureau. The bureau shall provide necessary technical assistance and training to all eligible reporting agencies in the appropriate procedures for completion of all forms and for submission of all information or statistics which the bureau may require. Upon request, the deputy secretary may direct employees or agents of the bureau to assist any criminal justice agency to establish a local system of identification and record management.

§581. Authorized audits and investigations.

With the written authorization of the deputy secretary, any employee or agent of the bureau, for purpose of audit or investigation of violations of any provisions herein, or any official rule or regulation of the bureau, shall be granted access by any public or private criminal justice agency collecting, processing, storing, or maintaining any documents, or automated, microfilmed, or manual records containing, or which may reasonably be expected to be used to substantiate and verify, any information or statistics the bureau is empowered to require from such public or private criminal justice agency. Upon written authorization of the deputy secretary, any employee or agent of the bureau may enter any institution to which persons have been committed, who have been convicted of crime, or declared to be criminally insane or to be feeble-minded delinquents, to take or cause to be taken fingerprints or photographs or to make investigations relative to any person confined therein, for the purpose of obtaining information which will lead to the identification of criminals.

§582. Civil identification files.

The bureau may accept and file the names, fingerprints, photographs, and other personal identification data submitted to local criminal justice agencies by the individuals or submitted by parents on behalf of their children for the purpose of securing a more certain and easy identification in case of death, injury, loss of memory, or change in appearance. Upon the application of a person identified under the provisions of this Section to the local criminal justice agency, all data received under this Section with relation to him shall be surrendered to the requesting criminal justice agency.

§583. Transmission of information.

The bureau may transmit any information in its possession which the deputy secretary shall designate, to any person or agency eligible to receive it under any provision of this Chapter. For this purpose the bureau shall operate and coordinate a modern system of communications which may be required in the normal conduct of its duties.

§584. Cooperation with federal and other state agencies.

The bureau shall cooperate with the United States Department of Justice and other federal criminal justice agencies and with similar agencies in other states and cities toward developing a comprehensive state, interstate, national, and international system of criminal information, identification, investigation, records, and statistics.

§585. Admissibility of bureau records in evidence.

Any original record including fingerprints, pictures, photographs, other documents or data, or any copy thereof, when certified by the deputy secretary or his authorized representative, shall be admissible as evidence in all criminal cases in courts of this state. Any certified record, or copy thereof, received by the court shall be received as prima facie proof of its contents and proper and accurate collection and custody; provided, when the record is presented for admission into evidence it is accompanied by a statement signed by the deputy secretary or his authorized representative which specifies:

(1) The date on which the record was received by the bureau.
(2) The agency of origin of each record.
(3) The nature or type of record received and by what method of transfer.
(4) The date the bureau compiles the record for the purpose of evidence.
(5) The name of the bureau employee who prepares the record for admission as evidence.

§586. Authority to purge records of the central repository.

Except for the provisions of R.S. 44:9, no records of the bureau may be permanently destroyed until five years after the person identified is known or reasonably believed to be dead. Upon the official issuance of appropriate rules and regulations, the bureau may retire or remove from active dissemination to eligible agencies records of any individual beyond the age of sixty, who has had no reported criminal arrest for a period of fifteen years from the last reported official release from the criminal justice system.

§587. Duty to provide information; processing fees; Louisiana Bureau of Criminal Identification and Information.

A. (1)(a) The bureau shall make available upon request, or at such other times as the deputy secretary shall designate, to any eligible criminal justice agency and the Department of Health and Hospitals, the Department of Social Services, the Department of Insurance, the Louisiana State Racing Commission, the Senate and Governmental Affairs Committee, the secretary of the Department of Labor or his designee, the Board of River Port Pilot Commissioners, the office of financial institutions of the Department of Economic Development, the municipal or parish department or personnel responsible for reviewing applications for alcoholic beverage outlet permits, and the legislative auditor any information contained in the criminal history record and identification files of the bureau. The Department of Social Services may provide information secured pursuant to this Subsection to all federal and state agencies providing child support enforcement services.

(b) The Louisiana State Board of Private Security Examiners shall be entitled to the criminal history record and identification files of the bureau on those persons seeking to be licensed as private security guards as a means of performing background checks on those individuals. An appropriate fee not to exceed ten dollars shall be charged for furnishing said records.

(c) The Louisiana State Board of Private Investigator Examiners shall be entitled to the criminal history record and identification files of the bureau on those persons seeking to be licensed or relicensed as a private investigator as a means of performing background checks on those individuals. An appropriate fee not to exceed ten dollars shall be charged for furnishing said records. The bureau shall, upon request and after receipt of fingerprint cards or other identifying information from the Louisiana State Board of Private Investigator

Examiners, make available to the board information contained in the bureau's criminal history record and identification files, which pertains to an applicant of the board. In addition, in order to determine an applicant's eligibility or suitability for licensure under the provisions of the Private Investigators Law (R.S. 37:3501 et seq.), each applicant shall be fingerprinted and the fingerprints shall be forwarded by the bureau to the Federal Bureau of Investigation for a national criminal history record check.

(2) (a) The bureau, in accordance with its powers to regulate and to enforce provisions herein, may further restrict those agencies eligible to receive information. However, the bureau shall make available to the Department of Social Services, office of community services, all criminal history record information as defined in R.S. 15:576 related to foster and adoptive parent applicants and adult members of foster and adoptive parent households. For the purposes in this Section, the bureau shall employ such methods and procedures and shall observe such duty hours as to provide information upon request within forty-eight hours from its receipt.

(b) The bureau shall facilitate national criminal history record checks of prospective foster and adoptive parent applicants and adult members of foster and adoptive parent households by receiving and forwarding fingerprint cards to the Federal Bureau of Investigation. The Department of Social Services, office of community services, is authorized to receive and screen the results of the state and national criminal history record checks in order to determine foster or adoptive parent applicants' eligibility for certification or recertification as a placement resource for children. The department shall maintain the confidentiality of criminal history information received in accordance with applicable federal or state law.

B. Pursuant to the Administrative Procedure Act* the bureau may charge a reasonable processing fee for information provided to any agency statutorily eligible to receive this information, except another state or local law enforcement agency, pursuant to a request to assist the agency in performing a screening function as part of any regulatory or licensing scheme. Payment of the processing fee shall accompany the request for such information and shall be deposited by the bureau immediately upon receipt into the state treasury.

**R.S. 49:950 et seq.*

C. The bureau shall, upon request and after receipt of fingerprint cards or other identifying information from the state police, make available to the state police gaming division, the Louisiana Riverboat Gaming Commission, and the Louisiana Economic Development and Gaming Corporation, information contained in the bureau's criminal history record and identification files, which pertains to an applicant or prospective employee of any of them. In addition, in order to determine an applicant's suitability for a gaming or employee license under the provisions of the Louisiana Video Draw Poker Devices Control Law (R.S. 33:4862.1 et seq.), the Louisiana Riverboat Economic Development and Gaming Control Act (R.S. 4:501 et seq.), the Louisiana Riverboat Economic Development and Gaming Corporation Act (R.S. 4:601 et seq.), the Louisiana Regulation of Gaming Equipment Law (R.S. 47:7001 et seq.), and the Regulation of Charitable Gaming Law (R.S. 40:1485.1 et seq.), each applicant shall be fingerprinted and the fingerprints shall be forwarded to the Federal Bureau of Investigation for a national criminal history record check.

D. Any local law enforcement agency may conduct any screening function conducted by the bureau, except those screening functions conducted for entities regulated by any office of the Department of Public Safety and Corrections, and also may charge a reasonable processing fee of not more than fifteen dollars per inquiry for information provided. The provisions of this Subsection shall also apply to any screening function provided for in R.S. 15:587.1.

(Chgd. by Acts 1990 No. 56, §1; Acts 1992 No. 576, §1, No. 984, §18; Acts 1993 No. 676, §1, No. 678, §1, No. 717, §1; Acts 1995 No. 1171, §1; Acts 1997 No. 334, §1, No. 901, §1, No. 1067, §1, No. 1172, §3, No. 1349, §1; Acts 1998 First Ex. Sess. No. 137, §1, eff. 5/5/98.)

§587.1. Provision of information to protect children.

A. As provided in R.S. 15:825.3, R.S. 17:15, Ch.C. Art. 424, and R.S. 46:51.2, any employer or others responsible for the actions of one or more persons who have been given or have applied to be considered for a position of supervisory or disciplinary authority over children shall request in writing that the bureau supply information to ascertain whether that person or persons has been convicted of, or pled nolo contendere to, any one or more of the crimes listed in Subsection C. The request must be on a form prepared by the bureau and signed by a responsible officer or official of the organization making the request. It must include a statement signed by the person about whom the request is made which gives his permission for such information to be released.

B. Upon receiving a request meeting the requirements of Subsection A, the bureau shall provide a report promptly and in writing, but provide only such information as is necessary to specify whether or not that person has been convicted of or pled nolo contendere to any such crime or crimes, the crime or crimes of which he has been convicted or to which he has pled nolo contendere, and the date or dates on which they occurred.

C. The crimes to be reported under this Section are those defined in:

(1) R.S. 14:30, R.S. 14:30.1, R.S. 14:31, R.S. 14:41 through R.S. 14:45, R.S. 14:74, R.S. 14:78, R.S. 14:79.1, R.S. 14:80 through R.S. 14:86, R.S. 14:89, R.S. 14:89.1, R.S. 14:92, R.S. 14:93, R.S. 14:93.2.1, R.S. 14:93.3, R.S. 14:106, R.S. 14:282, R.S. 14:286, R.S. 40:966(A), R.S. 40:967(A), R.S. 40:968(A), R.S. 40:969(A), and R.S. 40:970(A) or convictions for attempt or conspiracy to commit any of those offenses;

(2) Those of a jurisdiction other than Louisiana which, in the judgment of the bureau employee charged with responsibility for responding to the request, would constitute a crime under the provisions cited in this Subsection, and

(3) Those under the Federal Criminal Code having analogous elements of criminal and moral turpitude.

D. The costs of providing the information required under this Section shall be charged by the bureau to the private employer or to the department, office, or other agency of government which has given, or is considering giving, a person supervisory or disciplinary authority over children. Neither the individual applicant nor a judge exercising juvenile jurisdiction shall bear such costs.

E. In addition to any penalties otherwise imposed under the provisions of this Chapter, the head of or other responsible person for any public entity who fails to comply with the provisions of Subsection A of this Section or who employs any person in violation of the provisions of R.S. 15:825.3, R.S. 17:15, or R.S. 46:51.2(A) or (B), shall be fined not more than five hundred dollars.

F. This Section may be cited as the "Louisiana Child Protection Act".

(Chgd. by Acts 1991 No. 125, §1; Acts 1993 No. 923, §1; Acts 1995 No. 1171, §1; Acts 1997 No. 904, §2, eff. 7/10/97, No. 1067, §1, eff. 8/15/97.)

§587.2. Authority of university or college police officers; criminal history information.

A. University police officers commissioned pursuant to R.S. 17:1805 for the Louisiana State University System, after receipt of fingerprint cards or other identifying information from a prospective employee, may conduct criminal history background checks using prior conviction information in the bureau's criminal history record and identification files, which pertains to an applicant or prospective employee of the Louisiana State University System.

B. University police officers may conduct these background checks immediately upon receipt of the fingerprint cards or other identifying information and shall not be required to pay a processing fee to the bureau.

(Added by Acts 1997 No. 579, §1, eff. 8/15/97.)

§588. Right of individual access.

The bureau shall adopt rules and regulations which provide a means for any individual, or his authorized representative if he is physically incapable of appearing at the bureau, to view, make notes, and administratively challenge the accuracy and contents of his personal criminal history information record and to seek corrections. The bureau may levy a reasonable fee of not less than ten dollars for this purpose, which fees shall be collected by the bureau, paid into the state treasury, and appropriated to the bureau all in accordance with the provisions of R.S. 15:584 and shall be used by the bureau to supplement normal operating expenses and to expand the services which the bureau is required to furnish under the provisions of this Chapter. Any increase in such fee shall be adopted pursuant to R.S. 49:951 et seq. *(Chgd. by Acts 1992 No. 984, §5, eff. 8/21/92.)*

§589. Duty to maintain security.

The bureau shall adopt rules and regulations which shall establish necessary control over any data processing or telecommunication system, facilities and personnel recruitment and such processing or communication related assignment policies of the department as become necessary to ensure compliance with all applicable security standards at the state and national level for storage and transmission of criminal history record information. To the maximum extent feasible, the bureau shall regulate through the design, implementation, and operation of the criminal justice information system the privacy and security of information contained herein.

§590. Obtaining and filing fingerprint and identification data.

The bureau shall obtain and file the name, fingerprints, description, photographs, and any other pertinent identifying data as the deputy secretary deems necessary, of any person who:

(1) Has been or is hereafter arrested, formerly indicted, or taken into custody in this state;

(a) For any offense which is a felony and for certain misdemeanor offenses designated by the deputy secretary;

(b) For any violation of any ordinance which the bureau shall determine to be substantially related to or the equivalent of any offense described under state law as a felony offense; or

(c) For any other offense which the deputy secretary may designate.

(2) Is or becomes confined to any prison, penal institution, correctional facility, or institution for the criminally insane.

(3) After death, has become a human corpse which is unidentified or involved in any autopsy or inquest by a coroner.

(4) Is a fugitive from justice.

(5) Is or has been a habitual offender.

§591. Submission of information; statistics; data.

It shall be the obligation of every criminal justice agency to collect and submit the name, fingerprints, description, photographs, and other identifying data on persons lawfully arrested, indicted, or taken into custody in this state as required by the bureau with respect to all offenses described in R.S. 15:590. Upon notification, every criminal justice agency, coroner, correctional facility, prison, penal institution, institution for the criminally insane, or private criminal justice agency lawfully empowered to perform any arrest, detention, treatment, supervision, or any official function on behalf of the criminal justice system shall collect and report to the bureau in such manner as prescribed, any statistics, reports, lists of stolen property or fugitives, criminal history records, or any other information the deputy secretary may require under authority of any provision of this Chapter, rule, or regulation issued pursuant thereto. In addition, each coroner shall transmit to the bureau all statistics and information as prescribed regarding autopsies performed, inquests held, and verdicts rendered.

§592. Submission of fingerprints and identification data.

Each law enforcement agency empowered to arrest or take into custody any individual described in R.S. 15:590 shall obtain and forward to the bureau two sets of legible fingerprints and other identification data as required by the bureau within seventy-two hours after arrest and booking. However, this period may be extended to cover any intervening official holiday or weekend. *(Chgd. by Acts 1991 No. 106, §1, eff. 9/6/91.)*

§593. Prohibition against destruction of records.

Notwithstanding the provisions of Articles 893 and 894 of the Code of Criminal Procedure and R.S. 40:983 and except in accordance with the provisions set forth in R.S. 44:9, no judge, or other official shall order the expungement, alteration, or destruction of any record of the bureau or of any agency subject to reporting requirements of the bureau.

§594. Access to records.

Each criminal justice agency subject to reporting requirements of the bureau shall, upon request by any authorized agent of the bureau, provide reasonable access to any record of such agency for the purpose of audit or to substantiate the accuracy of any record or statistics which the bureau is empowered to collect.

§595. Duty to abide by regulations.

Each agency subject to reporting requirements of the bureau shall abide by all rules and regulations adopted by the bureau pursuant to its authority.

§596. Penalties.

A. Any head of an agency subject to the provisions of this Chapter who, after written notification by an authorized representative of the bureau, shall neglect or refuse to make any report or to do any act required by any provision of this Chapter shall be deemed guilty of nonfeasance in office and shall be subject to removal or a fine of not less than two thousand dollars nor more than five thousand dollars for each offense, or both.

B. Any individual who shall acquire or distribute any criminal history record, except as authorized by law and in accordance with applicable rules and regulations of the bureau, shall be fined not less than five hundred nor more than one thousand dollars, and may be imprisoned for not more than one year with or without hard labor for each offense, or both.

C. Any individual who transmits false information, withholds information, or prevents the transmission of information shall be fined not less than five hundred nor more than one thousand dollars, and may be imprisoned for not more than five years with or without hard labor for each offense, or both.

D. In addition to any criminal penalties, the deputy secretary is empowered to make reasonable administrative sanctions as he deems appropriate against those agencies who fail to comply with the provisions of this Chapter. Such sanctions may include, but are not limited to, loss of access to equipment and files maintained by the bureau.

§597. Disposition reporting.

A disposition report of all arrests shall be submitted to the bureau within thirty days following the termination of a case by the entity responsible for the termination. *(Added by Acts 1991 No. 131, §1, eff. 9/6/91.)*

CHAPTER 6-A. DNA DETECTION OF SEXUAL AND VIOLENT OFFENDERS

(Added by Acts 1997 No. 737, §1, eff. 9/1/99.)

(Note: Chapter 6-A was enacted with a delayed effective date of 9/1/99.)

Section

§601. Short title.

This Chapter shall be known as the "DNA Detection of Sexual and Violent Offenders Act". *(Added by Acts 1997 No. 737, §1, eff. 9/1/99.)*

§602. Legislative findings and objectives.

The Louisiana Legislature finds and declares that DNA data banks are important tools in criminal investigations, in the exclusion of individuals who are the subject of criminal investigations or prosecutions, and in deterring and detecting recidivist acts. More than forty states have enacted laws requiring persons arrested for or convicted of certain crimes, especially sex offenses, to provide genetic samples for DNA profiling. Moreover, it is the policy of this state to assist federal, state, and local criminal justice and law enforcement agencies in the identification and detection of individuals in criminal investigations and in the identification of missing persons, to assist in the recovery or identification of human remains from disasters, and to assist with other humanitarian identification purposes. It is therefore in the best interest of the state to establish a DNA data base and a DNA data bank containing DNA samples submitted by individuals arrested, convicted, or presently incarcerated for felony sex offenses and other specified offenses. *(Added by Acts 1997 No. 737, §1, eff. 9/1/99.)*

§603. Definitions.

For purposes of this Chapter, the following terms shall have the following meanings:

(1) "CODIS" means Combined DNA Index System, the Federal Bureau of Investigation's national DNA identification index system that allows the storage and exchange of DNA records submitted by state and local forensic DNA laboratories.

(2) "Criminal justice agency" means any criminal justice agency as defined in R.S. 15:576(3).

(3) "Deputy secretary" means the deputy secretary of the Department of Public Safety and Corrections, public safety services, or the commander of the Louisiana State Police.

(4) "DNA" means deoxyribonucleic acid, which is located in cells and provides an individual's personal genetic blueprint and which encodes genetic information that is the basis of human heredity and forensic identification.

(5) "DNA record" means DNA identification information stored in the state DNA data base or the Combined DNA Index System for the purpose of generating investigative leads or supporting statistical interpretation of DNA test results. The DNA record is the result obtained from the DNA typing tests. The DNA record is comprised of the characteristics of a DNA sample which is of value in establishing the identity of individuals.

(6) "DNA sample" means a blood, tissue, or bodily fluid sample provided by any person with respect to offenses covered by this Chapter or submitted to the state police criminalistics laboratory pursuant to this Chapter for analysis or storage, or both.

(7) "FBI" means the Federal Bureau of Investigation.

(8) "Felony sex offense" means a felony offense or an attempt to commit a felony offense in violation of R.S. 14:42 through 43.5 or R.S. 14:80 through 81.2.

(9) "Fund" means the DNA Detection Fund established in this Chapter.

(10) "Other specified offense" means a commission of the following:

(a) A violation of R.S. 14:30 through 32.7.

(b) A violation of R.S. 14:34 through 38.2.

(c) A violation of R.S. 14:40.1 through 40.2.

(d) A violation of R.S. 14:44 through 45.

(11) "State police" means the office of state police or the state police criminalistics laboratory.

(Added by Acts 1997 No. 737, §1, eff. 9/1/99.)

§604. Powers and duties of state police.

In addition to any other powers and duties conferred in this Chapter, the state police shall:

(1) Be responsible for the policy management and administration of the state DNA identification record system to support law enforcement agencies and other criminal justice agencies.

(2) Promulgate rules and regulations to carry out the provisions of this Chapter.

(3) Provide for liaison with the FBI and other criminal justice agencies in regard to the state's participation in CODIS or in any DNA data base designated by the state police.

(Added by Acts 1997 No. 737, §1, eff. 9/1/99.)

§605. State DNA data base.

There is hereby established the state DNA data base. It shall be administered by the state police and provide DNA records to the FBI for storage and maintenance by CODIS. The state DNA data base shall have the capability provided by computer software and procedures administered by the state police to store and maintain DNA records related to:

(1) Forensic casework.

(2) Offenders required to provide a DNA sample under this Chapter.

(3) Anonymous DNA records used for research or quality control.

(Added by Acts 1997 No. 737, §1, eff. 9/1/99.)

§606. State DNA data bank.

There is hereby established the state DNA data bank. It shall serve as the repository of DNA samples collected under this Chapter. *(Added by Acts 1997 No. 737, §1, eff. 9/1/99.)*

§607. State police recommendation of additional offenses.

The state police may recommend to the legislature that it enact legislation for the inclusion of additional offenses for which DNA samples shall be taken and otherwise subjected to the provisions of this Chapter. In determining whether to recommend additional offenses, the state police shall consider those offenses for which DNA testing will have a substantial impact on the detection and identification of sex offenders and violent offenders. *(Added by Acts 1997 No. 737, §1, eff. 9/1/99.)*

§608. Procedural compatibility with FBI.

The DNA identification system as established by the state police shall be compatible with the procedures specified by the FBI, including use of comparable test procedures, laboratory equipment, supplies, and computer software. *(Added by Acts 1997 No. 737, §1, eff. 9/1/99.)*

§609. Drawing or taking of DNA samples.

A. A person who is arrested for a felony sex offense or other specified offense on or after September 1, 1999, shall have a DNA sample drawn or taken at the same time he is fingerprinted pursuant to the booking procedure.

B. Any person who is convicted or enters into a plea agreement resulting in a conviction on or after September 1, 1999, for a felony sex offense or other specified offense committed prior to that date shall have a DNA sample drawn as follows:

(1) A person who is sentenced to a term of confinement for an offense covered by this Chapter shall have a DNA sample drawn upon intake to a prison, jail, or any other detention facility or institution. If the person is already confined at the time of sentencing, the person shall have a DNA sample drawn immediately after the sentencing.

(2) A person who is convicted or enters into a plea agreement resulting in a conviction for an offense covered by this Chapter shall have a DNA sample drawn as a condition of any sentence that will not involve an intake into a prison, jail, or any other detention facility or institution.

(3) Under no circumstances shall a person who is convicted or enters into a plea agreement resulting in a conviction for an offense covered by this Chapter be released in any manner after such disposition unless and until a DNA sample has been withdrawn.

C. A person who has been convicted or enters into a plea agreement resulting in a conviction for a felony sex offense or other specified offense before September 1, 1999, and who is still serving a term of confinement in connection therewith on that date shall not be released in any manner prior to the expiration of his maximum term of confinement unless and until a DNA sample has been withdrawn.

D. All DNA samples taken pursuant to this Chapter shall be taken in accordance with regulations promulgated by the state police.

E. As used in this Section, the term "released" means any release, parole, furlough, work release, prerelease, or release in any other manner from a prison, jail, juvenile detention facility, or any other place of confinement.
(Added by Acts 1997 No. 737, §1, eff. 9/1/99.)

§610. Procedures for withdrawal, collection, and transmission of DNA samples.

A. Each DNA sample required to be drawn under this Chapter from persons who are arrested, incarcerated, or confined shall be drawn at the place of booking, incarceration, or confinement. DNA samples from persons who are not ordered or sentenced to a term of confinement shall be drawn or taken at a prison, jail unit, juvenile facility, or other facility to be specified by the court. Only those individuals qualified to draw or take DNA samples in a medically approved manner shall draw or take a DNA sample to be submitted for DNA analysis. The DNA sample and a set of fingerprints taken upon booking shall be delivered to the state police in accordance with state police rules and regulations.

B. A person authorized to draw or take DNA samples under this Chapter shall not be criminally liable for withdrawing a DNA sample and transmitting test results pursuant to this Chapter if he performed these activities in good faith and shall not be civilly liable for such activities when he acted in a reasonable manner according to generally accepted medical and other professional practices.
(Added by Acts 1997 No. 737, §1, eff. 9/1/99.)

§611. Procedures for conduct, disposition, and use of DNA analysis.

A. The state police shall prescribe procedures to be used in the collection, submission, identification, analysis, storage, and disposition of DNA samples and typing results of DNA samples submitted pursuant to this Chapter. The DNA sample typing results shall be stored in the state DNA data base and records of testing shall be retained on file with the state police.

B. The state police may contract with third parties to effectuate the purposes of this Chapter.

C. Except as otherwise provided in R.S. 15:612(C), the tests to be performed on each DNA sample shall be used only for law enforcement identification purposes or to assist in the recovery or identification of human remains from disasters or for other humanitarian identification purposes, including identification of missing persons.

D. Any other party contracting to carry out the functions of this Chapter shall be subject to the same restrictions and requirements of this Chapter, insofar as applicable, as apply to the state police, and subject to any additional restrictions imposed by the state police.

(Added by Acts 1997 No. 737, §1, eff. 9/1/99.)

§612. DNA data base exchange.

A. The state police shall receive, store, and perform analysis on DNA samples or contract for DNA typing analysis with a qualified DNA laboratory that meets the guidelines as established by the state police, and shall classify and file the DNA record of identification characteristic profiles of DNA samples submitted under this Chapter and make such information available as provided in this Section. The state police may enter a contract for the storage of DNA typing analysis and for DNA typing analysis with a qualified DNA laboratory that meets guidelines as established by the state police. The results of the DNA profile of individuals in the state DNA data base shall be made available:

(1) To criminal justice agencies or approved crime laboratories which serve these agencies.

(2) Upon written or electronic request and in furtherance of an official investigation of a criminal offense or offender or suspected offender.

B. The state police shall adopt guidelines governing the methods of obtaining information from the state DNA data base and procedures for verification of the identity and authority of the requestor.

C. The state police may create a separate population data base comprised of DNA samples obtained under this Chapter after all personal identification is removed. The state police may share or disseminate the population data base with other criminal justice agencies or crime laboratories that serve to assist the state police with statistical data bases. The population data base may be made available to and searched by other agencies participating in the CODIS system.

(Added by Acts 1997 No. 737, §1, eff. 9/1/99.)

§613. Cancellation of authority to access or exchange DNA records.

The state police, for good cause shown, may revoke or suspend the right of a forensic DNA laboratory within this state to access or exchange DNA identification records with criminal justice agencies. *(Added by Acts 1997 No. 737, §1, eff. 9/1/99.)*

§614. Removal of records.

A. A person whose DNA record or profile has been included in the data base or data bank pursuant to this Chapter may request that his record or profile be removed on the following grounds:

(1) The arrest on which the authority for including his DNA record or profile was based does not result in a conviction or plea agreement resulting in a conviction.

(2) The conviction on which the authority for including his DNA record or profile was based has been reversed and the case dismissed.

B. The state police shall remove all records and identifiable information in the data base or data bank pertaining to the person and destroy all samples from the person upon receipt of a written request for the removal of the record and a certified court order of expungement properly obtained pursuant to the provisions of R.S. 44:9.

(Added by Acts 1997 No. 737, §1, eff. 9/1/99.)

§615. Mandatory cost.

Unless the defendant shows that undue hardship would result, a mandatory cost of two hundred fifty dollars, which shall be in addition to any other costs imposed pursuant to law, shall automatically be imposed on any person convicted of a felony sex offense or other specified offense, and all proceeds derived from this Section shall be transmitted to the fund. *(Added by Acts 1997 No. 737, §1, eff. 9/1/99.)*

§616. Confidentiality of records.

Unless otherwise provided, all DNA profiles and samples submitted to the state police pursuant to this Chapter shall be confidential. *(Added by Acts 1997 No. 737, §1, eff. 9/1/99.)*

§617. Disclosure prohibited.

A. Any person, by virtue of employment or official position, or any person contracting to carry out any functions under this Chapter, including any officer, employee, or agent of such contractor, who has possession of or access to individually identifiable DNA information contained in the state DNA data base or in the state DNA data bank shall not disclose it in any manner to any person or agency not authorized to receive it knowing that such person or agency is not authorized to receive it.

B. No person shall obtain individually identifiable DNA information from the state DNA data base or the state DNA data bank without authorization to do so.
(Added by Acts 1997 No. 737, §1, eff. 9/1/99.)

§618. Criminal penalties.

A. Any person who violates R.S. 15:617(A) shall be fined not more than five hundred dollars or imprisoned with or without hard labor for not more than six months, or both.

B. Any person who knowingly violates R.S. 15:617(B) shall be fined not more than five hundred dollars or imprisoned with or without hard labor for not more than six months, or both.

C. Any person who tampers or attempts to tamper with any sample of blood, tissue, or other bodily fluids or the collection container without lawful authority shall be fined not more than five hundred dollars or imprisoned with or without hard labor for not more than six months, or both.
(Added by Acts 1997 No. 737, §1, eff. 9/1/99.)

§619. DNA Detection Fund.

All monies collected as costs pursuant to R.S. 15:615 shall be deposited into the state treasury. After compliance with the requirements of Article VII, Section 9(B) of the Constitution of Louisiana relative to the Bond Security and Redemption Fund, and prior to monies being placed in the state general fund, an amount equal to that deposited as required in this Section shall be credited to a special fund hereby created in the state treasury to be known as the DNA Detection Fund. The monies in this fund shall be appropriated by the legislature to the state police to assist in carrying out the provisions of this Chapter. All unexpended and unencumbered monies in this fund at the end of the fiscal year shall remain in such fund. The monies in this fund shall be invested by the state treasurer in the same manner as monies in the state general fund and interest earned on the investment of monies shall be credited to this fund, again, following compliance with the requirements of Article VII, Section 9(B) relative to the Bond Security and Redemption Fund. *(Added by Acts 1997 No. 737, §1, eff. 9/1/99.)*

§620. Authority of law enforcement officers.

Nothing in this Chapter shall limit or abrogate any existing authority of law enforcement officers to take, maintain, store, and utilize DNA samples for law enforcement purposes. *(Added by Acts 1997 No. 737, §1, eff. 9/1/99.)*

CHAPTER 7. PRISONS AND CORRECTIONAL INSTITUTIONS

PART I. PRISONS AND PRISONERS IN GENERAL

PART I-A. PRISON INMATE TRAINING REFORM ACT

PART I-B. PRISON REFORM ACT OF 1995

PART II. BUILDING AND MAINTENANCE REGULATIONS FOR PRISONS

PART III. MULTIPARISH DISTRICTS

PART III-A. LOUISIANA DEPARTMENT OF CORRECTIONS

PART III-B. NORTHEAST LOUISIANA CORRECTIONAL CENTER

PART III-C. LINCOLN PARISH DETENTION CENTER

PART III-D. TERREBONNE PARISH DEPARTMENT OF CORRECTIONS AND REHABILITATION

PART III-E. UNION PARISH DETENTION CENTER

PART III-F. JACKSON PARISH DETENTION CENTER

PART IV. LOUISIANA STATE PENITENTIARY

PART IV-A. ADDITIONAL INSTITUTIONS

PART IV-B. JUVENILE INSTITUTIONS

SUBPART D. TRI-PARISH JUVENILE JUSTICE DISTRICT

SUBPART E. NORTHWEST LOUISIANA JUVENILE DETENTION CENTER AUTHORITY

SUBPART F. ST. JAMES PARISH YOUTH CENTER

SUBPART G. PARISH YOUTH CENTER

SUBPART H. ST. BERNARD PARISH JUVENILE DETENTION CENTER

SUBPART I. CENTRAL LOUISIANA JUVENILE DETENTION CENTER AUTHORITY

SUBPART J. BOSSIER/CADDO JUVENILE DETENTION CENTER AUTHORITY

PART XII. WORK RELEASE PROGRAM

PART XIII. COMMUNITY REHABILITATION CENTERS

PART XIV. PRISON ENTERPRISES

PART XV. CORRECTIONS ADMINISTRATIVE REMEDY PROCEDURE

PART XVI. PRISON LITIGATION REFORM ACT

PART I. PRISONS AND PRISONERS IN GENERAL

§701. Cities to provide covered patrol wagons; use of uncovered vehicles prohibited; penalty.

All cities with a population of twenty thousand or more, shall provide covers or canopies for all vehicles owned, controlled, or employed by the city for the purpose of conveying prisoners to any place of detention, in order to prevent the exposure of prisoners to public view.

City authorities or officers shall not compel any person who is under arrest, imprisoned, or detained, or in their custody, or charge to be conveyed in an open or uncovered vehicle, in or through any street or public place in this state.

Whoever violates this Section shall be fined not less than twenty dollars nor more than one hundred dollars, or imprisoned for not less than thirty days nor more than ninety days.

§702. Maintenance of parish jails.

The governing authority of each parish shall be responsible for the physical maintenance of all parish jails and prisons. In those parishes in which the governing authority operates the parish jail the governing authority shall pass all bylaws and regulations they may deem expedient for the police and good government of the jails and prisons being operated by the parish governing authority.

§703. Physician to be appointed for each parish; salary.

The governing authority of each parish shall appoint annually a physician who shall attend the prisoners whenever they are sick. His salary shall be fixed by the governing authority.

§704. Sheriff keeper of jail.

Each sheriff shall be the keeper of the public jail of his parish, and shall by all lawful means preserve the peace and apprehend all disturbers thereof, and other public offenders.

§705. Food and clothing provisions for prisoners; payment of incarceration expenses; payment of medical expenses.

A. (1) The sheriffs or jailkeepers shall supply each prisoner daily with wholesome food sufficient in quantity for the proper maintenance of life. They shall provide the prisoners with clothing suited to and sufficient for the season.

(2) (a) The governing authority of each parish may obtain reimbursement from an inmate for certain expenses incurred by reason of the inmate's incarceration in accordance with the requirements of Subparagraph (b) of this Paragraph.

(b) The sheriff of any parish may collect reimbursement for the costs of room and board from any inmate incarcerated in a parish facility provided such reimbursement is approved by the judge who sentenced the inmate and provided the amount of such reimbursement is a uniform and reasonable amount established by the Department of Public Safety and Corrections by rule.

B. The jailer shall be allowed twelve and one half cents per day for each and every prisoner who is sick in order that the sick prisoners may be taken care of as their situation may require.

C. (1) Notwithstanding the provisions of Subsection B, the governing authority of each parish is hereby authorized to obtain reimbursement from an inmate for his medical and dental expenses. In addition, each such governing authority may require that copayments be made by inmates upon receiving medical or dental treatment.

(2) The amount of reimbursement shall be the actual costs, or any portion thereof, of the medical or dental expenses incurred.

(3) (a) Each governing authority shall establish written rules for the collection of such expenses from the inmate, including freezing assets in his drawing account and prohibiting withdrawals therefrom until the expenses are paid. The drawing account may be frozen regardless of the source of the assets contained therein. Notwithstanding any other law to the contrary, the governing authority shall promulgate rules and regulations regarding reimbursement by the inmate for medical expenses incurred by the governing authority for the inmate's treatment, including a requirement that the inmate file a claim with his private medical or health care insurer or any public medical assistance program, under which he is covered and from which the inmate may make a claim for payment or reimbursement of the

cost of any such medical treatment. This Subsection shall not prohibit the withdrawal of funds for the purpose of payments under the Crime Victims Reparations Act*, court costs as authorized by law, and other withdrawals specifically authorized by the sheriff, in that order.

**R.S. 46:1801 et seq.*

(b) In addition, the governing authority for each parish shall establish written rules requiring that copayments be made by inmates upon receiving medical or dental treatment, which may include a sliding scale based on the inmates' ability to pay. These written rules shall include but not be limited to guidelines for payments for inmate visits to doctors, hospitals, psychiatrists, and dentists, and for receipt of prescription or nonprescription drugs. The procedures for collection of copayments shall follow the procedures for collection of other expenses as established in Subparagraph (a) of this Paragraph.

(4) Any inmate who is transferred to another facility or discharged shall remain liable for any reimbursement authorized under this Subsection.

(5) For purposes of this Subsection "inmate" means any prisoner confined to a parish correctional facility but shall not include inmates sentenced to the Department of Public Safety and Corrections who are in the custody of the sheriff.

(Chgd. by Acts 1990 No. 75, §1; Acts 1997 No. 626, §1, No. 665, §1, eff. 8/15/97.)

§706. Transfer of prisoners to jail of another parish.

A. (1) Whenever the jail of a parish is unsafe or unfit for the security of prisoners, or is held by judicial decree unfit for the detention of some or all of the inmates, or presents a security risk to a prisoner or other prisoners or to the public, or whenever a particular prisoner presents a security or health risk to himself or to other prisoners or to the public, the sheriff of the parish maintaining and keeping the prisoner or prisoners may transfer any prisoner or prisoners to the jail or jails of any other parish by written contract with the sheriff of the other parish.

(2) If the prisoner or prisoners to be transferred are not under sentence to the Department of Public Safety and Corrections, the sheriff proposing to make the transfer shall notify the court which set bail for the prisoner or prisoners at least seventy-two hours before making the transfer.

(3) If the prisoner or prisoners transferred are under sentence to the Department of Public Safety and Corrections, the sheriff transferring the prisoner or prisoners shall notify the department.

B. The sheriff to whom the transfer of the prisoner or prisoners is made shall receive, for the maintenance of such prisoner or prisoners, the same compensation authorized by law for the keeping and feeding of prisoners, which shall be paid by the parish transferring the prisoner or prisoners.

C. The sheriff of the parish to which the prisoner is conveyed shall keep the prisoner safe and secure, and subject to all orders or decrees issuing from the parish from which the prisoner was transferred.

§707. United States prisoners to be kept in custody; compensation of sheriff.

All the sheriffs, jailers, prison keepers, and their deputies to whom any person shall be sent or committed by United States marshals or their deputies, under the authority of the United States, whether on civil or criminal process, or upon any process or warrant which may be issued by the President of the United States, or those to whom he may delegate authority for any cause whatever under the law of the United States, shall take the prisoners into custody and keep them safely until their discharge by due course of law.

Any sheriff, jailer or prison keeper violating this Section shall be liable to the same penalties and the parties aggrieved shall be entitled to the same remedies as if the prisoners had been committed to their custody by virtue of legal process issued under the authority of Louisiana.

The sheriffs or jailers may contract with the U.S. Marshal of his district for the payment of a minimum rate of one dollar per day for the keeping of each federal prisoner. The sheriffs may use the funds for the proper care and safekeeping of the federal prisoners and to pay any expenses incurred in connection with their office or jail.

§708. Labor by prisoners permitted; workday release program; indemnification.

A. (1)(a) Whenever a prisoner sentenced to a parish prison of any parish of the state, by any court of competent jurisdiction, or a prisoner in a parish prison awaiting transfer to a state correctional facility shall be willing of his own free will to perform manual labor upon any of the public roads, levees, streets, or public buildings, works, or improvements inside or outside of the prison, the sheriff may set the prisoner to work. Work authorized pursuant to this Paragraph also specifically includes participation in litter abatement or collection programs to police and remove litter on public grounds, rights-of-way, lakes, streams, the shores of lakes and streams, public roads, levees, or streets. The prisoners shall always remain under the custody and control of the sheriffs.

(b) A prisoner, who participates in a litter abatement or collection program pursuant to this Paragraph, shall have no cause of action for damages against the sheriff conducting the program or supervising his participation therein, nor against any employee or agent of such sheriff, for any injury or loss suffered by him during or arising out of his participation in the program, if such injury or loss is a direct result of the lack of supervision or act or omission of the sheriff or his employee or agent, unless the injury or loss was caused by the intentional or grossly negligent act or omission of the sheriff or his employee or agent. The sheriff shall not be liable for any injury caused by the prisoner, unless the gross negligence or intentional act of the sheriff or his employee or agent was a substantial factor in causing the injury. No provision hereof shall negate the requirement to provide a prisoner with necessary medical treatment as statutorily required.

(2) Whenever a prisoner sentenced to the parish prison of any parish of this state, by any court of competent jurisdiction, or a prisoner in a parish prison awaiting transfer to a state correctional facility shall be willing of his own free will to perform manual labor upon any cemetery or graveyard or work in a solid waste recycling program administered by a state agency or political subdivision and approved by the sheriff, the criminal sheriff may set the prisoner to work upon labor determined by the governing authority of the parishes and the municipal authorities of the towns and cities. The prisoners shall always remain under the custody and control of the sheriffs.

(3) (a) Whenever a prisoner sentenced to the parish prison of any parish of the state, by any court of competent jurisdiction, or a prisoner in a parish prison awaiting transfer to a state correctional facility shall be willing of his own free will to perform manual labor by assisting the governing authority of any municipality to maintain the municipality in a safe and sanitary condition by cutting, destroying, or removing noxious weeds or grass or other deleterious, unhealthful, or noxious growths on any sidewalks or banquettes and on any lot, place, or area within the municipality and the sheriff has approved the work, the sheriff may set the prisoner to work upon labor determined by the governing authority of the municipalities to effectuate this purpose. The prisoners shall always remain under the custody and control of the sheriffs. The governing authority of any municipality shall comply with the provisions of R.S. 33:5062 and all other relevant provisions of law. R.S. 33:815 and 4766 are not affected by the provisions of this Paragraph. The Department of Transportation and Development is excluded from this Paragraph and is subject to the requirements of R.S. 48:261(B), (C), and (D) and all other relevant provisions of law.

(b) The use of prison labor shall in no way reduce the work force of any highway maintenance gang or cause the layoff of any classified employee.

(c) No sheriff shall be liable for any loss sustained by any such prisoner, except for those caused by the gross negligence or intentional acts of the sheriff or his deputies.

(4) Any prisoner in a parish prison awaiting transfer to a state correctional facility who is willing of his own free will to perform manual labor may be allowed to provide such services for work projects located within that parish which are performed by Prison Enterprises in accordance with the provisions of R.S. 15:1151 et seq. Any inmate performing work for Prison Enterprises pursuant to the provisions of this Paragraph shall be compensated in accordance with the provisions of R.S. 15:873. Such compensation shall be deposited in the same manner and in the appropriate accounts as provided in R.S. 15:874.

B. The sheriffs of the parishes shall establish regulations which they may deem necessary to carry into effect the provisions of this Section and for the discipline, working, and employment of the prisoners.

C. This Section shall not apply to criminals convicted of crimes of first or second degree murder, attempted first or second degree murder, aggravated rape, attempted aggravated rape, forcible rape, aggravated kidnapping, aggravated arson, armed robbery, or attempted armed robbery, or persons sentenced as habitual offenders under R.S. 15:529.1, except during the last six months of their terms.

D. (1)(a) Whenever a person is convicted of a misdemeanor for violation of any state law or any parish or municipal ordinance and is sentenced to imprisonment, the sentencing court may order the person so sentenced to report, during the term of imprisonment, to the sheriff to participate in a court-approved workday release program as established and administered by the sheriff.

(b) The person so sentenced shall pay the sum of fifty dollars to the sheriff to defray the cost of participation in the program. The payment of the costs shall be based upon the defendant's ability to pay.

(2) Each sheriff shall establish written rules for the administration of the workday release program. However, each participant shall be required to report for work for a period of time during daylight hours for not less than eight nor more than ten hours to be determined by the sheriff. Upon release each participant shall not be confined to jail, but shall return to his place of residence. The sheriff may determine that an inmate shall not participate in the program if such participation may result in harm to the community or to the participant.

(3) If any participant violates the rules of the workday release program prescribed by the sheriff, or if the sheriff determines that a person shall not participate in the program, the inmate shall be imprisoned for the remainder of his sentence. Failure to report to or return from the scheduled workday program shall be considered an escape under the provisions of R.S. 14:110.

E. The political subdivision which administers the solid waste recycling program or any other public work or nonprofit program shall indemnify and hold the sheriff, the state, and the state agency harmless for any injury caused by the inmate, unless the gross negligence or intentional act of the sheriff or the state or the state agency was a substantial factor in causing the injury.

(Chgd. by Acts 1990 No. 416, §1; Acts 1992 No. 402, §1; Acts 1995 No. 908, §1; Acts 1997 No. 509, §1, No. 656, §1, eff. 8/15/97.)

§710. Exchange of prisoners between parishes.

The governing authorities of the various parishes composing any one judicial district may arrange with each other or among themselves for the transfer of prisoners from one parish to another in the same judicial district for the purpose of performing any kind of work that may legally be required of them, under whatever conditions and upon whatever terms may be mutually agreed upon by the governing authorities.

§711. Work release program.

A. The sheriff of each parish, and in Orleans Parish, the criminal sheriff, is hereby authorized to establish and administer a work release program for inmates of any jail or prison under his jurisdiction. In the event that the inmate is confined to a parish correctional facility not operated by the sheriff, then the superintendent of the correction facility is hereby authorized to establish and administer a work release program for inmates of the correctional facility under his jurisdiction, and where the word sheriff is used herein it shall also mean superintendent of the correctional facility wherein the inmate is confined.

B. Each sheriff shall establish written rules for the administration of the work release program and shall determine those inmates who may participate in the release program, except that no inmate may participate in the program if his sentence so stipulates. Inmates sentenced to the Department of Corrections who are in the custody of the sheriff shall not be eligible for work release unless such inmates are in compliance with standards for work release within the department and written approval of the secretary of the department is obtained. If any inmate violates the conditions prescribed by the sheriff, his work release privileges may be withdrawn. Failure to report to or return from the planned employment shall be considered an escape under the provisions of R.S. 14:110. The sheriff may approve as work release privileges, placement in universities, colleges, technical, vocational or trade schools or in sheltered workshops or in training programs designed to improve the skills and abilities of the inmate.

C. Every inmate with work release privileges shall be liable for the cost of his room, board, clothing and other necessary expenses incident to his employment or placement.

D. The wages of any inmate so employed shall be collected by the sheriff or by his designated agent, and the sheriff shall deposit the same in a public banking institution and keep a ledger showing the financial status of each inmate on the program.

E. The wages of any such inmate shall be disbursed by the sheriff for the following purposes and in the order stated:

(1) The board of the inmate including food, clothing, medical, and dental expenses;

(2) Necessary travel expense to and from work and other incidental expenses of the inmate;

(3) Support of the inmate's dependents, if any;

(4) Payment, either in full or ratably of the inmate's obligations acknowledged by him in writing, or which have been reduced to judgment;

(5) The balance if any, to the inmate upon his discharge.

F. The wages of an inmate so employed shall be not less than the customary wages for an employee performing similar services.

G. Notwithstanding the provisions of Subsection B above or any other law to the contrary, any inmate who has been convicted for first degree murder (R.S. 14:30), second degree murder (R.S. 14:30.1), aggravated rape (R.S. 14:42), attempted aggravated rape (R.S. 14:27, 14:42), forcible rape (R.S. 14:42.1), aggravated kidnapping (R.S. 14:44), aggravated arson (R.S. 14:51), armed robbery (R.S. 14:64), attempted murder (R.S. 14:27, 14:29), attempted armed robbery (R.S. 14:27, 14:64), producing, manufacturing, distributing, or dispensing or possession with intent to produce, manufacture, distribute, or dispense a controlled dangerous substance classified in Schedule I or Schedule II of R.S. 40:964, and persons sentenced as habitual offenders under R.S. 15:529.1 shall be prohibited from participation in a work release program except during the last six months of their terms.

H. No inmate employed in the work release program shall be employed in a position which would necessitate his departure from the state.

§711.1. Jefferson Davis work-release program.

A. Notwithstanding the provisions of R.S. 15:711, and any other law to the contrary, the sheriff of the parish of Jefferson Davis is hereby authorized to establish and administer a work-release program for the inmates of any jail or prison under his jurisdiction who have been convicted of misdemeanors. The sheriff shall adopt rules and regulations providing for the administration of the program subject to the approval of the district attorney and the judge of the Thirty-First Judicial District Court. The rules and regulations, among other things, may provide:

(1) The criteria for eligibility of the inmates for participation in the program.

(2) The conditions to be observed by participants while released for work.

(3) The disposition of monies earned, including contribution to the expenses of confinement; support of any family; payment of fines, court costs, restitution, and judgments; and retention of earnings until release from confinement.

(4) Diminution of sentence for participation in the program which shall not exceed one and one-third days credit on the sentence for each day served on the work-release program, the diminution to be allowed only for inmates who spend each night in jail.

B. Beginning in 1979, and in every fourth year thereafter, on or before October 1 of the year, the sheriff shall disburse all monies collected under the program towards the expenses of administration by transferring one-half of such monies to the general fund of the parish governing authority of Jefferson Davis Parish and the remaining one-half to the operating fund of the sheriff.

PART I-A. PRISON INMATE TRAINING REFORM ACT

§731. Short title.

This Part may be cited as the "Prison Inmate Training Reform Act". *(Added by Acts 1994 Third Ex. Sess. No. 113, §1, eff. 8/27/94.)*

§732. Legislative findings and declaration.

The legislature finds that through inmate exercise programs, including karate, judo, and other types of martial arts, inmates are drastically improving their physical strength. The safety of law enforcement and correctional officers who guard and have contact with these inmates on a daily basis is being put at a greater and unnecessary risk. The safety of the public at large, as well as law enforcement personnel, may be put in increased jeopardy or increased physical risk upon an inmate's release because of the released prisoner's enhanced physical condition and training. It is therefore the intent of the legislature, for the protection of the public safety and for the protection of law enforcement and correctional personnel, to prohibit karate, judo, or martial arts programs of any form within jails, prisons, correctional facilities, juvenile facilities, temporary holding centers, halfway houses, or detention centers. *(Added by Acts 1994 Third Ex. Sess. No. 113, §1, eff. 8/27/94.)*

§733. Prohibition of karate, judo, or other martial arts programs.

A. No person who is incarcerated by a court of law and is being detained in any jail, prison, correctional facility, juvenile institution, temporary holding center, halfway house, or detention facility shall have access to or use any of the following programs, whether the programs are supported by state or local funds, or provided by incarcerated volunteers or employees or outside donations or volunteers:

(1) Karate.

(2) Judo.

(3) Martial arts of any form.

B. Nothing in this Section shall prohibit an inmate from participating in basketball, jogging, stationary bicycling, calisthenics supervised by correctional staff, and other forms of physical activities which correctional facility personnel approve.

(Added by Acts 1994 Third Ex. Sess. No. 113, §1, eff. 8/27/94.)

PART I-B. PRISON REFORM ACT OF 1995

(Added by Acts 1995 No. 810, §1, eff. 8/15/95.)

§737. Title.

This Part shall be known and may be cited as the "Prison Reform Act of 1995". *(Added by Acts 1995 No. 810, §1, eff. 8/15/95.)*

§738. Minimum standard of living.

No incarcerated state prisoner, whether before trial, during trial or on appeal, or after final conviction, who is housed in any jail, prison, correctional facility, juvenile institution, temporary holding center, or detention facility within the state shall have a standard of living above that required by the constitutions of the United States and the state of Louisiana, as ordered or interpreted by the appropriate courts of last resort, or by the standards set by the American Correctional Association. It is the intention of this legislature that, to the extent permitted by law, no inmate shall have a standard of living better than the state poverty level. Citizens should not be worse off economically and living in conditions that are below those granted to inmates whose living standards are being paid for and subsidized by the hard-working and law-abiding people of the state of Louisiana. *(Added by Acts 1995 No. 810, §1, eff. 8/15/95.)*

§739. Inmate blood and saliva testing.

A. (1) Any incarcerated prisoner, whether before trial, during trial, pending appeal, or after final conviction, who is housed in any jail, prison, correctional facility, juvenile institution, temporary holding center, or detention facility within the state who is involved in an incident in which another person is exposed to an infectious disease by the throwing of feces, urine, blood, saliva, any form of human waste, or bodily fluid on that other person shall submit to a test designed to determine whether the offender is infected with a sexually transmitted disease, or acquired immune deficiency syndrome (AIDS), the human immunodeficiency virus (HIV), HIV-1 antibodies, or any other probable causative agent of AIDS, viral hepatitis, or other infectious disease. Each incarcerated prisoner who is involved in an incident shall be deemed to be an offender and shall be subject to testing.

(2) The procedure or test shall be performed by a qualified physician or other qualified person who shall report any positive result to the chief administrator of the jail or correctional facility, if the offender is incarcerated, and shall also notify the offender, regardless of the results. If the offender is incarcerated, the test may be administered at the place of incarceration or the offender may be transferred to an appropriate testing facility and returned to incarceration following the testing procedure. If the offender tested under the provisions of this Subsection tests positive for a sexually transmitted disease, or AIDS, HIV, HIV-1 antibodies, or any other probable causative agent of AIDS, viral hepatitis, or other infectious disease, upon request, he shall be provided with the following services:

(a) Counseling regarding HIV, viral hepatitis, or other infectious disease.

(b) Referral to appropriate health care and support services. These services shall be provided in accordance with applicable state law and the regulations governing the specific programs under which the services are to be provided.

(3) The costs associated with this testing shall be paid by the offender.

B. A person who has been exposed to the feces, urine, blood, saliva, any form of human waste, or bodily fluid of an incarcerated prisoner housed in any jail, prison, correctional

facility, juvenile institution, temporary holding center, or detention facility within the state shall notify by affidavit, subject to penalty for false swearing, the chief administrator of the jail or correctional facility that the exposure has occurred and the administrator shall order the testing, as provided in this Section, of each incarcerated prisoner who was involved in the incident which resulted in the exposure.
(Added by Acts 1997 No. 1399, §1, eff. 8/15/97.)

PART II. BUILDING AND MAINTENANCE REGULATIONS FOR PRISONS

§751. State division of health standards required.

All jails, prisons, lockups and camps and all facilities, units and rooms of such jails, prisons, lockups and camps where prisoners are detained or confined must meet standards of health and decency which shall be established by the state division of health. The director of the Department of Corrections shall confer with the state health officer or his duly authorized representative concerning the establishment of such standards for all correctional institutions. The state health officer or his duly authorized representative shall periodically inspect all correctional institutions to determine if such institutions are in compliance with the established standards and he shall prepare and issue a report on his findings to the governor, the state hospital director and the administrators of the various institutions.

§760. Hospital quarters.

Where large numbers of prisoners are confined the proper authorities in charge shall provide hospital quarters with necessary arrangement, conveniences, attendants, etc.

§763. Procedure upon failure to comply with the provisions of this Part.

Whenever the governing authority of any parish or municipality or the authority in charge of any state prison, lockup, or camp shall fail to comply with the provisions of this part, the state health officer shall institute through the attorney general of the state, or through the district attorney of the district wherein the prison, lockup or camp is situated, proper legal proceedings to enjoin, restrain and prohibit the parish or municipal governing authority, or the authorities in charge of the state prison or camp from using the prison, lockup or camp for the purpose of confining prisoners until the provisions of this part have been complied with.

§764. Parish jail overcrowding; state of emergency.

A. If the prisoner population of a parish jail exceeds the rated design capacity of the parish jail for seven consecutive days, the sheriff of that parish shall certify that fact in writing, by first class mail or personal delivery, to each district, municipal and traffic court judge in the parish, to the district attorney and the chief of police of any municipality within the parish, and to the senior official of the parish governing authority. If this condition exists for seven consecutive days after notification of said officials, the sheriff shall declare a parish jail overcrowding state of emergency and shall notify such officials.

B. After the declaration of emergency is made in accordance with Subsection A of this Section, the sheriff may reduce overcrowding in the parish jail by any or all of the following means:

(1) The substitution of appearance tickets or summons for booking at the parish jail and the release or furlough of pre-trial arrestees, based on factors included in Code of Criminal Procedure Article 334 and on any other factors related to public safety or the likelihood of court appearance, however only persons charged with violations of municipal ordinances which are nonviolent offenses shall be eligible for such release.

(2) The furlough of individuals who have been convicted under municipal ordinance for nonviolent offenses who are within one year of release.
(Chgd. by Acts 1990 No. 397, §1, eff. 9/7/90.)

PART III. MULTIPARISH DISTRICTS

§801. Creation of multiparish prisons.

The governing authority of one or more parishes may create a multiparish prison whenever they shall, by joint resolution, deem it to be the best interest of the parish or parishes involved.

§802. Title of multiparish prison.

The multiparish prisons shall be known by the name of the parish in which the prison is domiciled, i.e., Ouachita Area Multiparish Prison.

§803. Organization and powers.

A. Every prison shall be a political corporation, with power to sue and be sued and shall be governed by a board of governors. The multiparish prison shall be domiciled at the parish seat in one of the parishes designated by the board of governors. It shall be sued at its domicile and service of all legal documents shall be made on the president or secretary of the board of governors.

B. Every multiparish prison may acquire title to property, real and personal, for public purposes by purchase or donation; may own, operate or maintain prison farms and other public works and may operate the farms or other public works in whole or in part with prison labor and persons sentenced to multiparish prisons by the courts.

§804. Board of governors.

A. The board of governors shall be composed of each sheriff and one member of each of the governing authorities appointed by the governing authority of each parish within the multiparish prison area.

B. The president of the board of governors shall be the sheriff of the parish in which the prison is domiciled. The president of the board of governors shall be the administrator of the multiparish prison. The appointed member of the governing authority of the parish where the multiparish prison is domiciled shall be the secretary of the board and the parish treasurer shall be ex officio treasurer.

C. In any parish having a population of not less than eight thousand nor more than thirteen thousand where only one parish governs and administers a prison district, the board of governors shall be composed of the president of the police jury of the administering parish and two other police jurors to be appointed by the police jury of the parish. The members of the board of governors shall elect one of their number president and one vice-president. The clerk of the police jury of the parish where the prison district is domiciled shall be the secretary of the board and the parish treasurer shall be ex officio treasurer.

D. The members of the board of governors other than the sheriffs shall be paid the same mileage and per diem in going to or returning from any regular or special meeting as is now paid to the members of the governing authorities of the parishes within the multiparish prison area, but they shall not receive pay for more than twelve meetings during any one year.

(Chgd. by Acts 1991 No. 122, §1, eff. 9/6/91.)

§805. Powers and duties of board of governors.

The board of governors:

(1) May inaugurate, conduct, and carry on farming vocational training programs, and other operations on behalf of the prison on property owned or leased by the prison for these purposes.

(2) Shall keep an accurate account of all revenues derived from the sale of the products of the labor of the prisoners. The accounts shall show the amount of money received from the sale of produce, the date of the sale, the name of the purchaser, and any other data which will enable the public to be in touch with its affairs.

(3) May acquire land by donation, purchase, or lease for multiparish prison farms. All purchases of real estate shall be ratified by a majority of the governing authorities of the parishes within the multiparish prison area on the basis of their assessed valuation. Whenever the purchase price is on terms of credit the land shall be the only security and the parishes involved shall not be liable for any part of the unpaid purchase price. The board of governors may remove any buildings or improvements on land acquired by them.

(4) May build, with the approval of the governing authorities of the parishes composing the multiparish prison area, jails or other places of imprisonment on the property of the

multiparish prison whenever they deem it advisable. They may dedicate a sum not to exceed one-half of one mill on the dollar assessment per year for a period of not more than ten years out of the regular alimony for this purpose. Their dedication of the money may be evidenced by certificates of indebtedness, payable annually with interest payable semi-annually, not to exceed the market rate of percent per annum, redeemable on maturity out of any excess revenues that may develop. No building shall be constructed on land not fully paid for.

(5) May grant security for debts incurred in the acquisition of lands for the multiparish prison for making improvements on the lands, for purchasing machinery, tools, equipment, or other property for the establishment, maintenance, operation, and administration of the multiparish prison or for obtaining funds to pay and extinguish any debt or debts incurred in the acquisition of the lands or the improvement thereof, by granting mortgages upon the immovable property of the district, where title thereto is in the public, mortgages upon its movables, or crop pledges and pawns upon the crops of the prison farms.

The acts of security shall stipulate that in case of default in the payment of any debt, secured thereby or any part of a debt, the property securing the debt shall be subject to seizure and sale with benefit of appraisement, in the same manner as private property subject to encumbrance may be seized and sold, notwithstanding the title of the property securing the debt is vested in the public. No security shall be granted unless sanctioned by the governing authorities of the parishes composing the multiparish prison area by ordinance or resolution fixing the maximum of the debt to be secured. The board of governors, the governing authorities of the parishes within the multiparish prison area, or the multiparish prisons shall never be obligated beyond the value of the property offered as security.

(6) Shall fix the salary to be paid the secretary and treasurer of the board of governors and shall fix the amount of bond with legal surety which the treasurer shall give, conditioned on a faithful accounting for all money and property entrusted to his care.

(7) May permit use of prisoners on public works at the request of any public body within the multiparish prison area, but only with the approval and under the supervision of the committing district judge having jurisdiction over the prisoners. The judge shall have full authority to recall any prisoner at any time.

(8) (a) May sell, dispose of, or lease any land owned by the multiparish prison which for any reason can no longer be used, or which is unused, or is unnecessary or unsuitable in the operations of the said multiparish prison.

(b) The board of governors of said multiparish prisons may lease said land upon such terms and conditions as may be most advantageous to the prison, but said lease shall not exceed five years.

(c) Should any multiparish prison lands be offered for sale, the board of governors thereof shall cause to be published for thirty days in the official journal of the parish in which said land is located, an advertisement setting forth a description of the land to be sold, and the time, place and terms of the sale.

(d) The land so advertised shall be sold by the sheriff of the parish where the land is located. The sale shall be at the principal door of the courthouse, between the hours of 11:00 o'clock A.M. and 4:00 o'clock P.M., and shall be to the last and highest bidder, except that the board of governors of the multiparish prison shall have the right to reject any and all bids. Should a bid be accepted for the sale of said land, then and in that event said board of governors, under the authority of a proper resolution, shall make and deliver to the purchaser a valid deed conveying title thereto.

§806. Budget and revenues.

A. The governing authorities of the parishes within the multiparish prison area shall appropriate, in proportion to the assessed valuation of the property of the parishes, an amount annually which, when added to the revenues of the multiparish prison will be sufficient to properly conduct the multiparish prison and to provide the necessary operational equipment. The first budget shall equal the amount expended for the keeping, feeding, and clothing of prisoners in each prison during the previous year and thereafter the annual budget shall be estimated on the basis of the budget of the preceding year.

B. The revenues derived from farming or other operations shall be applied to the operation of the multiparish prison. Any surplus revenues of the multiparish prison not needed for the succeeding calendar year may be paid into the general fund of the governing authorities of the parishes composing the multiparish prison area in proportion to the assessment of the parishes as shown by the last filed assessment roll of each.

§807. Municipalities may send prisoners to multiparish prisons for confinement.

A. A municipality, whenever it so desires, may have prisoners convicted by the municipal courts of violations of municipal ordinances sentenced to work on or be confined at the multiparish prison upon agreement by the governing authority of the municipality and the governing authorities of the parish farm for the charges and expenses of keeping the prisoners.

B. The governing authority of a municipality may enter into a contract with the governing authorities of a multiparish prison to determine the costs to be paid by the municipality to the multiparish prison for the keeping of prisoners. The charges shall be determined by mutual agreement.

§808. Prisoners confined in multiparish prisons.

All persons convicted of misdemeanors and felonies punishable with or without hard labor may be confined in the multiparish prisons, and in misdemeanor cases, may be ordered to participate in a court-approved work-day release program as provided in R.S. 15:708.

§809. Preexisting facilities.

The sheriff of a parish already the domicile of a prison facility may make the prison facilities under his jurisdiction available to one or more parishes on a per prisoner fee basis. The prison facilities shall in no way come under the requirement of this Part.

§810. Preexisting facilities operated by parish governing authorities.

In any parish in which there is presently located a prison, correctional institute or any other type of prison facility which is operated by the governing authority of the parish, the governing authority may make the said prison facilities under its jurisdiction and operation available to one or more other parishes on a per prisoner fee basis.

When any such parish governing authority does exercise its option to make any such prison facility so available, then the said prison facility shall not in any way come under the requirements of this part but it will be a multiparish prison, particularly for the purpose of receiving and working persons sentenced to imprisonment in said multiparish prison and such sentencing is hereby authorized for all misdemeanors and all offenses which are not capital and which are not necessarily punishable at hard labor.

§811. Inmate contact with persons outside of parish or multiparish prison; temporary release or furlough.

A. The sheriff of each parish prison and the administrator of each multiparish prison may authorize visits and correspondence under reasonable conditions, between an inmate and approved friends, relatives, and other persons. Notwithstanding any provision of law to the contrary, the sheriff or administrator may authorize the temporary release of an inmate only for serious illness or death of a member of the inmate's family or for an interview of the inmate by a prospective employer. For purposes of this Section an inmate is a person serving a sentence pursuant to a court judgment.

B. The sheriff or administrator may authorize a furlough to an inmate of a parish or multiparish prison. Such a furlough is intended as a rehabilitative tool to assist an inmate in maintaining family relationships during his incarceration.

C. An inmate sentenced to the Department of Corrections who is in the custody of the sheriff shall not be eligible for a furlough unless that inmate is in compliance with the Department of Corrections standards for such a furlough.

D. Failure to promptly report to destination or return from temporary release or furlough shall be considered an escape under the provisions of R.S. 14:110.

E. Except in cases of serious illness or death of a member of the inmate's family, or for an interview of the inmate by a prospective employer in which case the inmate may be released only in security escort with Department of Public Safety and Corrections authorized personnel, any inmate who has been convicted of first degree murder (R.S. 14:30), second degree murder (R.S. 14:30.1), aggravated rape (R.S. 14:42), attempted aggravated rape (R.S. 14:27, 14:42), forcible rape (R.S. 14:42.1), aggravated kidnapping (R.S. 14:44), aggravated arson (R.S. 14:51), armed robbery (R.S. 14:64), attempted murder (R.S. 14:27, 14:29), attempted armed robbery (R.S. 14:27, 14:64), producing, manufacturing, distributing, or dispensing or possession with intent to produce, manufacture, distribute, or dispense a controlled dangerous substance classified in Schedule I or Schedule II of R.S. 40:964, and persons sentenced as habitual offenders under R.S. 15:529.1 shall be ineligible for temporary release or furloughs as provided for herein, except during the last six months of their terms.

PART III-A. LOUISIANA DEPARTMENT OF CORRECTIONS

§821. Louisiana Department of Corrections; created; transfer of functions; functions of department.

In order to merge and consolidate into one department under authority of Section 32 of Article III of the Constitution of Louisiana, the executive and administrative offices, boards and commissions whose duties are of a similar nature or character there is hereby created and established the Louisiana Department of Corrections. The Louisiana Board of Institutions and the Department of Institutions are hereby merged and consolidated into the Louisiana Department of Corrections, and the functions of said board and department shall be transferred to the Louisiana Department of Corrections, hereinafter referred to as "the department". The functions of the department shall comprise administrative functions of the state now or hereafter authorized by law to be exercised in relation to the administration, management and operation of all state institutions for the care, custody and correction of persons sentenced for felonies or misdemeanors.

§821.1. Louisiana Department of Corrections; domicile.

The domicile of the department of corrections and its divisions shall be the parish of East Baton Rouge, city of Baton Rouge, Louisiana.

§823. Director of Corrections.

The director of corrections shall be the chief executive, administrative, budgetary and fiscal officer of the department. He shall attend all meetings of the Board of Corrections. He shall implement the policy determinations established by the board, and in so doing, he shall administer the department, prescribe rules and regulations for the operation thereof, and supervise the administration of all institutions, facilities and services under the jurisdiction of the department. The director shall be appointed by the governor and shall serve at his pleasure. He shall be qualified for his position by character, personality, ability, education, training and successful administrative experience in the correctional field, if possible. He need not be a resident of this state. The salary of the director shall be fixed by the Board of Corrections.

§824. Commitment of persons to the Department of Public Safety and Corrections.

A. Notwithstanding any provision of law to the contrary, any individual subject to confinement in a state adult penal or correctional institution shall be committed to the Louisiana Department of Public Safety and Corrections and not to any particular institution within the jurisdiction of the department. The director of corrections shall assign each newly committed inmate to an appropriate penal or correctional facility. The director may transfer an inmate from one such facility to another, insofar as the transfer is consistent with the commitment and in accordance with treatment, training and security needs established by the department; however, no juvenile may be transferred to a penal or correctional facility for persons committed by a court having criminal jurisdiction except in accordance with the provisions of R.S. 15:1062.

B. (1)(a) In the event any individual has been committed to the department for confinement which is or has been delayed or prevented after final sentence by court order restricting the department from institutionalizing the individual, or when the individual is not institutionalized in a state penal or corrections institution because of lack of facilities under the control of the department, or the department otherwise refused to accept the individual for confinement, which resulted or has resulted in the individual being confined in a parish jail or institution after final sentence, or when he is being held in the parish jail without bail, pending an appeal, the department shall pay to each parish sheriff, or to the governing authority of those parishes in which the governing authority operates the parish jail, for keeping and feeding the individual in the parish jail the sum of twenty-one dollars per day from date of sentencing until the individual is confined in a penal or correctional institution under the supervision of the department.

(b) In addition, the department shall reimburse only the cost of extraordinary medical expenses incurred in emergency circumstances when the health of the inmate requires the use of the closest services available. The department shall require an inmate to file a claim for reimbursement with any available health or medical insurer in accordance with R.S. 15:831.

(c) Each sheriff shall file a monthly report with the department to be paid on a monthly basis and shall include with any request for reimbursement for extraordinary medical expenses an explanation of why state provided services were not used.

(2) When the state makes payment in accordance with this Subsection, no additional compensation from the parish governing authority shall be paid to the sheriff for the care of those prisoners being held for the department.

(3) In any case in which a person has been committed to the department but is being confined in a parish jail or institution, the department shall accept into custody on a priority basis, as established by the Department of Public Safety and Corrections, any such individual who has been determined by the sheriff who has custody of the individual to be dangerous, an escape risk, or afflicted with a physical or mental disorder, upon the request of the sheriff.

(4) In the city of Shreveport, when the city jail holds prisoners for the sheriff of Caddo Parish, the increase in per diem provided for in Senate Bill No. 553 of the 1991 Regular Session shall be paid to the governing authority of the city of Shreveport.

(5) In the parish of Terrebonne, the monies received by the sheriff, pursuant to Paragraph (1) of this Subsection, may be used for the costs of a parish jail. Any contract, lease, sublease, obligation, agreement, or other instrument entered into by the sheriff of Terrebonne Parish shall be legal, valid, and binding upon the office monies of the sheriff, including any subsequent holder of the office of the sheriff, even though the term of the contract, agreement, lease, sublease, obligation, or other instrument extends beyond the expiration of the term of the sheriff who enters into it.

C. Notwithstanding any provision of law to the contrary, only individuals actually sentenced to death or confinement at hard labor shall be committed to the Department of Corrections.

D. In the event the Department of Public Safety and Corrections cannot accept an individual because of lack of facilities under the control of the department, the department may, subject to legislative appropriation, enter into a contract with a law enforcement district, municipal, or parish governing authority to house additional prisoners. If the contract requires the district, municipal, or parish governing authority to acquire additional bedspace by purchase or construction of new facilities, or renovation or addition to existing facilities, the department shall pay the sum of seven dollars per day for each prisoner provided for by such contract. This payment shall be in addition to any other payment required under this Section and shall be paid for the duration of the period necessary to service the debt incurred by the district, municipal, or parish governing authority in acquiring such bedspace by purchase or construction of new facilities or renovation or addition to existing facilities. Such debt service period shall be specified in the contract between the department and the district, municipal, or parish governing authority. Any such debt must receive the prior approval of the State Bond Commission of Louisiana.

(Chgd. by Acts 1990 No. 75, §1; Acts 1991 No. 175, §1, No. 520, §1, No. 988, §1; Acts 1992 No. 5, §1, No. 394, §1; Acts 1995 No. 978, §1, eff. 8/15/95.)

§824.1. Deputy marshals, town of Jackson; Department of Corrections to provide funds.

The Department of Corrections, out of its appropriated funds shall annually allocate fifteen thousand dollars to the governing authority of the town of Jackson, for use solely to provide funds for the employment of two additional deputy marshals to provide extra law enforcement in and around the town of Jackson made necessary by reason of the location of Dixon Correctional Institute.

§825. Personnel; employment; power of director.

The director of corrections, subject to the limitations of appropriations, and according to the laws regulating employment of public employees, shall appoint all personnel deemed necessary for the operation of the department, and in so doing, the director may establish positions within the department and make appointments thereto; abolish positions; transfer duties between positions; and shall assign duties to, direct and control the work of such personnel. He shall prescribe regulations governing the transfer of personnel from one institution or division of the department to another. He shall institute a program for the training and development of all personnel of the department. All personnel, other than the director and two assistants to the director shall be subject to the civil service laws of this state. Subject to civil service regulations, the director shall have the authority to suspend, discharge or otherwise discipline personnel for cause.

§825.1. Appointment of ex-officio notaries at state correctional institutions; scope of powers.

A. The secretary of corrections may designate, at each unit under the jurisdiction of the department, employees of the department to serve as ex-officio notaries public. All acts performed by such ex-officio notaries public as authorized herein shall be performed without charge or other compensation.

B. Appointees under this provision may take acknowledgements, administer oaths, and perform any other duty which notaries public are authorized by law to perform, provided that the authority of appointees under this provision is limited to acts and instruments to which the department of corrections or the secretary of corrections is a party, and to the administration of oaths, affidavits, and other documents concerning any matter in which the department of corrections has an interest.

C. The secretary of corrections may suspend or terminate any appointment made pursuant to this Section at any time. Separation from the employ of the department of corrections shall automatically terminate any authority granted pursuant to this Section.

D. The department of corrections shall pay the costs of notarial seals and bonds, if required, for ex-officio notaries public appointed pursuant to this Section.

§825.2. Special agents; appointment; carrying weapons.

A. The secretary of the Louisiana Department of Corrections shall be authorized at his discretion to appoint special agents. These agents shall be appointed from permanent status employees and may carry weapons exposed or concealed while in the performance of their duties in the same manner as law enforcement officers.

B. The secretary shall formulate and adopt appropriate rules and regulations governing the qualifications and duties of special agents.

§825.3. Criminal history review.

No operator, staff person, or employee of a juvenile detention, correction, or treatment facility shall be hired by the department until such person has submitted his fingerprints to the Louisiana Bureau of Criminal Identification and Information so that it may be determined whether or not such person has been convicted of or has pled nolo contendere to a crime listed in R.S. 15:587.1(C). If it is determined that such person has such a conviction or has entered a plea of nolo contendere to a crime listed in R.S. 15:587.1(C), that person shall not be hired.

§826. Services performed by department.

A. The department shall furnish a staff for the Board of Parole, and if such personnel are available, upon the request of any court of this state having criminal jurisdiction shall furnish probation and parole services for such court.

B. Upon the request of the appropriate parochial or municipal authority, the department shall perform the following services:

(1) It shall provide consultation services with respect to the design, construction, programs and administration of detention and correctional facilities for adults operated by parishes and municipalities;

(2) It shall make studies and surveys of the programs and administration of such detention and correctional facilities;

(3) It shall administer programs of grants-in-aid for construction and operation of approved local facilities; and

(4) It shall provide courses of training for the personnel of such detention and correctional facilities, shall inspect said facilities, and shall make recommendations to the respective authority to achieve compliance with standards established for such facilities.

§827. Duties of Department of Public Safety and Corrections.

A. In addition to other duties imposed upon the department it shall be the duty of the department to:

(1) Establish programs of research, statistics, and planning, which shall include but not be limited to studies of the efficacy and performance of the policies, plans and procedures of the department and studies of the treatment of offenders, and to provide information about other programs of the department.

(2) Make an annual report to the governor with respect to the work of the department, which shall include but not be limited to statistical and other data, accounts of research work performed by the department, the results of inspections of local detention and correctional

facilities and statistical and other data on persons detained in such facilities, and any recommendations for legislation affecting the department.

(3) Establish a diagnostic and treatment center, which may consist of one or more branches, which shall undertake medical, educational, psychiatric, and social studies of persons committed to facilities under the jurisdiction of the department and to provide for the training of such psychiatrists, neurologists, special educators, psychologists, nurses, technicians, social workers, occupational therapists, physicians, and other professional trainees whose services shall be utilized in the operation of said center.

(4) Establish rules and regulations for the detection of controlled dangerous substances upon the person or in the blood stream of inmates returning from any labor detail, pass, furlough, or emergency leave which required the inmate to leave the grounds of a correctional institution under the jurisdiction of the department. The methods which may be employed for the detection of controlled dangerous substances may include but are not limited to the use of a police dog trained to detect controlled dangerous substances and analysis of the inmate's breath or urine. If an inmate is found to be under the influence or in possession of a controlled dangerous substance upon returning to the facility from any labor detail, pass, furlough, or emergency leave, then the inmate shall be ineligible for Work Training Facility North.

B. No convicted felon whether in the custody of the Department of Public Safety and Corrections or in the physical custody of a parish sheriff shall be assigned to be housed or remain housed for any portion of his sentence at the correctional institution at Work Training Facility South. No person charged with the commission of a felony who is incarcerated pending trial shall be housed or remain housed pending trial at the Work Training Facility South.

(Chgd. by Acts 1994 Third Ex. Sess. No. 112, §1; Acts 1995 No. 320, §1, eff. 6/16/95, No. 914, §1, eff. 6/28/95.)

§828. Classification and treatment programs; qualified sex offender programs; reports; additional good time.

A. (1) Persons committed to and in the physical custody of the department shall be treated in a humane manner, and the department shall direct efforts toward the rehabilitation of such persons in order to effect their return to the community as promptly as practicable. In order to accomplish this purpose, the secretary of the Department of Public Safety and Corrections shall establish programs of classification and diagnosis, education, casework, counseling and psychotherapy, vocational training and guidance, work, library and religious services, and such other rehabilitation programs as are consistent with available resources, physical custody, and appropriate classification criteria. Such programs shall include but not be limited to the prison rehabilitation pilot program as set forth in R.S. 15:828.1. Additionally, he shall institute procedures to provide for the study and classification of all inmates of penal or correctional institutions under the jurisdiction of the department.

(2) (a) In cases where the offender has been convicted of a violation of any provision of Subpart C of Part II, Subpart B of Part IV, or Subpart A(1) or A(4) of Part V of Chapter 1 of Title 14 of the Louisiana Revised Statutes of 1950 and, in accordance with the penalty provisions of the particular statute, has been sentenced to hard labor in the custody of the Department of Public Safety and Corrections and is housed in a state correctional facility, the department, subject to the availability of resources and appropriate individual classification criteria, should provide counseling and therapy by institutional mental health staff in a sex offender program until successfully completed or until expiration of sentence, release on parole in accordance with and when permitted by R.S. 15:574.4, or other release in accordance with law, whichever comes first.

(b) For purposes of this Paragraph, a "sex offender program" means one which includes either or both group and individual therapy and may include arousal reconditioning. Group therapy should be conducted by two therapists, one male and one female, and, subject to availability of staff, at least one of whom should be licensed as a psychologist, board-certified as a psychiatrist, or a clinical social worker.

(c) The social worker, psychologist, or psychiatrist shall provide the Board of Parole with progress reports and information in accordance with R.S. 15:574.4(C)(2).

B. The secretary shall prescribe rules and regulations in the facilities and institutions under the jurisdiction of the department to encourage voluntary participation by inmates in vocational training, adult education, literacy, and reading programs. When funds are provided, such educational programs shall be available at each penal or correctional institution under the jurisdiction of the department. The rules and regulations may include provisions for furloughs or good time, in addition to the provisions of R.S. 15:571.3(B) and 571.14, for offenders who are otherwise eligible, but no offender shall receive more than ten additional days per month and one hundred eighty days total good time for program participation.

C. A prisoner who has been denied eligibility for diminution of sentence for good behavior as provided in R.S. 15:537 shall not be eligible for additional good time as provided in Subsection B of this Section.

(Chgd. by Acts 1991 No. 51, §1; No. 766, §1; Acts 1992 No. 723, §1; Acts 1993 No. 484, §1, No. 671, §1, No. 872, §1; Acts 1994 Third Ex. Sess. No. 110, §1, No. 138, §1, eff. 8/27/94.)

§828.1. Prison rehabilitation pilot program; establishment; participating correctional institutions; content; administration; implementation; reporting.

A. The "Prison Rehabilitation Pilot Program" is hereby created and established within the Department of Public Safety and Corrections.

B. Any state correctional institution may participate in the program.

C. The program shall consist of the following subprograms:

(1) An educational station, which shall utilize an educational system which first determines the most effective particular learning style of each inmate and then teaches each inmate using that particular learning style.

(2) A vocational station, which shall utilize a computer-based instruction program teaching basic academic skills in a job-related context.

(3) An after-care treatment program, which shall consist of the following:

(a) An in-prison case manager who shall prepare inmates for upcoming release.

(b) A community resource specialist who shall supervise and monitor former inmates for the first twelve months following release from the correctional institution.

(c) Participation in the post-release supervision segment of the after-care treatment program shall be voluntary for those former inmates who are released following fulfillment of their sentences or following an executive pardon. Participation shall be mandatory, as a condition of parole, for those former inmates who are released on parole.

(4) Participation shall be mandatory for those inmates who participate in the good time program.

D. The department shall adopt and promulgate rules and guidelines as it deems necessary for the administration and implementation of this program.

E. The program shall be introduced into the selected institutions on January 1, 1995.

F. Each in-prison case manager and community resource specialist shall present a comprehensive report on the progress of inmates and former inmates under their respective jurisdictions to the secretary within twenty-two months following initial implementation of the program. The secretary shall submit a report on the overall success of the program to the governor, the president of the Senate, and the speaker of the House of Representatives within twenty-four months following initial implementation of the program. This report shall include a recommendation that the program be continued, expanded, or terminated.

G. The provisions of this Section shall be implemented only to the extent that funds are appropriated for this purpose and to the extent that is consistent with available resources, physical custody, and appropriate classification criteria.

(Added by Acts 1994 Third Ex. Sess. No. 138, §1, eff. 8/27/94.)

§829. Discipline of inmates.

The director of corrections shall prescribe rules and regulations for the maintenance of good order and discipline in the facilities and institutions under the jurisdiction of the department, which rules and regulations shall include procedures for dealing with violations thereof. A copy of such rules and regulations shall be furnished each inmate. Corporal punishment is prohibited.

The director shall maintain a record of charges of infractions of the rules and regulations by inmates, any punishments imposed therefor, and of any medical examinations of inmates.

§830. Treatment of mentally ill and mentally retarded inmates.

A. The department may establish resources and programs for the treatment of mentally ill and mentally retarded inmates, either in a separate facility or as part of other institutions or facilities of the department.

B. On the recommendation of appropriate medical personnel and with the consent of the Department of Health and Human Resources or other appropriate department, the secretary of the Department of Corrections may transfer an inmate for observation and diagnosis to the Department of Health and Human Resources or other appropriate department or institution for a period not to exceed the length of his sentence. If the inmate is found to be subject to civil commitment for psychosis or other mental illness or retardation, the secretary of the Department of Corrections shall initiate legal proceedings for such commitment. If the inmate is not represented by counsel at such legal proceedings, the court shall appoint an attorney to represent him. Reasonable attorney fees shall be fixed by the judge and shall be paid by the state. While the inmate is in such other institution his sentence shall continue to run.

C. When, in the judgment of the administrator of the institution to which an inmate has been transferred, he has recovered from the condition which occasioned the transfer, he shall be returned to the department, unless his sentence has expired.

§830.1. Refusal of treatment by mentally ill or mentally retarded inmates.

A. Whenever a mentally ill or mentally retarded inmate refuses treatment and any staff physician, staff psychiatrist, or consulting psychiatrist of the institution certifies that the treatment is necessary to prevent harm or injury to the inmate or to others, such treatment will be permitted for a period not to exceed fifteen days. If treatment for a longer period is deemed necessary, a petition shall be filed in a court of competent jurisdiction setting forth the reasons for the treatment. Treatment shall continue while the hearing is pending. After a hearing at which the mentally ill or mentally retarded inmate is represented by counsel, the court shall determine whether the inmate is competent and, if not, he shall order that appropriate treatment be provided. If the inmate does not have counsel, the court shall appoint an attorney to represent him. Reasonable attorney fees shall be fixed by the judge and paid by the state.

B. Treatment shall be administered at a treatment facility as designated by law, or at a facility under the control or supervision of the Department of Public Safety and Corrections that has been designated by the Department of Health and Human Resources and the Department of Public Safety and Corrections as a treatment facility.

C. Commitments pursuant to this Section shall be in accord with all procedures required by law in the case of judicial commitment. Nothing herein shall be construed to preclude any person in the custody of the Department of Public Safety and Corrections from any commitment or admission as may be otherwise provided by law.

§830.2. Security for mental health patients.

The department may contract with the Department of Health and Human Resources to provide security personnel for mental health patients who are confined to forensic units or other facilities to which such patients may be temporarily referred for medical treatment under the jurisdiction of the Department of Health and Human Resources whenever it is deemed necessary by the Department of Health and Human Resources to establish forensic facilities in New Orleans, Baton Rouge, Shreveport, and Alexandria.

§831. Medical care of inmates; testing.

A. The secretary of public safety and corrections shall establish and shall prescribe standards for health, medical, and dental services for each institution, including preventive, diagnostic, and therapeutic measures on both an outpatient and a hospital basis, for all types of patients. An inmate may be taken to a medical facility outside the institution when deemed necessary by the director. However, in situations which are not life-threatening, the medical facility selected to treat the inmate shall be a part of the state's charity hospital system. No monies appropriated to the department from the state general fund or from dedicated funds shall be used for the purposes of providing cosmetic medical treatment of inmates, unless the condition necessitating such treatment arises or results from an accident or situation which was the fault of the department or resulted from an action or lack of action on the part of the department.

B. (1) Notwithstanding any other law to the contrary, the secretary shall promulgate rules and regulations regarding reimbursement by a state inmate for medical expenses incurred by the department or sheriff for the inmate's treatment, including a requirement that the inmate file a claim with his private medical or health care insurer or any public medical assistance program, under which he is covered and from which the inmate may make a claim for payment or reimbursement of the cost of any such medical treatment.

(2) In addition, the secretary shall promulgate rules and regulations requiring that copayments be made by inmates upon receiving medical or dental treatment, which may include a sliding scale based on the inmates' ability to pay. These rules and regulations shall

include but not be limited to guidelines for payments for inmate visits to doctors, hospitals, psychiatrists, and dentists, and for receipt of prescription or nonprescription drugs. The secretary shall also establish written guidelines for collection of copayments from an inmate's drawing account or savings account pursuant to R.S. 15:874.

C. The secretary may order that an inmate be tested for a contagious disease if the inmate has been in an altercation and there is reason to believe that an exchange of bodily fluids between the inmate and another person has taken place. In addition, the secretary may authorize the testing of a staff member for contagious diseases at state expense when such testing is in the best interest of the department, including consideration of its staff and inmate populations.

(Chgd. by Acts 1990 No. 75, §1; Acts 1993 No. 686, §1, No. 875, §1; Acts 1997 No. 626, §1, eff. 8/15/97.)

§832. Work by inmates; allowance.

A. The department shall provide employment opportunities and vocational training for all inmates, regardless of gender, consistent with available resources, physical custody, and appropriate classification criteria. Insofar as is possible, the equipment used in such programs, the conditions of employment, the management practices, and the general operating procedures thereof shall approximate those of private industry. The provisions of Part IX of Chapter 2 of Title 51 of the Louisiana Revised Statutes of 1950 with respect to prison-made goods shall be applicable to goods made, manufactured, or produced by the inmates of all institutions and facilities, under the jurisdiction of the department.

B. Inmates shall be compensated, within the limits in grades fixed by the secretary of the department for work performed, including institutional maintenance and attendance at training programs. Prisoners who are unable to work because of injury, illness, or other incapacity may be compensated at rates to be fixed by the secretary within the limits established by law. The inmate shall contribute to the support of his dependents who may be receiving public assistance during the period of commitment if funds available to him are adequate for such purpose.

C. The department may enter into contractual agreements for the use of inmate labor by any department, board, commission, or agency of this state responsible for the conservation of natural resources or the construction and maintenance of public works, subject to the following restrictions:

(1) No such contract shall be entered into with respect to the construction or maintenance of roads or highways, except as otherwise provided by law.

(2) No inmate shall be assigned to maintenance work at public facilities outside the department in accordance with this Section when such work requires housing the inmate in a parish prison or other local housing facility and the inmate has been convicted of first or second degree murder, attempted first or second degree murder, aggravated rape, attempted aggravated rape, forcible rape, aggravated kidnapping, aggravated arson, armed robbery, attempted armed robbery, or the inmate has been sentenced as an habitual offender under R.S. 15:529.1 except during the last six months of his term.

D. When inmates are assigned to maintenance work at public facilities outside the department, the contracting authority shall agree:

(1) To accept the physical custody of the inmate.

(2) To physically house the inmate in the parish jail or prison at all times and to allow the inmate to leave the parish jail or prison, or other housing facility, only to perform work to which he has been assigned.

(3) To notify the department prior to granting the inmate any pass, furlough, or emergency leave, said notification to include the reasons for the release and the duration thereof.

(4) To permit the inmate to engage only in work designed to conserve natural resources, maintain or improve public property or to assist with the daily functioning of the jail, prison, or courthouse and to prohibit the inmate from engaging in any work for a private individual or business entity whether said inmate is paid or not.

(5) To refer to the department for processing and approval in accordance with department regulations for the inmate to be transferred to a work release type program.

(6) To notify the department promptly of any escape, new offense, or conviction involving the inmate, or of any unusual occurrence involving the inmate.

(7) To maintain custody of the inmate until he is ordered released from custody or returned by the department; and to provide transportation of the inmate to and from any state correctional institution as may be required.

E. The department shall agree to compute the inmate's sentence and notify the sheriff when the inmate becomes eligible for parole or final discharge.

F. In addition, the department shall be responsible for monitoring such maintenance programs to assure that the above conditions are fulfilled. Should the contracting authority fail to abide by any condition of the agreement, the department shall have the right to terminate the agreement and all similar agreements between the department and the contracting authority.

G. Further, the department shall not assign an inmate on maintenance to the custody of any sheriff except the sheriff of the parish where the inmate is domiciled or sentenced, unless specifically authorized by the secretary.

H. The department shall reimburse the sheriff, for keeping and feeding any inmate assigned to his custody, in accordance with the amount set by R.S. 15:824(B).

The provisions of this Section shall not be construed to limit the applicability of R.S. 38:2212 to any work undertaken pursuant to this Section.

(Chgd. by Acts 1993 No. 872, §1; Acts 1997 No. 640, §1, eff. 7/3/97.)

§832.1. Work by inmates; construction, renovation, custodial, maintenance, or repairs.

A. Notwithstanding any other provision of law to the contrary, the governor, upon determining that it is appropriate and in furtherance of the rehabilitation and training of inmates, may, by executive order, authorize the use of inmates in a penal or correctional facility owned by the state of Louisiana for necessary labor in connection with a particular capital construction project on the grounds of the facility, when the estimated cost of the project or work, exclusive of labor costs, does not exceed two hundred thousand dollars for any new construction, or when the project involves renovation, maintenance, repair, or remodeling work on the grounds of the facility. Additionally the governor may authorize by executive order the use of inmates to perform custodial services on state grounds and buildings. For purposes of this Section, "penal or correctional facility" shall mean any location at which inmates are housed on a permanent basis.

B. Any requirement of law regarding the procurement of labor services in connection with public works projects or custodial services shall not apply to a project or work utilizing inmate laborers under the provisions of this Section. Nothing herein shall be construed to provide an exemption from any other requirement of law applicable to and regarding the purchase of or rental of materials, supplies, or equipment, or to the procurement of architectural or engineering services in connection with such projects or works except that the Department of Public Safety and Corrections may utilize, on such projects or work, the services of architects and engineers who are employees of the department, when the use of architects or engineers is otherwise required by law.

C. The provisions of this Section shall not affect any contract involving maintenance work performed by persons who are mentally or physically impaired. As far as practicable, the state shall utilize the services of persons mentally or physically impaired in any contract for maintenance of a public facility.

(Chgd. by Acts 1997 No. 1208, §1, eff. 7/15/97.)

§833. Inmate contact with persons outside institution; temporary release.

A. The secretary of the Department of Public Safety and Corrections may authorize visits and correspondence under reasonable conditions between inmates and approved friends, relatives, and other persons. Notwithstanding any provisions of law to the contrary, the secretary may authorize the temporary release of an inmate only for terminal illness, serious illness or death of a member of the inmate's family, or for an interview of the inmate by a prospective employer.

B. (1) The secretary may also, as herein provided, authorize furloughs to deserving inmates of any adult correctional institution. This type furlough is intended to serve as a rehabilitation tool to assist the inmate in maintaining family relationships during the period of his incarceration. A furlough, as provided herein, is not to be considered a reprieve and therefore will not extend the inmate's sentence.

(2) Prior to being recommended for furlough, the inmate shall submit a furlough plan to his supervising authority, stating the purpose of the furlough, the destination and with whom

he plans to stay, and otherwise comply with such rules and regulations as may be established by the secretary of corrections and adopted pursuant to the procedure as set forth in R.S. 49:953 et seq. No furloughs shall be granted until the plan has been approved by the secretary. A responsible member of the inmate's family or other previously approved person must sign a responsibility agreement and provide transportation for the inmate.

(3) (a) No inmate serving a sentence for conviction of first degree murder (R.S. 14:30), second degree murder (R.S. 14:30.1), attempted murder (R.S. 14:27, 14:29), aggravated rape (R.S. 14:42), attempted aggravated rape (R.S. 14:27, 14:42), forcible rape (R.S. 14:42.1), aggravated kidnapping (R.S. 14:44), aggravated arson (R.S. 14:51), armed robbery (R.S. 14:64), attempted armed robbery (R.S. 14:27, 14:64), or producing, manufacturing, distributing, or dispensing or possession with intent to produce, manufacture, distribute, or dispense a controlled dangerous substance classified in Schedule I or II of R.S. 40:964, nor any inmate sentenced as a habitual offender under R.S 15:529.1 shall be released from the institution to which he is assigned except under security escort and then only in the circumstances listed in Subparagraph (b) below.

(b) Treatment for serious illness; visits with dying family members; funerals of family members; participation in programs at other correctional institutions; speaking assignments; work details; court appearances; participation in charity boxing matches; performances of any organized vocal or instrumental group at any civic or charitable function; or religious services.

(c) However, notwithstanding any provisions of law to the contrary, inmates assigned to work duties at the governor's mansion and inmates within six months of discharge shall be eligible for furloughs and temporary releases.

C. The Department of Corrections shall compile statistical data on the incidence of furlough violations by participating inmates. Violations shall include the commission of new offenses as well as any transgressions that result in disciplinary action or removal from the program. The data shall indicate the nature of the incident, the age of the offender, his original offense, the length of his sentence, his prior criminal record, and any other characteristic found to be predictive of success or failure. This information shall be used by the department to guide it in formulating program policies and eligibility standards and shall be available to the legislature upon request.

§834. Lands under control of department; lease, rights of way, purchase.

The director of corrections shall have power and authority, with the approval of the Board of Corrections, to lease (but not for oil, gas or other minerals) any of the lands owned by the state and under the control of the department which is not being used, which lease shall not be for a longer period than January 1st after the inauguration of an incoming administration. The director shall have the right to grant rights of way across state owned lands under its jurisdiction for the purpose of laying pipe lines, gas lines, water lines and transmission of electricity for power and light and also for telephone and telegraph lines and to enter into the necessary contracts which shall provide for the payment of an adequate consideration. The director shall also have the authority, with the approval of the Board of Corrections and the governor, to buy lands needed for the proper use of any institution under the jurisdiction of the department; and also to sell and transfer to any other state agency real property belonging to the state and under the jurisdiction of the department.

§834.1. Free housing; employees living at correctional institutions.

The secretary of the Department of Public Safety and Corrections shall promulgate rules and regulations consistent with all other provisions of law to provide for free housing for persons who are not inmates, and who are employees living on the grounds of a state correctional institution. The secretary shall consider the cost-effectiveness of free housing as compared to housing at reduced costs and determine whether free housing would be more beneficial to such employees and to the state. In formulating the rules and regulations, the secretary shall also consider all other provisions of law, rules, or guidelines, particularly those pertaining to the regulation of employment, taxation, and compensation of state employees. *(Added by Acts 1997 No. 956, §1, eff. 8/15/97.)*

§835. Report of director to board.

The director of corrections shall submit an analysis of the institutions under the jurisdiction of, and services performed by the department and an analysis and evaluation of the adequacy and effectiveness of the personnel, programs and properties of the department to the Board of Corrections at least once a year.

§836. Cooperation and agreements with other agencies; federal government; local government.

The department shall cooperate with public and private agencies and officials to assist in fulfilling its functions. The department may enter into agreements with other departments of this state or any political subdivision thereof, with private agencies and with the federal government with respect to the discharge of their respective responsibilities.

§837. Transfer of functions; records, money and equipment; employees.

A. Upon the transfer of functions, any pending or unfinished business shall be taken over and completed by the Louisiana Department of Corrections with the same power and authority as the agency from which the functions are transferred. The department shall be the successor in every way to the agency from which such functions are transferred, and every act done in the exercise of such functions by the department shall be deemed to have the same force and effect under any provisions of law in effect as if done by the agency from which functions are transferred is referred to, or designated by any law or contract or other document, such reference or designation shall be deemed to apply to the department; provided that to the extent necessary to prevent the impairment of the contractual obligations of any agency heretofore existing, or of the state of Louisiana, the existence, organization and functions of any such agency shall be excluded from the provisions of the section, and like exclusion shall be made whenever necessary to prevent any violation of the provisions, terms, or conditions of any gift, donation, deed, will trust, or other instrument or disposition by which property of any nature or description has been vested in any agency affected by this section, or the diversion from the purposes for which such property was donated, deeded, divided or bequeathed, or otherwise vested in any such agency; provided further that the provisions of this section shall not be construed or applied in such a way as to prevent full compliance by the state or any agency of the federal government, by which federal aid or other financial assistance from the United States has been made available to this state or any subdivision or agency thereof, anything contained in this section to the contrary notwithstanding.

B. All books, papers, records, money, choses in action, and other property heretofore used or possessed by any agency in the exercise of functions hereby transferred, shall be transferred to the Department of Corrections.

C. All employees heretofore engaged in the performance of duties, in any agency in the exercise of functions transferred by this section to the Louisiana Department of Corrections shall be transferred with such functions to the department and shall, so far as practicable, continue to perform the duties heretofore performed.

§838. References to Board of Institutions, Department of Institutions, director of institutions.

Hereafter, all references in the laws of this state to the Louisiana Board of Institutions, the Department of Institutions, and the director of institutions shall be deemed to refer respectively to the Board of Corrections, the Louisiana Department of Corrections and the Director of Corrections.

§839. Effect of R.S. 40:2001 through 40:2017.9.

The provisions of Act No. 207 of 1956, as amended, providing for the organization and powers of the State Department of Hospitals, and incorporated into the Revised Statutes as Part I of Chapter 11 of Title 40, including R.S. 40:2001 through 40:2017.9, are hereby confirmed, ratified and continued in effect.

§840. Drug education and rehabilitation program.

The department of corrections shall establish and maintain a drug education and rehabilitation program at all juvenile correctional institutions under its jurisdiction. The director shall transmit a report to the legislature no later than ninety days after the effective date hereof regarding the establishment of the initial program. No later than April 1, 1975, the director shall transmit to the legislature a comprehensive plan regarding drug education and rehabilitation, and annually thereafter the director shall submit a report regarding such program to the legislature. In the establishment and maintenance of such program, the director may seek assistance from other state agencies involved in drug education and rehabilitation, and such agencies are authorized and directed to so cooperate with the director.

§840.1. Access to records; cooperation by other agencies; confidentiality; disclosure.

A. During the course of any investigation which the Department of Corrections is authorized by law to conduct, or any investigation necessary to the rehabilitation of persons in the custody of the Department of Corrections, said department shall have access to information and records under the control of any state or local agency which are reasonably related to the rehabilitation of the individual, which information shall be maintained in the file or case record of the offender. This information shall include circumstances attending the commission of the offense for which the offender was or is to be incarcerated, placed on probation, or released on parole, subsequent offenses that occur while under supervision, the offender's history of delinquency, or criminality as a juvenile and adult, his family situation and background, economic and employment status, education, personal habits, the condition of the offender's physical and mental health, and other matters deemed relevant to his rehabilitation.

B. Local and state law enforcement agencies, courts, welfare and social service agencies, juvenile agencies and mental, health and correctional institutions shall furnish to the Department of Corrections criminal or delinquency records, mental or health records, and such other relevant information as the department requests.

C. All information obtained under this provision shall be held as confidential and shall not be disclosed directly or indirectly to anyone except in accordance with R.S. 15:574.12.

§840.2. Louisiana Restitution Industries.

A. The director of the Louisiana Department of Corrections is hereby authorized to establish and carry out, outside the main restraining wall or structure but within the exterior boundary of the correctional facilities at Angola, St. Gabriel and DeQuincy, demonstration type projects involving the employment of inmates of such institutions; provided, however, that such projects shall not be conducted within one mile of any residential zone as so designated by the local governing authority. Such projects shall also provide for the provision of supportive services to inmates of the demonstration institutions, such as training, education, counseling, and the like. Such projects so established shall be known as Louisiana Restitution Industries. In establishing such projects, the director of the Louisiana Department of Corrections is authorized to enter into agreements, by contract, under the public bid laws of the state of Louisiana, with any private person, pursuant to which such person shall be authorized to establish, by construction, lease, or otherwise, facilities outside the main restraining wall or structure but within the exterior boundaries of such penal or correctional institutions for the purpose of carrying out industrial or other operations herein authorized. Such persons and company employees, excluding inmates, must be of good moral character. Such employment within such institutions of inmates shall, however, be on a voluntary basis.

B. Any such agreement shall contain provisions assuring that the wages paid to such inmate, shall be no less than minimum wage as established by the Fair Labor Standards Act.

C. Any inmate of any such institution so employed shall be entitled to receive, after deductions authorized in Subsection D of this Section or under any other law, wages earned by him in performing such work, except that such wages shall be made available to such inmate at such time or times as the director of the Louisiana Department of Corrections may by regulation prescribe, but in no event later than at the time of his release by parole or otherwise, from confinement in a state penal or correctional institution. Employers shall cover such inmate employees under worker's compensation but in no way shall such inmates be included in employment security.

D. Any inmate so employed shall be required, pursuant to regulations promulgated by the director of the Louisiana Department of Corrections, to pay from the wages received for work in accordance with this Section, and the director is authorized to deduct therefrom in the following order:

(1) Federal and state income taxes and social security deductions;

(2) Thirty percent of the remainder after the deductions for taxes and social security to the victims of any crimes committed by the inmate to the extent of their loss as determined by a written agreement or judgment and thereafter to any state fund established by law to compensate victims of crime;

(3) Twenty percent of the remainder after the deductions for taxes and social security to the Louisiana Department of Corrections to be returned to such state penal or correctional institutions in the same percentage as funds are contributed, less administrative expenses to the Louisiana Department of Corrections, for the purpose of defraying the costs of room and board of the inmate;

(4) Forty percent of the remainder after the deductions for taxes and social security to the spouse and children of the inmate or, if the inmate has no spouse and children, forty percent of the remainder after the deductions for taxes and social security to the victims of any crimes committed by the inmate to the extent of their loss as determined by a written agreement or judgment and thereafter to any state fund established by law to compensate victims of crime; and

(5) All remaining to the inmate's personal fund.

E. Any amounts so deducted pursuant to Subsection D of this Section shall be payable in such manner as the director of the Louisiana Department of Corrections may by regulation prescribe.

F. In administering the provisions of this Section, the director of the Louisiana Department of Corrections is authorized, as a part of, or in connection with, any agreement pursuant to Subsection A of this Section, to make available, by lease or otherwise, land, together with improvements thereon, located outside the main restraining wall or structure but within the exterior boundary of any state penal or correctional institution for use by the private party to such agreement for providing employment in accordance with this Section. Such lands, including improvements, shall be made available pursuant to such terms and conditions as the director of the Louisiana Department of Corrections, the Legislative Budget Committee and the Division of Administration may prescribe. Any such lease of land or of improvements or facilities entered into under authority of this Section shall be for a primary term not to exceed five years, and may be renewed from year to year after expiration of the primary term upon such terms and conditions as the director of the Louisiana Department of Corrections, the Legislative Budget Committee and the Division of Administration may prescribe.

G. As used in this Section, the term "person" means any individual, corporation, partnership, association, or other entity.

H. On or before October 1, 1978, the director of the Louisiana Department of Corrections shall submit a report to the Louisiana Legislature concerning the administration of the provisions of this Section, together with his views and recommendations with respect thereto.

PART III-B. NORTHEAST LOUISIANA CORRECTIONAL CENTER

§841. Establishment; purpose.

The Northeast Louisiana Correctional Center is hereby created as a political corporation, with power to sue and be sued. It shall be administered by a board of governors.

§842. Board of governors; membership, powers, duties; suits.

A. The board of governors shall be composed of the sheriff of Concordia Parish, the sheriff of Catahoula Parish, the chief judge of the Seventh Judicial District or a judge of the Seventh Judicial District designated by the chief judge as his representative, two members to be appointed by the chief judge of the Seventh Judicial District, one member of the Concordia Parish Police Jury to be elected by said policy jury, and one member of the Catahoula Parish Police Jury to be elected by said police jury.

B. The president of the board of governors shall be the sheriff of Concordia Parish and he shall be the administrator of the prison. A secretary shall be chosen by the board from among its members and the treasurer of Concordia Parish shall be the ex officio treasurer of the correctional center. The members of the board of governors shall receive no compensation.

§843. Powers of board of governors.

The board of governors:

(1) May inaugurate, conduct, and carry on farming vocational training programs, and other operations on behalf of the center on property owned or leased by the center for these purposes.

(2) Shall keep an accurate account of all revenues derived from the sale of the products of the labor of the prisoners. The accounts shall show the amount of money received from the

sale of produce, the date of the sale, the name of the purchaser, and any other data which will enable the public to be in touch with its affairs.

(3) May acquire land by donation, purchase, or lease for the site of the center. Whenever the purchase price is on terms of credit, the land shall be the only security and the parish shall not be liable for any part of the unpaid purchase price. The board of governors may remove any buildings or improvements on land acquired by them.

(4) May build jails or other places of imprisonment on the property of the center whenever they deem it advisable. They may dedicate a sum not to exceed one-half of one mill on the dollar assessment per year for a period of not more than ten years out of the regular alimony for this purpose. Their dedication of the money may be evidenced by certificates of indebtedness, payable annually with interest payable semiannually, not to exceed the market rate of percent per annum, redeemable on maturity out of any excess revenues that may develop. No building shall be constructed on land not fully paid for.

(5) (a) May grant security for debts incurred in the acquisition of lands for the center for making improvements on the lands, for purchasing machinery, tools, equipment, or other property for the establishment, maintenance, operation, and administration of the center or for obtaining funds to pay and extinguish any debt or debts incurred in the acquisition of the lands or the improvements thereof, by granting mortgages upon the immovable property of the district, where title thereto is in the public, mortgages upon its movables, or crop pledges and pawns upon the crops of the center.

(b) The acts of security shall stipulate that in case of default in the payment of any debt secured thereby or any part of a debt, the property securing the debt shall be subject to seizure and sale with benefit of appraisement, in the same manner as private property subject to encumbrance may be seized and sold, notwithstanding the title of the property securing the debt is vested in the public. The board of governors and the governing authorities of the parishes or the center shall never be obligated beyond the value of the property offered as security.

(6) Shall fix the amount of bond with legal surety which the treasurer shall give, conditioned on a faithful accounting for all money and property entrusted to his care.

(7) May permit use of prisoners on public works at the request of any public body within the center area, but only with the approval and under the supervision of the chief judge of the Seventh Judicial District or a judge of the Seventh Judicial District designated by the chief judge as his representative. The chief judge or such designated representative of said district shall have full authority to recall any prisoner at any time.

(8) (a) May sell, dispose of, or lease any land owned by the center which for any reason can no longer be used, or which is unused or is unnecessary or unsuitable for the operations of the said center.

(b) The board of governors of said center may lease said land upon such terms and conditions as may be most advantageous to the center, but said lease shall not exceed five years.

(c) Should any lands owned by the courts be offered for sale, the board of governors shall cause to be published for thirty days in the official journals of the parishes an advertisement setting forth a description of the land to be sold and the time, place, and terms of the sale.

(d) The land so advertised shall be sold by the sheriff. The sale shall be at the principal door of the courthouse of the Seventh Judicial District Court, between the hours of 11:00 o'clock A.M. and 4:00 o'clock P.M., and shall be to the last and highest bidder, except that the board of governors shall have the right to reject any and all bids. Should a bid be accepted for the sale of said land, then and in that event the board of governors, under the authority of a proper resolution, shall make and deliver to the purchaser a valid deed conveying title thereto.

§844. Suits; service of process.

Suit may be instituted against the Northeast Louisiana Correctional Center at its domicile and service of all legal documents shall be made on the president or secretary of the board of governors.

§845. Municipalities, agreements with for use.

A municipality, whenever it so desires, may have prisoners convicted by the municipal courts of violations of municipal ordinances sentenced to work on or be confined at the center upon agreement by the governing authority of the municipality and the governing authorities of the center for the charges and expenses of keeping the prisoners. The governing authority of a municipality may enter into a contract with the governing authorities of the center to determine the costs to be paid by the municipality to the center for the keeping of prisoners. The charges shall be determined by mutual agreement.

§846. Prisoners.

Any person convicted of misdemeanors and felonies not necessarily punishable by hard labor may be confined in the center. A judge of the Seventh Judicial District shall have full authority to sentence any party convicted of such offenses in the Seventh Judicial District to imprisonment in the center.

§847. Additional facilities.

Any prison, correctional institute, or other type of prison facility which is operated by the Concordia or Catahoula Parish Police Jury may be made available by said police jury to the Northeast Louisiana Correctional Center on a per prisoner fee basis. When any such facility is made available, the facility shall become a part of the Northeast Louisiana Correctional Center and subject to all the requirements of this Part.

PART III-C. LINCOLN PARISH DETENTION CENTER

§848. Establishment; purpose and title.

The governing authority of Lincoln Parish may create, establish, and construct a centralized, single-parish jail and prison for the purpose of providing for the maintenance and upkeep of all persons lawfully incarcerated in Lincoln Parish. If created, established, and constructed, under this Part, this jail and prison shall be known as the Lincoln Parish Detention Center. No other provision of this Part shall be effective and/or operative unless and until the Lincoln Parish Detention Center is created and established by the Lincoln Parish Police Jury under this Part.

§848.1. Organization and powers.

A. The Lincoln Parish Detention Center shall be a political corporation, with power to sue and be sued and shall be governed by a commission to be known as the Lincoln Parish Detention Center Commission. The Lincoln Parish Detention Center shall be domiciled at the parish seat. It shall be sued at its domicile and service of all legal documents shall be made on the chairman or vice-chairman of the commission.

B. The Lincoln Parish Detention Center may acquire title to movable property for public purposes by purchase or donation, may operate or maintain prison farms, and may operate or maintain the farms in whole or in part with prison labor and persons sentenced to the Lincoln Parish Detention Center by city or district courts.

C. Except only as hereinafter specifically provided, all persons lawfully incarcerated in Lincoln Parish shall be incarcerated in the Lincoln Parish Detention Center, subject to the exclusive jurisdiction and control of the Lincoln Parish Detention Center Commission.

§848.2. Lincoln Parish Detention Center Commission members.

A. The Lincoln Parish Detention Center Commission shall be composed of the president of the Lincoln Parish Policy Jury during his tenure as such; a member of the police jury, other than its president, who shall be selected by a majority vote of the Lincoln Parish Police Jury for a term of four years or until said juror's term of office ends, whichever occurs first; the sheriff of Lincoln Parish; the district attorney of Lincoln Parish; and the chief of police of the city of Ruston. The chairman of the commission shall be selected by majority vote of all members of the commission. It shall be the duty of the chairman to conduct all meetings of the commission in accordance with law and the resolutions adopted by a majority of the commission. In the same manner, the commission shall select a vice-chairman from among its number, who shall serve as chairman in the latter's absence.

B. The secretary of the Lincoln Parish Police Jury may serve as secretary of the commission and the Lincoln Parish treasurer may serve as ex officio treasurer of the commission.

C. The members of the Lincoln Parish Detention Center Commission shall receive no compensation.

D. Should any member of the Lincoln Parish Detention Center Commission be sued individually for damages arising out of or in any way connected with the performance of his duties as such commission member, it shall be the responsibility of the Lincoln Parish Police Jury to provide such member with a legal defense to such suit, including reasonable attorney's fees, investigating costs, and other related expenses not paid by any insurance. Should any such commission member be cast in judgment for damages in such a suit, it shall be the obligation of the Lincoln Parish Police Jury to indemnify him fully against such judgment, including all principal, interest, and costs in excess of that paid by any insurance company. Nothing in this Section shall require the Lincoln Parish Police Jury to indemnify a commission member against a judgment wherein there is a specific decree in the judgment that the action of the commission member was malicious, and willfully and deliberately intended to cause bodily harm.

§848.3. Powers and duties of commission.

A. The Lincoln Parish Detention Center Commission shall be keeper of the Lincoln Parish Detention Center, and the sheriff of Lincoln Parish is hereby specifically relieved of that duty in his official capacity as sheriff.

B. Any other provision of law to the contrary notwithstanding, upon relinquishing the custody of any prisoner, to any legally authorized agency, department, or body politic, neither the Lincoln Parish Detention Center nor the commission shall be responsible for the care, conduct, or control of such prisoner until his custody is returned to the Lincoln Parish Detention Center and the commission, or the agents and/or employees of either. The responsibility for the care, conduct, and control of such prisoner in such cases shall be transferred to the agency, department, or body politic to which custody of the prisoner has been relinquished.

C. The Lincoln Parish Detention Center Commission shall be responsible for the physical maintenance of the Lincoln Parish Detention Center, and the Lincoln Parish Police Jury is hereby specifically relieved of that duty in its official capacity as the governing authority of Lincoln Parish.

D. The Lincoln Parish Detention Center Commission shall have all other powers and duties of the sheriff and/or governing authority of a parish heretofore or hereafter provided by law for equipping, maintaining, operating, and/or supporting the public jail of a parish and the prisoners therein, which powers and duties include, but are not limited to the following:

(1) Adopting all rules and regulations necessary and proper for the governance and maintenance of proper operations and conduct of the Lincoln Parish Detention Center and the prisoners thereof.

(2) Appointing and employing all necessary superintendents, corrections officers, and other appropriate personnel, and fixing their salaries and adopting appropriate personnel policies and guidelines, which shall include policies and procedures for discipline and, if necessary, termination.

(3) Authorizing and permitting the use of prisoners of the Lincoln Parish Detention Center to maintain road rights of way, not to include construction, within the Parish of Lincoln and remove litter on public grounds, all under the supervision of the Lincoln Parish Police Jury or other appropriate authorities when such prisoners are committed for such purposes by appropriate courts.

(4) Creating, establishing, and conducting work release programs in accordance with law.

(5) Creating, establishing, and conducting any and all programs, including vocational, rehabilitative, and corrective, not inconsistent with law and consistent with the purposes of this Part.

E. Any construction project undertaken under the auspices of this act shall be performed in accordance with the provisions of R.S. 38:2212.

§848.4. Funding for operation and maintenance of Lincoln Parish Detention Center.

A. The expenses or costs of the operation and maintenance of the Lincoln Parish Detention Center, including salaries, wages, facility operating costs, and the feeding and maintenance of prisoners incarcerated there, shall be paid monthly by the Lincoln Parish Police Jury treasurer, upon approval of such expenses and costs by the Lincoln Parish Detention Center Commission, out of the funds derived from special taxes voted, levied, and collected, and/or budgeted for that purpose. The commission may by resolution delegate to the chairman or one of its other members the duty of approving such monthly expenses and maintenance costs.

B. The Lincoln Parish Police Jury and the Ruston City Council shall appropriate, in the respective proportions of eighty-five per cent and fifteen per cent, an amount necessary to properly maintain, operate, and provide necessary operational equipment or replacement equipment for the Lincoln Parish Detention Center whenever revenues from special taxes, and/or other available funds dedicated for those purposes, are insufficient.

§848.5. Use of other jail and prison facilities.

A. No person shall be incarcerated overnight in Lincoln Parish except in the Lincoln Parish Detention Center. Other jail and prison facilities in Lincoln Parish may be used only to hold prisoners for court during the day, except by express consent of the commission.

B. For good cause, the Lincoln Parish Detention Center Commission may at any time require the use of any jail or prison facility in Lincoln Parish for the purpose of keeping persons arrested for or convicted of crime in the parish.

§848.6. Superintendent and corrections officers.

A. The day-to-day operations of the Lincoln Parish Detention Center shall be conducted by a superintendent, corrections officers, and any other appropriate personnel, subject to the supervision and control of the commission.

B. The superintendent and all corrections officers shall have the power and authority to make arrests of any persons lawfully committed to the Lincoln Parish Detention Center when such persons have escaped, either from their custody or the custody of others; or when such persons have committed other criminal acts while incarcerated or while at large. This power and authority to arrest shall also extend to persons who aid or abet or otherwise interfere with the arrest of a prisoner of the Lincoln Parish Detention Center or who commit criminal acts while on or around the Lincoln Parish Detention Center.

PART III-D. TERREBONNE PARISH DEPARTMENT OF CORRECTIONS AND REHABILITATION

§849. Establishment; purpose and title.

A. The governing authority of Terrebonne Parish may create a department of corrections and rehabilitation. Said department shall have the authority to establish, and construct or designate a centralized, single-parish jail and prison for the purpose of providing for the maintenance and upkeep of all persons lawfully incarcerated in Terrebonne Parish. If created, established, and constructed or designated under this Part, this jail and prison shall be known as the Terrebonne Parish Detention Center.

B. No other provision of this Part shall become effective until and unless the Terrebonne Parish Consolidated Government creates and establishes, by resolution of the parish council of such body, a department of corrections and rehabilitation.

§849.1. Organization and powers.

A. The Terrebonne Parish Department of Corrections and Rehabilitation, hereinafter referred to as the "department", shall be a political subdivision with power to sue and be sued.

B. The department may acquire title to movable property for public purposes by purchase or donation, may operate or maintain prison farms, and may operate or maintain the farms in whole or in part with prison labor and persons sentenced to the department by city, parish or district courts.

C. Except only as hereinafter specifically provided, all persons lawfully incarcerated in Terrebonne Parish shall be incarcerated with the department subject to the exclusive jurisdiction and control of the commission.

§849.2. Terrebonne Parish Department of Corrections and Rehabilitation Commission; establishment; members.

A. The department shall be governed by the Terrebonne Parish Corrections and Rehabilitation Commission, hereinafter to be referred to as the "commission". It shall be domiciled at the parish seat. It shall be sued at its domicile. Service of all legal documents shall be made on the chairman and vice chairman of the commission.

B. (1) The commission shall be composed of the president of Terrebonne Parish during his tenure as such; a member of the Terrebonne Parish Consolidated Government other than its president who shall be selected by a majority vote of the Terrebonne Parish Consolidated Government Council for a term of four years or until his term of office ends, whichever occurs first; the sheriff of Terrebonne Parish; the chief of police of the city of Houma; and the coroner of the parish of Terrebonne.

(2) The chairman of the commission shall be selected by majority vote of all members of the commission. The chairman shall conduct all meetings of the commission in accordance with law and the resolutions adopted by a majority of the commission. In the same manner, the commission shall select a vice chairman from among its number, who shall serve as chairman in the latter's absence.

C. The council clerk of the Terrebonne Parish Consolidated Government may serve as ex officio secretary and treasurer of the commission, respectively.

D. The members of the Terrebonne Parish Detention Center Commission shall receive no compensation.

§849.3. Powers and duties of commission.

A. The commission shall be keeper of the Terrebonne Parish Detention Center or any other designated facility, and the sheriff of Terrebonne Parish is hereby specifically relieved of that duty in his official capacity as sheriff.

B. Any other provision of law to the contrary notwithstanding, upon relinquishing the custody of any prisoner to any legally authorized agency, department, or body politic, neither the department nor the commission shall be responsible for the care, conduct, or control of the prisoner until his custody is returned to the department and the commission, the agents, or the employees of either. The responsibility of the care, conduct, and control of the prisoner in those cases shall be transferred to the agency, department, or body politic to which custody of the prisoner has been relinquished.

C. The commission shall be responsible for the physical maintenance of the Terrebonne Parish Detention Center, and the Terrebonne Parish Consolidated Government is hereby specifically relieved of that duty in its official capacity as the governing authority of Terrebonne Parish.

D. The commission shall have all other powers and duties of the sheriff and/or governing authority of a parish heretofore or hereafter provided by law for equipping, maintaining, operating, and/or supporting the public jail of a parish and the prisoners therein, which powers and duties include but are not limited to the following:

(1) Adopting all rules and regulations necessary and proper for the governance and maintenance of proper operations and conduct of the Terrebonne Parish Detention Center and the prisoners thereof.

(2) Appointing and employing all necessary superintendents, corrections officers, and other appropriate personnel; fixing their salaries; and adopting appropriate personnel policies and guidelines which shall include policies and procedures for discipline and, if necessary, termination.

(3) Authorizing and permitting the use of prisoners of the department to maintain road rights of way, not to include construction, and such other maintenance functions as may be approved by the commission, when performing such tasks for the department, or other agencies or other appropriate authorities when the prisoners are committed for such purposes by appropriate courts.

(4) Creating, establishing, and conducting work-release programs in accordance with law.

(5) Creating, establishing, and conducting any and all programs, including vocational, rehabilitative, and corrective, not inconsistent with law and consistent with the purposes of this Part.

E. Any construction project undertaken under the auspices of this Part shall be performed in accordance with the provisions of R.S. 38:2212.

§849.4. Commission's right to incur debt; funding for operation and maintenance of Terrebonne Parish Department of Corrections and Rehabilitation; authority to levy ad valorem tax; tax election; approval by parish council.

A. The commission shall have the right to incur debt, enter into contracts, and to perform any act which is necessary or proper for carrying out the objects and purposes of the commission.

B. (1) Subject to the approval of a majority of the electors within the parish of Terrebonne, the commission is hereby authorized to levy an ad valorem tax on property located within the boundaries of the district without limit as to the amount of the tax.

(2) Before any tax is levied under the provisions of this Section, there shall be submitted to the qualified electors of the parish at a special election called for the purpose, the proposition to authorize the imposition of the ad valorem tax. Such proposition shall include the purpose, rate, and duration of the tax. Such election shall be conducted in accordance with the general election laws of the state of Louisiana, and a majority of those voting in the election shall have voted in favor of the proposition.

(3) No provision of this Subsection shall become effective until approved by resolution of the parish council of the Terrebonne Parish Consolidated Government.

(4) The funds collected from the imposition of such taxes shall be used for the costs or expenses of the operation and maintenance of the Terrebonne Parish Detention Center. They shall be paid by the commission, but only out of funds budgeted for that purpose. Such expenses or costs may include salaries, wages, facility operating costs, and costs necessary and proper to maintain or operate the facility, maintain or replace equipment, or maintain and feed prisoners incarcerated with the department. The commission may, by resolution, delegate to the chairman or one of the other members the duty of approving such monthly expenses and maintenance costs.

§849.5. Use of other jail and prison facilities.

The commission may designate the existing parish jail or subsequently acquired facility as a detention center under the department, and may use such in accordance with the provisions of this Part.

§849.6. Personnel.

A. The day-to-day operations of the department shall be conducted by a superintendent, corrections officers, and any other appropriate personnel, subject to the supervision and control of the commission.

B. The superintendent and all corrections officers may make arrests of any persons lawfully committed to the department when they have escaped, either from their custody or the custody of others, or when they have committed other criminal acts while incarcerated or while at large. This power and authority to arrest shall also extend to persons who aid or abet or otherwise interfere with the arrest of a prisoner of the department or who commit criminal acts while on or around the department or any of its facilities.

C. Department personnel shall have the authority to carry weapons. The superintendent shall have the authority, with approval of the commission, to establish guidelines for the limitation of carrying of weapons by department personnel.

PART III-E. UNION PARISH DETENTION CENTER

§850.1. Establishment; purpose and title.

The governing authority of Union Parish may create, establish, and construct a centralized, single-parish jail and prison for the purpose of providing for the maintenance and upkeep of all persons lawfully incarcerated in Union Parish. If created, established, and constructed, under this Part, this jail and prison shall be known as the "Union Parish Detention Center". No other provision of this Part shall be effective or operative unless and until the Union Parish Detention Center is created and established by the Union Parish Police Jury under this Part.

§850.2. Organization and powers.

A. The Union Parish Detention Center shall be a political corporation, with power to sue and be sued and shall be governed by a commission to be known as the "Union Parish Detention Center Commission". The Union Parish Detention Center shall be domiciled at the parish seat. It shall be sued at its domicile and service of all legal documents shall be made on the chairman or vice-chairman of the commission.

B. The Union Parish Detention Center may acquire title to movable property for the public purposes by purchase or donation, may operate or maintain prison farms, and may operate or maintain the farms in whole or in part with prison labor and persons sentenced to the Union Parish Detention Center by city or district courts.

C. Except only as hereinafter specifically provided, all persons lawfully incarcerated in Union Parish shall be incarcerated in the Union Parish Detention Center, subject to the exclusive jurisdiction and control of the Union Parish Detention Center Commission.

§850.3. Union Parish Detention Center Commission members.

A. The Union Parish Detention Center Commission shall be composed of the president of the Union Parish Police Jury during his tenure as such; a member of the police jury, other than its president, who shall be selected by a majority vote of the Union Parish Police Jury for a term of four years or until said juror's term of office ends, whichever occurs first; the sheriff of Union Parish; the district attorney of Union Parish; and the chief of police of the city of Farmerville. The chairman of the commission shall be selected by majority vote of all members of the commission. It shall be the duty of the chairman to conduct all meetings of the commission in accordance with law and the resolutions adopted by a majority of the commission. In the same manner, the commission shall select a vice-chairman from among its number, who shall serve as chairman in the latter's absence.

B. The secretary of the Union Parish Police Jury may serve as secretary of the commission and the Union Parish treasurer may serve as ex officio treasurer of the commission.

C. The members of the Union Parish Detention Center Commission shall receive no compensation.

D. Should any member of the Union Parish Detention Center Commission be sued individually for damages arising out of or in any way connected with the performance of his duties as such commission member, it shall be the responsibility of the Union Parish Police Jury to provide such member with a legal defense to such suit, including reasonable attorney's fees, investigating costs, and other related expenses not paid by any insurance. Should any such commission member be cast in judgment for damages in such a suit, it shall be the obligation of the Union Parish Police Jury to indemnify him fully against such judgment, including all principal, interest, and costs in excess of that paid by any insurance company. Nothing in this Section shall require the Union Parish Police Jury to indemnify a commission member against a judgment wherein there is a specific decree in the judgment that the action of the commission member was malicious, and willfully and deliberately intended to cause bodily harm.

§850.4. Powers and duties of commission.

A. The Union Parish Detention Center Commission shall be keeper of the Union Parish Detention Center, and the sheriff of Union Parish is hereby specifically relieved of that duty in his official capacity as sheriff.

B. Any other provision of law to the contrary notwithstanding, upon relinquishing the custody of any prisoner, to any legally authorized agency, department, or body politic, neither the Union Parish Detention Center nor the commission shall be responsible for the care, conduct, or control of such prisoner until his custody is returned to the Union Parish Detention Center and the commission, or the agents or employees of either. The responsibility for the care, conduct, and control of such prisoner in such cases shall be transferred to the agency, department, or body politic to which custody of the prisoner has been relinquished.

C. The Union Parish Detention Center Commission shall be responsible for the physical maintenance of the Union Parish Detention Center, and the Union Parish Police Jury is hereby specifically relieved of that duty in its official capacity as the governing authority of Union Parish.

D. The Union Parish Detention Center Commission shall have all other powers and duties of the sheriff or governing authority of a parish heretofore or hereafter provided by law for equipping, maintaining, operating, or supporting the public jail of a parish and the prisoners therein, which powers and duties include, but are not limited to the following:

(1) Adopting all rules and regulations necessary and proper for the governance and maintenance of proper operations and conduct of the Union Parish Detention Center and the prisoners thereof.

(2) Appointing and employing all necessary superintendents, corrections officers, and other appropriate personnel, and fixing their salaries and adopting appropriate personnel policies and guidelines, which shall include policies and procedures for discipline and, if necessary, termination.

(3) Authorizing and permitting the use of prisoners of the Union Parish Detention Center to maintain road rights of way, not to include construction, within the Parish of Union and remove litter on public grounds, all under the supervision of the Union Parish Police Jury or other appropriate authorities when such prisoners are committed for such purposes by appropriate courts.

(4) Creating, establishing, and conducting work release programs in accordance with law.

(5) Creating, establishing, and conducting any and all programs, including vocational, rehabilitative, and corrective, not inconsistent with law and consistent with the purposes of this Part.

E. Any construction project undertaken under the auspices of this Part shall be performed in accordance with the provisions of R.S. 38:2212.

§850.5. Funding for operation and maintenance of Union Parish Detention Center.

The expenses or costs of the operation and maintenance of the Union Parish Detention Center, including salaries, wages, facility operating costs, and the feeding and maintenance of prisoners incarcerated there, shall be paid monthly by the Union Parish Police Jury treasurer, upon approval of such expenses and costs by the Union Parish Detention Center Commission, out of the funds derived from special taxes voted, levied, and collected, or budgeted for that purpose. The commission may by resolution delegate to the chairman or one of its other members the duty of approving such monthly expenses and maintenance costs.

§850.6. Use of other jail and prison facilities.

A. No person shall be incarcerated overnight in Union Parish except in the Union Parish Detention Center. Other jail and prison facilities in Union Parish may be used only to hold prisoners for court during the day, except by express consent of the commission.

B. For good cause, the Union Parish Detention Center Commission may at any time require the use of any jail or prison facility in Union Parish for the purpose of keeping persons arrested for or convicted of crime in the parish.

§850.7. Superintendent and corrections officers.

A. The day-to-day operations of the Union Parish Detention Center shall be conducted by a superintendent, corrections officer, and any other appropriate personnel, subject to the supervision and control of the commission.

B. The superintendent and all corrections officers shall have the power and authority to make arrests of any persons lawfully committed to the Union Parish Detention Center when such persons have escaped, either from their custody or the custody of others, or when such persons have committed other criminal acts while incarcerated or while at large. This power and authority to arrest shall also extend to persons who aid or abet or otherwise interfere with the arrest of a prisoner of the Union Parish Detention Center or who commit criminal acts while on or around the Union Parish Detention Center.

PART III-F. JACKSON PARISH DETENTION CENTER

(Added by Acts 1995 No. 675, §1, eff. 8/15/95.)

§850.11. Establishment; purpose and title.

The governing authority of Jackson Parish may create, establish, and construct a centralized, single-parish jail and prison for the purpose of providing for the maintenance and upkeep of all persons lawfully incarcerated in Jackson Parish. If created, established, and constructed under this Part, this jail and prison shall be known as the Jackson Parish Detention Center. No other provision of this Part shall be effective or operative unless and until the Jackson Parish Detention Center is created and established by the Jackson Parish Police Jury under this Part. *(Added by Acts 1995 No. 675, §1, eff. 8/15/95.)*

§850.12. Organization and powers.

A. The Jackson Parish Detention Center shall be a political corporation, with power to sue and be sued and shall be governed by a commission to be known as the Jackson Parish Detention Center Commission. The Jackson Parish Detention Center shall be domiciled at the parish seat. It shall be sued at its domicile and service of all legal documents shall be made on the chairman or vice chairman of the commission.

B. The Jackson Parish Detention Center may acquire title to movable property for public purposes by purchase or donation, may operate or maintain prison farms, and may operate or maintain the farms in whole or in part with prison labor and persons sentenced to the Jackson Parish Detention Center by city or district courts.

C. Except only as hereinafter specifically provided, all persons lawfully incarcerated in Jackson Parish shall be incarcerated in the Jackson Parish Detention Center, subject to the exclusive jurisdiction and control of the Jackson Parish Detention Center Commission.
(Added by Acts 1995 No. 675, §1, eff. 8/15/95.)

§850.13. Commission members.

A. The Jackson Parish Detention Center Commission shall be composed of seven members including the president of the Jackson Parish Police Jury during his tenure as such; a member of the police jury, other than its president, who shall be elected by a majority vote of the police jury for a term of four years or until said juror's term of office ends, whichever occurs first; the sheriff of Jackson Parish; the chief of police of the town of Jonesboro; one mayor from a town or village within Jackson Parish, other than the town of Jonesboro, whose term shall be four years or until his term of office ends, the order of rotation for choosing a town or village shall be fixed by the commission; and two citizens who are to be appointed by the police jury. The chairman of the commission shall be selected by majority vote of all members of the commission. It shall be the duty of the chairman to conduct all meetings of the commission in accordance with law and the resolutions adopted by a majority of the commission. In the same manner, the commission shall select a vice chairman from among its number, who shall serve as chairman in the latter's absence.

B. The secretary of the police jury may serve as secretary of the commission and the Jackson Parish treasurer may serve as ex officio treasurer of the commission.

C. The members of the commission shall receive no compensation.

D. Should any member of the commission be sued individually for damages arising out of or in any way connected with the performance of his duties as such commission member, it shall be the responsibility of the commission to provide such member with a legal defense to such suit, including reasonable attorney fees, investigating costs, and other related expenses not paid by any insurance. Should any such commission member be cast in judgment for damages in such a suit, it shall be the obligation of the commission to indemnify him fully against such judgment, including all principal, interest, and costs in excess of that paid by any insurance company. Nothing in this Section shall require the commission to indemnify a commission member against a judgment wherein there is a specific decree in the judgment that the action of the commission member was malicious, and willfully and deliberately intended to cause bodily harm.
(Added by Acts 1995 No. 675, §1, eff. 8/15/95.)

§850.14. Powers and duties of commission.

A. The commission shall be keeper of the Jackson Parish Detention Center, and the sheriff of Jackson Parish is hereby specifically relieved of that duty in his official capacity as sheriff.

B. Any other provision of law to the contrary notwithstanding, upon relinquishing the custody of any prisoner to any legally authorized agency, department, or body politic, neither the Jackson Parish Detention Center nor the commission shall be responsible for the care, conduct, or control of such prisoner until his custody is returned to the Jackson Parish Detention Center and the commission, or the agents or employees of either. The responsibility for the care, conduct, and control of such prisoner in such cases shall be transferred to the agency, department, or body politic to which custody of the prisoner has been relinquished.

C. The commission shall be responsible for the physical maintenance of the Jackson Parish Detention Center, and the police jury is hereby specifically relieved of that duty in its official capacity as the governing authority of Jackson Parish.

D. The commission shall have all other powers and duties of the sheriff and governing authority of a parish heretofore or hereafter provided by law for equipping, maintaining, operating, and supporting the public jail of a parish and the prisoners therein, which powers and duties include but are not limited to the following:

(1) Adopting all rules and regulations necessary and proper for the governance and maintenance of proper operations and conduct of the Jackson Parish Detention Center and the prisoners thereof.

(2) Appointing and employing all necessary superintendents, corrections officers, and other appropriate personnel, and fixing their salaries and adopting appropriate personnel policies and guidelines, which shall include policies and procedures for discipline and, if necessary, termination.

(3) Authorizing and permitting the use of prisoners of the Jackson Parish Detention Center to maintain road rights-of-way, not to include construction, within the parish of Jackson and remove litter on public grounds, all under the supervision of the police jury or other appropriate authorities when such prisoners are committed for such purposes by appropriate courts.

(4) Creating, establishing, and conducting work release programs in accordance with law.

(5) Creating, establishing, and conducting any and all programs, including vocational, rehabilitative, and corrective, not inconsistent with law and consistent with the purposes of this Part.

E. Any construction project undertaken under the auspices of this Part shall be performed in accordance with the provisions of R.S. 38:2212.
(Added by Acts 1995 No. 675, §1, eff. 8/15/95.)

§850.15. Funding for operation and maintenance of Jackson Parish Detention Center.

The expenses or costs of the operation and maintenance of the Jackson Parish Detention Center, including salaries, wages, facility operating costs, and the feeding and maintenance of prisoners incarcerated there, shall be paid monthly by the police jury treasurer, upon approval of such expenses and costs by the Jackson Parish Detention Center Commission, out of the funds derived from special taxes voted, levied, collected, and budgeted for that purpose. The commission may by resolution delegate to the chairman or one of its other members the duty of approving such monthly expenses and maintenance costs. *(Added by Acts 1995 No. 675, §1, eff. 8/15/95.)*

§850.16. Use of other jail and prison facilities.

A. No person shall be incarcerated overnight in Jackson Parish except in the Jackson Parish Detention Center. Other jail and prison facilities in Jackson Parish may be used only to hold prisoners for court during the day, except by express consent of the commission.

B. For good cause, the commission may at any time require the use of any jail or prison facility in Jackson Parish for the purpose of keeping persons arrested for or convicted of crime in the parish.
(Added by Acts 1995 No. 675, §1, eff. 8/15/95.)

§850.17. Superintendent and corrections officers.

A. The day-to-day operations of the Jackson Parish Detention Center shall be conducted by a superintendent, corrections officers, and any other appropriate personnel, subject to the supervision and control of the commission.

B. The superintendent and all corrections officers shall have the power and authority to make arrests of any persons lawfully committed to the Jackson Parish Detention Center when such persons have escaped, either from their custody or from the custody of others, or when such persons have committed other criminal acts while incarcerated or while at large.
(Added by Acts 1995 No. 675, §1, eff. 8/15/95.)

PART IV. LOUISIANA STATE PENITENTIARY

§855. Road, street, highway, and right of way maintenance and litter removal, weed cutting, drug-free school zone sign posting, and solid waste recycling programs by convict labor; indemnification.

A. Notwithstanding the provisions of R.S. 15:1111, the wardens of state correctional facilities are authorized to assign convict labor from the correctional facilities as required in accordance with this Section to:

(1) Work and maintain, except for construction, parish roads, and rights of way not under the jurisdiction of the Department of Transportation and Development, and to police and remove litter on public grounds, rights of way, lakes, streams, and the shores of lakes and streams; and

(2) Police and remove litter on highways, rights of way, and road shoulders under the jurisdiction of the Department of Transportation and Development.

(3) Work in solid waste recycling programs under the auspices of a state agency or political subdivision as approved by the secretary of the Department of Public Safety and Corrections.

(4) Assist the governing authority of any municipality to maintain the municipality in a safe and sanitary condition by cutting, destroying, or removing noxious weeds or grass or other deleterious, unhealthful, or noxious growths on any sidewalks or banquettes and on any lot, place, or area within the municipality.

B. (1) The wardens shall furnish such convict labor when available and as authorized herein for all state, municipal, and parish roads, highways, streets, and rights of way when requested by the sheriff, municipal police, or governing authority of the parish or municipality in which the road, highway, street, or right of way is located. The wardens shall also furnish such convict labor when available and as authorized herein for state highways, road shoulders, and rights of way when requested by the Department of Transportation and Development. The department or parish or municipal governing authority or sheriff or municipal police shall not request such convict labor unless it has first certified that there are no free workers displaced because the convict labor is used. All work performed by convicts herein shall be without charge or expense to the department or parish or municipal governing authority or the sheriff or municipal police, except for transportation costs of the work unit, incentive pay as determined by the Department of Public Safety and Corrections, and road materials used in the work and maintenance of the state, municipal, or parish streets, roads, highways, or rights of way.

(2) The wardens shall also furnish available convict labor for the painting of markings and posting of signs indicating drug-free school zones pursuant to R.S. 17:405 and firearm-free zones pursuant to R.S. 14:95.6 when requested by a parish or city school board. All such work performed by convicts herein shall be without charge or expense to the school board, except for transportation costs of the work unit and the costs of signs and painting materials.

(3) The wardens shall also furnish available convict labor for solid waste recycling programs administered by a state agency or political subdivision and approved by the secretary of the department when requested by the agency or political subdivision. All such work performed by convicts herein shall be without charge or expense to the program, except for actual direct costs of the work unit.

(4) (a) The wardens may furnish such convict labor when available and as authorized herein to the governing authority of any municipality to maintain the municipality in a safe and sanitary condition by cutting, destroying, or removing noxious weeds or grass or other deleterious, unhealthful, or noxious growths on any sidewalks or banquettes and on any lot, place, or area within the municipality. The governing authority of the municipality shall comply with the provisions of R.S. 33:5062 and all other relevant provisions of law. R.S. 33:815 and 4766 are not affected by the provisions of this Paragraph. The Department of Transportation and Development is excluded from this Paragraph and is subject to the requirements of R.S. 48:261(B), (C), and (D) and all other relevant provisions of law.

(b) The use of prison labor shall in no way reduce the work force of any highway maintenance gang or cause the layoff of any classified employee.

(c) The Department of Public Safety and Corrections shall not be liable for any loss sustained by any such prisoner, except for those caused by the gross negligence or intentional acts of the warden, an assistant warden, or an employee of the department.

C. No more than one work unit composed of no more than twenty convicts shall be furnished by the warden in response to any request herein. Such work unit shall include sufficient guards and foremen as determined by the warden to be necessary to control the work unit. All convicts in such work unit shall be at least eighteen years of age.

D. The political subdivision which administers the solid waste recycling program shall indemnify and hold the sheriff, the state, and the state agency harmless for any injury caused by the inmate, unless the gross negligence or intentional act of the sheriff or the state or the state agency was a substantial factor in causing the injury.

(Chgd. by Acts 1990 No. 416, §1; Acts 1992 No. 197, §2, No. 402, §1, eff. 8/21/92.)

§857. Chaplains; access to inmates.

The warden shall provide for the services on a contractual basis of a full-time minister of the predominant non-Catholic denomination who shall serve as the Protestant chaplain. The inmates shall at all times have access to the Protestant chaplain. He shall be paid a monthly fee to be fixed by the warden to be paid out of the funds regularly appropriated for the state penitentiary. The warden may provide for the employment of additional part-time chaplains of any religious denomination on a contractual basis and shall have authority to fix their fees.

§858. Catholic priest for penitentiary; method of appointment; access to inmates.

The warden shall provide for the services on a contractual basis of a full-time Catholic priest who shall be appointed by and subject to the archbishop of New Orleans who shall serve as the Catholic chaplain. The inmates shall at all times have access to the Catholic chaplain. He shall be paid a monthly fee by the warden to be paid out of the funds regularly appropriated for the state penitentiary, which monthly fee shall be the same amount as the monthly fee paid the full-time minister serving as Protestant chaplain.

§859. Inmate spiritual and guidance services; leasing of property.

A. Notwithstanding any other provision of law to the contrary, the secretary of the Department of Public Safety and Corrections may lease land owned by the state and under the control of the department to a nonprofit corporation, on which land the lessee may construct a facility to be used for the purpose of providing spiritual and guidance services to inmates, subject to the rules and regulations of the department.

B. The lease shall be for a period not to exceed ninety-nine years and be subject to any such terms and conditions that the secretary deems appropriate and in accord with the rules and regulations of the department. The value of the facilities constructed shall be good and sufficient consideration for the lease granted by the department.

C. Contracts entered into by any such lessee for the performance of work or the erection, construction, or maintenance of improvements on the leased premises shall not constitute public works contracts.

D. The provisions of R.S. 39:1643 and Part I of Chapter 10 of Title 41 of the Louisiana Revised Statutes of 1950 shall not be applicable to leases authorized by this Section.
(Added by Acts 1997 No. 1113, §1, eff. 7/14/97.)

§860. Right of inmate to decline medical treatment.

Except as to compliance with the sanitary laws and all reasonable regulations relating to contagious and infectious diseases, any sane patient or sane inmate of the Louisiana State Penitentiary may decline any medical care or treatment offered or provided by the institution and provide other care for himself at his own expense.

§862. Officials and employees not to be personally interested in contracts; penalty.

No official or employee of the Louisiana State Penitentiary shall be personally interested, directly or indirectly, in any contract, purchase, lease, or sale of lands, materials or supplies, or in any contract for work to be done.

Whoever violates this Section shall be fined not more than five hundred dollars or imprisoned for not more than six months, or both.

All contracts or agreements of this nature shall be null and void and of no binding effect against the state.

§864. Trespass on state prison property prohibited; penalty; exceptions.

No person shall enter without permission of the superintendent of the Louisiana State Penitentiary upon any of the farms or properties which may be designated by the superintendent as state prisons.

Whoever violates this Section shall be fined not more than fifty dollars, or imprisoned for not more than thirty days, or both.

This Section shall not prohibit sheriffs, their deputies, and other officers of the law from entering the farms or properties in the performance of their official duties. No person shall be denied admittance to the farms or properties, at reasonable times and under the conditions fixed by the superintendent to insure the safety and proper discipline of inmates and prisoners for the transaction of legitimate business thereon.

§865. Solitary confinement abolished.

No prisoner in the state penitentiary shall be placed on solitary confinement, except in enforcing obedience to the police regulations of the penitentiary.

§866. Payment to released prisoners.

The secretary of the Department of Public Safety and Corrections shall promulgate rules and regulations to determine which prisoners are eligible upon release from prison to receive a temporary maintenance payment not to exceed the sum of twenty dollars. Payments shall be made from a source determined by the secretary.

§866.1. Transportation for released prisoners.

The secretary of the Department of Public Safety and Corrections shall promulgate rules and regulations to determine which prisoners shall be provided transportation to their residence upon release from prison. No inmate, otherwise eligible, shall be provided transportation to a residence outside of the state of Louisiana.

§866.2. Disposition of abandoned property of discharged inmates.

A. Any property abandoned by a prisoner in a penal institution under the jurisdiction of the Department of Public Safety and Corrections at the time of his discharge from the custody of the department shall, after ninety days from his release, be disposed of in the following manner:

(1) There shall be notice of the department's right to dispose of the property in accordance with this procedure on the data sheet listing the property of the person at the time he is transferred into the custody of the department; however, this requirement shall not apply to property in possession of the department prior to September 1, 1985.

(2) Ninety days after the release of the prisoner, if after notice to the prisoner within fourteen days after his release the property is unclaimed and not needed for any legal reason by the department, the secretary of the department may authorize the abandoned property to be destroyed, donated to a charitable organization, or put into lawful use within the institution from which it came. Any legal tender shall be placed in a fund for the benefit of all inmates. A record of the disposition of all abandoned property shall be maintained.

(3) Abandoned property, as defined in Subsection B below, in the possession of the department on September 1, 1985, shall, ninety days after September 1, 1985, be disposed of as set forth in Paragraph (A)(2) above, unless claimed by the prisoner before the ninety days has elapsed.

B. For the purposes of this Section, all property which the prisoner leaves at the institution or anywhere within the Department of Public Safety and Corrections, or which he fails to take with him upon discharge and to which he makes no claim prior to his discharge or within ninety days thereafter, shall be considered abandoned.

C. At the conclusion of a disciplinary proceeding against a prisoner, which proceeding indicates that property was obtained by the inmate through fraud or misrepresentation of his situation or his personal data such as his race, sex, age, marital status, offender class, nature of his conviction, or release dates, said property shall be returned to the complaining victim upon his submission of an affidavit setting forth the facts of the fraudulent or misrepresented transaction and his request that the property be returned to him. All such property allegedly obtained through fraud or misrepresentation may be suspended or held in the inmate's prison account or in inventory storage by the warden pending outcome of the disciplinary proceeding and receipt of the complainant's affidavit. Absent receipt of said affidavit within thirty days of its being requested of the complaining victim by the institution, said property shall be disposed of as set forth in Paragraph (A)(2) above.

§867. Compensation for damage or injury occasioned by escape.

A. The Louisiana Department of Public Safety and Corrections is hereby authorized to pay out of funds appropriated to any unit of the department compensation in an amount not to exceed two thousand dollars for the property damage or personal injury sustained, and medical expenses incurred therewith, by any person assisting or forced to assist in the pursuit of any prisoner who has escaped from the custody of any adult or juvenile institution of the department immediately following such escape and while in hot pursuit; or any such damage or injury sustained by persons, caused by any adult or juvenile who is in the physical custody of the department while in the course of such escape from any institution owned and operated by the department or the vicinity thereof.

B. Any contract entered into by the department for operation of a half-way house or similar facility which allows for physical custody of inmates by persons other than the department shall provide, as a condition of the contract, that the person assuming custody of the inmates shall be responsible for payment of damages caused as described in this Section.

C. A notarized statement, and such other information as may be required by the secretary of the department, shall be submitted prior to any reimbursement under this Section.

§867.1. Search teams; appointment and duties; training.

A. The warden of each state correctional facility may appoint search teams for the sole purpose of pursuing any prisoner who has escaped from the custody of the facility.

B. Search teams appointed by the wardens pursuant to this Section shall be composed of employees of the correctional facility. The search teams may set roadblocks and conduct limited inspections of motor vehicles for the sole purpose of locating and apprehending escapees.

C. For purposes of this Section, the wardens together with the secretary of the department shall design and implement sufficient training programs for persons appointed to the search teams. Training programs shall include proper and constitutionally allowable roadblock and inspection procedures, safety, reasonable means by which to conduct such stops and inspections, and other appropriate training. All proposed training and other guidelines for conducting search team activities pursuant to this Section shall be submitted in writing to the House Administration of Criminal Justice and Senate Judiciary B Committees prior to their implementation.

D. Nothing herein shall be construed as authorizing members of the search teams to interfere with state and local law enforcement officers conducting their duties pursuant to state law.

(Added by Acts 1997 No. 586, §1, eff. 8/15/97.)

§868. Appointment of attorney to represent inmates; fees.

Whenever it is necessary for a district court to appoint an attorney at law to represent any inmate who is charged with a crime alleged to have been committed while the inmate was in the actual physical custody and control of the Department of Public Safety and Corrections or when an inmate escapes from the actual physical custody and control of the department and during the period of escape is charged with committing a crime in the parish where the correctional institution from which he escaped is located, such attorney at law shall be paid a reasonable fee, fixed by the court, from funds appropriated to the department. *(Chgd. by Acts 1990 No. 231, §1, eff. 9/7/90.)*

§870. Work assignments not to be refused; overtime.

No inmate shall be permitted to refuse to accept or perform diligently any work assignment required of him because of any compensation rate herein imposed, nor shall extra or overtime compensation be paid for work required to be done.

§871. Inmates eligible for compensation.

Except as otherwise provided by law, compensation shall be paid to all inmates in accordance with rules established by the secretary of the department. The provisions of this Section shall be applicable to inmates received at the Adult Reception and Diagnostic Center on or after August 15, 1997. *(Chgd. by Acts 1991 No. 138, §1; Acts 1997 No. 1068, §1, eff. 7/14/97.)*

§873. Rate of inmate compensation; source of funding.

A. The secretary of the Department of Corrections shall establish various rates of compensation as an incentive to inmates incarcerated in state correctional facilities. The rates shall be according to the skill, industry and nature of the work performed by the inmate and shall be no more than twenty cents per hour and no less than two cents per hour.

B. This compensation shall be paid from the following sources:

(1) Inmates who are assigned to any state agency which operates from self-generated revenues shall be paid from those self-generated revenues.

(2) Inmates assigned to a certified Private Sector/Prison Industry Enhancement program shall be paid by the private sector company that employs them. Such wages shall be subject to state and federal taxes and mandatory deductions required for a Private Sector/Prison Industry Enhancement program.

(3) All other inmates shall be paid from the Department of Public Safety and Corrections, Prison Enterprises Fund.

(Chgd. by Acts 1992 No. 687, §1; Acts 1995 No. 644, §1, eff. 8/15/95.)

§874. Compensation account.

The inmate's compensation account shall be handled and accounted for as follows:

(1) Each foreman of inmates shall keep an accurate daily record, on forms provided, of the skill and industry of each inmate at his work and the time spent at such work. These records shall be submitted weekly to the accounting office of the penitentiary and shall serve as the basis for computing compensation.

(2) The inmate's compensation record, including a record of any wages earned working in a certified Private Sector/Prison Industry Enhancement program, shall be kept on forms prescribed and shall show the total amount earned by each inmate and shall show a distribution of said total on the basis of fifty percent for the inmate's drawing account and fifty percent for the inmate's savings account, except as otherwise provided in Paragraph (4) of this Section.

(3) Expenditures may be made for or on behalf of the inmate from his personal account in strict conformity with rules and regulations pertaining thereto.

(4) (a) All or any part of the amounts credited to the inmate's savings account may, upon written request, be expended for accredited educational courses or the purchase of bonds of the state of Louisiana or the United States. Any bonds so purchased shall be held for the inmate in the same manner as other money or personal property belonging to the inmate. The funds from bonds redeemed or cashed during the inmate's term of sentence shall revert to the account from which it originated.

(b) In addition, all or part of the amounts credited to any inmate's drawing or savings account may, upon the written request or authorization of the inmate or upon order of a court of competent jurisdiction, be expended for the payment of court costs in a matter in which the inmate is a party.

(c) When an inmate's savings account attains a balance of at least two hundred fifty dollars, the inmate may deposit future compensation into either his savings account or his personal drawing account. When an inmate selects to have future compensation deposited to his personal drawing account as provided herein, and subsequently a court of competent jurisdiction orders payment of court costs in a matter to which the inmate is a party causing the inmate's account balance to be less than two hundred fifty dollars, thirty percent of future compensation shall be deposited to his drawing account and seventy percent shall be distributed toward payment of the court costs.

(d) The funds credited to the inmate's drawing or savings account may be withdrawn to satisfy any medical or dental copayment in accordance with the provisions of R.S. 15:831(B)(2).

(e) The funds credited to the inmate's drawing or savings account may be withdrawn to satisfy any restitution imposed by the Department of Public Safety and Corrections and those accounts may be frozen by the warden until the amount of restitution due from the inmate has been withdrawn from the accounts and paid to the institution in accordance with the provisions of R.S. 15:875.

(f) Except as provided in Paragraph (7) of this Section, money may not be withdrawn from an inmate's savings account for any other reason prior to his discharge or parole, unless authorized by the secretary of the department.

(5) All past and present interest income earned from the investment of inmates' money shall be deposited in the fund established for the benefit of all inmates, pursuant to R.S. 15:866.2. The interest earned may be used to help defray administrative costs, to seed new institutions' inmate welfare funds, and to provide for other expenditures which will benefit the inmate population.

(6) All inmates released or discharged after payments are begun shall receive the total of accumulations due them in such installments and at such times as provided for by regulations.

(7) Upon the presentation to the Department of Public Safety and Corrections of a court order or a certified copy of an extract of the minutes of a court proceeding showing that an inmate was convicted and was assessed court costs, along with a letter from the sheriff itemizing the costs assessed and verifying which of the costs were not paid, the department shall withdraw funds from any of the inmate's accounts for the payment of the court costs due. All funds so collected shall be forwarded to the court that assessed the costs; however, if the inmate has not paid the costs assessed in accordance with Crime Victims Reparations Act, R.S. 46:1801 et seq., those costs shall be collected and shall be credited directly to the Crime Victims Reparations Fund, R.S. 46:1816, after all other costs are paid. The department shall notify the court if the costs for the Crime Victims Reparations Fund have been collected. The

funds in an inmate's accounts shall not be reduced by more than seventy-five percent in accordance with this Section.

(8) The warden, or his or her designee, shall make an accounting to the inmate showing each time the inmate's accounts are debited.

(Chgd. by Acts 1990 No. 329, §1; Acts 1994 Third Ex. Sess. No. 87, §1; Acts 1995 No. 644, §1; Acts 1997 No. 528, §1, eff. 8/15/97, No. 597, §1, eff. 7/3/97, No. 626, §1, eff. 8/15/97.)

§875. Imposition of restitution on offenders; procedures.

A. (1) Restitution may be obtained by the Department of Public Safety and Corrections from an offender who damages or destroys property, causes or attempts to cause injury to himself, civilians, other offenders, or department personnel, or who has a pattern of falsely alleging injury or illness with the result that medical expenses are incurred.

(2) The amount of restitution shall be the actual costs, or any portion thereof, of repairing or replacing the property or of the medical expenses incurred.

B. (1) Restitution may be obtained by corrections services from an offender for expenses incurred by the department or any other law enforcement agency in any escape or attempt to escape from the custody of any facility of the department.

2. The amount of restitution shall be the actual costs incurred, including but not limited to property damage, staff transportation and lodging, salaries for the duration of the chase, and costs of return of the inmate.

C. The determination of restitution by the department shall be by disciplinary proceeding in accordance with the rules and regulations of the department. The department may promulgate and adopt, in accordance with the Administrative Procedure Act*, specific rules and regulations governing the determination of restitution. The department shall not obtain restitution from an offender who appeals the findings of a determination proceeding until after the exhaustion of his remedies. The department shall render a report every calendar year to the division of administration detailing the amount withdrawn from each drawing or savings account, the purpose for which each withdrawal was made and the recipient, if any, of any funds so withdrawn for the payment of any expenses, other than to the department.

**R.S. 49:950 et seq.*

D. The amount of restitution may be obtained from an offender by freezing assets in his drawing and savings account and prohibiting withdrawals therefrom until the restitution is paid, whether from these accounts or from any other source by any other appropriate means. The accounts may be frozen regardless of the source of the assets contained therein and specifically including any assets of a juvenile sent to him by his parent or guardian and placed in his accounts. This Subsection shall not prohibit the withdrawal of funds for the purpose of payments under the Crime Victims Reparations Act*, court costs as authorized by law, and other withdrawals specifically authorized by the warden or by the superintendent if the warden is unavailable, in that order.

**R.S. 46:1801 et seq.*

E. The restitution collected from an offender under this Section shall be used to defray the expenses of his property damage or destruction, his medical expenses, or his escape or attempted escape.

F. Any offender who is transferred to another facility within or discharged from the department shall remain liable for any restitution authorized under this Section.

G. "Offender" means an adult or juvenile offender committed to the Department of Public Safety and Corrections at the time the property damage or destruction was sustained, or the medical expenses or escape costs were incurred.

H. This Section shall not be construed to prohibit or limit the imposition of any other disciplinary measures upon an offender as a result of his actions.

(Chgd. by Acts 1993 No. 103, §1; No. 685, §1; Acts 1994 Third Ex. Sess. No. 87, §1, eff. 8/27/94.)

PART IV-A. ADDITIONAL INSTITUTIONS

§891. Location of prison facilities.

A. No state prison (other than the Louisiana State Penitentiary at Angola), lockup, camp, quarter boat, or other state owned and operated correctional facility for the purpose of housing any prisoners or inmates shall be purchased, constructed, located, established, enlarged, or changed in character by the type or classification of prisoners or inmates housed therein within two miles of any residential area until the procedures required by Subsection B hereof have been complied with. An area shall be considered a residential area if it has been zoned or designated as such by the appropriate local governing authority or if within an area of one-quarter square mile or larger there is a population density of two thousand or more persons per square mile.

B. Prior to locating any prison facility in a residential area, the Department of Corrections shall:

(1) Notify the parish governing authority of the parish wherein the proposed site is located and, if the site is located within a municipality, the governing authority of the municipality. The notice shall specify the precise location of the proposed site, the exact type of criminals to be incarcerated at the facility, the general degree of security and the type of construction planned, and the date, time, and location of the public hearing required by Paragraph 3 below, which shall be held not less than thirty days after receipt of the notice by the appropriate governing authorities.

(2) Publish the notice required by Paragraph 1 hereof in the official parish journal at least once a week for the two consecutive weeks preceding the hearing.

(3) Hold a public hearing in the parish where the proposed site is located and, if the site is located within any municipality, hold a hearing within the municipality, at which any interested person or public official may appear.

(4) Consider the information received as a result of the public hearing for a period of not less than thirty days after the hearing before rendering a final decision on the location of the facility.

(5) Upon rendering its final decision, promptly notify the governing authorities specified in Paragraph 1 of the decision.

C. The provisions of this section shall not apply when the location of a prison facility in the parish has been approved by referendum.

§892. Women's correctional facility.

The Louisiana Department of Corrections is hereby authorized to create and establish and to operate and maintain a women's correctional facility in the vicinity of St. Gabriel for women convicted of felonies and sentenced to imprisonment in this state. This facility shall be known as "Louisiana Correctional Institute for Women".

§893. Adult correctional institutions.

A. The Department of Public Safety and Corrections, with the approval of the Board of Corrections and the governor, is hereby authorized to create, establish, operate, and maintain such adult correctional institutions as may be needed to fulfill the department's obligations, provided necessary funds have been appropriated by the Louisiana Legislature.

B. The Department of Public Safety and Corrections may house inmates in tent or tent-like structures unless prohibited by federal law or a specific court order.
(Chgd. by Acts 1997 No. 1272, §1, eff. 8/15/97.)

§893.1. Inmates who may not be assigned to Work Training Facility South and Work Training Facility North.

A. The Department of Public Safety and Corrections, corrections services, shall not assign any inmate included in the categories listed below to serve any portion of his term at the correctional institution at Work Training Facility North:

(1) Inmates who have been convicted of first or second degree murder, aggravated rape, aggravated kidnapping, armed robbery, sale of a controlled dangerous substance, other than marijuana, aggravated arson, or any provision of Subpart C of Part II, Subpart B of Part IV, or Subpart A(1) or A(4) of Part V of Chapter 1 of Title 14 of the Louisiana Revised Statutes of 1950.

(2) Inmates who have a balance of time extending beyond seven years to the earliest release date.

(3) Inmates sentenced pursuant to R.S. 15:529.1 et seq. if the instant offense is a third felony conviction or greater.

(4) Inmates who do not qualify for minimum custody status (trustee).

(5) Inmates with records, either arrest or institutional records, which reveal compulsive or habitual use of violence against the person.

(6) Inmates whose presence in the community are likely to evoke adverse public reaction.

(7) Persons who are currently under and/or who have demonstrated a need for extensive and/or intensive medical treatment. At the time treatment has been completed and such

termination of services has been documented by competent medical staff, persons may be considered as eligible for transfer.

(8) Persons who have escaped and/or who have abetted an escape and/or have attempted to escape within a period of the last seven years.

(9) Persons who have demonstrated an overt-aggressive pattern of homosexual behavior to the extent that it would disrupt the smooth daily operation of the institution.

(10) Inmates whose institutional records reflect habitual and compulsive violent behavior, consistent signs of bad work habits, lack of cooperation or good faith, or other undesirable behavior.

B. (1) The department shall not assign any inmate included in the category listed below to serve any portion of his term at the correctional institution at Work Training Facility North on work release.

(2) In addition to the requirement above for the maintenance program eligibility no persons shall be housed at Work Training Facility North on work release unless they are within six months of discharge and have had employment security verified in the area of the institution prior to assignment.

C. No convicted felon, whether in the custody of the Department of Public Safety and Corrections or in the physical custody of a parish sheriff, shall be assigned to be housed or remain housed while serving any portion of his sentence at the correctional institution at Work Training Facility South. No person charged with the commission of a felony who is incarcerated pending trial shall be housed or remain housed pending trial at the correctional institution at Work Training Facility South.

(Chgd. by Acts 1993 No. 133, §1; Acts 1995 No. 320, §1, eff. 6/16/95, No. 914, §1, eff. 6/28/95.)

§894. Diagnostic and treatment center.

The State Department of Institution is hereby authorized to create and establish and to operate and maintain a diagnostic and treatment center, which may consist of one or more branches and which shall undertake medical, educational, psychiatric and social studies of persons committed to facilities under the jurisdiction of the State Department of Institutions. The department also may provide for the training of psychiatrists, neurologists, special educators, psychologists, nurses, technicians, social workers, occupational therapists, physicians and other professional trainees whose services shall be utilized in the operation of said center.

§895. Geriatric correctional facilities; establishment as a pilot project; report.

A. In order to find ways to limit potentially high costs, to reduce the pressure on available high level security prison facilities, and to increase the efficiency and effectiveness of the correctional process relative to older prisoners, the state, through the Department of Public Safety and Corrections, shall undertake a planning process for the proper management of an increasingly older prison population.

B. At a minimum, the planning process required in this Section, shall include:

(1) A review of the status of the existing long-term adult prison population with regard to:

(a) Age.

(b) Health.

(c) Projected health care needs.

(d) Level of risk for violence or escape.

(2) A review of the mechanisms used to manage the incarceration of and health care needs of the geriatric long-term prisoner.

(3) A review of the alternatives to maintaining geriatric long-term prisoners in traditional prison settings.

(4) The conduct of a pilot project using an alternative prison setting, which pilot shall include the use of any state-owned facility available to house geriatric prisoners who present a low risk of violence or escape with a concomitant reduction in the level of security and an increase in the level of preventive health care.

(5) A summary and comparison of the anticipatable costs, short and long-term, of continuing traditional prison maintenance of the long-term geriatric prisoner versus the alternate presented by the pilot project required in Paragraph (4) of this Subsection.

(6) Report of the information generated as required in this Subsection to the Joint Legislative Committee on the Budget along with the department's recommendations regarding action. The first report required by this Paragraph shall be submitted no later than

one year after the establishment of the pilot project. Revisions or further reporting may occur thereafter as the department deems necessary.
(Added by Acts 1990 No. 407, §1, eff. 9/7/90.)

PART IV-B. JUVENILE INSTITUTIONS

§901. Juvenile reception and diagnostic center; establishment, commitment of juveniles, substance abuse inpatient program, order, report, fact of commitment.

A. The Department of Public Safety and Corrections may establish, operate, and maintain juvenile reception and diagnostic centers located on the premises of the Louisiana Training Institute in East Baton Rouge Parish and at other locations designated to meet the regional diagnostic needs of adjudicated youth.

B. The order of commitment shall be furnished to the department at or prior to the transfer of the child and shall include that the child has been adjudicated delinquent. The court shall also furnish at that time the information required by Article 903 of the Children's Code and, in addition, shall specify whether the child was represented by counsel, the counsel's name and address, or that the child waived the right to counsel, and the age of the child at the time of the offense. The court shall also specify, in years and months, the maximum period of confinement. The court at the time of transfer shall transmit all relevant reports in its possession concerning the child, including reports reflecting his social background, mode of living, family status, school records, behavior tendencies, psychological and psychiatric assessments or any one or combination of the foregoing.

C. The order of commitment may require the department to take physical custody of a child adjudicated a delinquent, committed to its custody pursuant to Article 897(D) or 899(D) of the Children's Code, and recommended by the court or the department for assignment to a secure program or facility, within fourteen days from the date of the court's signing of the judgment of disposition when the child is in or is going to be placed in the physical custody of a parish juvenile facility. If a court modifies a judgment of disposition, in accordance with Chapter 17 of Title VIII of the Children's Code, and gives the department custody of the adjudicated delinquent, the provisions of this Section and Article 903 of the Children's Code apply.

D. (1) Upon commitment to the Department of Public Safety and Corrections, the department shall have sole custody of the child and, except as provided for in Children's Code Article 897.1, shall determine the child's placement, care, and treatment, and the expenditures to be made therefor, through appropriate examinations, tests, or evaluations conducted under the supervision of the department. The department shall comply with Chapter 2 of Title VII-A and Chapter 17 of Title VIII of the Children's Code for any modification of the original disposition when the adjudicated juvenile has been placed in the custody of the department. The department shall not modify any disposition under Children's Code Article 897.1.

(2) Any child identified in the evaluation process as a substance abuser shall be counseled regarding the availability of the juvenile substance abuse inpatient facility provided for in R.S. 15:901.1 and its appropriateness for the particular child.

E. A court exercising juvenile court jurisdiction may, after exhausting all other state and local diagnostic, testing, and evaluation resources, temporarily assign a child to the Department of Public Safety and Corrections with recommendations for diagnostic testing and evaluation services in accordance with Articles 888 and 890 of the Children's Code. The court assigning a child to the department shall provide written findings indicating the need for such services. The department shall provide such services to the extent resources are available. Assignments to the department for such services shall not exceed thirty calendar days.

F. The Department of Public Safety and Corrections shall have an individualized plan for each child committed to the department except for a child committed to the department following adjudication for contempt. The plan shall be developed after consultation with the child and the family, if feasible. A copy may be forwarded to the court.

G. (1) Community placement services shall have authority and responsibilities for children adjudicated delinquent or in need of supervision, including but not limited to the following:

(a) To assess or arrange for the assessment of the needs of each child.

(b) To provide or arrange for the provision of comprehensive diagnosis and evaluation services as the needs of each child warrant.

(c) To develop comprehensive service plans for each child.

(d) With respect to children committed to the custody of the Department of Public Safety and Corrections pursuant to the provisions of Articles 672, 792.53, 897, 899, and 1509 of the Children's Code, the secretary of the department shall develop rules and regulations to govern the assignment of such children to specific facilities and institutions operated by the department directly or through contractual arrangements.

(e) To place children in the setting most appropriate to their needs, including any nonresidential, community-based residential, and institutional programs operated by the Department of Public Safety and Corrections, as well as programs operated by other public or private agencies with which the department enters into contractual or purchase of services arrangements.

(f) To periodically monitor and review the progress of each child, and modify the child's service plan as warranted, through a multidisciplinary panel.

(2) The following rules shall be followed with regard to client placement functions:

(a) No program or unit shall be required to provide services to a client if the provision of such services would place the program in violation of any state or federal statute or court order.

(b) The secretary of the department may overrule a decision of the client placement unit upon appeal by any program or unit on grounds that such placement would be inconsistent with the child's needs. For all cases which are appealed to the secretary, a notation shall be made in the child's file indicating the grounds for such appeal, the decision made by the secretary, and the secretary's reasons for upholding or failing to uphold the original placement decision.

(c) No public or private agency operating under contractual or purchase of service arrangements with the department shall be required to provide services to a child if the provision of such services is contradictory to the terms of the contractual or purchase of service arrangement or is in conflict with the policies of the agency or the decisions of its governing authority.

(Chgd. by Acts 1991 No. 467, §2; Acts 1992 No. 200, §2, No. 699, §1; Acts 1993 No. 430, §1, No. 873, §1; Acts 1995 No. 795, §1; Acts 1997 No. 615, §2, eff. 7/3/97.)

§901.1. Juvenile substance abuse programs; locations.

A. The Department of Public Safety and Corrections shall establish, operate, and maintain a juvenile substance abuse program on the premises of the Louisiana Training Institute in East Baton Rouge Parish, or at any other appropriate juvenile institution under the direction of the department, which shall be made available to all juveniles assigned to the institution.

B. The program shall be maintained as a specialized treatment service provided as a supplemental service to the regular rehabilitative counseling program being provided at the institution. The department shall assign appropriate staff with training and experience in the field of substance abuse counseling to design and implement this treatment service.

§902. Juvenile institutions.

The Department of Public Safety and Corrections shall establish, operate, and maintain the Louisiana Training Institute for juveniles, at locations situated to meet the regional needs of the state. *(Chgd. by Acts 1991 No. 467, §2, eff. 9/6/91.)*

§902.1. Transfer of adjudicated juvenile delinquents.

Notwithstanding Title VIII of the Louisiana Children's Code or any other provision of law, the secretary of the department may promulgate rules and regulations to authorize the transfer of adjudicated juvenile delinquents to adult correctional facilities when the delinquents have attained the age of seventeen years, the age of full criminal responsibility. *(Added by Acts 1997 No. 1063, §1, eff. 7/14/97.)*

§903. Separate facilities for males and females.

The Department of Corrections is authorized to provide separate facilities for male and female juveniles committed to it. These separate facilities may be provided at whatever location or locations the Department of Corrections deems advisable.

§904. Superintendent; powers and duties.

The secretary of public safety and corrections shall appoint a superintendent for each juvenile institution under the administration of the department and shall enumerate his powers and duties. *(Chgd. by Acts 1991 No. 467, §2, eff. 9/6/91.)*

§905. Rules and regulations; education; training and discipline, work opportunities, vocational training, contracts and agreements.

A. The Department of Public Safety and Corrections shall have full control of all juvenile institutions, facilities, and programs under its administration and the affairs of such institutions, facilities, and programs, and shall adopt all rules and regulations which it deems essential to the proper conduct of these institutions, facilities, and programs. All children in these juvenile institutions, facilities, and programs shall receive appropriate treatment, training, and education commensurate with their needs and abilities. The department may enter into contracts or cooperative agreements to fulfill its obligations to accomplish its goals in the most efficient manner possible.

B. The secretary of the department shall establish all rules and regulations for the placement, care, and treatment of a juvenile in the custody of the department.

C. Notwithstanding any other provisions of the law to the contrary, the secretary shall have the sole authority to establish the programmatic standards for juveniles assigned to the custody of the department.

D. Notwithstanding any other provisions of the law to the contrary, the department may enter into contracts or cooperative agreements in order to provide employment and vocational training for juveniles in the department's custody as part of the treatment plan for the juvenile. The secretary of the department shall establish all rules and regulations necessary for the operation of such programs consistent with the department's mission to protect public safety and to provide opportunities for the rehabilitation of juvenile offenders.

§906. Release from commitment.

A. (1) Except as provided for in Children's Code Article 897.1, the Department of Public Safety and Corrections may recommend to the committing court the release of any juvenile committed to its care, who, in the opinion of the department, is ready to be returned to his own home, or to a substitute home. Such juvenile may be discharged by the court without supervision or may be placed under supervision until further orders of the court.

(2) Except as provided for in Subsection B of this Section, it is hereby declared to be the public policy of this state that commitment of a juvenile to the care of the department is not punitive nor in anywise to be construed as a penal sentence, but as a step in the total treatment process toward rehabilitation of the juvenile and that, therefore, the recommendations of the department should be given careful consideration by the court in determining what is to the best interest of the juvenile. If, after release from the care of the department, but while the juvenile is still under the supervision of the court, the court deems it advisable to return the juvenile to the care of the department, a recommitment order shall be furnished the department.

B. In cases governed by Children's Code Article 897.1, it is hereby declared to be the public policy of this state that commitment of a juvenile to the custody of the Department of Public Safety and Corrections for placement in a secure facility without benefit of parole, probation, suspension of imposition or execution of sentence, modification, or furlough, is necessary and proper because for these very serious offenses the protection of society is the primary objective.

(Chgd. by Acts 1993 No. 430, §1, eff. 8/15/93.)

§907. Return of juvenile to committing court for transfer.

A. The Department of Corrections may recommend the return to the committing court, of any juvenile committed to the care of the Department of Corrections with recommendations for the transfer of the juvenile to such other agency or facility which may be available to best serve the needs of the juvenile.

B. *(Repealed.)*

§908. Student furlough program.

A. Except as provided for in Children's Code Article 897.1, the secretary for the Department of Public Safety and Corrections may authorize a temporary furlough to deserving students of any juvenile institution, unless, after receiving notification of the proposed furlough, the juvenile court having jurisdiction notifies the department of its objection. The temporary furlough is to serve as a rehabilitative tool to assist the child in maintaining family and community relations during the period of his commitment. A temporary furlough as provided herein is not to be considered a release from commitment and does not affect the jurisdiction of the juvenile court or the authority of the department as to the children granted a temporary furlough.

B. A responsible member of the child's family or other previously approved adult must sign a custody receipt and provide transportation for the child to and from the juvenile institution.

§909. Reporting of escapes from state juvenile institutions; records.

A. The superintendent or highest ranking employee of the Department of Public Safety and Corrections, Corrections Services, or the person acting on behalf of the department, who is physically present at and in charge of a juvenile institution at the time of an escape from that institution shall, within ten minutes after being notified that a child or offender has escaped from or left the premises or grounds of the institution without authority, notify or take necessary steps to insure the notification of every law enforcement agency as defined in this Section.

B. The superintendent or person in charge of a state juvenile institution shall maintain a record and description of every escape from the juvenile institution of which the superintendent has control. The record shall list the date and time of the escape, the number of offenders who escaped, the offenses for which the escapees were placed at the institution, the name of each law enforcement agency notified of the escape, the time each law enforcement agency was notified and the name of the person receiving the notice, and the name of the department employee or agent who notified that law enforcement agency. The report shall be available for public inspection and shall list all prior escapes, if any, from the institution within the last five years of the date of the last escape. A copy of the report shall be delivered to each law enforcement agency as defined in this Section.

C. The secretary of the department shall promulgate rules and regulations to insure the immediate reporting of all escapes from juvenile institutions as required by this Section.

D. As used in this Section, "law enforcement agency" means the sheriff's office, all police departments in the parish, and the office of state police.

(Added by Acts 1990 No. 977, §1, eff. 9/7/90.)

§910. Juvenile offenders; collection of parental support payments for cost of care.

A. When the Department of Public Safety and Corrections provides for care and treatment of a child assigned to a secure juvenile institution under the provisions of this Part, the parent or legal guardian for the juvenile offender shall be required to provide support for the cost of such care and treatment in a manner consistent with applicable federal and state regulations, and commensurate with ability to pay, in accordance with a sliding scale established by R.S. 9:315 through 9:315.15. Regulations established by the department to compute the parent's financial responsibility shall take into consideration other children living in the home. In assessing the amount of support, the department shall insure that the support payment does not exceed the cost to the department nor shall the cost basis include costs exclusively associated to confinement such as, but not necessarily limited to, security.

B. At the time the juvenile offender is assigned to the secure institution, the department shall notify the parent or legal guardian of his responsibility to provide support and shall bill him on a periodic basis, but no less than quarterly, for the amount due. The department shall make every reasonable effort to notify the person liable for support under the provisions of this Section as soon as possible after placement of the juvenile. Notice or receipt of notice shall not be a condition of liability.

C. Payments shall be made to the department and shall be deposited in the state treasury.

D. In the event of default, the department shall exercise all administrative and legal remedies provided by law or regulation to enforce the provisions of this Section, including the imposition of reasonable administrative costs, costs of court, and attorney fees. It is permissible for the department to enter into an agreement with other public agencies or to contract with the private sector for collection of debts owed to the state under provisions of this Section.

(Added by Acts 1990 No. 513, §1, eff. 9/1/90.)

PART V. YOUTHFUL OFFENDER MANAGEMENT FUND

(Added by Acts 1990 No. 324, §1, eff. 9/7/90.)

§921. Youthful Offender Management Fund; creation.

A. All probation and parole supervision fees received by the Department of Public Safety and Corrections pursuant to Code of Juvenile Procedure Art. 86.1 shall be deposited immediately upon receipt into the state treasury.

B. After compliance with the requirements of Article VII, Section 9(B) of the Constitution of Louisiana, relative to the Bond Security and Redemption Fund, and prior to monies being placed in the state general fund, an amount equal to that deposited as required by Subsection A of this Section shall be credited to the special fund hereby created in the state treasury to be known as the "Youthful Offender Management Fund." The monies in this fund shall be used solely as provided by Subsection C of this Section and only in the amounts appropriated by the legislature. All unexpended and unencumbered monies in this fund at the end of the fiscal year shall remain in such fund. All monies in this fund shall be invested by the state treasurer in the same manner as monies in the state general fund, with interest earned on the investment of these monies credited to this fund following compliance with the requirements of Article VII, Section 9(B), relative to the Bond Security and Redemption Fund.

C. The monies in the Youthful Offender Management Fund shall be used solely by the department to supplement appropriated funds for salaries and other category expenditures within the office of youth development deemed necessary by the secretary of the department, and to defray cost of collection and disbursement of monetary assessments imposed as a condition of probation and parole, including reasonable attorney fees.

D. The monies in the Youthful Offender Management Fund shall not exceed three million dollars and any monies received in excess of that amount shall be paid into the state general fund.

(Added by Acts 1990 No. 324, §1; chgd. by Acts 1992 No. 297, §1, eff. 8/21/92.)

PART VIII. PARISH INDUSTRIAL SCHOOLS FOR YOUTHS

§1031. Establishment of parish schools for youths authorized.

The governing authorities of the parishes may establish, within their parishes, an industrial school for male youths of the age seventeen years, and under, convicted in the juvenile court of the parish for offenses within the jurisdiction of the juvenile court. Where any school has been so established, it shall be employed only for the delinquent juveniles convicted within the parish, and shall be known as the "Parish Industrial School for Youths."

§1032. Commitment to parish school.

Where any parish school has been established the judge or judges of the juvenile court within the parish shall have the discretionary authority to commit any male youth tried and convicted under the laws of Louisiana, to the Parish Industrial School for Youths within the parish, for an indefinite period, but in no case beyond the majority of the person so convicted.

The fact that juveniles have been sentenced by the court to the school shall never be received in evidence by the court of this state in any proceeding involving or affecting the person.

§1033. Appointment of commissioners; compensation; term.

The governing authority of the parish in which any school for youths is established shall name and appoint by a majority vote, three commissioners to manage the affairs of the industrial school who shall serve without compensation or pay of any kind. The commissioners shall be appointed for a term of four years. Two commissioners shall constitute a quorum at meetings.

§1034. Board of commissioners; domicile; powers; officers.

The three commissioners shall be known as the Board of Commissioners of the Parish Industrial School for Youths. The board shall be a body politic and corporate, and shall be domiciled at the parish seat of the parish or parishes in which any school or schools are established. It shall have an official seal, may enter into contracts, and sue and be sued. It may hold, purchase, receive and accept by donation or otherwise, real and personal property for the use and benefit of the school, or for any use that may be helpful and beneficial to the accomplishment of the school's purposes.

The board of commissioners shall elect one of their number as president, one as vice president and one member as treasurer, and shall elect a secretary who may or may not be a member of the board.

§1035. Selection of site; construction.

The board shall select a central and convenient site within the parish for the parish industrial school and shall acquire the land by purchase or by donation or by lease in the name of the parish subject to the approval of the governing authority which shall accept or confirm the title thereto in the name of the parish. The board shall cause to be prepared plans and specifications for remodeling or erecting on the site the necessary buildings to provide a suitable plant for the industrial school and shall furnish and equip the building. The contracts shall be let by the board, and any contract calling for an expenditure of over five hundred dollars shall be advertised one time in the official journal of the parish, and shall after five days from the date of advertisement be awarded to the lowest responsible bidder by the board. The board may in its discretion reject all bids and readvertise the project anew. When the buildings have been prepared and equipped and the necessary staff of officers and employees has been organized, the board shall so certify to the governing authority of the parish and the governing authority shall notify the juvenile court that juvenile offenders may be committed to the institution.

§1036. Duties of board of commissioners; appointment, term, and compensation of superintendent; report.

The board of commissioners shall elect a superintendent for the school; fix his term of employment and his compensation, enumerate by proper by-laws his powers and duties, and employ and discharge the superintendent and all necessary employees at the will of the board. The board shall in each year render a full report to the governing authority of the parish of the operations of the industrial school accompanied by any recommendations which the board may desire to make in reference to management, expansion, and otherwise.

§1037. Rules and regulations; classification of inmates; education, training, and discipline.

The board of commissioners shall have full control and management of the industrial school and its affairs, and shall adopt all regulations which the board may deem essential to the proper conduct of the school. The inmates shall be classified according to rules which the board may deem best fitted to insure their reformation, and they shall receive educational, moral, industrial, and farm training. The discipline of the school shall be humane and of the most modern and reformatory nature.

§1038. Probation and parole; release of inmates.

The board of commissioners may release any inmate of the industrial school on probation or parole on conditions which the board may prescribe. If the conditions of parole or probation are violated the board may cause the paroled inmate to be rearrested wherever he may be found and to be returned to the industrial school.

The board shall provide a system of merits and demerits and shall provide for the unconditional release of the inmates of the school where by the system and by the judgment and discretion of the board it is determined that an inmate has entirely reformed and has definitely earned the right to release; and upon reaching this conclusion the board shall recommend to the juvenile court of the parish the unconditional release of the person. Upon approval by the court the inmate shall be unconditionally discharged from the industrial school.

§1039. Return of inmates to committing court for transfer.

The board of commissioners of the school may return to the juvenile court of the parish any inmate committed to the school with recommendation for the transfer of the inmate to the state reformatory, to a hospital for the insane, to an institution for the care of feeble minded or other appropriate institution to which the inmate might have been committed in the first instance, and thereupon, the court may cause the inmate to be committed to an appropriate institution or dealt with according to law.

PART X. PAYMENT FOR CARE OF CHILDREN IN NONSTATE OPERATED AGENCIES AND FACILITIES

§1081. Purpose.

Notwithstanding any other provision of law to the contrary, the provisions of this Part shall serve as the sole statutory authorization under which the Department of Health and Human Resources and the Department of Public Safety and Corrections shall make payments for the care and treatment of children in nonstate operated child caring agencies, child placing agencies, shelter care home facilities, and maternity homes.

§1082. Definitions.

The definitions provided in R.S. 13:1569 and in Article 13 of the code of juvenile procedure shall be applicable to this Part, unless the context clearly indicates otherwise.

§1083. Participation.

Nonstate operated agencies and facilities desiring to participate in payment under this Part shall:

(1) If otherwise required by statute or regulation, be duly licensed by the state of Louisiana through its agent, the Department of Health and Hospitals.

(2) Submit to the Department of Health and Hospitals, Department of Social Services or the Department of Public Safety and Corrections on or before August first, or at a time set by the department, a statement requesting participation and funding under this Part for the succeeding fiscal year.

(3) Submit programmatic and fiscal information within such time and to the extent as the Department of Health and Human Resources or the Department of Public Safety and Corrections may require. Agencies or facilities which operate multiple subprograms shall submit such information for each subprogram for which participation is being requested. The failure of an agency or facility to submit such a statement or to provide information required by these departments may, at their discretion, preclude that agency or facility from participating in funding under this Part for the fiscal year in question.

(4) Be subject to audit by the Department of Health and Human Resources or the Department of Public Safety and Corrections and the legislative auditor, and shall retain and make available such records and documents as are required to complete such audit.

§1084. Establishment of rates for payment for care in nonstate operated agencies and facilities.

A. For purposes of establishing rates of payment the Department of Health and Human Resources and the Department of Public Safety and Corrections shall develop a formula that bears a reasonable relationship to cost of care for children cared for by nonstate operated institutions and agencies and which incorporates a prospective budgeting methodology. For purposes of establishing such rates each department named herein shall develop criteria for budgeting that reflect established accounting practices and encourage cost containment.

B. On the basis of information provided in accordance with R.S. 15:1083, the Department of Health and Human Resources and the Department of Public Safety and Corrections shall pay monthly to each nonstate operated institution or agency a sum computed by these departments using a formula that bears a reasonable relationship to cost of care for children cared for by the nonstate operated institutions and agencies and which incorporates a prospective budgeting methodology.

C. The Department of Health and Human Resources and the Department of Public Safety and Corrections may make revisions to these rates provided that all of the following conditions are met:

(1) The Department of Health and Human Resources or the Department of Public Safety and Corrections submits a report to the legislature documenting the need for such revisions.

(2) The effective date of the revision shall be no earlier than the first day of the succeeding state fiscal year.

(3) The revised rate shall remain in effect for at least the entire state fiscal year for which the rate was revised; however, the rate paid to a facility may be reduced within such fiscal year when it fails to document approved adjustments properly or fails to follow the guidelines and regulations set forth by the departments.

(4) The legislature appropriates funds for implementation of the revised rates.

D. The Department of Health and Hospitals, Department of Social Services and the Department of Public Safety and Corrections shall promulgate under the Administrative Procedure Act* and publish in the State Register the criteria utilized in establishing the cost related formula that bears a reasonable relationship to cost of care for children cared for by nonstate operated institutions and agencies. Each department may set its own rates and make payment based on that rate.
R.S. 49:950 et seq.

§1084.1. *(Renumbered as R.S. 15:1087.)*

§1085. Payment for care and treatment.

A. The Department of Health and Human Resources is hereby authorized to make payments, at the rates established under R.S. 15:1084, for the care and treatment of children placed by the Department of Health and Human Resources in child caring agencies, child placing agencies, maternity homes, and shelter care facilities which conform to the requirements of this Part.

B. Payments shall be made on a monthly basis and shall represent reimbursements for services provided during the previous month. Participating agencies shall submit such information as the Department of Health and Human Resources may require to document claims for reimbursement.

C. Participating agencies and facilities shall receive one and only one monthly payment from the Department of Health and Human Resources for services rendered to each child under this Part except for such adjustments as may be necessary to rectify previous inaccurate payments.

D. The Department of Public Safety and Corrections may make payments, at the rates established under R.S. 15:1084, for the care and treatment of youth adjudicated delinquent or in need of supervision, who are assigned to the custody of the department and placed by the department in either nonstate operated residential or nonresidential treatment programs. Subject to the availability of agency resources and the availability of service providers, the department may make payments, at rates established under R.S. 15:1084, for services to adjudicated youth and their families who are at risk of having the youth removed from the legal custody and care of the parents or legal guardians.
(Chgd. by Acts 1990 No. 322, §1, eff. 9/7/90.)

§1086. Contribution to cost of care by parent or custodian.

A. When the Department of Health and Human Resources or the Department of Public Safety and Corrections provides payments for care and treatment of a child under the provisions of this Part, the parent or legal custodian will be required to contribute to the cost of care of the child in such a manner as is consistent with applicable federal and state regulations, as is commensurate with his ability to pay, and as is in accordance with a sliding scale which shall be established by the departments.

B. The department providing payment for the child shall notify the parent or legal custodian of his responsibility to contribute to the cost of care and shall bill him on a periodic basis, but no less than quarterly, for the amount due. The department shall make every reasonable effort to notify such person of his liability under this Section as soon as possible after placement of the juvenile; however, such notice or receipt thereof is not a condition for the imposition of liability for costs of care under this Section.

C. Such payments shall be made directly to department* providing payment for the child and shall be deposited in the state treasury.
**So in original. Probably should be "to the department".*

D. If a default occurs, the department providing payment for the child shall exercise all administrative and legal alternatives provided by law or regulation to enforce the provisions of this Section. This may include reasonable administrative costs, costs of court, and reasonable attorney fees. The department may enter into an agreement with other public agencies for collection of any debt owed to the state under provisions of this Section.
(Chgd. by Acts 1990 No. 536, §1, eff. 9/7/90.)

§1087. Non-state providers; contracts.

Notwithstanding any other law to the contrary, contracts with non-state providers for services to juvenile offenders assigned to the Department of Public Safety and Corrections, and/or to their families, shall not exceed a term of five years without renewal and renegotiation. Nothing in this Section shall prohibit the department from terminating or amending such contacts prior to their expiration as otherwise provided by law.

PART XI. REGIONAL JUVENILE FACILITIES

SUBPART A. IN GENERAL

§1091. Regional system of shelter care and detention facilities; alternative shelter care programs.

The Department of Public Safety and Corrections may develop or assist in the development of a regional system of approved and licensed shelter care and detention facilities and certified shelter care programs and may make payments for the care and treatment of children in approved and licensed detention and shelter facilities and programs.

§1092. Method of payment.

A. On the basis of information provided in accordance with R.S. 15:1083, the Department of Public Safety and Corrections will determine the actual cost of operating each facility or alternative shelter program. The Department of Public Safety and Corrections may enter into a contractual agreement with each regional detention facility, shelter care facility, or alternative shelter program specifying the services to be provided and based upon an annually approved operating budget. Up to twenty percent of the approved annual budget amount may be advanced to each participating contractor. Contract payments shall be made on a monthly installment basis as substantiated by expenditure claims from the contractor.

B. In order to develop the shelter care facilities and programs desperately needed in the state for juveniles who are clients of the Department of Public Safety and Corrections, the department may provide start-up funds for the establishment of such facilities and programs.

§1092.1. Other laws applicable.

The provisions of R.S. 15:1083, 1084, and 1086 shall apply to this Part.

§1093. Juvenile detention centers; special court costs.

A. The district court in any parish which is also contained within the jurisdiction of any juvenile detention center may levy special costs in the amount of fifty dollars against every defendant who is convicted of a felony after trial or who enters a plea of guilty or nolo contendere or forfeits bond, excluding traffic offenses and misdemeanors.

B. However, in lieu of imposing such special costs, the court may direct that a like amount be deducted from any fine imposed prior to disposition of the fine in accordance with law. In either event, any amounts so collected shall be remitted, by the tenth of the month following the month in which collected, by the proper officer of the court to the juvenile detention center in the parish in which the court resides to be used for the expenses of its operations as provided by law. Such costs shall be in addition to any otherwise imposed by law.

(Added by Acts 1990 No. 546, §1, eff. 9/7/90.)

SUBPART B. FLORIDA PARISHES JUVENILE JUSTICE DISTRICT

§1094. Florida Parishes Juvenile Justice District; creation; jurisdiction.

The Florida Parishes Juvenile District is hereby established as a political subdivision of the state, with a territorial jurisdiction throughout the Twenty-First and Twenty-Second Judicial Districts, including the parishes of Livingston, St. Helena, St. Tammany, Tangipahoa, and Washington.

§1094.1. Board of commissioners; appointment; terms.

A. The Florida Parishes Juvenile Justice Commission is hereby created to control, administer, and manage the affairs of the district. The commission shall be composed of a board of seven commissioners, who shall be qualified electors domiciled and residing in the district. Two commissioners shall be jointly appointed, for terms of four years, by the judges of the Twenty-First Judicial District; two commissioners shall be jointly appointed, for terms of four years, by the judges of the Twenty-Second Judicial District; one commissioner shall be jointly appointed, for a term of four years, by the judges of the city courts of the municipalities of Bogalusa and Slidell; one commissioner shall be jointly appointed, for a term of four years, by the judges of the city courts of the municipalities of Denham Springs and Hammond; and, on an alternating basis, one commissioner shall be appointed, for a two year term, by the district attorney of the Twenty-First Judicial District, and by the district attorney of the Twenty-Second Judicial District. All appointments shall be confirmed by the Senate.

B. The members of the board of commissioners shall serve without salary or per diem but the board may authorize a reasonable travel allowance for its members in the performance of their official duties.

(Chgd. by Acts 1990 No. 537, §1, eff. 7/19/90.)

§1094.2. Purpose.

The purpose of the commission shall be to assist and afford opportunities to children who enter the juvenile justice system, or who are children in need of care or supervision, to become productive, law-abiding citizens of the community, parish, and state by the establishment of rehabilitative programs within a structured environment and to provide physical facilities and related services for children throughout the parishes of Livingston, St. Helena, St. Tammany, Tangipahoa, and Washington.

§1094.3. Board of commissioners; officers; meetings.

A. The board of commissioners shall elect a president, a secretary, and a treasurer, whose duties in addition to those provided by this Subpart shall be established by the board. If the board so decides, one commissioner may serve as both secretary and treasurer, but in any event the treasurer shall furnish bond in an amount and in accordance with terms and conditions fixed by the board.

B. The board shall fix a time and place for the holding of its regular meetings and shall hold at least one regular meeting in each calendar month. Additional regular or special meetings may be held upon the call of the president or of three of the commissioners. All meetings of the board shall be held at the domicile of the board and shall be governed by the provisions of R.S. 42:4.1 through 12.

C. A majority of the current members of the board shall constitute a quorum. A quorum shall be required to transact business and all actions and resolutions of the board must be approved by a majority of the quorum present.

§1094.4. Board; general authority.

A. The board may purchase or otherwise acquire, construct, reconstruct, rehabilitate, improve, repair, operate, lease as lessor or lessee, manage, and administer or enter into contracts for the management, administration, and operation of a juvenile detention facility or facilities, shelter care facility or facilities, or such other juvenile justice facilities as are useful, necessary, expedient, or convenient to carry out the plans and purposes of the commission and for the orderly conduct of its business. Such facilities may include but are not limited to office facilities, parking facilities, diagnostic facilities, dormitories, and other residential facilities for delinquent, neglected, or abused children or children in need of care or supervision, as well as for employees, patrons, visitors, and relatives of children who may enter the juvenile justice system or who are in need of care or supervision. In addition, the commission may lease, purchase, or acquire by donation or otherwise, any property, immovable or movable, tangible or intangible, from any person, firm, or corporation, including the state and its agencies and political subdivisions.

B. The board may also authorize and approve, upon such terms as it may deem advisable, contracts of employment for a superintendent or administrator and other necessary personnel and contracts for legal, financial, engineering, and other professional services necessary or expedient for the conduct of its affairs.

§1094.5. Board; domicile; power to levy taxes, incur debt, issue bonds.

A. The board of commissioners shall be domiciled in the parish of Tangipahoa and shall have the power to sue and be sued. In the exercise of its powers to control, administer, and manage the affairs of the district, the board may incur debt and issue bonds, and it may levy taxes in the manner provided in this Subpart and pursuant to Article VI, Sections 30 and 32, of the Constitution of Louisiana or any other constitutional or statutory authority. The board generally may perform any function and exercise any power necessary, requisite, or proper for the administration and management of the affairs of the commission, and it specifically may cooperate with juvenile courts and other courts and public agencies within the Twenty-First and Twenty-Second Judicial Districts and aid and assist them in all ways authorized by law to carry out the purposes and responsibilities for which it is established.

B. In addition to the general powers conferred herein, in order to obtain the necessary funds to carry out its purposes, duties, and responsibilities, and in order to acquire, construct, maintain, and operate a juvenile facility or facilities and related services and programs throughout the Florida Parishes Juvenile Justice District, the commission may incur debt and issue general obligation bonds within the limitations prescribed by Article VI, Section 33, of the Constitution of Louisiana and other applicable constitutional or statutory authority, but only when authorized by a majority of the electors in the district who vote thereon in an election held for that purpose in accordance with laws governing such elections.
(Chgd. by Acts 1992 No. 693, §1, eff. 7/6/92.)

§1094.6. Method of payment; facility situated in Tangipahoa Parish.

A. On the basis of information provided in accordance with R.S. 15:1083, the Department of Public Safety and Corrections shall determine the actual cost of operating the juvenile detention facility situated in Tangipahoa Parish when the facility files a statement requesting participation and funding under this Part. The department shall enter into a contractual agreement with the participating regional detention facility, specifying the services to be provided and the dollar amount of the contractual agreement, which shall be the actual cost of operating the facility or program. This amount shall be paid in quarterly advances to the participating regional detention facility.

B. In order to develop the detention facility desperately needed in the state and region for juveniles who are clients of the Department of Public Safety and Corrections, the department shall provide start-up funds for the establishment of the facility or program.

§1094.7. Funding for the commission; criminal court costs.

A. In the parishes of Livingston, St. Helena, St. Tammany, Tangipahoa, and Washington, in all felony and misdemeanor prosecutions, including traffic offenses, under state law or parish or municipal ordinance, in any district, parish, city, or mayor's court, special costs in an amount not to exceed five dollars shall be levied against every defendant who is convicted after trial, enters a plea of guilty or nolo contendere, or forfeits bond. However, in lieu of imposing the special costs, the court may direct that a like amount be deducted from any fine imposed prior to disposition of the fine in accordance with other laws, but in either event any amounts so collected shall be remitted, by the tenth of the month following the month in which collected, by the proper officer of the court to the board of the Florida Parishes Juvenile Justice Commission to be used for the expenses of its operations as provided in this Subpart.

B. In the parishes of Livingston, St. Helena, St. Tammany, Tangipahoa, and Washington, in all courts exercising juvenile jurisdiction, special costs in an amount not to exceed five dollars shall be levied against every juvenile who is found to have committed a traffic violation, under state law or parish or municipal ordinance, and special costs in an amount not to exceed twenty-five dollars shall be levied against every juvenile who is adjudicated a delinquent. All or part of the costs may be suspended, but any amounts thereof collected shall be remitted, by the tenth of the month following the month in which collected, by the proper officer of the court in which the matter was heard to the board of the Florida Parishes Juvenile Justice Commission to be used for the expenses of its operations in this Subpart.

SUBPART C. TANGIPAHOA PARISH JUVENILE JUSTICE DISTRICT

§1095. Tangipahoa Parish Juvenile Justice District; creation; jurisdiction.

The Tangipahoa Parish Juvenile Justice District is hereby established as a political subdivision of the state, with a territorial jurisdiction throughout the parish.

§1095.1. Board of commissioners; appointment; terms.

A. The Tangipahoa Parish Juvenile Commission is hereby created to control, administer, and manage the affairs of the district. The commission shall be composed of a board of five commissioners, who shall be qualified electors domiciled and residing in the district. They shall be appointed for terms of four years. One commissioner shall be appointed by the district court judges who serve Tangipahoa Parish and the district attorney for the Twenty-First Judicial District; one commissioner shall be appointed by the judge of the City Court of Hammond; one commissioner shall be appointed by the state representative from District No.

72; one commissioner shall be appointed by the state representative from District No. 73; and one commissioner shall be appointed by the state representative from District No. 74.

B. The members of the board of commissioners shall serve without salary or per diem but the board may authorize a reasonable travel allowance for its members in the performance of their official duties.

§1095.2. Purpose.

The purpose of the commission shall be to assist and afford opportunities to children who enter the juvenile justice system, or who are children in need of care or supervision, to become productive, law-abiding citizens of the community, parish, and state by the establishment of rehabilitative programs within a structured environment and to provide physical facilities and related services for children throughout the area.

§1095.3. Board of commissioners; officers; meetings.

A. The board of commissioners shall elect a president, a secretary, and a treasurer, whose duties in addition to those provided by this Subpart shall be established by the board. If the board so decides, one commissioner may serve as both secretary and treasurer, but in any event the treasurer shall furnish bond in an amount and in accordance with terms and conditions fixed by the board.

B. The board shall fix a time and place for the holding of its regular meetings and shall hold at least one regular meeting in each calendar month. Additional regular or special meetings may be held upon the call of the president or of two of the commissioners. All meetings of the board shall be held at the domicile of the board and shall be governed by the provisions of R.S. 42:4.1 through 12.

C. A majority of the current members of the board shall constitute a quorum. A quorum shall be required to transact business and all actions and resolutions of the board must be approved by a majority of the quorum present.

§1095.4. Board; general authority.

A. The board may purchase or otherwise acquire, construct, reconstruct, rehabilitate, improve, repair, operate, lease as lessor or lessee, manage, and administer or enter into contracts for the management, administration, and operation of a juvenile detention facility or facilities, shelter care facility or facilities, or such other juvenile justice facilities as are useful, necessary, expedient, or convenient to carry out the plans and purposes of the commission and for the orderly conduct of its business. Such facilities may include but are not limited to office facilities, parking facilities, diagnostic facilities, dormitories, and other residential facilities for delinquent, neglected, or abused children or children in need of care or supervision, as well as for employees, patrons, visitors, and relatives of children who may enter the juvenile justice system or who are in need of care or supervision. In addition, the commission may lease, purchase, or acquire by donation or otherwise, any property, immovable or movable, tangible or intangible, from any person, firm, or corporation, including the state and its agencies and political subdivisions.

B. The board may also authorize and approve, upon such terms as it may deem advisable, contracts of employment for a superintendent or administrator and other necessary personnel and contracts for legal, financial, engineering, and other professional services necessary or expedient for the conduct of its affairs.

§1095.5. Board; domicile; power to levy taxes, incur debt, issue bonds.

A. The board of commissioners shall be domiciled in the city of Hammond and shall have the power to sue and be sued. In the exercise of its powers to control, administer, and manage the affairs of the district, the board may incur debt and issue bonds, and it may levy taxes in the manner provided in this Subpart and pursuant to Article VI, Sections 30 and 32, of the Constitution of Louisiana or any other constitutional or statutory authority. The board generally may perform any function and exercise any power necessary, requisite, or proper for the administration and management of the affairs of the commission, and it specifically may cooperate with juvenile courts and other courts and public agencies within the Twenty-First Judicial District and aid and assist them in all ways authorized by law to carry out the purposes and responsibilities for which it is established.

B. In addition to the general powers conferred herein, in order to obtain the necessary funds to carry out its purposes, duties, and responsibilities, and in order to acquire, construct, maintain, and operate a juvenile facility or facilities and related services and programs throughout the Tangipahoa Parish Juvenile Justice District, the commission may incur debt and issue general obligation bonds within the limitations prescribed by Article VI, Section 33, of the Constitution of Louisiana and other applicable constitutional or statutory authority, but only when authorized by a majority of the electors in the district who vote thereon in an election held for that purpose in accordance with laws governing such elections.

SUBPART D. TRI-PARISH JUVENILE JUSTICE DISTRICT

§1096. Tri-Parish Juvenile Justice District; creation; jurisdiction; definitions.

A. The Tri-Parish Juvenile Justice District is hereby established as a political subdivision of the state, with a territorial jurisdiction throughout the Eighteenth Judicial District, including the parishes of Iberville, Pointe Coupee, and West Baton Rouge.

B. As used in this Subpart, the following words and terms shall have the following meanings, unless the context clearly indicates and requires another or different meaning or intent:

(1) "Board" means the board of commissioners of the Tri-Parish Juvenile Justice Commission.

(2) "Commission" means the Tri-Parish Juvenile Justice Commission.

(3) "District" means the Tri-Parish Juvenile Justice District.

(4) "Facility" means any juvenile detention facility, shelter care facility, or such other juvenile justice facility.

(5) "Governing authority" means the governing authority of a parish.

(6) "Lease-purchase contract" is the financing and acquisition of property by a person pursuant to an arrangement under which such person acquires title to property, constructs a facility thereon, and enters into a lease-purchase contract with the commission providing for the leasing of the property, including a facility thereon, to the commission and the acquisition of title to the property by the commission at the end of the lease period. For the purposes of this Subpart, the term "lease-purchase contract" also means any agreement between a person and the commission providing for the acquisition, lease, custody of juveniles, or other form of operation of a newly constructed facility as may be provided in such agreement, provided that all policy and criteria matters for management shall be determined by the commission.

(7) "Participating parish" means any parish which has entered into a participation agreement with the commission by which certain space within the facility is subleased to house juveniles from the participating parish.

(Chgd. by Acts 1992 No. 1071, §1, eff. 7/14/92.)

§1096.1. Board of commissioners; appointment; terms.

A. The Tri-Parish Juvenile Justice Commission is hereby created to control, administer, and manage the affairs of the district. The commission shall be composed of a board of seven commissioners, who shall be qualified electors domiciled and residing in the Eighteenth Judicial District. They shall be appointed for terms of four years. Each of the three parish governing authorities shall appoint two commissioners from lists of not less than three nor more than five names of persons domiciled and residing in their respective parishes submitted by the district judges and the district attorney for the Eighteenth Judicial District. One commissioner shall be appointed at large by the district judges and the district attorney.

B. The members of the board of commissioners shall serve without salary or per diem but the board may authorize a reasonable travel allowance for its members in the performance of their official duties.

§1096.2. Purpose.

The purpose of the commission shall be to assist and afford opportunities to preadjudicatory and postadjudicatory children who enter the juvenile justice system, or who are children in need of care or supervision, to become productive, law-abiding citizens of the community, parish, and state by the establishment of rehabilitative programs within a structured environment and to provide physical facilities and related services for children, including the housing, care, supervision, maintenance, and education of juveniles under the age of seventeen years, and for juveniles seventeen years of age and over who were under seventeen years of age when they committed an alleged offense, throughout the parishes within the district and other participating parishes. *(Chgd. by Acts 1992 No. 1071, §1, eff. 7/14/92.)*

§1096.3. Board of commissioners; officers; meetings.

A. The board of commissioners shall elect a president, a secretary, and a treasurer, whose duties in addition to those provided by this Subpart shall be established by the board. If the board so decides, one commissioner may serve as both secretary and treasurer, but in any event the treasurer shall furnish bond in an amount and in accordance with terms and conditions fixed by the board.

B. The board shall fix a time and place for the holding of its regular meetings and shall hold at least one regular meeting in each calendar month. Additional regular or special meetings may be held upon the call of the president or of three of the commissioners. All meetings of the board shall be governed by the provisions of R.S. 42:4.1 through 12.

C. A majority of the current members of the board shall constitute a quorum. A quorum shall be required to transact business and all actions and resolutions of the board must be approved by a majority of the quorum present.

§1096.4. Board; general authority.

A. (1) The board may purchase or otherwise acquire, construct, reconstruct, rehabilitate, improve, repair, operate, lease as lessor or lessee, manage, and administer or enter into contracts for the management, administration, and operation of a juvenile detention facility or facilities, shelter care facility or facilities, or such other juvenile justice facilities as are useful, necessary, expedient, or convenient to carry out the plans and purposes of the commission and for the orderly conduct of its business. Such facilities may include but are not limited to office facilities, parking facilities, diagnostic facilities, dormitories, residential units, administration and social services buildings, cafeteria buildings, gymnasium and recreation buildings, education buildings, and other residential facilities for delinquent, neglected, or abused children or children in need of care or supervision, as well as for employees, patrons, visitors, and relatives of children who may enter the juvenile justice system or who are in need of care or supervision. In addition, the commission may lease, purchase, or acquire by donation or otherwise, any property, immovable or movable, tangible or intangible, from any person, firm, or corporation, including the state and its agencies and political subdivisions.

(2) In connection with the construction, reconstruction, rehabilitation, improvement, or repair of any facility and the equipping thereof, the board shall comply, or cause to be complied, with the applicable provisions of R.S. 38:2211 et seq., the Public Bid Law; however, the lease or lease-purchase contract need not additionally be advertised and bid by the board, and to that extent the board shall be exempt from the provisions of Chapter 10 of Title 41 of the Louisiana Revised Statutes of 1950.

(3) The purchase, reconstruction, rehabilitation, improvement, or repair of a facility and the equipping thereof by the lessor shall be subject to only those state and local sales and use taxes which the board would have been subject to if such purchase, reconstruction, rehabilitation, improvement, repair, or equipping had been contracted for directly by the board. If the board is subject to sales and use taxes upon a direct contract for such purchase, reconstruction, rehabilitation, improvement, repair, or equipping by the board, the lessor shall be so subject; however, in such cases the board shall not additionally be subject to a sales and use tax on the lease payments to the lessor under a lease or lease-purchase contract.

(4) The obligation to make payments under a lease-purchase contract and the obligation to pay other charges incident to any such contract shall not constitute or give rise to an indebtedness within the meaning of any constitutional, statutory, or home rule charter debt limitation. If the payments received from a lease or lease-purchase contract are security for any notes, certificates, bonds, or other similar instruments, the portion of such payments representing interest shall be exempt from all taxation by the state or any political subdivision thereof.

B. The board may:

(1) Enter into a lease or lease-purchase contract with any person, public or private, for the acquisition of a facility with a lease term not to exceed thirty years upon such terms and conditions as it shall deem proper; however, such contract shall contain the following annual appropriation dependency clause:

"The continuation of this contract is contingent upon the continuation of an appropriation of funds by the board to fulfill the requirements of the contract. If the board fails to appropriate sufficient monies to provide for the continuation of the contract or if such appropriation is reduced by any means provided in the appropriations resolution to prevent the total appropriations for the year from exceeding revenues for that last year or for any other lawful purpose and the effect of such reduction is to provide insufficient monies for the continuation of the contract, the contract shall terminate on the date of the beginning of the first fiscal year for which funds are not appropriated."

(2) Enter into a participation agreement with the parishes of Iberville, Pointe Coupee, and West Baton Rouge, and, subject to the approval of said parishes, with any other parish or other entity subleasing a portion of the facility, provided that no such sublease shall relieve the sublessor of obligations under its lease, and providing for the care and maintenance of juveniles from that parish at the facility.

(3) Generally do all things lawfully to provide temporary custodial care, supervision, and education of juveniles.

(4) Authorize and approve, upon such terms as it may deem advisable, contracts of employment for a superintendent or administrator and other necessary personnel and contracts for legal, financial, engineering, and other professional services necessary or expedient for the conduct of its affairs.

(5) Adopt rules and regulations for the operations and maintenance of the facility.

(6) Accept available federal, state or other public funds or private funds allocated for the purpose of establishing, improving, operating, or maintaining the facility.

(7) Perform any function and exercise any power necessary, requisite, or proper for the administration and management of its affairs pursuant to this Subpart.

(8) Cooperate with juvenile courts and other courts and public agencies of the parishes within the district and other participating parishes.

(9) Create pursuant to Chapter 2 of Title 12 of the Louisiana Revised Statutes of 1950, as amended, entities that are necessary or desirable in order to effect the issuance of notes, bonds, or certificates which will be secured by lease, lease-purchase contract, or participation agreement payments authorized by this Subpart.

(Chgd. by Acts 1992 No. 1071, §1, eff. 7/14/92.)

§1096.5. Board; domicile; power to levy taxes, incur debt, and issue bonds.

A. The board of commissioners shall be domiciled in the parish of West Baton Rouge and shall have the power to sue and be sued. In the exercise of its powers to control, administer, and manage the affairs of the district, the board may incur debt and issue bonds, and it may levy taxes in the manner provided in this Subpart and pursuant to Article VI, Sections 30 and 32, of the Constitution of Louisiana or any other constitutional or statutory authority. The board generally may perform any function and exercise any power necessary, requisite, or proper for the administration and management of the affairs of the commission, and it specifically may cooperate with juvenile courts and other courts and public agencies within the Eighteenth Judicial District and aid and assist them in all ways authorized by law to carry out the purposes and responsibilities for which it is established.

B. In addition to the general powers conferred herein, in order to obtain the necessary funds to carry out its purposes, duties, and responsibilities, and in order to acquire, construct, maintain, and operate a juvenile facility or facilities and related services and programs throughout the Tri-Parish Juvenile Justice District, the commission may, subject to the approval of the governing authorities of the parishes of Iberville, Pointe Coupee, and West Baton Rouge, incur debt and issue general obligation bonds within the limitations prescribed by Article VI, Section 33, of the Constitution of Louisiana and other applicable constitutional or statutory authority, but only when authorized by a majority of the electors in the district who vote thereon in an election held for that purpose in accordance with laws governing such elections.

C. The board, subject to the approval of the governing authorities of the parishes of Iberville, Pointe Coupee, and West Baton Rouge, may levy a special annual tax not to exceed one mill for a period of not more than twenty years for the purposes of acquiring, constructing, equipping, operating, maintaining, and managing a facility and providing rehabilitative programs within a structured environment for children who enter the juvenile justice system or who are children in need of care or supervision or making payments pursuant to a lease or lease-purchase contract pursuant to this Subpart by a two-thirds vote of total membership of the board, but only after a public hearing is held and when authorized by a majority of the electors who vote thereon in an election held for that purpose. In addition and subject to the approval of the governing authorities of the parishes of Iberville, Pointe Coupee, and West Baton Rouge, the board may also levy an additional tax not to exceed two mills for a period of not more than twenty years for such purposes by a two-thirds vote of the total membership of

the board, but only after a public hearing is held and when authorized by a majority of the electors who vote thereon in an election held for that purpose.
(Chgd. by Acts 1992 No. 1071, §1, eff. 7/14/92.)

§1096.6. Use of facilities.

The facility shall be used for the temporary detention of juveniles from the parishes within the district while awaiting trial or other disposition of their cases, runaways from parishes within the district, and juveniles awaiting transfer to the Department of Public Safety and Corrections. Subject to the approval of the governing authorities of the parishes of Iberville, Pointe Coupee, and West Baton Rouge, juveniles from parishes outside of the district may be accepted by the board in accordance with rules and regulations adopted therefor by the board and pursuant to a participation agreement between the board and the governing authority of the participating parish, but only upon payment or agreement of the participating parish to pay the charge established for the sublease of space in the facility and the fee for the care and maintenance of each juvenile. *(Added by Acts 1992 No. 1071, §1, eff. 7/14/92.)*

§1096.7. Participation by parishes; appropriations.

A. The governing authority of any parish may enter into a participation agreement with the board to sublease a portion of any facility and provide for the care and maintenance of juveniles from that participating parish at the facility pursuant to this Subpart.

B. The governing authority of each participating parish shall annually appropriate an amount which will be sufficient to fund the parish's obligation pursuant to the participation agreement entered into with the board pursuant to this Subpart.

C. For the purpose of obtaining necessary funds pursuant to Subsection B, each participating parish may levy a special annual tax not to exceed one mill for a period of not more than twenty years by a two-thirds vote of total membership of the parish governing authority, but only after a public hearing is held and when authorized by a majority of the electors who vote thereon in an election held for that purpose. In addition and if deemed necessary by the governing authority, a participating parish may levy a supplemental annual tax not to exceed two mills for a period of not more than twenty years for such purposes by a two-thirds vote of the total membership of the governing authority, but only after a public hearing is held and when authorized by a majority of the electors who vote thereon in an election held for that purpose.
(Added by Acts 1992 No. 1071, §1, eff. 7/14/92.)

SUBPART E. NORTHWEST LOUISIANA JUVENILE DETENTION CENTER AUTHORITY

§1097. Northwest Louisiana Juvenile Detention Center Authority; creation; jurisdiction.

A. The Northwest Louisiana Juvenile Detention Center Authority is hereby established as a political subdivision of the state, with a territorial jurisdiction throughout the parishes of Claiborne, DeSoto, Natchitoches, Red River, Sabine, and Webster. If the governing authority of Claiborne Parish or the governing authority of Webster Parish elects to withdraw its respective parish from the district, the territorial jurisdiction of the district shall not include such parish or parishes.

B. The local governing authority of Claiborne Parish or Webster Parish may elect to withdraw its respective parish from membership and participation in the Northwest Juvenile Detention Center upon majority vote of the governing authority during the period beginning September 1, 1991 and ending December 31, 1991.
(Chgd. by Acts 1991 No. 147, §1, eff. 7/2/91.)

§1097.1. Board of commissioners; appointment; terms.

A. The Northwest Louisiana Juvenile Detention Center Authority shall be governed by a commission which shall control, administer, and manage the affairs of the district. The commission shall be composed of a board of commissioners, who shall be qualified electors domiciled and residing in the district. They shall be appointed for terms of four years, as follows:

(1) Three commissioners shall be appointed by the judges exercising juvenile jurisdiction within the participating parish areas.

(2) Four commissioners shall be appointed by the sheriffs of the participating parishes and the chiefs of police of municipalities within the participating parish areas.

(3) One commissioner shall be appointed by the governing authority of each of the participating parishes.

(4) One commissioner shall be appointed by the district attorneys with jurisdiction in the participating parishes.

(5) Three commissioners shall be appointed by the assistant secretary of the office of youth development of the Department of Public Safety and Corrections.

B. The members of the board of commissioners shall serve without salary or per diem but the board may authorize a reasonable travel allowance for its members in the performance of their official duties.

(Chgd. by Acts 1991 No. 147, §1; Acts 1992 No. 297, §1, eff. 8/21/92.)

§1097.2. Purpose.

The purpose of the commission shall be to assist and afford opportunities to preadjudicatory and postadjudicatory children who enter the juvenile justice system to become productive, law-abiding citizens of the community, parish, and state by the establishment of rehabilitative programs within a structured environment and to provide physical facilities and related services for children throughout the parishes belonging to the authority. *(Chgd. by Acts 1991 No. 147, §1, eff. 7/2/91.)*

§1097.3. Board of commissioners; officers; meetings.

A. The board of commissioners shall elect a president, a secretary, and a treasurer, whose duties in addition to those provided by this Subpart shall be established by the board. If the board so decides, one commissioner may serve as both secretary and treasurer, but in any event the treasurer shall furnish bond in an amount and in accordance with terms and conditions fixed by the board. The board may also elect an executive board, composed of not more than seven members, and establish its duties and responsibilities.

B. The board shall fix a time and place for the holding of its regular meetings. Additional regular or special meetings may be held upon the call of the president or of three of the commissioners. All meetings of the board shall be held at the domicile of the board and shall be governed by the provisions of R.S. 42:4.1 through 12. The board shall hold at least one regular meeting in each calendar month; however, the board may meet less frequently but not less than once each calendar quarter if it establishes an executive board and requires it to hold regular meetings at least once in each calendar month.

C. A majority of the current members of the board shall constitute a quorum. A quorum shall be required to transact business and all actions and resolutions of the board must be approved by a majority of the quorum present.

§1097.4. Board; general authority.

A. The board may purchase or otherwise acquire, construct, reconstruct, rehabilitate, improve, repair, operate, lease as lessor or lessee, manage, and administer or enter into contracts for the management, administration, and operation of a juvenile detention facility or facilities, shelter care facility or facilities, or such other juvenile justice facilities as are useful, necessary, expedient, or convenient to carry out the plans and purposes of the commission and for the orderly conduct of its business. Such facilities may include but are not limited to office facilities, parking facilities, diagnostic facilities, dormitories, and other residential facilities for delinquent, neglected, or abused children or children in need of care or supervision, as well as for employees, patrons, visitors, and relatives of children who may enter the juvenile justice system or who are in need of care or supervision. In addition, the commission may lease, purchase, or acquire by donation or otherwise, any property, immovable or movable, tangible or intangible, from any person, firm, or corporation, including the state and its agencies and political subdivisions.

B. The board may also authorize and approve, upon such terms as it may deem advisable, contracts of employment for a superintendent or administrator and other necessary personnel and contracts for legal, financial, engineering, and other professional services necessary or expedient for the conduct of its affairs.

§1097.5. Board; domicile; power to levy taxes, incur debt, issue bonds.

A. The board of commissioners shall be domiciled in Red River Parish and shall have the power to sue and be sued. In the exercise of its powers to control, administer, and manage the affairs of the authority, the board may incur debt and issue bonds, and it may levy taxes in the manner provided in this Subpart and pursuant to Article VI, Sections 30 and 32, of the Constitution of Louisiana or any other constitutional or statutory authority. The board generally may perform any function and exercise any power necessary, requisite, or proper for the administration and management of the affairs of the commission, and it specifically may cooperate with juvenile courts and other courts and public agencies within the seven parish area and aid and assist them in all ways authorized by law to carry out the purposes and responsibilities for which it is established.

B. In addition to the general powers conferred herein, in order to obtain the necessary funds to carry out its purposes, duties, and responsibilities, and in order to acquire, construct, maintain, and operate a juvenile facility or facilities and related services and programs throughout the territorial jurisdiction of the Northwest Louisiana Juvenile Detention Center Authority, the commission may incur debt and issue general obligation bonds within the limitations prescribed by Article VI, Section 33, of the Constitution of Louisiana and other applicable constitutional or statutory authority, but only when authorized by a majority of the electors in the seven parish area who vote thereon in an election held for that purpose in accordance with laws governing such elections.

§1097.6. Funding for the authority; criminal court costs.

In the parishes of Bienville, Claiborne, DeSoto, Natchitoches, Red River, Sabine, and Webster, in all felony and misdemeanor prosecutions, including traffic offenses, under state law or parish or municipal ordinance, in any district, parish, city, or mayor's court, special costs in the amount of seven dollars and fifty cents shall be levied against every defendant who is convicted after trial or who enters a plea of guilty or nolo contendere or who forfeits bond. However, in lieu of imposing the special costs, the court may direct that a like amount be deducted from any fine imposed prior to disposition of the fine in accordance with other laws, but in either event any amounts so collected shall be remitted, by the tenth of the month following the month in which collected, by the proper officer of the court to the board of the Northwest Louisiana Juvenile Detention Center Authority to be used for the expenses of its operations as provided in this Subpart.

§1097.7. Funding for the authority; juvenile court costs.

In the parishes of Bienville, Claiborne, DeSoto, Natchitoches, Red River, Sabine, and Webster, in all court exercising juvenile jurisdiction, special costs in the amount of fifty dollars shall be levied against every juvenile who is found to have committed a traffic violation or who is adjudicated a delinquent. All or part of the costs may be suspended, but any amounts thereof collected shall be remitted, by the tenth of the month following the month in which collected, by the proper officer of the court in which the matter was heard to the board of the Northwest Louisiana Juvenile Detention Center Authority to be used for the expenses of its operations as provided in this Subpart.

SUBPART F. ST. JAMES PARISH YOUTH CENTER

§1098.1. Construction of Subpart; controlling law.

A. To the extent that the provisions of this Subpart are inconsistent with any other statutory law, the provisions of this Subpart shall be deemed controlling, except that all provisions of the Code of Juvenile Procedure relative to the placement of juveniles in shelter care facilities and detention centers shall be deemed controlling.

B. This Subpart does and shall be construed to provide a complete, additional, and alternative method for the doing of the things authorized hereby and shall be regarded as supplemental and additional to powers conferred by other laws. No notice to, consent, or approval by any governmental body or public officer shall be required as a prerequisite to the entering into of any lease or lease-purchase contract which contains an annual appropriation dependency clause, nor to the issuance of any participation certificates with respect thereto, or to the exercise of any other public function or corporate power of a governing authority except as is provided in this Subpart.

§1098.2. Definitions.

As used in this Subpart, the followings words and terms shall have the following meanings, unless the context clearly indicates and requires another or different meaning or intent:

(1) "Commission" means the governing authority of St. James Parish.

(2) "Lease-purchase contract" is the financing and acquisition of property by a person pursuant to an arrangement under which such person acquires title to property, constructs a youth center thereon, and enters into a lease-purchase contract with the commission providing for the leasing of the property, including a youth center, to the parish and the acquisition of title to the property by the parish at the end of the lease period. For the purposes of this Subpart, the term "lease-purchase contract" also means any agreement between a person and the parish providing for the acquisition, lease, custody of juveniles, or other form of operation of a newly constructed youth center as may be provided in such agreement, provided that all policy and criteria matters for management shall be determined by the parish.

(3) "Parish" means St. James Parish.

(4) "Participating parish" means any parish which has entered into a participation agreement with St. James Parish by which certain space within a youth center is subleased to house juveniles from the participating parish.

§1098.3. Purpose.

The commission may assist and afford opportunities to preadjudicatory and postadjudicatory children who enter the juvenile justice system to become productive, law-abiding citizens of the community, parish, and state by the establishment of rehabilitative programs within a structured environment and provide physical facilities and related services for children, including the housing, care, supervision, maintenance, and education of juveniles under the age of seventeen years, and for juveniles seventeen years of age and over who were under seventeen years of age when they committed an alleged offense, throughout St. James Parish and participating parishes.

§1098.4. General authority.

A. (1) The commission may purchase or otherwise acquire, construct, reconstruct, rehabilitate, improve, repair, operate, lease as lessor or lessee, manage, and administer, or enter into contracts for the management, administration, and operation of, a youth center useful, necessary, expedient, or convenient to carry out the plans and purposes of this Subpart. The center may include but is not limited to residential units, administration and social services building, cafeteria building, gymnasium and recreational building, education building, and other residential facilities for delinquent, neglected, or abused children or children in need of care or supervision, as well as for employees, patrons, visitors, and relatives of children who may enter the juvenile justice system or who are in need of care or supervision. In addition, the commission may lease, purchase, or acquire by donation or otherwise, any property, immovable or movable, corporeal or incorporeal, from any person, firm, or corporation, including the state and its agencies and political subdivisions.

(2) In connection with the construction, reconstruction, rehabilitation, improvement, and/or repair of a youth center and the equipping thereof, the parish shall comply, or cause to be complied, with the applicable provisions of R.S. 38:2211 et seq., the public bid law; however, the lease or lease-purchase contract need not additionally be advertised and bid by the parish, and to that extent the parish shall be exempt from the provisions of Chapter 10 of Title 41 of the Louisiana Revised Statutes of 1950.

(3) The purchase, reconstruction, rehabilitation, improvement, and/or repair of a youth center and the equipping thereof by the lessor shall be subject to only those state and local sales and use taxes which the parish would have been subject to if such purchase, reconstruction, rehabilitation, improvement, repair, and/or equipping had been contracted for directly by the parish. If the parish is subject to sales and use taxes upon a direct contract for such purchase, reconstruction, rehabilitation, improvement, repair, and/or equipping by the parish, the lessor shall be so subject; however, in such cases the parish shall not additionally be subject to a sales and use tax on the lease payments to the lessor under a lease or lease-purchase contract.

(4) The obligation to make payments under a lease-purchase contract and the obligation to pay other charges incident to any such contract shall not constitute or give rise to an indebtedness within the meaning of any constitutional, statutory, or home rule charter debt limitation. If the payments received from a lease or lease-purchase contract are security for any notes, certificates, bonds, or other similar instruments, the portion of such payments representing interest shall be exempt from all taxation by the state or any political subdivision thereof.

B. The commission may:

(1) Enter into a lease or lease-purchase contract with any person, public or private, for the acquisition of a youth center with a lease term not to exceed thirty years upon such terms and conditions as it shall deem proper; however, such contract shall contain the following annual appropriation dependency clause:

"The continuation of this contract is contingent upon the continuation of an appropriation of funds by the governing authority to fulfill the requirements of the contract. If the governing authority fails to appropriate sufficient monies to provide for the continuation of the contract or if such appropriation is reduced by any means provided in the appropriations ordinance to prevent the total appropriations for the year from exceeding revenues for that year or for any other lawful purpose and the effect of such reduction is to provide insufficient monies for the continuation of the contract, the contract shall terminate on the date of the beginning of the first fiscal year for which funds are not appropriated."

(2) Enter into a participation agreement with another parish or other entity subleasing a portion of the center, provided that no such sublease shall relieve the sublessor of obligations under its lease, and providing for the care and maintenance of juveniles from that parish at the center.

(3) Generally do all things lawful to provide temporary custodial care, supervision, and education of juveniles.

(4) Authorize and approve, upon such terms as it may deem advisable, contracts of employment for a superintendent or administrator and other necessary personnel and contracts for legal, financial, engineering, and other professional services necessary or expedient for the conduct of its affairs pursuant to this Subpart.

(5) Adopt rules and regulations for the operations and maintenance of the center.

(6) Accept available federal, state, or other public funds or private funds allocated for the purpose of establishing, improving, operating, or maintaining the center.

(7) Perform any function and exercise any power necessary, requisite, or proper for the administration and management of its affairs pursuant to this Subpart.

(8) Cooperate with juvenile courts and other courts and public agencies within St. James Parish and participating parishes.

(9) Create pursuant to the provisions of Chapter 2 of Title 12 of the Louisiana Revised Statutes of 1950, as amended, entitles that are necessary or desirable in order to effect the issuance of notes, bonds, or certificates which will be secured by lease, lease-purchase contract, or participation agreement payments authorized by this Subpart.

§1098.5. Power to levy taxes, incur debt, issue bonds.

A. The commission may incur debt and issue bonds, and it may levy taxes in the manner provided in this Subpart and pursuant to Article VI, Sections 30 and 32 of the Constitution of Louisiana or any other constitutional or statutory authority.

B. In order to obtain the necessary funds to carry out its purposes, duties, and responsibilities, and in order to acquire, construct, equip, maintain, and operate a youth center and related services and programs in St. James Parish, the commission may incur debt and issue general obligation bonds within the limitations prescribed by Article VI, Section 33, of the Constitution of Louisiana and other applicable constitutional or statutory authority, but only when authorized by a majority of the electors who vote thereon in an election held for that purpose.

C. (1) The commission may levy a special annual tax not to exceed one mill for a period of not more than twenty years for the purposes of:

(a) Acquiring, constructing, equipping, operating, maintaining, and managing a youth center and providing rehabilitative programs within a structured environment for children who enter the juvenile justice system or who are children in need of care or supervision, or

(b) Making payments pursuant to a lease or lease-purchase contract pursuant to this Subpart by a two-thirds vote of total membership of the commission, without voter approval, but only after a public hearing is held.

(2) In addition, the commission may also levy an additional tax not to exceed two mills for a period of not more than twenty years for such purposes by a two-thirds vote of the total membership of the commission, but only after a public hearing is held and when authorized by a majority of the electors who vote thereon in an election held for that purpose.

§1098.6. Use of youth center.

The youth center shall be used for the temporary detention of juveniles within St. James Parish while awaiting trial or other disposition of their cases, runaways within the parish, and juveniles awaiting transfer to the Department of Public Safety and Corrections. Juveniles from outside of St. James Parish may be accepted by the commission in accordance with rules and regulations adopted therefor by the commission and pursuant to a participation agreement between the commission and the governing authority of the participating parish, but only upon payment or agreement of the participating parish to pay the charge established for the sublease of space in the center and the fee for the care and maintenance of each juvenile.

§1098.7. Participation by other parishes; appropriations.

A. The governing authority of any parish may enter into a participation agreement with St. James Parish subleasing a portion of the youth center and providing for the care and maintenance of juveniles from that participating parish at the center pursuant to this Subpart.

B. The governing authority of each participating parish shall annually appropriate an amount which will be sufficient to fund the parish's obligation pursuant to the participation agreement entered into with St. James Parish pursuant to this Subpart.

C. For the purpose of obtaining necessary funds pursuant to Subsection B, each participating parish may levy a special annual tax not to exceed one mill for a period of not more than twenty years by a two-thirds vote of total membership of the parish governing authority, without voter approval, but only after a public hearing is held. In addition and if deemed necessary by the governing authority, a participating parish may levy a supplemental annual tax not to exceed two mills for a period of not more than twenty years for such purposes by a two-thirds vote of the total membership of the governing authority, but only after a public hearing held and when authorized by a majority of the electors who vote thereon in an election held for that purpose.

D. The governing authority of St. John the Baptist Parish may continue to levy the special annual tax not to exceed one mill for a period of twenty years to fund the costs of housing and detaining juveniles, but those tax proceeds shall not automatically be tied to the St. James Parish youth center. The parish council by majority vote may elect to utilize those funds at any other juvenile detention center approved by appropriate state and federal authorities in St. John the Baptist Parish or in any other parish.
(Chgd. by Acts 1995 No. 28, §1, eff. 8/15/95.)

SUBPART G. PARISH YOUTH CENTER

(Added by Acts 1991 No. 147, §2, eff. 7/2/91.)

§1099.1. Construction of Subpart; controlling law.

To the extent that the provisions of this Subpart are inconsistent with any other statutory law, the provisions of this Subpart shall be deemed controlling, except that all provisions of the Code of Juvenile Procedure relative to the placement of juveniles in shelter care facilities and detention centers shall be deemed controlling. *(Added by Acts 1991 No. 147, §2, eff. 7/2/91.)*

§1099.2. Definitions.

As used in this Subpart, the following words and terms shall have the following meanings, unless the context clearly indicates and requires another or different meaning or intent:

(1) "Governing authority" means the governing authority of a parish or parishes having a youth center or a juvenile detention center authority.

(2) "Lease-purchase contract" is the financing and acquisition of property by a person pursuant to an arrangement under which such person acquires title to property, constructs a youth center thereon, and enters into a lease-purchase contract with a governing authority providing for the leasing of the property, including a youth center, to the parish and the acquisition of title to the property by the parish at the end of the lease period. For the purposes of this Subpart, the term "lease-purchase contract" also means any agreement between a person and a parish providing for the acquisition, lease, custody of juveniles, or other form of operation of a newly constructed youth center as may be provided in such agreement, provided that all policy and criteria matters for management shall be determined by the parish.

(3) "Parish" means a parish in which a youth center is sited.

(4) "Participating parish" means any parish which has entered into a participation agreement with a parish having a youth center by which certain space within the center is subleased to house juveniles from the participating parish.
(Added by Acts 1991 No. 147, §2, eff. 7/2/91.)

§1099.3. Purpose.

A governing authority may assist and afford opportunities to preadjudicatory and postadjudicatory children who enter the juvenile justice system to become productive, law-abiding citizens of the community, parish, and state by the establishment of rehabilitative programs within a structured environment and provide physical facilities and related services for children, including the housing, care, supervision, maintenance, and education of juveniles under the age of seventeen years, and for juveniles seventeen years of age or over who were under seventeen years of age when they committed an alleged offense, throughout the parish and participating parishes. *(Added by Acts 1991 No. 147, §2, eff. 7/2/91.)*

§1099.4. General authority.

A. (1) A governing authority may purchase or otherwise acquire, construct, reconstruct, rehabilitate, improve, repair, operate, lease as lessor or lessee, manage, and administer or enter into contracts for the management, administration, and operation of a youth center useful, necessary, expedient, or convenient to carry out the plans and purposes of this Subpart. The center may include but is not limited to residential units, administration and social services building, cafeteria building, gymnasium and recreation building, education building, and other residential facilities for delinquent, neglected, or abused children or children in need of care or supervision, as well as for employees, patrons, visitors, and relatives of children who may enter the juvenile justice system or who are in need of care or supervision. In addition, a governing authority may lease, purchase, or acquire by donation or otherwise, any property, immovable or movable, tangible or intangible, from any person, firm, or corporation, including the state and its agencies and political subdivisions.

(2) In connection with the construction, reconstruction, rehabilitation, improvement, or repair of a youth center and the equipping thereof, the parish shall comply, or cause to be complied, with the applicable provisions of R.S. 38:2211 et seq., the public bid law; however, the lease or lease-purchase contract need not additionally be advertised and bid by the parish, and to that extent the parish shall be exempt from the provisions of Chapter 10 of Title 41 of the Louisiana Revised Statutes of 1950.

(3) The purchase, reconstruction, rehabilitation, improvement, or repair of a youth center and the equipping thereof by the lessor shall be subject to only those state and local sales and use taxes which the parish would have been subject to if such purchase, reconstruction, rehabilitation, improvement, repair, or equipping had been contracted for directly by the parish. If the parish is subject to sales and use taxes upon a direct contract for such purchase, reconstruction, rehabilitation, improvement, repair, or equipping by the parish, the lessor shall be so subject; however, in such cases the parish shall not additionally be subject to a sales and use tax on the lease payments to the lessor under a lease or lease-purchase contract.

(4) The obligation to make payments under a lease-purchase contract and the obligation to pay other charges incident to any such contract shall not constitute or give rise to an indebtedness within the meaning of any constitutional, statutory, or home rule charter debt limitation. If the payments received from a lease or lease-purchase contract are security for any notes, certificates, bonds, or other similar instruments, the portion of such payments representing interest shall be exempt from all taxation by the state or any political subdivision thereof.

B. A governing authority may:

(1) Enter into a lease or lease-purchase contract with any person, public or private, for the acquisition of a youth center with a lease term not to exceed thirty years upon such terms and conditions as it shall deem proper; however, such contract shall contain the following annual appropriation dependency clause:

"The continuation of this contract is contingent upon the continuation of an appropriation of funds by the governing authority to fulfill the requirements of the contract. If the governing authority fails to appropriate sufficient monies to provide for the continuation of the contract or if such appropriation is reduced by any means provided in the appropriations ordinance to prevent the total appropriations for the year from exceeding revenues for the last year or for any other lawful purpose and the effect of such reduction is to provide insufficient monies for the continuation of the contract, the contract shall terminate on the date of the beginning of the first fiscal year for which funds are not appropriated."

(2) Enter into a participation agreement with another parish or entity subleasing a portion of the center, provided that no such sublease shall relieve the sublessor of obligations under its lease, and providing for the care and maintenance of juveniles from that parish at the center.

(3) Generally do all things lawfully to provide temporary custodial care, supervision, and education of juveniles.

(4) Authorize and approve, upon such terms as it may deem advisable, contracts of employment for a superintendent or administrator and other necessary personnel and contracts for legal, financial, engineering, and other professional services necessary or expedient for the conduct of its affairs pursuant to this Subpart.

(5) Adopt rules and regulations for the operations and maintenance of the center.

(6) Accept available federal, state, or other public funds or private funds allocated for the purpose of establishing, improving, operating, or maintaining the center.

(7) Perform any function and exercise any power necessary, requisite, or proper for the administration and management of its affairs pursuant to this Subpart.

(8) Cooperate with juvenile courts and other courts and public agencies within the parish and participating parishes.

(9) Create pursuant to the provisions of Chapter 2 of Title 12 of the Louisiana Revised Statutes of 1950, as amended, entities that are necessary or desirable in order to effect the issuance of notes, bonds, or certificates which will be secured by lease, lease-purchase contract, or participation agreement payments authorized by this Subpart.

(Added by Acts 1991 No. 147, §2, eff. 7/2/91.)

§1099.5. Power to levy taxes, incur debt, issue bonds.

A. A governing authority may incur debt and issue bonds, and it may levy taxes in the manner provided in this Subpart and pursuant to Article VI, Sections 30 and 32 of the Constitution of Louisiana or any other constitutional or statutory authority.

B. In order to obtain the necessary funds to carry out its purposes, duties, and responsibilities, and in order to acquire, construct, equip, maintain, and operate a youth center and related services and programs in the parish, a governing authority may incur debt and issue general obligation bonds within the limitations prescribed by Article VI, Section 33, of the Constitution of Louisiana and other applicable constitutional or statutory authority, but only when authorized by a majority of the electors who vote thereon in an election held for that purpose.

C. (1) A governing authority may levy a special annual tax not to exceed one mill for a period of not more than twenty years for the purposes of acquiring, constructing, equipping, operating, maintaining, and managing a youth center and providing rehabilitative programs within a structured environment for children who enter the juvenile justice system or who are children in need of care or supervision or making payments pursuant to a lease or lease-purchase contract pursuant to this Subpart by a two-thirds vote of total membership of the governing authority, without voter approval, but only after a public hearing is held. In addition, a governing authority may also levy an additional tax not to exceed two mills for a period of not more than twenty years for such purposes by a two-thirds vote of the total membership of the governing authority, but only after a public hearing is held and when authorized by a majority of the electors who vote thereon in an election held for that purpose.

(2) In addition to the tax authorized by Paragraph (1) of this Subsection, the governing authority of Terrebonne Parish may levy an additional one-mill tax and use the proceeds of that tax for the purposes described in Paragraph (1) of this Subsection. The tax herein authorized shall be levied and collected only after the question of its imposition has been submitted to and approved by majority of the qualified voters of Terrebonne Parish voting thereon in an election for the purpose and conducted in accordance with the Louisiana Election Code. The authority granted by this Paragraph shall be effective upon the governing authority's withdrawal from the participation agreement entered into with St. James Parish pursuant to R.S. 15:1098.7.

D. The taxing authority provided for in this Section shall not apply to any governing authority with jurisdiction over a youth center located in the parishes of Acadia, Allen, Assumption, Beauregard, Bienville, Caddo, Caldwell, Cameron, Catahoula, Concordia, East Carroll, Evangeline, Franklin, Iberia, Jefferson, Lafayette, Lafourche, LaSalle, Madison, Orleans, Rapides, Richland, St. Bernard, St. Charles, St. Landry, St. Tammany, Tangipahoa, Tensas, Vermilion, Vernon, and West Carroll.

E. The taxing authority provided for in this Section shall apply to any governing authority with jurisdiction over a youth center located in the parishes of East Feliciana, Iberville, Pointe Coupee, West Baton Rouge, and West Feliciana, provided that any tax to be levied pursuant to this Section is authorized by a majority of the electors who vote thereon in an election held for that purpose.
(Added by Acts 1991 No. 147, §2; chgd. by Acts 1995 No. 28, §1, No. 781, §1, eff. 8/15/95.)

§1099.6. Use of youth center.

The youth center shall be used for the temporary detention of juveniles within the parish while awaiting trial or other disposition of their cases, runaways within the parish, and juveniles awaiting transfer to the Department of Public Safety and Corrections. Juveniles from outside of the parish may be accepted by the governing authority in accordance with rules and regulations adopted therefor by the governing authority and pursuant to a participation agreement between the governing authority and the governing authority of the participating parish, but only upon payment or agreement of the participating parish to pay the charge established for the sublease of space in the center and the fee for the care and maintenance of each juvenile. *(Added by Acts 1991 No. 147, §2, eff. 7/2/91.)*

§1099.7. Participation by other parishes; appropriations.

A. The governing authority of any parish may enter into a participation agreement with any parish having a youth center to sublease a portion of the center and provide for the care and maintenance of juveniles from that participating parish at the center pursuant to this Subpart.

B. The governing authority of each participating parish shall annually appropriate an amount which will be sufficient to fund the parish's obligation pursuant to the participation agreement entered into with a parish having a youth center pursuant to this Subpart.

C. For the purpose of obtaining necessary funds pursuant to Subsection B, each participating parish may levy a special annual tax not to exceed one mill for a period of not more than twenty years by a two-thirds vote of total membership of the parish governing authority, without voter approval, but only after a public hearing is held. In addition and if deemed necessary by the governing authority, a participating parish may levy a supplemental annual tax not to exceed two mills for a period of not more than twenty years for such purposes by a two-thirds vote of the total membership of the governing authority, but only after a public hearing is held and when authorized by a majority of the electors who vote thereon in an election held for that purpose.
(Added by Acts 1991 No. 147, §2, eff. 7/2/91.)

SUBPART H. ST. BERNARD PARISH JUVENILE DETENTION CENTER

(Added by Acts 1992 No. 713, §1, eff. 8/21/92.)

§1101. St. Bernard Parish Juvenile Detention Center; fee for keeping juveniles.

A. The sheriff of St. Bernard Parish shall receive the sum of forty-five dollars per day for the keeping, feeding, clothing, care, supervision, schooling, and maintenance of each juvenile assigned to the juvenile detention center in St. Bernard Parish.

B. The sheriff shall notify the party responsible for the maintenance of each juvenile assigned to the juvenile detention center of its responsibility to contribute to the cost of care and shall bill the responsible party on a periodic basis, but not less than quarterly, for the amount due. The sheriff shall make every reasonable effort to notify such party of its liability under this Section as soon as possible after the placement of the juvenile; however, such notice or receipt thereof is not a condition for the imposition of liability for costs of care under this Section.

C. Such payments shall be made directly to the sheriff and shall be deposited in the sheriff's salary fund for the costs of care of juveniles assigned to the juvenile detention center.

D. If default occurs, the sheriff shall exercise all administrative and legal alternatives provided by law or regulation to enforce the provisions of this Section. This may include an imposition of reasonable administrative costs, costs of court, and reasonable attorney fees. The sheriff may enter into an agreement with other public agencies or private entities for collection of any debt owed to the sheriff under the provisions of this Section.
(Added by Acts 1992 No. 713, §1, eff. 8/21/92.)

SUBPART I. CENTRAL LOUISIANA JUVENILE DETENTION CENTER AUTHORITY

(Added by Acts 1997 No. 1445, §1, eff. 7/15/97.)

§1105. Central Louisiana Juvenile Detention Center Authority; creation; jurisdiction.

The Central Louisiana Juvenile Detention Center Authority is hereby established as a political subdivision of the state, with a territorial jurisdiction throughout the parishes of Avoyelles, Catahoula, Concordia, Grant, LaSalle, Vernon, and Winn. *(Added by Acts 1997 No. 1445, §1, eff. 7/15/97.)*

§1105.1. Board of commissioners; appointment; terms.

A. The Central Louisiana Juvenile Detention Center Authority shall be governed by a commission which shall control, administer, and manage its affairs. The commission shall be composed of a board of seven commissioners. There shall be one commissioner appointed from each of the seven parishes within the territory of the authority and each shall be a qualified elector and domiciled in the parish for which he is appointed. They shall be appointed for terms of four years, as follows:

(1) Two commissioners shall be appointed by the judges exercising juvenile jurisdiction within the participating parishes.

(2) Two commissioners shall be appointed by the sheriffs of the participating parishes.

(3) One commissioner shall be appointed by the chiefs of police of municipalities within the participating parishes.

(4) Two commissioners shall be appointed by the district attorneys with jurisdiction in the participating parishes.

B. The members of the board of commissioners shall serve without salary or per diem but the board may authorize a reasonable travel allowance for its members in the performance of their official duties.

(Added by Acts 1997 No. 1445, §1, eff. 7/15/97.)

§1105.2. Purpose.

The purpose of the commission shall be to assist and afford opportunities to preadjudicatory and postadjudicatory children who enter the juvenile justice system to become productive, law-abiding citizens of the community, parish, and state through the establishment of rehabilitative programs within a structured environment and the provision of physical facilities and related services for children throughout the parishes belonging to the authority. *(Added by Acts 1997 No. 1445, §1, eff. 7/15/97.)*

§1105.3. Board of commissioners; officers; meetings.

A. The board of commissioners shall elect a president, a secretary, and a treasurer, whose duties in addition to those provided by this Subpart shall be established by the board. If the board so decides, one commissioner may serve as both secretary and treasurer, but in any event the treasurer shall furnish bond in an amount and in accordance with terms and conditions fixed by the board. The board may also elect an executive committee, composed of not more than five members, and establish its duties and responsibilities.

B. The board shall fix a time and place for the holding of its regular meetings. Additional regular or special meetings may be held upon the call of the president or of three of the commissioners. All meetings of the board shall be held at the domicile of the board and shall be governed by the provisions of R.S. 42:4.1 through 12. The board shall hold at least one regular meeting in each calendar month; however, the board may meet less frequently but not less than once each calendar quarter if it establishes an executive committee and requires it to hold regular meetings at least once in each calendar month.

C. A majority of the current members of the board shall constitute a quorum. A quorum shall be required to transact business and all actions and resolutions of the board must be approved by a majority of the quorum present.

(Added by Acts 1997 No. 1445, §1, eff. 7/15/97.)

§1105.4. Board; general authority.

A. The board may purchase or otherwise acquire, construct, reconstruct, rehabilitate, improve, repair, operate, lease as lessor or lessee, manage, and administer or enter into contracts for the management, administration, and operation of a juvenile detention facility or facilities, shelter care facility or facilities, or such other juvenile justice facilities as are useful, necessary, expedient, or convenient to carry out the plans and purposes of the commission and for the orderly conduct of its business. Such facilities may include but are not limited to office facilities, parking facilities, diagnostic facilities, dormitories, and other residential facilities for delinquent, neglected, or abused children or children in need of care or supervision, or in need of services as provided by Children's Code Articles 726 et seq., as well as for employees, patrons, visitors, and relatives of children who may enter the juvenile justice system or who are in need of care or supervision or services. In addition, the commission may lease, purchase, or acquire by donation or otherwise, any property, immovable or movable, tangible or intangible, from any person, firm, or corporation, including the state and its agencies and political subdivisions.

B. The board may also authorize and approve, upon such terms as it may deem advisable, contracts of employment for a superintendent or administrator and other necessary personnel and contracts for legal, financial, engineering, and other professional services necessary or expedient for the conduct of its affairs.
(Added by Acts 1997 No. 1445, §1, eff. 7/15/97.)

§1105.5. Board; domicile; power to levy taxes, incur debt, issue bonds.

A. The board of commissioners shall be domiciled in Grant Parish and shall have the power to sue and be sued. In the exercise of its powers to control, administer, and manage the affairs of the authority, the board may incur debt and issue bonds, and it may levy taxes in the manner provided in this Subpart and pursuant to Article VI, Sections 30 and 32 of the Constitution of Louisiana or any other constitutional or statutory authority. The board generally may perform any function and exercise any power necessary, requisite, or proper for the administration and management of the affairs of the commission, and it specifically may cooperate with juvenile courts and other courts and public agencies within the eight-parish area and aid and assist them in all ways authorized by law to carry out the purposes and responsibilities for which it is established.

B. In addition to the general powers conferred herein, in order to obtain the necessary funds to carry out its purposes, duties, and responsibilities, and in order to acquire, construct, maintain, and operate a juvenile facility or facilities and related services and programs throughout the territorial jurisdiction of the Central Louisiana Juvenile Detention Center Authority, the commission may incur debt and issue general obligation bonds within the limitations prescribed by Article VI, Section 33 of the Constitution of Louisiana and other applicable constitutional or statutory authority, but only when authorized by a majority of the electors in the eight-parish area who vote thereon in an election held for that purpose in accordance with laws governing such elections.
(Added by Acts 1997 No. 1445, §1, eff. 7/15/97.)

§1105.6. Funding for the authority; criminal court costs.

In the parishes within the jurisdiction of the authority, in all felony and misdemeanor prosecutions, including traffic offenses, under state law or parish or municipal ordinance, in any district, parish, city, or mayor's court, special costs in the amount of seven dollars and fifty cents shall be levied against every defendant who is convicted after trial or who enters a plea of guilty or nolo contendere or who forfeits bond. However, in lieu of imposing the special costs, the court may direct that a like amount be deducted from any fine imposed prior to disposition of the fine in accordance with other laws, but in either event any amounts so collected shall be remitted, by the tenth of the month following the month in which collected, by the proper officer of the court to the board to be used for the expenses of its operations as provided in this Subpart. *(Added by Acts 1997 No. 1445, §1, eff. 7/15/97.)*

§1105.7. Funding for the authority; juvenile court costs.

In the parishes within the jurisdiction of the authority, in all courts exercising juvenile jurisdiction, special costs in the amount of fifty dollars shall be levied against every juvenile who is found to have committed a traffic violation or who is adjudicated a delinquent. All or part of the costs may be suspended, but any amounts thereof collected shall be remitted, by the tenth of the month following the month in which collected, by the proper officer of the court in which the matter was heard to the board to be used for the expenses of its operations as provided in this Subpart. *(Added by Acts 1997 No. 1445, §1, eff. 7/15/97.)*

SUBPART J. BOSSIER/CADDO JUVENILE DETENTION CENTER AUTHORITY

(Added by Acts 1997 No. 1445, §1, eff. 7/15/97.)

§1106. Bossier/Caddo Juvenile Detention Center Authority; creation; jurisdiction.

The Bossier/Caddo Juvenile Detention Center Authority is hereby established as a political subdivision of the state, with a territorial jurisdiction throughout the parishes of Bossier and Caddo. *(Added by Acts 1997 No. 1445, §2, eff. 7/15/97.)*

§1106.1. Board of directors; appointment; terms.

A. (1) The Bossier/Caddo Juvenile Detention Center Authority shall be governed by a board of directors which shall control, administer, and manage the affairs of the district.

(2) The board shall be composed of eleven directors, who shall be qualified electors domiciled and residing in the district. The directors shall be appointed for terms coinciding with the position or agency that appoints that particular board member.

(a) One director shall be appointed by the Caddo Juvenile Court judges.

(b) One director shall be appointed by the Bossier Parish District and City Court judges.

(c) One director shall be appointed by Caddo Parish Commission.

(d) One director shall be appointed by the Bossier Police Jury.

(e) One director shall be appointed by the Shreveport City Council.

(f) One director shall be appointed by the Bossier City Council.

(g) One director shall be appointed by the Bossier Parish School Board.

(h) One director shall be appointed by the Caddo Parish School Board.

(i) One director shall be appointed by the Assistant Secretary of the Office of Youth Development of the Department of Public Safety and Corrections.

(j) One director shall be appointed by the Bossier Parish Sheriff.

(k) One director shall be appointed by the Caddo Parish Sheriff.

B. The members of the board of directors shall serve without salary or per diem but the board may authorize a reasonable travel allowance for its members in the performance of their official duties.

(Added by Acts 1997 No. 1445, §2, eff. 7/15/97.)

§1106.2. Purpose.

The purpose of the board of directors shall be to assist and afford opportunities to preadjudicatory and postadjudicatory children who enter the juvenile justice system to become productive, law-abiding citizens of the community, parish, and state through the establishment of rehabilitative programs within a structured environment and the provision of physical facilities and related services for children throughout Bossier and Caddo. *(Added by Acts 1997 No. 1445, §2, eff. 7/15/97.)*

§1106.3. Board of directors; officers; meetings.

A. The board of directors shall elect a chairman, a vice chairman, a secretary, and a treasurer, whose duties in addition to those provided by this Subpart shall be established by the board. If the board so decides, one director may serve as both secretary and treasurer, but in any event the treasurer shall furnish bond in an amount and in accordance with terms and conditions fixed by the board. The board may also elect an executive committee, composed of not more than five members, and establish its duties and responsibilities.

B. The board shall fix a time and place for the holding of its regular meetings. Additional regular or special meetings may be held upon the call of the chairman or of three of the directors. All meetings of the board shall be held at the domicile of the board and shall be governed by the provisions of R.S. 42:4.1 through 12. The board shall hold at least one regular meeting in each calendar month; however, the board may meet less frequently but not less than once each calendar quarter if it establishes an executive committee and requires it to hold regular meetings at least once in each calendar month.

C. A majority of the current members of the board shall constitute a quorum. A quorum shall be required to transact business and all actions and resolutions of the board must be approved by a majority of the quorum present.

(Added by Acts 1997 No. 1445, §2, eff. 7/15/97.)

§1106.4. Board; general authority.

A. The board may purchase or otherwise acquire, construct, reconstruct, rehabilitate, improve, repair, operate, lease as lessor or lessee, manage, and administer or enter into contracts for the management, administration, and operation of a juvenile detention facility or facilities, shelter care facility or facilities, or such other juvenile justice facilities as are useful, necessary, expedient, or convenient to carry out the plans and purposes of the board and for the orderly conduct of its business. Such facilities may include but are not limited to office facilities, parking facilities, diagnostic facilities, dormitories, and other residential facilities for delinquent, neglected, or abused children or children in need of care or supervision, or in need of services as provided by Children's Code Articles 726 et seq., as well as for employees, patrons, visitors, and relatives of children who may enter the juvenile justice system or who are in need of care or supervision or services. In addition, the board may lease, purchase, or acquire by donation or otherwise, any property, immovable or movable, tangible or intangible, from any person, firm, or corporation, including the state and its agencies and political subdivisions.

B. The board may also authorize and approve, upon such terms as it may deem advisable, contracts of employment for a superintendent or administrator and other necessary personnel and contracts for legal, financial, engineering, and other professional services necessary or expedient for the conduct of its affairs.

(Added by Acts 1997 No. 1445, §2, eff. 7/15/97.)

§1106.5. Board; domicile; power to levy taxes, incur debt, issue bonds.

A. The board of commissioners shall be domiciled in Caddo Parish and shall have the power to sue and be sued. In the exercise of its powers to control, administer, and manage the affairs of the authority, the board may incur debt and issue bonds, and it may levy taxes in the manner provided in this Subpart and pursuant to Article VI, Sections 30 and 32 of the Constitution of Louisiana or any other constitutional or statutory authority. The board generally may perform any function and exercise any power necessary, requisite, or proper for the administration and management of the affairs of the board, and it specifically may cooperate with juvenile courts and other courts and public agencies within the two-parish area and aid and assist them in all ways authorized by law to carry out the purposes and responsibilities for which it is established.

B. In addition to the general powers conferred herein, in order to obtain the necessary funds to carry out its purposes, duties, and responsibilities, and in order to acquire, construct, maintain, and operate a juvenile facility or facilities and related services and programs throughout the territorial jurisdiction of the Bossier/Caddo Juvenile Detention Center Authority, the board may incur debt and issue general obligation bonds within the limitations prescribed by Article VI, Section 33 of the Constitution of Louisiana and other applicable constitutional or statutory authority, but only when authorized by a majority of the electors in the two-parish area who vote thereon in an election held for that purpose in accordance with laws governing such elections.

(Added by Acts 1997 No. 1445, §2, eff. 7/15/97.)

PART XII. WORK RELEASE PROGRAM

§1111. Work release program.

A. The Louisiana Department of Institutions is hereby authorized to establish and administer a work release program for inmates of any institution under the jurisdiction of the department.

B. The department shall establish rules for the administration of the work release program and shall determine those inmates who may participate in the release program. Any convict sentenced to imprisonment at hard labor shall be eligible at any time during his sentence to participate in the work release program, subject to the provisions of this Part. If any inmate violates the conditions prescribed by the department, his work release privileges may be withdrawn. Failure to report to or return from the planned employment shall be considered an escape under the provisions of R.S. 14:110. The department may approve as work release privileges, placement in universities, colleges, technical, vocational or trade schools or in sheltered workshops or in training programs designed to improve the skills and abilities of the inmate.

C. The department shall designate and adapt facilities for the purpose of quartering inmates with work release privileges or it may arrange and contract for other facilities, including but not limited to portions of parish jails for inmates employed in the area. No inmate shall be granted work release privileges until: (1) such suitable quarters have been provided in the area of accepted or preferred employment, or educational or training placement, and (2) a position of employment or educational or training placement is available for the inmate.

D. Every inmate with work release privileges shall be liable for the cost of his room, board, clothing and other necessary expenses incident to his employment or placement unless other means of payment are approved by the department.

E. The wages of any inmate so employed shall be collected by the director of institutions or by his designated agent, and the director shall deposit the same in a public banking institution and keep a ledger showing the financial status of each inmate on the program.

F. The wages of any such inmate shall be disbursed by the department for the following purposes and in the order stated:

(1) The board of the inmate including food and clothing;

(2) Necessary travel expense to and from work and other incidental expenses of the inmate;

(3) Support of the inmate's dependents, if any;

(4) Payment, either in full or ratably of the inmate's obligations acknowledged by him in writing, or which have been reduced to judgment;

(5) The balance if any, to the inmate upon his discharge.

G. The wages of an inmate so employed shall be not less than the customary wages for an employee performing similar services.

H. No provision of this Act shall be construed to repeal the provisions of R.S. 15:855.1 or of R.S. 15:855.2.

I. Notwithstanding the provisions of Subsection B above or any other law to the contrary, any inmate who has been convicted of first degree murder (R.S. 14:30), second degree murder (R.S. 14:30.1), aggravated rape (R.S. 14:42), attempted aggravated rape (R.S. 14:27, 14:42), forcible rape (R.S. 14:42.1), aggravated kidnapping (R.S. 14:44), aggravated arson (R.S. 14:51), armed robbery (R.S. 14:64), attempted murder (R.S. 14:27, 14:29), attempted armed robbery (R.S. 14:27, 14:64), producing, manufacturing, distributing, or dispensing or possession with intent to produce, manufacture, distribute, or dispense a controlled dangerous substance classified in Schedule I or Schedule II of R.S. 40:964 and persons sentenced as habitual offenders under R.S. 15:529.1 shall be prohibited from participation in the work release program except during the last six months of their terms.

J. No inmate employed in the work release program shall be employed in a position which would necessitate his departure from the state.

K. The Department of Corrections shall compile statistical data on the incidence of work release violations by participating inmates. Violations shall include the commission of new offenses as well as any transgressions that result in disciplinary action or removal from the program. The data shall indicate the nature of the incident, the age of the offender, his original offense, the length of his sentence, his prior criminal record, and any other characteristic found to be predictive of success or failure. This information shall be used by the department to guide it in formulating program policies and eligibility standards and shall be available to the legislature upon request.

§1112. Reports to law enforcement agencies.

Probation and parole officers shall notify every law enforcement agency of any prisoner or parolees assigned to or presently working within the agency's jurisdiction under a work release program.

PART XIII. COMMUNITY REHABILITATION CENTERS

§1131. Community rehabilitation centers.

A. The Department of Corrections is hereby authorized to create, establish, operate and maintain community rehabilitation centers in such places throughout the state as are deemed necessary by the director. Such facilities shall be operated and maintained for prisoners who have strong rehabilitation potential.

B. The criminal sheriff of the parish of Orleans may create, establish, operate, and maintain community rehabilitation centers in such places within the parish of Orleans as he may deem necessary. Such facilities shall be operated and maintained for prisoners who have strong rehabilitation potential, as determined by said criminal sheriff. Residents of such facilities shall also include defendants ordered to reside in a community rehabilitation center as a condition of probation and prisoners released due to diminution of sentence where a condition of release is that the prisoner reside in such a center.

§1132. Pre-sentence investigations.

A. If a defendant is convicted of an offense, the court may order a pre-sentence investigation in accordance with the provisions of Code of Criminal Procedure Article 875. This investigation shall undertake educational, medical, physical fitness, psychiatric, and social studies of the defendant.

B. The Department of Corrections or, with court approval, the pre-sentence and probation officers of the various courts are hereby authorized to enter into contracts with professional personnel to perform the tests. The report of the investigation shall make recommendations to the court as to the rehabilitation potential of the defendant, the stages required to make the defendant useful and productive, and as to whether the defendant should be placed on probation and the terms thereof or whether the defendant should be committed to a community rehabilitation center or prison, or to the Department of Corrections for assignment to an appropriate penal or correctional facility.

C. The court may postpone sentence until this report is received.

D. Any expenses of these tests may be assessed and taxed as costs and shall be payable by the defendant benefiting by them. An additional civil action to collect these costs shall not prescribe for five years.

§1133. Sentence to community rehabilitation centers.

A. Notwithstanding any provision of law to the contrary, a court may order that an offender sentenced to not more than five years without hard labor be placed in a community rehabilitation center under terms and conditions established by the court, provided such placement receives the consent of the offender and the administrators in charge of the center. Upon the written request of the administrators of a community rehabilitation center, the court shall order that an offender placed pursuant to this Subsection be removed, and shall issue such other orders regarding the custody of the offender as are appropriate under the original sentence.

B. (1) Notwithstanding any law to the contrary, a court may recommend that an offender sentenced to imprisonment at hard labor in the custody of the Department of Public Safety and Corrections be placed in a community rehabilitation center. Upon such a recommendation, the secretary of the Department of Public Safety and Corrections or his designee may place the offender in a community rehabilitation center provided the following conditions are met:

(a) The placement is recommended in a presentence investigation report.

(b) The offender agrees to the placement.

(c) The sentence to imprisonment at hard labor is for five years or less.

(d) The offender has never been convicted of a sex-related offense.

(e) The offender has not exhibited and his record does not reveal an habitual or compulsive use of violence against persons.

(f) The secretary or his designee concludes, based upon evaluation conducted by the department, that the offender is likely to respond affirmatively to placement in a community rehabilitation center.

(2) Any offender placed in a community rehabilitation center pursuant to the provisions of this Subsection may be removed from the center and placed in a Department of Public Safety and Corrections facility at the discretion of the secretary or his designee.

C. The provisions of this Section shall not be applicable to a defendant who was convicted of any violation of R.S. 14:98.

§1134. Staff and facilities of community rehabilitation centers.

A. The Department of Corrections may employ psychiatrists, neurologists, special educators, guidance counselors, psychologists, nurses, technicians, social workers, occupational therapists, physicians and other professional personnel to staff community rehabilitation centers, or may contract for the services of such persons with community service organizations, religious groups, universities and medical schools.

B. The Department of Corrections and/or the criminal sheriff of the parish of Orleans, as the case may be may enter into contracts with other state agencies, local agencies, community service organizations or religious groups for the operation and maintenance of community rehabilitation centers or for the leasing of space for such facilities, or both. In addition, the criminal sheriff of the parish of Orleans, for the purposes of operating and maintaining such rehabilitation centers, programs and/or services for prisoners under his jurisdiction, shall have full power and authority as is provided for in Subsection A hereof, to retain such personnel as may be required for these purposes.

C. All community rehabilitation centers shall be minimum security structures and no such facility shall contain cells or barred windows, and no inmate of any such facility shall be locked in any room thereof. There shall be no armed guards at any such facility.

§1135. Work release program.

A. Except as otherwise provided in this Section, all inmates of a community rehabilitation center operated by the Department of Corrections shall be eligible to participate in the work release program provided for by R.S. 15:1111; provided however, that in no case shall inmates participating in such work release program be authorized or permitted to work or to continue working on a project or job involved in a labor dispute.

B. In those instances where a community rehabilitation center is not operated and maintained by the Louisiana Department of Corrections, the agency or organization administering such facility shall maintain a work release program to be administered as follows:

(1) Failure to report to or from the planned employment shall be considered an escape under the provisions of R.S. 14:110. Work release privileges may include placement in universities, colleges, technical vocational or trade schools or in sheltered workshops or in training programs designed to improve the skills and abilities of the inmate.

(2) Every inmate with work release privileges shall be liable for the cost of his room, board, clothing and other necessary expenses incident to his employment or placement unless other means of payment are approved by the Department of Corrections, excepting that this liability may be waived if the inmate is enrolled full time in a university, college, technical vocational or trade school or in sheltered workshops or training programs designed to improve the skills and abilities of the inmate.

(3) The wages of any inmate so employed shall be collected by the agency or organization operating the community rehabilitation center and deposited in a public banking institution and it shall keep a ledger showing the financial status of each inmate on the program, subject to the approval of the director of corrections.

(4) The wages of any such inmate shall be disbursed for the following purposes and in the order stated, subject to the approval of the director of corrections:

(a) The board of the inmate including food and clothing;

(b) Necessary travel expense to and from work and other incidental expenses of the inmate;

(c) Support of the inmate's dependents, if any;

(d) Payment, either in full or ratably of the inmate's obligations acknowledged by him in writing, or which have been reduced to judgment;

(e) The balance if any, to the inmate upon his discharge.

(5) The wages of an inmate so employed shall be not less than the customary wages for an employee performing similar services.

(6) In no case shall inmates participating in such program be authorized or permitted to work or to continue working on a project or job involved in a labor dispute.

C. Deductions for room, board and other administrative costs resulting from participation in a work release program authorized by this section shall not exceed fifty percentum of the wages received by an inmate.

D. Any inmate who has been convicted of first degree murder (R.S. 14:30), second degree murder (R.S. 14:30.1), aggravated rape (R.S. 14:42), attempted aggravated rape (R.S. 14:27, 14:42), forcible rape (R.S. 14:42.1), aggravated kidnapping (R.S. 14:44), aggravated arson (R.S. 14:51), armed robbery (R.S. 14:64), attempted murder (R.S. 14:27, 14:29), attempted armed robbery (R.S. 14:27, 14:64), producing, manufacturing, distributing, or dispensing or possession with intent to produce, manufacture, distribute, or dispense a controlled dangerous substance classified in Schedule I or Schedule II of R.S. 40:964 and persons sentenced as habitual offenders under R.S. 15:529.1 shall be prohibited from participation in the work release program except during the last six months of their terms.

E. No inmate employed in the work release program shall be employed in a position which would necessitate his departure from the state.

§1136. Rules and regulations of Department of Corrections.

The Department of Corrections shall adopt all regulations it deems essential to the proper conduct of community rehabilitation centers.

PART XIV. PRISON ENTERPRISES

§1151. Definitions.

As used in this Part, the following words shall have the following meanings ascribed to them:

(1) "Board" means the Prison Enterprises Board.

(2) "Department" means the Louisiana Department of Corrections.

(3) "Secretary" means the secretary of corrections.

§1152. Prison enterprises.

The department may engage in any agricultural, aquacultural, silvicultural, or industrial enterprise in accordance with the provisions of this Part.

§1153. Purposes.

A. The department shall operate prison enterprises for the following purposes, which shall be given priority in the order listed:

(1) To utilize the resources of the department in the production of food, fiber, and other necessary items used by the inmates in order to lower the cost of incarcerating the inmates.

(2) To provide products and services to state agencies and agencies of parishes, municipalities, and other political subdivisions. The products and services shall be provided at the cost to the department for providing the goods and services.

(3) To provide work opportunities for inmates in accordance with law.

B. (1) The department may enter into cooperative endeavors with and request studies or reports from private citizens, the Louisiana State University Cooperative Extension Service, and the public colleges and universities in this state for the purposes of encouraging and facilitating production and marketing of agricultural commodities and research in the area of production of agricultural commodities and for the purpose of acquiring advice on the most cost effective utilization of the products of its agricultural system.

(2) Should the department enter into such cooperative endeavors or receive such studies or reports as provided in Subsection A of this Section it shall do the following:

(a) Prepare an annual written summary of any recommendations made within three years preceding the date of the summary by any person or entity who has participated or is participating in a cooperative endeavor or who is making or has made a study or report, excluding any recommendations made prior to July 1, 1984, which summary shall be co-signed by such person or entity.

(b) Prepare a report of the specific actions taken by the department with regard to such recommendations.

(c) Prepare a report of the reasons why any such recommendation was not fully implemented.

(d) Transmit the summary and the reports to the committees on agriculture of the Senate and the House of Representatives, the Committee on Administration of Criminal Justice of the House of Representatives, the Legislative Fiscal Office, and the persons or entities which made the recommendations by the first of April of each year.

§1154. Administration.

A. The secretary shall administer the provisions of this Part.

B. The Prison Enterprises Board shall advise the secretary on all aspects of the administration of this Part.

C. The secretary shall administer the provisions of this Part in a manner which will insure the best long-range utilization of the resources of the department.

D. In the administration of the forest lands under the control of the department, no trees shall be cut or planted except in accordance with best management practices determined after consultation with the Louisiana State University School of Forestry.

E. The secretary shall develop the budgets and the plans of operation for the prison enterprises for the various institutions with the advice of the board and with the concurrence of the assistant secretaries of the offices of adult services and juvenile services, whichever may apply. The assistant secretaries shall consult with the warden or superintendent of each institution under their jurisdiction concerning proposed prison enterprises at the institutions. The warden or superintendent at each institution shall have the necessary authority and budgetary responsibility with respect to his respective institution to implement and execute the prison enterprises and for achieving the quantitative and qualitative production goals established by the secretary within the resources provided to each warden or superintendent.

§1155. Prison Enterprises Board.

A. The Prison Enterprises Board is hereby created within the Department of Corrections.

B. The board shall be domiciled in Baton Rouge.

C. The board shall consist of seven members who shall be appointed by the governor in accordance with the following provisions:

(1) One member shall be knowledgeable in agronomy and shall have experience as a farmer or farm manager in the actual production of field crops for commercial purposes.

(2) One member shall have technical and practical knowledge and experience in forest management.

(3) One member shall have knowledge and experience in livestock management, dairy operations, or both.

(4) One member shall be an owner or operator of a facility engaged in the processing of the types of agricultural products produced by prison enterprises.

(5) One member shall have knowledge of and experience in manufacturing.

(6) One member shall be appointed from a list of three nominees submitted by the Louisiana Association of Business and Industry.

(7) One member shall be appointed from a list of three members nominated by the Louisiana AFL-CIO.

D. Each appointment by the governor shall be submitted to the Senate for confirmation, and beginning in 1984 every appointment confirmed by the Senate shall again be submitted by the governor to the Senate for confirmation every two years after the initial confirmation.

E. Members shall serve at the pleasure of the governor.

F. Members shall receive a per diem of seventy-five dollars and shall be reimbursed for mileage at the rate established for state employees.

G. Four members shall constitute a quorum and all actions of the board shall require the affirmative vote of at least four members.

H. The board shall elect a chairman and a vice chairman from among its members who shall serve for terms of one year.

I. The board shall meet at least quarterly and may meet upon the call of the chairman or any three members. Meetings of the board shall be open to the public in accordance with law.

J. The secretary shall provide the board with necessary clerical personnel.

(Chgd. by Acts 1991 No. 137, §1, eff. 9/6/91.)

§1156. Rules.

A. The secretary, with the advice of the board, shall make such rules and regulations as are necessary to administer the provisions of this Part. All rules and regulations shall be made in accordance with the Administrative Procedure Act*.

**R.S. 49:950 et seq.*

B. In addition, the secretary with the advice of the board, shall make such rules and regulations as are necessary for the implementation and administration of the provisions of R.S. 15:708(A)(4). These rules and regulations shall include but shall not be limited to guidelines for transportation to and from work projects, supervision, custody, and control of such inmates, necessary security and safety provisions, and establishment and maintenance of inmate compensation and savings accounts.

(Chgd. by Acts 1997 No. 509, §1, eff. 8/15/97.)

§1157. Sales of goods and services; contractual powers.

A. (1) State agencies other than the Department of Public Safety and Corrections shall purchase, if available, goods and services from prison enterprises at a price which reflects the cost to the department of producing the goods or providing the services, or products manufactured in a certified Private Sector/Prison Industry Enhançement Program, if the prices are less than those of central purchasing.

(2) Goods and services may be sold to the governing authorities of parishes, municipalities, and other political subdivisions at a price which reflects the cost to the department of producing the goods or providing the services.

B. Agricultural commodities may be sold on the open market in accordance with rules adopted by the secretary when the sale will further the purposes of this Part.

C. The secretary may enter into contracts with private entities or govern-mental agencies for the sale, purchase, or barter of commodities to effectuate the purposes of this Part in accordance with rules adopted by the secretary.

D. Products of the type which are produced in foreign countries that are labor intensive may be produced and sold on the open market.

(Chgd. by Acts 1995 No. 644, §1, eff. 8/15/95.)

§1158. Inmate labor.

The department may use inmate labor to maintain existing facilities used in connection with agricultural or aquacultural production.

§1159. Proceeds of sales; Prison Enterprises Fund.

A. Subject to the exceptions contained in Article VII, Section 9(A) of the Constitution of Louisiana, all funds received by the department from the sale of products and services produced by the agricultural, silvicultural, and industrial prison enterprises operated by the department in accordance with the provisions of R.S. 15:1151, et seq., shall be deposited immediately upon receipt into the state treasury.

B to E. *(Repealed.)*

(Chgd. by Acts 1992 No. 984, §18, eff. 8/21/92.)

§1160. Used agricultural equipment purchases.

The secretary shall be allowed to purchase used agricultural and industrial equipment at public auction as provided by R.S. 39:1554(G)(2).

§1161. Sale of livestock breeding services; contractual powers.

A. The secretary may authorize the warden or superintendent of any institution under his jurisdiction to contract with private entities for the sale of the breeding services of any of the livestock owned by and under the control of the department.

B. Each private entity which contracts with any of the various institutions shall indemnify and hold the secretary, the warden or superintendent, the state agency, the state, and any employees of the same harmless for any injury caused by the animal, unless the gross negligence or intentional act of any of the above was a substantial factor in causing the injury.

C. The secretary shall have the authority to adopt, in accordance with the Administrative Procedure Act*, such rules and regulations as may be deemed necessary to provide for effective and efficient administration of this Section, including but not limited to specific contractual provisions.

**R.S. 49:950 et seq.*

D. The secretary may establish fees to be charged for all services provided at amounts which reflect the cost to the department providing the services.

(Added by Acts 1991 No. 93, §1, eff. 9/6/91.)

PART XV. CORRECTIONS ADMINISTRATIVE REMEDY PROCEDURE

§1171. Authority.

A. The Department of Public Safety and Corrections and each sheriff may adopt an administrative remedy procedure at each of their adult and juvenile institutions, including private prison facilities, in compliance with 42 United States Code 1997, the "Civil Rights of Institutionalized Persons Act", or CRIPA, and Part 40 of Title 28, Code of Federal Regulations.

B. The department or sheriff may also adopt, in accordance with the Administrative Procedure Act*, administrative remedy procedures for receiving, hearing, and disposing of any and all complaints and grievances by adult or juvenile offenders against the state, the governor, the department or any officials or employees thereof, the contractor operating a private prison facility or any of its employees, shareholders, directors, officers, or agents, or a sheriff, his deputies, or employees, which arise while an offender is within the custody or under the supervision of the department, a contractor operating a private prison facility, or a sheriff. Such complaints and grievances include but are not limited to any and all claims seeking monetary, injunctive, declaratory, or any other form of relief authorized by law and by way of illustration includes actions pertaining to conditions of confinement, personal injuries, medical malpractice, time computations, even though urged as a writ of habeas corpus, or challenges to rules, regulations, policies, or statutes. Such administrative procedures, when promulgated, shall provide the exclusive remedy available to the offender for complaints or grievances governed thereby insofar as federal law allows. All such procedures, including the adult and juvenile offender disciplinary process, promulgated and effective prior to June 30, 1989, shall be deemed to be the exclusive remedy for complaints and grievances to which they apply insofar as federal law allows.

**R.S. 49:950 et seq.*

C. The department or sheriff may also adopt procedures for adult or juvenile offenders to discover and produce evidence in order to substantiate their claims and promulgate rules and regulations governing the recommendation, review, and approval of an award for monetary relief.

D. For the purposes of this Part, status as an "offender" is determined as of the time the basis for a complaint or grievance arises. Subsequent events, including posttrial judicial action or release from custody, shall not affect status as an "offender" for the purposes of this Part.

(Chgd. by Acts 1993 No. 871, §1; Acts 1997 No. 575, §1, eff. 8/15/97.)

§1172. Effect.

A. Upon approval of the administrative remedy procedure by a federal court, as authorized and required by 42 USC 1997(C)(2), or as otherwise authorized by law, and the implementation of the procedure within the department or by the sheriff, this procedure shall constitute the administrative remedies available to offenders for the purpose of preserving any cause of action they may claim to have against the state of Louisiana, the Department of Public Safety and Corrections, or its employees, the contractor operating a private prison facility or any of its employees, shareholders, directors, or officers, or a sheriff, or his employees or deputies.

B. No state court shall entertain an offender's grievance or complaint which falls under the purview of the administrative remedy procedure unless and until the offender shall have exhausted the remedies as provided in said procedure. If the offender has failed timely to pursue administrative remedies through this procedure, any petition he files shall be dismissed. If at the time the petition is filed the administrative remedy process has not yet been completed, the court shall stay the proceedings for ninety days to allow for completion of the procedure and exhaustion of the remedies thereunder.

C. Any contractor operating a private prison facility shall adhere to all provisions of this Part and the administrative remedy procedures adopted by the department in accordance with this Part.

(Chgd. by Acts 1993 No. 871, §1, eff. 8/15/93.)

§1173. Publication of procedure.

The administrative remedy procedure shall be published in the State Register.

§1174. Definitions.

For purposes of this Part:

(1) "Contractor" means any entity entering into a contractual agreement to provide any correctional services pursuant to the provisions of the Louisiana Corrections Private Management Act, R.S. 39:1800.1 et seq.

(2) "Offender" means an adult or juvenile offender who is in the physical or legal custody of the Department of Public Safety and Corrections, a contractor operating a private prison facility, or a sheriff when the basis for the complaint or grievance arises. Any subsequent event, including posttrial judicial action or release from custody, shall not affect status as an "offender" for the purposes of this Part.

(3) "Private prison facility" means any institution operated pursuant to the provisions of the Louisiana Corrections Private Management Act, R.S. 39:1800.1 et seq.

(Chgd. by Acts 1993 No. 871, §1; Acts 1997 No. 575, §1, eff. 8/15/97.)

§1175. *(Repealed by Acts 1993 No. 871, §3, eff. 8/15/93.)*

§1176. Records, confidentiality.

Before any cause of action may be heard in any state or federal court, administrative remedies must be exhausted under the procedure authorized by this Part. Therefore, in addition to any other provisions of law providing for the confidentiality of records of the Department of Public Safety and Corrections, including any records maintained by a contractor of a private prison facility, or a sheriff, all reports, investigations, and like supporting documents prepared by the department, a contractor, or a sheriff for purposes of responding to the offender's request for an administrative remedy shall be deemed to be prepared in anticipation of litigation and are confidential and not subject to discovery by the offender in any civil action which may follow his request for an administrative remedy. All formal written responses to the offender's request shall be furnished to the offender as a matter of course, as required by the procedure. *(Chgd. by Acts 1993 No. 871, §1, eff. 8/15/93.)*

§1177. Judicial review.

A. Any offender who is aggrieved by an adverse decision by the Department of Public Safety and Corrections or a contractor operating a private prison facility rendered pursuant to any administrative remedy procedures under this Part may, within thirty days after receipt of the decision, seek judicial review of the decision only in the Nineteenth Judicial District Court or, if the offender is in the physical custody of the sheriff, in the district court having jurisdiction in the parish in which the sheriff is located, in the manner hereinafter provided:

(1) Proceedings for review may be instituted by filing a petition for review in the district court within thirty days after receipt of the notice of the final decision by the agency or, if a rehearing by the agency is had or ordered by the court, within thirty days after the decision thereon. Copies of the petition shall be served upon the agency and all defendants, as provided by law.

(2) The filing of the petition does not itself stay enforcement of the agency decision. The agency may grant, or the reviewing court may order, a stay ex parte upon appropriate terms.

(3) Within thirty days after service of the petition, or within further time allowed by the court, the agency shall transmit to the reviewing court the original or a certified copy of the entire record of the proceeding under review. By stipulation of all parties to the review proceedings, the record may be shortened. A party unreasonably refusing to stipulate to limit the record may be taxed by the court for the additional costs related thereto. The court may require or permit subsequent corrections or additions to the record.

(4) The court may order that additional evidence be taken before the agency upon conditions determined by the court. However, discovery provisions of the Code of Civil Procedure, pertaining to ordinary suits are inappropriate and not applicable in a suit for judicial review under this Part.

(5) The review shall be conducted by the court without a jury and shall be confined to the record. The review shall be limited to the issues presented in the petition for review and the administrative remedy request filed at the agency level. In cases of alleged irregularities in procedure before the agency, proof thereon may be taken in the court.

(6) A party or agency who desires oral argument shall make a timely request for oral argument, as hereinafter provided. The request shall include a brief statement of why oral argument should be had. The court, in its discretion, may hear oral argument.

(a) A request for oral argument must be made by the plaintiff with the petition for review or by the agency or defendant with the transmission of the administrative record or answer to the reviewing court, unless an extension of time is granted by the court.

(b) A request for oral argument on an exception or motion must be filed by the movant with the filing of the exception or motion, and by the non-movant with the filing of any timely opposition to the exception or motion.

(7) In the event that no oral argument is ordered, the court shall allow the parties, including the agency, a reasonable time for filing a brief or memorandum concerning the issues before the court.

(8) The court may affirm the decision of the agency or remand the case for further proceedings, or order that additional evidence be taken.

(9) The court may reverse or modify the decision only if substantial rights of the appellant have been prejudiced because the administrative findings, inferences, conclusions, or decisions are:

(a) In violation of constitutional or statutory provisions.

(b) In excess of the statutory authority of the agency.

(c) Made upon unlawful procedure.

(d) Affected by other error of law.

(e) Arbitrary or capricious or characterized by abuse of discretion or clearly unwarranted exercise of discretion.

(f) Manifestly erroneous in view of the reliable, probative and substantial evidence on the whole record. In the application of the rule, where the agency has the opportunity to judge the credibility of witnesses by firsthand observation of demeanor on the witness stand and the reviewing court does not, due regard shall be given to the agency's determination of credibility issues.

B. (1) If an offender who files a complaint or grievance which is the subject of an application for judicial review is not in the physical custody of the Department of Public Safety and Corrections, or of a contractor operating a private prison facility, or of a sheriff when the decision is rendered with respect to the application for judicial review, the person against whom the complaint or grievance was filed may deliver that decision to the person who filed the complaint or grievance by mailing the decision by first class United States mail to the person who filed the complaint or grievance, at the most recent address provided by that person.

(2) If the decision is mailed to that person and cannot be delivered by the United States Postal Service, the envelope in which the decision was mailed, together with the notations made on that envelope by the United States Postal Service concerning the inability to deliver that envelope, may be introduced into evidence for the purpose of showing compliance with the provisions of this Subsection.

(3) If the judge finds that the person against whom the complaint or grievance was filed has used due diligence in mailing the decision, the court may determine that person has complied with the provisions of this Subsection and has complied with the requirements of due process concerning notice of that decision.

C. This Section shall not apply to the commitment and transfer of children under R.S. 15:901.

D. This Section shall provide the exclusive procedure and standard for review for all offenders as defined seeking review under this Part.

(Chgd. by Acts 1993 No. 871, §§1, 3; Acts 1997 No. 575, §1, No. 1216, §1, eff. 8/15/97.)

§1178. Judicial screening.

A. When a clerk of court receives a petition for judicial review filed under the provisions of R.S. 15:1177, the clerk shall transmit the petition to the appropriate division or official of the court prior to taking any action on the petition.

B. The court, as soon as practicable after receiving the petition, shall review the petition to determine if the petition states a cognizable claim or if the petition, on its face, is frivolous or malicious, or fails to state a cause of action, or seeks monetary damages from a defendant who is immune from liability for monetary damages.

C. If the court determines that the petition states a cognizable claim, the court shall return the petition to the clerk of court for service of process.

D. If the court determines that the petition, on its face, is frivolous, or fails to state a cause of action, or seeks monetary damages from a defendant who is immune from liability for monetary damages, the court may dismiss the petition, or any portion of the petition, without requiring the exhaustion of administrative remedies.

(Added by Acts 1997 No. 716, §1, eff. 8/15/97.)

§1179. Service of process.

A. The clerk of court shall not order service of process with respect to any petition filed under the provisions of R.S. 15:1177 until the petition has been reviewed by the court and has been found to state a cognizable claim.

B. When the court returns a petition to the clerk for service:

(1) The secretary of the Department of Public Safety and Corrections shall be the agent for service of citation or other process with respect to any person who is an officer or employee of the department at the time the service is made.

(2) Service may be made by personal service on the secretary or his designee.

(3) The clerk of court may issue one citation addressed to all of the defendants being served through the secretary, and only one copy of the petition or other pleading need be served on the secretary, regardless of the number of defendants being served through the secretary.

(Added by Acts 1997 No. 716, §1, eff. 8/15/97.)

PART XVI. PRISON LITIGATION REFORM ACT

(Added by Acts 1997 No. 731, §1, eff. 7/9/97.)

§1181. Definitions.

In this Part the terms enumerated have the following meanings:

(1) "Consent decree" means any relief entered by the court that is based in whole or in part upon the consent or acquiescence of the parties but does not include private settlements.

(2) "Civil action with respect to prison conditions" or "prisoner suit" means any civil proceeding with respect to the conditions of confinement or the effects of actions by government officials on the lives of persons confined in prison, but does not include post conviction relief or habeas corpus proceedings challenging the fact or duration of confinement in prison.

(3) "Expert" means any person appointed by a court to exercise the powers of an expert, regardless of the title or description given by the court.

(4) "Fails to state a claim upon which relief can be granted" means the petition does not allege a set of facts in support of a claim which would entitle the petitioner to relief on that claim.

(5) "Prison" means any state or local jail, prison, or other correctional facility that incarcerates or detains juveniles or adults accused of, convicted of, sentenced for, or adjudicated delinquent for violations of criminal law.

(6) "Prisoner" means any person subject to incarceration, detention, or admission to any prison who is accused of, convicted of, sentenced for, or adjudicated delinquent for a violation of criminal law or the terms or conditions of parole, probation, pretrial release, or a diversionary program. Status as a "prisoner" is determined as of the time the cause of action arises. Subsequent events, including post trial judicial action or release from custody, shall not affect such status.

(7) "Prisoner release order" includes any order, including a temporary restraining order or preliminary injunctive relief, that has the purpose or effect of reducing or limiting the prison population, or that directs the release of prisoners from or prohibits the admission of prisoners to a prison.

(8) "Private settlement agreement" means an agreement entered into among the parties that is not subject to judicial enforcement other than the reinstatement of the civil proceeding that the agreement settled.

(9) "Prospective relief" means all relief other than compensatory monetary damages.

(10) "Relief" means all relief in any form that may be granted or approved by the court, and includes consent decrees but does not include private settlement agreements.

(Added by Acts 1997 No. 731, §1; chgd. by Acts 1998 First Ex. Sess. No. 110, §1, eff. 5/5/98.)

§1182. Appropriate remedies with respect to prison conditions.

A. Prospective relief in any civil action with respect to prison conditions shall extend no further than necessary to correct the violation of the state right of a particular plaintiff or plaintiffs. The court shall not grant or approve any prospective relief unless the court finds that such relief is narrowly drawn, extends no further than necessary to correct the violation of the state right, and is the least intrusive means necessary to correct the violation of the state right. The court shall give substantial weight to any adverse impact on public safety or the operation of a criminal justice system caused by the relief. The court shall not order any prospective relief that requires or permits a government official to exceed his or her authority under state or local law or otherwise violates state or local law unless state law permits such relief to be ordered, and the relief is necessary to correct the violation of a state right, and no other relief will correct the violation of the state right. Nothing in this Section shall be construed to authorize the courts, in exercising their remedial powers, to order the construction of prisons or the raising of taxes, or to repeal or detract from otherwise applicable limitations on the remedial powers of the courts.

B. In any civil action with respect to prison conditions, to the extent otherwise authorized by law, the court may enter a temporary restraining order or an order for preliminary injunctive relief. Preliminary injunctive relief must be narrowly drawn, extend no further than necessary to correct the harm the court finds requires preliminary relief, and be the least intrusive means necessary to correct that harm. The court shall give substantial weight to any adverse impact on public safety or the operation of a criminal justice system caused by the preliminary relief. Preliminary injunctive relief shall automatically expire ninety days after its entry, unless the court makes the findings required under Subsection A for the entry of prospective relief and makes the order final before the expiration of the ninety-day period.

C. In any civil action with respect to prison conditions, no prisoner release order shall be entered unless a court has previously entered an order for less intrusive relief that has failed to remedy the violation of the state right sought to be remedied through the prisoner release order and the defendant has had a reasonable amount of time to comply with the previous court order.

D. Any state or local official or unit of government whose jurisdiction or function includes the appropriation of funds for the construction, operation, or maintenance of prison facilities, or the prosecution or custody of persons who may be released from, or not admitted to, a prison as a result of a prisoner release order shall have standing to oppose the imposition or continuation in effect of such relief and to seek termination of such relief, and shall have the right to intervene in any proceeding relating to such relief.

E. (1) In any civil action with respect to prison conditions in which prospective relief is ordered, such relief shall be terminable upon the motion of any party or intervener two years after the date the court granted or approved the prospective relief, or one year after the date the court has entered an order denying termination of prospective relief under this Section, or, in the case of an order issued on or before the effective date of this Part, two years after such date.

(2) In any civil action with respect to prison conditions, a defendant or intervener shall be entitled to the immediate termination of any prospective relief if the relief was approved or granted in the absence of a finding by the court that the relief was narrowly drawn, extended no further than necessary to correct the violation of the state right, and was the least intrusive means necessary to correct the violation of the state right.

(3) Prospective relief shall not terminate if the court makes written findings based on the record that prospective relief remains necessary to correct a current or ongoing violation of the state right and that the prospective relief is narrowly drawn, extends no further than necessary to correct the violation of the state right, and is the least intrusive means to correct the violation.

(4) Nothing in this Section shall prevent any party or intervener from seeking modification or termination before the relief is terminable under this Subsection, to the extent that modification or termination would otherwise be legally permissible.

F. In any civil action with respect to prison conditions, the court shall not enter or approve a consent decree unless it complies with the limitations on relief set forth in Subsection A. Nothing in this Section shall preclude parties from entering into a private settlement agreement that does not comply with the limitations on relief set forth in Subsection A, if the terms of that agreement are not subject to court enforcement other than the reinstatement of the civil proceeding that the agreement settled.

G. The court shall promptly rule on any motion to modify or terminate prospective relief in a civil action with respect to prison conditions. Any prospective relief subject to a pending motion shall be automatically stayed during the period beginning on the thirtieth day after such motion is filed, in the case of a motion made under Subsection E, or beginning on the one hundred eightieth day after such motion is filed, in the case of a motion made under any other law, and ending on the date the court enters a final order ruling on the motion.

(Added by Acts 1997 No. 731, §1, eff. 7/9/97.)

§1183. Experts.

A. When otherwise specifically authorized by law, in any prisoner suit, the court may appoint an expert who shall be disinterested and objective and will give due regard to the public safety. If the court determines that the appointment of an expert is necessary, the court shall request that the defendant and the plaintiff each submit a list of not more than five persons to serve as an expert. Each party shall have the opportunity to remove up to three persons from the opposing party's list. The court shall select the expert from the persons remaining on the lists after all names have been removed. Any party shall have the right to an interlocutory appeal of the judge's selection of the expert under this Section on the ground of partiality.

B. An expert appointed under this Section may be authorized to conduct hearings and prepare proposed findings of fact on the record and may assist in the development of remedial plans. The expert shall not make any findings or communications ex parte. An expert may be appointed during the remedial phase of a civil action with respect to prison conditions only upon a finding that the remedial phase will be sufficiently complex to warrant such appointment.

C. In any civil action with respect to prison conditions in which an expert is appointed under this Section, the court shall review the appointment of the expert every six months to determine whether the services of the expert continue to be required. The expert may be removed at any time. In no event shall the appointment of an expert extend beyond the termination of the relief.

D. Notwithstanding any other law to the contrary, the compensation to be allowed to an expert shall not be greater than the hourly rate established for payment of court-appointed counsel, plus costs reasonably incurred by the expert. Such compensation and costs shall be paid with funds available to the court.

(Added by Acts 1997 No. 731, §1; chgd. by Acts 1998 First Ex. Sess. No. 110, §1, eff. 5/5/98.)

§1184. Suits by prisoners.

A. No prisoner suit shall assert a claim under state law until such administrative remedies as are available are exhausted.

B. The court, on its own motion or on the motion of a party, shall dismiss any prisoner suit if the court is satisfied that the action is frivolous, is malicious, fails to state a cause of action, seeks monetary relief from a defendant who is immune from such relief, or fails to state a claim upon which relief can be granted. If the court makes a determination to dismiss the suit based on the content, or lack thereof, of the petition, the court may dismiss the underlying claim without first requiring the exhaustion of administrative remedies.

C. Any defendant may waive the right to reply to any civil action brought by a person confined in any prison or to any prisoner suit. Notwithstanding any other law or rule of procedure, such waiver shall not constitute an admission of the allegations contained in the petition or waive any affirmative defenses available to the defendant. No relief shall be granted to the plaintiff unless an answer has been filed. The court may require any defendant to answer a petition brought under this Section if it finds that the plaintiff has a reasonable opportunity to prevail on the merits.

D. To the extent practicable, in any action brought with respect to prison conditions pursuant to the provisions of this Section, or any other law, by a prisoner confined in any prison, pretrial proceedings in which the prisoner's participation is required or permitted shall be conducted by telephone, video conference, or other communications technology without removing the prisoner from the facility in which he is confined. Subject to agreement by the state or local entity of government with custody over the prisoner, hearings may be conducted at the facility in which the prisoner is confined. To the extent practicable, the court shall allow counsel to participate by telephone, video conference, or other telecommunications technology in any hearing held at the facility.

E. No prisoner suit may assert a claim under state law for mental or emotional injury suffered while in custody without a prior showing of physical injury.

(Added by Acts 1997 No. 731, §1; chgd. by Acts 1998 First Ex. Sess. No. 110, §1, eff. 5/5/98.)

§1185. Attorney fees.

A. In any prisoner suit in which attorney fees are authorized, such fees shall not be awarded, except to the extent that the fee was directly and reasonably incurred in proving an actual violation of the plaintiff's rights protected by a statute pursuant to which a fee may be awarded, and the amount of the fee is proportionately related to the court-ordered relief for the violation or the fee was directly and reasonably incurred in enforcing the relief ordered for the violation.

B. Whenever a monetary judgment is awarded in an action described in Subsection A, a portion of the judgment, not to exceed twenty-five percent, shall be applied to satisfy the amount of attorney fees awarded against the defendant. If the award of attorney fees is not greater than one hundred fifty percent of the judgment, the excess shall be paid by the defendant. No award of attorney fees in an action shall be based on an hourly rate greater than the hourly rate established for payment of court-appointed counsel.

C. Nothing in this Section shall prohibit a prisoner from entering into an agreement to pay an attorney fee in an amount greater than the amount authorized under this Section, if the fee is paid by the individual rather than by the defendant.

(Added by Acts 1997 No. 731, §1; chgd. by Acts 1998 First Ex. Sess. No. 110, §1, eff. 5/5/98.)

§1186. Proceedings in forma pauperis.

A. (1) A prisoner seeking to bring a civil action or appeal a judgment in a civil action or proceeding without prepayment of fees or security therefor must comply with all requirements for proceeding in forma pauperis and shall submit a certified copy of the trust fund account statement or institutional equivalent for the six-month period immediately preceding the filing of the petition or notice of appeal, obtained from the appropriate official of each prison at which the prisoner is or was confined.

(2) If a prisoner brings a civil action or files an appeal in forma pauperis, the prisoner shall be required to pay the full amount of a filing fee. The court shall assess and, when funds exist, collect, as a partial payment of any court fees required by law, an initial partial filing fee of twenty percent of the greater of the average monthly deposits to the prisoner's account, or the average monthly balance in the prisoner's account for the six-month period immediately preceding the filing of the petition or notice of appeal.

B. After payment of the initial partial filing fee, the prisoner shall be required to make monthly payments of twenty percent of the preceding month's income credited to the prisoner's account. The agency having custody of the prisoner shall forward payments from the prisoner's account to the clerk of the court each time the amount in the account exceeds ten dollars until the filing fees are paid. In no event shall a prisoner be prohibited from bringing a civil action or appealing a civil or criminal judgment for the reason that the prisoner has no assets and no means by which to pay the initial partial filing fee. In no event shall the filing fee collected exceed the amount of fees permitted by statute for the commencement of a civil action or an appeal of a civil action or criminal judgment.

C. Notwithstanding any filing fee, or any portion thereof, that may have been paid, the court shall dismiss the case at any time if the court determines that the allegation of poverty is untrue, or the action or appeal is frivolous, is malicious, fails to state a cause of action, seeks monetary relief against a defendant who is immune from such relief, or fails to state a claim upon which relief can be granted.

D. If the judgment against a prisoner includes the payment of costs, the prisoner shall be required to pay the full amount of the costs ordered and in the same manner as is provided for filing fees. In no event shall the costs collected exceed the amount of the costs ordered by the court.

E. In actions to which this Part applies, the provisions of this Section, to the extent of any conflict with those of Code of Civil Procedure Article 5181 et seq., apply to the payment of filing fees and costs.

(Added by Acts 1997 No. 731, §1; chgd. by Acts 1998 First Ex. Sess. No 110, §1, eff. 5/5/98.)

§1187. Successive claims.

In no event shall a prisoner bring a civil action or appeal a judgment in a civil action or proceeding in forma pauperis if the prisoner has, on three or more prior occasions while incarcerated or detained in any facility, brought an action or appeal in a state court that was dismissed on the grounds that it was frivolous, was malicious, failed to state a cause of action, or failed to state a claim upon which relief may be granted, unless the prisoner is under imminent danger of serious physical injury. *(Added by Acts 1997 No. 731, §1; chgd. by Acts 1998 First Ex. Sess. No 110, §1, eff. 5/5/98.)*

§1188. Judicial screening.

The court shall review, before docketing if feasible or, in any event, as soon as practicable after docketing, a petition in a civil action in which a prisoner seeks redress from a governmental entity or officer or employee of a governmental entity. On review, the court shall identify cognizable claims or dismiss the petition, or any portion of the petition, if the petition is frivolous, is malicious, fails to state a cause of action, seeks monetary relief from a defendant who is immune from such relief, or fails to state a claim upon which relief can be granted. *(Added by Acts 1997 No. 731, §1; chgd. by Acts 1998 First Ex. Sess. No 110, §1, eff. 5/5/98.)*

§1189. Payment of damage award in satisfaction of pending restitution orders.

Any damages awarded to a prisoner in connection with a civil action brought against any prison or against any official or agent of such prison shall be paid directly to satisfy any outstanding restitution orders pending against the prisoner. The remainder of any such award after full payment of all pending restitution orders shall be forwarded to the prisoner. Prior to payment of any damages awarded under this Part, reasonable efforts shall be made to notify the victims of the crime for which the prisoner was convicted and incarcerated concerning the pending payment of any such damages. *(Added by Acts 1997 No. 731, §1; chgd. by Acts 1998 First Ex. Sess. No 110, §1, eff. 5/5/98.)*

§1190. Earned release credit or good time credit revocation.

In any civil action brought by any person convicted of a crime and confined in a prison, the court may order the revocation of such earned good time credit that has not yet been vested, if, on its own motion or the motion of any party, the court finds that the claim was filed for a malicious purpose, the claim was filed solely to harass the party against which it was filed, or the claimant testifies falsely or otherwise knowingly presents false evidence or information to the court. *(Added by Acts 1997 No. 731, §1, eff. 7/9/97.)*

CHAPTER 8. LOUISIANA COMMISSION ON LAW ENFORCEMENT AND THE ADMINISTRATION OF CRIMINAL JUSTICE

§1201. Louisiana Commission on Law Enforcement and Administration of Criminal Justice.

The Louisiana Commission on Law Enforcement and Administration of Criminal Justice is hereby created and established.

§1202. Composition of commission.

A. The commission shall consist of fifty-four* members as follows:

**So in original. Probably should be "fifty-three".*

(1) The chairman of the Senate Committee on the Judiciary, Section C, or his designee;

(2) The chairman of the House Committee on the Administration of Criminal Justice or his designee;

(3) The secretary of the Department of Public Safety and Corrections or his designee;

(4) The chief justice of the Louisiana Supreme Court or his designee;

(5) The chief judge of each of the courts of appeal;

(6) The president of the Louisiana Juvenile Judges' Association;

(7) The president of the Louisiana District Attorneys' Association;

(8) The president of the Louisiana State Troopers' Association;

(9) The president of the Louisiana Sheriffs' Association;

(10) The president of the Louisiana Municipal Association;

(11) The president of the Louisiana Chiefs of Police Association;

(12) The chairman of the Louisiana State Bar Association Section on Criminal Law;

(13) The director of the State Indigent Defender Board;

(14) The director of state police;

(15) Three district attorneys appointed by the governor;
(16) Three sheriffs appointed by the governor;
(17) Two chiefs of police appointed by the governor;
(18) A district court judge appointed by the governor;
(19) A juvenile court judge appointed by the governor;
(20) Three professional or lay persons appointed by the President of the Senate;
(21) Three professional or lay persons appointed by the Speaker of the House of Representatives; and
(22) Fifteen professional or lay persons appointed by the governor as may have a vital concern with law enforcement and the administration of criminal justice.
(23) The president of the Louisiana chapter of the National Constables Association.
(24) One person appointed by the governor from a list of at least three persons submitted by Victims and Citizens Against Crime, Inc.
(25) The president of the Louisiana Union of Police, or his designee.
(26) The attorney general or his designee.

B. Each member shall serve a term concurrent with that of the governor making the appointment. Every person who holds commission membership by virtue of his official position or employment shall cease to be a member at such time he no longer holds the position that qualified him for membership on the commission.

C. Each appointment by the governor shall be submitted to the Senate for confirmation. Members shall serve without compensation, per diem, or travel reimbursement; however, legislator-members may receive per diem or travel expense reimbursement.
(Chgd. by Acts 1991 No. 509, §1; Acts 1995 No. 856, §1, No. 1218, §1, eff. 8/15/95.)

§1203. Officers; meetings.

A. The commission shall elect a chairman and vice chairman from the commission members for two-year terms. The chairman shall be the chief executive officer of the commission. The vice chairman shall function as the chief executive officer of the commission upon direction of the chairman.

B. The domicile of the commission shall be in Baton Rouge. The commission shall hold public meetings monthly except as provided by vote of the commission or by order of the chairman.

§1204. Functions.

The functions of the commission shall be to:

(1) Bring together those persons most familiar with problems of law enforcement and the administration of criminal justice, including the disposition and treatment of persons convicted of crime, for the purpose of studying and encouraging the adoption of methods by which law enforcement can be made more effective and justice administered more efficiently and fairly, to the end that citizens may be more fully protected.

(2) Stimulate, promote, and organize citizen participation in the improvements and extension of law enforcement, corrections, rehabilitation, and the work of the courts.

(3) Recommend and assist in improvements with respect to the recruitment and training of law enforcement officers and other law enforcement personnel.

(4) Recommend methods by which cooperation may be furthered between federal, state, and local law enforcement officials.

(5) Assist in planning coordinated programs throughout the state in areas relating to the police, the courts, and corrections.

(6) Encourage public understanding of the responsibilities and problems of law enforcement officers and law enforcement and criminal justice agencies and the development of greater public support for their efforts.

(7) Aid in publicizing and promoting practices in the treatment of criminal offenders which will do most to prevent a return to criminal activity.

(8) Oversee, review, and approve the preparation of the state plan and its implementation.

(9) Approve or deny applications for grants of block funds provided for by the Justice Improvement Act of 1979*, the Juvenile and Delinquency Prevention Act of 1974*, and available state funds.

**42 U.S.C. §3701 et seq.*
***18 U.S.C. §5031 et seq.*

(10) Carry out the objectives of the Justice Improvement Act of 1979, the Juvenile Justice and Delinquency Prevention Act of 1974, and other federal and state programs which promote the improvement of criminal or juvenile justice as the governor or legislature may direct.

(11) Serve as the central coordinating agency for adult and juvenile correctional systems, in accordance with the requirements of this Chapter.

(12) Establish, implement, and develop a program to award annually a state medal of honor in the name of each law enforcement officer killed that year in the line of duty. The commission shall determine the nature or type of the award, the type of annual ceremony, and the recipient to whom the award is presented, shall gather necessary information from the appropriate state and local law enforcement agencies, procure funding for the program, and do all other things necessary or convenient to carry out the functions, powers, and duties set forth in this Paragraph.

(Chgd. by Acts 1997 No. 562, §1, eff. 8/15/97.)

§1204.1. Correctional coordination; duties of agency.

A. The commission shall serve as the central coordinating agency for adult and juvenile correctional systems, in conjunction with the Department of Public Safety and Corrections, the sheriffs of the state, and local juvenile justice officials.

B. The duties of the commission with regard to correctional coordination shall be to:

(1) Maintain accurate and timely statistical information relative to the operation of state and local correctional systems.

(2) Report the status of state and local correctional facilities and programs to the governor and legislature by April first of each year.

(3) Review and conduct needs analyses upon all state or local correctional facility construction projects which add capacity in the system and which require the expenditure of state funds, and report the analyses results to the governor and the legislature prior to their consideration of such funding.

(4) Prepare and present to the governor and legislature a policy impact statement on each major change to correctional law.

(5) Maintain prison population projections for all state or local correctional institutions and state probation and parole caseloads.

(6) Evaluate the cost and effectiveness of all correctional experimental programs approved by the legislature on an experimental basis and report the findings of such evaluations to the legislature.

(7) Recommend practical and realistic improvements in the state correctional system to the governor and the legislature by April first of each year.

(8) Aid state and local government in the development and exchange of information concerning correctional policies and programs, including the development of correctional information systems.

(9) Maintain the Parish Prison Information System.

(10) Assist state and local government in improving correctional decision making.

(11) Conduct evaluation of existing corrections programs or studies of proposed corrections programs, as requested by the governor, legislature, or Department of Public Safety and Corrections.

C. As used herein:

(1) "Agency" means the staff of the Louisiana Commission on Law Enforcement and Administration of Criminal Justice.

(2) "Commission" means the members of the Louisiana Commission on Law Enforcement and Administration of Criminal Justice.

(3) "Local government" means any political subdivision of the state.

(4) "State" means the state of Louisiana.

D. A majority vote of the commission membership present and voting shall be required for approval by the commission of a correctional construction or system improvement plan.

E. The agency shall have access to, and be provided upon request with, all statistical and other relevant information from any state or local correctional agency in order to perform the duties set forth in this Section. The agency shall also have access to all records maintained by any state agency for the purpose of correctional planning, policy decisions, and research activity. These records shall include information maintained by the Department of Public Safety and Corrections on adult and juvenile offenders, including inmate records, medical records, and student records. The agency shall maintain the confidentiality of any records required by law to be kept confidential.

§1204.2. Creation of system; functions; powers; duties.

A. There is hereby created within the Louisiana Commission on Law Enforcement and the Administration of Criminal Justice, hereinafter referred to as the "commission", a Louisiana Uniform Crime Reporting System, hereinafter referred to as the "system". The commission may appoint such employees, agents, consultants, and special committees as it may deem necessary to properly manage the system.

B. The system, by and through the commission, shall have the following functions, powers, and duties:

(1) To establish, through electronic data processing and related procedures, a system by which relevant information can be collected, coordinated, analyzed, and made readily available to serve qualified agencies concerned with the administration of criminal justice located anywhere in the state. The commission shall prescribe the terms and conditions under which such agencies shall contribute or gain access to information contained in the system files.

(2) To adopt such measures to assure the security of the system as may be specified in state and federal regulations.

(3) To adopt and publish for distribution to the system subscribers and other interested parties the operating policies, practices and procedures, and conditions of qualification for data access.

(4) To prepare and distribute, to all such persons and agencies, forms to be used in reporting data to the system. The forms shall provide for information regarding crimes which are directed against individuals or groups, or their property, by reason of their actual or perceived race, age, gender, religion, color, creed, disability, sexual orientation, national origin, or ancestry or by reason of their actual or perceived membership or service in, or employment with, an organization as defined in R.S. 14:107.2. The forms shall also provide for other items of information needed by federal and state bureaus or departments engaged in the development of national and state statistics.

(5) To instruct such persons and agencies in the installation, maintenance, and use of incident-based records and in the manner of reporting to the system.

(6) To tabulate, analyze, and interpret the data collected.

(7) To supply the data to federal bureaus or departments engaged in collecting national criminal statistics.

(8) (a) To present annually to the governor and members of the legislature, on or before May first, a printed report containing the criminal statistics of the preceding calendar year and to present at such other times as the commission may deem wise, or the governor or the chairman of the House Committee on Administration of Criminal Justice or the chairman of the Senate Committee on Judiciary C may request, reports on special aspects of criminal statistics.

(b) The report shall specifically contain a category entitled "gaming related offenses" and shall include statistics involving violations of R.S. 14:60, R.S. 14:62, R.S. 14:64 through 67, R.S. 14:70, R.S. 14:71, R.S. 14:71.1, and R.S. 14:72, in which the offender's gaming activity is a motive for commission of the crime. In addition, the report shall contain under the same category violations of prohibited acts and gaming offenses, as defined in R.S. 14:90, R.S. 14:90.2, R.S. 27:98 through 101, and R.S. 27:260 and 262 through 265.

(c) A sufficient number of copies of all reports shall be printed for distribution to all public officials in the state dealing with crimes or criminals and for general distribution in the interest of public enlightenment.

(9) To make, solicit, and request proposals and offers, and to execute and effectuate agreements or contracts for the operation of any part of the system.

(10) To do all other things necessary or convenient to carry out the functions, powers, and duties set forth in this Section.

(Added by Acts 1991 No. 509, §1; chgd. by Acts 1997 No. 488, §1, eff. 8/15/97, No. 1479, §1, eff. 7/15/97.)

§1204.3. Report to the system; duties of persons and agencies.

All law enforcement agencies, correctional agencies and institutions, district attorneys and municipal prosecutors, courts having criminal jurisdiction, or any other public agency dealing with crimes or criminals, when requested by the commission, shall:

(1) Install and maintain records needed for reporting crime incident and arrest information required by the commission.

(2) Report to the commission as and when the commission prescribes crime incident and arrest information required by the commission.

(3) Give the commission access to closed criminal case records for purposes of inspection.

(4) Upon the request of the commission, provide any other such assistance, information, and data which are reasonable and available as will enable the commission to properly carry out its powers and duties.
(Added by Acts 1991 No. 509, §1, eff. 9/6/91.)

§1204.4. Studies; surveys; report.

A. In the accomplishment of the purposes of this Chapter, the commission may undertake research and studies independently or in cooperation with any public or private agencies, including educational, civic, and research organizations, colleges, universities, institutions, or foundations.

B. The commission and the Louisiana Commission on Human Rights shall annually study data collected pursuant to this Chapter, relating to hate crimes, as defined by R.S. 14:107.2, occurring within the state. The results of the study shall be published in the annual report to the governor and the members of the legislature as required by R.S. 15:1204.2(B)(8).
(Added by Acts 1991 No. 509, §1; chgd. by Acts 1997 No. 1479, §1, eff. 7/15/97.)

§1204.5. Penalties.

The commission may impose reasonable administrative sanctions as it deems appropriate against those agencies who fail to comply with the reporting requirements of the Uniform Crime Reporting System. These sanctions include the preclusion of a subject agency's participation in any of the grant programs operated by the commission. *(Added by Acts 1991 No. 509, §1, eff. 9/6/91.)*

§1205. State Law Enforcement Planning Agency.

Within the Louisiana Commission on Law Enforcement and Administration of Criminal Justice, there shall be a State Law Enforcement Planning Agency (SLEPA), which shall serve as the staff of the commission.

§1206. Composition of State Law Enforcement Planning Agency.

A. The governor shall appoint an executive director of the planning agency who shall serve at the pleasure of the governor and who shall be the chief executive officer of the commission staff. He shall take all necessary action and devote his full time to assisting the commission in performing its duties and fulfilling its responsibilities, including staff recruitment, training and direction. The executive director shall be the appointing authority for commission staff and shall exercise administrative supervision over the district program directors, who shall be responsible to him for the accomplishment of all tasks assigned to the law enforcement planning district agencies by the State Law Enforcement Planning Agency, including the preparation of district plans and the preparation of projects in the respective law enforcement planning districts. The executive director shall have final authority on matters pertaining to the employment, termination of employment, and wages paid to professional staff members of the law enforcement planning district agencies, with the exception of such district staff as shall be covered by state or local civil service. The executive director shall fill vacancies which occur among professional staff of law enforcement planning districts from a list of at least three (3) names recommended by the local advisory council. Additionally, the executive director shall have the authority to award state agency grants in the amount of $10,000 or less with approval by the governor. Such grant awards must be consistent and compatible with the state plan.

B. The staff of the commission shall consist of necessary professional, administrative, and clerical personnel to accomplish required planning and plan implementation for each of the major law enforcement components, administration of the state subgrant program to local units of government, and for all other planning agency responsibilities. Staff members of the SLEPA shall be subject to the supervision of the executive director and shall perform duties directed by him.

§1207. Functions of the staff.

The functions of the staff of the commission shall include but not be limited to the following:

(1) Preparation, development, and revision of comprehensive plans based on an evaluation of law enforcement and criminal justice problems within the state.

(2) Definition, development, and correlation of action programs under such plans.

(3) Establishment of priorities for law enforcement and criminal justice improvement in the state.

(4) Providing information to prospective aid recipients on procedures for grant application.

(5) Encouraging grant proposals from local units of government for law enforcement and criminal justice planning and improvement efforts.

(6) Encouraging project proposals from state law enforcement and criminal justice agencies.

(7) Evaluation of applications for aid and awarding of funds to units of government and other eligible applicants.

(8) Monitoring progress and expenditures under grants to state law enforcement agencies, local units of government, and other recipients of Louisiana Commission on Law Enforcement grant funds.

(9) Encouraging regional, local, and metropolitan area planning efforts, action projects, and cooperative arrangement.

(10) Coordination of the state's law enforcement and criminal justice plan with other federally supported programs relating to or having an impact on law enforcement and criminal justice.

(11) Oversight and evaluation of the total state effort in plan implementation and law enforcement improvement.

(12) Provide technical assistance and services for programs and projects contemplated by the state plan and by units of general local government.

(13) Collecting and analyzing statistics and other data relevant to law enforcement and criminal justice in the state.

(14) Performing any other functions required by federal guidelines or state law.

§1208. Office of Peace Officer Standards and Training; program director.

A. An Office of Peace Officer Standards and Training is hereby created within the Louisiana Commission on Law Enforcement and Administration of Criminal Justice to be administered by a program director. He shall be a civil service employee selected by a majority vote of the Council on Peace Officer Standards and Training from a list of candidates certified by the Department of Civil Service. Retention of this position is subject to the rules of the Department of Civil Service.

B. The program director, in conjunction with the council members' advice and consent, shall develop a staffing plan for the office. Persons selected for this staff shall be civil service employees. Employees currently in the Louisiana Commission on Law Enforcement may be transferred to any position in the Office of Peace Officer Standards and Training.

C. The program director and administrative staff shall receive policy and direction from the council. No rules or regulations, statutes, or procedures initiated by the administrative staff shall be instituted without majority approval of the council.

§1209. Law enforcement planning district agencies.

A. The planning agencies for the planning districts shall be those heretofore or hereafter recognized as such by the governor.

B. The law enforcement planning district agency staff shall consist of a district program director and such other administrative and clerical personnel whose services are required on a full-time basis in the accomplishment of law enforcement planning and administrative functions.

C. The district planning agencies shall have all of the functions of the state planning agency that are applicable within their respective districts as may be approved by the State Law Enforcement Planning Agency.

§1210. Law enforcement planning district advisory councils; composition.

A law enforcement planning district advisory council is hereby created and established for each law enforcement planning district agency. These councils shall be composed in accordance with the guidelines prescribed by the Louisiana Commission on Law Enforcement.

§1211. Purpose and function of advisory councils.

Law enforcement planning district advisory councils shall perform functions similar to those prescribed for the commission in planning, developing, coordinating, and administering criminal justice improvement programs within their respective law enforcement planning districts. They shall:

(1) Review, approve, and submit the comprehensive district law enforcement plan and projects to implement that plan in accordance with district problems, needs, and goals, and with such format, schedule, description, and other specifics as the State Law Enforcement Planning Agency may require.

(2) Identify criminal justice problems and needs in the district and encourage, support, and assist with programs and projects proposed by appropriate public entitles toward resolving such problems and needs.

(3) Inform the SLEPA promptly and completely on all matters in the district affecting and/or affected by the SLEPA and its mission and advise the SLEPA in such matters.

(4) Inform public and private entities in the district affecting and/or affected by the SLEPA in any instance promptly and completely of the SLEPA's mission, policies, and action and advice such entities in criminal justice matters.

(5) Administer and monitor progress and/or changes in district projects on the basis of guidelines developed by the SLEPA.

(6) Make recommendations to the executive director of the State Law Enforcement Planning Agency on matters relating to the employment, termination of employment, and wages paid to professional staff members of the law enforcement planning district agency.

(7) Review and accept the district budget from the State Law Enforcement Planning Agency and assume responsibility for administering the district budget in conformity with state and federal requirements.

(8) Form task forces or committees to assist in planning, analysis, policy, and goal recommendations, and perform such other functions as the SLEPA deems necessary; appoint the chairmen of these task forces and committees and assure the satisfactory performance of each.

(9) Establish bylaws in compliance with the articles of incorporation specifically dealing with membership, including composition, method and duration of appointment; task force and special committee appointment, structure, and composition.

(10) Perform other functions in accordance with state and federal policy.

§1220. Authorization.

Parish governing bodies and the city of New Orleans are hereby authorized to create criminal justice information system policy boards established from representatives of all agencies who require service from the criminal justice information system, as well as such technical representatives as said local governing authorities may choose to appoint. Technical representation on the policy board shall be of an advisory nature and shall exist for the purpose of providing information to the policy board. Said technical representatives, however, shall not be voting or full members of the user group. Said policy boards shall be considered as a board of directors responsible for:

(1) The creation of a plan for the development of all information and statistical systems at the local level;

(2) Establishment of an operating policy for the criminal justice information system;

(3) Continued oversight over the development and operation of the criminal justice information system;

(4) And all other aspects of the planning, management, and operation of the system.

§1221. Information system's plan.

Each policy board shall establish a plan for the development of information and statistical systems.

(1) The plan shall specify systems, objectives, and services to be provided which shall include but not be limited to:

(a) Organization responsibilities;

(b) The scope of each system;

(c) Priorities for development; and

(d) A timetable for development.

(2) The plan shall indicate the appropriate funding source for both the development and operation of the system.

(3) The plan shall provide for the privacy, confidentiality, and security of data in the system.

(4) No plan for the department of said systems, however, shall be considered final or approved, nor shall implementation of said plan proceed until the plan has been reviewed and approved by the Louisiana Criminal Justice Information System and the local governing authority.

§1222. Staffing; funding; powers; and duties of policy boards.

Upon approval of the criminal justice information plan by the Louisiana Criminal Justice Information System and the local governing body, each policy board shall establish an operating policy for the criminal justice information system. The policy shall specify:

(1) The staffing required for the implementation of the plan;

(2) The level of hardware and software required for the implementation of the plan;

(3) The budget required to implement said plan;

(4) Standards and techniques for the protection of the privacy, security, and confidentiality of data and recommended sanctions and penalties for the violation of the rules and regulations adopted under it. The recommended sanctions and penalties shall apply to the improper collection, storage, uses and dissemination of criminal justice information; and

(5) The operating policy of each criminal justice information system policy board shall require, prior to any implementation of said policy, the specific approval of the local governing authority. Upon approval of the policy, local governing authorities may enact ordinances in accordance with said policies to enact its provisions, and to provide penalties for the violation of privacy, security, and confidentiality provisions.

§1223. Crime Victims Reparations Board.

The Crime Victims Reparations Board as further provided for in Chapter 21 of Title 46 of the Louisiana Revised Statutes of 1950 is hereby placed under the jurisdiction of the Louisiana Commission on Law Enforcement and Administration of Criminal Justice.

§1224. Drug Abuse Education and Treatment Fund; creation; purpose.

A. The Drug Abuse Education and Treatment Fund, hereafter referred to as the "fund", is hereby created as a special fund in the state treasury, which shall be the depository for all fees collected under the provisions of C.Cr.P. Art. 895.1(E).

B. After compliance with the requirements of Article VII, Section 9(B) of the Constitution of Louisiana relative to the Bond Security and Redemption Fund, and prior to monies being placed in the state general fund, an amount equal to that deposited as required by Subsection A hereof shall be credited to the fund. The monies in the fund shall be used solely as provided by Subsection C of this Section and only in the amounts appropriated by the legislature. The monies in this fund shall be invested by the state treasurer in the same manner as monies in the state general fund, and interest earned on the investment of these monies shall be credited to the fund, again following compliance with the requirement of Article VII, Section 9(B) relative to the Bond Security and Redemption Fund.

C. The monies available in the fund shall be used exclusively by the Louisiana Commission on Law Enforcement to administer a grant program to assist local public and private nonprofit agencies involved in drug abuse prevention and treatment in developing drug abuse and treatment programs. In addition, the commission shall allocate from the fund such monies as are necessary in administering this grant program.

D. The commission shall promulgate such rules, regulations, and procedures as are necessary in administering the assistance program, including procedures for application, audit and monitoring requirements, and annual report requirements. To this end, the commission may utilize resources and information developed pursuant to the provisions of R.S. 15:1255.

§1226. Juvenile Delinquency and Gang Prevention Act of 1993.

The Juvenile Delinquency and Gang Prevention Act of 1993, as provided for in Chapter 13 of Title 15 of the Louisiana Revised Statutes of 1950, and its administration are hereby placed under the jurisdiction of the Louisiana Commission on Law Enforcement and Administration of Criminal Justice. *(Added by Acts 1993 No. 461, §1, eff. 8/15/93.)*

§1227. Juvenile boot camp clearinghouse.

A. There is hereby created within the Louisiana Commission on Law Enforcement and Administration of Criminal Justice a juvenile boot camp clearinghouse, hereinafter referred to as the "clearinghouse". The commission may appoint such employees, agents, consultants, and special committees as it may deem necessary to properly establish the clearinghouse. The commission shall work with the appropriate local law enforcement personnel and juvenile court personnel or appropriate personnel from the court exercising juvenile jurisdiction in particular local areas in establishing, implementing, and reviewing the clearinghouse as well as local programs, as more fully set forth in Subsection B of this Section.

B. The clearinghouse, through the commission, shall have the following functions, powers, and duties:

(1) To develop general guidelines for local juvenile boot camp programs, sponsored by local government law enforcement agencies or courts exercising juvenile jurisdiction, hereinafter referred to as "local programs", which guidelines shall include and emphasize the following criteria:

(a) Military style discipline, excluding weapons training, martial arts training, or instruction in hand-to-hand combat.

(b) Education.

(c) Substance abuse.

(d) Psycho-social treatment.

(e) Extensive local community involvement, including but not limited to nongovernment groups such as boys clubs and volunteer groups, as well as appropriate local government law enforcement agencies and personnel from the appropriate courts exercising juvenile jurisdiction in that area.

(f) Intensive parole or aftercare supervision for an extended period of time, which supervision shall include organized after-school activities, counseling, and other organized efforts to promote the successful integration into society of juveniles who have been charged, with emphasis on prevention of the recurrence of any prior family and community problems which had a negative or detrimental effect on the juvenile initially.

(2) To set eligibility standards for local programs, including the age of the juvenile participants, and to include an enumeration of crimes for which a child has been charged and will be considered for admission to the program, so as to target the local programs for the appropriate class of offenders.

(3) To develop funding applications for local programs based on the developed guidelines.

(4) To analyze and grade funding applications for local programs objectively, based strictly on the developed guidelines.

(5) To distribute pilot program funds and federal funds derived from any appropriate and available source to approved local programs.

(6) To apply for, utilize, and maximize the use of any federal funding from any source now available or that becomes available in the future, including but not limited to government grants.

(7) To maintain data and statistics of details and results of local programs, including cost and recidivism.

(8) To make, solicit, and request proposals and offers and to execute and effectuate agreements or contracts for the operation of any part of the clearinghouse or a local program.

(9) To form task forces or committees to assist in the planning, analysis, policy, or goals of the clearinghouse and local programs and perform such other functions as the commission deems necessary, and to appoint the chairmen of the task forces or committees and assure their satisfactory performance.

(10) To do all other things necessary or convenient to carry out the functions, powers, and duties set forth in this Section.

C. The duties described in Paragraphs (1), (2), and (3) of Subsection B of this Section shall be accomplished by October 1, 1994.

D. Funding for additional local programs must come from federal revenues or grants and any private donations received. The commission may retain pilot program money received in the first year, if a pilot program is not yet in place, and hold the funds over until a pilot program is operational. All federal funding for local juvenile boot camp programs shall be received on behalf of the state by the commission, including funding from the Federal Omnibus Anti-Crime Bill of 1994, if and when passed by the Congress of the United States, and such

federal funding or grants received shall be disbursed through the clearinghouse's application process for disbursement.
(Added by Acts 1994 Third Ex. Sess. No. 147, §1, eff. 8/27/94.)

CHAPTER 8A. VICTIMIZATION OF SENIOR CITIZENS

(Added by Acts 1994 Third Ex. Sess. No. 19, §1, eff. 8/27/94.)

§1231. Short title.

R.S. 15:1231 through 1236 may be cited as the "Committee for the Coordination of Police Services to Elderly Persons Law". *(Added by Acts 1994 Third Ex. Sess. No. 19, §1, eff. 8/27/94.)*

§1232. Legislative findings and declaration.

A. The legislature hereby finds and declares that there are many efforts currently under way that work to coordinate criminal justice and social services partnerships to deal with the victimization of senior citizens. The Triad Program, sponsored by the National Sheriff's Association, hereafter referred to as "N.S.A.", the International Association of Chiefs of Police, hereafter referred to as "I.A.C.P.", and the American Association of Retired Persons, hereafter referred to as "A.A.R.P.", is one such effort. This program was replicated in Louisiana by the Louisiana Sheriff's Association, hereafter known as "L.S.A.", the Louisiana Association of Chiefs of Police, hereafter known as "L.A.C.P.", and the state A.A.R.P., with Louisiana being the first state to initiate such an agreement. This effort recognizes that senior citizens have the same fundamental desire as other members of society to live freely, without fear or restriction due to the criminal element, and that the state should seek to expand efforts to reduce crime against this growing and uniquely vulnerable segment of its population.

B. It is the intent of the legislature, therefore, to promote a coordinated effort among law enforcement and social services agencies to stem the tide of violence against senior citizens and support media and other strategies aimed at increasing both public understanding of the problem and the senior citizens' skills in preventing crime against themselves and their property. Further, it is the intent of the legislature to address the problem of crime against senior citizens in a systematic and effective manner by promoting and expanding collaborative crime prevention programs, such as the Triad model, that assist law enforcement agencies and senior citizens in implementing specific strategies for crime prevention, victim assistance, citizen involvement, and public education.
(Added by Acts 1994 Third Ex. Sess. No. 19, §1, eff. 8/27/94.)

§1233. Establishment of the committee.

There is hereby established within the jurisdiction of the Louisiana Commission on Law Enforcement and Administration of Criminal Justice, the Committee for the Coordination of Police Services of Elderly Persons, hereafter referred to as the "committee". *(Added by Acts 1994 Third Ex Sess. No. 19, §1, eff. 8/27/95.)*

§1234. Membership of committee; public office; compensation; meetings; quorum.

A. The committee shall consist of the following people:

(1) A representative of the Department of Public Safety and Corrections, office of state police, to be appointed by the deputy secretary of public safety services.

(2) Two representatives of the Louisiana Sheriff's Association, to be appointed by its president.

(3) Two representatives of the Louisiana Municipal Chiefs of Police Association, to be appointed by its president.

(4) One representative of the governor's Office of Elderly Affairs, to be appointed by its executive director.

(5) Two representatives from parish volunteer councils on aging, to be appointed by the executive director of the governor's Office of Elderly Affairs.

(6) One representative from the Louisiana Commission on Law Enforcement and Administration of Criminal Justice, to be appointed by its executive director.

(7) Two representatives from the American Association of Retired Persons, to be appointed by the president of the state American Association of Retired Persons.

(8) One representative from the Department of Justice, executive office of the attorney general, to be appointed by the attorney general.

B. In the performance of its functions, the committee shall, to the extent possible, solicit the participation and involvement of retired law enforcement personnel.

C. The committee shall elect a chairperson by a majority vote of the membership.

D. Members of the committee shall serve until the appropriately designated person in each representative organization selects another representative, and all persons on the committee shall be subject to the approval of the governor.

E. Membership on the committee shall not constitute the holding of a public office, and members of the committee shall not be required to take and file oaths of office before serving on the committee.

F. The members of the committee shall receive no compensation for their services as members.

G. No member of the committee shall be disqualified from holding any public office or employment, nor shall any member forfeit any employment or office by reason of his or her membership on the committee.

H. The committee shall meet as often as deemed necessary, but in no event less than four times annually. The chairman shall call the first meeting of the committee no later than January 1, 1995. A majority of the membership shall constitute a quorum for conducting business.

(Added by Acts 1994 Third Ex. Sess. No. 19, §1, eff. 8/27/94.)

§1235. Duties and responsibilities.

A. The committee shall advise the office of state police, sheriffs of the parishes in the state, and other local law enforcement agencies, senior advocates chosen in consultation with the governor's Office of Elderly Affairs and the parish volunteer councils on aging, and A.A.R.P. representatives in the study and evaluation of "Triad Programs" as an effective response to the problems of crime against elderly persons.

B. The committee may also consult with experts, service providers, and representative organizations engaged in the protection of the elderly and may recommend the development of "Triad Programs" in the state of Louisiana to assist the elderly to avoid criminal victimization through the coordinated efforts of state, parish, and local law enforcement agencies and organizations which provide services for the elderly.

C. The committee may also recommend policies and programs to assist law enforcement agencies to implement "Triad Programs", including training and crime prevention standards and technical assistance. Such recommendations may include the following:

(1) The establishment of a statewide central clearinghouse for information and education materials.

(2) The development of innovative community police programs for the elderly.

(3) The provision of assistance by the committee to the council on peace officers standards and training for the development and delivery of training to law enforcement professionals involved in the "Triad Programs", including but not limited to the following subjects:

(a) Crimes against the elderly and the protection of elderly persons.

(b) Police sensitivity to the needs of elderly persons as victims, witnesses, or victims of "vicarious victimization", which impairs their quality of life.

(c) Availability of social and human services.

(4) The provision of assistance to state and local law enforcement officials and to nonprofit corporations and organizations with respect to effective policies and responses to crimes against elderly persons.

(5) The promotion and facilitation of cooperation among state agencies and local government.

(6) The promotion of effective advocacy services to protect and assist elderly persons and elderly victims of crime.

(7) The evaluation of the relationship between crimes against elderly persons and other problems confronting elderly persons, and the making of recommendations for effective policy

(8) The collection of statistical data and research.

(9) The establishment of rules and regulations necessary to carry out the purposes of R.S. 15:1231 through 1236.

(Added by Acts 1994 Third Ex. Sess. No. 19. §1, eff. 8/27/94.)

§1236. "Triad Program" defined.

A. As used in R.S. 15:1231 through 1236, the "Triad Program" means the triad cooperative model developed by the American Association of Retired Persons, the National Sheriff's Association, and the International Association of Chiefs of Police, which calls for the participation of the sheriff, at least one police chief, and a representative of at least one senior citizens' organization within a parish and may include participation by coalitions of law enforcement, victims' services, and senior citizen advocate organizations.

B. If there is not both a sheriff and a police chief in a parish or if the sheriff or a police chief does not participate, a Triad Program may include in the place of the sheriff or police chief another member of the criminal justice system.

(Added by Acts 1994 Third Ex. Sess. No. 19, §1, eff. 8/27/94.)

CHAPTER 9. PARISH JAIL FACILITIES

Section

§1251. Short title.

This Chapter shall be known as and may be cited as the "Jail Standards and Assistance Act."

§1252. Statement of purpose.

The legislature enacts this Chapter to provide for a program to be administered by the Louisiana Commission on Law Enforcement and the Administration of Criminal Justice, hereinafter in this Chapter referred to as the commission, intended to upgrade parish jail facilities to standards promulgated by the commission.

§1253. Powers and duties of the commission.

The commission shall have the following powers and duties:

(1) To administer state grants programs to parish jails in conformity with jail standards and application procedures as developed by the commission.

(2) To develop, continually review, and update minimum standards for parish jail facilities.

(3) To review and approve or disapprove all plans for purposes of grant applications submitted to the commission.

(4) To approve or disapprove the use and allocation of funds.

(5) To advise and make recommendations to the secretary of the Department of Corrections concerning the coordination of correctional services between the state and the parishes.

(6) To establish annual priorities for the disbursement of funds pursuant to R.S. 15:1255.

(7) To provide technical assistance to parishes regarding minimum standards for parish jail facilities upon request of appropriate parish authorities.

(8) To inspect and prepare reports on jail conditions at the request of the parish governing authority, a court, or on the commission's own initiative.

§1254. Grant funds; appropriation; distribution and allocation of grant funds.

A. Funds appropriated for the purposes of this Chapter shall be appropriated by the legislature for the commission to issue as grants and such grants shall not be used to substitute for jail facility expenditures already allocated in the budget of a participating parish agency.

B. The amount which may be allocated and distributed annually to agencies in each parish shall be based on priorities established by the commission. All participating parish agencies are eligible to receive funds from other sources to supplement grants under the provisions of this Chapter.

§1255. Applications for grants; eligibility; standards; procedures.

A. Any parish governmental agency that has responsibility for a jail facility is eligible to apply for participation in the grant program herein authorized. Participation by any agency is voluntary; however, each recipient agency must comply with standards promulgated under this Chapter. The governmental agencies of adjoining parishes or two or more governmental agencies in the same parish which have responsibility for jail facilities may join together in implementing the provisions of this Section.

B. The commission shall promulgate the rules, regulations, and procedures by which the grants shall be distributed. Application forms shall be developed and submitted by the appropriate parish agency, and reviewed by the commission.

§1256. Program review, reports; on-site inspections.

A. The commission shall prepare and submit an annual report to the legislature and to the governor which shall include: (1) an overall assessment of the parish jail facilities grant program, and (2) an evaluation of the extent to which program goals and objectives are being met.

B. The commission shall require such monitoring of individual grants as it deems necessary and may provide by rule for such audit requirements for grants as it deems appropriate.

C. The commission shall prepare and submit a report of each on-site inspection to the appropriate state and parish government agencies.

CHAPTER 10. ELECTRONIC SURVEILLANCE

PART I. GENERAL

Section

PART II. INTERCEPTION OF COMMUNICATIONS AND RELATED MATTERS

PART III. PEN REGISTERS AND TRAP AND TRACE DEVICES

PART I. GENERAL

(Chgd. by Acts 1991 No. 795, §4, eff. 7/22/91.)

§1301. Short title.

This Chapter may be cited and referred to as the "Electronic Surveillance Act".

PART II. INTERCEPTION OF COMMUNICATIONS AND RELATED MATTERS

(Chgd. by Acts 1991 No. 795, §4, eff. 7/22/91.)

§1302. Definitions.

As used in this Chapter:

(1) "Aggrieved person" means a person who was party to any intercepted wire or oral communication or a person against whom the interception was directed.

(2) "Attorney for a government entity" means an attorney on the staff or under the direct supervision of the district attorney authorized by law to prosecute such offenses as are subject of the pen register or trap and trace device.

(3) "Aural transfer" means a transfer containing the human voice at any point between and including the point of origin and the point of reception.

(4) "Communications common carrier" means any person engaged as a common carrier for hire in communication by wire or radio; however, a person engaged in commercial radio broadcasting which is supervised by the Federal Communications Commission shall not, insofar as such person is so engaged, be deemed a common carrier.

(5) "Contents" when used with respect to any wire, electronic, or oral communication includes any information concerning the substance, purport, or meaning of that communication.

(6) "Court of competent jurisdiction" means state district courts of general criminal jurisdiction and those courts exercising appellate jurisdiction thereof.

(7) (a) "Electronic communication" means any transfer of signs, signals, writings, images, sounds, data, or intelligence of any nature transmitted in whole or in part by a wire, radio, electromagnetic, photoelectronic, or photo-optical system, but does not include any of the following:

(i) Any oral communication.

(ii) Any communication made through a tone-only paging device.

(iii) Any communication from a tracking device used to locate a mobile object by emission of a sound signal.

(b) "Electronic communication" specifically includes the radio portion of a cordless, portable, or cellular telephone communication that is transmitted between the cordless, portable, or cellular handset and the base or transmitting tower or unit.

(8) "Electronic communications service" means any service which provides the users thereof the ability to send or receive wire or electronic communications.

(9) "Electronic communications system" means any wire, radio, electromagnetic, photo-optical, or photoelectronic facilities used for the transmission of wire or electronic communications, and any computer facilities or related electronic equipment for the electronic storage of such communication.

(10) "Electronic, mechanical, or other device or means" denotes any device or apparatus which can be used in intercept a wire, electronic, or oral communication other than:

(a) Any telephone or telegraph instrument, equipment, or facility, or any component thereof, either:

(i) Furnished to the subscriber or user by a communications common carrier in the ordinary course of its business and being used by the subscriber or user in the ordinary course of its business, or

(ii) Being used by a communications common carrier in the ordinary course of its business, or by an investigative or law enforcement officer in the ordinary course of his duties.

(b) A hearing aid or similar device being used to correct subnormal hearing to not better than normal.

(11) "Intercept" means the aural acquisition of the contents of any wire or oral communication through the use of any electronic, mechanical, or other device.

(12) "Investigative or law enforcement officer" means any commissioned state police officer of the Department of Public Safety and Corrections who, in the normal course of his

law enforcement duties, is investigating an offense enumerated in this Chapter, and the district attorney authorized by law to prosecute or participate in the prosecution of such offense.

(13) "Judge" means the senior judge of a judicial district court of the state, any judge of the Orleans Parish Criminal District Court, or a judge designated by a majority vote of the court in writing in advance to consider applications for warrants under this Chapter.

(14) "Oral communication" means any oral communication uttered by a person exhibiting an expectation that such communication is not subject to interception under circumstances justifying such expectation, but such term does not include any electronic communication.

(15) "Pen register" means a device which records and decodes electronic or other impulses which identify the numbers dialed or otherwise transmitted on the telephone line to which such device is attached, but this term does not include any device used by a provider or customer of a wire or electronic communication service for billing, or recording as an incident to billing, for communications services provided by such provider or any device used by a provider or customer of a wire communication service for cost accounting or other like purposes in the ordinary course of its business.

(16) "Person" means any employee or agent of the state or a political subdivision thereof, and any individual, partnership, association, joint stock company, trust, or corporation.

(17) "Trap and trace device" means a device or electronic means which captures the incoming electronic or other impulses which identify the originating number of an instrument or device from which a wire or electronic communication was transmitted, except that it shall not include a service, device, or electronic means tariffed by the Louisiana Public Service Commission, used by a subscriber of telecommunicational services to receive the telephone numbers for calls placed to the subscriber.

(18) "Wire communication" or "communication by wire" means any aural transfer made in whole or in part through the use of facilities used for the transmission of communications by aid of wire, cable, or other like connection between the points of origin and reception, including the use of such connection in a switching station, furnished or operated by any person licensed to engage in providing or operating such facilities for the transmission of communications and such term includes any electronic storage of such communication, and such term includes the radio portion of a cordless, portable, or cellular telephone communication that is transmitted between the cordless, portable, or cellular handset and the base or transmitting tower or unit.

(Chgd. by Acts 1991 No. 795, §1; Acts 1995 No. 1193, §1, eff. 6/29/95.)

§1303. Interception and disclosure of wire, electronic, or oral communications.

A. Except as otherwise specifically provided in this Chapter, it shall be unlawful for any person to:

(1) Willfully intercept, endeavor to intercept, or procure any other person to intercept or endeavor to intercept, any wire or oral communication;

(2) Willfully use, endeavor to use, or procure any other person to use or endeavor to use, any electronic, mechanical, or other device to intercept any oral communication when:

(a) Such device is affixed to, or otherwise transmits a signal through, a wire, cable, or other like connection used in wire communication; or

(b) Such device transmits communications by radio or interferes with the transmission of such communication;

(3) Willfully disclose, or endeavor to disclose, to any other person the contents of any wire or oral communication, knowing or having reason to know that the information was obtained through the interception of a wire or oral communication in violation of this Subsection; or

(4) Willfully use, or endeavor to use, the contents of any wire or oral communication, knowing or having reason to know that the information was obtained through the interception of a wire or oral communication in violation of this Subsection.

B. Any person who violates the provisions of this Section shall be fined not more than ten thousand dollars and imprisoned for not less than two years nor more than ten years at hard labor, without benefit of probation, parole, or suspension of sentence.

C. (1) It shall not be unlawful under this Chapter for an operator of a switchboard, or any officer, employee, or agent of any communications common carrier, whose facilities are used in the transmission of a wire communication, to intercept, disclose, or use that communication in the normal course of his employment while engaged in any activity which is a necessary incident to the rendition of his service or to the protection of the rights or property of the carrier of such communication; however, such communications common carriers shall not utilize service observing or random monitoring, except for mechanical or service quality control checks.

(2) It shall not be unlawful under this Chapter for an officer, employee, or agent of the Federal Communications Commission, in the normal course of his employment and in discharge of the monitoring responsibilities exercised by the commission in the enforcement of Chapter 5 of Title 47 of the United States Code, to intercept a wire communication, or oral communication transmitted by radio, or to disclose or use the information thereby obtained.

(3) It shall not be unlawful under this Chapter for a person acting under color of law to intercept a wire or oral communication, where such person is a party to the communication or one of the parties to the communication has given prior consent to such interception. Such a person acting under color of law is authorized to possess equipment used under such circumstances.

(4) It shall not be unlawful under this Chapter for a person not acting under color of law to intercept a wire or oral communication where such person is a party to the communication or where one of the parties to the communication has given prior consent to such interception, unless such communication is intercepted for the purpose of committing any criminal or tortious act in violation of the constitution or laws of the United States or of the state or for the purpose of committing any other injurious act.

(5) It shall be unlawful under this Chapter:

(a) For the ultimate receiver of wire or electronic communication, or an investigative or law enforcement officer to use a pen register or trap and trace device as provided in Part III of this Chapter.

(b) For a provider of electronic communication services to record the fact that a wire or electronic communication was initiated or completed in order to protect such provider, or another provider furnishing service toward the completion of the wire or electronic communication, or a user of that service, from fraudulent, unlawful, or abusive use of such service.

(c) To use a device which captures the incoming electronic or other impulses which identify the numbers of an instrument from which a wire communication was transmitted.

(6) A person or entity providing electronic communication services to the public shall not intentionally divulge the contents of any communication while in transmission of that service to any person or entity other than an addressee or intended recipient of such communication or an agent of such addressee or intended recipient except:

(a) As otherwise authorized by federal or state law.

(b) To a person employed or authorized, or whose facilities are used, to forward such communication to its destination.

(c) Any electronic communication inadvertently obtained by the service provider and which appears to pertain to the commission of a crime, if such divulgence is made to a law enforcement agency.

D. Upon receipt of the information or evidence sought by the interception, the interception shall cease.

(Chgd. by Acts 1991 No. 795, §1, eff. 7/22/91.)

§1304. Manufacture, distribution, or possession of wire or oral communication intercepting devices prohibited.

A. Except as otherwise specifically provided in this Chapter, it shall be unlawful for any person willfully to manufacture, assemble, possess, or sell any electronic, mechanical, or other device, knowing or having reason to know that the design of such device renders it primarily useful for the purpose of surreptitious interception of wire or oral communications.

B. Any person who violates the provisions of this Section shall be fined not more than ten thousand dollars and imprisoned for not less than two years nor more than ten years at hard labor, without benefit of probation, parole, or suspension of sentence.

C. It shall not be unlawful under this Section for:

(1) A communications common carrier or an officer, agent, or employee of, or a person under contract with, a communications common carrier's business in the normal course of the communications common carrier's business, or

(2) An officer, agent, or employee of, or a person under contract with the United States or a commissioned state police officer of the Louisiana Department of Public Safety and Corrections specially authorized by the deputy secretary of public safety services in writing to

possess or use pursuant to court authorization, in the normal course of the activities of the Department of Public Safety and Corrections, to manufacture, assemble, possess, or sell any electronic, mechanical, or other device knowing or having reason to know that the design of such device renders it primarily useful for the purpose of surreptitious interception of wire or oral communications.

§1305. Confiscation of wire or oral communication intercepting devices.

Any electronic, mechanical, or other device used, manufactured, assembled, possessed, sold, or advertised in violation of R.S. 15:1304 may be seized. Upon seizure, it is forfeited to the state and may be disposed of by the state. No device shall be sold at public or private sale. Any competent judge in whose jurisdiction the device was seized or the judge of the trial court may order the device destroyed or may order it transferred without cost to the Department of Public Safety and Corrections.

§1306. Immunity of witnesses.

Whenever in the judgment of the attorney general or a district attorney, the testimony of any witness, or the production of books, papers, or other evidence by any witness, in any case or proceeding before any grand jury or court of the state involving any violation of this Chapter or any of the offenses enumerated in R.S. 15:1308, or any conspiracy to violate this Chapter or any of the offenses enumerated in R.S. 15:1308, is necessary to the public interest, the attorney general or such district attorney, with the approval of the attorney general, shall make application to the court that the witness shall be instructed to testify or produce evidence subject to the provisions of this Section, and upon order of the court such witness shall not be excused from testifying or from producing books, papers, or other evidence on the ground that the testimony or evidence required of him may tend to incriminate him or subject him to a penalty or forfeiture. No such witness shall be prosecuted or subjected to any penalty or forfeiture for or on account of any transaction, matter, or thing concerning which he is compelled, after having claimed his privilege against self-incrimination, to testify or produce evidence, nor shall testimony so compelled be used as evidence in any criminal proceeding against him in any court, except that no witness shall be exempt under this Section from prosecution for perjury or contempt of court committed while giving testimony or producing evidence under compulsion as provided in this Section. Failure to so testify shall be punishable as contempt of court.

§1307. Prohibition of use as evidence of intercepted wire or oral communications.

A. Whenever any wire or oral communication has been intercepted, no part of the contents of such communication and no evidence derived therefrom may be received in evidence in any trial, hearing, or other proceeding in or before any court, grand jury, department, officer, agency, regulatory body, legislative committee, or other authority of the state, or a political subdivision thereof, if the disclosure of that information would be in violation of this Chapter.

B. No person may broadcast, publish, disseminate, or otherwise distribute any part of the content of an electronic communication intercepted in violation of the provisions of this Chapter unless such dissemination or distribution is made to an investigator or law enforcement officer conducting an investigation into a violation of the provisions of this Section.

(Chgd. by Acts 1995 No. 1193, §1, eff. 6/29/95.)

§1308. Authorization for interception of wire or oral communications.

A. The attorney general, with the approval of the district attorney in whose district the interception of wire or oral communications shall take place, and the district attorney, with the approval of the attorney general, may authorize an application to a judge in whose district the interception of wire or oral communications shall take place, and such judge may grant in conformity with R.S. 15:1310 an order authorizing or approving the interception of wire or oral communications by an investigative or law enforcement officer having responsibility for the investigation of the offense as to which the application is made, when such interception may provide or has provided evidence of:

(1) Any violation of the Uniform Controlled Dangerous Substance Act by:

(a) Producing, manufacturing, distributing, or dispensing a controlled dangerous substance; or

(b) Possessing with intent to produce, manufacture, distribute, or dispense a controlled dangerous substance; or

(c) Creating, distributing, or possessing a counterfeit controlled dangerous substance; or

(d) Conspiring to commit any of the above enumerated offenses.

(2) The commission, attempted commission, or conspiracy to commit a crime involving any of the following offenses:

(a) First or second degree murder.

(b) Aggravated kidnapping.

(c) Aggravated arson.

(d) Manufacture and possession of delayed action incendiary device or manufacture and possession of a bomb.

(e) Armed robbery.

(f) Jury tampering.

(g) Solicitation for murder.

(h) Arson with intent to defraud.

(i) Extortion.

(j) Felony violations of the Uniform Controlled Dangerous Substances Law*.

**R.S. 40:961 et seq.*

(k) Intimidating, impeding, injuring witnesses or injuring officers.

(*l*) Any felony offense where the offense was or is to be committed against a law enforcement officer as a result of his official capacity or actions.

(m) Money laundering as defined in R.S. 14:230.

(n) Transactions involving proceeds from drug offenses as defined in R.S. 40:1049.

B. Failure of the district attorney to obtain approval for the interception of wire or oral communications as set forth in this Section shall constitute cause for the attorney general to institute, prosecute, or intervene in a criminal action or proceeding as authorized by law. *(Chgd. by Acts 1991 No. 121, §1; Acts 1995 No. 1130, §1, eff. 6/29/95.)*

§1309. Authorization for disclosure and use of intercepted wire or oral communications.

A. Any investigative or law enforcement officer who, by any means authorized by this Chapter, has obtained knowledge of the contents of any wire or oral communication, or evidence derived therefrom, may disclose such contents to another investigative or law enforcement officer to the extent that such disclosure is appropriate to the proper performance of the official duties of the officer making or receiving the disclosure, and provided that such disclosure of the contents of any wire or oral communication, or evidence derived therefrom, relates directly to the offense for which the order was granted.

B. Any investigative or law enforcement officer who, by any means authorized by this Chapter, has obtained knowledge of the contents of any wire or oral communication or evidence derived therefrom may use such contents to the extent such use is appropriate to the proper performance of his official duties.

C. Any person who has received, by any means authorized by this Chapter, any information concerning a wire or oral communication, or evidence derived therefrom, intercepted in accordance with the provisions of this Chapter may disclose the contents of that communication or such derivative evidence while giving testimony under oath or affirmation in any criminal proceeding in any court of the United States or of the state or in any federal or state grand jury proceeding.

D. No otherwise privileged wire or oral communication intercepted in accordance with, or in violation of, the provisions of this Chapter shall lose its privileged character.

E. When an investigative or law enforcement officer, while engaged in intercepting wire or oral communications, obtains knowledge of communications relating to offenses other than those specified in the order of authorization or approval, the contents thereof, and evidence derived therefrom, may be disclosed or used as provided in Subsections A, B and C of this Section.

§1310. Procedure for interception of wire or oral communications.

A. Each application for an order authorizing or approving the interception of a wire or oral communication shall be made in writing upon oath or affirmation to a judge in whose district such interception of wire or oral communication shall take place and shall state the applicant's authority to make such application. Each application shall include the following information:

(1) The identity of the investigative or law enforcement officer making the application and the person authorizing the application.

(2) A full and complete statement of the facts and circumstances relied upon by the applicant to justify his belief that an order should be issued, including:

(a) Details as to the particular offense that has been, is being, or is about to be committed,

(b) A particular description of the nature and location of the facilities from which or the place where the communication is to be intercepted,

(c) A particular description of the type of communications sought to be intercepted, and

(d) The identity of the person, if known, committing the offense and whose communications are to be intercepted.

(3) A full and complete statement as to whether or not other investigative procedures have been tried and failed or why they reasonably appear to be unlikely to succeed if tried or to be too dangerous, or that such circumstances exist that without immediate action a human life may be endangered.

(4) A statement of the period of time for which the interception is required to be maintained, which shall not exceed thirty days.

(5) When the application is for the extension of an order, a statement setting forth the results thus far obtained from the interception, or a reasonable explanation of the failure to obtain such results.

(6) A full and complete statement of the facts concerning previous applications for the past five years, known to the individuals authorizing and making the application, made to any judge for authorization to intercept, or for approval of interception of, wire or oral communications involving any of the same persons, facilities, or places specified in the application, and the action taken by the judge on each such application.

B. (1) If statements of an identified or unidentified informant are relied upon in the application as a basis for establishing that there are reasonable grounds to believe that an offense has been, is being, or is about to be committed, the application shall set forth the factual basis for the affiant's belief that the informant is credible and that the information has been obtained in a reliable manner. The informant shall be presented to the judge and be sworn to afford the judge opportunity to inquire if the statements made in the application are true. The application shall so state that the informant was presented to the judge and sworn for such purpose. This provision shall not affect the privileged character of the identity of an informant. Nothing herein shall be construed to require the identification of a confidential informant.

(2) The judge may require the applicant to furnish additional testimony or documentary evidence.

C. Upon such application the judge may enter an ex parte order, as requested or as modified, authorizing or approving interception of wire or oral communications within the territorial jurisdiction of the district in which the judge is sitting, if the judge determines on the basis of the facts submitted by the applicant that:

(1) There is probable cause for belief that an individual is committing, has committed, or is about to commit a particular offense enumerated in R.S. 15:1308.

(2) There is probable cause for belief that particular communications concerning that offense will be obtained through such interception.

(3) There is probable cause for belief that the facilities from which, or the place where, the wire or oral communications are to be intercepted are being used, or are about to be used, in connection with the commission of such offense or are leased to, listed in the name of, or commonly used by such person.

(4) There is reason to believe that investigative procedures have been tried and failed or they reasonably appear to be unlikely to succeed if tried or to be dangerous, or that such circumstances exist that without immediate action a human life may be endangered.

(5) The interception of wire or oral communications, as planned, is not reasonably expected to intercept privileged communications.

D. Each order authorizing or approving the interception of any wire or oral communication shall specify:

(1) The identity of the person, if known, whose communications are to be intercepted.

(2) The nature and location of the communications facilities as to which, or the place where, authority to intercept is granted.

(3) A particular description of the type of communication sought to be intercepted and a statement of the particular offense to which it relates.

(4) The identity of the agency authorized to intercept the communications, the person applying for the application, and the person authorizing the application.

(5) The period of time during which such interception is authorized.

E. No order entered under this Section may authorize or approve the interception of any wire or oral communication for any period longer than is necessary to achieve the objective of the investigation, and in no event longer than thirty days. Extensions of an order may be granted, but only upon application for an extension made in accordance with Subsection A of this Section and the court's making the findings required by Subsection C of this Section. The period of extension shall be no longer than the authorizing judge deems necessary to achieve the purposes for which it was granted and in no event for longer than thirty successive days or until the described type of communication has been obtained. Every order and extension thereof shall contain a provision that the authorization to intercept shall be executed as soon as practicable, shall be conducted in such a way as to minimize the interception of communications not otherwise subject to interception under this Chapter, and must terminate upon completion of the investigation or expiration of the order.

F. (1) The contents of any wire or oral communication intercepted by any means authorized by this Chapter shall be recorded on tape or wire or other comparable device. The recording of the contents of any wire or oral communication under this Subsection shall be done in such way as will protect the recording from editing or other alterations. Immediately upon the expiration of the period of the order, or extensions thereof, such recordings shall be made available to the judge issuing such order and sealed under his directions. Custody of the recording shall be wherever the judge orders. They shall not be destroyed except upon an order of the issuing or denying judge and in any event shall be kept for ten years. Duplicate recordings may be made for use or disclosure pursuant to the provisions of R.S. 15:1309(A) and (B) for investigations. The presence of the seal provided for by this Subsection, or a satisfactory explanation for the absence thereof, shall be a prerequisite for the use or disclosure of the contents of any wire or oral communication or evidence derived therefrom under R.S. 15:1309(C).

(2) Applications made and orders granted under this Chapter shall be sealed by the judge. Custody of the applications and orders shall be wherever the judge directs. Such applications and orders shall be disclosed only upon a showing of good cause before a judge in whose district the interception of wire or oral communication took place and shall not be destroyed, except on order of the issuing or denying judge, and in any event shall be kept for ten years.

(3) Any violation of the provisions of this Subsection may be punished as contempt of the issuing or denying judge.

(4) Within a reasonable time, but not later than ninety days after the filing of an application for an order of approval, the issuing judge shall cause to be served, on the persons named in the order of the application, and such other parties to intercepted communications as the judge may determine in his discretion to be in the interest of justice, an inventory which shall include notice of:

(a) The fact of the entry of the order or the application;

(b) The date of the entry and the period of authorized, approved, or disapproved interception, or the denial of the application; and

(c) The fact that during the period wire or oral communications were or were not intercepted. The judge, upon the filing of a motion, may in his discretion make available to such person or his counsel for inspection such portions of the intercepted communications, applications, and orders as the judge determines to be in the interest of justice. On an ex parte showing of good cause to a judge in whose district the interception of wire or oral communications took place, the serving of the inventory required by this Subsection may be postponed until such time as may be appropriate in the circumstances.

(5) Whenever an order authorizing the interceptions is entered pursuant to this Chapter, the order shall require reports to be made to the judge who issued the order showing what progress has been made toward achievement of the authorized objective and the need for continued interception. Such reports shall be made at such intervals as the judge may require.

G. The contents of any intercepted wire or oral communication or evidence derived therefrom shall not be received in evidence or otherwise disclosed in any trial, hearing, or other proceeding in any court unless each party, not less than thirty days before the trial, hearing, or proceeding, has been furnished with a copy of the court order, and accompanying application, under which the interception was authorized or approved. This thirty-day period may be waived by the judge if he finds that it was not possible to furnish the party with the above information thirty days before the trial, hearing, or proceeding and that the party will not be prejudiced by the delay in receiving such information.

H. (1) Any aggrieved person in any trial, hearing, or proceeding in or before any court, department, officer, agency, regulatory body, or other authority of the state, or a political subdivision thereof, may move to suppress the contents of any intercepted wire or oral communication, or evidence derived therefrom, on the grounds that:

(a) The communication was unlawfully intercepted;

(b) The order of authorization or approval under which it was intercepted is insufficient on its face; or

(c) The interception was not made in conformity with the order of authorization or approval.

(2) Such motion shall be made before the trial, hearing, or proceeding, unless there was not opportunity to make such motion or the person was not aware of the grounds of the motion. If the motion is granted, the contents of the intercepted wire or oral communication, or evidence derived therefrom, shall be treated as having been obtained in violation of this Chapter. The judge, upon the filing of such motion by the aggrieved person, may in his discretion make available to the aggrieved person or his counsel for inspection such portion of the intercepted communication or evidence derived therefrom as the judge determines to be in the interests of justice.

(3) In addition to any other right to appeal, the state shall have the right to appeal from an order granting a motion to suppress made under this Subsection, or the denial of any application for an order of approval, if the attorney general or district attorney shall certify to the judge or other official granting such motion or denying such application that the appeal is not taken for purposes of delay. Such appeal shall be taken within thirty days after the date the order was entered and shall be diligently prosecuted.

§1311. Reports concerning intercepted wire or oral communications.

A. Within twenty days after the expiration of an order, or such extension thereof, entered under R.S. 15:1310 or the denial of an order approving an interception, the issuing or denying judge shall report to the judicial administrator of the supreme court:

(1) The fact that an order or extension was applied for.

(2) The kind of order or extension applied for.

(3) The fact that the order or extension was granted as applied for, was modified, or was denied.

(4) The period of interceptions authorized by the order, and the number and duration of any extensions of the order.

(5) The offense specified in the order or application, or extension of an order.

(6) The identity of the applying investigative or law enforcement officer and agency making the application and the person authorizing the application.

(7) The nature of the facilities from which or the place where communications were to be intercepted.

B. In January of each year the district attorneys shall report to the attorney general and in March of each year the attorney general shall report to the judicial administrator of the supreme court the following information:

(1) The information required by Paragraphs (1) through (7) of Subsection A of this Section with respect to each application of an order or extension made during the preceding calendar year.

(2) A general description of the interceptions made under such order or extension, including:

(a) The approximate nature and frequency of incriminating communications intercepted,

(b) The approximate nature and frequency of other communications intercepted,

(c) The approximate number of persons whose communications were intercepted, and

(d) The approximate nature, amount, and cost of the manpower and other resources used in the interceptions.

(3) The number of arrests resulting from interceptions made under such order or extension, and the offenses for which arrests were made.

(4) The number of trials resulting from such interceptions.

(5) The number of motions to suppress made with respect to such interceptions, and the number granted or denied.

(6) The number of convictions resulting from such interceptions and the offenses for which the convictions were obtained and a general assessment of the importance of the interceptions.

(7) The information required by Paragraphs (2) through (6) of this Subsection with respect to orders or extensions obtained in the preceding calendar year.

C. In April of each year the judicial administrator of the supreme court shall transmit to the legislature a full and complete report concerning the number of applications for orders authorizing or approving the interception of wire or oral communications and the number of orders and extensions granted or denied during the preceding calendar year. Such report shall include a summary and analysis of the data required to be filed with the judicial administrator. The judicial administrator may issue binding regulations dealing with the content and form of the reports required to be filed by Subsections A and B of this Section.

§1312. Recovery of civil damages authorized.

A. Any person whose wire or oral communication is intercepted, disclosed, or used in violation of this Chapter shall have a civil cause of action against any person who intercepts, discloses, or uses, or procures any other person to intercept, disclose, or use such communications, and be entitled to recover from any such person:

(1) Actual damages, but not less than liquidated damages computed at the rate of one hundred dollars a day for each day of violation or one thousand dollars, whichever is greater.

(2) A reasonable attorney's fee and other litigation costs reasonably incurred.

(3) Punitive damages.

B. A good faith reliance on a court order shall constitute a complete defense to any civil or criminal action brought under this Chapter.

PART III. PEN REGISTERS AND TRAP AND TRACE DEVICES

(Added by Acts 1991 No. 795, §2, eff. 7/22/91.)

§1313. Pen registers and trap and trace devices, use prohibited.

A. Except as provided in this Section, no person may install or use a pen register or a trap and trace device without first obtaining a court order under R.S. 15:1315 of this Part.

B. The prohibition of this Section does not apply with respect to the use of a pen register or a trap and trace device by a provider of a wire or electronic communication service:

(1) Relating to the operation, maintenance and testing of a wire or electronic communication service or to the protection of the rights or property of such provider, or to the protection of users of that service from abuse of service or unlawful use of service.

(2) To record the fact that a wire or electronic communication was initiated or completed in order to protect such provider, another provider furnishing service toward the completion of the wire communication, or a user of that service, from fraudulent, unlawful, or abusive use of service, or with the consent of the user of that service.

C. Whoever intentionally violates Subsection A of this Section shall be fined not more than five thousand dollars, or imprisoned not more than one year, or both.
(Added by Acts 1991 No. 795, §2, eff. 7/22/91.)

§1314. Application for an order for a pen register or trap and trace device.

A. An investigative or law enforcement officer may make application for an order or an extension of an order under R.S. 15:1315 to a court of competent jurisdiction authorizing or approving the installation and use of a pen register or a trap and trace device under this Part, in writing under oath or equivalent affirmation, to a court of competent jurisdiction of this state. For the purposes of R.S. 15:1313 through 1316 only, "investigative or law enforcement officer" means:

(1) Any commissioned officer of the office of state police.

(2) Any full-time commissioned city police officer of a municipality of this state.

(3) Any sheriff or a deputy sheriff of a parish of this state which has been specifically designated by the sheriff of that parish as responsible for preparation of applications for installation and use of a pen register or trap and trace devices.

B. An application made pursuant to this Section shall include:

(1) The identity of the investigative or law enforcement officer making the application and the identity of the law enforcement agency conducting the investigation.

(2) A certification by the applicant attesting that the information sought is relevant to an ongoing felony criminal investigation being conducted by that agency, and includes in that

certification a recital of facts or information constituting the reasonable suspicion upon which the application is based.

(3) A certification by the appropriate agency head that he has reviewed the application and approves the use of the pen register or trap and trace device for that investigation.
(Added by Acts 1991 No. 795, §2, eff. 7/22/91.)

§1315. Issuance of an order for a pen register or a trap and trace device.

A. Upon an application made under R.S. 15:1314, the court may enter an ex parte order authorizing the installation and use of a pen register or a trap and trace device within the jurisdiction of the court if the court finds that the investigative or law enforcement officer has certified to the court that the information is likely to be obtained by such installation and use is relevant to an ongoing felony criminal investigation, and that the certification does include reasonable suspicion as required by R.S. 15:1314.

B. (1) An order issued under this Section shall specify:

(a) The identity, if known, of the person to whom is leased or in whose name is listed the telephone line to which the pen register or trap and trace device is to be attached.

(b) The identity, if known, of the person who is the subject of the criminal investigation.

(c) The number and, if known, physical location of the telephone line to which the pen register or trap and trace device is to be attached and, in the case of trap and trace, the geographic limits of the track and trace order.

(d) A statement of the offense to which the information likely to be obtained by the pen register or trap and trace device relates.

(2) An order issued under this Section shall direct, upon request of the applicant, the furnishing of information, facilities, and technical assistance necessary to accomplish the installation of the pen register or trap and trace device under R.S. 15:1316.

C. (1) An order issued under this Section shall authorize the installation and use of a pen register or a trap and trace device for a period not to exceed ten days.

(2) Extensions of such an order may be granted, but only upon an application for an order under R.S. 15:1314 and upon the judicial finding required by Subsection A of this Section. The period of extension shall be for a period not to exceed ten days.

D. An order authorizing or approving the installation and use of a pen register or a trap and trace device shall direct that:

(1) The order be sealed until otherwise ordered by the court, or until one hundred eighty days after the installation's authorized operation concludes, whichever is earlier.

(2) The person owning or leasing the line to which the pen register or trap and trace device is attached, or who has been ordered by the court to provide assistance to the applicant, not to disclose the existence of the pen register or trap and trace device or the existence of the investigation to the listed subscriber, or to any other person, unless or until otherwise ordered by the court.

E. The head of each law enforcement agency possessing or making application for the installation and use of a pen register or trap and trace device shall establish and implement procedures which shall provide for and ensure the following:

(1) Preparation and maintenance of such logs and records which record, after unsealing of the applications and orders, the approval of applications for installation and use of pen register or trap and trace devices and the duration thereof.

(2) That only the law enforcement agency chief officer or specifically authorized representative of the agency chief shall have the authority to authorize the installation and use of a pen register or trap and trace devices and only pursuant to court order.

(3) That no pen register or trap and trace device in the possession of the law enforcement agency shall be subject to unauthorized installation or use.

(4) That a designated sworn and commissioned officer of that law enforcement agency executes and transmits no later than March first of each calendar year to the deputy secretary of public safety services of the Department of Public Safety and Corrections, a sworn affidavit stating that, to the best of the affiant's knowledge, information and belief, all installations and uses of the pen register or trap and trace devices in the custody of that law enforcement agency have been in accordance with the provisions of this Part and further that no pen register or trap and trace device in the custody of that agency has been the subject of an unauthorized or illegal installation or use.
(Added by Acts 1991 No. 795, §2, eff. 7/22/91.)

§1316. Assistance in installation and use of a pen register or a trap and trace device.

A. Upon the request of an investigative or law enforcement agency authorized to install and use a pen register under this Part, a provider of a wire or electronic communication service, landlord, custodian, or other person shall furnish such investigative or law enforcement officer forthwith all information, facilities, and technical assistance necessary to accomplish the installation of the pen register unobtrusively and with a minimum of interference with the services that the person so ordered by the court accords the party with respect to whom the installation and use is to take place, if such assistance is directed by a court order as provided in R.S. 15:1315(B)(2).

B. Upon the request of an officer of a law enforcement agency authorized to receive the results of a trap and trace device under this Part, a provider of a wire or electronic communication service, landlord, custodian, or other person shall, if technically possible, install such device forthwith on the appropriate line and shall furnish such investigative or law enforcement officer all additional information, facilities, and technical assistance including installation and operation of the device unobtrusively and with a minimum of interference with the services that the person so ordered by the court accords the party with respect to whom the installation and use is to take place, if such installation and assistance is directed by a court order as provided in R.S. 15:1315(B)(2). Unless otherwise ordered by the court, the results of the trap and trace device shall be furnished to the investigative or law enforcement officer designated in the court order, at reasonable intervals during the regular business hours for the duration of the order.

C. A provider of a wire or electronic communication service, landlord, custodian, or other person who furnishes facilities or technical assistance pursuant to this Section shall be compensated for such reasonable expenses incurred in providing such facilities and assistance.

D. No cause of action shall lie in any Louisiana court against any provider of a wire or electronic communication service, its officers, employees, agents, or other specified persons for providing information, facilities, or assistance in accordance with the terms of a court order under this Part.

(Added by Acts 1991 No. 795, §2, eff. 7/22/91.)

CHAPTER 11. DRUG RACKETEERING AND RELATED ORGANIZATIONS

Section

§1351. Short title.

This Chapter may be cited and referred to as the "Louisiana Racketeering Act". *(Chgd. by Acts 1992 No. 918, §1, eff. 8/21/92.)*

§1352. Definitions.

As used in this Chapter:

A. "Racketeering activity" means committing, attempting to commit, conspiring to commit, or soliciting, coercing, or intimidating another person to commit any crime which is punishable under the following provisions of Title 14 of the Louisiana Revised Statutes of 1950 or the Uniform Controlled Dangerous Substances Law:

(1) R.S. 14:28.1
(2) R.S. 14:30
(3) R.S. 14:30.1
(4) R.S. 14:37.1
(5) R.S. 14:44
(6) R.S. 14:44.1
(7) R.S. 14:51
(8) R.S. 14:64.2

(9) R.S. 14:66
(10) R.S. 14:67
(11) R.S. 40:966(A)
(12) R.S. 40:966(E)
(13) R.S. 40:967(A)
(14) R.S. 40:968(A)
(15) R.S. 40:969(A)

B. "Enterprise" means any individual, sole proprietorship, partnership, corporation or other legal entity, or any unchartered association, or group of individuals associated in fact and includes unlawful as well as lawful enterprises and governmental as well as other entities.

C. "Pattern of racketeering activity" means engaging in at least two incidents of racketeering activity that have the same or similar intents, results, principals, victims, or methods of commission or otherwise are interrelated by distinguishing characteristics and are not isolated incidents, provided at least one of such incidents occurs after August 21, 1992 and that the last of such incidents occurs within five years after a prior incident of racketeering activity.

(Chgd. by Acts 1992 No. 918, §1; Acts 1994 Third Ex. Sess. No. 72, §1; Acts 1995 No. 955, §1, eff. 8/15/95.)

§1353. Prohibited activities.

A. It is unlawful for any person who has knowingly received any proceeds derived, directly or indirectly, from a pattern of racketeering activity to use or invest, whether directly or indirectly, any part of such proceeds, or the proceeds derived from the investment or use thereof, in the acquisition of any title to, or any right, interest, or equity in immovable property or in the establishment or operation of any enterprise.

B. It is unlawful for any person, through a pattern of racketeering activity, knowingly to acquire or maintain, directly or indirectly, any interest in or control of any enterprise or immovable property.

C. It is unlawful for any person employed by, or associated with, any enterprise knowingly to conduct or participate in, directly or indirectly, such enterprise through a pattern of racketeering activity.

D. It is unlawful for any person to conspire or attempt to violate any of the provisions of Subsections A, B, or C of this Section.

(Chgd. by Acts 1992 No. 918, §1, eff. 8/21/92.)

§1354. Penalties.

A. Any person who violates any provision of R.S. 15:1353 shall be fined not more than one million dollars, or imprisoned at hard labor for not more than fifty years, or both.

B. In lieu of a fine otherwise authorized by law, any person convicted of engaging in conduct in violation of the provisions of R.S. 15:1353 through which he derived pecuniary value, or by which he caused personal injury or property damage or other loss, may be sentenced to pay a fine that does not exceed three times the gross value gained or three times the gross loss caused, whichever is greater, plus court costs and the costs of investigation and prosecution reasonably incurred. The funds received for the costs of investigation shall be remitted to the law enforcement agency conducting such investigation. The funds received for the costs of prosecution shall be remitted to the district attorney.

C. The court shall hold a hearing to determine the amount of the fine authorized by Subsection B herein.

D. For the purposes of Subsection B herein, "pecuniary value" means anything of value, including any conceivable thing of the slightest value, movable or immovable, corporeal or incorporeal, public or private, and including transportation, telephone, telegraph, film, video, tape or other communication services, or any other service available for hire.

§1355. Arrest; warrant.

No person shall be arrested under the provisions of this Chapter without a warrant, except in emergency circumstances.

§1356. Civil remedies.

A. (1) All property, immovable or movable, including money, used in the course of, intended for use in the course of, derived from, or realized through, conduct in violation of a provision of R.S. 15:1353 is subject to civil forfeiture to the state. Any injured person shall have an in rem right or claim to forfeited property or to the proceeds derived therefrom superior to any right or claim the state has in the same property or proceeds. The state shall dispose of all forfeited property as soon as commercially feasible.

(2) All forfeitures or dispositions under this Section shall be made with due provisions for the rights of factually innocent persons. No mortgage, lien, privilege, or other security interest recognized under the laws of Louisiana and no ownership interest in indivision shall be affected by a forfeiture hereunder if the owner of such mortgage, lien, privilege, or other security interest, or owner in indivision establishes that he is a factually innocent person. No forfeiture or disposition under this Section shall affect the rights of factually innocent persons.

(3) The allocation of proceeds from such forfeiture and disposition shall be determined by the court in accordance with each law enforcement entity's participation in the investigation, seizure, and forfeiture process. Prior to such allocation, the costs of investigation shall be paid to the law enforcement agency conducting the investigation and twenty-five percent of the proceeds, including the costs of prosecution shall be paid to the district attorney's six percent fund, or in parishes where no such fund exists, to the district attorney's office. The court shall make an allocation of the remaining seventy-five percent of the proceeds based on the following determination:

(a) When more than one law enforcement agency has equally participated in the management of the investigation, seizure, and forfeiture, the proceeds shall be allocated equally among them.

(b) When one law enforcement agency has conducted or substantially conducted the investigation, the proceeds shall be allocated to such agency, with actual vouchered costs reimbursed to the other agencies, not to exceed ten per cent of the proceeds allocated to the primary law enforcement agency.

B. Property subject to forfeiture under this Section may be seized by a law enforcement officer upon court process. Seizure without court process may be made if:

(1) The seizure is incident to a lawful arrest or search.

(2) The property subject to seizure has been the subject of a prior judgment in favor of the state in a forfeiture proceeding based upon this Section.

C. In the event of a seizure under Subsection B of this Section, a forfeiture proceeding shall be instituted promptly. Property taken or detained under this Section shall not be subject to sequestration or attachment but is deemed to be in the custody of the law enforcement officer making the seizure, subject only to the order of the court. When property is seized under this Section, pending forfeiture and final disposition, the law enforcement officer making the seizure may:

(1) Place the property under seal;

(2) Remove the property to a place designated by the court; or

(3) Request another agency authorized by law to take custody of the property and remove it to an appropriate location.

D. The district attorney may institute civil proceedings under this Section. In any action brought under this Section, the district court shall proceed as soon as practicable to the hearing and determination. Pending final determination, the court may at any time enter such injunctions or restraining orders or take such actions, including the acceptance of satisfactory performance bonds, as the court may deem proper.

E. Any person who is injured by reason of any violation of the provisions of R.S. 15:1353 shall have a cause of action against any person engaged in a drug racketeering activity who violates a provision of R.S 15:1353. Such injured person shall be entitled to recover three times the actual damages sustained or ten thousand dollars, whichever is greater. Such person shall also recover attorneys' fees in the trial and appellate courts and costs of investigation and litigation reasonably incurred.

F. A final judgment or decree rendered in favor of the state in any criminal proceeding shall preclude the defendant from denying the essential facts established in that proceeding in any subsequent civil action.

G. The district attorney may upon timely application intervene in any civil action or proceeding brought under Subsection E herein if he certifies that in his opinion the action or proceeding is of general public importance. In such action or proceeding, the state shall be entitled to the same relief as if the district attorney had instituted the action or proceeding.

H. Notwithstanding any other provision of law, a criminal or civil action or proceeding under this Chapter may be commenced at any time within five years after the conduct in violation of a provision of this Chapter terminates or the cause of action accrues. If a criminal prosecution or civil action is brought under the provisions of this Chapter, the running of the period prescribed by this Section with respect to any cause of action arising under Subsection E of this Section which is based in whole or in part upon any matter complained of in any such prosecution or action shall be suspended during the pendency of such prosecution or action and for two years following its termination.

I. The application of one civil remedy under any provision of this Chapter shall not preclude the application of any other remedy, civil or criminal, under this Chapter or any other provision of law. Civil remedies under this Chapter are supplemental and not mutually exclusive.

J. Violations of the provisions of R.S. 15:1353 shall be treated as civil offenses or quasi offenses for the purpose of determining the proper venue for all civil actions instituted under this Section.

K. If two or more defendants have violated the provisions of R.S. 15:1353 they shall be liable in solido for all damages, attorney's fees, and costs of investigation and litigation.

CHAPTER 12. CRIMINAL STREET GANGS

(Added by Acts 1990 No. 230, §1, eff. 9/7/90.)

§1401. Citation.

This chapter shall be known and may be cited as the "Louisiana Street Terrorism Enforcement and Prevention Act". *(Added by Acts 1990 No. 230, §1, eff. 9/7/90.)*

§1402. Legislative findings and declaration.

A. The legislature hereby finds and declares that it is the right of every person, regardless of race, color, creed, religion, national origin, sex, age, or handicap, to be secure and protected from fear, intimidation, and physical harm caused by the activities of violent groups and individuals. It is not the intent of this Chapter to interfere with the constitutional exercise of the protected rights of freedom of expression and association. The legislature hereby recognizes the right of every citizen to harbor and constitutionally express beliefs on any lawful subject whatsoever, to associate lawfully with others who share similar beliefs, to petition lawfully constituted authority for a redress of perceived grievances, and to participate in the electoral process.

B. The legislature further finds that the state of Louisiana is in a state of crisis, which has been caused by violent street gangs whose members threaten, terrorize, and commit a multitude of crimes against the peaceful citizens of their neighborhoods. These activities, both individually and collectively, present a clear and present danger to public order and safety and are not constitutionally protected. The legislature finds that there are many criminal street gangs and gang members operating in Louisiana, and that the number of gang-related crimes is increasing. It is the intent of the legislature in enacting this Chapter to seek the eradication of criminal activity by street gangs by focusing upon patterns of criminal gang activity and upon the organized nature of street gangs, which together are the chief source of terror created by street gangs. The legislature also finds that an effective means of punishing and deterring the criminal activities of street gangs is through the elimination of the availability to criminal street gangs of premises, often referred to as crack houses, which are used almost exclusively for the commission of a pattern of criminal gang activity to the detriment of the law-abiding citizens of our state.

(Added by Acts 1990 No. 230, §1, eff. 9/7/90.)

§1403. Criminal street gangs and patterns of criminal street gang activity; prohibitions and criminal penalties.

A. Any person who intentionally directs, participates, conducts, furthers, or assists in the commission of a pattern of criminal gang activity as defined in this Chapter shall be punished by imprisonment for not less than one year nor more than one-half of the maximum term of imprisonment provided for an underlying offense committed in a pattern of criminal gang activity and may be fined an amount not to exceed ten thousand dollars. Any sentence of imprisonment imposed pursuant to this Section shall be in addition and consecutive to any sentence imposed for an underlying offense committed in the pattern of criminal gang activity.

B. Any person who is convicted of a felony or an attempted felony which is committed for the benefit of, at the direction of, or in association with any criminal street gang, with the intent to promote, further, or assist in the affairs of a criminal gang, shall, upon conviction of that felony, in addition and consecutive to the punishment prescribed for the felony or attempted felony of which he or she has been convicted, be imprisoned for not less than one year nor more than one-half of the maximum term of imprisonment provided for that offense.

C. Any person who is convicted of an offense other than a felony which is committed for the benefit of, at the direction of, or in association with, any criminal street gang, with the specific intent to promote, further, or assist in any criminal conduct or enterprise by gang members, shall, in addition and consecutive to the penalty provided for that offense, be imprisoned for an additional period of six months.

D. The court may elect top suspend all or a part of any additional mandatory punishment or enhanced punishment provided for in this Chapter only in an unusual case where the interests of justice would best be served, and if the court specifies on the record and enters into the minutes the circumstances and reasons that the interests of justice would best be served by that suspension of punishment.

(Added by Acts 1990 No. 230, §1, eff. 9/7/90.)

§1404. Definitions.

A. As used in this Chapter, "criminal street gang" means any ongoing organization, association, or group of three or more persons, whether formal or informal, which has as one of its primary activities the commission of one or more of the criminal acts enumerated in Paragraphs (1) through (8) of Subsection B of this Section or which has a common name or common identifying sign or symbol, whose members individually or collectively engage in or have engaged in a pattern of criminal gang activity.

B. As used in this Chapter, "pattern of criminal gang activity" means the commission or attempted commission of two or more of the following offenses, provided at least one of those offenses occurred after September 7, 1990 and the last of those offenses occurred within three years after a prior offense, and the offenses are committed on separate occasions or by two or more persons:

(1) Aggravated battery or second degree battery as defined in R.S. 14:34 and R.S. 14:34.1.

(2) Armed robbery as defined in R.S. 14:64.

(3) First or second degree murder or manslaughter, as defined in R.S. 14:30, 30.1, and 31.

(4) The sale, possession for sale, transportation, manufacture, offer for sale, or offer to manufacture controlled substances, as defined in R.S. 40:961 et seq.

(5) Illegal use of weapons or dangerous instrumentalities, as defined in R.S. 14:94.

(6) Aggravated arson as defined in R.S. 14:51.

(7) Intimidating, impeding, or injuring witnesses; or injuring officers, as defined in R.S. 14:129.1.

(8) Theft, as defined in R.S. 14:67, of any vehicle, trailer, or vessel.

(Added by Acts 1990 No. 230, §1, eff. 9/7/90.)

§1405. Premises used by criminal street gang; nuisances; actions for injunction, abatement, and damages; other remedies for unlawful use; exceptions.

A. Every private building or place used by members of a criminal street gang for the commission of a pattern of criminal gang activity is a nuisance and may be the subject of an injunction or cause of action for damages or for abatement of the nuisance as provided for in this Chapter.

B. Any person may file a petition for injunctive relief with the appropriate court seeking eviction from or closure of any premises used for commission of a pattern of criminal gang activity by a criminal street gang. Upon proof by the plaintiff that the premises are being used by members of a criminal street gang for the commission of a pattern of criminal gang activity, the court may order the owner of record or the lessee of the premises to remove or evict the persons from the premises and order the premises sealed, prohibit further use of the premises, or enter such order as may be necessary to prohibit the premises from being used for the commission of a pattern of criminal gang activity and to abate the nuisance.

C. Any action for injunction, damages, abatement, or other relief filed pursuant to this Section shall proceed according to the provisions of the Louisiana Code of Civil Procedure.

D. The court shall not issue an injunction or assess a civil penalty against any owner of record or the lessee of the private building or place, unless that person knew or should have known or had been notified of the use of the premises for a pattern of criminal gang activity. Any injunctive relief other than that specifically authorized in Subsection F of this Section shall be limited to that which is necessary to protect the health and safety of the residents or the public or that which is necessary to prevent further criminal activity. In addition to any other damages or injunction awarded, the court may assess a civil penalty not to exceed five thousand dollars against any or all of the defendants, as provided in Paragraph F(4) of this Section.

E. A petition for injunction shall not be filed until thirty days after notice of the unlawful use or criminal conduct has been provided to the owner of record or the lessee, by mail, return receipt requested, postage prepaid, to the last known address, or by personal service. If the premises are abandoned or closed, or if the whereabouts of the owner of record or lessee is unknown, all notices, process, pleadings, and orders required to be delivered or served under this Section may be attached to a door of the premises, and this shall have the same effect as personal service on the owner of record or lessee. No injunctive relief authorized by Subsection F of this Section shall be issued in the form of a temporary restraining order.

F. If the court has previously issued injunctive relief ordering the owner of record or the lessee of the premises to close the premises or otherwise to keep the premises from being used for the commission of a pattern of criminal gang activity, the court, upon proof of failure to comply with the terms of the injunction and that the premises continue to be used for the commission of a pattern of criminal gang activity, may do one or more of the following:

(1) Order the premises demolished and cleared at the cost of the owner.

(2) Order the premises sold at public auction and the proceeds from the sale, minus the costs of the sale and the expenses of bringing the action, delivered to the owner.

(3) Order the defendant to pay damages to persons or local governing authorities who have been damaged or injured or have incurred expense as a result of the defendant's failure to take reasonable steps or precautions to comply with the terms of any injunction issued pursuant to the provisions of this Chapter.

(4) Assess a civil penalty not to exceed five thousand dollars against the defendant based upon the severity of the nuisance and its duration. In establishing the amount of any civil penalty, the court shall consider all of the following factors:

(a) The actions taken by the defendant to mitigate or correct the problem at the private building or place or the reasons why no such action was taken.

(b) The failure of the plaintiff to provide notice as required by Subsection E.

(c) Any other factor deemed by the court to be relevant.

G. No nonprofit or charitable organization, which is conducting its affairs with ordinary care or skill, and no governmental entity shall be enjoined pursuant to the provisions of this Chapter.

H. Nothing in this Chapter shall preclude any aggrieved person from seeking any other remedy provided by law.

(Added by Acts 1990 No. 230, §1; chgd. by Acts 1994 Third Ex. Sess. No. 97, §1, eff. 7/7/94.)

§1405.1. Civil cause of action by state and political subdivisions against criminal street gangs.

A. A civil cause of action is hereby created in favor of the state of Louisiana, a parish, or municipality or other political subdivision, or an agency of any of them, sustaining any damage, impairment, or harm whatsoever, proximately caused by the commission of a pattern of criminal gang activity as defined in this Chapter. The cause of action created by this Section shall lie against any criminal street gang, as defined in this Chapter, and any person who intentionally directs, participates, conducts, furthers, or assists in the commission of a pattern of criminal gang activity.

B. Any action for injunction, damages, or other relief filed pursuant to this Section shall proceed according to the provisions of the Louisiana Code of Civil Procedure, except as otherwise specifically provided in this Section.

C. For purposes of venue, an action under this Section shall be considered as an action for the recovery of damages for an offense or quasi offense, and Code of Civil Procedure Article 74 is applicable. For purposes of service of process, service of process upon any member of a criminal street gang or any person representing him by appointment of court, operation of law, or mandate, shall constitute adequate service upon a criminal street gang.
(Chgd. by Acts 1993 No. 76, §1, eff. 8/15/93.)

§1405.2. Possession of firearms, ammunition, and dangerous weapons by criminal street gangs; forfeiture.

A. Any firearm, ammunition to be used in a firearm, or dangerous weapon in the possession of a member of a criminal street gang as defined by R.S. 15:1404, may be seized by any law enforcement agency or peace officer, when the law enforcement agency or peace officer reasonably believes that the firearm, ammunition to be used in a firearm, or dangerous weapon is or will be used in the commission of a pattern of criminal gang activity.

B. The district attorney shall initiate, in a civil action, forfeiture proceedings by petition in the district courts as to any property seized pursuant to the provisions of this Section within ninety days of seizure. The district attorney shall provide notice of the filing of the petition to those members of the gang who become known to law enforcement officials as a result of the seizure and any related arrests, and to any person learned by law enforcement officials to be the owner of any of the property involved. After initial notice of the filing of the petition, the court shall assure that all persons so notified continue to receive notice of all subsequent proceedings related to the property.

C. Any person who claims an interest in any seized property shall, in order to assert a claim that the property should not be forfeited, file a notice with the court, without necessity of paying costs, of the intent to establish either of the following:

(1) That the persons asserting the claim did not know and could not have known of its use in the commission of a pattern of criminal gang activity.

(2) That the law enforcement officer lacked the requisite reasonable belief that the property was or would be used in the commission of a pattern of criminal gang activity.

D. In any hearings held and determinations made pursuant to this Section, the court may receive and consider, in making any determination of reasonable cause, all evidence admissible in determining reasonable cause at a preliminary hearing or by a judge pursuant to C.Cr.P. Art. 162 together with inferences therefrom.

E. An acquittal or dismissal in a criminal proceeding shall not preclude civil proceedings under this Section; however, for good cause shown, on motion by the district attorney, the court may stay civil forfeiture proceedings during the criminal trial for a related criminal indictment or information alleging a violation of this Section. Such a stay shall not be available pending an appeal.

F. Except as otherwise provided by this Section, all proceedings hereunder shall be governed by the provisions of the Louisiana Code of Civil Procedure. Additionally, any action under the provisions of the Section may be consolidated with any other action or proceeding pursuant to the Section relating to the same property on motion of the district attorney.

G. The issue shall be determined by the court alone, and the hearing on the claim shall be held within sixty days after service of the petition unless continued for good cause. The district attorney shall have the initial burden of showing the existence of probable cause for forfeiture of the property. If the state shows probable cause, the claimant has the burden of showing by a preponderance of the evidence that the claimant's interest in the property is not subject to forfeiture.

H. Any person who asserts a successful claim in accordance with Subsection C of this Section, shall be awarded the seized property by the court. All property as to which no claim is filed, or as to which no successful claim is made, may be destroyed, sold at a private sale, retained for use by the seizing agency, or transferred without charge to any law enforcement agency of the state for use by it.
(Chgd. by Acts 1993 No. 439, §1, eff. 8/15/93.)

§1406. Mutual aid activities; labor organizations.

This Chapter does not apply to employees engaged in collective bargaining activities for their mutual aid and protection, or the activities of labor organizations or their members or agents. *(Added by Acts 1990 No. 230, §1, eff. 9/7/90.)*

§1407. Local laws; no preemption.

Nothing in this Chapter shall prevent the governing authority of a local governmental subdivision from adopting and enforcing ordinances consistent with this Chapter relating to gangs and gang violence. When local ordinances duplicate or supplement this Chapter, this Chapter shall be construed as providing alternative remedies and not as preempting the field. *(Added by Acts 1990 No. 230, §1, eff. 9/7/90.)*

CHAPTER 13. JUVENILE DELINQUENCY AND GANG PREVENTION

(Added by Acts 1993 No. 461, §1, eff. 8/15/93.)

§1421. Short Title.

This chapter may be cited as the "Juvenile Delinquency and Gang Prevention Act of 1993". *(Added by Acts 1993 No. 461, §1, eff. 8/15/95.)*

§1422. Legislative findings and declaration.

The legislature recognizes that, despite the large investment of resources committed to address the needs of the criminal justice system of this state, the crime rate continues to increase, overcrowding the state's juvenile detention centers, jails, and prisons and placing the state in jeopardy of being unable to effectively manage these facilities. The economic cost of crime to the state continues to drain existing resources, and the cost to victims, both economic and psychological, is traumatic and tragic. The legislature further recognizes that many adults in the criminal justice system were once delinquents in the juvenile justice system. The legislature also recognizes that the most effective juvenile delinquency programs are programs that not only prevent children from entering the juvenile justice system, but also meet local community needs and have substantial community involvement and support. Therefore, it is the belief of the legislature that one of the best investments of the scarce resources available to combat crime is in the prevention of delinquency with special emphasis on youth and street gang prevention. Juvenile involvement in gang activity is becoming more prevalent in certain areas of this state and continues to break down family and community support systems. The legislature recognizes that youth and street gangs may best be viewed as a symptom of underlying social and economic problems that reach far beyond the usual alienation found in youth subcultures in urban areas. The existence of an urban underclass, with its attendant socially disorganized and fragmented living conditions, gives rise to many social pathologies, of which the gang problem is just one. Youth and street gangs are symptomatic of many of the same social and economic problems as adult crime: substance abuse, alcoholism, mental illness, homelessness, unemployment, and multigeneration "welfare families" living in hopelessness and despair. The lure of juveniles into gangs stems from many factors, including extensive geographic mobility, rapid urbanization and population growth, substantial pockets of poverty, unemployment, increasing rates of dropouts and expulsions, a rich racial and ethnic mix, and a transient population of youth. Consequently, it is the intent of the legislature to authorize in each of the eight law enforcement planning districts the development of a comprehensive delinquency prevention plan, to be included in the state juvenile justice and delinquency prevention plan, including gang prevention where appropriate. It is further the intent of the legislature that cooperative agreements be developed among parishes within and between those districts and public and private agencies to implement such plans through effective local programs aimed at reducing juvenile crime and gangs and increasing the number of juveniles engaged in positive alternatives to crime. *(Added by Acts 1993 No. 461, §1, eff. 8/15/95.)*

§1423. Definitions.

In this Chapter, the following definitions apply:

(1) "Commission" means the Louisiana Commission on Law Enforcement and Administration of Criminal Justice.

(2) "Delinquency prevention programs" means programs designed for the purpose of reducing delinquent acts, including youth and street gang activity, and juvenile arrests. The term includes diversionary or mediation programs and community service work or other treatment available subsequent to the commission of a delinquent act.

(3) "Judicial administrator" means the judicial administrator of the judicial district and in those districts without a judicial administrator a person designated by the chief judge of the district.

(4) "Law Enforcement Planning District" means the eight districts established pursuant to R.S. 15:209 through 1210.

(5) "Minorities" means members of socially or economically disadvantaged groups, including Blacks, Hispanics, and Native Americans.

(Added by Acts 1993 No. 461, §1, eff. 8/15/95.)

§1424. Juvenile delinquency and gang prevention advisory boards; membership.

A. Within each law enforcement planning district advisory council a juvenile delinquency and gang prevention advisory board shall be established consisting of at least eleven members, at least three of whom shall be minorities. The chairman of the Louisiana Commission on Law Enforcement or his designee shall serve as a member and shall appoint at least four members representing child advocates in the community, business leaders, parents, and a student attending high school.

B. Each advisory board shall also include the following representatives:

(1) Two law enforcement officials appointed by the chairman of the Louisiana Commission on Law Enforcement from a list submitted by the Louisiana Sheriff's Association and the Louisiana Association of Chiefs of Police.

(2) An assistant district attorney assigned to a court having juvenile jurisdiction appointed by the chairman of the Louisiana Commission on Law Enforcement from a list submitted by the Louisiana District Attorney's Association.

(3) An assistant public defender or an attorney residing in the district who handles juvenile matters, appointed by the chairman of the indigent defender board.

(4) Two persons employed by the city or parish school board appointed by the chairman of the Louisiana Commission on Law Enforcement from a list furnished by the Louisiana Association of Educators and Louisiana Federation of Teachers.

(5) A judge who handles juvenile matters appointed by the chairman of the Louisiana Commission on Law Enforcement from a list submitted by the Louisiana Association of Juvenile and Family Court Judges.

(Added by Acts 1993 No. 461, §1, eff. 8/15/95.)

§1425. Purposes.

The purposes of each juvenile delinquency and gang prevention advisory board are to develop a delinquency prevention plan which meets the needs of each of the local communities in the law enforcement planning district, to advise the chairman of the commission on prevention and diversion programs in the district, to approve grants submitted to the governor's Juvenile Justice and Delinquency Prevention Advisory Board regarding juvenile delinquency and gang prevention program grant applications, and to act in an advisory capacity to each of the juvenile delinquency and gang prevention programs under such plan. The Juvenile Justice and Delinquency Prevention Advisory Board and the commission shall coordinate efforts among the councils and develop a comprehensive delinquency prevention state plan which shall conform to applicable federal and state laws and rules and regulations and shall coordinate funding between the two programs. *(Added by Acts 1993 No. 461, §1, eff. 8/15/95.)*

§1426. Powers and duties.

Each gang prevention council shall have the following powers and duties:

(1) Develop and implement a delinquency prevention plan for the provision and coordination of delinquency programs and services to meet the needs of the communities represented in the district.

(2) Advise and assist the judicial administrators or other local officials in the provision of optional, innovative delinquency services in the district to meet the unique needs of delinquent children.

(3) Develop, in consultation with the Law Enforcement Planning District Advisory Council, funding sources external to the commission for the provision and maintenance of additional programs and services in the district for delinquent children and their families in consultation with the Juvenile Justice and Delinquency Prevention and Advisory Board. The Juvenile Delinquency and Gang Prevention Advisory Board may apply for and receive funds, under contract or other funding arrangement, from federal, state, parish, city, and other public agencies, and from public and private foundations, agencies, and charities for the purpose of funding optional, innovative prevention, diversion, or treatment services in the district to meet the unique needs of delinquent children.

(4) Contract with city, parish, or other public agencies or private entities for the provision and maintenance of optional, innovative additional prevention and diversion programs and services in the district for delinquent children and their families, in consultation with the Law Enforcement Planning District Advisory Council. In contracting with public and private entities, the Juvenile Delinquency and Gang Prevention Advisory Board may use any funds available to it. The Juvenile Delinquency and Gang Prevention Advisory Board shall actively solicit proposals for new contract and purchase of service programs and services from community organizations, associations, and groups representing the racial and ethnic mix of the community which is being served.

(5) Programs may utilize up to fifteen percent of grant funds for audit costs, not to exceed the prorated share and shall require that each grant, contract, and purchase of service agreement entered into between the Juvenile Delinquency and Gang Prevention Advisory Board and any public or private entity to carry out any purpose or responsibility of the commission and of each program grant awarded by the commissioner. An evaluation component is required of each grantee. Evaluations must be submitted to the Juvenile Delinquency and Gang Prevention Advisory Board and Juvenile Justice and Delinquency Prevention Advisory Board.

(6) Collect information and statistical data helpful in assessing the need for delinquent children services in the district.

(7) Consult and coordinate with other districts and agencies dedicated to the provision of delinquent children services and the Juvenile Justice and Delinquency Prevention Advisory Board in order to ensure availability of sufficient services and prevent overlapping of services.

(8) Meet at least quarterly and convene special meetings at the call of the chair or the judicial administrator.

(9) Advise, assist, and approve juvenile delinquency and gang prevention program grants submitted by the local public or private entities and submit such applications as are approved for funding consideration by the Juvenile Justice and Delinquency Prevention Advisory Board and the commission.

(Added by Acts 1993 No. 461, §1, eff. 8/15/95.)

§1427. Establishment.

A. Each gang prevention council shall:

(1) Immediately after the members are appointed, elect a chair and a vice chair from among its members, and elect other officers as deemed necessary by the council. The judicial administrator or his designee may not serve as the chair, vice chair, or other officer.

(2) Immediately after the members are appointed and officers are elected, identify and assess the needs of delinquent children and their families in the district served by the council and submit to the Juvenile Justice and Delinquency Prevention Advisory Board a written description of:

(a) Existing services provided; the anticipated schedule for providing those services; and the manner in which the services are to be provided, including a description of arrangements and agreements with community organizations, state and local educational agencies, federal agencies, public assistance agencies, the juvenile courts, foster care agencies, and other applicable public and private agencies and organizations.

(b) The strategy to be used for service coordination.

(3) Make and adopt bylaws and rules for the operation of the Juvenile Delinquency and Gang Prevention Advisory Board, provided such bylaws and rules are not inconsistent with federal or state laws or parish ordinances. The bylaws and rules must be submitted to the Juvenile Justice and Delinquency Prevention Advisory Board for approval.

(4) Provide an annual written report to the chairman of the commission and the Juvenile Justice and Delinquency Prevention Advisory Board no later than October first of each year. The annual report shall contain such information as is required by the Juvenile Justice and Delinquency Prevention Advisory Board for effective program planning, for example: information on the effectiveness of delinquent children services in the district, including cost-effectiveness; detailed information on the various programs, services, and activities available in the district and the degree to which the programs, services, and activities have been successfully used; and information on programs, services, and activities that should be eliminated, continued, or added with respect to services in the district for delinquent children and their families.

B. Members of each Juvenile Delinquency and Gang Prevention Advisory Board shall serve without compensation and shall use existing available staff.

(Added by Acts 1993 No. 461, §1, eff. 8/15/95.)

§1428. Delinquency prevention plan; programs; grants.

A. A delinquency prevention plan submitted to and approved by the Juvenile Justice and Delinquency Prevention Advisory Board and the commission is authorized in each district for the purpose of reducing delinquent acts, juvenile arrests, and gang activity. Juvenile delinquency and gang prevention programs under such plan shall be administered by the commission in cooperation with other appropriate governmental organizations and public and private agencies.

B. Delinquency prevention plans that include youth and street gang prevention should be developed from a proactive policy stance regarding juveniles involved in gangs. Law enforcement should be active and aggressive against gang leaders and hard-core gang members by utilizing special gang units, centralized efforts, and statewide intelligence. Intervention programs should be used to initiate prevention efforts directed at marginal and potential gang members.

C. The Juvenile Delinquency and Gang Prevention Advisory Board may use public hearings and other appropriate processes to solicit input regarding the development and updating of the delinquency prevention plan. Input may be provided by parties which include but are not limited to:

(1) Local level public and private service providers, advocacy organizations, and other organizations working with delinquent children.

(2) Parish and municipal governments.

(3) The Department of Public Safety and Corrections, the Department of Social Services, and other departments or state agencies that provide services to delinquent children.

(4) University youth centers.

(5) Judges, district attorneys, public defenders, and the Louisiana State Bar Association.

(6) Victims of crimes committed by children.

(7) Law enforcement.

(8) Delinquent children and their families and caregivers.

D. The Juvenile Delinquency and Gang Prevention Advisory Board must develop its delinquency prevention plan in close cooperation with the commission, Department of Public Safety and Corrections, Department of Social Services, Department of Health and Hospitals, local school districts, and with local law enforcement in order to maximize services for delinquent children. The Juvenile Delinquency and Gang Prevention Advisory Board must update the plan for delinquent children policies and programs every year.

E. The commission shall develop a formula grant program based on such factors as population at risk, number of juvenile and young adult arrests, juvenile weapons and drug arrests, and other factors as may be found to be applicable.

F. Beginning with the 1993-1994 Fiscal Year, from funds specifically appropriated by the legislature for this purpose, the commission may award grants based on competitive basis. Local public or private entities interested in implementing juvenile delinquency and gang prevention programs may apply for these funds through the local Juvenile Delinquency and Gang Prevention Advisory Board. Such grants shall be awarded pursuant to R.S. 15:1429.

G. An amount not to exceed ten percent of the total appropriation may be used by the Louisiana Commission on Law Enforcement to administer the program.
(Added by Acts 1993 No. 461, §1, eff. 8/15/95.)

§1429. Grant application procedures.

A. An entity may apply for an annual juvenile delinquency and gang prevention program grant, which may be renewed for up to two additional years, if funding is available, by submitting a grant proposal for funding or continued funding to the Juvenile Delinquency and Gang Prevention Advisory Board by December 1, 1993, and by May first every year thereafter. The commission shall establish the grant application procedures, giving priority consideration to proposals which include a youth and street gang prevention component. In order to be considered for funding, the grant proposal shall include the following assurances and information:

(1) A letter from the chairman of the Juvenile Delinquency and Gang Prevention Advisory Board of the district confirming that the grant application has been reviewed and approved and that it conforms to the district's delinquency prevention plan as developed by the Juvenile Delinquency and Gang Prevention Advisory Board.

(2) A rationale and description of the program and the services to be provided, including goals and objectives.

(3) A method of identification for the appropriate clients in the program.

(4) Provisions for the participation of parents and custodians in the program.

(5) Coordination with other community-based and social service prevention efforts such as drug and alcohol abuse prevention, dropout prevention, and child abuse prevention, including hot lines and volunteers that serve the target neighborhood.

(6) An evaluation component to measure the effectiveness of the program in accordance with the provisions.

(7) A program budget, including the amount of local resources committed to the budget.

(8) The necessary program staff.

B. The department shall consider the following in awarding such grants:

(1) The number of juvenile arrests within the geographical area to be served by the program. Those geographical areas with the highest number of juvenile arrests shall have priority for selection.

(2) The extent to which the program targets high juvenile crime neighborhoods and those public schools serving juveniles from high crime neighborhoods.

(3) The validity and cost-effectiveness of the program.

(4) The degree to which the program is located in and managed by local leaders of the target neighborhoods and public schools serving the target neighborhoods.

C. The commission and Juvenile Justice and Delinquency Prevention Advisory Board shall make available to anyone wishing to apply for such a grant information on all of the criteria to be used by the commission and Juvenile Justice and Delinquency Prevention Advisory Board in the selection of the proposals for funding pursuant to the provisions of this Section.

D. The commission and Juvenile Justice and Delinquency Prevention Advisory Board shall review all program proposals submitted. Entities submitting proposals shall be notified of approval by March 2, 1994, for the 1993-1994 Fiscal Year and by September first of every fiscal year thereafter.

E. Each entity which is awarded a grant as provided for in this Chapter shall submit an annual evaluation report to the chairman of the commission and the chairman of the Juvenile Justice and Delinquency Prevention Advisory Board, and the chairman of the Juvenile Delinquency and Gang Prevention Advisory Board, by a date subsequent to the end of the contract period established by the commission, documenting the extent to which the program objectives have been met, the effect of the program on the juvenile arrest rate, and any other information required by the commission.

F. The commission may promulgate rules and regulations necessary to implement the provisions of this Chapter.
(Added by Acts 1993 No. 461, §1, eff. 8/15/95.)

§1430. Restrictions.

Nothing in this Chapter shall be construed to prevent a program initiated under a delinquency prevention plan established pursuant to this Chapter from continuing to operate beyond the three-year maximum funding period if it can find other funding sources. Likewise, nothing in this Chapter shall be construed to restrict the number of programs an entity may apply for or operate. *(Added by Acts 1993 No. 461, §1, eff. 8/15/95.)*

TITLE 32
MOTOR VEHICLE AND TRAFFIC REGULATIONS
(Complete Title)

CHAPTER 1. LOUISIANA HIGHWAY REGULATORY ACT

PART I. DEFINITIONS AND GENERAL AUTHORITY

PART II. UNIFORM APPLICABILITY OF CHAPTER; POWER OF LOCAL AUTHORITIES

SUBPART A. UNIFORMITY OF APPLICATION

SUBPART B. POWERS OF LOCAL AUTHORITIES

PART III. GENERAL PROHIBITIONS, PENALTIES

PART IV. TRAFFIC REGULATIONS

SUBPART A. SPEED RESTRICTIONS

SUBPART B. DRIVING ON THE RIGHT SIDE, OVERTAKING AND PASSING, ETC.

SUBPART C. TURNING, STARTING AND STOPPING AND SIGNALS THEREFOR

SUBPART D. RIGHT OF WAY

SUBPART E. PARKING, STANDING AND STOPPING

SUBPART F. RAILROAD GRADE CROSSINGS

SUBPART G. OPERATION OF MOTORCYCLES, MOTOR-DRIVEN CYCLES AND BICYCLES

SUBPART H. PEDESTRIANS' RIGHTS AND DUTIES

SUBPART I. SIGNS, MARKERS AND SIGNALS

SUBPART J. VEHICLES TRANSPORTING EXPLOSIVES OR INFLAMMABLES

SUBPART K. REGULATION OF CERTAIN HIGHWAYS AND ESTABLISHMENT OF THROUGH HIGHWAYS

SUBPART L. MISCELLANEOUS PROVISIONS

PART V. EQUIPMENT OF VEHICLES

SUBPART A. LAMPS AND OTHER LIGHTING EQUIPMENT

SUBPART B. BRAKES

SUBPART C. OTHER EQUIPMENT

PART VI. SIZE, WEIGHT, AND LOAD OF VEHICLE

379. Applicability; regulations in excess of R.S. 32:380 through R.S. 32:386 prohibited.

SUBPART A. SIZE, WIDTH, HEIGHT, LENGTH, WEIGHT AND LOAD OF VEHICLES IN REGULAR OPERATION

380. Width; projecting loads on vehicles.
381. Height.
382. Length; special length limits.
383. Loads on vehicles; care required thereto; penalties; definition.
383.1. Loads of loose materials on vehicles; care required thereto; penalties.
384. Trailers and towed vehicles.
385. Farm vehicles and equipment, exemption; other exemptions.
386. Weight.
386.1. Blanket oversize yearly permit; fees.

SUBPART B. SPECIAL PERMITS

387. Special permits.
387.1. Escort vehicles; permit to operate required.
387.2. Mobile homes; interstate highways.
387.3. Precast, fiberglass swimming pools and tanks; Interstate highways.
387.4. Equipment destined to or from any oil or gas facility or petrochemical complex; Interstate highways.
387.5. Special permits; authorization to travel on portions of Interstate 49.
387.6. Special permits; trucks hauling cotton modules.
387.7. Special permits; trucks hauling sugarcane.
387.8. Vehicles requiring steering axle permit; interstate highways.
387.9. Special permit; trucks hauling agronomic or horticultural crops.
387.10. Special permit; vehicles transporting timber cutting or logging equipment.

SUBPART C. PENALTIES

388. Penalties; payments.
388.1. Penalties; multiple violations.

SUBPART D. ENFORCEMENT, PAYMENT AND COLLECTION PROCEDURES

389. Weights and standards police; enforcement procedure; payment and collection procedures.

PART VI-A. WEIGH-IN-MOTION PHOTO ENFORCEMENT SYSTEM

390. Weigh-In-Motion (WIM) System.

PART VI-B. LOUISIANA TRUCK CENTER

390.21. Louisiana Truck Center; creation; purpose.
390.22. Services and assistance.
390.23. Agency representatives.
390.24. Coordinating authority; Louisiana Motor Carrier Advisory Committee.

PART VII. PROCEDURE AND REPORTS

391. Appearance upon arrest.
392. Impounding of vehicles authorized; prohibitions.
393. Persons charged with traffic violations; time for disposition, licenses, reports, and records to be sent to Department of Public Safety and Corrections, fee charged; penalties; record of unpaid traffic fines and parking fines; distribution prohibited.
393.1. Records of convictions; extracts; fees.
394. Flagrant violations; courts to give details on request of department.
395. Police officers not impeded by this chapter.

PART VII-A. UNIFORM TRAFFIC CITATIONS

PART VIII. METHOD OF CITATION

PART I. DEFINITIONS AND GENERAL AUTHORITY

§1. Definitions.

When used in this Chapter, the following words and phrases have the meaning ascribed to them in this Section, unless the context clearly indicates a different meaning:

(1) "Authorized emergency vehicle" means a vehicle of a fire department, a vehicle of the department's weights and standards police force, a police vehicle, a privately owned vehicle belonging to members of an organized volunteer fire department or fire district when so designated or authorized by the fire chief of that fire department or fire district, an industrial-owned vehicle assigned to members of a fire department or fire district when so designated or authorized by the fire chief of that fire department or fire district, a vehicle parked or stopped by elevator repair or construction personnel while responding to an elevator emergency, such ambulances and emergency medical response vehicles certified by the Department of Health and Hospitals that are operated by certified ambulance services, and emergency vehicles of municipal departments or public service corporations as are designated or authorized by the secretary of the Department of Transportation and Development or by the chief of police of any incorporated municipality. For purposes of this Section, elevator repair shall be limited to those elevators that move people.

(1.1) "Autocycle" means an enclosed motorcycle that is equipped with safety belts, rollbar, windshield wipers, steering wheel, and equipment otherwise required on a motorcycle and which has no more than three wheels in contact with the roadway at any one time.

(2) "Axle" means the common axis of rotation of one or more wheels whether power-driven or freely rotating, and whether in one or more segments, and regardless of the number of wheels carried thereon.

(3) "Axle group" means an assemblage of two or more consecutive axles considered together in determining their combined load effect on a highway.

(4) "Bicycle" means every device propelled by human power upon which any person may ride and designed to travel on two tandem wheels.

(5) "Bus" or "large passenger vehicle" means every motor propelled vehicle designed for carrying more than ten persons other than a taxicab constructed and designed for transporting persons for commercial purposes.

(6) "Business district" means the territory contiguous to and including a highway when within any six hundred feet along such highway there are buildings in use for business or industrial purposes, including but not limited to hotels, banks, or office buildings, railroad stations and public buildings which occupy at least three hundred feet frontage on one side or three hundred feet collectively on both sides of the highway.

(7) "Cargo" means the items or freight to be moved, including items placed on or in a vehicle, towed by a vehicle, or a vehicle itself.

(8) "Chauffeur" means every person who is employed by another for the principal purpose of driving a motor vehicle, and every person who drives a school bus transporting school children or any motor vehicle when in use for the transportation of persons or property for compensation.

(9) "Combination of vehicles" means every group of two or more vehicles howsoever joined together which are drawn or propelled by a single motor vehicle.

(10) "Commissioner" means the secretary of the Department of Public Safety.

(11) "Connecting mechanism" means an arrangement of parts interconnecting two or more consecutive axles to the frame of a vehicle in such a manner as to equalize the load between axles.

(12) "Controlled-access highway" means every highway, street, or roadway in respect to which owners or occupants of abutting lands and other persons have no legal right of access to or from the same except at such points only and in such manner as may be determined by the public authority having jurisdiction over such highway, street, or roadway.

(13) "Cross-walk" means: (a) That part of a roadway at an intersection included within the connections of the lateral lines of the sidewalks on opposite sides of the highway measured from the curbs or, in absence of curbs, from the edges of the traversable roadway.

(b) Any portion of a roadway at an intersection or elsewhere distinctly indicated for pedestrian crossing by lines or other markings on the surface.

(14) "Department" means the Department of Transportation and Development.

(15) "Divided highway" means any highway divided into roadways by a median, physical barrier, or clearly indicated dividing section so constructed as to impede vehicular traffic.

(16) "Driver" means every person who drives or is in actual physical control of a vehicle.

(17) "Dummy axle" means a single axle attached independently to the frame of a vehicle and so designed and placed as to indicate the appearance of and to carry a uniformly distributed load of a normal tandem axle.

(18) "Explosives" means any chemical compound or mechanical mixture that is commonly used or intended for the purpose of producing an explosion and which contains any oxidizing and combustive units or other ingredients in such proportions, quantities, or packing that an ignition by fire, by friction, by concussion, by percussion, or by detonator of any part of the compound or mixture may cause such a sudden generation of highly heated gases that the resultant gaseous pressures are capable of producing destructive effects on contiguous objects or of destroying life or limb.

(19) "Farm tractor" means every motor vehicle designed and used primarily as a farm implement, for drawing plows, mowing machines, and other implements of husbandry.

(20) "Flammable liquid" means any liquid which has a flash point of seventy degrees F., or less, as determined by a tagliabue or equivalent closed-cup test device.

(21) "Freight-carrying vehicle" means every motor vehicle designed for and used primarily as a carrier of freight transported for commercial purposes, which vehicle is licensed for six thousand pounds or more. This shall not include pick-up or panel trucks unless they are so heavily loaded with such freight as to exceed six thousand pounds gross weight and shall never include any passenger-carrying vehicle.

(22) "Gross weight" means the weight of a vehicle and/or combination of vehicles without load on all axles including the steering axle plus the weight of any load thereon.

(23) "Height" means the total vertical dimension of any vehicle above the ground surface including any load and load-holding devices thereon.

(24) "High pressure pneumatic tire" means a pneumatic tire designed for use and used when inflated with air to one hundred twenty pounds per square inch pressure or more.

(25) "Highway" means the entire width between the boundary lines of every way or place of whatever nature publicly maintained and open to the use of the public for the purpose of vehicular travel, including bridges, causeways, tunnels, and ferries; synonymous with the word "street."

(26) "Intersection" means: (a) The area embraced within the prolongation or connection of the lateral curb lines, or, if none, then the lateral boundary lines of the roadways of two highways which join one another at, or approximately at, right angles, or the area within which vehicles traveling upon different highways joining at any other angle may come in conflict.

(b) Where a highway includes two highways thirty feet or more apart, then every crossing of each highway of such divided highway by an intersecting highway shall be regarded as a separate intersection. In the event such intersecting highway also includes two highways thirty feet or more apart, then every crossing of two highways of such highways shall be regarded as a separate intersection.

(c) The junction of an alley with a street or highway shall not constitute an intersection.

(27) "Interstate highway" means a fully controlled access highway which is a part of the National System of Interstate and Defense Highways.

(28) "Laned roadway or highway" means a roadway or highway which is divided into two or more clearly marked lanes for vehicular traffic.

(29) "Length" means the total longitudinal dimension of a single vehicle, a trailer, or a semi-trailer. Length of a trailer or semi-trailer is measured from the front of the cargo-carrying unit to its rear and includes load-holding devices thereon.

(30) "Light trailer" means every vehicle of the trailer or semi-trailer type having a loaded gross weight of not more than five hundred pounds.

(31) "Load" means a weight or quantity of anything resting upon something else regarded as its support.

(32) "Local municipal authority" means every council, commission, or other board given authority by the constitution and laws of this state to govern the affairs of a municipality.

(33) "Local parish authority" means every police jury, commission, council, or other board given authority by the constitution and laws of this state to govern the affairs of a parish of this state.

(34) "Low pressure pneumatic tire" means a pneumatic tire designed for use and used when inflated with air to less than one hundred twenty pounds per square inch pressure.

(35) "Metal tire" means every tire, the surface of which is in contact with the highway, is wholly or partly of metal or other hard, nonresilient material.

(36) "Mobile home" means: (a) a trailer or semitrailer which is designed, constructed and equipped as a dwelling place, living abode, or sleeping place, either permanently or temporarily, and is equipped for use as a conveyance on highways; or, (b) a trailer or semitrailer whose chassis and exterior shell is designed and constructed for use as a mobile home, as defined in (a), but which is used instead permanently or temporarily for the advertising, sales, display, or promotion of merchandise or services, or for any other commercial purpose except the transportation of property for hire or the transportation of property for distribution by a private carrier.

(37) "Motor carrier" means any person owning, controlling, managing, operating, or causing to be used or operated any commercial motor vehicle used in the transportation of persons or property over the public highways of this state, whether as a transportation agency or howsoever utilizing said public facilities.

(38) "Motorcycle" means every motor vehicle having a seat or saddle for the use of the rider and designed to travel on not more than three wheels in contact with the ground, but excluding a tractor and excluding a motorized bicycle.

(39) "Motor driven cycle" means every motorcycle, including every motor scooter, with a motor of not to exceed five horsepower.

(40) "Motor vehicle" means every vehicle which is self-propelled, and every vehicle which is propelled by electric power obtained from overhead trolley wires, but not operated upon rails, but excluding a motorized bicycle.

(41) "Motorized bicycle" means a pedal bicycle which may be propelled by human power or helper motor, or by both, with a motor rated no more than one and one-half brake horsepower, a cylinder capacity not exceeding fifty cubic centimeters, an automatic transmission, and which produces a maximum design speed of no more than twenty-five miles per hour on a flat surface.

(42) "Multiple-lane highway" means any highway with two or more clearly marked lanes for traffic in each direction.

(43) "Municipality" means an incorporated village, town, or city created under the authority of the constitution or laws of this state.

(44) "Operator" means every person, other than a chauffeur, who drives or is in actual physical control of a motor vehicle upon a highway or who is exercising control over or steering a vehicle being towed by a motor vehicle.

(45) "Owner" means a person who holds a legal title to a vehicle or in the event a vehicle is the subject of an agreement for the conditional sale, lease, or transfer of possession thereof with the right of purchase upon the performance of the conditions stated in the agreement, with the right of immediate possession in the vendee, lessee, possessor, or in the event such similar transaction is had by means of mortgage and the mortgagor of a vehicle is entitled to possession, then the conditional vendee, lessee, possessor, or mortgagor shall be deemed the owner for the purposes of this Chapter.

(46) "Park" or "parking" means the standing of a vehicle, whether occupied or not, otherwise than temporarily for the purpose of and while actually engaged in loading or unloading merchandise or passengers.

(46.1) "Parking area" means an area used by the public as a means of access to and egress from, and for the free parking of motor vehicles by patrons of a shopping center, business, factory, hospital, institution, or similar building or location.

(46.2) "Passenger car" means any passenger car required to be equipped with safety belts by Federal Motor Vehicle Standard No. 208 (49 CFR 571.208).

(47) "Pavement structure" means the combination of subbase, base course, and surface course placed on an earth subgrade to support the traffic load and distribute it to the roadbed.

(48) "Pedestrian" means any person afoot.

(49) "Pneumatic tire" means every tire of rubber or other resilient material which depends upon compressed air for support of a load.

(50) "Police officer" means every officer authorized to direct or regulate traffic or to make arrests for violations of traffic regulations.

(51) "Private road or driveway" means every way or place in private ownership and used for vehicular travel by the owner and those having express or implied permission from the owner, but not by other persons.

(51a) "Quadrum axle" means any four consecutive axles whose centers are more than forty inches but not more than ninety-six inches apart, and are designed to equalize the load between axles.

(52) "Railroad" means a carrier of persons or property upon cars, other than streetcars, operated upon stationary rails.

(53) "Railroad sign or signal" means any sign, signal, or device erected by authority of a public body or official or by a railroad and intended to give notice of the presence of railroad tracks or the approach of a railroad train.

(54) "Railroad train" means a steam or diesel engine, electric or other motor, with or without cars coupled thereto, operated upon rails, except streetcars.

(55) "Regular operation" means movement over highways of vehicles, combinations of vehicles, and loads thereon, subject to the limitations contained in this Chapter governing maximum weights and dimensions for motor vehicles and loads thereon.

(56) "Residence district" means the territory contiguous to a highway not comprising a business district, when the frontage on such a highway for a distance of three hundred feet or more is mainly occupied by dwellings or by dwellings and buildings in use for business.

(57) "Right of way" means the privilege of the immediate use of the highway.

(58) "Road tractor" means every motor vehicle designed, constructed, or used either by itself or for drawing other vehicles used in the construction and maintenance of roads, highways, or streets, and not so constructed as to carry any load thereon, either independently or as a part of the weight of a vehicle or load so drawn.

(59) "Roadway" means that portion of a highway improved, designed, or ordinarily used for vehicular traffic, exclusive of the berm or shoulder. A divided highway has two or more roadways.

(60) "Rotary traffic island" means any circular area of ground, surrounded by a highway or roadway which is designed to prevent the crossing of traffic on four or more otherwise intersecting highways, in order to require all traffic approaching it to proceed for some distance around a portion of the island before entering one of the intersecting highways and to prevent left hand turns onto such otherwise intersecting highways.

(61) "Safety zone" means the area or space officially set apart within a highway for the exclusive use of pedestrians and which is protected or is so marked or indicated by adequate signs as to be plainly visible at all times while set apart as a safety zone.

(62) "School bus" means every motor vehicle that complies with the color, equipment, and identification requirements set forth in this Chapter and is used to transport children to and from school or in connection with school activities, but not including buses operated by common carriers in urban transportation of school children.

(a) "Type I school bus" means any school bus designed to carry more than sixteen pupils at one time.

(b) "Type II school bus" means any school bus designed to carry sixteen or less pupils at one time.

(62.1) "Seat belt" means the manual restraint system installed by the manufacturer as required by Federal Motor Vehicle Standard No. 208 which became effective January 1, 1968.

(63) "Secretary" means the secretary of the Department of Transportation and Development or his delegated or authorized representative.

(64) "Semitrailer" means every single vehicle without motive power designed for carrying property and passengers and so designed in conjunction and used with a motor vehicle that some part of its own weight and that of its own load rests or is carried by another vehicle and having one or more load-carrying axles.

(65) "Shoulder" means the portion of the highway contiguous with the roadway for accommodation of stopped vehicles, for emergency use, and for lateral support of base and surface.

(66) "Sidewalk" means that portion of a highway between the curb lines, or the lateral lines of a highway, and the adjacent property lines, intended for the use of pedestrians.

(67) "Single axle" means an assembly of two or more wheels, whose centers are in one transverse vertical plane or may be included between two parallel transverse vertical planes forty inches apart extending across the full width of the vehicle.

(68) "Single axle weight" means the total weight transmitted to the road by a single axle.

(69) "Special permit" means a written authorization to move or operate on a highway a vehicle or combination of vehicles with indivisible load of size and/or weight exceeding the limits prescribed for vehicles in regular operation.

(70) "Special permit applicant" means an individual, firm, partnership, corporation, or association making application for a special permit to transport a vehicle, combination of vehicles, and/or load which is oversize or overweight and under whose authority and responsibility such vehicle or load is transported.

(71) "Stand" or "standing" means the halting of a vehicle, whether occupied or not, otherwise than temporarily for the purpose of and while actually engaged in receiving or discharging passengers.

(72) "State maintained highway" means any highway in this state which is contained in the state highway system as defined by law or which is maintained by the department.

(73) "Steering axle" means the axle of a motor vehicle or combination of vehicles by which the same is guided or steered.

(74) "Stop" means, when required, the complete cessation from movement.

(75) "Stop" or "stopping" means, when prohibited, any halting, even momentarily of a vehicle, whether occupied or not, except when necessary to avoid conflict with other traffic or in compliance with the directions of a police officer, weights and standards police officer, or traffic control sign or signal.

(76) "Street" means the entire width between the boundary lines of every way or place of whatever nature publicly maintained and open to the use of the public for the purpose of vehicular travel, including bridges, causeways, tunnels, and ferries; synonymous with the word "highway."

(77) "Tandem axle" means any two consecutive axles whose centers are more than forty inches but not more than ninety-six inches apart, and are designed to equalize the load between axles.

(78) "Tandem axle weight" means the total weight transmitted to the road by a tandem axle.

(79) "Tandem truck" means every motor propelled single vehicle designed for the conveyance of property or things for hauling purposes and having one front or steering axle and two rear or load carrying axles, even though one of the load carrying axles is not permanently affixed to the frame of the vehicle and may be removed.

(80) "Through highway" means every highway or portion thereof on which vehicular traffic is given preferential right of way, and at the entrances to which vehicular traffic from intersecting highways is required by law to yield the right of way to vehicles on such through highway in obedience to either a stop sign or a yield sign, when such signs are erected as provided in this Chapter.

(81) "Traffic" means pedestrians, ridden or herded animals, vehicles, and other conveyances either singly or together while using any highway for purposes of travel.

(82) "Traffic control device" means all signs, signals, markings, and devices, not inconsistent with this Chapter, placed or erected by authority of a public body or official having jurisdiction, for the purpose of regulating, warning, or guiding traffic.

(83) "Traffic control signal" means a type of highway traffic signal, manually, electrically or mechanically operated, by which traffic is alternately directed to stop and permitted to proceed.

(84) "Trailer" means every single vehicle without motive power designed for carrying property or passengers wholly on its own structure, drawn by a motor vehicle which carries no part of the weight and load of the trailer on its own wheels and having two or more load carrying axles.

(85) "Tridum axle" means any three consecutive axles whose centers are more than forty inches but not more than ninety-six inches apart, and are designed to equalize the load between axles.

(86) "Tridum axle weight" means the total weight transmitted to the road by a tridum axle.

(87) "Truck" means every motor propelled single vehicle for the conveyance of property or things for hauling purposes and having one front steering axle and one rear or load carrying axle.

(88) "Truck-tractor" means every motor vehicle designed and used primarily for drawing other vehicles and not so constructed as to carry a load other than a part of the weight of the vehicle and load drawn.

(89) "Turning path" means the path of a designated point on a vehicle making a specified turn.

(90) "Turning track width" means the radial distance between the turning paths of the outside of the outer front tire and the outside of the rear tire which is nearest the center of the turn.

(91) "Urban district" means the territory contiguous to and including any street which is built up with structures devoted to business, industry, or dwelling houses situated at intervals of less than one hundred feet for a distance of a quarter of a mile or more.

(92) "Vehicle" means every device by which persons or things may be transported upon a public highway or bridge, except devices moved by human power or used exclusively upon stationary rails or tracks. A bicycle or a ridden animal shall be a vehicle, and a trailer or semitrailer shall be a separate vehicle.

(93) "Weights and standards mobile police officer" means an employee of the office of state police of the Department of Public Safety and Corrections with responsibilities and duties as provided by R.S. 40:1379.8.

(93.1) "Weights and standards stationary scale police officer" means an employee of the Department of Transportation and Development authorized to enforce the provisions of R.S. 32:380 through 389, both inclusive, and certain other specified statutes and regulations of the Department of Transportation and Development.

(94) "Width" means the total outside transverse dimension of a vehicle including any load or load holding devices thereon but excluding approved safety devices and tire bulge due to load.

(Chgd. by Acts 1995 No. 301, §1, No. 733, §1; Acts 1997 No. 297, §1, No. 1186, §1, eff. 8/15/97.)

§2. Authority of Department of Transportation and Development.

The department, as an exercise of the police power of this state, shall supervise and regulate all traffic on all highways within the state highway system and shall have the authority in its discretion to supervise and regulate all traffic on all highways within this state; promulgate rules and regulations not inconsistent with this Chapter and the general laws relative to highways and their construction, maintenance, and use, and the operation of vehicles and pedestrians thereon; and investigate the highways by utilizing surveys, traffic counts, etc., and effect methods and practices thereto, as in its judgment and experience it deems advisable.

Any regulation promulgated by the department pursuant to the authority granted by this Section or by any other provision of law shall become effective when filed with the clerks of court in the parishes in which such regulation is to be effective or upon the erection of signs on the affected highways giving notice thereof. All rules and regulations promulgated by the department relative to weight enforcement, payment and collection procedures, shall be adopted in accordance with the provisions of the Louisiana Administrative Procedure Act* and Act No. 279 of the 1976 Regular Session of the Louisiana Legislature. Such rules and regulations shall be referenced to the sections and/or subsections which they interpret or apply.

**R.S. 49:950 et seq.*

B.* The department shall enforce only the provisions of R.S. 32:380 through R.S. 32:389, both inclusive, and R.S. 47:718 and the provisions of Chapter 4 relating to trucks, trailers and semi-trailers and Part V of Chapter 7 of Subtitle II of Title 47 of the Revised Statutes and the department's regulations adopted pursuant thereto on all highways within this state and shall exercise such other power and authority as is specifically set forth in this Chapter or other laws of this state.

**So in original. No subsection A has been designated.*

C. (1) The Weights and Standards Stationary Scales Inspection Police Force is hereby created within the department. It may enforce only the provisions of R.S. 32:380 through R.S. 32:389; R.S. 47:718 and the provisions of Chapter 4 of Subtitle II of Title 47 relating to trucks, trailers and semitrailers; Part V of Chapter 7 of Subtitle II of Title 47; the provisions of R.S. 32:289; and the access laws and regulations relative to controlled access highways.

(2) Members of the Weights and Standards Stationary Scales Inspection Police Force are authorized to carry weapons and to make arrests in the enforcement of these laws and regulations, and in that regard, shall have the same authority and powers conferred by law upon other law enforcement officers of this state; however, no member of the Weights and Standards Stationary Scales Inspection Police Force shall be authorized to carry a weapon until the member has received P.O.S.T. certification training.

D. The Department of Transportation and Development shall have sole authority over the issuance of special permits as set forth in R.S. 32:387.

E. The secretary of the Department of Transportation and Development, through the office of the weights and standards police force, shall provide the personnel and equipment required to fully implement the provisions of R.S. 32:390.23 as it relates to the assessment and collection of fees and taxes of this department.

(Chgd. by Acts 1997 No. 273, §1, No. 1186, §1, eff. 8/15/97.)

§3. Authority of Department of Public Safety and Corrections.

A. The Department of Public Safety and Corrections shall enforce the provisions of this Chapter and the commissioner's regulations adopted pursuant thereto on all highways of this state within its jurisdiction and shall exercise such other power and authority as is specifically set forth in this Chapter or other laws of this state.

B. All rules and regulations promulgated by the commissioner relative to weight enforcement, payment, and collection of procedures shall be adopted in accordance with the provisions of the Administrative Procedure Act*. Such rules and regulations shall be referenced to the sections of law which they interpret or apply.

**R.S. 49:950 et seq.*

C. Members of the Weights and Standards Mobile Police Force are authorized to carry weapons and to make arrests in the enforcement of these laws and regulations, and in that regard, shall have the same authority and powers conferred by law upon other law enforcement officers of this state; however, no member of the Weights and Standards Mobile Police Force shall be authorized to carry a weapon until the member has received P.O.S.T. certification training.

D. The secretary of the Department of Public Safety and Corrections shall provide the personnel and equipment required to fully implement the provisions of R.S. 32:390.23 as it relates to the permit and licensing activities of the department.

(Chgd. by Acts 1997 No. 273, §1, No. 1186, §1, eff. 8/15/97.)

§4. Authority of departments to summon witnesses.

In administering laws and regulations relative to motor vehicles the secretary and the commissioner may summon witnesses in behalf of the state and may administer oaths and take testimony. They also may cause depositions to be taken and may order the production of books, papers, and documents. The fees for attendance and travel of witnesses shall be the same as for witnesses before the district courts and shall be paid by the state in the same manner as any other expenditure by the departments.

§5. Authority of other law enforcement officers.

All law enforcement officers of this state or of any political subdivision thereof invested by law with authority to direct, control, or regulate traffic are authorized to enforce the provisions of this Chapter and regulations of the department and the commissioner adopted pursuant hereto, within their respective territorial jurisdictions, except as otherwise provided by law or this Chapter.

§6. Authority of Department of Public Safety and Corrections to serve notices and subpoenas; procedure.

A. In administering laws and regulations under Title 32, unless otherwise provided, the Department of Public Safety and Corrections may serve notices and subpoenas by domiciliary service, personal service, or United States mail as provided in Subsection B of this Section. Personal service is made when a process server tenders the notice or subpoena to the addressee. Domiciliary service is made when a process server leaves the notice or subpoena at the dwelling house or usual abode of the addressee with a person of suitable age and discretion residing therein as a member of the domiciliary establishment of the addressee.

B. (1) The department may serve all notices and subpoenas by mailing the same in the United States Post Office, by either certified mail, return receipt request, or first-class mail to the addressee at the address most recently furnished to the department.

(2) Service by first-class mail shall include a request that the enclosed return form be signed by the addressee and mailed to the department. If a signed return is not received by the department within fifteen days after mailing, the notice or subpoena shall be served by domiciliary or personal service as provided in Subsection A of this Section.

(3) Service by mail shall be considered personal service if the certified return receipt or the return form is signed by the addressee. Service by mail shall be considered domiciliary service if the certified return receipt or the return form is signed by anyone other than the addressee.

C. The department may make service of notices or subpoenas on law enforcement officers through the law enforcement officer's ranking officers or their designated representative, which, upon service thereof, shall have the same legal effect as if domiciliary service had been made upon the law enforcement officer named therein. This service shall be made at the appropriate troop, region, or departmental headquarters of the law enforcement agency. Service may consist of individual notices or subpoenas or may consist of lists which include the officer's name and badge number, case title, and date of commanded appearance. Such lists may be served by the department by means of electronic transfer to printing devices located at the troop, region, or departmental headquarters. The ranking officer, or his designated representative, shall sign for such notices or subpoenas or indicate receipt by electronic verification code, and shall be required to notify the law enforcement officer named therein of receipt of the subpoenas or list. This type of service shall be known as departmental service on law enforcement officers, and shall not be construed to replace domiciliary or personal service on them but shall be an additional method of service.

D. For purposes of this Section:

(1) "Addressee" means the individual to whom the subpoena is directed.

(2) "Process server" means any person otherwise authorized by law to serve process, and shall also mean a chief process server or one of his deputies, which chief process server and as many deputy process servers as necessary shall be appointed by the department.

(3) "Subpoena" includes a subpoena issued for the attendance of an individual and a subpoena duces tecum.

(Added by Acts 1990 No. 319, §1, eff. 9/7/90.)

§7. Authority to operate joint weight enforcement scales with contiguous states; joint enforcement of laws.

A. The agency of the state which exercises authority over the state's stationary weight enforcement scale facilities may enter into interstate agreements with contiguous states through appropriate officials, departments, or agencies to jointly provide for the location, construction, staffing, and operation of scale facilities for the purpose of weighing vehicles and enforcement of the laws, rules, and regulations of this state and the laws, rules, and regulations of the contiguous state, its appropriate agencies, or departments.

B. The interstate agreement may authorize employees of either state to weigh vehicles under the jurisdiction of either state, issue permits, collect fees, taxes, interests, and penalties imposed by the laws, rules, or regulations of either state, its agencies, or departments, and enforce the laws, rules, and regulations of either state.

C. As part of an interstate agreement, the agency of this state may appoint employees of a contiguous state as duly authorized and empowered enforcement officers of that agency for the enforcement of tax, weight, size and load, equipment, safety, and all other state laws, rules, and regulations relating to vehicles entering into, exiting, or traveling upon the highways of this state and may allow employees of this state to accept similar positions or appointments with any contiguous state or appropriate agency or department of such state and to enforce the laws, rules, and regulations of such state, its agencies, and departments.

(1) Any employee of a contiguous state which enters into an interstate agreement pursuant to this Section shall not be considered an employee of this state, and as such, shall not be compensated by this state or entitled to any employment benefits either directly or indirectly from this state. Neither this state, nor its officers, agents, or employees shall be subject to civil or criminal liability for the actions or inactions of such persons.

(2) Employees of this state who accept appointments from a contiguous state shall not be considered an employee of that state, compensated by that state, or entitled to any employment rights from that state.

D. The agency of this state shall promulgate all rules and regulations necessary to implement the provisions of this Section in accordance with the Administrative Procedure Act.

E. For purposes of this Section, "agency of this state" shall mean either the Department of Transportation and Development or the Department of Public Safety and Corrections, based upon the authority granted to that department by this Chapter.

F. Any interstate agreement entered into pursuant to this Section shall be subject to oversight by the Joint Committee on Transportation, Highways and Public Works.

(Added by Acts 1998 First Ex. Sess. No. 37, §1, eff. 4/24/98.)

PART II. UNIFORM APPLICABILITY OF CHAPTER; POWER OF LOCAL AUTHORITIES

SUBPART A. UNIFORMITY OF APPLICATION

§21. Uniform application.

The provisions of this Chapter and the regulations of the department adopted pursuant thereto shall govern the operation of vehicles and pedestrians upon all highways within this state and other areas specifically set forth; provided, however, that local authorities may adopt local traffic regulations in accordance with the provisions of R.S. 32:41, 32:42.

§22. Persons riding animals or driving animal-drawn vehicles; application of part.

Every person riding an animal or driving any animal-drawn vehicle upon a roadway shall be granted all of the rights and be subject to all of the duties applicable to the driver of a vehicle by this Chapter, except those provisions which by their very nature can have no application.

§23. Persons and vehicles working on highways; exceptions.

Unless specifically made applicable, the provisions of this Chapter shall not apply to persons, teams, motor vehicles and other equipment while actually engaged in work upon a highway, but shall apply to such persons, teams, motor vehicles and other equipment when traveling to or from such work.

§24. Emergency vehicles; exceptions.

A. The driver of an authorized emergency vehicle, when responding to an emergency call, or when in the pursuit of an actual or suspected violator of the law, or when responding to, but not upon returning from, a fire alarm, may exercise the privileges set forth in this Section, but subject to the conditions herein stated.

B. The driver of an authorized emergency vehicle may:

(1) Park or stand, irrespective of the provisions of this Chapter;

(2) Proceed past a red or stop signal or stop sign, but only after slowing down or stopping as may be necessary for safe operation;

(3) Exceed the maximum speed limits so long as he does not endanger life or property;

(4) Disregard regulations governing the direction of movement or turning in specified directions.

C. The exceptions herein granted to an authorized emergency vehicle shall apply only when such vehicle is making use of audible or visual signals sufficient to warn motorists of their approach, except that a police vehicle need not be equipped with or display a red light from in front of the vehicle.

D. The foregoing provisions shall not relieve the driver of an authorized vehicle from the duty to drive with due regard for the safety of all persons, nor shall such provisions protect the driver from the consequences of his reckless disregard for the safety of others.

§25. Rights of owners of real property.

Nothing in this Chapter shall be construed to prevent the owner of real property used by the public for purposes of vehicular travel by permission of the owner, and not as a matter of right, from prohibiting such use, or from requiring other or different or additional conditions than those specified in this Chapter, or otherwise regulating such use as may seem best to such owner.

SUBPART B. POWERS OF LOCAL AUTHORITIES

§41. Power of local municipal authorities.

A. Except as otherwise provided by law, this Chapter shall not be deemed to prevent local municipal authorities, with respect to highways other than state maintained highways within their corporate limits, from adopting ordinances:

(1) Regulating the standing or parking of vehicles;

(2) Enforcing the provisions of this Chapter, regulations of the department and of the commissioner and local regulations adopted pursuant hereto, by means of police officers or by the use of traffic-control devices approved by the department;

(3) Regulating or prohibiting processions or assemblages on the highways;

(4) Designating particular highways as one-way highways, or through highways;

(5) Designating no passing zones;

(6) Designating routes for freight carrying vehicles;

(7) Requiring the registration and licensing of bicycles, including the requirement of a registration fee;

(8) Directing the flow of traffic by designating the places and direction in which turning movements may be made or prohibited;

(9) Establishing speed limits and speed zones, provided that no speed shall be permitted which is in excess of the specific maximum speed limits established by this Chapter;

(10) Restricting traffic on limited access highways, or, temporarily reducing the permissible weight of vehicles which may be operated thereon, on other highways, when, because of deterioration, rain, snow, other climatic conditions, or the making of repairs, the highway will be seriously damaged or destroyed unless the use of vehicles thereon is prohibited or permissible weight reduced;

(11) Erecting stop signs at particularly dangerous railroad crossings;

(12) Requiring pedestrians to comply strictly with the directions of any official traffic-control signal and prohibiting pedestrians from crossing any roadway within a business district or any designated highways except in a crosswalk;

(13) Creating additional regulations controlling traffic upon nonstate maintained highways within their corporate limits under their general police power so long as such regulations do not modify, or conflict with, the provisions of this Chapter or regulations of the department and the commissioner adopted pursuant hereto.

B. No ordinance or regulation enacted under paragraphs (4), (5), (6) or (10) of Sub-section A of this Section shall be effective until signs giving notice of such local traffic regulations are posted upon or at the entrances to the highway or part thereof affected, as may be most appropriate.

C. Local municipal authorities also may adopt ordinances regulating traffic on state maintained highways within their corporate limits, so long as such ordinances do not establish regulations different from, or in addition to, the provisions of this Chapter and the regulations of the department and the commissioner adopted pursuant thereto. In addition, local municipal authorities may adopt ordinances which supplement the provisions of this Chapter and regulations of the department and commissioner adopted pursuant thereto but only after such ordinances have been approved in writing by the department. However, the municipal ordinance may provide for such penalties as are consistent with the authority granted by the local municipal charter or state statute under which the municipal government operates and the penalties imposed need not necessarily be consistent with the penalties provided by Section 57 of this Title.

Furthermore, local municipal authorities may adopt by reference, all or any of the provisions of this Chapter and/or regulations of the department and commissioner adopted pursuant hereto with respect to any highways within their corporate limits.

D. Upon request of either the owner or the person in charge of the general operation and control of a parking area, local municipal authorities may adopt local ordinances to:

(1) Order stop signs, yield signs, or other traffic control devices erected at specified entrance or exit locations to a parking area or at an intersection in the parking area.

(2) Regulate traffic in the parking area, including regulation by means of traffic control signals.

(3) Prohibit or regulate the turning of vehicles or specified types of vehicles at intersections or other designated locations in the parking area.

(4) Regulate the crossing of a roadway in the parking area by pedestrians.

(5) Designate a separate roadway, drive, or lane in the parking area for one-way traffic.

(6) Prohibit, regulate, restrict, or limit the stopping, standing, or parking of vehicles in specified areas of the parking area.

(7) Designate safety zones, loading zones, and other restricted areas in the parking area.

(8) Provide for the removal and storage of vehicles parked or abandoned in the parking area during snowstorms, floods, fires, or other public emergencies, or found unattended in the parking area, if the vehicles constitute an obstruction to traffic or if stopping, standing, or parking is prohibited, and for the payment of reasonable charges for the removal and storage by the owner or the operator of the vehicle.

(9) Adopt additional reasonable rules with respect to traffic and parking in a parking area as local conditions may require for the safety and convenience of the public or users of the parking area.

§42. Power of local parish authorities.

A. Local parish authorities or lake commissioner shall, with respect to highways other than state maintained highways and with respect to public roads within their territorial limits, but outside corporate limits of any municipality therein, have henceforth, power to adopt ordinances regulating the matters enumerated in R.S. 32:41.

B. With respect to private roads when requested by the owner within recognized subdivisions within territorial limits but outside the corporate limits of any municipality therein, local parish authorities shall henceforth have power to adopt ordinances regulating matters enumerated in R.S. 32:41(A)(9) and provides for stop signs at certain intersections.

C. Local parish authorities shall with respect to parking areas located outside the corporate limits of any municipality have, henceforth, the power to adopt ordinances regulating the matters enumerated in R.S. 32:41(D).

PART III. GENERAL PROHIBITIONS, PENALTIES

§51. Vehicle license required.

No person shall operate, or permit to be operated, any motor vehicle upon the highways of this state unless it is registered with the commissioner, the license tax is paid thereon, and it is operated in accordance with the provisions of this Chapter and other laws of this state.

§52. Driver must be licensed.

No person shall drive or operate any vehicle upon any highway within this state unless and until he has been issued a license to so do as required by the laws of this state nor shall any person permit or allow any other person to drive or operate any vehicle owned or controlled by him upon highways of this state unless and until such other person has been issued a license to so do as required by the laws of this state.

§53. Proper equipment required on vehicles.

A. No person shall drive or move, nor cause or knowingly permit any vehicle owned or controlled by him to be driven or moved, on any highway of this state, at any time, any vehicle or combination of vehicles which is in such unsafe condition as to endanger any person or property, or which does not contain those parts or is not at all times equipped with such lamps and other equipment, in proper condition and adjustment, as required in this Chapter, or which is constructed or equipped in any manner in violation of this Chapter, and no person shall do any act forbidden or fail to perform any act required under this Chapter.

B. Nothing contained in this Chapter shall be construed to prohibit the use of additional parts and accessories on any vehicle not inconsistent with the provisions of this Chapter.

C. The provisions of this Chapter with respect to equipment on vehicles shall not apply to implements of husbandry, nor to vehicles used solely in building highways when they are temporarily upon the highways, except as herein made applicable. These exceptions shall not exclude any vehicle or combination of vehicles not used primarily for this purpose, or ordinary commercial vehicles upon which are placed removable machinery for such purposes, or vehicles designed for the purpose of evading the limitations of this Chapter.

D. No person shall drive a vehicle upon highways within this state, or permit or allow any vehicle owned by him or under his control to be driven on said highways, unless and until such vehicle bears an inspection tag showing it to have been inspected and approved as required by the provisions of R.S. 32:1301-32:1310, if such vehicle is required to be so inspected.

§54. Size, weight and load of vehicles limited.

A. No person shall drive or move any vehicle, nor cause or knowingly permit any vehicle owned, or controlled by him to be driven or moved, on any highway of this state when such vehicle is of a size or weight exceeding the limitations stated in this Chapter or otherwise in violation of this Chapter, and the maximum size and weight of vehicles herein specified shall be lawful throughout the state.

B. The provisions of this Chapter governing size, weight and load shall not apply to fire apparatus, vehicles and machinery used solely in the building of highways while actually temporarily engaged in work upon a highway, to implements of husbandry, including farm tractors temporarily moved upon a highway, or to a vehicle operated under the terms of a special permit issued as herein provided, or to trolley coaches or motor buses operated under a franchise of indeterminate permit wholly within the corporate limits of a municipality having a population of one hundred thousand or more inhabitants.

C. These exceptions shall not include any vehicle or combinations of vehicles not used primarily for such purposes, nor ordinary commercial vehicles upon which are placed removable machinery for such purposes, nor vehicles designed for the purpose of evading the limitations of this Part.

§55. Exclusion of vehicles from highways; notice required.

No person shall operate, or knowingly permit to be operated, a motor vehicle over any highway of this state from which it is by proper authority excluded, provided notice of such exclusion is conspicuously posted at the entrance to such highway.

§56. Obedience to police officers, weights and standards police officers, and traffic signs.

A. No person shall fail or refuse to comply with any lawful order or direction of any police officer or weights and standards police officer invested by law with authority to direct, control, or regulate traffic.

B. No person shall fail or refuse to comply with the instruction or direction of any traffic control device which has been created under authority of this Chapter or other law of this state.

§57. Penalties; alternatives to citation.

A. The first violation of the provisions of this Chapter or any regulation of the department, secretary, and commissioner made pursuant thereto shall be punished by a fine of not more than one hundred seventy-five dollars or by imprisonment for not more than thirty days, or both, unless otherwise specifically provided. A subsequent violation shall be punished by a fine of not more than five hundred dollars or by imprisonment for not more than ninety days, or both.

B. If the violator is other than an individual, there shall be no imprisonment but a double fine imposed.

C. (1) Each governing authority on whose behalf citations are issued for alleged violations of the provisions of this Chapter shall establish a procedure by which alleged offenders may promise, in writing, to appear in court to answer the charge or charges. The written promise to appear shall be accepted in lieu of posting bond or depositing a driver's license.

(2) Each city, parish, and district court for traffic offenses within their respective jurisdictions may also establish a procedure by court rule by which certain traffic offenses, as

determined by the court, constitute one-time-appearance violations. Alleged offenders who are charged with a one-time-appearance violation and who have not paid the fine prior to the date and time for appearance as indicated on the citation shall be presumed to plead not guilty. The alleged offender shall then, at the date and time indicated on the citation, appear in court, be arraigned and proceed to trial. If the trial is not held on the date indicated on the citation and no continuance has been granted, then the charges against the alleged offender may be dismissed.

D. Each governing authority on whose behalf citations are issued for alleged violations of the provisions of this Chapter shall establish a procedure by which alleged offenders may plead guilty to the alleged offense and pay the fine by mail; however, if the offender fails to pay the fine by mail in advance of adjudication and fails to appear at the time and date indicated on the citation, the court may impose an additional penalty in an amount not to exceed the amount of the fine for the original violation. In addition, each governing authority shall establish a procedure allowing for payment of the fine by credit cards as it may designate. However, the procedure shall not limit such payments to payment by credit card.

E. The provisions of Subsections C and D of this Section shall not apply to citations alleging that the operator of the motor vehicle was:

(1) Operating the motor vehicle under the influence of alcohol or controlled substances.
(2) Exceeding the speed limit by fifteen miles per hour or more.
(3) Exceeding the speed limit in a school zone.
(4) Driving with a suspended license.
(5) Drag racing.
(6) Cited for failure to maintain compulsory security.

F. The provisions of Subsections C and D of this Section shall not apply when the operator was involved in an accident in which a person was injured, nor shall those provisions apply when an operator is alleged to have committed the same offense twice within a period of one hour.

G. (1) Notwithstanding any provision of law to the contrary, any person who is found guilty, pleads guilty, or pleads nolo contendere to any motor vehicle offense when the citation was issued for a violation on the Huey P. Long Bridge or the Lake Pontchartrain Causeway Bridge or approaches to and from such bridges by police employed by the Greater New Orleans Expressway Commission shall pay an additional cost of five dollars.

(2) All proceeds generated by this additional cost shall be deposited into the state treasury. After compliance with the requirements of Article VII, Section 9(B) of the Constitution of Louisiana relative to the Bond Security and Redemption Fund, and prior to monies being placed in the state general fund, an amount equal to that deposited as required in this Subsection shall be credited to a special fund hereby created in the state treasury to be known as the Greater New Orleans Expressway Commission Additional Cost Fund. The monies in this fund shall be appropriated by the legislature to the Greater New Orleans Expressway Commission and shall be used by the commission to supplement the salaries of P.O.S.T. certified officers and for the acquisition or upkeep of police equipment. All unexpended and unencumbered monies in this fund at the end of the fiscal year shall remain in such fund. The monies in this fund shall be invested by the state treasurer in the same manner as monies in the state general fund and interest earned on the investment of monies shall be credited to this fund, again, following compliance with the requirements of Article VII, Section 9(B) of the Constitution, relative to the Bond Security and Redemption Fund. The monies appropriated by the legislature pursuant to this Paragraph shall not displace, replace, or supplant appropriations otherwise made from the general fund for the Greater New Orleans Expressway Commission.

H. If a person operating a motor vehicle exceeds the speed limit on the portion of a highway which is under active construction and construction workers are on site, or in the process of being repaired and construction workers are on site, the fine shall be an increase of fifty percent of the standard fine imposed.

(Chgd. by Acts 1995 No. 1036, §1; Acts 1997 No. 775, §1, No. 1011, §2, No. 1145, §1, eff. 8/15/97.)

§57.1. Failure to honor written promise to appear; penalty; disposition of fines.

A. Whenever an arrested person who was released on his written promise to appear before a magistrate at the place and time specified in a summons described in R.S. 32:391(B) fails to honor his written promise to appear, the magistrate or judge of the court exercising jurisdiction shall immediately forward to the Department of Public Safety and Corrections notice of the failure to appear, with information necessary for identification of the arrested person. Thereupon, unless the original charges have been disposed of, the Department of Public Safety and Corrections shall immediately notify the arrested person of suspension of his operator's license and the imposition of a fifty-dollar fee, regardless of the disposition of the original charge. The Department of Public Safety and Corrections likewise shall inform the arrested person that his operator's license cannot be renewed or reissued until the forwarding court exercising jurisdiction certifies that he had honored the appearance promise or paid an appropriate fine for the offense as determined by the forwarding court exercising jurisdiction.

B. Whenever the arrested person makes an appearance as required by Subsection A hereof or pays an appropriate fine for the offense committed, as determined by the court, the forwarding court exercising jurisdiction shall immediately notify the Department of Public Safety and Corrections thereof. Upon such notification and payment of an additional fifty dollars to the department, the operator's license of the arrested person shall be renewed or reissued for the purpose of this Section. Twelve dollars and fifty cents of the additional fine imposed by this Section shall be paid to the court exercising jurisdiction, to be deposited in that court's criminal court fund and to be used in the same manner as the other sums deposited in said fund.

(Chgd. by Acts 1995 No. 114, §1, eff. 8/15/95.)

§58. Careless operation.

Any person operating a motor vehicle on the public roads of this state shall drive in a careful and prudent manner, so as not to endanger the life, limb, or property of any person. Failure to drive in such a manner shall constitute careless operation. *(Chgd. by Acts 1992 No. 364, §1, eff. 8/21/92.)*

PART IV. TRAFFIC REGULATIONS

SUBPART A. SPEED RESTRICTIONS

§61. Maximum speed limit.

A. No person shall operate a vehicle on any highway of this state in excess of fifty-five miles per hour, unless a lower maximum speed is posted on the highway, except as follows:

(1) No person shall operate a vehicle on any Interstate or controlled access highway of this state in excess of seventy miles per hour.

(2) No person shall operate a vehicle on any multi-lane divided highway of this state which has partial or no control of access in excess of sixty-five miles per hour.

B. The Department of Transportation and Development shall develop criteria to determine which portions of a highway warrant a speed limit lower than the speed limits established by this Section. The criteria shall be based on an engineering study which shall consider, but not necessarily be limited to, the design speed of the road, the road geometry, the use of land surrounding the road, and the accident history of the road.

(Chgd. by Acts 1997 No. 1204, §1, eff. 8/15/97.)

§62. Maximum speed limit; certain vehicles.

A. No person shall operate any freight carrying vehicle upon the highways of this state at a speed in excess of fifty-five miles per hour except as follows:

(1) No person shall operate any freight carrying vehicle upon any Interstate or controlled access highway of this state at a speed in excess of seventy miles per hour.

(2) No person shall operate any freight carrying vehicle upon any multi-lane divided highway of this state which has partial or no control of access in excess of sixty-five miles per hour.

B. Forty-five miles per hour shall be the maximum speed at which a person shall be permitted to drive a vehicle which is towing a mobile home; however, when any such mobile home is not less than fifteen feet or more than thirty-two feet in length and is equipped with brakes or when such a mobile home is less than fifteen feet in length and is not equipped with brakes, a person may drive a vehicle towing any such mobile home at a speed not in excess of fifty-five miles per hour at any time between sunrise and sunset and not in excess of fifty miles per hour at any time between sunset and sunrise; however, if national speed limits are increased to an amount in excess of fifty-five miles per hour, the secretary is authorized to increase the maximum speed limit provided in this Subsection to a speed limit not in excess of such national speed limit.

C. No person pulling or towing upon any highway of this state, with another vehicle, any vehicle designed, equipped or intended to operate under its own power shall operate the towing vehicle at a speed in excess of forty-five miles per hour; except that a person operating a town truck meeting the requirements of R.S. 32:1711 et seq. may operate at the posted speed limit.

D. No person shall operate a school bus at a speed in excess of 55 miles per hour when transporting children, provided however, that the driver of a school bus transporting children under conditions which require frequent stops to receive and discharge such children shall not operate such school bus at a speed in excess of 35 miles per hour.

(Chgd. by Acts 1990 No. 963, §1; Acts 1997 No. 1204, §1, eff. 8/15/97.)

§63. Establishing of speed zones.

A. Whenever the department shall determine upon the basis of an engineering and traffic investigation that any maximum speed set forth in this Chapter is greater or less than is reasonable or safe under the conditions found to exist upon any highway of this state, or any part thereof, the department may determine and declare a reasonable and safe maximum speed limit thereat, which, when appropriate signs giving notice thereof are erected, shall be effective at all times or at such specific times as may be determined by the department.

B. Whenever the department determines on the basis of an engineering and traffic investigation that slow speeds on any highway of this state, or part thereof, consistently impede the normal and reasonable movement of traffic, the department may determine and declare a minimum speed limit thereat, below which no person shall drive a vehicle except when necessary for safe operation or in compliance with law. Minimum speeds so determined shall become effective upon the erection of signs giving notice thereof.

§63.1. Maximum speed limits; St. Tammany Parish and adjacent areas.

A. Any provisions of law to the contrary notwithstanding, the department shall declare the following maximum speed limits in effect on the westbound lanes of Interstate 10 in St. Tammany Parish and adjacent areas when hazardous driving conditions exist because of fog when there is visibility of one thousand feet or less:

(1) Fifty-five miles per hour from the intersection of Interstates 10, 12, and 59 west to Louisiana Highway 433 (Old Spanish Trail).

(2) Forty-five miles per hour west from the intersection of Interstate 10 and Louisiana Highway 433 to the north shore foot of the Interstate 10 bridge that crosses Lake Pontchartrain.

(3) Thirty-five miles per hour west from the north shore foot of the Interstate 10 bridge that crosses Lake Pontchartrain to one mile south of the foot of the bridge on the south shore.

B. The department shall erect signs and flags notifying the traveling public of the maximum speed limits provided for in Subsection A of this Section.

C. The department shall erect mile markers at one-tenth mile intervals on the portions of the highways listed in Subsection A of this Section.

D. The provisions of this Section shall be null and void at such time as permanent variable signs have been erected by the Department of Transportation and Development on the roads enumerated herein.

(Added by Acts 1997 No. 1022, §1, eff. 8/15/97.)

§64. General speed law.

A. No person shall drive a vehicle on the highway within this state at a speed greater than is reasonable and prudent under the conditions and potential hazards then existing, having due regard for the traffic on, and the surface and width of, the highway and the condition of the weather, and in no event at a speed in excess of the maximum speeds established by this Chapter or regulation of the department made pursuant thereto.

B. Except when a special hazard exists that requires lower speed for compliance with paragraph A of this section, no person shall operate or drive a motor vehicle upon the highways of this state at such a slow speed as to impede the normal and reasonable movement of traffic.

C. Rolling roadblocks shall be prohibited from operating on all Interstate highways in the state.

§65. Drag racing and racing on public roads; exemptions.

A. No person shall drive any vehicle upon the public roads in this state in any race, speed competition or contest, drag race or acceleration contest, test of physical endurance, exhibition of speed or acceleration, or for the purpose of making a speed record, and no person shall in any manner participate in any such race, speed competition, drag race, test of physical endurance, exhibition, or purpose of making a speed record.

B. For the purposes of this section drag race is defined as the operation of two or more vehicles from a point side by side at accelerating speeds in a competitive attempt to out distance each other, or the operation of one or more vehicles over a common selected course, from the same point to the same point, for the purpose of comparing the relative speeds or power of acceleration of such vehicle or vehicles within a certain distance or time limit on the public roads of this state.

C. For the purposes of this section racing is defined as the use of one or more vehicles in an attempt to out gain, out distance, or prevent another vehicle from passing, or to test the physical stamina or endurance of drivers over long distance driving routes on the public roads of this state.

D. Any person convicted of violating this section shall be punished as provided in R.S. 32:57.

E. The prohibitions contained in this Section do not apply to events sanctioned by local governing authorities.

SUBPART B. DRIVING ON THE RIGHT SIDE, OVERTAKING AND PASSING, ETC.

§71. Driving on right side of road; exceptions.

A. Upon all roadways of sufficient width of a vehicle shall be driven upon the right half of the roadway, except as follows:

(1) When overtaking and passing another vehicle proceeding in the same direction under the rules governing such movement, including passing lanes;

(2) When the right half of a roadway is closed to traffic while under construction or repair;

(3) Upon a roadway designated and signposted for one-way traffic.

B. (1) Upon all multilane highways any vehicle proceeding at less than the normal speed of traffic at the time and place and under the circumstances then existing, shall be driven in the right-hand lane then available for traffic except when preparing for a left turn at an intersection or into a private road or driveway, or passing or overtaking a vehicle proceeding in the same direction, if passing on the left side of it. Nothing herein contained shall be construed to authorize driving any vehicle in the left lane so as to prohibit, impede or block passage of an overtaking vehicle in such lane and in such event the vehicle in the left lane prohibiting, impeding or blocking passage of an overtaking vehicle shall expeditiously merge into the right lane of traffic.

(2) In addition to the requirement of Paragraph 1 hereof, any vehicle proceeding on a multilane highway at a speed slower than ten miles per hour less than the posted maximum speed limit shall be driven in the right hand lane then available for traffic, or as close as practicable to the right hand curb or edge of the roadway, except when overtaking and passing a vehicle proceeding in the same direction or when preparing for a left turn at an intersection or into a private road or driveway. Persons in violation of this Paragraph shall be punished by a fine of not more than one hundred dollars, or by imprisonment for not more than thirty days, or both.

§72. Passing vehicles proceeding in opposite directions.

Drivers of vehicles proceeding in opposite directions shall pass each other to the right, and upon roadways having width for not more than one line of traffic in each direction each driver shall give to the other at least one half of the main traveled portion of the roadway as nearly as possible.

§73. Passing a vehicle on the left.

The following rules shall govern the overtaking and passing of vehicles proceeding in the same direction, subject to those limitations, exceptions, and special rules hereinafter stated:

(1) Except when overtaking and passing on the right is permitted, the driver of a vehicle overtaking another vehicle proceeding in the same direction shall pass to the left thereof at a

safe distance, and shall not again drive to the right side of the roadway until safely clear of the overtaken vehicle.

(2) Except when overtaking and passing on the right is permitted, the driver of an overtaken vehicle shall give way to the right in favor of the overtaking vehicle on audible signal, and shall not increase the speed of his vehicle until completely passed by the overtaking vehicle.

§74. When passing on the right is permitted.

A. The driver of a vehicle may overtake and pass upon the right of another vehicle only under the following conditions:

(1) When the vehicle overtaken is making or about to make a left turn;

(2) Upon a one-way street, or upon a highway on which traffic is restricted to one direction of movement, where the highway is free from obstructions and of sufficient width for two or more lines of moving vehicles;

(3) Upon multiple-lane highways.

B. The driver of a vehicle may overtake and pass another vehicle upon the right only under conditions permitting such movement in safety. In no event shall such movement be made by driving off the pavement or main traveled portion of the highway.

§75. Limitations on passing on the left.

No vehicle shall be driven to the left side of the center of the highway in overtaking and passing another vehicle proceeding in the same direction unless such left side is clearly visible and is free of oncoming traffic for a sufficient distance ahead to permit such overtaking and passing to be completely made without interfering with the safe operation of any vehicle approaching from the opposite direction or any vehicle overtaken. In every event the overtaking vehicle must return to the right-hand side of the roadway before coming within one hundred feet of any vehicle approaching from the opposite direction.

§76. Further limitations on passing on the left.

A. No vehicle shall at any time be driven to the left side of the highway under the following conditions:

(1) When approaching the crest of a grade or upon a curve in the highway, where the driver's view is obstructed within such distance as to create a hazard in the event another vehicle might approach from the opposite direction;

(2) when approaching within one hundred feet of or traversing any intersection or railroad grade crossing;

(3) when the view is obstructed upon approaching within one hundred feet of any bridge, viaduct, or tunnel.

B. The foregoing limitations shall not apply upon a one-way roadway or a multiple lane highway nor to the driver of a vehicle turning left into or from an alley, private road or driveway.

§77. No passing zones.

A. The Department is hereby authorized to determine those portions of any highway where overtaking and passing or driving to the left of the roadway would be especially hazardous, and shall by appropriate signs or markings on the roadway indicate the beginning and end of such zones, and when such signs and markings are in place and are clearly visible to an ordinary observant person, every driver shall obey the directions thereof.

B. Where signs or markings are in place to define a no-passing zone as set forth in paragraph A, no driver shall at any time drive on the left side of the roadway within such zone, or on the left side of any pavement striping, designated to mark such no-passing zone, throughout its length.

§78. One-way roadways and rotary traffic islands.

A. The Department may designate any highway or any separate roadway for one-way traffic and shall erect appropriate signs giving notice thereof.

B. Upon a roadway designated and signposted for one-way traffic a vehicle shall be driven only in the direction designated, and a vehicle shall be driven as nearly as practicable entirely within a single line of traffic and shall not be moved from such line of traffic until the driver has first ascertained that such movement can be made with safety.

C. A vehicle passing around a rotary traffic island shall be driven only to the right of such island.

§79. Driving on roadway laned for traffic.

Whenever any roadway has been divided into two or more clearly marked lanes for traffic, the following rules, in addition to all others consistent herewith, shall apply.

(1) A vehicle shall be driven as nearly as practicable entirely within a single lane and shall not be moved from such lane until the driver has first ascertained that such movement can be made with safety.

(2) The department may erect signs directing slow moving traffic to use a designated lane or designating those lanes to be used by traffic moving in a particular direction, and drivers of vehicles shall obey the directions of such signs.

§80. Overtaking and passing school buses.

A. (1) The driver of a vehicle upon a highway meeting or overtaking from any direction any school bus that has stopped for the purpose of receiving or discharging any school children shall stop the vehicle not less than thirty feet from the school bus before reaching such school bus when there are in operation on said school bus visual signals as required by R.S. 32:318, and said driver shall not proceed until such bus resumes motion or the visual signals are no longer activated.

(2) The driver of any school bus is authorized to notify the appropriate law enforcement authority of any violation of this Subsection within twenty-four hours of the violation. The school bus driver by affidavit shall provide the authority with the color and license number of the vehicle involved in a violation.

(3) The appropriate authority may issue a citation to the owner or, in the case of a leased vehicle, the lessee of the vehicle involved, on the basis of this information. The owner or lessee shall not be cited if the vehicle is stolen, or if another driver is cited for the violation.

(4) Any person convicted of violating this Subsection shall be fined not less than one hundred dollars nor more than five hundred dollars or imprisoned for not more than six months, or both, in accordance with the provisions of R.S. 32:398.2, and shall have his driver's license suspended in accordance with the provisions of R.S. 32:414(A)(2).

B. (1) Every school bus used for the transportation of school children shall bear upon the front and rear thereof the words "SCHOOL BUS" in black letters not less than eight inches in height placed as high as possible without impairment of visibility, and no other lettering shall be visible from the front or rear except the words "emergency exit" shall be painted in black letters at least two inches in height and approximately located near such exit. In addition, every school bus shall be equipped with visual signs and signals as required in R.S. 32:318 which shall be activated by the driver of said school bus whenever, but only whenever, such vehicle is stopped, or is about to stop, on the roadway for the purpose of receiving or discharging school children. The driver of any school bus equipped only with signal lamps as provided in R.S. 32:318B(1) shall activate such lamps at least one hundred feet, but not more than five hundred feet, before every stop to receive or discharge any pupil; and upon stopping shall exhibit the semaphore sign or signs provided for in R.S. 32:318B(2) and upon resuming motion shall deactivate both the lamps and the semaphore sign or signs.

(2) The driver of any school bus equipped with signal lamps as provided in R.S. 32:318B(4) shall activate the yellow (amber) lights at least one hundred feet, but not more than five hundred feet, before stopping to receive or discharge any pupil, shall deactivate these lamps upon stopping, shall exhibit the red flashing lamps and semaphore sign or signs while stopped, and upon resuming motions shall deactivate both the lamps and the semaphore sign or signs.

C. The driver of a vehicle upon a highway with separate roadways need not stop upon meeting or passing a school bus which is on a different roadway or when upon a controlled access highway and the school bus is stopped in a loading zone which is a part of or adjacent to such highway and where pedestrians are not permitted to cross the roadway.

D. When, if, and on the date that the Department of Transportation and Development develops, adopts, and promulgates guidelines to establish school bus loading zones pursuant to Senate Concurrent Resolution No. 9 of the 1983 Regular Session of the Louisiana Legislature, the requirements of Subsection A of this Section regarding a vehicle stopping on a highway when meeting or overtaking a school bus and regarding the driver of a school bus activating the visual signs and signals shall be effective when a school bus stops on the shoulder of a highway for the purpose of receiving or discharging any school children as provided in the guidelines.

§81. Following vehicles.

A. The driver of a motor vehicle shall not follow another vehicle more closely than is reasonable and prudent, having due regard for the speed of such vehicle and the traffic upon and the condition of the highway.

B. The driver of a motor truck, when traveling upon a highway outside a business or residential district, shall not follow another motor truck within four hundred feet, but this shall not be so construed as to prevent one motor truck from overtaking and passing another.

C. Motor vehicles being driven upon any roadway outside of a business or residence district in a caravan or motorcade, whether or not towing other vehicles, shall be so operated as to allow sufficient space between each such vehicle or combination of vehicles so as to enable any other vehicle to enter and occupy such space without danger. This provision shall not apply to a funeral procession.

§82. Driving on divided highways.

A. Whenever any highway has been divided into two roadways by a median, physical barrier, or clearly indicated dividing section so constructed as to impede vehicular traffic, every vehicle shall be driven only upon the right hand roadway and no vehicle shall be driven over, across or within the median, barrier or section, except through an improved opening or at a cross over or intersection established under authority of this Chapter.

B. No vehicle shall cross the painted continuous center line of any multiple lane highway, except for the purpose of making a turn.

(Chgd. by Acts 1997 No. 186, §1, eff. 8/15/97.)

SUBPART C. TURNING, STARTING AND STOPPING AND SIGNALS THEREFOR

§101. Required position and method of turning at intersections.

A. The driver of a vehicle intending to turn at an intersection shall proceed as follows:

(1) Right turns. Both the approach for a right turn and a right turn shall be made as close as practicable to the right-hand curb or edge of the roadway.

(2) Left turns on two-way roadways. At any intersection where traffic is permitted to move in both directions on each roadway entering the intersection, an approach for a left turn shall be made in that portion of the right half of the roadway nearest the center line thereof and by passing to the right of such center line where it enters the intersection and after entering the intersection the left turn shall be made so as to leave the intersection to the right of the center line of the roadway being entered. Whenever practicable the left turn shall be made in that portion of the intersection to the left of the center of the intersection.

(3) Left turns on other than two-way roadways. At any intersection where traffic is restricted to one direction on one or more of the roadways, the driver of a vehicle intending to turn left at any such intersection shall approach the intersection in the extreme left-hand lane lawfully available to traffic moving in the direction of travel of such vehicle and after entering the intersection the left turn shall be made so as to leave the intersection in the safest lane lawfully available to traffic moving in such direction upon the roadway being entered.

B. The department may modify the foregoing methods of turning at intersections on highways of the state by signs directing the course to be followed by vehicles at those intersections, and no driver shall fail to follow such directions.

C. No person shall drive any vehicle through or over private property, including, but not limited to, any corner parking or driveway facility, from a highway solely for the purposes of entering another highway.

§102. Turning on curve or crest of grade prohibited.

No vehicle shall be turned so as to proceed in the opposite direction upon any curve, or upon the approach to or near the crest of a grade, where such vehicle cannot be seen by the driver of any other vehicle approaching from either direction within five hundred feet.

§103. Moving parked vehicles.
No person shall move a vehicle which is stopped, standing, or parked unless and until such movement can be made with reasonable safety.

§104. Turning movements and required signals.
A. No person shall turn a vehicle at an intersection unless the vehicle is in proper position upon the roadway as required in R.S. 32:101, or turn a vehicle to enter a private road or driveway, or otherwise turn a vehicle from a direct course or move right or left upon a roadway unless and until such movement can be made with reasonable safety.

B. Whenever a person intends to make a right or left turn which will take his vehicle from the highway it is then traveling, he shall give a signal of such intention in the manner described hereafter and such signal shall be given continuously during not less than the last one hundred (100) feet traveled by the vehicle before turning.

C. No person shall stop or suddenly decrease the speed of a vehicle without first giving an appropriate signal in the manner provided herein to the driver of any vehicle immediately to the rear when there is opportunity to give such signal.

D. The signals provided for in R.S. 32:105(B) shall be used to indicate an intention to turn, change lanes or start from a parked position and shall not be flashed on one side only on a parked or disabled vehicle, or flashed as a courtesy or "do pass" signal to operators of other vehicles approaching from the rear.

§105. Signals by hand and arm or signal lamps.
A. Any stop or turn signal when required herein shall be given either by means of the hand and arm as provided in R.S. 32:106 or by signal lamps, except as otherwise provided in Paragraph B.

B. Any motor vehicle in use on a highway shall be equipped with, and the required signal shall be given by, signal lamps when the vehicle is so constructed, loaded or operated as to prevent the hand and arm signal from being visible, both the front and to the rear.

§106. Methods of giving hand and arm signals.
All signals herein required to be given by hand and arm shall be given from the left side of the vehicle in the following manner, and such signals shall indicate as follows:

(1) Left turn—hand and arm extended horizontally, with the hand open and the back of the hand to the rear.

(2) Right turn—hand and arm extended upward at an angle of forty-five degrees from shoulder or elbow, with the hand open and the back of the hand to the rear.

(3) Stop or decrease speed—start—hand and arm extended downward at an angle of forty-five degrees from shoulder or elbow, with the hand open and the back of the hand to the rear.

(4) Pulling from curb or side of highway—same as for left turn.

SUBPART D. RIGHT OF WAY

§121. Vehicle approaching or entering intersection.
A. When the two vehicles approach or enter an intersection from different highways at approximately the same time, the driver of the vehicle on the left, shall yield the right of way to the vehicle on the right.

B. The right of way rule declared in Subsection A is modified at through highways and otherwise as hereinafter stated in this part.

§122. Vehicle turning left at intersection.
The driver of a vehicle within an intersection intending to turn to the left shall yield the right of way to all vehicles approaching from the opposite direction which are within the intersection or so close thereto as to constitute an immediate hazard.

§123. Stop signs and yield signs.
A. Preferential right of way at an intersection may be indicated by stop signs or yield signs.

B. Except when directed to proceed by a police officer or traffic control signal, every driver and operator of a vehicle approaching a stop intersection indicated by a stop sign shall stop before entering the cross walk on the near side at a clearly marked stop line, but if none, then at the point nearest the intersection roadway where the driver has a view of approaching traffic on the intersection roadway before entering the intersection. After having stopped, the driver shall yield the right of way to all vehicles which have entered the intersection from another highway or which are approaching so closely on said highway as to constitute an immediate hazard.

C. The driver or operator of a vehicle approaching a yield sign shall slow down to a speed reasonable for the existing conditions, or shall stop if necessary, before entering the cross walk on the near side of the intersection or, in the event there is no cross walk, at a clearly marked stop line, but if none, then at the point nearest the intersection roadway where the driver has a view of approaching traffic on the intersection roadway. Having slowed or stopped in this manner, the driver shall yield the right of way to any pedestrian legally crossing the roadway on which he is driving, and to any vehicle in the intersection or approaching on another highway so closely as to constitute an immediate hazard.

§124. Vehicle entering highway from private road, driveway, alley or building.

The driver of a vehicle about to enter or cross a highway from a private road, driveway, alley or building, shall stop such vehicle immediately prior to driving onto a sidewalk or onto the sidewalk area extending across any alleyway or driveway, and shall yield the right of way to any pedestrian as may be necessary to avoid collision, and shall yield the right of way to all approaching vehicles so close as to constitute an immediate hazard.

§125. Procedure on approach of an authorized emergency vehicle.

A. Upon the immediate approach of an authorized emergency vehicle making use of audible or visual signals, or of a police vehicle properly and lawfully making use of an audible signal only, the driver of every other vehicle shall yield the right of way and shall immediately drive to a position parallel to, and as close as possible to, the right hand edge or curb of the highway clear of any intersection, and shall stop and remain in such position until the authorized emergency vehicle has passed, except when otherwise directed by a police officer.

B. This section shall not operate to relieve the driver of an authorized emergency vehicle from the duty to drive with due regard for the safety of all persons using the highway.

§126. Cattle crossings.

A. All traffic on state highways shall stop and yield the right of way to cattle which are crossing the highway when all of the following apply:

(1) The cattle are crossing from one portion of property owned or leased by a person to another portion of property owned or leased by that person when such portions of the property are divided by the highway.

(2) A flagman is directing traffic.

(3) A cattle crossing sign is posted by the Department of Transportation and Development at the request of the person who owns or leases such property.

B. The Department of Transportation and Development shall adopt rules to determine where such cattle crossing signs shall be placed in accordance with the provisions of this Section.

C. The provisions of this Section are not intended and shall not be construed to impose any liability on the State of Louisiana for actions taken by the state under the provisions of this section.

(Added by Acts 1991 No. 364, §1, eff. 9/6/91.)

SUBPART E. PARKING, STANDING AND STOPPING

§141. Stopping, standing or parking outside business or residence districts.

A. Upon any highway outside of a business or residence district, no person shall stop, park, or leave standing any vehicle, whether attended or unattended, upon the paved or main traveled part of the highway when it is practicable to stop, park or so leave such vehicle off such part of said highway, but in every event an unobstructed width of the highway opposite a standing vehicle shall be left for the free passage of other vehicles and a clear view of such stopped vehicles shall be available from a distance of two hundred feet in each direction upon such highway.

B. The provisions of this Section shall not apply to the driver of any vehicle which is disabled while on the main traveled portion of a highway so that it is impossible to avoid stopping and temporarily leaving the vehicle in that position. However, the driver shall remove the vehicle as soon as possible, and until it is removed it is his responsibility to protect traffic.

C. The driver of any vehicle left parked, attended or unattended, on any highway, between sunset and sunrise, shall display appropriate signal lights thereon, sufficient to warn approaching traffic of its presence.

D. In the event of a motor vehicle accident on an interstate or four-lane highway, if the driver is not prevented by injury and the vehicle is not disabled by the accident, or the accident has not resulted in injury or death of any person, the driver shall remove the vehicle from the travel lane of the highway to the nearest safe shoulder. Compliance with the provisions of this Subsection shall in no way be interpreted as a violation of requirements to remain at the scene of an accident as provided for in the Highway Regulatory Act or by R.S. 32:414.
(Chgd. by Acts 1995 No. 1133, §1, eff. 8/15/95.)

§142. Officers authorized to remove illegally stopped vehicles.

A. Whenever any police officer finds a vehicle standing upon a highway in violation of any of the provisions of R.S. 32:141, he is hereby authorized to move such vehicle, or require the driver or other person in charge of the vehicle to move it to a position off the paved or main traveled part of the highway.

B. Whenever any police officer finds a vehicle unattended upon any bridge or causeway or in any tunnel where such vehicle constitutes an obstruction to traffic, the officer is hereby authorized to provide for the removal of the vehicle to the nearest garage or other place of safety.

C. Whenever any police officer finds a vehicle unattended upon any portion of the Crescent City Connection, whether on the traffic lane or shoulder, the officer is hereby authorized to provide for the immediate removal of the vehicle to the nearest garage or other place of safety.
(Chgd. by Acts 1997 No. 209, §1, eff. 6/16/97.)

§143. Stopping, standing or parking prohibited in specified places.

A. No person shall stand, or park a vehicle, except when necessary to avoid conflict with other traffic, or in compliance with law or the directions of a police officer or traffic control device, in any of the following places:

(1) On a sidewalk;

(2) In front of a public or private driveway;

(3) Within an intersection;

(4) Within fifteen feet of a fire hydrant;

(5) On a cross walk;

(6) Within twenty feet of a cross walk at an intersection;

(7) Within twenty feet upon the approach to any flashing beacon stop sign, or traffic control signal located at the side of a roadway;

(8) Between a safety zone and the adjacent curb, or within twenty feet of points on the curb immediately opposite the ends of a safety zone;

(9) Within fifty feet of the nearest rail of a railroad crossing;

(10) Within twenty feet of the driveway entrance to any fire station, and on the side of a street opposite the entrance to any fire station within seventy-five feet of said entrance, when properly posted;

(11) Alongside or opposite any street excavation or obstruction when stopping, standing, or parking would obstruct traffic;

(12) On the roadway side of any vehicle stopped or parked at the end or curb of a street;

(13) Upon any bridge or other elevated structure upon a highway or within a highway tunnel;

(14) At any place where official signs prohibit such;

(15) Any place where parking will obscure or obstruct visibility of any traffic control device.

B. No person shall move a vehicle not lawfully under his control into any such prohibited area or away from a curb such a distance as is unlawful.

§143.1. Blocking of private driveways, highways and state highway department right of ways, penalties.

A. No person shall park any vehicle along a highway or department right of way in any residential area so as to block private driveways.

B. Whenever any law enforcement officer finds such an unlawfully parked vehicle as described in Subsection A above, he may move the vehicle, or require the driver or other person in charge of the vehicle to move it to a legally permissible position away from the private driveway.

C. (1) The owner or operator of any vehicle parked in violation of Subsection A above may, within twenty days after the date when a ticket giving notice of such violation was attached to such vehicle, pay to the chief of police, sheriff, or other chief law enforcement officer, in full satisfaction of such violation, the sum of one dollar plus any towing charges for moving the vehicle.

(2) The owner or operator of any vehicle parked in violation of Subsection A above, who fails to pay the chief of police, sheriff or other chief law enforcement officer the sum of one dollar plus towing charges, as provided herein, shall upon conviction thereof, be fined, according to the discretion of the court, not less than two dollars and fifty cents nor more than twenty dollars plus any towing charges.

§144. Additional parking regulations.

A. Except as otherwise provided in this section, every vehicle standing or parked on a highway where there are adjacent curbs shall be so standing or parked with the right-hand wheels of such vehicle parallel to and within eighteen inches of the right-hand curb.

B. The department may place signs prohibiting or restricting the stopping, standing or parking of vehicles on any highway where in its opinion such stopping, standing or parking is dangerous to those using the highway, or where such would unduly interfere with the free movement of traffic thereon. Such signs shall be official signs, and no person shall stop, stand, or park any vehicle in violation of the restrictions stated on such signs.

§145. Unattended motor vehicles.

No person driving or in charge of any motor vehicle shall permit it to stand unattended without first stopping the motor, locking the ignition, removing the key, and effectively setting the brake thereon, and, when standing upon any grade, turning the front wheels to the curb or side of the highway.

§146. Prohibited parking; leased or rented motor vehicles.

A. Whenever a leased or rented motor vehicle, identified as provided in Subsection B of this Section, is parked in violation of any state law, local ordinance, or regulation, and a citation is issued at a time when the driver is not present to receive the citation, prior to any proceedings on the citation, the governing authority under whose jurisdiction the citation is issued shall request an affidavit from the registered owner attesting to the name, address, and driver's license number of the person to whom the vehicle was leased or rented at the time the citation was issued.

B. The owner of each leased or rented motor vehicle may place an identification tag attached to the inside of the bottom right side of the windshield of such vehicle. The identification tag shall state that the vehicle is rented or leased and shall list the name and address of the registered owner. All such information shall be clearly visible from the outside of the vehicle. The Department of Public Safety shall approve the forms for the identification tags.

C. Upon the request to furnish the affidavit pursuant to Subsection A of this Section, the owner shall within seven days after the receipt of the request, mail or deliver to the requesting authority an affidavit attesting to the name, address, and driver's license number of the person to whom the vehicle was rented or leased. The affidavit shall create the presumption that the person to whom the vehicle was leased or rented was the driver who parked the vehicle in violation of the law, ordinance or regulation, and the requesting authority shall notify the driver of his responsibility for the violation.

D. Whenever a leased or rented motor vehicle is not identified as provided in Subsection B of this Section or when the requested owner of a property identified leased or rented vehicle fails to furnish the affidavit, the presumption created under Subsection C of this Section shall not apply and the citation shall be treated as any other regular parking citation.

E. This Section shall supersede any conflicting provisions of R.S. 32:41 and 32:42 and any local ordinance or regulation adopted pursuant thereto or pursuant to any other authority.

SUBPART F. RAILROAD GRADE CROSSINGS

§168. Equipment of locomotive with bell and whistle or horn, sounding of signals.

(Effective only until 3/1/99. See other section 168 below.)

Every railroad company or person owning and operating a railroad in this state shall equip each locomotive engine with a bell and a whistle or horn which, under normal conditions, can be heard at a distance of three hundred yards and, upon engines approaching at grade any street or highway crossing, whether or not said crossing shall be otherwise protected, shall, for a distance of not less than three hundred yards and until the crossing is reached, cause either the bell to be sounded continuously or blasts of the whistle or horn to be sounded in the manner provided by the Uniform Code of Railroad Operating Rules, unless the distance from that crossing and the start of that movement or the distance between the crossings be less, in which event such warning signals shall be so sounded for that lesser distance; however, in cases of emergency said whistles or horn may be sounded in repeated short blasts.

§168. Equipment of locomotive with bell and whistle or horn, sounding of signals.

(Effective 3/1/99. See other section 168 above.)

A. Every railroad company or person owning and operating a railroad in this state shall equip each locomotive engine with a bell and a whistle or horn which, under normal conditions, can be heard at a distance of not less than one quarter mile.

B. Except as specifically exempted by law, any person controlling the motion of an engine on any railroad shall commence sounding the audible signal when such engine is approaching and not less than one quarter of a mile from the place where such railroad crosses any highway. Such sounding shall be prolonged either continuously or by blasts of the whistle or horn to be sounded in the manner provided by the Uniform Code of Railroad Operating Rules until the engine has crossed the roadway, unless the distance from that crossing and the start of the movement or the distance between the crossings is less than one quarter mile, in which event such warning signals shall be sounded for the lesser distance. In cases of emergency said whistles or horn may be sounded in repeated short blasts.

(Chgd. by Acts 1998 First Ex. Sess. No. 83 §1, eff. 3/1/99.)

§169. Cross buck, stop and warning signs.

A. Any person, firm, or corporation controlling any railroad track which intersects a public road or street at grade crossings, except those contained in the maintenance system of the office of highways, shall erect and maintain a "Railroad Cross Buck" sign at the crossings above referred to which shall be white with the "Railroad Crossing" in black letters. The sign shall be reflectorized. If there are two or more tracks, same shall be indicated on an auxiliary sign of inverted "T" shape mounted below the cross buck. This sign shall be erected on the right hand side of the roadway of such approach to the crossing not more than fifty feet nor less than fifteen feet from the nearest rail and not less than six feet or more than twelve feet from the edge of the roadway. The sign shall be ten feet above the level of the highway and said sign shall be constructed in accordance with the standards of the office of highways.

B. The person, firm, or corporation controlling any railroad track hereinabove referred to may with written approval of the office of highways, erect stop signs at any grade crossings of railroads on highways not contained in the state maintenance system. Said signs shall be octagonal in shape, shall have a red background, and carry the word "stop" in white letters all in accordance with the standards of the office of highways. Said signs shall be located not less than fifteen feet nor more than fifty feet from the nearest rail and shall be erected on the right hand side of the highway of each approach to the crossing and not less than six feet nor more than twelve feet from the edge of the roadway. Where "stop" signs are erected the said railroad shall also erect and maintain a railroad advance warning sign on the right side of the road not less than one hundred feet nor more than three hundred feet from the nearest rail of said crossing measured along the highway, said sign shall be a yellow disk thirty-six inches in diameter carrying a ninety degree cross buck x and the letters R.R. in black in accordance with the standards of the office of highways. When such signs are erected, the driver of any vehicle shall stop within fifty feet but not less than fifteen feet from the nearest rail of such railroad and shall proceed only upon the exercising of due care and being sure that it is safe to proceed.

C. All cross buck and warning signs provided for herein shall be installed by the person, firm or corporation controlling the railroad as the present signs are replaced.

D. Subsections A and B of this Section do not apply to grade crossings of any roadway which is contained in the state maintained highway system.

E. (1) A railroad company shall install a traffic control device or devices at a public railroad grade crossing pursuant to an agreement with the Department of Transportation and Development. Whenever the department determines that a particular traffic control device needs to be installed at a public highway railroad grade crossing, the railroad company shall cooperate with the department in the installation of such device or devices. In the case of a federally funded grade crossing project, the railroad company shall enter into an agreement with the department for the installation or upgrade of such traffic control device. A railroad company shall not be required to provide the non-federal share of costs involved in federally funded grade crossing improvement projects.

(2) A railroad company may install a traffic control device or make other improvements or modifications at a railroad grade crossing at its own expense under the following conditions:

(a) When such crossing upgrade, improvement, or modification will improve the safety of the traveling public, train crew members, or train passengers.

(b) When such crossing upgrade, improvement, or modification is needed due to the presence of hazardous conditions or certain operation factors or a combination of both.

(c) When such crossing upgrade, improvement, or modification is incidental to a railroad improvement project relating to track structures or train control systems.

(3) Any upgrade, improvement, or modification performed by a railroad company under the provisions of this Subsection shall comply with all conditions and requirements in the Manual on Uniform Traffic Control Devices.

F. Nothing in this Section shall relieve a railroad company of its responsibility to maintain safe crossings.

(Chgd. by Acts 1998 First Ex. Sess. No.122, §1, eff. 6/16/98.)

§170. Exemptions; Old Metairie railroad corridor; elimination of railroad liability.

A. The provisions of R.S. 32:168 and R.S. 32:169 shall not apply to crossings of public roads by house tracks, switch tracks, industry tracks, and plantation tracks, since the intention is that such provisions apply only to tracks over which trains are operated at high speed; also such provisions do not modify or repeal any parochial or municipal ordinance relating to signs or signals at public railroad crossings.

B. (1) The provisions of R.S. 32:168 requiring the sounding of a bell, whistle, or horn by a locomotive engine when it approaches a street or highway crossing shall not apply to crossings in the Old Metairie railroad corridor in Jefferson Parish between Airline Highway and the 17th Street Canal when train activated flashing light signals and gates are installed and operating at those crossings, and such soundings in the corridor are hereby prohibited except in cases of emergency.

(2) After train activated flashing light signals and gates are installed and operating at crossings in the Old Metairie railroad corridor in Jefferson Parish between Airline Highway and the 17th Street Canal, a railroad company or its employees shall not be liable to any person or other entity for civil damages for injury or death of persons or damage to property which occur due to failure of an oncoming train to sound an audible warning approaching or at such crossings.

(Chgd. by Acts 1990 No. 983, §1, eff. 9/7/90.)

§171. Obedience to signal indicating approach to train.

A. Whenever any person driving a motor vehicle approaches a railroad grade crossing under any of the circumstances stated in this Section, the driver of such vehicle shall stop within fifty feet but not less than fifteen feet from the nearest rail of such railroad, and shall not proceed until he can do so safely. The foregoing requirements shall apply when:

(1) A clearly visible electric or mechanical signal device gives warning of the immediate approach of a railroad train.

(2) A crossing gate is lowered or when a human flagman gives or continues to give a signal of the approach or passage of a railroad train.

(3) A railroad train approaching within approximately nine hundred feet of the highway crossing emits a signal in accordance with R.S. 32:168, and such railroad train, by reason of its speed or nearness to such crossing, is an immediate hazard.

(4) An approaching railroad train is plainly visible and is in hazardous proximity to such crossing.

(5) A stop sign is erected at the approach to a railroad grade crossing.

B. No person shall stop a motor vehicle upon any railroad crossing.

C. No person shall drive any vehicle through, around, or under any crossing gate or barrier at a railroad crossing while such gate or barrier is closed or is being opened or closed when an approaching railroad train is plainly visible and is in hazardous proximity to such crossing.

D. No person shall drive any vehicle across any railroad crossing while the signal devices are flashing when an approaching railroad train is plainly visible and is in hazardous proximity to such crossing.

E. At any railroad grade crossing provided with railroad cross buck signs, without automatic, electric, or mechanical signal devices, crossings gates, or a human flagman giving a signal of the approach or passage of a train, the driver of a vehicle shall in obedience to the railroad cross buck sign, yield the right-of-way and slow down to a speed reasonable for the existing conditions and shall stop, if required for safety, at a clearly marked stopped line or, if no line, within fifty feet but not less than fifteen feet from the nearest rail of the railroad and shall not proceed until he or she can do so safely. If a driver is involved in a collision at a railroad crossing or interferes with the movement of a train after driving past the railroad cross buck sign, the collision or interference is prima facie evidence of the driver's failure to yield right-of-way.

F. Any person who violates any provision of this Section shall be fined as follows:

(1) On first offense the fine shall be not more than one hundred seventy-five dollars or imprisonment for not more than thirty days, or both.

(2) On second and each subsequent offense the fine shall not be more than five hundred dollars or imprisonment for not more than ninety days, or both. Additionally on second offense, the person in violation shall be required to attend a court approved driver improvement course.

G. The governing authority of a municipality may enter into a cooperative endeavor agreement authorizing certified railroad law enforcement officers to assist in the enforcement of state laws and local ordinances pertaining to railroad grade crossings within its municipal limits.

(Chgd. by Acts 1998 First Ex. Sess. No.122, §1, eff. 6/16/98.)

§172. All vehicles must stop at certain railroad grade crossings.

A. (1) The department shall determine highway grade crossings of railroads on state maintained highways or roads which are of particular danger to public safety and shall erect stop signs thereat.

(2) The department shall also make a preliminary determination of highway grade crossings of railroads on non-state maintained public highways or roads which are of particular danger to public safety which shall be made available to parishes and municipalities. The governing authorities of such parishes and municipalities may erect stop signs at such crossings.

(3) The department shall promulgate rules and regulations, not later than December 15, 1998, which set forth criteria to determine those crossings which are particularly dangerous to include, but not be limited to, crossings where multiple collisions have occurred, crossings which are high profile crossings, and crossings with reduced sight distance or visibility. When such stop signs are erected, the driver of any vehicle shall stop within fifty feet, but not less than fifteen feet, from the nearest rail of such railroad and shall proceed only upon exercising due care.

B. The opinions and final report of the department promulgated or published pursuant to this Section shall not be subject to any discovery or production nor be admissible evidence in any judicial proceeding in this state.

C. A decision of the department relative to the placement of a stop sign at a crossing which possesses any other warning device shall not be considered as presumptive or conclusive evidence of fault on the part of the state or its agents or any political subdivision or its agents.

D. Nothing in this Section shall relieve the railroad of its responsibility to maintain safe crossings and operate their trains in a safe manner.

(Chgd. by Acts 1998 First Ex. Sess. No. 121, §1, eff. 6/16/98.)

§173. Certain vehicles must stop at all railroad grade crossings.

A. The driver of any motor vehicle carrying passengers for hire, or of any school bus whether carrying any school child or not, or of any vehicle carrying explosive substances or flammable liquids as a cargo or part of a cargo, before crossing at grade any track or tracks of a railroad, shall stop such vehicle within fifty feet but not less than fifteen feet from the nearest rail of such railroad and while so stopped shall listen and look in both directions along such track for any approaching train, and for signals indicating the approach of a train, except as hereinafter provided, and shall not proceed until he can do so safely. After stopping as required herein and upon proceeding when it is safe to do so the driver of any said vehicle shall cross only in such gear of the vehicle that there will be no necessity for changing gears while traversing such crossing and the driver shall not shift gears while crossing the track or tracks.

B. The driver of any school bus, in addition to the requirements of Sub-section A of this Section, after coming to a complete stop as required by Sub-section A of this Section, shall open the door of the school bus and shall leave it open while ascertaining that no train or other vehicle is approaching on the railroad track from either side and until immediately prior to proceeding across the railroad crossing.

C. No stop need be made at any such crossing where a police officer or a traffic-control signal directs traffic to proceed.

D. *(Repealed.)*

§174. Moving heavy equipment at railroad grade crossings.

A. No person shall operate or move any crawler-type tractor, steam shovel, derrick, roller, or any equipment or structure having a normal operating speed of ten or less miles per hour or a vertical body or load clearance of less than one-half inch per foot of the distance between any two adjacent axles or in any event of less than nine inches, measured above the level surface of a roadway, upon or across any tracks at a railroad grade crossing without first complying with this Section.

B. Notice of any such intended crossing shall be given to a station agent of such railroad and a reasonable time be given to such railroad to provide proper protection at such crossing.

C. Before making any such crossing the person operating or moving any such vehicle or equipment shall first stop the same not less than fifteen feet nor more than fifty feet from the nearest rail of such railroad and while so stopped shall listen and look in both directions, and shall not proceed until the crossing can be made safely.

D. No such crossing shall be made when warning is given by automatic signal or crossing gates or a flagman or otherwise of the immediate approach of a railroad train or car. If a flagman is provided by the railroad, movement over the crossing shall be under his direction.

§175. Vehicles must yield at railroad grade crossings; exceptions.

A. The driver or operator of a vehicle approaching a rail-highway grade crossing identified by the presence of a railroad cross buck sign shall slow down to a speed reasonable for the existing conditions, or shall stop if necessary, before entering the cross walk on the near side of the intersection or, in the event there is no cross walk, at a clearly marked stop line, or if none, then at the point nearest the intersecting rail of such railroad where the driver or operator has a clear view of any approaching train. The driver or operator shall listen and look in both directions along such track for any approaching train and for signals indicating the approach of a train. Having slowed or stopped in this manner, the driver or operator shall yield the right of way to any approaching train and then shall proceed only upon exercising due care and upon being sure that it is safe to proceed.

B. The driver or operator of a vehicle need not yield at any such rail-highway grade crossing where a police officer or traffic-control signal directs traffic to proceed.

C. The provisions of this Section do not relieve drivers or operators of the responsibility to comply with the provisions of R.S. 32:171 and 32:173.
(Added by Acts 1990 No. 143, §1, eff. 9/7/90.)

§176. Required notification of recording devices carried on railroad trains.

Immediately following a railroad crossing accident, the engineer or a responsible member of the crew, if the engineer is unable to provide the information, shall inform the law enforcement officer investigating such accident if the train possesses an event recorder which records and preserves any information which is relevant to the accident or may be of assistance in the investigation of the accident. Upon request of the law enforcement officer, the railroad or its representative shall provide, in a timely manner, any such information contained on the event recorder whose release is not prohibited by federal law, rule, or regulation. *(Added by Acts 1998 First Ex. Sess. No. 87, §1, eff. 6/16/98.)*

SUBPART G. OPERATION OF MOTORCYCLES, MOTOR-DRIVEN CYCLES AND BICYCLES

§190. Safety helmets.

A. No person shall operate or ride upon any motorcycle, motor driven cycle, or motorized bicycle unless the person is equipped with and is wearing on the head a safety helmet of the type and design manufactured for use by operators of such vehicles, which shall be secured properly with a chin strap while the vehicle is in motion. All such safety helmets shall consist of lining, padding, visor, and chin strap and shall meet such other specifications as shall be established by the commissioner.

B. It shall be unlawful to manufacture, sell, or distribute any protective helmet for use by the operator of a motorcycle, motor driven cycle, or motorized bicycle, or for use by the passenger thereon, unless such protective helmet is of a type and specification approved by the commissioner who shall publish a notice of such approval.

C. Notwithstanding the provisions of this Section, the police authorities of a village, town, city, or parish may issue a permit exempting members of organizations sponsoring, conducting, or participating in parades or other public exhibitions from the provisions of this Section while such members are actually participating in a parade or other public exhibition.

D. This Section does not apply to a person operating or riding in an autocycle if the vehicle is equipped with a roof which meets or exceeds standards for a safety helmet.

E. It shall be unlawful to manufacture, sell, or distribute any protective helmet for use by the operator of a motorcycle, motor driven cycle, or motorized bicycle, or for use by the passenger thereon, unless the manufacturer of the protective helmet obtains and maintains liability insurance of not less than one hundred thousand dollars for each occurrence of liability of the manufacturer for fault in the design, materials, or workmanship of the protective helmet. In addition to any other penalty provided in this Section, the commissioner may prohibit the movement, sale, or distribution of any protective helmet if the manufacturer is not covered by insurance as required by this Subsection.

F. Any person who violates any provision of this Section shall upon conviction be fined fifty dollars which shall include all costs of court. Notwithstanding any contrary provision of law, no other cost or fee shall be assessed against any person for a violation of this Section.

§190.1. Eye protective devices to be worn by motorcyclist; windshield on motorcycle.

A. No person shall operate a motorcycle or motor driven cycle unless the person is wearing an eye protective device of a type approved for such use by the secretary, except when the motorcycle or motor driven cycle is equipped with a windshield of sufficient height to afford adequate eye protection that meets the requirements of R.S. 32:358.

B. The secretary shall approve only goggles, face shields, or safety glasses which will meet performance specifications established by him.

C. Eye protective devices used at night shall not be tinted.

D. This Section shall not apply to persons riding within an enclosed cab.

§191. Riding on motorcycles.

A. A person operating a motorcycle shall ride only upon the permanent and regular seat attached thereto. Such operator shall not carry any other person nor shall any other person ride on a motorcycle unless such motorcycle is designed to carry more than one person, in which event a passenger may ride upon the permanent and regular seat if designed for two persons, or upon another seat firmly attached to the rear or side on the motorcycle.

B. A person shall ride upon a motorcycle only while sitting astride the seat, facing forward, with not more than one leg on each side of the motorcycle.

C. No person shall operate a motorcycle while carrying any package, bundle, or other article which prevents him from keeping both hands on the handlebars.

D. No operator shall carry any person, nor shall any person ride, in a position that will interfere with the operation or control of the motorcycle or the view of the operator.

§191.1. Operating motorcycles on roadways laned for traffic.

A. All motorcycles are entitled to full use of a lane and no motor vehicle shall be driven in such manner as to deprive any motorcycle of the full use of a lane. This subsection shall not apply to motorcycles operated two abreast in a single lane.

B. The operator of a motorcycle shall not overtake and pass in the same lane occupied by the vehicle being overtaken.

C. No person shall operate a motorcycle between lanes of traffic or between adjacent lines or rows of vehicles.

D. Motorcycles shall not be operated more than two abreast in a single lane.

E. Subsections (B) and (C) shall not apply to police officers in the performance of their official duties.

§191.2. Clinging to other vehicles.

No person riding upon a motorcycle shall attach himself or the motorcycle to any other vehicle (or streetcar) on a roadway.

§191.3. Footrests and handlebars.

A. Any motorcycle carrying a passenger, other than in a sidecar or enclosed cab, shall be equipped with footrests for such passenger.

B. No person shall operate any motorcycle with handlebars more than fifteen inches in height above the portion of the seat occupied by the operator.

§192. Riding on motor-driven cycles.

Not more than one person shall be allowed to ride upon a motor-driven cycle.

§193. Operation of bicycles; general provision.

The regulations applicable to bicycles shall apply whenever a bicycle is operated upon any highway or upon any path set aside for the exclusive use of bicycles, subject to those exceptions stated hereafter.

§194. Traffic laws apply to persons riding bicycles.

Every person riding a bicycle upon a highway of this state shall be granted all of the rights and shall be subject to all the duties applicable to the driver of a vehicle by this Chapter, except as to special regulations in this Part and except as to those provisions of this Chapter which by their very nature can have no application.

§195. Riding on bicycles.

A. A person propelling a bicycle shall not ride other than upon or astride a permanent or regular seat attached thereto.

B. No bicycle shall be used to carry more persons at one time than the number for which it is designed and equipped.

C. A person operating a bicycle shall at all times keep at least one hand upon the handle bars thereof.

§196. Clinging to vehicles.

No person riding upon any bicycle shall attach himself or the bicycle to any vehicle upon a highway.

§197. Riding on roadways and bicycle paths.

A. Every person operating a bicycle upon a roadway shall ride as near to the right side of the roadway as practicable, exercising due care when passing a standing vehicle or one proceeding in the same direction.

B. Persons riding bicycles upon a roadway shall not ride more than two abreast except on paths or parts of roadways set aside for the exclusive use of bicycles.

C. Whenever a usable path for bicycles has been provided adjacent to a roadway, bicycle riders shall use such path and shall not use the roadway.

§198. Operating motorized bicycles.

A motorized bicycle shall only be operated upon the roadway of the highways of this state by a person fifteen years of age or older who possesses a valid Louisiana driver's license and shall not be operated upon sidewalks or interstate highways.

SUBPART H. PEDESTRIANS' RIGHTS AND DUTIES

§211. Pedestrians subject to traffic regulations.

Pedestrians shall be subject to traffic-control signals at intersections as provided in R.S. 32:233 unless otherwise required by local ordinance, but at all other places pedestrians shall be accorded the privileges and shall be subject to the restrictions stated in this Part.

§212. Pedestrians right of way in cross-walks.

A. When traffic-control signals are not in place or not in operation the driver of a vehicle shall yield the right of way, slowing down or stopping if need be to so yield, to a pedestrian crossing the roadway within a cross walk when the pedestrian is upon the half of the roadway upon which the vehicle is traveling or when the pedestrian is approaching closely from the opposite half of the roadway as to be in danger.

B. No pedestrian shall suddenly leave a curb or other place of safety and walk or run into the path of a vehicle which is so close that it is impossible for the driver to yield.

C. Whenever any vehicle is stopped at a marked cross-walk or at any unmarked cross-walk at an intersection to permit a pedestrian to cross the roadway, the driver of any other vehicle approaching from the rear shall not overtake and pass such stopped vehicle.

D. Sub-section A of this section shall not apply where the pedestrian is crossing a roadway at a point where a pedestrian tunnel or overhead pedestrian crossing has been provided.

§213. Crossing at other than cross walks.

A. Every pedestrian crossing a roadway at any point other than within a marked cross walk or within an unmarked cross walk at an intersection shall yield the right of way to all vehicles upon the roadway.

B. Between adjacent intersections at which traffic-control signals are in operation pedestrians shall not cross at any place except in a marked cross walk.

§214. Drivers to exercise due care.

Notwithstanding the foregoing provisions of this Part, every driver of a vehicle shall exercise due care to avoid colliding with any pedestrian upon any roadway and shall give warning by sounding the horn when necessary and shall exercise proper precaution upon observing any child or any confused or incapacitated person upon a highway.

§215. Pedestrians to use right half of cross walks.

Pedestrians shall move, whenever practicable, upon the right half of cross walks.

§216. Pedestrians on highways.

A. Where sidewalks are provided, it shall be unlawful for any pedestrian to walk along and upon an adjacent highway.

B. Where sidewalks are not provided, any pedestrian walking along and upon a highway shall, when practicable, walk only on the left side of the highway or its shoulder, facing traffic which may approach from the opposite direction.

§217. Blind and incapacitated pedestrians; use of canes; vehicles.

A. It is unlawful for any person, unless totally or partially blind or otherwise incapacitated, while on any public street or highway, to carry in a raised or extended position a cane or walking stick which is metallic or white in color or white tipped with red.

B. Whenever a pedestrian is crossing or attempting to cross a public street or highway, at or near an intersection or crosswalk, guided by a guide dog, or carrying in a raised or extended position a cane or walking stick which is metallic or white in color, or white tipped with red, the driver of every vehicle approaching the said intersection or cross walk shall take such precautions as may be necessary to avoid injuring or endangering such pedestrian, and if injury or danger to such pedestrian can be avoided only by bringing his vehicle to a full stop, he shall bring his said vehicle to a full stop.

C. Nothing contained in this Section shall be construed to deprive any totally or partially blind or otherwise incapacitated person, not carrying such a cane or walking stick or not being guided by a dog, of the rights and privileges conferred by law upon pedestrians crossing streets or highways, nor shall the failure of such totally or partially blind or otherwise incapacitated person to carry a cane or walking stick, or to be guided by a guide dog upon the streets, highways or sidewalks of this state, be held to constitute nor be evidence of contributory negligence.

§218. Pedestrians soliciting rides or business.

No person shall stand on a roadway for the purpose of soliciting a ride, employment, or business from the occupant of any vehicle.

§219. Pedestrians right-of-way on sidewalks.

The driver of a motor vehicle emerging from or entering an alley, private road or driveway, or building shall yield the right-of-way to any pedestrian approaching on any sidewalk extending across such alley, road or driveway, or building entrance.

SUBPART I. SIGNS, MARKERS AND SIGNALS

§231. Obedience to and required traffic-control devices.

A. The driver of any vehicle shall obey the instructions of any official traffic-control device applicable thereto placed in accordance with the provisions of this Chapter, unless otherwise directed by a traffic or police officer, subject to the exceptions granted the driver of an authorized emergency vehicle in this Chapter.

B. No provision of this Chapter for which signs are required shall be enforced against an alleged violator if at the time and place of the alleged violation an official sign is not in a position and where it can be seen by an ordinarily observant person. Whenever a particular Section does not state that signs are required, such Section shall be effective even though no signs are erected or in place.

§232. Traffic-control signals.

Whenever traffic is controlled by traffic-control signals exhibiting different colored lights, or colored lighted arrows, successively one at a time or in combination, only the colors green, red and yellow shall be used, except for special pedestrian signals carrying a word legend, and said lights shall indicate and apply to drivers of vehicles and pedestrians as follows:

(1) GREEN indication:

(a) Vehicular traffic facing a circular green signal may proceed straight through or turn right or left unless a sign at such place prohibits either such turn. But vehicular traffic, including vehicles turning right, or left, shall yield the right-of-way to other vehicles and to pedestrians lawfully within the intersection or an adjacent crosswalk at the time such signal is exhibited.

(b) Vehicular traffic facing a green arrow signal, shown alone or in combination with another indication, may cautiously enter the intersection only to make the movement indicated by such arrow, or such other movement as is permitted by other indications shown at the same time. Such vehicular traffic shall yield the right-of-way to pedestrians lawfully within an adjacent crosswalk and to other traffic lawfully using the intersection.

(c) Unless otherwise directed by a pedestrian control signal as provided in R.S. 32:233, pedestrians facing any green signal, except when the sole green signal is a turn arrow, may proceed across the roadway within any marked or unmarked crosswalk.

(2) Steady YELLOW indication:

(a) Vehicular traffic facing a steady yellow signal alone is thereby warned that the related green signal is being terminated or that a red signal will be exhibited immediately thereafter and such vehicular traffic shall not enter or be crossing the intersection when the red signal is exhibited.

(b) Unless otherwise directed by a pedestrian control signal as provided in R.S. 32:233 a pedestrian facing a steady yellow signal is thereby advised that there is insufficient time to cross the roadway before a red signal is exhibited and no pedestrian shall then start to cross the roadway.

(3) Steady RED indication:

(a) Vehicular traffic facing a steady circular red signal alone shall stop at a clearly marked stop line, or if none, then before entering the crosswalk on the near side of the intersection, or if none, then before entering the intersection, and shall remain standing until an indication to proceed is shown except as provided in Subparagraph (c) of this Paragraph.

(b) Vehicular traffic facing a steady red arrow signal shall not enter the intersection to make the movement indicated by the arrow and, unless entering the intersection make a movement permitted by another signal, shall stop at a clearly marked stop line, or if none, then before entering the crosswalk on the near side of the intersection, or if none, then before entering the intersection, and shall remain standing until an indication permitting the movement indicated by such red arrow is shown except as provided in Subparagraph (c) of this Paragraph.

(c) Except when a sign prohibits a turn, vehicular traffic facing any steady red signal may cautiously enter the intersection to turn right, or to turn left from a one-way street into a one-way street, after stopping as required by Subparagraph (a) or Subparagraph (b) of this Paragraph. Such vehicular traffic shall yield the right-of-way to pedestrians lawfully within an adjacent crosswalk and to other traffic lawfully using the intersection.

(d) Unless otherwise directed by a pedestrian-control signal as provided in R.S. 32:233, a pedestrian facing a steady circular red or red arrow signal shall not enter the roadway.

(4) In the event an official traffic-control signal is erected and maintained at a place other than an intersection, the provisions of this Section shall be applicable except as to those provisions which by their nature can have no application. Any stop required shall be made at a sign or marking on the pavement indicating where the stop shall be made, but in the absence of any such sign or marking, the stop shall be made at the signal.

§233. Pedestrian-control signals.

Whenever special pedestrian-control signals exhibiting the words "Walk" or "Don't Walk" are in place, such signals shall indicate as follows:

(1) Flashing or Steady WALK—A pedestrian facing the signal may proceed across the roadway in the direction of the signal and shall be given the right-of-way by a driver of a vehicle.

(2) Flashing or Steady DON'T WALK—No pedestrian shall start to cross the roadway in the direction of the signal, but a pedestrian who has partially completed his crossing on the "Walk" signal shall proceed to a sidewalk or safety island while the "Don't Walk" signal is showing.

§234. Flashing signals.

A. Whenever an illuminated flashing red or yellow signal is used in a traffic sign or signal, it shall require obedience by vehicular traffic as follows:

(1) FLASHING RED (STOP SIGNAL)—When a red lane is illuminated with rapid intermittent flashes, drivers of vehicles shall stop before entering the nearest cross-walk at an intersection or at a limit line when marked, or, if none, then before entering the intersection, and the right to proceed shall be subject to the rules applicable after making a stop at a stop sign.

(2) FLASHING YELLOW OR AMBER (CAUTION SIGNAL)—When a yellow lens is illuminated with rapid intermittent flashes, drivers of vehicles may proceed through or past such signal only with caution.

B. This Section shall not apply at railroad grade crossings. Conduct of drivers of vehicles approaching railroad grade crossing shall be governed by the rules set forth in R.S. 32:171 through 32:174.

§235. Uniform highway marking system.

A. (1) The department shall adopt a manual and specifications for a uniform system of traffic control devices consistent with the provisions of this Chapter for use upon highways within this state. Such uniform system shall correlate with and so far as possible conform to the system then current as approved by the United States Department of Transportation, Federal Highway Administration, provided that the department is authorized to deviate from said system and to erect advisory signs only to post advisory weight limits on state bridges where a state bridge is scheduled for replacement or strengthening within three years from the date of approval by the chief engineer of the department's weight rating evaluation of any state bridge. In addition, the department may deviate from the criteria contained in said system for location of traffic signals to the extent that additional weighted consideration shall be given to pedestrian and vehicular traffic volumes associated with schools which are located on state highways.

(2) The department shall require that any signage on public highways which indicates maximum or minimum speed limits in kilometers also indicate such speed limits in miles per hour.

B. Local municipal and parish authorities in their respective jurisdictions shall place and maintain such traffic control devices upon highways under their jurisdiction as they may deem necessary to indicate and to carry out the provisions of this Chapter, regulations of the department and commissioner adopted pursuant hereto, and local traffic ordinances adopted pursuant to the authority granted by R.S. 32:41 and R.S. 32:42. All such traffic control devices hereafter erected shall conform to the department's manual or specifications. If any such device hereafter erected by a political subdivision of this state fails to conform to the manual or specifications, payment of any funds allocated to that political subdivision shall be withheld by the department until the standards established by the department are complied with.

C. No local municipal or parish authority shall place or maintain any traffic control device upon any state maintained highway without having first obtained the written approval of the department.

D. Wherever any highway crosses the boundaries of and enters into the state of Louisiana, the department may erect appropriate signs giving notice of the maximum speed limits authorized by law for each type of vehicle upon the highways of this state.

E. Proof that any state, parochial or municipal authority was at the time of any incident complained of in compliance with the provisions of the department's traffic control devices manual shall be prima facie evidence of discharge by such authority of its obligations to the motoring public.

(Chgd. by Acts 1995 No. 282, §1, No. 1125, §1, eff. 8/15/95.)

§236. Privately owned signs on public rights of way prohibited; exceptions; authority of municipalities and department of highways; advertising on convenience facilities at public transit stops.

A. No person, contractor, or public service corporation shall erect or maintain any sign of any nature or a traffic control device or any thing resembling a traffic control device within the right-of-way of any highway or street, without having official permission to install or maintain same in the public right-of-way under the provisions of R.S. 48:344 and R.S. 48:381, except the governing authority maintaining the highway or street.

B. Contractors may place such signs and warning devices and permit holders may place such temporary signs and warning devices as are authorized to warn the traveling public of dangers arising from the work being done within the right-of-way. The department may place such directional, regulatory, and warning signs, signals and barricades, or other traffic control devices as are desirable in its judgment to guide, inform, regulate, and warn the traveling public.

C. A public body, such as a parish or municipal governing authority maintaining a highway or street, may authorize and adopt rules to regulate advertising on convenience facilities such as benches, shelters, and kiosks, located within the public rights of way at designated stops of a public transit system, as designated or contracted for by the governing authority.

(Chgd. by Acts 1990 No. 220, §1; Acts 1992 No. 732, §1, eff. 8/21/92.)

§237. Barricades, signs, and signals; prohibition against tampering with, removing, possessing, and violating instructions; exceptions.

A. (1) No one shall in any way tamper with, move, damage, or destroy any barricade, sign, or signal placed upon any highway by the department or by any contractor or subcontractor doing highway construction or repair work under or by authority of the department; nor shall any person disobey the instructions, signals, warnings, or markings of any warning signs, signals, or barricades so placed upon any highway under construction or repair; nor shall any person disobey the instructions, signals, or warnings of any flagman; nor shall any person drive around or through any barricade or fences placed upon any closed highway by the department or any contractor or subcontractor doing highway construction or repair work under or by authority of the department unless at the time otherwise directed by a police officer.

(2) No individual shall without proper authority:

(a) Sell or purchase any official sign or signal of the department, or

(b) Remove or possess such sign or signal without the intention of returning the sign or signal to its original location.

B. Persons violating this Section shall be prima facie at fault and responsible for any damage to persons or property resulting from the said violation. Nothing contained in this

Section shall be construed to affect the liability of any other persons for failure to properly maintain warnings and markings of construction work.

C. The provisions of this Section shall not apply to the employees of the department or of any contractor or subcontractor or other person whose proper and lawful duties require them to go upon any portion of a highway which is under construction or in the process of being repaired, nor shall the presence of such persons, or that of machinery being operated by them, upon any portion of a highway, which is under construction or in the process of being repaired, by deemed negligent.

D. Nothing contained in this Section shall be construed to prevent or interfere with peaceful picketing by a labor organization.

E. Every person convicted of a violation of this Section shall be punished by a fine of not less than one hundred dollars nor more than five hundred dollars or by imprisonment for not more than thirty days or by both such fine and imprisonment.
(Chgd. by Acts 1997 No. 1145, §1, eff. 8/15/97.)

§238. Directional signs.

A. The governing authority of any parish, municipality, or school board may request the Department of Transportation and Development to place directional signs on the rights of way of the streets and highways which are within the state highway system and which are within the territorial jurisdiction of the governing authority making the request.

B. As used in this Section, a "directional sign" is a sign which serves the public purpose of directing vehicular traffic to or identifying thereat streets, highways, buildings, facilities, or other entities or locations which are of interest to the public. Entities or locations which are of interest to the public include but are not limited to governmental buildings, churches, libraries, public or private schools, hospitals, historic districts, and tourist attractions.

C. The request for directional signs shall be in writing, shall be in the form of a resolution unanimously passed by the governing authority making the request, and shall state the information which is to appear on the sign, the name and general location of the entity to which the public is to be directed, and the general location at which the sign is to be located.

D. The Department of Transportation and Development shall erect and maintain each sign requested under this Section in accordance with federal regulations.

E. The Department of Transportation and Development shall adopt administrative rules to implement the provisions of this Section as authorized by and in accordance with state law and federal regulations.

F. Any signing requested shall be paid for in advance, sign cost only, by the requester or public body making such request.
(Added by Acts 1990 No. 976, §1, eff. 9/7/90.)

SUBPART J. VEHICLES TRANSPORTING EXPLOSIVES OR INFLAMMABLES

§251. Permission for operation; crossing railroad grade crossings; markings.

A. The owner or operator of a vehicle transporting flammable liquids shall not, except where he is protected by a flagman then on duty, cross any railroad without coming to a full stop, before reaching it, in such manner and for such time as to make certain that no train or other facility is approaching, as provided in R.S. 32:173. If the vehicle is transporting explosives, the operator shall proceed across the tracks only under the protection of a competent flagman furnished by the owner or himself. Under no circumstances whatever shall any vehicle transporting explosives carry as part of its load any other commodity or thing.

B. The commissioner is authorized to adopt regulations concerning the markings and identification of vehicles transporting explosives and flammable liquids.

§252. Equipment and inspection.

A. A motor vehicle, when used in transporting explosives, shall be equipped with a minimum of one fire extinguisher having a rating of at least 10-BC, completely filled and in working condition, and placed at a convenient point on the motor vehicle.

B. *(Repealed.)*

§253. Commissioner; transportation of explosives.

The commissioner is hereby authorized and directed to promulgate such additional regulations as to the transportation of explosives by vehicles upon the highways of this state as he shall deem advisable for the protection of the public.

SUBPART K. REGULATION OF CERTAIN HIGHWAYS AND ESTABLISHMENT OF THROUGH HIGHWAYS

§261. Authority to prohibit use of road.

The department may prohibit the operation of vehicles upon any highway of this state or impose restrictions as to the weight of vehicles to be operated upon any highway whenever any such highway, because of its substandard condition or because of deterioration, rain, snow, or other climatic conditions, or construction thereof, or because of traffic conditions thereon, will be seriously damaged or destroyed, or the public endangered by the use of vehicles thereon unless such use is prohibited or the permissible weights thereof reduced.

§262. Controlled access highways.

A. The department may establish certain highways as controlled access highways and prohibit the entrance to, or exit from, such highways except at designated points.

B. When signs are erected giving notice thereof, no person shall drive a vehicle onto or from any controlled access highway except at such entrances and exits as have been designated by the department.

§263. Special restrictions on use of Louisiana interstate highways.

A. No person owning live stock, as defined in R.S. 3:2802, or having same under his care and control, shall knowingly, willfully or negligently permit such live stock to go upon any Louisiana interstate highway.

B. No person shall drive, or permit to be driven on any Louisiana interstate highway, any farm tractor, road tractor or other vehicle which is normally operated at a speed of less than 20 miles per hour.

C. The use of any Louisiana interstate highway by pedestrians, bicycles, or other non-motorized vehicles is prohibited.

§264. Authority to regulate traffic through tunnels.

A. The department may provide regulations to govern the use of all tunnels, including regulations excluding undesirable types of traffic or loads. No over-weight or over-sized permits may be granted for passage through a tunnel.

B. Regulations adopted pursuant to this Section shall be posted in a conspicuous place near each vehicular entrance to the tunnel.

§265. Designating through highways.

The department may designate through highways in the manner set forth in this Chapter, and when so designated, vehicles traveling thereon shall have the right of way over vehicles approaching or entering such highways.

SUBPART L. MISCELLANEOUS PROVISIONS

§281. Limitations on backing.

A. The driver of a vehicle shall not back the same unless such movement can be made with reasonable safety and without interfering with other traffic.

B. The driver of a vehicle shall not back the same upon any shoulder or roadway of any controlled-access highway except as a result of an emergency caused by an accident or breakdown of a motor vehicle.

§282. Obstruction to driver's view or driving mechanism.

A. No person shall drive a vehicle when it is so loaded, or when there are in the front seat such a number of persons, exceeding three, as to obstruct the view of the driver to the front sides or rear of the vehicle or as to interfere with the driver's control over the driving mechanism of the vehicle.

B. No passenger in a vehicle shall ride in such a position as to interfere with the view of the driver to the front, sides or rear of the vehicle or to interfere with his control over the driving mechanism of the vehicle.

C. No person shall drive any vehicle with any nontransparent material upon the windshield, side wings, side or rear windows, other than a certificate or other paper required to be so displayed by law, or permitted by regulation of the secretary of public safety.

§283. Opening and closing vehicle doors.

No person shall open the door of a motor vehicle on the side available to moving traffic unless and until it is reasonably safe to do so, nor shall any person leave a door open on the side of a vehicle available to moving traffic for a period of time longer than necessary to load or unload passengers.

§284. Riding in house trailers, on fenders, on running board or on rear racks prohibited; open pickup trucks; utility trailers.

A. No person or persons shall occupy a house trailer while it is being moved upon a highway of this state.

B. No person shall be allowed to ride on running boards, fenders, tail gates, or rear racks of motor vehicles while moving upon a highway of this state, provided, that this section shall not apply to emergency and public sanitation vehicles.

C. No person or persons under the age of twelve years shall be permitted to be a passenger in the open bed of a truck with a gross weight of six thousand pounds or less, commonly referred to as a pickup truck, or in a utility trailer while moving upon a highway of this state. The provisions of this Subsection shall not apply to a pickup truck traveling not more than fifteen miles per hour while participating in an authorized parade in a controlled situation. The provisions of this Section shall be inapplicable in an emergency situation if the child is accompanied within the truck bed by an adult.

(Chgd. by Acts 1997 No. 245, §1, eff. 8/15/97.)

§285. Coasting prohibited.

The driver of any motor vehicle when traveling upon a downgrade shall not coast with the gears of such vehicle in neutral or with the clutch disengaged.

§286. Following authorized emergency vehicles prohibited.

The driver of any vehicle other than one on official business shall not follow any authorized emergency vehicle traveling in response to an official call of duty closer than five hundred feet or drive into or park such vehicle within the block where such vehicle has stopped in answer to an official call.

§287. Crossing fire hoses.

No vehicle shall be driven over any unprotected hose of a fire department when laid on any highway, private driveway or streetcar track without the consent of the fire department official in command.

§288. Driving through safety zone prohibited.

No vehicle shall at any time be driven through or within a safety zone.

§289. *(Repealed by Acts 1998 First Ex. Sess. No. 148, §10, eff. 6/16/98.)*

§290. Driving across ditches; requirements.

No operator of any truck, tractor, bus, haywagon, or other heavy vehicle shall drive it across any ditch along the highways of this state without first constructing, at his own expense, a bridge over a ditch in such a way as not to in any way retard the drainage.

§291. Liability for damage to highway or structure.

A. Any person driving any vehicle, object or contrivance upon any highway or highway structure shall be liable for all damages which said highway or structure may sustain as a result of any illegal operation, driving or moving of such vehicle, object or contrivance, or as a result of operating, driving or moving any vehicle, object or contrivance weighing in excess of the maximum weight permitted in this Chapter even if authorized by a special permit issued as provided in R.S. 32:388.

B. Whenever such driver is not the owner of such vehicle, object or contrivance but is so operating, driving or moving the same with the express or implied permission of said owner, then said owner and driver shall be jointly and severally liable for any such damage.

§292. Hunting or discharge of firearms, when prohibited.

Hunting or the discharge of firearms on public roads or highways located in this state is hereby prohibited except by law enforcement officers when in the performance of their duties.

Whoever violates this Section shall be fined not more than fifty dollars or imprisoned for not more than thirty days or both.

§293. Seating capacity of school buses; prohibiting standing of school children under certain circumstances; limiting number of children transported at one time.

A. *(Repealed.)*

B. It shall be unlawful for the driver or operator of any school bus while transporting school children to permit any child to stand in said bus while same is in motion if there is seating space available for the use of such child.

C. It shall be unlawful for anyone responsible for the transportation of school children on school buses, including drivers or operators of buses, transportation supervisors, school superintendents, and members of parish and city school boards to permit a number of children exceeding the number of seats available on a bus to be transported at one time on such bus. *(Chgd. by Acts 1997 No. 620, §§1, 2, eff. 8/15/97.)*

§294. Mississippi River bridge crossings prohibited.

A. No motor vehicle or combination of motor vehicles other than vehicles operated by a public utility requiring a special overlength, overheight, or overwidth permit issued by the secretary of the department, as provided for in R.S. 32:387, shall enter upon or cross over any bridge which spans the Mississippi River or, within a distance of two miles of such bridge, park within 75 feet of the highway approaching such bridge, in any parish having a population in excess of two hundred and fifty thousand inhabitants, according to the latest federal census, between hours of six-thirty o'clock and nine o'clock a.m. and between the hours of three-thirty o'clock and six o'clock p.m. from Monday through Friday of each week, except on legal state holidays; however, this provision shall not apply to any such bridge spanning said river between the parishes of East Baton Rouge and West Baton Rouge.

B. Whoever violates the provisions of this Section shall be guilty of a misdemeanor and shall be fined fifty dollars or imprisoned for not more than ten days, or both. For any subsequent violations the penalty provided herein shall be doubled.

§295. Child Passenger Restraint System.

A. Every resident of this state who transports a child or children under the age of thirteen years in a motor vehicle which is equipped with safety belts at the time of manufacture or assembly, or is currently equipped with safety belts, shall have the child properly secured in accordance with the manufacturer's instructions in an age- or size-appropriate passenger restraint system which meets the applicable federal motor vehicle safety standards in effect, except as provided in Subsections (C), (D), and (E).

B. (1) The term "motor vehicle" as used in this Section, shall not mean the following: bicycle; farm tractor; motorcycle or motor-driven cycle; truck of manufacturer's rating carrying capacity of over 2,000 pounds; ambulance or other emergency vehicle; school bus as defined in R.S. 32:1(62)(a) and (b); church bus, private bus, or recreational vehicle which has a passenger capacity of over ten persons; or commercial truck, van, or taxi.

(2) The term "child restraint system" as used in this Section shall mean a lap belt, a shoulder harness, or an age- or size-appropriate child safety seat.

C. If such child is three to twelve years of age, securing the child in a lap belt or safety belt in a rear seat shall be sufficient to meet the requirements of this Section. If there are no rear seats, an age- or size-appropriate passenger restraint system shall be used.

D. When the number of children under the age of thirteen in the motor vehicle exceeds the number of age- or size-appropriate passenger restraint systems and seat belts available in the motor vehicle, the unrestrained children shall be seated in a rear seat.

E. The provisions of this Section shall not apply when one of the following conditions exists:

(1) The motor vehicle is being used as an ambulance or other emergency vehicle.

(2) An emergency exists which threatens the life of any person operating a motor vehicle to whom this Section otherwise would apply or the life of any child who otherwise would be required to be restrained under this Section.

(3) Any child who would otherwise be required to be restrained under this Section who is physically unable because of medical reasons to use a child passenger safety system or safety belt.

F. In no event shall failure to wear a child passenger safety seat system be considered as comparative negligence, nor shall such failure be admissible as evidence in the trial of any civil action with regard to negligence, nor shall such failure be considered a moving violation.

G. Any operator of a motor vehicle stopped for a violation of this Section and against whom enforcement action has been taken shall not be guilty of a subsequent violation of this Section until after twenty-four hours have elapsed from the date and time of the violation as indicated on the traffic ticket.

H. Any person who violates this Section shall upon conviction be fined fifty dollars for a first offense, one hundred dollars for a second offense, and one hundred dollars plus all costs of court for a third or subsequent offense. In addition to the fine, the license of a defendant in violation of this Section shall be confiscated and driving privileges suspended until such time as satisfactory proof is presented to the court that the defendant has acquired an approved age- or size-appropriate passenger restraint system where applicable.
(Chgd. by Acts 1997 No. 1037, §1, eff. 7/1/97.)

§295.1. Safety belt use; tags indicating exemption.

A. (1) Each driver of a passenger car, van, or truck having a gross weight of six thousand pounds or less, commonly referred to as a pickup truck, in this state shall have a safety belt properly fastened about his or her body at all times when the vehicle is in forward motion. The provisions of this Section shall not apply to those cars, vans, or pickups manufactured prior to January 1, 1981.

(2) A person operating or riding in an autocycle shall wear seatbelts while in forward motion.

B. Except as otherwise provided by law, each front seat occupant of a passenger car, van, or truck having a gross weight of six thousand pounds or less, commonly referred to as a pickup truck, in this state shall have a safety belt properly fastened about his or her body at all times when the vehicle is in forward motion, if a belt for his seating space has been provided by the manufacturer.

C. This Section shall not apply to a motor vehicle operated by a rural letter carrier of the United States Postal Service while performing his or her duties as a rural letter carrier, to a farm vehicle being operated within five miles of the place of its principal use, or to a motor vehicle being operated by a newspaper delivery person while he or she is engaged in the distribution of regularly published newspapers.

D. (1) This Section shall not apply to an occupant of a passenger car or operator with a physically or mentally disabling condition whose physical or mental disability would prevent appropriate restraint in the safety belt; however, the condition shall be duly certified by a physician who shall state the nature of the handicap, as well as the reason such restraint is inappropriate.

(2) (a) On the application of any mentally or physically disabled individual whose impairment is permanent and prevents use of a seat belt, the commissioner shall issue a special tag for the benefit of the applicant which indicates such condition. The fee for the tag shall be five dollars.

(b) Each application shall be accompanied by a physician's statement certifying that the applicant is permanently disabled and that such disability prevents the applicant's use of a seat belt.

(3) (a) On application of any mentally or physically disabled individual whose impairment prevents use of a seat belt, but is not permanent, the commissioner shall issue a special temporary tag for the benefit of the applicant which indicates such condition. The fee for the temporary tag shall be five dollars.

(b) Each application for a temporary tag shall be accompanied by a physician's statement certifying that the applicant is temporarily disabled and certifying a period of time for which the disability will prevent the applicant's use of a seat belt.

(c) Any individual who has been issued a temporary tag under the provisions of this Section and who desires to extend the time period for which the tag is valid shall provide to the office of motor vehicles a physician's statement certifying that the applicant continues to have a disability which prevents the applicant's use of a seat belt and certifying a period of time for which the tag should be renewed. Failure to provide recertification statements shall result in the suspension of such privilege.

(4) No individual to whom a tag has been issued shall do any of the following:

(a) Display or permit the display of the tag on any motor vehicle in which he is not a passenger.

(b) Refuse to return or surrender the tag when required.

(5) (a) If a tag is lost, destroyed, or mutilated, the individual to whom the card was issued may obtain a duplicate by doing all of the following:

(i) Furnish suitable proof of the loss, destruction, or mutilation to the secretary.

(ii) Complete an application as required by this Section for the issuance of an original tag.

(iii) Pay a fee of five dollars for reissuance.

(b) Any individual who loses a tag and, after obtaining a duplicate, finds the original, shall immediately surrender the original tag to the commissioner or to any field office of the office of motor vehicles and shall not display the original tag on any vehicle.

(6) Any individual who is not impaired as provided in this Section and who willfully and falsely represents himself as having the conditions to obtain a special tag authorized by this Section shall be fined not less than one hundred dollars nor more than two hundred and fifty dollars, or shall be imprisoned for not more than thirty days, or both, and on subsequent offenses, shall be fined not less than two hundred fifty dollars nor more than five hundred dollars, or shall be imprisoned for not more than ninety days, or both.

(7) Any individual who utilizes a tag authorized by this Section which was not legally issued to him and who is not transporting the individual to whom the tag was issued shall be fined not less than fifty dollars nor more than two hundred and fifty dollars or shall be imprisoned for not more than thirty days, or both, and on second and subsequent offenses, shall be fined not less than one hundred dollars nor more than five hundred dollars, or shall be imprisoned for not more than sixty days, or both.

(8) Any individual to whom a tag is issued under the provisions of this Section and who allows his tag to be used by an individual not entitled to the use of such tag shall have his tag suspended for six months and shall be fined not less than fifty dollars nor more than two hundred and fifty dollars, or shall be imprisoned for not more than thirty days for the first offense, or both. On the second and subsequent offenses, said suspension shall be for one year, and the individual shall be fined not less than two hundred and fifty dollars nor more than five hundred dollars, in addition to suspension of said privileges, or shall be imprisoned not more than thirty days, or both.

(9) Any physician who willfully and falsely certifies that an individual is impaired in order to allow that person to obtain the special tag authorized in this Section shall be fined one thousand dollars, or shall be imprisoned for not more than ninety days, or both.

(10) The commissioner shall promulgate rules and regulations in accordance with the Administrative Procedure Act* for the implementation of the provisions of this Section. The commissioner shall determine the design, color, and placement of the tag issued under the provisions of this Section, provided that such design, color, and placement is easily discernible to law enforcement officers as designating individuals who are exempted from seat belt usage and provided that the tag includes a photograph of the person entitled to the tag.

**R.S. 49:950 et seq.*

E. In any action to recover damages arising out of the ownership, common maintenance, or operation of a motor vehicle, failure to wear a safety belt in violation of this Section shall not be considered evidence of comparative negligence. Failure to wear a safety belt in violation of this Section shall not be admitted to mitigate damages.

F. No vehicle, the contents of the vehicle, driver, or passenger in a vehicle shall be inspected, detained, or searched solely because of a violation of this Section.

G. (1) Any person who violates this Section subsequent to August 31, 1995, and prior to November 1, 1995, shall be given a warning ticket only. Subsequent to October 31, 1995, any person who violates this Section shall be subject to the following penalties:

(a) Upon conviction of a first offense, the fine shall be twenty-five dollars which shall include all costs of court.

(b) Upon conviction of a second offense, the fine shall be fifty dollars which shall include all costs of court.

(c) Upon conviction of a third offense and any subsequent offense, the fine shall be fifty dollars plus all costs of court.

(2) Notwithstanding any contrary provision of law, no other cost or fee shall be assessed against any person for a violation of this Section.

H. The Department of Public Safety and Corrections shall initiate an educational program designed to encourage compliance with the safety belt usage requirements of this Section.

I. *(Repealed.)*

(Chgd. by Acts 1992 No. 1084, §1; Acts 1995 No. 643, §1; Acts 1997 No. 383, §1, No. 511, §1, No. 1085, §1, No. 1261, §1, eff. 8/15/97.)

§295.2. Wearing of headphones; prohibitions; exceptions.

A. The wearing of headphones by any operator of a motor vehicle is hereby prohibited. For purposes of this Section, "headphones" shall mean a headset, headphone, or listening device other than a hearing aid or instrument for the improvement of defective human hearing which covers both ears or which is inserted into both ears. Any headset, headphone, or other listening device which covers or which is inserted into only one ear may be used at any time.

B. The provisions of this Section shall not apply to:

(1) Any law enforcement officer or emergency vehicle operator equipped with any communication device necessary in performing his assigned duties.

(2) Any person operating a motorcycle who is using a headset that is installed in a helmet and worn so as to prevent the speakers from making direct contact with the user's ears so that the user can hear surrounding sounds.

C. The Department of Public Safety and Corrections, office of motor vehicles, shall adopt rules and regulations in accordance with the Administrative Procedure Act* to establish standards and specifications for headset equipment, the use of which is permitted under this Section. The department shall inspect and review all such devices submitted to it and shall publish a list by name and type of approved equipment.

**R.S. 49:950 et seq.*

D. No vehicle, contents of a vehicle, or driver in a vehicle shall be inspected, stopped, detained, or searched solely because of a violation of or to determine compliance with this Section.

E. The operation of a vehicle in violation of the provisions of this Section shall not be considered a moving violation as provided for under the provisions of Title 32 of the Louisiana Revised Statutes of 1950.

F. Whoever violates the provisions of this Section shall be fined twenty-five dollars in addition to court costs.

(Added by Acts 1995 No. 619, §1, eff. 8/15/95.)

§296. Stopping, parking, or standing upon the highway shoulder; driving upon the highway shoulder.

A. No person shall stop, park, or leave standing any unattended vehicle on any state highway shoulder when such stopping or parking on the highway shoulder shall obstruct the flow of traffic or is a hazard to public safety, unless such stopping, parking, or standing is made necessary by an emergency, except:

(1) In those areas designated as parking areas by the Department of Transportation and Development, or

(2) By any public utility personnel or public utility equipment engaged in the operation of the utility business, public vehicles owned by public bodies which are engaged in the conduct of official business, or privately-owned vehicles which are engaged in services authorized by the local governing authority.

B. In case of an emergency, the driver of a vehicle may lawfully operate the vehicle on any state highway shoulder in accordance with the normal standards of prudent conduct to protect himself and others from harm. When the emergency ends, the vehicle shall not be operated on the state highway shoulder.

(Chgd. by Acts 1997 No. 117, §1, eff. 8/15/97.)

§297. Low rider vehicles.

It shall be lawful to operate "low rider" vehicles on the streets and highways in this state, if the vehicle meets the following requirements:

(1) The vehicle complies with the minimum and maximum requirements for height of headlights.

(2) The vehicle has operational shock absorbers and springs and has at least three inches of suspension travel.

(3) The vehicle has at least four inches of ground clearance measured from the frame with the vehicle on a level surface.

(4) The vehicle complies with the general requirements for motor vehicles.

§298. Farm equipment on highway shoulders.

Except as otherwise prohibited by law, to allow for unrestricted flow of traffic, farm tractors and other types of farm equipment may operate on the shoulders of any publicly maintained highway with improved asphalt or concrete shoulders except an interstate highway. However, any farm equipment operating on the shoulders of a publicly maintained highway with improved asphalt on concrete shoulders except an interstate highway shall have in use hazard warning signals as provided in R.S. 32:320.1, or shall have displayed a slow-moving vehicle emblem as provided in R.S. 32:376 or any other hazard warning device which has been approved by the commissioner, or any combination thereof. *(Added by Acts 1992 No. 251, §1; chgd. by Acts 1993 No. 414, §1, eff. 8/15/93.)*

§298.1. Off-road vehicles; permits for use on the shoulders of certain public roads and highways; rules and regulations; fees.

A. (1) Operation of off-road vehicles, including but not limited to three wheelers, four wheelers, or other all-terrain vehicles, which are not specifically designated for road use are hereby permitted to travel on the shoulders of all public roads and highways except interstates in the manner provided for in this Section solely for the purposes of farm-related activities within a five-mile radius of a farmer's farm, provided that such operators possess a valid Class "E" driver's license. In addition, the owner or the operator of such off-road vehicle shall own at least one motor vehicle which is registered with the Department of Public Safety and Corrections, office of motor vehicles, as a vehicle which is engaged in the business of actual farming under the provisions of R.S. 47:462. As an alternative to the ownership of the motor vehicle, the owner or operator of such off-road vehicle may file a sworn affidavit that he is engaged in the business of actual farming under the provisions of R.S. 47:462.

(2) In addition, any agricultural consultant as defined in R.S. 3:3202 shall also be eligible to obtain a permit to operate off-road vehicles for the purposes of farm-related activities within a five-mile radius of a farmer's farm.

(3) The permits provided for in this Section shall authorize the operation of such off-road vehicles only on the shoulders of all public roads or highways except interstate highways during each day starting thirty minutes after sunrise and ending thirty minutes before sunset. Incidental crossing of such roads or highways shall also be authorized.

B. The provisions of this Section do not relieve drivers or operators of the responsibility to comply with all the other applicable provisions of R.S. 32:298 and 301. However , the provisions of R.S. 32:190 shall not apply to this Section.

C. Prior to October 1, 1998, the Department of Public Safety and Corrections, office of motor vehicles, shall promulgate rules and regulations for enforcement and administration of this Section, including the imposition of a permit fee not to exceed the sum of five dollars for issuance of any such permit to operate an off-road vehicle on the shoulders of public roads or highways which shall become effective November 1, 1998. Prior to the issuance of such permit, owners of off-road vehicles shall provide proof to the Department of Public Safety and Corrections, office of motor vehicles, that the off-road vehicle is covered by valid liability insurance.

D. The provisions of this Section shall not apply to roads and highways in Orleans Parish. *(Added by Acts 1998 First Ex. Sess. No. 98, §1, eff. 5/5/98.)*

PART V. EQUIPMENT OF VEHICLES

SUBPART A. LAMPS AND OTHER LIGHTING EQUIPMENT

§301. When lighted lamps are required.

Every vehicle upon a highway within this state shall display lighted lamps and illuminating devices as hereinafter respectively required for different classes of vehicles subject to exception with respect to parked vehicles at any of the following times:

(1) At any time between sunset and sunrise.

(2) When, due to insufficient light or unfavorable atmospheric conditions, persons and vehicles on the highway are not clearly discernable at a distance of five hundred feet ahead.

(3) When moisture in the air or precipitation necessitates the continuous use of windshield wipers. Any person found in violation of this Paragraph may be fined not more than twenty-five dollars. No court costs shall be assessed in addition to the fine authorized by this Paragraph. Violations of the provisions of this Paragraph shall not be considered moving violations.

(Chgd. by Acts 1997 No. 381, §1; Acts 1998 First Ex. Sess. No. 118, §1, eff. 5/5/98.)

§302. Visibility distance and mounted height of lamps.

A. Whenever requirement is hereinafter declared as to distance from which certain lamps and devices shall render objects visible or within which distance such lamps or devices shall be visible, said provisions shall apply during the times stated in R.S. 32:301, in respect to a vehicle without load when upon a straight, level, unlighted highway under normal atmospheric conditions unless a different time or condition is expressly stated.

B. Whenever requirement is hereinafter declared as to the mounted height of lamps or devices it shall mean from the center of such lamp or device to the level ground upon which the vehicle stands when such vehicle is without a load.

§303. Headlamps on motor vehicles; motorcycles and motordriven cycles.

A. Every motor vehicle other than a motorcycle or motordriven cycle shall be equipped with at least two headlamps with at least one on each side of the front of the motor vehicle, which headlamps shall comply with the requirements and limitations set forth in this Chapter.

B. Every motorcycle and every motor-driven cycle shall be equipped with at least one and not more than two headlamps which shall comply with the requirements and limitations in this Chapter.

C. Every headlamp upon every motor vehicle, including every motorcycle and motordriven cycle, shall be located at a height, measured from the center of the headlamp, of not more than 54 inches nor less than 24 inches to be measured as set forth in R.S. 32:302.

D. Every headlamp described in this section shall emit a white light only.

§304. Tail lamps.

A. Every motor vehicle, trailer, semi-trailer and pole trailer and any other vehicle which is being drawn at the end of a train of vehicles, shall be equipped with at least one tail lamp mounted on the rear, which, when lighted as hereinbefore required in R.S. 32:301, shall emit a red light plainly visible from a distance of one thousand feet to the rear, provided that in the case of a train of vehicles only the tail lamps on the rearmost vehicle need actually be seen from the distance specified. And further, every such above mentioned vehicle, other than a motorcycle or motor driven cycle registered in this state and manufactured or assembled after December 31, 1962, shall be equipped with at least two tail lamps mounted on the rear, on the same level and as widely spaced laterally at practicable, which, when lighted as herein required, shall comply with the provisions of this section.

B. Every tail lamp upon every vehicle shall be located at a height of not more than 72 inches nor less than 15 inches measured as provided in R.S. 32:302.

C. Either a tail lamp or a separate lamp shall be so constructed and placed as to illuminate with a white light the rear registration plate and render it clearly legible from a distance of 50 feet to the rear. Any tail lamp or tail lamps, together with any separate lamp for illuminating the rear registration plate, shall be so wired as to be lighted whenever the head lamps or auxiliary driving lamps are lighted.

§305. New motor vehicles to be equipped with reflectors.

A. Every new motor vehicle hereafter sold and operated upon a highway of this state other than a truck tractor shall carry on the rear, either as a part of the tail lamps or separately, two red reflectors, except that every motorcycle and every motor-driven cycle shall carry at least one reflector, meeting the requirements of this section, and except that vehicles of the type mentioned in R.S. 32:308 shall be equipped with reflectors as required in those Sections applicable thereto.

B. Every such reflector shall be mounted on the vehicle at a height of not less than 20 inches nor more than 60 inches measured as set forth in R.S. 32:302, and shall be of such size and characteristics and so mounted as to be visible at night from all distances within 350 feet to 100 feet from such vehicle when directly in front of lawful upper beams of head lamps, except that visibility from a greater distance is hereinafter required of reflectors on certain types of vehicles.

§306. Stop lamps and turn signals required on new motor vehicles.

A. No person shall sell or offer for sale or operate on the highways of this state any motor vehicle registered in this state and manufactured or assembled after December 31, 1962, unless it is equipped with at least two stop lamps meeting the requirements of R.S. 32:319, except that a motorcycle, motor-driven cycle or truck tractor manufactured or assembled after said date shall be equipped with at least one stop lamp meeting the requirements of said R.S. 32:319.

B. No person shall sell or offer for sale or operate on the highways of this state any motor vehicle, trailer or semi-trailer registered in this state and manufactured or assembled after December 31, 1962, unless it is equipped with electrical turn signals meeting the requirements of R.S. 32:319. This Sub-section shall not apply to any motorcycle or motor-driven cycle.

§307. Application of succeeding sections.

Those sections of this chapter which follow immediately, including R.S. 32:308, 32:309, 32:310, 32:311, 32:311.1, and 32:312, relating to clearance lamps, marker lamps and reflectors, shall apply as stated in said sections to vehicles of the types therein enumerated, namely; buses, trucks, truck tractors, motor homes, motor vehicles with mounted truck camper, and trailers, semitrailers and pole trailers, respectively, when operated upon any highway within this state and said vehicles shall be equipped as required and all lamp equipment required shall be lighted at the times mentioned in R.S. 32:301. For purposes of the sections enumerated herein, a truck camper, when mounted upon a motor vehicle, shall be considered part of the permanent structure of that motor vehicle.

§308. Additional equipment required on buses, trucks, truck tractors, trailers, semi-trailers and pole trailers.

In addition to other equipment required in this chapter, the following vehicles shall be equipped as herein stated under the conditions stated in R.S. 32:301.

A. Buses, trucks, motor homes, and motor vehicles with mounted truck camper, eighty or more inches in width shall meet equipment requirements as follows:

(1) On the front: two clearance lamps, one at each side, and all such vehicles manufactured or assembled after December 31, 1972 shall have three identification lamps meeting the specification of Subsection F of this section.

(2) On the rear: two clearance lamps, one at each side, and all such vehicles or manufactured after December 31, 1972 shall have three identification lamps meeting the specifications of Subsection F of this section.

(3) On each side: two side marker lamps and two reflectors one of each at or near the rear and at or near the front.

B. Trailers and semi-trailers eighty inches or more in width, except boat trailers, shall meet equipment requirements as follows:

(1) On the front: two clearance lamps, one at each side.

(2) On the rear: two clearance lamps, one at each side, and all such vehicles manufactured or assembled after December 31, 1972, three identification lamps meeting the specifications of Subsection F of this section.

(3) On each side: two side marker lamps and two reflectors one of each at or near the front and at or near the rear.

C. Truck tractors shall meet equipment requirements as follows:

(1) On the front: two cab clearance lamps, one at each side, and on vehicles manufactured or assembled after December 31, 1972, three identification lamps meeting the specifications of Subsection F of this section.

(2) On each side: two amber side marker lamps and two amber reflectors, one of each at or near the front and at or near the rear.

D. Trailers, semi-trailers and pole trailers thirty feet or more in length shall have one amber side marker lamp and one amber reflector, centrally located with respect to the length of the trailer, on each side. Pole trailers shall also have on each side, at the rearmost support for the load, one combination marker lamp showing amber to the front and red to the rear and side, mounted to indicate maximum width of the pole trailer.

E. Boat trailers eighty inches or more in width shall meet equipment requirements as follows:

(1) On each side: two side marker lamps and two reflectors, one of each at or near the front and at or near the rear, and at or near the midpoint, one clearance lamp performing the function of both a front and rear clearance lamp.

(2) On the rear of boat trailers manufactured or assembled after December 31, 1972, shall be three identification lamps meeting the specifications of Subsection F of this section.

F. Whenever required or permitted by this chapter, identification lamps shall be mounted as close as practicable to the top of the vehicle, and grouped in a horizontal row, one on the vertical center line and one on each side of the vertical center line with lamp centers spaced not less than six inches or more than twelve inches apart; provided, however, that where the cab of a vehicle is not more than forty-two inches wide at the front roof line, a single identification lamp at the center of the cab shall be deemed to comply with the requirements for front identification lamps.

§309. Color of clearance lamps, identification lamps, side marker lamps, backup lamps and reflectors.

A. Front clearance lamps, identification lamps and those marker lamps and reflectors on the front or on the side near the front of a vehicle shall display or reflect an amber color.

B. Rear clearance lamps, identification lamps and those marker lamps and reflectors mounted on the rear or on the sides near the rear of a vehicle shall display or reflect a red color.

C. All lighting devices and reflectors mounted on the rear of any vehicle shall display or reflect a red color, except the stop light, which must be red, or other signal device, which may be red, amber or yellow, and except that the light illuminating the license plate shall be white and the light emitted by a backup lamp shall be white.

§310. Mounting of reflectors, clearance lamps and side marker lamps.

A. Reflectors, when required by R.S. 32:308, shall be mounted at a height not less than 15 inches and not higher than 60 inches above the ground on which the vehicle stands, except that if the highest part of the permanent structure of the vehicle is less than 15 inches the reflector at such point shall be mounted as high as that part of the permanent structure will permit.

The rear reflectors on a pole trailer may be mounted on each side of the bolster or load.

The two red reflectors of a truck tractor may be mounted on the back of the cab at a minimum height of not less than four inches above the height of the rear tires.

Any required red reflector on the rear of the vehicle may be incorporated with the tail lamp, but such reflector shall meet all the other reflector requirements of this chapter.

B. Clearance lamps shall, so far as is practicable, be mounted on the permanent structure of the vehicle in such manner as to indicate the extreme height and width of the vehicle. Provided, that when rear identification lamps are required and are mounted as high as it is practicable, rear clearance lamps may be mounted at optional height and when the mounting of front clearance lamps results in such lamps failing to indicate the extreme width of the trailer, such lamps may be mounted at optional height but must indicate, as near as practicable, the extreme width of the trailer. Clearance lamps on truck tractors shall be located so as to indicate the extreme width of the truck tractor cab. Clearance lamps and side marker lamps may be mounted in combination provided illumination is given as required herein with reference to both.

§311. Visibility of reflectors, clearance lamps, identification lamps and marker lamps.

A. Every reflector upon any vehicle referred to in R.S. 32:308 shall be of such size and characteristics and so maintained as to be readily visible at nighttime from all distances, within 600 feet to 100 feet from the vehicle when directly in front of lawful lower beams of headlamps, except that the visibility for reflectors on vehicles manufactured or assembled prior to January 1, 1970, shall be measured in front of lawful upper beams of headlamps. Reflectors required to be mounted on the sides of the vehicle shall reflect the required color of light to the sides, and those mounted on the rear shall reflect a red color to the rear.

B. Front and rear clearance lamps and identification lamps shall be capable of being seen and distinguished under normal atmospheric conditions at the times lights are required in R.S. 32:301 at all distances between 500 feet and 50 feet from the front and rear, respectively, of the vehicle on which mounted.

C. Side marker lamps shall be capable of being seen and distinguished under normal atmospheric conditions at the times lights are required in R.S. 32:301 at all distances between 500 feet and 50 feet from the side of the vehicle on which mounted.

§311.1. Equipment combinations.

Two or more lamps, reflective devices, or items of associated equipment may be combined if the requirements of each lamp, reflective device, and item of associated equipment are met, except that no clearance lamp may be combined optically with any tail lamp or identification lamp.

§312. Obstructed lights not required.

Whenever motor and other vehicles are operated in combination during the time that lights are required, any lamp, except tail lamps, need not be lighted which, by reason of its location on a vehicle of the combination, would be obscured by another vehicle of the combination, but this shall not affect the requirement that lighted clearance lamps be displayed on the front of the foremost vehicle required to have clearance lamps, nor that all lights required on the rear of the rearmost vehicle of any combination shall be lighted.

§313. Lamp or flag on projecting load.

Whenever the load upon any vehicle extends to the rear four feet or more beyond the bed or body of such vehicle there shall be displayed at the extreme rear end of the load, at the time specified in R.S. 32:301, a red light or lantern plainly visible from a distance of at least 500 feet to the sides and rear. The red light or lantern required under this Section shall be in addition to the red rear light required upon every vehicle. At any other time there shall be displayed at the extreme rear end of such load a red flag or cloth not less than 12 inches square and so hung that the entire area is visible to the driver of a vehicle approaching from the rear.

§314. Lamps on parked vehicles.

A. Every vehicle shall be equipped with one or more lamps which, when lighted, shall display a white or amber light visible from a distance of 1,000 feet to the front of the vehicle, and a red light visible from a distance of 1,000 feet to the rear of the vehicle. The location of said lamp or lamps shall always be such that at least one lamp or combination of lamps meeting the requirements of this section is installed as near as practicable to the side of the vehicle which is closest to passing traffic.

B. Whenever a vehicle is lawfully parked upon a street or highway during the hours between a half hour after sunset and a half hour before sunrise and in the event there is sufficient light to reveal persons and vehicles within a distance of 1,000 feet upon such street or highway, no lights need be displayed upon such parked vehicle.

C. Whenever a vehicle is parked or stopped upon a roadway or shoulder adjacent thereto, whether attended or unattended, during the hours between a half hour after sunset and a half hour before sunrise and there is insufficient light to reveal any person or object within a distance of 1,000 feet upon such highway, such vehicle so parked or stopped shall be equipped with and shall display lamps meeting the requirements of Subsection A.

D. Any lighted head lamps upon a parked vehicle shall be depressed or dimmed.

E. When the parking lamps are activated, the tail lamps, license plate lamps, and side marker lamps shall also be activated.

F. The foregoing provisions shall not apply to motorcycles or motor driven cycles.

§315. Lamps on farm tractors, farm equipment and implements of husbandry.

A. Every farm tractor and every self-propelled farm equipment unit of husbandry not equipped with an electric lighting system shall at all times mentioned in R.S. 32:301 be equipped with at least one lamp displaying a white light visible when lighted from a distance of not less than 500 feet to the front of such vehicle and shall also be equipped with at least one lamp displaying a red light visible when lighted from a distance of not less than 500 feet to the rear of such vehicle.

B. Every self-propelled unit of farm equipment not equipped with an electric lighting system shall at all times mentioned in R.S. 32:301, in addition to the lamps required in Sub-section A, be equipped with two reflectors visible from all distances within 600 feet to 100 feet to the rear when directly in front of lawful upper beams of head lamps.

C. Every combination of farm tractor and towed unit of farm equipment or implement of husbandry not equipped with an electric lighting system at all times mentioned in R.S. 32:301 shall be equipped with the following lamps:

(1) At least one lamp mounted to indicate as nearly as practicable the extreme left projection of said combination and displaying a white light visible when lighted from a distance of not less than 500 feet to the front of said combination, and

(2) Two lamps each displaying a red light visible when lighted from a distance of not less than 500 feet to the rear thereof and two red reflectors visible from all distances within 600 feet to 100 feet to the rear thereof when illuminated by the upper beams of head lamps.

D. Every farm tractor and every self-propelled unit of farm equipment or implement of husbandry equipped with an electric lighting system shall at all times mentioned in R.S. 32:301 be equipped with two single beam or multiple beam head lamps meeting the requirements of R.S. 32:323 or 32:321 respectively or, as an alternative, R.S. 32:325, and at least one red lamp visible when lighted from a distance of not less than 500 feet to the rear provided, that every such self propelled unit of farm equipment other than a farm tractor shall have two such red lamps or, as an alternative, one such red lamp and two red reflectors visible from all distances within 600 feet to 100 feet when directly in front of lawful upper beams of head lamps.

E. Every combination of farm tractor and towed farm equipment or towed implement of husbandry equipped with an electric lighting system shall at all times mentioned in R.S. 32:301 be equipped with lamps as follows:

(1) The farm tractor element of every such combination shall be equipped as required in Sub-section D of this Section.

(2) The towed unit of farm equipment or implement of husbandry element of such combination shall be equipped with two red lamps visible when lighted from a distance of not less than 500 feet to the rear or, as an alternative, two red reflectors visible to the rear directly in front of lawful upper beams of head lamps.

(3) Said combinations shall also be equipped with a lamp displaying a white or amber light, or any shade of color between white and amber, visible when lighted from a distance of not less than 500 feet to the front and a lamp displaying a red light visible when lighted from a distance of not less than 500 feet to the rear.

F. The lamps and reflectors required in this Section shall be so positioned as to show from front and rear as nearly as practicable the extreme projection of the vehicle carrying them on the side of the roadway used in passing such vehicle. If a farm tractor, or a unit of farm equipment, whether self-propelled or towed, is equipped with two or more lamps or reflectors visible from the front or two or more lamps or reflectors visible from the rear, such lamps or reflectors shall be so positioned that the extreme projections both to the left and to the right of said vehicle shall be indicated as nearly as practicable.

§316. Lamps on other vehicles and equipment.

A. Every vehicle, including animal drawn vehicles and vehicles referred to in R.S. 32:53, not specifically required by the provisions of this article to be equipped with lamps or other lighting devices, shall at all times specified in R.S. 32:301 be equipped with at least one lamp displaying a white light visible from a distance of not less than 1,000 feet to the front of said vehicle, and shall also be equipped with two lamps displaying red light visible from a distance of not less than 1,000 feet to the rear of said vehicle, or as an alternative, one lamp displaying a red light visible from a distance of not less than 1,000 feet to the rear and two red reflectors visible from a distance of 100 to 600 feet to the rear when illuminated by lawful lower beams of head lamps.

B. After January 1, 1975, every animal drawn vehicle shall at all times be equipped with a slow-moving vehicle emblem complying with the provisions of R.S. 32:377.

§317. Spotlights and auxiliary lamps.

A. (1) A spotlight shall be authorized only on motor vehicles which meet one of the following conditions:

(a) The vehicle is a publicly owned emergency vehicle.

(b) The vehicle is operated by a public service corporation as approved by the secretary of the Department of Public Safety.

(c) The spotlight is for use within a municipality where such use is specifically permitted by special ordinance and such use shall be restricted to such municipalities.

(d) The vehicle is owned and operated by a farmer. A spotlight authorized by this Subparagraph:

(i) Shall only be mounted on the back panel of the cab of a pickup truck,

(ii) Shall not rotate more than 180 degrees at the rear of the cab,

(iii) Shall not face the front of the vehicle at any time,

(iv) Shall be used solely for agricultural purposes, and

(v) Shall not be operated on any state or local highway.

(2) When use of a spotlight is permitted, every such illuminated spotlight shall be operated upon approaching another vehicle so that no part of the high intensity portion of the beam will be directed to the left of the prolongation of the extreme left side of the vehicle nor more than one hundred feet ahead of the vehicle.

B. Any motor vehicle may be equipped with not more than two fog lamps mounted on the front of the vehicle at a height of not less than 12 inches nor more than 30 inches above the level surface upon which the vehicle stands and so aimed that when the vehicle is not loaded none of the high intensity portion of the light to the left of the center of the vehicle shall at a distance of 25 feet ahead project higher than a level of 4 inches below the level of the center of the lamp from which it comes. Lighted fog lamps meeting the above requirements may be used with lower head lamp beams as specified in R.S. 32:321.

C. Any motor vehicle may be equipped with not more than two auxiliary passing lamps mounted on the front of the vehicle at a height not less than 24 inches nor more than 42 inches above the level surface upon which the vehicle stands. The provisions of R.S. 32:321 shall apply to any combination of head lamps and auxiliary passing lamps.

D. Any motor vehicle may be equipped with not more than two auxiliary driving lamps mounted on the front of the vehicle at a height not less than 16 inches nor more than 42 inches above the level surface upon which the vehicle stands. The provisions of R.S. 32:321 shall apply to any combination of head lamps and auxiliary driving lamps.

§318. Audible and visual signals on certain vehicles.

A. Every authorized emergency vehicle, except privately owned vehicles belonging to members of an organized volunteer fire department or fire district shall, in addition to any other equipment and distinctive markings required by this Chapter, be equipped with a siren, exhaust whistle, or bell capable of giving an audible signal.

B. Every type I school bus purchased new after the effective date of this Act used for the transportation of school children shall, in addition to any other equipment and distinctive markings required by this Chapter, be equipped with the following signal lights and devices:

(1) Every type I school bus purchased new after the effective date of this Act shall be equipped with signal lamps mounted as high and as widely spaced laterally as practicable, which shall be capable of displaying to the front two alternately flashing red lights located at the same level and to the rear two alternately flashing red lights located at the same level, and these lights shall have sufficient intensity to be visible at five hundred feet in normal sunlight.

(2) Every type I school bus purchased new after the effective date of this Act shall be equipped with two semaphore signs mounted on the left side of the bus, one as near the front of the cab of the bus as practicable and one as near the rear of the body of the bus as practicable, said semaphore signs to be not less than eighteen inches in diameter, painted red, with the word "Stop" on each side thereof in white letters not less than six inches in height. Each semaphore sign shall be a standard octagonal sign containing two flashing red lamps which are visible from both sides of the extended sign. These signs shall be constructed so as to fold back against the side of the bus when at rest and capable of being extended perpendicular to the side of the bus with controls operated by the driver.

(3) Every type II school bus purchased new after the effective date of this Act shall be equipped with at least one semaphore sign which shall comply with the requirements in R.S. 32:318(B)(2).

(4) Every school bus purchased new after the effective date of this Act shall, in addition to the lights required by Subsection B(1), be equipped with yellow signal lamps mounted near each of the four red lamps and at the same level but closer to the vertical center line of the bus, which shall display two alternately flashing yellow lights to the front and two alternately flashing yellow lights to the rear, and these lights shall be visible at five hundred feet in normal sunlight. These lights shall be displayed by the school bus driver at least one hundred feet, but not more than five hundred feet, before (but not during) every stop at which the alternately flashing red lights required by Subsection B(1) shall be activated.

C. Every authorized emergency vehicle shall, in addition to any equipment and distinctive markings required by this Chapter, be equipped with signal lamps mounted as high and as widely spaced laterally as practicable, which shall be capable of displaying to the front two alternately flashing red lights located at the same level and to the rear two alternately flashing red lights located at the same level, and these lights shall have sufficient intensity to be visible at five hundred feet in normal sunlight. In lieu of the alternately flashing red lights in the front, an authorized emergency vehicle may be equipped with a large revolving red light on the roof which is discernable in all directions and which shall also have sufficient intensity to be visible at five hundred feet in normal sunlight. In lieu of the large revolving red light on the roof, authorized emergency vehicles of organized fire companies only shall be equipped with a large revolving alternating red and white light on the roof encased in a clear dome, which is discernible in all directions and which shall also have sufficient intensity to be visible at five hundred feet in normal sunlight.

D. A police vehicle when used as an authorized emergency vehicle may, but need not, be equipped with alternately flashing red lights specified herein.

E. The use of the signal equipment described herein shall impose upon drivers of other vehicles the obligation to yield the right of way and to stop as prescribed in R.S. 32:80 and 32:125.

F. In lieu of the alternating flashing red lights in the front of the vehicle, or of the large revolving red light on the roof of the vehicle, all law enforcement officers are hereby authorized to equip, operate and use motor vehicles with blue colored electric emergency lights in the exercise of their official duties. These lights shall have sufficient intensity to be visible at five hundred feet in normal sunlight.

All persons other than law enforcement officers on official duty are prohibited from equipping, operating or using motor vehicles with blue colored electric lights thereon.

G. (1) Notwithstanding any other provision of law to the contrary, privately owned motor vehicles belonging to members of the emergency medical team as designated by the commander of the United States Army Community Hospital at Fort Polk may be equipped with a large flashing red light which shall have sufficient intensity to be visible at five hundred feet in normal sunlight.

(2) The commander shall submit the name and motor vehicle license number of each member of the emergency medical team to the secretary of the Department of Public Safety and the secretary of the Department of Transportation and Development.

(3) The secretary of the Department of Public Safety shall issue, after review and recommendation of the secretary of the Department of Transportation and Development, to each team member a letter of authorization for the use of the light whenever the member is en route to the hospital in an emergency as declared by the hospital commander.

(4) The letter of authorization shall be located within the vehicle for which it has been issued. The provisions of R.S. 32:24 shall extend to the driver of any vehicle issued the letter of authorization under this Subsection.

§319. Signal lamps and signal devices.

A. Any vehicle may be equipped and when required under this chapter, shall be equipped with a stop lamp or lamps on the rear of the vehicle which shall display a red light, visible from a distance of not less than 300 feet to the rear in normal sunlight, and which shall be actuated upon application of the service (foot) brake, and which may, but need not be, incorporated with one or more other rear lamps.

B. Any vehicle may be equipped and when required under R.S. 32:306(C) shall be equipped with electric turn signals which shall indicate an intention to turn by flashing lights showing to the front and rear of a vehicle or on a combination of vehicles, on the side of the vehicle or combination toward which the turn is to be made. The lamps showing to the front shall be mounted on the same level and as widely spaced laterally as practicable and, when signaling, shall emit amber light, provided that on any vehicle manufactured prior to January 1, 1969, the lamps showing to the front may emit white or amber light, or any shade of light between white and amber. The lamps showing to the rear shall be mounted on the same level and as widely spaced laterally as practicable, and, when signaling, shall emit a red or amber light, or any shade of color between red and amber. Turn signal lamps on vehicles 80 inches or more in overall width shall be visible from a distance of not less than 500 feet to the front and rear in normal sunlight. Turn signal lamps on vehicles less than 80 inches wide shall be visible at a distance of not less than 300 feet to the front and rear in normal sunlight. Turn signal lamps may, but need not be, incorporated in other lamps on the vehicle.

C. A truck-tractor need not be equipped with turn signal lamps mounted on the rear provided the turn signal lamps mounted at or near the front are double-faced and so located as to be visible both to the front and to the rear from a distance of not less than 500 feet in normal sunlight.

§320. Additional lighting equipment.

A. Any motor vehicle may be equipped with not more than two side or fender lamps which shall emit an amber or white light without glare.

B. Any motor vehicle may be equipped with not more than one running board courtesy lamp on each side thereof which shall emit a white or amber light without glare.

C. Any motor vehicle may be equipped with not more than two backup lamps either separately or in combination with other lamps, but any such backup lamps shall not be lighted when the motor vehicle is in forward motion.

Backup lights are required on all passenger vehicles manufactured after January 1, 1969. The backup lamp shall be illuminated when the ignition switch is energized and reverse gear is engaged. Backup lamps shall not be lighted when the vehicle is in forward motion. Backup lamps shall be mounted on the rear so that the center of the lens, or at least one lamp is visible from any eye point elevation from at least six feet to two feet above the horizontal plane on which the vehicle is standing; and from any position in the area, rearward of a vertical plane perpendicular to the longitudinal axis of the vehicle, six feet to the rear of the vehicle and extending three feet beyond each side of the vehicle. Maximum candlepower is 300 cp total.

D. Any vehicle eighty inches or more in overall width, if not otherwise required by R.S. 32:308, may be equipped with not more than three identification lamps showing to the front which shall emit an amber light without glare and not more than three identification lamps showing to the rear which shall emit a red light without glare. Such lamps shall be mounted as specified in Subsection (F) of R.S. 32:308.

E. Any vehicle may be equipped with one or more side marker lamps and any such lamp may be flashed in conjunction with turn or vehicular hazard warning signals. Side marker lamps located toward the front of a vehicle shall be amber and side marker lamps located toward the rear shall be red.

§320.1. Vehicular hazard warning signals.

A. Any vehicle may be equipped with lamps for the purpose of warning the operators of other vehicles of the presence of a vehicular traffic hazard requiring the exercise of unusual care in approaching, overtaking or passing.

B. Every vehicle other than a motorcycle or motor-driven cycle registered in this state and manufactured or assembled after December 31, 1972, shall be equipped with vehicular hazard warning signal lamps meeting the requirements of this section.

C. Vehicular hazard warning signal lamps used to display such warning to the front shall be mounted at the same level and as widely spaced laterally as practicable and shall display simultaneously flashing amber lights, provided that on any vehicle manufactured prior to January 1, 1975, the lamps showing to the front may display simultaneously flashing white or amber lights, or any shade of color between white and amber. The lamps used to display such warning to the rear shall be mounted at the same level and as widely spaced laterally as practicable, and shall show simultaneously flashing amber or red lights, or any shade of color between amber and red. These warning lights shall be visible from a distance of not less than 500 feet in normal sunlight on vehicles 80 inches or more in overall width and 300 feet in normal sunlight on vehicles less than 80 inches in overall width.

§321. Multiple beam road lighting equipment.

Except as hereinafter provided, the head lamps or the auxiliary driving lamps or the auxiliary passing lamp or combinations thereof on motor vehicles other than motorcycles or motor-driven cycles shall be so arranged that the driver may control the selection between the distributions of light projected to different elevations, subject to the following requirements and limitations:

(1) There shall be an uppermost distribution of light, or composite beam, so aimed and of such intensity as to reveal persons and vehicles at a distance of at least 500 feet ahead for all conditions of loading.

(2) There shall be a lowermost distribution of light, or composite beam, so aimed and of such intensity to reveal persons and vehicles at a distance of at least 150 feet ahead; and on a

straight level road under any condition of loading none of the high intensity portion of the beam shall be directed to strike the eye of an approaching driver.

(3) Every new motor vehicle, other than a motorcycle or motor-driven cycle, registered in this state after January 1, 1955, which has multiple beam road lighting equipment shall be equipped with a beam indicator, which shall be lighted whenever the uppermost distribution of light from the head lamps is in use, and shall not otherwise be lighted. Said indicator shall be so designed and located that when lighted it will be readily visible without glare to the driver of the vehicle so equipped.

§322. Use of multiple beam road lighting equipment.

A. Whenever a motor vehicle is being operated on a roadway or shoulder adjacent thereto during the times specified in R.S. 32:301, the driver shall use a distribution of light or composite beam, directed high enough and of sufficient intensity to reveal persons and vehicles at safe distance in advance of the vehicle subject to the following requirements and limitations.

B. Whenever a driver of a vehicle approaches an oncoming vehicle within 500 feet, such driver shall use a distribution of light, or composite beam, so aimed that the glaring rays are not projected into the eyes of the oncoming driver. The lowermost distribution of light, or composite beam, specified in R.S. 32:321, shall be dimmed to avoid glare at all times, regardless of road contour and loading.

C. Whenever the driver of a vehicle follows another vehicle within 200 feet to the rear, except when engaged in the act of overtaking or passing, such driver shall use a distribution of light permissible under this Chapter other than the uppermost distribution of light specified in R.S. 32:321(1).

D. Whenever the driver of a vehicle approaches an oncoming vehicle within five hundred feet or follows another vehicle two hundred feet to the rear, such driver shall not use any fog lamps or other auxiliary driving or passing lamps, except during periods of inclement weather or fog.

§323. Single-beam road-lighting equipment.

Head lamps arranged to provide a single distribution of light shall be permitted on motor vehicles manufactured and sold prior to January 1, 1955 in lieu of multiple beam road lighting equipment herein specified if the single distribution of light complies with the following requirements and limitations:

(1) The head lamps shall be so aimed that when the vehicle is not loaded none of the high intensity portion of the light shall at a distance of 25 feet ahead project higher in than a level of 5 inches below the level of the center of the lamp from which it comes, and in no case higher than 42 inches above the level on which the vehicle stands at a distance of 75 feet ahead.

(2) The intensity shall be sufficient to reveal persons and vehicles at a distance of at least 200 feet.

§324. Lighting equipment on motor-driven cycles.

The head lamp or head lamps upon every motor-driven cycle may be of the single-beam or multiple-beam type but in either event shall comply with the requirements and limitations as follows:

(1) Every said head lamp or head lamps on a motor-driven cycle shall be of sufficient intensity to reveal a person or a vehicle at a distance of not less than 100 feet when the motor-driven cycle is operated at any speed less than 25 miles per hour and at a distance of not less than 200 feet when the motor-driven cycle is operated at a speed of 25 or more miles per hour, and at a distance of not less than 300 feet when the motor-driven cycle is operated at a speed of 35 or more miles per hour.

(2) In the event the motor-driven cycle is equipped with a multiple beam head lamp or head lamps the upper beam shall meet the minimum requirements set forth above and shall not exceed the limitations set forth in R.S. 32:321(1), and the lowermost beam shall meet the requirements applicable to a lowermost distribution of light as set forth in R.S. 32:321(2).

(3) In the event the motor-driven cycle is equipped with a single beam lamp or lamps, said lamp or lamps shall be so aimed that when the vehicle is loaded none of the high intensity portion of light, at a distance of 25 feet ahead, shall project higher than the level of the center of the lamp from which it comes.

§325. Alternate road-lighting equipment.

Any motor vehicle may be operated under the conditions specified in R.S. 32:301 when equipped with two lighted lamps upon the front thereof capable of revealing persons and objects 75 feet ahead in lieu of lamps required in R.S. 32:321 or 32:323, provided, however, that at no time shall it be operated at a speed in excess of 20 miles per hour but only on such highways, or parts thereof, that such slow speeds are permitted.

§326. Number of driving lamps required or permitted; parking lights.

A. At all times specified in R.S. 32:301, at least two lighted lamps shall be displayed, one on each side at the front of every motor vehicle other than a motorcycle or motor-driven cycle, except when such vehicle is parked subject to regulations governing lights on parked vehicles.

B. Whenever a motor vehicle equipped with head lamps as herein required is also equipped with any auxiliary lamps or any other lamp on the front thereof projecting a beam of intensity greater than 300 candlepower, not more than a total of four of any such lamps on the front of a vehicle shall be lighted at any one time when upon a highway of this state.

C. No moving vehicle upon any public highway within this state shall be operated with only the parking lights for illumination.

§327. Special restrictions on lamps.

A. Any lighted lamp or illuminating device upon a motor vehicle, other than head lamps, spotlamps, auxiliary lamps, flashing turn signals, emergency vehicle warning lamps and school bus warning lamps, which project a beam of light of an intensity greater than 300 candlepower shall be so directed that no part of the high intensity portion of the beam will strike the level of the roadway on which the vehicle stands at a distance of 75 feet from the vehicle.

B. No person shall drive or move any vehicular equipment upon any highway of this state with any lamp or device thereon displaying a red or green light visible from directly in front of the center thereof. This section shall not apply to any vehicle upon which a red or green light visible from the front is expressly authorized or required by this Chapter or by regulation of the department.

C. Flashing lights are prohibited except on authorized emergency vehicles, school buses, or on any vehicle as a means of indicating a right or left turn, or the presence of a vehicular traffic hazard requiring unusual care in approaching, overtaking or passing.

D. No person shall sell a dashboard, hood, vehicle front grill, or vehicle roof mounted emergency light that emits a blue or red glow, or that emits a glow in any combination of the colors red, white, and blue, to any person who is not a peace officer, a firefighter, or a person employed in the performance of emergency or public utility services. No person shall possess such an emergency light except peace officers, firefighters, public utility, and emergency personnel. However, vehicles which are owned and operated by members of nonprofit corporations as provided in R.S. 12:201 et seq. and which are tax exempt in accordance with Section 501(c) of the Internal Revenue Code, for exhibition in shows, parades, tours, and other special events and not for general transportation may be equipped with alternately flashing red lights and these lights may have sufficient intensity to be visible at five hundred feet in normal sunlight, provided that such use shall only be allowed when the vehicle is participating in exhibitions, shows, parades, tours, and other special events, and not for general transportation. The secretary by rule shall establish the criteria to be used in determining which persons, other than members of such nonprofit corporations, qualify to purchase or possess emergency lights as described in this Subsection.
(Chgd. by Acts 1993 No. 858, §1; Acts 1995 No. 56, §1, eff. 8/15/95.)

§328. Special lighting equipment on school buses.

A. The commissioner is hereby authorized to adopt standards and specifications applicable to lighting equipment on and special warning devices to be carried by school buses consistent with the provisions of this Chapter, but supplemental thereto. Such standards and specifications shall correlate with and, so far as possible, conform to the specifications then current as approved by the Society of Automotive Engineers.

B. It shall be unlawful to operate any flashing warning signal light on any school bus except when said school bus is stopped or is in the act of coming to a complete stop on a highway for the purpose of permitting school children to board or alight from said school bus, and also, except when any such school bus is stopped or coming to a complete stop on a highway at a crossing of a railroad.

§329. Bicycles; front lamps; side and rear reflectors.

A. Every bicycle when in use at nighttime shall be equipped with a lamp on the front which shall emit a white light visible from a distance of at least five hundred feet to the front and with a red reflector on the rear and a reflector on each side facing outward at a right angle to the bicycle frame, all of a type approved by the department which shall be visible from all distances within six hundred feet to one hundred feet to the rear when directly in front of lawful lower beams of headlamps on a motor vehicle. A lamp emitting a red light visible from a distance of five hundred feet to the rear may be used in addition to the red reflector.

B. After December 31, 1974, no person shall sell or offer for sale any bicycle unless such bicycle is equipped with at least one red reflector on the rear and one reflector on each side as required by this section. This section shall not apply to bicycles while engaged in sanctioned competition races.

§330. Selling or using lamps or equipment.

A. No person shall have for sale, sell, or offer for sale for use upon or as part of the equipment of a motor vehicle, trailer, or semitrailer, or for use upon any such vehicle any head lamp, auxiliary or fog lamp, rear lamp, signal lamp, or reflector, which reflector is required hereunder, or parts of any of the foregoing which tend to change the original design or performance, unless of a type which has been submitted to the commissioner and approved by him. This Section shall not apply to equipment in actual use on August 1, 1962, or replacement parts therefor.

B. No person shall have for sale, sell, or offer for sale for use upon or as a part of a motor vehicle, trailer, or semitrailer any lamp or device mentioned in this Section which has been approved by the commissioner unless such lamp or device bears thereon the trademark or name under which it is approved so as to be legible when installed.

C. No person shall use upon any motor vehicle, trailer, or semitrailer any lamps mentioned in this Section unless said lamps mentioned in this Section are equipped with bulbs of a rated candlepower and are mounted and adjusted so as to focus and aim in accordance with instructions of the commissioner.

§331. Authority of commissioner with reference to lighting devices.

A. The commissioner is hereby authorized to approve or disapprove lighting devices and to issue and enforce regulations establishing standards and specifications for the approval of such lighting devices, their installation, aiming, and readjusting. Such regulations shall correlate with and, so far as practicable, conform to the then current standards and specifications of the Society of Automotive Engineers applicable to such equipment.

B. The commissioner is hereby required to approve or disapprove any lighting device of a type on which approval is specifically required in this Chapter, within a reasonable time after such device has been submitted.

C. The commissioner is further authorized to set up the procedure which will be followed when any device is submitted for approval and to charge fees for the approval or disapproval of those lighting devices submitted. The fee shall not exceed twenty-five dollars for each type of lamp or lighting device submitted.

§332. Adjustment certificate.

A. The commissioner is authorized to designate, instruct, and supervise official stations for adjusting head lamps and auxiliary driving lamps to conform to the provisions of this Chapter.

B. When head lamps and auxiliary driving lamps have been adjusted in conformity with the instructions issued by the Department of Public Safety, a certificate of adjustment shall be issued by the Department of Public Safety to the driver of the motor vehicle on forms issued in duplicate and showing the date of issue, registration number of the motor vehicle, owner's name, make, and official designation of the adjusting station.

§333. Certain lights around license plates prohibited.

A. Except for antique automobiles, the use of neon lights around license plates, or the use of any other lights which obscure the clear view of motor vehicle license plates, for motor vehicles is prohibited.

B. Whoever violates the provisions of this Section shall be fined not more than one thousand dollars, or imprisoned not more than six months, or both.
(Added by Acts 1994 Third Ex. Sess. No. 106, §1, eff. 7/7/94.)

SUBPART B. BRAKES

§341. Brake equipment required.

A. Every motor vehicle, other than a motorcycle or motor-driven cycle, when operated upon a highway of this state, shall be equipped with brakes adequate to control the movement of and to stop and hold such vehicle, including two separate means of applying the brakes, each of which shall be effective to apply the brakes to at least two wheels. If these two separate means of applying the brakes are connected in any way, they shall be so constructed that the failure of any one part of the operating mechanism shall not leave the motor vehicle without brakes on at least two wheels.

B. Every motorcycle and every motor-driven cycle, when operated upon a highway of this state, shall be equipped with at least one brake, which may be operated by hand or foot.

C. Every trailer or semi-trailer of a gross weight of 3,000 pounds or more, when operated upon a highway of this state, shall be equipped with brakes adequate to control the movement of and to stop and hold such vehicle and so designed as to be applied by the driver of the towing motor vehicle from its cab, and said brakes shall be so designed and connected that in case of an accidental breakaway of the towed vehicle the brakes shall be automatically applied.

D. Every motor vehicle, trailer or semi-trailer manufactured or assembled after December 31, 1962, and thereafter sold in this state and operated upon the highways of this state shall be equipped with brakes upon all wheels of every such vehicle, except that no motorcycle, motor-driven cycle, or semi-trailer of less than 1,500 pounds gross weight, need be equipped with brakes.

E. Parking brakes—adequacy—Every such vehicle and combination of vehicles, except motorcycles and motor-driven cycles, shall be equipped with parking brakes adequate to hold the vehicle on any grade on which it is operated, under all conditions of loading, on a surface free from snow, ice, or loose material. The parking brakes shall be capable of being applied in conformance with the foregoing requirements by the driver's muscular effort or by spring action or by equivalent means. Their operation may be assisted by the service brakes or other source of power provided that failure of the service brake actuation system or other power assisting mechanism will not prevent the parking brakes from being applied in conformance with the foregoing requirements. The parking brakes shall be so designed that when once applied they shall remain applied with the required effectiveness despite exhaustion of any source of energy or leakage of any kind. The same brake drums, brake shoes and lining assemblies, brake shoe anchors and mechanical brake shoe actuation mechanism normally associated with the wheel brake assemblies may be used for both the service brakes and the parking brakes. If the means of applying the parking brakes and the service brakes are connected in any way, they shall be so constructed that failure of any one part shall not leave the vehicle without operative brakes.

F. The brake shoes operating within or upon the drums on the vehicle wheels of any motor vehicle may be used for both service and hand operation.

G. All sport, boat, or any other nonagricultural trailers and semi-trailers of less than 3,000 pounds gross weight need not be equipped with brakes.

H. Every trailer or semi-trailer of between three thousand and one and five thousand pounds gross weight need only have brakes on a single axle.

I. Vehicles carrying forest products in their natural state shall not be required to have a brake on the drag axle if the wheels of the axle touch the ground only when the vehicle is loaded; however, this provision does not apply to trailers or trucks with more than two axles.

§341.1. Exemptions; farm vehicles and equipment.

A. Any farm trailer, farm semi-trailer, rubber-tired farm wagon or cart, drawn rubber-tired farm equipment, or implement of husbandry manufactured or assembled prior to January 1, 1973 and operated or moved only incidentally on the highways of this state shall be exempt from the braking requirements imposed by the State of Louisiana, including more particularly but not exclusively those requirements set forth in this subpart, provided its gross weight does not exceed ten thousand pounds or when the speed of such vehicle does not exceed thirty miles per hour. The exemption for farm vehicles described herein shall apply only to those vehicles used exclusively in transporting farm produce, livestock, farm supplies and implements of husbandry.

B. All farm trailers or farm semi-trailers of a gross weight exceeding three thousand pounds manufactured or assembled after January 1, 1973, and used on the highways of this state shall be required to meet the braking requirements imposed by the state of Louisiana. Any rubber-tired farm wagon or cart, drawn rubber-tired farm equipment, or implement of husbandry, manufactured or assembled after January 1, 1973, and designed primarily for field use, and operated or moved only incidentally on the highways of this state, shall continue to be exempt from the braking requirements imposed by the state of Louisiana, including more particularly but not exclusively those requirements set forth in this subpart, provided its gross weight does not exceed ten thousand pounds or the speed of such vehicle does not exceed thirty miles per hour. The provisions of this paragraph shall be applicable only to vehicles used exclusively in transporting farm produce, livestock, farm supplies and implements of husbandry.

§342. Performance ability of brakes.

A. Every motor vehicle or combination of vehicles, at all times and under all conditions of loading, upon application of the service (foot) brake, shall be capable of:

(1) Developing a braking force that is not less than the percentage of its gross weight tabulated herein for its classification;

(2) Decelerating in a stop from not more than 20 miles per hour at not less than the feet per second tabulated herein for its classification; and

(3) Stopping from a speed of 20 miles per hour in not more than the distance tabulated herein for its classification, such distance to be measured from the point at which movement of the service brake pedal or control begins.

B. Test for declaration and stopping distance shall be made on a substantially level (not to exceed plus or minus one per cent grade), dry, smooth, hard surface that is free from loose material.

CLASSIFICATION TABLE FOR APPLICATION

Classification of vehicles and combinations	Braking force as a percentage of gross vehicle or combination wt.	Deceleration in feet per second	Brake system application and braking distance in feet per second
I	II	III	IV
(1) Passenger vehicles, not including buses	52.8%	17	25
(2) Single-unit vehicles with a manufacturer's gross weight rating of less than 10,000 pounds	43.5%	14	30
(3) Single-unit, 2 axle vehicles with a manufacturer's gross vehicle weight rating of 10,000 lbs. or more, and buses not having a manufacturer's gross vehicle weight rating	43.5%	14	40
(4) All other vehicles and combinations with a manufacturer's gross vehicle weight rating of 10,000 or more lbs.	43.5%	14	50

§343. Condition of brakes.

All brakes and component parts thereof shall be maintained in good condition and in good working order. The brakes shall be so adjusted as to operate as equally as practicable with respect to the wheels on opposite sides of the vehicle.

§344. Brakes after engine failure.

All motor vehicles shall be so equipped as to permit application of the brakes at least once for the purpose of bringing the vehicle to a stop within the legal stopping distance after the engine has become inoperative.

§345. Brakes on motor driven cycles.

A. The commissioner is hereby authorized to require an inspection of the brake on any motor driven cycle and to disapprove any such brake which he finds will not comply with the performance ability standard set forth in R.S. 32:342, or which in his opinion is not so designed or constructed as to insure reasonable and reliable performance in actual use.

B. The commissioner may refuse to register or may suspend or revoke the registration of any vehicle referred to in this Section when he determines that the brake thereon does not comply with the provisions of this Chapter.

C. No person shall operate on any highway of this state any vehicle referred to in this Section if the commissioner has disapproved the brake equipment upon such vehicle or type of vehicle.

§346. Brakes on bicycles.

Every bicycle shall be equipped with a brake which will enable the operator to make the braked wheels skid on dry, level, clean pavement.

SUBPART C. OTHER EQUIPMENT

§351. Horns and warning devices.

A. Every motor vehicle when operated upon a highway of this state shall be equipped with a horn in good working order and capable of emitting sound audible under normal conditions from a distance of not less than 200 feet, but no horn or other warning device shall emit an unreasonably loud or harsh sound or a whistle. The driver of a motor vehicle shall, when reasonably necessary to insure safe operation, give audible warning with his horn, but shall not otherwise use such horn when upon a highway of this state.

B. No vehicle shall be equipped with nor shall any person use upon a vehicle any siren, whistle or bell, except as otherwise permitted in this Section.

C. It is permissible but not required that any commercial vehicle be equipped with a theft alarm signal device which is so arranged that it cannot be used by the driver as an ordinary warning signal.

D. Any authorized emergency vehicle may be equipped with a siren, whistle, or bell capable of emitting sound audible under normal conditions from a distance of not less than five hundred feet and of a type approved by the commissioner, but such siren shall not be used except when such vehicle is operated in response to an emergency call or in the immediate pursuit of an actual or suspected violator of the law, in which events the driver of the vehicle shall sound the siren when reasonably necessary to warn pedestrians and other drivers of the approach thereof. However, motor vehicles which are owned and operated by members of nonprofit corporations as provided in R.S. 12:201 et seq. and which are tax exempt in accordance with Section 501(c) of the Internal Revenue Code, for exhibition in shows, parades, tours, and other special uses and not for general transportation may be equipped with a siren, whistle, or bell capable of emitting sound audible under normal conditions from a distance of up to five hundred feet but such sound equipment shall not be used except when such vehicle is participating in shows, parades, tours, and other special events.

(Chgd. by Acts 1995 No. 56, §1, eff. 8/15/95.)

§352. Mufflers; requirements; prevention of excessive noise, fumes and smoke.

A. Every motor vehicle shall at all times be equipped with a muffler in good working order and in constant operation to prevent excessive or unusual noise.

B. No person shall use a muffler cut-out, bypass or similar device upon a motor vehicle on a highway of this state.

C. The engine and power mechanism of every motor vehicle shall be so equipped and adjusted as to prevent the escape of excessive fumes or smoke.

§353. Modification of exhaust systems.

No person shall modify the exhaust system of a motor vehicle in a manner which will amplify or increase the noise emitted by the motor of such vehicle, above that emitted by the muffler originally installed on the vehicle and the original muffler shall comply with all of the requirements of R.S. 32:352.

§354. Mirrors.

A. After January 1, 1975, every motor vehicle manufactured or assembled after December 31, 1972, of a type subject to registration in this state shall be equipped with a mirror mounted on the left side of the vehicle and so located as to reflect to the driver a view of the highway for a distance of at least two hundred feet to the rear of the vehicle.

B. Every motor vehicle of a type subject to registration in this state, except a motorcycle or motor driven cycle, shall be equipped with an additional mirror mounted either inside the vehicle approximately in the center or outside the vehicle on the right side and so located as to reflect to the driver a view of the highway for a distance of at least two hundred feet to the rear of the vehicle. When the required view from the inside mirror is obstructed, an outside mirror on the right side of the vehicle shall be required.

C. All mirrors required by this section shall be maintained in good condition at all times.

D. In addition to the mirrors required in Subsection A and B of this Section, every school bus shall be equipped with a mirror on the right side of the vehicle and so located as to reflect to the driver a view of the highway for a distance of at least two hundred feet to the rear of the vehicle.

E. Every school bus shall be equipped with a mirror of a type and so located as to give the seated driver a view of the area immediately in front of the front bumper, provided, however, that any Type II school bus constructed in such a way that the seated driver has a view of the area immediately in front of the front bumper need not be equipped with the mirror otherwise required by this Subsection.

F. Notwithstanding any provision of this Section or any other provision of law to the contrary, motor vehicles which are used by rural mail carriers in the performance of their duties shall not be required to be equipped with a mirror on the passenger side of the vehicle.

G. In addition to the mirrors required in Subsection A and B of this Section, every delivery van which is part of an official state motor vehicle fleet shall be equipped with a mirror of a type and so located as to give the seated driver a view of the area immediately in the rear of the rear bumper.

(Chgd. by Acts 1993 No. 97, §1; Acts 1997 No. 187, §1, eff. 8/15/97.)

 72

§355. Fire extinguishers.

Every motor vehicle engaged in the transportation of passengers for hire on the highways shall be equipped with at least one quart of chemical type fire extinguisher, in good condition and conveniently located for immediate use.

§356. Windshields must be equipped with wiping and washing systems.

A. The windshield on every motor vehicle, other than motorcycles or motor-driven cycles, shall be equipped with a device for cleaning rain, snow or other moisture from the windshield, which device shall be so constructed as to be controlled or operated by the driver of the vehicle. In addition, every such motor vehicle manufactured or assembled after December 31, 1972, shall be equipped with a two-speed, power driven windshield wiping and washing system which will adequately clean rain, snow or other moisture from the windshield regardless of engine load and speed and so constructed as to be controlled and operated by the driver of the vehicle.

B. Every windshield wiping system upon a motor vehicle shall be maintained in good working order. The windshield washing system upon a vehicle that is not more than six years old from the date of manufacture or assembly shall be maintained in good working order.

(Chgd. by Acts 1992 No. 129, §1, eff. 8/21/92.)

§357. Windshields required.

Every passenger vehicle, other than a motorcycle, and every motor truck or truck tractor, and every authorized emergency vehicle shall be equipped with an adequate windshield.

§358. Motorcycle windshields.

The glazing material used as a windshield on motorcycles shall be of either approved safety glass or clear plastic which need not be of an approved type.

§359. Safety glass required.

No person shall sell or operate any new motor vehicle as specified herein, nor shall any motor vehicle be registered thereafter unless such vehicle is equipped with safety glazing materials of a type approved by the director of public safety whenever glazing materials are used in doors, windows and windshields. The foregoing provisions shall apply to all passenger type motor vehicles, including passenger buses and school buses, but in respect to trucks, including truck tractors, the requirements as to safety glazing material shall apply to all glazing material used in doors, windows and windshields in the driver's compartments of such vehicles.

§360. Safety glass defined.

The term "safety glass" as used in this Chapter shall mean glass so treated or combined with other materials as to reduce, in comparison with ordinary sheet glass or plate glass, the likelihood of injuries to persons by objects from external sources or by glass, when the glass is cracked or broken.

§361. Approved types of safety glass.

The commissioner shall approve and maintain a list of the approved types of safety glass, conforming to recognized specifications for safety glass, as defined in this Chapter, and the Department of Public Safety shall not issue a license for or relicense any motor vehicle subject to the provisions of this Chapter, unless such motor vehicle is equipped, as herein provided, with such approved type of glass.

§361.1. View outward or inward through windshield or windows; obscuring prohibited.

A. As used in this Section and regulations applicable thereto, the following terms shall have the following meanings, unless the context of use clearly indicates otherwise:

(1) "Sun screening device" means a film material or device that is designed to be used in conjunction with motor vehicle safety glazing materials for reducing the effects of the sun.

(2) "Light transmission" means the ratio of the amount of total light to pass through the product or material, including any glazing material, to the amount of total light falling on the product or material and the glazing.

(3) "Luminous reflectance" means the ratio of the amount of total light that is reflected outward by the product or material to the amount of total light falling on the product or material.

(4) "Manufacturer" means a person who engages in the manufacture or assembly of a vehicle sun screening device, or who fabricates, laminates, or tempers a safety glazing material, incorporating, during the manufacturing process, the capacity to reflect or reduce the transmission of light.

(5) "Installer" means any person or company who affixes, places, fastens, or secures any sun screening device to any windshield or window of a motor vehicle in Louisiana.

(6) "Seller" means any person or company who transfers in the contract of sale any sun screening device for windshields or windows of motor vehicles in Louisiana.

(7) "Distributor" means any person or company who markets, delivers, or distributes any sun screening device for motor vehicles in Louisiana.

B. Except as provided by R.S. 32:361.1(C), no person may operate a motor vehicle with any object or material placed on or affixed to the front windshield or to front side windows of the vehicle so as to obstruct or reduce the driver's clear view through the front windshield or front side windows, nor place on or affix to the front windshield or the front side windows of a motor vehicle, any transparent material if the material alters the color or reduces the light transmission of the windshield or front side windows.

C. The provisions of this Section do not apply to any of the following:

(1) A sun screening device when used in conjunction with automotive safety glazing materials on the front side window, with a light transmission of at least forty percent, all tolerances included, side window behind the driver with a light transmission of at least twenty-five percent, all tolerances included, and rearmost windows with a light transmission

of at least twelve percent, all tolerances included. All sun screening devices shall not have a luminous reflectance of more than twenty percent.

(2) A transparent material, not red or amber in color, affixed to the topmost portion of the windshield not to extend more than five inches down from the top.

(3) An adjustable nontransparent sun visor mounted forward of the side windows and not attached to the glass.

(4) Publicly owned law enforcement vehicles other than those vehicles owned or used by the Department of Wildlife and Fisheries.

D. (1) Each manufacturer shall certify to the Department of Public Safety and Corrections, office of motor vehicles, by independent test laboratory data, that a sun screening device marketed in this state is in compliance with the luminous reflectance and transmittance requirements of this section.

(2) Each installer shall provide a label not to exceed one and one-half square inches in size, with a means for the permanent and legible installation between the sun screening material and each glazing surface to which it is applied, which contains the installer's name and city where the business is located.

(3) The person placing the material on the glazing surface shall affix the label to the lower right corner of the drivers side window.

(4) The light transmittance requirement of this Section does not apply to windows behind the driver on trucks, busses, trailers, motor homes, multipurpose passenger vehicles, and all windows on vehicles used for law enforcement purposes and tinted in accordance with the provisions of this Section.

E. Except as provided in Subsections G and H of this Section, anyone who operates a motor vehicle registered in this state in violation of the provisions of this Section shall be fined not more than one hundred and fifty dollars for a first offense, not more than two hundred and fifty dollars for a second offense, and not more than three hundred and fifty dollars for a third or subsequent offense.

F. Except as provided in Subsections G and H of this Section, anyone who violates the provisions of this, or any rules or regulations applicable thereto shall be fined in accordance with the provisions of R.S. 32:57.

G. Any seller, installer, manufacturer, or distributor of a sun screening device who violates the provisions of this Section shall be fined not more than five hundred dollars for a first offense, not more than one thousand dollars for a second offense, and not more than one thousand and five hundred dollars for a third or subsequent offense.

H. The provisions of this Section shall apply to all vehicles manufactured on or after January 1, 1994, unless exempted in accordance with R.S. 32:361.1.

I. All vehicles that have windows tinted on or before December 31, 1993, in compliance with then existing provisions of law are exempt from the provisions of this Section, provided that a certificate is obtained by the owner, operator, or licensee certifying that the tinting was done prior to January 1, 1994. The office of motor vehicles shall adopt rules, regulations, and a form for proof of prior tinting in accordance with provisions of this Subsection. The certificate must be present in the vehicle at all times when being operated and presented upon demand by a law enforcement officer.

J. The provisions of this Section apply to any other vehicles not included in Subsections H and I of this Section on or after January 1, 1994.

(Chgd. by Acts 1992 No. 201, §1; Acts 1993 No. 519, §1, eff. 8/15/93.)

§361.2. Medical exemption.

The provisions of R.S. 32:361.1 do not apply to a motor vehicle registered in this state in the name of a person or his legal representative, who has an affidavit signed by a physician or an optometrist licensed to practice in this state stating that such person has a physical or medical condition, involving the effects of the sun that makes it necessary to equip the motor vehicle with sun screening material which would be of a light transmission or luminous reflectance in violation R.S. 32:361.1. The affidavit must include description of the vehicle and must be in the possession of the person so afflicted, or the person's legal representative, at all times while being transported in the motor vehicle or must be kept within the described vehicle. *(Chgd. by Acts 1993 No. 519, §1, eff. 8/15/93.)*

§361.3. Security exemption.

The provisions of R.S. 32:361.1 shall not apply to any motor vehicle registered in this state when the operator of the vehicle possesses an affidavit on a form issued by the

Department of Public Safety and Corrections stating that valid security reasons exist which make it necessary to equip the motor vehicle with sun screening material which would be of a light transmission or luminous reflectance in violation of R.S. 32:361.1. The affidavit shall include a description of the vehicle and be kept within the described vehicle. The department shall adopt rules and regulations in accordance with the Administrative Procedure Act* to implement the provisions of this Section. *(Added by Acts 1993 No. 519, §1, eff. 8/15/93.)*
**R.S. 49:950 et seq.*

§362. Restrictions as to tire equipment.

A. Every solid rubber tire on a vehicle moved on any highway of this state shall have rubber on its entire traction surface at least one inch thick above the edge of the flange of the entire periphery of the rim of the wheel.

B. No tire on a vehicle moved on a highway shall have on its periphery any protuberances of any material, other than rubber, which projects beyond the thread of the traction surface of the tire, except that it shall be permissible to:

(1) Use farm machinery with tires having protuberances which will not injure the highways; and

(2) Use tire chains of reasonable proportions upon any vehicle, when required for safety because of conditions tending to cause a vehicle to slide or skid.

C. The department may issue emergency permission authorizing the operation upon the highways of traction engines or tractors having movable tracks with transverse corrugations upon their periphery, or farm tractors or other farm machinery or instruments of husbandry.

D. No person shall operate or move on any highway of this state any motor vehicle, trailer, or semi-trailer having any metal tire in contact with the highway.

E. It shall be unlawful for any person to sell, offer to sell or trade, or knowingly use any motor vehicle tire not in compliance with Subsection A of this Section; or to sell, offer to sell, or trade, or knowingly use any motor vehicle tire the original tread of which has been worn, and which without additional treading being added, has been grooved so as to give the appearance of a new tire or a tire which has been recapped. Any person violating the provisions of this Sub-section upon conviction, shall be punished by a fine of fifty dollars or thirty days in jail for the first offense and, a fine of two hundred fifty dollars or three months in jail, or both, for a second offense, and for a third or subsequent offense, shall be fined five hundred dollars and shall be imprisoned for six months in jail.

§363. Fuel tank caps.

No motor vehicle shall be driven or moved upon any highway of this state if the filling spout for the fuel tank is closed or partially closed with a plug of wood, rags, or other combustible materials.

§364. Fenders and mudguards.

No person shall operate any truck, trailer, or semi-trailer registered and licensed under the provisions of R.S. 47:451 et seq. unless equipped with fenders, covers, or devices, including flaps or splash aprons, or unless the body of the vehicle or attachments thereto afford protection to effectively minimize the spray or splash of water or mud or loose material on the highways to the rear of the vehicle.

This section does not apply to those vehicles exempt from registrations, nor to any other vehicle having an unladen weight of under one thousand five hundred pounds, nor to trucks and farm vehicles handling and hauling agricultural and forestry products.

§365. Television.

A. Except as provided in Subsection B herein, no person shall drive a motor vehicle which is equipped with a television receiver, screen or other means of visually receiving a television broadcast, which is located in the motor vehicle at any point forward of the back of the driver's seat, or which is visible to the driver while operating the motor vehicle.

B. Law enforcement officers of the state or any political subdivision thereof shall be authorized to operate video recording equipment and monitors in their law enforcement vehicles while in the performance of their duties. However, this provision shall not be construed to allow law enforcement officers to record vehicles in violation of traffic safety laws with citations for such violations to be mailed to the alleged violator at a later date. *(Chgd. by Acts 1992 No. 834, §1, eff. 8/21/92.)*

§366. Required equipment of tow cars.

Tow cars shall be equipped with the following:

(1) One or more brooms, and the driver of the tow car engaged to remove a disabled vehicle from the scene of an accident shall remove all glass and debris deposited upon the roadway by the disabled vehicle which is to be towed.

(2) A shovel, and whenever practical the tow car driver engaged to remove any disabled vehicle shall spread dirt upon that portion of the roadway where oil or grease has been deposited by such disabled vehicle.

(3) A fire extinguisher of at least two quart capacity of a type capable of extinguishing a fire of flammable liquid.

§367. Certain vehicles to carry flares or other warning devices.

A. No person shall operate any freight carrying vehicle, passenger bus, truck-tractor or any motor vehicle towing a mobile home or other vehicle, upon any highway of this state at any time between sunset and sunrise, unless that is carried in such vehicle the following equipment, except as provided in Subsection B:

(1) At least three flares, three red electric lanterns, or three portable red emergency reflectors, each of which shall be capable of being seen and distinguished at a distance of not less than six hundred feet under normal atmospheric conditions at night time.

No flare, fuses, electric lantern, or cloth warning flag shall be used for the purpose of compliance with the requirements of this Subsection unless such equipment is of a type which has been submitted to the secretary of public safety and been approved by him.

No portable reflector unit shall be used for the purpose of compliance with the requirements of this Subsection unless it is so designed and constructed as to include two reflecting elements, one above the other, each of which shall be capable of reflecting red light clearly visible, from all distances within six hundred feet to one hundred feet under normal atmospheric conditions at night, when directly in front of lawful upper beams of headlamps, and unless it is of a type which has been submitted to the commissioner and been approved by him.

(2) At least three red burning fuses, unless red electric lanterns or red portable emergency reflectors are carried.

(3) At least two red cloth flags not less than twelve inches square, with standards to support such flags.

B. No person shall operate, at the time and under conditions stated in Sub-section A, any motor vehicle used for the transportation of explosives, any cargo tank truck used for the transportation of flammable liquids or compressed gases, or any motor vehicle using compressed gas as a fuel, unless there is carried in such vehicle three red electric lanterns or three red emergency reflectors meeting the requirements of Sub-section A of this section, and there shall not be carried in any such vehicle any flares, fuses or signals produced by flame.

§368. Display of warning devices when vehicle disabled.

A. Whenever any freight carrying vehicle, passenger bus, truck tractor, trailer, semi-trailer, or any motor vehicle pulling a house trailer or other vehicle, is disabled upon the traveled portion of any highway of this state, or the shoulder thereof, at any time when lighted lamps are required on vehicles, the driver of such vehicle shall display the following warning devices upon the highway during the time the vehicle is so disabled on the highway except as provided in Sub-section B of this Section:

(1) A lighted fuse, a lighted red electric lantern or a portable red emergency reflector shall be immediately placed at the traffic side of the vehicle in the direction of the nearest approaching traffic.

(2) As soon thereafter as possible, but in any event within the burning period of the fuse (15 minutes), the driver shall place three liquid burning flares (put torches), or three lighted red electric lanterns or three portable red emergency reflectors on the traveled portion of the highway in the following order:

(a) One, approximately 100 feet from the disabled vehicle in the center of the lane occupied by such vehicle and toward traffic approaching in that lane.

(b) One, approximately 100 feet in the opposite direction from the disabled vehicle and in the center of the traffic lane occupied by such vehicle.

(c) One at the traffic side of the disabled vehicle approximately 10 feet rearward or forward thereof in the direction of the nearest approaching traffic.

B. Whenever any vehicle referred to in this Section is disabled within 500 feet of a curve, hillcrest or other obstruction to view, the warning signal in that direction shall be placed as to afford ample warning to other users of the highway, but in no case less than 100 feet nor more than 500 feet from the disabled vehicle.

C. Whenever any vehicle of a type referred to in this Section is disabled upon any roadway of a divided highway of the state during the time that lights are required, the appropriate warning devices prescribed in Subsections A and E of this Section shall be placed as follows:

(1) One at a distance of approximately 200 feet from the vehicle in the center of the lane occupied by the stopped vehicle and in the direction of traffic approaching in that lane;

(2) One at a distance of approximately 100 feet from the vehicle in the center of the lane occupied by the vehicle and in the direction of traffic approaching in that lane;

(3) One at the traffic side of the vehicle and approximately 10 feet from the vehicle in the direction of the nearest approaching traffic.

D. Whenever any vehicle of a type referred to in this Section is disabled upon the traveled portion of a highway of this state or the shoulder thereof, outside of any municipality, at any time when the display of fuses, flares, red electric lanterns, or portable red emergency reflectors is not required, the driver of the vehicle shall display two red flags upon the roadway in the lane of traffic occupied by the disabled vehicle, one at a distance of approximately 100 feet in advance of the vehicle, and one at a distance of approximately 100 feet to the rear of the vehicle.

E. Whenever any motor vehicle used in the transportation of explosives, any cargo tank truck used for the transportation of any flammable liquid or compressed flammable gas, or any motor vehicle using compressed gas as a fuel, is disabled upon a highway of this state at any time or place mentioned in Sub-section A of this Section, the driver of such vehicle shall immediately display the following warning devices:

(1) One red electric lantern or portable red emergency reflector placed on the roadway at the traffic side of the vehicle; and

(2) Two red electric lanterns or portable red reflectors, one placed approximately 100 feet to the front and one placed approximately 100 feet to the rear of the disabled vehicle in the center of the traffic lane occupied by such vehicle.

Flares, fuses or signals produced by flame shall not be used as warning devices for disabled vehicles of the type mentioned in this Sub-section.

F. The flares, fuses, red electric lanterns, portable red emergency reflectors and flags to be displayed as required in this Section shall conform with the requirements of R.S. 32:367 applicable thereto.

§369. Red flags, use in parking certain vehicles.

Between sunrise and sunset, buses, cars for hire having a capacity for over ten passengers, cars or trucks used as wreckers or for other towing purposes, freight carrying vehicles and combinations thereof, shall be equipped with two red flags, one to be placed 100 feet behind and the other 100 feet ahead of said parked vehicles and in such a position as to be visible to all approaching traffic during the daylight hours.

§370. Warning devices must be approved by commissioner prior to sale or use thereof.

No person shall sell or offer for sale, either separately or as a part of the equipment of a motor vehicle, or use upon a motor vehicle on the highways in this state any warning device mentioned in this Chapter, unless such device has been submitted to the commissioner and been approved by him.

§371. Enforcement of Part.

The commissioner shall have charge of the enforcement of this Part and, in this respect, shall see that every motor vehicle is equipped with the flares, flags, or warning devices provided for, and he shall have the power to make and publish regulations and requirements with reference to the types of flares, flags, or warnings devices to be carried as equipment by motor vehicles.

§372. Warning devices, submission to commissioner; fee.

Any person desiring approval of a warning device shall submit to the commissioner two sets of each type of the device for which approval is desired, together with a fee of twenty-five dollars. This fee shall be used in making proper tests of the devices submitted and in issuing certificates of approval therefor in accordance with the requirements for oil burning flares or reflectors or similar devices as adopted by him.

§373. Removal of warning device.

No person shall willfully remove any warning device placed upon the highways under the provisions of R.S. 32:367 through R.S. 32:369 before the driver is ready to proceed upon the highway.

§374. Violation of regulations of commissioner.

No person shall violate any rule, regulation, or requirement adopted by the commissioner under the provisions of this Chapter.

§375. Air conditioning equipment.

A. Mechanical vapor compression refrigeration equipment which is used to cool the driver or passenger compartment of any motor vehicle shall be manufactured, installed and maintained with due regard for the safety of the occupants of the vehicle and the public, and shall not contain any refrigerant which is toxic to persons or which is flammable.

B. The commissioner may adopt and enforce safety requirements, regulations, and specifications consistent with the requirements of this Section applicable to such equipment, which shall correlate with and, so far as possible, conform to the current recommended practice or standard application to such equipment approved by the Society of Automotive Engineers.

C. No person shall have for sale, offer for sale, sell or equip any motor vehicle with any equipment unless it complies with the requirements of this Section.

D. No person shall operate on any highway of this state any motor vehicle equipped with any air conditioning equipment unless said equipment complies with the requirements of this Section.

§376. Special lights for certain department vehicles.

The Office of Highways of the department is authorized to install on vehicles used by it incidental to the painting of stripes on highways, two fixed white lights, directed to the rear, which lights may be illuminated while the vehicles are in use upon the highway.

§377. Slow moving vehicle, identification.

Every motor vehicle, combination of motor vehicle and towed equipment, every self-propelled unit of equipment, self-propelled implement of husbandry, or towed implement of husbandry normally operating at speeds not in excess of twenty-five miles per hour on public streets and roads at all times shall be equipped with a slow moving vehicle emblem as follows:

(1) Where the towed unit or any load thereon obscures the slow moving vehicle emblem on the towing unit, the towed unit shall be equipped with a slow moving vehicle emblem.

(2) Where the slow moving vehicle emblem on the towing unit is not obscured by the towed unit or its load, then either or both may be equipped with the required emblem, but it shall be sufficient if either has it.

(3) The emblem required shall comply with current standards and specifications as established by the American Society of Automotive Engineers and approved by the commissioner.

§378. School bus body, hood, bumpers; color of paint; back-up audible alarms.

A. Every school bus shall be painted national school bus glossy yellow except that the hood shall be painted the same color or lusterless black and its roof may be painted white. Bumpers shall be painted glossy black, except that for increased night visibility they may be covered with a retroflective material.

B. Any school bus acquired for any purpose other than transporting children to and from school shall be painted a color other than national school bus glossy yellow and all lights, signals, and other devices and any lettering identifying the vehicle as a school bus shall be removed.

C. Nothing contained in this Section shall prohibit a yellow school bus owned by a church from being used for other church related purposes.

D. Every new school bus ordered or purchased after August 15, 1993, and every used bus not in service as a school bus on that date, but put into service as a school bus thereafter, shall be equipped with an automatic back-up audible alarm which sounds on backing and which is capable of emitting sound audible under normal conditions from a distance of not less than one hundred feet. The alarm shall also be capable of operating automatically when the vehicle is in neutral or a forward gear but rolls backward.
(Chgd. by Acts 1990 No. 652, §2; Acts 1993 No. 493, §1, eff. 10/1/93.)

§378.1. Display of patently obscene words, photographs, and depictions.

A. No person owning or operating a Louisiana registered motor vehicle on any of the public streets in this state shall affix to any part of such motor vehicle any sticker, decal, emblem, or other device containing patently obscene words, photographs, or depictions that are displayed to members of the public not occupying such vehicle. For the purposes of this Section, "obscene" shall have the meaning of "obscenity" as contained in R.S. 14:106.

B. Any person who violates the provisions of R.S. 32:378.1, upon conviction, may be penalized by a fine not to exceed one hundred dollars.

§378.2. Ignition interlock devices; condition of probation for certain DWI offenders; restricted license.

A. (1) In addition to any other provisions of law and except as otherwise provided in Subsection I of this Section, the court may require that any person who is placed on probation as provided in R.S. 14:98(B), and the court shall require that any person who is placed on probation as provided by R.S. 14:98(C) and (D) not operate a motor vehicle during the period of probation unless the vehicle is equipped with a functioning ignition interlock device as provided in this Section.

(2) (a) Notwithstanding the provisions of R.S. 32:414, 415.1, 667, 668, or any other provisions of law to the contrary, any person who has had his driver's license suspended, revoked, or cancelled under any of the following conditions, shall, upon proof to the Department of Public Safety and Corrections that his motor vehicle has been equipped with a functioning ignition interlock device as provided in this Section, be issued a restricted driver's license:

(i) Upon first or subsequent conviction or entry of a plea of guilty or nolo contendere and sentence thereupon or the forfeiture of bail for the offense of operating a motor vehicle while under the influence of alcoholic beverages.

(ii) For the offense of driving while under suspension if the suspension was the result of a conviction or entry of a plea of guilty or nolo contendere and sentence thereupon or the forfeiture of bail for the offense of operating a motor vehicle while under the influence of alcoholic beverages.

(iii) For the refusal to submit to a chemical test for the purpose of determining the alcoholic content of his blood when arrested for any offense arising out of acts alleged to have been committed while the person was driving or in actual physical control of a motor vehicle while believed to be under the influence of alcoholic beverages.

(iv) For submitting to a chemical test to determine the alcohol content of blood where the test results showed over .10 grams percent by weight of alcohol in the blood, or where the results showed under .10 grams percent by weight of alcohol in the blood but the person was nevertheless convicted of a law or ordinance which prohibits operating a vehicle while intoxicated.

(b) The restricted license shall be designated as such by a large red "R" and shall be effective for the remaining period of suspension or as long as the functioning ignition interlock device is in place, whichever period is longer.

(c) The department shall designate in writing, and upon application of the person, amend as necessary, the routes over which and the times during which the restricted licensee shall be permitted to operate designated motor vehicles in order to earn his livelihood, which written restrictions shall be attached to the restricted license and kept with it at all times.

(d) Any person granted a restricted driver's license under the provisions of this Subsection who tampers with, circumvents the operation of, or removes the ignition interlock device during the period for which the restricted license is granted shall have his driving privileges suspended for a period of time not to exceed one year and may be punished by imprisonment of twenty days, such punishment to be in addition to other penalties provided by law for related offenses.

B. No person whose driving privilege has been restricted under a condition of probation as provided in this Section shall:

(1) Rent, lease, or borrow a motor vehicle unless that vehicle is equipped with a functioning ignition interlock device.

(2) Request or solicit any other person to blow into an ignition interlock device or to start a motor vehicle equipped with the device for the purpose of providing the person so restricted with an operable motor vehicle.

C. No person shall blow into an ignition interlock device or start a motor vehicle equipped with the device for the purpose of providing an operable motor vehicle to another person whose driving privilege is restricted.

D. No person shall tamper with or circumvent the operation of an ignition interlock device.

E. Any person convicted of a violation of this Section shall be punished by imprisonment for not more than six months or a fine of not more than five hundred dollars, or both.

F. If the court imposes the use of an ignition interlock device as a term of probation on a person whose driving privilege is not suspended or revoked, the court shall require the person to provide proof of compliance to the court or the probation officer within thirty days. If the person fails to provide proof of installation within that period, absent a finding by the court of good cause for that failure which is entered into the court record, the court shall revoke the person's probation.

G. Notwithstanding the provisions of R.S. 32:414, 415.1, or 667, if the court imposes the use of an ignition interlock device as a term of probation under this Section, the person shall be entitled to apply for restricted driving privileges. If the ensuing suspension period resulting from the offense committed extends beyond the probationary period set by the court, unless otherwise instructed by the court, the restricted driving privileges may be extended until the expiration of the suspension period.

H. The person whose driving privilege is restricted pursuant to this Section shall have the system monitored by the manufacturer, at the manufacturer's expense, for proper use at least semi-annually, and more frequently as the court may order, on the operation of each interlocking ignition device in the person's vehicles. A report of such monitoring shall be issued by the manufacturer to the court and the department within fourteen days after the system is monitored.

I. If a person is required to operate a motor vehicle in the course and scope of his employment which does not have an approved ignition interlock device, and if the vehicle is owned by the employer, the court may allow the person who is prohibited from operating a motor vehicle without such a device to operate the employer's vehicle while actually in the course and scope of employment, if the employer has been notified by the person that the person's driving privilege has been restricted and if the person has proof of that notification and evidence of court approval in his possession or the notice, or a facsimile copy thereof, is with this vehicle. The exemption provided by this Subsection shall not apply to any motor vehicle owned by a business entity which is all or partly owned or controlled by a person otherwise subject to this Subsection.

J. (1) The secretary of the Department of Public Safety and Corrections shall certify, or cause to be certified, ignition interlock devices required by this Section, and publish a list of approved devices. All reasonable costs of certification shall be borne by the manufacturer. The manufacturer of the system shall be responsible for the installation or the training of installers, and shall educate users and service and maintain the system.

(2) The secretary shall formulate and promulgate a set of standards for the proper use of ignition interlock devices in full compliance with this Section. The standards shall include, but not be limited to, requirements that the devices or systems:

(a) Do not impede the safe operation of the vehicle.

(b) Have features that make circumventing difficult and that do not interfere with the normal use of the vehicle.

(c) Correlate well with established measures of alcohol impairment.

(d) Work accurately and reliably in an unsupervised environment.

(e) Resist tampering and give evidence if tampering is attempted.

(f) Are difficult to circumvent, and require premeditation to do so.

(g) Minimize inconvenience to a sober user.

(h) Require a proper, deep lung breath sample or other accurate measure of blood alcohol content equivalence.

(i) Operate reliably over the range of automobile environments.

(j) Are manufactured by a party who will provide product liability insurance.

K. The Department of Public Safety and Corrections may, in its discretion, and consistent with this Section, adopt in whole or relevant part, the guidelines, rules, regulations, studies, or independent laboratory tests performed on and relied upon in the certification or approval of ignition interlock devices by other states, their agencies or commissions.

L. The secretary shall design and adopt by regulation a warning label which shall be affixed to each ignition interlock device upon installation. The label shall contain a warning that any person tampering, circumventing, or otherwise misusing the device is guilty of a misdemeanor and may be subject to civil liability.

M. As used in this Section, "ignition interlock device" means a constant monitoring device that prevents a motor vehicle from being started at any time without first determining the equivalent blood alcohol level of the operator through the taking of a breath sample for testing. The system shall be calibrated so that the motor vehicle may not be started if the blood alcohol level of the operator, as measured by the test, reaches a level established by the court, consistent with the rules promulgated by the Department of Public Safety and Corrections.
(Added by Acts 1992 No. 352, §2; chgd. by Acts 1995 No. 516, §1, No. 695, §1; Acts 1997 No. 581, §2, No. 1184, §1, eff. 8/15/97.)

PART VI. SIZE, WEIGHT, AND LOAD OF VEHICLE

§379. Applicability; regulations in excess of R.S. 32:380 through 32:386 prohibited.

A. The provisions of this Part governing width, height, length, tire pressure, weight, and load shall apply to vehicles in regular operation, as defined in R.S. 32:1. Vehicles operated under the terms of special permits are covered in R.S. 32:387.

B. The department shall not enact any regulation to allow any vehicle to travel the highways of this state in excess of the limits or requirements provided in R.S. 32:380 through R.S. 32:386, both inclusive.

SUBPART A. SIZE, WIDTH, HEIGHT, LENGTH, WEIGHT AND LOAD OF VEHICLES IN REGULAR OPERATION

§380. Width; projecting loads on vehicles.

A. The width of any vehicle shall not exceed ninety-six inches, exclusive of safety devices, except that on the Interstate System or other highways designated by the Secretary, the width of any vehicle shall not exceed one hundred two inches, exclusive of safety devices.

B. The load on any vehicle shall not project more than twelve inches beyond the width of its body.

C. The width of a farm tractor shall not exceed nine feet.

D. The secretary shall designate the qualifying highway system to which the foregoing width limitations shall apply.

E. Vehicles or combinations of vehicles in excess of ninety-six inches in width shall have reasonable access, not to exceed ten miles, and in the parish of Orleans, not to exceed three miles, between the interstate system or other highways designated by the secretary and terminals and facilities for food, fuel, repairs, and rest, unless otherwise prohibited. Household goods carriers shall have unrestricted access for loading and unloading purposes only, unless otherwise prohibited.
(Chgd. by Acts 1990 No. 51, §1, No. 896, §1, eff. 9/7/90.)

§381. Height.

A. The height of any vehicle shall not exceed thirteen feet, six inches.

B. Nothing in this Section shall be interpreted to require the state or any subdivision thereof or any person, firm, or corporation in this state to raise, alter, construct, or reconstruct any overpass, wire, pole, trestle, or other structure to provide such clearance.

§382. Length; special length limits.

A. LENGTH

(1) The length of a single vehicle shall not exceed forty-five feet. The length of a trailing unit on any single vehicle shall not exceed thirty feet. The length of the semitrailer portion of a tractor-semitrailer combination shall not exceed fifty-nine feet and six inches. The length of

the semitrailer or trailer portion of a tractor-semitrailer-trailer combination shall not exceed thirty feet. The length of the trailer portions of a tractor-trailer-trailer combination shall not exceed thirty feet. The length of the semitrailer portions of a tractor-semitrailer-semitrailer combination shall not exceed thirty feet.

(2) (a) The load carried by a combination of vehicles transporting timber poles and piling shall not exceed sixty-five feet plus one foot additional tolerance in length. The load carried by a combination of vehicles transporting forest products in their natural or treated state shall not exceed sixty-five feet plus one foot additional tolerance in length. Said combinations transporting poles and piling or forest products in their natural or treated state shall operate only during daylight hours and shall display a red flag or cloth not less than one foot square at the rear of the load. A combination of vehicles transporting forest products in their natural state shall be equipped with stationary vertical retaining poles on the driver's side of the trailer portion.

(b) No combination of vehicles shall consist of more than two vehicles, except as provided in R.S. 32:384(C) and R.S. 32:382(A)(3) and except that combinations of truck-tractor and two trailers; truck-tractor and two semi-trailers; or truck-tractor, semi-trailer, and trailer are permitted.

(c) The combination of vehicles consisting of three vehicles excepted in this Section by Subsection A(2)(b) shall be permitted to operate over all highways within the Interstate System and other highways designated by the secretary.

(d) No combination of vehicles operated on any parish road under the jurisdiction of the police jury shall consist of more than two vehicles, except as provided in R.S. 32:382(A)(3).

(3) (a) A vehicle having no more than two axles may tow any combination of two vehicles, provided the combination of vehicles does not exceed sixty-five feet.

(b) A vehicle having no more than two axles and owned and/or operated by a manufacturer or dealer of boats may tow two boat trailers.

B. SPECIAL LENGTH LIMITS

(1) Subject to the provisions of R.S. 32:380, R.S. 32:381, and Subsection A of this Section, the load upon any single vehicle or upon the front vehicle of a combination of vehicles shall not project more than four feet beyond the foremost part of said vehicle, and the load upon any single vehicle or upon the rear vehicle of a combination of vehicles shall not project more than eight feet beyond the rear of the bed or body of said vehicle, except that the load upon the rear vehicle of a combination of vehicles transporting poles and piling shall not project more than fifteen feet beyond the rear of the bed or rear tire of said vehicle, whichever is further from the cab, and the load upon the rear vehicle of a combination of vehicles transporting forest products in their natural state shall not project more than twenty feet beyond the rear of the bed or rear tire of said vehicle, whichever is further from the cab, and said load or loads must maintain a two foot clearance above the pavement structure, and provided further said combination of vehicles transporting forest products in their natural state with a rear projecting load in excess of fifteen feet shall operate only during daylight hours and shall display a red flag or cloth not less than one foot square at the rear of its projected load. A combination of vehicles transporting forest products in their natural state shall be equipped with stationary vertical retaining poles on the driver's side of the trailer portion.

(2) Equipment that is permanently attached to an cannot be readily removed from a vehicle shall not constitute load and the provisions of Subsection B(1) of this Section shall not apply to such vehicles if the following conditions exist:

(a) The vehicle meets requisite state safety standards to be and is licensed for use on state highways; and

(b) That portion of such equipment which extends in front of the foremost part of said vehicle has a minimum vertical clearance above the surface of the highway of six feet.

(c) The provisions of this Section shall not apply to vehicles collecting garbage, rubbish, refuse, or recyclable materials which are equipped with front-end loading attachments and containers provided that the vehicles are actively engaged in the collection of garbage, rubbish, refuse, or recyclable materials.

(3) Sportsmen coaches or vehicles obviously used solely for recreational purposes and registered therefor may tow a combination of no more than two vehicles and shall not exceed seventy feet in total length.

C. The combinations of vehicles consisting of three vehicles excepted in this Section by Subsection A(2)(b) shall have reasonable access, not to exceed ten miles, between the interstate system or other highways designated by the secretary and terminals and facilities for food, fuel, repairs and rest, unless otherwise prohibited. Household goods carriers shall have unrestricted access for loading and unloading purposes only, unless otherwise prohibited.

D. The secretary shall designate the qualifying highway system to which the foregoing length limitations shall apply.

E. The foregoing regulations of tractor-semi-trailer combinations shall not prohibit the operation, replacement, or reasonable business expansion of those types or lengths of vehicles which are in actual and lawful use on or before July 2, 1983.

F. All vehicles of legal length on the interstate system and other designated systems but which are not of legal length off of the interstate system and other designated systems shall have reasonable access, not to exceed ten miles, between the interstate system or other highways designated by the secretary and terminals and facilities for food, fuel, repairs, and rest, unless otherwise prohibited. Household goods carriers shall have unrestricted access for loading and unloading purposes only, unless otherwise prohibited.

(Chgd. by Acts 1990 No. 51, §1; Acts 1995 No. 1185, §1; Acts 1997 No. 764, §1, No. 940, §1, eff. 8/15/97.)

§383. Loads on vehicles; care required thereto; penalties; definition.

A. (1) The load on a vehicle shall not drop, sift, leak, or otherwise escape therefrom, except that sand may be dropped on a highway to secure traction or a liquid substance may be dropped on a highway to clean or maintain such highway.

(2) Any load of garbage, refuse, sludge, and other discarded material being transported by a commercial hauler shall be covered while being transported in such a manner as to prevent the load from spilling or dropping from the vehicle.

(3) Any violation of Paragraph (2) of this Subsection for failure to cover any load of garbage, refuse, sludge, and other discarded material shall be punishable by a fine of not more than five hundred dollars or by imprisonment for not more than six months, or both.

(4) The penalty provisions of Paragraph (3) of this Subsection shall not apply when the load was properly covered and subsequently became uncovered as the result of an accident or circumstances beyond the control of the operator of the vehicle.

B. (1) The load on any vehicle shall be securely fastened so as to prevent the covering or load from becoming loose, detached, or in any manner a hazard to other users of the highway.

(2) Freight containers, as defined in 49 CFR 171.8, used in both the waterborne transport of cargo and in the overland transport of cargo shall be properly secured so as to prevent the container from becoming loose, detached, or in any manner a hazard to other users of the highway.

(3) Any violation of Paragraph (2) of this Subsection shall be punishable by a fine of not more than five hundred dollars or by imprisonment for not more than six months, or both.

(4) The penalty provisions of R.S. 32:383(B)(3) shall not apply when the freight container was properly secured and subsequently became loose or detached as the result of an accident or circumstances beyond the control of the operator of the vehicle.

C. "Loose material" means dirt, sand, gravel, or other material that is capable of blowing or spilling from a vehicle as a result of movement or exposure to air, wind currents, or weather, but shall not include agricultural products in their natural state or wood chips.

(Chgd. by Acts 1990 No. 928, §1, eff. 9/7/90.)

§383.1. Loads of loose materials on vehicles; care required thereto; penalties.

A. Any load of loose material as defined in R.S. 32:383(C) being transported by a commercial hauler shall be covered in such a manner as to prevent the load from blowing, spilling, or dropping from the vehicle.

B. Any violation of this section for failure to cover a load of loose material while being transported shall be punishable by a fine of not less than one hundred dollars or more than two hundred dollars.

(Added by Acts 1991 No. 555, §1; chgd. by Acts 1995 No. 544, §1, eff. 8/15/95.)

§384. Trailers and towed vehicles.

A. The drawbar or connection between two vehicles, when one is towing the other, shall be of sufficient strength to pull all weight towed thereby and shall not exceed fifteen feet from one vehicle to the other, except that the drawbar or connection may exceed fifteen feet between any two vehicles transporting poles, pipes, machinery, or other objects of a structural nature which cannot be readily dismembered.

B. When the connection between a vehicle and a towed vehicle is a chain, rope, or cable, a red flag or cloth not less than one foot square shall be displayed upon such connection between sunrise and sunset, and a red light, plainly visible under ordinary atmospheric conditions for a distance of at least five hundred feet, shall be displayed upon such connection between sunset and sunrise.

C. Truck-tractors may be transported by a drawbar, pintle connection, or by the triple saddle mount method of transportation, consisting of a combination of four truck-tractors where the front axle of one truck-tractor is mounted on the fifth wheel of the lead truck-tractor, the front axle of the third truck-tractor is mounted on the fifth wheel of the second truck-tractor, and the front axle of the fourth truck-tractor is mounted on the fifth wheel of the third truck-tractor; and with the rear wheels of the second, third, and fourth truck-tractors trailing on the ground behind the operating motor unit, provided that:

(1) The combination of vehicles shall be equipped with necessary lights and signals in accordance with Louisiana law and Bureau of Motor Carrier Safety, United States Department of Transportation, Federal Highway Administration Safety Rules and Regulations;

(2) The rear wheels of the second, third, and fourth truck-tractors of the combination shall be equipped with adequate splash guards or mud flaps; and,

(3) It shall be unlawful to operate this combination of vehicles in excess of fifty-five miles per hour.

D. Every trailer and semi-trailer with a loaded gross weight capacity of up to six thousand pounds shall be equipped with safety chains. The safety chains shall be securely attached to the towing vehicle when the trailer or semi-trailer is in motion and shall be of sufficient strength to hold the trailer behind the towing vehicle in case the connection between the two vehicles detaches.

(Chgd. by Acts 1997 No. 940, §1, eff. 8/15/97.)

§385. Farm vehicles and equipment, exemption; other exemptions.

A. (1)(a) Farm vehicles and equipment, except draglines and bulldozers being operated and/or transported for bona fide agricultural purposes or the transportation of farm vehicles and equipment to be used for normal farm purposes by persons transporting such farm equipment or machinery for distances not to exceed fifty miles from the point of origin shall be exempt from the requirements of R.S. 32:380 through R.S. 32:382 and additionally farm equipment shall be exempt from the requirements of R.S. 32:384.

(b) Trailers and semi-trailers with a gross vehicle weight rating of not more than twelve thousand pounds, when owned and used by a retail business in this state and designed and used exclusively for the purposes of pick-up or delivery of new, used, or repaired farm equipment for distance not to exceed fifty miles from the point of origin shall be exempt from the requirements of R.S. 32:380.

(2) Vehicles being operated to transport timber cutting or logging equipment from one job site to another and the equipment being transported, when the trailer upon which the equipment is towed and the equipment are owned or leased by the same person, shall be exempt from the requirements of R.S. 32:380, 381, and 382.

(3) Such farm vehicles and vehicles transporting cutting or logging equipment may use any public highways other than those designated as part of the national system of interstate and defense highways during the period from thirty minutes after sunrise until thirty minutes before sunset without obtaining a special permit from the secretary, as provided in R.S. 32:387, or from any other agency or department of the state or political subdivisions, provided that such machinery or equipment being shipped by persons to be used for normal farm purposes shall be equipped with front and rear reflector lights and with a blinking hazard light clearly visible from the front and rear.

B. The provisions of R.S. 32:380, 381, and 382, relative to limitations on the width, height, and length of motor vehicles shall not apply to trucks which transport seed cotton modules or cotton from the field to the gin, or cotton seed from the gin to the mill, if the owner or operators of such trucks obtain an annual permit to be issued by the secretary for an annual fee of five dollars, according to rules and regulations to be promulgated by the secretary.

C. Notwithstanding any other provisions of law to the contrary, Part 393.86 of the Federal Motor Carrier Safety Regulations and state law as they pertain to the requirements of bumpers or devices serving similar purposes shall not apply to any vehicle transporting seed cotton modules if such vehicle was manufactured prior to September 1, 1991. *(Subsection C added by Acts 1991 No. 445, §1, eff. upon notification from the Federal Department of*

Transportation that an exemption to Part 393.86 of the Federal Motor Carrier Safety Regulations has been granted and that such exemption shall in no way limit the receipt of federal funding.)
(Chgd. by Acts 1991 No. 306, §1, No. 307, §1, No. 445, §1; Acts 1997 No. 113, §1, eff. 8/15/97.)

§386. Weight.

A. The total gross weight of any vehicle or combination of vehicles shall not exceed eighty thousand pounds, and no vehicle or combination of vehicles shall exceed its licensed gross weight.

B. No tire mounted on any axle attached to any vehicle or combination of vehicles shall impose a greater weight on the surface of a highway than six hundred fifty pounds per inch width of tire.

C. The total gross weight of any single axle attached to any vehicle and equipped with low pressure pneumatic tires shall not exceed twenty thousand pounds.

D. The total gross weight of any tandem axle or tandem steering axle attached to any vehicle and equipped with low pressure pneumatic tires shall not exceed thirty-four thousand pounds. However on any vehicle carrying forest products in their natural state, the weight limitation shall be thirty-seven thousand pounds per tandem axle and equipped with low pressure pneumatic tires except on the Interstate system.

E. The total gross weight of any tridum axle attached to any vehicle and equipped with low pressure pneumatic tires shall not exceed forty-two thousand pounds.

E-1. The total gross weight of any quadrum axle attached to any vehicle and equipped with low pressure pneumatic tires shall not exceed fifty thousand pounds.

F. The total gross weight of any single axle or any single steering axle attached to any vehicle and equipped with high pressure pneumatic, solid rubber or cushion tires shall not exceed eighteen thousand pounds.

G. The total gross weight of any tandem axle or any tandem steering axle attached to any vehicle and equipped with high pressure pneumatic, solid rubber or cushion tires shall not exceed thirty-two thousand pounds.

H. (1) For vehicles using the Interstate system, the overall maximum gross weight, including enforcement tolerances, on a group of two or more consecutive axles, shall be produced by application of the following formula:

$$W = 500(LN/(N - 1) + 12N + 36)$$

where W equals overall gross weight on any group of two or more consecutive axles to the nearest five hundred pounds, L equals distance in feet between the extreme of any group of two or more consecutive axles, and N equals number of axles in group under consideration, except that two consecutive sets of tandem axles may carry a gross load of thirty-four thousand pounds each provided the overall distance between the first and last axles of the consecutive sets of tandem axles is thirty-six feet or more. The overall gross weight shall not exceed eighty thousand pounds, including all enforcement tolerances, except for those vehicles and loads which cannot be easily dismantled or divided and which have been issued special permits.

(2) In accordance with 23 U.S.C. 127, certain vehicles carrying certain commodities shall be exempt from application of the formula. The exemptions shall include the following:

Vehicles with Type Two axle configuration (three axle combination with one single axle and one set of tandem axles) or Type Six axle configuration (five axle combination with one single axle and two sets of tandem axles); or a vehicle with Type Eight axle configuration (six axle combination with one single axle, one tandem axle, and one tridem* axle); or vehicles with Type Ten axle configuration (double bottom); or Type Eighteen axle configuration (four axle combination with one single axle and one set of tridem* axles) carrying any of the following bulk commodities thereof; forest products in their natural state, lumber, sand, gravel, agricultural products in their natural state, loose or mixed concrete (including asphaltic or Portland cement), or bulk liquid commodities.

**So in original. Probably should be "tridum".*

(3) All vehicles which are rendered economically useless by application of the bridge formula which are legal and operational on the effective date of this Subsection shall remain legal for a period of five years from the effective date of this Subsection. The trucking industry is hereby granted a phase-in period to extend for a period of five years from the

effective date of this Subsection, within which time it shall adjust, modify, or replace equipment to comply with the provisions of this Subsection.

I. Notwithstanding the provisions of Subsection (A) of this Section and subject to the provisions of Subsections (B), (C), (D), (E), and (E-1) of this section, the total gross weight of any combination of vehicles which has a tridum axle or a quadrum axle shall not exceed eighty-eight thousand pounds while operating on any state-maintained highway except the Interstate System and shall not exceed eighty-three thousand four hundred pounds while operating on the Interstate System within this state.

J. When by reason of the condition of the weather or other emergency, or the physical condition of any highway or its recent construction, or the making of repairs thereto, the secretary deems it necessary, then for such time as is reasonably necessary to remedy the situation, he may prohibit the use of such highway or specify lesser gross weights than those fixed in this Section, pursuant to the recommendations of the chief engineer of the department, in order to protect the public highways and the persons and property of the traveling public from unnecessary damage. Notice of such restrictions, prohibitions, or weight reductions shall be given by the secretary by posters at the terminal of the highway. However, failure to post such notice shall under no circumstances make either the state or the department liable for damages which may result because of such failure.

K. Vehicles and combinations of vehicles shall be loaded in such manner that the axle limitations set forth in Subsections C, D, E, E-1, F and G of this Section are not exceeded. However, while operating on any state-maintained highway except the Interstate System, the provisions of Subsections C, D, E, E-1, F and G of this section shall not be deemed to have been violated unless the axle weight exceeds by more than two thousand pounds Subsections C and F of this section or more than three thousand pounds Subsections D, E, E-1, and G of this section. This Subsection shall in no way be construed to allow the total gross weight in any vehicle or combination of vehicles to exceed the gross weight limits set forth in Subsection A or I of this Section.

§386.1. Blanket oversize yearly permit; fees.

Notwithstanding any other provision of law to the contrary, the Department of Transportation and Development shall establish a blanket oversize yearly permit for vehicles the width of which does not exceed twelve feet, the height of which does not exceed fourteen feet and four inches, a length not to exceed ninety feet, and the overhang of which does not exceed twenty-five feet. The fee for this yearly permit shall be five hundred dollars. The secretary shall promulgate rules and regulations to provide for the implementation of this Section. *(Added by Acts 1997 No. 292, §1, eff. 8/15/97.)*

SUBPART B. SPECIAL PERMITS

§387. Special permits.

A. No vehicle or combination of vehicles which does not meet the requirements of R.S. 32:380 through R.S. 32:386 shall use the public highways of this state without first obtaining a special permit from the department in addition to any other special permit which may be required from any other agency or department of the state or a political subdivision, and the special permit herein provided for shall be issued at the discretion of the secretary.

B. (1) The secretary may issue a special permit for the operation of vehicles or combination thereof having dimensions or weights in excess of the limits imposed by R.S. 32:380 through R.S. 32:386 if the shipment is not readily divided, broken, or dismantled, or the operation of such vehicles is otherwise prohibited by law, however, if the parts which have been divided, broken or dismantled from the shipment weigh in the aggregate of five hundred pounds, or less, then the shipment shall be considered as indivisible. Provided further, however, that the secretary may issue special overwidth permits for vehicles transporting pipe. In the exercise of his discretion, the secretary shall consider the following factors, as well as any other circumstances existing in the particular case:

(a) There is a vital and exceptional economic necessity therefor;

(b) The existence of a real necessity of transportation by public roads; or,

(c) The secretary considers the best interest of the state requires the issuance of the permit.

(2) Subject to the provisions of Paragraphs (3) and (4) of Subsection B of this Section, the secretary shall issue special permits to permit movement along the interstate highway system within Louisiana of mobile homes up to fourteen feet in width.

(3) When an application for a special permit is made, the secretary may require the special permit applicant to supply any information the secretary deems necessary for the protection of the interests of the state, the state highway system, and the public.

(4) The secretary may impose conditions upon the issuance of a special permit and may impose requirements upon its use, including but not restricted to the use of additional axles, so as to require that the axle weight conform as closely as possible to the weights provided in R.S. 32:386; the routing over the highways of the shipment under the special permit; the date, time of day, and speed limit; the furnishing of a bond with good and solvent surety to protect the state, the department, and all political corporations and subdivisions of the state from all liability and damage resulting from the use of such permit; the accompaniment of the vehicle and shipment by a proper escort, all at the expense of the permittee; and such other conditions or requirements as the secretary deems necessary and proper. When state police vehicles are required as a proper escort, there shall be a charge for the use thereof, and the secretary of the Department of Public Safety shall determine the fees charged for the use of the state police vehicles so used. Such charge shall be based on the mileage of the escort with a minimum charge of twenty five dollars. Any fees charged in excess of twenty-five dollars shall be adopted pursuant to R.S. 49:951, et seq.

(5) An overweight special permit shall be issued for the gross weight of the vehicle or combination of vehicles.

C. (1) The secretary may issue an annual special permit for the operation of those vehicles which are of such a particular design that they do not comply with R.S. 32:386. This type of annual special permit shall be issued only if:

(a) The vehicles are nonload carrying, primarily operate off the road and only occasionally use the state maintained highway system, or,

(b) The vehicle is a waste disposal truck that was in actual use in this state as of January 1, 1977, and,

(c) Such vehicles are mounted with a minimum size 10.00 tire or such size as is required by the secretary.

The secretary may establish and collect a reasonable fee for this annual special permit.

(2) In addition, subject to the provisions of Paragraphs (3), (4), and (5) of Subsection B of this Section, the secretary may issue special permits he finds essential and in the best interest of the state by reason of an emergency situation, unusual circumstances, natural catastrophes, or disasters affecting the transportation on the highways of the state of farm products in their natural state or forest products in their natural state. The weight limitations of any special farm or forest product permit so issued shall not exceed those set forth in Subsections B, C, D, E, F, and G of Section 386 of this Chapter; the gross weight of any combination of vehicles shall not exceed one hundred thousand pounds; and the length of any vehicle or combination of vehicles shall not exceed seventy-five feet. Each such special farm or forest product permit shall be issued for designated routes.

The secretary may establish and collect reasonable fees for each special farm or forest product permit issued. Permit fees shall be uniform for each classification of vehicle and/or purpose for which issued.

(3) (a) In addition, upon application of the owner or operator of any vehicle or combination of vehicles transporting farm and forest products in their natural state, transporting seed cotton modules, transporting cotton seed from the gin to the mill, or transporting raw sugar from the mill to the refinery, the secretary shall issue special harvest season permits within forty-eight hours of application and payment of fee for the transportation of farm and forest products in their natural state, for the transportation of seed cotton modules, for the transportation of cotton seed from the gin to the mill, or for the transportation of raw sugar from the mill to the refinery, on any state-maintained highway except the Interstate System for a total gross weight of eighty-six thousand six hundred pounds for any vehicle or combination of vehicles provided:

(i) The total weight of any single axle shall not exceed twenty-two thousand pounds.

(ii) The total gross weight of any tandem axle shall not exceed thirty-seven thousand pounds.

(b) Under the same special harvest season permit, the owners and operators shall be authorized to transport farm and forest products in their natural state, to transport seed cotton modules, to transport cotton seed from the gin to the mill, or to transport raw sugar from the mill to the refinery, on the Interstate System for a total gross weight of eighty-three thousand four hundred pounds for any vehicle or combination of vehicles provided:

(i) The total gross weight of any single axle shall not exceed twenty thousand pounds.

(ii) The total gross weight of any tandem axle shall not exceed thirty-five thousand two hundred pounds.

(c) The provisions of R.S. 32:387(B)(1), (2), and (3) and R.S. 32:388(D) shall not apply to special harvest season permits.

(d) The secretary shall collect a one-time fee of ten dollars for each harvest year for the issuance of the special harvest season permits.

(e) In addition, upon application of the owner or operator of any vehicle or combination of vehicles which has a minimum of eighteen wheels and which is engaged in the transfer of commercial and household trash, garbage, refuse waste, or recyclable waste material loaded exclusively from Louisiana Department of Environmental Quality authorized pickup stations, or transfer stations, or both, and upon payment of a fee of ten dollars, the secretary shall issue a special permit authorizing the vehicle or combination of vehicles to operate on any state-maintained highway except the interstate system at a total gross weight of eighty-six thousand six hundred pounds. The permit shall be valid for one year. Except as otherwise provided in this Subparagraph, all of the provisions of this Paragraph shall apply to permits issued under the provisions of this Subparagraph and to vehicles or combinations of vehicles for which permits are issued under the provisions of this Subparagraph.

(f) (i) In addition, upon application of the owner or operator of any vehicle or combination of vehicles which has a minimum of eighteen wheels, used to transfer commercial and household trash, garbage, refuse, or recyclable waste material loaded exclusively from the Department of Environmental Quality authorized pickup stations, or transfer stations, or both, and upon payment of a fee of one thousand dollars, the secretary shall issue a special permit authorizing the vehicle or combination of vehicles to operate at the maximum axle weights provided under the Department of Transportation and Development's regulations for overweight permit loads, on any state-maintained highway except the interstate system. The permit shall be valid for one year. Except as otherwise provided in this Subparagraph, all of the provisions of this Paragraph shall apply to permits issued under the provisions of this Subparagraph and to vehicles or combinations of vehicles for which permits are issued under the provisions of this Subparagraph.

(ii) In addition, upon application of the owner or operator of any vehicle or combination of vehicles which has a minimum of eighteen wheels used to transfer bundled or bailed* recyclable waste paper products and upon payment of a fee of one thousand dollars, the secretary shall issue a special permit authorizing the vehicle or combination of vehicles to operate at the maximum axle weights provided under the Department of Transportation and Development's regulations for overweight permit loads on any state-maintained highway except the interstate system. Such vehicles or the loads thereon shall not exceed a width of ten feet. The permit shall be valid for one year. Except as otherwise provided in this Subparagraph, all the provisions of this Paragraph shall apply to permits issued under the provisions of this Subparagraph and to vehicle** or combinations of vehicles for which permits are issued under the provisions of this Subparagraph.

**So in original. Probably should be "baled".*

***So in original. Probably should be "vehicles".*

(g) In addition, upon application of the owner or operator of any truck fitted with a compactor body which is engaged in the collecting and hauling of solid waste including residential solid waste, agricultural waste, commercial solid waste, construction or demolition debris, garbage, industrial solid waste, trash, white goods, woodwaste, and yard trash as defined by the Department of Environmental Quality's rules and regulations, and upon payment of a fee of fifty dollars, the secretary of the Department of Transportation and Development shall issue a special permit authorizing said single vehicles with tandem axles to operate on any state-maintained highway including the interstate system at a total gross weight not to exceed sixty-eight thousand pounds provided the federal government does not raise any objections to such permitted weight limitations and the secretary shall issue a special permit authorizing said single vehicles which have tridum axles to operate on any state-maintained highway including the interstate system at a total gross weight not to exceed eighty thousand pounds provided the federal government does not raise any objection to such permitted weight limitation. The permit shall be valid for one year. Except as otherwise provided herein, all of the provisions of this Paragraph shall apply to permits issued under the provisions herein and to said trucks for which permits are issued hereunder. Nothing herein shall preempt municipal or parish ordinances regulating weight limits on municipal or parish streets or roads.

(4) The secretary may issue an annual special overwidth permit for the operation of vehicles transporting pulpwood and plywood bolts not to exceed nine feet and forest management equipment except general construction equipment such as bulldozers, draglines, graders, etc. not to exceed ten feet. The secretary shall collect an annual fee of ten dollars for each pulpwood, plywood bolt, or forest management equipment special permit. This Paragraph does not apply to the operation of vehicles on the Interstate System.

(5) The secretary may issue a special overwidth permit for the transportation of privately owned pleasure craft together with its accompanying trailer when the width does not exceed ten feet. The permit shall be valid for a period of thirty days from the date of issuance. The secretary shall collect a fee of ten dollars for each permit issued. This permit shall not be issued to companies or individuals engaged in the business of buying, selling, or transporting pleasure craft. The permit shall not apply to the operation on the Interstate System or to other highways which may be designated by the secretary. The secretary may promulgate rules and regulations in accordance with the Administrative Procedure Act* as may be necessary to effectuate these provisions.

**R.S. 49:950 et seq.*

(6) The secretary may issue special permits to those vehicles transporting commodities between a port facility located outside the state of Louisiana on the Mississippi River and a manufacturing facility located within the state of Louisiana where the vehicle must enter the state via a bridge crossing the Mississippi River and transport commodities to a manufacturing facility located within the same parish as the bridge. The special permit issued shall provide for size and weight limitations and shall specify the roads or highways over which the vehicle may operate. The secretary may promulgate rules and regulations in accordance with the Administrative Procedure Act as may be necessary to effectuate the provisions of this Paragraph.

D. Neither the state nor the department shall incur any liability of any nature whatsoever to any permittee or any other person arising from the use of a special permit. Every special permit is issued upon the condition that the permittee accepts and uses it at his own risk, even though the directions and instructions of the secretary and particularly such instructions and requirements as those relating to routing, are faithfully complied with.

E. (1)(a) The secretary shall charge fees for special permits as provided in Subsection H of this Section for special permit applicants, if each permittee provides the department a surety bond or cash deposit in the minimum amount of one thousand dollars or any amount in excess thereof fixed by the secretary to guarantee payment of said account. To facilitate the use of such credit accounts, the department shall provide a sufficient number of Louisiana inbound wide area telephone service lines for use by the trucking industry.

(b) All of such special permit fees collected by the secretary shall be paid into the state treasury on or before the twenty-fifth day of each month following their collection and, in accordance with Article VII, Section 9 of the Constitution of Louisiana shall be credited, to the Bond Security and Redemption Fund.

(2) The department shall keep a set of books showing from whom every dollar is received and for what purpose and to whom every dollar is paid and for what purpose. It also shall keep in its file vouchers and receipts for all monies paid out.

F. Any special permit shall be carried with the vehicle using the same and shall be available at all times for inspection by the proper authorities.

G. The secretary may adopt rules and regulations necessary to carry out the purpose of this Section relating to the issuance of special permits.

H. SPECIAL PERMIT FEES.

(1) (a) Except as provided for mobile homes in Subparagraph (b) of this Paragraph, the fee for each overwidth, overheight, or overlength permit shall be ten dollars per trip or ten dollars per operating day for trips lasting more than one calendar day provided such vehicle or combination of vehicles is not also overweight; provided, however, that the fee for trailers or semitrailers hauling loads of the same product which exceed the legal limit shall be ten dollars per operating day provided such vehicles or combination of vehicles is also not overweight. Overwidth, overheight, and overlength permits may be issued on a monthly basis for a fee of ten dollars per operating day, except equipment used in an unloaded condition by companies engaged in the business of moving buildings may obtain one permit per company per month for a fee of fifteen dollars.

(b) The permit fee for the transporting of each overwidth, overheight, or overlength mobile home shall be a total of ten dollars per permit, provided the vehicle is not overweight, and each permit shall be issued for a consecutive seventy-two hour period.

(2) Fees for an overweight permit shall be as set forth in the following schedules:

(a) This schedule is for three types of vehicles:

(i) Vehicles and combinations of vehicles which do not exceed the legal gross weight, but which exceed the legal axle weight on one to three single or individual axles or on tandem, tridum, or quadrum axles, including the steering axles.

(ii) Vehicles or combinations of vehicles which have two or three single or individual axles total and which exceed both their legal gross weight and legal axle weight.

(iii) Off-road equipment with two or four single or individual axles, or tandem, or tridum axles.

EXCESS WEIGHT	PERMIT FEE DOLLARS DISTANCE IN MILES				
POUNDS	0-50	51-100	101-150	151-200	OVER 200
0-10,000	$ 20.00	$ 30.00	$ 35.00	$ 45.00	$ 55.00
10,001-20,000	35.00	65.00	90.00	115.00	140.00
20,001-30,000	55.00	100.00	140.00	185.00	230.00
30,001-40,000	70.00	135.00	195.00	255.00	315.00
40,001-50,000	90.00	170.00	245.00	325.00	405.00
50,001-60,000	105.00	205.00	300.00	395.00	490.00

Over 60,000—$10.00 permit fee plus $0.07 per ton-mile will be charged.

(b) This schedule is for combinations of vehicles with four single or individual axles including the steering axle.

FOUR AXLES, INCLUDING STEERING AXLE:

GROSS WEIGHT	PERMIT FEE DOLLARS DISTANCE IN MILES				
POUNDS	0-50	51-100	101-150	151-200	OVER 200
66,001-80,000	$ 20.00	$ 35.00	$ 45.00	$ 60.00	$ 70.00
80,001-90,000	45.00	75.00	110.00	145.00	175.00

(c) (i) This schedule is for combinations of vehicles with five or more single or individual axles, or tandem, or tridum axles, including the steering axle, where the gross weight exceeds eighty thousand pounds.

FIVE OR MORE AXLES INCLUDING STEERING AXLE
WHERE GROSS WEIGHT EXCEEDS 80,000 POUNDS

GROSS WEIGHT	PERMIT FEE DOLLARS DISTANCE IN MILES				
POUNDS	0-50	51-100	101-150	151-200	OVER 200
80,001-100,000	$ 30.00	$ 45.00	$ 65.00	$ 80.00	$ 100.00
100,001-108,000	50.00	95.00	135.00	180.00	220.00
108,001-120,000	70.00	130.00	190.00	250.00	310.00
120,001-132,000	90.00	170.00	250.00	330.00	415.00
132,001-152,000	120.00	225.00	335.00	445.00	555.00
152,001-172,000	155.00	295.00	440.00	585.00	730.00
172,001-192,000	190.00	365.00	545.00	725.00	905.00
192,001-212,000	225.00	435.00	650.00	865.00	1,080.00
212,001-232,000	260.00	505.00	755.00	1,005.00	1,250.00
232,001-254,000	295.00	575.00	860.00	1,145.00	1,420.00

(ii) Notwithstanding any other provision of law to the contrary, any combination vehicle with a gross weight greater than 212,000 pounds, but not in excess of 254,000 pounds shall be authorized a maximum tandem axle weight of forty-five thousand pounds and a maximum steering axle weight of thirteen thousand pounds, provided the spread between axle groups is a minimum of twelve feet and the spread between tires in a group is a minimum of four feet.

(iii) Loads exceeding 232,001 pounds, but not greater than 254,000 pounds shall be allowed statewide movement on the Department of Transportation and Development selected and approved routes, the majority of which are Interstate highways only, however, those portions of their route from the load's origin to the National Highway System and that portion from the National Highway System to its destination shall be subject to the structural evaluation provided for in this Subparagraph.

(iv) OVER 254,000—$10.00 permit fee, plus $0.50 per ton-mile of weight in excess of 80,000 pounds, plus a fee for structural evaluation based on the following schedule:

(aa) $125.00—for evaluation of treated timber, concrete slab, and precast concrete slab bridge.

(bb) $850.00—for evaluation of truss, continuous span, and movable bridges and for all Mississippi River structures.

(cc) $500.00—for all other structures.

(3) A permit granted under the provisions of Paragraph (2) of this Subsection shall include the operation of vehicles or combination of vehicles having both dimensions and weights in excess of the limits imposed in Subpart A of this Part, without the payment of any fee other than that imposed in the schedules above set forth in Paragraph (2) of this Subsection.

I. All vehicles or combinations of vehicles utilizing a balance type utility trailer or a fifth-wheel type utility trailer engaged in the transportation of utility poles shall be deemed to have a special permit by operation of law and may use the public highways of this state for the transportation of utility poles by a utility, its representative, or its contractor for the normal operation of its facilities to provide service to the area it serves. Such vehicles or combinations of vehicles shall be subject to the restriction that no load consisting of such poles shall extend more than thirty-five feet past the rear of the vehicle or combination of vehicles carrying the load, and the load shall maintain a minimum clearance of one and one-half feet above the ground. These restrictions shall be deemed to be in lieu of those set forth in R.S. 32:382.

J. Notwithstanding other provisions of this Subpart or other provisions of law to the contrary, vehicles hauling prepackaged products in international trade originating from or destined to an intermodal facility, which are containerized in such a manner as to make subdivision thereof impractical, shall be authorized special container permits. For the purposes of this Subsection, the contents of a sealed container being used in international trade in conjunction with a maritime shipment shall be considered nondivisible. The special container permits shall be subject to the following provisions:

(1) Upon application of the owner or operator of any vehicle transporting intermodal containers, the secretary shall issue a Class I Ocean Container Permit for the transportation of such containers with the gross vehicle weight limitation not to exceed eighty thousand pounds and the axle weight not to exceed forty thousand pounds per tandem axle group. The applicant shall indicate on the application the VIN number of the vehicle for which the permit shall be issued. The annual fee for the permit shall be fifty dollars per vehicle. If the Vehicle for which the permit is issued is no longer usable by the owner or operator, the permit may be transferred to a replacement vehicle. However, such transfer shall be authorized only one time during the year for which the permit is in effect.

(2) Upon application of the owner or operator of any vehicle transporting sealed intermodal containers within a fifty-mile radius of a statutorily defined port or harbor district, the secretary shall issue a Class II Ocean Container Permit for the transportation of such containers with the gross vehicle weight limitation not to exceed ninety-five thousand pounds and the axle weight not exceed twenty thousand pounds per axle provided the rear axle set is in tridem*. The applicant shall indicate on the application the VIN number of the vehicle for which the permit shall be issued. The annual fee for the permit shall be five hundred dollars per vehicle. If the vehicle for which the permit is issued is no longer usable by the owner or operator, the permit may be transferred to a replacement vehicle. However, such transfer shall be authorized only one time during the year for which the permit is in effect.

(3) Upon application of the owner or operator of any vehicle transporting a liquid bulk container within a fifty-mile radius of a statutorily defined port or harbor district, the secretary shall issue a Liquid Bulk Container Permit with the gross vehicle weight limitation not to exceed ninety-five thousand pounds and the axle weight not to exceed twenty thousand pounds per axle provided the rear axle set is in tridem*. Each vehicle issued such a permit shall be equipped with a standard intermodal drop-frame chassis with twist locks to secure the liquid bulk container on the chassis. The applicant shall indicate on the application the VIN number for the power unit of the vehicle for which the permit shall be issued. The annual fee for the permit shall be two hundred dollars per vehicle. If the vehicle for which the permit is issued is no longer usable by the owner or operator, the permit may be transferred to a

replacement vehicle. However, such transfer shall be authorized only one time during the year for which the permit is in effect.

**So in original. Probably should be "tridum".*

(Chgd. by Acts 1990 No. 822, §1; Acts 1991 No. 445, §1, No. 839, §1; Acts 1992 No. 186, §1, No. 243, §1, No. 734, §1, No. 984, §10; Acts 1993 No. 13, §1, No. 340, §1; Acts 1995 No. 228, §1, No. 254, §1, No. 474, §1; Acts 1997 No. 86, §1, eff. 6/11/97, No. 432, §1, eff. 8/15/97, No. 1342, §1, eff. 7/15/97.)

§387.1. Escort vehicles; permit to operate required.

A. Notwithstanding any contrary provision of R.S. 32:388 and except for those vehicles provided for in R.S. 32:385, or any rule or regulation adopted under authority thereof, or of any other provision of law or rule or regulation, all motor vehicles excluding motorcycles, shall be proper escorts in accordance with the provisions of R.S. 32:388 and any other laws and rules or regulations providing with respect to motor vehicles and traffic regulation, for the moving of house trailers on the roads, streets and highways of this state.

B. (1) Each company which operates an escort service in this state and which is domiciled in another state shall register annually with the secretary in accordance with rules and regulations adopted by the secretary. The oversight review of the rules and regulations adopted under this Section shall be conducted by the House and Senate Committees on Transportation, Highways and Public Works. The secretary shall establish a permit fee sufficient to cover the costs of the service. The fee shall not be less than ten dollars.

(2) Each application for registration shall be accompanied by each of the following:

(a) The name and address of the agent for service of process. The agent shall reside in and shall be domiciled in this state.

(b) Proof that each vehicle operated in this state by the applicant is insured in the same amount as is required for escort companies which are domiciled in this state.

(c) Proof that each driver of an escort vehicle has a valid operator's license issued by a state or territory of the United States.

(d) Such other information as the secretary by rule may require.

C. The secretary may revoke, suspend, or refuse to issue a registration for any violation of Subsection B hereof.

D. Whoever violates Subsection B hereof shall be fined one hundred dollars for each offense.

§387.2. Mobile homes; interstate highways.

A. Notwithstanding any other provision of law to the contrary, the secretary may issue special permits for the movement of mobile homes, not to exceed sixteen feet in width, on Interstate highways located in this state. Vehicles transporting mobile homes on Interstate highways shall not exceed a speed of fifty-five miles per hour.

B. The provisions of R.S. 32:387 which are not in conflict herewith, are applicable to the issuance of special permits under this Section.

C. The secretary may refuse to issue a special permit under this Section whenever, because of construction or the condition of the highway or because of traffic conditions thereon, the public would be endangered by the use sought to be permitted.

§387.3. Precast, fiberglass swimming pools and tanks; Interstate highways.

A. Notwithstanding any other provision of law to the contrary, the secretary may issue special permits for the movement of precast, fiberglass swimming pools and tanks, not to exceed sixteen feet in width, on Interstate highways located in this state. Vehicles transporting precast, fiberglass swimming pools on Interstate highways shall not exceed a speed of forty-five miles per hour.

B. The provisions of R.S. 32:387 which are not in conflict herewith are applicable to the issuance of special permits under this Section.

C. The secretary may refuse to issue a special permit under this Section whenever, because of construction or the condition of the highway or because of traffic conditions thereon, the public would be endangered by the use sought to be permitted.

§387.4. Equipment destined to or from any oil or gas facility or petrochemical complex; Interstate highways.

A. Notwithstanding any other provision of law to the contrary, the secretary may issue special permits for the movement of equipment destined to or from any oil or gas facility and/or petrochemical complex on Interstate highways located in this state. Vehicles transporting such equipment on interstate highways shall not exceed a speed of forty-five miles per hour and shall be accompanied by a state police escort.

B. The provisions of R.S. 32:387 which are not in conflict herewith are applicable to the issuance of special permits under this Section.

C. The secretary may refuse to issue a special permit under this Section whenever, because of construction or the condition of the highway or because of traffic conditions thereon, the public would be endangered by the use sought to be permitted.

(Added by Acts 1992 No. 219, §1, eff. 8/21/92.)

§387.5. Special permits; authorization to travel on portions of Interstate 49.

Notwithstanding any other provisions of the law to the contrary, and provided the federal government does not raise any objection to such permitted weight limitations, Interstate 49 from its northern intersection with U.S. Highway No. 167 near Meeker in Rapides Parish to its southern intersection with U.S. Highway No. 167 near Washington in St. Landry Parish is hereby deemed as an alternate route for U.S. Highway No. 167. Any vehicle traveling under a special permit issued under the provisions of this Subpart, the conditions of which permit travel on U.S. Highway No. 167, is hereby authorized to travel Interstate 49 under the same conditions and restrictions as those applicable to its permit to travel on U.S. Highway No. 167. *(Added by Acts 1995 No. 254, §1, eff. 8/15/95.)*

§387.6. Special permits; trucks hauling cotton modules.

Notwithstanding any other provision of law to the contrary, the secretary shall issue annual special permits to persons who operate trucks which haul cotton modules and are in compliance with the provisions of the Federal Motor Carrier Safety Regulations. These permits shall be issued in accordance with the following provisions:

(1) The permits shall be issued at the truck permit office of the Department of Transportation and Development.

(2) The fee for the permits shall be fifty dollars per permit per year.

(3) The permit shall authorize the operation of a three-axle vehicle at a gross weight of sixty-eight thousand pounds; with a tandem axle not to exceed forty-eight thousand pounds; and a single axle not to exceed twenty thousand pounds. These permits shall allow travel on any state-maintained highway with the exception of interstates.

(4) The secretary may impose a civil penalty of up to five cents per pound for each violation of the limit established by this Subsection. The secretary, by rule, shall establish procedures for enforcing the provisions of this Subsection, including a procedure by which persons accused of violations may contest those accusations.

(Added by Acts 1995 No. 790, §1, eff. 8/15/95.)

§387.7. Special permits; trucks hauling sugarcane.

Notwithstanding any other provision of law to the contrary and provided that there are no objections raised by the federal government, the secretary shall issue annual special permits to persons who operate trucks which haul sugarcane. These permits shall be issued in accordance with the following provisions:

(1) The permits shall be issued at the truck permit office of the Department of Transportation and Development.

(2) The fee for the permits shall be one hundred dollars per permit per year.

(3) The permit shall authorize the operation of the truck at a gross vehicle weight not to exceed one hundred thousand pounds.

(4) The secretary may impose a civil penalty of up to five cents per pound for each violation of the limit established in this Subsection. The secretary, by rule, shall establish procedures for enforcing the provisions of this Subsection, including a procedure by which persons accused of violations may contest those accusations.

(Added by Acts 1995 No. 584, §1, eff. 8/15/95.)

§387.8. Vehicles requiring steering axle permit; interstate highways.

All vehicles requiring a steering axle permit to travel on state highways shall also be entitled to travel on interstate highways without an additional permit, provided the single axle vehicles requiring such permit do not exceed twenty-four thousand pounds in weight. *(Added by Acts 1997 No. 176, §1, eff. 8/15/97.)*

§387.9. Special permit; trucks hauling agronomic or horticultural crops.

Notwithstanding any other provision of law to the contrary, the secretary shall issue annual special permits to persons who operate trucks hauling agronomic or horticultural crops in their natural state. These permits shall be issued in accordance with the following provisions:

(1) The permits shall be issued at the truck permit office of the Department of Transportation and Development.

(2) The fee for the permits shall be one hundred dollars per permit per year.

(3) The permit shall authorize the operation of the truck at a gross vehicle weight not to exceed one hundred thousand pounds.

(4) The secretary may impose a civil penalty of up to five cents per pound for each violation of the limit established in this Section. The secretary, by rule, shall establish procedures for enforcing the provisions of this Section, including a procedure by which persons accused of violations may contest those accusations.

(5) Trucks permitted under the provisions of this Section shall be prohibited from traveling on the Interstate System.

(Added by Acts 1997 No. 420, §1, eff. 8/15/97.)

§387.10. Special permit; vehicles transporting timber cutting or logging equipment.

A. Notwithstanding any other provision of law to the contrary, whenever a vehicle is being operated to transport two, but not more than two, pieces of timber cutting or logging equipment from one job site to another, the secretary shall issue an annual special overweight permit to the person who operates the vehicle. The permit shall be issued in accordance with the following provisions:

(1) The permit shall be issued at the truck permit office of the Department of Transportation and Development.

(2) The fee for the permit shall be one hundred dollars per permit per year.

(3) The permit shall authorize the operation of the truck, trailer and load thereon to operate at the maximum axle weights provided for overweight permit loads, with a gross vehicle weight not to exceed one hundred and five thousand pounds. The maximum width on such truck, trailer, and the load thereon shall not exceed twelve feet.

B. The special permit shall not authorize the operation of the vehicle on the Interstate system of the state.

C. The special permit authorizes operation of the vehicle during daylight hours and prohibits such operation during heavy rain or when visibility is less than five hundred feet.

(Added by Acts 1997 No. 1193, §1, eff. 8/15/97.)

SUBPART C. PENALTIES

§388. Penalties; payments.

A. Whoever owns or drives any vehicle or combination of vehicles in violation of any rule, regulation, directive, or requirement of the secretary adopted pursuant to R.S. 32:380 through R.S. 32:385 or in violation of R.S. 32:380 through R.S. 32:385 shall be assessed a penalty of one hundred dollars for each violation.

B. (1) Whoever owns or drives any vehicle or combination of vehicles in violation of any rule, regulation, directive, or requirement of the secretary adopted under R.S. 32:386 or in violation of R.S. 32:386 shall be required to reduce the load to the maximum permissible gross weight and shall be assessed a penalty on such weight which exceeds the maximum permissible gross weight as defined by R.S. 32:386 or maximum allowable axle weights, whichever results in the higher fine, in accordance with the following schedule:

OVERWEIGHT POUNDS	PENALTY OVER GROSS WEIGHT	PENALTY UNDER GROSS WEIGHT BUT OVER INDIVIDUAL AXLE WEIGHT
0 to 3,000	2¢ per pound	1¢ per pound
3,001 to 5,000	3¢ per pound	1.5¢ per pound
5,001 to 10,000	4¢ per pound	2¢ per pound
10,001 and over	$100 plus 5¢ per pound	$100 plus 5¢ per pound

(2) Whoever owns or drives any vehicle or combination of vehicles with a gross weight in excess of its licensed weight but less than or equal to its legal maximum gross weight may be assessed a penalty of one hundred dollars and shall be required to increase its license to the weight being carried not to exceed the legal maximum.

(3) The owner or driver of a vehicle or combination of vehicles in violation of the bridge formula axle spacing requirements of R.S. 32:386(H) shall be fined fifty dollars for each violation.

(4) (a) Whoever owns any business entity engaged in the sale or shipment of construction aggregates requiring a weighmaster, not including asphalt, or transfer sales or shipment from rail, barge, or ship to wholesale stockpiles or inventories within a five-mile radius of the point where the shipment was transferred, who violates, or whose driver or contract driver violates any rule, regulation, directive, or requirement of the secretary adopted under R.S. 32:386 or violates R.S. 32:386 shall also be assessed a separate penalty for each violation in accordance with the schedule set forth in Paragraph B(1). However, notwithstanding any other provision of this Chapter or any law to the contrary, any such business, or weighmaster thereof, who releases a vehicle that is within the maximum permissible gross weight limitations for travel on a state highway shall not be assessed any penalty when said vehicle is found in violation of gross maximum weight limitations while traveling on any interstate highway. For purposes of enforcing this paragraph, any weights and standards and state policeman having reason to believe that such owner is in violation of R.S. 32:386 is authorized to enter and go upon, without formal warrant, any vehicle, stand, place, building, or premises, for the purpose of inspecting only the shipping ticket or tickets issued in connection with the particular load found in violation of R.S. 32:386 by the Weights and Standards Police in order to determine whether such sales at the origin of shipment contain the amounts represented and are offered for sale or sold in a manner in accordance with law. The discovery of an overweight vehicle after proper weighing shall constitute "reason to believe" for purposes of this Paragraph.

(b) When used in this Paragraph, "construction aggregates" means any of the following:

(i) Sand.

(ii) Gravel.

(iii) Crushed stone.

(iv) Reef shell.

(v) Clam shell.

(vi) Sand-clam shell mixture.

(vii) Sand-reef shell mixture.

(viii) Sand clay gravel.

(ix) Clam-reef shell mixture.

(x) Crushed concrete.

(xi) Expanded clay.

(xii) Calcium sulfate hemihydrate.

(xiii) Asphalt.

C. Whoever owns or drives any vehicle or combination of vehicles in violation of any rule, regulation, directive, or requirement of the secretary adopted pursuant to R.S. 32:387 or in violation of the terms and conditions of any special permit issued under R.S. 32:387 shall be assessed a penalty of one hundred dollars.

Whoever owns or drives a vehicle or combination of vehicles in violation of an overweight special permit shall be assessed a penalty for each pound of weight in excess of the special permit weight in accordance with the following schedule and may increase his special permit if he shall satisfy any special conditions imposed by the secretary or otherwise shall reduce his load to the maximum weight allowed under his special permit:

POUNDS OVER PERMIT GROSS WEIGHT	PENALTY
0 to 3,000	2¢ per pound
3,001 to 5,000	3¢ per pound
5,001 to 10,000	4¢ per pound
10,001 and over	$100 plus 5¢ per pound

Nothing contained in this Subsection shall authorize the department to assess any penalty provided for herein for both the failure to possess a required special permit and for operating a vehicle in violation of R.S. 32:386 when arising out of the same activity, and to this extent the penalties provided for in this Subsection shall not be cumulative in nature.

C–1. Whoever owns or drives any vehicle or combination of vehicles in violation of Subsection F of Section 387 shall be assessed a penalty of twenty-five dollars.

D. Whoever owns or drives a vehicle or combination of vehicles without a proper escort when such escort is required by a special permit shall be assessed a penalty of one hundred dollars and the vehicle or combination of vehicles shall be impounded until a proper escort is secured by the permittee.

E. Payments for penalties shall be remitted to the Louisiana Department of Transportation and Development or to the Department of Public Safety and Corrections, as applicable. However, any payments for citations for weight limit violations on parish roads in a parish shall be paid to the public works department of said parish.

F. (1) All of such penalties collected by the secretary shall be paid into the state treasury on or before the twenty-fifth day of each month following their collection and, in accordance with Article VII, Section 9 of the Constitution of Louisiana, shall be credited to the Bond Security and Redemption Fund. However, after a sufficient amount of the penalties collected by the Department of Public Safety and Corrections is allocated from the fund to pay all obligations secured by the full faith and credit of the state within any fiscal year, the treasurer shall pay an amount equal to the fees paid into the Bond Security and Redemption Fund pursuant to this Paragraph into the Weights and Standards Mobile Police Force Fund created under the provisions of R.S. 47:718(C).

(2) The department shall keep a set of books showing from whom every dollar is paid and for what purpose. It shall keep in its file vouchers or receipts for all moneys paid out. *(Chgd. by Acts 1992 No. 902, §1, No. 984, §10; Acts 1993 No. 847, §1; Acts 1997 No. 1186, §1, eff. 8/15/97.)*

§388.1. Penalties; multiple violations.

Whoever owns or drives any vehicle or combination of vehicles in violation of two or more of the provisions of this Part at any one time shall be assessed the greater or the greatest of the penalties, in the full amount of the penalty. The department is hereby authorized to promulgate rules and regulations to provide that in addition to assessment of the greater or greatest penalty, the owner or driver shall be assessed a penalty not to exceed ten dollars for each other violation committed at the same time; however, such rules and regulations shall only be promulgated provided the Federal Highway Administration initiates official sanctions which would result in the loss of National Highway System apportionment or other federal funds should such penalties for multiple violations not be provided. *(Chgd. by Acts 1993 No. 692, §1, eff. 6/21/93.)*

SUBPART D. ENFORCEMENT, PAYMENT AND COLLECTION PROCEDURES

§389. Weights and standards police; enforcement procedure; payment and collection procedures.

A. The weights and standards police force and the state police shall have concurrent authority to enforce the provisions of R.S. 32:380 through 388.

B. Any weights and standards police officer having reason to believe that any vehicle or combination of vehicles exceeds or is in violation of the provisions of R.S. 32:380 through R.S. 32:386 or the terms and conditions of a special permit issued under R.S. 32:387 or regulations of the department or secretary adopted pursuant to this Part is authorized to stop such vehicle or combination of vehicles and to inspect, measure, or weight such vehicle, either by means of portable or stationary scales, or to require that such vehicle be driven to the nearest available location equipped with facilities to inspect, measure, or weight such vehicle.

(1)* Any state policeman having reason to believe that any vehicle or combination of vehicles exceeds or is in violation of the provisions of R.S. 32:380 through 32:386 or the terms and conditions of a special permit issued under R.S. 32:387 or regulations of the department or secretary adopted pursuant to this Part is authorized to stop such vehicle or combination of vehicles and to inspect or measure such vehicle or to require that such vehicle be driven to the nearest available location equipped with facilities to inspect or measure such vehicle, provided that any state policeman having reason to believe that any vehicle or combination of vehicles exceeds or is in violation of the provisions of R.S. 32:386, any overweight special permit as provided in R.S. 32:387, or the department's regulations adopted pursuant thereto, may escort such vehicle to the nearest permanent or portable scale operated by the department's weights and standards police force, where a weights and standards police officer shall weigh such vehicle and if such vehicle is overweight, is in violation of an overweight special permit, or the department's or secretary's regulations adopted pursuant thereto, shall issue a violation ticket in accordance with Subsection C of this Section.

**So in original. No Paragraph B.(2) has been enacted.*

C. (1) Whenever any vehicle or combination of vehicles is found in violation of any provision of this Part or any regulation of the department or secretary adopted pursuant thereto, the weights and standards police officer or any state policeman shall take the name and address of the owner and driver and the license number of the vehicle and shall issue a violation ticket assessing a penalty for such violation in accordance with R.S. 32:388.

(2) Upon issuance of the violation ticket, the owner or driver shall pay forthwith the penalty assessed with certified check, cashier's check, money order or department approved credit card to the weights and standard* police officer or state policeman. The secretary may establish credit accounts for violators, if each violator provides the department a cash deposit in the minimum amount of five thousand dollars or any amount in excess thereof fixed by the secretary to guarantee payment of said account. However, any driver of any vehicle registered in Louisiana, who is lawfully possessed of a valid Louisiana driver's license, as provided in Subsection A of R.S. 32:411, in lieu of immediate payment may deposit said license with the state policeman or the weights and standards police officer, who shall issue said driver a receipt for the license on a form approved or provided by the department. The receipt shall notify the owner and driver in writing to appear at a time and place to pay the penalty assessed and secure the return of the driver's license. This receipt shall be considered as a valid driver's license for a period not to exceed thirty days.

**So in original. Probably should be "standards".*

(3) Whoever violates his promise to appear and pay a penalty assessed under this Part shall be punished as provided in R.S. 32:57, and the driver's license shall be forwarded to the Department of Public Safety for suspension, revocation, and cancellation and the weights and standards police force or the state policeman shall locate and remove the owner's license plate(s) from said vehicle(s) until any penalty assessed is paid in accordance with this Part.

(4) (a) Any owner or driver resisting the payment of the penalty found due, or the enforcement of any provision of this Part in relation thereto, shall pay the amount of the penalty assessed to the weights and standards police officer, state policeman or other person designated in a license receipt and shall give this officer, state policeman or person notice at the time of payment of his intention to file suit for the recovery of such penalty.

(b) Any owner or driver who pays an assessed penalty under protest in accordance with the provisions of this Section shall have a period of ninety days after the date of payment to institute a civil suit against the department to recover the penalty so paid.

(c) The right to sue for recovery of a penalty paid under protest shall afford a legal remedy and right of action in any state district court for a full and complete adjudication of any questions arising in the enforcement of a penalty respecting the legality of any penalty assessed or the method of enforcement thereof. Any such suit may be instituted either in the parish in which the violation occurred, the domicile of vehicles, provided the domicile is within the state of Louisiana, or in East Baton Rouge Parish. In any such suit, service of process shall be made on the department, through the secretary. The department shall be a necessary and proper party defendant in any such suit.

(5) No court of this state shall issue any process whatsoever to restrain the collection of any penalty assessed by the department pursuant to this Part.

(6) If upon expiration of the ninety day period provided in Subparagraph (b) of Paragraph (4) of this Subsection any penalty assessed remains unpaid, the department may institute a civil suit in the parish in which the violation occurred or in the domicile of the owner or driver to collect any penalty assessed but unpaid. The department shall have one year from the date of expiration of the ninety day period to institute such a suit.

(7) Notwithstanding the above provisions, any member of the armed forces, who is in uniform or presents an order for duty and who is operating a military vehicle in the line of duty in violation of any provision of R.S. 32:380 through R.S. 32:387 or any regulation of the department or secretary adopted pursuant thereto shall not be required to pay the penalty

assessed, nor shall he be required to surrender his Louisiana driver's license. However, the owner of the vehicle or the federal government shall pay the penalty within thirty days.

(8) Failure of any vehicle or combination of vehicles to stop at a weigh facility may be excused if stopping the vehicle or combination of vehicles would create a serious traffic hazard. The Department of Transportation and Development shall promulgate rules under the provisions of the Administrative Procedure Act* for the implementation of this Paragraph. Such rules shall define "serious traffic hazard" and shall authorize the use of green traffic signal lights to allow vehicles to pass the weigh facility at such times as vehicles have accumulated on the entrance ramp to the weigh facility to the extent that the vehicles present a traffic hazard. Rules adopted hereunder shall be subject to oversight by the House and Senate Committees on Transportation, Highways and Public Works.

**R.S. 49:950 et seq.*

D. The secretary shall establish a procedure for the administrative review of citations issued by weights and standards police. The secretary may take appropriate actions based on the findings of any administrative review held under the provisions of this Subsection. The secretary shall adopt rules to govern administrative review and any actions taken based on the findings of an administrative review. All rules shall be adopted in accordance with the Administrative Procedure Act.

(Chgd. by Acts 1995 No. 429, §1, No. 1024, §1; Acts 1997 No. 1186, §1, eff. 8/15/97.)

PART VI-A. WEIGH-IN-MOTION PHOTO ENFORCEMENT SYSTEM

§390. Weigh-In-Motion (WIM) System.

A. A pilot program incorporating a Weigh-In-Motion (WIM) System and an Enforcement Camera System (ECS) shall be established in St. Martin Parish in the westbound lane of Interstate 10 at the foot of the Atchafalaya Spillway and on Interstate 10 East between Ambassador Caffery Parkway and University Avenue, when sufficient funds are available for the program.

B. The Weigh-In-Motion (WIM) System shall provide integrated functions of traffic management, weight enforcement, and data collection for a weigh station bypass monitoring system, which shall include an Enforcement Camera System (ECS).

C. All trucks attempting to bypass weigh station facilities using certain off-ramp bypass routes will be screened and monitored by a Weigh-In-Motion (WIM) Photo Enforcement System. Trucks which do not exit to the weigh station shall be weighed and classified by a highly accurate Single Load Cell Weigh-In-Motion (WIM) Photo Enforcement System. As trucks traverse the Weigh-In-Motion (WIM) site a camera will capture an image of the truck and match it with the truck's weight. Its images shall be captured and stored by the Roadside Weigh-In-Motion (WIM) Electronics and shall be transmitted to the central office station computer via a communication modem. At the central office, a station computer with monitor will display the image of the violating truck, with the truck's gross weight indicated on the screen. This image can then be printed using a laser printer located in the central office and used for enforcement purposes.

D. When it is determined that a truck is in violation, the driver shall stop at the weigh station within twenty-four hours of the violation.

E. Whoever violates the provisions of this Part shall be subject to the penalties provided in R.S. 32:388.

(Added by Acts 1997 No. 1071, §1, eff. 8/15/97.)

PART VI-B. LOUISIANA TRUCK CENTER

§390.21. Louisiana Truck Center; creation; purpose.

A. Within the Department of Public Safety and Corrections there shall be established and is hereby created the Louisiana Truck Center, hereinafter referred to as the "truck center". The purpose of this truck center shall be to serve as the headquarters and central location for motor carriers in obtaining all permits and for payment of any fees or charges required to engage in the motor carrier trade in the state of Louisiana.

B. (1) For the purposes of this Section, "permit" means any license, certificate, registration, permit, or any other form of authorization required by a state agency to engage in the motor carrier trade in the state of Louisiana.

(2) However, the provisions of this Part shall not apply to any permit or other form of authorization which requires the approval of the Public Service Commission after notification and public hearings.

C. The truck center shall provide centralized services to assist motor carriers in identifying and securing all appropriate permits required to operate a motor carrier business in the state. The goal of the truck center shall be to enable interested parties to secure permits and information regarding such permits at a single location.

(Added by Acts 1997 No. 273, §1, eff. 8/15/97.)

§390.22. Services and assistance.

A. The truck center shall serve as a centralized licensing and information center.

B. The truck center shall have the responsibility of developing, implementing, managing, and operating a system of:

(1) Assisting the trucking interests by providing both general and specific information on permitting and by furnishing permit application forms pertaining to their specific businesses.

(2) Compiling a list of all state permits and categorizing the required permits into a comprehensive handbook that is readily available to persons interested in establishing a motor carrier trade.

(3) Providing an applicant with on-site contacts with the proper state agency representative responsible for processing and reviewing the respective permit application.

(4) Assisting the applicant in the following:

(a) Clarification of licensing requirements and standards.

(b) Preparation of applications and forms.

(c) Determination of the status of an application during the review process, including the resolution of disputes.

(d) General coordination of the various aspects of the permitting or licensing process.

(5) Coordinating federal, state, and local permit review actions to the extent practicable.

(6) Allow trucking interest to procure and pay for needed authorizations at a one-stop site.

(Added by Acts 1997 No. 273, §1, eff. 8/15/97.)

§390.23. Agency representatives.

A. Located within the truck center shall be representatives of the following agencies:

(1) The Public Service Commission.

(2) The Department of Public Safety and Corrections, public safety services.

(3) The Department of Revenue and Taxation*.

**The former Department of Revenue and Taxation was reorganized and incorporated into the Department of Revenue by Acts 1997 No. 658, §1, eff. 7/7/97.)*

(4) The Department of Transportation and Development, office of weights and standards.

B. All state agencies involved in the regulation and licensing of motor carriers shall provide at their own expense all personnel and equipment necessary for the following:

(1) The issuance of all permits, licenses, certificates, or other authorizations.

(2) The provision of both general and specific information as may be required by the respective state agency to adequately provide the services as set out in this Part.

(Added by Acts 1997 No. 273, §1, eff. 8/15/97.)

§390.24. Coordinating authority; Louisiana Motor Carrier Advisory Committee.

A. The Louisiana Motor Carrier Advisory Committee as created under the provisions of R.S. 40:1486.1 shall be the coordinating authority of the Louisiana Truck Center.

B. It shall be the function of the committee to:

(1) Periodically review the operations of the truck center and to provide advice and recommendations for appropriate administration of the truck center to the coordinating agencies and the appropriate oversight legislative committees.

(2) Facilitate and assist as necessary in providing uniform, consistent, and coordinated administration of the activities at the truck center.

(3) Offer advice and information as requested by the component agencies of the truck center as to the efficiency and timeliness of the permits or registration process.

(4) Assist in any other coordination activities as requested by the coordinating agencies of the truck center.

(Added by Acts 1997 No. 273, §1, eff. 8/15/97.)

PART VII. PROCEDURE AND REPORTS

§391. Appearance upon arrest.

A. Whenever any person is arrested for a violation of any provision of this Chapter or any regulation of the department or of the secretary of the Department of Public Safety adopted pursuant thereto, except as otherwise provided in this Section, the arresting officer shall take his name, address, the license number of his motor vehicle, and the number of his operator's license, and shall issue a summons or otherwise notify him in writing to appear at a time and place to be specified in such summons and notice. The time shall be at least five days after arrest, unless the person arrested demands an earlier hearing. If the person arrested demands an earlier hearing, he shall have a right to an immediate hearing or a hearing within twenty-four hours, at a convenient hour, to be before a magistrate within the parish where the offense was committed. Except as otherwise provided in this Section, the person arrested shall have the option of remaining in custody pending his furnishing bail as fixed by a magistrate or depositing his operator's license with the arresting officer, as provided in R.S. 32:411.

B. If the person arrested holds a Louisiana operator's license and gives his written promise to appear at the time and place stated, the officer may release him from custody or take him immediately before a magistrate, but shall not require the person arrested to deposit his operator's license. Any such person refusing to give the written promise to appear shall be taken immediately by the arresting officer before the nearest or most accessible magistrate having jurisdiction. Any person who willfully violates his written promise to appear shall be punished as provided in R.S. 32:57.1, regardless of the disposition of the charge upon which he was arrested originally. The arresting officer shall fully inform the arrested person of the consequences of failing to honor a written promise to appear pursuant to R.S. 32:57.1.

C. This Section does not apply to any person charged with an offense involving or contributing to an accident resulting in injury or death to any person, or to any person charged with driving while under the influence of intoxicants or narcotics, or to any person whom the arresting officer has good cause to believe has committed any felony or misdemeanor, and in any of these cases the arresting officer shall immediately take the person arrested before the nearest or most accessible magistrate having jurisdiction.

D. This Section does not apply to any person owning or operating a vehicle or combination of vehicles found in violation of R.S. 32:380 through R.S. 32:387.

§392. Impounding of vehicles authorized; prohibitions.

A. (1) Upon discovery of any vehicle operated in violation of this Chapter, except in any case in which the offense is a minor traffic violation only, the vehicle may be impounded forthwith by any state policeman, any authorized representative of the commissioner, any peace officer, or weights and standards police officer of the department except that any overweight or oversize vehicle registered in Louisiana and carrying perishable products or products once loaded which become indivisible shall not be impounded but shall be directed to and followed by the weights and standards police officer or state policeman to the nearest appropriate place suitable for unloading to its licensed gross weight or maximum size requirements as provided in this Chapter and storage of said product to preserve it for its intended use in commerce and in either case shall be detained or unloaded at the expense and responsibility of the owner or driver.

(2) When used in this Subsection, the following words and phrases have the following meanings:

(a) "Minor traffic violation" means any violation of the Highway Regulatory Act as provided for in Title 32 of the Louisiana Revised Statutes of 1950. However, R.S. 32:380 through 387, inclusively, are exempted from this definition.

(b) "Perishable products" means products which are subject to lose their commercial value or decay in a short period of time, including but not limited to agricultural or seafood products and concrete.

(c) "Products once loaded which become indivisible" means products divisible by nature, but which become indivisible once loaded upon a vehicle because of the required manner or method of unloading would be such that the entire load or portion of the load required to be unloaded could not be preserved for its intended use in commerce, or which endangers the public safety, including but not limited to forest products in their natural state.

B. A vehicle impounded for violations of the provisions of this Chapter other than R.S. 32:380 through R.S. 32:387 shall be detained until released by any court or committing magistrate having jurisdiction over the offense. The court or committing magistrate having jurisdiction over an offense involving a vehicle shall not order or allow the release of the vehicle prior to the full satisfaction of all penalties or charges assessed on account of the offense, except upon the execution of an appearance bond in the maximum amount of such penalties and charges, with good and solvent surety approved by the court or committing magistrate.

C. Vehicles impounded for violations of the provisions of R.S. 32:380 through R.S. 32:387 shall be detained until all penalties or charges assessed on account of the violation have been paid as provided in R.S. 32:389, except as provided in Subsection A of this Section. *(Chgd. by Acts 1995 No. 527, §1, eff. 8/15/95.)*

§393. Persons charged with traffic violations; time for disposition, licenses, reports, and records to be sent to Department of Public Safety and Corrections, fee charged; penalties; record of unpaid traffic fines and parking fines; distribution prohibited.

A. Whenever any person is charged with a violation of any provision of this Chapter or regulation of the department final disposition thereof shall be made as soon as feasibly possible. "Final disposition" shall be defined in this Section as a final conviction, not capable of appeal or review and not subject to dismissal.

B. (1) Whenever any person is convicted of an offense for which this Chapter makes mandatory the revocation of the license of such person, the court in which such conviction is had must require the surrender of the license then held by the person convicted and must thereupon forward the same, together with a record of the conviction, to the commissioner.

(2) Whenever the driver's license of any person is mandatorily suspended under the provisions of R.S. 32:414, the court in which the conviction is had or in which bail is forfeited shall attach the license to a record of the conviction or bail forfeiture and shall forward both to the Department of Public Safety.

C. (1)(a) Every court in this state shall keep a full report of every case in which a person is charged with violation of any provision of this Chapter or any regulation of the department or the commissioner adopted pursuant thereto, or any law of this state or of any municipal or parish governing authority lawfully established for regulating the operation of motor vehicles on highways.

(b) If such person is convicted and sentenced thereupon, and such conviction is a final disposition as defined in R.S. 32:853(A)(1)(a), or his bail is forfeited as a result of a final judgment of forfeiture, or other final disposition be made, an abstract of the report, all parking convictions only excepted, shall be sent by the court or the district attorney, as the case may be, to the commissioner not later than thirty days after the date of such person's conviction and sentencing thereupon, forfeiture of his bail and final judgement of forfeiture, or the final disposition of his case. This report shall not be a court record.

(2) No state agency or political subdivision, nor any law enforcement agency of either, nor any officer, official, or employee thereof, shall transfer, disseminate, distribute, or otherwise communicate a record or other compilation of an individual's unpaid fines for traffic violations or parking violations to any credit bureau, credit information agency or bureau, or a subsidiary entity operating such a business in this state, or to a collection agency or firm. No such state agency or political subdivision, nor law enforcement agency of either, nor any officer, official, or employee thereof, shall confect, enter into, or maintain a contract or agreement to provide such a record or compilation to any credit bureau, credit information agency or bureau, or subsidiary entity, or to a collection agency or firm.

(3) Whoever violates the provisions of Paragraph (2) of this Subsection is liable to the individual, whose record of unpaid fines was disclosed, for the amount of his actual damages or five hundred dollars, whichever is greater, and for reasonable attorney fees and costs incurred by the individual in prosecuting his claim. Each separate act of transfer, dissemination, distribution or communication which is prohibited by Paragraph (2) of this Subsection constitutes a separate violation.

D. Abstracts required by this Section shall be made on forms prepared by the commissioner and may include all necessary information as to the parties to the case, the nature of the offense, the date of hearing, the plea, the judgment, the amount of the fine or forfeiture, as the case may be, or the final disposition. When the nature of the offense is specified as speeding, the abstract shall also include a statement of the miles per hour in excess of the speed limit that the person charged was alleged to have been traveling. Every such abstract shall be certified by the judge or the clerk of such court as a true abstract of the records of the court. If the abstract is sent by the district attorney, it shall be certified by him as a true abstract of the final disposition of the case as contained or found in the files of his office.

E. Certified copies of the judgment also shall be forwarded to the commissioner upon the conviction of any person of any felony in the commission of which a vehicle was used. The commissioner shall keep these records in his office, and they shall be open to public inspection during reasonable business hours.

F. (1) For each conviction or forfeiture of bail as outlined above, a fee of two dollars shall be added to the fine of the person convicted, except in a parish having a population of four hundred seventy-five thousand or more where for each such conviction or forfeiture of bail a fee of ten dollars shall be added to the fine of the person convicted. This fee shall be retained by the respective court to cover the cost of preparing and submitting the abstract of the report to the commissioner.

(2) In addition to the two dollar fee provided for in Subsection F of this Section, the City Court of Bossier City is hereby authorized to collect an additional fee of one dollar for each conviction or forfeiture of bail which shall be added to the fine of the person convicted.

G. Whenever a certified statement of revocation or suspension of a driver's license from the Department of Public Safety is offered in evidence in any court of competent jurisdiction, it shall be received in evidence by such court as prima facie proof of its contents, provided that the party against whom the certificate is sought to be used may summon and examine those making the said certificate as witnesses under cross-examination.

H. Whenever any person is charged with a violation of any provision of this Chapter or regulation of the department, and the law enforcement officer issuing the citation has reason to believe that there exists a medical condition which constitutes cause for revocation or suspension under the provisions of R.S. 32:414(E), notification of such medical condition shall be made to the medical/conviction unit of the office of motor vehicles of the Department of Public Safety and Corrections at the same time and in the same manner as notification of the violation, provided that the law enforcement officer first consult with his superior officer as to his specific observations and such superior officer concurs with the issuing officer's belief. *(Chgd. by Acts 1991 No. 289, §9, No. 901, §1; Acts 1997 No. 1280, §1, No. 1288, §1, No. 1343, §1, eff. 8/15/97.)*

§393.1. Records of convictions; extracts; fees.

A. The commissioner shall prepare and maintain records of the convictions of any persons for the violation of traffic offenses which the courts of this state or federal court and magistrates have forwarded to the Department of Public Safety. Extract copies of such records shall be available through the Baton Rouge office and at least two offices in every district.

B. The commissioner shall furnish an extract copy of license records required to be kept by Subsection A hereof to state, parish, municipal, and court officials of this state for official use only, without charge.

C. The commissioner shall charge a fee of five dollars for furnishing extract copies from the Baton Rouge office of license records required to be kept by Subsection A to other persons, firms, or corporations for uses other than official. The fee for extract copies furnished from local field offices shall be ten dollars.

D. All fees collected by the department's local field offices shall be paid into the state treasury on or before the twenty-fifth day of each month following their collection and, in accordance with Article VII, Section 9 of the Constitution of Louisiana shall be credited to the Bond Security and Redemption Fund.
(Chgd. by Acts 1992 No. 984, §10, eff. 8/21/92.)

§394. Flagrant violations; courts to give details on request of department.

The court shall, upon the request of the commissioner or his agents, furnish to the secretary the details of all particularly flagrant cases which may be heard before them. They may make recommendations to the commissioner as to the suspension or revocation of the licenses and the certificates of registration of the defendant in such cases as they deem necessary.

§395. Police officers not impeded by this chapter.

Except as otherwise provided by law or by this Chapter, authorized agents of the commissioner shall not be impeded from exercising the functions of their office or performing their duties in the enforcement of this Chapter, the regulations of the department or of the commissioner adopted pursuant hereto, or any other law of this state within the scope of their authority upon any highway, whether or not the highway is located in whole or in part within the corporate limits of any incorporated municipality of whatsoever population or within any parish of this state. However, in doing so, they shall observe the traffic and police regulations of such municipalities and parishes and, whenever practicably possible, shall cooperate with the police departments of such municipalities or parish officials who shall aid and assist them in the enforcement of this Chapter.

§396. Commissioner to publish records.

As often as practicable, but at least once each month, the commissioner shall either publish or post upon public bulletin boards in each of his offices, a record of stolen and recovered motor vehicles and of suspensions and revocations of operators' and chauffeurs' licenses. He also shall furnish copies of such records to the police departments and sheriffs' offices throughout the state.

§397. Commissioner to furnish forms and receive accident reports.

A. The commissioner shall prepare, and may supply to police and sheriff offices and other suitable agencies, forms for accident reports calling for sufficiently detailed information to disclose, with reference to a highway accident, the cause, the conditions then existing, the persons and vehicles involved, the names of the liability carriers and policy numbers for the vehicles, and the name, address, and telephone number of the insurance agents who procured the liability policies providing coverage for the vehicles.

B. The commissioner shall receive accident reports required to be made by law and shall tabulate and analyze such reports and publish, annually or at more frequent intervals, statistical information based thereon as to the number, cause, and location of highway accidents.

(Chgd. by Acts 1995 No. 527, §1, eff. 8/15/95.)

§397.1. Accident reports; citizens right to privacy.

A. The Legislature of Louisiana hereby finds that the provisions of Title 44 of the Louisiana Revised Statutes of 1950, relating to public records, were enacted to serve the public purpose of providing the citizens of the state with access to information which affects the citizens of the state. The Legislature of Louisiana further finds that the salutory purpose which underlies the provisions of Title 44 has become subverted by certain businesses which use information which appears in the public record solely because a citizen had the misfortune to become involved in a traffic accident as a means of aggressively soliciting that citizen for the commercial gain of that business. The legislature further finds that this aggressive commercial solicitation violates the provisions of Article I, Section 5 of the Constitution of Louisiana, which establishes the right of citizens of this state to be free from unreasonable invasion of privacy.

B. The Legislature of Louisiana hereby declares that the provisions of this Section are enacted for the purpose of implementing the right to privacy found in Article I, Section 5 of the Constitution of Louisiana, by establishing a procedure by which citizens who are involved in traffic accidents can prohibit commercial solicitation connected with that accident.

C. The office of motor vehicles shall establish a form which shall be made available, at cost, to all law enforcement agencies. The form shall provide each person who is involved in a traffic accident with a method of stating that the person does not wish to be solicited by specific commercial businesses. The businesses shall include but shall not be limited to attorneys, health care providers, motor vehicle repair businesses, and insurance businesses. The form shall allow the person who was involved in the accident to state that the person does not wish to be solicited by specific businesses or does not wish to be solicited by any businesses.

D. Each law enforcement officer who investigates and writes up a traffic accident shall furnish a form provided for in this Section to each person whose name appears in the accident report.

E. Each such form which is returned to the law enforcement officer shall be filed with the accident report.

F. Upon filing, the form shall become public record, and under the "public records doctrine" shall become binding on all businesses which are listed on the form.

G. When a form has been executed by a person who was involved in a traffic accident, and the form has been filed with an accident report, the solicitation of that citizen by a business with regard to any commercial activity which is reasonably related to the accident which is the subject of the report, in contravention of the statement on the form, is hereby declared to be an unreasonable invasion of privacy as denounced by the provisions of Article I, Section 5 of the Constitution of Louisiana, and is hereby prohibited.

H. Whoever violates the prohibition of Subsection G of this Section shall be fined not more than one thousand dollars, or imprisoned for not more than six months, or both.

I. In addition to the criminal penalties of Subsection H of this Section, a violation of the prohibition of Subsection G of this Section may be considered a violation of the ethical requirements of any profession or business which is regulated by a governing body which is created or recognized by law, and may subject the violator to sanctions by that governing body, including suspension or revocation of any license, permit, certificate, or similar document held by the offender.

J. The provisions of this Section shall not prohibit the sale of police accident reports or other driving record information to consumers of on-line driving records under written contracts with the Department of Public Safety and Corrections. The department shall include a clause in all such contracts which preclude the release of information in contravention of this section.

(Chgd. by Acts 1993 No. 924, §1, eff. 8/15/93.)

§398. Accident reports; when and to whom made; information aid; fees for copies; fees for accident photographs.

A. The driver of a vehicle involved in an accident resulting in injury to or death of any person or property damage in excess of five hundred dollars shall:

(1) Immediately, by the quickest means of communication, give notice of the accident to the local police department if the accident occurs within an incorporated city or town or, if the accident occurs outside of an incorporated city or town, to the nearest sheriff's office or state police station.

(2) Give his name, address, and the registration number of the vehicle he was driving and, upon request and if available, exhibit his license or permit to drive to any person injured in such accident or to the driver or occupant of or person attending any vehicle or other property damaged in the accident.

(3) Give such information and, upon request, exhibit such license or permit to any police officer at the scene of the accident or who is investigating the accident.

(4) If the accident occurs in a geographical area under order of evacuation by a competent authority or is under a declared state of emergency, comply with the provisions of Paragraphs (1) and (2) herein within seventy-two hours after the occurrence of the accident.

B. The driver of any vehicle involved in an accident resulting in injury to or death of any person or total property damage to an apparent extent of one hundred dollars or more shall, within twenty-four hours after the accident, forward a written report of the accident to the Department of Public Safety and Corrections. Any person who violates the provisions of this Subsection may be imprisoned for not more than sixty days or fined not more than one hundred dollars, or both.

C. The Department of Public Safety and Corrections may require the driver of a vehicle involved in an accident, which is required to be reported by this Section, to file a supplemental report when the original report is insufficient in the opinion of the department and may require witnesses of an accident to render reports.

D. It shall be the duty of the state police or the sheriff's office to investigate all accidents required to be reported by this Section when the accident occurs outside the corporate limits of a city or town, and it shall be the duty of the police department of each city or town to investigate all accidents required to be reported by this Section when the accidents occur within the corporate limits of the city or town. Every law enforcement officer who investigates an accident, as required by this Subsection, shall instruct the driver of each vehicle involved in the accident to report the following to all parties suffering injury or property damage as an apparent result of the accident:

(1) The name and address of the owner and the driver of the vehicle.

(2) The license number of the vehicle.

(3) The name of the liability carrier for the vehicle, the name, address, and telephone number of the insurance agent who procured the liability policy providing coverage for the vehicle.

E. (1) Every law enforcement officer who investigates an accident shall initial the accident report form to show that the officer has complied with the provisions of Subsection D of this Section, and shall indicate on the accident report form whether the investigation is made at the scene of the accident or by subsequent investigation and interviews. Every law enforcement officer who investigates an accident, within forty-eight hours after completing the investigation, shall forward a written report of the accident to the Department of Public Safety and Corrections if the accident occurred outside the corporate limits of a city or town, or to the police department of the city or town if the accident occurred within the corporate limits of such city or town. Police departments shall forward such reports to the Department of Public Safety and Corrections within six days of the date of the accident.

(2) Within forty-eight hours after completing the investigation, the investigating law enforcement officer shall forward a written report of the accident to the Department of Public Safety and Corrections. However, if the accident occurred within the corporate limits of a city or town, the enforcement office shall forward a written report of the accident to the police department of the city or town and a duplicate report to the Department of Public Safety and Corrections within forty-eight hours after completing the investigation.

F. The state police, any local police department, or any sheriff's office shall provide copies of accident reports to any interested person upon request and may charge a fee, not to exceed the sum of five dollars per report that does not exceed two pages, and seven dollars and fifty cents per report that exceeds two pages.

G. The state police, any local police department, or any sheriff's office shall provide copies of photographs of accidents or other photographs required of the investigating agency to any interested person upon request and may charge a reasonable fee, adopted pursuant to R.S. 49:950 et seq., for copies of photographs actually received.

H. Every person holding the office of coroner in this state, or, in the event of a vacancy in the office, the person performing the duties of coroner, shall report to the Department of Public Safety and Corrections and to the Louisiana Highway Safety Commission the death of any person as a result of an accident involving a motor vehicle, and the circumstances of the accident within five days following such death. Such reports shall be made on forms supplied or approved by the department as provided for in Subsection I of this Section. Every hospital shall notify the coroner of the parish in which it is located of any death occurring in the hospital as a result of injuries sustained in a motor vehicle accident.

I. The Department of Public Safety and Corrections shall prepare and, upon request, shall supply to police, coroners, sheriffs, and other suitable agencies or individuals, forms for accident reports, calling for sufficient detailed information to disclose, with reference to a highway accident, the cause, conditions then existing, and the persons and vehicles involved. All accident reports required by this Section shall be made on forms supplied or approved by the Department of Public Safety and Corrections. Each accident report form supplied or approved by the department shall contain directions to the investigating officer to instruct the parties to the accidents to exchange information as required in Subsection D herein and shall contain a place for the investigating officer to initial the report to indicate that he has given those instructions.

J. The Department of Public Safety and Corrections shall receive accident reports required to be made by this Section and may tabulate and analyze such reports and publish annually, or at more frequent intervals, statistical information based thereon as to the number, cause, and location of highway accidents. Based upon its findings after analysis, the department may conduct further necessary detailed research to determine more fully the cause and control of highway accidents. It may further conduct experimental field tests within areas in the state from time to time to prove the practicality of various ideas advanced in traffic control and accident prevention.

K. The reports required by this Section, and the information contained in the reports, shall be confidential, shall be exempt from the provisions of R.S. 44:1 et seq., and shall be made available only to the parties to the accident, parents or guardians of a minor who is a party to the accident, and insurers of any party which is the subject of the report, or to the succession representatives of those parties, or to the attorneys of the parties or succession representatives, or to a news-gathering organization that requests documents related to the accident. All persons and their agents are prohibited from screening accident reports if the person or his agent does not represent any of the persons involved in a particular accident, the report for which could reasonably be expected to be available. However, this limitation shall not prevent any person from requesting particular reports regardless of whether the person represents any party in the accident. The information in the reports may be tabulated and included in the statistical information published under the provisions of Subsection J of this Section. Nothing in this Section shall prohibit the sale of police accident reports or other driving record information to consumers of on-line driving records under written contract for purchase of records with the Department of Public Safety and Corrections. Further, the information in the reports may be used by the office of motor vehicles for the purpose of maintaining operating records.

L. Whenever any person is involved in an accident resulting in injury to or death of any person, or property damage in excess of five hundred dollars and the law enforcement officer investigating the accident has reason to believe that there exists a medical condition which constitutes cause for revocation or suspension under the provisions of R.S. 32:414(E), notification of such medical condition shall be made to the medical/conviction unit of the office of motor vehicles of the Department of Public Safety and Corrections, provided that the law enforcement officer first consult with his superior officer as to his specific observations and such superior officer concurs with the issuing officer's belief.

M. (1) All police, state or local, shall immediately contact the Department of Transportation and Development district office when called to the scene of an accident where that department's property has been damaged in an amount which is estimated to exceed five hundred dollars.

(2) All police, state or local, shall forward copies of accident reports which indicate damage to property of the Department of Transportation and Development in an amount which is estimated to exceed five hundred dollars to the department's headquarters maintenance division within six days of the date of the accident without cost to the department.

(Chgd. by Acts 1990 No. 960, §1; Acts 1992 No. 878, §1; Acts 1993 No. 538, §1; Acts 1995 No. 527, §1, No. 1071, §1; Acts 1997 No. 112, §1, eff. 8/15/97, No. 1036, §1, eff. 7/1/97, No. 1288, §1, No. 1442, §1, eff. 8/15/97.)

PART VII-A. UNIFORM TRAFFIC CITATIONS

§398.1. Traffic citations; form; issuance.

A. All traffic enforcement agencies in this state shall provide traffic citations in appropriate form containing notices to appear, which shall be issued in books with citations in quadruplicate and meeting the requirements of this Part and approved by the commissioner.

B. The chief administrative officer of each traffic-enforcement agency shall issue these books, maintain a record of each book and each citation contained therein issued to all individual members of the traffic enforcement agency and shall require and retain a receipt for each book issued.

C. The issuance of warning citations for violations of the motor vehicle laws of this state is hereby specifically prohibited. However, nothing herein shall prohibit a peace officer from issuing a violation ticket which compels or instructs the motorist to comply with administrative or other legal requirements of Title 32 or Title 47 of the Louisiana Revised Statutes of 1950.

(Chgd. by Acts 1997 No. 759, §1, eff. 7/10/97.)

§398.2. Disposition of traffic citations; unlawful acts; records.

A. Each traffic enforcement officer upon issuing a traffic citation to an alleged violator of any provision of the motor vehicle laws of this state or of any traffic ordinance of any city or town shall deposit the original citation or a copy of such traffic citation with a court having jurisdiction over the alleged offense or with the appropriate traffic violations bureau. However, a citation for a violation of R.S. 32:80(A) shall be deposited only with a court and not with a traffic violations bureau.

B. Upon the deposit of the original citation or a copy of the traffic citation with a court having jurisdiction over the alleged offense or with the traffic violations bureau as set forth herein, the original citation or copy of such traffic citation shall be disposed of only by trial in the court of proper jurisdiction or any other official action by a judge of the court, including forfeiture of the bail, or by the deposit of sufficient bail with the traffic violations bureau or payment of a fine to said bureau by the person to whom such traffic citation has been issued. However, a citation or its copy alleging a violation of R.S. 32:80(A) shall be disposed of only by trial or acceptance of a plea in open court.

C. It shall be unlawful for any traffic enforcement officer or any other officer or public employee to dispose of a traffic citation or copies thereof or of the record of the issuance of the citation in a manner other than as required herein.

D. The chief administrative officer of each traffic enforcement agency in the state shall require all traffic officers under his supervision to return to him a copy of every traffic citation which was issued by the officer for the violation of a traffic law or ordinance, and in addition shall require the return of all copies of every traffic citation which has been spoiled or upon which an entry has been made without having issued the citation to the alleged violator.

E. The chief administrative officer shall also maintain or cause to be maintained in connection with every traffic citation issued by an officer under his supervision a record of the disposition of the charge by the court or its traffic violations bureau in which the original or a copy of the traffic citation was deposited.

F. Nothing herein shall be construed as prohibiting or interfering with the authority of a district attorney or other prosecuting attorney to dismiss a traffic citation or charge by entry of a nolle prosequi.

§398.3. Illegal cancellation of traffic citation; penalty; audit of citation records; publication.

A. Any person who cancels or solicits the cancellation of any traffic citation, in any manner other than as provided in this Part, shall be guilty of a misdemeanor, and shall, upon conviction, be fined not more than five hundred dollars or imprisoned for not more than six months or both.

B. Each record of traffic citations required in this Part shall be audited quarterly by the appropriate fiscal officer of the governmental agency to which the traffic enforcement agency is responsible.

§398.4. When copy of citation shall be deemed a lawful complaint.

In the event the citation form provided for in this Part is sworn to and includes the necessary information required under the general laws of this state with respect to a complaint which charges commission of the offense alleged in said citation to have been committed, then such citation, when filed with a court of proper jurisdiction, shall be deemed to be a lawful complaint for the purpose of prosecution under this Part.

§398.5. Applicability.

The provisions of this Part are to be considered as supplementing any and all other provisions of law relating to the same subject matter or which can be given full force and effect in accomplishing the purposes set forth in this Part and which are not in direct conflict with any of the provisions of this Part.

PART VIII. METHOD OF CITATION

§399. Citation.

Chapter I* of Title 32 of the Louisiana Revised Statutes as amended and revised shall be known as the Louisiana Highway Regulatory Act. The provisions hereinafter may be referred to or cited either as Sections of the Highway Regulatory Act or as Sections of the Revised Statutes. Thus Section 5 of the Highway Regulatory Act may also be referred to or cited as R.S. 32:5.

**So in original. Probably should be "Chapter 1".*

Whenever reference is made herein to a Section of the Highway Regulatory Act, the same shall also relate to the corresponding Section of the Revised Statutes.

CHAPTER 2. DRIVER'S LICENSE LAW

Section

§401. Definitions.

The following words and phrases when used in this Chapter shall have the meaning herein assigned unless the context clearly indicates otherwise.

(1) "Agricultural movements" means the operation of a motor vehicle or combination of vehicles by a farmer to transport agricultural products, farm machinery, and farm supplies; or agricultural crop production fertilizers, agricultural chemicals, or agricultural related fuels, found to be hazardous under the provisions of the Hazardous Materials Transportation Act which requires the motor vehicle to bear a placard under the provisions of the Hazardous Materials Regulations (99 CFR Part 172, Subpart F); to and from a farm within one hundred fifty air miles of the owner's or operator's farm, and which is not used in the operation of a common or contract carrier or used to transport passengers or property for hire.

(2) "Cancellation" means that a driver's license is annulled because of some error or defect or because the licensee is no longer entitled to such license, but the cancellation of a license is without prejudice and application for a new license may be made at any time after such cancellation.

(3) "Commerce" means transportation for the purpose of compensation, remuneration, employment, trade, or payment of any thing of value.

(4) "Commercial driver's license" means a driver's license to operate a commercial motor vehicle.

(5) "Commercial motor vehicle" means a motor vehicle or combination of motor vehicles used in commerce to transport passengers or property if the motor vehicle meets one of the following requirements:

(a) Has a gross combination weight rating of twenty-six thousand one or more pounds inclusive of a towed unit with a gross vehicle weight rating of more than ten thousand pounds.

(b) Has a gross vehicle weight rating of twenty-six thousand one or more pounds.

(c) Is designed to transport sixteen or more passengers, including the driver.

(d) Is of any size and is used in the transportation of materials found to be hazardous under the provisions of the Hazardous Materials Transportation Act which requires the motor vehicle to bear a placard under the provision of the Hazardous Materials Regulations (CFR 49 Part 172, Subpart F). This shall not include hazardous materials used in agricultural movements as defined in this Chapter.

(6) "Convicted" or "conviction" includes the entry of a plea of guilty or nolo contendere to an offense; the forfeiture of bail of any person charged with an offense; and the adjudication of a person as a delinquent for the commission of an offense pursuant to juvenile proceedings.

(7) "Department" means the Department of Public Safety and Corrections.

(8) "Driver's license division" means the driver's license division of the Department of Public Safety and Corrections.

(9) "Driver rehabilitation specialist" means an individual who provides comprehensive services in clinical evaluation of physical functioning, visual/perceptual/cognitive screening, as it pertains to the driving test, and wheelchair/seating assessment, driving assessment, vehicle modification prescription, and driver education; possesses at a minimum an undergraduate degree in a rehabilitation, education, health, safety, physical, occupational, kinesio, or recreational therapy, or related profession or an equivalent of eight years experience in driver rehabilitation/education; and has a minimum of one year of experience in the area of driver evaluation and training for persons with disabilities or possesses current recognition from the Association of Driver Educators for the Disabled (ADED) as a driver rehabilitation specialist.

(10) "Drug offense" means any criminal offense which includes:

(a) The possession, distribution, manufacture, cultivation, sale, transfer, or the attempt or conspiracy to possess, distribute, manufacture, cultivate, sell, or transfer any substance the possession of which is prohibited under the Controlled Dangerous Substances Law*, or

(b) The operation of a motor vehicle under the influence of such a substance.

**R.S. 40:961 et seq.*

(11) "Farmer" means any person who operates a farm or is directly involved in the cultivation of land, crops, or livestock which are owned by that person, or are under the direct control of that person.

(12) "Gross vehicle weight rating" (GVWR) means that value specified by the manufacturer as the maximum loaded weight of a single or combination (articulated) vehicle. The gross vehicle weight rating of a combination (articulated) vehicle, commonly referred to as the "gross combination weight rating" (GVWR)*, is the gross vehicle weight rating of the power unit plus the gross vehicle weight rating of the towed unit or units. In the absence of a value specified for the towed unit or units by the manufacturer, the gross vehicle weight rating of a combination (articulated) vehicle is the gross vehicle weight rating of the power unit plus the total weight of the towed unit or units, including their loads.

**So in original. Probably should be "(GCWR)".*

(13) "Light vehicle" means any motor vehicle or combination of motor vehicles used to transport passengers or property if the motor vehicle has a gross combination weight rating of less than twenty-six thousand and one pounds inclusive of a towed unit with a gross vehicle weight rating of ten thousand pounds or less; or has a gross vehicle weight rating of less than twenty-six thousand and one pounds; or is designed to carry fewer than sixteen passengers, including the driver, and is not used in the transportation of materials found to be hazardous under the provisions of the Hazardous Materials Transportation Act, or a state law or

regulation, which requires the vehicle to bear a placard under the provision of the Federal Hazardous Materials Regulations or under state law or regulation.

(14) "License" or "driver's license" means any license secured from the Department of Public Safety and Corrections, in accordance with this Chapter to operate a motor vehicle on the highways of this state.

(15) "License fee" means the privilege, tax, or fee imposed by this Chapter.

(16) "Motor driven cycle" means every motorcycle, including every motor scooter, with a motor of not to exceed five horsepower.

(17) "Motor vehicle" means and includes automobiles, trucks, truck-tractors, trailers, semitrailers, and motorcycles, propelled by steam, gasoline, electricity, or any other source of energy other than muscular power, except farm implements temporarily operated or moved on a highway or vehicles operated only on rails or tracks constructed therefor.

(18) "Motorcycle" means every motor vehicle having a seat or saddle for use of the rider and designed to travel on not more than three wheels in contact with the ground, but excluding a tractor and a motorized bicycle.

(19) "Motorized bicycle" means a pedal bicycle which may be propelled by human power or helper motor, or by both, with a motor rated no more than one and one-half horsepower, a cylinder capacity not exceeding fifty cubic centimeters, an automatic transmission, and which produces a maximum design speed of no more than twenty-five miles per hour on a flat surface.

(20) "Power cycle" means every motor vehicle propelled by an engine developing not more than five brake horse power, designed to travel on not more than three wheels, at a speed under thirty-five miles per hour, and equipped with brakes adequate to stop such vehicle upon a reasonably clean, dry, level surface within forty-five feet from the spot where the brakes were first applied when the vehicle is travelling at twenty miles per hour.

(21) "Revocation" means that the driver's license to drive a motor vehicle on the highways is terminated and shall not be renewed, except that an application for a new license may be presented and acted upon by the department after the expiration of at least one year after revocation.

(22) "Suspension" means that the driver's license to drive a motor vehicle on the highways is temporarily withdrawn during the period of such suspension.

(23) "Transportation of passengers for hire or fee" means the movement of passengers by motor vehicle for direct monetary payment to a taxicab, limousine service, livery, and/or any common carrier of passengers.

(Chgd. by Acts 1992 No. 277, §1, No. 629, §1; Acts 1993 No. 218, §1, No. 382, §1; Acts 1995 No. 694, §1, eff. 8/15/95.)

§402. All drivers must secure license; emergency vehicle exceptions.

A. Every person who operates a motor vehicle which is designated as being in either Class "A", "B", "C", "D", or "E" under R.S. 32:408, before driving or operating any such motor vehicle on any public street, road, or highway of this state, shall secure from the department an appropriately classified driver's license with all necessary endorsements.

B. It shall be unlawful for any person to drive a motor vehicle on any public street road, or highway of this state unless he has been issued a license by the department in accordance with the provisions of this Chapter. It shall also be unlawful for any person to apply for or obtain more than one valid license.

C. (1) Notwithstanding any provision of this Section or any other law to the contrary, the only driver's license required of a full-time, regularly paid operator of an emergency medical vehicle or firefighting equipment employed by a municipality, parish, fire protection district, or other political subdivision of this state, or civilian employees of the U.S. military who are required to operate emergency vehicles, shall be a Class "E" driver's license when operating such vehicle or equipment in the course and scope of his employment.

(2) Notwithstanding any provision of this Section or any other law to the contrary, the only driver's license required of a driver for an industrial mutual aid response team or a volunteer operator of an emergency medical vehicle or firefighting equipment shall be a Class "E" driver's license when operating such vehicle or equipment.

D. (1) Upon the written request of a licensed physician for driver assessment, the secretary may authorize a driver rehabilitation specialist as defined in this Chapter to issue a temporary Class "E" driving permit for the purpose of driver assessment and training to an individual who is not licensed to drive under the provisions of this Chapter or who has an expired license provided such license is not currently under suspension or revocation. If a

 ZL

license has been suspended or revoked, the temporary medical assessment permit only be issued upon receipt of special authorization from the department.

(2) The temporary permit shall be issued for a total time period of six weeks; however, such period of time shall begin on the first date of evaluation which shall be indicated on the permit and signed by the driver rehabilitation specialist. The temporary permit shall only be issued to those who are sixteen years of age or older.

(3) The temporary permit shall be valid only during the individual's participation in an actual in-car evaluation process during which time the evaluator shall be present.

(4) The department shall promulgate rules and regulations necessary to the administration and enforcement of this Subsection, to include, but not be limited to the design of the application and the permit.

(Chgd. by Acts 1993 No. 218, §1; Acts 1995 No. 1221, §1; Acts 1997 No. 37, §1, eff. 8/15/97.)

§402.1. Driver education; required.

A. No application for a license for the operation of a motor vehicle shall be received from any person seventeen years or older making application for the first time unless there is also submitted with the application, on a form approved by the secretary of the Department of Public Safety and Corrections, written evidence of the successful completion by the applicant of:

(1) A "driver education course", which shall include training of railroad and highway grade crossing safety, approved by the Department of Public Safety and Corrections or the Department of Education.

(2) A "prelicensing training course" if a behind-the-wheel course is not completed. The prelicensing training course shall consist of a minimum of six hours of instruction in the National Safety Council's defensive driving course, Louisiana's traffic safety laws, and substance abuse education, or shall be an equivalent course approved and certified by the Department of Public Safety and Corrections. The course shall include training of railroad and highway grade crossing safety. The secretary of the Department of Public Safety and Corrections shall adopt rules relating to the "prelicensing training course." Oversight review of these rules shall be conducted by the House and Senate Committees on Transportation, Highways and Public Works. The rules shall provide for:

(a) Licensing of training agencies.

(b) Course content and presentation.

(c) Instructor qualifications and certification.

(d) Classroom size and facilities.

(e) Certificates of completion.

(f) Required records and reporting.

(g) Fees, which shall not exceed twenty-five dollars per student.

(h) Penalties.

B. The provisions of this Section shall not apply to any person applying for a renewal license under the provisions of this Chapter or to any person living twenty-five miles or more distant from a location providing a "prelicensing training course".

C. Beginning one year after the appropriation of funds by the Legislature to the State Department of Education for the implementation of a driver education and training program for all children of secondary school age in each parish of this state, and upon the certification by the state superintendent of public education to the secretary of public safety that such program is operating in each parish of this state, no application for the operation of a motor vehicle shall be received from a minor sixteen years of age or older unless there is also submitted with the application, on a form approved by the secretary of public safety, written evidence of the successful completion by the applicant of a "driver education course" approved by the Board of Elementary and Secondary Education or the Department of Public Safety and Corrections.

(Chgd. by Acts 1992 No. 246, §1, No. 382, §1, No. 1009, §1; Acts 1993 No. 225, §1; Acts 1997 No. 725, §1; Acts 1998 First Ex. Sess. No. 80, §2, eff. 6/16/98.)

§402.2. Driver improvement program for remediation.

The Department of Public Safety and Corrections, office of motor vehicles may approve court-ordered driver remediation courses or programs, in the same manner as "prelicensing training courses" are approved in R.S. 32:402.1(A)(2). All such approved driver remediation courses or programs shall include instruction on railroad grade crossing safety. The department shall compile and maintain a list of all department-approved courses which shall be delivered to all persons who are decreed by a court to be traffic violators and who are ordered by a court to attend a driver improvement course for remediation purposes. The court shall allow a violator to select a course within the judicial district in which he resides if there is no court-approved driving course in such district provided that it is one of the courses on the department-approved list. *(Added by Acts 1997 No. 1336, §2; chgd. by Acts 1998 First Ex. Sess. No. 82, §2, eff. 6/16/98.)*

§403. Application; fee; duration of license.

Each application shall be accompanied by the proper license fee, and the license when issued shall be valid for the period prescribed in R.S. 32:412 unless revoked, cancelled, or suspended. Application for license shall be made to the department on a form and in a manner prescribed by the department. No license shall be issued until the application has been approved by the driver's license division.

§403.1. Application of persons sixty years of age or above.

Every person, sixty years of age or above, applying for a license under the provisions of this Chapter shall attach to his application a detailed report from a duly licensed physician or optometrist indicating his visual ability and a detailed medical report from a duly licensed physician indicating his physical condition and specifying any defects in connection therewith which might impair the applicant's ability to exercise ordinary and reasonable control in the operation of a motor vehicle. The provisions of this Section shall not apply to persons applying for a renewal license except for those persons subject to R.S. 32:403.4. However, it shall not be a breach of duty to the public or the individual if the department inadvertently fails to require a report from such applicant or if the department issues a license under the mistaken belief that such applicant is capable of driving safely.

§403.2. Application of persons with physical disability or mental disability.

Every physically or mentally handicapped person applying for a license under the provisions of this Chapter for the first time shall attach to his application a detailed medical report, or a report from an optometrist if it is a visual defect, from a duly licensed physician indicating the severity of his disability and the limitations imposed thereby which might impair the applicant's ability to exercise ordinary and reasonable control in the operation of a motor vehicle. The department may waive the furnishing of said report by any person applying for a renewal license under the provisions of this Chapter, except for a person subject to R.S. 32:403.4.

§403.3. Identification stickers for the deaf and hard of hearing; license label.

The office of motor vehicles of the Department of Public Safety is hereby authorized to issue an identification sticker or decal which shall be the international symbol of deafness at no cost for use by deaf persons and hard of hearing who are granted a driver's license. Every deaf or hard of hearing person applying for a driver's license with an identification decal or sticker shall attach to the application a statement indicating a hearing loss attested by one of the following: a medical physician, audiologist, or speech pathologist. The sticker or decal is to be offered at the time the driver's license is issued and shall be prepared so that it may at the option of the user be applied to the windshield and viewed from the outside of the vehicle or on the license plate, or both. The same sticker or decal identifying the licensee as deaf or hard of hearing shall be offered and imprinted on the back of the driver's license under the lamination. *(Chgd. by Acts 1993 No. 231, §1, eff. 8/15/93.)*

§403.4. Medical evaluation report required of persons driving a commercial motor vehicle.

A. A person applying for a Class "A", "B", or "C" commercial driver's license shall not have any physical or mental disability affecting the ability to exercise ordinary and reasonable control in the operation of a commercial motor vehicle. Such person, unless exempted by the office of motor vehicles or by a rule or regulation, shall provide a current medical report, on a form approved by the office of motor vehicles, prepared by a duly licensed medical examiner, certifying that he is capable of exercising ordinary and reasonable control in the operation of a commercial motor vehicle. Such person shall submit a valid medical report at every renewal and shall carry a current medical certificate on his person at all times when driving a commercial motor vehicle requiring either a Class "A", "B", or "C" commercial driver's license as defined herein.

B. "Medical examiner" means a person who is licensed, certified, or registered to perform physical examinations.
(Chgd. by Acts 1995 No. 1086, §1, eff. 8/15/95.)

§404. Operation of motor vehicles by nonresidents, students, and military dependents; reciprocity agreements with foreign countries.

A. A nonresident or a nonresident minor, who has been licensed to drive or operate a motor vehicle under the laws of his home state and who has in his immediate possession a valid license issued to him by his home state, shall be permitted to drive a motor vehicle in this state without examination or license for a period not to exceed ninety days. The department is authorized to promulgate rules and regulations covering the case of any person whose home states does not require a license, and they shall have the full force and effect of law.

B. A student attending a Louisiana school but who is domiciled in another state, and who has in his immediate possession both a valid license issued to him by his home state and a current student identification card, shall be permitted to drive a motor vehicle in this state without examination or Louisiana license during his enrollment as a student and for not more than ninety days thereafter.

C. A resident dependent of any person on active duty with the Armed Forces of the United States and stationed within Louisiana, but who is domiciled in another state, and who has in his immediate possession both a valid license issued to him by his home state and a current military dependent identification card, shall be permitted to drive a motor vehicle in this state without examination or Louisiana license during the period of residency with the supporting member of the Armed Forces while stationed in Louisiana and for not more than ninety days thereafter.

D. A nonresident, a student, or a military dependent who has in his immediate possession a license not valid in his home state, but which has not been revoked or suspended, may be issued a temporary license for a period not to exceed ten days for the purpose of allowing such nonresident a period of time sufficient to acquire a valid license in his home state. Only one temporary license shall be issued to the same individual within the twelve month period immediately following the issue of a temporary license.

E. Except as provided herein each nonresident or student or military dependent must meet all the requirements set forth in Chapter 2 of Title 32 of the Louisiana Revised Statutes of 1950 except as to residence.

F. The deputy secretary of public safety services of the Department of Public Safety and Corrections is hereby authorized to promulgate rules and regulations as may be necessary to enter into reciprocity agreements with foreign countries. The rules shall specify that the driver's license standards of a foreign country shall be comparable to those of this state. The rules shall also require foreign drivers, who are operating a motor vehicle in Louisiana under such a reciprocity agreement, to comply with the compulsory motor vehicle liability security laws of this state.
(Chgd. by Acts 1997 No. 265, §1, eff. 8/15/97.)

§404.1. Commercial driver's license applicant; domiciliary of state requirement; time limits; reciprocity.

An applicant for a commercial driver's license must be a domiciliary of this state, unless applying for a nonresident commercial driver's license. A person domiciled in and holding a valid commercial driver's license from another jurisdiction meeting the standards contained in 49 Code of Federal Regulations Part 383, shall not be required to obtain a Louisiana driver's license while operating in this state. However, a holder of a commercial driver's license who has been a resident of this state for thirty days or longer shall be considered a domiciliary of this state for purposes of this Chapter and shall obtain a Louisiana commercial driver's license within the time period* specified in R.S. 32:404. An applicant for a Louisiana commercial driver's license shall surrender any driver's license from this or any other state or any jurisdiction meeting the requirements contained in 49 Code of Federal Regulations Part 383. A driver holding a commercial driver's license from any other jurisdiction shall apply for a Louisiana commercial driver's license within no more than thirty days* after establishing a domicile in this state.
**So in original.*

§405. Application must be verified.

Every application shall be verified by the applicant, and by any other person required by this Chapter to sign such application, before a person authorized to administer oaths. The officers and employees of the drivers' license division are authorized to administer oaths without fee, and notaries public or other officers shall not charge in excess of twenty-five cents for the administration of such oath.

§405.1. Age requirements.

Subject to R.S. 32:407, a Class "E" driver's license or a Class "D" chauffeur's license shall be granted to a person seventeen years of age or above. Class "A", "B", or "C" licenses shall be granted only to persons eighteen years of age or above. However, hazardous materials endorsements shall be issued only to persons twenty-one years of age or above. The age limitations are subject to the minimum age requirements set forth in the Federal Motor Carrier Safety Act of 1986* and the regulations promulgated thereunder relative to licensing of carriers in interstate commerce. *(Chgd. by Acts 1992 No. 382, §1; Acts 1993 No. 382, §1; Acts 1995 No. 692, §1; Acts 1997 No. 725, §1, eff. 1/1/98.)*

**So in original. Probably should be "Motor Carrier Safety Act of 1984".*

§406. Licensee must give notice of change of address.

Whenever any person after applying for or receiving license shall move permanently from the address or place of residence named in the application he shall, within ten days thereafter, notify the driver's license division, in writing, of such change and of his new address.

§407. Application of minors; revocation.

A. (1) The application of any minor applying for operating privileges shall not be granted, unless it is signed by either the father or mother of the applicant, who has custody of the applicant, otherwise, by the tutor or other person having custody of him. A license issued to a minor shall be issued upon compliance with the other provisions of this Chapter.

(2) Upon completion of a driver's education course approved by the Department of Public Safety and Corrections or the Department of Education and upon passing a visual examination and a road knowledge test, including rules of the road, signs and signals and not less than two questions relative to railroad and highway grade railroad safety, an applicant at least fifteen years of age, but less than seventeen years of age, applying for the first time may be issued a Class "E" learner's license. The license may be issued for a four-year period at the same fee as a Class "E" driver's license and must be maintained for at least ninety days prior to being converted to a Class "E" intermediate driver's license. The Class "E" learner's license shall authorize the holder to drive while being accompanied by a licensed parent, guardian, or adult at least age twenty-one or older.

(3) The Class "E" learner's license may be converted to a Class "E" intermediate license upon the applicant being at least sixteen years of age and passing an on-road driving test. The intermediate license shall restrict those under the age of seventeen from driving between 11 p.m. and 5 a.m. unless otherwise accompanied by a licensed parent, guardian, or adult at least twenty-one years of age.

(4) Upon completing the Class "E" intermediate licensing stage, and upon demonstrating that the licensee has remained accident free, except in cases where the licensee was not at fault, has received no convictions for moving violations, and has received no convictions for violations of the seat belt or curfew laws of this state for twelve consecutive months after being issued his intermediate license, an applicant may be issued full Class "E" driving privileges.

(5) The department may establish rules and regulations to extend the term of the intermediate license if an applicant's license has been suspended, the applicant has been placed on probation by a court due to a driving violation, or the applicant has violated any of the provisions of Paragraph (4) of this Subsection. The term of the extension of the intermediate license shall be for no less than thirty days nor more than one hundred eighty days from the end of any suspension or probation period, or from the date he would otherwise have been eligible to apply for a Class "E" permanent license in the case of a violation of Paragraph (4) of this Subsection. The licensee shall have the right to an administrative hearing to appeal the determination of the department to extend the applicant's intermediate license. The provisions of this Paragraph shall apply to any licensee who has not attained the age of eighteen.

B. Notwithstanding any provision of law to the contrary, the department may deny the application or revoke the license of a minor upon the forwarding of a written request to the department by the parent, tutor, or other person having legal custody who has not signed the application for a license.

C. The department may promulgate rules and regulations for the enforcement and administration of this Section.

D. The driver's licenses issued pursuant to this Section shall be of a distinctive color to ensure ease of identification as a license issued to a minor.

(Chgd. by Acts 1990 No. 962, §1; Acts 1992 No. 382, §1; Acts 1993 No. 382, §1; Acts 1997 No. 725, §1; Acts 1998 First Ex. Sess. No. 80 §2, eff. 6/16/98.)

§408. Examination of applicants required; classes of licenses.

A. (1) Except as otherwise provided, every applicant must pass a knowledge and skills test for a motor vehicle representative of the type of motor vehicle he operates or expects to operate, or provide evidence on a form approved by the department that he has successfully passed a driving or skills test administered by an authorized third party. In addition to the specialized knowledge and skills tests, each such examination shall include a test of the applicant's eyesight; his ability to understand highway signs regulating, warning, and directing traffic; his knowledge of railroad and highway grade crossing safety; and his knowledge of all relevant traffic regulations.

(2) All tests shall be constructed in such a way as to determine if the applicant possesses the required knowledge and skills for the group of motor vehicles that will be operated. The department shall develop specifications for tests for each vehicle group and endorsement, which shall be at least as stringent as the standards established by the Federal Highway Administration in 49 Code of Federal Regulations Part 383. The department shall determine specific methods for scoring the knowledge and skills tests. The department shall develop standardized scoring sheets for the skills tests, as well as standardized driving instructions for the applicant. Knowledge and skills tests shall be based solely on information contained in the driver's manual. Each test shall have administrative procedures, designed to achieve inter-examiner reliability, that are sufficient to ensure fair pass/fail rates. The knowledge tests may be given in oral, written, or automated form. A simulator or off-road course may be used for skills testing as long as such testing is combined with actual on-the-road testing. If the applicant does not obey traffic laws or causes an accident during the test, he shall automatically fail the test.

(3) Each knowledge test for a Group "D" or "E" vehicle shall contain at least thirty items, exclusive of the number of items testing airbrake knowledge. Not less than two of the thirty items shall be relative to railroad and highway grade crossing safety. For each endorsement, the knowledge test and the airbrake component of the basic knowledge test shall contain a number of questions that is sufficient to test the applicant's knowledge of the required subject matter with validity and reliability. The applicant for a Class "A", "B", "C", "D", or "E" license shall correctly answer at least eighty percent of the questions on each knowledge test in order to achieve a passing score on such knowledge test. To achieve a passing score on the skills test, an applicant for a Class "A", "B", "C", "D", or "E" license shall demonstrate that he can successfully perform all of the required skills. If an applicant for a Class "A", "B", or "C" commercial driver's license scores less than eighty percent on the airbrake component of the basic knowledge test, the driver shall fail the airbrake component and, if the driver is issued a driver's license, an airbrake restriction shall be indicated on the commercial driver's license. If an applicant for a Class "A", "B", or "C" commercial driver's license performs the skills test in a vehicle not equipped with air brakes, the driver shall have omitted the airbrake component of the skills test and, if the driver is issued a driver's license, the airbrake restriction shall be indicated on the license.

(4) The knowledge test for all applicants must be administered by the department. However, the department may elect to administer skills tests itself or to authorize a third party, including another state, an employer, a private training facility or other private institution, or a department, agency or instrumentality of state or local government, to administer the skills tests. The department may contract with or enter into agreements with such third parties or certify or license them to perform the testing. However, the department shall ensure that examiners are qualified to administer the tests on the basis of training or other experience. The department shall establish minimum qualifications for persons administering driver's license tests and prescribe the procedures to be used. The tests given the third party shall be the same as those that would otherwise be given by the department. The Federal Highway

Administration, or its representative, and the department, or its representative, may conduct random examinations, inspections, and audits without prior notice. The department, or its representative, shall conduct a random inspection at least annually. All third party examiners shall meet the same qualifications and training as state examiners to the extent necessary to conduct skills tests in compliance with this Subsection. Department employees shall at least annually take the tests actually administered by the third party as if the employee were a test applicant, or the department shall at least annually test a sample of drivers who were examined by the third party to compare pass/fail results. These requirements and conditions shall be included in any third party contract or agreement and shall be a part of any license, certificate, or permit issued to such third parties. The department shall devise a system to regulate such third parties and the regulations shall have the full force and effect of law. In addition to any other applicable sanction, improper issuance of proof of successful completion of the skills tests shall subject the third party to the penalties imposed by this Chapter, up to a five thousand dollar civil penalty per violation, or revocation or suspension of the privilege to test applicants, or both. The department shall set the cost of any license, permit, or certificate to test applicants and may set any maximum fee that such third parties may charge applicants. The department shall submit any such third party contract or agreement to the commissioner of the division of administration for his approval. The third party shall provide evidence to the applicant who has successfully passed the driving skills tests on a form approved by the department. The applicant shall provide this form to the department before being issued a commercial driver's license.

(5) *(Repealed.)*

(6) At the discretion of the department, the driving skills tests may be waived for a driver who is licensed prior to the institution of the new testing program and substituted with either an applicant's driving record and previous passage of an acceptable skills test, or an applicant's record in combination with at least two years of driving experience in a vehicle representative of the vehicle he operates or expects to operate.

(7) In addition to the exemptions granted in Subsection (A)(6) of this Section, the department may exempt the drivers of the vehicles listed in Subsection (A)(8) of this Section from the retest requirements.

(8) The department may exempt the drivers of the following vehicles from the test specifications contained in Subsection (A)(3) of this Section and devise substitute test specifications for such drivers:

(a) A vehicle designed for personal use unless used for commercial purposes or used to transport hazardous materials required to be placarded.

(b) A farm vehicle controlled and operated by a farmer and used to transport agricultural products, farm machinery, or farm supplies within one hundred and fifty miles of the farm and which is not used as a contract or common carrier.

(9) The department is authorized to promulgate rules and regulations necessary to administer and enforce this Subsection, in accordance with the Administrative Procedure Act*, subject to oversight by the Joint Legislative Committee on Transportation, Highways, and Public Works. The department may delegate the duties and authority imposed by this Subsection.

**R.S. 49:950 et seq.*

(10) Provision shall be made for examination in the parish wherein an applicant resides, except for commercial driver skill and knowledge testing. The department shall locate testing centers for driver skill and knowledge testing in locations convenient to applicants.

(11) One of the motor vehicle field offices established within a parish shall be located in the parish seat. If an existing office is not in the parish seat, an additional office shall be located in the parish seat.

B. (1) There shall be three general types of driver's licenses:

(a) The "Commercial Driver's License" (Classes "A", "B", and "C").

(b) The "Chauffeur's License" (Class "D").

(c) The "Personal Vehicle Driver's License" (Class "E").

(2) A commercial driver's license shall be required when a vehicle is used in commerce as defined in this Chapter, and is a commercial motor vehicle as defined in this Chapter. A farmer shall not need a commercial driver's license when operating a motor vehicle as provided for in R.S. 32:408(B)(2)(e). The department may elect to or, if required by the Federal Highway Administration, shall change the weight and passenger limits expressed herein to conform to regulations by the Federal Highway Administration. The department shall do so by regulations promulgated in accordance with the Administrative Procedure Act subject to

oversight by the Joint Legislative Committee on Transportation, Highways and Public Works. The different classes of driver's licenses to be issued shall be as follows:

(a) Class "A" "Commercial Driver's License"—"Combination Vehicle"

Permits the operation of all vehicles within Classes "B", "C", "D", and "E", with any appropriate endorsements, and any combination of vehicles with a gross combination weight rating of twenty-six thousand and one or more pounds, provided that the gross vehicle weight rating of the vehicle or vehicles being towed is in excess of ten thousand pounds. This class of vehicles does not include the operation of motorcycles and motor scooters except as an endorsement to the basic license.

(b) Class "B" Commercial Driver's License—"Heavy Straight Vehicle"

Permits the operation of any vehicle within Classes "C", "D", and "E", with any appropriate endorsements, plus any single vehicle with a gross vehicle weight rating of twenty-six thousand and one or more pounds, or any such vehicle towing a vehicle not in excess of ten thousand pounds gross vehicle weight rating. A "straight vehicle" is defined for the purpose of this class as being one that does not bend or have any moveable joint in its frame between the driver's seat and the cargo or passenger compartment. This class does not include the operation of motorcycles and motor scooters except as an endorsement to the basic license.

(c) Class "C" Commercial Driver's License—"Light Vehicle"

Permits the operation of any vehicle within Classes "D" and "E", with any appropriate endorsements, plus any single vehicle less than twenty-six thousand and one pounds gross vehicle weight rating, or any such vehicle towing a vehicle not in excess of ten thousand pounds gross vehicle weight rating. This group includes vehicles designed to transport sixteen or more passengers including the driver and which are not within the definition of a Group "A" or "B" vehicle, and vehicles used in the transportation of materials found to be hazardous for purposes of the Federal Hazardous Materials Transportation Act, 49 United States Code 1801 et seq. or under state law or regulation and which require the motor vehicle to be placarded under the Federal Hazardous Materials Regulations (49 Code of Federal Regulations Part 172, Subpart F) or under state law or regulation. This class does not include the operation of motorcycles and motor scooters except as an endorsement to the basic license.

(d) Class "D" Chauffeur's License

Permits the operation of all vehicles included in Class "E" plus any single motor vehicle used in commerce to transport passengers or property if the motor vehicle has a gross vehicle weight rating of ten thousand one or more pounds but less than twenty-six thousand one pounds, or any such vehicle towing a vehicle not in excess of ten thousand pounds gross vehicle weight rating; or any vehicle designed or utilized for the transportation of passengers for hire or fee; and not utilized in the transportation of materials found to be hazardous under the provisions of the Hazardous Materials Transportation Act which requires the vehicle to bear a placard under the provisions of Hazardous Materials Regulations (49 CFR Part 172, Subpart F).

(e) Class "E" Driver's License—"Personal Vehicle"

Permits the operation of any single motor vehicle under ten thousand one pounds gross vehicle weight rating or any such vehicle towing a vehicle not in excess of ten thousand pounds gross vehicle weight rating; any personal use of recreational vehicle or combination of vehicles; any farm vehicle utilized in agricultural movements as defined in this Chapter; or any vehicle which is not within the definition of Group "A", "B", "C", or "D" and not utilized in the transportation of materials found to be hazardous under the provision of the Hazardous Materials Transportation Act which requires the vehicle to bear a placard under provisions of the Hazardous Materials Regulations (49 CFR Part 178, Subpart F). This class of vehicles does not include the operation of motorcycles and motor scooters except as an endorsement to the basic license.

(3) There shall be the following endorsements possible to the classes of commercial driver's licenses:

(a) "T"—double/triple trailers. This endorsement shall not be construed so as to allow operation of triple trailer combinations in this state.

(b) "P"—passenger vehicle.

(c) "N"—tank vehicle.

(d) "H"—hazardous materials.

(e) "X"—combination tank vehicle and hazardous materials.

(f) Any other endorsement required by the department as long as it is fully explained on the license.

(4) There shall be the following restrictions possible to the classes of commercial driver's license:

(a) "L"—airbrake restriction.

(b) Any other restriction required by the department as long as it is fully explained on the license.

(5) The department may elect to issue a "nonresident commercial driver's license" to a person domiciled in a foreign country if the Federal Highway Administrator has determined that the commercial motor vehicle testing and licensing standards in the foreign domicile do not meet the standards contained in 49 Code of Federal Regulations Part 383. If the department elects to issue nonresident commercial drivers' licenses, the procedures for issuance and the notification to the Commercial Driver's License Information System shall be the same as those pertaining to any other commercial driver's license. Prior to issuing any nonresident commercial driver's license, the department shall establish enforcement procedures for disqualifying the holder of a nonresident commercial driver's license and for withdrawing, suspending, canceling, or revoking the nonresident commercial driver's license under the same conditions applicable to a commercial driver's license issued to a resident of this state. The department may set the fees to be charged for such license and the duration of such license by regulation in accordance with the Administrative Procedure Act subject to oversight by the Joint Legislative Committee on Transportation, Highways and Public Works.

C. Motorcycles, motor driven cycles, and motorized bicycles shall not be given a separate class, as such, but their use shall be provided for by making an endorsement on one of the basic classes outlined in this Section. Such an endorsement shall be made only after the applicant has taken and successfully passed tests specifically designed for the operation of such vehicles. No operator's skill test shall be required if an applicant has successfully completed the Motorcycle Safety, Awareness, and Operator Training Program provided in R.S. 17:282.

D. Authorized emergency vehicles shall not be given a special class, as such, but their lawful operation shall be provided for by an appropriate special endorsement on a class "E" license indicating the group or groups of motor vehicles the driver is authorized to operate.

E. The license or special certificate of each applicant shall be endorsed appropriately with respect to his qualifications to operate said vehicles. Any applicable restriction shall be noted on the driver's license or special certificate.

F. (1) The department shall make provisions for testing driver's license or special certificate applicants in languages other than English and for testing deaf applicants. However, this shall not be construed to require the department to furnish an interpreter.

(2) Notwithstanding Subsection (G)(1) of this Section, a driver, unless exempted by the department by rule or regulations, who transports hazardous materials required to be placarded or who is otherwise subject to the English literacy requirement of 49 Code of Federal Regulations Part 391, shall be able to read and speak the English language sufficiently to converse with the general public, to understand highway traffic signs and signals in the English language, to respond to official inquiries, and to make entries on reports and records.

G. The deputy secretary of public safety services shall adopt and promulgate any rules and regulations relative to motor carrier operator qualifications, including minimum qualifications of operators of motor rules and regulations in accordance with the Administrative Procedure Act. Oversight review shall be conducted by the Joint Legislative Committee on Transportation, Highways, and Public Works. All rules and regulations adopted by the deputy secretary relative to motor carrier vehicle operator qualifications shall be consistent with the regulations of the United States Department of Transportation contained in Title 46 and Title 49 of the Code of Federal Regulations relative to motor carrier safety and the transportation of hazardous materials.

H. (1) Information on how to obtain a driver's license and endorsements shall be included in manuals made available by the office of motor vehicles to applicants at a cost to be established by regulation. The information provided to the applicant shall include:

(a) Information on the requirements and qualifications for obtaining a driver's license.

(b) The procedure for issuance of a driver's license.

(c) Information on third party testing.

(d) Information on the experience substitute for the skills tests.

(e) Information on any exemptions to the retest requirements.

(f) Any special test specification modifications for certain drivers.

(g) Information on the vehicle groups and endorsements.

(h) The substance of the knowledge and skills which drivers must have for the different vehicle groups and endorsements, including information on railroad and highway grade crossing signage and safety procedures.

(i) Information on the airbrake restriction.

(j) Details of testing procedures, including the purpose of the test, how to respond, any time limits for taking the test, and any other special procedures determined by the department.

(k) Directions on taking the tests.

(*l*) Information on the implied consent provision to be tested for alcohol or drugs.

(m) Information on the criminal and civil penalties imposed on drivers of commercial motor vehicles, including the disqualifications offenses.

(2) A supply of guides shall be furnished to libraries and schools in each parish and shall be available for use in the library or school at no cost to the applicant.

(3) Details on testing and other requirements established by the department shall be included in driver examiner manuals and made available to examiners and third party testers at a cost to be established by regulation. The information made available to the examiner shall include:

(a) Information on driver application procedures.

(b) Information on third party testing.

(c) Information on the procedures for issuance of the driver's license.

(d) Information on the experience substitute for the skills tests.

(e) Information on any exemption to the retest requirement.

(f) Details on the information which must be given to the applicant, including information on the implied consent provision to be tested for alcohol or drugs, the criminal and civil penalties faced by persons who operate commercial motor vehicles, and on the disqualification offenses.

(g) Details on how to conduct the tests.

(h) Scoring procedures and minimum passing scores.

(i) Information for selecting driving test routes.

(j) A list of skills to be tested.

(k) Instructions on where and how the skills will be tested.

(*l*) How performance of the skills will be scored.

(m) Criteria for automatic failures of the skills test.

(4) Information on any special procedures for applying for any other special endorsement, any special qualifications required of such persons, and any special knowledge or skills drivers are required to possess shall be included in a manual or manuals, unless such information is included in the driver's manual, and shall be made available to the applicant at a cost to be established by regulation. However, a supply of guides shall be furnished to libraries and schools in each parish, where they shall be available for use at no cost to the applicant.

(Chgd. by Acts 1992 No. 629, §1; Acts 1993 No. 34, §1; No. 382, §§1, 2; Acts 1995 No. 801, §1; Acts 1998 First Ex. Sess. No. 80, §2, eff. 6/16/98.)

§408.1. Third party testing; proof of testing.

The Department of Public Safety and Corrections may authorize another state, an employer, a private driver training facility or other private institution, or a department, agency or instrumentality of a local government to administer the skills test as specified herein if all of the following conditions are met:

(1) The tests given by the third party are the same as those which would otherwise be given by the department.

(2) The third party has an agreement with the department containing, at a minimum, provisions which:

(a) Allow the Department of Public Safety and Corrections or its representative to conduct random examinations, inspections, and audits without prior notice;

(b) Require the Department of Public Safety and Corrections to conduct on-site inspections at least annually;

(c) Require that all third party examiners meet the same qualification and training standards as Department of Public Safety and Corrections examiners to the extent necessary to conduct skills tests in compliance herein;

(d) Require that, at least on an annual basis, designated Department of Public Safety and Corrections employees take the tests actually administered by the third party as if said employee were a test applicant, or that the Department of Public Safety and Corrections test a sample of drivers who were examined by the third party to compare pass/fail results; and

(e) Reserve unto the Department of Public Safety and Corrections the right to take prompt and appropriate remedial action against the third-party testers in the event that the third-party fails to comply with state or federal standards for the commercial driver's license testing program or with any other terms of the third-party contract.

(3) A driver applicant who takes and passes driving tests administered by an authorized third party shall provide evidence to the state licensing agency that he has successfully passed the driving tests administered by the third party on a form approved by the department.

(4) Any third party or department employee authorized under the provisions of this Chapter to administer tests to applicants for commercial driver's licenses who falsifies information regarding test results or applicant qualification or who in any way participates in, aids, or abets the fraudulent testing or issuance to an applicant of a commercial driver's license or endorsement thereon shall be liable under this Chapter for civil penalties of not less than five hundred nor more than five thousand dollars per act. Furthermore, the department may establish procedures to void all transactions and any licenses issued as a result of such falsification or fraud, such procedures to be established pursuant to the Administrative Procedure Act*. Any authorized third party tester suffering a sanction under the provisions of this Chapter shall forfeit his authorized third party testing status and contract and shall not qualify for such status henceforth.

**R.S. 49:950 et seq.*

§408.2. Third party testing; limitation of liability.

The third party tester, its agents, or its employees shall not be liable for any and all claims, losses, damages, costs, and other proceedings made, sustained, brought, or prosecuted in any manner based upon, occasioned by, or attributable to any injury, infringement, or damage arising from, or claimed to have arisen from, acts committed by a driver who has been given a skills test by such third party tester provided the test was administered in accordance with Louisiana rules, regulations, and laws. *(Added by Acts 1990 No. 994, §1, eff. 9/7/90.)*

§409. Filing of applications; use of abbreviations; release of information.

A. The driver's license division shall file every application approved by it and arrange them alphabetically under the name of the applicant, including only applications granted, and shall assign to each applicant a distinguishing number. The driver's license division shall also maintain an alphabetical file containing the names of all persons whose licenses have been suspended, cancelled, or revoked by it or by a court of competent jurisdiction and the reason therefor. For purposes of the driver's license law the department may, by regulation, require the use of an abbreviated form of an excessively lengthy name.

B. Upon written request, the department may provide information contained in these files to any interested party for a reasonable fee. These fees shall be adopted pursuant to R.S. 49:950 et seq.

§409.1. Application or special certificate applications; penalties for false information.

A. (1) If the department does not develop alternate means of ensuring that the applicant meets the requirements of the certifications listed below, the department shall require applicants for a driver's license to make the following certifications:

(a) An applicant for a commercial driver's license who operates or expects to operate in interstate or foreign commerce or who is otherwise subject to 49 Code of Federal Regulations Part 391, shall certify that he meets the qualification requirements contained in 49 Code of Federal Regulations Part 391, including twenty-one year age requirement, English literacy requirement, special knowledge and skills, reporting violations, and employment history.

(b) An applicant for a commercial driver's license who operates or expects to operate entirely in intrastate commerce and who is not otherwise subject to 49 Code of Federal Regulations Part 391 shall certify that he is not subject to such provisions.

(c) An applicant shall certify and the department shall verify that the motor vehicle in which he will take or has taken the driving or skills test is representative of the type of motor vehicle he operates or expects to operate.

(d) An applicant shall certify that his driver's license is not suspended, revoked, or cancelled; that he is not disqualified from operating a motor vehicle; and the he has not otherwise lost the privilege to drive.

(e) An applicant for a commercial driver's license shall certify that he does not have a driver's license from more than one state or jurisdiction.

(f) Any other certification required by the department.

(2) An applicant for a driver's license shall provide the following information:

(a) Full name.

(b) Current mailing address.

(c) Current residential address.

(d) Identifying information including:

(i) Date of birth (month, day, and year).

(ii) Sex.

(iii) Height.

(iv) Weight.

(v) Eye and hair color.

(vi) Social security number. The department shall maintain confidentiality of an applicant's social security number.

(vii) Signature or a mark attested to by at least one witness if the applicant cannot make a signature.

(viii) Any other information required by the department.

(ix) *(Repealed.)*

(x) Unless applying for renewal of a license or the replacement of an expired license under this Chapter, one primary and two secondary documents of identification or two primary documents of identification from a list of acceptable documents determined by the department. However, such documentation shall include at least one of the following:

(aa) Certified copy of a birth certificate, original certificate of birth, or birth registration card or certificate issued by a state or county bureau of vital statistics with raised agency seal.

(bb) Certification of birth abroad issued by the United States Department of State.

(cc) Certificate of citizenship.

(dd) Current out-of-state driver's license.

(ee) Current U.S. military identification card or draft record or military dependent identification card.

(ff) U.S. Coast Guard Merchant Mariner card.

(gg) Identification card issued by federal, state, or local government agency or entity provided it contains a photograph or information such as name, date of birth, sex, height, and address.

(hh) Passport. Foreign passports must be appropriately stamped and accompanied by proper immigration documents.

(ii) Native American tribal document.

(jj) In cases where none of the above are available, some document of equal significance considered by the secretary of the department or his designee to assure sufficient proof of identity.

(3) An applicant falling within the provisions of R.S. 32:403.1, 403.2, or 403.4 shall provide a medical report and all applicants shall pass a vision test.

(4) An applicant for a driver's license shall pass a knowledge test for the type of motor vehicle he operates or expects to operate and, except as otherwise provided herein, the department has authority to waive said skills test. Every applicant shall pass a driving or skills test taken in a motor vehicle which is representative of the type of motor vehicle the applicant operates or expects to operate, or provide evidence on a form approved by the department that he has successfully passed a driving or skills test administered by an authorized third party in such a representative vehicle.

(5) An applicant for a commercial driver's license or a chauffeur's license shall surrender any driver's license issued by this or any other state or jurisdiction. An applicant for a Class "E", "Personal Vehicle" driver's license, shall surrender any driver's license issued by this or any other state or jurisdiction, unless such state or jurisdiction requires him to have a local driver's license.

(6) The department shall initiate and complete a check of the applicant's driving record to ensure that the person is not subject to any disqualifications, suspensions, revocations, or cancellations and that the driver does not have a driver's license from more than one state. The record check for a commercial driver's license shall include:

(a) A check of the applicant's driving record as maintained by his current state of licensure, if any.

(b) A check with the Commercial Driver's License Information System (CDLIS) to determine if the applicant has a commercial driver's license, if the applicant's license has been suspended, revoked, or cancelled, or if the applicant has been disqualified from operating a commercial motor vehicle.

(c) A check with the National Driver Register (NDR), if it is determined to be operational by the Federal Highway Administrator, to determine if the applicant:

(i) Has been disqualified from operating a motor vehicle other than a commercial motor vehicle.

(ii) Has had a license other than a commercial driver's license suspended, revoked, or cancelled for cause in the three year period ending on the date of application.

(iii) Has been convicted of any of the offenses contained in Section 205(A)(3) of the National Drivers Register Act of 1982. The department may perform a similar record check for all applicants of a Class "D" chauffeur's license or a Class "E" personal vehicle driver's license and may charge such applicant a record check fee equal to the application for a commercial driver's license. The department shall give full weight and consideration to such information in deciding whether to issue a driver's license to such applicant. The department shall not issue a driver's license to an applicant who is disqualified from operating a motor vehicle, whose driver's license has been suspended, revoked, or canceled, or who has otherwise lost the privilege to drive in another state or jurisdiction, except for the limited exception provided in R.S. 32:404. However, inadvertent issuance of a driver's license to such an applicant shall not be considered a breach of duty on the part of the department to the public or the individual.

(7) The department shall inform all applicants for a commercial driver's license, subject to R.S. 32:414.2, of the implied consent provision to be tested for alcohol, controlled substances, or for any other substance which may impair his ability to safety drive and of the resultant exposures and penalties. The department shall also inform such an applicant that he may be subject to stiffer criminal and civil penalties for offenses involving a commercial motor vehicle or a commercial driver's license. However, inadvertent failure of the department to so inform the applicant shall not be a breach of duty on the part of the department to the public or to the applicant and shall not constitute a defense in a subsequent criminal or civil action against the applicant.

(8) Any other requirement of the department established by rule or regulation.

B. Prior to renewing a driver's license, the department shall require the certifications specified in Subsection (A)(1); complete a check of the applicant's record as specified in Subsection (A)(6); request and receive updates of the information specified in Subsection (A)(2); require the applicant to pass the test for a hazardous materials endorsement if he wishes to retain the endorsement; require the applicant to furnish a current medical report and pass a vision test as specified in Subsection (A)(3); require the applicant to be tested with respect to his qualifications at least every four years, provided, however, that the department may waive the actual demonstration of the applicant's ability to operate the vehicle; and, any other requirement of the department established by rule or regulation.

C. Prior to issuing an upgrade of a driver's license or issuing a special certificate, the department shall require the applicant to provide the certifications specified in Subsection (A)(1), complete a check of the applicant's record as specified in Subsection (A)(6), request and receive updates of the information specified in Subsection (A)(2), and require the applicant to pass the tests related to the new vehicle group or endorsements or special certificate. The department shall require a medical report or vision test as specified in Subsection (A)(3) and any other requirement established by rule or regulation.

D. When applying to transfer a driver's license from a previous state of domicile to this state, an applicant shall apply for a driver's license from this state within no more than thirty days after establishing a domicile in this state. Prior to issuing a driver's license to a person who wishes to transfer his driver's license from another state, the department shall require the applicant to provide the certifications specified in Subsection (A)(1), complete a check of the applicant's record as specified in Subsection (A)(6), and request updates of the information specified in Subsection (A)(2). If the applicant wishes to retain a hazardous materials endorsement, the department shall ensure that the applicant has, within two years preceding the transfer, either passed the test for such endorsement or successfully completed a hazardous materials test or training given by a third party deemed by the department to cover the same knowledge base as the state-administered test. The department shall further require the applicant to submit a medical report and to take a vision test as specified in Subsection (A)(3), to obtain the driver's license issued by the applicant's previous state of domicile, to require the applicant to submit to a knowledge or skills test if the department so provides by rule or regulation, and to meet any other requirements of the department established by rule or regulation.

E. If the department determines in its check of an applicant's license status and record prior to issuing a driver's license, or at any time after the driver's license is issued, that the applicant has falsified information specified in Subsection (A)(2) or any of the certifications specified in Subsection (A)(1), the department shall, within thirty days after discovering the falsification, suspend, revoke, or cancel the person's driver's license or his pending application. The provisions of this Subsection shall be in addition to any other penalties imposed by this Chapter.

(Chgd. by Acts 1992 No. 1009, §2; Acts 1993 No. 382, §1; Acts 1995 No. 801, §1; Acts 1997 No. 111, §1, No. 274, §1, No. 864, §§1, 2; Acts 1998 First Ex. Sess. No. 8, §2, eff. 4/24/98.)

§410. Form of license; photograph, signature of licensee, anatomical gift statement, declaration of life-sustaining procedures, and additional information on license.

A. (1) Every application for a driver's license and the license issued as a result of such application shall contain the photograph of the applicant or licensee, as the case may be. At the time of renewal of a license, the expired or expiring license shall be surrendered to the office of motor vehicles of the Department of Public Safety and Corrections.

(2) The Department of Public Safety and Corrections shall use such process or processes in the issuance of licenses that prohibit as nearly as possible the ability to alter or reproduce a license or to superimpose a photograph on such license without ready detection. All licenses and photo attachments shall be processed in color.

(3) (a) Every license issued shall bear thereon:

(i) The distinguishing number assigned to the applicant and shall contain the name of the state.

(ii) The applicant's full legal name.

(iii) The applicant's mailing address and residential address, if different from the mailing address.

(iv) The dates of issuance and expiration.

(v) The group or groups of motor vehicles the applicant is authorized to operate.

(vi) The endorsements for which the driver has qualified.

(vii) Any applicable restrictions to which the applicant is subject.

(viii) Other information to identify the applicant including date of birth (month, day, and year), sex, height, weight, and eye and hair color. An applicant's license may bear his social security number at his option.

(ix) Parish of residence code number. The parish code shall be consistent with the numerical code as designated by the secretary of state.

(b) Every applicant for a license shall write his usual signature with pen and ink in the space provided for that purpose on the license issued to him immediately upon receipt of such license, and such license shall not be valid until so signed, except in the case of a person who cannot write his or her name, and in such case he may make his mark in the presence of one attesting witness and any other information requested by the department.

(c) Every license issued shall bear thereon the words "DON'T DRINK AND DRIVE; DON'T LITTER LOUISIANA".

(4) Every commercial driver's license must contain a prominent statement that the license is a "Commercial Driver's License" or "CDL". The word "nonresident" shall be added to the face of a nonresident commercial driver's license. The word "nonresident" shall be conspicuously and unmistakenly displayed but may be noncontiguous with the words "Commercial Driver's License" or "CDL". Additionally, every commercial driver's license must state: "Holder of this license must be twenty-one years of age or older to utilize the privileges of this license in interstate commerce pursuant to 49 Code of Federal Regulations 391.11."

B. (1)(a) The Department of Public Safety and Corrections shall give the widest possible dissemination to the anatomical donation program relating to eyes, kidneys, entire bodies, etc., and shall make whatever provisions are feasible and desirable, through its drivers licensing examining offices, to enable persons desiring to make such anatomical donations to confirm their desires and intentions through the use of suitable documents to be maintained and issued in all driver's license examining offices. Additionally the license issued by the department shall contain an indication thereon whether or not the named applicant has elected to make an anatomical gift pursuant to the provisions of this Chapter or R.S. 17:2351 et seq., said indication to be by placing an "X" in the appropriate box marked "Yes" or "No" under or adjacent to the term "anatomical gift".

(b) The following information shall be made available free of charge to applicants for a driver's license on a form to be promulgated by the department and maintained on file with the department:

(i) An anatomical gift statement indicating the organs donated for the purpose of transplantation or transplantation research;

(ii) A space for indicating any limitation or special wish of the donor; and

(iii) The signature of the donor and the witnesses to the signature of the donor.

(c) If the applicant elects not to execute an anatomical gift statement at the time of application, the statement shall remain blank when presented to the licensee so it can be executed by the licensee at any time after the license is issued. No other form or statement shall be required for the purpose of providing for the donation of organs.

(2) The applicant shall be asked at the time of application if he would like to be an organ donor and informed that the gift may be made either to a named donee or without the naming of a donee and the effect thereof as provided in R.S. 17:2354(D).

(3) An anatomical gift made pursuant to this Subsection may be revoked as provided in R.S. 17:2351 et seq.

(4) The state or any of its agencies, departments, or political subdivisions shall not be liable in damages or otherwise for any removal or use of any anatomical gift made pursuant to this Subsection.

(5) The attending physician, and the hospital where an anatomical gift is made or was to be made, shall not be liable for the removal, use, or the failure to remove or use any anatomical gift made pursuant to this Subsection.

(6) Except as otherwise provided in this Subsection, the document of donation and the donation shall be made pursuant to R.S. 17:2351 et seq.

(7) The department shall furnish upon request, written information to each applicant for a driver's license or renewal thereof at the time of the application, stating that if such applicant has executed a document of gift pursuant to the Anatomical Gift Act, and if the document has been deposited in any hospital, registry office, or depository that accepts such documents for safekeeping or for facilitation of procedures after death, he may authorize the department to include on an organ donor card a notification disclosing that a document has been executed including the file number for the document. When so authorized by the applicant, the department shall in such manner and form as it determines include on the donor card a notification disclosing that a document has been executed, and disclosing the place where the document is deposited including the file number for the document, in order to provide the widest possible dissemination of the information.

C. (1)(a) The Department of Public Safety and Corrections shall give the widest possible dissemination to the declarations concerning life-sustaining procedures under the provisions of R.S. 40:1299.58.1 et seq., and shall make whatever provisions are feasible and desirable, through its driver's licensing examining offices, to enable persons desiring to make such declarations to confirm their desires and intentions through the use of suitable documents to be maintained and issued in all driver's license examining offices. Additionally, the license issued by the department shall contain an indication thereon whether or not the named applicant has elected to make such a declaration, said indication to be by placing an "X" in the appropriate box marked "Yes" or "No" under or adjacent to the term "living will".

(b) If the applicant elects not to execute a declaration concerning life-sustaining procedures at the time of application, the statement shall remain blank when presented to the licensee so it can be executed by the licensee at any time after the license is issued.

(2) The applicant shall be asked at the time of application if he would like to make a declaration concerning life-sustaining procedures or a living will.

(3) The state or any of its agencies, departments, or political subdivisions shall not be liable in damages or otherwise for any declaration made pursuant to this Subsection.

(Chgd. by Acts 1990 No. 866, §1, No. 934, §1; Acts 1995 No. 554, §1; Acts 1997 No. 864, §1, No. 934, §1; Acts 1998 First Ex. Sess. No. 8, §2, eff. 4/24/98.)

§411. Deposit of license in lieu of security upon arrest; receipt; licensee to have license or receipt in immediate possession; notification to vehicle owner; surrender of license; issuance of temporary permits.

A. Except as is otherwise specifically provided in this Section, the deposit of a driver's license in connection with the issuance of a citation alleging the commission of a traffic offense is prohibited.

B. (1) An arresting officer may retain the driver's license of an operator of a motor vehicle when that operator has been issued a citation alleging that the operator was:

(a) Operating the motor vehicle under the influence of alcohol or controlled substances.

(b) Exceeding the speed limit by twenty-five miles per hour or more.

(c) Exceeding the speed limit in a school zone.

(d) Driving with a suspended license.

(e) Drag racing.

(f) Cited for failure to maintain compulsory security.

(2) An arresting officer may retain the driver's license of an operator when the operator was involved in an accident in which a person was injured, or when an operator:

(a) Is alleged to have committed the same offense twice within a period of one hour.

(b) Is alleged by the investigating law enforcement officer to have a medical condition which could result in suspension or revocation of his driver's license under the provisions of R.S. 32:414(E), provided that the arresting officer first consult with his superior officer as to his specific observations and such superior officer concurs with the issuing officer's belief.

(3) In each instance listed in this Subsection, the provisions of Subsections C through H of this Section shall apply.

C. Whenever any person lawfully possessed of a driver's license issued to him by either:

(1) The Department of Public Safety and Corrections; or

(2) The appropriate agency of another state if such person resides in this state and either:

(a) Is on active duty with the armed forces of the United States or is a dependent of any person described in this Subparagraph; or

(b) Is enrolled in a Louisiana college or university

is arrested and charged with a violation of the Louisiana Highway Regulatory Act* or any municipal or parish ordinance regulating traffic in any municipality or in any parish he shall have the option of depositing his driver's license with the arresting officer in lieu of bail.

**R.S. 32:1 et seq.*

(3) The arresting officer shall immediately forward any license so deposited to the sheriff, district attorney, or the city court clerk of the parish in which the charge is filed, except the parish of Orleans, where the license shall be forwarded to the clerk of the traffic court. Additionally, any person described in Paragraph (2) of this Subsection must also furnish satisfactory proof of his residence in this state by either providing the arresting officer with a copy of orders assigning him, or the person whose dependent he is, to an area inside Louisiana or with a valid student identification card issued by a Louisiana college or university.

(4) This Subsection does not apply when the arresting officer has probable cause to believe that the person charged has committed an offense as defined in Title 14 of the Louisiana Revised Statutes of 1950. The arresting officer shall take these persons forthwith before the nearest or most accessible magistrate having jurisdiction.

D. Whenever any person as described in Subsection C of this Section deposits his driver's license as provided in said Subsection, the arresting officer shall issue said person a receipt for said license upon a form approved or provided by the Department of Public Safety and Corrections, and thereafter said person shall be permitted to operate a motor vehicle upon the public highways of this state during the pendency of the case in which the license was deposited.

E. The district attorney, sheriff, or clerk of a court accepting the license as provided in Subsection C of this section, shall forward as soon as practicable to the Department of Public Safety and Corrections, the license of a driver deposited in lieu of bail if the driver fails to appear in answer to the charge filed against him. The department shall not return, reissue, or renew the license until authorized to do so by the forwarding court.

F. (1) The licensee shall have his license in his immediate possession at all times when driving a motor vehicle and shall display it upon demand of any officer or agent of the department or any police officer of the state, parish, or municipality, except that where the licensee has previously deposited his license as provided in Subsection C of this Section, and has received a receipt, as provided in Subsection D of this Section, the licensee shall display the receipt upon demand of any officer or agent of the department or any police officer of the state, parish, or municipality, the same to serve as a substitute for the license until the license is returned to the licensee. However, when an officer or agent of the department or any police officer of the state, or any parish or municipality has reasonable grounds to believe a person has committed an offense of driving without a valid driver's license in his possession, the police officer shall make every practical attempt based on identifying information provided by the person to confirm that the person has been issued a valid driver's license. If the police officer determines that the person has been issued a valid driver's license which is neither under revocation, suspension, or cancellation, but that the license is not in his possession, the peace officer shall issue a written summons to the offender in accordance with law, commanding him to appear and answer the charge.

(2) The provisions of this Subsection shall in no way limit the peace officer from issuing a citation for operating a motor vehicle without physical possession of a valid driver's license.

G. When a person is arrested or issued a summons for a violation of R.S. 14:98 or 98.1, the arresting officer shall determine whether the person is the owner of the vehicle used. If the person is not the owner, the arresting officer, his agency of employment, or the Department of Public Safety and Corrections shall take all reasonable measures to identify and locate the registered owner and notify him of the arrest or summons. Such notification may be oral or written. A record shall be kept of whether or not such notification was given.

H. (1) When a fine is levied against a person convicted of any offense as described in Subsection C and the defendant is granted an extension of time to pay the fine, the judge of the court having jurisdiction may order the driver's license to be surrendered to the sheriff or official of the court collecting fines for a period of time not to exceed one hundred eighty days. If, after expiration of one hundred eighty days, the defendant has not paid the fine, the sheriff or official of the court designated to collect fines shall forward the license to the Department of Public Safety and Corrections.

(2) Upon receipt of a surrendered driver's license, the sheriff or court official responsible for collection of such fines shall issue a temporary permit for a period not to exceed one hundred eighty days or for a period of time set forth by the judge having jurisdiction. The Department of Public Safety and Corrections shall devise such temporary permits and provide for a procedure for distributing such permits, all by the promulgation of rules and regulations according to the Administrative Procedure Act*. After final promulgation of such rules and regulations, or after six months from August 15, 1995, whichever occurs first, the temporary permits shall be distributed to the courts or other agencies responsible for the collection of the fines and court costs for such violations.

**R.S. 49:950 et seq.*

(3) The department shall not return, reissue, or renew a driver's license in its possession pursuant to this Section until payment of the fine and any additional administrative cost, fee, or penalty required by the judge having the jurisdiction and any other cost, fee, or penalty required by the department.

(Chgd. by Acts 1993 No. 600, §1; Acts 1995 No. 1036, §1; Acts 1997 No. 807, §1, No. 1288, §1, eff. 8/15/97, No. 1296, §3, eff. 7/15/97.)

§411.1. Licensee to have license in immediate possession; notification to vehicle owner; surrender of license; issuance of temporary permits.

A. (1) Any person lawfully possessed of a driver's license issued to him by either the Department of Public Safety and Corrections or the appropriate agency of another state if such person resides in this state shall have such license in his immediate possession at all times when driving a motor vehicle and shall display it upon demand of any officer or agent of the department or any police officer of the state, parish, or municipality.

(2) However if the person is on active duty with the armed forces of the United States or is a dependent thereof, or is enrolled in a Louisiana college or university and is charged with a violation of the Louisiana Highway Regulatory Act* or any municipal or parish ordinance regulating traffic in any municipality or in any parish the provisions of C.Cr.P. Article 211.4 shall apply.

**R.S. 32:1 et seq.*

(3) Additionally, any person described in Paragraph (2) of this Subsection shall also furnish, upon demand, satisfactory proof of his residency in this state by either providing the arresting officer with a copy of orders assigning him, or the person whose dependent he is, to an area inside Louisiana or with a valid student identification card issued by a Louisiana college or university.

(4) Whenever any person who resides in this state is arrested and charged with a violation of the Louisiana Highway Regulatory Act or any municipal or parish ordinance regulating traffic in any parish or municipality such person shall be released on his own recognizance upon signing the promise to appear section of the traffic citation. This shall only apply to such persons who are not wanted for failure to appear in connection with other traffic citations or for whom a warrant has been issued for any other reason. If the offender fails to pay the fine by mail in advance of adjudication and fails to appear at the time and date indicated on the citation, the court may impose an additional penalty in an amount not to exceed the amount of the fine for the original violation.

B. When the arresting officer has probable cause to believe that the person charged has committed an offense as defined in Title 14 of the Louisiana Revised Statutes of 1950 he shall take such person forthwith before the nearest or most accessible magistrate having jurisdiction.

C. (1) When an officer or agent of the department or any police officer of the state, or any parish or municipality has reasonable grounds to believe a person has committed an offense of driving without a valid driver's license in his possession, the police officer shall make every practical attempt based on identifying information provided by the person to confirm that the person has been issued a valid driver's license. If the police officer determines that the person has been issued a valid driver's license which is neither under revocation, suspension, or cancellation, but that the license is not in his possession, the peace officer shall issue a written summons to the offender in accordance with law, commanding him to appear and answer the charge.

(2) The provisions of this Subsection shall in no way limit the peace officer from issuing a citation for operating a motor vehicle without physical possession of a valid driver's license.

D. When a person is arrested or issued a summons for a violation of R.S. 14:98 or 98.1, the arresting officer shall determine whether the person is the owner of the vehicle used. If the person is not the owner, the arresting officer, his agency of employment, or the Department of Public Safety and Corrections shall take all reasonable measures to identify and locate the registered owner and notify him of the arrest or summons. Such notification may be oral or written. A record shall be kept of whether or not such notification was given.

E. (1) When a fine is levied against a person convicted of any violation of the Louisiana Highway Regulatory Act or any municipal or parish ordinance regulating traffic in any municipality or in any parish and the defendant is granted an extension of time to pay the fine, the judge of the court having jurisdiction may order the driver's license to be surrendered to the sheriff or official of the court collecting fines for a period of time not to exceed one hundred eighty days. If, after expiration of one hundred eighty days, the defendant has not paid the fine, the sheriff or official of the court designated to collect fines shall forward the license to the Department of Public Safety and Corrections.

(2) Upon receipt of a surrendered driver's license, the sheriff or court official responsible for collection of such fines shall issue a temporary permit for a period not to exceed one hundred eighty days or for a period of time set forth by the judge having jurisdiction. The Department of Public Safety and Corrections shall devise such temporary permits and provide for a procedure for distributing such permits, all by the promulgation of rules and regulations according to the Administrative Procedure Act*. After final promulgation of such rules and regulations the temporary permits shall be distributed to the courts or other agencies responsible for the collection of the fines and court costs for such violations.

**R.S. 49:950 et seq.*

(3) The department shall not return, reissue, or renew a driver's license in its possession pursuant to this Subsection until payment of the fine and any additional administrative cost, fee, or penalty required by the judge having the jurisdiction and any other cost, fee, or penalty required by the department.

(Added by Acts 1995 No. 995, §1; chgd. by Acts 1997 No. 1296, §3, eff. 7/15/97.)

§412. Amount of fees; credit or refund; duration of license; disbursement of funds; renewal by mail of Class "D" or "E" drivers' licenses.

A. (1) Every applicant for a Class "D" driver's license, or for a renewal of a Class "D" driver's license, except those bona fide residents of cities having a population in excess of four hundred and fifty thousand, shall pay for such basic license a fee of twenty-seven dollars and fifty cents, twenty-seven percent of which fee shall be paid to the State Police Pension and Retirement Fund.

(2) The fee for Class "D" driver's licenses, or renewal of a Class "D" driver's license, issued to bona fide residents of municipalities having a population in excess of four hundred and fifty thousand shall be thirty-five dollars, ten dollars of which fee shall be payable by the department to the board of trustees of the police pension fund of such municipalities and three and one-half percent of which fee shall be paid to the State Police Pension and Retirement Fund.

(3) There shall be a fee of five dollars for an emergency vehicle endorsement for any vehicle group.

(4) A Class "D" driver's license shall expire on the anniversary of the birthday of the applicant which is nearest to a period of four years subsequent to the issuing of the license, unless suspended, revoked or cancelled prior to that time.

(5) Every applicant for a Class "E" driver's license, or for a renewal of a Class "E" driver's license, except those bona fide residents of cities having a population in excess of four hundred and fifty thousand, shall pay for such basic license a fee of twelve dollars and fifty cents, which shall be the cost of such basic license, thirty percent of which fee shall be paid to the State Police Pension and Retirement Fund.

(6) The fee for a Class "E" driver's license, or renewal of a Class "E" driver's license, issued to bona fide residents of municipalities having a population in excess of four hundred and fifty thousand shall be twelve dollars and fifty cents, two dollars and fifty cents of which fee shall be paid by the department to the board of trustees of the police pension funds of such municipalities and twenty percent of which fee shall be paid to the State Police Pension and Retirement Fund.

(7) A Class "E" driver's license shall expire on the anniversary of the birthday of the applicant which is nearest to a period of four years subsequent to the issuing of the license, unless suspended, revoked or cancelled.

B. (1) Every applicant for a Class "A", "B", or "C" commercial driver's license, or for a renewal of a basic Class "A", "B", or "C" commercial driver's license, except for those bona fide residents of cities having a population in excess of four hundred and fifty thousand, shall pay for such basic license a fee of forty dollars, twenty-seven percent of which fee shall be paid to the State Police Pension and Retirement Fund.

(2) The fee for a basic Class "A", "B", or "C" commercial driver's license, or for the renewal of a basic Class "A", "B", or "C" commercial driver's license, issued to bona fide residents of municipalities having a population in excess of four hundred and fifty thousand shall be fifty dollars, ten dollars of which fee shall be paid by the department to the board of trustees of the police pension fund of such municipalities and twenty percent of which fee shall be paid to the State Police Pension and Retirement Fund.

(3) In addition to the basic fee, there shall be a skills test fee of not more than sixty dollars for commercial drivers' licenses in Classes "A", "B", or "C". This fee shall be charged by the department or by a third party tester, whichever administers the test. The department may increase the maximum amount of this fee to reflect increased costs. The increased maximum fee shall be established by rule adopted in accordance with the Administrative Procedure Act*, subject to oversight by the House of Representatives and Senate Committees on Transportation, Highways and Public Works. If the department elects to administer skills tests for commercial drivers' licenses in Class "A", "B", or "C", the department may charge fees for those tests. The amount of those fees shall be established in accordance with the provisions of this Paragraph. If an applicant for a commercial driver's license in Class "A", "B", or "C" has successfully completed a skills test administered by a third party, the department shall not charge a skills test fee.

**R.S. 49:950 et seq.*

(4) The application fee shall be fifteen dollars which is nonrefundable.

(5) There shall be a fee of five dollars for each endorsement to the basic licenses listed in R.S. 32:408(B).

(6) *(Repealed.)*

(7) (a) A Class "C" commercial driver's license not carrying an endorsement permitting the transportation of material found to be hazardous for purposes of the Federal Hazardous Material Act, 49 United States Code 1801 et seq. or under state law or regulation shall expire on the anniversary of the birthday of the applicant which is nearest to a date of four years subsequent to the issuing of the license, unless revoked, cancelled, or suspended prior to that time.

(b) A Class "C" commercial driver's license carrying an endorsement permitting the transportation of materials found to be hazardous for purposes of the Federal Hazardous

Material Act, 49 United States Code 1801 et seq. or under state law or regulation shall expire on the anniversary of the birthday of the applicant which is nearest to a date of four years subsequent to the issuing of the license, unless revoked, cancelled, or suspended prior to that time.

(c) A Class "B" commercial driver's license shall expire on the anniversary of the birthday of the applicant which is nearest to a date of four years subsequent to the issuing of the license, unless revoked, cancelled, or suspended prior to that time.

(d) A Class "A" commercial driver's license shall expire on the anniversary of the birthday of the applicant which is nearest to a date of four years subsequent to the issuing of the license, unless revoked, cancelled or suspended prior to that time.

(e) (i) Every applicant seventy years of age or older for a Class "E" driver's license, or for the renewal of a Class "E" driver's license, except those bona fide residents of cities having a population in excess of four hundred and fifty thousand, shall pay for such basic license a fee of three dollars and fifty cents, which shall be the cost of the license. The license shall expire on the anniversary of the birthday of the applicant which is nearest to a date of four years subsequent to the issuing of the license, unless revoked, cancelled or suspended. Fifty cents of the fee shall be paid to the office of state police and one dollar and fifty cents of the fee shall be paid to the State Police Pension and Retirement Fund. Every applicant seventy years of age or older for a Class "D" driver's license or for the renewal of a Class "D" driver's license, except those bona fide residents of cities having a population in excess of four hundred and fifty thousand, shall pay for such basic license a fee of thirteen dollars and seventy-five cents, which shall be the cost of the license. The license shall expire on the anniversary of the birthday of the applicant which is nearest to the date of four years subsequent to the issuing of the license, unless revoked, cancelled, or suspended. Twenty-seven percent of the fee shall be paid to the State Police Pension and Retirement Fund.

(ii) Every applicant seventy years of age or older for a Class "E" driver's license, or for the renewal of a Class "E" driver's license, issued to bona fide residents of cities having a population in excess of four hundred fifty thousand, shall pay for such basic license a fee of three dollars and fifty cents, which shall be the cost of the license. This license shall expire on the anniversary of the birthday of the applicant which is nearest to a date of four years subsequent to the issuing of the license, unless revoked, cancelled, or suspended. One dollar of the fee shall be paid to the Board of Trustees of the Police Pension Fund of said municipalities and one dollar of the fee shall be paid to the State Police Pension and Retirement Fund. Every applicant seventy years of age and older for a Class "D" driver's license, or for the renewal of a Class "D" driver's license, issued to bona fide residents of cities having a population in excess of four hundred fifty thousand, shall pay for such basic license a fee of seventeen dollars and fifty cents, which shall be the cost of the license. This license shall expire on the anniversary of the birthday of the applicant which is nearest to a date to four years subsequent to the issuing of the license, unless revoked, cancelled, or suspended. Five dollars of the fee shall be payable by the department to the board of trustees of the police pension fund of such municipalities and three and one-half percent of which fee shall be paid to the State Police Pension and Retirement Fund.

(8) Persons who hold certain specified licenses issued by the office of motor vehicles and who apply for other specified licenses issued by the office of motor vehicles shall receive credit for the unexpired portion of the first license. The credit shall be computed in accordance with the provisions of Paragraph (9) of this Subsection. As used in this Paragraph, the phrase "prior provisions of law" means provisions of law in effect prior to the effectiveness of Act No. 293 of the 1989 Regular Session of the Legislature (the "Commercial Drivers License Law"). The three circumstances in which credit shall be given are as follows:

(a) When a person who holds a Class "B", "C", or "D" license issued under prior provisions of law applies for a Class "A", "B", or "C," commercial driver's license issued under current provisions of law.

(b) When a person who holds a Class "B", "C", or "D", license issued under current provisions of law applies for a commercial driver's license of a higher class.

(c) When a person who holds a Class A driver's license issued under prior provisions of law or a Class E personal vehicle driver's license issued under current provisions of law applies for any commercial driver's license or chauffeur's license.

(9) The credit shall be computed on a basis under which each month from the date of issuance of the existing license to the date of the expiration of the license shall be given an equal monetary value. The applicant shall be given credit toward the fee for the license for

which the applicant has applied based on the monetary value of the remaining months of validity of the existing license. In computing the credit, only whole months shall be used.

C. (1) The addition of a motorcycle or motor scooter endorsement to a basic license will require, besides the specific examination for such vehicles, the payment of an additional fee of eight dollars. If the motorcycle endorsement is to any license which is valid for less than four years, the fee for the endorsement will be four dollars.

(2) Notwithstanding any provisions of law to the contrary and subject to the exceptions contained in Article VII, Section 9(A) of the Constitution of Louisiana, the amount of five dollars from the fee for a motorcycle or motor scooter endorsement to a basic license, or the amount of two dollars from the fee if the motorcycle endorsement for any person is to a license that is valid for only less than four years shall be credited to the Bond Security and Redemption Fund. After a sufficient amount is allocated from that fund to pay all obligations secured by the full faith and credit of the state which become due and payable within any fiscal years, the treasurer shall pay an amount equal to the fees paid into the Bond Security and Redemption Fund pursuant to this Paragraph into a special fund which is hereby created in the state treasury and designated as the "Motorcycle Safety, Awareness, and Operator Training Program Fund," hereinafter referred to as the "fund". The monies credited to the fund shall be used solely for operator training, instructor training, and motorcycle safety and awareness programs. Any unexpended and unencumbered monies remaining to the credit of the fund on June thirtieth of each year, after all appropriations of the preceding fiscal year have been made, shall revert to the state general fund. The monies in the fund shall be expended solely from year to year as appropriated by the legislature for the purposes of motorcycle safety and awareness and operator training. Any amounts earned through investment of the monies in the fund shall revert to the state general fund.

D. (1) Upon application and payment of the fee imposed by this Chapter and subject to the requirements of R.S. 32:408, a license shall be renewable on or before its expiration. An application for renewal may be made at any time within ninety days prior to expiration.

(2) Each person who is less than seventy years of age and who applies for the renewal of a license which expired more than ten days prior to the date of the application shall pay a late fee of fifteen dollars. The late fee shall not affect the criminal penalties imposed by R.S. 32:402 and 427.

(3) A Class "E" or "D" operator's license may be renewed by mail, except as follows:

(a) No renewal by mail shall be granted if the applicant's individual driving record indicates that within two years preceding the date of the application the individual has been convicted of a moving violation, as the department defines by rule, committed in this state or of an offense described in R.S. 32:414.

(b) No renewal by mail shall be granted to any person who is seventy years of age or older.

(c) No renewal by mail shall be granted if the license was renewed by mail at the last occurrence of its expiration.

(d) No renewal by mail shall be granted if the previously issue license is expired, or has been suspended, revoked, canceled, or lost, or if it is in the possession of a law enforcement agency as a result of an accusation that the driver has violated a traffic law.

(e) The department may establish rules and regulations to grant or deny renewal by mail in cases where a Louisiana resident is temporarily domiciled out of state or out of country, or temporarily residing, employed, or attending school in another state or foreign country, even if the resident does not meet the qualification criteria under this Section.

(4) The renewal by mail shall include the following:

(a) A statement from the applicant that he has not experienced any loss of consciousness other than normal sleep and has no current physical or mental condition which would impair his ability to operate a motor vehicle safely.

(b) *(Repealed.)*

(c) A statement from the applicant indicating that all motor vehicles owned by the applicant are covered by liability insurance or security and said coverage will be maintained until such time as a vehicle is no longer utilized on the highways of this state, or until a vehicle is transferred to another.

(5) Upon receipt of the required statements by the department and upon renewal of the license, the state shall not be liable for any property damages, injuries, or deaths that may arise from an applicant's involvement in an accident where said accident can be attributed to the applicant's medical condition that may have existed which rendered him incapable of operating a motor vehicle safely.

(6) When a license is renewed by mail, the secretary shall issue evidence of renewal which shall be affixed to the previously issued license to indicate the date the license expires in the future.

(7) The secretary of the department, in accordance with the Administrative Procedure Act, shall promulgate rules and regulations to implement the provisions of Paragraphs (3), (4), (5), and (6) of this Subsection.

E. If the failure to make timely application is attributable to the fact that the applicant has had no occasion to operate a motor vehicle since the expiration date, then the additional fee shall be waived upon the filing of an affidavit by the applicant to evidence this fact.

F. (1) The Louisiana driver's license, regardless of its class, issued to any person who serves in the Peace Corps or the armed forces of the United States stationed outside the state of Louisiana, and his dependents who are residing with him, if such license has not been revoked or suspended, shall be considered valid during the period of service in the armed forces or Peace Corps and for a period of sixty days after discharge from such service. Any person to whom this Subsection applies shall be exempt from any late fees provided the person makes an application for renewal within sixty days of the date in which the applicant, or the person upon whom the applicant is dependent, is discharged from the armed forces or terminates his service with the Peace Corps.

(2) Any person to whom this Subsection applies, while operating a motor vehicle, shall carry upon his person the last license issued to him and conclusive evidence that he is a member of the United States armed forces or the Peace Corps, and if discharged from the armed forces, a copy of such discharge or proof of his last date of service with the Peace Corps. The dependent of a person in such service shall carry upon his person the last license issued to him and copies of conclusive evidence that the person upon whom they are dependent is a member of the armed forces or the Peace Corps, and if such person has been discharged or has terminated his position with the Peace Corps, a copy of such discharge or proof of his last date of service with the Peace Corps, respectively.

(3) As used in this Subsection, the term "dependent" means a spouse or minor child.

G. It shall be unlawful for any person to drive a motor vehicle on any public street, road, or highway of this state with an expired driver's license.

H. Each person who takes a test a second or subsequent time, whether written or driving, which is administered by the office of motor vehicles in connection with an application for the issuance or renewal of a driver's license shall pay a testing fee. The fee shall not be refundable. The office of motor vehicles shall establish the fee by rule adopted in accordance with the Administrative Procedure Act. The amount of the fee shall not exceed ten dollars. The fees collected under the provisions of this Subsection shall be subject to the following provisions:

(1) The fee shall be deposited immediately upon receipt into the state treasury.

(2) After compliance with the provisions of Article VII, Section 9(B) of the Constitution of Louisiana relative to the Bond Security and Redemption Fund, and prior to monies being placed in the state general fund, an amount equal to the fees collected under this subsection shall be credited to a special fund which is hereby created in the state treasury to be known as the Office of Motor Vehicles Testing Fund. The monies in this fund shall be used solely as provided in Paragraph (3) of this Subsection, and only in the amounts appropriated by the legislature. The monies in this fund shall be invested by the state treasurer in the same manner as monies in the state general fund and interest earned on those investments shall be credited to this fund, after compliance with the requirements of Article VII, Subsection 9(B) of the Constitution of Louisiana.

(3) The monies in the Office of Motor Vehicles Testing Fund shall be used solely for the purpose of funding the operation of the office of motor vehicles.

(Chgd. by Acts 1990 No. 40, §1; Acts 1991 No. 351, §1, No. 389, §1, No. 936, §1; Acts 1993 No. 227, §1, No. 348, §1, No. 382, §1, No. 578, §1, No. 1027, §1; Acts 1995 No. 151, §§1, 2, No. 1015, §§1, 2; Acts 1997 No. 786, §1, eff. 8/15/97.)

§412.1. Handling charges.

A. The office of motor vehicles shall collect, in addition to any fee authorized by law, a handling charge of five dollars and fifty cents for each of the following transactions:

(1) Class D and Class E drivers' licenses:

(a) New applications.

(b) Renewals.

(c) Duplicates.

(d) Valid without photo.
(2) Identification cards:
(a) New applications.
(b) Renewals.
(c) Duplicates.
(3) Vehicle titling and registration:
(a) New vehicle or out of state title.
(b) Transfer of ownership.
(c) Record and cancel mortgage.
(d) Lost plate and stickers.
(e) Conversion of license plate.
(f) Duplicate title.
(g) Letter of authorization to operate an unregistered vehicle.
(h) Motor vehicle inspection sticker and rejection stickers.
(i) Motor vehicle inspection station permits.
(j) Duplicate motor vehicle inspection station permits.
(k) Motor vehicle inspection station signs.
(*l*) Motor vehicle inspection mechanic inspection license.
(m) Duplicate motor vehicle inspection mechanic inspection license.
(n) Sheriff's certificate of chattel mortgages.
(*o*) Recordation of floor plans.
(p) Dealer temporary marker.
(q) Agriculture permits.
(r) Refunds—driver's license and vehicle registration.
(s) Certified copies.
(t) Claims against dealer bonds.
(u) Titles, certificates, or similar documents for salvaged vehicles.
(v) Department of Transportation and Development ticket assessment.
(w) Nonresident cab cards.
(x) Reciprocity cab cards.

B. Additional handling charges of five dollars and fifty cents may be established by the office of motor vehicles upon transactions not specifically named in Subsection A of this Section in accordance with procedures in the Administrative Procedure Act*.
(Added by Acts 1990 No. 291, §1, eff. 9/7/90.)
**R.S. 49:950 et seq.*

§413. Loss or destruction of licenses.

A. If any license shall be lost or destroyed, the person to whom it was issued shall submit satisfactory proof to the office of motor vehicles of such loss or destruction and shall apply for, within ten days after such loss or destruction, a duplicate license.

B. For each duplicate license so issued there shall be collected the sum of five dollars.

C. If any license which was issued to a Louisiana domiciliary or resident who is temporarily out of state, or who is a domiciliary or resident who is an active member of the Armed Forces, or who is a domiciliary resident dependent of a member of the active Armed Forces, in lieu thereof has been lost or destroyed, the person to whom the license was issued, or a person who has power of attorney for the person to whom the license was issued, may submit satisfactory proof to the office of motor vehicles of such loss or destruction and may apply for a duplicate license.
(Chgd. by Acts 1993 No. 464, §1, eff. 8/15/93.)

§414. Suspension, revocation, and cancellation of licenses; judicial review.

A. (1)(a) The department shall suspend the license of any person for a period of ninety days upon receiving, from any district, city, or municipal court, of this state or of any other state, having traffic jurisdiction, or from any federal court or magistrate having traffic jurisdiction, satisfactory evidence of the conviction or of the entry of a plea of guilty or nolo contendere and sentence thereupon or of the forfeiture of bail of any such person charged with the first offense for vehicular negligent injuring, R.S. 14:39.1, or for operating a motor vehicle while under the influence of beverages of high alcoholic content, of low alcoholic content, of narcotic drugs, or of central nervous system stimulants. However, if the offender was under the age of twenty-one years at the time of the offense, the suspension provided for in this Subsection shall be in effect for one hundred eighty days from the date of suspension.

The department shall promptly investigate an allegation made by such licensee that the suspension of his driving privileges will deprive him or his family of the necessities of life, or will prevent him from earning a livelihood. If the department so finds, it may reinstate the license of such licensee; however, such suspension and reinstatement shall be considered as a first suspension and grant of restricted driving privileges for the purposes of R.S. 32:415.1, and the driving privileges of the licensee shall be restricted as provided in R.S. 32:415.1 for a period of ninety days from the date of conviction or the entry of a plea of guilty or nolo contendere and sentence thereupon or of the forfeiture of bail. Notice of the restriction shall be attached to the license.

(b) Any licensee who has had his driver's license suspended for operating a motor vehicle while under the influence of alcoholic beverages under the provisions of this Section shall, upon proof to the Department of Public Safety and Corrections that his motor vehicle has been equipped with a functioning ignition interlock device, be issued a restricted driver's license. In the event that the department fails or refuses to issue the restricted driver's license, the district court for the parish in which the licensee resides may issue an order directing the department to issue the restricted license either by ex parte order or after contradictory hearing.

(2) The department shall suspend the license of any person for a period of thirty days upon a first conviction; sixty days upon a second conviction; and, one year upon a third conviction for violation of R.S. 32:80(A)(1) relative to a failure to stop or passing a school bus which is stopped for loading or unloading children.

(3) (a) The department shall forthwith suspend the license of any person thirty days upon third violation, and sixty days upon fourth and any subsequent violation of R.S. 30:2531 or 2531.1 relative to litter violations.

(b) When a person in violation of the provisions of R.S. 30:2531 or 2531.1 has failed to pay any penalty assessed in any previous violation of such Sections, his driver's license shall be suspended sixty days upon third violation and one hundred and twenty days upon fourth and subsequent violation.

(c) The department shall promptly investigate an allegation made by such licensee that the suspension of his driving privileges will deprive him or his family of the necessities of life or will prevent him from earning a livelihood. If the department so finds, it may reinstate the license of such licensee; however, such suspension and reinstatement shall be considered as a first suspension and grant of restricted driving privileges for the purposes of R.S. 32:415.1. However, nothing contained in this Paragraph (3) shall be construed as limiting or prohibiting a district court from granting a hardship or restricted driver's license for the full period of the suspension.

B. The department shall forthwith suspend the license of any person, for a period of twelve months, upon receiving satisfactory evidence of the conviction or of the entry of a plea of guilty and sentence thereupon or of the forfeiture of bail of any such person charged with any of the following crimes:

(1) Manslaughter or negligent homicide resulting from the operation of a motor vehicle.

(2) (a) Conviction or the entry of a plea of guilty and sentence thereupon, or of the forfeiture of bail of any such person on the second offense for vehicular negligent injuring or for operating or being in actual physical control of a motor vehicle while under the influence of intoxicating beverages, of central nervous system stimulants or depressants, or of narcotic drugs or any other drug or substance to a degree which renders him incapable of safely operating a motor vehicle, when any or all of the offenses were the result of violations of a state law, a municipal ordinance, a federal law, or any combination of them; however, any offense for vehicular negligent injuring or for operating or being in actual physical control of a motor vehicle while under the influence of alcoholic beverages which was committed more than five years prior to the commission of a subsequent such offense of operating or being in actual physical control of a motor vehicle while under the influence of alcoholic beverages shall not be considered in determining the number of such offenses of operating or controlling a motor vehicle while under the influence of alcoholic beverages which the person has committed.

(b) Any licensee who has had his license suspended for operating a motor vehicle while under the influence of alcoholic beverages under the provisions of this Section shall, upon proof that his motor vehicle has been equipped with a functioning ignition interlock device, be issued a restricted driver's license. In the event that the department fails or refuses to issue the restricted driver's license the district court for the parish in which the licensee resides may issue an order directing the department to issue the restricted license by ex parte order or after contradictory hearing.

(3) Any felony in the commission of which a motor vehicle is used.

(4) Failure to stop and render aid as required under the laws of this state in the event of a motor vehicle accident resulting in the death or personal injury of another.

(5) Conviction or forfeiture of bail upon three charges of reckless driving committed within a period of twelve months.

C. The department shall forthwith suspend the license of any person upon receipt of evidence satisfactory to the department of such person's violation of any of the provisions of R.S. 32:414.1 constituting an unlawful use of a driver's license. The suspension for a first violation shall be for a period of ninety days. The suspension for a second or subsequent violation shall be for a period of twelve months. On a first offense violation, the department is hereby authorized to issue a hardship driver's license to any person who has violated the provisions of R.S. 32:414.1.

D. (1)(a) The department shall suspend the license of any person for a period of twenty-four months upon receiving satisfactory evidence of conviction, plea of guilty, or plea of nolo contendere, and sentence thereon, or of the forfeiture of bail of any such person as determined by any court of jurisdiction as set forth in this Section, with regard to a third or subsequent offense for vehicular negligent injuring or for operating a motor vehicle while under the influence of beverages of alcoholic content, of narcotic drugs, or of central nervous system stimulants. Third or subsequent offenses for purposes for this Subsection does* not refer to the criminal charge but rather to the number of offenses resulting in conviction, guilty pleas, nolo contendere pleas, or bond forfeitures within five years from date of first offense to the date of third offense.

**So in original. Probably should be "do".*

(b) Any licensee who has had his license suspended for operating a motor vehicle while under the influence of alcoholic beverages under the provisions of this Section shall, upon proof that his motor vehicle has been equipped with a functioning ignition interlock device, be issued a restricted driver's license in accordance. In the event that the department fails or refuses to issue the restricted driver's license the district court for the parish in which the licensee resides may issue an order directing the department to issue the restricted license either by ex parte order or after contradictory hearing.

(2) Upon termination of the twenty-four month suspension set forth in this Subsection, the person whose license has been suspended shall be reinstated, provided no other suspension of license is outstanding and upon satisfaction of any financial responsibility law requirements and upon payment of a reinstatement fee as required by this Section.

E. The department may conduct an investigation to determine whether the license shall be suspended, cancelled, or revoked upon a showing by its records or other sufficient evidence that the licensee:

(1) Has committed an offense for which mandatory revocation of license is required.

(2) Has been involved as a driver in any accident resulting in the death or personal injury of another or serious property damage.

(3) Has been convicted of or has forfeited bail for traffic offenses involving movement of vehicles with such frequency as to indicate a disrespect for traffic laws and a disregard for the safety of others.

(4) Is habitually reckless or negligent driver of a motor vehicle.

(5) Is incompetent to drive a motor vehicle.

(6) Has permitted an unlawful or fraudulent use of such license.

(7) Has committed an offense in another state or federal jurisdiction which if committed in this state would be grounds for suspension or revocation.

(8) Is afflicted with such mental or physical infirmities or disabilities as would constitute grounds for refusal of a license.

F. (1) Upon the conclusion of such investigation, the person holding such investigation shall prepare findings based upon the evidence received and considered. If the findings are to the effect that the person referred to herein is incompetent or is unfit to operate a motor vehicle upon any grounds upon which license may be refused as stated in this Chapter, the department upon a review of such findings shall have authority to forthwith revoke the license of such person, or if the findings are to the effect that the person therein referred to has by reason of negligence or reckless driving endangered life, limb, or property or has thereby caused loss of life or injury to person or property, the department upon a review of such findings shall have power to suspend the license of such person for a period not to exceed six months or may revoke such license and in either event shall require that such license be surrendered to the department.

(2) For cause satisfactory to the department, it is hereby authorized to suspend, cancel, or revoke the license of any person for a period of not more than one year.

(3) Any person whose license has been suspended, cancelled, or revoked by the department shall be notified of such suspension, cancellation, or revocation in writing by the department. This notice shall be sent by certified mail to the last address furnished by such person, and the person within five days shall return his or her license to the department. The notice shall also advise such person that he or she may obtain a special identification card from the driver's license division of the Department of Public Safety and Corrections pursuant to R.S. 40:1321.

(4) The failure on the part of any person to comply with this provision shall be punishable as herein provided. Any person denied a license or whose license has been suspended, cancelled, or revoked shall have the right to file an application within thirty days thereafter for a hearing before the district court of the parish in which the applicant resides. The court is vested with jurisdiction to set the matter for hearing in open court upon ten days' written notice to the department and thereupon to determine whether the person is entitled to a license or is subject to suspension, cancellation, or revocation of license under the provisions of this Chapter. Appeal from the decision of the district court may be taken to any court of competent appellate jurisdiction.

G. Any period of suspension or revocation under this Chapter shall begin upon receipt by the department of the operator's license of the person affected, upon the expiration of the operator's license, or upon proof of its loss.

H. Except as provided in Subsections I and J of this Section, upon the expiration of the period of the suspension or revocation of any license, the department shall return the license to the licensee or in its discretion may issue him a new license but only after a reinstatement fee of sixty dollars has been paid to the department and the requirements of R.S. 32:896 relative to proof of financial responsibility have been satisfied. Ten dollars of this fee shall be appropriated annually by the legislature for emergency medical services (EMS) needs and expenses. The collecting agency shall make a monthly report of the EMS funds collected under this provision to the state treasurer. The legislature shall appropriate the total as follows: fifty percent to the Department of Health and Hospitals for the operation of emergency medical services, forty-five percent to the governing authority of the parish or municipality of origin to be used for the governing authority's emergency medical services and public safety needs, and five percent to the Department of Public Safety and Corrections for expenses incurred in the administration of these fees.

I. (1) The reinstatement fee for a license of a person who has been convicted of or forfeited bond on or entered a plea of guilty or nolo contendere to a charge of operating a motor vehicle while under the influence of beverages of high alcoholic content, of low alcoholic content, of narcotic drugs, or of central nervous system stimulants shall be one hundred dollars if one conviction appears listed on his record prior to application for reinstatement; two hundred dollars if two such convictions appear on his record prior to application for reinstatement; and three hundred dollars for each conviction on his record after the second conviction prior to application for reinstatement, and the requirements of R.S. 32:896 relative to proof of financial responsibility have been satisfied.

(2) After deposit in the Bond Security and Redemption Fund under the provisions of Article VII, Section 9 of the Constitution of Louisiana, an amount equal to forty dollars of each reinstatement fee for a single conviction and ninety dollars of each reinstatement fee for two or more convictions is hereby dedicated to the Department of Public Safety and Corrections, public safety services, for traffic control and DWI programs and shall be appropriated by the legislature each year for that purpose.

(3) Ten dollars of the fee levied under the provisions of this Subsection shall be paid into the state general fund to be appropriated annually by the legislature for emergency medical services (EMS) needs and expenses. The collecting agency shall make a monthly report of the EMS funds collected under this provision to the state treasurer. The legislature shall appropriate the total as follows: fifty percent to the Department of Health and Hospitals for the operation of emergency medical services, forty-five percent to the governing authority of the parish or municipality of origin to be used for the governing authority's emergency medical services and public safety needs, and five percent to the Department of Public Safety and Corrections for expenses incurred in the administration of these fees.

J. If the suspension or revocation was due to mental or physical infirmities or disabilities, when such physical infirmities or disabilities are not the result of alcohol or drug abuse, upon the expiration of the period of the revocation of the license, the department shall return the license to the licensee or in its discretion may issue him a new license but only after a reinstatement fee in an amount equal to the issuance fees provided in R.S. 32:412 has been paid to the department.

K. (1) When any person's driver's license has been seized, suspended, or revoked, and the seizure, suspension, or revocation is connected to a charge or charges of violation of a criminal law, and the charge or charges do not result in a conviction, plea of guilty, or bond forfeiture, the person charged shall not be required to pay any reinstatement fee if at the time for reinstatement of driver's license, it can be shown that the criminal charges have been dismissed or that there has been a permanent refusal to charge a crime by the appropriate prosecutor or there has been an acquittal. If however, at the time for reinstatement, the licensee has pending against him criminal charges arising from the arrest which led to his suspension or revocation of driver's license, the reinstatement fee shall be collected. Upon subsequent proof of final dismissal or acquittal, other than under Articles 893 or 894 of the Code of Criminal Procedure, the licensee shall be entitled to a reimbursement of the reinstatement fee previously paid. In no event shall exemption from this reinstatement fee or reimbursement of a reinstatement fee affect the validity of the underlying suspension or revocation.

(2) If a licensee qualifies for the exemption from the reinstatement fee or for a reimbursement of the reinstatement fee as provided in Paragraph (1), the licensee shall receive credit for the unexpired portion of the license which was seized, and shall be exempt from the payment of, or shall receive reimbursement for the payment of, the duplicate license fee and the handling fee with regard to the license which was seized.

L. The department shall forthwith suspend the license of any person, for a period of ninety days, upon receiving satisfactory evidence of conviction, plea of guilty, or nolo contendere of any person charged with a violation of R.S. 14:333, if the court has ordered, as part of the sentence, the suspension of such person's driving privileges.

M. (1) The department shall forthwith suspend the driving privileges of and confiscate any driver's license held by any person who is convicted of violating any law or rule while operating any commercial vehicle without holding the commercial driver's license which is required for the operation of that vehicle. The offender's driving privileges shall be suspended for sixty days on a first conviction, for one hundred eighty days on a second conviction, and for one year on a third or subsequent conviction.

(2) Any person whose license is suspended pursuant to the provisions of this Subsection shall be eligible to apply for and receive a hardship license in accordance with the provisions of R.S. 32:415.1.

N. The department may suspend the driving and motor vehicle registration privileges of any person who pays taxes or fees to the office of motor vehicles with a check which is subsequently dishonored for insufficient funds, if the person fails to redeem the check within thirty days of receipt of notice that it has been dishonored. Any license so suspended shall remain suspended until all pending assessments against the person, including a reinstatement fee provided for in Subsection H of this Section, have been paid in cash. No economic hardship license shall be issued when a person's driving and motor vehicle registration privileges have been suspended under the provisions of this Paragraph.

(Chgd. by Acts 1990 No. 933, §1; Acts 1992 No. 327, §2, No. 605, §1, No. 831, §1, No. 941, §1; No. 947, §2; Acts 1993 No. 842, §1; Acts 1994 Third Ex. Sess. No. 20, §2; Acts 1995 No. 198, §1, No. 516, §1, No. 520, §2, No. 797, §1; Acts 1997 No. 1184, §1, No. 1296, §3, No. 1455, §1; Acts 1998 First Ex. Sess. No. 148, §4, eff. 6/16/98.)

§414.1. Unlawful use of license.

It shall be unlawful for any person:

1. To display or cause or permit to be displayed or have in his possession any cancelled, revoked, suspended, or fictitious operator's or chauffeur's license, or an operator's or chauffeur's license which has been intentionally altered, or has been caused to be altered, by such person;

2. To lend his operator's or chauffeur's license to any person or knowingly permit the use thereof by another;

3. To display or represent as one's own any operator's or chauffeur's license not issued to him;

4. To fail or refuse to surrender to the department upon its lawful demand any operator's or chauffeur's license which has been suspended, revoked or cancelled;

5. To use a false or fictitious name in any application for an operator's or chauffeur's license or to knowingly make a false statement or to knowingly conceal a material fact or otherwise commit a fraud in any such application, or to commit perjury by making any false affidavit, or knowingly swearing or affirming falsely to any matter or thing required by the terms of this Chapter to be sworn to or affirmed;

6. To permit any unlawful use of an operator's or chauffeur's license issued to him; or

7. To do any act forbidden or fail to perform any act required by this Chapter.

§414.2. Commercial motor vehicle drivers; disqualification; issuance of Group "E" license; alcohol content in breath and blood; implied consent.

A. (1)(a) Notwithstanding any other law to the contrary, any person is disqualified from driving for the offenses specified in Paragraphs (A)(2) through (5) of this Subsection when committed in a commercial motor vehicle. The disqualification offenses apply to violations occurring in this or any other state or in any foreign jurisdiction meeting the requirement of 49 Code of Federal Regulations Part 383. The department shall suspend, revoke, or cancel the driver's license of a person who is disqualified to drive pursuant to this Section. If the Federal Highway Administration so provides, the department may establish procedures by which a driver with a lifetime disqualification under Paragraph (A)(2) of this Subsection may apply to have the disqualification reduced to a period of not less than ten years. If a driver is disqualified from operating a Group "D" or "E" motor vehicle, he shall also be disqualified from operating a commercial motor vehicle.

(b) (i) There shall be no economic hardship license to operate a commercial motor vehicle; however, an economic hardship license may be granted to operate a Group "D" license provided the applicant for an economic hardship license is otherwise eligible for such license. These disqualifications shall supplement and be in addition to any other sanctions that may be imposed.

(ii) Whenever a person has been disqualified from driving a commercial motor vehicle, such person shall be issued a Group "E", "Personal Use Motor Vehicle" driving license upon expiration of any Group "E" or "D" license suspension, revocation, or cancellation resulting from the disqualifying offense and provided his Group "E" driving privileges are otherwise valid. The license shall be valid for the duration of the disqualification of his commercial motor vehicle privileges. When the license becomes invalid, the licensee shall apply for a renewal of the license if he desires to retain his Group "E" driving privileges. The license shall not be issued until the licensee's commercial driver's license has been surrendered to the office of motor vehicles. The driving record shall reflect the class of license previously held. When the licensee's privilege to operate a commercial motor vehicle has been restored, his commercial driver's license shall be returned to him if it has not expired during the duration of the disqualification. If the commercial driver's license has expired, the licensee shall report to a driver's license office for renewal of the commercial driver's license. There shall be no fee for the initial Group "E" license provided under the provisions of this Subparagraph or the return of the commercial driver's license to the licensee if the commercial driver's license has not expired during the period of disqualification.

(iii) The department shall promulgate rules and regulations necessary to the administration and enforcement of this Subparagraph.

(c) As used in this Section, "alcohol concentration" shall mean the concentration of alcohol in a person's blood, breath, or urine, or other bodily substance. When expressed as a percentage, alcohol concentration means the numbers of grams of alcohol per one hundred milliliters of blood, the number of grams of alcohol per two hundred ten liters of breath, the number of grams of alcohol per sixty-seven milliliters of urine, or their equivalents.

(d) For the purposes of this Section, when operating a commercial motor vehicle, "serious traffic violation" means conviction of any of the following:

(i) Excessive speeding, involving any single offense for any speed of fifteen miles per hour or more above the posted speed limit.

(ii) Reckless driving, as defined by state or local law or regulation, including, but not limited to, offenses of driving a commercial motor vehicle in willful or wanton disregard for the safety of persons or property.

(iii) Improper or erratic traffic lane changes.

(iv) Following the vehicle ahead too closely.

(v) A violation, arising in connection with a fatal accident, or of a state or local law relating to motor vehicle traffic control, other than a parking violation. Serious traffic violations shall not include vehicle weight and defect violations.

(2) Any person shall be disqualified for life from operating a commercial motor vehicle for:

(a) Use of a commercial motor vehicle in the commission of a felony involving the manufacture, distribution, or dispensing of a controlled substance or possession with intent to manufacture, distribute, or dispense a controlled substance;

(b) Use of a commercial motor vehicle in the commission of more than one felony arising out of different crime episodes;

(c) Conviction of a second offense of driving under the influence of alcohol or a controlled substance while operating a commercial motor vehicle, or a second offense of operating a commercial motor vehicle with an alcohol concentration of 0.04 or more;

(d) A second offense of leaving the scene of an accident in a commercial motor vehicle;

(e) A second offense of refusal to submit to an alcohol concentration or drug test, while operating a commercial motor vehicle;

(f) Two or more of any combination of the offenses listed in Paragraph (A)(4), which arise from different episodes;

(3) Any person shall be disqualified from operating a commercial motor vehicle for a minimum period of three years for any of the offenses listed in Paragraph (A)(4), while transporting hazardous materials required to be placarded, or any other disqualification established by the department by regulation.

(4) Except as provided in Subparagraph A(2)(a) for lifetime disqualification, and in Paragraph A(3) for three years disqualification for offenses committed while transporting hazardous materials, any person shall be disqualified from operating a commercial motor vehicle for a minimum period of one year for:

(a) A conviction of driving under the influence of alcohol or a controlled substance, while operating a commercial motor vehicle, operating a commercial motor vehicle with an alcohol concentration of 0.04 or more, or operating a commercial motor vehicle under the influence of a controlled dangerous substance;

(b) Using a commercial motor vehicle in the commission of a felony;

(c) A first offense of leaving the scene of an accident in a commercial motor vehicle;

(d) A first offense of refusal to submit to an alcohol concentration or drug test, while operating a commercial motor vehicle;

(e) *(Repealed.)*

(5) Any person shall be disqualified from operating a commercial motor vehicle for a period of not less than sixty days if convicted of two serious traffic violations, or one hundred twenty days if convicted of three serious traffic violations, arising from separate incidents occurring within a three-year period.

(6) For purposes of Paragraph A(5) of this Subsection, any person who commits a serious traffic offense as defined in Paragraph A(1), including driving under the influence of alcohol or a controlled substance with an alcohol concentration of four one-hundredths or more, while operating a Class "A", "B", or "C" motor vehicle, shall be subject to the reporting, suspension, revocation, or enhancement penalties provided for in this Section and R.S. 32:1471 et seq.

B. (1) Notwithstanding any other law to the contrary or Subsection A of this Section, an operator of a commercial motor vehicle shall not have any measured alcohol concentration or any detected presence of alcohol or a controlled dangerous substance while operating or taking part in operating, or in physical control of, a commercial motor vehicle. Violation of this Subsection or refusal to submit to an alcohol concentration or drug test shall subject the person to a minimum twenty-four hour out-of-service period.

(2) Any driver who is found in violation of an out-of-service order while driving a commercial motor vehicle shall be subject to the following penalties:

(a) Upon a first conviction, the driver shall be subject to disqualification for a period of not less than ninety days nor more than one year. Any driver who is found in violation twice within a ten-year period shall be subject to disqualification for not less than one year nor more than five years. If a driver is found in violation three or more separate times within a ten-year period, the driver shall be subject to disqualification for not less than three years nor more than five years.

(b) Upon a first conviction, if the driver was transporting hazardous materials required to be placarded under the Hazardous Materials Transportation Act (49 App. U.S.C.A.

1801—1813) or a vehicle designed to transport more than fifteen persons, the driver shall be subject to disqualification for a period of not less than one hundred eighty days nor more than two years. If a driver is found in violation two or more separate times within a ten-year period while transporting hazardous materials or while operating a vehicle designed to transport more than fifteen persons, the driver shall be subject to disqualification for not less than three years nor more than five years.

C. (1) The act of operating a commercial motor vehicle shall constitute implied consent to be tested for any trace of alcohol, or controlled substances.

(2) The procedures for testing commercial motor vehicle operators for alcohol or controlled substances, and for reporting the results shall, with any appropriate modifications, be the same as for other drivers. The department may enact special provisions by regulation to take into account the unique requirements imposed by this Section. An officer need only have a reasonable belief that such a driver is under the influence of alcohol or drugs which may impair the driver's ability to safely drive to place him out-of-service. If a person operating a commercial motor vehicle refuses to submit to an alcohol concentration or drug test, the officer shall inform him that he may be disqualified from driving for the time periods specified in this Section and may be subject to stiffer criminal and civil penalties.

D. For purposes of this Section, the term "conviction" shall mean receipt of satisfactory evidence of a conviction, or of the entry of a plea of guilty or nolo contendere and sentence thereupon, or the forfeiture of bail.

(Chgd. by Acts 1990 No. 931, §1; Acts 1993 No. 382, §§1, 2; Acts 1995 No. 286, §1, No. 693, §1; Acts 1997 No. 264, §1, eff. 8/15/97.)

§414.3. Commercial motor vehicle drivers; employer responsibilities.

A. For purposes of this Section and R.S. 32:414.4 "employee" means an operator of a commercial motor vehicle, including an independent contractor while in the course of operating a commercial motor vehicle, who is employed by an employer.

B. For purposes of this Section and R.S. 32:414.4, "employer" means any person, including the United States, a state, or a political subdivision of a state, who owns or leases a commercial motor vehicle, or assigns employees to operate a commercial motor vehicle.

§414.4. Commercial motor vehicle operator; notification requirements.

A. (1) Any driver of a commercial motor vehicle who violates a state or local law or a law of a foreign jurisdiction meeting the requirements of 49 Code of Federal Regulations Part 383 relating to motor vehicle traffic control, other than a parking violation, in any other state, or such foreign jurisdiction, shall notify the department, in the manner specified by the secretary (unless exempted by the department by rule or regulation), of such violation within thirty days after the date he is adjudicated guilty in a court of competent jurisdiction, enters a plea of nolo contendere or guilty, suffers a forfeiture in connection with any such violations, or suffers a conviction as defined herein. The department may waive this requirement if permitted by the Federal Highway Administration.

(2) The driver of a commercial motor vehicle who drives for hire or compensation or who operates a commercial motor vehicle as a part of his employment, even if such operation is only occasional and who violates a state or local law relating to motor vehicle traffic control other than a parking violation, in any other state, shall notify his employer, in the manner specified by the department and the employer, of such violation within thirty days after he is adjudicated guilty in a court of competent jurisdiction, enters a plea of nolo contendere, or suffers a forfeiture in connection with any such violation. The department or the employer may require the driver to report violations of foreign law relating to motor vehicle traffic control, other than a parking violation. A violation includes an administrative action.

B. A driver of a commercial motor vehicle who drives for hire or who operates a commercial motor vehicle as part of his employment, even if such operation is only occasional; whose driver's license is suspended, revoked, or cancelled by any state; who loses the privilege to drive in any state for any period; or who is disqualified from driving for any period, including out-of-service orders, shall notify his employer in the manner specified by the department before the end of the next business day following the day the driver received notice of the fact. A nonresident commercial driver shall report any such suspension, revocations, or cancellation by any foreign jurisdiction. An employer or the department shall require the driver to report such actions taken by foreign authorities.

C. A driver applying for employment as a commercial motor vehicle operator or who operates a commercial motor vehicle in the course and scope of his employment, even if such operation is only occasional, shall notify his prospective employer of any previous employment. This information shall include a list of names and addresses of the driver's previous employers for which he drove a commercial motor vehicle, the dates the applicant drove for such employer, and the reason for leaving the employment. The applicant shall certify that such information is true and correct. The department or the employer may require the applicant to furnish additional information.

§415. Operating vehicle while license is suspended; offenses in other states; record of offenses given other states.

A. It shall be unlawful for any person to operate a motor vehicle upon any public highway of this state during the period of suspension, revocation or cancellation of any license which may have been issued to him by this state or by any other state.

B. Any period of suspension or revocation shall automatically be extended for a period of one year from the date the licensee would otherwise have been entitled to apply for a new license upon his conviction for any offense involving the operation of a motor vehicle committed during such period. No driver shall use a license issued to him in another state or the privilege of a nonresident to drive a motor vehicle in this state, upon receiving notice of his conviction, or of the entry of a plea of guilty and sentence thereupon, or of the forfeiture of bail in another state of federal jurisdiction for any offense, which if committed in this state, would be grounds for suspension or revocation of the license.

C. (1) A person with a Class "D" or Class "E" driver's license who violates the provisions of Subsection A of this Section may be fined up to five hundred dollars or imprisoned for not more than six months, or both and may be subject to a civil penalty of up to one thousand two hundred fifty dollars.

(2) A person with a Class "A", "B", or "C" driver's license who violates the provisions of Subsection A of this Section may be fined up to five thousand dollars or imprisoned for not more than six months or both and may be subject to a civil penalty of up to two thousand five hundred dollars.

D. (1) If the court finds that the defendant violated Subsection A at the time of conduct resulting in a conviction for a second or subsequent offense violation of R.S. 14:98, the offender shall be fined not less than three hundred dollars nor more than five hundred dollars and imprisoned for not less than seven days nor more than six months. At least seven days of such imprisonment shall be without benefit of probation, parole, or suspension of sentence and shall be consecutive to any sentence imposed for the violation of R.S. 14:98. In addition the person may be subject to a civil penalty of up to one thousand two hundred fifty dollars.

(2) If the person is operating a Group "A", "B", or "C" vehicle, and the court finds that the defendant violated Subsection A of this Section, at the time of conduct resulting in a conviction for a second or subsequent offense in violation of R.S. 14:98, the offender shall be fined not less than three hundred dollars nor more than five thousand dollars and imprisoned for not less than seven days nor more than six months. At least seven days of such imprisonment shall be without benefit of probation, parole, or suspension of sentence and shall be consecutive to any sentence imposed for the violation of R.S. 14:98. In addition, the person may be subject to a civil fine of up to two thousand five hundred dollars.
(Chgd. by Acts 1993 No. 382, §1, eff. 8/15/93.)

§415.1. Economic hardship appeal of driver's license suspension.

A. (1) Except as provided in R.S. 32:378.2(A), upon suspension, revocation, or cancellation of a person's driver's license for the first time only as provided for under R.S. 32:414 and R.S. 32:415, said person, after initial notice from the department, shall have the right to file a petition in the district court of the parish in which the applicant is domiciled alleging that revocation of his driving privileges will deprive him or his family of the necessities of life or will prevent him from earning a livelihood. The district court is vested with jurisdiction to set the matter for contradictory hearing in open court upon ten days written notice to the department, and thereupon to determine whether the allegations of hardship have merit. Upon determination by the court that the lack of a license would deprive the person or his family of the necessities of life, the court may order that the person be granted, by the department, a restricted license to enable the person to continue to support his family. The restrictions of said license shall be determined by the court and shall include the following:

(a) Licensee shall only be permitted to operate a motor vehicle on such streets as would enable him to earn his livelihood.

(b) Such operation is restricted to such times during which he is involved in earning a livelihood.

(c) During the period of suspension, licensee shall be responsible for applying to the court in the event that earning his livelihood necessitates a change in the original restrictions proposed by the court.

(d) Any other restrictions that the court determines to be necessary and proper.

(2) Notwithstanding the restrictions contained in Paragraph (1) of this Subsection, in any case in which the applicant for a restricted driver's license has had his driver's license suspended, revoked, or cancelled upon conviction or entry of plea of guilty and sentence thereupon, or the forfeiture of bail if the offense involved constituted operating or being in actual physical control of a motor vehicle while under the influence of intoxicating beverages, the court may additionally order that the applicant's restricted license include permission to operate a motor vehicle on such streets as would enable him to go to and from meetings of Alcoholics Anonymous and to go to and from approved group therapy or special education courses for or about the disease of alcoholism, alcohol abuse or drug abuse, in a suitable public or private institution or program approved by the appropriate state authority; provided however, that the receipt of such a restricted license may be conditioned upon (1) a medical evaluation and a recommendation that the convicted person is pathologically addicted to alcohol and/or a habitual alcoholic or other drug offender and (2) on the condition that such convicted individual submit to medical treatment and/or medically approved group therapy or special education courses for or about the disease of alcoholism, alcohol abuse or drug abuse, in a suitable public or private institution or program approved by the appropriate state authority; and the provisions of this Paragraph shall apply only to persons never previously convicted of operating or being in actual physical control of a motor vehicle while under the influence of intoxicating beverages.

B. A copy of the order shall be sent to the department along with a copy of the conviction notice. A copy of the order containing the restrictions shall be attached to the license of the person convicted and must be in possession of the person whenever he is operating a motor vehicle. A restricted license shall be issued by the department and designated by a large red R printed on the face of the license. The term of the restrictions shall be the same as the term of the original suspension, cancellation, or revocation.

C. A violation of the restrictions or a subsequent conviction of any offense involving the operation of a motor vehicle during the term of the restricted license shall result in the extension of the period of suspension, revocation, or cancellation for one year from the date upon which the licensee would otherwise have been able to apply for new license and shall also constitute contempt of court. Suspension, revocation, or cancellation that results from such a violation shall not be subject to appeal as set forth in this Section. Except as provided in R.S. 32:378.2(A)(2), restricted driving privileges for this Section may be allowed to a person only once.

D. The provisions of this Section shall apply to Class "D" and Class "E" licenses. *(Chgd. by Acts 1991 No. 936, §1; Acts 1995 No. 516, §1, eff. 8/15/95.)*

§416. Unlawful operation by persons under the age of seventeen; parents responsible.

No person shall cause or knowingly permit his child or ward, under the age of seventeen years, to drive a motor vehicle or a power cycle upon any highway unless such child or ward is licensed by the state to do so. *(Chgd. by Acts 1992 No. 382, §1; Acts 1997 No. 725, §1, eff. 1/1/98.)*

§416.1. Unlawful operation by persons less than seventeen years of age; operation of motor vehicles and power cycles between certain hours prohibited.

It shall be unlawful for any person who is less than seventeen years of age to drive a motor vehicle or a power cycle upon any highway, street, public road, or public thoroughfare at any time between 11 p.m. and 5 a.m. except when accompanied by a parent, tutor, or any other person twenty-one years of age or older, having custody of the minor. *(Chgd. by Acts 1997 No. 725, §1, eff. 1/1/98.)*

§417. Allowing unlicensed person under the age of seventeen to drive.

A. It shall be unlawful for any person to cause or knowingly permit his or her minor child or ward under the age of seventeen to drive a motor vehicle or a power cycle upon any public highway in this state unless such child or ward shall have first obtained a license to drive a motor vehicle or a power cycle.

B. It shall be unlawful for any person knowingly to rent for hire a motor vehicle to be operated by any person who does not have a current license or, in the case of a non-resident who has not been licensed to drive a motor vehicle under the laws of his resident state, if the laws of his resident state so require.

C. It shall be unlawful for any person or entity to employ any person as a driver of a motor vehicle if said person being employed does not have a current, valid license issued by the department in accordance with the provisions of this Chapter.

(Chgd. by Acts 1992 No. 382, §1; Acts 1997 No. 725, §1, eff. 1/1/98.)

§419. Department may for cause refuse to license applicant; judicial review.

The department is hereby authorized to refuse to issue a license under this Chapter to any person for any cause satisfactory to said department, but the applicant for said license in such case shall have a right of action in the same manner as is provided for in R.S. 32:414 of this Chapter.

§420. Exemptions.

No person shall be required to obtain a license for the purpose of operating implements of husbandry temporarily on the highways. A license shall not be required of the members of the armed forces of the United States in the operation of vehicles belonging to such agency when they have operator's licenses issued by such agency and are on official duty for the United States. However, a previously valid resident or nonresident commercial driver's license issued to a member of the armed forces of the United States which expires during the enlistment of the holder shall be valid for Class "E" operation only while the holder is still a full-time member of said armed forces and for not more than sixty days thereafter.

§421. False swearing; obtaining two licenses; unlawful.

Every person making application for a license under the provisions of this Chapter shall give and furnish such information as may be required by the department. The giving or furnishing of false, erroneous, or incorrect information shall be deemed a violation of this Chapter. It shall be unlawful to apply for or obtain more than one valid license. In addition to the other penalties imposed by this Chapter, if the department determines, in its check of an applicant's license status and record prior to issuing a driver's license, or at any time after the driver's license is issued, that the applicant has falsified information, the department shall, and within no more than thirty days of discovering the falsification, suspend, revoke, or cancel the person's driver's license for up to sixty days or shall cancel his pending application and may prohibit his reapplication for up to sixty days.

§422. Learner's license; school instruction permit; special restrictions on motorcycles.

A. Any person who is at least seventeen years of age may apply to the department for a learner's license to drive motor vehicles or power cycles, provided such person has completed a driving course in accordance with R.S. 32:402.1. The department may, in its discretion, after the applicant has successfully passed all parts of the examination, other than the driving test, issue to the applicant a learner's license at the regular fee of a Class "E" driver's license, which shall entitle the applicant while having such license in his immediate possession to drive a motor vehicle upon public highways when accompanied by one licensed driver at least twenty-one years of age, or when accompanied by a parent or parents, and it shall be unlawful for any other person to accompany the beginner and licensed driver, except in the event the applicant is operating a motorcycle. Any person under the age of seventeen who has a valid learner's license and is operating a motorcycle is restricted to a distance of three miles from the applicant's residence, unless a parent, tutor, or other person having custody is temporarily staying or residing at another location, where the applicant would be restricted to within three miles of that location. Any person seventeen years of age or older being issued a learner's license may apply for a regular Class "E" license thirty days after the issuance of a learner's license, or at any time after the issuance of the learner's license provided the applicant provides proof that the applicant has completed an approved thirty-six hour driver education course, and there shall not be any additional fee for the regular license.

B. Any person who is at least fifteen years of age may apply to the department for a school instruction permit if he is enrolled in a driver education course conducted by a person who meets certification requirements as established by the State Board of Elementary and Secondary Education or the Department of Public Safety and Corrections for teachers of driver education and traffic safety. The department may, in its discretion, after the applicant has successfully passed all parts of the examination, other than the driving test, issue to the applicant a school instruction permit for which no fee shall be charged. Such school instruction permit shall be valid only during the period of such instruction, and when the person to whom the permit is issued is accompanied by the high school instructor of driver education and traffic safety. Such permit shall be in the possession of the instructor during the period of its validity and shall be presented at any time for examination, when so requested by any law enforcement officer. Upon completion of such course of instruction, it shall be the responsibility of the instructor, as directed by the department, to return for cancellation any and all permits which have been issued and are held by him.

(Chgd. by Acts 1992 No. 382, §1; Acts 1994 Third Ex. Sess. No. 119, §1; Acts 1995 No. 163, §1, No. 1247, §1; Acts 1997 No. 725, §1, eff. 1/1/98.)

§422.1. Driver training school permits.

Persons licensed by the Department of Public Safety and Corrections to engage in the business of operating a driver training school or licensed instructors for such schools shall be authorized to issue Class "E" student driving permits on forms provided by the Department of Public Safety and Corrections in accordance with rules and regulations of the department. The Class "E" driving training school permits may be issued to persons who meet the age requirement for public school driver education courses. Such permit shall be valid only when the student is accompanied by a licensed instructor, and the licensed instructor shall maintain possession of the permit. A copy of the same permit shall be given to the student upon completion of the course with certification thereon of the instructor as to the student's qualification to drive. Improper issuance of such permit shall subject both the driving instructor training school and the instructor to suspension or revocation of license.

§423. Restricted license.

A. The department upon issuing a Class "A", "B", "C", "D", and "E" license shall have authority whenever good cause appears to impose restrictions suitable to the licensee's driving ability with respect to the type of, or special mechanical control devices required on, a motor vehicle which the licensee may operate or of such other restrictions applicable to the licensee as the department may determine to be appropriate to assure the safe operation of a motor vehicle by the licensee.

B. The department may either issue a special restricted license, or may set forth such restrictions upon the usual license form.

C. The department may, upon receiving satisfactory evidence of any violation of the restrictions of such license suspend or revoke the same, but the licensee shall be entitled to a hearing as upon a suspension or revocation under this Chapter.

D. No person shall operate a motor vehicle in violation of the restrictions imposed in the license issued to him.

§424. Department may compel examination of suspected incompetents.

The department having good cause to believe that a licensed driver or chauffeur is incompetent or otherwise not qualified to be licensed, may upon written notice of at least ten days to the licensee require him to submit to an examination. Upon the conclusion of such examination the department shall take action as may be appropriate and may suspend or revoke the license of such person or permit him to retain such license, or may issue a license subject to restrictions as permitted under R.S. 32:423. Refusal or neglect of the licensee to submit to examination shall be ground for suspension or revocation of his license.

§425. *(Repealed.)*

§426. Disposition of fees; surplus funds.

A. (1) The license fees collected under this Chapter shall be used by the Department of Public Safety and Corrections for the operation of said department and for the furtherance of highway safety education, except those funds payable to the board of trustees for certain police funds and the division of state police or to other specially dedicated funds.

(2) All other fees collected under this Chapter, except for specially dedicated funds, shall be used by the office of motor vehicles for the operation of said department and the furtherance of highway safety education.

(3) All civil penalties collected pursuant to this Chapter shall be used by the department for the operation of said agency except for those civil penalties payable to specially dedicated funds.

B. Any surplus in the fees and civil penalties allocated for use by the office of motor vehicles and the office of state police or the department under the provisions of this Chapter shall be paid into the general fund at the end of each biennium after July 1, 1991.

C. The general provision that dedicated funds shall be expended before appropriated funds shall not apply to expenditures made by these agencies of the fees and civil penalties collected under this Chapter.

§427. Penalty.

A. (1) Violation of a provision of this Chapter, or of a regulation promulgated thereunder, while operating a Group "D" or Group "E" vehicle or involving a Class "D" or "E" license or application for a Class "D" or "E" license, shall subject the person to criminal penalties of a fine of not less than ten nor more than five hundred dollars or imprisonment for up to six months, or both and civil penalties of up to a one thousand two hundred fifty dollar fine.

(2) Violation of a provision of this Chapter, or of a regulation promulgated thereunder, while operating a commercial motor vehicle or involving a commercial driver's license shall subject the person to criminal penalties of a fine of not less than ten nor more than five thousand dollars or imprisonment for up to six months, or both and civil penalties of up to a two thousand five hundred dollar fine.

(3) Any commercial motor vehicle driver who is convicted of a violation of an out-of-service order as provided in this Chapter, shall be subject to a civil penalty of not less than one thousand dollars nor more than two thousand five hundred dollars for each occurrence. Any employer who is convicted of violation of an out-of-service order shall be subject to a civil penalty of not less than two thousand five hundred dollars nor more than ten thousand dollars for each occurrence.

B. (1) For purposes of this Chapter and particularly R.S. 32:414.2, "conviction" means an unvacated adjudication of guilt or a determination that a person has violated or failed to comply with the law in a court of original jurisdiction or by an authorized administrative tribunal, an unvacated forfeiture of bail or collateral deposited to secure the person's appearance in court, a plea of guilty or nolo contendere accepted by the court, the payment of a fine or court costs, or a violation of a condition of release without bail, regardless of whether or not the penalty is rebated, suspended, or probated. A conviction will occur even if a person is referred to a remedial program as a substitute for the imposition of a penalty, fine, or other sanction.

(2) The assistant secretary of the office of motor vehicles shall notify any person found to be in violation of a civil penalty imposed by this Chapter of the penalty or disqualification to drive levied after due process either by mail or in person. Upon passage of thirty days without receipt of fine, the assistant secretary of the office of motor vehicles may order the removal of the offending vehicle's license tag if the registration is from Louisiana. For vehicles not registered within the state, any vehicle owned by the person or company may be seized. For offenses by the driver or operator, the driver's or operator's license shall be suspended. Upon receipt of the fine, the license tags, vehicle, or driver's license shall be returned.

(3) The amount of any civil penalty or duration of a disqualification to drive, or suspension, revocation, or cancellation imposed under this Chapter shall be determined by taking into account the nature, circumstances, extent, and gravity of the violation committed and, with respect to the violator, the degree of culpability, history of prior offenses, ability to pay, effect on the ability to continue to do business, and any other matters as justice and public safety may require. In each case, the assessment shall be calculated to induce further compliance.

(Chgd. by Acts 1993 No. 382, §1; Acts 1995 No. 693, §1, eff. 8/15/95.)

§428. Failure to enforce requirement.

Notwithstanding the testing, licensing, and reporting requirements herein, it shall not be a breach of duty to the public or any individual if the department inadvertently fails to enforce said requirements or waives same pursuant to the authority granted herein.

§429. Motor vehicle field offices; authorization of fees.

A. The governing authority of any local governmental subdivision is hereby authorized to levy, by resolution, a fee for each service or transaction carried out as an operation of a local field office of the office of motor vehicles of the Department of Public Safety and Corrections which local field office is not fully funded by the state. The fee shall not exceed two dollars per service or transaction, shall not apply to the procurement or renewal of a motor vehicle registration license, and shall be used solely to defray the cost of operations of that local field office supported by the governing authority of any local governmental subdivision including but not limited to facility rental, utilities, and maintenance.

B. Any fee levied under the authority of Subsection A of this Section shall be considered nonstate funds and shall be collected by the motor vehicle commissioner on behalf of the governing authority of any local governmental subdivision pursuant to an agreement to be executed by and between the motor vehicle commissioner and the governing authority of any local governmental subdivision. Any such fees collected by the motor vehicle commissioner shall be deposited in the state treasury in the Escrow Fund and held for the account of the governing authority of any local governmental subdivision levying such fee. The office of the motor vehicle commissioner shall distribute any such fees to the appropriate governing authorities of local governmental subdivisions.

(Chgd. by Acts 1990 No. 275, §1, eff. 7/5/90.)

CHAPTER 2-A. DENIAL OF DRIVING PRIVILEGES

Section

§430. Suspension, revocation, and denial of driving privileges; hardship license; insurance rates.

A. (1) Whenever any person who has not yet attained the age of nineteen, but who is not younger than thirteen years of age, is convicted of any crime, offense, violation, or infraction involving the possession, use, or abuse of alcohol or one or more controlled dangerous substances, is convicted of any provision of R.S. 40:966 through 970 of the Uniform Controlled Dangerous Substances Law, is convicted of any provision of the Louisiana Racketeering Act*, or is adjudicated delinquent for the commission of such offense, the court in which the person was so convicted or adjudicated delinquent shall prepare and send to the Department of Public Safety and Corrections, within ten days of the conviction or adjudication, an order of denial of driving privileges for not less than ninety days but not more than one year for the person convicted or adjudicated delinquent, or until he has reached the age of eighteen years, whichever is longer. If the person convicted or adjudicated delinquent is older than eighteen years, the order of denial shall be for not less than ninety days nor more than one year.

**R.S. 15:1351 et seq.*

(2) Whenever any person who has attained the age of nineteen is convicted of any crime, offense, violation, or infraction involving the possession, use, or abuse of one or more controlled dangerous substances, the court in which the person was convicted shall prepare and send to the Department of Public Safety and Corrections, within ten days of the conviction, an order of denial of driving privileges for not less than ninety days but not more than one year for the person convicted.

(3) Whenever a person nineteen years of age or older is convicted of any felony offense involving a possession violation of any provision of R.S. 40:966 through 970 of the Uniform Controlled Dangerous Substances Law, or a violation of the Louisiana Racketeering Act, the court in which the person is so convicted shall prepare and send to the Department of Public Safety and Corrections, within ten days of the conviction, an order of denial of driving privileges for the person so convicted.

B. In addition to any other authority to suspend driving privileges, the department shall suspend all driving privileges or the right to apply for driving privileges of any person upon receipt of an order of denial of driving privileges under this Section.

C. The suspension of driving privileges shall be imposed without hearing. Driving privileges, or the right to apply for driving privileges, of the person shall be suspended as provided in the following Paragraphs:

(1) Upon receipt of the first order denying driving privileges to a person under Paragraph A(1) of this Section, the department shall suspend the driving privileges of that person for not less than ninety days nor more than one year, or until the person whose driving privileges were suspended reaches eighteen years of age, whichever is longer. If he is older than eighteen years, his driving privileges shall be suspended for not less than ninety days nor more than one year.

(2) Upon receipt of a second or subsequent order denying driving privileges to a person under Subsection A(1) of this Section, the department shall suspend the driving privileges of that person for one year or until the person whose driving privileges were suspended reaches nineteen years of age, whichever is longer.

(3) Upon receipt of an order denying driving privileges to a person under Subsection A(2) of this Section, the department shall suspend the driving privileges of that person for not less than ninety days nor more than one year.

D. If the department receives notice from a court that it has withdrawn an order issued under this Section, the department shall immediately reinstate any driving privileges that have been suspended under this Section because of the issuance of the order.

E. The court, in addition to any other authority granted under this Section, may issue an order which authorizes the department to issue a restricted driver's license after the first thirty days of the suspension period upon a demonstration to the court's satisfaction that a hardship would result from being unable to commute to either school or to work. The restrictions of said license shall be determined by the court.

F. (1) Notwithstanding any restrictions imposed, in any case in which the applicant for a restricted driver's license has had his driver's license suspended, revoked, or cancelled upon conviction or entry of plea of guilty and sentence thereupon, or the forfeiture of bail if the offense involved constituted operating or being in actual physical control of a motor vehicle while under the influence of intoxicating beverages, or if the offense involved possession, in violation of R.S. 40:966 through R.S. 40:970, of any controlled dangerous substance listed in Schedules I, II, III, IV or V of the Uniform Controlled Dangerous Substances Law, or any drug offense as defined in R.S. 32:401(20), the court may, after the first thirty days of the suspension period, additionally order that the applicant's restricted license include permission to operate a motor vehicle on such streets as would enable him to go to and from meetings of Alcoholics Anonymous and to go to and from approved group therapy or special education courses for or about the disease of alcoholism, alcohol abuse, or drug abuse, in a suitable public or private institution or program approved by the appropriate state authority.

(2) The receipt of such a restricted license may be conditioned upon:

(a) A medical evaluation and a recommendation that the convicted person is pathologically addicted to alcohol and/or is a habitual alcoholic or other drug offender, and

(b) On the condition that such convicted individual submit to medical treatment and/or medically approved group therapy or special education courses for or about the disease of alcoholism, alcohol abuse or drug abuse, in a suitable public or private institution or program approved by the appropriate state authority.

G. The provisions of this Subsection F shall apply only to persons never previously convicted of any offense listed in Subsection A of this Section. The provisions of Subsection F shall apply to Class "D" and Class "E" licenses.

H. A copy of an order issued under Subsections F and G of this Section shall be sent to the department along with a copy of the conviction or adjudication notice. A copy of the order containing the restrictions shall be attached to the license of the person convicted or adjudicated and shall be in the possession of the person whenever he is operating a motor vehicle. A restricted license shall be issued by the department and designated by a large red "R" printed on the face of the license. The term of the restrictions shall be the same as the term of the original suspension, cancellation, or revocation.

I. A violation of the restrictions or a subsequent conviction or adjudication of delinquency for the offenses stated in this Section during the term of the restricted license shall result in the extension of the period of suspension for one year from the date upon which the licensee would otherwise have been able to apply for a new license and shall also constitute contempt of court. A suspension which results from such a violation, conviction, or adjudication of delinquency shall not be subject to appeal as set forth in this Section. The restricted driving privileges authorized by Subsection F and G of this Section may be allowed to a person only once.

J. Any person whose license has been suspended by the department shall be notified of such suspension in writing by the department. This notice shall be sent by certified mail to the last address furnished by such person, and the person shall return his or her license to the department within five days of receiving the notice. The notice shall also advise such person that he or she may obtain a special identification card from the driver's license division of the Department of Public Safety and Corrections pursuant to R.S. 40:1321.

K. Any period of suspension under this Chapter shall begin upon receipt by the department of the operator's license of the person affected.

L. Upon the expiration of the period of the suspension of any license, the department shall return the license to the licensee or in its discretion may issue him a new license, but only after a reinstatement fee of sixty dollars has been paid to the department and the requirements of R.S. 32:896 relative to proof of financial responsibility have been satisfied. Monies derived from this reinstatement fee shall be disbursed as set out in R.S. 32:414(G)(1)(b).

M. No insurer issuing a policy of automobile insurance covering property damages, personal injury, or accidental death shall increase any rate or premium charges for insurance coverage because of any suspension or revocation of a license under the provisions of this Section unless the crime, offense, violation, or infraction is directly related to the operation of a motor vehicle. The provisions of this Subsection shall not be construed to prohibit the increase of any automobile insurance rate or premium, pursuant to a rate increase which is approved by the Louisiana Insurance Rating Commission, for a class of insurance of which the person whose license has been suspended or revoked pursuant to this Section is or becomes a member.

N. (1) When any person's driver's license has been seized, suspended, or revoked, and the seizure, suspension, or revocation is connected to a charge or charges of violation of a criminal law, and the charge or charges do not result in a conviction, plea of guilty, or bond forfeiture, the person charged shall not be required to pay any reinstatement fee if at the time for reinstatement of driver's license, it can be shown that the criminal charges have been dismissed or that there has been a permanent refusal to charge a crime by the appropriate prosecutor or there has been an acquittal. If however, at the time for reinstatement, the licensee has pending against him criminal charges arising from the arrest which led to his suspension or revocation of driver's license, the reinstatement fee shall be collected. Upon subsequent proof of final dismissal or acquittal, other than under Articles 893 or 894 of the Code of Criminal Procedure, the licensee shall be entitled to a reimbursement of the reinstatement fee previously paid. In no event shall exemption from this reinstatement fee or reimbursement of a reinstatement fee affect the validity of the underlying suspension or revocation.

(2) If a licensee qualifies for the exemption from the reinstatement fee or for a reimbursement of the reinstatement fee as provided in Paragraph (1), the licensee shall receive credit for the unexpired portion of the license which was seized, and shall be exempt from the payment of, or shall receive reimbursement for the payment of, the duplicate license fee and the handling fee with regard to the license which was seized.

(Chgd. by Acts 1991 No. 936, §1; Acts 1992 No. 277, §1; No. 605, §1, No. 1096, §1; Acts 1995 No. 520, §2, eff. 8/15/95.)

§431. *(Repealed by Acts 1997 No. 725, §2, eff. 1/1/98.)*

§432. Suspension or denial of driving privileges; failure to pay child support.

A. Regardless of the requirements for the issuance or renewal of a license to operate a motor vehicle on the highways of this state, or suspension or revocation thereof, all drivers' licenses issued pursuant to this Chapter are also subject to the provisions of R.S. 9:315.30 et seq., suspension of license for nonpayment of child support.

B. The Department of Public Safety and Corrections, office of motor vehicles, shall adopt rules and regulations in accordance with the provisions of the Administrative Procedure Act* to effectuate the orderly and expeditious suspension and reissuance of drivers' licenses in accordance with R.S. 9:315.30 et seq.

(Added by Acts 1995 No. 1078, §2, eff. 1/1/96.)

**R.S. 49:950 et seq.*

CHAPTER 3. MISCELLANEOUS PROVISIONS

PART I. MOTOR VEHICLES OF HISTORIC OR SPECIAL INTEREST

PART II. STREET RODS AND STREET CRUISERS

PART III. PARKING MOTOR VEHICLES

PART VI. STEEL TIRES, CLEATS OR LUGS

PART VII. STORED MOTOR VEHICLES

PART IX. GARAGES AND OIL STATIONS

PART X. PUBLIC LIABILITY CONTRACTS BY SCHOOL BOARDS AND OTHER PUBLIC BODIES

PART XI. BRAKE FLUID

PART XII. TRAFFIC VIOLATIONS

PART XIII. HEAVY EQUIPMENT

PART XIV. TESTS FOR SUSPECTED DRUNKEN DRIVERS

PART XV. RESPONSIBILITIES OF DEPARTMENT OF PUBLIC SAFETY AND CORRECTIONS, OFFICE OF STATE POLICE

PART I. MOTOR VEHICLES OF HISTORIC OR SPECIAL INTEREST

§441. Declaration of purpose.

This Part is enacted in recognition of the importance of constructive leisure pursuits by Louisiana citizens, for the purpose of encouraging responsible participation in the hobby of collecting, preserving, restoring, operating and maintaining motor vehicles of historic or special interest. Further, the legislature of Louisiana, recognizing that the current pattern of resource recycling leads to an ever shortening period of existence for vehicles of historic or special interest, enacts this Part to ensure the preservation of our American heritage as it relates to the motor vehicle manufacturing industry. The legislature further recognizes that a vehicle representative of this heritage, being held by a hobbyist, finds significance as a motor vehicle of historic or special interest through a personal relevance to the life of the collector holding it and, or, through a general relevance as an example-artifact of the transportation history of Louisiana.

§442. Definitions.

As used in this Part, the following words and phrases have the meaning ascribed to them in this Section, unless the context requires otherwise:

(1) "Collector" means the owner of one or more motor vehicles of historic or special interest who collects, purchases, acquires, trades, or disposes of such motor vehicles or the parts thereof for his own use in order to preserve, restore, and maintain such a motor vehicle for hobby purposes.

(2) "Commissioner" means the director of public safety as provided in R.S. 47:451(5).

(3) "Parts car" means a motor vehicle of historic or special interest which is generally in inoperable condition and which is owned by a collector to furnish parts that are usually not obtainable from normal sources, thus enabling a collector to preserve, restore or maintain a motor vehicle of historic or special interest.

(4) "Motor vehicle of historic or special interest" means a motor vehicle, including a motorcycle as defined in R.S. 32:1(38), of any age which, because of its significances, is being collected, preserved, restored, operated, or maintained by a hobbyist as a leisure pursuit.

§443. Storage on collector's property.

A collector may store unlicensed, operable or inoperable motor vehicles of historic or special interest or parts cars on his property provided such vehicles and parts cars and the storage area are maintained in such a manner that they do not constitute a health, safety or fire hazard.

§444. Equipment requirements.

Any other provision of law, particularly Part V of Chapter 1 of this Title, to the contrary notwithstanding, unless the presence of equipment on a motor vehicle was a prior condition to the sale, to the offering for sale or to the operation of a motor vehicle on the highways of this state at the time the motor vehicle was manufactured for sale or use, the absence of equipment now or hereafter required by law from motor vehicles of historic or special interest shall not be construed as prohibiting the sale, the offering for sale or the legal operation on the highways of this state of any motor vehicle of historic or special interest. Notwithstanding the provisions of Chapter 7 of this Title, any motor vehicle of historic or special interest manufactured prior to the date on which emission control devices were standard equipment on that particular make or model of motor vehicle shall be exempt from all state and local requirements relative to the inspection and use of such emission control devices. Any safety equipment that was manufactured as part of such vehicle's original equipment shall be maintained in proper operating condition whenever the vehicle is operated on the highways of this state.

§445. Sale or trade; not contingent upon vehicle being in operating condition.

The sale or trade and subsequent legal transfer of a motor vehicle of historic or special interest or parts car shall not be contingent upon any condition that would require the vehicle or parts car to be in operating condition at the time of sale or transfer of ownership.

§446. Abandoned or stored motor vehicles of historic or special interest.

Notwithstanding any provision of law relating to abandoned or stored motor vehicles to the contrary, no motor vehicle of historic or special interest or parts car which, because of its age, would be eligible for the special license plates issued by the commissioner to the owner of such vehicles shall be considered as an abandoned or an unclaimed, stored motor vehicle unless and until the provisions herein have been complied with. If no action has been taken by the last known owner or by others entitled to ownership of the motor vehicle so that such abandoned or unclaimed, stored motor vehicle may be reclaimed, the municipality, parish or department of public safety, whichever intends to provide for the disposal of such vehicle, shall notify by certified letter or by other suitable means the nearest club or chapter of any national organization which has at its purpose the restoration of motor vehicles of historic or special interest of its intention to dispose of such motor vehicle. Such notice shall allow adequate time for such club or chapter, or any individual member thereof, to buy or bid for such motor vehicle.

§447. Rules and regulations.

The commissioner shall adopt rules and regulations not inconsistent with this Part in order to fully effectuate the purpose and intent hereof.

PART II. STREET RODS AND STREET CRUISERS

(Chgd. by Acts 1992 No. 189, §1, eff. 6/8/92.)

§451. Declaration of purpose.

This Part is enacted for the purpose of enhancing the recreational and leisure pursuits of Louisiana citizens by facilitating participation in the hobby of collecting, preserving, modifying, operating, and maintaining street rods and street cruisers and thus providing the following: preservation of modified antique motor vehicles known as street rods or of other vehicles known as street cruisers; recognition for the automobile hobbyist in Louisiana; promotion of vehicle safety through self-policing; additional revenue to the state through sales tax paid upon the purchase of such vehicles and parts therefor; and family-oriented recreation for Louisiana citizens. *(Chgd. by Acts 1992 No. 189, §1, eff. 6/8/92.)*

§452. Street rod; definition.

As used in this Part, the phrase "street rod" means any antique automobile or truck produced in 1948 or earlier, which is an automobile or truck that is recognized as a street rod by the National Street Rod Association, and which has undergone some type of modernizing, to include modernizing of engine, transmission, drivetrain, interior refinements, and any other modifications the builder desires, which vehicle is to be driven to events under its own power and to be used as a safe, nonracing vehicle for total family enjoyment.

§453. Licensing requirements; exemptions.

No vehicle which has been registered and licensed as a street rod pursuant to this Section and to R.S. 47:463.12 shall be subject to the regular motor vehicle licensing requirements.

§454. Rules and regulations.

The Secretary of the Department of Public Safety and Corrections shall adopt rules and regulations not inconsistent with this Part in order to fully effectuate the purpose and intent hereof. Oversight review of the secretary's rules and regulations shall be conducted by the Joint Legislative Committee on Transportation, Highways, and Public Works.

§455. Street cruiser; definition.

As used in this Part, the phrase "street cruiser" means any automobile or truck twenty-five years or older, and which has undergone some type of modernizing, to include modernizing of the engine, transmission, drive train, and interior refinements, and any other modifications the builder desires, which vehicle is to be driven to events under its own power and to be used as a safe, nonracing vehicle for total family enjoyment. *(Added by Acts 1992 No. 189, §1, eff. 6/8/92.)*

§456. Registration; licensing.

No vehicle which has been registered and licensed as a street cruiser pursuant to this Part and R.S. 47:463.33 shall be subject to the regular motor vehicle licensing requirements. *(Added by Acts 1992 No. 189, §1, eff. 6/8/92.)*

§457. Authorized rules.

The secretary of the Department of Public Safety and Corrections shall adopt rules not inconsistent with this Part in order to fully effectuate the purpose and intent hereof. *(Added by Acts 1992 No. 189, §1, eff. 6/8/92.)*

PART III. PARKING MOTOR VEHICLES

§471. Definitions.

The following words and phrases, when used in this Chapter, shall have the meanings herein assigned unless the context clearly indicates otherwise:

(1) "Abandoned motor vehicle" means a motor vehicle that is inoperable and is left unattended on public property for more than three days, or is inoperable and left unattended on the shoulder or right-of-way of an interstate or a four-lane highway for more than three days, or a motor vehicle that has remained illegally on public property for a period of more than three days, or a motor vehicle that has remained on private property without the consent of the owner or person in control of the property for more than three days.

(2) "Department" means the Louisiana Department of Public Safety.

(3) "Policing authority," or "authority" means, with respect to the city of New Orleans, the police board of the city of New Orleans and in all other municipalities and parishes means the police department, sheriff or such other authority as is vested with police authority. All costs or fees arising from seizures in said city shall be transmitted to the city treasurer, to be deposited in the general fund.

(Chgd. by Acts 1995 No. 1072, §1, eff. 8/15/95.)

§472. Parking motor vehicles; seizure of; payment of costs.

If any motor vehicle, in any municipality in this state, is seized or otherwise held by any policeman or other officer employed by said municipality for illegal parking, stationing or abandoning of such motor vehicle or for the violation of any traffic ordinance or regulation of the municipality, the owner shall be entitled to regain possession thereof upon payment of such costs as may be fixed by the policing authority of the municipality for the violation. The costs so fixed shall cover all charges for removing the vehicle to the place of holding and all other costs incurred during the period of holding.

§473. Seized vehicles; penalties for illegal parking and for the impounding and detention of vehicles illegally parked.

A. All municipalities may adopt ordinances imposing fines, imprisonment, or other penalties on any person for parking, stationing, or abandoning any automobile or other vehicle on the municipal streets in violation of any municipal ordinance or other regulatory law, and such municipalities may further charge for the impounding and detention of vehicles illegally parked in loading, reserved or otherwise restricted zones, no parking areas, or public carrier stands, but the total of such charges, including the charge for its removal from the street where it may have been situated, and all other charges during the period of storage, shall not exceed thirty dollars.

B. The limitations in this Section shall not apply to the parish of Orleans.

§474. Authority to take possession of abandoned motor vehicles.

The department or any municipality or any parochial authority may take into custody any motor vehicle found abandoned on public or private property. The department or any municipality or parochial authority may employ its own personnel, equipment and facilities or may employ persons, equipment and facilities for the purpose of removing, preserving and storing abandoned motor vehicles.

§475. Notification of owners and mortgage holders.

A. Whenever any motor vehicle is found to be abandoned by the department or any municipality or any parochial authority by reason of the illegal parking or the stationing of such motor vehicle on a public street, way, road or highway within the state, said department, municipality or parochial authority shall send a registered or certified letter, return receipt requested, to the last known owner of said vehicle at his last known address informing him to remove said vehicle within ten working days from date of receipt of notice, as herein provided. The department, municipality or parochial authority shall notify the owner of such vehicle that, in lieu of removal, said owner may remit fifteen dollars, together with a completed certificate of authority to the department, municipality or parochial authority to remove and dispose of said abandoned motor vehicle. The certificate or authority shall be on a form prescribed and furnished by the department, municipality or parochial authority, along with a self-addressed return envelope.

B. If the abandoned motor vehicle is not removed within ten working days from date of receipt of notice and the fifteen dollar removal fee has not been returned as provided above, the motor vehicle may be removed and disposed of by the department, municipality or parochial authority forthwith, and in such case the department, municipality or parochial authority may assess a penalty in the amount of twenty dollars for the failure of an owner to remove an abandoned motor vehicle. If the penalty is not paid within thirty days, and upon receipt, from within the department or from any municipality or any parochial authority, of satisfactory evidence of the failure to pay the penalty as assessed, the department shall revoke the license of the owner of the vehicle. Upon recommendation from within the department or from any municipality or any parochial authority, the department may suspend or revoke the certificates of registration of motor vehicles owned by persons or corporations who fail to comply with the provisions of this Chapter. The department may continue such suspension or revocation, in its discretion, until the payment of the penalties assessed herein.

§476. Abandoned motor vehicles; sale by municipalities and parochial authorities; procedure.

A. Whenever any motor vehicle belonging to a known or unknown person has been seized or is otherwise held by any municipality or any parochial authority for illegal parking, stationing, or abandoning of such motor vehicle on the public streets, ways, roads, and highways within the state, and the same has not been claimed for a period of three months or more, then the motor vehicle shall be considered as having been abandoned to the municipality or parochial authority and the municipality or parochial authority may dispose of such motor vehicle and collect the costs and charges of removing and storing said vehicle in the following manner:

(1) The municipality or parochial authority shall send a registered or certified letter, return receipt requested, to the owner of said vehicle, within ten days of the date the vehicle was seized. Said governing authority shall send a second letter to the vehicle owner upon the expiration of the three-month period provided for in this Section. Any such letter shall be sent to the owner of the vehicle at his last known address informing him that the municipality or parochial authority is holding said vehicle. The owner shall also be informed in such letter that the vehicle shall be sold to the highest bidder unless said owner, on or before the date of sale, claims the vehicle and pays to the municipality or parochial authority all costs and charges imposed by the municipality or parochial authority for the removal and detention of the vehicle. A copy of the letters shall also be sent to any person or firm known to the holder of a mortgage on said vehicle.

(2) Before the sale of any such vehicles, the municipality or parochial authority shall have them appraised by a competent appraiser and shall publish a notice of the proposed sale of said vehicle or vehicles in the official journal of the municipality or parish not less than three times within a ten-day period prior to the date of said sale. The published notice shall contain a complete list of the vehicles to be sold, the date and place of said sale, and notification that said vehicles will be sold either individually or in globo to the highest bidder therefor, all in the discretion of the municipality or parochial authority.

(3) All funds received from the sale of a motor vehicle under the provisions hereof shall be set aside and placed in a separate account established therefor by the municipality or parochial authority. If, within one year following the date of the sale, the owner or lienholders of any of said vehicles shall present sufficient proof to the municipality or parochial authority of his ownership or lien, the said owner or lienholder shall be entitled to the amount received for his individual vehicle less his pro rata share of the costs and expenses of the sale, as well as all charges and costs due and owing for removal and storage of said vehicle. Any funds not claimed within one year following the date of sale shall be deposited to the general fund of the municipality or parish.

B. Parishes and municipalities are authorized to adopt local ordinances defining derelict or junk vehicles and adopting procedures for the towing away and selling of the same and shall not be required to comply with Subsection A hereof as to derelict or junk vehicles.

(Chgd. by Acts 1992 No. 1040, §1, eff. 8/21/92.)

PART VI. STEEL TIRES, CLEATS OR LUGS

§501. Motor trucks, etc., with lugs, not to be used on hard-surfaced roads; exceptions.

No motor truck or trailer with steel tires, or tractors with cleats or lugs on the wheels shall be operated over any public road in the state which has been hard-surfaced with any kind of material, or improved, in any manner by public funds, proceeds of bond issues, or with revenues of the state highway department, or of the United States. Nothing contained in this Section shall prevent the use of trucks or trailers equipped with steel tires by persons engaged in farming or agricultural pursuits when transporting their products to and from plantations abutting any improved highway of this state, or to persons operating under certificates of permission by the police jury of the parish, or of the municipal authorities of the city or town in which they may be operating.

§503. Penalty.

Whoever violates R.S. 32:501 and 32:502 shall be fined not less than two hundred and fifty dollars nor more than five hundred dollars, or imprisoned in the parish jail for not less than thirty nor more than ninety days, or both.

PART VII. STORED MOTOR VEHICLES

§523. Record of sales proceedings to be kept for year.

The person obtaining the sale of a motor vehicle under R.S. 32:521 shall keep a record of all proceedings of all sales made thereunder for a period of one year after the sale.

§524. Parish of Orleans, list of motor vehicles held in storage to be furnished public administrator; administration as vacant estates.

In the parish of Orleans all persons shall on the first day of September and March of each year furnish the public administrator of the parish of Orleans with a list of all motor vehicles held by them in storage together with a description thereof and the name of the last owner and the storage and cost due. The public administrator of the parish of Orleans shall then proceed to take them into his possession and administrate them as vacant estates and as estates of unknown owners.

PART IX. GARAGES AND OIL STATIONS

§531. Garage or oil businesses, petition for location; consent of property owners.

Any person desiring to conduct a garage or oil business in this state, prior to the issuance to him of any permit by either state, town, parish, or municipal authorities, shall, when such business is to be located in any incorporated city, town, or village, address a petition to the city council or board of alderman, or when it is to be located without such limits, to the police jury of the parish in which it is to be located, stating the name of the owner, its exact location, and must be accompanied with the written assent of a majority of the property owners within three hundred feet, to be measured along the street or road fronts, of the proposed location.

§532. Restrictions as to location.

No town council, board of aldermen, or police jury shall grant any permit for the conducting of such a business within three hundred feet of any bridge over a river on any state highway, when in their discretion the conducting of such a business so located is dangerous to public safety.

§533. Application of Part.

This Part shall not become effective in any city, town, village or parish, until an ordinance of the governing authority adopting it has been passed and has been published in the official journal of the parish for at least thirty days.

§534. Construction of Part; zoning.

This Part shall in no way conflict with R.S. 33:4721 through 33:4730. However, if zoning ordinances are now in operation in any municipality allowing the erection and operation of filling stations in zoned areas, such municipality is prohibited from enacting any ordinance regulating the hour of their closing, and other zoning laws.

§535. Return of parts to customer; exceptions.

A. Unless the customer stipulates otherwise, it shall be the duty of any repairman employed by a customer to repair a motor vehicle to offer to return all replaced parts upon completion of the work if such parts are not required to be returned to the manufacturer or distributor pursuant to a warranty agreement. If such parts are required to be returned to the manufacturer or distributor, the repairman, at the time the work is authorized, shall offer to, or if requested by the customer, display the parts upon completion of the work. However, the repairman shall not be required to display a part when there is no charge for the replacement part. If the customer accepts the repairman's offer to either return or display replaced parts as provided in this Section, it shall be the duty of the repairman to return or display such parts. The provisions of this Section shall not apply to the replacement of parts on the exterior or interior of the vehicle the damage to which is apparent to the customer upon examination.

B. Anyone who violates this Section shall be fined not more than one hundred dollars and assessed all costs of court.

(Added by Acts 1995 No. 1122, §1, eff. 8/15/95.)

§535.1. Required invoice.

A. It shall be the duty of any repairman employed by a customer to repair a motor vehicle to provide the customer with an invoice containing the following information:

(1) A description of all work done including any warranty work.

(2) An itemization of all parts supplied.

(3) A clear statement of what new original or nonoriginal manufacturer parts, or used, rebuilt, or reconditioned parts have been supplied or that a part of a component system that has been supplied is composed of new original or nonoriginal manufacturer parts, or used, rebuilt, or reconditioned parts.

(4) A description of the vehicle identification number, make, model, and mileage.

B. The repairman shall provide the customer with a copy of the invoice and shall retain a copy for his records.

C. Anyone who violates the provisions of this Section shall be fined not more than one hundred dollars.

(Added by Acts 1997 No. 496, §1, eff. 8/15/97.)

PART X. PUBLIC LIABILITY CONTRACTS BY SCHOOL BOARDS AND OTHER PUBLIC BODIES

§601. Public liability, bodily injury, and property damage insurance.

Parish school boards, levee boards, and other public bodies be and they are hereby authorized, in their discretion, to enter into and consummate contracts for public liability and/or bodily injury insurance, and property damage insurance, covering the operation, use or maintenance of motor vehicles owned and operated by such boards.

§602. Tort liability.

The action of any such parish school board, levee board, or other public body in contracting for such insurance shall not be construed by the courts as a waiver of the governmental immunity of such boards or bodies from liability for torts committed by its agents or employees.

§603. Contract provisions.

All such contracts of insurance shall contain a clause whereby the insurance companies issuing said insurance shall not assert as a defense to any suit against them, the governmental immunity of such school board, levee board or other public body.

§604. Actions; parties.

Any suit by an injured party under such a contract of insurance shall be against the insurance company alone and the parish school board that is insured shall not be made a party to the suit.

PART XI. BRAKE FLUID

§621. Definitions.

The following definitions shall apply for purposes of this Part:

(1) "Brake fluid" means the fluid intended for use as the liquid medium through which force is transmitted in the hydraulic brake system of a vehicle operated upon the highways.

(2) "Person" includes any individual, firm, corporation, partnership or association.

(3) "Department" means the Department of Public Safety.

(4) "Labeling" includes all written, printed, or graphic representations, in any form whatsoever, imprinted upon or affixed to any container of brake fluid or accompanying any brake fluid.

(5) "Container" means any receptacle in which brake fluid is immediately contained when sold, but does not mean a carton or wrapping in which a number of such receptacles are shipped or stored or a tank car or truck.

(6) "Permit period" means the period set by the department validating the permit.

§622. Manufacture, sale or distribution of brake fluid; registration; permits.

It shall be unlawful to manufacture or distribute any brake fluid for sale in this state unless such brake fluid has first been registered as required by this Part. No person shall manufacture, or distribute any brake fluid for sale in this state unless he has first applied to the department for the registration of such brake fluid to be handled by applicant and has received a written permit authorizing the sale, use, manufacture, or distribution of such brake fluid for sale in this state during the period and under the conditions stated in R.S. 32:623.

§623. Application for registration; forms; contents; issuance of permit; renewal.

Application for registration of each brand of brake fluid shall be made on forms to be supplied by the department. Each form shall include space for the name and address of the applicant, the brand name of the brake fluid and for certification that the brake fluid to be sold under such brand name conforms to the specifications established by the department for brake fluids. Upon receipt and approval of the application the department shall issue to the applicant a permit authorizing the manufacture or wholesale and retail sale and distribution of the brake fluid in this state during the permit period specified in the permit. Permits shall be renewed at the discretion of the department, provided, such renewals shall not be required more frequently than once every two years.

§624. Cancellation, refusal to issue, or refusal to renew permit, grounds; procedure; powers of department.

The department may cancel, refuse to issue, or refuse to renew any permit, if it finds, after due notice and a hearing, that the brake fluid is adulterated or misbranded, or that the registrant has failed to comply with the provisions of this Part or the rules and regulations of the department. The proceedings shall be conducted in accordance with rules and regulations to be promulgated by the department.

§625. When brake fluid adulterated; specifications; amendment of specifications.

Any brake fluid is adulterated if its quality or characteristics fall below the specifications for brake fluid established by the department as minimum standards.

The department shall establish specifications for brake fluid which shall promote the public safety in the operation of automotive vehicles and may amend such specifications by regulation, after a hearing, but in no event shall the specifications for brake fluid fall below the minimum standard specifications established by the Society of Automotive Engineers for hydraulic brake fluid, heavy duty type. Hydraulic brake fluid which meets or exceeds the standard of specifications established by the Society of Automotive Engineers for heavy duty brake fluid shall prima facie be deemed to meet the requirements of this section.

§626. When brake fluid deemed misbranded; words and letters to be in legible type.

Brake fluid shall be deemed to be misbranded if:

(1) The container does not bear a label on which is printed the name and place of business of the manufacturer, packer, or distributor, the words "Brake Fluid", and, if required by regulation established by the department, the type of classification.

(2) The container does not bear an accurate statement of the quantity of the contents in terms of liquid measure.

(3) The labeling on the container is false or misleading in any particular. The words and letters required by this Section shall appear on the label in legible type and the fact that same meets or exceeds SAE specifications shall be stated.

§627. Enforcement; inspection; access to premises; authority to open boxes, cartons and other containers.

The department and its duly authorized agents shall enforce the provisions of this Part and may sample, inspect, analyze and test any brake fluid manufactured, used, packed, sold or distributed within this state. The department, through its agents, shall have free access by all legal means during business hours to all premises, buildings, vehicles, cars, and vessels used in the manufacture, packing, storage, sale or transportation of brake fluid, and may by legal means open any box, carton, parcel or container of brake fluid and take therefrom samples for analysis or for evidence.

§628. Promulgation and enforcement of rules and regulations.

The department shall have authority to promulgate and enforce such rules and regulations as are necessary to carry out the provisions of this Part.

§629. Fees.

The department shall collect from the applicant seeking a permit to manufacture or distribute brake fluid as defined in this Part, a fee of $50.00 for each permit or renewal which fee shall be used by the department to administer the provisions of this Part.

§630. Violations; penalties.

It is unlawful to manufacture, sell or distribute any brake fluid which is adulterated or misbranded, or which is not registered, or which is without a valid permit as required by this Part. Violation of any provision of this Part is a misdemeanor. The first offense shall be punishable by a fine of not more than $1,000.00 and the permanent cancellation of the offender's permit.

PART XII. TRAFFIC VIOLATIONS

§641. Parishwide schedule of fines, penalties and costs; written pleas of guilty; payment; exceptions.

A. The judges of any judicial district, the parish of Orleans excepted, with the consent of the district attorney, may adopt a parish-wide schedule of fines, penalties and costs for violations of the traffic laws and regulations of the state of Louisiana or any parish under their jurisdiction, within the limits of such penalties as are set by law, and such schedules shall be applicable as provided hereafter.

B. Any person apprehended for or charged with the violation of a law or regulation contained in such schedule may enter a written plea of guilty to the same by signing a declaration to that effect, which declaration shall specify the issue charged and the time and place thereof, and deposit with the sheriff of the parish a sum of money corresponding to the schedule of fines and costs for the violation of the particular traffic offense charged. The said declaration shall authorize the sheriff to pay the amount of such fine, penalty and costs from money deposited in escrow for that purpose with the sheriff. Such declarations and the deposit of money in escrow shall be executed and transferred only in the courthouse, parish jail or such other place as is designated by the judges, and within such time limits as is set by the judges.

C. The judge or district attorney may refuse to accept such written plea of guilty in any case and in the event of refusal, the written plea of guilty shall not be admissible in evidence for any reason whatsoever.

D. This Section does not apply to any person charged with any offense under Title 14 of the Louisiana Revised Statutes of 1950, except reckless operation of a motor vehicle where no accident is involved.

E. For traffic offenses, the fines for which are scheduled under the provisions of this Section, clerks of the judicial district courts shall not be required to keep and transcribe minutes for proceedings involving offenders who plead guilty and pay fines before their scheduled trial, thereby waiving their court appearance. This provision may be modified by rule of court.

PART XIII. HEAVY EQUIPMENT

§651. Emblem or name of owner to appear on equipment; penalties.

A. Every owner of any heavy equipment, except those coming within the provisions of R.S. 47:478, which weighs in excess of three tons and is capable of transporting itself or being transported on the highways of this state shall have inscribed, painted, stenciled, or affixed by means of magnetic plastic signs, decals or other secured signs conspicuously thereon the emblem or name of such owner in letters not less than two and one-half inches in height and not less than one-quarter inch in width. Nothing contained herein shall apply to watercraft or farming equipment.

B. Whoever violates the provisions of this section shall be punished by a fine of not more than two hundred dollars or be imprisoned for not more than six months, or both.

PART XIV. TESTS FOR SUSPECTED DRUNKEN DRIVERS

§661. Operating a vehicle under the influence of alcoholic beverages or illegal substance or controlled dangerous substances; implied consent to chemical tests; administering of test and presumptions; effect of refusal to submit to tests; informing person of consequences of submission or refusal and his rights; furnishing information to person tested.

A. (1) Any person, regardless of age, who operates a motor vehicle upon the public highways of this state shall be deemed to have given consent, subject to the provisions of R.S. 32:662, to a chemical test or tests of his blood, breath, urine, or other bodily substance for the purpose of determining the alcoholic content of his blood, and the presence of any abused substance or controlled dangerous substance as set forth in R.S. 40:964 in his blood if arrested for any offense arising out of acts alleged to have been committed while the person was driving or in actual physical control of a motor vehicle while believed to be under the influence of alcoholic beverages or any abused substance or controlled dangerous substance as set forth in R.S. 40:964.

(2) The test or tests shall be administered at the direction of a law enforcement officer having reasonable grounds to believe the person, regardless of age, to have been driving or in actual physical control of a motor vehicle upon the public highways of this state while under the influence of either alcoholic beverages or any abused substance or controlled dangerous substance as set forth in R.S. 40:964. The law enforcement agency by which such officer is employed shall designate in writing and under what conditions which of the aforesaid tests shall be administered.

(3) If the person is under twenty-one years of age, the test or tests shall be administered at the direction of a law enforcement officer having reasonable grounds to believe the person to have been driving or in actual physical control of a motor vehicle upon the public highways of this state after having consumed alcoholic beverages. The law enforcement agency by which the officer is employed shall designate in writing and under what conditions which of the tests shall be administered.

B. Any person who is dead, unconscious or otherwise in a condition rendering him incapable of refusal shall be deemed not to have withdrawn the consent provided by Subsection (A) of this section, and the test or tests may be administered subject to the provisions of R.S. 32:662.

C. (1) When a law enforcement officer requests that a person submit to a chemical test as provided for above, he shall first read to the person a standardized form approved by the Department of Public Safety and Corrections. The department is authorized to use such language in the form as it, in its sole discretion, deems proper, provided that the form does inform the person of the following:

(a) His constitutional rights under *Miranda v. Arizona.*

(b) That his driving privileges can be suspended for refusing to submit to the chemical test.

(c) That his driving privileges can be suspended if he submits to the chemical test and such test results show a blood alcohol level of 0.10 percent or above or, if he is under the age of twenty-one years, a blood alcohol level of 0.02 percent or above.

(d) That his driving privileges can be suspended if he submits to the chemical test and the test results show a positive reading indicating the presence of any controlled dangerous substance listed in R.S. 40:964.

(e) The name and employing agency of all law enforcement officers involved in the stop, detention, investigation, or arrest of the person.

(2) In addition, the arresting officer shall, after reading said form, request the arrested person to sign the form. If the person is unable or unwilling to sign, the officer shall certify that the arrestee was advised of the information contained in the form and that the person was unable to sign or refused to sign.

(Chgd. by Acts 1994 Third Ex. Sess. No. 20, §2; Acts 1997 No. 1296, §3, No. 1297, §1, eff. 7/15/97.)

§661.1. Operating a watercraft under the influence of alcoholic beverages or controlled dangerous substances; implied consent to chemical tests; administering of test and presumptions.

A. (1) Any person, regardless of age, who operates a motor powered watercraft upon the public navigable waterways of this state shall be deemed to have given consent, subject to the provisions of R.S. 32:662, to a chemical test or tests of his blood, breath, urine, or other bodily substance for the purpose of determining the alcoholic content of his blood and the presence of any abused substance or controlled dangerous substance as set forth in R.S. 40:964 in his blood if arrested for any offense arising out of acts alleged to have been committed while the person was driving or in actual physical control of a motor powered watercraft, while believed to be under the influence of alcoholic beverages or any abused substance or controlled dangerous substance as set forth in R.S. 40:964.

(2) The test or tests shall be administered at the direction of a law enforcement officer having reasonable grounds to believe the person, regardless of age, to have been driving or in actual physical control of a motor powered watercraft upon the public navigable waterways of this state, while under the influence of either alcoholic beverages or any abused substance or controlled dangerous substance as set forth in R.S. 40:964. The law enforcement agency by which such officer is employed shall designate which of the aforesaid tests shall be administered.

B. Any person who is dead, unconscious, or otherwise in a condition rendering him incapable of refusal or who has been involved in an accident involving bodily injury or death shall be deemed not to have withdrawn the consent provided by Subsection A of this Section, and the test or tests may be administered subject to the provisions of R.S. 32:662.

C. (1) When a law enforcement officer requests that a person submit to a chemical test as provided for in this Section, he shall first read to the person a standardized form approved by the Department of Public Safety and Corrections. The department is authorized to use such language in the form as it, in its sole discretion, deems proper, provided that the form does inform the person of the following:

(a) His constitutional rights under *Miranda v. Arizona* and subsequent applicable jurisprudence.

(b) That his driving privileges can be suspended for refusing to submit to the chemical test.

(c) That his driving privileges can be suspended if he submits to the chemical test and such test results show a blood alcohol level of 0.10 percent or above or, if he is under the age of twenty-one years, a blood alcohol level of 0.02 percent or above.

(d) The name and employing agency of all law enforcement officers involved in the stop, detention, investigation, or arrest of the person.

(2) In addition, the law enforcement officer, after reading the form, shall request the arrested person to sign the form. If the person is unable or unwilling to sign, the officer shall certify that the arrestee was advised of the information contained in the form and that the person was unable to sign or refused to sign.

(Chgd. by Acts 1994 Third Ex. Sess. No. 20, §2; Acts 1997 No. 1296, §3, No. 1297, §1, eff. 7/15/97.)

§661.2. Operation of a locomotive engine under the influence of alcoholic beverages or controlled dangerous substances; implied consent to chemical tests; administering of test and presumptions.

A. (1) Any person who operates a locomotive engine upon the railroad tracks of this state shall be deemed to have given consent, subject to the provisions of R.S. 32:662, to a chemical test or tests of his blood, breath, urine, or other bodily substance for the purpose of determining the alcoholic content of his blood and the presence of any abused or illegal controlled dangerous substance as set forth in R.S. 40:964 in his blood if he is involved in a collision at a railroad crossing at any roadway of this state alleged to have occurred when he was driving or in actual physical control of the locomotive engine while believed to be under the influence of alcoholic beverage or any abused or illegal controlled dangerous substance as set forth in R.S. 40:964.

(2) The test or tests shall be administered at the direction of the law enforcement officer having reasonable grounds to believe the person to have been operating or in physical control of the locomotive engine while under the influence of either alcoholic beverage or any abused or illegal controlled dangerous substance as set forth in R.S. 40:964. The law enforcement agency by which such officer is employed shall designate which of the aforesaid tests shall be administered.

B. Any person who is dead, unconscious, or otherwise in a condition rendering him incapable of refusal or who has been involved in a railroad crossing collision involving bodily injury or death shall be deemed not to have withdrawn the consent provided by Subsection A of this Section, and the test or tests may be administered subject to the provisions of R.S. 32:662.

C. (1) When a law enforcement officer requests that a person submit to a chemical test as provided for in this Section, he shall first read to the person a standardized form approved by the Department of Public Safety and Corrections. The department is authorized to use such language in the form as it, in its sole discretion, deems proper, provided that the form does inform the person of the following:

(a) His constitutional rights under *Miranda v. Arizona* and subsequent applicable jurisprudence.

(b) The consequences of his refusal to submit to the chemical test.

(c) The name and employing agency of all law enforcement officers involved in the detention, investigation, or arrest of the person.

(2) In addition, the law enforcement officer, after reading the form, shall request the arrested person to sign the form. If the person is unable or unwilling to sign, the officer shall certify that the arrestee was advised of the information contained in the form and that the person was unable to sign or refused to sign.

D. If a person refuses the request of the law enforcement officer to submit to a chemical test offered pursuant to the provisions of this Section, a test shall not be given without a court order. A written report shall be forwarded by the enforcement officer to the United States Department of Transportation. The report shall state that the officer had reasonable grounds to believe that the person had committed a crime pursuant to the provisions of R.S. 14:98 and that the person had refused to submit to the test upon the request of the peace officer and had been advised of the consequences of the refusal.

(Added by Acts 1998 First Ex. Sess. No. 81, §1, eff. 6/16/98.)

§662. Administering chemical tests; use of results as evidence.

A. The chemical test or tests as provided for by this Part shall be subject to the following rules and shall be administered as provided for hereafter:

(1) Upon the trial of any criminal action or proceeding arising out of acts alleged to have been committed by any person while driving or in actual physical control of a vehicle while under the influence of alcoholic beverages the amount of alcohol in the person's blood at the time alleged as shown by chemical analysis of the person's blood, urine, breath, or other bodily substance shall give rise to the following presumptions:

(a) Except as provided in Subparagraph (d), if the person had a blood alcohol concentration at that time 0.05 percent or less by weight, it shall be presumed that the person was not under the influence of alcoholic beverages.

(b) Except as provided in Subparagraph (d), if the person had a blood alcohol concentration at that time in excess of 0.05 percent but less than 0.10 percent by weight, such fact shall not give rise to any presumption that the person was or was not under the influence of alcoholic beverages, but such fact may be considered with other competent evidence in determining whether the person was under the influence of alcoholic beverages.

(c) If the person had a blood alcohol concentration at that time of 0.10 percent or more by weight, it shall be presumed that the person was under the influence of alcoholic beverages.

(d) If the person was under the age of twenty-one years at the time of the test and had a blood alcohol concentration at that time of 0.02 percent or more by weight, it shall be presumed that the person had consumed alcoholic beverages.

(2) The blood alcohol concentration or level shall be based upon grams of alcohol per one hundred cubic centimeters of blood. Individuals measured through breath shall be afforded the timely option of the administration of a blood test for alcohol content.

B. The provisions of Subsection A of this Section shall not be construed as limiting the introduction of any other competent evidence bearing upon the question whether the person was under the influence of alcoholic beverages or any abused substance or controlled dangerous substance as set forth in R.S. 40:964.

C. Except as provided in Paragraph A(2) of this Section, this Section has no application to a civil action or proceeding.

(Chgd. by Acts 1994 Third Ex. Sess. No. 20, §2; Acts 1997 No. 1296, §3, No. 1297, §1, eff. 7/15/97.)

§663. Approval of testing methods by Department of Public Safety.

Chemical analyses of the person's blood, urine, breath or other bodily substance, to be considered valid under the provisions of this Part, shall have been performed according to methods approved by the Department of Public Safety and by an individual possessing a valid permit issued by said department for this purpose. The Department of Public Safety in authorized to approve satisfactory techniques or methods, to ascertain the qualifications and competence of individuals to conduct such analyses, and to issue permits which shall be subject to termination or revocation at the discretion of the department.

§664. Persons qualified to make test.

A. When a person submits to a blood test at the request of a law enforcement officer under the provisions of this Part, only a physician, registered nurse, qualified technician, or chemist may withdraw blood for the purpose of determining the alcoholic content or presence of any abused or illegal controlled dangerous substances therein. No law enforcement officer who is not otherwise qualified as a physician, registered nurse, qualified technician, or chemist may withdraw blood for the purpose of determining, or of having determined, the alcoholic content or presence of any abused or illegal controlled dangerous substances therein. This limitation shall not apply to the taking of breath specimens.

B. The person tested may have a physician or a qualified technician, chemical, registered nurse or other qualified person of his own choosing administer a chemical test or tests in addition to any administered at the direction of a law enforcement officer. After being advised of this right as provided in R.S. 32:661(C), he shall be given the opportunity to telephone and request the qualified person to administer such test. The failure or inability to obtain an additional test by a person shall not preclude the admission of evidence relating to the test or tests taken at the direction of a law enforcement officer.

C. No person who administers any such test upon the request of a law enforcement officer as herein defined, no hospital in or with which such person is employed or otherwise associated or in which such test is administered, and no other person, firm or corporation by whom or which such person is employed or is in any way associated, shall be in any wise criminally liable for the administration of such test, or civilly liable in damages to the person tested.

(Chgd. by Acts 1990 No. 68, §1, eff. 9/7/90.)

§665. Furnishing of information to person tested.

Upon the request of the person who submits to a chemical test or tests at the request of a law enforcement officer, results concerning the test or tests shall be made available to him or his attorney.

§666. Refusal to submit to chemical test; exception; effects of.

A. A person under arrest for a violation of R.S. 14:98, R.S. 14:98.1, or any other law or ordinance that prohibits operating a vehicle while intoxicated may not refuse to submit to a chemical test in any case wherein a traffic fatality has occurred or a person has sustained serious bodily injury. The law enforcement officer shall direct that a chemical test be conducted in such circumstances. A physician, registered nurse, qualified technician, or chemist shall perform a chemical test in accordance with the provisions of R.S. 32:664 when directed to do so by a law enforcement officer. In all other cases, a person under arrest for a violation of R.S. 14:98, R.S. 14:98.1, or other law or ordinance that prohibits operating a vehicle while intoxicated may refuse to submit to such chemical test, after being advised of the consequences of such refusal as provided for in R.S. 32:661(C), subject to the following:

(1) His license shall be seized under the circumstances provided in R.S. 32:667.

(2) If he is a resident without a license or permit to operate a motor vehicle in this state, the department shall deny the issuance of a license or permit to such person for a period of six months after the date of the alleged violation.

(3) Evidence of his refusal shall be admissible in any criminal action or proceeding arising out of acts alleged to have been committed while the person, regardless of age, was driving or in actual physical control of a motor vehicle upon the public highways of this state while under the influence of alcoholic beverages or any abused substance or controlled dangerous substance as set forth in R.S. 40:964. Additionally, evidence of his refusal shall be admissible in any criminal action or proceeding arising out of acts alleged to have been committed while the person under twenty-one years of age was driving or in actual physical control of a motor vehicle upon the public highways of this state after having consumed alcoholic beverages. However, such evidence shall not be admissible in a civil action or proceeding other than to suspend, revoke, or cancel his driving privileges.

B. In each instance that a person refuses to submit to a chemical test, after being advised of the consequences of such refusal as provided for in R.S. 32:661(C), the officer shall submit a sworn report in a form approved by the secretary that he had reasonable grounds to believe that the arrested person had been driving or was in actual physical control of a motor vehicle upon the public highways of this state while under the influence of alcoholic beverages or any abused or illegal controlled dangerous substance as set forth in R.S. 40:964, that he had followed the procedure in informing such person of his rights under R.S. 32:661(C), and that such person had refused to submit to the test upon the request of the officer.

(Chgd. by Acts 1992 No. 671, §1; Acts 1993 No. 987, §1; Acts 1997 No. 1296, §3, No. 1297, §1, eff. 7/15/97.)

§667. Seizure of license; circumstances; temporary license.

A. When a law enforcement officer places a person under arrest for a violation of R.S. 14:98, R.S. 14:98.1, or a violation of a parish or municipal ordinance that prohibits operating a vehicle while intoxicated, and the person either refuses to submit to an approved chemical test for intoxication, or submits to such test and such test results show a blood alcohol level of 0.10 percent or above by weight or, if the person is under the age of twenty-one years, a blood alcohol level of 0.02 percent or above by weight, the following procedures shall apply:

(1) The officer shall seize the driver's license of the person under arrest and shall issue in its place a temporary receipt of license on a form approved by the Department of Public Safety and Corrections. Such temporary receipt shall authorize the person to whom it has been issued to operate a motor vehicle upon the public highways of this state for a period not to exceed thirty days from the date of arrest or as otherwise provided herein.

(2) The temporary receipt shall also provide and serve as notice to the person that he has not more than ten days from the date of arrest to make written request to the Department of Public Safety and Corrections for an administrative hearing in accordance with the provisions of R.S. 32:668.

(3) In a case where a person submits to an approved chemical test for intoxication, but the results of the test are not immediately available, the law enforcement officer shall comply with Paragraphs (1) and (2) of this Subsection, and the person shall have ten days from the date of arrest to make written request for an administrative hearing. If after thirty days from the date of arrest the test results have not been received or if the person was twenty-one years of age or older on the date of arrest and the test results show a blood alcohol level of less than 0.10 percent by weight, then no hearing shall be held and the license shall be returned without the payment of a reinstatement fee. If the person was under the age of twenty-one years on the date of arrest and the test results show a blood alcohol level of less than 0.02 percent by weight, then no hearing shall be held and the license shall be returned without the payment of a reinstatement fee.

(4) If the vehicle is operable and a passenger in the vehicle who is not under the influence of alcohol has a valid driver's license, the officer shall allow the passenger to take control of the vehicle and shall not order or procure towing services for the vehicle. Provided the vehicle does not create a hazard or obstruction to traffic and the motoring public, if there is no such passenger, the officer, before ordering or procuring towing service, shall allow the arrestee a reasonable time and opportunity to contact another person to take possession or control of the vehicle on behalf of the arrestee. Reasonable time to notify and take possession of the vehicle shall be in the sole discretion of the officer. However, the law enforcement agency, the law

enforcement officer, the state, and the political subdivision shall not be liable for damages, injuries, or deaths occasioned by the vehicle not being towed immediately or by another person taking possession or control of the vehicle on behalf of the arrestee. If a law enforcement officer violates the provisions of this Paragraph, his employing agency rather than the arrestee shall be responsible for the payment of any towing charges incurred.

B. If such written request is not made by the end of the ten-day period, the person's license shall be suspended as follows:

(1) If the person submitted to the test and the test results show a blood alcohol level of 0.10 percent or above by weight, his driving privileges shall be suspended for ninety days from the date of suspension on first offense violation, without eligibility for a hardship license for the first thirty days, and for three hundred sixty-five days from the date of suspension, without eligibility for a hardship license, on second and subsequent violations occurring within five years of the first offense. If the person was under the age of twenty-one years on the date of the test and the test results show a blood alcohol level of 0.02 percent or above by weight, his driving privileges shall be suspended for one hundred eighty days from the date of suspension.

(2) If the person had refused to submit to the test, his driving privileges shall be suspended for one hundred eighty days from the date of suspension on first refusal and five hundred forty-five days from the date of suspension without benefit of eligibility for a hardship license on the second and subsequent refusals occurring within five years of the first refusal. However, if the person was under the age of twenty-one years at the time of first refusal, his driver's license shall be suspended one hundred eighty days from the date of suspension.

(3) However, any licensee who has had his license suspended for operating a motor vehicle while under the influence of alcoholic beverages under the provisions of this Subsection shall, upon proof to the Department of Public Safety and Corrections that his motor vehicle has been equipped with a functioning ignition interlock device, be immediately eligible for and shall be granted a restricted license. In the event that the department fails or refuses to issue the restricted driver's license, the district court for the parish in which the licensee resides may issue an order directing the department to issue the restricted license either by ex parte order or after contradictory hearing.

(4) If the person had refused to submit to the test in any case wherein a fatality occurred or a person sustained serious bodily injury as a result of an accident, his driving privileges shall be suspended for five hundred forty-five days from the date of suspension without benefit of eligibility for a hardship license.

C. The department shall develop a uniform statewide form for temporary receipt of licenses which shall be used by all state and local law enforcement officials. The form shall be issued in duplicate to the person arrested to provide a means for him to request an administrative hearing.

D. Upon receipt of a request for an administrative hearing, the department shall issue a document extending the temporary license, which shall remain in effect until the completion of administrative suspension, revocation, or cancellation proceedings. The department shall promptly schedule such request for hearing. No delay of the hearing shall be granted by the department, unless requested in writing at least three days prior to such hearing, and upon a showing of good cause for the delay. However, in the case of an unforeseen emergency the secretary, or his designee, may waive the requirement for a written request to be submitted three days prior to the hearing in order to grant a delay. A hearing granted by the department may be rescheduled only once by the person seeking such hearing and in no event shall a hearing be rescheduled for a date later than ninety days from the date of the arrest. Oversight review of rules and regulations promulgated by the secretary under the provisions of this Part shall be conducted by the House Committee on Transportation, Highways, and Public Works and the Senate Committee on Transportation, Highways, and Public Works.

E. The department shall develop a plan as soon as practicable and no later than by January 1, 1991, to provide for prompt suspension or revocation of driving privileges within an average of forty-five days of the date of arrest in cases.

F. When a license has been suspended under the provisions of this Section and the person is also convicted of or pleads guilty to an offense arising out of the same occurrence, any suspension of license imposed for such offense shall run concurrently with the suspension provided by this Section and the total period of suspension shall not exceed the longer of the two periods.

G. Notwithstanding the provisions of any other law, any person whose license has been suspended under the provisions of this Section shall, after completion of the period of suspension, be required to pay a reinstatement fee of fifty dollars to the department for the return of his license.

H. (1) When any person's driver's license has been seized, suspended, or revoked, and the seizure, suspension, or revocation is connected to a charge or charges of violation of a criminal law, and the charge or charges do not result in a conviction, plea of guilty, or bond forfeiture, the person charged shall have his license immediately reinstated and shall not be required to pay any reinstatement fee if at the time for reinstatement of driver's license, it can be shown that the criminal charges have been dismissed or that there has been a permanent refusal to charge a crime by the appropriate prosecutor or there has been an acquittal. If however, at the time for reinstatement, the licensee has pending against him criminal charges arising from the arrest which led to his suspension or revocation of driver's license, the reinstatement fee shall be collected. Upon subsequent proof of final dismissal or acquittal, other than under Articles 893 or 894 of the Code of Criminal Procedure, the licensee shall be entitled to a reimbursement of the reinstatement fee previously paid. In no event shall exemption from this reinstatement fee or reimbursement of a reinstatement fee affect the validity of the underlying suspension or revocation.

(2) If a licensee qualifies for the exemption from the reinstatement fee or for a reimbursement of the reinstatement fee as provided in Paragraph (1), the licensee shall receive credit for the unexpired portion of the license which was seized, and shall be exempt from the payment of, or shall receive reimbursement for the payment of, the duplicate license fee and the handling fee with regard to the license which was seized.

(Chgd. by Acts 1990 No. 932, §1; Acts 1992 No. 605, §1; Acts 1993 No. 17, §1, No. 453, §1; Acts 1994 Third Ex. Sess. No. 20, §2; Acts 1995 No. 516, §1, No. 520, §2, No. 1070, §1; Acts 1997 No. 1184, §1, eff. 8/15/97, No. 1296, §3, No. 1297, §1, eff. 7/15/97.)

§668. Procedure following revocation or denial of license; hearing; court review; review of final order; restricted licenses.

A. Upon suspending the license or permit to drive or nonresident operating privilege of any person or upon determining that the issuance of a license or permit shall be denied to the person, the Department of Public Safety and Corrections shall immediately notify the person in writing and upon his request shall afford him an opportunity for a hearing in the same manner and under the same conditions as is provided in R.S. 32:414 for notification and hearings in the case of suspension of licenses, except that the scope of such a hearing for the purposes of this Part shall cover the following issues:

(1) Whether a law enforcement officer had reasonable grounds to believe the person, regardless of age, had been driving or was in actual physical control of a motor vehicle upon the public highways of this state while under the influence of either alcoholic beverages or any abused substance or controlled dangerous substance as set forth in R.S. 40:964.

(2) Whether the person was placed under arrest.

(3) Whether he was warned by the officer as provided in R.S. 32:661(C).

(4) Whether he voluntarily submitted to an approved chemical test and whether the test resulted in a blood alcohol reading of 0.10 percent or above by weight, or of 0.02 percent or above if he was under the age of twenty-one years on the date of the test.

(5) Whether he refused to submit to the test upon the request of the officer.

(6) Such additional matters as may relate to the reasonableness of a suspension of the license.

B. (1)(a) In a case of first refusal or first submission to a test for intoxication and when there has been no prior suspension of the driver's license, if suspension is otherwise proper, upon a showing of proof satisfactory to the department that the suspension of driving privileges would prevent the person from earning a livelihood, the department may:

(i) Require the licensee to surrender his regular license and issue in its stead at a cost to the person of fifty dollars plus the cost of the license a special restricted operator's license designated as such by a large red *R* printed on the face of the license, to be effective for the remaining period of suspension.

(ii) Designate in writing, and upon application of the person to amend as necessary, the routes over which and the times during which the restricted license shall be permitted to operate designated motor vehicles in order to earn his livelihood, which written restrictions shall be attached to the restricted license and kept with it at all times.

(b) No person who has refused a chemical test for intoxication is eligible for a restricted license for the first ninety days of the suspension. When a person submits to a chemical test and the results show a blood alcohol level of 0.10 percent or above by weight, or of 0.02 percent or above if the person was under the age of twenty-one years on the date of the test, he is not eligible for a restricted license for the first thirty days of the suspension.

(c) However, any licensee who has had his license suspended for operating a motor vehicle while under the influence of alcoholic beverages under the provisions of this Subsection, shall, upon proof to the Department of Public Safety and Corrections, be immediately eligible for and shall be issued a restricted license. In the event that the department fails or refuses to issue the restricted driver's license, the district court for the parish in which the licensee resides may issue an order directing the department to issue the restricted license either by ex parte order or after contradictory hearing.

(2) However, the department shall immediately cancel and seize the restricted license upon receiving satisfactory evidence of violation of the restrictions, and no person shall have driving privileges of any kind for a period of six months from the receipt by the department of the cancelled restricted license.

C. After a person has exhausted his remedies with the department, he shall have the right to file a petition in the appropriate court for a review of the final order of suspension or denial by the Department of Public Safety and Corrections in the same manner and under the same conditions as is provided in R.S. 32:414 in the cases of suspension, revocation, and cancellation of licenses. The court in its review of the final order of suspension or denial by the Department of Public Safety and Corrections may exercise any action it deems necessary under the law including ordering the department to grant the person restricted driving privileges where appropriate as provided in Subsection B.
(Chgd. by Acts 1994 Third Ex. Sess. No. 20, §2; Acts 1995 No. 516, §1; Acts 1997 No. 1184, §1, eff. 8/15/97, No. 1296, §3, No. 1297, §1, eff. 7/15/97.)

§669. Suspension of nonresident's operating privilege; notification to state of residence.

A. When a nonresident driver refuses to take an approved chemical test as provided for in R.S. 32:666, the arresting officer or agency shall notify the department, which shall give information, in writing, to the motor vehicle administrator of the state of the person's residence and of any state in which he has a license.

B. When it has been finally determined that a nonresident's privilege to operate a motor vehicle in this state has been suspended, the Department of Public Safety shall give information in writing of the action taken to the motor vehicle administrator of the state of the person's residence and of any state in which he has a license.

PART XV. RESPONSIBILITIES OF DEPARTMENT OF PUBLIC SAFETY AND CORRECTIONS, OFFICE OF STATE POLICE

§671. Responsibilities of the Department of Public Safety and Corrections, office of state police; interstate highways.

The Department of Public Safety and Corrections, office of state police, shall use its best efforts to respond to calls placed by motorists from call boxes located along Interstate 10 as it crosses the Atchafalaya River Basin between the West Atchafalaya Basin Protection Levee and the East Atchafalaya Basin Protection Levee, or to relay the calls to the appropriate law enforcement agency. *(Added by Acts 1993 No. 122, §1, eff. 8/15/93.)*

CHAPTER 4. VEHICLE CERTIFICATE OF TITLE LAW

Section

§702. Definitions.

As used in this Chapter:

(1) "Person" shall mean any individual, firm, corporation, partnership or association.

(2) "Dealer" shall mean any person engaged in the business of buying, selling or exchanging motor vehicles which are subject to license under Chapter 4 of the Subtitle II of Title 47 of the Louisiana Revised Statutes of 1950.

The term dealer shall also mean any person engaged in the business of buying, selling or exchanging used parts or used accessories of motor vehicles.

Any person who buys, sells, or deals in ten or more motor vehicles in any twelve month period shall be prima facie presumed to be engaged in such business.

The term "Dealer" does not include: public officers while performing their official duties; receivers, trustees, administrators, executors, guardians or other persons appointed by or acting under the judgment or order of any court; banks, finance companies or other loan agencies that acquire motor vehicles as an incident to their regular business; motor vehicle rental and leasing companies that sell motor vehicles to motor vehicle dealers licensed under this Section; and bona fide fleet purchasers of motor vehicles.

(3) "User" shall mean any person who acquires a vehicle for purposes other than resale and is required to register same under the provisions of the Louisiana Vehicle Registration License Tax Law, Chapter 4 of Subtitle II of Title 47 of the Louisiana Revised Statutes of 1950.

(4) "Commissioner" shall mean the director of public safety as provided for in Section 1301 of Title 40 of the Louisiana Revised Statutes of 1950, who, in addition to all other powers granted and duties imposed by law, shall have all powers granted and perform such duties as are imposed on the commissioner by this chapter.

Any duly authorized representative of the commissioner when acting under his authority and direction, shall have the same power as is conferred on the commissioner by this chapter.

(5) The term "floor plan loan" shall mean any loan made to a licensed vehicle dealer and secured by a chattel mortgage entered into prior to the effective date [January 1, 1990]* of Chapter 9 of the Louisiana Commercial Laws (R.S. 10:9–101, et seq.) which constitute a part of the dealer's stock in trade, and which may change in specifics, held for sale in the ordinary course of business.

**Matter in brackets editorially supplied.*

(6) The term "manufacturer" means any person regularly engaged in the business of manufacturing or assembling new motor vehicles, either within or without this state.

(7) The term "manufacturer's certificate" means a certificate on a form to be prescribed by the commissioner, and furnished by the manufacturer, showing the original transfer of a new vehicle from the manufacturer to the original purchaser, and each subsequent transfer between distributor and dealer, dealer and dealer, and dealer to owner, through and including the transfer to the title applicant.

(8) The term "salesman" shall mean any person who for a compensation of valuable consideration is employed or engaged either directly or indirectly by a "dealer" to sell or offer to sell, buy or offer to buy, exchange or offer to exchange, or negotiate the purchase or sale or exchange, or assist in negotiating the purchase or sale or exchange, either as a whole or partial vocation, of motor vehicles which are subject to license under Chapter 4 or Subtitle II of Title 47 of the Louisiana Revised Statutes of 1950.

(9) The term "vehicle" shall include those devices sometimes referred to as mobile homes as defined in R.S. 9:1149.2(3), whether or not they may be required to be registered or licensed under other laws, and except as otherwise expressly provided herein, the provisions of this Chapter shall apply to the sale and mortgaging thereof. Neither the inclusion or exclusion of any property in or from the definition of vehicle for purposes of this Chapter, nor any other provision in this Chapter, is intended to affect in any way the status, as determined under other laws, of such property for purposes of ad valorem property taxation, or for any other taxes presently levied, or for the purposes of insurance classification.

(10) The term "certificate of salvage" shall mean a certificate used to evidence the transfer of a "total loss" motor vehicle as provided in this Chapter, to be prescribed and distributed by the office of motor vehicles, to an insurance company, its authorized agent, or the owner of a "total loss" motor vehicle.

(11) The term "total loss" means a motor vehicle which has sustained damages equivalent to seventy-five percent or more of the market value as determined by the most current National Automobile Dealers Association Handbook.

(12) "Auto title company" means any person, firm, association, or corporation which is engaged primarily in the transfer and recordation of sales, leases, or mortgages of vehicles including but not limited to mobile homes, trailers, and motor vehicles. The term "auto title company" also means any person, firm, association, or corporation which has been licensed in accordance with the provisions of R.S. 32:735 et seq. An auto title company shall not mean an insurance company transferring titles to wrecked vehicles, or a licensed motor vehicle dealer, lending institution, financial institution regulated by state or federal authorities, notary, attorney, or individual applicant unless it or he is doing business as an auto title company.

(13) "Antique vehicle" shall mean a vehicle twenty-five years old or older.

(Chgd. by Acts 1990 No. 964, §1; Acts 1993 No. 737, §1, No. 1005, §1, eff. 8/15/93.)

§703. Offices of commissioner.

The vehicle commissioner shall maintain an office in the State Capitol at Baton Rouge and such other places in this state as he shall deem necessary, to properly carry out the provisions of this Chapter. The custodian of the capitol building shall provide therein adequate quarters for the offices and records of the vehicle commissioner.

§703.1. *(Repealed by Acts 1997 No. 1116, §2, eff. 8/15/97.)*

§704. Applicability.

A. The provisions of this Chapter shall apply to the sale and chattel mortgaging of and the granting of a security interest on vehicles of the sort and kind required to be registered and licensed under the provisions of Chapter 4 of Subtitle II of Title 47 of the Louisiana Revised Statutes of 1950, and prior to the time Chapter 9 of the Louisiana Commercial Laws (R.S. 10:9–101, et seq.) becomes effective [January 1, 1990]*, to the chattel mortgaging of vehicles by dealers to secure floor plan loans, except that there is specifically excluded from the provisions of this Chapter the sale, but not the chattel mortgaging of or the granting of a security interest on a new vehicle prior to the first sale of such new vehicle to a user, as defined herein. Such exclusion, however, does not exempt from the provisions of this Chapter such first sale made to a user as defined herein. Floor plan loans entered into after Chapter 9 of the Louisiana Commercial Laws become effective may be secured as provided therein.

**Matter in brackets editorially supplied.*

B. This Chapter does not apply to the mortgaging of movables by corporations for the purposes of and under the provisions contained in R.S. 12:701 and R.S. 12:702.

C. The Department of Public Safety and Corrections shall promulgate rules and regulations to govern this Chapter pursuant to R.S. 49:950 et seq.

(Chgd. by Acts 1990 No. 964, §1, eff. 9/7/90.)

§705. Delivery of certificate to purchaser of vehicle.

A. No person shall sell a vehicle without delivery to the purchaser thereof, whether such purchaser be a dealer or otherwise, a certificate of title issued under this Chapter in the name of the seller with such signed endorsement of sale and assignment thereon as may be necessary to show title in the purchaser; provided:

(1) A bonded dealer shall provide the purchaser the certificate of title within twenty days.

(2) A dealer who is reselling a vehicle that he purchased for stock purposes from an owner who, at the time of such purchase, delivered to the dealer an existing certificate of title issued under this Chapter in the name of such owner, properly endorsed, may, in lieu of applying for and obtaining a new certificate of title in his own, the dealer's, name, and delivering the same to the purchaser, instead execute a resale and reassignment of such existing certificate of title, with warranty of title.

(3) A dealer who is reselling a vehicle that he purchased for stock purposes, and for which no certificate of title exists under this Chapter shall, in lieu of applying for and obtaining a certificate of title in his own, the dealer's, name, and delivering same to the purchaser, note the fact of nonexistence and the reasons therefor, including name and address of the party, whether factory, distributor, or other person, from whom the vehicle was obtained, on a form to be prescribed and furnished by the commissioner, and deliver said form duly signed to such purchaser at the time of sale; however, as to vehicles of the model year 1957 or any later model year, the dealer shall, if the vehicle is of the model year current at the time, in lieu of furnishing said form, deliver to such purchaser at the time of sale a "manufacturer's certificate" duly endorsed to the applicant.

(4) A dealer who is selling a vehicle that was consigned to him for sale by the registered owner may, in lieu of applying for and obtaining a new certificate of title in the dealer's own name, and delivering the same to the purchaser, execute a sale and reassignment of such existing certificate of title, with warranty of title if:

(a) There is a written agreement between the dealer and the consignor, executed on a form provided or approved by the commissioner, as to the terms and conditions of the consignment.

(b) Pursuant to the consignment agreement, the consignor has assigned title to the dealer.

(c) There are no liens or encumbrances affecting the vehicle except those about which the purchaser is actually and specifically informed.

B. For purposes of this Section, an "endorsement" means either of the following:

(1) The signature of the seller in the presence of a notary who shall subscribe his name thereon.

(2) The signature of the seller in the presence of two witnesses who shall subscribe their names thereon, which signature shall be acknowledged by a subscribing witness in substantially the following manner:

ACKNOWLEDGMENT OF WITNESS

State of Louisiana
Parish of_________

Before me, personally came and appeared the undersigned, who, after being duly sworn, said that he subscribed his name to the certificate of title as a witness to the signature(s) of seller(s) and he saw seller(s) sign his name as his voluntary act and deed.

______________________ ______________________
(Witness) Notary Public

C. All new certificates of title issued by the Department of Public Safety and Corrections, office of motor vehicles, shall include thereon language not inconsistent with the provisions of Subsection B hereof.

(Chgd. by Acts 1992 No. 1082, §1, eff. 7/1/93.)

§706. Marketable title.

A. On and after December 15, 1950, except as provided in R.S. 32:705 and 32:712, no person buying a vehicle from the owner thereof, whether such owner be a dealer or otherwise, hereafter shall acquire a marketable title in or to the vehicle until the purchaser shall have obtained a certificate of title to the vehicle; however, neither the foregoing nor any other provisions of this Vehicle Certificate of Title Law shall be construed to have the effect of delaying, suspending or preventing the negotiation of a note secured by a chattel mortgage or security interest on a vehicle from being complete until the purchaser shall have obtained a certificate of title to the vehicle, the actual intention and effect of this section being that such a chattel mortgage or security interest filed before September 1, 1990, shall be complete and effective as to all persons from the time of its execution by the parties if the mortgage or security agreement or a financing statement in the form approved by the commissioner is received and such receipt is validated by the office of the commissioner within fifteen days after such date of execution.

B. In the case of an authentic act of mortgage, the time of execution shall be the date of execution before a notary public or other duly authorized officer and, if by duly acknowledged private act of mortgage, the date of signing by the parties shall be the time of execution.

C. Until September 1, 1990, if the chattel mortgage, security agreement, or financing statement is not received and such receipt is not validated by the office of the commissioner within fifteen days after such date of execution it shall be complete and effective as to all persons from the date of notation of the chattel mortgage or security interest on the face of the certificate of title for such vehicle by the commissioner.

D. Notwithstanding the foregoing provisions, any security interest affecting a titled motor vehicle under a security agreement or financing statement filed hereunder on or after September 1, 1990, shall be complete and effective as to all persons and shall take its rank and priority as provided in Chapter 9 of the Louisiana Commercial Laws, R.S. 10:9–101, et seq. A financing statement is filed when received and such receipt is validated by the secretary of the department.

E. The transfer of ownership of vehicles shall be governed by the following provisions:

(1) Except as otherwise provided in this Subsection, no person shall sell, exchange, donate, or otherwise transfer any ownership interest in any vehicle unless a title to that vehicle has been issued in that person's name.

(2) The provisions of this Section shall not apply to circumstances in which the title to a vehicle has been issued in the name of a person who is deceased. The provisions of R.S. 32:707.1 shall continue to apply to those circumstances.

(3) The provisions of this Section shall not apply to licensed new or used motor vehicle dealers, and supervised financial organizations or licensed lenders as defined in R.S. 9:3516, when they acquire or dispose of such vehicles in connection with enforcement of any security interest held therein.

(4) Whoever violates the provisions of this Subsection shall be fined not more than one thousand dollars, or imprisoned for not more than six months, or both.

(5) Each person to whom an ownership interest in a vehicle is transferred in violation of the provisions of this Subsection shall be entitled to rescind the contract of transfer, shall be entitled to the return of any consideration paid or delivered by that person as part of the contract of transfer, and shall be entitled to reimbursement for any taxes and fees paid by that person in connection with the transfer of ownership of the vehicle. In addition, should the person to whom an ownership interest in a vehicle is transferred in violation of the provisions of this Subsection be forced to file a civil action in order to enforce the remedies provided by this Subsection, that person shall be entitled to reasonable attorney fees.

(Chgd. by Acts 1990 No. 1079, §5; Acts 1995 No. 791, §1, eff. 8/15/95.)

§706.1. Disclosure by persons who transfer ownership of vehicles with salvage or reconstructed titles.

A. Each person who sells, exchanges, donates, or otherwise transfers any interest in any vehicle for which a salvage title or a reconstructed title has been issued shall disclose the existence of that title to the prospective purchaser, recipient in exchange, recipient by donation, or recipient by other act of transfer. The disclosure shall be made by a conspicuous written document, and shall be made prior to the completion of the sale, exchange, donation, or other act of transfer.

B. If any person sells, exchanges, donates, or otherwise transfers any interest in any vehicle for which a salvage title or a reconstructed title has been issued and does not make the disclosures required by this Section, the person to whom the interest in that vehicle was transferred may demand the rescission of the sale, exchange, donation, or other act of transfer, and, in that event, shall be entitled to recover the price or other consideration for the transaction and any fees or taxes paid to any governmental agency in connection with that transaction.
(Added by Acts 1995 No. 848, §1, eff. 8/15/95.)

§707. Application for certificates of title; exception; salvage title; antique vehicles; reconstructed title.

A. Any purchaser of a vehicle, other than a mobile home, as defined by R.S. 9:1149.2(3), shall file an application for a new certificate of title within five days after the delivery of a previously issued certificate of title for such vehicle, or within five days of the delivery of the vehicle, if a certificate of title has not been previously issued. However, dealers need not apply for certificates of title for any vehicle acquired for stock purposes, if upon reselling such vehicle, the dealer complies with the requirements of R.S. 32:705. A purchaser of a mobile home, as defined by R.S. 9:1149.2(3), shall apply for a new certificate of title on or before the twentieth day of the month following the month of delivery of the home.

B. Application for a certificate of title shall be made upon a form to be prescribed by the secretary of the Department of Public Safety and Corrections, and shall be filed with the secretary of the Department of Public Safety and Corrections. Such application shall be accompanied by the fee prescribed in this Chapter, except where the secretary of the Department of Public Safety and Corrections has received an authorization from the secretary of the Department of Revenue under the provisions of R.S. 47:303(B)(5). If a certificate of title has previously been issued for such vehicle in this state, such application shall be accompanied by said certificate of title duly endorsed with the sale and assignment or duly endorsed with sale and assignment and resale and reassignment, unless otherwise provided for in this Chapter.

C. For the purposes of this Chapter, the commissioner or his aides and assistants, shall be qualified to take the acknowledgments herein required, for which no charge shall be made.

D. (1) If a certificate of title has not previously been issued for such vehicle in this state, said application, unless otherwise provided for in this Chapter, shall be accompanied by:

(a) A proper bill of sale, or sworn statement of ownership, or a duly certified copy thereof, or such other evidence of ownership as the commissioner may in his discretion require; or

(b) By a certificate of title, bill of sale or other evidence of ownership required by the law of another state from which such vehicle was brought into this state;

(2) As to vehicles of the model year 1957 or any later model year, if the vehicle is of the model year current at the time, and the application is not accompanied by a certificate of title issued under the law of another state, the application must, in addition to the foregoing, also be accompanied by a "manufacturer's certificate" as herein defined.

(3) Applications of a certificate of title for motor vehicles as defined in R.S. 32:1252(1), except a chassis cab purchased by truck equipment installers who are considered final stage manufacturers by the National Highway Traffic Safety Administration and the United States Department of Transportation, for the purpose of installing heavy duty mechanized truck mounted machinery and subsequent resale only, which are required to be accompanied by a manufacturer's certificate by this Subsection, shall also be accompanied by a final and proper bill of sale to the applicant from a motor vehicle dealer licensed by the Louisiana Motor Vehicle Commission to sell that brand of motor vehicle. The provisions of this Subsection shall apply only to sellers doing business and/or domiciled in this state.

E. Upon application for certificate of title of a vehicle previously titled or registered outside of this state, the application shall show on its face such fact and the time and place of the last issuance of certificate of title, or registration, or such vehicle outside this state, and the name and address of the governmental officer, agency, or authority making such registration, together with such further information relative to its previous registration, together with such further information relative to its previous registration as may reasonably be required by the commissioner, including the time and place of original registration, if known, and if different from such last foreign registration. The applicant shall surrender to the commissioner all unexpired seals, certificates, registration cards, or other evidence of foreign registration pertaining to the vehicles. The certificate of title issued by the commissioner for a vehicle previously registered outside the state shall give the name of the state or country in which such vehicle was last previously registered outside this state.

F. Where in the course of interstate operation of a vehicle registered in another state it is desirable to retain registration of said vehicle, in such other state, such applicant need not surrender but shall exhibit said evidences of such foreign registration and the commissioner, upon a proper showing, shall register said vehicle in this state but shall not issue a certificate of title for such vehicle.

G. The commissioner shall retain the evidence of title presented by every applicant and on which the certificate of title is issued. The commissioner shall use reasonable diligence in ascertaining whether or not the facts in said application are true by checking the application and documents accompanying same with the records of vehicles in his office, and, if satisfied that the applicant is the owner of such vehicle and that the application is in the proper form he shall issue a certificate of title over his signature, but not otherwise.

H. The purchaser of a used vehicle from a private individual, for a period of sixty days, shall be protected from citations for failure to have a current license tag during the interval between the date of purchase and the receipt of title, provided proof of application can be shown.

I. (1) If, as a result of a "total loss", as defined in R.S. 32:702(11), insurance settlement on a motor vehicle, the vehicle is transferred as a total loss, the insurance company, its authorized agent, or the vehicle owner shall, within thirty days from the settlement of the property damages claim, send the certificate of title to the office of motor vehicles along with an application for a salvage title in the name of the insurance company, or its authorized agent, or the vehicle owner. Upon receipt of the salvage title, the insurance company, its authorized agent, or the vehicle owner may proceed to dismantle the vehicle, sell it, or rebuild and restore it to operation. A rebuilder of a salvaged title motor vehicle may upon completion of rebuilding the vehicle demonstrate the rebuilt motor vehicle to a prospective purchaser without applying for a reconstructed vehicle title. Except for the purposes of this demonstration, no rebuilt and restored vehicle shall be operated upon any public street, roadway, or highway until it is registered with the office of motor vehicles, and a reconstructed vehicle title is issued.

(2) No further documentation is required for dismantling; however, the dismantler shall retain possession of the salvage title for five years following dismantling. The vehicle may be sold, assigned, or donated by endorsing the salvage title and delivering it along with the vehicle to the new owner; however, dealers, salvage pools, and dismantlers shall keep a register of such transfers.

J. (1) If a vehicle with a salvage title is rebuilt and restored to operation, such vehicle shall not be titled and registered for operation until a certificate of inspection is submitted to office of motor vehicles by a member of the city, parish, or state police force, authorized by the police chief, sheriff, or commander to make such inspections.

(2) On receipt of the required certificate of inspection and the salvage title, together with receipts for the major component parts that have been replaced on the vehicle, the office of motor vehicles shall issue a new certificate of title, which shall indicate on its face it has been reconstructed.

K. The office of motor vehicles, may assess civil penalties of up to one thousand dollars per violation in accordance with the Administrative Procedure Act* to anyone who has sold or dismantled a total loss vehicle in violation of this Section.

**R.S. 49:950 et seq.*

L. The office of motor vehicles shall issue a certificate of title for antique, classic, or vintage vehicles as defined in this Chapter when there is no current record of ownership to base the issuance of a new title on, provided:

(1) The applicant has provided to the office of motor vehicles a statement from the state police auto theft division obtained by a local law enforcement agency confirming that based upon a check by photo or rub of a vehicle body identification plate the vehicle is not listed as stolen.

(2) The sales tax based upon purchase price is paid.

(3) The applicant has provided a statement attesting to his membership in an organized automobile club.

M. (1) Notwithstanding any provision of law to the contrary, the office of motor vehicles shall issue to a person in good faith possession of a vehicle a certificate of title for the vehicle even if there is no bill of sale and no current record of ownership upon which to base the issuance of a new title, provided:

(a) The vehicle is twenty-five years old or older.

(b) The vehicle has not had its registration renewed in this state or any other state for a period of three years immediately prior to the application for the title.

(c) The applicant has submitted the sworn affidavit or affidavits of two people who shall attest on their own personal knowledge that the vehicle has been abandoned for three or more years.

(d) The applicant has provided to the office of motor vehicles a statement from the state police auto theft division obtained by a local law enforcement agency confirming that, based upon a check by photo or rub of a vehicle body identification plate, the vehicle is not listed as stolen.

(e) The person is not otherwise subject to the provisions of Chapter 4-A of this Title.

(2) The applicant for the title shall apply to the office of motor vehicles for registration. No title shall be issued for one year, during which time the applicant may have the vehicle in his possession, but shall not have official title to the vehicle. If, at the end of one year, no one has proven ownership of the vehicle, the applicant shall be issued a certificate of title.
(Chgd. by Acts 1990 No. 823, §1, No. 1079, §5; Acts 1992 No. 273, §1; Acts 1993 No. 20, §1; Acts 1997 No. 272, §1, eff. 7/1/97, No. 872, §1, eff. 7/10/97.)

§707.1. Deceased persons; titles to vehicles.

A. The office of motor vehicles shall establish a procedure by which surviving spouses, heirs, and legatees of deceased persons may obtain title to a vehicle or vehicles which is, or are, titled in the name of the deceased person.

B. The procedure established under the provisions of this Section shall contain but shall not be limited to the following provisions:

(1) Any person who has an ownership interest in a vehicle which is titled in the name of a deceased person may apply for a title to the vehicle.

(2) The applicant shall attach to the application a copy of the death certificate of the deceased person, or other proof of death acceptable to the office of motor vehicles.

(3) The applicant shall attach to the application either a copy of the will, if any, which was executed by the deceased person or a notarized statement summarizing the disposition of vehicles contained in the will.

(4) The applicant shall attach to the application the title and the registration certificate of the vehicle, if available. If the title or registration certificate is not available, the applicant shall include a declaration of that fact in the affidavit executed by the applicant under Paragraph (5) of this Subsection.

(5) The applicant and each other person who has an ownership interest in the vehicle shall execute an affidavit which shall contain:

(a) A declaration establishing the relationship of each affiant to the deceased person.

(b) A declaration of each affiant's knowledge, or lack of knowledge, of a will executed by the deceased person.

(c) A declaration by each affiant, other than the applicant, by which the affiant donates, sells or otherwise transfers to the applicant all ownership interest which the affiant has in the vehicle.

(6) The affidavits required by Paragraph (5) above may be executed in one or more documents. The affidavits shall be attached to the application.

(7) The office of motor vehicles may require applicants and other persons who have an ownership interest in the vehicle to provide specific information, or to make specific declarations, or to submit copies of specific documents in connection with applications for titles under the provisions of this Section. The information, declarations, or documents of this Paragraph shall be limited to information, declarations, and documents which are necessary to insure the integrity of the title to the vehicle.

C. The office of motor vehicles shall adopt administrative rules to implement the provisions of this Section. The rules shall be adopted in accordance with the provisions of the Administrative Procedure Act*.
(Added by Acts 1992 No. 992, §1, eff. 7/9/92.)
**R.S. 49:950 et seq.*

§708. Issuance of certificates; satisfaction of lien or security interest; security measures.

A. The commissioner, when issuing a certificate of title or a corrected certificate, shall maintain sufficient records and information in his possession to produce a duplicate copy of the certificate of title or the corrected certificate of title. Where there are no liens shown on the title certificate, such certificate shall be signed by the motor vehicle commissioner and forwarded to the applicant. When a lien is shown in the certificate, the certificate of title, which shall be signed by the motor vehicle commissioner, shall be forwarded to the lien holder of first rank who shall retain it until the full amount of such mortgage is liquidated. The first lien holder shall then deliver the title with proper release of the lien executed in the title to the registered owner if no other lien exists, or to the next ranking lien holder as shown in the files of the commissioner.

B. (1) Upon the final discharge of any chattel mortgage or security interest, the owner or any lien holder may present the certificate of title with the fee prescribed by law, if not prepaid, to the commissioner and request that the commissioner note on the face of the certificate of title and his records a cancellation of notation of said lien so endorsed as satisfied by the holder thereof on the face of the certificate of title. The commissioner shall comply with such request, if the satisfaction appears genuine.

(2) When the certificate of title endorsed to evidence satisfaction of a lien noted thereon has been lost or stolen, the commissioner may issue a duplicate certificate of title noted on its face to show cancellation of notice of lien so endorsed, only when all the following conditions have been satisfied:

(a) The owner establishes to the satisfaction of the commissioner on a form satisfactory to him, that he is unable to obtain a duplicate certificate of title endorsed by the lien holder as provided in Paragraph (1) of this Subsection, due to the fact that the lien holder is no longer in existence.

(b) The secured party of record has filed a termination statement as provided in R.S. 10:9–404.

C. The commissioner, when issuing a certificate of title, or a duplicate certificate, for a motor vehicle shall use security procedures, processes, and materials in the preparation and issuance of each certificate of title to prevent, to the greatest extent possible, the ability of a person to alter, counterfeit, duplicate, or modify the certificate of title. The commissioner shall charge an additional fee of fifty cents per certificate of title or duplicate certificate to cover the cost of security measures.

(Chgd. by Acts 1990 No. 917, §1, No. 1079, §5; Acts 1995 No. 1201, §4, eff. 6/29/95.)

§709. Numbers assigned; indices; files.

The commissioner shall assign a number for each certificate of title and shall maintain in his office indices for such certificates of title. The commissioner shall not be required to retain on file any bill of sale or duplicate thereof covering any vehicle for a period longer than seven years after the date of the filing thereof and thereafter the same may be destroyed.

§710. Chattel mortgages, form and contents; priority; notation on certificate; fraud; enforcement.

On and after December 15, 1950, until the time Chapter 9 of the Louisiana Commercial Laws (R.S. 10:9–101, et seq.) becomes effective [January 1, 1990]*, the sole and exclusive method of executing and recording chattel mortgages and the priority of such mortgages which are subject to this Chapter, shall be through compliance with the provisions of this Chapter. All other chattel mortgages do not come within the provisions of this Chapter and shall continue to be governed exclusively by existing laws, particularly R.S. 9:5351–9:5365.

A. (1) Every chattel mortgage subject to this Chapter, except as hereinafter provided for floor plan loans, entered into prior to the time Chapter 9 of the Louisiana Commercial Laws (R.S. 10:9–101, et seq.) becomes effective [January 1, 1990]*, shall be in writing and the obligation secured thereby shall be described, and there shall also be stated whether the same be payable on demand or at what fixed or determinable future time, and a full description of the vehicle to be mortgaged or encumbered, must be set forth, including the following data insofar as it may exist with respect to the particular vehicle:

(a) The make,

(b) The year (as designated by the manufacturer),

(c) The model,

(d) The type of body,

(e) The motor number, if a year model prior to 1957,

(f) The manufacturer's serial or identification number,

(g) The license number and year of the Louisiana plates currently in effect on the vehicle at the date of the mortgage, and

(h) The location at which the mortgaged or secured vehicle will be primarily kept when not in use elsewhere; provided, that the failure to recite the location of the vehicle shall not affect the validity of the mortgage.

(2) (a) Every chattel mortgage given by a dealer to secure a floor plan loan shall be in writing and the obligations secured thereby shall be described and the exact sum secured thereby shall be stated, or, if the same is to secure future advances then the maximum amount thereof, shall be stated, and there shall also be stated whether the same be payable on demand or at what fixed or determinable future time.

(b) For the purposes of floor plan loans, it shall be lawful to mortgage in bulk, but changing in specific, the entire new or used or both motor vehicle inventory of a dealer, even though the same may not be all of a similar nature or kind, and even though the motor vehicles be described as a mass or assemblage of vehicles or as a stock or inventory of vehicles to be sold in the ordinary course of business at a specified place or specified places of business of the dealer in the ordinary course of business.

(c) Nothing of the above is to preclude a dealer from entering into a floor plan mortgage which specifies the parts of vehicles to be covered by such mortgage.

B. (1)(a) In order to affect third persons, a chattel mortgage executed prior to the time Chapter 9 of the Louisiana Commercial Laws (R.S. 10:9–101, et seq.) becomes effective [January 1, 1990]* must be by authentic act or by private act duly authenticated in any manner provided by law. A security agreement subject to Chapter 9 of the Louisiana Commercial Laws (R.S. 10:9–101, et seq.) affecting a titled motor vehicle subject to this Chapter is not required to be witnessed or notarized.

(b) Until September 1, 1990, every such chattel mortgage other than one securing a floor plan loan, as well as every security agreement covering a titled motor vehicle subject to this Chapter, shall be effective as against third persons as of the time of its execution by the parties if the chattel mortgage or security agreement or a financing statement in the form approved by the commissioner is received and such receipt is validated by the secretary of the Department of Public Safety and Corrections within fifteen days after such date of execution. However, in the case of an authentic act of mortgage, the time of execution shall be the date of execution before a notary public or other duly authorized officer; but if by duly acknowledged private act of mortgage, the date of signing by the parties shall be the time of execution. The date on which a security agreement subject to Chapter 9 of the Louisiana Commercial Laws (R.S. 10:9–101, et seq.) is signed by the debtor shall be the time of execution for purposes of this Subsection.

(c) Until September 1, 1990, if the chattel mortgage, security agreement or financing statement is not received and such receipt is not validated by the secretary of the Department of Public Safety within fifteen days after such date of execution, it shall be effective as to all persons from the date such chattel mortgage, security agreement or financing statement is delivered to the secretary, and the same shall be superior in rank to any privilege or preference arising subsequently thereto.

(d) The secretary shall, upon the request of any person, issue a certification whenever the chattel mortgage, security agreement or financing statement is delivered to his office. Such certification receipt may include one or more chattel mortgage or security agreement applications.

(e) All mortgages or security interests filed on and before August 31, 1990, noted upon a certificate of title shall take priority according to the order of time in which same have been effective as provided in this Subsection B. Security interests affecting titled motor vehicles, perfected by filing with the Department of Public Safety and Corrections, office of motor vehicles on and after September 1, 1990, shall take priority in accordance with Chapter 9 of the Louisiana Commercial Law.

(2) (a) A floor plan mortgage shall be effective against third persons as of the time it is executed if it is received and such receipt is validated by the secretary of the Department of Public Safety within fifteen days after such date of execution; otherwise, it shall be effective as of the time it is entered in the register of floor plan mortgages by the commissioner or his duly authorized representative.

(b) A mortgage given by a dealer to secure a floor plan loan may be by authentic act, by private act duly authenticated, or by act under private signature.

(c) Every mortgage given by a dealer to secure a floor plan loan by act under private signature shall contain an accurate description of the note or other evidence of indebtedness and need not be paraphed by a notary.

C. The holders of mortgages on motor vehicles, who expressly or impliedly consent to such vehicles being placed on sale by the owners thereof in the State of Louisiana in the ordinary course of business shall be precluded from asserting the said floor plan mortgage or the lien created by it against bona fide retail purchasers in actual good faith of said vehicles. Holders of such mortgages shall be deemed to have impliedly consented to sales of the mortgaged property free and clear of such mortgages to bona fide retail purchasers in actual good faith whenever the mortgagor is a dealer duly licensed to sell the type of vehicles covered by the floor plan mortgage. Such consent may not be negated or withheld by any express provision in the mortgage when the mortgagor holds such an occupational license. For purposes of this section, a bona fide retail purchaser in actual good faith shall be deemed to be any person, firm, partnership or corporation purchasing a vehicle, for individual or business use and not for resale from a licensed dealer, who does not in fact know of a mortgage existing on the property purchased; provided, however, that the holders of mortgages on vehicles who expressly or impliedly consent to such vehicles being placed on sale by the owner thereof in the ordinary course of business shall not be precluded from asserting said mortgage or the lien created by it against group or bulk purchases whether said purchase is in good faith or not.

D. The holder of a chattel mortgage or security interest covering a vehicle, upon presentation of a multiple original or certified copy of such act of mortgage or a multiple original, or photographic copy of the debtor's security agreement or financing statement, together with any respective certificate of title issued in this state or, if no certificate of title exists on such vehicle in this state, together with a proper application for certificate of title pursuant to the provisions of this Chapter, and the fee prescribed by law, may have a notation of such chattel mortgage or security interest made on the face of such certificate of title in the order in which it was filed. The commissioner shall enter said notation over his signature and seal of office, and he also shall note such chattel mortgage or security interest and the date receipt thereof was validated, on the duplicate of said certificate in his file. The commissioner also shall indicate by appropriate notation on the instrument itself the fact that such chattel mortgage or security interest has been noted on the certificate of title.

E. When such chattel mortgage or security interest is discharged, the requirements of R.S. 32:708, Subsection B, shall be complied with.

F. (1) Provided, however, that the effect of the notation of the chattel mortgage or security interest filed on or before August 31, 1990, or of the registration of the floor plan mortgage by the commissioner shall cease if the notation or registration thereof has not been renewed in the same manner in which it was first made by the commissioner within one year after the date of the last installment provided for in such mortgage or security agreement or within six years after the date of execution of the act of mortgage or of the security agreement, whichever date is later. Such renewal shall renew the effect of the mortgage or security interest for the amount unpaid for a period of two years from the date of renewal, and further renewals may be made thereafter from time to time, the effect of each renewal being for two years from its date. The effect of such notation of any security interest affecting a titled motor vehicle, filed on or after September 1, 1990, shall cease only upon satisfaction as provided in R.S. 32:708(B).

(2) Notwithstanding any other provision of law to the contrary, on or after September 1, 1990, the sole method of reinscribing a chattel mortgage, security agreement, financing statement, or notice of security interest affecting a titled motor vehicle, effective as to third persons, shall be by filing with the commissioner a continuation statement under R.S. 10:9–403. Such a continuation statement need be signed only by the mortgagee/secured party and must include the information set forth in R.S. 9:5356(J)(1)(a) through (g), and may be filed at any time within the applicable time period established in Subparagraph (1) above. Upon timely filing of the continuation statement, the effectiveness of the original inscription is continued until satisfaction thereof as provided in R.S. 32:708(B).

(3) Notwithstanding any other provision of law to the contrary, on or after September 1, 1990, the sole method of reinscribing a floor plan mortgage originally subject to this Chapter prior to January 1, 1990 (the effective date of Chapter 9 of the Louisiana Commercial Laws, R.S. 10:9–101, et seq.), shall be by filing a continuation statement under R.S. 10:9–403 in the location provided in R.S. 10:9–401(1)(b) without regard to R.S. 10:9–401(2). Such a continuation statement need be signed only by the mortgagee/secured party and must include the information set forth in R.S. 9:5356(J)(1)(a) through (g), and may be filed at any time within the applicable time period established in Subparagraph (1) above. Upon timely filing of the continuation statement, the effectiveness of the original inscription is continued for

five years after the date of filing of the continuation statement, notwithstanding R.S. 32:710(F)(1) or any other provision of law to the contrary, whereupon the original floor plan mortgage inscription lapses unless another continuation statement is filed within six months prior to such lapse in accordance with R.S. 10:9–403. Succeeding continuation statements may be filed within six months prior to the expiration of each five-year period in the same manner to continue the effectiveness of the inscription of the original floor plan mortgage.

G. Any person who, having executed a mortgage or granted a security interest on a vehicle, sells, assigns, exchanges, injures, destroys, conceals, or otherwise disposes of any part of the vehicle with fraudulent intent to defeat the mortgage or security interest, or removes the vehicle from the state without the written consent of the mortgagee or secured party and with fraudulent intent to defeat the mortgage or security interest, shall be guilty of a misdemeanor and shall be fined not more than five hundred dollars, or imprisoned for not more than six months, or both.

H. If any person shall fraudulently give or attempt to give a mortgage or security interest on a vehicle without being the lawful owner, or without having the proper authority to represent the lawful owner of said vehicle, or if any person shall fraudulently give a mortgage or security interest under this Chapter or under Chapter 9 of the Louisiana Commercial Laws without fully disclosing the description and amount of any existing liens, privileges or encumbrances on the vehicle mortgaged, he shall be deemed guilty of a misdemeanor and shall be fined not more than five hundred dollars, or imprisoned for not more than six months, or both.

I. Provided further, that the obligation secured by the act of mortgage or security interest shall, at the option of the creditor or holder of the mortgage note or secured indebtedness, forthwith mature and become due and payable and the mortgagee or secured party shall be entitled to enforce the collection of the obligation secured by the mortgage or security agreement immediately and in the manner provided, in any case where the mortgagor or debtor shall have committed any of the fraudulent practices denounced by Subsection G and H of this Section. These provisions for acceleration of the mortgage or secured debt shall not be construed as excluding the operation of any other statutory provisions, or any lawful stipulation existing between the parties, accelerating the maturity of the obligation secured by the mortgage.

J. If any mortgagee named in a chattel mortgage or secured party named in a security agreement, and not being at the time the owner and holder of the debt secured, shall fraudulently execute a release of satisfaction of said chattel mortgage or security interest, he shall be deemed guilty of a misdemeanor and shall be fined not more than five hundred dollars, or imprisoned for not more than six months, or both.

K. All laws and rules and all remedies and processes, including executory process under confessions of judgment as well as proceedings via ordinaria, now or hereafter made available to creditors for the protection or enforcement of their rights under mortgages affecting immovables are available to creditors of obligations secured by mortgages or security agreements affecting vehicles, whether evidenced by authentic acts or by acts under private signature duly acknowledged, or in the case of a security agreement subject to Chapter 9 of the Louisiana Commercial Laws (R.S. 10:9–101, et seq.), by acts under private signature alone.

L. It shall be unlawful for the owner of a vehicle which is mortgaged or secured under the provisions of this Chapter or under Chapter 9 of the Louisiana Commercial Laws (R.S. 10:9–101, et seq.) to drive, carry, transport, or otherwise move said vehicle permanently beyond the territorial limits of the state of Louisiana without the written consent of the holder of said mortgage or security interest, and whoever shall violate such provisions of this Chapter shall be guilty of a felony and upon conviction thereof shall be sentenced to imprisonment in the state penitentiary for a period not to exceed one year.

M. Nothing in the provisions of this Chapter shall in any way affect the validity of chattel mortgages executed prior to December 15, 1950, or the method of enforcing them.

N. If a dealer executes more than one chattel mortgage on the inventory, the subsequently executed and recorded chattel mortgage shall be inferior in ranking to the prior recorded chattel mortgage except as hereinafter provided:

(1) If the holder of an inferior chattel mortgage gives advance written notice to the superior chattel mortgage holder that the dealer has executed a chattel mortgage on specifically identifiable motor vehicles or mass or assemblage of motor vehicles and such chattel mortgage is properly executed and recorded, such inferior mortgage shall be superior in ranking as to the motor vehicles or property the dealer receives possession of after

execution and recordation of such chattel mortgage on which the holder sells or advances funds for the purchase thereof.

(2) If an assignee or pledgee of a retail installment contract retakes possession of the mortgaged property by judicial foreclosure or otherwise, the mortgaged property may be placed on a dealer's premises with the dealer's permission and thereafter, the property shall not be affected by a prior recorded chattel mortgage not held by the assignee or pledgee covering the dealer's inventory.

O. (1) Notwithstanding the domicile of the grantor of a foreign security interest or Louisiana chattel mortgage, the provisions of this Section shall not apply to a foreign security interest or Louisiana chattel mortgage created and recorded on movable property that is subject to titling under the provisions of a foreign motor vehicle statute, provided that a certificate of title has been issued and clearly shows that a security interest has been created pursuant to the laws of the state in which the title was issued or that a Louisiana chattel mortgage has been recorded on such foreign certificate of title.

(2) However, nothing herein shall be construed to repeal the laws of this state protecting the interests of bona fide retail purchasers of motor vehicles from retail motor vehicle dealers domiciled or doing business in this state, and nothing herein shall be construed to repeal the laws of this state requiring persons to comply with the provisions of Title 32 of the Louisiana Revised Statutes of 1950.

(Chgd. by Acts 1990 No. 1079, §5, eff. 9/1/90.)

**Matter in brackets editorially supplied.*

§711. Sale subject to mortgage or security interest; act of sale and assignment of certificate; corrected certificate.

A. In the event the certificate of title is held by a lien holder and sale is contemplated subject to the existing chattel mortgage or security interest and it is impractical for the owner to produce and deliver the certificate of title at the time possession is delivered to the purchaser, then the owner shall make and deliver to the purchaser at the time of delivery of the vehicle an act of sale of such vehicle and assignment of the certificate of title, subject to all existing chattel mortgages and security interests, on a form to be prescribed and furnished by the commissioner. The purchaser shall within five days of the transaction forward the act of sale and assignment to the commissioner accompanied by the fee prescribed by this Chapter and also accompanied by an application for a certificate of title as hereafter set forth.

B. Upon receipt of the act of sale and assignment and the application, the commissioner shall notify all lien holders in writing of the sale and request the holder of the certificate of title to surrender it, and shall issue in lieu thereof a corrected certificate of title in the name of the new owner and deliver it to the first ranking mortgage holder or owner. The corrected certificate of title shall show on its face all existing chattel mortgages or security interests. It shall be the duty of any holder of a certificate of title, on request of the commissioner, to return same, within five days, in order that correction might be made thereon; provided however, the provisions of this Section shall not be construed as impairing any rights which a mortgage or lien holder may have by virtue of a chattel which existed prior to December 15, 1950.

§712. Ownership of vehicle passing otherwise than by voluntary transfer.

On and after December 15, 1950, whenever the ownership of any vehicle shall pass otherwise than by voluntary transfer, the new owner shall obtain a certificate of title therefor upon presentation of an application for certificate of title and payment of the fee prescribed by this Chapter, accompanied by the prior certificate, if possible, and accompanied by such instruments or documents of authority, or certified copies thereof, as may be required by law to evidence or effect a transfer of title in movables in such case. If the applicant obtains possession of a vehicle in accordance with the provisions of R.S. 6:965 et seq., he must present a certified copy of the order entitling him to take possession of the vehicle and an affidavit of possession verifying that he has, in fact, obtained possession of the vehicle in accordance with the terms of the judgment. The commissioner, when satisfied of the genuineness of regularity of such transfer, shall issue a certificate of title to the person entitled thereto. Such certificate of title shall contain a statement of any chattel mortgages of record in the office of the commissioner, unless such application is accompanied by proper evidence of their satisfaction or extinction. *(Chgd. by Acts 1992 No. 235, §3; Acts 1993 No. 927, §2, eff. 8/15/93.)*

§713. Lost or destroyed certificate.

In the event of a lost or destroyed certificate of title, application shall be made to the commissioner by the owner of said vehicle in whose name the original title was issued for a certified copy of the same upon a prescribed form duly sworn to by the owner and accompanied by a fee prescribed by this Chapter. Thereupon the commissioner shall issue a certified copy of said certificate of title to the person entitled to receive the certificate of title under the provisions of this Chapter. Said certified copy and all subsequent certificates of title issued in the chain of title originated by said certified copy shall be plainly marked across their face "duplicate copy", and any subsequent purchaser of said vehicle in the chain of title originating through such certified copy shall acquire only such rights in such vehicle as the original holder of said certified copy himself had. Any purchaser of such vehicle may at the time of such purchase require the seller of same to indemnify him and all subsequent purchasers of said vehicle against any loss which he or they may suffer by reason of any claim or claims presented upon the original certificate. In the event of the recovery of the original certificate of title by said owner, he shall forthwith surrender same to the commissioner for cancellation.

§715. Change of engine in vehicle.

The commissioner is authorized to adopt and enforce such registration rules and regulations with respect to the change or substitution of one engine or motor in place of another in any vehicle as may be deemed necessary and consistent with the purposes of this Chapter.

§716. Dismantling registered vehicle.

Any owner dismantling or wrecking any registered vehicle shall immediately forward to the commissioner the certificate of title or permit to sell, registration card, and the registration plate or plates last issued for such vehicle, whether such plates and documents were issued by the vehicle commissioner of this state or of any other state.

§717. Sale of motor vehicle as scrap.

A. Any owner who sells a motor vehicle as scrap to be dismantled or destroyed shall assign a certificate of title thereto to the purchaser, whether the certificate was issued by the vehicle commissioner of this state or any other state, and the purchaser shall deliver the certificate of title to the commissioner with an application for a permit to dismantle such vehicle. The commissioner shall thereupon issue to the purchaser a permit to dismantle the vehicle, which shall authorize the purchaser to possess or transport the motor vehicle or to transfer ownership thereto by an endorsement upon the permit. A certificate of title shall not again be issued for the motor vehicle in the event it is scrapped, dismantled, or destroyed.

B. Notwithstanding Subsection A, of this Section the commissioner may issue, without the delivery of the certificate of title, a permit to dismantle any vehicle which is more than ten years old and has not had its registration renewed in this state or any other state for a period of three years immediately prior to the application for a permit to dismantle the vehicle.
(Chgd. by Acts 1991 No. 883, §1, eff. 9/6/91.)

§721. Stolen vehicles; report of theft and recovery.

The Department of Public Safety and every sheriff, chief of police, or peace officer upon receiving reliable information that any vehicle registered hereunder has been stolen shall immediately or not later than one week after receiving such information report such theft to the commissioner, unless prior thereto information has been received of the recovery of such vehicle. Any said officer upon receiving information that any vehicle, which he has previously reported as stolen, has been recovered, shall immediately report the fact of such recovery to the local sheriff's office or police department and to the commissioner.

§722. Stolen or embezzled vehicles; liens and encumbrances.

The owner, or person having a lien or encumbrance upon a registered vehicle which has been stolen or embezzled, may notify the commissioner of such theft or embezzlement, but, in the event of an embezzlement, may make such report only after having procured the issuance of a warrant for the arrest of the person charged with such embezzlement. Every owner or other person who has given such notice must notify the commissioner of a recovery of such vehicle.

§723. Stolen or embezzled vehicles; suspension of registration; lists.

A. The commissioner upon receiving a report of a stolen or embezzled vehicle as hereinbefore provided shall file and appropriately index the same and shall immediately suspend the registration of the vehicle so reported and shall not transfer the registration of the same until such time as it is notified in writing that such vehicle has been recovered.

B. The commissioner shall at least once each week compile and mention at his headquarters office a list of all vehicles which have been stolen or embezzled or recovered as reported to it during the preceding week and such lists shall be open to inspection by any peace officer or other person interested in any such vehicle.

§724. Transfer and possession of stolen vehicles.

Any person who, with intent to procure or pass title to a vehicle which he knows or has reason to believe has been stolen or unlawfully taken, received, or transfers possession of the same from one to another, or who has in his possession any vehicle which he knows or has reason to believe has been stolen or unlawfully taken, and who is not an officer of the law engaged at the time in the performance of his duty as such officer, is guilty of a felony.

§725. Concealing or misrepresenting identity of motor vehicle or engine.

Any person who knowingly buys, receives, disposes of, sells, offers for sale, or has in his possession any motor vehicle, or engine removed from a vehicle, from which the manufacturer's serial or engine number or other distinguishing number or identification mark or number placed thereon under assignment from the commissioner has been removed, defaced, covered, altered, or destroyed for the purpose of concealing or misrepresenting the identity of said motor vehicle or engine is guilty of a misdemeanor.

§726. Destruction or alteration of distinguishing number or mark.

A. No person shall with fraudulent intent deface, destroy or alter the manufacturer's serial or engine number or other distinguishing number or identification mark of a motor vehicle nor shall any person place or stamp any serial, engine, or other number or mark upon a motor vehicle, except one assigned thereto by the commissioner. Any violation of this provision is a misdemeanor.

B. This section shall not prohibit the restoration by an owner of an original serial, engine, or other number or mark when such restoration is made under permit issued by the commissioner, nor prevent any manufacturer from placing in the ordinary course of business numbers or marks upon motor vehicles or parts thereof.

§726.1. Tampering with or altering odometers prohibited; penalties.

A. No person shall knowingly tamper with, adjust, alter, change, set back, disconnect or fail to connect the odometer of any motor vehicle, or cause any of the foregoing to occur to an odometer of a motor vehicle, so as to reflect a lower mileage than the true mileage driven by the motor vehicle.

B. No person shall with intent to defraud operate a motor vehicle on any street or highway knowing that the odometer of the motor vehicle is disconnected or nonfunctional.

C. No person shall advertise for sale, sell, use or install on any part of a motor vehicle or on any odometer in a motor vehicle any device which causes the odometer to register any mileage other than the true mileage.

D. In the event any odometer is repaired or replaced, the reading of the repaired or replaced odometer shall be set at the reading of the odometer repaired or replaced immediately prior to repair or replacement, and the adjustment shall not be deemed a violation of any provision of this section. If the odometer cannot be repaired or replaced a written notice shall be posted on the vehicle that the odometer has been reset at zero, the date of the repair and the mileage indicated at the time of repair.

E. No certificate of title shall be issued for a motor vehicle which was equipped with an odometer by the manufacturer unless the statement required in Subsection F of this section has been furnished by the transferor. However, a certificate of title may be issued for a motor vehicle to a person who moves into this state if such person acquired ownership of the motor vehicle prior to moving to this state.

F. Except where a transfer is made by operation of law the transferor of any motor vehicle which was equipped with an odometer by the manufacturer, shall provide to the buyer a statement signed by the transferor which shall set forth the mileage on the odometer at the time of transfer and which shall state that to the transferor's best knowledge and belief it is the true mileage. If the transferor has knowledge that the mileage shown on the odometer is not the true mileage traveled by the motor vehicle, he shall so indicate on the statement and he shall state the true mileage to his best knowledge and belief. The mileage disclosed on such statement shall be included in the application for certificate of title and the new certificate issued in the name of the buyer shall have the mileage recorded on the face thereof.

G. Any transferee of a motor vehicle reassigning the certificate of title to such motor vehicle pursuant to the provisions of the Certificate of Title Law shall not be guilty of a violation of this section if such transferee has in his possession the statement signed by his transferor as required by Subsection F of this section and if he has no knowledge that the odometer does not reflect the true mileage of such motor vehicle.

H. (1) Any person, except a new or used car dealer, who violates the provisions of this Section shall be guilty of a misdemeanor and shall be punished by a fine not to exceed five hundred dollars or by imprisonment not to exceed ninety days or both. On each subsequent conviction, the offender shall be fined not more than fifty thousand dollars, or imprisoned for not more than one year, or both.

(2) A new or used car dealer who violates the provisions of this Section shall be fined not more than fifty thousand dollars, or imprisoned for not more than one year, or both.

(3) A new or used car dealer who violates the provisions of this Section shall be subject to a civil penalty of not more than one thousand dollars.

(Chgd. by Acts 1995 No. 1048, §1, eff. 8/15/95.)

§727. Rules and regulations; forms; cancellation of certificates; copies of and reports as to records.

A. The commissioner may adopt such reasonable rules and regulations as he may deem necessary to insure uniform and orderly operation of this Chapter.

B. The commissioner shall provide and furnish the forms required by this Chapter. The commissioner shall keep on hand a sufficient supply of blank forms, which, except certificate of title and memorandum certificate forms, shall be furnished and distributed without charge to all persons residing within the state.

C. If it appears that a certificate of title has been improperly issued, the commissioner shall have the power, and it shall be his duty, to cancel same. Upon cancellation of any certificate of title, the commissioner shall notify the person to whom such certificate of title was issued as well as any chattel mortgage holders appearing thereon of said cancellation and shall demand the surrender of such certificate of title, but said cancellation shall not affect the validity of any chattel mortgage noted thereon. The holder of such certificate of title shall return same to the commissioner forthwith.

D. The commissioner is authorized upon application of any person and payment of the proper fees, to search the records of the bureau and make reports thereof, and to make photographic copies of the bureau records and attestations thereof.

E. The commissioner shall charge two dollars a page for photographic copies of records and attestations thereof, under the signature and seal of the commissioner. Such copy or copies shall be taken as prima facie evidence of the facts therein stated, in any court of the state of Louisiana. The commissioner shall furnish without charge to the Department of Public Safety, sheriffs, or chiefs of police, information on any title.

§728. Fees.

The commissioner shall charge the following fees and no others:

(1) Each certificate of title — eighteen dollars and fifty cents.

(2) Each certified copy of a certificate of title — fifteen dollars.

(3) Each memorandum certificate — one dollar; provided, that if the application for a memorandum certificate is made at the time of application for a certificate of title, the commissioner shall charge only the three dollar and fifty cent fee for the certificate of title and no fee shall be required for the memorandum certificate.

(4) Each certified copy of memorandum certificate — one dollar.

(5) Each notation of a security interest, whether a chattel mortgage, other security agreement, or other financing statement evidencing such security interest is filed, on a vehicle certificate of title — five dollars.

(6) Each cancellation of a notation of any chattel mortgage or security interest on a certificate of title or a cancellation of a floor plan mortgage — five dollars.

(7) Each permit to sell or duplicate permit to sell a motor vehicle — fifteen dollars.

(8) Each salvage title — eighteen dollars and fifty cents.

(9) The fees authorized under R.S. 10:9–401, et seq.
(Chgd. by Acts 1990 No. 823, §1, No. 1079, §5; Acts 1991 No. 377, §6, No. 483, §1; Acts 1992 No. 272, §1, eff. 8/21/92.)

§729. Necessity for certificate.

After July 1, 1951, no owner of any vehicle registered and licensed under the Louisiana Vehicle Registration License Tax Law, Chapter 4 of Subtitle II of Title 47 of the Louisiana Revised Statutes of 1950 shall operate any such vehicle upon any public road, highway or bridge in this state, without first applying for a certificate of title therefor, nor shall he so operate any such vehicle upon which the certificate of title has been cancelled; nor shall any other person operate such vehicle upon any public road, highway or bridge in this state, knowing or having reason to believe that the owner has failed to obtain a certificate of title therefor, or that same has been cancelled.

Provided, however, that the commissioner is hereby vested with discretion to grant extension of such general compliance date, upon reasonable grounds, for a reasonable period not exceeding three months, and may thereafter grant a further extension, upon reasonable grounds, not exceeding two months.

§730. Alteration and forgery; false name, address, or statement; other fraud.

Whoever alters or forges any certificate of title to a vehicle, or any endorsement or sale and assignment thereof, or resale or reassignment thereof, or any cancellation of any chattel mortgage on a vehicle is guilty of forgery and punishable as provided by law. Whoever holds or uses such certificate or endorsement of sale and assignment or cancellation knowing the same to have been altered or forged; or whoever uses a false or fictitious name or gives a false or fictitious address or makes any false statement in any application or affidavit required under the provisions of this Chapter, or in a bill of sale or sworn statement of ownership or otherwise commits a fraud in any application, shall, upon conviction thereof be punished by imprisonment not exceeding four years, or by fine not exceeding five thousand dollars, or both, in the discretion of the court.

§731. Violations; penalty.

Whoever shall, except as otherwise provided for in this Chapter, purport to sell or transfer a vehicle without delivery to the purchaser or transferee thereof a certificate of title thereto duly endorsed and assigned to such purchaser as provided in this Chapter; or, being the owner thereof, shall operate on any public road, highway or bridge in this state a vehicle for which a certificate of title is required by the provisions of this Chapter without such certificate having been applied for in accordance with the provisions of this Chapter, or upon which the certificate of title has been cancelled; or any person other than the owner thereof who shall operate on any public road, highway or bridge in this state a vehicle for which a certificate of title is required by the provisions of this Chapter, knowing or having reason to believe that the owner has failed to obtain a certificate of title therefor, or that same has been cancelled; or whoever shall fail to surrender any certificate of title or memorandum certificate upon cancellation of the same by the commissioner and notice thereof as prescribed in this Chapter; or whoever fails to surrender the certificate of title to the commissioner as provided in this Chapter in case of the destruction or dismantling or change of a vehicle in such respect that it is not the vehicle described in the certificate of title; or whoever shall violate any of the other provisions of this Chapter, or any lawful rule or regulation promulgated pursuant to the provisions of this Chapter shall be guilty of a misdemeanor, and upon conviction, shall for each offense be punished by imprisonment for not more than ninety days, or by fine not exceeding five hundred dollars, or both, in the discretion of the court.

§732. Additional penalties.

A. Unless another penalty is in this Chapter or by the laws of this state provided, every person convicted of a misdemeanor for the violation of any provisions of this Chapter shall be punished by a fine of not more than five hundred dollars or by imprisonment for not more than six months, or by both such fine and imprisonment.

B. Any person who is convicted of a violation of any of the provisions of this Chapter herein or by the laws of this state declared to constitute a felony shall be punished by imprisonment for not less than one year nor more than five years, or by a fine of not less than five hundred dollars nor more than five thousand dollars, or by both such fine and imprisonment.

§733. *(Repealed by Acts 1992 No. 984, §18, eff. 8/21/92.)*

§734. Signature to documents.

Whenever the commissioner is required to sign any document under this Chapter he may, at his discretion, perform the act of signing in person or by duly authorized agent, and may use or cause to be used a signature machine for the purpose of affixing his signature to such documents.

§735. Auto title companies; licensing; regulation; fees, suspension and revocation; domicile; surety bonds; expiration and renewal dates.

A. All auto title companies, as defined by R.S. 32:702(12), shall be licensed by the Department of Public Safety and Corrections, office of motor vehicles. Eligibility for a license under the provisions of this Section shall be limited to those persons of good moral character, who maintain an office within the state, have executed a good and sufficient surety bond that meets the requirements of R.S. 32:736, and have paid the annual fee required by Subsection C of this Section.

B. Rules for eligibility, suspension, revocation, or cancellation of a license to operate an auto title company shall be reasonably related to the public interest, shall be consistent with all provisions of this Chapter, and shall be adopted in accordance with the Administrative Procedure Act*.

**R.S. 49:950 et seq.*

C. An annual license fee of two hundred dollars shall be collected from an applicant prior to the initial issuance or renewal of the license. The license and bond shall be valid for additional locations when such locations are under the same ownership, management, and control as that of the licensed auto title company. However, for the initial application period and for each renewal period, the auto title company shall pay an additional fifty dollars for each additional location. These fees and renewal fees shall be considered a title certificate fee for the purposes of R.S. 32:733*.

**R.S. 32:733 was repealed.*

D. Every license issued pursuant to this section shall expire as of the first day of June following the year in which such license was issued.

E. Each license issued pursuant to this Section shall be renewed annually at least sixty days in advance of the expiration date of the license by submitting to the office of motor vehicles an application for renewal upon a form supplied by that office, together with the license renewal fee and surety bond for the renewal period.

(Added by Acts 1992 No. 626, §2; chgd. by Acts 1993 No. 463, §1, No. 737, §1, No. 1005, §1, eff. 8/15/93.)

§736. Surety bond required; amount and conditions of surety bond; filing of bond.

A. Each auto title company shall execute a good and sufficient surety bond with a surety company qualified to do business in Louisiana as surety, in the sum of ten thousand dollars, if such surety bond is available for purchase. Such bond shall name the Department of Public Safety and Corrections, office of motor vehicles as obligee and shall be subject to the condition that, if the auto title company shall, throughout the entire term of the bond, timely file with office of motor vehicles all applications delivered to the auto title company for filing, and timely remit all fees and taxes collected, the obligation shall be void. If the company fails to meet the conditions of the bond, the obligation of the surety shall remain in full force and effect. An auto title company having multiple locations need furnish only a single twenty thousand dollar surety bond.

B. The surety bond furnished as required herein shall be delivered to and filed with the office of motor vehicles.

(Added by Acts 1993 No. 737, §1, eff. 8/15/93.)

§737. Causes for nonissuance, suspension, revocation, cancellation, or restrictions; reinstatement.

A. The office of motor vehicles may refuse to issue, or may suspend, revoke, cancel or impose other restrictions on any license issued under this Chapter for the following causes:

(1) Failure to remit taxes and fees collected from applicants for title transfers.

(2) Operating as an auto title company without a license for each location, with an expired license, or without a valid surety bond on file with the office of motor vehicles.

(3) Issuance of more than one temporary registration (T-Marker) to a title applicant, or issuing a T-Marker without first collecting all taxes and fees.

(4) Operating from an unlicensed location.

(5) Changing the ownership of the auto title company and not reporting in writing to the office of motor vehicles within thirty days from the date of such change.

(6) Changing the officers or directors of the auto title company and not reporting in writing to the office of motor vehicles within thirty days from the date of such change.

(7) Being a principal or accessory to the alteration of documents relevant to a registration or titling transaction that results in a material injury to the public records or a shortfall in the collection of taxes owed.

(8) The forwarding to the office of motor vehicles by an auto title company of a document relevant to a registration or titling transaction that results in a material injury to the public records, or a shortfall in the collection of taxes owed when the auto title company had knowledge of facts causing such injury or shortfall, and failed to disclose same to the office of motor vehicles.

(9) Conviction of, or entry of plea of guilty or nolo contendere to, any felony or conviction of, or entry of a plea of guilty or nolo contendere to, any criminal charge an element of which is fraud.

(10) Fraud, deceit, or perjury in obtaining any license issued under this chapter.

(11) Failure to maintain at all times during the existence of the license all qualifications required for issuance or renewal of a license.

B. Any proceeding to suspend, revoke, cancel or otherwise restrict a license granted under this Chapter shall be brought by the office of motor vehicles in the district court having civil jurisdiction in any parish in which such person resides, or is domiciled or has his principal place of business. If the person whose license is to be suspended, revoked, canceled or otherwise restricted is a non-resident and is not domiciled within the state, such proceeding may be brought in the Nineteenth Judicial District Court for the parish of East Baton Rouge. Upon a proper showing by the office of motor vehicles that such person has engaged or is engaged in any activity, conduct or practice proscribed by this Chapter, the court shall suspend, revoke, cancel or otherwise restrict such person's license as may be necessary to protect the interests of the public and the state of Louisiana. The trial of the proceeding shall be a summary proceeding, and shall be by the judge alone without a jury.

C. Any license suspended, revoked, canceled, or otherwise restricted by the office of motor vehicles may be reinstated by the office of motor vehicles.

(Added by Acts 1993 No. 737, §1, eff. 8/15/93.)

§738. Cease and desist order; injunctive relief.

A. In addition to or in lieu of the administrative sanctions provided in this Chapter, and any criminal sanctions otherwise provided by law, the office of motor vehicles is empowered to issue an order to any person engaged in any activity, conduct, or practice constituting a violation of any provision of this Chapter, directing such person to cease and desist from such activity, conduct, or practice. Such order shall be issued in the name of the state of Louisiana under the official seal of the Department of Public safety and Corrections, office of motor vehicles.

B. If the person to whom the office of motor vehicles directs a cease and desist order does not cease and desist the proscribed activity, conduct, or practice within ten days from service of such cease and desist order by certified mail, the office of motor vehicles may cause to issue a writ of injunction enjoining such person from engaging in any activity, conduct, or practice proscribed by this Chapter. Such proceeding shall be brought in the district court having civil jurisdiction in any parish in which such person resides, or is domiciled or has his principal place of business. If the person whose license is to be suspended, revoked, canceled, or otherwise restricted is a non-resident and is not domiciled within the state, such proceeding may be brought in the Nineteenth Judicial District Court for the parish of East Baton Rouge.

C. Upon a proper showing by the office of motor vehicles that such person has engaged or is engaged in any activity, conduct, or practice proscribed by this Chapter, the court shall issue a temporary restraining order restraining the person from engaging in unlawful activity, conduct, or practices pending the hearing on a preliminary injunction, and in due course a permanent injunction shall issue after hearing, commanding the cessation of the unlawful activity, conduct, or practice complained of, all without the necessity of the office of motor vehicles having to give bond as usually required in such cases.

D. The trial of the proceeding by injunction shall be a summary proceeding, and shall be by judge alone without a jury.
(Chgd. by Acts 1993 No. 737, §1, eff. 8/15/93.)

CHAPTER 4-A. AUTOMOTIVE DISMANTLERS AND PARTS RECYCLERS; MOTOR VEHICLE CRUSHERS; AND SCRAPPED MOTOR VEHICLE DEALERS

(Chgd. by Acts 1990 No. 905, §1, eff. 9/7/90.)

§751. Definitions.

As used in this Chapter:

(1) "Automotive dismantler and parts recycler" means a person, firm, or corporation engaged in whole or in part in the business of acquiring and dismantling, disassembling, or repairing wrecked, abandoned, or repairable motor vehicles or selling the usable parts thereof, or selling such wrecked, abandoned, or repairable motor vehicles as a unit of wholesale, or selling such repaired motor vehicles as a unit at wholesale. For purposes of this Chapter, a person, firm, or corporation shall be presumed to be engaging in the business of an automotive dismantler and parts recycler if such person, firm, or corporation possesses ten or more inoperable motor vehicles for more than thirty days, except when such inoperable motor vehicles are being held:

(a) By a licensed tow truck owner or operator.

(b) By a scrap metal processor to recycle the scrap metal.

(c) By a bona fide repair business awaiting repairs.

(2) "Automotive dismantler and parts recycler salesman" shall include anyone who for compensation of any kind sells or brokers any used motor vehicle parts.

(3) "Commission" means the Louisiana Used Motor Vehicle and Parts Commission.

(4) "Motor vehicle" means every automobile, motor home, motorcycle, all-terrain vehicle, recreational vehicle trailer, boat trailer, semitrailer, truck, truck-tractor, and any other device which is self-propelled and drawn, in, upon, or by which any person or property is or may be transported or drawn either upon or off a public highway, except such as is moved by animal power, or is used exclusively upon stationary rails or tracks, or is an implement of husbandry.

(5) "Motor vehicle crusher" means any person, firm, or corporation engaged in whole or in part in the business of purchasing and crushing or compacting motor vehicles and selling the crushed or compacted vehicle for scrap.

(6) "Place of business" means the place owned or leased and regularly occupied by a person, firm, or corporation, licensed under the provisions of this Chapter for the principal purpose of engaging in the business of an automotive dismantler and parts recycler, where the products for sale are displayed and offered for sale, and where the books and records required for the conduct of the business are maintained and kept.

(7) "Salvage pool or salvage disposal sale" means a scheduled sale at auction or by private bid of wrecked or repairable motor vehicles by insurance companies or by used motor vehicle dealers or automotive dismantlers and parts recyclers licensed by the commission.

(8) "Scrap metal processor" means any person, firm, or corporation engaged in whole or in part in the business of obtaining scrap metal whose origin may have included abandoned, wrecked, or junked motor vehicles for scrap, shredding, or recycling as scrap metal.

(9) "Used motor vehicle dealer" shall have the meaning set forth in R.S. 32:771 et seq.

(Chgd. by Acts 1990 No. 905, §1; Acts 1991 No. 883, §1; Acts 1992 No. 205, §1, eff. 8/21/92.)

§752. License required.

A. It shall be unlawful and shall constitute a misdemeanor for any person, firm, association, corporation, or trust to engage in business in whole or in part as, or serve in the capacity of, or act as an automotive dismantler and parts recycler, automotive dismantler and parts recycler salesman, or motor vehicle crusher in this state without first obtaining a license therefor from the Louisiana Used Motor Vehicle and Parts Commission.

B. Any person, firm, association, corporation, or trust engaging, acting, or serving in more than one of the capacities or having more than one place where the business is carried on or conducted shall be required to obtain and hold a current license for each thereof in which he, it, or they shall engage.

(Chgd. by Acts 1990 No. 905, §1; Acts 1991 No. 883, §1; Acts 1992 No. 205, §1, eff. 8/21/92.)

§753. Application.

Every person, firm, or corporation desiring to engage in the business of an automotive dismantler and parts recycler, automotive dismantler and parts recycler salesman, or motor vehicle crusher shall apply in writing, on a form to be prescribed by the commission, which form shall contain:

(1) The name of the applicant.

(2) The street address of applicant's principal place of business.

(3) The type of business organization of applicant.

(4) The applicant's financial standing.

(5) The applicant's business integrity.

(6) Whether the applicant has an established place of business and is engaged in the pursuit, avocation, or business for which a license or licenses is applied.

(7) Whether the applicant is able to properly conduct the business for which a license or licenses is applied.

(8) Such additional information as may be required by the commission.

(Chgd. by Acts 1990 No. 905, §1; Acts 1991 No. 883, §1; Acts 1992 No. 205, §1, eff. 8/21/92.)

§754. Fee.

Every application for license as an automotive dismantler and parts recycler, automotive dismantler and parts recycler salesman, or motor vehicle crusher shall be accompanied by the following fee:

(1) A maximum of two hundred dollars for an applicant's established place of business.

(2) One hundred dollars for each place of business in addition to the principal place of business.

(Chgd. by Acts 1990 No. 905, §1; Acts 1991 No. 883, §1; Acts 1992 No. 205, §1, eff. 8/21/92.)

§755. *(Repealed by Acts 1997 No. 1388, §2, eff. 8/15/97.)*

§756. Duration.

A. All bonds and licenses issued under the provisions of this Chapter shall expire on the first anniversary of the date of issue and shall be nontransferable.

B. All applications for renewal of licenses hereunder shall be submitted on or before sixty days prior to the date on which the existing license will expire. If application has not been made for renewal of licenses, such licenses shall expire one year from the date issued and it shall be a violation of this Chapter for any person to represent himself and act thereafter in the capacity and business for which he was formerly licensed hereunder.

C. Any licensee who submits a renewal application after the expiration date of an existing license shall be subject to a late penalty of one hundred dollars and shall be presumed to be a renewal applicant.

D. Any licensee changing the name of the business, the business address, the ownership of the business, or opening any additional place of business shall notify the commission within ten days of such change or be in violation of this Chapter.

E. Any licensee ceasing to maintain its business shall surrender the license to the commission within ten days and any failure to do so shall constitute a misdemeanor criminal violation and also subject the licensee to civil penalties as further defined in this Chapter.

F. The commission is authorized to adopt rules to implement the provisions of this Section.

(Chgd. by Acts 1990 No. 905, §1; Acts 1991 No. 883, §1, eff. 9/6/91.)

§757. Requirement to keep records.

A. Every used motor vehicle dealer, automotive dismantler and parts recycler, motor vehicle crusher, and scrap metal processor shall keep a register of all purchases and sales of motor vehicles for three years from the date of purchase or sale indicating the make, model, year, body style, vehicle identification number, odometer reading, and name and address of the purchaser and sellers, provided that any person, firm, or corporation purchasing a motor vehicle from a licensee of this commission is exempted from the requirement of keeping records on such purchases as are required in this Section. Scrap metal processors shall provide the information concerning the vehicle purchased, as required in this Section, only to the extent the information is readily available or ascertainable from the motor vehicle itself, as determined by the scrap metal processor.

B. Such registers and any vehicles or parts of vehicles still in the possession of the used motor vehicle dealer or automotive dismantler and parts recycler, motor vehicle crusher, and scrap metal processor shall be made available for inspection to identified representatives of the commission and to identified law enforcement officers of the state, parish, and municipality during reasonable business hours on business days.

(Chgd. by Acts 1990 No. 905, §1; Acts 1991 No. 883, §1, eff. 9/6/91.)

§758. Other licenses not required.

A licensed automotive dismantler and parts recycler shall not be required to obtain a separate license as a used motor vehicle dealer, an automobile accessory dealer, an automobile garage or shop, or a storage garage or yard, to engage in the business of an automotive dismantler and parts recycler as set forth herein. *(Chgd. by Acts 1990 No. 905, §1; Acts 1991 No. 883, §1, eff. 9/6/91.)*

§759. Transfer of motor vehicle certificate of title to or from an automotive dismantler and parts recycler.

In all transfers of motor vehicles at wholesale as authorized herein, an automotive dismantler and parts recycler, duly licensed hereunder, shall have the authority to transfer the certificates of title to such motor vehicles as a dealer under the Louisiana certificate of title law. *(Chgd. by Acts 1991 No. 883, §1, eff. 9/6/91.)*

§759.1. Transfers of scrapped motor vehicles.

A. Unless transferred by an automotive dismantler and parts recycler or motor vehicle crusher licensed by this commission, all transfers of motor vehicles shall be accompanied by the delivery of possession of the certificate of title, a permit to sell, or the permit to dismantle the motor vehicle, as required under R.S. 32:716 or 717, whichever is applicable, by the transferor to the transferee thereof.

B. No motor vehicle crusher or scrap metal processor acquiring a motor vehicle from any person, firm, or corporation who is not licensed under the provisions of this Chapter as an automotive dismantler and parts recycler or as a motor vehicle crusher shall crush, compact, demolish, shred, or otherwise recycle for scrap such motor vehicle until after applying with the Department of Public Safety and Corrections, office of motor vehicles, for a permit to dismantle the motor vehicle for scrap in accordance with the applicable provisions and procedures set forth in R.S. 32:716 or 717, unless a permit to dismantle or a permit to sell such motor vehicle has previously been issued to the seller and transferred to the purchaser of the motor vehicle.

C. A scrap metal processor, upon receiving a copy of the license from a used motor vehicle dealer, automotive dismantler and parts recycler, or motor vehicle crusher, shall be authorized to rely on the validity of said license for the term of said license unless and until the

scrap metal processor receives actual written notice from the commission that said license has been revoked, suspended, and/or cancelled.
(Added by Acts 1990 No. 905, §1; chgd. by Acts 1991 No. 883, §1, eff. 9/6/91.)

§760. Refusal, cancellation, or revocation of license.

A. Except as otherwise provided in this Section, the commission may deny an application for a license or revoke, or suspend, or cancel a license after it has been granted for any of the following reasons:

(1) On satisfactory proof of unfitness of the applicant or the licensee, as the case may be, under the standards established by this Chapter.

(2) For fraudulent practices or any material misstatement made by an applicant in any application for license under the provisions of this Chapter.

(3) For any willful failure to comply with any provisions of this Chapter, any provision relating to the proper disposition of certificates of title or permits to dismantle in connection with the purchase or sale of any motor vehicle, or with any rule or regulation adopted and promulgated by the commission under authority vested in it by this Chapter.

(4) Change of condition after license is granted resulting in failure to maintain the qualifications for licensure.

(5) Continued or flagrant violation of any of the rules or regulations of the commission.

(6) Being an automotive dismantler and parts recycler, automotive dismantler or parts recycler salesman, or motor vehicle crusher who:

(a) Resorts to or uses any false or misleading advertising in connection with his business.

(b) Has committed any unlawful act which resulted in the revocation of any similar license in another state.

(c) Has been convicted of a crime involving moral turpitude.

(d) Has committed a fraudulent act in selling, purchasing, or otherwise dealing in motor vehicles or motor vehicle parts, or has misrepresented the terms and conditions of a sale, purchase, or contract for sale or purchase of used motor vehicle parts, motor vehicles, or any interest therein including an option to purchase such motor vehicles.

(e) Has engaged in his business under a past or present license issued pursuant to this Chapter or in any other course of conduct in such a manner as to cause injury to the public or to those with whom he is dealing.

(f) Has failed to meet or maintain the conditions and requirements necessary to qualify for the issuance of a license.

(g) Has failed or refused to furnish and keep in force any bond required under this Chapter.

(h) Has knowingly engaged in tampering with, adjusting, altering, changing, setting back, disconnecting, or failing to connect the odometer of any motor vehicle, or causing any of the foregoing to occur in an odometer of a motor vehicle, so as to reflect a lower mileage than the true mileage driven by the motor vehicle. The foregoing shall be applicable to any motor vehicle whether sold wholesale or retail or whether or not the foregoing occurred within or without the state of Louisiana.

(7) Being an automotive dismantler and parts recycler, or motor vehicle crusher who:

(a) Does not have an established place of business.

(b) Is not operating from the address shown on his license if this change has not been reported to the commission.

B. The commission shall not deny an application for a license or revoke or suspend a license based upon consideration of an existing or anticipated economic or competitive effect on other licensees in the surrounding community or territory.

C. Each of the aforementioned grounds for suspension, revocation, cancellation, or denial of issuance or renewal of license shall also constitute a violation of this Chapter, unless the person involved has been tried and acquitted of the offense constituting such grounds.

D. The suspension, revocation, cancellation, or refusal to issue or renew a license or the imposition of any other penalty by the commission shall be in addition to any penalty which might be imposed upon any licensee upon a conviction at law for any violation of this Chapter.

E. In the performance of its duties under this Section the commission shall have the authority to obtain from the Department of Public Safety and Corrections and other governmental agencies information relating to the criminal records of applicants for licensure under this Chapter.
(Chgd. by Acts 1991 No. 883, §1; Acts 1992 No. 205, §1, eff. 8/21/92.)

§761. Denial, suspension, cancellation, or revocation of license; procedure.

A. (1) The commission may, without prior notice, deny any application for a license within sixty days after receipt thereof by written notice to the applicant stating the grounds for such denial. Upon request by the applicant whose application has been so denied, the commission shall set the time and place of a hearing to review such denial, the same to be heard with reasonable promptness. The commission may suspend or revoke a license only after a hearing of which the licensee affected shall be given at least fifteen days written notice specifying the grounds or reasons for revocation or suspension.

(2) Notices may be served as provided by law for the service of notices, or by mailing a copy by certified mail to the last known residence or business address of such applicant or licensee. A copy of such notice shall be mailed by certified mail to the surety on the licensee's bond at the address of the surety given in the bond. The hearing on charges shall be at such time and place as the commission may prescribe and the aforementioned notice shall further specify the time and place.

(3) The commission shall have the power to compel the production of records and papers bearing upon the issues to be presented for hearing. The commission shall have the power to subpoena and bring before it any person in this state, or take testimony of any such person by deposition, with the same fees and mileage and in the same manner as prescribed by law in judicial procedure before courts of the state in civil cases. Any party to the hearing shall have the right to the attendance of witnesses in his behalf upon designating to the commission the person or persons sought to be subpoenaed.

(4) If the commission determines that any applicant is not qualified to receive a license, a license shall not be granted to the applicant, and, if the commission determines that any licensee is guilty of violation of any of the provisions of this Chapter, his or its license may be suspended or revoked.

(5) Upon the determination by the commission that either the applicant is not qualified to receive a license or that a licensee is guilty of violating any of the provisions of this Chapter, all costs of the hearing procedure shall be charged to and borne by the applicant or licensee so affected. These costs shall include but not be limited to attorney fees, court reporter fees, and mileage and per diem of the commissioners, as well as other applicable and reasonable costs.

B. (1) The decision of the commission granting or refusing to grant an application for a license or suspending or revoking a license shall not become final for a period of thirty days from the date thereof, during which time said applicant or licensee may appeal from the decision of the commission to the Nineteenth Judicial District Court by:

(a) Filing a petition in the court setting forth the facts relied upon and praying for a review of the decision, and

(b) Mailing by certified mail a copy of the petition to the executive director of the commission or causing service of summons directed to the executive director of the commission to be issued, the petition to be mailed or the summons to be issued within thirty days from the date of the decision of the commission from which appeal is taken.

(2) On appeal, the issues shall be tried de novo, and the court shall enter an order with respect thereto as it shall deem just and equitable. Nothing herein shall be construed to limit the authority of the court to grant relief as the circumstances may require. If the issues involved were first presented to the commission by a complaint filed with the commission, the complainant may appeal from the decision of the commission in the same manner as hereinabove prescribed.

C. (1) In holding and conducting hearings on complaints of violations of the provisions of this Chapter or hearings on the imposition of a civil penalty for any such violation, the commission shall give the licensee or other person, firm, association, corporation, or trust alleged to have committed such violation at least fifteen days written notice specifying the violation charged.

(2) Notices may be served as provided by law for the service of notices, or by mailing a copy by certified mail to the last known residence or business address of the party charged with such violation. Hearings shall be at such time and place as the commission may prescribe and the aforementioned notice shall specify the time and place thereof.

(3) (a) The commission shall have the power to compel the production of records and papers bearing upon the issues to be presented for hearing.

(b) The commission shall have the power to subpoena and bring before it any person in this state, or take testimony of any such person by deposition, with the same fees and mileage and in the same manner as prescribed by law in judicial procedure before courts of the state in civil cases.

(c) Any party to the hearing shall have the right to the attendance of witnesses in his behalf upon designating to the commission the person or persons sought to be subpoenaed.

(4) Upon the determination by the commission that the party charged is guilty of violating any of the provisions of this Chapter, then all costs of the hearing procedure shall be charged to and borne by the parties so affected. The costs shall include but not be limited to attorney's fees, court reporter fees, and mileage and per diem of commissioners, as well as other applicable and reasonable costs.
(Chgd. by Acts 1990 No. 905, §1; Acts 1991 No. 883, §1, eff. 9/6/91.)

§762. Salvage pools.

A. Sales of motor vehicles at a salvage pool, salvage disposal sale, or through an insurance company shall be opened only to persons possessing a Louisiana buyer's identification card to buy such motor vehicles as provided in this Section.

B. (1) Buyer's identification cards to bid or buy motor vehicles at salvage pools, salvage disposal sales, or through insurance companies shall be available to any person, business, or corporation, or licensed employee thereof, possessing a valid used motor vehicle dealer license, or a valid automotive dismantlers and recyclers license. Buyer's identification cards to bid or buy salvage shall be issued by the commission on a form prescribed by it and shall contain as a minimum the name, address, driver's license number, any one of the aforementioned dealers' license numbers, physical description, and signature of the applicant and the name and address of the employer of the applicant.

(2) The commission may exact a fee not to exceed twenty-five dollars for the issuing of the buyer's identification card to a resident of Louisiana and a fee not to exceed two hundred dollars for the issuing of a buyer's identification card to an out-of-state resident.

(3) The buyer's identification card shall be renewable each year for a fee of twenty-five dollars for a resident of Louisiana and for a fee not to exceed two hundred dollars for an out-of-state resident.

C. It shall be the duty of the owner, manager, or person in charge of any salvage pool or salvage disposal sale, to prohibit the bidding by any person who does not display a buyer's identification card, to refuse to sell to any person any wrecked or repairable motor vehicle if such person does not display a valid buyer's identification card and to prohibit any person without a buyer's identification card to be present at the bidding site during a sale. Each buyer's identification card holder may be accompanied by a mechanic or other technical expert of his choice.

D. The permit may be refused, cancelled, or revoked for the same reasons a license under this Chapter may be refused, cancelled, or revoked. Any person whose permit is refused, cancelled, or revoked shall enjoy the same review and appeal procedures as a person whose license is refused, cancelled, or revoked.

E. (1) The owner, manager, or person in charge of a salvage pool or salvage disposal sale shall keep a register of all sales of motor vehicles for three years from the date of sale, showing the make, model, year, body style, vehicle identification number, odometer reading, and the name and address of the seller and buyer. In addition the sale transaction register shall contain the buyer's identification card number issued by the commission.

(2) The register shall be made available for inspection by identified law enforcement officers of the state, parish, or municipality or agents of the commission at the salvage pool or salvage disposal sale business location during regular business hours on business days.
(Chgd. by Acts 1991 No. 883, §1, eff. 9/6/91.)

§763. Salvage dealers licensed in other states.

Nothing herein shall prohibit salvage dealers licensed in other states from buying at a salvage pool or salvage disposal sale provided that the state in which they are licensed extends the same privileges to salvage dealers licensed under this law and provided that they obtain a buyer's identification card and number as required in R.S. 32:762. *(Chgd. by Acts 1991 No. 883, §1, eff. 9/6/91.)*

§764. Criminal penalties.

Any person, firm, association, corporation, or trust committing a violation of this Chapter shall, upon conviction, be fined not less than five hundred dollars and each day that a person, firm, association, corporation, or trust violates this Chapter shall constitute a separate offense. *(Chgd. by Acts 1990 No. 905, §1, eff. 9/7/90.)*

§765. Civil penalties.

A. If the commission shall determine that any applicant is not qualified to receive a license, a license shall not be granted to said applicant, and if the commission shall determine that any licensee is guilty of a violation of any of the provisions of this Chapter or the rules and regulations of the commission, his or its license may be suspended or revoked, or a civil penalty may be imposed by the commission. The commission may also impose a civil penalty against any person, firm, association, corporation, or trust which is determined by the commission to have violated any of the provisions of this Chapter or the rules and regulations of the commission.

B. (1) No civil penalty imposed for the violation of the provisions of this Chapter or the rules and regulations of the commission shall exceed five hundred dollars for each day such violation continues.

(2) On a second or subsequent violation, no civil penalty imposed shall exceed one thousand dollars for each day such second or subsequent violation continues. In order to constitute a second or subsequent violation, there must occur a lapse of at least one day following the first or previous violation.

C. Any civil penalty imposed by the commission may, in the discretion of the commission, be suspended in whole or in part.

D. Upon the failure of a person, firm, association, corporation, or trust to timely pay any civil penalty imposed by the commission when due, the commission shall be entitled to recover, by suit or otherwise, from such party all costs of collection, including court costs, deposition and other discovery costs, and reasonable attorney's fees incurred by the commission in collecting such civil penalty.

(Chgd. by Acts 1990 No. 905, §1; Acts 1991 No. 883, §1, eff. 9/6/91.)

§766. Injunction.

A. The commission is hereby authorized without cost, bond, or deposit to institute injunctive actions in courts of competent jurisdiction in the name of the state on the relation of the commission to enforce the provisions of this Chapter.

B. Any licensee or other person who violates or threatens to violate any provision of this Chapter or rule or regulation promulgated thereunder may be enjoined from committing or continuing the violation or engaging in any business for which a license has been issued under this Chapter. In addition to any other proper venue, the parish of East Baton Rouge shall constitute a proper venue for the institution by the commission of judicial actions authorized under this Chapter.

C. The court shall impose all costs on the person or persons enjoined, and shall award reasonable attorney fees to the commission as a cost of court.

(Chgd. by Acts 1991 No. 883, §1, eff. 9/6/91.)

CHAPTER 4-B. USED MOTOR VEHICLE DEALERS AND MARINE PRODUCT DEALERS

Section

§771. Definitions.

As used in this Chapter:

(1) "All-terrain vehicle" commonly referred to as "ATV" means any vehicle with three or more low pressure flotation type tires with a seat which is designed to be straddled by the operator.

(2) "Commission" means the Louisiana Used Motor Vehicle and Parts Commission, or its designee.

(3) "Distributor" means any person, firm, association, corporation, or trust, resident or nonresident, who in whole or in part sells or distributes new and unused motorcycles, all-terrain vehicles, trailers, motor homes, buses, recreational vehicles, travel trailers, and/or marine products to dealers, or who maintains distributor representatives.

(4) "Distributor sales representative" means any officer, agent, or employee employed by a distributor for the purpose of promoting the sale of his, its, or their motorcycles, all-terrain vehicles, trailers, motor homes, buses, recreational vehicles, travel trailers, or marine products, or for supervising or contacting his, its, or their dealers or prospective dealers.

(5) "Fire truck" means any motorized vehicle utilized by a fire department in transporting firefighters and/or equipment to fires and emergency calls and supports extinguishing operations such as water, pumps, ladders, special service apparatus, hoses, foam, air, lights, rescue equipment, and utility equipment.

(6) "Manufacturer" means any person, firm, association, corporation, or trust, resident or nonresident, who fabricates, manufactures, or assembles new and unused motorcycles, all-terrain vehicles, trailers, motor homes, buses, recreational vehicles, travel trailers, or marine products. It does not include a person, firm, association, corporation, or trust which converts, modifies, or otherwise alters a motor vehicle manufactured by another person, firm, association, corporation, or trust.

(7) "Manufacturer sales representative" means any officer, agent, or employee employed by a person, firm, association, corporation, or trust who fabricates, manufactures, or assembles motorcycles, all-terrain vehicles, trailers, motor homes, buses, recreational vehicles, travel trailers, or marine products, or by a factory branch for the purpose of making or promoting the sale of his, its, or their vehicles, or marine products, or for supervising or contacting his, its, or their dealers or prospective dealers.

(8) "Marine dealer" means any person who holds a bona fide contract or franchise with a manufacturer or distributor of marine products, except for a person engaged in the business of renting and/or selling new or used watercraft or boats adapted to be powered only by occupant's energy, and who holds a license as a marine dealer under the provisions of this Chapter.

(9) "Marine product" means a new or used watercraft, boat, or motor designed for recreational or commercial use on water. The term also includes an outboard motor or a boat with an inboard/outboard motor attached thereto. The term shall not mean a watercraft designed for use primarily for commercial purposes or new or used watercraft or boats adapted to be powered only by occupant's energy.

(10) "Motorcycle" means a motor vehicle having a seat or saddle for the use of the rider and designed to travel on not more than three wheels in contact with the ground, but excluding a tractor.

(11) "Motor home" means a motor vehicle designed as an integral unit to be used as a conveyance upon the public streets and highways and for use as a temporary or recreational dwelling and having at least four of the following permanently installed systems which meet American National Standards Institute and National Fire Protection Association standards in effect as of the date of manufacture, two of which shall be systems specified below in Subparagraph (a), (d), or (e) of this Paragraph:

(a) Cooking facilities.

(b) Ice box or mechanical refrigerators.

(c) Potable water supply including plumbing and a sink with faucet either self-contained or with connections for an external source, or both.

(d) Self-contained toilet or toilet connected to a plumbing system with connection for external water disposal, or both.

(e) Heating or air conditioning system, or both, separate from the vehicle engine or the vehicle engine electrical system.

(f) A one hundred ten/one hundred fifteen volt alternating current electrical system either with its own power supply or with a connection for an external source, or both, or a liquefied petroleum system and supply.

(12) "Motor vehicle" means any motor driven car, van, or truck required to be registered which is used, or is designed to be used, for the transporting of passengers or goods for public, private, commercial, or for hire purposes and includes new and used motor homes, new and used motorcycles, new and used all-terrain vehicles, new and used recreational trailers, new and used boat trailers, and new and used semitrailers.

(13) "Recreational vehicle" means a motorized or towable vehicle that combines transportation and temporary living quarters for travel, recreation, and camping. For purposes of this Chapter, a "recreational vehicle" includes new and used motor homes, new and used travel trailers, new and used fifth-wheel travel trailers, and new and used folding camper trailers.

(14) "Ultimate purchaser" means the first person or corporate entity, other than a dealer purchasing in his capacity as a dealer, who in good faith purchases a new motor vehicle for purposes other than resale. "Ultimate purchaser" shall not include a person who purchases a vehicle for purposes of altering or remanufacturing the motor vehicle for future resale.

(15) "Used motor vehicle" means a motor vehicle, the legal title of which has been transferred by a manufacturer, distributor, or dealer to an ultimate purchaser. For purposes of this Chapter a "used motor vehicle" includes new and used motor homes, new and used motorcycles, new and used all-terrain vehicles, new and used recreational trailers, new and used boat trailers, and new and used semitrailers.

(16) (a)(i) "Used motor vehicle dealer" means any person who, for a commission or with intent to make a profit or gain of money or other thing of value, sells, brokers, exchanges, rents with option to purchase, offers or attempts to negotiate a sale or exchange of an interest in five or more used motor vehicles in any twelve-month period and who is engaged wholly or in part in the business of selling used motor vehicles, whether or not such motor vehicles are owned by such person.

(ii) The term shall also include anyone not licensed under Chapter 6 of Title 32 of the Louisiana Revised Statutes of 1950 who sells used cars and trucks, new and used motorcycles, new and used trailers, new and used semitrailers, new and used travel trailers, new and used buses, new and used fire trucks, new and used wreckers, new and used recreational vehicles, new and used motor homes, used hearses, used ambulances and who rents on a daily basis motor vehicles, not of the current year or immediate prior year models, that have been titled previously to an ultimate purchaser.

(b) "Used motor vehicle dealer" shall not include any of the following:

(i) Receivers, trustees, administrators, executors, guardians, or other persons appointed by or acting under the judgment or order of any court.

(ii) Public officers while performing their official duties.

(iii) Employees of persons enumerated in the definition of "used motor vehicle dealer" when engaged in the specific performance of their duties as such employees.

(iv) Mortgagees or secured parties as to sales of motor vehicles constituting collateral on a mortgage or security agreement.

(v) Insurance companies.

(17) "Used motor vehicle salesman" shall include anyone who for compensation of any kind operates as a broker or is compensated for any referral of a prospective buyer to a dealer. "Compensation" for purposes of this Chapter means anything of value including money, merchandise, rebates on purchases, trading stamps, or any other thing of value.

(18) "Wrecker" means a truck with a hoist and towing apparatus used in towing wrecked or disabled vehicles.

(Chgd. by Acts 1990 No. 905, §1; Acts 1991 No. 915, §1, No. 965, §1; Acts 1997 No. 754, §1, No. 1388, §1, eff. 8/15/97.)

§772. Used Motor Vehicle and Parts Commission.

A. (1) There is hereby created the Louisiana Used Motor Vehicle and Parts Commission within the Department of Economic Development to be composed of twelve members all appointed by the governor with the consent of the Senate. Five members shall be licensed used motor vehicle dealers, one selected from each Public Service Commission district. One member shall be a licensed automotive dismantler or parts recycler, two members shall be consumers selected from the state at large, one member shall be a licensed motorcycle dealer, one member shall be a licensed marine dealer, one member shall be a representative of the recycling industry, and one member shall be a representative of a manufacturer licensed by this commission. Such manufacturer representative shall be a resident of Louisiana. The chairman shall be designated by the governor.

(2) Of the five members who shall be licensed used motor vehicle dealers, one member shall be a new or used motor home dealer or a new or used travel trailer dealer, or both. The first vacancy occurring on the commission after September 6, 1991 shall be filled by the appointment of a new or used motor home dealer or a new or used travel trailer dealer or both.

(3) *(Repealed.)*

B. (1) The terms of the chairman and commissioners shall be coterminous with that of the governor making the appointment and until his successor is appointed and is qualified. The term of office of any member will automatically expire if the member moves out of the public service commission district from which he was appointed. In the event of death, resignation, removal, or automatic expiration of term of any person serving on the commission, the vacancy shall be filled for the unexpired portion of the term in the manner of original appointment.

(2) The commission shall meet at Baton Rouge and complete its organization immediately after the entire membership has been appointed and qualified.

(3) The chairman and each member of the commission shall take and subscribe to the oath of office required of public officers.

C. (1) The chairman and members of the commission shall receive seventy-five dollars for each and every day actually and necessarily spent in attending the meetings of the commission, including any commission committee meetings, and shall be reimbursed for subsistence and traveling expenses incurred in the performance of their duties hereunder as provided by the commissioner of the division of administration.

(2) Such meeting payments shall not exceed the sum of eighteen hundred dollars per annum to any one person.

D. (1) The commission shall appoint a qualified person to serve as executive director who shall have had sufficient management and organizational experience in the automotive industry to direct the functions of the commission. The commission shall fix his salary and shall define and prescribe his duties.

(2) The executive director shall be in charge of the commission's office and shall devote such time as necessary to fulfill the duties thereof, and before entering upon his duties he shall take and subscribe to the oath of office.

(3) The commission may employ such clerical, technical, legal, and other help and incur such expenses as may be necessary for the proper discharge of its duties under this Chapter.

(4) The commission shall maintain its office and transact its business in Baton Rouge and is authorized to adopt and use a seal.

E. The commission is hereby vested with the powers and duties necessary and proper to enable it to fully and effectively carry out and enforce the provisions and objectives of this Chapter, and is hereby authorized and empowered to make and enforce all reasonable rules and regulations and to adopt and prescribe all forms necessary to accomplish said purpose. The enumeration of any power or authority herein shall not be construed to deny, impair, disparage, or limit any others necessary to the attainment thereof. All rules and regulations shall be adopted in accordance with the provisions of the Administrative Procedure Act*. Oversight review shall be conducted by the House Committee on Commerce and the Senate Committee on Transportation, Highways, and Public Works.

**R.S. 49:950 et seq.*

F. The commission's powers and duties shall include but are not limited to the following:

(1) Licensing used motor vehicle dealers and salesmen, motor vehicle crushers, motor vehicle shredders, scrap motor vehicle processors, dealers of used parts and accessories, and automotive dismantlers and parts recyclers.

(2) Inspecting used motor vehicle dealer, motor vehicle crusher, motor vehicle shredder, scrap motor vehicle processors, dealers of used parts and accessories locations and automotive dismantlers and parts recyclers locations to ensure that they are in an approved location, meet local zoning or other municipal requirements, and have sufficient facilities which shall include but not be limited to a business sign, a listed and usable telephone number, and a sales office.

(3) Requiring all dealer sales to have a condition of sale, such as warranty disclaimer, implied or written warranty, or a service contract approved by the commission.

(4) Working with consumers and dealers to hear complaints on used vehicles and parts and to establish a Used Car Consumer Action Panel to hear complaints on a condition of sale, implied and written warranties, and service complaints.

(5) Requiring all dismantlers, motor vehicle crushers, motor vehicle shredders, scrap motor vehicle processors, dealers of used parts and accessories, recyclers, and dealers to maintain their records for a period of three years and to keep their records, vehicles and places of business open to inspection by any peace officer or agent of the Department of Public Safety and Corrections or of the commission during reasonable hours.

(6) Regulating the selling of performance warranties or guarantees by sellers of motor vehicles and promulgating rules and regulations to effect such regulation.

(7) Holding and conducting hearings on any violation of the provisions of this Chapter or of the provisions of Chapter 4-A and on the imposition of a civil penalty for any such violation.

(8) To regulate the conduct of trade shows at which used motor vehicles sold by used motor vehicle dealers licensed pursuant to this Chapter, new and used marine products, new and used motorcycles, new and used all-terrain vehicles, new and used motor homes, new and used recreational vehicles, new and used buses, new and used travel trailers, new and used fire trucks, new and used wreckers, used hearses, used ambulances, and new and used semitrailers are displayed, auctioned, or sold.

G. All fees and charges under the provisions of this Chapter shall be collected and received by the executive director to the commission and deposited by him in a special fund with the state treasury to be known as the Louisiana Used Motor Vehicle and Parts Commission Fund. The proceeds of the fund shall be disbursed by him at the direction of the commission in administering and enforcing the provisions of this Chapter.

H. All expenses incurred by the commission in carrying out the provisions of this Chapter including but not limited to per diem, wages, salaries, rent, postage, supplies, bond premiums, travel and subsistence for the commissioners and the executive director, printing, and utilities shall be a proper charge against the fund.

I. The commission shall, in addition to the powers herein conferred, be constituted a body politic or political corporation, invested with the powers inherent in corporations. It may sue and be sued under the style of the Louisiana Used Motor Vehicle and Parts Commission, and all process against the corporation shall be served on the chairman or executive director, and all suits on behalf of the commission shall be brought by the chairman or his designee. The domicile for the purpose of being sued shall be in East Baton Rouge Parish. Service of process shall be made upon the chairman or upon the executive director of the commission in person. No member of the board shall be held liable as an individual in any suit against the board. *(Chgd. by Acts 1990 No. 905, §1; Acts 1991 No. 80, §1, No. 451, §1, No. 883, §1, No. 965, §1; Acts 1992 No. 83, §§1, 2; Acts 1997 No. 941, §1, No. 1388, §1, eff. 8/15/97.)*

§773. Dealers, manufacturers, and distributors to be licensed; exception.

A. No person, firm, or corporation, unless licensed to do so by the commission under the provisions of this Chapter, shall carry on or conduct the business of:

(1) A used motor vehicle dealer.

(2) A dealer in used parts or used accessories of motor vehicles.

(3) An auto dismantler and parts recycler.

(4) Used motor vehicle auctions and salvage pools that deal in used motor vehicles.

(5) Any person, partnership, corporation, or other entity dealing in motor vehicles who is not licensed by the Louisiana Motor Vehicle Commission.

(6) A dealer in marine products.

(7) (a) A manufacturer or distributor, who holds a current contract, selling, or franchise agreement with a licensed new motorcycle, all terrain vehicle, marine, trailer, motor home, or bus dealer.

(b) Upon application for license or renewal, the manufacturer or distributor shall furnish the commission with a list of all current dealers and shall notify the commission within thirty days of any cancellations or additional contract, selling, or franchise agreements granted.

(8) Any manufacturer or distributor sales representative; however, the provisions of this Subsection shall not apply if the manufacturer is also the dealer and both operations are conducted at the same location. Multiple locations shall not be exempt.

B. Any motor vehicle dealer, not licensed under the provisions of Chapter 6 of Title 32, who rents on a daily basis, motor vehicles not of the current year or immediate prior year

models, that have been titled previously to an ultimate purchaser, shall be subject to the regulation of the Louisiana Used Motor Vehicle and Parts Commission.
(Chgd. by Acts 1990 No. 905, §1; Acts 1991 No. 965, §1; Acts 1995 No. 758, §1; Acts 1997 No. 322, §1, eff. 8/15/97.)

§773.1. Manufacturers and distributors; unlawful acts.

A. It shall be unlawful and constitute a violation of this Chapter:

(1) For a manufacturer, distributor, wholesaler, distributor branch or factory branch, or officer, agent, or other representative thereof, to induce by unreasonable coercion, or attempt to induce by unreasonable coercion, any motorcycle, all-terrain vehicle, trailer, motor home, bus, recreational vehicle, travel trailer, or marine dealer:

(a) To order or accept delivery of any motorcycle, all-terrain vehicle, trailer, motor home, bus, recreational vehicle, travel trailer or marine product, or vehicles, appliances, equipment, parts, or accessories therefor, or any other commodity or commodities which have not been voluntarily ordered by said motorcycle, all-terrain vehicle, trailer, motor home, bus, recreational vehicle, travel trailer, or marine product dealer.

(b) To order or accept delivery of any motorcycle, all-terrain vehicle, trailer, motor home, bus, recreational vehicle, travel trailer, or marine product with special features, appliances, accessories, or equipment not included in the list price thereof as publicly advertised by the manufacturer thereof.

(c) To order for any person any parts, accessories, equipment, machinery, tools, appliances, or any commodity whatsoever.

(2) For a manufacturer, distributor, wholesaler, distributor branch or factory branch, or officer, agent, or other representative thereof:

(a) Unless otherwise provided by contract, to refuse without just cause to deliver to any duly licensed motorcycle, all-terrain vehicle, trailer, motor home, bus, recreational vehicle, travel trailer, or marine dealer having a franchise, selling, or other contractual arrangement for the retail sale of new and unused motorcycles, all-terrain vehicles, trailers, motor homes, buses, recreational vehicles, travel trailers, or marine products sold or distributed by such manufacturer, distributor, wholesaler, distributor branch or factory branch, any motorcycle, all-terrain vehicle, trailer, motor home, bus, recreational vehicle, travel trailer, or marine product publicly advertised for immediate delivery, within sixty days after such dealer's order has been received.

(b) To attempt to unreasonably coerce or to unreasonably coerce, any motorcycle, all-terrain vehicle, trailer, motor home, bus, recreational vehicle, travel trailer, or marine dealer to enter into any agreement with such manufacturer, distributor, wholesaler, distributor branch or factory branch or representative thereof, or to do any other act unfair to said dealer; or to threaten to cancel without just cause any franchise or any contractual agreement existing between such manufacturer, distributor, wholesaler, distributor branch or factory branch and said dealer.

(c) To unfairly, without due regard to the equities in favor of any such dealer and without just provocation, cancel any franchise, selling, or other contractual arrangement with any motorcycle, all-terrain vehicle, trailer, motor home, bus, recreational vehicle, travel trailer, or marine dealer without just cause and without ninety days notice prior thereto, unless such cancellation arises out of financial default of the dealer or fraudulent activity of the dealer principal which results in the conviction of a crime punishable by imprisonment. The nonrenewal of a franchise, selling, or other agreement with such dealer or his successor without just provocation or cause, and without ninety days prior notice, or the refusal to approve a qualified transferee or qualified successor to the dealer-operator as provided for in the franchise, selling, or other contractual agreement shall be deemed an evasion of this Paragraph and shall constitute an unfair cancellation, notwithstanding any contrary terms or provisions of such franchise, selling, or other contractual agreement. Any such prohibited cancellation, nonrenewal, or refusal to approve the transfer of such agreements without any just provocation or cause shall further constitute a violation of the Unfair Trade Practices and Consumer Protection Law*.

**R.S. 51:1401 et seq.*

(d) Unless otherwise provided by contract, to refuse to extend to a motorcycle, all-terrain vehicle, trailer, motor home, bus, recreational vehicle, travel trailer, or marine dealer the privilege of determining the mode or manner of available transportation facility that such dealer desires to be used or employed in making deliveries of new motorcycles, all-terrain vehicle, trailer, motor home, bus, recreational vehicles, travel trailers, or marine products to him or it.

(e) To resort to or use any false or misleading advertisement in connection with his business as such manufacturer, distributor, wholesaler, distributor branch or factory branch, or officer, agent, or other representative thereof.

(f) Unless otherwise provided by contract, to fail or refuse to pay a motorcycle, all-terrain vehicle, trailer, motor home, bus, recreational vehicle, travel trailer, or marine dealer doing warranty work under the manufacturer's published warranty a labor rate equal to but not in excess of the labor rate in effect in the particular dealership for such work when done for the public in general, that is, nonwarranty work.

(g) Unless otherwise provided by contract, to delay, refuse, or fail to deliver motorcycles, all-terrain vehicles, trailers, motor homes, buses, recreational vehicles, travel trailers, or marine products in reasonable quantities relative to the new motorcycle, all-terrain vehicle, trailer, motor home, bus, recreational vehicle, travel trailer, or marine dealer's facilities and sales potential in the relevant market area. It shall not be a violation, however, if such failure is caused by acts or causes beyond the control of the manufacturer, distributor, or other such party.

(h) To hold a motorcycle, all-terrain vehicle, trailer, motor home, bus, recreational vehicle, travel trailer, or marine dealer liable for any sums determined to be owed to a manufacturer, distributor, wholesaler, distributor branch, or factory branch by virtue of an audit of the books of such dealer, when said sums owed are a result of transactions which occurred more than two years prior to the commencement date of such an audit, unless such sums are owed as a result of fraudulent practices of such dealer. However, a dealer shall not be held liable by virtue of an audit for failure to retain parts for a period in excess of six months.

(i) To ship or sell motorcycles, all-terrain vehicles, trailers, motor homes, buses, recreational vehicles, travel trailers, or marine products to a motorcycle, all-terrain vehicle, trailer, motor home, bus, recreational vehicle, travel trailer, or marine dealer prior to the dealer having been granted a license by the commission.

(j) To unreasonably withhold consent to the sale, transfer, or exchange of a franchise to a qualified transferee capable of being licensed as a new motorcycle, all-terrain vehicle, trailer, motor home, bus, recreational vehicle, travel trailer, or marine dealer in this state, provided the transferee meets the criteria generally applied by the manufacturer in approving new dealers and agrees to be bound by all the terms and conditions of the standard franchises.

(k) To fail to respond in writing to a written request for consent as specified in Subparagraph (j) above within sixty days of receipt of a written request on the forms, if any, generally utilized by the manufacturer or distributor for such purposes and containing the information required therein. Failure to respond shall be deemed to be consent to the request.

(*l*) Unless otherwise provided by contract, to compete with a new motorcycle, all-terrain vehicle, trailer, motor home, bus, recreational vehicle, travel trailer, or marine dealer in the same line make operating under an agreement or franchise from the aforementioned manufacturer or distributor. A manufacturer or distributor shall not, however, be deemed to be competing when any of the following conditions are met:

(i) Operating a dealership temporarily for a reasonable period, not to exceed two years;

(ii) Operating a bona fide retail dealership which is for sale to any qualified independent person at a fair and reasonable price, not to exceed two years;

(iii) Operating in a bona fide relationship in which an independent person has made a significant investment subject to loss in the dealership and can reasonably expect to acquire full ownership of such dealership on reasonable terms and conditions.

B. Any person, firm, association, corporation, or trust which sells or offers to sell new and unused motorcycles, all-terrain vehicles, trailers, motor homes, buses, recreational vehicles, travel trailers or marine products or leases, rents, or offers to lease or rent motorcycles, all-terrain vehicles, trailers, motor homes, buses, recreational vehicles, travel trailers, or marine products, and which is not a licensee of the commission shall, nonetheless, be subject to the provisions of this Chapter and the rules and regulations of the commission which pertain to the regulation of advertising.

(Chgd. by Acts 1990 No. 905, §1; Acts 1991 No. 915, §1; Acts 1997 No. 1388, §1, eff. 8/15/97.)

§773.2. New motorcycle, all-terrain vehicle, trailer, motor home, bus, recreational vehicle, travel trailer, and marine dealer/manufacturer relationship; requirements upon termination; penalty; indemnity.

A. (1) In the event that a dealer ceases to engage in the business of being a motorcycle, all-terrain vehicle, trailer, motor home, bus, recreational vehicle, travel trailer, or marine dealer or ceases to sell a particular make of motorcycle, all-terrain vehicle, trailer, motor home, bus, recreational vehicle, travel trailer, or marine product, and after notice thereof to the manufacturer by registered or certified mail return receipt requested within thirty days thereafter, the manufacturer, at a minimum, shall repurchase all new and unused motorcycles, all-terrain vehicles, trailers, motor homes, buses, recreational vehicles, travel trailers, or marine products of the current or immediate prior model year and parts on hand that have not been damaged or substantially altered to the prejudice of the manufacturer while in the possession of the dealer and all required demonstrators.

(2) The manufacturer shall make the required repurchase after the dealer terminates his franchise, selling, or other contractual agreement and within sixty days of the submission by the dealer to the manufacturer, by registered or certified mail return receipt requested, of a final inventory of motorcycles, all-terrain vehicles, trailers, motor homes, buses, recreational vehicles, travel trailers, or marine products and parts on hand.

B. Failure to make said repurchase without just cause shall subject the manufacturer to a penalty of one and one-half percent per month or fraction thereof of the inventory value of returnable motorcycles, all-terrain vehicles, trailers, motor homes, buses, recreational vehicles, travel trailers, or marine products and parts, payable to the dealer, as long as said repurchase is not made.

C. Notwithstanding the terms of any franchise, selling, or other contractual agreement, each manufacturer shall indemnify and hold harmless its dealers against any judgment for damages, including but not limited to court costs and reasonable attorney fees of the dealer, arising out of complaints, claims, or lawsuits including but not limited to strict liability, negligence, misrepresentation, express or implied warranty or rescission of sale to the extent that the judgment arises out of alleged defective or negligent manufacture, assembly or design of motorcycles, all-terrain vehicles, trailers, motor homes, buses, recreational vehicles, travel trailers, marine products, parts, or accessories or other functions by the manufacturer, which are beyond the control of the dealer.

D. Prior to making a change in the area of responsibility described in the franchise, selling, or other contractual agreement or sales and service agreement of a dealer, the franchisor or manufacturer shall give said dealer and the commission no less than sixty days prior written notice by certified or registered mail.

(Chgd. by Acts 1990 No. 905, §1; Acts 1997 No. 1388, §1, eff. 8/15/97.)

§774. License; fee; liability insurance; filing of franchise agreement; requirement upon termination; penalty; indemnity; marine, new motorcycle, trailer, motor home, bus, recreational vehicle, travel trailers, or all-terrain product franchise cancellation.

A. (1) It shall be unlawful and shall constitute a misdemeanor for any person, firm, association, corporation, or trust to engage in business as, or serve in the capacity of, or act as a used motor vehicle dealer or used motor vehicle salesman, or as an all-terrain vehicle dealer, trailer, motor home, bus, recreational vehicle, travel trailer, fire truck, wrecker, used hearse, used ambulance, or marine dealer in this state without first obtaining a license therefor as provided in this Section.

(2) Any person, firm, association, corporation, or trust engaging, acting, or serving in more than one of the foregoing capacities or having more than one place where the business is carried on or conducted shall be required to obtain and hold a current license for each capacity or location in which he, it, or they shall engage in such business provided that all used motor vehicle dealers shall have at least one licensed salesman per location.

(3) Any person, firm, association, corporation, or trust which violates Paragraph (1) of this Subsection or Subparagraph (f) of Paragraph (4) of Subsection B of this Section shall be fined not less than three hundred dollars nor more than one thousand dollars or imprisoned for not more than ninety days, or both.

B. (1) Applications for licenses required under the provisions of this Section shall be verified by the oath or affirmation of the applicant, shall be on forms prescribed by the commission and furnished to such applicants, and shall contain such information as the commission deems necessary to enable it to fully determine the qualifications and eligibility of the several applicants to receive the license or licenses.

(2) The commission shall require in such application, or otherwise, information relating to:

(a) The applicant's financial standing.

(b) The applicant's business integrity.

(c) Whether the applicant has an established place of business and is engaged in the pursuit, avocation, or business for which each license is applied for.

(d) Whether the applicant is able to properly conduct the business for which each license is applied for.

(e) Such other pertinent information consistent with the safeguarding of the public interest and the public welfare.

(f) The name of the applicant.

(g) The street address of applicant's principal place of business and each additional place of business.

(h) The type of business organization of applicant.

(3) All applications for license or licenses shall be accompanied by the appropriate fee or fees in accordance with the schedule hereinafter provided. In the event any application is denied and the license applied for is not issued, the entire license fee shall be returned to the applicant.

(4) (a) All bonds and licenses issued under the provisions of this Chapter shall expire on December thirty-first following the date of issue and shall be nontransferable.

(b) All applications for renewal of dealers' licenses shall be submitted on or before sixty days prior to the date on which the existing license will expire. If applications have not been made for renewal of licenses, such licenses shall expire one year from the date of issue and it shall be illegal for any person to represent himself and act as a dealer thereafter.

(c) Any dealer who submits a renewal application after the expiration date of an existing license shall be subject to a late penalty of one hundred dollars which shall be paid to the commission.

(d) Any dealer having a previous annual license shall be presumed to be a renewal applicant.

(e) Any dealer changing the name of the dealership, the dealership's address, the ownership of the dealership, or opening any additional place of business shall notify the commission within ten days of such change or be in violation of this Chapter.

(f) Any dealership ceasing to maintain its business shall surrender the dealership license to the commission within ten days and any failure to do so shall constitute a misdemeanor. Violations of this Subparagraph shall be punished as provided in Paragraph (3) of Subsection A of this Section.

(g) The commission is authorized to adopt rules to implement the provisions of this Section.

(5) The office of motor vehicles of the Department of Public Safety and Corrections shall be notified not to accept dealers' titles until such time as licenses have been issued.

C. A used motor vehicle salesman's license shall permit the licensee to engage in the activities of a used motor vehicle salesman. Salesmen shall not be allowed to sell vehicles unless applications and fees are on file with the commission and the motor vehicle salesman's or temporary salesman's license has been issued. No person shall hold more than one salesman's license at a time.

D. The schedule of license fees to be charged and received by the commission for the licenses issued hereunder shall be as follows:

(1) For each used motor vehicle, motorcycle, all terrain vehicle, or marine dealer's license, a maximum of two hundred dollars.

(2) For a used motor vehicle, trailer, motor home, bus, recreational vehicle, travel trailer, fire truck, wrecker, used hearse, used ambulance, motorcycle, all-terrain vehicle or marine dealer's license and for each place of business in addition to the principal place of business, one hundred dollars.

(3) For each used motor vehicle salesman's license, no more than twenty-five dollars.

(4) For each manufacturer or distributor, one hundred dollars.

(5) For each manufacturer or distributor sales representative, one hundred dollars.

E. The license issued to each used motor vehicle, trailer, motor home, bus, recreational vehicle, travel trailer, fire truck, wrecker, used hearse, used ambulance, motorcycle, all-terrain vehicle, and marine dealer shall specify the location of the place of business. If the business location is changed, the commission shall be notified immediately of the change and the commission may endorse the change of location on the license without charge. The license of each dealer shall be posted in a conspicuous place in the dealer's place or places of business.

F. Every used motor vehicle salesman shall have his license upon his person when engaged in his business and shall display same upon request. The name of the employer of the salesman shall be stated on the license.

G. (1) Every person, firm, or corporation before being licensed hereunder as a used motor vehicle, trailer, motor home, bus, recreational vehicle, travel trailer, fire truck, wrecker, used hearse, used ambulance, new motorcycle, all-terrain vehicle, or marine dealer shall show proof of responsibility by depositing with the commission a continuing bond in the amount of ten thousand dollars with surety thereon of a company authorized to do business in the state, which bond shall be approved by the commission, payable to the state of Louisiana through the commission, and shall be conditioned upon faithful observance of all laws relating to the proper disposition of licenses, tags, or titles and shall also indemnify any person who suffers any loss by reason of a failure to observe the provisions of the law relating to sales tax, licenses, tags, or titles and shall also indemnify any person who suffers any loss, damages, and expenses by reason of a failure to deliver title and for the proper disposition of all taxes, licenses, and registration fees.

(2) Such bond shall be for the license period and a new bond or a proper continuation certificate shall be delivered to the commission at the beginning of each license period; provided, however, the aggregate liability of the surety in any one year shall in no event exceed the sum of such bond.

(3) Such bond shall be made payable to the state of Louisiana through the commission for the use, benefit, and indemnity of any persons who shall suffer any loss as a result of any violation of the conditions hereinabove contained and for the proper disposition of all taxes and registration fees.

(4) *(Repealed.)*

H. The bond required by this Section shall be maintained throughout the period of licensure. Should the bond be cancelled for any reason, the dealer license shall be revoked as of the date of cancellation unless a new bond is furnished prior to such date.

I. All used motor vehicle dealers are required to furnish and keep in force the minimum required liability insurance coverage on all vehicles offered for sale or used in any other capacity in demonstrating or utilizing the streets and roadways in accordance with the financial responsibility laws of this state. Should the liability insurance coverage be allowed to lapse or be cancelled for any reason, the dealer license shall be revoked as of the date of cancellation unless proof of a new policy of insurance is furnished prior to such date.

J. (1) Applications for license as a marine dealer, new motorcycle, trailer, motor home, bus, recreational vehicle, travel trailer, or all-terrain vehicle dealer must, in addition to the foregoing, also be accompanied by the filing with the commission of any bona fide contract or franchise in effect between the applicant and a manufacturer or distributor of the marine products, new and unused motorcycle, trailer, motor home, bus, recreational vehicle, travel trailer, or all-terrain vehicle or vehicles proposed to be dealt in; unless such contract or franchise has already been filed with the commission in connection with a previous application made by such applicant, in which event the applicant shall, in lieu of again filing the contract or franchise, identify same by appropriate reference and file all revisions and additions, if any, which have been made to said contract or franchise; and the applicant must furnish satisfactory evidence that the applicant maintains adequate space in the building or structure wherein the applicant's established business is conducted for the display of marine products, new and unused motorcycles, trailers, motor homes, buses, recreational vehicles, travel trailers, or all-terrain vehicles, together with adequate facilities for the repair and servicing of marine products, motorcycles, trailers, motor homes, buses, recreational vehicles, travel trailers, or all-terrain vehicles and the storage of new parts and accessories for same.

(2) The application shall also identify the individual named as dealer-operator, and shall contain such information as the commission considers necessary to enable it to fully determine his qualifications and eligibility to serve in that capacity.

(3) The venue for any arbitration proceeding and the jurisdiction and venue for any action concerning the franchise, selling, or other contractual agreement between any motorcycle, trailer, motor home, bus, recreational vehicle, travel trailer, all-terrain vehicle, or marine products dealer and any manufacturer or distributor shall be in Louisiana in the parish of East

Baton Rouge. It is the public policy of this state that the venue and jurisdiction provided for herein shall not be modified by contract.

(4) No person, firm, association, corporation, or trust can sell, offer or attempt to negotiate a sale, or make deliveries of five or more new and unused motorcycles, trailers, motor homes, buses, recreational vehicles, travel trailers, or all-terrain vehicles in, or into, this state, other than by common or contract carrier, unless licensed by this commission. *(Chgd. by Acts 1990 No. 905, §§1, 2; Acts 1991 No. 965, §1; Acts 1995 No. 758, §1; Acts 1997 No. 1388, §1, eff. 8/15/97.)*

§774.1. Extended warranty contracts; requirements.

A. A used motor vehicle dealer shall not sell an extended warranty contract or a product warrant contract covering a used motor vehicle unless all of the following requirements are met:

(1) The company issuing the extended warranty contract or product warranty contract has posted with the Louisiana Used Motor Vehicle and Parts Commission a bond in the amount of one hundred fifty thousand dollars issued by a surety company authorized to do business in this state.

(2) The company issuing the extended warranty contract or product warranty contract has appointed an agent for service of process in this state.

(3) The dealer gives the prospective purchaser of the extended warranty contract or product warranty contract a copy of the contract of warranty prior to the sale.

B. (1) Any company issuing the extended warranty contract or product warranty contract who does not comply with the provisions of Paragraphs (A)(1) and (2) shall be punished by a fine of not more than one thousand dollars.

(2) Any used motor vehicle dealer who sells the extended warranty contract or product warranty contract without meeting the requirements of Paragraphs (A)(3) shall be punished by a fine of not more than one thousand dollars.

C. For the purposes of this Section, "extended warranty contract" shall mean any contract which insures the purchaser against any of the following:

(1) Breach of warranty by manufacturers, wholesalers, distributors, retailers, or dealers during the initial warranty period.

(2) Mechanical failure, breakdown, or required repairs.

(3) Expense of repairs during a contractual period.

D. For the purposes of this Section, "product warranty contract" shall mean any contract which insures the purchaser against mechanical failure, breakdown, or required repairs or the expenses thereof as a result of the failure, in proper performance or nonperformance of a product intended to maintain or extend the useful life of the engine, transmission, drive axle, assembly, power steering, or air conditioner components of a used motor vehicle.
(Chgd. by Acts 1990 No. 905, §1, eff. 9/7/90.)

§774.2. Sale of used water damaged vehicles.

A. No used motor vehicle dealer, nor any private person, shall sell, transfer, or convey any used motor vehicle to any person without notifying the buyer or receiver of the vehicle in writing of the extent of any water damage from flooding which occurred to the vehicle prior to the transaction.

B. If a sale, transfer, or conveyance of a used motor vehicle occurs in violation of Subsection A, the person receiving ownership and title to the vehicle who is not otherwise aware of the damage at the time of the transaction may bring an action to set aside the transaction within one year from the date of the transaction and receive all monies or other property given as consideration for the vehicle less a reasonable assessment for miles driven.
(Added by Acts 1995 No. 758, §1, eff. 6/27/95.)

§775. Denial, revocation or suspension of license; grounds; unauthorized acts.

A. Except as otherwise provided in this Section, the commission may deny an application for a license or revoke or suspend a license after it has been granted for any of the following reasons:

(1) On satisfactory proof of unfitness of the applicant or the licensee, as the case may be, under the standards established by this Chapter.

(2) For fraudulent practices or any material misstatement made by an applicant in any application for license under the provisions of this Chapter.

(3) For any willful failure to comply with any provision of this Chapter or Chapter 4-A of this Title, any provision relating to the proper disposition of license tags or registrations, transfers of title, or payment of sales taxes in connection with the purchase or sale of any new or used motor vehicle, trailer, motor home, bus, recreational vehicle, travel trailer, fire truck, wrecker, used hearse, used ambulance, motorcycle, all-terrain vehicle, or trailer, or with any rule or regulation adopted and promulgated by the commission under authority vested in it by this Chapter.

(4) Change of condition after license is granted resulting in failure to maintain the qualifications for licensure.

(5) Continued or flagrant violation of any of the rules or regulations of the commission.

(6) Being a used motor vehicle dealer or used motor vehicle salesman who:

(a) Resorts to or uses any false or misleading advertising in connection with his business.

(b) Has committed any unlawful act which resulted in the revocation of any similar license in another state.

(c) Has been convicted of a crime involving moral turpitude.

(d) Has committed a fraudulent act in selling, purchasing, or otherwise dealing in motor vehicles or has misrepresented the terms and conditions of a sale, purchase, or contract for sale or purchase of a motor vehicle or any interest therein including an option to purchase such motor vehicles.

(e) Has engaged in his business under a past or present license issued pursuant to this Chapter or in any other course of conduct in such a manner as to cause injury to the public or to those with whom he is dealing.

(f) Has failed to meet or maintain the conditions and requirements necessary to qualify for the issuance of a license.

(g) Has failed or refused to furnish and keep in force any bond required under this Chapter.

(h) Has knowingly engaged in tampering with, adjusting, altering, changing, setting back, disconnecting, or failure to connect the odometer of any motor vehicle, or causing any of the foregoing to occur to an odometer of a motor vehicle, so as to reflect a lower mileage than the true mileage driven by the motor vehicle. The foregoing shall be applicable to any motor vehicle whether sold wholesale or retail or whether or not the foregoing occurred within or without the state of Louisiana.

(7) Being a used motor vehicle dealer who:

(a) Does not have an established place of business.

(b) Employs unlicensed salesmen or other unlicensed persons in connection with the sale of used vehicles.

(c) Fails or refuses to furnish or keep in force liability insurance on any vehicle offered for sale and otherwise required under the financial responsibility laws of this state.

(d) Is not operating from the address shown on his license if this change has not been reported to the commission or is not restricting the location of the display of motor vehicles for sale exclusively to the address shown on his license.

(e) Is found to be parking vehicles on any public roadway or right-of-way for the purpose of displaying such vehicles for sale.

(8) Being a used motor vehicle dealer who has used false or misleading advertising in connection with the sale of used motor vehicles as defined in this Chapter.

B. The commission shall not deny an application for a license or revoke or suspend a license based upon consideration of an existing or anticipated economic or competitive effect on other licensees in the surrounding community or territory.

C. Each of the aforementioned grounds for suspension, revocation, or denial of issuance or renewal of license shall also constitute a violation of this Chapter, unless the person involved has been tried and acquitted of the offense constituting such grounds.

D. The suspension, revocation, or refusal to issue or renew a license of the imposition of any other penalty by the commission shall be in addition to any penalty which might be imposed upon any licensee upon a conviction at law for any violation of this Chapter.

E. In the performance of its duties under this Section the commission shall have the authority to obtain from the Department of Public Safety and Corrections and other governmental agencies information relating to the criminal records of applicants for licenses under this Chapter.

F. A manufacturer or distributor who violates any of the following provisions shall be subject to the fine or penalty provided in R.S. 32:780. It shall be unlawful for a manufacturer or distributor or representative thereof:

(1) To attempt to induce or coerce, or to induce or coerce, any dealer to enter into any agreement with such manufacturer, distributor, or representative thereof, or to do any other act unfair to said dealer; or to threaten to cancel any franchise or any contractual agreement existing between such manufacturer or distributor and said dealer.

(2) To resort or to use any false or misleading advertisement in connection with his business as manufacturer or distributor of motorcycles, trailers, motor homes, buses, recreational vehicles, travel trailers, all-terrain vehicles, or marine products.

(3) To ship or sell vehicles, trailers, motor homes, buses, recreational vehicles, travel trailers, or marine products to a dealer prior to the dealer having been granted a license by the commission.

(Chgd. by Acts 1990 No. 905, §1; Acts 1991 No. 915, §1, No. 965, §1; Acts 1995 No. 758, §1; Acts 1997 No. 1388, §1, eff. 8/15/97.)

§776. Denial, suspension, or revocation of license; procedure.

A. (1) The commission, without prior notice, may deny any application for a license within sixty days after receipt thereof by written notice to the applicant stating the grounds for such denial. Upon request by the applicant whose application has been so denied, the commission shall set the time and place of a hearing to review such denial, the same to be heard with reasonable promptness. The commission may suspend or revoke a license only after a hearing of which the licensee affected shall be given at least fifteen days written notice specifying the grounds or reasons for revocation or suspension.

(2) Notices may be served as provided by law for the service of notices, or by mailing a copy by certified mail to the last known residence or business address of such applicant or licensee. A copy of such notice shall be mailed by certified mail to the surety on the licensee's bond at the address of the surety given in the bond. The hearing on charges shall be at such time and place as the commission may prescribe and the aforementioned notice shall further specify the time and place. If the applicant or licensee is a used motor vehicle salesman, the commission shall in like manner also notify the person, firm, association, corporation, or trust with whom the licensee is associated or in whose association he is about to enter.

(3) (a) The commission shall have the power to compel the production of records and papers bearing upon the issues to be presented for hearing.

(b) The commission shall have the power to subpoena and bring before it any person in this state, or take testimony of any such person by deposition, with the same fees and mileage and in the same manner as prescribed by law in judicial procedure before courts of the state in civil cases.

(c) Any party to the hearing shall have the right to the attendance of witnesses in his behalf upon designating to the commission the person or persons sought to be subpoenaed.

(4) If the commission determines that any applicant is not qualified to receive a license, a license shall not be granted to the applicant, and, if the commission determines that any licensee is guilty of violation of any of the provisions of this Chapter, his or its license shall be suspended or revoked.

(5) Upon the determination by the commission that either the applicant is not qualified to receive a license or that a licensee is guilty of violating any of the provisions of this Chapter, then all costs of the hearing procedure shall be charged to and borne by the applicant or licensee so affected. These costs shall include but not be limited to attorney fees, court reporter fees, and mileage and per diem of commissioners, as well as other applicable and reasonable costs.

B. (1) The decision of the commission imposing a civil penalty, granting or refusing to grant an application for a license, or suspending or revoking a license shall not become final for a period of thirty days from the date thereof, during which time said applicant or licensee may appeal from the decision of the commission to the Nineteenth Judicial District Court by:

(a) Filing a petition in the court setting forth the facts relied upon and praying for a review of the decision, and

(b) Mailing by certified mail a copy of the petition to the executive director of the commission or causing service of summons directed to the executive director of the commission to be issued, the petition to be mailed or the summons to be issued within thirty days from the date of the decision of the commission from which appeal is taken.

(2) On appeal, the issue shall be heard in accordance with the Administrative Procedure Act*. Nothing herein shall be construed to limit the authority of the court to grant relief as prescribed by R.S. 49:964. If the issues involved were first presented to the commission by a

complaint filed with the commission, the complainant may appeal from the decision of the commission in the same manner as hereinabove prescribed.

**R.S. 49:950 et seq.*

C. (1)(a) Except as provided by Subparagraph (b) of this Paragraph, in holding and conducting hearings on complaints of violations of the provisions of this Chapter or hearings on the imposition of a civil penalty for any such violation, the commission shall give the licensee or other person, firm, association, corporation, or trust alleged to have committed such violation at least fifteen days written notice specifying the violation charged.

(b) (i) In the event disputes arise between a marine dealer and a manufacturer or distributor of marine products concerning a violation of this Chapter, the notification period shall be a minimum of twenty-one days and either party may elect within the twenty-one day notification period to have the complaint or violation determined by any court of competent jurisdiction by notifying the commission by certified or registered mail of its intent to invoke the jurisdiction of any competent court. This election shall be made within the twenty-one day notification period.

(ii) If either party fails to institute legal proceedings in a court of competent jurisdiction within thirty days of its notification to the commission, the commission shall proceed with its scheduled hearing after renotifying the parties and providing them with at least fifteen days notice of the new hearing date.

(iii) During the notice period provided in Item (b)(i) and the delay provided for in Item (b)(ii), and provided either party seeks judicial relief during either of those time periods and takes reasonable steps to pursue such relief, the commission shall withhold any further action on the complaint.

(iv) The provisions of Items (i), (ii), and (iii) of this Subparagraph shall not apply to hearings involving complaints of violations of R.S. 32:773(A) and (B), 774, 774.1, and 775.

(2) Notices may be served as provided by law for the service of notices, or by mailing a copy by certified mail to the last known residence or business address of the party charged with such violation. Hearings shall be at such time and place as the commission may prescribe and the aforementioned notice shall specify the time and place thereof.

(3) (a) The commission shall have the power to compel the production of records and papers bearing upon the issues to be presented for hearing.

(b) The commission shall have the power to subpoena and bring before it any person in this state, or take testimony of any such person by deposition, with the same fees and mileage and in the same manner as prescribed by law in judicial procedure before courts of the state in civil cases.

(c) Any party to the hearing shall have the right to the attendance of witnesses in his behalf upon designating to the commission the person or persons sought to be subpoenaed.

(4) Upon the determination by the commission that the party charged is guilty of violating any of the provisions of this Chapter, then all costs of the hearing procedure shall be charged to and borne by the parties so affected. The costs shall include but not be limited to attorney's fees, court reporter fees, and mileage and per diem of commissioners, as well as other applicable and reasonable costs.

D. When the licensed premises of a used motor vehicle dealer are abandoned, the dealer is no longer in business, there are no salesmen on the premises, and all attempts to locate the dealer have been exhausted, then the used motor vehicle dealer's license and the salesmen's licenses shall be revoked without a hearing.

(Chgd. by Acts 1990 No. 905, §1; Acts 1991 No. 915, §1, No. 965, §1; Acts 1995 No. 758, §1, eff. 6/27/95.)

§777. Injunctions.

A. The commission is hereby authorized without cost, bond, or deposit to institute injunctive actions in courts of competent jurisdiction in the name of the state on the relation of the commission to enforce the provisions of this Chapter.

B. Any licensee or other person who violates or threatens to violate any provision of this Chapter or Chapter 4-A of this Title or rule or regulation promulgated thereunder may be enjoined from committing or continuing the violation or engaging in any business for which a license has been issued under this Chapter. In addition to any other proper venue, the parish of East Baton Rouge shall constitute a proper venue for the institution by the commission of judicial actions authorized under this chapter and under Chapter 4-A of this Title.

(Chgd. by Acts 1990 No. 905, §1; Acts 1991 No. 965, §1, eff. 9/6/91.)

§778. Louisiana Motor Vehicle Commission licensees; exemptions.

The provisions of this Chapter shall not apply to any person, partnership, corporation, or other entity that is licensed or regulated by the Louisiana Motor Vehicle Commission. If any provision of this Chapter conflicts with any provision of Chapter 6 of Title 32 of the Louisiana Revised Statutes of 1950, the provisions of Chapter 6 of Title 32 of the Louisiana Revised Statutes of 1950 shall prevail.

§779. Criminal penalties.

Any person, firm, association, corporation, or trust, except a manufacturer or distributor which is required to be licensed under the provisions of this Chapter, committing a violation of this Chapter shall, upon conviction, be fined not less than five hundred dollars, nor more than one thousand dollars, and each day that a person, firm, association, corporation, or trust violates this Chapter shall constitute a separate offense. *(Chgd. by Acts 1990 No. 905, §1; Acts 1991 No. 915, §1; Acts 1995 No. 758, §1, eff. 6/27/95.)*

§780. Civil penalties.

A. If the commission shall determine that any applicant is not qualified to receive a license, a license shall not be granted to said applicant, and if the commission shall determine that any licensee is guilty of a violation of any of the provisions of this Chapter or the rules and regulations of the commission, his or its license may be suspended or revoked, or a civil penalty may be imposed by the commission. The commission may also impose a civil penalty against any person, firm, association, corporation, or trust which is determined by the commission to have violated any of the provisions of this Chapter or the rules and regulations of the commission.

B. (1) No civil penalty imposed for the violation of the provisions of this Chapter or the rules and regulations of the commission shall exceed five hundred dollars for each day such violation continues.

(2) On a second or subsequent violation, no civil penalty imposed shall exceed one thousand dollars for each day such second or subsequent violation continues. In order to constitute a second or subsequent violation there must occur a lapse of at least one day following the first or previous violation.

C. Any civil penalty imposed by the commission may, in the discretion of the commission, be suspended in whole or in part.

D. Upon the failure of any person, firm, association, corporation or trust to timely pay any civil penalty imposed by the commission when due, the commission shall be entitled to recover by suit or otherwise, from such party all costs of collection, including court costs, deposition, and other discovery costs, and reasonable attorney's fees incurred by the commission in collecting such civil penalty.
(Chgd. by Acts 1990 No. 905, §1; Acts 1991 No. 965, §1, eff. 9/6/91.)

CHAPTER 5. MOTOR VEHICLE SAFETY RESPONSIBILITY LAW

PART I. GENERAL PROVISIONS

Section

PART I-A. COMPULSORY MOTOR VEHICLE LIABILITY SECURITY

PART II. SECURITY FOLLOWING ACCIDENT

PART III. PROOF OF FINANCIAL RESPONSIBILITY

PART IV. PENAL PROVISIONS

PART V. MISCELLANEOUS PROVISIONS

PART I. GENERAL PROVISIONS

§851. Definitions.

The following words and phrases, when used in this Chapter, shall, for the purposes of this Chapter, have the meanings respectively ascribed to them in this Section, except in those instances where the context clearly indicates a different meaning.

(1) "Commissioner"—The term "Commissioner" means the Department of Public Safety of Louisiana.

(2) "Judgment"—Any judgment which shall have become final by expiration without appeal of the time within which a suspensive appeal might have been perfected or by final affirmation on appeal, rendered by a court of competent jurisdiction of any state or of the United States, upon a cause of action arising out of the ownership, maintenance or use of any motor vehicle, for damages, including damages for care and loss of services, because of bodily injury to or death of any person, or for damages because of injury to or destruction of property including the loss of use thereof, or upon a cause of action on an agreement of settlement for such damages.

(3) "License"—Any license, temporary instruction permit or temporary license issued under the laws of this state to the licensing of persons to operate motor vehicles.

(4) "Motor vehicle"—Every self-propelled vehicle (except traction engines; road rollers, farm tractors, tractor cranes, power shovels and well drillers) and every vehicle which is propelled by electric power obtained from overhead wires but not operated upon rails.

(5) "Non-resident"—Every person who is not a resident of this state; but does not include persons dwelling outside of this state whose occupation or business requires them to spend one-half or more of their working hours in this state in pursuance of their business or employment.

(6) "Non-resident's operating privileges"—The privilege conferred upon a non-resident by the laws of this state pertaining to the operation by him of a motor vehicle, or the use of a motor vehicle owned by him, in this state.

(7) "Operator"—Every person who is in actual physical control of a motor vehicle.

(8) "Owner"—Every person who holds the legal title to a motor vehicle or in the event a motor vehicle is the subject of an agreement for the conditional sale, lease or transfer of the possession, however, thereof, with the right of purchase upon performance of the condition stated in the agreement and with an immediate right of possession vested in the conditional vendee, lessee, possessor or in the event such or similar transaction is had by means of a mortgage, and the mortgagor of a vehicle is entitled to possession, then such conditional vendee, lessee, possessor or mortgagor shall be deemed the owner for the purpose of this Chapter.

(9) "Person"—Every natural person, firm, co-partnership, association or corporation.

(10) "Proof of financial responsibility" means proof of ability to respond in damages for liability, on account of accidents occurring subsequent to the effective date of the proof, arising out of the ownership, maintenance, or use of a motor vehicle in the amounts specified in R.S. 32:872 in reference to the acceptable limits of a policy or bond.

(11) "Registration"—Registration certificate or certificates and registration plates issued under the laws of this state pertaining to the registration of motor vehicles.

(12) "State"—Any state, territory, or possession of the United States, the District of Columbia, or any province of the Dominion of Canada.

§852. Commissioner to administer law; hearings; notice to injured parties; appeal to court.

A. The commissioner shall administer and enforce the provisions of this Chapter and may make rules and regulations necessary for its administration and shall provide for hearings upon request of persons aggrieved by orders or acts of the commissioner under the provisions of this Chapter.

B. Any other provision of law to the contrary notwithstanding, whenever a person is involved in an accident and as a result thereof, whether directly or indirectly, the director of public safety is requested or required to hold an administrative hearing to determine whether or not that person's driver's license or driving privilege is to be suspended, cancelled, or revoked, the director shall, in addition, notify each party who suffered personal injury or property damage in such accident of the hearing. Such notification shall be made by regular or first class mail to the last known address of the party. The notification shall state therein that the hearing will be held, for what purpose the hearing will be held, that the party to whom the notification is made may attend the hearing, and that the hearing shall in addition be held for the purpose of determining whether or not compensation has been made for damages.

C. Any order or act of the commissioner, under the provisions of this Chapter, shall be subject to review by appeal to the district court of the parish of East Baton Rouge or by appeal to the district court of the domicile of appellant, provided an appeal is filed in the district court within thirty days from the effective dates of the order or act of the commissioner, at the instance of any party in interest. The court shall determine whether the filing of the appeal shall operate as a stay of any such order or decision of the commissioner. The court may, in disposing of the issue before it, modify, affirm or reverse the order or decision of the commissioner in whole or in part.

D. The deputy secretary for the office of public safety services shall annually include in his budget a provision for the expenditure of funds to improve the enforcement of the Motor Vehicle Safety Responsibility Law. Ten days prior to the beginning of each regular session of the legislature, he shall submit a written report to each house of the legislature on the effectiveness of the law and his enforcement efforts, for amending the law, and for additional authority or financial assistance he requires to enforce the law effectively.

E. Notwithstanding any other provision of the law to the contrary, no fine, fee, or other monetary sanction shall be imposed for failure to respond to any notice required as provided in this Chapter as it provides for notices of suspension or revocation of driving privileges or motor vehicle registration privileges unless the notice was transmitted by certified or registered mail, return receipt requested.

(Chgd. by Acts 1991 No. 1020, §1; Acts 1992 No. 984, §10, eff. 8/21/92.)

§853. Commissioner to furnish operating records; other information; fees; withdrawal of forms or information.

A. (1)(a) The commissioner shall, upon request, furnish any person a certified abstract of the operating record of any person subject to the provisions of this Chapter. The abstract shall also fully designate the motor vehicles, if any, registered in the name of such person. The operating record of an individual driver shall only include those offenses where an individual has pled guilty and been sentenced thereupon, forfeited bond resulting in a final judgment of forfeiture, or been found guilty in a final disposition by a court of competent jurisdiction of violating a law in the operation of a motor vehicle, or civil actions in which an individual has been adjudged at fault, and all accidents. "Final disposition" shall be defined in this Section as a final conviction, not capable of appeal or review, and not subject to dismissal.

(b) On accidents occurring after December 31, 1984, it shall be noted on the record whether or not such person was issued a citation, or whether an individual has pled guilty, forfeited bond, or been found guilty by a court of competent jurisdiction of violating a law in the operation of a motor vehicle, or civil actions in which an individual has been adjudged at fault.

(c) The operating record of a person shall not include those arrests for a first or second violation of any ordinance or statute making criminal the driving of a motor vehicle while under the influence of alcoholic beverages nor shall it include any record of any civil sanction imposed, including the suspension of a license, as a result of such an arrest when any of the following occurs:

(i) The person submitted to an approved chemical test and the test resulted in a blood alcohol reading of less than 0.10 percent by weight, or of less than 0.02 percent by weight, if the person was under the age of twenty-one years on the date of the test, and the person is found not guilty.

(ii) The person was found not guilty whether or not he submitted to a test.

(iii) The person was convicted or entered a plea, and such conviction or plea was subject to the provisions of Code of Criminal Procedure Article 894.

(d) The operating record shall not include those arrests or convictions for a first or second violation of R.S. 14:98.1, if at least two years have elapsed since the date of conviction and the offender has not been convicted of an additional offense for violation of R.S. 14:98 or 98.1. If he has been convicted of one or more of these additional offenses during the two-year period, then the earlier offense shall remain on his record for a period of four years from the date of that conviction.

(2) The commissioner shall also, upon request, advise as to whether any person subject to the provisions of this Chapter has complied with the requirements concerning the deposit of security, and, if so, shall designate the manner of compliance, the nature and amount of

security deposited, or the name and address of the liability insurance company insuring such person.

(3) (a) No insurance company shall use the certified abstract of the operating record to increase an insured's premium without complying with the following conditions:

(i) Furnish a copy of the abstract to the insured.

(ii) Determine that the insured is over fifty percent at fault in any accident shown on the abstract.

(iii) Provide the insured a notice in writing that the insured has a right to appeal the determination of fault by requesting a hearing before the Department of Public Safety and Corrections. The notice shall contain the procedure for requesting the hearing and the address to which the request is to be transmitted.

(b) Should the insured not agree that the insured is over fifty percent at fault, the insured may appeal the matter to the Department of Public Safety and Corrections for determination. The department shall provide notice of the hearing to the insured, to the insurance company of the insured, and to each person who suffered personal injury or property damage as a result of the accident. The notice shall be transmitted by first class mail to the last known address of the person.

(c) The Department of Public Safety and Corrections shall notify the insured and insurance company of their findings. If the Department of Public Safety and Corrections finds the insured not over fifty percent at fault in the accident, the insurance company shall remove any additional premium charged to the insured for that accident.

(4) Whenever it is determined that the person is not over 50% at fault, the department shall note such finding on the person's operating record.

(5) No insurance company shall increase an insured's premium for an accident in which he was not over 50% at fault.

(6) (a) The provisions of this Subsection shall not apply to accidents involving publicly owned emergency vehicles operated by any public safety or law enforcement officer, whether fulltime, parttime, or volunteer, including but not limited to firefighters in the employ of any municipality, parish or fire protection district; deputy sheriffs; municipal police officers; officers of the Louisiana State Police; officers of the enforcement division of the Department of Wildlife and Fisheries; and emergency medical vehicle operators with respect to accidents in which these persons are involved while engaged in the operation of a publicly owned emergency vehicle in the course and scope of their employment.

(b) No accident involving the operation of a publicly owned emergency vehicle by any of the persons described in this Paragraph shall be included on the individual officer's operating record nor shall any insurance company increase the premium on that person's privately owned vehicle because of that accident.

B. (1) The commissioner shall be entitled to charge and collect a fee of six dollars for each copy of a certified abstract and for each copy of any information furnished upon request of any person from the files of the financial responsibility division of the Department of Public Safety and Corrections. Notwithstanding any other fees as stipulated herein, the fee for furnishing motor vehicle reports that are derived from computer generated requests shall not exceed six dollars for records from all sources.

(2) (a) Subject to the exceptions contained in Article VII, Section 9(B) of the Constitution of Louisiana, all fees, fines, or other monies collected under the provisions of this Chapter or dedicated to the enforcement of the provisions of this Chapter shall be paid to the state treasury and shall be credited to the Bond Security and Redemption Fund.

(b), (c) *(Repealed.)*

C. When any person files a form, or furnishes information, which is provided for under this Chapter, and the person was not at that time required by law to file the form or furnish the information, that person may request that the form, and all of the information contained in the form, and any other information furnished by him be withdrawn from the files maintained by the commissioner. If the commissioner determines that the law as it existed at that time did not require the form to be filed, or the information to be submitted, he shall return the form to the person who filed it and shall delete from the files of the commissioner any information concerning the form and any other information furnished by that person.

(Chgd. by Acts 1990 No. 871, §1; Acts 1991 No. 980, §1; Acts 1992 No. 984, §18; Acts 1994 Third Ex. Sess. No. 20, §2; Acts 1997 No. 1296, §3, eff. 7/15/97, No. 1343, §1, eff. 8/15/97.)

§854. Chapter supplemental to motor vehicle laws.

This Chapter shall in no respect be considered as a repeal of the state motor vehicle laws but shall be construed as supplemental thereto.

§855. Past application of chapter.

This Chapter shall not apply with respect to any accident, or judgment arising therefrom, or violation of the motor vehicle laws of this state, occurring prior to the effective date of this Chapter.

§856. Chapter not to prevent other process.

Nothing in this Chapter shall be construed as preventing the plaintiff in any action at law from relying for relief upon the other processes provided by law.

§857. Uniformity of interpretation.

This Chapter shall be so interpreted and construed as to effectuate its general purpose to make uniform the laws of those states which enact it.

§858. Short title.

This Chapter may be cited as the Motor Vehicle Safety Responsibility Law.

PART I-A. COMPULSORY MOTOR VEHICLE LIABILITY SECURITY

§861. Security required.

A. (1) Every self-propelled motor vehicle registered in this state except those motor vehicles used as agricultural or forest vehicles during seasons when they are not used on the highway, those used primarily for exhibit or kept primarily for use in parades, exhibits, or shows, and lease-bound mobile rig haulers as defined in Subsection D of this Section, shall be covered by an automobile liability policy with liability limits as defined by R.S. 32:900(B)(2) or 900(M), or a binder for same, or by a motor vehicle liability bond as defined by Subsection B of this Section, or by a certificate of the state treasurer stating that cash or securities have been deposited with said treasurer as provided by Subsection C of this Section, or by a certificate of self-insurance as provided by R.S. 32:1042.

(2) It shall be the duty of the registered owner of a motor vehicle to maintain the security hereinabove required. Failure to maintain said security shall subject the registered owner to the sanctions hereinafter provided in Sections 863, 864, and 865 of this Part.

(3) If the owner or lessee wishes to discontinue the use of a vehicle registered in his name, he shall notify the secretary by sworn affidavit that the vehicle is no longer in use and the proposed period of nonuse, and shall have the agent who had previously issued the policy of insurance on the vehicle submit an affidavit that the insurance on the vehicle has been cancelled during the period of time that the vehicle will not be in use.

B. "Motor vehicle liability bond" means a bond conditioned:

(1) That the obligor shall, within thirty days after the rendition thereof, satisfy:

(a) (i) All judgments rendered against him or against any person responsible for the operation of the obligor's motor vehicle with his express or implied consent in actions to recover damages for property damage or for bodily injuries, including death at any time resulting therefrom, and

(ii) Judgments rendered as aforesaid for consequential damages consisting of expenses incurred by a husband, wife, parent, or tutor for medical, nursing, hospital, or surgical services in connection with or on account of such bodily injuries or death sustained during the term of the bond by any person, and

(b) Arising out of the ownership, operation, maintenance, control, or use upon the highways and roads of the state of such motor vehicle,

(2) To the amount or limit of:

(a) Not less than ten thousand dollars for damages to the property of others, and

(b) Of not less than ten thousand dollars on account of injury to or death of any one person, and

(c) Subject to such limits as respects injury to or death of one person, of not less than twenty thousand dollars on account of any one accident resulting in injury to or death of more than one person.

C. (1)(a) The applicant for registration may, in lieu of procuring a motor vehicle liability bond or policy, deposit with the state treasurer cash in the amount of thirty thousand dollars or bonds, stocks, or other evidences of indebtedness satisfactory to said treasurer of a market value of not less than thirty thousand dollars as security for the payment by such applicant or by any person responsible for the operation of such applicant's motor vehicle with his express or implied consent of all judgments rendered against such applicant or against such person in actions to recover damages to property or for bodily injuries, including death at any time resulting therefrom, and judgments rendered as aforesaid for consequential damages consisting of expenses incurred by a husband, wife, parent, or tutor for medical, nursing, hospital, or surgical services in connection with or on account of such bodily injuries or death sustained during the term of registration by any person and arising out of the ownership, operation, maintenance, control, or use upon the highways and roads of the state of such motor vehicle to the amount or limit of at least ten thousand dollars on account of any such judgment for damages to property or to the amount of ten thousand dollars for bodily injury or death to any one person or to the amount of twenty thousand dollars for bodily injury or death to more than one person.

(b) Upon presentation to the state treasurer by an officer qualified to serve civil process of an execution issued on any such judgment against the registrant or other person responsible as aforesaid, the treasurer shall pay, out of the cash deposited by the registrant as herein provided, the amount of the execution, including costs and interest, up to but not in excess of ten thousand dollars for damages to property or ten thousand dollars to any one person for damages for bodily injury or death or twenty thousand dollars for bodily injury or death to more than one person.

(c) If the registrant has deposited bonds, stocks, or other evidences of indebtedness, the state treasurer shall, on presentation of an execution as aforesaid, cause the securities, or such part thereof as may be necessary to satisfy the judgment, to be sold at public auction giving the registrant three days notice in writing of the time and place of the sale. From the proceeds of the sale the state treasurer shall, after paying the expenses thereof, satisfy the execution as hereinbefore provided when a cash deposit has been made.

(d) Any payment upon an execution by the state treasurer in accordance with the provisions of this Section shall discharge him from all official and personal liability whatever to the registrant to the extent of such payment.

(e) The state treasurer shall deposit any cash received under the provisions of this Section in a savings bank or savings department of a trust company or of a national bank within the state.

(f) The depositor shall be entitled to the interest accruing on his deposit and to the income payable on the securities deposited. He may from time to time change such securities with the approval of the state treasurer.

(g) The state treasurer, whenever for any reason the amount of such deposit falls below the amount required by this Section, shall require, at the option of the registrant, the deposit of additional cash or securities up to the amount required by this Section or a motor vehicle liability bond or policy as provided in this Chapter.

(h) Money or securities deposited with the state treasurer under the provisions of this Section shall not be subject to attachment or execution except as provided in this Section.

(2) The state treasurer shall give to the applicant for registration a receipt on a form prescribed by the treasurer for the amount of cash or securities deposited by him with the treasurer under this Chapter. The state treasurer shall retain such cash or securities deposited as aforesaid and shall not deliver the same or the balance thereof to the registrant on his order until the expiration of the time within which actions, the payment of judgments in which are secured by such deposit, may be brought against the registrant or the person responsible for the operation of the registrant's motor vehicle with his express or implied consent, nor in any case if a written notice is filed with the state treasurer stating that such an action has been brought against the registrant or other person responsible as aforesaid, until payment is made as provided in this Subsection or satisfactory evidence is presented to the treasurer that final disposition of the action has been made.

D. "Lease-bound mobile rig hauler" as used in this Chapter means a winch or crew truck in excess of twenty-six thousand pounds which meets the following description:

(1) The hauler is operated on the highways of Louisiana only for the purpose of hauling mobile work over rigs or any accessories for a mobile work over rig within a ten mile radius of the operator's oil and gas lease.

(2) The haulers are covered under a general liability policy, issued by an insurance company authorized to do business in the state, with liability coverage and limits equal to or greater than those defined R.S. 32:900(B)(2), and such proof of the coverage is provided to the secretary as he may, by rule, require.
(Chgd. by Acts 1992 No. 830, §1; Acts 1995 No. 301, §1, eff. 6/15/95.)

§862. Proof of compliance.

A. As used in this Section, the phrase "proof of compliance" means proof of compliance with the requirements of the Motor Vehicle Safety Responsibility Law, R.S. 32:851 et seq., and the rules adopted under that law.

B. (1) The commissioner shall adopt rules to implement the provisions of this Section. The rules shall provide that documentation of insurance or other security shall be required for proof of compliance. The rules shall require that the original or a copy of one of the following documents be produced as documentation of insurance: an insurance card; an insurance policy; or the declarations page of the insurance policy showing coverages. The rules shall require insurance and security companies to issue cards or similar documents which indicate the existence of insurance or security coverage, may establish the form for the cards or similar documents, and may establish the form for the written declarations required by this Section.

(2) The provisions of this Subsection with regard to the documentation of insurance requirements shall not apply to new and used automobile dealers as defined by law. However, the rules shall provide for the use of affidavits to prove compliance when registration is sought by a licensed new or used motor vehicle dealer on behalf of a customer.

(3) The provisions of this Subsection shall not apply to renewals of registration by mail.

C. Each person who applies for the registration of a motor vehicle, or who applies for the renewal of a registration of a motor vehicle, or who applies for a motor vehicle inspection certificate shall provide proof of compliance and shall declare in writing that the applicant will remain in compliance during the time for which the registration, the renewal of registration, or the certificate is issued.

D. Each adult person who applies for a driver's license shall:

(1) Provide proof of compliance and declare in writing that the applicant will remain in compliance during the time for which the license is issued; or

(2) Declare in writing that the applicant does not own a motor vehicle which is currently registered or licensed in this state or any other state or in any territory.

E. When a minor person applies for a driver's license, the parent or guardian who has custody of the minor applicant shall:

(1) Provide proof of compliance for both the minor applicant and the parent or guardian, and declare in writing that the minor applicant and the parent or guardian will remain in compliance during the time for which the license is issued; or

(2) Declare in writing that the parent or guardian does not own a motor vehicle which is currently registered or licensed in this state or in any other state or in any territory.

F. As used in Subsections D and E of this Section, an application for a driver's license includes an initial application, an application for renewal, and an application for reissue to change the address of the applicant, to change any other information concerning the applicant, or to change the endorsements held by the applicant.

G. The prohibited actions and penalties for violations thereof are as follows:

(1) No person shall provide false or fraudulent information or documents or make false or fraudulent representations in connection with any application for the registration of a motor vehicle, or for a renewal of a registration of a motor vehicle, or for a motor vehicle inspection certificate, or for a driver's license.

(2) No person shall make a false declaration or execute a false affidavit in response to the requirements of this Section.

(3) No person shall alter or counterfeit any card or similar document used to show proof of compliance.

(4) Whoever violates the provisions of this Subsection shall be fined not more than one thousand dollars and shall be required to perform not less than forty hours nor more than two hundred hours of community service.

(5) When the commissioner finds that any person has violated the provisions of this Subsection, the commissioner may suspend, revoke, or cancel the driver's license held by the offender and may suspend, revoke, or cancel the registration of each motor vehicle owned by the offender.

H. No action taken by any person, whether private citizen or public officer or employee, with regard to any license, registration, or inspection certificate, or with regard to any document which indicates compliance with this Part, shall create a presumption of the existence of insurance coverage, or be construed by any court as a warranty of the reliability or accuracy of the document, or create any liability on the part of the state, or on the part of any department, office, or agency of the state, or on the part of any officer, employee, or agent of the state.

(Chgd. by Acts 1990 No. 25, §1; Acts 1995 No. 423, §§1, 2, No. 756, §1, eff. 8/15/95.)

§863. Sanctions for false declaration; reinstatement fees; revocation; suspension of driving privileges; review.

A. (1) Except as provided herein below, when the secretary determines that a vehicle is not covered by security as required by this Chapter or that the owner or lessee has allowed the required security to lapse, he shall revoke the registration of the vehicle, impound or cancel the vehicle's license plate.

(2) Should the secretary determine that any person, whether in his application for registration of a motor vehicle or in his application for a motor vehicle inspection or otherwise, has submitted false information that the motor vehicle was covered by the security required by Section 861 of this Part, the secretary shall impose upon the owner or owner's lessee the sanctions set forth in Subsection A(1), but for a longer minimum period, as set forth hereinafter.

(3) (a) In the case of a first violation of Paragraph (1), sanctions shall be imposed for a period of three days. In the case of a second or subsequent violation of Paragraph (1), sanctions shall be imposed for a period of not less than thirty days nor more than twelve months. In the case of a first or subsequent violation of Paragraph (2) above, sanctions shall be imposed for a period of not less than six months nor more than eighteen months. However, in no event shall these sanctions be removed until such time as proof of the required security is provided to the secretary along with all appropriate fees required by law, including a reinstatement fee of twenty-five dollars for a first violation, one hundred dollars for a second violation, and two hundred dollars for a third or subsequent violation, provided the offenses occurred within a five-year period. The reinstatement fee shall not be owed for an alleged violation when proof of the required security is provided. The first offense occurring after five years from the prior first offense shall be deemed to be a first offense, until completion of the new capital immovables and related movables as described in Subparagraph (b). The minimum term of a liability insurance policy or other security obtained to comply with this Section shall be six months.

(b) Notwithstanding any other provision of this Chapter to the contrary, and after satisfying the requirements of the Bond Security and Redemption Fund, and upon the creation of a fund to secure the bonded indebtedness of the Department of Public Safety and Corrections for the construction and maintenance of new capital immovables and related movables for the office of motor vehicles, the office of state police, or any other office, agency, board, or commission within the Department of Public Safety and Corrections, public safety services, thirty-six percent of the revenue from reinstatement fees imposed by this Paragraph shall be deposited in the bond fund. In addition, fourteen percent of the revenues from the reinstatement fees shall be dedicated for obtaining equipment and related supplies to be used in connection with the issuance of validation stickers. In addition, twenty-six percent of the revenue from reinstatement fees shall be dedicated to increase the salaries of all full-time employees of the Department of Public Safety and Corrections, office of motor vehicles. In the event no bond fund is created, thirty-six percent of the revenues from the reinstatement fees shall be used as provided by law for the construction and maintenance of the new capital immovables and related movables described in this Paragraph.

(c) Upon completion of the construction of the new capital immovables and related movables described in this Paragraph and payment of the debt obligation related to such construction, the forty percent of the revenue from reinstatement fees imposed by this Paragraph shall be deposited in the state general fund. However, fifteen percent of such revenues shall be reserved for maintenance of the complex.

(4) Fees shall be paid to the secretary, who shall remit them to the state treasurer to be credited to the Bond Security and Redemption Fund as provided in R.S. 32:853(B)(2).

B. The sanctions of Paragraph (1) of Subsection A shall not be imposed, and any fine, fee, or other monetary sanction which has been remitted to the secretary pursuant to the sanctions of this Section, specifically including any reinstatement fee paid pursuant to Paragraph (3) of

Subsection A and any fee paid pursuant to Paragraph (5) of Subsection C, shall be promptly refunded by the secretary to the person who paid it, if the owner or lessee furnishes:

(1) An original or photocopy of a Louisiana auto insurance identification card showing that the required security is in effect on the vehicle and has been continuous without lapse or an original or photocopy of any written communication from an insurer either to the insured or to the secretary stating that the required security is in effect on the vehicle and has been continuous without lapse, any one of which shall constitute sufficient evidence that the required security on the vehicle has not lapsed; or

(2) If such evidence is not furnished by the owner or lessee, any other evidence satisfactory to the secretary, that:

(a) The vehicle was at the time in question in fact covered by the required security or else has newly been covered by security as required by R.S. 32:861 within ten days of the initiation of termination or cancellation of previous security; and

(b) The vehicle is currently covered by security as required by R.S. 32:861; and

(c) The vehicle was not involved in an accident during the period when it was not covered by security as required by R.S. 32:861; or

(3) If the person applies for a registration during the same period for which the surrendered plate would have been valid, credit shall be applied toward the purchase of a new plate. The credit shall be equal to the amount paid for the most recent registration of the motor vehicle multiplied by a fraction, the numerator of which is the unused months of said registration and the denominator of which is the number of months for which said registration was issued.

C. (1) When the secretary seeks to impose the sanctions required in this Section, he shall send written notice to the owner, lessee, or other person against whom sanctions are intended at the last address furnished to the department. A notice of noncompliance, issued by a law enforcement officer under the provisions of R.S. 32:863.1(C)(1), shall serve as notice to the owner, lessee, or other person. Prior to imposition of such sanctions, a hearing may be requested within ten days from the date of notice. Sanctions shall not be imposed until all rights for appeal have expired or been exhausted.

(2) At the hearing, the commissioner shall consider the correctness of his initial determination with regard to petitioner's violation of any provision of Subsection A or B of this Section. Should the commissioner find that his initial determination with regard to such a violation was correct, the suspension and revocation ordered by him shall be maintained and given effect. The commissioner shall rescind an ordered revocation and suspension only if he finds that the petitioner violated no provision of Subsection A or B of this Section, and that the initial determination made by the commissioner was incorrect.

(3) If revocation and suspension is proper, upon a showing of proof satisfactory to the commissioner that a person's livelihood requires the use of a motor vehicle for purposes other than transportation to and from the workplace, that use of such motor vehicle is an integral and inseparable aspect of his job, and that suspension of driving privileges would thereby prevent the earning of a livelihood; the commissioner may, after revocation of the registration of the vehicle, suspension of the driving privileges, and after confiscating the driver's license and license plate of such persons, issue to first offenders a special operator's permit, appropriately identified as such, which would authorized* the holder to drive a vehicle belonging to his employer, and only in the regular course of his duties, provided that:

**So in original. Probably should be "authorize".*

(a) The licensee shall be permitted to operate his employer's vehicle only within the geographic area identified in the special permit required for the earning of a livelihood.

(b) Such operation shall be restricted to regular hours of employment, which hours shall be indicated on the special permit; and

(c) Required security is demonstrated covering both the vehicle and the driver, and proof of such security is kept with operator and vehicle during operation.

A violation of the restrictions of the special permit or a subsequent determination of non-compliance with any provision of this Section by the commissioner during the term of the restricted license shall result in the extension of the period of revocation and suspension for one year from the date upon which the licensee would otherwise have been able to apply for a new license.

(4) Within ten days after a person has exhausted his remedies with the commissioner, he shall have the right to file a petition in the district court in the parish of his domicile for a review of the final order of revocation and suspension. The court may exercise any action it deems appropriate.

(5) The department may promulgate rules and regulations necessary to offset the administrative cost of this Section not to exceed twenty-five dollars.

D. (1) When the driving privileges or vehicle registration of a person are suspended or revoked under the provisions of this Section, his driving privileges shall remain suspended and his vehicle registration shall remain revoked, and no driving privileges, including a special operator's permit as provided in Subsection C of this Section, shall be issued or motor vehicle registered to that person unless the person files proof of future financial responsibility on Form SR 22 accompanied by a fee of twenty-five dollars with the secretary with respect to all motor vehicles registered in his name. There shall be no filing fee required if the owner shows that he had, and presently has, liability insurance as provided by this Chapter, or if he shows that there was a lapse in liability insurance for a period not in excess of ten calendar days.

(2) Such proof of future financial responsibility shall be maintained for three years after the date of filing.

(3) *(Repealed.)*

(Chgd. by Acts 1991 No. 391, §1; Acts 1992 No. 984, §18; Acts 1994 Third Ex. Sess. No. 119, §1; Acts 1998 First Ex. Sess. No. 159, §1, eff. 6/16/98.)

§863.1. Evidence of compulsory motor vehicle liability security contained in vehicle; enforcement; penalty; fees; out-of-state vehicles.

A. No owner or lessee of a self-propelled motor vehicle registered in this state, except a motor vehicle used primarily for exhibit or kept primarily for use in parades, exhibits, or shows, or agricultural or forest use vehicles during seasons when they are not used on the highways, shall operate or allow the operation of such vehicle upon any public road, street, or highway in this state unless there is contained within the vehicle one of the following documents evidencing that the motor vehicle is in compliance with R.S. 32:861 relative to compulsory motor vehicle liability security:

(1) A certificate of insurance. "Certificate" means the written evidence of motor vehicle liability insurance as defined in R.S. 32:900 that is in the form of one of the following:

(a) An identification card issued by an insurer to its insured which shall contain the following information:

(i) The name and address of the insurance company.

(ii) The insurance policy number.

(iii) A description of the motor vehicle insured under the policy.

(iv) The effective date and the expiration date of the policy.

(v) The name of any person who is excluded from coverage as authorized by R.S. 32:900(L).

(b) A motor vehicle liability insurance policy or a duplicate original thereof.

(c) A motor vehicle liability insurance policy binder or a duplicate original thereof.

(2) A duplicate original of a motor vehicle liability bond which complies with the requirements for a motor vehicle liability bond set forth in R.S. 32:861(B).

(3) A certificate of the state treasurer stating that cash or securities have been deposited with said treasurer as provided for under the provisions of R.S. 32:861(C).

(4) A certificate of self-insurance issued by the secretary under the provisions of R.S. 32:1042 qualifying the owner of the vehicle as a self-insurer.

B. When a law enforcement officer stops a vehicle at an administrative violations checkpoint, or in connection with an alleged violation of the law, or for any other reason, or when a law enforcement officer investigates an accident, the law enforcement officer shall determine if the owner or lessee of each vehicle is in compliance with the provisions of this Section which require evidence of liability insurance or other security to be contained in the vehicle. If the owner or lessee is not in compliance with those provisions, the law enforcement officer shall take the actions specified in this Section.

C. (1)(a) If the operator of a motor vehicle is unable to show compliance with the provisions of this Part by displaying the required document when requested to do so, the motor vehicle shall be impounded and the operator shall be issued a notice of noncompliance with the provisions of this Part on a form to be provided by the department. A copy of the notice of noncompliance shall be provided to the towing or storage company and a copy shall be forwarded to the office of motor vehicles within three calendar days after the notice on noncompliance was served. The notice of noncompliance shall serve as notice of administrative hearings rights. In addition, the law enforcement officer shall remove the license plate from the vehicle if the vehicle is registered in Louisiana. The law enforcement officer shall deliver the vehicle license plate to the chief of the agency which employs the officer, or to a person in that agency designated to receive such license plates. In those cases in which a motor vehicle is not impounded, a copy of the notice of noncompliance shall be attached to the vehicle license plate and both shall be delivered to the nearest office of motor vehicles within three calendar days after the notice of noncompliance was served.

(b) The owner of the vehicle shall have three calendar days from the date that the notice of noncompliance was issued to present to the office of motor vehicles proof of insurance coverage or security in effect at the time of the issuance of the notice of noncompliance. If the vehicle was properly insured at the time the notice was issued, any valid license plate shall be returned within forty-eight hours, exclusive of legal holidays, to the owner of the vehicle at no cost to the owner. However, if the owner fails to provide proof of the fact that the vehicle was properly insured at the time the notice of noncompliance was issued, the chief administrative officer of the office of motor vehicles shall destroy, or shall cause to be destroyed, the license plate removed from that owner's vehicle and shall notify the secretary that the owner of the vehicle is not in compliance with the compulsory liability law. Upon receipt of such notification, the secretary shall revoke the registration of such vehicle.

(c) For a first offense there shall be a reinstatement fee of fifty dollars, for a second offense there shall be a reinstatement fee of one hundred fifty dollars, and for any subsequent offense there shall be a reinstatement fee of five hundred dollars. The reinstatement fee contained herein shall be in addition to other appropriate registration fees allowed by law and reinstatement shall depend upon proof of compliance with the compulsory liability law.

(2) In those cases in which the motor vehicle is not impounded, any law enforcement officer who removes and takes a license plate pursuant to the provisions of this Section shall issue for attachment to the rear end of the vehicle, a temporary sticker denoting its use in lieu of an official license plate. The sticker shall bear the date upon which it was issued in written or stamped numerals or letters not less than three inches in height. This temporary sticker shall only be effective for a period of three calendar days beginning from the day on which the license plate is taken.

(3) The temporary stickers required by Paragraph (2) of this Subsection shall be designed and produced by the Department of Public Safety and Corrections, and the department shall supply such stickers, at no cost, to all law enforcement agencies authorized by law to enforce traffic laws.

(4) The Department of Public Safety and Corrections shall formulate and promulgate rules and regulations for the implementation of the provisions of this Section. To this end, no license* shall be taken or destroyed pursuant to the authority granted in Paragraph (1) of this Subsection until such rules are properly promulgated in accordance with law. However, this limitation shall not be construed so as to otherwise limit the enforcement of laws relative to operating a vehicle without proper insurance or security.

**So in original. Probably should be "license plate".*

(5)(a) The administrative hearing shall be limited to a review of the issue of whether the vehicle was covered by a valid policy of insurance at the time of the alleged violation. The records of the department on the particular violation shall be prima facie proof of the violation, and the owner or operator shall have the burden of proving that the vehicle was covered by a valid policy of insurance or was self-insured pursuant to this Chapter at the time of the violation. The owner or operator may subpoena any witness to appear at the hearing, including the officer issuing the violation, to establish that the owner or operator was in compliance with the law at the time of the alleged violation. A request for a hearing shall not stay the sanctions required by this Part. If it is determined at the administrative hearing that the vehicle was covered by a valid policy of insurance or was self-insured pursuant to this Chapter at the time of the violation, but that such proof was not presented to the law enforcement officer at the time the vehicle was impounded, then the vehicle owner shall be required to pay the storage and wrecker fees of the person or company who impounded and towed the subject vehicle.

(b) The department or other agency that conducts the hearings, shall promulgate such rules and regulations as are necessary to implement the requirements of this Section. Any action for judicial review of the decision from the administrative hearing shall be in the same manner and under the same conditions as provided in R.S. 32:414. No court shall issue an injunction, stay or other process preventing the enforcement of the sanctions required by this Part pending the hearing provided for in this Part, except as provided by R.S. 49:964.

(6) The impounded vehicle shall remain impounded and the registration shall remain suspended until such time as proof of valid insurance is given to the Department of Public

Safety and Corrections. Notwithstanding any other provision of law to the contrary, in no event shall a car be released from impoundment until such time as proof, in writing, has been presented from the Department of Public Safety and Corrections that all penalties, fees, fines and requirements of this Section have been met.

(7) In those instances when there is a passenger in the motor vehicle under the age of twelve or when the driver or a passenger in the motor vehicle is handicapped or when considering the location and the time of day of the stop, the law enforcement officer perceives that there would be a threat to the public safety or to the occupants in the motor vehicle, such law enforcement officer enforcing the provision of this Section may in lieu of the impoundment provisions of this Section, seize the license plate and issue a temporary sticker valid for three calendar days. Upon expiration of the sticker, the vehicle shall not be driven until the owner has complied with the requirements of this Section. In the event the vehicle is being driven after the expiration of the temporary sticker provided for herein, the vehicle shall be immediately impounded pursuant to the provisions of this Section.

D. Prior to reinstatement of registration and license plate privileges to any individual who cannot prove the required insurance coverage or security in effect at the time of the offense within three calendar days after the offense, the Department of Public Safety and Corrections shall collect a reinstatement fee of ten dollars to offset the costs of administering this Section. This ten dollar fee shall be in addition to any other fines, fees, or penalties owed prior to reinstatement of privileges.

E. The legislature hereby declares that the presence of a current license plate on a motor vehicle has become one indication that the motor vehicle is covered by liability security. The legislature further declares that the provisions of R.S. 47:505(B), which require owners of motor vehicles to surrender the license plates of motor vehicles when the lawful use of the motor vehicle by the owner has terminated has become an integral part of the enforcement of the laws requiring all motor vehicles to be covered by liability security. In order to inform the public of the requirements of R.S. 47:505(B) and to facilitate the enforcement of the laws requiring motor vehicle liability security, the office of motor vehicles shall provide notice of the requirements of R.S. 47:505(B) to each person to whom a motor vehicle registration is delivered or transmitted.

F. In the case where the driver is a minor child, the owner of the vehicle shall be responsible under this Section. If the owner of the vehicle is the minor child, the parents of the minor child shall be jointly subject to the provisions of this Section along with the minor child, unless the minor has been adjudicated emancipated, or is in the sole custody of another or only one parent under the law. If the minor is in the sole custody of another or only one parent under the law, the person or parent in whose sole custody the child has been placed will be jointly responsible with the minor child under this Section.

G. The only acceptable means of proof of a valid and current policy of insurance shall be one of the following:

(1) The insurance identification card, declaration page, or policy issued by the insurer.

(2) In the case of a self-insured vehicle as provided in R.S. 32:851 et seq., the certificate of self-insurance issued by the Department of Public Safety and Corrections.

(3) The records of the Department of Public Safety and Corrections, if such records reflect that the motor vehicle is covered by a valid and current policy of liability insurance.

(4) The law enforcement officer making the stop has a reasonable belief that the motor vehicle is covered by a valid and current policy of liability insurance.

H. (1) In addition to the other requirements of this Section, every insurer issuing policies on motor vehicles in Louisiana or in the case of self-insured vehicles pursuant to R.S. 32:851 et seq., the Department of Public Safety and Corrections, may be required to issue stickers to those persons owning valid and current insurance as required in R.S. 32:851 et seq., within five working days of binding coverage. The Department of Public Safety and Corrections, in consultation with the Department of Insurance, may adopt rules and regulations to implement the provisions of this Subsection. The proposed rules and regulations shall be submitted to the House Committee on Transportation, Highways and Public Works, the Senate Committee on the Judiciary, Section B, the House Committee on Insurance, and the Senate Committee on Insurance pursuant to the Administrative Procedure Act*.

**R.S. 49:950 et seq.*

(2) If such rules and regulations are promulgated, the insured shall be required to place the decal in the upper left corner of the windshield of the driver's side of the insured motor vehicle or in such other location on the motor vehicle as set forth by rules and regulations that shall be established by the Department of Public Safety and Corrections. The rules and

regulations shall provide that the failure to display the decal in an approved location on the vehicle or the displaying of an expired decal may subject the vehicle to being towed and impounded, unless the driver can show that the vehicle is covered by a valid policy of insurance or is self-insured pursuant to this Chapter before towing of the vehicle. The only acceptable means of proof of a valid policy of insurance shall be those provided in this Section.

(3) There will be a fifteen day grace period on the expiration of a decal before any law enforcement action may be taken. All penalties and exceptions contained in this Section shall be applicable to this Subsection, and the decal required herein shall be required in addition to the other requirements contained in this Section.

I. (1) Every owner or lessee of a self-propelled motor vehicle registered in another state which is involved in a traffic accident or collision in Louisiana shall provide one of the documents comparable to those listed in Subsection A evidencing that the motor vehicle is covered by a valid policy of automobile insurance. If the operator of the motor vehicle is unable to show such proof, a notice of noncompliance shall be issued.

(2) If the operator of the motor vehicle is issued a notice of noncompliance, the owner of the vehicle shall have thirty working days from the date that the notice of noncompliance was issued to present to the office of motor vehicles proof that insurance coverage was in effect at the time of the issuance of the notice of noncompliance or proof that insurance coverage was not required by the state in which the vehicle was registered.

(3) If the owner fails to provide the proof required in Paragraph (2), there shall be a fine of fifty dollars for a first offense, a fine of one hundred fifty dollars for a second offense, and a fine of five hundred dollars for any subsequent offense.

(Chgd. by Acts 1992 No. 805, §1; Acts 1993 No. 100, §1, No. 259, §1; Acts 1994 Third Ex. Sess. No. 119, §1; Acts 1995 No. 209, §1, No. 423, §1, No. 759, §1; Acts 1997 No. 835, §1, eff. 7/10/97, No. 1486, §1, eff. 1/1/98.)

§863.2. Notification of the cancellation or issuance of security; penalties.

A. (1) *(As enacted by Acts 1997 No. 1077, §1. See other paragraph A(1) below.)* Beginning July 1, 1998, all entities providing security in compliance with R.S. 32:861 et seq., hereinafter referred to as "security providers", whether admitted or nonadmitted (surplus line underwriter) insurance companies providing automobile liability policies, or sales representatives or agents of surety companies issuing motor vehicle liability bonds, or the state treasurer holding deposits, shall notify the secretary of the effective dates of each liability policy, liability bond, deposit, or other security within fifteen working days from the date such policy, bond, deposit, or other security was issued or made.

A. (1) *(Contingent effective date; as enacted by Acts 1997 No. 1476, §4*. See other paragraph A(1) above.)* All entities providing security in compliance with R.S. 32:861 et seq., hereinafter referred to as "security providers", whether admitted or nonadmitted (surplus line underwriter) insurance companies providing automobile liability policies, or sales representatives or agents of surety companies issuing motor vehicle liability bonds, or the state treasurer holding deposits, shall notify the secretary of the effective dates of each liability policy, liability bond, deposit, or other security within fifteen business days from the date such policy, bond, deposit, or other security was issued or made.

(2) *(As enacted by Acts 1997 No. 1077, §1. See other paragraph A(2) below.)* Except as otherwise provided for motor carriers in R.S. 32:900(M), in addition, all such security providers, beginning July 9, 1998, shall notify the secretary when any policy, bond, deposit, or other item of security is terminated, withdrawn, canceled, lapsed, or otherwise made ineffective within fifteen working days of the date the security became ineffective.

(2) *(Contingent effective date; as enacted by Acts 1997 No. 1476, §4*. See other paragraph A(2) above.)* Except as otherwise provided for motor carriers in R.S. 32:900(M), in addition, all such security providers shall notify the secretary when any policy, bond, deposit, or other item of security is terminated, withdrawn, canceled, lapsed, or otherwise made ineffective within fifteen business days of the date the security became ineffective.

(3) Beginning January 1, 1990, the information required by this Section shall be in the form required by the secretary, who may require by regulation such information as the driver's license number of the owner or lessee of the vehicle and of the named insureds, together with the complete vehicle identification number and a description of each vehicle.

(4) The information required by this Section shall be in the form required by the secretary, who may require by regulation such information as the driver's license number of

the owner or lessee or the vehicle and of the named insureds, together with the complete vehicle identification number and description of each vehicle.

(5) *(Contingent effective date; as enacted by Acts 1997 No. 1476, §4*.)* If any cancellation of a motor vehicle liability policy occurs at the request of the insured, the insurer is not obligated to cancel such policy earlier than ten days prior to actual receipt by the insurer of such request.

B. Upon failure of a security provider to provide the secretary with the information required by this Section, the insurance company, sales representative or agent, state treasurer, or other provider shall be assessed a fee of not more than fifty dollars per policy, bond, or deposit, or other security item concerning which information is not supplied. All fees collected under this Subsection shall be deposited in the Bond Security and Redemption Fund as provided in R.S. 32:853(B)(2).

C. The secretary shall keep a record of the information received from security providers concerning coverage of vehicles and persons by security required by R.S. 32:861, which information may be stored through automated electronic data processing means. After the department has complete vehicle liability security records, upon written request including the driver's license number for each person, the vehicle identification number for each vehicle, and the payment of a fee of fifteen dollars for each vehicle owned by a person about which inquiry is made, the secretary shall forward to the inquiring party such vehicle and driver liability security information as is contained in the records of the department. If the department's search of its records fails to show the existence of any liability insurance or other security as of the date about which inquiry is made, an official of the department will issue a sworn, notarized affidavit to that effect. Such an affidavit shall be prima facie evidence that on the date in question, the person or vehicle about which inquiry was made did not have in effect a policy of liability insurance or other security as required by law. The fee collected pursuant to this Section shall be remitted by the secretary to the state treasurer to be credited to the Bond Security and Redemption Fund as provided in R.S. 32:853(B)(2).

D. *(Deleted.)*

E. Notwithstanding any provision of law to the contrary, when there is a question of fact as to the existence of liability insurance coverage on a motor vehicle, and the owner of that motor vehicle has in fact maintained that coverage without lapse, and the question results from a mistake made by an insurance company or agent, or by any other entity, the owner of the motor vehicle shall not be required to pay any reinstatement fee in connection with any actions taken based on that question of coverage. If a reinstatement fee is imposed by the state, the reinstatement fee shall be paid by the agent, company, or other entity which made the mistake.

F. (1) Prior to taking any administrative action based on the receipt of a notice of cancellation of insurance or other security, the secretary shall notify the person who is the subject of the notice at his last known driver's license address, of cancellation of the receipt of that notice. The notice of receipt of a notice of cancellation shall be in writing. The person to whom the notice is addressed shall have thirty days to respond to the notice. The response may be made by mail.

(2) If the person to whom the notice is addressed is able to show that the insurance or other security was canceled for a legitimate reason, the secretary shall take no administrative action against that person. Legitimate reasons for cancellation of insurance or other security shall include but shall not be limited to the transfer of ownership of the vehicle by sale, donation, exchange, surrender to a salvage yard, or other transaction. The transfer of ownership of the vehicle may be established by presenting to the secretary a copy of the title transfer or a copy of the act of sale, donation, exchange, surrender to a salvage yard, or other transaction.

(3) If the original of the document presented as proof of transfer of ownership has not been notarized, the authenticity of the document may be established by an affidavit executed by the person to whom the notice is addressed in which that person recites the circumstances of the transfer of ownership of the vehicle and attests to the truthfulness and accuracy of the document presented as proof of transfer of ownership.

(Chgd. by Acts 1995 No. 183, §1, No. 301, §1, No. 423, §1; Acts 1997 No. 1077, §1, eff. 8/15/97, No. 1476, §4.)*

**Acts 1997 No. 1476, §8(B) provides:*

(1) Sections 2 through 4 of this Act shall become effective one hundred twenty days after "rate reduction day" and shall apply to all causes of action which occur on or after the effective date thereof.

(2) If, however, during the time prescribed in Subsection 5(C) of this Act, the Louisiana Insurance Rating Commission approves rates of insurers selling more than twenty-five percent of the automobile insurance in this state, as measured by earned premium volume for the calendar year of 1996, which rates are not in compliance with the mandatory percentage rate reduction provisions of Subsection 5(A) or (B) or, if applicable, the actuarial provision of Section 7(B) of this Act, all as determined and certified by the commissioner of the Department of Insurance within ten days of the rate approval, then Sections 2 through 4 of the Omnibus Premium Reduction Act shall never take effect.

§863.3. Proof of motorcycle endorsement.

A. Each person who makes an application for issuance of a policy of insurance covering a motorcycle shall provide proof of the appropriate license endorsement required by R.S. 32:408(c). Such proof shall be provided to the insurer or its agent at the time of application for such policy. If the policy of insurance is issued by an insurer which does not maintain an office in this state, then the person may submit a sworn affidavit that he has the proper license endorsement to the insurer.

B. No insurer or agent of an insurer shall issue a policy of insurance which will cover a motorcycle unless the applicant has provided proof of the appropriate license endorsement required by R.S. 32:408(c).

C. In addition to any other applicable penalties, anyone in violation of this section shall be subject to a fine of no more than five hundred dollars.

(Chgd. by Acts 1993 No. 40, §1, eff. 8/15/93.)

§864. Criminal sanctions for false declaration.

Any person, firm or corporation which violates R.S. 32:863(A)(2) shall be guilty of a misdemeanor and upon conviction shall be fined not more than one hundred twenty-five dollars or imprisoned for a period of not more than thirty days.

§865. Criminal sanctions for operating motor vehicle not covered by security.

A. Any person knowingly operating a motor vehicle and any owner allowing a motor vehicle to be operated, when such motor vehicle is not covered by the security required under R.S. 32:861 shall, upon conviction, be fined not more than five hundred dollars.

B. (1) If the vehicle is in any manner involved in an accident within this state, when such motor vehicle is not covered by the security required under R.S. 32:861, the owner thereof shall, upon conviction, be fined not more than five hundred dollars, shall have the registration of the vehicle revoked for a period of sixty days, and shall have his driving privileges suspended for a period of sixty days.

(2) Notwithstanding Paragraph (1) of this Subsection and except as provided in Paragraph (3) of this Subsection, any person operating a motor vehicle when that person knows the vehicle is not covered by the security required under R.S. 32:861, and any owner allowing a motor vehicle to be operated which is in any way involved in an accident within this state in which any person is killed or injured or in which damage to the property of any one person in excess of five hundred dollars is sustained, when such motor vehicle is not covered by the security required under R.S. 32:861, the owner thereof knows or has been notified by the department of the absence of the required security, and at least thirty days has elapsed after such knowledge has been acquired or notification received by the owner, shall, upon conviction, be fined not less than one thousand dollars, nor more than ten thousand dollars, shall have the registration of his vehicle revoked for a period of twelve months, shall have his driving privileges suspended for a period of twelve months, and shall be required to perform not less than forty hours nor more than two hundred hours of community service. After deposit in the Bond Security and Redemption Fund, an amount equal to all fines collected under the provisions of this Paragraph shall be credited to the Crime Victims Reparations Fund, R.S. 46:1816.

(3) The criminal sanction provisions of Paragraph (2) of this Subsection, shall not apply:

(a) To the operator or the owner of a motor vehicle involved in an accident wherein no injury or damage was caused to the person or property of any one* other than such operator or owner or the immediate family members of such operator or owner.

**So in original. Probably should be "anyone".*

(b) To the owner of a motor vehicle if at the time of the accident the vehicle was being operated without his permission, express or implied, or was parked by a person who had been operating such motor vehicle without such permission.

(c) To the operator or the owner of a motor vehicle involved in a collision with another vehicle, in which the operator of the other vehicle is found guilty of or pleads guilty to a charge of operating a vehicle while intoxicated, negligent injuring, vehicular negligent injuring, vehicular homicide, or negligent homicide.

(4) Any such owner or operator described in Paragraph (1) or (2) of this Subsection shall be able to use the procedures described in R.S. 32:415.1 to obtain a temporary driver's license, registration, and plate, upon showing undue economic or personal hardship that would result from the suspension of his driving privileges.
(Chgd. by Acts 1992 No. 1060, §1, eff. 8/21/92.)

§866. Compulsory motor vehicle liability security; failure to comply; limitation of damages.

(Contingent effective date.)

A. (1) There shall be no recovery for the first ten thousand dollars of bodily injury and no recovery for the first ten thousand dollars of property damage based on any cause or right of action arising out of a motor vehicle accident, for such injury or damages occasioned by an owner or operator of a motor vehicle involved in such accident who fails to own or maintain compulsory motor vehicle liability security.

(2) For purposes of this Section, the meaning of "bodily injury" and "property damage" is governed by the applicable motor vehicle liability insurance policy or, in the event of security other than an insurance policy, the meaning of such terms is that which is commonly ascribed thereto.

(3) The limitation of recovery provisions of this Subsection do not apply if the driver of the other vehicle:

(a) Is cited for a violation of R.S. 14:98 as a result of the accident and is subsequently convicted of or pleads nolo contendere to such offense.

(b) Intentionally causes the accident.

(c) Flees from the scene of the accident.

(d) At the time of the accident, is in furtherance of the commission of a felony offense under the law.

B. Each person who is involved in an accident in which the other motor vehicle was not covered by compulsory motor vehicle liability security and who is found to be liable for damages to the owner or operator of the other motor vehicle may assert as an affirmative defense the limitation of recovery provisions of Subsection A of this Section.

C. If the owner of a motor vehicle, who fails to own or maintain compulsory motor vehicle liability security, institutes an action to recover damages in any amount, regardless of whether such owner or operator is at fault, and is awarded an amount equal to or less than the minimum amount of compulsory motor vehicle liability security, then such owner or operator shall be assessed and held liable for all court costs incurred by all parties to the action.

D. Each person who applies for a driver's license, registers a motor vehicle, or operates or owns a motor vehicle in this state is deemed to have given his consent to be subject to and governed by the provisions of this Section. All persons who apply for the issuance or renewal of a driver's license, motor vehicle title, or motor vehicle registration shall sign a declaration on a form developed by the Department of Public Safety and Corrections pursuant to rule and regulation that the person acknowledges and gives consent to the requirements and provisions of this Section and that the person will comply with all provisions of this Section and the Motor Vehicle Safety Responsibility Law. Proof of whether the person obtained or signed such declaration is irrelevant to the application of this Section.

E. Nothing in this Section shall preclude a passenger in a vehicle from asserting a claim to recover damages for injury, death, or loss which he occasioned, in whole or in part, by the negligence of another person arising out of the operation or use of a motor vehicle. This Subsection shall not apply to a passenger who is also the owner of the uninsured motor vehicle involved in the accident.

F. (1) Notwithstanding any provision of law to the contrary, no insurer shall lose any rights of subrogation for claims paid under the applicable insurance policy for the recovery of any sum in excess of the first ten thousand dollars of bodily injury and the first ten thousand dollars of property damages.

(2) In claims where no suit is filed, the claimant's insurer shall have all rights to recover any amount paid by the claimant's insurer on behalf of the insured for the recovery of any sum

in excess of the first ten thousand dollars of bodily injury and the first ten thousand dollars of property damages.

(Added by Acts 1997 No. 1476, §4.)*

**Acts 1997 No. 1476, §8(B) provides:*

(1) Sections 2 through 4 of this Act shall become effective one hundred twenty days after "rate reduction day" and shall apply to all causes of action which occur on or after the effective date thereof.

(2) If, however, during the time prescribed in Subsection 5(C) of this Act, the Louisiana Insurance Rating Commission approves rates of insurers selling more than twenty-five percent of the automobile insurance in this state, as measured by earned premium volume for the calendar year of 1996, which rates are not in compliance with the mandatory percentage rate reduction provisions of Subsection 5(A) or (B) or, if applicable, the actuarial provision of Section 7(B) of this Act, all as determined and certified by the commissioner of the Department of Insurance within ten days of the rate approval, then Sections 2 through 4 of the Omnibus Premium Reduction Act shall never take effect.

PART II. SECURITY FOLLOWING ACCIDENT

§871. Report required following accident; availability.

A. The operator of every motor vehicle which is in any manner involved in an accident within this state, in which any person is killed or injured or in which damage to the property of any one person, including himself, in excess of five hundred dollars is sustained, shall within ten days after such accident report the matter in writing to the commissioner. Such report, the form of which shall be prescribed by the commissioner, shall declare in writing that the motor vehicle is covered by security as required by this Chapter, including the name of the insurance company, policy number, effective dates of the policy, and the amount of said security, listing the liability limits as well as bodily injury and property damage limits if also maintained, and such other information as the commissioner may require to enable him to determine whether the requirements for the deposit of security under R.S. 32:872 are applicable by reason of the existence of insurance or other exceptions specified in this Chapter. The commissioner may rely upon the accuracy of the information unless and until he has reason to believe that the information is erroneous. If such operator is physically incapable of making such report, the owner of the motor vehicle involved in such accident, shall, within ten days after learning of the accident, make such report. The operator or the owner shall furnish such additional relevant information as the commissioner shall require.

B. The Department of Public Safety and Corrections shall keep a record of information concerning insurance coverage or security declared pursuant to Subsection A. Upon the written request of and the payment of a fifteen dollar fee by an interested person, the Department of Public Safety and Corrections shall forward this information as to insurance coverage or security as required by this Chapter.

C. In such case that the Department of Public Safety does not have a record of the requested information, the department shall direct a written inquiry as to insurance coverage or security as required by this Chapter by registered or certified mail to the owner or operator, or both, of a motor vehicle involved in any accident in this state. After the lapse of fifteen days, the department shall provide an affidavit to said interested person as to the response or lack thereof received from said owner or operator, or both.

D. In the event that the damage described in Subsection A of this Section is to property owned by the state, then the report required by Subsection A shall be submitted if the amount of damage exceeds fifty dollars.

§872. Security and proof of financial responsibility required unless evidence of insurance; when security determined; suspension; exception.

A. If, twenty days after the receipt of a report of a motor vehicle accident within this state which has resulted in bodily injury or death, or damage to property of any one person in excess of two hundred dollars, or if the damage is to property owned by the state of Louisiana in an amount in excess of fifty dollars, the secretary does not have on file evidence satisfactory to him that the person who would otherwise be required to file security and give proof of financial responsibility under Subsection B of this Section has been released from liability, or has been finally adjudicated not to be liable, or has executed a duly acknowledged written agreement providing for the payment of an agreed amount in installments with respect to all claims for injuries or damages resulting from the accident, the secretary shall determine the amount of security which shall be sufficient in his judgment to satisfy any judgment or judgments for damages resulting from such accidents as may be recovered against each operator or owner.

B. The commissioner shall suspend the license and all registrations of each operator and owner of a motor vehicle in any manner involved in such accident, and if such operator is a nonresident, the privilege of operating a motor vehicle within this state, and if such owner is a nonresident, the privilege of the use within this state of any motor vehicle owned by him, unless such operator or owner, or both, shall deposit security in the sum determined by the commissioner. Notice of such a suspension shall be sent by the commissioner to such operator and owner not less than ten days prior to the effective date of such suspension and shall state the amount required as security. The notice shall also advise such owner or operator that he or she may obtain a special identification card from the drivers license division of the Department of Public Safety pursuant to R.S. 40:1321. Where erroneous information is given the commissioner with respect to the matter set forth in Paragraph (1), (2), or (3) of Subsection C of this Section, he shall take appropriate action as hereinbefore provided within sixty days after receipt by him of correct information with respect to said matters.

C. This Section shall not apply under the conditions stated in R.S. 32:873, nor:

(1) To such operator or owner if such owner had in effect at the time of such accident an automobile liability policy with respect to the motor vehicle involved in such accident.

(2) To such operator, if not the owner of such motor vehicle, if there was in effect at the time of such accident an automobile liability policy or bond with respect to his operation of motor vehicles not owned by him.

(3) To such operator or owner if the liability of such operator or owner for damages resulting from such accident is, in the judgment of the commissioner, covered by any other form of liability insurance policy or bond.

(4) To any person qualifying as a self-insurer under R.S. 32:1042 or to any person operating a motor vehicle for such self-insurer.

(5) To any operator of a "lease-bound mobile rig hauler" as provided for in R.S. 32:861(D).

D. (1) No such policy or bond shall be effective under this Section unless issued by an insurance company or surety company authorized to do business in the state of Louisiana, except that if such motor vehicle was not registered in this state or was a motor vehicle which was registered elsewhere than in this state at the effective date of the policy or bond, or the most recent renewal thereof, such policy or bond shall not be effective under this Section unless the insurance company or surety company, if not authorized to do business in this state, shall execute a power of attorney authorizing the commissioner to accept service on its behalf of notice of process in any action upon such policy or bond arising out of such accident;

(2) Provided, however, every such policy or bond is subject, if the accident has resulted in bodily injury or death, to a limit, exclusive of interest and costs, of not less than ten thousand dollars because of bodily injury to or death of one person in any one accident and, subject to the limit for one person, to a limit of not less than twenty thousand dollars because of bodily injury to or death of two or more persons in any one accident and, if the accident has resulted in injury to or destruction of property, to a limit of not less than ten thousand dollars because of injury to or destruction of property of others in any one accident.

(Chgd. by Acts 1992 No. 830, §1, eff. 7/8/92.)

§873. Further exceptions to requirements of security.

The requirements as to security and suspension in R.S. 32:872 shall not apply:

(1) To the operator or the owner of a motor vehicle involved in an accident wherein no injury or damage was caused to the person or property of any one other than such operator or owner;

(2) To the operator or the owner of a motor vehicle legally parked at the time of the accident;

(3) To the owner of a motor vehicle if at the time of the accident the vehicle was being operated without his permission, express or implied, or was parked by a person who had been operating such motor vehicle without such permission;

(4) To the operator or the owner of a motor vehicle involved in a collision with another vehicle, the operator of which other vehicle is found guilty or pleads guilty to a charge of drunk driving, negligent injury or negligent homicide;

(5) To any person who would otherwise be required to file security, when the adverse party has been charged with negligent homicide; provided however, that this exemption shall not apply if and when the adverse party so charged has been tried and found not guilty; nor

(6) If, prior to the date that the commissioner would otherwise suspend license and registration or non-resident's operating privilege under R.S. 32:872, there is filed with the commissioner evidence satisfactory to him that the person who would otherwise have to file security has been released from liability or been finally adjudicated not to be liable or has executed a duly acknowledged written agreement providing for the payment of an agreed amount in installments, with respect to all claims for injuries or damages resulting from the accident.

However, notwithstanding any of the provisions of this Chapter, the commissioner shall never suspend any registration of any owner of a motor vehicle involved in any accident where under the law of this state such owner is not legally liable for damages arising from such accident.

§874. Duration of suspension, revocation, or withdrawal; reinstatement fees.

A. The license and registration and nonresident's operating privilege suspended as provided in R.S. 32:872 shall remain so suspended and shall not be renewed nor shall any such license or registration be issued to such person until:

(1) Such person shall deposit or there shall be deposited on his behalf, the security required under R.S. 32:872; or

(2) One year shall have elapsed following the date of the accident and evidence satisfactory to the commissioner has been filed with him that during such period no action for damages arising out of the accident has been instituted; or

(3) Evidence satisfactory to the commissioner has been filed with him of a release from liability, or a final adjudication of nonliability, or a duly acknowledged written agreement, in accordance with Paragraph (6) of R.S. 32:873, provided however, in the event that there shall be any default in the payment of any installment under any duly acknowledged written agreement, then, upon written notice of such default, the commissioner shall forthwith suspend the license and registration or nonresident's operating privilege of such person defaulting which shall not be restored unless and until:

(a) Such person deposits and thereafter maintains security as required under R.S. 32:872 in such amount as the commissioner may then determine, or

(b) One year shall have elapsed following the date when such security was required and during such period no action upon such agreement has been instituted in a court in this state.

B. (1)(a) Any person whose license has been suspended, revoked, or withdrawn under any provision of this Chapter shall, after complying with the requirements of this Chapter, be required to pay a reinstatement fee or to show proof, in the instance in which the loss of license was predicated on failure to file the necessary reports that adequate insurance coverage existed, that in fact such coverage did timely exist, before such license may be returned; and the license shall remain withdrawn and shall not be renewed, nor shall any such license be issued to such person, until payment of this reinstatement fee has been made or the proof shown. Upon receipt of said fee or proof, such license shall be returned within ten days.

(b) For a first offense there shall be a reinstatement fee of twenty-five dollars, for a second offense there shall be a reinstatement fee of one hundred dollars, and for any subsequent offense there shall be a reinstatement fee of two hundred dollars, provided the offenses occurred within a five-year period. The first offense occurring after five years from the prior first offense shall be deemed to be a first offense. The reinstatement fee contained herein shall be in addition to other appropriate registration fees allowed by law and reinstatement shall depend upon proof of compliance with the compulsory liability law.

(2) Proof of coverage in this Section shall include an original or photocopy of a Louisiana auto insurance identification card showing that the required security is in effect on the vehicle and has been continuous without lapse or an original or photocopy of any written communication from an insurer either to the insured or to the secretary stating that the required security is in effect on the vehicle and has been continuous without lapse. The original or photocopy of either the insurance card or the written communication specified above shall constitute sufficient proof of coverage in this Section and, upon receipt of any of these documents, the license shall be returned within ten days, no reinstatement fee shall be charged, and any reinstatement fee which has been paid shall be refunded at the same time that the license is returned.

C. *(Repealed.)*

D. The department's local field offices are hereby authorized to reinstate suspended driver's licenses when the only requirements for reinstatement are proof of insurance and the payment of a reinstatement fee. The field offices are also authorized to reinstate suspended driver's licenses when proof of coverage, pursuant to Subsection B of this Section, is presented and such reinstatement shall be made without payment of a reinstatement fee. Any reinstatement fee paid shall be refunded as provided in Subsection B of this Section.
(Chgd. by Acts 1992 No. 984, §18; Acts 1998 First Ex. Sess. No. 40, §1, eff. 6/16/98.)

§875. Application to non-residents, unlicensed drivers, unregistered motor vehicles and accidents in other states.

A. In case the operator or the owner of a motor vehicle involved in an accident within this state has no license or registration, or is a non-resident, he shall not be allowed a license or registration until he has complied with the requirements of this Chapter to the same extent that would be necessary if, at the time of the accident, he had held a license and registration.

B. When a non-resident's operating privilege is suspended pursuant to R.S. 32:872, or 32:874, the commissioner shall transmit a certified copy of the record of such action to the official in charge of the issuance of licenses and registration certificates in the state in which such non-resident resides, if the law of such other state provides for action in relation thereto similar to that provided for in Subsection C of this Section.

C. Upon receipt of such certification that the operating privilege of a resident of this state has been suspended or revoked in any such other state pursuant to a law providing for its suspension or revocation for failure to deposit security for the payment of judgments arising out of a motor vehicle accident, under circumstances which would require the commissioner to suspend a non-resident's operating privilege had the accident occurred in this state, the commissioner shall suspend the license of such resident if he was the operator, and all of his registrations if he was the owner of a motor vehicle involved in such accident. Such suspension shall continue until such resident furnishes evidence of his compliance with the law of such other state relating to the deposit of such security.

§876. Form and amount of security.

The security required under this Part shall be in such form and in such amount as the commissioner may require but in no case in excess of the limits specified in R.S. 32:872 in reference to the acceptable limits of a policy or bond. The person depositing security shall specify in writing the person or persons on whose behalf the deposit is made, and at any time while such deposit is in the custody of the commissioner or state treasurer, the person depositing it may in writing amend the specification of the person or persons on whose behalf the deposit is made to include an additional person or persons; provided, however, that any single deposit of security shall be applicable only on behalf of persons required to furnish security because of the same accident.

The commissioner may reduce the amount of security ordered in any case if, in his judgment, the amount ordered is excessive. In case the security originally ordered has been deposited, the excess deposited over the reduced amount ordered shall be returned to the depositor or his personal representative forthwith, notwithstanding the provisions of R.S. 32:877.

§877. Custody, distribution and return of security.

Cash security deposited in compliance with the requirements of this Part shall be deposited by the commissioner in an escrow account of the Department of Public Safety. Surety bonds issued by a surety company duly authorized to transact business in the state and negotiable securities (subject to R.S. 32:876) shall be held by the commissioner. Such deposits shall be applicable to the payment of a judgment or judgments rendered against the person or persons on whose behalf the deposit was made, for damages arising out of the accident in question in an action at law, begun not later than one year after the date of such accident, or within one year after the date of deposit of any security under Paragraph (3) of R.S. 32:874. Deposits of security in cash or negotiable securities shall be applicable also to the payment in settlement, agreed to by the depositor, of a claim or claims arising out of such accident. Such deposit of cash or negotiable securities or any balance thereof shall be returned to the depositor or his personal representative and any surety bond shall be cancelled and returned, when evidence satisfactory to the commissioner has been filed with him that there has been a full release from liability, or a final adjudication of nonliability, or a duly acknowledged agreement in accordance with Paragraph (6) of R.S. 32:873, or whenever, after the expiration of one year (1) from the date of the accident, or (2) from the date of deposit of any security under Paragraph (3) of R.S. 32:874, the commissioner shall be given reasonable evidence that there is no such action pending and no judgment rendered in such action left unpaid.

§878. Matters not to be evidence in civil suits.

Neither the report required by R.S. 32:871, the action taken by the commissioner pursuant to this Part, the findings, if any, of the commissioner upon which such action is based, nor the security filed as provided in this Part shall be referred to in any way, nor be any evidence of the negligence of due care of either party, at the trial of any action at law to recover damages.

§879. Registration after suspension of inoperable vehicle.

A. Any owner of a vehicle that is no longer in use or operable due to damage sustained in an accident and the registration for which has been suspended, revoked, or withdrawn under any provision of this Chapter because of the accident, after complying with the requirements of this Chapter, shall be allowed to apply to register another vehicle when he furnishes to the commissioner one of the following:

(1) A copy of any sale, transfer, or assignment of the vehicle that is no longer in use or operable.

(2) The registration plate and registration certificate for the vehicle that is no longer in use or operable.

B. In the event the owner has no copy of the sale, transfer, or assignment or a registration plate and registration certificate for the vehicle, the owner may furnish the commissioner an affidavit stating that the vehicle with the suspended registration is no longer in use or operable due to damage sustained in the accident. The affidavit shall be in the form required by the commissioner.

§880. Nonresident drivers; accidents.

A. Whenever a nonresident driver is involved in an accident in this state, and is issued a traffic citation in connection with that accident, the nonresident driver shall:

(1) Show proof of liability insurance coverage as required by law,

(2) Post a bond in an amount sufficient to cover the damage caused in the accident, or

(3) Deposit his driver's license with the law enforcement agency which investigates the accident.

B. As used in this Section, the phrase "nonresident driver" means a person who operates a motor vehicle in this state and who has a foreign driver's license, or a foreign registration for the motor vehicle, or both.

(Added by Acts 1990 No. 93, §1, eff. 9/7/90.)

PART III. PROOF OF FINANCIAL RESPONSIBILITY

§891. Courts to report non-payment of judgments and convictions.

Whenever any person fails within sixty days to satisfy any final judgment, upon the written request of the judgment creditor or his attorney, it shall be the duty of the clerk of the court, or of the judge of a court which has no clerk, in which any such judgment is rendered within this state, to forward to the commissioner immediately after the expiration of said sixty days, a certified copy of such judgment.

If the defendant named in any certified copy of a judgment reported to the commissioner is a non-resident, the commissioner shall transmit a certified copy of the judgment to the official in charge of the issuance of licenses and registration certificates of the state of which the defendant is a resident.

§892. Suspension for non-payment of judgment; exceptions.

A. The commissioner, upon the receipt of a certified copy of a final judgment shall forthwith suspend the license and registration and any non-resident's operating privilege of any person against whom such judgment was rendered, except as hereinafter otherwise provided in this Section and in R.S. 32:895.

B. If the judgment creditor consents in writing, in such form as the commissioner may prescribe, that the judgment debtor be allowed license and registration or non-resident's operating privilege, the same may be allowed by the commissioner, in his discretion, for six months from the date of such consent and thereafter until such consent is revoked in writing, notwithstanding default in the payment of such judgment, or of any installments thereof prescribed in R.S. 32:895 provided the judgment debtor furnished proof of financial responsibility.

C. However, notwithstanding any provisions of this Part, satisfaction of any judgment or the giving of future proof shall not be required of a judgment debtor whose insurance company became insolvent subsequent to the accident from which the judgment arose. Furnishing of acceptable written proof of such insolvency shall rest with such judgment debtor.

§893. Suspension to continue until judgments paid and proof given.

Such license, registration and non-resident's operating privilege shall remain so suspended and shall not be renewed, nor shall any such license or registration be thereafter issued in the name of such person, including any such person not previously licensed, unless and until every such judgment is stayed, satisfied in full or to the extent hereinafter provided and until the said person gives proof of financial responsibility subject to the exemption stated in R.S. 32:892 and 32:895.

A discharge in bankruptcy following the rendering of any such judgment shall not relieve the judgment debtor from any of the requirements of this Part.

§894. Payments sufficient to satisfy requirements.

A. Judgments herein referred to shall, for the purpose of this Chapter only, be deemed satisfied:

(1) When ten thousand dollars has been credited upon any judgment or judgments rendered in excess of that amount because of bodily injury to or death of one person as the result of any one accident.

(2) When, subject to such limit of ten thousand dollars because of bodily injury to or death of one person, the sum of twenty thousand dollars has been credited upon any judgment, or judgments, rendered in excess of that amount because of bodily injury to or death of two or more persons as the result of any one accident.

(3) When ten thousand dollars has been credited upon any judgment or judgments rendered in excess of that amount because of injury to or destruction of property of others as a result of any one accident.

B. Payments made in settlement of any claims because of bodily injury, death, or property damage arising from a motor vehicle accident shall be credited in reduction of the amounts provided for in this Section.

§895. Installment payment of judgments; default.

A. A judgment debtor upon due notice to the judgment creditor may apply to the court in which such judgment was rendered for the privilege of paying such judgment in installments and the court, in its discretion and without prejudice to any other legal remedies which the judgment creditor may have, may so order and fix the amounts and times of payment of the installments.

B. The commissioner shall not suspend a license, registration or a non-resident's operating privilege, and shall restore any license, registration or non-resident's operating privilege suspended following non-payment of a judgment, when the judgment debtor gives proof of financial responsibility and obtains such an order permitting the payment of such judgment in installments, and while the payment of any said installment is not a default.

C. In the event the judgment debtor fails to pay and installment as specified by such order, then upon notice of such default, the commissioner shall forthwith suspend the license, registration or non-resident's operating privilege of the judgment debtor until such judgment is satisfied, as provided in this Chapter.

§896. Proof required upon certain convictions.

A. When the director under Section 414(B)(2) of this Title suspends the license or nonresident operating privilege of any person upon receipt of evidence of conviction, entry of guilty plea, or forfeiture of bond of any person charged with operating a motor vehicle while under the influence of intoxicating beverages or narcotic drugs or stimulants of the central nervous system, or under Section 667 of this Title for refusal to submit to chemical tests of blood, breath, urine, or other bodily substance for determining the alcoholic content of his blood, no license shall be reinstated or reissued to the person unless such person previously has given or immediately gives and thereafter maintains proof of financial responsibility with respect to all motor vehicles registered by him and shall show financial responsibility individually as a non-owner for a period of three years.

B. If a person is not licensed, but by final order or judgment is convicted of or forfeits any bail or collateral deposited to secure an appearance for trial for any offense requiring the suspension or revocation of license, or for operating a motor vehicle upon the highways without being licensed to do so, or for operating an unregistered motor vehicle upon the highways, no license shall be thereafter issued to such person until he shall give and thereafter maintain proof of financial responsibility, when required.

§897. Alternate methods of giving proof.

Proof of financial responsibility when required under this Chapter with respect to a motor vehicle or with respect to a person who is not the owner of a motor vehicle may be given by filing:

(1) A certificate of insurance as provided in R.S. 32:898 or 32:899, or

(2) A bond as provided in R.S. 32:903 or

(3) A certificate of deposit of money or securities as provided in R.S. 32:904 or

(4) A certificate of self-insurance, as provided in R.S. 32:1042, supplemented by an agreement by the self-insurer that, with respect to accidents occurring while the certificate is in force, he will pay the same judgments and in the same amounts that an insurer would have been obligated to pay under an owner's motor vehicle liability policy if it has been issued such a policy to said self-insurer.

No motor vehicle shall be or continue to be registered in the name of any person required to file proof of financial responsibility unless such proof shall be furnished for such motor vehicle.

§898. Certificate of insurance as proof.

A. Proof of financial responsibility may be furnished by filing with the commissioner the written certificate of any insurance carrier duly authorized to do business in this state certifying that there is in effect a motor vehicle liability policy for the benefit of the person required to furnish proof of financial responsibility. Such certificate shall give the effective date of such motor vehicle liability policy, which date shall be the same as the effective date of the certificate, and shall designate by explicit description or by appropriate reference all motor vehicles covered thereby, unless the policy is issued to a person who is not the owner of a motor vehicle.

B. No motor vehicle shall be or continue to be registered in the name of any person required to file proof of financial responsibility unless such motor vehicle is so designated in such a certificate.

§899. Certificate furnished by non-resident as proof.

A. The non-resident owner of a motor vehicle not registered in this state may give proof of financial responsibility by filing with the commissioner a written certificate or certificates of an insurance carrier authorized to transact business in the state in which the motor vehicle or motor vehicles described in such certificates is registered, or if such non-resident does not own a motor vehicle, then in the state in which the insured resides, provided such certificate otherwise conforms to the provisions of this Chapter, and the commissioner shall accept the same upon condition that said insurance carrier complies with the following provisions with respect to the policies so certified:

(1) Said insurance carrier shall execute a power of attorney authorizing the commissioner to accept service on its behalf of notice or process in any action arising out of a motor vehicle accident in this state; and

(2) Said insurance carrier shall agree in writing that such policies shall be deemed to conform with the laws of this state relating to the terms of motor vehicle liability policies issued herein.

B. If any insurance carrier not authorized to transact business in this state, which has qualified to furnish proof of financial responsibility, defaults in any said undertakings or agreements, the commissioner shall not thereafter accept as proof any certificate of said carrier whether theretofore filed or thereafter tendered as proof, so long as such default continues.

§900. "Motor Vehicle Liability Policy" defined.

A. A "Motor Vehicle Liability Policy" as said term is used in this Chapter, shall mean an owner's or an operator's policy of liability insurance, certified as provided in R.S. 32:898 or 32:899 as proof of financial responsibility, and issued except as otherwise provided in R.S. 32:899, by an insurance carrier duly authorized to transact business in this state, to or for the benefit of the person named therein as insured.

B. Such owner's policy of liability insurance:

(1) Shall designate by explicit description or by appropriate reference all motor vehicles with respect to which coverage is thereby to be granted; and

(2) Shall insure the person named therein and any other person, as insured, using any such motor vehicle or motor vehicles with the express or implied permission of such named insured against loss from the liability imposed by law for damages arising out of the ownership, maintenance, or use of such motor vehicle or motor vehicles within the United States of America or the Dominion of Canada, subject to limits exclusive of interest and costs with respect to each such motor vehicle as follows:

(a) Ten thousand dollars because of bodily injury to or death of one person in any one accident and,

(b) Subject to said limit for one person, twenty thousand dollars because of bodily injury to or death of two or more persons in any one accident, and

(c) Ten thousand dollars because of bodily injury to or destruction of property of others in any one accident.

(d) An owner may exclude a named person as an insured under a commercial policy if the owner obtains and maintains in force another policy of motor vehicle insurance which provides coverage for the person so excluded which is equal to that coverage provided in the policy for which the person was excluded. The alternative coverage is required for both primary and excess insurance.

C. Such operator's policy of liability insurance shall insure the person named as insured therein against loss from the liability imposed upon him by law for damages arising out of the use by him of any motor vehicle not owned by him, within the same territorial limits and subject to the same limits of liability as are set forth above with respect to an owner's policy of liability insurance.

D. Such motor vehicle liability policy shall state the name and address of the named insured, the coverage afforded by the policy, the premium charged therefor, the policy period and the limits of liability, and shall contain an agreement or be endorsed that insurance is provided thereunder in accordance with the coverage defined in this Chapter as respects bodily injury and death or property damage, or both, and is subject to all the provisions of this Chapter.

E. Such motor vehicle liability policy need not insure any liability under any worker's compensation law nor any liability on account of bodily injury to or death of an employee of the insured while engaged in the employment, other than domestic, of the insured, or while engaged in the operation, maintenance or repair of any such motor vehicle nor any liability for damage to property owned by, rented to, in charge of or transported by the insured.

F. Every motor vehicle liability policy shall be subject to the following provisions which need not be contained therein:

(1) The liability of the insurance carrier with respect to the insurance required by this Chapter shall become absolute whenever injury or damage covered by said motor vehicle liability policy occurs; said policy may not be cancelled or annulled as to such liability by an agreement between the insurance carrier and the insured after the occurrence of the injury or damage; no statement made by the insured or on his behalf and no violation of said policy shall defeat or void said policy;

(2) The satisfaction by the insured of a judgment for such injury or damage shall not be a condition precedent to the right or duty of the insurance carrier to make payment on account of such injury or damage;

(3) The insurance carrier shall have the right to settle any claim covered by the policy, and if such settlement is made in good faith, the amount thereof shall be deductible from the limits of liability specified in paragraph (2) of Subsection B of this Section;

(4) The policy, the written application therefor, if any, and any rider or endorsement which does not conflict with the provisions of the Chapter shall constitute the entire contract between the parties.

G. Any policy which grants the coverage required for a motor vehicle liability policy may also grant any lawful coverage in excess of or in addition to the coverage specified for a motor vehicle liability policy and such excess or additional coverage shall not be subject to the provisions of this Chapter. With respect to a policy which grants such excess or additional coverage the term "motor vehicle liability policy" shall apply only to that part of the coverage which is required by this Section.

H. Any motor vehicle liability policy may provide that the insured shall reimburse the insurance carrier for any payment the insurance carrier would not have been obligated to make under the terms of the policy except for the provisions of this Chapter.

I. Any motor vehicle liability policy may provide for the prorating of the insurance thereunder with other valid and collectible insurance.

J. The requirements for a motor vehicle liability policy may be fulfilled by the policies of one or more insurance carriers which policies together meet such requirements.

K. Any binder issued pending the issuance of a motor vehicle liability policy shall be deemed to fulfill the requirements for such a policy.

L. Notwithstanding the provisions of Paragraph (B)(2) of this Section, an insurer and an insured may by written agreement exclude from coverage any named person who is a resident of the same household as the named insured.

M. (1) Except for those tow trucks carrying liability coverage under the provisions of R.S. 32:1717, for those motor vehicles owned or operated by persons engaged in the business of actual farming and used primarily, but not exclusively, in carrying farm produce from farm to market or returning therefrom carrying goods and merchandise back to the farms, individually or cooperatively, where such carrying is not primarily for hire, or for motor vehicles being used for the transportation of forest products in their natural state, every motor carrier as defined in R.S. 32:1(37) shall be covered by a liability policy. Public liability and property damage insurance on motor carriers operating a vehicle that has a gross vehicle weight or gross combined weight rating in excess of twenty thousand pounds shall have the following liability limits:

(a) Those vehicles with a gross vehicle weight of more than twenty thousand pounds, but not more than fifty thousand pounds shall have:

(i) Twenty-five thousand dollars because of bodily injury or death of one person in any one accident, and

(ii) Subject to said limit for one person, fifty thousand dollars because of bodily injury to or death of two or more persons in any one accident, and

(iii) Twenty-five thousand dollars because of damage to or destruction of property of others in any one accident.

(b) Those vehicles with a gross vehicle weight of more than fifty thousand pounds shall provide a combined minimum single coverage limit of three hundred thousand dollars or the equivalent coverage of one hundred thousand dollars for injury or death to any one person, with a required minimum of not less than three hundred thousand dollars per occurrence, and twenty-five thousand dollars property damage.

(2) If, however, the motor carrier has qualified with the United States Department of Transportation (Interstate Commerce Commission) as a self-insurer, as authorized by 49 U.S.C. 10927, or has qualified for self-insurance under the provisions of R.S. 32:1042, the carrier shall be authorized as a self-insurer in Louisiana.

(3) The department may impose a fee not to exceed one dollar per vehicle to cover the expenses resulting from the administration of the provisions of this Subsection.

(4) In addition, all security providers for motor carriers, beginning June 15, 1995, shall notify the secretary, on a form required by the secretary, within forty-five calendar days from the date when any policy, bond, deposit, or other item of security is terminated, withdrawn, canceled, lapsed, or otherwise made ineffective.

(Chgd. by Acts 1992 No. 979, §1; Acts 1995 No. 301, §1; Acts 1996 First Ex. Sess. No. 34, §1, eff. 5/7/96.)

§901. Notice of cancellation or termination of certified policy.

When an insurance carrier has certified a motor vehicle liability policy under R.S. 32:898 or a policy under R.S. 32:899, the insurance so certified shall not be cancelled or terminated until at least ten days after a notice of cancellation or termination of the insurance so certified shall be filed in the office of the commissioner, except that such a policy subsequently procured and certified shall, on the effective date of its certification, terminate the insurance previously certified with respect to any motor vehicle designated in both certificates.

§902. Chapter not to affect other policies.

A. This Chapter shall not be held to apply to or affect policies of automobile insurance against liability which may now or hereafter be required by any other law of this state, and such policies, if they contain an agreement or are endorsed to conform to the requirements of this Chapter, may be certified as proof of financial responsibility under this Chapter.

B. This Chapter shall not be held to apply to or affect policies insuring solely the insured named in the policy against liability resulting from the maintenance or use by persons in the insured's employ or on his behalf of motor vehicle not owned by the insured.

§903. Bond as proof.

A. Proof of financial responsibility may be furnished by filing with the commissioner the bond of a surety company duly authorized to transact business in the state, or a bond with at least two individual sureties each owning real estate within this state, and together having equities equal in value to at least twice the amount of such bond, which real estate shall be scheduled in the bond approved by a judge of a court of record. Such bond shall be conditioned for payments in amounts and under the same circumstances as would be required in a motor vehicle liability policy, and shall not be cancelable except after ten days' written notice to the commissioner. Upon the filing of notice to such effect by the commissioner in the office of the proper clerk or court of the county of city where such real estate shall be located, such bond shall constitute a lien in favor of the state upon the real estate so scheduled of any surety, which lien shall exist in favor of any holder of a judgment against the person who has filed such bond.

B. If such a judgment, rendered against the principal on such bond shall not be satisfied within sixty days after it has become final, the judgment creditor may, for his own use and benefit and at his sole expense, bring an action or actions in the name of the state against the company or persons executing such bond, including an action or proceeding to foreclose any lien that may exist upon the real estate of a person who has executed such bond.

§904. Money or securities as proof.

A. (1) Proof of financial responsibility may be evidenced by the certificate of the state treasurer that the person named therein has deposited with him thirty thousand dollars in cash or securities such as may legally be purchased by savings banks or for trust funds of a market value of thirty thousand dollars.

(2) The state treasurer shall not accept any such deposit and issue a certificate therefor and the commissioner shall not accept such certificate unless accompanied by evidence that there are no unsatisfied judgments of any character against the depositor in the parish where the depositor resides.

B. Such deposit shall be held by the State Treasurer to satisfy, in accordance with the provisions of this Chapter, any execution on a judgment issued against such person making the deposit, for damages, including damages for care and loss of services, because of bodily injury to or death of any person, or for damages because of injury to or destruction of property, including the loss of use thereof, resulting from the ownership, maintenance, use or operation of a motor vehicle after such deposit was made. Money or securities so deposited shall not be subject to attachment or execution unless such attachment or execution shall arise out of a suit for damages as aforesaid.

§905. Owner may give proof for others.

Whenever any person required to give proof of financial responsibility hereunder is or later becomes an operator in the employ of any owner, or is or later becomes a member of the immediate family or household of the owner, the commissioner shall accept proof given by such owner in lieu of proof by such other person to permit such other person to operate a motor vehicle for which the owner has given proof as herein provided. The commissioner shall designate the restrictions imposed by this Section on the face of such person's license.

§906. Substitution of proof.

The commissioner shall consent to the cancellation of any bond or certificate of insurance or the commissioner shall direct and the State Treasurer shall return any money or securities to the person entitled thereto upon the substitution and acceptance of other adequate proof of financial responsibility pursuant to this Chapter.

§907. Other proof may be required.

Whenever any proof of financial responsibility filed under the provisions of this Chapter no longer fulfills the purposes for which required, the commissioner shall for the purpose of this Chapter, require other proof as required by this Chapter, and shall suspend the license and registration or the non-resident's operating privileges pending the filing of such other proof.

§908. Duration of proof; when proof may be cancelled or returned.

A. The commissioner shall, upon request, consent to the immediate cancellation of any bond or certificate of insurance, or the commissioner shall direct and the state treasurer shall return to the person entitled thereto, any money or securities deposited pursuant to this Chapter as proof of financial responsibility, or the commissioner shall waive the requirement of filing proof, in any of the following events:

(1) At any time after three years from the date such proof was required when during the three year period preceding the request, the commissioner has not received record of a conviction or a forfeiture of bail which would require or permit the suspension or revocation of the license; registration or non-resident's operating privilege of the person by or for whom such proof was furnished; or

(2) In the event of the death of the person on whose behalf such proof was filed or the permanent incapacity of such person to operate a motor vehicle; or

(3) In the event that the person who has given proof surrenders his license and registration to the commissioner;

B. However, the commissioner shall not consent to the cancellation of any bond or the return of any money or securities in the event any action for damages upon a liability covered by such proof is then pending or any judgment upon such liability is then unsatisfied, or in the event the person who has filed such bond or deposited such money or securities, has, within one year immediately preceding such request been involved as an operator or owner in any motor vehicle accident resulting in injury or damage to the person or property of others. An affidavit of the applicant as to the non-existence of such facts, or that he has been released from all of his liability, or has been finally adjudicated not to be liable, for such injury or damage, shall be sufficient evidence thereof in the absence of evidence to the contrary in the records of the commissioner.

C. Whenever any person whose proof has been cancelled or returned under paragraph (3) of this Section applies for a license or registration within a period of three years from the date proof was originally required, any such application shall be refused unless the applicant shall reestablish such proof for the remainder of such three year period.

§909. Proof to be maintained for three years.

In all cases, under this Chapter, in which a person is required to give proof of financial responsibility, he shall maintain such proof for a period of three years.

§910. Driver's license; immediate reinstatement, reissuance, or issuance of restricted license.

Whenever any person who is eligible for the reinstatement of a license, reissuance of a license, or issuance of a restricted license due to economic hardship, upon presentation of proof of financial responsibility under the provisions of this Chapter, presents a certified copy of the judgment ordering the reinstatement, reissuance, or issuance at the driver's license office for the parish in which he resides, the Department of Public Safety shall immediately reinstate, reissue, or issue the license to which the person is entitled without any additional administrative delays. If at a later date the Department of Public Safety determines that the proof given was false or fraudulent, the license previously reinstated, reissued, or issued shall immediately be suspended for a period of time in accordance with the original order of suspension and the person shall be prosecuted as otherwise provided by law.

PART IV. PENAL PROVISIONS

§1021. Transfer of registration to defeat purpose of chapter prohibited.

If an owner's registration has been suspended hereunder, such registration shall not be transferred nor the motor vehicle in respect of which such registration was issued registered in any other name until the commissioner is satisfied that such transfer of registration is proposed in good faith and not for the purpose or with the effect of defeating the purposes of this Chapter. Nothing in this Section shall in any way affect the rights of any conditional vendor, chattel mortgagee or lessor of a motor vehicle registered in the name of another as owner who becomes subject to the provisions of this Section.

§1022. Surrender of license and registration.

Any person whose license or registration shall have been suspended as herein provided, or whose policy of insurance or bond, when required under this Chapter, shall have been cancelled or terminated, or who shall neglect to furnish other proof upon request of the commissioner, shall immediately return his license and registration to the commissioner. If any person shall fail to return to the commissioner the license or registration as provided herein, the commissioner shall forthwith direct any peace officer to secure possession thereof and to return the same to the commissioner.

§1023. Other violations; penalties.

A. Failure to report an accident as required in R.S. 32:871 shall be punished by a fine not in excess of twenty-five dollars, and in the event of injury or damage to the person or property of another in such accident, the commissioner shall suspend the license of the person failing to make such report, or the non-resident's operating privilege of such person, until such report has been filed and for such further period not to exceed thirty days as the commissioner may file.

B. Any person who gives information required in a report provided for in R.S 32:398 or 32:871 knowing or having reason to believe that such information is false, or who shall forge or, without authority, sign any evidence of proof of financial responsibility, or who files or offers for filing any such evidence of proof knowing or having reason to believe that it is forged or signed without authority, shall be fined not more than one thousand dollars or imprisoned for not more than one year, or both.

C. Any person whose license or registration or non-resident's operating privilege has been suspended or revoked under this Chapter, and who, during such suspension or revocation drives any motor vehicle upon any highway or knowingly permits any motor vehicle owned by such person to be operated by another upon any highway, except as permitted under this Chapter, shall be fined not more than five hundred dollars or imprisoned not exceeding six months, or both.

D. Any person willfully failing to return license or registration as required in R.S. 32:1022 shall be fined not more than five hundred dollars or imprisoned not to exceed thirty days, or both.

E. Any person who shall violate any provision of this Chapter for which no penalty is otherwise provided shall be fined not more than five hundred dollars or imprisoned not more than ninety days, or both.

PART V. MISCELLANEOUS PROVISIONS

§1041. Exceptions.

A. This Chapter shall not apply with respect to any motor vehicle owned by the United States, this state or any political subdivision of this state, or any municipality therein, a bona fide organized public volunteer fire department which owns and operates those specially equipped motor vehicles for fire fighting purposes, nor, except for R.S. 32:871 and 905, with respect to any motor vehicle which is subject to the jurisdiction of the Louisiana Public Service Commission, or to any motor vehicle subject to registration under the single state registration for motor carriers authorized by 49 U.S.C. 11506, or as otherwise permitted by federal law, or to carriers of persons operating over specified routes with fixed termini and predominantly under franchises or indeterminate permits granted by an incorporated municipality and who are subject to the regulatory jurisdiction of such municipality.

B. Any person, firm, association or corporation licensed and engaged in the business of renting or leasing motor vehicles to be operated on the public highways shall only be required to furnish proof of financial ability to satisfy any judgment or judgments rendered against said person, firm, association or corporation in his or its capacity as owner of the said motor vehicles, and shall not be required to furnish proof of its financial ability to satisfy any judgment or judgments rendered against the person to whom the motor vehicle was rented or leased at the time of the accident.

(Chgd. by Acts 1990 No. 862, §1; Acts 1995 No. 301, §1, eff. 6/15/95.)

§1042. Self-insurers.

A. Any person in whose name more than twenty-five motor vehicles are registered or who owns property in Louisiana assessed in his name having a value of one hundred thousand dollars or more after deducting any encumbrances thereon from its assessed valuation may qualify as a self-insurer by obtaining a certificate of self-insurance issued by the assistant secretary of the office of motor vehicles as provided in Subsection B of this Section.

B. The assistant secretary may, at his discretion, upon the application of such a person, issue a certificate of self-insurance when he is satisfied that such person is possessed and will continue to be possessed of ability to pay judgments obtained against such person. The assistant secretary shall assess a fee of one hundred dollars for each certificate.

C. Upon not less than five days notice and a hearing pursuant to such notice, the commissioner may cancel upon reasonable grounds a certificate of self-insurance. Failure to pay any judgment within sixty days after such judgment has become final shall constitute a reasonable ground for the cancellation of a certificate of self-insurance. The commissioner, upon receipt of certified copy of a final judgment, shall forthwith suspend the license and registration, or any non-resident's operating privileges, of any person, or any legal entity, against whom such judgment was rendered, except as otherwise provided in R.S. 32:892 and R.S. 32:895.

D. Any person or any legal entity whose certificate of self-insurance has been cancelled for his failure to pay a final judgment shall not be eligible for the renewal or reissuance of a certificate of self-insurance for a period of five years from the date of cancellation.

§1043. Residual market plans.

A. After consultation with insurance companies authorized to issue motor vehicle insurance in this state, the commissioner of insurance shall approve a reasonable plan for insuring commercial motor vehicles, including garage liability insurance, called the Commercial Automobile Insurance Procedures and a separate reasonable assigned risk plan for insuring private passenger automobiles and other motor vehicles, called the Louisiana Automobile Insurance Plan. These plans shall provide insurance to those who are in good faith entitled to but are unable to procure such policies through ordinary methods. The Louisiana Automobile Insurance Plan shall not subsidize losses or participate in the profits of the members of the Commercial Automobile Insurance Procedures. All actuarially adequate rates for insurance provided by the plans shall be approved by the Louisiana Insurance Rating Commission. All insurers writing insurance for commercial motor vehicle insurance, private passenger automobiles, or other motor vehicles in the state shall be members of the plans authorized by this Section and share in the administrative expenses for the operation of the plans based on the market share of premiums for the preceding calendar year. The exceptions provided in R.S. 32:1041(A) shall not apply to this Section.

B. Any applicant for any such policy, any person insured under any such plan, and any insurance company affected may appeal to the commissioner of insurance from any ruling or decision of the manager or committee designated to operate such plan. Any person aggrieved hereunder by any order or act of the commissioner of insurance may, within ten days after notice thereof, file a petition in the district court of the parish of East Baton Rouge or in the district court of the domicile of the aggrieved person, for a review thereof. The court shall summarily hear the petition and may make any appropriate order or decree.

(Chgd. by Acts 1995 No. 431, §1, eff. 8/15/95.)

CHAPTER 6. DISTRIBUTION AND SALE OF MOTOR VEHICLES

§1251. Declaration of public policy.

The legislature funds and declares that the distribution and sale of motor vehicles in the state of Louisiana vitally affects the general economy of the state, the public interest, and the public welfare, and that in order to promote the public interest, and the public welfare, and in the exercise of its police power, it is necessary to regulate and to license motor vehicle manufacturers, distributors, dealers, and lessors doing business in Louisiana, in order to prevent frauds, impositions, and other abuses upon its citizens, and avoid undue control of the independent motor vehicle dealer by the motor vehicle manufacturing and distributive organizations and foster and keep alive vigorous and healthy competition, by prohibiting unfair practices by which fair and honest competition is destroyed or prevented, and to protect the public against the creation or perpetuation of monopolies and practices detrimental to the public welfare, to prevent the practice of requiring the buying, leasing, or renting of special features, appliances, and equipment not desired or requested by the purchaser, lessee, or renter, to prevent false and misleading advertising, to prevent unfair practices by motor vehicle dealers, lessors, manufacturers, and distributing organizations, to promote the public safety and prevent disruption of the system of distribution of motor vehicles to the public and prevent deterioration of facilities for servicing motor vehicles and keeping same safe and properly functioning, and prevent bankrupting of motor vehicle dealers and lessors, who might otherwise be caused to fail because of such unfair practices and competition, thereby resulting in unemployment, disruption of leases, and nonpayment of taxes and loans, and contribute to an inevitable train of undesirable consequences, including economic depression.

§1252. Definitions.

The following words, terms, and phrases, when used in this Chapter, shall have the meanings respectively ascribed to them in this Section, except where the context clearly indicates a different meaning:

(1) "Commission"means the Louisiana Motor Vehicle Commission created by this Chapter or its designee.

(2) "Community or territory" shall mean the motor vehicle dealer's area of principal sales and service responsibility as specified by the contract or franchise in effect with the manufacturer or distributor.

(3) "Dealer-operator" shall mean the individual (natural person) designated as the operator of a motor vehicle dealership.

(3.1) "Designated successor" means the spouse, child, grandchild, parent, brother, or sister, of a dealer who, in the case of a deceased dealer, is entitled to inherit the dealer's ownership interest in the dealership under the terms of the dealer's will; the spouse, or other person who has otherwise been designated in writing by a deceased dealer to succeed him in the motor vehicle dealership, such designation having been furnished to the manufacturer; or the spouse, or other person who, under the laws of intestate succession of this state is entitled to inherit the interest; or who, in the case of an incapacitated dealer, has been appointed by a court in a proceeding interdicting the dealer as the legal representative of the dealer's property. The term shall also include the appointed and qualified personal representative and testamentary trustee of a deceased dealer.

(4) "Distributor" or "wholesaler" means any person, firm, association, corporation, or trust, resident or nonresident, who in whole or in part sells or distributes new and unused motor vehicles or new and unused motor vehicle motors to motor vehicle dealers, or who maintains distributor representatives.

(5) "Distributor branch" means a branch office maintained by a person, firm, association, corporation, or trust, resident or nonresident, who in whole or in part sells or distributes new and unused motor vehicles to motor vehicle dealers, or for directing or supervising, in whole or in part, its representatives.

(6) "Distributor representative" means any officer, agent, or employee employed by a distributor, distributor branch, or wholesaler.

(7) "Established place or established place of business" shall mean a permanently enclosed building or structure either owned, leased, or rented, which meets local zoning or municipal requirements, and regularly occupied by a person, firm, association, corporation, or trust, easily accessible to the public at which a regular business of selling new or used motor vehicles, or of leasing or renting motor vehicles will be carried on in good faith, and, at which place of business shall be kept and maintained the books, records, and files necessary to conduct the business; and shall not mean residences, tents, temporary stands, lots, or any temporary quarters.

(8) "Factory branch" means a branch office maintained by a person, firm, association, corporation, or trust who fabricates, manufacturers, or assembles motor vehicles, for the sale of motor vehicles to distributors, or for the sale of motor vehicles to motor vehicle dealers, or for directing or supervising, in whole or in part, its representatives.

(9) "Factory representative" means any officer, agent, or employee employed by a person, firm, association, corporation, or trust who fabricates, manufactures, or assembles motor vehicles, or by a factory branch, for the purpose of making or promoting the sale of his, its, or their motor vehicles, or for supervising or contracting his, its, or their dealers or prospective dealers.

(9.1) "Financial institution" means any person organized to engage in the business of banking pursuant to the laws of the United States or Title 6 of the Louisiana Revised Statutes of 1950.

(10) "Franchise" means any written contract or agreement between a motor vehicle dealer and a manufacturer of a new motor vehicle or its distributor or factory branch by which the dealer is authorized to engage in the business of selling the specific makes, models, or classifications of new motor vehicles marketed by the manufacturer and designated in the franchise agreement or any addendum thereto.

(11) "Manufacturer" means any person, firm, association, corporation, or trust, resident or nonresident, who fabricates, manufactures, or assembles new and unused motor vehicles and new and unused motor vehicle motors. It does not include a person, firm, association, corporation, or trust which converts, modifies, or otherwise alters a motor vehicle or motor vehicle motor manufactured by another person, firm, association, corporation, or trust, or one who uses a motor vehicle or motor vehicle motor manufactured by another person, to construct a motor home as defined in this Section.

(12) "Motor home" means a motor vehicle designed as an integral unit to be used as a conveyance upon the public streets and highways and for use as a temporary or recreational dwelling and having at least four of the following permanently installed systems which meet American National Standards Institute and National Fire Protection Association standards in effect as of the date of manufacture, two of which shall be systems specified below in Subparagraphs (a), (d), or (e) of this Paragraph:

(a) Cooking facilities.

(b) Ice box or mechanical refrigerator.

(c) Potable water supply including plumbing and a sink with faucet either self-contained or with connections for an external source, or both.

(d) Self-contained toilet or a toilet connected to a plumbing system with connection for external water disposal, or both.

(e) Heating or air conditioning system, or both, separate from the vehicle engine or the vehicle engine electrical system.

(f) A one hundred ten/one hundred fifteen volt alternating current electrical system either with its own power supply or with a connection for an external source, or both, or a liquefied petroleum system and supply.

(13) "Motor vehicle" means any motor driven car, van, or truck required to be registered which is used, or is designed to be used, for the transporting of passengers or goods for public, private, commercial, or for hire purposes; but does not include those vehicles which are commonly known as motor homes, mobile homes, trailers, semitrailers, boat trailers, or motorcycles. Such term specifically does not include any chassis for the purpose of bus body or fire truck body installation and ultimate use as a bus or a fire truck, if the seller of such bus assumes warranty liability that would otherwise be the obligation of a motor vehicle dealer authorized to sell that make of vehicle.

(14) (a) "Motor vehicle dealer" means any person, firm, association, corporation, or trust not excluded by Subparagraph (b) of Paragraph (14) of this Section who holds a bona fide

franchise in effect with a manufacturer or distributor of new or unused motor vehicles, and a license under the provisions of this Chapter or a subsidiary corporation of any such corporation. Such duly franchised and licensed motor vehicle dealers shall be the sole and only persons, firms, associations, corporations, or trusts entitled to sell, publicly solicit, and advertise the sale of new and unused motor vehicles as such.

(b) The term "motor vehicle dealer" does not include:

(i) Receivers, trustees, administrators, executors, guardians, or other persons appointed by or acting under judgment or order of any court;

(ii) Public officers while performing or in operation of their duties;

(iii) Employees of persons, corporations, or associations enumerated in Subparagraph (b)(i) of this Paragraph when engaged in the specific performance of their duties as such employees; or

(iv) Financial institutions engaged in the sale of motor vehicles for the collection of debts secured thereby.

(15) (a) "Motor vehicle lessor" shall mean any person, firm, association, corporation, or trust, not excluded by R.S. 32:1252(14)(b), engaged in the motor vehicle leasing or rental business. It shall also include a subsidiary corporation of any such corporation.

(b) The term "motor vehicle lessor" does not include:

(i) Receivers, trustees, administrators, executors, guardians, or other persons appointed by or acting under judgment or order of any court; or

(ii) Public officers while performing or in the operation of their duties; or

(iii) Employees of persons, corporations, or associations enumerated in Paragraph 15(b)(i) when engaged in the specific performance of their duties as such employees.

(iv) A motor vehicle lessor who is an agent of or for a person, firm, corporation, partnership, proprietorship, or association which rents or leases a motor vehicle for the transportation of movable property.

(v) Financial institutions engaged in the leasing of motor vehicles.

(c) Any motor vehicle lessor who rents on a daily basis motor vehicles not of the current year or immediate prior year models that have been titled previously to an ultimate purchaser, and who is otherwise not required to obtain a license under this Chapter, shall be subject to the regulation of the Louisiana Used Motor Vehicle and Parts Commission.

(16) "Motor vehicle salesman/agent" means any person, other than a daily rental person, employed by a licensee of the Louisiana Motor Vehicle Commission whose duties include the selling, leasing, renting, or offering for sale, lease, or rent motor vehicles on behalf of said licensee.

(17) "New and unused motor vehicle" means a motor vehicle, the legal title to which has never been transferred by a manufacturer, distributor, or dealer to an ultimate purchaser.

(18) "Person" shall mean any individual, firm, corporation, partnership, or association.

(19) Retail sale" or "sale at retail" means the act or attempted act of selling, bartering, exchanging, or otherwise disposing of a motor vehicle to an ultimate purchaser for use as a consumer.

(20) "Subsidiary corporation" shall mean a corporation engaged in the business of selling, or leasing motor vehicles, in which a majority of the outstanding stock is owned by a corporation or the majority shareholders of a corporation that holds a license issued by the commission.

(21) "Ultimate purchaser" means, with respect to any new and unused motor vehicle, the first person, other than a dealer purchasing in his capacity as a dealer, who in good faith purchases such new motor vehicles for purposes other than resale. "Ultimate purchaser" shall not include a person who purchases a vehicle for purposes of altering or remanufacturing the motor vehicle for future resale.

(22) "Used motor vehicle" means a motor vehicle, the legal title of which has been transferred by a manufacturer, distributor, or dealer to an ultimate purchaser.

(23) (a) "Used motor vehicle dealer" means any person, firm, association, corporation, or trust whose business is to sell or offer for sale, display, or advertise used motor vehicles, or any person, firm, association, corporation, or trust who holds a new motor vehicle dealer's license and is not excluded by Paragraph 23(b) of this Section.

(b) "Used motor vehicle dealer" shall not include any of the following:

(i) Receivers, trustees, administrators, executors, guardians, or other persons appointed by or acting under the judgment or order of any court.

(ii) Public officers while performing their official duties.

(iii) Employees of persons, corporations, or associations enumerated in the definition of "used motor vehicle dealer" when engaged in the specific performance of their duties as such employees.

(iv) Mortgagees or secured parties as to sales of motor vehicles constituting collateral on a mortgage or security agreement and who do not maintain a used car lot or building with one or more employed motor vehicle salesman.

(v) Insurance companies who sell motor vehicles to which they have taken title as an incident of payments made under policies of insurance and who do not maintain a used car lot or building with one or more employed motor vehicle salesman.

(vi) Used motor vehicle dealers licensed pursuant to R.S. 32:771, et seq.

(Chgd. by Acts 1990 No. 283, §1; Acts 1991 No. 937, §1; Acts 1995 No. 51, §1, eff. 6/9/95.)

§1253. Motor Vehicle Commission; appointment and qualifications of members; terms of office; organization; oath; official bond; compensation; powers and duties.

A. There is hereby created the Louisiana Motor Vehicle Commission, to be composed of fourteen members appointed by the governor, as follows:

(1) A chairman of the commission shall be appointed from the state at large. Ten members shall be appointed in such manner that at least one, but no more than two, shall be from each of the commission districts as listed below:

(a) Commission District 1 shall consist of the following parishes: Orleans, Plaquemine, St. Bernard, St. Tammany, and Washington.

(b) Commission District 2 shall consist of the following parishes: Jefferson, St. Charles, St. John, St. James, and Tangipahoa.

(c) Commission District 3 shall consist of the following parishes: East Baton Rouge, West Baton Rouge, Iberville, Ascension, East Feliciana, West Feliciana, St. Helena, Livingston, Assumption, and Pointe Coupee.

(d) Commission District 4 shall consist of the following parishes: Richland, Franklin, Union, Lincoln, Jackson, Winn, Caldwell, Ouachita, Morehouse, West Carroll, East Carroll, and Madison.

(e) Commission District 5 shall consist of the following parishes: Caddo, Bossier, Webster, DeSoto, Red River, Bienville, Claiborne. and Sabine.

(f) Commission District 6 shall consist of the following parishes: Rapides, Grant, LaSalle, Catahoula, Concordia, Avoyelles, Vernon, Tensas, and Natchitoches.

(g) Commission District 7 shall consist of the following parishes: Beauregard, Allen, Calcasieu, Cameron, Jefferson Davis, Acadia, and Evangeline.

(h) Commission District 8 shall consist of the following parishes: Lafayette, St. Landry, St. Martin, St. Mary, Iberia, Terrebonne, Lafourche, and Vermilion.

(2) Each of the commissioners appointed under the provisions of Paragraph (1) of this Subsection shall have been actively engaged in the manufacture, distribution, sale, lease, rental, or financing of motor vehicles in this state under a license issued by the Louisiana Motor Vehicle Commission for not less than five consecutive years prior to such appointment and be a holder of such a license at all times while a member of the commission. Being engaged in more than one such pursuit shall not disqualify a person otherwise qualified from serving on the commission. Of these members one member shall be primarily engaged in the business of lease or rental and one member shall be primarily engaged in the business of sales finance.

(3) Each of the three remaining appointive members shall be a public member who is not a licensee under this Chapter and shall be appointed from the state at large. These three commissioners shall have the sole function of hearing and deciding disputes between manufacturers, distributors, or representatives and dealers. This function shall be performed only when so requested in writing at the time of the filing of the initial protest or initial answer to the protest by a manufacturer, distributor, representative, or dealer who is a party to a dispute. If no party requests a hearing before these commissioners, the commissioners appointed pursuant to Paragraph (1) of this Subsection shall retain jurisdiction over the dispute. Should a manufacturer, distributor, representative, or dealer make the request as set forth above, the commissioners appointed pursuant to Paragraph (1) of this Subsection shall not participate, deliberate, or in any way take part in the hearing. The three commissioners shall elect among themselves a chairman to serve as presiding officer of the hearing.

(4) Each appointment to the commission by the governor shall be submitted to the Senate for confirmation. Each commissioner shall at the time of appointment be a resident of this state and shall be of good moral character.

B. (1) The members shall serve at the pleasure of the governor. In the event of the death, resignation, or removal of any person serving on the commission, the vacancy shall be filled in the manner of the original appointment.

(2) The commission shall meet in Jefferson Parish and complete its organization immediately after the entire membership thereof has been appointed and has qualified.

(3) The chairman and each member of the commission shall take and subscribe to the oath of office required of public officers.

C. The chairman and members of said commission shall receive fifty dollars per diem for each and every day actually and necessarily spent in attending the meetings of the commission, and shall be reimbursed for actual expenses incurred in the performance of their duties hereunder.

D. The commission shall appoint a qualified person to serve as executive director thereof, to serve at the pleasure of the commission and shall fix his salary and shall define and prescribe his duties. The executive director shall be in charge of the commission's office and shall devote such time to the duties thereof, as may be necessary. Said commission may employ such clerical and professional help and incur such expenses as may be necessary for the proper discharge of its duties under this Chapter. The commission shall maintain its office and transact its business in Jefferson Parish, and it is authorized to adopt and use a seal.

E. The commission is hereby vested with the powers and duties necessary and proper to enable it to fully and effectively carry out the provisions and objects of this Chapter, and is hereby authorized and empowered to make and enforce all reasonable rules and regulations and to adopt and prescribe all forms necessary to accomplish said purpose, and the enumeration of any power or authority herein shall not be construed to deny, impair, disparage, or limit any others necessary to the attainment thereof. A copy of all rules and regulations adopted by the commission shall be published in the Louisiana Register, and same may be amended, modified, or repealed from time to time.

F. All fees and charges under the provisions of this Chapter shall be collected and received by the executive director of the commission and shall be disbursed by him at the direction of the commission in administering and enforcing the provisions of this Chapter.

G. All expenses incurred by the commission in carrying out the provisions of this Chapter, including but not limited to per diem, wages, salaries, rent, postage, supplies, bond premiums, travel and subsistence, and printing and utilities, shall be a proper charge against said fund.

H. *(Repealed.)*

I. The commission shall, in addition to the powers herein conferred, be constituted a body politic or political corporation, invested with the powers inherent in corporations, including but not limited to the power and authority to own immovable property. It may sue and be sued under the style of the Louisiana Motor Vehicle Commission, and all process against the corporation shall be served on the chairman or executive director, and all suits on behalf of the commission shall be brought by the chairman. The domicile for the purpose of being sued shall be Jefferson Parish. Service of process shall be made upon the chairman or upon the executive director of the commission in person. No member of the board, or the executive director, shall be subject to suit or be held liable as an individual in any suit against the board. *(Chgd. by Acts 1990 No. 124, §1; Acts 1991 No. 296, §1; Acts 1993 No. 536, §1; Acts 1995 No. 51, §1; Acts 1997 No. 211, §1, eff. 8/15/97.)*

§1254. Application for license; contents; notices of intent; fees; license; boards; unauthorized acts; auto shows.

A. (1) All applications for licenses required to be obtained under provisions of this Chapter shall be verified by the oath or affirmation of the applicant and shall be on forms prescribed by the commission and furnished to such applicants, and shall contain such information as the commission deems necessary to enable it to fully determine the qualifications and eligibility of the several applicants to receive the license or licenses applied for.

(2) The commission shall require, in such application or otherwise, information relating to the applicant's financial standing, the applicant's business integrity, whether the applicant has an established place of business and is primarily engaged in the pursuit, avocation, or business for which a license or licenses is applied, the particular qualifications, and

requirements pertaining to the license or licenses sought, and whether the applicant is able to properly conduct the business for which a license or licenses is applied, and such other pertinent information consistent with the safeguarding of the public interest and public welfare.

(3) In the performance of its duties under this Section, the commission shall have the authority to obtain from the Department of Public Safety and Corrections and other governmental agencies information relating to the criminal records of applicants for licenses under this Chapter. The information in such records shall be kept confidential by the commission.

B. In determining whether or not to issue a license to any applicant, the commission shall consider the information provided above, the declaration of public policy set forth in Section 1251, as well as all of the following:

(1) Financial standing and business integrity of the applicant.

(2) Ability of the applicant to conduct properly the business for which a license is sought.

(3) Adequacy of the applicant's established place of business for the purpose for which a license is sought.

(4) Effect on the retail motor vehicle business and the consuming public in the community or territory and the state of Louisiana.

(5) Effect on the motor vehicle leasing/rental business and the consuming public in the state of Louisiana.

C. Applications for license as motor vehicle dealer must, in addition to the foregoing, also be accompanied by the filing with the commission of a bona fide contract or franchise in effect between the applicant and a manufacturer or distributor of the new and unused motor vehicle or vehicles proposed to be dealt in for a specific location in the state of Louisiana; unless such contract or franchise has already been filed with the commission in connection with a previous application made by such applicant, in which event the applicant shall, in lieu of again filing the contract or franchise, identify same by appropriate reference and file all revisions and additions, if any, which have been made to said contract or franchise; and the applicant must furnish satisfactory evidence that the applicant maintains adequate space in the building or structure wherein the applicant's established business is conducted for the display of new and unused motor vehicles, together with adequate facilities for the repair and servicing of motor vehicles and the storage of new parts and accessories for same. The application shall also identify the individual named as dealer-operator, and shall contain such information as the commission deems necessary to enable it to fully determine his qualifications and eligibility to serve in that capacity.

D. The commission may authorize or prohibit motor vehicle sales and shows at off-site locations. The commission may, in its discretion, allow such sales and shows provided all of the following conditions are met:

(1) The request is received by the commission forty-five days prior to the opening date of the event.

(2) Only new motor vehicle franchised, licensed dealers may conduct sales of motor vehicles at such sales and shows.

(3) The event is conducted for not more than six days.

(4) All local new motor vehicle dealers shall be offered the opportunity to participate.

(5) A majority of new motor vehicle dealers offered the opportunity to participate must participate in the event.

(6) Each respective manufacturer has granted authority to the respective dealers participating to conduct the sale or show of motor vehicles at the proposed off-site location.

(7) Such events are limited to two times per calendar year per new car dealer.

E. At least sixty days prior to the receipt by the commission of an application for the establishment of a new motor vehicle dealership, for a change of location, change in corporate ownership or majority ownership, change in the name of a licensee, change in the makes, models, or classifications of motor vehicles designated in the franchise or any addendum thereto and manufactured, distributed, or sold, the addition of makes, models, or classifications of motor vehicles designated in the franchise or any addendum thereto and manufactured, distributed, or sold, or a change in the identity of the designated dealer-operator of a licensee the commission must receive written notice from the person seeking to effect such change, said sixty-day notice to provide such information as the commission in its discretion may require. Said notice may be waived by the commission when, in its discretion, the commission feels that such waiver would be in the best interest of the public welfare.

F. (1) Whenever the commission receives an application for a motor vehicle dealer's license which would add a new motor vehicle dealership or authorize an existing motor vehicle dealership to deal in a new or additional make of motor vehicle which would establish an additional franchise in that area, or which would authorize an existing motor vehicle dealership to deal in additional makes, models, or classifications of motor vehicles designated in the franchise or any addendum thereto, it shall first notify the existing licensed motor vehicle dealership or dealerships selling the same line makes, models, or classifications within the community or territory in which the applicant proposes to conduct business. Any same line makes, models, or classifications dealership whose assigned community or territory includes the location of the proposed new motor vehicle dealership may object to the granting of the license.

(2) Whenever the commission receives an application for a motor vehicle dealer's license which would relocate an existing motor vehicle dealership, including the transfer of a franchise and relocation to an existing motor vehicle dealership, it shall first notify the existing licensed motor vehicle dealership or dealerships selling the same line makes, models, or classifications within the community or territory in which the applicant proposes to conduct business. The existing same line makes, models, or classifications dealership or dealerships shall have the right to object to the granting of the license only if the proposed relocation is within a radius of five miles of its facility. However, without regard to distance, whenever the commission receives an application for the relocation of a motor vehicle dealership which would add an additional franchise to an existing same line makes, models, or classifications dealership's community or territory, the affected dealership shall have the right to object.

(3) The objection shall be in writing, and shall be received by the commission within a fifteen-day period after receipt of the notice. Said fifteen-day objection period shall be waived upon written notification to the commission from all licensees entitled to object, that said licensees have no objections to the proposed change or addition for which said notice of intent was issued. If timely objection is lodged, and prior to the issuance of the license, the commission shall hold a hearing within thirty days after receipt of the objection and issue its decision within ninety days after date of said hearing. Notice of the hearing, and an opportunity to participate therein, shall be given to the manufacturer or distributor, to the applicant for the license as a motor vehicle dealer, and to the protesting dealer or dealers. The absence of a timely protest shall not prevent the commission from considering the effect of the issuance of a license on other motor vehicle dealerships located either within or on other motor vehicle dealerships, located either within or outside the community or territory as part of its determination of whether or not the license sought should be issued.

(4) Whenever the commission receives a protest pursuant to the provisions of Paragraph (1) of this Subsection, the commission shall consider the following in determining whether there is good cause to issue a license:

(a) Whether the community or territory can support an additional dealership.

(b) Notwithstanding the provisions of R.S. 32:1251 to the contrary, the financial impact on both the applicant and the existing dealership or dealerships.

(c) Whether the existing motor vehicle dealerships of the same line makes, models, or classifications in the dealership's community or territory are providing adequate representation and convenient consumer care for the motor vehicles of the same line makes, models, or classifications located within that area.

(d) Whether the issuance of the license would increase competition or be in the public interest, or both.

The applicant and manufacturer or distributor shall have the burden of proof in demonstrating good cause by preponderance of the evidence.

(5) Whenever the commission receives a protest pursuant to the provisions of Paragraph (2) of this Subsection, the applicant and the manufacturer or distributor shall show, by a preponderance of the evidence, that the existing same line makes, models, or classifications motor vehicle dealership or dealerships will not be substantially harmed by locating the dealership within the five-mile area. Notwithstanding the provisions of R.S. 32:1251 to the contrary, the commission shall consider the financial impact on both the applicant and the existing dealership or dealerships.

(6) The reopening or replacement of a dealership at a location where the same line makes, models, or classifications has* been sold by a licensed motor vehicle dealer within the previous two years shall not be considered an additional motor vehicle dealer under Paragraph (1) of this Subsection.

**So in original. Probably should be "have".*

G. *(Repealed.)*

H. (1) All applications for license or licenses shall be accompanied by the appropriate fee or fees in accordance with the schedule set out. In the event any application is denied and the license applied for is not issued, the entire license fee shall be returned to the applicant. Except as set out in Paragraph (2) of this Subsection, all licenses issued under the provisions of this Chapter in accordance with the geographical location of the licensee will be for the year beginning and ending as follows:

1st Commission District—April 1 through March 31
2nd Commission District—May 1 through April 30
3rd Commission District—June 1 through May 31
4th Commission District—July 1 through June 30
5th Commission District—August 1 through July 31
6th Commission District—September 1 through August 31
7th Commission District—October 1 through September 30
8th Commission District—November 1 through October 31

(2) The license of any licensee who does not maintain a place of business in this state shall expire on December thirty-first of each year.

(3) *(Repealed.)*

I. To defray the cost of issuing licenses and administering this Chapter, the commission shall fix reasonable fees to be assessed under this Chapter; however, the license for each manufacturer, distributor, or wholesaler, and factory branch or distributor branch, shall not exceed one thousand dollars; the license for each motor vehicle dealer, motor vehicle lessor, used motor vehicle dealer, factory representative, or distributor representative shall not exceed three hundred dollars; and the license fee for each motor vehicle salesman/agent shall not exceed thirty dollars.

J. Any person, firm, or corporation required to be licensed hereunder, who fails to make application for such license at the time required herein, or required by the rules and regulations of the commission shall, in addition to the aforesaid fees, pay a penalty of fifty percent of the amount of the license fee. The penalty, however, may be waived in whole or in part within the discretion of the commission.

K. (1) The license issued to each motor vehicle dealer, manufacturer, distributor, wholesaler, factory branch, or distributor branch shall specify the location of the office or factory, or branch thereof, and the makes, models, or classifications of motor vehicles to be sold, manufactured, or distributed, and, in the case of a motor vehicle dealer, the name of the dealer-operator. The license issued to any licensee shall specify the location of such licensee's established place of business.

(2) A change of location, or a change in corporate ownership or majority ownership, or a change in the name of a licensee, or a change by a licensee in the makes, models, or classifications, requiring an addendum to a franchise agreement, of motor vehicles manufactured, distributed, or sold, or the addition of a make of motor vehicle manufactured, distributed, or sold, or a change in the identity of the designated dealer-operator shall require a new license and application therefor.

L. Every motor vehicle salesman/agent, factory representative, or distributor representative shall have his license upon his person when engaged in his business, and shall display same upon request. The name of the employer of such salesman/agent, factory representative, or distributor representative shall be stated on said license.

M. Applicants for and holders of motor vehicle dealers' licenses and used motor vehicle dealers' licenses shall obtain and maintain bonds in accordance with the following provisions:

(1) Before any motor vehicle dealer's license is issued to an applicant under the provisions of this Chapter, a good and sufficient surety bond, executed by the applicant as principal and by a surety company qualified to do business in Louisiana as surety, in the sum of twenty thousand dollars, shall be delivered to the Louisiana Motor Vehicle Commission.

(2) Before any used motor vehicle dealer's license is issued to an applicant under the provisions of this Chapter, a good and sufficient surety bond, executed by the applicant as principal and by a surety company qualified to do business in Louisiana as surety, in the sum of ten thousand dollars, shall be delivered to the Louisiana Motor Vehicle Commission. If a used motor vehicle dealer operates from more than one location, a bond in the amount of ten thousand dollars shall be required for each location.

(3) Such bonds shall be in a form to be approved by the commission and shall be conditioned so that the dealer shall comply with the conditions of any written contract made

by such dealer in connection with the sale or exchange of any motor vehicle and shall not violate any of the provisions of this Chapter or any other law of Louisiana in the conduct of the business for which he is licensed. Such bond shall be made payable to the secretary of the Department of Public Safety and Corrections or to his successor in office, for the use, benefit, and indemnity of any persons who shall suffer any loss as a result of any violation of the conditions hereinabove contained. Such bond shall be for the license period and a new bond or a proper continuation certificate shall be delivered to the Louisiana Motor Vehicle Commission at the beginning of each license period; however, the aggregate liability of the surety in any one year shall in no event exceed the sum of such bond. Upon notification to the commission of the termination of such bond, the license of the affected licensee shall be revoked or suspended at the discretion of the commission.

(4), (5) *(Repealed.)*

N. It shall be a violation of this Chapter:

(1) (a) Any person, firm, association, corporation, or trust engaging in business as, or serving or acting as a motor vehicle dealer, used motor vehicle dealer, motor vehicle lessor, or motor vehicle salesman/agent, or manufacturer, distributor, or wholesaler of motor vehicles, or factory branch, distributor branch, or factory representative or distributor representative, as such, in this state must first obtain a license therefor as provided in this Chapter, regardless of whether or not said person, firm, association, corporation, or trust maintains or has a place or places of business in this state.

(b) (i) Any person, firm, association, corporation, or trust engaging, acting, or serving in more than one of the capacities or having more than one place where such business is carried on or conducted shall be required to obtain and hold a current license for each capacity and place of business.

(ii) *(Repealed.)*

(c) However, notwithstanding any other provisions of law to the contrary, any motor vehicle dealer holding a license hereunder shall not be required to obtain a license as a motor vehicle lessor or used motor vehicle dealer provided such operations are conducted from the location from which said motor vehicle dealer is licensed to do business.

(2) (a) All licensees must operate from an established place of business properly zoned in the municipality, provide a suitable office, have a permanently affixed sign in front of the establishment, which denotes that vehicles are offered for sale, lease, or rent at the location to which the sign is affixed.

(b) All licensees must have a usable telephone at the place of business, the number of which should be listed on the application for license and in a local directory accessible to the public. The commission must be notified of any change in the telephone number.

(c) All licensees are required to furnish and keep in force the minimum required liability insurance coverage on all vehicles offered for sale, rental, lease, or used in any other capacity in demonstrating or utilizing the streets and roadways in accordance with the financial responsibility laws of the state of Louisiana. Failure to maintain such insurance shall result in the immediate suspension of license, which suspension shall be effective as of the date of said failure to maintain said liability insurance coverage until proof of the required liability insurance is furnished to the commission. Should no proof of insurance be furnished to the commission within thirty days, the license of said licensee shall be revoked.

(d) Any person licensed under this Subsection shall furnish evidence that he currently has garage liability insurance covering his place of business. The policy must have limits of not less than one hundred thousand dollars for bodily injury to one person, three hundred thousand dollars per accident and fifty thousand for property damage. Said insurance must be maintained throughout the period of licensure. Failure to maintain such insurance shall result in the immediate suspension of license, which suspension shall be effective as of the date of said failure to maintain said liability insurance coverage until proof of the required garage liability insurance is furnished to the commission. Should no proof of insurance be furnished to the commission within thirty days, the license of the said licensee shall be revoked.

(3) For a motor vehicle dealer, used motor vehicle dealer, or a motor vehicle salesman/agent:

(a) To require a purchaser of a new motor vehicle, as a condition of sale and delivery thereof, to also purchase special features, appliances, accessories, or equipment not desired or requested by the purchaser; provided, however, that this prohibition shall not apply as to special features, appliances, accessories, or equipment which is already installed on the car when received by the dealer;

(b) To represent and sell as a new and unused motor vehicle any motor vehicle which has been used and operated for demonstration purposes or which is otherwise a used motor vehicle; or

(c) To resort to or use any false or misleading advertisement in connection with his business as such motor vehicle dealer or motor vehicle salesman/agent; or

(d) To sell or offer to sell makes, models, or classifications of new and unused motor vehicles for which no franchise and license to sell is held.

(e) Except as otherwise approved by the commission, to sell or offer to sell a motor vehicle from an unlicensed location.

(f) To deliver to a prospective purchaser a new and unused or a used motor vehicle on a sale conditioned on financing, i.e., a spot delivery, except on the following terms and conditions which shall be in writing and shall be a part of the conditional sales contract:

(i) That if the sale is not concluded by the financing of the sale to the purchaser within seven days of the delivery, the sale contract shall be null and void.

(ii) That the motor vehicle being offered for trade-in by the purchaser shall not be sold by the motor vehicle dealer until the conditional sale is complete.

(iii) That there shall be no charge to the purchaser should the conditional sale not be complete, including, but not limited to, mileage charges or charges to refurbish the vehicle offered for trade-in.

(iv) That if the conditional sale is not completed, the motor vehicle dealer shall refund to the purchaser all sums placed with the dealership as a deposit or any other purpose associated with the attempted sale of the vehicle.

(v) That the prospective purchaser shall return the vehicle to the dealership within forty-eight hours of notification by the dealer that the conditional sale will not be completed.

(4) For a motor vehicle lessor:

(a) To represent and sell as a new and unused motor vehicle any motor vehicle which has been used or intended to be used and operated for leasing and rental purposes or which is otherwise a used motor vehicle; or

(b) To resort to or use any false or misleading advertising in connection with the business of leasing or renting motor vehicles.

(c) To lease, rent, sell, or offer to sell a motor vehicle from a location not licensed for such activity.

(d) To rent or lease any motor vehicle which has been located within the state of Louisiana for a period of thirty days or more, unless such motor vehicle has been issued a Louisiana license plate by, and all license fees and taxes have been paid to, the state of Louisiana.

(5) For a manufacturer of motor vehicles, a distributor, a wholesaler, distributor branch or factory branch, or officer, agent, or other representative thereof, to induce or coerce, or attempt to induce or coerce, any motor vehicle dealer:

(a) To order or accept delivery of any motor vehicle or vehicles, appliances, equipment, parts or accessories therefor, or any other commodity or commodities which shall not have been voluntarily ordered by said motor vehicle dealer;

(b) To order or accept delivery of any motor vehicle with special features, appliances, accessories, or equipment not included in the list price of said motor vehicles as publicly advertised by the manufacturer thereof; or

(c) To order for any person any parts, accessories, equipment, machinery, tools, appliances, or any commodity whatsoever.

(d) To assent to a release, assignment, novation, waiver, or estoppel which would relieve any person from liability to be imposed by law, unless done in connection with a settlement agreement to resolve a matter pending a commission hearing or pending litigation between a manufacturer, distributor, wholesaler, distributor branch or factory branch, or officer, agent, or other representative thereof, or to require any controversy between a dealer and a manufacturer to be referred to any person or entity other than the commission, duly constituted courts of this state or the United States, if such referral would be binding upon the dealer.

(e) To enter into a franchise with a new motor vehicle dealer or during the franchise term, use any written instrument, agreement, or waiver, to attempt to nullify or modify any provision of this Chapter, or prevent a new motor vehicle dealer from bringing an action in a particular forum otherwise available under law. Such instruments, agreements, and waivers are null and void, unless done in connection with a settlement agreement to resolve a matter pending a commission hearing or pending litigation between a manufacturer, distributor, wholesaler, distributor branch or factory branch, or officer, agent, or other representative.

(6) For a manufacturer of motor vehicles, a distributor, a wholesaler, distributor branch or factory branch, or officer, agent, or other representative thereof:

(a) To refuse to deliver to any duly licensed motor vehicle dealer having a franchise or contractual arrangement for the retail sale of new and unused motor vehicles sold or distributed by such manufacturer, distributor, wholesaler, distributor branch or factory branch, any motor vehicle, publicly advertised for immediate delivery, within sixty days after such dealer's order shall have been received;

(b) To attempt to induce or coerce, or to induce or coerce, any motor vehicle dealer to enter into any agreement with such manufacturer, distributor, wholesaler, distributor branch or factory branch or representative thereof, or to do any other act unfair to said dealer; or to threaten to cancel any franchise or any contractual agreement existing between such manufacturer, distributor, wholesaler, distributor branch or factory branch and said dealer;

(c) To unfairly, without just cause and due regard to the equities of said dealer, cancel the franchise of any motor vehicle dealer without ninety days' notice prior thereto, unless such cancellation arises out of financial default of the motor vehicle dealer or fraudulent activity of the dealer principal which results in the conviction of a crime punishable by imprisonment. The nonrenewal of a franchise or selling agreement with said dealer or his successor without just provocation or cause, or the refusal to approve a qualified transferee or qualified successor to the dealer-operator as provided for in the franchise or selling agreement shall be deemed an evasion of this Paragraph and shall constitute an unfair cancellation, regardless of the terms or provisions of such franchise or selling agreement;

(d) To refuse to extend to a motor vehicle dealer the privilege of determining the mode or manner of available transportation facility that said dealer desires to be used or employed in making deliveries of new motor vehicles to him or it;

(e) To resort to or use any false or misleading advertisement in connection with his business as such manufacturer of motor vehicles, distributor, wholesaler, distributor branch or factory branch, or officer, agent, or other representative thereof; or

(f) To fail or refuse to pay a franchise dealer doing warranty work under the manufacturer's published warranty a labor rate equal to but not in excess of the labor rate in effect in the particular dealership for such work when done for the public in general, i.e., nonwarranty work.

(g) To delay, refuse, or fail to deliver motor vehicles in reasonable quantities relative to the new motor vehicle dealer's facilities and sales potential in the relevant market area. This Subparagraph shall not be valid, however, if such failure is caused by acts or causes beyond the control of the manufacturer, distributor, or other such party.

(h) To hold a franchised dealer liable for any sums determined to be owed to a manufacturer, distributor, wholesaler, distributor branch, or factory branch by virtue of an audit of the books of such franchised dealer, when said sums owed are a result of transactions which occurred more than two years prior to the commencement date of such an audit, unless such sums are owed as a result of fraudulent practices of such franchise dealers. Provided however, a dealer shall not be held liable by virtue of an audit for failure to retain parts for a period in excess of six months.

(i) To ship or sell motor vehicles to a motor vehicle dealer prior to the motor vehicle dealer having been granted a license by the commission to sell such motor vehicles.

(j) To unreasonably withhold consent to the sale, transfer, or exchange of the franchise to a qualified transferee capable of being licensed as a new motor vehicle dealer in this state, provided the transferee meets the criteria generally applied by the manufacturer in approving new motor vehicle dealers and agrees to be bound by all the terms and conditions of the standard franchises.

(k) To fail to respond in writing to a written request for consent as specified in Subparagraph (j) above within sixty days of receipt of a written request on the forms, if any, generally utilized by the manufacturer or distributor for such purposes and containing the information required therein. Failure to respond shall be deemed to be consent to the request.

(*l*) To compete with a new motor vehicle dealer in the same line makes, models, or classifications operating under an agreement or franchise from the aforementioned manufacturer. A manufacturer shall not, however, be deemed to be competing when any of the following conditions are met:

(i) Operating a dealership temporarily for a reasonable period, not to exceed two years;

(ii) Operating a bona fide retail dealership which is for sale to any qualified independent person at a fair and reasonable price, not to exceed two years;

(iii) Operating in a bona fide relationship in which an independent person has made a significant investment subject to loss in the dealership and can reasonably expect to acquire full ownership of such dealership on reasonable terms and conditions.

(m) To condition the renewal or extension of a franchise on a new motor vehicle dealer's substantial renovation of the dealer's place of business or on the construction, purchase, acquisition, or rental of a new place of business by the new motor vehicle dealer, unless the manufacturer has advised the new motor vehicle dealer in writing of its intent to impose such a condition within a reasonable time prior to the effective date of the proposed date of renewal or extension, but in no case less than one hundred eighty days, and provided the manufacturer demonstrates the need for such demand in view of the need to service the public and the economic conditions existing in the automobile industry at the time such action would be required of the new motor vehicle dealer. As part of any such condition the manufacturer shall agree, in writing, to supply the dealer with an adequate supply and marketable model mix of automobiles to meet the sales levels necessary to support the increased overhead incurred by the dealer by reason of such renovation, construction, purchase or rental of a new place of business.

(n) To fail to compensate its dealers for the work and services they are required to perform in connection with the dealer's delivery and preparation obligations according to the terms of compensation that shall be filed with the commission on or before October first of each year. The commission shall find the compensation to be reasonable or the manufacturer shall remedy any deficiencies.

(*o*) To fail to adequately and fairly compensate its dealers for labor, parts, and other expenses incurred by such dealer to perform under and comply with a manufacturer's or a distributor's warranty agreement. In no event shall any manufacturer or distributor pay its dealers at a price or rate for warranty work that is less than that charged by the dealer to the retail customers of the dealer for nonwarranty work of like kind. Warranty work includes parts and labor performed. All claims made by the dealer for compensation under this Subparagraph shall be paid within thirty days after approval and shall be approved or disapproved within thirty days after receipt. When any claim is disapproved, the dealer shall be notified in writing of the grounds for disapproval. No claim which has been approved and paid may be charged back to the dealer unless it can be shown that the claim was false or fraudulent, that the repairs were not properly made or were unnecessary to correct a defective condition, or that the dealer failed to reasonably substantiate or properly submit the claim.

(p) To coerce, or attempt to coerce, any franchised dealer to participate in an advertising group or to participate monetarily in an advertising campaign or contest or to purchase any promotional materials, showroom or other display decorations or materials at the expense of such dealer.

(q) To fail to designate and provide to the commission in writing the community or territory assigned to a motor vehicle dealer.

(7) Any person, firm, association, corporation, or trust which sells or offers to sell new and unused motor vehicles, or leases, rents, or offers to lease or rent motor vehicles, and which is not a licensee of the commission shall, nonetheless, be subject to the provisions of Chapter 6 of Title 32 and the rules and regulations of the commission which pertain to the regulation of advertising.

O. After any of the conditions have been met under R.S. 32:1254(N)(6)(*l*)(i) or (ii), the commission shall allow the manufacturer of new motor vehicles to compete with new motor vehicle dealers of the same-line makes, models, or classifications under an agreement or franchise from said manufacturer for longer than two years when, in the discretion of the commission, the best interest of the manufacturer, consuming public, and new motor vehicle dealer are best served.

P. (1) Under the terms of the franchise notwithstanding, any dealer may appoint by will, or other written instrument, a designated successor to succeed in the ownership interest of the dealer in the dealership upon the death or incapacity of the dealer.

(2) Unless good cause exists for refusal to honor the succession on the part of the manufacturer or distributor, any designated successor of a deceased or incapacitated dealer of a dealership may succeed to the ownership of the dealership under the existing franchise if:

(i) The designated successor gives the manufacturer or distributor written notice of his or her intention to succeed to the ownership of the dealer within sixty days of the dealer's death or incapacity, and

(ii) The designated successor agrees to be bound by all the terms and conditions of the franchise.

(3) The manufacturer or distributor may request, and the designated successor shall provide, promptly upon such request, personal and financial data reasonably necessary to determine whether the succession should be honored.

(4) If a manufacturer or distributor believes that good cause exists for refusing to honor the succession of a deceased or incapacitated dealer, the manufacturer or distributor may, not more than six months following receipt of notice of the designated successor's intent to succeed and receipt of such personal or financial data, serve upon the designated successor notice of its refusal to honor the succession and of its intent to discontinue the existing franchise with the dealer not earlier than six months from the date such notice is served.

(5) The notice must state the specific grounds for the refusal to honor the succession.

(6) If notice of refusal and discontinuance is not timely served upon the designated successor, the franchise shall continue in effect subject to termination only as otherwise permitted by this Chapter.

(7) In determining whether good cause for the refusal to honor the succession exists, the manufacturer or distributor has the burden of proving that the designated successor is not of good moral character or does not otherwise meet the manufacturer's or distributor's reasonable standards as a franchise.

(8) If a manufacturer or distributor refuses to honor the succession to the ownership interest of a deceased or incapacitated owner for good cause, then and in such event:

(i) The manufacturer or distributor shall allow the designated successor a reasonable period of time which shall not be less than six months in which to consummate a sale of the dealership. Any such sale shall be subject to R.S. 32:1254(N)(6)(c); and

(ii) Upon termination of the franchise pursuant to such refusal, the provisions of R.S. 32:1257 shall apply.

Q. All foreign corporations seeking or maintaining a license under this Chapter must be registered to do business in this state with the secretary of state. Evidence showing such registration shall be furnished by such applicant or licensee upon request by the commission.

R. No person shall modify a motor vehicle dealer agreement during the term of the agreement or upon its renewal if the modification substantially and adversely affects the motor vehicles dealer's rights, obligations, investment or return on investment without giving sixty day written notice of the proposed modification to the motor vehicle dealer unless the modifications are required by law, court order, or the commission. Within the sixty day notice period the motor vehicle dealer may file with the commission a complaint for a determination whether there is good cause for permitting the proposed modification. The commission shall schedule a hearing within sixty days to decide the matter. Multiple complaints pertaining to the same proposed modifications shall be consolidated for hearing. The proposed modification may not take effect pending the determination of the matter.

(1) In making a determination of whether there is good cause for permitting a proposed modification, the commission may consider any relevant factor including;

(a) The reasons for the proposed modification.

(b) Whether the proposed modification is applied to or affects all motor vehicle dealers in a nondiscriminating manner.

(c) The degree to which the proposed modification will have a substantial and adverse effect upon the motor vehicle dealer's investment or return on investment.

(d) Whether the proposed modification is in the public interest.

(e) The degree to which the proposed modification is necessary to the orderly and profitable distribution of motor vehicles by the motor vehicle dealer.

(f) Whether the proposed modification is offset by other modifications beneficial to the motor vehicle dealer.

(2) The decision of the commission shall be in writing and shall contain findings of fact and a determination of whether there is good cause for permitting the proposed modification. The commission shall deliver copies of the decision to the parties personally or by registered mail.

(3) *(Repealed.)*

(Chgd. by Acts 1990 No. 124, §1, No. 283, §1; Acts 1991 No. 296, §1; Acts 1992 No. 258, §1; Acts 1993 No. 536, §§1, 2; Acts 1995 No. 51, §§1, 2; Acts 1997 No. 87, §1, No. 211, §1, eff. 8/15/97.)

§1254.1. *(Renumbered as R.S. 32:1260.)*

§1255. Denial, revocation, imposition of a civil penalty, or suspension of license; grounds.

The commission may, in addition to imposing a civil penalty under the provisions of this Chapter, deny an application for a license, or revoke or suspend a license after it has been granted for any of the following reasons:

(1) On satisfactory proof of unfitness of the applicant or the licensee, as the case may be, under the standards established and set out in this Chapter.

(2) For fraud practiced or any material misstatement made by an applicant in any application for license under the provisions of this Chapter.

(3) For any willful failure to comply with any provision of this Chapter or with any rule or regulation adopted and promulgated by the commission under authority vested in it by this Chapter.

(4) Change of condition after license is granted or failure to maintain the qualifications for license.

(5) Continued or flagrant violation of any of the rules or regulations of the commission.

(6) For any willful violation of any law relating to the sale, lease or rental, distribution or financing of motor vehicles.

(7) Upon a finding that, considering the matters set forth in the applicable paragraphs of Subsections A through J of Section 1254, the public interest is not served by the issuance of the license sought or continuance of the license previously granted.

(Chgd. by Acts 1995 No. 51, §1, eff. 6/9/95.)

§1256. Denial, revocation, suspension, or expiration of license; penalties; injunctive relief; cease and desist orders.

A. The commission may without prior notice deny the application for a license within thirty days after receipt thereof by written notice to the applicant stating the grounds for such denial. Upon request by the applicant whose license has been so denied, the commission shall set the time and place of hearing a review of such denial, the same to be heard with reasonable promptness.

B. The commission may suspend or revoke a license issued or impose a civil penalty only after a hearing of which the licensee affected shall be given at least ten days written notice specifying the grounds or reasons for suspension, revocation, or penalty. Such notice may be served as provided by law for the service of notices or by mailing a copy by registered or certified mail to the last known residence or business address of such licensee.

C. (1) The hearing on denial of a license, suspension or revocation of a license, or imposition of a civil penalty shall be at such time and place as the commission may prescribe and the affected applicant or licensee shall be notified of such time and place at least ten days prior to the date of hearing. The hearing shall be scheduled to be held within sixty days of notification to the licensee or applicant of the violation. The commission shall in like manner also notify the person, firm, association, corporation, or trust with whom the applicant or licensee is associated, or in whose association he is about to enter. The commission shall have the power to compel the production of records and papers bearing upon the application or complaints. The commission shall have the power to subpoena and bring before it any person in this state, or take testimony of any such person by deposition in the same manner as prescribed by law in judicial procedure before courts of the state in civil cases. Any party to such hearing shall have the right to procure the attendance of witnesses in his behalf upon designating to the commission the person or persons sought to be subpoenaed.

(2) If the commissioner shall determine that any applicant is not qualified to receive a license, a license shall not be granted to said applicant, and if the commission shall determine that any licensee is guilty of a violation of any of the provisions of this Chapter or the rules and regulations of the Louisiana Motor Vehicle Commission his or its license may be suspended or revoked, or a civil penalty may be imposed, or both.

(3) (a) No civil penalty imposed for the violation of the provisions of this Chapter or the rules and regulations of the Louisiana Motor Vehicle Commission shall exceed five thousand dollars for each day such violation continues.

(b) On a second or subsequent violation, no civil penalty imposed shall exceed ten thousand dollars for each day such second or subsequent violation continues.

(c) In order to constitute a second or subsequent violation there must occur a lapse of at least one day following the first or previous violation.

(d) Any civil penalty imposed by the commission may, in the discretion of the commission, be suspended in whole or in part.

(e) No civil penalty imposed for the negligent filing or the untimely updating of information as required under the provisions of this Chapter or under the rules and regulations of the Louisiana Motor Vehicle Commission shall exceed one hundred dollars per day.

D. All licenses shall be granted or refused within thirty days after application therefor, and shall expire as provided in this Chapter, unless sooner revoked or suspended, except that where a complaint of unfair cancellation of a dealer franchise is in process of being heard, no replacement application for such franchise shall be considered until a decision is rendered by the commission.

E. (1) The decision of the commission to grant or refuse to grant an application for a license, to suspend or revoke a license, or to impose a civil penalty shall not become final for a period of thirty days from the date thereof, except when revocation is a result of the failure of the licensee to maintain a valid surety bond, in which case the period shall be twenty-four hours, during which time said applicant or licensee may appeal devolutively or suspensively in accordance with law from the decision of the commission in accordance with the Administrative Procedure Act* by mailing to the executive director of the commission a copy of the petition, or causing service of summons directed to the executive director of the commission to be issued; said petition to be deposited in the United States mail or said summons to be issued within thirty days from the date of the decision of the commission from which appeal is taken, except when the decision is to revoke a license as a result of the failure of the licensee to maintain a valid surety bond, in which case the aforedirected action must be taken within twenty-four hours. All appeals of commission decisions shall be made in compliance with Louisiana Code of Civil Procedure Article 2124.

**R.S. 49:950 et seq.*

(2) If the issues involved were first presented to the commission by a complaint filed with the commission, such complainant may appeal from the decision of the commission in the same manner as hereinbefore prescribed.

F. The commission is hereby authorized without posting of cost, bond, or deposit to institute an injunctive action in the district court for the parish in which the commission office is located or the district court for the parish in which the alleged offender is domiciled to enforce the provisions of R.S. 32:1251 through 1257 and any other law, rule, or regulation relating to the sale, leasing, renting, distribution, or financing of a motor vehicle.

G. (1) In addition to the penalties provided under this Chapter, the commission is expressly empowered and authorized to order the renewal or reinstatement, as the case may be, of any franchise of a motor vehicle dealer which, after following the procedures under this Chapter, is found by the commission to have been unfairly cancelled or not renewed due to lack of just provocation or cause.

(2) The commission's authority to order a renewal or reinstatement, as the case may be, shall be consistent with the terms of the unfairly cancelled franchise agreement.

(3) The commission shall order the renewal for an additional full franchise term or reinstatement for the remaining term of the franchise, as the case may be, under the franchise agreement.

H. The commission may render judgment for costs, or any part thereof, against any party to proceedings held or scheduled to be held before the commission as it may consider equitable. These costs shall include but not be limited to court reporter fees, commission attorney fees, the mileage and per diem of the commissioners, and other applicable and reasonable costs.

I. (1) If it appears to the commission at any time that a person is violating the provisions of this Chapter or any rule or order of the commission issued pursuant to this Chapter, it shall notify the person engaged in such conduct to appear and show cause why a cease and desist order should not be issued prohibiting the proscribed conduct. An interlocutory cease and desist order may be granted with or without bond or other undertaking if:

(a) Such an order is necessary to the performance of the duties delegated to the commission by this Chapter or is otherwise necessary or convenient to maintaining the status quo between two or more adverse parties before the commission;

(b) A party before the commission is entitled to relief demanded of the commission and all or part of the relief requires the restraint of some act prejudicial to the party;

(c) A person is performing or is about to perform or is procuring or allowing the performance of an act relating to the subject of a contested case pending before the commission, in violation of the rights of a party before the commission, and the act would tend to render the commission's order in that case ineffectual; or

(d) Substantial injury to the rights of a person subject to the commission's jurisdiction is threatened irrespective of any remedy at law.

(2) Interlocutory cease and desist orders shall remain in effect until vacated or until incorporated into a final commission order. Permanent cease and desist orders may issue without regard to the enumerations in Paragraph 1 of this Subsection, but only in accordance with the provisions of this Chapter pertaining to the issuance of final commission orders. Appeal of any interlocutory cease and desist order shall be made to the commission prior to seeking judicial review under the provisions of this Chapter. Appeal of a permanent cease and desist order shall be conducted pursuant to the provisions of this Chapter pertaining to judicial review of final orders.

(Chgd. by Acts 1990 No. 519, §1; Acts 1995 No. 51, §1, No. 458, §1, No. 758, §1, No. 1133, §2; Acts 1997 No. 211, §1, eff. 8/15/97.)

§1256.1. Venue for arbitration.

The venue for an arbitration proceeding required by the motor vehicle dealer sales and service agreement with the manufacturer shall be in Louisiana and not inconsistent with Louisiana law. It is the public policy of this state that the venue provided for herein may not be modified by contract.

§1257. Requirements upon termination; penalty; indemnity.

A. (1) In the event the licensee ceases to engage in the business of being a motor vehicle dealer, or ceases to sell a particular make of motor vehicle and after notice to the manufacturer, distributor, or representative by registered or certified mail, within thirty days of the receipt of the notice by the manufacturer, distributor, or representative, the manufacturer, distributor, or representative shall repurchase:

(a) All new and unused motor vehicles of the current and last prior model year delivered to the licensee and parts on hand that have not been damaged or substantially altered to the prejudice of the manufacturer while in the possession of the licensee. The motor vehicles and parts shall be repurchased at the cost to the licensee which shall include without limitation freight and advertising costs, except that new and unused automobiles shall be purchased on the following schedule:

(i) Vehicles with 0—1,000 miles at the cost to the licensee.

(ii) Vehicles with 1,001—6,000 miles at the cost to the licensee reduced by the net discount value of each mile in excess of 1,000 miles, where "net discount value" is determined according to the following formula: cost to the licensee multiplied by total mileage in excess of 1,000 miles divided by 100,000, and where "net cost" equals the dealer cost plus any charges by the manufacturer, distributor, or representative for distribution, delivery, advertising, and taxes, less all allowances paid to the dealer by the manufacturer, distributor, or representative for new, unsold, undamaged, and complete motor vehicles.

(iii) Vehicles with 6,001 miles or over—no obligation to repurchase.

(b) At fair market value, each undamaged sign owned by the dealer which bears a trademark or trade name used or claimed by the manufacturer, distributor, or representative if the sign was purchased from or purchased at the request of the manufacturer, distributor, or representative.

(c) At fair market value, all special tools and automotive service equipment owned by the dealer which were recommended in writing and designated as special tools and equipment and purchased from or purchased at the request of the manufacturer, distributor, or representative, if the tools and equipment are in usable and good condition except for reasonable wear and tear.

(d) The manufacturer, distributor, or representative shall pay to the dealer the costs of transporting, handling, packing, and loading of motor vehicle or parts, signs, tools, and equipment subject to repurchase.

(2) The manufacturer shall make the required repurchase after the dealer terminates his franchise and within thirty days of the submission to it, by registered or certified mail return receipt requested, of a final inventory of motor vehicles and parts on hand.

B. Failure to make said repurchase without just cause shall subject the manufacturer to a penalty of one and one-half percent per month or fraction thereof of the inventory value or returnable motor vehicles and parts, signs, special tools, and automotive service equipment, payable to the dealer, as long as said repurchase is not made.

C. Notwithstanding the terms of any franchise agreement, each manufacturer shall indemnify and hold harmless its franchised dealers against any judgment for damages, including but not limited to court costs and reasonable attorney fees of the dealer, arising out of complaints, claims or lawsuits including, but not limited to, strict liability, negligence, misrepresentation, express or implied warranty or rescission of sale to the extent that the judgment arises out of alleged defective or negligent manufacture, assembly or design of motor vehicles, parts or accessories or other functions by the manufacturer, which are beyond the control of the dealer.

D. Prior to making a change in the area of responsibility described in the franchise agreement or sales and service agreement of a dealer, the franchisor or manufacturer shall give said dealer and the commission no less than sixty days prior written notice by certified or registered mail.

E. Upon the involuntary termination, nonrenewal or cancellation of any franchise by the manufacturer, except for termination, nonrenewal, or cancellation resulting from a felony conviction, notwithstanding the terms of any franchise, whether entered into before or after the enactment of this Chapter or any of its provisions, the new motor vehicle dealer shall be allowed fair and reasonable compensation by the manufacturer as agreed by the parties, or lacking agreement, as determined by the commission, for the following:

(1) The dealership facilities if the facilities were required to be purchased or constructed as a precondition to obtaining the franchise or to its renewal; provided that if such facilities were leased and the lease were required as a precondition to obtaining the franchise or to its renewal, then the manufacturer shall be liable for one year's payment of the rent or the remainder of the term of the lease, whichever is less.

(2) Payment under this Section shall entitle the manufacturers or distributors to possession and use of the facility.

(3) As used in this Section, "manufacturer" shall include a manufacturer, a distributor, a factory branch, distributor branch, or other subsidiary thereof.

(Chgd. by Acts 1991 No. 296, §1; Acts 1995 No. 51, §1, eff. 6/9/95.)

§1258. *(Repealed by Acts 1995 No. 51, §2, eff. 6/9/95.)*

§1259. Cumulative effect of law; remedial action; retroactive application of certain provisions.

A. The provisions of this Chapter shall be cumulative to existing laws.

B. The provisions of R.S. 32:1254(N)(6)(g) and R.S. 32:1256(F) and (G) are declared to be remedial and shall be applied retroactively.

§1260. Damage disclosure.

Whenever a new and unused motor vehicle is sold to any person, the seller shall notify the purchaser of any body damage or mechanical damage which the vehicle has sustained that exceeds six percent of the manufacturer's suggested retail price. Such notice shall be in writing and a copy thereof shall be delivered to the purchaser prior to or simultaneous with transfer of the vehicle title.

CHAPTER 7. MOTOR VEHICLE INSPECTION

§1301. Vehicles without required equipment or in unsafe condition.

No person shall drive or move on any highway any motor vehicle, trailer, semitrailer, or pole trailer, or any combination thereof, unless the equipment upon any such vehicle is in good working order and adjustment as required in this Chapter and said vehicle is in such safe mechanical condition as not to endanger the driver or other occupant or any person upon the highway. Every motor vehicle, trailer, semitrailer, and pole trailer registered in this state shall bear a valid safety inspection certificate issued in the state of Louisiana, except as otherwise provided by R.S. 32:1305(G). *(Chgd. by Acts 1995 No. 475, §1; Acts 1997 No. 77, §1, No. 288, §1, eff. 8/15/97.)*

§1302. Inspection by officers of the department.

A. The Director of Public Safety, members of the State Police and such other officers and employees of the department as the director may designate, may at any time upon reasonable cause to believe that a vehicle is unsafe or not equipped as required by law, or that its equipment is not in proper adjustment or repair, require the driver of such vehicle to stop and submit such vehicle to an inspection and such test with reference thereto as may be appropriate.

B. In the event such vehicle is found to be in unsafe condition or any required part or equipment is not present or is not in proper repair and adjustment the officer shall give a written notice to the driver and shall send a copy to the department. Said notice shall require that such vehicle be placed in safe condition and its equipment in proper repair and adjustment specifying the particulars with reference thereto and that a certificate of inspection and approval be obtained within 5 days.

§1303. Owners and drivers to comply with inspection laws.

A. No person driving a vehicle shall refuse to submit such vehicle to an inspection and test when required to do so by the director or an authorized officer or employee of the department.

B. Every owner or driver, upon receiving a notice as provided in R.S. 32:1302 shall comply therewith and shall within 5 days secure an official certificate of inspection and approval which shall be issued in duplicate, one copy to be retained by the owner or driver and the other copy to be forwarded to the department. In lieu of compliance with this Sub-section the vehicle shall not be operated, except as provided in Sub-section C of this Section.

C. No person shall operate any vehicle after receiving a notice with reference thereto as above provided, except as may be necessary to return such vehicle to the residence or place of business of the owner or driver, if within a distance of 20 miles, or to a garage, until said vehicle and its equipment has been placed in proper repair and adjustment and otherwise made to conform to the requirements of this act and a certificate of inspection and approval shall be obtained as promptly as possible thereafter.

D. In the event repair or adjustment of any vehicle or its equipment is found necessary upon inspection, the owner of said vehicle may obtain such repair or adjustment at any place he may choose, but in every event an official certificate of inspection and approval must be obtained otherwise such vehicle shall not be operated upon the highways of this State.

§1304. Secretary to require periodical inspection.

A. (1) The secretary shall at least once every other year, but not more frequently than twice each year, require that every motor vehicle, trailer, semitrailer, and pole trailer registered in this state be inspected and that an official certificate of inspection and approval be obtained for such vehicle. However, overweight and oversize mobile homes requiring a state permit shall not be required to bear a certificate of approved inspection when being moved by a bonded carrier as defined by law nor shall used motor vehicles in transit by a dealer be required to have a certificate of inspection and approval.

(2) Such inspection should be made and such certificates obtained with respect to the mechanism, brakes and equipment of every vehicle as shall be designated by the secretary. The secretary shall require the inspection of all approved automotive emission control devices installed on motor vehicles produced after model year 1980 to insure that such devices are operative and have not been tampered with.

(3) (a) The secretary shall formulate and promulgate a set of standards for the control and regulation of emission control devices on all automobiles and other motor vehicles which standards shall be consistent with other federal and state regulations for the installation and operation of approved emission control devices.

(b) The secretary is hereby authorized to make necessary rules and regulations for the administration and enforcement of this Section and to designate any periods of time during which owners of vehicles, subject to this Section, shall display upon such vehicles certificates of inspection and approval and shall produce the same on demand of any officer or employee of the department designated by the secretary or any police or peace officer when authorized by the secretary.

(4) The rules and regulations adopted for the administration and enforcement of this Section shall include standards for windshields as follows:

(a) In the eight and one-half inch by eleven inch "acute area" directly in the driver's line of vision there shall be no cracks and there shall be no more than two stars, nicks, chips, bullseyes, or half-moons in excess of one-half inch.

(b) In the "critical area" cleaned by the normal sweep of the windshield wiper blade on the driver's side of the windshield there shall be no star which is larger than two inches in diameter; there shall be no more than two stars larger than one and one-half inches in diameter; and there shall be no more than two cracks longer than eight inches; or any combination thereof.

(c) In the remaining areas of the windshield, only those cracks which jeopardize the integrity of the windshield shall be cause for rejection.

B. The secretary is hereby authorized to make necessary rules and regulations for the administration and enforcement of this Section and to designate any periods of time during which owners of vehicles, subject to this Section, shall display upon such vehicles certificates of inspection and approval or shall produce the same on demand of any officer or employee of the department designated by the secretary or any police or peace officer when authorized by the secretary. Owners and operators of all motor vehicles required to be equipped with windshields shall display on the lower left hand corner of the windshield a certificate of inspection affixed thereto by a duly authorized motor vehicle inspection station. The secretary shall accept the certificate of inspection and approval issued by any municipality pursuant to any municipal ordinance adopted prior to July 27, 1960. However, each person who applies for a motor vehicle inspection tag in the city of New Orleans shall produce written proof of insurance from an insurer that the motor vehicle is covered by security and shall declare in writing that he or she intends to maintain said security at all times while said vehicle is used upon the highways of Louisiana.

C. The director may authorize the acceptance in this state of a certificate of inspection and approval issued in another state having an inspection law similar to this Chapter and may extend the time within which a certificate shall be obtained by the resident owner of a vehicle which was not in this state during the time an inspection was required.

D. (1) The secretary may suspend the registration of any vehicle which he determines is in such unsafe condition as to constitute a menace to safety, or which after notice and demand is not equipped as required in this Chapter, or for which a required certificate has not been obtained.

(2) In accordance with the rules and regulations adopted by the Department of Environmental Quality pursuant to R.S. 30:2054(B)(8), when a vehicle has failed an emission inspection conducted pursuant to such rules, the registered owner shall have a stipulated amount of time of not less than thirty days to make the necessary repairs to the vehicle. The owner shall be required to submit the vehicle to be reinspected no later than the last day of the stipulated amount of time. If the vehicle fails the reinspection and the owner shows evidence of expending four hundred fifty dollars for repairs made for the purpose of causing the vehicle to be capable of passing the reinspection, the vehicle shall not be required to be submitted for an emission inspection for a period of two years. The four hundred fifty dollar minimum expenditure required for a two-year waiver shall be adjusted in January of each year by the percentage, if any, by which the consumer price index for the preceding calendar year differs from the consumer price index for 1989. If the vehicle fails the reinspection and the owner does not show evidence of expending an amount specified in rules for repairs made for the purpose of causing the vehicle to be capable of passing the reinspection, or the vehicle has not been submitted to an emission inspection as required by R.S. 30:2054(B)(8), the secretary shall suspend or revoke the registration of the vehicle and impound or cancel the vehicle's license plate. The secretary shall adopt rules and regulations in accordance with the Administrative Procedure Act* in order to effectuate the suspension or revocation of the registration of the vehicle and impoundment or cancellation of the vehicle's license plate.

**R.S. 49:950 et seq.*

(3) Motor vehicles being titled for the first time may be registered for up to two years without being subject to an emissions inspection, and the four immediately preceding model years, that are being held in a motor vehicle dealer's inventory for resale, may be registered in the localities provided for under this Paragraph for up to one year without being subject to an emissions inspection, provided that the dealer states in writing that the emissions equipment on the motor vehicle was operating in accordance with the manufacturer's and distributor's warranty at the time of resale.

E. (1) The mere failure of the owner or operator of a motor vehicle required by this Section to be inspected to obtain a current and valid inspection certificate shall not be in violation, provided that the certificate has been expired less than one calendar month; nor shall an owner or operator be in violation if he shall produce on demand, under Subsection B of this Section, a certificate of inspection for the vehicle valid and effective for not more than six months and not in current display on the windshield by reason of replacement of the windshield glass.

(2) However, when a certificate of inspection is removed from a windshield by reason of replacement of windshield glass, the owner of the vehicle may be issued, for a fee of twenty-five cents and return of the original certificate to an inspection certificate station, a certificate which shall be valid for the time remaining on the original certificate.

F. The purchaser of a used vehicle from a private individual shall be protected from citations for failure to have an inspection tag during the interval between the date of purchase and the receipt of title, provided proof of application can be shown.

G. In order to enforce the provisions of this Section as applicable to motor vehicles which are propelled by an internal combustion engine or motor capable of using liquefied petroleum gas or compressed natural gas, no such vehicle shall be issued a motor vehicle inspection certificate without a current decal as evidence of tax payment, as required by R.S. 47:802.3. *(Chgd. by Acts 1990 No. 166, §1; Acts 1991 No. 416, §1; Acts 1993 No. 570, §1; Acts 1994 Third Ex. Sess. No. 128, §1, eff. 7/7/94.)*

§1304.1. *(Redesignated as R.S. 32:1311(A).)*

§1304.2. *(Redesignated as R.S. 32:1311(B) to (D).)*

§1305. Appointment of official inspection stations.

A. For the purpose of making inspections and issuing official certificates of inspection and approval as provided herein the director shall issue permits for and furnish instructions and all necessary forms to official inspection stations for the inspection of vehicles as herein required and the issuance of official certificates of inspection and approval.

B. Application for permit shall be made upon an official form and shall be granted only when the director is satisfied that the station is properly equipped and has competent personnel to make such inspections and adjustments and that inspection will be properly conducted. The director shall not issue a permit as an official inspection station unless the applicant business has been in operation for not less than ninety days prior to the issuance. However, if there is no other official inspection station for use by the general public within twenty-five miles of the business making application, this required prior operation period shall not be less than thirty days. The director before issuing a permit may require the applicant to file a bond conditioned that it will make compensation for any damage to a vehicle during an inspection or adjustment due to negligence on the part of such applicant or its employees. The aggregate liability of the surety for all such damages shall in no event exceed the amount of such bond.

C. The director shall properly supervise and cause inspections to be made of such stations and shall revoke and require the surrender of the permit issued to a station which he finds is not properly equipped or conducted. The director shall maintain and post at the office of the department lists of all stations holding permits and of those whose permits have been revoked.

D. Permits for inspecting and issuing official certificates of inspection and approval shall be issued for a period of one year upon payment to the director of an annual fee of twenty-five dollars, plus an annual fee of five dollars for each mechanic inspector named in the permit application.

E. Any motor vehicle repair or maintenance shop operated or maintained by a person, firm or corporation in whose name there is licensed under the provisions of R.S. 47:462, ten or more vehicles, shall be, at his or its request, designated as an official inspection station, for the purpose of inspecting and certifying vehicles operated by such person.

F. Any motor vehicle repair shop or maintenance shop operated by a school board of any city or parish in whose name there are licensed under the provisions of R.S. 47:462 ten or more vehicles, or which has ten or more vehicles under contract, or which has a combination of owned and contract vehicles totaling ten or more, shall be, at their request, designated as an official inspection station for the purpose of inspecting and certifying vehicles operated or contracted for such board.

G. (1) Any person, corporation, partnership, or other business entity owning more than forty motor vehicles registered in Louisiana pursuant to the International Registration Plan, and operating at least one vehicle repair and maintenance shop, shall, upon request in writing to the Department of Public Safety and Corrections, have one or more of his vehicle repair and maintenance shops designated as official inspection stations for the purpose of inspecting and certifying those motor vehicles which are owned by him. Such duly designated vehicle repair and maintenance shops may be located within or without the state of Louisiana.

(2) The secretary shall adopt and promulgate rules and regulations in accordance with the Administrative Procedure Act* necessary to implement the provisions of this Subsection. These rules shall include provisions for total reimbursement by the business entity of any costs incurred by the state for the administration of this Subsection. Reimbursement shall be made by the business entity availing itself of this program within thirty days after submission by the state of the total costs incurred.

(3) The venue for any civil action arising out of this Subsection shall be East Baton Rouge Parish.

(Chgd. by Acts 1991 No. 571, §1; Acts 1995 No. 267, §1; Acts 1997 No. 77, §1, No. 288, §1, eff. 8/15/97.)

**R.S. 49:950 et seq.*

§1306. Operation of official inspection stations.

A. No permit for an official station shall be assigned or transferred or used at any location other than therein designated and every said permit shall be posted in a conspicuous place at the location designated.

B. The person operating an official inspection station shall issue a certificate of inspection and approval upon an official form to the owner of a vehicle upon inspecting such vehicle and determining that its equipment required under the provisions of this act is in good condition and proper adjustment, otherwise no certificate shall be issued. When required by the director a record and report shall be made of every inspection and every certificate so issued.

C. (1) An annual charge or fee shall be charged for each certificate of inspection and approval issued, as provided in this Subsection.

(2) Except as otherwise provided in Paragraph (3) of this Subsection, an annual charge or fee of ten dollars shall be charged for each certificate of inspection and approval issued, four dollars and seventy-five cents of which shall be retained by the operator of the motor vehicle inspection station conducting the inspection, four dollars of which shall be transferred to the office of state police for use in traffic law enforcement and one dollar and twenty-five cents shall be transferred to the office of motor vehicles for expenses associated with the motor vehicle inspection and financial responsibility programs. Included in the inspection shall be the adjustment of headlights when needed and mechanically practical, at no additional cost to the operator of the motor vehicle inspected.

(3) An annual charge or fee of thirty dollars shall be charged for the inspection of all commercial motor vehicles which are required to be inspected under the provisions of Part 396 of Title 49 of the Code of Federal Regulations, including Part 396.17 and "Appendix G" thereof. No charges or fees other than the thirty dollar fee shall be charged for a commercial motor vehicle inspection. Of the thirty dollar fee, the motor vehicle inspection station operator who performs this inspection shall retain twenty-three dollars and seventy-five cents; two dollars and twenty-five cents shall be transferred to the office of motor vehicles for expenses associated with motor vehicle and financial responsibility programs; and four dollars of which shall be transferred to the office of state police for use in traffic law enforcement. Included in the inspection shall be the adjustment of headlights at no additional cost to the operator of the motor vehicle being inspected. The Legislature of Louisiana hereby declares that a commercial motor vehicle inspection is much more extensive than the inspection mandated in Paragraph (2) of this Subsection and that the increase in the fee or charge for the inspection of commercial vehicles is based on the difference in the two types of inspection.

D. The Department of Public Safety shall adopt guidelines for the certification of motor vehicle inspection stations. Any applicant meeting the guidelines shall be certified as a motor vehicle inspection station. Geographical location shall not be a criteria for certification.

E. The office of motor vehicles shall distribute motor vehicle inspection stickers to each district office throughout the state and shall make such stickers available for purchase by certified motor vehicle inspection stations during normal business hours. The stickers shall be in convenient book form and shall be sold in such practical increments as will not present a financial hardship to low volume stations.

F. Each certified motor vehicle inspection station shall replace motor vehicle inspection stickers which are damaged, or which are attached to windshields which have become damaged, upon the presentation of proof of purchase of the damaged sticker, the presentation of identification of the person applying for the replacement sticker, and the payment of a fee of five dollars and twenty-five cents. The deputy secretary of public safety services shall design a notice that shall be posted in public view at all certified motor vehicle inspection stations, which shall include the availability and cost of the replacement of a damaged motor vehicle inspection sticker.

G. Notwithstanding any law or rule or administrative policy to the contrary, official motor vehicle inspection stations shall not be required to reserve a service bay or stall for the exclusive purpose of conducting motor vehicle inspections. Each official motor vehicle inspection station shall give priority to customers seeking motor vehicle inspections.
(Chgd. by Acts 1991 No. 929, §1; Acts 1994 Third Ex. Sess. No. 129, §1; Acts 1995 No. 267, §1, eff. 8/15/95.)

§1307. Improper representation as official station.

A. No person shall in any manner represent any place as an official inspection station unless such station is operating under a valid permit issued by the department.

B. No person other than a duly authorized officer or employee of inspection station shall issue a certificate of inspection and approval.

§1308. False certificates.

A. No person shall make, issue or knowingly use any imitation or counterfeit of an official certificate of inspection.

B. No person shall display or cause or permit to be displayed upon any vehicle any certificate of inspection and approval knowing the same to be fictitious or issued for another vehicle or issued without an inspection having been made.

§1309. Fee for inspection certificates.

The fees collected for the issuance of certificates of inspection and approval shall be deposited in the state treasury upon receipt and shall be credited to the Bond Security and Redemption Fund as required by Article VII, Section 9 of the Constitution of Louisiana. *(Chgd. by Acts 1992 No. 984, §10, eff. 8/21/92.)*

§1310. Penalty for violation.

Any person violating any of the provisions of R.S. 32:1301 through 32:1308 or of any rules and regulations established by the director as herein provided shall, upon conviction, be punished by a fine of not more than five hundred dollars or by imprisonment of not more than six months or by both such fine and imprisonment.

§1311. Exemptions.

A. Farm tractors, self-propelled farm equipment, rubber-tired farm wagons and carts, drawn rubber-tired farm equipment, and implements of husbandry which are designed primarily for field use and which are operated or moved only incidentally on the highways of this state, and which are used for farm purposes only, are exempt from the inspection requirements of this chapter.

B. Motor vehicles which are forty years old or older and which are used primarily for exhibition in shows, parades, tours, and other special uses and not for general transportation and which are registered and licensed as antique as provided in R.S. 32:707(L) shall be exempt from the inspection requirements of this Chapter.

C. Motor vehicles which display a current safety inspection sticker as certified by the Department of Public Safety and Corrections shall be exempt from the inspection requirements of this Chapter.

D. Commercial motor vehicles in interstate and intrastate commerce which are subject to the Federal Motor Carrier Safety Regulations shall be exempt from the inspection requirements of this Chapter provided, however, that these inspection requirements are determined by the Federal Highway Administration as not being as effective or comparable to the Periodic Motor Vehicle Inspection requisites contained in the Code of Federal Regulations (49 CFR Part 396). As used in this Subsection, "commercial motor vehicle" means any self-propelled or towed vehicle which is used on public highways in one of the following circumstances:

(1) The vehicle is used to transport passengers or property in interstate commerce, and

(a) Has a gross vehicle weight rating (GVWR) or gross combination weight rating (GCWR) of 10,001 pounds or more; or

(b) Is designed to transport more than fifteen passengers including the driver; or

(c) Is used in the transportation of hazardous materials in a quantity requiring placarding under regulations issued by the Secretary under the Hazardous Transportation Act (49 USC app. 1801—1813).

(2) The vehicle is used to transport passengers or property in intrastate commerce, and

(a) Has a gross vehicle weight rating (GVWR) or gross combination weight rating (GCWR) of 20,001 pounds or more; or

(b) Is designed to transport more than fifteen passengers, including the driver; or

(c) Is used in the transportation of hazardous materials and has a gross vehicle weight rating (GVWR) or gross combination weight rating (GCWR) of 10,001 pounds or more.
(Chgd. by Acts 1990 No. 725, §1, eff. 9/7/90.)

§1312. Civil penalties.

A. After reasonable notice and opportunity for a fair and impartial hearing to be held in accordance with the Administrative Procedure Act*, any person who is determined by the secretary to have committed an act that is in violation of the provisions of this Chapter relative to the operation of an official inspection station or the actual conduct of a motor vehicle safety inspection, or any rule adopted under the provisions of this Chapter for such activities, is subject to a civil penalty of not more than one thousand dollars.
**R.S. 49:950 et seq.*

B. The secretary shall determine and assess the amount of any civil penalty. In determining the amount of the penalty, the secretary shall take into account the nature, circumstances, extent, and gravity of the violation; the degree of culpability of the person charged; the person's history of previous offenses and ability to pay; the effect of the penalty on the person's ability to continue to operate his business or maintain his employment; and any other matter that justice requires.
(Added by Acts 1994 Third Ex. Sess. No. 128, §1, eff. 7/7/94.)

§1313. Recovery of civil penalties; Motor Vehicle Safety Inspection Fund.

A. After due process, the secretary shall notify, either by certified mail or in person, any person found in violation of the provisions of this Chapter relative to the operation of an official inspection station or the actual conduct of a motor vehicle safety inspection, or in violation of any rules adopted under the provisions of this Chapter for such activities, of the penalty assessed. If the penalty assessed has not been received by the secretary within thirty calendar days after notification of the assessment, the secretary may order the suspension of the motor vehicle inspection station license. For offenses involving the mechanic inspector rather than the station, the secretary may order the suspension of the certificate authorizing the mechanic to inspect motor vehicles. Upon receipt by the secretary of the penalty assessed, the license or certificate shall be reinstated.

B. All civil penalties collected pursuant to the provisions of this Chapter shall be deposited into the state treasury and, in accordance with Article VII, Section 9 of the Constitution of Louisiana, shall be credited to the Bond Security and Redemption Fund. After a sufficient amount is allocated from that fund to pay all obligations secured by the full faith and credit of the state which become due and payable within each fiscal year, the state treasurer shall pay into a special fund that is hereby created in the state treasury an amount equal to the amount of penalties deposited. Such special fund shall be designated as the Motor Vehicle Safety Inspection Fund. The monies deposited in the fund shall be used solely for the purpose of the motor vehicle inspection program and only in the amounts appropriated by the legislature each year.

C. The secretary shall adopt and promulgate rules and regulations in accordance with the Administrative Procedure Act* to implement the assessment of the civil penalty.
(Added by Acts 1994 Third Ex. Sess. No. 128, §1, eff. 7/7/94.)
**R.S. 49:950 et seq.*

CHAPTER 9. DRIVER LICENSE COMPACT

Section

§1420. Enactment; text.

The Driver License Compact is hereby enacted into law and entered into with all other jurisdictions legally joining therein in the form substantially as follows:

DRIVER LICENSE COMPACT

ARTICLE I
FINDINGS AND DECLARATION OF POLICY

(a) The party states find that:

(1) The safety of their streets and highways is materially affected by the degree of compliance with state and local ordinances relating to the operation of motor vehicles.

(2) Violation of such a law or ordinance is evidence that the violator engages in conduct which is likely to endanger the safety of persons and property.

(3) The continuance in force of a license to drive is predicated upon compliance with laws and ordinances relating to the operation of motor vehicles, in whichever jurisdiction the vehicle is operated.

(b) It is the policy of each of the party states to:

(1) Promote compliance with the laws, ordinances, and administrative rules and regulations relating to the operation of motor vehicles by their operators in each of the jurisdictions where such operators drive motor vehicles.

(2) Make the reciprocal recognition of licenses to drive and eligibility therefor more just and equitable by considering the overall compliance with motor vehicle laws, ordinances and administrative rules and regulations as a condition precedent to the continuance or issuance of any license by reason of which the licensee is authorized or permitted to operate a motor vehicle in any of the party states.

ARTICLE II
DEFINITIONS

As used in this compact:

(a) "State" means a state, territory or possession of the United States, the District of Columbia, or the Commonwealth of Puerto Rico.

(b) "Home state" means the state which has issued and has the power to suspend or revoke the use of the license or permit to operate a motor vehicle.

(c) "Conviction" means a conviction of any offense related to the use or operation of a motor vehicle which is prohibited by state law, municipal ordinance or administrative rule or regulation, or a forfeiture of bail, bond or other security deposited to secure appearance by a person charged with having committed any such offense, and which conviction or forfeiture is required to be reported to the licensing authority.

ARTICLE III
REPORTS OF CONVICTION

The licensing authority of a party state shall report each conviction of a person from another party state occurring within its jurisdiction to the licensing authority of the home state of the licensee. Such report shall clearly identify the person convicted; describe the violation specifying the section of the statute, code or ordinance violated; identify the court in which action was taken; indicate whether a plea of guilty or not guilty was entered, or the conviction was a result of the forfeiture of bail, bond or other security; and shall include any special findings made in connection therewith.

ARTICLE IV
EFFECT OF CONVICTION

(a) The licensing authority in the home state, for the purposes of suspension, revocation or limitation of the license to operate a motor vehicle, shall give the same effect to the conduct reported, pursuant to Article III of this compact, as it would if such conduct had occurred in the home state, in the case of convictions for:

(1) Manslaughter or negligent homicide resulting from the operation of a motor vehicle;

(2) Driving a motor vehicle while under the influence of intoxicating liquor or a narcotic drug, or under the influence of any other drug to a degree which renders the driver incapable of safely driving a motor vehicle;

(3) Any felony in the commission of which a motor vehicle is used;

(4) Failure to stop and render aid in the event of a motor vehicle accident resulting in the death or personal injury of another.

(b) As to other convictions, reported pursuant to Article III, the licensing authority in the home state shall give such effect to the conduct as is provided by the laws of the home state.

(c) If the laws of a party state do not provide for offenses or violations denominated or described in precisely the words employed in subdivision (a) of this Article, such party state shall construe the denominations and descriptions appearing in subdivision (a) hereof as being applicable to and identifying those offenses or violations of a substantially similar nature and the laws of such party state shall contain such provisions as may be necessary to ensure that full force and effect is given to this Article.

ARTICLE V
APPLICATION FOR NEW LICENSES

Upon application for a license to drive, the licensing authority in a party state shall ascertain whether the applicant has ever held, or is the holder of a license to drive issued by any other party state. The licensing authority in the state where application is made shall not issue a license to drive to the applicant if:

(1) The applicant has held such a license, but the same has been suspended by reason, in whole or in part, of a violation and if such suspension period has not terminated.

(2) The applicant has held such a license, but the same has been revoked by reason, in whole or in part, of a violation and if such revocation has not terminated, except that after the expiration of one year from the date the license was revoked, such person may make application for a new license if permitted by law. The licensing authority may refuse to issue a license to any such applicant if, after investigation, the licensing authority determines that it will not be safe to grant to such person the privilege of driving a motor vehicle on the public highways.

(3) The applicant is the holder of a license to drive issued by another party state and currently in force unless the applicant surrenders such license.

ARTICLE VI
APPLICABILITY OF OTHER LAWS

Except as expressly required by provisions of this compact, nothing contained herein shall be construed to affect the right of any party state to apply any of its other laws relating to licenses to drive to any person or circumstance, not to invalidate or prevent any driver license agreement or other cooperative arrangement between a party state and a nonparty state.

ARTICLE VII
COMPACT ADMINISTRATOR AND INTERCHANGE OF INFORMATION

(a) The head of the licensing authority of each party state shall be the administrator of this compact for his state. The administrators, acting jointly, shall have the power to formulate all necessary and proper procedures for the exchange of information under this compact.

(b) The administrator of each party state shall furnish to the administrator of each other party state any information or documents reasonably necessary to facilitate the administration of this compact.

ARTICLE VIII
ENTRY INTO FORCE AND WITHDRAWAL

(a) This compact shall enter into force and become effective as to any state when it is enacted the same into law.

(b) Any party state may withdraw from this compact by enacting a statute repealing the same, but no such withdrawal shall take effect until six months after the executive head of the withdrawing state has given notice of the withdrawal to the executive heads of all other party states. No withdrawal shall affect the validity or applicability by the licensing authorities of states remaining party to the compact of any report of conviction occurring to withdrawal.

ARTICLE IX
CONSTRUCTION SEVERABILITY

This compact shall be liberally constructed so as to effectuate the purposes thereof. The provisions of this compact shall be severable and if any phrase, clause, sentence or provision of this compact is declared to be contrary to the constitution of any party state or the United States or the applicability thereof to any government, agency, person or circumstance is held invalid, the validity of the remainder of this compact and the applicability thereof to any government, agency, person or circumstance shall not be affected thereby. If this compact shall be held contrary to the constitution of any state party thereto, the compact shall remain in full force and effect as to the remaining states and in full force and effect as to the state affected as to the severable matters.

§1421. "Licensing authority" defined.

As used in the compact, the term "licensing authority" with reference to this state, shall mean the Department of Public Safety. Said department shall furnish to the appropriate authorities of any other party state any information or documents reasonably necessary to facilitate the administration of Articles III, IV and V of the compact.

§1422. Administrator; compensation.

The Compact administrator provided for in Article VII of the compact shall be the director of public safety. The director shall not be entitled to any additional compensation on account of his service as such administrator, but shall be entitled to expenses incurred in connection with his duties and responsibilities as such administrator, in the same manner as for expenses incurred in connection with any other duties or responsibilities of his office or employment.

§1423. "Executive head" defined.

As used in the compact, with reference to this state, the term "executive head" shall mean the governor.

§1424. "Intoxicating liquor" defined.

As used in the compact, the term "intoxicating liquor" with reference to this state shall mean alcoholic beverages.

§1425. "Narcotic drug" defined.

As used in the compact, the term "narcotic drug" with reference to this state shall mean in addition to narcotic drugs, central nervous system stimulants and hallucinogenic drugs.

CHAPTER 10. NONRESIDENT VIOLATOR COMPACT

(Chgd. by Acts 1991 No. 498, §1, eff. 9/6/91.)

§1441. Enactment and text of the Nonresident Violator Compact.

The Nonresident Violator Compact, hereinafter called the "compact" is recognized as substantially the same as its predecessor, the Traffic Violations Compact of which Louisiana has been a member since 1970. Louisiana hereby adopts the correct name of the compact as the Nonresident Violator Compact and ratifies continuous past, present, and future membership in the compact in the form substantially as follows:

NONRESIDENT VIOLATOR COMPACT

ARTICLE I
FINDINGS AND DECLARATION OF POLICY AND PURPOSE

A. The party jurisdictions find that:

(1) In most instances, a motorist who is cited for a traffic violation in a jurisdiction other than his home jurisdiction:

(a) Must post collateral or bond to secure appearance for trial at a later date;

(b) If unable to post collateral or bond, is taken into custody until the collateral bond is posted; or

(c) Is taken directly to court for trial.

(2) In some instances, the motorist's driver's license may be deposited as collateral to be returned after he has complied with the terms of the citation.

(3) The purpose of the practices described in Subparagraphs (1) and (2) above is to ensure compliance with the terms of a traffic citation by the motorist who, if permitted to continue on his way after receiving the traffic citation, could return to his or her home jurisdiction and disregard his or her duty under the terms of the traffic citation.

(4) A motorist receiving a traffic citation in his or her home jurisdiction is permitted, except for certain violations, to accept the citation from the officer at the scene of the violation and to immediately continue on his way after promising or being instructed to comply with the terms of the citation.

(5) The practice described in Subparagraph (1) above causes unnecessary inconvenience and, at times, a hardship for the motorist who at the time is unable to post collateral, furnish a bond, stand trial, or pay the fine and is thus compelled to remain in custody until some arrangement can be made.

(6) The deposit of a driver's license as a bail bond as directed in Subparagraph (2) above is viewed with disfavor.

(7) The practices described consume an undue amount of law enforcement time.

B. It is the policy of the party jurisdictions to:

(1) Seek compliance with the laws, ordinances, and administrative rules and regulations relating to the operation of motor vehicles in each of the jurisdictions.

(2) Allow motorists to accept a traffic citation for certain violations and to proceed on their way without delay whether or not the motorist is a resident of the jurisdiction in which the citation is issued.

(3) Extend cooperation to its fullest extent among the jurisdictions for obtaining compliance with the terms of a traffic citation issued in one jurisdiction to a resident of another jurisdiction.

(4) Maximize effective utilization of law enforcement personnel and assist court systems in the efficient disposition of traffic violations.

C. The purpose of this compact is to:

(1) Provide a means through which the party jurisdictions may participate in a reciprocal program to effectuate the policies enumerated in Paragraph B above in a uniform and orderly manner.

(2) Provide for the fair and impartial treatment of traffic violators operating within party jurisdictions and recognition of the motorist's right of due process and the sovereign status of a party jurisdiction.

ARTICLE II
DEFINITIONS

A.* In the Nonresident Violator Compact, the following words have the meaning indicated unless the context requires otherwise:

**So in original. No subsection B has been enacted.*

(1) "Citation" means any summons, ticket, or other official document issued by a police officer for a traffic violation containing an order which requires the motorist to respond.

(2) "Collateral" means any cash or other security deposited to secure an appearance for trial following the issuance by a police officer of a citation for a traffic violation.

(3) "Compliance" means the act of answering a citation, summons, or subpoena through appearance at court or payment of fines and costs. This includes the recall or dismissal of a citation, summons, or subpoena.

(4) "Court" means a court of law or equity with jurisdiction over traffic violations.

(5) "Driver's license" means any license or privilege to operate a motor vehicle issued under the laws of the home jurisdiction.

(6) "Home jurisdiction" means the jurisdiction which issued the driver's license of the traffic violator.

(7) "Issuing jurisdiction" means the jurisdiction in which the traffic citation was issued to the motorist.

(8) "Jurisdiction" or "party jurisdiction" means a state, territory, possession, district, or commonwealth of the United States, province of Canada, or other nation which is or becomes a member of this compact.

(9) "Motorist" means a driver of a motor vehicle operating in a party jurisdiction other than the home jurisdiction.

(10) "Personal recognizance" means an agreement by a motorist at the time of issuance of a traffic citation that he or she will comply with the terms of that traffic citation. Physical receipt of the citation by the motorist implies the agreement.

(11) "Police officer" means any individual authorized by the party jurisdiction to issue a citation for a traffic violation.

(12) "Terms of the citation" means those options expressly stated upon the citation.

ARTICLE III
PROCEDURE FOR ISSUING JURISDICTION

A. Unless prohibited by law, a police officer when issuing a citation to a motorist licensed by a party jurisdiction shall not require the motorist to post collateral or a driver's license to secure appearance if the officer receives the motorist's personal recognizance.

B. Upon failure of a motorist to comply with the terms of a traffic citation, the appropriate official shall report the failure to comply to the driver's license authority of the jurisdiction in which the traffic citation was issued. The report must, at a minimum, contain the name, address, driver's license number, date of birth, sex, type and/or citation of violation, date of violation, and court address and telephone number.

C. Upon receipt of the report as provided in Paragraph B above, the licensing authority of the issuing jurisdiction shall transmit a report containing the information to the licensing authority of the home jurisdiction containing at least the minimum information received in the report.

D. The licensing authority of the issuing jurisdiction shall not transmit a report on any violation if the date of transmission would be more than six months after the date on which the traffic citation was issued.

ARTICLE IV
PROCEDURE FOR HOME JURISDICTION

A. Upon receipt of a report of a failure to comply, from the licensing authority of the issuing jurisdiction, the home jurisdiction shall notify the motorist and initiate a suspension action as hereinafter provided.

B. The notice referred to in Paragraph A above shall be sent, as soon as possible after the receipt by the home jurisdiction, to the motorist at his last known address by regular mail. The notice shall inform the motorist of his right to a presuspension hearing upon request within thirty days of the date of notice.

C. If the motorist furnishes satisfactory evidence of compliance or that he is not the person who gave personal recognizance or presents another valid defense at the administrative hearing, no driver's license suspension shall occur.

D. If after thirty days from the date of notice, the motorist has not responded to the office of motor vehicles, the Louisiana driver's license of the motorist shall be immediately suspended until proof of compliance is furnished or for one year, whichever is the lesser period.

E. Nothing in this Article shall be construed to require application of the financial responsibility laws of any jurisdiction if those laws would otherwise be inapplicable.

ARTICLE V
APPLICABILITY OF OTHER LAWS

Except as expressly required by provisions of the compact, nothing contained herein shall be construed to affect the right of any party jurisdiction to apply any of its other laws relating to licenses to operate motor vehicles or to invalidate or prevent any driver-license agreement or cooperative agreement between a party jurisdiction and a nonparty jurisdiction.

ARTICLE VI
COMPACT ADMINISTRATION AND INTERCHANGE OF INFORMATION

A. The head of the licensing authority for Louisiana is the administrator of this compact for this jurisdiction.

B. The administrators of this compact for each party jurisdiction, acting jointly may formulate all necessary and proper procedures for the exchange of information under this compact.

C. The administrator of each party jurisdiction shall furnish to the administrator of each other party jurisdiction any information or documents necessary to facilitate the administration of this compact.

ARTICLE VII
ENTRY INTO AND WITHDRAWAL FROM COMPACT

A. The head of the licensing authority for Louisiana is the administrator of this compact for this jurisdiction.

B. The administrator of this compact for each party jurisdiction acting jointly may formulate all necessary and proper procedures for the exchange of information under this compact.

C. The administrator of each party jurisdiction shall furnish to the administrator of each other party jurisdiction any information or documents necessary to facilitate the administration of this compact.

ARTICLE VIII
EXCEPTIONS TO JURISDICTION

The provisions of this compact shall not apply to parking of other nonmoving violations, highway weight limit violations, or violations of law governing transportation of hazardous materials.

ARTICLE IX
CONSTRUCTION SEVERABILITY

This compact shall be liberally construed as to effectuate the purposes stated herein. The provisions of this compact shall be severable and if any phrase, clause, sentence, or provision of this compact is declared contrary to the constitution, laws, ordinances, rules, or regulations of any party jurisdiction or of the United States, the applicability thereof to any government, agency, person, or circumstance shall not be affected thereby. If this compact shall be declared in any part or way invalid in any party jurisdiction, the compact shall remain in full force and

effect as to the remaining states and in full force and effect as to the objecting jurisdiction as to all severable matters.
(Chgd. by Acts 1991 No. 498, §1, eff. 9/6/91.)

§1442. "Licensing authority" defined.

As used in the compact, the term "licensing authority" shall mean the Louisiana Department of Public Safety and Corrections, office of motor vehicles. *(Chgd. by Acts 1991 No. 498, §1, eff. 9/6/91.)*

§1443. Administrator; no compensation.

The compact administrator provided for in Article VI of the compact shall serve without pay but is entitled to reimbursement of expenses incurred in performance of his duties as administrator, in the same manner as for expenses incurred in connection with other duties of his office. *(Chgd. by Acts 1991 No. 498, §1, eff. 9/6/91.)*

§§1444 to 1446. *(Deleted to conform with Acts 1991 No. 498, §1, eff. 9/6/91.)*

CHAPTER 11. MOTOR VEHICLE HABITUAL OFFENDER LAW

§1471. Declaration of policy.

It is hereby declared to be the policy of this state:

(1) To provide maximum safety for all persons who travel or otherwise use the public highways of this state; and

(2) To deny the privilege of operating motor vehicles on such highways to persons who by their conduct and record have demonstrated their indifference to the safety and welfare of others and their disrespect for the laws of this state, the orders of its courts, and the statutorily required acts of its administrative agencies; and

(3) To discourage repetition of criminal acts by individuals against the peace and dignity of this state and her political subdivisions and to impose increased and added deprivation of the privilege to operate motor vehicles upon habitual offenders who have been convicted repeatedly of violations of the traffic laws.

§1472. Habitual offender defined.

A. A "habitual offender" shall be any person, resident or non-resident, whose record, as maintained in the office of the Department of Public Safety and Corrections, shows that such person has accumulated ten or more convictions of separate and distinct offenses, committed within three years of the date on which the last offense is committed, involving moving violations, singularly or in combination, in the operation of a motor vehicle which are required to be reported to the department. However, when more than one included offense is committed within a twelve-hour period, such multiple offenses shall be treated for the purposes of this Chapter as one offense.

B. The offenses included in Subsection A shall be deemed to include offenses under any federal law, any law of another state or any valid town, city or county ordinance of another state substantially conforming to the aforesaid state statutory provision.

C. For the purpose of this chapter, the term "conviction" means a final conviction. Also for the purpose of this Section, a forfeiture of bail or collateral deposited to secure a

defendant's appearance in court, which forfeiture has not been vacated or a plea of nolo contendere shall be equivalent to a conviction.
(Chgd. by Acts 1990 No. 933, §1, eff. 9/7/90.)

§1473. Department of Public Safety to certify record to court.

The Department of Public Safety shall certify the conviction record as maintained in its office of any person whose record brings him within the definition of a habitual offender, as defined above, and such abstract shall be competent evidence that the person named therein was duly convicted by the court wherein such conviction or holding was made by each offense shown by such abstract.

§1474. Time limitation.

No person shall be declared a habitual offender under the provisions of this Chapter unless the department certifies the offender's conviction record as provided in R.S. 32:1473 and serves the notice required in R.S. 32:1475 on such person within one year of the date of last conviction which brings that person within the definition of a habitual offender.

§1475. Service of petition; order to show cause.

The department shall issue a written notice along with a copy of the abstract to the person named in the abstract, directing him to show cause why he should not be declared a habitual offender. The notice shall state the time, place, and cause of the hearing which shall be not less than ten nor more than thirty calendar days from the date of the notice. All notices shall be served on the person named in the abstract in accordance with the provisions of R.S. 32:6.
(Chgd. by Acts 1990 No. 319, §1, eff. 9/7/90.)

§1476. Hearing; procedure.

The matter shall be heard by an adjudication officer of the Department of Public Safety. If the person named in the abstract denies that he was convicted of any offense shown in the abstract and necessary for a holding that he is a habitual offender, and if the department cannot, on the evidence available to it, determine the issue, the department may request the decision of such issue from the court in which such conviction was reportedly made. The court to which such request is made shall send to the department certified copies of its records determining such issue. The department in its discretion, may rely on certified copies of convictions adjudged by courts outside of this state, or federal courts, or may request such a court to make a determination.

§1477. Department's findings; order.

A. If the department finds that such person is not the same person named in the aforesaid abstract, or that he is not a habitual offender under this chapter, the proceeding shall be dismissed, but if the department finds that such person is the same person named in the abstract and that such person is a habitual offender, the department shall so find, and by appropriate order, shall direct that such person not operate a motor vehicle upon the highways of this state and shall surrender to the department all licenses or permits to operate a motor vehicle upon the highways of this state.

B. (1) Upon revocation of a driver's license for the first time as provided for under this Section the person whose license has been revoked, upon administrative determination that he is a habitual offender, shall have the right to file a petition in the district court of the parish in which the applicant is domiciled alleging that revocation of his driving privileges will deprive him or his family of the necessities of life or will prevent him from earning a livelihood.

(2) The district court is vested with jurisdiction to set the matter for contradictory hearing in open court upon ten days written notice to the department, and thereupon to determine whether the allegations of hardship have merit.

(3) Upon determination by the court that the lack of a license would deprive the person or his family of the necessities of life, the court may order that the person be granted a restricted license to enable the person to continue to support his family. The restrictions on the license shall be determined by the court and shall include the following:

(a) Licensee shall only be permitted to operate a motor vehicle on such streets as would enable him to earn his livelihood.

(b) Such operation is restricted to times during which he is involved in earning a livelihood.

(c) During the period of revocation, licensee shall be responsible for applying to the court in the event earning his livelihood necessitates a change in the original restrictions imposed by the court.

(d) Any other restrictions that the court determines are necessary and proper.

C. (1) A violation of the restrictions or a subsequent conviction of any offense involving the operation of a motor vehicle during the terms of the restricted license shall result in the forfeiture of the restricted license and the reimposition of the full three year term of revocation and shall also constitute contempt of court.

(2) Suspension, revocation, or cancellation that results from such a violation shall not be subject to appeal.

(3) The restricted driving privileges for this Section shall be allowed to a person only once.

(Chgd. by Acts 1990 No. 933, §1, eff. 9/7/90.)

§1478. Appeals.

An appeal may be taken from any final order entered under the provisions of this Chapter by petition to the district court of the parish in which the person named in the abstract resides. Appeal from the decision of the district court may be taken to any court of competent appellate jurisdiction.

§1479. Prohibition.

No license to operate motor vehicles in this state shall be issued to a habitual offender, nor shall a nonresident habitual offender operate a motor vehicle in this state until all of the following requirements have been complied with:

(1) A period of three years has elapsed since the date of the order finding such person to be a habitual offender.

(2) Financial responsibility requirements are met.

(3) If after the lapse of the three-year period provided above, the department determines that the person has faithfully complied with the order declaring him to be a habitual offender, the department shall restore to such person the privilege to operate a motor vehicle in this state, upon the payment of a one hundred dollar reinstatement fee.

(Chgd. by Acts 1990 No. 933, §1, eff. 9/7/90.)

§§1480, 1481. *(Repealed by Acts 1990 No. 933, §2, eff. 9/7/90.)*

CHAPTER 12. TRANSPORTATION OF HAZARDOUS MATERIALS

Section

§1501. Declaration of policy.

It is hereby declared to be the policy of this state:

(1) That hazardous materials are essential for various industrial, commercial, and other purposes, that their transportation is a necessary incident to their use, and that the transportation is required for the economic prosperity of the people of the state of Louisiana.

(2) That the offering or accepting for transportation, loading or unloading, or transporting, handling, and movement of hazardous materials, because of their capacity for injury to human health, the environment, or property, poses a substantial danger to the health and safety of the citizens of this state unless such materials are loaded and transported in a safe and prudent manner.

(3) That all carrier transportation, including offering and accepting for transportation, loading or unloading, or transportation of hazardous materials, freight, or passengers, should comply with minimum state standards of safe operation, manufacture, and maintenance due to the size and momentum of the transport vehicles involved, the adverse impact on economic welfare posed to the citizens of this state when these transport vehicles are involved in accidents, the threat to public safety caused by these accidents, and the huge volume of shipments in which carriers are involved.

(4) That the offering or accepting for transportation, loading or unloading, or transporting of hazardous materials, freight, and passengers in accordance with minimum state standards of safety is the responsibility of the state.

(Chgd. by Acts 1992 No. 340, §1, eff. 8/21/92.)

§1502. Definitions.

For all purposes of this Chapter and regulations applicable thereto, the terms defined in this Section shall have the following meanings unless the context or use clearly indicates otherwise:

(1) "Carrier" means any person who transports in a transport vehicle hazardous materials, freight or passengers subject to this Chapter and includes a common, contract, or private carrier.

(2) "Common carrier" means any carrier other than a contract carrier or private carrier.

(3) "Contract carrier" means a for-hire carrier who transports hazardous materials, freight, or passengers tendered exclusively by shippers under special contract and whose services are not available to the public.

(4) "Department" means the Department of Public Safety and Corrections.

(5) (a) "Hazardous materials" means any gaseous, liquid, or solid material which because of its quantity, concentration, or physical, chemical, or biological composition poses a substantial present or potential hazard to human health, the environment, or property when transported in commerce, or which material is identified or designated as being hazardous by rules and regulations adopted and promulgated by the secretary of the Department of Public Safety and Corrections pursuant to the Louisiana Administrative Procedure Act*. The secretary, in finding that a material is hazardous, shall consider the following factors with respect to each material:

**R.S. 49:950 et seq.*

(i) Actual or relative potential for harm to human health, the environment, or property when transported in commerce.

(ii) Scientific evidence of its potential for harm based upon quantity, concentration, or chemical or biological composition.

(iii) State of current scientific knowledge regarding the material.

(iv) Its history and current pattern of harm.

(v) Actual or potential volatility when combined with other common substances likely to be encountered during transportation in commerce.

(vi) Actual or relative potential for harm to human health if allowed to escape its containment.

(b) The rules and regulations adopted by the secretary of the Department of Public Safety and Corrections shall be consistent with the Code of Federal Regulations Title 49. "Explosives" as defined and regulated by R.S. 40:1471.1 through 1471.22 shall be considered to be hazardous material subject to regulation by this Chapter.

(6) "Person" means a natural person, firm, association, partnership, copartnership, joint venture, corporation, or other legal entity.

(7) "Private carrier" means a carrier who transports hazardous materials, freight, or passengers for its use or for other purpose without reward or compensation.

(8) "Transport vehicle" means a motor vehicle, rail freight car, freight container, cargo tank, portable tank, aircraft, or vessel used to transport hazardous materials, freight, or passengers.

(9) "Hazardous waste" shall be defined as provided in R.S. 30:1133.

(10) "Freight" means anything that is loaded for transportation.

(11) "Secretary" means the secretary of the Department of Public Safety and Corrections or his designee.

§1503. General provisions; carrier liability insurance; carrier placards.

A. This Chapter implements and is supplementary to the Louisiana motor vehicle laws.

B. Whenever in this Chapter or regulations issued pursuant thereto a reference is made to another law or regulation, the reference also applies to any amendment of the referenced law or regulation.

C. Each carrier, other than a rail carrier, which transports hazardous materials or hazardous waste in any vehicle, and each carrier, other than a rail carrier, which transports freight in a vehicle with a gross vehicle weight rating of twenty-four thousand pounds or more shall acquire a minimum continuous coverage of three hundred thousand dollars public liability and two hundred thousand dollars property damage insurance for each unit regulated by this Chapter. The financial responsibility required may be established by any one or a combination of the following:

(1) Evidence of liability insurance.

(2) Self-insurance, but the level of self-insurance may not be less than twenty percent of equity.

(3) Other evidence of financial responsibility acceptable to the secretary.

D. Each carrier transporting hazardous materials shall indicate the proper hazard class by placing a placard stating such class on all four sides of each vehicle as required by the rules and regulations promulgated by the secretary.

(Chgd. by Acts 1990 No. 922, §1; Acts 1992 No. 567, §1, eff. 8/21/92.)

§1504. Powers of the secretary.

A. The secretary of the department may adopt and promulgate any rules and regulations necessary to carry out the provisions of this Chapter. The secretary shall adopt and promulgate all such rules and regulations in accordance with the Administrative Procedure Act, Chapter 13 of Title 49 of the Louisiana Revised Statutes of 1950. Oversight review shall be conducted by the Joint Legislative Committee on Transportation, Highways and Public Works. All rules and regulations adopted by the secretary shall be compatible with this Chapter and the regulations of the United States Department of Transportation contained in Title 49 and Title 46 of the Code of Federal Regulations relative to the transportation of hazardous materials, freight, or passengers.

B. The secretary may conduct investigations; make reports; issue subpoenas; conduct hearings; require the production of relevant documents, records, and property; take depositions; and conduct, directly and indirectly, research, development, demonstration, or training activities.

C. The secretary shall provide for the periodic inspection of rail cars transporting hazardous material prior to the departure of those rail cars from a railroad switching yard located outside of the property boundaries of chemical manufacturing or processing plants.

(Chgd. by Acts 1997 No. 529, §1, eff. 8/15/97.)

§1505. Authority of officers, employees, and agents.

A. The secretary may authorize any officer, employee, or agent of the department to:

(1) Enter, inspect, and examine at reasonable times and in a reasonable manner the property or records of any person or carrier, to the extent those records or properties relate to this Chapter and the transportation of hazardous materials, freight, or passengers; and

(2) Stop and inspect any transport vehicle or part thereof for any violation of this Chapter or any regulation issued pursuant thereto.

B. Upon request of the owner or operator, the officer, employee, or agent shall display proper credentials issued under this Chapter.

(Chgd. by Acts 1990 No. 935, §1, eff. 9/7/90.)

§1506. Alternate means of compliance.

A. Upon a finding by the secretary that an alternate means of compliance with this Chapter or any regulation issued pursuant thereto provides protection to the public equal to or greater than that which would be derived from compliance with the Chapter or regulation, the secretary may authorize in writing the use of that alternate method.

B. The carrier shall carry a copy of the authorization in or on each transport vehicle to which it applies.

C. The secretary shall not issue an authorization for any interstate transportation or for any transportation for which a special permit has been issued by the United States Department of Transportation.

§1507. Special permits and exemptions.

A. The secretary shall exempt any carrier from compliance with this Chapter or any regulation issued pursuant thereto if that exemption is identical to an exemption or special permit issued by the United States Department of Transportation. However, the secretary shall enforce the exemption or special permit if it pertains to transportation subject to this Chapter.

B. The number of each exemption granted shall be conspicuously marked on the vehicle to which it applied.

§1508. Declaration and marking of unsafe vehicles and containers.

A. An officer, employee, or agent of the department may declare and mark any transport vehicle or container as out-of-service if its condition, filling, equipment, or protective devices would be hazardous to life or property during the transportation of hazardous material, freight or passengers.

B. No person shall operate, authorize, or require the operation of any vehicle or container that has been marked out-of-service until all required corrections have been made.

C. No person shall remove an out-of-service marking from a transport vehicle or container unless all required corrections have been made and the vehicle or container has been inspected and approved by an officer, employee, or agent of the department.

§1509. Shipping documents.

A. No carrier shall transport any hazardous material unless shipping documents describing the lading are provided to the operator of the vehicle prior to departure and shall be carried in the vehicle or combination of vehicles. The description of lading shall include at least the shipping name, classification, and weight or volume of the material. The carrier shall make each shipping document available for inspection whenever requested by an officer, employee, or agent of the department.

B. If the tractor of a tractor-trailer combination is detached from the trailer, a copy of the shipping documents must be placed in a holder by the left front of the trailer.

§1510. Reporting of incidents, accidents, and cleanups.

A. Each person involved in an incident, accident, or the cleanup of an incident or accident during the transportation, loading, unloading, or related storage in any place of a hazardous material subject to this Chapter shall report immediately by telephone to the department if that incident, accident, or cleanup of an incident or accident involves:

(1) A fatality due to fire, explosion, or exposure to any hazardous material.

(2) The hospitalization of any person due to fire, explosion, or exposure to any hazardous material.

(3) A continuing danger to life, health, or property at the place of the incident or accident.

(4) An estimated property damage of more than ten thousand dollars.

B. A written report shall be submitted to the department on an approved form. Each report submitted shall contain the time and date of the incident or accident, a description of any injuries to persons or property, any continuing danger to life at the place of the accident or incident, the identity and classification of the material, and any other pertinent details.

C. In the case of an incident or accident involving hazardous materials which is not subject to this Chapter but which is subject to Title 49 and Title 46 of the Code of Federal Regulations, the carrier shall send a copy of the report filed with the United States Department of Transportation to the department.

D. The secretary shall adopt and promulgate rules and regulations in accordance with the Administrative Procedures Act* to coordinate the implementation of a transportation emergency response system.
**R.S. 49:950 et seq.*

§1511. Illegal discharge of hazardous materials.

No person shall intentionally discharge or cause to be discharged the contents of any transport vehicle containing hazardous material between the points of origin and the points of billed destination, except as authorized by representatives of the Department of Public Safety or the Department of Natural Resources.

§1512. Civil penalties; assessment.

A. Any person who is determined by the secretary, after reasonable notice and opportunity for a fair and impartial hearing held in accordance with the Administrative Procedure Act*, to have committed an act that is a violation of this Chapter or any regulation issued thereunder, is subject to a civil penalty of not more than twenty-five thousand dollars. If the violation is a continuing one, each day of violation shall constitute a separate offense.
**R.S. 49:950 et seq.*

B. In determining the amount of penalty, the secretary shall take into account the nature, circumstances, extent, and gravity of the violation; the degree of culpability of the person charged; the person's history of previous offenses and ability to pay; the effect of the penalty on the person's ability to continue to operate; and any other matters that justice requires.

C. The secretary shall assess the amount of any civil penalty by a written notice to the violator.

D. Before referral under Section 1513, the secretary may compromise any civil penalty.

§1513. Civil penalties; recovery.

A. The secretary shall notify any person found in violation of this Chapter of the penalty levied after due process either by mail or in person. Upon passage of thirty days without receipt of the fine, the secretary may order the removal of the offending vehicle's license tag if the registration is from Louisiana. For vehicles not registered within the state, any vehicle owned by the person or company in violation may be seized. For offenses by the driver or operator, the driver or operator's license shall be suspended. Upon receipt of the fine, the license tags, vehicle, or driver's license shall be returned.

B. The amount of any civil penalty compromised or collected by court action may be deducted from any amount owed to the state by the person charged.

C. All civil penalties collected pursuant to this Chapter shall be paid into the state treasury and, in accordance with Article VII, Section 9 of the Constitution of Louisiana, shall be credited to the Bond Security and Redemption Fund.
(Chgd. by Acts 1992 No. 984, §10, eff. 8/21/92.)

§1513.1. Immunity from civil liability; limitations.

A. A person qualified by training, education, or experience, shall be immune from civil liability for the rendering of care, assistance, or advice, in the area of these qualifications, if responding to an emergency dealing with the prevention or management of an incident resulting from the storage or transportation of hazardous materials at the request of the local civil defense director or his designee, the chief local law enforcement officer in the jurisdiction where the incident occurs or his designee, the state police, or the hazardous waste division's emergency response section within the Department of Natural Resources.

B. The immunity provided for in Subsections A or D or both of this Section shall not apply to any person who is under a legal duty to respond to the emergency incident, or anyone who receives compensation for responding to the emergency incident other than reimbursement for actual out-of-pocket expenses while rendering assistance or advice.

C. Nothing herein shall be construed to limit or otherwise affect the liability of any person for damages resulting from such person's gross negligence, or from his reckless, wanton, or intentional misconduct.

D. The immunity provided for in Subsection A of this Section shall also apply to the employer of such person when no compensation except reimbursement of out-of-pocket expenses is received, but nothing herein shall provide immunity from workers' compensation liability.

E. The immunity provided for in Subsections A or D or both of this Section shall apply only to a situation that occurs outside the physical boundaries of a manufacturing establishment whose primary business is the utilization, handling and processing, of hazardous materials.

F. The immunity provided for in Subsections A or D or both of this Section shall not apply so as to afford any immunity to any common carrier relative to its handling or transporting of hazardous materials or hazardous waste.

G. Any act or omission of any person granted immunity under Subsections A or D or both of this Section shall not be available as a defense to liability by any other person responsible for causing damages in connection with the emergency incident.

§1514. Criminal penalties.

A. Any person who violates any provision of this Chapter, or any regulation issued thereunder, shall, upon conviction, be guilty of a misdemeanor and be fined not more than one thousand dollars per day of violation or imprisoned for not more than one year, or both.

B. Any person who willfully violates any provision of this Chapter shall, upon conviction, be guilty of a felony and be fined not less than five thousand dollars nor more than ten thousand dollars per day of violation, or be imprisoned with or without hard labor for not less than five years nor more than ten years, or both.

§1515. Injunctions.

A. If the secretary considers that an imminent hazard exists with respect to the transportation of a hazardous material, he may petition the district court in the parish in which the person sought to be enjoined resides or in the parish in which the danger exists for a restraining order to restrain that person from performing any act creating the hazard, or for any other order necessary to eliminate or ameliorate the hazard. Such actions may be taken without the necessity of posting bond, and actions taken by the secretary in good faith shall make him exempt from suit for civil damage.

B. For the purposes of this Section, an "imminent hazard" exists with respect to the transportation of hazardous materials, when the transportation may present an imminent and substantial endangerment to health or the environment.

§1516. Driver qualifications.

A. The secretary shall adopt and promulgate rules and regulations for the qualifications and licensing of each person driving, piloting, or otherwise in charge of any transport vehicle transporting hazardous material, freight or passengers or any material designated as hazardous waste under regulations issued in this state. Oversight review shall be conducted by the Joint Legislative Committee on Transportation, Highways, and Public Works. The regulations shall cover physical ability, a written examination, and an examination of the skill necessary for the operation or supervision of the transport vehicle.

B. No person having any disorder characterized by a lapse of consciousness or other mental or physical disability affecting the ability to drive or pilot safely shall be granted a license under this Section. The secretary of the Department of Health and Human Resources shall provide a medical evaluation and recommendation as to which disorders are characterized by a lapse of consciousness and which types of mental or physical disability will affect the ability of a person to drive or pilot safely. Based upon these recommendations the secretary shall adopt and promulgate a listing of disorders and disabilities which make a person ineligible to receive a license pursuant to this Section.

C. (1) No person shall operate or take part in operating, or be in physical control of a transport vehicle if he possesses, is under the influence of, or is using, any substance controlled under the Uniform Controlled Dangerous Substance Law (R.S. 40:963), nor may that person do so with any substance which renders him incapable of performing his duties.

(2) No carrier shall knowingly require or permit a person to violate this Section.

(3) The provisions of this Paragraph do not apply to the possession or use of a substance administered to a person by a physician or under the care of a physician when the physician has advised the person that the substance will not affect his ability to operate a transport vehicle.

(4) As used in this Section, "possession" does not include possession of a substance which is manifested and transported as part of a shipment.

D. (1) No person shall:

(a) Consume an intoxicating beverage, regardless of its alcoholic content, or be under the influence of an intoxicating beverage, within four hours of going on duty or operating, or participating in the operation of or having physical control of, a transport vehicle; or

(b) Consume an intoxicating beverage regardless of its alcoholic content, or be under the influence of an intoxicating beverage, while on duty, or operating, or participating in the operating of or in physical control of, a transport vehicle; or

(c) Be on duty or operate a transport vehicle while having in his possession an intoxicating beverage regardless of its alcoholic content. The provisions of this Paragraph do not apply to possession of an intoxicating beverage which is manifested and transported as part of a shipment.

(d) Be on duty, operate, or participate in the operation of a transport vehicle under the influence of alcohol.

(2) No carrier shall require or permit a person to:

(a) Violate any provision of Paragraph (a) of this Subsection; or

(b) Be on duty or operate a transport vehicle if, by the person's general appearance or conduct or by other substantiating evidence, the person appears to have consumed an intoxicating beverage within the preceding four hours or have alcohol in his system.

E. (1) With a reasonable suspicion, any officer of the office of state police may require anyone operating or participating in the operation of a transport vehicle to take a chemical test or tests of his blood, breath, or urine to determine the alcohol content and/or content in his system of any Schedule I, II, III, IV, and V drugs, as defined in R.S. 40:964.

(2) Pursuant to rules and regulations promulgated by the Deputy Secretary of Public Safety refusal to submit to the chemical test may result in the loss for one year of the individual's privileges to operate a transport vehicle.

§1517. Personnel and expenses.

A. The secretary shall employ such persons as he considers qualified, consistent with applicable civil service regulations, to carry out the provisions of this Chapter.

B. The secretary may incur such expenses as may be required to carry out the provisions of this Chapter.

§1518. Reckless handling of hazardous materials.

A. No person shall offer or accept for transportation, load or unload, or transport a hazardous waste or hazardous material as defined in R.S. 32:1502, in a manner that endangers or could endanger human life or health.

B. Any person who willfully violates this Section shall, upon conviction, be guilty of a felony and be fined or imprisoned in accordance with R.S. 32:1514(B) or may be subject to a civil penalty in accordance with R.S. 32:1512(A).

(Chgd. by Acts 1992 No. 270, §1, eff. 8/21/92.)

§1519. Reimbursement of remedial costs.

A. Any person who has transported a hazardous material as defined in this Chapter, a hazardous substance as defined in R.S. 30:1149.9(4), or a hazardous waste as defined in R.S. 30:1133 shall be liable to the state for undertaking remedial action or for all costs of remedial actions taken in cleaning up any discharge or disposal at a pollution source or facility if it can be shown that the hazardous material, hazardous substance or hazardous waste was discharged or disposed of directly by the transporter and the transporter directly caused the discharge or disposal for which remedial action must be undertaken.

B. (1) The secretary may order any transporter causing a discharge or disposal of a hazardous material, hazardous substance, or hazardous waste at a pollution source or facility to take any remedial actions necessary to contain, abate, cleanup, restore, or remove the discharge or disposal.

(2) When the secretary must file suit against a transporter to recover remedial costs or to obtain remedial action, the court shall also award to the state a penalty of twenty-five percent of the amount determined to be remedial costs.

C. (1) When the secretary orders one transporter to undertake remedial action and other transporters or persons have caused or contributed to the discharge or disposal, the transporter undertaking remedial action may sue for reimbursement from any other transporter or person for the costs of remedial actions attributable to that transporter or person.

(2) When the remedial action is undertaken voluntarily, in accordance with an agreement entered into with the secretary, the person undertaking such remedial action may sue other responsible parties and may recover twice their share of the remedial costs.

(3) Prior to the filing of any suit by a person undertaking remedial action, a written demand must be made on the person from whom remedial costs are being demanded.

D. As used in this Section, the following terms shall have the following meanings:

(1) "Discharge" means:

(a) The placing, releasing, spilling, percolating, draining, pumping, leaking, seeping, emitting or other escaping of pollutants into the air, waters, subsurface water, or the ground as the result of a prior act or omission; or

(b) The placing of pollutants into pits, drums, barrels, or similar containers under conditions and circumstances that leaking, seeping, draining, or escaping of the pollutants can be reasonably anticipated.

(2) "Disposal" means the discharge, deposit, injection, dumping, spilling, leaking, or placing of any hazardous waste into or on any land or water so that such waste, or any constituent thereof, may enter the environment or be emitted into the air or discharged into any waters, including ground waters.

(3) "Facility" means a pollution source or any public or private property or facility where an activity is conducted which is required to be regulated under this Chapter and which does or has the potential to do any of the following:

(a) Emit air contaminants into the atmosphere.

(b) Discharge pollutant into waters of the state.

(c) Use or control radioactive materials and waste.

(d) Transport, process, or dispose of solid wastes.

(e) Generate, transport, treat, store or dispose of hazardous wastes.

(4) "Pollution source" means the immediate site or location of a discharge or potential discharge, including such surrounding property necessary to secure or quarantine the area from access by the general public.

(5) "Remedial cost" means, after the discharge or disposal of a hazardous substance, the cost of:

(a) Removing, confining, or storing any hazardous substance;

(b) Constructing barriers, securing the site, encapsulating in clay or other impermeable material;

(c) Cleaning up a contamination, recycling, or reuse of a hazardous substance;

(d) Diversion, destruction, or segregation of reactive or other wastes;

(e) Dredging or excavating a site;

(f) Repairing or replacing leaking containers;

(g) Collection of leachate and runoff;

(h) Onsite treatment or incineration of a substance;

(i) Provision of alternative water supplies;

(j) Monitoring, testing, or analyzing;

(k) Employing legal, engineering, chemical, biological, architectural, or other professional consultants or personnel;

(*l*) Investigation, initiation, or prosecution of lawsuits to final judgment;

(m) Transporting and disposing of waste from the site;

(n) Or any other action the secretary deems necessary to restore the site or remove the hazardous substance.

§1520. Careless handling of hazardous material.

A. Any person who offers or accepts for transportation, loads or unloads, or transports a hazardous material or a hazardous waste in a careless or imprudent manner without regard for the hazards of the material or the circumstances of such actions shall be guilty of careless handling.

B. Any person who violates this Section shall, upon conviction, be guilty of a misdemeanor and be fined or imprisoned in accordance with R.S. 32:1514(A) or may be civilly penalized in accordance with R.S. 32:1512(A).

(Chgd. by Acts 1992 No. 269, §1, eff. 8/21/92.)

§1521. Restrictions on transportation of hazardous materials.

A. No carrier shall transport hazardous materials on Louisiana Highway 73 between Interstate 10 and Louisiana Highway 74 and within three hundred yards or less of any building used as a public or private elementary or secondary school, except for carriers making local deliveries on this portion of Highway 73.

B. (1) Whoever violates the provisions of Subsection A of this Section shall be fined not more than two hundred dollars, or imprisoned for not more than ninety days, or both.

(2) On a second or subsequent violation the offender shall be fined not less than twenty-five nor more than five hundred dollars, or imprisoned for not less than ten days nor more than six months, or both.

(Added by Acts 1991 No. 556, §1, eff. 9/6/91.)

CHAPTER 13. SEIZURE AND FORFEITURE OF CONTRABAND

(Repealed by Acts 1997 No. 1334, §2, eff. 8/15/97.)

§§1550 to 1553. *(Repealed by Acts 1997 No. 1334, §2, eff. 8/15/97.)*

CHAPTER 14. HYDROCARBON GAS POWERED VEHICLES

Section

§1601. Definitions.

When used in this Chapter, the following words and phrases shall have the following meanings ascribed to them, unless the context clearly indicates a different meaning:

(1) "Hydrocarbon gas" means a combustible organic gas containing only one carbon and hydrogen. Hydrocarbon gas includes, but is not limited to, propane, compressed natural gas, liquified* petroleum gas, methane, or any chemically similar gas, but does not include gasoline or diesel fuel.

**So in original. Probably should be "liquefied".*

(2) "Motor vehicle" means every vehicle which is self-propelled, excluding a motorized bicycle.

§1602. Hydrocarbon gas powered motor vehicles, placard required.

It shall be unlawful to operate any hydrocarbon gas powered motor vehicle, registered in Louisiana, with a concealed tank for the fuel, upon any public highway or street in this state, which does not have conspicuously displayed, a placard stating that the motor vehicle is powered by hydrocarbon gas.

§1603. Placard, rules and regulations.

The secretary of the department may adopt and promulgate any rules and regulations necessary to carry out the provisions of this Chapter. The secretary shall adopt and promulgate all rules and regulations in accordance with the Administrative Procedure Act*.

**R.S. 49:950 et seq.*

§1604. Penalty.

Any person who violates any provision of this Chapter, or any regulation issued thereunder shall be fined in accordance with the provisions of R.S. 32:57.

CHAPTER 15. NOTIFICATION OF OWNERS

PART I*. CHANGES IN STATUTORY PROVISIONS

PART I*. CHANGES IN STATUTORY PROVISIONS

**No Part II has been enacted.*

§1700. Secretary of Department of Public Safety and Corrections to notify.

A. The secretary of the Department of Public Safety and Corrections is authorized to notify, in writing, owners of all motor vehicles as provided in R.S. 47:462 except those also classified as farm trucks, farm tractors, and other farm vehicles of all changes in the provisions of R.S. 32:311.11 through 398.5, R.S. 32:1501 through 1520, R.S. 47:711 through 727, R.S. 47:771 through 789, and R.S. 801 through 815, which affect the operation on state highways and public roads of those vehicles.

B. Notices of any changes described in Subsection A above shall be in writing in a form to be determined by the secretary of the Department of Public Safety and Corrections, or his designee, and shall be mailed to the owner of such vehicles at the address listed on the registration certificate for that vehicle. The secretary shall determine the cost of providing a notice of change, and, in accordance with rules and regulations promulgated by the secretary, such costs shall be paid by the recipients of the notice.

C. Oversight review of all rules and regulations promulgated by the secretary under the provisions of this Chapter shall be conducted by the House Committee on Transportation, Highways and Public Works and the Senate Committee on Transportation, Highways and Public Works.

CHAPTER 16. THE LOUISIANA TOWING AND STORAGE ACT

§1711. Declaration of public policy.

The legislature finds and declares that the towing and storage of motor vehicles in the state of Louisiana vitally affects the general economy of the state, the public interest, and the public welfare, and that in order to promote the public interest and the public welfare, and in the exercise of its police power, it is necessary to regulate and to license those who conduct towing and storage businesses in Louisiana, in order to prevent frauds, impositions, and other abuses upon its citizens, and to provide maximum safety for all persons who travel or otherwise use the public highways of this state.

§1712. Short title.

This Chapter shall be known and may be cited as the "Louisiana Towing and Storage Act."

§1713. Definitions.

For the purposes of this Section, the following terms shall have the following meaning:

(1) "Department" means the Department of Public Safety and Corrections.

(2) "Indirect compensation" means any benefit derived by the tow truck owner or operator as a result of barter, payment, or fees charged for repair work performed on the towed vehicle.

(3) "Owner" means the last registered owner of a vehicle and the holder of any lien on the vehicle, as shown on the records of the office of motor vehicles.

(4) "Tow" means pull, winch, carry, or otherwise move a vehicle or equipment other than under its own power with the use of a tow truck.

(5) "Tow truck" means any motor vehicle equipped with a boom or booms, winches, slings, tilt beds, and/or similar equipment designed for the towing and/or recovery of vehicles and other objects which cannot operate under their own power or for some reason must be transported by means of towing.

(6) "Tow truck owner or operator" means any person or entity owning or operating a tow truck service.

§1714. Powers and duties of the office of state police.

The Department of Public Safety and Corrections, office of state police, subject to the provisions of the Administrative Procedure Act*, shall:

**R.S. 49:950 et seq.*

(1) Adopt rules and regulations to govern the towing and storage industry in Louisiana.

(2) Adopt rules and regulations to insure that no person shall operate a towing business when they arrive at the scene of a vehicle accident without being called by the police or by the owner of the vehicle or his representative. Any rules and regulations adopted to implement the provisions of this Paragraph, whether directly or indirectly, shall not apply to municipalities which have a population of four hundred and fifty thousand or more and which have established procedures which pertain to the subject matter of this Paragraph and which also satisfy the requirements and standards of R.S. 32:1711 et seq.

(3) Adopt and levy fines for violation of this Chapter or any rule or regulation adopted pursuant to this Chapter.

(4) Make recommendations to the office of motor vehicles in reference to the examination, issuance, suspension, or revocation of licenses for tow trucks and operators.

(5) Adopt a schedule of maximum fees which may be charged for the notifications required by this Chapter.

(6) Adopt a schedule of maximum fees which may be charged for the storage of vehicles which are stored under the authority of this Chapter.

(Chgd. by Acts 1990 No. 907, §1, eff. 7/25/90.)

§1715. Towing of motor vehicles in the state of Louisiana.

A. It shall be unlawful for any tow truck or carrier to tow or to carry a vehicle on the highways and roadways of the state of Louisiana without the towing vehicle or carrier having displayed a towing license plate and complying with the rules and regulations adopted pursuant to this Chapter.

B. This Section shall apply to every commercial entity that receives direct or indirect compensation for the towing of a vehicle.

C. This Section shall not apply to:

(1) Car carriers that are capable of carrying five or more vehicles and have Interstate Commerce Commission authority.

(2) Tow trucks that are registered in another state with Interstate Commerce Commission authority.

(3) Tow trucks that are owned by a governmental entity and that are not used for commercial purposes.

(4) Tow trucks that are owned by an owner of a garage, automotive mechanic shop, or other place where motor vehicles are repaired, are operated by an employee or an owner of such a shop, and are operated solely to transport motor vehicles to such shop for maintenance or repair work, but only when such owners or operators:

(a) Have insurance coverage as required by this Chapter.

(b) Obtain the license plate as required by this Chapter.

(c) Shall not respond to accident scenes or participate in a police rotation system or conduct private property tows.

(d) Shall not offer towing services for hire or store any motor vehicles.

(Chgd. by Acts 1991 No. 305, §1, eff. 9/6/91.)

§1716. Licensing; special license plates.

A. In addition to the fee charged by Title 47, each tow truck owner shall pay an annual fee of one hundred dollars per tow truck, not to include those tow trucks owned by public agencies.

B. The assistant secretary for the office of motor vehicles shall establish and issue a special tow truck license plate for vehicles which are designed to tow or carry any other vehicle.

C. The assistant secretary for the office of motor vehicles shall establish by rules promulgated under the Administrative Procedure Act* the implementation of this Section.

**R.S. 49:950 et seq.*

§1717. Qualifications of licensee; proof of financial responsibility in lieu of insurance.

(A) A tow truck license plate shall not be issued to a tow truck owner unless:

(1) The applicant has never been convicted of a felony relating to vehicle thefts.

(2) The applicant and all drivers who operate the tow truck possess the proper driver's license as required.

(3) The vehicle is properly equipped as required by this Title and any rules promulgated by the Department of Public Safety and Corrections.

(B) Proof of financial responsibility satisfactory to the office of motor vehicles or certificates of insurance issued by an insurer licensed to do business in the state of Louisiana or a federally authorized insurance group licensed in their state of domicile and attesting to carriage with coverage in the amounts hereinbelow listed shall be submitted with the application:

(1) Automobile liability coverage in an amount of not less than three hundred thousand dollars combined single limits coverage.

(2) Garage keeper's legal liability insurance in an amount of not less than fifty thousand dollars which shall include on-hook coverage in an amount of not less than twenty-five thousand dollars.

(3) Garage liability insurance in an amount of not less than fifty thousand dollars.

(4) Self-insurance as contemplated under the provisions of R.S. 32:1042, when property owned in Louisiana in the tow truck owner's name has a value of three hundred thousand dollars or more after deducting encumbrances thereon from its assessed valuation.

(C) All certificates shall contain the initial and the expiration dates of carriage and coverage and the serial number of the vehicle that the license is being applied for and the following statement:

"The insurance covered by this certificate shall not be cancelled or materially altered except after twenty days prior written notice of such cancellation or alteration has been sent to the Department of Public Safety and Corrections, office of state police, by certified letter, return receipt requested."

(Chgd. by Acts 1990 No. 956, §1; Acts 1997 No. 402, §1, eff. 8/15/97.)

§1718. Law enforcement notification of a vehicle towed to a storage facility; outdoor storage facility.

A. Whenever any vehicle has been towed to a storage facility where fees are charged for such storage or parking, the owner or operator of the storage facility shall, within twenty-four hours of the time such vehicle is towed to a storage facility, notify the office of the sheriff or the municipal police or their assigned designees from whose jurisdiction the vehicle is towed that the vehicle has been towed for storage. Except when the vehicle is stored by or upon request from a law enforcement agency, the storage operator shall provide to the law enforcement authorities or their designees:

(1) The location from which the vehicle was towed.

(2) A description of the vehicle.

(3) The license plate number of the vehicle.

(4) The name and address of the location to which the vehicle was towed.

B. Each law enforcement authority or designee receiving information pursuant to the provisions of this Section shall accept, record, and file the information in order to be reasonably obtainable for responding to requests from the public.

C. If the storage facility is an outdoor facility, it shall provide a reasonable security barrier or safety apparatus suitable to the premises of the facility which will assure security to the property contained therein.

(Chgd. by Acts 1990 No. 956, §1, eff. 9/7/90.)

§1719. Notification to Department of Public Safety and Corrections.

A. Whenever any vehicle of a type subject to registration in this state has been stored, parked, or left in a garage, or any type of public storage or parking lot, where fees are charged for such storage or parking, the owner of the storage garage or parking facility shall, within a period of three working days, report in writing to the Department of Public Safety and Corrections the make, model, serial, and license numbers, and the date of storage of such vehicle, on a form prescribed and furnished by the office and shall secure from the Department of Public Safety and Corrections, or the department's authorized agent, the most current registration information available on the vehicle, along with any chattel mortgages that may be on file with the department.

B. When the tow truck owner or operator has complied with this Section, he shall not be held liable, civilly or criminally, when the state or its agent has failed to return the information requested in a timely manner so that notification cannot be made within the seven-day period as required in R.S. 32:1720, as long as he does make the notification, as provided in R.S. 32:1720, within three days of receiving the information.

§1720. Owner notification of a stored vehicle.

A. Within seven days of the time that a vehicle is placed in a storage facility, the operator of the storage facility shall notify in writing, by certified letter, return receipt requested, the last registered owner of the vehicle at the owner's last known address and the mortgage holder, should there be any.

B. The storage operator shall provide to the owner:

(1) The location and name of the storage facility.

(2) The vehicle identification number.

(3) The vehicle license plate number.

(4) A description of the vehicle.

(5) The name of the person or agency that had the vehicle towed and/or placed in storage.

(6) The date that the vehicle was placed in storage.

(7) The condition of the vehicle.

(8) The notice of the owner's right to an administrative hearing.

(9) The address to which the request for a hearing must be sent.

(10) The date by which the request must be mailed, by certified letter, return receipt requested, which shall be ten days from the date that the owner notification is mailed.

§1721. Self-park storage facility notification procedure.

A. If the storage garage or parking lot is of the type where vehicles are driven in and left in storage and the entrance to the facility is controlled manually or mechanically similar to parking facilities usually found at airports and railway stations, the garage or parking lot shall operate under some system whereby the length of time the vehicle has been in storage can readily be determined within one week of the time the vehicle was left, and should a vehicle be brought to such a garage or parking facility with the intent to remain there over twenty days, arrangement must be made in writing with the operator of the parking facility.

B. Any vehicle left at such a garage or parking facility for more than twenty days which has no written arrangements recorded must be reported to the Department of Public Safety and Corrections as outlined in R.S. 32:1719 and must be reported to the owner as outlined in R.S. 32:1720.

§1722. Exemption from provisions of R.S. 32:1718 through R.S. 32:1721.

A. Except when summoned to a location by a law enforcement agency from a call allocation system, the provisions of R.S. 32:1718 through R.S. 32:1721 shall not apply where the owner of the vehicle or the legal representative of the owner has entered into a contract, in writing on a form herein described, for the continuous storage or parking of the vehicle.

B. For the purposes of this Section, when a vehicle is stored as a result of a court order, the court shall act as a representative of the owner, thus the notifications of R.S. 32:1718 through R.S. 32:1721 are not required.

C. The written storage contract shall contain the following:

(1) The name, address, and driver's license number of the owner or legal representative of the owner that is making the storage arrangements.

(2) The name and address of the owner if different from the above person.

(3) The cost of storage and any other costs that will be accrued to the vehicle. Any costs not set forth within the storage agreement may not be charged.

(4) A description of the vehicle.

(5) The vehicle identification number.

(6) The vehicle license plate number.

(7) The condition of the vehicle.

(8) The date that the vehicle is placed in storage.

(9) The date after which time the vehicle will be considered abandoned, not to exceed six months from the date of storage.

(10) Notice that when the vehicle is considered abandoned, it will be subject to sale by the storage facility owner.

(11) The signature of the owner or legal representative of the owner that is making the storage arrangements.

§1723. Maintenance of records.

The owner of the place of business shall maintain adequate records on storage of all vehicles, describing the vehicle, the date brought into storage, and the name of the person and/or department authorizing such storage. These records and any vehicle remaining in storage shall be open to inspection by any peace officer any time the business is open. All records of storage shall be maintained for a period of at least five years.

§1724. Administrative penalties.

A. Any person who fails to comply with any provision required by this Chapter shall forfeit all claims for towing services and storage of such vehicles and shall be subject to an administrative fine. Each day's failure to make such a report as required hereunder shall constitute a separate offense.

B. In accordance with the rules and regulations adopted pursuant to the Administrative Procedure Act*, administrative fines shall be assessed by the deputy secretary of the Department of Public Safety and Corrections and payable to the Louisiana Towing and Storage Fund.

**R.S. 49:950 et seq.*

§1725. Criminal penalties.

Any violation of this Chapter shall be punishable by a fine of not more than five hundred dollars or by imprisonment for not more than six months, or both.

§1726. Abandoned automobiles; stored or in possession of dealer or repairman; right to sell; procedure.

A. Whenever any vehicle of a type subject to registration in this state has been stored or left in possession of a motor vehicle dealer or repairman for repair or otherwise and the same has not been claimed after a vehicle has been placed in storage as a result of nonpayment, the repair shop shall make the notifications required in R.S. 32:1719 and R.S. 32:1720.

B. After a period of forty-five days from the notice required in R.S. 32:1720 and no payment of the cost of storage or repair has been made for that period, the motor vehicle dealer or repairman with whom the vehicle has been left for storage or repair may dispose of it and collect the charges and cost of storage, not to exceed ten dollars per day and cost of repair in the manner set forth in R.S. 32:1728(B).

§1727. Hearings.

A. The owner of any vehicle that was stored by a public agency shall have the right to an administrative hearing to determine if towing and storage of said vehicle was proper. The owner of the vehicle must make a request for a hearing within ten days of the date that the owner notification is mailed as described in R.S. 32:1720 to the agency that had the vehicle towed.

B. The hearing shall be conducted by the public agency authorizing the tow or other body authorized to do so within three days after receipt of the request for a hearing.

§1728. Disposal of a stored motor vehicle.

A. Whenever any such vehicle has been left in storage with any person engaged in the business of public storage of motor vehicles and the same has not been claimed for a period of forty-five days or more, and no payment for the costs of storage has been made for that period, the persons with whom the vehicle has been left for storage may dispose of it and collect the charges and costs of storage in the manner set forth hereinafter.

B. After the forty-five day period has lapsed, he shall forward a certified letter, return receipt requested, to the owner at the owner's last known address and to the mortgage holder, should there be any, advising in the letter the exact location of the vehicle, the date it was placed in storage, and by whom so placed, the outstanding charges against the vehicle, and the general condition of the vehicle. The letter shall also include a statement placing the registered owner and mortgage holder, if any, on notice that, unless action is taken on their part to claim the vehicle from the possession of the place of storage or unless an agreement is made by either or both of them to pay outstanding storage charges and to pay storage charges for continued storage of the vehicle and all costs incurred for the notification required by this Chapter, not to exceed the cost authorized by R.S. 32:1714(5), within fifteen days from the receipt of the letter, the vehicle will be advertised for sale at public auction and the proceeds disposed of as hereinafter provided.

C. After the lapse of the fifteen days above set out, the person in whose possession the vehicle has been left for storage may then, if it has not been claimed and the costs and charges have not been paid, insert an advertisement in a local newspaper with general circulation describing the vehicle and stating that the vehicle will be sold to the highest bidder for cash for not less than two-thirds of its appraised value, free from all liens, privileges, and chattel mortgages. This advertisement must be published once and the sale shall be made not less than ten days nor more than fifteen days from the date of the advertisement, which shall fix the time and place of the sale. Prior to the sale, the vehicle shall be appraised in the same manner that personal property is appraised for judicial sales, and it shall then be offered at public auction on the terms as advertised. The person causing said vehicle to be sold shall make a process verbal in writing in duplicate originals of the proceedings leading up to the sale, one original to be kept for his own records and one to be delivered to the purchaser.

D. Upon presentation of said process verbal and to which there shall be attached:

(1) A copy of the original report, if applicable, which is required to be filed with the Department of Public Safety and Corrections.

(2) A copy of the letter which has been sent to the owner, lien holder, and chattel mortgage holder, if applicable, as required by this Section.

(3) The original post office receipt of delivery if the letter required to be sent by this Section has been delivered or the unopened envelope with the postal markings indicating attempt to deliver the letter required by this Section.

(4) Copies of two separate appraisals required by this Section.

(5) Statement by the newspaper publisher or the publisher's authorized representative setting forth the contents of the advertisement and the date on which such advertisement was placed; and such other evidence as the department may require, a title certificate shall be issued by the department to the said purchaser free from all liens, privileges, and chattel mortgages.

E. If, however, the vehicle is in a wrecked or salvaged condition, and has been reduced in value below one-half the NADA Book Value of a similar vehicle in average operable condition, or if the storage or wrecker service costs and charges have been equal to or surpassed the higher of two appraisals made by a competent, qualified, independent appraiser, the forty-five day waiting period hereinabove set out may be reduced to thirty days. The owner or operator of the storage or parking facility, having secured from the Department of Public Safety and Corrections, as set forth in this Chapter, or from whatever source necessary, the most current registration information available on the vehicle, along with any chattel mortgages that may be on file with the department, shall forward a certified letter, return receipt requested, to the owner at the last known address, the content of the letter being the same as aforementioned in this Chapter. After the fifteen-day notice given in the letter has lapsed, which date shall be not less than thirty days from date of storage as required in this Section, and no action has been taken on the part of the owner or mortgage holder to claim the vehicle from the possession of the storage garage or parking facility and no arrangements have been made in writing for continued storage, the owner of said garage or parking facility shall then make a process verbal in writing in duplicate originals with supporting data, excluding advertisement which is not to be required by this Subsection. Upon presentation of said process verbal and other evidence required by this Section, a permit to sell the vehicle shall be granted by the department to the person storing said vehicle allowing him to sell the vehicle for the protection of his interest. In the event the storage garage or parking lot operator desires a certificate of title to be issued in lieu of the permit to sell, he shall include an affidavit of physical inspection by a full-time P.O.S.T. certified law enforcement officer of this state wherein the general condition of the vehicle is stated in detail.

F. *(Repealed.)*

(Chgd. by Acts 1993 No. 412, §2, eff. 8/15/93.)

§1728.1. Alternative procedure for disposal of certain vehicles.

A. The provisions of this Section shall provide a procedure for disposing of certain vehicles. The procedure provided for in this Section shall be an alternative to the procedure set forth in R.S. 32:1728. When a vehicle is eligible for disposal under the provisions of this Section, the provisions of R.S. 32:1720 and 1728 shall not apply to the disposal of that vehicle.

B. As used in this Section, "owner-operator" means a person or legal entity who owns or operates a business which is engaged in the towing or storage, or both, of vehicles.

C. The provisions of this Section shall apply to vehicles which meet each of the following criteria:

(1) The vehicle is ten years old or older.

(2) The vehicle has a fair market value of five thousand dollars or less.

(3) The vehicle has not been registered in this state or in any other state for a period of three years or more immediately preceding the filing of a notice under R.S. 32:1719.

D. Each owner-operator who is holding a vehicle which meets the criteria set forth in Subsection C above may apply for a permit to sell that vehicle provided the owner-operator satisfies each of the following requirements:

(1) The owner-operator has complied with the provisions of R.S. 32:1718 and 1719.

(2) The owner-operator has received from the office of motor vehicles a statement that the vehicle has not been registered in this state or in any other state for a period of three years or more immediately preceding the filing of the notice under R.S. 32:1719.

(3) The owner-operator has the vehicle physically inspected by a full-time P.O.S.T. certified law enforcement officer.

(4) The owner-operator obtains two estimates from competent estimators showing that the vehicle has a fair market value of five thousand dollars or less.

(5) The owner-operator applies to the office of motor vehicles for a permit to sell the vehicle.

(6) The owner-operator attaches to the application each of the following documents:

(a) A statement by the owner-operator affirming that the owner-operator has complied with the provisions of R.S. 32:1718 and 1719.

(b) A statement by the owner-operator affirming that the owner-operator has received from the office of motor vehicles a statement that the vehicle has not been registered in this state or in any other state for a period of three years or more immediately preceding the filing of the notice under R.S. 32:1719.

(c) The two estimates made by competent estimators showing that the vehicle has a fair market value of five thousand dollars or less.

(d) An affidavit executed by the full-time P.O.S.T. certified law enforcement officer who physically inspected the vehicle. The affidavit shall state the make and year of the vehicle, the vehicle identification number, and the general description of the vehicle.

(7) The owner-operator has notified the last person to whom the vehicle was registered of the intention to sell. The notification shall be sent, by registered mail, to the last known address of such person.

E. The office of motor vehicles shall issue a permit to sell in response to each application which satisfies the requirements set forth in Subsection D.

F. No owner-operator shall incur any liability for disposing of a vehicle under a permit to sell which was acquired in good faith under the provisions of this Section.

G. Neither the state of Louisiana nor the office of motor vehicles shall incur any liability as a result of the disposal of a vehicle under a permit to sell which was issued in good faith under the provisions of this Section.

H. When the office of motor vehicles issues a statement concerning whether or not a vehicle is or has been registered in another state, the statement shall mean only that the office of motor vehicles has used due diligence in obtaining that information from the most reliable of the nationwide databases which are reasonably available to the office of motor vehicles.

I. The office of motor vehicles shall adopt administrative rules to implement the provisions of this Section. All rules shall be adopted in accordance with the Administrative Procedure Act*.

(Chgd. by Acts 1993 No. 412, §1, eff. 8/15/93.)

**R.S. 49:950 et seq.*

§1728.2. Procedure for disposal of junk vehicles.

A. The provisions of this Section shall provide a procedure for disposing of certain vehicles. The procedure provided for in this Section shall be an alternative to the procedures set forth in R.S. 32:1728 and 1728.1. When a vehicle is eligible for disposal under the provisions of this Section, the provisions of R.S. 32:1728 and 1728.1 shall not apply to the disposal of that vehicle.

B. As used in this Section, "owner-operator" means a person or legal entity who owns or operates a business which is engaged in the towing or storage of vehicles, and has a vehicle licensed as a towing vehicle under R.S. 32:1716.

C. As used in this Section:

(1) "Crush or dismantle" means to render the vehicle in such a state that it cannot ever be used or be rebuilt for use as a motor vehicle.

(2) "Junk vehicle" means a vehicle which is in such a state of deterioration that it cannot be profitably restored and the vehicle has a fair market value of two hundred dollars or less.

D. Each owner-operator who possesses a vehicle which meets the criteria set forth in Paragraph C(2) of this Section may crush or dismantle that vehicle at the expiration of thirty days from mailing of the final certified notice provided the owner-operator satisfies each of the following requirements:

(1) The owner-operator has complied with the provisions of R.S. 32:1719 and R.S. 32:1720.

(2) The owner-operator has the vehicle physically inspected by a full-time Peace Officer Standards and Training (P.O.S.T.) certified law enforcement officer.

(3) The vehicle is over ten years old.

(4) The owner-operator obtains two appraisals from competent appraisers showing that the vehicle has a fair market value of two hundred dollars or less.

(5) The owner-operator takes a picture of each and every side of the vehicle prior to crushing or dismantling which is a clear, color photograph.

E. Within seven days after the time that a vehicle is crushed or dismantled the owner-operator shall execute an affidavit, and forward it to the office of motor vehicles, by certified mail, return receipt requested, stating:

(1) That a vehicle has been crushed or dismantled.

(2) A description of each vehicle.

(3) The vehicle identification number.

F. The owner-operator shall maintain the following records on all vehicles crushed or dismantled under the provisions of this Section.

(1) Completed physical inspection form.

(2) Two appraisals showing a fair market value of two hundred dollars or less.

(3) A picture of each and every side of the vehicle prior to crushing or dismantling which is a clear, color photograph.

(4) A copy of the original report as required in R.S. 32:1719.

(5) A copy of the letter which has been sent to the owner, lien holder, and chattel mortgage holder, if applicable.

(6) The original post office receipt of delivery if the letter required to be sent by this Section has been delivered; or the unopened envelope with the postal marking indicating attempt to deliver the letter required by this Section. These records shall be open to inspection by any peace officer any time the business is open. All records required by this Section shall be maintained for a period of at least five years.

G. Neither the state of Louisiana nor the office of motor vehicles shall incur any liability as a result of the disposal of a vehicle under these provisions.
(Added by Acts 1997 No. 892, §1, eff. 8/15/97.)

§1729. Waiver of fee; disposal of law enforcement storage.

After complying with the provisions of this Chapter, a wrecker operator may obtain from the department, without the payment of fees otherwise required by R.S. 32:728, a certificate of title, or certified copy thereof, or a permit to sell in order to dispose of a vehicle in a wrecked or salvaged condition or having a value of less than the amount of the accrued towing and storage charges, which he removed, pursuant to a request from a law enforcement agency, as an abandoned vehicle or from the scene of an accident.

§1730. Proceeds of sale; disposition of.

All funds received from the sale of a vehicle under this Chapter shall be set aside into separate accounts by the person making the sale and he shall deduct therefrom the full amount due and owing him for the storage and other charges, which shall be at the customary rates charged for such service, together with the costs of appraisal and advertisement, the balance, if any, to be credited on the books of such person to the credit of the owner for six months from the date of the sale; provided, however, that if the funds so credited are not claimed by the owner within the time specified herein they shall be deemed forfeited to the person making the sale, who may credit such funds to his own account free and clear of all claims.

§1731. The Louisiana Towing and Storage Fund.

All fees and fines collected under the provisions of this Chapter shall be paid into the state treasury on or before the twenty-fifth day of the month following their collection and, in accordance with Article VII, Section 9 of the Constitution of Louisiana, shall be credited to the Bond Security and Redemption Fund. Out of the funds remaining in the Bond Security and Redemption Fund, after a sufficient amount is allocated therefrom to pay all obligations secured by the full faith and credit of the state which become due and payable within each fiscal year, the treasurer shall pay an amount equal to the total amount of funds paid into the treasury into a special fund, which is hereby created in the state treasury and designated as the "Louisiana Towing and Storage Fund." All funds collected or received pursuant to this Chapter and deposited in the Louisiana Towing and Storage Fund shall be administered by the deputy secretary of public safety services. The fund shall be used solely to fund the activities and enforcement of this Chapter by the office of state police and only in the amount appropriated by the legislature with all remaining funds to be deposited in the state general fund.

§1732. Third party surcharges.

Whenever a motor vehicle is towed to a location other than a facility owned and operated by the tow company, the surcharge levied by the third party receiving the motor vehicle shall not exceed twenty-five percent of the amount charged for the towing of the vehicle. *(Added by Acts 1992 No. 1089, §1, eff. 8/21/92.)*

§1733. Fees charged for towing; certain parishes.

A. When, in parishes with a population of four hundred thousand or more, an individual parks a vehicle on private property and the owner or lessee of that property requests a towing company to remove and store the parked vehicle, the fee charged by the towing company shall not exceed the towing fee which the local governing authority would have charged had the vehicle been towed for a violation while parked on public property.

B. If the towing company charges an excessive fee, the owner of the vehicle shall have a right and cause of action to recover the amount of the excess fee, plus reasonable attorney fees, and all costs of court.
(Added by Acts 1997 No. 349, §1, eff. 8/15/97.)

CHAPTER 17. TRI-STATE CORRIDOR COMMISSION

(Added by Acts 1990 No. 912, §1, eff. 7/25/90.)

§1751. Powers of the commission.

The Tri-State Corridor Commission is hereby declared to constitute and is declared to be a body politic and political subdivision of the state of Louisiana, as defined in Article VI, Section 44 of the Constitution of Louisiana. The commission is hereby granted all of the rights, powers, privileges, and immunities granted to political subdivisions, including but not limited to the following:

(1) The commission is declared to constitute and be a body politic and political subdivision of the state and is empowered to, among other things:

(a) Sue and be sued;

(b) Adopt, use, and alter a corporate seal;

(c) Initiate or coordinate research, studies and the gathering of information pertaining to the four laning, construction, expansion, improvement or extension of Louisiana Highway 1; and

(d) Provide for the long-term economic/industrial development and tourism development of the corridor area.

(2) Further provision is hereby authorized that the boundary of the commission shall be the geographical boundaries of the parish of Caddo in Louisiana and the counties of Marion, Cass, and Bowie in Texas and Miller and Little River Counties in Arkansas.

(3) The management and control of the commission shall be vested in a twelve member board of commissioners, who shall serve without compensation, and shall be appointed by the municipalities, parish, or county government within the boundaries of the commission with three members who shall be appointed by the three highway departments, one each from Louisiana, Texas, and Arkansas, and who shall serve as an ex officio-nonvoting member.

(4) The commission shall have the authority to undertake and perform economic development, industrial development, and tourism development in the corridor and in behalf of the membership comprising those political subdivisions (city, town, village, county, parish) within the boundaries of the commission's authority.

(5) The commission shall be designated as an official depository for all research, analyses, and information relating to the project area and shall receive and preserve all such information. It shall further be the depository for maps, aerial photography, and other study and survey materials.

(6) The commission is authorized to receive monies from any public or private body which may so desire to appropriate, donate, or transfer funds, real property or other items of value to be used by the commission to defray costs of operation and expenses of the commission. Further, the commission has the authority to apply for, receive, and accept from any public agency or private entity, group, or its designee any grant, contribution, or loan of money, property, or other things of value for purposes authorized by the commission.

(7) The commission shall abide by all provisions of Louisiana and federal law pertaining to open meetings, public records, fiscal agents, official journals, dual office holding and employment, public bid law, and the Code of Governmental Ethics.

(8) The commission shall have the authority to levy and cause to be collected any taxes, except ad valorem taxes, fees, or charges authorized under the constitution or laws of this state, which shall be limited to those taxes, fees, or charges that are commonly referred to as user fees or charges and which bear relationship to the proposed four laning highway project or highway usage, including motor vehicle transfer fees and annual road use charges or license fees, and to pledge the proceeds of such levy to the reimbursement of debt service payments for bonds issued on the behalf of the commission by the state of Louisiana. Provided, however, that no tax, fee, or charge may be levied or imposed unless first approved by a majority of the qualified electors who vote in an election called for such purposes within the commission and by a majority of the qualified electors within Caddo Parish.

(9) The commission shall have the authority to enter into cooperative agreements and arrangements or a cooperative endeavor with the state as authorized by Article VII, Section 14(C) of the Constitution of Louisiana, under which the state will agree to issue bonds for the completion of the project, and in return, the commission shall agree to reimburse the state for a portion of the total cost of said highway project which portion shall not exceed twenty-five percent of the total cost to the state, from the revenues of the commission, for debt service payments of those bonds.

(10) No tax, fee, or charge shall be proposed unless and until public notice of the intention to submit such tax, fee, or charge for voter approval is published in the official journal of the parish included within the boundaries of the commission at least thirty days prior to the date on which the board of commissioners shall consider and vote on a resolution calling for said tax election. Such notice must set forth:

(a) A general description of the highway project to be funded through bonds to be serviced by said tax.

(b) The total approximate cost of the highway project.

(c) The portion of the total cost of said highway project which will be funded through revenues of the commission.

(d) The date on which construction is anticipated to begin and the anticipated date of completion.

(e) The date, time, and place of the meeting at which said resolution shall be considered. *(Added by Acts 1990 No. 912, §1, eff. 7/25/90.)*

CHAPTER 18. LOUISIANA MOTOR VEHICLE THEFT PREVENTION AUTHORITY

(Repealed by Acts 1997 No. 1116, §2, eff. 8/15/97.)

§§1801 to 1805. *(Repealed by Acts 1997 No. 1116, §2, eff. 8/15/97.)*

TITLE 37
PROFESSIONS AND OCCUPATIONS
(Selected Chapter)

CHAPTER 47. PRIVATE CONTRACT SECURITY COMPANIES
(Complete Chapter)

§3270. Declaration of purpose.
A. The Legislature of Louisiana declares that it is necessary to require the licensure of private security agents and businesses to be in the best interest of the citizens of this state.

B. The purpose of this Chapter is to require qualifying criteria in a professional field in which unqualified individuals may injure the public. The requirements of this Chapter will contribute to the safety, health, and welfare of the people of Louisiana.
(Chgd. by Acts 1991 No. 315, §1.)

§3271. Private security law; short title.
This Chapter shall be known and may be cited as the Private Security Regulatory and Licensing Law.

§3272. General definition of terms.

A. As used in this Chapter, the following terms shall have the following meanings ascribed to them:

(1) "Applicant" means a person who seeks to be examined for licensure or registration by the board.

(2) "Armed security officer" is an individual who provides security services and who at any time wears, carries, possesses, or has access to a firearm or any other weapon defined by the board. All other defensive or offensive weapons not approved by the board are prohibited.

(3) "Armored car company or armed courier company" means any person that provides secured transportation and protection from one place or point to another place or point involving money, currency, coins, bullion, securities, bonds, jewelry, or other valuables.

(4) "Board" means the Louisiana State Board of Private Security Examiners, an agency in the Department of Public Safety and Corrections.

(5) "Branch manager" means the individual endowed with the responsibility and liability for a branch office.

(6) "Branch office" means a separate office which is part of a company licensed by the board.

(7) "Instructor" means any person approved and licensed by the board to administer and certify the successful completion of the required minimum training requirements for security officers.

(8) "Contract security company" means any person engaging in the business of providing, or which undertakes to provide, a security officer on a contractual basis for another person.

(9) "Department" means the Louisiana Department of Public Safety and Corrections.

(10) "Executive secretary" means the chief administrative officer of the board.

(11) "Licensee" means any person to whom a license is granted in accordance with the provisions of this Chapter.

(12) "Person" means an individual, firm, association, company, partnership, corporation, nonprofit organization, or other legal entity.

(13) "Principal corporate officer" means the president, vice president, treasurer, secretary, or comptroller or any other person who performs functions for the corporation corresponding to those performed by the foregoing officers.

(14) "Private security business" is any entity that provides protection to persons and property, excluding any law enforcement agency, but including any:

(a) Contract security company; or

(b) Armored car company or armed courier company.

(15) "Qualifying agent" means a responsible officer or executive employee meeting the experience qualifications set forth herein.

(16) "Registrant" means an individual who holds a valid registration card issued by the board.

(17) "Registration card" means the identification card issued by the board to a registrant as evidence that the registrant has met the required minimum qualifications.

(18) "Security officer" means an individual who is principally employed by a contract security company whether armed or unarmed, to protect a person or persons or property or both, and whose duties include but are not limited to the following:

(a) Prevention of unlawful intrusion or entry.

(b) Prevention of larceny.

(c) Prevention of vandalism.

(d) Protection of property or person.

(e) Prevention of abuse.

(f) Prevention of arson.

(g) Prevention of trespass on private property.

(h) Control, regulation, or direction of the flow or movements of the public, except on public streets, whether by vehicle, on foot, or otherwise.

(i) Street patrol service or merchant patrol service, which is any contract security company that utilizes foot patrols, motor vehicles, or any other means of transportation in public areas or on public thoroughfares in the performance of its security functions.

B. The board by rule may define terms only pursuant to and consistent with the provisions of this Chapter.

C. The provisions of this Chapter shall not apply to persons and corporations exempted by R.S. 37:3298.
(Chgd. by Acts 1991 No. 315, §1.)

§3273. Louisiana State Board of Private Security Examiners; creation; qualification; domicile; term of office; confirmation; oath of office; compensation.

A. The Louisiana State Board of Private Security Examiners is hereby created as an agency of the state government in the Department of Public Safety and Corrections. The board shall be a body corporate and may sue and be sued.

B. The board shall consist of nine members appointed by the governor. One member shall be appointed from and shall reside in each of the five public service commission districts established by law. Four members shall be appointed from the state at large. Each member shall be a citizen of the United States of America, a resident of Louisiana, at least thirty years of age, and shall have been actively engaged in the private security business for at least five years. One of the members appointed at large shall be a representative of a nationally operated security company. Each member shall be licensed or registered with the board or a corporate officer of a licensed company.

C. The board shall be domiciled in Baton Rouge, but shall be authorized to meet elsewhere in the state.

D. Each appointed member shall serve at the pleasure of the governor for a term concurrent with the term of office of the governor appointing him, except that each member shall serve until his successor has been appointed and begins serving.

E. Each appointment by the governor shall be submitted to the Senate for confirmation. No appointee shall serve more than two consecutive terms.

F. In the event of death, resignation, or disability of a member of the board, the governor shall fill the vacancy by appointing a qualified person for the remainder of the unexpired term.

G. Each member of the board shall receive a certificate of appointment from the governor, and before beginning his term of office, shall file with the secretary of state his written oath or affirmation for faithful discharge of his official duty.

H. (1) No member of the board shall receive a per diem but shall be reimbursed for actual expenses when actually attending a meeting of the board or any of its committees, and for time spent on behalf of the board on official business not to exceed ten days in any month.

(2) Additionally, each member shall be reimbursed for all necessary travel and incidental, and clerical expenses incurred in carrying out the provisions of this Chapter and upon approval of the board as evidenced by voucher.
(Chgd. by Acts 1991 No. 315, §1.)

§3274. Powers, duties, authorities, and responsibilities; meetings; quorum.

A. The board shall:

(1) Examine all applicants to be licensed and regulated under the provisions of this Chapter

(2) Administer a written examination for prospective licensees at least twice each year.

(3) Adopt rules and regulations to govern the practice of private security in the state of Louisiana.

(4) Issue, suspend, modify, or revoke licenses or certificates to provide private security in the state of Louisiana.

(5) Report to the attorney general of the state of Louisiana all persons violating the provisions of this Chapter.

(6) Elect a chairman and a vice chairman, each to serve two-year terms.

(7) Report annually, no later than March 1, to the governor, the secretary of the department, and the legislature on its activities.

(8) Adopt its official seal.

(9) Investigate alleged violations of the provisions of this Chapter and any rules and regulations adopted by the board.

(10) Govern in accordance with the Louisiana Administrative Procedure Act*.
**R.S. 49:950 et seq.*

(11) Adopt rules to authorize the assessment of administrative penalties in the form of fines not to exceed five hundred dollars per violation and cost of the board's proceedings.

B. The board may:

(1) Adopt and enforce rules and regulations, bylaws, and rules of professional conduct as the board may deem necessary and proper to regulate private security businesses in the state of Louisiana, to provide for the efficient operation of the board, and otherwise to discharge its duties and powers under this Chapter.

(2) Prescribe and adopt regulations, standards, procedures, and policies governing the manner and conditions under which credit shall be given by the board for participation in a program of continuing professional education such as the board may consider necessary and appropriate to maintain the highest standards of the private security industry in the state of Louisiana.

(3) Authorize any member of the board to make any affidavit necessary for the issuance of any injunction or other legal process authorized under this Chapter or under the rules and regulations of the board.

(4) Issue subpoenas to require attendance and testimony and the production of documents, for the purpose of enforcing the laws relative to the private security industry and securing evidence of violations thereof.

(5) Maintain a current list of all businesses and persons licensed by the board.

(6) Appoint a qualified executive secretary.

(7) Employ clerical assistance necessary to carry out the administrative work of the board.

(8) Employ legal counsel to carry out the provisions of this Chapter, provided that the fees of such counsel and the costs of all proceedings except criminal prosecutions shall be paid by the board from its own funds.

(9) Incur all necessary and proper expenses.

(10) Purchase or otherwise acquire any real or personal property, including making or entering mortgages, as may be necessary or convenient to the exercise of its powers in order to accomplish the purposes of this Chapter. The board shall take title to and hold such property in its name as an agency of the state.

C. The chairman and executive secretary of the board, or in their absence any other member of the board, may administer oaths in the taking of testimony upon any matter appertaining to the duties and powers of the board.

D. The board shall meet quarterly at regular meetings each year. A special meeting may be held at such time and place as specified by the executive secretary on call of the chairman or any four members. The executive secretary shall give written notice of all meetings to the members of the board and to the interested public.

E. A majority of the voting members of the board shall constitute a quorum for all purposes, including the granting or issuance of licenses and the rulemaking and adjudicative functions of the board.

(Chgd. by Acts 1991 No. 315, §1; Acts 1994 Third Ex. Sess. No. 96, §1, eff. 8/27/94.)

§3275. Executive secretary; duties.

The position of executive secretary of the board is hereby created. The executive secretary shall be appointed by the board and shall serve as its chief administrator. He shall not be a member of the board, but shall be a full-time employee of the board, to be paid compensation in an amount to be determined by the board. The executive secretary shall perform such duties as may be prescribed by the board, and shall employ such persons as he deems necessary and fix their compensation. He shall have no financial or business interests, contingent dealings or otherwise, in the security services investigative business, watch, guard, or patrol agency while so employed or for a period of five years thereafter. *(Chgd. by Acts 1991 No. 315, §1.)*

§3276. Qualifications of licensee.

A. The board shall base the determination of the satisfactory minimum qualifications for licensing on whether or not the applicant meets the following criteria:

(1) Is of good moral character.

(2) Is of legal age.

(3) Is a citizen of the United States.

(4) Has not been convicted in any jurisdiction of any felony or any crime involving moral turpitude, or illegal use or possession of a dangerous weapon for any of which a full pardon or similar relief has not been granted under the laws of the United States, the state of Louisiana, or any state or country.

(5) Has not been declared by any court of competent jurisdiction incompetent by reason of mental defect or disease which has not been restored.

(6) Does not suffer from habitual drunkenness or from narcotics addiction or dependence.

(7) A corporation seeking a license shall be incorporated under the laws of this state, or shall be duly qualified to do business within this state with a valid certificate of authority issued by the secretary of state, and shall have an agent for service of process designated as required by law.

B. If, in the opinion of the board, the applicant provides inadequate information to allow the board to ascertain whether the applicant satisfies the qualifications for licensing, the applicant shall be required to provide additional information for purposes of the application, or may be required to present himself for an interview for this purpose.

C. An applicant for licensing shall fill out and file with the board an application form provided by the board. The form shall require relevant information about the applicant's character, experience, and background.

D. (1) If the applicant is an individual, the application shall be subscribed and sworn to by such person.

(2) If the applicant is a partnership, the application shall be subscribed and sworn to by each partner.

(3) If the applicant is a corporation, it shall be subscribed and sworn to by at least two principal corporate officers.

(4) Any individual signing a license application shall submit with the license application classifiable impressions of his fingerprints on a form approved by the board.

E. The licensee shall be required to have in effect general liability insurance of at least five hundred thousand dollars with the state of Louisiana named as an additional insured and shall provide to the board a certificate of insurance issued by the carrier.

F. Every person in the private security business shall apply to the board for a license prior to operating a business or soliciting business in Louisiana. Any such person filing a timely application may continue to engage in business pending a final determination of such application.

G. An applicant and/or qualifying agent for a security business shall have three years' consecutive experience as an employee, manager, or owner of a security company, or three years' experience as a law enforcement officer with any federal, state or local agency.

(Chgd. by Acts 1991 No. 315, §1; Acts 1992 No. 266, §1; Acts 1997 No. 155, §1, eff. 8/15/97.)

§3277. Investigation; time; procedure.

A. (1) After receipt of an application for a license, the board shall conduct an investigation to determine whether the facts set forth in the application are true.

(2) Within sixty days after receipt of an application, the board shall either issue a license to the applicant or notify the applicant of a denial of the license application.

(3) In the event that the board requires additional information from the applicant to complete its investigation, or otherwise to satisfy the requirements of this Chapter, or if the applicant has not submitted all of the required information with the application, the board shall notify the applicant by certified mail of the additional information required and the applicant shall have thirty days from the date of said notice to submit the additional information to the board, or the application shall be denied.

(4) The board shall deny the application for a license if it finds that the applicant, or the qualifying agent, or any of the applicant's owners, partners, or principal corporate officers have committed any of the following:

(a) Violated any of the provisions of this Chapter or the rules and regulations promulgated by the board.

(b) Practiced fraud, deceit, or misrepresentation.

(c) Knowingly made a material misstatement in the application for a license.

(d) Failed to meet the qualifications as outlined in R.S. 37:3276; and any other qualifications set forth in this Chapter and any other rules and regulations adopted by the board.

(e) *(Repealed.)*

B. The board may refuse to issue a license for good cause shown.

(Chgd. by Acts 1997 No. 155, §1, eff. 8/15/97.)

§3278. Examination.

The board shall determine the scope, form, and content of the examinations for licensure. The examination, which shall be written, shall test the applicant's knowledge of the private security business and his ability to apply that knowledge and to assume responsible charge in the practice of private security.

§3279. Approval; denial; procedure; appeals; prior qualifications.

A. The procedure of the board in approving or denying an application shall be as follows:

(1) If the application is approved, the board shall notify the applicant in writing that a license will be issued.

(2) If the application is denied, the board shall notify the applicant in writing and shall set forth the grounds for denial.

(3) (a) If the grounds for denial are subject to correction by the applicant, the notice of denial shall so state and the applicant shall be given ten days after receipt of such notice or, upon application, a reasonable additional period of time within which to make the required correction.

(b) If the application is denied, the applicant, within thirty days after receipt of notice of denial from the board, may request a hearing on the denial. Within ten days after the filing of such request for hearing by the applicant, the board shall schedule a hearing to be held after due notice to the applicant. The hearing shall be conducted in accordance with the Administrative Procedure Act*.

**R.S. 49:950 et seq.*

B. The board shall issue a license to each applicant who meets the requirements of this Chapter, passes satisfactorily the examination administered by the board, and pays the required fee.

C. An applicant who fails an examination may be examined again upon filing a reexamination application and the payment of the reexamination fee fixed by this Chapter.

D, E. *(Repealed.)*

(Chgd. by Acts 1991 No. 315, §§1, 2; Acts 1997 No. 155, §1, eff. 8/15/97.)

§3280. License form; information; assignment or transfer.

A. The license, when issued, shall be in a form prescribed by the board and shall include the following:

(1) Name of the licensee.

(2) Business name under which the licensee is to operate.

(3) Addresses of the locations where the licensee is authorized to operate.

(4) Number and date of the license, and its date of expiration.

B. (1) No license shall be assigned or transferred, either by operation of law or otherwise.

(2) If a sale, assignment, transfer, merger, or consolidation of a business licensed under this Chapter is consummated, the purchaser, assignee, transferee, or surviving or new corporation, who is not already a licensee, shall immediately apply for a license on a form prescribed by the board which shall include the general information required of this Chapter.

(3) The purchaser, assignee, transferee, or surviving or new corporation shall be subject to the same general requirements and procedures set forth in this Chapter to the extent such sections are applicable, and may continue the operation of that licensed business until notified by the board of its final decision on the new application for a license.

(4) For good cause shown, the board may extend the period of time for filing the application required.

§3281. Posting; unlawful posting; surrender of license.

A. (1) Within seventy-two hours after receipt of the license certificate, the licensee shall cause the license certificate to be posted and to be displayed at all times in a conspicuous place in the principal office of the licensee within the state.

(2) Copies of the license certificate shall be displayed at all times in any other office within the state where the licensee transacts business.

(3) Such license certificates, or copies thereof, shall be subject to inspection at all reasonable times by the board.

B. It shall be unlawful for any person holding such a license certificate knowingly and willfully to post such license certificates, or permit such license certificate to be posted, upon premises other than those described in the license certificate, or knowingly and willfully to alter such license certificate.

C. (1) Each license certificate shall be surrendered to the board within seventy-two hours after it has been revoked or after the licensee ceases to do business.

(2) If, however, the board or a court of competent jurisdiction has pending before it any matter relating to the renewal, revocation, or transfer of a license, the licensee shall not be required to surrender the license until the matter has been adjudicated and all appeals have been exhausted.

(3) *(Repealed.)*

(Chgd. by Acts 1991 No. 315, §2.)

§3282. Notification of changes.

The licensee shall notify the board within ten days of any change in its officers, directors, or other material change in the information previously furnished or required to be furnished to the board, or immediately upon any occurrence which could reasonably be expected to affect the licensee's right to a license under this Chapter. *(Chgd. by Acts 1991 No. 315, §1.)*

§3283. Security officer registrant; card; application; qualifications; investigation; denial, suspension, or revocation; validity; renewal; change of address.

A. (1) Each person who performs the functions and duties of a security officer within this state as defined in this Chapter shall apply to the board for a registration card.

(2) The portion of the board application indicating temporary registration shall be carried by the applicant when he is within the scope of his employment until such time as he receives his permanent registration card from the board.

(3) Individuals required to obtain a registration card under this Chapter shall file for a registration card and, upon completion thereof, the licensee shall immediately forward the application to the board.

(4) (a) Every applicant for a registration card shall make and deliver to the licensee a sworn application in writing upon a form prescribed by the board.

(b) The board shall prescribe by rule the form for such application and procedures for their submission, consideration and disposition, including the fee to accompany the application.

(c) To be eligible to apply for a registration card an individual shall have the same qualifications required of an applicant provided in R.S. 37:3276 but may be a resident alien.

B. Every person required to be registered by the board shall carry his registration card when performing the duties for which he is registered, and it shall be exhibited upon request by any authorized representative of the board or any law enforcement officer. The registration card shall entitle the registrant to perform the duties as described therein as long as the registrant maintains his eligibility under the provisions of this Chapter.

C. The registration card shall bear the name or license number of the employer, an identifying number, photograph, and any other identifying data required by the board.

D. After receipt of an application for a registration card, the board shall conduct an investigation to determine whether the facts set forth in the application are true. Actions by the board to approve or deny an application for a registration card shall be the same as that action taken to deny or approve an application for license as provided in R.S. 37:3279.

E. (1) If the board denies, suspends, or revokes a registration card, the cardholder, upon receipt of the notice of denial, suspension, or revocation, shall immediately cease to perform the duties for which he is registered, unless specifically authorized to continue work by order of the board, or by a court of competent jurisdiction within the state.

(2) Both the cardholder and the employer shall be notified by the board of its final action to deny, suspend, or revoke a registration card.

F. (1) Registration cards issued by the board shall be valid for a period of two years. The registrant shall be required to advise the board of any changes in his status or permanent address during the valid period. The cardholder shall file a registration card renewal form with the board not less than thirty days prior to the expiration of the card, together with the fee for renewal. The renewal application shall include a statement by the registrant that the registrant continues to meet the qualifications as set forth by the board.

(2) The board may refuse to renew a registration card, and shall promptly notify the cardholder of its intent to refuse to renew. The cardholder, within fifteen days after receipt of such notice, may request a hearing on such refusal, in the same manner and in accordance with the same procedure as that provided in R.S. 37:3279.

(3) A licensee or employer shall notify the board within ten days after the death or termination of employment of any of its employees who are registrants. Licensees or employers subject to this Chapter shall notify the board within ten days upon receipt of information relating to a registrant's loss of eligibility to hold such a card.

G. (1) Any individual who changes his permanent residence to this state from any other state which the board determines has selection, training, and all other similar requirements at least equal to those required under this Chapter, and who holds a valid registration, commission, identification, or similar card issued by said other state through a licensee which is licensed by this state, and who wishes to continue to be employed by said licensee, may apply for a registration card on a form prescribed by the board upon the payment of a transfer fee. Upon certification by said licensee that such individual has completed the training prescribed by said state, the board shall issue the individual a registration card.

(2) If a person who holds a registration card terminates employment with one employer and is reemployed within thirty calendar days in the same classification as registered with the board, the new employer, within ten days of such reemployment shall submit to the board a notice of the change on a form prescribed by the board, together with a transfer fee paid by the new employer. The board shall then issue a new registration card reflecting the name or license number, or both, of the new employer.

(3) The cardholder may continue to work for the new employer while the board is processing the transfer application. The holder of a registration card who terminates employment shall surrender within forty-eight hours the registration card to the former employer. The employer shall return the cancelled registration card to the board within ten calendar days of effective termination date.

H. A registration card shall be subject to expiration and renewal during the period in which the holder of the card is subject to an order of suspension.

(Chgd. by Acts 1991 No. 315, §1; Acts 1995 No. 489, §1; Acts 1997 No. 155, §1, eff. 8/15/97.)

§3284. Training of security officers; requirements.

A. The board shall approve all training programs and shall develop training criteria outlining specific curriculum to be used in the instructing and training of all security officers.

B. (1) Any security officer employed after the effective date of this Chapter shall complete, within thirty days of his first work assignment, eight hours classroom training under a licensed instructor and successfully pass an examination on the prescribed material which shall include the following topics:

(a) Orientation to R.S. 37:3270 through 3298 and the board's rules and regulations: two hours.

(b) Legal powers and limitations of a security officer: two hours.

(c) Emergency procedures: two hours.

(d) General duties/field notes/report writing: two hours.

(2) Armed security officers in addition to the training requirements outlined in Paragraphs (B)(1) and (4) of this Section shall complete twelve hours firearms training and range qualifications prior to armed work assignment. The nature and extent of firearms training shall be adequately described, approved, and monitored by the board to include at a minimum the following:

(a) Legal limitations on use of weapons.

(b) Handling of a weapon.

(c) Safety and maintenance.

(d) Dim light firing.

(e) A shoot, don't shoot program.

(f) Stress factors.

(3) Marksmanship requirement shall be a minimum of seventy-five percent on any silhouette target course approved by the board.

(4) Security officers shall have three months to complete an additional eight hours training under a licensed instructor, as prescribed by the board, and successfully pass a fifty question test administered by the licensed instructor by achieving a minimum score of seventy percent.

C. Failure to complete the required training within the prescribed time period may preclude future consideration for a license for a period of one year.

D. (1) All armed security officers must complete an annual firearms retraining course of at least four hours, which includes two hours of refresher courses on subjects previously specified, and at least two hours aggregate retraining in firearms instructions, to include minimum marksmanship qualification of seventy-five percent on an approved silhouette target course approved by the board.

(2) Upon a registrant's completion of any training required, the licensee or employer, as the case may be, shall furnish to the board a documented training verification form of such completion signed by a licensed instructor within fifteen calendar days from said training.

E. All classroom training required by this Chapter shall be administered by a licensed instructor who:

(1) Is approved by the board.

(2) Meets the qualifications of an applicant as required by R.S. 37:3276(A)(1) through (6);

(3) Has a minimum of three years supervisory experience with a contract security company, proprietary security organization, or with any federal, state, parochial, or municipal law enforcement agency; or

(4) Degree in administration of justice or the equivalent thereof from an accredited college or university;

(5) P.O.S.T. certified instructor; or

(6) Teaching certificate issued by the state of Louisiana, Department of Education, or the equivalent thereof, and one year supervisory experience in the security field.

F. All firearms training required by this Chapter shall be administered by a licensed instructor who:

(1) Meets the same qualifications of a classroom instructor as required by Subsection E; and

(2) Has successfully completed training and possesses a National Rifle Association Security or Police Firearms Instructor certificate; or a P.O.S.T. Firearm Instructor Certificate, or a Department of Energy Firearms Instructor Certificate.

G. A board-licensed instructor may be held accountable for improperly certifying security officers, and upon showing of cause, his license as an instructor may be suspended or revoked.

H. All board-licensed instructors shall be required to carry a minimum of one hundred thousand dollars general liability insurance with the state of Louisiana named as the additional insured and provide the board with a certificate of insurance as proof of coverage.

I. All applicants who apply to the board to become licensed as an instructor are required to pass a written examination administered by the board. The passing grade of the examination shall be seventy percent.

J. Current and former law enforcement officers who have successfully completed a P.O.S.T. certification and firearms training program within one year prior to application may submit proof of such documentation to the board as proof of training and shall be considered the equivalent of the classroom training for security officers as required in Paragraphs (B)(1), (2), and (4) of this Section, but shall not exempt them from the requirements of Paragraph D(1) of this Section.

(Chgd. by Acts 1991 No. 315, §1; Acts 1995 No. 489, §1; Acts 1997 No. 155, §1, eff. 8/15/97.)

§3285. Transportation of firearms.

An armed security officer whose duties require the transporting of a firearm to and from the work assignment and his residence, or between assignments, shall be required to have in his possession an armed registration card issued by the board. This registration card does not permit the carrying of concealed weapons.

§3286. Fees.

A. The board may assess the following schedule of fees, which shall not be refundable:

(1) Company licensee:

(a) Application fee—$20.00.
(b) Examination fee—$50.00.
(c) Reexamination fee—$20.00.
(d) Initial license fee—$200.00.
(e) Renewal license fee—$200.00.
(f) Replacement fee for a lost, destroyed, or mutilated license—$10.00.

(2) Registrant:

(a) Application fee—$20.00.
(b) Renewal fee—$20.00.
(c) Transfer fee—$10.00.
(d) Replacement fee for a lost, destroyed, or mutilated card—$10.00.
(e) Reinstatement fee—$10.00.
(f) Status change fee—$10.00.

(3) Instructor licensee:

(a) Application fee—$20.00.
(b) Inhouse/outside classroom license fee—$50.00.
(c) Inhouse/outside firearms license fee—$75.00.
(d) Transfer application fee—$20.00.
(e) Inhouse/outside classroom renewal license fee—$50.00.
(f) Inhouse/outside firearms renewal license fee—$75.00.
(g) Examination fee—$25.00.
(h) Reexamination fee—$15.00.
(i) Replacement fee for a lost, destroyed, or mutilated license—$10.00.

B. All fees shall be paid by check or money order made payable to the board.

C. Any fees payable by a registrant under this Chapter, or paid by a licensee on the registrant's behalf, or any deposits which may be required by a licensee from a registrant under this Chapter, may be deducted from any wages payable to the registrant by the licensee; provided that such deduction does not reduce the hourly wage below the applicable minimum wage law.

D. After complying with the Administrative Procedure Act*, fees may be assessed on licensees and registrants in addition to the above stated fees as may be required to cover administrative costs.

(Chgd. by Acts 1991 No. 315, §1.)
**R.S. 49:950 et seq.*

§3287. Renewal of license, certificate; penalty.

A. A license shall expire annually on the date of issuance unless renewed by payment of the required renewal fee at least thirty days prior to its expiration. The board shall notify the licensee of the renewal at the last known address at least sixty days in advance of the expiration. If a license is not renewed upon its expiration date, it shall be deemed to have lapsed and to be invalid. The delinquent licensee shall apply again for initial licensure.

B. The board shall issue the same number for the renewed license as that number issued for the original license or shall deny renewal within thirty days. The board shall promptly notify the licensee if it refuses to renew the license.

C. The licensee, within fifteen days after receipt of such notice of intent to refuse to renew a license, may request a hearing on such refusal. A licensee shall be permitted to continue to be engaged in business while his renewal application is pending.

(Chgd. by Acts 1991 No. 315, §1.)

§3288. Administrative penalties.

A. Any person who is determined by the board, after reasonable notice and opportunity for a fair and impartial hearing held in accordance with the Administrative Procedure Act*, to have committed an act that is a violation of this Chapter or any regulation or rule issued thereunder is subject to an administrative penalty of not more than five hundred dollars per violation.

**R.S. 49:950 et seq.*

B. The board, in accordance with the Administrative Procedure Act, may adopt a schedule of administrative penalties for minor violations that can be assessed by the executive secretary when the violator waives the right to an administrative hearing.

(Chgd. by Acts 1991 No. 315, §1.)

§3289. Causes for nonissuance, suspension, revocation, or restrictions; fines; reinstatement.

A. The board may refuse to issue or may suspend, revoke, or impose probationary or other restrictions on any license issued under this Chapter for good cause shown which shall include the following:

(1) Conviction of a felony or entry of a plea of guilty or nolo contendere to a felony charge under the laws of the United States of America or of any state.

(2) Deceit or perjury in obtaining any certificate or license issued under this Chapter.

(3) Providing false testimony before the board.

(4) Efforts to deceive or defraud the public.

(5) Professional incompetency or gross negligence.

(6) Rendering, submitting, subscribing, or verifying false, deceptive, misleading, or unfounded opinions or reports.

(7) The refusal of the licensing authority of another state to issue or renew a license, permit, or certificate to practice in that state, or the revocation or suspension of or other restriction imposed on a license, permit, or certificate issued by such licensing authority.

(8) Aiding or abetting a person to evade the provisions of this Chapter or knowingly combining or conspiring with an unlicensed person, or acting as an agent, partner, associate or otherwise, of an unlicensed person with intent to evade provisions of this Chapter.

(9) Violation of any provision of this Chapter or any rules or regulations of the board or rules of professional conduct promulgated by the board.

B. The board, as a probationary condition or as a condition of the reinstatement of any license suspended or revoked hereunder, may require the holder to pay all costs of the board proceedings, including investigators', stenographers', and attorneys' fees and assess administrative penalties not to exceed five hundred dollars per violation.

C. Four concurring votes of the board shall be required for the revocation of any license. Four concurring votes shall be required for suspension of any license or the imposition of costs or fines in excess of five hundred dollars.

D. Any certificate or license suspended, revoked, or otherwise restricted by the board may be reinstated by majority vote of a quorum.

(Chgd. by Acts 1991 No. 315, §1.)

§3290. Insignias; markings; clothing; restrictions.

A. (1) With the exception of sworn peace officers in police uniform, no individual, while performing the duties of a security officer, shall wear or display any badge, insignia, device, shield, patch, or pattern which shall indicate or tend to indicate that he is a sworn peace officer, or which contains or includes the word "police", or the equivalent thereof, or is similar in wording to any law enforcement agency in this state.

(2) A copy of such badges and insignias of the licensee shall be submitted for approval to the board at the time of filing for initial and renewable license application.

(3) Security officer uniforms shall be specifically described and a full length picture of said uniform shall be submitted to the board for approval.

B. No person, while performing any private security services, shall have or utilize any vehicle or equipment displaying the words "police", "law enforcement officer", or the equivalent thereof, or have any sign, shield, marking, accessory, or insignia that may indicate that such vehicle is a vehicle of a public law enforcement agency.

C. (1) *(Repealed.)*

(2) All military or police-style uniforms, except for rainwear or other foul weather clothing, shall have affixed over the left breast pocket or on the sleeve of the shirt, blouse, or the outermost garment, and on all caps worn by such persons, badges, or insignias distinct in design from those utilized by law enforcement agencies within the state, and approved by the board.

(3) Suppliers of uniforms shall be prohibited from the sale or rental of uniforms, badges, and insignia of a licensee or law enforcement agency without appropriate certification from such licensees or agencies that the intended purchaser is properly authorized to use those items.

D. An employer may require a reasonable deposit to secure the return of the uniform, weapon, or any equipment provided by the employer, provided that such deduction does not reduce the hourly wage below the applicable minimum wage law.
(Chgd. by Acts 1997 No. 155, §§1, 2, eff. 8/15/97.)

§3291. Unlawful commissions.

A. It shall be unlawful for any person to knowingly commit any of the following acts:

(1) Provide contract security services without possessing a valid license.

(2) Employ any individual to perform the duties that are regulated by this Chapter, who is not the holder of a valid registration card.

(3) Publish any advertisement, letterhead, circular, statement, or phrase of any sort which suggests that the licensee is an official police agency or any other agency, instrumentality, or division of this state or any of its political subdivisions, or of the federal government.

(4) Issue any badge or shield not in conformance with R.S. 37:3290.

(5) Designate an individual as other than one defined in R.S. 37:3272 to circumvent the requirements of this Chapter.

(6) Knowingly make any false statement or material omission in any application filed with the board.

(7) Falsely represent that a person is the holder of a valid license or registration; or

(8) Violate any provision of this Chapter or any rule or regulation of the board.

(9) Provide security for any obvious criminal conduct.

B. It shall be unlawful for any person to knowingly commit any of the following:

(1) Provide or perform security services without a valid registration card.

(2) Fail to return immediately on demand or within twenty-four hours of termination of employment a firearm issued by an employer.

(3) Carry a firearm in the performance of his duties without a valid registration card.

(4) Fail to return immediately on demand or within seven days of termination of employment any uniform, badge, or other item of equipment issued to the security officer by an employer.

(5) Make any statement which would reasonably cause another person to believe that the security officer functions as a sworn peace officer or other official of this state, or of any of its political subdivisions, or an agency of the federal government.

(6) Fail to comply with the regulations issued by the board, or with any other requirements under the provisions of this Chapter.

(7) Divulge to anyone, other than his employer, or to such persons as his employer may direct, or as may be required by law, any information acquired during such employment that may compromise the security of any premises or assignment to which he shall have been assigned by such employer.

(8) Fail to return to the employer or the board a registration card as required by the provisions of this Chapter.

(9) Possess a license or registration card issued to another person.

(10) Use any uniform, badge, or shield not in conformance with this Chapter.

(11) Provide security for any obvious criminal conduct.
(Chgd. by Acts 1991 No. 315, §1.)

§3292. Violations; penalties.

A. No person shall engage in the private security business except in accordance with this Chapter and the rules and regulations adopted by the board hereunder.

B. Whoever willfully violates any provisions of this Chapter shall be fined not less than one hundred dollars nor more than five hundred dollars, or imprisoned for not less than ten days nor more than five months, or both.

§3293. Cease and desist order; injunctive relief.

A. In addition to or in lieu of the criminal penalties and administrative sanctions provided in this Chapter, the board is empowered to issue an order to any person or firm engaged in any activity, conduct, or practice constituting a violation of any provision of this Chapter, directing such person or firm to forthwith cease and desist from such activity, conduct, or practice. Such order shall be issued in the name of the state of Louisiana, under the official seal of the board.

B. If the person or firm to whom the board directs a cease and desist order does not cease and desist the prohibited activity, conduct, or practice within three working days from service of such cease and desist order by certified mail, the board may seek, in any court of competent jurisdiction and proper venue, a writ of injunction enjoining such person or firm from engaging in any activity, conduct, or practice prohibited by this Chapter.

C. (1) Upon a proper showing by the board that such person or firm has engaged in any activity, conduct, or practice prohibited by this Chapter, the court shall issue a temporary restraining order restraining the person or firm from engaging in unlawful activity, conduct, or practices pending the hearing on a preliminary injunction, and in due course a permanent injunction shall be issued after a hearing, commanding the cessation of the unlawful activity, conduct, or practices complained of, all without the necessity of the board having to give bond as usually required in such cases.

(2) A temporary restraining order, preliminary injunction, or permanent injunction issued hereunder shall not be subject to being released upon bond.

§3294. Sole proprietorship, partnership, corporation, association with licensed business.

A. This Chapter shall not prohibit one or more businesses from practicing through a partnership, corporation, or association.

B. In any partnership, corporation, or association whose primary activity consists of providing services regulated by this Chapter, at least one partner or corporate officer shall be licensed as a business under this Chapter.

§3295. Fund of the board of private security examiners.

All fees, administrative fines and cost collected under the provisions of this Chapter shall be paid into the state treasury on or before the twenty-fifth day of the month following their collection and, in accordance with Article VII, Section 9 of the Constitution of Louisiana, shall be credited to the Bond Security and Redemption Fund. Out of the funds remaining in the Bond Security and Redemption Fund, after a sufficient amount is allocated therefrom to pay all obligations secured by the full faith and credit of the state which become due and payable within each fiscal year, the treasurer shall pay an amount equal to the total amount of funds paid into the treasury into a special fund, which is hereby created in the state treasury and designated as the Louisiana State Board of Private Security Examiners Fund. In addition, all other money made available for use as provided in this Chapter shall be credited to this fund. *(Chgd. by Acts 1991 No. 315, §1.).*

§3296. Adoption of rules.

The adoption of any rule or regulation, guideline, substantive procedure, or code of conduct shall be subject to the provisions of the Administrative Procedure Act*.

**R.S. 49:950 et seq.*

§3297. Local governmental restrictions; superseded local governmental laws, code, or ordinances.

A. From and after the effective date of this Chapter, no governmental subdivision of this state shall enact any legislation, code, or ordinance or promulgate any rules or regulations relating to the licensing, training, or regulations of contract security companies other than the imposition of a bona fide business tax.

B. Upon said effective date, any provisions of any legislation, code, or ordinance, or rules promulgated by any local governmental subdivision of this state which relates to licensing, training, or regulation of licensees and registrants, as defined herein, shall be superseded by this Chapter.

§3298. Inapplicability.

A. This Chapter shall not apply to a person or corporation which employs persons who do private security work in connection with the affairs of such employer only and who have an employer-employee relationship with such employer. Neither such persons or corporations nor their employees shall be required to register or be licensed under this Chapter.

B. This Chapter shall not apply to a peace officer employed by a state, parish, or local law enforcement agency who contracts directly with an employer to work during his off-duty hours and whose off-duty employment is conducted on an independent contractor basis with an employer other than a peace officer engaged in the private detective or private security business or a private detective or private security agency.

C. This Chapter shall not be construed to apply to a federal peace officer or federal law enforcement officer.

TITLE 40
PUBLIC HEALTH AND SAFETY
(Selected Chapters)

CHAPTER 4. FOOD AND DRUGS
(Selected Parts)

PART I. ADULTERATION, SUBSTITUTION, MISBRANDING, OR FALSE ADVERTISING

PART X. UNIFORM CONTROLLED DANGEROUS SUBSTANCES LAW

PART X-A. THERAPEUTIC USE OF MARIJUANA

PART X-B. TRANSACTIONS IN DRUG RELATED OBJECTS PROHIBITED

PART X-C. ANIMAL EUTHANASIA WITH SODIUM PENTOBARBITAL

PART X-D. TRANSACTIONS INVOLVING PROCEEDS FROM CONTROLLED DANGEROUS SUBSTANCES ACTIVITY

PART XIII. SUBSTANCE ABUSE/ADDICTION TREATMENT FACILITIES

PART I. ADULTERATION, SUBSTITUTION, MISBRANDING, OR FALSE ADVERTISING

(Selected Section)

§617.1. Distribution of imitation controlled dangerous substances to a person under eighteen.

A. A person eighteen years of age or over shall not knowingly or intentionally distribute or possess with intent to distribute an imitation controlled dangerous substance representing it to be a controlled dangerous substance to a person under eighteen years of age.

B. A person eighteen years of age or over shall not knowingly or intentionally distribute or possess with intent to distribute an imitation controlled dangerous substance intending it to be used or distributed as a controlled dangerous substance or under circumstances in which the person has reasonable cause to believe that the imitation controlled dangerous substance will be used or distributed for use as a controlled dangerous substance.

C. "Imitation controlled dangerous substance" means a substance that is a noncontrolled substance, but which by appearance or operation, including color, shape, size, markings, or packaging, or by representations made, or by its pharmacological effect, would lead a reasonable person to believe that the substance is a controlled dangerous substance.

D. It is not a defense that the accused believed the imitation controlled dangerous substance to be a controlled dangerous substance.

E. Whoever commits the crime of distribution of an imitation controlled dangerous substance to a person under eighteen shall be imprisoned with or without hard labor for not more than five years and may be fined not more than five thousand dollars.
(Added by Acts 1992 No. 1059, §1; chgd. by Acts 1993 No. 154, §1, eff. 5/31/93.)

PART X. UNIFORM CONTROLLED DANGEROUS SUBSTANCES LAW

(Complete Part)

§961. Definitions.

As used in this Part, the following terms shall have the meaning ascribed to them in this Section unless the context clearly indicates otherwise:

(1) "Addict" means a drug dependent person who habitually uses any narcotic drugs as to have lost the power of self-control with reference to his use of said drugs.

(2) "Administer" means to deliver under the auspices of a registered practitioner a controlled dangerous substance to the ultimate user or human research subject by injection, or for inhalation, or ingestion, or by any other means except where otherwise provided by law.

(3) "Agent" means an authorized person who acts on behalf of or at the direction of a manufacturer, distributor, or dispenser but does not include a common or contract carrier, public warehouseman, or employee thereof.

(4) "Apothecary" means a licensed pharmacist as defined by the laws of this state and, where the context so requires, the owner of the store or other place of business where narcotic drugs are compounded or dispensed by a licensed pharmacist; but nothing in this Part shall be construed as conferring on a person who is not registered nor licensed as a pharmacist any authority, right or privilege that is not granted to him by the pharmacy laws of this state.

(5) "Cannabis" includes all parts of plants of the genus Cannabis, whether growing or not; the seeds thereof; the resin extracted from any part of such plant, and every compound, manufacture, salt, derivative, mixture, or preparation of such plant, its seeds or resin, but shall not include the mature stalks of such plant, fiber produced from such stalks, oil or cake made from the seeds of such plant, any other compound, manufacture, salt, derivative, mixture, or preparation of such mature stalks (except the resin extracted therefrom), fiber, oil, or cake or the sterilized seed of such plant which is incapable of germination.

(6) "Control" means to add a drug or other substance, or immediate precursor, to a schedule under R.S. 40:964, whether by transfer from another schedule or otherwise.

(7) "Controlled dangerous substance" means a drug, substance or immediate precursor in Schedule I through V of R.S. 40:964. The term shall not include distilled spirits, wine, malt beverages, or tobacco.

(8) "Controlled substance analogue" means a substance the chemical structure of which is substantially similar to the chemical structure of a controlled dangerous substance in Schedule I or II of R.S. 40:964; which has a stimulant, depressant, or hallucinogenic effect on the central nervous system that is substantially similar to or greater than the stimulant, depressant, or hallucinogenic effect on the central nervous system of a controlled dangerous substance in Schedule I or II; or with respect to a particular person, which such person represents or intends to have a stimulant, depressant, or hallucinogenic effect on the central nervous system that is substantially similar to or greater than the stimulant, depressant, or hallucinogenic effect on the central nervous system of a controlled dangerous substance in Schedule I or II. Such term shall not include a controlled dangerous substance; any substance for which there is an approved new drug application; with respect to a particular person any substance, if an exemption is in effect for investigational use, for that person, under the federal Food, Drug, and Cosmetic Act (21 U.S.C.A. §355) to the extent conduct with respect to such substance is pursuant to such exemption; or any substance to the extent not intended for human consumption before an exception takes effect with respect to that substance.

(9) "Counterfeit Controlled Dangerous Substance" means a controlled dangerous substance which, without authorization, bears the trademark, trade name or other identifying mark, imprint, number, or device, or any likeness thereof, of a manufacturer, distributor, or dispenser other than the person or persons who in fact manufactured, distributed, or dispensed such substance and which thereby falsely purports or is represented to be the product of, or to have been distributed by, such other manufacturer, distributor, or dispenser.

(10) "Deliver" or "delivery" means the transfer of a controlled dangerous substance whether or not there exists an agency relationship.

(11) "Dentist" means a person licensed and authorized by law to practice dentistry in this state.

(12) "Depressant" means a drug which contains any quantity of barbituric acid or any of the salts of barbituric acid; or any derivatives of barbituric acid; or any substance listed in Schedule I(d), Schedule II(d) or Schedule III(b) of R.S. 40:964, or which has been designated by the secretary of the Department of Health and Hospitals as habit forming because of its depressant effect on the central nervous system.

(13) "Dispense" means to deliver a controlled dangerous substance to the ultimate user or human research subject by or pursuant to the lawful order of a practitioner, including the packaging, labeling, or compounding necessary to prepare the substance for such delivery.

(14) "Distribute" means to deliver a controlled dangerous substance whether by physical delivery, administering, subterfuge, furnishing a prescription, or by filling, packaging, labeling or compounding the substance pursuant to the lawful order of a practitioner.

(15) "Distributor" means a person who delivers a controlled dangerous substance as herein defined.

(16) "Drug" means:

(a) Articles recognized in the official United States Pharmacopoeia, official Homeopathic Pharmacopoeia of the United States, or official National Formulary, or any supplement to any of them.

(b) Articles intended for use in the diagnosis, cure, mitigation, treatment, or prevention of disease in man or other animals.

(c) Articles other than food intended to affect the structure of any function of the body of man or other animals.

(d) Articles intended for use as a component of any article specified in Subparagraph (a), (b) or (c) of this Paragraph, but does not include devices or their components, parts, or accessories.

(17) "Drug Enforcement Administration" means the Drug Enforcement Administration, United States Department of Justice or its successor.

(18) "Drug dependent person" means a person who is using a controlled dangerous substance and who is in a state of psychic or physical dependence, or both, arising from administration of that controlled dangerous substance on a continuous basis. Drug dependence is characterized by behavioral and other responses which include a strong compulsion to take the substance on a continuous basis in order to experience its psychic effects, or to avoid the discomfort of its absence.

(19) "Hallucinogen" means a drug which contains any quantity of LSD (Lysergic acid diethylamide), its isomers, salts, salts of isomers, or any quantity of a substance listed in Schedule I(C) of R.S. 40:964, or any substance which the secretary of the Department of Health and Hospitals after investigation has found to have, and by regulation designates as having, a potential for abuse because of its depressant or stimulant effect on the central nervous system, or hallucinogenic effect.

(20) "Imitation controlled dangerous substance" means a noncontrolled substance which by appearance or operation, including color, shape, size, markings, or packaging, or by representations made, or by its pharmacological effect, would lead a reasonable person to believe that the substance is a controlled dangerous substance.

(21) "Immediate precursor" means a substance which the secretary of the Department of Health and Hospitals has found to be and by regulation designates as being the principal compound commonly used or produced primarily for use, and which is an immediate chemical intermediary used or likely to be used in the manufacture of a controlled dangerous substance, the control of which is necessary to prevent, curtail, or limit such manufacture.

(22) "Isomers" refers to optical isomers and/or stereoisomers and mixtures thereof, unless specifically excepted in this Part. Optical isomers or stereoisomers are molecules which differ from each other only in the way the constituent atoms are oriented in space.

(23) "Legend drug" means any drug or drug product bearing on the label of the manufacturer or distributor, as required by the Federal Food and Drug Administration, the statement "Caution: Federal law prohibits dispensing without prescription".

(24) "Manufacture" means the production, preparation, propagation, compounding or processing of a controlled dangerous substance, either directly or indirectly by extraction from substances of natural origin, or independently by means of chemical synthesis, or by a combination of extraction and chemical synthesis. Manufacturer includes any person who packages, repackages, or labels any container of any controlled dangerous substance, except

practitioners who dispense or compound prescription orders for delivery to the ultimate consumer.

(25) "Marijuana" means all parts of plants of the genus Cannabis, whether growing or not; the seeds thereof; the resin extracted from any part of such plant; and every compound, manufacture, salt, derivative, mixture, or preparation of such plant, its seeds or resin, but shall not include the mature stalks of such plant, fiber produced from such stalks, oil or cake made from the seeds of such plant, any other compound, manufacture, salt, derivative, mixture, or preparation of such mature stalks (except the resin extracted therefrom), fiber, oil, or cake, or the sterilized seed of such plant which is incapable of germination.

(26) "Narcotic drug" means any of the following, whether produced directly or indirectly by extraction from substances of vegetable origin, or independently by means of chemical synthesis, or by a combination of extraction and chemical synthesis:

(a) Opium, coca leaves, and opiates.

(b) A compound, manufacture, salt, derivatives, or preparation of opium, coca leaves, or opiates.

(c) A substance and any compound, manufacture, salt, derivative, or preparation thereof which is chemically identical with any of the substances referred to in Subparagraphs (a) and (b) of this Paragraph, except that the words "narcotic drug" as used in this Part shall not include decocainized coca leaves or extracts of coca leaves, which extracts do not contain cocaine or ecgonine.

(27) "Opiate" means any dangerous substance having an addiction-forming or addiction-sustaining liability similar to morphine or being capable of conversion into a drug having such addiction-forming or addiction-sustaining liability. It does not include, unless specifically designated as controlled under R.S. 40:963, the dextrorotatory isomer of 3-methoxy-n-methylmorphinan and its salts (dextromethorphan). It does include its racemic and levorotatory forms.

(28) "Opium poppy" means the plant of the species Papaver somniferum, except the seeds thereof.

(29) "Person" includes any institution whether public or private, hospitals or clinics operated by the state or any of its political subdivisions, and any corporation, association, partnership or one or more individuals.

(30) "Poppy straw" means all parts, except the seeds, of the opium poppy, after mowing.

(31) "Practitioner" means a physician, dentist, veterinarian, scientific investigator, pharmacy, hospital, or other person licensed, registered, or otherwise permitted to distribute, dispense, conduct research with respect to, or administer a controlled dangerous substance in the course of professional practice or research in this state.

(32) "Prescribe" means to issue a written request or order for a controlled dangerous substance by a person licensed under this Part for a legitimate medical purpose. The act of prescribing must be in good faith and in the usual course of the licensee's professional practice.

(33) "Prescription" means a written request for a drug or therapeutic aid issued by a licensed physician, dentist, veterinarian, osteopath, or podiatrist for a legitimate medical purpose, for the purpose of correcting a physical, mental, or bodily ailment, and acting in good faith in the usual course of his professional practice.

(34) "Production" includes the manufacture, planting, cultivation, growing, or harvesting of a controlled dangerous substance.

(35) "Secretary" means the secretary of the Department of Health and Hospitals or his successor.

(36) "State" means the state of Louisiana.

(37) "Stimulant" means a drug which contains a quantity of amphetamine or any of its isomers; any salt of amphetamine or any salt of an isomer of amphetamine; or any substance listed in Schedules II(C) or III(A) of R.S. 40:964 or any substance which the secretary of the Department of Health and Hospitals after investigation, has found to be and by regulation designated as habit forming because of its stimulant effect on the central nervous system.

(38) "Ultimate user" means a person who lawfully possesses a controlled dangerous substance for his own use or for the use of a member of his household or for administration to an animal owned by him or by a member of his household.

(Chgd. by Acts 1992 No. 1059, §1; Acts 1993 No. 154, §1; Acts 1994 Third Ex. Sess. No. 34, §1, eff. 8/27/94.)

§962. Authority to control.

A. All controlled dangerous substances listed in R.S. 40:964 are hereby controlled.

B. The secretary of the Department of Health and Human Resources shall add a substance as a controlled dangerous substance if it is classified as a controlled dangerous substance by the Drug Enforcement Administration of the United States government.

C. The secretary may by rule add to the schedules provided in Section 964 of this Part any drug or other substance if he finds that such drug or other substance has a high potential for abuse, and after such a finding by the secretary, the drug shall be added in the appropriate schedule under the criteria provided under Section 963 of this Part. In making a finding that a drug or other substance has a high potential for abuse, the secretary of the Department of Health and Human Resources shall consider the following factors with respect to each drug or other substance proposed to be controlled:

(1) Its actual or relative potential for abuse.

(2) Scientific evidence of its pharmacological effect, if known.

(3) State of current scientific knowledge regarding the substance.

(4) Its history and current pattern of abuse.

(5) The scope, duration and significance of abuse.

(6) What, if any, risk there is to public health.

(7) Its psychic or physiological dependence liability.

(8) Whether the substance is an immediate precursor of a substance already controlled by this Section.

D. In an adjudication the secretary of the Department of Health and Human Resources may transfer a controlled substance from one schedule to another schedule upon the basis of a finding that the characteristics of the controlled drug or substances are such that under the criteria in Section 963 of this Part the controlled substances should be transferred or that a transfer of any substance listed under Section 964 from one schedule to another schedule should be made in order to conform with the schedule in which the drug is placed by the Drug Enforcement Administration of the United States government.

E. If the secretary of the Department of Health and Human Resources designates a substance as an immediate precursor, substances which are precursors of the controlled precursor shall not be subject to control solely because they are precursors of the controlled precursor.

F. The secretary of the Department of Health and Human Resources shall exclude any nonnarcotic substance from a schedule if the substance may, under the Federal Food, Drug and Cosmetic Act* and the law of this state, be lawfully sold over the counter without a prescription.

**21 U.S.C. §301 et seq.*

G. The reclassification of any controlled dangerous substance or its transfer from one schedule to another by the secretary of the Department of Health and Human Resources or the state health officer shall not affect the penalties provided by this Part.

H. If the scheduling of a substance in Schedule I is necessary to avoid an imminent peril to the public health, safety or welfare, the secretary may adopt an emergency rule adding the substance to Schedule I pursuant to R.S. 49:953(B). In determining whether the substance poses an imminent peril to the public health, safety or welfare, the secretary shall consider the factors set forth in Paragraphs (C)(4), (5) and (6) of this Section.

(Chgd. by Acts 1994 Third Ex. Sess. No. 34, §2, eff. 8/27/94.)

§962.1. Ephedrine products.

A. Except as provided in Subsection B, any product that contains any quantity of ephedrine, a salt of ephedrine, an optical isomer of ephedrine, or a salt of an optical isomer of ephedrine may be dispensed only upon the prescription of a duly licensed practitioner authorized by the laws of the state to prescribe prescription drugs.

B. The following products containing ephedrine shall be exempt from the provisions of Subsection A provided that such product may lawfully be sold over the counter without a prescription under the federal Food, Drug, and Cosmetic Act, is labeled and marketed in a manner consistent with the pertinent OTC Tentative Final or Final Monograph, and is manufactured and distributed for legitimate medicinal use in a manner that reduces or eliminates the likelihood of abuse:

(1) Solid oral dosage forms (including soft gelatin caplets) that combine active ingredients in the following ranges for each dosage unit:

(a) Theophylline (100—130 mg), Ephedrine (12.56—24 mg).

(b) Theophylline (60—100 mg), Ephedrine (12.5—24 mg), Guaifenesin (200—400 mg).

(c) Ephedrine (12.5—25 mg), Guaifenesin (200—400 mg).

(d) Phenobarbital (not greater than 8 mg) in combination with ingredients of Subparagraph (a) or (b) of this Paragraph.

(2) Liquid oral dosage forms that combine active ingredients in the following ranges for each (5 ml) dose:

(a) Theophylline (not greater than 45 mg), Ephedrine (not greater than 36 mg), Guaifenesin (not greater than 100 mg), Phenobarbital (not greater than 12 mg).

(b) Phenylephephrine (not greater than 5 mg), Ephedrine (not greater than 5 mg), chlorpheniramine (not greater than 2 mg), dextromethorphan (not greater than 10 mg), ammonium C1 (not greater than 40 mg), ipecac fluid extract (not greater than 0.005 ml).

(3) Anorectal preparations containing less than five percent ephedrine.

(4) Any liquid compound, mixture, or preparation containing one-half percent or less of ephedrine.

C. The marketing, advertising, or labeling of any nonprescription product containing ephedrine, a salt of ephedrine, an optical isomer of ephedrine, or a salt of an optical isomer of ephedrine for the indication of stimulation, mental alertness, weight loss, appetite control, or energy is prohibited. The Department of Health and Hospitals, office of public health is authorized to adopt rules and regulations in accordance with the Administrative Procedure Act* to exempt other nonprescription products from the prohibition contained herein. Such rules and regulations shall require a distributor or manufacturer seeking an exemption from the prohibition contained herein to clearly demonstrate that the nonprescription product is intended for use for a valid medicinal purpose and that the marketing of that product does not encourage, promote, or abet the abuse or misuse of ephedrine. In addition, such rules and regulations shall include the following factors for purposes of determining whether or not such an exemption should be granted:

(1) The packing of the product.

(2) The name and labeling of the product.

(3) The manner of distribution, advertising, and promotion of the product.

(4) Verbal representations made concerning the product.

(5) The duration, scope, and significance of abuse or misuse of the particular product.

**R.S. 49:950 et seq.*

D. Whoever violates any provision of this Section shall be fined not more than one thousand dollars or imprisoned for not more than six months, or both.

(Added by Acts 1995 No. 1253, §1, eff. 1/1/96.)

§963. Schedules of controlled dangerous substances.

There are established five schedules of controlled substances, to be known as Schedules I, II, III, IV, and V. Such schedules shall initially consist of the substances listed in R.S. 40:964. In determining that a substance is to be added to these schedules, the secretary of the Department of Health and Human Resources shall find the following:

A. As to Schedule I:

(1) The drug or other substance has a high potential for abuse.

(2) The drug or other substance has no currently accepted medical use in treatment in the United States, and

(3) There is a lack of accepted safety for use of the drug or other substance under medical supervision.

B. As to Schedule II:

(1) The drug or other substance has a high potential for abuse.

(2) The drug or other substance has a currently accepted medical use in treatment in the United States or a currently accepted medical use with severe restrictions, and

(3) Abuse of the drug or other substances may lead to severe psychological or physical dependence.

C. As to Schedule III:

(1) The drug or other substance has a potential for abuse less than the drugs or other substances listed in Schedules I and II.

(2) The drug or other substance has a currently accepted medical use in treatment in the United States, and

(3) Abuse of the drug or other substance may lead to moderate or low physical dependence or high psychological dependence.

D. As to Schedule IV:

(1) The drug or other substance has a low potential for abuse relative to the drugs or other substances listed in Schedule III.

(2) The drug or other substance has a currently accepted medical use in treatment in the United States, and

(3) Abuse of the drug or other substance may lead to limited physical dependence or psychological dependence relative to the drugs or other substances listed in Schedule III.

E. As to Schedule V:

(1) The drug or other substance has a low potential for abuse relative to the drugs or other substances listed in Schedule IV.

(2) The drug or other substance has a currently accepted medical use in treatment in the United States, and

(3) Abuse of the drug or other substance may lead to limited physical dependence or psychological dependence relative to the drugs or other substances listed in Schedule IV.

§964. Composition of schedules.

Schedules I, II, III, IV, and V shall, unless and until added to pursuant to R.S. 40:962, consist of the following drugs or other substances, by whatever official name, common or usual name, chemical name, or brand name designated:

SCHEDULE I

A. Opiates. Unless specifically excepted or unless listed in another schedule, any of the following opiates, including their isomers, esters, ethers, salts, or salts of isomers, esters, and ethers, whenever the existence of such isomers, esters, ethers, or salts is possible within the specific chemical designation:

*(1) Acetylmethadol
*(2) Allylprodine
*(3) Alphacetylmethadol
*(4) Alphameprodine
*(5) Alphamethadol
*(6) Benzethidine
*(7) Betacetylmethadol
*(8) Betameprodine
*(9) Betamethadol
*(10) Betaprodine
*(11) Clonitazene
*(12) Dextromoramide
*(13) Dextrorphan
*(14) Diampromide
*(15) Diethylthiambutene
*(16) Difenoxin
*(17) Dimenoxadol
*(18) Dimepheptanol
*(19) Dimethylthiambutene
*(20) Dioxaphetyl butyrate
*(21) Dipipanone
*(22) Ethylmethylthiambutene
*(23) Etonitazene
*(24) Etoxeridine
*(25) Furethidine
*(26) Hydroxypethidine
*(27) Ketobemidone
*(28) Levomoramide
*(29) Levophenacylmorphan
*(30) Morpheridine
*(31) Noracymethadol
*(32) Norlevorphanol
*(33) Normethadone
*(34) Norpipanone
*(35) Phenadoxone

*(36) Phenampromide
*(37) Phenomorphan
*(38) Phenoperidine
*(39) Piritramide
*(40) Proheptazine
*(41) Properidine
*(42) Propiram
*(43) Racemoramide
*(44) Trimeperidine

Editor's note: See section 966(B)(1) and section 979(B) for references to substances preceded by an asterisk "".*

B. Opium derivatives. Unless specifically excepted or unless listed in another schedule, any of the following opium derivatives, its salts, isomers, and salts of isomers whenever the existence of such salts, isomers, and salts of isomers is possible within the specific chemical designation:

*(1) Acetorphine
*(2) Acetyldihydrocodeine
*(3) Benzylmorphine
*(4) Codeine methylbromide
*(5) Codeine-N-Oxide
*(6) Cyprenorphine
*(7) Desomorphine
*(8) Dihydromorphine
*(9) Drotebanol
*(10) Etorphine, except hydrochloride salt
*(11) Heroin
*(12) Hydromorphinol
*(13) Methyldesorphine
*(14) Methylhydromorphine
*(15) Morphine methylbromide
*(16) Morphine methylsulfonate
*(17) Morphine-N-Oxide
*(18) Myrophine
*(19) Nicocodeine
*(20) Nicomorphine
*(21) Normorphine
*(22) Pholcodine
*(23) Thebacon

Editor's note: See section 966(B)(1) and section 979(B) for references to Schedule I substances preceded by an asterisk "".*

C. Hallucinogenic substances. Unless specifically excepted or unless listed in another schedule, any material, compound, mixture, or preparation, which contains any quantity of the following hallucinogenic substances, or which contains any of their salts, isomers, or salts of isomers, whenever the existence of such salts, isomers, or salts of isomers is possible within the specific chemical designation, for purposes of this Paragraph only, the term "isomer" includes the optical, position, and geometric isomers:

(1) 3, 4-methylenedioxy amphetamine.
(2) 5-methoxy-3, 4-methylenedioxy amphetamine.
(3) 3, 4, 5-trimethoxy amphetamine.
(4) Bufotenine.
(5) Diethyltryptamine.
(6) Dimethyltryptamine.
(7) 4-methyl-2, 5-dimethoxyamphetamine.
(8) Ibogaine.
(9) Lysergic acid diethylamide.
(10) Mescaline.
(11) Peyote.
(12) N-ethyl-3-piperidyl benzilate.
(13) N-methyl-3-piperidyl benzilate.

(14) Psilocybin.
(15) Psilocyn.
(16) 2, 5-dimethoxyamphetamine.
(17) 4-bromo-2, 5-dimethoxyamphetamine.
(18) 4-methoxyamphetamine.
(19) 1-[1-(2-Thienyl) Cyclohexyl] Piperidine.
(20) Cyclohexamine.
(21) 1-Piperidinocyclohexanecarbonitrile.
(22) Marijuana, tetrahydrocannabinols, or chemical derivatives of tetrahydrocannabinols.
(23) 3,4-methylenedioxymethamphetamine (MDMA).
(24) N-ethyl 3,4-methylenedioxyamphetamine.
(25) N-Hydroxy Methylenedioxyamphetamine.

D. Depressants. Unless specifically excepted or unless listed in another schedule, any material, compound, mixture, or preparation which contains any quantity of the following substances having a depressant effect on the central nervous system, including its salts, isomers, and salts of isomers whenever the existence of such salts, isomers, and salts of isomers is possible within the specific chemical designation:

(1) Mecloqualone
(2) Phencyclidine

E. Stimulants. Unless specifically excepted or unless listed in another schedule, any material, compound, mixture, or preparation which contains any quantity of the following substances having a stimulant effect on the central nervous system including its salts, isomers, and salts of isomers whenever the existence of such salts, isomers, and salts of isomers is possible within the specific chemical designation:

(1) N-ethylamphetamine
(2) Fenethylline

SCHEDULE II

A. Substances of vegetable origin or chemical synthesis. Unless specifically excepted or unless listed in another schedule, any of the following substances whether produced directly or indirectly by extraction from substances of vegetable origin, or independently by means of chemical synthesis, or by a combination of extraction and chemical synthesis:

(1) Opinion and opiate, and any salt, compound, isomer, derivative, or preparation of opium or opiate, excluding naloxone, and its salts, and excluding naltrexone and its salts but including the following:
(a) Raw opium
(b) Opium extracts
(c) Opium fluid extracts
(d) Powdered opium
(e) Granulated opium
(f) Tincture of opium
(g) Apomorphine
(h) Codeine
(i) Ethylmorphine
(j) Etorphine hydrochloride
(k) Hydrocodone
(*l*) Hydromorphone—also commonly known as Dilaudid
(m) Metopone
(n) Morphine
(*o*) Oxycodone
(p) Oxymorphone
(q) Thebaine
(2) Any salt, compound, isomer, derivative, or preparation thereof which is chemically equivalent or identical with any of the substances referred to in Paragraph (1), except that these substances shall not include the isoquinoline alkaloids of opium.
(3) Opium poppy and poppy straw.

(4) Coca leaves, cocaine, ecgonine and any salt, isomer, salt of an isomer, compound, derivative, or preparation of coca leaves, cocaine or ecgonine and any salt, isomer, salt of an isomer, compound, derivative, or preparation thereof which is chemically equivalent or identical with any of these substances, except that the substances shall not include decocainized coca leaves or extraction of coca leaves, which extractions do not contain cocaine or ecgonine.

(5) Synthetic Dronabinol [delta-9-(trans) tetrahydrocannabinol] in sesame oil and encapsulated in a soft gelatin capsule in a U.S. Food and Drug Administration approved product.

B. Opiates. Unless specifically excepted or unless in another schedule any of the following opiates, including its isomers, esters, ethers, salts, and salts of isomers, esters and ethers whenever the existence of such isomers, esters and ethers, and salts is possible within the specific chemical designation:

(1) Alphaprodine
(2) Anileridine
(3) Bezitramide
(4) Dihydrocodeine
(5) Diphenoxylate
(6) Fentanyl
(7) Isomethadone
(8) Levomethorphan
(9) Levorphanol
(10) Metazocine
(11) Methadone
(12) Methadone-Intermediate, 4-cyano-2-dimethylamino-4, 4-diphenyl butane
(13) Moramide-Intermediate, 2-methyl-3-morpholino-1, 1-diphenylpropane-carboxylic acid
(14) Pethidine
(15) Pethidine-Intermediate-A, 4-cyano-1-methyl-4-phenyl-piperidine
(16) Pethidine-Intermediate-B, ethyl-4-phenylpiperidine-4-carboxylate
(17) Pethidine-Intermediate-C, 1-methyl-4-phenylpiperidine-4-carboxylic acid
(18) Phenazocine
(19) Piminodine
(20) Racemethorphan
(21) Racemorphan
(22) Sufentanil

C. Stimulants. Unless specifically excepted or unless listed in another schedule, any material, compound, mixture, or preparation which contains any quantity of the following substances having a stimulant effect on the central nervous system, including their salts, isomers and salts of isomers, whenever the existence of such salts, isomers, and salts of isomers is possible within the specific chemical designation:

(1) Amphetamine
(2) Methamphetamine
(3) Phenmetrazine
(4) Methylphenidate
(5) Phendimetrazine
(6) Phentermine

D. Depressants. Unless specifically excepted or unless listed in another schedule, any material, compound, mixture, or preparation which contains any quantity of the following substances having a depressant effect on the central nervous system, including their salts, isomers, or salts of isomers whenever the existence of such salts, isomers, or salts of isomers is possible within the specific chemical designation:

(1) Methaqualone
(2) Gamma Hydroxybutyric Acid

E. Immediate precursors. Unless specifically excepted or unless listed in another schedule, any material, compound, mixture, or preparation which contains any quantity of the following substances, including their salts, isomers, and salts of isomers, whenever the existence of such salts, isomers, and salts of isomers is possible within the specific chemical designation:

(1) Immediate precursors to methamphetamine: (a) phenylacetone and methylamine or (b) hydriodic acid, and ephedrine or pseudoephedrine, if possessed together with intent to manufacture methamphetamine.

(2) Immediate precursors to phencyclidine and 1-piperidino-cyclohexane-carbonitrile (PCC):

(a) 1-phenylcyclohexylamine;

(b) Piperidine and cyclohexanone, if possessed together, or a combination product thereof, with intent to manufacture phencyclidine.

(3) Immediate precursors to phenylacetone: phenylacetic acid and acetic anhydride, if possessed together with intent to manufacture phenylacetone.

For purposes of this Subsection, possession of immediate precursors sufficient for the manufacture of methylamine, phenylacetone, piperidine, or cyclohexanone shall be deemed to be possession of such a derivative substance.

F. *(Repealed.)*

SCHEDULE III

A. Stimulants. Unless specifically excepted or unless listed in another schedule, any material, compound, mixture, or preparation which contains any quantity of the following substances having a stimulant effect on the central nervous system, including their salts, isomers, or salts of isomers whenever the existence of such salts, isomers, or salts of isomers is within the specific chemical designation:

(1) Benzphetamine
(2) Chlorphentermine
(3) Clortermine

B. Depressants. Unless specifically excepted or unless listed in another schedule, any material, compound, mixture, or preparation which contains any quantity of the following substances having a depressant effect on the central nervous system:

(1) Any substance which contains any quantity of a derivative of barbituric acid, or any salt of a derivative of barbituric acid, but not including butalbital when in combination with at least three hundred twenty-five milligrams of acetaminophen per dosage unit.
(2) Chlorexadol
(3) Glutethimide
(4) Lysergic Acid
(5) Lysergic acid amide
(6) Methyprylon
(7) Sulfondiethylmethane
(8) Sulfonethylmethane
(9) Ketamine hydrochloride

C. Nalorphine

D. Limited narcotic drugs. Unless specifically excepted or unless listed in another schedule, any material, compound, mixture, or preparation containing limited quantities of any of the following narcotic drugs, or any salts thereof:

(1) Not more than 1.8 grams of codeine per 100 milliliters or not more than 90 milligrams per dosage unit with an equal or greater quantity of an isoquinoline alkaloid of opium.

(2) Not more than 1.8 grams of codeine per 100 milliliters or not more than 90 milligrams per dosage unit, with one or more active, nonnarcotic ingredients in recognized therapeutic amounts.

(3) Not more than 300 milligrams of dihydrocodeinone per 100 milliliters or not more than 15 milligrams per dosage unit, with a fourfold or greater quantity of an isoquinoline alkaloid of opium.

(4) Not more than 300 milligrams of dihydrocodeinone per 100 milliliters or not more than 15 milligrams per dosage unit, with one or more active, nonnarcotic ingredients in recognized therapeutic amounts.

(5) Not more than 1.8 grams of dihydrocodeine per 100 milliliters or not more than 90 milligrams per dosage unit, with one or more active, nonnarcotic ingredients in recognized therapeutic amounts.

(6) Not more than 300 milligrams of ethylmorphine per 100 milliliters or not more than 15 milligrams per dosage unit, with one or more active, nonnarcotic ingredients in recognized therapeutic amounts.

(7) Not more than 500 milligrams of opium per 100 milliliters or per 100 grams, or not more than 25 milligrams per dosage unit, with one or more active, nonnarcotic ingredients in recognized therapeutic amounts.

(8) Not more than 50 milligrams of morphine per 100 milliliters or per 100 grams, with one or more active nonnarcotic ingredients in recognized therapeutic amounts.

E. Anabolic steroids and muscle building substances. Unless specifically excepted or unless listed in another schedule, any material compound, mixture, or preparation, which contains any quantity of anabolic steroids including but not limited to the following substances, or material which contains any of their salts, esters, isomers, or salts of isomers whenever the existence of such salts, esters, isomers, or salts of isomers is possible within the specific chemical designation. The term anabolic steroid means any drug or hormonal substance, chemically and pharmacologically related to testosterone other than estrogens, progestins, and corticosteroids that promote muscle growth and include the following:

(1) Boldenone
(2) Clostebol (Chlorotestosterone)
(3) Dehydrochlormethyltestosterone
(4) Drostanolone
(5) Ethylestrenol
(6) Fluoxymesterone
(7) Formebolone
(8) Mesterolone
(9) Methandienone (Methandrostenolone)
(10) Methandriol
(11) Methenolone
(12) Methlytestosterone
(13) Mibolerone
(14) Nandrolone
(15) Norethandrolone
(16) Oxandrolone
(17) Oxymesterone
(18) Oxymetholone
(19) Stanolone (Dihydrotestosterone)
(20) Stanozolol
(21) Testolactone
(22) Testosterone
(23) Trenbolone

F. (1) Except as provided in Paragraph (2) of this Subsection, the term anabolic steroid does not include a substance listed in Subsection E above but which is expressly intended for administration to livestock or other nonhuman species and which has been approved by the secretary of health and hospitals for such administration.

(2) If any person prescribes, dispenses, or distributes such steroid for human use, such person shall be considered to have prescribed, dispensed, or distributed an anabolic steroid within the meaning of Subsection E above.

(3) A physician, dentist, or veterinarian shall not prescribe, dispense, deliver, or administer an anabolic steroid for human use or cause an anabolic steroid to be administered under his direction or supervision for human use except for a valid medical purpose and when required by demonstrable generally accepted medical indications. Bodybuilding, muscle enhancement, or increasing muscle bulk or strength through the use of an anabolic steroid by a person who is in good health is hereby declared not a valid medical purpose.

SCHEDULE IV

Unless specifically excepted or unless listed in another schedule, any material, compound, mixture, or preparation which contains any quantity of the following substances, including their salts, isomers, or salts of isomers whenever the existence of such salts, isomers, or salts of isomers is possible within the specific chemical designation:

(1) Barbital
(2) Chloral Betaine
(3) Chloral Hydrate
(4) Ethchlorvynol
(5) Ethinamate
(6) Methohexital
(7) Meprobamate
(8) Methylphenobarbital
(9) Paraldehyde
(10) Petrichloral
(11) Phenobarbital
(12) Fenfluramine
(13) Diethylpropion
(14) Mebutamate
(15) Clonazepam
(16) Chlordiazepoxide but not including chlordiazepoxide hydrochloride in combination with clindinium bromide, or chlordiazepoxide and water soluble esterfied estrogens.
(17) Diazepam
(18) Flurazepam
(19) Chlorazepate
(20) Oxazepam
(21) Nitrazepam
(22) Desmethyldiazepam
(23) Dextropropoxyphene
(24) Prazepam
(25) Pemoline
(26) Halazepam
(27) Lorazepam
(28) Alprazolam
(29) Mazindol
(30) Pentazocine
(31) Temazepam
(32) Triazolam
(33) Nubaine
(34) Flunitrazepam

SCHEDULE V

A. Narcotic drugs containing non-narcotic active medicinal ingredients. Any compound, mixture, or preparation containing any of the following limited quantities of narcotic drugs or salts thereof, which shall include one or more nonnarcotic active medicinal ingredients in sufficient proportion to confer upon the compound, mixture, or preparation valuable medicinal qualities other than those possessed by the narcotic drug alone:

(1) Not more than 200 milligrams of codeine per 100 milliliters or per 100 grams.
(2) Not more than 100 milligrams of dihydrocodeine per 100 milliliters or per 100 grams.
(3) Not more than 100 milligrams of ethylmorphine per 100 milliliters or per 100 grams.
(4) Not more than 2.5 milligrams of diphenoxylate and not less than 25 micrograms of atropine sulphate per dosage unit.
(5) Not more than 100 milligrams of opium per 100 milliliters or per 100 grams.

B. Narcotic drugs. Unless specifically excepted or unless listed in another schedule, any material, compound, mixture, or preparation containing any of the following narcotic drugs and their salts, as set forth below:

(1)* Buprenorphine.

(Chgd. by Acts 1991 No. 513, §§1, 3, No. 842, §1; Acts 1993 No. 156, §§1, 2, No. 288, §1, No. 616, §1; Acts 1997 No. 398, §1; Acts 1998 First Ex. Sess. No. 129, §1, eff. 6/16/98.)

**No paragraph B(2) has been enacted.*

§964.1. Treatment of controlled analogues.

A controlled substance analogue shall be treated, for the purposes of any state law and to the extent intended for human consumption, as a controlled dangerous substance in Schedule I of R.S. 40:964. *(Added by Acts 1994 Third Ex. Sess. No. 34, §2, eff. 8/27/94.)*

§965. Secretary of health and hospitals; authority to except.

A. The secretary of health and hospitals may by regulation except any material, compound, mixture, or preparation containing any depressant or stimulant substance listed in Subsection A, B, C, or D of Schedule III or in Schedule IV or V from the application of all or any part of this Part if the material, compound, mixture, or preparation contains one or more active medicinal ingredients not having a depressant or stimulant effect on the central nervous system, provided that such ingredients are included therein in such combinations, quantity, proportion, or concentration as to vitiate the potential for abuse of the substances which do have a depressant or stimulant effect on the central nervous system.

B. The secretary of health and hospitals, may, by regulation, exempt any compound, mixture, or preparation containing any anabolic steroids substances listed in Schedule III(E) of R.S. 40:964 from the application of all or any part of this Part if, because of its concentration, preparation, mixture, or delivery system, it has no significant potential for abuse.

(Chgd. by Acts 1991 No. 513, §1, eff. 9/6/91.)

§966. Penalty for distribution or possession with intent to distribute narcotic drugs listed in Schedule I; possession of marijuana.

A. MANUFACTURE; DISTRIBUTION. Except as authorized by this part, it shall be unlawful for any person knowingly or intentionally:

(1) To produce, manufacture, distribute or dispense or possess with intent to produce, manufacture, distribute, or dispense, a controlled dangerous substance classified in Schedule I;

(2) To create, distribute, or possess with intent to distribute, a counterfeit controlled dangerous substance classified in Schedule I.

B. PENALTIES FOR VIOLATION OF SUBSECTION A. Any person who violates Subsection A with respect to:

(1) A substance classified in Schedule I which is a narcotic drug (all substances in Schedule I preceded by an asterisk "*"), upon conviction shall be sentenced to life imprisonment at hard labor without benefit of probation, or suspension of sentence, and may, in addition, be required to pay a fine of not more than fifty thousand dollars.

(2) Any other controlled dangerous substance classified in Schedule I, shall upon conviction be sentenced to a term of imprisonment at hard labor for not less than five years nor more than thirty years and pay a fine of not more than fifty thousand dollars.

C. POSSESSION. It is unlawful for any person knowingly or intentionally to possess a controlled dangerous substance classified in Schedule I unless such substance was obtained directly, or pursuant to a valid prescription or order, from a practitioner or as provided in R.S. 40:978, while acting in the course of his professional practice, or except as otherwise authorized by this Part. Any person who violates this Subsection with respect to:

(1) A substance classified in Schedule I which is a narcotic drug (all substances in Schedule I preceded by an asterisk), shall be imprisoned at hard labor for not less than four years nor more than ten years without benefit of probation or suspension of sentence and may, in addition, be required to pay a fine of not more than five thousand dollars.

(2) Phencyclidine, shall be sentenced to imprisonment with or without hard labor for not less than five nor more than twenty years and may be sentenced to pay a fine of not more than five thousand dollars, or both.

(3) Any other controlled dangerous substance classified in Schedule I, shall be imprisoned at hard labor for not more than ten years, and may in addition, be required to pay a fine of not more than five thousand dollars.

D. POSSESSION OF MARIJUANA. (1) Except as provided in Subsections E and F hereof, on a first conviction for violation of Subsection C of this Section with regard to marijuana, tetrahydrocannabinol or chemical derivatives thereof, the offender shall be fined not more than five hundred dollars, imprisoned in the parish jail for not more than six months, or both.

(2) Except as provided in Subsections E and F hereof, on a second conviction for violation of Subsection C of this Section with regard to marijuana, tetrahydrocannabinol or chemical derivatives thereof, the offender shall be fined not more than two thousand dollars, imprisoned with or without hard labor for not more than five years, or both.

(3) Except as provided in Subsections E and F hereof, on a third or subsequent conviction for violation of Subsection C of this Section with regard to marijuana, tetrahydrocannabinol or chemical derivatives thereof, the offender shall be sentenced to imprisonment with or without hard labor for not more than twenty years.

(4) A conviction for the violation of any other statute or ordinance with the same elements as R.S. 40:966(C) prohibiting the possession of marijuana, tetrahydrocannabinol or chemical derivatives thereof, shall be considered as a prior conviction for the purposes of this Subsection relating to penalties for second, third, or subsequent offenders.

E. Except as otherwise authorized in this Part:

(1) Any person who knowingly or intentionally possesses sixty pounds or more, but less than two thousand pounds of marijuana, tetrahydrocannabinol, or chemical derivatives thereof, shall be sentenced to serve a term of imprisonment at hard labor of not less than ten years, nor more than sixty years, and to pay a fine of not less than fifty thousand dollars nor more than one hundred thousand dollars.

(2) Any person who knowingly or intentionally possesses two thousand pounds or more, but less than ten thousand pounds of marijuana, tetrahydrocannabinol, or chemical derivatives thereof, shall be sentenced to serve a term of imprisonment at hard labor of not less than twenty years nor more than eighty years, and to pay a fine of not less than one hundred thousand dollars nor more than four hundred thousand dollars.

(3) Any person who knowingly or intentionally possesses ten thousand pounds or more of marijuana, tetrahydrocannabinol, or chemical derivatives thereof, shall be sentenced to serve a term of imprisonment at hard labor of not less than fifty years, nor more than eighty years, and to pay a fine of not less than four hundred thousand dollars nor more than one million dollars.

F. With respect to any person to whom the provisions of Subsection E are applicable, the adjudication of guilt or imposition of sentence shall not be suspended, deferred, or withheld, nor shall such person be eligible for probation or parole prior to serving the minimum sentences provided by Subsection E.

(Chgd. by Acts 1991 No. 99, §1; Acts 1993 No. 969, §1; Acts 1994 Third Ex. Sess. No. 77, §1, eff. 8/27/94.)

§967. Prohibited acts—Schedule II, penalties.

A. MANUFACTURE; DISTRIBUTION. Except as authorized by this part or by Part VII-B of Chapter 5 of Title 40 of the Louisiana Revised Statutes of 1950, it shall be unlawful for any person knowingly or intentionally:

(1) To produce, manufacture, distribute, or dispense or possess with intent to produce, manufacture, distribute, or dispense, a controlled dangerous substance classified in Schedule II;

(2) To create, distribute, or possess with intent to distribute, a counterfeit controlled dangerous substance classified in Schedule II.

B. PENALTIES FOR VIOLATION OF SUBSECTION A. Except as provided in Subsection F, any person who violates Subsection A with respect to:

(1) A substance classified in Schedule II which is a narcotic drug, except cocaine or cocaine base or a mixture or substance containing cocaine or its analogues as provided in Schedule II(A)(4) of R.S. 40:964, or which is an amphetamine or methamphetamine, shall be sentenced to a term of imprisonment at hard labor for not less than five years nor more than thirty years; and may, in addition, be sentenced to pay a fine of not more than fifty thousand dollars.

(2) Pentazocine, shall be sentenced to imprisonment at hard labor for not less than seven years nor more than ten years, without benefit of parole, probation, or suspension of sentence; and, in addition, may be sentenced to pay a fine of not more than fifteen thousand dollars.

(3) Production or manufacturing of amphetamine or methamphetamine shall be sentenced to imprisonment at hard labor for not less than forty years nor more than ninety-nine years, without benefit of parole, probation, or suspension of sentence, and in addition may be sentenced to pay a fine of not more than five hundred thousand dollars.

(4) (a) Production or manufacturing of cocaine or cocaine base or a mixture or substance containing cocaine or its analogues as provided in Schedule II(A)(4) of R.S. 40:964 shall be sentenced to life imprisonment at hard labor without benefit of parole, probation, or suspension of sentence and may be fined not more than five hundred thousand dollars.

(b) Distribution, dispensing, or possession with intent to produce, manufacture, distribute or dispense cocaine or cocaine base or a mixture or substance containing cocaine or its analogues as provided in Schedule II(A)(4) of R.S. 40:964 shall be sentenced to a term of imprisonment at hard labor for not less than five years nor more than thirty years, with the first five years of said sentence being without benefit of parole, probation, or suspension of sentence; and may, in addition, be sentenced to pay a fine of not more than fifty thousand dollars.

(5) Any other controlled dangerous substance classified in Schedule II except pentazocine, amphetamine, methamphetamine, or cocaine shall be sentenced to a term of imprisonment at hard labor for not more than ten years, and in addition may be sentenced to pay a fine of not more than fifteen thousand dollars.

C. POSSESSION. It is unlawful for any person knowingly or intentionally to possess a controlled dangerous substance as classified in Schedule II unless such substance was obtained directly or pursuant to a valid prescription or order from a practitioner, as provided in R.S. 40:978 while acting in the course of his professional practice, or except as otherwise authorized in this Part.

(1) Any person who violates this Subsection with respect to pentazocine shall be imprisoned with or without hard labor for not less than two years and for not more than five years and, in addition, may be sentenced to pay a fine of not more than five thousand dollars.

(2) Any person who violates this Subsection as to any other controlled dangerous substance shall be imprisoned with or without hard labor for not more than five years and, in addition, may be sentenced to pay a fine of not more than five thousand dollars.

D, E. *(Repealed.)*

F. OTHER PENALTIES FOR POSSESSION. (1) Except as otherwise authorized in this Part:

(a) Any person who knowingly or intentionally possesses twenty-eight grams or more, but less than two hundred grams, of cocaine or of a mixture or substance containing a detectable amount of cocaine or of its analogues as provided in Schedule II(A)(4) of R.S. 40:964, shall be sentenced to serve a term of imprisonment at hard labor of not less than ten years, nor more than sixty years, and to pay a fine of not less than fifty thousand dollars, nor more than one hundred fifty thousand dollars.

(b) Any person who knowingly or intentionally possesses two hundred grams or more, but less than four hundred grams, of cocaine or of a mixture or substance containing a detectable amount of cocaine or of its analogues as provided in Schedule II(A)(4) of R.S. 40:964, shall be sentenced to serve a term of imprisonment at hard labor of not less than twenty years, nor more than sixty years, and to pay a fine of not less than one hundred thousand dollars, nor more than three hundred fifty thousand dollars.

(c) Any person who knowingly or intentionally possesses four hundred grams or more of cocaine or of a mixture or substance containing a detectable amount of cocaine or of its analogues as provided in Schedule II(A)(4) of R.S. 40:964, shall be sentenced to serve a term of imprisonment at hard labor of not less than thirty years, nor more than sixty years and to pay a fine of not less than two hundred fifty thousand dollars, nor more than six hundred thousand dollars.

(2) Except as otherwise authorized in this Part:

(a) Any person who knowingly or intentionally possesses twenty-eight grams or more, but less than two hundred grams, of amphetamine or methamphetamine or of a mixture or substance containing a detectable amount of amphetamine or methamphetamine or any of their analogues as provided in Schedule II(C) of R.S. 40:964, shall be sentenced to serve a term of imprisonment at hard labor of not less than ten years, nor more than sixty years, and to pay a fine of not less than fifty thousand dollars, nor more than one hundred fifty thousand dollars.

(b) Any person who knowingly or intentionally possesses two hundred grams or more, but less than four hundred grams, of amphetamine or methamphetamine or of a mixture or substance containing a detectable amount of amphetamine or methamphetamine or any of their analogues as provided in Schedule II(C) of R.S. 40:964, shall be sentenced to serve a term of imprisonment at hard labor of not less than twenty years, nor more than sixty years, and to pay a fine of not less than one hundred thousand dollars, nor more than three hundred fifty thousand dollars.

(c) Any person who knowingly or intentionally possesses four hundred grams or more of amphetamine or methamphetamine or of a mixture or substance containing a detectable amount of amphetamine or methamphetamine or any of its analogues as provided in Schedule II(C) of R.S. 40:964, shall be sentenced to serve a term of imprisonment at hard labor of not less than thirty years, nor more than sixty years and to pay a fine of not less than two hundred fifty thousand dollars, nor more than six hundred thousand dollars.

G. With respect to any person to whom the provisions of Subsection F are applicable, the adjudication of guilt or imposition of sentence shall not be suspended, deferred, or withheld, nor shall such person be eligible for probation or parole prior to serving the minimum sentences provided by Subsection F.

(Chgd. by Acts 1990 No. 542, §1; Acts 1991 No. 100, §1, No. 513, §2; Acts 1991 1st Ex. Sess. No. 2, §1; Acts 1993 No. 969, §1; Acts 1994 Third Ex. Sess. No. 77, §1; Acts 1997 No. 1284, §1, eff. 8/15/97.)

§968. Prohibited acts—Schedule III; penalties.

A. MANUFACTURE; DISTRIBUTION. Except as authorized by this part, it shall be unlawful for any person knowingly or intentionally:

(1) To produce, manufacture, distribute or dispense or possess with intent to produce, manufacture, distribute, or dispense, a controlled dangerous substance classified in Schedule III;

(2) To create, distribute, or possess with intent to distribute, a counterfeit controlled dangerous substance classified in Schedule III.

B. PENALTIES FOR VIOLATION OF SUBSECTION A. Any person who violates Subsection A with respect to any controlled dangerous substance classified in Schedule III shall be sentenced to a term of imprisonment at hard labor for not more than ten years; and, in addition, may be sentenced to pay a fine of not more than fifteen thousand dollars.

C. POSSESSION. It is unlawful for any person knowingly or intentionally to possess a controlled dangerous substance classified in Schedule III unless such substance was obtained directly or pursuant to a valid prescription or order from a practitioner, or as provided in R.S. 40:978 or R.S. 40:1239, while acting in the course of his professional practice or except as otherwise authorized by this Part. Any person who violates this Subsection shall be imprisoned with or without hard labor for not more than five years and, in addition, may be required to pay a fine of not more than five thousand dollars.

(Chgd. by Acts 1991 No. 513, §2, eff. 9/6/91.)

§969. Prohibited acts—Schedule IV; penalties.

A. MANUFACTURE; DISTRIBUTION. Except as authorized by this part, it shall be unlawful for any person knowingly or intentionally:

(1) To produce, manufacture, distribute or dispense or possess with intent to produce, manufacture, distribute, or dispense, a controlled dangerous substance classified in Schedule IV;

(2) To create, distribute, or possess with intent to distribute, a counterfeit controlled dangerous substance classified in Schedule IV.

B. PENALTIES FOR VIOLATION OF SUBSECTION A. Any person who violates Subsection A with respect to:

(1) Flunitrazepam shall be sentenced to a term of imprisonment at hard labor for not less than five years nor more than thirty years and pay a fine of not more than fifty thousand dollars.

(2) Any other controlled dangerous substance classified in Schedule IV, except flunitrazepam, shall be sentenced to a term of imprisonment at hard labor for not more than ten years; and in addition, may be sentenced to pay a fine of not more than fifteen thousand dollars.

C. POSSESSION. It is unlawful for any person unknowingly* or intentionally to possess a controlled dangerous substance classified in Schedule IV unless such substance was obtained directly or pursuant to a valid prescription or order from a practitioner, or as provided in R.S. 40:978, while acting in the course of his professional practice or except as otherwise authorized by this Part.

**So in original.*

(1) Any person who violates this Subsection with respect to flunitrazepam shall be imprisoned at hard labor for not more than ten years, and may in addition, be required to pay a fine of not more than five thousand dollars.

(2) Any person who violates this Subsection as to any other controlled dangerous substance shall be imprisoned with or without hard labor for not more than five years and, in addition, may be required to pay a fine of not more than five thousand dollars.

D. Whoever, with the intent to commit a crime of violence as defined in R.S. 14:2(13)(j) against an individual, violates Subsection A of this Section by administering a controlled dangerous substance to a person who is unaware that the controlled dangerous substance has been or is being administered to him, shall be sentenced to a term of imprisonment at hard labor for not less than five years nor more than forty years and may be fined not more than one hundred thousand dollars.

(Chgd. by Acts 1997 No. 1191, §1, eff. 8/15/97.)

§970. Prohibited acts—Schedule V; penalties.

A. MANUFACTURE; DISTRIBUTION. Except as authorized by this part, it shall be unlawful for any person knowingly or intentionally:

(1) To produce, manufacture, distribute or dispense or possess with intent to produce, manufacture, distribute, or dispense, a controlled dangerous substance classified in Schedule V;

(2) To create, distribute, or possess with intent to distribute, a counterfeit controlled dangerous substance classified in Schedule V.

B. PENALTIES FOR VIOLATION OF SUBSECTION A. Any person who violates Subsection A with respect to any controlled dangerous substance classified in Schedule V shall be sentenced to a term of imprisonment at hard labor for not more than five years; and, in addition, may be sentenced to pay a fine of not more than five thousand dollars.

C. POSSESSION. It is unlawful for any person unknowingly* or intentionally to possess a controlled dangerous substance classified in Schedule V unless such substance was obtained directly or pursuant to a valid prescription or order from a practitioner, or as provided in R.S. 40:978, while acting in the course of his professional practice or except as otherwise authorized by this part. Any person who violates this section shall be imprisoned with or without hard labor for not more than five years; and in addition, may be required to pay a fine of not more than five thousand dollars.

**So in original.*

§971. Prohibited acts; all schedules.

A. (1) It shall be unlawful for any person:

(a) Who is subject to the requirements of this part to distribute or dispense a controlled dangerous substance in violation of this part; or

(b) Who is a licensee to manufacture, distribute, or dispense a controlled dangerous substance to another licensee or other authorized person not authorized by his license; or

(c) To omit, remove, alter, or obliterate a symbol required by the Uniform Controlled Dangerous Substances Law; or

(d) To refuse or fail to make, keep, or furnish any record, notification, order form, statement, invoice or information required under this part; or

(e) To refuse entry into any premise for inspection as authorized by this part; or

(f) To keep or maintain any store, shop, warehouse, dwelling house, building, vehicle, boat, aircraft, or any place whatever, which is frequented by persons using controlled dangerous substances in violation of this part for the purpose of using such substances, or which is used for the keeping or selling of the same in violation of this part.

(2) Any person who violates this subsection shall be fined not more than fifteen thousand dollars. Such proceeding shall be independent, and not in lieu of, other proceedings under this part or any other law of this state. If the violation is prosecuted by a bill of information or an indictment which alleges that the violation was committed knowingly or intentionally, such

person, upon conviction, shall be imprisoned for not more than six months; and, in addition, may be sentenced to pay a fine of not more than five hundred dollars.

B. (1) It shall be unlawful for any person knowingly or intentionally:

(a) To use in the course of the manufacture or distribution of a controlled dangerous substance a license number which is fictitious, revoked, suspended or issued to another person; or

(b) To acquire or obtain possession of a controlled dangerous substance by misrepresentation, fraud, forgery, deception or subterfuge; or

(c) To furnish false or fraudulent material, information in any application, report or other document required to be kept by this part.

(d) To make, distribute, or possess any punch, die, plate, stone, or other thing designed to print, imprint, or reproduce the trademark, trade name, or other identifying mark, imprint, or device of another of* any likeness of any of the foregoing upon any drug or container or labeling thereof so as to render such drug a counterfeit controlled dangerous substance; or

**So in original. Probably should be "or".*

(e) To alter any controlled dangerous substance obtained by prescription without prior approval of the department; or

(f) To alter any prescription for a controlled dangerous substance; provided that this shall not apply to the person issuing the original prescription or the pharmacist pursuant to instructions from the physician; or

(g) To obtain or attempt to obtain a prescription or prescription blank form from a doctor, dentist, or veterinarian for a controlled dangerous substance and/or legend drug by fraud, theft, misrepresentation, deception or subterfuge.

(h) To possess a prescription for a controlled dangerous substance and/or legend drugs without the express consent of the party for whom such prescription was written. For the purposes hereof a legend drug is any drug or drug product bearing on the label of the manufacturer or distributor as required by the Federal Food and Drug Administration the statement "Caution: Federal law prohibits dispensing without prescription."

(2) Any person who violates this subsection shall be imprisoned, with or without hard labor, for not more than five years; and, in addition may be sentenced to pay a fine of not more than five thousand dollars.

C. (1) It shall be unlawful for a person, including a physician, dentist, podiatrist, or veterinarian, to prescribe, dispense, or administer legally controlled substances beyond his respective prescribing authority or for a purpose other than accepted medical treatment of a disease, condition, or illness.

(2) It shall be unlawful for a pharmacist to dispense legally controlled substances beyond his dispensing authority.

(3) Any person who violates this Subsection shall be subject to the penalties as established for the controlled dangerous substance and the particular criminal act committed in R.S. 40:966 through 967.

§971.1. Prohibited acts; false representation.

A. It shall be unlawful for any person to produce, manufacture, distribute, or dispense any substance which is represented to be a controlled dangerous substance and which is an imitation controlled dangerous substance, or any controlled dangerous substance which is a counterfeit controlled dangerous substance.

B. The provisions of this Section shall not apply to a law enforcement officer acting in the course and scope of his employment or to a medical practitioner, pharmacist, or other person authorized to dispense or administer controlled dangerous substances pursuant to Part X of Chapter 4 of Title 40 of the Revised Statutes of 1950.

C. Any person who violates the provisions of this Section shall be imprisoned with or without hard labor for not more than five years, and in addition may be fined not more than five thousand dollars.

(Chgd. by Acts 1993 No. 154, §1; Acts 1994 Third Ex. Sess. No. 34, §1, eff. 8/27/94.)

§972. Rules and regulations and fees.

The department is authorized to promulgate rules and regulations and to charge reasonable fees relating to the registration and control of the manufacture, distribution and dispensing of controlled dangerous substances within this state. The fees collected by the department for registration and licensing shall be retained by said department except in the case of those fees collectible from pharmacies registered and licensed by the state board of pharmacy, which latter fees shall be collected and retained by said board of pharmacy. All said fees collected in accordance with the provisions of this Chapter shall be deposited in a separate fund and used for the administration and enforcement of this Part, and for education and research as provided by R.S. 40:992, together with any supplemental funds appropriated by the legislature or federal funds or grants received.

§973. Licensing requirements.

A. Every person who manufactures, distributes, or dispenses any controlled dangerous substance within this state or who proposes to engage in the manufacture, distribution, or dispensing of any controlled dangerous substance within this state, shall obtain a license issued by the department in accordance with the rules and regulations promulgated by it.

B. The following persons shall not be required to obtain a license and may lawfully possess controlled dangerous substances under the provisions of this part:

(1) An agent, or an employee thereof, of any registered manufacturer, distributor, or dispenser of any controlled dangerous substance if such agent is acting in the usual course of his business or employment;

(2) A common or contract carrier or warehouseman, or an employee thereof, whose possession of any controlled dangerous substance is in the usual course of his business or employment;

(3) An ultimate user or person in possession of any controlled dangerous substance pursuant to a lawful order of a practitioner.

C. The department may, by regulation, waive the requirement for licensing of certain manufacturers, distributors, or dispensers if it finds it consistent with the public health and safety.

D. A separate license shall be required at each principal place of business or professional practice where the applicant manufactures, distributes, or dispenses controlled dangerous substances.

E. The department is authorized to inspect the establishment of a licensee or applicant for licensing in accordance with the rules and regulations promulgated by it.

F. (1) Any person licensed by the department to manufacture, distribute, or dispense controlled dangerous substances shall submit to the Department of Health and Human Resources data on transactions involving the disbursement of Schedule II controlled dangerous substances to licensed Louisiana registrants except as provided in R.S. 40:972 and R.S. 40:988(B).

(2) The department is authorized to promulgate rules and regulations necessary to implement the provisions of this Subsection including but not limited to the scope of such data, the form in which it is to be submitted, and the time requirements for such submission.

G. (1) The department shall disseminate its findings concerning possible violations to the respective boards for action in correcting violations on the part of licensed Louisiana registrants.

(2) (a) Such supervisory board shall receive the findings of the department concerning possible violations and shall disseminate such findings to the respective boards for action in correcting violations on the part of licensed Louisiana registrants.

(b) All expenses for the operation of the supervisory board shall be borne by the licensing boards which make up said supervisory boards.

§974. Licensing.

A. The department shall license an applicant to manufacture or distribute controlled dangerous substances included in Schedules I through V of R.S. 40:964 at such fees as it shall determine to be reasonable, unless it determines that the issuance of such license is inconsistent with the public interest. In determining the public interest, the following factors shall be considered:

(1) Maintenance of effective controls against diversion of particular controlled dangerous substances and any Schedule I or II substance compounded therefrom into other than legitimate medical, scientific, or industrial channels.

(2) Compliance with applicable state and local laws.

(3) Prior conviction record of applicant under federal or state laws relating to the manufacture, distribution, or dispensing of such substances.

(4) Past experience in the manufacture of controlled dangerous substances, and the existence in the establishment of effective controls against diversion.

(5) Such other factors as are relevant to and consistent with the public health and safety.

B. Licenses granted under Subsection A of this Section shall not entitle a licensee to manufacture and distribute controlled dangerous substances in Schedule I or II other than those specified in the license.

C. A license application by a practitioner who wishes to conduct research with a controlled substance shall be referred to the department. Licensing by the department for the purpose of bona fide research with a controlled dangerous substance by a practitioner deemed qualified by the department may be denied only on a ground specified in R.S. 40:975(A) or on the ground that the applicant's past practice or proposed procedures furnish grounds for the belief that the applicant will abuse or unlawfully transfer such substances from legitimate medical or scientific use.

§975. Denial, revocation, suspension, or termination of license.

A. A license pursuant to R.S. 40:974 to manufacturer, distribute, or dispense a controlled dangerous substance may be suspended or revoked by the department upon a finding that the applicant or licensee:

(1) Has materially falsified any application filed pursuant to this Part or required by this Part, or

(2) Has been convicted of a felony under this Part or any law of the United States, or of any state, relating to any substances defined herein as a controlled dangerous substance, or any felony under any other law of the United States or of any state within five years of the date of the issuance of the license, or

(3) Has had his federal license suspended or revoked by competent federal authority and is no longer authorized by federal law to engage in the manufacturing, distribution, or dispensing of controlled dangerous substances.

(4) Has manufactured, distributed or dispensed controlled dangerous substances in violation of any provision of this Part or any other state or federal laws pertaining to the manufacture, distribution or dispensing of controlled dangerous substances.

(5) Has repeatedly failed to submit to the Department of Health and Human Resources data on transactions involving the disbursement of Schedule II controlled dangerous substances to licensed Louisiana registrants as required by R.S. 40:973(F) and by rules promulgated pursuant thereto.

B. The department may limit revocation or suspension of a license to the particular controlled dangerous substance with respect to which grounds for revocation or suspension exist.

C. Before taking action pursuant to this Section or pursuant to a denial of license under R.S. 40:974, the department shall serve upon the applicant or licensee an order to show cause why the license should not be denied, revoked, or suspended. The order to show cause shall contain a statement of the basis thereof and shall call upon the applicant or licensee to appear before the department at a time and place stated in the order, but in no event less than thirty days after the date of receipt of the order. Proceedings to deny, revoke, or suspend shall be conducted pursuant to this Section in accordance with R.S. 49:951 et seq. Such proceedings shall be independent of, and not in lieu of, criminal prosecution or other proceedings under this Part or any law of the state.

D. The department may, in its discretion, suspend any license simultaneously with the institution of proceedings under this Section in cases where it finds that there is an imminent danger to the public health or safety. Such suspension shall continue in effect until the conclusion of such proceedings, including judicial review thereof, unless sooner withdrawn by the department or dissolved by a court of competent jurisdiction.

E. In the event the department suspends or revokes a license granted under R.S. 40:974, all controlled dangerous substances owned or possessed by the licensee pursuant to such license at the time of suspension or the effective date of the revocation order, as the case may be, may in the discretion of the department, be placed under seal. No disposition may be made of substances under seal until the time for taking an appeal has elapsed or until all appeals have been concluded unless a court, upon application therefor, orders the sale of perishable substances and the deposit of the proceeds of the sale with the court. Upon a revocation order becoming final, all such controlled dangerous substances shall be forfeited to the state.

F. The Bureau of Narcotics and Dangerous Drugs shall promptly be notified of all orders suspending or revoking license and all forfeitures of controlled dangerous substances.

G. (1) A license pursuant to R.S. 40:974 to manufacture, distribute, or dispense a controlled dangerous substance shall be terminated by the department if the licensee has failed to timely renew the license and submit the applicable fee, and thirty days have elapsed since the date of expiration.

(2) Any appeal from the provisions of this Subsection shall be governed by the Administrative Procedure Act*.

R.S. 49:950 et seq.

(3) The Department of Health and Hospitals shall promulgate rules, regulations, and standards to implement the provisions of this Subsection. The rules, regulations, and standards shall be promulgated in accordance with the Administrative Procedure Act.

(Chgd. by Acts 1997 No. 62, §1, eff. 8/15/97.)

§976. Records of licensees.

Each licensee manufacturing, distributing or dispensing controlled dangerous substances in Schedules I, II, III, IV or V shall make a complete and accurate record of all stocks of such dangerous substances on hand. Thereafter, complete and accurate records of all such dangerous substances shall be maintained until the next inventory is made for the next two-year period as required by this Section. At each two-year period after July 29, 1970, at the time of his regular physical inventory, each licensee manufacturing, distributing, or dispensing controlled dangerous substances shall prepare an inventory of each dangerous substance in his possession. Records and inventories shall contain such information as shall be provided by rules and regulations promulgated by the department. This Section shall not apply to practitioners who lawfully prescribe or administer, but do not otherwise dispense, controlled dangerous substances listed in Schedules II, III, IV or V of this Part.

§976.1. Chemical precursor, recordkeeping requirements.

A. A manufacturer, wholesaler, retailer, or other person who sells, transfers, or otherwise furnishes any of the following precursor substances shall make an accurate and legible record of the transaction and maintain the record for a period of at least five years after the date of the transaction:

(1) Methylamine.
(2) Ethylamine.
(3) D-lysergic acid.
(4) Ergotamine tartrate.
(5) Diethyl malonate.
(6) Malonic acid.
(7) Ethyl malonate.
(8) Barbituric acid.
(9) Piperidine.
(10) N-acetylanthranilic acid.
(11) Pyrrolidine.
(12) Phenylacetic acid.
(13) Anthranilic acid.
(14) Morpholine.
(15) Ephedrine.
(16) Pseudoephedrine or norpseudoephedrine.
(17) Phenylpropanolamine.
(18) Acetic anhydride
(19) Anthranilic acid, its esters and its salts
(20) Benzaldehyde
(21) Benzyl chloride
(22) Benzyl cyanide
(23) Ergonovine and its salts
(24) Hydriodic acid
(25) Isosafrole
(26) 3,4-methylenedioxyphenyl-2-propanone
(27) N-ethylephedrine, it salts, optical isomers, and salts of optical isomers
(28) N-ethylpseudoephedrine, its salts, optical isomers, and salts of optical isomers
(29) N-methylephedrine, its salts, optical isomers, and salts of optical isomers
(30) N-methylpseudoephedrine, its salts, optical isomers, and salts of optical isomers
(31) Nitroethane
(32) 1-phenyl-1-chloro-2-methylaminopropanone (chlorephedrine; chloro-pseudoephedrine), their salts, optical isomers, and salts of optical isomers

(33) Phenyl-2-propanone
(34) Piperonal
(35) Propionic anhydride
(36) Safrole
(37) Thionylchloride

B. (1) Before selling, transferring, or otherwise furnishing to a person in this state a precursor substance designated in Subsection A of this Section, a manufacturer, wholesaler, retailer, or other person shall obtain from the buyer or recipient not representing a business the following information:

(a) The recipient's driver's license number or other personal identification certificate number, date of birth, and residential or mailing address, other than post office box number. This information shall be obtained from a driver's license or other personal identification card issued by the Department of Public Safety and Corrections that contains a photograph of the recipient.

(b) The year, state, and number of the motor vehicle license of the motor vehicle owned or operated by the recipient.

(c) A complete description of how the substance is to be used.

(d) The recipient's signature.

(2) Before selling, transferring, or otherwise furnishing to a person in this state a precursor substance designated in Subsection A of this Section, a manufacturer, wholesaler, retailer, or other person shall obtain from the buyer or recipient representing a business the following information:

(a) A letter of authorization from the business that includes the business license or comptroller tax identification number, address, area code, and telephone number and a complete description of how the substance is to be used.

(b) The signature of the recipient.

(3) For any recipient, the seller, manufacturer, or retailer shall sign as a witness to the signature and identification of the recipient.

C. Except as provided by Subsection E of this Section, a manufacturer, wholesaler, retailer, or other person who sells, transfers, or otherwise furnishes to a person in this state a precursor substance designated in Subsection A of this Section shall, at least twenty-one days before the delivery of the substance, submit a report of the transaction on a form obtained from the deputy secretary that includes the information required by Subsection B of this Section.

D. The deputy secretary shall supply to a manufacturer, wholesaler, retailer, or other person who sells, transfers, or otherwise furnishes a precursor substance subject to Subsection A of this Section a form for the submission of:

(1) The report required by Subsection C of this Section.

(2) The name and measured amount of the precursor substance, delivered.

(3) Any other information required by the deputy secretary.

E. The deputy secretary shall require a manufacturer, wholesaler, retailer, or other person to submit a comprehensive monthly report instead of the report required by Subsection C of this Section if the deputy secretary determines either of the following:

(1) That there is a pattern of regular supply and purchase of the substance between the furnisher and the recipient.

(2) That the recipient has established a record of utilization of the substance solely for a lawful purpose.

F. A manufacturer, wholesaler, retailer, or other person who received from a source outside this state a substance designated in Subsection A of this Section or who discovers a loss or theft of a substance designated in Subsection A of this Section shall submit a report of the transaction to the deputy secretary in accordance with rules adopted pursuant to administrative procedure, and shall include in the report any difference between the amount of the substance actually received and the amount of the substance shipped according to the shipping statement or invoice or the amount of the loss or theft.

G. A report required under Subsection F of this Section shall:

(1) Be made not later than the third day after the date that the manufacturer, wholesaler, retailer, or other person learns of the discrepancy, loss, or theft.

(2) If the discrepancy, loss, or theft occurred during a shipment of the substance, include the name of the common carrier or person who transported the substance and the date that the substance was shipped.

H. The provisions of this Section shall not apply to the sale or transfer of a nonnarcotic product that includes a precursor substance listed in Subsection A, if the product may otherwise be sold lawfully with a prescription or over the counter without a prescription under the Federal Food, Drug, and Cosmetic Act (21 U.S.C. Sec. 301, et seq.) or a rule adopted thereunder.

I. Any person who violates the provisions of this Section shall be imprisoned with or without hard labor for not more than one year, and in addition may be fined not more than one thousand dollars.

(Chgd. by Acts 1993 No. 994, §1, eff. 8/15/93.)

§977. Order forms.

Controlled dangerous substances in Schedules I and II shall be distributed only pursuant to an order form. Compliance with the regulations of the department respecting order forms shall be deemed compliance with this Section.

§978. Prescriptions.

A. Except when dispensed or administered directly by a medical practitioner or administered by a person authorized to administer by such practitioner, other than a pharmacist, to an ultimate user, no controlled dangerous substance included in Schedule II, which is a prescription drug as determined under the Louisiana Revised Statutes, of 1950, may be dispensed or administered without the written prescription of a practitioner, except that in emergency situations, as prescribed by the department by regulation, such drug may be dispensed or administered upon oral prescription reduced promptly to writing and filed by the pharmacist. Prescriptions shall be retained in conformity with the requirements of R.S. 40:976. No prescription for a Schedule II substance may be refilled.

B. Except when dispensed or administered directly by a practitioner or administered by a person authorized to administer by such practitioner, other than a pharmacist, to an ultimate user, no controlled dangerous substance included in Schedule III and IV which is a prescription drug as determined under the Louisiana Revised Statutes may be dispensed or administered without a written or oral prescription. Such prescription may not be filled or refilled more than six months after the date thereof or refilled more than five times after the date of the prescription, unless renewed by the practitioner.

C. No controlled dangerous substance included in Schedule V may be distributed, administered or dispensed other than for a medical purpose by prescription of a licensed practitioner or as otherwise permitted by the provisions of this Part. However, nothing contained in this Subsection shall prohibit a practitioner from delegating the authority to administer controlled dangerous substances in Schedule V to a person authorized by such practitioner.

§979. Attempt and conspiracy.

A. Except as otherwise provided herein, any person who attempts or conspires to commit any offense denounced and or made unlawful by the provisions of this Part shall, upon conviction, be fined or imprisoned in the same manner as for the offense planned or attempted, but such fine or imprisonment shall not exceed one-half of the punishment prescribed for the offense, the commission of which was the object of the attempt or conspiracy.

B. Any person who attempts or conspires to distribute or possess with intent to distribute any substance classified in Schedule I, as provided for in R.S. 40:963 and R.S. 40:964, which is a narcotic drug (all substances in Schedule I preceded by an asterisk "*") shall, upon conviction, be imprisoned at hard labor for not less than eight nor more than fifty years without benefit of parole, probation or suspension of sentence and may, in addition, be required to pay a fine of not more than ten thousand dollars.

§980. Additional penalties.

Any penalty imposed for violation of this part shall be in addition to, and not in lieu of, any civil or administrative penalty or sanction authorized by law.

§981. Distribution to persons under age eighteen.

A. Persons over twenty-five to persons under eighteen. Any person who is at least twenty-five years of age, or more, who violates R.S. 40:966 or R.S. 40:967 by distributing a substance, listed in Schedules I or II, which is a narcotic drug, to a person under eighteen years of age, shall, upon conviction, be punished by life imprisonment at hard labor.

B. Any person who is at least eighteen years of age who violates R.S 40:966 or R.S. 40:967 by distributing a substance listed in Schedules I or II which is a narcotic drug to a person under eighteen years of age who is at least three years his junior shall, upon conviction, be punished by a term of imprisonment of up to twice that authorized by R.S. 40:966 or R.S. 40:967 or by payment of not more than twice the fine authorized by R.S. 40:966 or R.S. 40:967, or both.

C. Any person who is at least eighteen years of age who violates R.S. 40:966—R.S. 40:970 by distributing any other controlled dangerous substance listed in Schedules I, II, III, IV and V to a person under eighteen years of age who is at least three years his junior shall, upon conviction, be punished by a term of imprisonment up to twice that authorized by R.S. 40:966—R.S. 40:970 or by payment of not more than twice the fine authorized by R.S. 40:966—R.S. 40:970, or both.

§981.1. Distribution to a student.

Any person who violates any provision of R.S. 40:966 through R.S. 40:970 by distributing any controlled dangerous substance listed in Schedules I, II, III, IV, and V to any student enrolled in any public or private elementary, secondary, vocational-technical training, special, or post-secondary school or institution in Louisiana shall, upon conviction, be punished by a term of imprisonment of not more than twice that authorized by the applicable provisions of R.S. 40:966 through R.S. 40:970 or by payment of not more than twice the fine authorized by the applicable provisions of R.S. 40:966 through R.S. 40:970, or both.

§981.2. Soliciting minors to distribute controlled dangerous substances.

A. No person eighteen years of age or older shall solicit, procure, or counsel any person under eighteen years of age to distribute or attempt to distribute, in violation of any provision of R.S. 40:966 through R.S. 40:970, any controlled dangerous substance listed in Schedules I, II, III, IV, or V, or to distribute or attempt to distribute, in violation of R.S. 40:989, a chemical substance commonly known as "rush".

B. Except as provided in Subsection C of this Section, any person who violates the provisions of this Section shall upon conviction be punished by a term of imprisonment of not more than twice that authorized by the applicable provision of R.S. 40:966 through 970, or by a fine of not more than twice that authorized by such applicable provision, or both.

C. Any person eighteen years of age or older who violates the provisions of this Section by soliciting, procuring, or counseling a person under eighteen years of age to distribute or to attempt to distribute cocaine in violation of R.S. 40:967(A) shall be sentenced to a term of imprisonment at hard labor for not less than twenty years nor more than twice that authorized by R.S. 40:967(B)(1), without benefit of probation, parole, or suspension of sentence. *(Chgd. by Acts 1991 No. 837, §1, eff. 9/6/91.)*

§981.3. Violation of Controlled Dangerous Substances Law.

A. (1) Any person who violates a felony provision of R.S. 40:966 through R.S. 40:970 of the Uniform Controlled Dangerous Substances Law while on any property used for school purposes by any school, within one thousand feet of any such property, or while on a school bus, shall, upon conviction, be punished in accordance with Subsection E.

(2) Any person who violates a felony provision of R.S. 40:966(A), 967(A), 968(A), 969(A), or 970(A) while on property used as a drug treatment facility or within one thousand feet of any such property, when included within an area marked as a drug free zone pursuant to R.S. 40:1058.10 shall, upon conviction, be punished in accordance with Subsection E.

(3)(a) Any person who violates a felony provision of R.S. 40:966 through R.S. 40:970 of the Uniform Controlled Dangerous Substances Law while on any religious building property or within one thousand feet of any such property, if the area is posted as a drug-free zone, shall, upon conviction, be punished in accordance with Subsection E.

(b) In order for the provisions of this Section to apply to religious buildings, the building must be posted as a drug-free zone as provided herein. The design and posting of the signs shall be at the discretion of the entity that owns or has authority over the religious building. In order to post the area as a drug-free zone, the signs shall be located in a visible manner on or near each religious building indicating that such area is a drug-free zone, that such zone extends for a distance of one thousand feet, and that a felony violation of the Uniform Controlled Dangerous Substances Law will subject the offender to severe penalties under law.

B. Lack of knowledge that the prohibited act occurred on or within one thousand feet of school or drug treatment facility property shall not be a defense.

C. For purposes of this Section:

(1) "School" means any public or private elementary, secondary, vocational-technical school, or any public or private college or university in Louisiana.

(2) "School property" means all property used for school purposes, including but not limited to school playgrounds, as well as any building or area owned by the state or by a political subdivision and used or operated as a playground or recreational facility and all parks and recreational areas administered by the office of state parks.

(3) "Drug treatment facility" means all property used for diagnostic, treatment, and rehabilitative services to patients and their families with problems related to alcohol, drug, or substance abuse.

(4) "Religious building property" means property on which is located any church, synagogue, mosque, or other building, structure, or place used for religious worship or other religious purpose.

D. A violation of this Section within one thousand feet of school property, a drug treatment facility, or religious building property shall not include an act which occurs entirely within a private residence wherein no person seventeen years of age or under was present.

E. (1) On a first conviction, whoever violates a provision of this Section shall be punished by the imposition of the maximum fine and not less than one-half nor more than the maximum term of imprisonment authorized by the applicable provisions of R.S 40:966 through R.S. 40:970, with the minimum mandatory term of imprisonment being served without benefit of parole, probation, or suspension of sentence, provided in no case shall the term of imprisonment be less than the minimum term provided in R.S. 40:966 through R.S. 40:970.

(2) On a second or subsequent conviction, whoever violates a provision of this Section shall be punished by the imposition of the maximum fine and maximum term of imprisonment authorized by the applicable provisions of R.S. 40:966 through R.S 40:970, without benefit of parole, probation, or suspension of sentence. An offense shall be considered a second or subsequent offense, if, prior to the commission of such offense, the offender had at any time been convicted of any felony violation of this state, the United States, any other state, or any foreign country, relating to an act prohibited by the Uniform Controlled Dangerous Substances Law.

(Chgd. by Acts 1990 No. 293, §2, No. 1027, §2; Acts 1994 Third Ex. Sess. No. 46, §1; Acts 1997 No. 355, §1, eff. 6/20/97.)

§981.4. Drug-traffic loitering.

A. Drug-traffic loitering is the remaining in a public place in a manner and under circumstances manifesting the purpose to engage in unlawful conduct in violation of R.S. 40:966 through 995 or R.S. 40:1031 through 1036.

B. Whoever commits the crime of drug-traffic loitering shall be fined not less than one hundred dollars nor more than one thousand dollars or imprisoned for not more than six months, or sentenced to community service not to exceed one hundred twenty hours, or any combination of or all three.

C. For the purpose of this Section, the following words have the following meanings:

(1) "Drug paraphernalia" means and includes the items enumerated and described in R.S. 40:1031.

(2) "Illegal drug activity" means unlawful conduct which violates any provision of this Part or the equivalent federal statute or ordinance of any political subdivision of this state.

(3) "Known drug trafficker" means any person who has, within the knowledge of the arresting police officer, been convicted of, or pled guilty or nolo contendere to, within the last two years in any court, any illegal drug activity.

(4) "Public place" means any area generally visible to public view and includes but is not limited to streets, sidewalks, bridges, alleys, plazas, parks, driveways, parking lots, transit stations, shelters, automobiles, and buildings, including those which serve food or drink or provide entertainment, and the doorways and entrances to buildings or dwellings and the grounds enclosing them.

D. Among the circumstances which may be considered in determining whether the person is manifesting a purpose to engage in unlawful drug-related activity are that the person is:

(1) Seen by the officer to be in possession of drug paraphernalia.

(2) A known drug trafficker.

(3) Behaving in such a manner as to raise a reasonable suspicion that he is about to engage in or is engaging in unlawful drug-related activity and such activity includes any of the following actions:

(a) Acting as a "lookout".

(b) Being physically identified by an officer as a member of a criminal street gang or association, which has as its purpose illegal drug activity.

(c) Transferring small objects or packages for currency in a furtive fashion.

(d) Being in an area known for unlawful drug use and drug trafficking.

(e) Being on or in premises that have been reported to law enforcement as a place suspected of unlawful drug activity.

(f) Being within six feet of any vehicle registered to a known unlawful drug user, possessor, or seller, or a person for whom there is an outstanding warrant for a crime involving drug-related activity.

(g) Repeatedly beckoning to, stopping, or attempting to stop passersby or engaging passersby in conversation.

(h) Repeatedly stopping or attempting to stop motor vehicle operators by hailing, waving of arms, or any bodily gesture.

(i) Circling an area in a motor vehicle and repeatedly beckoning to, contacting, or attempting to stop pedestrians.

(4) The subject of any court order, which directs the person to stay out of any specified area as a condition of release from custody, a condition of probation, parole, or other supervision or any court order, in a criminal or civil case involving illegal drug activity.

(5) Evicted as the result of his illegal drug activity and ordered to stay out of a specified area affected by drug-related activity.

(6) Taking flight upon the appearance of a police officer.

(7) Trying to conceal himself or any object within his possession that reasonably could be involved in an unlawful drug-related activity.

(Added by Acts 1995 No. 1067, §1, eff. 8/15/95.)

§982. Second or subsequent offenses.

A. Any person convicted of any offense under this part, if the offense is a second or subsequent offense, shall be sentenced to a term of imprisonment that is twice that otherwise authorized or to payment of a fine that is twice that otherwise authorized, or both. If the conviction is for an offense punishable under R.S. 40:966(B), R.S. 40:967(B), R.S 40:968(B) or R.S. 40:969(B), and if it is the offender's second or subsequent offense, the court may impose in addition to any term of imprisonment and fine, twice the special parole term otherwise authorized.

B. For purposes of this section, an offense shall be considered a second or subsequent offense, if, prior to the commission of such offense, the offender had at any time been convicted of any violation of this state, the United States, any other state of or any foreign country, relating to the unlawful use, possession, production, manufacturing, distribution, or dispensation of any narcotic drug, marijuana, depressant, stimulant, or hallucinogenic drugs.

§983. *(Repealed by Acts 1995 No. 1251, §2, eff. 8/15/95.)*

§984. Powers of enforcement personnel.

The secretary of the department and his designated employees may:

(1) Carry firearms.

(2) Execute and serve search warrants, arrest warrants, administrative inspection warrants, subpoenas, and summonses issued under the authority of this state.

(3) Make arrests without warrant for any offense under this Part on the same basis as provided in Code of Criminal Procedure Article 213.

(4) Make seizures of property pursuant to the authority granted under the provisions of this Part.

§985. Search warrants.

A search warrant relating to offenses involving controlled dangerous substances may be authorized to be served at any time of the day or night if the judge or magistrate issuing the warrant is satisfied that there is probable cause to believe that grounds exist for the warrant.

§986. Administrative inspections and warrants.

A. Issuance and execution of administrative inspection warrants shall be as follows:

(1) Any judge of a state court of record, or any state magistrate of any court of record may, within his jurisdiction and upon proper oath or affirmation after being satisfied there is probable cause to believe that legal grounds exist for the issuance of such warrant, issue warrants for the purpose of conducting administrative inspections authorized by this part or regulations thereunder, and may authorize seizure of property related to such inspections.

(2) A warrant shall issue only upon an affidavit of any law enforcement officer or employee designated in R.S. 40:984 having knowledge of the facts alleged, sworn to before a judge or magistrate of any court of record and establishing the grounds for issuing the warrant. If the judge or magistrate of any court of record is satisfied that grounds for the application exist or that there is probable cause to believe they exist, he shall issue a warrant identifying the area, premises, building, or conveyance to be inspected, the purpose of such inspection, and, where appropriate, the type of property to be inspected, if any. The warrant shall also identify the item or types of property to be seized, if any. The warrant shall be directed to a person authorized by R.S. 40:984 to execute it. The warrant shall state the grounds for its issuance and the name of the person or persons whose affidavit has been taken in support thereof. It shall command the person to whom it is directed to inspect the area, premises, building, or conveyance identified for the purposes specified, and, where appropriate, shall also direct the seizure of the property specified. The warrant shall direct that it be served during normal business hours. It shall designate the judge or magistrate of any court of record to whom it shall be returned.

(3) A warrant issued pursuant to this section must be executed and returned within ten days of its date. If property is seized pursuant to a warrant, the person executing the warrant shall give to the person from whom or from whose premises the property was taken a copy of the warrant and a receipt for the property taken. The return of the warrant shall be made promptly and shall be accompanied by a written inventory of any property taken. The inventory shall be made in the presence of the person executing the warrant and of the person from whose possession or premises the property was taken. The judge or magistrate of any court of record, upon request, shall deliver a copy of the inventory to the person from whom or from whose premises the property was taken and to the applicant for the warrant.

(4) The judge or magistrate of any court of record who has issued a warrant under this section shall attach to the warrant a copy of the return and all papers filed in connection therewith and shall file them with the clerk of the state court for the judicial district in which the inspection was made.

B. The secretary of the department is authorized to make administrative inspections of controlled premises in accordance with the following provisions:

(1) For purposes of this section only, "controlled premises" means:

(a) Places where persons licensed or exempted from licensing requirements under this part are required to keep records; and

(b) Places including factories, warehouses, establishments, and conveyances where persons licensed or exempted from licensing requirements under this part are permitted to possess, manufacture, compound, process, sell, deliver, or otherwise dispose of any controlled dangerous substance.

(2) When so authorized by an administrative inspection warrant issued pursuant to Subsection A of this Section a law enforcement officer or an employee as designated in R.S. 40:984 hereof, upon presenting the warrant and appropriate credentials to the owner, operator, or agent in charge, shall have the right to enter controlled premises for the purpose of conducting such an administrative inspection.

(3) When so authorized by an administrative inspection warrant, a law enforcement officer or an employee as designated in R.S. 40:984 hereof shall have the right:

(a) To inspect and copy records required by this Part to be kept.

(b) To inspect, within reasonable limits and in a reasonable manner, the controlled premises and all pertinent equipment, finished and unfinished material, containers and labeling found therein, and except as provided in Subsection B(5) of this Section, all other things therein including records, files, papers, processes, controls, and facilities subject to regulation and control by the provisions of this Part or by regulations promulgated by the secretary of the department.

(c) To inventory any stock of any controlled dangerous substance therein and obtain samples of any such substance.

(4) This section shall not be construed to prevent the inspection without a warrant of books and records pursuant to an administrative subpoena issued in accordance with R.S. 40:986 nor shall this section be construed to prevent entries and administrative inspections including seizures of property without a warrant:

(a) With the written consent of the owner, operator, or agent in charge of the controlled premises;

(b) In situations involving inspection of conveyances where there is probable cause to believe that the mobility of the conveyance makes it impracticable to obtain a warrant;

(5) Except when the owner, operator, or agent in charge of the controlled premises so consents in writing, no inspection authorized by this section shall extend to:

(a) Financial data;

(b) Sales data other than shipment data; or

(c) Pricing data.

§987. Injunctions.

Any district court of this state shall have jurisdiction in proceedings in accordance with the rules of such courts to enjoin violations of this part and in accordance with the Code of Civil Procedure and other laws of this state.

§988. Cooperative arrangements; inspections.

A. The department may cooperate with federal and other state agencies in discharging its responsibilities concerning dangerous substances. To this end, it is authorized to:

(1) Arrange for the exchange of information between governmental officials concerning the use and abuse of dangerous substances.

(2) Coordinate and cooperate in training programs on dangerous substance law enforcement at the local and state levels.

(3) Cooperate with the Federal Bureau of Narcotics and Dangerous Drugs by establishing a centralized unit which will receive, catalogue, file, and collect statistics, including records of drug dependent persons and other dangerous substance law offenders within the state, and make such information available for federal, state, and local law enforcement purposes.

(4) Conduct programs of eradication aimed at destroying wild or illicit growth of plant species from which controlled dangerous substances may be extracted.

B. Anything contained in any other provision of Part X of Chapter 4 of Title 40 of the Louisiana Revised Statutes of 1950 to the contrary notwithstanding, the inspections authorized or required by said law, insofar as pharmacists and pharmacies registered and licensed under the Louisiana Board of Pharmacy only are concerned, shall be conducted by the Louisiana Board of Pharmacy, through its duly authorized officers, members, inspectors, agents and representatives, insofar as pharmacists and pharmacies registered and licensed under the Louisiana Board of Pharmacy are concerned; and compliance with requirements involving security measures, inventories, records and reports required by said law and/or the regulations promulgated from time to time in connection therewith shall be administratively determined by the Louisiana Board of Pharmacy in cooperation with the department, insofar as pharmacists and pharmacies registered and licensed under the Louisiana Board of Pharmacy only are concerned.

C. Anything contained in any other provision of Part X of Chapter 4 of Title 40 of the Louisiana Revised Statutes of 1950 to the contrary notwithstanding, the inspections authorized or required by said law, insofar as persons licensed by the department including physicians, dentists, veterinarians, scientific investigators, hospitals, or other persons licensed, registered, or otherwise permitted to distribute, dispense, conduct research with respect to, or administer a controlled dangerous substance in the course of professional practice or research in this state, shall be conducted and furnished exclusively by the department, through its duly authorized officers, members, inspectors, agents and representatives, insofar as physicians, dentists, veterinarians, scientific investigators, hospitals, or other persons licensed, registered, or otherwise permitted to distribute, dispense, conduct research with respect to, or administer a controlled dangerous substance in the course of professional practice or research in this state registered and licensed under the department are concerned; and compliance with requirements involving security measures, inventories, records and reports required by said law and/or the regulations promulgated from time to time in connection therewith shall be administratively determined by the department.

§989. Dangerous chemical substances; butyl nitrite, nitrous oxide, and amyl nitrite; use and transference; penalties.

A. (1) It shall be unlawful for any person to inhale, ingest, use, or possess any compound, liquid, or chemical which contains butyl nitrite, isobutyl nitrite, secondary butyl nitrite, tertiary butyl nitrite, and mixtures containing butyl nitrite, isobutyl nitrite, secondary butyl nitrite, or tertiary butyl nitrite.

(2) It shall be unlawful for any person to inhale, ingest, use, or possess any compound, liquid, or chemical which contains nitrous oxide, commonly known as "laughing gas" and any amyl nitrite, commonly known as "poppers" or "snappers".

(3) The provisions hereof do not apply to the possession and use of these substances prescribed as part of the care or treatment of a disease, condition, or injury by a licensed medical or dental practitioner or to the use as part of a manufacturing process or industrial operation.

(4) The provisions of this Section do not apply to the possession, use, or sale of nitrous oxide as a propellant in food preparation for restaurant, food service, or houseware products.

B. It shall be unlawful for any person to possess, buy, sell, or otherwise transfer any substance specified in Subsection A of this Section for the purpose of inducing or aiding any other person to inhale or ingest such substance or otherwise violate the provisions of Subsection A.

C. Whoever violates the provisions of this Section shall be fined not more than five hundred dollars or imprisoned for not more than six months, or both.

D. Any person who violates any of the provisions of this Section may, in the discretion of the trial judge, be required to participate in an approved drug rehabilitation program, as a condition of probation.

(Chgd. by Acts 1992 No. 933, §1; Acts 1993 No. 500, §1, eff. 8/15/93.)

§990. Burden of proof; liabilities.

A. It shall not be necessary for the state to negate any exemption or exception set forth in this part in any complaint, information, indictment or other pleading or in any trial, hearing, or other proceeding under this part, and the burden of proof of any such exemption or exception shall be upon the person claiming its benefit.

B. In the absence of proof that a person is the duly authorized holder of an appropriate registration or order form issued under this part, he shall be presumed not to be the holder of such registration or form, and the burden of proof shall be upon him to rebut such presumption.

C. No liability shall be imposed by virtue of this part upon any duly authorized law enforcement officer, the president of the department of health, or his designated agents as provided in R.S. 40:984 engaged in the enforcement of any law or municipal ordinance relating to controlled dangerous substances, the regulation and control of which is herein provided for.

§991. *(Repealed.)*

§992. Education and research.

A. The department is authorized to carry out educational programs designed to prevent and deter misuse and abuse of controlled dangerous substances. In connection with such programs it is authorized to:

(1) Promote better recognition of the problems of misuse and abuse of controlled dangerous substances within the regulated industry and among interested groups and organizations.

(2) Assist the regulated industry and interested groups and organizations in contributing to the reduction of misuse and abuse of controlled dangerous substances.

(3) Consult with interested groups and organizations to aid them in solving administrative and organizational problems.

(4) Evaluate procedures, projects, techniques, and controls conducted or proposed as part of educational programs on misuse and abuse of controlled dangerous substances.

(5) Disseminate to the industry and the general public the results of research on misuse and abuse of controlled dangerous substances to promote a better public understanding of what problems exist and what can be done to combat them.

(6) Assist in the education and training of state and local law enforcement officials in their efforts to control misuse and abuse of controlled dangerous substances.

B. The department is authorized to encourage research on misuse and abuse of controlled dangerous substances. In connection with such research and in furtherance of the enforcement of this Part, it is authorized to:

(1) Establish methods to assess accurately the effects of controlled dangerous substances and to identify and characterize controlled dangerous substances with potential for abuse.

(2) Make studies and undertake programs of research to:

(a) Develop new or improved approaches, techniques, systems, equipment and devices to strengthen the enforcement of this Part.

(b) Determine patterns of misuse and abuse of controlled dangerous substances and the social effects thereof.

(c) Improve methods for preventing, predicting, understanding and dealing with the misuse and abuse of controlled dangerous substances.

(3) Enter into contracts with public agencies or institutions of higher education, for the purpose of conducting research, demonstrations, or special projects which bear directly on misuse and abuse of controlled dangerous substances.

C. The department may authorize persons engaged in research on the use and effects of dangerous substances to withhold the names and other identifying characteristics of persons who are the subjects of such research. Persons who obtain this authorization shall not be compelled, in any civil, criminal, administrative, legislative, or other proceeding to identify the subjects of research for which authorization was obtained.

D. The department may authorize the possession and distribution of controlled dangerous substances by persons engaged in research in accordance with rules promulgated by the department. Persons who obtained this authorization shall be exempt from state prosecution for possession and distribution of dangerous substances to the extent authorized by the department.

E. The department, with the concurrence and under the supervision and control of the chief law enforcement officer of the jurisdiction wherein the program is conducted, may authorize the possession and exhibition for educational purposes only of controlled dangerous substances by persons employed by local and state law enforcement agencies engaged in educational programs in accordance with rules promulgated by the department. Persons acting pursuant to this authorization shall be exempt from state and local prosecution for the possession and distribution of dangerous substances to the extent authorized by the department. The department shall coordinate and evaluate the training programs of the various law enforcement agencies to ensure compliance with the rules promulgated regulating the possession and exhibition of controlled dangerous substances for educational purposes.

§993. Pending proceedings.

A. Prosecutions, for any violation of law occurring prior to July 26, 1972, shall not be affected by this part or abated by reason thereof.

B. Civil seizures, forfeitures and injunctive proceedings commenced prior to July 26, 1972 shall not be affected by this part or abated by reason thereof.

C. All administrative proceedings pending before the department on July 26, 1972 shall be continued and brought to final determination in accordance with laws and regulations in effect prior to July 26, 1972. Such drugs placed under control prior to enactment of this Part, which are not listed within Schedules I through V, shall automatically be controlled and listed in the appropriate schedule.

D. The provisions of this part shall be applicable to violations of law, seizures and forfeiture, injunctive proceedings, administrative proceedings and investigations which occur following July 26, 1972.

§994. Continuation of regulations.

Any orders, rules, and regulations which have been promulgated under any law affected by this Part, and which are in effect on the day preceding enactment of this Section, shall continue in effect until modified, superseded or repealed by the secretary, Department of Health and Human Resources.

§995. Short title.

This part may be cited as the Uniform Controlled Dangerous Substances Law.

PART X-A. THERAPEUTIC USE OF MARIJUANA

(Added by Acts 1991 No. 874, §1, eff. 9/6/91.)
(Complete Part)

§1021. Prescription of marijuana for therapeutic use; rules and regulations; secretary of health and hospitals.

A. Notwithstanding any other provision of this Part, a physician licensed to practice medicine in this state and who is also registered to prescribe Schedule I substances with the Drug Enforcement Administration may prescribe marijuana, tetrahydrocannabinols, or a chemical derivative of tetrahydrocannabinols for therapeutic use by patients clinically diagnosed as suffering from glaucoma, symptoms resulting from the administration of chemotherapy cancer treatment, and spastic quadriplegia in accordance with rules and regulations promulgated by the secretary of health and hospitals and in accordance with FDA and DEA administrative guidelines for procurement of the controlled substance from the National Institute on Drug Abuse.

B. The secretary of health and hospitals, by January 1, 1992, shall promulgate rules and regulations, authorizing physicians licensed to practice in this state to prescribe marijuana for therapeutic use by patients as described in Subsection A of this Section.
(Added by Acts 1991 No. 874, §1, eff. 9/6/91.)

PART X-B. TRANSACTIONS IN DRUG RELATED OBJECTS PROHIBITED

(Complete Part)

§1031. Definitions.

A.* As used in this Part, unless the context clearly otherwise indicates, the term "drug paraphernalia" shall mean and include, but not be limited to:
**So in original. No subsection B has been enacted.*

(1) All equipment, products, and materials of any kind which are used, intended for use, or designed for use in planting, propagating, cultivating, growing, harvesting, manufacturing, compounding, converting, producing, processing, preparing, testing, analyzing, packaging, repackaging, storing, containing, concealing, injecting, ingesting, inhaling, or otherwise introducing into the human body a controlled substance in violation of the Uniform Controlled Dangerous Substances Law, as scheduled in R.S. 40:964.

(2) Kits used, intended for use, or designed for use in planting, propagating, cultivating, growing, or harvesting of any species of plant which is a controlled substance or from which a controlled substance can be derived.

(3) Kits used, intended for use, or designed for use in manufacturing, compounding, converting, producing, processing, or preparing controlled substances.

(4) Isomerization devices used, intended for use, or designed for use in increasing the potency of any species of plant which is a controlled substance.

(5) Testing equipment used, intended for use, or designed for use in identifying, or in analyzing the strength, effectiveness, or purity of controlled substances.

(6) Diluents and adulterants, such as quinine, hydrochloride, mannitol, mannite, dextrose, and lactose, used, intended for use, or designed for use in cutting controlled substances.

(7) Separation gins and sifters used, intended for use, or designed for use in removing twigs and seeds from, or in otherwise cleaning or refining, marijuana.

(8) Blenders, bowls, containers, spoons, and mixing devices used, intended for use, or designed for use in compounding controlled substances.

(9) Capsules, balloons, envelopes, and other containers used, intended for use, or designed for use in packaging small quantities of controlled substances.

(10) Containers and other objects used, intended for use, or designed for use in storing or concealing controlled substances.

(11) Hypodermic syringes, needles, and other objects used, intended for use, or designed for use in parenterally injecting controlled substances into the human body.

(12) Objects used, intended for use, or designed for use in ingesting, inhaling, or otherwise introducing marijuana, cocaine, hashish, or hashish oil into the human body, such as:

(a) Metal, wooden, acrylic, glass, stone, plastic, or ceramic pipes with or without screens, permanent screens, hashish heads, or punctured metal bowls.

(b) Water pipes.

(c) Carburetion tubes and devices.

(d) Smoking and carburetion masks.

(e) Roach clips, meaning objects used to hold burning material such as a marijuana cigarette, that has become too small or too short to be held in the hand.

(f) Miniature cocaine spoons, and cocaine vials.

(g) Chamber pipes.

(h) Carburetor pipes.

(i) Electric pipes.

(j) Air-driven pipes.

(k) Chillums.

(*l*) Bongs.

(m) Ice pipes or chillers.

§1032. Determination of drug paraphernalia.

In determining whether an object is drug paraphernalia, a court or other authority shall consider, in addition to all other legally relevant factors, the following:

(1) Statements by an owner or by anyone in control of the object concerning its use.

(2) The proximity of the object, in time and space, to a direct violation of the Uniform Controlled Dangerous Substances Law*.

**R.S. 40:961 et seq.*

(3) The proximity of the object to controlled substances.

(4) The existence of any residue of controlled substances on the object.

(5) Direct or circumstantial evidence of the intent of an owner, or of anyone in control of the object, to deliver it to persons whom he knows or should reasonably know intend to use the object to facilitate a violation of the Uniform Controlled Dangerous Substances Law; the innocence of an owner, or of anyone in control of the object, as to a direct violation of the Uniform Controlled Dangerous Substances Law shall not prevent a finding that the object is intended for use or designed for use as drug paraphernalia.

(6) Instructions, oral or written, provided with the object concerning its use.

(7) Descriptive materials accompanying the object which explain or depict its use.

(8) National and local advertising concerning its use.

(9) The manner in which the object is displayed for sale.

(10) Direct or circumstantial evidence of the ratio of sales of the object(s) to the total sales of the business enterprise.

(11) The existence and scope of legitimate use for the object in the community.

(12) Expert testimony concerning its use.

§1033. Prohibited acts.

A. It is unlawful for any person or corporation, knowing, or under circumstances where one reasonably should know, to sell, lend, rent, lease, give, exchange, or otherwise distribute to any person any drug paraphernalia.

B. It is unlawful for any person or corporation, knowing, or under circumstances where one reasonably should know, to display for sale or possess with the intent to distribute, any drug paraphernalia.

C. It is unlawful for any person to use, or to possess with intent to use, any drug paraphernalia, to plant, propagate, cultivate, grow, harvest, manufacture, compound, convert, produce, process, prepare, test, analyze, pack, repack, store, contain, conceal, inject, ingest, inhale, or otherwise introduce into the human body a controlled substance in violation of this Part.

D. *(Repealed.)*

(Chgd. by Acts 1990 No. 517, §§1, 2, eff. 7/18/90.)

§1033.1. Prohibited acts; unmarried persons under seventeen years of age.

A. It is unlawful for any person, corporation, or association to sell, lend, rent, lease, give, exchange, exhibit, display, or distribute to any unmarried person under the age of seventeen any drug paraphernalia.

B. The unlawful sale, loan, rent, lease, gift, exchange, exhibition, display, or distribution of drug paraphernalia to any unmarried person under the age of seventeen is the intentional sale, loan, rent, lease, gift, exchange, exhibition, display, or distribution of drug paraphernalia to any unmarried person under the age of seventeen years, at any newsstand, record store, tape store or any other commercial establishment which is open to persons under the age of seventeen years.

C. It shall be unlawful to invite or permit any unmarried person under the age of seventeen to be in any commercial establishment that exhibits or displays any item, material, work, or object of any kind that is defined as drug paraphernalia pursuant to this Part.

D. Lack of knowledge of age or marital status shall not constitute a defense, unless the defendant shows that he had reasonable cause to believe that the minor involved was either married or seventeen years of age or more and that the minor exhibited to the defendant a draft card, driver's license, birth certificate, or other official or apparently official document purporting to establish that such person was either married or seventeen years of age or more. *(Added by Acts 1990 No. 398, §1, eff. 7/18/90.)*

§1034. Exceptions; defenses.

A. Any provision of law to the contrary herein notwithstanding, the provisions of this Part shall not apply to the manufacture, sale, distribution, or advertisement of any product or object designed and sold primarily for scientific research, industrial, veterinary, or agricultural purposes, or for bona fide medical or clinical use.

B. It shall be an affirmative defense that the person to whom the drug related object or advertisement or notice was distributed had a prescription from a licensed medical practitioner or psychiatrist for marijuana or the controlled substance for which the object is primarily intended to be used. It is also an affirmative defense that the drug related object was designed or marketed as useful primarily for veterinary or agricultural purposes.

§1035. Penalties.

A. The first violation of or failure to comply with any provision of this Part shall subject the offender to a fine not in excess of five hundred dollars, or imprisonment of not more than six months, or both.

B. On second conviction, the offender shall be fined not more than one thousand dollars, or imprisoned for not more than one year, or both.

C. On third conviction, the offender shall be fined not more than five thousand dollars, or imprisoned, with or without hard labor, for not more than five years.

D. If the second or subsequent conviction is by any person licensed under the occupational license tax law, as provided in R.S. 47:341, et seq., or by such person's manager, agent, servant, or employee, then such person shall forfeit the right to any permit issued thereunder and such permit may be suspended or revoked.

§1036. Contraband; condemnation proceedings.

All instruments, devices, and objects which are seized after the effective date of this Section, on condemnation as being distributed or possessed in violation of this Part, may be destroyed by the authorities making the seizure, but only after compliance with the following procedure. Within ninety days after any seizure is made after the effective date of this Section, the district attorney shall institute condemnation proceedings in district court by petition, a copy of which shall be served upon the owner of the seized items, if known. If the owner is unknown, notice of the proceedings shall be published once a week for two weeks in the official journal of the parish. The petition shall allege that the seized items were distributed or possessed in violation of this Part. Fifteen days after the filing of the petition, judgment by default shall be entered by the court, and the court shall order the seized items to be destroyed. Otherwise, the case shall proceed as other civil cases in said court. If the prosecution proves, by a preponderance of the evidence, that the seized items were distributed or possessed in violation of the law, the court shall order the seized items to be destroyed.

PART X-C. ANIMAL EUTHANASIA WITH SODIUM PENTOBARBITAL

(Complete Part)

§1041. Purpose.

It is the purpose of this Part to establish a permit system to allow animal control facilities to acquire and administer sodium pentobarbital for the humane euthanasia of sick, homeless, and abandoned animals.

§1042. Permit.

No animal control agency or facility shall purchase, possess, or administer sodium pentobarbital to sick, homeless, injured, or unwanted pets or other domestic and wild animals for their humane euthanasia without the permit required by this Part.

§1043. Permit application.

Any duly incorporated humane society contracted to perform animal control services by a parish or municipality or any parish or municipal animal control agency may apply to the secretary of the Department of Health and Human Resources for a permit to purchase, possess, and administer sodium pentobarbital for the humane euthanasia of animals.

§1044. Permit issuance and conditions.

A. The secretary shall not issue a permit to purchase, possess, or administer sodium pentobarbital for the humane euthanasia of animals unless the following criteria have been met:

(1) The animal control agency or facility is a duly incorporated humane society contracted to perform animal control services by a parish or municipality or a parish or municipal animal control agency.

(2) The animal control agency has on staff a certified euthanasia technician, as provided in R.S. 37:1551 et seq.

(3) Any other criteria which may be established by the department pursuant to R.S. 40:1046.

B. The permit shall designate a sole responsible person for the duration of the permit to oversee the purchase, possession, and administration of sodium pentobarbital, which such person shall be a certified euthanasia technician.

§1045. Permit revocation or suspension; inspections.

A. The secretary may revoke or suspend any permit issued hereunder if it is determined that sodium pentobarbital is being used for any purpose other than humane animal euthanasia or that the permitted facility has failed to abide by the regulations promulgated by the secretary for the safe and efficient purchase, possession, or administration of sodium pentobarbital.

B. The department shall inspect any permitted animal control facility to determine compliance with this Chapter or any rules or regulations promulgated pursuant thereto.

§1046. Rules and regulations.

The department may promulgate any rules and regulations necessary to effectuate the purposes of this Chapter.

PART X-D. TRANSACTIONS INVOLVING PROCEEDS FROM CONTROLLED DANGEROUS SUBSTANCES ACTIVITY

(Complete Part)

§1049. Transactions involving proceeds from drug offenses.

A. It is unlawful for any person knowingly or intentionally to conduct a financial transaction involving proceeds known to be derived from a violation of R.S. 40:966 et seq. when the transaction is designed in whole or in part to conceal or disguise the nature, location, source, ownership, or the control of the proceeds known to be derived from such violation or to avoid a transaction reporting requirement under state or federal law.

B. It is unlawful for any person knowingly or intentionally to give, sell, transfer, trade, invest, conceal, transport, maintain an interest in, or otherwise make available anything of value known to be for the purpose of committing or furthering the commission of any violation of R.S. 40:966 et seq.

C. It is unlawful for any person knowingly or intentionally to direct, plan, organize, initiate, finance, manage, supervise, or facilitate the transportation or transfer of proceeds known to be derived from any violation of R.S. 40:966 et seq.

D. It is unlawful for any person to knowingly or intentionally receive or acquire proceeds derived from any violation of R.S. 40:966 et seq., or to knowingly or intentionally engage in any transaction involving proceeds from any such violations. The provisions of this Section shall not include any transaction between an individual and his attorney, that is necessary to preserve that individual's right to representation by counsel, as guaranteed by the Sixth amendment of the United States Constitution, and Article I Section 13 of the Constitution of Louisiana. However, this shall not affect the right of the state to seek and obtain forfeiture of any proceeds derived from a violation of R.S. 40:966 et seq., as provided by R.S. 40:2601 through 2622.

E. Any person who is convicted of violating this Section shall be imprisoned for not more than ten years, or fined not more than ten thousand dollars, or both.

PART XIII. SUBSTANCE ABUSE/ADDICTION TREATMENT FACILITIES

(Chgd. by Acts 1997 No. 1000, §1, eff. 8/15/97.)
(Selected Section)

§1058.10. Drug free zone; notice; signs.

A. A drug free zone is an area inclusive of any property used as a drug treatment facility or within one thousand feet of such property. For the purposes of this Section, "drug treatment facility" means all property used for the diagnostic, treatment, and rehabilitative services to patients and their families with problems related to alcohol, drug or substance abuse.

B. The local governing authority which has jurisdiction over zoning matters in which each drug free zone is located shall publish a map clearly indicating the boundaries of each drug free zone in accordance with the specifications in Subsection A. The drug free zone map shall be made an official public document and placed with the clerk of court for the parish or parishes in which the drug free zone is located.

C. (1) The secretary of the Department of Health and Hospitals shall develop a method by which to mark drug free zones, including the use of signs or other marking suitable to the situation. Signs or other markings shall be located in a visible manner on or near each drug treatment facility indicating that such area is a drug free zone, that such zone extends for a distance of one thousand feet, and that a felony violation of the Uniform Controlled Dangerous Substances Law* will subject the offender to severe penalties under law. The Department of Health and Hospitals shall assist each drug treatment facility with providing for the posting required in this Subsection.

**R.S. 40:961 et seq.*

(2) The Department of Public Safety and Corrections shall coordinate and provide rules for the establishment of toll free telephone numbers for use in submitting anonymous information regarding drug activity to local law enforcement agencies. Such telephone numbers shall be displayed on the drug free zone signs which shall be manufactured in correctional institutions subject to the regulations of the office of corrections in the Department of Public Safety and Corrections.

D. (1) It shall be unlawful for any person to cover, remove, deface, alter, or destroy any sign or other marking identifying a drug free zone as provided in this Section.

(2) Any violation of this Subsection shall be punishable by a fine of not more than one thousand dollars or by a jail sentence of not more than six months, or both.

(Added by Acts 1994 Third Ex. Sess. No. 46, §1, eff. 7/7/94.)

CHAPTER 5. MISCELLANEOUS HEALTH PROVISIONS
(Selected Sections)

PART I-A. MINOR'S CONSENT TO MEDICAL TREATMENT AND RELATED PROCEDURES

SUBPART A. MINOR'S CONSENT; MISCELLANEOUS PROVISIONS

SUBPART B. PREVENTIVE ALCOHOLISM AND ADDICTION COUNSELING AND TREATMENT FOR ALCOHOL OR DRUG ABUSE FOR MINOR CHILDREN

PART VII-B. ANABOLIC STEROID

PART I-A. MINOR'S CONSENT TO MEDICAL TREATMENT AND RELATED PROCEDURES
(Complete Part)

SUBPART A. MINOR'S CONSENT; MISCELLANEOUS PROVISIONS
(Chgd. by Acts 1994 Third Ex. Sess. No. 18, §2, eff. 7/6/94.)

§1095. Medical treatment.

A. Consent to the provision of medical or surgical care or services by a hospital or public clinic, or to the performance of medical or surgical care or services by a physician, licensed to practice medicine in this state, when executed by a minor who is or believes himself to be afflicted with an illness or disease, shall be valid and binding as if the minor had achieved his majority. Any such consent shall not be subject to a later disaffirmance by reason of his minority.

B. The consent of a spouse, parent, guardian or any other person standing in a fiduciary capacity to the minor shall not be necessary in order to authorize such hospital care or services or medical or surgical care or services to be provided by a physician licensed to practice medicine to such a minor.

C. Upon the advice and direction of a treating physician, or, in the case of a medical staff, any one of them, a physician or member of a medical staff may, but shall not be obligated to, inform the spouse, parent or guardian of any such minor as to the treatment given or needed, and such information may be given to, or withheld from the spouse, parent or guardian without the consent and over the express objection of the minor.

D. No hospital and no physician licensed to practice medicine in this state shall incur civil or criminal liability in connection with any examination, diagnosis and treatment authorized by this Section except for negligence.

§1096. Treatment for drug abuse.

A. Consent to the provision of medical or surgical care or services by a hospital or public clinic, or to the performance of medical or surgical care or services by a physician, licensed to practice medicine in this state, when executed by a minor who is or believes himself to be addicted to a narcotic or other drug, shall be valid and binding as if the minor had achieved his majority. Any such consent shall not be subject to a later disaffirmance by reason of his minority.

B. The consent of a spouse, parent, guardian or any other person standing in a fiduciary capacity to the minor shall not be necessary in order to authorize such hospital care or services or medical or surgical care or services to be provided by a physician licensed to practice medicine to such a minor.

C. Upon the advice and direction of a treating physician, or, in the case of a medical staff, any one of them, a physician or member of a medical staff may, but shall not be obligated to, inform the spouse, parent or guardian of any such minor as to the treatment given or needed, and such information may be given to, or withheld from the spouse, parent or guardian without the consent and over the express objection of the minor.

D. No hospital and no physician licensed to practice medicine in this state shall incur civil or criminal liability in connection with any examination, diagnosis and treatment authorized by this Section except for negligence.

§1097. Donation of blood.

Notwithstanding any other provision of the laws of the state of Louisiana, a minor who has reached the age of seventeen years may give consent to the donation of his or her blood and to the penetration of tissue necessary to accomplish such donation, but such minor shall not be compensated therefor. Such consent shall not be subject to deferments because of minority, and the consent of the parents or guardian of such a minor shall not be required in order to authorize such donation and penetration of tissue.

SUBPART B. PREVENTIVE ALCOHOLISM AND ADDICTION COUNSELING AND TREATMENT FOR ALCOHOL OR DRUG ABUSE FOR MINOR CHILDREN

(Added by Acts 1994 Third Ex. Sess. No. 18, §1, eff. 7/6/94.)

§1098.1. Statement of purpose.

It is the purpose of this Subpart to provide for accessibility to preventive alcoholism and addiction counseling or treatment by qualified professionals for minor children. *(Added by Acts 1994 Third Ex. Sess. No. 18, §1, eff. 7/6/94.)*

§1098.2. Definitions.

As used in this Subpart, the following terms shall have the following meanings:

(1) "Child" means an unmarried individual under the age of eighteen.

(2) "Facility" means an entity licensed by the Department of Health and Hospitals that provides a broad range of diagnostic, treatment, and rehabilitation services on both a scheduled and nonscheduled basis in an accessible residential or nonresidential setting by qualified professionals to persons and their families in need of counseling or treatment related to alcohol abuse and alcoholism, or drug abuse, or both.

(3) "Parent" shall be defined as provided in Ch.C. Article 116.

(4) "Preventive alcoholism and addiction counseling", hereinafter referred to as "preventive counseling", means services, general guidance and support, or service coordination, including but not limited to individual and group counseling, support services, and education about alcohol and other drugs and their effects, which are provided by a qualified professional to prevent the child from developing or suffering from alcoholism, alcohol or drug addiction, alcohol or drug abuse, or related physical, emotional, or mental health problems.

(5) "Qualified professional" shall include:

(a) A substance abuse counselor who has been certified and has worked in a licensed substance abuse treatment program for a minimum of two years.

(b) A board-certified social worker, psychologist licensed under R.S. 37:2351 et seq., or licensed physician.

(c) A registered nurse who has at least one year of experience in the treatment of alcoholism, addiction, or other alcohol and drug-related problems.

(d) A teacher or other educational professional who has completed training through the Substance Abuse Prevention Education Program of the state Department of Education.

(6) "School" means any public elementary or secondary school in the state of Louisiana operated by a city or parish school board or any nonpublic school approved by the State Board of Elementary and Secondary Education.

(7) "Treatment" means an active effort to accomplish an improvement in the mental condition or behavior of a child or to prevent deterioration in his condition or behavior as it relates to drug or alcohol abuse. Treatment includes but is not limited to hospitalization, partial hospitalization, outpatient services, examination, diagnosis, training, the use of pharmaceuticals, and other services as necessary to treat such abuse.
(Added by Acts 1994 Third Ex. Sess. No. 18, §1, eff. 7/6/94.)

§1098.3. Consent requirements.

A. A school or a facility may provide preventive counseling or treatment to a child without parental consent if all of the following conditions are met:

(1) The child requests such preventive counseling or treatment.

(2) The child withholds permission to contact a parent or parents to seek consent.

(3) A qualified professional reasonably determines in good faith and based on independent evidence that seeking parental consent would not be helpful and would be harmful to the child.

(4) The child provides a statement of his or her reason for seeking preventive counseling or treatment and provides written consent for such services.

B. When requesting a child's written consent for providing preventive counseling or treatment, the school or facility shall comply with all of the following:

(1) Advise the child of the purpose and nature of the preventive counseling or treatment.

(2) Inform the child that the school or facility will maintain a confidential written record of the services provided.

(3) Inform the child that he or she may withdraw consent and cease participating in the preventive counseling or treatment at any time.
(Added by Acts 1994 Third Ex. Sess. No. 18, §1, eff. 7/6/94.)

§1098.4. Facility requirements.

Any school or facility that provides preventive counseling or treatment services to a child, without parental consent, shall at a minimum:

(1) Maintain a written record of the reason for the preventive counseling or treatment without parental consent and a record of the attempts, if any, made to obtain such consent.

(2) Conduct an initial assessment and evaluation of the child to determine the extent of preventive counseling or treatment services needed.

(3) Prepare a written plan for the provision of preventive counseling or treatment based on the individual assessment and evaluation of the child's needs.

(4) Provide preventive counseling or treatment in accordance with the written plan.

(5) Maintain a written record of the services provided to the child including periodic notes relating to the child's progress.

(6) When it has been determined such services are no longer necessary or the child withdraws from the program, prepare a written summary of the preventive counseling or treatment provided to the child and a statement of the child's progress and maintain such summary and statement as a part of the child's records.
(Added by Acts 1994 Third Ex. Sess. No. 18, §1, eff. 7/6/94.)

§1098.5. Parental involvement in counseling.

Any school or facility that provides preventive counseling or treatment to a child shall seek, only with the written consent of the child, the involvement of a parent, family member, or other individual close to the child. Such involvement shall be in conformity with the confidentiality requirements of R.S. 40:1098.8. *(Added by Acts 1994 Third Ex. Sess. No. 18, §1, eff. 7/6/94.)*

§1098.6. Limitation of liability.

A. Any qualified professional who provides services in accordance with the provisions of this Subpart without the permission of one or both of the child's parents shall be presumed to be acting in good faith.

B. Any qualified professional found to be acting in good faith and in compliance with the provisions of this Subpart, and absent willful and wanton misconduct, shall be immune from

any liability, civil or criminal, that might otherwise be incurred or imposed as a result of action taken pursuant to this Subpart.
(Added by Acts 1994 Third Ex. Sess. No. 18, §1, eff. 7/6/94.)

§1098.7. Authorized resources.

A school or facility may solicit and use any available state, federal, or private resources, which may include but shall not be limited to funds, in-kind resources, or volunteer services, for the purpose of providing preventive counseling services or treatment for alcohol or drug abuse. *(Added by Acts 1994 Third Ex. Sess. No. 18, §1, eff. 7/6/94.)*

§1098.8. Confidentiality.

Notwithstanding any other provision of law to the contrary, the identity of persons receiving preventive counseling or treatment and all records containing information regarding the provision of preventive counseling or treatment shall be confidential. No qualified professional or employee of a school or facility providing preventive counseling or treatment shall disclose any records or information in such records containing the identity of any child receiving preventive counseling or treatment except in compliance with state and federal laws and regulations. *(Added by Acts 1994 Third Ex. Sess. No. 18, §1, eff. 7/6/94.)*

PART VII-B. ANABOLIC STEROID

(Complete Part)

§1239. Uses authorized; regulation; penalties.

A. The provisions of this Section and of the Uniform Controlled Dangerous Substances Law* do not apply to anabolic steroids that are expressly intended for administration to livestock or other nonhuman species, that are approved by the federal Food and Drug Administration for such use.

**R.S. 40:961 et seq.*

B. "Anabolic steroid" as used herein means any anabolic steroid or synthetic derivative of testosterone, including but not limited to the following:

(1) Bodenone.
(2) Chlorotestosterone.
(3) Clostebol.
(4) Chorionic gonadotropin.
(5) Dehydrochlormethyltestosterone.
(6) Dihydrotestosterone.
(7) Drostanolone.
(8) Ethylestrenol.
(9) Fluoxymesterone.
(10) Mesterolone.
(11) Methandienone.
(12) Methandranone.
(13) Methandriol.
(14) Methandrostenolone.
(15) Methyltestosterone.
(16) Mibolerone.
(17) Nandrolone.
(18) Norethandrolone.
(19) Oxandrolone.
(20) Oxymesterone.
(21) Oxymetholone.
(22) Stanolone.
(23) Stanozolol.
(24) Testolactone.
(25) Testosterone.
(26) Trenbolone.

C. (1) A physician, dentist, or veterinarian shall not prescribe, dispense, deliver, or administer an anabolic steroid for human use or cause an anabolic steroid to be administered under his direction or supervision for human use except for a valid medical purpose and when required by demonstrable generally accepted medical indications. Bodybuilding, muscle enhancement, or increasing muscle bulk or strength through the use of an anabolic steroid by a person who is in good health is not a valid medical purpose.

(2) Whoever violates the provisions of this Subsection shall be subject to suspension or revocation of his license to practice medicine, dentistry, or veterinary medicine by his governing board.

(3) Whoever violates the provisions of this Subsection shall also be fined not more than five thousand dollars or imprisoned with or without hard labor for not more than five years, or both.

(Chgd. by Acts 1990 No. 542, §1; Acts 1991 1st Ex. Sess., No. 2, §1, eff. 6/7/91.)

CHAPTER 8. BUILDING REGULATIONS

(Selected Section)

PART V. EQUAL ACCESS TO GOVERNMENTAL AND PUBLIC FACILITIES FOR PHYSICALLY HANDICAPPED

PART V. EQUAL ACCESS TO GOVERNMENTAL AND PUBLIC FACILITIES FOR PHYSICALLY HANDICAPPED

(Chgd. by Acts 1995 No. 880, §1, eff. 8/15/95.)

(Selected Section)

§1742. Parking spaces for certain disabled persons.

A. (1) Each state agency and political subdivision having jurisdiction over street parking or publicly owned and operated parking facilities shall provide a minimum number of specially designed and marked motor vehicle parking spaces for the exclusive use of persons whose vehicles are identified by license plates or parking cards for the mobility impaired which contain the word "handicapped" embossed on the license plate or parking card. The motor vehicle parking spaces shall adhere to the ADAAG specifications. The minimum number of such parking spaces shall be as established by ADAAG.

(2) The fire marshal may, in cases of extreme hardship, waive any provisions of this Section after consultation with the office of rehabilitative services.

(3) Any owner or lessee of a public facility who fails to maintain spaces reserved and designated for the exclusive use of vehicles bearing a special license plate or parking card issued to a mobility-impaired driver free of obstructions shall be fined not more than five hundred dollars.

B. (1) Each state agency and political subdivision having jurisdiction over state parking, publicly owned and operated parking facilities, public facilities or public facilities for accommodation shall provide for and enforce a penalty of two hundred seventy-five dollars for persons who park in spaces for the mobility impaired who do not have a license plate for the mobility impaired which contains the word "handicapped" embossed on the license plate or a properly displayed parking card issued pursuant to R.S. 47:463.4 or 463.4.1.

(2) In addition to such fine, the offender may also be required to pay the towing fee and any storage costs which are incurred.

(3)(a) In addition to all fines, fees, costs, and punishment authorized by this Subsection, any parish which institutes a formal program of utilizing disabled volunteers to assist the law enforcement agency in enforcing the provisions of this Subsection may provide for and enforce an additional twenty-five dollar fine for each violation of such provisions.

(b) All monies collected by the court from such additional fine shall be forwarded by the officer of the court who collects the same to the parish governing authority within thirty days after the fine is collected.

(c) The proceeds of such additional fine shall be used by the parish governing authority exclusively to fund the formal program of utilizing volunteers to aid in enforcing the provisions of this Subsection.

(Chgd. by Acts 1995 No. 573, §1, No. 880, §1; Acts 1997 No. 278, §1, eff. 6/17/97.)

CHAPTER 9. WEAPONS

(Complete Chapter)

PART I. MACHINE GUNS

PART II. REGISTRATION

PART II-A. MISCELLANEOUS PROVISIONS

PART III. PURCHASE OF RIFLES AND SHOTGUNS

PART IV. ARMOR-PIERCING BULLETS

PART I. MACHINE GUNS

§1751. Definitions.

For purposes of this Part, "machine gun" includes all firearms of any calibre, commonly known as machine rifles, machine guns, and sub-machine guns, capable of automatically discharging more than eight cartridges successfully without reloading, in which the ammunition is fed to the gun from or by means of clips, disks, belts, or some other separable mechanical device. "Manufacturer" includes all persons manufacturing machine guns; "Merchant" includes all persons dealing with machine guns as merchandise.

§1752. Handling of machine guns unlawful; exceptions.

No person shall sell, keep or offer for sale, loan or give away, purchase, possess, carry, or transport any machine gun within this state, except that:

(1) All duly appointed peace officers may purchase, possess, carry, and transport machine guns.

(2) This Part does not apply to the Army, Navy, or Marine Corps of the United States, the National Guard, and organizations authorized by law to purchase or receive machine guns

from the United States or from this state. The members of such Corps, National Guard, and organizations may possess, carry, and transport machine guns while on duty.

(3) Persons possessing war relics may purchase and possess machine guns which are relics of any war in which the United States was involved, may exhibit and carry the machine guns in the parades of any military organization, and may sell, offer to sell, loan, or give the machine guns to other persons possessing war relics.

(4) Guards or messengers employed by common carriers, banks, and trust companies, and pay-roll guards or messengers may possess and carry machine guns while actually employed in and about the shipment, transportation, or delivery, or in the guarding of any money, treasure, bullion, bonds, or other thing of value. Their employers may purchase or receive machine guns and keep them in their possession when the guns are not being used by their guards or messengers.

(5) Manufacturers and merchants may sell, keep or offer for sale, loan or give away, purchase, possess, and transport machine guns in the same manner as other merchandise except as otherwise provided in this Part. Common carriers may possess and transport unloaded machine guns as other merchandise.

§1753. Transfers of possessions permitted in certain cases; method.

No manufacturer or merchant shall permit any machine gun to pass from his possession to the possession of any person other than:

(1) A manufacturer or a merchant.

(2) A common carrier for shipment to a manufacturer or merchant.

(3) A duly authorized agent of the government of the United States or of this state, acting in his official capacity.

(4) A person authorized to purchase a machine gun under the provisions of paragraphs (1) and (4) of R.S. 40:1752.

Manufacturers or merchants shall not deliver a machine gun to any of the persons authorized to purchase it under the provisions of paragraphs (1) and (4) of R.S. 40:1752 unless the person presents a written permit to purchase and possess a machine gun, signed by the sheriff of the parish in which the manufacturer or merchant has his place of business or delivers the machine gun. The manufacturer or merchant shall retain the written permit and keep it on file in his place of business. Each sheriff shall keep a record of all permits issued by him.

§1754. Registers to be kept; inspection thereof.

Every manufacturer or merchant shall keep a register of all machine guns manufactured or handled by him. This register shall show:

(1) The date of the sale, loan, gift, delivery, or receipt of any machine gun;

(2) The name, address, and occupation of the person to whom the machine gun was sold, loaned, given, or delivered, or from whom it was received; and

(3) The purpose for which the person, to whom the machine gun was sold, loaned, given, or delivered, purchased or obtained it.

Upon demand, every manufacturer or merchant shall permit any sheriff or deputy sheriff or any police officer to inspect his entire stock of machine guns, and parts and supplies therefor, and shall produce the register required in this Section and all written permits to purchase or possess a machine gun, which he has retained and filed in his place of business.

§1755. Penalty.

A. Any manufacturer who:

(1) Passes possession of or delivers a machine gun to any person in violation of R.S. 40:1753; or

(2) Fails to keep an accurate register, as required in R.S. 40:1754; or

(3) Fails to produce or account for a sheriff's permit for each machine gun sold by him for which a permit is necessary under the provisions of R.S. 40:1753, shall be imprisoned at hard labor for not less than one year nor more than five years.

B. Any person who violates R.S. 40:1752 shall be imprisoned at hard labor for not less than one year nor more than ten years.

C. Whoever, having been convicted of murder, armed or simple robbery, aggravated or simple burglary, or aggravated battery, or an attempt to commit any one of those crimes, thereafter violates any of the provisions of this Part shall be imprisoned at hard labor for not less than three years nor more than ten years.

PART II. REGISTRATION

§1781. Definitions.

For the purpose of this Part, the following terms have the meanings ascribed to them in this Section:

(1) "Dealer" means any person not a manufacturer or importer engaged in this state in the business of selling any firearm. The term includes wholesalers, pawnbrokers, and other persons dealing in used firearms.

(2) "Department" means the Department of Public Safety*.

**The former Department of Public Safety was renamed the Department of Public Safety and Corrections.*

(3) "Firearm" means a shotgun having a barrel of less than eighteen inches in length; a rifle having a barrel of less than sixteen inches in length; any weapon made from either a rifle or a shotgun if said weapon has been modified to have an overall length of less than twenty-six inches; any other firearm, pistol, revolver, or shotgun from which the serial number or mark of identification has been obliterated, from which a shot is discharged by an explosive, if that weapon is capable of being concealed on the person; or a machine gun, grenade launcher, flame thrower, bazooka, rocket launcher, excluding black powder weapons, or gas grenade; and includes a muffler or silencer for any firearm, whether or not the firearm is included within this definition. Pistols and revolvers and those rifles and shotguns which have not previously been defined in this Paragraph as firearms from which serial numbers or marks of identification have not been obliterated are specifically exempt from this definition.

(4) "Importer" means any person who imports or brings into the state any firearm.

(5) "Machine gun" means any weapon, including a submachine gun, which shoots or is designed to shoot automatically more than one shot without manual reloading, by a single function of the trigger.

(6) "Manufacturer" means any person who is engaged in this state in the manufacture, assembling, alteration, or repair of any firearm.

(7) "Muffler" or "silencer" includes any device for silencing or diminishing the report of any portable weapon such as a rifle, carbine, pistol, revolver, machine gun, submachine gun, shotgun, fowling piece, or other device from which a shot, bullet, or projectile may be discharged by an explosive and is not limited to mufflers and silencers for firearms as defined in this Section.

(8) "Transfer" includes the sale, assignment, pledge, lease, loan, gift, or other disposition of any firearm.

§1782. Exemptions from Part.

This Part does not apply to the following persons and things:

(1) Sheriffs or equivalent municipal officers in municipalities of over ten thousand, when they are acting in their official capacity.

(2) The arms, accoutrements, and equipment of the military and naval forces of the United States or of other officers of the United States authorized by law to possess weapons of any kind.

(3) The arms, accoutrements, and equipment of the militia.

(4) Any firearm which is unserviceable and which is transferred as a curiosity or ornament.

§1783. Registration with department of public safety*.

Every person possessing any firearm shall register with the department the number or other mark identifying the firearm, together with his name, address, and place of business or employment, the place where the firearm is usually kept, and, if the person is other than a natural person, the name and home address of the executive officer thereof having control of the firearm and the name and home address of the person having actual possession thereof.

**The former Department of Public Safety was renamed the Department of Public Safety and Corrections.*

§1784. Application to possess or transfer; use of information or evidence.

No person shall continue to possess or shall transfer any firearm without the prior approval of the department. Interested persons shall file written applications in duplicate on application forms issued in blank for those purposes by the department. In the case of transfers of any firearm, applications shall be filed by both the proposed vendor and the proposed vendee.

The applications shall set forth, in the original and duplicate, the manufacturer's number or other mark identifying the firearm. Both the original and duplicate shall be forwarded to the department. If approved, the original shall be returned to the applicant.

No information or evidence obtained from an application, registration or records required to be submitted or retained by a natural person in order to comply with any provision of this Part or regulations issued thereunder shall, except as provided by the laws on perjury or false swearing, be used, directly or indirectly, as evidence against that person in a criminal proceeding with respect to a violation of law occurring prior to or concurrently with the filing of the application or registration, or the compiling of the records containing the information or evidence.

§1785. Possession or dealing in unregistered or illegally transferred weapons.

No person shall receive, possess, carry, conceal, buy, sell, or transport any firearm which has not been registered or transferred in accordance with this Part.

§1786. Seizure and forfeiture of weapons; disposition thereof.

Any firearm possessed or transferred in violation of the provisions of this Part may be seized by the department. Upon seizure, it is forfeited to the state and may be disposed of by the department as follows:

No firearm shall be sold at public sale; the department may order the firearm destroyed or may sell it at private sale to any political subdivision of the state or to any officer thereof, or may retain it for its own use, or may transfer it without charge to any executive department or independent establishment of the state for use by it.

§1787. Importation, manufacture, or dealing in without registration.

Upon first engaging in business, every importer, manufacturer, and dealer in firearms shall register with the department his name or style, principal place of business and other places of business in this state. No person required to register under the provisions of this Section shall import, manufacture, or deal in any firearm without having registered as required by this Section.

§1788. Identification with number or other mark; obliteration or alteration of number or mark.

A. Each manufacturer, importer, and dealer in any firearm shall identify it with a number or other identification mark approved by the department and shall mark or stamp or otherwise place the number or mark thereon in a manner approved by the department.

B. No one shall obliterate, remove, change, or alter this number or mark. Whenever, in a trial for a violation of this Subsection, the defendant is shown to have or to have had possession of any firearm upon which the number or mark was obliterated, removed, changed, or altered, that possession is sufficient evidence to authorize conviction unless the defendant explains it to the satisfaction of the court.

§1789. Records of importers, manufacturers, or dealers.

Importers, manufacturers, and dealers shall deep* such books and records and render such returns in relation to the transactions in firearms specified in this Part as the department requires.

**So in original. Probably should be "keep".*

§1790. Rules and regulations; importation of firearms.

The department may prescribe such rules and regulations as are necessary for carrying out the provisions of this Part.

Under regulations prescribed by the department, any firearm may be imported or brought into this state or possessed or transferred when the purpose thereof is shown to be lawful.

§1791. Penalty.

Upon the first violation of any provision of this Part the penalty shall be a fine of not less than five hundred dollars nor more than two thousand dollars and imprisonment with or without hard labor for not less than one nor more than five years. For any subsequent violation of this Part the penalty shall be a fine of not less than two thousand dollars nor more than five thousand dollars and imprisonment at hard labor for not less than five years nor more than ten years.

§1792. Possession of unidentifiable firearm; particular penalties; identification of source of firearm.

A. No person shall intentionally receive, possess, carry, conceal, buy, sell, transfer, or transport any firearm which has been illegally obtained or from which the serial number or individual identifying mark, as required by R.S. 40:1788, has been intentionally obliterated, altered, removed, or concealed.

B. The provisions of this Section shall not apply to any firearm which is an antique or war relic and is inoperable or for which ammunition is no longer manufactured in the United States and is not readily available in the ordinary channels of commercial trade, or which was originally manufactured without such a number.

C. Except as otherwise provided in this Section, whoever violates the provisions of this Section may be fined not more than one thousand dollars and shall be imprisoned at hard labor for five years without benefit of probation, parole, or suspension of sentence.

D. Prior to sentencing for a conviction under this Section, the defendant shall be given the opportunity to identify the source of the firearm upon which the conviction was based. If the defendant reveals the identity of the source of the weapon and the identity of the source is confirmed by the prosecutor or the court, the defendant shall be fined not more than one thousand dollars or imprisoned for not more than six months, or both.

E. Nothing in this Section shall be construed to prevent the prosecution of an individual who obtained the firearm by theft, robbery, deception, or by other unlawful means from the lawful owner of the firearm.

F. Any illegally obtained firearm or a firearm from which the serial number or identifying mark required by R.S. 40:1788 has been obliterated or altered is hereby declared to be contraband and shall be seized by the law enforcement agency of jurisdiction. If it is determined that a person other than the owner was responsible for removing, altering, or obliterating the serial number or identifying mark, the firearm shall be returned to its lawful owner or may be disposed of according to law but only after a new serial number has been permanently fixed on the firearm. If a new serial number is not so affixed, the firearm shall be destroyed by the law enforcement agency in possession of the firearm.

(Added by Acts 1994 Third Ex. Sess. No. 29, §1, eff. 8/27/94.)

PART II-A. MISCELLANEOUS PROVISIONS

§1796. Preemption of state law.

No governing authority of a political subdivision shall enact after July 15, 1985, any ordinance or regulation more restrictive than state law concerning in any way the sale, purchase, possession, ownership, transfer, transportation, license, or registration of firearms, ammunition, or components of firearms or ammunition; provided, however, that this Section shall not apply to the levy and collection of sales and use taxes, license fees and taxes and permit fees, nor shall it affect the authority of political subdivisions to prohibit the possession of a weapon or firearm in certain commercial establishments and public buildings.

PART III. PURCHASE OF RIFLES AND SHOTGUNS

§1801. Declaration of policy.

It is declared that it is in the public interest to authorize residents of this state to purchase or otherwise obtain rifles and shotguns or ammunition in states contiguous to this state in compliance with such other laws of this state or its political subdivisions as may be applicable and in compliance with Section 102 of the Gun Control Act of 1968, Public Law 90–618, 18 U.S.C. §921 et seq. and it is the declared intention of this state that the sale of shotguns and rifles and the sale of ammunition in this state to residents of adjacent states is hereby authorized pursuant to regulations issued under the Gun Control Act of 1968.

§1802. Definitions.

As used in this Part:

(1) "A state contiguous to this state" shall mean any state having a common border with this state.

(2) All other terms shall be given the meaning prescribed in 18 U.S.C. §921 (the Gun Control Act of 1968, Public Law 90–618) and the regulations duty* promulgated thereunder as presently enacted or promulgated and as hereafter modified.
**So in original. Probably should be "duly".*

§1803. Purchase of rifle or shotgun or ammunition.

It shall be lawful for any person residing in this state, including any corporation or other business entity maintaining a place of business in this state, to purchase or otherwise obtain a rifle or shotgun or ammunition in any state which is contiguous to this state and to receive or transport such rifle or shotgun or ammunition into this state and to permit any person residing in a contiguous state to purchase shotguns, rifles or ammunition in this state and to receive or transport such rifles, shotguns or ammunition in this state.

§1804. Application.

This Part shall not apply or be construed to affect in any way the purchase, receipt or transportation of rifles or shotguns or ammunition by federally licensed firearms manufacturers, importers, dealers or collectors except to permit such purchase, receipt or transportation.

PART IV. ARMOR-PIERCING BULLETS

§1810. Definitions.

As used in this Part, "armor-piercing bullet" shall mean any bullet, except a shotgun shell or ammunition primarily designed for use in rifles, that:

(1) Has a steel inner core or core of equivalent density and hardness, truncated cone, and is designed for use in a pistol or revolver as a body armor or metal piercing bullet; or

(2) Has been primarily manufactured or designed, by virtue of its shape, cross-sectional density, or any coating applied thereto, to breach or penetrate body armor when fired from a handgun.

§1811. Prohibitions.

A. No person shall import, manufacture, sell, purchase, possess, or transfer armor-piercing bullets.

B. Whoever violates the provisions of this Section shall be fined not more than one thousand dollars or imprisoned with or without hard labor for not more than one year, or both.

§1812. Exemptions.

The provisions of this Part shall not apply to:

(1) Law enforcement officers and employees acting in the lawful performance of their duties.

(2) Law enforcement or other authorized agencies conducting a firearms training course, operating a forensic ballistics laboratory, or specializing in the development of ammunition or explosive ordinance.

(3) Department of Corrections officials and employees authorized to carry firearms while engaged in the performance of their official duties.

(4) Members of the armed services or reserve forces of the United States or Louisiana National Guard while engaged in the performance of their official duties.

(5) Federal officials authorized to carry firearms while engaged in the performance of their official duties.

(6) The lawful manufacture, importation, sale, purchase, possession, or transfer of armor-piercing bullets exclusively to or for persons authorized by law to possess such bullets.

(7) A bona fide collector licensed by the Department of Public Safety*.
**The former Department of Public Safety was renamed the Department of Public Safety and Corrections.*

TITLE 47
REVENUE AND TAXATION

SUBTITLE II. PROVISIONS RELATING TO TAXES COLLECTED AND ADMINISTERED BY THE COLLECTOR OF REVENUE
(Selected Chapter)

CHAPTER 4. VEHICLE REGISTRATION LICENSE TAX
(Selected Sections)

PART II. LEVY OF REGISTRATION LICENSE FEE OR TAX

PART III. REGISTRATION OF VEHICLES

PART IV. ADMINISTRATIVE PROVISIONS

PART II. LEVY OF REGISTRATION LICENSE FEE OR TAX
(Selected Section)

§478. Trucks to bear name and address of owner or lessee; exceptions.

A. (1) All interstate motor carriers registered with the Interstate Commerce Commission which operate on the highways shall bear the name or trade name of the motor carrier under whose authority the vehicle is being operated. Such a name or trade name shall be placed on the outside of both truck doors and may be placed thereon by any means permitted by R.S. 32:651.

(2) All other trucks operated on the highways shall bear the name and address or equivalent identification of the owner or lessee. Such a name and address shall be placed on the outside of both truck doors and may be placed thereon by any means permitted by R.S. 32:651.

B. The requirement provided for in Subsection A of this Section shall apply to only those trucks licensed and registered for four thousand pounds or more and which are used for commercial purposes.

PART III. REGISTRATION OF VEHICLES

(Selected Sections)

§501. Owner to secure registration.

A. Every owner of a motor vehicle, trailer, or semi-trailer, or other vehicle intended to be operated upon the public highways in this state shall, before operating the same, apply to the secretary of the Department of Public Safety and Corrections for and obtain the registration thereof and pay the state registration or license tax imposed by this Chapter, except where the secretary of the Department of Revenue has found that the registration and license taxes have been previously paid to a motor vehicle dealer pursuant to R.S. 47:303(B)(5). This Section does not apply to the owner of any vehicle which is exempted by this Chapter, nor to the owner who is permitted to operate a vehicle under the special provisions relating to lienholders, manufacturers, dealers, and nonresidents, as provided in this Chapter.

B. Every vehicle required to be registered under the provisions of this Chapter shall be registered in the parish of domicile of the owner, or if the owner is not domiciled in Louisiana, in a parish in which the owner has a residence.

(Chgd. by Acts 1995 No. 393, §2, eff. 6/16/95.)

§501.1. Duties of employees and employers.

A. Any person who is a resident of a state which requires registration of the motor vehicle or motor vehicles of a person who is employed in that state within thirty days of such employment, and who is employed in and maintains a residence in Louisiana and who operates one or more vehicles on the public streets and roads in Louisiana shall apply for a certificate of registration for each of those vehicles within thirty days of the date on which the person was employed in Louisiana.

B. Each employer in this state shall notify each person employed by that employer of the requirement of Subsection A of this Section. The notice shall be by direct communication at the time of employment and by posting a notice in a prominent location at the place of employment.

C. The provisions of this Section shall not be applicable to members actively serving in the armed forces of the United States.

(Added by Acts 1993 No. 765, §1, eff. 8/15/93.)

§502. Exemption from registration.

Farm tractors, self-propelled farm equipment, rubber-tired farm wagons and carts and drawn rubber-tired farm equipment which are designed primarily for field use and which are operated or moved only incidentally on the highways of this state, and which are used for farm purposes only need not be registered under this chapter. Road rollers and road machinery temporarily moved upon the highways are also exempt from registration.

§502.1. Exemption from registration; log loaders.

A. The provisions of this section shall apply to log loaders which are used exclusively for loading logs upon another vehicle and are not used to haul logs, and which are operated or moved only incidentally on the highways of this state. Such log loaders are exempt from the registration and registration tax provided for by Chapter 4 of Title 47 of the Louisiana Revised Statutes of 1950 and are exempt from the provisions of Chapter 7 of Title 32 of the Louisiana Revised Statutes of 1950.

B. No such log loader shall be operated at a speed in excess of forty miles per hour.

Violations of the provisions of this subsection shall be punished by a fine of not more than one hundred dollars, or by imprisonment for not more than thirty days, or both. A subsequent violation shall be punished by a fine of not more than five hundred dollars, or by imprisonment for not more than ninety days, or both.

If the violator is other than an individual, imprisonment shall be dispensed with and a double fine imposed.

§506. Registration certificates.

A. The registration certificate issued for a vehicle required to be registered, or a photostatic or other similar copy thereof, shall at all times, while the vehicle is being operated upon a public highway in this state, be carried in a registration certificate holder of a type and design approved by the department, in or on said vehicle, in an accessible place, in plain view of and subject to inspection by any members of the division of state police or any officer, agent or representative of the department or of the commissioner or other public officer; provided, however, that no fine or other penalty shall apply for failure to comply with the aforesaid provisions if, within five days after an authorized officer's request to inspect a registration certificate, that certificate is presented at the office or headquarters of the requesting officer.

B. Registration certificates must, at all times and under all conditions, correspond with the license plates being used upon the vehicle.

C. Whenever the owner, purchaser, transferee or assignee of any vehicle seeks to procure the issuance of any registration certificate, the commissioner may require, as a condition precedent thereto, the production of the old certificate issued to the former owner of the vehicle, or proof satisfactory to him as to the change of ownership or title and the transactions by which such change of ownership was effected.

D. Every manufacturer, dealer or other person selling or disposing of any motor vehicle in this state shall equip the same with a registration certificate holder.

§507. Display of plate.

A. The registration license plate assigned to a trailer, semitrailer, motorcycle, or other motor vehicle shall be attached to the rear thereof. Notwithstanding the foregoing, the registration license plate assigned to any truck having a gross vehicle weight in excess of six thousand pounds or to any dump truck may be attached to either the front or rear thereof. For the purposes of this Section, dump truck means any truck with a bed that raises to dump a load. The registration license plate shall be so displayed during the current registration year, except as otherwise provided herein.

B. Every registration license plate shall at all times be securely fastened to the vehicle to which it is assigned, so as to prevent the plate from swinging, and at a height not less than twelve inches from the ground, measuring from the bottom of such plate, in a place and position to be clearly visible, and shall be maintained free from foreign materials and in a condition to be clearly legible.

§508. Registration; commercial vehicles; exemption.

A. (1) Except as provided in Paragraph (2) of this Subsection, every vehicle registration under this Chapter other than those licensed under R.S. 47:463(A), R.S. 47:511(B), and those included, by regulation of the secretary, in the staggered registration system, shall expire on June thirtieth of each year. The registrations shall be renewed annually between May first and June thirtieth of each year.

(2) Notwithstanding any other provision of law to the contrary, every registration of an automobile or truck to be used as a commercial rental or leased vehicle shall expire one year from the date of issuance and shall be renewed annually thereafter.

B. In odd numbered years every registration of a private passenger carrying automobile, registered or to be registered under R.S. 47:463(A), shall expire on December 31 and shall be renewed on or before February 6 of the year immediately following that in which the registration expires, except that the expiration date for vehicles registered under R.S. 47:463(A) which are included in a staggered registration system by rules and regulations of the secretary shall be those established in such rules and regulations.

C. Failure to make application and payment of registration fees, as provided herein, on or before the renewal dates provided in this Section, or on or before renewal dates established by rule of the secretary, shall cause the license to become delinquent and subject to penalties and interest charges as provided in Chapter 18 of this Title.

D. (1) Except as provided in Paragraph (2) of this Subsection, any person acquiring any vehicle subject to registration and license subsequent to July first of any year in which renewal of registration is required shall, before operating the same, make the required application for registration and shall pay the license. Failure to make application and payment as herein directed shall cause the license on any such vehicle to become delinquent and subject to the penalties fixed in Chapter 18 of this Subtitle. New vehicles purchased subsequent to July first of any year in which renewal of registration is required shall be entitled to a monthly pro rata reduction of license as hereinafter provided. Any person owning a vehicle other than those licensed by R.S. 47:463(A) during any part of the current registration period and not having used it on the highways during the period commencing July first of the year in which renewal of registration is required shall be entitled to a monthly pro rata reduction of the license after July thirty-first, upon furnishing sworn proof satisfactory to the secretary that the vehicle had not been used as hereinabove stated or that any sale, transfer, or assignment thereof was bona fide and not for the purpose of evading the provisions of the

Chapter. In no event, however, shall the amount of the license tax payable hereunder be less than the minimums as fixed in R.S. 47:475.

(2) Notwithstanding any other provision of law to the contrary, every person acquiring an automobile or truck to be used as a commercial rental or leased vehicle shall, before operating the same as a commercial rental or leased vehicle, make the required application for registration and shall pay the license fee which shall expire one year from the date of issuance. Failure to make application and payment as herein directed shall cause the commercial license on such automobile or truck to become delinquent and subject to the penalties fixed in Chapter 18 of this Subtitle.

E. Any owner who has made proper application and paid the proper license tax for the renewal of registration of a vehicle but who has not received the number plates or registration certificate for the current registration period, shall be entitled to operate or permit the operation of such vehicle upon the public highways by displaying upon said vehicle the number plate or plates issued for the preceding registration period, upon furnishing sworn proof satisfactory to the secretary or the division of state police of his timely application and failure to receive the number plate or plates or registration certificate for the current registration period. This privilege shall be limited to and extended no further than September 1 of the year in which the registration period begins.

F. Notwithstanding the provisions of Subsection A of this Section, every registration of a motor truck or tandem truck having a gross weight per load carrying axle up to and including six thousand pounds or less and motorcycles for which the registration or license tax is paid for two years as provided for in R.S. 47:462B(6) shall expire two years from the date the registration or license tax is paid and shall be renewed every second year on or before the last day of the month.

G. Notwithstanding the provisions of Subsection A of this Section, every registration of a boat trailer having a gross weight per load carrying axle of one thousand five hundred pounds or less, a farm use trailer having a gross weight per load carrying axle of six thousand pounds or less, or a privately owned trailer having a gross weight per load carrying axle of five hundred pounds or less for which the registration or license tax is paid for two years as provided for in R.S. 47:462B(7) shall expire two years from the date the registration or license tax is paid and shall be renewed every second year on or before the last day of the month immediately following the month in which the previous registration expired.

H. The secretary of the Department of Public Safety is hereby authorized to issue permanent license plates at the time of first issuance for a commercial vehicle. Said registration thereafter shall be renewed annually by the affixing of a registration sticker on the license plate. The secretary shall promulgate rules and regulations necessary to carry out the provisions of this Section. Such vehicles registered under the Interstate Registration Plan are exempt from the provision of this Section.

(Chgd. by Acts 1995 No. 256, §1; Acts 1997 No. 1386, §1, eff. 8/15/97.)

§513. Vehicle of nonresident owner used regularly in business in Louisiana.

Every nonresident person, regularly employed in or carrying on a business within this state for a period of at least thirty consecutive days and owning or leasing and regularly operating, in such business or in connection therewith, any motor vehicle, trailer or semitrailer within this state, shall be required to register each vehicle and pay the same license taxes therefore as is required with reference to like vehicles owned by residents of this state. This Section shall not apply to vehicles which are covered by reciprocal agreements in effect between Louisiana and other jurisdictions.

§519.2. Temporary license plates; lending institutions; auto title companies.

A. Subject to the provisions of this Section, the commissioner may sell temporary license plates to lending institutions which are chartered by the office of financial institutions or by an agency of the federal government and to auto title companies which are defined in R.S. 32:702(12).

B. The purpose of this Section is to provide lending institutions and auto title companies an opportunity to obtain temporary license plates to be issued to a person who purchases a vehicle for which the lending institution has provided financing and with regard to which the financial institution or auto title company handles the applications for a title and for registration.

C. Lending institutions and auto title companies may purchase and issue temporary license plates for the purpose stated in Subsection B of this Section. All other uses of the temporary plates authorized under this Section are prohibited.

D. Temporary license plates may be issued under this Section for any vehicle for which the commissioner issues permanent license plates.

E. The fee for each temporary license plate is four dollars.

F. The commissioner shall design the temporary plates and shall design and furnish all forms required under this Section.

G. Temporary license plates shall expire on the date the permanent license plate is received, or on the ninetieth day after the temporary license plate is issued, even if the permanent license plate has not been received, whichever is sooner.

H. Each person to whom a temporary license plate has been issued shall destroy the temporary license plate on the day the temporary license plate expires.

I. The commissioner shall adopt rules to implement the provisions of this Section. The rules shall include, but shall not be limited to:

(1) Rules establishing requirements for being eligible to participate in the program.

(2) Rules establishing grounds and procedures for suspending or revoking eligibility to participate in the program and for reclaiming temporary license plates.

(3) Rules establishing requirements for information which the lending institutions shall transmit to the commissioner with regard to each temporary license which the lending institution purchases and uses.

(4) Rules establishing procedures for issuing temporary license plates.

(5) Rules establishing requirements for keeping records concerning temporary license plates, including the information in the records and access to the records.

J. The provisions of this Section shall not apply to temporary license plates issued for commercial motor vehicles for which the taxes are apportioned.

(Added by Acts 1990 No. 125, §1; chgd. by Acts 1992 No. 626, §1; Acts 1993 No. 33, §1, eff. 5/18/93.)

§520. Dealers temporary demonstration and transportation identification plate.

A. As used in this Section, the word "dealership" means any legal entity which is licensed to do business as a motor vehicle dealer by the Louisiana Motor Vehicle Commission, R.S. 32:1251 et seq., or by the Louisiana Used Motor Vehicle and Parts Commission, R.S. 32:771 et seq.

B. Each dealership may print and utilize dealers temporary demonstration and transportation identification plates, hereinafter referred to as identification plates, in lieu of motor vehicle registration plates in accordance with the provisions of this Section.

C. Each identification plate shall be green and shall contain the following information:

(1) The name of the dealership which is using the identification plate.

(2) The telephone number of the dealership which is using the identification plate.

(3) The number on the license issued by the Motor Vehicle Commission or by the Used Motor Vehicle and Parts Commission to the dealership which is using the identification plate.

(4) The date on which the identification plate was placed in service.

D. Subject to the provisions of Subsection B of this Section, the office of motor vehicles shall establish the size, design, and other characteristics of the identification plate.

E. Each identification plate shall be valid for five days from the date on which the identification plate was placed in service.

F. Each dealership which places an identification plate in service on a motor vehicle may use that motor vehicle for any business purpose of the dealership, including but not limited to the demonstration or transportation of that vehicle.

(Added by Acts 1995 No. 229, §1, eff. 6/14/95.)

PART IV. ADMINISTRATIVE PROVISIONS

(Selected Section)

§536. Violations of registration provisions.

Except as otherwise specifically provided herein, no person shall do, omit to do, permit, or cause to be done or omitted, any of the things required or prohibited by this Chapter, or to commit any of the following acts:

(1) To operate, or for the owner thereof knowingly to permit the operation of any motor or other vehicle, trailer or semi-trailer, which is not registered or which does not have attached thereto and displayed thereon, in accordance with the provisions of R.S. 47:507, the number plates assigned to it for the current year, subject to the exemptions provided in this Chapter.

(2) To display or cause or permit to be displayed or have in possession any registration certificate, or registration number plate, knowing the same to be fictitious or to have become cancelled, revoked, suspended or altered.

(3) To lend to or knowingly permit the use of by any one not entitled thereto, any registration number plate issued to the person so lending or permitting the use thereof.

(4) To fail or refuse to surrender to the commissioner or officers of the Division of State Police, upon demand, any registration certificate or registration number plate which has been suspended, cancelled or revoked, as provided in this Chapter.

(5) To use a false or fictitious name or address in any application for the registration of any vehicle or for any renewal or duplicate thereof, or to make a false statement or knowingly to conceal a material fact or otherwise commit a fraud in any such application.

(6) For the owner, purchaser, assignee or transferee of a vehicle formerly registered in the name of another, to neglect, fail or refuse to surrender to the commissioner or officer of the Division of State Police the registration certificate of the former owner, or to fail or refuse to furnish the commissioner with satisfactory proof as to the transfer thereof and his ownership of the vehicle.

(7) To use or operate, or permit to be used or operated, any vehicle on the highways of the state carrying a net load in excess of that for which it is registered and the tax thereon paid. Each use of said vehicle shall constitute a separate offense.

Whoever violates the provisions of this paragraph shall be fined not more than one hundred dollars, or imprisoned for not more than thirty days, or both.

For the purposes of paragraph (7) of this Section and of R.S. 47:516, where the weight of a vehicle does not exceed by ten per centum the weight for which it is licensed or registered, and where such overloading is bona fide, such overloading shall not constitute a violation and shall not subject the owner or operator of the vehicle to the penalties and requirements therein provided.

(8) To obtain or use an improper registration certificate, license or license plates, or to make improper use of a properly obtained registration license or license plate, or to use upon one vehicle the license plates issued for another vehicle, or to register and attach license plates to and use on the highways of this State a vehicle unsafe or unfit to be operated, or one that is not equipped as required by law, or for a manufacturer or dealer to make or permit to be made any unlawful use of the same or permit the use thereof by a person not entitled thereto.

CODE OF CRIMINAL PROCEDURE

(Complete Code)

Title

TITLE I. PRELIMINARY PROVISIONS AND GENERAL POWERS OF COURTS

Chapter

CHAPTER 1. PRELIMINARY PROVISIONS AND RULES OF CONSTRUCTION

Article

Art. 1. Short title; citation of Code.

This Code shall be known as the Louisiana Code of Criminal Procedure and may be cited officially: C.Cr.P.

Art. 2. Purpose and construction.

The provisions of this Code are intended to provide for the just determination of criminal proceedings. They shall be construed to secure simplicity in procedure, fairness in administration, and the elimination of unjustifiable delay.

Art. 3. Procedures not otherwise specified.

Where no procedure is specifically prescribed by this Code or by statute, the court may proceed in a manner consistent with the spirit of the provisions of this Code and other applicable statutory and constitutional provisions.

Art. 4. Number; gender.

Unless the context clearly indicates otherwise:

(1) Words used in the singular number apply also to the plural; words used in the plural number include the singular; and

(2) Words used in one gender apply also to the other.

Art. 5. Mandatory and permissive language.

The word "shall" is mandatory, and the word "may" is permissive.

Art. 6. Conjunctive, disjunctive, or both.

Unless the context clearly indicates otherwise:

(1) The word "and" indicates the conjunctive;

(2) The word "or" indicates the disjunctive;

(3) When the article is phrased in the disjunctive, followed by the words "or both," both the conjunctive and disjunctive are intended; and

(4) The word "and" or "or" between the last two items in a series applies to the entire series.

Art. 7. Municipal and parochial officers included.

Unless the context clearly indicates the contrary, the term "district attorney" includes a municipal prosecuting officer; the term "sheriff" includes a city or municipal police chief or a city marshall; and other official titles include their counterparts in municipal and parochial governments.

Art. 8. Assistants and deputies included.

Unless the context clearly indicates the contrary, official titles, such as clerk of court, coroner, district attorney, and sheriff, include assistants and deputies.

Art. 9. References to Code articles or statutory sections.

Unless the context clearly indicates the contrary:

(1) A reference in this Code to a title, chapter, or article, without further designation, means a title, chapter, or article of this Code; and

(2) A reference in this Code to a title, chapter, or article of a code, or to any statutory or constitutional provision, applies to subsequent amendments thereof.

Art. 10. Article headings, source notes, and comments not part of law.

The headings of the articles of this Code, and the source notes and comments thereunder do not constitute parts of the law.

Art. 11. Clerical and typographical errors disregarded.

Clerical and typographical errors in this Code shall be disregarded when the legislative intent is clear.

Art. 12. Pleading a statute.

In pleading a state statute of Louisiana or an ordinance of a political subdivision thereof, a state statute of another state of the United States, or a federal statute, or a right derived therefrom or an obligation created thereby, it is sufficient to refer to the statute or ordinance by an official method of citation, by its title, or in any other manner which identifies the statute or ordinance.

Art. 13. Computation of time.

In computing a period of time allowed or prescribed by law or by order of court, the date of the act, event, or default after which the period begins to run is not to be included. The last day of the period is to be included, unless it is a legal holiday, in which event the period runs until the end of the next day which is not a legal holiday.

A half-holiday is considered as a legal holiday.

A legal holiday is to be included in the computation of a period of time allowed or prescribed, except when:

(1) It is expressly excluded;

(2) It would otherwise be the last day of the period; or

(3) The period is less than seven days.

Art. 14. Oath or affirmation in criminal proceedings; witness.

A. If a person refuses to take an oath or to make a sworn statement or affidavit required in connection with any criminal proceedings, he may affirm in lieu of swearing, and his affirmation shall fulfill the requirement and shall have the same legal effect as an oath, sworn statement, or affidavit.

B. Before testifying every witness shall be required to declare that he will testify truthfully, by oath or affirmation administered in a form calculated to awaken his conscience and impress his mind with his duty to do so.

CHAPTER 2. APPLICATION OF CODE

Art. 15. Courts to which applicable; military not affected.

A. The provisions of this Code, except as otherwise specially provided by other statutes, shall govern and regulate the procedure in criminal prosecutions and proceedings in district courts. They also shall govern criminal prosecutions in city, parish, juvenile, and family courts, except insofar as a particular provision is incompatible with the general nature and organization of, or special procedures established or authorized by law for, those courts.

B. This Code shall not affect any power conferred by law upon any court martial, military authority, or military officer to impose or inflict punishment upon offenders.

CHAPTER 3. INHERENT POWERS OF COURTS; CONTEMPT

Art. 16. Jurisdiction and powers of courts.

Courts have the jurisdiction and powers over criminal proceedings that are conferred upon them by the constitution and statutes of this state, except as their statutory jurisdiction and powers are restricted, enlarged, or modified by the provisions of this Code.

Art. 17. Inherent power and authority of courts.

A court possesses inherently all powers necessary for the exercise of its jurisdiction and the enforcement of its lawful orders, including authority to issue such writs and orders as may be necessary or proper in aid of its jurisdiction. It has the duty to require that criminal proceedings shall be conducted with dignity and in an orderly and expeditious manner and to so control the proceedings that justice is done. A court has the power to punish for contempt.

Art. 18. Adoption of local rules of court.

A court may adopt rules for the conduct of criminal proceedings before it, not in conflict with provisions of this Code or of other laws. When a court has more than one judge, its rules shall be adopted or amended by a majority of the judges thereof, sitting en banc.

The rules shall be entered on the minutes of the court, and a copy shall be furnished on request to any attorney licensed to practice law in this state.

Art. 19. Special sessions of court.

A court may call a special criminal session at any time, including vacation, and any criminal proceeding or prosecution may be tried or heard during the special session.

Art. 20. Contempt of court; kinds of contempt.

A contempt of court is an act or omission tending to obstruct or interfere with the orderly administration of justice, or to impair the dignity of the court or respect for its authority.

Contempts of court are of two kinds, direct and constructive.

Art. 21. Direct contempt.

A direct contempt of court is one committed in the immediate view and presence of the court and of which it has personal knowledge; or, a contumacious failure to comply with a subpoena, summons or order to appear in court, proof of service of which appears of record; or, a contumacious failure to comply with an order sequestering a witness.

A direct contempt includes, but is not limited to, any of the following acts:

(1) Contumacious failure, after notice, to appear for arraignment or trial on the day fixed therefor;

(2) Contumacious failure to comply with a subpoena or summons to appear in court, proof of service of which appears of record;

(3) Contumacious violation of an order excluding, separating, or sequestering a witness;

(4) Refusal to take the oath or affirmation as a witness, or refusal of a witness to answer a nonincriminating question when ordered to do so by the court;

(5) Contumacious, insolent, or disorderly behavior toward the judge or an attorney or other officer of the court, tending to interrupt or interfere with the business of the court or to impair its dignity or respect for its authority;

(6) Breach of the peace, boisterous conduct, or violent disturbance tending to interrupt or interfere with the business of the court or to impair its dignity or respect for its authority;

(7) Use of insulting, abusive, or discourteous language by an attorney or other person in open court, or in a motion, plea, brief, or other document, filed with the court, in irrelevant criticism of another attorney or of a judge or officer of the court;

(8) Violation of a rule of the court adopted to maintain order and decorum in the court room; or

(9) Contumacious failure to attend court as a member of a jury venire or to serve as a juror after being accepted as such when proof of service of the subpoena appears of record.

Art. 22. Procedure for punishing direct contempt.

A person who has committed a direct contempt of court may be found guilty and punished therefor by the court without any trial, after affording him an opportunity to be heard orally by way of defense or mitigation. The court shall render an order reciting the facts constituting the contempt, adjudging the person guilty thereof, and specifying the punishment imposed.

Art. 22.1. Direct contempt; fingerprinting and photographing; exceptions.

No person arrested or found guilty for the first offense of direct contempt of court either for failure to attend court as a member of a jury venire when proof of service of the summons appears on the record or for failure to comply with a subpoena to attend court to serve as a witness when proof of service of the subpoena appears on the record shall be subject to fingerprinting or have his photograph taken in any arrest or postsentence procedure.

Art. 23. Constructive contempt.

A constructive contempt of court is any contempt other than a direct one.

A constructive contempt includes, but is not limited to any of the following acts:

(1) Willful neglect or violation of duty by a clerk, sheriff, or other person elected, appointed, or employed to assist the court in the administration of justice;

(2) Willful disobedience of any lawful judgment, order, mandate, writ, or process of court;

(3) Removal or attempted removal of any person or of property in the custody of an officer acting under the authority of a judgment, order, mandate, writ, or process of the court;

(4) Unlawful detention of a witness, the defendant or his attorney, or the district attorney, while going to, remaining at, or returning from the court;

(5) Improper conversation by a juror or venireman with any person relative to the merits of a case which is being, or may be, tried by a jury of which the juror is a member, or of which the venireman may become a member; or receipt by a juror or venireman of a communication from any person with reference to such a case without making an immediate disclosure to the court of the substance thereof;

(6) Assuming to act as a juror, or as an attorney or other officer of the court, without lawful authority;

(7) Willful disobedience by an inferior court, judge, or other official thereof, of the lawful judgment, order, mandate, writ, or process of an appellate court, rendered in connection with an appeal from a judgment or order of the inferior court, or in connection with a review of such judgment or order under a supervisory writ.

Art. 24. Procedure for punishing constructive contempt.

A. When a person is charged with committing a constructive contempt, he shall be tried by the judge on a rule to show cause alleging the facts constituting the contempt. The rule may be issued by the court on its own motion or on motion of the district attorney.

B. A certified copy of the motion and of the rule shall be served on the person charged in the manner of a subpoena not less than forty-eight hours prior to the time assigned for trial of the rule.

C. A person charged with committing a constructive contempt of a court of appeal may be found guilty thereof and punished therefor after receiving a notice to show cause, by brief, to be filed not less than forty-eight hours from the date the person receives such notice, why he should not be found guilty of contempt and punished accordingly. Such notice may be sent by certified or registered mail or may be served by the sheriff. The person so charged shall be granted an oral hearing on the charge if he submits a written request to the clerk of the appellate court within forty-eight hours after receiving notice of the charge.

D. If the person charged with contempt is found guilty, the court shall render an order reciting the facts constituting the contempt, adjudging the person charged with the contempt guilty thereof, and specifying the punishment imposed.

Art. 25. Penalties for contempt.

A. A person may not be adjudged guilty of a contempt of court except for misconduct defined as such, or made punishable as such, expressly by law.

B. Except as otherwise provided in this Article, a court may punish a person adjudged guilty of contempt of court in connection with a criminal proceeding by a fine of not more than five hundred dollars, or by imprisonment for not more than six months, or both.

C. When an attorney is adjudged guilty of a direct contempt of court, the punishment shall be limited to a fine of not more than one hundred dollars, or imprisonment for not more than twenty-four hours, or both; and, for any subsequent direct contempt of the same court by the same offender, a fine of not more than two hundred dollars, or imprisonment for not more than ten days, or both.

D. A justice of the peace may punish a person adjudged guilty of a direct contempt of court by a fine of not more than fifty dollars, or imprisonment in the parish jail for not more than twenty-four hours, or both.

E. When a contempt of court consists of the omission to perform an act which is yet in the power of the person charged with contempt to perform, he may be imprisoned until he performs it, and in such a case this shall be specified in the court's order.
(Chgd. by Acts 1991 No. 508, §1, eff. 9/6/91.)

CHAPTER 4. PEACE BONDS

Article

Art. 26. Power to order peace bonds.

A magistrate may order a peace bond in conformity with the provisions of this Chapter.

Art. 27. Application for peace bond; examination.

An applicant for a peace bond shall file an affidavit charging that the defendant has threatened or is about to commit a specified breach of the peace. The magistrate with whom the application is filed may examine under oath the complainant and any witnesses produced.

Art. 28. Issuance of summons or warrant of arrest.

If the magistrate is satisfied that there is just cause to fear that the defendant is about to commit the threatened offense, he shall issue a summons ordering the defendant to appear before him at a specified time and date. The magistrate may issue a warrant of arrest when imminent and serious harm is threatened.

Art. 29. Peace bond hearing; costs.

A. When a defendant appears before the magistrate, a contradictory hearing to determine the validity of the complaint shall be held immediately either in chambers or in open court. If the magistrate determines that there is just cause to fear that the defendant is about to commit the threatened offense, he may order the defendant to give a peace bond. Otherwise, he shall discharge the defendant.

B. The applicant for a peace bond shall pay as advanced court costs a fee of fifteen dollars for each defendant summoned to a hearing. If the magistrate discharges the defendant, the costs shall be paid by the applicant. If the magistrate orders the defendant to give a peace bond, the costs shall be paid instead by the defendant. However, the court may assess those costs, or any part thereof, against any party, as it may consider equitable.

C. Costs may be waived for an indigent applicant or defendant who complies with the provisions of Chapter 5 of Book IX of the Louisiana Code of Civil Procedure. The proceeds derived from these costs shall be deposited and used by the court in accordance with the provisions of R.S. 13:1899(B).

Art. 30. The peace bond.

The peace bond shall be for a specified period, not to exceed six months, and its condition shall be that the defendant will not commit the threatened or any related breach of the peace. The bond shall be for a sum fixed by the magistrate. When fixed by a justice of the peace, the maximum amount of the bond shall not exceed one thousand dollars.

The peace bond obligation shall run in favor of the clerk or judge of the court ordering the bond, in favor of the city when ordered by the mayor of a mayor's court, or in favor of the police jury when the bond is ordered by a justice of the peace. The proceeds shall be disposed of in the manner provided by law.

The types of security for a peace bond shall be governed by the bail bond rules set forth in Title VIII, as far as applicable.

Art. 31. Failure to give peace bond; effect.

If the defendant fails to give the peace bond required under Articles 29 and 30, he shall be committed to jail. The defendant may be discharged by the committing or some other magistrate upon giving bond as ordered. The committing magistrate may revoke or modify his order for a peace bond.

A defendant who has been committed for failure to give a peace bond ordered by a justice of the peace may not be held longer than five days.

Art. 32. Forfeiture of peace bond.

When the magistrate determines that a breach of peace in violation of a peace bond has been committed, he shall order a forfeiture of the bond and send notice of the forfeiture by certified mail to the defendant and to his surety. If neither the defendant nor his surety appears within fifteen days to contest the forfeiture, the order shall become final and executory.

Art. 33. Automatic discharge.

A peace bond is automatically discharged at the end of thirty days from the expiration of the period specified therein, unless a proceeding to declare a forfeiture has been brought within that time.

TITLE II. DISTRICT ATTORNEY AND ATTORNEY GENERAL

Art. 61. District attorney; powers and duties.

Subject to the supervision of the attorney general, as provided in Article 62, the district attorney has entire charge and control of every criminal prosecution instituted or pending in his district, and determines whom, when, and how he shall prosecute.

Art. 62. Authority of attorney general; supervision of district attorney.

The attorney general shall exercise supervision over all district attorneys in the state.

The attorney general has authority to institute and prosecute, or to intervene in any proceeding, as he may deem necessary for the assertion or protection of the rights and interests of the state.

Art. 63. District attorney; assistance of other counsel.

The district attorney may employ or accept the assistance of other counsel in the conduct of a criminal case.

Art. 64. Relationship of district attorney with grand jury.

The district attorney is the representative of the state before the grand jury and is its legal advisor. He shall be notified of and has the right to be present at all sessions of the grand jury, except while it is deliberating and voting. He shall examine witnesses before the grand jury.

Art. 65. Defense of prosecution unlawful.

It is unlawful for the following officers or their law partners to defend or assist in the defense of any person charged with an offense in any parish of the state:

(1) Any district attorney or assistant district attorney; or

(2) The attorney general or any assistant attorney general, provided that the provisions of this article shall not apply to the law partners of any assistant attorney general not employed to handle criminal matters for the attorney general, when any such law partner is judicially appointed to defend an indigent defendant.

Art. 66. Subpoena of witness to appear before attorney general and district attorney.

Upon written motion of the attorney general or district attorney setting forth reasonable grounds therefor, the court may order the clerk to issue subpoenas directed to the persons named in the motion, ordering them to appear at a time and place designated in the order for questioning by the attorney general or district attorney respectively, concerning any offense under investigation by him. The court may also order the issuance of a subpoena duces tecum.

The contumacious failure or refusal of the person subpoenaed to appear is punishable as a contempt of court.

The attorney general or district attorney, respectively, may determine who shall be present during the examination and may order all persons excluded, except counsel for the person subpoenaed.

Art. 67. Report of appeals; preparation of briefs; appellate representation.

The district attorney shall immediately notify the attorney general in writing when an appeal has been taken to the supreme court, or when the supervisory jurisdiction of the supreme court has been invoked. The district attorney shall prepare a brief and forward it to the attorney general, who may revise the brief for use in the supreme court.

The attorney general shall represent the state in criminal cases before the supreme court.

TITLE III. THE CORONER AND OTHER OFFICERS

Chapter

CHAPTER 1. THE CORONER

Article

Art. 101. Abolition of coroner's jury and inquest; investigation by coroner.

The coroner's jury and inquest are abolished.

The coroner shall conduct an investigation concerning the manner and cause of any death when informed that death has resulted from violence or accident, or under suspicious circumstances.

The coroner may conduct an investigation concerning the medical aspects of any case that may involve medical evidence and in which there is a reasonable probability that a criminal statute has been violated and shall do so when ordered by the court. This order may be issued ex parte by the court either on its own motion or on application by the district attorney.

Art. 102. Autopsy.

The coroner may perform an autopsy in any death case or cause one to be performed by a competent physician. He shall do so:

(1) When there is a reasonable probability that the violation of a criminal statute has contributed to the death;

(2) When ordered by the court, which order may be issued ex parte by the court either on its own motion or on application by the district attorney; or

(3) In all other cases provided by law.

Art. 103. Subpoena of witnesses; testimony; subpoena duces tecum; issuance.

A. The coroner may issue a subpoena or a subpoena duces tecum in the course of an investigation, directing a witness to appear and testify at an open hearing to be held at a time and place designated in the subpoena or directing the production of medical records and other documents relating to a deceased person which are necessary to classify the cause and manner of death. The subpoena shall be served in the same manner and with the same effect as a subpoena for a witness at a trial.

B. (1) The subpoena duces tecum shall be filed in and issued by the district court in the domicile of the coroner, and may be served by a coroner investigator.

(2) Production of the records, or a copy thereof, shall be made at the office of the coroner within five days of service of the subpoena duces tecum.

(3) All records produced pursuant to a subpoena duces tecum issued in accordance with this Paragraph are confidential unless otherwise ordered by the court. However, a subpoena duces tecum for the production of a public record does not alter the public nature of that record.

(4) Any person acting pursuant to and in accordance with the provisions hereof shall be immune from liability for production or disclosure to the coroner of the records identified in the subpoena duces tecum.

(5) Failure to comply with a subpoena duces tecum issued under this Article is punishable as contempt of court.

C. The witness shall be sworn, in accordance with Article 14, by the coroner or another person authorized to administer oaths, and the testimony may be reduced to writing. If the testimony is reduced to writing, the transcript shall be available for inspection by a person requesting it. Failure of a witness to appear is punishable as a constructive contempt of court.

D. No provision of this Article shall be deemed to amend, supersede, or repeal the provisions of R.S. 45:1455 et seq.

(Chgd. by Acts 1995 No. 887, §1, eff. 8/15/95.)

Art. 104. Employment of expert assistants.

The coroner may use expert assistants in the conduct of an investigation, or in the performance of an autopsy.

Art. 105. Coroner's report; admissibility in evidence.

In a case involving the apparent commission of a crime, the coroner shall make a written report of his investigation to the district attorney within ten days after the completion thereof. In homicide cases the coroner's report shall certify the cause of death.

The report shall be in addition to the procès verbal of an autopsy required by R.S. 33:1565.

A coroner's report and a procès verbal of an autopsy shall be competent evidence of death and the cause thereof, but not of any other fact.

Art. 106. Arrest of criminal suspect.

If an investigation by the coroner indicates that a crime has been committed by a person who is not in custody, the coroner may arrest him. The coroner shall deliver the person arrested to a peace officer.

CHAPTER 2. CLERKS, SHERIFFS, CONSTABLES, AND MARSHALS

Art. 131. Duties and powers.

Clerks, sheriffs, constables, marshals, stenographers, and other court officers have such powers and perform such duties as are conferred upon them by law.

TITLE IV. SEARCH WARRANTS

Art. 161. Property subject to seizure.

A. A judge may issue a warrant authorizing the search for and seizure of any thing within the territorial jurisdiction of the court which:

(1) Has been the subject of theft.

(2) Is intended for use or has been used as a means of committing an offense.

(3) May constitute evidence tending to prove the commission of an offense.

B. A judge of a city court located in a municipality with a population of between twelve thousand and fifteen thousand, in a parish the population of which is between twenty-five thousand and thirty-five thousand, within a judicial district composed of two parishes may, only with the consent of the judicial district court, issue a warrant authorizing the search for and seizure of anything within the territorial jurisdiction of the district court.

C. A judge may also issue a search warrant in all other cases specifically provided by law. A justice of the peace may issue a search warrant only in those cases specifically provided by law.

(Chgd. by Acts 1993 No. 846, §1, eff. 8/15/93.)

Art. 162. Issuance of warrant; affidavit; description.

A search warrant may issue only upon probable cause established to the satisfaction of the judge, by the affidavit of a credible person, reciting facts establishing the cause for issuance of the warrant.

A search warrant shall particularly describe the person or place to be searched, the persons or things to be seized, and the lawful purpose or reason for the search or seizure.

Art. 162.1. Warrant issued upon oral testimony.

A. In addition to the provisions of Article 162, a search warrant may issue only upon probable cause established to the satisfaction of the judge by the sworn oral testimony of a credible person reciting facts establishing the cause for issuance of the warrant.

B. The sworn oral testimony may be communicated to the judge, and the oath may be administered by the judge, by telephone, radio, or such other electronic method of communication deemed appropriate by the judge. If the judge determines that the warrant should issue, he shall order the applicant to affix a facsimile of his signature to the warrant which the applicant has prepared and to note thereon the date and time of the determination. The sworn oral testimony, the contents of the warrant issued, the order to affix the signature facsimile, and the date and time of the determination shall be electronically recorded by the judge, who shall cause the recording to be transcribed and fixed in the record within seven days. The judge shall certify the accuracy of the transcription.

C. A search warrant shall particularly describe the person or place to be searched, the persons or things to be seized, and the lawful purpose or reason for the search or seizure.

(Chgd. by Acts 1991 No. 84, §1, eff. 9/6/91.)

Art. 163. Officer to whom directed; time for execution.

A search warrant shall be directed to any peace officer, who shall execute it and bring any property seized into the court issuing the warrant.

A search or seizure shall not be made during the nighttime or on Sunday, unless the warrant expressly so directs.

A search warrant cannot be lawfully executed after the expiration of the tenth day after its issuance.

Art. 164. Means and force in executing warrant.

In order to execute a search warrant a peace officer may use such means and force as are authorized for arrest by Title V.

Art. 165. Authority of peace officer in executing a search warrant.

While in the course of executing a search warrant, a peace officer may make photographs, lift fingerprints, seize things whether or not described in the warrant that may constitute evidence tending to prove the commission of any offense, and perform all other acts pursuant to his duties.

Art. 166. Receipt for seized property.

When a peace officer seizes property under a warrant he shall give a receipt to the person from whom the property is taken, describing the property in detail. In the absence of such person, the peace officer shall leave the receipt in the place where the property was seized.

Art. 167. Custody of seized property; disposition.

When property is seized pursuant to a search warrant, it shall be retained under the direction of the judge. If seized property is not to be used as evidence or is no longer needed as evidence, it shall be disposed of according to law, under the direction of the judge.

TITLE V. ARREST

Art. 201. Arrest defined.

Arrest is the taking of one person into custody by another. To constitute arrest there must be an actual restraint of the person. The restraint may be imposed by force or may result from the submission of the person arrested to the custody of the one arresting him.

Art. 202. Warrant of arrest; issuance.

A. A warrant of arrest may be issued by any magistrate, and, except where a summons is issued under Article 209, shall be issued when:

(1) The person making the complaint executes an affidavit specifying, to his best knowledge and belief, the nature, date, and place of the offense, and the name and surname of the offender if known, and of the person injured if there be any; and

(2) The magistrate has probable cause to believe that an offense was committed and that the person against whom the complaint was made committed it.

B. (1) A justice of the peace shall not have the authority to issue a warrant for the arrest of a peace officer for acts performed while in the course and scope of his official duties.

(2) A justice of the peace shall not issue a warrant for the arrest of an administrator of any public or private elementary, secondary, high school, vocational-technical school, college, university, or licensed child day care center in this state who is acting in the course and scope of his official duties, unless an independent investigation into the allegations has been conducted and the investigator's findings support the allegations contained in the affidavit required in Subparagraph A(1) of this Article.

C. When complaint is made before a magistrate of the commission of an offense in another parish, the magistrate shall also immediately notify the district attorney of the parish in which the offense is alleged to have been committed.

(Chgd. by Acts 1997 No. 783, §1, eff. 8/15/97.)

Art. 203. Form and contents of warrant.

The warrant of arrest shall:

(1) Be in writing and be in the name of the State of Louisiana;

(2) State the date when issued and the municipality or parish where issued;

(3) State the name of the person to be arrested, or, if his name is unknown, designate the person by any name or description by which he can be identified with reasonable certainty;

(4) State the offense charged against the person to be arrested;

(5) Command that the person against whom the complaint was made be arrested and booked; and

(6) Be signed by the magistrate with the title of his office.

The warrant of arrest may specify the amount of bail in noncapital cases when the magistrate has authority to fix bail.

Art. 204. Execution of warrant.

The warrant shall be directed to all peace officers in the state. It shall be executed only by a peace officer, and may be executed in any parish by any peace officer having authority in the territorial jurisdiction where the person arrested is found, or by any peace officer having authority in one territorial jurisdiction in this state who enters another jurisdiction in close pursuit of the person arrested.

Art. 205. Effective period.

A warrant of arrest remains in effect until executed.

Art. 206. Procedure when warrant defective.

A warrant of arrest shall not be quashed or abated, and a person in custody for an offense shall not be discharged from custody, because of any informality or defect in the warrant, but the warrant may be amended, so as to remedy the informality or defect.

Art. 207. Procedure when arrest made for offense triable in another parish.

When an arrest under a warrant occurs in a parish other than that in which the alleged offense was committed, the person arrested shall be booked and imprisoned in the parish where he was arrested until he gives bail or is transferred to the parish where the offense is alleged to have been committed. A person awaiting transfer shall not be detained in custody in the parish of his arrest for a longer period than ten days.

Art. 208. Summons; defined.

A summons is an order in writing, issued and signed by a magistrate or peace officer in the name of the state, stating the offense charged and the name of the alleged offender, and commanding him to appear before the court designated in the summons at the time and place stated in the summons.

Art. 209. When summons may be issued by magistrate.

When a complaint is made of the commission of a misdemeanor and the requirements of Article 202 are met, the magistrate may issue a summons instead of a warrant of arrest, if he has reasonable ground to believe that the person against whom the complaint is made will appear upon a summons. In a case where a summons has been issued, a warrant of arrest may be issued later in its place.

Art. 210. Service of summons.

The service of a summons is made in the same manner as a citation in a civil action.

Art. 211. Summons by officer instead of arrest and booking.

A. When it is lawful for a peace officer to arrest a person without a warrant for a misdemeanor, or for a felony charge of theft or illegal possession of stolen things when the thing of value is one hundred dollars or more but less than five hundred dollars, he may give a written summons instead of making an arrest if all of the following exist:

(1) The officer has reasonable grounds to believe that the person will appear upon summons;

(2) The officer has no reasonable grounds to believe that the person will cause injury to himself or another or damage to property or will continue in the same or a similar offense unless immediately arrested and booked;

(3) There is no necessity to book the person to comply with routine identification procedures.

(4) If an officer issues a summons for a felony described in this Paragraph, the officer issuing the summons shall ascertain that the person has no prior criminal convictions.

B. In any case in which a summons has been issued, a warrant of arrest may later be issued in its place.

(Chgd. by Acts 1995 No. 769, §1, eff. 8/15/95.)

Art. 211.1. Criminal trespass; summons by officer instead of arrest.

When a peace officer has reasonable grounds to believe a person has committed criminal trespass as defined by Section 63 of Title 14 of the Louisiana Revised Statutes of 1950, he shall give a written summons instead of making an arrest if:

(1) He has reasonable grounds to believe that the person will appear upon summons, and

(2) He has no reasonable grounds to believe that the person will cause injury to himself or another or damage to property unless immediately arrested.

In any case in which a summons has been issued, a warrant of arrest may later be issued in its place.

Art. 211.2. Issuing worthless checks; summons by peace officer instead of arrest.

A. When a peace officer has reasonable grounds to believe a person has committed the offense of issuing worthless checks as defined by R.S. 14:71, he may give a written summons instead of making an arrest if:

(1) He has reasonable grounds to believe that the person will appear upon summons, and

(2) He has no reasonable grounds to believe that the person will cause injury to himself or another or damage to property unless immediately arrested.

B. In any case in which a summons has been issued, a warrant of arrest may later be issued in its place.

Art. 211.3. Littering; citation or summons by peace officer instead of arrest; affidavits.

A. When a peace officer has reasonable grounds to believe a person has committed an offense of littering under the provisions of R.S. 30:2531 through 2531.3 he shall issue a written citation or summons to the offender in accordance with law, commanding him to appear and answer the charge.

B. For the purposes of this Section, reasonable belief may be based upon an affidavit completed on a form provided by any sheriff or the chief of police of the city of New Orleans for such purpose, containing the sworn statement of any Louisiana citizen of the age of majority, deposing that the citizen witnessed an act of littering, and particularly describing the offender and any vehicle or watercraft involved. Any form provided by a sheriff or the chief shall be pre-addressed and returnable to such sheriff or chief of police.
(Chgd. by Acts 1992 No. 360, §2; Acts 1998 First Ex. Sess. No. 148, §9, eff. 6/16/98.)

Art. 211.4. Driving without possession of a driver's license; summons by peace officer instead of arrest.

A. When a peace officer has reasonable grounds to believe a person has committed an offense of driving without a valid driver's license in his possession, the police officer shall make every practical attempt based on identifying information provided by the person to confirm that the person has been issued a valid driver's license. If the police officer determines that the person has been issued a valid driver's license which is neither under revocation, suspension, or cancellation, but that the license is not in his possession, the peace officer shall issue a written summons to the offender in accordance with law, commanding him to appear and answer the charge.

B. The provisions of this Article shall in no way limit the peace officer from issuing a citation for operating a motor vehicle without physical possession of a valid driver's license.
(Chgd. by Acts 1993 No. 537, §1, eff. 8/15/93.)

Art. 212. Securing jurisdiction over corporation, partnership, or other unincorporated association.

A. When a corporation, or partnership, or other association of persons not incorporated, is charged with the commission of an offense, the court before which the case is to be tried shall issue a summons stating the offense charged and ordering the defendant to appear before the court at a time and place stated in the summons.

B. The summons is served in the same manner as the citation of a corporation, or partnership, or other association of persons not incorporated, in a civil action.

C. If the corporation, or partnership, or other association of persons not incorporated, fails to appear as ordered, a plea of not guilty shall be entered by the court. Without further process, the trial shall be held and the court shall proceed to judgment and sentence as though the defendant had appeared.

Art. 213. Arrest by officer without warrant; when lawful.

A peace officer may, without a warrant, arrest a person when:

(1) The person to be arrested has committed an offense in his presence; and if the arrest is for a misdemeanor, it must be made immediately or on close pursuit;

(2) The person to be arrested has committed a felony, although not in the presence of the officer;

(3) The peace officer has reasonable cause to believe that the person to be arrested has committed an offense, although not in the presence of the officer; or

(4) The peace officer has received positive and reliable information that another peace officer from this state holds an arrest warrant, or a peace officer of another state or the United States holds an arrest warrant for a felony offense.

A peace officer in close pursuit of a person to be arrested, who is making an arrest pursuant to this Article may enter another jurisdiction in this state and make the arrest.

Art. 214. Arrest by private person; when lawful.

A private person may make an arrest when the person arrested has committed a felony, whether in or out of his presence.

Art. 215. Detention and arrest of shoplifters.

A. (1) A peace officer, merchant, or a specifically authorized employee or agent of a merchant, may use reasonable force to detain a person for questioning on the merchant's premises, for a length of time, not to exceed sixty minutes, unless it is reasonable under the circumstances that the person be detained longer, when he has reasonable cause to believe that the person has committed a theft of goods held for sale by the merchant, regardless of the actual value of the goods. The merchant or his employee or agent may also detain such a person for arrest by a peace officer. The detention shall not constitute an arrest.

(2) A peace officer may, without a warrant, arrest a person when he has reasonable grounds to believe the person has committed a theft of goods held for sale by a merchant, regardless of the actual value of the goods. A complaint made to a peace officer by a merchant or a merchant's employee or agent shall constitute reasonable cause for the officer making the arrest.

B. If a merchant utilizes electronic devices which are designed to detect the unauthorized removal of marked merchandise from the store, and if sufficient notice has been posted to advise the patrons that such a device is being utilized, a signal from the device to the merchant or his employee or agent indicating the removal of specially marked merchandise shall constitute a sufficient basis for reasonable cause to detain the person.

C. As used in this Article, "reasonable under the circumstances" shall be construed in such a manner so as to include the value of the merchandise in question, the location of the store, the length of time taken for law enforcement personnel to respond, the cooperation of the person detained, and any other relevant circumstances to be considered with respect to the length of time a person is detained.

Art. 215.1. Temporary questioning of persons in public places; frisk and search for weapons.

A. A law enforcement officer may stop a person in a public place whom he reasonably suspects is committing, has committed, or is about to commit an offense and may demand of him his name, address, and an explanation of his actions.

B. When a law enforcement officer has stopped a person for questioning pursuant to this Article and reasonably suspects that he is in danger, he may frisk the outer clothing of such person for a dangerous weapon. If the law enforcement officer reasonably suspects the person possesses a dangerous weapon, he may search the person.

C. If the law enforcement officer finds a dangerous weapon, he may take and keep it until the completion of the questioning, at which time he shall either return it, if lawfully possessed, or arrest such person.

D. During detention of an alleged violator of any provision of the motor vehicle laws of this state, an officer may not detain a motorist for a period of time longer than reasonably necessary to complete the investigation of the violation and issuance of a citation for the violation, absent reasonable suspicion of additional criminal activity. However, nothing herein shall prohibit a peace officer from compelling or instructing the motorist to comply with administrative or other legal requirements of Title 32 or Title 47 of the Louisiana Revised Statutes of 1950.

(Chgd. by Acts 1997 No. 759, §3, eff. 7/10/97.)

Art. 215.2. Detaining of persons on premises of correctional institution for questioning about contraband; detention for arrest.

A. A specifically authorized employee of a correctional institution may use reasonable force to detain a person for questioning on the premises of a correctional institution for a length of time not to exceed one hour, when he has reasonable cause to believe that the person is carrying contraband as defined in R.S. 14:402(A).

B. The specifically authorized employee, when he has reasonable cause to believe that the person is carrying contraband as defined in R.S. 14:402(A), may also detain such a person for arrest by a peace officer or for the procurement of a search warrant. The detention shall not constitute an arrest.

Art. 216. Time and place of making arrest.

An arrest may be made on any day and at any time of the day or night, and at any place.

Art. 217. Method of arrest by officer under warrant.

A peace officer, when making an arrest by virtue of a warrant, shall inform the person to be arrested of his authority and of the fact that a warrant has been issued for his arrest, unless he flees or forcibly resists before the officer has an opportunity to inform him, or unless the giving of such information would imperil the arrest. The officer need not have the warrant in his possession at the time of the arrest, but after the arrest, if the person arrested so requests, the warrant shall be shown to him as soon as practicable.

Art. 218. Method of arrest without warrant.

A peace officer, when making an arrest without a warrant, shall inform the person to be arrested of his intention to arrest him, of his authority, and of the cause of the arrest. A private person, when making an arrest, shall inform the person to be arrested of his intention to arrest him and of the cause of the arrest.

The officer or private person making the arrest need not so inform the person to be arrested if the person is then engaged in the commission of an offense, or is pursued immediately after its commission or after an escape, or flees or forcibly resists before the officer or person making the arrest has an opportunity to so inform him, or when the giving of the information would imperil the arrest.

Art. 218.1. Advice of reasons for arrest or detention and of rights.

When any person has been arrested or detained in connection with the investigation or commission of any offense, he shall be advised fully of the reason for his arrest or detention, his right to remain silent, his right against self incrimination, his right to the assistance of counsel and, if indigent, his right to court appointed counsel.

Art. 219. Officer may summon assistance.

A peace officer making a lawful arrest may call upon as many persons has he considers necessary to aid him in making the arrest. A person thus called upon shall be considered a peace officer for such purposes.

Art. 220. Submission to arrest; use of force.

A person shall submit peaceably to a lawful arrest. The person making a lawful arrest may use reasonable force to effect the arrest and detention, and also to overcome any resistance or threatened resistance of the person being arrested or detained.

Art. 221. Blood and saliva testing.

A. (1) Following arrest if an offender is charged by bill of information or indicted by a grand jury for intentionally exposing a police officer to AIDS virus as defined in R.S. 14:43.5, or battery upon a police officer as defined in R.S. 14:34.2, the police officer may be tested to determine whether the police officer is infected with a sexually transmitted disease, or is infected with acquired immune deficiency syndrome (AIDS), the human immunodeficiency virus (HIV), HIV-1 antibodies, or any other probable causative agent of AIDS, or other infectious disease resulting from this exposure, or viral hepatitis.

(2) For purposes of this Section, "police officer" means a commissioned police officer, sheriff, deputy sheriff, marshal, deputy marshal, correctional officer, constable, wildlife enforcement agent, and probation and parole officer.

B. (1) If testing is requested by the police officer, as provided in Subsection A of this Section, the testing shall be performed at a state hospital or other facility as determined by the Department of Health and Hospitals or as provided by law.

(2) If the police officer tested under the provisions of this Subsection tests positive for AIDS, HIV, HIV-1 antibodies, or any other probable causative agent of AIDS, viral hepatitis, or other infectious disease, the police officer, upon request, shall be provided with the following services:

(a) Counseling regarding HIV, viral hepatitis, or other infectious disease.

(b) Referral to appropriate health care and support services. These services shall be provided in accordance with applicable state law and the regulations governing the specific programs under which the services are to be provided.

(3) The cost associated with this testing and services shall be paid by the employing law enforcement agency of the police officer. The agency may seek reimbursement for these expenses from the offender.

C. (1) If the police officer tested under the provisions of Subsection B tests positive for AIDS, HIV, HIV-1 antibodies, or any other probable causative agent of AIDS, viral hepatitis, or other infectious disease, then the offender who may have exposed the officer shall submit to a test designed to determine whether the offender is infected with a sexually transmitted disease, or is infected with acquired immune deficiency syndrome (AIDS), the human immunodeficiency virus (HIV), HIV-1 antibodies, or any other probable causative agent of AIDS, viral hepatitis, or other infectious disease.

(2) The procedure or test shall be performed by a qualified physician or other qualified person who shall report any positive result to the chief administrator of the jail or correctional facility, if the offender is incarcerated, and shall also notify the offender, regardless of the results. If the offender is incarcerated, the test may be administered at the place of incarceration or the offender may be transferred to an appropriate testing facility and returned to incarceration following the testing procedure.

(3) If the offender tested under the provisions of this Subsection tests positive for AIDS, HIV, HIV-1 antibodies, or any other probable causative agent of AIDS, viral hepatitis, or other infectious disease, upon request, he shall be provided with the following services:

(a) Counseling regarding HIV, viral hepatitis, or other infectious disease.

(b) Referral to appropriate health care and support services. These services shall be provided in accordance with applicable state law and the regulations governing the specific programs under which the services are to be provided.

(4) The costs associated with this testing shall be paid by the offender.

(Added by Acts 1997 No. 1012, §1, eff. 8/15/97.)

Art. 224. Forcible entry in making arrest.

In order to make an arrest, a peace officer, who has announced his authority and purpose, may break open an outer or inner door or window of any vehicle, watercraft, aircraft, dwelling or other structure, movable or immovable, where the person to be arrested is or is reasonably believed to be, if he is refused or otherwise obstructed from admittance. The peace officer need not announce his authority and purpose when to do so would imperil the arrest.

Art. 225. Duty of peace officer as to weapons and incriminating articles.

A peace officer making an arrest shall take from the person arrested all weapons and incriminating articles which he may have about his person. He shall deliver these articles and all other evidence seized incidental to the arrest to the sheriff, chief of police, or other officer before whom the person arrested is taken.

Art. 226. Duty of private person after making arrest.

A private person who has made an arrest shall immediately turn the prisoner and all effects removed from him over to a peace officer.

Art. 227. Rearrest after escape.

If a person lawfully arrested escapes or is rescued, the person from whose custody he escaped or was rescued may pursue and retake him immediately without a warrant at any time and in any place within the state. He may use the same means to retake as are authorized for an arrest.

Art. 227.1. Prevention of escape; use of force.

A guard or other law enforcement officer is justified in the reasonable use of force, to prevent the escape from a state correctional facility, parish prison, or the physical custody of a guard or other law enforcement officer of a person under sentence or awaiting trial.

Art. 228. Booking of arrested person, submission of booking information summary.

A. It is the duty of every peace officer making an arrest, or having an arrested person in his custody, promptly to conduct the person arrested to the nearest jail or police station and cause him to be booked.

B. A person is booked by an entry, in a book kept for that purpose, showing his name and address, a list of any property taken from him, the date and time of booking, and the submission of a booking information summary as provided for in Paragraph C of this Article to the person making the entry in the police or jail book. Every jail and police station shall keep a book for the listing of the above information as to each prisoner received. The book and booking information summaries shall always be open for public inspection. The person booked shall be imprisoned unless he is released on bail.

C. (1) At the time of booking, the peace officer causing the arrested person to be booked shall deliver to the person at the jail or police station who accepts custody of the arrestee a booking information summary which shall include at least the following information:

(a) The proper legal name of the arrestee, if known.

(b) The charge or charges upon which the person was arrested and the name of the person making the arrest.

(c) A short recitation of the facts or events which caused the defendant to be arrested.

(d) The names of all other persons arrested as a result of the same events or facts.

(2) If the peace officer presenting an arrestee for booking is unable to submit a complete booking information summary, he shall provide the person receiving custody of the arrestee a written statement or form, explaining why a complete booking information summary cannot be presented.

(Chgd. by Acts 1992 No. 672, §1, eff. 8/21/92.)

Art. 228.1. Disposal of property of prisoners; Orleans Parish.

Any property taken from a prisoner in any of the penal institutions under jurisdiction of the criminal sheriff for the parish of Orleans shall, after 90 days from the release of said prisoner, be disposed of in the following manner:

(1) There shall be notice of the sheriff's right to dispose of the property in ninety days on the entry of the list of property made at the time the person is incarcerated. Provided however, this provision shall not apply to property in possession of the sheriff at the effective date of this Act.

(2) After the passage of ninety days from the release of the prisoner, and providing the property is not needed for any legal reason by the sheriff, and it remains unclaimed, the criminal sheriff of Orleans Parish may petition the Criminal District Court for the parish of Orleans or any court of proper jurisdiction for the disposal of said property in any lawful manner, at his discretion.

(3) Before the criminal sheriff petitions said court he shall cause an advertisement of his intention to seek approval of the court to be placed in the newspaper designated as the official journal of the city of New Orleans one time at least ten days prior to filing of his petition. In the petition for disposal the sheriff shall set forth a brief description of the items to be disposed of, the court in which the proceedings will be filed, the title of the proceedings, and method or methods of intended disposal.

(4) The petition of the sheriff shall make specific recommendations as to the method of disposal for each item of unclaimed property and pray for the court to order its disposal.

(5) The court shall order the property disposed of in the manner contained in the sheriff's petition or order the disposal of the property in any legal manner within the sole discretion of the court.

(6) The costs of the proceeding to dispose of unclaimed property shall be derived from the disposal of the property as provided under this subsection.

(7) Any funds remaining after payment of the cost of the proceedings to dispose of unclaimed property shall be deposited in the criminal court fund account which shall be used in defraying the expenses of the criminal district courts of Orleans Parish.

Art. 228.2. Disposal of property of prisoners; Orleans Parish excepted.

Any property taken from a prisoner in any of the penal institutions under the jurisdiction of any sheriff, Orleans excepted, shall, after ninety days from the release of said prisoner, be disposed of, if unclaimed, in the following manner:

(1) There shall be notice of the sheriff's right to dispose of the property in ninety days on the entry of the list of property made at the time the person was incarcerated. Provided however, this provision shall not apply to property in possession of the sheriff on September 12, 1975.

(2) After the passage of ninety days from the release of the prisoner, any sheriff may petition the court having proper jurisdiction for the disposal of said property in any lawful manner, at his discretion.

(3) Before any sheriff petitions said court he shall cause an advertisement of his intention to seek approval of the court to be placed in the newspaper designated as the official journal of the parish one time at least ten days prior to filing of his petition, and shall mail a copy of the advertisement to the prisoner at his last known address, postage prepaid. In the petition for disposal the sheriff shall set forth a brief description of the items to be disposed of, the court in which the proceedings will be filed, the title of the proceedings, and method or methods of intended disposal.

(4) The petition of the sheriff shall make specific recommendations as to the method of disposal for each item of unclaimed property and pray for the court to order its disposal.

(5) The court shall order the property disposed of in the manner contained in the sheriff's petition or order the disposal of the property in any legal manner within the sole discretion of the court.

(6) The costs of the proceedings to dispose of unclaimed property shall be derived from the disposal of the property as provided under this subsection.

(7) Any funds remaining after payment of the cost of the proceedings to dispose of unclaimed property shall be deposited in the Sheriff's salary fund.

Art. 228.3. Disposal of unclaimed property seized in any criminal investigation; Orleans Parish excepted.

Any unclaimed property seized in connection with any criminal investigation under the jurisdiction of any sheriff, Orleans excepted, shall, if it remains unclaimed for more than one year after its use or from the time it was last used in connection with any criminal proceeding, be disposed of in the following manner:

(1) After the lapse of one year any sheriff may petition the court having proper jurisdiction for the disposal of said property in any lawful manner.

(2) Before any sheriff petitions said court he shall cause an advertisement of his intention to seek approval of the court to be placed in the newspaper designated as the official journal of the parish one time at least ten days prior to filing of his petition, and shall mail a copy of the advertisement to the last known owner at his last known address, postage prepaid. In the petition for disposal the sheriff shall set forth a brief description of the items to be disposed of, the court in which the proceedings will be filed, the title of the proceedings, and method or methods of intended disposal.

(3) The petition of the sheriff shall make specific recommendations as to the method of disposal for each item of unclaimed property and pray for the court to order its disposal.

(4) The court shall order the property disposed of in the manner contained in the sheriff's petition or order the disposal of the property in any legal manner within the sole discretion of the court.

(5) The costs of the proceedings to dispose of unclaimed property shall be derived from the disposal of the property as provided under this Subsection.

(6) Any funds remaining after payment of the cost of the proceedings to dispose of unclaimed property shall be deposited in the sheriffs' salary fund.

Art. 229. Duties of officer in charge.

The officer in charge of the jail or police station shall immediately inform the prisoner booked:

(1) Of the charge against him;

(2) Of his rights to communicate with and procure counsel; and

(3) Of his right to request a preliminary examination when he is charged with a felony.

The officer in charge shall, within forty-eight hours from the time of the booking, notify the district attorney in writing of all persons booked for violation of state statutes, and shall furnish without cost a certified copy of any booking entry to any person requesting it.

Art. 230. Rights of person arrested.

The person arrested has, from the moment of his arrest, a right to procure and confer with counsel and to use a telephone or send a messenger for the purpose of communicating with his friends or with counsel.

Art. 230.1. Maximum time for appearance before judge for the purpose of appointment of counsel; court discretion to fix bail at the appearance; extension of time limit for cause; effect of failure of appearance.

A. The sheriff or law enforcement officer having custody of an arrested person shall bring him promptly, and in any case within seventy-two hours from the time of the arrest, before a judge for the purpose of appointment of counsel. Saturdays, Sundays, and legal holidays shall be excluded in computing the seventy-two hour period referred to herein. The defendant shall appear in person unless the court by local rule provides for such appearance by telephone or audio-video electronic equipment.

B. At this appearance, if a defendant has the right to have the court appoint counsel to defend him, the court shall assign counsel to the defendant. The court may also, in its discretion, determine or review a prior determination of the amount of bail.

C. If the arrested person is not brought before a judge in accordance with the provisions of Paragraph A of this Article, he shall be released forthwith.

D. The failure of the sheriff or law enforcement officer to comply with the requirements herein shall have no effect whatsoever upon the validity of the proceedings thereafter against the defendant.

Art. 230.2. Probable cause determination; persons arrested without a warrant and continued in custody.

A. A law enforcement officer effecting the arrest of a person without a warrant shall promptly complete an affidavit of probable cause supporting the arrest of the person and submit the same to a magistrate. Persons continued or remaining in custody pursuant to an arrest made without a warrant shall be entitled to a determination of probable cause within forty-eight hours of arrest. The probable cause determination shall be made by a magistrate and shall not be an adversary proceeding. The determination may be made without the presence of the defendant and may be made upon affidavits or other written evidence. A magistrate's determination of probable cause hereunder shall not act as a waiver of a person's right to a preliminary examination pursuant to Article 292.

B. If a probable cause determination is not timely made in accordance with the provisions of Paragraph A of this Article, the arrested person shall be released on his own recognizance. *(Added by Acts 1992 No. 674, §1, eff. 8/21/92.)*

Art. 231. Close pursuit of person from another state; authority to arrest.

A state, county, or city peace officer of another state of the United States who enters this state in close pursuit of a person and continues within this state in close pursuit to arrest him on the ground that he is reasonably believed to have committed a felony in the other state, shall have the same authority to arrest and hold the person in custody as has a peace officer of this state to arrest and hold a person in custody on the ground that he is reasonably believed to have committed a felony in this state.

This article shall not be construed so as to make unlawful any arrest in this state that would otherwise be lawful.

Art. 232. Same; arrested person taken before judge for hearing.

An officer making an arrest under Article 231 shall, without unnecessary delay, take the person arrested before a judge of the parish in which the arrest was made, who shall conduct a hearing for the purpose of determining the lawfulness of the arrest. If the judge determines that the arrest was lawful he shall, subject to rights of bail as stated in Article 271, commit the person arrested to jail for a period of time, not exceeding thirty days, to await the issuance of an extradition warrant by the governor of this state. If the judge determines that the arrest was unlawful he shall discharge the person arrested.

TITLE VI. EXTRADITION

Art. 261. Special definitions.

In this Title:

(1) "Crime" means any offense denounced by a state statute and does not include an offense denounced by a local ordinance.

(2) "Governor" includes any person performing the functions of governor by authority of the law of this state.

(3) "Executive authority" includes the governor, and any person performing the functions of governor in a state other than this state.

(4) "Indictment" is limited in meaning to the finding of a grand jury.

(5) "Judge" means any judge of a district court with criminal jurisdiction.

(6) "State," when used with reference to a state other than this state, means any state or territory of the United States of America, and includes the District of Columbia.

Art. 262. Extradition of wanted criminals.

Subject to the provisions of this Title, the governor may, in his discretion, have arrested and delivered to the executive authority of any other state any person wanted in that state to be tried for a crime, or wanted for sentencing or to serve sentence after conviction of a crime, who is found in this state.

Art. 263. Form of demand for extradition; necessary papers.

A demand for the extradition of a person wanted in another state shall not be recognized by the governor unless the demand is in writing and states the purpose for which he is wanted. The demand must be accompanied by:

(1) A statement of facts by the prosecuting officer having jurisdiction of the crime, and by a copy of an indictment found or of an information filed in the state having jurisdiction of the crime, or by a copy of an affidavit made before a magistrate there, together with a copy of any warrant which was issued thereupon; or

(2) A copy of a judgment of conviction or of a sentence imposed in execution thereof, together with a statement by the executive authority of the demanding state that the person claimed has escaped from confinement or has broken the terms of his bail, probation, parole, furlough, or reprieve.

The indictment, information, or affidavit made before the magistrate must substantially charge the person demanded with having committed a crime under the law of that state; and the copy of the indictment, information, affidavit, judgment of conviction, or sentence must be authenticated by the executive authority making the demand.

Art. 264. Investigation of demand by governor.

When a demand is made upon the governor of this state by the executive authority of another state for surrender of a person wanted by the other state, the governor may call upon the attorney general, a district attorney, or other official or agency in this state to investigate or assist in investigating the demand, and to report to him the situation of and circumstances surrounding the person so demanded, and whether or not he ought to be surrendered.

Art. 265. Governor's warrant; issuance and recitals.

If the governor decides that a demand for extradition should be complied with, he shall sign a warrant of arrest directed to any peace officer for execution. The warrant shall recite facts showing substantial compliance with Article 263, but an incomplete recital of facts shall not invalidate the warrant if a proper basis for its issuance exists.

Art. 266. Execution, recall, and expiration of governor's warrant.

The governor's warrant authorizes any peace officer to arrest the accused at any time and at any place he may be found in the state. The peace officer shall have authority to command the aid of other peace officers or persons in the execution of the warrant, and to deliver the accused, subject to the provisions of this Title, to the designated agent of the demanding state. The governor may recall his warrant of arrest or may issue another warrant at any time. A warrant issued by the governor shall expire when not executed within six months from the date of its issuance.

Art. 267. Rights of accused; extradition hearing.

A person arrested upon the governor's warrant shall not be delivered over to the agent appointed by the executive authority to receive him unless he shall first be taken before a judge, or in Orleans Parish, before a judge, a magistrate judge, or a commissioner of the magistrate section of the criminal district court, who shall inform him of the demand made for his surrender, of the crime with which he is charged, of his right to procure legal counsel, and of his right to an extradition hearing. If the prisoner or his counsel states that he desires an extradition hearing, the court shall assign as early a day as practicable for the hearing, to be held in open court. At least one full day shall intervene between the assignment and the day fixed for the hearing. Notice of the time and place of the hearing shall be given to the district attorney of the parish in which the hearing is to be held. If an extradition hearing is not requested, the prisoner shall be delivered promptly to the agent of the demanding state.

Art. 268. Issues at extradition hearing; resulting orders.

A. The grounds for discharge at the extradition hearing are that:

(1) The accused is not the person mentioned in the governor's warrant, in the requisition, or in the judgment of conviction, sentence, indictment, information, or affidavit which is the basis of the requisition;

(2) The governor's warrant is not signed; or

(3) A requirement of Art. 263 has not been met.

B. The guilt or innocence of the accused as to the crime of which he is charged is not an issue at the hearing. Unless one of the grounds for discharge is proven, the accused shall, without further delay, be delivered into the custody of the designated agent of the demanding state.

C. The court may commit the accused for an additional thirty-day period, to enable the demanding state to furnish the proper and necessary papers, if a ground for discharge under Subparagraph (2) or (3) under Paragraph (A) has been established. If some other ground for discharge is established the accused shall, without further delay, be released.

Art. 269. Arrest prior to demand for extradition; issuance of warrant.

A judge may issue a warrant for the arrest of a person in this state, prior to a demand for extradition in conformity with Article 263, when on the oath or affidavit of a credible person, taken before a judge or clerk of court, the person to be arrested is charged with:

(1) Being a fugitive from justice of another state;

(2) Commission of a crime in another state; or

(3) Having been convicted of a crime in another state, and having escaped from confinement or having broken the terms of his bail, probation, parole, furlough, or reprieve.

In this article, "judge" means any judge of a district, city, or parish court with criminal jurisdiction.

Art. 270. Commitment to await extradition.

A. The judge shall commit the accused for thirty days if it appears, after a hearing in open court, that there is reasonable ground to hold him awaiting extradition. The order of commitment shall recite the accusation. The accused shall be imprisoned in the parish jail until the term of his commitment expires or he is otherwise legally discharged, unless he gives bail as provided in Article 271.

B. The judge may extend the commitment of the accused for an additional period, not to exceed sixty days, if such additional period of commitment is for the purpose of awaiting receipt of the extradition requisition or other necessary or proper papers needed for the extradition of the accused.

Art. 271. Bail in extradition cases.

A judge shall admit to bail a person arrested for extradition, or to await extradition, unless the offense with which the accused is charged is punishable by death or by life imprisonment under the laws of the state in which it was committed or unless the offender is charged as a parole violator or a convict charged with escape.

Art. 272. Persons under criminal prosecution or sentence in this state at time of requisition.

If a criminal prosecution against the demanded person is pending under the laws of this state, or if he has been convicted in a court of this state but has not completely satisfied his sentence, the governor may, in his discretion, surrender him on demand of the executive authority of the other state. The surrender must be pursuant to a re-extradition agreement, and:

(1) If a prosecution is pending the district attorney must agree to the surrender; or

(2) If the person demanded has been convicted, but has not been sentenced or has not completely satisfied his sentence, the court of the conviction must agree to the surrender.

Art. 273. Waiver of extradition proceedings.

A. A demanded person arrested in this state may waive the issuance and service of the warrant required by Articles 265 and 266 and all other requirements incidental to extradition proceedings, by consenting in writing in the presence of the judge to return to the demanding state. Before such waiver is executed or subscribed to by the demanded person, the judge shall inform him of his rights to the issuance and service of a warrant of extradition and to an extradition hearing. When a waiver has been executed the judge shall direct the officer having the person in custody to deliver him immediately to the accredited agent of the demanding state, with a copy of the waiver.

B. The waiver procedure of Paragraph A of this Article is not exclusive and does not in any way preclude the state's return of a probationer or parolee to another state with which the state of Louisiana has entered into a compact for out-of-state probation and parole supervision, under the authority of R.S. 15:574.14(3), or a probation or parole absconder who has signed a waiver of extradition as a condition of probation or parole.

Art. 274. Application for issuance of requisition.

When a district attorney desires the return to this state of a person wanted to be tried for a crime, he shall present to the governor a written application for a requisition for the return of the person charged. The application shall state the name of the person wanted, the crime with which he is charged, and the approximate time, place, and circumstances of its commission. It shall also specify the state in which he is believed to be and his probable location in that state at the time the application is made. The application shall recommend a peace officer or other person as agent to receive the accused. It shall certify that, in the opinion of the district attorney the ends of justice require the arrest and return of the accused to this state for trial and that the proceeding is not instituted to enforce a private claim.

Art. 275. Application for return of wanted fugitive.

When the return to this state of a person convicted of a crime who has escaped from confinement or broken the terms of his bail, probation, parole, furlough, or reprieve is desired, the governor shall be presented with a written application for a requisition for his return. The application may be made by a district attorney or the attorney general, and shall state the name of the person, the crime of which he was convicted, the circumstances of his escape from confinement or of the breach of the terms of his bail, probation, parole, furlough, or reprieve.

It shall specify the state in which he is believed to be and his probable location in that state at the time the application is made. It shall also recommend a peace officer or other person as agent to receive the person sought.

Art. 276. Documents to be filed with application for requisition.
The application for a requisition shall be verified by affidavit, executed in duplicate, and accompanied by two certified copies of all documents that are required for extradition by the law of the state from which the wanted person is to be returned. One copy of the application, with the action of the governor indicated by endorsement thereon, and one of the certified copies of the required documents, shall be filed in the office of the secretary of state. The other copies of all papers shall be forwarded with the governor's requisition. Failure to meet the requirements of this article, or of Articles 274 and 275, will not invalidate a requisition issued by the governor.

Art. 277. Appointment of agents to receive prisoner.
When the governor issues a requisition for extradition he shall also issue a warrant under the seal of the state, to an agent, commanding him to receive the person to be extradited and to deliver him to the proper authority.

Art. 278. Re-extradition agreements.
When the return to this state of a person wanted in this state to be tried for a crime is desired, and the person is imprisoned or is held under criminal proceedings pending against him in another state, the governor may enter into a re-extradition agreement with the executive authority of the other state for the purpose of procuring the extradition of the person before the conclusion of the proceedings or his term of sentence in the other state. The agreement shall be upon the condition that the person extradited will be returned to the other state without further extradition proceedings, upon the request of the executive authority of that state and at the expense of this state.

Art. 279. Extradition costs and expenses.
Necessary and reasonable expenses connected with an extradition shall be paid by the authority for whom it was requested.

Art. 280. Immunity of extradited person from service of process in civil actions.
A person brought into this state by, or after waiver of, extradition based on a criminal charge shall not be subject to service of personal process in civil actions until he has been convicted or has pleaded guilty in the criminal proceeding, or, if acquitted or otherwise discharged, until three days after the acquittal or discharge.

TITLE VII. PRELIMINARY EXAMINATION

Art. 291. Authority to conduct preliminary examinations.
The following magistrates, throughout their several territorial jurisdictions, shall have authority to conduct preliminary examinations of persons accused of felonies, with authority to bail or discharge, as follows:
(1) District courts having criminal jurisdiction, in all cases;
(2) City or parish courts having criminal jurisdiction, in cases not capital; and
(3) Justices of the peace in cases not capital or necessarily punishable at hard labor.

Art. 292. Order for preliminary examination before and after indictment.

The court, on request of the state or the defendant, shall immediately order a preliminary examination in felony cases unless the defendant has been indicted by a grand jury.

After the defendant has been indicted by a grand jury, the court may rescind its order for a preliminary examination.

An order for a preliminary examination in felony cases may be granted by the court at any time, either on its own motion or on request of the state or of the defendant before or after the defendant has been indicted by a grand jury.

Art. 293. Time for examination; procurement of counsel.

When a preliminary examination is ordered, the court shall conduct the examination promptly but shall allow the defendant a reasonable time to procure counsel.

Art. 294. Examination of witnesses; transcript of testimony.

A. At the preliminary examination the state and the defendant may produce witnesses, who shall be examined in the presence of the defendant and shall be subject to cross-examination. The defendant may also testify, subject to cross-examination. A record of the preliminary examination proceedings shall be made.

B. Except upon an order issued by the court pursuant to a motion filed by the defendant, a defendant who is charged with a crime against a juvenile may not subpoena the victim to testify at the preliminary examination.

C. A transcript of the testimony of the witnesses, including that of the defendant, may be made by the court or under its direction and, if made, shall be signed and certified by the person taking the testimony.

D. Upon motion of the state or the defendant, a transcript of the preliminary examination proceedings may be made. The cost of the transcript preparation under this Paragraph shall be paid by the party making the motion, unless the party is an indigent defendant.

E. The procedures set forth in Articles 322 through 329 of the Louisiana Children's Code and R.S. 15:440.1 and 283, relative to those procedures which provide protection for children who are victims of physical or sexual abuse, shall apply to all trial and pretrial procedures. *(Chgd. by Acts 1994 Third Ex. Sess. No. 142, §1, eff. 8/27/94.)*

Art. 295. Admissibility of transcripts in other proceedings.

A. The transcript of the testimony of a defendant who testified at the preliminary examination is admissible against him upon the trial of the case or, if relevant, in any subsequent judicial proceeding.

B. The transcript of testimony of any other witness who testified at the preliminary examination is admissible for any purpose in any subsequent proceeding in the case, on behalf of either party, if the court finds that the witness is dead, too ill to testify, cannot be found, or is otherwise unavailable for testimony, and that the absence of the witness was not procured by the party offering the testimony.

C. The transcript of testimony given by a person at a preliminary examination may be used by any party in a subsequent judicial proceeding for the purpose of impeaching or contradicting the testimony of such person as a witness.

Art. 296. Scope of preliminary examination before and after indictment.

If the defendant has not been indicted by a grand jury for the offense charged, the court shall, at the preliminary examination, order his release from custody or bail if, from the evidence adduced, it appears that there is not probable cause to charge him with the offense or with a lesser included offense. If the defendant is ordered held upon a finding of probable cause, the court shall fix his bail if he is entitled to bail.

After an indictment has been found by a grand jury, the preliminary examination shall be limited to the perpetuation of testimony and the fixing of bail.

Art. 297. Transmission of transcripts and other evidence.

After the preliminary examination, unless the court has ordered the release of the defendant upon a finding that there is not probable cause to charge him with an offense, the court shall transmit, without delay, to the clerk of the court having jurisdiction of the offense:

(1) The transcript of the testimony of the witnesses, including that of the defendant if he testified;

(2) The order rendered after the examination, or a certified copy thereof; and

(3) All articles or objects admitted in evidence.

Art. 298. Effect of informality in proceeding.

A person ordered held in custody following a preliminary examination shall not be discharged on a writ of habeas corpus or by other process because of any informality or error in the commitment or the proceedings prior thereto that does not substantially prejudice him. No preliminary examination shall be held invalid for any purpose because of an informality or error that does not substantially prejudice the defendant.

TITLE VIII. BAIL

Art. 311. Bail defined.

Bail is the security given by a person to assure his appearance before the proper court whenever required.

Art. 312. Types of bail.

A. There are three types or forms of bail in Louisiana:

(1) Bail through surety.

(2) Bail through cash deposits.

(3) Bail without surety.

B. All bail must be posted in the full amount set by the court.
(Chgd. by Acts 1993 No. 834, §1; Acts 1994 Third Ex. Sess. No. 52, §1, eff. 9/1/94.)

Art. 313. Surety.

Surety is defined as a legal suretyship pursuant to the provisions of Civil Code Art. 3035 et seq. *(Chgd. by Acts 1993 No. 834, §1, eff. 6/22/93.)*

Art. 314. Commercial surety.

A surety company authorized to do business in the state of Louisiana may become surety for the release of a person on bail. The sufficiency of security posted in the form of an appearance bond by a surety company, as required by the provisions of Title 22 of the Louisiana Revised Statutes of 1950, shall be determined solely by the commissioner of insurance. *(Chgd. by Acts 1993 No. 834, §1, eff. 6/22/93.)*

Art. 315. Personal surety.

A personal surety must be a citizen and resident of Louisiana, and worth, considering all his property whether incorporeal movable or immovable property, the amount specified in the bail bond. The worth of the surety shall be exclusive of the amount of any other bail bond on which he may be principal or surety, exclusive of property exempt from execution, and over and above all his other liabilities. When there is more than one surety the above requirements shall apply to their aggregate worth. No personal surety shall charge a fee or receive any compensation for posting a personal surety bond on behalf of any person. *(Chgd. by Acts 1993 No. 834, §1; Acts 1994 Third Ex. Sess. No. 52, §1, eff. 9/1/94.)*

Art. 316. Types of personal surety.

There are two types of personal surety in Louisiana: unsecured, and secured. *(Chgd. by Acts 1993 No. 834, §1, eff. 6/22/93.)*

Art. 317. Unsecured personal surety.

A person in custody may be released by order of the court on an unsecured personal surety bond. An unsecured personal surety is a personal surety where the surety meets all the qualifications of law and lives and resides in the judicial district where the criminal proceeding is pending without specifically mortgaging or giving a security interest in any property as security to guarantee the surety's performance. *(Chgd. by Acts 1991 No. 72, §1; Acts 1992 No. 401, §1; Acts 1993 No. 834, §1, eff. 6/22/93.)*

Art. 318. Secured personal surety.

A secured personal surety is a personal surety who meets all the qualifications of law and specifically mortgages or gives security interest in immovable property located in the state of Louisiana to secure the bail obligation. *(Chgd. by Acts 1993 No. 834, §1, eff. 6/22/93.)*

Art. 319. Proof of security interest.

Prior to the release of any criminal defendant on a secured personal surety bond, the personal surety shall present to the officer authorized to accept the bond recorded proof of a security interest in immovable property in favor of the state of Louisiana or the proper political subdivision, as proof that the value of the security interest less any encumbrances is equal to or greater than the full amount of the bail as set by the court. These requirements shall not be waived, except on weekends or holidays, and then only when sufficient proof shall be submitted to the officer authorized to accept the bond. *(Chgd. by Acts 1993 No. 834, §1; Acts 1994 Third Ex. Sess. No. 52, §1, eff. 9/1/94.)*

Art. 320. Those who may not be sureties.

A person shall not be released on bail for which an attorney at law, a judge, or ministerial officer of a court becomes a surety or provides money or property for bail; but the invalidity of such bail shall not be a defense to an action to forfeit and enforce the bail. *(Chgd. by Acts 1993 No. 834, §1, eff. 6/22/93.)*

Art. 321. Affidavit of surety.

A personal surety shall execute an affidavit that he possesses the sufficiency and qualifications prescribed by Article 315 and that he is not disqualified from becoming a surety by Article 320. The affidavit shall list the number and amount of undischarged bail bonds, if any, entered into by the surety. The officer accepting the bail may require the surety to state in his affidavit the nature and value of his property not exempt from execution, and the amount of his liabilities. An officer authorized to accept the bail shall have authority to administer any affidavit required of the person signing a bail bond. *(Chgd. by Acts 1993 No. 834, §1, eff. 6/22/93.)*

Art. 322. Declaration of residence by defendant and surety; waiver of notice.

A. The defendant when signing a bail bond shall write under his signature the address at which he resides. The address shall be conclusively presumed to continue for all proceedings on the bond, until he files in the proceeding in which the bond was given a written declaration changing the address.

B. A personal surety signing a bail bond shall write under his signature the address at which he resides. The address shall be conclusively presumed to continue for all proceedings on the bond, until he files in the proceeding in which the bond was given a written declaration changing the address.

C. A commercial surety shall inscribe on the face of the power of attorney used the execute the bond its proper mailing address. The address shall be conclusively presumed to continue for all proceedings on the bond, until a written declaration changing the address is filed in the proceeding in which the bond was given.

D. The agent or bondsman posting the bond shall write under his signature his proper mailing address. The address shall be conclusively presumed to continue for all proceedings on the bond, until a written declaration changing the address is filed in the proceeding in which the bond was given.

E. By signing the bail bond, the defendant and his surety waive any right to notice, except the notice provided for in Article 344 and R.S. 15:85.
(Chgd. by Acts 1993 No. 834, §1, eff. 6/22/93.)

Art. 323. Signature or declaration of person unable to write.

When a person who is required to sign his name or to make a declaration in writing under the provisions of this Code swears that he cannot sign or write, the officer authorized to receive the signature or declaration in writing may, at the request of the person, sign for him or make for him the declaration in writing, with the same binding effect as if the person had himself signed or himself made the declaration in writing; provided that the declaration and signature shall be witnessed and signed by at least two competent witnesses. *(Chgd. by Acts 1993 No. 834, §1, eff. 6/22/93.)*

Art. 324. Cash deposits.

A. (1) In lieu of a surety the defendant may furnish his personal undertaking, secured by a deposit with an officer authorized to accept the bail.

(2) The deposit shall consist of any of the following which are equal to the amount of the bail:

(a) Cash.

(b) A certified or cashier's check on any state or national bank.

(c) Bonds of the United States government negotiable by delivery.

(d) Bonds of the state of Louisiana or any political subdivision thereof negotiable by delivery.

(e) United States postal money orders or money orders issued by any state or national bank.

(3) The court in the parishes of St. John the Baptist and St. Charles, by written rule, may alter the percentage amount of bail to be deposited with the officer authorized to accept the bond and authorize the officer to charge an administrative fee, not to exceed fifteen dollars, for processing the bond.

B. Upon final disposition of all cases in which a deposit of money, checks, bonds or money orders has been made pursuant to this Article, and said deposits have remained unclaimed for a period of one year from the date of said final disposition, the officer authorized to accept said bail shall apply and use one-half of said funds for the operation and maintenance of the office of the clerk of court, or the office of the clerk of the criminal district court, or the office of the clerk of the criminal district court in parishes having a population of four hundred fifty thousand or more, and one-half to the local governing authority after advertising his intention to so utilize said funds by publication in the official parish journal of a notice to the public containing an itemized list of all of said funds on deposit, containing the names and last known addresses of defendants and the docket numbers of the cases involved. Said publication shall be made once within thirty days after the final disposition of the case as aforesaid. The clerk shall also send a notice by certified mail to each of said defendants at the last known address of said defendant.

C. After said publication and mailing of said notice by certified mail, the clerk of court, or the clerk of the criminal district court in parishes having a population of four hundred fifty thousand or more shall petition the court of proper jurisdiction for permission to utilize said funds for the use, operation, and maintenance of the office of the clerk of court or the clerk of criminal district court in parishes having a population of four hundred fifty thousand or more.

D. When bail has been given in conformity with this Article, the money, check, bond, or money order shall not be subject to garnishment, attachment, or seizure under any legal process. An assignment or sale thereof by the owner, to be valid, must be in the form of an authentic act and filed in the proceedings in the court having jurisdiction to discharge the bail. The property shall remain on deposit and the assignment or sale shall be contingent upon the nonforfeiture of the bail.

(Chgd. by Acts 1993 No. 834, §1; Acts 1994 Third Ex. Sess. No. 52, §1, eff. 9/1/94.)

Art. 325. Bail without surety.

A person in custody may be released by order of the court on his personal bail undertaking without the necessity of furnishing a surety. *(Chgd. by Acts 1993 No. 834, §1, eff. 6/22/93.)*

Art. 326. Condition of the bail undertaking.

A. Except as provided in Paragraph B, the condition of the bail undertaking in district, juvenile, parish, and city courts shall be that the defendant will appear at all stages of the proceedings to answer the charge before the court in which he may be prosecuted, will submit himself to the orders and process of the court, and will not leave the state without written permission of the court. The bail obligation shall run, subject to the provisions of Article 626, in favor of the state of Louisiana, or the city or parish whose ordinance is charged to have been violated, with the proceeds to be disposed of according to law. No error, inaccuracy, or omission in naming the obligee on the bond is a defense to an action thereon.

B. Upon conviction and imposition of sentence or the pronouncement of sentence or condition of probation pursuant to Articles 893 and 894 and R.S. 40:983, the bail undertaking shall cease and the surety shall be relieved of all obligations under the bond. If necessary to assure the presence of the defendant at all future stages of the proceedings, if any, the court may in its discretion require the defendant to post another bond or other acceptable security, or may release the defendant on bail without surety as provided for in Article 325. The court may continue the existing bail undertaking with the written approval of the surety on the bond. Such approval must be obtained after conviction and imposition of sentence or the pronouncement of sentence or conditions of probation pursuant to Articles 893 and 894 and R.S. 40:983.

(Chgd. by Acts 1993 No. 834, §1, eff. 6/22/93.)

Art. 327. Requisites of the bail undertaking.

A. The bail undertaking shall:

(1) Be in writing.

(2) State the court before which the defendant is bound to appear.

(3) Be entered into before an officer who is authorized to take it.

(4) State the amount of the bail.

B. The bail undertaking shall be enforceable if the above requirements are met; and a person shall not be discharged from his bail undertaking, nor shall a judgment of forfeiture be stayed, set aside, or reversed, nor the collection of any such judgment be barred or defeated by reason of any defect of form, omission of a recital, or of a condition of the undertaking, by reason of a failure to note or record the default of any defendant or surety, or because of any other irregularity.

(Chgd. by Acts 1993 No. 834, §1, eff. 6/22/93.)

Art. 327.1. Bail restrictions to be transmitted to Louisiana Protective Order Registry.

If, as part of a bail restriction, an order is issued for the purpose of preventing violent or threatening acts or harassment against, or contact or communication with or physical proximity to, another person for the purpose of preventing domestic violence, the judge shall cause to have prepared a Uniform Abuse Prevention Order, as provided in R.S. 46:2136.2(C), shall sign such order, and shall forward it to the clerk of court for filing, all without delay. The clerk of the issuing court shall transmit the Uniform Abuse Prevention Order to the Louisiana Protective Order Registry, R.S. 46:2136.2(A), by facsimile transmission, mail, or direct electronic input, where available, as expeditiously as possible, but no later than the end of the next business day after the order is filed with the clerk of court. *(Added by Acts 1997 No. 1156, §3, eff. 8/15/97.)*

Art. 328. Substitution of security.

The defendant or his surety may, at any time before a breach of the bail undertaking and with approval of the court in which the prosecution is pending, substitute another form of security authorized by this Code. The original security, including a surety, shall be released when the substitution of security is made. *(Chgd. by Acts 1993 No. 834, §1, eff. 6/22/93.)*

Art. 329. Contract to indemnify surety.

A contract to indemnify a surety against loss on a bail bond is valid and enforceable. *(Chgd. by Acts 1993 No. 834, §1, eff. 6/22/93.)*

Art. 330. Bail before conviction.

(See other article 330 below.)

A person in custody charged with the commission of an offense is entitled to be admitted to bail before conviction, except as provided in Article 331. *(Chgd. by Acts 1990 No. 483, §1; Acts 1992 No. 254, §1; Acts 1993 No. 834, §1, eff. 6/22/93.)*

Art. 330. Bail before conviction.

(Contingent effective date. See other article 330 above.)

Except as provided in Article 331, a person in custody charged with the commission of an offense is entitled to be admitted to bail before conviction unless the person is charged with a crime of violence as defined by law or with production, manufacture, distribution, or dispensing or possession with intent to produce, manufacture, distribute, or dispense a controlled dangerous substance as defined by the Louisiana Controlled Dangerous Substances Law, and after a contradictory hearing, conducted pursuant to the provisions of Article 330.1, the judge or magistrate finds by clear and convincing evidence that the defendant may flee or poses an imminent danger to any other person or the community. *(Chgd. by Acts 1990 No. 483, §1; Acts 1992 No. 254, §1; Acts 1993 No. 834, §1, eff. 6/22/93; Acts 1997 No. 1305, §1*.)*

**Effective only if and when the proposed amendment of Article I, Section 18 of the Constitution of Louisiana contained in Acts 1997 No. 1498 is adopted at the congressional primary election to be held in 1998 and becomes effective.*

Art. 330.1. Detention; bail hearing.

(Contingent effective date.)

A. Upon motion of the prosecutor, the judge or magistrate may order the temporary detention of the defendant, for a period of not more than five days, exclusive of weekends and legal holidays, pending the conducting of a contradictory bail hearing.

B. Following the contradictory hearing, upon proof by clear and convincing evidence either that there is a substantial risk that the defendant might flee or that the defendant poses an imminent danger to any other person or the community, the judge or magistrate may order the defendant held without bail pending trial.

(Added by Acts 1997 No. 1305, §1.)*

**Effective only if and when the proposed amendment of Article I, Section 18 of the Constitution of Louisiana contained in Acts 1997 No. 1498 is adopted at the congressional primary election to be held in 1998 and becomes effective.*

Art. 331. Capital offenses.

A. A person charged with the commission of a capital offense shall not be admitted to bail if the proof is evident and the presumption great that he is guilty of the capital offense.

B. When a person charged with the commission of a capital offense makes an application for admission to bail, the judge shall hold a hearing contradictorily with the state.

C. The burden of proof:

(1) Prior to indictment is on the state to show that the proof is evident and the presumption great that the defendant is guilty of the capital offense.

(2) After indictment is on the defendant to show that the proof is not evident or the presumption is not great that he is guilty of the capital offense.

(Chgd. by Acts 1993 No. 834, §1, eff. 6/22/93.)

Art. 332. Bail after conviction.

(See other article 332 below.)

A. A convicted person shall be remanded to jail to await sentence unless he is released on bail in accordance with this Article.

B. After conviction and before sentence, bail shall be allowed if the maximum sentence which may be imposed is imprisonment for five years or less. Bail may be allowed pending sentence if the maximum sentence which may be imposed is imprisonment exceeding five years, except when the court has reason to believe, based on competent evidence, that the release of the person convicted will pose a danger to any other person or the community.

C. After sentence and until final judgment, bail shall be allowed if a sentence of five years or less is actually imposed. Bail may be allowed after sentence and until final judgment if the sentence actually imposed exceeds imprisonment for five years, except when the court has reason to believe, based on competent evidence, that the release of the person convicted will pose a danger to any other person or the community.

D. In those instances above in which bail shall be allowed, the court shall consider whether the release of the person convicted or sentenced will pose a danger to any other person or the community in determining the amount of bail.

E. After conviction of a capital offense, a defendant shall not be allowed bail.

(Chgd. by Acts 1993 No. 834, §1, eff. 6/22/93.)

Art. 332. Bail after conviction.

(Contingent effective date. See other article 332 above.)

A. A convicted person shall be remanded to jail to await sentence unless he is released on bail in accordance with this Article.

B. After conviction and before sentence, bail shall be allowed if the maximum sentence which may be imposed is imprisonment for five years or less. Bail may be allowed pending sentence if the maximum sentence which may be imposed is imprisonment exceeding five years, except when the court has reason to believe, based on competent evidence, that the release of the person convicted will pose a danger to any other person or the community, or that there is a substantial risk that the person convicted might flee.

C. After sentence and until final judgment, bail shall be allowed if a sentence of five years or less is actually imposed. Bail may be allowed after sentence and until final judgment if the sentence actually imposed exceeds imprisonment for five years, except when the court has reason to believe, based on competent evidence, that the release of the person convicted will pose a danger to any other person or the community, or that there is a substantial risk that the person convicted might flee.

D. In those instances above in which bail shall be allowed, the court shall consider whether the release of the person convicted or sentenced will pose a danger to any other person or the community in determining the amount of bail.

E. After conviction of a capital offense, a defendant shall not be allowed bail.

(Chgd. by Acts 1993 No. 834, §1, eff. 6/22/93; Acts 1997 No. 1305, §1.)*

**Effective only if and when the proposed amendment of Article I, Section 18 of the Constitution of Louisiana contained in Acts 1997 No. 1498 is adopted at the congressional primary election to be held in 1998 and becomes effective.*

Art. 333. Authority to fix bail.

The following magistrates, throughout their several territorial jurisdictions, shall have authority to fix bail:

(1) District courts having criminal jurisdiction, in all cases.

(2) City or parish courts having criminal jurisdiction, in cases not capital.

(3) Mayor's courts and traffic courts in criminal cases within their trial jurisdiction.

(4) Juvenile and family courts in criminal cases within their trial jurisdiction.

(5) Justices of the peace in cases not capital or necessarily punishable by hard labor.

(Chgd. by Acts 1993 No. 834, §1, eff. 6/22/93.)

Art. 334. Factors in determining amount of bail.

The amount of bail shall be such that, in the judgment of the court, commissioner, or magistrate, it will insure the presence of the defendant, as required, and the safety of any other person and the community, having regard to:

(1) The seriousness of the offense charged, including but not limited to whether the offense is a crime of violence or involves a controlled dangerous substance.

(2) The weight of the evidence against the defendant.

(3) The previous criminal record of the defendant.

(4) The ability of the defendant to give bail.

(5) The nature and seriousness of the danger to any other person or the community that would be posed by the defendant's release.

(6) The defendant's voluntary participation in a pretrial drug testing program.

(7) The absence or presence of any controlled dangerous substance in the defendant's blood at the time of arrest.

(8) Whether the defendant is currently out on bond on a previous felony arrest for which he is awaiting institution of prosecution, arraignment, trial, or sentencing.

(9) Any other circumstances affecting the probability of defendant's appearance.

(10) The type or form of bail.

(Chgd. by Acts 1993 No. 834, §1; Acts 1995 No. 853, §1, eff. 8/15/95.)

Art. 335. Other conditions related to appearance of defendant.

The court may impose any additional condition of release that is reasonably related to assuring the appearance of the defendant before the court. Violation of such condition by the defendant shall be considered as a constructive contempt of court, and shall be grounds for revocation of bail, but does not give rise to a forfeiture. *(Chgd. by Acts 1993 No. 834, §1, eff. 6/22/93.)*

Art. 335.1. Offenses against a family or household member; provisions for forfeiture, arrest, modification.

A. In determining conditions of release of a defendant who is alleged to have committed an offense against the defendant's family or household member, as defined in R.S. 46:2132(4), the court shall consider whether the defendant poses a threat or danger to the victim. If the court determines that the defendant poses such threat or danger, it shall require as a condition of bail that the defendant refrain from going to the residence or household of the victim, the victim's school, and the victim's place of employment or otherwise contacting the victim in any manner whatsoever, and shall refrain from having any further contact with the victim.

B. A violation of the conditions of release may be punishable by the forfeiture of bail and the issuance of a bench warrant for the defendant's arrest or remanding the defendant to custody or a modification of the terms of bail.

(Added by Acts 1994 Third Ex. Sess. No. 70, §3, eff. 8/27/94.)

Art. 336. Release conditioned on participation in pretrial drug testing program.

A. (1) Every person arrested for a violation of the Uniform Controlled Dangerous Substances Law* or a crime of violence as provided in R.S. 14:2(13) shall be required to submit to a pretrial drug test for the presence of designated substances in accordance with the provisions of this Article and rules of court governing such testing. A person arrested for the above referenced crimes, who tests positive for the presence of one or more of the designated substances set forth in Subparagraph (2) of Paragraph B of this Article or any person arrested for a violation of R.S. 40:961 through 1036, if released by order of court on his personal surety, shall meet the requirements of Article 315 for a personal surety and shall, as a condition of bail, be required to participate in a pretrial drug testing program.

**R.S. 40:961 et seq.*

(2) Every person arrested for a misdemeanor may be required to submit to a pretrial drug test for the presence of designated substances in accordance with the provisions of this Article and rules of court governing such testing. A person arrested for a misdemeanor who tests positive for the presence of one or more of the designated substances set forth in Subparagraph (2) of Paragraph B of this Article or any person arrested for a violation of R.S. 40:961 through 1036, if released by order of court on his personal surety, shall meet the requirements of Article 315 for a personal surety and may, as a condition of bail, be required to participate in a pretrial drug testing program.

(3) The provisions of this Paragraph requiring mandatory pretrial drug testing shall be contingent upon receipt of adequate funding to cover the costs of such testing, as provided in Paragraph E of this Article.

B. The court may, and in all parishes with a population of four hundred thousand or more persons shall, implement a pretrial drug testing program which shall provide for the following:

(1) Mandatory participation for all persons arrested for violations of state law.

(2) Drug testing to determine the presence of phencyclidine (PCP), opiates (heroin), cocaine, methadone, amphetamines, or marijuana, prior to first court appearance and random testing thereafter to verify that the person is drug free.

(3) Restrictions on the use of any and all test results to ensure that they are used only for the benefit of the court to determine appropriate conditions of release, monitoring compliance with court orders, and assisting in determining appropriate sentences. A form statement shall be signed by the law enforcement agency and the person in custody stipulating that under no circumstances shall the information be used as evidence or as the basis for additional charges.

(4) Reasonable testing procedures to ensure the fair administration of the test and protection for the chain of custody for any evidence obtained.

C. If the person fails to comply with the pretrial drug testing program rules, the court may hold him in contempt and impose sanctions the court deems appropriate, including the posting of additional bail.

D. No person shall be released under the provisions of the pretrial drug testing program unless he agrees to do the following:

(1) Submit to continued random testing to verify that he is drug free.

(2) Refrain from the use or possession of any controlled dangerous substance or any substance designated by the court.

E. The implementation of any pretrial drug testing program authorized pursuant to the provisions of this Article shall be contingent upon receipt by the court requiring the test of sufficient federal or other funding to conduct the testing program in accordance with the provisions of this Article and any rules of court.

F. No elected official who is in any way connected with the administration of the pretrial drug testing program provided for in this Article, either directly or indirectly, shall have any financial interest, either directly or indirectly, in any drug testing company participating in such pretrial drug testing program.

G. All contracts awarded to any drug testing company authorized to conduct the pretrial drug testing program provided for in this Article shall be awarded in accordance with the provisions governing public bids, R.S. 38:2181 et seq.

(Chgd. by Acts 1991 No. 1039, §1; Acts 1993 No. 834, §1; Acts 1997 No. 1189, §1, eff. 8/15/97.)

Art. 337. Juvenile records to determine bail.

A. For the purpose of fixing bail, a magistrate may make a written request of any juvenile court for an abstract containing only the delinquent acts of a defendant currently before the requesting magistrate. The request shall be promptly complied with; however, not more than forty-eight hours, exclusive of Saturdays, Sundays and legal holidays, shall lapse before the requested information is deposited in the mail, addressed to the requesting court.

B. The requesting court shall not copy, duplicate or otherwise reproduce such juvenile records, and these shall be deposited in the mail and addressed to the issuing juvenile court within seventy-two hours, exclusive of Saturdays, Sundays and legal holidays, after bail is determined.

C. Failure to comply with the provisions of this Article shall subject the violating court to disciplinary action by the Supreme Court of Louisiana upon receipt by the judicial administrator of the supreme court of a written complaint, subsequently substantiated.

(Chgd. by Acts 1993 No. 834, §1, eff. 6/22/93.)

Art. 338. Form and contents of bail order.

An order fixing bail shall be in writing, specify the amount and type of the bail, and designate the officer or officers authorized to accept the bail, and shall be signed by the magistrate. The order may issue on motion of the state or defendant, or on the magistrate's own initiative. In any parish with a population in excess of four hundred ninety thousand, the magistrate or district court shall hold a contradictory hearing prior to fixing bail in any felony case. *(Chgd. by Acts 1993 No. 834, §1; Acts 1995 No. 989, §1, eff. 8/15/95.)*

Art. 339. Elections of types of bail.

Once the amount of bail has been fixed by the court, the defendant, in posting the bond, shall have the right to select either a commercial surety, a secured personal surety, or a cash deposit. However, the court may elect to release the defendant on an unsecured personal surety or a bail without surety. The election of the unsecured personal surety or bail without surety by the court shall be expressed in the bail order. *(Chgd. by Acts 1993 No. 834, §1, eff. 6/22/93.)*

Art. 340. Amount of bail in felony cases; schedules of bail in noncapital cases.

A. Unless the bail is fixed by a schedule in accordance with Paragraph B, the amount of bail in felony cases shall be specifically fixed in each case. A person shall not be released on bail pursuant to a general order which authorizes the sheriff, or other officers, to take bail and fixes the amount thereof at a certain sum for particular felonies.

B. A schedule of bail according to the offense charged in noncapital felony cases may be fixed by a district court. The court order setting the bail schedule shall fix the amount of bail for each offense listed, designate the officer or officers authorized to accept the bail, and order that bail be taken in conformity with the schedule. It may also contain a general provision designating the amount of bail for any noncapital felony not listed in the schedule. A copy of the schedule shall be sent to all jails, sheriff's offices, and police stations within the judicial district. A bail schedule may be revised or rescinded at any time.

C. A person charged with the commission of a felony for which bail is fixed by a schedule may give bail according to the schedule or demand a special order fixing bail.

D. Bail herein may be set above the scheduled amount if the court deems it appropriate or the district attorney moves for good cause to have the bail set above the scheduled amount and the court finds it appropriate.

E. In any parish with a population in excess of four hundred ninety thousand, the magistrate or district court shall hold a contradictory hearing prior to fixing bail in any felony case.

(Chgd. by Acts 1993 No. 850, §1; Acts 1995 No. 989, §1, eff. 8/15/95.)

Art. 341. Schedules of bail in misdemeanor cases.

A. Schedules of bail according to the offense charged in misdemeanor cases may be fixed by district, parish, and city courts for offenses within their respective trial jurisdictions. The type or form of bail shall not be set in the bail schedule. When more than one court has trial jurisdiction over an offense, the applicable bail schedule shall be that of the court in which the case is to be tried.

B. The court order setting the bail schedule shall fix the amount of bail for each offense listed, designate the officer or officers authorized to accept the bail, and order that bail be taken in conformity with the schedule. It may also contain a general provision designating the amount of bail for any misdemeanor not listed in the schedule. A copy of the schedule shall be sent to all jails, sheriff's offices, and police stations within the judicial district, parish, or city, respectively. A bail schedule may be revised or rescinded at any time.

C. If a bail schedule has been set up and bail has not previously been specially fixed, a person charged with the commission of a misdemeanor has the right either to give bail according to the bail schedule, or to demand a special order fixing type or form of bail and amount of bail.

(Chgd. by Acts 1993 No. 834, §1, eff. 6/22/93.)

Art. 342. Increase or reduction of bail; sufficiency of security.

The court having trial jurisdiction over the offense charged, on its own motion or on motion of the state or defendant, for good cause may either increase or reduce the amount of bail, or require new or additional security. For purposes of this Article, good cause for increase of bail specifically includes but is not limited to the rearrest of the defendant on offenses alleged to have been committed while out on bond. However, in any parish with a population in excess of four hundred ninety thousand, the district court shall hold a contradictory hearing prior to a modification of the bail order. The modification of any bail order wherein a bail bond has been posted by a criminal defendant and his sureties shall upon said modification terminate the liability of the defendant and his sureties under the previously existing bail contract. A new bail must be posted in the amount of the new bail order. *(Chgd. by Acts 1993 No. 834, §1, eff. 6/22/93.)*

Art. 343. Remedy for refusal of bail or excessive bail.

A person held may invoke the supervisory jurisdiction of the court of appeal on a claim that the trial court has improperly refused bail or a reduction of bail in a bailable case. *(Chgd. by Acts 1993 No. 834, §1, eff. 6/22/93.)*

Art. 344. Right to notice of time and place of defendant's required appearance.

A. When a bail bond fixes the initial appearance date, no additional notice is required to be given to the defendant or the personal surety or the commercial surety or the agent or bondsman who posted the bond for the commercial surety, if the defendant appears as ordered. If a defendant fails to appear when a bail bond fixes the initial appearance date, no additional preforfeiture notice for that date is required to be given to the defendant or the personal surety or the commercial surety or the agent or bondsman who posted the bond for the commercial surety. The bond shall be forfeited forthwith as per R.S. 15:85.

B. (1) When a bail bond does not fix the appearance date, and the presence is required of a person who has been released on bail, the defendant and his personal surety or the commercial surety or the agent or bondsman who posted the bond for the commercial surety, shall be given written notice of the time, date, and place the principal is required to appear.

(2) The notice may be delivered to the defendant and the personal surety or the commercial surety or the agent or bondsman who posted the bond for the commercial surety by an officer designated by the court, at least two days prior to the day set for the appearance; or this notice may be mailed by United States first class mail to the defendant and his personal surety or the commercial surety or the agent or bondsman who posted the bond for the commercial surety, at least three days prior to the day set for the appearance. The notice shall be mailed to the defendant and his personal surety or the commercial surety or the agent or bondsman who posted the bond for the commercial surety to the address designated pursuant to Article 322.

(3) If the defendant appears as ordered and the proceeding is continued to a specific date, the defendant and the personal surety or the commercial surety or the agent or bondsman who posted the bond for the commercial surety need not be given notice of the new appearance date. If the defendant fails to appear as ordered, or the proceeding is not continued to a specific date, the personal surety or the agent or bondsman who posted the bond for the commercial surety shall be given notice of the new appearance date.

(4) Failure to give notice, as required by this Paragraph, relieves the surety from liability on a judgment of bond forfeiture for the defendant's nonappearance on that particular date. *(Chgd. by Acts 1993 No. 834, §1; Acts 1995 No. 927, §1, eff. 8/15/95.)*

Art. 345. Surrender of defendant.

A. A surety may surrender the defendant or the defendant may surrender himself, in open court or to the officer charged with his detention, at any time prior to forfeiture or within the time allowed by law for setting aside a judgment of forfeiture of the bail bond. For the purpose of surrendering the defendant, the surety may arrest him. Upon surrender of the defendant, the officer shall detain the defendant in his custody as upon the original commitment and shall acknowledge the surrender by a certificate signed by him and delivered to the surety. Thereafter, the surety shall be fully and finally discharged and relieved of any and all obligation under the bond.

B. If the defendant is incarcerated by the officer originally charged with his detention at any time prior to forfeiture or within the time allowed by law for setting aside a judgment for forfeiture of the bail bond, the surety may apply for and receive from the officer charged with the detention of the defendant a letter verifying that the defendant is incarcerated, but only after the surety verifies to the satisfaction of the officer charged with the detention of the defendant as to the identity of the defendant. Thereafter, the surety shall be fully and finally discharged and relieved of any and all obligation under the bond.

C. When a surety receives either a certificate of surrender provided for in Paragraph A or a letter of verification as provided for in Paragraph B, the surety shall pay a fee of twenty-five dollars to the officer charged with the defendant's detention for recalling the capias, accepting the surrender or verifying the incarceration, processing the paperwork, and giving the surety a certificate of surrender or a letter of verification of incarceration releasing him from his obligation under the defendant's bond.

D. If during the six-month period allowed for the surrender of the defendant, the defendant is found to be incarcerated in another parish of the state of Louisiana or a foreign jurisdiction, the judgment of bond forfeiture is deemed satisfied if all of the following conditions are met:

(1) The defendant or his sureties file a motion in summary proceeding within the six month period.

(2) The defendant's sureties produce to the court adequate proof of defendant's incarceration, or the officer originally charged with defendant's detention verifies the defendant's incarceration.

(3) The defendant's sureties pay the officer originally charged with the defendant's detention, the reasonable cost of returning the defendant to the officer originally charged with the defendant's detention.

E. At any time prior to forfeiture or within the time allowed by law for setting aside a judgment for forfeiture of the bail bond, the surety may present to the court a certificate of death naming the defendant as the deceased party. The certificate shall be under seal of the authority confirming the defendant's death. Thereafter, the surety shall be fully and finally discharged and relieved of any and all obligation under the bond.

F. When the defendant has been surrendered in conformity with this Article or a letter of verification of incarceration has been issued to the surety as provided for in Paragraph B of this Article, the court shall, upon presentation of the certificate of surrender or the letter of verification of incarceration, order that the surety be exonerated from liability on his bail undertaking and shall order any judgment of forfeiture set aside.

(Chgd. by Acts 1993 No. 834, §1, eff. 6/22/93.)

Art. 346. Court order for arrest of defendant.

The court in which the defendant is held to answer may issue a warrant for the arrest and commitment of the defendant who is at large on bail when any of the following are true:

(1) There has been a breach of the bail undertaking.

(2) It appears that a surety has become insufficient, is dead, cannot be found, or has ceased to meet the qualifications of law or does not own adequate immovable property within the state.

(3) The court is satisfied that the bail should be increased or new or additional security required.

(Chgd. by Acts 1993 No. 834, §1, eff. 6/22/93.)

Art. 347. Bail after surrender.

A defendant who has surrendered himself under the provisions of Article 345, or has been rearrested under the provisions of Article 346 is entitled to bail in accordance with this Code.

(Added by Acts 1993 No. 834, §1, eff. 6/22/93.)

Art. 348. Cancellation of bail bond.

The court shall order the bail bond canceled when there is no further liability thereon.

(Added by Acts 1993 No. 834, §1, eff. 6/22/93.)

TITLE IX. HABEAS CORPUS

Article

Art. 351. Habeas corpus; definition.

Habeas corpus is a writ commanding a person who has another in his custody to produce him before the court and to state the authority for the custody.

"Custody" as used in this Title means detention or confinement as a result of or incidental to an instituted or anticipated criminal proceeding.

The provisions of this Title are not available to persons entitled to file an application for post conviction relief under Title XXXI-A.

Art. 352. Venue.

Habeas corpus proceedings by or on behalf of a person in custody shall be instituted in the parish in which the person is in custody.

Art. 353. Application for writ; form and contents.

An application for a writ of habeas corpus shall be by written petition addressed to a competent court by the person in custody or by some other person in his behalf. If the custody is by virtue of or under pretext of a court order, a copy of such order shall be annexed to the petition, or the petition shall allege that a copy of it has been demanded and refused. The petition shall further allege:

(1) The name of the person in custody and the place of custody if known, or if not known, a statement to that effect;

(2) The name of the custodian, if known, or if not known, a designation or description of him as far as possible; and

(3) A statement of facts upon which the petition is based, which statement may be supported by affidavits filed with the petition.

The application shall conclude with a prayer for the issuance of the writ. It shall be signed by the applicant and be accompanied by an affidavit that the allegations contained in the petition are true to the best of the affiant's information and belief.

Art. 354. Granting of writ; time and place for answer.

The court to which the application is presented shall immediately grant a writ of habeas corpus, unless it appears by the petition itself or by the documents annexed to it that the person in custody is not entitled to be set at liberty. The writ may issue at any time on any day, in term time or vacation, and shall fix the place and time for the answer, which shall be as early as practicable, and shall not exceed seventy-two hours from the time of the issuance of the writ.

Art. 355. Persons authorized to make service; proof of service.

A writ of habeas corpus may be served by a person over the age of twenty-one who is capable of testifying. If the writ is served by someone other than a sheriff, the affidavit of the person who served it shall be prima facie proof of such service.

Art. 356. Method of service.

Service of the writ may be made on any day by:

(1) Delivering it to the person to whom it is addressed;

(2) Informing him of its contents if he refuses to receive it; or

(3) Attaching the writ to an entrance door of the residence of the person to be served or of the place of custody if such person conceals himself or cannot be found or refuses admittance to the person attempting service.

A writ of habeas corpus, although addressed to a particular person, may be served in the manner provided by this article upon any person who has custody of the person whose release is sought.

Art. 357. Answer; production of person in custody.

The person upon whom the writ has been served, whether it is directed to him or not, shall file a written answer, signed and sworn to by him stating whether he has custody of the person named in the writ. If the person is in his custody, he shall produce him and state in his answer his authority for holding the person in custody. If the custody is by virtue of a court order, the document in the possession of the custodian shall be annexed to the answer. The answer and the production of the person in custody shall be made at the place and time designated by the writ.

Art. 358. Transfer of custody; answer.

If the custody has been transferred prior to service of the writ, the person upon whom the writ was served shall state in his answer the name and address of the person to whom custody was transferred, the time of and the authority for the transfer, and the place where the person is then in custody.

Art. 359. Nonproduction of person confined; justification.

If the person in custody cannot for any reason be brought before the court, the reasons therefor shall be stated in the answer. If the court is satisfied with the reasons stated, the hearing may proceed without his presence. If the court is not satisfied with the reasons stated, it may require the immediate production of the person in custody.

Art. 360. Hearing.

At the time and place fixed in the writ for the answer thereto, the court shall proceed summarily to hear the evidence and reasons adduced by the person in custody and by the custodian. The hearing shall be held in open court and may be held in term time or in vacation, or on a legal holiday.

Art. 361. Custody without court order.

If the person in custody is being held not by virtue of a court order, the court, after the hearing, shall discharge or refuse to discharge the person from custody as justice may require.

Art. 362. Custody with court order.

If the person in custody is being held by virtue of a court order, relief shall be granted only on the following grounds:

(1) The court has exceeded its jurisdiction;

(2) The original custody was lawful, but by some act, omission, or event which has since occurred, the custody has become unlawful;

(3) The order for the custody is deficient in some legal requisite;

(4) The order for the custody, although legal in form, imposes an illegal custody;

(5) The custodian is not the person allowed by law to detain the person in custody;

(6) He has been denied his right to a hearing in an extradition case, as provided in Article 267; or

(7) He is being held in custody prior to trial in violation of due process of law.

Art. 363. Effect of appeal.

The writ of habeas corpus shall not be granted to a convicted person for a cause under Article 362, if he may appeal, or has done so and the appeal is pending.

Art. 364. New warrant; when issued.

The court shall issue a new warrant of arrest when it appears that there exists sufficient legal ground for the custody of the person based on an offense with which he may be charged, although the order for the custody may have been rendered in an irregular or unauthorized manner, or may have been executed by an unauthorized person.

Art. 365. Burden of proof.

If the person in custody is being held not by virtue of a court order, the custodian shall have the burden of proving the legality of the custody and of showing good cause why the person in custody should not be released.

If the person in custody is being held by virtue of a court order, he shall have the burden of proving the illegality of the custody and that he is entitled to be released.

Art. 366. Custody pendente lite.

At the time of issuing the writ the court may render a special order concerning the custody of the person from the time the writ is served until rendition of judgment.

Art. 367. Rearrest after discharge.

A person discharged from custody in a habeas corpus proceeding may be rearrested if a legal ground exists therefor.

Art. 368. Disobedience of writ or judgment; contempt.

A person who fails to comply with the writ of habeas corpus, or with a judgment rendered on a petition for a writ of habeas corpus may be punished for contempt.

Art. 369. Appeal not permitted.

There shall be no appeal from a judgment granting or refusing to grant release upon a petition for a writ of habeas corpus.

Art. 370. Custody pending application for writs.

A person in custody shall not be released upon a writ of habeas corpus until forty-eight hours after the judgment ordering the release has been entered or until an application by the state for supervisory writs has been denied, whichever occurs first, if:

(1) The state has announced its intention to apply for supervisory writs; and

(2) The person is being held in custody by virtue of a court order or in connection with a felony.

TITLE X. INSTITUTING CRIMINAL PROSECUTIONS

Art. 381. Nature of criminal prosecution.

A criminal prosecution is brought in the name of the state in a court of criminal jurisdiction, for the purpose of bringing to punishment one who has violated a criminal law.

The person injured by the commission of an offense is not a party to the criminal prosecution, and his rights are not affected thereby.

Art. 382. Methods of instituting criminal prosecutions.

A. A prosecution for an offense punishable by death, or for an offense punishable by life imprisonment, shall be instituted by indictment by a grand jury. Other criminal prosecutions in a district court shall be instituted by indictment or by information.

B. (1) A prosecution for violation of an ordinance and other criminal prosecutions in a parish court shall be instituted by affidavit or information charging any offense.

(2) A prosecution for violation of an ordinance and other criminal prosecutions in a city court shall be instituted by affidavit or information charging any offense supported by affidavit.

(3) Criminal prosecutions in a juvenile court or family court shall be instituted by affidavit, information, or indictment.

(Chgd. by Acts 1994 Third Ex. Sess. No. 83, §1, eff. 8/27/94.)

Art. 383. Indictment.

An indictment is a written accusation of crime made by a grand jury. It must be concurred in by not less than nine of the grand jurors, indorsed "a true bill," and the indorsement must be signed by the foreman. Indictments shall be returned into the district court in open court; but when an indictment has been returned for an offense which is within the trial jurisdiction of another court in the parish, the indictment may be transferred to that court.

Art. 384. Information.

An information is a written accusation of crime made by the district attorney or the city prosecutor and signed by him. It must be filed in open court in a court having jurisdiction to try the offense, or in the office of the clerk thereof.

Art. 385. Affidavit.

An affidavit is a written accusation of crime made under oath and signed by the affiant. It must be filed in open court in a court having jurisdiction to try the offense, or in the office of the clerk thereof.

Art. 386. Institution of prosecution after discharge at preliminary examination; after failure of grand jury to indict.

Discharge of a defendant after a preliminary examination does not preclude the subsequent filing of an indictment, information, or affidavit against him for the same offense.

The failure or refusal of a grand jury to indict a defendant does not preclude a subsequent indictment by the same or another grand jury, or the subsequent filing of an information or affidavit against him, for the same offense.

TITLE XI. QUALIFICATIONS AND SELECTION OF GRAND AND PETIT JURORS

Art. 401. General qualifications of jurors.

A. In order to qualify to serve as a juror, a person must:

(1) Be a citizen of the United States and of this state who has resided within the parish in which he is to serve as a juror for at least one year immediately preceding his jury service.

(2) Be at least eighteen years of age.

(3) Be able to read, write, and speak the English language and be possessed of sufficient knowledge of the English language.

(4) Not be under interdiction or incapable of serving as a juror because of a mental or physical infirmity, provided that no person shall be deemed incompetent solely because of the loss of hearing in any degree.

(5) Not be under indictment for a felony nor have been convicted of a felony for which he has not been pardoned.

B. Notwithstanding any provision in Subsection A, a person may be challenged for cause on one or more of the following:

(1) A loss of hearing or the existence of any other incapacity which satisfies the court that the challenged person is incapable of performing the duties of a juror in the particular action without prejudice to the substantial rights of the challenging party.

(2) When reasonable doubt exists as to the competency of the prospective juror to serve as provided for in Code of Criminal Procedure Art. 787.

Art. 401.1. Court instructions for interpreter.

A. When a person with a hearing loss is among the petit jury venire, the court shall:

(1) Provide an interpreter for the deaf prospective juror. The interpreter shall be sworn in as an officer of the court.

(2) Permit the interpreter to be present and assist a deaf prospective juror during voir dire.

B. When a hard of hearing or hearing impaired person is summoned for jury duty, the court shall:

(1) Provide an interpreter for the deaf juror. The interpreter shall be sworn in as an officer of the court.

(2) Instruct the interpreter, in the presence of the jury, to:

(a) Make true, literal, and complete translations of all testimony and other relevant colloquy to the deaf juror during the deliberations of the jury.

(b) Refrain from participating in any manner in the deliberations of the jury.

(c) Refrain from having any communications, oral or visual, with any member of the jury regarding the deliberations of the jury except for literal translations of jurors' remarks made during deliberations.

(3) Permit the interpreter to be present and assist a deaf juror during the deliberations of the jury.

(4) Give a special instruction to the interpreter not to disclose any portion of the deliberations with any person following a verdict.

(5) Direct all costs relating to the interpreting services provided, including summoning, voir dire process, and empaneling of a juror in all trials, to be paid by the clerk of court's office through the juror and witness fee account.

C. The verdict of the jury shall be valid notwithstanding the presence of the interpreter during deliberations.

D. All costs relating to the interpreting services provided herein shall be paid by the clerk of court's office through the juror and witness fee account.

Art. 403. Exemption from jury service.

Exemptions from jury service shall be as provided by rules of the Louisiana Supreme Court pursuant to Section 33(B) of Article V of the Louisiana Constitution of 1974.

Art. 403.1. Disqualification for undue hardship.

If the judge who presided over the impaneling of the grand jury finds that a grand juror can no longer serve without undue hardship, he may disqualify such juror and a substitute juror shall be selected in the same manner as for the filling of a vacancy.

Art. 404. Appointment of jury commission; term of office; oath; quorum; performance of function in the parish of East Baton Rouge by the judicial administrator; performance of function in the parish of Lafourche by the clerk of court.

A. Except in the parish of East Baton Rouge:

(1) The jury commission of each parish shall consist of five members, each having the qualifications set forth in Article 401.

(2) In Orleans Parish the jury commission shall be appointed by the governor, and the commissioners shall serve at his pleasure. In other parishes the jury commission shall consist of the clerk of court or a deputy clerk designated by him in writing to act in his stead in all

matters affecting the jury commission, and four other persons appointed by written order of the district court, who shall serve at the court's pleasure.

(3) Before entering upon their duties, members of the jury commission shall take an oath to discharge their duties faithfully.

(4) Three members of the jury commission shall constitute a quorum.

(5) Meetings of the jury commission shall be open to the public.

B. In the parish of East Baton Rouge the function of the jury commission shall be performed by the judicial administrator of the Nineteenth Judicial District Court or by a deputy judicial administrator designated by him in writing to act in his stead in all matters affecting the jury commission. The judicial administrator or his designated deputy shall have the same powers, duties and responsibilities, and be governed by those provisions of law as presently pertain to jury commissioners which are applicable, including the taking of an oath to discharge their duties faithfully. The clerk of court of the parish of East Baton Rouge shall perform the duties and responsibilities otherwise imposed upon him by law with respect to jury venires, shall coordinate the jury venire process, and shall receive the compensation generally authorized for a jury commissioner.

C. In the parish of Lafourche the function of the jury commission may be performed by the clerk of court of the parish of Lafourche or by a deputy clerk of court designated by him in writing to act in his stead in all matters affecting the jury commission. The clerk of court or his designated deputy shall have the same powers, duties, and responsibilities, and shall be governed by applicable provisions of law pertaining to jury commissioners. The clerk of court of the parish of Lafourche shall perform the duties and responsibilities otherwise imposed upon him by law with respect to jury venires, shall coordinate the jury venire process, and shall receive the compensation generally authorized for a jury commissioner.

(Chgd. by Acts 1993 No. 632, §1, eff. 8/15/93.)

Art. 404.1. Powers, duties and functions of the board of jury commissioners in parishes of four hundred seventy-five thousand or more.

A. Notwithstanding any other law to the contrary, this Article shall apply to the board of jury commissioners in parishes of four hundred seventy-five thousand or more in population. In such parishes, there shall be a board of jury commissioners, hereinafter referred to as "the board", composed of five members appointed by the governor, subject to confirmation of the Senate, to serve at his pleasure. The board shall meet at least once every six months and when it is ordered to do so by the court, and may meet to select or supplement the general venire for grand and petit jurors. Three members shall constitute a quorum. The board may select a new general venire at any meeting and shall do so when ordered by the court.

B. The board in such parishes may, with the concurrence of the judges of the criminal district court, have subpoenas served through personal or domiciliary service by depositing same in the United States mail, regular, certified, or registered, addressed to the juror at his usual residence or business address. The date of mailing shall be not less than fifteen days prior to the date on which the addressee is subpoenaed to appear. When service is by regular mail, the board of jury commissioners shall retain a record of the date of mailing. In cases of service by regular mail, prior to any contempt citation, the person shall be served by registered or certified mail with return receipt requested. If service is made by registered or certified mail with return receipt requested, the return receipt shall be retained by the jury commission as proof of proper service and failure of the person to respond to the subpoena so served shall constitute contempt of court.

C. The municipality which the board serves in such parishes shall cooperate with the board to provide the board with records, computer and other equipment, voter registration rolls, tapes, and other items which it needs to compile the general venire of grand jurors and petit jurors at no cost to the board.

D. The board in such parishes shall develop a plan to govern its operation. Such plan shall be approved by a majority of the judges of the criminal district court of such parishes.

E. The board shall have authority over all its employees, subject to supervision by the criminal district court. The board, by majority vote, shall determine all matters relating to its jurisdiction, subject only to the approval of the judges of the district court or criminal district court.

F. The accounting functions of the board and of the jury commission shall be transferred to the judicial administrator of the criminal district court.

G. All procedures and policies developed by the jury commission shall be under the direction and subject to the approval of the criminal district court, en banc.
(Chgd. by Acts 1991 No. 289, §2, eff. 9/6/91.)

Art. 405. Notice of jury commission meetings.
Each member of the jury commission shall be notified in writing of the time and place designated for a meeting of the commission, at least twenty-four hours prior to the meeting.
The notice shall be issued by one of the members or the secretary of the jury commission in Orleans Parish, and by the clerk of court in all other parishes, and shall be served in the manner provided for service of subpoenas.

Art. 406. Powers of jury commission; penalty for disobedience of commission process.
In order to secure qualified jurors, the jury commission may issue subpoenas to compel the attendance of witnesses and the production of evidence relative to the qualifications of prospective jurors.
Disobedience of a subpoena of a jury commission is punishable as contempt of court.

Art. 407. Administration of oath to witnesses.
A jury commissioner shall administer an oath to each witness appearing before the commission, in accordance with Article 14.

Art. 408. Selection of general venire in parishes other than Orleans.
A. In parishes other than Orleans, the jury commission shall select impartially at least three hundred persons having the qualifications to serve as jurors, who shall constitute the general venire. A list of persons so selected shall be prepared and certified by the clerk of court as the general venire list, and said list shall be kept as part of the records of the commission. The name and address of each person on the list shall be written on a separate slip of paper, with no designation as to race or color, which shall be placed in a box labeled "General Venire Box."
B. After the jury commission has selected the general venire, it shall lock and seal the general venire box and deliver it to the clerk of court, as the custodian thereof. Alternatively, the list of persons so selected may be retained in a form suitable for use by a properly programmed electronic device commonly known as a computer.
C. The jury commission shall meet at least once every six months and when ordered by the court, and may meet at any time to select or supplement the general venire. The commission may select a new general venire at any meeting and shall do so when ordered by the court.

Art. 408.1. Initial selection of general venire; source.
A. In developing a list of all persons who may be called for grand or petit jury duty:
(1) It shall be determined by each judicial district whether or not the names of prospective jurors shall be drawn exclusively from voter registration lists or also from other sources or lists.
(2) If the district judges of the judicial district, in their discretion, authorize the use of sources other than voter registration lists in developing grand and petit jury lists, a jury commission shall not draw the names of prospective jurors exclusively from voter registration lists, but shall use other sources or lists of prospective jurors as may be legally available.
B. If the district judges authorize the use of a list of persons issued driver's licenses, as a source from which to choose prospective jurors, such list of drivers shall be provided annually at no cost by the Department of Public Safety and Corrections to the respective clerks of court or jury commissions responsible for preparing the list of prospective jurors. However, such a list shall only be provided to parishes that make written request through the parish clerk of court or jury commission.
(Added by Acts 1995 No. 933, §1, No. 1102, §1; chgd. by Acts 1997 No. 886, §1; Acts 1998 First Ex. Sess. No. 124, §1, eff. 6/16/98.)

Art. 409. Selection of general venire in Orleans Parish.

In the Parish of Orleans, the jury commission shall select impartially at least seven hundred fifty persons having the qualifications to serve as jurors, who shall constitute the general venire.

A list of the persons so selected shall be prepared and certified by the commission as the general venire list and shall be kept as part of the records of the commission.

The name and address of each person on the list shall be written on a separate slip of paper, with no designation as to race or color, which shall be placed in a box labeled "General Venire Box."

No drawing shall be made from a general venire containing fewer than seven hundred fifty names, except when the court orders the drawing of tales jurors.

After the jury commission has selected the general venire, it shall lock and seal the general venire box and deliver it to the secretary of the commission, as the custodian thereof.

Art. 409.1. Orleans parish central jury pool.

A. There is hereby created a central jury pool for the Criminal District Court for the Parish of Orleans which shall be administered by the Jury Commission of the Parish of Orleans as hereinafter provided.

B. In order to properly and adequately administer and operate the central jury pool for the Criminal District Court for the Parish of Orleans, the chairman of the Jury Commissioners for the Parish of Orleans shall designate two jury commissioners each month who shall be specifically charged with the responsibility for administering and operating the central jury pool. The chairman of the jury commissioners shall rotate the responsibility for the administration and operation of the central jury pool amongst the other four jury commissioners so that no jury commissioner shall be assigned to the central jury pool for more than six months out of every twelve months.

C. The Criminal District Court for the Parish of Orleans acting en banc shall by majority vote determine the number of jurors to serve in the central jury pool in any given month, the jury days for that month, and all other matters relative to the operating procedures of the central jury pool.

D. The jury commission shall select the number of jurors to serve in the central jury pool as hereinabove determined by the criminal district court acting en banc and by the method now prescribed by law.

E. The provisions of this Act shall be cumulative of and in addition to the method now prescribed by law for the selection of a jury panel for the Criminal District Court for the Parish of Orleans except that those provisions in conflict with this Act are hereby repealed and declared invalid insofar as they apply to the Criminal District Court for the Parish of Orleans.

Art. 409.2. Jefferson Parish central jury pool.

A. The judges of the Twenty-Fourth Judicial District Court for the parish of Jefferson, sitting en banc by majority vote may create a central jury pool for criminal and/or civil juries for the Twenty-Fourth Judicial District Court for the parish of Jefferson, which shall be administered by the jury commission for the parish of Jefferson as hereinafter provided.

B. The jury selection shall be administered by the jury commission for the parish of Jefferson as provided by law, except that the provisions of Article 417(B) shall not apply to Jefferson Parish.

C. The judges of the Twenty-Fourth Judicial District Court for the parish of Jefferson, acting en banc shall by majority vote determine the system, method, and number of jurors to serve in the central jury pool for criminal and/or civil juries for a given term whether daily, weekly, or monthly, and may specify jury days for a particular term. Likewise, all other matters relative to the operating procedures of the central jury pool shall be determined by the judges of the Twenty-Fourth Judicial District Court for the parish of Jefferson, acting en banc by a majority vote, including the designation of persons to administer the central jury pool.

D. The jury commission shall select the number of jurors to serve in the central jury pool as hereinabove determined by the judges of the Twenty-Fourth Judicial District Court, acting en banc and by the method now prescribed by law for jury selection.

E. The jurors so selected may serve as jurors in either criminal and/or civil matters in the method and manner prescribed by majority vote of the judges of the Twenty-Fourth Judicial District Court for the parish of Jefferson sitting en banc.

F. The provisions of this section shall be cumulative of and in addition to the method now prescribed by law for the selection of jury panels for the Twenty-Fourth Judicial District

Court for the parish of Jefferson, except that those provisions in conflict with this Act are hereby repealed and declared invalid insofar as they apply to the Twenty-Fourth Judicial District Court for the parish of Jefferson.
(Chgd. by Acts 1995 No. 1012, §1, eff. 6/29/95, No. 1273, §1, No. 1277, §1, eff. 8/15/95.)

Art. 409.3. Central jury pools; local rules.

A. A district court may, by local rules adopted by majority vote of the judges, create and provide for the manner of administering a central jury pool for criminal and civil cases. The combined Orleans criminal and civil district courts shall be considered a district court for purposes of this Article.

B. Jurors selected to serve in the central jury pool may serve as jurors in either civil or criminal matters, or both.

C. The central jury pool shall be selected at random from persons included within the general venire. The number of persons selected to comprise the central jury pool and their length of service shall be determined pursuant to local court rules.

D. A panel of the central jury pool shall be selected at random from persons in the central jury pool. The number of persons selected to comprise the panel shall be determined pursuant to local court rules but the number shall be no less than three times the number of persons needed to complete the jury and in no event less than ten.

E. The petit jury shall be selected from the one or more central jury pool panels assigned to the court. Persons shall be called from the central jury pool panel at random.

F. Persons selected to serve on a central jury pool panel and not selected to serve on a jury may, pursuant to local court rules, be returned to the central jury pool.

G. The provisions of this Article supplement the methods presently provided by law for selecting jurors.

Art. 409.4. Nineteenth Judicial District Court central jury pool.

A. The Nineteenth Judicial District Court may, by local rules adopted by majority vote of the judges, create and provide for the manner of administering a central jury pool for criminal and civil cases.

B. The central jury pool shall be selected from persons included within the general venire. The number of persons selected to comprise the central jury pool and their length of service shall be determined pursuant to local court rules.

C. Jurors selected to serve in the central jury pool may serve as jurors in either civil or criminal matters, or both.

D. The provisions of this Article supplement the methods presently provided by law for selecting jurors.

Art. 409.5. One day/one trial jury system.

A. A district court may, by local rules adopted by a majority vote of all the judges of that district, create and provide for the manner of administering a one day/one trial jury system for criminal and civil cases. The combined Orleans criminal and civil district courts shall be considered a district court for the purposes of this Article.

B. Unless otherwise provided in this Article, the jurors shall be selected and shall serve in accordance with the provisions of Code of Criminal Procedure Article 409.3.

C. Any juror selected pursuant to this Article shall serve in the central jury pool for a period of not more than one day unless he is selected to serve on a jury or unless extraordinary circumstances warrant, pursuant to local court rules, that he be held over for the continuation of voir dire. Any juror selected to serve on a jury shall serve until he is discharged from the jury.

D. Any district court which adopts rules pursuant to this Article is hereby authorized to provide for (1) audio-visual presentations for the purpose of orienting new jurors and (2) prequalification questionnaires to prospective jurors in order to assist those public officials responsible for selecting qualified jurors for the general venire and central jury pool.

E. No district court may adopt rules pursuant to this Article unless the court has previously determined by majority vote of all the judges that it has sufficient computer availability to assist in the overall management of a one day/one trial jury system.

Art. 410. Revising and supplementing the general venire.

At each commission meeting to revise and supplement the general venire, the commission shall examine the general venire list prepared at the previous selection of the general venire and shall delete therefrom the names of those persons who:

(1) Have served as civil or criminal jurors since the previous selection of the general venire; or

(2) Are known to have died or who have become disqualified to serve as jurors since their selection on the general venire.

The slips bearing the names of those persons deleted from the general venire list shall be removed from the general venire box.

The commission shall then supplement the list prepared at the previous commission meeting and the corresponding slips in the box by selecting a sufficient number of additional persons in compliance with Article 408 or Article 409, whichever is applicable. Where the general venire list is maintained in a form suitable for use by an electronic device commonly known as a computer, the general venire shall likewise as hereinabove provided be deleted and supplemented.

Art. 411. Drawing of grand jury venire in parishes other than Orleans; disposition of slips; jury box; subpoena of persons on grand jury venire.

A. Upon order of the court the jury commission in parishes other than Orleans shall select by drawing indiscriminately and by lot from the general venire box the names of at least twenty but not more than one hundred persons, with the number to be specified by the court in its order, who shall constitute the grand jury venire. Alternatively, the grand jury venire may be drawn with the use of a properly programmed electronic device commonly known as a computer. A grand jury venire shall not be drawn from a general venire containing fewer than three hundred names.

B. The slips containing the names of the persons so drawn shall be placed in an envelope which shall be sealed and the words "Grand Jury Venire" written thereon.

C. The sealed envelope shall be placed in a box labeled "Grand Jury Box", which shall be locked and sealed and placed in the custody of the clerk of court for use at the next term of court, subject to the orders of the district court, as hereinafter provided.

D. (1) The clerk shall prepare subpoenas directed to the persons on the grand jury venire, ordering their appearance in court on the date set by the court for the selection of the grand jury, and shall deliver the subpoenas to the sheriff for service.

(2) The sheriff, at the election of the district judges of the judicial district in which the parish lies, may serve such subpoenas by:

(a) Personal or domiciliary service, or by registered, certified, or regular mail addressed to the juror at his usual residence or business address.

(b) When the service is by mail, the date of mailing shall be not less than fifteen days prior to the date on which the addressee is subpoenaed to appear.

(c) When service is by registered or certified mail, the sheriff shall attach to his return the return receipt of delivery from the United States Post Office showing the disposition of the envelope bearing the summons to the juror.

(d) When service is by regular mail, the return shall show the date of mailing. In case of service by regular mail, prior to any contempt citation, the person shall be served by registered or certified mail with return receipt requested.

(3) The return, with the attached return receipt of delivery, when received by the clerk, shall form part of the record and shall be considered prima facie correct and shall constitute sufficient basis for an action to cite persons for contempt for failure to appear in response thereto.

Art. 412. Drawing grand jury venire and subpoena of veniremen; Orleans Parish.

A. In Orleans Parish, upon order of the court, the commission shall draw indiscriminately and by lot from the general venire box the names of seventy-five qualified persons, who shall constitute the grand jury venire.

B. The commission shall prepare and certify a list containing the names so drawn, and the list shall be delivered to the judge who ordered the drawing.

C. The court may direct the jury commission to prepare subpoenas directed to the persons on the grand jury venire, ordering their appearance in court on the date set by the court for the selection of the grand jury, and the jury commission shall then cause the subpoenas to be served in accordance with the provisions of Article 404.1(B) or R.S. 15:112, as directed by the court.

Art. 413. Method of impaneling of grand jury; selection of foreman.

A. The grand jury shall consist of twelve persons plus a first and second alternate for a total of fourteen persons qualified to serve as jurors, selected or drawn from the grand jury venire.

B. In parishes other than Orleans, the court shall select one person from the grand jury venire to serve as foreman of the grand jury. The sheriff shall draw indiscriminately and by lot from the envelope containing the remaining names on the grand jury venire a sufficient number of names to complete the grand jury. The envelope containing the remaining names shall be replaced into the grand jury box for use in filling vacancies as provided in Article 415.

C. In the Parish of Orleans, the court shall select twelve persons plus a first and second alternate for a total of fourteen persons from the grand jury venire, who shall constitute the grand jury. The court shall thereupon select one of the jurors to serve as foreman.

D. The first and second alternates shall receive the charge as provided in Article 432 but shall not be sworn nor become members of the grand jury except as provided in Article 415.
(Chgd. by Acts 1990 No. 47, §1, eff. 9/7/90.)

Art. 414. Time for impaneling grand juries; period of service.

A. A grand jury shall be impaneled twice a year in each parish, except in the parish of Cameron in which at least one grand jury shall be impaneled each year.

B. In parishes other than Orleans, the court shall fix the time at which a grand jury shall be impaneled, but no grand jury shall be impaneled for more than eight months, nor less than four months, except in the parish of Cameron in which the grand jury may be impaneled for a year.

C. In Orleans Parish, a grand jury venire shall be drawn by the jury commission on the date set by the presiding judge. On the next legal day following the drawing, the jury commission shall submit the grand jury venire to the presiding judge, who shall impanel the grand jury, A grand jury in Orleans Parish shall be impaneled on the first Wednesday of March and September of each year.

D. A grand jury shall remain in office until a succeeding grand jury is impaneled. A court may not discharge a grand jury or any of its members before the time for the impaneling of a new grand jury, except for legal cause.

Art. 415. Method of filling vacancies on grand jury.

A. When a vacancy occurs on a grand jury, the court shall fill the vacancy as follows:

(1) In parishes other than Orleans, by administering the oath to and seating the first alternate if he is still legally qualified and available, or if he is not, by administering the oath to and seating the second alternate, if still legally qualified and available. If a vacancy occurs after the second alternate has been seated on the grand jury to fill a vacancy or if the second alternate cannot be seated, the vacancy shall be filled by ordering the sheriff to draw indiscriminately and by lot from the envelope containing the remaining names on the grand jury venire a sufficient number of names to complete the grand jury. If the names in the envelope be exhausted before the grand jury is completed, or if a vacancy occurs on the grand jury and no names remain in the envelope, the court shall order the jury commission to withdraw indiscriminately and by lot from the general venire box an additional number of names sufficient to complete the grand jury.

(2) In Orleans Parish, by administering the oath to and seating the first alternate if he is still legally qualified and available, or if he is not, by administering the oath to and seating the second alternate, if still legally qualified and available. If a vacancy occurs after the second alternate has been seated to fill a vacancy or if the second alternate cannot be seated, the vacancy shall be filled by ordering the jury commission to draw indiscriminately and by lot from the general venire box twelve or more names, as specified by the court, from which the court shall select the persons necessary to fill the vacancy.

B. If the foreman of the grand jury is, for any reason, unable to act, the court shall designate some member of the grand jury to serve as acting foreman or to serve as a new foreman of that grand jury. An acting foreman has the powers and duties of the foreman.
(Chgd. by Acts 1990 No. 47, §1, eff. 9/7/90.)

Art. 415.1. Selection of additional grand juries.

Upon the request of the district attorney, the court shall order one additional grand jury to be impaneled. Such additional grand jury shall be selected in the same manner and have the same qualifications, duties, powers, and responsibilities, and be subject to the same provisions of law which presently govern grand juries, except as to duration and the duty to inspect facilities as provided by R.S. 15:121. However, no grand jury may concurrently conduct an inquiry into any offense or matter or receive evidence of any offense or matter which is under investigation by another grand jury impaneled in the same parish. This additional grand jury shall be impaneled and presided over by the judge who impaneled the existing regular grand jury or a judge appointed by him to act in his absence. *(Chgd. by Acts 1990 No. 74, §1, eff. 9/7/90.)*

Art. 415.2. Duration of additional grand juries; extension of impanelment.

Grand juries impaneled in accordance with Article 415.1 shall remain impaneled for a period not to exceed one year unless discharged sooner by the court upon motion of the district attorney. Provided, however, that prior to the discharge of a grand jury by the court, a grand jury shall return its report on all offenses and matters presented or pending before it as authorized by the provisions of Article 444. Upon the request of the district attorney, the court may extend this time limit for an extra six months.

Art. 416. Drawing petit jury venire in parishes other than Orleans; term of service.

A. Upon order of court the jury commission in parishes other than Orleans shall draw a petit jury venire. The commission shall draw indiscriminately and by lot thirty name slips from the general venire box, unless directed by the court order to draw a larger number. The persons whose names are so drawn shall be subject to serve as petit jurors for the first week of the next criminal session of court.

The court also may order the commission to draw indiscriminately and by lot as many additional name slips, not less than thirty, as it may direct for each additional week that a petit jury venire may be required, not to exceed two additional weeks. The persons whose names are so drawn shall be subject to serve as petit jurors for the week for which their names were drawn.

Alternatively, for the purpose of drawing a petit jury venire, the jury commission may use an electronic device, commonly known as a computer, which is programmed to draw indiscriminately and by lot.

B. A petit jury venire for the first week of a session shall not be drawn from a general venire containing less than two hundred fifty names, and no petit jury venire for any subsequent week shall be drawn from a general venire containing less than one hundred fifty names.

The commission shall place the slips bearing the names of the petit jury venire for each week in a separate envelope. It shall seal each envelope and write thereon the words "Petit Jury Venire No. 1," "Petit Jury Venire No. 2," and "Petit Jury Venire No. 3." Each envelope shall be placed in a box labeled "Petit Jury Box."

If a petit jury venire does not serve during the week for which it was drawn, the court may order that it serve during any other week of that session of court.

Art. 416.1. One-step qualification/summoning.

A. In parishes other than Orleans, at the election of the judges of the judicial district in which the parish lies, the qualification questionnaire, subpoena, and return envelope for each person who may be selected for the petit jury venire shall be prepared by the clerk and delivered in the same computer-generated envelope to the sheriff for service. The sheriff may serve such questionnaire and subpoena by first class mail addressed to such person at his usual residence or business address. The subpoena shall state an appearance date for such person not later than three weeks after the date on which the questionnaire is to be returned.

B. The questionnaire shall contain a section for signature to acknowledge receipt of the accompanying subpoena. The addressee of the subpoena and questionnaire shall fill out, sign, and return the questionnaire in the return envelope by first class mail, within five days of receipt thereof. The signing of the questionnaire shall constitute acknowledgment of receipt of the subpoena and personal service of the subpoena on the addressee.

C. The questionnaire may constitute part of the sheriff's return and may be made part of the record. When served in accordance with this Section, a person may be cited for contempt for failing to appear in response to the subpoena.

Art. 417. Process verbal; summoning of petit jurors; parishes other than Orleans.

A. In parishes other than Orleans, the clerk of court shall make a process verbal of the selection of the general venire and of the drawing of the grand jury venire and of the petit jury venire. It shall be certified to by a member of the commission and shall be filed in the clerk's office as a public record.

The clerk shall make a list of the names on the grand jury venire and on the petit jury venire, showing the week for which each petit jury venire is to serve. The lists, together with the general venire list, shall be a part of the process verbal.

B. The clerk shall cause a copy of the petit jury venire list and grand jury venire list to be published in the official journal of the parish, if there be one, or in some other newspaper published in the parish, or, if there is no official journal or other newspaper in said parish, he shall post a copy of the lists on the door of the courthouse.

C. (1) The clerk shall prepare subpoenas directed to the persons on the petit jury venire and deliver them to the sheriff for service.

(2) The sheriff, at the election of the district judges of the judicial district in which the parish lies, may serve such subpoenas by:

(a) Personal or domiciliary service, or by registered, certified, or regular mail addressed to such juror at his usual residence or business address.

(b) When the service is by mail, the date of mailing shall not be less than fifteen days prior to the date on which the addressee is subpoenaed to appear.

(c) When service is by registered or certified mail, the sheriff shall attach to his return the return receipt of delivery from the United States Post Office showing the disposition of the envelope bearing the summons to the juror.

(d) When service is by regular mail, the return shall show the date of mailing. In case of service by regular mail, prior to any contempt citation, the person shall be served by registered or certified mail with return receipt requested.

(3) The return, with the attached return receipt of delivery, when received by the clerk, shall form part of the record and shall be considered prima facie correct and shall constitute sufficient basis for an action to cite persons for contempt for failure to appear in response thereto.

Art. 418. Drawing petit jury venire in Orleans parish; number chosen; term of service; petit jury venire list.

A. In Orleans Parish upon order of the court the jury commission shall draw a petit jury venire.

B. The jury commission shall draw indiscriminately and by lot as many name slips from the general venire box as a court may direct, not less than seventy-five, for service as petit jurors during the next monthly session of that judge's section of court.

C. The commission shall prepare a list of the persons drawn which shall constitute the petit jury venire list. This list, together with the name slips drawn, shall be delivered to the judge ordering the drawing.

D. The commission shall prepare subpoenas directed to the persons on the petit jury venire and cause them to be served in accordance with the provisions of Article 404.1(B) or R.S. 15:112, as directed by the court.

Art. 419. Challenge of venire not permitted except for fraud or irreparable injury or systematic exclusion based on race.

A. A general venire, grand jury venire, or petit jury venire shall not be set aside for any reason unless fraud has been practiced, some great wrong committed that would work irreparable injury to the defendant, or unless persons were systematically excluded from the venires solely upon the basis of race.

B. This Article does not affect the right to challenge for cause, a juror who is not qualified to serve.

TITLE XII. THE GRAND JURY

Art. 431. Oath of grand jury.

The grand jurors shall take the following oath when impaneled:

"As members of the grand jury, do you solemnly swear or affirm that you will diligently inquire into and true presentment make of all indictable offenses triable within this parish which shall be given you in charge, or which shall otherwise come to your knowledge; that you will keep secret your own counsel and that of your fellows and of the state, and will not, except when authorized by law, disclose testimony of any witness examined before you, nor disclose anything which any grand juror may have said, or how any grand juror may have voted on any matter before you; that you will not indict any person through malice, hatred, or ill will, nor fail to indict any person through fear, favor, affection, or hope of reward or gain; but in all of your indictments you will present the truth, according to the best of your skill and understanding?"

The oath shall be read to the grand jury by the clerk, who shall then ask each juror: "Do you take this oath or affirmation?"

The oath shall be administered to every grand juror appointed to fill a vacancy in the grand jury and to every grand juror who was not present at the taking of the oath by the grand jury.

Art. 432. Charge to grand jury.

After the oath is administered to the members of the grand jury, the judge shall charge them orally in open court upon their duties, rights, and powers. Upon completion of the charge the judge shall give the grand jury a written copy of the charge.

At any time thereafter, the judge, on his own initiative or on request of the grand jury, may give the grand jury additional charges concerning their duties, rights, and powers. Such additional charges shall be given in open court, and a written copy thereof shall thereafter be given to the grand jury.

Art. 433. Persons present during grand jury sessions.

A. (1) Only the following persons may be present at the sessions of the grand jury:

(a) The district attorney and assistant district attorneys or any one or more of them;

(b) The attorney general and assistant attorneys general or any one of them;

(c) The witness under examination;

(d) A person sworn to record the proceedings of and the testimony given before the grand jury; and

(e) An interpreter sworn to translate the testimony of a witness who is unable to speak the English language.

(2) An attorney for a target of the grand jury's investigation may be present during the testimony of said target. The attorney shall be prohibited from objecting, addressing or arguing before the grand jury; however he may consult with his client at anytime. The court shall remove such attorney for violation of these conditions. If a witness becomes a target because of his testimony, the legal advisor to the grand jury shall inform him of his right to counsel and cease questioning until such witness has obtained counsel or voluntarily and intelligently waived his right to counsel. Any evidence or testimony obtained under the

provisions of this Subparagraph from a witness who later becomes a target shall not be admissible in a proceeding against him.

B. No person, other than a grand juror, shall be present while the grand jury is deliberating and voting.

C. A person who is intentionally present at a meeting of the grand jury, except as authorized by Paragraph A of this article, shall be in constructive contempt of court.

(Chgd. by Acts 1992 No. 308, §1, eff. 8/21/92.)

Art. 434. Secrecy of grand jury meetings; procedures for crimes in other parishes.

A. Members of the grand jury, all other persons present at a grand jury meeting, and all persons having confidential access to information concerning grand jury proceedings, shall keep secret the testimony of witnesses and all other matters occurring at, or directly connected with, a meeting of the grand jury. However, after the indictment, such persons may reveal statutory irregularities in grand jury proceedings to defense counsel, the attorney general, the district attorney, or the court, and may testify concerning them. Such persons may disclose testimony given before the grand jury, at any time when permitted by the court, to show that a witness committed perjury in his testimony before the grand jury. A witness may discuss his testimony given before the grand jury with counsel for a person under investigation or indicted, with the attorney general or the district attorney, or with the court.

B. Whenever a grand jury of one parish discovers that a crime may have been committed in another parish of the state, the foreman of that grand jury, after notifying his district attorney, shall make that discovery known to the attorney general. The district attorney or the attorney general may direct to the district attorney of another parish any and all evidence, testimony, and transcripts thereof, received or prepared by the grand jury of the former parish, concerning any offense that may have been committed in the latter parish, for use in such latter parish.

C. Any person who violates the provisions of this article shall be in constructive contempt of court.

Art. 435. Meetings of grand jury.

The grand jury shall meet as directed by the court, or may meet on its own initiative at the direction of nine of its members, at any time and place within the parish. Nine grand jurors shall constitute a quorum, and nine grand jurors must concur to find an indictment.

Art. 436. The foreman; rules of procedure.

The foreman of the grand jury shall preside over all hearings. He may delegate duties to other grand jurors and may determine rules of procedure. A grand juror who objects to a rule of procedure made by the foreman may apply to the court for a determination of the matter.

Art. 437. Inquiry into offenses; authority and duties.

The grand jury shall inquire into all capital offenses triable within the parish. It may inquire into other offenses triable by the district court of the parish, and shall inquire into such offenses when requested to do so by the district attorney or ordered to do so by the court.

Art. 438. Duty of grand juror having knowledge of offense; investigation.

If a grand juror knows or has reason to believe that an offense triable by the district court of the parish has been committed, he shall declare such fact to his fellow jurors, who may investigate it. In such investigation or any subsequent criminal proceeding the grand juror shall be a competent witness.

Art. 439. Subpoena of witnesses to appear before the grand jury.

Upon request of the grand jury or the district attorney, the court shall issue a subpoena for a witness to appear before the grand jury to testify when questioned by the grand jury or district attorney, or both, concerning an offense under investigation. Upon request of the grand jury or the district attorney, the court may also issue a subpoena duces tecum. The issuance, service, and return of a subpoena provided for in this article and the effect of the return and the enforcement of the subpoena shall be as provided in Articles 731 through 737.

Art. 439.1. Witnesses; authority to compel testimony and evidence.

A. In the case of any individual who has been or may be called to testify or provide other information at any proceeding before or ancillary to a grand jury of the state, at any proceeding before a court of this state, or in response to any subpoena by the attorney general or district attorney, the judicial district court of the district in which the proceeding is or may be held shall issue, in accordance with Subsection B of this article, upon the request of the attorney general together with the district attorney for such district, an order requiring such individual to give testimony or provide other information which he refuses to give or provide on the basis of his privilege against self-incrimination, such order to become effective as provided in Subsection C of this article.

B. The attorney general together with the district attorney may request an order under Subsection A of this article when in his judgment

(1) the testimony or other information from such individual may be necessary to the public interest; and

(2) such individual has refused or is likely to refuse to testify or provide other information on the basis of his privilege against self incrimination.

C. The witness may not refuse to comply with the order on the basis of his privilege against self incrimination, but no testimony or other information compelled under the order, or any information directly or indirectly derived from such testimony or other information, may be used against the witness in any criminal case, except a prosecution for perjury, giving a false statement or otherwise failing to comply with the order.

D. Whoever refuses to comply with an order as hereinabove provided shall be adjudged in contempt of court and punished as provided by law.

Art. 440. Administration of oath to witnesses.

A witness who is to testify before the grand jury shall first be sworn by the foreman, in accordance with Article 14, to testify truthfully and to keep secret, except as authorized by law, matters which he learns at the grand jury meeting.

Art. 441. Administration of oath to other persons.

Before being permitted to function in their respective capacities, the court shall administer an oath, to persons employed to record and transcribe the testimony and proceedings, and to interpreters, to faithfully perform their duties and keep secret the grand jury proceedings.

Art. 442. Evidence to be received by grand jury.

A grand jury shall hear all evidence presented by the district attorney. It may hear evidence for the defendant, but is under no duty to do so.

When the grand jury has reason to believe that other available evidence will explain the charge, it should order the evidence produced.

A grand jury should receive only legal evidence and such as is given by witnesses produced, or furnished by documents and other physical evidence. However, no indictment shall be quashed or conviction reversed on the ground that the indictment was based, in whole or in part, on illegal evidence, or on the ground that the grand jury has violated a provision of this article.

Art. 443. When indictment to be found.

The grand jury shall find an indictment, charging the defendant with the commission of an offense, when, in its judgment, the evidence considered by it, if unexplained and uncontradicted, warrants a conviction.

Art. 444. Action by grand jury.

A. A grand jury shall have power to act, concerning a matter, only in one of the following ways:

(1) By returning a true bill;
(2) By returning not a true bill; or
(3) By pretermitting entirely the matter investigated.

The grand jury is an accusatory body and not a censor of public morals. It shall make no report or recommendation, other than to report its action as aforesaid.

B. At least nine members of the grand jury must concur in returning "a true bill" or "not a true bill." A matter may be pretermitted by a vote of at least nine members of the grand jury, or as a consequence of the failure of nine of the grand jury members to agree on a finding.

C. A grand jury may make such reports or requests as are authorized by law.

TITLE XIII. INDICTMENT AND INFORMATION

CHAPTER 1. INDICTMENT FORMS

Art. 461. Special definitions.

In this Title the terms enumerated shall have the designated meanings:

"Writing" and "written" include words printed, painted, typed, engraved, lithographed, photographed, or otherwise copied, traced, or made visible to the eye.

"Indictment" includes affidavit and information, unless it is the clear intent to restrict that word to the finding of a grand jury.

Art. 462. Form of grand jury indictment.

The indictment by a grand jury may be in substantially the following form:

In the (Here state the name of the court.) on the __ day of _____, 19__. State of Louisiana v. A.B. (Here state the name or description of the accused.).

The grand jury of the Parish of _____, charges that A.B. (Here state the name or description of the accused.) committed the offense of _____, in that (Here set forth the offense and transaction according to the rules stated in this Title. The particulars of the offense may be added with a view to avoiding the necessity for a bill of particulars.) contrary to the law of the State of Louisiana and against the peace and dignity of the same.

Art. 463. Form of information.

The information may be in substantially the following form:

In the (Here state the name of the court.) on the ___ day of _____, 19__. State of Louisiana v. A.B. (Here state the name or description of the accused.).

X.Y., District Attorney for the Parish of _____, charges that A.B. (Here state the name or description of the accused.) committed the offense of _____, in that (Here set forth the offense and transaction according to the rules stated in this Title. The particulars of the offense may be added with a view to avoiding the necessity for a bill of particulars.) contrary to the law of the state of Louisiana and against the peace and dignity of the same.

Art. 464. Nature and contents of indictment.

The indictment shall be a plain, concise, and definite written statement of the essential facts constituting the offense charged. It shall state for each count the official or customary citation of the statute which the defendant is alleged to have violated. Error in the citation or its omission shall not be ground for dismissal of the indictment or for reversal of a conviction if the error or omission did not mislead the defendant to his prejudice.

Art. 465. Specific indictment forms.

A. The following forms of charging offenses may be used, but any other forms authorized by this title may also be used:

1. Abortion—A.B. committed abortion on C.D.

2. Aggravated Arson—A.B. committed aggravated arson of a dwelling (or structure, watercraft, or movable, as the case may be). If the words "belonging to another and with the damage amounting to ___ dollars" are added, simple arson will be included in the charge.

3. Simple Arson—A.B. committed simple arson of _____ (state the property burned or damaged) with the damage amounting to ___ dollars.

4. Arson with Intent to Defraud—A.B. committed arson of _____ (state the property burned or damaged) with intent to defraud C.D.

5. Aggravated Assault—A.B. assaulted C.D. with a dangerous weapon.

6. Simple Assault—A.B. assaulted C.D.

7. Attempt—A.B. attempted to _____ (commit theft of one rifle—state property subject of the theft; rob C.D.; or murder C.D.; as the case may be).

8. Aggravated Battery—A.B. committed a battery with a dangerous weapon upon C.D.

9. Simple Battery—A.B. committed a battery upon C.D.

10. Bigamy—A.B. committed bigamy with C.D.

11. Public Bribery—A.B. committed public bribery by giving (or offering to give) ___ dollars (or describe property) to C.D., _____, (state official status of person bribed); or, A.B., _____, (state official status of A.B.) committed public bribery by receiving (or offering to receive) ___ dollars (or describe property) from C.D.

12. Bribery of Voters—A.B. bribed C.D., a voter, by giving him (or offering him) ___ dollars (or describe property); or A.B., a voter, committed bribery of voters by receiving (or offering to receive) ___ dollars (or describe property) from C.D.

13. Aggravated Burglary—A.B. committed aggravated burglary of the dwelling of C.D.; or A.B. committed aggravated burglary of a warehouse (or other structure, watercraft, or movable, as the case may be) belonging to C.D.

14. Simple Burglary—A.B. committed simple burglary of the houseboat (or other structure, watercraft, or movable, as the case may be) belonging to C.D.

15. Carnal Knowledge of a Juvenile—A.B. committed carnal knowledge of C.D., a juvenile.

16. Crime Against Nature—A.B. committed crime against nature with C.D. by ____ (describe the act).

17. Criminal Conspiracy—A.B. conspired with C.D. to _____ (commit theft of one rifle—state property subject of the theft; murder E.F.; or rob E.F.; as the case may be).

18. Aggravated Criminal Damage to Property—A.B. committed aggravated criminal damage to _____ (state the structure, watercraft, or movable). If the words "belonging to another and with the damage amounting to ___ dollars" are added, simple criminal damage to property will be included in the charge.

19. Simple Criminal Damage to Property—A.B. committed simple criminal damage to ____ (state the property damaged) with the damage amounting to ___ dollars.

20. Damage to Property with Intent to Defraud—A.B. damaged _____ (state the property damaged) with intent to defraud C.D.

21. Cruelty to Juveniles—A.B. committed cruelty to C.D., a juvenile, by _____ (describe act of cruelty).

22. Aggravated Escape—A.B. committed aggravated escape from C.D., a _____ (state official status of person escaped from); or A.B. committed aggravated escape from _____ (state place of official detention).

23. Simple Escape—A.B. escaped from C.D., a _____ (state official status of person escaped from); or A.B. escaped from _____ (state place of official detention).

24. Forgery—A.B. forged a _____ (promissory note, or other instrument) by _____ (state nature of defendant's act).

25. False Imprisonment—A.B. falsely imprisoned C.D.

26. Incest—A.B. committed incest with C.D., his _____ (state relationship).

27. Public Intimidation—A.B. committed public intimidation upon C.D., a _____ (state official status of person intimidated).

28. Issuing Worthless Checks—A.B. issued a worthless check to _____ (state name of payee) in the amount of ___ dollars.

29. Aggravated Kidnapping—A.B. committed aggravated kidnapping of C.D.

30. Simple Kidnapping—A.B. kidnapped C.D.

31. First Degree Murder—A.B. committed first degree murder of C.D.
32. Second Degree Murder—A.B. committed second degree murder of C.D.
33. Manslaughter—A.B. unlawfully killed C.D.
34. Negligent Homicide—A.B. negligently killed C.D.
35. Negligent Injuring—A.B. negligently injured C.D.
36. Perjury—A.B. committed perjury on the trial of C.D. for a felony (or on the trial of C.D. for a misdemeanor; or in a civil case between C.D. and E.F.; or at a _____ hearing; as the case may be) by testifying as follows: _____ (set forth the testimony).
37. False Swearing—A.B. made a false statement under oath for _____ (set forth purpose of making the statement) as follows: _____ (set forth the false statement).
38. Prostitution—A.B. committed prostitution.
39. Aggravated Rape—A.B. committed aggravated rape upon C.D.
40. Simple Rape—A.B. committed simple rape upon C.D.
41. Receiving Stolen Things—A.B. received stolen things, viz., _____ (state property received) of a value of ___ dollars.
42. Armed Robbery—A.B., while armed with a dangerous weapon, robbed C.D.
43. Simple Robbery—A.B. robbed C.D.
44. Theft—A.B. committed theft of _____ (state property stolen) of a value of ___ dollars.
45. Theft of Cattle, etc.—A.B. committed theft of _____ (describe animal or animals stolen).
46. Unauthorized Use of Movables—A.B. committed unauthorized use of _____ (describe the movable).

B. The indictment, in additional to the necessary averments of the appropriate specific form hereinbefore set forth, may also include a statement of additional facts pertaining to the offense charged. If this is done it shall not affect the sufficiency of the specific indictment form authorized by this article.

CHAPTER 2. SPECIAL ALLEGATIONS

Article

Art. 466. Name of defendant.

In an indictment it is sufficient for the purpose of identifying the defendant to state his true name, or to state the name, appellation, or nickname by which he is known, or if no better way of identifying him is practicable, to state a fictitious name, or to describe him as a person whose name is unknown, or in any other manner. In stating the true name or the name by which the defendant is known or a fictitious name, it is sufficient to state a surname, a surname and one or more given names, or a surname and one or more abbreviations or initials of a given name or names.

If the true name of a defendant identified in the indictment otherwise than by his true name is disclosed by the evidence or is otherwise discovered, the court shall cause the indictment to be amended to show his true name, and the proceedings shall continue against the defendant in his true name.

In no case is it necessary to aver or prove that the true name of the defendant is unknown to the grand jury, complainant, or prosecuting officer.

Art. 467. Naming corporation, partnership or other unincorporated association.

If the defendant is a corporation, it is sufficient to state the corporate name of the defendant in an indictment, or to state any name or designation by which it has been or is known or by which it may be identified, without an averment that it is a corporation or that it was incorporated according to law.

If the defendant is a partnership or other association of persons not incorporated, it is sufficient to state any proper name of the partnership or association, or to state any name or designation by which it is known, or to state the names of all the persons in the partnership or association, or to state the name of one or more persons in the partnership or association referring to the other or others as "another" or "others." It is not necessary to state the legal form of the partnership or association.

Art. 468. Date and time.

The date or time of the commission of the offense need not be alleged in the indictment, unless the date or time is essential to the offense.

If the date or time is not essential to the offense, an indictment shall not be held insufficient if it does not state the proper date or time, or if it states the offense to have been committed on a day subsequent to the finding of the indictment, or on an impossible day.

All allegations of the indictment and bill of particulars shall be considered as referring to the same date or time, unless otherwise stated.

Art. 469. Venue and place.

It is not necessary to state any venue in the body of the indictment, but the state, parish, or other jurisdiction where the indictment is filed shall be taken to be the venue for the offense charged in the indictment.

The place of the commission of the offense need not be alleged in the indictment unless the place of commission is essential to the offense. All allegations in the indictment and bill of particulars shall be considered as referring to the same place, unless stated otherwise.

Art. 470. Value, price, or damage.

Value, price, or amount of damage need not be alleged in the indictment, unless such allegation is essential to the charge or determine the grade of the offense.

Art. 471. Ownership.

Ownership, or the name of the owner of property, need not be alleged in the indictment, unless such ownership or name of the owner is essential to the offense.

Art. 472. General intent.

In offenses requiring only a general criminal intent, the indictment need not allege that the act was intentionally done.

Art. 473. Identification of victim.

When the name of the person injured is substantial and not merely descriptive, such as when the injury is to the person, as in murder, rape, or battery, the indictment shall state the true name of the victim or the name, appellation, or nickname by which he is known. If the name, appellation, or nickname of the victim is not known, it is sufficient to so state and to describe him as far as possible. In stating any name of a victim it is sufficient to state a surname, a surname and one or more given names, or a surname and one or more abbreviations or initials of a given name or names.

Art. 474. Property described as money.

When it is necessary to make an averment in an indictment as to money, treasury notes or certificates, banknotes or other securities intended to circulate as money, it is sufficient to describe them or any of them as money, without specifying the particular character, denomination, kind, species, or nature thereof.

Art. 475. Description of written instruments and printed objects.

When it is necessary to make an averment in an indictment relative to any instrument or object which consists wholly or in part of writing or figures, pictures or designs, it is sufficient to describe the instrument or object by any name or description by which it is usually known or by which it may be identified, or by its purport, without setting forth a copy or facsimile of the whole or any part thereof.

Art. 476. Description of spoken or written matter.

When it is necessary to make an averment in an indictment relative to any words, whether spoken, written or otherwise recorded, or to any plan, map, or picture, it is sufficient to set forth the words by their general purport, or to describe the plan, map, or picture generally, without setting forth a copy or facsimile thereof.

Art. 477. Meaning of words and phrases.

The words and phrases used in an indictment or bill of particulars are to be construed according to their usual meaning and acceptation. Words and phrases which have been defined by law or which have otherwise acquired a legal meaning are to be construed according to their legal meaning.

Art. 478. Judgments and other determinations.

Where a judgment or other determination of, or a proceeding before, any court or official, civil or military, is referred to in an indictment, it is unnecessary to allege the facts conferring jurisdiction on the court or official. It is sufficient to allege generally that the judgment or determination was given or made or the proceeding had, in such manner as identifies the judgment, determination or proceeding.

Art. 479. Exceptions.

An indictment shall not be invalid or insufficient for the reason that it fails to negative an exception, excuse, or proviso contained in the statute creating or defining the offense. An exception, excuse, or proviso must be urged by way of defense.

Art. 480. Conjunctive charging.

If an offense may be committed by doing one or more of several acts, or by one or more of several means, or with one or more of several intents, or with one or more of several results, two or more of such acts, means, intents, or results may be charged conjunctively in a single count of an indictment, or set forth conjunctively in a bill of particulars, and proof of any one of the acts, means, intents, or results so charged or set forth will support a conviction.

Art. 481. Theft.

An indictment for theft may include several counts against the same defendant for distinct acts of theft, and the aggregate amount of the thefts shall determine the grade of the offense charged. If a defendant misappropriates money or other things of value, which were entrusted to him by virtue of his office, employment, or any fiduciary relationship, he may be charged in one count with theft of the aggregate amount misappropriated by him during the entire time of his holding the office, employment, or fiduciary relationship.

Art. 482. Alternative offenses; special joinder rules.

A. An indictment for theft may also contain a count for receiving stolen things, and the defendant may be convicted of either offense. When two or more persons are jointly indicted for these offenses, any or all of the persons indicted may be found guilty of either of the offenses charged. The district attorney shall not be required to elect between the two offenses charged.

B. An indictment for manslaughter may also contain a count for abortion and the jury may convict of either offense. The district attorney shall not be required to elect between the two offenses charged.

Art. 483. Allegations of prior convictions.

If it is necessary to allege a prior conviction in an indictment, it is sufficient to allege the name or nature of the offense and the fact, date, and court of the conviction.

An indictment shall not contain an allegation of a prior conviction of the defendant unless such allegation is necessary to fully charge the offense.

CHAPTER 3. BILL OF PARTICULARS

Art. 484. Bill of particulars.

A motion for a bill of particulars may be filed of right in accordance with Article 521. The court, on its own motion or on motion of the defendant, may require the district attorney to furnish a bill of particulars setting forth more specifically the nature and cause of the charge against the defendant.

Supplemental bills of particulars or a new bill may be ordered by the court at least seven days before the trial begins.

When a bill of particulars is furnished, it shall be filed of record and a copy of the bill shall be given to the defendant.

Art. 485. Effect of inconsistent or limiting allegations of bill of particulars.

If it appears from the bill of particulars furnished under Article 484, together with any particulars appearing in the indictment, that the offense charged in the indictment was not committed, or that the defendant did not commit it, or that there is a ground for quashing the indictment, the court may on its own motion, and on motion of the defendant shall, order that the indictment be quashed unless the defect is cured. The defect will be cured if the district attorney furnishes, within a period fixed by the court and not to exceed three days from the order, another bill of particulars which either by itself or together with any particulars appearing in the indictment so states the particulars as to make it appear that the offense charged was committed by the defendant, or that there is no ground for quashing the indictment, as the case may be.

CHAPTER 4. DEFECTS; AMENDMENT

Art. 486. Repugnancy; surplusage.

An indictment that charges an offense in accordance with the provisions of this Title shall not be invalid or insufficient because it contains repugnant allegations. Unnecessary allegations may be disregarded as surplusage.

Art. 487. Defective indictment; amendment.

A. An indictment that charges an offense in accordance with the provisions of this Title shall not be invalid or insufficient because of any defect or imperfection in, or omission of, any matter of form only, or because of any miswriting, misspelling, or improper English, or because of the use of any sign, symbol, figure, or abbreviation, or because any similar defect, imperfection, omission, or uncertainty exists therein. The court may at any time cause the indictment to be amended in respect to any such formal defect, imperfection, omission, or uncertainty.

Before the trial begins the court may order an indictment amended with respect to a defect of substance. After the trial begins a mistrial shall be ordered on the ground of a defect of substance.

B. Nothing contained herein shall be construed to prohibit the defendant from entering a plea of guilty to a crime nonresponsive to the original indictment when such a plea is acceptable to the district attorney, and in such case, the district attorney shall not be required to file a new indictment to charge the crime to which the plea is offered.

Art. 487.1. Indictment for driving while intoxicated; amendment.

An indictment which charges operating a vehicle while intoxicated may be amended at any time prior to commencement of the trial to charge a second, third, or fourth offense thereof regardless of whether such second, third, or fourth offense occurred before or after an earlier conviction of operating a vehicle while intoxicated.

Art. 488. Variances; amendment.

When there is a variance between the allegations of an indictment or bill of particulars which state the particulars of the offense, and the evidence offered in support thereof, the court may order the indictment or bill of particulars amended in respect to the variance, and then admit the evidence.

Art. 489. Continuance where amendment prejudicial.

If it is shown, on motion of the defendant, that the defendant has been prejudiced in his defense on the merits by the defect, imperfection, omission, uncertainty, or variance, with respect to which an amendment is made, the court shall grant a continuance for a reasonable time. In determining whether the defendant has been prejudiced in his defense upon the merits, the court shall consider all the circumstances of the case and the entire course of the prosecution. If it becomes necessary to discharge the original jury from further consideration of the case, the trial before a new jury will not constitute double jeopardy.

CHAPTER 5. JOINDER RULES

Art. 490. Counts.

Counts are charges of crime joined in the same indictment. Recitals in one count may be incorporated in subsequent counts by means of a clear and distinct reference. The conclusion of the indictment applies to all counts stated therein.

Art. 493. Joinder of offenses.

Two or more offenses may be charged in the same indictment or information in a separate count for each offense if the offenses charged, whether felonies or misdemeanors, are of the same or similar character or are based on the same act or transaction or on two or more acts or transactions connected together or constituting parts of a common scheme or plan; provided that the offenses joined must be triable by the same mode of trial.

Art. 493.1. Joinder of misdemeanors; penalties.

Whenever two or more misdemeanors are joined in accordance with Article 493 in the same indictment or information, the maximum aggregate penalty that may be imposed for the misdemeanors shall not exceed imprisonment for more than six months or a fine of more than one thousand dollars, or both. *(Chgd. by Acts 1992 No. 313, §1, eff. 6/17/92.)*

Art. 493.2. Joinder of felonies; mode of trial.

Notwithstanding the provisions of Article 493, offenses in which punishment is necessarily confinement at hard labor may be charged in the same indictment or information with offenses in which the punishment may be confinement at hard labor, provided that the joined offenses are of the same or similar character or are based on the same act or transaction or on two or more acts or transactions connected together or constituting parts of a common scheme or plan. Cases so joined shall be tried by a jury composed of twelve jurors, ten of whom must concur to render a verdict. *(Added by Acts 1997 No. 559, §1, eff. 8/15/97.)*

Art. 494. Joinder of defendants.

Two or more defendants may be charged in the same indictment or information if they are alleged to have participated in the same act or transaction or in the same series of acts or transactions constituting an offense or offenses. Such defendants may be charged in one or more counts together or separately and all of the defendants need not be charged in each count.

Art. 495. Objections to misjoinder.

The objections of misjoinder of defendants or misjoinder of offenses may be urged only by a motion to quash the indictment.

Art. 495.1. Severance of offenses.

If it appears that a defendant or the state is prejudiced by a joinder of offenses in an indictment or bill of information or by such joinder for trial together, the court may order separate trials, grant a severance of offenses, or provide whatever other relief justice requires.

CHAPTER 6. PROCEDURE AFTER INDICTMENT

Art. 496. Warrant of arrest on indictment or information.

When an indictment has been found or an information filed against a defendant who is not in custody or at large on bail for the offense charged, the court shall issue a warrant for the defendant's arrest, unless it issues a summons under Article 497.

Art. 497. Summons in misdemeanor cases.

If an offense charged by indictment or information is a misdemeanor, the court may issue a summons, instead of a warrant of arrest, if it has reasonable ground to believe that the person will appear in response to a summons. If the court issues a summons, it may later issue a warrant of arrest in place of the summons.

Art. 498. Copy of indictment or information.

A certified copy of the indictment or information shall be furnished by the clerk of court to a defendant upon his request. Failure to furnish a correct copy of the indictment or information shall not affect the validity of the criminal prosecution, unless the defendant was substantially prejudiced thereby.

Art. 499. Release conditioned on AIDS testing.

A. A person indicted by a grand jury for a sexual offense as defined in R.S. 14:42 through 43.4 shall, at the direction of the court, undergo a medical procedure or test designed to determine or aid in determining whether the person has a sexually transmitted disease, or is infected with the acquired immune deficiency syndrome (AIDS) virus, the human immuno deficiency virus (HIV-1) infection, any antibodies to such viruses, or with any other probable causative agent of AIDS.

B. The court shall include in its order the designation of an appropriate facility for the procedure, and shall require that the result be reported to the court. The court may in its discretion provide the results to the victim of the offense, and shall provide them to health authorities in accordance with law.

C. The state shall not use the fact that the medical procedure or test was performed on the alleged offender under this Article, or the results thereof, in any criminal proceeding arising out of the alleged offense.

(Added by Acts 1991 No. 316, §1, eff. 9/6/91.)

TITLE XIV. RIGHT TO COUNSEL

Art. 511. Right to counsel.

The accused in every instance has the right to defend himself and to have the assistance of counsel. His counsel shall have free access to him, in private, at reasonable hours.

Art. 512. Assignment of counsel in capital cases.

When a defendant charged with a capital offense appears for arraignment without counsel, the court shall provide counsel for his defense in accordance with the provisions of R.S. 15:145. Such counsel must be assigned before the defendant pleads to the indictment, but may be assigned earlier. Counsel assigned in a capital case must have been admitted to the bar for at least five years. An attorney with less experience may be assigned as assistant counsel.

Art. 513. Assignment of counsel in other cases.

In the case of an offense punishable by imprisonment, when the defendant appears for arraignment without counsel, the court shall inform him before he pleads to the indictment of his right to have counsel appointed to defend him if he is indigent. When a defendant states under oath that he desires counsel but is indigent, and the court finds the statement of indigency to be true, the court shall provide for counsel in accordance with the provisions of R.S. 15:145 to the defendant before he pleads to the indictment.

Art. 514. Minute entry regarding counsel.

The minutes of the court must show either that the defendant was represented by counsel or that he was informed by the court of the defendant's right to counsel, including the right to court-appointed counsel, and that he waived such right.

Art. 515. Substitution of counsel.

Assignment of counsel shall not deprive the defendant of the right to engage other counsel at any stage of the proceedings in substitution of counsel assigned by the court. The court may assign other counsel in substitution of counsel previously assigned or specially assigned to assist the defendant at the arraignment.

Art. 516. Belated pleas and motions; when authorized.

When a defendant has pleaded at the arraignment without counsel, counsel subsequently appointed or procured before trial shall be given a reasonable time within which to withdraw any motion, plea, or waiver made by the defendant, and to enter any other motion or plea.

Art. 517. Joint representation of co-defendants; duty of court.

A. Whenever two or more defendants have been jointly charged in a single indictment or have moved to consolidate their indictments for a joint trial, and are represented by the same retained or appointed counsel or by retained or appointed counsel who are associated in the practice of law, the court shall inquire with respect to such joint representation and shall advise each defendant on the record of his right to separate representation.

B. Unless it appears that there is good cause to believe that no conflict of interest is likely to arise, the court shall take such measures as may be appropriate to protect each defendant's right to counsel.

(Added by Acts 1997 No. 889, §1, eff. 8/15/97.)

TITLE XIV-A. PRETRIAL MOTIONS

Art. 521. Time for filing of pretrial motions.

Pretrial motions shall be made or filed within fifteen days after arraignment, unless a different time is provided by law or fixed by the court at arraignment upon a showing of good cause why fifteen days is inadequate.

Upon written motion at any time and a showing of good cause, the court shall allow additional time to file pretrial motions.

Art. 522. Hearings on motions; audio-visual appearance.

A. If provided by local rule of the court, a defendant's appearance at the seventy-two hour hearing and the initial setting of bail may be by simultaneous transmission through audio-visual electronic equipment.

B. If provided by local rule of the court and approved by the defense counsel, a defendant's appearance at any pretrial motion or at any hearing on a pretrial motion except as provided in Paragraph A of this Article, may be by simultaneous transmission through audio-visual electronic equipment.

(Added by Acts 1997 No. 1015, §1, eff. 8/15/97.)

TITLE XV. MOTION TO QUASH

Art. 531. Motion to quash; nature of motion.

All pleas or defenses raised before trial, other than mental incapacity to proceed, or pleas of "not guilty" and of "not guilty and not guilty by reason of insanity," shall be urged by a motion to quash.

Art. 532. General grounds for motion to quash.

A motion to quash may be based on one or more of the following grounds:

(1) The indictment fails to charge an offense which is punishable under a valid statute.

(2) The indictment fails to conform to the requirements of Chapters 1 and 2 of Title XIII. In such case the court may permit the district attorney to amend the indictment to correct the defect.

(3) The indictment is duplicitous or contains a misjoinder of defendants or offenses. In such case the court may permit the district attorney to sever the indictment into separate counts or separate indictments.

(4) The district attorney failed to furnish a sufficient bill of particulars when ordered to do so by the court. In such case the court may overrule the motion if a sufficient bill of particulars is furnished within the delay fixed by the court.

(5) A bill of particulars has shown a ground for quashing the indictment under Article 485.

(6) Trial for the offense charged would constitute double jeopardy.

(7) The time limitation for the institution of prosecution or for the commencement of trial has expired.

(8) The court has no jurisdiction of the offense charged.

(9) The general venire or the petit jury venire was improperly drawn, selected, or constituted.

Art. 533. Special grounds for motion to quash grand jury indictment.

A motion to quash an indictment by a grand jury may also be based on one or more of the following grounds:

(1) The manner of selection of the general venire, the grand jury venire, or the grand jury was illegal.

(2) An individual grand juror was not qualified under Article 401.

(3) A person, other than a grand juror, was present while the grand jurors were deliberating or voting, or an unauthorized person was present when the grand jury was examining a witness.

(4) Less than nine grand jurors were present when the indictment was found.

(5) The indictment was not indorsed "a true bill," or the endorsement was not signed by the foreman of the grand jury.

Art. 534. Special grounds for motion to quash information.

A motion to quash an information may also be based on one or more of the following grounds:

(1) The information was not signed by the district attorney; or was not properly filed.

(2) The offense is not one for which prosecution can be instituted by an information.

Art. 535. Time to file motion to quash.

A. A motion to quash may be filed of right at any time before commencement of the trial, when based on the ground that:

(1) The offense charged is not punishable under a valid statute;

(2) The indictment does not conform with the requirements of Chapters 1 and 2 of Title XIII;

(3) Trial for the offense charged would constitute double jeopardy;

(4) The time limitation for the institution of prosecution has expired;

(5) The court has no jurisdiction of the offense charged; or

(6) The information charges an offense for which prosecution can be instituted only by a grand jury indictment.

These grounds may be urged at a later state of the proceedings in accordance with other provisions of this Code.

B. A motion to quash on the ground that the time limitation for commencement of trial has expired may be filed at any time before commencement of trial.

C. A motion to quash on grounds other than those stated in Paragraphs A and B of this Article shall be filed in accordance with Article 521.

D. The grounds for a motion to quash under Paragraphs B and C are waived unless a motion to quash is filed in conformity with those provisions.

E. The court may, in order to avoid a continuance, defer a hearing on a motion to quash until the end of the trial.

Art. 536. Form and contents of motion to quash; place to file.

A motion to quash shall be in writing, signed by the defendant or his attorney, and filed in open court or in the office of the clerk of court. It shall specify distinctly the grounds on which it is based. The court shall hear no objection based on grounds not stated in the motion.

Art. 537. Trial of issues arising on motion to quash.

All issues, whether of law or fact, that arise on a motion to quash shall be tried by the court without a jury.

Art. 538. Effect of sustaining motion to quash.

The court shall order the defendant discharged from custody or bail, as to that charge, when it sustains a motion to quash based upon the ground that:

(1) The offense is not punishable under a valid statute;

(2) Trial for the offense charged would constitute double jeopardy;

(3) The time limitation for the institution of prosecution or for the commencement of trial has expired; or

(4) The court has no jurisdiction of the offense charged.

In other cases, when a motion to quash is sustained, the court may order that the defendant be held in custody or that his bail be continued for a specified time, pending the filing of a new indictment.

TITLE XVI. ARRAIGNMENT AND PLEAS

Article

Art. 551. Arraignment of defendant.

A. The arraignment consists of the reading of the indictment to the defendant by the clerk in open court, and the court calling upon the defendant to plead. Reading of the indictment may be waived by the defendant at the discretion and with the permission of the court. The arraignment and the defendant's plea shall be entered in the minutes of the court and shall constitute a part of the record.

B. Nothing in this Article shall prohibit the court, by local rule, or the defense counsel from providing for a defendant's appearance at his arraignment by simultaneous audio-visual transmission. The court may, by local rule, provide for the defendant's appearance at the arraignment and the entry of his plea by way of simultaneous transmission through audio-visual electronic equipment.

(Chgd. by Acts 1990 No. 543, §1, No. 593, §1, eff. 9/7/90.)

Art. 551.1. Substitution of railroad defendant at arraignment.

A. Subject to the provisions of Paragraph D, at arraignment and upon verified motion of the railroad employer of an employee-defendant charged with a violation of a parish or municipal ordinance, the railroad employer shall be substituted as defendant in the proceedings in accordance with the provisions of Paragraphs B and C.

B. Any railroad employer seeking to be substituted as the defendant in any proceeding citing its employee for a violation of any parish or municipal ordinance must file a verified motion setting forth the facts that the defendant is its employee, and at the time of the violation, the defendant was in the employ of the railroad employer and was performing his duties and functions in the course and scope of his employment which caused the violation, in accordance with the rules and regulations or instructions of the employer.

C. Subject to the provisions of Paragraph D, upon the timely filing of the motion to substitute defendant by the railroad employer, the railroad employer shall be substituted as the defendant in the proceedings, the individual employee shall be dismissed as a defendant, and the charges against the individual employee shall be erased from the record, at which time the railroad defendant shall be the sole defendant and entity responsible for the violation of the parish or municipal ordinance as originally cited.

D. The provisions of this Article shall not apply to or be available in prosecutions involving the alleged consumption of alcohol or controlled dangerous substances.

(Added by Acts 1993 No. 360, §1, eff. 6/3/93.)

Art. 552. Pleas at the arraignment.

There are four kinds of pleas to the indictment at the arraignment:

(1) Guilty;

(2) Not guilty;

(3) Not guilty and not guilty by reason of insanity; or

(4) Nolo contendere, which plea a court may in its discretion accept only if the offense charged is not a capital offense. If a court accepts such a plea, it shall impose sentence or place the defendant on probation, or release him during his good behavior, in accordance with the laws applicable to the offense. A sentence imposed upon a plea of nolo contendere is a

conviction and may be considered as a prior conviction and provide a basis for prosecution or sentencing under laws pertaining to multiple offenses, and shall be a conviction for purposes of laws providing for the granting, suspension or revocation of licenses to operate motor vehicles.

Art. 553. Method of pleading.

A. Except when otherwise provided under Paragraph B of this Article or by local rule in accordance with Article 551, the defendant in a felony case shall plead in person. In misdemeanor cases, the defendant may plead not guilty through counsel, plead guilty through counsel with consent of the court, may appear at arraignment by way of simultaneous audio-visual transmission in accordance with local rules of court, and may plead and be arraigned in accordance with procedures established according to R.S. 32:57(C). A corporation may plead through counsel in all cases. The plea shall be made in open court and shall be immediately entered in the minutes of the court. A failure to enter a plea in the minutes shall not affect the validity of any proceeding in the case.

B. By rule adopted pursuant to R.S. 13:472, the judge of the district court or a majority of the judges in a multi-district court may permit the defendant in a noncapital felony case to waive formal arraignment and enter a plea of not guilty without pleading in person. The rule shall require that the plea be in writing and shall set forth the filing procedure. Any formal defect shall not affect the validity of the proceeding.

C. Nothing in this Article shall prohibit the court, by local rule, from providing for a defendant's appearance at his arraignment by simultaneous audio-visual transmission, except when defense counsel requests the defendant's appearance in open court.

(Chgd. by Acts 1990 No. 543, §1, No. 593, §1; Acts 1997 No. 1011, §1, eff. 8/15/97.)

Art. 554. Effect of failure to plead.

A defendant shall plead when arraigned. If he stands mute, refuses to plead, or pleads evasively, a plea of not guilty shall be entered of record. When a defendant is a corporation and fails to appear for arraignment when summoned, a plea of not guilty shall be entered of record.

Art. 555. Waivers.

Any irregularity in the arraignment, including a failure to read the indictment, is waived if the defendant pleads to the indictment without objecting thereto. A failure to arraign the defendant or the fact that he did not plead, is waived if the defendant enters upon the trial without objecting thereto, and it shall be considered as if he had pleaded not guilty.

Art. 556. Plea of guilty; duty of court.

Where the defendant is not represented by counsel in a felony case, the courts shall not accept a plea of guilty without first determining that the plea is made voluntarily with understanding of the nature of the charge.

Art. 556.1. Plea of guilty or nolo contendere in a criminal case; duty of court.

A. In any criminal case, the court shall not accept a plea of guilty or nolo contendere, without first addressing the defendant personally in open court and informing him of, and determining that he understands, all of the following:

(1) The nature of the charge to which the plea is offered, the mandatory minimum penalty provided by law, if any, and the maximum possible penalty provided by law.

(2) If the defendant is not represented by an attorney, that he has the right to be represented by an attorney at every stage of the proceeding against him and, if financially unable to employ counsel, one will be appointed to represent him.

(3) That he has the right to plead not guilty or to persist in that plea if it has already been made, and that he has the right to be tried by a jury and at that trial has the right to the assistance of counsel, the right to confront and cross-examine witnesses against him, and the right not to be compelled to incriminate himself.

(4) That if he pleads guilty or nolo contendere there will not be a further trial of any kind, so that by pleading guilty or nolo contendere he waives the right to a trial.

B. In any criminal case, the court shall not accept a plea of guilty or nolo contendere without first addressing the defendant personally in open court and determining that the plea is voluntary and not the result of force or threats or of promises apart from a plea agreement, and that the waiver of all constitutional and legal rights are knowingly and intelligently waived.

C. The court shall also inquire as to whether the defendant's willingness to plead guilty or nolo contendere results from prior discussions between the district attorney and the defendant or his attorney. If a plea agreement has been reached by the parties, the court, on the record, shall require the disclosure of the agreement in open court or, on a showing of good cause, in camera, at the time the plea is offered.

D. A verbatim record shall be made of the proceedings at which the defendant enters a plea of guilty or nolo contendere.

E. In any case where a subsequent offense carries an enhanced penalty, the court shall inform the defendant of the penalties for subsequent offenses.

(Added by Acts 1997 No. 1061, §1, eff. 8/15/97.)

Art. 557. Plea of guilty in capital cases.

A. A court shall not receive an unqualified plea of guilty in a capital case. However, with the consent of the court and the state, a defendant may plead guilty with the stipulation either that the court shall impose a sentence of life imprisonment without benefit of probation, parole, or suspension of sentence without conducting a sentencing hearing, or that the court shall impanel a jury for the purpose of conducting a hearing to determine the issue of penalty in accordance with the applicable provisions of this Code.

B. If a defendant makes an unqualified plea, the court shall order a plea of not guilty entered for him.

(Chgd. by Acts 1995 No. 434, §1, eff. 8/15/95.)

Art. 558. Plea of guilty of lesser included offense.

The defendant, with the consent of the district attorney, may plead guilty of a lesser offense that is included in the offense charged in the indictment.

Art. 558.1. Adjudication of not guilty by reason of insanity.

The court may adjudicate a defendant not guilty by reason of insanity without trial, when the district attorney consents and the court makes a finding based upon expert testimony that there is a factual basis for the plea.

Art. 559. Withdrawal or setting aside of plea of guilty.

A. The court may permit a plea of guilty to be withdrawn at any time before sentence.

B. The court shall not accept a plea of guilty of a felony within forty-eight hours of the defendant's arrest. When such a plea has been accepted within the forty-eight hour period, the court, upon a motion filed by the defendant within thirty days after the plea was entered, shall set aside the plea and any sentence imposed thereon.

C. The admissibility of a withdrawn plea of guilty and the facts surrounding it, is governed by Louisiana Code of Evidence Article 410.

Art. 560. Change of plea of not guilty to guilty.

A defendant may at any time withdraw a plea of not guilty and plead guilty, subject to the limitations stated in Articles 556 through 559.

Art. 561. Change of plea of "not guilty" to "not guilty and not guilty by reason of insanity".

The defendant may withdraw a plea of "not guilty" and enter a plea of "not guilty and not guilty by reason of insanity," within ten days after arraignment. Thereafter, the court may, for good cause shown, allow such a change of plea at any time before the commencement of the trial.

TITLE XVII. TIME LIMITATIONS

Chapter

CHAPTER 1. LIMITATIONS UPON INSTITUTION OF PROSECUTION

Art. 571. Crimes for which there is no time limitation.

There is no time limitation upon the institution of prosecution for any crime for which the punishment may be death or life imprisonment.

Art. 571.1. Time limitation for certain sex offenses.

The time within which to institute prosecution of the following sex offenses: forcible rape (R.S. 14:42.1), sexual battery (R.S. 14:43.1), aggravated sexual battery (R.S. 14:43.2), oral sexual battery (R.S. 14:43.3), aggravated oral sexual battery (R.S. 14:43.4), carnal knowledge of a juvenile (R.S. 14:80), indecent behavior with juveniles (R.S. 14:81), molestation of a juvenile (R.S. 14:81.2), crime against nature (R.S. 14:89), or aggravated crime against nature (R.S. 14:89.1), which involves a victim under seventeen years of age, regardless of whether the crime involves force, serious physical injury, death, or is punishable by imprisonment at hard labor shall be ten years. This ten-year period begins to run when the victim attains the age of seventeen. *(Added by Acts 1993 No. 592, §1, eff. 6/15/93.)*

Art. 572. Limitation of prosecution of noncapital offenses.

No person shall be prosecuted, tried, or punished for an offense not punishable by death or life imprisonment, unless the prosecution is instituted within the following periods of time after the offense has been committed:

(1) Six years, for a felony necessarily punishable by imprisonment at hard labor;
(2) Four years, for a felony not necessarily punishable by imprisonment at hard labor;
(3) Two years, for a misdemeanor punishable by a fine or imprisonment or both; or
(4) Six months, for a misdemeanor punishable only by a fine or forfeiture.

Art. 573. Running of time limitations; exception.

The time limitations established by Article 572 shall not commence to run as to the following offenses until the relationship or status involved has ceased to exist when:

(1) The offense charged is based on the misappropriation of any money or thing of value by one who, by virtue of his office, employment, or fiduciary relationship, has been entrusted therewith or has control thereof.

(2) The offense charged is extortion or false accounting committed by a public officer or employee in his official capacity.

(3) The offense charged is public bribery.

(4) The offense charged is aggravated battery (R.S. 14:34) and the victim is under seventeen years of age.

(Chgd. by Acts 1993 No. 592, §1, eff. 6/15/93.)

Art. 574. Conviction and punishment for lesser offenses; limitations applicable.

The time limitations applicable to the offense for which a person is prosecuted apply to a conviction or punishment for a lesser and included offense.

Art. 575. Interruption of time limitations.

The periods of limitation established by this Chapter shall be interrupted when the defendant:

(1) For the purpose of avoiding detection, apprehension or prosecution, flees from the state, is outside the state, or is absent from his usual place of abode within the state; or

(2) Lacks mental capacity to proceed at trial and is committed in accordance with Article 648 of this Code.

Art. 576. Filing of new charges upon dismissal of prosecution.

When a criminal prosecution is timely instituted in a court of proper jurisdiction and the prosecution is dismissed by the district attorney with the defendant's consent, or before the first witness is sworn at the trial on the merits, or the indictment is dismissed by a court for any error, defect, irregularity, or deficiency, a new prosecution for the same offense or for a lesser offense based on the same facts may be instituted within the time established by this Chapter or within six months from the date of dismissal, whichever is longer.

A new prosecution shall not be instituted under this article following a dismissal of the prosecution by the district attorney unless the state shows that the dismissal was not for the purpose of avoiding the time limitation for commencement of trial established by Article 578.

Art. 577. Pleading of limitation; burden of proof.

The issue that a prosecution was not timely instituted may be raised at any time, but only once, and shall be tried by the court alone. If raised during the trial, a hearing thereon may be deferred until the end of the trial.

The state shall not be required to allege facts showing that the time limitation has not expired, but when the issue is raised, the state has the burden of proving the facts necessary to show that the prosecution was timely instituted.

CHAPTER 2. LIMITATIONS UPON TRIAL

Art. 578. General rule.

Except as otherwise provided in this Chapter, no trial shall be commenced:

(1) In capital cases after three years from the date of institution of the prosecution;

(2) In other felony cases after two years from the date of institution of the prosecution; and

(3) In misdemeanor cases after one year from the date of institution of the prosecution.

The offense charged shall determine the applicable limitation.

Art. 579. Interruption of time limitation.

A. The period of limitation established by Article 578 shall be interrupted if:

(1) The defendant at any time, with the purpose to avoid detection, apprehension, or prosecution, flees from the state, is outside the state, or is absent from his usual place of abode within the state; or

(2) The defendant cannot be tried because of insanity or because his presence for trial cannot be obtained by legal process, or for any other cause beyond the control of the state; or

(3) The defendant fails to appear at any proceeding pursuant to actual notice, proof of which appears of record.

B. The periods of limitation established by Article 578 shall commence to run anew from the date the cause of interruption no longer exists.

Art. 580. Suspension of time limitations.

When a defendant files a motion to quash or other preliminary plea, the running of the periods of limitation established by Article 578 shall be suspended until the ruling of the court thereon; but in no case shall the state have less than one year after the ruling to commence the trial.

Art. 581. Expiration of limitations; motion to quash; effect.

Upon the expiration of the limitations established by this Chapter, the court shall, upon motion of the defendant, dismiss the indictment. This right of dismissal is waived unless the motion to quash is made prior to trial.

If the indictment is dismissed under this article, there shall be no further prosecution against the defendant for the same or a lesser offense based on the same facts.

Art. 582. Time limitations; effect of new trial.

When a defendant obtains a new trial or there is a mistrial, the state must commence the second trial within one year from the date the new trial is granted, or the mistrial is ordered, or within the period established by Article 578, whichever is longer.

Art. 583. Interruption of time limitation where new trial.

The period of limitation established by Article 582 shall be interrupted by any of the causes stated in Article 579. Where such interruption occurs, the state must commence the new trial within one year from the date the cause of interruption no longer exists.

TITLE XVIII. DOUBLE JEOPARDY

Art. 591. Double jeopardy; definition.

No person shall be twice put in jeopardy of life or liberty for the same offense, except, when on his own motion, a new trial has been granted or judgment has been arrested, or where there has been a mistrial legally ordered under the provisions of Article 775 or ordered with the express consent of the defendant.

Art. 592. When jeopardy begins.

When a defendant pleads not guilty and is tried by jury, jeopardy begins when the jury panel is sworn pursuant to Article 790. When a defendant pleads not guilty, and is tried without a jury, jeopardy begins when the first witness is sworn at the trial on the merits. When a defendant pleads guilty, jeopardy begins when a valid sentence is imposed. *(Chgd. by Acts 1990 No. 525, §1, eff. 9/7/90.)*

Art. 593. Method of pleading.

Double jeopardy shall be raised by a written motion setting forth the name of the court, the proceeding in which the defendant was in jeopardy, and the facts constituting double jeopardy.

Art. 594. Method of trial; time for disposition.

Double jeopardy may be raised at any time, but only once, and shall be tried by the court alone. If raised during the trial, a hearing thereon may be deferred until the end of the trial.

Art. 595. Double jeopardy; when not applicable.

A person shall not be considered as having been in jeopardy in a trial in which:

(1) The court was illegally constituted or lacked jurisdiction;

(2) The prosecution was dismissed because it was instituted in an improper venue; or

(3) The indictment was invalid.

Art. 596. Requirements for double jeopardy.

Double jeopardy exists in a second trial only when the charge in that trial is:

(1) Identical with or a different grade of the same offense for which the defendant was in jeopardy in the first trial, whether or not a responsive verdict could have been rendered in the first trial as to the charge in the second trial; or

(2) Based on a part of a continuous offense for which offense the defendant was in jeopardy in the first trial.

Art. 597. Prosecution in other jurisdiction.

Double jeopardy does not apply to a prosecution under a law enacted by the Louisiana Legislature if the prior jeopardy was in a prosecution under the laws of another state or the United States.

Art. 598. Effect of verdict.

A. When a person is found guilty of a lesser degree of the offense charged, the verdict or judgment of the court is an acquittal of all greater offenses charged in the indictment and the defendant cannot thereafter be tried for those offenses on a new trial.

B. When a jury returns a verdict in the sentencing hearing in a capital case determining that the defendant should be sentenced to life imprisonment, the defendant cannot thereafter be sentenced to death for that offense on a new trial.

TITLE XIX. JURISDICTION AND VENUE

Article

Art. 611. Venue; trial where offense committed.

All trials shall take place in the parish where the offense has been committed, unless the venue is changed. If acts constituting an offense or if the elements of an offense occurred in more than one place, in or out of the parish or state, the offense is deemed to have been committed in any parish in this state in which any such act or element occurred.

Art. 612. Offenses on railway trains, vessels, aircraft, or other vehicles.

If an offense is committed on a train, vessel, aircraft, or other public or private vehicle while in transit in this state and the exact place of the offense in this state cannot be established, the offense is deemed to have been committed in any parish through or over which the train, vessel, aircraft, or other vehicle passed, and in which the crime could have been committed.

Art. 613. Jurisdiction of court where body of water is parish boundary.

When a river, bayou, lake, water course, or other body of water is the boundary of any parish, the jurisdiction of the court of such parish extends to the middle of such river, bayou, lake, water course, or other body of water.

Art. 614. Venue where offense committed within one hundred feet of parish boundary.

An offense committed on the boundary line of two parishes or within one hundred feet thereof is deemed to have been committed in either parish.

Art. 615. Improper venue; pleading.

Improper venue shall be raised in advance of trial by motion to quash, and shall be tried by the judge alone. Venue shall not be considered an essential element to be proven by the state at trial, rather it shall be a jurisdictional matter to be proven by the state by a preponderance of the evidence and decided by the court in advance of trial.

TITLE XX. CHANGE OF VENUE

Art. 621. Motion; form; time for filing.

A motion for a change of venue may be filed by either the state or the defendant. It shall be filed in accordance with Article 521; or thereafter, in the discretion of the court, any time before the first witness is sworn at the trial of the merits. The motion shall be in writing, sworn to by mover or his counsel, and shall contain:

(1) Allegations of fact upon which the motion is based; and

(2) A statement that the motion is not made for the purpose of delay, but to obtain a fair and impartial trial.

A contradictory hearing shall be held upon the motion.

Art. 622. Grounds for change of venue.

A change of venue shall be granted when the applicant proves that by reason of prejudice existing in the public mind or because of undue influence, or that for any other reason, a fair and impartial trial cannot be obtained in the parish where the prosecution is pending.

In deciding whether to grant a change of venue the court shall consider whether the prejudice, the influence, or the other reasons are such that they will affect the answers of jurors on the voir dire examination or the testimony of witnesses at the trial.

Art. 623. Change granted; transfer.

When a change of venue is granted, the court shall transfer the case to another parish.

Art. 623.1. Capital cases; transfer of jury.

In a case involving a capital offense, upon motion to transfer a jury or on its own motion, if the court determines it is in the interest of justice, the court may as an alternative to transferring the case to another parish after a change of venue is granted, select a jury in the parish to which venue would otherwise have been transferred, and thereafter, transfer such jury to the court in which the case is pending. *(Added by Acts 1991 No. 82, §1, eff. 9/6/91.)*

Art. 624. Grant of change of venue; procedure.

When a change of venue is granted, the clerk of the court in which the case is pending shall make and retain copies of all documents relating to the case. He shall deliver the original documents together with certified copies of all minute entries of the case to the clerk of the court to which the case is transferred, who shall enter the case upon the docket of the court, and the case shall be proceeded with in the same manner as if the proceedings had originally been instituted therein.

Art. 625. Transfer of defendant in custody.

If a defendant is in custody when a change of venue is granted, the sheriff shall immediately deliver him to the sheriff of the parish to which the case is transferred, who shall hold him in custody until otherwise ordered by the court.

Art. 626. Change of venue where defendant is on bail.

If a defendant has furnished bail prior to a change of venue, his obligation and that of the surety on his bond shall be the same as if the prosecution had been instituted in the court to which the case is transferred.

Art. 627. Appeals.

If a change of venue is granted to the defendant over the objection of the state, or if the court denies an application by the state for a change of venue, the state shall have the right to appeal from the ruling, within the legal delays for making a motion for an appeal, before a trial on the merits. Prior to sentence the defendant may not appeal from a ruling changing or refusing to change the venue.

TITLE XXI. INSANITY PROCEEDINGS

Chapter

CHAPTER 1. MENTAL INCAPACITY TO PROCEED

Article

Art. 641. Mental incapacity to proceed defined.

Mental incapacity to proceed exists when, as a result of mental disease or defect, a defendant presently lacks the capacity to understand the proceedings against him or to assist in his defense.

Art. 642. How mental incapacity is raised; effect.

The defendant's mental incapacity to proceed may be raised at any time by the defense, the district attorney, or the court. When the question of the defendant's mental incapacity to proceed is raised, there shall be no further steps in the criminal prosecution, except the institution of prosecution, until the defendant is found to have the mental capacity to proceed.

Art. 643. Order for mental examination.

The court shall order a mental examination of the defendant when it has reasonable ground to doubt the defendant's mental capacity to proceed. Prior to the ordering of any such mental examination, the court shall appoint counsel to represent the defendant if he has not already retained counsel.

Art. 644. Appointment of sanity commission; examination of defendant.

A. Within seven days after a mental examination is ordered, the court shall appoint a sanity commission to examine and report upon the mental condition of the defendant. The sanity commission shall consist of at least two and not more than three members who are licensed to practice medicine in Louisiana, who have been in the actual practice of medicine for not less than three consecutive years immediately preceding the appointment, and who are qualified by training or experience in forensic evaluations. The court may appoint, in lieu of one physician, a clinical psychologist who is licensed to practice psychology in Louisiana, who has been engaged in the practice of clinical or counseling psychology for not less than three consecutive years immediately preceding the appointment, and who is qualified by training or experience in forensic evaluations. Every sanity commission shall have at least one psychiatrist as a member of the commission, unless one is not reasonably available, in which case, the commission shall have at least one clinical psychologist as a member of the commission. No more than one member of the sanity commission shall be the coroner or any of his deputies.

B. The members of the sanity commission appointed to make the examination shall have free access to the defendant at all reasonable times. The court shall subpoena witnesses to attend the examination at the request of the defendant, the commission, or any member thereof.

C. For the purpose of the mental examination, the court may order a defendant previously released on bail to appear for mental examinations and hearings in the same manner as other criminal proceedings.

D. (1) The court, in any judicial district which enters into a cooperative endeavor agreement with the local mental health unit, in lieu of appointing a sanity commission as provided in Paragraph A, may appoint the local mental health unit to examine and report on the mental condition of the defendant. If the local mental health unit is ordered to conduct the examination, it shall form a clinical team, consisting of at least two but not more than three members, to conduct the examination. The clinical team shall be composed of one or more licensed physicians with at least three years experience in the study of psychiatry in an approved United States General Psychiatry Residency Program; if only one such licensed physician is a member of the clinical team, the remaining members of the clinical team may be composed of clinical psychologists, or psychiatric social workers, who are qualified by training or experience in forensic evaluations.

(2) (a) With respect to all other provisions of the Code of Criminal Procedure in which the term "sanity commission" is designated, it shall also mean and include, for the exclusive purpose of this Article, a clinical team designated by the local health unit to conduct the examination of the defendant in accordance with this Paragraph.

(b) "Local mental health unit" as used in this Paragraph shall mean a legislatively created Human Services Authority.

(Chgd. by Acts 1990 No. 488, §1; Acts 1994 Third Ex. Sess. No. 67, §1; Acts 1997 No. 1222, §1, eff. 8/15/97.)

Art. 645. Report of sanity commission.

A. (1) The report of the sanity commission members shall address their specific findings with regard to all of the following:

(a) The defendant's capacity to understand the proceedings against him.

(b) His ability to assist in his defense.

(c) His need for inpatient hospitalization in the event he is found incompetent.

(2) The fact that the defendant claims to be unable to remember the time period surrounding the alleged offense shall not, by itself, bar a finding of competency if the defendant otherwise understands the charges against him and can assist in his defense.

B. The report of the sanity commission shall be filed in triplicate with the presiding judge within thirty days after the date of the order of appointment. The time for filing may be extended by the court. The clerk shall make copies of the report available to the district attorney and to the defendant or his counsel without cost.

(Chgd. by Acts 1990 No. 436, §1, eff. 9/7/90.)

Art. 646. Examination by physician retained by defense or district attorney.

The court order for a mental examination shall not deprive the defendant or the district attorney of the right to an independent mental examination by a physician of his choice, and such physician shall be permitted to have reasonable access to the defendant for the purposes of the examination.

Art. 647. Determination of mental capacity to proceed.

The issue of the defendant's mental capacity to proceed shall be determined by the court in a contradictory hearing. The report of the sanity commission is admissible in evidence at the hearing, and members of the sanity commission may be called as witnesses by the court, the defense, or the district attorney. Regardless of who calls them as witnesses, the members of the commission are subject to cross-examination by the defense, by the district attorney, and by the court. Other evidence pertaining to the defendant's mental capacity to proceed may be introduced at the hearing by the defense and by the district attorney.

Art. 648. Procedure after determination of mental capacity or incapacity.

A. The criminal prosecution shall be resumed unless the court determines by clear and convincing evidence that the defendant does not have the mental capacity to proceed. If the court determines that the defendant lacks mental capacity to proceed, the proceedings shall be suspended and one of the following dispositions made:

(1) If the court determines that the defendant's mental capacity is likely to be restored within ninety days by outpatient care and treatment at an institution as defined by R.S. 28:2(28) while remaining in the custody of the criminal authorities, and if the person is not charged with a felony or a misdemeanor classified as an offense against the person and is considered by the court to be unlikely to commit crimes of violence, then the court may order outpatient care and treatment at any institution as defined by R.S. 28:2(28).

(2)(a) If the person is charged with a felony or a misdemeanor classified as an offense against the person and considered by the court to be likely to commit crimes of violence, and if the court determines that his mental capacity is likely to be restored within ninety days as a result of treatment, the court may order immediate jail-based treatment by the Department of Health and Hospitals not to exceed ninety days; otherwise, if his capacity cannot be restored within ninety days and inpatient treatment is recommended, the court shall commit the defendant to the Feliciana Forensic Facility.

(b) If a defendant committed to the Feliciana Forensic Facility is held in a parish jail for one hundred eighty days after the court's determination that he lacks the mental capacity to proceed, the court shall order a status conference to be held with the defense and the district attorney present, and for good cause shown and on motion of the defendant or the district attorney or on the court's own motion, the court shall order a contradictory hearing to determine whether there has been a change in the defendant's condition or other circumstances sufficient to warrant a modification of the previous order.

B. (1) In no instance shall such custody, care, and treatment exceed the time of the maximum sentence the defendant could receive if convicted of the crime with which he is charged. At any time after commitment and on the recommendation of the superintendent of the institution that the defendant will not attain the capacity to proceed with his trial in the foreseeable future, the court shall, within sixty days and after at least ten days notice to the district attorney and defendant's counsel, conduct a contradictory hearing to determine whether the mentally defective defendant is, and will in the foreseeable future be, incapable of standing trial and whether he is a danger to himself or others.

(2) If, after the hearing, the court determines the defendant is, and will in the foreseeable future be, incapable of standing trial and may be released without danger to himself or others, the court shall release the defendant on probation. The probationer shall be under the supervision of the Department of Public Safety and Corrections, division of probation and parole, and subject to such conditions as may be imposed by the court.

(3) If, after the hearing, the court determines the mentally defective defendant incapable of standing trial, is a danger to himself or others, and is unlikely in the foreseeable future to be capable of standing trial, the court shall order commitment to a designated and medically suitable treatment facility. Such a judgment shall constitute an order of civil commitment. However, the director of the institution designated for the patient's treatment shall, in writing, notify the court and the district attorney when the patient is to be discharged or conditionally discharged.

C. The superintendent of the forensic unit of the Feliciana Forensic Facility shall admit only those persons specified in R.S. 28:25.1 and those persons found not guilty by reason of insanity on conditional release who have a physician's emergency certificate or who seek voluntary admission pursuant to Article 658(B)(4).

(Chgd. by Acts 1990 No. 755, §1; Acts 1992 No. 400, §1; Acts 1995 No. 800, §1; Acts 1997 No. 723, §1, eff. 8/15/97.)

Art. 648.1. Information required prior to admission.

No superintendent of an institution shall admit a defendant found by the court to lack the mental capacity to proceed pursuant to Article 648 unless he is furnished by the court the following information:

(1) The name and address of the defendant's attorney.

(2) The crime or crimes with which the defendant is charged and the date of such charge or charges.

(3) A copy of the report of the sanity commission.

(4) Any other pertinent information concerning the defendant's health which has come to the attention of the court such as injuries sustained at the time of arrest or injuries sustained following incarceration.

(5) A copy of the defendant's criminal history record.

(6) A copy of the police report concerning the charged offense.

(7) A copy of the judgment and order specifying the nature and purpose of the commitment or recommitment to the state institution.
(Chgd. by Acts 1990 No. 754, §1; Acts 1992 No. 399, §1, eff. 8/21/92.)

Art. 649. Procedure when capacity regained.

A. At any time after a defendant's commitment, if either the superintendent of the mental institution or the administrator of outreach forensic services reports to the committing court that the defendant presently has the mental capacity to proceed, the defendant, if hospitalized, shall be discharged from the mental institution and released to the custody of the sheriff of the parish from which the defendant was committed, and the court shall hold a contradictory hearing within thirty days on that issue. No defendant shall be released prior to the holding of the contradictory hearing on his release unless the office of the district attorney in charge of the prosecution of the defendant receives seven days notice of the pending release of the defendant.

B. Prior to such a hearing, the court shall appoint counsel to represent the defendant, if the defendant does not have counsel, and may order a mental examination by a sanity commission appointed in conformity with Article 644. The report of the superintendent of the mental institution or the administrator of outreach services may be stipulated to and submitted by the state and the defense in lieu of a mental examination by a sanity commission. If the committing court does not hold a hearing within thirty days, the sheriff of the parish from which the defendant was committed shall appear at the institution within seven days thereafter and shall receive and hold the defendant in custody pending further orders of the committing court. If the sheriff fails to appear with a court order and accept custody of the defendant, the superintendent of the state mental institution or the director of the mental health unit shall notify the judicial administrator and the attorney general of such fact. Thereafter the Criminal Court Fund of the parish from which the defendant was committed shall pay to the general fund of the state the sum of one hundred dollars a day until the sheriff appears and accepts custody of the defendant for the court.

C. The district attorney or the defense may apply to the court to have the proceedings resumed, on the ground that the defendant presently has the mental capacity to proceed. Upon receipt of such application the court shall hold a contradictory hearing to determine if there is reasonable ground to believe that the defendant presently has the mental capacity to proceed. The court may direct the superintendent of the mental institution where the defendant is committed or the administrator of outreach forensic services, if treatment is initiated in jail, to make a report and recommendation prior to such hearing as to whether the defendant presently has capacity to proceed, or may order an independent mental examination by a sanity commission appointed in conformity with Article 644.

D. Reports as to present mental capacity to proceed shall be filed in conformity with Article 645, and the court's determination of present mental capacity to proceed shall be made in conformity with the appropriate provisions of Articles 646 and 647.

E. If the court determines that the defendant has the mental capacity to proceed, the proceedings shall be promptly resumed.
(Chgd. by Acts 1990 No. 490, §1; Acts 1992 No. 397, §1, eff. 8/21/92.)

Art. 649.1. Prescribed medication; administration.

When a person is returned to the committing court from an institution pursuant to Article 649 pending a sanity hearing, and the superintendent of the committing institution deems it necessary that the patient receive prescribed medication, it shall be the duty of the chief administrative officer of the parish jail to make such medication available to the person until such time as the coroner or another physician finds that the medication or its prescribed dosage is no longer necessary.

CHAPTER 2. DEFENSE OF INSANITY AT TIME OF OFFENSE

Article

Art. 650. Mental examination after plea of insanity.

When a defendant enters a combined plea of "not guilty and not guilty by reason of insanity," the court may appoint a sanity commission as provided in Article 644 to make an examination as to the defendant's mental condition at the time of the offense. The court may also order the commission to make an examination as to the defendant's present mental capacity to proceed. Mental examinations and reports under this article shall be conducted and filed in conformity with Articles 644 through 646.

Art. 651. When defense of insanity at time of offense is available; method of trial.

When a defendant is tried upon a plea of "not guilty", evidence of insanity or mental defect at the time of the offense shall not be admissible.

The defenses available under a combined plea of "not guilty and not guilty by reason of insanity" shall be tried together.

Art. 652. Burden of proof.

The defendant has the burden of establishing the defense of insanity at the time of the offense by a preponderance of the evidence.

Art. 653. Testimony of members of sanity commission.

Upon the trial of the defense of insanity at the time of the offense, the members of the sanity commission may be called as witnesses by the court, the defense, or the district attorney. Regardless of who calls them as witnesses, the members of the commission are subject to cross-examination by the defense, by the district attorney, and by the court. Other evidence pertaining to the defense of insanity at the time of the offense may be introduced at the trial by the defense and by the district attorney.

Art. 654. Legal effect of acquittal on ground of insanity; commitment.

When a verdict of not guilty by reason of insanity is returned in a capital case, the court shall commit the defendant to a proper state mental institution or to a private mental institution approved by the court for custody, care, and treatment.

When a defendant is found not guilty by reason of insanity in any other felony case, the court shall remand him to the parish jail or to a private mental institution approved by the court and shall promptly hold a contradictory hearing at which the defendant shall have the burden of proof, to determine whether the defendant can be discharged or can be released on probation, without danger to others or to himself. If the court determines that the defendant cannot be released without danger to others or to himself, it shall order him committed to a proper state mental institution or to a private mental institution approved by the court for custody, care, and treatment. If the court determines that the defendant can be discharged or released on probation without danger to others or to himself, the court shall either order his discharge, or order his release on probation subject to specified conditions for a fixed or an indeterminate period. The court shall assign written findings of fact and conclusions of law; however, the assignment of reasons shall not delay the implementation of judgment.

Art. 654.1. Information required prior to admission.

No superintendent of a mental institution shall admit a defendant found not guilty by reason of insanity pursuant to Article 654 unless the court furnishes the following information:

(1) The defendant's commitment order specifying not guilty by reason of insanity.

(2) A copy of the defendant's criminal history record.

(3) A police report concerning the charged offense.

(4) Victim and witness statements, if any.

(5) The name, address, and telephone number of the district attorney who prosecuted the defendant.

(Added by Acts 1990 No. 753, §1, eff. 9/7/90.)

Art. 655. Application for discharge or release on probation; review panel.

A. When the superintendent of a mental institution is of the opinion that a person committed pursuant to Article 654 can be discharged or can be released on probation, without danger to others or to himself, he shall recommend the discharge or release of the person in a report to a review panel comprised of the person's treating physician, the clinical director of the facility to which the person is committed, and a physician or psychologist who served on the sanity commission which recommended commitment of the person. If any member of the panel is unable to serve, a physician or a psychologist engaged in the practice of clinical or counseling psychology with at least three years' experience in the field of mental health shall be appointed by the remaining members. The panel shall review all reports received promptly. After review, the panel shall make a recommendation to the court by which the person was committed as to the person's mental condition and whether he can be discharged, conditionally or unconditionally, or placed on probation, without being a danger to others or himself. If the review panel recommends to the court that the person be discharged, conditionally or unconditionally, or placed on probation, the court shall conduct a contradictory hearing following notice to the district attorney.

B. A person committed pursuant to Article 654 may make application to the review panel for discharge or for release on probation. Such application by a committed person may not be filed until the committed person has been confined for a period of at least six months after the original commitment. If the review panel recommends to the court that the person be discharged, conditionally or unconditionally, or placed on probation, the court shall conduct a hearing following notice to the district attorney. If the recommendation of the review panel or the court is adverse, the applicant shall not be permitted to file another application until one year has elapsed from the date of determination.

C. The superintendent of the mental institution shall, under both Paragraphs A and B of this article, transmit a copy of this report and recommendation to the person committed or his attorney and to the district attorney of the parish from which the person was committed.

Art. 656. Additional mental examinations.

A. Upon receipt of the superintendent's report, filed in conformity with Article 655, the review panel may examine the committed person and report, to the court promptly, whether he can be safely discharged, conditionally or unconditionally, or be safely released on probation, without danger to others or to himself.

B. The committed person or the district attorney may also retain a physician to examine the committed person for the same purpose. The physician's report shall be filed with the court.

C. Upon receipt by the superintendent of the state hospital or other treatment facility to which the person has been committed on the recommendation of the hospital-based treatment team that the person is appropriate for probated outpatient status as set forth in this Chapter, the superintendent shall immediately forward such recommendation to the administrator of the conditional release program, together with the proposed aftercare plans. The administrator or a designee shall submit to the review panel a recommended plan, if appropriate, for outpatient supervision and monitoring. The plan shall set forth any additional terms and conditions to be followed during outpatient status, if recommended.

(Chgd. by Acts 1995 No. 800, §1, eff. 8/15/95.)

Art. 657. Discharge or release; hearing.

After considering the report or reports filed pursuant to Articles 655 and 656, the court may either continue the commitment or hold a contradictory hearing to determine whether the committed person is no longer mentally ill as defined by R.S. 28:2(14) and can be discharged, or can be released on probation, without danger to others or to himself as defined by R.S. 28:2(3) and (4). At the hearing the burden shall be upon the state to seek continuance of the confinement by proving by clear and convincing evidence that the committed person is currently both mentally ill and dangerous. After the hearing, and upon filing written findings of fact and conclusions of law, the court may order the committed person discharged, released on probation subject to specified conditions for a fixed or an indeterminate period, or recommitted to the state mental institution. A copy of the judgment and order containing the written findings of fact and conclusions of law shall be forwarded to the administrator of the forensic facility. Notice to the counsel for the committed person and the district attorney of the contradictory hearing shall be given at least thirty days prior to the hearing. *(Chgd. by Acts 1992 No. 398, §1; Acts 1993 No. 700, §1, eff. 8/15/93.)*

Art. 657.1. Conditional release; criteria.

A. At any time the court considers a recommendation from the hospital-based review panel that the person may be discharged or released on probation, it may place the insanity acquitee on conditional release if it finds the following:

(1) Based on the factors which the court shall consider pursuant to Article 657, he does not need impatient hospitalization but needs outpatient treatment, supervision, and monitoring to prevent his condition from deteriorating to a degree that he would likely become dangerous to self and others.

(2) Appropriate outpatient treatment, supervision, and monitoring are reasonably available.

(3) There is significant reason to believe that the insanity acquitee, if conditionally released, would comply with the conditions specified.

(4) Conditional release will not present an undue risk of danger to others or self, as defined in R.S. 28:2(3) and (4).

B. The court shall subject a conditionally released insanity acquittee to such orders and conditions it deems will best meet the acquittee's need for treatment, supervision, and monitoring and will best serve the interests of justice and society.

C. These provisions for conditional release may also be applied to discharges of pretrial defendants found unrestorably incompetent to proceed pursuant to Article 648(B).
(Added by Acts 1995 No. 800, §1, eff. 8/15/95.)

Art. 657.2. Conditional release; additional requirements.

A. Upon an application for conditional release of a person, who has been committed to a state hospital or other treatment facility pursuant to this Chapter upon the grounds that the adverse effects of a mental illness are in remission, and if after a hearing the court determines that the applicant will not likely be a danger to others or himself, as defined in R.S. 28:2(3) and (4), if he is under supervision and his treatment is monitored in the community, the court shall not consider the applicant to be in stable remission from the adverse effects of a mental illness until the applicant is placed with an appropriate forensic conditional release program for at least one year but not more than five years.

B. For good cause shown, placement in a conditional release program may be extended after five years in one-year increments at a yearly contradictory hearing with the state.

C. All or a substantial portion of the program shall include outpatient treatment, supervision, and monitoring.

D. At the termination of conditional release, the person may continue to receive appropriate treatment services, if recommended by the treating psychiatrist, from public or private mental health agencies, with inactive supervision provided by the division of probation and parole of the Department of Public Safety and Corrections.
(Added by Acts 1995 No. 800, §1, eff. 8/15/95.)

Art. 658. Probation; conditional release; reporting.

A. When the committed person is released on probation, which shall also be known as conditional release, the clerk of court shall deliver to him a certificate setting forth the period and the conditions of his probation. It shall be a condition of every such probation that the person released shall be recommitted if he becomes dangerous to others or to himself for reasons of mental illness, substance abuse, or mental retardation. The probationer shall be required to agree in writing to the conditions of his probation.

B. (1) The probationer shall be under the supervision of the division of probation and parole. When the probationer violates or is about to violate the conditions of his probation, he may be arrested and detained in conformity with the applicable provisions of Article 899.

(2) The Department of Health and Hospitals shall be responsible for the community treatment and monitoring of persons placed on outpatient status under this Chapter. These services shall be available on a parish or regional basis. The department may provide treatment services directly or through contracts with private providers or local jurisdictions.

(3) The department shall designate for each parish or for each region comprised of two or more parishes a conditional release program coordinator, who shall be responsible for the provisions specified in this Chapter. The coordinator shall monitor the forensic aftercare provider's implementation of the conditional release order and the forensic aftercare provider's submission to the court of written reports on the acquittee's progress, adjustment in the community, and compliance with the order no less frequently than ninety days after admission to the program and every one hundred eighty days thereafter.

(4) If a person on conditional release or otherwise probated under this Chapter is in need of acute, i.e. short-term, hospitalization and is not charged with a new criminal offense, he may be voluntarily admitted pursuant to R.S. 28:52 or admitted by emergency certificate pursuant to R.S. 28:53 to the Feliciana Forensic Facility or to another suitable treatment facility, with subsequent notice to the court. Transportation to and from the receiving hospital may be effected by the Feliciana Forensic Facility or the sheriff of the parish of incarceration. Hospital discharge of the person under this provision shall be at the discretion of the clinical director of the facility and a hospital admission pursuant to this provision will not be grounds for revocation or recommitment under Subparagraph C(4) of this Article. However, the discharge of a person based on the need for indefinite hospitalization or noncompliance with treatment recommendations shall be grounds for revocation or recommitment.

(5) The division of probation and parole or the Department of Health and Hospitals through the conditional release program coordinator or a designee shall immediately notify the court of any substantive violations or imminent violations of the conditions of a person's probated release and shall present recommendations to the court regarding whether the court should revoke the probation and recommit the probationer to a state mental institution or other recommendations as may be appropriate.

(6) The court, on its own motion or that of the district attorney or probation officer, or upon receiving a report recommending revocation or other disposition from the conditional release program coordinator, may cause the person to be arrested, if he is not already in custody, and shall immediately hold a hearing to consider the violations listed or transfer the case to the parish of commitment, if different from that of the arrest, at which place the hearing should be held as soon as possible.

C. If the court determines that there has been a violation or that the probationer was about to violate the conditions of release or probation it may do any of the following:

(1) Reprimand and warn the probationer.

(2) Order that supervision be intensified.

(3) Modify or add additional conditions to the probation.

(4) Revoke the probation and recommit the probationer to a state mental institution, subject to consideration for discharge or release on probation only after one year has elapsed from the date of revocation and in accordance with the procedure prescribed in Articles 655 through 657 for a first application and hearing. If the probation is revoked and the probationer recommitted, the court shall provide the hospital with the report of the probation officer or forensic aftercare provider regarding the details of the violations involved.

D. The court may completely discharge the probationer after the expiration of one year in a supervised conditional release program only on recommendation of the director of the division of probation and parole or the administrator of the conditional release program or on other proper evidence of expected outpatient compliance with any continued treatment recommendations, and after a contradictory hearing with the district attorney.

E. No person who is on outpatient conditional release status pursuant to this Chapter shall leave this state without first obtaining written approval to do so from the director of the division of probation and parole and the administrator of the conditional release program. Any person who violates the provisions of this Paragraph may be fined not more than one thousand dollars or imprisoned with or without hard labor for not more than one year, or both. *(Chgd. by Acts 1995 No. 800, §1, eff. 8/15/95.)*

CHAPTER 3. COSTS

Art. 659. Costs of mental examinations prior to commitment.

The fees and expenses of physicians, including coroners and other physicians in the employ of the state or its political subdivisions, appointed by a court to make a mental examination and report prior to commitment shall be fixed by the court and shall be paid by the parish where the prosecution was instituted. The fee paid to the coroner or other physician in the employ of the state shall be in addition to his salary. Use of the facilities of a state mental institution in making the mental examination shall be without cost to the parish.

Art. 660. Institutional costs after commitment.

The custody, care, and treatment of a defendant committed under the provisions of this Title, and mental examinations and reports subsequent thereto by physicians on the medical staff of the institution, shall be without cost to the parish from which the defendant was committed. When a physician on the medical staff of the institution is called to testify at a hearing or trial concerning a mental examination made by him, he shall be entitled to a reasonable expert witness fee to be fixed by the court, and to reimbursement for traveling expenses in conformity with law, with such fees and expenses to be paid by the parish where the prosecution was instituted.

CHAPTER 4. PROGRESS REPORTS

Art. 661. Progress reports; responsibility to furnish.

The superintendent of each mental institution and the director of each mental health unit throughout the state shall furnish progress reports every six months on each patient committed under the provisions of this Title. Copies of such reports shall be furnished to the committing court, the judicial administrator, and the attorney general of the state.

TITLE XXII. RECUSATION OF JUDGES AND DISTRICT ATTORNEYS

CHAPTER 1. RECUSATION OF JUDGES

Art. 671. Grounds for recusation of judge.

A. In a criminal case a judge of any court, trial or appellate, shall be recused when he:

(1) Is biased, prejudiced, or personally interested in the cause to such an extent that he would be unable to conduct a fair and impartial trial;

(2) Is the spouse of the accused, of the party injured, of an attorney employed in the cause, or of the district attorney; or is related to the accused or the party injured, or to the spouse of the accused or party injured, within the fourth degree; or is related to an attorney employed in the cause or to the district attorney, or to the spouse of either, within the second degree;

(3) Has been employed or consulted as an attorney in the cause, or has been associated with an attorney during the latter's employment in the cause;

(4) Is a witness in the cause;

(5) Has performed a judicial act in the case in another court; or

(6) Would be unable, for any other reason, to conduct a fair and impartial trial.

B. In any cause in which the state, or a political subdivision thereof, or a religious body is interested, the fact that the judge is a citizen of the state or a resident of the political subdivision, or pays taxes thereto, or is a member of the religious body is not of itself a ground for recusation.

Art. 672. Recusation on court's own motion; by supreme court.

A judge may recuse himself, whether a motion for his recusation has been filed by a party or not, in any case in which a ground for recusation exists.

On the written application of a trial judge, the supreme court may recuse him for any reason that it considers sufficient.

Art. 673. Judge may act until recused.

A judge has full power and authority to act, even though a ground for recusation exists, until he is recused, or a motion for his recusation is filed.

Art. 674. Procedure for recusation of trial judge.

A party desiring to recuse a trial judge shall file a written motion therefor assigning the ground for recusation. The motion shall be filed prior to commencement of the trial unless the party discovers the facts constituting the ground for recusation thereafter, in which event it shall be filed immediately after the facts are discovered, but prior to verdict or judgment. If a valid ground for recusation is set forth in the motion, the judge shall either recuse himself, or refer the motion for hearing to another judge or to a judge ad hoc, as provided in Article 675.

Art. 675. Selection of judge ad hoc to try motion to recuse.

In a court having two or more judges, the judge who is sought to be recused shall refer the motion to recuse to another judge of that court.

When the ground assigned for the recusation of the judge of a district court having one judge is that he is biased, prejudiced, or personally interested in the cause, the judge shall appoint a district judge of an adjoining district to try the motion to recuse. When any other ground is assigned for the recusation of such a district judge, he may appoint either a district judge of an adjoining district, or a lawyer domiciled in the judicial district who has the qualifications of a district judge, to try the motion to recuse. In a city court, a separate juvenile court, or a family court, when the court has a single judge, the judge shall refer the motion to recuse to a district judge of his district.

The order of the court appointing a judge ad hoc shall be entered on the minutes of the court, and the clerk of court shall forward a certified copy of the order to the appointed judge ad hoc. The motion to recuse shall be tried promptly in a contradictory hearing in the court in which the case is pending.

Art. 676. Judge ad hoc to try case when judge recused.

A. When a district court judge, or a judge of a separate juvenile court or of a family court, recuses himself, he shall appoint a judge ad hoc to try the case in the manner provided by Article 675 for the appointment of a judge ad hoc to try a motion to recuse. When a city court judge of a court having a single judge recuses himself, he shall appoint to try the case either a city court judge from an adjoining parish or a lawyer, who is domiciled in the parish and has the qualifications of a city court judge.

B. When a district court judge, or a judge of a separate juvenile court or of a family court, is recused after a trial of the motion, the judge ad hoc who tried the motion to recuse shall continue to act as judge ad hoc for the trial of the case. When a city court judge of a court having a single judge is recused after a trial on the motion, the judge ad hoc who tried the motion to recuse shall appoint to try the case either a city court judge from an adjoining parish or a lawyer, who is domiciled in the parish and has the qualifications of a city court judge.

C. When a city court has two or more judges, if a judge recuses himself or is recused, the case shall be tried by another judge of that court.

D. The judge ad hoc has the same power and authority to dispose of the case as the recused judge would have.

Art. 677. Supreme court appointment of judge ad hoc.

In a case in which the district judge is recused, even when a judge ad hoc has been appointed for the trial of the case under Article 676, the defendant or the district attorney may apply to the supreme court for the appointment of another district judge as judge ad hoc to try the case. If the supreme court deems it in the interest of justice, it shall make such appointment.

The order of the supreme court appointing a judge ad hoc shall be entered on its minutes. The clerk of the supreme court shall forward a certified copy of the order to the appointed judge ad hoc, and a certified copy to the clerk of the district court where the case is pending, for entry in its minutes.

Art. 678. Recusation of judge ad hoc.

A judge ad hoc appointed to try a motion to recuse a judge, or appointed to try the case, may be recused on the grounds and in the manner provided in this Chapter for the recusation of judges.

Art. 679. Recusation of an appellate judge and a supreme court justice.

A. When a written motion is filed to recuse a judge of a court of appeal, he may recuse himself or the motion shall be heard by the other judges on the panel to which the cause is assigned, or by all judges of the court, except the judge sought to be recused, sitting en banc.

B. When a judge of a court of appeal recuses himself or is recused, the court shall appoint another of its judges to act for the recused judge in the hearing and disposition of the case.

C. When a written motion is filed to recuse a justice of the supreme court, he may recuse himself or the motion shall be heard by the other justices of the court.

D. When a justice of the supreme court recuses himself, or is recused, the court may have the case argued before and disposed of by the other justices or appoint a judge of a district court or of a court of appeal to sit as a member of the court in the hearing and disposition of the case.

(Chgd. by Acts 1997 No. 887, §1, eff. 8/15/97.)

CHAPTER 2. RECUSATION OF DISTRICT ATTORNEYS; DISTRICT ATTORNEY AD HOC

Article

Art. 680. Grounds for recusation of district attorney.

A district attorney shall be recused when he:

(1) Has a personal interest in the cause or grand jury proceeding which is in conflict with fair and impartial administration of justice;

(2) Is related to the party accused or to the party injured, or to the spouse of the accused or party injured, or to a party who is a focus of a grand jury investigation, to such an extent that it may appreciably influence him in the performance of the duties of his office; or

(3) Has been employed or consulted in the case as attorney for the defendant before his election or appointment as district attorney.

Art. 681. Procedure for recusation of district attorney.

A district attorney may recuse himself, whether a motion for his recusation has been filed or not, in any case in which a ground for recusation exists. A motion to recuse the district attorney shall be in writing and shall set forth the grounds therefor. The motion shall be filed in accordance with Article 521, and shall be tried in a contradictory hearing. If a ground for recusation is established the judge shall recuse the district attorney.

Art. 682. Appointment of substitute for a recused district attorney.

When a district attorney is recused, or recuses himself, the trial judge shall either appoint an attorney at law of that district, who has the qualifications of a district attorney and is not an assistant to the recused district attorney, to act in the place of the district attorney in the case, or shall notify the attorney general in writing of the recusation. In the latter instance, it shall be the duty of the attorney general to appoint a member of his staff or a district attorney of another district to act in the place of the recused district attorney. The substitute appointed for the recused district attorney shall have all powers of the recused district attorney with reference to the case.

Art. 683. Disability or absence of district attorney.

When a district attorney is unable to perform his duties for any cause, other than recusation, death, or resignation or removal from office, an assistant district attorney shall act in his place. When the district attorney still holds office and there is no assistant district attorney, the trial judge shall appoint an attorney at law of that district, having the qualifications of a district attorney, to act in his place during his disability or absence. If the trial judge is unable to make the appointment, he shall certify the fact in writing to the attorney general, who shall appoint a district attorney of another district to act in place of the regular district attorney. The temporary district attorney shall have all powers of the district attorney during the time of his disability or absence.

Art. 683.1. Costs of prosecution and investigation.

A. Whenever the district attorney of the parish of original jurisdiction and venue is recused or requests another district attorney or the attorney general to undertake a prosecution or an investigation reasonably related to a possible prosecution and such other district attorney or the attorney general actually undertakes same, the costs of such prosecution and investigation shall be borne by the parish of original jurisdiction and venue, which shall reimburse such other district attorney or the attorney general therefor.

B. For the purposes of this Article, "costs of prosecution and investigation" include not only unreimbursed court costs but also the actual costs of travel, including mileage or transportation costs, lodging, and meals, all in accord with the travel regulations of the Division of Administration; the actual costs of experts and expert witnesses, their actual costs of travel, including mileage or transportation costs, lodging, and meals; laboratory fees, and all other actual costs of performing the prosecution and investigation.

CHAPTER 3. APPEAL FROM RECUSATION RULING

Art. 684. Review of recusation ruling.

If a judge or a district attorney is recused over the objection of the state, or if an application by the state for recusation of a judge is denied, the state may apply for a review of the ruling by supervisory writs. The defendant may not appeal prior to sentence from a ruling recusing or refusing to recuse the judge or the district attorney. *(Chgd. by Acts 1997 No. 887, §1, eff. 8/15/97.)*

TITLE XXIII. DISMISSAL OF PROSECUTION

Art. 691. Dismissal of prosecution by district attorney.

The district attorney has the power, in his discretion, to dismiss an indictment or a count in an indictment, and in order to exercise that power it is not necessary that he obtain consent of the court. The dismissal may be made orally by the district attorney in open court, or by a written statement of the dismissal signed by the district attorney and filed with the clerk of court. The clerk of court shall cause the dismissal to be entered on the minutes of the court.

Art. 692. Dismissal of indictment after conviction.

After conviction, the district attorney is authorized to dismiss an indictment or count thereof only:

(1) When a new trial has been granted.

(2) When a motion in arrest of judgment has been sustained.

Art. 693. Effect of dismissal.

Dismissal by the district attorney of an indictment or of a count of an indictment, discharges that particular indictment or count. The dismissal is not a bar to a subsequent prosecution, except that:

(1) A dismissal entered without the defendant's consent after the first witness is sworn at the trial on the merits, shall operate as an acquittal and bar a subsequent prosecution for the charge dismissed; and

(2) A dismissal entered after a city court conviction has been appealed to the district court for a trial de novo, shall operate as an acquittal and bar a subsequent prosecution for the charge dismissed.

TITLE XXIV. PROCEDURES PRIOR TO TRIAL

CHAPTER 1. SETTING CASES FOR TRIAL

Art. 701. Right to a speedy trial.

A. The state and the defendant have the right to a speedy trial.

B. The time period for filing a bill of information or indictment after arrest shall be as follows:

(1) When the defendant is continued in custody subsequent to an arrest, an indictment or information shall be filed within forty-five days of the arrest if the defendant is being held for a misdemeanor and within sixty days of the arrest if the defendant is being held for a felony.

(2) When the defendant is not continued in custody subsequent to arrest, an indictment or information shall be filed within ninety days of the arrest if the defendant is booked with a misdemeanor and one hundred fifty days of the arrest if the defendant is booked with a felony.

Failure to institute prosecution as provided in Subparagraph (1) shall result in release of the defendant if, after contradictory hearing with the district attorney, just cause for the failure is not shown. If just cause is shown, the court shall reconsider bail for the defendant. Failure to institute prosecution as provided in Subparagraph (2) shall result in the release of the bail obligation if, after contradictory hearing with the district attorney, just cause for the delay is not shown.

C. Upon filing of a bill of information or indictment, the district attorney shall set the matter for arraignment within thirty days unless just cause for a longer delay is shown.

D. (1) A motion by the defendant for a speedy trial, in order to be valid, must be accompanied by an affidavit by defendant's counsel certifying that the defendant and his counsel are prepared to proceed to trial within the delays set forth in this Article. After the filing of a motion for a speedy trial by the defendant and his counsel the time period for commencement of trial shall be as follows:

(a) The trial of a defendant charged with a felony shall commence within one hundred twenty days if he is continued in custody and within one hundred eighty days if he is not continued in custody.

(b) The trial of a defendant charged with a misdemeanor shall commence within thirty days if he is continued in custody and within sixty days if he is not continued in custody.

(2) Failure to commence trial within the time periods provided above shall result in the release of the defendant without bail or in the discharge of the bail obligation, if after contradictory hearing with the district attorney, just cause for the delay is not shown.

E. "Just cause" as used in this Article shall include any grounds beyond the control of the State or the Court.

F. A motion for a speedy trial filed by the defendant, but not verified by the affidavit of his counsel, shall be set for contradictory hearing within thirty days.

(Chgd. by Acts 1993 No. 682, §1, eff. 8/15/93.)

Art. 702. Setting cases for trial.

Cases shall be set for trial by the court on motion of the state, and may be set for trial on motion of the defendant.

Courts shall adopt rules governing the procedure for setting cases for trial and giving notice thereof. The defendant shall be given notice of trial sufficiently in advance thereof so that he may summon his witnesses.

CHAPTER 2. MOTION TO SUPPRESS EVIDENCE

Art. 703. Motion to suppress evidence.

A. A defendant adversely affected may move to suppress any evidence from use at the trial on the merits on the ground that it was unconstitutionally obtained.

B. A defendant may move on any constitutional ground to suppress a confession or statement of any nature made by the defendant.

C. A motion filed under the provisions of this Article must be filed in accordance with Article 521, unless opportunity therefor did not exist or neither the defendant nor his counsel was aware of the existence of the evidence or the ground of the motion, or unless the failure to file the motion was otherwise excusable. The court in its discretion may permit the filing of a motion to suppress at any time before or during the trial.

D. On the trial of a motion to suppress filed under the provisions of this Article, the burden of proof is on the defendant to prove the ground of his motion, except that the state shall have the burden of proving the admissibility of a purported confession or statement by the defendant or of any evidence seized without a warrant.

E. (1) An evidentiary hearing on a motion to suppress shall be held only when the defendant alleges facts that would require the granting of relief. The state may file an answer to the motion. The defendant may testify in support of a motion to suppress without being subject to examination on other matters. The defendant's testimony cannot be used by the state except for the purpose of attacking the credibility of the defendant's testimony at the trial on the merits.

(2) If the defendant testifies before the jury at the trial on the merits, he can be cross-examined on the whole case.

F. A ruling prior to trial on the merits, upon a motion to suppress, is binding at the trial. Failure to file a motion to suppress evidence in accordance with this Article prevents the defendant from objecting to its admissibility at the trial on the merits on a ground assertable by a motion to suppress.

G. When a ruling on a motion to suppress a confession or statement is adverse to the defendant, the state shall be required, prior to presenting the confession or statement to the jury, to introduce evidence concerning the circumstances surrounding the making of the confession or statement for the purpose of enabling the jury to determine the weight to be given the confession or statement.

A ruling made adversely to the defendant prior to trial upon a motion to suppress a confession or statement does not prevent the defendant from introducing evidence during the trial concerning the circumstances surrounding the making of the confession or statement for the purpose of enabling the jury to determine the weight to be given the confession or statement.

CHAPTER 3. SEVERANCE AND CONSOLIDATION

Article

Art. 704. Severance.

Jointly indicted defendants shall be tried jointly unless:

(1) The state elects to try them separately; or

(2) The court, on motion of the defendant, and after contradictory hearing with the district attorney, is satisfied that justice requires a severance.

Art. 705. Effects of severance.

When the court has ordered severance of an indictment, the district attorney shall file separate indictments.

In the case of a grand jury indictment, no further action by the grand jury is required. Severed indictments shall be considered as filed on the date of the filing of the original indictment. Proceedings under the original indictment are not affected by the severance except insofar as they may be inconsistent with some other provision of this Code. The effects of a severance, as stated in this article, apply to severances under Articles 532(3) and 704.

Art. 706. Consolidation for trial.

Upon motion of a defendant, or of all defendants if there are more than one, the court may order two or more indictments consolidated for trial if the offenses and the defendants, if there are more than one, could have been joined in a single indictment. The procedure thereafter shall be the same as if the prosecution were under a single indictment.

CHAPTER 4. CONTINUANCE

Article

Art. 707. Motion for continuance; time for filing.

A motion for a continuance shall be in writing and shall allege specifically the grounds upon which it is based and, when made by a defendant, must be verified by his affidavit or that of his counsel. It shall be filed at least seven days prior to the commencement of trial.

Upon written motion at any time and after contradictory hearing, the court may grant a continuance, but only upon a showing that such motion is in the interest of justice.

Art. 708. Continuance and recess; definitions.

A continuance is the postponement of a scheduled trial or hearing, and shall not be granted after the trial or hearing has commenced. A recess is a temporary adjournment of a trial or hearing that occurs after a trial or hearing has commenced.

Art. 709. Continuance based on absence of a witness.

A motion for a continuance based upon the absence of a witness must state:

(1) Facts to which the absent witness is expected to testify, showing the materiality of the testimony and the necessity for the presence of the witness at the trial;

(2) Facts and circumstances showing a probability that the witness will be available at the time to which the trial is deferred; and

(3) Facts showing due diligence used in an effort to procure attendance of the witness.

Art. 710. Prevention of continuance by admission of adverse party.

When a motion for a continuance is based on the absence of a material witness, and the adverse party admits that if the witness were present he would testify as stated in the motion, the court may proceed to the trial of the case. If the court is of the opinion that despite the admission, the case cannot be tried with justice to the applicant, it may require the adverse party to admit also the truth of the testimony as a condition of refusing to grant the continuance.

Art. 711. Trial of motion.

A motion for continuance, unless consented to, shall be tried summarily and contradictorily with the adverse party.

Art. 712. Discretionary grounds.

A motion for continuance, if timely filed, may be granted, in the discretion of the court, in any case if there is good ground therefor.

Art. 713. Peremptory grounds.

A motion for a continuance based upon peremptory grounds as provided by law shall be granted.

Art. 714. Continuance to defendants jointly indicted.

When defendants are jointly indicted and a continuance is granted to one of them, the court may grant a continuance to any of the others, on his motion. However, a continuance granted to one defendant shall not deprive other jointly indicted defendants of a prompt trial unless the state can show good ground for continuance as to them.

Art. 715. Continuance to definite date or indefinitely.

In granting the continuance, the judge shall fix the date upon which the trial or hearing shall proceed, if then practicable, except when both parties ask that no date be set.

CHAPTER 5. DISCOVERY AND INSPECTION

PART A. DISCOVERY BY THE DEFENDANT

PART B. DISCOVERY BY THE STATE

PART C. REGULATION OF DISCOVERY

PART A. DISCOVERY BY THE DEFENDANT

Art. 716. Statements by the defendant.

A. Upon motion of the defendant, the court shall order the district attorney to permit or authorize the defendant to inspect and copy, photograph or otherwise reproduce any relevant written or recorded confession or statement of any nature, including recorded testimony before a grand jury, or copy thereof, of the defendant in the possession, custody, control, or knowledge of the district attorney.

B. Upon motion of the defendant, the court shall order the district attorney to inform the defendant of the existence, but not the contents, of any oral confession or statement of any nature, made by the defendant, which the district attorney intends to offer in evidence at the trial, with the information as to when, where and to whom such oral confession or statement was made.

C. Upon motion of the defendant, the court shall order the district attorney to inform the defendant of the substance of any oral statement which the state intends to offer in evidence made by the defendant, whether before or after arrest, in response to interrogation by any person then known to the defendant to be a law enforcement officer.

Art. 717. Defendant's prior criminal record.

Upon motion of the defendant, the court shall order the district attorney or the appropriate law enforcement agency to furnish to defendant a copy of any record of his criminal arrests and convictions that is in their possession or custody.

Art. 718. Documents and tangible objects.

Subject to the limitation of Article 723, on motion of the defendant, the court shall order the district attorney to permit or authorize the defendant to inspect, copy, examine, test scientifically, photograph, or otherwise reproduce books, papers, documents, photographs, tangible objects, buildings, places, or copies or portions thereof, which are within the possession, custody, or control of the state, and which:

(1) are favorable to the defendant and which are material and relevant to the issue of guilt or punishment, or

(2) are intended for use by the state as evidence at the trial, or

(3) were obtained from or belong to the defendant.

The court may determine whether evidence is subject to the provisions of Paragraph (1) hereof by in camera inspection.

Art. 719. Reports of examinations and tests.

A. Upon motion of the defendant, the court shall order the district attorney to permit or authorize the defendant to inspect and copy, photograph, or otherwise reproduce any results or reports, or copies thereof, of a physical or mental examination, and of scientific tests or experiments, made in connection with or material to the particular case, that are in the possession, custody, control, or knowledge of the district attorney and intended for use at trial. Exculpatory evidence shall be produced under this Article even though it is not intended for use at trial.

B. In addition, upon motion of the defendant, whenever the court orders the defendant to provide urine, blood, saliva, or hair samples or samples of other bodily substances for deoxyribonucleic acid testing in a criminal case, the defendant shall be authorized to acquire one-half of the deoxyribonucleic acid sample to be tested separately by the defendant at his expense.
(Chgd. by Acts 1997 No. 1074, §1, eff. 8/15/97.)

Art. 720. Evidence of other crimes.

Upon motion of defendant, the court shall order the district attorney to inform the defendant of the state's intent to offer evidence of the commission of any other crime admissible under the authority of Louisiana Code of Evidence Article 404. Provided however, that such order shall not require the district attorney to inform the defendant of the state's intent to offer evidence of offenses which relates to conduct that constitutes an integral part of the act or transaction that is the subject of the present proceeding or other crimes for which the accused was previously convicted.

Art. 721. Statements of coconspirators.

Upon motion of the defendant, the court shall order the district attorney to inform the defendant of the state's intent to use statements of coconspirators pursuant to Louisiana Code of Evidence Article 801(d)(3)(b).

Art. 722. Confessions and inculpatory statements of codefendants.

Upon motion of the defendant, the court shall order the district attorney to permit or authorize the defendant to inspect and copy, photograph or otherwise reproduce any relevant written or recorded confessions or inculpatory statements made by a codefendant and intended for use at trial. Exculpatory evidence shall be produced under this article even though it is not intended for use at trial.

Art. 723. State reports and other matters not subject to disclosure.

Except as provided in Articles 716, 718, 721, and 722, this Chapter does not authorize the discovery or inspection of reports, memoranda or other internal state documents made by the district attorney or by agents of the state in connection with the investigation or prosecution of the case; or of statements made by witnesses or prospective witnesses, other than the defendant, to the district attorney, or to agents of the state.

PART B. DISCOVERY BY THE STATE

Art. 724. Documents and tangible objects.

When the court grants relief sought by the defendant under Article 718, it shall upon the motion of the district attorney, condition its order by requiring that the defendant permit or authorize the district attorney to inspect and copy, examine, test scientifically, photograph, or otherwise reproduce books, papers, documents, photographs, tangible objects, copies, or portions thereof, that are in the possession, custody, or control of the defendant, and that the defendant intends to use in evidence at the trial.

Art. 725. Reports of examinations and tests.

When the court grants the relief sought by the defendant under Article 719 it shall, upon the motion of the state, condition its order by requiring that the defendant permit or authorize the state to inspect and copy, photograph or otherwise reproduce any results of reports, or copies thereof, of physical and mental examinations and of scientific tests or experiments, of a similar nature, made in connection with the case, that are in the possession, custody, or control of the defendant, and that the defendant intends to use as evidence at the trial or were prepared by a witness whom the defendant intends to call at the trial when such results or reports relate to his testimony.

Art. 726. Notice of defense based upon mental condition.

A. If a defendant intends to introduce testimony relating to a mental disease, defect, or other condition bearing upon the issue of whether he had the mental state required for the offense charged, he shall not later than ten days prior to trial or such reasonable time as the court may permit, notify the district attorney in writing of such intention and file a copy of such notice with the clerk. The court may for cause shown allow late filing of the notice or grant additional time to the parties to prepare for trial or make such other orders as may be appropriate.

B. If there is a failure to give notice as required by Subsection A of this Article, the court may exclude the testimony of any witness offered by the defendant on the issue of mental condition.

Art. 727. Notice of alibi.

A. Upon written demand of the district attorney stating the time, date, and place at which the alleged offense was committed, the defendant shall serve within ten days, or at such different time as the court may direct, upon the district attorney a written notice of his intention to offer a defense of alibi. Such notice by the defendant shall state the specific place or places at which the defendant claims to have been at the time of the alleged offense and the names and addresses of the witnesses upon whom he intends to rely to establish such alibi.

B. Within ten days thereafter, but in no event less than ten days before trial, unless the court otherwise directs, the district attorney shall serve upon the defendant or his attorney a written notice stating the names and addresses of the witnesses upon whom the state intends to rely to establish the defendant's presence at the scene of the alleged offense and any other witnesses to be relied on to rebut testimony of any of the defendant's alibi witnesses.

C. If prior to or during trial, a party learns of an additional witness whose identity, if known, should have been included in the information furnished under Subsection A or B, the party shall promptly notify the other party or his attorney of the existence and identity of such additional witness.

D. Upon the failure of either party to comply with the requirements of this rule, the court may exclude the testimony of any undisclosed witness offered by such party as to the defendant's absence from or presence at, the scene of the alleged offense. This rule shall not limit the right of the defendant to testify in his own behalf.

E. For good cause shown, the court may grant an exception to any of the requirements of Subsections A through D of this Section.

F. Evidence of an intention to rely upon an alibi defense, later withdrawn, or of statements made in connection with such intention, is not admissible in any civil or criminal proceeding against the person who gave notice of the intention.

Art. 728. Defense information and other matters not subject to disclosure.

Except as to scientific or medical reports, this Chapter does not authorize the discovery or inspection of reports, memoranda, or other internal defense documents made by the defendant or his attorneys or agents in connection with the investigation or defense of the case; or of statements made by the defendant, or by witnesses or prospective witnesses to the defendant, his agents or attorneys; or of the names of defense witnesses or prospective defense witnesses.

PART C. REGULATION OF DISCOVERY

Art. 729. Time and scope of motion by defendant.

A motion for discovery by a defendant under this Chapter may be filed in accordance with Article 521 or within such reasonable time as the court may permit. The motion shall include all relief sought under this Chapter. A subsequent motion may be considered before trial, but only upon a showing that such motion would be in the interest of justice.

Art. 729.1. Court's disposition of motion for discovery; vacation or restriction of order.

A. A motion for discovery shall not be denied without a contradictory hearing unless it appears on the face of the motion that, as a matter of law, the moving party is not entitled to the relief sought.

B. Upon a sufficient showing by either party, the court may at any time vacate, restrict or defer an order for discovery, or make such other order as is appropriate.

Art. 729.2. Time, place and manner of discovery and inspection.

An order of the court granting relief under this Chapter shall specify the time, place, and manner of making the discovery and inspection and may prescribe such terms and conditions as are appropriate.

Art. 729.3. Continuing duty to disclose.

If, subsequent to compliance with an order issued pursuant to this Chapter and prior to or during trial, a party discovers additional evidence or decides to use additional evidence and such evidence is or may be, subject to discovery or inspection under the order issued, he shall promptly notify the other party and the court of the existence of the additional evidence, so that the court may modify its previous order or allow the other party to make an appropriate motion for additional discovery or inspection.

Art. 729.4. Pretrial conferences.

The court may by special order or pursuant to local rules require the district attorney and defense counsel to participate in a pretrial conference for the purpose of:

(1) Disposing of discovery motions without formal hearing when there is no objection and no prior voluntary compliance with the provisions hereof; and

(2) Consideration of such other matters as may aid in the prompt and fair disposition of the charge.

Art. 729.5. Failure to comply; sanctions.

A. If at any time during the course of the proceedings it is brought to the attention of the court that a party has failed to comply with this Chapter or with an order issued pursuant to this Chapter, the court may order such party to permit the discovery or inspection, grant a continuance, order a mistrial on motion of the defendant, prohibit the party from introducing into evidence the subject matter not disclosed, or enter such other order, other than dismissal, as may be appropriate.

B. In addition to the sanctions authorized in Part A hereof, if at any time prior or subsequent to final disposition the court finds that either the state through the district attorney or assistant district attorney or the defendant or his counsel has willfully failed to comply with this Chapter or with an order issued pursuant to this Chapter, such failure shall be deemed to be a constructive contempt of court.

Art. 729.6. Applicability of discovery.

The rules of this Chapter shall be applied in all criminal cases which are to be tried in the district court. They shall be applicable following institution of the criminal prosecution by the return of a grand jury indictment or the filing of a bill of information by the district attorney.

TITLE XXV. COMPULSORY PROCESS

Chapter

CHAPTER 1. GENERAL SECTION; SUBPOENAS

Article

Art. 731. Issuance of subpoenas.

The court shall issue subpoenas for the compulsory attendance of witnesses at hearings or trials when requested to do so by the state or the defendant. Clerks of court may issue subpoenas except as provided in Article 739.

Art. 732. Subpoena duces tecum.

A subpoena may order a person to produce at the trial or hearing, books, papers, documents, or any other tangible things in his possession or under his control, if a reasonably accurate description thereof is given; but the court shall vacate or modify the subpoena if it is unreasonable or oppressive.

Art. 733. Form.

A subpoena shall state the name of the court and the title of the case and shall command the attendance of a witness at a time and place specified.

Art. 734. Service of subpoena by sheriff.

The sheriff of any parish in which the witness may be found, or of the parish in which the proceeding is pending, shall serve the subpoena and make a return thereof without delay.

Art. 735. Types of service.

A. Unless otherwise directed by the state or defendant, subpoenas shall be served by domiciliary service, personal service, or United States mail as provided in Paragraph B. Personal service is made when the sheriff tenders the subpoena to the witness. Domiciliary service is made when the sheriff leaves the subpoena at the dwelling house or usual abode of the witness with a person of suitable age and discretion residing therein as a member of the domiciliary establishment of the witness.

B. (1) The criminal sheriff for the parish of Orleans and all other sheriffs throughout the state may serve all subpoenas directed to him to be served by mailing the said subpoenas in the United States Post Office, by either certified mail, return receipt requested, or first class mail to the addressee at the address listed on the subpoena.

(2) Service by first class mail shall include a request that the enclosed return form be signed by the addressee and mailed to the sheriff. If a signed return is not received by the sheriff, the subpoena shall be served by domiciliary or personal service as provided in Paragraph A.

(3) Service by mail shall be considered personal service if the certified return receipt or the return form is signed by the addressee. Service by mail shall be considered domiciliary service if the certified return receipt or the return form is signed by anyone other than the addressee.

C. The criminal sheriff of the parish of Orleans and all other sheriffs throughout the state are hereby authorized to make service of subpoenas to law enforcement officers through the law enforcement officer's ranking officers or their designated representative, which, upon service thereof, shall have the same legal effect as if domiciliary service had been made upon the law enforcement officer named therein. This service shall be made at the district stations or departmental headquarters of said law enforcement agency. Service may consist of individual subpoenas or may consist of lists which include officer's name and badge number, case title, name of court, and date of commanded appearance. Such lists may be served by the sheriff or his deputies by means of electronic transfer to printing devices located in the district stations or departmental headquarters. The ranking officer, or his designated representative, shall sign for such subpoenas or indicate receipt by electronic verification code, and shall be required to notify the law enforcement officer named therein of receipt of the subpoenas or list.

D. This type of subpoena service shall be known as departmental subpoena service of law enforcement officers, and shall not be construed to replace domiciliary or personal service for said officers, but shall be an additional method of service.

Art. 736. Return of subpoena by sheriff.

A. The sheriff shall endorse on a copy of the subpoena the date, place, type of service, and sufficient other data to show service in compliance with law. When the witness cannot be found, the sheriff must set out in his return every fact that in his opinion justifies the return. He shall sign and return the copy promptly after the service to the court that issued the subpoena. The return, when received by the clerk, shall form part of the record and shall be considered prima facie correct.

B. The criminal sheriff for the Parish of Orleans when serving subpoenas under the provisions of Paragraph A of Article 735 of the Louisiana Code of Criminal Procedure shall endorse on a copy of the subpoena the date and time of mailing, and shall attach the return receipt of delivery from the United States Post Office showing the disposition of the envelope bearing the subpoena. He shall return the copy and the attached receipt to the court that issued the subpoena. The return, when received by the clerk, shall form part of the record and shall be considered prima facie correct and shall constitute sufficient basis for an action to cite persons for contempt for failure to appear in response thereto.

Art. 737. Contempt; attachment of witnesses failing to appear.

Contumacious failure to comply with a subpoena, proof of service of which appears of record, constitutes a direct contempt of the court which issued the subpoena, and the court may order the witness attached and brought to court immediately.

If an order of attachment is issued, it may be executed in any parish by the sheriff of the parish from which the attachment was issued, or by the sheriff of the parish where the witness is found.

CHAPTER 2. RESTRICTIONS ON SUBPOENAS

Art. 738. Number of witnesses allowed.

At a trial or hearing, each defendant in a misdemeanor case shall be allowed to summon six witnesses at the expense of the parish, and in a felony case twelve witnesses. A defendant shall have the right of compulsory process for additional witnesses at his own expense.

Art. 739. Indigent defendant.

If a defendant is indigent and unable to pay for witnesses desired by him in addition to those summoned at the expense of the parish, he shall make a sworn application to the court for the additional witnesses. The application must allege that the testimony is relevant and material and not cumulative and that the defendant cannot safely go to trial without it.

The court shall make a private inquiry into the facts, and if satisfied that the defendant is entitled to the privilege, it shall render an order permitting the defendant to subpoena additional witnesses at the expense of the parish. If the application is denied, the court shall state the reasons for the denial in writing, which shall become part of the record.

CHAPTER 3. OBTAINING WITNESSES FROM OUTSIDE THE STATE

Art. 741. Method of obtaining a witness from another state.

If a person in any state, which by its laws has made provision for commanding persons within its borders to attend and testify in criminal prosecutions or grand jury investigations commenced or about to commence in this state, is a material witness in a prosecution pending in a court of record in this state, or in a grand jury investigation which has commenced or is about to commence, a judge of such court may issue a certificate under the seal of the court stating these facts and specifying the number of days the witness shall be required. This certificate shall be presented to a judge of a court of record in the county (parish) in which the witness is found.

If the certificate recommends that the witness be taken into immediate custody and delivered to an officer of this state to assure his attendance in this state, the judge may direct that the witness be forthwith brought before him. The judge being satisfied of the desirability of custody and delivery, for which determination the certificate shall be prima facie proof, may order that the witness be forthwith taken into custody and delivered to an officer of this state. The order shall be sufficient authority for the officer to take the witness into custody and hold him unless and until he may be released by bail, recognizance, or order of the judge issuing the certificate.

If the witness is summoned to attend and testify in this state he shall be tendered the sum of ten cents a mile for each mile and five dollars for each day that he is required to travel and attend as a witness. A witness who has appeared in accordance with the provisions of the summons shall not be required to remain within the state a longer period of time than the period mentioned in the certificate, unless otherwise ordered by the court. If the witness fails without good cause to attend and testify as directed in the summons, he shall be punished in the manner provided for the punishment of any witness who disobeys a summons issued from a court of record of this state.

Art. 742. Method of summoning a witness in this state to testify in another state.

If a judge of a court of record in any state which by its laws has made provision for commanding persons within that state to attend and testify in this state, certifies under seal of court that there is a criminal prosecution pending in that court, or that a grand jury investigation has commenced or is about to commence, that a person being within this state is a material witness in the prosecution or grand jury investigation, and that his presence will be required for a specified number of days, upon presentation of the certificate to any judge of a court of record in the parish (county) in which the person is, the judge shall fix a time and place for a hearing and shall make an order directing the witness to appear at a time and place certain for the hearing.

If at a hearing the judge determines that the witness is material and necessary, that it will not cause undue hardship to the witness to be compelled to attend and testify in the prosecution or grand jury investigation in the other state, and that the laws of the state in which the prosecution is pending, or grand jury investigation has commenced or is about to commence, will give to him protection from arrest and the service of civil and criminal process, he shall issue a summons, with a copy of the certificate attached, directing the witness to attend and testify in the court where the prosecution is pending, or where a grand jury investigation has commenced or is about to commence at a time and place specified in the summons. In any such hearing the certificate shall be prima facie evidence of all the facts stated therein.

If the certificate recommends that the witness be taken into immediate custody and delivered to an officer of the requesting state to assure his attendance in the requesting state, the judge may, in lieu of notification of the hearing, direct that the witness be forthwith brought before him for the hearing. The judge at the hearing being satisfied of the desirability of custody and delivery, for which determination the certificate shall be prima facie proof of desirability may, in lieu of issuing subpoena or summons, order that the witness be forthwith taken into custody and delivered to an officer of the requesting state.

If the witness, who is summoned as above provided, after being paid or tendered by some properly authorized person the sum of ten cents a mile for each mile and five dollars for each day, that he is required to travel and attend as a witness, fails without good cause to attend and testify as directed in the summons, he shall be punished in the manner provided by law for the punishment of any witness who disobeys a summons issued from a court of record in this state.

Art. 743. Exemption from arrest and service of process.

If a person comes into this state in obedience to a summons directing him to attend and testify in this state, he shall not, while in this state pursuant to such summons or order, be subject to arrest or the service of process, civil or criminal, in connection with matters which arose before his entrance into this state under the summons.

If a person passes through this state while going to another state in obedience to a summons or order to attend and testify in that state or while returning therefrom, he shall not, while so passing through this state be subject to arrest, or the service of process, civil or criminal, in connection with matters which arose before his entrance into this state under the summons or order.

Art. 744. Witness; state; defined.

"Witness" as used in Articles 741 through 743 shall include a person whose testimony is relevant and material and desired in any proceeding or investigation by a grand jury or in a criminal action, prosecution, or proceeding.

"State" shall include any territory of the United States and the District of Columbia.

Art. 745. Uniformity of interpretation.

Articles 741 through 744 shall be so interpreted and construed as to effect their general purpose to make uniform the law of the states which enact similar provisions.

TITLE XXVI. TRIAL PROCEDURE

CHAPTER 1. GENERAL PROVISIONS

Art. 761. Commencement of trial.

A jury trial commences when the first prospective juror is called for examination. A trial by a judge alone commences when the first witness is sworn.

Art. 762. Place of sessions of court.

Sessions of court shall be held at the parish courthouse and, if there is more than one courthouse in a parish, sessions may be held at any such courthouse, or sessions may be held at places within the parish other than the courthouse or courthouses in the discretion of the court:

(1) To take the testimony of witnesses who are so incapacitated that they cannot attend the trial in the parish courthouse;

(2) To allow the jury or judge to view the place where the crime or any material part thereof is alleged to have occurred, or to view an object which is admissible in evidence but which is difficult to produce in court. At this view, the court shall not permit the taking of evidence except in connection with the place or object; or

(3) When the courthouse in which the sessions are usually held is unsuitable for use, or there is no courthouse.

Art. 763. Proceedings on holidays.

Trials and hearings may commence or continue on a holiday or half-holiday in the discretion of the court.

Art. 764. Exclusion of witnesses.

The exclusion of witnesses is governed by Louisiana Code of Evidence Article 615.

Art. 765. Normal order of trial.

The normal order of trial shall be as follows:

(1) The selection and swearing of the jury;
(2) The reading of the indictment;
(3) The reading of the defendant's plea on arraignment;
(4) The opening statements of the state and of the defendant;

(5) The presentation of the evidence of the state, and of the defendant, and of the state in rebuttal. The court in its discretion may permit the introduction of additional evidence prior to argument;

(6) The argument of the state, the defendant, and the state in rebuttal;

(7) The court's charge;

(8) The announcement of the verdict or mistrial in jury cases, or of the judgment in nonjury cases; and

(9) The discharge of the jury in jury cases.

When there is more than one defendant, the court shall determine the order of trial as between them.

A defendant may waive his opening statement.

Art. 766. Opening statement by state; scope.

The opening statement of the state shall explain the nature of the charge, and set forth, in general terms, the nature of the evidence by which the state expects to prove the charge.

Art. 767. Same; prohibition against adverting to confessions.

The state shall not, in the opening statement, advert in any way to a confession or inculpatory statement made by the defendant unless the statement has been previously ruled admissible in the case. *(Chgd. by Acts 1995 No. 1278, §1, eff. 8/15/95.)*

Art. 768. Same; use of confession or inculpatory statement; notice to defendant prior to opening statement.

Unless the defendant has been granted pretrial discovery, if the state intends to introduce a confession or inculpatory statement in evidence, it shall so advise the defendant in writing prior to beginning the state's opening statement. If it fails to do so a confession or inculpatory statement shall not be admissible in evidence.

Art. 769. Same; effect on introduction of evidence.

Evidence not fairly within the scope of the opening statement of the state shall not be admitted in evidence.

If the state offers evidence that was inadvertently and in good faith omitted from the opening statement, the court, in its discretion may admit the evidence if it finds that the defendant is not taken by surprise or prejudiced in the preparation of his defense.

Art. 770. Prejudicial remarks; basis of mistrial.

Upon motion of a defendant, a mistrial shall be ordered when a remark or comment, made within the hearing of the jury by the judge, district attorney, or a court official, during the trial or in argument, refers directly or indirectly to:

(1) Race, religion, color or national origin, if the remark or comment is not material and relevant and might create prejudice against the defendant in the mind of the jury;

(2) Another crime committed or alleged to have been committed by the defendant as to which evidence is not admissible;

(3) The failure of the defendant to testify in his own defense; or

(4) The refusal of the judge to direct a verdict.

An admonition to the jury to disregard the remark or comment shall not be sufficient to prevent a mistrial. If the defendant, however, requests that only an admonition be given, the court shall admonish the jury to disregard the remark or comment but shall not declare a mistrial.

Art. 771. Admonition.

In the following cases, upon the request of the defendant or the state, the court shall promptly admonish the jury to disregard a remark or comment made during the trial, or in argument within the hearing of the jury, when the remark is irrelevant or immaterial and of such a nature that it might create prejudice against the defendant, or the state, in the mind of the jury:

(1) When the remark or comment is made by the judge, the district attorney, or a court official, and the remark is not within the scope of Article 770; or

(2) When the remark or comment is made by a witness or person other than the judge, district attorney, or a court official, regardless of whether the remark or comment is within the scope of Article 770.

In such cases, on motion of the defendant, the court may grant a mistrial if it is satisfied that an admonition is not sufficient to assure the defendant a fair trial.

Art. 772. Comment on facts by judge in jury's presence prohibited.

The judge in the presence of the jury shall not comment upon the facts of the case, either by commenting upon or recapitulating the evidence, repeating the testimony of any witness, or giving an opinion as to what has been proved, not proved, or refuted.

Art. 773. Order of evidence; foundation.

Neither the state nor the defendant can be controlled by the court as to the order in which evidence shall be adduced. The procedure for laying a foundation is provided in the Louisiana Code of Evidence.

Art. 774. Argument; scope.

The argument shall be confined to evidence admitted, to the lack of evidence, to conclusions of fact that the state or defendant may draw therefrom, and to the law applicable to the case.

The argument shall not appeal to prejudice.

The state's rebuttal shall be confined to answering the argument of the defendant.

Art. 775. Mistrial; grounds for.

A mistrial may be ordered, and in a jury case the jury dismissed, when:

(1) The defendant consents thereto;

(2) The jury is unable to agree upon a verdict;

(3) There is a legal defect in the proceedings which would make any judgment entered upon a verdict reversible as a matter of law;

(4) The court finds that the defendant does not have the mental capacity to proceed;

(5) It is physically impossible to proceed with the trial in conformity with law; or

(6) False statements of a juror on voir dire prevent a fair trial.

Upon motion of a defendant, a mistrial shall be ordered, and in a jury case the jury dismissed, when prejudicial conduct in or outside the courtroom makes it impossible for the defendant to obtain a fair trial, or when authorized by Article 770 or 771.

A mistrial shall be ordered, and in a jury case the jury dismissed, when the state and the defendant jointly move for a mistrial.

Art. 776. Oath of witness.

Before a witness is permitted to testify he shall be sworn, in accordance with Article 14.

Art. 777. Recordation of proceedings.

A record of the trial proceedings shall be made in accordance with other provisions of law.

Art. 778. Motion for acquittal.

In a trial by the judge alone the court shall enter a judgment of acquittal on one or more of the offenses charged, on its own motion or on that of defendant, after the close of the state's evidence or of all the evidence, if the evidence is insufficient to sustain a conviction.

If the court denies a defendant's motion for a judgment of acquittal at the close of the state's case, the defendant may offer its evidence in defense.

CHAPTER 2. TRIAL WITHOUT JURY

Art. 779. Trial of misdemeanors.

A. A defendant charged with a misdemeanor in which the punishment, as set forth in the statute defining the offense, may be a fine in excess of one thousand dollars or imprisonment for more than six months shall be tried by a jury of six jurors, all of whom must concur to render a verdict.

B. The defendant charged with any other misdemeanor shall be tried by the court without a jury.

Art. 780. Right to waive trial by jury.

A. A defendant charged with an offense other than one punishable by death may knowingly and intelligently waive a trial by jury and elect to be tried by the judge. At the time of arraignment, the defendant in such cases shall be informed by the court of his right to waive trial by jury.

B. The defendant shall exercise his right to waive trial by jury in accordance with the time limits set forth in Article 521. However, with permission of the court, he may exercise his right to waive trial by jury at any time prior to the commencement of trial.

C. The defendant may withdraw a waiver of trial by jury unless the court finds that withdrawal of the waiver would result in interference with the administration of justice, unnecessary delay, unnecessary inconvenience to witnesses, or prejudice to the state.

Art. 781. Charges in cases tried without a jury.

When a case is tried without a jury the state or the defendant may request the court to charge itself in accordance with written charges presented to the court. The requested charges shall be governed by the rules of procedure relative to requested charges in jury cases.

CHAPTER 3. TRIAL BY JURY

SECTION 1. GENERAL PROVISIONS

Article

SECTION 2. CHALLENGES

SECTION 3. CHARGING THE JURY

SECTION 1. GENERAL PROVISIONS

Art. 782. Number of jurors composing jury; number which must concur; waiver.

A. Cases in which punishment may be capital shall be tried by a jury of twelve jurors, all of whom must concur to render a verdict. Cases in which punishment is necessarily confinement at hard labor shall be tried by a jury composed of twelve jurors, ten of whom must concur to render a verdict. Cases in which the punishment may be confinement at hard labor shall be tried by a jury composed of six jurors, all of whom must concur to render a verdict.

B. Trial by jury may be knowingly and intelligently waived by the defendant except in capital cases.

Art. 783. Excusing, tendering, and attachment of members of the venire.

A. The court may excuse a member of the petit jury venire at any time prior to the time he is sworn as a juror to try a particular case. The panel shall be selected from the remaining members of the petit jury venire. The court, either on its own motion, or that of the state or a defendant, may order the attachment of an absent and unexcused petit jury venireman.

B. If jury service, whether criminal or civil, would result in undue hardship or extreme inconvenience, the district court may excuse a person from such service either prior to or after his selection for the general venire, jury pool, or jury wheel. The court may take such action on its own initiative or on recommendation of an official or employee designated by the court.

C. No person or group of persons shall be automatically excused.

D. In the event a person is excused because jury service would result in undue hardship or extreme inconvenience, the court may order that person's name be placed again in the general venire or in a central jury pool.

Art. 784. Method of selecting panel.

In selecting a panel, names shall be drawn from the petit jury venire indiscriminately and by lot in open court and in a manner to be determined by the court.

In those judicial district courts, including the Criminal District Court for the parish of Orleans, wherein use of a jury pool has been authorized by law, the petit jury panel shall be selected by random, indiscriminate choice in a manner to be determined by the rules of the court in which the jury panel is selected.

Art. 785. Tales jurors.

A. In a parish other than Orleans having more than one division of court, holding petit jury terms simultaneously, when a petit jury venire of one division is or is about to be exhausted before a trial jury is impaneled, the judge of that division, with the consent of the judge of a division that has not exhausted its petit jury venire, may order the petit jury venire of the latter division or such portion thereof not being used by the latter division, to report to his division to serve as tales jurors. The names of the petit jury veniremen so ordered to report shall be drawn as provided by Article 784 for examination as prospective trial jurors. Those who are impaneled as trial jurors shall serve as though regularly selected as tales jurors. Those who are not selected as trial jurors shall be ordered to report back to the division of court in which they were previously serving as petit jury veniremen.

B. In all other instances, except as provided in Article 409.1 of this code, when the petit jury venire is or is about to be exhausted before a trial jury is impaneled, the judge may order the secretary of the jury commission or the clerk of court to draw indiscriminately and by lot such number of tales jurors from the general venire box as in the opinion of the court may be necessary to complete the impaneling of the trial jury.

C. Immediately after the drawing of tales jurors, they shall be summoned to attend court at such time as the court may direct, and shall be subject to the same duties as petit jurors.

D. In parishes other than Orleans, the judge may order the summoning of tales jurors from among the bystanders or persons in or about the courthouse, in place of the drawing of tales jurors.

E. When called, tales jurors shall be selected for completion of the panel in accordance with Article 784.

Art. 786. Examination of jurors.

The court, the state, and the defendant shall have the right to examine prospective jurors. The scope of the examination shall be within the discretion of the court. A prospective juror, before being examined, shall be sworn to answer truthfully questions asked him relative to his qualifications to serve as a juror in the case.

Art. 787. Disqualification of petit jurors in particular cases.

The court may disqualify a prospective petit juror from service in a particular case when for any reason doubt exists as to the competency of the prospective juror to serve in the case.

Art. 788. Tendering jurors.

A. After the examination provided by Article 786, a prospective juror may be tendered first to the state, which shall accept or challenge him. If the state accepts the prospective juror, he shall be tendered to the defendant, who shall accept or challenge him. When a prospective juror is accepted by the state and the defendant, he shall be sworn immediately as a juror. This Article is subject to the provisions of Articles 795 and 796.

B. If the court does not require tendering of jurors, it shall by local rule provide for a system of simultaneous exercise of challenges.

Art. 789. Alternate jurors.

A. The court may direct that not more than six jurors in addition to the regular panel be called and impaneled to sit as alternate jurors. Alternate jurors, in the order in which they are called, shall replace jurors who become unable to perform or disqualified from performing their duties. Alternate jurors shall be drawn in the same manner, shall have the same qualifications, shall be subject to the same examination and challenges for cause, shall take the same oath, and shall have the same functions, powers, facilities, and privileges as the principal jurors. If the court determines that alternate jurors are desirable in the case, the court shall determine the number to be chosen. The regular peremptory challenges allowed by law shall not be used against the alternate jurors. The court shall determine how many additional peremptory challenges shall be allowed, and each defendant shall have an equal number of such challenges. The state shall have as many peremptory challenges as the defense. The additional peremptory challenges may be used only against alternate jurors. Except in capital cases, an alternate juror who does not replace a principal juror may be discharged when the jury retires to consider its verdict.

B. In a capital case, at the conclusion of the guilt phase of the trial, alternate jurors that have not replaced principal jurors shall not be discharged, but shall be sequestered from other members of the jury until the jury has reached a verdict. If a sentencing hearing is mandated, the alternate jurors will be returned to the jury and will hear the evidence presented at the sentencing hearing and will be available to replace principal jurors.

C. If the court, as provided in Paragraph A, replaces a principal juror with an alternate juror after deliberations have begun, the court shall order the jury to begin deliberations anew. *(Chgd. by Acts 1995 No. 364, §1, No. 1273, §1, eff. 8/15/95.)*

Art. 790. Swearing of jurors.

When selection of jurors and alternate jurors has been completed, and all issues properly raised under Article 795 have been resolved, the jurors shall then be sworn together to try the case in a just and impartial manner, each to the best of his judgment, and to render a verdict according to the law and the evidence. *(Chgd. by Acts 1990 No. 524, §1, eff. 9/7/90.)*

Art. 791. Sequestration of jurors and jury.

A. A jury is sequestered by being kept together in the charge of an officer of the court so as to be secluded from outside communication, except as permitted by R.S. 18:1307.2.

B. *(As amended by Acts 1995 No. 1277, §1. See other subsection B below.)* (1) In capital cases, after each juror is sworn he shall be sequestered, unless the state and the defense have jointly moved that the jury not be sequestered.

B. *(As amended by Acts 1995 No. 1172, §1. See other subsection B above.)* (1) In capital cases, after each juror is sworn he shall be sequestered, unless the court grants a joint state and defense motion that the jury not be sequestered.

(2) When the court grants the state and defense motion as provided for in Subparagraph (1) of this Paragraph, the jury shall be sequestered after the court's charge until the completion of the sentencing hearing. The jury may be sequestered at any time upon order of the court.

C. In noncapital cases, the jury shall be sequestered after the court's charge and may be sequestered at any time upon order of the court.
(Chgd. by Acts 1995 No. 1172, §1, No. 1277, §1, eff. 8/15/95.)

Art. 792. Selection of foreman.

When the jury has retired, the jurors shall select a foreman who shall preside over their deliberations and sign the verdict.

Art. 793. Use of evidence in jury room; reading of recorded testimony.

A juror must rely upon his memory in reaching a verdict. He shall not be permitted to refer to notes or to have access to any written evidence. Testimony shall not be repeated to the jury. Upon the request of a juror and in the discretion of the court, the jury may take with it or have sent to it any object or document received in evidence when a physical examination thereof is required to enable the jury to arrive at a verdict.

Art. 794. Removal of jury.

A. The court may, and at the request of the state or a defendant shall, remove the jury from the courtroom when the court hears matters to be decided by the court alone. The court may remove the jury from the courtroom at any time when considered in the best interest of justice.

B. The removal of the jury when the court is asked to make rulings on evidentiary matters is controlled by the Louisiana Code of Evidence.

SECTION 2. CHALLENGES

Art. 795. Time for challenges; method; racially based peremptory challenges; restrictions.

A. A juror shall not be challenged for cause after having been temporarily accepted pursuant to Paragraph A of Article 788 unless the challenging party shows that the cause was not known to him prior to that time.

B. (1) Peremptory challenges shall be exercised prior to the swearing of the jury panel.

(2) Peremptory challenges of jurors shall be made and communicated to the court in a side bar conference of the judge, the attorneys conducting the examination and selection of jurors, and the defendant in a case in which the defendant chooses to represent himself. The conference shall be conducted in a manner that only the court, the attorneys, and the defendant in a case in which the defendant chooses to represent himself, are aware of the challenges made until the court announces the challenges without reference to any party or attorney in the case.

C. No peremptory challenge made by the state or the defendant shall be based solely upon the race of the juror. If an objection is made that the state or defense has excluded a juror solely on the basis of race, and a prima facie case supporting that objection is made by the objecting party, the court may demand a satisfactory racially neutral reason for the exercise of the challenge, unless the court is satisfied that such reason is apparent from the voir dire examination of the juror. Such demand and disclosure, if required by the court, shall be made outside of the hearing of any juror or prospective juror.

D. The court shall allow to stand each peremptory challenge exercised for a racially neutral reason either apparent from the examination or disclosed by counsel when required by the court. The provisions of Subsection C and this Subsection shall not apply when both the state and the defense have exercised a challenge against the same juror.

E. The court shall allow to stand each peremptory challenge for which a satisfactory racially neutral reason is given. Those jurors who have been peremptorily challenged and for whom no satisfactory racially neutral reason is apparent or given may be ordered returned to the panel, or the court may take such other corrective action as it deems appropriate under the circumstances. The court shall make specific findings regarding each such challenge.

(Chgd. by Acts 1990 No. 547, §1, No. 713, §1; Acts 1993 No. 1019, §1, eff. 8/15/93.)

Art. 796. Removal of juror after swearing.

If it is discovered after a juror has been accepted and sworn, that he is incompetent to serve, the court may, at any time before the first witness is sworn, order the juror removed and the panel completed in the ordinary course.

Art. 797. Challenge for cause.

The state or the defendant may challenge a juror for cause on the ground that:

(1) The juror lacks a qualification required by law;

(2) The juror is not impartial, whatever the cause of his partiality. An opinion or impression as to the guilt or innocence of the defendant shall not of itself be sufficient ground of challenge to a juror, if he declares, and the court is satisfied, that he can render an impartial verdict according to the law and the evidence;

(3) The relationship, whether by blood, marriage, employment, friendship, or enmity between the juror and the defendant, the person injured by the offense, the district attorney, or defense counsel, is such that it is reasonable to conclude that it would influence the juror in arriving at a verdict;

(4) The juror will not accept the law as given to him by the court; or

(5) The juror served on the grand jury that found the indictment, or on a petit jury that once tried the defendant for the same or any other offense.

Art. 798. Causes for challenge by the state.

It is good cause for challenge on the part of the state, but not on the part of the defendant, that:

(1) The juror is biased against the enforcement of the statute charged to have been violated, or is of the fixed opinion that the statute is invalid or unconstitutional;

(2) The juror tendered in a capital case who has conscientious scruples against the infliction of capital punishment and makes it known:

(a) That he would automatically vote against the imposition of capital punishment without regard to any evidence that might be developed at the trial of the case before him;

(b) That his attitude toward the death penalty would prevent or substantially impair him from making an impartial decision as a juror in accordance with his instructions and his oath; or

(c) That his attitude toward the death penalty would prevent him from making an impartial decision as to the defendant's guilt; or

(3) The juror would not convict upon circumstantial evidence.

(Chgd. by Acts 1990 No. 366, §1, eff. 9/7/90.)

Art. 799. Number of peremptory challenges.

In trials of offenses punishable by death or necessarily by imprisonment at hard labor, each defendant shall have twelve peremptory challenges, and the state twelve for each defendant. In all other cases, each defendant shall have six peremptory challenges, and the state six for each defendant.

Art. 800. Objection to ruling on challenge for cause.

A. A defendant may not assign as error a ruling refusing to sustain a challenge for cause made by him, unless an objection thereto is made at the time of the ruling. The nature of the objection and grounds therefor shall be stated at the time of objection.

B. The erroneous allowance to the state of a challenge for cause does not afford the defendant a ground for complaint, unless the effect of such ruling is the exercise by the state of more peremptory challenges than it is entitled to by law.

SECTION 3. CHARGING THE JURY

Art. 801. Time for charge; when written charge required.

The court shall charge the jury after the presentation of all evidence and arguments. The court shall reduce its charge to writing if it is requested to do so by either a defendant or the state prior to the swearing of the first witness at the trial on the merits. The court's written charge shall be read to the jury. The court shall deliver a copy thereof to the defendant and to the state prior to reading it to the jury.

A party may not assign as error the giving or failure to give a jury charge or any portion thereof unless an objection thereto is made before the jury retires or within such time as the court may reasonably cure the alleged error. The nature of the objection and grounds therefor shall be stated at the time of objection. The court shall give the party an opportunity to make the objection out of the presence of the jury.

Art. 802. General charge; scope.

The court shall charge the jury:

(1) As to the law applicable to the case;

(2) That the jury is the judge of the law and of the facts on the question of guilt or innocence, but that it has the duty to accept and to apply the law as given by the court; and

(3) That the jury alone shall determine the weight and credibility of the evidence.

Art. 803. Same; charge as to included minor offenses and plea of insanity.

When a count in an indictment sets out an offense which includes other offenses of which the accused could be found guilty under the provisions of Article 814 or 815, the court shall charge the jury as to the law applicable to each offense.

When a defendant has specially pleaded insanity in accordance with Article 552, the court shall charge the jury with respect to the law applicable thereto.

Art. 804. Same; charge as to presumption of innocence, reasonable doubt, and several grades of offense.

A. In all cases the court shall charge the jury that:

(1) A person accused of crime is presumed by law to be innocent until each element of the crime, necessary to constitute his guilt, is proven beyond a reasonable doubt;

(2) It is the duty of the jury, in considering the evidence and in applying to that evidence the law as given by the court, to give the defendant the benefit of every reasonable doubt arising out of the evidence or out of the lack of evidence in the case; and

(3) It is the duty of the jury if not convinced of the guilt of a defendant beyond a reasonable doubt, to find him not guilty.

The court may, but is not required to, define "the presumption of innocence" or "reasonable doubt" or give any other or further charge upon the same than that contained in this article.

B. When there are several grades of an offense contained in a single count, the court shall charge the jury as to each grade of which the defendant could be found guilty. The court shall in that case also charge the jury that if it has a reasonable doubt as to any or all grades of the offense charged it shall find the defendant not guilty of that grade, or all grades of the offense, as the case may be.

Art. 805. Same; charge as to verdict acquitting on account of insanity.

The court shall charge the jury that if it acquits a defendant on account of a plea of insanity it shall state that the defendant was found not guilty by reason of insanity.

Art. 806. Prohibited charges.

The court shall not charge the jury concerning the facts of the case and shall not comment upon the facts of the case, either by commenting upon or recapitulating the evidence, repeating the testimony of any witness, or giving an opinion as to what has been proved, not proved, or refuted.

Art. 807. Special written charges.

The state and the defendant shall have the right before argument to submit to the court special written charges for the jury. Such charges may be received by the court in its discretion after argument has begun. The party submitting the charges shall furnish a copy of the charges to the other party when the charges are submitted to the court.

A requested special charge shall be given by the court if it does not require qualification, limitation, or explanation, and if it is wholly correct and pertinent. It need not be given if it is included in the general charge or in another special charge to be given.

Art. 808. Manner of giving further charges after jury retires.

If the jury or any member thereof, after having retired to deliberate upon the verdict, desires further charges, the officer in charge shall bring the jury into the courtroom, and the court shall in the presence of the defendant, his counsel, and the district attorney, further charge the jury. The further charge may be verbal.

CHAPTER 4. VERDICTS

Art. 809. Judge to give jury written list of responsive verdicts.

After charging the jury, the judge shall give the jury a written list of the verdicts responsive to each offense charged, with each separately stated. The list shall be taken into the jury room for use by the jury during its deliberation.

Art. 810. Form of verdict; delivery of verdict.

When a verdict has been agreed upon, the foreman shall write the verdict on the back of the list of responsive verdicts given to the jury and shall sign it. There shall be no formal requirement as to the language of the verdict except that it shall clearly convey the intention of the jury.

The foreman of the jury shall deliver the verdict to the judge in open court.

Art. 811. Receipt and recordation of verdict.

If the verdict is correct in form and responsive to the indictment, the court shall order the clerk to receive the verdict, to read it to the jury, and to ask: "Is that your verdict?" If the jury answer "Yes," the court shall order the clerk to record the verdict and shall discharge the jury.

Art. 812. Same; polling and disposition of jury.

The court shall order the clerk to poll the jury if requested by the state or the defendant. It shall be within the discretion of the court whether such poll shall be conducted orally or in writing by applying the procedures of Paragraph (1) or Paragraph (2) of this Article.

(1) Oral polling of the jury shall consist of the clerk's calling each juror, one at a time, by name. He shall announce to each juror the verdict returned, and ask him, "Is this your verdict?" Upon receiving the juror's answer to the question, the clerk shall record the answer.

If, upon polling all of the jurors, the number of jurors required by law to find a verdict answer "Yes," the court shall order the clerk to record the verdict and the jury shall be discharged. If, upon polling all of the jurors, the number required to find a verdict do not answer "Yes," the jury may be remanded for further deliberation, or the court may declare a mistrial in accordance with Article 775.

(2) The procedure for the written polling of the jury shall require that the clerk hand to each juror a separate piece of paper containing the name of the juror and the words "Is this your verdict?" Each juror shall write on the slip of paper the words "Yes" or "No" along with his signature. The clerk shall collect the slips of paper, make them available for inspection by the court and counsel, and record the results. If a sufficient number of jurors as required by law to reach a verdict answer "yes" the clerk shall so inform the court. Upon verification of the results, the court shall order the clerk to record the verdict and order the jury discharged. If an insufficient number required to find a verdict answer "Yes," the court may remand the jury for further deliberation, or the court may declare a mistrial in accordance with Article 775.

Art. 813. Improper verdict; procedure.

If the court finds that the verdict is incorrect in form or is not responsive to the indictment, it shall refuse to receive it, and shall remand the jury with the necessary oral instructions. In such a case the court shall read the verdict, and record the reasons for refusal.

Art. 814. Responsive verdicts; in particular.

A. The only responsive verdicts which may be rendered when the indictment charges the following offenses are:

1. FIRST DEGREE MURDER:
   Guilty.
   Guilty of second degree murder.
   Guilty of manslaughter.
   Not guilty.

2. ATTEMPTED FIRST DEGREE MURDER:
   Guilty.
   Guilty of attempted second degree murder.
   Guilty of attempted manslaughter.
   Guilty of aggravated battery.
   Not guilty.

3. SECOND DEGREE MURDER:
   Guilty.
   Guilty of manslaughter.
   Not guilty.

4. ATTEMPTED SECOND DEGREE MURDER:
   Guilty.
   Guilty of attempted manslaughter.
   Guilty of aggravated battery.
   Not guilty.

5. MANSLAUGHTER:
   Guilty.
   Not guilty.

6. ATTEMPTED MANSLAUGHTER:
   Guilty.
   Guilty of aggravated battery.
   Not guilty.

7. NEGLIGENT HOMICIDE:
   Guilty.
   Not guilty.

7.1. VEHICULAR HOMICIDE:
   Guilty.
   Guilty of negligent homicide.
   Not guilty.

7.2. VEHICULAR NEGLIGENT INJURING:
   Guilty.
   Guilty of operating a vehicle while intoxicated.
   Not guilty.

7.3. FIRST DEGREE VEHICULAR NEGLIGENT INJURING:
   Guilty.
   Guilty of vehicular negligent injuring.
   Guilty of operating a vehicle while intoxicated.
   Not guilty.

8. AGGRAVATED RAPE:
   Guilty.
   Guilty of attempted aggravated rape.
   Guilty of forcible rape.
   Guilty of attempted forcible rape.
   Guilty of sexual battery.
   Guilty of simple rape.
   Guilty of attempted simple rape.
   Not guilty.

9. ATTEMPTED AGGRAVATED RAPE:
Guilty.
Guilty of attempted forcible rape.
Guilty of attempted simple rape.
Not guilty.

10. FORCIBLE RAPE:
Guilty.
Guilty of attempted forcible rape.
Guilty of simple rape.
Guilty of attempted simple rape.
Guilty of sexual battery.
Not guilty.

11. ATTEMPTED FORCIBLE RAPE:
Guilty.
Guilty of attempted simple rape.
Not Guilty.

12. SIMPLE RAPE:
Guilty.
Guilty of attempted simple rape.
Guilty of sexual battery.
Not guilty.

13. ATTEMPTED SIMPLE RAPE:
Guilty.
Not guilty.

14. AGGRAVATED BATTERY:
Guilty.
Guilty of second degree battery.
Guilty of simple battery.
Not guilty.

14.1. DISARMING OF A PEACE OFFICER:
Guilty.
Guilty of attempted disarming of a peace officer.
Guilty of battery of a police officer.
Guilty of aggravated assault.
Not guilty.

15. SECOND DEGREE BATTERY:
Guilty.
Guilty of simple battery.
Not guilty.

15.1. VEHICULAR NEGLIGENT INJURING:
Guilty.
Not guilty.

16. AGGRAVATED ASSAULT:
Guilty.
Guilty of simple assault.
Not guilty.

17. SIMPLE BATTERY:
Guilty.
Not guilty.

18. AGGRAVATED KIDNAPPING:
Guilty.
Guilty of attempted aggravated kidnapping.
Guilty of second degree kidnapping.
Guilty of attempted second degree kidnapping.
Guilty of simple kidnapping.

Guilty of attempted simple kidnapping.
Not guilty.

19. ATTEMPTED AGGRAVATED KIDNAPPING:
Guilty.
Guilty of attempted second degree kidnapping.
Guilty of attempted simple kidnapping.
Not guilty.

20. SIMPLE KIDNAPPING:
Guilty.
Guilty of attempted simple kidnapping.
Not guilty.

21. ATTEMPTED SIMPLE KIDNAPPING:
Guilty.
Not guilty.

22. ARMED ROBBERY:
Guilty.
Guilty of attempted armed robbery.
Guilty of first degree robbery.
Guilty of attempted first degree robbery.
Guilty of simple robbery.
Guilty of attempted simple robbery.
Not guilty.

23. ATTEMPTED ARMED ROBBERY:
Guilty.
Guilty of attempted first degree robbery.
Guilty of attempted simple robbery.
Not guilty.

23.1. FIRST DEGREE ROBBERY:
Guilty.
Guilty of attempted first degree robbery.
Guilty of simple robbery.
Guilty of attempted simple robbery.
Not guilty.

24. SIMPLE ROBBERY:
Guilty.
Guilty of attempted simple robbery.
Not guilty.

25. ATTEMPTED SIMPLE ROBBERY:
Guilty.
Not guilty.

26. THEFT:
Guilty of theft of property having a value of five hundred dollars or more.
Guilty of theft of property having a value of one hundred dollars or more, but less than five hundred dollars.
Guilty of theft of property having a value of less than one hundred dollars.
Guilty of attempted theft of property having a value of one hundred dollars or more.
Guilty of attempted theft of property having a value of less than one hundred dollars.
Guilty of unauthorized use of movables having a value in excess of one thousand dollars, but only if a value in excess of one thousand dollars is stated in the indictment.
Guilty of unauthorized use of movables having a value of one thousand dollars or less.
Not guilty.

27. ATTEMPTED THEFT:
Guilty of attempted theft of property having a value of one hundred dollars or more.
Guilty of attempted theft of property having a value of less than one hundred dollars.
Guilty of attempted unauthorized use of movables having a value of less than one hundred dollars.
Guilty of attempted unauthorized use of movables having a value in excess of one thousand dollars, but only if a value in excess of one thousand dollars is stated in the indictment.
Guilty of attempted unauthorized use of movables having a value of one thousand dollars or less.
Not guilty.

28. THEFT OF CATTLE, HORSES, MULES, SHEEP, HOGS, OR GOATS:
Guilty.
Guilty of attempted theft of cattle, horses, mules, sheep, hogs, or goats.
Not guilty.

29. ATTEMPTED THEFT OF CATTLE, HORSES, MULES, SHEEP, HOGS, OR GOATS:
Guilty.
Not guilty.

30. AGGRAVATED ARSON:
Guilty.
Guilty of simple arson where the damage amounted to five hundred dollars or more.
Guilty of simple arson where the damage amounted to less than five hundred dollars.

The simple arson verdicts are responsive only if the words "belonging to another and with damage amounting to ______ dollars" are included in the indictment.

Not guilty.

31. ATTEMPTED AGGRAVATED ARSON:
Guilty.
Guilty of attempted simple arson where the damage would have amounted to five hundred dollars or more.
Guilty of attempted simple arson where the damage would have amounted to less than five hundred dollars.

The attempted simple arson verdicts are responsive only if the words "belonging to another and with damage that would have amounted to ______ dollars" are included in the indictment.

Not guilty.

32. SIMPLE ARSON:
Guilty of simple arson where the damage done amounted to five hundred dollars or more.
Guilty of simple arson where the damage done amounted to less than five hundred dollars.
Not guilty.

33. ATTEMPTED SIMPLE ARSON:
Guilty of attempted arson where the damage would have amounted to five hundred dollars or more.
Guilty of attempted simple arson where the damage would have amounted to less than five hundred dollars.
Not guilty.

34. ARSON WITH INTENT TO DEFRAUD:
Guilty.
Not guilty.

35. ATTEMPTED ARSON WITH INTENT TO DEFRAUD:
Guilty.
Not guilty.

36. AGGRAVATED CRIMINAL DAMAGE TO PROPERTY:
Guilty.
Guilty of simple criminal damage to property where the damage amounted to fifty thousand dollars or more.
Guilty of simple criminal damage to property where the damage amounted to five hundred dollars or more, but less than fifty thousand dollars.
Guilty of simple criminal damage to property where the damage amounted to less than five hundred dollars.

The simple criminal damage to property verdicts are responsive only if the words "belonging to another and with damage amounting to ______ dollars" are included in the indictment.

Not guilty.

37. ATTEMPTED AGGRAVATED CRIMINAL DAMAGE TO PROPERTY:
Guilty.
Guilty of attempted simple criminal damage to property where the damage would have amounted to fifty thousand dollars or more.
Guilty of attempted simple criminal damage to property where the damage would have amounted to five hundred dollars or more, but less than fifty thousand dollars.
Guilty of attempted simple criminal damage to property where the damage would have amounted to less than five hundred dollars.

The attempted simple criminal damage to property verdicts are responsive only if the words "belonging to another and with damage that would have amounted to ______ dollars" are included in the indictment.

Not guilty.

38. SIMPLE CRIMINAL DAMAGE TO PROPERTY:
Guilty of simple criminal damage to property where the damage done amounted to fifty thousand dollars or more.
Guilty of simple criminal damage to property where the damage done amounted to five hundred dollars or more, but less than fifty thousand dollars.
Guilty of simple criminal damage to property where the damage done amounted to less than five hundred dollars.
Not guilty.

39. ATTEMPTED SIMPLE CRIMINAL DAMAGE TO PROPERTY:
Guilty of attempted simple criminal damage to property where the damage would have amounted to five hundred dollars or more, but less than fifty thousand dollars.
Guilty of attempted simple criminal damage to property where the damage would have amounted to less than five hundred dollars.
Not guilty.

40. DAMAGE TO PROPERTY WITH INTENT TO DEFRAUD:
Guilty.
Not guilty.

41. ATTEMPTED DAMAGE TO PROPERTY WITH INTENT TO DEFRAUD:
Guilty.
Not guilty.

42. AGGRAVATED BURGLARY:
Guilty.
Guilty of attempted aggravated burglary.
Guilty of simple burglary.
Guilty of attempted simple burglary.
Guilty of simple burglary of an inhabited dwelling.

Guilty of attempted simple burglary of an inhabited dwelling.
Guilty of unauthorized entry of an inhabited dwelling.
Guilty of attempted unauthorized entry of an inhabited dwelling.
Not guilty.

43. ATTEMPTED AGGRAVATED BURGLARY:
Guilty.
Guilty of attempted simple burglary.
Guilty of attempted simple burglary of an inhabited dwelling.
Guilty of attempted unauthorized entry of an inhabited dwelling.
Not guilty.

44. SIMPLE BURGLARY:
Guilty.
Guilty of attempted simple burglary.
Guilty of unauthorized entry of a place of business.
Guilty of attempted unauthorized entry of a place of business.
Not guilty.

44.1. SIMPLE BURGLARY OF AN INHABITED DWELLING:
Guilty.
Guilty of attempted simple burglary of an inhabited dwelling.
Guilty of unauthorized entry of an inhabited dwelling.
Guilty of attempted unauthorized entry of an inhabited dwelling.
Not guilty.

45. ATTEMPTED SIMPLE BURGLARY:
Guilty.
Not guilty.

45.1. AGGRAVATED FLIGHT FROM AN OFFICER:
Guilty.
Guilty of flight from an officer.
Not guilty.

46. CONTAMINATION OF WATER SUPPLIES:
Guilty of contaminating water supplies when the act foreseeably endangered the life or health of human beings.
Guilty of contaminating water supplies when the act did not foreseeably endanger the life or health of human beings.
Not guilty.

47. ATTEMPTED CONTAMINATION OF WATER SUPPLIES:
Guilty of attempted contamination of water supplies when the act would foreseeably endanger the life or health of human beings.
Guilty of attempted contamination of water supplies when the act would not foreseeably endanger the life or health of human beings.
Not guilty.

48. PRODUCTION, MANUFACTURE, DISTRIBUTION OR DISPENSATION OF CONTROLLED DANGEROUS SUBSTANCES:
Guilty.
Guilty of attempted production, manufacture, distribution or dispensation of controlled dangerous substances.
Guilty of possession of controlled dangerous substances.
Guilty of attempted possession of controlled dangerous substances.
Not guilty.

49. POSSESSION OF CONTROLLED DANGEROUS SUBSTANCES WITH INTENT TO PRODUCE, MANUFACTURE, DISTRIBUTE, OR DISPENSE:
Guilty.
Guilty of attempted possession of controlled dangerous substances with intent to produce, manufacture, distribute or dispense.
Guilty of possession of controlled dangerous substances.

Guilty of attempted possession of controlled dangerous substances.
Not guilty.

50. POSSESSION OF CONTROLLED DANGEROUS SUBSTANCES:
Guilty.
Guilty of attempted possession of controlled dangerous substances.
Not guilty.

51. ATTEMPTED PRODUCTION OR MANUFACTURE OF CONTROLLED DANGEROUS SUBSTANCES:
Guilty.
Guilty of attempted possession of controlled dangerous substances.
Not guilty.

52. ATTEMPTED DISTRIBUTION OR DISPENSATION OF CONTROLLED DANGEROUS SUBSTANCES:
Guilty.
Guilty of possession of controlled dangerous substances.
Guilty of attempted possession of controlled dangerous substances.
Not guilty.

53. ATTEMPTED POSSESSION OF CONTROLLED DANGEROUS SUBSTANCES WITH INTENT TO PRODUCE, MANUFACTURE, DISTRIBUTE OR DISPENSE:
Guilty.
Guilty of attempted possession of controlled dangerous substances.
Not guilty.

54. CREATION OR DISTRIBUTION OF COUNTERFEIT CONTROLLED DANGEROUS SUBSTANCES:
Guilty.
Guilty of attempted creation or distribution of counterfeit controlled dangerous substances.
Not guilty.

55. POSSESSION OF COUNTERFEIT CONTROLLED DANGEROUS SUBSTANCES WITH INTENT TO DISTRIBUTE:
Guilty.
Guilty of attempted possession of counterfeit controlled dangerous substances with intent to distribute.
Not guilty.

56. ATTEMPTED CREATION, DISTRIBUTION, OR POSSESSION OF COUNTERFEIT CONTROLLED DANGEROUS SUBSTANCES WITH INTENT TO DISTRIBUTE:
Guilty.
Not guilty.

57. CONSPIRACY TO VIOLATE ANY PROVISION OF THE UNIFORM CONTROLLED DANGEROUS SUBSTANCES LAW*:
Guilty.
Not guilty.

58. CRUELTY TO THE INFIRM:
Guilty.
Guilty of attempted cruelty to the infirm.
Guilty of simple battery.
Guilty of assault.
Guilty of negligent injuring.
Not guilty.

B. Except as provided in Subarticle A, responsive verdicts in any other cases arising under the Uniform Controlled Dangerous Substances Law shall be governed by Article 815 of the Code of Criminal Procedure.

C. Upon motion of the state or the defendant, or on its own motion, the court shall exclude a responsive verdict listed in Paragraph A if, after all the evidence has been submitted, the evidence, viewed in a light most favorable to the state, is not sufficient reasonably to permit a finding of guilty of the responsive offense.

D. Where an offense is graded according to property value or amount of damage, the responsive verdicts shall not include a grade of the offense that is greater than the property value or amount of damage charged in the indictment.

(Chgd. by Acts 1991 No. 465, §1; Acts 1992 No. 307, §1; Acts 1995 No. 403, §2; Acts 1997 No. 400, §1, No. 558, §1, No. 865, §1, eff. 8/15/97.)

**R.S. 40:961 et seq.*

Art. 815. Responsive verdicts; in general.

In all cases not provided for in Article 814, the following verdicts are responsive:

(1) Guilty;

(2) Guilty of a lesser and included grade of the offense even though the offense charged is a felony, and the lesser offense a misdemeanor; or

(3) Not Guilty.

Art. 816. Verdict acquitting on account of insanity.

In addition to the responsive verdicts in Articles 814 and 815, a verdict of not guilty by reason of insanity is responsive if a defendant has specially pleaded insanity in accordance with Article 552.

Art. 817. Qualifying verdicts.

Any qualification of or addition to a verdict of guilty, beyond a specification of the offense as to which the verdict is found, is without effect upon the finding.

Art. 818. Separate verdict for each defendant.

If there is more than one defendant on trial, the verdict shall name each defendant and the finding as to him.

Art. 819. Separate verdict for each count.

If there is more than one count in an indictment, the jury must find a verdict as to each count, unless it cannot agree on a verdict as to a count.

Art. 820. Application of chapter to cases tried without a jury.

All provisions of this Chapter regulating the responsiveness and effect of verdicts shall apply to cases tried without a jury.

Art. 821. Motion for post verdict judgment of acquittal.

A. The defendant may move for a post verdict judgment of acquittal following the verdict. A motion for a post verdict judgment of acquittal must be made and disposed of before sentence.

B. A post verdict judgment of acquittal shall be granted only if the court finds that the evidence, viewed in a light most favorable to the state, does not reasonably permit a finding of guilty.

C. If the court finds that the evidence, viewed in a light most favorable to the state, supports only a conviction of a lesser included responsive offense, the court, in lieu of granting a post verdict judgment of acquittal, may modify the verdict and render a judgment of conviction on the lesser included responsive offense.

D. If a post verdict judgment of acquittal is granted or if a verdict is modified, the state may seek review by invoking the supervisory jurisdiction of or by appealing to the appropriate appellate court.

E. If the appellate court finds that the evidence, viewed in a light most favorable to the state, supports only a conviction of a lesser included responsive offense, the court, in lieu of granting a post verdict judgment of acquittal, may modify the verdict and render a judgment of conviction on the lesser included responsive offense.

Art. 822. Motion for amending or modifying sentence.

A. (1) Should the court on its own motion or on motion of the defendant consider setting aside a guilty verdict or a plea of guilty or, after the sentence is imposed, consider amending or modifying the sentence imposed, the district attorney shall be notified and the motion shall be tried contradictorily with the district attorney unless the district attorney waives such contradictory hearing.

(2) Such motions include but are not limited to motions for a new trial, motions in arrest of judgment, motions for amendment, modification, or reconsideration of sentence, and motions for modification of conditions of probation or termination of probation.

B. Additionally, if at any time after sentence is imposed, the defendant seeks the production of all or any portion of the district attorney's file in a criminal proceeding, the request for production shall be presented by written motion, which shall be tried contradictorily with the district attorney.

(Added by Acts 1997 No. 1321, §1, eff. 8/15/97.)

TITLE XXVII. PRESENCE OF DEFENDANT

Article

Art. 831. Presence of defendant when prosecution is for felony.

A. Except as may be provided by local rules of court in accordance with Articles 522 and 551, a defendant charged with a felony shall be present:

(1) At arraignment;

(2) When a plea of guilty, not guilty, or not guilty and not guilty by reason of insanity is made;

(3) At the calling, examination, challenging, impanelling, and swearing of the jury, and at any subsequent proceedings for the discharge of the jury or of a juror;

(4) At all times during the trial when the court is determining and ruling on the admissibility of evidence;

(5) In trials by jury, at all proceedings when the jury is present, and in trials without a jury, at all times when evidence is being adduced; and

(6) At the rendition of the verdict or judgment, unless he voluntarily absents himself.

B. Nothing in this Article shall prohibit the court, by local rule, from providing for a defendant's appearance at his arraignment by simultaneous audio-visual transmission, except when the defense counsel requests the defendant's appearance in open court.

(Chgd. by Acts 1990 No. 543, §1, No. 593, §1; Acts 1997 No. 1015, §1, eff. 8/15/97.)

Art. 832. Continued presence not required.

A. A defendant initially present for the commencement of trial shall not prevent the further progress of the trial, including the return of the verdict, and shall be considered to have waived his right to be present if his counsel is present or if the right to counsel has been waived and:

(1) He voluntarily absents himself after the trial has commenced, whether or not he has been informed by the court of his obligation to be present during the trial; or

(2) After being warned by the court that disruptive conduct will cause him to be removed from the courtroom, he persists in conduct which justifies his exclusion from the courtroom.

B. Nothing in this Article shall prohibit the court, by local rule, from providing for a defendant's appearance at his arraignment by simultaneous audio-visual transmission, except when the defense counsel requests the defendant's appearance in open court. Any appearance made by way of simultaneous audio-visual transmission under applicable local rules of court in accordance with the provisions of Article 551 shall not constitute absence for the purposes of this Article.

(Chgd. by Acts 1990 No. 543, §1, No. 593, §1; Acts 1997 No. 718, §1, eff. 8/15/97.)

Art. 833. Presence of defendant when prosecution is for misdemeanor.

A. The court may permit a defendant charged with a misdemeanor to be arraigned, plead guilty, or be tried, in his absence. Otherwise he must be present, provided that he may appear at arraignment by way of simultaneous audio-visual transmission under applicable local rules in accordance with the provisions of Articles 522 and 551.

B. A plea of not guilty of a misdemeanor may always be entered through counsel and in the absence of the defendant.

C. Nothing in this Article shall prohibit the court, by local rule, from providing for a defendant's appearance at his arraignment by simultaneous audio-visual transmission, except when the defense counsel requests the defendant's appearance in open court.

(Chgd. by Acts 1990 No. 543, §1, No. 593, §1; Acts 1997 No. 1015, §1, eff. 8/15/97.)

Art. 834. When presence of defendant not necessary.

The defendant has a right to be present, but his presence is not essential to the validity of any of the following proceedings in a criminal prosecution:

(1) The making, hearing of, or ruling on a preliminary motion or application addressed to the court;

(2) The making, hearing of, or ruling on a motion or application addressed to the court during the trial when the jury is not present; except as provided in Clause (4) of Article 831; and

(3) The making, hearing of, or ruling on a motion or application made after his conviction.

Art. 835. Presence of defendant at pronouncement of sentence.

In felony cases the defendant shall always be present when sentence is pronounced. In misdemeanor cases the defendant shall be present when sentence is pronounced, unless excused by the court. If a sentence is improperly pronounced in the defendant's absence, he shall be resentenced when his presence is secured.

Art. 836. Presence of corporation or association.

When a corporation, partnership, or other association is a defendant, the requirements of this Title are fulfilled if its counsel is present.

TITLE XXVIII. BILL OF EXCEPTIONS

Art. 841. Bill of exceptions unnecessary; objections required.

A. An irregularity or error cannot be availed of after verdict unless it was objected to at the time of occurrence. A bill of exceptions to rulings or orders is unnecessary. It is sufficient that a party, at the time the ruling or order of the court is made or sought, makes known to the court the action which he desires the court to take, or of his objections to the action of the court, and the grounds therefor.

B. The requirement of an objection shall not apply to the court's ruling on any written motion.

C. The necessity for and specificity of evidentiary objections are governed by the Louisiana Code of Evidence.

Art. 842. Codefendants; presumption as to objections.

If an objection has been made when more than one defendant is on trial, it shall be presumed, unless the contrary appears, that the objection has been made by all the defendants.

Art. 843. Recording of proceedings.

In felony cases, and on motion of the court, the state, or the defendant in misdemeanor cases tried in a district, parish, or city court, the clerk or court stenographer shall record all of the proceedings, including the examination of prospective jurors, the testimony of witnesses, statements, rulings, orders, and charges by the court, and objections, questions, statements, and arguments of counsel.

Art. 844. Assignment of errors; sanctions for failure to file timely.

A. The party appealing shall file with the appellate court a written designation of those errors which are to be urged on appeal and furnish a copy to the trial judge and all counsel. This assignment of errors shall be filed in accordance with the uniform rules of the appropriate appellate court.

B. If the appellant fails to comply with these provisions and fails to secure an extension in accordance with Article 916(1), the trial judge on his own motion or motion of the clerk or any party or upon referral by the appellate court and after hearing shall either:

(1) Extend the time within which the assignment of errors shall be filed.

(2) Impose a fine not to exceed five hundred dollars upon the appellant or his attorney or both if the failure is found by the court to be arbitrary and capricious.

C. If the record is not lodged in the appellate court within sixty days after the motion for the appeal is made or within the extended time granted by the proper court or if the record is lodged in the appellate court without an assignment of errors, the appellate court may adjudge the appellant, his attorney, or both guilty of contempt of court and impose a punishment authorized by law.

D. The trial judge may submit such per curiam comments as he desires.

(Chgd. by Acts 1997 No. 642, §1, eff. 8/15/97.)

TITLE XXIX. MOTIONS FOR NEW TRIAL AND IN ARREST OF JUDGMENT

Chapter

CHAPTER 1. MOTION FOR NEW TRIAL

Article

Art. 851. Grounds for new trial.

The motion for a new trial is based on the supposition that injustice has been done the defendant, and, unless such is shown to have been the case the motion shall be denied, no matter upon what allegations it is grounded.

The court, on motion of the defendant, shall grant a new trial whenever:

(1) The verdict is contrary to the law and the evidence;

(2) The court's ruling on a written motion, or an objection made during the proceedings, shows prejudicial error;

(3) New and material evidence that, notwithstanding the exercise of reasonable diligence by the defendant, was not discovered before or during the trial, is available, and if the evidence had been introduced at the trial it would probably have changed the verdict or judgment of guilty;

(4) The defendant has discovered, since the verdict or judgment of guilty, a prejudicial error or defect in the proceedings that, notwithstanding the exercise of reasonable diligence by the defendant, was not discovered before the verdict or judgment; or

(5) The court is of the opinion that the ends of justice would be served by the granting of a new trial, although the defendant may not be entitled to a new trial as a matter of strict legal right.

Art. 852. Form, content, and trial of motion for new trial.

A motion for a new trial shall be in writing, shall state the grounds upon which it is based, and shall be tried contradictorily with the district attorney.

Art. 853. Time for filing motion for new trial.

A motion for a new trial must be filed and disposed of before sentence. The court, on motion of the defendant and for good cause shown, may postpone the imposition of sentence for a specified period in order to give the defendant additional time to prepare and file a motion for a new trial.

When the motion for a new trial is based on ground (3) of Article 851, the motion may be filed within one year after verdict or judgment of the trial court, although a sentence has been imposed or a motion for a new trial has been previously filed; but if an appeal is pending the court may hear the motion only on remand of the case.

Art. 854. Newly discovered evidence; necessary allegations.

A motion for a new trial based on ground (3) of Article 851 shall contain allegations of fact, sworn to by the defendant or his counsel, showing:

(1) That notwithstanding the exercise of reasonable diligence by the defendant, the new evidence was not discovered before or during the trial;

(2) The names of the witnesses who will testify and a concise statement of the newly discovered evidence;

(3) The facts which the witnesses or evidence will establish; and

(4) That the witnesses or evidence are not beyond the process of the court, or are otherwise available.

The newly discovered whereabouts or residence of a witness do not constitute newly discovered evidence.

Art. 855. Errors discovered after verdict or judgment of guilty; necessary allegations.

A motion for a new trial based on ground (4) of Article 851 shall contain allegations of fact sworn to by the defendant or his counsel, showing:

(1) The specific nature of the error or defect complained of; and

(2) That, notwithstanding the exercise of reasonable diligence by the defense, the error or defect was not discovered before or during the trial.

Art. 856. Motion to urge all available grounds; exceptions.

A motion for a new trial shall urge all grounds known and available to the defendant at the time of the filing of the motion. However, the court may permit the defendant to supplement his original motion by urging an additional ground, or may permit the defendant to file an additional motion for a new trial, prior to the court's ruling on the motion.

Art. 857. Effect of granting new trial.

The effect of granting a new trial is to set aside the verdict or judgment and to permit retrial of the case with as little prejudice to either party as if it had never been tried.

Art. 858. Review of ruling on motion for new trial.

Neither the appellate nor supervisory jurisdiction of the supreme court may be invoked to review the granting or the refusal to grant a new trial, except for error of law.

CHAPTER 2. MOTION IN ARREST OF JUDGMENT

Article

Art. 859. Grounds for arrest of judgment.

The court shall arrest the judgment only on one or more of the following grounds:

(1) The indictment is substantially defective, in that an essential averment is omitted;

(2) The offense charged is not punishable under a valid statute;

(3) The court is without jurisdiction of the case;

(4) The tribunal that tried the case did not conform with the requirements of Articles 779, 780 and 782 of this code;

(5) The verdict is not responsive to the indictment, or is otherwise so defective that it will not form the basis of a valid judgment;

(6) Double jeopardy, if not previously urged; or

(7) The prosecution was not timely instituted, if not previously urged.

(8) The prosecution was for capital offense or for an offense punishable by life imprisonment, but was not instituted by a grand jury indictment.

Improper venue may not be urged by a motion in arrest of judgment.

Art. 860. Form, content, and trial of motion in arrest.

A motion in arrest of judgment shall be in writing, shall state the ground upon which it is based, and shall be tried contradictorily with the district attorney.

Art. 861. Time for filing motion in arrest.

A motion in arrest of judgment must be filed and disposed of before sentence. The court, on motion of the defendant and for cause shown, may postpone the imposition of sentence for a specified period in order to give the defense additional time to prepare and file a motion in arrest of judgment.

Art. 862. Effect of sustaining motion in arrest of judgment.

If the judgment is arrested because of a defect in the indictment, the indictment shall be dismissed and the defendant shall be discharged as to that indictment. However, a new indictment may be filed within the time limitation stated in Article 576.

If the judgment is arrested because the court is without jurisdiction of the case, the defendant shall be discharged, but may be tried by a court of proper jurisdiction.

If the judgment is arrested because the wrong type of tribunal tried the case, or because the verdict is not responsive to the indictment or is otherwise fatally defective, the defendant shall be remanded to custody or bail to await a new trial.

If the judgment is arrested on any other ground, the defendant shall be discharged.

TITLE XXX. SENTENCE

Chapter

CHAPTER 1. GENERAL SENTENCING PROVISIONS

Article

Art. 871. Sentence defined; pronouncing and recording of sentence; certification of conviction.

A. A sentence is the penalty imposed by the court on a defendant upon a plea of guilty, upon a verdict of guilty, or upon a judgment of guilt. Sentence shall be pronounced orally in open court and recorded in the minutes of the court.

B. (1)(a) In every judgment of guilty of a felony or of one of the misdemeanors enumerated in Subparagraph (2) of this Paragraph, the sheriff shall cause to be affixed to the bill of indictment or information the fingerprints of the defendant against whom such judgment is rendered.

(b) (i) Beneath such fingerprints shall be appended a certificate to the following effect:

"I hereby certify that the above and foregoing fingerprints on this bill are the fingerprints of the defendant, and that they were placed thereon by said defendant this ___ day of ___, ___."

(ii) The certificate shall be signed by the sheriff or other law enforcement officer who has custody of the defendant.

(2) In addition to judgments of guilty of a felony, the sheriff shall cause the fingerprints of the defendant to be so affixed for every judgment of guilty of the following misdemeanors:

(a) First or second offense operating a vehicle while intoxicated in violation of R.S. 14:98.

(b) First offense possession of marijuana, tetrahydrocannabinol, or chemical derivatives thereof, pursuant to a sentence imposed under R.S. 40:966(D)(1).

(c) A first or second offense involving drug paraphernalia pursuant to a sentence imposed under R.S. 40:1035(A) and (B).

(d) First or second offense theft pursuant to a sentence imposed under R.S. 14:67(B)(3) and first or second offense theft of goods pursuant to a sentence imposed under R.S. 14:67.10(B)(3).

(e) First offense prostitution pursuant to a sentence imposed under R.S. 14:82(B)(1).

C. The certificate required by Paragraph B of this Article shall be admissible in evidence in the courts of this state as prima facie evidence that the fingerprints appearing thereon are the fingerprints of the defendant against whom the judgment of guilty of a felony or one of the enumerated misdemeanors was rendered.

(Chgd. by Acts 1997 No. 852, §1, eff. 8/15/97.)

Art. 871.1. Sentencing orders to be sent to Louisiana Protective Order Registry.

If part of the sentence contains an order for the purpose of preventing violent or threatening acts or harassment against, contact or communication with, or physical proximity to, another person in order to prevent domestic violence, the judge shall cause to have prepared a Uniform Abuse Prevention Order, as provided in R.S. 46:2136.2(C), shall sign such order, and shall forward it to the clerk of court for filing, all without delay. The clerk of the issuing court shall transmit the Uniform Abuse Prevention Order to the Louisiana Protective Order Registry, R.S. 46:2136.2(A), by facsimile transmission, mail, or direct electronic input, where available, as expeditiously as possible, but no later than the end of the next business day after the order is filed with the clerk of court. *(Added by Acts 1997 No. 1156, §3, eff. 8/15/97.)*

Art. 872. Basis for valid sentence.

A valid sentence must rest upon a valid and sufficient:

(1) Statute;

(2) Indictment; and

(3) Verdict, judgment, or plea of guilty.

Art. 873. Delay between conviction and sentence.

If a defendant is convicted of a felony, at least three days shall elapse between conviction and sentence. If a motion for a new trial, or in arrest of judgment, is filed, sentence shall not be imposed until at least twenty-four hours after the motion is overruled. If the defendant expressly waives a delay provided for in this article or pleads guilty, sentence may be imposed immediately.

Art. 874. Prompt sentence required; relief by writs.

Sentence shall be imposed without unreasonable delay. If a defendant claims that the sentence has been unreasonably delayed, he may invoke the supervisory jurisdiction of the appellate court. *(Chgd. by Acts 1993 No. 975, §1, eff. 8/15/93.)*

Art. 875. Presentence investigation; juvenile records; drug screening.

A. (1) If a defendant is convicted of a felony offense or a misdemeanor offense that has been reduced from a felony, the court may order the Department of Public Safety and Corrections, division of probation and parole, to make a presentence investigation. All such reports shall be made within sixty days of conviction except that when the defendant is released on bond pending imposition of sentence, such reports shall be made within ninety days of conviction. In making the investigation, the probation officer shall inquire into the circumstances attending the commission of the offense, the defendant's history of delinquency or criminality, his family situation and background, economic and employment status, education, and personal habits.

(2) The probation officer shall also indicate specifically those resources available in the community which could provide needed assistance to the defendant should he be released on probation and shall inquire into other matters deemed relevant by the officer or ordered investigated by the court. The court may postpone imposition of sentence until the report is received.

(3) Local and state law enforcement agencies and mental and correctional institutions shall furnish to the probation officer criminal records and such other information and data as the probation officer requests. The court may order a physical and mental examination of the defendant.

B. If a defendant is convicted or pleads guilty to an offense involving a victim, the court shall require that a victim impact statement be included in the presentence report. The victim impact statement shall include factual information as to whether the victim or his family has suffered, as a result of the offense, any monetary loss, medical expense, physical impairment, and any other information deemed relevant. The district attorney may also file a victim impact statement with the court.

C. (1) The court may also make a written request of any juvenile court for an abstract containing only the delinquent acts of a convicted defendant currently before the requesting judge. The request shall be promptly complied with; provided, however, not more than ten days, exclusive of Saturdays, Sundays and legal holidays, shall lapse before the requested information is deposited in the mail, addressed to the requesting court. The court may postpone imposition of sentence until the report is received.

(2) The requesting court shall not copy, duplicate or otherwise reproduce such juvenile records, and these records shall be deposited in the mail and addressed to the issuing juvenile court within seventy-two hours, exclusive of Saturdays, Sundays and legal holidays, after sentencing.

(3) Failure to comply with the provisions of this Subsection shall subject the violating court to disciplinary action by the Supreme Court of Louisiana upon receipt by the judicial administrator of the supreme court of a written complaint, subsequently substantiated.

D. If the defendant is sentenced to imprisonment, a copy of the report* shall be transmitted by the division of probation and parole to the institution to which he is committed.
**So in original.*

E. (1) If a defendant is convicted of a second or subsequent violation of the Controlled Dangerous Substances Law* as provided in R.S. 40:982, the court may order that the

defendant submit to a chemical test to determine the presence or use of any controlled dangerous substance. The result of any such test shall be a part of the presentence investigation report.
**R.S. 40:961 et seq.*

(2) Any test so ordered shall be conducted at the cost of the defendant. The court's order shall include guidelines that will assure a test approved by the court and protection for the chain of custody for the test results.

(3) The test results shall be used exclusively by the court for guidance in determining the sentence or conditions of release of the defendant. Thereafter, the court shall order that this part of the record be sealed, to be opened pursuant only to court order. To this end, the test results shall not be duplicated by the court for any reason, provided that the defendant and his counsel shall have access to them prior to sentencing. Under no circumstances shall the information contained in the results be used as evidence or as the basis of any additional charge against the defendant.
(Chgd. by Acts 1990 No. 1028, §1, eff. 9/7/90.)

Art. 875.1. *(Repealed by Acts 1995 No. 942, §3, eff. 8/15/95.)*

Art. 876. Post-sentence investigation.

If a court has not ordered a presentence investigation in a felony case and has committed the offender to the Department of Public Safety and Corrections, the division of probation and parole within the office of adult services shall make a post-sentence investigation and report within sixty days from the date the sentence is imposed. The post-sentence investigation report shall be delivered to the sentencing judge and to the district attorney in order that each may supplement it with appropriate comments. The report shall then be forwarded to the officer in charge of the penal or correctional institution in which the convicted person is incarcerated and shall become a part of the records pertaining to that person. *(Added by Acts 1995 No. 942, §1, eff. 8/15/95. Former Article 876 repealed by Acts 1992 No. 300, §2, eff. 8/21/92.)*

Art. 877. Protection of investigation reports.

(As chgd. by Acts 1985 No. 200, §1 and Acts 1992 No. 300, §1. See other article 877 below.)

A. The presentence investigation report shall be privileged and shall not be disclosed directly or indirectly to anyone other than the sentencing court, members of the division of probation and parole within the office of adult services, the officer in charge of the institution to which the defendant is committed, the Board of Parole, the probation or the parole officer if the defendant is placed on probation or released on parole, medical authorities directly involved in the defendant's rehabilitation or treatment if the defendant is committed to a hospital or a substance abuse program, the Board of Pardons, and the governor or his representative.

B. Before imposing sentence the court may advise the defendant or his counsel of the factual contents and conclusions of any presentence investigation report. The sources of confidential information shall not, however, be disclosed.
(Chgd. by Acts 1992 No. 300, §1, eff. 8/21/92.)

Art. 877. Protection of investigation reports.

(As chgd. by Acts 1985 No. 384, §1 and Acts 1992 No. 300, §1. See other article 877 above.)

A. The presentence investigation report shall be privileged and shall not be disclosed directly or indirectly to anyone other than the sentencing court, members of the division of probation and parole within the office of adult supervision, the officer in charge of the institution to which the defendant is committed, the Board of Parole, the probation or the parole officer if the defendant is placed on probation or released on parole, medical authorities directly involved in the defendant's rehabilitation or treatment if the defendant is committed to a hospital or a substance abuse program, the Board of Pardons, and the governor or his representative.

B. Before imposing sentence the court may advise the defendant or his counsel of the factual contents and conclusions of any presentence investigation report. The sources of confidential information shall not, however, be disclosed. If the defendant contests any information contained in the presentence report, the court shall provide the district attorney the same access to the report as was given to the defendant or his counsel. The district attorney may respond to the defendant's contentions concerning the information in the presentence report.

C. The presentence investigation report, edited to protect sources of confidential information, shall be made a part of the record if the defendant seeks post-conviction relief only on the grounds of an excessive sentence imposed by the court.
(Chgd. by Acts 1992 No. 300, §1, eff. 8/21/92.)

Art. 878. Cruel or unusual punishment.

A sentence shall not be set aside on the ground that it inflicts cruel or unusual punishment unless the statute under which it is imposed is found unconstitutional.

Art. 879. Determinate sentence required.

If a defendant who has been convicted of an offense is sentenced to imprisonment, the court shall impose a determinate sentence.

Art. 880. Credit for prior custody.

A defendant shall receive credit toward service of his sentence for time spent in actual custody prior to the imposition of sentence. *(Chgd. by Acts 1997 No. 788, §1, eff. 8/15/97.)*

Art. 881. Amendment of sentence.

A. Although the sentence imposed is legal in every respect, the court may amend or change the sentence, within the legal limits of its discretion, prior to the beginning of execution of the sentence.

B. (1) After commencement of execution of sentence, in felony cases in which the defendant has been sentenced to imprisonment without hard labor and in misdemeanor cases, the sentencing judge may reduce the sentence or may amend the sentence to place the defendant on supervised probation. Should the court consider any motion amending or changing the sentence imposed, either prior to or after execution of the sentence, the district attorney shall be notified and, if such motion is filed by the defendant, it shall be tried contradictorily with the district attorney, unless the district attorney waives such contradictory hearing.

(2) Such motions include but are not limited to motions for a new trial, motions in arrest of judgment, motions for amendment, modification, or reconsideration of sentence, and motions for modification of conditions of probation or termination of probation.

(3) If a sentence is reduced or amended, a copy of the minute entry reflecting the judgment reducing or amending the sentence shall be furnished to the district attorney and the arresting law enforcement agency.

C. If the sentence imposed by the court is consecutive to a sentence imposed in a different criminal proceeding, for purposes of this Article only, commencement of the execution of sentence begins when the defendant is remanded by the sentencing court to the Department of Public Safety and Corrections, to begin serving either the imposed sentence or a prior sentence to which the imposed sentence is consecutive.
(Chgd. by Acts 1997 No. 1321, §1, eff. 8/15/97.)

Art. 881.1. Motion to reconsider sentence.

A. (1) Within thirty days following the imposition of sentence or within such longer period as the trial court may set at sentence, the state or the defendant may make or file a motion to reconsider sentence.

(2) The motion shall be oral at the time of sentencing or in writing thereafter and shall set forth the specific grounds on which the motion is based.

B. If a motion is made or filed under Paragraph A of this Article, the trial court may resentence the defendant despite the pendency of an appeal or the commencement of execution of the sentence.

C. The trial court may deny a motion to reconsider sentence without a contradictory hearing.

D. Failure to make or file a motion to reconsider sentence or to include a specific ground upon which a motion to reconsider sentence may be based, including a claim of excessiveness, shall preclude the state or the defendant from raising an objection to the sentence or from urging any ground not raised in the motion on appeal or review.
(Added by Acts 1991 No. 38, §1, eff. 1/31/92.)

Art. 881.2. Review of sentence.

A. (1) The defendant may appeal or seek review of a sentence based on any ground asserted in a motion to reconsider sentence. The defendant also may seek review of a sentence which exceeds the maximum sentence authorized by the statute under which the defendant was convicted and any applicable statutory enhancement provisions.

(2) The defendant cannot appeal or seek review of a sentence imposed in conformity with a plea agreement which was set forth in the record at the time of the plea.

B. The state may appeal or seek review of a sentence:

(1) If the sentence imposed was not in conformity with:

(a) Mandatory requirements of the statute under which the defendant was convicted, or any other applicable mandatory sentence provisions; or

(b) The applicable enhancement provisions under the Habitual Offender Law, R.S. 15:529.1; and

(2) If the state objected at the time the sentence was imposed or made or filed a motion to reconsider sentence under this Article.

(Added by Acts 1991 No. 38, §1, eff. 6/19/92.)

Art. 881.3. Record on review of sentence.

In reviewing a sentence the appellate court may consider the record of the case which shall include any evidence or relevant information introduced at preliminary hearings, hearings on motions, arraignments, or sentencing proceedings, and any relevant information included in a presentence investigation report filed into the record at sentencing. In order to preserve confidentiality, in appropriate cases, the court may order that the presentence report, or any portion thereof, be held under seal. *(Added by Acts 1991 No. 38, §1, eff. 1/31/92.)*

Art. 881.4. Action by appellate court.

A. If the appellate court finds that a sentence must be set aside on any ground, the court shall remand for resentence by the trial court. The appellate court may give direction to the trial court concerning the proper sentence to impose.

B. In the interest of justice, the appellate court may remand the case for resentencing before a judge other than the judge who imposed the initial sentence.

C. If necessary to an appropriate disposition of a motion to reconsider sentence, the appellate court may remand the case to the trial court with instructions to supplement the record or to hold an evidentiary hearing.

D. The appellate court shall not set aside a sentence for excessiveness if the record supports the sentence imposed.

(Added by Acts 1991 No. 38, §1; chgd. by Acts 1995 No. 942, §1, eff. 8/15/95.)

Art. 881.5. Correction of illegal sentence by trial court.

On motion of the state or the defendant, or on its own motion, at any time, the court may correct a sentence imposed by that court which exceeds the maximum sentence authorized by law. *(Added by Acts 1991 No. 38, §1, eff. 1/31/92.)*

Art. 881.6. *(Repealed by Acts 1995 No. 942, §3, eff. 8/15/95.)*

Art. 882. Correction of illegal sentence; review of illegal sentence.

A. An illegal sentence may be corrected at any time by the court that imposed the sentence or by an appellate court on review.

B. A sentence may be reviewed as to its legality on the application of the defendant or of the state:

(1) In an appealable case by appeal; or

(2) In an unappealable case by writs of certiorari and prohibition.

C. Nothing in this Article shall be construed to deprive any defendant of his right, in a proper case, to the writ of habeas corpus.

Art. 883. Concurrent and consecutive sentences.

If the defendant is convicted of two or more offenses based on the same act or transaction, or constituting parts of a common scheme or plan, the terms of imprisonment shall be served concurrently unless the court expressly directs that some or all be served consecutively. Other sentences of imprisonment shall be served consecutively unless the court expressly directs that some or all of them be served concurrently. In the case of the concurrent sentence, the judge shall specify, and the court minutes shall reflect, the date from which the sentences are to run concurrently.

Art. 883.1. Sentences concurrent with sentences of other jurisdictions.

A. The sentencing court may specify that the sentence imposed be served concurrently with a sentence imposed by a federal court or a court of any other state and that service of the concurrent terms of imprisonment in a federal correctional institution or a correctional institution of another state shall be in satisfaction of the sentence imposed in this state in the manner and to the same extent as if the defendant had been committed to the Louisiana Department of Public Safety and Corrections for the term of years served in a federal correctional institution or a correctional institution of another state. When serving a concurrent sentence in a federal correctional institution or a correctional institution of another state, the defendant shall receive credit for time served as allowed under the laws of this state.

B. Whenever sentence is imposed under the provisions of this Article, the court shall order that the defendant be remanded to the custody of the sheriff of the parish in which the conviction was had in the event that the terms of imprisonment to which the defendant is sentenced in the foreign jurisdiction terminates prior to the date on which the sentence imposed in this state is to terminate.

C. In every case where a sentence at hard labor is imposed under the provisions of this Article, the court shall order that a certified copy of the court minutes and court order be forwarded to the Louisiana Department of Corrections. Should the defendant complete his term of imprisonment during his incarceration in the other jurisdiction, the department shall forward a copy of the discharge papers to the sheriff in the parish of conviction and to the appropriate authorities having physical custody of the defendant.
(Chgd. by Acts 1991 No. 138, §2, eff. 1/31/92.)

Art. 884. Sentence of fine with imprisonment for default.

If a sentence imposed includes a fine or costs, the sentence shall provide that in default of payment thereof the defendant shall be imprisoned for a specified period not to exceed one year; provided that where the maximum prison sentence which may be imposed as a penalty for a misdemeanor is six months or less, the total period of imprisonment upon conviction of the offense, including imprisonment for default in payment of a fine or costs, shall not exceed six months for that offense.

Art. 885. Release on payment of fine and costs.

A defendant who has been imprisoned for default in the payment of a fine, or fine and costs, under a sentence imposed pursuant to Article 884, may, at any time before expiration of the term of imprisonment, obtain his release by paying to his custodian all of the costs imposed and a sum of money that bears the same proportion to the imposed fine as the term of alternate imprisonment yet to run bears to the whole of such term of imprisonment.

Art. 886. Enforcement of fine by civil process; offset of tax refund.

A. In the event of nonpayment of a fine, or of a fine and costs, within sixty days after the sentence was imposed, and if no appeal is pending, the court which imposed the sentence may sign a judgment against the defendant in a sum equal to the fine plus judicial interest to begin sixty days after the sentence was imposed, plus all costs of criminal proceeding and subsequent proceedings necessary to enforce the judgment in either civil or criminal court. Collection of the judgment may be enforced in either criminal or civil court in the same manner as a money judgment in a civil case. In addition, particular courts may provide by court rule for enforcement by the filing of an offset claim against the defendant, in accordance with R.S. 47:299.1 through 299.19.

B. The provisions of Paragraph A of this Article shall apply to all fines and costs due and owing, regardless of whether they become due and owing prior to September 6, 1991.
(Chgd. by Acts 1991 No. 85, §1, eff. 9/6/91.)

Art. 886.1. Judgment for fines and costs declared executory; required notice.

If a civil judgment is signed in accordance with Article 886, the judgment shall be executory upon rendition by the court provided the defendant was notified at the time of sentencing of the possible rendition of a civil judgment in the event of his failure to pay the fine and costs. In all other cases, the judgment shall be executory immediately upon service of the notice of judgment upon the defendant in accordance with Code of Civil Procedure Article 1913. *(Added by Acts 1991 No. 85, §1, eff. 9/6/91.)*

Art. 887. Defendant's liability for costs; suspension of costs; no advance costs.

A. A defendant who is convicted of an offense or is the person owing a duty of support in a support proceeding shall be liable for all costs of the prosecution or proceeding, whether or not costs are assessed by the court, and such costs are recoverable by the party or parties who incurred the expense. However, such defendant or person shall not be liable for costs if acquitted or if the prosecution or proceeding is dismissed. In addition, any judge of a district court, parish court, city court, traffic court, juvenile court, or family court within the state shall be authorized to suspend court costs.

B. All processes of the court shall issue without the payment of advance costs.

C. In addition to the costs provided in Paragraph A, a person convicted of a violation of R.S. 14:98, R.S. 14:98.1, or of any municipal or parochial ordinance defining the offense of operating a motor vehicle, aircraft, watercraft, vessel, or other motorized means of conveyance under the influence of alcohol or drugs, who was subjected to a blood, breath, or urine analysis for alcohol or any controlled dangerous substance listed in R.S. 40:964, Schedule I, II, III, IV, or V, shall be assessed an additional seventy-five dollars as special costs. Such costs shall be paid in the following manner: twenty-five dollars to the governing authority owning the instrument used to perform the analysis, and fifty dollars to the governing authority whose agency performed the analysis. If the office of state police performed or participated in a blood, breath, or urine analysis for which these costs are assessed, that portion of the costs applicable to the office of state police shall be forwarded to the applied technology unit within the office of state police and forwarded for disposition in accordance with R.S. 40:1379.7. In the event the person is unable to pay the fine when assessed, the court may allow payment within certain time limits, based on the person's ability to pay such costs.

D. In addition to the costs provided in Paragraphs A and C, a person convicted of a violation of R.S. 14:98, R.S. 14:98.1, or of any municipal or parochial ordinance defining the offense of operating a motor vehicle while under the influence of alcohol or drugs, shall be assessed an additional fifty dollars as special costs to be used to defray expenses of administering conditions of probation or of incarceration. If the offender is incarcerated, such costs shall be paid to the sheriff or other custodian of the facility in which the offender is incarcerated. If the offender is placed on probation as provided in R.S. 14:98(B) or (C) or R.S. 14:98.1(D) or (E), the court may order the apportionment and payment of all or a part of such costs to the agencies or persons responsible for administering the prescribed substance abuse program, driver improvement program, or community service activities. In addition, the person convicted of a violation of R.S. 14:98, R.S. 14:98.1, or of any such municipal or parochial ordinance shall be assessed costs of the witness fee provided by R.S. 15:255.

E. In addition to the costs provided in Paragraphs A, C, and D, a person convicted of a felony, a misdemeanor, or ordinance of any local government shall be assessed an additional two dollars as special costs. Such special costs shall be imposed by all courts, including mayor's courts and magistrate courts, and shall be used for the purpose of training local law enforcement officers as directed by the council on peace officer standards and training. The proceeds of the special costs shall be paid to the Louisiana Commission on Law Enforcement and Administration of Criminal Justice to be used to train local law enforcement officers and to provide assistance to local law enforcement agencies. The court, public office, or local governing body collecting the special costs imposed herein shall retain two percent of such costs to defray the administrative expenses of collecting and remitting the special costs.

F. (1) In addition to the costs provided in Paragraphs A, C, D, and E, a person convicted of a felony, a misdemeanor, or ordinance of any local government, including a traffic felony, a traffic misdemeanor, or a local traffic violation, shall be assessed an additional two dollars as a special court cost; provided that such additional cost shall be one dollar in mayor's courts in municipalities with a population of two thousand or less. Such special costs shall be imposed by all courts, including mayor's courts and magistrate courts, and shall be used for implementation of the master plan for the development of a trial court case management information system and for the fast-tracked prototype development of the criminal disposition component thereof in order to define and meet the needs of clerks of court, trial court judges, law enforcement and corrections officials, the supreme court, the legislature, and the general public. The proceeds of the special cost shall be deposited in the state treasury monthly on or before the tenth day of each calendar month. After compliance with the requirements of Article VII, Section 9(B) of the Constitution of Louisiana, relative to the Bond Security and Redemption Fund, and prior to monies being placed in the state general fund, an amount equal to that deposited in the state treasury, as required above, shall be credited to the special fund hereby created in the state treasury to be known as the Trial Court Case Management Information Fund. The disbursement of the proceeds from the fund shall be made on the warrant of the judicial administrator of the supreme court drawn on the state treasury. The monies in this fund shall be used solely for the purposes identified in this Paragraph, including necessary and associated administrative expenses. All unexpended and unencumbered monies in this fund at the end of the fiscal year shall remain in such fund. All monies in this fund shall be invested by the state treasurer in the same manner as monies in the general fund with interest earned on the investment of these monies credited to this fund following compliance with the requirements of Article VII, Section 9(B), relative to the Bond Security and Redemption Fund.

(2) In Jefferson Parish, in addition to the costs in Paragraphs A, C, D, and E, a person convicted of an offense against the state of Louisiana shall be assessed a special court cost in the following amounts: in the case of a misdemeanor, an additional twenty-five dollars, and in the case of a felony, an additional fifty dollars. The amount so assessed shall be collected on behalf of the clerk of court's office, in the manner that fines are collected in criminal cases. The funds shall be transmitted to the clerk of court's office to be used by the clerk in his discretion to defray the expenses of his office.

G. In addition to the costs provided in Paragraphs A, C, D, E, and F, a person convicted of a violation of the Uniform Controlled Dangerous Substances Law* may be assessed an additional one hundred dollars as special costs of court. Such special costs shall be imposed by all courts and shall be used for the development or maintenance of Drug Abuse Resistance Education (D.A.R.E.) programs. The amount so assessed shall be collected on behalf of the parish sheriff's office, to be distributed among agencies providing the D.A.R.E. programs based upon the number of programs each agency offers within the public and private educational systems of the parish.

**R.S. 40:961 et seq.*

H. In addition to the costs provided in Paragraphs A, C, D, E, F, and G, a person convicted of a felony, a misdemeanor, or ordinance of any local government, may be assessed additional reasonable costs, to cover the costs expended by the sheriff, marshal, constable, or municipal police in the execution of a bench warrant, or a fugitive warrant, or both effecting the arrest. An itemized statement of expenses shall be prepared and submitted for review and assessment by the court at the time of sentencing. Such costs shall be paid to the sheriff, marshal, constable, or municipal police as reimbursement of expenses incurred in the execution of such warrant.

(Chgd. by Acts 1990 No. 320, §1; Acts 1993 No. 151, §1, No. 152, §1, No. 440, §1; Acts 1994 Third Ex. Sess. No. 109, §1; Acts 1995 No. 1064, §1, No. 1276, §1; Acts 1997 No. 1296, §1, eff. 7/15/97.)

Art. 888. Costs and fines; payment.

Costs and any fine imposed shall be payable immediately; provided, however, that in cases involving the violation of any traffic law or ordinance, the court having jurisdiction may grant the defendant five judicial days after rendition of judgment to pay any costs and any fine imposed.

Art. 889. Collection and disposition of fines, costs, and forfeitures.

The collection and disposition of fines, costs, and forfeitures shall be as provided by law.

Art. 890. Method of service of sentence of imprisonment; labor and confinement; workday release program.

A. A sentence of imprisonment in the state penitentiary shall be served in conformity with the applicable provisions of Title 15 of the Louisiana Revised Statutes of 1950 that govern the state penitentiary.

B. Except in misdemeanor cases, any other sentence of imprisonment subjects the defendant to confinement, and to labor unless otherwise specified.

C. In all misdemeanor cases in which a sentence of imprisonment is imposed and the sentencing court has ordered the defendant to report to the sheriff for participation in a court-approved workday release program during the term of imprisonment, the defendant shall be subjected to confinement and costs as provided for in R.S. 15:708.

Art. 890.1. Sentence imposed on crimes of violence.

A. When the court imposes a sentence, the court shall designate whether the crime involved is a crime of violence or an attempted crime of violence as defined or enumerated in R.S. 14:2(13).

B. Notwithstanding any provision of law to the contrary, if a person is convicted of or pleads guilty to a crime of violence as defined or enumerated in R.S. 14:2(13) and is sentenced to imprisonment for a stated number of years or months, the sentencing court may deny or place conditions on eligibility for diminution of sentence for good behavior unless diminution of sentence is prohibited by R.S. 15:571.3(C) or (D).

(Added by Acts 1995 No. 946, §1; chgd. by Acts 1997 No. 697, §1, eff. 8/15/97.)

Art. 890.2. Fines for individual defendants.

A. When a defendant has been convicted of a felony, and upon a determination that a defendant has the ability and resources available to pay an additional fine and that such a fine would not unduly burden the defendant's dependents, the court may impose as an additional fine or as a component of a fine the expected costs to the state of any imprisonment ordered by the court and prescribe the manner in which the fine shall be enforced and paid.

B. The additional fine or component of the fine may be imposed contingent upon the defendant's ability to pay the fine while incarcerated from any future sources of income the defendant may receive while incarcerated.

C. The Department of Public Safety and Corrections may determine the amount due the state in cases where the defendant is confined in a penal or correctional institution under the supervision of the department and render statements thereof, and such sworn statements shall be considered prima facie evidence of the amount due. If the defendant is committed to the department and confined in a parish jail or institution as provided for in R.S. 15:824(B), the amount of the additional fine or component of the fine shall be equal to the amount paid by the department to the parish sheriff or governing authority of those parishes in which the governing authority operates the parish jail, for keeping and feeding the individual in the parish jail.

D. The amount of reimbursement under this Article shall not be in excess of the per capita cost of care for maintaining inmates in the state correctional facility in which the inmate is housed. The funds collected from the fines imposed pursuant to this Article shall be distributed to the entity that expended the funds. However, ten percent of the funds shall go to the Crime Victims' Reparation Fund as provided in R.S. 46:1816.

(Added by Acts 1997 No. 751, §1, eff. 8/15/97.)

Art. 891. Forfeiture of weapons.

A. For purposes of this Article, a firearm or other dangerous weapon either used in the commission of a felony offense or the use of which constitutes an element of a felony offense may be declared to be crime-related contraband which may be seized by a law enforcement officer in the course of an arrest or issuance of summons or may be seized by order of court pursuant to other provisions of law. The district attorney of the parish where the arrest or seizure occurred may petition the district court to forfeit to the seizing agency an item or thing seized, or may petition the court for seizure, upon showing that the item or thing seized or to be seized constitutes crime-related contraband.

B. Forfeiture under this Article may be initiated within sixty days of receipt or publication of notice of seizure. The law enforcement agency effecting the seizure shall send notice to the registered owner if known and possessor of the item or thing by certified mail, return receipt requested, at the address provided to the law enforcement agency by any known or believed registered owner or possessor; and if returned unclaimed, notice shall be by an advertisement placed for publication by the seizing agency in the official journal of the parish of the place of seizure.

C. The notice provided for in Paragraph B must state or contain all of the following:

(1) A description of the item or thing to be forfeited.

(2) The name of the registered or believed owner, if any.

(3) A statement regarding the nature and circumstances surrounding the forfeiture.

(4) That the seizing law enforcement agency seeks to forfeit the described item or thing.

(5) That a claim to the item must be made within sixty days from date of receipt or publication of notice in order to interrupt or prevent the forfeiture.

D. The claimant of the item or thing to be forfeited must file a written affidavit with the court wherein the petition was filed within the time period provided for in Paragraph C of this

Article. The affidavit shall allege or establish the owner's or possessor's lack of knowledge or lack of duty to know that the thing or item was used or intended for use in the commission of an offense. The claimant must also be legally entitled to the ownership or possession of the thing or item and must establish, to the satisfaction of the court, proof of ownership or dominion. If no legitimate claim is made within sixty days, the thing or item shall be declared crime-related contraband by the court and all rights, title, and interest to the thing or item seized shall be transferred to and vested with the seizing law enforcement agency making the seizure. Discretion as to the disposition of crime-related contraband which is a firearm or dangerous weapon shall rest with the court.

E. In addition to ordering the forfeiture of a firearm or dangerous weapon as crime-related contraband as otherwise provided in this Article or by any other provision of law, when a court sentences a defendant, it may order the forfeiture of any weapon used in connection with the offense or found in the possession or under the immediate control of the defendant at the time of the arrest. The court may provide for the destruction, sale, or other disposition of the weapons forfeited.

(Chgd. by Acts 1994 Third Ex. Sess. No. 21, §1, eff. 8/27/94.)

Art. 892. Post-sentence statement by sheriff; accompanying documents.

A. The sheriff shall prepare a statement indicating the amount of time a defendant has spent in custody prior to conviction when such defendant is committed to the Department of Corrections, sentenced for a term of one year or more to any penal institution, or ordered committed to any mental institution or mental hospital. The sheriff shall retain a copy of the statement and submit the original to the officer in charge of the institution or department to which the defendant is sentenced.

B. (1) When a sheriff's statement is required as set forth above, the clerk of court shall also prepare the following documents:

(a) A copy of the indictment under which the defendant was convicted.

(b) A copy of the sentence as recorded in the minutes of the court.

(c) The name and address of the judge and of the district attorney who participated in the trial.

(2) The clerk shall retain a copy of the statement and documents and send the original to the officer in charge of the department or penal institution to which the defendant has been sentenced, where they shall be preserved. The documents, or copies thereof, shall be made available to the governor, the pardon board, and the parole board.

C. All statements and documents required by this Article shall physically accompany any defendant when said defendant is transferred to a penal institution or a mental institution or mental hospital. Said documents and statements shall be tendered to the officer in charge of the institution at the time that the defendant is presented for admittance thereto.

D. Failure to comply with the provisions of this Article shall not affect the validity of a prosecution, conviction, or sentence.

Art. 892.1. Driver improvement programs.

A. Whenever, in a misdemeanor case, a person is convicted of violating any law of this state that regulates traffic or any parish or municipal ordinance that regulates traffic, or when a child is decreed by a court to be a traffic violator, regardless of any sentence imposed, the court imposing sentence may order the person or child to attend and participate in a driver education, training, or improvement program approved by the court or the violator may choose a program approved by the Department of Public Safety and Corrections, office of motor vehicles as provided and pursuant to the conditions in R.S. 32:402.2.

B. Notwithstanding the provision of any other law to the contrary, upon conviction for the first time only of a misdemeanor offense under Title 32 of the Louisiana Revised Statutes of 1950 that regulates traffic or of any similar parish or municipal ordinance that regulates traffic, the court may suspend the sentence for such offense and order the defendant to attend, at his cost, a driver education, training, or improvement program as provided for in Paragraph A of this Article.

C. Upon completion by the defendant of the driver program, the court may set the conviction aside and dismiss the prosecution.

D. All driver improvement courses under this Article shall include instruction on railroad and highway grade crossing safety.

E. The court in its discretion may defer sentencing and allow the defendant ninety days to present a certificate of course completion as evidence that, subsequent to the alleged act, the person has successfully completed a driver education, training, or improvement course as provided in Paragraph A of this Article when all of the following conditions are met:

(1) The person, except as provided in Paragraph F of this Article, enters a plea in person or in writing of nolo contendere or guilty and presents to the court an oral request or a written request, in person or by mail postmarked on or before the appearance date on the citation, to take a driving course.

(2) The court enters judgment on the defendant's plea of nolo contendere or guilty at the time the plea is made, but defers the imposition of the whole or any part of the sentence for ninety days.

(3) The defendant has a valid driver's license or permit.

(4) The defendant's driving record as maintained by the Department of Public Safety and Corrections does not indicate successful completion of a driver's education, training, or improvement course under this Article within the two years immediately preceding the date of the alleged offense.

(5) The defendant files an affidavit with the court stating that he is not in the process of taking a course under this Article and he has not completed a course under this Article that is not yet reflected on his driving record.

(6) The offense charged is for a misdemeanor offense under Title 32 of the Louisiana Revised Statutes of 1950, except when the offense involves speeding twenty-five miles per hour or more over the posted speed limit at the place where the alleged offense occurred.

F. A written request to take a driving course under Subparagraph E(1) of this Article is timely if it is postmarked on or before the appearance date on the citation.

G. A court shall not require a minor who is sixteen years of age or younger to enter a plea of nolo contendere or guilty under Subparagraph E(1) of this Article.

H. (1) When a person complies with Paragraph E of this Article and a certificate of course completion is accepted by the court, the court shall set the conviction aside and dismiss the charge, but the court may only dismiss one charge for completion of each course.

(2) When a charge is dismissed under this Paragraph, the charge shall not be part of the person's driving record or used for any purpose; however, the court shall report that the person has successfully completed the driving course and the date of completion to the Department of Public Safety and Corrections for inclusion in his driving record. The report shall indicate that the course was taken under the provisions of this Article to determine eligibility to take a subsequent course under such provisions.

(3) No insurance company shall increase the premium or cancel an insured's policy merely because of an offense dismissed under this Article or because the insured completed a driving course under this Article.

I. The court may require the person requesting a driving course to pay a fee set by the court at an amount that does not exceed ten dollars to cover the cost of administering this Article. Fees collected by a municipal court shall be deposited in the municipal treasury. Fees collected by other courts shall be deposited in the criminal court fund of the parish in which the court is located. If the person requesting a driving course does not take the course, he is not entitled to a refund of the court fee. In addition to the cost of the driving course, the person shall pay any fines and costs for the driving offense.

J. The authority vested in courts by this Article is in addition to any authority granted by other laws with respect to persons convicted of traffic violations and children decreed to be traffic violators.

(Chgd. by Acts 1990 No. 834, §1; Acts 1991 No. 485, §§1, 2; Acts 1993 No. 225, §2; Acts 1995 No. 1091, §1; Acts 1996 First Ex. Sess. No. 93, §1; Acts 1997 No. 1336, §1, eff. 8/15/97.)

Art. 892.2. Notice of controlled dangerous substance conviction; licensing authority.

When a person is convicted of violating any felony provision of the Uniform Controlled Dangerous Substances Law*, the court imposing sentence shall determine if the defendant possesses a license to practice a trade, occupation, or profession in this state and, if so, the court shall cause notice of the conviction to be forwarded to the appropriate licensing authority.

**R.S. 40:961 et seq.*

Art. 892.3. Transfer of foreign nationals or citizens; treaty.

When a treaty is in effect between the United States and a foreign country providing for the transfer of a convicted offender who is a citizen or national of the foreign country to the foreign country or the transfer of a citizen of the United States convicted as an offender in the foreign country to the United States, the governor is authorized, subject to the terms of such treaty, to act on behalf of the state and to consent to the transfer of such convicted offenders under the provisions of Article IV, Section 5(A) of the Constitution of Louisiana. *(Added by Acts 1990 No. 514, §1, eff. 7/18/90.)*

CHAPTER 2. SUSPENDED SENTENCE AND PROBATION

Art. 893. Suspension and deferral of sentence and probation in felony cases.

A. When it appears that the best interest of the public and of the defendant will be served, the court, after a first or second conviction of a noncapital felony, may suspend, in whole or in part, the imposition or execution of either or both sentences, where suspension is allowed under the law, and in either or both cases place the defendant on probation under the supervision of the division of probation and parole. The court shall not suspend the sentence of a conviction for a crime of violence as defined in R.S. 14:2(13)(a), (b), (c), (d), (e), (i), (j), (k), (*l*), (m), (n), (*o*), (p), (q), (r), (t), (v), (w), (x), (bb), (cc), or (dd), or of a second conviction if the second conviction is for a violation of R.S. 14:73.5, R.S. 14:81.1, or R.S. 14:81.2, or for a violation of the Uniform Controlled Dangerous Substances Law* punishable by a term of imprisonment for more than five years. The period of probation shall be specified and shall not be less than one year nor more than five years. The suspended sentence shall be regarded as a sentence for the purpose of granting or denying a new trial or appeal.

**R.S. 40:961 et seq.*

B. If the sentence consists of both a fine and imprisonment, the court may impose the fine and suspend the sentence or place the defendant on probation as to the imprisonment.

C. Except as otherwise provided by law, the court shall not suspend a felony sentence after the defendant has begun to serve the sentence.

D. (1)(a) When it appears that the best interest of the public and of the defendant will be served, the court may defer, in whole or in part, the imposition of a sentence after conviction of a first offense noncapital felony under the conditions set forth in this Paragraph. When a conviction is entered under this Paragraph, the court may defer the imposition of sentence and place the defendant on probation under the supervision of the division of probation and parole.

(b) The court shall not defer a sentence under this provision for an offense or an attempted offense which is defined or enumerated as a crime of violence under R.S. 14:2(13) or a sex offense as defined by R.S. 15:542(E), involving a child under the age of seventeen years or for a violation of the Uniform Controlled Dangerous Substances Law punishable by a term of imprisonment of more than five years or for a violation of R.S. 40:966(A), 967(A), 968(A), 969(A), or 970(A).

(2) Upon motion of the defendant, if the court finds at the conclusion of the probationary period that the probation of the defendant has been satisfactory, the court may set the conviction aside and dismiss the prosecution. The dismissal of the prosecution shall have the same effect as acquittal, except that the conviction may be considered as a first offense and provide the basis for subsequent prosecution of the party as a multiple offender, and further shall be considered as a first offense for purposes of any other law or laws relating to cumulation of offenses. Dismissal under this Paragraph shall occur only once with respect to any person.

E. Nothing contained herein shall be construed as being a basis for destruction of records of the arrest and prosecution of any person convicted of a felony.

(Chgd. by Acts 1991 No. 89, §1, No. 91, §1; Acts 1992 No. 303, §1; Acts 1994 Third Ex. Sess. No. 100, §1, No. 123, §1; Acts 1995 No. 990, §1, No. 1251, §4; Acts 1996 First Ex. Sess. No. 5, §1; Acts 1997 No. 696, §1, eff. 8/15/97.)

Art. 893.1. Motion to invoke firearm sentencing provision.

A. If the district attorney intends to move for imposition of sentence under the provisions of Article 893.3, he shall file a motion within a reasonable period of time prior to commencement of trial of the felony in which the firearm was used.

B. The motion shall contain a plain, concise, and definite written statement of the essential facts constituting the basis for the motion.

Art. 893.2. Use of firearm in commission of a felony; hearing.

A. If a motion was filed by the state in compliance with Article 893.1, the court shall conduct a contradictory hearing following conviction to determine whether a firearm was used in the commission of the felony.

B. The court may consider any evidence introduced at the trial on the merits, at defendant's guilty plea, or at the hearing of any motion filed in the case. The court may also consider any other relevant evidence presented by either party at the contradictory hearing. The hearsay rule shall not be applicable at such contradictory hearings.

C. The motion shall be heard and disposed of prior to the imposition of sentence.

Art. 893.3. Sentence imposed on felony in which firearm was used.

A. If the court finds by clear and convincing evidence that a firearm was actually used by the defendant in the commission of the felony for which he was convicted, the court shall impose the maximum sentence of imprisonment provided by law if the maximum sentence is less than five years and shall impose a sentence of at least five years if the maximum sentence exceeds five years.

B. A sentence imposed under this provision shall not be suspended and shall be imposed in the same manner as provided in the felony for which the defendant was convicted.

C. The court may order that a defendant sentenced under this provision shall not be eligible for parole for a specified period of time not to exceed five years.

D. If the court finds that a sentence imposed under provisions of this Article would be excessive, the court shall state for the record the reasons for such finding and shall impose the most severe sentence which is not excessive.

E. (1)(a) Notwithstanding any other provision of law to the contrary, if the defendant commits a felony with a firearm as provided for in this Article, and the crime is considered a violent felony, the court shall impose a minimum term of imprisonment of ten years.

(b) A "violent felony" for the purposes of this Paragraph is: first degree murder, second degree murder, aggravated rape, aggravated sexual battery, aggravated kidnapping, aggravated burglary, carjacking, or armed robbery.

(2) A sentence imposed under this Paragraph shall be without benefit of parole, probation or suspension of sentence.

(Chgd. by Acts 1994 Third Ex. Sess. No. 41, §1, eff. 8/27/94.)

Art. 893.4. Inapplicability to unintentional felonies.

The provisions of Article 893.3 shall not apply to a conviction for a felony in which criminal negligence is an element of the offense.

Art. 893.5. Community service in lieu of imprisonment.

A. Except as otherwise prohibited by law, the court may suspend, in whole or in part, the imposition or execution of sentence if:

(1) The defendant has not previously been convicted of a felony.

(2) The maximum term of imprisonment for the offense is thirty years or less.

(3) The court imposes a period of court-approved community service of not less than two nor more than five years.

(4) The court specifies in written form in the court record the reason for the imposition of community service in lieu of imprisonment.

B. An offender sentenced under the provisions of this Article shall be subject to all conditions of supervised probation imposed by the court or as set forth by law. The offender may have his probation revoked or modified as provided by law and shall not be allowed credit for time spent doing community service or for the time elapsed during suspension of the sentence.

(Added by Acts 1990 No. 462, §1; chgd. by Acts 1991 No. 406, §1, eff. 9/6/91.)

Art. 894. Suspension and deferral of sentence; probation in misdemeanor cases.

A. (1) Notwithstanding any other provision of this Article to the contrary, when a defendant has been convicted of a misdemeanor, except criminal neglect of family, the court may suspend the imposition or the execution of the whole or any part of the sentence imposed, provided suspension is not prohibited by law, and place the defendant on unsupervised probation or probation supervised by a probation office, agency, or officer designated by the court, other than the division of probation and parole of the Department of Public Safety and Corrections, upon such conditions as the court may fix. Such suspension of sentence and probation shall be for a period of two years or such shorter period as the court may specify.

(2) When a suspended sentence in excess of six months is imposed, the court may place the defendant on probation under the supervision of the Department of Public Safety and Corrections, division of probation and parole, for a period of not more than two years and under such conditions as the court may specify.

(3) When a defendant has been convicted of the misdemeanor offense of operating a vehicle while intoxicated, second offense, the court may suspend the imposition or the execution of the whole or any part of the sentence imposed and place the defendant on unsupervised or supervised probation upon such conditions as the court may fix, where suspension is not prohibited under the law. Such suspension of sentence and probation shall be for a period of two years or such shorter period as the court may specify.

(4) The court may suspend, reduce, or amend a misdemeanor sentence after the defendant has begun to serve the sentence.

B. When the imposition of sentence has been deferred by the court, as authorized by this Article, and the court finds at the conclusion of the period of deferral that the defendant has not been convicted of any other offense during the period of the deferred sentence, and that no criminal charge is pending against him, the court may set the conviction aside and dismiss the prosecution. The dismissal of the prosecution shall have the same effect as an acquittal, except that the conviction may be considered as a first offense and provide the basis for subsequent prosecution of the party as a multiple offender. Discharge and dismissal under this provision may occur only once with respect to any person during a five-year period. However, discharge and dismissal under this provision for the offense of operating a vehicle while intoxicated may occur only once with respect to any person during a ten-year period.

C. Nothing contained herein shall be construed as being a basis for destruction of records of the arrest and prosecution of any person convicted of a misdemeanor.

(Chgd. by Acts 1990 No. 89, §1; Acts 1995 No. 1251, §4; Acts 1996 First Ex. Sess. No. 5, §1, eff. 4/23/96, oper. 8/15/95.)

Art. 894.1. Sentencing guidelines; generally.

A. When a defendant has been convicted of a felony or misdemeanor, the court should impose a sentence of imprisonment if any of the following occurs:

(1) There is an undue risk that during the period of a suspended sentence or probation the defendant will commit another crime.

(2) The defendant is in need of correctional treatment or a custodial environment that can be provided most effectively by his commitment to an institution.

(3) A lesser sentence will deprecate the seriousness of the defendant's crime.

B. The following grounds, while not controlling the discretion of the court, shall be accorded weight in its determination of suspension of sentence or probation:

(1) The offender's conduct during the commission of the offense manifested deliberate cruelty to the victim.

(2) The offender knew or should have known that the victim of the offense was particularly vulnerable or incapable of resistance due to extreme youth, advanced age, disability, or ill health.

(3) The offender offered or has been offered or has given or received anything of value for the commission of the offense.

(4) The offender used his or her position or status to facilitate the commission of the offense.

(5) The offender knowingly created a risk of death or great bodily harm to more than one person.

(6) The offender used threats of or actual violence in the commission of the offense.

(7) Subsequent to the offense, the offender used or caused others to use violence, force, or threats with the intent to influence the institution, conduct, or outcome of the criminal proceedings.

(8) The offender committed the offense in order to facilitate or conceal the commission of another offense.

(9) The offense resulted in a significant permanent injury or significant economic loss to the victim or his family.

(10) The offender used a dangerous weapon in the commission of the offense.

(11) The offense involved multiple victims or incidents for which separate sentences have not been imposed.

(12) The offender was persistently involved in similar offenses not already considered as criminal history or as a part of a multiple offender adjudication.

(13) The offender was a leader or his violation was in concert with one or more other persons with respect to whom the offender occupied a position of organizer, a supervisory position, or any other position of management.

(14) The offense was a major economic offense.

(15) The offense was a controlled dangerous substance offense and the offender obtained substantial income or resources from ongoing drug activities.

(16) The offense was a controlled dangerous substance offense in which the offender involved juveniles in the trafficking or distribution of drugs.

(17) The offender committed the offense in furtherance of a terrorist action.

(18) The offender foreseeably endangered human life by discharging a firearm during the commission of an offense which has, as an element, the use, attempted use, or threatened use of physical force against the person or property of another, and which, by its very nature, involves a substantial risk that physical force may be used in the course of committing the offense.

(19) The offender used a firearm or other dangerous weapon while committing or attempting to commit an offense which has, as an element, the use, attempted use, or threatened use of physical force against the person or property of another, and which by its very nature, involves a substantial risk that physical force may be used in the course of committing the offense.

(20) The offender used a firearm or other dangerous weapon while committing or attempting to commit a controlled dangerous substance offense.

(21) Any other relevant aggravating circumstances.

(22) The defendant's criminal conduct neither caused nor threatened serious harm.

(23) The defendant did not contemplate that his criminal conduct would cause or threaten serious harm.

(24) The defendant acted under strong provocation.

(25) There were substantial grounds tending to excuse or justify the defendant's criminal conduct, though failing to establish a defense.

(26) The victim of the defendant's criminal conduct induced or facilitated its commission.

(27) The defendant has compensated or will compensate the victim of his criminal conduct for the damage or injury that he has sustained.

(28) The defendant has no history of prior delinquency or criminal activity or has led a law-abiding life for a substantial period of time before the commission of the instant crime.

(29) The defendant's criminal conduct was the result of circumstances unlikely to recur.

(30) The defendant is particularly likely to respond affirmatively to probationary treatment.

(31) The imprisonment of the defendant would entail excessive hardship to himself or his dependents.

(32) The defendant has voluntarily participated in a pretrial drug testing program.

(33) Any other relevant mitigating circumstance.

C. The court shall state for the record the considerations taken into account and the factual basis therefor in imposing sentence.

D. Immediately following the imposition of a felony sentence pursuant to this Article, the sentencing court shall advise the offender in open court of each of the following:

(1) Whether, pursuant to the provisions of R.S. 15:571.3, the offender's sentence is subject to diminution for good behavior.

(2) Whether the sentence imposed was enhanced pursuant to R.S. 15:529.1 et seq., Article 893.3, or any other relevant provision of law.

(3)–(5) *(Repealed.)*

E. All victims of felonies who provide a written request to the Department of Public Safety and Corrections, which includes a mailing address, are entitled to receive a written report of the prospective term of imprisonment of their offenders. The Department of Public Safety and Corrections shall furnish to the victim and the sentencing judge within ninety days of commitment a report which includes the following information, in a format to be determined by the Department of Public Safety and Corrections:

(1) The prospective release date of the offender should his sentence be subject to diminution of sentence for good behavior, to the extent that the report shall advise the offender that he may be released upon serving the certain percentage of his sentence as provided for by law.

(2) The prospective parole eligibility date of the offender should he be eligible for parole pursuant to R.S. 15:574.4 et seq., to the extent that the report shall advise the offender that he may be eligible for release upon serving a certain percentage of his sentence as provided by law.

F. However, no sentence shall be declared unlawful or inadequate for failure to comply with the provisions of Paragraph D.

(Chgd. by Acts 1991 No. 22, §1; Acts 1995 No. 942, §1; Acts 1997 No. 750, §1, No. 1199, §§1, 2, eff. 8/15/97.)

Art. 894.2. Home incarceration; requirements.

A. Notwithstanding any other provision of law to the contrary, a defendant may be sentenced to home incarceration in lieu of imprisonment under the following conditions:

(1) The defendant is eligible for probation or was convicted of a misdemeanor or a felony punishable with or without hard labor.

(2) In felony cases, the Department of Public Safety and Corrections, through the division of probation and parole, recommends home incarceration of the defendant and specific conditions of that home incarceration, or the district attorney recommends home incarceration, or, after contradictory hearing, the court determines that home incarceration would serve the best interests of justice.

(3) The court determines that home incarceration of the defendant is more suitable than imprisonment or supervised probation without home incarceration.

B. A defendant sentenced to home incarceration shall be supervised and may be subject to any of the conditions of probation.

C. The court shall specify the conditions of home incarceration when it imposes such sentence upon the defendant. The conditions may include any condition reasonably related to implementing or monitoring a sentence of home incarceration, including curfew, electronic or telephone monitoring, home visitation by persons designated by the court, and limitation of the defendant's activities outside of the home.

D. The defendant shall be given a certificate setting forth the conditions of his home incarceration and shall be required to agree in writing to the conditions.

E. The court may require the defendant to obtain employment and may require the defendant to pay a reasonable supervision fee to the supervising agency to defray the cost of his home incarceration supervision.

F. The court may, at any time during the period of home incarceration, modify, change, or add to the conditions of such incarceration.

G. The sentence of home incarceration shall be for a period of not more than two years in felony cases and for a period not to exceed six months in misdemeanor cases.

H. If the defendant violates the conditions of home incarceration, the court, on motion of the state or its own motion, may, after contradictory hearing modify the sentence to impose a sentence of imprisonment.

I. In the event of revocation and sentence to imprisonment, the defendant shall not receive credit for time served under home incarceration.

J. The provisions of this Article shall not be applicable to a defendant who has been convicted of any second or subsequent violation of any state or local driving-while-intoxicated law committed within five years of the commission of any prior driving-while-intoxicated violation until the defendant has first served a minimum of forty-eight consecutive hours of imprisonment.

(Chgd. by Acts 1991 No. 431, §1; Acts 1992 No. 653, §1; Acts 1997 No. 663, §1, eff. 8/15/97.)

Art. 894.3. Notice to victim for sentencing.

A. Before sentencing a defendant who has been convicted of a violation of any provision of R.S. 14:92(A)(7), Subpart C of Part II, Subpart B of Part IV, or Subpart A(1) or A(4) of Part V of Chapter 1 of Title 14 of the Louisiana Revised Statutes of 1950, if the victim was under eighteen years of age at the time of the offense, the office of the district attorney shall notify the clerk of court of the name and the address of the victim, and the clerk of court shall give written notice of the date and time of sentencing at least three days prior to the hearing, when the sentencing is not immediately following the finding of guilt, to the victim or the victim's parent or guardian, unless the victim, parent, or guardian has advised the office of the district attorney in writing that such notification is not desired.

B. The victim or the victim's parent or guardian who desires to do so shall be given a reasonable opportunity to attend the hearing and to be heard.

(Added by Acts 1992 No. 962, §1; chgd. by Acts 1995 No. 1290, §3, eff. 8/15/95.)

Art. 895. Conditions of probation.

A. When the court places a defendant on probation, it shall require the defendant to refrain from criminal conduct and to pay a supervision fee to defray the costs of probation supervision, and it may impose any specific conditions reasonably related to his rehabilitation, including any of the following. That the defendant shall:

(1) Make a full and truthful report at the end of each month;

(2) Meet his specified family responsibilities, including any obligations imposed in a court order of child support;

(3) Report to the probation officer as directed;

(4) Permit the probation officer to visit him at his home or elsewhere;

(5) Devote himself to an approved employment or occupation;

(6) Refrain from owning or possessing firearms or other dangerous weapons;

(7) Make reasonable reparation or restitution to the aggrieved party for damage or loss caused by his offense in an amount to be determined by the court;

(8) Refrain from frequenting unlawful or disreputable places or consorting with disreputable persons;

(9) Remain within the jurisdiction of the court and get the permission of the probation officer before making any change in his address or his employment; and

(10) Devote himself to an approved reading program at his cost if he is unable to read the English language.

(11) Perform community service work.

(12) Submit himself to available medical, psychiatric, mental health, or substance abuse examination or treatment or both when deemed appropriate and ordered to do so by the probation and parole officer.

B. In felony cases, an additional condition of the probation may be that the defendant shall serve a term of imprisonment without hard labor for a period not to exceed two years.

C. In cases of violations of the Uniform Controlled Dangerous Substances Law*, the court may order the suspension or restriction of the defendant's driving privileges, if any, for all or part of the period of probation. In such cases, a copy of the order shall be forwarded to the Department of Public Safety and Corrections, which shall suspend the defendant's driver's license or issue a restricted license in accordance with the orders of the court. Additionally, the court may order the defendant to:

(1) Submit to and pay all costs for drug testing by an approved laboratory at the direction of his probation officer.

(2) Perform not less than one hundred sixty hours nor more than nine hundred sixty hours of community service work.

**R.S. 40:961 et seq.*

D. The court may, in lieu of the monthly supervision fee provided for in Paragraph A, require the defendant to perform a specified amount of community service work each month if the court finds the defendant is unable to pay the supervision fee provided for in Paragraph A.

E. Before the court places a sexual offender on probation, it shall order the offender who has not previously been tested to submit to a blood and saliva test in accordance with R.S. 15:535. All costs shall be paid by the offender.

F. In cases of any violation of Subpart (A)(1) of Part V of Chapter 1 of Title 14 of the Louisiana Revised Statutes of 1950 or R.S. 14:92(7), the court may order the defendant to submit to psychological evaluation and, if indicated, order him to obtain psychiatric or psychological counseling for all or part of the period of probation. All costs shall be paid by the defendant.

G. Before the court places the defendant on probation, it shall determine if the defendant has a high school degree or its equivalent and, if the defendant does not, it shall order the defendant to take a reading proficiency test. If the defendant scores below a sixth grade level on the reading proficiency test, the court shall condition probation upon the defendant's enrolling in and attending an adult education or reading program until he attains a sixth grade reading level or until his term of probation expires, whichever occurs first. All costs shall be paid by the defendant. If the court finds that there are no adult education or reading programs in the parish in which the defendant is domiciled, the defendant is unable to afford such a program, or attendance would create an undue hardship on the defendant, the court may suspend this condition of probation. The provisions of this Paragraph shall not apply to those defendants who are mentally, physically, or by reason of age, infirmity, dyslexia or other such learning disorders unable to participate.

H. In cases where the defendant has been convicted of the perpetration or attempted perpetration of any provision of R.S. 14:92(A)(7), Subpart C of Part II, Subpart B of Part IV, or Subpart A(1) or A(4) of Part V of Chapter 1 of Title 14 of the Louisiana Revised Statutes of 1950, and probation is permitted by law and when the court places a defendant on probation, the court shall order the following:

(1) As a condition of probation, that the defendant give notice of the crime for which he was convicted, his name, and address to:

(a) People who live within a one-mile radius in a rural area or a three-square block area in an urban or suburban area of the address where the defendant will reside upon release on probation.

(b) (i) The superintendent of the school district within the designated area where the defendant will reside, who shall notify the principal of whichever schools the superintendent thinks should be notified of the defendant's name, address, and the crime for which he was convicted. The superintendent shall also notify the principal and headmaster of each nonpublic school located within the designated area where the defendant will reside. The notice sent by the superintendent shall be accompanied by two clear, recent photographs or a clear photocopy of the defendant.

(ii) The photographs, which shall be provided by the defendant, shall be taken after release and within sufficient time to accompany the notification which is a required condition of probation.

(c) (i) The superintendent of the park, playground, and recreation districts within the designated area where the defendant will reside, who shall notify the custodians of whichever parks, playgrounds, and recreational facilities of the defendant's name, address, and the crime for which he was convicted. The notice sent by the superintendent shall be accompanied by two clear, recent photographs or a clear photocopy of the defendant.

(ii) The photographs, which shall be provided by the defendant, shall be taken after release and within sufficient time to accompany the notification which is a required condition of probation.

(2)(a) That the defendant give notice of the crime for which he was convicted, his name, and his address by mail to all people residing within the designated area, including the superintendent of the park, playground, and recreation districts and the superintendent of the school district within the designated area, within thirty days of the sentencing or within thirty days of setting up residency in the locale where the defendant plans to have his domicile, and that the notice shall be published on two separate days within this thirty-day period of time, without cost to the state, in the official journal of the governing authority of the parish where the defendant will reside and, if ordered by the court, in a newspaper which meets the requirements of R.S. 43:140(3) for qualification as an official journal and which has a larger or smaller circulation in the parish than the official journal. This notice which shall be provided to the superintendent of the school district, the superintendent of the park, playground, and recreation districts and the official journal or other designated newspaper shall also include a recent photograph and a clear photocopy of the defendant. The court may order any other form of notice which it deems appropriate, including but not limited to signs, handbills, bumper stickers, or clothing labeled to that effect.

(b) In the parish of St. Tammany, the court may order that the notice be published in a newspaper which meets the requirements of R.S. 43:140(3) for qualification as an official journal and which has a larger circulation in the parish than the official journal.

(3) That the defendant state under oath where he will reside after sentencing and that he will advise the court of any subsequent change of address during the probationary period.

(4) No offender, who is the parent, stepparent, or has legal custody and physical custody of the child who is the victim, shall be released on probation unless the victim has received psychological counseling prior to the offender's release if the offender is returning to the residence or community in which the child resides. Such psychological counseling shall include an attempt by the health care provider to ease the psychological impact upon the child of the notice required under Subparagraphs (1) and (2) of this Paragraph, including assisting the child in coping with potential insensitive comments and actions by the child's neighbors and peers. The cost of such counseling shall be paid by the offender.

(5) In cases where the defendant has been convicted of a violation of R.S. 14:80(A)(1), the defendant may petition the court to be relieved of or have modified certain conditions of probation required in Paragraph H of this Article. The petition shall be made a part of the original record of the court in which the petitioner was convicted of the offense that subjects him to the conditions of probation or, in the case of convictions in other states, the defendant shall petition the district court of the parish in which the person is registered. The district attorney of the parish shall be served with a copy of the petition. The court shall order a contradictory hearing and shall consider the nature of the sex offense committed and the criminal and relevant noncriminal behavior of the petitioner, both before and after conviction, and may consider other factors. The court may relieve the petitioner of certain conditions of probation or modify certain conditions of probation only if the petitioner shows, with clear and convincing evidence, that modifying the condition of probation will not serve the purposes of this Chapter. The state may appeal or seek review of the court's ruling.

(6) The court may order that the conditions of probation as provided for in Subparagraphs (1) and (2) of this Paragraph shall apply for each subsequent change of address made by the defendant during the probationary period.

I. The defendant shall be given a certificate setting forth the conditions of his probation and shall be required to agree in writing to the conditions.

J. In cases where the defendant has been convicted of an offense involving criminal sexual activity, the court shall order as a condition of probation that the defendant successfully complete a sex offender treatment program. As part of the sex offender treatment program, the offender shall participate with a victim impact panel or program providing a forum for victims of criminal sexual activity and sex offenders to share experiences on the impact of the criminal sexual activity in their lives. The Department of Public Safety and Corrections shall establish guidelines to implement victim impact panels where, in the judgment of the licensed professional responsible for the sexual treatment program, appropriate victims are available, and shall establish guidelines for other programs where such victims are not available. All costs for the sex offender treatment program shall be paid by the offender.

K. A conviction for any offense involving criminal sexual activity as provided for in Paragraph H of this Article, includes a conviction for an equivalent offense under the laws of another state. Criminal sexual offenders under the supervision and legal authority of the Department of Public Safety and Corrections pursuant to the terms and conditions of the interstate compact agreement provided for in R.S. 15:574.14 shall be notified of the registration requirements provided for in this Article at the time the department accepts supervision and has legal authority of the individual.

L. In all cases where the defendant has been convicted of an offense of domestic abuse as provided in R.S. 46:2132(3) to a family or household member as provided in R.S. 46:2132(4), the court shall order that the defendant submit to and successfully complete a court approved course of counseling or therapy related to family violence, for all or part of the period of probation. If the defendant has already completed such a counseling program, said counseling requirement shall be required only upon a finding by the court that such counseling or therapy would be effective in preventing future domestic violence. All costs for the counseling or therapy shall be paid by the offender.

M. If a defendant is injured or suffers other loss in the performance of community service work required as a condition of probation, neither the state nor any political subdivision, nor any officer, agent, or employee of the state or political subdivision shall be liable for any such injury or loss, unless the injury or loss was caused by the gross negligence or intentional acts of the officer, agent, or employee of the state or political subdivision. No provision of this Paragraph shall negate any requirement that an officer, agent, or employee secure proper and appropriate medical assistance for a defendant who is injured while performing community service work and in need of immediate medical attention.

(Chgd. by Acts 1992 No. 311, §1, No. 962, §1; Acts 1993 No. 510, §1, No. 874, §2, No. 922, §2; Acts 1994 Third Ex. Sess. No. 57, §1, No. 58, §2, No. 70, §2; Acts 1995 No. 605, §1, No. 906, §1, No. 928, §2, No. 1266, §1, No. 1290, §3, No. 1291, §1, No. 1303, §2; Acts 1997 No. 134, §1, No. 137, §1, No. 520, §1, No. 602, §1, eff. 8/15/97, No. 1148, §1, eff. 7/14/97.)

Art. 895.1. Probation; restitution; judgment for restitution; fees.

A. (1) When a court places the defendant on probation, it shall, as a condition of probation, order the payment of restitution in cases where the victim or his family has suffered any direct loss of actual cash, any monetary loss pursuant to damage to or loss of property, or medical expense. The court shall order restitution in a reasonable sum not to exceed the actual pecuniary loss to the victim in an amount certain. However, any additional or other damages sought by the victim and available under the law shall be pursued in an action separate from the establishment of the restitution order as a civil money judgment provided for in Subparagraph (2) of this Paragraph. The restitution payment shall be made, in discretion of the court, either in a lump sum or in monthly installments based on the earning capacity and assets of the defendant.

(2) (a) The order to pay restitution, as provided in this Article, is deemed a civil money judgment in favor of the person to whom restitution is owed, if the defendant is informed of his right to have a judicial determination of the amount and is provided with a hearing, waived a hearing, or stipulated to the amount of the restitution ordered. In addition to proceedings had by the court which orders the restitution, the judgment may be enforced in the same manner as a money judgment in a civil case. Likewise, the judgment may be filed as a lien as provided by law for judgment creditors. Prior to the enforcement of the restitution order, the defendant shall be notified of his right to have a judicial determination of the amount of restitution. Such notice shall be served personally by the district attorney's office of the respective judicial district in which the restitution is ordered.

(b) In addition to the powers under R.S. 13:1336, the Criminal District Court for the Parish of Orleans shall have the authority to order the payment of restitution as provided in this Paragraph. The enforcement of the judgment for restitution shall be filed in the Civil District Court for the Parish of Orleans.

(3) The court which orders the restitution shall provide written evidence of the order which constitutes the judgment.

(4) The court may suspend payment of any amount awarded hereunder and may suspend recordation of any judgment hereunder during the pendency of any civil suit instituted to recover damages, from said defendant brought by the victim or victims which arises out of the same act or acts which are the subject of the criminal offense contemplated hereunder.

(5) The amount of any judgment by the court hereunder, shall be credited against the amount of any subsequent civil judgment against the defendant and in favor of the victim or victims, which arises out of the same act or acts which are the subject of the criminal offense contemplated hereunder.

B. When a court suspends the imposition or the execution of a sentence and places the defendant on probation, it may in its discretion, order placed, as a condition of probation, an amount of money to be paid by the defendant to any or all of the following:

(1) To the indigent defender program for that court.

(2) To the criminal court fund to defray the costs of operation of that court.

(3) To the sheriff and clerk of court for costs incurred.

(4) To a law enforcement agency for the reasonable costs incurred in arresting the defendant, in felony cases involving the distribution of or intent to distribute controlled dangerous substances.

(5) To the victim to compensate him for his loss and inconvenience. Such an amount may be in addition to any amounts ordered to be paid by the defendant under Paragraph A herein.

(6) To a duly incorporated crime stoppers organization for the reasonable costs incurred in obtaining information which leads to the arrest of the defendant.

(7) To a local public or private nonprofit agency involved in drug abuse prevention and treatment for supervising a treatment program ordered by the court for a particular defendant, provided that such agency is qualified as a tax exempt organization under Section 501(c) of the Internal Revenue Code of the United States. Any nonprofit agency receiving money under the provisions of this Paragraph, must be licensed by the Department of Health and Hospitals in the supervision of drug abuse prevention and treatment.

C. When the court places the defendant on supervised probation, it shall order as a condition of probation a monthly fee of not less than twenty nor more than one hundred dollars payable to the Department of Public Safety and Corrections or such other probation office, agency, or officer as designated by the court, to defray the cost of supervision. If the probation supervision services are rendered by an agency other than the department, the fee may be ordered payable to that agency. These fees are only to supplement the level of funds that would ordinarily be available from regular state appropriations or any other source of funding.

D. The court may, in lieu of the monthly supervision fee provided for in Paragraph C, require the defendant to perform a specified amount of community service work each month if the court finds the defendant is unable to pay the minimum supervision fee provided for in Paragraph C.

E. When the court places any defendant convicted of a violation of the controlled dangerous substances law, R.S. 40:966 through 1034, on any type of probation, it shall order as a condition of probation a fee of not less than fifty nor more than one hundred dollars, payable to the Louisiana Commission on Law Enforcement to be credited to the Drug Abuse Education and Treatment Fund and used for the purposes provided in R.S. 15:1224.
(Chgd. by Acts 1990 No. 53, §1, No. 89, §1, No. 188, §1; Acts 1994 Third Ex. Sess. No. 60, §1; Acts 1998 First Ex. Sess. No. 138, §1, eff. 6/16/98.)

Art. 895.2. Probation; restitution for values of wildlife.

A. In all cases in which the defendant has been convicted of a crime which involves the illegal taking of wild birds, wild quadrupeds, or fish or other aquatic life in violation of the provisions of Title 56 of the Louisiana Revised Statutes of 1950 or of any rules and regulations promulgated thereunder, or any rules and regulations adopted by the Louisiana Wildlife and Fisheries Commission, the court shall, as a condition of probation, order civil restitution to the state of Louisiana, Department of Wildlife and Fisheries Conservation Fund, for the value of the said wild birds, wild quadrupeds, or fish or other aquatic life illegally taken. This restitution shall be in accordance with a schedule of wildlife and aquatic life species values promulgated by the Louisiana Wildlife and Fisheries Commission in accordance with the Administrative Procedure Act*.

**R.S. 49:950 et seq.*

B. If any assessment of civil penalties has been made or a civil action instituted pursuant to R.S. 56:40.1 et seq., then the court shall not order the restitution provided for in Paragraph A as a condition of probation.

Art. 895.3. Probationer transferred between states; fees.

The collection of the supervision fee imposed pursuant to C.Cr.P. Art. 895 and 895.1 shall be suspended upon the transfer of an offender to another state for probation supervision in that state, pursuant to the provisions of the interstate compact for out of state parolee supervision as provided in R.S. 15:574.14. *(Added by Acts 1991 No. 119, §2, eff. 9/6/91.)*

Art. 895.4. Probation; fees; crime stoppers organizations.

A. When a court places a person upon probation for any offense except for a violation of Chapters 1, 2, 2-A, and 3 of Title 32 of the Louisiana Revised Statutes of 1950 or a comparable parish or municipal ordinance, and a crime stoppers organization, as defined by R.S. 15:477.1, exists within the territorial jurisdiction of the court, the court shall order the defendant as a condition of probation to pay a fee, of not less than one dollar nor more than three dollars for each offense for which the defendant is sentenced, to that crime stoppers organization. The proceeds from payment of the fee shall be used by crime stoppers organizations in accordance with the corporate charter, bylaws, and rules and regulations of crime stoppers organizations to defray reasonable costs incurred in obtaining information relating to criminal acts conducted in that parish.

B. The payment of the fee as required by Paragraph A shall be in addition to any amounts ordered paid by the court in accordance with the provisions of Article 895.1(B)(6) or R.S. 32:1550(L)(3)*.

(Added by Acts 1991 No. 921, §1, eff. 9/6/91.)

**Section 32:1550 was repealed.*

Art. 896. Modifying or changing conditions of probation.

The court may, at any time during the probation period, modify, change, or discharge the conditions of probation, or add further conditions authorized by Article 895.

Art. 897. Termination of probation or suspended sentence; discharge of defendant.

In a felony case the court may terminate the defendant's probation and discharge him at any time after the expiration of one year of probation.

In a misdemeanor case the court may terminate the defendant's suspended sentence or probation and discharge him at any time.

Art. 898. Satisfaction of suspended sentence and probation.

Upon completion of the period of suspension of sentence or probation, or an earlier discharge of the defendant pursuant to Article 897, the defendant shall have satisfied the sentence imposed. Where part of a sentence is suspended, this provision shall not apply until the unsuspended part has been satisfied.

Art. 899. Arrest or summons for violation of probation.

A. At any time during probation and suspension of sentence the court may issue a warrant for the arrest of a defendant for violation of any of the conditions of probation, or may issue a summons to appear to answer to a charge of violation or threatened violation.

The warrant of arrest may be executed by any peace officer and shall direct that the defendant be returned to the custody of the court or to a designated detention facility. The summons shall be personally served upon the defendant.

B. If a probation officer has reasonable cause to believe that a defendant has violated or is about to violate a condition of his probation or that an emergency exists so that awaiting an order of the court would create an undue risk to the public or to the probationer, the probation officer may arrest the defendant without a warrant, or may authorize a peace officer to do so. The authorization may be in writing or oral, but if not written, shall be subsequently confirmed by a written statement. The written authorization or subsequent confirmation delivered with the defendant to the official in charge of a parish jail or other place of detention shall be sufficient authority for the detention of the defendant. The probation officer shall immediately notify the proper court of the arrest and shall submit a written report showing in what manner the defendant violated, or was about to violate, a condition of his probation.

C. The court may grant bail to a defendant who is arrested under this article.

D. When a warrant for a defendant's arrest or a summons for defendant's appearance is issued under Paragraph A or a detainer is issued under Paragraph B of this Article, the running of the period of probation shall cease as of the time the warrant, summons, or detainer is issued.

E. An offender arrested under this article shall be given a prerevocation hearing within a reasonable time after his arrest to determine if there is probable cause to detain him pending a final violation hearing.

F. Incidental to the supervision of probationers, probation officers shall be deemed to be peace officers and shall have the same powers with respect to criminal matters and the enforcement of the law relating thereto as sheriffs, constables, and police officers have in their respective jurisdictions. They have all the immunities and defenses now or hereafter made available to sheriffs, constables, and police officers in any suit brought against them in consequence of acts done in the course of their employment.

Art. 900. Violation hearing; sanctions.

A. After an arrest or service of a summons pursuant to Article 899, the court shall cause the defendant to be brought before it within ten days for a hearing. The hearing may be informal or summary. If the court decides that the defendant has violated, or was about to violate, a condition of his probation it may:

(1) Reprimand and warn the defendant.

(2) Order that supervision be intensified.

(3) Add additional conditions to the probation.

(4) Order the defendant, as an additional condition of probation, to be committed to a community rehabilitation center operated by, or under contract with, the Department of Public Safety and Corrections for a period of time not to exceed six months, without benefit of parole or good time, if:

(a) There is bed space available.

(b) The offender has been sentenced to the department, and the sentence has been suspended pursuant to Article 893.

(c) Such commitment does not extend the period of probation beyond the maximum period of probation provided by law.

(d) The violation of probation did not involve the commission of another felony.

(e) The placement in a community rehabilitation center is recommended by the division of probation and parole.

(5) Order that the probation be revoked. In the event of revocation the defendant shall serve the sentence suspended, with or without credit for the time served on probation in the discretion of the court. If the imposition of sentence was suspended, the defendant shall serve the sentence imposed by the court at the revocation hearing.

(6) Extend the period of probation, provided the total amount of time served by the defendant on probation for any one offense shall not exceed the maximum period of probation provided by law.

B. When a defendant has been committed to a community rehabilitation center pursuant to Subparagraph (4) of Paragraph A of this Article, upon written request of the department that an offender be removed for violating the rules or regulations of the community rehabilitation center, the court shall cause the defendant to be brought before it and order that probation be revoked with credit for the time served in the community rehabilitation center.

C. The department may pay a per diem for offenders placed in a community rehabilitation center pursuant to the provisions of Subparagraph (4) of Paragraph A of this Article.

D. When a court considers the revocation of probation, the court shall consider aggravating and mitigating circumstances in the case, including but not limited to the circumstances stated in Article 894.1. If the court revokes the probation of the defendant, the court shall issue oral or written reasons for revocation which shall be entered into the record. The oral or written reasons for revocation shall state the allegations made by the probation officer concerning a violation or threatened violation of the conditions of probation, the findings of the court concerning those allegations, the factual basis or bases for those findings, and the aggravating circumstances, or mitigating circumstances, or both, considered by the court.

(Chgd. by Acts 1991 No. 96, §1; Acts 1995 No. 335, §1; Acts 1997 No. 1323, §1, eff. 8/15/97.)

Art. 901. Revocation for commission of another offense.

A. In addition to the grounds for revocation of probation enumerated in Louisiana Code of Criminal Procedure Article 900, when a defendant who is on probation for a felony commits or is convicted of a felony under the laws of this state, or under the laws of another state, the United States, or the District of Columbia, or is convicted of a misdemeanor under the provisions of Title 14 of the Louisiana Revised Statutes of 1950, or is convicted of a misdemeanor under the provisions of the Uniform Controlled Dangerous Substances Law* contained in Title 40 of the Louisiana Revised Statutes of 1950, his probation may be revoked as of the date of the commission of the felony or final conviction of the felony or misdemeanor.

**R.S. 40:961 et seq.*

B. When a defendant who is under a suspended sentence or on probation for a misdemeanor commits or is convicted of any offense under the laws of this state, a political subdivision thereof, another state or a political subdivision thereof, the United States, or the District of Columbia, his suspended sentence or probation may be revoked as of the date of the commission or final conviction of the offense.

C. In cases of revocation provided for in this Article:

(1) No credit shall be allowed for time spent on probation or for the time elapsed during suspension of the sentence; and

(2) When the new conviction is a Louisiana conviction, the sentence shall run consecutively with the sentence for the new conviction, unless the court originally imposing the suspension or probation specifically orders that said sentences are to be served concurrently, in which case the court minutes shall reflect the date from which the sentences are to run concurrently.

Art. 901.1. Additional sanctions for probation revocation.

A. Notwithstanding any other provision of law, when a defendant, who is a first offender on probation with a suspended sentence for a term of seven years or less at hard labor, or a second offender on probation and having never served time in a state prison, has his probation revoked for any reason other than a subsequent felony conviction, the court, upon the recommendation of the division of probation and parole, may order that the offender be committed to the Department of Public Safety and Corrections and be considered for participation in the intensive incarceration and intensive parole supervision program as provided for in R.S. 15:574.4 or R.S. 15:574.5. If the offender committed to the custody of the department participates in an intensive incarceration program of an eligible parish, the department shall reimburse the sheriff's office of the parish conducting the program in the amount appropriated by the legislature.

B. If the imposition of the sentence was suspended, the defendant shall serve the sentence imposed by the court at the revocation hearing. If the defendant is a first offender and receives a sentence of seven years or less at hard labor, or a second offender on probation and having never served time in a state prison, the court, upon recommendation of the division of probation and parole, may order that the offender be committed to the department and be considered for participation in the intensive incarceration and intensive parole supervision program as provided for in R.S. 15:574.4 or R.S. 15:574.5. If the offender committed to the custody of the department participates in an intensive incarceration program as provided for in R.S. 15:574.5, the department shall reimburse the sheriff's office of the parish conducting the program in the amount appropriated by the legislature.

(Chgd. by Acts 1990 No. 83, §1, eff. 9/7/90.)

Art. 902. Drug addict; pre-sentence investigation; voluntary treatment; conditions of probation.

A. Upon the rendering of a guilty verdict or judgment, the district attorney, with the written consent of the division of probation and parole, may, by ex parte motion, stating the belief that the defendant is a drug addict, whether the crime charged is related to drug abuse or not, request the court to order the division of probation and parole to conduct a presentence investigation for the purpose of determining whether or not the defendant is a drug addict. The presentence investigation may be ordered in the discretion of the court.

B. Upon receiving the report of the presentence investigation, the court may, in its discretion, if it finds probable cause from such report to believe the defendant to be a drug addict, order a contradictory hearing for the purpose of making a judicial determination of such issue.

C. If, at such contradictory hearing, the court finds that the defendant is a drug addict, and it is the court's desire to suspend any sentence which it may impose and place the defendant on probation, it may require as a condition of probation that the defendant submit to urinalysis or any acknowledged recognized test given at reasonable intervals, not to exceed once a week, and at reasonable times in accordance with the request of the division of probation and parole. If the defendant refuses to submit to the tests, the sentencing court may revoke the probation. If the defendant submits to the tests, upon the first instance of a test proving positive for the presence of a controlled dangerous substance, as defined in R.S. 40:963, the sentencing court may commit the defendant to a medical clinic for treatment for a period not to exceed the period of probation. Upon a second positive result, the sentencing court shall revoke the probation and impose the sentence.

D. If the conviction is for a violation of the Uniform Controlled Dangerous Substances Law*, and the sentence consists of both a fine and imprisonment, the court, if it wishes to suspend the sentence and place the defendant on probation, may, with the consent of the defendant, order that the defendant enter a residential drug treatment facility licensed in accordance with R.S. 40:1058.1 et seq., or R.S. 40:2100 et seq., or one operated by the federal

government, and approved by the court. The defendant's consent in such cases shall include consent to pay the cost of treatment for the duration of time ordered by the court. The court may, in its discretion, also suspend the payment of the applicable fine in an amount equal to all or some portion of the cost of the ordered treatment. Upon the successful completion of the treatment program and the termination of probation, the court may order that the fine be reduced in accordance with any amount by which it was reduced. However, if the defendant does not successfully complete the treatment program, or otherwise violates the conditions of probation, the court shall include among any orders issued, that the defendant pay the entire fine imposed by the court. Nothing in this Paragraph shall be construed to grant a defendant a right to probation in cases in which probation is otherwise denied by law.
(Chgd. by Acts 1990 No. 1035, §1, eff. 9/7/90.)
**R.S. 40:961 et seq.*

CHAPTER 3. SENTENCING IN CAPITAL CASES

Article

Art. 905. Capital cases; sentencing hearing required; delay; waiver.

A. Following a verdict or plea of guilty in a capital case, a sentence of death may be imposed only after a sentencing hearing as provided herein.

B. Following a conviction by trial or guilty plea in a capital case, on joint motion of the state and the defendant, the court may impose a sentence of life imprisonment without benefit of parole, probation, or suspension of sentence without conducting a sentencing hearing. The court may refuse to grant the joint motion and order that a sentencing hearing be conducted.

C. If a sentencing hearing will be conducted, the hearing shall not commence sooner than twelve hours after a verdict or plea of guilty, except on joint motion of the state and the defendant.
(Chgd. by Acts 1993 No. 935, §1; Acts 1995 No. 434, §1, eff. 8/15/95.)

Art. 905.1. Sentencing hearing jury; commencement.

A. Except as provided in Part B herein, the sentencing hearing shall be conducted before the same jury that determined the issue of guilt. The order of sequestration shall remain in effect until the completion of the sentencing hearing.

B. If an error occurs only during the sentencing hearing which would necessitate the declaration of a mistrial, or the granting of a new trial by the trial court, or if an appellate court finds an error that occurred only in the sentencing hearing which would necessitate a remand and a new trial, then the trial court shall be empowered to empanel a new jury under the same procedure set out in Title XXVI, Chapter 3 of The Louisiana Code of Criminal Procedure for determining only the issue of penalty, and the rule of sequestration shall apply to the new jury so empanelled.

Art. 905.2. Sentencing hearing; procedure and evidence; jury instructions.

A. The sentencing hearing shall focus on the circumstances of the offense, the character and propensities of the offender, and the impact that the death of the victim has had on the family members. Family members may decline the right to testify but, after testifying for the state, shall be subject to cross-examination. The hearing shall be conducted according to the rules of evidence. Evidence relative to aggravating or mitigating circumstances shall be relevant irrespective of whether the defendant places his character at issue. Insofar as applicable, the procedure shall be the same as that provided for trial in the Code of Criminal Procedure. The jury may consider any evidence offered at the trial on the issue of guilt. The defendant may testify in his own behalf. In the event of retrial the defendant's testimony shall not be admissible except for purposes of impeachment.

B. Notwithstanding any provision to the contrary, the court shall instruct the jury that under the provisions of the state constitution, the governor is empowered to grant a reprieve, pardon, or commutation of sentence following conviction of a crime, and the governor may, in exercising such authority, commute or modify a sentence of life imprisonment without benefit of parole to a lesser sentence including the possibility of parole, and may commute a sentence of death to a lesser sentence of life imprisonment without benefit of parole. The court shall also instruct the jury that under this authority the governor may allow the release of an offender either by reducing a life imprisonment or death sentence to the time already served by the offender or by granting the offender a pardon. The defense may argue or present evidence to the jury on the frequency and extent of use by the governor of his authority. *(Chgd. by Acts 1993 No. 436, §1; Acts 1994 Third Ex. Sess. No. 14, §1; Acts 1995 No. 551, §1, eff. 12/23/95.)*

Art. 905.3. Sentence of death; jury findings.

A sentence of death shall not be imposed unless the jury finds beyond a reasonable doubt that at least one statutory aggravating circumstance exists and, after consideration of any mitigating circumstances, determines that the sentence of death should be imposed. The court shall instruct the jury concerning all of the statutory mitigating circumstances. The court shall also instruct the jury concerning the statutory aggravating circumstances but may decline to instruct the jury on any aggravating circumstance not supported by evidence. The court may provide the jury with a list of the mitigating and aggravating circumstances upon which the jury was instructed.

Art. 905.4. Aggravating circumstances.

A. The following shall be considered aggravating circumstances:

(1) The offender was engaged in the perpetration or attempted perpetration of aggravated rape, forcible rape, aggravated kidnapping, second degree kidnapping, aggravated burglary, aggravated arson, aggravated escape, assault by drive-by shooting, armed robbery, first degree robbery, or simple robbery.

(2) The victim was a fireman or peace officer engaged in his lawful duties.

(3) The offender has been previously convicted of an unrelated murder, aggravated rape, aggravated burglary, aggravated arson, aggravated escape, armed robbery, or aggravated kidnapping.

(4) The offender knowingly created a risk of death or great bodily harm to more than one person.

(5) The offender offered or has been offered or has given or received anything of value for the commission of the offense.

(6) The offender at the time of the commission of the offense was imprisoned after sentence for the commission of an unrelated forcible felony.

(7) The offense was committed in an especially heinous, atrocious or cruel manner.

(8) The victim was a witness in a prosecution against the defendant, gave material assistance to the state in any investigation or prosecution of the defendant, or was an eye witness to a crime alleged to have been committed by the defendant or possessed other material evidence against the defendant.

(9) The victim was a correctional officer or any employee of the Department of Public Safety and Corrections who, in the normal course of his employment was required to come in close contact with persons incarcerated in a state prison facility, and the victim was engaged in his lawful duties at the time of the offense.

(10) The victim was under the age of twelve years or sixty-five years of age or older.

(11) The offender was engaged in the distribution, exchange, sale, or purchase, or any attempt thereof, of a controlled dangerous substance listed in Schedule I, II, III, IV, or V of the Uniform Controlled Dangerous Substances Law*.

**R.S. 40:961 et seq.*

(12) The offender was engaged in the activities prohibited by R.S. 14:107.1(C)(1).

B. For the purposes of Paragraph A(2) herein, the term "peace officer" is defined to include any constable, marshal, deputy marshal, sheriff, deputy sheriff, local or state policeman, commissioned wildlife enforcement agent, federal law enforcement officer, jail or prison guard, parole officer, probation officer, judge, attorney general, assistant attorney

general, attorney general's investigator, district attorney, assistant district attorney, or district attorney's investigator.
(Chgd. by Acts 1995 No. 1179, §1, No. 1274, §1, eff. 8/15/95.)

Art. 905.5. Mitigating circumstances.
The following shall be considered mitigating circumstances:
(a) The offender has no significant prior history of criminal activity;
(b) The offense was committed while the offender was under the influence of extreme mental or emotional disturbance;
(c) The offense was committed while the offender was under the influence or under the domination of another person;
(d) The offense was committed under circumstances which the offender reasonably believed to provide a moral justification or extenuation for his conduct;
(e) At the time of the offense the capacity of the offender to appreciate the criminality of his conduct or to conform his conduct to the requirements of law was impaired as a result of mental disease or defect or intoxication;
(f) The youth of the offender at the time of the offense;
(g) The offender was a principal whose participation was relatively minor;
(h) Any other relevant mitigating circumstance.

Art. 905.6. Jury; unanimous determination.
A sentence of death shall be imposed only upon a unanimous determination of the jury. If the jury unanimously finds the sentence of death inappropriate, it shall render a determination of a sentence of life imprisonment without benefit of probation, parole or suspension of sentence.

Art. 905.7. Form of determination.
The form of jury determination shall be as follows:

"Having found the below listed statutory aggravating circumstance or circumstances and, after consideration of the mitigating circumstances offered, the jury unanimously determines that the defendant should be sentenced to death.

Aggravating circumstance or circumstances found:

s/____________
Foreman"

or

"The jury unanimously determines that the defendant should be sentenced to life imprisonment without benefit of probation, parole or suspension of sentence.

s/____________
Foreman"

Art. 905.8. Imposition of sentence.
The court shall sentence the defendant in accordance with the determination of the jury. If the jury is unable to unanimously agree on a determination, the court shall impose a sentence of life imprisonment without benefit of probation, parole or suspension of sentence.

Art. 905.9. Review on appeal.
The Supreme Court of Louisiana shall review every sentence of death to determine if it is excessive. The court by rules shall establish such procedures as are necessary to satisfy constitutional criteria for review.

TITLE XXXI. APPEAL

CHAPTER 1. GENERAL DISPOSITIONS

Art. 911. Right to appeal from judgment.

Appeal is the exercise of the right of the state or the defendant to have a judgment or ruling reviewed by the proper appellate court. An appeal bond is not required.

Art. 912. Judgments or rulings appealable.

A. Only a final judgment or ruling is appealable.

B. The state cannot appeal from a verdict of acquittal. Adverse judgments or rulings from which the state may appeal include, but are not limited to, judgments or rulings on:

(1) A motion to quash an indictment or any count thereof;
(2) A plea of time limitation;
(3) A plea of double jeopardy;
(4) A motion in arrest of judgment;
(5) A motion to change the venue;
(6) A motion to recuse; and*
(7) *(Repealed.)*

C. The judgments or rulings from which the defendant may appeal include, but are not limited to:

(1) A judgment which imposes sentence;
(2) A ruling upon a motion by the state declaring the present insanity of the defendant; and*
(3) *(Repealed.)*

**So in original.*

Art. 912.1. Right of appeal and application for review; defendant.

A. The defendant may appeal to the supreme court from a judgment in a capital case in which a sentence of death actually has been imposed.

B. The defendant may appeal to the court of appeal from a judgment in a criminal case triable by jury, except as provided in Paragraph A of this Article.

C. (1) In all other cases not otherwise provided by law, the defendant has the right of judicial review by application to the court of appeal for a writ of review. This application shall be accompanied by a complete record of all evidence upon which the judgment is based unless the defendant intelligently waives the right to cause all or any portion of the record to accompany the application.

(2) An application for review by the defendant shall not suspend the execution of sentence, unless the defendant is admitted to postconviction bail.

Art. 913. Effect of appeal.

A. An appeal by the state suspends the ruling or judgment from which the appeal is taken, except when the ruling or judgment requires the release of the defendant.

B. An appeal by the defendant shall not suspend the execution of sentence, unless the defendant is admitted to postconviction bail.

CHAPTER 2. PROCEDURE IN LOWER COURT FOR APPEAL

Art. 914. Method and time of appeal.

A. A motion for an appeal may be made orally in open court or by filing a written motion with the clerk. The motion shall be entered in the minutes of the court.

B. The motion for an appeal must be made no later than:

(1) Five days after the rendition of the judgment or ruling from which the appeal is taken.

(2) Five days from the ruling on a motion to reconsider sentence filed pursuant to Article 881.1, should such a motion be filed.

(Chgd. by Acts 1993 No. 490, §1, eff. 6/10/93.)

Art. 914.1. Designation of record; payment of costs; sanction.

A. The party making the motion for appeal shall, at the time the motion is made, request the transcript of that portion of the proceedings necessary, in light of the assignment of errors to be urged. Not later than five days after the motion, the opposing party may designate in writing the transcript of that portion or portions of the proceedings necessary to oppose the appeal.

B. A transcript of any portion of the proceedings which does not relate to anticipated assignment of errors shall not be furnished to a party for purposes of appeal and shall not result in delay of preparation of the appeal record.

C. (1) An attorney who requests a transcript in accordance with this Article must certify there are good grounds for such request in light of the assignment of errors to be urged.

(2) Except in indigent cases, the costs for preparing the transcript must be paid to the court reporter or the appropriate agency and the costs as required for filing the appeal must be paid in the appellate court, both within twenty days of the mailing of notice, including the payment of any additional costs owed upon notice.

(3) Where applicable, if the appellant or appellant's counsel fails to pay the estimated cost for preparing the record including the transcript within the time specified, the trial judge, on his own motion or upon motion by the clerk or by any party, and after a hearing, may do one of the following:

(a) Extend the time within which the costs may be paid not to exceed thirty days with or without penalty to the appellant or his attorney.

(b) Impose a fine not to exceed five hundred dollars upon the appellant or his attorney, or both.

(c) Dismiss the appeal.

D. The trial court or the appellate court may designate additional portions of the transcript of the proceedings which it feels are necessary for full and fair review of the assignment of errors.

Art. 915. Action on a motion for appeal; return; notice.

A. When a motion for an appeal is made in conformity with Articles 912, 914, and 914.1 the trial court shall grant or deny the motion within seventy-two hours, exclusive of legal holidays, after the motion is made. The return date shall be sixty days from the date the motion for appeal is granted, unless the trial judge fixes a lesser period. When a motion for an appeal has been timely made, the appeal shall not be affected by any fault or omission on the part of the trial court.

B. The minute clerk for each section of the trial court shall forward a copy of the notice of appeal to the clerk of the trial court and to the court reporters responsible for preparing the necessary transcripts, within twenty-four hours, exclusive of legal holidays, of the date the appeal is ordered. The clerk of the trial court shall forward a copy of the notice of appeal to the sheriff having custody of the defendant, to the appropriate appellate court, and to each party, within seven days of the date the appeal is ordered. The party moving for the appeal must forward notice that a motion for appeal has been made to the appropriate appellate court within seven days of the date the motion is made. Failure of the minute clerk, the clerk of court, or the party moving for the appeal, to provide notice shall not affect the validity of the appeal.

Art. 915.1. Appeals; extension of return date; notice.

A. The trial court may grant one extension of the return date of not more than thirty days. An extension may not be granted after the return date has passed. The extension may be granted only upon proof presented by the moving party that additional time is necessary due to extenuating circumstances beyond the control of the moving party and that, without the extension, an unusual and undue hardship would be created. A copy of the extension shall be filed with the appellate court and the clerk of the trial court.

B. Subsequent extensions may be granted by the appellate court for sufficient cause or at the request of the court reporter as provided in Article 919. When a subsequent extension is granted by the appellate court, notice thereof shall be given by mail by the clerk of the trial court to all parties. Failure of the clerk of the trial court to mail such notice shall not affect the validity of the appeal nor will any error or defect which is not imputable to the appellant affect the validity of the appeal.

Art. 916. Divesting of jurisdiction of trial court.

The jurisdiction of the trial court is divested and that of the appellate court attaches upon the entering of the order of appeal. Thereafter, the trial court has no jurisdiction to take any action except as otherwise provided by law and to:

(1) Extend the return day of the appeal, the time for filing assignments of error, or the time for filing per curiam comments in accordance with Articles 844 and 919.

(2) Correct an error or deficiency in the record.

(3) Correct an illegal sentence or take other appropriate action pursuant to a properly made or filed motion to reconsider sentence.

(4) Take all action concerning bail permitted by Title VIII.

(5) Furnish per curiam comments.

(6) Render an interlocutory order or a definitive judgment concerning a ministerial matter not in controversy on appeal.

(7) Impose the penalty provided by Article 844.

(8) Sentence the defendant pursuant to a conviction under the Habitual Offender Law as set forth in R.S. 15:529.1.

(Chgd. by Acts 1991 No. 38, §2; Acts 1997 No. 642, §1, eff. 8/15/97.)

Art. 917. Record on appeal; preparation.

The clerk of the trial court shall prepare the record on appeal and lodge it with the appellate court on or before the return date or any extension thereof. The clerk of the trial court shall prepare the record in accordance with the rules of the appellate court. Failure of the Clerk to prepare and lodge the record on appeal either correctly or timely shall not prejudice the appeal, unless such defect or delay is imputable to the appellant.

Art. 918. Record on appeal; certified and dated.

A. All records and supplemental records prepared for filing in any appellate court shall be certified and dated by the clerk upon completion. The certification shall include the date any transcript was received for inclusion in the record.

B. All transcripts or parts thereof completed for inclusion in the record shall be dated and certified by the court reporter who prepares them. The date of certification by the court reporter shall be the date on which the transcript was completed and furnished to the clerk for inclusion in the record.

Art. 919. Record on appeal; preparation and delivery of transcripts.

A. Each court reporter assigned to prepare any transcript necessary to complete the appeal record shall deliver the transcript to the clerk of the trial court who has the duty of preparing the record for appeal on or before the return date.

B. Whenever the court reporter cannot deliver the transcript to the clerk of the trial court on or before the return date, the reporter shall file a request for an extension of the return date with the trial court or the appellate court as provided by Article 915.1. Whenever a court reporter has not delivered a transcript on or before the return date, the clerk of the trial court shall file a certificate with the court of appeal, not later than seven days after the return date, advising that the record is ready for lodging except for the lack of delivery of the transcript. In such certificate, the clerk shall include the name and address of each reporter who has failed to deliver a transcript and whether any of the court reporters have requested an extension of the return date.

C. Upon the request of the appellate court when the transcript has not been delivered to the clerk of court, but the record is otherwise ready for lodging, the record shall be lodged. The clerk of the trial court shall include with the record a certificate stating the name and address of each court reporter who is required to prepare and deliver a transcript. Thereafter, the appellate court may issue appropriate orders to any named reporter to expedite the preparation and delivery of any necessary transcripts.

Art. 919.1. Record on appeal; contempt.

A. Failure of any person to comply with Articles 914 through 919 may subject such person to contempt of court. Such contempt charges may be initiated by the trial court or by the appellate court on the court's own motion or by motion of any party.

B. In any court where the duty of preparing the appellate record is delegated to, or assumed by, an official other than the clerk of court, by court rule or by custom, all of the provisions applicable to the clerk of court regarding the preparation of such a record are equally applicable to such court official.

CHAPTER 3. PROCEDURE IN APPELLATE COURT

Art. 920. Scope of appellate review.

The following matters and no others shall be considered on appeal:

(1) An error designated in the assignment of errors; and

(2) An error that is discoverable by a mere inspection of the pleadings and proceedings and without inspection of the evidence.

Art. 921. Matters not grounds for reversal.

A judgment or ruling shall not be reversed by an appellate court because of any error, defect, irregularity, or variance which does not affect substantial rights of the accused.

Art. 922. Finality of judgment on appeal.

A. Within fourteen days of rendition of the judgment of the supreme court or any appellate court, in term time or out, a party may apply to the appropriate court for a rehearing. The court may act upon the application at any time.

B. A judgment rendered by the supreme court or other appellate court becomes final when the delay for applying for a rehearing has expired and no application therefor has been made.

C. If an application for a rehearing has been made timely, a judgment of the appellate court becomes final when the application is denied.

D. If an application for a writ of review is timely filed with the supreme court, the judgment of the appellate court from which the writ of review is sought becomes final when the supreme court denies the writ.

(Chgd. by Acts 1993 No. 976, §1, eff. 8/15/93.)

Art. 923. Duty of clerk as to final decisions in appellate court.

When a decision of an appellate court becomes final, the clerk of court shall transmit a certified copy of the decree to the court from which the appeal was taken.

When the judgment is received by the lower court, it shall be filed and executed.

TITLE XXXI-A. POST CONVICTION RELIEF

Art. 924. Application for post conviction relief.

An application for post conviction relief is a petition filed by a person in custody after sentence following conviction for the commission of an offense seeking to have the conviction and sentence set aside.

"Custody" as used in this Title means detention or confinement, or probation or parole supervision, after sentence following conviction for the commission of an offense.

Art. 924.1. Effect of appeal.

An application for post conviction relief shall not be entertained if the petitioner may appeal the conviction and sentence which he seeks to challenge, or if an appeal is pending.

Art. 925. Venue.

Applications for post conviction relief shall be filed in the parish in which the petitioner was convicted.

Art. 926. Petition.

A. An application for post conviction relief shall be by written petition addressed to the district court for the parish in which the petitioner was convicted. A copy of the judgment of conviction and sentence shall be annexed to the petition, or the petition shall allege that a copy has been demanded and refused.

B. The petition shall allege:

(1) The name of the person in custody and the place of custody, if known, or if not known, a statement to that effect;

(2) The name of the custodian, if known, or if not known, a designation or description of him as far as possible;

(3) A statement of the grounds upon which relief is sought, specifying with reasonable particularity the factual basis for such relief;

(4) A statement of all prior applications for writs of habeas corpus or for post conviction relief filed by or on behalf of the person in custody in connection with his present custody; and

(5) All errors known or discoverable by the exercise of due diligence.

C. The application shall be signed by the petitioner and be accompanied by his affidavit that the allegations contained in the petition are true to the best of his information and belief.

D. The petitioner shall use the uniform application for post conviction relief approved by the Supreme Court of Louisiana. If the petitioner fails to use the uniform application, the court may provide the petitioner with the uniform application and require its use.

E. Inexcusable failure of the petitioner to comply with the provisions of this Article may be a basis for dismissal of his application.

Art. 927. Procedural objections; answer.

A. If an application alleges a claim which, if established, would entitle the petitioner to relief, the court shall order the custodian, through the district attorney in the parish in which the defendant was convicted, to file any procedural objections he may have, or an answer on the merits if there are no procedural objections, within a specified period not in excess of thirty days. If procedural objections are timely filed, no answer on the merits of the claim may be ordered until such objections have been considered and rulings thereon have become final.

B. In any order of the court requiring a response by the district attorney pursuant to this Article, the court shall render specific rulings dismissing any claim which, if established as alleged, would not entitle the petitioner to relief, and shall order a response only as to such claim or claims which, if established as alleged, would entitle the petitioner to relief.

C. If the court orders an answer filed, the court need not order production of the petitioner except as provided in Article 930.

(Chgd. by Acts 1990 No. 523, §1, eff. 9/7/90.)

Art. 928. Dismissal upon the pleadings.

The application may be dismissed without an answer if the application fails to allege a claim which, if established, would entitle the petitioner to relief.

Art. 929. Summary disposition.

A. If the court determines that the factual and legal issues can be resolved based upon the application and answer, and supporting documents, including relevant transcripts, depositions, and other reliable documents submitted by either party or available to the court, the court may grant or deny relief without further proceedings.

B. For good cause, oral depositions of the petitioner and witnesses may be taken under conditions specified by the court. The court may authorize requests for admissions of fact and of genuineness of documents. In such matters, the court shall be guided by the Code of Civil Procedure.

Art. 930. Evidentiary hearing.

A. An evidentiary hearing for the taking of testimony or other evidence shall be ordered whenever there are questions of fact which cannot properly be resolved pursuant to Articles 928 and 929. The petitioner, in absence of an express waiver, is entitled to be present at such hearing, unless the only evidence to be received is evidence as permitted pursuant to Subsection B of this Section, and the petitioner has been or will be provided with copies of such evidence and an opportunity to respond thereto in writing.

B. Duly authenticated records, transcripts, depositions, documents, or portions thereof, or admissions of facts may be received in evidence.

C. No evidentiary hearing on the merits of a claim shall be ordered or conducted, nor shall any proffer of evidence be received over the objection of the respondent, and no ruling upon procedural objections to the petition shall purport to address the merits of the claim over the objection of the respondent, unless the court has first ruled upon all procedural objections raised by the respondent, and such rulings have become final. Any language in a ruling on procedural objections raised by the respondent which purports to address the merits of the claim shall be deemed as null, void, and of no effect.

(Chgd. by Acts 1990 No. 523, §1, eff. 9/7/90.)

Art. 930.1. Judgment granting or denying relief under Articles 928, 929, and 930.

A copy of the judgment granting or denying relief and written or transcribed reasons for the judgment shall be furnished to the petitioner, the district attorney, and the custodian.

Art. 930.2. Burden of proof.

The petitioner in an application for post conviction relief shall have the burden of proving that relief should be granted.

Art. 930.3. Grounds.

If the petitioner is in custody after sentence for conviction for an offense, relief shall be granted only on the following grounds:

(1) The conviction was obtained in violation of the constitution of the United States or the state of Louisiana;

(2) The court exceeded its jurisdiction;

(3) The conviction or sentence subjected him to double jeopardy;

(4) The limitations on the institution of prosecution had expired;

(5) The statute creating the offense for which he was convicted and sentenced is unconstitutional; or

(6) The conviction or sentence constitute the ex post facto application of law in violation of the constitution of the United States or the state of Louisiana.

Art. 930.4. Repetitive applications.

A. Unless required in the interest of justice, any claim for relief which was fully litigated in an appeal from the proceedings leading to the judgment of conviction and sentence shall not be considered.

B. If the application alleges a claim of which the petitioner had knowledge and inexcusably failed to raise in the proceedings leading to conviction, the court may deny relief.

C. If the application alleges a claim which the petitioner raised in the trial court and inexcusably failed to pursue on appeal, the court may deny relief.

D. A successive application may be dismissed if it fails to raise a new or different claim.

E. A successive application may be dismissed if it raises a new or different claim that was inexcusably omitted from a prior application.

F. If the court considers dismissing an application for failure of the petitioner to raise the claim in the proceedings leading to conviction, failure to urge the claim on appeal, or failure to include the claim in a prior application, the court shall order the petitioner to state reasons for his failure. If the court finds that the failure was excusable, it shall consider the merits of the claim.

Art. 930.5. Custody pending retrial; bail.

If a court grants relief under an application for post conviction relief, the court shall order that the petitioner be held in custody pending a new trial if it appears that there are legally sufficient grounds upon which to reprosecute the petitioner.

In such a case, the petitioner shall be entitled to bail on the offense as though he has not been convicted of the offense.

Art. 930.6. Review of trial court judgments.

A. The petitioner may invoke the supervisory jurisdiction of the court of appeal if the trial court dismisses the application or otherwise denies relief on an application for post conviction relief. No appeal lies from a judgment dismissing an application or otherwise denying relief.

B. If a statute or ordinance is declared unconstitutional, the state may appeal to the supreme court. If relief is granted on any other ground, the state may invoke the supervisory jurisdiction of the court of appeal.

C. Pending the state's application for writs, or pending the state's appeal, the district court or the court of appeal may stay the judgment granting relief.

Art. 930.7. Right to counsel.

A. If the petitioner is indigent and alleges a claim which, if established, would entitle him to relief, the court may appoint counsel.

B. The court may appoint counsel for an indigent petitioner when it orders an evidentiary hearing, authorizes the taking of depositions, or authorizes requests for admissions of fact or genuineness of documents, when such evidence is necessary for the disposition of procedural objections raised by the respondent.

C. The court shall appoint counsel for an indigent petitioner when it orders an evidentiary hearing on the merits of a claim, or authorizes the taking of depositions or requests for admissions of fact or genuineness of documents for use as evidence in ruling upon the merits of the claim.

(Chgd. by Acts 1990 No. 523, §1, eff. 9/7/90.)

Art. 930.8. Time limitations; exceptions; prejudicial delay.

A. No application for post conviction relief, including applications which seek an out-of-time appeal, shall be considered if it is filed more than three years after the judgment of conviction and sentence has become final under the provisions of Article 914 or 922, unless any of the following apply:

(1) The application alleges, and the petitioner proves or the state admits, that the facts upon which the claim is predicated were not known to the petitioner or his attorney.

(2) The claim asserted in the petition is based upon a final ruling of an appellate court establishing a theretofore unknown interpretation of constitutional law and petitioner establishes that this interpretation is retroactively applicable to his case, and the petition is filed within one year of the finality of such ruling.

(3) The application would already be barred by the provisions of this Article, but the application is filed on or before October 1, 1991.

(4) The person asserting the claim has been sentenced to death.

B. An application for post conviction relief which is timely filed, or which is allowed under an exception to the time limitation as set forth in Paragraph A of this Article, shall be dismissed upon a showing by the state of prejudice to its ability to respond to, negate, or rebut the allegations of the petition caused by events not under the control of the state which have transpired since the date of original conviction, if the court finds, after a hearing limited to that issue, that the state's ability to respond to, negate, or rebut such allegations has been materially prejudiced thereby.

C. At the time of sentencing, the trial court shall inform the defendant of the prescriptive period for post conviction relief.

(Added by Acts 1990 No. 1023, §1, eff. 10/1/90.)

TITLE XXXII. DEFINITIONS

Article

Art. 931. Courts, judges, and magistrates.

Except where the context clearly indicates otherwise, as used in this Code:

(1) "Court" means a court with criminal jurisdiction or its judge. It does not include a mayor's court or a justice of the peace.

(2) "City court" means a city, town, village, or other municipal court, with criminal jurisdiction. It does not include a mayor's court or a justice of the peace.

(3) "Judge" means a judge of a court, as defined in this article.

(4) "Magistrate" means any judge, a justice of the peace, or a mayor of a mayor's court.

Art. 932. Jurors, juries, and jury venires.

Except where the context clearly indicates otherwise, as used in this Code:

(1) "Juror" means a grand or a petit juror.

(2) "Petit jury" means the jury that tries a defendant.

(3) "Panel" is a group of persons selected according to law from a grand jury or petit jury venire to serve as a grand jury, or as a petit jury.

Art. 933. Offenses.

Except where the context clearly indicates otherwise, as used in this Code:

(1) "Offense" includes both a felony and a misdemeanor.

(2) "Capital offense" means an offense that may be punished by death.

(3) "Felony" means an offense that may be punished by death or by imprisonment at hard labor.

(4) "Misdemeanor" means any offense other than a felony, and includes the violation of an ordinance providing a penal sanction.

Art. 934. Miscellaneous definitions.

Except where the context clearly indicates otherwise, as used in this Code:

(1) "Act" includes a failure or omission to perform a legal duty.

(2) "City" means a city, town, village, or other municipality.

(3) "Convicted" means adjudicated guilty after a plea or after trial on the merits.

(4) "Defendant" means a person who has been charged with or accused of an offense.

(5) "District Attorney" includes an assistant district attorney, and where the prosecution is in a city court, includes the prosecuting officer of that court.

(6) "Indictment" includes information and affidavit, unless it is the clear intent to restrict that word to the finding of a grand jury.

(7) "Institution of prosecution" means the finding of an indictment, or the filing of an information, or affidavit, which is designed to serve as the basis of a trial.

(8) "Oath" includes affirmation.

(9) "Person" includes an individual, partnership, unincorporated association of individuals, joint stock company, or corporation.

(10) "State" includes a city or other political subdivision of the state.

(11) "Statute" and "criminal law" mean a criminal statute, a constitutional provision, or an ordinance of a city or other political subdivision of the state.

(12) "Trial on the merits" means trial on the issue of guilt or innocence.

LOUISIANA CHILDREN'S CODE

(Added by Acts 1991 No. 235, §§1 to 16, eff. 1/1/92.)

(Complete Code)

TITLE I. GENERAL PROVISIONS

Art. 100. Short title; citation of Code.

This Code shall be known as the "Louisiana Children's Code" and may be officially cited: Ch.C. *(Added by Acts 1991 No. 235, §1, eff. 1/1/92.)*

Art. 101. Preamble.

The people of Louisiana recognize the family as the most fundamental unit of human society; that preserving families is essential to a free society; that the relationship between parent and child is preeminent in establishing and maintaining the well-being of the child; that parents have the responsibility for providing the basic necessities of life as well as love and affection to their children; that parents have the paramount right to raise their children in accordance with their own values and traditions; that parents should make the decisions regarding where and with whom the child shall reside, the educational, moral, ethical, and religious training of the child, the medical, psychiatric, surgical, and preventive health care of the child, and the discipline of the child; that children owe to their parents respect, obedience, and affection; that the role of the state in the family is limited and should only be asserted when there is a serious threat to the family, the parents, or the child; and that extraordinary procedures established by law are meant to be used only when required by necessity and then with due respect for the rights of the parents, the children, and the institution of the family. *(Added by Acts 1991 No. 235, §1, eff. 1/1/92.)*

Art. 102. Purpose and construction.

The provisions of this Code shall be liberally construed to the end that each child and parent coming within the jurisdiction of the court shall be accorded due process and that each child shall receive, preferably in his own home, the care, guidance, and control that will be conducive to his welfare. In those instances when he is removed from the control of his parents, the court shall secure for him care as nearly as possible equivalent to that which the parents should have given him. These Code provisions shall be construed to promote the stability of the family and to secure simplicity in procedure, fairness in adjudication and administration, and the elimination of unjustifiable delay. *(Added by Acts 1991 No. 235, §1, eff. 1/1/92.)*

Art. 103. General applicability.

Except as otherwise specified in any Title of this Code, the provisions of the Children's Code shall be applicable in all juvenile court proceedings, and only to such proceedings. *(Added by Acts 1991 No. 235, §1; chgd. by Acts 1992 No. 705, §1, eff. 7/6/92.)*

Art. 104. Applicability of Code of Criminal Procedure; Code of Civil Procedure.

Where procedures are not provided in this Code, or otherwise by law, the court shall proceed in accordance with:

(1) The Code of Criminal Procedure in a delinquency proceeding and in a criminal trial of an adult.

(2) The Code of Civil Procedure in all other matters.

(Added by Acts 1991 No. 235, §1, eff. 1/1/92.)

Art. 105. Applicability of Code of Evidence.

Except as otherwise specially provided by this Code, the rules of evidence applicable to juvenile adjudication hearings in nondelinquency proceedings are those provisions of the Louisiana Code of Evidence applicable to civil cases. The rules of evidence applicable to delinquency proceedings and criminal trials of adults are those provisions of the Louisiana Code of Evidence applicable to criminal cases. *(Added by Acts 1991 No. 235, §1; chgd. by Acts 1992 No. 705, §1, eff. 7/6/92.)*

Art. 106. Number, gender.

Unless the context clearly indicates otherwise:

(1) Words used in the singular number apply also to the plural; words used in the plural number include the singular.

(2) Words used in one gender apply also to the other.

(Added by Acts 1991 No. 235, §1, eff. 1/1/92.)

Art. 107. Mandatory and permissive language.

The word "shall" is mandatory, and the word "may" is permissive. *(Added by Acts 1991 No. 235, §1, eff. 1/1/92.)*

Art. 108. Conjunctive, disjunctive, or both.

Unless the context clearly indicates otherwise:

(1) The word "and" indicates the conjunctive.

(2) The word "or" indicates the disjunctive.

(3) When the Article is phrased in the disjunctive, followed by the words "or both", both the conjunctive and disjunctive are intended.

(Added by Acts 1991 No. 235, §1, eff. 1/1/92.)

Art. 109. Assistants and deputies included.

Unless the context clearly indicates the contrary, official titles, such as clerk of court, district attorney, and sheriff, include assistants and deputies. *(Added by Acts 1991 No. 235, §1, eff. 1/1/92.)*

Art. 110. References to code articles or statutory sections.

Unless the context clearly indicates the contrary:

(1) A reference in this Code to a Title, Chapter, or Article without further designation, means a Title, Chapter, or Article of this Code.

(2) A reference in this Code to an Article of a code or to a statutory section applies to subsequent amendments thereof.

(Added by Acts 1991 No. 235, §1, eff. 1/1/92.)

Art. 111. Article headings and comments not part of law.

The headings of the Articles of this Code and any comments thereto are for convenient reference and do not constitute parts of the law. *(Added by Acts 1991 No. 235, §1, eff. 1/1/92.)*

Art. 112. Clerical and typographical errors disregarded.

Clerical and typographical errors in this Code shall be disregarded when the legislative intent is clear from the context in which the provision or word is found. *(Added by Acts 1991 No. 235, §1, eff. 1/1/92.)*

Art. 113. Pleading a statute or ordinance.

In the course of any proceeding under this Code, when pleading a statute of Louisiana or an ordinance of a political subdivision thereof, a statute of another state of the United States, or a federal statute, or a right derived therefrom, it is sufficient to refer to the statute or ordinance by an official method of citation, by its title, or in any other manner which identifies the statute or ordinance. A copy of any ordinance pleaded shall be furnished to the court and filed with the record of the proceeding. *(Added by Acts 1991 No. 235, §1, eff. 1/1/92.)*

Art. 114. Computation of time.

A. In computing a period of time allowed or prescribed by law or by order of court, the date of the act, event, or default after which the period begins to run is not to be included. The last day of the period is to be included, unless it is a legal holiday, in which event the period runs until the end of the next day which is not a legal holiday.

B. A half-holiday is considered as a legal holiday.

C. A legal holiday is to be included in the computation of a period of time allowed or prescribed, except in any one of the following instances:

(1) It is expressly excluded.

(2) It would otherwise be the last day of the period, except that, for purposes of calculating a release date from an order of commitment, a legal holiday shall be included if it is the last day of the period.

(3) The period is less than seven days.

D. All Saturdays and Sundays are also considered as legal holidays.

(Added by Acts 1991 No. 235, §1, eff. 1/1/92.)

Art. 115. Oath or affirmation in juvenile proceedings.

A. Witnesses shall swear or affirm to speak the truth and nothing but the truth.

B. A child witness need not be placed under oath or be required to make an affirmation if the court can otherwise assure that the child understands his obligation to speak the truth.

(Added by Acts 1991 No. 235, §1, eff. 1/1/92.)

Art. 116. Definitions.

Except where the context clearly indicates otherwise, these definitions apply for the following terms used throughout this Code.

(1) "Act" includes a failure or omission to perform a legal duty.

(2) "Capital offense" means an offense that may be punished by death.

(3) "Child" means a person who has not attained the age of seventeen years, except as it is specially defined by a Title of this Code.

(4) "Court" means any city, parish, district, or juvenile, or its judge, when exercising juvenile jurisdiction as provided for in this code. It does not include a judge of a mayor's court or a justice of the peace.

(5) "Felony" means an offense that may be punished by death or by imprisonment at hard labor.

(6) "Guardianship of the person of a child" means the duty and authority to make important decisions in matters having a permanent effect on the life and development of the

child and the responsibility for the child's general welfare until he reaches the age of majority, subject to any residual rights possessed by the child's parents. It shall include but not necessarily be limited to:

(a) The authority to consent to marriage, to enlistment in the armed forces of the United States, to represent the minor in legal actions, to make other decisions of substantial legal significance concerning the minor.

(b) The authority and duty of reasonable visitation, except to the extent that such right of visitation has been limited by court order.

(c) The rights and responsibilities of legal custody.

(7) "Indictment" means a written accusation of crime made by a grand jury.

(8) "Information" means a written accusation of crime made by the district attorney or the city prosecutor and signed by him. It must be filed in open court in a court having jurisdiction to try the offense, or in the office of the clerk thereof.

(9) "Judge" means the judge of a court exercising juvenile jurisdiction.

(9.1) "Juvenile crime victim" means a person, under the age of seventeen, against whom an offense against the person that is a felony has been committed.

(10) "Juvenile detention center" means a facility providing care for children under circumstances which are physically restricting.

(11) "Juvenile proceeding" or "juvenile case" means a proceeding or case in which the court is exercising juvenile jurisdiction.

(12) "Legal custody" means the right to have physical custody of the child and to determine where and with whom the child shall reside; to exercise the rights and duty to protect, train, and discipline the child; the authority to consent to major medical, psychiatric, and surgical treatment; and to provide the child with food, shelter, education, and ordinary medical care, all subject to any residual rights possessed by the child's parents.

(13) "Licensed institution", "licensed facility", or "licensed agency" means an institution or agency that has been licensed under state law, if licensure is required by law for such an institution or agency.

(14) "Minor" means a person who has not attained the age of eighteen years.

(15) "Misdemeanor" means an offense other than a felony, and includes the violation of an ordinance providing a penal sanction.

(16) "Offense" includes both felony and misdemeanor.

(17) "Parent" means any living person who is presumed to be a parent under Civil Code Articles 184 through 190, a biological or adoptive mother or father of a child.

(18) "Parole" means the legal status created by court order whereby a child is conditionally released from a juvenile correctional institution to a less restrictive setting where continued supervision will be provided by a probation officer and standards of conduct will be imposed by the court.

(19) "Peace officer" means any sheriff, police officer, or other person deputized by proper authority to serve as a peace officer.

(20) "Physician" means a person permitted to practice and in active practice as a physician under the laws of Louisiana or a person in a postgraduate medical training program of an accredited medical school in Louisiana or a medical officer similarly qualified by the government of the United States while in this state in the performance of official duties.

(21) "Probation" means the legal status created by court order following an adjudication of delinquency or an adjudication that a family is in need of services or that the child is in need of supervision, whereby a child is permitted to remain in a community subject to supervision by a probation officer and to standards of conduct imposed by the court.

(22) "Probation officer" is a representative of the agency providing supervision services to a court exercising juvenile jurisdiction. It also includes any person designated by the court to serve as the court's probation officer.

(23) "Psychiatrist" means a physician who has at least three years of formal training or primary experience in the diagnosis and treatment of mental illness.

(24) "Residual parental rights" means those rights and responsibilities remaining with the parents after the legal transfer of custody of their child, including but not necessarily limited to right of visitation, consent to adoption, right to determine religious affiliation, responsibility of support, and the right of inheritance from the child.

(25) "Shelter care facility" means a physically unrestricting child caring facility providing temporary care for children.

(26) "State" includes a city or other political subdivision of the state.

(27) "Statute" or "law" means a statute, a constitutional provision, or an ordinance of a city or other political subdivision of the state.

(28) "Tutor" means one other than a parent who has qualified for the office and has been confirmed or appointed by a court.

(Added by Acts 1991 No. 235, §1; chgd. by Acts 1992 No. 705, §1; Acts 1997 No. 732, §2, eff. 8/15/97.)

TITLE II. LEGAL STATUS OF CHILDREN

(Reserved.)

TITLE III. JURISDICTION, GENERAL AUTHORITY, AND APPEALS

Chapter

CHAPTER 1. DEFINITIONS

Article

Art. 301. Definitions.

As used in this Title:

"Nonmetropolitan area" means a parish whose largest city has a population of fifty thousand or less and where the population of the entire parish is less than one hundred thousand.

(Added by Acts 1991 No. 235, §3, eff. 1/1/92.)

CHAPTER 2. JUVENILE JURISDICTION OF COURTS

Article

Art. 302. Juvenile jurisdiction of courts.

Juvenile jurisdiction shall be exercised as follows:

(1) Special juvenile courts created by law for Caddo, Orleans, Jefferson, and East Baton Rouge Parishes shall have exclusive original juvenile jurisdiction, and any other jurisdiction conferred by the statute creating them, in the parish or parishes for which they are created. Judges of these courts shall exercise their juvenile jurisdiction according to the provisions of this Code.

(2) District courts, except where a separate juvenile court with exclusive original juvenile jurisdiction is established by law, shall have original juvenile jurisdiction for the parish or parishes within their district.

(3) Parish courts, except where a separate juvenile court with exclusive original juvenile jurisdiction is established by law, shall have original juvenile jurisdiction for their parish. This jurisdiction shall be concurrent with that of the district court.

(4) City courts, except where a separate juvenile court with exclusive original juvenile jurisdiction is established by law, shall have original juvenile jurisdiction for their territorial jurisdiction. This jurisdiction shall be concurrent with that of the district court.

(Added by Acts 1991 No. 235, §3, eff. 1/1/92.)

CHAPTER 3. JURISDICTION OVER CHILDREN AND MINORS

Art. 303. Exclusive jurisdiction over children and minors; exceptions.

A court exercising juvenile jurisdiction shall have exclusive original jurisdiction over:

(1) Delinquency proceedings pursuant to Title VIII, except when a child either:

(a) Is subject to the jurisdiction of the criminal courts for prosecution and liability as an adult pursuant to Chapter 4 of this Title.

(b) Has been transferred by the juvenile court for criminal prosecution and liability as an adult pursuant to Chapter 11 of Title VIII.

(2) Child in need of care proceedings pursuant to Title VI.

(3) Families in need of services proceedings pursuant to Title VII.

(4) Traffic proceedings pursuant to Title IX.

(5) Involuntary termination of parental rights proceedings pursuant to Title X.

(6) Voluntary termination of parental rights proceedings pursuant to Title XI.

(7) Adoption proceedings pursuant to Title XII.

(8) Mental health proceedings pursuant to Title XIV.

(9) Any special proceeding authorized by Title XV, except domestic abuse assistance proceedings brought in a district court pursuant to R.S. 46:2131 et seq.

(10) Any proceeding necessary to implement the provisions of interstate compacts affecting children pursuant to Title XVI.

(11) Such other jurisdiction over children as may be provided by law.

(Added by Acts 1991 No. 235, §3; chgd. by Acts 1992 No. 705, §1, eff. 7/6/92.)

Art. 304. Transfer of child adjudicated in another state for disposition.

A. (1) Upon request of a court of another state, a court of this state shall accept jurisdiction of a child provided both the following occur:

(a) The child is about to become a resident of or is domiciled in the parish.

(b) The child has been adjudicated in the other state under circumstances which would confer jurisdiction in this state.

(2) The request shall include a certified copy of the judgment of the requesting court and a copy of the record.

B. The order of adjudication of the requesting state is not subject to attack.

C. Within fourteen days of receiving such request, the court shall determine whether the conditions of transfer are met. If the conditions of transfer have not been met, the court shall immediately advise the requesting court in writing. If the conditions of transfer are met, the court shall immediately issue written notice of its intent to accept jurisdiction of the child.

D. Upon receipt of an order of the requesting court transferring jurisdiction of the child, the court shall direct its probation officer or other person to take custody of the child or otherwise provide for his appearance before the court.

E. Upon acceptance, the court shall promptly hold a hearing to determine the proper disposition. The disposition hearing and judgment of disposition shall be in accordance with the provisions of this Code.

(Added by Acts 1991 No. 235, §3, eff. 1/1/92.)

CHAPTER 4. ORIGINAL CRIMINAL COURT JURISDICTION OVER CHILDREN

Art. 305. Divestiture of juvenile court jurisdiction; original criminal court jurisdiction over children; when acquired.

A. (1) When a child is fifteen years of age or older at the time of the commission of first degree murder, second degree murder, aggravated rape, or aggravated kidnapping, he is subject to the exclusive jurisdiction of the juvenile court until either:

(a) An indictment charging one of these offenses is returned.

(b) The juvenile court holds a continued custody hearing pursuant to Articles 819 and 820 and finds probable cause that he committed one of these offenses, whichever occurs first.

(2) Thereafter, the child is subject to the exclusive jurisdiction of the appropriate court exercising criminal jurisdiction for all subsequent procedures, including the review of bail applications, and the child shall be transferred forthwith to the appropriate adult facility for detention prior to his trial as an adult.

B. (1) When a child is fifteen years of age or older at the time of the commission of any of the offenses listed in Subparagraph (2) of this Paragraph, he is subject to the exclusive jurisdiction of the juvenile court until whichever of the following occurs first:

(a) An indictment charging one of the offenses listed in Subparagraph (2) of this Paragraph is returned.

(b) The juvenile court holds a continued custody hearing and finds probable cause that the child has committed any of the offenses listed in Subparagraph (2) of this Paragraph and a bill of information charging any of the offenses listed in Subparagraph (2) of this Paragraph is filed.

(2) (a) Attempted first degree murder.

(b) Attempted second degree murder.

(c) Manslaughter.

(d) Armed robbery.

(e) Aggravated burglary.

(f) Forcible rape.

(g) Simple rape.

(h) Second degree kidnapping.

(i) Aggravated oral sexual battery.

(j) Aggravated battery committed with a firearm.

(k) A second or subsequent aggravated battery.

(*l*) A second or subsequent aggravated burglary.

(m) A second or subsequent offense of burglary of an inhabited dwelling.

(n) A second or subsequent felony-grade violation of Part X or X-B of Chapter 4 of Title 40 of the Louisiana Revised Statutes of 1950 involving the manufacture, distribution, or possession with intent to distribute controlled dangerous substances.

(3) The district attorney shall have the discretion to file a petition alleging any of the offenses listed in Subparagraph (2) of this Paragraph in the juvenile court or, alternatively, to obtain an indictment or file a bill of information. If the child is being held in detention, the district attorney shall make his election and file the indictment, bill of information, or petition in the appropriate court within thirty calendar days after the child's arrest, unless the child waives this right.

(4) If an indictment is returned or a bill of information is filed, the child is subject to the exclusive jurisdiction of the appropriate court exercising criminal jurisdiction for all subsequent procedures, including the review of bail applications, and the child shall be transferred forthwith to the appropriate adult facility for detention prior to his trial as an adult.

C. Except when a juvenile is held in an adult jail or lockup, the time limitations for the conduct of a continued custody hearing are those provided by Article 819.

D. The court exercising criminal jurisdiction shall retain jurisdiction over the child's case, even though he pleads guilty to or is convicted of a lesser included offense. A plea to or conviction of a lesser included offense shall not revest jurisdiction in the court exercising juvenile jurisdiction over such a child.

(Added by Acts 1991 No. 235, §3, No. 501, §1; chgd. by Acts 1992 No. 705, §4; Acts 1994 Third Ex. Sess. No. 15, §1; Acts 1995 No. 367, §1, No. 959, §1, No. 979, §1, eff. 8/15/95.)

Art. 306. Places of detention; juveniles subject to criminal court jurisdiction.

A. Prior to the divesting events specified in Paragraphs A through D of Article 305, the child shall be held in custody in a juvenile detention center, except as hereinafter provided.

B. If a detention facility for juveniles is not available, he may be held in an adult jail or lockup for identification or processing procedures or while awaiting transportation only as long as necessary to complete these activities for up to six hours, except that in nonmetropolitan areas, he may be held for up to twenty-four hours if all of the following occur:

(1) The child meets the age and offense criteria set out in Article 305.

(2) A continued custody hearing in accordance with Articles 820 and 821 is held within twenty-four hours after his arrest.

(3) There is no acceptable alternative placement to the jail or lockup in which he is being held.

(4) The sheriff or the administrator of the adult jail or lockup has certified to the court that facilities exist providing for sight and sound separation of the juvenile from adult offenders and that he can be given continuous visual supervision while placed in the jail or lockup.

C. If an indictment has not been returned, a bill of information filed, or a continued custody hearing not held within twenty-four hours, the child held in an adult jail or lockup in a nonmetropolitan area shall be released or removed to a juvenile detention facility.

D. If at the conclusion of the continued custody hearing, the court determines that the child meets the age requirements and that there is probable cause that the child has committed one of the offenses enumerated in Article 305, the court shall order him held for trial as an adult for the appropriate court of criminal jurisdiction. The child shall thereafter be held in any facility used for the pretrial detention of accused adults and shall apply to the appropriate court of criminal jurisdiction for a preliminary hearing, bail, and for any other rights to which he may be entitled under the Code of Criminal Procedure.

E. If for any reason the court determines that the child is not subject to the jurisdiction of the criminal courts, it may continue him in custody only in those places authorized by Article 822.

F. The court authorizing the detention of the child in an adult jail or lockup pursuant to Paragraph B or D of this Article shall submit a written report delineating appropriate reasons for the continued custody to the judicial administrator of the supreme court for review and shall submit copies to the Louisiana Commission on Law Enforcement and Administration of Criminal Justice and to the sheriff or chief of police of the facility in which the child is being detained within seven working days of the court's decision.
(Added by Acts 1991 No. 235, §3; chgd. by Acts 1992 No. 705, §1, eff. 7/6/92.)

Art. 306.1. Transmission of order; transcripts.

A. If the child has been ordered held for trial as an adult as a result of a continued custody hearing convened pursuant to Article 305(A)(1)(b) or Article 305(B)(1)(b), the court shall transmit the order rendered after the hearing, or a certified copy thereof, without delay, to the clerk of the court having jurisdiction of the offense.

B. Any party may request the court to provide a complete or partial transcript of the testimony of the witnesses; however, neither the record of the hearing not the reasons for the transfer shall be admissible in evidence in any subsequent criminal proceedings, except for the purpose of impeachment of a witness.
(Added by Acts 1992 No. 705, §1, eff. 7/6/92.)

CHAPTER 5. JUVENILE JURISDICTION OVER ADULTS

Art. 307. Juvenile jurisdiction over adults in proceedings involving the care, custody, or control of a child.

A. A court exercising juvenile jurisdiction shall have exclusive original jurisdiction over adult parties in the following cases involving the care, custody or control of a child:

(1) Child in need of care proceedings pursuant to Title VI.

(2) Families in need of services proceedings pursuant to Title VII.
(3) Involuntary termination of parental rights proceedings pursuant to Title X.
(4) Voluntary termination of parental rights proceedings pursuant to Title XI.
(5) Adoption proceedings pursuant to Title XII.
(6) Special proceedings pursuant to Title XV.

B. In aid of its jurisdiction over children, a court exercising juvenile jurisdiction shall also have jurisdiction over any natural person who is a parent or caretaker of the child or other adult lawfully before it to secure his full cooperation and assistance in the entire rehabilitative program prescribed by the court for the child, including conditions or incidents of probation, supervision, protection, custody, or release on parole in:

(1) Delinquency proceedings pursuant to Title VIII.
(2) Traffic violation proceedings pursuant to Title IX.
(3) Mental health proceedings pursuant to Title XIV.
(4) Any special proceeding authorized by Title XV.
(5) Any proceeding necessary to implement the provisions of interstate compacts affecting children pursuant to Title XVI.

C. Nothing in this Article shall be construed to deprive other courts of jurisdiction over domestic abuse assistance proceedings brought pursuant to R.S. 46:2131 et seq. or over contempt proceedings.

(Added by Acts 1991 No. 235, §3; chgd. by Acts 1992 No. 705, §1, eff. 7/6/92.)

Art. 308. Authority of courts to refer child abuse, neglect.

A. Whenever any court of this state in the trial of any proceeding has cause to believe that a child's physical or mental health or welfare is endangered by abuse or neglect, it may report and refer the charges to the local child protection unit of the Department of Social Services in accordance with Article 610.

B. If from its investigation the department determines that the report is validated or if it has obtained an instanter order from the juvenile court, it shall file appropriate written notice in the civil proceeding in which the complaint arose. Thereafter, the juvenile court shall have jurisdiction to resolve the case as a child in need of care proceeding pursuant to the provisions of Title VI.

(Added by Acts 1991 No. 235, §3, eff. 1/1/92.)

Art. 309. Continuing jurisdiction over custody disputes.

A. Except as provided in Article 313, a court exercising juvenile jurisdiction shall have continuing jurisdiction over the following proceedings and the exclusive authority to modify any custody determination rendered, including the consideration of visitation rights:

(1) Child in need of care proceedings pursuant to Title VI.
(2) Families in need of services proceedings pursuant to Title VII.
(3) Involuntary termination of parental rights proceedings pursuant to Title X.
(4) Voluntary termination of parental rights proceedings pursuant to Title XI.
(5) Adoption proceedings pursuant to Title XII.
(6) Parental transfer of custody proceedings pursuant to Chapter 3 of Title XV.

B. In exercise of its jurisdiction to determine the custody of a child under writs of habeas corpus or when custody is incidental to the determination of pending cases, a district court may enter an order of custody or modify any prior order of custody rendered by a juvenile court concerning the same child in any proceeding except those enumerated in Paragraph A of this Article.

(Added by Acts 1991 No. 235, §3, eff. 1/1/92.)

Art. 310. Jurisdiction under the Uniform Child Custody Jurisdiction Act.

A. Unless declined, a court exercising juvenile court jurisdiction shall have exclusive original jurisdiction over cases subject to the provisions of the Uniform Child Custody Jurisdiction Act, pursuant to R.S. 13:1701 et seq., when in such interstate custody disputes any of the following occur:

(1) A claim of emergency jurisdiction is made pursuant to R.S. 13:1702(A)(3).
(2) A petition alleges that a child is in need of care as defined by Title VI.
(3) A petition otherwise alleges facts that would bring the proceedings within the exclusive original jurisdiction of the juvenile courts pursuant to this Code.

B. The district courts shall have exclusive original jurisdiction over all other claims of jurisdiction under the Uniform Child Custody Jurisdiction Act* and claims of emergency jurisdiction when declined by the juvenile court.
(Added by Acts 1991 No. 235, §3, eff. 1/1/92.)
**R.S. 13:1700 et seq.*

Art. 311. Juvenile jurisdiction over adults; support proceedings; coexistent orders.

A. (1) A court exercising juvenile jurisdiction shall have exclusive original jurisdiction in the following cases involving support of family:

(a) Proceedings involving criminal neglect of a child by either parent, or of one spouse by the other spouse.

(b) Proceedings under the Uniform Interstate Family Support Act*.
**Ch.C. arts. 1301.1 et seq.*

(c) Proceedings brought by the Department of Social Services on its own behalf or on behalf of any person for whom support has been ordered to enforce support by interstate income assignment pursuant to R.S. 46:236.4.

(2) A support order rendered pursuant to an action brought under this Paragraph shall not modify a prior judgment of a district court or be modified by a district court having appropriate jurisdiction over support, unless the court rendering the original support order has transferred jurisdiction.

B. (1) A court exercising juvenile jurisdiction shall have concurrent jurisdiction in the following cases involving support of family:

(a) Proceedings brought by the district attorney pursuant to the provisions of Article 1303.7 of the Uniform Interstate Family Support Act.

(b) Proceedings brought by the district attorney to establish paternity or to establish or enforce support pursuant to provisions of R.S. 46:236.1(F).

(c) Proceedings brought by the district attorney to enforce support pursuant to R.S. 46:236.2.

(d) Proceedings brought by the district attorney under any state law to register, enforce, or modify any order of support issued by any court in this state.

(2) A support order rendered pursuant to an action brought under Item (1)(b) or (c) of this Paragraph B shall not modify a prior judgment of a district court or be modified by a district court having appropriate jurisdiction over support, unless the court rendering the original support order has transferred jurisdiction.

C. Upon proof thereof, amounts paid for a particular period pursuant to a support order rendered by either court shall be credited against the amounts accruing or accrued for the same period under any support order rendered by the other court.
(Added by Acts 1991 No. 235, §3; chgd. by Acts 1992 No. 865, §1; Acts 1997 No. 601, §1, eff. 8/15/97.)

Art. 312. Juvenile jurisdiction over adults; criminal proceedings.

A. Except as provided in Paragraph B of this Article, a court exercising juvenile jurisdiction shall have exclusive original jurisdiction, in conformity with any special rules prescribed by law, to try an adult for:

(1) The crime of contributing to the delinquency of children as authorized by R.S. 14:92, except R.S. 14:92(A)(7).

(2) The crime of contributing to the delinquency or dependency of children as authorized by R.S. 14:92.1.

(3) Any other misdemeanor enacted for the protection of the physical, moral, or mental well-being of children.

(4) Criminal neglect of family.

(5) The crime of improper supervision of a minor by parents or legal custodian as authorized by R.S. 14:92.2.

B. In any parish with a population of three hundred fifty thousand or more, jurisdiction pursuant to Subparagraphs A(1) and (3) of this Article is vested in the district court, or, in the parish of Orleans, in the criminal district court for that parish or the Municipal Court of New Orleans.

C. If the defendant in any case within this Article is entitled to trial by jury and does not waive that right, the court shall transfer the case to its criminal docket or to the appropriate court having criminal jurisdiction.
(Added by Acts 1991 No. 235, §3; chgd. by Acts 1995 No. 702, §1; Acts 1997 No. 569, §1, eff. 8/15/97.)

Art. 313. Duration of jurisdiction over proceedings.

A court exercising juvenile jurisdiction no longer exercises such jurisdiction in any proceeding authorized by this Code upon:

(1) Declination of jurisdiction.
(2) Transfer of the proceeding.
(3) Expiration or satisfaction of an informal adjustment agreement.
(4) Expiration or satisfaction of an informal family services plan agreement.
(5) Expiration, satisfaction, or vacation of a juvenile disposition or adult sentence.
(6) Dismissal of the proceeding.

(Added by Acts 1991 No. 235, §3; chgd. by Acts 1992 No. 705, §1, eff. 7/6/92.)

CHAPTER 6. VENUE

Art. 314. Venue.

Except when a special venue rule is provided by a Title of this Code, any proceeding may be commenced in the parish in which the child is domiciled with his parent or tutor, the parish in which the child is residing, the parish in which the act complained of took place or the conditions complained of existed, or the parish in which the child is found. *(Added by Acts 1991 No. 235, §3; chgd. by Acts 1992 No. 705, §1, eff. 7/6/92.)*

Art. 314.1. Special venue in proceedings concerning child support.

Proceedings to modify an order for child support, medical support, and income assignment, or any one or combination of such orders, brought pursuant to Article 311 shall be brought only in the proper parish specified by Code of Civil Procedure Article 74.2. *(Added by Acts 1997 No. 603, §3, eff. 8/15/97.)*

Art. 315. Transfer of proper venue.

A. At any time, the court in which a petition is filed may transfer the case for the convenience of the parties and the witnesses and in the interests of justice to another court having venue according to Article 314.

B. After adjudication, the court in which a petition is filed shall transfer the proceeding if it receives information at any time that both of the following exist:

(1) The child is domiciled with his parent or tutor in another parish.
(2) The court of the child's domicile has proceedings currently pending before it.

C. Certified copies of all legal and social documents and records pertaining to the case which are on file with the clerk of the court shall accompany the transfer.
(Added by Acts 1991 No. 235, §3, eff. 1/1/92.)

Art. 316. Improper venue; transfer.

When a petition is filed in a court of improper venue, the court shall either dismiss the petition or transfer it to a court of proper venue. *(Added by Acts 1991 No. 235, §3, eff. 1/1/92.)*

Art. 317. Change of proper venue.

Any party by contradictory motion may obtain a change of venue upon proof that he cannot obtain a fair and impartial trial because of the undue influence of an adverse party, prejudice existing in the public mind, or some other sufficient cause. *(Added by Acts 1991 No. 235, §3, eff. 1/1/92.)*

CHAPTER 7. GENERAL AUTHORITY OF COURTS

Article

Art. 318. Inherent power and authority of courts.

A court inherently possesses all powers necessary for the exercise of its juvenile jurisdiction and the enforcement of its lawful orders. It has authority to issue such writs and orders as may be necessary or proper in aid of its jurisdiction. It has the duty to require that the juvenile proceedings be conducted with dignity and in an orderly and expeditious manner.
(Added by Acts 1991 No. 235, §3, eff. 1/1/92.)

Art. 319. Contempt.

A. Any person who willfully violates, neglects, or refuses to obey or perform any lawful order of a court may be proceeded against for contempt of court. This general contempt authority shall not detract from or prevent the application of specific contempt provisions contained elsewhere in this Code.

B. Any parent, guardian, custodian, or other person entrusted with the care of a child coming within the jurisdiction of the juvenile court may be proceeded against for contempt of court for the failure, unwillingness, or neglect, without just cause, to fully cooperate in the rehabilitative program ordered by the court as a part of any protective order or disposition judgment authorized by a Title of this Code, including but not limited to:

(1) Participation in a counseling or instructional program.

(2) Participation in family counseling sessions.

(3) Participation in mental health sessions.

(4) Assistance in obtaining vocational training for the child.

(5) Assistance in obtaining a special educational placement for the child.

(6) Participation in such other adjustment programs that the court finds beneficial and remedial in the rehabilitation of the child.

C. Contempt proceedings shall be conducted in accordance with the provisions of Chapter 2 of Title XV.
(Added by Acts 1991 No. 235, §3, eff. 1/1/92.)

Art. 320. Indigency determination.

A. The determination of the indigency of any person entitled to counsel under this Code may be made by the court at any stage of the proceedings. If necessary, the person shall be allowed to summon witnesses to testify before the court concerning his financial ability to employ counsel.

B. (1) In determining whether or not a person is indigent and entitled to the appointment of counsel, the court shall consider whether the person is a needy person and the extent of his ability to pay. The court shall consider such factors as income, property owned, outstanding obligations, and the number and ages of dependents.

(2) Release on bail alone shall not disqualify a person for appointment of counsel.

C. In each case, the person subject to the penalty of perjury, shall certify in writing such material factors relating to his ability to pay as the court prescribes.
(Added by Acts 1991 No. 235, §3, eff. 1/1/92.)

Art. 321. Partial reimbursement by indigents.

A. To the extent that a person is financially able to provide for an attorney, other necessary services and facilities of representation, and court costs, the court shall order him to pay for these items. The court may order payment in installments or in any manner which it believes reasonable and compatible with the defendant's financial ability.

B. Payments so made shall be transmitted to and become a part of the indigent defender fund of the district in which the proceeding is pending.

C. When an individual is initially determined to be indigent and is appointed counsel but subsequently hires private counsel, the court shall conduct a contradictory hearing to first determine if the person was in fact initially indigent and if not, then secondly to determine the charges incurred in retaining counsel which, if not disclosed, will constitute grounds for contempt of court, then lastly to determine the expenses of representing the individual which have been incurred by the indigent defender board or other appointed counsel.

D. Upon determining the expenses incurred, the court may hold the individual liable to the board or other appointed counsel for reimbursement of all or part of those expenses, and a judgment for the amount owed may be recorded in the mortgage records in favor of the board or other appointed counsel and may be enforced as provided by law.

(Added by Acts 1991 No. 235, §3, eff. 1/1/92.)

CHAPTER 8. SPECIAL AUTHORITY OF COURTS; CHILD ABUSE VICTIMS; VIDEOTAPING; CLOSED CIRCUIT TELEVISION

Article

Art. 322. Purpose.

The purpose of this Chapter is to provide further protection for children who are victims of physical or sexual abuse and to permit the trial concerning such abuse to proceed with a minimum of additional intrusion into the lives of such children. To effect this purpose, the need for a special exception to the hearsay rule allowing receipt of videotaped statements of the child's account and the need for closed-circuit television for transmitting certain child victims' testimony is recognized. *(Added by Acts 1991 No. 235, §3, eff. 1/1/92.)*

Art. 323. Definitions.

(1) "Department" means the Department of Social Services.

(2) "Videotape" means the visual recording on a magnetic tape together with the associated oral record.

(Added by Acts 1991 No. 235, §3, eff. 1/1/92.)

Art. 324. Authorization.

A. A court exercising juvenile jurisdiction may, on its own motion or on the motion of the district attorney, a parish welfare unit or agency, or the department, require that a statement of a child be recorded on videotape in conformity with Article 326.

B. The coroner may, in conjunction with the district attorney and appropriate hospital personnel and pursuant to their duties in R.S. 40:2109.1 and R.S. 40:2113.4, provide for the videotaping of the statements of children under the age of sixteen who present themselves or who are brought to a hospital for treatment as victims of rape or who have been otherwise physically or sexually abused.

C. Such a videotape shall be available for introduction into evidence in any juvenile proceeding under this Code in which it is relevant.

(Added by Acts 1991 No. 235, §3, eff. 1/1/92.)

Art. 325. Exception to hearsay rule.

The videotape authorized by this Chapter is hereby admissible in evidence as an exception to the hearsay rule. *(Added by Acts 1991 No. 235, §3, eff. 1/1/92.)*

Art. 326. Competent evidence; procedures for making videotape.

A. A videotape of the statements of a child fourteen years of age or younger who is alleged to be the victim of physical or sexual abuse or rape may be offered in evidence for or against such abuse. To render such a videotape competent evidence, all of the following must be satisfactorily proved:

(1) Such electronic recording was voluntarily made by the child.

(2) No relative of the child was present in the room in which the recording was made.

(3) No attorney for either party was present when the statement was made.

(4) Such recording was not made of answers to questions calculated to lead the child to make any particular statement.

(5) Such recording is both visual and oral and is recorded on film or videotape or by other electronic means.

(6) Such recording is accurate, has not been altered, and reflects what the child said.

(7) The taking of the child's statement was supervised by a physician, a board-certified social worker, a law enforcement officer, a licensed psychologist, or an authorized representative of the department.

(8) Every voice on the recording is identified.

B. The department shall develop and promulgate regulations regarding training requirements and certification for department personnel who are authorized to supervise the taking of the child's statement.

(Added by Acts 1991 No. 235, §3, eff. 1/1/92.)

Art. 327. Admissibility.

A. A prehearing videotape which meets all the requirements of Article 326 may be admissible into evidence if all of the following occur:

(1) The parties to the proceeding are afforded an opportunity to view the recording before it is offered into evidence.

(2) The person conducting the interview of the child in the recording is present at the proceeding and available to testify or be cross-examined by either party.

(3) The child is available to testify.

B. The admission into evidence of the videotape as authorized herein shall not preclude the state from calling the child as a witness or taking the child's testimony outside the courtroom as otherwise authorized by law.

C. Nothing in this Chapter shall be construed to prohibit the right of confrontation of a defendant in a criminal proceeding before the court.

(Added by Acts 1991 No. 235, §3, eff. 1/1/92.)

Art. 328. Confidentiality.

Videotapes which are a part of the court record shall be preserved under a protective order of the court in order to protect the privacy of the child. The court shall order the destruction of the videotapes after five years have elapsed from the date of entry of judgment. However, if an appeal is filed, the videotapes shall not be destroyed until a final judgment on appeal has been rendered. *(Added by Acts 1991 No. 235, §3, eff. 1/1/92.)*

Art. 329. Closed circuit television; testimony taken outside courtroom.

A. On its own motion or on the motion of the attorney for any party, a court may order that the testimony of a child under fourteen years of age who may have been physically or sexually abused be taken in a room other than the courtroom and be simultaneously televised by closed circuit television to the court when the court makes a specific finding of necessity based upon both the following:

(1) Expert testimony that the child would be likely to suffer serious emotional distress if forced to give testimony in open court.

(2) Expert testimony that without such special shielding procedures, the child cannot reasonably communicate his testimony to the court.

B. The court shall ensure that the child cannot see or hear the accused unless such viewing or hearing is requested for purposes of identification. However, the court shall ensure that the accused is afforded the ability to consult with his attorney during the testimony of the child.

C. The only persons who may be present in the room with the child are the person or persons operating the audio-video equipment, the presiding judge, the attorneys for the state and the accused, and any person, other than a relative of the child, whose presence is determined by the court to be necessary to the welfare and well-being of the child during his testimony. The persons operating the equipment shall be confined to an adjacent room or behind a screen or mirror that permits them to see and hear the child during his testimony but does not permit the child to see or hear them.

D. Only the attorneys, or the presiding judge as authorized by law, may question the child.

(Added by Acts 1991 No. 235, §3, eff. 1/1/92.)

CHAPTER 9. APPEALS AND SUPERVISORY JURISDICTION

Art. 330. Judgments appealable.

A. An appeal may be taken from any final judgment of a court and shall be to the appropriate court of appeal.

B. In delinquency proceedings pursuant to Title VIII, child in need of care proceedings pursuant to Title VI, and families in need of services proceedings pursuant to Title VII, an appeal may be taken only after a judgment of disposition. The appeal shall include all errors assigned concerning the adjudication and disposition.

(Added by Acts 1991 No. 235, §3, eff. 1/1/92.)

Art. 331. Right of appeal.

A. Except when the court is exercising its jurisdiction pursuant to Article 960, a party to the proceedings or any other party in interest shall have the right to appeal.

B. The state may not appeal from a judgment refusing to adjudicate a child to be delinquent or from a judgment of acquittal.

(Added by Acts 1991 No. 235, §3, eff. 1/1/92.)

Art. 332. Notice of judgment; new trials; time for appeal.

A. Except as otherwise provided within a particular Title of this Code, appeals shall be taken within fifteen days from the signing of a judgment or from the mailing of notice of the judgment when required. However, if a timely application for a new trial is made pursuant to Paragraph C, the delay for appeal commences to run from the date of the mailing of notice of denial of the new trial motion.

B. Notice of judgment, including notice of orders or judgments taken under advisement, shall be as provided in the Code of Civil Procedure, except no notice is required for counsel or parties not represented by counsel who are present when the judgment is rendered and signed.

C. After judgment is signed, a party may make a written request for a motion for new trial on any ground provided by law. The delay for applying for a new trial is three days, exclusive of holidays, and shall commence to run from the signing of the judgment or the mailing of notice of judgment, when required. A motion for new trial shall be decided expeditiously and within seven days from the date of submission for decision.

(Added by Acts 1991 No. 235, §3; chgd. by Acts 1995 No. 1095, §1, eff. 8/15/95.)

Art. 333. Perfecting the appeal.

A. An appeal is taken by obtaining an order therefor from the court which rendered the judgment.

B. An order of appeal may be granted on oral motion in open court, on written motion, or on petition. The order shall show the return day of the appeal in the appellate court.

C. When the order is granted, the clerk of court shall mail a notice of appeal to counsel of record for all parties represented by counsel, and to parties not represented by counsel. Upon request, notice shall be mailed to counsel for the party seeking the appeal.

(Added by Acts 1991 No. 235, §3, eff. 1/1/92.)

Art. 334. Return day.

A. Except as otherwise provided in this Code, the return day of the appeal shall be thirty days from the date the appeal is granted, if no costs are required, or from the date estimated costs are paid, unless the trial court fixes a lesser period.

B. The trial court may grant only one extension of the return day, and such extension shall not exceed thirty days. Subsequent extensions of the return day may be granted by the appellate court for sufficient cause.
(Added by Acts 1991 No. 235, §3, eff. 1/1/92.)

Art. 335. Preparation of record; costs.

A. The clerk of the trial court shall cause the record on appeal to be prepared and lodged with the appellate court on or before the return day or extension thereof.

B. All records and supplemental records prepared for filing in any appellate court shall be certified and dated by the clerk upon completion. The certification shall include the date any transcript was received for inclusion in the record.

C. All transcripts or parts thereof completed for inclusion in the record shall be dated and certified by the court reporter who prepares them. The date of certification by the court reporter shall be the date on which the transcript was concluded and furnished to the clerk for inclusion in the record.

D. If a child desires a transcript for appeal, he or his parents shall pay the cost of transcription of the record unless the court determines that the child and his parents lack means to pay such cost.

E. Failure of the clerk to prepare and lodge the record on appeal either timely or correctly shall not prejudice the appeal.
(Added by Acts 1991 No. 235, §3, eff. 1/1/92.)

Art. 336. Effect of appeal.

A. Except as provided by Paragraphs B and C of this Article, the effect of a judgment shall not be suspended by an appeal, unless the trial court or a court of appeal directs otherwise.

B. A parent shall have the right to appeal suspensively from any ruling terminating his parental rights, including a judgment of adoption, notwithstanding the power of the court to order the commencement or continuation of temporary custody of the child with persons other than the parents.

C. A suspensive appeal shall not suspend the execution of the judgment insofar as the judgment relates to custody or child support.
(Added by Acts 1991 No. 235, §3, eff. 1/1/92.)

Art. 337. Preference.

Appeals authorized by Titles VI, VII, VIII, X, XI, and XII and Chapter 7 of Title XV shall be accorded preference in the court of appeal and shall be determined at the earliest practicable time. *(Added by Acts 1991 No. 235, §3, eff. 1/1/92.)*

Art. 338. Supervisory jurisdiction.

Applications for supervisory writs may be made to the appropriate court of appeal in accordance with applicable rules of court. *(Added by Acts 1991 No. 235, §3, eff. 1/1/92.)*

TITLE IV. JUVENILE COURT ADMINISTRATION

Chapter

CHAPTER 1. LOCAL RULES OF COURT

Article

Art. 401. Adoption of local rules of court.

A. A court may adopt rules not in conflict with provisions of this Code, or of other laws for the conduct of proceedings before it. When a court has more than one judge, its rules shall be adopted or amended by a majority of the judges thereof sitting en banc.

B. The rules shall be entered on the minutes of the court, and a copy shall be furnished on request to any attorney licensed to practice law in this state.
(Added by Acts 1991 No. 235, §4, eff. 1/1/92.)

CHAPTER 2. SCHEDULING AND CONDUCT OF CASES

Art. 402. Court of record.

A court exercising juvenile jurisdiction is a court of record. *(Added by Acts 1991 No. 235, §4, eff. 1/1/92.)*

Art. 403. Sessions of court.

A. When a court is exercising its juvenile jurisdiction it may sit in chambers and hold its sessions irrespective of regular terms of court.

B. Juvenile courts shall be in continuous session, provided that the judges of said courts shall be entitled to a vacation as provided by existing laws.
(Added by Acts 1991 No. 235, §4, eff. 1/1/92.)

Art. 404. Docketing of juvenile cases.

Juvenile cases shall be docketed and handled separately from regular criminal and civil cases, and juvenile case records shall be confidential and kept separately. *(Added by Acts 1991 No. 235, §4, eff. 1/1/92.)*

Art. 405. Court or witness fees; travel expenses.

A. Except as otherwise provided by law, no court or witness fees shall be allowed against any party to a petition, and no salaried officer of the state or of any parish or municipality therein shall be entitled to receive any fee for the service or for attendance in court in any such proceedings. All other persons acting under orders of the court may be paid in the same manner as in the district court for services or service of process and attendance or serving as witnesses, the fees provided by law for like services in cases before the district court.

B. The court may authorize the payment of necessary travel expenses to witnesses attending in response to summons and the payment of curator fees to be fixed by the court. Such expenses, when authorized by the court, shall be paid from the general fund of the parish or other funds available to the court.

C. The court may charge a reasonable court cost or charge fees for adoption cases which shall be payable in the same manner as fees in ordinary civil proceedings.

D. In municipalities with a population in excess of four hundred thousand inhabitants, in all proceedings under Chapter 1 of Title XIII after a conviction or plea of guilty, the court in its discretion, instead of imposing the punishment or fine, or both, provided therein, having issued an order directing the defendant to pay a certain sum weekly or at such periods as the court may direct, may assess costs against the defendant not to exceed five percent of all sums paid weekly or periodically through the registry of the court.

E. In parishes having a population between two hundred twenty-five thousand and four hundred fifty thousand, in all proceedings under Chapter 1 of Title XIII where the defendant has violated the terms of such order as provided therein and the defendant is adjudged guilty of contempt by failing to comply with the judgment or order of the court by paying the support assessed, the court may assess costs against the defendant in an amount not to exceed five percent of the fine imposed by the court for the contempt of its order or judgment; however, in no case shall the fine and costs together exceed the sum of five hundred dollars.

F. All such costs so assessed and collected shall remain with the court and shall be deposited in the judicial expense fund of such court.

G. In all cases in which support rights have been assigned to the Department of Social Services as a condition of eligibility for Family Independence Temporary Assistance Program (FITAP) and in all civil, criminal, or juvenile support proceedings initiated by the department on its own behalf or on behalf of a non-FITAP applicant, the provisions of Chapter 2 of Title XIII shall apply as to imposition of a collection fee against the person owing the support obligation.

(Added by Acts 1991 No. 235, §4, eff. 1/1/92.)

Art. 406. Waiver of court costs and fees.

A. In its discretion, the court may waive costs and fees to the extent that a party is unable to pay such costs and fees due to poverty or lack of means.

B. In determining whether or to what extent a party is unable to pay, the court shall consider the party's income, property owned, outstanding obligations, and the number and ages of dependents.

C. The court may order payments in installments over time, or in any manner which it believes reasonable and compatible with the financial ability of the party.

(Added by Acts 1991 No. 235, §4; chgd. by Acts 1992 No. 705, §1, eff. 7/6/92.)

Art. 407. Confidentiality of hearings.

A. With the exceptions of delinquency proceedings pursuant to Article 879, child support proceedings, traffic violations pursuant to Chapter 2 of Title IX in parishes with a population between three hundred eighty thousand and four hundred thousand, and misdemeanor trials of adults pursuant to Chapter 4 of Title XV, proceedings before the juvenile court shall not be public. However, the court shall allow the proceedings to be open to the public when the alleged delinquent act committed by the child would be considered a crime of violence as defined in R.S. 14:2(13), or when the alleged delinquent act would be a second or subsequent felony-grade adjudication.

B. The child, his parents, counsel, the district attorney, authorized officers of the court, and witnesses called by the parties may be present at an adjudication hearing. The court may admit any other person who has a proper interest in the proceedings or the work of the court. In delinquency proceedings involving the violation of R.S. 14:30, first degree murder; R.S. 14:30.1, second degree murder; R.S. 14:42, aggravated rape; R.S. 14:44, aggravated kidnapping; or R.S. 14:64, armed robbery; the court shall admit the victim and the victim's spouse, children, siblings, and parents.

(Added by Acts 1991 No. 235, §4; chgd. by Acts 1992 No. 705, §1; Acts 1993 No. 769, §1; Acts 1994 Third Ex. Sess. No. 120, §1; Acts 1995 No. 1261, §1, eff. 8/15/95.)

Art. 408. Duty of court to control proceedings.

The court shall require that the proceedings be conducted with dignity and in an orderly and expeditious manner, and shall control the proceedings so that justice is done. The court may exclude any person whose conduct is disruptive if the person fails promptly to heed the court's admonition to refrain from such conduct. *(Added by Acts 1991 No. 235, §4, eff. 1/1/92.)*

Art. 409. Sequestration of witnesses.

On its own motion the court may, and on request of a party the court shall, order that the witnesses, other than parties, be excluded from the courtroom or from a place where they can see or hear the proceedings and refrain from discussing the facts of the case with anyone other than counsel in the case. In the interests of justice, the court may exempt any witness from its order. *(Added by Acts 1991 No. 235, §4, eff. 1/1/92.)*

Art. 410. Recording of proceedings.

Juvenile proceedings, except in cases of traffic violations pursuant to Title IX, shall be recorded. *(Added by Acts 1991 No. 235, §4, eff. 1/1/92.)*

CHAPTER 3. RECORDS

Article

Art. 411. Records; forms.

A. The court shall make, or have made, and keep records of all cases brought before it.

B. The court shall devise and cause to be printed such forms for social and legal records or such other papers as may be required.

(Added by Acts 1991 No. 235, §4, eff. 1/1/92.)

Art. 412. Confidentiality of records; disclosure exceptions; sanctions.

A. (1) The information in Subparagraph (2) of this Paragraph shall be made available to the public by the appropriate law enforcement agency only when a child has been taken into custody, pursuant to Articles 812 through 814 of this Code, a court of competent jurisdiction has made a pretrial determination regarding the probity of the evidence and the basis of the probable cause, and there is probable cause to believe either of the following:

(a) That the alleged delinquent act committed by the child would be considered a crime of violence as defined in R.S. 14:2(13).

(b) That the alleged delinquent act would be a second or subsequent felony-grade adjudication for the alleged offender.

(2) (a) The name of the child.

(b) The age of the child.

(c) The crime for which the child is charged.

B. Except as provided in Paragraph A of this Article, records and reports of the court, probation officers, and law enforcement agencies concerning matters or proceedings in court are confidential and shall not be disclosed, except:

(1) Statistical information and information of a general nature.

(2) Upon motion and order of the court for discovery as authorized by any Title of this Code.

(3) Traffic violation proceedings, which shall be open to public inspection pursuant to Title IX.

(4) Certain adoption records upon order of the court pursuant to Chapter 4 of Title XII.

(5) The delinquency record upon written waiver by a person seventeen years of age or older who has been the subject of a delinquency proceeding pursuant to Title VIII.

(6) The delinquency record of a person, adjudicated delinquent under Title VIII for the commission of a felony-grade violation of either the Louisiana Controlled Dangerous Substances Law* or a crime of violence as listed in R.S. 15:529.1(A)(2), upon request of the district attorney for purposes of charging that person as a habitual offender pursuant to R.S. 15:529.1.

**R.S. 40:961 et seq.*

(7) The court record of a person adjudicated delinquent for a crime of violence as defined in R.S. 14:2(13).

C. The court may authorize a designated person to review confidential reports and records for the purpose of collecting statistical information and information of a general nature. Such authorization shall be in writing and state specifically the type of information which may be reviewed.

D. The court may also release to a peace officer, probation officer, district attorney, or employee of the office of community services or office of juvenile services, in connection with the performance of his duties, the record of arrests, convictions, adjudications, or dispositions of:

(1) Anyone previously adjudicated a delinquent and who is subsequently arrested or charged with any crime or delinquent act.

(2) Any child adjudicated a delinquent for committing a felony-grade delinquent act or a misdemeanor-grade delinquent act involving an offense against the person or involving a dangerous weapon.

E. Reports and records concerning matters or proceedings under the juvenile jurisdiction of the court may also be released to a peace officer, probation officer, district attorney, or employee of the office of community services or office of juvenile services in connection with the performance of his duties.

F. For good cause, the court may also order disclosure of records and reports of the court, probation officers, and law enforcement agencies to:

(1) A child, who has been the subject of any juvenile court proceeding, except an adoption, after he has reached majority, or to his representative.

(2) Any person, agency, institution, or other court upon a particular showing that the information is relevant to a specific investigation or proceeding.

G. In accordance with Article 811.1, the district attorney may release information concerning the results of an adjudication and disposition hearing in court to the victim of the delinquent act or his legal representative.

H. (1) Within twenty-four hours, exclusive of holidays and weekends, after receiving a predisposition report, the sentencing court shall order the release of any portion of a predisposition report containing and limited to conviction, adjudication, or disposition of a child in grades seven through twelve, who is arrested, charged, or adjudicated a delinquent for committing a felony-grade delinquent act or a misdemeanor-grade delinquent act involving distribution or possession with intent to distribute a controlled dangerous substance in violation of the Uniform Controlled Dangerous Substances Law or any violent offense against the person, to the principal of the school in which the child is registered and enrolled or registered and enrolled but suspended. Such notification to the principal shall be a continuing responsibility of the court through adjudication and disposition. The principal shall have a continuing responsibility to advise each teacher who has that student assigned to his class of the notification, within two school days, after the principal receives it. Such information shall be strictly confidential within the school environment. Failure to maintain confidentiality of the information will result in a fine of two hundred fifty dollars per violation. Such release shall be done in compliance with the provisions of this Code.

(2) For purposes of this Subsection, crime of violence against the person or involving weapons shall include but not be limited to any homicide and any violation of R.S. 14:34, 34.2, 34.3, 37, 37.1, 40.1, 40.2, 42, 42.1, 43.2, 44, 44.1, 45, 64, 64.1, 64.2, 65, 94, 95, and 95.2.

I. Notwithstanding any other provisions of any Title of this Code, or any other provision of law to the contrary, the district attorney may release the name of a juvenile arrested after a pretrial determination regarding the probity of the evidence and the basis of the probable cause, and there is probable cause to believe either of the following:

(1) That the alleged delinquent act committed by the child would be considered a crime of violence as defined in R.S. 14:2(13).

(2) That the alleged delinquent act would be a second or subsequent felony-grade adjudication for the alleged offender.

J. (1) Identifying information of a juvenile wanted for the commission of a felony-grade delinquent act may be publicly disseminated by any law enforcement agency in a way calculated to assist such agency in arresting the absent juvenile.

(2) For purposes of this Subsection:

(a) "Delinquent act" means a felony-grade delinquent act involving an offense against the person or involving a dangerous weapon.

(b) "Identifying information" may include the juvenile's name or alias, address, social security number, driver's license number, physical description, age, and photograph.

K. A violation of the provisions of this Article shall be punishable as a constructive contempt of court, pursuant to Articles 1507 through 1509.

(Added by Acts 1991 No. 235, §4; chgd. by Acts 1993 No. 596, §1, No. 634, §1, No. 840, §1; Acts 1994 Third Ex. Sess. No. 23, §2, No. 76, §1, No. 120, §1, No. 140, §1; Acts 1995 No. 1313, §1, eff. 6/29/95.)

Art. 413. Records; intercourt transfer.

A. When any court of this state makes a written request, including telegraphic, teletyped, or facsimile transmission requests, hereinafter "requesting court", of any other court, hereinafter "responding court", for the arrest, disposition, and other records relating to a juvenile currently within the jurisdiction of the requesting court, the responding court shall promptly comply with such requests by depositing the requested information in the mail, addressed to the requesting court, within ten days exclusive of legal holidays.

B. Failure to comply with the provisions of this Article shall subject the violating court to disciplinary action by the Supreme Court of Louisiana upon receipt by the judicial administrator of the supreme court of a written complaint, subsequently substantiated, by the requesting court.

(Added by Acts 1991 No. 235, §4; chgd. by Acts 1992 No. 705, §1, eff. 7/6/92.)

Art. 414. Disclosure of records for sentencing; habitual offender proceedings.

A. Notwithstanding any provision of law to the contrary, upon written request, reports and records concerning juvenile court proceedings shall be released to the sentencing judge when necessary for sentencing and released to the district attorney for purposes of charging a person as a habitual offender pursuant to R.S. 15:529.1.

B. The request shall be complied with promptly; however, not more than ten days, exclusive of legal holidays, shall lapse after receipt of the request before the requested information is deposited in the mail, addressed to the requesting court. The court may postpone imposition of sentence until the report is received.

C. Except as provided for in Articles 412(G) and 891(D), the sentencing court shall not copy, duplicate, or otherwise reproduce such juvenile records, and the records shall be deposited in the mail, addressed to the issuing court, within three days after sentencing.

(Added by Acts 1991 No. 235, §4; chgd. by Acts 1993 No. 634, §1, No. 840, §1; Acts 1994 Third Ex. Sess. No. 23, §2, eff. 8/27/94.)

Art. 415. Destruction of inactive and closed files.

A. On its own motion, after a contradictory hearing with the district attorney, the court may order the destruction of:

(1) Any reports or records of criminal neglect of family proceedings brought pursuant to Chapter 1 of Title XIII of this Code, which have been inactive or closed for five years.

(2) Any other reports or records concerning matters or proceedings under its juvenile jurisdiction which have been inactive or closed for ten years.

B. Nothing in this Article shall authorize the destruction of adoption or domestic relations reports or records.

(Added by Acts 1991 No. 235, §4, eff. 1/1/92.)

Art. 416. Service of motion to destroy reports and records.

A. A motion to destroy reports and records shall be served upon all of the following:

(1) The district attorney.

(2) The clerk of the court whose records are sought to be destroyed.

(3) The head of any agency whose reports and records are sought to be destroyed.

B. Service shall be in the manner provided for service of a petition.

(Added by Acts 1991 No. 235, §4, eff. 1/1/92.)

Art. 417. Judgment ordering destruction of reports and records.

A. A judgment ordering destruction of reports and records shall be in writing and shall be served upon all of the following:

(1) The district attorney.

(2) The clerk of the court whose reports and records are to be destroyed.

(3) The head of the agency whose reports and records are to be destroyed.

B. Service shall be in the manner provided for service of a petition.

C. The judgment shall specify the manner and time within which the destruction is to be effected and shall also specify the limitations of Paragraph E of this Article.

D. The judgment may require the custodian of records to submit an affidavit to the court attesting that the reports and records have been destroyed.

E. Although the custodian of the records or report may keep a copy of the judgment ordering destruction, he shall not disclose the fact that such judgment is maintained or that the destroyed reports or records previously existed to anyone except upon written order of the court.

(Added by Acts 1991 No. 235, §4, eff. 1/1/92.)

CHAPTER 4. COURT PERSONNEL

Article

Art. 418. Juvenile court; juvenile judge.

When another statute uses the term "juvenile court" or "juvenile judge" for purposes of proceedings under this Code, those terms shall be construed to mean "court" or "judge" as defined in Article 116. *(Added by Acts 1991 No. 235, §4, eff. 1/1/92.)*

Art. 419. Court personnel.

A. The judge of the court may employ such stenographic, secretarial, and other personnel deemed necessary to make the functions of the court effective and provide adequate service.

B. The employment of such persons shall be at the expense of the court and, unless otherwise provided by law, shall be paid by the respective parishes.
(Added by Acts 1991 No. 235, §4, eff. 1/1/92.)

Art. 420. Law clerks.

Each judge of the juvenile court is hereby authorized to employ a law clerk, provided funds are available, to perform such research duties as the judge who employs the law clerk may assign. The salary of each such law clerk shall be fixed and paid on the warrant of the employing judge. *(Added by Acts 1991 No. 235, §4, eff. 1/1/92.)*

Art. 421. Probation officers.

A. The judge of the court shall have the authority to commission probation officers, one of whom may be designated as chief probation officer or director of probation.

B. Probation officers shall have the power and authority to make arrests, serve notices, orders, subpoenas, and writs, and to execute all orders and perform any other duties incident to their office. Nothing herein contained shall be construed to relieve the sheriff from the duties as set forth in R.S. 33:1435.

C. Employment of such personnel by any court for its exclusive service shall in no wise be affected by or limit the court in availing itself of the services of such officers or other employees as may be provided by the state.
(Added by Acts 1991 No. 235, §4, eff. 1/1/92.)

Art. 422. Juvenile traffic referee.

A. The judge, or a majority of the judges of a court, may appoint persons to serve as juvenile traffic referees to adjudicate and dispose of traffic violations, when authorized by local rule of court under Article 401. The adjudication and disposition shall be held in the parish where the juvenile is domiciled with his parent or tutor or the parish in which the child is residing. If the violation occurred in a different parish, the court in that parish shall transfer the case to the juvenile court in the parish where the child is domiciled or resides for adjudication and disposition.

B. Any person appointed to serve as a juvenile traffic referee shall have been admitted to the practice of law in this state for at least five years prior to his appointment and shall be domiciled in the district or parish in which the court is located.

C. Any person who is serving and, since September 6, 1985, has served as a juvenile traffic referee without having had the qualifications set forth in this Article may continue to serve in that capacity and all acts performed by such a person in that capacity from and after September 6, 1985, are hereby ratified, confirmed, and validated.
(Added by Acts 1991 No. 235, §4; chgd. by Acts 1993 No. 684, §1, eff. 8/15/93.)

Art. 423. Child support hearing officers.

A. The judge or judges of the court may appoint one or more hearing officers to hear child support and support related matters.

B. The hearing officer shall act as a finder of fact and shall make recommendations to the court pursuant to Article 1331.

(Added by Acts 1991 No. 235, §4, eff. 1/1/92.)

Art. 424. Court-appointed special advocates (CASA).

A. The judge of the court exercising juvenile jurisdiction is authorized to appoint one or more court-appointed special advocates, hereinafter referred to as "CASA volunteer", to assist the court in fulfilling its duties and responsibilities to children brought into court. The CASA volunteer shall have as his special duty and responsibility the advocacy of the best interests of the child involved in the juvenile proceeding in which he is appointed.

B. (1) CASA volunteers serve without compensation and at the pleasure of the court exercising juvenile jurisdiction. The judge of the court will first satisfy himself of the volunteer's qualifications, training, and ability to serve as a CASA volunteer, including his ability to represent and advocate the best interest of children assigned to him. Pursuant to R.S. 15:587.1, no volunteer shall be appointed until the volunteer has submitted fingerprints to the Louisiana Bureau of Criminal Identification and Information to determine whether the volunteer has been convicted of or has pled nolo contendere to a crime listed in R.S. 15:587.1(C).

(2) All CASA volunteers shall:

(a) Be sworn by the judge making the appointment.

(b) Swear or affirm to abide by all the laws, regulations, and orders of court.

(c) Swear or affirm to advocate what he perceives to be in the best interests of the child for whom he is appointed in all matters pending before the court.

C. It shall be the duty of a CASA volunteer to:

(1) Provide independent, factual information to the court regarding the children and cases to which they are appointed.

(2) Advocate on behalf of the children involved in the cases in which they are appointed what they perceive to be in the best interest of the children.

(3) Monitor proceedings in cases in which they have been appointed and advise and assist the court in its determination of the best interest of the children involved.

D. (1) To accomplish the appointment of a CASA volunteer, the court shall issue an order of appointment which shall grant the CASA volunteer the authority to review all relevant documents and interview all parties and witnesses involved in the proceeding in which he is appointed.

(2) The CASA volunteer shall be notified by the court of all court proceedings and hearings of any kind pertaining to a child for whom he is appointed and shall be entitled to attend such hearings. He shall also be given access to all portions of the court record relating to that proceeding, and upon application to the court and notice to all parties, the court may grant the CASA volunteer access to other information, including the department records as provided in R.S. 46:56, relating to the child and to other matters involved in the proceeding in which he is appointed.

(3) The CASA volunteer shall be notified by the department of all administrative review hearings concerning the case to which he has been appointed.

(4) The CASA volunteer may be called as a witness in the proceedings by any party or by the court and may request of the court the opportunity to appear as a witness.

E. (1) All reports of the CASA volunteer shall be directed to the presiding judge and will be made available to counsel for the parties but the reports may be subject to a protective order upon the request of the CASA volunteer, a party or party's attorney, or by the action of the judge.

(2) All records and information requested or reviewed by the CASA volunteer in the course of his appointment shall be deemed confidential and shall not be disclosed by him except pursuant to court order, and such materials will only be disclosed as directed by court order and will be subject to whatever protective order the court deems appropriate.

F. The CASA volunteer may request a hearing before the court when any of the following occur:

(1) The case plan on behalf of the child is not being implemented or adhered to by any party.

(2) The plan is not meeting the child's needs.

(3) For other reasons in the best interests of the child.

G. No cause of action shall exist against any CASA volunteer, director, employee, staff, or volunteer who in good faith makes a report, cooperates in an investigation by an agency, or participates in judicial proceedings and each such person shall have immunity from civil or criminal liability that might otherwise be incurred or imposed. This immunity from liability shall not extend to:

(1) Any alleged principal, conspirator, or accessory to an offense involving the abuse or neglect or sexual exploitation of a child.

(2) Any person who makes a report known to be false or with reckless disregard for the truth of the report.

(3) The unauthorized divulging of confidential information occasioned by the CASA volunteer's gross fault or gross neglect.

(Added by Acts 1991 No. 235, §4; chgd. by Acts 1997 No. 904, §1, eff. 7/10/97.)

Art. 425. Rules for conduct of officers, employees.

Each court shall have power to frame and publish rules of procedure for the conduct of its officers and employees. *(Added by Acts 1991 No. 235, §4, eff. 1/1/92.)*

Art. 426. Compensation to courts.

Provisions for extra compensation and for extra expense allowances for courts serving as juvenile courts shall apply to courts exercising juvenile jurisdiction under this Code. *(Added by Acts 1991 No. 235, §4, eff. 1/1/92.)*

CHAPTER 5. DUTIES OF COURT CLERKS

Art. 427. Clerks; duties; authority.

A. Court clerks shall perform all duties generally required by law of clerks and all duties specifically required under the provisions of this Code.

B. Court clerks shall have all powers and authority granted by law.

(Added by Acts 1991 No. 235, §4, eff. 1/1/92.)

TITLE V. SERVICES TO FAMILIES

CHAPTER 1. CHILDREN'S ADVOCACY CLEARINGHOUSE

(Chgd. by Acts 1995 No. 1305, §1, eff. 6/29/95.)

Art. 501. Children's Advocacy Clearinghouse; establishment; purpose.

The legislature finds that the establishment of the Children's Advocacy Clearinghouse and the development of a coordinated protocol by the Louisiana Commission on Law Enforcement and Administration of Criminal Justice for the processing of child sex abuse cases among the various responsible agencies is in the best interest of the children of Louisiana. *(Added by Acts 1994 Third Ex. Sess. No. 69, §1; chgd. by Acts 1995 No. 1305, §1, eff. 6/29/95.)*

Art. 502. Creation.

The Children's Advocacy Clearinghouse is hereby created and established under the jurisdiction of the Louisiana Commission on Law Enforcement and Administration of Criminal Justice in the office of the governor. *(Added by Acts 1994 Third Ex. Sess. No. 69, §1; chgd. by Acts 1995 No. 1305, §1, eff. 6/29/95.)*

Art. 503. Duties of the Louisiana Commission on Law Enforcement and Administration of Criminal Justice.

The Louisiana Commission on Law Enforcement and Administration of Criminal Justice shall:

(1) Assist local law enforcement and prosecutorial agencies in the development of programs, resources, or expertise which promote the detection and prosecution of offenders committing crimes of sexual abuse against children.

(2) Provide information, relative to child sexual abuse, child sexual abuse programs, including programs dealing with prevention, detection, and treatment of sex abuse to various units of state and local government and other interested parties.

(3) Assist units of local government and qualified private non-profit institutions in identifying sources of funding to begin the operation of coordinated children's advocacy programs in the state.

(4) Report findings and recommendations to the Interagency Council on the Prevention of Sex Offenses prior to the 1996 Regular Session of the Legislature.

(Added by Acts 1994 Third Ex. Sess. No. 69, §1; chgd. by Acts 1995 No. 1305, §1, eff. 6/29/95.)

Arts. 504, 505. *(Repealed by Acts 1995 No. 1305, §1, eff. 6/29/95.)*

TITLE VI. CHILD IN NEED OF CARE

Chapter

CHAPTER 1. PRELIMINARY PROVISIONS; DEFINITIONS

Article

Art. 601. Purpose.

The purpose of this Title is to protect children whose physical or mental health and welfare is substantially at risk of harm by physical abuse, neglect, or exploitation and who may be further threatened by the conduct of others, by providing for the reporting of suspected cases of abuse, exploitation, or neglect of children; by providing for the investigation of such complaints; and by providing, if necessary, for the resolution of child in need of care proceedings in the courts. This Title is intended to provide the greatest possible protection as promptly as possible for such children. This Title shall be administered and interpreted to avoid unnecessary interference with family privacy and trauma to the child, and yet, at the same time, authorize the protective and preventive intervention needed to safeguard and enhance the health and well-being of children. *(Added by Acts 1991 No. 235, §6, eff. 1/1/92.)*

Art. 602. General applicability.

Except as otherwise specified in this Title, all provisions of the Code remain applicable. *(Added by Acts 1991 No. 235, §6, eff. 1/1/92.)*

Art. 603. Definitions.

As used in this Title:

(1) "Abuse" means any one of the following acts which seriously endanger the physical, mental, or emotional health of the child:

(a) The infliction, attempted infliction, or, as a result of inadequate supervision, the allowance of the infliction or attempted infliction of physical or mental injury upon the child by a parent or any other person.

(b) The exploitation or overwork of a child by a parent or any other person.

(c) The involvement of the child in any sexual act with a parent or any other person, or the aiding or toleration by the parent or the caretaker of the child's sexual involvement with any other person or of the child's involvement in pornographic displays, or any other involvement of a child in sexual activity constituting a crime under the laws of this state.

(2) "Administrative review body" means a panel of appropriate persons, at least one of whom is not responsible for the case management of or delivery of services to either the child or the parents who are the subject of the review, including the citizen review boards, state hearing examiners, special department reviewers, or department personnel.

(3) "Caretaker" means any person legally obligated to provide or secure adequate care for a child, including a parent, tutor, guardian, legal custodian, foster home parent, an employee of a public or private day care center, or other person providing a residence for the child.

(4) "Case review hearing" means a review hearing by a court or administrative review body for the purpose of determining the continuing necessity for and appropriateness of the child's placement, to determine the extent of compliance with the case plan, to determine the extent of progress which has been made toward alleviating or mitigating the causes necessitating placement, and to project a likely date by which the child may be permanently placed.

(5) "Child" means a person under eighteen years of age who, prior to juvenile proceedings, has not been judicially emancipated under Civil Code Article 385 or emancipated by marriage under Civil Code Articles 379 through 384.

(6) "Child care agency" means any public or private agency exercising custody of a child.

(7) "Child pornography" means visual depiction of a child engaged in actual or simulated sexual intercourse, deviate sexual intercourse, sexual bestiality, masturbation, sadomasochistic abuse, or lewd exhibition of the genitals.

(8) "Court-appointed or court-approved administrative body" means a body appointed or approved by a court and subject to the court's supervision for the purposes of assisting the court with dispositional review hearings, including magistrates or other court or noncourt personnel.

(9) "Crime against the child" shall include the commission of or the attempted commission of any of the following crimes against the child as provided by federal or state statutes:

(a) Homicide.
(b) Battery.
(c) Assault.
(d) Rape.
(e) Sexual battery.
(f) Kidnapping.
(g) Criminal neglect.
(h) Criminal abandonment.
(i) Incest.
(j) Carnal knowledge of a juvenile.
(k) Indecent behavior with juveniles.

(*l*) Pornography involving juveniles.

(m) Molestation of a juvenile.

(n) Crime against nature.

(*o*) Cruelty to juveniles.

(p) Contributing to the delinquency or dependency of children.

(q) Sale of minor children.

(10) "Department" means the Louisiana Department of Social Services.

(11) "Dispositional review hearing" means a hearing for the purpose of determining the future status of the child.

(12) "Foster care" means placement in a foster family home, a relative's home, a residential child caring facility, or other living arrangement approved and supervised by the state for provision of substitute care for a child in the department's custody. Such placement shall not include a detention facility.

(13) "Mandatory reporter" is any of the following individuals performing their occupational duties:

(a) "Health practitioner" is any individual who provides health care services, including a physician, surgeon, physical therapist, dentist, resident, intern, hospital staff member, podiatrist, chiropractor, licensed nurse, nursing aide, dental hygienist, any emergency medical technician, a paramedic, optometrist, medical examiner, or coroner, who diagnoses, examines, or treats a child or his family.

(b) "Mental health/social service practitioner" is any individual who provides mental health care or social service diagnosis, assessment, counseling, or treatment, including a psychiatrist, psychologist, marriage or family counselor, social worker, aide, or other individual who provides counseling services to a child or his family. However, when a priest, rabbi, duly ordained minister, or Christian Science practitioner has acquired knowledge of abuse or neglect from a person during a confession or other sacred communication, he shall encourage that person to report but shall not be a mandatory reporter of that information given in confession or sacred communication.

(c) "Teaching or child care provider" is any person who provides training and supervision of a child, including any public or private teacher, teacher's aide, instructional aide, school principal, school staff member, social worker, probation officer, foster home parent, group home or other child care institutional staff member, personnel of residential home facilities, a licensed or unlicensed day care provider, or any individual who provides such services to a child.

(d) Police officers or law enforcement officials.

(e) "Commercial film and photographic print processor" is any person who develops exposed photographic film into negatives, slides, or prints, or who makes prints from negatives or slides for compensation.

(14) "Neglect" means the refusal or willful failure of a parent or caretaker to supply the child with necessary food, clothing, shelter, care, treatment, or counseling for any injury, illness, or condition of the child, as a result of which the child's physical, mental, or emotional health is substantially threatened or impaired. Consistent with Article 606(B), the inability of a parent or caretaker to provide for a child due to inadequate financial resources shall not, for that reason alone, be considered neglect. Whenever, in lieu of medical care, a child is being provided treatment in accordance with the tenets of a well-recognized religious method of healing which has a reasonable, proven record of success, the child shall not, for that reason alone, be considered to be neglected or maltreated. However, nothing herein shall prohibit the court from ordering medical services for the child when there is substantial risk of harm to the child's health or welfare.

(15) "Permanent placement" means:

(a) Return of the legal custody of a child to his parent(s).

(b) Placement of the child under a guardianship of the person.

(c) Placement of the child with adoptive parents pursuant to a final decree of adoption.

(16) "Person" means any individual, partnership, association, agency, or corporation, and specifically shall include city, parish, or state law enforcement agencies, and a parish or city school board or a person employed by a parish or city school board.

(17) "Reasonable efforts" means the exercise of ordinary diligence and care by department caseworkers and supervisors and shall assume the availability of a reasonable program of services to children and their families.

(Added by Acts 1991 No. 235, §6; chgd. by Acts 1992 No. 705, §1; Acts 1993 No. 634, §1; Acts 1995 No. 444, §1, eff. 6/17/95.)

Art. 604. Persons subject to proceedings.

A court exercising juvenile jurisdiction shall have exclusive original jurisdiction, in conformity with any special rules prescribed by law, over any child alleged to be in need of care and the parents of any such child. *(Added by Acts 1991 No. 235, §6, eff. 1/1/92.)*

CHAPTER 2. VENUE

Art. 605. Venue.

A. A proceeding under this Title may be commenced in the parish in which the child is domiciled with his parent or tutor, the parish in which the child was present when an act alleged took place or conditions alleged existed, or the parish in which the child is found.

B. When a petition is filed in a parish other than that of the child's domicile, the court in which the proceeding is filed, upon motion of a party or upon the court's own motion, may transfer the proceeding to the court for the parish in which the child is domiciled. A transfer under this Paragraph may be made at any time.

C. When a petition is filed in a parish other than that of the child's domicile and the proceeding is not transferred under Paragraph B of this Article, the court in which the proceeding is filed shall immediately notify the appropriate court for the parish in which the child is domiciled, and if the court for the parish in which the child is domiciled requests a transfer within five days after receipt of the notification, the court in which the proceeding was filed may transfer the proceeding. A transfer under this Paragraph shall be made prior to the adjudication hearing.

D. When a petition is filed in a parish other than that of the child's domicile, and the proceeding is not transferred under Paragraph B or C of this Article, the court in which the proceeding was filed may, after the adjudication hearing, transfer the proceeding to the court of the parish where the child is domiciled for the disposition hearing.

(Added by Acts 1991 No. 235, §6; chgd. by Acts 1992 No. 705, §1, eff. 7/6/92.)

CHAPTER 3. GROUNDS; CHILD IN NEED OF CARE

Art. 606. Grounds; child in need of care.

A. Allegations that a child is in need of care must assert one or more of the following grounds:

(1) The child is the victim of abuse perpetrated, aided, or tolerated by the parent or caretaker, and his welfare is seriously endangered if he is left within the custody or control of that parent or caretaker.

(2) The child is a victim of neglect.

(3) The child is without necessary food, clothing, shelter, medical care, or supervision because of the disappearance or prolonged absence of his parent or when, for any other reason, the child is placed at substantial risk of imminent harm because of the continuing absence of the parent.

(4) As a result of a criminal prosecution, the parent has been convicted of a crime against the child who is the subject of this proceeding, or against another child of the parent, and the parent is now unable to retain custody or control or the child's welfare is otherwise endangered if left within the parent's custody or control.

(5) The conduct of the parent, either as principal or accessory, constitutes a crime against the child or against any other child of that parent.

B. A child whose parent is unable to provide basic support, supervision, treatment, or services due to inadequate financial resources shall not, for that reason alone, be determined to be a child in need of care.

(Added by Acts 1991 No. 235, §6; chgd. by Acts 1992 No. 705, §1; Acts 1995 No. 1095, §2, eff. 8/15/95.)

CHAPTER 4. RIGHT TO COUNSEL

Article

Art. 607. Child's right to appointed counsel; payment.

A. In every proceeding under this Title, the court shall appoint independent counsel for the child, or refer the child for representation by the indigent defender board. Neither the child nor anyone purporting to act on his behalf may be permitted to waive this right.

B. If the court finds that the parents of the child are financially able, it may order the parents to pay some or all of the costs of the child's representation.

C. In any dispositional or postdispositional hearing which may result in the mental health institutionalization of a child who is in the custody of the state, the child shall be entitled to representation by an attorney appointed by the Mental Health Advocacy Service, unless unavailable as determined by the director, or representation by retained private counsel who shall represent only the interest of the child.

(Added by Acts 1991 No. 235, §6; chgd. by Acts 1992 No. 705, §1, eff. 7/6/92.)

Art. 608. Parents' right to counsel; payment.

A. The parents of a child who is the subject of a child in need of care proceeding shall be entitled to counsel, which right may be waived by the parents.

B. If the parents of a child are financially unable to afford counsel, the court shall appoint counsel, or refer the parents for representation by the indigent defender board.

(Added by Acts 1991 No. 235, §6; chgd. by Acts 1992 No. 705, §1, eff. 7/6/92.)

CHAPTER 5. CHILD ABUSE REPORTING AND INVESTIGATION

Article

Art. 609. Mandatory and permitted reporting.

A. With respect to mandatory reporters:

(1) Notwithstanding any claim of privileged communication, any mandatory reporter who has cause to believe that a child's physical or mental health or welfare is endangered as a result of abuse or neglect or that abuse or neglect was a contributing factor in a child's death shall report in accordance with Article 610.

(2) Violation of the duties imposed upon a mandatory reporter subjects the offender to criminal prosecution authorized by R.S. 14:403(A)(1).

B. With respect to permitted reporters, any other person having cause to believe that a child's physical or mental health or welfare is endangered as a result of abuse or neglect, including a judge of any court of this state, may report in accordance with Article 610.

C. The filing of a report, known to be false, may subject the offender to criminal prosecution authorized by R.S. 14:403(A)(3).

(Added by Acts 1991 No. 235, §6; chgd. by Acts 1993 No. 637, §1, eff. 6/15/93.)

Art. 610. Reporting procedure.

A. Reports of child abuse or neglect or that such was a contributing factor in a child's death, where the abuser is believed to be a parent or caretaker, shall be made immediately to the local child protection unit of the department. Reports in which the abuse or neglect is believed to be perpetrated by someone other than a caretaker and the caretaker is not believed to have any responsibility for the abuse or neglect shall be made immediately to a local or state law enforcement agency.

B. The report shall contain the following information, if known:

(1) The name, address, age, sex, and race of the child.

(2) The nature, extent, and cause of the child's injuries or endangered condition, including any previous known or suspected abuse to this child or the child's siblings.

(3) The name and address of the child's parent(s) or other caretaker.

(4) The names and ages of all other members of the child's household.

(5) The name and address of the reporter.

(6) An account of how this child came to the reporter's attention.

(7) Any explanation of the cause of the child's injury or condition offered by the child, the caretaker, or any other person.

(8) Any other information which the reporter believes might be important or relevant.

C. The report shall also name the person or persons who are thought to have caused or contributed to the child's condition, if known, and the report shall contain the name of such person if he is named by the child.

D. If the initial report was in oral form by a mandatory reporter, it shall be followed by a written report made within five days to the local child protection unit of the department or, if necessary to the local law enforcement agency.

E. All reports received by any local or state law enforcement agency involving abuse or neglect in which the child's parent or caretaker is believed responsible shall be referred to the local child protection unit of the department. A local child protection unit shall refer abuse or neglect cases not involving a parent, caretaker, or occupant of the household to the appropriate law enforcement agency and also shall report all cases of child death which involve a suspicion of abuse or neglect as a contributing factor in the child's death to the local and state law enforcement agencies, the office of the district attorney, and the coroner.

F. Any commercial film or photographic print processor who has knowledge of or observes, within the scope of this professional capacity or employment, any film, photograph, video tape, negative, or slide depicting a child who he knows or should know is under the age of seventeen years, which constitutes child pornography as defined in Article 603, shall report immediately to the local law enforcement agency having jurisdiction over the case. The reporter shall provide a copy of the film, photograph, videotape, negative, or slide to the agency receiving the report.

(Added by Acts 1991 No. 235, §6; chgd. by Acts 1997 No. 1103, §1, eff. 7/14/97.)

Art. 611. Immunity from civil or criminal liability.

A. Any person who in good faith makes a report, cooperates in any investigation arising as a result of such report, or participates in judicial proceedings authorized under the provisions of this Chapter, or any caseworker who in good faith conducts an investigation, makes an investigative judgment or disposition, or releases or uses information contained in the central registry for the purpose of protecting a child, shall have immunity from civil or criminal liability that otherwise might be incurred or imposed.

B. This immunity shall not be extended to:

(1) Any alleged principal, conspirator, or accessory to an offense involving the abuse or neglect of the child.

(2) Any person who makes a report known to be false or with reckless disregard for the truth of the report.

(Added by Acts 1991 No. 235, §6; chgd. by Acts 1993 No. 675, §1, eff. 8/15/93.)

Art. 612. Assignment of reports for investigation and assessment.

A. Upon receiving a report of abuse or neglect of a child who is not in the custody of the state, the local child protection unit of the department shall promptly assign a level of risk to the child based on the information provided by the reporter. Reports of high and intermediate levels of risk shall be investigated promptly. This investigation shall include a preliminary investigation as to the nature, extent, and cause of the abuse or neglect and the identity of the person actually responsible for the child's condition. This preliminary investigation shall include an interview with the child and his parent or parents or other caretaker. Admission of the investigator on school premises or access to the child in school shall not be denied by school personnel. Reports of low levels of risk shall be assessed promptly through interviews with the family to identify needs and available match to community resources. If during this assessment, it is determined that a child is at immediate substantial risk of harm, the local child protection unit shall promptly conduct or participate in an intensive investigation.

B. All persons, including without limitation mandatory and permissive reporters, shall cooperate fully with investigative procedures, including independent investigations and psychological evaluations of the child initiated by the parent on behalf of the child. The provisions of this Paragraph shall not require the disclosure of any communications between an attorney and his client or any confession or other sacred communication between priest, rabbi, duly ordained minister, or Christian Science practitioner and his communicant.

C. All interviews of the child or his parents conducted in the course of a child protective investigation shall be tape-recorded, if requested by the parent or parents.

D. Upon determination that there is reason to believe that the child has been abused or neglected, the local child protection unit shall conduct a more intensive investigation. If necessary, the investigator may apply for an evaluation order authorized by Article 614.

E. When the report concerns a facility under the supervision of the department, the secretary of the department may assign the duties and powers enumerated herein to any office within the department to carry out the purposes of this Chapter or may enter into cooperative agreements with other state agencies to conduct investigations in accordance with this Article.

F. Violation of the duties imposed by this Article subjects the offender to criminal prosecution authorized by R.S. 14:403(A)(2).

G. The Department of Social Services shall set priorities for case response and allocate staff resources to cases identified by reporters as presenting immediate substantial risk of harm to children. Absent evidence of willful or intentional misconduct or gross negligence in carrying out the investigative functions of the state child protection program, caseworkers, supervisors, program managers, and agency heads shall be immune from civil and criminal liability in any legal action arising from the department's decisions made relative to the setting of priorities for cases and targeting of staff resources.

(Added by Acts 1991 No. 235, §6; chgd. by Acts 1992 No. 705, §1; Acts 1993 No. 675, §1; Acts 1995 No. 444, §1, eff. 6/17/95.)

Art. 613. Entry orders.

A. If in the course of an investigation of a report, admission cannot be obtained to the home, school, or any other place where the child may be found, the investigator shall apply to the juvenile court for an order authorizing an entry for the purposes of interviewing the child and other members of the household, for the visual inspection of the child, and for an inspection of the home to the extent such an inspection is essential to the investigation of specific allegations. The affidavit of the applicant must demonstrate:

(1) That reasonable suspicion exists that the child has been abused or neglected.

(2) That entry has been denied.

B. The court may grant such an order on an ex parte application and may also order a law enforcement officer to accompany the applicant in executing the entry order.

(Added by Acts 1991 No. 235, §6; chgd. by Acts 1992 No. 705, §1, eff. 7/6/92.)

Art. 614. Evaluation orders.

A. If necessary, the investigator may apply to the court for certain medical examinations and evaluations of the child or other children in the household.

B. Upon a showing of good cause in an affidavit executed by the applicant, the court may order a physical examination and evaluation of the child or other children in the household by any physician. Such an order may be granted ex parte.

C. Upon a showing of good cause in an affidavit executed by the applicant and after a contradictory hearing, the court may order a psychological or psychiatric examination and evaluation of the child or other children in the household by a psychologist or psychiatrist.

D. Upon a showing of good cause in an affidavit executed by the applicant and after a contradictory hearing, the court may order a physical, psychological, or psychiatric examination of the parent or caretaker.

(Added by Acts 1991 No. 235, §6; chgd. by Acts 1992 No. 705, §1; chgd. by Acts 1995 No. 1095, §2, eff. 8/15/95.)

Art. 615. Disposition of reports.

A. In determining the disposition of the report, the agency shall take into account, in mitigation, the possibility of accidental injury or condition, or that the injury resulted from what might be considered a reasonable exercise of discipline for the child's misbehavior.

B. After investigation, the local child protection unit shall make one of the following determinations:

(1) The child appears to be a child in need of care and his immediate removal is necessary for his protection from further abuse or neglect, in which case, whenever such extraordinary justification arises, it shall apply for an instanter removal order authorized under Articles 619 and 620 and shall notify the district attorney as soon as possible.

(2) The report appears to be justified, in that there is evidence of child abuse, and a protective order would eliminate the need for removal of the child in order to protect him from further abuse, in which case it may apply for a temporary restraining order or protective order authorized by Article 617 and Article 618.

(3) The report appears to be justified, in that there is evidence of child abuse or neglect, in which case it shall report all pertinent information to the district attorney, as soon as possible but in no case more than thirty days after such determination, for evaluation of whether a child in need of care petition should be filed in the court with juvenile jurisdiction.

(4) The report does not appear justified as the evidence does not support a finding of child abuse or neglect.

(5) The investigation indicates the report appears to be false and that the reporter knowingly made a false report in which case all pertinent information shall be forwarded to the district attorney for a determination of whether the evidence supports a finding of a false public report.

(6) *(Repealed.)*

C. In addition to investigation or assessment of reports, or both, the local child protection family services unit may offer available information, referrals, or services to the family when there appears to be some need for medical, mental health, social, basic support, supervision, or other services. Assignments for case response and allocation of resources shall be made in the order of children at greatest risk of harm to the lowest risk of harm.

D. Violation of the duties imposed by this Article subjects the offender to criminal prosecution authorized by R.S. 14:403(A)(2).

E. When, after the investigation of a report, the determination is made that the report does not appear to be justified, as provided in Paragraph B(4), or appears to be false, as provided in Paragraph B(5) of this Article, all files, records, and pertinent information regarding the report and investigation shall be destroyed following the three-year period required by federal law for audit purposes. During the three-year record retention period, such records shall be sealed and all identifying information removed, and shall be accessible only to the financial auditors. Records shall be maintained during the pendency of any litigation or prosecution involving those records.

(Added by Acts 1991 No. 235, §6; chgd. by Acts 1993 No. 505, §1; Acts 1995 No. 444, §§1, 2, eff. 6/17/95, No. 625, §1, eff. 6/19/95.)

Art. 616. Central registry; screening court-appointed special advocates volunteers; confidentiality.

A. (1) The department shall maintain a central registry of all reports of abuse and neglect. When, after the investigation, the determination is made by the department that the report does appear to be justified, any subsequent adjudication by a court exercising juvenile jurisdiction which dismisses the child in need of care petition involving this report shall be added to the central registry.

(2) When, after the investigation, the determination is made that the report does not appear to be justified as provided in Paragraph B(4) or is false as provided in Paragraph B(5) of Article 615, all files, records, and pertinent information regarding the report and investigation shall be destroyed following the three-year period required by federal law for audit purposes. During the three-year record retention period, such records shall be sealed and all identifying information removed, and shall be accessible only to the financial auditors. Records shall be maintained during the pendency of any litigation involving those records.

(3) The purpose of a central registry is to provide information of past reports of child abuse or neglect of children to assist in the proper evaluation of current reports of abuse or neglect which may include a pattern of incidents.

B. (1) All records of reports of child abuse or neglect are confidential. The department shall promulgate rules regarding the maintenance, deletion, and release of information in the central registry, determined by the types of dispositions made pursuant to Article 615.

(2) A judge of a court exercising juvenile jurisdiction may request, in writing from the department, a central registry check of an individual applying to work as a court-appointed special advocate volunteer provided the judge of a court exercising juvenile jurisdiction has obtained the individual's written consent to the registry check.

(3) The department shall search the central registry to determine whether a justified report of abuse or neglect exists naming the individual as an alleged perpetrator and report the results of the search to the judge of a court exercising juvenile jurisdiction who made the request.

C. Violation of the confidentiality provisions of Paragraph B of this Article or the lawful regulations of the department subjects the offender to criminal prosecution authorized by R.S. 14:403(I)(2).

(Added by Acts 1991 No. 235, §6; chgd. by Acts 1993 No. 505, §1; Acts 1995 No. 625, §1; Acts 1997 No. 903, §2, eff. 7/10/97.)

Art. 616.1. Correction of central registry entries; procedure.

A. When a report alleging abuse or neglect is recorded as justified by the department in the central registry but when no petition is subsequently filed alleging that the child is in need of care, the individual who is the subject of the finding may file a written motion seeking correction of that entry and all related department records in the court exercising juvenile jurisdiction in the parish in which the finding was made.

B. Prior to the hearing, the motion shall be served on the department and the district attorney.

C. If neither the department nor the district attorney files a written objection, the court may enter an order in accordance with Paragraph D.

D. If after a contradictory hearing with the department and the district attorney the court finds that the report was not justified, in accordance with Article 615(B)(4) or (5), and correction of the record is not contrary to the best interest of the child, it may order the department to correct the central registry entry. If the central registry entry is ordered to be corrected, the department and any law enforcement offices having any record of the report shall be ordered to correct those records and any other records, notations, or references thereto, and the court shall order the department and other custodians of such records to file a sworn affidavit to the effect that their records have been corrected. The affidavit of the department shall also attest to the correction of the central registry entry.

E. The originals of the affidavits required in Paragraph D shall be kept by the court and a copy shall be retained by the affiant. The copy shall not be a public record and shall not be open for public inspection but rather shall be kept under lock and key and maintained only for internal recordkeeping purposes and to preserve the integrity of the files of the department or office and shall not be used for any investigative purpose.

(Added by Acts 1997 No. 612, §1, eff. 8/15/97.)

CHAPTER 6. PROCEDURES FOR THE PROTECTION OF A CHILD

Art. 617. Temporary restraining order.

A. Upon good cause shown in an ex parte proceeding, the court may enter a temporary restraining order, without bond, as it deems necessary to protect from abuse the petitioner, any children, or any person alleged to be an incompetent. Immediate and present danger of abuse shall constitute good cause for purposes of this Article. The order may include but is not limited to the following:

(1) Directing the defendant to refrain from abusing, harassing, or interfering with the person or employment or going near the residence or place of employment of the petitioner, the children, or any person alleged to be incompetent, on whose behalf a petition was filed.

(2) Awarding to a party use and possession of specified community property, such as an automobile.

(3) Granting possession to the petitioner of the residence or household to the exclusion of the defendant, by evicting the defendant or restoring possession to the petitioner where:

(a) The residence is jointly owned in equal proportion or leased by the defendant and the petitioner or the person on whose behalf the petition is brought.

(b) The residence is solely owned by the petitioner of the person on whose behalf the petition is brought.

(c) The residence is solely leased by defendant and defendant has a duty to support the petitioner or the person on whose behalf the petition is brought.

(4) Prohibiting either party from transferring, encumbering, or otherwise disposing of property mutually owned or leased by the parties, except when in the ordinary course of business, or for the necessary support of the party or the minor children.

B. If a temporary restraining order is granted without notice, the matter shall be set within ten days for a rule to show cause why the protective order should not be issued, at which time the petitioner must prove the allegations of abuse by a preponderance of the evidence. The defendant shall be given notice of the temporary restraining order and the hearing on the rule to show cause by service of process as required by law.

C. During the existence of the temporary restraining order, a party shall have the right to return to the family residence once to recover his or her personal clothing and necessities, provided that the party is accompanied by a law enforcement officer to insure the protection and safety of the parties.

D. If no temporary restraining order has been granted, the court shall issue a rule to show cause why the protective order should not be issued, and set the rule for hearing on the earliest day that the business of the court will permit, but in any case within ten days from the date of service of the petition, at which time the petitioner must prove the allegations of abuse by a preponderance of the evidence. The defendant shall be given notice by service of process as required by law.

E. If the hearing pursuant to Paragraph B or D of this Article is continued, the court shall make or extend such temporary restraining orders as it deems necessary. Such continuance shall not exceed ten days.

F. The court may, in its discretion, grant an emergency temporary restraining order outside regular court hours.

G. Immediately upon rendering a decision granting the relief requested by the petitioner, the judge shall cause to have prepared a Uniform Abuse Prevention Order, as provided in R.S. 46:2136.2(C), shall sign such order, and shall forward it to the clerk of court for filing, all without delay.

H. If a temporary restraining order is issued or extended, the clerk of the issuing court shall transmit the Uniform Abuse Prevention Order to the Louisiana Protective Order Registry, R.S. 46:2136.2(A), by facsimile transmission, mail, or direct electronic input, where available, as expeditiously as possible, but no later than the end of the next business day after the order is filed with the clerk of court.

(Added by Acts 1991 No. 235, §6; chgd. by Acts 1997 No. 1156, §1, eff. 8/15/97.)

Art. 618. Protective orders; content; modification; service.

A. The court may grant any protective order or approve any consent agreement to bring about a cessation of abuse of a party, any minor children, or any person alleged to be incompetent, which relief may include but is not limited to:

(1) Granting the relief enumerated in Article 617.

(2) When there is a duty to support a party, any minor children, or any person alleged to be incompetent living in the residence or household, ordering payment of temporary support or provision of suitable housing for them.

(3) Awarding temporary custody of or establishing temporary visitation rights and conditions with regard to any minor children or person alleged to be incompetent.

(4) Ordering counseling or professional medical treatment for either the defendant or the abused person, or both.

B. A protective order may be rendered pursuant to this Chapter if the court has jurisdiction over the parties and subject matter and either of the following occurs:

(1) The parties enter into a consent agreement.

(2) Reasonable notice and opportunity to be heard is given to the person against whom the order is sought sufficient to protect that person's right to due process.

C. Any protective order issued within this state or outside this state that is consistent with Paragraph B of this Article shall be accorded full faith and credit by the courts of this state and enforced as if it were the order of the enforcing court.

D. On the motion of any party, the court, after notice to the other parties and a hearing, may modify a prior order to exclude any item included in the prior order or to include any item that could have been included in the prior order.

E. A protective order made under this Article shall be served on the person to whom the order applies in open court at the close of the hearing, or in the same manner as a writ of injunction. The clerk of the issuing court shall send a copy of the order or any modification thereof to the chief law enforcement official of the parish where the person or persons protected by the order reside. A copy of the protective order shall be retained on file in the office of the chief law enforcement officer as provided herein until otherwise directed by the court.

F. Any final protective order or approved consent agreement shall be for a fixed period of time, not to exceed six months, and may be extended by the court, after a contradictory hearing, in its discretion. Such protective order or extension thereof shall be subject to a devolutive appeal only.

G. Immediately upon rendering a decision granting the relief requested by the petitioner, the judge shall cause to have prepared a Uniform Abuse Prevention Order, as provided in R.S. 46:2136.2(C), shall sign such order, and shall forward it to the clerk of court for filing, all without delay.

H. If a protective order is issued or modified, or a consent agreement is agreed to or modified, the clerk of the issuing court shall transmit the Uniform Abuse Prevention Order to the Louisiana Protective Order Registry, R.S. 46:2136.2(A), by facsimile transmission, mail, or direct electronic input, where available, as expeditiously as possible, but no later than the end of the next business day after the order is filed with the clerk of court.

(Added by Acts 1991 No. 235, §6; chgd. by Acts 1995 No. 1095, §2; Acts 1997 No. 1156, §1, eff. 8/15/97.)

Art. 619. Instanter orders of custody.

A. A peace officer, district attorney, or employee of the local child protection unit of the department may file a verified complaint alleging facts showing that there are reasonable grounds to believe that the child is in need of care and that emergency removal is necessary to secure the child's protection.

B. The court shall determine whether reasonable efforts have been made by the department to prevent or eliminate the need for the child's removal, including whether the department has requested a temporary restraining order pursuant to Article 617 or a protective order pursuant to Article 618. However, the court may authorize the removal of the child even if the department's efforts have not been reasonable.

C. If the court determines that the child's welfare cannot be safeguarded without removal, the court may issue an instanter order directing that the child be taken into custody of the state.

D. An instanter order shall be executed by either an employee of the local child protection unit or any peace officer having territorial jurisdiction over the child.

E. An employee of the local child protection unit or any peace officer having territorial jurisdiction over the child is authorized to serve a summons upon a parent or caretaker, commanding him to appear at court for a continued custody hearing. A copy of the summons shall be filed in the record as proof of service.

(Added by Acts 1991 No. 235, §6; chgd. by Acts 1993 No. 634, §1; Acts 1995 No. 1095, §2, eff. 8/15/95.)

Art. 620. Oral instanter orders.

A. In exceptional circumstances, the facts supporting the issuance of an instanter order and the exceptional circumstances may be relayed orally, including telephonically, to the judge and his order directing that a child be taken into custody may be issued orally.

B. In such cases, an affidavit containing the information previously relayed orally, including telephonically, shall be filed with the clerk of the court within twenty-four hours and a written order shall be issued.

C. If the affidavit is filed after the child has been taken into custody, it shall indicate whether the child was released to his parents or continued in custody.

D. The department shall promptly notify the parents or caretaker of the nature of the allegations and, if the child is not released, of the time and place of the continued custody hearing.

(Added by Acts 1991 No. 235, §6; chgd. by Acts 1993 No. 634, §1, eff. 6/15/93.)

Art. 621. Taking child into custody without a court order.

A. A peace officer or probation officer of the court may take a child into custody without a court order if he has reasonable grounds to believe that the child's surroundings are such as to endanger his welfare and immediate removal appears to be necessary for his protection.

B. Employees of the department must secure an instanter order before taking a child into custody.

C. A peace officer, having taken a child into custody without a court order, shall have the responsibility to promptly notify and release the child to the department.

D. The department may release the child or secure an instanter order.

E. The department shall promptly notify the parents or caretaker of the nature of the allegations and, if the child is not released, of the time and place of the continued custody hearing.

(Added by Acts 1991 No. 235, §6; chgd. by Acts 1993 No. 634, §1, eff. 6/15/93.)

Art. 622. Rules for placement.

A. (1) GENERAL RULE. A child who is taken into custody as a child in need of care shall be placed in the home of a suitable relative who is of the age of majority and who is willing to assume such care of the child if such placement is in the best interest of the child. The following are those relatives to whom care of the child may be entrusted and are listed in the order of priority:

(a) Grandparent.
(b) Aunt or uncle.
(c) Sibling.
(d) Cousin.

(2) Notwithstanding any other provision of law to the contrary and prior to the continued custody hearing required in Article 624, any relative designated in this Paragraph may seek and obtain an ex parte court order to take immediate physical custody of the child under the provisions and requirements of this Paragraph and pending the continued custody hearing. The provisions of Code of Civil Procedure Article 3945 are inapplicable to an ex parte order rendered pursuant hereto.

B. EXCEPTION. A child shall be placed in a foster care home or facility approved by the department only if:

(1) No ex parte court order has been rendered pursuant to Paragraph A of this Article.

(2) The continued custody hearing has been held, the court has continued the child in the custody of the department, and the court has made a specific finding, by clear and convincing evidence, that the placement of the child with a relative seeking physical custody of the child is not in the best interest of the child.

C. The department shall supervise the child's placement for the duration of the time the department has custody of the child.

D. In the event that a child is placed with nonrelatives pursuant to Paragraph B of this Article, any suitable relative of the age of majority may petition the court for the physical custody of the child.

(Added by Acts 1991 No. 235, §6; chgd. by Acts 1992 No. 705, §1; Acts 1997 No. 1152, §1, eff. 8/15/97.)

Art. 623. Shelter care facility records; access.

A. Every juvenile shelter care facility shall maintain a permanent record of certain information as to each child received. The record shall include:

(1) The child's name and address.

(2) The date and time of the child's entry into the facility.

(3) The name of the person who brought the child to the facility.

B. The record in which such information is kept shall not be open for public inspection. Peace officers, counsel representing the child or the parents, the district attorney, the department, persons collecting statistical information, and authorized officers of the court shall have access to the record.

(Added by Acts 1991 No. 235, §6, eff. 1/1/92.)

Art. 624. Continued custody hearing.

A. If a child is not released to the care of his parents, a hearing shall be held by the court within three days after the child's entry into custody. The hearing may be continued for up to three additional days upon motion and with good cause shown.

B. If it appears from the record that the parent cannot be found or has been served a summons to appear at the continued custody hearing and fails to appear at the hearing, then the hearing may be held in the parent's absence.

C. At this hearing, the state has the burden to prove the existence of a ground for continued custody pursuant to Article 626.

D. The child and his parents may introduce evidence, call witnesses, be heard on their own behalf, and cross-examine witnesses called by the state.

E. Hearsay evidence shall be admissible at this hearing.

(Added by Acts 1991 No. 235, §6; chgd. by Acts 1993 No. 634, §1, eff. 6/15/93.)

Art. 625. Advice of rights.

A. At the continued custody hearing, the court shall advise the parents and may advise the child, insofar as practicable, of:

(1) The nature of the proceedings in terms understandable to the child.

(2) The nature of the allegations in terms understandable to the child.

(3) The right to an adjudication hearing.

(4) The right to be represented by an attorney and the right to have counsel appointed as provided in Chapter 4.

B. If at the time of the hearing a petition has been filed, the court may also call upon the parent to answer its allegations in accordance with Chapter 9.

(Added by Acts 1991 No. 235, §6, eff. 1/1/92.)

Art. 626. Grounds for continued custody; reasonable efforts.

A. The court may authorize continued custody of a child prior to adjudication if there are reasonable grounds to believe the child is in need of care and that continued custody is necessary for his safety and protection.

B. The court shall determine whether the department has made reasonable efforts as defined in Article 603(17) to prevent or eliminate the need for removal of the child from his home and, after removal, to make it possible for the child to return home.

C. If the department's first contact with the family occurred during an emergency in which the child could not safely remain at home even with reasonable in-home services provided to the family, the department shall be deemed to have made reasonable efforts to prevent or eliminate the need for removal.

D. The court may authorize the removal of the child even if the department's efforts have not been reasonable, and may impose such sanctions it deems appropriate pursuant to Article 712.

(Added by Acts 1991 No. 235, §6, eff. 1/1/92.)

Art. 627. Continued custody order.

A. Following a hearing, the court may return the child to the parents, continue the child in the custody of the department, or place the legal custody of the child with a suitable person, preferably a relative. If the court continues the child in the custody of the department and a suitable relative of the child is seeking the physical custody of the child, the court shall grant the relative physical custody unless the court has made a specific finding, by clear and convincing evidence, that such placement is not in the best interest of the child. The court shall give specific oral and written reasons for its findings, which shall be made a part of the record of the proceeding. For purposes of this Paragraph, a relative includes any person listed in Article 622(A)(1) who shall be given priority in the designated order, and also includes any other relative although not included in the order of priority.

B. If the court finds that the child can be safely returned home under a protective order pending adjudication, the court may order return of the child and issue such protective orders as are deemed necessary for the protection and welfare of the child.

C. If a protective order is issued or modified, the judge shall cause to have prepared a Uniform Abuse Prevention Order, as provided in R.S. 46:2136.2(C), shall sign such order, and shall forward it to the clerk of court for filing, all without delay, and the clerk of the issuing court shall transmit the Uniform Abuse Prevention Order to the Louisiana Protective Order Registry, R.S. 46:2136.2(A), by facsimile transmission, mail, or direct electronic input, where available, as expeditiously as possible, but no later than the end of the next business day after the order is filed with the clerk of court.

(Added by Acts 1991 No. 235, §6; chgd. by Acts 1997 No. 1152, §1, No. 1156, §1, eff. 8/15/97.)

CHAPTER 7. INFORMAL ADJUSTMENT PROCEDURE

Article

Art. 628. Informal adjustment agreement.

A. Prior to the filing of a petition, the court or district attorney may authorize an informal adjustment agreement or refer the matter to an intake officer as a families in need of services case.

B. After the filing of a petition, the court may authorize the district attorney to effect an informal adjustment agreement. The court may dismiss the petition or allow the petition to remain pending during the period of informal adjustment.

(Added by Acts 1991 No. 235, §6, eff. 1/1/92.)

Art. 629. Form of agreement; duration.

An informal adjustment agreement shall set forth in writing its terms and conditions and shall be signed by the district attorney, by the child's parents, and by the child or counsel for the child. The period of informal adjustment shall not exceed six months; however, the court may extend the agreement for one additional period not to exceed six months. *(Added by Acts 1991 No. 235, §6; chgd. by Acts 1992 No. 705, §1, eff. 7/6/92.)*

Art. 630. Effect of an agreement.

An informal adjustment agreement shall not be considered an adjudication. Evidence of such an agreement shall not be admissible in any subsequent proceeding. *(Added by Acts 1991 No. 235, §6, eff. 1/1/92.)*

CHAPTER 8. PETITIONS; SERVICE; SUMMONS

Article

Art. 631. Authority to file petition.

A child in need of care proceeding shall be commenced by petition filed by the district attorney. Any other person authorized by the court may file a petition if there are reasonable grounds to believe that the child is a child in need of care. *(Added by Acts 1991 No. 235, §6; chgd. by Acts 1992 No. 705, §1, eff. 7/6/92.)*

Art. 632. Time for filing of petition; child in custody.

A. If a child is continued in custody prior to adjudication, or if a protective order is issued, a petition requesting that the child be adjudicated in need of care shall be filed within thirty days of the hearing to determine continued custody.

B. Upon motion and good cause shown, the time for filing a petition may be extended by the court.

C. If no petition is filed within the applicable time period, the child shall be returned to the parent.

(Added by Acts 1991 No. 235, §6, eff. 1/1/92.)

Art. 633. Form of petition.

A. The petition shall contain a caption setting forth the name of the court and the title of the action. The petition shall be entitled, "The State of Louisiana in the Interest of______."

B. Allegations of fact shall be simple, concise, and direct and shall be set forth in numbered paragraphs. As far as practicable, each paragraph shall be limited to a single set of circumstances.

C. The petition shall be verified. Allegations of fact may be made on information and belief.

D. Failure to comply with formal requirements of this Article shall not be grounds for dismissal of a petition or invalidation of the proceedings unless it results in substantial prejudice.

(Added by Acts 1991 No. 235, §6, eff. 1/1/92.)

Art. 634. Contents of petition.

A. The petition shall set forth with specificity:

(1) The name, date and place of birth, sex, race, and address of the child. If the child is in a foster home, the identification of the parish in which he resides shall suffice for his address.

(2) The name and current address of each parent.

(3) Facts which show that the child is a child in need of care, including the acts or omissions of either parent which caused or contributed to the child's condition.

B. If any of the information required by Subparagraph A(1) or (2) is unknown, the petition shall so allege. Any defects in the information required by Subparagraph A(1) shall be considered defects of form.

C. The petition shall conclude with a request that the court adjudicate the child to be a child in need of care.

(Added by Acts 1991 No. 235, §6; chgd. by Acts 1997 No. 612, §1, eff. 8/15/97.)

Art. 635. Amendment of petition.

A. With leave of court, the petitioner may amend the petition at any time to cure defects of form.

B. With leave of court, prior to the adjudication hearing, the petitioner may amend the petition to include new allegations of fact or requests for adjudication. However, if such leave is granted, the child or parent may request a continuance of the adjudication hearing. A continuance may be granted for such period as is required in the interest of justice.

(Added by Acts 1991 No. 235, §6, eff. 1/1/92.)

Art. 636. Summons.

When the petition is filed, the court shall issue a summons commanding that the child, his resident parents, and such other persons, including a nonresident parent, as the court deems proper appear before the court at a designated time and place. *(Added by Acts 1991 No. 235, §6, eff. 1/1/92.)*

Art. 637. Failure to appear as summoned.

If a properly served person fails to appear in response to a summons, the court may order that such person be taken into custody and immediately brought before the court. *(Added by Acts 1991 No. 235, §6, eff. 1/1/92.)*

Art. 638. Service of petition.

A copy of the petition and the notice of the nature of the hearing and the rights of the parent, as provided for in Article 639, shall be served upon every parent of the child. *(Added by Acts 1991 No. 235, §6, eff. 1/1/92.)*

Art. 639. Notice of nature of hearing; parental rights; form.

The following notice shall be served with a petition and summons on every parent whose child is the subject of a child in need of care proceeding:

"NOTICE

Louisiana law provides that you can lose some of your parental rights regarding your child under certain circumstances. Suit has been filed which claims that your child is in need of care, and a hearing will be held to determine whether these circumstances exist. If the court rules that your child is being abused or neglected, as defined by Louisiana law, your rights to have custody of your child, to visit your child, or to make decisions affecting your child will be seriously affected. You may also become liable for paying for the costs of your child's care if custody is awarded to some other individual or to the state.

You have the right to hire an attorney and are encouraged to do so. When you come to court, if you cannot afford to hire an attorney, you may qualify to have the court appoint one for you at state expense.

Whether or not you decide to hire an attorney, you have the right to attend the hearing of your case and must attend as summoned, and the right to call witnesses on your behalf, and to question those witnesses brought against you."

(Added by Acts 1991 No. 235, §6, eff. 1/1/92.)

Art. 640. Service and return; resident parent.

A. If a parent resides within the state, service of the petition, summons, and notice shall be made personally or by domiciliary service or by certified mail as soon as possible and not less than fifteen days prior to commencement of the adjudication hearing on the matter.

B. The person effecting service shall execute a return and, if service was made by certified mail, the return receipt shall be attached thereto.

(Added by Acts 1991 No. 235, §6, eff. 1/1/92.)

Art. 641. Service and return; nonresident parent.

A. If a parent does not reside within this state, service of the petition and notice, and summons if issued by the court, shall be made by certified mail, return receipt requested, to the address indicated in the petition, not less than five days prior to commencement of the adjudication hearing on the matter.

B. The person effecting the service shall file the return receipt as proof of service.

(Added by Acts 1991 No. 235, §6, eff. 1/1/92.)

Art. 642. Effect of nonappearance by a parent.

If it appears from the record that the parent has been served in accordance with Article 640 or 641 and summoned to any hearing, and the parent fails to appear at the hearing, then the hearing may be held in the parent's absence and petitioner shall be required to establish prima facie proof of the allegations contained in the petition. *(Added by Acts 1991 No. 235, §6, eff. 1/1/92.)*

Art. 643. Service; absentee parent; curator ad hoc.

A. If the parent against whom a proceeding is instituted cannot be served in accordance with Article 640 or 641, the court shall appoint an attorney at law as curator ad hoc for the parent and service shall be made upon the curator ad hoc.

B. Upon appointment of the curator ad hoc, a copy of the letter of appointment shall be forwarded to the department and the district attorney.

(Added by Acts 1991 No. 235, §6, eff. 1/1/92.)

Art. 644. Duties of curator ad hoc.

A. The curator ad hoc shall make a diligent effort to locate the parent and notify him of the pendency and nature of the proceedings. Such notice shall include:

(1) The allegations made against the parent.

(2) The right of the parent to appear at the hearing, to defend against the allegations, and to compel the attendance of witnesses in his behalf.

(3) The right of the parent to retain counsel.

B. If the curator ad hoc fails to locate the parent, the curator ad hoc shall attend the hearing of this matter, submit a note of evidence on the record indicating the efforts made to locate the parent, and proceed contradictorily unless the parent is subsequently served or waives objection to jurisdiction. Proceedings held contradictorily with the curator ad hoc shall be of full force and legal effect against the parent.

C. If the parent is subsequently served in accordance with either Article 640 or Article 641 or is located by the curator ad hoc, the curator ad hoc shall be required only to attend the hearing and submit a note of evidence on the record indicating the efforts made to locate the parent.

(Added by Acts 1991 No. 235, §6; chgd. by Acts 1997 No. 578, §4, eff. 8/15/97.)

Art. 645. Department of Social Services to provide information concerning the parents' location.

Notwithstanding any other provision of the law to the contrary, the department shall obtain and provide to the district attorney with any request for a petition all available information pertinent to the location of every parent, including names and addresses of known relatives. If a curator ad hoc is appointed, the department shall supply this information to him within fifteen days of its receipt of a copy of the order appointing the curator ad hoc. This duty shall be a continuing one as long as the child remains subject to the jurisdiction of the court. *(Added by Acts 1991 No. 235, §6, eff. 1/1/92.)*

CHAPTER 9. ANSWER TO PETITION

Art. 646. Appearance to answer petition or stipulation.

A. The court may require the parents to appear to answer the petition at any time prior to the adjudication hearing but no later than fifteen days after the filing of the petition.

B. The court may also permit the parents to stipulate that the child is in need of care.

C. If the petition is filed prior to or during the hearing to determine continued custody, the court may order the parent to answer the petition upon completion of the hearing or permit the entry of a stipulation that the child is in need of care.

(Added by Acts 1991 No. 235, §6, eff. 1/1/92.)

Art. 647. Stipulation; consent to judgment.

With the approval of the petitioner, a parent whose child is the subject of pending proceedings may, with or without admitting the allegations of the petition, stipulate that the child is in need of care according to Article 606, provided that:

(1) The parent personally appears before the court.

(2) The court fully informs the parent of his rights as required by Article 625.

(3) The court fully informs the parent of the consequences of such a stipulation.

(4) The parent knowingly and voluntarily consents to the judgment.

(Added by Acts 1991 No. 235, §6; chgd. by Acts 1992 No. 705, §1, eff. 7/6/92.)

Art. 648. Advice of rights at appearance to answer petition.

If an appearance to answer the petition is required, the court shall advise the parent of his rights pursuant to Article 625, unless they were so advised at a previous hearing. *(Added by Acts 1991 No. 235, §6, eff. 1/1/92.)*

Art. 649. Answer to petition.

After the parent has been advised of his rights and if the parent has not stipulated pursuant to Article 647, the court shall determine whether the parent admits or denies the allegations of the petition.

(1) If the parent denies the allegations of the petition, the court shall set the matter for adjudication.

(2) If the parent admits the allegations of the petition, the court shall determine whether there is a factual basis for adjudication and whether the parent consents to adjudication. *(Added by Acts 1991 No. 235, §6, eff. 1/1/92.)*

Art. 650. Objection of child.

A child may object, in writing or in open court, to an answer of his parent, which objection shall be noted by the court. *(Added by Acts 1991 No. 235, §6, eff. 1/1/92.)*

CHAPTER 10. SPECIAL MOTIONS AND DISCOVERY

Art. 651. Preadjudication motions; time for filing; hearings.

A. All motions prior to the adjudication hearing shall be made by written motion filed no later than fifteen days before any scheduled adjudication hearing. In the interest of justice, the court may allow additional time within which to make or file such motions or may permit such requests to be made by oral motion.

B. The motion shall state with particularity the grounds therefor and shall set forth the relief sought.

C. A motion may be granted without a contradictory hearing when mover is clearly entitled thereto without supporting proof. A motion shall not be denied without a contradictory hearing unless, assuming the facts alleged to be true, mover is not entitled to relief.

(Added by Acts 1991 No. 235, §6, eff. 1/1/92.)

Art. 652. Discovery.

A. At any stage of the proceeding, upon written motion of counsel for the child or his parent, the court may order the district attorney or the department to permit counsel to inspect:

(1) Reports of investigation in the possession or control of the district attorney or the department.

(2) Reports of evaluations or tests pertaining to the child in the possession or control of the district attorney or the department.

(3) The case records maintained by the department pertaining to the child and the parent, except information otherwise protected under R.S. 46:56 or by restrictive order pursuant to Article 653.

(4) Any videotape of a child who has been physically or sexually abused made in compliance with Chapter 8 of Title III which is in the possession or control of the district attorney.

B. The court shall order the district attorney or the department to permit counsel to inspect and copy any physical evidence, documents, or photographs which the state intends to offer into evidence at the adjudication hearing as provided for in Paragraph A(1), (2), and (4). However, the court may, in its discretion, permit the inspection of evidence provided for in Paragraph A(3).

C. If counsel for the child or his parents is granted relief* under Paragraph A, the court may condition that order upon reciprocal discovery by the state.

**So in original.*

D. The court shall not order the production or inspection of any part of a writing that reflects the mental impressions, conclusions, or theories of an attorney.

E. The duties imposed by a discovery order are continuing in nature as long as the child is subject to the jurisdiction of the court, unless the order provides to the contrary.
(Added by Acts 1991 No. 235, §6, eff. 1/1/92.)

Art. 653. Restrictive orders; discovery.

A. The court may limit, modify, or restrict discovery upon written motion and a showing of good cause, such as a claim of confidentiality under R.S. 46:56. Such showing may be made ex parte if the interests of justice so require.

B. If the court restricts, limits, or modifies its order, the written motion showing good cause may be sealed and shall be placed in the record of the proceeding.
(Added by Acts 1991 No. 235, §6, eff. 1/1/92.)

Art. 654. Medical, sensory, psychological, and psychiatric examinations.

A. On its own motion, or on the motion of the child, the parent, or the petitioner, the court may order any child concerning whom a petition has been filed to be examined by a physician, optometrist, or audiologist.

B. On its own motion or on motion of the parent or the petitioner, after a contradictory hearing and a showing of good cause, the court may order any child alleged to be in need of care to be examined by a psychologist or a psychiatrist.

C. On the motion of the child, the court may order a child concerning whom a petition has been filed, to be examined by a psychologist or a psychiatrist.

D. Any examination as herein provided shall be made and the findings submitted to the court within thirty days of the date the order is entered. Such period may be extended by the court for good cause.

E. Copies of any reports of findings submitted to the court shall be available to counsel for all parties.
(Added by Acts 1991 No. 235, §6; chgd. by Acts 1992 No. 705, §1, eff. 7/6/92.)

Art. 655. Medical treatment of children; costs.

A. On its own motion, or on the motion of the child or the petitioner, the court may order the parent of a child concerning whom a petition has been filed to provide necessary medical or surgical care.

B. If the parent fails to provide such care, the court may, after due notice to the parent, order the care and order the parent to pay all or part of the expense.
(Added by Acts 1991 No. 235, §6; chgd. by Acts 1992 No. 705, §1, eff. 7/6/92.)

Art. 656. Motions for severance.

On its own motion, or on the motion of the child, the parent, or the petitioner, if the petition also alleges that the child is a delinquent or that the family is in need of services, the court may, in the interest of justice, order separate adjudication hearings. *(Added by Acts 1991 No. 235, §6; chgd. by Acts 1992 No. 705, §1, eff. 7/6/92.)*

Art. 657. Motions to dismiss.

All objections to the proceedings, including objections based on defects in the petition and defenses capable of determination as a matter of law, may be raised by a motion to dismiss. *(Added by Acts 1991 No. 235, §6, eff. 1/1/92.)*

Art. 658. Dismissal of petition.

A. For good cause, the court may dismiss a petition on its own motion, or on the motion of the child or the parent.

B. The court shall dismiss a petition on the motion of the petitioner.
(Added by Acts 1991 No. 235, §6; chgd. by Acts 1992 No. 705, §1, eff. 7/6/92.)

CHAPTER 11. ADJUDICATION

Art. 659. Time for adjudication hearing.

A. If the child is in continued custody pursuant to Article 627, the adjudication hearing shall commence within forty-five days of the filing of the petition. If the child is not continued in custody, the adjudication hearing shall commence within one hundred five days of the filing of the petition.

B. Upon a showing of good cause and notice to the opposing party, the court may grant, deny or restrict a requested continuance of the proceeding in accordance with the best interests of the child.

C. If the hearing has not been commenced timely, upon motion of the child, the court shall release a child continued in custody and may dismiss the petition.

(Added by Acts 1991 No. 235, §6; chgd. by Acts 1992 No. 705, §1, eff. 7/6/92.)

Art. 660. Order of adjudication hearing.

The court shall determine the order of the presentation of evidence at an adjudication hearing. *(Added by Acts 1991 No. 235, §6, eff. 1/1/92.)*

Art. 661. Presence at adjudication hearing; exclusion of witnesses.

A. The child, his parents, counsel, the district attorney, authorized officials* of the court, and witnesses called by the parties may be present at the adjudication hearing.

**So in original. Probably should be "officers".*

B. The court may admit any other person who has a proper interest in the proceedings or the work of the court.

C. On its own motion the court may, and on the request of a party the court shall, order that the witnesses, other than parties, be excluded from the courtroom or from a place where they can see or hear the proceedings, and refrain from discussing the facts of the case with anyone other than counsel in the case. In the interest of justice, the court may exempt any witness from its order.

(Added by Acts 1991 No. 235, §6, eff. 1/1/92.)

Art. 662. Right to present evidence and examine witnesses.

The child and his parents may introduce evidence, call witnesses, be heard on their own behalf, and cross-examine witnesses called by the state. *(Added by Acts 1991 No. 235, §6, eff. 1/1/92.)*

Art. 663. Evidence; suspension of privileges.

A. Except as otherwise hereinafter provided, the adjudication hearing shall be conducted according to the rules of evidence applicable to civil proceedings.

B. The court may consider as evidence any videotape which is prepared in compliance with Chapter 8 of Title III and which is relevant to the proceeding.

C. Evidence of a prior criminal conviction shall be admissible in proceedings brought under this Title in order to prove allegations made under Article 606. Such proof shall be by certified copy of the judgment of conviction or certified copy of the minute entry of conviction in accordance with the Louisiana Code of Evidence.

D. Testimony or other evidence relevant to the abuse or neglect of a child or the cause of such condition may not be excluded on any ground of privilege, except in the case of confessions or communications between an attorney and his client or confidential communications between a priest, rabbi, duly ordained minister, or Christian Science practitioner and his confidential communicant.

(Added by Acts 1991 No. 235, §6; chgd. by Acts 1997 No. 612, §1, eff. 8/15/97.)

Art. 664. Adjudication by the court.

The adjudication hearing shall be held before the court without a jury. *(Added by Acts 1991 No. 235, §6, eff. 1/1/92.)*

Art. 665. Burden of proof.

The state shall have the burden to prove the allegations of the petition by a preponderance of evidence. *(Added by Acts 1991 No. 235, §6, eff. 1/1/92.)*

Art. 666. Adjudication order.

A. Following the adjudication hearing, the court shall immediately declare whether the evidence warrants an adjudication of child in need of care. In exceptional circumstances, the court may take the matter under advisement.

B. If the evidence warrants such an adjudication, the court may find that the family is in need of services according to Title VII.

C. If the court finds that the evidence does not warrant an adjudication that either the child is in need of care or the family is in need of services, it shall dismiss the petition. *(Added by Acts 1991 No. 235, §6, eff. 1/1/92.)*

Art. 667. Vacation of adjudication.

A. On motion of the child or the parent, an adjudication shall be vacated and a new adjudication hearing ordered if, after contradictory hearing, the court finds that:

(1) The adjudication was obtained by fraud or mistake sufficient to justify vacating the adjudication.

(2) The court making the adjudication lacked jurisdiction.

(3) New evidence not previously discoverable by due diligence requires vacating the adjudication in the interest of justice. A motion based upon this ground must be brought within one year of the adjudication.

B. In the interest of justice, the court may vacate an adjudication prior to disposition. *(Added by Acts 1991 No. 235, §6, eff. 1/1/92.)*

CHAPTER 12. PREDISPOSITION INVESTIGATION

Article

Art. 668. Predisposition investigation and report.

Following adjudication, the court may order a predisposition investigation. The investigation shall include the circumstances, needs, and social history of the child and his family, and also the circumstances surrounding the factual allegations of the petition. A written report of the investigation and findings shall be submitted to the court prior to the disposition hearing. *(Added by Acts 1991 No. 235, §6, eff. 1/1/92.)*

Art. 669. Physical and mental examination for disposition.

A. Following the adjudication, the court may order such physical and mental examination and evaluation of the child and his parents as may be helpful in determining a fair and just disposition.

B. After giving the parent a reasonable opportunity to be heard, the court may order that such parent shall contribute to the cost of the examination or evaluation in an amount commensurate with the parent's ability to pay. *(Added by Acts 1991 No. 235, §6, eff. 1/1/92.)*

Art. 670. Notice of predisposition report and examination.

A. Prior to or during the disposition hearing, the court shall advise the petitioner, counsel for the child, and counsel for the parents of the factual contents and the conclusions of the predisposition report authorized by Article 668 and any other reports considered by the court. The court need not, but may, disclose sources of factual information to counsel for the child.

B. If the court has ordered a mental examination of the child or his parents pursuant to Article 669, the court, prior to the disposition hearing, shall provide the petitioner and counsel for the child and parent with copies of reports submitted in connection with such mental examination.

C. The court shall afford the petitioner and counsel for the child and parent fair opportunity to controvert factual contents and conclusions disclosed pursuant to Paragraphs A and B of this Article.
(Added by Acts 1991 No. 235, §6, eff. 1/1/92.)

CHAPTER 13. PERMANENCY PLANNING REPORTS

Article

Art. 671. Applicability.

If at any point in a child in need of care proceeding a child enters the custody of a child care agency, the provisions of this Chapter shall also be applicable. *(Added by Acts 1991 No. 235, §6, eff. 1/1/92.)*

Art. 672. Care and treatment by department.

A. When custody of a child adjudicated in need of care is assigned to the Department of Social Services, the child shall be assigned to the custody of the department rather than to a particular placement setting. The department shall have sole authority over the placements within its resources and sole authority over the allocation of other available resources within the department for children judicially committed to the department's custody.

B. The court shall not divide legal and physical custody of a child whenever assigning custody to a department in accordance with this Article, Articles 619, 681, 700, or 716, or any other statute or provision of law. The court shall specify other public agencies or institutions that have legal or financial responsibility, or both, to provide their particular services identified at disposition or subsequent case review. Placing custody of a child with one state department shall not remove the obligation of any other state department to provide services to that child from their resources for which the child is eligible under state or federal statute or state or federal appropriation.
(Added by Acts 1991 No. 235, §6; chgd. by Acts 1993 No. 634, §1, No. 866, §1; Acts 1997, No. 612, §1, eff. 8/15/97, No. 671, §1, eff. 7/7/97.)

Art. 673. Case plan.

Within sixty days after a child enters the custody of a child care agency, the custodian shall develop a case plan detailing the custodian's efforts toward achieving a permanent placement for the child. *(Added by Acts 1991 No. 235, §6, eff. 1/1/92.)*

Art. 674. Filing.

Copies of the case plan shall be filed with the court ten days before any scheduled dispositional or case review hearing. Upon filing, the department shall mail copies of the case plan to counsel of record and shall mail them by certified mail to any unrepresented parent at his last known address, unless otherwise ordered by the court for good cause. *(Added by Acts 1991 No. 235, §6; chgd. by Acts 1993 No. 634, §1; Acts 1997 No. 612, §1, eff. 8/15/97.)*

Art. 675. Case plan purpose; contents.

A. The case plan shall be designed to achieve placement in the least restrictive, most family-like and most appropriate setting available, and in close proximity to the parents' homes, consistent with the best interest and special needs of the child.

B. The case plan shall include at least the following:

(1) A description of the type of home or institution in which the child is placed, including a discussion of the appropriateness of the placement, the reasons why the placement, if a substantial distance from the home of the parents or in a different state, is in the best interests

of the child, and how the agency which is responsible for the child plans to carry out the judicial determination of reasonable efforts made with respect to the return of the child home.

(2) A plan for assuring that the child receives proper care and that services are provided to the parents, child, and foster parents in order to improve the conditions in the parents' home, facilitate return of the child to his own home or the permanent placement of the child, and address the needs of the child while in foster care, including a plan for visitation and a discussion of the appropriateness of the services that have been provided to the child under the plan.

(Added by Acts 1991 No. 235, §6; chgd. by Acts 1997 No. 612, §1, eff. 8/15/97.)

Art. 676. Response to case plan.

Any party may file a written response to the case plan as submitted. *(Added by Acts 1991 No. 235, §6, eff. 1/1/92.)*

Art. 677. Case plan review.

A. At any hearing held subsequent to the filing of the case plan, on its own motion or upon motion of any party for good cause shown, the court may consider the content or implementation of the case plan or of any response filed concerning it.

B. If no party files a written response objecting to the case plan and the court finds the plan to be in the best interest of the child, the court shall render an order approving the plan.

(Added by Acts 1991 No. 235, §6; chgd. by Acts 1997 No. 612, §1, eff. 8/15/97.)

CHAPTER 14. DISPOSITION

Art. 678. Disposition hearing; time.

A. Prior to entering a judgment of disposition, the court shall conduct a disposition hearing.

B. The disposition hearing may be conducted immediately after the adjudication and shall be conducted within thirty days after the adjudication. Such period may be extended for good cause.

(Added by Acts 1991 No. 235, §6, eff. 1/1/92.)

Art. 679. Presence at disposition.

The child need not be present when the court enters a judgment of disposition. *(Added by Acts 1991 No. 235, §6, eff. 1/1/92.)*

Art. 680. Disposition hearing; evidence.

The court may consider the report of the predisposition investigation, any reports of mental evaluation, and all other evidence offered by the child or the state relating to the proper disposition. The court may consider evidence which would not be admissible at the adjudication hearing. *(Added by Acts 1991 No. 235, §6, eff. 1/1/92.)*

Art. 681. Dispositional alternatives.

A. In a case in which a child has been adjudicated to be in need of care, the court may:

(1) Place the child in the custody of a parent or such other suitable person on such terms and conditions as deemed in the best interest of the child including but not limited to the issuance of a protective order pursuant to Article 618.

(2) Place the child in the custody of a private or public institution or agency.

(3) Commit a child found to be mentally ill to a public or private mental institution or institution for the mentally ill.

(4) Grant guardianship of the person of the child to any individual.

(5) Make such other disposition or combination of the above dispositions as the court deems to be in the best interest of the child.

B. A child in need of care shall not be committed to the Department of Public Safety and Corrections, nor shall such department accept a child in need of care.
(Added by Acts 1991 No. 235, §6, eff. 1/1/92.)

Art. 682. Removal of a child from parental custody or control.

A. The court shall not remove a child from the custody of his parents unless his welfare cannot, in the opinion of the court, be adequately safeguarded without such removal. In support of any such disposition removing a child from the parental home, the court shall determine whether the department has made reasonable efforts, as defined by this Title, to prevent or eliminate the need for removal of the child from his home and, after removal, to make it possible for the child to return home. The department shall have the burden of demonstrating reasonable efforts.

B. If the court concludes that the child is to be removed from his parents' custody, it shall:

(1) Inform the parents about the case review and disposition review procedure, as provided for in Chapters 15 and 16 of this Title.

(2) Inform the parents that it is their obligation to comply with the requirements of the case plan, including their duty to keep the department apprised of their current address.

(3) Inform the parents that a termination of parental rights petition may be filed by the department for the parents' failure to comply with the requirements of the case plan within one year after the child's initial removal from their home, or sooner with leave of court.
(Added by Acts 1991 No. 235, §6; chgd. by Acts 1997 No. 612, §1, eff. 8/15/97.)

Art. 683. Disposition; generally.

A. The court shall impose the least restrictive disposition which the court finds is consistent with the circumstances of the case, the needs of the child, and the best interest of society.

B. If the court commits a child to a private institution or agency, it shall select one that has been licensed under state law, if licensure is required by law for such an institution or agency. When no institution, social agency, or association so licensed for care or placement of children is available to the court, the court may commit the child to some other institution, social agency, or association which in the court s judgment is suitable for such child.

C. In committing a child to the custody of an individual or a private agency or institution, the court shall, whenever practicable, select a person agency, or institution of the same religious affiliation as the child or his parents.

D. A child shall not be committed to a public or private mental institution or institution for the mentally ill unless the court finds, based on psychological or psychiatric evaluation, that the child has a mental disorder, other than mental retardation, which has a substantial adverse effect on his ability to function and requires care and treatment in an institution. When the child is in the custody of the state of Louisiana, this finding shall not be made without the representation of the child by an attorney appointed from the Mental Health Advocacy Service, unless such attorneys are unavailable as determined by the director or the child retains private counsel who shall represent only the interest of the child. The Mental Health Advocacy Service's attorney so appointed shall continue to represent the child in any proceeding relating to admission, change of status, or discharge from the mental hospital or psychiatric unit. Upon modification of the disposition to a placement other than a mental hospital or psychiatric unit, the Mental Health Advocacy Service's attorney shall be relieved of representation of the child.

E. A child shall not be committed to a public or private institution for the mentally retarded unless the court finds, based on psychological or psychiatric evaluation, that the child is mentally retarded and such condition has a substantial adverse effect on his ability to function and requires care and treatment in an institution.
(Added by Acts 1991 No. 235, §6, eff. 1/1/92.)

Art. 684. Judgment of disposition.

A. The court shall enter into the record a written judgment of disposition specifying the following:

(1) The nature of the disposition.

(2) The maximum duration of the disposition.

(3) The agency, institution, or person to whom the child is assigned, including the responsibilities of any other agency, institution, or person having legal responsibility to secure or provide services to the child which the court has determined are needed.

(4) Any other applicable terms and conditions regarding the disposition.

B. In addition, when the child is to be removed from his parents' custody, in support of its determination of whether reasonable efforts have been made to prevent removal, the court shall enter findings, including a brief description of what preventive and reunification efforts, or both, were made and why further efforts could or could not have prevented or shortened the separation of the family. If a child is to be or has been placed out-of-state, the court shall determine and enter findings on whether the placement is appropriate and in the best interest of the child.

C. In all cases in which the child is removed from his parents' custody and assigned to the department, the order shall recite:

(1) Information about the case plan, case review, and disposition review procedure, as provided for in Chapters 15 and 16 of this Title.

(2) That it is the obligation of the parents to comply with the requirements of the case plan, including their duty to keep the department apprised of their current address.

(3) That a determination of parental rights petition may be filed by the department for the parents' failure to comply with the requirements of the case plan within one year after the child's initial removal from their home, or sooner with leave of court.

D. An extract of minutes of court specifying the information in Paragraph A of this Article and signed by the court shall be considered a written judgment of disposition.

E. The date of entry of the judgment of disposition shall be recorded on the judgment.

F. A copy of the judgment of disposition shall be furnished to the parents, their counsel, or curator.

(Added by Acts 1991 No. 235, §6; chgd. by Acts 1993 No. 865, §1; Acts 1997 No. 612, §1, eff. 8/15/97.)

Art. 685. Parent's contribution to costs of care and treatment.

A. As a part of any judgment of disposition committing a child to custody other than that of the child's parents, the court may, after giving the parent a reasonable opportunity to be heard, order that such parent contribute to the cost of care of the child in an amount commensurate with the parent's ability to pay for such care.

B. When the department has provided or will provide payment for care and treatment of the child, the payments by the parent shall be made directly to the department and shall, immediately upon receipt, be deposited in the state treasury. In the event of default in the payment of costs of care by the parent, the department may exercise all administrative and legal alternatives provided by law or regulation to enforce the provisions of this Article.

C. When care and treatment of the child is to be provided by some caretaker other than the department, the payments by the parent shall be made according to the court's order. In the event of default in the payment of costs of care by the parent, he may be proceeded against as provided by law for cases of desertion or failure to provide subsistence.

(Added by Acts 1991 No. 235, §6, eff. 1/1/92.)

Art. 686. Duration of disposition.

A judgment of disposition shall remain in force only until a child reaches his eighteenth birthday. It may expire earlier by its own terms, if it is modified, or if it is vacated. *(Added by Acts 1991 No. 235, §6, eff. 1/1/92.)*

CHAPTER 15. CASE REVIEW PROCEDURE; REPORTS; REVIEW HEARINGS

Article

Art. 687. Applicability.

If at any point in child in need of care proceedings, the child is removed from his parents' care and control and placed in the custody of the department, the provisions of this Chapter shall govern the subsequent case review process until such time as the child achieves a permanent placement as defined in Article 603(15). *(Added by Acts 1991 No. 235, §6, eff. 1/1/92.)*

Art. 688. Case review reports; filing.

The custodial agency shall file a case review report with the court or, if appropriate, with the administrative review body ten days prior to every scheduled review hearing. *(Added by Acts 1991 No. 235, §6, eff. 1/1/92.)*

Art. 689. Case review reports; service.

Copies of the report shall be served by certified mail to the last known address upon counsel of record and any unrepresented party prior to or at the same time it is filed with the court. *(Added by Acts 1991 No. 235, §6; chgd. by Acts 1993 No. 634, §1, eff. 6/15/93.)*

Art. 690. Case review report purpose; contents.

A. The case review report shall review the status of the child.

B. The case review report shall address the following:

(1) The continuing necessity for and appropriateness of the placement.

(2) The extent of compliance with the case plan.

(3) The extent of progress which has been made toward alleviating or mitigating the causes necessitating placement in foster care.

(4) A likely date by which the child may be returned to the home or placed for adoption or guardianship of the person of the child.

(Added by Acts 1991 No. 235, §6, eff. 1/1/92.)

Art. 691. Response.

Parties may file with the court a written response to the case review report, as long as the response is submitted to counsel of record and any unrepresented party at least five days prior to the review hearing. *(Added by Acts 1991 No. 235, §6; chgd. by Acts 1993 No. 634, §1, eff. 6/15/93.)*

Art. 692. Case review hearings.

A. A review hearing shall be conducted by the court or administrative review body three months after the disposition hearing if the child was removed prior to disposition or within six months after the disposition hearing if the child was removed at disposition, but in no case more than six months after removal of the child from his parent(s).

B. Case reviews shall continue to be held at least once every six months thereafter until the child is permanently placed, or earlier upon the motion of a party for good cause shown or upon the court's own motion.

(Added by Acts 1991 No. 235, §6, eff. 1/1/92.)

Art. 693. Notice.

Written notice of the date, time, and place of the case review hearing shall be served and a return made in the same manner as a petition on all parties and counsel of record at least fifteen days prior to the hearing, unless the parties have been previously notified in open court at a prior hearing. *(Added by Acts 1991 No. 235, §6, eff. 1/1/92.)*

Art. 694. Notice; absent parents.

A. The court may permit a case review hearing to be held in the absence of any parent if it is established on the record that the parent was served but is not in attendance or that there have been diligent but unsuccessful efforts to serve the parent.

B. The department shall make continuing diligent efforts to locate the absent parent and notify him of the nature and outcome of the case review hearing and shall promptly inform the court of any known or discovered address.
(Added by Acts 1991 No. 235, §6, eff. 1/1/92.)

Art. 695. Notice; foster parent.
A. The department shall give notice of the right to appear at each case review hearing to all foster parents who have exercised physical custody of the child since the last hearing.
B. The notice shall inform the foster parent of the day, time, and place of the case review hearing and inform the foster parent of his right to attend the hearing and be available as a witness.
C. If a foster parent fails to appear at a case review hearing, the department shall report to the court whether notice was given or, if not, what diligent efforts were made to locate and notify the absent foster parent.
(Added by Acts 1991 No. 235, §6, eff. 1/1/92.)

Art. 696. Rights of parties.
A. All parties have the right to testify, the right to confront and cross-examine adverse witnesses, the right to present evidence and witnesses, and the right to counsel.
B. Any party who has received notice of the case review hearing and does not appear shall be deemed to have waived his right to be present.
(Added by Acts 1991 No. 235, §6, eff. 1/1/92.)

Art. 697. Intervention.
A. For good cause shown, the court or administrative review body may allow any interested person, agency, or organization to intervene in the case review proceedings to facilitate the permanent placement of the child and to insure that the best interests of the child are protected.
B. Upon motion of a party and for good cause shown, the court or administrative review body may limit the nature and extent of intervenor's participation in the case review hearing.
(Added by Acts 1991 No. 235, §6, eff. 1/1/92.)

Art. 698. Presence at case review.
A. All parties, authorized officers of the court, and witnesses called by parties may be present at a case review hearing. The court or administrative review body may admit any other person who has a proper interest in the proceedings or the work of the court.
B. On its own motion or the motion of any party, the court or administrative review body may order that witnesses, other than parties, be excluded from the courtroom and refrain from discussing the facts of the case with anyone other than counsel in the case.
(Added by Acts 1991 No. 235, §6, eff. 1/1/92.)

Art. 699. Evidence.
The court or administrative review body shall consider all relevant evidence offered by the parties and may limit the admissibility or weight of any evidence which it deems unreliable, cumulative, or unduly dilatory. *(Added by Acts 1991 No. 235, §6, eff. 1/1/92.)*

Art. 700. Order; appeal.
A. At the conclusion of the case review hearing, the court may:
(1) Approve the plan and order compliance by all parties.
(2) Find that the case plan is not appropriate, in whole or in part, based on the evidence presented at the contradictory hearing and order the department to revise the case plan accordingly.
B. Any person directly affected may appeal the findings or orders of the court rendered pursuant to this Article.
(Added by Acts 1991 No. 235, §6, eff. 1/1/92.)

CHAPTER 16. DISPOSITIONAL REVIEWS

Art. 701. Applicability.

If at any point in child in need of care proceedings, the child is removed from his parents' care and control and placed in the custody of the department, the provisions of this Chapter shall govern the subsequent review process until such time as the child achieves a permanent placement as defined in Article 603(15). *(Added by Acts 1991 No. 235, §6, eff. 1/1/92.)*

Art. 702. Dispositional review hearing.

A. The court shall conduct a dispositional review hearing within nine months after the disposition hearing if the child was removed prior to disposition or within twelve months if the child was removed at disposition, but in no case more than twelve months after the removal. Dispositional reviews shall continue to be held at least once every twelve months thereafter until the child is permanently placed or earlier upon motion of a party for good cause shown or on the court's own motion.

B. If a child is in an out-of-state placement, the court shall determine and enter findings on whether the placement is appropriate and in the best interests of the child.

C. In the discretion of the court, dispositional review hearings need not be conducted for a child who the court has determined should remain permanently in foster care with a specific foster family or for a child who has been placed in an adoptive home.

D. The court may appoint or approve an administrative body to conduct these dispositional review hearings.

(Added by Acts 1991 No. 235, §6; chgd. by Acts 1997 No. 612, §1, eff. 8/15/97.)

Art. 703. Notice.

Written notice of the date, time, and place of the dispositional hearing shall be served and a return made in the same manner as a petition on all parties and counsel of record at least fifteen days prior to the hearing, unless the parties have been previously notified in open court at a prior hearing. *(Added by Acts 1991 No. 235, §6, eff. 1/1/92.)*

Art. 704. Notice; absent parents.

A. The court may permit a dispositional review hearing to be held in the absence of any parent if it is established on the record that the parent was served but failed to attend or that there have been diligent but unsuccessful efforts to serve the parent.

B. The department shall make continuing diligent efforts to locate the absent parent and notify him of the nature and outcome of the dispositional review hearing and shall promptly inform the court of any known or discovered address.

(Added by Acts 1991 No. 235, §6, eff. 1/1/92.)

Art. 705. Notice; foster parent.

A. The department shall give notice of the right to appear at each dispositional review hearing to all foster parents who have exercised physical custody of the child since the last hearing.

B. The notice shall inform the foster parent of the day, time, and place of the dispositional review hearing and inform the foster parent of his right to attend the hearing and be available as a witness.

C. If a foster parent fails to appear at a dispositional review hearing, the department shall report to the court whether notice was given or, if not, what diligent efforts were made to locate and notify the absent foster parent.
(Added by Acts 1991 No. 235, §6, eff. 1/1/92.)

Art. 706. Rights of parties.
A. All parties have the right to testify, the right to confront and cross-examine adverse witnesses, the right to present evidence and witnesses, and the right to counsel.
B. Any party who has received notice of the dispositional review hearing and does not appear shall be deemed to have waived his right to be present.
(Added by Acts 1991 No. 235, §6, eff. 1/1/92.)

Art. 707. Intervention.
A. For good cause shown, the court or administrative review body may allow any interested person, agency, or organization to intervene in the dispositional review proceedings to facilitate the permanent placement of the child and to insure that the best interests of the child are protected.
B. Upon motion of a party and for good cause shown, the court or administrative review body may limit the nature and extent of intervenor's participation in the hearing.
(Added by Acts 1991 No. 235, §6, eff. 1/1/92.)

Art. 708. Presence at dispositional review.
A. All parties, authorized officers of the court, and witnesses called by parties may be present at a dispositional review hearing. The court or administrative review body may admit any other person who has a proper interest in the proceedings or the work of the court.
B. On its own motion or the motion of any party, the court or administrative review body may order that witnesses, other than parties, be excluded from the courtroom and refrain from discussing the facts of the case with anyone other than counsel in the case.
(Added by Acts 1991 No. 235, §6, eff. 1/1/92.)

Art. 709. Evidence.
The court shall consider all relevant evidence offered by the parties and may limit the admissibility or weight of any evidence which it deems unreliable, cumulative, or unduly dilatory. *(Added by Acts 1991 No. 235, §6, eff. 1/1/92.)*

Art. 710. Order; appeal.
A. In writing or on the record, the court shall determine the permanent plan for the child:
(1) Whether the child should be returned to the parent.
(2) Whether the child should be continued in foster care for a specified period.
(3) Whether the child should be freed for adoption.
(4) Whether the child should be placed for guardianship of the person of the child.
(5) Whether the child should, because of the child's special needs or circumstances, be continued in foster care on a permanent or long-term basis.
B. Any person directly affected may appeal the findings or orders of the court rendered pursuant to this Article.
(Added by Acts 1991 No. 235, §6, eff. 1/1/92.)

Art. 711. Simultaneous hearings.
When appropriate, case review hearings and dispositional review hearings may be scheduled to be heard simultaneously, so long as the record reflects that the appropriate findings and orders are made pursuant to Chapters 15 and 16 of this Title. *(Added by Acts 1991 No. 235, §6, eff. 1/1/92.)*

CHAPTER 17. SANCTIONS FOR FAILURE TO COMPLY WITH PERMANENCY PLANNING REQUIREMENTS

Art. 712. Sanctions for failure to comply with permanency planning requirements.

Upon determination by the court that the department has failed to comply with any permanency planning requirements, including but not necessarily limited to Chapters 13, 15, and 16 of this Title, the court may:

(1) Subpoena agency witnesses to testify regarding the failure to comply.

(2) Order the agency or appropriate representatives to show cause why a contempt order should not issue.

(3) Order that the agency not seek federal reimbursement for the cost of the child's care where the court finds that reasonable efforts were not made.

(4) Submit a report of noncompliance to appropriate state and federal agencies.

(5) Refer the agency representative found responsible for the failure to comply to the appropriate department personnel for administrative reprimand or other administrative sanctions.

(Added by Acts 1991 No. 235, §6, eff. 1/1/92.)

CHAPTER 18. MODIFICATION OF DISPOSITION

Art. 713. Applicability.

In all cases the provisions of this Chapter shall be applicable. *(Added by Acts 1991 No. 235, §6, eff. 1/1/92.)*

Art. 714. Motion to modify judgment of disposition.

A. The court may modify a judgment of disposition on its own motion or on the motion of the district attorney, the department, the child, or his parents. When a child has been committed to a mental hospital, psychiatric unit, or substance abuse facility, the court may modify the judgment of disposition, for good cause shown, on the filing of a proper motion by the director of the mental hospital, psychiatric unit, or substance abuse facility.

B. (1) A motion to modify a judgment of disposition may be denied without a contradictory hearing, except when made by the director of a mental hospital, psychiatric unit, or substance abuse facility to which a child has been committed. In such instances, the director shall be permitted to show that the continued commitment would not be in the child's best interest because the facility cannot provide proper treatment or that the child has received the maximum benefit from the treatment available at the facility. The director shall make specific written recommendations regarding proper treatment or placement of the child, or both, in the motion filed with the court. The court shall hold a hearing on the motion for modification of a disposition filed by the director of a mental health hospital, psychiatric unit, or substance abuse facility within ten days of the filing of the motion unless continued for cause shown. An attorney from the Mental Health Advocacy Service shall be appointed to represent the child's interest at such a hearing unless attorneys from such agency are unavailable or the child has retained private counsel who shall represent only the interest of the child.

(2) A motion to modify to impose more restrictive conditions may not be granted without a contradictory hearing unless the parties consent.

C. On its own motion or on oral or written motion of the department, the court may modify a judgment of disposition without a contradictory hearing when the conditions of the disposition are sought to be made less restrictive.

D. Except as provided in Paragraph C of this Article, the motion shall be in writing and set forth in plain and concise terms the facts supporting the modification.
(Added by Acts 1991 No. 235, §6, eff. 1/1/92.)

Art. 715. Service of motion to modify.
A. A copy of a motion to modify shall be served upon the child, his parent, the petitioner, and any person, institution, or agency to whom the custody of the child has been assigned.
B. Service shall be in the manner provided for service of the petition.
(Added by Acts 1991 No. 235, §6, eff. 1/1/92.)

Art. 716. Modification of judgment of disposition.
A judgment of disposition may be modified if the court finds that the conditions and circumstances justify the modification. *(Added by Acts 1991 No. 235, §6, eff. 1/1/92.)*

Art. 717. Notice of modification.
If a judgment of disposition is modified, a copy of the minute entry reflecting the modification shall be served upon the petitioner, the child, his parent, and any person, institution, or agency to whom custody of the child is assigned. *(Added by Acts 1991 No. 235, §6, eff. 1/1/92.)*

TITLE VII. FAMILIES IN NEED OF SERVICES

Chapter

CHAPTER 1. PRELIMINARY PROVISIONS; DEFINITIONS

Article

Art. 726. Purpose.
The purpose of this Title is to define self-destructive behaviors by the child and conduct by other family members which contribute to the child's harm and which warrant court intervention in the family's life so that appropriate services to remedy the family's dysfunction can be secured; to secure the effectiveness of the court's intervention by explicitly confirming its duty to obtain the cooperation and coordination of all public institutions or agencies having responsibility to supply services to any member of the family referred to the court; to establish a family service plan binding upon all family members and the appropriate service providers; and to protect the integrity of the family by authorizing adjudication and the imposition of a dispositional judgment requiring participation in a plan of services only after all available voluntary alternatives have been exhausted. *(Added by Acts 1991 No. 235, §7, eff. 7/1/92 in the parishes of Caddo, East Baton Rouge, Jefferson, and Orleans, eff. 7/1/93 in all remaining parishes.)*

Art. 727. General applicability.

Except as otherwise specified in this Title, all provisions of the Children's Code remain applicable. *(Added by Acts 1991 No. 235, §7, eff. 7/1/92 in the parishes of Caddo, East Baton Rouge, Jefferson, and Orleans, eff. 7/1/93 in all remaining parishes.)*

Art. 728. Definitions.

As used in this Title:

(1) "Caretaker" means any person legally obligated to provide or secure adequate care for a child, including a parent, tutor, guardian, or legal custodian.

(2) "Child" means a person under eighteen years of age who, prior to juvenile proceedings, has not been judicially emancipated or emancipated by marriage.

(3) "Runaway" means the continued absence of the child from the home of his caretaker without the caretaker's consent.

(4) "Truant" means the repeated or habitual unauthorized absence of a child from school by a child who is subject to the compulsory attendance laws of this state.

(5) "Ungovernable" means the child's habitual disregard of the lawful and reasonable demands of his caretakers and that the child is beyond their control.

(Added by Acts 1991 No. 235, §7, eff. 7/1/92 in the parishes of Caddo, East Baton Rouge, Jefferson, and Orleans, eff. 7/1/93 in all remaining parishes; chgd. by Acts 1992 No. 705, §1, eff. 7/6/92.)

CHAPTER 2. PERSONS SUBJECT TO PROCEEDINGS; GROUNDS; COMPLAINT

Art. 729. Persons subject to proceedings.

A court exercising juvenile jurisdiction shall have exclusive original jurisdiction, in conformity with any special rules prescribed by law, over any child, his caretaker, or any other member of the child's family, who is alleged to be in need of services, as well as over any employee of a public institution or agency having legal responsibility and ability to supply the needed services. *(Added by Acts 1991 No. 235, §7, eff. 7/1/92 in the parishes of Caddo, East Baton Rouge, Jefferson, and Orleans, eff. 7/1/93 in all remaining parishes.)*

Art. 730. Grounds.

Allegations that a family is in need of services must assert one or more of the following grounds:

(1) That a child is truant or has willfully and repeatedly violated lawful school rules.

(2) That a child is ungovernable.

(3) That a child is a runaway.

(4) That a child has repeatedly possessed or consumed intoxicating beverages, or that he has misrepresented or deceived his age for the purpose of purchasing or receiving such beverages from any person, or has repeatedly loitered around any place where such beverages are the principal commodities sold or handled.

(5) That a child has committed an offense applicable only to children.

(6) That a child under ten years of age has committed any act which if committed by an adult would be a crime under any federal, state, or local law.

(7) That a caretaker has caused, encouraged, or contributed to the child's behaviors enumerated in this Article or to the commission of delinquent acts as defined in Title VIII.

(8) That, after notice, a caretaker has willfully failed to attend a meeting with the child's teacher, school principal, or other appropriate school employee to discuss the child's truancy, the child's repeated violation of school rules, or other serious educational problems of the child.

(9) Subsequent to the investigation or assessment conducted pursuant to Article 612, it is determined that a parent or caretaker is failing to provide for a child, the child's health or safety, or both, will be substantially threatened without intervention, and the court's authority is needed to effect a mandatory conference and informal family services plan agreement in

accordance with Articles 743 and 744, the court may designate a referring agency's staff as the intake officer for a referred family in accordance with Article 732. This ground shall become available on a discretionary basis to all courts exercising juvenile jurisdiction on October 1, 1996, following written agreement by the courts, the district attorney, and referring agencies to effect this discretionary provision within a jurisdiction. Prior to the effective date, the district attorney, the juvenile court of a parish whose population is between four hundred thousand and four hundred fifty thousand persons, and one non-metropolitan area as defined in Article 301 may engage in a pilot program consistent with written agreement by the district attorney, the court, and referring agencies.
(Added by Acts 1991 No. 235, §7; chgd. by Acts 1994 Third Ex. Sess. No. 45, §3; Acts 1995 No. 444, §1, eff. 6/17/95.)

Art. 731. Complaint.

A. A caretaker, other adult family member, any representative of an agency having the responsibility or ability to supply services to a family, or any other person authorized by the court may file a complaint which alleges one or more of the grounds enumerated in Article 730.

B. The complaint shall be in writing but may make allegations of fact on information and belief.

C. The complaint shall set forth with specificity:

(1) The name, date and place of birth, sex, race, address, and present location of the child.

(2) The name, age, sex, and current address of the child's parents or other caretakers.

(3) The name, age, and sex of any other family members living within the child's home.

(4) The name of any public institution or agency having the responsibility or ability to supply services alleged to be needed by the family.

D. If any of the information required by Paragraph C of this Article is unknown, the complaint shall so allege.
(Added by Acts 1991 No. 235, §7; chgd. by Acts 1997 No. 612, §2, eff. 8/15/97.)

CHAPTER 3. DUTIES OF INTAKE OFFICER

Art. 732. Duties of intake officer.

A. The court shall designate someone who will serve as the intake officer for the court in families in need of services cases.

B. Unless otherwise specified by the court, the duties of the intake officer shall include:

(1) Responsibility for receiving all complaints alleging that a family is in need of services.

(2) Responsibility for conducting a preliminary investigation into the merits of the allegations.

(3) Responsibility for identifying any public institutions or agencies having the legal responsibility and ability to supply any needed services.

(4) Scheduling the conference authorized by Article 743 and notifying all parties of the time and place of the conference.

(5) Conducting the Informal Family Services Plan conference and writing the resulting agreement, if any.

(6) Coordinating the implementation of the resulting agreement, if any.

(7) Referring the case for petition and an adjudication hearing, if necessary.
(Added by Acts 1991 No. 235, §7, eff. 7/1/92 in the parishes of Caddo, East Baton Rouge, Jefferson, and Orleans, eff. 7/1/93 in all remaining parishes.)

CHAPTER 4. PREADJUDICATION CUSTODY AND RELEASE OF CHILDREN

Art. 733. Instanter orders of custody.

A. A peace officer, probation officer, district attorney, or other person designated by the court may file a verified complaint alleging facts showing that there are reasonable grounds to believe that the family is in need of services and that emergency removal of the child from his home is necessary to secure the child's protection.

B. If the court determines that the child's welfare cannot be safeguarded without removal, the court may issue an instanter order directing that the child be taken into custody.

C. An instanter order may be executed by any peace officer having territorial jurisdiction over the child or any other person designated by the court.

D. Any peace officer having territorial jurisdiction over the child or any other person designated by the court may serve a summons upon a caretaker to appear at court for a hearing. A copy of the summons shall be filed in the record as proof of service.

(Added by Acts 1991 No. 235, §7, eff. 7/1/92 in the parishes of Caddo, East Baton Rouge, Jefferson, and Orleans, eff. 7/1/93 in all remaining parishes.)

Art. 733.1. Stop of child absent from school; transportation to school facility.

A. In addition to the authority provided in Article 736, a peace officer, probation officer, or school attendance officer may briefly detain any child from the age of seven through sixteen whom the officer reasonably believes to be absent from school during normal school hours and the officer may question the child about his reasons for being absent.

B. If based on this inquiry the officer has reasonable grounds to believe that the child is absent from school without justification, the officer may release the child to his parents or transport the child to the appropriate administrator of the child's assigned school or to a receiving center designated by the parish school board for acceptance of such children.

C. Upon the child's transportation to either school or receiving center, the administrator shall promptly notify the child's parents.

D. If the officer has reasonable grounds to believe that the child is truant or that the family is otherwise in need of services, the officer or administrator may file a complaint pursuant to Article 731.

(Added by Acts 1994 Third Ex. Sess. No. 114, §1; chgd. by Acts 1995 No. 1095, §3, eff. 8/15/95.)

Art. 734. Oral instanter orders.

A. In exceptional circumstances, the facts supporting the issuance of an instanter order and the exceptional circumstances may be relayed orally, including telephonically, to the judge and his order directing that a child be taken into custody may be issued orally.

B. In such cases, an affidavit containing the information previously relayed orally, including telephonically, shall be filed with the clerk of the court within twenty-four hours and a written order shall be issued.

C. If the affidavit is filed after the child has been taken into custody, it shall indicate whether the child was released to his parents or continued in custody.

(Added by Acts 1991 No. 235, §7, eff. 7/1/92 in the parishes of Caddo, East Baton Rouge, Jefferson, and Orleans, eff. 7/1/93 in all remaining parishes.)

Art. 735. Taking child into custody with a court order.

A. The court may issue an order directing that a child be taken into custody upon presentation to the court of a written verified complaint by a peace officer, probation officer, district attorney, or other person designated by the court alleging facts showing that there are reasonable grounds to believe that the child's family is in need of services and that the child's surroundings are such as to endanger his welfare and that immediate removal appears to be necessary for his protection.

B. In exceptional cases, the facts supporting the issuance of this order may be relayed telephonically or orally to the judge and his order directing that a child be taken into custody may be issued orally. In such cases, the requirements of Article 734(B) and (C) must be followed.

C. An order directing that a child be taken into custody may be executed by a peace officer or probation officer having territorial jurisdiction over the child.

(Added by Acts 1991 No. 235, §7; chgd. by Acts 1995 No. 1095, §3, eff. 8/15/95.)

Art. 736. Taking child into custody without a court order.

A. A peace officer or probation officer of the court may take a child into custody without a court order if he has reasonable grounds to believe that the child's family is in need of services and that the child's surroundings are such as to endanger his welfare and that immediate removal appears to be necessary for his protection.

B. If a child is taken into custody without a court order or warrant, the peace officer shall have the responsibility to:

(1) Counsel and release the child to the care of his parents upon their written promise to bring the child to court at such time as may be fixed by the court.

(2) Promptly conduct the child to the appropriate facility in accordance with Article 737.

C. If the officer does not release the child to the care of his parents, the officer promptly shall notify the child's parents that he has been taken into custody.

D. The officer shall submit a report to the district attorney or the officer designated by the court to receive such reports. The report shall include:

(1) The name, address, date of birth, sex, and race of the child.

(2) The name and address of the parents, or spouse, if any, of the child.

(3) A plain and concise statement of the facts and circumstances of the officer's taking the child into custody.

(4) A plain and concise statement of facts and circumstances showing probable cause that the child committed a delinquent act.

(5) A statement indicating whether the child was released or conducted to a shelter care facility.

E. If the child is released pursuant to Paragraph B of this Article, the report shall be submitted by the officer within seven days from the child's release. If the child is not so released, the report shall be submitted within twenty-four hours of the child being taken into custody.

(Added by Acts 1991 No. 235, §7, eff. 7/1/92 in the parishes of Caddo, East Baton Rouge, Jefferson, and Orleans, eff. 7/1/93 in all remaining parishes.)

Art. 737. Place of detention upon a taking into custody.

When taken into custody, the child shall be housed in a shelter care facility for juveniles. The peace officer or an appropriate representative of the arresting agency shall have the authority and responsibility to transport the child to a shelter care facility. *(Added by Acts 1991 No. 235, §7; chgd. by Acts 1995 No. 1095, §3, eff. 8/15/95.)*

Art. 738. Release from custody.

A. As soon as practicable after a child is received by a shelter care facility, the court or a probation officer employed and authorized by the court, upon determining it to be appropriate, shall release the child to the care of his parents or other relatives upon their written promise to bring him to court at such times as may be fixed by the court. The court may also impose reasonable restrictions upon the child's travel, place of abode, association with other people, or employment during this period of release.

B. If the court finds that these conditions are insufficient to assure the presence of the child at later proceedings, the court may require the posting of bail in accordance with Title VIII.

C. If the court finds that release under neither Paragraph A nor B of this Article is appropriate, it may authorize the continued custody of the child pending a continued custody hearing.

D. An appropriate representative of the arresting agency shall be responsible for transporting the child to the adjudication or dispositional hearing, or both, and transporting the child back to the shelter care facility or to such state or local facility as determined by the court through its order or judgment of disposition.
(Added by Acts 1991 No. 235, §7, eff. 7/1/92 in the parishes of Caddo, East Baton Rouge, Jefferson, and Orleans, eff. 7/1/93 in all remaining parishes.)

Art. 739. Continued custody hearing; time limitations.

A. If a child is not released to the care of his parents, a hearing shall be held by the court within three days after the child's entry into custody. The hearing may be continued for up to three additional days upon motion and with good cause shown. If the hearing is not held, the child shall be released unless the hearing is continued at the request of the child.

B. At this hearing the state has the burden to prove the existence of a ground for continued custody pursuant to Article 741.

C. Hearsay evidence shall be admissible at this hearing.
(Added by Acts 1991 No. 235, §7, eff. 7/1/92 in the parishes of Caddo, East Baton Rouge, Jefferson, and Orleans, eff. 7/1/93 in all remaining parishes; chgd. by Acts 1993 No. 634, §1, eff. 6/15/93.)

Art. 740. Advice of rights.

A. At the continued custody hearing, the court shall advise the parents and the child, in terms understandable by the child, of:

(1) The nature of the proceedings.
(2) The nature of the allegations.
(3) The right to an adjudication hearing.
(4) The right to retain and be represented by an attorney.

B. If the child is not released from custody, the court shall also advise the child of his right to have counsel appointed if he or his caretaker is unable to afford counsel.
(Added by Acts 1991 No. 235, §7, eff. 7/1/92 in the parishes of Caddo, East Baton Rouge, Jefferson, and Orleans, eff. 7/1/93 in all remaining parishes.)

Art. 741. Grounds for continued custody.

The court may authorize the continued custody of a child prior to adjudication if there are reasonable grounds to believe that the child is in need of services and that the child will not appear as ordered, based upon any of the following circumstances:

(1) The child is a runaway.
(2) The child is ungovernable.
(3) The child has previously failed to appear at a scheduled juvenile court hearing.

(Added by Acts 1991 No. 235, §7, eff. 7/1/92 in the parishes of Caddo, East Baton Rouge, Jefferson, and Orleans, eff. 7/1/93 in all remaining parishes.)

Art. 742. Place of continued custody.

Following the hearing required by Article 739, the court may order the child continued in custody in a licensed public or private shelter care facility for juveniles, if licensure is required by law, or in a private home subject to the supervision of the court. *(Added by Acts 1991 No. 235, §7, eff. 7/1/92 in the parishes of Caddo, East Baton Rouge, Jefferson, and Orleans, eff. 7/1/93 in all remaining parishes.)*

CHAPTER 5. INFORMAL FAMILY SERVICES PLAN PROCEDURE

Article

Art. 743. Mandatory conference.

A. Except in emergencies or where the court determines it to be inappropriate, the court, its officer, or any person it designates shall convene a conference to be attended by the child, his parents or other legal custodian, and representatives of any public institution or agency having legal responsibility or discretionary ability to supply services to the family, which according to the petition are needed.

B. This conference may be held at any time before or after a petition is filed but shall be held before any appearance to answer is made.

(Added by Acts 1991 No. 235, §7, eff. 7/1/92 in the parishes of Caddo, East Baton Rouge, Jefferson, and Orleans, eff. 7/1/93 in all remaining parishes.)

Art. 744. Informal family services plan agreement.

A. After any preadjudication conference, the child, his caretakers, and any service provider may effect an informal family services plan agreement.

B. An informal family services plan agreement shall include:

(1) The identification of the conduct of the child, caretaker, or any family member which is causing serious harm to the child and the services needed by that individual to mitigate or eliminate the problems within the family unit.

(2) A description of the services which are needed for the child, his caretakers, or other family members, the availability of such services within the community, and a plan for ensuring that any such services that are available will be secured and delivered.

(3) A description of all expected action to be taken by the child, his caretakers, or other family members.

(4) The name of the person within the affected public service agency who is directly responsible for assuring that the informal family services plan agreement is implemented.

(5) An estimate of the time anticipated to be necessary in order to accomplish the goals set out in the agreement.

C. An informal family services plan agreement shall set forth in writing the terms and conditions agreed to by the parties. It shall be signed by the convenor of the Informal adjustment conference and all parties.

D. The informal family services plan agreement must demonstrate that the child and his caretakers understand their right to an adjudication hearing on their need for services. It must also demonstrate that they consent to its terms with knowledge that their consent is not obligatory and with knowledge of the effect of the agreement as set out hereinafter in Article 745.

E. The duration of the informal family services plan agreement shall not exceed six months; however, the court may extend the agreement for one additional period not to exceed six months.

F. If a petition has been filed, the informal family services plan agreement shall be filed in the record.

(Added by Acts 1991 No. 235, §7, eff. 7/1/92 in the parishes of Caddo, East Baton Rouge, Jefferson, and Orleans, eff. 7/1/93 in all remaining parishes; chgd. by Acts 1992 No. 705, §1, eff. 7/6/92.)

Art. 745. Effect of informal family services plan agreement.

A. An informal family services plan agreement shall not be considered an adjudication. Evidence of the existence of such an agreement shall not be used against the child, the caretaker, or other family member over objection in any adjudication hearing or criminal trial. Such evidence may, however, be used in a disposition hearing in the juvenile court or for the purpose of a presentence investigation after a criminal conviction.

B. An informal family services plan agreement suspends the proceedings on the conduct charged in a family in need of services complaint or petition. If any of the terms of the agreement are violated, the case may proceed to an adjudication hearing on the charges. If the child, caretaker, or other family member satisfies the terms of the agreement, he shall be discharged from further services or supervision, and the pending complaint or petition shall be dismissed with prejudice.

C. After the confection of the agreement, an incriminating statement made by the child, caretaker, or other family member during discussions or conferences incident to the informal adjustment agreement shall not be used against the declarant, over objection, in an adjudication hearing or criminal trial. Any such statement may be used in a disposition

hearing in the juvenile court or for the purpose of a presentence investigation after a criminal conviction.
(Added by Acts 1991 No. 235, §7, eff. 7/1/92 in the parishes of Caddo, East Baton Rouge, Jefferson, and Orleans, eff. 7/1/93 in all remaining parishes.)

CHAPTER 6. PETITION AND SUMMONS

Article

Art. 746. Authority to file petition.

A family in need of services proceeding shall be commenced by a petition filed by the district attorney, any representative of an agency having the responsibility or ability to supply services to the family, or any other person authorized by the court, provided there are reasonable grounds to believe that the family is in need of services. *(Added by Acts 1991 No. 235, §7, eff. 7/1/92 in the parishes of Caddo, East Baton Rouge, Jefferson, and Orleans, eff. 7/1/93 in all remaining parishes.)*

Art. 747. Time for filing of petition; child in custody.

A. If a child is continued in custody prior to adjudication, a petition requesting that the family be adjudicated in need of services shall be filed within thirty days of the hearing to determine continued custody.

B. Upon motion and good cause shown, the time for filing a petition may be extended by the court.

C. If no petition is filed within the applicable time period, the child shall be returned to the parent.
(Added by Acts 1991 No. 235, §7, eff. 7/1/92 in the parishes of Caddo, East Baton Rouge, Jefferson, and Orleans, eff. 7/1/93 in all remaining parishes.)

Art. 748. Form of petition.

A. The petition shall contain a caption setting forth the name of the court and the title of the action. The petition shall be entitled, "The State of Louisiana in the Interest of . . .".

B. Allegations of fact shall be simple, concise, and direct and shall be set forth in numbered paragraphs. As far as practicable, each paragraph shall be limited to a single set of circumstances.

C. The petition shall be verified. Allegations of fact may be made on information and belief.

D. Failure to comply with formal requirements of this Article shall not be grounds for dismissal of a petition or invalidation of the proceedings unless it results in substantial prejudice.
(Added by Acts 1991 No. 235, §7, eff. 7/1/92 in the parishes of Caddo, East Baton Rouge, Jefferson, and Orleans, eff. 7/1/93 in all remaining parishes.)

Art. 749. Contents of petition.

A. The petition shall set forth with specificity:

(1) The name, date and place of birth, sex, race, address, and present location of the child.

(2) The name, age, sex, race, and current address of the child's parents and caretakers.

(3) The name, age, sex, and race of any other family members living within the child's home.

(4) The name of any public institution or agency having the responsibility or ability to supply services alleged to be needed by the family.

B. If any of the information required by Paragraph A of this Article is unknown, the petition shall so allege. Any defects in the allegations required by Paragraph A of this Article shall be considered defects of form.

C. The petition shall aver one or more of the grounds set out in Article 730.

D. The petition shall also aver that all available and appropriate attempts to encourage voluntary use of community services by the family have been exhausted.

E. The petition shall conclude with a request that the court intervene to adjudicate the family to be in need of services.

(Added by Acts 1991 No. 235, §7, eff. 7/1/92 in the parishes of Caddo, East Baton Rouge, Jefferson, and Orleans, eff. 7/1/93 in all remaining parishes.)

Art. 750. Amendment of petition.

A. Without leave of court, the court's designate may amend the petition at any time prior to the adjudication hearing to add new names of agencies or institutions having the legal responsibility to provide services to the family or to delete the names of agencies or institutions named in the original petition.

B. With leave of court, the petitioner may amend the petition at any time to cure defects of form.

C. With leave of court, prior to the adjudication hearing, the petitioner may amend the petition to include new allegations of fact or requests for adjudication. However, if such leave is granted, the child or parent may request a continuance of the adjudication hearing. A continuance may be granted for such period as is required in the interest of justice.

D. With leave of court, prior to the adjudication hearing, the petitioner may dismiss the family in need of services petition and instead file a petition which alleges delinquency pursuant to Title VIII or that a child is in need of care pursuant to Title VI.

(Added by Acts 1991 No. 235, §7, eff. 7/1/92 in the parishes of Caddo, East Baton Rouge, Jefferson, and Orleans, eff. 7/1/93 in all remaining parishes.)

Art. 751. Service of petition.

A copy of the petition shall be served upon any member of the family who is alleged to be in need of services and upon any public institutions or agencies identified in the petition as providing these services. *(Added by Acts 1991 No. 235, §7, eff. 7/1/92 in the parishes of Caddo, East Baton Rouge, Jefferson, and Orleans, eff. 7/1/93 in all remaining parishes.)*

Art. 752. Service and return; resident caretaker.

A. If a caretaker resides within the state, service shall be made personally or by domiciliary service or by certified mail as soon as possible and not less than fifteen days prior to commencement of the adjudication hearing on the matter.

B. The person effecting service shall execute a return and, if service was made by certified mail, the return receipt shall be attached thereto.

(Added by Acts 1991 No. 235, §7, eff. 7/1/92 in the parishes of Caddo, East Baton Rouge, Jefferson, and Orleans, eff. 7/1/93 in all remaining parishes.)

Art. 753. Summons; resident caretaker.

A. When any petition involves a child whose caretaker is a resident of this state, the court shall issue a summons commanding that the child, his caretaker, and such other persons as the court deems proper appear before the court at a designated time and place.

B. If the petition identifies a public agency having the responsibility or ability to provide services needed by any family member, a summons shall also be served upon the director of the agency or any employee designated by the director to the court to receive notice of family in need of services petitions.

(Added by Acts 1991 No. 235, §7, eff. 7/1/92 in the parishes of Caddo, East Baton Rouge, Jefferson, and Orleans, eff. 7/1/93 in all remaining parishes.)

Art. 754. Failure to appear as summoned.

If a properly served person fails to appear in response to a summons, the court may order that such person be taken into custody and immediately brought before the court. *(Added by Acts 1991 No. 235, §7, eff. 7/1/92 in the parishes of Caddo, East Baton Rouge, Jefferson, and Orleans, eff. 7/1/93 in all remaining parishes.)*

Art. 755. Service; nonresident caretaker.

A. If a caretaker does not reside within this state, service shall be made by certified mail to the address indicated in the petition, return receipt requested, not less than fifteen days prior to commencement of the adjudication hearing on the matter.

B. The person effecting the service shall file the return receipt as proof of service. *(Added by Acts 1991 No. 235, §7, eff. 7/1/92 in the parishes of Caddo, East Baton Rouge, Jefferson, and Orleans, eff. 7/1/93 in all remaining parishes.)*

CHAPTER 7. ANSWER TO PETITION

Article

Art. 756. Appearance to answer petition; time.

A. If no informal family services plan agreement has been made, the court shall require the child, the child's caretaker, or other family member served with the petition to appear to answer the petition at any time prior to the adjudication hearing but no later than forty-five days after the filing of the petition.

B. The court may also permit the parties to stipulate that the family is in need of services.

C. If the petition is filed prior to or during the hearing to determine continued custody, the court may order any party to answer the petition upon completion of the hearing or permit the entry of a stipulation that the family is in need of services.
(Added by Acts 1991 No. 235, §7, eff. 7/1/92 in the parishes of Caddo, East Baton Rouge, Jefferson, and Orleans, eff. 7/1/93 in all remaining parishes.)

Art. 757. Stipulation; consent to judgment.

With the consent of the petitioner and district attorney, any party may stipulate that the family is in need of services, with or without admitting the allegations of the petition, provided that:

(1) The person so stipulating personally appears before the court unless absent with the court's approval.

(2) The court fully informs the person of rights, if any, as required by Article 740.

(3) The court fully informs the person of the consequences of such a stipulation.

(4) The person knowingly and voluntarily consents to the judgment.
(Added by Acts 1991 No. 235, §7, eff. 7/1/92 in the parishes of Caddo, East Baton Rouge, Jefferson, and Orleans, eff. 7/1/93 in all remaining parishes.)

Art. 758. Advice of rights at appearance to answer petition.

If an appearance to answer the petition is required, the court shall advise the child and the child's caretaker of their rights pursuant to Article 740, unless they were so advised at a previous hearing. *(Added by Acts 1991 No. 235, §7, eff. 7/1/92 in the parishes of Caddo, East Baton Rouge, Jefferson, and Orleans, eff. 7/1/93 in all remaining parishes.)*

Art. 759. Answer to petition.

After the child and his caretaker have been advised pursuant to Article 740, the court shall determine whether each admits or denies the allegations of the petition.

(1) If either the caretaker or child denies the allegations, the court shall set the matter for adjudication.

(2) If both the child and the caretaker admit that the allegations of the petition are true or stipulate that the family is in need of services, the court shall determine whether there is a factual basis for adjudication and if the child and caretaker consent to adjudication. If so, the court may accept a consent judgment and order a predisposition investigation.
(Added by Acts 1991 No. 235, §7, eff. 7/1/92 in the parishes of Caddo, East Baton Rouge, Jefferson, and Orleans, eff. 7/1/93 in all remaining parishes.)

CHAPTER 8. SPECIAL MOTIONS AND DISCOVERY

Art. 760. Medical, sensory, psychological, and psychiatric examinations.

A. On its own motion or on the motion of any party, the court may order any child of the family or the caretaker to be examined by a physician, optometrist, or audiologist.

B. On its own motion or on motion of any party, after a contradictory hearing and a showing of good cause, the court may order any child of the family or the caretaker to be examined by a psychologist or a psychiatrist.

C. Any examination as herein provided shall be made and the findings submitted to the court within thirty days of the date the order is entered. Such period may be extended by the court for good cause.

D. Copies of any reports of findings submitted to the court shall be available to counsel for all parties.
(Added by Acts 1991 No. 235, §7, eff. 7/1/92 in the parishes of Caddo, East Baton Rouge, Jefferson, and Orleans, eff. 7/1/93 in all remaining parishes.)

Art. 761. Medical treatment of children; costs.

A. On its own motion or on the motion of any party, the court may order the caretaker to provide medical or surgical care needed by the child.

B. If the caretaker fails to provide such care, the court may order such care or treatment and, after due notice to the caretaker, order him to pay all or part of the expense.
(Added by Acts 1991 No. 235, §7, eff. 7/1/92 in the parishes of Caddo, East Baton Rouge, Jefferson, and Orleans, eff. 7/1/93 in all remaining parishes.)

Art. 762. Consolidation of hearings.

The hearing on the petition to declare the family in need of services may be consolidated with a hearing on a petition to declare a child delinquent or a petition to declare a child in need of care. *(Added by Acts 1991 No. 235, §7, eff. 7/1/92 in the parishes of Caddo, East Baton Rouge, Jefferson, and Orleans, eff. 7/1/93 in all remaining parishes.)*

Art. 763. Motions to dismiss.

All objections to the proceedings, including objections based on defects in the petition and defenses capable of determination as a matter of law, may be raised by motion to dismiss.
(Added by Acts 1991 No. 235, §7, eff. 7/1/92 in the parishes of Caddo, East Baton Rouge, Jefferson, and Orleans, eff. 7/1/93 in all remaining parishes.)

Art. 764. Dismissal of petition.

A. For good cause, the court may dismiss a petition on its own motion, or on the motion of the child, the caretaker, or the person filing the petition.

B. The court shall dismiss a petition on the motion of the district attorney.
(Added by Acts 1991 No. 235, §7, eff. 7/1/92 in the parishes of Caddo, East Baton Rouge, Jefferson, and Orleans, eff. 7/1/93 in all remaining parishes.)

CHAPTER 9. ADJUDICATION

Art. 765. Time for setting adjudication hearing.

A. If the child is in continued custody pursuant to Chapter 4 of this Title, the adjudication hearing shall commence within thirty days of the appearance to answer the petition. If the child is not continued in custody, the adjudication hearing shall commence within ninety days of the appearance to answer the petition.

B. For good cause, the court may extend such period.

C. If the hearing has not been commenced timely, upon motion of the child, the court shall release a child continued in custody and may dismiss the petition.

(Added by Acts 1991 No. 235, §7, eff. 7/1/92 in the parishes of Caddo, East Baton Rouge, Jefferson, and Orleans, eff. 7/1/93 in all remaining parishes.)

Art. 766. Order of adjudication hearing.

The court shall determine the order of the presentation of evidence at an adjudication hearing. *(Added by Acts 1991 No. 235, §7, eff. 7/1/92 in the parishes of Caddo, East Baton Rouge, Jefferson, and Orleans, eff. 7/1/93 in all remaining parishes.)*

Art. 767. Presence at adjudication hearing; exclusion of witnesses.

A. The child, his caretakers, counsel, the petitioner, the district attorney, authorized officials of the court, and witnesses called by the parties may be present at the adjudication hearing.

B. The court may admit any other person who has a proper interest in the proceedings or the work of the court.

C. On its own motion the court may, and on the request of a party the court shall, order that the witnesses, other than parties, be excluded from the courtroom or from a place where they can see or hear the proceedings, and refrain from discussing the facts of the case with anyone other than counsel in the case. In the interest of justice, the court may exempt any witness from its order.

(Added by Acts 1991 No. 235, §7, eff. 7/1/92 in the parishes of Caddo, East Baton Rouge, Jefferson, and Orleans, eff. 7/1/93 in all remaining parishes.)

Art. 768. Right to present evidence and examine witnesses.

The adjudication hearing shall be conducted according to the rules of evidence applicable to civil proceedings. *(Added by Acts 1991 No. 235, §7, eff. 7/1/92 in the parishes of Caddo, East Baton Rouge, Jefferson, and Orleans, eff. 7/1/93 in all remaining parishes.)*

Art. 769. Adjudication by the court.

The adjudication hearing shall be held before the court without a jury. *(Added by Acts 1991 No. 235, §7, eff. 7/1/92 in the parishes of Caddo, East Baton Rouge, Jefferson, and Orleans, eff. 7/1/93 in all remaining parishes.)*

Art. 770. Burden of proof.

The petitioner shall prove the allegations of the petition by a preponderance of evidence. *(Added by Acts 1991 No. 235, §7, eff. 7/1/92 in the parishes of Caddo, East Baton Rouge, Jefferson, and Orleans, eff. 7/1/93 in all remaining parishes.)*

Art. 771. Adjudication order.

A. Following the adjudication, the court shall immediately declare whether the evidence warrants an adjudication that the family is in need of services. In exceptional circumstances, the court may take the matter under advisement.

B. If the court finds that the evidence does not warrant an adjudication that the family is in need of services, it shall dismiss the petition.

(Added by Acts 1991 No. 235, §7, eff. 7/1/92 in the parishes of Caddo, East Baton Rouge, Jefferson, and Orleans, eff. 7/1/93 in all remaining parishes.)

Art. 772. Vacation of adjudication.

A. On motion of the child or his caretaker, an adjudication shall be vacated and a new adjudication hearing ordered if, after contradictory hearing, the court finds that:

(1) The adjudication was obtained by fraud or mistake sufficient to justify vacating the adjudication.

(2) The court making the adjudication lacked jurisdiction.

(3) New evidence not previously discoverable by due diligence requires vacating the adjudication in the interest of justice. A motion based upon this ground must be brought within one year of the adjudication.

B. In the interest of justice, the court may vacate an adjudication prior to disposition. *(Added by Acts 1991 No. 235, §7, eff. 7/1/92 in the parishes of Caddo, East Baton Rouge, Jefferson, and Orleans, eff. 7/1/93 in all remaining parishes.)*

CHAPTER 10. PREDISPOSITION INVESTIGATION

Art. 773. Predisposition investigation and report.

Following adjudication, the court may order a predisposition investigation. The investigation shall include inquiring into the circumstances surrounding the factual allegations of the petition and shall gather the information required by Article 744(B). A written report of the investigation and findings shall be submitted to the court prior to the disposition hearing. *(Added by Acts 1991 No. 235, §7, eff. 7/1/92 in the parishes of Caddo, East Baton Rouge, Jefferson, and Orleans, eff. 7/1/93 in all remaining parishes.)*

Art. 774. Physical and mental examination for disposition.

A. Following the adjudication, the court may order such physical and mental examination and evaluation of any child of the family and his caretaker as may be helpful in determining a fair and just disposition.

B. After giving the caretaker a reasonable opportunity to be heard, the court may order that he shall contribute to the cost of any court-ordered examination or evaluation in an amount commensurate with his ability to pay.

(Added by Acts 1991 No. 235, §7, eff. 7/1/92 in the parishes of Caddo, East Baton Rouge, Jefferson, and Orleans, eff. 7/1/93 in all remaining parishes.)

Art. 775. Notice of predisposition report and examination.

A. Prior to or during the disposition hearing, the court shall advise the child and his caretaker of the factual contents and the conclusions of the predisposition report authorized by Article 773 and any other reports considered by the court.

B. If the court has ordered a mental examination of the child or his caretaker pursuant to Article 774, the court, prior to the disposition hearing, shall provide the counsel for the child and caretaker with copies of reports submitted in connection with such mental examination.

C. The court shall afford the child and his caretaker fair opportunity to controvert factual contents and conclusions disclosed pursuant to Paragraphs A and B of this Article.

D. A copy of any reports relevant to the dispositional plan of services shall also be provided to any agency named in the disposition order as having responsibility to provide services to the child or his caretaker.

(Added by Acts 1991 No. 235, §7, eff. 7/1/92 in the parishes of Caddo, East Baton Rouge, Jefferson, and Orleans, eff. 7/1/93 in all remaining parishes.)

CHAPTER 11. PERMANENCY PLANNING REPORTS

Art. 776. Permanency planning reports.

A. If at any point in Family in Need of Services proceedings, a child enters the custody of the state, the provisions of Chapters 13, 15, and 16 of Title VI shall be applicable.

B. When the department of Public Safety and Corrections is the custodian, the provisions of Chapter 14 of Title VI shall be applicable only as provided in Article 907.

(Added by Acts 1991 No. 235, §7, eff. 7/1/92 in the parishes of Caddo, East Baton Rouge, Jefferson, and Orleans, eff. 7/1/93 in all remaining parishes; chgd. by Acts 1993 No. 634, §1, eff. 6/15/93.)

CHAPTER 12. DISPOSITION

Art. 777. Disposition hearing; time; obligation of agency representative.

A. Prior to entering a judgment of disposition, the court shall conduct a disposition hearing.

B. This hearing may be conducted immediately after the adjudication and shall be conducted within thirty days after the adjudication. Such period may be extended for good cause.

C. At the hearing, the court shall inform any employee of a public institution or agency designated by its director to represent the agency in this matter that he will be deemed personally responsible for his agency's cooperation in the providing of services to the family unless in writing, the director of the institution or agency subsequently informs the court that some other individual within its administration is to be substituted for him.

(Added by Acts 1991 No. 235, §7, eff. 7/1/92 in the parishes of Caddo, East Baton Rouge, Jefferson, and Orleans, eff. 7/1/93 in all remaining parishes.)

Art. 778. Disposition hearing; evidence.

The court may consider the report of the predisposition investigation, any reports of mental evaluation, and all other evidence offered by the child, his caretaker or the state relating to the proper disposition. The court may consider evidence which would not be admissible at the adjudication hearing. *(Added by Acts 1991 No. 235, §7, eff. 7/1/92 in the parishes of Caddo, East Baton Rouge, Jefferson, and Orleans, eff. 7/1/93 in all remaining parishes.)*

Art. 779. Dispositional alternatives.

A. In any case in which the family has been adjudicated to be in need of services, the court may impose the following orders directly affecting any child of the family:

(1) Order the child to submit to counseling or to psychiatric or psychological examination or treatment.

(2) Order the child to cooperate in accepting particular services from any public institution or agency or from any private institution or agency willing and able to provide him with needed services.

(3) Place the child in the custody of a caretaker or other suitable person on such terms and conditions as deemed in the best interests of the child and the public.

(4) Place the child on probation on such terms and conditions as deemed in the best interests of the child and the public.

(5) Assign the child to the custody of a private or public institution or agency, except that the child shall not be placed in a correctional facility designed and operated exclusively for delinquent children, nor shall such facility accept the child.

(6) Make such other disposition or combination of the above dispositions as the court deems to be in the best interests of the child and the public.

B. In any case in which the family has been adjudicated to be in need of services, the court may impose any of the following orders directly affecting a caretaker:

(1) Order the caretaker to submit to counseling or to psychiatric or psychological examination or treatment.

(2) Order the caretaker to cooperate in accepting particular services from any public institution or agency or from any private institution or agency willing and able to provide him with needed services.

(3) Order the caretaker to cooperate in connection with any part of the disposition order directly affecting the child.

(4) Impose any other conditions reasonably related to improving the family relationship.

C. In any case in which the family has been adjudicated to be in need of services, the court may order any public institution or agency and its representatives to:

(1) Provide any services specified in its order as necessary to improve the family relationships or reunite the family in the best interests of the child, provided only that such services are available within the agency or institution.

(2) Report at least once every six months in writing concerning the progress of the family in receiving and accepting the services ordered.

(Added by Acts 1991 No. 235, §7; chgd. by Acts 1995 No. 1095, §3, eff. 8/15/95.)

Art. 780. Removal of a child from parental custody or control; limitations.

A. The court shall not remove a child from the custody of his caretakers unless his welfare cannot, in the opinion of the court, be adequately safeguarded without such removal.

B. In support of any disposition removing a child from the caretaker's home, the court shall determine whether reasonable efforts have been made by public institutions and agencies to prevent or eliminate the need for removal of the child from his home and, after removal, to make it possible for the child to return home.

C. If a child is assigned to the custody of a public or private institution or agency, the court shall transmit with the judgment of disposition all relevant reports concerning the child and his family.

D. Any institution or agency to which a child is assigned shall:

(1) Report at least once every six months in writing concerning the whereabouts and condition of the child to the judge who rendered the judgment of disposition.

(2) Upon request, provide the court any information concerning the condition, supervision, treatment, or rehabilitation program of the child.

(Added by Acts 1991 No. 235, §7, eff. 7/1/92 in the parishes of Caddo, East Baton Rouge, Jefferson, and Orleans, eff. 7/1/93 in all remaining parishes.)

Art. 781. Disposition; generally.

A. The court shall impose the least restrictive disposition which the court finds is consistent with the circumstances of the case, the needs of the child, and the best interest of society.

B. If the court commits a child to a private institution or agency, it shall select one that has been licensed under state law, if licensure is required by law for such an institution or agency.

C. In committing a child to the custody of an individual or a private agency or institution, the court shall, whenever practicable, select a person, agency, or institution of the same religious affiliation as the child or his parents.

D. A child shall not be committed to a public or private mental institution or institution for the mentally ill unless the court finds, based on psychological or psychiatric evaluation, that the child has a mental disorder, other than mental retardation, which has a substantial adverse effect on his ability to function and requires care and treatment in an institution. When the child is in the custody of the state of Louisiana, this finding shall not be made without the representation of the child by an attorney appointed from the Mental Health Advocacy Service, unless such attorneys are unavailable as determined by the director or the child retains private counsel who shall represent only the interest of the child. The Mental Health Advocacy Service's attorney so appointed shall continue to represent the child in any proceeding relating to admission, change of status, or discharge from the mental hospital or psychiatric unit. Upon modification of the disposition to a placement other than a mental hospital or psychiatric unit, the Mental Health Advocacy Service's attorney shall be relieved of representation of the child.

E. A child shall not be committed to a public or private institution for the mentally retarded unless the court finds, based on psychological or psychiatric evaluation, that the child is mentally retarded and such condition has a substantial adverse effect on his ability to function and requires care and treatment in an institution.

(Added by Acts 1991 No. 235, §7; chgd. by Acts 1995 No. 1095, §3, eff. 8/15/95.)

Art. 781.1. Probation and parole supervision fees.

A. When the court suspends the imposition or execution of sentence and places the child or his parent or both on supervised probation or grants the child supervised parole, and the probationer or parolee is to be supervised by the Department of Public Safety and Corrections or any other agency, the court shall order payment, as a condition of probation or parole, of a monthly supervision fee. The supervision fee imposed shall be not less than ten nor more than one hundred dollars per month and shall be payable to the department or other supervising agency to defray the costs of supervision. These funds are only to supplement the level of funds that would ordinarily be available from regular state or other appropriations.

B. The parent is responsible for payment of any supervision fee imposed and is subject to contempt of court for failure to pay such fees. The parent shall not be subject to judicial sanctions for failure to pay supervision fees if the failure was due to financial inability to pay based upon reasonable expenses for the necessities of life.

(Added by Acts 1992 No. 705, §1; chgd. by Acts 1995 No. 794, §1, eff. 8/15/95.)

Art. 782. Judgment of disposition.

A. The court shall enter into the record a written judgment of disposition specifying the following:

(1) The nature of the disposition, including the responsibilities of the child, his caretakers, and public providers in securing or providing needed, particularized services for the family members.

(2) The maximum duration of the disposition.

(3) The agency, institution, or person to whom the child is assigned.

(4) How the needed services are to be paid for.

(5) Any other applicable terms and conditions regarding the disposition.

(6) A warning in substantially the following form: "If you do not obey each and every condition and rule of this order, you may be placed in a juvenile shelter or detention facility."

B. If the child is to remain within his family's home, the order shall also reflect the name of the representative of any institution or agency required to provide services who is to be held personally responsible for their provision.

C. An extract of minutes of court specifying the information in Paragraph A of this Article and signed by the court shall be considered a written judgment of disposition.

D. The date of entry of the judgment of disposition shall be recorded on the judgment.

E. A copy of the judgment shall be furnished to all parties.

(Added by Acts 1991 No. 235, §7; chgd. by Acts 1995 No. 1095, §3, eff. 8/15/95.)

Art. 783. Parent's contribution to costs of care and treatment.

A. As a part of any judgment of disposition assigning a child to custody other than that of the child's parents, the court may, after giving the parent a reasonable opportunity to be heard, order that such parent contribute to the cost of care of the child in an amount commensurate with the parent's ability to pay for such care.

B. When any public agency or institution has provided or will provide payment for care and treatment of the child, the payments by the parent shall be made directly to that public agency or institution and shall, immediately upon receipt, be deposited in the state treasury. In the event of default in the payment of costs of care by the parent, the agency or institution may exercise all administrative and legal alternatives provided by law or regulation to enforce the provisions of this Article.

C. When care and treatment of the child is to be provided by some caretaker other than a public agency or institution, the payments by the parent shall be made according to the court's order. In the event of default in the payment of costs of care by the parent, he may be proceeded against as provided by Chapter 2 or 4 of Title XV, Chapter 1 of Title XIII, or Title X.

(Added by Acts 1991 No. 235, §7, eff. 7/1/92 in the parishes of Caddo, East Baton Rouge, Jefferson, and Orleans, eff. 7/1/93 in all remaining parishes.)

Art. 784. Duration of disposition.

A judgment of disposition shall remain in force only until a child reaches his eighteenth birthday. It may expire earlier by its own terms, if it is modified, or if it is vacated. *(Added by Acts 1991 No. 235, §7, eff. 7/1/92 in the parishes of Caddo, East Baton Rouge, Jefferson, and Orleans, eff. 7/1/93 in all remaining parishes.)*

CHAPTER 13. CASE REVIEW PROCEDURE; REPORTS; REVIEW HEARINGS

Art. 785. Applicability.

If at any point in families in need of services proceedings the child is removed from his caretaker's care and control and placed in the custody of a child care agency, the provisions of Chapters 15 and 16 of Title VI shall govern the subsequent review process until such time as the child achieves a permanent placement as defined by that Title. *(Added by Acts 1991 No. 235, §7, eff. 7/1/92 in the parishes of Caddo, East Baton Rouge, Jefferson, and Orleans, eff. 7/1/93 in all remaining parishes.)*

CHAPTER 14. MODIFICATION OF DISPOSITION

Art. 786. Applicability.

In all cases except a disposition committing the child to the custody of a child care agency, the provisions of this Chapter shall be applicable. *(Added by Acts 1991 No. 235, §7, eff. 7/1/92 in the parishes of Caddo, East Baton Rouge, Jefferson, and Orleans, eff. 7/1/93 in all remaining parishes.)*

Art. 787. Motion to modify judgment of disposition.

A. The court may modify a judgment of disposition on its own motion or on the motion of the district attorney, a probation officer, any child of the family, a caretaker, any individual or agency to whom the child's custody has been assigned, or the duly authorized representative of an institution or agency providing services to the family under the court's disposition order.

B. A motion to modify a judgment of disposition to impose less restrictive conditions may be denied without a contradictory hearing. A motion to modify to impose more restrictive conditions may not be granted without a contradictory hearing unless the parties consent.

C. On its own motion or on oral or written motion of a probation officer, the court may modify a judgment of disposition without a contradictory hearing when the conditions of the disposition are sought to be made less restrictive.

D. Except as provided in Paragraph C of this Article, the motion shall be in writing and set forth in plain and concise terms the facts supporting the modification.

(Added by Acts 1991 No. 235, §7, eff. 7/1/92 in the parishes of Caddo, East Baton Rouge, Jefferson, and Orleans, eff. 7/1/93 in all remaining parishes.)

Art. 788. Service of motion to modify.

A. A copy of a motion to modify shall be served upon any affected child, his caretaker, the district attorney, the duly authorized representative of any affected institution or agency providing services, and any person, institution, or agency to whom the custody of the child has been assigned.

B. Service shall be in the manner provided for service of the petition.

(Added by Acts 1991 No. 235, §7, eff. 7/1/92 in the parishes of Caddo, East Baton Rouge, Jefferson, and Orleans, eff. 7/1/93 in all remaining parishes.)

Art. 789. Modification of judgment of disposition.

A judgment of disposition may be modified if the court finds that the conditions and circumstances justify the modification. *(Added by Acts 1991 No. 235, §7, eff. 7/1/92 in the parishes of Caddo, East Baton Rouge, Jefferson, and Orleans, eff. 7/1/93 in all remaining parishes.)*

Art. 790. Notice of modification.

If a judgment of disposition is modified, a copy of the minute entry reflecting the modification shall be served upon the petitioner, the child, his parent, and any person, institution, or agency to whom custody of the child is assigned. *(Added by Acts 1991 No. 235, §7, eff. 7/1/92 in the parishes of Caddo, East Baton Rouge, Jefferson, and Orleans, eff. 7/1/93 in all remaining parishes.)*

Art. 791. Contempt; prehearing detention.

A. If there are reasonable grounds to believe that the child has violated the terms of a judgment of disposition, the child may be taken into custody in accordance with Article 735 or 736.

B. The child may be taken to a shelter care facility or a juvenile detention facility. The peace officer, probation officer, or an appropriate representative of the arresting agency shall have the authority and responsibility to transport the child to such juvenile facility.

C. If the child is taken to a shelter care facility or detention facility, there shall be a hearing within twenty-four hours, exclusive of legal holidays, to determine whether probable cause exists that the child has violated the judgment of disposition.

D. If the court finds probable cause, the child may be detained for protective purposes or to assure the child's appearance at the contempt hearing.

E. If the child is detained, he may be held for up to three days pending a hearing on the rule for contempt. This time limitation shall run from the time of the probable cause determination or the taking into custody, whichever is later.

(Added by Acts 1995 No. 1095, §3, eff. 8/15/95.)

TITLE VII-A. TRANSITIONAL PROVISIONS OF CHILDREN AND PARENTS IN NEED OF SUPERVISION

(Repealed by the terms of former article 791(C) and Acts 1993 No. 36, §§1, 2, eff. 7/1/94.)

§§791 to 793.7. *(Repealed by the terms of former article 791(C) and Acts 1993 No. 36, §§1, 2, eff. 7/1/94.)*

TITLE VIII. DELINQUENCY

Chapter

CHAPTER 1. PRELIMINARY PROVISIONS; DEFINITIONS

Art. 801. Purpose.

The purpose of this Title is to accord due process to each child who is accused of having committed a delinquent act and, except as provided for in Article 897.1, to insure that he shall receive, preferably in his own home, the care, guidance, and control that will be conducive to his welfare and the best interests of the state and that in those instances when he is removed from the control of his parents, the court shall secure for him care as nearly as possible equivalent to that which the parents should have given him. *(Added by Acts 1991 No. 235, §8; chgd. by Acts 1993 No. 430, §2, eff. 8/15/93.)*

Art. 802. General applicability.

Except as otherwise specified in this Title, all provisions of the Children's Code remain applicable. *(Added by Acts 1991 No. 235, §8, eff. 1/1/92.)*

Art. 803. Applicability of Title procedures; supplemental procedures.

The provisions of this Title shall govern and regulate delinquency proceedings of courts exercising juvenile jurisdiction. Where procedures are not provided in this Title, or otherwise by this Code, the court shall proceed in accordance with the Code of Criminal Procedure. *(Added by Acts 1991 No. 235, §8, eff. 1/1/92.)*

Art. 804. Definitions.

As used in this Title:

(1) "Child" means any person under the age of twenty-one, including an emancipated minor, who commits a delinquent act before attaining seventeen years of age.

(2) "Child care institution" means a nonprofit, licensed private or public institution which accommodates no more than twenty-five children and which is not a detention facility, a forestry camp, a training school, or any other facility operated primarily for the detention of children who are determined to be delinquent.

(3) "Delinquent act" means an act committed by a child of ten years of age or older which if committed by an adult is designated an offense under the statutes or ordinances of this state, or of another state if the act occurred in another state, or under federal law, except traffic violations. It includes a direct contempt of court committed by a child.

(4) "Delinquent child" means a child who has committed a delinquent act.

(5) "Felony-grade delinquent act" means an offense that if committed by an adult, may be punished by death or by imprisonment at hard labor.

(6) "Insanity" means a mental disease or mental illness which renders the child incapable of distinguishing between right and wrong with reference to the conduct in question, as a result of which the child is exempt from criminal responsibility.

(7) "Mental incapacity to proceed" means that, as a result of mental disease or illness, a child presently lacks the capacity to understand the nature of proceedings against him or to assist in his defense.

(8) "Misdemeanor-grade delinquent act" means any offense which if committed by an adult is other than a felony and includes the violation of an ordinance providing a penal sanction.

(Added by Acts 1991 No. 235, §8, eff. 1/1/92.)

CHAPTER 2. VENUE

Art. 805. Venue.

A. A delinquency proceeding shall be commenced in the parish in which the offense complained of took place. The juvenile court shall conduct the adjudication hearing and may also conduct the disposition hearing unless it decides to transfer the case as provided for in Paragraph B of this Article.

B. Upon motion of the district attorney, the child, or upon the court's own motion, after the confection of an informal adjustment agreement or an adjudication that the child is delinquent, the court may transfer the proceeding to the parish in which the child is domiciled. *(Added by Acts 1991 No. 235, §8, eff. 1/1/92.)*

Art. 806. Change of venue; improper venue.

When a petition is filed in a court of improper venue, on the court's own motion or upon written motion of a party and after contradictory hearing, the court may dismiss the petition or transfer the proceedings to a court of proper venue. *(Added by Acts 1991 No. 235, §8, eff. 1/1/92.)*

Art. 807. Change of venue; proper venue.

A. A request for change of venue must be made by written motion of the district attorney or the child, sworn to by mover or his counsel, before jeopardy begins. The motion shall contain allegations of facts upon which the motion is based and a statement that the motion is not made for the purpose of delay but to obtain a fair and impartial trial. The motion must be resolved after a contradictory hearing unless waived by the district attorney and the child.

B. A change of venue shall be granted if the court finds that, because of undue influence of an adverse party, prejudice existing in the public mind, or for any other reason, a fair and impartial trial cannot be obtained. The court shall consider whether the reasons are such that they will effect the testimony of witnesses at the trial.

C. The court may order a change of venue in accordance with Articles 623 through 627 of the Code of Criminal Procedure, except that the proceedings may be transferred to any parish. *(Added by Acts 1991 No. 235, §8, eff. 1/1/92.)*

CHAPTER 3. CONSTITUTIONAL RIGHTS

Art. 808. Constitutional rights of accused delinquents.

All rights guaranteed to criminal defendants by the Constitution of the United States or the Constitution of Louisiana, except the right to jury trial, shall be applicable in juvenile court proceedings brought under this Title. *(Added by Acts 1991 No. 235, §8, eff. 1/1/92.)*

Art. 809. Right to counsel.

A. At every stage of proceedings under this Title, the accused child shall be entitled to counsel.

B. No child in the custody of the state shall be committed to a public or private mental institution or institution for the mentally ill unless he has been represented by retained private counsel who represents only the child's interest or by an attorney from the Mental Health Advocacy Service, unless its executive director has determined that its attorneys are unavailable. Any attorney from the Mental Health Advocacy Service so appointed shall continue to represent the child in any proceeding relating to admission, change of status, or discharge from the mental hospital or psychiatric unit. Upon modification of the disposition to placement other than a mental hospital or psychiatric unit, the Mental Health Advocacy Service's attorney shall be relieved of representation of the child.

C. If the court finds that the parents of the child are financially unable to afford counsel for the child, the court shall appoint counsel, or refer the child for representation by the indigent defender board.

D. If the court finds that the parents of the child are financially able, it may order the parents to pay some or all of the costs of the child's representation.
(Added by Acts 1991 No. 235, §8; chgd. by Acts 1992 No. 705, §1, eff. 7/6/92.)

Art. 810. Waiver of right to counsel.

A. The court may allow a child to waive the assistance of counsel if the court determines that all of the following exists:

(1) The child has consulted with an attorney or other adult interested in the child's welfare.

(2) That both the child and the adult advisor have been instructed by the court about the child's rights and the possible consequences of waiver.

(3) That the child is voluntarily waiving his right to counsel.

B. Such waiver may be accepted at any stage in the proceedings and shall be evidenced by a writing reciting the requirements contained in Paragraph A of this Article and signed by the child and his attorney or other interested adult and filed in the record, or by a verbatim transcript of the proceedings which demonstrates compliance with Paragraph A of this Article.

C. The court shall appoint an attorney in any case in which the interests of the child and his parent or other adult advisor conflict or whenever appointment of counsel is otherwise required in the interests of justice.

D. The child shall not be permitted to waive assistance of counsel in proceedings in which it has been recommended to the court that the child be placed in a mental hospital, psychiatric unit, or substance abuse facility, nor in proceedings to modify said dispositions.
(Added by Acts 1991 No. 235, §8, eff. 1/1/92.)

Art. 811. When jeopardy begins.

When a child enters a denial to the petition, jeopardy begins when the first witness is sworn at the adjudication hearing. When he enters an admission to the petition, jeopardy begins when a valid disposition is made the judgment of the court. *(Added by Acts 1991 No. 235, §8, eff. 1/1/92.)*

CHAPTER 3-A. RIGHTS OF THE VICTIM

Art. 811.1. Rights of the victim of alleged delinquent act.

A. The juvenile court, district attorneys, and law enforcement agencies shall provide the following services to victims of alleged delinquent acts, providing the victim reported the act to law enforcement authorities within seventy-two hours of its occurrence or discovery, unless extenuating circumstances exist for later reporting:

(1) The district attorney shall, whenever practical, inform the victim or his legal representative of judicial proceedings relating to their case including:

(a) The taking into custody of the alleged delinquent.

(b) Adjudication hearings and disposition hearings relating to the alleged delinquent.

(c) The release pending adjudication after a continued custody hearing whenever an alleged delinquent is accused of a violent offense, such as attempted murder, rape, or a crime against another child.

(2) The district attorney shall, whenever practical, notify the victim or his legal representative if a court proceeding to which he has been subpoenaed will not go on as scheduled, in order to save the person an unnecessary trip to court.

(3) The district attorney shall notify the victim or his legal representative whenever he is notified that a child accused of a violent offense such as attempted murder, rape, or a crime against another child, has escaped from lawful confinement or has been released in

accordance with Chapter 6 of this Title, and whenever a child committed to the Department of Public Safety and Corrections has escaped or has been released from a secure institution. The district attorney shall also inform the victim that the sheriff shall provide information relative to victim assistance.

(4) The sheriff shall inform the victim or his legal representative of financial assistance, fees, or other social services available as a result of being a victim of a crime, including information on how to apply for the financial assistance and services.

(5) The court should provide, whenever possible, a secure waiting area during court proceedings that does not require victims and their legal representatives to be in close proximity to accused children and their families and friends. The juvenile court shall provide a secure waiting area in cases involving violent crime.

(6) All judicial and law enforcement agencies shall expeditiously return any stolen or other personal property to victims when no longer needed as evidence.

(7) The appropriate law enforcement agency shall ensure that the victim receives emergency, social, and medical services as soon as possible. The appropriate law enforcement agency shall also distribute to the victim, or to the family of a homicide victim, a crime victim's brochure prepared by the Crime Victims Reparations Board as provided in R.S. 46:1844(T), and supplemented as necessary by the district attorney with victim information specific to the parish in which the delinquent act is alleged to have occurred, as provided in R.S. 46:1844(A).

(8) All law enforcement agencies shall provide a private setting for all interviewing of victims of crime. "Private setting" shall mean an enclosed room from which the occupants are not visible or otherwise identifiable and whose conversations cannot be heard from outside such room. Only those persons directly and immediately related to the interviewing of the victim, specifically the victim, a social worker, psychologist, or other professional, the victim advocate designated by the sheriff's office, or a representative from a not-for-profit victim service organization, including but not limited to rape crisis centers, domestic violence advocacy groups, and alcohol abuse or substance abuse groups providing emotional support to the victim, shall be present, unless the victim requests the exclusion of such person from the interview, and, where appropriate, the parent or parents of the victim.

(9) The victim or the family of the victim shall have the right to retain counsel to confer with law enforcement and judicial agencies on the disposition of the victim's case. The prosecutor, in accordance with the provisions of Code of Criminal Procedure Article 63, may confer with the counsel retained by the victim or victim's family in the prosecution of the case.

(10) If requested, the victim of a violent felony-grade offense and the designated member of the victim's family in the case of homicide or injury to a minor shall be consulted by the prosecutor in order to obtain their view regarding:

(a) The disposition of the delinquency case by dismissal, plea bargaining, or adjudication hearing.

(b) The use of available disposition alternatives such as placement in secure detention, probation, community service, and the payment of restitution to the victim.

(11) The victim or a member of the victim's family may file a victim notice form as provided in R.S. 46:1842(8). Upon filing of a victim notice form by a victim or a family member, it shall be the duty of the Department of Public Safety and Corrections to notify the victim or family member by certified mail of appeal or release at the time of such appeal, discharge, or parole of a delinquent named in that form. Such form shall be included in the delinquent's commitment documents to be delivered to the state training facility where such delinquent has been confined or transferred.

(12) The victim or witness who so requests shall be assisted by judicial and law enforcement agencies in informing employers that the need for victim and witness cooperation in the prosecution of the case may necessitate absence of the victim or witness from work.

B. The family members of all homicide victims shall be afforded all of the rights under this Article accruing to victims. Communication with the appropriate law enforcement or judicial agencies concerning the rights of the victim's family members shall be made through a designated family member. A designated family member is a member of the victim's family designated by a majority of the victim's family members to make such communications.

C. No order or disposition shall be invalidated because of failure to comply with the provisions of this Article.

D. The juvenile court, the district attorney, the sheriff, and law enforcement agencies are exempt from the requirements of this Section in any case in which either:

(1) The victim has failed to provide a current address.

(2) The victim refuses the services offered.

E. Nothing in this Article shall be construed as creating a right of appeal on behalf of any person nor as creating a cause of action on behalf of any person against any public employee, office, or department responsible for the provision of services set forth in this Article.

F. Any information about the status of the case in juvenile court which is received by the victim or his legal representative shall remain subject to the confidentiality restrictions of Article 412 and shall not be further disclosed by him.

G. (1) In order to protect the identity and provide for the safety and welfare of juvenile crime victims under the age of seventeen years, all public officials, officers, and public agencies, including but not limited to, all law enforcement agencies, sheriffs, district attorneys, judicial officers, clerks of court, and the Department of Social Services or any division thereof shall not publicly disclose the name, address, or identity of a juvenile victim of crime who at the time of the commission of the offense is under seventeen years of age.

(2) Notwithstanding any other provision of law to the contrary, all public officials, officers, and public agencies, including but not limited to, all law enforcement agencies, sheriffs, district attorneys, judicial officers, clerks of court, and the Department of Social Services or any division thereof charged with the responsibility of knowing the name, address and identity of juvenile crime victims as a necessary part of their duties shall have full and complete access to this information regarding a juvenile crime victim and they may lawfully utilize initials, abbreviations, or other forms of indefinite descriptions on all public documents used in the performance of their duties to whatever extent they deem necessary, to prevent the public disclosure of the name, address, or identity of a juvenile victim of crime under the age of seventeen years.

(Added by Acts 1993 No. 634, §1; chgd. by Acts 1995 No. 522, §1, No. 835, §1; Acts 1997 No. 732, §2, eff. 8/15/97.)

Art. 811.2. Victims of juvenile crime compensation fund; established; disbursements.

A. All courts exercising juvenile jurisdiction may levy a special cost in an amount not to exceed fifteen dollars against any juvenile defendant, other than an indigent, who is found to have committed a traffic violation resulting in injury or property loss, or who pleads guilty to or is adjudicated convicted of a juvenile offense. Such cost shall be in addition to any fine, clerk's fees or costs, or any other fees or costs provided by law.

B. The clerk of court shall remit two-thirds of the sums collected or received pursuant to this Article for deposit in a special account which is hereby designated as the Victims of Juvenile Crime Compensation Fund. The fund shall be used to compensate victims of juvenile crimes who do not otherwise receive restitution or reparation. The judges of the courts exercising juvenile jurisdiction shall have control over the fund and disbursements made therefrom. The judges shall cause to be conducted annually an audit of the fund and the books and accounts relating thereto and shall file the same with the office of the legislative auditor, where it shall be available for public inspection.

C. The judges shall provide by court rule for the collection, administration, and distribution of the fund in order to implement the purpose of this Article. However, no amount greater than five hundred dollars shall be disbursed from the fund to any one claimant.

D. The clerk of court shall remit one-third of the total sums collected or received pursuant to this Article monthly to the Crime Victims Reparations Fund as provided in R.S. 46:1801 et seq.

(Added by Acts 1993 No. 634, §1, eff. 6/15/93.)

Art. 811.3. Definitions.

In this Chapter:

(1) "Victim" means a person against whom an offense that is a felony-grade delinquent act has been committed.

(2) "Victim's family" means a spouse, parent, child, stepchild, sibling, or legal representative of the victim, except when the person is in custody for an offense or is the defendant.

(3) "Juvenile crime victim" means a person, under the age of seventeen, against whom an offense against the person that is a felony has been committed.

(Added by Acts 1995 No. 522, §1, No. 835, §1; chgd. by Acts 1997 No. 732, §2, eff. 8/15/97.)

CHAPTER 4. PREADJUDICATION CUSTODY AND RELEASE OF CHILDREN

Art. 812. Taking child into custody.

A. A child may be taken into custody pursuant to an order of the court under this Title or pursuant to the laws governing arrest.

B. The taking of a child into custody is not an arrest, except for the purpose of determining its validity under the Constitution of the United States or the Constitution of Louisiana.

(Added by Acts 1991 No. 235, §8, eff. 1/1/92.)

Art. 813. Taking child into custody with a court order; filing of verified complaint; execution.

A. The court may issue an order directing that a child be taken into custody upon presentation to the court of a written statement of facts sworn to before an officer authorized by law to administer oaths, by a peace officer, probation officer, district attorney, or other person designated by the court alleging facts showing that there is probable cause to believe either that:

(1) The child has committed a delinquent act.

(2) The child has violated the terms of his probation or otherwise has violated the terms of his release.

B. The verified complaint shall be filed with the clerk of court. If it is filed after the child has been taken into custody, the complaint shall indicate whether the child was released to his parents or continued in custody.

C. An order directing that a child be taken into custody may be executed by a peace officer or the child's probation officer having territorial jurisdiction over the child. The officer shall promptly notify the child's parents that their child has been taken into custody. The officer shall also promptly conduct the child to the appropriate facility in accordance with Article 815.

(Added by Acts 1991 No. 235, §8; chgd. by Acts 1995 No. 1158, §1, eff. 8/15/95.)

Art. 814. Taking child into custody without a court order; duties of the officer; duties of the court.

A. A child may be taken into custody without a court order or warrant by a peace officer or probation officer if the officer has probable cause to believe that the child has committed a delinquent act.

B. If a child is taken into custody without a court order or warrant, the officer shall have the responsibility to either:

(1) Counsel and release the child to the care of his parents upon their written promise to bring the child to court at such time as may be fixed by the court.

(2) Promptly escort the child to the appropriate facility in accordance with Article 815.

C. If the officer does not release the child to the care of his parents, the officer shall promptly notify the child's parents that he has been taken into custody.

D. The officer shall immediately execute a written statement of facts, sworn to before an officer authorized by law to administer oaths, supporting the existence of probable cause to believe either that the child committed a delinquent act or that the child has violated the terms of his probation or otherwise has violated the terms of his release. This affidavit shall be submitted to the juvenile court. Within forty-eight hours after the child has been taken into custody, including legal holidays within the time computation, the court shall review the affidavit and if it determines that probable cause exists, the child shall be held for a continued custody hearing pursuant to Article 819. If the court determines that probable cause does not exist, the child shall be released from custody.

E. The officer shall submit a report to the district attorney or an officer designated by the court to receive such reports. The report shall include:

(1) The name, address, date of birth, sex, and race of the child.

(2) The name and address of the parents, or spouse, if any, of the child.

(3) A plain and concise statement of the facts and circumstances of the officer's taking the child into custody.

(4) A plain and concise statement of facts and circumstances showing probable cause that the child committed a delinquent act.

(5) A statement indicating whether the child was released, or escorted to a juvenile detention center, or placed in a shelter care facility.

F. If the child is released pursuant to Paragraph B or D of this Article, the report shall be submitted by the officer within seven days from the child's release. If the child is not so released, the report shall be submitted within twenty-four hours of the child being taken into custody.

(Added by Acts 1991 No. 235, §8; chgd. by Acts 1992 No. 705, §1; Acts 1993 No. 634, §1; Acts 1995 No. 1158, §1, eff. 8/15/95.)

Art. 815. Child taken into custody; place of detention.

A. The peace officer or an appropriate representative of the arresting agency shall have the authority and responsibility to transport the child to the appropriate place of detention specified in Paragraphs B and C of this Article, unless the child has been released to the care of his parents pursuant to Article 814(B)(1).

B. If the child has been taken into custody for the commission of a felony-grade delinquent act or of a misdemeanor-grade delinquent act based upon an offense against the person of another, the child shall be taken to a juvenile detention center.

C. For the commission of any other misdemeanor-grade delinquent act, the child shall be taken to either a shelter care facility or a juvenile detention center.

D. By order of a judge, a youth taken into custody for a felony-grade delinquent act or for a misdemeanor-grade delinquent act based upon an offense against the person of another, may be placed in a shelter care facility provided all of the following conditions are met:

(1) No detention facility is available and, in the opinion of the requesting authority, the youth is not considered a threat to himself, staff, or others.

(2) The administrator of the shelter care facility is willing to allow the youth to enter the program and is able to provide proper supervision and safety for the youth, staff, and all others in the care facility.

(3) The governing authority of the parish or municipality requesting such placement and the administrator of the facility enter into a mutual agreement for reimbursement to the facility for the cost of the care provided.

(Added. by Acts 1991 No. 235, §8; chgd. by Acts 1993 No. 818, §1; Acts 1995 No. 1158, §1, eff. 8/15/95.)

Art. 816. Record of detention center; access.

A. Every juvenile detention center shall maintain a permanent record of certain information as to each child received. The record shall include:

(1) The child's name, age, sex, race, and address.

(2) The reason the child is being taken into custody.

(3) The date and time of the child's entry into and exit from the juvenile detention center.

(4) The name of the officer and the law enforcement agency employing the officer who brings the child to the juvenile detention center.

B. The record in which such information is kept shall not be open for public inspection. Peace officers, probation officers, counsel representing the child, the district attorney, persons collecting statistical information, and authorized officers of the court shall have access to the record.

(Added by Acts 1991 No. 235, §8; chgd. by Acts 1992 No. 705, §1, eff. 7/6/92.)

Art. 817. Release from custody.

A. As soon as practicable after a child is received by a juvenile detention center or shelter care facility, the court or a probation officer employed and authorized by the court, upon determining it to be appropriate, shall release the child to the care of his parents or other relatives upon their written promise to bring him to court at such times as may be fixed by the court. The court may also impose reasonable restrictions upon the child's travel, place of abode, association with other people, or employment during the period of this release.

B. If the court finds that these conditions are insufficient to assure the presence of the child at later proceedings, the court may require the posting of bail in accordance with Chapter 6 of this Title.

C. If the court finds that release under neither Paragraph A or B of this Article is appropriate, it may authorize the continued custody of a child pending a hearing in accordance with Chapter 5 of this Title.

D. If custody is continued, an appropriate representative of the arresting agency shall be responsible for transporting the child to the adjudication or dispositional hearing, or both, and transporting the child back to the juvenile detention center or to such state or local facility as determined by the court through its order or judgment or disposition.

(Added by Acts 1991 No. 235, §8, eff. 1/1/92.)

Art. 818. Identification procedures.

A. A child may be photographed or fingerprinted only in connection with being taken into custody for the commission of either:

(1) A felony-grade delinquent act.

(2) A misdemeanor-grade delinquent act involving the use of a dangerous weapon.

B. Any child other than those described in Paragraph A of this Article can be photographed or fingerprinted only upon motion of the district attorney and court order.

C. Upon motion of the district attorney, the court in its discretion can order any child to submit to other reasonable identification procedures, such as, to provide handwriting exemplars or to stand in a lineup.

D. Fingerprints and photographs taken pursuant to Paragraph A or B of this Article shall be maintained and indexed separately from those of adults. They shall be made available only to law enforcement and correctional agencies for purposes related to their official functions. Fingerprints taken pursuant to Paragraph A or B shall be submitted to the central fingerprint repository maintained by the Louisiana Bureau of Criminal Identification and Information as specified under R.S. 15:590 et seq., and to the fingerprint repository, if any, maintained by the local law enforcement agency.

(Added by Acts 1991 No. 235, §8; chgd. by Acts 1992 No. 1078, §1, eff. 8/21/92.)

CHAPTER 5. CONTINUED CUSTODY PRIOR TO ADJUDICATION

Article

Art. 819. Continued custody hearing; time limitations.

If a child is not released to the care of his parents, a hearing shall be held by the court within three days after the child's entry into the juvenile detention center or shelter care facility. If the hearing is not held, the child shall be released unless the hearing is continued at the request of the child. *(Added by Acts 1991 No. 235, §8; chgd. by Acts 1993 No. 634, §1, eff. 6/15/93.)*

Art. 820. Grounds for continued custody prior to adjudication.

At the continued custody hearing, the state shall prove that there is probable cause that the child has committed a delinquent act or has violated a condition of his probation or release. *(Added by Acts 1991 No. 235, §8; chgd. by Acts 1992 No. 705, §1, eff. 7/6/92.)*

Art. 821. Continued custody hearing.

A. At the outset of the continued custody hearing, if not before, the court shall advise the child of his rights to counsel pursuant to Articles 809 and 810.

B. At the continued custody hearing, the state and the child may produce witnesses, who shall be examined in the presence of the child and shall be subject to cross-examination. The child may also testify, subject to cross-examination.

C. Hearsay evidence shall be admissible.

D. If probable cause has not been demonstrated, the court shall order the child's release.

E. If probable cause has been demonstrated, the court may release the child. The court may also require bail or other security pursuant to Articles 823 through 825 if the court finds that such is necessary to secure the child's appearance for subsequent hearings.
(Added by Acts 1991 No. 235, §8; chgd. by Acts 1992 No. 705, §1, eff. 7/6/92.)

Art. 822. Place of continued custody prior to adjudication.

A. Following the hearing required by Article 819, the court may order a child alleged to have committed a delinquent act or alleged to have violated probation or parole for a delinquent act, continued in custody in a licensed public or private facility for juveniles, if licensure is required by law for such a facility, or in a private home subject to the supervision of the court or in a juvenile detention center.

B. The court shall not place a child alleged to be delinquent in the custody of either the department of Social Services or the department of Public Safety and Corrections prior to adjudication.

C. No child subject to the jurisdiction of the juvenile court shall be held in an adult jail or lockup.
(Added by Acts 1991 No. 235, §8, eff. 1/1/92.)

CHAPTER 6. BAIL, SECURITY DEPOSITS, CONDITIONS OF RELEASE, AND BREACH OF BAIL CONDITIONS

Article

Art. 823. Right to bail or other security for release.

A. Except as provided for in Paragraph C of this Article, upon application by the child, parent, guardian, or legal custodian, a child shall have a right to bail for release from custody prior to adjudication by the deposit of a bond or other security as determined by the court and upon agreeing to any other reasonable conditions found necessary to insure appearance of the child for adjudication.

B. In any case when the child has appeared as ordered and otherwise met the conditions of the bail, the bail shall not be used to satisfy fines and costs except as specified by this Chapter or unless agreed to by the person who executed the bail.

C. A child charged with the commission of a delinquent act which would otherwise be deemed a capital offense under Title 14 of the Louisiana Revised Statutes of 1950 shall not be admitted to bail if the state shows that the proof is evident and the presumption great that the child is guilty of the capital offense. The court shall hold a contradictory hearing to resolve the child's application for bail in these circumstances.
(Added by Acts 1991 No. 235, §8, eff. 1/1/92.)

Art. 824. Criteria for setting bail or alternative forms of security.

In determining the amount of bail, alternative security deposits, and conditions of release, the court shall consider:

(1) The nature and circumstances of the delinquent act.
(2) The weight of the evidence.
(3) The child's prior delinquency record, if any.
(4) The financial ability of the child and family to post money bail.

(5) The probability of the child's appearance at any scheduled hearing, considering the following:

(a) The child has failed to appear at some previously scheduled hearing.

(b) The child has violated a condition of his probation or release.

(c) The child has absented himself from home or his usual place of abode without the consent of his parent.

(d) The child is habitually disobedient and is ungovernable and beyond the control of his parent.

(e) The potential danger of release to the child and to the public as it affects the probability of appearance.

(Added by Acts 1991 No. 235, §8, eff. 1/1/92.)

Art. 825. Types of security.

If the court determines that some sort of security is required to insure the child's presence for the adjudication, it shall set bail and may require any of the following forms of security:

(1) The child, parent, guardian, or legal custodian may have executed a bail bond in accordance with Article 314 of the Code of Criminal Procedure and deposit with the clerk the full amount of the bail secured by a deposit in cash or other authorized security, all of which shall be returnable upon satisfactory performance of the bail conditions.

(2) The child, parent, guardian, or legal custodian may have executed a bail bond and may deposit with the court or its designee a sum of money equal to ten percent of the bail, but in no event shall such deposit be less than twenty-five dollars. When the conditions of the bail bond have been discharged, the clerk shall return to the accused, unless the court orders otherwise, ninety percent of the sum which had been deposited and shall retain as bail bond costs ten percent of the amount deposited. However, in no event shall the amount retained by the clerk as bail bond costs be less than five dollars.

(3) The court may in the best interests of the child and his family agree to the deposit of other reasonable items of value or to the encumbrance of property as security to insure appearance for adjudication. These items will be returned to the child or other obligor upon the child's appearance for adjudication and the court's notice to the clerk for return.

(4) The child and his parents may sign a personal bail undertaking without the necessity of furnishing a surety, without depositing any special security, or without meeting any of the requirements for a personal surety as defined by Article 315 of the Code of Criminal Procedure.

(Added by Acts 1991 No. 235, §8; chgd. by Acts 1995 No. 1158, §1, eff. 8/15/95.)

Art. 826. Conditions of release.

A. A condition of every type of bail authorized in Article 825, and the only condition for which a security on the bail bond may be subject to forfeiture, is that the released child appear at any place and upon any date to which the proceeding is transferred or continued.

B. Every bail order shall also contain the condition that the released child not commit any further delinquent acts while at liberty on such bail bond or security deposit.

C. The court may also impose as a condition of release:

(1) That the child regularly attend school.

(2) That the child voluntarily participate in a pretrial drug testing program which meets the requirements of Article 336 of the Code of Criminal Procedure.

(3) Any other condition of release that is reasonably related to assuring the child's appearance before the court.

D. A violation of any condition by the child or his parents, guardian, or legal custodian shall be considered as a constructive contempt of court.

(Added by Acts 1991 No. 235, §8; chgd. by Acts 1995 No. 1158, §1, eff. 8/15/95.)

Art. 827. Judgment of release from continued custody.

A. The court authorizing a child's release from continued custody shall issue an order containing bail provisions, if any, and a statement of conditions imposed upon the child. This order shall also set forth the date of the child's next court appearance.

B. The court shall advise the child and his parents, guardian, or legal custodian of the child's duty to appear as well as of any conditions specified in the order.

C. The child and his parent, guardian, or legal custodian shall sign the agreement of security and release and acknowledge the conditions of release imposed by the court.

(Added by Acts 1991 No. 235, §8, eff. 1/1/92.)

Art. 828. Violation of conditions of release.

A. Any failure to comply with the conditions of release, including failure to appear before the court as scheduled, may constitute a breach of the bail agreement. Any such breach of the agreement constitutes constructive contempt of court and failure to appear constitutes the offense of bail jumping.

B. Where there is a breach of the bail agreement or the court is satisfied with good cause that the bail agreement should be modified, the court may order the child and his parent, guardian, legal counsel, and the surety, if any, to appear before the court, or the court may issue an order directing that the child be taken into custody and brought before the court.

C. When the child's parents, guardian, legal custodian, or the child's counsel has good cause to believe that the child has violated or will violate the conditions of the bail agreement, which violation will result in the child's failure to appear before the court as directed, he may report the breach or impending violation to the court, surrender the child, and request revocation of the bail agreement.

D. If a surety obligated under a bail bond, executed pursuant to Article 825(1), has good cause to believe that the child has violated or will violate the conditions of the bail agreement, which will result in the child's failure to appear before the court as directed, he may report the breach and apply to the court for an instanter order for the child to be taken into custody. Unless authorized by the court, the surety shall not arrest or take the child into custody. *(Added by Acts 1991 No. 235, §8, eff. 1/1/92.)*

Art. 829. Cancellation of bail bond.

The court shall order the bail bond cancelled or other security released when there is no further liability thereon. *(Added by Acts 1991 No. 235, §8, eff. 1/1/92.)*

Art. 830. Modification of bail.

The court on its own motion or on motion of the state or upon subsequent application by the child or his parent, guardian, or legal custodian, for good cause may either increase or reduce the amount of bail or other security. *(Added by Acts 1991 No. 235, §8, eff. 1/1/92.)*

Art. 831. Review of bail orders.

A child refused bail, or as a remedy for excessive bail, may invoke the supervisory jurisdiction of the court of appeal. *(Added by Acts 1991 No. 235, §8, eff. 1/1/92.)*

CHAPTER 7. MENTAL INCAPACITY TO PROCEED

Art. 832. How mental incapacity is raised; effect.

A child's mental incapacity to proceed, as defined by this Title, may be raised at any time by the child, the district attorney, or the court. When the question of the child's mental incapacity to proceed is raised, there shall be no further steps in the delinquency proceeding, except the filing of a delinquency petition, until counsel is appointed in accordance with Article 809(B) and the child is found to have the mental capacity to proceed. *(Added by Acts 1991 No. 235, §8, eff. 1/1/92.)*

Art. 833. Mental examinations.

A. The court shall order a mental examination of the child when it has reasonable ground to doubt the child's mental capacity to proceed. Prior to the ordering of any such mental examination, the court shall appoint counsel to represent the child if the child is not yet represented.

B. The court order for a mental examination shall not deprive the child or the district attorney of the right to an independent mental examination by a physician of his choice. Such

physician shall be permitted to have reasonable access to the child for the purposes of the examination.
(Added by Acts 1991 No. 235, §8, eff. 1/1/92.)

Art. 834. Appointment of sanity commission; qualifications.

A. Within seven days after a mental examination is ordered, the court shall appoint a sanity commission to examine and report upon the mental condition of the child. The sanity commission shall consist of at least two and not more than three physicians who are licensed to practice medicine in Louisiana, who have been in the actual practice of medicine for not less than three consecutive years immediately preceding the appointment and who are qualified by training or experience in forensic evaluations. No more than one member of the commission shall be the coroner or any one of his deputies. The court may appoint, in lieu of one physician, a psychologist who is licensed to practice psychology in Louisiana, who has been engaged in the practice of clinical or counseling psychology for not less than three consecutive years immediately preceding the appointment, and who is qualified by training or experience in forensic evaluations.

B. The physicians appointed to make the examination shall have free access to the child at all reasonable times. The court shall subpoena witnesses to attend the examination at the request of the child, the commission, or any member thereof.

C. For the purpose of the mental examination, the court may order a child who has been previously released on bail to appear for any mental examinations and hearings authorized by this Chapter.
(Added by Acts 1991 No. 235, §8; chgd. by Acts 1992 No. 705, §1, eff. 7/6/92.)

Art. 835. Report of sanity commission; filing.

A. The report of the sanity commission shall be filed with the court within thirty days after the date of the order of appointment. The time for filing may be extended by the court.

B. The clerk shall make copies of the report available to the district attorney and to the child or his counsel without cost.
(Added by Acts 1991 No. 235, §8, eff. 1/1/92.)

Art. 836. Determination of mental capacity to proceed.

A. The issue of the child's mental capacity to proceed shall be determined by the court in a contradictory hearing.

B. The report of the sanity commission is admissible in evidence at the hearing. Members of the sanity commission may be called as witnesses by the court, the child, or the district attorney. Regardless of who calls them as witnesses, the members of the commission are subject to cross-examination by the child, by the district attorney, and by the court. Other evidence pertaining to the child's capacity to proceed may be introduced at the hearing by the child and by the district attorney.
(Added by Acts 1991 No. 235, §8, eff. 1/1/92.)

Art. 837. Procedure after determination of mental capacity.

A. If the court determines that the child has the mental capacity to proceed, the delinquency proceedings shall be resumed.

B. If the court determines that the child lacks mental capacity to proceed, the proceedings shall be suspended and the court may either:

(1) Commit the child to the Department of Health and Hospitals, a private mental institution, or an institution for the mentally ill.

(2) Place the child in the custody of his parents or other suitable person under such terms and conditions as deemed in the best interests of the child and the public, which conditions may include the provision of outpatient services by the Department of Health and Hospitals, office of mental health.

C. In no instance shall a commitment ordered pursuant to Paragraph B(1) of this Article exceed the time of the maximum disposition the child could receive if adjudicated delinquent for the alleged delinquent act.

D. At any time after commitment and on recommendation of the department or the superintendent of the private institution that the child will not attain the capacity to proceed with his adjudication in the foreseeable future, the court shall, within a reasonable time and after at least ten days' notice to the district attorney and the counsel for the child, conduct a contradictory hearing to determine whether the mentally ill child is and will, in the foreseeable future, be incapable of standing adjudication and whether he is a danger to himself or others.

E. If, after the hearing, the court determines that the child is and will, in the foreseeable future, be incapable of proceeding and that he may be released without danger to himself or others, the court may either:

(1) Release the child on probation, subject to such conditions as may be imposed by the court.

(2) Place the child in the custody of his parents or other suitable person under such terms and conditions as deemed in the best interests of the child and the public, which conditions may include the provision of outpatient services by the Department of Health and Hospitals.

F. If, after the hearing, the court determines that the mentally ill child is incapable of proceeding, is a danger to himself or others, and is unlikely in the foreseeable future to be capable of proceeding, the court shall order commitment to a designated and medically suitable treatment facility. Such a judgment shall constitute an order of civil commitment as provided in Title XIV on the civil commitment of children. However, no child shall be discharged or conditionally discharged except upon order of court after motion and contradictory hearing.

G. Upon commitment, the court shall furnish to the institution the following information:

(1) The name and address of the child's attorney.

(2) The offense with which the child is charged and the date of such charges.

(3) A copy of the sanity commission report.

(4) Any other pertinent information concerning the child's health which has come to the attention of the court.

(Added by Acts 1991 No. 235, §8, eff. 1/1/92.)

Art. 838. Procedure when capacity regained.

A. At any time after a child's commitment, if the Department of Health and Hospitals or the superintendent of the mental institution reports to the committing court that the child presently has the mental capacity to proceed, the court shall hold a contradictory hearing within thirty days on that issue.

B. Prior to such a hearing, the court shall appoint counsel to represent the child if the child does not have counsel, and shall order a mental examination by a sanity commission appointed in conformity with Article 834.

C. The district attorney or the child may apply to the court to have the proceedings resumed, on the ground that the child presently has the mental capacity to proceed. Upon receipt of such application the court shall hold a contradictory hearing to determine if there is reasonable ground to believe that the child presently has the mental capacity to proceed. The court may direct the Department of Health and Hospitals or superintendent of the mental institution where the child is committed to make a report and recommendation prior to such hearing as to whether the child presently has capacity to proceed, or may order an independent mental examination by a sanity commission appointed in conformity with Article 834.

D. Reports as to present mental capacity to proceed shall be filed in conformity with Article 835, and the court's determination of present mental capacity to proceed shall be made in conformity with the provisions of Article 836.

E. If the court determines that the child has the mental capacity to proceed, the proceedings shall be promptly resumed.

(Added by Acts 1991 No. 235, §8, eff. 1/1/92.)

CHAPTER 8. INFORMAL ADJUSTMENT PROCEDURE

Article

Art. 839. Availability of an informal adjustment agreement.

A. Prior to the filing of a petition, the district attorney or the court with the consent of the district attorney may authorize an informal adjustment agreement.

B. After the filing of a petition but before the attachment of jeopardy pursuant to Article 811, the court may authorize the district attorney or probation officer to effect an informal adjustment agreement if the child and district attorney have no objection. The court may, with

concurrence of the district attorney, dismiss the petition or allow the petition to remain pending during the period of informal adjustment.
(Added by Acts 1991 No. 235, §8; chgd. by Acts 1993 No. 897, §1, eff. 8/15/93.)

Art. 840. Form of agreement.

A. An informal adjustment agreement shall set forth in writing the terms and conditions of the child's supervision during the term specified in the agreement. It shall be signed by the district attorney or the probation officer and by the child and his parents.

B. It must demonstrate that the child and his parents understand the child's right to an adjudication hearing on the offense. It must also demonstrate that they consent to the terms of the adjustment agreement with knowledge that their consent is not obligatory and with knowledge of the effect of the agreement as set out hereinafter in Article 841.

C. The period of informal adjustment shall not exceed six months; however, the court may extend the agreement for one additional period not to exceed six months.

D. If a petition has been filed, the adjustment agreement shall be filed in the record.
(Added by Acts 1991 No. 235, §8; chgd. by Acts 1992 No. 705, §1, eff. 7/6/92.)

Art. 841. Effect of agreement.

A. An informal adjustment agreement shall not be considered an adjudication. Evidence of the existence of such an agreement shall not be used against the child over objection in any adjudication hearing or criminal trial. Such evidence may be used in a disposition hearing in the juvenile court or for the purpose of a presentence investigation after a criminal conviction.

B. An informal adjustment agreement suspends the proceedings on the delinquent acts charged in the complaint or petition. If any of the terms of the agreement are violated, the case may proceed to an adjudication hearing on the charges. If the child satisfies the terms of the agreement, he shall be discharged from further supervision, and the pending complaint or petition shall be dismissed with prejudice.

C. After the confection of the agreement, any incriminating statement made by the child to the person giving counsel or advice and in the discussions or conferences incident to the informal adjustment agreement shall not be used against the declarant over objection in an adjudication hearing or criminal trial. Any such statement may be used in a disposition hearing in the court or for the purpose of a presentence investigation after a criminal conviction.
(Added by Acts 1991 No. 235, §8, eff. 1/1/92.)

CHAPTER 9. PETITION AND SUMMONS

Article

Art. 842. Authority to file petition.

A delinquency proceeding shall be commenced by a petition. The district attorney may file a petition without leave of court. Any person authorized by the court may file a petition if there are reasonable grounds to believe that the child is a delinquent child. *(Added by Acts 1991 No. 235, §8, eff. 1/1/92.)*

Art. 843. Time for filing of petition; child in custody.

A. If a child is continued in custody prior to adjudication, the delinquency petition shall be filed within forty-eight hours of the hearing to determine continued custody.

B. If no petition is filed within the applicable time period, the child shall be released.
(Added by Acts 1991 No. 235, §8, eff. 1/1/92.)

Art. 844. Form of petition.

A. The petition shall contain a caption setting forth the name of the court and the title of the action. The petition shall be entitled, "The State of Louisiana in the Interest of . . .".

B. Allegations of fact shall be simple, concise, and direct and shall be set forth in numbered paragraphs. As far as practicable, each paragraph shall be limited to a single set of circumstances.

C. The petition shall be verified. Allegations of fact may be made on information and belief.

D. Failure to comply with formal requirements of this Article shall not be grounds for dismissal of a petition or invalidation of the proceedings unless it results in substantial prejudice.
(Added by Acts 1991 No. 235, §8, eff. 1/1/92.)

Art. 845. Contents of petition.

A. The petition shall set forth with specificity:

(1) The name, date, and place of birth, sex, race, address, and present location of the child.

(2) The names and addresses of the parents and spouse, if any, of the child. If the parents are not within the state or cannot be located, the name and address of the child's closest adult relative within the state, or, if there be none, the known adult relative residing nearest to the court.

(3) Facts which show that the child is a delinquent child.

(4) The statute or ordinance which the child is alleged to have violated.

B. If the information required by Paragraph A(1) or (2) of this Article is unknown, the petition shall so allege. Any defects in the allegations required by Paragraphs A(1) and (2) of this Article and in the citation of the statute or ordinance required by Paragraph A(4) of this Article shall be considered defects of form.

C. Two or more delinquent acts may be charged in the same petition in a separate count for each act if the acts charged, whether based upon felony or misdemeanor offenses, are of the same or similar character or are based on the same act or transaction or on two or more acts or transactions connected together or constituting parts of a common scheme or plan.

D. The petition shall conclude with a request that the court adjudicate the child to be delinquent.
(Added by Acts 1991 No. 235, §8, eff. 1/1/92.)

Art. 846. Amendment of petition.

A. With leave of court, the petitioner may amend the petition at any time to cure defects of form.

B. With leave of court, prior to the adjudication hearing, the petitioner may amend the petition to include new allegations of fact or requests for adjudication. However, if such leave is granted, the child may request a continuance of the adjudication hearing. A continuance may be granted for such period as is required in the interest of justice.

C. After jeopardy begins pursuant to Article 811, a petition shall not be amended to include new allegations of fact or requests for adjudication.
(Added by Acts 1991 No. 235, §8, eff. 1/1/92.)

Art. 847. Service of petition.

A. A copy of the petition and the right to counsel form specified in Article 848 shall be served upon the child.

B. A copy of the petition and the right to counsel form specified in Article 848 shall also be served upon every parent whose address is known or can be determined after due diligence.
(Added by Acts 1991 No. 235, §8, eff. 1/1/92.)

Art. 848. Notice of right to counsel; form.

*"NOTICE

RIGHT TO COUNSEL

Under the laws of Louisiana, every child accused of delinquency is entitled to have a lawyer to be present and to assist the child to answer the attached petition. A child is entitled to be represented by a lawyer at every stage of proceedings in the juvenile court, including the right to appeal from any judgment of disposition which might be ordered by the court.

If the parents of an accused child are completely financially unable to afford to employ a lawyer, the court will appoint a lawyer and the state will pay for his services.

If the parents are found to be financially able to afford to employ a lawyer but fail to employ one, the juvenile court may appoint a lawyer for the child and require the parents to pay for the lawyer's services.

The financial ability or inability of the parents to employ a lawyer will be determined by the court after a hearing. The court may require the parents to pay for some or all of the costs of lawyer's services on behalf of the child.

After consulting with parents or other adult interested in the child's welfare, the child may be permitted by the court to proceed without the assistance of a lawyer. This decision can be made at any time during the proceedings in the juvenile court."

(Added by Acts 1991 No. 235, §8, eff. 1/1/92.)

**So in original. No introductory paragraph has been enacted.*

Art. 849. Service and return; resident parent.

A. If a parent resides within the state, service shall be made personally or by domiciliary service or by certified mail as soon as possible and not less than forty-eight hours prior to commencement of the adjudication hearing on the matter.

B. The person effecting service shall execute a return and, if service was made by certified mail, the return receipt shall be attached thereto.

(Added by Acts 1991 No. 235, §8, eff. 1/1/92.)

Art. 850. Summons; child and resident parent.

A. Except as provided in Paragraph B of this Article, when a delinquency petition involves a child whose parent is a resident, the court shall issue a summons commanding that the child, his parents, and such other persons as the court deems proper appear before the court at a designated time and place.

B. In its discretion the court may decline to issue a summons to appear at any hearing for the parents of any child who is eighteen years of age or older.

(Added by Acts 1991 No. 235, §8, eff. 1/1/92.)

Art. 851. Failure to appear as summoned.

If a properly served person fails to appear in response to a summons, the court may order that such person be taken into custody and immediately brought before the court. *(Added by Acts 1991 No. 235, §8, eff. 1/1/92.)*

Art. 852. Service; nonresident parent.

A. If a parent does not reside within this state, service shall be made by personal service or by certified mail to the address indicated in the petition, return receipt requested, not less than five days prior to the commencement of the adjudication hearing on the matter.

B. The person effecting the service shall file the return receipt as proof of service.

(Added by Acts 1991 No. 235, §8, eff. 1/1/92.)

Art. 853. Effect of nonappearance by a parent.

If it appears from the record that the parent has been served in accordance with Article 849 or 852 and summoned to any hearing, or cannot be found, and the parent fails to appear, the hearing may be held in the parent's absence. Should the court decide to proceed, it may appoint a Court Appointed Special Advocate in accordance with Article 424 for the child. The court shall appoint counsel for the child if neither parent appears. *(Added by Acts 1991 No. 235, §8, eff. 1/1/92.)*

CHAPTER 10. ANSWER TO PETITION

Art. 854. Appearance to answer petition; time.

A. If the petition is filed prior to or during the hearing to determine continued custody, the court may order the child to answer the petition upon completion of the hearing. If not so ordered and the child is continued in custody, he shall be ordered to appear to answer the petition within five days after the filing of the petition.

B. In all other cases, the child shall be ordered to appear to answer the petition within fifteen days after the filing of the petition.

C. For good cause, the court may extend such period.

(Added by Acts 1991 No. 235, §8, eff. 1/1/92.)

Art. 855. Advice of rights at appearance to answer.

A. When the child appears to answer the petition, the court shall first determine that the child is capable of understanding statements about his rights under this Code.

B. If the child is capable, the court shall then advise the child of the following items in terms understandable to the child:

(1) The nature of this delinquency proceeding.

(2) The nature of the allegations of the petition.

(3) His right to an adjudication hearing.

(4) His right to be represented by an attorney, his right to have counsel appointed as provided in Article 809, and his right in certain circumstances authorized by Article 810 to waive counsel.

(5) His privilege against self-incrimination.

(6) The range of responses authorized under Article 856.

(7) The possible consequences of his admission that the allegations are true, including the maximum and minimal dispositions which the court might impose pursuant to Articles 897 through 900.

(Added by Acts 1991 No. 235, §8, eff. 1/1/92.)

Art. 856. Answer to petition.

A. After the child has been advised pursuant to Article 855, the court shall inquire how the child responds. The child may:

(1) Deny the allegations of the petition, in which case the court shall set the matter for an adjudication hearing.

(2) Deny the allegations of the petition and contest the request for adjudication due to insanity as defined in this Title, in which case the court shall not adjudicate the child without a hearing, at which time the child has the burden of establishing this defense.

(3) Admit the allegations of the petition, in which case the court shall further inquire to determine whether there is a factual basis for adjudication. If so, the court may then adjudicate the child delinquent.

(4) With the court's permission, enter a response of nolo contendere. If, in its discretion, the court accepts such response, the court shall further inquire to determine whether there is a factual basis for adjudication, and it may then adjudicate the child delinquent.

B. A child shall plead when called upon to answer. If he stands mute, refuses to plead, or pleads evasively, a denial of the petition shall be entered of record.

(Added by Acts 1991 No. 235, §8, eff. 1/1/92.)

CHAPTER 11. TRANSFERS FOR CRIMINAL PROSECUTION

Art. 857. Transfers for criminal prosecution; authority.

A. The court on its own motion or on motion of the district attorney may conduct a hearing to consider whether to transfer a child for prosecution to the appropriate court exercising criminal jurisdiction if a delinquency petition has been filed which alleges that a child who is fourteen years of age or older at the time of the commission of the alleged offense but is not otherwise subject to the original jurisdiction of a court exercising criminal jurisdiction has committed any one or more of the following crimes:

(1) First degree murder.

(2) Second degree murder.

(3) Aggravated kidnapping.

(4) Aggravated rape.

(5) Aggravated battery when committed by the discharge of a firearm.

(6) Armed robbery when committed with a firearm.

(7) Aggravated oral sexual battery.

(8) Forcible rape if the rape is committed upon a child at least two years younger than the rapist.

B. Notwithstanding any other provision of law to the contrary, a fourteen-year-old who is transferred pursuant to this Article and subsequently convicted shall not be confined for such conviction beyond his thirty-first birthday.

(Added by Acts 1991 No. 235, §8; chgd. by Acts 1993 No. 634, §1; Acts 1994 Third Ex. Sess. No. 15, §1; Acts 1997 No. 1137, §1, eff. 7/14/97.)

Art. 858. Motion for transfer; notice.

A. On motion of the district attorney, the child, or on its own motion, the court may conduct a transfer hearing. Such motion may be filed at any time following the filing of a delinquency petition but shall be heard prior to the adjudication hearing or acceptance of an admission to the delinquency petition.

B. Notice in writing of the time, place, and purpose of the hearing must be given to the child and his parents and other custodian, if any, at least ten days before the hearing.

(Added by Acts 1991 No. 235, §8; chgd. by Acts 1993 No. 634, §1, eff. 6/15/93.)

Art. 859. Conduct of transfer hearing.

A. The transfer hearing shall be conducted in accordance with the provisions of Chapter 13 of this Title governing the conduct of an adjudication hearing, except as otherwise provided herein.

B. Only such evidence which pertains to the transfer criteria set out in Article 862 may be introduced.

(Added by Acts 1991 No. 235, §8, eff. 1/1/92.)

Art. 860. Medical, sensory, psychological, and psychiatric examinations.

A. On its own motion or on the motion of the child or district attorney, the court may order any child subject to a motion to transfer to be examined by a physician, optometrist, audiologist, psychologist, or psychiatrist.

B. Any examination shall be made and the findings submitted to the court within three days of the transfer hearing. Such period may be extended by the court for good cause.

C. Copies of any reports of findings submitted to the court shall be made available to counsel for all parties.

D. Unless the child has sought the examination or otherwise waives his privilege against self-incrimination, neither testimony about the report nor any of its contents is admissible in an adjudication hearing or later criminal trial, if any, which would violate the child's privilege against self-incrimination.
(Added by Acts 1991 No. 235, §8, eff. 1/1/92.)

Art. 861. Access to evidence; reports.

A. The child shall have all rights to discovery as provided for in Article 866.

B. In addition to the rights to review any report submitted pursuant to Article 860, the child shall have the right to review any report prepared regarding the transfer.
(Added by Acts 1991 No. 235, §8, eff. 1/1/92.)

Art. 862. Transfer hearing; required findings.

A. In order for a motion to transfer a child to be granted, the burden shall be upon the state to prove all of the following:

(1) Probable cause exists that the child meets the requirements of Article 857.

(2) By clear and convincing proof, there is no substantial opportunity for the child's rehabilitation through facilities available to the court, based upon the following criteria:

(a) The age, maturity, both mental and physical, and sophistication of the child.

(b) The nature and seriousness of the alleged offense to the community and whether the protection of the community requires transfer.

(c) The child's prior acts of delinquency, if any, and their nature and seriousness.

(d) Past efforts at rehabilitation and treatment, if any, and the child's response.

(e) Whether the child's behavior might be related to physical or mental problems.

(f) Techniques, programs, personnel, and facilities available to the juvenile court which might be competent to deal with the child's particular problems.

B. The court shall state for the record its reasons for judgment.

C. (1) The court shall transmit the order rendered after the hearing or a certified copy thereof, without delay, to the clerk of court having jurisdiction of the offense.

(2) Any party may request the court to provide a complete or partial transcript of the testimony of the witnesses; however, neither the record of the hearing nor the reasons for the transfer shall be admissible in evidence in any subsequent criminal proceedings, except for the purpose of impeachment of a witness.
(Added by Acts 1991 No. 235, §8; chgd. by Acts 1992 No. 705, §1; Acts 1993 No. 634, §1, eff. 6/15/93.)

Art. 863. Effect of transfer order; review.

A. An order of transfer terminates the jurisdiction of the court exercising juvenile jurisdiction over the child with respect to the delinquent acts alleged in the petition. The appropriate court exercising criminal jurisdiction shall retain jurisdiction over the case, even though the child pleads guilty to, or is convicted of, a lesser included offense. The plea to, or conviction of, a lesser included offense shall not revest juvenile jurisdiction over such child.

B. The decision of the court regarding transfer of the case to the court exercising criminal jurisdiction is only an interlocutory judgment which either the child or the state, or both, have the right to have reviewed summarily by the appropriate court of appeal. Such review shall be by preference.
(Added by Acts 1991 No. 235, §8, eff. 1/1/92.)

Art. 864. Places of detention; before and after transfer.

A. Prior to the entry of a judgment ordering his transfer, the child shall be held in custody only in those places authorized for the preadjudication detention of children as specified in Article 822.

B. After the entry of a judgment ordering his transfer, the child shall be held in any facility used for the pretrial detention of accused adults and shall apply to the appropriate court of criminal jurisdiction for a preliminary hearing, bail, and for any other rights to which he may be entitled under the Code of Criminal Procedure.
(Added by Acts 1991 No. 235, §8, eff. 1/1/92.)

CHAPTER 12. PREADJUDICATION MOTIONS AND RELIEF

Art. 865. Preadjudication requests for relief; general provisions.

A. All motions or other requests for relief prior to the adjudication hearing shall be made by written motion filed within fifteen days after the child or his counsel has appeared to answer the petition. In the interest of justice, the court may allow additional time within which to make or file such motions or may permit such requests to be made by oral motion.

B. The motion shall state with particularity the grounds therefor and shall set forth the relief sought.

C. A motion may be granted without a contradictory hearing when mover is clearly entitled thereto without supporting proof. A motion shall not be denied without a contradictory hearing unless, assuming the facts alleged to be true, mover is not entitled to relief.

(Added by Acts 1991 No. 235, §8, eff. 1/1/92.)

Art. 866. Discovery.

Discovery shall be as provided in the Louisiana Code of Criminal Procedure. *(Added by Acts 1991 No. 235, §8, eff. 1/1/92.)*

Art. 867. Medical, sensory, psychological, and psychiatric examinations.

A. On its own motion or on the motion of the child or district attorney, the court may order any child concerning whom a petition has been filed to be examined by a physician, optometrist, or audiologist.

B. On motion of the child, the court may order a child concerning whom a petition has been filed, to be examined by a psychologist or a psychiatrist.

C. Any examination as herein provided shall be made and the findings submitted to the court within thirty days of the date the order is entered. Such period may be extended by the court for good cause.

D. Copies of any reports of findings submitted to the court shall be available to counsel for all parties.

(Added by Acts 1991 No. 235, §8, eff. 1/1/92.)

Art. 868. Medical treatment of children; costs.

A. On its own motion, or on the motion of the child or the district attorney, the court may order the parent of a child concerning whom a petition has been filed to provide necessary medical or surgical care.

B. If the parent fails to provide such care, the court may, after due notice to the parent, order the care and order the parent to pay all or part of the expense.

(Added by Acts 1991 No. 235, §8, eff. 1/1/92.)

Art. 869. Insanity plea; appointment of sanity commission.

A. In addition to the provisions of Article 867, when a child contests an adjudication based on his insanity, the court shall appoint counsel in accordance with Article 809(B) and may appoint a sanity commission as provided for in Article 834 to make an examination as to the child's mental condition at the time of the offense. The court may also order the commission to make an examination as to the child's present mental capacity to proceed.

B. Mental examinations and reports under this Article shall be conducted and filed in conformity with Chapter 7 of this Title.

C. The costs of such court ordered mental examinations shall be paid in accordance with Chapter 3 of Title XXI (Article 659 et seq.) of the Code of Criminal Procedure.
(Added by Acts 1991 No. 235, §8, eff. 1/1/92.)

Art. 870. Motion for a bill of particulars.

A. On motion of the child or on its own motion, the court may require the district attorney to furnish a bill of particulars setting forth more specifically the nature and cause of the allegations charging that the child committed a delinquent act.

B. When a bill of particulars is furnished, it shall be filed with the clerk of court and a copy shall be given to the child or his counsel.

C. Supplemental bills of particulars may be ordered by the court at any time before the adjudication hearing.
(Added by Acts 1991 No. 235, §8, eff. 1/1/92.)

Art. 871. Effect of inconsistent or limiting allegations of a bill of particulars.

A. The court shall dismiss the petition unless its defects are cured by a supplemental bill of particulars if it finds from the bill of particulars and the petition either that:

(1) No delinquent act cognizable under the provisions of this Code was committed.

(2) The child named in the petition did not commit the delinquent act charged.

B. The defect will be cured if the district attorney furnishes, within a period fixed by the court, not to exceed three days from the order, another bill of particulars which either by itself or together with any particulars appearing in the petition so states the particulars as to make it appear that the offense charged was committed by the defendant.

C. If the district attorney fails to furnish a sufficient bill of particulars when ordered to do so by the court, the court may dismiss the petition.
(Added by Acts 1991 No. 235, §8, eff. 1/1/92.)

Art. 872. Motion to suppress.

The child may move to suppress evidence obtained in violation of the Constitution of the United States or the Constitution of Louisiana. *(Added by Acts 1991 No. 235, §8, eff. 1/1/92.)*

Art. 873. Severance of causes for adjudication.

A. If it appears that the child or the state is prejudiced by a joinder of delinquent acts in the petition or by such joinder for trial together, the court may order separate adjudication hearings, grant severance, or provide whatever other relief justice requires.

B. If a petition joins a request to adjudicate the child delinquent with a request for adjudication on any other jurisdictional ground authorized by this Code, the court may, in the interests of justice, order separate adjudication hearings.
(Added by Acts 1991 No. 235, §8, eff. 1/1/92.)

Art. 874. Severance of individual cases for adjudication.

Where petitions have been filed which allege that one or more children were involved in the commission of the same delinquent act or acts, the children shall be tried jointly unless either:

(1) The state elects to try them separately.

(2) The court, on motion of the child and after contradictory hearing with the district attorney, is satisfied that justice requires a severance.
(Added by Acts 1991 No. 235, §8, eff. 1/1/92.)

Art. 875. Motions to dismiss.

All objections to the proceedings, including objections based on defects in the petition and defenses capable of determination as a matter of law, may be raised by motion to dismiss.
(Added by Acts 1991 No. 235, §8, eff. 1/1/92.)

Art. 876. Dismissal of petition.

For good cause, the court may dismiss a petition on its own motion, on the motion of the child, or on motion of the petitioner. The court shall dismiss a petition on the motion of the district attorney. *(Added by Acts 1991 No. 235, §8, eff. 1/1/92.)*

CHAPTER 13. ADJUDICATION

Art. 877. Adjudication hearing; time limitations.

A. If the child is continued in custody pursuant to Chapter 5 of this Title, the adjudication hearing shall commence within thirty days of the appearance to answer the petition.

B. If the child is not continued in custody, the adjudication hearing shall commence within ninety days of the appearance to answer the petition.

C. If the hearing has not been commenced timely, upon motion of the child, the court shall release a child continued in custody and shall dismiss the petition.

D. For good cause, the court may extend such period.

(Added by Acts 1991 No. 235, §8, eff. 1/1/92.)

Art. 878. Order of adjudication hearing.

A. The normal order of an adjudication hearing shall be:

(1) Presentation of evidence offered by the state.

(2) Presentation of evidence offered on behalf of the child.

(3) Presentation of evidence to rebut evidence offered on behalf of the child.

(4) Closing arguments of counsel.

B. With consent of counsel, the order may be varied. When the child is not represented by counsel, the order may not be varied.

C. The court may permit opening statements of the state and of counsel representing the child.

(Added by Acts 1991 No. 235, §8, eff. 1/1/92.)

Art. 879. Presence at adjudication hearing; exclusion of witnesses.

A. The child, his parents, counsel, the district attorney, authorized officials of the court, and witnesses called by the parties may be present at the adjudication hearing.

B. All proceedings in a juvenile delinquency case involving a crime of violence as defined in R.S. 14:2(13) or a delinquent act which is a second or subsequent felony-grade adjudication shall be open to the public.

C. On its own motion the court may, and on the request of a party the court shall, order that the witnesses, other than parties, be excluded from the courtroom or from a place where they can see or hear the proceedings, and refrain from discussing the facts of the case with anyone other than counsel in the case. In the interest of justice, the court may exempt any witness from its order.

(Added by Acts 1991 No. 235, §8; chgd. by Acts 1993 No. 769, §1; Acts 1994 Third Ex. Sess. No. 120, §1; Acts 1995 No. 1313, §1, eff. 6/29/95.)

Art. 880. Right to present evidence and examine witnesses.

A. Among other rights guaranteed by Chapter 3 of this Title, at the adjudication hearing the child may introduce evidence, call witnesses, be heard on his own behalf, and cross-examine witnesses called by the state.

B. When a child has contested an adjudication based on his insanity, the members of the sanity commission may be called as witnesses by the court, the child, or the district attorney. Regardless of who calls them as witnesses, the members of the commission are subject to cross-examination by the child, by the district attorney, and by the court.

C. Other evidence pertaining to the defense of insanity at the time of the offense may be introduced at the adjudication hearing by the child and by the district attorney.

(Added by Acts 1991 No. 235, §8, eff. 1/1/92.)

Art. 881. Evidence.

A. The adjudication hearing in delinquency proceedings shall be conducted according to the provisions of the Code of Evidence applicable to criminal cases.

B. The child shall not be required to testify, and evidence obtained in violation of the child's rights under the Constitution of the United States or the Constitution of Louisiana shall not be admitted over objection.

(Added by Acts 1991 No. 235, §8, eff. 1/1/92.)

Art. 882. Adjudication by the court.

The adjudication hearing shall be held before the court without a jury. *(Added by Acts 1991 No. 235, §8, eff. 1/1/92.)*

Art. 883. Burden of proof.

In order for the court to adjudicate a child delinquent, the state must prove beyond a reasonable doubt that the child committed a delinquent act alleged in the petition. *(Added by Acts 1991 No. 235, §8, eff. 1/1/92.)*

Art. 884. Adjudication order.

A. Following the adjudication hearing, the court shall immediately declare whether the evidence warrants an adjudication that the child is delinquent. In exceptional circumstances, the court may take the matter under advisement.

B. If the evidence warrants such an adjudication, the court may find that the family is in need of services according to Title VII.

C. If the court finds that the evidence does not warrant any requested or authorized adjudication, it shall dismiss the petition.

(Added by Acts 1991 No. 235, §8, eff. 1/1/92.)

Art. 885. Denial of driving privileges; restricted driver's license.

A. Without any further hearing, whenever any child over the age of thirteen is adjudicated delinquent for the commission of any offense involving the possession, use, or abuse of alcohol or one or more controlled dangerous substances, any offense in violation of the Uniform Controlled Dangerous Substances Law*, or any offense in violation of any provision of the Louisiana Drug Racketeering Act**, the court shall order the child to relinquish his driver's license, if any, and shall order a denial of driving privileges, including the right to apply for driving privileges, by the child for a period of not less than thirty days but not more than one year.

**R.S. 40:961 et seq.*

***R.S. 15:1351 et seq.*

B. In addition to any other authority granted by this Article, the court may issue an order which authorizes the Department of Public Safety and Corrections to issue a restricted driver's license to the child after the first thirty days of the suspension period upon a demonstration to the court's satisfaction that a hardship would result from the child being unable to commute to either school or work. In its discretion, the court shall determine the appropriate restrictions which shall last for the term of the suspension of driving privileges.

C. (1) In addition to any other authority granted by this Article, the court may order that upon the expiration of the first thirty days of the suspension period, the terms of the restricted driver's license include permission during the term of the suspension for the child to operate a motor vehicle for the purpose of going to and from meetings of Alcoholics Anonymous, approved group therapy, or special education courses for or about the disease of alcoholism, alcohol abuse, or drug use in a suitable public or private institution or state approved program if either:

(a) Bail was forfeited by the child for an offense of operating or being in actual physical control of a motor vehicle while under the influence of intoxicating beverages.

(b) The adjudication was the child's first adjudication of an offense involving the possession of any controlled dangerous substance in violation of the Uniform Controlled Dangerous Substances Law.

(2) If ordered by the court, a medical evaluation and recommendation is submitted which demonstrates that the child is pathologically addicted to alcohol or is a habitual alcoholic or other drug offender; or

(3) If ordered by the court, the child agrees to submit to medical treatment or medically approved group therapy or special education courses for or about the disease of alcoholism,

alcohol abuse, or drug abuse, in a suitable public or private institution or state-approved program.

D. The privilege of driving with a restricted driver's license authorized by Paragraph B or C of this Article may be allowed only once to each child. A copy of the order containing the restrictions authorized by Paragraph B or C of this Article shall be attached to the license of the child and shall be in his possession whenever he is operating a motor vehicle.

E. A subsequent adjudication of delinquency for the offenses set out in Paragraph A of this Article or a violation of the restrictions imposed pursuant to either Paragraph B or C of this Article during the period of suspension shall result in the extension of the period of suspension for one year from the date upon which the child would otherwise have been able to apply for a new license. Such an adjudication or violation shall also constitute contempt of court.

F. The court shall prepare and send a copy of the order of denial of driving privileges, together with any special restrictions, to the Department of Public Safety and Corrections within ten days of the adjudication.

G. Any period of suspension imposed pursuant to this Article shall begin upon receipt by the Department of Public Safety and Corrections of the child's driver's license.

(Added by Acts 1991 No. 235, §8, eff. 1/1/92.)

Art. 886. Continued custody pending disposition; bail; places of detention.

A. At the conclusion of the hearing if the child has been adjudicated delinquent, the court shall consider whether the child should be released or held in custody pending a disposition hearing.

B. If the adjudication was based upon a misdemeanor-grade delinquent act, the child shall have a right to bail in accordance with the procedures established in Chapter 6 of this Title.

C. If the adjudication was based upon a felony-grade delinquent act, there is a presumption in favor of the child's right to bail unless the court has reason to believe, based upon competent evidence, that the release of the child will pose a danger to any other person or the community. If the child is to be released, the court shall set bail according to the procedures established in Chapter 6 of this Title.

D. If the child is held in custody, the court may place him in a juvenile detention center, in a public or private facility for juveniles, in a private home subject to the supervision of the court, or in any other suitable facility for juveniles authorized by the court.

(Added by Acts 1991 No. 235, §8, eff. 1/1/92.)

CHAPTER 14. VACATION OF ADJUDICATION

Art. 887. Vacation of adjudication; grounds.

A. On motion of the child prior to disposition, a delinquency adjudication shall be vacated and the child discharged if, after contradictory hearing, the court finds that:

(1) The petition is substantially defective, in that an essential averment is omitted, although the child may be recharged by a new petition within the time limitations provided by law for that offense.

(2) The delinquent act charged in the petition is not based upon an offense which is punishable under a valid statute.

(3) The court making the adjudication lacked jurisdiction.

(4) The act charged constitutes double jeopardy, if not previously urged.

(5) The prosecution was not timely instituted, if not previously urged.

B. On motion of the child before disposition, an adjudication shall be vacated and a new adjudication hearing ordered if, after a contradictory hearing, the court finds that:

(1) The adjudication is not responsive to the petition, or is otherwise so defective that it will not form the basis of a valid judgment, in which case the child shall be remanded to custody or bail to await a new adjudication hearing.

(2) The adjudication was obtained by fraud or mistake sufficient to justify vacating the adjudication.

(3) The child and his counsel satisfy the requirements of Articles 851(3), 853, and 854 of the Code of Criminal Procedure regarding the discovery of new and material evidence.

(4) The adjudication judgment is contrary to the law and evidence.

C. If the court is of the opinion that the ends of justice would be served, it may vacate the adjudication prior to disposition, although the child may not be entitled to such relief as a matter of strict legal right.
(Added by Acts 1991 No. 235, §8, eff. 1/1/92.)

CHAPTER 15. PREDISPOSITION INVESTIGATION

Article

Art. 888. Physical and mental examination for disposition; costs.

A. Following the adjudication, the court may order such physical and mental examination and evaluation of the child as may be helpful in determining a fair and just disposition.

B. In conjunction with such an examination or evaluation, the court may order the preparation of a social summary and case history about the child, including otherwise confidential information within the court's records, for submission to the evaluator.

C. The court may, after due notice to the parent, order the parent to pay all or part of the expense of any evaluation or examination. The court shall make a determination of the parent's ability to pay according to the procedures of Article 406.
(Added by Acts 1991 No. 235, §8, eff. 1/1/92.)

Art. 889. Disclosure of resulting evaluation report.

Copies of any reports of findings submitted to the court pursuant to Article 888 shall be made available to the district attorney and counsel for the child. *(Added by Acts 1991 No. 235, §8, eff. 1/1/92.)*

Art. 890. Predisposition report; contents.

A. In making the investigation, the probation officer shall investigate and report to the court regarding:

(1) The circumstances attending the commission of the offense; the attitudes of the child and his parents toward the offense; the prior offenses committed by the child, including other referrals or contacts not resulting in juvenile court petitions; and, when applicable, the disposition of companion cases arising out of this offense.

(2) The impact on the victim, if a child is adjudicated of or admits to a delinquent act involving a victim. The court shall require that a victim impact statement be included in the predisposition report. The victim impact statement shall include factual information as to whether the victim or his family has suffered, as a result of the offense, any monetary loss, medical expense, or physical impairment, and shall include any other information deemed relevant. The district attorney may also file a victim impact statement with the court.

(3) The child's home environment including his family's composition and dynamics, stability, economic status, participation in community or religious activities, and any physical, mental, or emotional handicaps, substance abuse, or criminal history of any of its members.

(4) The child's current physical description, developmental and medical history, social adjustment in the community, school record, including the name and address of the school where the child is registered and enrolled, employment or vocational interest, significant behavior patterns, or other personality traits relevant to his rehabilitation.

B. The report shall contain a list of all persons contacted in completing the investigation and their relationship to the child.

C. The report shall contain a brief statement of the child's identified behavioral problems and the probation officer's assessment of cause and potential for rehabilitation, indicating specifically those resources available in the community or within the child's extended family which could provide needed assistance to the child and his family.

D. The report shall contain recommendations for suggested disposition, including, if applicable, special conditions of supervision.
(Added by Acts 1991 No. 235, §8; chgd. by Acts 1993 No. 634, §1, No. 840, §1, eff. 6/15/93.)

Art. 891. Disclosure of predisposition report.

A. Copies of the predisposition report shall be made available to the district attorney and counsel for the child at least three days in advance of any scheduled disposition hearing. Such period may be extended for good cause.

B. The court may order that the predisposition report be edited to protect the identity of confidential sources or to exclude the recommendations of the probation officer. In addition, the court may caution the district attorney or counsel for the child not to disclose any such information contained within the report which may prove harmful to the child.

C. If the child is unrepresented by counsel, the court shall disclose to the child the factual contents of the predisposition report.

D. After August 15, 1993, and within thirty days after receiving a predisposition report, the sentencing court shall order the release of any portion of a predisposition report containing and limited to the instant arrest, conviction, adjudication, or disposition of a child in grades nine through twelve, who is arrested, charged, or adjudicated a delinquent for committing a felony-grade delinquent act or a misdemeanor-grade delinquent act involving distribution or possession with intent to distribute a controlled dangerous substance in violation of the Uniform Controlled Dangerous Substances Law*, to the principal of the school in which the child is registered and enrolled or registered and enrolled but suspended.

**R.S. 40:961 et seq.*

(Added by Acts 1991 No. 235, §8; chgd. by Acts 1993 No. 840, §1, eff. 8/15/93.)

CHAPTER 16. DISPOSITION HEARINGS

Art. 892. Disposition hearing; time.

Prior to entering a judgment of disposition, the court shall conduct a disposition hearing. The disposition hearing may be conducted immediately after the adjudication and shall be conducted within thirty days after the adjudication. Such period may be extended for good cause. *(Added by Acts 1991 No. 235, §8, eff. 1/1/92.)*

Art. 893. Disposition hearing; evidence.

A. At the disposition hearing, unless the child waives the presentation, the court shall hear evidence as to whether the child is in need of treatment or rehabilitation and shall make and file its findings.

B. All evidence helpful in determining the proper disposition, including oral and written reports, the report of the predisposition investigation, any reports of mental evaluation, and all other evidence offered by the child or the state shall be received by the court and may be relied upon to the extent of its probative value even though not admissible at the adjudication hearing. Upon motion of the district attorney or the child, the court may hear testimony from the victim of the offense.

C. Counsel for the state and for the child shall be afforded an opportunity to present evidence and to examine and controvert written reports so received and to cross-examine individuals preparing the reports or other witnesses who give testimony at the hearing. Sources of confidential information need not be disclosed.

D. If the court finds that the child is in need of treatment or rehabilitation as a delinquent child, the court shall proceed immediately to make any appropriate disposition authorized by Articles 895 through 899.

(Added by Acts 1991 No. 235, §8; chgd. by Acts 1993 No. 634, §1, eff. 6/15/93.)

Art. 894. Disposition after finding of insanity.

In cases in which a child has not been adjudicated a delinquent and has been found to be insane at the time of the offense, the court may either:

(1) Place the child in the custody of his parents or other suitable person under such terms and conditions as deemed in the best interests of the child and the public.

(2) Place the child on probation in the custody of his parents or other suitable person under such terms and conditions as deemed in the best interests of the child and the public.

(3) Commit the child to the Department of Health and Hospitals, office of mental health or a private mental institution or an institution for the mentally ill pursuant to Article 895.

(Added by Acts 1991 No. 235, §8, eff. 1/1/92.)

Art. 895. Commitment to mental institution.

A. In cases in which a child has been adjudicated a delinquent, the court may commit him to a public or private mental institution or institution for the mentally ill if the court finds, based on psychological or psychiatric evaluation, that the child has a mental disorder, other than mental retardation, which has a substantial adverse effect on his ability to function and requires care and treatment in an institution.

B. This finding shall not be made unless the child is accorded his right to special counsel in accordance with Article 809(B).

(Added by Acts 1991 No. 235, §8, eff. 1/1/92.)

Art. 896. Deferred dispositional agreement.

A. At any time after the entry of an adjudication order, the court may, on motion of the district attorney or of counsel for the child, suspend further proceedings and place the child on supervised or unsupervised probation, with or without any of the conditions authorized by Article 897(B)(1) or Article 899(B)(1).

B. The child and his parent must consent to this special type of disposition. If the child has waived counsel, the court must advise the child and his parent concerning the consequences of a deferred dispositional agreement and of the child's right to have a disposition imposed by the court in accordance with Articles 897 through 900.

C. A deferred dispositional agreement order shall comply with all the requirements of Article 903.

D. A deferred dispositional agreement shall remain in force for six months unless the child is discharged sooner by the court. Upon application of the district attorney or by any agency supervising the child made before the expiration of the six-month period, a deferred dispositional agreement order may be extended by the court for an additional period not to exceed six months.

E. If prior to the expiration of the order a new petition alleging the commission of a delinquent act is filed against the child, or the child otherwise fails to fulfill the express terms and conditions of the order, the court may proceed to impose any disposition authorized by this Title and the child may be held accountable as if the deferred dispositional agreement order had never been entered.

F. If the child satisfactorily completes the court ordered period of supervision, the court shall discharge the child from any further supervision or conditions, set aside the adjudication, and dismiss the petition with prejudice.

(Added by Acts 1991 No. 235, §8, eff. 1/1/92.)

Art. 897. Disposition after adjudication of a felony-grade delinquent act.

A. After adjudication of any felony-grade delinquent act other than those described in Article 897.1, the court may:

(1) Reprimand and warn the child and release him into the custody of his parents either unconditionally or subject to such terms and conditions as deemed in the best interests of the child and the public.

(2) Reprimand and warn the child and release him into the custody of some other suitable person either unconditionally or subject to such terms and conditions as deemed in the best interests of the child and the public. The court shall, whenever practicable, select a person of the same religious faith as the child or his parents.

(3) Place the child on probation in the custody of his parents or other suitable person.

B. As conditions of probation, if ordered pursuant to Subparagraph A(3) of this Article:

(1) The court shall impose all of the following restrictions:

(a) Prohibit the child from possessing any drugs or alcohol.

(b) Prohibit the child from engaging in any further delinquent or criminal activity.

(c) Prohibit the child from possessing a firearm or carrying a concealed weapon, if he has been adjudicated for any of the following offenses and probation is not otherwise prohibited: first or second degree murder; manslaughter; aggravated battery; aggravated, forcible, or simple rape; aggravated crime against nature; aggravated kidnapping; aggravated arson; aggravated or simple burglary; armed or simple robbery; burglary of a pharmacy; burglary of an inhabited dwelling; unauthorized entry of an inhabited dwelling; or any violation of the Uniform Controlled Dangerous Substances Law* which is a felony or any crime defined as an attempt to commit one of these enumerated offenses.

**R.S. 40:961 et seq.*

(2) The court may impose any other term and condition deemed in the best interests of the child and the public, including:

(a) A requirement that the child attend school, if the school admits the child.

(b) A requirement that the child perform court-approved community service activities.

(c) A requirement that the child make reasonable restitution to any victim for any personal or property damage caused by the child in the commission of the delinquent act.

(d) A requirement that the child participate in any program of medical or psychological or other treatment found necessary for his rehabilitation.

(e) A requirement suspending or restricting the child's driving privileges, if any, for all or part of the period of probation. In such cases, a copy of the order shall be forwarded to the Department of Public Safety and Corrections, which shall suspend the child's driver's license or issue a restricted license in accordance with the order of the court.

(f) A requirement prohibiting the child from possessing a firearm or carrying a concealed weapon.

(g) A requirement that the child pay a supervision fee of not less than ten nor more than one hundred dollars per month, payable to the Department of Public Safety and Corrections or other supervising agency, to defray the costs of supervision. The amount of the fee shall be based upon the financial ability of the payor to pay such a fee. The court may order a parent, tutor, guardian, or other person who is financially responsible for the care of the child to be responsible for payment of all or part of any supervision fee imposed.

C. Except as provided for in Article 897.1, the court may commit the child to the custody of a private or public institution or agency. When commitment is to be made to a private institution or agency, the court shall:

(1) Select one that has been licensed under state law, if licensure is required by law for such an institution or agency.

(2) Whenever practicable, select an agency or institution of the same religious faith as the child or his parents.

D. Except as provided for in Article 897.1, the court may commit the child to the custody of the Department of Public Safety and Corrections, with or without a recommendation that the child be placed in alternative care facilities through the department's client placement process or be referred to appropriate placement resources in the Department of Social Services.

E. Except as provided for in Article 897.1, the court may impose but suspend the execution of the whole or part of any order of commitment and place the child on probation subject to any of the terms and conditions authorized under Paragraph B of this Article.

(Added by Acts 1991 No. 235, §8; chgd. by Acts 1992 No. 299, §1; Acts 1993 No. 430, §2, eff. 8/15/93.)

Art. 897.1. Disposition after adjudication of certain felony-grade delinquent acts.

A. Notwithstanding any other provision of law to the contrary, after adjudication of a felony-grade delinquent act based upon a violation of R.S. 14:30, first degree murder; R.S. 14:30.1, second degree murder; R.S. 14:42, aggravated rape; R.S. 14:44, aggravated kidnapping; R.S. 14:64, armed robbery; or R.S. 14:113, treason; the court shall commit the child to the custody of the Department of Public Safety and Corrections to be placed within a secure detention facility until the child attains the age of twenty-one years without benefit of parole, probation, suspension of imposition or execution of sentence, modification, or furlough.

B. Notwithstanding any other provision of law to the contrary, after adjudication of a felony-grade delinquent act based upon a violation of R.S. 14:64, armed robbery, the court shall commit the child to the custody of the Department of Public Safety and Corrections to be placed within a secure detention facility for the length of the term imposed by the court at the disposition hearing without benefit of parole, probation, suspension of imposition or execution of sentence, modification, or furlough.

(Added by Acts 1993 No. 430, §2, eff. 8/15/93.)

Art. 898. Duration of a disposition based on a felony-grade adjudication.

A. No judgment of disposition shall remain in force for a period exceeding the maximum term of imprisonment for the felony forming the basis for the adjudication. The court shall give a child credit for time spent in secure detention prior to the imposition of disposition.

B. When modification and parole is not prohibited by Article 897.1, if an order of commitment to custody of the Department of Public Safety and Corrections is subsequently modified and the child is placed on parole, the maximum term of parole shall be the remainder of the sentence originally imposed.

C. These maximums do not apply if:

(1) The child was under thirteen at the time of a commitment to custody of the Department of Public Safety and Corrections, in which case the judgment shall terminate upon the child's reaching age eighteen.

(2) A portion of an order of commitment was suspended, when permitted by law, in which case the term of parole shall end when the time period so suspended has elapsed.

(3) The child is tried as an adult and is convicted of, or pleads guilty to a felony after having been committed to the Department of Public Safety and Corrections. In this instance, after sentencing, the department shall have the authority to keep the offender in custody according to terms of the juvenile disposition, or to transfer him to serve his adult sentence. The department shall retain such authority until the expiration of the juvenile commitment when, if not effected earlier, the individual will be transferred to begin serving the adult sentence.

(4) The judgment expires by its own terms, is modified when permitted by law, or is vacated.

(5) The child reaches age twenty-one.

(Added by Acts 1991 No. 235, §8; chgd. by Acts 1992 No. 705, §1; Acts 1993 No. 430, §2; Acts 1995 No. 969, §1, No. 1158, §1, eff. 8/15/95.)

Art. 899. Disposition after adjudication of a misdemeanor-grade delinquent act.

A. After adjudication of a misdemeanor-grade delinquent act, the court may:

(1) Reprimand and warn the child and release him into the custody of his parents either unconditionally or subject to such terms and conditions as deemed in the best interests of the child and the public.

(2) Reprimand and warn the child and release him into the custody of some other suitable person either unconditionally or subject to such terms and conditions as deemed in the best interests of the child and the public. The court shall, whenever practicable, select a person of the same religious faith as the child or his parents.

(3) Place the child on probation in the custody of his parents or other suitable person.

B. As conditions of probation, if ordered pursuant to Subparagraph A(3) of this Article:

(1) The court shall impose all of the following restrictions:

(a) Prohibit the child from possessing any drugs or alcohol.

(b) Prohibit the child from engaging in any further delinquent or criminal activity.

(2) The court may impose any other term and condition deemed in the best interests of the child and the public, including:

(a) A requirement that the child attend school, if the school admits the child.

(b) A requirement that the child perform court-approved community service activities.

(c) A requirement that the child make reasonable restitution to any victim for any personal or property damage caused by the child in the commission of the delinquent act.

(d) A requirement that the child participate in any program of medical or psychological or other treatment found necessary for his rehabilitation.

(e) A requirement suspending or restricting the child's driving privileges, if any, for all or part of the period of probation. In such cases, a copy of the order shall be forwarded to the Department of Public Safety and Corrections, which shall suspend the child's driver's license or issue a restricted license in accordance with the order of the court.

(f) A requirement prohibiting the child from possessing a firearm or carrying a concealed weapon.

(g) A requirement that the child pay a monthly supervision fee of not less than ten nor more than one hundred dollars per month, payable to the Department of Public Safety and Corrections or other supervising agency, to defray the cost of supervision. The court may order a parent, tutor, guardian, or other person who is financially responsible for the care of the child to be responsible for payment of all or part of any supervision fee imposed.

C. The court may commit the child to the custody of a private or public institution or agency. When commitment is to be made to a private institution or agency, the court shall:

(1) Select one that has been licensed under state law, if licensure is required by law for such an institution or agency.

(2) Whenever practicable, select an agency or institution of the same religious faith as the child or his parents.

D. If the child is thirteen years of age or older at the time of the commission of the delinquent act, the court may commit the child to the custody of the Department of Public Safety and Corrections, with or without a recommendation that the child be placed in alternative care facilities through the department's client placement process or be referred to appropriate placement resources in the Department of Social Services.

E. The court may impose but suspend the execution of the whole or part of any authorized order of commitment and place the child on probation subject to any of the terms and conditions authorized under Paragraph B of this Article.

(Added by Acts 1991 No. 235, §8; chgd. by Acts 1992 No. 299, §1, eff. 8/21/92, No. 705, §1, eff. 7/6/92.)

Art. 900. Duration of a disposition based on a misdemeanor-grade adjudication.

A. No judgment of disposition shall remain in force for a period exceeding the maximum term of imprisonment for the offense which forms the basis for the adjudication, except that if the child is placed on probation, the term of probation may extend for a maximum of two years. The court shall give a child credit for time spent in secure detention prior to the imposition of disposition.

B. If an order of commitment to the custody of the Department of Public Safety and Corrections is subsequently modified and the child is placed on parole, the maximum term of parole shall be the remainder of the sentence originally imposed.

C. These maximums do not apply if:

(1) A portion of an order of commitment was suspended, in which case the term of parole shall end when the time period so suspended has elapsed.

(2) The child commits a felony after having been committed to the custody of the Department of Public Safety and Corrections or while on probation and is tried as an adult and convicted or pleads guilty, in which case the judgment of disposition in the juvenile court shall terminate as of the date of conviction. The child shall earn no diminution of his felony sentence based upon time served under the order of disposition.

(3) The judgment expires by its own terms, is modified, or is vacated.

(4) The child reaches age twenty-one.

(Added by Acts 1991 No. 235, §8; chgd. by Acts 1992 No. 705, §1, eff. 7/6/92.)

Art. 901. Disposition guidelines; generally.

A. In considering dispositional options, the court shall not remove a child from the custody of his parents unless his welfare or the safety and protection of the public cannot, in the opinion of the court, be adequately safeguarded without such removal.

B. The court should impose the least restrictive disposition authorized by Articles 897 through 900 of this Title which the court finds is consistent with the circumstances of the case, the needs of the child, and the best interest of society.

C. Commitment of the child to the custody of the Department of Public Safety and Corrections may be appropriate if any of the following exists:

(1) There is an undue risk that during the period of a suspended commitment or probation the child will commit another crime.

(2) The child is in need of correctional treatment or a custodial environment that can be provided most effectively by his commitment.

(3) A lesser disposition will deprecate the seriousness of the child's delinquent act.

(4) The delinquent act involved the illegal carrying, use, or possession of a firearm.

D. The following grounds, while not controlling the discretion of the court, shall be accorded weight in its determination of suspension of the disposition or probation:

(1) The child's delinquent conduct neither caused nor threatened serious harm.

(2) The child did not contemplate that his delinquent conduct would cause or threaten serious harm.

(3) The child acted under strong provocation.

(4) There were substantial grounds tending to excuse or justify the child's delinquent conduct, though failing to establish a defense.

(5) The victim of the child's delinquent conduct induced or facilitated its commission.

(6) The child or his family has compensated or will compensate the victim of his delinquent conduct for the damage or injury that the victim sustained.

(7) The child has no history of prior delinquency or has led a law-abiding life for a substantial period of time before the commission of the instant delinquent act.

(8) The child's delinquent conduct was the result of circumstances unlikely to recur.

(9) The character and attitudes of the child indicate that he is unlikely to commit another delinquent act or crime.

(10) The child is particularly likely to respond affirmatively to probationary treatment.

(11) The commitment of the child would entail excessive hardship to himself or his family.

E. The general disposition guidelines set forth in Paragraphs A through D of this Article do not apply when a child has been adjudicated a delinquent for the violation of R.S. 14:30, first degree murder; R.S. 14:30.1, second degree murder; R.S. 14:42, aggravated rape; R.S. 14:44, aggravated kidnapping; R.S. 14:64, armed robbery; or R.S. 14:113, treason; in accordance with Article 897.1.

(Added by Acts 1991 No. 235, §8; chgd. by Acts 1993 No. 430, §2, eff. 8/15/93, No. 634, §1, eff. 6/15/93.)

Art. 901.1. Probation and parole supervision fees.

A. When the court suspends the imposition or execution of sentence and places the child or his parent or both on supervised probation or grants the child supervised parole, and the probationer or parolee is to be supervised by the Department of Public Safety and Corrections or any other agency, the court shall order payment, as a condition of probation or parole, of a monthly supervision fee. The supervision fee imposed shall be not less than ten nor more than one hundred dollars per month and shall be payable to the department or other supervising agency to defray the costs of supervision. These funds are only to supplement the level of funds that would ordinarily be available from regular state or other appropriations.

B. The parent is responsible for payment of any supervision fee imposed and is subject to contempt of court for failure to pay such fees. The parent shall not be subject to judicial sanctions for failure to pay supervision fees if the failure was due to financial inability to pay based upon reasonable expenses for the necessities of life.

(Added by Acts 1992 No. 705, §1; chgd. by Acts 1995 No. 794, §1, eff. 8/15/95.)

Art. 902. Presence at disposition.

All parties shall be present when the court enters a judgment of disposition. Witnesses need not be present. *(Added by Acts 1991 No. 235, §8, eff. 1/1/92.)*

Art. 903. Judgment of disposition.

A. Before entering a judgment of disposition, the court shall orally inform the child and shall state for the record the considerations taken into account and the factual basis therefor in imposing the particular disposition chosen.

B. The court shall enter into the record a written judgment of disposition specifying all of the following:

(1) The offense for which the child has been adjudicated a delinquent.

(2) The nature of the disposition.
(3) The agency, institution, or person to whom the child is assigned.
(4) The conditions of probation, if applicable.
(5) Any other applicable terms and conditions regarding the disposition.
(6) The maximum duration of the disposition and, if committed to the custody of the Department of Public Safety and Corrections, the maximum term of the commitment.

C. The order of commitment may require the department to take physical custody of a child adjudicated a delinquent, committed to its custody pursuant to Article 897(D) or Article 899(D), and recommended by the court or the department for assignment to a secure program or facility, within fourteen days from the date of the court's signing of the judgment of disposition when the child is in or is going to be placed in the physical custody of a parish juvenile facility. If a court modifies a judgment of disposition, in accordance with Chapter 17, and gives the department custody of the adjudicated delinquent, the provisions of this Article and R.S. 15:901 apply.

D. An extract of the minutes of court specifying the information required by Paragraph B of this Article and signed by the court shall be considered a written judgment of disposition.

E. The date of entry of the judgment of disposition shall be recorded on the judgment.

F. Upon request, a copy of the judgment of disposition shall be furnished to the parent. *(Added by Acts 1991 No. 235, §8; chgd. by Acts 1992 No. 200, §1; Acts 1993 No. 873, §2; Acts 1997 No. 615, §1, eff. 7/3/97.)*

Art. 904. Court transmission of reports.

If the child is assigned to the custody of the Department of Public Safety and Corrections or to the custody of a public or private institution or agency, the court shall transmit with the judgment of disposition all relevant reports concerning the child. *(Added by Acts 1991 No. 235, §8, eff. 1/1/92.)*

Art. 905. Progress reports to court.

A. Any institution or agency to which a child is assigned, upon request, shall provide the court any information concerning the condition, supervision, treatment, or rehabilitation program of the child.

B. Any institution, agency, or person to which a child is assigned shall, not less than once every six months, report in writing the whereabouts and condition of the child to the judge who rendered the judgment of disposition.

(Added by Acts 1991 No. 235, §8, eff. 1/1/92.)

Art. 906. Required review hearings; commitment to mental institution.

A. The medical staff of a mental institution to which a child is committed or placed by the Department of Health and Hospitals after the child has been found not guilty by reason of insanity or after a court determines that the child lacks mental capacity to proceed shall review the child's record after the first sixty days, again after one hundred twenty days of commitment, and every one hundred eighty days thereafter.

B. The purpose of these reviews is to determine the child's present mental condition and whether he is presently capable of being discharged, conditionally or unconditionally, or being placed on probation, without being a danger to others or himself, or is presently capable of proceeding.

C. The department or the superintendent of the private institution shall make such recommendations to the court as provided in Article 835 or Article 838.

(Added by Acts 1991 No. 235, §8, eff. 1/1/92.)

Art. 907. Permanency planning for children committed to the Department of Public Safety and Corrections.

If the Department of Public Safety and Corrections makes a placement of a child committed to its legal custody in a foster home or child care institution for which the department claims funding under 42 U.S.C. §672(c), it shall be subject to the permanency planning requirements of Chapters 13, 15, and 16 of Title VI, except that the time limitations for the preparation of case plans, and administrative and judicial reviews shall date from the time when such an initial placement is made. *(Added by Acts 1991 No. 235, §8, eff. 1/1/92.)*

Art. 908. Care and treatment by Department of Public Safety and Corrections.

A. Except as provided in Article 906, the Department of Public Safety and Corrections shall have sole authority over the placement, care, treatment, or any other considerations deemed necessary from the resources that are available for children judicially committed to the department.

B. When care and treatment are to be provided by the department, either through facilities and programs operated by it or through contractual arrangements or through purchase of service arrangements for which the department provides funding, the child shall be committed to the department rather than to a particular institution or facility.

C. The court shall not divide legal and physical custody of a child when assigning custody to the department in accordance with this Article or in accordance with any other statute or provision of law.

(Added by Acts 1991 No. 235, §8, eff. 1/1/92.)

Art. 908.1. AIDS and sexually transmitted diseases; victim's testing and services.

When a juvenile is adjudicated a delinquent for a sexual offense as defined in R.S. 14:42 through 43.4, the provisions of R.S. 15:535(C) and (D) shall apply. *(Added by Acts 1993 No. 904, §2, eff. 8/15/93.)*

CHAPTER 17. MODIFICATION OF DISPOSITION

Article

Art. 909. Modification authority; in general.

Except as provided for in Article 897.1, after the entry of any order of disposition, the court retains the power to modify it, including changing the child's legal custody, suspending all or part of any order of commitment, discharging conditions of probation, or adding any further condition authorized by Article 897(B) or 899(B). It may also terminate an order of disposition at any time while it is still in force. *(Added by Acts 1991 No. 235, §8; chgd. by Acts 1993 No. 430, §2, eff. 8/15/93.)*

Art. 910. Modification procedure; generally applicable.

A. Except as specially provided hereinafter in Articles 911 through 916, a motion for modification may be filed by the district attorney, the child, his parents, the custodian of the child, a probation officer, or the court. A motion for modification shall be in writing and shall set forth in plain and concise terms the facts supporting the modification.

B. Any motion to modify may be denied without a hearing.

C. When the motion to modify seeks the imposition of less restrictive conditions, the court may modify a judgment without a contradictory hearing.

D. When the motion to modify seeks the imposition of more restrictive conditions, the court shall conduct a contradictory hearing, except upon the waiver of the parties.

E. A judgment of disposition shall not be modified to release a child from the custody of a public or private mental institution or an institution for the mentally ill without three days prior notice to the district attorney and the institution.

F. If a judgment of disposition is modified, a copy of the minute entry reflecting the modification shall be served upon the district attorney, the child, his parent, and any person, institution, or agency to whom custody of the child is assigned.

(Added by Acts 1991 No. 235, §8, eff. 1/1/92.)

Art. 911. Modification of dispositions while in custody of the Department of Public Safety and Corrections.

A. A motion filed by the Department of Public Safety and Corrections whereby the conditions of the disposition are sought to be made less restrictive shall be tried contradictorily against the district attorney, unless the district attorney files in the record an affidavit averring no opposition to the motion.

B. A judgment of disposition shall not be modified to release a child from the custody of the Department of Public Safety and Corrections unless three days' prior notice is given to the district attorney and to the Department of Public Safety and Corrections.
(Added by Acts 1991 No. 235, §8, eff. 1/1/92.)

Art. 912. Resolution of grievances while under an order of commitment.

A. When committed to the custody of the department of Public Safety and Corrections, a child shall have the right to file a grievance concerning his care, custody, and control and have it resolved pursuant to Louisiana Administrative Code Section 22:I:325, the administrative remedy procedure.

B. Upon exhausting his administrative remedies, any child who is still aggrieved by an adverse decision by the department may seek judicial review of that decision by applying, within thirty days after receipt of the department's decision, to the juvenile court which entered the order of commitment.

C. If represented by counsel, the application shall be in the form of a petition. If unrepresented, the child may secure court review by writing a letter to the court outlining the facts of his complaint and the steps he had taken to secure administrative redress of his grievance.

D. If the court concludes that all administrative remedies have been exhausted and that the child's grievance appears to have merit, it shall proceed to schedule a contradictory hearing to resolve the grievance.
(Added by Acts 1991 No. 235, §8, eff. 1/1/92.)

Art. 913. Revocation of probation; procedure; evidence.

A. A motion filed to revoke a child's probation shall be accompanied by a supporting affidavit specifying the claimed violations which form the basis of the revocation. The child shall be entitled to a copy of the motion and supporting affidavit.

B. Unless the child waives his right, the court shall conduct a contradictory hearing. At this hearing, the child shall be entitled to:

(1) The right to confront and cross-examine adverse witnesses.

(2) The right to appear in person and to present witnesses in his own behalf.

(3) The right to have the state bear the burden of providing by clear and convincing evidence that he violated a condition of his probation which was contained in the order of disposition.

C. The hearing may be more informal and summary than an adjudication hearing. Consistent with the child's constitutional rights and the burdens upon the prosecution which full compliance with the Code of Evidence might otherwise entail, the court shall have discretion in the receipt and consideration of proffered evidence.

D. An order revoking probation shall comply with the requirements of Article 903.
(Added by Acts 1991 No. 235, §8; chgd. by Acts 1995 No. 1158, §1, eff. 8/15/95.)

Art. 914. Probation violation; sanctions including revocation.

A. Except as provided in Paragraph B of this Article, if the court finds that the child has violated a condition of his probation, it may, consistent with the best interests of the child and the public, do any of the following:

(1) Reprimand and warn the child.

(2) Order that supervision be intensified.

(3) Impose additional conditions to the probation.

(4) Extend the period of probation, provided the total amount of time served by the child on probation for any one offense shall not exceed the maximum period of probation authorized by Articles 898 and 900.

(5) Order that probation be revoked and execute the suspended sentence.

B. If the probation violation is the illegal or unlawful possession of a firearm, probation revocation is mandatory, and the child shall be committed to the custody of the Department of Public Safety and Corrections.

C. For repeated violations of a judgment of disposition, the court may also find the child in direct or constructive contempt of court and commit him to a juvenile detention center or other licensed facility, provided that the child shall not be physically housed in the same dormitory, room, or area used to house children adjudicated delinquent for behavior other than direct or constructive contempt.
(Added by Acts 1991 No. 235, §8, eff. 1/1/92.)

Art. 915. Probation revocation; limitations upon restraint.

A. When revoking a previous order of probation, the court may reinstate the original suspended or deferred disposition order and commit the child to the Department of Public Safety and Corrections for the term of that order, with credit for any time served in secure detention prior to the revocation hearing and with or without credit for time served on probation, in the discretion of the court. In no event shall the term of commitment exceed the maximum term of imprisonment for the offense forming the basis for the original adjudication.

B. When finding a child in direct or constructive contempt of court, commitment for each contempt shall not exceed fifteen days, including time spent in detention for the contempt prior to adjudication for contempt.

C. When the conduct alleged as the basis for probation revocation also constitutes a delinquent act, a petition shall be filed and an adjudication hearing scheduled for resolution of the new offense. If the child is adjudicated delinquent on the new petition, the order of disposition may include any sanction authorized by this Title as well as the revocation of the child's probation and imposition of any suspended disposition originally ordered.
(Added by Acts 1991 No. 235, §8; chgd. by Acts 1992 No. 705, §1, eff. 7/6/92.)

Art. 916. Modification of a mental health commitment.

A. In cases where a child has been committed to the Department of Health and Hospitals, office of mental health, or private mental institution, or an institution for the mentally ill, the court may also modify the judgment on motion of the department or superintendent of a private mental institution.

B. In cases in which a child has been adjudicated a delinquent, a judgment of disposition shall not be modified to release a child from the custody of the Department of Health and Hospitals, office of mental health, or private mental institution or an institution for the mentally ill without three days prior notice to the district attorney and the department or other institution.

C. Notwithstanding any provisions of law to the contrary, in cases in which a child has not been adjudicated a delinquent and has been found to be insane at the time of the offense, a child shall not be released from the custody of the Department of Health and Hospitals, office of mental health, or private mental institution, or an institution for the mentally ill except upon order of the court after motion and contradictory hearing.
(Added by Acts 1991 No. 235, §8, eff. 1/1/92.)

CHAPTER 18. EXPUNGEMENT

(Added by Acts 1997 No. 1127, §1, eff. 7/14/97. Former Chapter 18 was repealed by Acts 1995 No. 1251, §5, eff. 8/15/95.)

Article

Art. 917. Expungement; generally.

A person seventeen years of age or older may move for expungement of records of juvenile criminal conduct pursuant to this Chapter. *(Added by Acts 1997 No. 1127, §1, eff. 7/14/97. Former article 917 was repealed by Acts 1995 No. 1251, §5, eff. 8/15/95.)*

Art. 918. Grounds.

A. Records concerning conduct or conditions that did not result in adjudication may be expunged.

B. Records concerning conduct or conditions that resulted in a misdemeanor adjudication may be expunged only if two or more years have elapsed since the person satisfied the most recent judgment against him.

C. Records concerning conduct or conditions that resulted in a felony adjudication may be expunged only if:

(1) The adjudication was not for murder, manslaughter, any sexual crime, kidnapping, or armed robbery.

(2) Five or more years have elapsed since the person satisfied the most recent judgment against him.

(3) The person has no criminal court felony convictions and no criminal court convictions for misdemeanors involving a weapon.

(4) The person has no outstanding indictment or bill of information charging him.

(Added by Acts 1997 No. 1127, §1, eff. 7/14/97. Former article 918 was repealed by Acts 1995 No. 1251, §5, eff. 8/15/95.)

Art. 919. Procedure for expungement.

A. A person seventeen years of age or older may move for the expungement of records and reports concerning the person's juvenile criminal conduct or conditions.

B. The motion for expungement must be in writing and must state facts that constitute grounds for expungement under Article 918.

C. The motion for expungement must be filed with the court possessing the records the person seeks to expunge, or with the court having jurisdiction over the arresting agency.

D. The motion must be served personally or by domiciliary service or by certified mail on the district attorney, the clerk of the court whose records are sought to be expunged, and the head of any agency whose reports and records are sought to be expunged, including but not limited to the Federal Bureau of Investigation, the Louisiana Bureau of Criminal Identification, the Department of Public Safety and Corrections, and local law enforcement agencies.

E. Unless waived by consent of the parties, a contradictory hearing must be conducted with the district attorney and any agency whose records are sought to be expunged.

F. If the court finds that the grounds have been established, and that the person is entitled to expungement, the court may order expungement.

(Added by Acts 1997 No. 1127, §1, eff. 7/14/97. Former article 919 was repealed by Acts 1995 No. 1251, §5, eff. 8/15/95.)

Art. 920. Order of expungement; court records.

A. An order for the expungement of juvenile court records must be in writing and, except as hereinafter provided, must require that the clerk of court destroy all records relating to the conduct or condition referred to in the motion of expungement, including but not limited to pleadings, exhibits, reports, minute entries, correspondence, and all other documents.

B. References, documents, recordings, or other materials that cannot be destroyed may be maintained. Under no circumstances may any undestroyed information be released.

C. The court may maintain a confidential record, such as a minute entry, of the fact of an adjudication. This information may be released only upon written motion of a court exercising criminal jurisdiction over the person whose record is sought and then only for the purposes authorized by the Code of Criminal Procedure.

(Added by Acts 1997 No. 1127, §1, eff. 7/14/97. Former article 920 was repealed by Acts 1995 No. 1251, §5, eff. 8/15/95.)

Art. 921. Order of expungement; agency records.

A. An order for the expungement of juvenile records must be in writing and must require that both of the following occur:

(1) Except as otherwise provided by law, all officials, agencies, institutions, boards, systems, and law enforcement offices, and their employees, agents, and consultants, destroy all reports and records whether on microfilm, computer memory device, or tape, or any other photographic, fingerprint, or any other information of any kind and all kinds or descriptions relating to the conduct or condition referred to in the motion of expungement.

(2) Any and all such agencies and law enforcement offices file an affidavit with the court attesting to the fact that such records have been destroyed and that no notation or references have been retained in any central depository which will or might lead to the inference that any record ever was on file with that agency or law enforcement office.

B. The order must specify the time within which the destruction is to be effected. The order must also specify the limitations on information which may be maintained in accordance with this Article.

C. An order for expungement must be served in the manner provided for service of the motion on both the district attorney and the head of the agency whose reports or records are to be destroyed.

D. A copy of the judgment ordering destruction may be maintained by the custodian of reports and records of the agency or office. However, the custodian must not disclose the fact that such judgment is maintained or that the destroyed reports or records previously existed to anyone except upon written order of the court.

(Added by Acts 1997 No. 1127, §1, eff. 7/14/97. Former article 921 was repealed by Acts 1995 No. 1251, §5, eff. 8/15/95.)

Art. 922. Expungement order; effect.

Except for the limited purposes stated in Articles 920 and 921, upon an order of expungement, the conduct and conditions expunged are considered nonexistent and are to be treated as such upon inquiry. *(Added by Acts 1997 No. 1127, §1, eff. 7/14/97. Former article 922 was repealed by Acts 1995 No. 1251, §5, eff. 8/15/95.)*

TITLE IX. TRAFFIC VIOLATIONS

CHAPTER 1. PRELIMINARY PROVISIONS

Art. 951. Purpose.

The purpose of this Title is to facilitate and expedite proceedings involving minor traffic offenses. The intent of this Title is to recognize both the state's strong interest in protecting the public safety through the imposition of reasonable regulations on the operation of motor vehicles and the due process rights of children accused of traffic violations. *(Added by Acts 1991 No. 235, §9, eff. 1/1/92.)*

Art. 952. General applicability.

Except as otherwise specified in this Title, all provisions of the Children's Code remain applicable. *(Added by Acts 1991 No. 235, §9, eff. 1/1/92.)*

CHAPTER 2. TRAFFIC JURISDICTION; CITATION

Art. 953. Scope of traffic jurisdiction.

Traffic violation means any violation of a statute or ordinance regulating traffic, except the following criminal offenses:

(1) Vehicular homicide.
(2) Vehicular negligent injuring.
(3) Unauthorized use of a movable.
(4) Operating a vehicle while intoxicated.
(5) Reckless operation of a vehicle.
(6) Hit and run driving.

(Added by Acts 1991 No. 235, §9, eff. 1/1/92.)

Art. 954. Traffic violations adjudicated on citation; petition not required.

In cases of traffic violations, a petition is not required. The child may be summoned to appear and the case may be instituted with a uniform traffic citation. The citation shall describe in general terms the nature of the violation. The citation or summons may direct the child to bring a parent with him when he appears. *(Added by Acts 1991 No. 235, §9, eff. 1/1/92.)*

CHAPTER 3. JUVENILE TRAFFIC REFEREES

Art. 955. Traffic violations; referral to juvenile traffic referee.

The court may, by local rule, refer cases of traffic violations to a juvenile traffic referee for adjudication and disposition. *(Added by Acts 1991 No. 235, §9, eff. 1/1/92.)*

Art. 956. Authority of juvenile traffic referee.

A. A juvenile traffic referee shall have the authority including but not limited to the following:

(1) To administer oaths.
(2) To compel the attendance of witnesses and issue subpoenas.
(3) To take testimony.
(4) To make a record of the hearing.

B. The referee's exercise of control over traffic proceedings through punishment for contempt of court shall be limited to the following:

(1) The referee may make a recommendation to any judge of the court exercising juvenile jurisdiction that the child be charged with a direct or constructive contempt of court, as otherwise governed by Chapter 2 of Title XV.

(2) Failure to comply with a subpoena, without reasonable excuse, proof of service of which appears of record, constitutes a direct contempt of the court which issued the subpoena. The referee may order the witness attached and brought to court forthwith or on a designated day. If an order of attachment is issued, it may be executed in any parish by the sheriff of the parish from which the attachment was issued, or by the sheriff of the parish where the witness is found.

(Added by Acts 1991 No. 235, §9, eff. 1/1/92.)

CHAPTER 4. APPOINTMENT OF COUNSEL

Art. 957. Appointment of counsel.

The juvenile court or traffic referee may appoint an attorney to represent the child whenever appointment of counsel is required in the interests of justice. *(Added by Acts 1991 No. 235, §9, eff. 1/1/92.)*

CHAPTER 5. DISPOSITION

Art. 958. Disposition immediately following adjudication.

A. In cases of traffic violations, the court or juvenile traffic referee may dispense with a predisposition investigation and enter a judgment of disposition immediately following adjudication if there is sufficient information in the record to enable the court or referee to determine a fair and just disposition of the case.

B. Judgments of disposition in traffic cases may be evidenced by a minute entry.

(Added by Acts 1991 No. 235, §9, eff. 1/1/92.)

Art. 959. Disposition of traffic violations.

If the court or juvenile traffic referee finds that the child committed a traffic violation, the court or referee may:

(1) Suspend the child's driver's license for a specific or indefinite period.

(2) Revoke the child's driver's license.

(3) Restrict the child's driving privileges to driving at specified times, under specified conditions, or for specified purposes.

(4) Order the child to attend traffic school or to receive additional driving instruction.

(5) Order inspection of a motor vehicle and correction of any deficiencies.

(6) Require public liability insurance coverage as a condition of the child's driving.

(7) Impose a fine not exceeding two hundred dollars payable immediately or over a period of time.

(8) Place the child on probation.

(9) Make such other disposition or combination of dispositions as it deems to be in the best interests of the child.

(Added by Acts 1991 No. 235, §9, eff. 1/1/92.)

CHAPTER 6. TRAFFIC CASES HEARD BEFORE JUVENILE TRAFFIC REFEREE; APPEAL TO COURT

Art. 960. Traffic cases heard before juvenile traffic referee; appeal to court.

A. In cases of traffic violations, the child may appeal to the court from a judgment of the juvenile traffic referee. Such an appeal shall be filed within three days of the judgment of disposition.

B. On appeal, the case shall be tried de novo, and there shall be no further appeal.

(Added by Acts 1991 No. 235, §9, eff. 1/1/92.)

TITLE X. JUDICIAL CERTIFICATION OF CHILDREN FOR ADOPTION

(Chgd. by Acts 1997 No. 256, §2, eff. 8/15/97.)

CHAPTER 1. PRELIMINARY PROVISIONS; DEFINITIONS

Art. 1001. Purpose.

The purpose of this Title is to protect children whose parents are unwilling or unable to provide care adequate to meet their physical, emotional, and mental health needs, by providing a judicial process for the termination of all parental rights and responsibilities and for the certification of the child for adoption. In all proceedings, the primary concern is to secure the best interest of the child if a ground justifying termination of parental rights is proved. Termination of parental rights is to be considered the first step toward permanent placement of the child in a suitable home, and if at all possible, to achieve the child's adoption. The procedural provisions of this Title shall be construed liberally. The proceedings shall be conducted expeditiously to avoid delays in resolving the status of the parent and in achieving permanency for children. *(Added by Acts 1991 No. 235, §10; chgd. by Acts 1997 No. 256, §1, eff. 8/15/97.)*

Art. 1001.1. Priority of docketing; adjudication.

Any petition filed and any proceeding held under the provisions of this Title shall be given priority, to the extent practicable, over any other civil action before the court, except emergency proceedings for the protection of the child under Articles 617 through 627, or Domestic Abuse Assistance proceedings under Chapter 8 of Title XV. Any petition filed under the provisions of this Title shall be docketed immediately upon filing, and hearings shall be scheduled for the earliest dates practicable. *(Added by Acts 1997 No. 256, §1, eff. 8/15/97.)*

Art. 1002. General applicability.

Except as otherwise specified in this Title, all provisions of the Children's Code remain applicable. *(Added by Acts 1991 No. 235, §10, eff. 1/1/92.)*

Art. 1003. Definitions.

(1) "Abuse" means any of the following acts which seriously endanger the physical, mental, or emotional health of the child:

(a) The infliction or attempted infliction, or, as a result of inadequate supervision, the allowance or toleration of the infliction or attempted infliction of physical or mental injury upon the child by a parent or any other person.

(b) The exploitation or overwork of a child by a parent or any other person.

(c) The involvement of the child in any sexual act with a parent or any other person, or the aiding or toleration by the parent or the caretaker of the child's sexual involvement with any other person or of the child's involvement in pornographic displays, or any other involvement of a child in sexual activity constituting a crime under the laws of this state.

(2) "Agency" shall include the Department of Social Services, the corresponding department of any other state, and those private agencies and institutions licensed for the placement of children for adoption by the Department of Social Services or by the corresponding department of any other state.

(3) "Child in need of care" means a child adjudicated as such under Title VI.

(4) "Dangerous to others" means the condition of a person whose behavior or significant threats support a reasonable expectation that there is a substantial risk that he will inflict physical harm upon another person in the near future.

(5) "Dangerous to self" means the condition of a person whose behavior, significant threats, or inaction supports a reasonable expectation that there is a substantial risk that he will inflict physical or severe emotional harm upon his own person.

(6) "Department" means the Louisiana Department of Social Services.

(7) "Grave disability" means the condition of a person who is unable to provide for his own basic physical needs, such as essential food, clothing, medical care, and shelter, as a result of serious mental illness or substance abuse and is unable to survive safely in freedom or protect himself from serious harm. The term also includes incapacitation by alcohol, which means the condition of a person who, as a result of the use of alcohol, is unconscious or whose judgment is otherwise so impaired that he is incapable of realizing and making a rational decision with respect to his need for treatment.

(8) "Mental deficiency" means significantly subaverage intellectual functioning existing concurrently with deficits in adaptive behavior, as determined by a psychiatrist or psychologist and manifested during the developmental period.

(9) "Mental illness" means a psychiatric disorder which has substantial adverse effects on the parent's ability to function and which requires care and treatment as determined by a psychiatrist or psychologist. It does not include a person suffering solely from mental retardation, epilepsy, alcoholism, or drug abuse.

(10) "Neglect" means the refusal or failure of a parent or caretaker to supply the child with necessary food, clothing, shelter, care, treatment, or counseling for any injury, illness, or condition of the child, as a result of which the child's physical, mental, or emotional health is substantially threatened or impaired. Whenever, in lieu of medical care, a child is being provided treatment in accordance with the tenets of a well-recognized religious method of healing which has a reasonable, proven record of success, the child shall not, for that reason alone, be considered to be neglected or abused. Disagreement by the parent regarding the need for medical care shall not, by itself, be grounds for termination of parental rights. However, nothing herein shall prohibit the court from ordering medical services for the child when there is substantial risk of harm to the child's health or welfare.

(11) "Permanent placement" means either placement of the child under a guardianship of the person or placement of the child with adoptive parents pursuant to a final decree of adoption.

(12) "Starvation" means mistreatment causing suffering from extreme hunger or malnourishment.

(13) "Substance abuse" means the condition of a person who uses narcotic, stimulant, depressant, soporific, tranquilizing, or hallucinogenic drugs or alcohol to the extent that it renders the person dangerous to himself or others or renders the person gravely disabled.

(14) "Torture" means torment, maiming, mutilation, or ritualistic or malicious acts causing extreme and unjustifiable physical or mental pain or suffering, disfigurement, or injury.

(Added by Acts 1991 No. 235, §10; chgd. by Acts 1992 No. 705, §1; Acts 1997 No. 256, §1, eff. 8/15/97.)

Art. 1004. Who may file.

A. At any time, including in any hearing in a child in need of care proceeding, the court on its own motion may order the filing of a petition on any ground authorized by Article 1015.

B. Counsel appointed for the child pursuant to Article 607 may petition for the termination of parental rights of the parent of the child if the petition alleges a ground authorized by Article 1015(4), (5), or (6) and, although eighteen months have elapsed since the date of the child's adjudication as a child in need of care, no petition has been filed by the district attorney or the department.

C. The district attorney may petition for the termination of parental rights of the parent of the child on any ground authorized by Article 1015.

D. The department may petition for the termination of parental rights of the parent of the child when the child has been abandoned and termination is authorized by Article 1015(4), when as a result of a prior child in need of care disposition, termination is authorized by Article 1015(5), or when the child is in foster care because the parent is incarcerated and termination is authorized by Article 1015(6).

E. When termination is authorized by Article 1015, other than on the grounds specified by Paragraph D of this Article, by special appointment, the district attorney may designate counsel for the department as a special assistant authorized to act in his stead in all such termination actions or in a particular case.

F. By special appointment for a particular case, the court or the district attorney may designate private counsel authorized to petition for the termination of parental rights of the parent of the child on the ground of abandonment authorized by Article 1015(4).

(Added by Acts 1991 No. 235, §10; chgd. by Acts 1992 No. 705, §1; Acts 1997 No. 256, §1, eff. 8/15/97.)

Art. 1005. Persons subject to proceedings.

Any parent may be subject to proceedings under this Title and shall have juridical capacity for such proceedings regardless of age or matrimonial status. *(Added by Acts 1991 No. 235, §10, eff. 1/1/92.)*

CHAPTER 2. VENUE

Art. 1006. Venue.

A proceeding under this Title may be commenced in the parish in which the child is domiciled with his parent or tutor, the parish in which the child was present when an act alleged in the petition took place or conditions alleged in the petition existed, or the parish in which the child is found. *(Added by Acts 1991 No. 235, §10; chgd. by Acts 1992 No. 705, §1, eff. 7/6/92.)*

CHAPTER 3. CONFIDENTIALITY OF RECORDS; DUTIES OF COURT CLERKS; DISCLOSURE PROCEEDINGS

Art. 1007. Court records of proceedings.

All records and reports which result from proceedings held pursuant to the provisions of this Title are confidential and shall not be disclosed except as otherwise provided by this Chapter, by Chapter 7 of this Title, or as may be necessary to facilitate any order for continued contact as authorized by Article 1037.1. *(Added by Acts 1991 No. 235, §10; chgd. by Acts 1997 No. 256, §1, eff. 8/15/97.)*

Art. 1008. Duties of court clerks.

The clerks of the courts having proper jurisdiction over proceedings under this Title shall keep separate indices of all suits filed in accordance with this Title and shall index such suits in the name of the parents and in the name of the child. These records are subject to the confidentiality requirements of this Chapter. *(Added by Acts 1991 No. 235, §10; chgd. by Acts 1992 No. 705, §1, eff. 7/6/92.)*

Art. 1009. Disclosure of information in court records.

A. A child whose parent's rights have been terminated and who has not been subsequently adopted may have access to the records of the termination of parental rights action as provided by Chapter 3 of Title IV.

B. A child whose parent's rights have been terminated and who has been subsequently adopted may have access to the records of the termination of parental rights action only as provided by Articles 1010 through 1013.

(Added by Acts 1991 No. 235, §10; chgd. by Acts 1997 No. 256, §1, eff. 8/15/97.)

Art. 1010. Petitions for disclosure.

The child or if still a minor, his legal representative on his behalf, may file a petition for disclosure of information pertaining to the termination of parental rights proceeding. The action shall be styled: "In re the termination of parental rights to _____." *(Added by Acts 1991 No. 235, §10, eff. 1/1/92.)*

Art. 1011. Grounds for disclosure.

The petition must show compelling necessity overriding the general policy of confidentiality for termination of parental rights records by demonstrating any of the following:

(1) That there are inheritance rights which are or may be due from his biological parents under Civil Code Article 214.

(2) That there is a medical necessity requiring information about his biological family or his own health history in order to treat the petitioner or his descendants.

(3) That both he and a person reasonably believed to be his biological parent have registered with the department pursuant to Chapter 14 of Title XII.

(4) That such information is otherwise required to be disclosed by federal or state law. *(Added by Acts 1991 No. 235, §10; chgd. by Acts 1992 No. 705, §1, eff. 7/6/92.)*

Art. 1012. Authority of the court.

Upon reviewing a petition for disclosure, the court may deny it for lack of a proper showing of compelling necessity. Before granting a petition, the court may appoint a curator ad hoc and shall set the petition for a hearing. *(Added by Acts 1991 No. 235, §10; chgd. by Acts 1992 No. 705, §1, eff. 7/6/92.)*

Art. 1013. Duties of a curator ad hoc.

A. Upon appointment, the curator ad hoc shall be responsible for all of the following:

(1) Securing all records pertaining to the petitioner's request through subpoenas duces tecum or other discovery process, if necessary.

(2) Reviewing all records pertaining to the termination of parental rights proceeding.

(3) Reporting to the court any objections to disclosure which he may have received from a custodian of records.

(4) After the records review is completed, recommending the granting or denial of the petitioner's request and particularizing the necessary scope of any disclosure order for the court's consideration.

B. A person proceeding in forma pauperis shall receive the services of the curator ad hoc without having to pay the curator's fees. However, in all cases, the curator shall be entitled to a reasonable fee for his services, and the court shall fix the fee commensurate with the services performed.

(Added by Acts 1991 No. 235, §10; chgd. by Acts 1992 No. 705, §1, eff. 7/6/92.)

Art. 1014. Orders of disclosure.

After hearing the petitioner, the court may order disclosure. Insofar as possible, an order disclosing information from the court's own records or any records obtained by the curator ad hoc shall contain nonidentifying information about the biological family. If identifying information must be disclosed, the court may release such information to the person requiring it and order that its confidentiality be maintained without disclosure to the petitioner. *(Added by Acts 1991 No. 235, §10, eff. 1/1/92.)*

CHAPTER 4. GROUNDS OF INVOLUNTARY TERMINATION

Article

Art. 1015. Grounds.

The grounds for termination of parental rights are:

(1) Conviction of murder of the child's other parent.

(2) Unjustified intentional killing of the child's other parent.

(3) Misconduct of the parent toward this child or any other child in his household which constitutes extreme abuse, cruel and inhuman treatment, or grossly negligent behavior below a reasonable standard of human decency, including but not limited to any of the following:

(a) Conviction of murder.

(b) Unjustified intentional killing.

(c) Aggravated incest.

(d) Rape.

(e) Sodomy.
(f) Torture.
(g) Starvation.
(h) Abuse or neglect which is life threatening or results in gravely disabling physical or psychological injury or disfigurement.
(i) Abuse or neglect after the child is returned to the parent's care and custody while under department supervision, when the child had previously been removed for his safety from the parent pursuant to a disposition judgment in a child in need of care proceeding.
(j) The parent's parental rights to one or more of the child's siblings have been terminated due to neglect or abuse and prior attempts to rehabilitate the parent have been unsuccessful.
(4) Abandonment of the child by placing him in the physical custody of a nonparent or by otherwise leaving him under circumstances demonstrating an intention to permanently avoid parental responsibility by any of the following:
(a) For a period of at least four months as of the time of the hearing, despite a diligent search, the whereabouts of the child's parent continue to be unknown.
(b) As of the time the petition is filed, the parent has failed to provide significant contributions to the child's care and support for any period of six consecutive months.
(c) As of the time the petition is filed, the parent has failed to maintain significant contact with the child by visiting him or communicating with him for any period of six consecutive months.
(5) Unless sooner permitted by the court, at least one year has elapsed since a child was removed from the parent's custody pursuant to a court order; there has been no substantial parental compliance with a case plan for services which has been previously filed by the department and approved by the court as necessary for the safe return of the child; and despite earlier intervention, there is no reasonable expectation of significant improvement in the parent's condition or conduct in the near future, considering the child's age and his needs for a stable and permanent home.
(6) The child is in the custody of the department pursuant to a court order or placement by the parent; the parent has been convicted and sentenced to a period of incarceration of such duration that the parent will not be able to care for the child for an extended period of time; and despite notice by the department, the parent has refused or failed to provide a reasonable plan for the appropriate care of the child other than foster care.
(Added by Acts 1991 No. 235, §10; chgd. by Acts 1997 No. 256, §1, eff. 8/15/97.)

CHAPTER 5. RIGHT TO COUNSEL

Art. 1016. Right to counsel.

A. The child and the parent shall each have the right to be represented by separate counsel in a termination proceeding brought under this Title.
B. The court shall appoint an attorney to represent the child in such a proceeding.
C. If the court determines that the parent is indigent and unable to employ counsel solely for that reason, an attorney shall be appointed to represent the parent in accordance with Article 320.
(Added by Acts 1991 No. 235, §10, eff. 1/1/92.)

CHAPTER 6. PREHEARING PROCEDURE

Art. 1017. Petition.

A proceeding under this Title shall be commenced by petition. *(Added by Acts 1991 No. 235, §10, eff. 1/1/92.)*

Art. 1018. Form of petition.

A. The petition shall contain a caption setting forth the name of the court and the title of the action. The petition shall be entitled, "The State of Louisiana in the Interest of . . .".

B. Allegations of fact shall be simple, concise, and direct and shall be set forth in numbered paragraphs. As far as practicable, each paragraph shall be limited to a single set of circumstances.

C. The petition shall be verified. Allegations of fact may be made on information and belief.

D. Failure to comply with formal requirements of this Article shall not be grounds for dismissal of a petition or invalidation of the proceedings unless it results in substantial prejudice.

(Added by Acts 1991 No. 235, §10, eff. 1/1/92.)

Art. 1019. Contents of the petition.

A. The petition shall set forth with specificity:

(1) The name, date, and place of birth, sex, race, and address of the child. If the child is in a foster home, the identification of the parish in which he resides shall suffice for his address.

(2) The name and current address of the child's parents.

(3) The name, age, and sex of any other biological relatives of the child who are currently living with the child in his home.

(4) The name of any public institution or agency having the responsibility or ability to supply services alleged to be needed by the family.

B. If any of the information required by Paragraph A of this Article is unknown, the petition shall so allege. Any defects in the information required by Paragraph A of this Article shall be considered defects of form.

C. The petition shall allege facts which constitute the grounds necessary for the termination of parental rights as set forth in Article 1015.

(Added by Acts 1991 No. 235, §10; chgd. by Acts 1997 No. 256, §1, eff. 8/15/97.)

Art. 1020. Notice of right to counsel and effect of termination judgment; form.

Notice shall be issued by the clerk and served, together with a copy of the petition, on every parent against whom a proceeding is instituted under this Title and shall state:

"NOTICE

Louisiana law provides that you can permanently lose your rights as a parent. A petition has been filed requesting the court to terminate your parental rights to your child. A copy of the petition is attached to this notice. A court hearing of your case has been scheduled for the ____ day of ______, ____, at the ______ division of ______ court in the parish of ______. At this hearing, you will be asked to answer the petition by either admitting or denying the truth of the facts stated in the petition. If you admit those facts, you may also consent to the termination of your parental rights at this hearing. If you deny any or all of those facts, you will be given a date to return for a trial. If you fail to appear, the court can terminate your rights despite your absence. If the court at the trial finds that the facts set out in the petition are true and that termination of your rights will serve the best interests of your child, the court can enter a judgment ending your rights to your child. If the judgment terminates your parental rights, you will no longer have any rights to visit or to have custody of your child, or make any decisions affecting your child. Your child will be legally freed to be adopted by someone else. This is a very serious matter. You should contact a lawyer immediately so that you can be prepared for the court hearing. You have the right to hire a lawyer and to have him or her represent you. If you cannot afford to hire a lawyer, you may call the telephone number on the attached form for information concerning free legal aid. If free legal aid is not available, the court will appoint a lawyer at the scheduled hearing if the court finds that you are unable to pay some or all of the costs. Whether or not you decide to hire an attorney, you have the right to attend the hearing of your case, to call witnesses on your behalf, and to question those witnesses brought against you. If you have any questions concerning this notice, you may call the telephone number of the clerk's office which is _________ ."

(Added by Acts 1991 No. 235, §10; chgd. by Acts 1993 No. 634, §1; Acts 1997 No. 256, §1, eff. 8/15/97.)

Art. 1021. Service; resident parent.

If a parent against whom a proceeding is instituted resides within the state, service of citation shall be made either personally or by domiciliary service not less than five days prior to commencement of the hearing on the matter. *(Added by Acts 1991 No. 235, §10, eff. 1/1/92.)*

Art. 1022. Service; nonresident parent.

If a parent against whom a proceeding is instituted does not reside within this state, service of citation shall be made by registered mail to the address indicated in the petition, return receipt required, not less than five days prior to commencement of the hearing on the matter. *(Added by Acts 1991 No. 235, §10, eff. 1/1/92.)*

Art. 1023. Service; absentee parent.

A. If the parent against whom a proceeding is instituted cannot be served in accordance with either Article 1021 or 1022, the court shall appoint an attorney at law as curator ad hoc for the parent and service of citation shall be made upon the curator ad hoc.

B. Upon appointment of the curator ad hoc, a copy of the order of appointment shall be forwarded to the department.

C. The fee and costs of the curator ad hoc shall be paid by the petitioner, any law to the contrary notwithstanding.

(Added by Acts 1991 No. 235, §10; chgd. by Acts 1993 No. 634, §1, eff. 6/15/93.)

Art. 1024. Duties of curator ad hoc.

A. The curator ad hoc shall make a diligent effort to locate the parent and notify him of the pendency and nature of the proceedings. Such notice shall include:

(1) The allegations made against the parent.

(2) The right of the parent to appear at the hearing, to defend against the allegations, and to compel the attendance of witnesses on his behalf.

(3) The right of the parent to retain counsel.

B. If the curator ad hoc fails to locate the parent, the curator ad hoc shall attend the hearing of this matter, submit a note of evidence on the record indicating the efforts made to locate the parent, and proceed contradictorily unless the parent is subsequently served or waives objection to jurisdiction. Proceedings held contradictorily with the curator ad hoc shall be of full force and legal effect against the parent.

C. If the parent is served in accordance with either Article 1021 or 1022 or is located by the curator ad hoc, the curator ad hoc shall attend the hearing and submit a note of evidence on the record indicating the efforts made to locate the parent.

(Added by Acts 1991 No. 235, §10; chgd. by Acts 1997 No. 578, §4, eff. 8/15/97.)

Art. 1025. Duty of department to provide information concerning the parent's location.

Notwithstanding any provision of the law to the contrary, the department shall provide to the curator ad hoc all available information pertinent to the location of an absentee parent, including names and addresses of known relatives, within fifteen days of receipt of a copy of the court order appointing the curator ad hoc. *(Added by Acts 1991 No. 235, §10, eff. 1/1/92.)*

Art. 1025.1. Appearance to answer petition.

A. The court shall require the parent to appear in person to answer the petition within fifteen days after the filing of the petition.

B. The court may also permit the parent to consent to judgment in accordance with Article 1025.2 or execute a surrender for adoption in accordance with Article 1122.

C. At the appearance the court may either convene immediately the pre-hearing conference required by Article 1025.4 or set a date for the conference.

(Added by Acts 1997 No. 256, §1, eff. 8/15/97.)

Art. 1025.2. Stipulation; consent to judgment; resident, nonresident parents.

The parent whose rights are sought to be terminated may stipulate that the grounds alleged in the petition are true provided that all of the following occur:

(1) He personally appears before the court. A parent who resides either in another parish or in another state may personally appear before the court exercising juvenile court jurisdiction in his place of residence.

(2) The court fully informs him of his rights and the consequences of such a stipulation.

(3) The parent knowingly and voluntarily consents to the judgment.

(Added by Acts 1991 No. 235, §10; redesignated from article 1033 and chgd. by Acts 1997 No. 256, §1, eff. 8/15/97.)

Art. 1025.3. Failure to appear at appearance to answer.

A. If, after proper service, the parent fails to appear before the court to answer the petition as required by Article 1025.1(A), the court shall set the date for the termination of parental rights hearing as required by Article 1031.

B. Notice of the hearing date shall be sent to the nonappearing parent by either registered or certified mail, return receipt requested, postage prepaid, to the addressee only.

(Added by Acts 1997 No. 256, §1, eff. 8/15/97.)

Art. 1025.4. Pre-hearing and scheduling conference; order.

A. At the appearance, on its own motion or on motion of counsel, the court shall direct counsel for the petitioner, for the parents, and for the child to appear before it for a conference to consider the following:

(1) The simplification of the issues including the elimination of frivolous claims or defenses.

(2) The necessity or desirability of amendments to the petition.

(3) What material facts and issues exist without substantial controversy, and what material facts and issues are actually and in good faith controverted.

(4) Proof, stipulations regarding the authenticity of documents, and advance rulings from the court on the admissibility of evidence.

(5) Limitations or restrictions on or regulation of the use of expert testimony under Louisiana Code of Evidence Article 702.

(6) The control and scheduling of discovery.

(7) The identification of witnesses, documents, and exhibits.

(8) Such other matters as may aid in the disposition of the action.

B. The court shall render an order which recites the action taken at the conference, the amendments allowed to the petition, and the agreements made by the parties as to any of the matters considered, and which limits the issues for adjudication to those not disposed of by admissions or agreements of counsel. Such order controls the subsequent course of the action, unless modified at the termination of parental rights hearing to prevent manifest injustice.

C. If a party's attorney fails to obey a pre-hearing order, or to appear at the pre-hearing and scheduling conference, or is substantially unprepared to participate in the conference, or fails to participate in good faith, the court, upon its own motion or on the motion of a party, after hearing, may make such orders as are just, including orders provided in Code of Civil Procedure Article 1471(2), (3), and (4). In lieu of or in addition to any other sanction, the court may require the party or the attorney representing the party or both to pay the reasonable expenses incurred by noncompliance with this Paragraph, including attorney fees.

(Added by Acts 1997 No. 256, §1, eff. 8/15/97.)

CHAPTER 7. SPECIAL MOTIONS AND DISCOVERY

Article

Art. 1026. Medical examinations.

A. Upon motion of any party or the court, the court may order physical or mental examination or evaluation of any party whose mental or physical condition is in controversy in accordance with the provisions of Article 1464 of the Louisiana Code of Civil Procedure.

B. The cost of any ordered examination or evaluation shall be paid by the moving party unless apportioned by the court, in its discretion, to any other party or parties.

C. The information obtained by an examination or evaluation ordered pursuant to this Article shall not be admissible in any subsequent proceeding for any purpose including impeachment.

(Added by Acts 1991 No. 235, §10, eff. 1/1/92.)

Art. 1027. Discovery rights; access to department records.

A. Counsel for any child who is the subject of these proceedings shall have access to records of the department in accordance with R.S. 46:56(F).

B. A parent against whom proceedings are instituted in accordance with this Title shall have access to records of the department except the identity of the reporter of child abuse or neglect and the work product or writing reflecting the mental impressions, conclusions, opinions, or theories of an attorney or expert.

(Added by Acts 1991 No. 235, §10, eff. 1/1/92.)

Art. 1028. Restrictive order.

The department may move, showing good cause, to limit parental access to particular information. After a contradictory hearing, if the court determines that the information is protected or that the need for confidentiality outweighs the needs of the parent to prepare adequately for trial, the court may issue an appropriate restrictive order. *(Added by Acts 1991 No. 235, §10; chgd. by Acts 1992 No. 705, §1, eff. 7/6/92.)*

Art. 1029. Intervention.

No person shall be allowed to intervene in a proceeding brought under this Title. *(Added by Acts 1991 No. 235, §10, eff. 1/1/92.)*

Art. 1030. Suspension of right of voluntary surrender of parental rights by initiation of termination proceeding.

Once a petition to terminate parental rights has been filed, the parent is thereafter without authority to execute an act of surrender or otherwise to affect the custody of the child except:

(1) The parent may execute an act of surrender in favor of the department with the approval of the court.

(2) The parent may consent to a judgment terminating his parental rights as provided in Article 1033*.

**Former article 1033 was redesignated as article 1025.2.*
(Added by Acts 1991 No. 235, §10, eff. 1/1/92.)

CHAPTER 8. HEARING

Art. 1031. Time for setting termination of parental rights hearing.

The termination of parental rights hearing shall commence within sixty days after the date set for the appearance to answer the petition. *(Added by Acts 1991 No. 235, §10; chgd. by Acts 1992 No. 705, §1; Acts 1997 No. 256, §1, eff. 8/15/97.)*

Art. 1032. Continuances.

Upon a showing of good cause and notice to the opposing party, the court may grant, deny, or restrict a requested continuance of the proceeding. The court shall avoid delays in resolving the status of the parent and in achieving permanency for the child. *(Added by Acts 1991 No. 235, §10; chgd. by Acts 1997 No. 256, §1, eff. 8/15/97.)*

Art. 1033. Effect of nonappearance.

If it appears from the record that the parent has been served in accordance with Article 1021 or 1022 or has been located and notified in accordance with Article 1020 and the parent fails to appear at the hearing, then the hearing shall be held in the parent's absence and the petitioner shall be required to establish prima facie proof of the allegations contained in the petition. *(Added by Acts 1991 No. 235, §10, eff. 1/1/92; redesignated from article 1034 by Acts 1997 No. 256, §1, eff. 8/15/97. Former article 1033 was redesignated as article 1025.2 by Acts 1997 No. 256, §1, eff. 8/15/97.)*

Art. 1034. Right to present evidence and examine witnesses.

A. Among other rights expressly guaranteed by this Title or by due process of law, at the hearing the parent may introduce evidence, call witnesses, be heard on his own behalf, and cross-examine witnesses called by the petitioner or the child.

B. Among other rights expressly guaranteed by this Title or by due process of law, at the hearing the child may introduce evidence, call witnesses, and cross-examine witnesses called by the petitioner or by the parent.

C. If competent, the child may be heard on his own behalf. Any testimony given by a child may be taken by a videotaped interview or by closed circuit television, as authorized by Title 3, Chapter 8 of this Code, or by an in-chambers conference attended only by the judge and court reporter and by counsel for the child, for the petitioner, and for the parents.

D. Testimony or other evidence relevant to the abuse or neglect of a child or the cause of such condition may not be excluded on any ground of privilege, except in the case of communications between an attorney and his client or communications between a priest, rabbi, duly ordained minister, or Christian Science practitioner and his communicant.

(Added by Acts 1997 No. 256, §1, eff. 8/15/97. Former article 1034 was redesignated as article 1033 by Acts 1997 No. 256, §1, eff. 8/15/97.)

Art. 1035. Burden of proof.

A. The petitioner bears the burden of establishing each element of a ground for termination of parental rights by clear and convincing evidence.

B. The parent asserting a mental or physical disability as an affirmative defense to abandonment under Article 1015(4) bears the burden of proof by a preponderance of the evidence.

(Added by Acts 1991 No. 235, §10; chgd. by Acts 1997 No. 256, §1, eff. 8/15/97.)

Art. 1036. Proof of parental misconduct.

A. The admissibility of the conviction of a parent is governed by the Code of Evidence.

B. A prior conviction may be proved by certified copy of the judgment of conviction or certified copy of the minute entry of conviction.

C. Under Article 1015(5), lack of parental compliance with a case plan may be evidenced by one or more of the following:

(1) The parent's failure to attend court-approved scheduled visitations with the child.

(2) The parent's failure to communicate with the child.

(3) The parent's failure to keep the department apprised of the parent's whereabouts and significant changes affecting the parent's ability to comply with the case plan for services.

(4) The parent's failure to contribute to the costs of the child's foster care, if ordered to do so by the court when approving the case plan.

(5) The parent's repeated failure to comply with the required program of treatment and rehabilitation services provided in the case plan.

(6) The parent's lack of substantial improvement in redressing the problems preventing reunification.

(7) The persistence of conditions that led to removal or similar potentially harmful conditions.

D. Under Article 1015(5), lack of any reasonable expectation of significant improvement in the parent's conduct in the near future may be evidenced by one or more of the following:

(1) Any physical or mental illness, mental deficiency, substance abuse, or chemical dependency that renders the parent unable or incapable of exercising parental responsibilities without exposing the child to a substantial risk of serious harm, based upon expert opinion or based upon an established pattern of behavior.

(2) A pattern of repeated incarceration of the parent that has rendered the parent unable to care for the immediate and continuing physical or emotional needs of the child for extended periods of time.

(3) Any other condition or conduct that reasonably indicates that the parent is unable or unwilling to provide an adequate permanent home for the child, based upon expert opinion or based upon an established pattern of behavior.

E. Under Article 1015(6), a sentence of at least five years of imprisonment raises a presumption of the parent's inability to care for the child for an extended period of time, although the incarceration of a parent shall not in and of itself be sufficient to deprive a parent of his parental rights.

(Added by Acts 1991 No. 235, §10; chgd. by Acts 1997 No. 256, §1, eff. 8/15/97.)

Art. 1036.1. Proof of prior child in need of care judgment, stipulation; record.

A. Evidence of a prior adjudication or a parent's prior stipulation that a child is in need of care and an instanter order or disposition judgment removing the child from the parent's custody shall be admissible in proceedings brought under this Title. If the prior adjudication judgment was entered by the same court, it may take judicial notice of its own records. If the prior order or judgment was entered by another court, a certified copy of the order or judgment or certified copy of the minute entry shall be admissible in accordance with the Louisiana Code of Evidence.

B. The court record of a prior child in need of care proceeding involving the child who is the subject of the termination proceeding may be introduced into evidence at the hearing on the termination of parental rights.

(Added by Acts 1997 No. 256, §1, eff. 8/15/97.)

CHAPTER 9. JUDGMENTS

Art. 1037. Findings and contents of termination judgment.

A. When the court finds that the alleged grounds set out in any Paragraph of Article 1015 are proven true by the evidentiary standards required by Article 1035 and that it is in the best interest of the child, it shall order the termination of the parental rights of the parent against whom the allegations are proven.

B. A judgment terminating the parental rights of the parent shall inform the parent of his right to use the services of the voluntary registry as provided in Chapter 15 of Title XII. Failure to include such information shall not affect the validity of the termination judgment.

C. A judgment terminating the parental rights of the parent shall grant custody of the child to the department or other suitable person.

D. The judgment shall also certify the child for adoption if, as a result of proceedings pursuant to this Title or Titles XI and XII, the rights of all parents as defined by Article 1193 have been terminated or relinquished.

(Added by Acts 1991 No. 235, §10; chgd. by Acts 1992 No. 705, §1; Acts 1997 No. 256, §1, eff. 8/15/97.)

Art. 1037.1. Continued contact with biological relatives.

A. Subsequent to a termination of parental rights judgment when custody is granted to the department, counsel for the child or for the department on behalf of the child may move for an order providing for continued contact between the child and the parent, sibling, or other biological relative. The court may provide for such continued contact if it finds that it would serve the best interests of the child. The court may receive expert testimony on the issue of continued contact.

B. Any order of continued contact remains modifiable and shall be reviewed in the subsequent hearings required by Chapter 10 of this Title.
(Added by Acts 1997 No. 256, §1, eff. 8/15/97.)

Art. 1038. Effects of termination judgment.

A final judgment terminating parental rights relieves the child and the parent against whom the judgment is rendered of all of their legal duties and divests them of all of their legal rights with regard to one another except as provided in Article 1037.1, and except:

(1) The right of the child to inherit from his biological parents and other relatives.

(2) The right of the child to benefits due him from any third person, agency, state, or the United States based on his status as a child of his biological parents or the rights and benefits that a native American derives from his descent from a member of a federally recognized Indian Tribe.

(3) The right of the child to pursue any civil action, other than future child support, against his biological parents.
(Added by Acts 1991 No. 235, §10; chgd. by Acts 1997 No. 256, §1, eff. 8/15/97.)

Art. 1039. Other dispositions.

If the court finds that the alleged grounds are not proven in accordance with the evidentiary standards set forth in Article 1035 or if the court finds that termination of parental rights is not in the best interests of the child, the court may:

(1) Dismiss the petition.

(2) Reinstate the parent to full care and custody of the child.

(3) If the child has been previously adjudicated as a child in need of care, reinstate that proceeding pursuant to Title VI.

(4) Upon a showing of sufficient facts, adjudicate the child in need of care in accordance with Title VI.

(5) Upon a showing of sufficient facts, adjudicate the family in need of services in accordance with Title VII.

(6) Make any other disposition that is in the best interest of the child.
(Added by Acts 1991 No. 235, §10, eff. 1/1/92.)

CHAPTER 10. PERMANENT PLACEMENT

Art. 1040. Report.

Following a judgment terminating all parental rights pursuant to this Title, when the department is the legal custodian of the child, the department shall report to the court in detail upon the effecting of a permanent placement for the child. *(Added by Acts 1991 No. 235, §10, eff. 1/1/92.)*

Art. 1041. Registration.

A. If no permanent placement has been made within ninety days of such a judgment, the child shall be registered by the appropriate child placement agency involved or the state child placement agency with the Louisiana Adoption Resource Exchange within the department. Any such registration shall not include the surname of the child or otherwise reveal the identities of the blood parents of the child.

B. The department shall maintain a list of the registered children. Such list shall be updated quarterly and made available to all licensed child placement agencies in the state. Subject to the confidentiality requirements of all adoption matters, the department shall use every reasonable method of effecting a permanent placement. Media presentation of available children and other means of public solicitation for the purpose of matching potential adoptive parents with available children shall be used only in cases involving a child who is difficult to

place for adoption, subject to rules and regulations adopted pursuant to the Administrative Procedure Act*.
**R.S. 49:950 et seq.*
(Added by Acts 1991 No. 235, §10, eff. 1/1/92.)

Art. 1042. Review; counsel for child.
A. If no permanent placement has been made within ninety days of such a judgment, review hearings shall be held in accordance with the provisions of Chapters 15 and 16 of Title VI.
B. Any attorney appointed to represent the child in the termination action shall continue to represent the child in all subsequent review hearings until the child is permanently placed. *(Added by Acts 1991 No. 235, §10; chgd. by Acts 1995 No. 1095, §4, eff. 8/15/95.)*

Art. 1043. Adoption; voluntary registration by child and parents whose parental rights have been terminated.
Parents whose rights have been terminated and an adopted child are permitted to use the services of the voluntary registry as provided in Chapter 15 of Title XII. *(Added by Acts 1991 No. 235, §10, eff. 1/1/92.)*

TITLE XI. SURRENDER OF PARENTAL RIGHTS

Chapter

CHAPTER 1. PRELIMINARY PROVISIONS; DEFINITIONS

Article

Art. 1101. Purpose.
Except as otherwise provided in Articles 1195 and 1196, this Title provides the exclusive means by which a parent can voluntarily relinquish his parental rights to a child for the ultimate purpose of adoption. *(Added by Acts 1991 No. 235, §11, eff. 1/1/92.)*

Art. 1102. General applicability.
Except as otherwise specified in this Title, all provisions of the Children's Code remain applicable. *(Added by Acts 1991 No. 235, §11, eff. 1/1/92.)*

Art. 1103. Definitions.
As used in this Title:
(1) "Agency" includes the Department of Social Services, the corresponding department of any other state, and those private agencies and institutions licensed for the placement of children for adoption by the Department of Social Services or by the corresponding department of any other state.

(2) "Birth certificate" means the child's official birth certificate or a true copy of a prefiled version of the birth certificate in the event the official birth certificate has not yet been issued.

(3) "Child" means a person under seventeen years of age and not emancipated by marriage.

(4) "Department" means the Louisiana Department of Social Services.

(5) "Parental fitness" means:

(a) That a parent has not abused the child. For purposes of this Paragraph, abuse means the infliction of physical or mental injury which causes deterioration to the child, sexual abuse, exploitation, or overworking of a child to such an extent that his health or moral or emotional well-being is endangered.

(b) That a parent has consistently offered to provide reasonably necessary food, clothing, appropriate shelter, or treatment for the child. For purposes of this Paragraph, treatment means medical care or other health services provided in accordance with the tenets of a well-recognized religious method of healing with a reasonable, proven record of success.

(c) That a parent suffers from no medical or emotional illness, mental deficiency, behavior or conduct disorder, severe physical disability, substance abuse, or chemical dependency which makes him unable or unwilling to provide an adequate permanent home for the child at the present time or in the reasonably near future based upon expert opinion or based upon an established pattern of behavior.

(d) Viewed in its entirety, the parent's past or present conduct, including his criminal convictions, would not pose a risk of substantial harm to the physical, mental, or emotional health of the child.

(6) "Putative father registry" means the Louisiana putative father registry established in Part I-C of Chapter 1 of Code Title VII of Code Book I of Title 9 of the Louisiana Revised Statutes of 1950, comprised of R.S. 9:400 and 400.1.

(Added by Acts 1991 No. 235, §11; chgd. by Acts 1992 No. 705, §1; Acts 1997 No. 797, §1, eff. 8/15/97.)

Art. 1104. Nature of surrender.

A. To the extent there are special provisions set forth in this Title, a voluntary act of surrender executed pursuant to this Title is subject to the provisions herein and not to conventional obligations law.

B. The act of surrender shall be presumptive evidence of a legal and voluntary surrender only if it contains every element required by Article 1122, and is in all other respects executed in accordance with the provisions of this Title.

(Added by Acts 1991 No. 235, §11; chgd. by Acts 1993 No. 634, §1, eff. 6/15/93.)

CHAPTER 2. DUTIES OF COURT CLERKS; CONFIDENTIALITY

Article

Art. 1105. Recordkeeping generally.

The clerks of the respective juvenile courts shall open separate records and keep separate indices of all documents filed in accordance with this Title. All such records shall be indexed in the name of the child and shall be subject to disclosure only as provided in this Title. *(Added by Acts 1991 No. 235, §11, eff. 1/1/92.)*

Art. 1106. Recordation of acknowledgment by authentic act, legitimation by authentic act, and judgments of filiation.

A. Acknowledgment of a child by authentic act or legitimation by authentic act of a child may be evidenced by proof of its filing. If the child is born in Louisiana, and the acknowledgment or legitimation is by authentic act, it must be recorded in the office of the clerk of court in the parish in which the child is born in order for the father to be accorded the rights afforded by Article 1193.

B. All acknowledgments by authentic act or legitimations by authentic act recorded pursuant to this Article shall indicate the name of the child, the child's date of birth, if known, the name of the mother, and the full name and address of the acknowledging or legitimating father.

C. A judgment of filiation rendered by a court which recognizes a father as having either formally or informally acknowledged an illegitimate child and in which the father is adjudged the parent of the child shall also be filed and recorded in the office of the clerk of court in the parish in which the child is born, if born in this state, or if the child was born in another state, in the parish in which the child is domiciled at the time of the judgment.

D. The clerk of court shall issue, on request, a certificate indicating whether any act of acknowledgment, legitimation by authentic act, or any filiation judgment has been recorded relative to a particular child. If such an act has been recorded, the clerk shall include on the certificate the name and address of the father, the name of the notary, and the date of recordation of the certificate. Records of requests for certificates and copies of certificates issued shall be maintained in confidential records and shall not be open to public inspection. The acts recorded, however, shall be made available only upon motion and order for good cause shown. Certifications shall be issued to the department, other adoption agencies, and the courts of this state at no charge. The clerk may assess reasonable charges for copies of the certificate requested by other persons or agencies.

E. For purposes of this Article, "clerk of court" means the clerk of court in the parish in which the child was born. However, "clerk of court" means only the following clerks of court in the following parishes:

(1) In the parish of Caddo, the clerk of the Caddo Parish Juvenile Court.
(2) In the parish of East Baton Rouge, the clerk of the East Baton Rouge Juvenile Court.
(3) In the parish of Jefferson, the clerk of the Jefferson Parish Juvenile Court.
(4) In the parish of Orleans, the clerk of the Orleans Parish Juvenile Court.

(Added by Acts 1991 No. 235, §11; chgd. by Acts 1993 No. 634, §1, eff. 6/15/93.)

Art. 1107. Confidentiality of records.

A. All records maintained in accordance with this Title shall be confidential and shall not be open to inspection except on written authorization by the court and there shall be no publication.

B. Such written authorization shall be granted only upon a showing of compelling reasons and then only to the extent necessary to satisfy the compelling necessity pursuant to the procedures contained in Articles 1188 through 1192.

(Added by Acts 1991 No. 235, §11, eff. 1/1/92.)

CHAPTER 3. AUTHORITY TO SURRENDER

Art. 1108. Authority to surrender.

A. Subject to the provisions for capacity found in Chapter 4 of this Title any parent may execute a voluntary act of surrender.

B. If the parents are dead or are unknown, the child's tutor may execute the act of surrender for adoption.

(Added by Acts 1991 No. 235, §11, eff. 1/1/92.)

Art. 1109. Domiciliary requirements.

A surrendering parent must be domiciled in this state, unless the person or agency to whom the child is surrendered is domiciled in this state. *(Added by Acts 1991 No. 235, §11, eff. 1/1/92.)*

Art. 1110. Nature of authority.

The surrender of a child for adoption by one parent shall have no effect upon the parental rights of any other parent. *(Added by Acts 1991 No. 235, §11, eff. 1/1/92.)*

CHAPTER 4. CAPACITY TO SURRENDER

Art. 1111. Capacity generally.

Except as provided hereinafter in this Chapter, any parent has the capacity to surrender his or her child for adoption. *(Added by Acts 1991 No. 235, §11, eff. 1/1/92.)*

Art. 1112. Inability due to court intervention.

A. Except as provided herein, a parent may not execute a private surrender once custody of that child has been removed from the parent by order of a juvenile court and the child has been placed in the legal custody of any person or agency or if the child is the subject of a pending termination of parental rights proceeding.

B. Upon notice to the department and after a contradictory hearing, if requested by the department, a parent may, with approval of the court, execute a private surrender of a child in the legal custody of the department to the foster parent with whom the child was placed by the department.

(Added by Acts 1991 No. 235, §11; chgd. by Acts 1992 No. 705, §1, eff. 7/6/92.)

Art. 1113. Minor parents.

A. Except as otherwise provided herein, if a parent executing a surrender is a minor, the parents or tutor of the minor must join in the surrender.

B. When the parents of the minor are separated or divorced, only the parent who has legal custody of the minor must join in the surrender.

C. When the minor's parents or tutor refuse to join in the act or cannot be located, the court may authorize the minor to surrender without the required consent if it finds that the minor is sufficiently mature and well-informed to surrender his child for adoption or that the surrender is otherwise in the child's best interest.

D. When the minor's parents are the parties to whom the child is being surrendered, the court shall authorize the minor to surrender without the required consent if it finds that the minor is sufficiently mature and well-informed to surrender his child for adoption or that the surrender is otherwise in the child's best interest.

E. A minor may surrender to an agency without the consent of the parents or tutor of the minor.

(Added by Acts 1991 No. 235, §11, eff. 1/1/92.)

Art. 1114. Mentally incapacitated parents.

Any parent who has been interdicted or who the court finds to be mentally incapable of giving a knowing and voluntary surrender shall not execute an act of surrender. Any act of surrender executed by an interdicted or mentally incapacitated parent is subject to annulment under Chapter 12 of this Title. *(Added by Acts 1991 No. 235, §11, eff. 1/1/92.)*

CHAPTER 5. AUTHORITY TO ACCEPT SURRENDER

Art. 1115. Authority generally; preplacement approval.

A. A surrender may be made to any person or agency qualified to petition for the adoption of the child.

B. Prior to the execution of a surrender for private adoption pursuant to Chapter 10 of Title XII, each prospective adoptive parent shall obtain preplacement approval as required by Chapter 2 of Title XII.

C. Either a certification for adoption or a court order approving the adoptive placement shall be provided to the attorney for the prospective adoptive parents for filing with the surrender.
(Added by Acts 1991 No. 235, §11, eff. 1/1/92.)

Art. 1116. Agency adoption; acceptance by agency.
In order for a surrender to an agency to be effective, the surrender shall be accepted in writing by the agency in the form of an authentic act. *(Added by Acts 1991 No. 235, §11, eff. 1/1/92.)*

Art. 1117. Domiciliary requirements.
If the surrendering parent is not domiciled in this state, then the agency must be a licensed child placing agency authorized to do business in this state. *(Added by Acts 1991 No. 235, §11, eff. 1/1/92.)*

Art. 1118. Effect of acceptance.
The person or agency to whom a child is surrendered shall exercise all rights and responsibilities as legal custodian of the child. *(Added by Acts 1991 No. 235, §11, eff. 1/1/92.)*

Art. 1119. Anonymity; limitations upon attorney as representative.
A. For purposes of insuring anonymity in private adoptions, an attorney at law licensed to practice in this state may be named in the surrender as representative of the accepting person. The named attorney may facilitate transfer of the child to the accepting person.

B. The attorney shall not be deemed the legal custodian of the child for any reason, including the satisfaction of the domiciliary requirement of Article 1117 of this Title or for the determination of jurisdiction or venue in any subsequent adoption proceeding.

C. The prospective adoptive parent need not be informed of the identity of the surrendering parent nor be shown the petition or other documents connected with the adoption proceeding, including any certification for adoption or court order approving the adoptive placement as required by Chapter 2 of Title XII.
(Added by Acts 1991 No. 235, §11, eff. 1/1/92.)

CHAPTER 6. COUNSELING REQUIREMENTS

Article

Art. 1120. Mental health counseling; affidavit.
A. Prior to the execution of any surrender, a surrendering parent shall submit to a minimum of two counseling sessions relative to the surrender with a licensed social worker, licensed psychologist, licensed psychiatrist, or licensed counselor or a counselor employed by a hospital, accredited mental health center, or licensed child placing agency.

B. The counselor shall execute an affidavit attesting that the surrendering parent attended a minimum of two sessions, and that the surrendering parent appeared to understand the nature of his act.

C. Any surrendering father of a child may waive the counseling otherwise mandated by Paragraph A of this Article. In this case, the attorney or counselor shall execute an affidavit attesting to his waiver.

D. The affidavit of the counselor or attorney shall be attached to the act of surrender.
(Added by Acts 1991 No. 235, §11, eff. 1/1/92.)

Art. 1121. Legal counseling; affidavit.
A. In all private surrenders, the surrendering parent and his representative, if applicable, or the child's tutor, as provided in Article 1108, shall be represented at the execution of the act by an attorney at law licensed to practice law in Louisiana; however, the attorney representing such person shall not be the attorney who represents the person who is the prospective adoptive parent, or an attorney who is an associate, partner, shareholder, or employee of the attorney, law firm, or corporation representing the prospective adoptive parent.

B. Counsel for the surrendering parent shall execute an affidavit of counsel, which shall be attached to the act of surrender.

C. The affidavit of counsel shall recite that counsel for the surrendering parent has fully explained to the parent the nature and effect of the act of surrender and that the parent appeared to understand the explanation given; that the parent freely and voluntarily executed the surrender; and that a copy of the act as executed has been provided to the surrendering parent.

(Added by Acts 1991 No. 235, §11; chgd. by Acts 1993 No. 634, §1, eff. 6/15/93.)

CHAPTER 7. SURRENDER REQUIREMENTS

Art. 1122. Contents of surrender; form.

A. Every act of surrender shall contain the following information:

(1) The name, parish of domicile, age, and marital status of the surrendering parent.

(2) The name and last address, if known, of any other legal or natural parent of the child or a statement that the name or address is not known.

(3) The birth name, place, and date of birth of the child.

(4) The name and address of the person, agency, or representative to whom surrender is made.

(5) The court in which the surrender is to be filed as required by Article 1131.

B. The act of surrender shall also recite the following declarations:

(1) That the act is not being executed earlier than the fifth day following the birth of the child; or, when a father is surrendering earlier than the fifth day following the birth of the child, that the act is being executed earlier than the fifth day following the birth of the child.

(2) That the parent has no mental incapacity and is under no interdiction.

(3) That the parent who is a minor is joined in the act of surrender by the parents or tutor or has written consent of the court, except in acts of surrender to an agency.

(4) That the parent has been informed and understands that upon its execution, his act of surrender is irrevocable, and that his rights as a parent of the child are permanently terminated by execution of the act of surrender unless it is nullified due to fraud or duress or is dissolved by a court of competent jurisdiction.

(5) That the parent freely and voluntarily surrenders custody of the child for the purpose of placement and adoption.

(6) That the parent consents to an adoption which consent is final and irrevocable.

(7) That the parent waives notice and service of any subsequent adoption proceedings.

(8) That the parent has been informed of the provisions of the voluntary registration law, as provided for in Chapter 15 of Title XII, whereby contact can be established between the parent and the surrendered child upon the child's reaching majority.

C. The act of surrender shall recite that the parent has received a minimum of two mental health counseling sessions relative to the surrender with a licensed counselor or a counselor employed by a hospital or accredited mental health center, or that the father has waived such counseling in accordance with the requirements of Article 1120.

D. An act of private surrender shall also recite that the parent has consulted with and been fully advised by an attorney, other than the attorney, associate, partner, shareholder, or employee of the attorney's law firm or corporation for the prospective adoptive parent, about the meaning of these declarations and the effects of the act of surrender in accordance with Article 1123.

E. The act of surrender shall be in authentic form and shall be dated and signed by the surrendering parent, the attorney for the surrendering parent, if applicable, and either the adoptive parent or attorney representing the adoptive parent who wishes to remain anonymous, or a representative of the agency. If required by Article 1113, it shall also be signed by the minor's parents or tutor, or the written consent of the court shall be attached.

F. The Act of Surrender shall contain the requirements in substantially the following form, depending upon whether the surrendering parent is the child's mother or father:

"VOLUNTARY ACT OF SURRENDER FOR ADOPTION
(FOR A SURRENDERING MOTHER OF A CHILD)

STATE OF LOUISIANA

PARISH OF (NAME OF PARISH)

BEFORE ME, the undersigned notary public, and in the presence of the two undersigned competent witnesses who are over the age of eighteen, personally came and appeared:

(NAME OF SURRENDERING MOTHER)

a female of the age of (AGE), who is (MARITAL STATUS), and domiciled in the Parish of (NAME OF PARISH), who being first duly sworn, did depose and state:

(1) She is the mother of (CHILD'S NAME), born on (DATE OF BIRTH) in the (PARISH/COUNTY OF BIRTH), State of (STATE OF BIRTH).

(2) She was married at the birth or conception of the child, or has married subsequent to the child's birth and her husband has acknowledged his paternity of the child. The husband's name is (HUSBAND'S NAME) and his last known address was (ADDRESS OR UNKNOWN).

OR

She was not married at the birth or conception of the child, nor has she, subsequent to the child's birth, married any man who has acknowledged his paternity of the child. To the best of her knowledge, the alleged father has/has not executed a notarial act of acknowledgement/a notarial act of legitimation/a registration with the putative father registry which admitted his paternity of this child. He has/has not informally acknowledged his paternity of this child. His paternity of this child has/has not been established by court judgment.

(3) The other natural/alleged father of the child is (FATHER'S NAME), and his last known address was (ADDRESS OR UNKNOWN).

(4) The person, agency or representative to whom this child is hereby surrendered is (NAME OF PERSON, AGENCY OR REPRESENTATIVE), whose address is (ADDRESS), who hereby accepts this surrender.

(5) The court in which this surrender is to be filed is (NAME OF JUVENILE COURT) located in (CITY AND PARISH OF COURT).

(6) Affiant declares that this Act of Surrender is not being executed earlier than the fifth day following the birth of the child.

(7) Affiant declares that she has no mental incapacity and is under no interdiction.

(8) Affiant declares that she has been informed and understands that her rights as a parent of the child are permanently and irrevocably terminated by execution of this Act of Surrender; however, she understands that it may be declared null due to fraud or duress and may be dissolved if the adoption cannot be accomplished.

(9) Affiant declares that she freely and voluntarily surrenders custody of the child for the purpose of placement and adoption.

(10) Affiant declares that she consents to an adoption, which consent is final and irrevocable upon execution of this surrender.

(11) Affiant declares that she waives notice of the filing and service of any pleading of any sort in any subsequent adoption proceeding regarding the child surrendered.

(12) Affiant declares that she has been informed of the provisions of the voluntary registration law, whereby contact may be established with the surrendered child upon the child's reaching the age of eighteen years.

(13) Affiant declares that she has attended a minimum of two mental health counseling sessions relative to this surrender of her child for adoption.

(ADDITIONAL DECLARATIONS IF THE SURRENDER IS FOR A PRIVATE ADOPTION)

(14) Affiant declares that she is eighteen years of age or older.

OR

Affiant declares that she is under the age of eighteen and that (NAME OF PARENTS OR TUTOR) join in this surrender.

OR

Affiant declares that she is under the age of eighteen and that (NAME OF JUVENILE COURT) located in (CITY AND PARISH OF COURT) has given its written consent for her surrender.

(15) Affiant declares that she has consulted with and been fully advised by an attorney other than the attorney for the prospective adoptive parents about the meaning of these declarations and the consequences of this Act of Surrender.

Sworn to, signed, and notarized, after being carefully read and explained to (NAME OF SURRENDERING PARENT) in the presence of the undersigned notary and witnesses on this _____ day of ______, 19___.

WITNESSES:

____

____

(If agency adoption:)

____
SURRENDERING MOTHER

____
AGENCY REPRESENTATIVE

(If private adoption:)

____
SURRENDERING MOTHER

____
ATTORNEY FOR SURRENDERING MOTHER

____
ADOPTING PARENTS
or

____
ATTORNEY FOR ADOPTIVE PARENTS
(if anonymity to be protected)

(Additional signature(s) in private adoption if the surrendering mother is a minor

____
PARENT(S)/TUTOR OF MINOR
SURRENDERING MOTHER)

____
NOTARY PUBLIC AND SEAL

ATTACHMENTS:
( ) AFFIDAVIT OF MENTAL HEALTH COUNSELOR
( ) STATEMENT OF FAMILY HISTORY

(Required additional attachment if the surrender is for private adoption:
( ) AFFIDAVIT OF ATTORNEY FOR SURRENDERING PARENT)

Required additional attachment if the surrender is by a minor mother whose parent(s) or tutor refuse to join in the Act of Surrender for a private adoption:
( ) (WRITTEN CONSENT OF COURT)"

****

"VOLUNTARY ACT OF SURRENDER FOR ADOPTION
(FOR A SURRENDERING FATHER OF A CHILD)

STATE OF LOUISIANA

PARISH OF (NAME OF PARISH)

BEFORE ME, the undersigned notary public, and in the presence of the two undersigned competent witnesses who are over the age of eighteen, personally came and appeared:

<u>(NAME OF SURRENDERING FATHER)</u>

a male of the age of (AGE), who is (MARITAL STATUS), and domiciled in the Parish of (NAME OF PARISH), who being first duly sworn, did depose and state:

(1) He is the natural/alleged father of (CHILD'S NAME), born on (DATE OF BIRTH) in the (PARISH/COUNTY OF BIRTH), State of (STATE OF BIRTH).

OR

He is the natural/alleged father of the child to be born on or about (PROJECTED DATE OF BIRTH) to (MOTHER'S NAME)

(2) He was not married to the child's mother at the time of the child's birth or conception nor has he subsequently married this child's mother and acknowledged his paternity of the child.

OR

He was married to the child's mother at the time of the child's birth or conception.

OR

He has married this child's mother subsequent to the child's birth and had acknowledged his paternity of the child.

OR

He was not married to and has not married the mother of this child/expected child. He has/has not executed a notarial act of acknowledgement/a notarial act of legitimation/a registration with the putative father registry which admitted his paternity of this child/expected child. He has/has not informally acknowledged his paternity of this child/expected child. His paternity of this child/expected child has/has not been established by court judgment.

(3) The natural mother of the child/expected child is (MOTHER'S NAME), and her last known address was (ADDRESS OR UNKNOWN).

(4) The person, agency or representative to whom this child is hereby surrendered is (NAME OF PERSON, AGENCY OR REPRESENTATIVE), whose address is (ADDRESS), who hereby accepts this surrender.

(5) The court in which this surrender is to be filed is (NAME OF JUVENILE COURT) located in (CITY AND PARISH).

(6) Affiant declares that this Act of Surrender is/is not being executed earlier than the fifth day following the birth of the child.

(7) Affiant declares that he has no mental incapacity and is under no interdiction.

(8) Affiant declares that he has been informed and understands that his rights as a natural parent/alleged parent of the child/expected child less than five days old are permanently and irrevocably terminated on the fifth day following the birth of the child; however, he understands that this Act of Surrender may be declared null due to fraud or duress and may be dissolved if the adoption cannot be accomplished.

OR

Affiant declares that he has been informed and understands that his rights as a natural parent/alleged parent of the child are permanently and irrevocably terminated by execution of this Act of Surrender; however, he understands that it may be declared null due to fraud or duress and may be dissolved if the adoption cannot be accomplished.

(9) Affiant declares that he freely and voluntarily surrenders custody of this child for the purpose of placement and adoption.

(10) Affiant declares that he consents to an adoption, which consent is final and irrevocable on the fifth day following the birth of this child/expected child less than five days old.

OR

Affiant declares that he consents to an adoption, which consent is final and irrevocable upon the execution of this surrender.

(11) Affiant declares that he waives notice of the filing and service of any pleading of any sort in any subsequent adoption proceeding regarding the child surrendered.

(12) Affiant declares that he has been informed of the provisions of the voluntary registration law, whereby contact may be established with the surrendered child upon the child's reaching the age of eighteen years.

(13) Affiant declares that he has attended a minimum of two mental health counseling sessions relative to the surrender of this child for adoption.

OR

Affiant declares that he waives mental health counseling relative to the surrender of this child for adoption.

(ADDITIONAL DECLARATIONS IF THE SURRENDER IS FOR A PRIVATE ADOPTION)

[(14) Affiant declares that he is eighteen years of age or older.

OR

Affiant declares that he is under the age of eighteen and that (NAME OF PARENTS OR TUTOR) join in this surrender.

OR

Affiant declares that he is under the age of eighteen and that (NAME OF JUVENILE COURT) located in (CITY AND PARISH OF COURT) has given its written consent for his surrender.

(15) Affiant declares that he has consulted with and been fully advised by an attorney other than the attorney for the prospective adoptive parents about the meaning of these declarations and the consequences of this Act of Surrender.]

Sworn to, signed, and notarized, after being carefully read and explained to (NAME OF SURRENDERING PARENT) in the presence of the undersigned notary and witnesses on this _____ day of ______, 19___ .

WITNESSES:

____

____

(If agency adoption:)

____
SURRENDERING FATHER

____
AGENCY REPRESENTATIVE

(If private adoption:)

____
SURRENDERING FATHER

____
ATTORNEY FOR SURRENDERING FATHER

____
ADOPTING PARENTS

or

____
ATTORNEY FOR ADOPTIVE PARENTS
(if anonymity to be protected)

[Additional signature(s) in private adoption if the surrendering father is a minor

____
PARENT(S)/TUTOR OF MINOR SURRENDERING FATHER]

____
NOTARY PUBLIC AND SEAL

ATTACHMENTS:
( ) AFFIDAVIT OF MENTAL HEALTH COUNSELOR or AFFIDAVIT OF WAIVER OF COUNSELING
( ) STATEMENT OF FAMILY HISTORY

[Required additional attachment if the surrender is for private adoption:
( ) AFFIDAVIT OF ATTORNEY FOR SURRENDERING PARENT]

[Required additional attachment if the surrender is by a minor father whose parent(s) or tutor refuse to join in the Act of Surrender for a private adoption:
( ) WRITTEN CONSENT OF COURT]"

(Added by Acts 1991 No. 235, §11; chgd. by Acts 1992 No. 705, §1; Acts 1993 No. 634, §1; Acts 1995 No. 1095, §5, eff. 8/15/95.)

Art. 1123. Effect of surrender.

A. An act of surrender shall be irrevocable upon execution except as provided in Article 1130.

B. An authentic act of voluntary surrender executed by a parent grants the legal custody of the child identified in the act to the agency or person named or represented in the act and grants the irrevocable consent of the surrendering parent and his representative, if applicable, or the child's tutor, to the subsequent adoption of the child surrendered to the agency or to the adoption of the child by the person named or represented in the act except as provided in Paragraph C.

C. If for any reason an adoption cannot be accomplished, the act of surrender may be dissolved by a court of competent jurisdiction.

(Added by Acts 1991 No. 235, §11; chgd. by Acts 1992 No. 705, §1; Acts 1993 No. 634, §1, eff. 6/15/93.)

CHAPTER 8. STATEMENT OF FAMILY HISTORY

Art. 1124. Requirement of family information.

A. A surrendering parent shall execute a Statement of Family History which shall be attached to the act of surrender, shall be included in the sealed adoption record, and shall be given to the prospective adoptive parents at the time of placement.

B. A surrendering parent shall execute an affidavit attesting to the parent's execution of the Statement of Family History which shall be included in the sealed adoption record only and shall not be given to the prospective adoptive parents or the adopted child. The affidavit may also indicate the parent's wishes concerning the future release of identifying information in the event of a medical necessity for which information is needed in order to treat the child.

C. The form for the affidavit shall be substantially as follows:

STATE OF ____________________

PARISH/COUNTY OF ______________________________

AFFIDAVIT

BEFORE ME, the undersigned authority, personally came and appeared

____
SURRENDERING PARENT

who declares that he/she has executed a true and correct Statement of Family History to provide the adoptive parents of the minor child with nonidentifying medical genetic information in accordance with the provisions of Louisiana Children's Code Articles 1124 through 1127.

Affiant understands and agrees that the nonidentifying Statement of Family History will be attached to the act of surrender and included in the sealed adoption record. Affiant further understands that the Statement of Family History will be given to the prospective adoptive parent(s) at the time of placement.

Affiant has been informed that this affidavit shall be included in the sealed adoption record only, and will not be given to the adoptive parents or the minor child.

(Affiant declares that, in the event of a future medical necessity for which information is needed in order to treat the child, he does/does not desire that identifying information be released.)

SIGNATURE OF SURRENDERING PARENT

NAME OF SURRENDERING PARENT

SWORN TO AND SUBSCRIBED
BEFORE ME THIS __________ DAY
OF , 199 .

NOTARY PUBLIC

(Added by Acts 1991 No. 235, §11; chgd. by Acts 1993 No. 634, §1, eff. 6/15/93.)

Art. 1125. Statement of family history; contents; form.

A. The Statement of Family History shall contain the following nonidentifying information, if known:

(1) Date of birth of biological parents.

(2) Explicit and extensive medical genetic history of biological parents and their immediate families.

B. The form for the Statement of Family History shall be substantially as follows:

"STATEMENT OF FAMILY HISTORY

(1) State ages of biological parents: MOTHER ________ FATHER ________
(2) Race of biological parents: MOTHER ________ FATHER ________

(3) State whether either of the biological parents or any of their immediate families have ever had the following:

YES	NO	YES	NO
( )	( ) Cancer	( )	( ) Mental Illness ________ (Specify)
( )	( ) Heart trouble	( )	( ) Allergies________ (Specify)
( )	( ) Diabetes	( )	( ) Blood Disease ________ (Specify)
( )	( ) Epilepsy	( )	( ) Venereal Disease________ (Specify)
( )	( ) Stroke	( )	( ) Mental Retardation ________ (Specify)
( )	( ) Asthma	( )	( ) Glandular Disturbance ________ (Specify)
( )	( ) Arthritis	( )	( ) High Blood Pressure
( )	( ) Kidney Ailments		
( )	( ) Tuberculosis		
( )	( ) Alcoholism		
( )	( ) Blindness		
( )	( ) Deafness		
( )	( ) Neurological and Muscular________ (Specify)		
( )	( ) Drug Abuse ________ (Specify)		

(4) Please state whether the minor child has had the following shots:

YES	NO	YES	NO
( )	( ) 2 mos. DPT + OPV	( )	( ) 18 mos. DPT + OPV Booster
( )	( ) 4 mos. DPT + OPV	( )	( ) 24 mos. TB
( )	( ) 6 mos. DPT	( )	( ) 36 mos. TB
( )	( ) 9 mos. MGB	( )	( ) 48 mos. TB
( )	( ) 12 mos. TB	( )	( ) 5 yrs. DPT + OPV Booster
( )	( ) 15 mos. MMR	( )	( ) 5 yrs. TB

(5) Please state whether the minor child has had the following illness:

YES	NO	YES	NO
( )	( ) Pertussis	( )	( ) Appendicitis
( )	( ) Rubella	( )	( ) Rheumatic Fever
( )	( ) Mumps	( )	( ) Tonsillitis
( )	( ) Chicken Pox	( )	( ) Convulsions
( )	( ) Scarlet Fever	( )	( ) Asthma
( )	( ) Diphtheria	( )	( ) Allergies ____________
( )	( ) Operations ________		____________ (Specify)
	____________	( )	( ) Glandular Disturbance ________
	____________ (Specify)		____________ (Specify)"

(Added by Acts 1991 No. 235, §11, eff. 1/1/92.)

Art. 1126. Fiduciary duty; breach; good faith exception.

A. The agency or person to whom a surrender is made shall have the duty to make a good faith effort to obtain the Statement of Family History required by Articles 1124 and 1125, to deliver it to prospective adoptive parents upon placement, and to disclose the Statement of Family History upon request of the adopted child upon his attaining the age of eighteen in the event that such information was never otherwise made available to him.

B. Failure to comply with the provision of this Chapter shall constitute a breach of fiduciary duty, punishable by a fine of not less than one hundred nor more than five hundred dollars. Should the agency or person to whom a surrender is made fail to obtain all information required for the Statement of Family History, the agency or person shall document by affidavit the good faith efforts made to obtain such information and that such efforts were unproductive.

(Added by Acts 1991 No. 235, §11; chgd. by Acts 1992 No. 705, §1; Acts 1995 No. 1108, §1, eff. 8/15/95.)

Art. 1127. Request for disclosure of nonidentifying medical records; adoptions prior to September 11, 1981.

A. Any child who was surrendered to an agency prior to September 11, 1981, or, if still a minor, his legal representative on his behalf, may, upon written request to an agency, obtain nonidentifying medical history from the agency without the necessity of filing a petition for disclosure as required by the provisions of Chapter 5 of Title XII of this Code.

B. Upon written request, the agency shall make a good faith effort to review its records and abstract nonidentifying medical history, similar in content to the Statement of Family History.

C. Such nonidentifying medical history shall be made available to the adopted child, or his legal representative, for a reasonable charge.

D. For the purposes of this Article, an "agency" shall include an agency or institution that is no longer licensed by the state for the placement of children for adoption, but was licensed by the state to perform such service at the time the child was surrendered to the agency or institution.

(Added by Acts 1991 No. 235, §11; chgd. by Acts 1992 No. 705, §1; Acts 1995 No. 1108, §1, eff. 8/15/95.)

CHAPTER 9. FOREIGN SURRENDERS

Article

Art. 1128. Validity.

A surrender or consent to adoption executed by a nondomiciliary parent in accordance with the laws of the state of his domicile shall be recognized as valid and given the force and effect accorded it by the laws of the foreign state. *(Added by Acts 1991 No. 235, §11, eff. 1/1/92.)*

Art. 1129. Proof of law.

A person asserting the validity of a surrender or consent executed in a foreign state shall produce sufficient proof of the laws of the foreign state governing the requirements for form and content and the force and effect accorded a properly executed act. *(Added by Acts 1991 No. 235, §11, eff. 1/1/92.)*

CHAPTER 10. SURRENDER PROCEDURE IN GENERAL

Art. 1130. Time limitations.

A. No act of surrender by a mother shall be executed earlier than five days following the birth of the child.

B. A father may execute an act of surrender prior to the birth of the child or at any time after the birth. However, any surrender executed by a father earlier than the fifth day following the birth of the child shall not be irrevocable until the fifth day following the birth of the child.

C. In making these time calculations, the date of birth shall not be included, and the days shall be consecutive calendar days, including weekends and holidays.

D. An alleged or adjudicated father may execute an act of surrender prior to the birth of the child or at any time after the birth. His surrender shall be irrevocable upon execution. *(Added by Acts 1991 No. 235, §11; chgd. by Acts 1992 No. 705, §1; Acts 1993 No. 634, §1, eff. 6/15/93.)*

Art. 1131. Filing; institution of records check.

A. Within three days after the surrender becomes irrevocable under Article 1123, exclusive of legal holidays, the agency or attorney for the prospective adoptive parents shall file the authentic act of voluntary surrender, together with any certification for adoption or court order approving the adoptive placement required by Chapter 2 of Title XII in a court of proper venue as authorized by Article 1180.

B. The surrender, and certification for adoption or court order approving the adoptive placement if required, may be filed later than three days after execution only with leave of court for good cause shown.

C. Upon the filing of any court order approving the adoptive placement pursuant to Article 1178, the court shall immediately issue both of the following orders:

(1) That the local sheriff conduct a records check for all federal arrests and convictions and all state arrests and convictions in this and any other states in which either of the prospective adoptive parents has been domiciled.

(2) That the department conduct a records check for validated complaints of child abuse or neglect in this or any other state in which either of the prospective adoptive parents has been domiciled since becoming a major, involving either prospective adoptive parent.

D. Each order shall state the full name, date of birth, social security number, and former and current state(s) of domicile since becoming a major of each prospective adoptive parent.

E. The sheriff and the department shall accord priority to these orders and shall provide a certificate indicating all information discovered or that no information has been found. *(Added by Acts 1991 No. 235, §11; chgd. by Acts 1992 No. 705, §1; Acts 1993 No. 634, §1, eff. 6/15/93.)*

Art. 1132. Notice of filing of surrender; form.

A. If a mother of an illegitimate child has executed a surrender and identifies the child's alleged or adjudicated father, notice of the filing of her surrender shall be served upon the alleged or adjudicated father unless any of the following apply:

(1) His potential parental rights have been terminated by a judgment in accordance with Title X.

(2) He has executed a surrender in accordance with this Title.

(3) He has given his consent in open court in accordance with Article 1195.

(4) He has executed a release of claims in accordance with Article 1196.

B. The notice of filing of a surrender shall be issued by the clerk and shall contain the following information in substantially the following form:

"NOTICE OF FILING OF SURRENDER

Be advised that on the _____ day of ________, 19___, an authentic Act of Surrender executed by __________ was filed wherein she surrendered for adoption her minor child, namely _______, born on the _____ day of ________, 19___, in the Parish of _________, State of ___________.

The Act of Surrender alleges that you are the father of this child. You may attempt to oppose the adoption of this child only by filing a written objection with this court within fifteen days after you receive this notice.

If you file a written objection timely, the court will then hold a hearing within twenty days of the filing of the opposition, to determine whether you have established or forfeited your parental rights.

To establish your parental right to oppose the adoption, you must demonstrate to the court the affirmative efforts you have made to establish or maintain a parental relationship with the child. This may include attempted legitimation of the child, formal acknowledgment of the child with the clerk of court in the parish in which the child was born, declaration of paternity filed in the Louisiana putative father registry (after July 1, 1992), or provision of substantial parental care and support to the child.

If you fail to file a written motion of opposition, or if, after a hearing on a motion timely filed, the court finds that you have failed to establish your parental right to oppose the adoption, the court will order the termination of any and all parental rights you may have and the child may be subject to adoption."

(Added by Acts 1991 No. 235, §11; chgd. by Acts 1993 No. 634 §1, eff. 6/15/93.)

Art. 1133. Notice of filing of surrender; service upon resident alleged or adjudicated father.

Notice of the filing of a mother's surrender shall be promptly served upon the alleged or adjudicated father. Notice of the filing shall not be required if an alleged or adjudicated father waives notice of service. If he resides within this state, service shall be made by either registered or certified mail, return receipt requested, postage prepaid and properly addressed to his last known address. *(Added by Acts 1991 No. 235, §11; chgd. by Acts 1992 No. 705, §1; Acts 1993 No. 634, §1, eff. 6/15/93.)*

Art. 1134. Notice of filing of surrender; service upon nonresident alleged or adjudicated father.

Notice of the filing of a mother's surrender shall be promptly served upon the alleged or adjudicated father. Notice of the filing shall not be required if an alleged or adjudicated father waives notice of service. If he does not reside within this state, service shall be made by either registered or certified mail, return receipt requested, postage prepaid and properly addressed to his last known address. *(Added by Acts 1991 No. 235, §11; chgd. by Acts 1992 No. 705, §1; Acts 1993 No. 634, §1, eff. 6/15/93.)*

Art. 1135. Unidentified fathers; diligent effort; order.

A. If the father of the child is unknown, the court, upon motion of the agency or attorney for the prospective adoptive parent and upon finding that a diligent effort has been made to identify the father, shall terminate the father's parental rights.

B. For purposes of this Article, the existence of all of the following is sufficient proof that the father is unknown and a diligent effort was made to identify him:

(1) A declaration by the surrendering mother in the act of surrender that the father is unknown.

(2) A certified copy of the child's birth certificate with no one indicated thereon as the father of the child.

(3) A certificate from the putative father registry indicating that no person is listed or registered as the child's father, which certificate must be dated more than fifteen days after the date the act of surrender was executed by the surrendering mother.

(4) A certificate from the clerk of court in the parish in which the child was born indicating that no acknowledgment with respect to this child has been recorded, which certificate must be dated more than fifteen days after the date the act of surrender was executed by the surrendering mother.

(Added by Acts 1991 No. 235, §11, eff. 1/1/92.)

Art. 1136. Absentee alleged or adjudicated fathers; curator.

A. If the alleged or adjudicated father of the child is identified but his whereabouts are unknown, as indicated in a surrender or in a return on service, the court shall appoint a curator and notice of filing of a surrender shall be served upon him.

B. The court must appoint a curator for an alleged or adjudicated father whose whereabouts are unknown within five days, exclusive of legal holidays, from the date of the filing of an act of surrender indicating that his whereabouts are unknown or from the receipt of a return indicating that he cannot be served. The curator shall begin a diligent effort to locate the alleged or adjudicated father within seven days, exclusive of legal holidays, from the date of his appointment.

C. Upon motion of the agency or attorney for the prospective adoptive parent, which motion may be filed thirty days after the appointment of the curator, and upon finding that a diligent effort has been made to locate the alleged or adjudicated father, but that he has not been located within thirty days from the appointment of the curator, the court shall terminate the alleged or adjudicated father's parental rights.

D. For purposes of this Article, the following is sufficient proof that the alleged or adjudicated father's whereabouts are unknown and that a diligent effort was made to locate him:

(1) A declaration by the surrendering mother in the act of surrender that his address is unknown or evidence that attempts to contact him at the address indicated in the act of surrender have been unsuccessful.

(2) A certified copy of the child's birth certificate, with no one indicated thereon as the father of the child.

(3) A certificate from the putative father registry indicating whether any person is listed registered as the child's father and if so registered, proof that no address is stated thereon or evidence that attempts to contact him at the address indicated on the registration form have been unsuccessful, which certificate must be dated more than fifteen days after the date the act of surrender was executed by the surrendering mother.

(4) A certificate from the clerk of court where the child was born indicating whether any act of acknowledgment with respect to this child has been recorded and if so recorded, proof that no address is stated thereon or evidence that attempts to contact the alleged or adjudicated father at the address indicated on the acknowledgment have been unsuccessful, which certificate must be dated after fifteen days from the date the act of surrender was executed by the surrendering mother.

(5) An affidavit executed by the curator detailing efforts made to locate the alleged or adjudicated father, including but not limited to proof of publication seeking his whereabouts.

E. If the alleged or adjudicated father of the child is located by the curator within thirty days of his appointment, the curator shall promptly file an affidavit with the court detailing efforts made to locate the him, disclosing his location, and, certifying that he has been given oral or written notice of filing of surrender in conformity with Article 1132.

(Added by Acts 1991 No. 235, §11; chgd. by Acts 1992 No. 705, §1; Acts 1993 No. 634, §1, eff. 6/15/93.)

Art. 1137. Notice of opposition to adoption by alleged or adjudicated father; time limitations; appointment of counsel for the child; scheduling of hearing; paternity testing.

A. An alleged or adjudicated father or his representative, if applicable, may oppose the adoption of his child by filing a clear and written declaration of intention to oppose the adoption. The notice of opposition shall be filed with the court indicated in the notice of filing of surrender within fifteen days after the time he was served with the notice of surrender, or from the time he was served with notice of the filing of an adoption petition in the event that no surrender was executed or filed.

B. Upon receipt of the notice of opposition, the court shall appoint an attorney to represent the child, subject to the limitations set out in Article 1121. Neither the child nor anyone purporting to act on his behalf may be permitted to waive this right. The costs of the child's representation shall be taxed as costs of court.

C. The court shall set the opposition for contradictory hearing, which hearing shall be held within twenty days of the filing of the opposition.

D. Notice of the hearing shall be served in accordance with Articles 1133 and 1134 on the opposing father, the legal custodian, and counsel appointed for the child.

E. If paternity is at issue, on its own motion or motion of any party, the court shall issue an order for immediate blood or tissue sampling in accordance with the provisions of R.S. 9:396 et seq. and shall order an expedited report. The hearing resolving this issue shall be held at the earliest time that the results of the testing can be reported to the court.

(Added by Acts 1991 No. 235, §11; chgd. by Acts 1993 No. 634, §1; Acts 1997 No. 797, §1, eff. 8/15/97.)

Art. 1138. Hearing of opposition to adoption; establishment of parental rights.

A. At the hearing of the opposition, the alleged or adjudicated father must establish his parental rights by acknowledging that he is the father of the child and by proving that he has manifested a substantial commitment to his parental responsibilities and that he is a fit parent of his child.

B. Proof of the father's substantial commitment to his parental responsibilities requires a showing, in accordance with his means and knowledge of the mother's pregnancy or the child's birth, that he either:

(1) Provided financial support, including but not limited to the payment of consistent support to the mother during her pregnancy, contributions to the payment of the medical expenses of pregnancy and birth, or contributions of consistent support of the child after birth; that he frequently and consistently visited the child after birth; and that he is now willing and able to assume legal and physical care of the child.

(2) Was willing to provide such support and to visit the child and that he made reasonable attempts to manifest such a parental commitment, but was thwarted in his efforts by the mother or her agents, and that he is now willing and able to assume legal and physical care of the child.

C. The child and the legal custodian may offer rebuttal evidence limited to the issues enumerated in Paragraphs A and B of this Article.

D. If the court finds that the alleged or adjudicated father has failed to establish his parental rights, it shall decree that his rights are terminated.

E. If the court finds that the alleged or adjudicated father has established his parental rights, the court shall declare that no adoption may be granted without his consent and shall order the child to be in his legal custody. The court may also order the alleged or adjudicated father to reimburse the department, or the licensed private adoption agency, or other agency, or whoever has assumed liability for such costs, all or part of the medical expenses incurred for the mother and the child in connection with the birth of the child.

(Added by Acts 1991 No. 235, §11; chgd. by Acts 1992 No. 705, §1; Acts 1993 No. 634, §1; Acts 1997 No. 797, §1, eff. 8/15/97.)

Art. 1139. Order maintaining opposition; effect on other surrendering parent; service.

A. If the court maintains an opposition and declares that no adoption can take place without the consent of the opposing parent, a surrender executed by the other parent of the child shall be dissolved.

B. The order shall be served on the surrendering parent in the manner for service of process provided in civil proceedings.
(Added by Acts 1991 No. 235, §11; chgd. by Acts 1993 No. 634, §1, eff. 6/15/93.)

Art. 1140. Continuing jurisdiction.
The court rendering an order pursuant to this Chapter shall have exclusive, original jurisdiction to modify that order. *(Added by Acts 1991 No. 235, §11, eff. 1/1/92.)*

Art. 1141. Prior clearance on original birth certificate; putative father registry; acknowledgment by authentic act, legitimation by authentic act, and judgment of filiation.
A. Prior to the entry of any order terminating parental rights pursuant to this Chapter, the attorney for the prospective adoptive parents shall obtain a certified copy of all of the following:
(1) The child's birth certificate.
(2) A certificate indicating the name and address of any person listed with the putative father registry, or a certificate that no registration or listing has occurred, relative to this child.
(3) A certificate from the clerk of court in and for the parish in which the child was born indicating whether any acknowledgment by authentic act or legitimation by authentic act, or judgment of filiation has been recorded relative to this child.
B. The vital records registry of the office of public health of the Department of Health and Hospitals, or its counterpart in any other state, shall, upon request of the attorney for the prospective adoptive parent, provide him with a certified copy of the information in its custody that is required in this Article.
(Added by Acts 1991 No. 235, §11; chgd. by Acts 1993 No. 634, §1, eff. 6/15/93.)

Art. 1142. Order declaring parental rights terminated; motion; certificates.
A. If no opposition is timely received by the court, the court shall, upon motion, render an order approving the surrender, if any, and declaring the rights of the parents terminated.
B. The motion shall be accompanied by a certified copy of the child's birth certificate, a certificate from the putative father registry indicating whether any act of acknowledgment by authentic act has been recorded, and a certificate from the clerk of court in and for the parish in which the child was born indicating whether any acknowledgement by authentic act, legitimation by authentic act, or judgment of filiation has been recorded relative to this child.
C. If the clerk reports that a legitimation by authentic act has been duly recorded by a father, the court shall deny the motion unless the father's parental rights have been terminated in accordance with Title X or the father has executed a surrender in accordance with this Title or has given his consent to the adoption in accordance with Article 1195.
D. If any of these certificates identify an alleged or adjudicated father who has not previously been served with notice of the mother's act of surrender, the alleged or adjudicated father shall be served with a copy of the motion to terminate his parental rights and given an opportunity to be heard in accordance with Articles 1132 through 1141 unless any of the following occur:
(1) The alleged or adjudicated father's parental rights have been terminated by a judgment in accordance with Title X.
(2) The alleged or adjudicated father has executed an act of surrender in accordance with this Title.
(3) The alleged or adjudicated father has consented to the child's adoption in accordance with Article 1195.
(4) The alleged or adjudicated father has executed a release of claims in accordance with Article 1196.
(Added by Acts 1991 No. 235, §11; chgd. by Acts 1993 No. 634, §1, eff. 6/15/93.)

Art. 1143. Appeal.
A. An appeal from or application for a rehearing on any order or judgment rendered relative to a provision of this Title shall be in accordance with the provisions of this Article to the extent that the provisions hereof conflict with the provisions of the Code of Civil Procedure.
B. An appeal from an order or judgment of a district, family, or juvenile court shall be to the court of appeal on both law and fact. The court shall fix the return date of the appeal no more than twenty days after the day the estimated costs are paid. Emergency supplemental

court reporting services may be applied for with the judicial administrator. The court of appeal shall hear and decide the appeal within twenty days after the lodging of the record on appeal.

C. (1) Within seven days after the mailing of the notice of the judgment and opinion of the court of appeal, a party may apply to the court of appeal for a rehearing. Within ten days after the mailing of the notice of the judgment and opinion of the court of appeal, a party may apply to the supreme court for a writ of certiorari. The judgment of a court of appeal becomes final and definitive if neither an application to the court of appeal for rehearing nor an application to the supreme court for a writ of certiorari is timely filed.

(2) If any party files a timely application to the court of appeal for a rehearing, then the time within which any other party may apply to the supreme court for a writ of certiorari shall be extended until ten days after the mailing of the notice of a denial of rehearing.

(3) If a timely application for rehearing has been filed in the court of appeal and the court of appeal denies the application, the judgment becomes final and definitive unless an application for writ of certiorari to the supreme court is filed within ten days after the mailing of the notice of a denial of rehearing.

(4) If an application for certiorari to the supreme court is timely filed, a judgment of the court of appeal becomes final and definitive when the supreme court denies the application for certiorari. The supreme court may stay the execution of the judgment of the court of appeal pending a timely application for certiorari or an appeal to the United States Supreme Court.

D. (1) Within seven days after the mailing of the notice of judgment in the supreme court, a party may apply to the court for a rehearing.

(2) A judgment of the supreme court becomes final and definitive when the delay for application for rehearing has expired and no timely application therefor has been made.

(3) When an application for rehearing has been applied for timely, a judgment of the supreme court becomes final and definitive when the application is denied. The supreme court may stay the execution of the judgment pending a timely application for certiorari or an appeal to the United States Supreme Court.

(Added by Acts 1991 No. 235, §11; chgd. by Acts 1997 No. 797, §1, eff. 8/15/97.)

CHAPTER 11. PERMANENCY PLANNING

Article

Art. 1144. Placement report.

After filing of a surrender in accordance with the provisions of Article 1131, when the department has effected a permanent placement of the child, the department shall report such placement in detail to the court. *(Added by Acts 1991 No. 235, §11, eff. 1/1/92.)*

Art. 1145. Registration.

A. If no permanent placement has been made within ninety days after a voluntary surrender to a child care agency, the child shall be registered by the appropriate child placement agency with the Louisiana Adoption Resource Exchange within the office of community resources of the department.

B. Any such registration shall not include the surname of the child or otherwise reveal the identities of the blood parents of the child.

C. The department shall maintain a list of the registered children. Such a list shall be updated quarterly and made available to all licensed child placement agencies in the state. Subject to the confidentiality requirements of all adoption matters, the department shall use every reasonable method of effecting a permanent placement.

D. Media presentation of available children and other means of public solicitation for the purpose of matching potential adoptive parents with available children shall be used only in cases involving a child who is difficult to place for adoption, subject to rules and regulations adopted pursuant to the Administrative Procedure Act*.

**R.S. 49:950 et seq.*

(Added by Acts 1991 No. 235, §11, eff. 1/1/92.)

Art. 1146. Permanency planning review; counsel for child.

A. If no permanent placement has been made within ninety days after a voluntary surrender to a child care agency, review hearings shall be held in accordance with the provisions of Chapters 15 and 16 of Title VI.

B. Any attorney previously appointed to represent the child shall continue to represent the child in all subsequent review hearings until the child is permanently placed. If no attorney was previously appointed, the court shall appoint an attorney to represent the child for the purposes of facilitating permanent placement.
(Added by Acts 1991 No. 235, §11, eff. 1/1/92.)

CHAPTER 12. ANNULMENT OF SURRENDER

Art. 1147. Grounds.

No act of surrender shall be subject to annulment except upon proof of duress or fraud, notwithstanding any provision of law to the contrary. *(Added by Acts 1991 No. 235, §11, eff. 1/1/92.)*

Art. 1148. Time limitations; finality.

No action to annul a surrender shall be brought for any reason after ninety days from its execution or after a decree of adoption has been entered, whichever is earlier. *(Added by Acts 1991 No. 235, §11, eff. 1/1/92.)*

TITLE XII. ADOPTION OF CHILDREN

CHAPTER 1. PRELIMINARY PROVISIONS; DEFINITIONS

Art. 1167. Purpose.

The purpose of this Title is to promote the permanent placement of available children into suitable homes through the procedures described herein. *(Added by Acts 1991 No. 235, §12, eff. 1/1/92.)*

Art. 1168. General applicability of other Children's Code provisions.

Except as otherwise specified in this Title, all provisions of the Children's Code remain applicable. *(Added by Acts 1991 No. 235, §12, eff. 1/1/92.)*

Art. 1169. Definitions.

As used in this Title:

(1) "Agency" or "child placing agency" includes the Department of Social Services, the corresponding department of any other state, and those private agencies and institutions licensed for the placement of children for adoption by the Department of Social Services or by the corresponding department of any other state.

(2) "Birth certificate" means the child's official birth certificate or a true copy of a prefiled version of the birth certificate in the event the official birth certificate has not been issued.

(3) "Child" means a person under seventeen years of age and not emancipated by marriage.

(4) "Department" means the Louisiana Department of Social Services.

(5) "Putative father registry" means the Louisiana putative father registry established in Part I-C of Chapter 1 of Code Title VII of Code Book I of Title 9 of the Louisiana Revised Statutes of 1950, comprised of R.S. 9:400 and 400.1.

(Added by Acts 1991 No. 235, §12; chgd. by Acts 1992 No. 705, §1, eff. 7/6/92.)

Art. 1170. Types of adoption.

A. This Title sets forth the exclusive procedures for adoption of minor children in Louisiana. There are three types of adoption of minor children in Louisiana:

(1) Agency adoption.

(2) Private adoption.

(3) Intrafamily adoption.

B. The procedures governing each type of adoption are set forth in the following Articles. *(Added by Acts 1991 No. 235, §12, eff. 1/1/92.)*

CHAPTER 2. PREPLACEMENT APPROVAL OF ADOPTIVE HOME IN PRIVATE ADOPTIONS

Article

Art. 1171. Prior approval of private adoptive placement; exceptions.

Except when the child is the stepchild, grandchild, sibling, niece, or nephew of one of the prospective adopting parents, no child who is the subject of a private adoption shall be placed in the home of the prospective adoptive parents prior to their either obtaining a certification for adoption, as provided for in Articles 1171 through 1173, or by their obtaining an order of a court of competent jurisdiction approving the adoptive placement, as provided for in Articles 1175 through 1177. *(Added by Acts 1991 No. 235, §12, eff. 1/1/92.)*

Art. 1172. Certification for adoption; authority to conduct preplacement home study.

Any person qualified to adopt a child pursuant to Article 1221 may request a licensed agency, board certified social worker, licensed counselor, psychologist, or psychiatrist to conduct a preplacement home study for the purpose of obtaining a certification for adoption. *(Added by Acts 1991 No. 235, §12, eff. 1/1/92.)*

Art. 1173. Preplacement home study; requirements.

A. The department shall promulgate rules and regulations for preplacement home studies in private adoptions in accordance with the Administrative Procedure Act* and official review and approval of the Louisiana Advisory Committee on Licensing of Child Day Care Facilities and Child-Placing Agencies as provided in R.S. 46:1406 et seq., which rules and regulations shall not be inconsistent with the following:

**R.S. 49:950 et seq.*

(1) The rules and regulations governing the licensing of adoption agencies relative to preplacement home studies, specifically adoptive home studies, notification regarding application, access to records, updating home studies, review procedures, and adoptive parents' records, to the extent that such provisions are compatible with procedural laws governing private surrenders and adoptions.

(2) Such study shall be conducted by a social worker in the employ of a licensed agency, a board certified social worker, or a licensed counselor, psychologist, or psychiatrist, except that a prospective adoptive parent who is domiciled outside the state shall obtain a preplacement home study in accordance with the provisions of Chapter 2 of Title XVI.

(3) A certification for adoption obtained pursuant to a favorable preplacement home study shall be valid for a minimum of two years.

B. The sheriff and department shall conduct and accord priority to requests for a criminal records check for all federal and state arrests and convictions and validated complaints of child abuse or neglect, respectively, in this or any other state of each prospective adoptive parent, and shall provide a certificate indicating all information discovered or that no information has been found, all in accordance with the applicable rules and regulations promulgated by the department.

C. The department shall promulgate and submit for approval such rules and regulations governing placement home studies in private adoptions in accordance with the Administrative Procedure Act no later than October 1, 1991, and such rules and regulations shall become effective upon its publication in the Louisiana Register.

(Added by Acts 1991 No. 235, §12, eff. 1/1/92.)

Art. 1174. Issuance of Certification for Adoption.

A. If the preplacement home study is favorable, the professional who conducted it shall issue a certification for adoption to the prospective adoptive parents.

B. The certification for adoption shall be valid for a minimum of two years.

(Added by Acts 1991 No. 235, §12, eff. 1/1/92.)

Art. 1175. Court approval of uncertified adoptive placement.

Prospective adoptive parents who have not previously obtained a certification for adoption may apply for a court order approving the placement of a child in their home. *(Added by Acts 1991 No. 235, §12, eff. 1/1/92.)*

Art. 1176. Application for court approval of adoptive placement; contents; filing.

A. An application for court approval of adoptive placement shall be verified and shall contain the following:

(1) The name, address, age, occupation, and marital status of the prospective adoptive parents.

(2) The expected date of the child's placement.

(3) The relationship between the child and the prospective adoptive parents, if any.

(4) The name of the child whose placement is requested, if known.

B. An application for court approval of adoptive placement shall be filed with the clerk of a court of appropriate venue as authorized by Article 1180.

(Added by Acts 1991 No. 235, §12, eff. 1/1/92.)

Art. 1177. Hearing.

A. The application for court approval of adoptive placement shall be set for hearing in chambers, confidentially, and in a summary manner within forty-eight hours of its filing.

B. At the hearing, the prospective adoptive parents shall testify under oath concerning their fitness to receive the child into their care and custody, including but not limited to:

(1) Their moral fitness, previous criminal records or validated complaints of child abuse or neglect, if any.

(2) Their mental and physical health.

(3) Their financial capacity and disposition to provide the child with food, clothing, medical care, and other material needs.

(4) Their capacity and disposition to give the child love, affection, and guidance and to undertake the responsibilities of becoming the child's parents.

(5) The adequacy of the physical environment of their home and neighborhood for the placement of the child.

(6) The names and ages of other family members who would reside with the child in the prospective adoptive home and their attitude toward the proposed adoption.

(7) The stability and permanence, as a family unit, of the proposed adoptive home.

(Added by Acts 1991 No. 235, §12, eff. 1/1/92.)

Art. 1178. Order and revocation.

A. At the conclusion of the hearing, the court shall render an order approving or disapproving the placement of the child with the prospective adoptive parents.

B. The order shall be in writing and signed by the judge.

C. A certified copy of a court order approving the adoptive placement shall be given to the prospective adoptive parents.

D. Any order disapproving the adoptive placement shall include specific reasons therefor.

E. Subsequent to the entry of an order approving an adoptive placement, if the result of a criminal records check or the results of abuse or neglect validated complaint records check indicate that the prospective adoptive parents failed to disclose such unfavorable information at the hearing, the court may issue an instanter order taking protective custody of the child, pursuant to Article 619, if this information, if known, together with other evidence presented at the hearing would have resulted in the court's disapproval of the adoptive placement.

(Added by Acts 1991 No. 235, §12, eff. 1/1/92.)

Art. 1179. Appeal.

A. Appeal from an order disapproving the adoptive placement shall be trial de novo in the court of appeal, based upon the criteria set out in Article 1177.

B. The appeal shall be heard in chambers, confidentially, in a summary manner, and within forty-eight hours of its filing.

(Added by Acts 1991 No. 235, §12, eff. 1/1/92.)

CHAPTER 3. VENUE

Article

Art. 1180. Venue in adoption.

A. A proceeding for the adoption of a child may be commenced in either:

(1) The juvenile court in the parish of the domicile of the petitioner.

(2) The juvenile court in the parish of the domicile of the custodian of the child.

(3) The juvenile court in the parish in which a voluntary act of surrender has been executed with respect to the child to be adopted.

(4) The juvenile court which previously terminated parental rights of a parent with respect to the child to be adopted.

B. An attorney at law named as representative of the prospective adoptive parent shall not be deemed the legal custodian of the child for purposes of proper jurisdiction or venue.

(Added by Acts 1991 No. 235, §12, eff. 1/1/92.)

CHAPTER 4. DUTIES OF COURT CLERKS

Art. 1181. Adoption records.

The clerks of court shall keep separate indices of all suits filed in accordance with this Title, and shall index these suits in the name of the parties filing the petition and in the name of the child to be adopted. *(Added by Acts 1991 No. 235, §12, eff. 1/1/92.)*

Art. 1182. Records of adoption decrees.

A. Whenever an interlocutory decree of adoption has been granted, the clerk of court shall forward a certified copy of the decree to the Department of Social Services.

B. Whenever a final decree of adoption has been granted with regard to a child born in Louisiana, the clerk of court shall forward, on a form supplied by the Department of Social Services, a certificate of the decree to the state registrar of vital records.

(Added by Acts 1991 No. 235, §12, eff. 1/1/92.)

Art. 1183. Reports of annulments of adoption decrees.

The clerk of court shall prepare, within ten days after a decree of annulment of adoption becomes final, a certificate of the decree of annulment on forms furnished by the state registrar of vital records. On or before the fifteenth day of each month, the clerk shall forward any certificates prepared by him during the preceding calendar month to the state registrar of vital records. *(Added by Acts 1991 No. 235, §12, eff. 1/1/92.)*

CHAPTER 5. CONFIDENTIALITY

Art. 1184. Admission to hearings.

All adoption proceedings shall be heard by the judge in chambers, and no one shall be admitted to the hearings except the parties in interest, their attorneys, and officers of the court. The court, in its discretion, may grant the request of a petitioner to permit others to be present at the hearing. *(Added by Acts 1991 No. 235, §12, eff. 1/1/92.)*

Art. 1185. Confidential reports.

No one except the judge presiding in the case, his successor, or a curator ad hoc, as provided for in Article 1191, shall have access to the confidential reports rendered to the court pursuant to this Title. Following final disposition of an adoption case, all confidential reports submitted by the department to the judge shall be retained in the court's confidential adoption record. *(Added by Acts 1991 No. 235, §12, eff. 1/1/92.)*

Art. 1186. Records of adoption agencies.

A. All adoption records of agencies shall be retained in confidential files and it shall be unlawful, except for purposes directly connected with the agencies' responsibilities in relation to adoption work, and then subject to the agencies' rules and regulations, or to a duly appointed curator ad hoc, as provided for in Article 1191, to disclose any information concerning any individual adoption case.

B. Any person who violates this requirement of confidentiality shall be fined not more than five hundred dollars or imprisoned for not more than ninety days, or both.
(Added by Acts 1991 No. 235, §12, eff. 1/1/92.)

Art. 1187. Court records of proceedings.
All court records of adoption proceedings shall be confidential and shall not be open to inspection except on written authorization by the court and there shall be no publication thereof. *(Added by Acts 1991 No. 235, §12, eff. 1/1/92.)*

Art. 1188. Petitions for disclosure.
A. An adopted child or, if still a minor, his legal representative on his behalf, may file a petition for disclosure of information pertaining to his adoption. The action shall be styled: "In re the Adoption of_____."

B. This action and the limited medical exception provision of Article 1127 shall be the exclusive means for gaining access to records of adoptions whether maintained by this court, some other court, an adoption agency, any state agency, or private individual, notwithstanding provisions of laws to the contrary.
(Added by Acts 1991 No. 235, §12; chgd. by Acts 1995 No. 1108, §1, eff. 8/15/95.)

Art. 1189. Grounds for disclosure.
The petition for disclosure must show compelling necessity overriding the general policy of confidentiality for adoption records by demonstrating any of the following:

(1) That there are inheritance rights which are or may be due from his biological parents under Civil Code Article 214.

(2) By proof that there is a medical necessity requiring information about his biological family or his own preadoption health history in order to treat the petitioner or his descendants.

(3) By proof that both he and a person reasonably believed to be his biological parent or biological sibling have registered with the department pursuant to Chapter 15 of this Title.

(4) That such information is otherwise required to be disclosed by federal or state law.
(Added by Acts 1991 No. 235, §12; chgd. by Acts 1997 No. 715, §1, eff. 8/15/97.)

Art. 1190. Authority of the court.
A. Upon reviewing a petition for disclosure on grounds of either inheritance rights or medical necessity, the court may deny it for lack of a proper showing of compelling necessity. Before granting a petition, the court may appoint a curator ad hoc and shall set the petition for a hearing.

B. A petition seeking information to verify a match of voluntary registration pursuant to Chapter 15 of this Title of other information required by law to be disclosed shall be granted. The court may appoint a curator ad hoc to open and review the adoption record and original birth certificate. The curator shall report back to the court with his findings within thirty days of the date of his acceptance of his appointments.
(Added by Acts 1991 No. 235, §12; chgd. by Acts 1992 No. 705, §1, eff. 7/6/92.)

Art. 1191. Duties of a curator ad hoc.
A. Upon appointment, the curator ad hoc shall be responsible for:

(1) Securing all records pertaining to the petitioner's request through subpoenas duces tecum or other discovery process, if necessary.

(2) Reviewing all records pertaining to the adoption.

(3) Reporting to the court any objections to disclosure which he may have received from a custodian of records.

(4) After the records review is completed, recommending the granting or denial of the petitioner's request and particularizing the necessary scope of any disclosure order for the court's consideration.

B. A person proceeding in forma pauperis shall receive the services of the curator ad hoc without having to pay the curator's fees. However, in all cases, the curator shall be entitled to a reasonable fee for his services, and the court shall fix the fee commensurate with the services performed.
(Added by Acts 1991 No. 235, §12; chgd. by Acts 1992 No. 705, §1, eff. 7/6/92.)

Art. 1192. Orders of disclosure.

After hearing the petitioner, the court may order disclosure. Insofar as possible, an order disclosing information from the court's own records or any records obtained by the curator ad hoc shall contain nonidentifying information about the biological family. If identifying information must be disclosed, the court may release such information to the person requiring it and order that its confidentiality be maintained without disclosure to the petitioner. *(Added by Acts 1991 No. 235, §12, eff. 1/1/92.)*

CHAPTER 6. RIGHTS OF PARENTS; CONSENT; RELINQUISHMENT

Article

Art. 1193. Persons whose consent or relinquishment is required.

Unless rights have been terminated in accordance with Title X or XI, consent to the adoption of a child or relinquishment of parental rights shall be required of the following:

(1) The mother of the child.

(2) The father of the child, regardless of the child's actual paternity, if any of the following apply:

(a) The child is legitimate in accordance with Article 179 or Article 198 of the Louisiana Civil Code or their legal equivalents in another state.

(b) The father has executed a legitimation by authentic act as authorized by Article 200 of the Louisiana Civil Code or its legal equivalent in another state and has further recorded the act of legitimation in the parish of the child's birth or on the child's birth certificate.

(c) The father is presumed to be the father of the child in accordance with Articles 184 through 186 of the Louisiana Civil Code or their legal equivalents in another state.

(3) The alleged father of the child who has established his parental rights in accordance with Chapter 10 of Title XI.

(4) The biological father of the child whose paternity has been determined by a judgment of filiation in accordance with Civil Code Article 209 and who has established his parental rights in accordance with Chapter 10 of Title XI.

(5) The custodial agency which has placed the child for adoption, except that the court may grant the adoption without the consent of the agency if the adoption is in the best interest of the child and there is a finding that the agency has unreasonably withheld its consent. *(Added by Acts 1991 No. 235, §12; chgd. by Acts 1993 No. 634, §1; Acts 1995 No. 1095, §6, eff. 8/15/95.)*

Art. 1194. Granting adoption over objection of incarcerated parent.

A. Notwithstanding provisions of law to the contrary, an adoption may be granted over the objection of a parent or parents incarcerated in a state or federal penal institution, following conviction of a felony which has not been appealed, or which has been affirmed at least once on appeal, when all of the following exist:

(1) The nonincarcerated parent has executed an act of surrender for adoption of the child pursuant to Title XI; the nonincarcerated parent is deceased; or the nonincarcerated parent's rights have been terminated.

(2) The incarcerated parent has not developed or maintained a significant relationship with the child.

(3) The adoption is manifestly in the best interest of the child. In determining the best interest of a child, the court shall consider the following factors:

(a) The nature of the offense resulting in the incarceration of the parent, including all prior criminal activity.

(b) The length of the sentence imposed upon the parent, and the impact of such on the parent's ability to provide a stable, permanent home for the child during the times in the child's life when permanence and stability are important.

(c) Expert testimony concerning the fitness of the adoptive parent or parents and their relationship with the child, the child's relationship with the incarcerated parent, the fitness of the incarcerated parent, and the needs of the child.

(d) Any relevant history of the incarcerated parent, including his or her relationship with the other parent, the child at issue or other children, any history of violence, substance abuse, sexual deviance, mental illness, or personality disorder.

(e) The physical, psychological, and emotional needs of the child, considering the child's entire history and age.

B. The incarcerated parent shall be served and cited as in any adoption proceeding, and shall have the right to attend the adoption hearing and to present any relevant evidence.

C. Unless agreed to by the adoptive parent or parents, the incarcerated parent shall not be allowed to see the adoptive parent or to acquire any identifying information concerning the adoptive parents.

D. The court shall give specific reasons for judgment should the court grant an adoption over the objection of an incarcerated parent under the provisions of this Article.
(Added by Acts 1991 No. 235, §12, eff. 1/1/92.)

CHAPTER 7. FORM OF PARENTAL CONSENT

Art. 1195. Consent to adoption given in open court; effect.

A. Any parent may give consent to the adoption of his child in open court, provided that all of the following occur:

(1) The parent appears before the court in person.

(2) The court informs the parent of the consequences of his consent.

(3) The parent voluntarily consents to the adoption.

B. Upon acceptance by the court, the parent's consent to the adoption is irrevocable.

C. Upon acceptance by the court, the parent shall execute the Statement of Family History set out in Article 1125.
(Added by Acts 1991 No. 235, §12; chgd. by Acts 1992 No. 705, §1, eff. 7/6/92.)

Art. 1196. Release of claims by alleged father; consent to adoption.

A. At any time following the birth of the child, any alleged or adjudicated father may execute an authentic act of consent to the adoption of his child, releasing any real or potential claims to the child, including a waiver of service for any subsequent adoption proceeding.

B. Such a consent shall be irrevocable upon execution.

C. Such a consent shall not be evidence of a confession, admission, or acknowledgment of paternity in any proceeding.

D. A father as described by Article 1193(2) shall not be authorized to execute a release of claims but may execute a surrender in accordance with Article 1122.
(Added by Acts 1991 No. 235, §12; chgd. by Acts 1992 No. 705, §1; Acts 1993 No. 634, §1, eff. 6/15/93.)

CHAPTER 8. PRIOR CLEARANCE OF ORIGINAL BIRTH CERTIFICATE

Art. 1197. Birth certificate requirement.

Prior to the initiation of any adoption under the provisions of this Title, the attorney for the petitioners shall obtain a certified copy of the child's birth certificate, which shall be attached to the petition for adoption. *(Added by Acts 1991 No. 235, §12, eff. 1/1/92.)*

CHAPTER 9. AGENCY ADOPTIONS

Art. 1198. Persons who may petition for adoption.

A single person, eighteen years or older, or a married couple jointly may petition to adopt a child through an agency. When one joint petitioner dies after the petition has been filed, the adoption proceedings may continue as though the survivor was a single original petitioner. *(Added by Acts 1991 No. 235, §12, eff. 1/1/92.)*

Art. 1199. Agency adoption; petition; contents; form.

A. The petition for an agency adoption shall be styled: "In re ______, Applying for Agency Adoption." The petition or an attached exhibit shall state:

(1) The full name, address, age, occupation, and marital status of each petitioner.

(2) The name by which the child is known to petitioners as well as the name under which the birth of the child is recorded.

(3) The place and date of the birth of the child if known; if not known, then the approximate age of the child.

(4) If known, the name of every parent whose consent to the adoption is required pursuant to Article 1193(1) and (2) and proof of their consent, or the name of every parent and the reason such consent is not required.

(5) The diligent efforts made in accordance with Article 1135(B), if the alleged father of the child is unknown, which establish that his rights should be terminated in accordance with Article 1135(A).

(6) The date and circumstances under which the child entered the home of the petitioner.

(7) Any relationship existing between the petitioner and the child.

B. The petition shall be accompanied by a certified copy of any order terminating the rights of the child's parents.
(Added by Acts 1991 No. 235, §12; chgd. by Acts 1993 No. 634, §1, eff. 6/15/93.)

Art. 1200. Permissible reimbursement of expenses.

A. Payments made by the adoptive parents to the department of Social Services, or to a child-placing agency for reimbursement of the following expenses are permissible and not a violation of R.S. 14:286:

(1) Medical and hospital expenses incurred by the natural mother for prenatal care and those medical and hospital expenses incurred by the natural mother and child incident to birth.

(2) Medical, hospital, and foster care expenses incurred on behalf of the child prior to the decree of adoption.

(3) Reasonable expenses incurred by the department or the agency for adjustment counseling and training services provided to the adoptive parents and for home studies or investigations.

(4) Reasonable administrative expenses incurred by the department or the agency, including overhead costs and attorney fees.

B. Adoptive parents shall pay to the Department of Social Services any of the expenses listed in Paragraph A of this Article which may be imposed by the department. Such payments shall be imposed solely at the discretion of the department. The department shall not include payment of the expenses listed in Paragraph A of this Article as a requirement for adoption. *(Added by Acts 1991 No. 235, §12, eff. 1/1/92.)*

Art. 1201. Adoption disclosure affidavit of fees and charges.

A. Each petition for an agency adoption shall be accompanied by an affidavit executed by the petitioner and petitioner's attorney containing an accounting of fees and charges paid or agreed to be paid by or on behalf of the petitioner in connection with the adoption.

B. The affidavit shall not include any identifying information as to the biological parents, their families, or the child's birth name.

C. The form for the affidavit shall be as follows:

"ADOPTION DISCLOSURE AFFIDAVIT

BEFORE ME, the undersigned authority, personally came and appeared _____ (petitioner) and _____ (attorney for petitioner), who, being first duly sworn, did depose and state:

In the matter of the adoption by _____ (petitioner's name):

1. We report the following fees and charges, or other things of value given in connection with this adoption:

	Actual	Estimated	Due or paid to
A. Attorney fees:	$	$	
B. Adoption agency fees:			
C. Medical costs:			
1. Child			
2. Birth mother			
D. Birth mother's expenses:			
1. Room and board			
2. Travel			
3. Mental health counseling			
E. Other: fees, charges, or other things of value (specify):			
	Actual total $	Estimated total $	

2. We certify that no other fees, charges, or things of value other than court costs have been given or shall be given by any party in this adoption proceeding.
3. We declare that this disclosure statement has been examined by each of us and that its contents are true to the best of our information, knowledge, and belief.
4. We understand that each of us has a continuing obligation to supplement and amend this affidavit as necessary.
5. We understand that this information may be released by written authorization of the court for purposes of a grand jury investigation pursuant to R.S. 14:286 or for an ethical investigation by the Committee on Professional Responsibility of the Louisiana Bar Association.

____________________ ____________________

Signature of Petitioner Signature of Attorney

____________________ ____________________

Address Address

SWORN TO AND SUBSCRIBED BEFORE ME ON THIS _____ DAY OF ____________, 19____.

____

(NOTARY PUBLIC)"

D. The adoption disclosure affidavit shall not be included as an exhibit for service with a copy of the petition under Article 1202.

E. Confidentiality of the information contained in the adoption disclosure affidavit shall be maintained as provided in Chapter 5 of this Title, and shall be released only on written authorization of the court for the purposes of a grand jury investigation of a violation of R.S. 14:286 or an ethical investigation by the Committee on Professional Responsibility of the Louisiana Bar Association.

(Added by Acts 1991 No. 235, §12; chgd. by Acts 1993 No. 634, §1, eff. 6/15/93.)

Art. 1202. Service of process.

A. A copy of the petition for an agency adoption together with all exhibits shall be served by registered or certified mail, return receipt requested, postage prepaid and properly addressed to the department and on any agency having legal custody of the child. Two copies of the same petition need not be served on the department.

B. Except when waived, notice of the filing of the petition shall be served on any parent whose parental rights have not been terminated by a court of competent jurisdiction.

C. If the adoption petition names an alleged or adjudicated father and his parental rights have not been terminated by a court of competent jurisdiction, he shall be served with notice of the filing of the petition in accordance with Articles 1133, 1134, and 1136 and thereafter, his rights shall be determined in accordance with the provisions of Articles 1137 through 1143.

(Added by Acts 1991 No. 235, §12; chgd. by Acts 1992 No. 705, §1; Acts 1993 No. 634, §1, eff. 6/15/93.)

Art. 1203. Service; resident parent.

If a parent upon whom service is required under Article 1202 resides within this state, service shall be made either personally or by domiciliary service not less than thirty days prior to the commencement of the hearing on the petition. *(Added by Acts 1991 No. 235, §12, eff. 1/1/92.)*

Art. 1204. Service; nonresident parent.

If a parent upon whom service is required under Article 1202 does not reside within this state, service shall be made by registered or certified mail, return receipt requested, postage prepaid and properly addressed to the address indicated in the petition not less than thirty days prior to commencement of the hearing on the petition. *(Added by Acts 1991 No. 235, §12; chgd. by Acts 1992 No. 705, §1, eff. 7/6/92.)*

Art. 1205. Service; absentee parent; curator ad hoc.

A. If a parent upon whom service is required under Article 1202 cannot be served in accordance with the provisions of Article 1203 or 1204, the court shall appoint an attorney at law as curator ad hoc for the parent and service shall be made upon the curator ad hoc.

B. Upon appointment of the curator ad hoc, a copy of the court order shall be forwarded to the department.

C. The fees and costs of the curator ad hoc shall be paid by the petitioner, notwithstanding any provision of law to the contrary.

(Added by Acts 1991 No. 235, §12, eff. 1/1/92.)

Art. 1206. Duties of curator ad hoc.

A. The curator ad hoc shall make a diligent effort to locate the parent and notify him of the pendency and nature of the proceedings. Any appearances or acceptances of service by the curator ad hoc shall be valid, but he shall not be allowed to waive any rights of notice.

B. The curator ad hoc shall submit to the court a note of evidence indicating the efforts made to locate the parent and shall receive an appropriate fee.

(Added by Acts 1991 No. 235, §12, eff. 1/1/92.)

Art. 1207. Duties of department; home study; confidential report.

A. The department shall investigate the proposed agency adoption and submit a confidential report of its findings to the court. The findings shall include:

(1) The conditions with respect to the availability of the child for adoption.

(2) The physical and mental condition of the child.

(3) Other factors regarding the suitability of the child for adoption in petitioner's home.

(4) The moral and financial fitness of the petitioner.

(5) The conditions of the proposed adoptive home with respect to health, adjustment, and other advantages or disadvantages to the child.

B. The department shall make every effort to locate any living parent whose consent is required under Article 1193 to determine the parent's attitude toward the proposed adoption. If a curator ad hoc has been appointed by the court pursuant to Article 1205, the department shall supply him with all information pertinent to the location of an absentee parent within fifteen days of its receipt of a copy of the order appointing the curator ad hoc.
(Added by Acts 1991 No. 235, §12, eff. 1/1/92.)

Art. 1208. Hearing.

A. The court shall set a time and place for the hearing of the petition for agency adoption not less than thirty nor more than sixty days after the filing of the adoption petition. The court may extend this time for good cause, which may include a showing by the department that it has been impossible to gather the necessary data within the time prescribed. The court may reduce the time to a minimum of fifteen days with written approval of the department and the petitioner.

B. At this hearing the court shall consider:

(1) Any motion to intervene which has been filed.

(2) Any other issues in dispute.

(3) The confidential report of the department.

(4) The testimony of the parties.

C. If the child to be adopted is twelve years of age or older, the court shall solicit and consider his wishes in the matter.
(Added by Acts 1991 No. 235, §12; chgd. by Acts 1993 No. 634, §1, eff. 6/15/93.)

Art. 1209. Intervention.

A. Intervention in agency adoption proceedings shall not be allowed except on motion to the court and a showing of good cause.

B. Such intervention shall be limited to persons having a substantial caretaking relationship with the child for one year or longer, or any other person that the court finds to be a party in interest.

C. The intervention of a party in interest shall be for the limited purpose of presenting evidence as to the best interests of the child.
(Added by Acts 1991 No. 235, §12, eff. 1/1/92.)

Art. 1210. Interlocutory decree.

Upon due consideration of the factors enumerated in Article 1208(B), the court may grant or refuse to grant an interlocutory decree during or after the hearing. The basic consideration for this decree shall be the best interests of the child. *(Added by Acts 1991 No. 235, §12, eff. 1/1/92.)*

Art. 1211. Final decree at first hearing.

The court, upon due consideration of the factors enumerated in Article 1208(B), may render a final decree of agency adoption at the first hearing, without the necessity of first entering an interlocutory decree, if either:

(1) The child was placed in the petitioner's home by an agency and the child has lived in that home for at least six months prior to the hearing for adoption.

(2) The rights of the child's parents have been terminated pursuant to Titles X or XI and the child has lived in the petitioner's home for at least one year.
(Added by Acts 1991 No. 235, §12, eff. 1/1/92.)

Art. 1212. Effect of interlocutory decree.

Upon issuance of an interlocutory decree; the period that must elapse prior to application for final decree of adoption begins to run. *(Added by Acts 1991 No. 235, §12, eff. 1/1/92.)*

Art. 1213. Continuing duties of department.

A. After an interlocutory decree has been entered, the department shall maintain contact with the proposed adoptive home directly or through another agency. The number of visits to the home and the time for them shall be within the discretion of the department. However, no less than two visits shall be made to the home, one of which shall occur within thirty days before the final decree of agency adoption.

B. A second confidential report must be presented to the court preceding the hearing on the final decree of agency adoption. The findings of this report shall be based upon the same considerations as prescribed in Article 1207 and shall disclose any changed conditions and all new pertinent information.
(Added by Acts 1991 No. 235, §12, eff. 1/1/92.)

Art. 1214. Expiration of interlocutory decree.

If no petition for a final decree is filed within two years after the granting of an interlocutory decree, the latter shall become null and void unless good cause is shown why an extension should be granted. *(Added by Acts 1991 No. 235, §12, eff. 1/1/92.)*

Art. 1215. Revocation of interlocutory decree.

A. At any time before the entry of the final decree of agency adoption, the court for good cause may revoke its interlocutory decree either on its own motion or on the motion of the department or on the motion of the petitioner or any person interested in the child.

B. All parties upon whom service was originally made shall be notified at least ten days prior to the signing of the order of revocation and shall be given an opportunity to be heard upon their written request.
(Added by Acts 1991 No. 235, §12, eff. 1/1/92.)

Art. 1216. Petition for final decree.

A. The child shall have lived with the petitioner for at least one year and at least six months shall have elapsed after the granting of an interlocutory decree before the petitioner may file a petition for final decree of agency adoption.

B. The court shall set a time and place for the hearing of the petition for final decree. The petition for final decree need not be served upon anyone except the department.
(Added by Acts 1991 No. 235, §12, eff. 1/1/92.)

Art. 1217. Final decree; standard.

The court, after hearing and after taking into consideration information from all sources concerning the adoption, may enter a final decree of agency adoption, or it may deny the adoption. The basic consideration shall be the best interests of the child. *(Added by Acts 1991 No. 235, §12, eff. 1/1/92.)*

Art. 1218. Effect of final decree.

A. Except as otherwise provided in this Title, upon a final decree of agency adoption, the parents of the child whose rights have not been previously terminated by a surrender or a judgment of termination are relieved of all their legal duties and divested of all their legal rights with regard to the adopted child, and the adopted child is relieved of all of his legal duties and divested of all his legal rights with regard to the parents, except the right of the child to inherit from his parents.

B. Under the circumstances and pursuant to the procedures authorized by Chapter 14 of this Title, grandparents may obtain limited visitation rights to the adopted child.
(Added by Acts 1991 No. 235, §12, eff. 1/1/92.)

Art. 1219. Change of name.

The full name of the adopted child may be changed in the final decree of agency adoption and, if changed, the surname shall be the same as that of the adoptive parent. *(Added by Acts 1991 No. 235, §12, eff. 1/1/92.)*

Art. 1220. Refusal of interlocutory or final decree.

Upon refusal to grant an interlocutory or final decree to the petitioners for the reason that the agency adoption is not in the best interests of the child, the court may remove the child from the petitioner and reinstate the legal custodian or appoint a custodian. *(Added by Acts 1991 No. 235, §12, eff. 1/1/92.)*

CHAPTER 10. PRIVATE ADOPTIONS

Article

Art. 1221. Persons who may petition for adoption.

A single person, eighteen years or older, or a married couple jointly may petition to privately adopt a child. When one joint petitioner dies after the petition has been filed, the adoption proceedings may continue as though the survivor was a single original petitioner.
(Added by Acts 1991 No. 235, §12, eff. 1/1/92.)

Art. 1222. Private adoptions; petition; contents.

A. The petition shall be styled: "In re _____, Applying for Private Adoption." The petition or an attached exhibit shall state:

(1) The full name, address, age, occupation, and marital status of each petitioner.

(2) The name by which the child is known to petitioners as well as the name under which the birth of the child is recorded.

(3) The place and date of the birth of the child if known; if not known, then the approximate age of the child.

(4) If known, the name of every parent whose consent to the adoption is required pursuant to Article 1193(1) and (2) and proof of their consent, or the name of every parent and the reason such consent is not required.

(5) The diligent efforts made in accordance with Article 1135(B), if the alleged father of the child is unknown, which establish that his rights should be terminated in accordance with Article 1135(A).

(6) The date and circumstances under which the child entered the home of the petitioner.

(7) Any relationship existing between the petitioner and the child.

B. The petition shall be accompanied by a certified copy of any order terminating the rights of the child's parents.
(Added by Acts 1991 No. 235, §12; chgd. by Acts 1993 No. 634, §1, eff. 6/15/93.)

Art. 1223. Adoption disclosure affidavit of fees and charges; form.

A. Each petition for private adoption shall be accompanied by an affidavit executed by petitioner and petitioner's attorney containing an accounting of fees and charges paid or agreed to be paid by or on behalf of the petitioner in connection with the adoption.

B. The affidavit shall not include any identifying information as to the biological parents, their families, or the child's birth name.

C. The form for the affidavit shall be as follows:

"ADOPTION DISCLOSURE AFFIDAVIT

BEFORE ME, the undersigned authority, personally came and appeared _______________ (petitioner) and __________________ (attorney for petitioner), who, being first duly sworn, did depose and state:

In the matter of the adoption of _______________ (adoptee's name), __________ (court number), by _________________ (petitioner's name):

1. We report the following fees and charges, or other things of value given in connection with this adoption:

	Actual	Estimated	Due or paid to
A. Attorney fees:	$	$	
B. Adoption agency fees:			
C. Medical costs:			
1. Child			
2. Birth mother			
D. Birth mother's expenses:			
1. Room and board			
2. Travel			
3. Mental health counseling			
E. Other: fees, charges or other things of value (specify):			
	Actual total $	Estimated total $	

2. We certify that no other fees, charges, or things of value other than court costs have been given or shall be given by any party in this adoption proceeding.
3. We declare that this disclosure statement has been examined by both of us and that its contents are true to the best of our information, knowledge, and belief.
4. We understand that each of us has a continuing obligation to supplement and amend this affidavit as necessary.
5. We understand that this information may be released by written authorization of the court for purposes of a grand jury investigation pursuant to R.S. 14:286 or for an ethical investigation by the Committee on Professional Responsibility of the Louisiana Bar Association.

_____________________ _____________________
Signature of Petitioner Signature of Attorney

_____________________ _____________________
Address Address

SWORN TO AND SUBSCRIBED BEFORE ME ON THIS _____ DAY OF ___________, 19____.

____
(NOTARY PUBLIC)"

D. The adoption disclosure affidavit shall not be included as an exhibit for service with a copy of the petition under Article 1224.

E. Confidentiality of the information contained in the adoption disclosure affidavit shall be maintained as provided in Chapter 5 of this Title, and shall be released only on written authorization of the court for the purposes of a grand jury investigation of a violation of R.S. 14:286 or an ethical investigation by the Committee on Professional Responsibility of the Louisiana Bar Association.

(Added by Acts 1991 No. 235, §12, eff. 1/1/92.)

Art. 1224. Service of process.

A. A copy of the petition for private adoption together with all exhibits shall be served by registered or certified mail, return receipt requested, postage prepaid and properly addressed to the department.

B. Except when waived, notice of the filing of the petition shall be served on any parent whose parental rights have not been terminated by a court of competent jurisdiction.

C. If the adoption petition names an alleged or adjudicated father and his parental rights have not been terminated by a court of competent jurisdiction, he shall be served with notice of the filing of the petition in accordance with Articles 1133, 1134, and 1136 and thereafter, his rights shall be determined in accordance with the provisions of Articles 1137 through 1143.
(Added by Acts 1991 No. 235, §12; chgd. by Acts 1993 No. 634, §1, eff. 6/15/93.)

Art. 1225. Service; resident parent.

If a parent upon whom service is required under Article 1224 resides within this state, service shall be made either personally or by domiciliary service not less than thirty days prior to the commencement of the hearing on the petition.
(Added by Acts 1991 No. 235, §12, eff. 1/1/92.)

Art. 1226. Service; nonresident parent.

If a parent upon whom service is required under Article 1224 does not reside within this state, service shall be made by registered mail to the address indicated in the petition, return receipt required, not less than thirty days prior to commencement of the hearing on the petition. *(Added by Acts 1991 No. 235, §12, eff. 1/1/92.)*

Art. 1227. Service; absentee parent; curator ad hoc.

A. If a parent upon whom service is required under Article 1224 cannot be served in accordance with the provisions of Article 1225 or 1226, the court shall appoint an attorney at law as curator ad hoc for the parent and service shall be made upon the curator ad hoc.

B. Upon appointment of the curator ad hoc, a copy of the letter of appointment shall be forwarded to the department.

C. The fees and costs of the curator ad hoc shall be paid by the petitioner notwithstanding any provision of law to the contrary.
(Added by Acts 1991 No. 235, §12, eff. 1/1/92.)

Art. 1228. Duties of curator ad hoc.

A. The curator ad hoc shall make a diligent effort to locate the parent and notify him of the pendency and nature of the proceedings. Any appearances or acceptances of service by the curator ad hoc shall be valid but he shall not be allowed to waive any rights of notice.

B. The curator ad hoc shall submit to the court a note of evidence indicating the efforts made to locate the parent and shall receive an appropriate fee.
(Added by Acts 1991 No. 235, §12, eff. 1/1/92.)

Art. 1229. Duties of department; home study; confidential report.

A. The department shall investigate the proposed private adoption and submit a confidential report of its findings to the court. The findings shall include:

(1) The conditions with respect to the availability of the child for adoption.
(2) The physical and mental condition of the child.
(3) Other factors regarding the suitability of the child for adoption in petitioner's home.
(4) The moral and financial fitness of the petitioner.
(5) The conditions of the proposed adoptive home with respect to health, adjustment, and other advantages or disadvantages to the child.

B. The department shall make every effort to locate any living parent whose consent is required under Article 1193 to determine the parent's attitude toward the proposed adoption. If a curator ad hoc has been appointed by the court pursuant to Article 1227 the department shall supply him with all information pertinent to the location of an absentee parent within fifteen days of its receipt of a copy of the order appointing the curator ad hoc.
(Added by Acts 1991 No. 235, §12, eff. 1/1/92.)

Art. 1230. Hearing.

A. The court shall set a time and place for the hearing of the petition for private adoption not less than thirty nor more than sixty days after the filing of the adoption petition. The court may extend this time for good cause, which may include a showing by the department that it has been impossible to gather the necessary data within the time prescribed. The court may reduce the time to a minimum of fifteen days with written approval of the department and the petitioner.

B. At this hearing the court shall consider:
(1) Any motion to intervene which has been filed.
(2) Any other issues in dispute.
(3) The confidential report of the department.
(4) The testimony of the parties.
C. If the child to be adopted is twelve years of age or older, the court shall solicit and consider his wishes in the matter.
(Added by Acts 1991 No. 235, §12; chgd. by Acts 1993 No. 634, §1, eff. 6/15/93.)

Art. 1231. Intervention.
A. Intervention in private adoption proceedings shall not be allowed except on motion to the court and a showing of good cause.
B. Such intervention shall be limited to persons having a substantial caretaking relationship with the child for one year or longer, or any other person that the court finds to be a party in interest.
C. The intervention of a party in interest shall be for the limited purpose of presenting evidence as to the best interests of the child.
(Added by Acts 1991 No. 235, §12, eff. 1/1/92.)

Art. 1232. Interlocutory decree.
Upon due consideration of the factors enumerated in Article 1230(B), the court may grant or refuse to grant an interlocutory decree during or after the hearing. The basic consideration for this decree shall be the best interests of the child. *(Added by Acts 1991 No. 235, §12, eff. 1/1/92.)*

Art. 1233. Final decree at first hearing.
The court, upon due consideration of the factors enumerated in Article 1230(B), may render a final decree of private adoption at the first hearing, without the necessity of first entering an interlocutory decree, if either:
(1) The rights of the child's parents have been terminated pursuant to Title X or XI and the child has lived in the petitioner's home for one year.
(2) A parent petitions to adopt his child born out of wedlock.
(Added by Acts 1991 No. 235, §12; chgd. by Acts 1993 No. 634, §1, eff. 6/15/93.)

Art. 1234. Effect of interlocutory decree.
Upon issuance of an interlocutory decree, the period that must elapse prior to application for final decree of private adoption begins to run. *(Added by Acts 1991 No. 235, §12, eff. 1/1/92.)*

Art. 1235. Continuing duties of department.
A. After an interlocutory decree has been entered, the department shall maintain contact with the proposed adoptive home directly or through another agency. The number of visits to the home and the time for them shall be within the discretion of the department. However, no less than two visits shall be made to the home, one of which shall occur within thirty days before the final decree of private adoption.
B. A second confidential report must be presented to the court preceding the hearing on the final decree of private adoption. The findings of this report shall be based upon the same considerations as prescribed in Article 1229 and shall disclose any changed conditions and all new pertinent information.
(Added by Acts 1991 No. 235, §12, eff. 1/1/92.)

Art. 1236. Expiration of interlocutory decree.
If no petition for a final decree is filed within two years after the granting of an interlocutory decree, the latter shall become null and void unless good cause is shown why an extension should be granted. *(Added by Acts 1991 No. 235, §12, eff. 1/1/92.)*

Art. 1237. Revocation of interlocutory decree.
A. At any time before the entry of the final decree of private adoption, the court for good cause may revoke its interlocutory decree either on its own motion or on the motion of the department or on the motion of the petitioner or any person interested in the child.

B. All parties upon whom service was originally made shall be notified at least ten days prior to the signing of the order of revocation and shall be given an opportunity to be heard upon their written request.
(Added by Acts 1991 No. 235, §12, eff. 1/1/92.)

Art. 1238. Petition for final decree.

A. The child shall have lived with the petitioner for at least one year and at least six months shall have elapsed after the granting of an interlocutory decree before the petitioner may file a petition for final decree of private adoption.

B. The court shall set a time and place for the hearing of the petition for final decree. The petition for final decree need not be served upon anyone except the department.
(Added by Acts 1991 No. 235, §12, eff. 1/1/92.)

Art. 1239. Final decree; standard.

The court, after hearing and after taking into consideration information from all sources concerning the adoption, may enter a final decree of private adoption, or it may deny the adoption. The basic consideration shall be the best interests of the child. *(Added by Acts 1991 No. 235, §12, eff. 1/1/92.)*

Art. 1240. Effect of final decree.

A. Except as otherwise provided in this Title, upon a final decree of private adoption, the parents of the child whose rights have not been previously terminated by a surrender or a judgment of termination are relieved of all their legal duties and divested of all their legal rights with regard to the adopted child, and the adopted child is relieved of all of his legal duties and divested of all his legal rights with regard to the parents, except the right of the child to inherit from his parents.

B. Under the circumstances and pursuant to the procedures authorized by Chapter 14 of this Title, grandparents may obtain limited visitation rights to the adopted child.
(Added by Acts 1991 No. 235, §12, eff. 1/1/92.)

Art. 1241. Change of name.

The full name of the adopted child may be changed in the final decree of private adoption and, if changed, the surname shall be the same as that of the adoptive parent. *(Added by Acts 1991 No. 235, §12, eff. 1/1/92.)*

Art. 1242. Refusal of interlocutory or final decree.

Upon refusal to grant an interlocutory or final decree to the petitioners for the reason that the private adoption is not in the best interests of the child, the court may remove the child from the petitioner and reinstate the legal custodian or appoint a custodian. *(Added by Acts 1991 No. 235, §12, eff. 1/1/92.)*

CHAPTER 11. INTRAFAMILY ADOPTIONS

Art. 1243. Persons who may petition for intrafamily adoption.

A. The following persons may petition for an intrafamily adoption:

(1) A stepparent married to the parent of a child, provided that the parent is recognized as having parental rights in accordance with Article 1193.

(2) A single grandparent, married grandparents, or aunt or uncle, of a child, provided all the following exist:

(a) The parent through whom the grandparent, aunt, or uncle is claiming the right to petition is a parent recognized as having parental rights in accordance with Article 1193.

(b) The child has been in the home of the grandparent, aunt, or uncle for six months prior to the filing of a petition for adoption.

B. When the spouse of the stepparent or one joint petitioner dies after the petition has been filed, the adoption proceedings may continue as though the survivor was a single original petitioner.

C. For purposes of this Chapter:

(a) "Aunt" or "uncle" means a sibling of a parent of the child.

(b) "Grandparent" includes a great grandparent.

(Added by Acts 1991 No. 235, §12; chgd. by Acts 1992 No. 733, §1; Acts 1993 No. 634, §1; Acts 1997 No. 256, §1, eff. 8/15/97.)

Art. 1244. Consent of parent.

A. Notwithstanding any provision of law to the contrary, any parent may execute an authentic act consenting to the adoption of his child, including a waiver of service for any subsequent adoption proceeding.

B. If the parent of a legitimate child is married to the stepparent petitioner and executes an authentic act of consent, he need not join in the petition nor be served with a copy thereof.

C. The parent of an illegitimate child who is married to the petitioning spouse shall join in the petition.

D. No surrender of parental rights pursuant to Title XI, including the requirements thereunder, is required for a valid consent under the provisions of this Chapter.

(Added by Acts 1991 No. 235, §12; chgd. by Acts 1992 No. 705, §1; Acts 1993 No. 634, §1; Acts 1997 No. 256, §1, eff. 8/15/97.)

Art. 1245. Parental consent not necessary.

A. The consent of a parent as required by Article 1193 may be dispensed with upon proof of the required elements of either Paragraph B, C, or D.

B. When a grandparent, aunt, or uncle has been granted custody of the child by a court of competent jurisdiction and any one of the following conditions exist:

(1) A parent has refused or failed to comply with a court order of support for a period of one year.

(2) A parent is a nonresident of this state and has failed to support the child for a period of one year after a judgment awarding custody to the grandparent, aunt, or uncle.

(3) A parent has refused or failed to visit, communicate, or attempt to communicate with the child without just cause for a period of two years.

C. When a parent is married to a stepparent petitioner and both of the following conditions exist:

(1) The parent married to the stepparent petitioner has been granted sole or joint custody of the child by a court of competent jurisdiction.

(2) The noncustodial parent is a nonresident of this state and has failed to support the child for a period of one year after the judgment awarding custody.

D. When a parent lawfully exercising actual custody of the child is married to a stepparent petitioner and either of the following conditions exist:

(1) The other parent has refused or failed to comply with a court order of support for a period of one year.

(2) The other parent has refused or failed to visit, communicate, or attempt to communicate with the child without just cause for a period of two years.

(Added by Acts 1991 No. 235, §12; chgd. by Acts 1997 No. 256, §1, eff. 8/15/97.)

Art. 1246. Intrafamily adoptions; petition; contents; form.

The petition shall be styled: "In re _____, Applying for Intrafamily Adoption." The petition or an attached exhibit shall state:

(1) The full name, address, age, occupation, and marital status of each petitioner.

(2) The name by which the child is known to petitioners as well as the name under which the birth of the child is recorded.

(3) The place and date of the birth of the child if known; if not known, then the approximate age of the child.

(4) If known, the name of every parent whose consent to the adoption is required pursuant to Article 1193(1) and (2) and proof of their consent, or the name of every parent and the reason such consent is not required as authorized by Article 1245.

(5) The diligent efforts made in accordance with Article 1135(B), if the alleged father of the child in unknown, which establish that his rights should be terminated in accordance with Article 1135(A).

(6) The date and circumstances under which the child entered the home of the petitioner.

(7) Any relationship existing between the petitioner and the child.

(Added by Acts 1991 No. 235, §12; chgd. by Acts 1993 No. 634, §1, eff. 6/15/93.)

Art. 1247. Service of process.

A. A copy of the petition for intrafamily adoption together with all exhibits shall be served by registered or certified mail, return receipt requested, postage prepaid, and properly addressed to the department.

B. Except when waived in accordance with the provision of Title XI or XII, notice of the filing of the petition shall be served on any parent whose parental rights have not been terminated by a court of competent jurisdiction.

C. If the adoption petition names an alleged or adjudicated father and his parental rights have not been terminated by a court of competent jurisdiction, he shall be served with notice of the filing of the petition in accordance with Articles 1133, 1134, and 1136 and thereafter, his rights shall be determined in accordance with the provision of Articles 1137 through 1143. *(Added by Acts 1991 No. 235, §12; chgd. by Acts 1993 No. 634, §1; Acts 1995 No. 1095, §6, eff. 8/15/95.)*

Art. 1248. Service; resident parent.

If a parent upon whom service is required under Article 1247 resides within this state, service shall be made either personally or by domiciliary service not less than thirty days prior to the commencement of the hearing on the petition. *(Added by Acts 1991 No. 235, §12, eff. 1/1/92.)*

Art. 1249. Service; nonresident parent.

If a parent upon whom service is required under Article 1247 does not reside within this state, service shall be made by registered mail to the address indicated in the petition, return receipt required, not less than thirty days prior to commencement of the hearing on the petition. *(Added by Acts 1991 No. 235, §12, eff. 1/1/92.)*

Art. 1250. Service; absentee parent; curator ad hoc.

A. If a parent upon whom service is required under Article 1247 cannot be served in accordance with the provisions of Article 1248 or 1249, the court shall appoint an attorney at law as curator ad hoc for the parent and service shall be made upon the curator ad hoc.

B. Upon appointment of the curator ad hoc, a copy of the letter of appointment shall be forwarded to the department.

C. The fees and costs of the curator ad hoc shall be paid by the petitioner, notwithstanding any provision of law to the contrary.

(Added by Acts 1991 No. 235, §12, eff. 1/1/92.)

Art. 1251. Duties of curator ad hoc.

A. The curator ad hoc shall make a diligent effort to locate the parent and notify him of the pendency and nature of the proceedings. Any appearances or acceptances of service by the curator ad hoc shall be valid, but he shall not be allowed to waive any rights of notice.

B. The curator ad hoc shall submit to the court a note of evidence indicating the efforts made to locate the parent and shall receive an appropriate fee.

(Added by Acts 1991 No. 235, §12, eff. 1/1/92.)

Art. 1252. Duties of department; home study; confidential report.

A. The department need not investigate the proposed intrafamily adoption except upon order of the court. If the court orders an investigation, it may request any information which it deems relevant and require that the department submit a confidential report of its findings to the court.

B. The department shall make every effort to locate any living parent whose consent is required under Article 1193 to determine the parent's attitude toward the proposed adoption. If a curator ad hoc has been appointed by the court pursuant to Article 1250, the department shall supply him with all information pertinent to the location of an absentee parent within fifteen days of its receipt of a copy of the order appointing the curator ad hoc.

(Added by Acts 1991 No. 235, §12, eff. 1/1/92.)

Art. 1253. Hearing.

A. The court shall set a time and place for the hearing of the petition for intrafamily adoption not less than thirty nor more than sixty days after the filing of the adoption petition. The court may extend this time for good cause, which may include a showing by the department that it has been impossible to gather the necessary data within the time prescribed. The court may reduce the time to a minimum of fifteen days with written approval of the department and the petitioner.

B. At this hearing the court shall consider:

(1) Any motion to intervene which has been filed.

(2) Any other issues in dispute.

(3) The confidential report of the department, if any.

(4) The testimony of the parties.

C. If the child to be adopted is twelve years of age or older, the court shall solicit and consider his wishes in the matter.

(Added by Acts 1991 No. 235, §12; chgd. by Acts 1993 No. 634, §1, eff. 6/15/93.)

Art. 1254. Intervention.

A. Intervention in intrafamily adoption proceedings shall not be allowed except on motion to the court and a showing of good cause.

B. Such intervention shall be limited to persons having a substantial caretaking relationship with the child for one year or longer, or any other person that the court finds to be a party in interest.

C. The intervention of a party in interest shall be for the limited purpose of presenting evidence as to the best interests of the child.

(Added by Acts 1991 No. 235, §12, eff. 1/1/92.)

Art. 1255. Final decree; standard.

A. The court, after hearing and after taking into consideration information from all sources concerning the intrafamily adoption, may enter a final decree of adoption, or it may deny the adoption. The basic consideration shall be the best interests of the child.

B. When a court has granted custody to either the child's grandparents or his parent married to the stepparent petitioner, there shall be a rebuttable presumption that this adoption is in the best interests of the child.

(Added by Acts 1991 No. 235, §12, eff. 1/1/92.)

Art. 1256. Effect of final decree.

A. Except as otherwise provided by Paragraph C of this Article, upon a final decree of adoption, the parents of the child whose rights have not been previously terminated by a surrender or a judgment of termination and all other blood relatives of the adopted child are relieved of all their legal duties and divested of all their legal rights with regard to the adopted child including the right of inheritance from the adopted child and his lawful descendants, and the adopted child and his lawful descendants are relieved of all legal duties and divested of all legal rights with regard to the parents and other blood relatives.

B. The right of the child to inherit from his parents and other blood relatives is unaffected by the adoption.

C. If the adoptive parent is married to a blood parent of the adopted child, the relationship of that blood parent and his blood relatives to the adopted child shall remain unaltered and unaffected by the adoption.

D. Under the circumstances and pursuant to the procedures authorized by Chapter 14 of this Title, grandparents may obtain limited visitation rights to the adopted child.
(Added by Acts 1991 No. 235, §12, eff. 1/1/92.)

Art. 1257. Change of name.

The full name of the adopted child may be changed in the final decree of intrafamily adoption and, if changed, the surname shall be the same as that of the adoptive parent. *(Added by Acts 1991 No. 235, §12, eff. 1/1/92.)*

Art. 1258. Refusal of interlocutory or final decree.

Upon refusal to grant an interlocutory or final decree to the petitioners for the reason that the intrafamily adoption is not in the best interests of the child, the court may remove the child from the petitioner and reinstate the legal custodian or appoint a custodian. *(Added by Acts 1991 No. 235, §12, eff. 1/1/92.)*

CHAPTER 12. APPEAL

Article

Art. 1259. Appeal of judgment; time limitations.

A. Any party to the proceedings or any other party in interest shall have the right to appeal a judgment granting or refusing to grant an interlocutory or final decree regarding any type of adoption within thirty days after the rendition of a judgment or decree.

B. If no appeal is perfected within thirty days after a judgment is rendered, the judgment shall be final.
(Added by Acts 1991 No. 235, §12, eff. 1/1/92.)

Art. 1260. Appellate jurisdiction.

All appeals from any judgment rendered in accordance with this Title shall be to the proper court of appeal on both law and fact. *(Added by Acts 1991 No. 235, §12, eff. 1/1/92.)*

Art. 1261. Suspensive nature.

All appeals from any judgment rendered in accordance with this Title shall be suspensive in nature. There shall be no requirement for posting of bond. Otherwise, the appeal shall be governed by Chapter 9 of Title III. *(Added by Acts 1991 No. 235, §12, eff. 1/1/92.)*

CHAPTER 13. ANNULMENT OF FINAL DECREES

Article

Art. 1262. Grounds.

No action to annul a final decree of adoption of any type may be brought except on the grounds of fraud or duress. *(Added by Acts 1991 No. 235, §12, eff. 1/1/92.)*

Art. 1263. Time limitations; finality.

A. (1) No action to annul a final decree of adoption of any type may be brought for any reason after a lapse of six months from discovery of the fraud or duress.

(2) However, even as to actions filed within six months from the date of such discovery, in all events such actions to annul a final decree of adoption shall be filed at the latest within a period of four years from the date of the signing of the final decree or mailing of the notice of judgment when required.

B. In an action to annul a final decree of adoption based on fraud or duress perpetrated by the adoptive parent or parents on the petitioning biological parent, the peremptive provisions of Subparagraph A(2) of this Article do not apply.
(Added by Acts 1991 No. 235, §12; chgd. by Acts 1997 No. 796, §1, eff. 7/1/97.)

CHAPTER 14. VISITATION RIGHTS OF GRANDPARENTS

Art. 1264. Post-adoption visitation rights of grandparents.

Notwithstanding any provision of law to the contrary, the natural parents of a deceased party to a marriage dissolved by death whose child is thereafter adopted, and the parents of a party who has forfeited the right to object to the adoption of his child pursuant to Article 1245 may have limited visitation rights to the minor child so adopted. *(Added by Acts 1991 No. 235, §12, eff. 1/1/92.)*

Art. 1265. Motion; filing.

Any request for limited visitation rights shall be made by written motion of the grandparents and filed with the court which rendered the final decree of adoption. *(Added by Acts 1991 No. 235, §12, eff. 1/1/92.)*

Art. 1266. Hearing.

The motion for limited visitation rights shall be set for hearing contradictorily with the adoptive parents. *(Added by Acts 1991 No. 235, §12, eff. 1/1/92.)*

Art. 1267. Burden of proof.

The grandparents requesting limited visitation rights shall prove both of the following:

(1) That they have been unreasonably denied visitation rights.

(2) That such limited visitation rights would be in the best interests of the minor child.

(Added by Acts 1991 No. 235, §12, eff. 1/1/92.)

Art. 1268. Evidence.

A. The court, on its own motion or on motion of any party, may order an investigation to be conducted by the department or may order such psychological evaluations as deemed necessary.

B. The court shall consider all relevant factors in making its determination, including but not limited to reports of psychological evaluations.

(Added by Acts 1991 No. 235, §12, eff. 1/1/92.)

Art. 1269. Order.

The court may issue any limited visitation order that is consistent with the findings of the court and the best interests of the child. *(Added by Acts 1991 No. 235, §12, eff. 1/1/92.)*

CHAPTER 15. VOLUNTARY REGISTRATION

Art. 1270. Legislative findings; purpose.

A. Adoption is based upon the legal termination of parental rights and responsibilities of birth parents and the creation of such a relationship of parent and child between an adoptee and his adoptive parents. These legal and social premises underlying adoption must be maintained. The legislature recognizes that some adults who were adopted as children have a strong interest in identifying information about their birth parents or biological siblings, or both, while other such adult adoptees have no such interest. The legislature further recognizes that some birth parents and biological siblings have a strong interest in identifying information about their biological children or siblings who were surrendered for adoption, while others have no such interest. The legislature fully recognizes the right to privacy and confidentiality of birth parents whose children were adopted, of siblings, and of the adoptees, as well as that of the adoptive family.

B. There is hereby created within the office of community services of the Department of Social Services a voluntary registry for the matching of adopted persons and biological parents or siblings, or both. The purpose of this registry shall be to facilitate voluntary contact between the adopted person and the biological parents or siblings, or both.

C. The use of the registry shall be limited to the adopted person who is at least eighteen years of age, the biological mother, and the biological father, if the biological father has legitimated or formally acknowledged the child as provided by law or has executed a voluntary surrender or consent to the child's adoption regardless of whether the parent's rights were terminated in accordance with Title X or surrendered in accordance with Titles XI and XII, and any biological sibling who is at least eighteen years of age.

D. No registration by an adopted person shall be permitted until all biological siblings who were adopted by the same adoptive parents have reached the age of eighteen years.

E. The registry shall not release any information from adoption records in violation of the privacy or confidentiality rights of a biological parent who has not authorized the release of any information.

(Added by Acts 1991 No. 235, §12; chgd. by Acts 1992 No. 705, §1; Acts 1997 No. 715, §1, eff. 8/15/97.)

Art. 1271. Registration.

A. Registration shall be by affidavit filed with the office of community services, which office shall develop and furnish standardized affidavit forms appropriate for effecting the purpose of this Chapter.

B. Registration shall remain effective indefinitely after filing, unless withdrawn by the affiant by written request.

C. The department may establish registration and renewal fees not to exceed twenty-five dollars.

(Added by Acts 1991 No. 235, §12; chgd. by Acts 1992 No. 705, §1; Acts 1997 No. 715, §1, eff. 8/15/97.)

Art. 1272. Matching; verification by original documents; mandatory counseling.

A. The office of community services shall regularly monitor registrant affidavits, utilizing computer services if necessary, to determine whether or not affidavits have been filed by an adopted person and his biological parents or biological sibling.

B. If there appears to be a match between an adopted person and a biological parent or biological sibling, the office of community services shall notify the respective parties of the match and that each of them must participate in the counseling requirements of Paragraph D of this Article. Upon satisfaction of these requirements and provided none of the parties subsequently withdraws his registration, the office of community services shall provide the details of the match to the licensed social worker or adoption agency that provided counseling for the adopted person, and the social worker or agency shall then contact the registered and matched parties in a careful and confidential manner and give them the information necessary to contact each other.

C. If doubt exists that the adopted person registered and the biological parents or biological sibling registered are indeed biologically related, the office of community services shall advise the parties to petition the court having jurisdiction to open the sealed adoption record for verification. Such verification shall be a compelling reason, within the meaning of Article 1189, to open the adoption records for the limited purpose of verification.

D. Each party shall participate in not less than one hour of counseling with a board-certified social worker or a social worker employed by a licensed adoption agency before they will be put into contact with one another. An adopted person, a biological parent, or a biological sibling who is domiciled outside the state may obtain the required counseling from a social worker or adoption agency, board-certified or licensed in his state of domicile. *(Added by Acts 1991 No. 235, §12; chgd. by Acts 1997 No. 715, §1, eff. 8/15/97.)*

Art. 1273. Confidentiality.

Documents filed with the office of human development, pursuant to this Chapter, shall be confidential and shall not be available for inspection, except under the procedures set forth in this Chapter. *(Added by Acts 1991 No. 235, §12, eff. 1/1/92.)*

Art. 1274. Penalties.

Any employee or former employee of the Department of Social Services, or a licensed adoption agency, or any employee or appointee or former employee or appointee of a court who discloses identifying information other than pursuant to judicial order or through the registry, as provided in this Chapter, shall be guilty of a misdemeanor and shall be fined not less than five hundred dollars and not more than five thousand dollars, or imprisoned for not more than six months, or both. *(Added by Acts 1991 No. 235, §12, eff. 1/1/92.)*

Art. 1275. Nondisclosure.

A. Notwithstanding any provision of law to the contrary, the information acquired by the voluntary registry of Louisiana shall not be disclosed under any sunshine or freedom of information legislation, rules, or practice.

B. Notwithstanding any provision of law to the contrary, no person, group of persons, or entity, including an agency, may file a class action to force the voluntary registry to disclose identifying information.

(Added by Acts 1991 No. 235, §12, eff. 1/1/92.)

Art. 1276. Disclosure of death of birth parents.

In any case where one or both of the birth parents are deceased, and when this fact is known by the voluntary registry or by the licensed adoption agency which originally placed the adult adoptee for adoption, this information shall be disclosed to the adult adoptee who has registered with the office of human development under the provisions of this Chapter. *(Added by Acts 1991 No. 235, §12, eff. 1/1/92.)*

Art. 1277. Other remedies not affected.

Nothing contained in this Chapter shall limit a person's right to proceed under Chapter 5 of this Title to obtain confidential adoption information. *(Added by Acts 1991 No. 235, §12, eff. 1/1/92.)*

Art. 1278. Rules and regulations.

The department shall adopt such reasonable rules and regulations as are necessary to implement the provisions of this Chapter. *(Added by Acts 1991 No. 235, §12, eff. 1/1/92.)*

TITLE XIII. SUPPORT OF FAMILY

CHAPTER 1. UNIFORM INTERSTATE FAMILY SUPPORT ACT

(Chgd. by Acts 1995 No. 251, §1, eff. 1/1/96.)

Section 1. General Provisions

Section 2. Jurisdiction

Subsection A. Extended Personal Jurisdiction

Subsection B. Proceedings Involving Two or More States

Subsection C. Reconciliation of Multiple Orders

Section 3. Provisions of General Application

Section 4. Establishment of Support Order

Section 5. Enforcement of Order of Another State Without Registration

Section 6. Enforcement and Modification of Support Order After Registration

Subsection A. Registration and Enforcement of Support Order

Subsection B. Contest of Validity or Enforcement

Subsection C. Registration and Modification of Child Support Order

Section 7. Determination of Parentage

Section 8. Interstate Rendition

Section 1. General Provisions

(Added by Acts 1995 No. 251, §1, eff. 1/1/96.)

Art. 1301. *(Repealed by Acts 1995 No. 251, §2, eff. 1/1/96.)*

Art. 1301.1. Short title.

This Chapter may be cited as the "Uniform Interstate Family Support Act". *(Added by Acts 1995 No. 251, §1, eff. 1/1/96.)*

Art. 1301.2. Uniformity of application and construction.

This Chapter shall be applied and construed to effectuate its general purpose to make uniform the law with respect to the subject of this Chapter among states enacting it. *(Added by Acts 1995 No. 251, §1, eff. 1/1/96.)*

Art. 1301.3. Definitions.

As used in this Chapter:

(1) "Act" means the Uniform Interstate Family Support Act.

(2) "Child" means an individual, whether over or under the age of majority, who is or is alleged to be owed a duty of support by the individual's parent or who is or is alleged to be the beneficiary of a support order directed to the parent.

(3) "Child support order" means a support order for a child, including a child who has attained the age of majority under the law of the issuing state.

(4) "Department" means the Department of Social Services.

(5) "Duty of support" means an obligation imposed or imposable by law to provide support for a child, spouse, or former spouse, including an unsatisfied obligation to provide support.

(6) "Home state" means the state in which a child lived with a parent or a person acting as parent for at least six consecutive months immediately preceding the time of filing of a petition or comparable pleading for support and, if a child is less than six months old, the state in which the child lived from birth with any of them. A period of temporary absence of any of them is counted as part of the six-month or other period.

(7) "Income" includes earnings or other periodic entitlements to money from any source and any other property subject to withholding for support under the laws of this state.

(8) "Income-withholding order" means an order or other legal process directed to an obligor's employer or other debtor, as defined by the income-withholding law of this state, to withhold support from the income of the obligor.

(9) "Initiating state" means a state from which a proceeding is forwarded or in which a proceeding is filed for forwarding to a responding state under this Chapter or a law or procedure substantially similar to this Chapter, the Uniform Reciprocal Enforcement of Support Act, or the Revised Uniform Reciprocal Enforcement of Support Act.

(10) "Initiating tribunal" means the authorized tribunal in an initiating state.

(11) "Issuing state" means the state in which a tribunal issues a support order or renders a judgment determining parentage.

(12) "Issuing tribunal" means the tribunal that issues a support order or renders a judgment determining parentage.

(13) "Law" includes decisional and statutory law and rules and regulations having the force of law.

(14) "Obligee" means any of the following:

(a) An individual to whom a duty of support is owed or is alleged to be owed or in whose favor a support order has been issued or a judgment determining parentage has been rendered.

(b) A state or political subdivision to which the rights under a duty of support or support order have been assigned or which has independent claims based on financial assistance provided to an individual obligee.

(c) An individual seeking a judgment determining parentage of the individual's child.

(15) "Obligor" means an individual or the estate of a decedent who, with respect to any of the following:

(a) Owes or is alleged to owe a duty of support.

(b) Is alleged, but has not been adjudicated, to be a parent of a child.

(c) Is liable under a support order.

(16) "Register" means to record or file a support order or judgment determining parentage in the registry of foreign support orders.

(17) "Registering tribunal" means a tribunal in which a support order is registered.

(18) "Registry of foreign support orders" means any place where a clerk of court records all support orders rendered in another state and enforced within this state.

(19) "Responding state" means a state in which a proceeding is filed or to which a proceeding is forwarded for filing from an initiating state under this Chapter or a law or procedure substantially similar to this Chapter, the Uniform Reciprocal Enforcement of Support Act, or the Revised Uniform Reciprocal Enforcement of Support Act.

(20) "Responding tribunal" means the authorized tribunal in a responding state.

(21) "Spousal support order" means a support order for a spouse or former spouse of the obligor.

(22) "State" means a state of the United States, the District of Columbia, Puerto Rico, the United States Virgin Islands, or any territory or insular possession subject to the jurisdiction of the United States. The term "state" includes both of the following:

(a) An Indian tribe.

(b) A foreign jurisdiction that has enacted a law or established procedures for issuance and enforcement of support orders that are substantially similar to the procedures under this Chapter, the Uniform Reciprocal Enforcement of Support Act, or the Revised Uniform Reciprocal Enforcement of Support Act.

(23) "Support enforcement agency" means a public official or an agency authorized to seek any of the following:

(a) Enforcement of support orders or laws relating to the duty of support.

(b) Establishment or modification of child support.

(c) Determination of parentage.

(d) Location of obligors or their assets.

(24) "Support order" means a judgment, decree, or order, whether temporary, final, or subject to modification, for the benefit of a child, a spouse, or a former spouse, which provides for monetary support, health care, arrearages, or reimbursement, and may include related costs and fees, interest, income withholding, attorney fees, and other relief.

(25) "Tribunal" means a court, administrative agency, or quasi judicial entity authorized to establish, enforce, or modify support orders or to determine parentage. However, with respect to the establishment, enforcement, or modification of support orders or the determination of parentage in Louisiana, a "tribunal" is limited to a state court of competent jurisdiction.

(Added by Acts 1995 No. 251, §1; chgd. by Acts 1997 No. 1241, §1, eff. 7/15/97.)

Art. 1301.4. Tribunals of state.

The district courts or, if applicable, the family or juvenile courts, and the division of administrative review, office of the secretary, Department of Social Services, or other administrative law division authorized by law, are the tribunals of this state for purposes of this Chapter. *(Added by Acts 1995 No. 251, §1; chgd. by Acts 1997 No. 1241, §1, eff. 7/15/97.)*

Art. 1301.5. Remedies cumulative.

Remedies provided by this Chapter are cumulative and do not affect the availability of remedies under other law. *(Added by Acts 1995 No. 251, §1; chgd. by Acts 1997 No. 1241, §1, eff. 7/15/97.)*

Section 2. Jurisdiction

(Added by Acts 1995 No. 251, §1, eff. 1/1/96.)

Subsection A. Extended Personal Jurisdiction

Art. 1302. *(Repealed by Acts 1995 No. 251, §2, eff. 1/1/96.)*

Art. 1302.1. Basis for jurisdiction over nonresident.

In a proceeding to establish, enforce, or modify a support order or to determine parentage, a tribunal of this state may exercise personal jurisdiction over a nonresident individual, or his tutor, in any of the following situations:

(1) The individual is personally served with citation, summons, or notice within this state.

(2) The individual submits to the jurisdiction of this state by consent, by entering a general appearance, or by filing a responsive document having the effect of waiving any exception or contest to personal jurisdiction.

(3) The individual resided with the child in this state.

(4) The individual resided in this state and provided prenatal expenses or support for the child.

(5) The child resides in this state as a result of the acts or directives of the individual.

(6) The individual engaged in sexual intercourse in this state and the child may have been conceived by that act of intercourse.

(7) The individual asserted parentage in the putative father registry maintained in this state by the Department of Health and Hospitals, office of preventive and public health services.

(8) There is any other basis consistent with the constitutions of this state and the United States for the exercise of personal jurisdiction.

(Added by Acts 1995 No. 251, §1; chgd. by Acts 1997 No. 1241, §1, eff. 7/15/97.)

Art.1302.2. Procedure when exercising jurisdiction over nonresident.

A tribunal of this state exercising personal jurisdiction over a nonresident under Article 1302.1 (Basis for jurisdiction over nonresident) may apply Article 1303.16 (Special rules of evidence and procedure) to receive evidence from another state, and Article 1303.18 (Assistance with discovery) to obtain discovery through a tribunal of another state. In all other respects, the provisions of Sections 3 through 7 of this Chapter do not apply and the tribunal shall apply the procedural and substantive laws of this state, including the rules on choice of law other than those established by this Chapter. *(Added by Acts 1995 No. 251, §1; chgd. by Acts 1997 No. 1241, §1, eff. 7/15/97.)*

Subsection B. Proceedings Involving Two or More States

Art. 1302.3. Initiating and responding tribunal of state.

Under this Chapter, a tribunal of this state may serve as an initiating tribunal to forward proceedings to another state and as a responding tribunal for proceedings initiated in another state. *(Added by Acts 1995 No. 251, §1; chgd. by Acts 1997 No. 1241, §1, eff. 7/15/97.)*

Art. 1302.4. Simultaneous proceedings in another state.

A. A tribunal of this state may exercise jurisdiction to establish a support order if the petition or comparable pleading is filed after a pleading* or a comparable pleading is filed in another state only if all of the following exist:

**So in original. Probably should be "petition".*

(1) The petition or comparable pleading in this state is filed before the expiration of the time allowed in the other state for filing a responsive pleading challenging the exercise of jurisdiction by the other state.

(2) The contesting party timely challenges the exercise of jurisdiction in the other state.

(3) If relevant, this state is the home state of the child.

B. A tribunal of this state may not exercise jurisdiction to establish a support order if the petition or comparable pleading is filed before a petition or comparable pleading is filed in another state if all of the following exist:

(1) The petition or comparable pleading in the other state is filed before the expiration of the time allowed in this state for filing a responsive pleading challenging the exercise of jurisdiction by this state.

(2) The contesting party timely challenges the exercise of jurisdiction in this state.

(3) If relevant, the other state is the home state of the child.

(Added by Acts 1995 No. 251, §1; chgd. by Acts 1997 No. 1241, §1, eff. 7/15/97.)

Art. 1302.5. Continuing, exclusive jurisdiction.

A. A tribunal of this state issuing a support order consistent with the laws of this state has continuing, exclusive jurisdiction over a child support order as follows:

(1) As long as this state remains the residence of the obligor, the individual obligee, or the child for whose benefit the support order is issued.

(2) Until all of the parties who are individuals have filed written consent with the tribunal of this state for a tribunal of another state to modify the order and assume continuing, exclusive jurisdiction.

B. A tribunal of this state issuing a child support order consistent with the law of this state may not exercise its continuing jurisdiction to modify the order if the order has been modified by a tribunal of another state pursuant to this Chapter or a law substantially similar to this Chapter.

C. If a child support order of this state is modified by a tribunal of another state pursuant to this Chapter or a law substantially similar to this Chapter, a tribunal of this state loses its continuing, exclusive jurisdiction with regard to prospective enforcement of the order issued in this state, and may only:

(1) Enforce the order that was modified as to amounts accruing before the modification.

(2) Enforce nonmodifiable aspects of that order.

(3) Provide other appropriate relief for violations of that order which occurred before the effective date of the modification.

D. A tribunal of this state shall recognize the continuing, exclusive jurisdiction of a tribunal of another state which has issued a child support order pursuant to this Chapter or a law substantially similar to this Chapter.

E. A temporary support order issued ex parte or pending resolution of a jurisdictional conflict does not create continuing, exclusive jurisdiction in the issuing tribunal.

F. A tribunal of this state issuing a support order consistent with the laws of this state has continuing, exclusive jurisdiction over a spousal support order throughout the existence of the support obligation. A tribunal of this state may not modify a spousal support order issued by a tribunal of another state having continuing, exclusive jurisdiction over that order under the laws of that state.

(Added by Acts 1995 No. 251, §1; chgd. by Acts 1997 No. 1241, §1, eff. 7/15/97.)

Art. 1302.6. Enforcement and modification of support order by tribunal having continuing jurisdiction.

A. A tribunal of this state may serve as an initiating tribunal to request a tribunal of another state to enforce or modify a support order issued in that state.

B. A tribunal of this state having continuing, exclusive jurisdiction over a support order may act as a responding tribunal to enforce or modify the order. If a party subject to the continuing, exclusive jurisdiction of the tribunal no longer resides in the issuing state, in subsequent proceedings the tribunal may apply Article 1303.16 (Special rules of evidence and procedure) to receive evidence from another state and Article 1303.18 (Assistance with discovery) to obtain discovery through a tribunal of another state.

C. A tribunal of this state which lacks continuing, exclusive jurisdiction over a spousal support order may not serve as a responding tribunal to modify a spousal support order of another state.

(Added by Acts 1995 No. 251, §1; chgd. by Acts 1997 No. 1241, §1, eff. 7/15/97.)

Subsection C. Reconciliation of Multiple Orders

(Chgd. by Acts 1997 No. 1241, §1, eff. 7/15/97.)

Art. 1302.7. Recognition of controlling child support order.

A. If a proceeding is brought under this Chapter, and only one tribunal has issued a child support order, the order of that tribunal controls and must be so recognized.

B. If a proceeding is brought under this Chapter, and two or more child support orders have been issued by tribunals of this state or another state with regard to the same obligor and child, a tribunal of this state shall apply the following rules in determining which order to recognize for purposes of continuing, exclusive jurisdiction:

(1) If only one of the tribunals would have continuing, exclusive jurisdiction under this Chapter, the order of that tribunal controls and must be so recognized.

(2) If more than one of the tribunals would have continuing, exclusive jurisdiction under this Chapter, an order issued by a tribunal in the current home state of the child controls and must be so recognized, but if an order has not been issued in the current home state of the child, the order most recently issued controls and must be so recognized.

(3) If none of the tribunals would have continuing, exclusive jurisdiction under this Chapter, the tribunal of this state having jurisdiction over the parties shall issue a child support order, which controls and must be so recognized.

C. If two or more child support orders have been issued for the same obligor and child and if the obligor or the individual obligee resides in the state, a party may request a tribunal of this state to determine which order controls and must be so recognized under Paragraph B hereof.

The request must be accompanied by a certified copy of every support order in effect. The requesting party shall give notice of the request to each party whose rights may be affected by the determination.

D. The tribunal that issued the controlling order under Paragraph A, B, or C of this Article is the tribunal that has continuing, exclusive jurisdiction in accordance with Article 1302.5 (Continuing, exclusive jurisdiction).

E. A tribunal of this state that determines by order the identity of the controlling order under Subparagraph B(1) or (2) or that issues a new controlling order under Subparagraph B(3) shall state in that order the basis upon which the tribunal made its determination.

F. Within thirty days after issuance of an order determining the identity of the controlling order, the party obtaining the order shall file a certified copy of it with each tribunal that issued or registered an earlier order of child support. A party who obtains the order and fails to file a certified copy is subject to appropriate sanctions by a tribunal in which the issue of failure to file arises. The failure to file does not affect the validity or enforceability of the controlling order.

(Added by Acts 1995 No. 251, §1; chgd. by Acts 1997 No. 1241, §1, eff. 7/15/97.)

Art. 1302.8. Multiple child support orders for two or more obligees.

In responding to multiple registrations or petitions for enforcement of two or more child support orders in effect at the same time with regard to the same obligor and different individual obligees, at least one of which was issued by a tribunal of another state, a tribunal of this state shall enforce those orders in the same manner as if the multiple orders had been issued by a tribunal of this state. *(Added by Acts 1995 No. 251, §1; chgd. by Acts 1997 No. 1241, §1, eff. 7/15/97.)*

Art. 1302.9. Credit for payments.

Amounts collected and credited for a particular period pursuant to a support order issued by a tribunal of another state must be credited against the amounts accruing or accrued for the same period under a support order issued by the tribunal of this state. *(Added by Acts 1995 No. 251, §1; chgd. by Acts 1997 No. 1241, §1, eff. 7/15/97.)*

Section 3. Civil Provisions of General Application

(Added by Acts 1995 No. 251, §1; chgd. by Acts 1997 No. 1241, §1, eff. 7/15/97.)

Art. 1303. *(Repealed by Acts 1995 No. 251, §2, eff. 1/1/96.)*

Art. 1303.1. Proceedings under Chapter.

A. Except as otherwise provided by this Chapter, this Section applies to all proceedings under this Chapter.

B. This Chapter provides for the following proceedings:

(1) Establishment of an order for spousal support or child support pursuant to Section 4 of this Chapter.

(2) Enforcement of a support order and income-withholding order of another state without registration pursuant to Section 5 of this Chapter.

(3) Registration of an order for spousal support or child support of another state for enforcement pursuant to Section 7 of this Chapter.

(4) Modification of an order for child support or spousal support issued by a tribunal of this state pursuant to Subsection B of Section 2 of this Chapter.

(5) Registration of an order for child support for another state for modification pursuant to Section 6 of this Chapter.

(6) Determination of parentage pursuant to Section 7 of this Chapter.

(7) Assertion of jurisdiction over nonresidents pursuant to Subsection A of Section 2 of this Chapter.

C. An individual petitioner or a support enforcement agency may commence a proceeding authorized under this Chapter by filing a petition in an initiating tribunal for forwarding to a responding tribunal or by filing a petition or a comparable pleading directly in a tribunal of another state which has or can obtain personal jurisdiction over the respondent. *(Added by Acts 1995 No. 251, §1; chgd. by Acts 1997 No. 1241, §1, eff. 7/15/97.)*

Art. 1303.2. Action by minor parent.

A minor parent or a tutor or other legal representative of a minor parent may maintain a proceeding on behalf of or for the benefit of the minor's child. *(Added by Acts 1995 No. 251, §1, eff. 1/1/96.)*

Art. 1303.3. Application of law of state.

Except as otherwise provided by this Chapter, a responding tribunal of this state shall:

(1) Apply the procedural and substantive law, including the rules on choice of law, generally applicable to similar proceedings originating in this state and may exercise all powers and provide all remedies available in those proceedings.

(2) Determine the duty of support and the amounts payable in accordance with the law and support guidelines of this state.

(Added by Acts 1995 No. 251, §1; chgd. by Acts 1997 No. 1241, §1, eff. 7/15/97.)

Art. 1303.4. Duties of initiating tribunal.

A. Upon the filing of a petition authorized by this Chapter, an initiating tribunal of this state shall forward three copies of the petition and its accompanying documents as follows:

(1) To the responding tribunal or appropriate support enforcement agency in the responding state.

(2) If the identity of the responding tribunal is unknown, to the state information agency of the responding state with a request that the documents be forwarded to the appropriate tribunal and that receipt be acknowledged.

B. If a responding state has not enacted this Chapter or a law or procedure substantially similar to this Chapter, a tribunal of this state may issue a certificate or other document and make findings required by the law of the responding state. If the responding state is a foreign jurisdiction, the tribunal may specify the amount of support sought and provide other documents necessary to satisfy the requirements of the responding state.

(Added by Acts 1995 No. 251, §1; chgd. by Acts 1997 No. 1241, §1, eff. 7/15/97.)

Art. 1303.5. Duties and powers of responding tribunal.

A. When a responding tribunal of this state receives a petition or comparable pleading from an initiating tribunal or directly pursuant to Article 1303.1(C) (Proceeding under this Chapter), it shall cause the petition or pleading to be filed and notify the petitioner where and when it was filed.

B. A responding tribunal of this state, to the extent otherwise authorized by law, may do one or more of the following:

(1) Issue or enforce a support order, modify a child support order, or render a judgment to determine parentage.

(2) Order an obligor to comply with a support order, specifying the amount and the manner of compliance.

(3) Order income withholding.

(4) Determine the amount of any arrearages and specify a method of payment.

(5) Enforce orders by civil or criminal contempt, or both.

(6) Set aside property for satisfaction of the support order.

(7) Place liens and order execution on the obligor's property.

(8) Order an obligor to keep the tribunal informed of the obligor's current residential address, telephone number, employer, address of employment, and telephone number at the place of employment.

(9) Issue an order of contempt or a bench warrant, or both, for an obligor who has failed, after proper notice, to appear at a hearing ordered by the tribunal and enter the order of contempt and bench warrant in any local and state computer systems for criminal warrants.

(10) Order the obligor to seek appropriate employment by specified methods.

(11) Award reasonable attorney fees and other fees and costs.

(12) Grant any other available remedy.

C. A responding tribunal of this state shall include in a support order issued under this Chapter, or in the documents accompanying the order, the calculations on which the support order is based.

D. A responding tribunal of this state may not condition the payment of a support order issued under this Chapter upon compliance by a party with provisions for visitation.

E. If a responding tribunal of this state issues an order under this Chapter, the tribunal shall send a copy of the order to the petitioner and the respondent and to the initiating tribunal, if any.
(Added by Acts 1995 No. 251, §1; chgd. by Acts 1997 No. 1241, §1, eff. 7/15/97.)

Art. 1303.6. Inappropriate tribunal.

If a petition or comparable pleading is received by an inappropriate tribunal of this state, it shall forward the pleading and accompanying documents to an appropriate tribunal in this state or another state and notify the petitioner where and when the pleading was sent. *(Added by Acts 1995 No. 251, §1; chgd. by Acts 1997 No. 1241, §1, eff. 7/15/97.)*

Art. 1303.7. Duties of the support enforcement agency.

A. A support enforcement agency of this state, upon request, shall provide services to a petitioner in a proceeding under this Chapter.

B. A support enforcement agency that is providing services to the petitioner, as appropriate, shall:

(1) Take all steps necessary to enable an appropriate tribunal in this state or another state to obtain jurisdiction over the respondent.

(2) Request an appropriate tribunal to set a date, time, and place for a hearing.

(3) Make a reasonable effort to obtain all relevant information, including information as to income and property of the parties.

(4) Within two days, exclusive of Saturdays, Sundays, and legal holidays, after receipt of a written notice from an initiating, responding, or registering tribunal, send a copy of the notice to the petitioner.

(5) Within two days, exclusive of Saturdays, Sundays, and legal holidays, after receipt of a written communication from the respondent or the respondent's attorney, send a copy of the communication to the petitioner.

(6) Notify the petitioner if jurisdiction over the respondent cannot be obtained.

C. This Chapter does not create or negate a relationship of attorney and client or other fiduciary relationship between a support enforcement agency or the attorney for the agency and the individual being assisted by the agency.
(Added by Acts 1995 No. 251, §1; chgd. by Acts 1997 No. 1241, §1, eff. 7/15/97.)

Art. 1303.8. Duty of attorney general.

If the attorney general determines that the support enforcement agency is neglecting or refusing to provide services to an individual, the attorney general may order the agency to perform its duties under this Chapter or may provide those services directly to the individual. *(Added by Acts 1995 No. 251, §1; chgd. by Acts 1997 No. 1241, §1, eff. 7/15/97.)*

Art. 1303.9. Private counsel.

An individual may employ private counsel to represent the individual in proceedings authorized by this Chapter. *(Added by Acts 1995 No. 251, §1, eff. 1/1/96.)*

Art. 1303.10. Duties of the Department of Social Services; state information agency.

A. The department is the state information agency under this Chapter.

B. The state information agency shall:

(1) Compile and maintain a current list, including addresses, of the tribunals in this state that have jurisdiction under this Chapter and any support enforcement agencies in this state and transmit a copy to the state information agency of every other state.

(2) Maintain a register of tribunals and support enforcement agencies received from other states.

(3) Forward to the appropriate tribunal in the place in this state in which the individual obligee or the obligor resides, or where the obligor's property is believed to be located, all documents concerning a proceeding under this Chapter received from an initiating tribunal or the state information agency of the initiating state.

(4) Obtain information concerning the location of the obligor and the obligor's property within this state not exempt from execution, by such means as postal verification and federal or state locator services, examination of telephone directories, requests for the obligor's address from employers, and examination of governmental records, including, to the extent

not prohibited by other law, those relating to real property, vital statistics, law enforcement, taxation, motor vehicles, drivers' licenses, and social security.
(Added by Acts 1995 No. 251, §1; chgd. by Acts 1997 No. 1241, §1, eff. 7/15/97.)

Art. 1303.11. Pleadings and accompanying documents.

A. A petitioner seeking to establish or modify a support order or to determine parentage in a proceeding under this Chapter must verify the petition. Unless otherwise ordered under Article 1303.12 (Nondisclosure of information in exceptional circumstances), the petition or accompanying documents must provide, so far as known, the name, residential address, and social security number of the obligor and the obligee, and the name, sex, residential address, social security number, and the date of birth of each child for whom support is sought. The petition must be accompanied by a certified copy of any support order in effect. The petition may include any other information that may assist in locating or identifying the respondent.

B. The petition must specify the relief sought. The petition and accompanying documents must conform substantially with the requirements imposed by the forms mandated by federal law for use in cases filed by a support enforcement agency.
(Added by Acts 1995 No. 251, §1; chgd. by Acts 1997 No. 1241, §1, eff. 7/15/97.)

Art. 1303.12. Nondisclosure of information in exceptional circumstances.

Upon a finding, which may be made ex parte, that the health, safety, or liberty of a party or child would be unreasonably put at risk by the disclosure of identifying information, or if an existing order so provides, a tribunal shall order that the address of the child or party or other identifying information not be disclosed in a pleading or other document filed in a proceeding under this Chapter. *(Added by Acts 1995 No. 251, §1; chgd. by Acts 1997 No. 1241, §1, eff. 7/15/97.)*

Art. 1303.13. Costs and fees.

A. The petitioner may not be required to pay a filing fee or other costs.

B. If an obligee prevails, a responding tribunal may assess against an obligor filing fees, reasonable attorney fees, other costs, and necessary travel and other reasonable expenses incurred by the obligee and the obligee's witnesses. The tribunal may not assess fees, costs, or expenses against the obligee or the support enforcement agency of either the initiating or the responding state, except as provided by other law. Attorney fees may be taxed as costs and may be ordered paid directly to the attorney, who may enforce the order in the attorney's own name. Payment of support owed to the obligee has priority over fees, costs, and expenses.

C. The tribunal shall order the payment of costs and reasonable attorney fees if it determines that a hearing was requested primarily for delay. In a proceeding under Section 6 of this Chapter (Enforcement and modification of support order after registration), a hearing is presumed to have been requested primarily for delay if a registered support order is confirmed or enforced without change.
(Added by Acts 1995 No. 251, §1; chgd. by Acts 1997 No. 1241, §1, eff. 7/15/97.)

Art. 1303.14. Limited immunity of petitioner.

A. Participation by a petitioner in a proceeding before a responding tribunal, whether in person, by private attorney, or through services provided by the support enforcement agency, does not confer personal jurisdiction over the petitioner in another proceeding.

B. A petitioner is not amenable to services of civil process while physically present in this state to participate in a proceeding under this Chapter.

C. The immunity granted by this Article does not extend to civil litigation based on acts unrelated to a proceeding under this Chapter committed by a party while present in this state to participate in the proceeding.
(Added by Acts 1995 No. 251, §1; chgd. by Acts 1997 No. 1241, §1, eff. 7/15/97.)

Art. 1303.15. Nonparentage as defense.

A party whose parentage of a child has been previously determined by or pursuant to law may not plead nonparentage as a defense to a proceeding under this Chapter. *(Added by Acts 1995 No. 251, §1, eff. 1/1/96.)*

Art. 1303.16. Special rules of evidence and procedures.

A. The physical presence of the petitioner in a responding tribunal of this state is not required for the establishment, enforcement, or modification of a support order or the rendition of a judgment determining parentage.

B. A verified petition, affidavit, document substantially complying with federally mandated forms, and a document incorporated by reference in any of them, not excluded under the hearsay rule if given in person, is admissible in evidence if given under oath by a party or witness residing in another state.

C. A copy of the record of child support payments certified as a true copy of the original by the custodian of the record may be forwarded to a responding tribunal. The copy is evidence of facts asserted in it and is admissible to show whether payments were made.

D. Copies of bills for testing for parentage and for prenatal and postnatal health care of the mother and child, furnished to the adverse party at least ten days before trial, are admissible in evidence to prove the amount of the charges billed and that the charges were reasonable, necessary, and customary.

E. Documentary evidence transmitted from another state to a tribunal of this state by telephone, telecopier, or other means that do not provide an original writing may not be excluded from evidence on an objection based on the means of transmission.

F. In a proceeding under this Chapter, a tribunal of this state may permit a party or witness residing in another state to be deposed or to testify by telephone, audiovisual means, or other electronic means at a designated tribunal or other location in that state. A tribunal of this state shall cooperate with tribunals of other states in designating an appropriate location for the deposition or testimony.

G. If a party called to testify at a civil hearing refuses to answer on the ground that the testimony may be self-incriminating, the trier of fact may draw an adverse inference from the refusal.

H. A privilege against disclosure of communications between spouses does not apply in a proceeding under this Chapter.

I. The defense of immunity based on the relationship of husband and wife or parent and child does not apply in a proceeding under this Chapter.

(Added by Acts 1995 No. 251, §1; chgd. by Acts 1997 No. 1241, §1, eff. 7/15/97.)

Art. 1303.17. Communications between tribunals.

A tribunal of this state may communicate with a tribunal of another state in writing, or by telephone or other means, to obtain information concerning the laws of that state, the legal effect of a judgment, decree, or order of that tribunal, and the status of a proceeding in the other state. A tribunal of this state may furnish similar information by similar means to a tribunal of another state. *(Added by Acts 1995 No. 251, §1; chgd. by Acts 1997 No. 1241, §1, eff. 7/15/97.)*

Art. 1303.18. Assistance with discovery.

A tribunal of this state may do all of the following:

(1) Request a tribunal of another state to assist in obtaining discovery.

(2) On request, compel a person over whom it has jurisdiction to respond to a discovery order issued by a tribunal of another state.

(Added by Acts 1995 No. 251, §1; chgd. by Acts 1997 No. 1241, §1, eff. 7/15/97.)

Art. 1303.19. Receipt and disbursement of payments.

A support enforcement agency or tribunal of this state shall disburse promptly any amounts received pursuant to a support order, as directed by the order. The agency or tribunal shall furnish to a requesting party or tribunal of another state a certified statement by the custodian of the record of the amounts and dates of all payments received. *(Added by Acts 1995 No. 251, §1; chgd. by Acts 1997 No. 1241, §1, eff. 7/15/97.)*

Section 4. Establishment of Support Order

(Added by Acts 1995 No. 251, §1, eff. 1/1/96.)

Art. 1304. *(Repealed by Acts 1995 No. 251, §2, eff. 1/1/96.)*

Art. 1304.1. Petition to establish support order.

A. If a support order entitled to recognition under this Chapter has not been issued, a responding tribunal of this state may issue a support order if either:

(1) The individual seeking the order resides in another state.

(2) The support enforcement agency seeking the order is located in another state.

B. The tribunal may issue a temporary child support order in the event of any of the following:

(1) The respondent has signed a verified statement acknowledging parentage.

(2) The respondent has been determined by or pursuant to law to be the parent.

(3) There is other clear and convincing evidence that the respondent is the child's parent.

C. Upon finding, after notice and opportunity to be heard, that an obligor owes a duty of support, the tribunal shall issue a support order directed to the obligor and may issue other orders pursuant to Article 1303.5 (Duties and powers of responding tribunal).

(Added by Acts 1995 No. 251, §1; chgd. by Acts 1997 No. 1241, §1, eff. 7/15/97.)

Section 5. Enforcement of Order of Another State Without Registration

(Added by Acts 1995 No. 251, §1; chgd. by Acts 1997 No. 1241, §1, eff. 7/15/97.)

Art. 1305. *(Repealed by Acts 1995 No. 251, §2, eff. 1/1/96.)*

Art. 1305.1. Employer's receipt of income-withholding order of another state.

An income-withholding order issued in another state may be sent to the person or entity defined as the obligor's employer under the income withholding law of this state without first filing a petition or comparable pleading or registering the order with a tribunal of this state.

(Added by Acts 1995 No. 251, §1; chgd. by Acts 1997 No. 1241, §1, eff. 7/15/97.)

Art. 1305.2. *(Redesignated as article 1305.7 by Acts 1997 No. 1241, §1, eff. 7/15/97. See also article 1305.2 below.)*

Art. 1305.2. Employer's compliance with income-withholding order of another state.

(See also former article 1305.2 above.)

A. Upon receipt of an income withholding order, the obligor's employer shall immediately provide a copy of the order to the obligor.

B. The employer shall treat an income withholding order issued in another state which appears regular on its face as if it had been issued by a tribunal of this state.

C. Except as otherwise provided in Paragraph D hereof and Article 1305.3, the employer shall withhold and distribute the funds as directed in the withholding order by complying with the terms of the order, which specifies all of the following:

(1) The duration and the amount of periodic payments of current child support, stated as a sum certain.

(2) The person or agency designated to receive payments and the address to which the payments are to be forwarded.

(3) Medical support, whether in the form of periodic cash payment, stated as a sum certain, or ordering the obligor to provide health insurance coverage for the child under a policy available through the obligor's employment.

(4) The amount of periodic payments of fees and costs for a support enforcement agency, the issuing tribunal, and the obligee's attorney, stated as sums certain.

(5) The amount of periodic payments of arrearages and interest on arrearages, stated as sums certain.

D. An employer shall comply with the law of the state of the obligor's principal place of employment for withholding from income with respect to all of the following:

(1) The employer's fee for processing an income-withholding order.

(2) The maximum amount permitted to be withheld from the obligor's income.

(3) The times within which the employer must implement the withholding order and forward the child support payment.

(Added by Acts 1997 No. 1241, §1, eff. 7/15/97.)

Art. 1305.3. Compliance with multiple income withholding orders.

If the obligor's employer receives multiple income withholding orders with respect to the earnings of the same obligor, the employer satisfies the terms of the multiple orders if the employer complies with the law of the state of the obligor's principal place of employment to establish the priorities for withholding and allocating income withheld for multiple child support obligees. *(Added by Acts 1997 No. 1241, §1, eff. 7/15/97.)*

Art. 1305.4. Immunity from civil liability.

An employer who complies with an income-withholding order issued in another state in accordance with this Section is not subject to civil liability to any individual or agency with regard to the employer's withholding of child support from the obligor's income. *(Added by Acts 1997 No. 1241, §1, eff. 7/15/97.)*

Art. 1305.5. Penalties for noncompliance.

An employer who willfully fails to comply with an income-withholding order issued by another state and received for enforcement is subject to the same penalties that may be imposed for noncompliance with an order issued by a tribunal of this state. *(Added by Acts 1997 No. 1241, §1, eff. 7/15/97.)*

Art. 1305.6. Contest by obligor.

A. An obligor may contest the validity or enforcement of an income-withholding order issued in another state and received directly by an employer in this state in the same manner as if the order had been issued by a tribunal of this state. Article 1306.4 (Choice of law) applies to the contest.

B. The obligor shall give notice of the contest to all of the following:

(1) A support enforcement agency providing services to the obligee.

(2) Each employer that has directly received an income-withholding order.

(3) The person or agency designated to receive payments in the income-withholding order or, if no person or agency is designated, to the obligee.

(Added by Acts 1997 No. 1241, §1, eff. 7/15/97.)

Art. 1305.7. Administrative enforcement of orders.

A. A party seeking to enforce a support order or an income-withholding order, or both, issued by a tribunal of another state may send the documents required for registering the order to a support enforcement agency of this state.

B. Upon receipt of the documents, the support enforcement agency, without initially seeking to register the order, shall consider and, if appropriate, use any administrative procedure authorized by the law of this state to enforce a support order or an income-withholding order, or both. If the obligor does not contest administrative enforcement, the order need not be registered. If the obligor contests the validity or administrative enforcement of the order, the support enforcement agency shall register the order pursuant to this Chapter.

(Added by Acts 1995 No. 251, §1; redesignated from article 1305.2 and chgd. by Acts 1997 No. 1241, §1, eff. 7/15/97.)

Section 6. Enforcement and Modification of Support Order After Registration

(Added by Acts 1995 No. 251, §1, eff. 1/1/96.)

Subsection A. Registration and Enforcement of Support Order

Art. 1306. *(Repealed by Acts 1995 No. 251, §2, eff. 1/1/96.)*

Art. 1306.1. Registration of order for enforcement.

A support order or an income-withholding order issued by a tribunal of another state may be registered in this state for enforcement. *(Added by Acts 1995 No. 251, §1; chgd. by Acts 1997 No. 1241, §1, eff. 7/15/97.)*

Art. 1306.2. Procedure to register order for enforcement.

A. A support order or income-withholding order of another state may be registered in this state by sending the following documents and information to the appropriate tribunal in this state:

(1) A letter of transmittal to the tribunal requesting registration and enforcement.

(2) Two copies, including one certified copy, of all orders to be registered, including any modification of an order.

(3) A sworn statement by the party seeking registration or a certified statement by the custodian of the records showing the amount of any arrearage.

(4) The name of the obligor and, if known:

(a) The obligor's address and social security number.

(b) The name and address of the obligor's employer and any other source of income of the obligor.

(c) A description and the location of property of the obligor in this state not exempt from execution.

(5) The name and address of the obligee and, if applicable, the agency or person to whom support payments are to be remitted.

B. On receipt of a request for registration, the registering tribunal shall cause the order to be filed as a foreign judgment, together with one copy of the documents and information, regardless of their form.

C. A petition or comparable pleading seeking a remedy that must be affirmatively sought under other law of this state may be filed at the same time as the request for registration or later. The pleading must specify the grounds for the remedy sought.

(Added by Acts 1995 No. 251, §1; chgd. by Acts 1997 No. 1241, §1, eff. 7/15/97.)

Art. 1306.3. Effect of registration for enforcement.

A. A support order or income-withholding order issued in another state is registered when the order is filed in the registering tribunal of this state.

B. A registered order issued in another state is enforceable in the same manner and is subject to the same procedures as an order issued by a tribunal of this state.

C. Except as otherwise provided in this Section, a tribunal of this state shall recognize and enforce, but may not modify, a registered order if the issuing tribunal had jurisdiction.

(Added by Acts 1995 No. 251, §1; chgd. by Acts 1997 No. 1241, §1, eff. 7/15/97.)

Art. 1306.4. Choice of law.

A. The law of the issuing state governs the notice, extent, amount, and duration of current payments and other obligations of support and the payment of arrearages under the order.

B. In a proceeding for arrearages, the prescriptive period under the laws of this state or of the issuing state, whichever is longer, applies.

(Added by Acts 1995 No. 251, §1, eff. 1/1/96.)

Subsection B. Contest of Validity or Enforcement

Art. 1306.5. Notice of registration of order.

A. When a support order or income-withholding order issued in another state is registered, the registering tribunal shall notify the nonregistering party. The notice must be accompanied by a copy of the registered order and the documents and relevant information accompanying the order.

B. The notice must inform the nonregistering party of all of the following:

(1) That a registered order is enforceable as of the date of registration in the same manner as an order issued by a tribunal of this state.

(2) That a hearing to contest the validity or enforcement of the registered order must be requested within twenty days after notice.

(3) That failure to contest the validity or enforcement of the registered order in a timely manner will result in confirmation of the order and enforcement of the order and the alleged arrearages and precludes further contest of that order with respect to any matter that could have been asserted.

(4) Of the amount of any alleged arrearages.

C. Upon registration of an income-withholding order for enforcement, the registering tribunal shall notify the obligor's employer pursuant to the income-withholding laws of this state.

(Added by Acts 1995 No. 251, §1; chgd. by Acts 1997 No. 1241, §1, eff. 7/15/97.)

Art. 1306.6. Procedure to contest validity or enforcement of registered order.

A. A nonregistering party seeking to contest the validity or enforcement of a registered order in this state shall request a hearing within twenty days after notice of the registration. The nonregistering party may seek to vacate the registration, to assert any defense to an allegation of noncompliance with the registered order, or to contest the remedies being sought or the amount of any alleged arrearages pursuant to Article 1306.7 (Contest of registration or enforcement).

B. If the nonregistering party fails to contest the validity or enforcement of the registered order in a timely manner, the order is confirmed by operation of law.

C. If a nonregistering party requests a hearing to contest the validity or enforcement of the registered order, the registering tribunal shall schedule the matter for hearing and give notice to the parties of the date, time, and place of the hearing.

(Added by Acts 1995 No. 251, §1; chgd. by Acts 1997 No. 1241, §1, eff. 7/15/97.)

Art. 1306.7. Contest of registration or enforcement.

A. A party contesting the validity or enforcement of a registered order or seeking to vacate the registration has the burden of proving one or more of the following defenses:

(1) The issuing tribunal lacked personal jurisdiction over the contesting party.

(2) The order was obtained by fraud.

(3) The order has been vacated, suspended, or modified by a later order.

(4) The issuing tribunal has stayed the order pending appeal.

(5) There is a defense under the law of this state to the remedy sought.

(6) Full or partial payment has been made.

(7) The prescriptive period under Article 1306.4 (Choice of law) precludes enforcement of some or all of the arrearages.

B. If a party presents evidence establishing a full or partial defense under Paragraph A of this Article, a tribunal may stay enforcement of the registered order, continue the proceeding to permit production of additional relevant evidence, and issue other appropriate orders. An uncontested portion of the registered order may be enforced by all remedies available under the laws of this state.

C. If the contesting party does not establish a defense under Paragraph A of this Article to the validity or enforcement of the order, the registering tribunal shall issue an order confirming the order.

(Added by Acts 1995 No. 251, §1; chgd. by Acts 1997 No. 1241, §1, eff. 7/15/97.)

Art. 1306.8. Confirmed order.

Confirmation of a registered order, whether by operation of law or after notice and hearing, precludes further contest of the order with respect to any matter that could have been asserted at the time of registration. *(Added by Acts 1995 No. 251, §1, eff. 1/1/96.)*

Subsection C. Registration and Modification of Child Support Order

Art. 1306.9. Procedure to register child support order of another state for modification.

A party or support enforcement agency seeking to modify, or to modify and enforce, a child support order issued in another state shall register that order in this state in the same manner provided in Subsection A of this Section if the order has not been registered. A petition for modification may be filed at the same time as a request for registration, or later. The pleading must specify the grounds for modification. *(Added by Acts 1995 No. 251, §1, eff. 1/1/96.)*

Art. 1306.10. Effect of registration for modification.

A tribunal of this state may enforce a child support order of another state registered for purposes of modification, in the same manner as if the order had been issued by a tribunal of this state, but the registered order may be modified only if the requirements of Article 1306.11 (Modification of child support order of another state) have been met. *(Added by Acts 1995 No. 251, §1; chgd. by Acts 1997 No. 1241, §1, eff. 7/15/97.)*

Art. 1306.11. Modification of child support order of another state.

A. After a child support order issued in another state has been registered in this state, the responding tribunal of this state may modify that order only if Article 1306.13 (Jurisdiction to modify child support order of another state when individual parties reside in this state) does not apply and, after notice and hearing it finds that either:

(1) All of the following requirements are met:

(a) The child, the individual obligee, and the obligor do not reside in the issuing state.

(b) A petitioner who is a nonresident of this state seeks modification.

(c) The respondent is subject to the personal jurisdiction of the tribunal of this state.

(2) The child or a party who is an individual is subject to the personal jurisdiction of the tribunal of this state and all of the parties who are individuals have filed a written consent in the issuing tribunal for a tribunal of this state to modify the support order and assume continuing, exclusive jurisdiction over the order. However, if the issuing state is a foreign jurisdiction that has not enacted a law or established procedures substantially similar to the procedures under this Chapter, the consent otherwise required of an individual residing in this state is not required for the tribunal to assume jurisdiction to modify the child support order.

B. Modification of a registered child support order is subject to the same requirements, procedures, and defenses that apply to the modification of an order issued by a tribunal of this state and the order may be enforced and satisfied in the same manner.

C. A tribunal of this state may not modify any aspect of a child support order that may not be modified under the law of the issuing state. If two or more tribunals have issued child support orders for the same obligor and child, the order that controls and must be so recognized under the provisions of Article 1302.7 (Recognition of controlling child support order) establishes the aspects of the support order that are nonmodifiable.

D. On issuance of an order modifying a child support order issued in another state, a tribunal of this state becomes the tribunal having continuing, exclusive jurisdiction.
(Added by Acts 1995 No. 251, §1; chgd. by Acts 1997 No. 1241, §1, eff. 7/15/97.)

Art. 1306.12. Recognition of order modified in another state.

A tribunal of this state shall recognize a modification of its earlier child support order by a tribunal of another state, which assumed jurisdiction pursuant to this Chapter or a law substantially similar to this Chapter, and, upon request, except as otherwise provided in this Chapter, shall do all of the following:

(1) Enforce the order that was modified only as to amounts accruing before the modification.

(2) Enforce only nonmodifiable aspects of that order.

(3) Provide other appropriate relief only for violations of that order that occurred before the effective date of the modification.

(4) Recognize the modifying order of the other state, upon registration, for the purpose of enforcement.
(Added by Acts 1995 No. 251, §1; chgd. by Acts 1997 No. 1241, §1, eff. 7/15/97.)

Art. 1306.13. Jurisdiction to modify child-support order of another state when individual parties reside in this state.

A. If all of the parties who are individuals reside in this state and the child does not reside in the issuing state, a tribunal of this state has jurisdiction to enforce and to modify the issuing state's child support order in a proceeding to register that order.

B. A tribunal of this state exercising jurisdiction as provided in this Article shall apply the provisions of Sections 1 and 2 of this Chapter, this Article, and the procedural and substantive laws of this state to the proceeding for enforcement or modification. Sections 3, 4, 5, 7, and 8 of this Chapter do not apply.

(Added by Acts 1997 No. 1241, §1, eff. 7/15/97.)

Art. 1306.14. Notice to issuing tribunal of modification.

Within thirty days after issuance of a modified child support order, the party obtaining the modification shall file a certified copy of the order with the issuing tribunal that had continuing, exclusive jurisdiction over the earlier order, and in each tribunal in which the party knows the earlier order has been registered. A party who obtains the order and fails to file a certified copy is subject to appropriate sanctions by a tribunal in which the issue of failure to file arises. The failure to file does not affect the validity or enforceability of the modified order of the new tribunal having continuing, exclusive jurisdiction. *(Added by Acts 1997 No. 1241, §1, eff. 7/15/97.)*

Section 7. Determination of Parentage

(Added by Acts 1995 No. 251, §1, eff. 1/1/96.)

Art. 1307. *(Repealed by Acts 1995 No. 251, §2, eff. 1/1/96.)*

Art. 1307.1. Proceeding to determine parentage.

A. A tribunal of this state may serve as an initiating or responding tribunal in a proceeding brought under this Chapter or a law or procedure substantially similar to this Chapter, the Uniform Reciprocal Enforcement of Support Act, or the Revised Uniform Reciprocal Enforcement of Support Act to determine that the petitioner is a parent of a particular child or to determine that a respondent is a parent of that child.

B. In a proceeding to determine parentage, a responding tribunal of this state shall apply the procedural and substantive law of this state and the rules of this state on choice of law.

(Added by Acts 1995 No. 251, §1; chgd. by Acts 1997 No. 1241, §1, eff. 7/15/97.)

Section 8. Interstate Rendition

(Added by Acts 1995 No. 251, §1, eff. 1/1/96.)

Art. 1308. *(Repealed by Acts 1995 No. 251, §2, eff. 1/1/96.)*

Art. 1308.1. Grounds for rendition.

A. For purposes of this Section, "governor" includes an individual performing the functions of governor or the executive authority of a state covered by this Chapter.

B. The governor of this state may either:

(1) Demand that the governor of another state surrender an individual found in the other state who is charged criminally in this state with having failed to provide for the support of an obligee.

(2) On the demand by the governor of another state, surrender an individual found in this state who is charged criminally in the other state with having failed to provide for the support of an obligee.

C. A provision for extradition of individuals not inconsistent with this Chapter applies to the demand even if the individual whose surrender is demanded was not in the demanding state when the crime was allegedly committed and has not fled therefrom.

(Added by Acts 1995 No. 251, §1, eff. 1/1/96.)

Art. 1308.2. Conditions of rendition.

A. Before making demand that the governor of another state surrender an individual charged criminally in this state with having failed to provide for the support of an obligee, the governor of this state may require a prosecutor of this state to demonstrate that at least sixty days previously the obligee had initiated proceedings for support pursuant to this Chapter or that the proceeding would be of no avail.

B. If, under this Chapter or a law substantially similar to this Chapter, the Uniform Reciprocal Enforcement of Support Act, or the Revised Uniform Reciprocal Enforcement of Support Act, the governor of another state makes a demand that the governor of this state surrender an individual charged criminally in that state with having failed to provide for the support of a child or other individual to whom a duty of support is owed, the governor may require a prosecutor to investigate the demand and report whether a proceeding for support has been initiated or would be effective. If it appears that a proceeding would be effective but has not been initiated, the governor may delay honoring the demand for a reasonable time to permit the initiation of a proceeding.

C. If a proceeding for support has been initiated and the individual whose rendition is demanded prevails, the governor may decline to honor the demand. If the petitioner prevails and the individual whose rendition is demanded is subject to a support order, the governor may decline to honor the demand if the individual is complying with the support order.
(Added by Acts 1995 No. 251, §1; chgd. by Acts 1997 No. 1241, §1, eff. 7/15/97.)

Arts. 1309 to 1342. *(Repealed by Acts 1995 No. 251, §2, eff. 1/1/96.)*

CHAPTER 2. CRIMINAL NEGLECT OF FAMILY

Article

Art. 1351. Definitions.

As used in this Chapter:

(1) "Child" means a person under the age of eighteen or an eighteen year old who is a full-time student in a secondary school and who is dependent on either parent.

(2) "Criminal neglect of family" means the desertion or intentional nonsupport by a spouse of his or her spouse who is in destitute or necessitous circumstances or by either parent of his minor child who is in destitute or necessitous circumstances.

(3) "Department" means the Department of Social Services.

(4) "Spouse" shall mean a husband or wife.

(5) "FITAP" means Family Independence Temporary Assistance Program.

(6) "Applicable payee" means the spouse, the tutor or custodian of the child, the court-approved fiduciary of the spouse or child, or the department in an FITAP case or in a non-FITAP case in which the department is rendering services as designated by the court to be the payee.
(Added by Acts 1993 No. 442, §2, eff. 6/9/93.)

Art. 1352. Diversion; support provisions.

A. With the consent of the defendant, at any time prior to a trial on a charge of criminal neglect of family brought pursuant to R.S. 14:74 the court, in lieu of imposing the punishment herein before provided, may issue a support order, after considering the circumstances and financial ability of the defendant, directing the defendant to pay a certain sum, at such periods as the court directs, and to maintain health care insurance.

B. This support shall be ordered payable to the applicable payee.

C. The amount of support as set by the court may be increased or decreased as the circumstances may require.

D. The court may also require the defendant to enter into a recognizance, with or without surety, in order to insure the payment of support and the maintenance of health care insurance. The condition of the recognizance shall be that the defendant shall make his or her personal appearance in court whenever required to do so, and shall further comply with the terms of the order or of any subsequent modification thereof.
(Added by Acts 1993 No. 442, §2, eff. 6/9/93.)

Art. 1353. Support provisions; contempt; penalties.

A. If the defendant violates the terms of the court order, the court, upon motion, may issue an order directing the defendant to show cause why he or she should not be found in contempt of court for failure to pay the court ordered support or maintain health care insurance, which rule shall be tried in a summary manner.

B. If on the hearing of such rule the court finds the accused guilty of contempt for failure to comply with the judgment of the court in paying the support assessed, the court may punish for such contempt as follows, either:

(1) The court may sentence the defendant to be imprisoned for not more than six months. The court in it discretion may suspend this term of imprisonment in whole or in part on condition that the defendant pay the total amount of unpaid support and obtain health care insurance in a manner to be determined by the court and on such other conditions as set by the court. If the court suspends the sentence in whole or in part, the court may place the defendant on probation under R.S. 15:305 with conditions of probation to be set by the court. In addition, the court may fine the defendant an amount not to exceed one hundred dollars to be paid to the applicable payee.

(2) The court may order the defendant to pay the total amount of unpaid support to the applicable payee and obtain health care insurance within a period of time fixed by the court. During this period of time, the defendant may be released upon giving bond for his appearance in court if he fails to comply with the order of the court within the period of time fixed. Should the defendant not pay the total amount of unpaid support which the court has ordered, the defendant shall be imprisoned for not more than six months.

C. Upon a second or subsequent finding of contempt, the court shall sentence the defendant to imprisonment for not more than six months. At the discretion of the judge, the sentence may be suspended by the court upon the occurrence of all of the following:

(1) Payment of the amount of unpaid support.
(2) Payment of the amount of unpaid support accrued since the date of the said order.
(3) Payment of the amount of all attendant court costs.
(4) Proof of health care insurance.

D. Upon recommendation of the state attorney or the support enforcement officer, or both, the remainder of the sentence may be suspended upon payment of a lesser amount, plus attendant court costs. Such payment shall apply toward but not extinguish the total amount due.

E. If the court finds the accused guilty of contempt, the court shall also render judgment directing the defendant to obtain health care insurance and to pay the total amount of unpaid support to the applicable payee, and attendant court costs. Such judgment for the payment of unpaid support and court costs shall have the same force and effect as a final judgment for money damages against the defendant. This judgment may be made executory by any Louisiana court of competent jurisdiction on petition of the department or the district attorney.

F. If the defendant has entered into a recognizance in the amount fixed by the court to insure the payment of the support and maintenance of health care insurance, the court may order the forfeiture of the recognizance and enforcement thereof by execution. The sum recovered shall be paid in whole or in part to the applicable payee. However, should the court order both the forfeiture of the recognizance and at the same time order the defendant to pay all unpaid support under the sentence for contempt, the amount of unpaid support plus attendant court costs and fines shall be the maximum payable.
(Added by Acts 1993 No. 442, §2, eff. 6/9/93.)

Art. 1354. Persons adjudged guilty of criminal neglect.

Whenever a person has been ordered to pay a fixed sum of money as support to an individual following a plea or adjudication for the offense of criminal neglect of family, pursuant to R.S. 14:74, and such person has absconded or fled the jurisdiction of the court or has violated the terms of his probation relating to that support obligation, or both, if such conduct necessitates help and support to the individual by the office of family security of the department and should such person be apprehended and arrearages of his support payments are collected from him, the arrearage collected from the person will go to the department as reimbursement to the extent allowed by federal law. *(Added by Acts 1993 No. 442, §2, eff. 6/9/93.)*

Art. 1355. Stipulation to order of support.

In cases in which the responsible parent or other person owing a duty of support and the district attorney stipulate to an order of support, the court shall have the power to issue an order of support under the provisions of Article 1352 without the necessity of instituting criminal proceedings pursuant to R.S. 14:74. *(Added by Acts 1993 No. 442, §2, eff. 6/9/93.)*

TITLE XIV. MENTAL HEALTH PROCEEDINGS

Chapter

CHAPTER 1. PRELIMINARY PROVISIONS; DEFINITIONS

Article

Art. 1401. Purpose.

The purpose of this Title is to facilitate the proper treatment of children suffering from mental illness or substance abuse. The manner of treatment should be medically appropriate, least restrictive of the child's liberty, and respectful of the child's individual rights. A preference for outpatient treatment should prevail unless the admission to a treatment facility is determined necessary for the recovery of the child from the mental illness or substance abuse. *(Added by Acts 1991 No. 235, §14, eff. 1/1/92.)*

Art. 1402. Declaration of policy.

The underlying policy of this Title is as follows:

(1) That mentally ill minors and minors suffering from substance abuse and their caretakers on their behalf be encouraged to seek voluntary treatment.

(2) That any involuntary treatment or evaluation be accomplished in a setting which is medically appropriate, most likely to facilitate proper care and treatment that will return the minor patient to the community as soon as possible, and is the least restrictive of the minor's liberty.

(3) That continuity of care for the mentally ill and minors suffering from substance abuse be provided.

(4) That mental health and substance abuse treatment services be delivered as near to the place of residence of the minor receiving such services as is reasonably possible and medically appropriate.

(5) That individual rights of minor patients be safeguarded.

(6) That no minor solely as a result of mental illness or alcoholism or incapacitation by alcohol shall be confined in any jail, prison, correctional facility, or juvenile detention center.

(7) That no minor shall be denied treatment solely because he has withdrawn from treatment against medical advice on a prior occasion or because he has relapsed after an earlier treatment.

(8) That minors be protected from unnecessary institutionalization and be afforded proper treatment for their special mental health needs.

(9) That, in view of the liberty interest at issue in any commitment decision, proper respect for the parental decisionmaking role be balanced with the individual rights of the minor.
(Added by Acts 1991 No. 235, §14, eff. 1/1/92.)

Art. 1403. General applicability.

Except as otherwise specified in this Title, all provisions of the Children's Code remain applicable. *(Added by Acts 1991 No. 235, §14, eff. 1/1/92.)*

Art. 1404. Definitions.

As used in this Title:

(1) "Caretaker" means any person legally obligated to provide or secure adequate care for a child, including a parent, tutor, guardian, legal custodian, foster home parent, or other person providing a residence for the child.

(2) "Conditional discharge" means the physical release of a judicially committed minor from a treatment facility by the director or by the court.

(3) "Dangerous to others" means the condition of a person whose behavior or significant threats support a reasonable expectation that there is a substantial risk that he will inflict physical harm upon another person in the near future.

(4) "Dangerous to self" means the condition of a person whose behavior, significant threats, or inaction supports a reasonable expectation that there is a substantial risk that he will inflict physical or severe emotional harm upon his own person.

(5) "Department" means the Department of Health and Hospitals.

(6) "Diagnosis" means the art and science of determining the presence of disease in an individual and distinguishing one disease from another.

(7) "Director" or "superintendent" means a person in charge of a treatment facility or his deputy.

(8) "Discharge" means the full or conditional release from a treatment facility of any minor admitted or otherwise detained under this Title.

(9) "Formal voluntary admission" means the admission of a minor suffering from mental illness or substance abuse desiring admission to a treatment facility for diagnosis or treatment of such condition, or both, who may be formally admitted upon his written request.

(10) "Grave disability" means the condition of a person who is unable to provide for his own basic physical needs, such as essential food, clothing, medical care, and shelter, as a result of serious mental illness or substance abuse and is unable to survive safely in freedom or protect himself from serious harm; the term also includes incapacitation by alcohol, which means the condition of a person who, as a result of the use of alcohol, is unconscious or whose judgment is otherwise so impaired that he is incapable of realizing and making a rational decision with respect to his need for treatment.

(11) "Informal voluntary admission" means the admission of a minor suffering from mental illness or substance abuse, desiring admission to a treatment facility for diagnosis or treatment of such condition, or both, who may be admitted upon his request without making formal application.

(12) "MHAS" means Mental Health Advocacy Service, as established by R.S. 28:64.

(13) "Major surgical procedure" means an invasive procedure of a serious nature with incision upon the body or parts thereof under general, local, or spinal anesthesia, utilizing surgical instruments, for the purpose of diagnosis or treatment of a medical condition. Diagnostic procedures, including but not limited to the following, shall not be considered as major surgical procedures:

(a) Endoscopy through natural body openings, such as the mouth, anus, or urethra, to view the trachea, bronchi, esophagus, stomach, pancreas, small or large intestine, urethra, urinary bladder, or ureters, and to obtain from such organs specimens of fluids or tissues for chemical or microscopic analysis.

(b) Subcutaneous percutaneous liver biopsy.

(c) Punch biopsy of skeletal muscles.

(d) Bone marrow biopsy.

(e) Lumbar puncture.

(f) Myelogram.

(g) Abdominocentesis.

(h) Conization of the uterine cervix.

(i) Renal angiography.
(j) Femoral angiography.
(k) Carotid angiography.
(*l*) Vertebral angiography.

(14) "Mental Health Advocacy Service" means a service established by the state of Louisiana for the purpose of providing legal counsel and representation for mentally disabled persons and to insure that their legal rights are protected.

(15) "Mentally ill person" means any person with a psychiatric disorder which has substantial adverse effects on his ability to function and who requires care and treatment. It does not include a person suffering solely from mental retardation, epilepsy, alcoholism, or drug abuse.

(16) "Patient" means any person detained and taken care of as a mentally ill person or person suffering from substance abuse.

(17) "Respondent" means a person alleged to be mentally ill or suffering from substance abuse and for whom an application for commitment to a treatment facility has been filed.

(18) "Restraint" means the partial or total immobilization of any or all of the extremities or the torso by mechanical means for psychiatric indications. Restraint does not include the use of mechanisms usually and customarily used during medical or surgical procedures, including but not limited to body immobilization during surgery and arm immobilization during intravenous administration. Restraint does not include orthopedic appliances used to posturally support the patient, such as posies.

(19) "Seclusion" means the involuntary confinement of a patient alone in a room, which the patient is physically prevented from leaving, for any period of time, except that seclusion does not include the placement of a patient alone in a room or other area for no more than thirty minutes at a time and no more than three hours in any twenty-four hour time period pursuant to behavior-shaping techniques such as "time-out".

(20) "Substance abuse" means the condition of a person who uses narcotic, stimulant, depressant, soporific, tranquilizing, or hallucinogenic drugs or alcohol to the extent that it renders the person dangerous to himself or others or renders the person gravely disabled.

(21) "Treatment" means an active effort to accomplish an improvement in the mental condition or behavior of a patient or to prevent deterioration in his condition or behavior. Treatment includes, but is not limited to hospitalization, partial hospitalization, outpatient services, examination, diagnosis, training, the use of pharmaceutical, and other services provided for patients by a treatment facility.

(22) "Treatment facility" means any public or private hospital, retreat, institution, mental health center, or facility licensed by the state of Louisiana in which any mentally ill minor or minor suffering from substance abuse is received or detained as a patient except a facility under the control or supervision of the Department of Public Safety and Corrections unless otherwise provided in Title VIII of this Code.

(Added by Acts 1991 No. 235, §14; chgd. by Acts 1995 No. 1287, §2. eff. 6/29/95.)

Art. 1405. Mental Health Advocacy Service (MHAS); representation; fees.

A. MHAS shall provide legal counsel to all patients who request such service and who are admitted for treatment pursuant to this Title, including but not limited to voluntary or involuntary admission, commitment, legal competency, change of status, transfer, and discharge.

B. MHAS shall provide legal counsel, as availability is determined by its executive director, to minors admitted for mental health or substance abuse treatment pursuant to the dispositional alternatives as provided in the other Titles of this Code, including but not limited to Titles VI and VIII.

C. Nothing in this Title shall be construed to prohibit a mentally ill person or respondent from being represented by privately retained counsel. If a MHAS attorney has been appointed by the court and the mentally ill minor or respondent secures his own counsel, the court shall discharge the MHAS attorney.

D. MHAS shall establish official rules and regulations for evaluating a client's financial resources, for the purpose of determining whether a client has the ability to pay for services received. A client found to have sufficient financial resources shall be required to pay in accordance with standards established by the executive director. An indigent client shall be provided legal counsel and representation without charge.

E. MHAS shall be empowered with all of the same rights and responsibilities to represent their clients whether appointed through the provisions of this Code or Title 28 of the Louisiana Revised Statutes of 1950. These rights include but are not limited to:

(1) A request for a judicial hearing pursuant to Article 1411.

(2) An independent medical examination as requested and approved by the MHAS executive director.

(Added by Acts 1991 No. 235, §14, eff. 1/1/92.)

CHAPTER 2. TREATMENT FACILITIES

Art. 1406. Selection of facilities; judicial commitments.

A. Any treatment facility, except a forensic facility, shall be selected with a consideration for the following:

(1) Medical suitability.

(2) Least restriction of the minor's liberty.

(3) Nearness to the minor patient's usual residence.

(4) Financial status of the minor patient.

B. Treatment facilities include but are not limited to the following:

(1) Community mental health centers.

(2) Private clinics.

(3) Public or private halfway houses.

(4) Public or private group homes.

(5) Residential facilities for children.

(6) Public or private general hospitals.

(7) Public or private mental hospitals.

(8) Detoxification canters.

(9) Substance abuse clinics.

(10) Substance abuse inpatient facilities.

(11) Forensic facilities.

C. Judicial commitments may be made to any facility, except forensic facilities, which is listed in Paragraph B of this Article.

(Added by Acts 1991 No. 235, §14, eff. 1/1/92.)

Art. 1407. Facilities prohibited; emergency certificate for mental health treatment.

A. Minor patients involuntarily hospitalized by emergency certificate for mental health treatment shall not be admitted to the following facilities:

(1) Private clinics.

(2) Public or private halfway houses.

(3) Public or private group homes.

(4) Substance abuse clinics.

(5) Forensic facilities.

(6) Residential facilities for children.

B. Minor patients in the custody of the Department of Public Safety and Corrections may be admitted to forensic facilities by emergency certificate provided that judicial commitment proceedings are initiated during the period of treatment at the forensic facility authorized by emergency certificate.

(Added by Acts 1991 No. 235, §14, eff. 1/1/92.)

Art. 1408. Facilities prohibited; emergency certificate for substance abuse treatment.

A. Minor patients involuntarily hospitalized by emergency certificate for substance abuse treatment shall not be admitted to the following facilities:

(1) Private clinics.

(2) Public or private halfway houses.

(3) Public or private group homes.
(4) Forensic facilities.
(5) Residential facilities for children.

B. Judicial commitment or hospitalization by emergency certificate may be made to any facility listed in Article 1406(B), except forensic facilities, provided that such facility has a substance abuse inpatient operation maintained separate and apart from any mental health inpatient operation in such facility.

(Added by Acts 1991 No. 235, §14, eff. 1/1/92.)

CHAPTER 3. RIGHTS OF MINOR PATIENTS

Art. 1409. Rights guaranteed.

A. Each minor patient has a right to care provided in a dignified and humane manner, and to such privacy as is possible consistent with the minor's treatment plan.

B. The confinement of a minor to an institution shall not of itself cause him to lose any of the rights enjoyed by citizens of Louisiana and of the United States. No minor patient shall be deprived of these rights except when the determination is made by an appropriate court.

C. (1) The minor patient in a treatment facility shall be permitted unimpeded, private, and uncensored communication with persons of his choice by mail, telephone, and visitation. These rights may be restricted by the director of the treatment facility if sufficient cause exists and is so documented in the minor's medical records. The minor's legal counsel, as well as his next of kin or responsible party, must be notified in writing of any such restrictions and the reasons therefor. When the cause for any restriction ceases to exist, the minor's full rights shall be reinstated. A minor shall have the right to communicate in any manner in private with his attorney at all times.

(2) The director of a treatment facility shall ensure that correspondence can be conveniently received and mailed, that telephones are reasonably accessible, and that space for visits is available. Writing materials, postage, and telephone usage funds shall be provided in reasonable amounts to minor patients who are unable to procure such items.

(3) Reasonable times and places for the use of telephones and for visits may be established in writing by the director of any treatment facility. However, the times and places established by the director must allow patients, at a minimum, reasonable daily communication by telephone and visitation. These rights may be restricted by the director of the treatment facility if sufficient cause exists and is so documented in the patient's medical records. The patient's legal counsel, as well as his next of kin or responsible party, must be notified in writing of any such restrictions and the reasons therefor. When the cause for any restriction ceases to exist, the patient's full rights shall be reinstated.

(4) (a) The director of any substance abuse treatment facility may restrict the visitation rights of a minor who is voluntarily admitted to such treatment facility for substance abuse treatment under provisions of this Title for the initial phase of treatment but no longer than seven days unless good cause exists to extend the restriction and is so documented in the patient's record. This restriction shall not apply to visitation by the minor's attorney, or if he is not represented by counsel, the MHAS attorney or the minor's minister. This restriction shall also not apply to the parent or legal guardian of a minor unless the director determines that good cause exists that such restriction shall be in the best interests of the minor and is so documented in the minor's record. When the facility director determines the need to restrict visitation of new minor patients, he shall post notice of such restriction in places prominent to all new admissions, and shall inform each new patient of the restriction prior to his admission and the length and duration thereof, and further that such restriction may be extended on an individual basis as determined to be in the minor's interest by the treatment staff with the concurrence of the medical director.

(b) Nothing herein shall be construed to further restrict other forms of patient communication by and to minor patients as permitted in this Article nor shall this restriction apply to mental health treatment facilities.

D. Physical restraints or seclusion shall only be used to prevent a minor patient from physically injuring himself or others. Physical restraints or seclusion may not be used to punish or discipline a patient or used as a convenience to the staff of the treatment facility. Restraint and seclusion shall be used only in accordance with the following standards:

(1) Restraint or seclusion shall only be used when verbal intervention or less restrictive measures fail. Use of restraint or seclusion shall require documentation in the patient's record of the clinical justification for such use as well as the inadequacy of less restrictive intervention techniques.

(2) A written order from a physician or a psychologist acting within the scope of his institutional privileges shall be required for any use of restraint or seclusion. If, however, no physician or psychologist is immediately available, a registered nurse who has been trained in management of disturbed behavior may utilize restraint or seclusion. The nurse or the nursing supervisor shall then immediately notify a physician or a psychologist with institutional authority to order seclusion and provide him with sufficient information to determine whether restraints or seclusion are necessary and whether less restrictive interventions have been tried or considered. The physician or psychologist may then issue a telephone order for seclusion or restraint, if such order is indicated.

(3) Written orders for the use of restraint or seclusion shall be time limited and not more than twelve hours in duration. The written order shall include the date and time of the actual examination of the patient, the date and time that the patient was placed in restraint or seclusion, and the date and time that the order was signed.

(4) A renewal order for up to twelve hours of restraint or seclusion may be issued by a physician or a psychologist with institutional authority to order seclusion or restraint after determining that there is no less restrictive means of preventing injury to the patient or others. If any patient is held in restraint or seclusion for twenty-four hours, the physician or psychologist with institutional authority shall conduct an actual examination of the patient and document the reason why the use of seclusion or restraint beyond twenty-four hours is necessary, and the parent, tutor, or caretaker shall be notified by the twenty-sixth hour.

(5) Staff who implement written orders for restraints and seclusion shall have documented training in the proper use of the procedure for which the order was written.

(6) Periodic monitoring and care of the patient shall be provided by responsible staff. A patient in restraint or seclusion shall be evaluated every fifteen minutes, especially in regard to regular meals, water, and snacks, bathing, the need for motion and exercise, and use of the bathroom, and documentation of these evaluations shall be entered in the patient's record.

(7) Patients shall be released from restraint or seclusion as soon as the reasons justifying the use of restraints or seclusion subside. If at any time during the period of restraint or seclusion a registered nurse determines that the emergency which justified the seclusion or restraint has subsided and a physician or psychologist is not immediately available, the patient shall be released. At the end of the period of restraint or seclusion ordered by the physician or psychologist the patient shall be released unless a renewal order is issued.

(8) Mechanical restraints shall be designed and used so as not to cause physical injury to the patient and so to cause the least possible discomfort.

(9) Facilities using seclusion or restraint shall have written policies concerning their use. These policies shall include standards and procedures for placing a patient in seclusion or restraint, and for informing him of the reason he was put in seclusion or restraint and the means of terminating such seclusion or restraint.

(10) Nothing in this Article shall be construed to expand the scope of practice of psychology as defined in R.S. 37:2351 et seq. to authorize the ordering, administering, or dispensing of medications, or to authorize any practice not permitted under the privileges granted by the institution.

(11) The department shall adopt rules and regulations in accordance with the Administrative Procedure Act* to govern the use of seclusion and restraint. Such rules and regulations shall respect the minor patient's individual rights, protect the minor patient's health, safety, and welfare, and be the least restrictive of the minor patient's liberty. The department shall adopt rules and regulations to provide for enforcement procedures and penalties applicable to a person who violates the requirements of this Section.

**R.S. 49:950 et seq.*

E. A patient may be placed alone in a room or other area pursuant to behavior shaping techniques such as "time-out". Such placement may only be used as part of a written treatment plan, shall not be used for the convenience of staff, and may be used only according to the following standards and procedures:

(1) Placement alone in a room or other area shall be imposed only when less restrictive measures are inadequate.

(2) Placement alone in a room or other area shall only be ordered by a qualified professional trained in behavior-shaping techniques and authorized in accordance with written policies and procedures of the facility to order the use of behavior-shaping techniques.

(3) The period of placement alone in a room or other area shall not exceed thirty minutes.

(4) The patient shall be observed and supervised by a staff member.

(5) The period of placement alone in a room or other area shall not exceed a total of three hours in any twenty-four hour time period. If the placement alone in a room or other area exceeds a total of three hours in any twenty-four hour time period, it shall then be considered seclusion and shall be governed by the procedures and standards set forth in Paragraph D of this Article.

(6) The date, time, and duration of the placement shall be documented.

(7) In treatment facilities where patients are placed alone in a room or other area as a behavior-shaping technique, there shall be written policies and procedures governing use of such behavior-shaping technique.

F. No minor patient confined by emergency certificate, judicial commitment, court order, or noncontested status shall receive major surgical procedures or electroshock therapy without the written consent of a court of competent jurisdiction after a hearing. However, if the director of the treatment facility, in consultation with two physicians, determines that the condition of the minor is of such a critical nature that it may be life threatening unless major surgical procedures or electroshock therapy are administered, such emergency measures may be performed without the consent otherwise provided for in this Paragraph. No physician shall be liable for a good faith determination that a medical emergency exists.

G. Every minor patient shall have the right to wear his own clothes and keep and use his personal possessions, including toilet articles, unless determined by a physician that these are medically inappropriate and the reasons therefor are documented in his medical record. The minor shall also be allowed to spend a reasonable sum of his own money for canteen expenses and small purchases, and to have access to individual storage spaces for his private use. If the minor is financially unable to provide these articles for himself, the treatment facility shall provide a reasonable supply of clothing and toiletries.

H. The following rules shall govern performance of work by minor patients:

(1) No minor shall be required to perform work of any kind that involves the operation and maintenance of an institution, nor shall privileges or release from an institution be conditioned upon performance of any work, except as follows:

(a) A minor patient may be required to perform vocational training tasks, provided each task is:

(i) Part of the minor's individual treatment plan and has been approved as a program activity by a professional responsible for supervising the program.

(ii) Supervised by a qualified professional.

(iii) Not continued for longer than six months, unless it is specifically reinstated by the minor's treatment plan.

(b) A minor patient may be required to perform without compensation such housekeeping tasks as would be performed by a minor in a natural home, foster home, or group home, provided that nothing in the minor's individual treatment plan forbids such work. In no case, however, may a minor be required to perform housekeeping tasks for more than twelve other people.

(2) A minor may voluntarily engage in work during nonprogram hours, provided that:

(a) The minor's individual treatment plan does not forbid it.

(b) The particular work has been approved by the qualified professional responsible for supervising the implementation of the minor treatment plan.

(c) The particular work is supervised by qualified staff.

(d) The conditions of employment and the compensation are in full compliance with all applicable federal laws.

(3) No minor patient shall be involved in the care, feeding, clothing, training, or supervision of other minors unless the qualified professional responsible for supervising the implementation of the treatment plan certifies in writing in the minor's record that the particular task will not in any way endanger the life or health or be detrimental to the development of the particular children who receive such care or of the minor patient providing it.

I. Under appropriate supervision, each minor patient shall be provided with suitable opportunities for interaction with members of the opposite sex, except where a qualified professional responsible for the formulation of a particular minor's treatment plan writes an order to the contrary and explains the reasons therefor.

J. Every minor patient shall have the right to be discharged from a treatment facility when his condition has changed or improved to the extent that confinement and treatment at the treatment facility are no longer required. The director of the treatment facility shall have the authority to discharge a patient admitted by judicial commitment pursuant to Chapter 9 of this Title without the approval of the court which committed him to the treatment facility. The court shall be advised of any such discharge. The director shall not be legally responsible to any person for the subsequent acts of behavior of a patient discharged by him in good faith.

K. Every minor patient shall have the right to engage a private attorney. If the minor is indigent, he shall be provided an attorney by the MHAS, if he so requests. The attorneys provided by the MHAS or appointed by a court shall be interested in and qualified by training or experience, or both, in the field of mental health statutes and jurisprudence.

L. Every minor patient shall have the right to request a court hearing pursuant to Article 1411. The purpose of the hearing shall be to determine whether or not he should be discharged from the treatment facility or transferred to a less restrictive and medically suitable treatment facility.

M. No provision hereof shall abridge or diminish the right of any minor patient to avail himself of the right of habeas corpus at any time.

N. Every minor patient shall have the right to be visited and examined at his own expense by a physician designated by him, a member of his family, or an interested party. The physician may consult and confer with the medical staff of the treatment facility and have the benefit of all information contained in the patient's medical record.

O. Prefrontal lobotomy shall be prohibited as a treatment solely for medical or emotional illness of a minor patient.

P. No medication shall be administered to a minor patient unless a written order of a physician prescribes it in writing. The physician is responsible for all medications which he has ordered and which are administered to a minor patient. The medication prescribed shall be noted in the minor patient's records. At least monthly, the attending physician shall review the drug regimen of each minor patient under his care. All prescriptions shall be written with a termination date, which shall not exceed thirty days. The minor's records shall state the effects of psychoactive medication on him. Unnecessary or excessive medication shall not be administered to any minor patient. Medication shall not be used as punishment, for the convenience of staff, as a substitute for a treatment program, or in quantities that interfere with the minor's treatment program. No medication shall be administered except by persons who have been appropriately trained.

Q. A minor patient admitted to a treatment facility has the right to an individualized treatment plan and periodic review to determine his progress. The appropriate staff of the facility shall review the minor's progress at least at intervals of thirty days. The staff shall enter into the minor's medical record his response to medical treatment, his current mental status, and specific reasons why continued treatment is necessary in the current setting or whether a treatment facility is available which is medically suitable and less restrictive of the minor patient's liberty.

R. A minor patient admitted to a treatment facility has the right to have available such treatment as is medically appropriate to his condition. Should the treatment facility be unable to provide an active and appropriate medical treatment program, the minor shall be discharged.

S. Each minor patient shall have the right to receive prompt and adequate medical treatment for any physical ailments and for the prevention of any illness or disability. Such medical treatment shall meet the standards of medical practice in the community.

T. The institution shall prohibit the mistreatment, neglect, or abuse of any minor child in any way.

(Added by Acts 1991 No. 235, §14; chgd. by Acts 1995 No. 436, §2, No. 1287, §2; Acts 1997 No. 985, §2, eff. 8/15/97.)

Art. 1410. Violation of rights; reports; reports of abuse or neglect.

A. Alleged violations of the rights established by Article 1409 shall be reported immediately to the superintendent and there shall be a written record that:

(1) Each alleged violation has been thoroughly investigated and findings stated.

(2) The results of such investigation were reported to the superintendent within twenty-four hours of the report of the incident.

B. Abuse or neglect of any child shall be reported to a child protection agency in accordance with Chapter 5 of Title VI.
(Added by Acts 1991 No. 235, §14, eff. 1/1/92.)

CHAPTER 4. HOSPITALIZED MINORS' RIGHT TO HEARING

Art. 1411. Right to hearing.

A minor or his attorney shall have the right to demand a hearing to determine whether the minor should receive treatment on an inpatient basis, be discharged from the treatment facility, or placed in a less restrictive setting. *(Added by Acts 1991 No. 235, §14, eff. 1/1/92.)*

Art. 1412. Petition; venue.

A. The petition shall be filed in the court of the jurisdiction in which the patient is confined or, if the minor is currently under a disposition by a juvenile court, the hearing shall be held in that juvenile court.

B. The hearing shall be held in that court and no other except for good cause shown.

C. The judge of the court where the petition was filed may hold the hearing at the treatment facility where the minor is confined, if in the opinion of the director of the treatment facility it will be detrimental to the patient's health, welfare, or dignity to travel to the court where the petition was filed.
(Added by Acts 1991 No. 235, §14, eff. 1/1/92.)

Art. 1413. Time for hearing.

The hearing shall be held within five days of the filing of the petition. *(Added by Acts 1991 No. 235, §14; chgd. by Acts 1997 No. 612, §3, eff. 8/15/97.)*

Art. 1414. Order of hearing.

A. Witnesses and evidence tending to show that the child needs to be in a treatment facility shall be presented first.

B. Counsel for the child shall have the opportunity to present evidence and to cross-examine witnesses.
(Added by Acts 1991 No. 235, §14, eff. 1/1/92.)

Art. 1415. Burden of proof; order.

If the court finds by clear and convincing evidence that the minor has a mental illness or suffers from substance abuse of such severity that hospitalization is necessary and that he can benefit from inpatient treatment, it shall order his continued confinement in a designated treatment facility which is medically suitable and least restrictive of his liberty. *(Added by Acts 1991 No. 235, §14, eff. 1/1/92.)*

CHAPTER 5. RECORDS

Art. 1416. Facility records; confidentiality; disclosure; destruction.

A. Complete records for each minor shall be maintained and all information contained in a minor patient's records shall be considered privileged and confidential and shall not be disclosed except as provided herein.

B. A minor patient's record shall be readily available to both the qualified professionals and the residential care workers who are directly involved with the minor.

C. The parent or tutor of the minor shall be permitted access to his records. These records shall include:

(1) Identification data, including the minor's legal status.

(2) The minor's history, including but not limited to:

(a) Family data, educational background, and employment record.

(b) Prior medical history, both physical and mental, including prior institutionalization.

(3) The minor patient's grievances if any.

(4) An inventory of the minor's life skills.

(5) A record of each physical examination describing the results of the examination.

(6) A copy of the minor's individual plan and any modifications thereto and an appropriate summary to guide and assist resident care workers in implementing the minor's program.

(7) The findings made in periodic reviews of the plan, including an analysis of the successes and failures of the minor patient's program and recommendations for any modifications deemed necessary.

(8) A copy of the post-institutionalization plan and any modifications thereto, and a summary of the steps that have been taken to implement that plan.

(9) History and present status with respect to medication.

(10) A summary of each significant contact with the minor by a qualified professional.

(11) A summary of the minor patient's response to his program, prepared by a qualified professional involved in his treatment and recorded at least monthly. Such response wherever possible, shall be scientifically documented.

(12) A signed order by a qualified professional for any physical restraints or seclusion, and documentation of the clinical justification for the use of restraints, seclusion, and placement as required by Article 1409(D) and (E).

(13) A description of any extraordinary incident or accident in the institution involving the minor, to be entered by a staff member noting personal knowledge of the incident or accident or other source of information, including any reports of investigations of mistreatment of the child, as required by Article 1410.

(14) A summary of family visits and contacts.

(15) A summary of attendance and leaves from the institution.

(16) A record of any seizures, illnesses, treatments thereof, and immunizations.

D. Any attorney representing a mentally ill minor or a respondent as defined herein shall have ready access to view and copy all mental health and developmental disability records pertaining to his client unless the client objects. The attorney shall return all copies of his client's medical record to the treatment facility upon completion of their use. If the patient or respondent later retains a private attorney to represent him, the MHAS shall destroy all copies of records pertaining to his case.

E. Any respondent or mentally disabled minor shall have the right to demand that the records in the possession of his attorney regarding his mental condition be destroyed or returned to the treatment facility and he shall have the right to assurance by the director that such records have been so destroyed by the MHAS attorney.

(Added by Acts 1991 No. 235, §14; chgd. by Acts 1995 No. 1287, §2, eff. 6/29/95.)

Art. 1417. Court records.

A. Each court shall keep a record of the cases relating to mentally ill minors coming before it under this Title and the disposition of them. It shall also keep on file the original petition and certificates of physicians required by this Chapter, or a microfilm duplicate of such records.

B. All records maintained in the courts under the provisions of this Article shall be sealed and available only to the respondent or his attorney unless the court, after a hearing held with notice to the respondent, determines such records should be disclosed to a petitioner for cause shown.

(Added by Acts 1991 No. 235, §14, eff. 1/1/92.)

CHAPTER 6. IMMUNITY FROM LIABILITY

Art. 1418. Physician's standard of care.

Any licensed physician who acts pursuant to the provisions of this Title, including execution of an emergency certificate, shall be held to that degree of skill and care ordinarily employed under similar circumstances by members of his profession in good standing in the same community or locality and using reasonable care and diligence with his best judgment in the application of his skill. *(Added by Acts 1991 No. 235, §14, eff. 1/1/92.)*

Art. 1419. Immunity.

A. Any licensed physician exercising that degree of skill and care ordinarily employed under similar circumstances by members of his profession in good standing in the same community or locality and using reasonable care and diligence with his best judgment in the application of his skill, shall not be held civilly liable or subject to criminal prosecution for acts arising from his medical opinions, judgments, actions, or duties pursuant to any of the provisions of this Title.

B. Any person who acts in good faith to assist in the apprehension or taking into protective custody and examination of a minor patient will not be subject to civil or criminal penalties. However, a person who willfully advises or participates in the making of a false application or certificate shall be imprisoned with or without hard labor for not more than two years or fined not more than ten thousand dollars, or both.

C. Any apprehension or taking into protective custody and confinement made by law enforcement officers, ordered by a court or upon the certificate of a physician under the procedures provided in this Title, is hereby declared to be an administrative act relative to the functions of their office, as required by law, and for which act they are specifically granted personal immunity, but not thereby relieved of their official responsibilities.

D. Coroners and assistant coroners who act in good faith to order persons to be taken into protective custody and transported for examination in accordance with Article 1432 shall not be civilly liable for damages to such persons resulting from those actions.

(Added by Acts 1991 No. 235, §14; chgd. by Acts 1992 No. 705, §1, eff. 7/6/92.)

CHAPTER 7. EMERGENCY CERTIFICATE ADMISSION PROCEDURE

Art. 1420. Admission by emergency certificate; extension.

A. A mentally ill minor or a minor suffering from substance abuse may be admitted and detained at a treatment facility for observation, diagnosis, and treatment for a period not to exceed fifteen days under an emergency certificate.

B. A minor suffering from substance abuse may be detained at a treatment facility for one additional period, not to exceed fifteen days, provided that a second emergency certificate is executed. A second certificate may be executed only if and when a physician at the treatment facility and any other physician have examined the detained minor within seventy-two hours prior to the termination of the initial fifteen-day period and certified in writing on the second certificate that the minor remains dangerous to himself or others or gravely disabled, and that his condition is likely to improve during the extended period. The director shall inform the minor patient of the execution of the second certificate, the length of the extended period, and the specific reasons therefor, and shall also give notice of the same to the minor's nearest relative or other designated responsible party initially notified pursuant to Article 1428. *(Added by Acts 1991 No. 235, §14, eff. 1/1/92.)*

Art. 1421. Examination required.

Any physician may execute an emergency certificate only after an actual examination of a minor alleged to be mentally ill or suffering from substance abuse who is determined to be in need of immediate medical treatment in a treatment facility because the examining physician determines him to be dangerous to himself or others or to be gravely disabled. Failure to conduct an examination prior to the execution of the certificate will be evidence of gross negligence. *(Added by Acts 1991 No. 235, §14, eff. 1/1/92.)*

Art. 1422. Certificate; contents.

A. The emergency certificate shall state all of the following:

(1) The date of the physician's examination of the minor, which shall not be more than seventy-two hours prior to the date of the signature of the certificate.

(2) The objective findings of the physician relative to the physical and mental condition of the minor, leading to the conclusion that he is dangerous to himself or others or is gravely disabled as a result of substance abuse or mental illness.

(3) The history of the case, if known.

(4) The determination of whether the minor examined is in need of immediate psychiatric treatment in a treatment facility because he is either:

(a) Dangerous to himself.

(b) Dangerous to others.

(c) Gravely disabled.

(5) A statement that the minor is unwilling or unable to seek voluntary admission.

B. The certificate shall be dated and executed under the penalty of perjury, but need not be notarized. The certificate shall be valid for seventy-two hours and shall be delivered to the director of the treatment facility where the person is to be further evaluated and treated. *(Added by Acts 1991 No. 235, §14, eff. 1/1/92.)*

Art. 1423. Coroner; notice; independent examination; discharge.

A. Upon admission of any minor by emergency certificate to a treatment facility, it shall be the duty of the director of the treatment facility immediately to notify the coroner of the parish in which the treatment facility is located of the admission, giving the following information if known:

(1) The minor's name, address, date of birth.

(2) Name of certifying physician.

(3) Date and time of admission.

(4) The name and address of the treatment facility.

B. Within seventy-two hours of admission, the minor patient shall be independently examined by the coroner or his deputy who shall execute an emergency certificate pursuant to Article 1422, which shall be a necessary precondition to the person's continued confinement.

C. However, in the event that the coroner has made the initial examination and executed the first emergency commitment certificate, then a second examination shall be made within the seventy-two hour period set forth in this Article by any physician at the treatment facility where the minor patient is confined.

D. If from his examination the coroner concludes that the minor is not a proper subject for emergency admission, then the minor shall not be further detained in the treatment facility and shall be discharged by the director forthwith.
(Added by Acts 1991 No. 235, §14, eff. 1/1/92.)

Art. 1424. Coroner; fees; records.

A. In making either the initial examination or the second examination, when the coroner or his deputy examines the patient and executes an emergency certificate and a reexamination of the minor and reexecution of a certificate is necessary for any reason to insure the validity of the certificate, both the first examiner and the reexaminer shall be entitled to a fee for the service, unless they are one and the same.

B. When a minor patient is confined in a treatment facility other than a state mental institution, the examining coroner in the parish where the minor is confined shall be entitled to the usual fee paid for this service to the coroner of the parish in which the patient is domiciled or residing.

C. When a minor patient is confined in a state mental institution in a parish other than his parish of domicile or residence, the examining coroner shall be entitled to the fee authorized by law in his parish for the service.

D. In either case, the fee shall be paid and accurate records of such payments kept by the governing authority of the parish in which the minor patient is domiciled or residing from parish funds designated for the purpose of payment to the coroner.

E. All coroners shall keep accurate records showing the number of patients confined in their parishes pursuant to this Article.
(Added by Acts 1991 No. 235, §14, eff. 1/1/92.)

Art. 1425. Request for MHAS representation.

Upon admission by emergency certificate, a patient may request the director of the treatment facility to advise the executive director of MHAS of his admission and may request representation. *(Added by Acts 1991 No. 235, §14, eff. 1/1/92.)*

Art. 1426. Right to hearing.

A. Prior to or during confinement under the provisions of this Title, any minor or his attorney shall have the right to demand a judicial hearing to determine if probable cause exists for his continued confinement under an emergency certificate.

B. The hearing shall be held within five days of the filing of the petition.

C. Pending the decision of the court, the minor patient shall remain confined unless the court orders release or a less restrictive status.
(Added by Acts 1991 No. 235, §14, eff. 1/1/92.)

Art. 1427. Authority to transport and detain.

A. An emergency certificate shall constitute legal authority to transport a patient to a treatment facility and shall permit the director of such treatment facility to detain the minor patient for diagnosis and treatment for a period not to exceed fifteen days, and to return him to the facility if he is absent with or without permission during authorized periods of detention.

B. If necessary, peace officers shall apprehend and transport, or ambulance services, under appropriate circumstances, may locate and transport a minor patient on whom an emergency certificate has been completed to a treatment facility at the request of either the director of the facility, the certifying physician, the minor's next of kin or tutor, or the agency legally responsible for his welfare.
(Added by Acts 1991 No. 235, §14, eff. 1/1/92.)

Art. 1428. Notice of admission.

The director of the treatment facility shall notify the minor patient's nearest relative, if known, or designated responsible party, if any, in writing of the minor's admission by emergency certificate as soon as reasonably possible. *(Added by Acts 1991 No. 235, §14, eff. 1/1/92.)*

Art. 1429. Application for judicial commitment.

A. If the minor patient admitted to a treatment facility pursuant to this Chapter is a proper candidate for judicial commitment pursuant to Chapter 9 of this Title, the director of the treatment facility, or any interested party, may apply for such commitment under provisions of Chapter 9 of this Title.

B. Such a minor patient, hospitalized on an emergency certificate, for whom a petition for judicial commitment has been filed in court may continue to be detained for a further period on order of the court.
(Added by Acts 1991 No. 235, §14, eff. 1/1/92.)

Art. 1430. Advice of rights.

A. Every minor patient admitted by emergency certificate shall be informed in writing at the time of his admission of the procedures of requesting release from the treatment facility, the availability of counsel, information about MHAS, the rights enumerated in Chapter 3 of this Title, and the rules and regulations applicable to or concerning his conduct while a patient is in the treatment facility.

B. If the minor is illiterate or does not read or understand English, appropriate provisions should be made to supply him this information.

C. In addition, a copy of the information mentioned in this Article must be posted in any area where patients are confined and treated.

(Added by Acts 1991 No. 235, §14, eff. 1/1/92.)

Art. 1431. Coroner's examination; emergency certificate.

A. Upon the request of a credible adult who is financially unable to afford a private physician or who cannot immediately obtain an examination by a physician, the parish coroner may render, or the coroner or a judge of a court of competent jurisdiction may cause to be rendered by a physician, an actual examination of a minor alleged to be mentally ill or suffering from substance abuse and in need of immediate medical treatment because he is dangerous to self or others or gravely disabled. If the coroner is not a physician he may deputize a physician to perform this examination.

B. Failure to render an actual examination prior to execution of the emergency certificate shall be evidence of gross negligence.

C. To accomplish the examination authorized by this Article, if the coroner or the judge is apprehensive that his own safety or that of the deputy or other physician may be endangered thereby, he shall issue a protective custody order pursuant to Chapter 8 of this Title.

D. If the examining physician determines that the provisions of this Article are met, he shall execute an emergency certificate and shall transport or cause to be transported the minor named in the emergency certificate to a treatment facility.

(Added by Acts 1991 No. 235, §14, eff. 1/1/92.)

CHAPTER 8. PROTECTIVE CUSTODY

Article

Art. 1432. Order for custody; grounds.

A. Any parish coroner or judge of a court of competent jurisdiction may order a minor to be taken into protective custody and transported to a treatment facility or the office of the coroner for immediate examination when a peace officer or other credible person executes a statement under private signature specifying that, to the best of his knowledge and belief, the minor is mentally ill or suffering from substance abuse and is in need of immediate treatment to protect the minor patient or others from physical harm. The statement may include the following information:

(1) A statement of facts, including the affiant's observations leading to the conclusion that the minor is mentally ill or suffering from substance abuse and dangerous to himself or others or gravely disabled.

(2) The date and place of any dangerous acts or threats.

(3) The name and surname, if known, of any other person who is in danger.

(4) Facts showing that the minor sought has been encouraged to seek treatment and is unwilling to be evaluated on a voluntary basis.

(5) Facts showing that the affiant has attempted to contact a specific treatment facility or a specific physician in order to obtain an examination of the minor sought to be treated.

B. The order for custody shall be in writing, in the name of the state of Louisiana, signed by the judge or parish coroner, and shall state all of the following:

(1) The date and hour of issuance and the municipality or parish where issued.

(2) The name of the minor to be taken into custody or, if his name is not known, a designation of the minor by any name or description by which he can be identified with reasonable certainty.

(3) A description of the acts or threats which have led to the belief that the minor is mentally ill or suffering from substance abuse and is in need of immediate hospitalization to protect the person or others from physical harm.

(4) That the minor shall be taken to a community mental health center, a public or private general hospital, a public or private mental hospital, coroner's office, or a detoxification center.

C. The order for custody shall be effective for seventy-two hours from its issuance and shall be delivered to the coroner or director of the treatment facility by the individual who has transported the minor. The date and hour that the minor is taken into protective custody shall be written on the order. Without delay, and in no event more than twelve hours after being taken into protective custody, the minor shall be delivered to a treatment facility or the office of the coroner or he shall be released. Upon arrival, the minor in custody shall be examined immediately by the coroner or, if at a treatment facility, by a physician, preferably a psychiatrist, who shall determine if the minor shall be voluntarily admitted, admitted by emergency certificate, admitted as a noncontested admission, or discharged. The minor in custody shall be examined within eight hours of his arrival at the treatment facility or coroner's office or he shall be released.
(Added by Acts 1991 No. 235, §14, eff. 1/1/92.)

Art. 1433. Protective custody without court order.

A. A peace officer or a peace officer accompanied by an emergency medical service trained technician may take a minor into protective custody and transport him to a treatment facility for a medical evaluation when, as a result of his personal observation, the peace officer or emergency medical service technician has reasonable grounds to believe the minor is a proper subject for involuntary admission to a treatment facility because he is acting in a manner dangerous to himself or dangerous to others, is gravely disabled, and is in need of immediate hospitalization to protect the minor or others from physical harm.

B. The minor may only be transported to one of the following:

(1) A community mental health center.
(2) A public or private general hospital.
(3) A public or private mental hospital.
(4) A detoxification center.
(5) A substance abuse clinic.
(6) A substance abuse inpatient facility.

C. Upon arrival at the treatment facility, the escorting peace officer shall then be relieved of any further responsibility and the minor shall be immediately examined by a physician, preferably a psychiatrist, who shall determine if the minor shall be voluntarily admitted, admitted by emergency certificate, or discharged.

D. In the case of a minor suffering from substance abuse and where any of the facilities stated in Paragraph B of this Article are unavailable, the peace officer and emergency medical service technician may use whatever means or facilities available to protect the health and safety of the minor suffering from substance abuse until such time as any of the above facilities become available. In taking a minor into protective custody, the peace officer and emergency medical service technician may take reasonable steps to protect themselves. A peace officer or emergency medical service technician who acts in compliance with this Article is acting in the course of his official duty and cannot be subjected to criminal or civil liability as a result thereof.

E. Under the provisions of this Article no minor shall be placed in protective custody for a period in excess of seventy-two hours. Any minor placed in protective custody under the provisions of this Article shall be considered as an inmate for maintenance purposes only.
(Added by Acts 1991 No. 235, §14, eff. 1/1/92.)

CHAPTER 9. JUDICIAL COMMITMENT PROCEDURE

Art. 1434. Judicial commitment; petition.

A. Any adult may file with the court a petition which asserts his belief that a minor is suffering from mental illness which contributes or causes him to be a danger to himself or others or to be gravely disabled, or is suffering from substance abuse which contributes or causes the minor to be a danger to himself or others or to be gravely disabled, and may thereby request a hearing.

B. The petition shall contain the facts which are the basis of the assertion and provide the minor respondent with adequate notice and knowledge relative to the nature of the proceedings.

C. A petitioner who is unable to afford an attorney may seek the assistance of any legal aid society or similar agency if available.

(Added by Acts 1991 No. 235, §14, eff. 1/1/92.)

Art. 1435. Filing; venue.

A. The petition may be filed in the judicial district in which the minor respondent is confined or, if not confined, in the judicial district where he resides or may be found.

B. Before the hearing, the minor respondent may move for a change of venue to the parish of his domicile, which motion shall be granted only for compelling reasons. If the minor respondent is confined to a hospital, the judge of the court where the petition was filed may hold the hearing on such commitment at the treatment facility where he is confined, if in the opinion of at least one of the physicians appointed by the court to examine him, it will be detrimental to the minor's health, welfare, or dignity to travel to the court where the petition was filed.

(Added by Acts 1991 No. 235, §14, eff. 1/1/92.)

Art. 1436. Hearing; notice.

A. Upon the filing of the petition, the court shall assign a time, not later than eighteen calendar days thereafter, shall assign a place for a hearing upon the petition, and shall cause reasonable notice thereof to be given to the minor, his attorney, and the petitioner.

B. The notice shall inform the minor respondent that he has a right to be present at the hearing, that he has a right to counsel, that he, if indigent or otherwise qualified, has the right to have counsel appointed to represent him by the MHAS, and that he has the right to cross examine witnesses testifying at any hearing on such application.

(Added by Acts 1991 No. 235, §14, eff. 1/1/92.)

Art. 1437. Probable cause; order for examination.

A. As soon as practical after the filing of the petition, the court shall review the petition and supporting documents and determine whether there exists probable cause to believe that the minor respondent is suffering from mental illness which contributes or causes him to be a danger to himself or others, or to be gravely disabled, or is suffering from substance abuse which contributes or causes him to be a danger to himself or others or to be gravely disabled.

B. If the court determines that probable cause exists, the court may appoint the minor respondent's treating physician if available or, if none, then another physician, preferably a psychiatrist, to examine the minor and make a written report to the court and respondent's attorney on the form provided by the office of human services of the Department of Health and Hospitals.

(Added by Acts 1991 No. 235, §14, eff. 1/1/92.)

Art. 1438. Report of examination.

A. Any report ordered pursuant to Article 1437 shall set forth specifically the objective factors leading to the conclusion that the minor has a mental illness or suffers from substance abuse, the actions or statements by the person leading to the conclusion that the mental illness or substance abuse causes the minor to be dangerous to himself or others or to be gravely disabled and in need of immediate treatment as a result of such illness or abuse, and why involuntary confinement and treatment are indicated.

B. The following criteria should be considered by the physician:

(1) The minor is suffering from serious mental illness which contributes or causes him to be dangerous to himself or others or to be gravely disabled or from substance abuse which contributes or causes him to be dangerous to himself or others or to be gravely disabled.

(2) The minor's condition is likely to deteriorate needlessly unless he is provided appropriate medical treatment.

(3) The minor's condition is likely to improve if he is provided appropriate medical treatment.

(Added by Acts 1991 No. 235, §14, eff. 1/1/92.)

Art. 1439. Independent examination.

A. The minor respondent or his attorney shall have the right to seek an additional independent medical opinion, when necessary, in their discretion.

B. If the respondent is indigent, this opinion may be paid for by the MHAS, upon the approval of its executive director.

C. Reasonable compensation of the appointed examining physicians and all court costs shall be established by the court and ordered paid by the minor respondent or the petitioner in the discretion of the court. If it is determined by the court that the costs shall not be borne by the minor respondent or the petitioner, then compensation to the physicians and all court costs shall be paid from funds appropriated to the judiciary, but such court costs shall not exceed the sum of seventy-five dollars.

(Added by Acts 1991 No. 235, §14, eff. 1/1/92.)

Art. 1440. Order for custody and detention.

A. If the minor respondent refuses to be examined by the court appointed physician as herein provided or if the judge, after reviewing the petition and an affidavit filed pursuant to Article 1432, the report of the treating physician, or the court-appointed physician, finds that the minor is mentally ill or suffering from substance abuse and is in need of immediate hospitalization to protect himself or others from physical harm, or that the minor respondent's condition may be markedly worsened by delay, then the court may issue a court order for custody of the minor and a peace officer shall deliver him to a treatment facility designated by the court.

B. The court shall also issue an order to the treatment facility authorizing detention of the minor until the commitment hearing is completed, unless he is discharged by the director.

(Added by Acts 1991 No. 235, §14, eff. 1/1/92.)

Art. 1441. Placement pending hearing.

A. Unless the minor is currently hospitalized or under an emergency certificate, he shall be allowed to remain in his home or other place of residence pending an ordered examination and to return to his home or other place of residence upon completion of the examination.

B. An examining physician may execute an emergency certificate pursuant to Article 1422 if he deems that action appropriate. In such a case, the respondent shall be admitted pursuant to Article 1420 pending the hearing on the petition.

(Added by Acts 1991 No. 235, §14, eff. 1/1/92.)

Art. 1442. Right to counsel.

A. The court shall provide the minor respondent a reasonable opportunity to select his own counsel. In the event he does not select counsel and is unable to pay for counsel or in the event counsel selected by him refuses to represent said minor or is not available for such representation, then the court shall appoint counsel for him provided by the MHAS.

B. Reasonable compensation of appointed counsel shall be established by the court and may be ordered paid by the minor respondent or petitioner in the discretion of the court if either is found financially capable. If it is determined by the court that the costs shall not be borne by the respondent or the petitioner, then compensation to the attorney shall be paid from funds appropriated to the judiciary.

C. The minor respondent shall have the right to privately retained and paid counsel at any time. However, all minor respondents must be represented by counsel as early as possible in every proceeding. If attorneys are available through the MHAS, the court shall contact the MHAS and request the assignment of an attorney who will be appointed.

D. In cases where the service is unable to provide representation, the court shall select and appoint an attorney to represent the minor respondent, whose fee shall be set by the court.

E. An attorney appointed by a court to represent a minor respondent pursuant to this Chapter has a continuing duty toward that minor even after admission. That duty shall include but not be limited to follow-up investigation of the circumstances of the person and representation in subsequent proceedings relating to admission, status, and discharge. The duty shall continue until it is terminated by the court making the appointment.
(Added by Acts 1991 No. 235, §14, eff. 1/1/92.)

Art. 1443. Hearing; priority.

On the day appointed, the hearing shall take precedence over all other matters, except pending cases of the same type. *(Added by Acts 1991 No. 235, §14, eff. 1/1/92.)*

Art. 1444. Nature of hearing; evidence.

The court shall conduct the hearing in as formal a manner as is possible under the circumstances and shall admit evidence according to the usual rules of evidence. *(Added by Acts 1991 No. 235, §14, eff. 1/1/92.)*

Art. 1445. Order of hearing.

A. Witnesses and evidence tending to show that the minor who is the subject of the petition is a proper subject for judicial commitment shall be presented first.

B. The minor respondent or his counsel shall have the right to present evidence and cross-examine witnesses who may testify at the hearing.

C. If the minor respondent or his attorney notified the court not less than three days before the hearing that he wishes to cross-examine the examining physicians, the court shall order such physicians to appear in person or by deposition.

D. If the minor respondent is present at the hearing and is medicated, the court shall be informed of the medication and its common effects.
(Added by Acts 1991 No. 235, §14, eff. 1/1/92.)

Art. 1446. Record; transcription.

A. The court shall cause a recording of the testimony of the hearing to be made, which shall be transcribed only in the event of an appeal from the judgment.

B. A copy of such transcript shall be furnished without charge, to any appellant whom the court finds unable to pay for the same.

C. The cost of such transcript shall be paid from funds appropriated to the judicial department.
(Added by Acts 1991 No. 235, §14, eff. 1/1/92.)

Art. 1447. Burden of proof; order.

A. If the court finds by clear and convincing evidence that the minor respondent is dangerous to himself or others or is gravely disabled as a result of substance abuse or mental illness, it shall render a judgment for his commitment to a designated treatment facility which is medically suitable and least restrictive of his liberty.

B. The court order shall order a suitable person to convey the minor to the treatment facility and deliver respondent, together with a copy of the judgment and certificates, to the director.

C. In appointing a person to execute the order, the court should give preference to a near relative or friend of the minor.
(Added by Acts 1991 No. 235, §14, eff. 1/1/92.)

Art. 1448. Discharge; revocation.

A. The director shall notify the court in writing when a minor patient has been discharged or conditionally discharged.

B. The court may, if it finds it to be in the best interests of the minor, revoke the certificate or judgment of commitment.
(Added by Acts 1991 No. 235, §14, eff. 1/1/92.)

Art. 1449. Notice of court action.

Notice of any action taken by the court shall be given to the minor respondent and his attorney as well as to the director of the designated treatment facility in such manner as the court concludes would be appropriate under the circumstances. *(Added by Acts 1991 No. 235, §14, eff. 1/1/92.)*

Art. 1450. Advisement of rights.

A. Every minor patient admitted by judicial commitment shall be informed in writing at the time of his admission of the procedures for requesting release from the treatment facility, the availability of counsel, information about the MHAS, the rights enumerated in Article 1409, and the rules and regulations applicable to or concerning his conduct while a patient in the treatment facility.

B. If the minor patient is illiterate or does not read or understand English, appropriate provisions should be made to supply him this information.

C. In addition, a copy of the information listed in this Article must be posted in any area where patients are confined and treated.
(Added by Acts 1991 No. 235, §14, eff. 1/1/92.)

Art. 1451. Conversion to voluntary status.

A. No director of a treatment facility shall prohibit any mentally ill minor or minor suffering from substance abuse from applying for conversion of involuntary or emergency admission status to voluntary admission status.

B. Any minor patient on an involuntary admission status shall have the right to apply for a writ of habeas corpus to have his admission status changed to voluntary status.
(Added by Acts 1991 No. 235, §14, eff. 1/1/92.)

Art. 1452. Mandatory review of commitments.

A. All judicial commitments, except those for alcoholism, shall be reviewed by the court issuing the order for commitment every ninety days.

B. A commitment for alcoholism shall expire after forty-five days and the minor patient, if not converted to a voluntary status, shall be discharged, unless the court, upon application by the director of the treatment facility, finds that continued involuntary treatment is necessary and orders the minor patient recommitted for a period not to exceed sixty days; provided, that not more than two such sixty-day recommitments may be ordered in connection with the same continuous confinement.

C. All judicial commitments involving a minor patient who has been found not guilty by reason of insanity or who has been found to lack the capacity to proceed, shall be reviewed in the manner as set forth in Title VIII.
(Added by Acts 1991 No. 235, §14; chgd. by Acts 1997 No. 985, §2, eff. 8/15/97.)

Art. 1453. Reports to court.

A. The director of the treatment facility to which the minor has been judicially committed shall issue reports to the court at the intervals provided in Article 1452, setting forth the minor patient's response to the treatment, his current condition, and the reasons why continued involuntary treatment is necessary to improve his condition or to prevent it from deteriorating.

B. These reports shall be treated by the court as confidential and shall not be available for public examination, nor shall they be subject to discovery in any proceedings other than those initiated pursuant to this Title.
(Added by Acts 1991 No. 235, §14, eff. 1/1/92.)

Art. 1454. Hearing to determine continued involuntary commitment.

A. The court may at any time upon application or upon its own motion order a new hearing to be held in order to determine whether the involuntary status of the minor patient should be continued.

B. Minor patients committed judicially shall have their cases reviewed in a hearing every one hundred twenty days.

C. The review hearing shall be conducted according to the procedures and standards set forth in this Chapter and may be held by the juvenile court in the parish in which the minor patient is being confined or, if not confined, by the juvenile court in the parish in which he resides or may be found. The hearing shall not be transferred to another district except for good cause shown.
(Added by Acts 1991 No. 235, §14; chgd. by Acts 1997 No. 985, §2, eff. 8/15/97.)

Art. 1455. Discretion of director.

A. Notwithstanding an order of judicial commitment, the director of the treatment facility to which the minor patient is committed is encouraged to explore treatment measures that are medically appropriate and less restrictive.

B. The director may at any time convert an involuntary commitment to a voluntary one should he deem that action medically appropriate. He shall inform the court of any action in that regard.

C. The director may discharge any minor patient if in his opinion discharge is appropriate. The director shall not be legally responsible to any person for the subsequent acts of behavior of a patient discharged in good faith.
(Added by Acts 1991 No. 235, §14, eff. 1/1/92.)

Art. 1456. Appeal; writs.

A. A minor who is judicially committed shall be allowed to appeal devolutively from the order to the court of appeal. If the lower court finds the minor indigent, it shall allow the appeal to be taken in forma pauperis.

B. Upon perfection of an appeal, it shall be heard in a summary manner, taking preference over all other cases except similar matters.

C. Upon affirmation of the order of commitment, the minor may apply for appropriate writs from the supreme court which shall be heard in a summary manner.
(Added by Acts 1991 No. 235, §14, eff. 1/1/92.)

Art. 1457. Right of habeas corpus.

Nothing in this Title shall deny the right of habeas corpus, including an application based upon a change of circumstances. *(Added by Acts 1991 No. 235, §14, eff. 1/1/92.)*

Art. 1458. Conditional discharge.

A. A minor who is judicially committed as a result of mental illness may be conditionally discharged for a period of up to one hundred twenty days by the director or by the court during which time the judicial commitment of the minor shall remain in effect. The minor patient may be required to report for outpatient treatment as a condition of his release. The terms and conditions of the conditional discharge shall be specifically set forth in writing and signed by the minor patient. A copy of the conditional discharge shall be given to him and explained to him before he is discharged.

B. If the minor patient is conditionally discharged by the director, a copy of the conditional discharge shall be sent to the court which judicially committed him. If the minor patient is conditionally discharged by the court, a copy of the conditional discharge shall be sent to the facility to which he has been committed.

C. If a minor patient does not comply with the terms and conditions of his conditional discharge, he is subject to any of the procedures for involuntary treatment, including but not limited to the issuance of an order for custody and the execution of an emergency certificate. A conditionally discharged minor patient who is confined pursuant to any of these involuntary procedures shall have all rights of an involuntary patient, including the right to demand a probable cause hearing, the right to periodic reports and review, and a review hearing pursuant to Article 1454.

D. An extension of a conditional discharge may be granted upon application by the director of the treatment facility to the court and notification to the minor's counsel of record. The court may grant the extension of the conditional discharge for an additional period of up to one hundred twenty days. No further extension may be made without a contradictory hearing. The burden of proof is on the director of the treatment facility to show why continued treatment is necessary.
(Added by Acts 1991 No. 235, §14; chgd. by Acts 1997 No. 985, §2, eff. 8/15/97.)

Art. 1459. Review by MHAS.

All minor patients presently unrepresented by privately retained counsel and who are the subject of involuntary commitment under any prior statute shall have their cases reviewed by attorneys provided by the MHAS within one year from the effective date of this Code, or be discharged or be committed again according to the provisions of this Chapter. *(Added by Acts 1991 No. 235, §14, eff. 1/1/92.)*

CHAPTER 10. PARENTAL ADMISSION

Art. 1460. Parental admission of minor; objection request for discharge.

A. Any minor may be admitted to a treatment facility for inpatient care and treatment upon application of a parent, tutor, or, in the absence of a parent or tutor, of a caretaker to the director of a treatment facility if the director finds that the minor has a mental illness or suffers from substance abuse which has a substantial adverse effect on his ability to function and requires care and treatment in an institution. Within twenty-four hours of admission, the minor shall be examined by a physician who shall set forth in detail in the patient's medical record the reasons for the continued need of confinement and treatment of the minor. The parent, tutor, or caretaker may request the minor's discharge pursuant to the provisions of Paragraph C.

B. A minor who is eligible for admission pursuant to Paragraph A of this Article and who is in such a condition that immediate hospitalization is necessary may be admitted upon the application of any interested adult, when after diligent effort the minor's parent, tutor, or caretaker cannot be located. Following the admission of the minor, the director of the treatment facility shall continue efforts to locate the minor's parent, tutor, or caretaker. If such person is located and consents in writing to the admission, the minor may continue to be hospitalized. However, upon notification of the admission, the parent, tutor, or caretaker, may request the minor's discharge pursuant to the provisions of Paragraph C.

C. Upon receipt of a request for discharge, the director of the treatment facility shall release such minor within seventy-two hours unless proceedings are begun pursuant to Chapter 7 or 9 of this Title.

(Added by Acts 1991 No. 235, §14; chgd. by Acts 1992 No. 705, §1; Acts 1993 No. 634, §1, eff. 6/15/93.)

Art. 1461. Advice of rights.

A. On admission to a treatment facility, the minor and the minor's parent, tutor, or caretaker, if the minor is admitted pursuant to Article 1460, shall be informed in writing of the procedures for requesting release and of the availability of counsel, information about the MHAS, the rights enumerated in Article 1409, and the rules and regulations applicable to or concerning his conduct while a patient in the program or facility.

B. This information shall also be prominently posted in any area where the patient is to be confined or treated.

(Added by Acts 1991 No. 235, §14; chgd. by Acts 1997 No. 612, §3, eff. 8/15/97.)

Art. 1462. Objection to admission by the minor who has been admitted.

A. Objection may be made by the minor who has been admitted if the minor is sixteen years of age or older.

B. If the minor informs any staff person of his desire to object to the admission, a staff person shall assist him in preparing and submitting his objection.

C. Upon receipt of an objection, the director of the treatment facility shall release such minor within seventy-two hours unless proceedings are begun pursuant to Chapter 7 or 9 of this Title.

(Added by Acts 1991 No. 235, §14, eff. 1/1/92.)

Art. 1463. Physician's certificate for a minor.

A. A minor shall not be detained at a treatment facility pursuant to parental admission more than seventy-two hours unless a physician's certificate for a minor has been executed and delivered to the MHAS.

B. The certificate may be executed by any licensed physician after an actual examination.

C. Failure to conduct an actual examination prior to the execution of the certificate will be evidence of gross negligence.

D. The certificate shall be dated and executed under penalty of perjury, but need not be notarized. The certificate shall state:

(1) The date and time of the physician's examination of the minor, which shall not be more than seventy-two hours prior to the signature of the certificate.

(2) The name and age of the minor and the patient's identification number, if known.

(3) The date and time of admission.

(4) The name and address of the parent, tutor, caretaker, or responsible person admitting the minor.

(5) The objective findings of the physician relative to the physical and mental condition of the minor, leading to the determination of whether the minor examined is in need of inpatient psychiatric treatment because all of the following conditions exist:

(a) The minor suffers from mental illness or substance abuse which has a substantial adverse effect on his ability to function and requires care and treatment in an institution.

(b) The minor can benefit from inpatient treatment.

(c) The treatment facility where the minor is confined is medically appropriate.

(6) The history pertinent to this admission.

(7) A statement as to whether the minor wishes to remain in the treatment facility.

E. The certificate shall be delivered to the MHAS located nearest to the treatment facility. Delivery may be accomplished either by:

(1) Personal delivery to any MHAS employee.

(2) Mailing a copy of the certificate to the nearest MHAS, certified mail, return receipt requested.

F. MHAS shall have the authority to represent the interests of any minor they suspect has been inappropriately placed or who had requested their services. Services may be rendered as deemed necessary including but not limited to the provisions of Article 1405.

(Added by Acts 1991 No. 235, §14; chgd. by Acts 1992 No. 705, §1; Acts 1993 No. 187, §1, No. 634, §1; Acts 1997 No. 612, §3, eff. 8/15/97.)

CHAPTER 11. VOLUNTARY ADMISSION

Article

Art. 1464. Voluntary admission of minors.

A. Any minor sixteen years of age or older may apply for voluntary admission to a treatment facility pursuant to this Chapter.

B. A minor so admitted shall have the same rights as an adult patient.

C. The admitting physician may admit the person on either a formal or informal basis, as hereinafter provided.

(Added by Acts 1991 No. 235, §14, eff. 1/1/92.)

Art. 1465. Voluntary admissions favored.

A. Admitting physicians are encouraged to admit mentally ill minors or minors suffering from substance abuse to treatment facilities on voluntary admission status whenever medically feasible.

B. No director of a treatment facility shall prohibit any mentally ill minor or minor suffering from substance abuse from applying for conversion of involuntary or emergency admission status to voluntary admission status. Any minor patient on an involuntary admission status shall have the right to apply for a writ of habeas corpus in order to have his admission status changed to voluntary status.

C. No employee of a mental health care program or treatment facility, peace officer, or physician shall state to any person that involuntary admission may result if the minor does not voluntarily admit himself to a mental health care program or treatment facility unless the employee, peace officer, or physician is prepared to execute a certificate pursuant to Chapter 7 or a petition pursuant to Chapter 9 of this Title.

(Added by Acts 1991 No. 235, §14, eff. 1/1/92.)

Art. 1466. Advice of rights.

A. Each minor admitted on a voluntary basis shall be informed of any other medically appropriate alternative treatment programs and treatment facilities known to the admitting physician and be given an opportunity to seek admission to alternative treatment programs or facilities.

B. Every minor patient admitted on a voluntary admission status shall be informed in writing at the time of admission of the procedures for requesting release from the treatment facility, the availability of counsel, information about the mental health advocacy service, the rights enumerated in Article 1409, and rules and regulations applicable to or concerning his conduct while a patient in the treatment facility.

C. If the minor is illiterate or does not read or understand English, appropriate provisions should be made to supply him this information.

D. In addition, a copy of the information listed in this Article must be posted in any area where minor patients are confined and treated.

(Added by Acts 1991 No. 235, §14, eff. 1/1/92.)

Art. 1467. Capacity required.

A. No admission may be deemed voluntary unless the admitting physician determines that the minor to be admitted has the capacity to make a knowing and voluntary consent to the admission.

B. Knowing and voluntary consent shall be determined by the ability of the minor to understand:

(1) That the treatment facility to which the minor patient is requesting admission is one for mentally ill persons or persons suffering from substance abuse.

(2) That he is making an application for admission.

(3) The nature of his status and the provisions governing discharge or conversion to an involuntary status.

(Added by Acts 1991 No. 235, §14, eff. 1/1/92.)

Art. 1468. Informal voluntary admission.

A. In the discretion of the director, any mentally ill minor or minor suffering from substance abuse, who is sixteen years of age or older and who desires admission to a treatment facility for diagnosis or treatment of a psychiatric disorder or substance abuse, may be admitted upon the minor patient's request without a formal application.

B. Any minor patient admitted pursuant to this Article shall have the right to leave the treatment facility at any time during the normal day-shift hours of operation, which shall include but not be limited to nine a.m. to five p.m.

(Added by Acts 1991 No. 235, §14, eff. 1/1/92.)

Art. 1469. Formal voluntary admission.

A. Any mentally ill minor or minor suffering from substance abuse who is sixteen years old or older and who desires admission to a treatment facility for diagnosis and/or treatment of a psychiatric disorder or substance abuse and who is deemed suitable for formal voluntary admission by the admitting physician may be so admitted upon his written request.

B. A minor patient admitted under the provisions of this Article shall not be detained in the treatment facility for longer than seventy-two hours after making a valid written request for discharge to the director of the treatment facility unless an emergency certificate is executed pursuant to Article 1422 or unless judicial commitment is instituted pursuant to Chapter 9 of this Title.

(Added by Acts 1991 No. 235, §14, eff. 1/1/92.)

CHAPTER 12. SUBSTANCE ABUSE TREATMENT PROCEDURE

Art. 1470. Admission by parent.

A. A minor suffering from substance abuse may be admitted and detained at a public or private general hospital or a substance abuse inpatient facility for observation, diagnosis, and treatment for a period not to exceed twenty-eight days, when a parent has admitted the person or caused him to be admitted pursuant to the provisions of Chapter 10 of this Title.

B. At the time of admission, the parent shall execute or provide a written statement of facts, including personal observations, leading to the conclusion that the minor is suffering from substance abuse and is dangerous to himself or others or is gravely disabled, specifically describing any dangerous acts or threats, and stating that the minor has been encouraged to seek treatment but is unwilling to be evaluated on a voluntary basis.

C. As soon as practicable, but in no event more than eight hours after admission to the hospital or inpatient facility, a physician shall examine the minor and either execute an emergency certificate in accordance with Article 1422 or order the minor discharged. If an emergency certificate is executed, the physician or the director of the hospital or inpatient facility shall immediately notify the coroner and the coroner or his deputy shall conduct an independent examination in accordance with Article 1423. If the coroner or his deputy executes a second emergency certificate, the minor patient may be detained for treatment for a period not to exceed twenty-eight days from the date of his admission. Otherwise, he shall be discharged.

D. Except as inconsistent with the provisions of this Article, all other provisions of this Title applicable to persons admitted by emergency certificate shall be applicable.

(Added by Acts 1991 No. 235, §14, eff. 1/1/92.)

CHAPTER 13. TRANSFER OF PATIENTS COMMITTED TO THE DEPARTMENT

Art. 1471. Transfer of patients between institutions.

A. Except as otherwise provided in this Article, the department may transfer any patient from one mental institution to another. Moreover, the superintendent of an institution may request the department to transfer a patient when he believes that a transfer is necessary.

(1) A patient may be transferred to or from a private mental institution only upon the joint application of the superintendent of that institution and of the legal or natural guardian or the person liable for the support of the minor patient. However, no private mental institution shall be obligated to retain a minor patient because of the refusal to sign the application by the guardian or the person liable for support.

(2) A person under an order of commitment or acquitted of a delinquent act on the ground of mental illness shall be transferred only upon authority of the committing court.

(3) A minor patient voluntarily admitted pursuant to Article 1464 shall be transferred only with his written consent.

(4) A minor patient admitted by a parental commitment pursuant to Article 1460 shall be transferred only upon the written consent of the parent, tutor, or caretaker who originally sought his admission.

B. The following documents, as applicable, shall accompany a minor patient upon his transfer:

(1) The transfer order of the department.

(2) Certified copies of the application for admission, the physician's certificate, the report of the commission, and the order of the committing court.

(3) All of the minor patient's clinical records or a full abstract thereof, including the results of medical, physical, and laboratory examinations.

(Added by Acts 1991 No. 235, §14, eff. 1/1/92.)

TITLE XV. SPECIAL PROCEEDINGS

CHAPTER 1. PRELIMINARY PROVISIONS

Art. 1501. Purpose.

The purpose of this Title is to establish the substantive and procedural guidelines governing the juvenile court's exercise of jurisdiction over contempt proceedings, voluntary transfer of custody proceedings, proceedings seeking judicial authorization for minors' abortions, proceedings seeking judicial authorization for minors' marriages, declaratory judgment proceedings involving medical treatment for terminally ill children, domestic abuse assistance proceedings, and such other types of proceedings as may hereafter be added by the legislature to the jurisdiction of the juvenile courts of this state. *(Added by Acts 1991 No. 235, §15, eff. 1/1/92.)*

Art. 1502. General applicability.

Except as otherwise specified in this Title, all provisions of the Children's Code remain applicable. *(Added by Acts 1991 No. 235, §15, eff. 1/1/92.)*

CHAPTER 2. CONTEMPT

Art. 1503. Purpose.

The purpose of this Chapter is to provide procedures for allowing each juvenile court to enforce its orders and maintain proper court decorum. *(Added by Acts 1991 No. 235, §15, eff. 1/1/92.)*

Art. 1504. Kinds of contempt.

A. A contempt of court is any act or omission tending to obstruct or interfere with the orderly administration of justice, or to impair the dignity of the court or respect for its authority.

B. Contempts of court are of two kinds, direct and constructive.

(Added by Acts 1991 No. 235, §15, eff. 1/1/92.)

Art. 1505. Direct contempt.

A. A direct contempt of court is one committed in the immediate view and presence of the court and of which it has personal knowledge.

B. A direct contempt includes but is not limited to any of the following acts:

(1) Contumacious failure, after notice, to appear for a hearing on the day fixed therefor.

(2) Contumacious failure to comply with a subpoena or summons to appear in court, proof of service of which appears of record.

(3) Contumacious violation of an order excluding, separating, or sequestering a witness.

(4) Refusal to take the oath or affirmation as a witness, or refusal of a witness to answer a nonincriminating question when ordered to do so by the court.

(5) Contumacious, insolent, or disorderly behavior toward the judge or an attorney or other officer of the court, tending to interrupt or interfere with the business of the court or to impair its dignity or respect for its authority.

(6) Breach of the peace, boisterous conduct, or violent disturbance tending to interrupt or interfere with the business of the court or to impair its dignity or respect for its authority.

(7) Use of insulting, abusive, or discourteous language by an attorney or other person in open court, or in a motion, plea, brief, or other document, filed with the court, in irrelevant criticism of another attorney or officer of the court.

(8) Violation of a rule of the court adopted to maintain order and decorum in the courtroom.

(Added by Acts 1991 No. 235, §15, eff. 1/1/92.)

Art. 1506. Procedure for punishing direct contempt.

A person who has committed a direct contempt of court may be found guilty and punished therefor by the court without any trial, after affording him an opportunity to be heard orally by way of defense or mitigation. The court shall render an order reciting the facts constituting the contempt, adjudging the person guilty thereof, and specifying the punishment imposed. *(Added by Acts 1991 No. 235, §15, eff. 1/1/92.)*

Art. 1507. Constructive contempt.

A constructive contempt of court is any contempt other than a direct one, including but not limited to the following:

(1) Willful neglect or violation of duty by a clerk, sheriff, or other person elected, appointed, or employed to assist the court in the administration of justice.

(2) Willful disobedience of any lawful judgment, order, mandate, writ, or process of the court.

(3) Removal or attempted removal of any person or property in the custody of an officer acting under authority of a judgment, order, mandate, writ, or process of the court.

(4) Deceit or abuse of the process or procedure of the court by a party to an action or proceeding, or by his attorney.

(5) Unlawful detention of a witness, party, or his attorney, while going to, remaining at, or returning from the court where the action or proceeding is to be tried.

(6) Assuming to act as an attorney or other officer of the court, without lawful authority.

(7) Comment by a newspaper or other medium for the dissemination of news upon a case or proceeding, then pending and undecided, which constitutes a clear, present, and imminent danger of obstructing or interfering with the orderly administration of justice, by either influencing the court to reach a particular decision, or embarrassing it in the discharge of its judicial duties.

(8) Willful disobedience by an inferior court, judge, or other officer thereof, of the lawful judgment, order, mandate, writ, or process of an appellate court, rendered in connection with an appeal from a judgment or order of the inferior court, or in connection with a review of such judgment or order under a supervisory writ issued by the appellate court.

(9) Willful disobedience of the confidentiality provisions of Article 412.

(10) Any other act or omission punishable by law as a contempt of court, or intended to obstruct or interfere with the orderly administration of justice, or to impair the dignity of the court or respect for its authority, and which is not a direct contempt.

(Added by Acts 1991 No. 235, §15; chgd. by Acts 1993 No. 634, §1, eff. 6/15/93.)

Art. 1508. Procedure for punishing constructive contempt.

A. When a person is charged with committing a constructive contempt, he shall be tried by the judge on a rule to show cause alleging the facts constituting the contempt. The rule may be issued by the court on its own motion or on motion of any party.

B. A certified copy of the motion and of the rule shall be served on the person charged, in the manner of a subpoena, not less than forty-eight hours prior to the time assigned for trial of the rule.

C. If the person charged with contempt is found guilty, the court shall render an order reciting the facts constituting the contempt, adjudging the person charged with the contempt guilty thereof, and specifying the punishment imposed.
(Added by Acts 1991 No. 235, §15, eff. 1/1/92.)

Art. 1509. Penalties.

A. A person may not be adjudged guilty of a contempt of court except for misconduct defined as such, or made punishable as such, expressly by law.

B. When a child is adjudged guilty of direct contempt of court or when an adjudicated child is adjudged guilty of constructive contempt of court for repeated disobedience of the court's judgment of disposition, the court may commit the child to a juvenile detention center or other suitable facility for not more than fifteen days, including time spent in detention for the contempt prior to the contempt hearing. However:

(1) A child in need of care who is adjudged to be in contempt shall not be placed in secure detention, nor shall such detention facility accept a child in need of care.

(2) A child committed under this provision shall not be physically housed in the same room or area used to house children adjudicated delinquent.

C. When a contempt of court consists of the omission to perform an act which is yet in the power of an adult person charged with contempt to perform, he may be imprisoned until he performs it and in such a case this shall be specified in the court's order.

D. When an attorney is adjudged guilty of a direct contempt of court, the punishment shall be limited to a fine of not more than one hundred dollars or imprisonment for not more than twenty-four hours, or both; and, for any subsequent direct contempt of the same court by the same offender, a fine of not more than two hundred dollars or imprisonment for not more than ten days, or both.

E. Except as otherwise provided in this Article, a court may punish an adult person adjudged guilty of contempt of court in connection with a juvenile proceeding by a fine of not more than five hundred dollars or by imprisonment for not more than six months, or both.
(Added by Acts 1991 No. 235, §15; chgd. by Acts 1995 No. 1095, §8, eff. 8/15/95.)

CHAPTER 3. VOLUNTARY TRANSFER OF CUSTODY

Article

Art. 1510. Purpose.

The purpose of this Chapter is to protect the health and welfare of children by providing, in addition to any other provisions of law, for juvenile court procedure to govern a voluntary transfer of custody of a child by parents to other responsible adults for the purpose of enabling the child to receive adequate care and treatment. The provisions of this Chapter are intended to promote mutual understanding of the rights and responsibilities of the parents and custodians and of any terms or conditions which may be set forth by agreement of the parties.
(Added by Acts 1991 No. 235, §15, eff. 1/1/92.)

Art. 1511. Definitions.

As used in this Chapter:

(1) "Guardianship of the person of a child" means the duty and authority to make important decisions in matters having a permanent effect on the life and development of the minor and to be concerned about his general welfare. It shall include but shall not necessarily be limited in either number or kind to:

(a) The authority to consent to marriage, to enlistment in the armed forces of the United States, or to major medical, psychiatric, and surgical treatment, to represent the minor in legal actions, to make other decisions of substantial legal significance concerning the minor.

(b) The authority and duty of reasonable visitation, except to the extent that such right of visitation has been limited by court order.

(c) The rights and responsibilities of legal custody, including the right to have physical custody of the child and to exercise the rights and duty to protect, train, and discipline him and to provide him with food, shelter, education, and ordinary medical care, all subject to any residual rights possessed by the child's parents.

(2) "Legal custody" means a legal status created by court order which vests in a custodian the right to have physical custody of the child and the right and duty to protect, train, and discipline him and to provide him with food, shelter, education, and ordinary medical care, all subject to the powers, rights, and duties and responsibilities of the guardian of the person of the child and subject to any residual parental rights and responsibilities.

(3) "Physical custody" means the duty and authority to provide care for a child in the home of the custodian.

(4) "Voluntary transfer of custody" is a parent's knowing and voluntary relinquishment of legal custody or guardianship to an agency, institution, or individual, subject to residual parental rights retained by the parent and under such terms and conditions that enable the child to receive adequate care and treatment.

(Added by Acts 1991 No. 235, §15, eff. 1/1/92.)

Art. 1512. Continuing jurisdiction.

The court exercising juvenile jurisdiction shall have continuing jurisdiction and the exclusive authority to modify its orders rendered pursuant to this Chapter. *(Added by Acts 1991 No. 235, §15, eff. 1/1/92.)*

Art. 1513. Venue.

A proceeding brought pursuant to this Chapter may be commenced in the parish in which either:

(1) The parents requesting transfer of custody reside.

(2) The person, agency, or institution to whom the transfer of custody is intended resides.

(Added by Acts 1991 No. 235, §15, eff. 1/1/92.)

Art. 1514. Petition for voluntary transfer.

A. A proceeding under this Chapter shall be commenced by written petition.

B. Except as otherwise provided in this Article, all persons or organizations lawfully exercising legal custody of the child shall join in the petition.

C. If a legal custodian is unable or unwilling to join in the petition, the petition shall state with particularity the reasons therefor.

(Added by Acts 1991 No. 235, §15, eff. 1/1/92.)

Art. 1515. Petition; contents; form.

A. A petition for voluntary transfer of custody shall set forth specifically:

(1) The name and address of all parents and legal custodians.

(2) An affirmation that the parents are knowingly and voluntarily transferring custody.

(3) The full name and date of birth of the child whose custody is sought to be transferred.

(4) The factual basis for the transfer of custody.

(5) The nature, duration, and extent of the transfer of custody including any terms and conditions.

(6) The name and address of the agency, institution, or individual to whom the child is sought to be transferred and the relationship, if any, to the child.

B. The form for the petition shall be as follows:

"PETITION FOR VOLUNTARY TRANSFER OF CUSTODY

The petition of _________ (all legal custodians of the child unless otherwise indicated in Paragraph III of the petition), domiciled in the parish of _________ , respectfully represent(s):

I.

That petitioner(s) reside at the following address(es):

____

____

II.

That petitioner(s) is/are the parent(s) and legal custodian(s) of the minor child(ren), namely _________ , whose date of birth is _________ (add same information for all children subject to the petition), as more fully appears from the attached certificate(s) of birth.

III.

That there are no other legal custodians of the child(ren) OR that a legal custodian, namely _________ , is unable to join in this petition for the following reasons:

____

____

____

____.

IV.

That petitioner(s) desire(s) to knowingly and voluntarily transfer custody of the above named children to _________ , which individual(s), institution or agency reside(s) at the following address: _________ and who have the following relationship with the children:

____

____.

V.

That petitioner(s) desire* to transfer physical custody OR legal custody OR guardianship of the person of the children (indicate one) for the period of time _________ (specify intended duration) in accordance with the following terms and conditions:

____

____

____

____

(may include provisions for support and/or visitation).

**So in original. Probably should be "desire(s)".*

VI.

That petitioners desire* this transfer of custody for the following reason:

____

____

____

____

____.

**So in original. Probably should be "petitioner(s) desire(s)".*

VII.

That _________ has/have agreed to and does/do desire to accept custody of the child(ren) to the extent and under the terms and conditions stated in this petition, as more fully appears in the attached Affidavit of Acceptance.

WHEREFORE, petitioner(s) pray(s) that there be judgment herein transferring custody of the child(ren), ______ , ______ , ______ , ______ , to _________ , to the extent and under the terms and conditions set forth in this petition.

____
(Signature and address of Petitioner(s) or counsel for Petitioner(s))

(If in proper person, petition should be signed in presence of a notary.)

SWORN TO AND SUBSCRIBED BEFORE ME ON THIS THE ____ DAY OF _____, 19___.

____
NOTARY PUBLIC"

(Added by Acts 1991 No. 235, §15, eff. 1/1/92.)

Art. 1516. Affidavit of acceptance; contents; form.

A. An Affidavit of Acceptance shall be executed by the agency, institution, or individual accepting custody and shall state that the agency, institution, or individual knowingly and voluntarily accepts custody of the child to the extent and under the terms and conditions custody is transferred from the parents.

B. The form for the Affidavit of Acceptance shall be as follows:

"AFFIDAVIT OF ACCEPTANCE

BEFORE ME, the undersigned Notary Public, personally came and appeared: _______, individual(s) OR a representative of __________ (name of agency or institution) who, being first duly sworn, did depose and state:

That affiant is a person of the full age of majority and resides at ___________ (address of individual(s), agency, or institution) in _________ Parish, Louisiana.

That affiant does knowingly and voluntarily accept physical custody OR legal custody OR guardianship of the person of the children (indicate one) of ______, ______, ______, ______ (name(s) of child(ren)) for the period of time _________ (specify intended period) in accordance with the following terms and conditions:

____

____

____

____.

(may include provisions for support and/or visitation)

____
AFFIANT

SWORN TO AND SUBSCRIBED BEFORE ME ON THIS THE ____ DAY OF _____, 19___.

____
NOTARY PUBLIC"

(Added by Acts 1991 No. 235, §15, eff. 1/1/92.)

Art. 1517. Notice; service; curator; reservation of rights.

A. Notice of the proceedings shall be served on any parent or legal custodian who has not joined in the petition.

B. Notice may be served by personal or domiciliary service or by certified mail, proof of which shall be filed in the record.

C. If a parent or legal custodian cannot be served, the court may appoint an attorney at law as curator for him and service shall be made upon the curator.

D. If a parent or legal custodian cannot be served and a curator is not appointed for him, the court shall specifically reserve the absentee's rights in any order transferring custody pursuant to this Chapter.

(Added by Acts 1991 No. 235, §15, eff. 1/1/92.)

Art. 1518. Pretrial orders; contribution to costs.

A. On its own motion or the motion of any party to the proceedings, the court may render such orders it deems necessary to protect the best interests of the child, including but not limited to the following:

(1) A home study of the proposed placement.

(2) A physical or mental examination of any party.

(3) An appointment of counsel for the child.

B. After giving the parent a reasonable opportunity to be heard, the court may order that such parent shall contribute to the cost of the home study, examination, or of the child's representation.
(Added by Acts 1991 No. 235, §15, eff. 1/1/92.)

Art. 1519. Hearing.

The petition shall be set for hearing on the record unless specifically waived by the court.
(Added by Acts 1991 No. 235, §15, eff. 1/1/92.)

Art. 1520. Judgment.

A. The court shall render a written judgment granting or denying the transfer of custody.

B. If the court grants the transfer of custody, the judgment shall recite that:

(1) All necessary parties are involved.

(2) The transfer is knowing and voluntary.

(3) There is a legitimate purpose and a factual basis to support that purpose.

(4) All parties have been advised of and understand the nature and extent of the transfer, including any terms and conditions, and of their respective rights.

(5) The proposed change of custody is in the best interests of the child.

C. In addition, if the order grants the transfer of custody, the judgment shall order the transfer of custody and recite such terms and conditions as requested by the parties.
(Added by Acts 1991 No. 235, §15, eff. 1/1/92.)

Art. 1521. Review; permanency planning.

A. On its own motion or on the motion of any party, the court may order a hearing to be set for review of the transfer of custody.

B. Judgments transferring custody pursuant to this Chapter are exempt from the permanency planning requirements mandated in Title VI including the provisions of Chapters 13, 15 and 16 of that Title.
(Added by Acts 1991 No. 235, §15; chgd. by Acts 1992 No. 705, §1, eff. 7/6/92.)

Art. 1522. Modification.

A. Except when the parties jointly desire to dismiss the proceedings and return custody of the child to the parents, modification or enforcement of a judgment transferring custody shall be upon motion of any party and by order of the court according to the provisions of this Chapter.

B. If the parties jointly desire to dismiss the proceedings and return the custody of the child to the parents, the court should be notified. A court so notified shall then render an ex parte dismissal of the proceedings.
(Added by Acts 1991 No. 235, §15, eff. 1/1/92.)

Art. 1523. Revocation.

A. Upon failure of a custodian to return a child after revocation of the parent's consent, the parent may move for dismissal of the proceedings and for the return of the child to their custody.

B. The motion to dismiss shall be set for contradictory hearing with the custodians.

C. In making its determination of the best interests of the child, the court shall consider the following:

(1) The length of the parent/child separation.

(2) The current fitness of the parent.

(3) The frequency of contact between the parent and child during the separation.

(4) The efforts made by the parent to exercise parental responsibilities during the separation, including support.

(5) The terms and conditions of the judgment.
(Added by Acts 1991 No. 235, §15, eff. 1/1/92.)

CHAPTER 4. MISDEMEANOR PROSECUTION OF ADULTS

Article

Art. 1524. Purpose.

The purpose of this Chapter is to set out the substantive principles and procedures by which the juvenile court tries adults for misdemeanors when the law violated was enacted for the protection of the physical, moral, or mental well-being of children. *(Added by Acts 1991 No. 235, §15, eff. 1/1/92.)*

Art. 1525. Scope of jurisdiction.

The juvenile court shall have jurisdiction to try any adult who is charged with any of the following misdemeanors:

(1) Interference with the custody of a child.

(2) Criminal abandonment.

(3) Unlawful sales to minors.

(4) Unlawful purchase of alcoholic beverages for minors.

(5) Unlawful distribution of sample tobacco products to minors.

(6) Sale, exhibition or distribution of material harmful to minors.

(7) Sale, distribution, or making available to minors publications encouraging, advocating, or facilitating the illegal use of controlled substances.

(8) Illegal use of controlled dangerous substances in the presence of children.

(9) Sale of poisonous reptiles to minors.

(10) Contributing to the delinquency of juveniles or encouraging or contributing to child delinquency, dependency, or neglect.

(11) Unlawful use and sale of model glue to minors.

(12) Tatooing minors.

(13) Child desertion.

(14) Abandoning ice boxes or other air tight containers in a place accessible to children.

(15) Failure of a mandatory reporter to report abuse of children.

(16) Violation of the requirements for the investigation of reports of child abuse.

(17) Knowingly making a false report of child abuse.

(18) Making a false report of a missing child.

(19) Violation of the compulsory school attendance law.

(20) Any offense affecting the physical, moral, or mental well-being of children as provided in Section 2 of Subpart B of Part V of Chapter 1 of Title 14 of the Louisiana Revised Statutes of 1950.

(Added by Acts 1991 No. 235, §15; chgd. by Acts 1995 No. 1095, §8, eff. 8/15/95.)

Art. 1526. Definitions.

Except when the context clearly indicates otherwise, as used in this Chapter:

(1) "Affidavit" means a written accusation of crime made under oath and signed by the affiant. It must be filed in open court in a court having jurisdiction to try the offense or in the office of the clerk thereof.

(2) "Institution of prosecution" means the filing of an information or affidavit, which is designed to serve as the basis of a trial.

(Added by Acts 1991 No. 235, §15, eff. 1/1/92.)

Art. 1527. Venue.

Proceedings pursuant to this Chapter shall be commenced in the parish in which the offense is alleged to have been committed. If acts constituting an offense or if the elements of an offense occurred in more than one place, the offense is deemed to have been committed in any parish in which any such act or element occurred. *(Added by Acts 1991 No. 235, §15, eff. 1/1/92.)*

Art. 1528. Method of instituting prosecution.

Criminal prosecutions in a juvenile court shall be instituted by affidavit, information, or indictment. *(Added by Acts 1991 No. 235, §15, eff. 1/1/92.)*

Art. 1529. Procedure.

Proceedings pursuant to this Chapter shall be conducted in accordance with the Louisiana Code of Criminal Procedure. *(Added by Acts 1991 No. 235, §15, eff. 1/1/92.)*

Art. 1530. Trial of misdemeanors.

A. A defendant charged with a misdemeanor in which the punishment, as set forth in the statute defining the offense, may be a fine in excess of one thousand dollars or imprisonment for more than six months, shall be tried by a jury of six jurors, all of whom must concur to render a verdict.

B. The defendant charged with any other misdemeanor shall be tried by the court without a jury.

(Added by Acts 1991 No. 235, §15, eff. 1/1/92.)

Art. 1531. Right to waive trial by jury.

A. A defendant charged in juvenile court with a misdemeanor triable by jury may knowingly and intelligently waive a trial by jury and elect to be tried by the judge. At the time of arraignment, the defendant in such cases shall be informed by the court of his right to waive trial by jury.

B. The defendant shall exercise his right to waive trial by jury within fifteen days after the arraignment. However, with permission of the court, he may exercise his right to waive trial by jury at any time prior to the commencement of trial.

C. The defendant may withdraw a waiver of trial by jury unless the court finds that withdrawal of the waiver would result in interference with the administration of justice, unnecessary delay, unnecessary inconvenience to witnesses, or prejudice to the state.

(Added by Acts 1991 No. 235, §15, eff. 1/1/92.)

Art. 1532. Transfers to courts exercising criminal jurisdiction.

A. When the defendant is entitled to a trial by a jury, as defined in Article 1530, but knowingly and intelligently waives that right pursuant to Article 1531, the juvenile court may proceed with trial.

B. In cases where the defendant elects to exercise his right to a trial by jury, the court shall transfer the case to the proper court exercising criminal jurisdiction.

(Added by Acts 1991 No. 235, §15, eff. 1/1/92.)

CHAPTER 5. *(Reserved.)*

CHAPTER 6. AUTHORIZATION OF MINORS' MARRIAGES

Art. 1543. Purpose.

The purpose of this Chapter is to set out the substantive law and procedures for securing the authorization of the juvenile court for the marriage of a minor. *(Added by Acts 1991 No. 235, §15, eff. 1/1/92.)*

Art. 1544. Definitions.

Except when the context clearly indicates otherwise, as used in this Chapter, "officiant" is a person authorized by law to perform marriage ceremonies. *(Added by Acts 1991 No. 235, §15, eff. 1/1/92.)*

Art. 1545. Necessary consent; parents; judicial authorization.

A. An officiant may not perform a marriage ceremony in which a minor is a party unless the minor has the written consent to marry of either:

(1) Both of his parents.

(2) The tutor of his person.

(3) A person who has been awarded custody of the minor.

(4) The juvenile court as provided in Article 1547.

B. A minor under the age of sixteen must also obtain written authorization to marry from the judge of the court exercising juvenile jurisdiction in the parish in which the minor resides or the marriage ceremony is to be performed.

(Added by Acts 1991 No. 235, §15, eff. 1/1/92.)

Art. 1546. Venue.

A proceeding brought pursuant to this Chapter may be commenced in the parish in which the minor resides or the marriage ceremony is to be performed. *(Added by Acts 1991 No. 235, §15, eff. 1/1/92.)*

Art. 1547. Judicial authorization; compelling reasons.

Upon application by the minor, the judge may authorize the marriage when there is a compelling reason why the marriage should take place. *(Added by Acts 1991 No. 235, §15, eff. 1/1/92.)*

Art. 1548. Hearing; confidentiality.

The court shall hear a request for authorization for a minor to marry in chambers. *(Added by Acts 1991 No. 235, §15, eff. 1/1/92.)*

Art. 1549. Authorization; copies; filing.

A. The authorization must be in writing but may not give the court's reasons for granting it.

B. A copy of the authorization must be attached to the copy of the marriage certificate given to the parties and the original of the authorization must be presented to the official who issues the marriage license.

C. A copy of the authorization must also be filed with the marriage certificate as required by law.

(Added by Acts 1991 No. 235, §15, eff. 1/1/92.)

Art. 1550. Penalty for officiant who performs a marriage ceremony in violation of this Chapter.

Any officiant, other than a judge or justice of the peace, who knowingly performs a marriage ceremony at which one of the parties is a minor when the officiant does not have the necessary consent or authorization to marry required by Article 1545 shall be permanently deprived of his right to perform marriage ceremonies. *(Added by Acts 1991 No. 235, §15, eff. 1/1/92.)*

CHAPTER 7. PROTECTION OF TERMINALLY ILL CHILDREN

Art. 1551. Purpose.

The purpose of this Chapter is to recognize the right of a parent or guardian to make a declaration pursuant to which life-sustaining procedures or other medical care may be withheld or withdrawn from certain terminally ill children and to authorize judicial review, if needed, by the juvenile courts of such decisions if a child's parents or physician cannot agree that the requirements of this Chapter have been met. The procedures authorized by this Chapter are in addition to the existing remedies of Title VI. *(Added by Acts 1991 No. 235, §15, eff. 1/1/92.)*

Art. 1552. Definitions.

As used in this Chapter:

(1) "Attending physician" means the physician who has primary responsibility for the treatment and care of the child patient.

(2) "Child" means a person under eighteen years of age who has not been judicially emancipated under Civil Code Article 385 or emancipated by marriage under Civil Code Articles 379 through 384.

(3) "Continual profound comatose state" means that there is no reasonable medical possibility of ever achieving a cognitive state of conscious perception.

(4) "Death" means that in the announced opinion of a physician, based on ordinary standards of approved medical practice, the child has experienced an irreversible cessation of spontaneous respiratory and circulatory functions. In the event that artificial means of support preclude a determination that these functions have ceased, a child will be considered dead if, in the announced opinion of a physician based on ordinary standards of approved medical practice, the child has experienced an irreversible total cessation of brain function. Death will have occurred at the time when the relevant functions ceased. In any case when organs are to be used in a transplant, then an additional physician who is not a member of the transplant team must make the pronouncement of death.

(5) "Declaration" means a written and witnessed document voluntarily made by the declarant, authorizing the withholding or withdrawal of life-sustaining procedures for a child, in accordance with the requirements of this Chapter.

(6) "Life-sustaining procedure" means any medical procedure or intervention which, within reasonable medical judgment, would serve only to prolong the dying process. It does not include any measure deemed necessary to provide comfort care.

(7) "Terminal and irreversible condition" means a condition, injury, disease, or illness which, within reasonable medical judgment, would produce death and for which the application of a life-support system would serve only to postpone the moment of death. *(Added by Acts 1991 No. 235, §15, eff. 1/1/92.)*

Art. 1553. Deprivation of comfort care prohibited.

No child, including any infant born alive, shall be denied or deprived of food or nutrients, water, oxygen, or comfort care by any person with the intent to cause or allow the death of the child for any reason, including but not limited to the following situations:

(1) The child was born with physical or mental handicapping conditions which, in the opinion of the parent, the physician, or other persons, diminishes the quality of the child's life.

(2) The child was born alive in the course of an attempted abortion.

(3) The child is not wanted by the parent.

(Added by Acts 1991 No. 235, §15, eff. 1/1/92.)

Art. 1554. Deprivation of medical or surgical care prohibited; exceptions.

No child, including any infant born alive, shall be intentionally denied or deprived of any medical or surgical care by his parent, physician, or any other person when such medical or surgical care is necessary to attempt to save the life of the child in the opinion of a physician exercising competent medical judgment, except:

(1) When a child is in a continual profound comatose state and in the opinion of the child's physician, exercising competent medical judgment, he has no reasonable chance of recovery from that state despite every appropriate medical treatment to correct such condition, the child's parents and physician may discontinue the use of life-support systems or other medical treatment.

(2) When a child suffers from a terminal and irreversible condition despite every appropriate medical treatment to correct such condition, the child's parents and physician may discontinue the use of life-sustaining procedures or other medical treatment.

(3) When the potential risks to the child's life or health inherent in any treatment or surgery outweigh the potential benefits for survival from the treatment or surgery, a child's parents and physician may decline to provide potentially lifesaving medical or surgical care for the child.

(Added by Acts 1991 No. 235, §15, eff. 1/1/92.)

Art. 1555. Certification of child's terminal status.

Before the discontinuation of any medical care or treatment, the child must be diagnosed and certified in writing as qualifying within one or more of the exceptions authorized by Article 1554 by two physicians who have personally examined the child, one of whom shall be the child's attending physician. *(Added by Acts 1991 No. 235, §15, eff. 1/1/92.)*

Art. 1556. Declaration for the benefit of a terminally ill child.

If a child has been certified as required by Article 1555, the child's parent or his guardian may make a declaration to document the decision concerning the withholding or withdrawal of medical treatment or life-sustaining procedures on the child's behalf, except where either:

(1) The parent or guardian has actual notice of contrary indications by the affected child.

(2) The parent or guardian has actual notice of opposition to the decision by the other parent or by the child's guardian.

(Added by Acts 1991 No. 235, §15, eff. 1/1/92.)

Art. 1557. Making of declaration; notification; illustrative form.

A. At any time, a parent or guardian may make a written declaration directing the withholding or withdrawal of life-sustaining procedures for his child in the event the child should have a terminal and irreversible condition.

B. The declaration shall be signed by the parent or guardian in the presence of two witnesses.

C. It shall be the responsibility of the parent or guardian to notify the child's attending physician that a declaration has been made.

D. Any attending physician who is so notified shall promptly make the declaration or copy of the declaration a part of the child's medical record.

E. Nothing in this Article shall be construed to require the making of a declaration for a terminally ill minor. The legislature intends that the provisions of this Chapter are permissive and voluntary. The legislature further intends that the making of a declaration pursuant to this Chapter merely illustrates a means of documenting the decision relative to withholding or withdrawal of medical treatment or life-sustaining procedures by a parent or guardian on behalf of his child.

F. The declaration may but need not be in the following illustrative form and may include other specific directions:

"DECLARATION

Declaration made this _____ day of ___________ (month, year)

I, ___________, being of sound mind, willfully and voluntarily make known my desire that the death of my dying child, ________, shall not be artificially prolonged under the circumstances set forth below and do hereby declare:

Because my child has an incurable condition, injury, disease, or illness certified to be terminal and irreversible by two physicians who have personally examined my child, one of whom is his attending physician, and the physicians have determined that my child's death will occur whether or not life-sustaining procedures are utilized and that the application of life-sustaining procedures will serve only to prolong artificially the dying process, I direct that such procedures be withheld or withdrawn and that my child be permitted to die naturally with only the administration of medication or the performance of any medical procedure deemed necessary to provide him with comfort care.

I understand the full import of this declaration, and I am emotionally and mentally competent to make this declaration on behalf of my child.

Signed ____________________

City, Parish, and State of Residence ____________________________

The declarant has been personally known to me and I believe him or her to be of sound mind.

____
Witness

____
Witness"

(Added by Acts 1991 No. 235, §15, eff. 1/1/92.)

Art. 1558. Revocation of declaration.

A. A declaration by a parent or guardian pursuant to Article 1557 may be revoked at any time by the declarant without regard to his or her mental state or competency by any of the following methods:

(1) By being cancelled, defaced, obliterated, burned, torn, or otherwise destroyed by the declarant or by some person in the presence of and at the direction of the declarant.

(2) By a written revocation of the declarant expressing the intent to revoke, signed and dated by the declarant.

(3) By an oral or nonverbal expression by the declarant of the intent to revoke the declaration.

B. Such revocation by any method enumerated in Paragraph A of this Article shall become effective upon communication to the attending physician.

C. The attending physician shall record in the child's medical records the time and date when notification of the revocation was received.
(Added by Acts 1991 No. 235, §15, eff. 1/1/92.)

Art. 1559. Surrender of parental rights to a terminally ill child.

A. A parent or guardian who refuses to consent to the medical care and treatment of his child as required by this Chapter may at any time execute a voluntary act of surrender pursuant to Title XI and place the child in the legal custody of the department or a licensed adoption agency.

B. The department or agency shall immediately provide the treatment necessary for the child and shall make every effort to find an adoptive home for the child.
(Added by Acts 1991 No. 235, §15, eff. 1/1/92.)

Art. 1560. Wrongful refusal to consent to medical care and treatment of a child.

Whenever the parent or guardian of a child wrongfully refuses to consent to the medical care and treatment of his child as required by this Chapter, the physician may report the child as a child in need of care in accordance with the provisions of Title VI. *(Added by Acts 1991 No. 235, §15, eff. 1/1/92.)*

Art. 1561. Medical insurer's liability.

No medical insurer of a parent or guardian of a child who would have otherwise been liable for such medical expenses may deny liability to their insured solely because the insured parent or guardian desires to withhold medical or surgical treatment for the child. *(Added by Acts 1991 No. 235, §15, eff. 1/1/92.)*

Art. 1562. Immunity.

No hospital, physician, or other person authorized by law to provide medical or surgical care shall be held liable for providing such care for a terminally ill child protected by this Chapter when both:

(1) In the opinion of the hospital, physician, or other person authorized by law to provide medical or surgical care, exercising competent medical judgment, the child's life would be threatened by delaying the provision of medical care or treatment.

(2) The child's parent or guardian has wrongfully refused to consent to such medical care or treatment.

(Added by Acts 1991 No. 235, §15, eff. 1/1/92.)

Art. 1563. Declaratory judgment; appeal.

A. An action seeking a declaratory judgment may be brought by any parent, guardian, physician, or hospital in the juvenile court in the parish in which the child is present or is domiciled for the purposes of resolving any issue arising out of a dispute whether certain medical care or treatment should be extended in accordance with this Chapter.

B. An attorney shall be appointed to represent the child in all trial and appellate proceedings.

C. This proceeding shall be heard in chambers, confidentially and within forty-eight hours of the filing thereof.

D. Before entering any judgment approving the refusal or discontinuance of any medical or surgical care for a child, the court must find by clear and convincing evidence that the requirements of Article 1554 have been met.

E. Any appeal or application for writs to review the juvenile court's judgment in any appellate court shall be heard in chambers, confidentially and within forty-eight hours of the filing thereof.

F. Nothing in this Article shall be construed to require any court proceeding when a declaration authorized by Article 1557 has been executed or when the parent and the child's physician agree concerning the child's care, consistent with the requirements of this Chapter.

(Added by Acts 1991 No. 235, §15, eff. 1/1/92.)

CHAPTER 8. DOMESTIC ABUSE ASSISTANCE

Article

Art. 1564. Purpose.

The purpose of this Chapter is to recognize and address the complex legal and social problems created by domestic violence and to provide a civil remedy in the juvenile courts for domestic violence in homes in which children reside which will afford the victim immediate and easily accessible protection. *(Added by Acts 1991 No. 235, §15, eff. 1/1/92.)*

Art. 1565. Definitions.

As used in this Chapter:

(1) "Domestic abuse" includes but is not limited to physical or sexual abuse and any offense against the person as defined in the Chapter 1 of Title 14 of the Louisiana Revised Statutes of 1950, except negligent injury and defamation, committed by one family or household member against another.

(2) "Family or household member" means spouses, former spouses, parents and children, stepparents, stepchildren, foster parents, foster children, and any person living in the same residence with the defendant as a spouse whether married or not if a child or children also live in the residence, who are seeking protection under this Chapter.

(Added by Acts 1991 No. 235, §15; chgd. by Acts 1997 No. 1156, §1, eff. 8/15/97.)

Art. 1566. Assistance of clerk of court.

The clerk of court shall make forms available for making application for protective orders under this Chapter, provide clerical assistance to the petitioner when necessary, advise indigent applicants of the availability of filing in forma pauperis, provide the necessary forms, and provide the services of a notary, where available, for completion of the affidavit required in Article 1568. The forms shall be prepared by the Judicial Administrator's Office, Louisiana Supreme Court. *(Added by Acts 1991 No. 235, §15; chgd. by Acts 1997 No. 1156, §1, eff. 8/15/97.)*

Art. 1567. Venue; standing.

A. Venue lies in either:

(1) The parish in which the marital domicile is located or in which the household is located.

(2) The parish in which the defendant resides.

(3) The parish in which the abuse is alleged to have been committed.

(4) For purposes of issuing an order pursuant to Article 1569(A)(1) only, the parish in which the petitioner resides.

(5) The parish in which an action for an annulment of marriage or for a divorce could be brought pursuant to the Code of Civil Procedure.

B. An adult may seek relief under this Chapter by filing a petition with the court alleging abuse by the defendant. Any parent, adult household member, local child protection unit of the Department of Social Services, or district attorney may seek relief on behalf of any child or any person alleged to be incompetent by filing a petition with the court alleging abuse by the defendant. A petitioner's right to relief under this Chapter shall not be affected by his leaving the residence or household to avoid further abuse.

(Added by Acts 1991 No. 235, §15; chgd. by Acts 1995 No. 1095, §8; Acts 1997 No. 1156, §1, eff. 8/15/97.)

Art. 1568. Petition.

A. A petition filed under the provisions of this Chapter shall contain the following:

(1) The name of each petitioner and each person on whose behalf the petition is filed and the name, address, and parish of residence of each individual alleged to have committed abuse, if known.

(2) If the petition is being filed on behalf of a child or person alleged to be incompetent, the relationship between that person and the petitioner.

(3) The facts and circumstances concerning the alleged abuse.

(4) The relationship between each petitioner and each individual alleged to have committed abuse.

(5) A request for one or more protective orders or a temporary restraining order.

B. The address and parish of residence of each petitioner and each person on whose behalf the petition is filed, may remain confidential with the court.

C. If the petition requests a protective order for a spouse and alleges that the other spouse has committed abuse, the petition shall state whether a suit for divorce is pending.

D. If the petition requests the issuance of an ex parte temporary restraining order, the petition shall contain an affidavit signed by each petitioner that the facts and circumstances contained in the petition are true and correct to the best knowledge, information, and belief of the petitioner. Any false statement under oath contained in the affidavit shall constitute perjury and shall be punishable by a fine of not more than one thousand dollars or by imprisonment with or without hard labor for not more than five years, or both.

E. If a suit for divorce is pending, any application for a protective order shall be filed in that proceeding and shall be heard within the delays provided by this Chapter. Any decree issued in a divorce proceeding filed subsequent to the filing of a petition or an order issued pursuant to this Chapter may, in the discretion of the court hearing the divorce proceeding, supersede in whole or in part the orders issued pursuant to this Chapter. Such subsequent decree shall be forwarded by the rendering court to the court having jurisdiction of the petition for a protective order and shall be made a part of the record thereof. The findings and rulings made in connection with such protective orders shall not be res judicata in any subsequent proceeding.
(Added by Acts 1991 No. 235, §15; chgd. by Acts 1997 No. 1156, §1, eff. 8/15/97.)

Art. 1569. Temporary restraining order.

A. Upon good cause shown in an ex parte proceeding, the court may enter a temporary restraining order, without bond, as it deems necessary to protect from abuse the petitioner, any children, or any person alleged to be an incompetent. Immediate and present danger of abuse shall constitute good cause for purposes of this Article. The order may include but is not limited to the following:

(1) Directing the defendant to refrain from abusing, harassing, or interfering with the person or employment or going near the residence or place of employment of the petitioner, the children, or any person alleged to be incompetent, on whose behalf a petition was filed under this Chapter.

(2) Awarding to a party the use and possession of specified community property, such as an automobile.

(3) Granting possession to the petitioner of the residence or household to the exclusion of the defendant, by evicting the defendant or restoring possession to the petitioner when either:

(a) The residence is jointly owned in equal proportion or leased by the defendant and the petitioner or the person on whose behalf the petition is brought.

(b) The residence is solely owned by the petitioner or the person on whose behalf the petition is brought.

(c) The residence is solely leased by defendant and defendant has a duty to support the petitioner or the person on whose behalf the petition is brought.

(4) Prohibiting either party from the transferring, encumbering, or otherwise disposing of property mutually owned or leased by the parties, except when in the ordinary course of business, or for the necessary support of the party or the minor children.

(5) Awarding temporary custody of children or persons alleged to be incompetent.

B. If a temporary restraining order is granted without notice, the matter shall be set within ten days for a rule to show cause why the protective order should not be issued, at which time the petitioner must prove the allegations of abuse by a preponderance of the evidence. The defendant shall be given notice of the temporary restraining order and the hearing on the rule to show cause by service of process as required by law.

C. During the existence of the temporary restraining order, a party shall have the right to return to the family residence once to recover his or her personal clothing and necessities, provided that the party is accompanied by a law enforcement officer to insure the protection and safety of the parties.

D. If no temporary restraining order has been granted, the court shall issue a rule to show cause why the protective order should not be issued, and set the rule for hearing on the earliest day that the business of the court will permit, but in any case within ten days from the date of service of the petition, at which time the petitioner must prove the allegations of abuse by a preponderance of the evidence. The defendant shall be given notice by service of process as required by law.

E. If the hearing pursuant to Article 1570(B) or (D) is continued, the court shall make or extend such temporary restraining order as it deems necessary. Any continuance of a hearing ordered pursuant to Article 1570(B) or (D) shall not exceed ten days.

F. The court may, in its discretion, grant an emergency temporary restraining order outside regular court hours.

G. No ex parte order for a temporary restraining order shall be granted by a court until the court has questioned the petitioner seeking the order and the court believes good cause exists for the issuance of the temporary restraining order. The court shall require a bond for any temporary restraining order unless the petitioner demonstrates indigency in accordance with the provisions of Code of Civil Procedure Art. 5181 et seq.

H. Immediately upon rendering a decision granting the relief requested by the petitioner, the judge shall cause to have prepared a Uniform Abuse Prevention Order, as provided in R.S. 46:2136.2(C), shall sign such order, and shall forward it to the clerk of court for filing, all without delay.

I. If a temporary restraining order is issued or extended, the clerk of the issuing court shall transmit the Uniform Abuse Prevention Order to the Louisiana Protective Order Registry, R.S. 46:2136.2(A), by facsimile transmission, mail, or direct electronic input, where available, as expeditiously as possible, but no later than the end of the next business day after the order is filed with the clerk of court.

(Added by Acts 1991 No. 235, §15; chgd. by Acts 1997 No. 1156, §1, eff. 8/15/97.)

Art. 1570. Protective orders; content; modification; service.

A. The court may grant any protective order or approve any consent agreement to bring about a cessation of abuse of a party, any children, or any person alleged to be incompetent, which relief may include but is not limited to:

(1) Granting the relief enumerated in Article 1569.

(2) When there is a duty to support a party, any minor children, or any person alleged to be incompetent living in the residence or household, ordering payment of temporary support or provision of suitable housing for them.

(3) Awarding temporary custody of or establishing temporary visitation rights and conditions with regard to any children or person alleged to be incompetent.

(4) Ordering counseling or professional medical treatment for the defendant or the abused person, or both.

B. A protective order may be rendered pursuant to this Chapter if the court has jurisdiction over the parties and subject matter and either of the following occurs:

(1) The parties enter into a consent agreement.

(2) Reasonable notice and opportunity to be heard is given to the person against whom the order is sought sufficient to protect that person's right to due process.

C. Any protective order issued within this state or outside this state that is consistent with Paragraph B shall be accorded full faith and credit by the courts of this state and enforced as if it were the order of the enforcing court.

D. On the motion of any party, the court, after notice to the other parties and a hearing, may modify a prior order to exclude any item included in the prior order or to include any item that could have been included in the prior order.

E. A protective order made under this Chapter shall be served on the person to whom the order applied in open court at the close of the hearing, or in the same manner as a writ of injunction. The clerk of the issuing court shall send a copy of the Uniform Abuse Prevention Order, R.S. 46:2136.2(C), or any modification thereof to the chief law enforcement official of the parish where the person or persons protected by the order reside. A copy of the Louisiana Abuse Prevention Order shall be retained on file in the office of the chief law enforcement officer as provided herein until otherwise directed by the court.

F. Any final protective order or approved consent agreement shall be for a fixed period of time, not to exceed six months, and may be extended by the court, after a contradictory hearing, in its discretion. Such protective order or extension thereof shall be subject to a devolutive appeal only.

G. Immediately upon rendering a decision granting the relief requested by the petitioner, the judge shall cause to have prepared a Uniform Abuse Prevention Order, as provided in R.S. 46:2136.2(C), shall sign such order, and shall forward it to the clerk of court for filing, all without delay.

H. If a protective order is issued or modified, or a consent agreement is agreed to or modified, the clerk of the issuing court shall transmit the Uniform Abuse Prevention Order to the Louisiana Protective Order Registry, R.S. 46:2136.2(A), by facsimile transmission, mail, or direct electronic input, where available, as expeditiously as possible, but no later than the end of the next business day after the order is filed with the clerk of court.

(Added by Acts 1991 No. 235, §15; chgd. by Acts 1994 Third Ex. Sess. No. 22, §1; Acts 1997 No. 1156, §1, eff. 8/15/97.)

Art. 1570.1. Costs paid by abuser.

All court costs, attorney fees, evaluation fees, and expert witness fees incurred in furtherance of this Chapter shall be paid by the perpetrator of the domestic violence, including all costs of medical and psychological care for the abused adult, or for any of the children, necessitated by the domestic violence. *(Added by Acts 1997 No. 1156, §1, eff. 8/15/97.)*

Art. 1571. Penalties; notice of penalty in order.

A. Upon violation of a temporary restraining order, a protective order, or a court-approved consent agreement, the court may hold the defendant in contempt of court and punish the defendant by imprisonment in the parish jail for not more than six months or a fine of not more than five hundred dollars, or both, and may order that all or a part of any fine be forwarded for the support of petitioner and dependents, in the discretion of the court.

B. Such sentence shall be imposed only after trial by the judge of a rule against the defendant to show cause why he should not be adjudged guilty of contempt and punished accordingly. The rule to show cause may issue on the court's own motion or on motion of a party to the action or proceeding, and shall state the facts alleged to constitute the contempt. A certified copy of the motion and of the rule to show cause shall be served upon the person charged with contempt in the same manner as a subpoena, at least forty-eight hours before the time assigned for the trial of the rule, which shall be scheduled within five days of the filing of the motion for contempt.

C. Each protective order issued under this Chapter, including a temporary ex parte order, shall have the following statement printed in bold-faced type or in capital letters: "A PERSON WHO VIOLATES THIS ORDER MAY BE PUNISHED FOR CONTEMPT OF COURT BY A FINE OF NOT MORE THAN $500 OR BY CONFINEMENT IN JAIL FOR AS LONG AS SIX MONTHS, OR BOTH, AND MAY BE FURTHER PUNISHED UNDER THE CRIMINAL LAWS OF THE STATE OF LOUISIANA. THIS ORDER SHALL BE ENFORCED BY ALL LAW ENFORCEMENT OFFICERS AND COURTS OF THE STATE OF LOUISIANA."

D. Nothing contained herein shall be construed as a limitation on any applicable provisions of Title 14 of the Louisiana Revised Statutes of 1950.
(Added by Acts 1991 No. 235, §15, eff. 1/1/92.)

Art. 1572. Other relief not affected.

The granting of any relief authorized under this Chapter shall not preclude any other relief authorized by law. *(Added by Acts 1991 No. 235, §15, eff. 1/1/92.)*

Art. 1573. Law enforcement officers; duties.

Whenever a law enforcement officer has reason to believe that a family or household member has been abused, the officer shall immediately use all reasonable means to prevent further abuse, including:

(1) Arresting the abusive party with a warrant or without a warrant pursuant to Article 213 of the Code of Criminal Procedure, if probable cause exists to believe that aggravated or second degree battery has been committed by that person, whether or not the offense occurred in the officer's presence.

(2) Arresting the abusive party in case of simple assault, aggravated assault, or simple battery, whether or not the offense occurred in the presence of the officer, when the officer reasonably believes there is impending danger to the physical safety of the abused person in the officer's absence. If there is no cause to believe there is impending danger, arresting the abusive party is at the officer's discretion.

(3) Assisting the abused person in obtaining medical treatment necessitated by the battery, or arranging for, or providing or assisting in the procurement of transportation for the abused person to a place of shelter or safety.

(4) Notifying the abused, person of his right to initiate criminal or civil proceedings, the availability of the protective order pursuant to Article 1570, and the availability of community assistance for domestic violence victims.
(Added by Acts 1991 No. 235, §15, eff. 1/1/92.)

Art. 1574. Reporting.

Whenever a law enforcement officer investigates an allegation of domestic abuse, whether or not an arrest is made, the officer shall make a written report of the alleged incident, including a statement of the complainant and the disposition of the case. *(Added by Acts 1991 No. 235, §15, eff. 1/1/92.)*

Art. 1575. Immunity.

Any law enforcement officer reporting in good faith, exercising due care in the making of an arrest, or providing assistance pursuant to the provisions of Articles 1573 and 1574 shall have immunity from any civil liability that otherwise might be incurred or imposed because of the report, arrest, or assistance provided. *(Added by Acts 1991 No. 235, §15, eff. 1/1/92.)*

TITLE XVI. INTERSTATE COMPACTS AFFECTING CHILDREN

Chapter

CHAPTER 1. INTERSTATE COMPACT ON ADOPTION AND MEDICAL ASSISTANCE

Article

Art. 1601. Enactment.

The Interstate Compact on Adoption and Medical Assistance is hereby enacted into law and entered into with all other jurisdictions legally joining therein in form substantially as follows. *(Added by Acts 1991 No. 235, §16, eff. 1/1/92.)*

Art. 1602. Findings.

The party states find that:

(1) In order to obtain adoptive families for children with special needs, prospective adoptive parents must be assured of substantial assistance, usually on a continuing basis, in meeting the high costs of supporting and providing for the special needs and services required by such children.

(2) The states have a fundamental interest in promoting adoption for children with special needs because the care, emotional stability, and general support and encouragement required by such children to surmount their physical, mental, or emotional conditions can be best, and often only, obtained in family homes with a normal parent-child relationship.

(3) The states obtain advantages from providing adoption assistance because the customary alternative is for the state to defray the entire cost of meeting all the needs of such children.

(4) The special needs involved are for the emotional, physical maintenance of the child, and medical support and services.

(5) The necessary assurances of adoption assistance for children with special needs, in those instances where children and adoptive parents are in states other than the one undertaking to provide the assistance, is to establish and maintain suitable substantive guarantees and workable procedures for interstate payments to assist with the necessary child maintenance, procurement of services, and medical assistance.
(Added by Acts 1991 No. 235, §16, eff. 1/1/92.)

Art. 1603. Purposes.

The purposes of this compact are to:

(1) Strengthen protections for the interests of the children with special needs on behalf of whom adoptive assistance is committed to be paid, when such children are in or move to states other than the one committed to make adoption assistance payments.

(2) Provide substantive assurances and procedures which will promote the delivery of medical and other services on an interstate basis to children through programs of adoption assistance established by the laws of the party states.
(Added by Acts 1991 No. 235, §16, eff. 1/1/92.)

Art. 1604. Definitions.

As used in this compact, unless the context clearly requires a different construction:

(1) "Adoption assistance" means the payment or payments for maintenance of a child, which payment or payments are made or committed to be made pursuant to the adoption assistance program established by the laws of a party state.

(2) "Adoption assistance state" means the state that is signatory to an adoption assistance agreement in a particular case.

(3) "Child with special needs" means a minor who has not yet attained the age at which the state normally discontinues children's services or twenty-one, where the state determines that the child's mental or physical handicaps warrant the continuation of assistance, for whom the state has determined the following:

(a) That the child cannot or should not be returned to the home of his parents.

(b) That there exists with respect to the child a specific factor or condition, such as his ethnic background, age, or membership in a minority or sibling group, or the presence of factors such as medical condition or physical, mental, or emotional handicaps, because of which it is reasonable to conclude that such child cannot be placed with adoptive parents without providing adoption assistance.

(c) That, except where it would be against the best interests of the child because of such factors as the existence of significant emotional ties with prospective adoptive parents while in the care of such parents as a foster child, a reasonable but unsuccessful effort has been made to place the child with appropriate adoptive parents without providing adoption assistance payments.

(4) "Parents" means either the singular or plural of the word "parent".

(5) "Residence state" means the state of which the child is a resident by virtue of the residence of the adoptive parents.

(6) "State" means a state of the United States, the District of Columbia, the Commonwealth of Puerto Rico, the Virgin Islands, Guam, the Commonwealth of the Northern Mariana Islands, or a territory or possession of the United States.
(Added by Acts 1991 No. 235, §16, eff. 1/1/92.)

Art. 1605. Adoption assistance.

A. Each state shall determine the amounts of adoption assistance and other aid which it will give to children with special needs and their adoptive parents in accordance with its own laws and programs. The adoption assistance and other aid may be made subject to periodic reevaluation of eligibility by the adoption assistance state in accordance with its laws. The provisions of this Article and of Article 1606 are subject to the limitation set forth in this Paragraph.

B. The adoption assistance and medical assistance services and benefits to which this compact applies are those provided to children with special needs and their adoptive parents from the time of the final decree of adoption or the interlocutory decree of adoption, as the case may be, pursuant to the laws of the adoption assistance state. In addition to the content required by subsequent provisions of this Article for adoption assistance agreements, each such agreement shall state whether the initial adoption assistance period thereunder begins with the final or interlocutory decree of adoption. Aid provided by party states to children with special needs during the preadoptive placement period or earlier shall be under the foster care or other programs of the states and, except as provided in Paragraph C of this Article, shall not be governed by the provisions of this compact.

C. Every case of adoption assistance shall include an adoption assistance agreement between the adoptive parents and the agency of the state undertaking to provide the adoption assistance. Every such agreement shall contain provisions for the fixing of actual or potential interstate aspects of the adoption assistance as follows:

(1) An express commitment that the adoption assistance shall be payable without regard for the state of residence of the adoptive parents, both at the outset of the agreement period and at all times during its continuance.

(2) A provision setting forth with particularity the types of child care and services toward which the adoption assistance state will make payments.

(3) A commitment to make medical assistance available to the child in accordance with Article 1606.

(4) An express declaration that the agreement is for the benefit of the child, the adoptive parents, and that state and that it is enforceable by any or all of them.

D. Any services or benefits provided by the residence state and the adoption assistance state for a child may be facilitated by the party states on each other's behalf. To this end, the personnel of the child welfare agencies of the party states will assist each other and beneficiaries of adoption assistance agreements with other party states in implementing benefits expressly included in adoption assistance agreements. However, it is recognized and agreed that, in general, children to whom adoption assistance agreements apply are eligible for benefits under the child welfare, education, rehabilitation, mental health, and other programs of their state of residence on the same basis as other resident children.

E. Adoption assistance payments, when made on behalf of a child in another state, shall be made on the same basis and in the same amounts as they would be made if the child were in the state making the payments.

(Added by Acts 1991 No. 235, §16, eff. 1/1/92.)

Art. 1606. Medical assistance.

A. Children for whom a party state is committed in accordance with the terms of an adoption assistance agreement to make adoption assistance payments are eligible for medical assistance during the entire period for which such payments are to be provided. Upon application therefor, the adoptive parents of a child on whose behalf a party state's duly constituted authorities have entered into an adoption assistance agreement shall receive a medical assistance identification made out in the child's name. The identification shall be issued by the medical assistance program of the residence state and shall entitle the child to the same benefits, pursuant to the same procedures, as any other child who is a resident of the state and covered by medical assistance, whether or not the adoptive parents are eligible for medical assistance.

B. The identification shall bear no indication that an adoption assistance agreement with another state is the basis for issuance. However, if the identification is issued on account of an outstanding adoption assistance agreement to which another state is a signatory, the records of the issuing state and the adoption assistance state shall show the fact and shall contain a copy of the adoption assistance agreement and any amendment or replacement therefor, and all other pertinent information. The adoption assistance and medical assistance programs of the adoption assistance state shall be notified of the identification issuance.

C. A state which has issued a medical assistance identification pursuant to this compact, which identification is valid and currently in force, shall accept, process, and pay medical assistance claims thereon as on any other medical assistance eligibilities of residents.

D. An adoption assistance state which provides medical services or benefits to children covered by its adoption assistance agreements, which services or benefits are not provided for those children under the medical assistance program of the residence state, may enter into cooperative arrangements with the residence state to facilitate the delivery and administration of such services and benefits. However, any such arrangements shall not be inconsistent with this compact nor shall they relieve the residence state of any obligation to provide medical assistance in accordance with its laws and this compact.

E. A child whose residence is changed from one party state to another party state shall be eligible for medical assistance under the medical assistance program of the new state of residence.

(Added by Acts 1991 No. 235, §16, eff. 1/1/92.)

Art. 1607. Joinder and withdrawal.

A. This compact shall be open to joinder by any state. It shall enter into force as to a state when its duly constituted and empowered authority has executed it.

B. In order that the provisions of this compact may be accessible to and known by the general public and so that its status as law in each of the party states may be fully implemented, the full text of the compact, together with a notice of its execution shall be caused to be published by the authority which has executed it in each party state. Copies of the compact shall be made available upon request made of the executing authority in any state.

C. Withdrawal from this compact shall be by written notice sent by the authority which executed it to the appropriate officials of all other party states, but no such notice shall take effect until one year after it is given in accordance with the requirements of this Paragraph.

D. All adoption assistance agreements outstanding and to which a party state is signatory at the time when its withdrawal from this compact takes effect shall continue to have the effects given to them pursuant to this compact, until they expire or are terminated in accordance with their provisions. Until such expiration or termination, all beneficiaries of the agreements involved shall continue to have all rights and obligations conferred or imposed by this compact, and the withdrawing state shall continue to administer the compact to the extent necessary to accord and implement fully the rights and protections preserved hereby.
(Added by Acts 1991 No. 235, §16, eff. 1/1/92.)

CHAPTER 2. INTERSTATE COMPACT ON THE PLACEMENT OF CHILDREN

Art. 1608. Interstate compact on the placement of children, adoption; enactment; purpose and policy.

A. The Interstate Compact on the Placement of Children is hereby enacted into law and entered into with all other jurisdictions legally joining therein as set out herein in Articles 1608 through 1617.

B. It is the purpose and policy of the party states to cooperate with each other in the interstate placement of children to the end that:

(1) Each child requiring placement shall receive the maximum opportunity to be placed in a suitable environment and with persons or institutions having appropriate qualifications and facilities to provide a necessary and desirable degree and type of care.

(2) The appropriate authorities in a state where a child is to be placed may have full opportunity to ascertain the circumstances of the proposed placement, thereby promoting full compliance with applicable requirements for the protection of the child.

(3) The proper authorities of the state from which the placement is made may obtain the most complete information on the basis of which to evaluate a projected placement before it is made.

(4) Appropriate jurisdictional arrangements for the care of children will be promoted.
(Added by Acts 1991 No. 235, §16, eff. 1/1/92.)

Art. 1609. Compact definitions.

As used in this compact:

(1) "Child" means a person who, by reason of minority, is legally subject to parental, guardianship, or similar control.

(2) "Placement" means the arrangement for the care of a child in a family free or boarding home or in a child-caring agency or institution but does not include any institution caring for the mentally ill, mentally defective, or epileptic, or any institution primarily educational in character, and any hospital or other medical facility.

(3) "Receiving state" means the state to which a child is sent, brought, or caused to be sent or brought, whether by public authorities or private persons or agencies, and whether for placement with state or local public authorities or for placement with private agencies or persons.

(4) "Sending agency" means a party state, officer or employee thereof; a subdivision of a party state, or officer or employee thereof; a court of a party state; a person, corporation, association, charitable agency, or other entity which sends, brings, or causes to be sent or brought any child to another party state.
(Added by Acts 1991 No. 235, §16, eff. 1/1/92.)

Art. 1610. Conditions for placement.

A. No sending agency shall send, bring, or cause to be sent or brought into any other party state any child for placement in foster care or as a preliminary to a possible adoption unless the sending agency shall comply with each and every requirement set forth in this Article and with the applicable laws of the receiving state governing the placement of children therein.

B. Prior to sending, bringing, or causing any child to be sent or brought into a receiving state for placement in foster care or as a preliminary to a possible adoption, the sending agency shall furnish the appropriate public authorities in the receiving state written notice of the intention to send, bring, or place the child in the receiving state. The notice shall contain:

(1) The name, date, and place of birth of the child.

(2) The identity and address or addresses of the parents or legal guardian.

(3) The name and address of the person, agency, or institution to or with which the sending agency proposes to send, bring, or place the child.

(4) A full statement of the reasons for such proposed action and evidence of the authority pursuant to which the placement is proposed to be made.

C. Any public officer or agency in a receiving state which is in receipt of a notice pursuant to Paragraph B of this Article may request the sending agency or any other appropriate officer or agency of or in the sending agency's state, and shall be entitled to receive therefrom, such supporting or additional information as it may deem necessary under the circumstances to carry out the purpose and policy of this compact.

D. The child shall not be sent, brought, or caused to be sent or brought into the receiving state until the appropriate public authorities in the receiving state shall notify the sending agency, in writing, to the effect that the proposed placement does not appear to be contrary to the interests of the child.
(Added by Acts 1991 No. 235, §16, eff. 1/1/92.)

Art. 1611. Illegal placement; penalty.

A. The sending, bringing or causing to be sent or brought into any receiving state of a child in violation of the terms of this compact shall constitute a violation of the laws respecting the placement of children of both the state in which the sending agency is located or from which it sends or brings the child and of the receiving state.

B. Such violation may be punished or subjected to penalty in either jurisdiction in accordance with its laws.

C. In addition to liability for any such punishment or penalty, any such violation shall constitute full and sufficient grounds for the suspension or revocation of any license, permit, or other legal authorization held by the sending agency which empowers or allows it to place or care for children.
(Added by Acts 1991 No. 235, §16, eff. 1/1/92.)

Art. 1612. Retention of jurisdiction.

A. The sending agency shall retain jurisdiction over the child sufficient to determine all matters in relation to the custody, supervision, care, treatment, and disposition of the child which it would have had if the child had remained in the sending agency's state, until the child is adopted, reaches majority, becomes self-supporting, or is discharged with the concurrence of the appropriate authority in the receiving state. Such jurisdiction shall also include the power to effect or cause the return of the child or its transfer to another location and custody pursuant to law. The sending agency shall continue to have financial responsibility for support and maintenance of the child during the period of the placement. Nothing contained herein shall defeat a claim of jurisdiction by a receiving state sufficient to deal with an act of delinquency or crime committed therein.

B. When the sending agency is a public agency, it may enter into an agreement with an authorized public or private agency in the receiving state providing for the performance of one or more services in respect of such case by the latter as agent for the sending agency.

C. Nothing in this compact shall be construed to prevent a private charitable agency authorized to place children in the receiving state from performing services or acting as agent in that state for a private charitable agency of the sending state, nor to prevent the agency in the receiving state from discharging financial responsibility for the support and maintenance of a child who has been placed on behalf of the sending agency without relieving the responsibility set forth in Paragraph A of this Article.
(Added by Acts 1991 No. 235, §16, eff. 1/1/92.)

Art. 1613. Institutional care of delinquent children.

A child adjudicated delinquent may be placed in an institution in another party jurisdiction pursuant to this compact, but no such placement shall be made unless the child is given a court hearing on notice to the parent or guardian with opportunity to be heard, prior to his being sent to such other party jurisdiction for institutional care, and the court finds both that:

(1) Equivalent facilities for the child are not available in the sending agency's jurisdiction.

(2) Institutional care in the other jurisdiction is in the best interest of the child and will not produce undue hardship.
(Added by Acts 1991 No. 235, §16, eff. 1/1/92.)

Art. 1614. Compact administrator.

The executive head of each jurisdiction party to this compact shall designate an officer who shall be general coordinator of activities under this compact in his jurisdiction and who, acting jointly with like officers of other party jurisdictions, shall have power to promulgate rules and regulations to carry out more effectively the terms and provisions of this compact.
(Added by Acts 1991 No. 235, §16, eff. 1/1/92.)

Art. 1615. Limitations upon applicability.

This compact shall not apply to:

(1) The sending or bringing of a child into a receiving state by his parent, stepparent, grandparent, adult brother or sister, adult uncle or aunt, or his guardian and leaving the child with any such relative or nonagency guardian in the receiving state.

(2) Any placement, sending, or bringing of a child into a receiving state pursuant to any other interstate compact to which both the state from which the child is sent or brought and the receiving state are party, or to any other agreement between said states which has the force of law.
(Added by Acts 1991 No. 235, §16, eff. 1/1/92.)

Art. 1616. Enactment and withdrawal.

A. This compact shall be open to joinder by any state, territory, or possession of the United States, the District of Columbia, the Commonwealth of Puerto Rico, and, with the consent of congress, the government of Canada or any province thereof. It shall become effective with respect to any such jurisdiction when such jurisdiction has enacted the same into law.

B. Withdrawal from this compact shall be by the enactment of a statute repealing the same, but shall not take effect until two years after the effective date of such statute and until written notice of the withdrawal has been given by the withdrawing state to the governor of each other party jurisdiction.

C. Withdrawal of a party state shall not affect the rights, duties, and obligations under this compact of any sending agency herein with respect to a placement made prior to the effective date of withdrawal.
(Added by Acts 1991 No. 235, §16, eff. 1/1/92.)

Art. 1617. Construction and severability.

A. The provisions of this compact shall be liberally construed to effectuate the purposes thereof.

B. The provisions of this compact shall be severable, and if any phrase, clause, sentence, or provision of this compact is declared to be contrary to the constitution of any party state or of the United States or the applicability thereof to any government, agency, person, or circumstance is held invalid, the validity of the remainder of this compact and the applicability thereof to any government, agency, person, or circumstance shall not be affected

thereby. If this compact shall be held contrary to the constitution of any state party thereto, the compact shall remain in full force and effect as to the remaining states and in full force and effect as to the state affected as to all severable matters.
(Added by Acts 1991 No. 235, §16, eff. 1/1/92.)

Art. 1618. Supplementary definitions applicable only to this state.

A. As used in Article 1610, when referring to this state, "appropriate public authorities" means the Louisiana Department of Social Services.

B. As used in Article 1612, "appropriate authority in the receiving state" means any licensed child welfare agency in Louisiana.

C. As used in Article 1614, "executive head" means the governor of Louisiana.
(Added by Acts 1991 No. 235, §16, eff. 1/1/92.)

Art. 1619. Financial responsibility for children.

Financial responsibility for any child placed pursuant to the provisions of this compact shall be determined in accordance with the provisions of Article 1612 in the first instance. However, in the event of partial or complete default of performance thereunder, the provisions of Louisiana's laws fixing the responsibility for the support of children also may be invoked. *(Added by Acts 1991 No. 235, §16, eff. 1/1/92.)*

Art. 1620. Authority to enter into agreements; approval of state treasurer.

A. The officers and agencies of this state and its political subdivisions having authority to place children are hereby empowered to enter into agreements with appropriate officers or agencies of or in other party states pursuant to Paragraph B of Article 1612.

B. Any such agreement which contains a financial commitment or imposes a financial obligation on this state or subdivision or agency thereof shall not be binding unless it has the approval in writing of the state treasurer in the case of the state and of the chief local fiscal officer in the case of a subdivision of the state.
(Added by Acts 1991 No. 235, §16, eff. 1/1/92.)

Art. 1621. Jurisdiction.

Any court having jurisdiction to place delinquent children may place such a child in an institution or in another state pursuant to Article 1613 and shall retain jurisdiction as provided in Article 1612. *(Added by Acts 1991 No. 235, §16, eff. 1/1/92.)*

Art. 1622. Appointment of compact administrator.

The governor is hereby authorized to appoint a compact administrator in accordance with the terms of Article 1614. *(Added by Acts 1991 No. 235, §16, eff. 1/1/92.)*

CHAPTER 3. INTERSTATE COMPACT ON JUVENILES

Article

Art. 1623. Authorization to enter into compact; form of compact.

The governor of this state is hereby authorized and directed to execute an Interstate Compact on Juveniles on behalf of this state with any other state or states legally joining therein in the form substantially as follows. *(Added by Acts 1991 No. 235, §16, eff. 1/1/92.)*

Art. 1624. Findings; purpose; policy.

A. The contracting states solemnly agree:

(1) That juveniles who are not under proper supervision and control, or who have absconded, escaped, or run away, are likely to endanger their own health, morals, and welfare, and the health, morals, and welfare of others.

(2) That the cooperation of the states party to this compact is therefore necessary to provide for the welfare and protection of juveniles and of the public with respect to:

(a) Cooperative supervision of delinquent juveniles on probation or parole.

(b) The return from one state to another of delinquent juveniles who have escaped or absconded.

(c) The return from one state to another of nondelinquent juveniles who have run away from home.

(d) Additional measures for the protection of juveniles and of the public, which any two or more of the party states may find desirable to undertake cooperatively.

B. In carrying out the provisions of this compact the party states shall be guided by the noncriminal reformative and protective policies which guide their laws concerning delinquent, neglected, or dependent juveniles generally. It shall be the policy of the states party to this compact to cooperate and observe their respective responsibilities for the prompt return and acceptance of juveniles and delinquent juveniles who become subject to the provisions of this compact.

C. To every extent possible, it shall be the policy of states party to this compact that no juvenile or delinquent juvenile shall be placed or detained in any prison, jail, or lockup nor be detained or transported in association with criminal, vicious, or dissolute persons.
(Added by Acts 1991 No. 235, §16, eff. 1/1/92.)

Art. 1625. Construction.

The provisions of this compact shall be reasonably and literally construed to accomplish the foregoing purpose. *(Added by Acts 1991 No. 235, §16, eff. 1/1/92.)*

Art. 1626. Nature of remedies.

All remedies and procedures provided by this compact shall be in addition to and not in substitution for other rights, remedies, and procedures, and shall not be in derogation of parental rights and responsibilities. *(Added by Acts 1991 No. 235, §16, eff. 1/1/92.)*

Art. 1627. Definitions.

For the purposes of this compact, the following definitions shall be used:

(1) "Court" means any court having jurisdiction over delinquent, neglected, or dependent children.

(2) "Delinquent juvenile" means any juvenile who has been adjudged delinquent and who, at the time the provisions of this compact are invoked, is still subject to the jurisdiction

of the court that has made such adjudication or to the jurisdiction or supervision of an agency or institution pursuant to an order of such court.

(3) "Juvenile" means any person who is a minor under the law of the state of residence of the parent, guardian, person, or agency entitled to the legal custody of such minor.

(4) "Probation or parole" means any kind of conditional release of juveniles authorized under the laws of the states party hereto.

(5) "Residence" or any variant thereof means a place at which a home or regular place of abode is maintained.

(6) "State" means any state, territory, or possession of the United States, the District of Columbia, and the Commonwealth of Puerto Rico.

(Added by Acts 1991 No. 235, §16, eff. 1/1/92.)

Art. 1628. Runaway juveniles; petition for requisition for return.

A. The parent, guardian, person, or agency entitled to legal custody of a juvenile who has not been adjudged delinquent but who has run away without the consent of such parent, guardian, person, or agency may petition the appropriate court in the demanding state for the issuance of a requisition for his return.

B. The petition shall state:

(1) The name and age of the juvenile.

(2) The name of the petitioner and the basis of entitlement to the juvenile's custody.

(3) The circumstances of his running away.

(4) His location if known at the time application is made.

(5) Such other facts as may tend to show that the juvenile who has run away is endangering his own welfare or the welfare of others and is not an emancipated minor.

C. The petition shall be verified by affidavit, shall be executed in duplicate, and shall be accomplished by two certified copies of the document or documents on which the petitioner's entitlement to the juvenile's custody is based, such as birth certificates, letters of guardianship, or custody decrees.

D. Such further affidavits and other documents as may be deemed proper may be submitted with such petition.

(Added by Acts 1991 No. 235, §16, eff. 1/1/92.)

Art. 1629. Runaway juveniles; hearing on petition.

The judge of the court to which this application is made may hold a hearing thereon to determine whether for the purposes of this compact the petitioner is entitled to the legal custody of the juvenile, whether or not it appears that the juvenile has in fact run away without consent, whether or not he is an emancipated minor, and whether or not it is in the best interest of the juvenile to compel his return to the state. *(Added by Acts 1991 No. 235, §16, eff. 1/1/92.)*

Art. 1630. Runaway juveniles; requisition for return.

A. If the judge determines either with or without a hearing that the juvenile should be returned, he shall present to the appropriate court or to the executive authority of the state where the juvenile is alleged to be located a written requisition for the return of such juvenile.

B. Such requisition shall set forth:

(1) The name and age of the juvenile.

(2) The determination of the court that the juvenile has run away without the consent of a parent, guardian, person, or agency entitled to his legal custody, and that it is in the best interest and for the protection of such juvenile that he be returned.

(Added by Acts 1991 No. 235, §16, eff. 1/1/92.)

Art. 1631. Runaway juveniles; requisition when adjudication is pending.

A. In the event that a proceeding for the adjudication of the juvenile as a delinquent, neglected, or dependent juvenile is pending in the court at the time when such juvenile runs away, the court may issue a requisition for the return of such juvenile upon its own action, regardless of the consent of the parent, guardian, person, or agency entitled to legal custody.

B. The requisition shall recite the nature and circumstances of the pending proceeding.

C. The requisition shall in every case be executed in duplicate and shall be signed by the judge.

D. One copy of the requisition shall be filed with the compact administrator of the demanding state, there to remain on file subject to the provisions of law governing records of such court.

(Added by Acts 1991 No. 235, §16, eff. 1/1/92.)

Art. 1632. Runaway juveniles; duties of state upon receipt of requisition.

A. Upon the receipt of a requisition demanding the return of a juvenile who has run away, the court or the executive authority to whom the requisition is addressed shall issue an order to any peace officer or other appropriate person directing him to take into custody and detain such juvenile.

B. Such detention order must substantially recite the facts necessary to the validity of its issuance hereunder.

C. No juvenile detained upon such order shall be delivered over to the officer whom the court demanding him shall have appointed to receive him, unless he shall first be taken forthwith before a judge of a court in the state, who shall inform him of the demand made for his return, and who may appoint counsel or a guardian ad litem for him.

D. If the judge of such court shall find that the requisition is in order, he shall deliver such juvenile over to the officer whom the court demanding him shall have appointed to receive him. The judge, however, may fix a reasonable time to be allowed for the purpose of testing the legality of the proceedings.

(Added by Acts 1991 No. 235, §16, eff. 1/1/92.)

Art. 1633. Report of runaway status; no requisition.

A. Upon reasonable information that a person is a juvenile who has run away from another state party to this compact without the consent of a parent, guardian, person, or agency entitled to his legal custody, such juvenile may be taken into custody without a requisition and brought forthwith before a judge of the appropriate court.

B. The court may appoint counsel or a guardian ad litem for such juvenile and shall determine after a hearing whether sufficient cause exists to hold the person, subject to the order of the court, for his own protection and welfare.

C. The child may be held for such a time not exceeding ninety days as will enable his return to another state party to this compact pursuant to a requisition for his return from a court of that state.

D. If, at the time when a state seeks the return of a juvenile who has run away, there is pending in the state wherein he is found any criminal charge, or any proceeding to have him adjudicated a delinquent juvenile for an act committed in such state, or if he is suspected of having committed within such state a criminal offense or an act of juvenile delinquency, he shall not be returned without the consent of such state until discharged from prosecution or other form of proceeding, imprisonment, detention, or supervision for such offense or juvenile delinquency.

(Added by Acts 1991 No. 235, §16, eff. 1/1/92.)

Art. 1634. Transportation of runaway juveniles.

A. The duly accredited officers of any state party to this compact, upon the establishment of their authority and the identity of the juvenile being returned, shall be permitted to transport such juvenile through any and all states party to this compact, without interference.

B. The state to which a juvenile is returned under this compact shall be responsible for payment of the transportation costs of such return.

(Added by Acts 1991 No. 235, §16, eff. 1/1/92.)

Art. 1635. Proceedings in home state upon return.

Upon his return to the state from which he ran away, the juvenile shall be subject to such further proceedings as may be appropriate under the laws of that state. *(Added by Acts 1991 No. 235, §16, eff. 1/1/92.)*

Art. 1636. Requisition for absconding or escaped delinquent juvenile.

A. The appropriate person or authority from whose probation or parole supervision a delinquent juvenile has absconded or from whose institutional custody he has escaped shall present to the appropriate court or to the executive authority of the state where the delinquent juvenile is alleged to be located a written requisition for the return of such delinquent juvenile.

B. Such requisition shall state:

(1) The name and age of the delinquent juvenile.

(2) The particulars of his adjudication as a delinquent juvenile.

(3) The circumstances of the breach of the terms of his probation or parole or of his escape from an institution or agency vested with his legal custody or supervision.

(4) The location of such delinquent juvenile, if known, at the time the requisition is made.

C. The requisition shall be verified by affidavit, shall be executed in duplicate, and shall be accompanied by two certified copies of the judgment, formal adjudication, or order of commitment which subjects such delinquent juvenile to probation or parole or to the legal custody of the institution or agency concerned.

D. Such further affidavits and other documents as may be deemed proper may be submitted with such requisition.

E. One copy of the requisition shall be filed with the compact administrator of the demanding state, there to remain on file subject to the provisions of law governing records of the appropriate court.

(Added by Acts 1991 No. 235, §16, eff. 1/1/92.)

Art. 1637. Duties of state receiving requisition.

A. Upon the receipt of a requisition demanding the return of a delinquent juvenile who has absconded or escaped, the court or the executive authority to whom the requisition is addressed shall issue an order to any peace officer or other appropriate person directing him to take into custody and detain such delinquent juvenile.

B. Such detention order must substantially recite the facts necessary to the validity of its issuance hereunder.

C. No delinquent juvenile detained upon such order shall be delivered over to the officer whom the appropriate person or authority demanding him shall have appointed to receive him, unless he shall first be taken forthwith before a judge of an appropriate court in the state, who shall inform him of the demand made for his return and who may appoint counsel or a guardian ad litem for him.

D. If the judge of such court shall find that the requisition is in order, he shall deliver such delinquent juvenile over to the officer whom the appropriate person or authority demanding him shall have appointed to receive him. The judge, however, may fix a reasonable time to be allowed for the purpose of testing the legality of the proceeding.

(Added by Acts 1991 No. 235, §16, eff. 1/1/92.)

Art. 1638. Report of absconding or escaped juvenile.

A. Upon reasonable information that a person is a delinquent juvenile who had absconded while on probation or parole, or escaped from an institution or agency vested with his legal custody or supervision in any state party to this compact, such person may be taken into custody in any other state party to this compact without a requisition.

B. In such event, he must be taken forthwith before a judge of the appropriate court, who may appoint counsel or a guardian ad litem for such person.

C. The court shall determine after a hearing whether sufficient cause exists to hold the person.

D. The court may order the person for such a time, not exceeding ninety days, as will enable his detention under a detention order issued on a requisition pursuant to Article 1636.

E. If, at the time when a state seeks the return of a delinquent juvenile who has either absconded while on probation or parole or escaped from an institution or agency vested with his legal custody or supervision, there is pending in the state wherein he is detained any criminal charge or any proceeding to have him adjudicated a delinquent juvenile for an act committed in such state, or if he is suspected of having committed within such state a criminal offense or an act of juvenile delinquency, he shall not be returned without the consent of such state until discharged from prosecution or other form of proceeding, imprisonment, detention, or supervision for such offense or juvenile delinquency.

(Added by Acts 1991 No. 235, §16, eff. 1/1/92.)

Art. 1639. Transportation of absconding or escaped juvenile.

A. The duly accredited officers of any state party to this compact, upon the establishment of their authority and the identity of the delinquent juvenile being returned, shall be permitted to transport such delinquent juvenile through any and all states party to this compact, without interference.

B. The state to which a delinquent juvenile is returned under this Article shall be responsible for payment of the transportation costs of such return.

(Added by Acts 1991 No. 235, §16, eff. 1/1/92.)

Art. 1640. Further proceedings in home state upon return.

Upon his return to the state from which he escaped or absconded, the delinquent juvenile shall be subject to such further proceedings as may be appropriate under the laws of that state. *(Added by Acts 1991 No. 235, §16, eff. 1/1/92.)*

Art. 1641. Juvenile's consent to return.

A. Any delinquent juvenile who has absconded while on probation or parole, or escaped from an institution or agency vested with his legal custody or supervision in any state party to this compact, and any juvenile who has run away from any state party to this compact, who is taken into custody without a requisition in another state party to this compact under the provisions of Article 1633 or 1638, may consent to his immediate return to the state from which he absconded, escaped, or ran away.

B. Before such consent shall be executed or subscribed, however, the judge, in the presence of counsel or guardian ad litem, if any, shall inform the juvenile or delinquent juvenile of his rights under this compact.

C. Such consent shall be given by the juvenile or delinquent juvenile and his counsel or guardian ad litem if any, by executing or subscribing a writing, in the presence of a judge of the appropriate court, which states that the juvenile or delinquent juvenile and his counsel or guardian ad litem, if any, consent to his return to the demanding state.

D. When the consent has been duly executed, it shall be forwarded to and filed with the compact administrator of the state in which the court is located and the judge shall direct the officer having the juvenile or delinquent juvenile in custody to deliver him to the duly accredited officer or officers of the state demanding his return, and shall cause to be delivered to such officer or officers a copy of the consent.

E. The court may, however, upon the request of the state to which the juvenile or delinquent juvenile is being returned, order him to return unaccompanied to such state and shall provide him with a copy of such court order. In such event, a copy of the consent shall be forwarded to, the compact administrator of the state to which said juvenile or delinquent juvenile is ordered to return.
(Added by Acts 1991 No. 235, §16, eff. 1/1/92.)

Art. 1642. Additional plans or procedures for return of runaway juveniles.

In addition to any procedure provided in Articles 1628 through 1635 and 1641 for the return of any runaway juvenile, the particular states, the juvenile or his parents, the courts, or other legal custodian involved may agree upon and adopt any other plan or procedure legally authorized under the laws of this state and the other respective party states for the return of any such runaway juvenile. *(Added by Acts 1991 No. 235, §16, eff. 1/1/92.)*

Art. 1643. Delinquency charges; nonresident juvenile; additional remedies.

A. Any juvenile charged with being a delinquent by reason of violating any criminal law shall be returned to the requesting state upon a requisition to the state where the juvenile may be found.

B. A petition in such case shall be filed in a court of competent jurisdiction in the requesting state where the violation of criminal law is alleged to have been committed. The petition may be filed regardless of whether the juvenile has left the state before or after the filing of the petition.

C. The requisition described in Article 1636 shall be forwarded by the judge of the court in which the petition has been filed.

D. All provisions and procedures of Articles 1636 through 1641 shall be construed to apply to any juvenile charged with being a delinquent by reason of a violation of any criminal law.

E. This Article shall provide additional remedies, and shall be binding only as among and between these party states which specifically execute the same.
(Added by Acts 1991 No. 235, §16, eff. 1/1/92.)

Art. 1644. Permission for juvenile to relocate; transfer of supervisory responsibility.

A. The duly constituted judicial and administrative authorities of a state party to this compact, herein called "sending state" may permit any delinquent juvenile within such state, placed on probation or parole, to reside in any other state party to this compact, herein called "receiving state", while on probation or parole. The receiving state shall accept such delinquent juvenile, if the parent, guardian, or person entitled to the legal custody of such delinquent juvenile is residing or undertakes to reside within the receiving state.

B. Before granting such permission, opportunity shall be given to the receiving state to make such investigations as it deems necessary. The authorities of the sending state shall send to the authorities of the receiving state copies of pertinent court orders, social case studies, and all other available information which may be of value to and assist the receiving state in supervising a probationer or parolee under this compact.

C. A receiving state, in its discretion, may agree to accept supervision of a probationer or parolee in cases where the parent, guardian, or person entitled to the legal custody of the delinquent juvenile is not a resident of the receiving state, and if so accepted, the sending state may transfer supervision accordingly.

(Added by Acts 1991 No. 235, §16, eff. 1/1/92.)

Art. 1645. Standards of supervision.

Each receiving state will assume the duties of visitation and of supervision over any such delinquent juvenile and in the exercise of those duties will be governed by the same standards of visitation and supervision that prevail for its own delinquent juveniles released on probation or parole. *(Added by Acts 1991 No. 235, §16, eff. 1/1/92.)*

Art. 1646. Retaking of delinquent on probation or parole.

A. After consultation between the appropriate authorities of the sending state and of the receiving state as to the desirability and necessity of returning such a delinquent juvenile, the duly accredited officers of a sending state may enter a receiving state and there apprehend and retake any such delinquent juvenile on probation or parole.

B. For this purpose, no formalities will be required other than establishing the authority of the officer and the identity of the delinquent juvenile to be retaken and returned.

C. The decision of the sending state to retake a delinquent juvenile on probation or parole shall be conclusive upon and not reviewable within the receiving state, except at the time the sending state seeks to retake a delinquent juvenile on probation or parole if either:

(1) There is pending against him within the receiving state any criminal charge or any proceeding to have him adjudicated a delinquent juvenile for any act committed in such state.

(2) He is suspected of having committed within such state a criminal offense or an act of juvenile delinquency.

D. In these two exceptional cases, as set forth in Paragraph C of this Article, the juvenile shall not be returned without the consent of the receiving state until discharged from prosecution or other form of proceeding, imprisonment, detention, or supervision for such offense or juvenile delinquency.

(Added by Acts 1991 No. 235, §16, eff. 1/1/92.)

Art. 1647. Transportation of retaken juveniles; costs.

A. The duly accredited officers of the sending state shall be permitted to transport delinquent juveniles being so returned through any and all states party to this compact, without interference.

B. The sending state shall be responsible under this Article for paying the costs of transporting any delinquent juvenile to the receiving state or returning any delinquent juvenile to the sending state.

(Added by Acts 1991 No. 235, §16, eff. 1/1/92.)

Art. 1648. Allocation of costs; collection.

A. The provisions of Articles 1634, 1639, and 1647 authorizing interstate cooperation shall not be construed to alter or affect any internal relationship among the departments, agencies, and officers of and in the government of a party state, or between a party state and its subdivisions, as to the payment of costs or responsibilities therefor.

B. Nothing in this compact shall be construed to prevent any party state or subdivision thereof from asserting any right against any person, agency, or other entity in regard to costs for which such party state or subdivision thereof may be responsible pursuant to Articles 1634, 1639, and 1647.

(Added by Acts 1991 No. 235, §16, eff. 1/1/92.)

Art. 1649. Supplementary agreements between states; authorization; requirements.

A. The duly constituted administrative authorities of a state party to this compact may enter into supplementary agreements with any other state or states party hereto for the cooperative care, treatment, and rehabilitation of delinquent juveniles whenever they shall find that such agreements will improve the facilities or programs available for such care, treatment, and rehabilitation.

B. Such care, treatment and rehabilitation may be provided in an institution located within any state entering into such supplementary agreement.

C. Such supplementary agreements shall:

(1) Provide the rates to be paid for the care, treatment, and custody of such delinquent juveniles, taking into consideration the character of facilities, services, and subsistence furnished.

(2) Provide that the delinquent juvenile shall be given a court hearing prior to his being sent to another state for care, treatment, and custody.

(3) Provide that the state receiving such a delinquent juvenile in one of its institutions shall act solely as agent for the state sending such delinquent juvenile.

(4) Provide that the sending state shall at all times retain jurisdiction over delinquent juveniles sent to an institution in another state.

(5) Provide for reasonable inspection of such institutions by the sending state.

(6) Provide that the consent of the parent, guardian, person, or agency entitled to the legal custody of said delinquent juvenile shall be secured prior to his being sent to another state.

(7) Make provision for such other matters and details as shall be necessary to protect the rights and equities of such delinquent juveniles and of the cooperating states.

(Added by Acts 1991 No. 235, §16, eff. 1/1/92.)

Art. 1650. Acceptance of gifts and grants.

Any state party to this compact may accept any and all donations, gifts, and grants of money, equipment, and services from the federal or any local government, or any agency thereof and from any person, firm, or corporation, for any of the purposes and functions of this compact, and may receive and utilize the same subject to the terms, conditions, and regulations governing such donations, gifts, and grants. *(Added by Acts 1991 No. 235, §16, eff. 1/1/92.)*

Art. 1651. Compact administrator; rules and regulations; term of office; authority.

A. Pursuant to said compact, the governor is hereby authorized and empowered to designate an officer who shall be the compact administrator and who, acting jointly with like officers of other party states, shall promulgate rules and regulations to carry out more effectively the terms of the compact. Said compact administrator shall serve subject to the pleasure of the governor. The compact administrator is hereby authorized, empowered, and directed to cooperate with all departments, agencies, and officers of and in the government of this state and its subdivisions in facilitating the proper administration of the compact or of any supplementary agreement or agreements entered into by this state thereunder.

B. The compact administrator, subject to the approval of the secretary of the Department of Public Safety and Corrections, may make or arrange for any payments necessary to discharge any financial obligations imposed upon this state by the compact or by any supplementary agreement entered into thereunder.

(Added by Acts 1991 No. 235, §16, eff. 1/1/92.)

Art. 1652. Supplementary agreements by compact administrator.

A. The compact administrator is hereby authorized and empowered to enter into supplementary agreements with appropriate officials of other states pursuant to the compact.

B. In the event that such supplementary agreement shall require or contemplate the use of any institution or facility of this state or require or contemplate the provision of any service by this state, said supplementary agreement shall have no force or effect until approved by the head of the department or agency under whose jurisdiction said institution or facility is operated or whose department or agency will be charged with the rendering of such service.

(Added by Acts 1991 No. 235, §16, eff. 1/1/92.)

Art. 1653. Effect of compact.

This compact shall become operative immediately upon its execution by any state as between it and any other state or states so executing. When executed it shall have the full force and effect of law within such state, the form of execution to be in accordance with the laws of the executing state. *(Added by Acts 1991 No. 235, §16, eff. 1/1/92.)*

Art. 1654. Renunciation; effect.

A. This compact shall continue in force and remain binding upon each executing state until renounced by it. Renunciation of this compact shall be by the same authority which executed it, by sending six months' notice in writing of its intention to withdraw from the compact to the other states party hereto.

B. The duties and obligations of a renouncing state under Articles 1644 through 1647 shall continue as to parolees and probationers residing therein at the time of withdrawal until retaken or finally discharged.

C. Supplementary agreements entered into under Article 1649 shall be subject to renunciation as provided by such supplementary agreements, and shall not be subject to the six months' renunciation notice of this Article.

(Added by Acts 1991 No. 235, §16, eff. 1/1/92.)

Art. 1655. Severability.

The provisions of this compact shall be severable and if any phrase, clause, sentence, or provision of this compact is declared to be contrary to the constitution of any participating state or of the United States or the applicability thereof to any government, agency, person, or circumstance is held invalid, the validity of the remainder of this compact and the applicability thereof to any government, agency, person, or circumstance shall not be affected thereby. If this compact shall be held contrary to the constitution of any state participating therein, the compact shall remain in full force and effect as to the remaining states and in full force and effect as to the state affected as to all severable matters. *(Added by Acts 1991 No. 235, §16, eff. 1/1/92.)*

Art. 1656. Additional remedies; appearance of nonresident child before court.

A. When any child is brought before a court of a state of which the child is not a resident, and that state is willing to permit the child's return to his home state, the home state, upon being so advised by the state in which such proceeding is pending, shall immediately institute proceedings to determine the residence and jurisdictional facts as to the child and his home state.

B. Upon finding that the child is in fact its resident and subject to the jurisdiction of the court thereof, the home state shall within five days authorize the return of the child to the home state and to the parent or custodial agency legally authorized to accept custody in the home state, and at the expense of the home state, to be paid from such funds as the home state may procure, designate, or provide, prompt action being of the essence.

C. For the purposes of this Article, "child" means any minor within the jurisdictional age limits of any court in the home state.

(Added by Acts 1991 No. 235, §16, eff. 1/1/92.)

Art. 1657. Enforcement.

The courts, departments, agencies, and officers of this state and its subdivision shall enforce this compact and shall do all things appropriate to the effectuation of its purposes and intent which may be within their respective jurisdictions. *(Added by Acts 1991 No. 235, §16, eff. 1/1/92.)*

This page intentionally left blank.

Louisiana Criminal Law and Motor Vehicle Handbook—Index

(Unless otherwise noted, all references are to Titles 14, 15, 32, 37, 40 and 47 of the Louisiana Revised Statutes; the Code of Criminal Procedure (CCrP) and the Children's Code (ChC).)

large passenger vehicle - 32:1
lease-bound mobile rig hauler - 32:861
lease-purchase contract - 15:1096, 1098.2
legend drug - 40:961
length - 32:1
license - 32:401, 851
license fee - 32:401
licensing authority - 32:1421, 1442
light trailer - 32:1
light transmission - 32:361.1
light vehicle - 32:401
load - 32:1
local municipal authority - 32:1
local parish authority - 32:1
loose material - 32:383
low pressure pneumatic tire - 32:1
luminous reflectance - 32:361.1
mandatory reporter - 14:403
manufacture - 40:961
manufacturer - 32:361.1, 702, 771, 1252
manufacturer or distributor of marine products - 32:771
manufacturer sales representative - 32:771
manufacturer's certificate - 32:702
marijuana - 40:961
marine dealer - 32:771
marine product - 32:771
mental health/social service practitioner - 14:403
metal tire - 32:1
misdemeanor - 14:2
mobile home - 32:1
motor carrier - 32:1
motor driven cycle - 32:1, 401
motor home - 32:1252
motor vehicle - 32:1, 401, 751, 851, 1252, 1601, 1801
motor vehicle dealer - 32:1252
motor vehicle lessor - 32:1252
motor vehicle liability policy - 32:900
motor vehicle of historic or special interest - 32:442
motor vehicle salesman/agent - 32:1252
motorcycle - 32:1, 401, 771
motorized bicycle - 32:1, 32:401
multiple-lane highway - 32:1
municipality - 32:1
narcotic drug - 32:1425, 1446, 40:961
neglect - 14:403, 403.2
new and unused motor vehicle - 32:1252
non-resident - 32:851
non-resident's operating privileges - 32:851
nonconviction data - 15:541
offender - 15:1174
operator - 32:1, 851
opiate - 40:961
opium poppy - 40:961
oral communication - 15:1302
organization - 14:359
owner - 14:223.1, 32:1, 851, 1713
parish - 15:1098.2
park - 32:1
parking area - 32:1
participating parish - 15:1096, 1098.2
parts car - 32:442
passenger car - 32:1
pattern of racketeering activity - 15:1352
pavement structure - 32:1
pedestrian - 32:1
permit period - 32:621
person - 14:2, 67.3, 403.1, 15:1302, 32:621, 702, 851, 1252, 1502, 40:961
place of business - 32:751
pneumatic tire - 32:1
police officer - 32:1
policing authority - 32:471
poppy straw - 40:961
position of public authority - 14:2
power cycle - 32:401
practitioner - 40:961
prescribe - 40:961
prescription - 40:961
private carrier - 32:1502
private road - 32:1
production - 40:961
proof of financial responsibility - 32:851
proper food - 14:102
proper means - 14:73.1
proper shelter - 14:102
proper veterinary care - 14:102
proper water - 14:102
property - 14:2, 73.1
prostitution - 14:82
public employee - 14:2
public office - 14:2
public officer - 14:2
public official - 14:122.2
quadrum axle - 32:1
racketeering activity - 15:1352
railroad - 32:1
railroad sign or signal - 32:1
railroad train - 32:1
rape - 14:41
registration - 32:851
regular operation - 32:1
residence district - 32:1
restrictive rating - 14:330
retail sale - 32:1252
revocation - 32:401
revoked access card - 14:67.3
right of way - 32:1
road tractor - 32:1
roadway - 32:1
rotary traffic island - 32:1
runaway - ChC 728
safety glass - 32:360
safety zone - 32:1
sale at retail - 32:1252
salesman - 32:702
salvage disposal sale - 32:751
salvage pool - 32:751
school - 14:403.1

This page intentionally left blank.

NEW from GOULD!

Disabled Offenders (Stop, Search and Arrest)

by Sheila A. Bolin, Richard A. Flesch, and Fanchon F. Funk

Presents proper awareness and suggested procedures for law enforcement officers dealing with offenders with disabilities. Also includes related materials from Title 42, Chapter 126 of the United States Code, the Code of Federal Regulations, selected state statutes and relevant cases. Softcover, 8½" x 11", approximately 200 pages.

ONLY $24.95

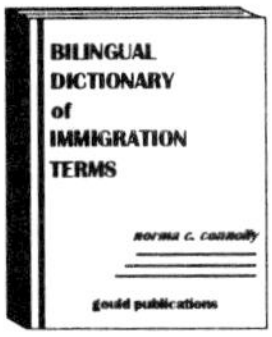

Bilingual Dictionary of Immigration Terms

(English/Spanish) by Norma Connolly

A current comprehensive compilation of significant procedural and substantive immigration terms and concepts defined in Spanish and English. Also includes flow charts of immigration procedures such as visa application, deportation and exclusion, as well as a Spanish-English index. Looseleaf or Softcover, approximately 110 pages.

ONLY $19.95

Bilingual Dictionary of Domestic Relations and Juvenile Terms

(English/Spanish) by Norma Connolly

A comprehensive collection of significant procedural and substantive family law and juvenile justice terms defined in Spanish and English. Also includes flow charts of juvenile justice procedures from the commission of the offense to disposition, as well as a Spanish-English index. Looseleaf or Softcover, approximately 270 pages. (Available Fall 1998)

ONLY $19.95

Gould's DRUG LAWS on CD-ROM

Immediate, inexpensive and user-friendly access to all 50 States and Federal laws covering Criminal Violations, Misdemeanors and Felonies of drug-related offenses. This is the only publication of its kind available on the market. Discs are updated by Gould's editorial staff with all changes enacted. The single-user subscription price per year, including updated discs, is only $249. Multiple-user/network pricing is available as follows-$249 for the first user plus: $99 each per user for more than 99 users; $129 each per user for 50 to 99 users; $149 each per user for 2 to 49 users.

ONLY $249

Gould's FIREARMS LAWS on CD-ROM

Immediate, inexpensive and user-friendly access to all 50 States and Federal laws covering Weapons, Arms, Crimes, Devices, and Ammunition. This is the only publication of its kind available on the market. Discs are updated by Gould's editorial staff with all changes enacted. The single-user subscription price per year, including updated discs, is only $349. Multiple-user/network pricing is available as follows-$349 for the first user plus: $129 each per user for more than 99 users; $179 each per user for 50 to 99 users; $199 each per user for 2 to 49 users.

ONLY $349

Gould's VEHICLE LAWS on CD-ROM

Immediate, inexpensive and user-friendly access to all 50 States and Federal laws covering Traffic, Transportation, Vessels and Motor Vehicles. This is the only publication of its kind available on the market. Discs are updated by Gould's editorial staff with all changes enacted. The single-user subscription price per year, including updated discs, is only $499. Multiple-user/network pricing is available as follows-$499 for the first user plus: $199 each per user for more than 99 users; $250 each per user for 50 to 99 users; $350 each per user for 2 to 49 users.

ONLY $499

Criminal and Vehicle Laws of your state on computer disk — only $49.95!

GOULD PUBLICATIONS • (800) 847-6502 • Quantity Discounts Available

World Wide Web — http://www.gouldlaw.com E-mail — info@gouldlaw.com

Want more information? Point your browser to www.gouldlaw.com
Sample software and Search Engine • Complete Catalog • Table of Contents for each publication • Links and Legal Resources
For Quick Credit Card Purchases, try our Internet Shopping Cart.

GouldLaw™—*We give you the Law, You Choose the Medium℠*

GOULD'S QUICK FIND LOCATOR™

HOW TO USE: Bend the edge and follow the arrow to the corresponding black mark.